AMERICAN INDIAN LAW

CONTEMPORARY LEGAL EDUCATION SERIES

American Indian Law

CASES AND MATERIALS

Third Edition

ROBERT N. CLINTON

Wiley B. Rutledge Distinguished Professor of Law
University of Iowa College of Law

NELL JESSUP NEWTON

Professor of Law
American University, Washington College of Law

MONROE E. PRICE

Joseph and Sadie Danciger Professor of Law
Benjamin Cardozo School of Law
  of Yeshiva University

THE MICHIE COMPANY
Law Publishers
CHARLOTTESVILLE, VIRGINIA

Preface

In the preface to the second edition of this book, the authors noted the explosive development of federal Indian law that occurred between 1973, when the first edition of this book was published, and 1983, when the second edition appeared. We noted that during that period the Supreme Court had decided thirty-two cases and Congress enacted a large number of statutes of vital importance to Indians and others in Indian country. The years since publication of the second edition have also been an active and volatile period for Indian law, albeit one with remarkably more mixed results for Native American peoples. The decade preceding publication of the second edition was characterized by a rising crescendo of success for the efforts of Indian peoples to enforce their rights and secure redress for their grievances in federal legislative and judicial forums. While there were certainly many notable losses, on balance Indian tribes and members were winning more cases than they were losing.

The period since the second edition was published, however, has demonstrated that the rising expectations created by the previous legislative and judicial successes only represented a prelude to a more bumpy roller coaster ride for the resolution of many Indian issues, particularly in federal and state courts. Some very important new legislative initiatives were adopted during this period, such as the Indian Land Consolidation Act of 1982, the Indian Tribal Government Tax Status Act of 1982, the Indian Mineral Development Act of 1982, and the Indian Gaming Regulatory Act of 1988. During this time the nation experienced the effects of declining federal program budgets. This impact was felt disproportionately in Indian country, however, where some of the nation's poorest citizens reside. The primary developments in Indian law during this period occurred on the reservations through the increased sophistication and development of tribal governments and their courts and through their efforts to cope with increased federal regulations and decreased federal financial support. Other significant developments continued in the federal and state courts where Indian efforts to develop their tribal governments and exploit their remaining resources often collided with the regulatory, taxing, or adjudicative preferences of state and municipal governments.

Since the last edition of this book was published, the United States Supreme Court has decided thirty-one new Indian law cases, most of them with lengthy opinions and many by narrowly divided votes. Obviously hundreds of other cases were decided by lower federal, state, and tribal courts during this time. The volatility of legal doctrine in this area is reflected both by the closeness of many of the recent votes on cases decided by the Supreme Court and by the fact that the shifting pluralities that recently have tended to comprise the Court majority often treat each case as a new and unique opportunity to develop novel or original doctrines in Indian law, making doctrinal predictability or governmental stability in Indian country quite tenuous. Thus, many landmark decisions have been distinguished, and new and uncertain doctrines have emerged to replace them.

While casebooks obviously tend to focus on reported appellate cases to search for predictably stable decisional patterns, other developments during the past decade outside the courts have further complicated any effort to accurately survey the discipline of Indian law. These developments resulted from important new intellectual cross-currents among scholars and lawyers in Indian law. The emergence of the Critical Legal Studies Movement in the academy and the increased focus in Indian country on tribal or supra-tribal nationalism during this period created important, illuminating dialogues and disagreements between academics and attorneys with reform objectives bent on applying existing federal Indian law doctrines to the benefit of Indian tribes and their people and others who believe that such changes cannot come about without a fundamental transformation in the structure and vision one has of Indian law.[1] The reformers see the existing federal legal structure as the best, or most practical, forum for the resolution of many Indian grievances. By contrast, lawyers and scholars who espouse transformative objectives have attacked many of the basic tenets of federal Indian law and sometimes employ rejectionist legal arguments, suggesting the colonial illegitimacy and intellectual bankruptcy of federal Indian law doctrines. Those from the transformative school of thought often argue in favor of resolving Indian rights disputes outside of the context of the existing doctrines of federal Indian law. Thus, many scholars and lawyers increasingly looked to international, comparative, and tribal law models to inform and resolve the concerns of Native Americans.

The cross-currents and inconsistencies of such legislative developments, case decisions, and intellectual ferment present formidable challenges to anyone who sets out in a casebook format to capture the depth and richness of the intellectual efforts of tribal people and others, including judges, legislators, lawyers, and academics, to build a coherent body of Indian law. From its inception in Professor Monroe Price's hands, this book always has sought to present a broad jurisprudential and comparative perspective that transcended mere efforts to accurately portray existing federal Indian law doctrine. The book not only has repeatedly questioned and challenged those doctrines, it also has aspired to place federal Indian law in a larger historical and global context and to tie federal legal doctrines affecting indigenous peoples to other similar problems of preserving autonomous cultures and nationalities in South America, Africa, Canada, New Zealand, and Australia, to name but a few. Editors of a book in such a rich field are faced with an exacting task. They can ignore the breadth and richness of the field and devote extended attention to a small part of the panorama of Indian law, such as federal court doctrine, or they can attempt to survey the various cross-currents and expose the reader to a broad, but not necessarily in-depth, treatment of the major issues and perspectives in the field. We deliberately have chosen the second approach. In our preface to the second edition, we indicated that the book had two purposes — (1) to survey

---

[1] The authors are indebted to Professor Stephen Cornell of the Harvard University's Sociology Department for the classifications employed here. In his fine book The Return of the Native: American Indian Political Resurgence (Oxford Press 1988), Professor Cornell explores the political, historical, and sociological background surrounding the emergence of the supra-tribal political identity evident today on many Indian law issues and further cogently probes and describes the differences in the political techniques employed by tribal political activists and their lawyers.

the major doctrines in the field of Indian law and (2) to provide a wide-ranging inquiry into the role of law and legal processes, both domestic and international, in protecting or frustrating the desires for political and cultural autonomy of various racial, cultural, religious, or national subgroups within a society. These twin perspectives may reflect the underlying ambivalence of the authors, since we share many of the views of both reformist and transformative scholars in Native American law. Thus, we continue to hold to these twin objectives, although the increasingly diverse directions of the scholarship, decisions, and legislation in Indian law has made it increasingly difficult to remain firmly astride both steeds.

By choosing to survey some of the broad currents in federal Indian law, we have been forced to make certain basic decisions about the organization and structure of this book. First, we have concluded that richness and diversity of the cases and scholarship relating to Native Americans called for a book that was larger and deeper than would be possible to teach in any single two- or three-hour Native American law course or seminar. Rather, we chose to present an organized smorgasbord of sources from which an instructor could select the ingredients to craft his or her own course to suit individual objectives. Thus, teachers and students most interested in questions of political authority, sovereignty, legitimacy, and jurisdiction may focus the primary attention of their courses on chapters 1 through 4. Those primarily interested in the protection of Indian property and natural resources may find their time most profitably spent concentrating primarily on chapters 1 and 5-7. Instructors or students interested in transformative models of Native American rights and increasingly important international regimes of protection may find their primary attention captured by chapters 1 and 9. Similarly, students or faculty whose interests or location suggest the need to focus considerable attention on atypical patterns of federal Native American law, such as those found in Hawaii, eastern Oklahoma, Alaska, and on terminated or nonrecognized reservations, may find careful attention to chapter 8 particularly useful. In short, we organized the materials in this book on the assumption that no course could or would survey the book cover to cover. Rather, we sought to present a rich and diverse collection of readings in an organized fashion that would offer considerable variety in presenting and selecting course materials.

As in prior editions of this book, chapter 1 of this edition immediately confronts the basic policy and legal questions posed by federal Indian law — the tension between the integrative, assimilationist objectives of the American "melting pot" model of cultural, racial, and other subgroup relations and the separatist, nationalist model of political and cultural autonomy espoused by Indian leaders and protected by federal treaties and law. The chapter reviews this dichotomy from jurisprudential, historical, and policy perspectives and explores important constitutional equal protection questions surrounding the body of federal Indian law that sometimes protects Native American political and cultural autonomy. This chapter also explores the prerequisites of such a body of law by probing the varying federal definitions assigned to the terms "Indian tribe," "Indian," and "Indian country" — the historical terms of art employed in defining the outer reaches of federal Indian law. Finally, chapter 1 introduces the need to place the domestic legal debate over Indian law within a broader international context, a theme to which the last chapter returns, by exploring the details of the new International Labor Organization Convention on the legal rights of indigenous peoples.

Chapters 2 through 4 focus attention on the competition for legal authority and power in Indian country between the three sovereign authorities, each of which asserts claims to political dominion and sovereignty over Indian country and its people — the federal government, the tribal government, and the state government. These chapters examine in that order the history and legal doctrines surrounding each respective government's claim to exercise legitimate political power and authority over the people and resources of Indian country. These chapters explore the historical evolution of each sovereign's claim to authority and the prevailing legal doctrines that shape those claims. These materials also question the historical or political legitimacy of some of those claims to political authority. In short, these chapters explore the limits of sovereignty. They provide a test of the extent to which the original self-government and political authority of the aboriginal tribes of the North American continent have been eroded by the dominant colonial power.

Sovereignty and political authority are not ends unto themselves, however. Rather, political authority is a means to structure society to maximize production and distribution of goods and services in an orderly and culturally appropriate manner. Allocating political authority or sovereignty also delegates decisionmaking responsibilities and thereby determines whether the political, economic, or cultural destinies of Native American peoples and those who enter onto their reservations will be decided by Native Americans or by non-Indian federal or state governments. In order to give meaning to such decisionmaking, however, the very existence of Indian resources, goods, and services must be assured by legal protections. Chapters 5 through 7 focus attention on the legal protections afforded Indian property rights and the manner in which the law facilitates or frustrates the development of those resources. Chapter 5 focuses attention on the legal protection of the one resource that simultaneously is often the tribe's most valued cultural resource and sometimes its only major remaining economic resource — tribal land and resources appurtenant thereto, such as oil and gas, minerals, or timber. It also explores issues dealing with a special kind of tribal property — skeletal remains and artifacts.

Chapter 6 focuses on important hunting and fishing, food gathering, and water rights. The protection and enforcement of such Indian rights are critical to Indian survival in the harsh terrains that characterize some reservations. This chapter illustrates the manner in which the political, cultural, and economic facets of Indian autonomy are interwoven with each other and how the Euro-American legal system's concepts of property and sovereignty have been used to protect or frustrate concerns central to Indian survival.

Chapter 7 explores the modern problems of economic development of Indian country — problems that are logistical, economic, and cultural. It probes the legal doctrines and practical economic problems surrounding different strategies for Indian economic development, including surface and mineral leasing, tribal development of mineral resources, timber operations, and gaming, in the context of tribal desires to preserve their culture and peoplehood. In the process, this chapter raises important questions about the compatibility of modern western-style economic development with the values of tribal cultures through-out the world.

Chapter 8 focuses attention on the legal protections accorded certain special indigenous communities within the United States, including the Alaska Natives, the Indians of eastern Oklahoma, Native Hawaiians, and Indians from termi-nated or nonrecognized Indian tribes. While much of the rest of the book assumes a paradigm model in Indian country, chapter 8 points out that the legal protections accorded many Indian communities depart from that model for historical, political, or other reasons. The chapter also poses questions, particu-larly with regard to Native Hawaiians and Alaskans, as to whether such depar-tures are historically legitimate or represent sound contemporary policy.

Chapter 9 turns the spotlight on international legal protections and compara-tive models of the treatment of indigenous peoples. It provides a transformative and comparative focus for the book. This chapter was placed at the end of the volume to encourage those attracted to reformative visions of federal Indian law to challenge their ideas from a broader global perspective. Similarly, its placement was designed to encourage those committed to transformative models to compare international protections and processes with those available under domestic law. Furthermore, the chapter raises important questions about the extent to which domestic Indian law should be informed by both interna-tional law on the treatment of indigenous peoples and comparative perspectives available from other societies which have sought to provide separate legal pro-tections for culturally and politically autonomous peoples.

A further problem for the creation of this volume was imposed by size con-straints dictated by both our publisher and the concessions that unfortunately must be made to the length of the academic calendar. As the decisions from the courts grow longer and more ponderous and the richness, depth, and diversity of the literature increases, casebook editors are forced to make very difficult editing decisions — decisions on which we did not always agree even among ourselves. Significant problems emerge in paring down extensive, sometimes convoluted, often carefully integrated opinions from the Supreme Court into a few pages manageable for a class session. Similarly, the historical, political, and legal arguments found in the secondary literature often do not lend themselves to brief encapsulation, either by way of paraphrased description or through inclusion of a carefully pruned snippet or two. Nevertheless, employing these techniques, we have sought to present some very complicated material in a more condensed form.

Editing of cases and source materials, of course, poses its own technical dan-gers and pitfalls. For example, how is a reader to know where editing in a text has occurred? On this question, we have opted for visual readability, rather than detailed technical cues. Thus, we have liberally deleted citations and footnotes from both primary cases and secondary works without any indication in text of the omission. Similarly, we have tried to use ellipses sparingly, preferring in-stead when possible to use brackets to indicate where minor editing was neces-sary to smooth transitions required by omissions. Furthermore, in an effort to increase readability, we have chosen not to indicate each deletion of interstitial paragraphs by indented hanging ellipses, relying instead primarily on brackets which begin or end a paragraph to indicate that some editing was done with the

intervening material. That editing may represent a short phrase or many paragraphs omitted from the original source. We believe that this casebook should
be designed as an instructional volume in which readability is an important
asset. Those interested in the details of the complete opinion or source should
consult the original rather than relying on our abridged version of those materials.

Robert N. Clinton
Iowa City, Iowa

Nell Jessup Newton
Washington, DC

Monroe E. Price
New York, New York

Acknowledgments

Preparation of this edition took several years. The authors are deeply indebted to many people who assisted either directly or indirectly in the preparation of this book. First, the authors acknowledge S. James Anaya, Milner Ball, Reid Chambers, Ralph Johnson, Russel Barsh, Derrick Bell, Margery Brown, Richard Collins, Philip S. Deloria, Philip Frickey, David Getches, Frank Pommersheim, Rennard Strickland, Charles Wilkinson, Robert Williams, and Alvin Ziontz, together with many others, some of whose works appear or are cited in this volume, for their major contributions to the development of Indian law which have enriched us all in innumerable ways. John Leshy is owed a particular debt of gratitude for teaching from these materials when they were in a very rough stage and providing thorough feedback based on his experience. In addition, we wish to thank the following persons who contributed valuable insights on specific issues: Curtis Berkey, Virginia Boylan, Robert T. Coulter, Toby Grossman, Kenneth Guido, Charles Hobbes, Rene Kuppe, Bettie Rushing, Sarah Sneed, and Pete Taylor. Finally, we wish to pay tribute to the memory of Denise Carty-Bennia of the Northeastern School of Law, whose early death deprived the field of critical race theory of one of the most eloquent adherents.

We also appreciate the support of our deans, N. William Hines of the University of Iowa College of Law, and the Nellie Ball Trust, who supported Professor Clinton's work with generous summer grants; Ralph J. Rohner of Catholic University School of Law, who supported Professor Newton's work with two summer research grants, and Dean Elliot Milstein, who has generously provided assistance to Professor Newton while she was visiting at the American University, Washington College of Law. Dean Theodore Parnall at the University of New Mexico and Sam Deloria at the American Indian Law Center at the University of New Mexico provided Professor Newton with a laptop computer and facilities at the Law School and the Law Center during the summer of 1990. Likewise, we acknowledge the patience and support of the staff of our publisher, including Don Selby, who smoothed out the rough spots in the publication process, and Don Whitenack, who smoothed out the rougher edges in our manuscript.

Many of the cases included in this book were downloaded through Mead Data Central's LEXIS electronic information retrieval services or West Publishing Company's WESTLAW service. We acknowledge the kind cooperation of these firms in making these services available. As requested by West Publishing Company, we also note that insofar as this volume contains any work in which West Publishing Company can claim a valid copyright, they have asked us to include for those portions the following notice: Copyright © 1991, West Publishing Company.

We also deeply appreciate the kind cooperation of the many authors, law reviews, and publishers who have graciously agreed to permit us to use or reproduce their work in this volume. Their permissions are acknowledged in the book.

In particular, Professor Clinton gratefully acknowledges various law students at the University of Iowa Law School for providing invaluable research assistance, copyreading, and other help. They include Scott Morrison, John D. Gates, Helen Adams, Robin Hulshizer, Charlotte Williams, Robert Ethridge, Kate Varlas, Linda Bennett, and Mark Hostager. In addition, the professional secretarial staff at the University of Iowa College of Law, including Jan Barnes and Debbie Cowherd, typed portions of this manuscript.

Professor Newton wishes to thank her research assistants, James Votaw, Maureen Donohue, and Lynn Balcar at Catholic University and Pamela DeMent at the Washington College of Law. The work of Nancy Dunn and Aline Henderson as research assistants for Professor Newton several years ago bore fruit in this work, for which she is grateful. Her brothers, Robert Mier and Fred Boehm, and Alice Haller, Jack Harris, Suzanne Lipsett, William Mullen, and Natasha Reatig, provided the kind of support without which a long project of this type could never have been finished.

Finally, we express our appreciation to Patricia K. Clinton who always provided support and a model of professional caring, diligence, and pride that contributed greatly to this project.

Robert N. Clinton
Iowa City, Iowa

Nell Jessup Newton
Washington, DC

Monroe E. Price
New York, New York

Summary Table of Contents

Table of Contents

Chapter 1

LEGAL PROTECTION OF NATIVE AMERICAN TRIBAL AUTONOMY AND SELF-GOVERNMENT

The body of jurisprudence in the United States surrounding the legal rights of Native Americans affords them a special protected status in the American legal structure. Unlike other minority groups, whose primary legal protections arise from laws prohibiting discrimination designed to facilitate their complete integration into the social, political, and economic fabric of the country, Indians have enjoyed a legal status that was, at the outset, designed primarily to protect their cultural separateness and political autonomy. Modern Indian law in the United States involves a special protection of a separate minority population that is currently designed to facilitate Indian group autonomy.

In a nation that has prided itself on its role as a melting pot of diverse cultural traditions, Indian separatism and legal autonomy may appear to some to be a political aberration. Why should the law protect Indian autonomy? Why should not the Indians be forced to assimilate into the economic, social, and political structure of the larger society and abandon their tribal traditions and autonomy? How can the special legal protection of Indians be squared with the equal protection and due process clauses of the fifth and fourteenth amendments? This chapter is devoted to consideration of these issues.

CORNELL, THE RETURN OF THE NATIVE: AMERICAN INDIAN POLITICAL RESURGENCE 6-7 (1988)*

For four centuries non-Indians in North America have had an "Indian problem." In its most basic form this problem has had three aspects. First, it has been an economic problem: how best to secure access to Indian resources, land in particular. Second, it has been a problem in cultural transformation: how best to accomplish the cultural transformation of Indians into non-Indians. Third, and consequently, it has been a political problem: how to maintain an effective system of controls over Indian groups so that problems one and two could be satisfactorily resolved.

These concerns have been more prominent during some historical periods than others — pressures on Indian lands, for example, diminished substantially in the 1920s and 1930s — and from time to time other issues have been more salient, particularly in the twentieth century. Today, policy-makers tend to be preoccupied with problems of reservation poverty and ill-health, urban Indian adjustment, education, economic development, and related topics. But these problems are themselves part of the legacy of the centuries-old effort to solve the more fundamental "Indian problem," a problem that has by no means

---

*Copyright © 1988 by Oxford University Press. Reprinted by permission.

disappeared, as contemporary efforts to gain access to Indian natural resources testify.

Indians, on the other hand, have had what might be called a "Euro-American problem." In its essence this problem seems to have been tribal survival: the maintenance of particular sets of social relations, more or less distinct cultural orders, and some measure of political autonomy in the face of invasion, conquest, and loss of power. Again, many Native Americans, particularly in recent years, have had other concerns than these. In the face of often astonishing poverty they, too, have focused much of their energy on jobs, improved standards of living, and the rewards offered by the larger society. Few, however, have been willing to sacrifice the goal of tribal survival — itself a social and political as much as an economic objective — for purely economic gains.

The working out of these two inverse and conflictual agendas has given context and shape to Indian-White relations. The history of those relations can be viewed as a record of the attempts of each group — Indians and Whites — to solve the particular problem they have had to face. Those attempts have not proceeded independently. On the contrary, they have conditioned each other. In the long drama of Indian-White interaction, each actor has been forced to respond to the actions of the other or to the consequences of those actions, manifest in concrete social conditions and relationships.

While mutual, this conditioning process has been uneven. Although in the early years Native Americans on occasion exerted considerable influence over the actions of the invaders and the shape of events, over time they found themselves increasingly constrained, caught in an ever more elaborate mesh of circumstances and relationships beyond their control.

In the pattern of their subjugation lies the shape of their resistance.

A. THE RESPONSE OF AMERICAN LAW TO CULTURAL CONTACT WITH THE AMERICAN INDIAN

1. THE ROOTS OF FEDERAL INDIAN LAW: CHIEF JUSTICE MARSHALL'S TRILOGY

JOHNSON v. M'INTOSH

21 U.S. (8 Wheat.) 543 (1823)

Mr. Chief Justice MARSHALL delivered the opinion of the court. — The plaintiffs in this cause claim the land in their declaration mentioned, under two grants, purporting to be made, the first in 1773, and the last in 1775, by the chiefs of certain Indian tribes, constituting the Illinois and the Piankeshaw nations; and the question is, whether this title can be recognised in the courts of the United States? The facts, as stated in the case agreed, show the authority of the chiefs who executed this conveyance, so far as it could be given by their own people; and likewise show, that the particular tribes for whom these chiefs acted were in rightful possession of the land they sold. The inquiry, therefore, is, in a great measure, confined to the power of Indians to give, and of private individuals to receive, a title, which can be sustained in the courts of this country.

As the right of society to prescribe those rules by which property may be acquired and preserved is not, and cannot, be drawn into question; as the title to lands, especially, is, and must be, admitted, to depend entirely on the law of the nation in which they lie; it will be necessary, in pursuing this inquiry, to examine, not simply those principles of abstract justice, which the Creator of all things has impressed on the mind of his creature man, and which are admitted to regulate, in a great degree, the rights of civilized nations, whose perfect independence is acknowledged; but those principles also which our own government has adopted in the particular case, and given us as the rule for our decision.

On the discovery of this immense continent, the great nations of Europe were eager to appropriate to themselves so much of it as they could respectively acquire. Its vast extent offered an ample field to the ambition and enterprise of all; and the character and religion of its inhabitants afforded an apology for considering them as a people over whom the superior genius of Europe might claim an ascendency. The potentates of the old world found no difficulty in convincing themselves, that they made ample compensation to the inhabitants of the new, by bestowing on them civilization and Christianity, in exchange for unlimited independence. But as they were all in pursuit of nearly the same object, it was necessary, in order to avoid conflicting settlements, and consequent war with each other, to establish a principle, which all should acknowledge as the law by which the right of acquisition, which they all asserted, should be regulated, as between themselves. This principle was, that discovery gave title to the government by whose subjects, or by whose authority, it was made, against all other European governments, which title might be consummated by possession. The exclusion of all other Europeans, necessarily gave to the nation making the discovery the sole right of acquiring the soil from the natives, and establishing settlements upon it. It was a right with which no Europeans could interfere. It was a right which all asserted for themselves, and to the assertion of which, by others, all assented. Those relations which were to exist between the discoverer and the natives, were to be regulated by themselves. The rights thus acquired being exclusive, no other power could interpose between them.

In the establishment of these relations, the rights of the original inhabitants were, in no instance, entirely disregarded; but were, necessarily, to a considerable extent, impaired. They were admitted to be the rightful occupants of the soil, with a legal as well as just claim to retain possession of it, and to use it according to their own discretion; but their rights to complete sovereignty, as independent nations, were necessarily diminished, and their power to dispose of the soil, at their own will, to whomsoever they pleased, was denied by the original fundamental principle, that discovery gave exclusive title to those who made it. While the different nations of Europe respected the right of the natives, as occupants, they asserted the ultimate dominion to be in themselves; and claimed and exercised, as a consequence of this ultimate dominion, a power to grant the soil, while yet in possession of the natives. These grants have been understood by all, to convey a title to the grantees, subject only to the Indian right of occupancy....

The United States, then, have unequivocally acceded to that great and broad rule by which its civilized inhabitants now hold this country. They hold, and assert in themselves, the title by which it was acquired. They maintain, as all others have maintained, that discovery gave an exclusive right to extinguish the

Indian title of occupancy, either by purchase or by conquest; and gave also a right to such a degree of sovereignty, as the circumstances of the people would allow them to exercise. The power now possessed by the government of the United States to grant lands, resided, while we were colonies, in the crown or its grantees. The validity of the titles given by either has never been questioned in our courts. It has been exercised uniformly over territory in possession of the Indians. The existence of this power must negative the existence of any right which may conflict with and control it. An absolute title to lands cannot exist, at the same time, in different persons, or in different governments. An absolute, must be an exclusive title, or at least a title which excludes all others not compatible with it. All our institutions recognise the absolute title of the crown, subject only to the Indian right of occupancy, and recognise the absolute title of the crown to extinguish that right. This is incompatible with an absolute and complete title in the Indians.

We will not enter into the controversy, whether agriculturists, merchants and manufacturers, have a right, on abstract principles, to expel hunters from the territory they possess, or to contract their limits. Conquest gives a title which the courts of the conqueror cannot deny, whatever the private and speculative opinions of individuals may be, respecting the original justice of the claim which has been successfully asserted. The British government, which was then our government, and whose rights have passed to the United States, asserted a title to all the lands occupied by Indians, within the chartered limits of the British colonies. It asserted also a limited sovereignty over them, and the exclusive right of extinguishing the titles which occupancy gave to them. These claims have been maintained and established as far west as the river Mississippi, by the sword. The title to a vast portion of the lands we now hold, originates in them. It is not for the courts of this country to question the validity of this title, or to sustain one which is incompatible with it.

Although we do not mean to engage in the defence of those principles which Europeans have applied to Indian title, they may, we think, find some excuse, if not justification, in the character and habits of the people whose rights have been wrested from them. The title by conquest is acquired and maintained by force. The conqueror prescribes its limits. Humanity, however, acting on public opinion, has established, as a general rule, that the conquered shall not be wantonly oppressed, and that their condition shall remain as eligible as is compatible with the objects of the conquest. Most usually, they are incorporated with the victorious nation, and become subjects or citizens of the government with which they are connected. The new and old members of the society mingle with each other; the distinction between them is gradually lost, and they make one people. Where this incorporation is practicable, humanity demands, and a wise policy requires, that the rights of the conquered to property should remain unimpaired; that the new subjects should be governed as equitably as the old, and that confidence in their security should gradually banish the painful sense of being separated from their ancient connections, and united by force to strangers. When the conquest is complete, and the conquered inhabitants can be blended with the conquerors, or safely governed as a distinct people, public opinion, which not even the conqueror can disregard, imposes these restraints upon him; and he cannot neglect them, without injury to his fame, and hazard to his power.

But the tribes of Indians inhabiting this country were fierce savages, whose occupation was war, and whose subsistence was drawn chiefly from the forest. To leave them in possession of their country, was to leave the country a wilderness; to govern them as a distinct people, was impossible, because they were as brave and as high-spirited as they were fierce, and were ready to repel by arms every attempt on their independence. What was the inevitable consequence of this state of things? The Europeans were under the necessity either of abandoning the country, and relinquishing their pompous claims to it, or of enforcing those claims by the sword, and by the adoption of principles adapted to the condition of a people with whom it was impossible to mix, and who could not be governed as a distinct society, or of remaining in their neighborhood, and exposing themselves and their families to the perpetual hazard of being massacred. Frequent and bloody wars, in which the whites were not always the aggressors, unavoidably ensued. European policy, numbers and skill prevailed; as the white population advanced, that of the Indians necessarily receded; the country in the immediate neighborhood of agriculturists became unfit for them; the game fled into thicker and more unbroken forests, and the Indians followed. The soil, to which the crown originally claimed title, being no longer occupied by its ancient inhabitants, was parcelled out according to the will of the sovereign power, and taken possession of by persons who claimed immediately from the crown, or mediately, through its grantees or deputies.

That law which regulates, and ought to regulate in general, the relations between the conqueror and conquered, was incapable of application to a people under such circumstances. The resort to some new and different rule, better adapted to the actual state of things, was unavoidable. Every rule which can be suggested will be found to be attended with great difficulty. However extravagant the pretension of converting the discovery of an inhabited country into conquest may appear; if the principle has been asserted in the first instance, and afterwards sustained; if a country has been acquired and held under it; if the property of the great mass of the community originates in it, it becomes the law of the land, and cannot be questioned. So too, with respect to the concomitant principle, that the Indian inhabitants are to be considered merely as occupants, to be protected, indeed, while in peace, in the possession of their lands, but to be deemed incapable of transferring the absolute title to others. However this restriction may be opposed to natural right, and to the usages of civilized nations, yet, if it be indispensable to that system under which the country has been settled, and be adapted to the actual condition of the two people, it may, perhaps, be supported by reason, and certainly cannot be rejected by courts of justice.

This question is not entirely new in this court. The case of *Fletcher v. Peck*, grew out of a sale made by the state of Georgia, of a large tract of country within the limits of that state, the grant of which was afterwards resumed. The action was brought by a sub-purchaser, on the contract of sale, and one of the covenants in the deed was, that the state of Georgia was, at the time of sale, seised in fee of the premises. The real question presented by the issue was, whether the seisin in fee was in the state of Georgia, or in the United States.

After stating, that this controversy between the several states and the United States had been compromised, the court thought it necessary to notice the Indian title, which, although entitled to the respect of all courts, until it should be legitimately extinguished, was declared not to be such as to be absolutely repugnant to a seisin in fee on the part of the state. This opinion conforms precisely to the principle which has been supposed to be recognised by all European governments, from the first settlement of America. The absolute ultimate title has been considered as acquired by discovery, subject only to the Indian title of occupancy, which title the discoverers possessed the exclusive right of acquiring. Such a right is no more incompatible with a seisin in fee, than a lease for years, and might as effectually bar an ejectment.

Another view has been taken of this question, which deserves to be considered. The title of the crown, whatever it might be, could be acquired only by a conveyance from the crown. If an individual might extinguish the Indian title, for his own benefit, or, in other words, might purchase it, still he could acquire only that title. Admitting their power to change their laws or usages, so far as to allow an individual to separate a portion of their lands from the common stock, and hold it in severalty, still it is a part of their territory, and is held under them, by a title dependent on their laws. The grant derives its efficacy from their will; and, if they choose to resume it, and make a different disposition of the land, the courts of the United States cannot interpose for the protection of the title. The person who purchases lands from the Indians, within their territory, incorporates himself with them, so far as respects the property purchased; holds their title under their protection, and subject to their laws. If they annul the grant, we know of no tribunal which can revise and set aside [their decision].

The acts of the several colonial assemblies, prohibiting purchases from the Indians, have also been relied on, as proving, that, independent of such prohibitions, Indian deeds would be valid. But, we think, this fact, at most, equivocal. While the existence of such purchases would justify their prohibition, even by colonies which considered Indian deeds as previously invalid, the fact that such acts have been generally passed, is strong evidence of the general opinion, that such purchases are opposed by the soundest principles of wisdom and national policy.

After bestowing on this subject a degree of attention which was more required by the magnitude of the interest in litigation, and the able and elaborate arguments of the bar, than by its intrinsic difficulty, the court is decidedly of opinion, that the plaintiffs do not exhibit a title which can be sustained in the courts of the United States; and that there is no error in the judgment which was rendered against them in the district court of Illinois.

Judgment affirmed, with costs.

NOTE: SAVAGISM IN INDIAN POLICY

In *M'Intosh* Chief Justice Marshall suggested that the reason for the policy of separate autonomous treatment of Indians was that the natives were "fierce savages, whose occupation was war, and whose subsistence was drawn chiefly from the forest" and therefore could not be subjected to the usual policy of assimilation of conquered peoples into the dominant population. The characterization of Indians as savages fit well with the Euro-American myths that had developed in the Americas regarding Native American populations. Recall that Chief Justice Marshall is writing almost contemporaneously with the appearance of important literary works by James Fenimore Cooper extolling and romanticizing savagism, such as THE LAST OF THE MOHICANS. Some recent scholarship, on the other hand, paints a very different view of the process of contact between Euro-American and native civilizations. For example, in F. JENNINGS, THE INVASION OF AMERICA: INDIANS, COLONIALISM AND THE CANT OF CONQUEST 15-16, 32 (1975),* the author suggests:

> European explorers and invaders discovered an inhabited land. Had it been pristine wilderness then, it would possibly be so still today, for neither the technology nor the social organization of Europe in the sixteenth and seventeenth centuries had the capacity to maintain, of its own resources, outpost colonies thousands of miles from home. Incapable of conquering true wilderness, the Europeans were highly competent in the skill of conquering other people, and that is what they did. They did not settle a virgin land. They invaded and displaced a resident population.
>
> This is so simple a fact that it seems self-evident. All historians of the European colonies in America begin by describing the natives' reception of the newcomers. Yet, paradoxically, most of the same historians also repeat identical mythical phrases purporting that the land-starved people of Europe had found magnificent opportunity to pioneer in a savage wilderness and to bring civilization to it. As rationalization for the invasion and conquest of unoffending peoples, such phrases function to smother retroactive moral scruples that have been dismissed as irrelevant to objective history. Unfortunately, however, the price of repressing scruples has been the suppression of facts.
>
> The basic conquest myth postulates that America was virgin land, or wilderness, inhabited by nonpeople called savages; that these savages were creatures sometimes defined as demons, sometimes as beasts "in the shape of men"; that their mode of existence and cast of mind were such as to make them incapable of civilization and therefore of full humanity; that civilization was required by divine sanction or the imperative of progress to conquer the wilderness and make it a garden; that the savage creatures of the wilderness, being unable to adapt to any environment other than the wild, stubbornly and viciously resisted God or fate, and thereby incurred their suicidal extermination; that civilization and its bearers were refined and ennobled in their contest with the dark powers of the wilderness; and that it all was inevitable.
>
> Allowing for reasonable qualification and modification, the grand myth is fallacious because there never were such absolutes as "savagery" and "civilization" (considered as savagery's antithesis) that play the myth's active roles; there was accordingly no triumph of civilization and no death of savagery; there was nothing in the product of the events to make their survivors inherently superior to mankind elsewhere; and only the events unwilled by human agency were inevitable. Historians have now begun to examine and analyze the origins of the myth.
>
> It is customary for our histories to dwell at some length on the immensity of the task of "settling" North America, mentioning the hazards of vast wilderness, the logistical problems of supplying colonists from faraway Europe, the strangeness of the flora and fauna, and the hostilities that the natives were sooner or later bound to display. The implications of this use of the word *settlement* are worth notice. First, it vaguely implies that preexisting populations did not classify as humanity, for it is not used to apply to Indians; only Europeans "settle." It also dismisses the Indians' ability to wrest a generally satisfactory living from the "wilderness" and to travel over established trails to known destinations. Most inaccurate is the word's bland misdirection about the Europeans' intentions, for their common purpose was to exploit rather than to settle.

---

*Copyright 1975 by The University of North Carolina Press. Published for the Institute of Early American History and Culture, Williamsburg. Reprinted by permission.

Among the early European visitors, residence was merely a means of increasing the efficiency of exploitation. A taste for permanent habitation came later. Regularly the first Europeans were welcomed by natives with gifts of food and tokens of honor until the moment came when the gifts were demanded as tribute and the honors were commanded as homage — a moment that sometimes came very rapidly. At the outset native hostility was never directed against European settlement as such; what made trouble was the European purpose of settling on top.*

Many others have attacked this notion of savagism. One noted commentator has suggested that the saga of the history of contact between Indians and Euro-Americans best can be described as a struggle for human survival by Indians against genocidal extermination. Strickland, *Genocide-At-Law: An Historical and Contemporary View of the Native American Experience*, 34 U. KAN. L. REV. 713 (1986). In this struggle law has played important roles. In Professor Strickland's terms, law has been an important instrument "both as a factor in the genocidal extermination and as a weapon in the contemporary struggle for survival." *Id.* at 714. Thus, Strickland argues that, for most of the nineteenth century, the law constituted both a formal and informal agent of genocide. As he put it, "I share de Tocqueville's conclusion that it would be impossible to destroy men with more respect for the law." *Id.* at 719. Are the two cases involving the Cherokee Nation that follow exceptions to that trend or do they merely regularize the process of Euro-American appropriation and genocide?

CHEROKEE NATION v. GEORGIA

30 U.S. (5 Pet.) 1 (1831)

Mr. Chief Justice MARSHALL delivered the opinion of the court. — This bill is brought by the Cherokee nation, praying an injunction to restrain the state of Georgia from the execution of certain laws of that state, which, as is alleged, go directly to annihilate the Cherokee as a political society, and to seize for the use of Georgia, the lands of the nation which have been assured to them by the United States, in solemn treaties repeatedly made and still in force.

If courts were permitted to indulge their sympathies, a case better calculated to excite them can scarcely be imagined. A people, once numerous, powerful, and truly independent, found by our ancestors in the quiet and uncontrolled possession of an ample domain, gradually sinking beneath our superior policy, our arts and our arms, have yielded their lands, by successive treaties, each of which contains a solemn guarantee of the residue, until they retain no more of their formerly extensive territory than is deemed necessary to their comfortable subsistence. To preserve this remnant, the present application is made.

Before we can look into the merits of the case, a preliminary inquiry presents itself. Has this court jurisdiction of the cause? The third article of the constitution describes the extent of the judicial power. The second section closes an enumeration of the cases to which it is extended, with "controversies" "between a state or citizens thereof, and foreign states, citizens or subjects." A subsequent

---

*The "frontier of settlement" idea which Francis Jennings' work attacks was the concept with which Frederick Jackson Turner began his famous essay "The Significance of the Frontier in American History," and it remains prominent throughout all his works. His disciple Ray Allen Billington properly stresses the idea as central to Turner's thought. TURNER, FRONTIER IN AMERICAN HISTORY 1; BILLINGTON, WESTWARD EXPANSION 1-3. [Eds.]

clause of the same section gives the supreme court original jurisdiction, in all cases in which a state shall be a party. The party defendant may then unquestionably be sued in this court. May the plaintiff sue in it? Is the Cherokee nation a foreign state, in the sense in which that term is used in the·constitution? The counsel for the plaintiffs have maintained the affirmative of this proposition with great earnestness and ability. So much of the argument as was intended to prove the character of the Cherokees as a state, as a distinct political society, separated from others, capable of managing its own affairs and governing itself, has, in the opinion of a majority of the judges, been completely successful. They have been uniformly treated as a state, from the settlement of our country. The numerous treaties made with them by the United States, recognise them as a people capable of maintaining the relations of peace and war, of being responsible in their political character for any violation of their engagements, or for any aggression committed on the citizens of the United States, by any individual of their community. Laws have been enacted in the spirit of these treaties. The acts of our government plainly recognise the Cherokee nation as a state, and the courts are bound by those acts.

A question of much more difficulty remains. Do the Cherokees constitute a *foreign* state in the sense of the constitution? The counsel have shown conclusively, that they are not a state of the Union, and have insisted that, individually, they are aliens, not owing allegiance to the United States. An aggregate of aliens composing a state must, they say, be a foreign state; each individual being foreign, the whole must be foreign.

This argument is imposing, but we must examine it more closely, before we yield to it. The condition of the Indians in relation to the United States is, perhaps, unlike that of any other two people in existence. In general, nations not owing a common allegiance, are foreign to each other. The term *foreign nation* is, with strict propriety, applicable by either to the other. But the relation of the Indians to the United States is marked by peculiar and cardinal distinctions which exist nowhere else. The Indian territory is admitted to compose a part of the United States. In all our maps, geographical treatises, histories and laws, it is so considered. In all our intercourse with foreign nations, in our commercial regulations, in any attempt at intercourse between Indians and foreign nations, they are considered as within the jurisdictional limits of the United States, subject to many of those restraints which are imposed upon our own citizens. They acknowledge themselves, in their treaties, to be under the protection of the United States; they admit, that the United States shall have the sole and exclusive right of regulating the trade with them, and managing all their affairs as they think proper; and the Cherokees in particular were allowed by the treaty of Hopewell, which preceded the constitution, "to send a deputy of their choice, whenever they think fit, to Congress." Treaties were made with some tribes, by the state of New York, under a then unsettled construction of the confederation, by which they ceded all their lands to that state, taking back a limited grant to themselves, in which they admit their dependence. Though the Indians are acknowledged to have an unquestionable, and, heretofore, unquestioned, right to the lands they occupy, until that right shall be extinguished by a voluntary cession to our government; yet it may well be doubted, whether those tribes which reside within the acknowledged boundaries of the

United States can, with strict accuracy, be denominated foreign nations. They may, more correctly, perhaps, be denominated domestic dependent nations. They occupy a territory to which we assert a title independent of their will, which must take effect in point of possession, when their right of possession ceases. Meanwhile, they are in a state of pupilage. Their relation to the United States resembles that of a ward to his guardian. They look to our government for protection; rely upon its kindness and its power; appeal to it for relief to their wants; and address the president as their great father. They and their country are considered by foreign nations, as well as by ourselves, as being so completely under the sovereignty and dominion of the United States, that any attempt to acquire their lands, or to form a political connection with them, would be considered by all as an invasion of our territory and an act of hostility. These considerations go far to support the opinion, that the framers of our constitution had not the Indian tribes in view, when they opened the courts of the Union to controversies between a state or the citizens thereof and foreign states.

In considering this subject, the habits and usages of the Indians, in their intercourse with their white neighbors, ought not to be entirely disregarded. At the time the constitution was framed, the idea of appealing to an American court of justice for an assertion of right or a redress of wrong, had perhaps never entered the mind of an Indian or of his tribe. Their appeal was to the tomahawk, or to the government. This was well understood by the statesmen who framed the constitution of the United States, and might furnish some reason for omitting to enumerate them among the parties who might sue in the courts of the Union. Be this as it may, the peculiar relations between the United States and the Indians occupying our territory are such, that we should feel much difficulty in considering them as designated by the term *foreign state*, were there no other part of the constitution which might shed light on the meaning of these words. But we think that in construing them, considerable aid is furnished by the clause in the eighth section of the [first] article, which empowers congress to "regulate commerce with foreign nations, and among the several states, and with the Indian tribes." In this clause, they are as clearly contradistinguished, by a name appropriate to themselves, from foreign nations, as from the several states composing the Union. They are designated by a distinct appellation; and as this appellation can be applied to neither of the others, neither can the application distinguishing either of the others be, in fair construction, applied to them. The objects to which the power of regulating commerce might be directed, are divided into three distinct classes — foreign nations, the several states, and Indian tribes. When forming this article, the convention considered them as entirely distinct. We cannot assume that the distinction was lost, in framing a subsequent article, unless there be something in its language to authorize the assumption.

The counsel for the plaintiffs contend, that the words "Indian tribes" were introduced into the article, empowering congress to regulate commerce, for the purpose of removing those doubts in which the management of Indian affairs was involved by the language of the ninth article of the confederation. Intending to give the whole power of managing those affairs to the government about to be instituted, the convention conferred it explicitly; and omitted those qualifications which embarrassed the exercise of it as granted in the confederation. This may be admitted without weakening the construction which has been intimated. Had the Indian tribes been foreign nations, in the view of the convention, this exclusive power of regulating intercourse with them might have been, and most probably would have been, specifically given, in language indicating that idea, not in language contradistinguishing them from foreign nations. Congress might have been empowered "to regulate commerce with foreign nations, including the Indian tribes, and among the several states." This language would have suggested itself to statesmen who considered the Indian tribes as foreign nations, and were yet desirous of mentioning them [specifically].

If it be true that the Cherokee nation have rights, this is not the tribunal in which those rights are to be asserted. If it be true that wrongs have been inflicted, and that still greater are to be apprehended, this is not the tribunal which can redress the past or prevent the future.

The motion for an injunction is denied.

[Separate concurring opinions of Justices Johnson and Baldwin omitted.]

Mr. Justice THOMPSON, dissenting [joined by Justice Story.]

[There] is a rule which has been repeatedly sanctioned by this court, that the judicial department is to consider as sovereign and independent states or nations those powers, that are recognized as such by the executive and legislative departments of the government; they being more particularly entrusted with our foreign relations.

If we look to the whole course of treatment by this country of the Indians, from the year 1775, to the present day, when dealing with them in their aggregate capacity as nations or tribes, and regarding the mode and manner in which all negotiations have been carried on and concluded with them; the conclusion appears to me irresistible, that they have been regarded, by the executive and legislative branches of the government, not only as sovereign and independent, but as foreign nations or tribes, not within the jurisdiction nor under the government of the states within which they were located....

Upon the whole, I am of opinion:

1. That the Cherokees compose a foreign State, within the sense and meaning of the Constitution, and constitute a competent party to maintain a suit against the State of Georgia.

2. That the bill presents a case for judicial consideration, arising under the laws of the United States and treaties made under their authority with the Cherokee Nation, and which laws and treaties have been and are threatened to be still further violated by the laws of the State of Georgia referred to in this opinion.

3. That an injunction is a fit and proper writ to be issued to prevent the further execution of such laws, and ought therefore to be awarded.

NOTES

1. Historical Background: During the early nineteenth century and, especially, after the War of 1812, the Cherokee experienced a major national revitalization movement that profoundly affected Cherokee society. As early as 1802,

President Jefferson had urged the Cherokee to adopt a republican form of government, and the then-prevailing federal Indian policy encouraged bringing the benefits of Euro-American civilization to the Indians. Due to their traditional agricultural organization, their comparatively greater reliance on hierarchical political structures, and their general receptiveness to Euro-American society, including intermarriage with Scottish traders, the Cherokee were the most successful product of this policy. In 1808, the Cherokee National Council adopted the first written law in an effort to control horse stealing and robbery. Among other things, the law created a national police force, the "Light Horse Guard." In order to ameliorate the adverse effects of the blood feud — the traditional Cherokee system of clan revenge also used by many other tribes — this law provided that if an accused resisted and killed a member of the guard no retaliation should be required from the guard's clan. Ultimately, in 1810 the Cherokee Council formally abolished the system of clan revenge. During the subsequent period missionary activity increased in the Cherokee Nation and brought with it more widespread literacy. In 1821, Sequoyah, also known as George Guess (or Gist), revealed a Cherokee syllabary that permitted the transcribing of Cherokee, thereby producing the first written Indian language in the United States and further accelerating Cherokee literacy. By 1828, a national newspaper, *The Cherokee Phoenix*, was being published at the national capitol of New Echota in both English and Cherokee. The first set of Cherokee written laws was published in 1821, and the Supreme Court of the Cherokee Nation was created by the Cherokee legislature in 1822 and held its first sessions in 1823. Finally, in 1827, the Cherokee Nation created a written tribal constitution, patterned after the United States Constitution, which asserted exclusive "Sovereignty and Jurisdiction" over all lands of the Cherokee Nation. *See generally* H. MALONE, CHEROKEES OF THE OLD SOUTH: A PEOPLE IN TRANSITION (1956).

The late 1820's, however, brought a new dimension to Cherokee relations with the state of Georgia. Georgia had long had designs on the valuable Cherokee land. As early as 1802 the United States entered into an agreement with the state of Georgia in which Georgia ceded her western land claims to the federal government in exchange for the promise that the United States would extinguish as soon as possible the Indian title to lands within the state on peaceable and reasonable terms. Sporadic federal efforts were made to fulfill this agreement by attempting to secure Cherokee and Creek agreement to remove voluntarily from Georgia to lands west of the Mississippi River, but little was actually accomplished to execute the removal promise until after the end of the War of 1812. Thereafter, the United States encouraged the southern tribes to remove westward to an area that would become known as the Indian Territory, an area now encompassing eastern Oklahoma and portions of southern Kansas. The Treaty with the Cherokees, July 8, 1817, 7 Stat. 156, provided that those who wanted to continue the hunting way of life could voluntarily remove to the west side of the Mississippi River to do so, while those who wished to remain in their ancestral homelands were permitted to remain. Major General Andrew Jackson, who recently had commanded brigades of Cherokee and loyal Creek warriors against hostile Creeks during the War of 1812, led the American treaty commissioners. Insofar as Cherokees residing east of the Mississippi River resided on lands surrendered to the United States, article 8 of the treaty provided that if they "may wish to become citizens of the United States, the United States do agree to give [to each head of household] a reservation of six hundred and forty acres of land, in square, to include their improvements ... in which they will have a life estate, with a reversion in fee simple to their children, reserving to the widow her dower." *See also* Treaty with the Cherokee, Feb. 27, 1819, 7 Stat. 195. Within two years approximately one-third of the Cherokees, principally those from the upper towns in Tennessee, did remove across the Mississippi under the terms of this treaty, but many, including those of the lower towns in northern Georgia, remained.

In the 1820's Georgia land policies came into conflict with Cherokee national political development and produced the first great constitutional conflict in United States history over Indian policy. Georgians came increasingly to covet Indian land and resources. This sentiment was fueled both by the fact that Creeks and Cherokees were located on fertile river valley land and by a Georgia land lottery system that made valuable land readily available to the common man in small tracts at very low prices, thereby increasing political pressure for expansionist land policies. Georgian demands for Indian resources were further fueled by the discovery of gold in the Cherokee Nation in July, 1829. By the summer of 1830, over 3,000 miners had illegally entered the Cherokee Nation to dig for gold.

The political and economic development of the Cherokee Nation was too much for Georgia. Having lost patience with federal efforts to remove the Cherokee, Georgia enacted legislation on December 29, 1828, that annexed the lands of the Cherokee Nation to Georgia counties. This act thereby opened Indian lands to settlement under the land lottery system and, under threat of criminal penalties, annulled all laws, ordinances, or orders enacted by the Cherokees and made it illegal to enforce them. Drawing on then-existing slave laws, the legislation also provided that no Indian "shall be deemed a competent witness in any court of this state to which a white person may be a party, except when such white person resides within the said nation." This provision effectively made Cherokees outlaws in their own lands. Their own courts had been declared illegal by Georgia, and they were unable to call upon the Georgia court system for redress of any wrongs done them by whites. Later Georgia legislation established an entry permit system by which all whites residing in the Cherokee Nation were required to swear an oath to support Georgia law, including these oppressive measures. In Congress and elsewhere, Georgia defended these measures as exercises of state sovereignty. As then Senator, later Governor, Wilson Lumpkin put it in his speech to the Senate on removal legislation, "Georgia ... is one of the good old thirteen States; she entered the Union upon an equal footing with any of her sisters.... Within the limits therein defined and pointed out, our State authorities claim entire and complete jurisdiction over soil and population, regardless of complexion." Indeed, in both *Cherokee Nation* and *Worcester*, which follows, Georgia claimed sovereign immunity and did not respond or otherwise argue the case in the Supreme Court. What was Chief Justice Marshall's response in *Cherokee Nation* to Georgia's claim of sovereign immunity, and what does that response suggest about the scope of state sovereign immunity Marshall thought was protected by the eleventh amendment?

Even before the decision in *Cherokee Nation*, the Cherokee tribal government, relying on federal treaty guarantees of their land, protested the Georgia measures to the federal government. While former President John Quincy Adams had defended the Indians, the newly elected President was Andrew Jackson, their former military ally. Jackson, however, was a staunch states righter and defender of the common "western" man. He said that he was powerless to protect them from the sovereign State of Georgia. Thereafter, the debate moved to Congress where the removal legislation, declaring national policy to support removal of the Indians from within state boundaries, narrowly passed the Congress over vocal protests from northeastern legislators outside New York. The vote in the House was 102 to 97. Thus, by the time the Supreme Court decided *Cherokee Nation*, the political branches of the federal government already had rejected the Cherokees' claims. Marshall's statements in the case regarding the state of pupilage that existed between the *federal government* and the tribes and his argument that their recourse was to the political branches of the federal government, therefore, must be placed in their historical context. In light of this context, should Marshall's opinion in *Cherokee Nation* be read, like his equally famous opinion a quarter of a century earlier in *Marbury v. Madison*, as an effort to resolve the merits of the dispute without formally deciding the case? Indeed, can the *Cherokee Nation* opinion be seen as an attack on the Georgia legislation and on the federal government's response thereto?

While its efforts produced the most controversial reaction, in great part due to Northern sympathy for the "civilized" Cherokees, Georgia was not alone either in its reaction or its legislation. Similar laws had been passed in other southern states, including Tennessee and Mississippi, often patterned on the Georgia laws. New York also reacted adversely to efforts at political revitalization and development among tribes of the Iroquois Confederation. In 1822 New York enacted the following statute:

> *Whereas* the Seneca, and other tribes of Indians residing within this state, have assumed the power and authority of trying and punishing, and in some cases capitally, members of their respective tribes, for supposed crimes by them done and committed in their respective reservations, and within this state. And whereas the sole and exclusive cognizance of all crimes and offences committed within this state, belongs of right to courts holden under the constitution and laws thereof, as a necessary attribute of sovereignty, except only crimes and offences cognizable in the courts deriving jurisdiction under the constitution and laws of the United States. And whereas it has become necessary, as well to protect the said Indian tribes, as to assert and maintain the jurisdiction of the courts of this state, that provision should be made in the premises: Therefore,
>
> 1. *Be it enacted by the People of the state of New York, represented in Senate and Assembly,* That the sole and exclusive jurisdiction, of trying and punishing all and every person, of whatsoever nation or tribe, for crimes and offences committed within any part of this state, except only such crimes and offences as are or may be cognizable in courts deriving jurisdiction under the constitution and laws of the United States, of right belongs to, and is exclusively vested in the courts of justice of this state, organized under the constitution and laws thereof.

New York Laws, ch. 204 (1822). For an excellent survey of the jurisdictional cases in New York, see Gunther, *Governmental Power and New York Indian Lands — A Reassessment of a Persistent Problem in Federal-State Relations*, 8 BUFF. L. REV. 1 (1958).

Even before *Cherokee Nation* and *Worcester*, many of the southeastern tribes had recognized the inability or unwillingness of the federal government to protect them from state-supported white encroachments and had signed removal treaties to emigrate west of the Mississippi River. The Creeks, for example, had been removed from Georgia a half-decade before the Cherokee removal controversy. Treaty with the Creeks, Feb. 12, 1825, 7 Stat. 237. The Choctaws and Chickasaws also had agreed to remove from other southeastern states. The Cherokees were not only the most controversial, they also were among the last tribes in the southeast to confront removal. Significantly, while the Cherokees had gone to war as recently as the War of 1812, they never seriously considered adopting the military option to resist removal that was adopted by some Seminoles in Florida.

For a brief collection of the primary historical documents surrounding the removal controversy, *see* L. FILLER & A. GUTTMAN, THE REMOVAL OF THE CHEROKEE: MANIFEST DESTINY OR NATIONAL DISHONOR (1962). For an in-depth treatment of the history surrounding the Cherokee cases, see Burke, *The Cherokee Cases, A Study in Law, Politics and Morality*, 21 STAN. L. REV. 500 (1969); Swindler, *Politics as Law: The Cherokee Cases*, 3 AM. INDIAN L. REV. 7 (1975); 2 C. WARREN, THE SUPREME COURT IN UNITED STATES HISTORY 189-239 (1923).

2. The Federal Trusteeship Over Indian Affairs: While Chief Justice Marshall's opinion in *Cherokee Nation* never uses the term, that opinion is the origin in the Supreme Court of an important and controversial notion in federal Indian law, the federal trusteeship over Indian affairs. What precisely did Marshall have in mind when he described the Indian tribes as "in a state of pupilage. Their relation to the United States resembles that of a ward to his guardian"? Did Marshall contemplate that the federal trusteeship over Indian affairs would constitute an independent source of federal authority over Indian affairs, as it was later invoked in the cases of *United States v. Kagama*, 118 U.S. 375 (1886) and *Lone Wolf v. Hitchcock*, 187 U.S. 553 (1903), both discussed in Chapter 2? Did Marshall intend the trusteeship to limit the exercise of federal authority over Indian affairs? Why, then, did he describe the Indian commerce clause as "intending to give the whole power of managing those [Indian] affairs to the government about to be instituted"? Was Marshall's description of the guardian-ward relationship between the federal government and the Indian tribes conceived to create enforceable fiduciary obligations between the parties? Was Marshall merely attempting to explain that Indian allegiance and control of Indian affairs rested in the federal government, rather than the state of Georgia?

Fiduciary relationships generally are created to protect the ward or beneficiary in a described fashion and to marshal trust assets toward a designated objective. From whom did the Indian tribes need protection? Toward what end did Chief Justice Marshall conceive that the federal trust responsibility was created?

3. Origins of the Trusteeship Concept: The concept of trust supervision over indigenous populations is not unique to the United States. Furthermore, the seeds of this legal status did not originate in Chief Justice Marshall's opinion in *Cherokee Nation*. Rather, Marshall only imparted into American law an idea that had been prevalent, if not uniformly accepted, since the sixteenth century. *See generally* Cohen, *The Spanish Origin of Indian Rights in the Law of the United States*, 31 GEO. L.J. 1 (1942); Cohen, *Original Indian Title*, 32 MINN. L. REV. 28, 44-45 (1947). In 1532 Francisco de Vitoria, a Spanish cleric and professor of theology at the University of Salamanca in Spain, delivered a series of dissertations responding to the then-prevalent arguments that the Indians were heathens and heretics who did not enjoy the rights of other humans. He advanced a series of arguments regarding Indian rights and the legitimate scope of European powers over the Indians. *See generally* F. VICTORIA, DE INDIS ET DE IURE BELLI RELECTIONES (E. Nys. ed., J. Bate trans. 1917). In a chapter entitled "On the lawful titles whereby the aborigines of America could have come into the power of Spain," Vitoria concluded his analysis of the methods by which the European powers could assume power over the Indian as follows:

> There is another title which can indeed not be asserted, but brought up for discussion, and some think it a lawful one. I dare not affirm it at all, nor do I entirely

condemn it. It is this: Although the aborigines in question are (as has been said above) not wholly unintelligent, yet they are little short of that condition, and so are unfit to found or administer a lawful State up to the standard required by human and civil claims. Accordingly they have no proper laws nor magistrates, and are not even capable of controlling their family affairs; they are without any literature or arts, not only the liberal arts, but the mechanical arts also; they have no careful agriculture and no artisans; and they lack many other conveniences, yea necessaries, of human life. It might, therefore, be maintained that in their own interests the sovereigns of Spain might undertake the administration of their country, providing them with prefects and governors for their towns, and might even give them new lords, so long as this was clearly for their benefit. I say there would be some force in this contention; for if they were all wanting in intelligence, there is no doubt that this would not only be a permissible, but also a highly proper, course to take; nay, our sovereigns would be bound to take it, just as if the natives were infants. The same principle seems to apply here to them as to people of defective intelligence; and indeed they are no whit or little better than such so far as self-government is concerned, or even than the wild beasts, for their food is not more pleasant and hardly better than that of beasts. Therefore their governance should in the same way be entrusted to people of intelligence.

Id. at 160-61. The seed of the famous English colonial phrase "the white man's burden," of course, can be found in these early clerical debates over Spanish Indian policy.

The conception of the Indians as ignorant savages without law or governance in need of supervision and protection had some popularity in America even prior to Chief Justice Marshall's ruling in *Cherokee Nation*. Ridiculing a ruling of an English tribunal that the Mohegan tribe of Connecticut was a sovereign state, William Samuel Johnson had written during the colonial period of the eighteenth century:

When the English Treated with [the Indians] it was not with Independent States (for they had no such thing as a Land Policy, nor hardly any one Circumstance essential to the existence of a state) but as with savages, whom they were to quiet and manage as well as they could, sometimes by flattery, but oftener by force. [Certainly], the English have taken Infinite Pains to Civilize and Christianize the Indians, and they sometimes flattered themselves with hopes of success, and that they should by degrees make them Men and Christians, but after all their Endeavours (except in a very few Instances) they remain but little superior in point of Civilization, to the Beasts of the Field. This notion of their being free States is perfectly ridiculous and absurd. Without Polity, laws etc. there can be no such thing as a State. The Indian had neither in any proper sense of the words. It is also Inconsistent with their own Ideas that they were always under the Guardianship of the Masons [trustees appointed by the Connecticut government to manage the affairs of the Indians].

Quoted in J. SMITH, APPEALS TO THE PRIVY COUNCIL FROM THE AMERICAN PLANTATION 434-35 n.109 (1965). Of course, this view of the Indians was the product of an ethnocentric conception of governance and laws on the part of the colonial powers. The Indian tribes did in fact have clear social, political, and legal institutions. *See, e.g.,* J. REID, A LAW OF BLOOD: THE PRIMITIVE LAW OF THE CHEROKEE NATION (1970); J. REID, A BETTER KIND OF HATCHET: LAW, TRADE, AND DIPLOMACY IN THE CHEROKEE NATION DURING THE EARLY YEARS OF EUROPEAN CONTACT (1976); K. LLEWELLYN & E. HOEBEL, THE CHEYENNE WAY: CONFLICT AND CASE LAW IN PRIMITIVE JURISPRUDENCE (1941). Nevertheless, the non-Indian perception of the uncivilized formlessness of Indian society helped create the federal trusteeship over Indian affairs. Myths, nevertheless, die hard. For Senator Lumpkin and many Georgians, it appeared that only white men and their descendants were capable of Anglo-American style western government and that, if the Cherokee had adopted such forms, it must be because non-Indians or mixed-bloods had assumed leadership roles in the tribe. Even as the Cherokees were adopting western forms of governance, Lumpkin defended their removal by erroneously arguing that "[a] large portion of the full blooded Cherokee still remain a poor degraded race of human beings. [However], a very small portion of the real Indians are in a state of improvement, whilst their lords and rulers are white men, and the descendants of white men, enjoying the fat of the land, and enjoying exclusively the Government annuities, upon which they foster, feed, and clothe the most violent and dangerous enemies of our civil institutions." Quoted in FILLER & GUTTMAN, *supra*, at 37. While some mixed-bloods certainly had risen to positions of prominence during the post-war Cherokee revitalization, many Cherokee political leaders of the day, such as Elias Boudinot, the first editor of *The Cherokee Phoenix* and a member of the Cherokee National Council, were full bloods educated by Christian missionaries or in eastern schools.

During the colonial period, Massachusetts Bay, Connecticut, and other colonies sometimes formally appointed non-Indian trustees to supervise Indian lands, particularly lands of tribes conquered during King Philip's War of 1675 and earlier Indian conflicts. Indeed, after similar Indian wars in Virginia, the Commonwealth entered into treaties that established the conquered tribes of that region, principally remnants of the Powhatan Confederation, as "tributary tribes," formally paying feudal tribute to the colonial government. Jefferson specifically referred to the Virginia tributary or feudatory tribes when he proposed the somewhat confused Indian affairs clause of the Articles of Confederation to the Continental Congress. In *Worcester v. Georgia*, decided the year after *Cherokee Nation*, Chief Justice Marshall further clarified his "domestic dependent nation" phrase as follows:

> A weak state, in order to provide for its safety, may place itself under the protection of one more powerful, without stripping itself of the right of government, and ceasing to be a state. Examples of this kind are not wanting in Europe. "Tributary and feudatory states," says Vattel, "do not thereby cease to be sovereign and independent states, so long as self-government and sovereign and independent authority are left in the administration of the state." At the present day, more than one state may be considered as holding its right of self-government under the guarantee and protection of one or more allies.

Today, perhaps the best and most well-known remaining European feudatory state is the Principality of Monaco, which relies on the protection of France. While Chief Justice Marshall's description of Indian tribes as tributary or feudatory tribes was not new, what was novel in Marshall's argument was that he seemed to refer to *all* tribes, rather than merely tribes that had been conquered or had otherwise affirmatively, voluntarily established a dependency relationship with the federal government. While language in the Treaty of Hopewell of 1784 and Treaty of Holston of 1791 arguably might have supported such claims for the Cherokees, Marshall seems to phrase his argument in *Cherokee Nation* and in *Worcester*, which follows, as if it applied to all Indian tribes irrespective of the history of their dealings with the United States. What national concerns might have animated such pretentious claims?

Given the modern progress Indians in the United States have made toward governmental institutions structured along Anglo-American models (see Chapter 3), does the federal trusteeship over Indian affairs have a continued viable role to play in the regulation of Indian affairs? Did it make sense even as applied to the Cherokee in 1830? As you review the remainder of the materials in this book, analyze what role, if any, the federal trusteeship should play in Indian law.

4. The Trusteeship as a Source of Rights: In light of the last paragraph of the opinion in *Cherokee Nation*, can it be said that Chief Justice Marshall intended the federal trusteeship over Indian affairs to create enforceable legal rights and obligations? By what agency could such legal rights and obligations be enforced? If the trusteeship creates no enforceable legal relationships, what role does it play in federal Indian law?

WORCESTER v. GEORGIA

31 U.S. (6 Pet.) 515 (1832)

[The *Worcester* case involved the criminal prosecution and conviction of a number of white missionaries to the Cherokees, including Samuel A. Worcester, for violating an 1830 law enacted by the legislature of the state of Georgia that required any person residing within the Cherokee Nation to have a license or permit from the Georgia governor and to take an oath of loyalty. Georgia law also purported to annex the Cherokee Nation to the state, extend state law over the Cherokees, and disqualify Indians from testifying in state court. Similar laws were passed in other southeastern states, including Mississippi and Tennessee. The appeal of Worcester's criminal conviction reached the Court after the tribe failed in *Cherokee Nation* to establish original jurisdiction in the United States Supreme Court to contest the legality of Georgia's unilateral efforts to extend its laws to that portion of the Cherokee Nation located within its boundaries and to appropriate Cherokee lands.

[As a missionary, Worcester was in the Cherokee Nation expending federal "civilization" funds under the Indian Trade and Intercourse Act of 1802. He also was the United States postmaster at New Echota. When Worcester, other missionaries, and certain other whites living in the Cherokee Nation were again arrested for violating the Georgia laws, the local court dismissed the prosecution, believing that they were agents of the federal government since they were expending federal funds. After the Governor of Georgia consulted federal authorities, a ruling was issued that they were not federal agents and Worcester was further dismissed, at Georgia's request, from his position as federal postmaster in order to clear the way for his prosecution. After approximately 10 whites residing in the Cherokee Nation without entry permits from Georgia were arrested, all were offered pardons on condition of swearing an oath to uphold Georgia law and leaving the Cherokee Nation. All accepted the pardons except two missionaries — Worcester and Butler. They were convicted of violating the Georgia legislation and sentenced to 4 years in prison. They ultimately appealed their criminal convictions to the Supreme Court, claiming that the state of Georgia had no legitimate authority over the Cherokee Nation.

[Even before *Worcester* was decided, the Court had good reason to doubt that Georgia would comply with its mandate. Earlier, another Cherokee removal test case involving the murder conviction of a Cherokee named Corn, or George, Tassel had come before the Court. Notwithstanding a Supreme Court stay of execution, Georgia had hung Tassel, thereby mooting the case.]

Mr. Chief Justice MARSHALL delivered the opinion of the Court.

This cause, in every point of view in which it can be placed, is of the deepest interest. The defendant is a state, a member of the Union, which has exercised the powers of government over a people who deny its jurisdiction, and are under the protection of the United States. The plaintiff is a citizen of the State of Vermont, condemned to hard labour for four years in the penitentiary of Georgia; under colour of an act which he alleges to be repugnant to the Constitution, laws, and treaties of the United States. The legislative power of a state, the controlling power of the Constitution and laws of the United States, the rights, if they have any, the political existence of a once numerous and powerful people, the personal liberty of a citizen, are all involved in the subject now to be considered.

[It has been argued] that the acts of the Legislature of Georgia seize on the whole Cherokee country, parcel it out among the neighbouring counties of the state, extend her code over the whole country, abolish its institutions and its laws, and annihilate its political existence. [E]xtra-territorial power of every legislature being limited in its action to its own citizens or subjects, the very passage of this act is an assertion of jurisdiction over the Cherokee Nation, and of the rights and powers consequent on jurisdiction. The first step, then, in the inquiry which the Constitution and laws impose on this Court, is an examination of the rightfulness of this claim.

America, separated from Europe by a wide ocean, was inhabited by a distinct people, divided into separate nations, independent of each other and of the rest of the world, having institutions of their own, and governing themselves by their own laws. It is difficult to comprehend the proposition that the inhabitants of either quarter of the globe could have rightful original claims of dominion over the inhabitants of the other, or over the lands they occupied; or that the discovery of either by the other should give the discoverer rights in the country discovered which annulled the pre-existing rights of its ancient possessors. After lying concealed for a series of ages, the enterprise of Europe, guided by nautical science, conducted some of her adventurous sons into this western world. They found it in possession of a people who had made small progress in agriculture or manufactures, and whose general employment was war, hunting, and fishing. Did these adventurers, by sailing along the coast and occasionally landing on it, acquire for the several governments to whom they belonged, or by whom they were commissioned, a rightful property in the soil from the Atlantic to the Pacific; or rightful dominion over the numerous people who occupied it? Or has nature, or the great Creator of all things, conferred these rights over hunters and fishermen, on agriculturists and manufacturers? But power, war, conquest, give rights, which, after possession, are conceded by the world; and which can never be controverted by those on whom they descend. We proceed, then, to the actual state of things, having glanced at their origin, because holding it in our recollection might shed some light on existing pretensions....

Certain it is, that our history furnishes no example, from the first settlement of our country, of any attempt on the part of the crown, to interfere with the internal affairs of the Indians, further than to keep out the agents of foreign powers, who, as traders or otherwise, might seduce them into foreign alliances. The king purchased their lands, when they were willing to sell, at a price they were willing to take, but never coerced a surrender of them. He also purchased their alliance and dependence by subsidies, but never intruded into the interior of their affairs, nor interfered with their self-government, so far as respected themselves only.

The general views of Great Britain, with regard to the Indians, were detailed by Mr. Stuart, superintendent of Indian affairs, in a speech delivered at Mobile, in presence of several persons of distinction, soon after the peace of 1763. Towards the conclusion he says, "Lastly, I inform you that it is the king's order to all his governors and subjects, to treat Indians with justice and humanity, and to forbear all encroachments on the territories allotted to them; accordingly, all individuals are prohibited from purchasing any of your lands; but as you know that, as your white brethren cannot feed you when you visit them, unless you give them ground to plant, it is expected that you will cede lands to the king for that purpose. But whenever you shall be pleased to surrender any of your territories to his majesty, it must be done, for the future, at a public meeting of your nation, when the governors of the provinces, or the superintendent shall be present, and obtain the consent of all your people. The boundaries of your hunting-grounds will be accurately fixed, and no settlement permitted to be made upon them. As you may be assured that all treaties with your people will be faithfully kept, so it is expected that you, also, will be careful strictly to observe them."

The proclamation issued by the King of Great Britain, in 1763, soon after the ratification of the articles of peace, forbids the governors of any of the colonies to grant warrants of survey, or pass patents upon any lands whatever, which, not having been ceded to, or purchased by, us (the king), as aforesaid, are reserved to the said Indians, or any of them. The proclamation proceeds: "And we do further declare it to be our royal will and pleasure, for the present, as aforesaid, to reserve, under our sovereignty, protection and dominion, for the use of the said Indians, all the lands and territories lying to the westward of the sources of the rivers which fall into the sea from the west and northwest as aforesaid; and we do hereby strictly forbid on pain of our displeasure, all our loving subjects from making any purchases or settlements whatever, or taking possession of any of the lands above reserved, without our special leave and license for that purpose first obtained. And we do further strictly enjoin and require all persons whatever, who have, either wilfully or inadvertently, seated themselves upon any lands within the countries above described, or upon any other lands which, not having been ceded to, or purchased by us, are still reserved to the said Indians, as aforesaid, forthwith to remove themselves from such settlements."

[In 1783 the Cherokee Nations and the United States concluded the Treaty of Hopewell.] The third article acknowledges the Cherokees to be under the protection of the United States of America, and of no other power.

This stipulation is found in Indian treaties, generally. It was introduced into their treaties with Great Britain; and may probably be found in those with other European powers. Its origin may be traced to the nature of their connexion with those powers; and its true meaning is discerned in their relative situation.

The general law of European sovereigns, respecting their claims in America, limited the intercourse of Indians, in a great degree, to the particular potentate whose ultimate right of domain was acknowledged by the others. This was the general state of things in time of peace. It was sometimes changed in war. The consequence was, that their supplies were derived chiefly from that nation, and their trade confined to it. Goods, indispensable to their comfort, in the shape of presents, were received from the same hand. What was of still more importance, the strong hand of government was interposed to restrain the disorderly and licentious from intrusions into their country, from encroachments on their lands, and from those acts of violence which were often attended by reciprocal murder. The Indians perceived in this protection only what was beneficial to themselves — an engagement to punish aggressions on them. It involved, practically, no claim to their lands, no dominion over their persons. It merely bound the nation to the British crown, as a dependent ally, claiming the protection of a powerful friend and neighbour, and receiving the advantages of that protection, without involving a surrender of their national character.

This is the true meaning of the stipulation, and is undoubtedly the sense in which it was made. Neither the British government, nor the Cherokees, ever understood it otherwise.

The same stipulation entered into with the United States, is undoubtedly to be construed in the same manner. They receive the Cherokee nation into their favor and protection. The Cherokees acknowledge themselves to be under the protection of the United States, and of no other power. Protection does not imply the destruction of the protected. The manner in which this stipulation was understood by the American government, is explained by the language and acts of our first president.

The fourth article draws the boundary between the Indians and the citizens of the United States. But, in describing this boundary, the term "allotted" and the term "hunting ground" are used.

Is it reasonable to suppose, that the Indians, who could not write, and most probably could not read, who certainly were not critical judges of our language, should distinguish the word "allotted" from the words "marked out." The actual subject of contract was the dividing line between the two nations, and their attention may very well be supposed to have been confined to that subject. When, in fact, they were ceding lands to the United States, and describing the extent of their cession, it may very well be supposed that they might not understand the term employed, as indicating that, instead of granting, they were receiving lands. If the term would admit of no other signification, which is not conceded, its being misunderstood is so apparent, results so necessarily from the whole transaction; that it must, we think, be taken in the sense in which it was most obviously used.

So with respect to the words "hunting grounds." Hunting was at that time the principal occupation of the Indians, and their land was more used for that purpose than for any other. It could not, however, be supposed, that any intention existed of restricting the full use of the lands they reserved.

To the United States, it could be a matter of no concern, whether their whole territory was devoted to hunting grounds, or whether an occasional village, and an occasional corn field, interrupted, and gave some variety to the scene.

These terms had been used in their treaties with Great Britain, and had never been misunderstood. They had never been supposed to imply a right in the

British government to take their lands, or to interfere with their internal government.

The fifth article withdraws the protection of the United States from any citizen who has settled, or shall settle, on the lands allotted to the Indians, for their hunting grounds; and stipulates that if he shall not remove within six months the Indians may punish him.

The sixth and seventh articles stipulate for the punishment of the citizens of either country, who may commit offences on or against the citizens of the other. The only inference to be drawn from them is, that the United States considered the Cherokees as a nation.

The ninth article is in these words: "For the benefit and comfort of the Indians, and for the prevention of injuries or oppressions on the part of the citizens or Indians, the United States in Congress assembled, shall have the sole and exclusive right of regulating the trade with the Indians, and managing all their affairs, as they think proper."

To construe the expression "managing all their affairs," into a surrender of self-government, would be, we think, a perversion of their necessary meaning, and a departure from the construction which has been uniformly put on them. The great subject of the article is the Indian trade. The influence it gave, made it desirable that Congress should possess it. The commissioners brought forward the claim, with the profession that their motive was "the benefit and comfort of the Indians, and the prevention of injuries or oppressions." This may be true, as respects the regulation of their trade, and as respects the regulation of all affairs connected with their trade, but cannot be true, as respects the management of all their affairs. The most important of these, are the cession of their lands, and security against intruders. Is it credible, that they should have considered themselves as surrendering to the United States the right to dictate their future cessions, and the terms on which they should be made? or to compel their submission to the violence of disorderly and licentious intruders? It is equally inconceivable that they could have supposed themselves, by a phrase thus slipped into an article, on another and most interesting subject, to have divested themselves of the right of self-government on subjects not connected with trade. Such a measure could not be "for their benefit and comfort," or for "the prevention of injuries and oppression." Such a construction would be inconsistent with the spirit of this and of all subsequent treaties; especially of those articles which recognise the right of the Cherokees to declare hostilities, and to make war. It would convert a treaty of peace covertly into an act, annihilating the political existence of one of the parties. Had such a result been intended, it would have been openly avowed.

[Article 2 of the Treaty of Holston of July 1791] repeats the important acknowledgement, that the Cherokee nation is under the protection of the United States of America, and of no other sovereign whosoever.

The meaning of this has already been explained. The Indian nations were, from their situation, necessarily dependent on some foreign potentate for the supply of their essential wants, and for their protection from lawless and injurious intrusions into their country. That power was naturally termed their protector. They had been arranged under the protection of Great Britain: but the extinguishment of the British power in their neighborhood, and the establishment of that of the United States in its place, lead naturally to the declaration, on the part of the Cherokees, that they were under the protection of the United States, and no other power. They assumed the relation with the United States, which had before subsisted with Great Britain. This relation was that of a nation claiming and receiving the protection of one more powerful, not that of individuals abandoning their national character, and submitting as subjects to the laws of a master.

[The] treaty [of Holston], thus explicitly recognizing the national character of the Cherokees, and their right of self government; thus guarantying their lands; assuming the duty of protection, and of course pledging the faith of the United States for that protection; has been frequently renewed, and is now in full force.

To the general pledge of protection have been added several specific pledges, deemed valuable by the Indians. Some of these restrain the citizens of the United States from encroachments on the Cherokee country, and provide for the punishment of intruders.

From the commencement of our government, Congress has passed acts to regulate trade and intercourse with the Indians; which treat them as nations, respect their rights, and manifest a firm purpose to afford that protection which treaties stipulate. All these acts, and especially that of 1802, which is still in force, manifestly consider the several Indian nations as distinct political communities, having territorial boundaries, within which their authority is exclusive, and having a right to all the lands within those boundaries, which is not only acknowledged, but guarantied by the United States.

[These] treaties and the laws of the United States contemplate the Indian territory as completely separated from that of the states; and provide that all intercourse with them shall be carried on exclusively by the government of the Union. Is this the rightful exercise of power, or is it usurpation?

While these states were colonies, this power, in its utmost extent, was admitted to reside in the crown. When our revolutionary struggle commenced, Congress was composed of an assemblage of deputies acting under specific powers granted by the legislatures, or conventions of the several colonies. It was a great popular movement, not perfectly organized; nor were the respective powers of those who were intrusted with the management of affairs accurately defined. The necessities of our situation produced a general conviction that those measures which concerned all, must be transacted by a body in which the representatives of all were assembled, and which could command the confidence of all: Congress, therefore, was considered as invested with all the powers of war and peace, and Congress dissolved our connection with the mother country, and declared these United Colonies to be independent states. Without any written definition of powers, they employed diplomatic agents to represent the United States at the several courts of England; offered to negotiate treaties with them, and did actually negotiate treaties with France. From the same necessity, and on the same principles, Congress assumed the management of Indian affairs; first in the name of these United Colonies, and afterwards in the name of the United States. Early attempts were made at negotiation, and to regulate trade with them. These not proving successful, war was carried on under the direction, and with the forces of the United States, and the efforts to make peace by treaty were earnest and incessant. The confederation found Congress in the exercise of the same powers of peace and war, in our relations with Indian nations, as with those of Europe.

Such was the state of things when the confederation was adopted. That instrument surrendered the powers of peace and war to Congress and prohibited them to the states, respectively, unless a state be actually invaded, "or shall have received certain advice of a resolution being formed by some nation of Indians to invade such state, and the danger is so imminent as not to admit of delay till the United States in Congress assembled can be consulted." This instrument also gave the United States in Congress assembled the sole and exclusive right of "regulating the trade and managing all the affairs with the Indians, not members of any of the states: provided, that the legislative power of any state within its own limits be not infringed or violated."

The ambiguous phrases which follow the grant of power to the United States were so construed by the States of North Carolina and Georgia as to annul the power itself. The discontents and confusion resulting from these conflicting claims produced representations to Congress, which were referred to a committee, who made their report in 1787. The report does not assent to the construction of the two states, but recommends an accommodation, by liberal cessions of territory, or by an admission on their part of the powers claimed by Congress. The correct exposition of this article is rendered unnecessary by the adoption of our existing Constitution. That instrument confers on Congress the powers of war and peace; of making treaties, and of regulating commerce with foreign nations, and among the several states, and with the Indian tribes. These powers comprehend all that is required for the regulation of our intercourse with the Indians. They are not limited by any restrictions on their free actions. The shackles imposed on this power, in the confederation, are discarded.

The Indian nations had always been considered as distinct, independent political communities, retaining their original natural rights, as the undisputed possessors of the soil from time immemorial, with the single exception of that imposed by irresistible power, which excluded them from intercourse with any other European potentate than the first discoverer of the coast of the particular region claimed; and this was a restriction which those European potentates imposed on themselves, as well as on the Indians. The very term "nation," so generally applied to them, means "a people distinct from others." The Constitution, by declaring treaties already made, as well as those to be made, to be the supreme law of the land, has adopted and sanctioned the previous treaties with the Indian nations, and consequently admits their rank among those powers who are capable of making treaties. The words "treaty" and "nation" are words of our own language, selected in our diplomatic and legislative proceedings, by ourselves, having each a definite and well understood meaning. We have applied them to Indians, as we have applied them to the other nations of the earth. They are applied to all in the same sense.

[The articles repeated in treaties with the Cherokee Nation] are associated with others, recognizing their title to self government. The very fact of repeated treaties with them recognizes it; and the settled doctrine of the law of nations is, that a weaker power does not surrender its independence — its right to self government, by associating with a stronger, and taking its protection. A weak state, in order to provide for its safety, may place itself under the protection of one more powerful, without stripping itself of the right of government, and ceasing to be a state. Examples of this kind are not wanting in Europe. "Tributary and feudatory states," says Vattel, "do not thereby cease to be sovereign and independent states, so long as self government and sovereign and independent authority are left in the administration of the state." At the present day, more than one state may be considered as holding its right of self government under the guarantee and protection of one or more allies.

The Cherokee nation, then, is a distinct community, occupying its own territory, with boundaries accurately described, in which the laws of Georgia can have no force, and which the citizens of Georgia have no right to enter, but with the assent of the Cherokees themselves, or in conformity with treaties, and with the acts of Congress. The whole intercourse between the United States and this nation, is, by our Constitution and laws, vested in the government of the United States. The act of the state of Georgia, under which the plaintiff in error was prosecuted, is, consequently, void, and the judgment a nullity. Can this court revise and reverse it?

If the objection to the system of legislation, lately adopted by the legislature of Georgia, in relation to the Cherokee nation, was confined to its extra-territorial operation, the objection, though complete, so far as respected mere right, would give this court no power over the subject. But it goes much further. If the view which has been taken be correct, and we think it is, the acts of Georgia are repugnant to the Constitution, laws and treaties of the United States. They interfere forcibly with the relations established between the United States and the Cherokee nation, the regulation of which, according to the settled principles of our Constitution, are committed exclusively to the government of the Union.

They are in direct hostility with treaties, repeated in a succession of years, which mark out the boundary that separates the Cherokee country from Georgia; guaranty to them all the land within their boundary; solemnly pledge the faith of the United States to restrain their citizens from trespassing on it; and recognize the pre-existing power of the nation to govern itself. They are in hostility with the acts of Congress for regulating this intercourse, and giving effect to the treaties. The forcible seizure and abduction of the plaintiff in error, who was residing in the nation, with its permission, and by authority of the President of the United States, is also a violation of the acts which authorize the chief magistrate to exercise this authority.

[T]he judgment of the superior court for the county of Gwinnett, in the state of Georgia, condemning Samuel A. Worcester to hard labor in the penitentiary of the state of Georgia, for four years, was pronounced by that court under color of a law which is void, as being repugnant to the Constitution, treaties and laws of the United States, and ought, therefore, to be reversed and annulled.

Mr. Justice McLean. As this case involves principles of the highest importance, and may lead to consequences which shall have an enduring influence on the institutions of this country; and as there are some points in the case on which I wish to state, distinctly, my opinion, I embrace the privilege of doing so. With the decision just given, I concur.

[T]he Indians sustain a peculiar relation to the United States. They do not constitute, as was decided at the last term, a foreign state, so as to claim the right to sue in the supreme court of the United States; and yet, having the right of self-government, they, in some sense, form a state. In the management of their internal concerns, they are dependent on no power. They punish offences, under their own laws, and in doing so, they are responsible to no earthly tribunal. They make war, and form treaties of peace. The exercise of these and other powers, gives to them a distinct character as a people, and constitutes them, in some respects, a state, although they may not be admitted to possess the right of soil.

By various treaties, the Cherokees have placed themselves under the protection of the United States; they have agreed to trade with no other people, nor to invoke the protection of any other sovereignty. But such engagements do not divest them of the right of self-government, nor destroy their capacity to enter into treaties or compacts. Every state is more or less dependent on those which surround it; but, unless this dependence shall extend so far as to merge the political existence of the protected people into that of their protectors, they may still constitute a state. They may exercise the powers not relinquished, and bind themselves as a distinct and separate community.

[No one would doubt] that, so far as the Indians, as distinct communities, have formed a connection with the federal government, by treaties; that such connection is political, and is equally binding on both parties. This cannot be questioned, except upon the ground, that in making these treaties, the federal government has transcended the treaty-making power. Such an objection, it is true, has been stated, but it is one of modern invention, which arises out of local circumstances; and is not only opposed to the uniform practice of the government, but also to the letter and spirit of the constitution.

But the inquiry may be made, is there no end to the exercise of this power over Indians, within the limits of a state, by the general government? The answer is, that, in its nature, it must be limited by circumstances. If a tribe of Indians shall become so degraded or reduced in numbers, as to lose the power of self-government, the protection of the local law, of necessity, must be extended over them. The point at which this exercise of power by a state would be proper, need not now be considered; if, indeed, it be a judicial question. Such a question does not seem to arise in this case. So long as treaties and laws remain in full force, and apply to Indian nations, exercising the right of self-government, within the limits of a state, the judicial power can exercise no discretion in refusing to give effect to those laws, when questions arise under them, unless they shall be deemed unconstitutional. The exercise of the power of self-government by the Indians, within a state, is undoubtedly contemplated to be temporary. This is shown by the settled policy of the government, in the extinguishment of their title, and especially, by the compact with the state of Georgia. It is a question, not of abstract right, but of public policy. I do not mean to say, that the same moral rule which should regulate the affairs of private life, should not be regarded by communities or nations. But a sound national policy does require, that the Indian tribes within our states should exchange their territories, upon equitable principles, or eventually consent to become amalgamated in our political communities. At best, they can enjoy a very limited independence within the boundaries of a state, and such a residence must always subject them to encroachments from the settlements around them; and their existence within a state, as a separate and independent community, may seriously embarrass or obstruct the operation of the state laws. If, therefore, it would be inconsistent with the political welfare of the states, and the social advance of their citizens, that an independent and permanent power should exist within their limits, this power must give way to the greater power which surrounds it, or seek its exercise beyond the sphere of state authority.

This state of things can only be produced by a co-operation of the state and federal governments. The latter has the exclusive regulation of intercourse with the Indians; and so long as this power shall be exercised, it cannot be obstructed by the state. It is a power given by the constitution, and sanctioned by the most solemn acts of both the federal and state governments; consequently, it cannot be abrogated at the will of a state. It is one of the powers parted with by the states, and vested in the federal government. But if a contingency shall occur, which shall render the Indians who reside in a state, incapable of self-government, either by moral degradation, or a reduction of their numbers, it would undoubtedly be in the power of a state government, to extend to them the *aegis* of its laws. Under such circumstances, the agency of the general government, of necessity, must cease. But if it shall be the policy of the government, to withdraw its protection from the Indians who reside within the limits of the respective states, and who not only claim the right of self-government, but have uniformly exercised it; the laws and treaties which impose duties and obligations on the general government should be abrogated by the powers competent to do so. So long as those laws and treaties exist, having been formed within the sphere of the federal powers, they must be respected and enforced by the appropriate organs of the federal government.

[Dissenting opinion of Justice Baldwin omitted.]

NOTES

1. **The *Worcester* Decision:** In *Worcester* what was it that rendered the state law invalid and unconstitutional? Was it merely the continued existence of Cherokee tribal sovereignty, or was it the federal law and policy protecting that tribal sovereignty? If the latter, what federal law controls the legal issue? Was the commitment to the federal government of the power over Indian affairs in the Indian commerce clause sufficient to control the issue of the scope of state authority? In the absence of affirmative congressional legislation or treaties, would the negative implications of the Indian commerce clause preclude state control over resident Indian tribal populations under Chief Justice Marshall's analysis? What about under Justice McLean's analysis?

What role did the treaties with the Cherokee play in the Marshall opinion? Did the treaties expressly purport to resolve the jurisdictional question with which the Court was confronted? How did Chief Justice Marshall approach the problem of construction of the treaties with the Cherokee for the purposes of resolving the jurisdictional question?

What role did the Trade and Intercourse Acts play in the Marshall opinion? Did they explicitly resolve the jurisdictional question posed by the case? How, then, were they relevant to the final outcome of the litigation?

2. Indians as Litigants: Together with the *Cherokee Nation* decision, *Worcester* marks an important constitutional milestone. In these two cases an Indian tribe, a domestic dependent nation, had initially gone to court, relying upon American judicial processes to prevent white encroachment and preserve its culture and government, and ultimately prevailed, albeit in a test case resulting from state criminal prosecution of non-Indian missionaries. Only once before, in the *Mohegan Indians* case, a land title litigation conducted for 70 years before the Privy Council during the colonial period, had an Indian tribe or its allies resorted to litigation rather than war or diplomacy to protect its cultural and political heritage.

That the Cherokee Nation should set this precedent is not surprising since, as noted above, it was the tribe that was the most open to absorbing and applying in a tribal context the elements of European civilization that it found valuable.

3. The Cherokee Removal Cases and Constitutional Crisis: Conflict between state and tribal government was not, however, all that was involved in *Worcester.* The unilateral legislative action of the state of Georgia, and similar actions taken simultaneously by Mississippi, Tennessee, and other states, were in part attributable to the election of Andrew Jackson as President. Jackson was perceived as an avowed enemy of Indian interests in the affected states (despite his military alliances with some of the affected tribes), and these states properly perceived that the federal government under Jackson's stewardship would not interfere in their unilateral extension of state authority over the tribes. Indeed, at least one historian has attributed to Jackson the following famous retort to the *Worcester* decision: "John Marshall has made his decision; now let him enforce it." H. GREELEY, AMERICAN CONFLICT 106 (1884). While the story about the remark is probably apocryphal, the statement accurately captures the prevailing political climate and the conflict between the executive and judicial branches wrought by the *Worcester* case. *See* 2 C. WARREN, THE SUPREME COURT IN UNITED STATES HISTORY 189-239 (1923); M. JAMES, THE LIFE OF ANDREW JACKSON 603-04 (1938). Indeed, writing in 1923, Professor Charles Warren called the Cherokee cases "the most serious crises in the history of the Court." *Id.* at 189. For several years the Supreme Court decision was simply ignored — an unprecedented constitutional phenomena, then and now. Immediate constitutional crisis was averted, however, when the Court adjourned in 1832, a few days after issuing the opinion and special mandate in *Worcester,* without issuing the necessary order to a federal marshal to secure Worcester's release. During the interim, until the Court reconvened for its 1833 Term, successful efforts were made to secure a pardon from the Georgia governor in order to compromise the litigation and avert a constitutional confrontation. At the same time, the nation was also embroiled in the South Carolina tariff nullification controversy, and the Jackson administration sought to avoid constitutional confrontation on Cherokee removal.

While Worcester and the Cherokee Nation won the battle of legal doctrine, they ultimately lost the war of federal policy in the halls of Congress and in the White House. Despite Chief Justice Marshall's ringing rhetoric about the legally protected separate sovereign status of the Cherokee Nation, the Cherokees were finally forced to assent to removal when the federal government refused to protect the tribe from political, cultural, and physical encroachment by the state of Georgia and its citizens. Treaty with the Cherokees, Dec. 29, 1835, 7 Stat. 478. *See generally* F. PRUCHA, AMERICAN INDIAN POLICY IN THE FORMATIVE YEARS 213-73 (1962); G. FOREMAN, INDIAN REMOVAL 229-312 (1932); R. STRICKLAND, FIRE AND THE SPIRITS 40-72 (1975). This removal led to the Cherokee's famous Trail of Tears, during which many Cherokee died on the harsh winter road to the Indian Territory. The last Cherokee party left on December 4, 1838, but some Cherokee literally headed for the hills in North Carolina to escape removal, and their descendants can still be found there comprising the only remaining Cherokee reservation — the Eastern Band of the Cherokee. The racism of the Cherokee removal controversy is evident by the fate of articles 12 and 13 of the Treaty of New Echota. Those provisions guaranteed that Cherokees in North Carolina, Tennessee, and Alabama who wished to remain and become citizens of the state could retain a farm of 160 acres, including their improvements, and become subject to state law and that similar reservations under prior treaties would be honored. President Jackson refused to accede even to these provisions, and they were abrogated in a supplemental agreement with the Cherokee dated March 1, 1836.

Article 5 of the Treaty of New Echota provided:

The United States hereby covenant and agree that the lands ceded to the Cherokee nation ... in no future time without their consent, be included within the territorial limits or jurisdiction of any State or Territory. But they shall secure to the Cherokee nation the right by their national councils to make and carry into effect all such laws as they may deem necessary for the government and protection of the persons and property within their country belonging to their people or such persons as have connected themselves with them: provided always that they shall not be inconsistent with the Constitution of the United States and such acts of Congress as have been or may be passed regulating trade and intercourse with the Indians; and also, that they shall not be considered as extending to such citizens and army of the United States as may travel or reside in the Indian country by permission according to the laws and regulations established by the Government of the same.

While the government of the Cherokee Nation, like the governments of most of the removed tribes in the Indian Territory, flourished and became quite westernized during the last half of the nineteenth century, this treaty promise was broken by the Curtis Act of 1898, ch. 517, 30 Stat. 495, which, as prelude to Oklahoma statehood, purported to suspend the Cherokee government and nullify the force of Cherokee law. It purported to do the same for the governments of the other four members of the so-called Five Civilized Tribes (Creek, Choctaw, Chickasaw, and Seminole).

4. Indian Islands and State Sovereignty: What significance should be attached to Justice McLean's suggestion that if "a tribe of Indians shall become so degraded or reduced in numbers, as to lose the power of self-government, the protection of the local law, of necessity, must be extended over them." Does this principle of state sovereignty by "necessity" make sense? If so, which government or branch of government has the responsibility of ascertaining the degraded status of the tribe and its loss of self-governing powers? Can the state legislatures or governors be trusted with final authority to ascertain the Indian's abandonment of tribal status? Is a finding of detribalization of an Indian society a proper function for the federal courts?

Not all jurists of Marshall's time perceived the Indian tribes as separate, autonomous, self-governing political groups. Justice McLean's ambivalent position doubted the long-term ability of Indian tribes to survive as separate sovereign entities when surrounded by the governments of non-Indian communities. While sitting as a circuit judge, Justice McLean later had an opportunity to implement his ideas partially. In *United States v. Cisna*, 25 F. Cas. 422 (C.C. Ohio 1835) (No. 14,795), he held that the federal courts lacked jurisdiction over an offense committed against an Indian on the Wyandot reserve in Ohio because the Wyandot reservation had become surrounded by and intermixed with white settlements and had become subject to state law, at least for white inhabitants, through the passage of a state statute. Thus, McLean held that the provisions of the 1802 Trade and Intercourse Act proscribing larceny of Indian property governed only non-Indians who committed crimes on remote Indian settlements and were therefore inoperative on the Wyandot reserve. Similarly, in *United States v. Bailey*, 24 F. Cas. 937 (C.C. Tenn. 1834) (No. 14,495), Justice McLean, sitting as a circuit judge, dismissed a murder indictment against a white person for the murder of another white person in Cherokee country, stating that the federal power to regulate commerce with the Indian tribes could not constitutionally reach such a crime. Significantly, in each of these cases the accused was a non-Indian. Note that in implementing his earlier dicta McLean was not holding that state laws could be extended to Indians within the states. Indeed, in *Bailey* McLean said, "The power of Congress is limited to the regulation of a commercial intercourse, with such tribes that exist, as a distinct community, governed by their own laws, and resting for their protection on the faith of treaties and laws of the Union." 24 F. Cas. at 939.

While Justice McLean's efforts to extend state laws to Indian lands were limited to non-Indians, some of the state courts that sought to implement his views during the nineteenth century extended the principle to Indians as well. In *State v. Foreman*, 16 Tenn. 256 (1835), the court affirmed the jurisdiction of the state courts over a murder committed by a Cherokee Indian in Indian country, basing its decision primarily on the principle that the Cherokee Nation had been conquered and, under accepted principles of international law was thereby subjected to the laws of the conquering nation. Similarly, in *State v. Doxtater*, 47 Wis. 278, 2 N.W. 439 (1879), the court affirmed the jurisdiction of state authorities to try an Oneida Indian for the crime of adultery occurring on the Oneida reservation.* Reasoning that the power to punish Indians for crimes committed against white persons had been exercised by the Wisconsin territorial courts prior to statehood, the court concluded that these Indians were therefore not an independent tribe subject only to their own laws. Consequently, the court concluded that punishment of offenses committed by Indians in Indian country fell within the reserved rights of the states.

While these examples do not reflect the modern state of the law on state jurisdiction, they highlight the continuing debate during the early nineteenth century over the legal status of Indian tribes within the Union and the states and suggest that Chief Justice Marshall's assumptions about Indian legal autonomy were not uniformly shared.

5. Proposals for Indian Statehood: In light of Chief Justice Marshall's comments in *Johnson v. M'Intosh* and *Worcester* regarding the inability of the European colonists to absorb the native population, consider the historical fact that proposals for the formation of an Indian state frequently were voiced in the late eighteenth and nineteenth centuries. The idea of an Indian state, while never fulfilled, is almost as old as the nation. Article VI of the Treaty of Sept. 17, 1778, with the Delawares, 7 Stat. 13, one of the first treaties the newly independent government of the United States entered into with an Indian tribe, provided:

> And it is further agreed on between the contracting parties should it for the future be
> found conducive for the mutual interest of both parties to invite any other tribes who

---

*The Wisconsin Supreme Court later recognized the error of its decision in *Doxtater* and overruled that decision in *State v. Rufus*, 205 Wis. 317, 237 N.W. 67 (1931).

have been friends to the interest of the United States, to join the present confederation, and to form a state whereof the Delaware nation shall be the head, and have a
representation in Congress ....

Echoing an earlier treaty promise to the Delaware in 1778, article 7 of the
Treaty of New Echota also contained the promise that the removed Cherokees
"shall be entitled to a delegate in the House of Representatives of the United
States whenever Congress shall make provision for the same." Like the similar
promise made to the Delawares, this guarantee was never carried into force.

In Abel, *Proposals for an Indian State 1778-1878*, ANNUAL REPORT OF THE
AMERICAN HISTORICAL ASSOCIATION 89, 94-102 (1907), the author traces the
later nineteenth century shift from the idea of an Indian territory or state
under the governance of Indians to a territory of mixed populations. These
debates for the most part centered on the history of unsuccessful late nineteenth century ideas for an organized territorial government and later an Indian state, proposed to be named for the Cherokee linguist Sequoyah, to be
formed out of the former Indian Territory in what is now eastern Oklahoma.

[Early] Congressional action [shows] how clearly defined was the idea that the Indian
country to the westward should constitute a regular Territory, and that for the red
men only. On the former point, the House resolution of December 27, 1825, was
especially explicit, and on the latter, an earlier one of December 17, 1824. There was
no mistaking the character of the Territory. It was to be "of the same kind and
regulated by the same rules" as other "Territories of the U.S." Inferentially, then, it
was to be a State in embryo....

During Jackson's presidency Indian removal became a promising political issue; but
if it is to be regarded as akin in any sense to colonization, the act of 1830, which made it
a part of the nation's policy, was legislation ill advised, ill considered, and incomplete.
Under it the whole body of eastern Indians were to be taken, if possible, west of
Missouri and left there totally unorganized. Each tribe, it is true, was to retain, presumably, its own native government; but had not that government already proved its
insufficiency by revealing traits incompatible with economic development in the
United States? Professions of a desire to civilize the Indians necessarily presupposed
admittance at some future time to citizenship. The Cherokees, as we have seen, had
already adopted Anglo-Saxon institutions, and *all* the tribes *might* be *induced* to do
the same. No more fitting time for making a change in their political status could have
been found than this when a change of homes was to be made and the old associations
cast aside. Removal was in itself iconoclastic. Why not have gone a step further?

[The titles of these bills] — the preservation of the Indians and the protection of the
western frontier — offers a possible clue to the underlying motive of the government.
The motley crowd of Indians, predisposed, by reason of their being advanced each to a
different stage of civilization, to quarrel among themselves, were a menace to the
peace of adjoining states. Many of these, being enraged at the grievous wrong that had
been done them, were suspected of plotting revenge. Remember, these were the years
when the Texas question was beginning to be agitated. Should war with Mexico come
on this or on any other pretext, the Indian might find his opportunity. Closer military
supervision, therefore, under pretense of giving training in republican self-government, was deemed the wisest course. Strange to say, certain army men, consulted as to
ways of fortifying the frontier, declaimed against the organization of the Indian Territory on the ground that the tribes would realize the force of the old saying, "In union
there is strength."

[Thereafter], during the next three decades individuals found time and opportunity
to discuss the Indian situation. Meanwhile the great question of establishing a territory
for the tribes found favor, or would have found favor had it been sufficiently agitated,
with at least two of President Tyler's Secretaries of War, viz., John C. Spencer, and
William Wilkins. In the session of 1845-46 Congress took up the subject again, moved
thereto by a stirring memorial from a missionary association. On that occasion the

House Committee on Indian Affairs went so far as to report a bill defining such a territory, but it was not acted upon. In 1848, the safety of Texas in view, Representative McIlvane, from the Indian Committee, made an exhaustive report, quite on a par with Everett's and Tipton's of earlier years, in which he urged territorial organization, but he urged in vain. He also reported a bill "embracing the general principles of the bill of 1834."

[In 1853], Schoolcraft manifested some slight interest in the general subject of Indian welfare, but opposed the formation of a territory since, like Doty, he deemed the political consolidation of the tribes impracticable. To him a series of small colonies from the Rockies to the Pacific, presumably like the reservation farms of California, would be a better solution of the Indian problem. The fact is, the time was not propitious for organization. The United States Government was even then breaking away from the rash promises it had made in the twenties and thirties; for it was looking forward, as was evidenced in the consideration of the question of Wyandott citizenship, to the Kansas-Nebraska bill, to the passage of which organization along the original lines, i.e., southward from the Platte, might have proved an insurmountable obstacle.

[When], after the civil war, the Federal Government was calling the Five Civilized Tribes to account for their recent alliance with the southern Confederacy, it made a desperate effort to force territorial organization upon them; but they stood out firmly and unanimously against it, yet in their position as conquered rebels perforce had finally to accept a halfway measure in the shape of a general council. The Indian understanding of this was well expressed in 1874 when territorial bills were before Congress and the Indians were memorializing against them. "We do hereby most solemnly and emphatically declare that the articles of the treaties of 1866, *do not authorize the formation* by *Congress* of a *Territorial government* of the *United States* over the *Indians* of the *Indian Territory*. On the contrary the agreement on our part in assenting to the establishment of said council was entered into for the very purpose of obviating the alleged necessity for such a Territorial government.... We held that country was exclusively an Indian country, as contradistinguished from a Territory of the United States, and we treated upon that basis." [The Creek] general council indicated was organized at Okmulgee, in the Creek country, in 1869, and formed of itself a constituent assembly, drawing up and provisionally adopting a constitution, which, however, failed of ratification by the Indians.

[After Grant became President], no time was lost in urging territorial government for the Indians, notwithstanding the fact that the several treaties of 1866 had stipulated explicitly that the legislation of Congress in the direction of a civil administration for the Indian country should not interfere with or annul tribal organization, rights, laws, privileges, or customs. The exigencies of the times demanded a change, however, and, as Grant said in his first annual message, economic growth, as seen in the building of large railways that brought the white settlements ever nearer to the red, made it expedient. The application of the suggestion to the country south of Kansas was not specific until two years later (1871), when Grant recommended the establishment of a territory there as a possible "means of collecting most of the Indians now between the Missouri and the Pacific and south of the British possessions into one Territory or one State." That he had not a mixed state in mind is seen from his fourth annual message, his policy being definite, to collect as many Indians as he could and protect them from the incursions of white men. Later messages in his second administration emphasized this point of view, but sentiment in the country at large steadily drifted toward the exclusion of the old notion. Thus the resolution of the National Commercial Convention at St. Louis in 1872 pointed unerringly toward a mixed state. Bills in Congress, for the most part, did likewise and hence the determined opposition of the Indians. During this time also the separate organization of Oklahoma came to be talked of and no pretense was ever made that Oklahoma was to be exclusively Indian. After 1878 there was practically no thought whatsoever of allowing the aborigines a separate existence as an integral part of the Union, and the spasmodic efforts of a hundred years had failed.

What political or social advantages would a separate Indian state have afforded to the Indians? What advantages, if any, would have accrued to the non-Indian portion of the nation from such proposals? Would a separate Indian state have been compatible with nineteenth-century American constitutional notions of federalism? Would it be compatible with twentieth-century concepts of federalism? Has acceptance of the doctrine that the due process clause of the fourteenth amendment incorporates the bill of rights and makes them applicable to the states and the revolution in federal-state relations since the New Deal undermined the value of statehood in protecting Indian autonomy? As you review the materials in this book, consider to what extent federal law now accomplishes the objectives behind these early proposals for an Indian state.

2. THE POLICY DILEMMA — THE PARADIGMS OF AUTONOMY AND ASSIMILATION

EX PARTE CROW DOG

109 U.S. 556 (1883)

Mr. Justice MATTHEWS delivered the opinion of the Court.

The petitioner is in the custody of the Marshal of the United States for the Territory of Dakota, imprisoned in the jail of Lawrence County in the First Judicial District of that Territory, under sentence of death, adjudged against him by the district court for that district, to be carried into execution January 14th, 1884. That judgment was rendered upon a conviction for the murder of an Indian of the Brule Sioux Band of the Sioux Nation of Indians by the name of Sin-ta-ge-le-Scka, or in English, Spotted Tail, the prisoner also being an Indian, of the same band and nation, and the homicide having occurred, as alleged in the indictment, in the Indian country, within a place and district of country under the exclusive jurisdiction of the United States and within the said judicial district. The judgment was affirmed, on a writ of error, by the Supreme Court of the Territory. It is claimed on behalf of the prisoner that the crime charged against him, and of which he stands convicted, is not an offense under the laws of the United States; that the district court had no jurisdiction to try him, and that its judgment and sentence are void. He, therefore, prays for a writ of habeas corpus, that he may be delivered from an imprisonment which he asserts to be illegal.

[Title 28] of the Revised Statutes relates to Indians, and the sub-title of chapter four is, Government of Indian Country. It embraces many provisions regulating the subject of intercourse and trade with the Indians in the Indian country, and imposes penalties and punishments for various violations of them. Section 2142 provides for the punishment of assaults with deadly weapons and intent, by Indians upon white persons, and by white persons upon Indians; section 2143, for the case of arson, in like cases; and section 2144 provides that "the general laws of the United States defining and prescribing punishments for forgery and depredations upon the mails shall extend to the Indian country."

The next two sections are as follows:

Sec. 2145. Except as to crimes, the punishment of which is expressly provided for in this title, the general laws of the United States as to the punishment of crimes committed in any place within the sole and exclusive jurisdiction of the United States, except the District of Columbia, shall extend to the Indian country.

Sec. 2146. The preceding section shall not be construed to extend to [crimes committed by one Indian against the person or property of another Indian, nor to] any Indian committing any offence in the Indian country who has been punished by the local law of the tribe, or to any case where by treaty stipulations the exclusive jurisdiction over such offences is or may be secured to the Indian tribes respectively.

[This] argument in support of the jurisdiction and conviction is, that the exception contained in § 2146 Rev. Stat. is repealed by the operation and legal effect of the treaty with the different tribes of the Sioux Indians of April 29th, 1868, 15 Stat. 635; and an act of Congress, approved February 28th, 1877, to ratify an agreement with certain bands of the Sioux Indians, &c., 19 Stat. 254. The following provisions of the treaty of 1868 are relied on:

Article I. From this day forward all war between the parties to this agreement shall forever cease. The government of the United States desires peace, and its honor is hereby pledged to keep it. The Indians desire peace, and they now pledge their honor to maintain it.

If bad men among the whites, or among other people subject to the authority of the United States, shall commit any wrong upon the person or property of the Indians, the United States will, upon proof made to the agent and forwarded to the commissioner of Indian affairs at Washington City, proceed at once to cause the offender to be arrested and punished according to the laws of the United States, and also reimburse the injured person for the loss sustained.

If bad men among the Indians shall commit a wrong or depredation upon the person or property of any one, white, black, or Indian, subject to the authority of the United States and at peace therewith, the Indians herein named solemnly agree that they will, upon proof made to their agent and notice by him, deliver up the wrongdoer to the United States, to be tried and punished according to its laws; and in case they wilfully refuse so to do, the person injured shall be reimbursed for his loss from the annuities or other moneys due or to become due to them under this or other treaties made with the United States. And the President, on advising with the commissioner of Indian affairs, shall prescribe such rules and regulations for ascertaining damages under the provisions of this article as in his judgment may be proper. But no one sustaining loss while violating the provisions of this treaty or the laws of the United States shall be reimbursed therefor.

[If these agreements] have the effect contended for, to support the conviction in the present case, it also makes punishable, when committed within the Indian country by one Indian against the person or property of another Indian, the following offences, defined by the general laws of the United States as to crimes committed in places within their exclusive jurisdiction, viz.: manslaughter, § 5341; attempt to commit murder or manslaughter, § 5342; rape, § 5345; mayhem, § 5348; bigamy, § 5352; larceny, § 5356; and receiving stolen goods, § 5357. That this legislation could constitutionally be extended to embrace Indians in the Indian country, by the mere force of a treaty, whenever it operates of itself, without the aid of any legislative provision, was decided by this court in the case of *The United States v. 43 Gallons of Whiskey*, 93 U.S. 188. *See Holden v. Joy,* 17 Wall. [83 U.S.] 211; *The Cherokee Tobacco*, 11 Wall. [78 U.S.] 616. It becomes necessary, therefore, to examine the particular provisions that are supposed to work this result.

The first of these is contained in the first article of the treaty of 1868, that "if bad men among the Indians shall commit a wrong or depredation upon the person or property of any one, white, black, or Indian, subject to the authority of the United States and at peace therewith, the Indians herein named solemnly agree that they will, upon proof made to their agent and notice by him, deliver up the wrong-doer to the United States, to be tried and punished according to its laws."

But it is quite clear from the context that this does not cover the present case of an alleged wrong committed by one Indian upon the person of another of the same tribe. [The second provision used to] justify the jurisdiction asserted in the present case, is the eighth article of the agreement, embodied in the act of 1877, in which it is declared:

> And Congress shall, by appropriate legislation, secure to them an orderly government; they shall be subject to the laws of the United States, and each individual shall be protected in his rights of property, person, and life.

It is equally clear, in our opinion, that the words can have no such effect as that claimed for them. The pledge to secure to these people, with whom the United States was contracting as a distinct political body, an orderly government, by appropriate legislation thereafter to be framed and enacted, necessarily implies, having regard to all the circumstances attending the transaction, that among the arts of civilized life, which it was the very purpose of all these arrangements to introduce and naturalize among them, was the highest and best of all, that of self-government, the regulation by themselves of their own domestic affairs, the maintenance of order and peace among their own members by the administration of their own laws and customs. They were nevertheless to be subject to the laws of the United States, not in the sense of citizens, but, as they had always been, as wards subject to a guardian; not as individuals, constituted members of the political community of the United States, with a voice in the selection of representatives and the framing of the laws, but as a dependent community who were in a state of pupilage, advancing from the condition of a savage tribe to that of a people who, through the discipline of labor and by education, it was hoped might become a self-supporting and self-governed society....

The nature and circumstances of this case strongly reinforce this rule of interpretation in its present application. It is a case involving the judgment of a court of special and limited jurisdiction, not to be assumed without clear warrant of law. It is a case of life and death. It is a case where, against an express exception in the law itself, that law, by argument and inference only, is sought to be extended over aliens and strangers; over the members of a community separated by race, by tradition, by the instincts of a free though savage life, from the authority and power which seeks to impose upon them the restraints of an external and unknown code, and to subject them to the responsibilities of civil conduct, according to rules and penalties of which they could have no previous warning; which judges them by a standard made by others and not for them, which takes no account of the conditions which should except them from its exactions, and makes no allowance for their inability to understand it. It tries them, not by their peers, nor by the customs of their people, nor the law of their land, but by superiors of a different race, according to the law of a social state of which they have an imperfect conception, and which is opposed to the traditions of their history, to the habits of their lives, to the strongest prejudices of their savage nature; one which measures the red man's revenge by the maxims of the white man's morality. [As stated] by Mr. Justice Miller, delivering the opinion of the court in *United States v. Joseph*, 94 U.S. 614, 617:

> The tribes for whom the act of 1834 was made were those semi-independent tribes whom our government has always recognized as exempt from our laws, whether within or without the limits of an organized state or territory, and, in regard to their domestic government, left to their own rules and traditions, in whom we have recognized the capacity to make treaties, and with whom the governments, state and national, deal, with a few exceptions only, in their national or tribal character, and not as individuals.

[Thus], the First District Court of Dakota was without jurisdiction to find or try the indictment against the prisoner, that the conviction and sentence are void, and that his imprisonment is illegal.

The writs of habeas corpus and certiorari prayed for will accordingly be issued.

NOTES

1. Indian Political Autonomy: The themes of Justice Matthews's opinion in *Ex parte Crow Dog* offer a framework for discussion of the legally protected political autonomy of Indian tribes. Most enticing are the broadest questions. What are the qualities of a group that allow it the privilege of establishing its own criminal code? While *Crow Dog* presents the question in its starkest form, the Indian context, it proliferates throughout the legal system. How are the geographic and subject matter boundary lines drawn which settle the extent of power? Boundaries are sometimes drawn to preserve certain legal systems, see *Gomillion v. Lightfoot*, 364 U.S. 339 (1960) (redistricting scheme intended to exclude blacks from city), and sometimes they are destroyed to abolish a society, see *The Late Corp. of Church of Jesus Christ of Latter-Day Saints v. United States*, 136 U.S. 1 (1890) (Mormon efforts to physically separate themselves from the dominant society to further their atypical religious practices, including polygamy, frustrated by territorial and federal laws). *Crow Dog* presents the issue in a striking fashion: one Indian murders another, and by his act stirs up a whirlpool of culture, history, and federalism. What is it about the Sioux that furnishes them the opportunity to regulate, if they so desire, the conduct of the alleged murderer? Why the Sioux in South Dakota and not the nineteenth century Mormons in Utah or the resettled Swedes or Italians? Is it wholly a matter of historical accident that one group can exercise power and another cannot? Are there other principles that emerge from Justice Matthews's opinion that justify the historical fact? What is it, in short, about the Sioux Nation that makes it a wise policy to allow it the authority to establish a criminal code for its citizens?

2. Federal Major Crimes Act and Non-Indian Responses to *Crow Dog*: As a consequence of *Ex parte Crow Dog*, serious disputes among Indians in the Indian country would be resolved according to tribal custom. Subsequent protests by Indian agents and others resulted in the passage of the federal legislation that specifically listed seven major crimes that would be punishable under federal law.

A typical complaint is contained in this statement by the Commissioner of Indian Affairs in his annual report for 1884:

> I again desire to call attention to the necessity for legislation for the punishment of crimes on the Indian reservations. Since my last report the Supreme Court of the

United States decided in the case of *Ex parte Crow Dog*, indicted for murder, that the District Court of Dakota was without jurisdiction, when the crime was committed on the reservation by one Indian against another. If offenses of this character cannot be tried in the courts of the United States, there is no tribunal in which the crime of murder can be punished. Minor offenses may be punished through the agency of the "court of Indian offenses," but it will hardly do to leave the punishment of the crime of murder to a tribunal that exists only by the consent of the Indians of the reservation. If the murderer is left to be punished according to the old Indian custom, it becomes the duty of the next of kin to avenge the death of his relative by either killing the murderer or some one of his kinsmen. The laws of the state or territory wherein the reservation is situated ought to be extended over the reservation, and the Indians should be compelled to obey such laws and be allowed to claim the protection thereof.

Within two years of *Ex parte Crow Dog* the Congress enacted the Major Crimes Act (23 Stat. 362, 385, codified as amended at 18 U.S.C. § 1153), which was the first major declaration of a split in power between the tribes and the federal government where crimes among Indians were involved. The principle of the split has yielded peculiar results; for how should Congress decide which offenses are federal and which offenses are tribal?

Under the Major Crimes Act, Congress preserved the idea that the tribe is the exclusive proper authority to regulate conduct (by defining crimes and then trying offenders) for lesser crimes. As to lesser offenses, the exercise of tribal sovereignty may there take place without discomfort. But Congress apparently believed the risk of defining and enforcing major crimes is too great to leave to chance tribal enactment. Without expressly divesting the tribes of concurrent jurisdiction over such offenses, Congress turned the primary resolution of such matters over to federal authority. What are the criteria which dispose a legislature to ensure that certain conduct is proscribed — even where a tribal legislature may have purposely set different standards — in defining the crime and prescribing the punishment? Is it a standard of danger or seriousness to people outside the relevant community? Would it be a matter of concern to the people of Arizona if the Navajo reservation, in its wisdom, considered certain homicides (such as euthanasia) not murder; or if it gave much lighter sentences for inter-Indian violence than Arizona would inflict (perhaps by having a different form of punishment, such as banishment, rather than a period of time in the penitentiary)? Notice, for example, that by making murder a federal offense, the decision whether capital punishment is an appropriate punishment is a matter for the federal Congress rather than the local tribal council. *United States v. Whaley*, 37 Fed. 145 (C.C.S.D. Cal. 1888) (tribal members executing a tribally imposed death sentence convicted of murder under the Federal Major Crimes Act). Moreover, note the enforcement and guilt-determining problems. By making major crimes federal offenses, the defendants must be tried in federal courts by federally selected juries often a hundred miles or more from the scene of the crime or their home. What are the problems in jury discrimination posed by such a system? Might the distances preclude many tribesmen from appearing as witnesses or on the jury?

Nothing in the language of the Act compels the conclusion that the tribe lost concurrent jurisdiction over these major offenses, and, in fact, concurrent jurisdiction has been confirmed through administrative practice. But so has the treatment of Indian courts as educational devices that should not have too much power. Indeed, the Civil Rights Act of 1968 now limits, for the first time, the term of imprisonment that can be meted out by the tribe to six months, no matter how serious the offense. 25 U.S.C. § 1302(7). Should the Act be read as only a temporary measure — an intervention by Congress that was necessary only so long as the tribes did not develop adequate judicial machinery more in conformity with American traditions? As to offenses that were not included in the Major Crimes Act, the authority of the tribe was unchanged. *See United States v. Quiver*, 241 U.S. 602 (1916).

UNITED STATES v. CLAPOX

35 F. 575 (D.C. Or. 1888)

DEADY, J. The defendants are accused by this information of a violation of section 5401 of the Revised Statutes, which provides:

> Every person who by force sets at liberty or rescues any person who, before conviction, stands committed for any capital crime against the United States, or who by force sets at liberty or rescues any person committed for or convicted of any offense other than capital, shall be fined not more than $500, and imprisoned not more than one year.

It is alleged in the information that on March 27, 1888, the defendants were Indians residing on the Umatilla Indian reservation, and under the charge of a United States Indian agent; that one Minnie was then an Indian woman, married to an Indian, both of whom then resided on said reservation, and were under the charge of said agent; that prior to said date the Secretary of the Interior, under the authority and by the direction of the President, [promulgated] certain rules providing for a "court of Indian offenses" and an Indian police force on said reservation, and caused to be erected thereon a jail for the safe-keeping of such persons as might be committed thereto by said court, either for examination or punishment; that no written warrants are issued by said court, and no written record is kept of its findings or judgments; that under the rules establishing said court and police, and the direction of said agent, the officers of said police force had then and there the authority to arrest any Indian whom they might have cause to believe had "committed a crime or an Indian offense" on said reservation, and commit him to jail for examination or trial before said court. On March 27, 1888, said Minnie was arrested on said reservation by said police force for the "offense of living and cohabiting" thereon with an Indian other than her husband, and placed in said jail, to await her trial for said offense before said court; and that said defendants did then and there "unlawfully and with force and arms break open the said jail, enter the same, rescue and set at liberty" said Minnie, contrary to the statute, etc.

[The rules] prescribe the punishment for certain acts called therein "Indian offenses," such as the "sun," the "scalp," and the "war dance," polygamy, "the usual practices of so-called 'medicine men,'" the destruction or theft of Indian property, and buying or selling Indian women for the purpose of cohabitation. In addition to these, rule 9 provides that said court shall have "jurisdiction of misdemeanors committed by Indians belonging to the reservation."

[Defendants question] whether the interior department has authority to define "Indian offenses," or establish courts for the punishment of Indian offenders, as set forth in said rules.

And first, as to the authority of the department in the premises.

By article 8 of the treaty of June 9, 1855 (12 St. 948) between the United States and certain tribes and bands of Indians of eastern Oregon and Washington, of which the Umatilla Indians are one, it is provided:

The confederate bands acknowledge their dependence on the government of the United States, ... and engage to submit to and observe all laws, rules and regulations which may be prescribed by the United States for the government of said Indians.

The Revised Statutes provide:

Sec. 441. The secretary of the interior is charged with the supervision of the public business relating to the ... Indians.

Sec. 463. The commissioner of Indian affairs shall, under the direction of the secretary of the interior, and agreeably to such regulations as the President may prescribe, have the management of all Indian affairs, and of all matters arising out of the Indian relations.

Sec. 465. The President may prescribe such regulations as he may think fit for carrying into effect the various provisions of any act relating to Indian affairs.

By this treaty the Umatilla Indians engaged to submit to any rule that might be prescribed by the United States for their government. This obviously includes the power to organize and maintain this Indian court and police, and to specify the acts or conduct concerning which it shall have jurisdiction. This treaty is an "act" or law "relating to Indian affairs" — the affairs of these Indians; and by said section 465 the power to prescribe a rule for carrying the same into effect is given to the President, who has exercised the same in this case through the proper instrumentality — the Secretary of the Interior.

Then there is the general power given by said sections 441 and 463 to the President, acting through the Secretary of the Interior and the Commissioner of Indian Affairs, to make regulations for the "management of all Indian affairs, and of all matters arising out of the Indian relations."

These "courts of Indian offenses" are not the constitutional courts provided for in section I, art. 3, Const., which Congress only has the power to "ordain and establish," but mere educational and disciplinary instrumentalities, by which the government of the United States is endeavoring to improve and elevate the condition of these dependent tribes to whom it sustains the relation of guardian. In fact, the reservation itself is in the nature of a school, and the Indians are gathered there, under the charge of an agent, for the purpose of acquiring the habits, ideas, and aspirations which distinguish the civilized from the uncivilized man.

[I]n conclusion, the act with which these defendants are charged is in flagrant opposition to the authority of the United States on this reservation, and directly subversive of this laudable effort to accustom and educate these Indians in the habit and knowledge of self-government. It is therefore appropriate and needful that the power and name of the government of the United States should be invoked to restrain and punish them. The case falls within the letter of the statute providing for the punishment of persons who are guilty of rescuing any one committed for an offense against the United States.

Demurrer overruled.

NOTE: THE ASSIMILATIVE GOALS OF RESERVATIONS

The federal government saw legal institutions as educational tools in the nineteenth-century reservation context. Self-governance was good not only because it enhanced the possibility of order, but also because it provided a special classroom for Indian wards, in the ideology of the times, to absorb the methods of the mainstream of society. In this view, the reservation was a way-station between the society prior to the advent of the European settlers and the society when reservations would no longer be needed. It is not uncommon in the intellectual history of the United States that there be faith in democratic law-making activity as being civilizing and educational in itself. John Collier, as Commissioner of Indian Affairs in the 1930's, stated that the "experience of responsible democracy is, of all experiences, the most therapeutic, the most disciplinary, the most dynamogenic and the most productive of efficiency." *See* Dobyns, *Therapeutic Experience of Responsible Democracy*, in S. Levine & N. Lurie, The American Indian Today 268, 269 (Pelican rev. ed. 1968). Thus, Judge Deady states a familiar view of the reservation: it is "in the nature of a school, and the Indians are gathered there, under the charge of an agent, for the purpose of acquiring the habits, ideas, and aspirations which distinguish the civilized from the uncivilized man." If the rules on the reservation are designed to civilize, then to what extent is it deleterious for such rules to reflect Indian ways and customs? If the agent is the "teacher," should the agent or the federal government write the rules, or is it part of the lesson that the Indian tribes themselves engage in legislative activity? Should rules that are designed to educate be different from rules that are designed to discipline? Are there implications, for example, for the length of sentence an offender should sustain?

If *Clapox* is correct, if the predominant basis for the reservation concept was its educational function (as opposed to a notion of entitlement to land and right to a culture), the sovereignty tolerated by the dominant society would have certain constraints and temporal limitations. Most obvious are the limits that would be placed on the power of the tribe to assert jurisdiction over non-Indians within its midst, at least in criminal matters. *See Oliphant v. Suquamish Indian Tribe*, 435 U.S. 191 (1978). If the federal government established tribal courts for the purpose of teaching self-government, it might determine that the learning function could adequately be achieved without practicing on non-Indians. Indeed, one view long has suggested that tribal government does not have criminal jurisdiction over non-Indians, a position confirmed in *Duro v. Reina*, 110 S. Ct. 2053 (1990), set forth in Chapter 3, section D1, *infra*. Furthermore, if the reservation is a school, and only a school, then the federal government, as teacher, has control over the scope of activities of the tribe. If the lawmaking power is to be merely educational, it need not be comprehensive. All that is wanted is that a group go through the forms of government if that is the best way for its membership to learn about institutional responses to breaches of law. Thus, for example, in the 1968 Civil Rights Act, 25 U.S.C. § 1302, the inherent power of Indian tribes to regulate the conduct of their members, albeit subject to significant limitations on penalties, was reaffirmed but made subject to certain quasi-constitutional limitations. Most of these issues are more fully discussed in Chapter 3.

Perhaps the most serious implication of the *Clapox* view is the suggestion that when the lesson has been learned, the school might be dissolved. Reservation as classroom, rather than entitlement, means that the federal government can determine (a) when individual Indians "graduate" and (b) when the reservation itself is no longer needed. Indeed, this process in fact occurs, under the dread name of "termination." Termination, usually the ending of the federal trust status of Indian land, means the imposition of local taxes, the ending of federal benefits, and the conclusion of the special associational status that permitted the group to live under a differentiated legal system. In the 1950's, as a matter of national policy (and before that sporadically), Congress determined which reservations were "ready" for termination, theoretically on the basis that its members had learned, well enough, how to become subject to the laws of the dominant society. Partial terminations, such as Public Law No. 280, codified as amended at 18 U.S.C. § 1162, 25 U.S.C. §§ 1321-26, 28 U.S.C. § 1360, maintained the trust status but generally substituted state criminal and civil laws for federal and tribal enactments. Conceptually, termination flows smoothly from the idea of reservation as classroom rather than tribal government as an entitlement.

REGINA v. MUDDARUBBA

Unpublished (Australia 1956)*

[This case involved an Australian aborigine of the Pitjintara tribe accused of murdering a woman with a spear after she used a native word referring to the male genitalia in the accused's presence. The material below is from the unreported transcript of the judge's charge to the jury.]

KRIEWALDT, J.: Gentlemen of the Jury,

[I am sorry to say that in my six years on the bench] I have heard many people say that on the trial of a native, some members of the jury come into court with their minds made up and that it can be predicted before the trial whether there will be a conviction or an acquittal[;] other people say it is a waste of time to try natives according to the law applicable to white men. I hope that none of you think so. You are all citizens of the Northern Territory. You have taken an oath to bring in a true verdict according to the evidence. The words of the oath are that you will "hearken to the evidence and true deliverance make between our Sovereign Lady the Queen and the Prisoner at the Bar."

[The prevailing law] is that the trial of natives is to be conducted in exactly the same manner and under the same rules as the trial of a white man. There is only one difference. If a white man is found guilty of murder, that I must sentence him to death. That is the law. It is then the province of the Queen's advisors whether or not the prerogative of mercy will be exercised. But, if an aboriginal is found guilty of murder the responsibility of deciding the penalty lies entirely on my shoulders. The prerogative of mercy vested in the Queen still exists. It is possible to reduce the penalty but the penalty I impose cannot be increased.

[The evidence] brought by the Crown as proof that the accused is the killer is the confession he made to Sgt. Kelly or rather, should I say, the two confessions he made....

When a white person is interrogated by police and admits an offense, you generally accept the admission as true. The average person's confession is usually true. But here we are dealing with a native and the question for you is

---

*Delivered 2nd February, 1956, Northern Territory of Australia in the Supreme Court, Alice Springs Sittings.

whether this native would have said he killed the woman if it was not true. You must consider the circumstances. There were present two Native Affairs protectors, two interpreters and a third interpreter. You will ask whether there is any reason for an untrue confession. The decision lies with you....

If you come to the conclusion that there was a confession by the accused and that his confession is reliable, then you must consider the second of the three major questions I outlined to you some time ago. Are there in this case any circumstances which will excuse the throwing of the spear? I direct you as a matter of law that nothing disclosed by the evidence excuses the throwing of a spear by the accused at the woman. A tribal custom or tribal law permitting the accused to inflict punishment on the woman is not regarded by the law as an excuse.

The third question is, was the killing of the woman by the accused (if you decide that he killed her) murder or manslaughter? I need not give you a full explanation of the law applicable to manslaughter. In this case it will suffice if I say that the law takes notice of human temper and human frailty and decrees that in some cases the unlawful killing of one person by another person is not murder but manslaughter. In the eyes of the law, if something happens which would make the ordinary reasonable person react with violence and death ensues as a result of that violence, the crime is not murder but manslaughter. That is a concession by the law to human nature and is called killing under provocation.

The test in law is: would what happened have caused an average human being so to lose his self control that he would have done that which the accused did? I ask you to note that the yard stick is the reaction of the average person not the reaction of the particular accused. Let me give a few examples. A hot tempered person who reacts with violence when the average person would not have so reacted is guilty of murder if death ensues as a result of his violence. My second example some of you may consider a little bit rude. It concerns a young man who was sexually impotent, or so he suspected. Driven by his suspicions one night he sought out a harlot. When he was unable to take advantage of her proffered favours, she mocked at his impotence. The young man lost his temper and killed her. The court decided that her actions were not sufficient to amount to provocation and hence the crime was not reduced to manslaughter. The average person would not have reacted with violence and therefore in law the harlot's gibe was not provocation. There is another rule relating to provocation, namely that the reaction of the provoked person must bear a reasonable proportion to the provocation he receives. I mentioned to you earlier that the same rules which apply to the trial of a white person apply in the trial of a native. The rules relating to provocation have given me some worry in native trials. After much thought I have when summing up to a jury in a case where a native is on trial perhaps departed somewhat from the strict rule applied in trials of white persons. Perhaps my view is not correct, perhaps the white rule should be applied strictly to natives, but whatever the law may be it is your duty to accept today what I tell you to be the law. Perhaps I should also say that I believe the law to be as I shall put it to you.

In my opinion, in any discussion of provocation, the general principle of law is to create a standard which would be observed by the average person in the community in which the accused person lives. It is clear from the cases decided by Courts whose decisions bind me that in white communities matters regarded as sufficient provocation a century ago would not be regarded as sufficient today. This suggests that the standard is not a fixed and unchanging standard[;] it leaves it open, and I think properly so, to regard the Pitjintara tribe as a separate community for purposes of considering the reaction of the average man. I tell you that if you think the average member of the Pitjintara tribe (and you must remember that these are "Myall" blacks) would have retaliated to the words and actions of the woman, by spearing her, then the act of spearing is not murder but manslaughter. If provocation sufficient for the average reasonable person in his community to lose his self control exists, then the unlawful killing is manslaughter and not murder. I may be wrong, but until put right by a higher court I shall continue to tell juries that the members of the Pitjintara tribe are to be considered as a separate community for the purposes of the rules relating to provocation. I shall not apply to them the standard applied to the white citizens of the Northern Territory.

Now let us consider the nature of the provocation in this case. For a white person, it has been laid down that mere words are not provocation under any circumstances. In this case, if the aboriginal word "karlu" was used by the woman, I have no doubt that you will regard the use of this word as a serious insult. But whether or not it was sufficiently serious to cause a person to whom it was used to retaliate by throwing a spear (and remember that you must consider how the average member of the Pitjintara tribe would react), is a matter for you to decide, and it would be unwise for me to express my own view.

[T]hree verdicts [are] open and it is one of these you will bring in: (1) Not guilty (2) Guilty of murder (3) Guilty of manslaughter....

Verdict: Guilty of manslaughter.

Sentenced to nine months' imprisonment with hard labour.

NOTES

1. Separate Cultures and Uniform Law: How can one reconcile Judge Kriewaldt's view that the native population constitutes "a separate community for purposes of considering the reaction of the average man" with his statement that "the trial of natives is to be conducted in exactly the same manner and under the same rules as the trial of a white man"? Assuming the jury in the *Muddarubba* case consisted primarily of nonnatives, could they effectively apply the Judge's instructions? How? Do these problems suggest that the natives should not be treated as separate legal communities or, rather, do they indicate that they should not be tried in the same manner and under the same rules as the nonnative population?

2. A Canadian Response: In *Regina v. Machekequonabe*, 28 Ont. 309 (1898), the accused, an Indian, was convicted of manslaughter for the killing of another Indian. The jury specifically found that when the accused shot the Indian he acted under the belief that the victim was a Windigo embodied in human form. The accused's tribe (probably Northern Ojibwa) believed that a Windigo was an evil spirit clothed in human form that ate human beings. Persons believed to be Windigoes were therefore commonly killed to prevent such cannibalism. The trial judge instructed the jury that, under the facts of the case, there was no justification for the murder. Counsel for the accused contested this instruction, arguing that the killing took place under a reasonable mistake. Furthermore, he urged that, under common law, religious belief was an excuse for homicide. The appellate court summarily affirmed the conviction.

3. Separate Cultures and National Integration — A Jurisprudential Perspective: *Crow Dog, Muddarubba,* and *Machekequonabe* raise a number of fundamental questions regarding the extent to which a society or a state can be built upon or even tolerate divergent cultures, traditions, morals, and social control mechanisms. The extent to which nationhood is the product of shared or imposed uniformity of culture and social thought and the extent to which the legal fabric of a nation can tolerate cultural pluralism is a particularly acute one in Anglo-American jurisprudence. In western legal thought, such issues cut to the core of questions about the force of law, and impinge on the realm of moral and ethical, as well as legal, philosophy.

For example, in his treatise on the common law, Sir William Blackstone identified Natural Law and Divine Law as the foundations of *all* human law. As Blackstone would have understood these sources of law, definite and recognizable moral principle lay at their core. 1 W. BLACKSTONE, COMMENTARIES ON THE LAWS OF ENGLAND *40-44. Anglo-American jurisprudence at the time was thus heavily freighted with the understanding that immutable moral precepts grounded social organization. Human happiness, or good, could be discovered only by adherence to Natural Law.

Even as this system of ethics and jurisprudence was at its zenith, however, it was under attack. Jeremy Bentham, in assaulting Blackstone's work, argued that there was no need to appeal to Natural Law or any other moral principle in defining and establishing a legal framework for social relations. *See* J. BENTHAM, A FRAGMENT ON GOVERNMENT, COMMENT ON THE COMMENTARIES. Bentham turned the approach used by the Natural Law philosophers on its head, reasoning that since "happiness" was the goal of all social organization, even in the eyes of the Natural Law theorists, law should be simply directed toward increasing happiness, regardless of whether or not the activity being engaged in was undergirded by moral precept.

The debate between utilitarian pragmatists like Bentham and "moral sense" idealists continued throughout the nineteenth and twentieth centuries, though the focus of the latter group shifted away from Natural Law toward different sources of immutable principles. *See* G. HEGEL, PHENOMENOLOGY OF SPIRIT (A. Miller trans. 1977). In the field of law, formalism was enormously attractive to nineteenth century jurists, and carried over the Natural Law principle that held law to be a discoverable commodity, in the form of basic principles. *See* Pound, *Mechanical Jurisprudence*, 8 COLUM. L. REV. 605 (1908). In reformist England during the middle to late nineteenth century, and gradually in the United States, "Benthamic" theories of jurisprudence and ethics began to influence judicial opinion and legislation, though they played a minor role. *See* P. KING, UTILITARIAN JURISPRUDENCE IN AMERICA: THE INFLUENCE OF BENTHAM AND AUSTIN ON AMERICAN LEGAL THOUGHT IN THE NINETEENTH CENTURY (1986).

The vision one has of the appropriate goals for federal Indian policy may vary quite radically depending on whether one sees law as enforcing some moral sense of the community or merely as a social institution designed to maximize pleasure and reduce harm. The educational goal of federal Indian policy reflected in the *Clapox* case obviously is closer to the moral sense school of jurisprudence than any vision of law based on utilitarian objects. Likewise, efforts to protect Indian autonomy and assure Indian tribes separate self-governing status on their reservations may derive, in part, from the utilitarian notion that the persons most affected by government will have the best idea how to maximize the pleasure it produces while reducing social harm to a minimum.

Felix S. Cohen, who wrote the HANDBOOK OF FEDERAL INDIAN LAW (1942), one of the first treatises on Indian law and a fundamental document in the field, was also a legal philosopher, being a central figure in the most distinctively American school of jurisprudence — twentieth century judicial realism. For Cohen and other legal realists, it was impossible to believe that one set of rules could be found that should be applicable to all cultures and situations. Cohen believed that the search for and use of absolute principles resulted in law disconnected from social reality, and argued strongly for balancing pleasures against harms as a means to decide individual disputes. All law, including federal Indian law, must be adapted to the social and cultural realities under which it is applied. *See* F. COHEN, ETHICAL SYSTEMS AND LEGAL IDEAS (1933). *See also* Feldman, *Felix S. Cohen and His Jurisprudence: Reflections on Federal Indian Law*, 35 BUFFALO L. REV. 479, 481-97 (1986).

The debate between utilitarian visions of law and concepts of jurisprudence that focus on the collective enforcement of moral norms of the society is still alive, and remains a critical factor in determining the objectives of legislative policy and law in many situations. *Compare* P. DEVLIN, THE ENFORCEMENT OF MORALS (1965) *with* H.L.A. HART, LAW, LIBERTY, AND MORALITY (1963).

Has *Crow Dog* been decided in conformity with the utilitarian principle, or is there another reason for that decision? How would a natural lawyer and a legal realist view the decision in *Clapox*? Is utilitarianism of any use in determining how the law should deal with Native Americans? Would the consequences that would flow from a utilitarian approach *always* benefit Indians or their tribes? *See* Feldman, *Felix S. Cohen and His Jurisprudence: Reflections on Federal Indian Law*, supra, at 518-25.

4. Toleration of Atypical Communities: In *Wisconsin v. Yoder*, 406 U.S. 205 (1972), the Court dealt with the right of an Amish community, acting on its religiously derived beliefs, to resist generally applicable state compulsory education laws. In somewhat grudging fashion, the Court recognized the right of the Amish community to some zone of immunity in order to fulfill their special beliefs.

> Aided by a history of three centuries as an identifiable religious sect and a long history as a successful and self-sufficient segment of American society, the Amish in this case have convincingly demonstrated the sincerity of their religious beliefs, the interrelationship of belief with their mode of life, the vital role which belief and daily conduct play in the continued survival of Old Order Amish communities and their religious organization, and the hazards presented by the state's enforcement of a statute generally valid as to others. Beyond this, they have carried the even more difficult burden of demonstrating the adequacy of their alternative mode of continuing informal vocational education in terms of precisely those over-all interests that the state advances in support of its program of compulsory high school education. In light of this convincing showing, one which probably few other religious groups or sects could make, and weighing the minimal difference between what the state would require and what the Amish already accept, it was incumbent on the state to show with more particularity how its admittedly strong interest in compulsory education would be adversely affected by granting an exemption to the Amish.

Does the holding in *Yoder* suggest a swing toward a utilitarian view of the force of law and away from the types of views expressed by natural lawyers? As reflected in the next case, later first amendment cases have been less supportive of the demands of atypical cultural communities. In *Bowen v. Roy*, 476 U.S. 693

(1986), for example, a divided Supreme Court held that a state could legitimately require Native American parents to provide the social security number of a child when applying for welfare benefits. Based on conversations with an Abenaki chief, the father, an Indian of Abenaki descent, claimed that control over one's life was essential to spiritual purity. He asserted that securing a social security number for his child, Little Bird of the Snow, would involve her in the degrading, dehumanizing technology that is associated with such numbers and prevent her from attaining greater spiritual power. Finding that computer matching techniques employing social security numbers were critical to administration of such benefit programs and the prevention of fraud, the Court rejected the father's first amendment claim. In particular, Chief Justice Burger's opinion stated: "To maintain an organized society that guarantees religious freedom to a great variety of faiths requires that some religious practices yield to the common good. Religious beliefs can be accommodated, but there is a point at which accommodation would 'radically restrict the operating latitude of the legislature.'" 476 U.S. at 702, quoting *United States v. Lee*, 455 U.S. 252, at 259 (1982). Justice O'Connor filed a dissenting opinion, joined by Justices Brennan and Marshall, arguing that "[g]ranting an exemption to Little Bird of the Snow and to the handful of others who can be expected to make similar religious objection to providing the social security number in conjunction with the receipt of welfare benefits, will not demonstrably diminish the Government's ability to combat welfare fraud." 476 U.S. at 728.

EMPLOYMENT DIVISION, DEPARTMENT OF HUMAN RESOURCES OF OREGON v. SMITH

110 S. Ct. 1595 (1990)

Justice SCALIA delivered the opinion of the Court.

This case requires us to decide whether the Free Exercise Clause of the First Amendment permits the State of Oregon to include religiously inspired peyote use within the reach of its general criminal prohibition on use of that drug, and thus permits the State to deny unemployment benefits to persons dismissed from their jobs because of such religiously inspired use.

I

Oregon law prohibits the knowing or intentional possession of a "controlled substance" unless the substance has been prescribed by a medical practitioner. Ore. Rev. Stat. § 475.992(4) (1987). The law defines "controlled substance" as a drug classified in Schedules I through V of the Federal Controlled Substances Act, 21 U.S.C. §§ 811-812 (1982 ed. and Supp. V), as modified by the State Board of Pharmacy. Ore. Rev. Stat. § 475.005(6) (1987). Persons who violate this provision by possessing a controlled substance listed on Schedule I are "guilty of a Class B felony." § 475.992(4)(a). As compiled by the State Board of Pharmacy under its statutory authority, see Ore. Rev. Stat. § 475.035 (1987), Schedule I contains the drug peyote, a hallucinogen derived from the plant Lophophorawilliamsii Lemaire. Ore. Admin. Rule 855-80-021(3)(s) (1988).

Respondents Alfred Smith and Galen Black were fired from their jobs with a private drug rehabilitation organization because they ingested peyote for sacramental purposes at a ceremony of the Native American Church, of which both are members. When respondents applied to petitioner Employment Division for unemployment compensation, they were determined to be ineligible for benefits because they had been discharged for work-related "misconduct." The Oregon Court of Appeals reversed that determination, holding that the denial of benefits violated respondents' free exercise rights under the First Amendment.

On appeal to the Oregon Supreme Court, petitioner argued that the denial of benefits was permissible because respondents' consumption of peyote was a crime under Oregon law. The Oregon Supreme Court reasoned, however, that the criminality of respondents' peyote use was irrelevant to resolution of their constitutional claim — since the purpose of the "misconduct" provision under which respondents had been disqualified was not to enforce the State's criminal laws but to preserve the financial integrity of the compensation fund, and since that purpose was inadequate to justify the burden that disqualification imposed on respondents' religious practice. Citing our decisions in *Sherbert v. Verner*, 374 U.S. 398 (1963), and *Thomas v. Review Board, Indiana Employment Security Div.*, 450 U.S. 707 (1981), the court concluded that respondents were entitled to payment of unemployment benefits. We granted certiorari. Before this Court in 1987, petitioner continued to maintain that the illegality of respondents' peyote consumption was relevant to their constitutional claim. We agreed, concluding that "if a State has prohibited through its criminal laws certain kinds of religiously motivated conduct without violating the First Amendment, it certainly follows that it may impose the lesser burden of denying unemployment compensation benefits to persons who engage in that conduct." *Employment Div., Dept. of Human Resources of Oregon v. Smith*, 485 U.S. 660, 670 (1988) (*Smith I*). We vacated the judgment of the Oregon Supreme Court and remanded for further proceedings [to determine the legality of religious use under Oregon law].

On remand, the Oregon Supreme Court held that respondents' religiously inspired use of peyote fell within the prohibition of the Oregon statute, which "makes no exception for the sacramental use" of the drug. It then considered whether that prohibition was valid under the Free Exercise Clause, and concluded that it was not. The court therefore reaffirmed its previous ruling that the State could not deny unemployment benefits to respondents for having engaged in that practice.

We again granted certiorari.

II

Respondents' claim for relief rests on our decisions in *Sherbert v. Verner, supra, Thomas v. Review Board, Indiana Employment Security Div., supra*, and *Hobbie v. Unemployment Appeals Comm'n of Florida*, 480 U.S. 136 (1987), in which we held that a State could not condition the availability of unemployment insurance on an individual's willingness to forgo conduct required by his religion. As we observed in *Smith I*, however, the conduct at issue in those cases was not prohibited by law. We held that distinction to be critical, for "if Oregon does prohibit the religious use of peyote, and if that prohibition is consistent with the Federal Constitution, there is no federal right to engage in that conduct in Oregon," and "the State is free to withhold unemployment compensation from respondents for engaging in work-related misconduct, despite its religious motivation." Now that the Oregon Supreme Court has confirmed that Oregon does prohibit the religious use of peyote, we proceed to consider whether that prohibition is permissible under the Free Exercise Clause.

A

The Free Exercise Clause of the First Amendment, which has been made applicable to the States by incorporation into the Fourteenth Amendment, *see Cantwell v. Connecticut*, 310 U.S. 296, 303 (1940), provides that "Congress shall make no law respecting an establishment of religion, or prohibiting the *free exercise* thereof ...." U.S. Const. Am. I (emphasis added). The free exercise of religion means, first and foremost, the right to believe and profess whatever religious doctrine one desires. Thus, the First Amendment obviously excludes all "governmental regulation of religious beliefs as such." *Sherbert v. Verner*, *supra*, at 402. The government may not compel affirmation of religious belief, *see Torcaso v. Watkins*, 367 U.S. 488 (1961), punish the expression of religious doctrines it believes to be false, *United States v. Ballard*, 322 U.S. 78, 86-88 (1944), impose special disabilities on the basis of religious views or religious status, [*e.g., McDaniel v. Paty*, 435 U.S. 618 (1978)], or lend its power to one or the other side in controversies over religious authority or dogma, [*e.g., Presbyterian Church v. Hull Church*, 393 U.S. 440, 445-452 (1969)].

But the "exercise of religion" often involves not only belief and profession but the performance of (or abstention from) physical acts: assembling with others for a worship service, participating in sacramental use of bread and wine, proselytizing, abstaining from certain foods or certain modes of transportation. It would be true, we think (though no case of ours has involved the point), that a state would be "prohibiting the free exercise [of religion]" if it sought to ban such acts or abstentions only when they are engaged in for religious reasons, or only because of the religious belief that they display. It would doubtless be unconstitutional, for example, to ban the casting of "statues that are to be used for worship purposes," or to prohibit bowing down before a golden calf.

Respondents in the present case, however, seek to carry the meaning of "prohibiting the free exercise [of religion]" one large step further. They contend that their religious motivation for using peyote places them beyond the reach of a criminal law that is not specifically directed at their religious practice, and that is concededly constitutional as applied to those who use the drug for other reasons. They assert, in other words, that "prohibiting the free exercise [of religion]" includes requiring any individual to observe a generally applicable law that requires (or forbids) the performance of an act that his religious belief forbids (or requires). As a textual matter, we do not think the words must be given that meaning. It is no more necessary to regard the collection of a general tax, for example, as "prohibiting the free exercise [of religion]" by those citizens who believe support of organized government to be sinful, than it is to regard the same tax as "abridging the freedom ... of the press" of those publishing companies that must pay the tax as a condition of staying in business. It is a permissible reading of the text, in the one case as in the other, to say that if prohibiting the exercise of religion (or burdening the activity of printing) is not the object of the tax but merely the incidental effect of a generally applicable and otherwise valid provision, the First Amendment has not been offended. *Compare Citizen Publishing Co. v. United States*, 394 U.S. 131, 139 (1969) (upholding application of antitrust laws to press), with *Grosjean v. American Press Co.*, 297 U.S. 233, 250-251 (1936) (striking down license tax applied only to newspapers with weekly circulation above a specified level); *see generally Minneapolis Star & Tribune Co. v. Minnesota Commissioner of Revenue*, 460 U.S. 575, 581 (1983).

Our decisions reveal that the latter reading is the correct one. We have never held that an individual's religious beliefs excuse him from compliance with an otherwise valid law prohibiting conduct that the State is free to regulate. On the contrary, the record of more than a century of our free exercise jurisprudence contradicts that proposition. As described succinctly by Justice Frankfurter in *Minersville School Dist. Bd. of Educ. v. Gobitis*, 310 U.S. 586, 594-595 (1940): "Conscientious scruples have not, in the course of the long struggle for religious toleration, relieved the individual from obedience to a general law not aimed at the promotion or restriction of religious beliefs. The mere possession of religious convictions which contradict the relevant concerns of a political society does not relieve the citizen from the discharge of political responsibilities (footnote omitted)." We first had occasion to assert that principle in *Reynolds v. United States*, 98 U.S. 145 (1879), where we rejected the claim that criminal laws against polygamy could not be constitutionally applied to those whose religion commanded the practice. "Laws," we said, "are made for the government of actions, and while they cannot interfere with mere religious belief and opinions, they may with practices.... Can man excuse his practices to the contrary because of his religious belief? To permit this would be to make the professed doctrines of religious belief superior to the law of the land, and in effect to permit every citizen to become a law unto himself."

Subsequent decisions have consistently held that the right of free exercise does not relieve an individual of the obligation to comply with a "valid and neutral law of general applicability on the ground that the law proscribes (or prescribes) conduct that his religion prescribes (or proscribes)." *United States v. Lee*, 455 U.S. 252, 263, n. 3 (1982) (STEVENS, J., concurring in judgment); *see Minersville School Dist. Bd. of Educ. v. Gobitis, supra*, at 595 (collecting cases). In *Prince v. Massachusetts*, 321 U.S. 158 (1944), we held that a mother could be prosecuted under the child labor laws for using her children to dispense literature in the streets, her religious motivation notwithstanding. We found no constitutional infirmity in "excluding [these children] from doing there what no other children may do." In *Braunfield v. Brown*, 366 U.S. 599 (1961) (plurality opinion), we upheld Sunday-closing laws against the claim that they burdened the religious practices of persons whose religions compelled them to refrain from work on other days. In *Gillette v. United States*, 401 U.S. 437, 461 (1971), we sustained the military selective service system against the claim that it violated free exercise by conscripting persons who opposed a particular war on religious grounds.

Our most recent decision involving a neutral, generally applicable regulatory law that compelled activity forbidden by an individual's religion was *United States v. Lee*, 455 U.S. at 258-261. There, an Amish employer, on behalf of

himself and his employees, sought exemption from collection and payment of
Social Security taxes on the ground that the Amish faith prohibited participation in governmental support programs. We rejected the claim that an exemption was constitutionally required. There would be no way, we observed, to
distinguish the Amish believer's objection to Social Security taxes from the
religious objections that others might have to the collection or use of other
taxes. "If, for example, a religious adherent believes war is a sin, and if a certain
percentage of the federal budget can be identified as devoted to war-related
activities, such individuals would have a similarly valid claim to be exempted
from paying that percentage of the income tax. The tax system could not function if denominations were allowed to challenge the tax system because tax
payments were spent in a manner that violates their religious belief." *Id.*

The only decisions in which we have held that the First Amendment bars
application of a neutral, generally applicable law to religiously motivated action
have involved not the Free Exercise Clause alone, but the Free Exercise Clause
in conjunction with other constitutional protections, such as freedom of speech
and of the press, *see Cantwell v. Connecticut*, 310 U.S. at 304-307 (invalidating
a licensing system for religious and charitable solicitations under which the
administrator had discretion to deny a license to any cause he deemed nonreligious); *Murdock v. Pennsylvania*, 319 U.S. 105 (1943) (invalidating a flat tax on
solicitation as applied to the dissemination of religious ideas); *Follett v.
McCormick*, 321 U.S. 573 (1944) (same), or the right of parents, acknowledged
in *Pierce v. Society of Sisters*, 268 U.S. 510 (1925), to direct the education of
their children, *see Wisconsin v. Yoder*, 406 U.S. 205 (1972) (invalidating compulsory school-attendance laws as applied to Amish parents who refused on
religious grounds to send their children to school). Some of our cases prohibiting compelled expression, decided exclusively upon free speech grounds, have
also involved freedom of religion, *cf. Wooley v. Maynard*, 430 U.S. 705 (1977)
(invalidating compelled display of a license plate slogan that offended individual religious beliefs); *West Virginia Board of Education v. Barnette*, 319 U.S.
624 (1943) (invalidating compulsory flag salute statute challenged by religious
objectors). And it is easy to envision a case in which a challenge on freedom of
association grounds would likewise be reinforced by Free Exercise Clause concerns.

The present case does not present such a hybrid situation, but a free exercise
claim unconnected with any communicative activity or parental right. Respondents urge us to hold, quite simply, that when otherwise prohibitable conduct is
accompanied by religious convictions, not only the convictions but the conduct
itself must be free from governmental regulation. We have never held that, and
decline to do so now. There being no contention that Oregon's drug law represents an attempt to regulate religious beliefs, the communication of religious
beliefs, or the raising of one's children in those beliefs, the rule to which we
have adhered ever since *Reynolds* plainly controls. "Our cases do not at their
farthest reach support the proposition that a stance of conscientious opposition
relieves an objector from any colliding duty fixed by a democratic government."
Gillette v. United States, supra, at 461.

B

Respondents argue that even though exemption from generally applicable criminal laws need not automatically be extended to religiously motivated actors, at least the claim for a religious exemption must be evaluated under the balancing test set forth in *Sherbert v. Verner*, 374 U.S. 398 (1963). Under the *Sherbert* test, governmental actions that substantially burden a religious practice must be justified by a compelling governmental interest. [While we have applied this test three times to unemployment compensation cases, we] have never invalidated any governmental action on the basis of the *Sherbert* test except the denial of unemployment compensation. Although we have sometimes purported to apply the *Sherbert* test in contexts other than that, we have always found the test satisfied, *see United States v. Lee*, 455 U.S. 252 (1982); *Gillette v. United States*, 401 U.S. 437 (1971). In recent years we have abstained from applying the *Sherbert* test (outside the unemployment compensation field) at all. In *Bowen v. Roy*, 476 U.S. 693 (1986), we declined to apply *Sherbert* analysis to a federal statutory scheme that required benefit applicants and recipients to provide their Social Security numbers. The plaintiffs in that case asserted that it would violate their religious beliefs to obtain and provide a Social Security number for their daughter. We held the statute's application to the plaintiffs valid regardless of whether it was necessary to effectuate a compelling interest. In *Lyng v. Northwest Indian Cemetery Protective Assn.*, 485 U.S. 439 (1988), we declined to apply *Sherbert* analysis to the Government's logging and road construction activities on lands used for religious purposes by several Native American Tribes, even though it was undisputed that the activities "could have devastating effects on traditional Indian religious practices."

Even if we were inclined to breathe into *Sherbert* some life beyond the unemployment compensation field, we would not apply it to require exemptions from a generally applicable criminal law. The *Sherbert* test, it must be recalled, was developed in a context that lent itself to individualized governmental assessment of the reasons for the relevant conduct. As a plurality of the Court noted in *Roy*, a distinctive feature of unemployment compensation programs is that their eligibility criteria invite consideration of the particular circumstances behind an applicant's unemployment: "The statutory conditions [in *Sherbert* and *Thomas*] provided that a person was not eligible for unemployment compensation benefits if, 'without good cause,' he had quit work or refused available work. The 'good cause' standard created a mechanism for individualized exemptions." As the plurality pointed out in *Roy*, our decisions in the unemployment cases stand for the proposition that where the State has in place a system of individual exemptions, it may not refuse to extend that system to cases of "religious hardship" without compelling reason. *Bowen v. Roy, supra*, at 708.

Whether or not the decisions are that limited, they at least have nothing to do with an across-the-board criminal prohibition on a particular form of conduct. Although, as noted earlier, we have sometimes used the *Sherbert* test to analyze free exercise challenges to such laws, we have never applied the test to invalidate one. We conclude today that the sounder approach, and the approach in accord with the vast majority of our precedents, is to hold the test inapplicable to such challenges. The government's ability to enforce generally applicable prohibitions of socially harmful conduct, like its ability to carry out other aspects of public policy, "cannot depend on measuring the effects of a governmental action on a religious objector's spiritual development." *Lyng, supra*, at 451. To make an individual's obligation to obey such a law contingent upon the law's coincidence with his religious beliefs, except where the State's interest is "compelling" — permitting him, by virtue of his beliefs, "to become a law unto himself," *Reynolds v. United States*, 98 U.S., at 167 — contradicts both constitutional tradition and common sense.[2]

The "compelling government interest" requirement seems benign, because it is familiar from other fields. But using it as the standard that must be met before the government may accord different treatment on the basis of race, or before the government may regulate the content of speech, is not remotely comparable to using it for the purpose asserted here. What it produces in those other fields — equality of treatment, and an unrestricted flow of contending speech — are constitutional norms; what it would produce here — a private right to ignore generally applicable laws — is a constitutional anomaly.[3]

Nor is it possible to limit the impact of respondents' proposal by requiring a "compelling state interest" only when the conduct prohibited is "central" to the individual's religion. Cf. *Lyng v. Northwest Indian Cemetery Protective Assn., supra*, at __ (BRENNAN, J., dissenting). It is no more appropriate for judges to determine the "centrality" of religious beliefs before applying a "compelling interest" test in the free exercise field, than it would be for them to determine the "importance" of ideas before applying the "compelling interest" test in the free speech field. What principle of law or logic can be brought to bear to

---

[2] Justice O'CONNOR seeks to distinguish *Lyng v. Northwest Indian Cemetery Protective Assn., supra*, and *Bowen v. Roy, supra*, on the ground that those cases involved the government's conduct of "its own internal affairs," which is different because, as Justice Douglas said in *Sherbert*, "'the Free Exercise Clause is written in terms of what the government cannot do to the individual, not in terms of what the individual can exact from the government.'" (O'Connor, J., concurring), quoting *Sherbert, supra*, at 412 (Douglas, J., concurring). But since Justice Douglas voted with the majority in *Sherbert*, that quote obviously envisioned that what "the government cannot do to the individual" includes not just the prohibition of an individual's freedom of action through criminal laws but also the running of its programs (in *Sherbert*, state unemployment compensation) in such fashion as to harm the individual's religious interests. Moreover, it is hard to see any reason in principle or practicality why the government should have to tailor its health and safety laws to conform to the diversity of religious belief, but should not have to tailor its management of public lands, *Lyng, supra*, or its administration of welfare programs, *Roy, supra*.

[3] Justice O'CONNOR suggests that "[t]here is nothing talismanic about neutral laws of general applicability," and that all laws burdening religious practices should be subject to compelling-interest scrutiny because "the First Amendment unequivocally makes freedom of religion, like freedom from race discrimination and freedom of speech, a 'constitutional norm,' not an 'anomaly.'" (O'CONNOR, J., concurring). But this comparison with other fields supports, rather than undermines, the conclusion we draw today. Just as we subject to the most exacting scrutiny laws that make classifications based on race, or on the content of speech, so too we strictly scrutinize governmental classifications based on religion, see *McDaniel v. Paty*, 435 U.S. 618 (1978); see also *Torcaso v. Watkins*, 367 U.S. 488 (1961). But we have held that race-neutral laws that have the effect of disproportionately disadvantaging a particular racial group do not thereby become subject to compelling-interest analysis under the Equal Protection Clause, see *Washington v. Davis*, 426 U.S. 229 (1976) (police employment examination); and we have held that generally applicable laws unconcerned with regulating speech that have the effect of interfering with speech do not thereby become subject to compelling-interest analysis under the First Amendment, see *Citizen Publishing Co. v. United States*, 394 U.S. 131, 139 (1969) (antitrust laws). Our conclusion that generally applicable, religion-neutral laws that have the effect of burdening a particular religious practice need not be justified by a compelling governmental interest is the only approach compatible with these precedents.

contradict a believer's assertion that a particular act is "central" to his personal faith? Judging the centrality of different religious practices is akin to the unacceptable "business of evaluating the relative merits of differing religious claims." *United States v. Lee*, 455 U.S., at 263 n. 2 (STEVENS, J., concurring). As we reaffirmed only last Term, "[i]t is not within the judicial ken to question the centrality of particular beliefs or practices to a faith, or the validity of particular litigants' interpretation of those creeds." *Hernandez v. Commissioner*, [109 S. Ct. 2136, 2149]. Repeatedly and in many different contexts, we have warned that courts must not presume to determine the place of a particular belief in a religion or the plausibility of a religious claim.[4]

Nor is this difficulty avoided by Justice BLACKMUN's assertion that "although courts should refrain from delving into questions of whether, as a matter of religious doctrine, a particular practice is 'central' to the religion, I do not think this means that the courts must turn a blind eye to the severe impact of a State's restrictions on the adherents of a minority religion." (BLACKMUN, J. dissenting). As Justice BLACKMUN's opinion proceeds to make clear, inquiry into "severe impact" is no different from inquiry into centrality. He has merely substituted for the question "How important is X to the religious adherent?" the question "How great will be the harm to the religious adherent if X is taken away?" There is no material difference.

If the "compelling interest" test is to be applied at all, then, it must be applied across the board, to all actions thought to be religiously commanded. Moreover, if "compelling interest" really means what it says (and watering it down here would subvert its rigor in the other fields where it is applied), many laws will not meet the test. Any society adopting such a system would be courting anarchy, but that danger increases in direct proportion to the society's diversity of religious beliefs, and its determination to coerce or suppress none of them. Precisely because "we are a cosmopolitan nation made up of people of almost every conceivable religious preference," and precisely because we value and protect that religious divergence, we cannot afford the luxury of deeming presumptively invalid, as applied to the religious objector, every regulation of conduct that does not protect an interest of the highest order. The rule respondents favor would open the prospect of constitutionally required religious exemptions from civic obligations of almost every conceivable kind — ranging from compulsory military service, to the payment of taxes, to health and safety regulation such as manslaughter and child neglect laws, compulsory vaccination laws, drug

---

[4] While arguing that we should apply the compelling interest test in this case, Justice O'CONNOR nonetheless agrees that "our determination of the constitutionality of Oregon's general criminal prohibition cannot, and should not, turn on the centrality of the particular religious practice at issue," (O'CONNOR, J., concurring). This means, presumably, that compelling interest scrutiny must be applied to generally applicable laws that regulate or prohibit any religiously motivated activity, no matter how unimportant to the claimant's religion. Earlier in her opinion, however, Justice O'CONNOR appears to contradict this, saying that the proper approach is "to determine whether the burden on the specific plaintiffs before us is constitutionally significant and whether the particular criminal interest asserted by the State before us is compelling." "Constitutionally significant burden" would seem to be "centrality" under another name. In any case, dispensing with a "centrality" inquiry is utterly unworkable. It would require, for example, the same degree of "compelling state interest" to impede the practice of throwing rice at church weddings as to impede the practice of getting married in church. There is no way out of the difficulty that, if general laws are to be subjected to a "religious practice" exception, both the importance of the law at issue and the centrality of the practice at issue must reasonably be considered.

laws, and traffic laws; to social welfare legislation such as minimum wage laws, child labor laws, animal cruelty laws, environmental protection laws, and laws providing for equality of opportunity for the races. The First Amendment's protection of religious liberty does not require this.[5]

Values that are protected against government interference through enshrinement in the Bill of Rights are not thereby banished from the political process. Just as a society that believes in the negative protection accorded to the press by the First Amendment is likely to enact laws that affirmatively foster the dissemination of the printed word, so also a society that believes in the negative protection accorded to religious belief can be expected to be solicitous of that value in its legislation as well. It is therefore not surprising that a number of States have made an exception to their drug laws for sacramental peyote use. See, e. g., Ariz. Rev. Stat. Ann. § 13-3402(b)(1)-(3) (1989); Colo. Rev. Stat. § 12-22-317(3) (1985); N. M. Stat. Ann. § 30-31-6(D) (Supp. 1989). But to say that a nondiscriminatory religious-practice exemption is permitted, or even that it is desirable, is not to say that it is constitutionally required, and that the appropriate occasions for its creation can be discerned by the courts. It may fairly be said that leaving accommodation to the political process will place at a relative disadvantage those religious practices that are not widely engaged in; but that unavoidable consequence of democratic government must be preferred to a system in which each conscience is a law unto itself or in which judges weigh the social importance of all laws against the centrality of all religious beliefs.

. . . .

Because respondents' ingestion of peyote was prohibited under Oregon law, and because that prohibition is constitutional, Oregon may, consistent with the Free Exercise Clause, deny respondents unemployment compensation when their dismissal results from use of the drug. The decision of the Oregon Supreme Court is accordingly *reversed*.

It is so ordered.

Justice O'CONNOR, with whom Justice BRENNAN, Justice MARSHALL, and Justice BLACKMUN join as to Parts I and II, concurring in the judgment.[*]

Although I agree with the result the Court reaches in this case, I cannot join its opinion. In my view, today's holding dramatically departs from well-settled First Amendment jurisprudence, appears unnecessary to resolve the question presented, and is incompatible with our Nation's fundamental commitment to individual religious liberty.

---

[5] Justice O'CONNOR contends that the "parade of horribles" in the text only "demonstrates . . . that courts have been quite capable of strik[ing] sensible balances between religious liberty and competing state interests." (O'CONNOR, J., concurring). But the cases we cite have struck "sensible balances" only because they have all applied the general laws, despite the claims for religious exemption. In any event, Justice O'CONNOR mistakes the purpose of our parade: it is not to suggest that courts would necessarily permit harmful exemptions from these laws (though they might), but to suggest that courts would constantly be in the business of determining whether the "severe impact" of various laws on religious practice (to use Justice BLACKMUN's terminology) or the "constitutiona[l] significan[ce]" of the "burden on the particular plaintiffs" (to use Justice O'CONNOR's terminology) suffices to permit us to confer an exemption. It is a parade of horribles because it is horrible to contemplate that federal judges will regularly balance against the importance of general laws the significance of religious practice.

[*] Although Justice BRENNAN, Justice MARSHALL, and Justice BLACKMUN join Parts I and II of this opinion, they do not concur in the judgment.

I

At the outset, I note that I agree with the Court's implicit determination that the constitutional question upon which we granted review — whether the Free Exercise Clause protects a person's religiously motivated use of peyote from the reach of a State's general criminal law prohibition — is properly presented [here].

II

The Court today extracts from our long history of free exercise precedents the single categorical rule that "if prohibiting the exercise of religion ... is ... merely the incidental effect of a generally applicable and otherwise valid provision, the First Amendment has not been offended." Indeed, the Court holds that where the law is a generally applicable criminal prohibition, our usual free exercise jurisprudence does not even apply. To reach this sweeping result, however, the Court must not only give a strained reading of the First Amendment but must also disregard our consistent application of free exercise doctrine to cases involving generally applicable regulations that burden religious conduct.

A

The Free Exercise Clause of the First Amendment commands that "Congress shall make no law ... prohibiting the free exercise [of religion]." In *Cantwell v. Connecticut*, 310 U.S. 296 (1940), we held that this prohibition applies to the States by incorporation into the Fourteenth Amendment and that it categorically forbids government regulation of religious beliefs. As the Court recognizes, however, the "free exercise" of religion often, if not invariably, requires the performance of (or abstention from) certain acts. [3 A New English Dictionary on Historical Principles 401-402 (J. Murray, ed. 1897) (defining "exercise" to include "[t]he practice and performance of rites and ceremonies, worship, etc.; the right or permission to celebrate the observances (of a religion)" and religious observances such as acts of public and private worship, preaching, and prophesying)]. "[B]elief and action cannot be neatly confined in logic-tight compartments." *Wisconsin v. Yoder*, 406 U.S. 205, 220 (1972). Because the First Amendment does not distinguish between religious belief and religious conduct, conduct motivated by sincere religious belief, like the belief itself, must therefore be at least presumptively protected by the Free Exercise Clause.

The Court today, however, interprets the Clause to permit the government to prohibit, without justification, conduct mandated by an individual's religious beliefs, so long as that prohibition is generally applicable. But a law that prohibits certain conduct — conduct that happens to be an act of worship for someone — manifestly does prohibit that person's free exercise of his religion. A person who is barred from engaging in religiously motivated conduct is barred from freely exercising his religion. Moreover, that person is barred from freely exercising his religion regardless of whether the law prohibits the conduct only when engaged in for religious reasons, only by members of that religion, or by all persons. It is difficult to deny that a law that prohibits religiously motivated conduct, even if the law is generally applicable, does not at least implicate First Amendment concerns.

The Court responds that generally applicable laws are "one large step" removed from laws aimed at specific religious practices. The First Amendment, however, does not distinguish between laws that are generally applicable and laws that target particular religious practices. Indeed, few States would be so naive as to enact a law directly prohibiting or burdening a religious practice as such. Our free exercise cases have all concerned generally applicable laws that had the effect of significantly burdening a religious practice. If the First Amendment is to have any vitality, it ought not be construed to cover only the extreme and hypothetical situation in which a State directly targets a religious practice. As we have noted in a slightly different context, "'[s]uch a test has no basis in precedent and relegates a serious First Amendment value to the barest level of minimum scrutiny that the Equal Protection Clause already provides.'" *Hobbie v. Unemployment Appeals Comm'n of Florida*, 480 U.S. 136, 141-142 (1987) (quoting *Bowen v. Roy*, 476 U.S. 693, 727 (1986) (opinion concurring in part and dissenting in part)).

To say that a person's right to free exercise has been burdened, of course, does not mean that he has an absolute right to engage in the conduct. Under our established First Amendment jurisprudence, we have recognized that the freedom to act, unlike the freedom to believe, cannot be absolute. *See, e.g., Cantwell, supra,* at 304; *Reynolds v. United States,* 98 U.S. 145, 161-167 (1879). Instead, we have respected both the First Amendment's express textual mandate and the governmental interest in regulation of conduct by requiring the Government to justify any substantial burden on religiously motivated conduct by a compelling state interest and by means narrowly tailored to achieve that interest. The compelling interest test effectuates the First Amendment's command that religious liberty is an independent liberty, that it occupies a preferred position, and that the Court will not permit encroachments upon this liberty, whether direct or indirect, unless required by clear and compelling governmental interests "of the highest order," *Yoder, supra,* at 215. "Only an especially important governmental interest pursued by narrowly tailored means can justify exacting a sacrifice of First Amendment freedoms as the price for an equal share of the rights, benefits, and privileges enjoyed by other citizens." *Roy, supra,* at 728 (opinion concurring in part and dissenting in part).

The Court attempts to support its narrow reading of the Clause by claiming that "[w]e have never held that an individual's religious beliefs excuse him from compliance with an otherwise valid law prohibiting conduct that the State is free to regulate." But as the Court later notes, as it must, in cases such as *Cantwell* and *Yoder* we have in fact interpreted the Free Exercise Clause to forbid application of a generally applicable prohibition to religiously motivated conduct. Indeed, in *Yoder* we expressly rejected the interpretation the Court now adopts:

> "[O]ur decisions have rejected the idea that religiously grounded conduct is always outside the protection of the Free Exercise Clause. It is true that activities of individuals, even when religiously based, are often subject to regulation by the States in the exercise of their undoubted power to promote the health, safety, and general welfare, or the Federal Government in the exercise of its delegated powers. But to agree that

religiously grounded conduct must often be subject to the broad police power of the State is not to deny that there are areas of conduct protected by the Free Exercise Clause of the First Amendment and thus beyond the power of the State to control, even under regulations of general applicability....

"... A regulation neutral on its face may, in its application, nonetheless offend the constitutional requirement for government neutrality if it unduly burdens the free exercise of religion." 406 U.S., at 219-220 (emphasis added; citations omitted).

The Court endeavors to escape from our decisions in *Cantwell* and *Yoder* by labeling them "hybrid" decisions, but there is no denying that both cases expressly relied on the Free Exercise Clause, and that we have consistently regarded those cases as part of the mainstream of our free exercise jurisprudence. Moreover, in each of the other cases cited by the Court to support its categorical rule, we rejected the particular constitutional claims before us only after carefully weighing the competing interests. [*See Prince v. Massachusetts*, 321 U.S. 158, 168-170 (1944) (state interest in regulating children's activities justifies denial of religious exemption from child labor laws); *Braunfield v. Brown*, 366 U.S. 599, 608-609 (1961) (plurality opinion) (state interest in uniform day of rest justifies denial of religious exemption from Sunday closing law)]. That we rejected the free exercise claims in those cases hardly calls into question the applicability of First Amendment doctrine in the first place. Indeed, it is surely unusual to judge the vitality of a constitutional doctrine by looking to the win-loss record of the plaintiffs who happen to come before us.

B

Respondents, of course, do not contend that their conduct is automatically immune from all governmental regulation simply because it is motivated by their sincere religious beliefs. The Court's rejection of that argument, might therefore be regarded as merely harmless dictum. Rather, respondents invoke our traditional compelling interest test to argue that the Free Exercise Clause requires the State to grant them a limited exemption from its general criminal prohibition against the possession of peyote. The Court today, however, denies them even the opportunity to make that argument, concluding that "the sounder approach, and the approach in accord with the vast majority of our precedents, is to hold the [compelling interest] test inapplicable to" challenges to general criminal prohibitions.

In my view, however, the essence of a free exercise claim is relief from a burden imposed by government on religious practices or beliefs, whether the burden is imposed directly through laws that prohibit or compel specific religious practices, or indirectly through laws that, in effect, make abandonment of one's own religion or conformity to the religious beliefs of others the price of an equal place in the civil community. As we explained in *Thomas*:

"Where the state conditions receipt of an important benefit upon conduct proscribed by a religious faith, or where it denies such a benefit because of conduct mandated by religious belief, thereby putting substantial pressure on an adherent to modify his behavior and to violate his beliefs, a burden upon religion exists." 450 U.S., at 717-718.

A State that makes criminal an individual's religiously motivated conduct burdens that individual's free exercise of religion in the severest manner possible, for it "results in the choice to the individual of either abandoning his religious principle or facing criminal prosecution." I would have thought it beyond argument that such laws implicate free exercise concerns.

Indeed, we have never distinguished between cases in which a State conditions receipt of a benefit on conduct prohibited by religious beliefs and cases in which a State affirmatively prohibits such conduct. The *Sherbert* compelling interest test applies in both kinds of cases. [Hence] I would reaffirm that principle today: a neutral criminal law prohibiting conduct that a State may legitimately regulate is, if anything, more burdensome than a neutral civil statute placing legitimate conditions on the award of a state benefit.

Legislatures, of course, have always been "left free to reach actions which were in violation of social duties or subversive of good order." *Reynolds*, 98 U.S., at 164; *see also Yoder*, 406 U.S., at 219-220; *Braunfield*, 366 U.S., at 603-604. Yet because of the close relationship between conduct and religious belief, "[i]n every case the power to regulate must be so exercised as not, in attaining a permissible end, unduly to infringe the protected freedom." *Cantwell*, 310 U.S., at 304. Once it has been shown that a government regulation or criminal prohibition burdens the free exercise of religion, we have consistently asked the Government to demonstrate that unbending application of its regulation to the religious objector "is essential to accomplish an overriding governmental interest," *Lee, supra*, at 257-258, or represents "the least restrictive means of achieving some compelling state interest," *Thomas*, 450 U.S., at 718. To me, the sounder approach — the approach more consistent with our role as judges to decide each case on its individual merits — is to apply this test in each case to determine whether the burden on the specific plaintiffs before us is constitutionally significant and whether the particular criminal interest asserted by the State before us is compelling. Even if, as an empirical matter, a government's criminal laws might usually serve a compelling interest in health, safety, or public order, the First Amendment at least requires a case-by-case determination of the question, sensitive to the facts of each particular claim. Given the range of conduct that a State might legitimately make criminal, we cannot assume, merely because a law carries criminal sanctions and is generally applicable, that the First Amendment never requires the State to grant a limited exemption for religiously motivated conduct.

[Today, the Court] gives no convincing reason to depart from settled First Amendment jurisprudence. There is nothing talismanic about neutral laws of general applicability or general criminal prohibitions, for laws neutral toward religion can coerce a person to violate his religious conscience or intrude upon his religious duties just as effectively as laws aimed at religion. Although the Court suggests that the compelling interest test, as applied to generally applicable laws, would result in a "constitutional anomaly," the First Amendment unequivocally makes freedom of religion, like freedom from race discrimination and freedom of speech, a "constitutional nor[m]," not an "anomaly." Nor would application of our established free exercise doctrine to this case necessarily be incompatible with our equal protection cases. [See, e.g., McConnell, Accommodation of Religion, 1985 Sup. Ct. Rev. 1, 9 ("[T]he text of the First Amendment itself 'singles out' religion for special protections"); P. Kauper, Religion and the Constitution 17 (1964)]. A law that makes criminal such an activity therefore triggers constitutional concern — and heightened judicial scrutiny — even if it does not target the particular religious conduct at issue. Our free speech cases similarly recognize that neutral regulations that affect free speech values are subject to a balancing, rather than categorical, approach. The Court's parade of horribles, not only fails as a reason for discarding the compelling interest test, it instead demonstrates just the opposite: that courts have been quite capable of applying our free exercise jurisprudence to strike sensible balances between religious liberty and competing state interests.

Finally, the Court today suggests that the disfavoring of minority religions is an "unavoidable consequence" under our system of government and that accommodation of such religions must be left to the political process. In my view, however, the First Amendment was enacted precisely to protect the rights of those whose religious practices are not shared by the majority and may be viewed with hostility. The history of our free exercise doctrine amply demonstrates the harsh impact majoritarian rule has had on unpopular or emerging religious groups such as the Jehovah's Witnesses and the Amish. Indeed, the words of Justice Jackson in *West Virginia Board of Education v. Barnette* (overruling *Minersville School District v. Gobitis*, 310 U.S. 586 (1940)) are apt:

> "The very purpose of a Bill of Rights was to withdraw certain subjects from the vicissitudes of political controversy, to place them beyond the reach of majorities and officials and to establish them as legal principles to be applied by the courts. One's right to life, liberty, and property, to free speech, a free press, freedom of worship and assembly, and other fundamental rights may not be submitted to vote; they depend on the outcome of no elections." 319 U.S., at 638.

The compelling interest test reflects the First Amendment's mandate of preserving religious liberty to the fullest extent possible in a pluralistic society. For the Court to deem this command a "luxury," is to denigrate "[t]he very purpose of a Bill of Rights."

III

The Court's holding today not only misreads settled First Amendment precedent; it appears to be unnecessary to this case. I would reach the same result applying our established free exercise jurisprudence.

A

There is no dispute that Oregon's criminal prohibition of peyote places a severe burden on the ability of respondents to freely exercise their religion. Peyote is a sacrament of the Native American Church, and is regarded as vital to respondents' ability to practice their religion. [In addition, there] is also no dispute that Oregon has a significant interest in enforcing laws that control the possession and use of controlled substances by its citizens. As we recently noted, drug abuse is "one of the greatest problems affecting the health and welfare of our population" and thus "one of the most serious problems confronting our society today." [P]eyote is specifically regulated as a Schedule I controlled substance [because] Congress has found that it has a high potential for abuse, that there is no currently accepted medical use, and that there is a lack of accepted safety [*sic*] for use of the drug under medical supervision. [R]espondents do not seriously dispute that Oregon has a compelling interest in prohibiting the possession of peyote by its citizens.

B

Thus, the critical question in this case is whether exempting respondents from the State's general criminal prohibition "will unduly interfere with fulfillment of the governmental interest." Although the question is close, I would conclude that uniform application of Oregon's criminal prohibition is "essential to accomplish" *Lee, supra,* at 257, its overriding interest in preventing the physical harm caused by the use of a Schedule I controlled substance. Oregon's criminal prohibition represents that State's judgment that the possession and use of controlled substances, even by only one person, is inherently harmful and dangerous. Because the health effects caused by the use of controlled substances exist regardless of the motivation of the user, the use of such substances, even for religious purposes, violates the very purpose of the laws that prohibit them....

For these reasons, I believe that granting a selective exemption in this case would seriously impair Oregon's compelling interest in prohibiting possession of peyote by its citizens. Under such circumstances, the Free Exercise Clause does not require the State to accommodate respondents' religiously motivated conduct....

I would therefore adhere to our established free exercise jurisprudence and hold that the State in this case has a compelling interest in regulating peyote use by its citizens and that accommodating respondents' religiously motivated conduct "will unduly interfere with fulfillment of the governmental interest." *Lee,* 455 U.S., at 259. Accordingly, I concur in the judgment of the Court.

Justice BLACKMUN, with whom Justice BRENNAN and Justice MARSHALL join, dissenting.

This Court over the years painstakingly has developed a consistent and exacting standard to test the constitutionality of a state statute that burdens the free exercise of religion. Such a statute may stand only if the law in general, and the State's refusal to allow a religious exemption in particular, are justified by a compelling interest that cannot be served by less restrictive means.

Until today, I thought this was a settled and inviolate principle of this Court's First Amendment jurisprudence. The majority, however, perfunctorily dismisses it as a "constitutional anomaly." As carefully detailed in Justice O'CONNOR's concurring opinion, the majority is able to arrive at this view only by mischaracterizing this Court's precedents. The Court discards leading free exercise cases such as *Cantwell v. Connecticut,* 310 U.S. 296 (1940), and *Wisconsin v. Yoder,* 406 U.S. 205 (1972), as "hybrid." The Court views traditional free exercise analysis as somehow inapplicable to criminal prohibitions (as opposed to conditions on the receipt of benefits), and to state laws of general applicability (as opposed, presumably, to laws that expressly single out religious practices). The Court cites cases in which, due to various exceptional circumstances, we found strict scrutiny inapposite, to hint that the Court has repudiated that standard altogether. In short, it effectuates a wholesale overturning of settled law concerning the Religion Clauses of our Constitution. One hopes that the

Court is aware of the consequences, and that its result is not a product of overreaction to the serious problems the country's drug crisis has generated.

This distorted view of our precedents leads the majority to conclude that strict scrutiny of a state law burdening the free exercise of religion is a "luxury" that a well-ordered society cannot afford, and that the repression of minority religions is an "unavoidable consequence of democratic government." I do not believe the Founders thought their dearly bought freedom from religious persecution a "luxury," but an essential element of liberty — and they could not have thought religious intolerance "unavoidable," for they drafted the Religion Clauses precisely in order to avoid that intolerance.

For these reasons, I agree with Justice O'CONNOR's analysis of the applicable free exercise doctrine, and I join Parts I and II of her opinion. As she points out, "the critical question in this case is whether exempting respondents from the State's general criminal prohibition 'will unduly interfere with fulfillment of the governmental interest.'" I do disagree, however, with her specific answer to that question.

I

In weighing respondents' clear interest in the free exercise of their religion against Oregon's asserted interest in enforcing its drug laws, it is important to articulate in precise terms the state interest involved. It is not the State's broad interest in fighting the critical "war on drugs" that must be weighed against respondents' claim, but the State's narrow interest in refusing to make an exception for the religious, ceremonial use of peyote. Failure to reduce the competing interests to the same plane of generality tends to distort the weighing process in the State's favor. See Clark, *Guidelines for the Free Exercise Clause*, 83 Harv. L. Rev. 327, 330-331 (1969) ("The purpose of almost any law can be traced back to one or another of the fundamental concerns of government: public health and safety, public peace and order, defense, revenue. To measure an individual interest directly against one of these rarified values inevitably makes the individual interest appear the less significant"); Pound, *A Survey of Social Interests,* 57 Harv. L. Rev. 1, 2 (1943) ("When it comes to weighing or valuing claims or demands with respect to other claims or demands, we must be careful to compare them on the same plane ... [or else] we may decide the question in advance in our very way of putting it").

It is surprising, to say the least, that this Court which so often prides itself about principles of judicial restraint and reduction of federal control over matters of state law would stretch its jurisdiction to the limit in order to reach, in this abstract setting, the constitutionality of Oregon's criminal prohibition of peyote use.

The State's interest in enforcing its prohibition, in order to be sufficiently compelling to outweigh a free exercise claim, cannot be merely abstract or symbolic. The State cannot plausibly assert that unbending application of a criminal prohibition is essential to fulfill any compelling interest, if it does not, in fact, attempt to enforce that prohibition. In this case, the State actually has not evinced any concrete interest in enforcing its drug laws against religious users of peyote. Oregon has never sought to prosecute respondents, and does not claim that it has made significant enforcement efforts against other religious users of peyote. The State's asserted interest thus amounts only to the symbolic preservation of an unenforced prohibition. But a government interest in "symbolism, even symbolism for so worthy a cause as the abolition of unlawful drugs," cannot suffice to abrogate the constitutional rights of individuals.

Similarly, this Court's prior decisions have not allowed a government to rely on mere speculation about potential harms, but have demanded evidentiary support for a refusal to allow a religious exception. In this case, the State's justification for refusing to recognize an exception to its criminal laws for religious peyote use is entirely speculative.

The State proclaims an interest in protecting the health and safety of its citizens from the dangers of unlawful drugs. It offers, however, no evidence that the religious use of peyote has ever harmed anyone. The factual findings of other courts cast doubt on the State's assumption that religious use of peyote is harmful. See *State v. Whittingham,* 19 Ariz. App. 27, 30, 504 P.2d 950, 953 (1973) ("the State failed to prove that the quantities of peyote used in the sacraments of the Native American Church are sufficiently harmful to the health and welfare of the participants so as to permit a legitimate intrusion under the State's police power"); *People v. Woody,* 61 Cal. 2d 716, 722-723, 394 P.2d 813, 818 (1964) ("as the Attorney General ... admits, the opinion of scientists and other experts is 'that peyote ... works no permanent deleterious injury to the Indian'").

The fact that peyote is classified as a Schedule I controlled substance does not, by itself, show that any and all uses of peyote, in any circumstance, are inherently harmful and dangerous. The Federal Government, which created the classifications of unlawful drugs from which Oregon's drug laws are derived, apparently does not find peyote so dangerous as to preclude an exemption for religious use.[5] Moreover, other Schedule I drugs have lawful uses.

[Furthermore], 23 States, including many that have significant Native American populations, have statutory or judicially crafted exemptions in their drug laws for religious use of peyote. *See Smith v. Employment Division,* 307 Ore. 68, 73, n. 2, 763 P.2d 146, 148, n. 2 (1988). Although this does not prove that Oregon must have such an exception too, it is significant that these States, and the Federal Government, all find their (presumably compelling) interests in controlling the use of dangerous drugs compatible with an exemption for religious use of peyote.

The carefully circumscribed ritual context in which respondents used peyote is far removed from the irresponsible and unrestricted recreational use of unlawful drugs.[6] The Native American Church's internal restrictions on, and

---

[5]See 21 CFR § 1307.31 (1989) ("The listing of peyote as a controlled substance in Schedule I does not apply to the nondrug use of peyote in bona fide religious ceremonies of the Native American Church, and members of the Native American Church so using peyote are exempt from registration. Any person who manufactures peyote for or distributes peyote to the Native American Church, however, is required to obtain registration annually and to comply with all other requirements of law"); *see Olsen v. Drug Enforcement Admin.,* [878 F.2d 1458, 1463-1464 (D.C. Cir. (1989)] (explaining DEA's rationale for the exception).

[6]In this respect, respondents' use of peyote seems closely analogous to the sacramental use of wine by the Roman Catholic Church. During Prohibition, the Federal Government exempted such use of wine from its general ban on possession and use of alcohol. See National Prohibition Act, Title II, § 3, 41 Stat. 308. However compelling the Government's then general interest in prohibit-

supervision of, its members' use of peyote substantially obviate the State's health and safety concerns.[7]

Moreover, just as in *Yoder*, the values and interests of those seeking a religious exemption in this case are congruent, to a great degree, with those the State seeks to promote through its drug laws. Not only does the Church's doctrine forbid nonreligious use of peyote; it also generally advocates self-reliance, familial responsibility, and abstinence from alcohol. There is considerable evidence that the spiritual and social support provided by the Church has been effective in combatting the tragic effects of alcoholism on the Native American population. Two noted experts on peyotism, Dr. Omer C. Stewart and Dr. Robert Bergman, testified by affidavit to this effect on behalf of respondent Smith before the Employment Appeal Board. Far from promoting the lawless and irresponsible use of drugs, Native American Church members' spiritual code exemplifies values that Oregon's drug laws are presumably intended to foster.

The State also seeks to support its refusal to make an exception for religious use of peyote by invoking its interest in abolishing drug trafficking. There is, however, practically no illegal traffic in peyote.

[Lastly,] the State argues that granting an exception for religious peyote use would erode its interest in the uniform, fair, and certain enforcement of its drug laws. The State fears that, if it grants an exemption for religious peyote use, a flood of other claims to religious exemptions will follow. It would then be placed in a dilemma, it says, between allowing a patchwork of exemptions that would hinder its law enforcement efforts, and risking a violation of the Establishment Clause by arbitrarily limiting its religious exemptions. This argument, however, could be made in almost any free exercise case. See Lupu, *Where Rights Begin: The Problem of Burdens on the Free Exercise of Religion*, 102 Harv. L. Rev. 933, 947 (1989) ("Behind every free exercise claim is a spectral march; grant this one, a voice whispers to each judge, and you will be confronted with an endless chain of exemption demands from religious deviants of every stripe"). This Court, however, consistently has rejected similar arguments in past free exercise cases, and it should do so here as well.

The State's apprehension of a flood of other religious claims is purely speculative. Almost half the States, and the Federal Government, have maintained an exemption for religious peyote use for many years, and apparently have not found themselves overwhelmed by claims to other religious exemptions. Allowing an exemption for religious peyote use would not necessarily oblige the State to grant a similar exemption to other religious groups. The unusual circumstances that make the religious use of peyote compatible with the State's interests in health and safety and in preventing drug trafficking would not apply to

---

ing the use of alcohol may have been, it could not plausibly have asserted an interest sufficiently compelling to outweigh Catholics' right to take communion.

[7] The use of peyote is, to some degree, self-limiting. The peyote plant is extremely bitter, and eating it is an unpleasant experience, which would tend to discourage casual or recreational use. *See State v. Whittingham*, 19 Ariz. App. 27, 30, 504 P.2d 950, 953 (1973) ("peyote can cause vomiting by reason of its bitter taste"); E. Anderson, Peyote: The Divine Cactus 161 (1980) ("[T]he eating of peyote usually is a difficult ordeal in that nausea and other unpleasant physical manifestations occur regularly. Repeated use is likely, therefore, only if one is a serious researcher or is devoutly involved in taking peyote as part of a religious ceremony"); Slotkin, The Peyote Way, at 98 ("many find it bitter, inducing indigestion or nausea").

other religious claims. Some religions, for example, might not restrict drug use to a limited ceremonial context, as does the Native American Church. Some religious claims involve drugs such as marijuana and heroin, in which there is significant illegal traffic, with its attendant greed and violence, so that it would be difficult to grant a religious exemption without seriously compromising law enforcement efforts. That the State might grant an exemption for religious peyote use, but deny other religious claims arising in different circumstances, would not violate the Establishment Clause. Though the State must treat all religions equally, and not favor one over another, this obligation is fulfilled by the uniform application of the "compelling interest" test to all free exercise claims, not by reaching uniform results as to all claims. A showing that religious peyote use does not unduly interfere with the State's interests is "one that probably few other religious groups or sects could make," *Yoder*, 406 U.S., at 236; this does not mean that an exemption limited to peyote use is tantamount to an establishment of religion.

III

Finally, although I agree with Justice O'CONNOR that courts should refrain from delving into questions of whether, as a matter of religious doctrine, a particular practice is "central" to the religion, I do not think this means that the courts must turn a blind eye to the severe impact of a State's restrictions on the adherents of a minority religion. *Cf. Yoder*, 406 U.S., at 219 (since "education is inseparable from and a part of the basic tenets of their religion ... [just as] baptism, the confessional, or a sabbath may be for others," enforcement of State's compulsory education law would "gravely endanger if not destroy the free exercise of respondents' religious beliefs").

Respondents believe, and their sincerity has never been at issue, that the peyote plant embodies their deity, and eating it is an act of worship and communion. Without peyote, they could not enact the essential ritual of their religion.

If Oregon can constitutionally prosecute them for this act of worship, they, like the Amish, may be "forced to migrate to some other and more tolerant region." *Yoder*, 406 U.S., at 218. This potentially devastating impact must be viewed in light of the federal policy — reached in reaction to many years of religious persecution and intolerance — of protecting the religious freedom of Native Americans. See American Indian Religious Freedom Act, 92 Stat. 469, 42 U.S.C. § 1996 ("it shall be the policy of the United States to protect and preserve for American Indians their inherent right of freedom to believe, express, and exercise the traditional religions ..., including but not limited to access to sites, use and possession of sacred objects, and the freedom to worship through ceremonials and traditional rites"). Congress recognized that certain substances, such as peyote, "have religious significance because they are sacred, they have power, they heal, they are necessary to the exercise of the rites of the religion, they are necessary to the cultural integrity of the tribe, and, therefore, religious survival." H. R. Rep. No. 95-1308, p. 2 (1978).

Indeed, Oregon's attitude toward respondents' religious peyote use harkens back to the repressive federal policies pursued a century ago:

"In the government's view, traditional practices were not only morally degrading, but unhealthy. 'Indians are fond of gatherings of every description,' a 1913 public health study complained, advocating the restriction of dances and 'sings' to stem contagious diseases. In 1921, the Commissioner of Indian Affairs Charles Burke reminded his staff to punish any Indian engaged in 'any dance which involves ... the reckless giving away of property ... frequent or prolonged periods of celebration ... in fact, any disorderly or plainly excessive performance that promotes superstitious cruelty, licentiousness, idleness, danger to health, and shiftless indifference to family welfare.' Two years later, he [forbade] Indians under the age of 50 from participating in any dances of any kind, and directed federal employees 'to educate public opinion' against them." *Id.*, at 370-371 (footnotes omitted).

The American Indian Religious Freedom Act, in itself, may not create rights enforceable against government action restricting religious freedom, but this Court must scrupulously apply its free exercise analysis to the religious claims of Native Americans, however unorthodox they may be. Otherwise, both the First Amendment and the stated policy of Congress will offer to Native Americans merely an unfulfilled and hollow promise.

IV

For these reasons, I conclude that Oregon's interest in enforcing its drug laws against religious use of peyote is not sufficiently compelling to outweigh respondents' right to the free exercise of their religion. Since the State could not constitutionally enforce its criminal prohibition against respondents, the interests underlying the State's drug laws cannot justify its denial of unemployment benefits. Absent such justification, the State's regulatory interest in denying benefits for religiously motivated "misconduct," is indistinguishable from the state interests this Court has rejected in *Frazee, Hobbie, Thomas*, and *Sherbert*. The State of Oregon cannot, consistently with the Free Exercise Clause, deny respondents unemployment benefits.

I dissent.

NOTES

1. Peyote, the Native American Church and the First Amendment: Prior to the Court's decision in *Smith*, many decisions that considered the question of ceremonial peyote use by the Native American Church had permitted such ceremonial use. The classic case was *People v. Woody*, 61 Cal. 2d 716, 394 P.2d 813, 40 Cal. Rptr. 69 (1964), in which the Court reversed the convictions of several Navajo Indians who had been convicted under state controlled substances laws for the ceremonial use of peyote at a Native American Church meeting in a remote California desert area. The court held that the first amendment free exercise clause protected the ritual, clearly applying a compelling government interest test. In response to the state's assertion of an interest that echoes those suggested in the *Clapox* decision, the California Supreme Court noted:

[Further the Attorney General] argues that since "peyote could be regarded as a symbol, one that obstructs enlightenment and shackles the Indian to primitive conditions" the responsibility rests with the state to eliminate its use. We know of no doctrine that the state, in its asserted omniscience, should undertake to deny to defendants the observance of their religion in order to free them from the superstitious "shackles" of their "unenlightened" and "primitive condition."

The court distinguished the *Reynolds* polygamy case, as relied upon in *Smith*, as follows:

> *Reynolds v. United States* must be distinguished from the instant case for two funda-
> mental reasons. The test of constitutionality calls for an examination of the degree of
> abridgement of religious freedom involved in each case. Polygamy, although a basic
> tenet in the theology of Mormonism, is not essential to the practice of the religion;
> peyote, on the other hand, is the *sine qua non* of defendants' faith. It is the sole means
> by which defendants are able to experience their religion; without peyote defendants
> cannot practice their faith. Second, the degree of danger to state interests in *Reynolds*
> far exceeded that in the instant case. The Court in *Reynolds* considered polygamy as a
> serious threat to democratic institutions and injurious to the morals and well-being of
> its practitioners. As we have heretofore indicated, no such compelling state interest
> supports the prohibition of the use of peyote.

Thus, the arguments made in *Woody* closely paralleled some of the arguments
made by Justice Blackmun's dissenting opinion and Justice O'Connor's concur-
ring opinion in *Smith*. After *Woody* the legal practice of permitting the Native
American Church to pursue the ceremonial use of peyote seemed reasonably
well accepted. *Native American Church of New York v. United States*, 468 F.
Supp. 1247 (S.D.N.Y. 1979), aff'd, 633 F.2d 205 (2d Cir. 1980); *In re Grady*, 61
Cal. 2d 887, 39 Cal. Rptr. 912, 394 P.2d 728 (1964); *State v. Whittingham*, 19
Ariz. App. 27, 504 P.2d 950 (1973), *cert. denied*, 417 U.S. 946 (1974); *but see
State v. Big Sheep*, 75 Mont. 219, 243 P. 1067 (1926) (dicta suggesting that state
has power to prohibit use of peyote by members of Native American Church as
inconsistent with the peace, safety, and order of the state). While a number of
other *bona fide* and less sincere claims to religious protection of controlled
substances thereafter were made by other groups, none proved successful. *See,
e.g., Olsen v. Iowa*, 808 F.2d 652 (8th Cir. 1986) (marijuana use by Ethiopian
Zion Coptic Church); *Peyote Way of God, Inc. v. Smith*, 742 F.2d 193 (5th Cir.
1984) (nonrestrictive church utilizing peyote not entitled to protection); *Whyte
v. United States*, 471 A.2d 1018 (D.C. App. 1984) (marijuana use by
Rastafarian). As reflected in both the majority and dissenting opinions, both the
federal regulations and a large number of state statutes explicitly exempt ceremonial use of peyote by the Native American Church from the controlled substances restrictions. *E.g.,* 21 C.F.R. § 1307.31 (1989) ("The listing of peyote as a
controlled substance in Schedule I does not apply to the nondrug use of peyote
in bona fide religious ceremonies of the Native American Church, and members of the Native American Church so using peyote are exempt from registration. Any person who manufactures peyote for or distributes peyote to the
Native American Church, however, is required to obtain registration annually
and to comply with all other requirements of law."); *see generally Olsen v. Drug
Enforcement Admin.*, 878 F.2d 1458, 1463-64 (D.C. Cir. 1989) (explaining the
basis for the exemption). In light of Justice Scalia's approval, toward the end of
the majority opinion, of "a nondiscriminatory religious-practice exemption," are
the federal and state regulatory exemptions for the Native American Church
still valid?

2. The Scope of Tribal Control of Religious Claims: At the time the California Supreme Court decided *Woody*, the Navajo tribe prohibited the possession,
use, and sale of peyote on the reservation. 17 Navajo Tribal Code § 1251 (1962).
This proscription had been unsuccessfully attacked in federal litigation, although the litigation predated the statutory imposition on tribal governments of
a requirement that they respect the free exercise of religion in the Indian Civil
Rights Act of 1968. *See Oliver v. Udall*, 306 F.2d 819 (D.C. Cir. 1962); *Native*

American Church v. Navajo Tribal Council, 272 F.2d 131 (10th Cir. 1959). The defendants in *Woody* were Navajo but their crime did not occur on Navajo land. Why did not the Navajo tribal laws proscribing peyote dispose of the case? Was it merely because the incident occurred outside the Navajo reservation? In 1967 the Navajo Tribe amended its tribal ordinances to provide an exemption from its peyote regulations for use and possession by members of the Native American Church in connection with religious practices, 17 Navajo Tribal Code § 1201 (1977).

3. Religious Protections in a Pantheistic Tradition: To what extent are other attributes of Indian culture and religious life exempted on religious grounds under the first and fourteenth amendments from state or federal laws of general application? For example, may Indians claim a right to hunt or fish free from state conservation regulations when such regulations are inconsistent with the capture or use of wildlife for Indian religious purposes? In *Frank v. Alaska*, 604 P.2d 1068 (Alaska 1979), the Supreme Court of Alaska, over two dissents, sustained the right of Athabascan Indians to kill and possess a moose out of season when fresh moose meat was found to be a very important part of the religious funeral feast (potlatch) given to honor a deceased member of the tribe. In a dissent, one member of the court stressed that while such fresh moose meat was important, it was not indispensable and was not "central to a religious observance." This dissenting judge pointed out that other native foods might have sufficed and that other such foods, including moose, were "already available" to the tribe to some extent, presumably preserved. 604 P.2d at 1076. *See also* WIS. STAT. ANN. § 29.106 (creating an exemption for Winnebago Indians taking deer out of season for religious ceremonies).

In *Teterud v. Burns*, 522 F.2d 357 (8th Cir. 1975), the court struck down on first amendment free exercise grounds the application to an Indian of a prison regulation mandating short hair length. *Contrast New Rider v. Board of Educ.*, 480 F.2d 693 (10th Cir.), *cert. denied*, 414 U.S. 1097 (1973) (long hair as an expression of cultural pride rather than religious observance).

Can precedents like *Teterud* or *Frank* survive the *Smith* decision?

NOTE: THE AMERICAN INDIAN RELIGIOUS FREEDOM ACT

In an effort to safeguard traditional Indian religious activity, Congress passed the American Indian Religious Freedom Act of 1978, Pub. L. No. 95-341, 92 Stat. 469, codified at 42 U.S.C. § 1996. This Act provides in relevant part:

> [I]t shall be the policy of the United States to protect and preserve for American Indians their inherent right of freedom to believe, express, and exercise the traditional religions of the American Indian, Eskimo, Aleut, and Native Hawaiians, including but not limited to access to sites, use and possession of sacred objects, and the freedom to worship through ceremonial and traditional rites.

The Act also required the President to survey the various federal departments and agencies to evaluate in consultation with Indian religious leaders what changes, if any, were needed in their policies and procedures and to report to Congress within a year. Senate Select Committee on Indian Affairs, Hearings Before Senate Select Committee on Indian Affairs on S.J. Res. 102 (American Indian Religious Freedom), 95th Cong., 2d Sess. (1978); Federal Agencies Task Force, U.S. Department of the Interior, American Indian Religious Freedom Act Report, P.L. 95-341, (1979). *See generally, e.g.,* Michaelsen, Is the Miner's Canary Silent? Implications of the Supreme Court's Denial of American Indian

Free Exercise of Religion, 6 J.L. & RELIGION 97-114; Comment, *The First Amendment and the American Indian Religious Freedom Act: An Approach to Protecting Native American Religion*, 71 IOWA L. REV. 631 (1986); Comment, *Indian Religious Freedom and Governmental Development of Public Lands*, 94 YALE L.J. 1447 (1985). As reflected in the *Lyng* case which follows, efforts to invoke the Act to limit federal policies adversely affecting Indian access to religious sites have proven notably unsuccessful. *Badoni v. Higginson*, 638 F.2d 172 (10th Cir. 1980), *cert. denied*, 452 U.S. 954 (1981) (unsuccessful challenge under Act to federal operation of Rainbow Bridge National Monument); *Sequoyah v. Tennessee Valley Auth.*, 620 F.2d 1159 (6th Cir.), *cert. denied*, 449 U.S. 953 (1980) (unsuccessful effort to halt flooding of Indian burial site through federal construction of Tellico Dam); *Wilson v. Block*, 708 F.2d 735 (D.C. Cir.), *cert. denied*, 464 U.S. 956 (1983) (unsuccessful effort to halt expansion of ski facilities of the Arizona Snow Bowl in the San Francisco Peaks, an area that is sacred to members of both the Hopi and Navajo Tribes); *Crow v. Gullet*, 541 F. Supp. 785 (D.S.D. 1982), *aff'd*, 706 F.2d 856 (8th Cir.), *cert. denied*, 464 U.S. 977 (1983) (unsuccessful challenge to restrictions on Indian access to and public desecration of ceremonial sites located in Bear Butte State Park in the Black Hills).

LYNG v. NORTHWEST INDIAN CEMETERY PROTECTIVE ASSOCIATION

485 U.S. 439 (1988)

Justice O'CONNOR delivered the opinion of the Court.

This case requires us to consider whether the First Amendment's Free Exercise Clause forbids the Government from permitting timber harvesting in, or constructing a road through, a portion of a National Forest that has traditionally been used for religious purposes by members of three American Indian tribes in northwestern California. We conclude that it does not.

I

As part of a project to create a paved 75-mile road linking two California towns, Gasquet and Orleans, the United States Forest Service has upgraded 49 miles of previously unpaved roads on federal land. In order to complete this project (the G-O road), the Forest Service must build a 6-mile paved segment through the Chimney Rock section of the Six Rivers National Forest. That section of the forest is situated between two other portions of the road that are already complete.

In 1977, the Forest Service issued a draft environmental impact statement that discussed proposals for upgrading an existing unpaved road that runs through the Chimney Rock area. In response to comments on the draft statement, the Forest Service commissioned a study of American Indian cultural and religious sites in the area. The Hoopa Valley Indian reservation adjoins the Six Rivers National Forest, and the Chimney Rock area has historically been used for religious purposes by Yurok, Karok, and Tolowa Indians. The commissioned study, which was completed in 1979, found that the entire area "is significant as an integral and indispensable (sic) part of Indian religious conceptualization and practice." [Certain] sites are used for certain rituals, and "successful use of the (area) is dependent upon and facilitated by certain qualities of the physical environment, the most important of which are privacy, silence, and an undisturbed natural setting." [The commissioned] study concluded that constructing a road along any of the available routes "would cause serious and irreparable damage to the sacred areas which are an integral and necessary part of the belief systems and lifeway of Northwest California Indian peoples." Accordingly, the report recommended that the G-O road not be completed.

In 1982, the Forest Service decided not to adopt this recommendation, and it prepared a final environmental impact statement for construction of the road. The Regional Forester selected a route that avoided archeological sites and was removed as far as possible from the sites used by contemporary Indians for specific spiritual activities. Alternative routes that would have avoided the Chimney Rock area altogether were rejected because they would have required the acquisition of private land, had serious soil stability problems, and would in any event have traversed areas having ritualistic value to American Indians. [Simultaneously], the Forest Service adopted a management plan allowing for the harvesting of significant amounts of timber in this area of the forest. The management plan provided for one-half mile protective zones around all the religious sites identified in the report that had been commissioned in connection with the G-O road.

After exhausting their administrative remedies, respondents — an Indian organization, individual Indians, nature organizations and individual members of those organizations, and the State of California — challenged both the road-building and timber-harvesting decisions in the United States District Court for the Northern District of California. Respondents claimed that the Forest Service's decisions violated the Free Exercise Clause, the Federal Water Pollution Control Act (FWPCA), 86 Stat. 896, as amended, 33 U.S.C. section 1251 et seq., the National Environment Policy Act of 1969 (NEPA), 83 Stat. 852, 42 U.S.C. section 4321 et seq., several other federal statutes, and governmental trust responsibilities to Indians living on the Hoopa Valley Reservation.

After a trial, the District Court issued a permanent injunction forbidding the Government from constructing the Chimney Rock section of the G-O road or putting the timber-harvesting management plan into effect. See *Northwest Indian Cemetery Protective Assn. v. Peterson*, 565 F. Supp. 586 (ND Cal. 1983). The court found that both actions would violate the Free Exercise Clause because they "would seriously damage the salient visual, aural, and environmental qualities of the high country." *Id.,* at 594-595. The court also found that both proposed actions would violate the FWPCA, and that the environmental impact statements for construction of the road were deficient under the National Environmental Policy Act. Finally, the court concluded that both projects would breach the Government's trust responsibilities to protect water and fishing rights reserved to the Hoopa Valley Indians.

[T]he Ninth Circuit affirmed in part. *Northwest Indian Cemetery Protective Assn. v. Peterson*, 795 F.2d 688 (1986). The panel unanimously rejected the District Court's conclusion that the Government's proposed actions would breach its trust responsibilities to Indians on the Hoopa Valley Reservation [and affirmed the District Court's constitutional ruling by a divided decision].

II

We begin by noting that the courts below did not articulate the bases of their decisions with perfect clarity. A fundamental and long-standing principle of judicial restraint requires that courts avoid reaching constitutional questions in advance of the necessity of deciding them. *See* [, *e.g.,*] Three Affiliated Tribes of Ft. Berthold Reservation v. Wold Engineering, P. C., 467 U.S. 138, 157-158 (1984). This principle required the courts below to determine, before addressing the constitutional issue, whether a decision on that question could have entitled respondents to relief beyond that to which they were entitled on their statutory claims. If no additional relief would have been warranted, a constitutional decision would have been unnecessary and therefore inappropriate.

Neither the District Court nor the Court of Appeals explained or expressly articulated the necessity for their constitutional holdings. Were we persuaded that those holdings were unnecessary, we could simply vacate the relevant portions of the judgment below without discussing the merits of the constitutional issue. The structure and wording of the District Court's injunctive order, however, suggests that the statutory holdings would not have supported all the relief granted.

[Since] it appears reasonably likely that the First Amendment issue was necessary to the decisions below, we believe that it would be inadvisable to vacate and remand without addressing that issue on the merits. This conclusion is strengthened by considerations of judicial economy [and convenience].

III

A

The Free Exercise Clause of the First Amendment provides that "Congress shall make no law ... prohibiting the free exercise [of religion]." U.S. Const., Amdt. 1. It is undisputed that the Indian respondents' beliefs are sincere and that the Government's proposed actions will have severe adverse effects on the practice of their religion. Respondents contend that the burden on their religious practices is heavy enough to violate the Free Exercise Clause unless the Government can demonstrate a compelling need to complete the G-O road or to engage in timber harvesting in the Chimney Rock area. We disagree.

In *Bowen v. Roy*, 476 U.S. 693 (1986), we considered a challenge to a federal statute that required the States to use Social Security numbers in administering certain welfare programs. Two applicants for benefits under these programs contended that their religious beliefs prevented them from acceding to the use of a Social Security number for their two-year-old daughter because the use of a numerical identifier would "'rob the spirit' of (their) daughter and prevent her from attaining greater spiritual power." Similarly, in this case, it is said that disruption of the natural environment caused by the G-O road will diminish the sacredness of the area in question and create distractions that will interfere with "training and ongoing religious experience of individuals using (sites within) the area for personal medicine and growth ... and as integrated parts of a system of religious belief and practice which correlates ascending degrees of personal power with a geographic hierarchy of power." ("Scarred hills and mountains, and disturbed rocks destroy the purity of the sacred areas, and (Indian) consultants repeatedly stressed the need of a training doctor to be undistracted by such disturbance"). The Court rejected this kind of challenge in *Roy*.

> The Free Exercise Clause simply cannot be understood to require the Government to conduct its own internal affairs in ways that comport with the religious beliefs of particular citizens. Just as the government may not insist that (the Roys) engage in any set form of religious observance, so (they) may not demand that the Government join in their chosen religious practices by refraining from using a number to identify their daughter ....
>
> ... The Free Exercise Clause affords an individual protection from certain forms of governmental compulsion; it does not afford an individual a right to dictate the conduct of the Government's internal procedures. 476 U.S., at 699-700.

The building of a road or the harvesting of timber on publicly owned land cannot meaningfully be distinguished from the use of a Social Security number in *Roy*. In both cases, the challenged government action would interfere significantly with private persons' ability to pursue spiritual fulfillment according to their own religious beliefs. In neither case, however, would the affected individuals be coerced by the Government's action into violating their religious beliefs; nor would either governmental action penalize religious activity by denying any person an equal share of the rights, benefits, and privileges enjoyed by other citizens.

We are asked to distinguish this case from *Roy* on the ground that the infringement on religious liberty here is "significantly greater," or on the ground that the government practice in *Roy* was "purely mechanical" whereas this case involves "a case-by-case substantive determination as to how a particular unit of land will be managed." [W]e are [also] told that this case can be distinguished from *Roy* because "the government action is not at some physically removed location where it places no restriction on what a practitioner may do." [The State argues] that the Social Security number in *Roy* "could be characterized as interfering with Roy's religious tenets from a subjective point of view, where the government's conduct of 'its own internal affairs' was known to him only secondhand and did not interfere with his ability to practice his religion." [Here], however, it is said that the proposed road will "physically destro(y) the environmental conditions and the privacy without which the (religious) practices cannot be conducted."

[The plaintiffs'] efforts to distinguish *Roy* are unavailing. This Court cannot determine the truth of the underlying beliefs that led to the religious objections here or in *Roy*, [and therefore] cannot weigh the adverse effects on the Roys and compare them with the adverse effects on respondents. Without the ability to make such comparisons, we cannot say that the one form of incidental interference with an individual's spiritual activities should be subjected to a different constitutional analysis than the other. Respondents insist, nonetheless, that the courts below properly relied on a factual inquiry into the degree to which the Indians' spiritual practices would become ineffectual if the G-O road were built. They rely on several cases in which this Court has sustained free exercise challenges to government programs that interfered with individuals' ability to practice their religion. See *Wisconsin v. Yoder*, 406 U.S. 205 (1972) (compulsory school-attendance law) ....

Even apart from the inconsistency between *Roy* and respondents' reading of these cases, their interpretation will not withstand analysis. It is true that this Court has repeatedly held that indirect coercion or penalties on the free exercise of religion, not just outright prohibitions, are subject to scrutiny under the First Amendment. [This point] does not and cannot imply that incidental effects of government programs, which may make it more difficult to practice certain religions but which have no tendency to coerce individuals into acting contrary to their religious beliefs, require government to bring forward a compelling justification for its otherwise lawful actions. The crucial word in the constitutional text is "prohibit": "For the Free Exercise Clause is written in terms of what the government cannot do to the individual, not in terms of what the individual can exact from the government." ...

Whatever may be the exact line between unconstitutional prohibitions on the free exercise of religion and the legitimate conduct by government of its own affairs, the location of the line cannot depend on measuring the effects of a governmental action on a religious objector's spiritual development. The Government does not dispute, and we have no reason to doubt, that the logging and road-building projects at issue in this case could have devastating effects on traditional Indian religious practices. Those practices are intimately and inextricably bound up with the unique features of the Chimney Rock area, which is known to the Indians as the "high country." Individual practitioners use this area for personal spiritual development; some of their activities are believed to be critically important in advancing the welfare of the tribe, and indeed, of mankind itself. The Indians use this area, as they have used it for a very long time, to conduct a wide variety of specific rituals that aim to accomplish their religious goals. According to their beliefs, the rituals would not be efficacious if conducted at other sites than the ones traditionally used, and too much disturbance of the area's natural state would clearly render any meaningful continuation of traditional practices impossible. [We] assume that the threat to the efficacy of at least some religious practices is extremely grave.

Even if we assume that we should accept the Ninth Circuit's prediction, according to which the G-O road will "virtually destroy the Indians' ability to practice their religion" 795 F.2d, at 693 (opinion below), the Constitution simply does not provide a principle that could justify upholding respondents' legal claims. However much we might wish that it were otherwise, government simply could not operate if it were required to satisfy every citizen's religious needs and desires. A broad range of government activities — from social welfare programs to foreign aid to conservation projects — will always be considered essential to the spiritual well-being of some citizens, often on the basis of sincerely held religious beliefs. Others will find the very same activities deeply offensive, and perhaps incompatible with their own search for spiritual fulfillment and with the tenets of their religion. The First Amendment must apply to all citizens alike, and it can give to none of them a veto over public programs that do not prohibit the free exercise of religion. The Constitution does not, and courts cannot, offer to reconcile the various competing demands on government, many of them rooted in sincere religious belief, that inevitably arise in so diverse a society as ours. That task, to the extent that it is feasible, is for the legislatures and other institutions. Cf. The Federalist No. 10 (suggesting that the effects of religious factionalism are best restrained through competition among a multiplicity of religious sects).

One need not look far beyond the present case to see why the analysis in *Roy* [advances] a sound reading of the Constitution. Respondents attempt to stress the limits of the religious servitude that they are now seeking to impose on the Chimney Rock area of the Six Rivers National Forest. While defending an injunction against logging operations and the construction of a road, they apparently do not at present object to the area's being used by recreational visitors, other Indians, or forest rangers. Nothing in the principle for which they contend, however, would distinguish this case from another lawsuit in which they (or similarly situated religious objectors) might seek to exclude all human activity but their own from sacred areas of the public lands. The Indian respondents insist that "*(p)rivacy* during the power quests is required for the practitioners to maintain the purity needed for a successful journey." [Likewise]: "The practices conducted in the high country entail intense meditation and require the practitioner to achieve a profound awareness of the natural environment. Prayer seats are oriented so there is an unobstructed view, and the practitioner must be surrounded by *undisturbed* naturalness." No disrespect for these practices is implied when one notes that such beliefs could easily require de facto beneficial ownership of some rather spacious tracts of public property. Even without anticipating future cases, the diminution of the Government's property rights, and the concomitant subsidy of the Indian religion, would in this case be far from trivial: the District Court's order permanently forbade commercial timber harvesting, or the construction of a two-lane road, anywhere within an area covering a full 27 sections (i.e. more than 17,000 acres) of public land.

The Constitution does not permit government to discriminate against religions that treat particular physical sites as sacred, and a law forbidding the Indian respondents from visiting the Chimney Rock area would raise a different set of constitutional questions. Whatever rights the Indians may have to the use of the area, however, those rights do not divest the Government of its right to use what is, after all, its land. *Cf. Bowen v. Roy*, 476 U.S., at 724-727 (O'CONNOR, J., concurring in part and dissenting in part) (distinguishing between the Government's use of information in its possession and the Government's requiring an individual to provide such information).

B

Nothing in our opinion should be read to encourage governmental insensitivity to the religious needs of any citizen. The Government's rights to the use of its own land, for example, need not and should not discourage it from accommodating religious practices like those engaged in by the Indian respondents. [T]he Government has taken numerous steps in this very case to minimize the impact that construction of the G-O road will have on the Indians' religious [practices].

Except for abandoning its project entirely, and thereby leaving the two existing segments of road to deadend in the middle of a National Forest, it is difficult to see how the Government could have been more solicitous. Such solicitude accords with "the policy of the United States to protect and preserve for

American Indians their inherent right of freedom to believe, express, and exercise the traditional religions of the American Indian ... including but not limited to access to sites, use and possession of sacred objects, and the freedom to worship through ceremonials and traditional rites." American Indian Religious Freedom Act (AIRFA), Pub. L. 95-341, 92 Stat. 469, 42 U.S.C. section 1996.

Respondents, however, suggest that AIRFA goes further and in effect enacts their interpretation of the First Amendment into statutory law. Although this contention was rejected by the District Court, they seek to defend the judgment below by arguing that AIRFA authorizes the injunction against completion of the G-O road. This argument is without merit. After reciting several legislative findings, AIRFA "resolves" upon the policy quoted above. A second section of the statute, 92 Stat. 470, required an evaluation of federal policies and procedures, in consultation with native religious leaders, of changes necessary to protect and preserve the rights and practices in question. The required report dealing with this evaluation was completed and released in 1979. Reply Brief for Petitioners 2, n. 3. Nowhere in the law is there so much as a hint of any intent to create a cause of action or any judicially enforceable individual rights.

What is obvious from the face of the statute is confirmed by numerous indications in the legislative history. The sponsor of the bill that became AIRFA, Representative Udall, called it "a sense of Congress joint resolution," aimed at ensuring that "the basic right of the Indian people to exercise their traditional religious practices is not infringed without a clear decision on the part of the Congress or the administrators that such religious practices must yield to some higher consideration." 124 Cong. Rec. 21444 (1978). Representative Udall emphasized that the bill would not "confer special religious rights on Indians," would "not change any existing State or Federal law," and in fact "has no teeth in it." Id., at 21444-21445.

C

The dissent proposes an approach to the First Amendment that is fundamentally inconsistent with the principles on which our decision rests. Notwithstanding the sympathy that we all must feel for the plight of the Indian respondents, it is plain that the approach taken by the dissent cannot withstand analysis. On the contrary, the path towards which it points us is incompatible with the text of the Constitution, with the precedents of this Court, and with a responsible sense of our own institutional role.

The dissent begins by asserting that the "constitutional guarantee we interpret today ... is directed against any form of government action that frustrates or inhibits religious practice." ... The Constitution, however, says no such thing. Rather, it states: "Congress shall make no law ... *prohibiting* the free exercise (of religion)." U.S. Const., Amdt. 1 (emphasis added).

[So that] the District Court's injunction may be reconsidered in light of this holding, and in light of any other relevant events that may have intervened since the injunction issued, the case is remanded for further proceedings consistent with this opinion.

It is so ordered.

Justice Brennan, with whom Justice Marshall and Justice Blackmun join, dissenting.

"[T]he Free Exercise Clause," the Court explains today, "is written in terms of what the government cannot do to the individual, not in terms of what the individual can exact from the government." [Claiming] fidelity to the unremarkable constitutional principle, the Court nevertheless concludes that even where the Government uses federal land in a manner that threatens the very existence of a Native American religion, the Government is simply not "*doing*" anything to the practitioners of that faith. Instead, the Court believes that Native Americans who request that the Government refrain from destroying their religion effectively seek to exact from the Government *de facto* beneficial ownership of federal property. These two astonishing conclusions follow naturally from the Court's determination that federal land-use decisions that render the practice of a given religion impossible do not burden that religion in a manner cognizable under the Free Exercise Clause, because such decisions neither coerce conduct inconsistent with religious belief nor penalize religious activity. The constitutional guarantee we interpret today, however, draws no such fine distinctions between types of restraints on religious exercise, but rather is directed against any form of governmental action that frustrates or inhibits religious practice. Because the Court today refuses even to acknowledge the constitutional injury respondents will suffer, and because this refusal essentially leaves Native Americans with absolutely no constitutional protection against perhaps the gravest threat to their religious practices, I dissent.

I

For at least 200 years and probably much longer, the Yurok, Karok, and Tolowa Indians have held sacred an approximately 25 square-mile area of land situated in what is today the Blue Creek Unit of Six Rivers National Forest in northwestern California. As the Government readily concedes, regular visits to this area, known to respondent Indians as the "high country," have played and continue to play a "critical" role in the religious practices and rituals of these tribes. [Such] beliefs, only briefly described in the Court's opinion, are crucial to a proper understanding of respondents' claims.

As the Forest Service's commissioned study, the Theodoratus Report, explains, for Native Americans religion is not a discrete sphere of activity separate from all others, and any attempt to isolate the religious aspects of Indian life "is in reality an exercise which forces Indian concepts into *non*-Indian categories." [To] most Native Americans, "(t)he area of worship cannot be delineated from social, political, cultural and other aspects of Indian lifestyle." American Indian Religious Freedom, Hearings on S. J. Res. 102 Before the Select Comm. on Indian Affairs, U.S. Sen. 95th Cong., 2d Sess. at 86 (Statement of Barney Old Coyote, Crow Tribe). A pervasive feature of this lifestyle is the individual's relationship with the natural world; this relationship, which can accurately though somewhat incompletely be characterized as one of stewardship, forms the core of what might be called, for want of a better nomenclature, the Indian religious experience. While traditional western religions view creation as the work of a deity "who institutes natural laws which then govern the operation of physical nature," tribal religions regard creation as an ongoing process in which they are morally and religiously obligated to participate. [The] Native Americans fulfill this duty through ceremonies and rituals designed to preserve and stabilize the earth and to protect humankind from disease and other catastrophes. Failure to conduct these ceremonies in the manner and place specified, adherents believe, will result in great harm to the earth and to the people whose welfare depends upon it.

In marked contrast to traditional western religions, the belief systems of Native Americans do not rely on doctrines, creeds, or dogmas. Established or universal truths — the mainstay of western religions — play no part in Indian faith. Ceremonies are communal efforts undertaken for specific purposes in accordance with instructions handed down from generation to generation. Commentaries on or interpretations of the rituals themselves are deemed absolute violations of the ceremonies, whose value lies not in their ability to explain the natural world or to enlighten individual believers but in their efficacy as protectors and enhancers of tribal existence. *Ibid.* Where dogma lies at the heart of western religions, Native American faith is inextricably bound to the use of land. The site-specific nature of Indian religious practice derives from the Native American perception that land is itself a sacred, living being. See Suagee, American Indian Religious Freedom and Cultural Resources Management: Protecting Mother Earth's Caretakers, 10 Amer. Ind. L. Rev. 1, 10 (1982). Rituals are performed in prescribed locations not merely as a matter of traditional orthodoxy, but because land, like all other living things, is unique, and specific sites possess different spiritual properties and significance. Within this belief system, therefore, land is not fungible; indeed, at the time of the Spanish colonization of the American southwest, "all ... Indians held in some form a belief in a sacred and indissoluble bond between themselves and the land in which their settlements were located." E. Spicer, Cycle of Conquest: The Impact of Spain, Mexico, and the United States on the Indians of the United States 576 (1962).

For respondent Indians, the most sacred of lands is the high country where, they believe, pre-human spirits moved with the coming of humans to the earth. Because these spirits are seen as the source of religious power, or "medicine," many of the tribes' rituals and practices require frequent journeys to the [high country].

Recognizing that the high country is "indispensable" to the religious lives of the approximately 5,000 tribe members who reside in that area, [the Court of Appeals] concluded "that the proposed government operations would *virtually destroy the Indians' ability to practice their religion.*" [Like the district court], the Court of Appeals found the Government's interests in building the road and permitting limited timber harvesting — interests which of course were considerably undermined by passage of the California Wilderness Act — did not justify the destruction of respondents' religion.

II

The Court does not for a moment suggest that the interests served by the G-O road are in any way compelling, or that they outweigh the destructive effect construction of the road will have on respondents' religious practices. Instead, the Court embraces the Government's contention that its prerogative as landowner should always take precedence over a claim that a particular use of federal property infringes religious practices. Attempting to justify this rule, the Court argues that the First Amendment bars only outright prohibitions, indirect coercion, and penalties on the free exercise of religion. All other "incidental effects of government programs," it concludes, even those "which may make it more difficult to practice certain religions but which have no tendency to coerce individuals into acting contrary to their religious beliefs," simply do not give rise to constitutional concerns. [Ever since] our recognition nearly half a century ago that restraints on religious conduct implicate the concerns of the Free Exercise Clause, [this Court has] never suggested that the protections of the guarantee are limited to so narrow a range of governmental burdens....

A

[I cannot] accept the Court's premise that the form of the Government's restraint on religious practice, rather than its effect, controls our constitutional analysis. [T]he proposed logging and construction activities will virtually destroy respondents' religion, and will therefore necessarily force them into abandoning those practices [completely].

B

Federal land-use decisions, [in contrast to the demand for social security numbers involved in *Roy*], are likely to have substantial external effects that government decisions concerning office furniture and information storage obviously will not, and they are correspondingly subject to public scrutiny and public challenge in a host of ways that office equipment purchases are not.[3] Indeed, in the American Indian Religious Freedom Act (AIRFA), 42 U.S.C. section 1996, Congress expressly recognized the adverse impact land-use decisions and other governmental actions frequently have on the site-specific religious practices of Native Americans, and the Act accordingly directs agencies to consult with Native American religious leaders before taking actions that might impair those practices. Although I agree that the Act does not create any judicially enforceable rights, [the] absence of any private right of action in no way undermines the statute's significance as an express congressional determination that federal land management decisions are not "internal" governmental "procedures," but are instead governmental actions that can and indeed are likely to burden Native American religious practices. That such decisions should be

---

[3] Remarkably, the Court treats this factual determination as nothing more than an assumption predicated on a "Worst-case hypothesis," [and therefore] suggests that it is "less than certain that construction of the road will be so disruptive that it will doom (respondents') religion." *Ibid.* Such speculation flies in the face of the most basic principles of appellate review [and furthermore] is wholly at odds with the well-settled rule that this Court will not disturb findings of facts agreed upon by both lower courts unless those findings are clearly in error. [Nevertheless], the mere fact that a handful of Native Americans who reside in the affected area do not oppose the road in no way casts doubt upon the validity of the lower courts' amply supported factual findings, particularly where the members of this minority did not indicate whether their lack of objection reflected their assessment of the religious significance of the high country, or their own apathy towards religious matters generally.

subject to constitutional challenge, and potential constitutional limitations, should hardly come as a surprise.

C

[Before] today's decision, several courts of appeals had attempted to fashion a test that accommodates the competing "demands" placed on federal property by the two cultures. Recognizing that the Government normally enjoys plenary authority over federal lands, the courts of appeals required Native Americans to demonstrate that any land-use decisions they challenged involved lands that were "central" or "indispensable" to their religious practices. *See, e.g., [Wilson v. Block*, 708 F.2d 735 (DC Cir.), cert. denied, 464 U.S. 956 (1983)]. Although this requirement limits the potential number of free exercise claims that might be brought to federal land management decisions, and thus forestalls the possibility that the Government will find itself ensnared in a host of lilliputian lawsuits, it has been criticized as inherently ethnocentric, for it incorrectly assumes that Native American belief systems ascribe religious significance to land in a traditionally western hierarchical manner. See Michaelsen, American Indian Religious Freedom Litigation: Promise and Perils, 3 J. Law & Rel. 47 (1985); Pepper, Conundrum of the Free Exercise Clause — Some Reflections on Recent Cases, 9 N. Ky. L. Rev. 265, 283-284 (1982). It is frequently the case in constitutional litigation, however, that courts are called upon to balance interests that are not readily translated into rough equivalents. At their most absolute, the competing claims that both the Government and Native Americans assert in federal land are fundamentally incompatible, and unless they are tempered by compromise, mutual accommodation will remain impossible.

I believe it appropriate, therefore, to require some showing of "centrality" before the Government can be required either to come forward with a compelling justification for its proposed use of federal land or to forego that use altogether. "Centrality," however, should not be equated with the survival or extinction of the religion itself. [W]hile Native Americans need not demonstrate, as respondents did here, that the Government's land-use decision will assuredly eradicate their faith, I do not think it is enough to allege simply that the land in question is held sacred. Rather, adherents challenging a proposed use of federal land should be required to show that the decision poses a substantial and realistic threat of frustrating their religious practices. Once such a showing is made, the burden should shift to the Government to come forward with a compelling state interest sufficient to justify the infringement of those practices.

III

[It is hard] to imagine conduct more insensitive to religious needs than the Government's determination to build a marginally useful road in the face of uncontradicted evidence that the road will render the practice of respondents' religion impossible. Nor do I believe that respondents will derive any solace from the knowledge that although the practice of their religion will become "more difficult" as a result of the Government's actions, they remain free to maintain their religious beliefs. Given today's ruling, that freedom amounts to nothing more than the right to believe that their religion will be destroyed. The safeguarding of such a hollow freedom not only makes a mockery of the "policy of the United States to protect and preserve for American Indians their inherent right of freedom to believe, express, and exercise the(ir) traditional religions," [the decision] fails utterly to accord with the dictates of the First Amendment.

I dissent.

NOTE

In light of the *Northwest Cemetery* case, does the American Indian Religious Freedom Act of 1978 (AIRFA) offer any protections to Native Americans that would otherwise not be afforded by the first amendment religion clauses? Does AIRFA inform or affect the first amendment analysis in any way?

The *Yoder* case, relied upon in *Northwest Cemetery*, suggested that the first amendment protects a "traditional way of life [involving] deep religious conviction, shared by an organized group, and intimately related to daily living." In light of *Northwest Cemetery* and the AIRFA cases that it discusses, to what extent can Indians rely upon such protections? To what extent was the Court concerned about the pantheistic nature of Indian religious experience and the problems of accommodating such a world view with the implicit assumptions of the first amendment that require a separation of the religious and secular aspects of public life?

B. CONTEMPORARY FEDERAL INDIAN LAW: OVERVIEW QUESTIONS

The existence of a legal regime specially protecting the rights to legal autonomy and self-determination of indigenous peoples requires the existence of a body of rules defining the people and groups to which that law applies and the geographic reach of the powers attendant to this special status. In federal Indian law, it is therefore critical to define which groups constitute Indian tribes, who is an Indian, and precisely what area falls within the geographic reach of Indian country. This section is devoted to these legal questions, as well as important equal protection and due process questions that emerge from drawing such lines of political demarcation that are so closely defined by race and ethnology.

1. DEFINING WHICH GROUPS CONSTITUTE INDIAN TRIBES AND WHO IS AN INDIAN

Like many legal terms, the definition of the terms "Indian tribe" and "Indian" may shift depending on the purpose for which the definition is used.

a. Indian Tribe

The term "Indian tribe," for example, has an ethnological as well as legal meaning. A terminated tribe may exist to an anthropologist, but not for the purpose of interpreting a statute granting statutory benefits only to recognized tribes. Congress can and has granted some benefits to members of terminated tribes, but only when it has chosen to define the term "tribe" as including them.

On the other hand, some tribes are legal entities only. A congressionally created confederated or consolidated tribe can be made up of different ethnological tribes presently occupying the same reservation because of federal policies, such as the Wind River Tribes (Shoshone and Arapaho).

When the term is used to denote a recognized tribe, it is necessary to determine which tribes are federally recognized. According to *Cohen's Handbook of Federal Indian Law**:

> Although there is broad federal authority to recognize tribes, the question may arise whether that power has been exercised in a particular instance. Normally a group will be treated as a tribe or a "recognized" tribe if (a) Congress or the Executive has created a reservation for the group by treaty, agreement, statute, executive order, or valid administrative action; and (b) the United States has had some continuing political relationship with the group, such as by providing services through the Bureau of Indian Affairs. Accordingly, reservation tribes with continuing federal contact are considered tribes under virtually every statute that refers to Indian tribes.

Id. at 6 (citations omitted).

In 1978, the Department of the Interior adopted regulations creating an administrative procedure to be invoked by tribes seeking recognition. 25 C.F.R. Part 83. This process has involved significant research into ethnohistory and anthropology. The core requirements for recognition are set forth in the required elements of a petition for recognition in 25 C.F.R. § 83.7:

> All the criteria in paragraphs (a) through (g) of this section are mandatory in order for tribal existence to be acknowledged and must be included in the petition.
>
> (a) A statement of facts establishing that the petitioner has been identified from historical times until the present on a substantially continuous basis, as "American Indian," or "aboriginal." A petitioner shall not fail to satisfy any criteria herein merely because of fluctuations of tribal activity during various years. Evidence to be relied upon in determining the group's substantially continuous Indian identity shall include one or more of the following:
>
> (1) Repeated identification by Federal authorities;
>
> (2) Longstanding relationships with State governments based on identification of the group as Indian;
>
> (3) Repeated dealings with a county, parish, or other local government in a relationship based on the group's Indian identity;
>
> (4) Identification as an Indian entity by records in courthouses, churches, or schools;
>
> (5) Identification as an Indian entity by anthropologists, historians, or other scholars;
>
> (6) Repeated identification as an Indian entity in newspapers and books;
>
> (7) Repeated identification and dealings as an Indian entity with recognized Indian tribes or national Indian organizations.
>
> (b) Evidence that a substantial portion of the petitioning group inhabits a specific area or lives in a community viewed as American Indian and distinct from other populations in the area, and that its members are descendants of an Indian tribe which historically inhabited a specific area.
>
> (c) A statement of facts which establishes that the petitioner has maintained tribal political influence or other authority over its members as an autonomous entity throughout history until the present.
>
> (d) A copy of the group's present governing document, or in the absence of a written document, a statement describing in full the membership criteria and the procedures through which the group currently governs its affairs and its members.

(e) A list of all known current members of the group and a copy of each available former list of members based on the tribe's own defined criteria. The membership must consist of individuals who have established, using evidence acceptable to the Secretary, descendancy from a tribe which existed historically or from historical tribes which combined and functioned as a single autonomous entity. Evidence acceptable to the Secretary of tribal membership for this purpose includes but is not limited to:

(1) Descendancy rolls prepared by the Secretary for the petitioner for purposes of distributing claims money, providing allotments, or other purposes;

(2) State, Federal, or other official records or evidence identifying present members or ancestors of present members as being an Indian descendant and a member of the petitioning group;

(3) Church, school, and other similar enrollment records indicating the person as being a member of the petitioning entity;

(4) Affidavits of recognition by tribal elders, leaders, or the tribal governing body, as being an Indian descendant of the tribe and a member of the petitioning entity;

(5) Other records or evidence identifying the person as a member of the petitioning entity.

(f) The membership of the petitioning group is composed principally of persons who are not members of any other North American Indian tribe.

(g) The petitioner is not, nor are its members, the subject of congressional legislation which has expressly terminated or forbidden the Federal relationship.

Federal recognition is not essential to tribal status, however. Federal statutes before 1934 rarely defined the term "Indian tribe." For example, the Indian Depredation Act of 1891, 26 Stat. 851, granted jurisdiction to the Court of Claims to compensate settlers whose property was "taken or destroyed by Indians belonging to any band, tribe, or nation, in amity with the United States." In *Montoya v. United States*, 180 U.S. 261, 266 (1901), the Supreme Court established the following definitions of tribe and band for purposes of applying the Depredation Act:

By a "tribe" we understand a body of Indians of the same or a similar race, united in a community under one leadership or government, and inhabiting a particular though sometimes ill-defined territory; by a "band," a company of Indians not necessarily, though often of the same race or tribe, but united under the same leadership in a common design. While a "band" does not imply the separate racial origin characteristic of a tribe, of which it is usually an offshoot, it does imply a leadership and a concert of action.

This definition came to be used to determine whether a tribe was a tribe for purposes of the Nonintercourse Act, which invalidates transfers of lands "from any Indian nation or tribe of Indians" if made without federal approval. 25 U.S.C. § 177. In 1972, the Passamaquoddy Tribe sought to force the government to represent them in their claim that treaties the tribe made with Maine's predecessor, Massachusetts, were void because they violated the Nonintercourse Act. The government's sole reason for refusing to represent the tribe was the argument that since the tribe had never been federally recognized, the federal government had no obligations to the tribe. The First Circuit Court of Appeals disagreed, holding that federal recognition was not necessary for Nonintercourse Act purposes, and that the tribe met the definition developed in the *Montoya* case. *Joint Tribal Council of Passamaquoddy Tribe v. Morton*, 528 F.2d 370 (1st Cir. 1975).

The present trend to define the term "tribe" in particular statutes began with the Indian Reorganization Act, which extended its benefits to "any Indian tribe, organized band, pueblo, or the Indians residing on a reservation." 25 U.S.C. § 479. Because the purpose of the Act was to permit the greatest number of Indian peoples to gain the Act's benefits, the Department of the Interior has interpreted the provision broadly. According to *Cohen's Handbook of Federal Indian Law**:

> The considerations which, singly or jointly, have been particularly relied upon by the Department in reaching the conclusion that a group constitutes a tribe or band [for purposes of the IRA] have been:
> (1) That the group has had treaty relations with the United States;
> (2) That the group has been denominated a tribe by act of Congress or executive order;
> (3) That the group has been treated as having collective rights in tribal lands or funds, even though not expressly designated a tribe.
> (4) That the group has been treated as a tribe or band by other Indian tribes; and
> (5) That the group has exercised political authority over its members, through a tribal council or other governmental forms.
> Other factors considered, although not seen as conclusive, are the existence of special appropriation items for the group and the social solidarity of the group. Ethnological and historical considerations, although not conclusive, are also entitled to great weight in determining the question of tribal existence under the Act.

Id. at 13.

Recent statutes have also begun to define "tribe" more broadly. For example, the Indian Tribal Tax Status Act defines tribe as "any Indian tribe, band, nation, or other organized group or community which is recognized as eligible for the special programs and services provided by the United States to Indians because of their status as Indians." 26 U.S.C. § 7871(E)(ii). *See also, e.g.,* the Indian Financing Act of 1974, 25 U.S.C. § 1452(c). Under these definitions, if a tribe has received any services from the government as a tribe, it would be eligible for the benefits of the statute.

The Supreme Court has upheld Congress's broad power to determine tribal status for purposes of the political relationship between the United States government and Indian tribes. *United States v. Sandoval,* 231 U.S. 28, 46 (1913), set forth and discussed in Chapter 2, section A2. Concomitantly, the Court has recognized congressional power to terminate tribal status. In addressing the question of termination of tribal status, however, should it make any difference to the courts whether the affected tribe had previously been recognized in dealings with the United States by treaty or statute as a domestic dependent nation? Should Congress be able to unilaterally declare the detribalization of an Indian society with consequent expansion of state jurisdiction over them? While dicta in *McClanahan v. Arizona Tax Comm'n,* 411 U.S. 164, 173 n.12 (1973), and *The Kansas Indians,* 72 U.S. (5 Wall.) 737, 757 (1866), suggest that the sovereign legal status of an Indian tribe may be relinquished by voluntary abandonment of tribal status, neither case addresses the important question of which government or branch of government can find such a voluntary abandonment. While the cases are reasonably clear that only the federal government can find such a voluntary relinquishment of sovereign authority and consequent extension of state law to Indian lands, there is some disagreement as to which branch of the federal government may properly conduct such an inquiry. In *Mashpee*

---

*Copyright © 1982, The Michie Company. Reprinted with permission.

Tribe v. New Seabury Corp., 592 F.2d 575 (1st Cir.), *cert. denied*, 444 U.S. 866 (1979), the First Circuit affirmed the dismissal of one of the eastern land claims cases predicated on a judicial determination (resting on a jury finding) that the Mashpee Indians had voluntarily abandoned their tribal existence and were, therefore, not within the protection of the restraints on alienation of Indian land contained in the Trade and Intercourse Acts. The court said:

> [Any] tribe, even if it is federally recognized, however, can choose to terminate tribal existence .... Certainly individual Indians or portions of tribes may choose to give up tribal status. [When] all or nearly all members of a tribe [choose] to abandon the tribe, it follows, the tribe would disappear.

Id. at 586-87. In the *Mashpee* case the Indians in question had never specifically been federally recognized. Although the court's determination that the tribe no longer existed may have been correct in its interpretation of the Nonintercourse Act definition of "tribe", was its extension of the principle that a tribe can abandon its status to recognized tribes correct in the absence of a congressional finding that a tribe was no longer recognized?

When Congress or the executive has recognized an Indian tribe as a domestic, dependent nation, should inquiry into its continued sovereign status generally be barred by the political question doctrine under the test of *Baker v. Carr*, 369 U.S. 186, 215-18 (1962)? In *Tiger v. Western Inv. Co.*, 221 U.S. 286, 315 (1911), the Supreme Court noted:

> [I]t may be taken as the settled doctrine of this Court that Congress, in pursuance of the long-established policy of the Government, has a right to determine for itself when the guardianship which has been maintained over the Indian shall cease. It is for that body, and not the courts, to determine when the true interests of the Indian require his release from such condition of tutelage.

b. Indian

As with the concept of tribe, the question of who is an Indian within the sphere of federal Indian law can only be answered with reference to the varying purposes for which it is necessary to ask the question. This determination implicates the added dimensions of race and descendance, the fluid concept of tribal membership, which is essentially a political and ethnological determination, the varying purposes for which membership determinations must be made, and the role of individual choice in the affiliation process. In short, the ethnological and political considerations at issue in determining tribal membership are essential inquiries in determining who is an Indian for federal Indian law purposes, but race is almost always an essential, although not dispositive, element of the inquiry. A person of complete Indian ancestry may be considered a non-Indian; at the same time a person of very little, or even no, Indian ancestry can be considered an Indian.

According to the authors of *Cohen's Handbook of Federal Indian Law*, a person can usually be considered an Indian for most purposes if he or she meets two qualifications:

> (a) that some of the individual's ancestors lived in what is now the United States before its discovery by Europeans, and (b) that the individual is recognized as an Indian by his or her tribe or community.

As this synthesis indicates, many statutory or common law references to the concept "Indian" refer to a person's status as a member of an Indian tribe. The concept of tribal membership itself is elusive, because it can refer to formal enrollment on a tribal roll of a federally recognized tribe or to a more informal status as one recognized to be a member of the tribal community. Furthermore, a person regarded as a member by the tribe may not be so regarded by the Secretary of the Interior, who claims the authority to determine membership for purposes of distributing property rights. BIA Manual, Release 83-4, Part 8, *Enrollment*, § 8.2 (1959).

This concept of formal enrollment is relatively recent in Indian law. Historically, some Indian tribes treated all participating members of their community as tribal members and were therefore willing to incorporate into the tribal community non-Indians who married tribal members. Although the term "adoption" is often used to describe this process, extending the benefits of tribal membership is more akin to the statist notion of naturalization. While such persons might be considered tribal members by the Indians, federal law was not immediately receptive to the idea of treating such persons as being properly within the realm of federal Indian law. For example, in *United States v. Rogers*, 45 U.S. (4 How.) 567 (1846), the Court held that a white man who had voluntarily moved to the Cherokee Nation in the Indian Territory, who made his home there, and who had become a member of the tribe with its assent could be prosecuted in federal court despite provisions in the federal jurisdictional statutes exempting intra-Indian crimes from federal court jurisdiction. The Court ruled that adoption by the tribe did not bring the accused within the statutory exemption since "[h]e was still a white man, of the white race." 45 U.S. (4 How.) at 573. Is *Rogers* consistent with the rationale of *Morton v. Mancari*, set forth in the next section? In *Nofire v. United States*, 164 U.S. 657 (1897), the Court partially backed away from its approach in *Rogers* and held that non-Indian defendants who were members of the tribe could not be prosecuted in federal court for the murder of a white person who had been adopted by the Cherokee Nation, since the jurisdiction over offenses that solely involved tribal members was vested exclusively in the tribal courts under the laws of the United States and the treaties with the Cherokee Nation.

The requirement of formal tribal rolls can be traced to the allotment policy. To lay the groundwork for the allotment of tribal property, it was necessary to clearly identify the persons who were tribal members entitled to participate in the anticipated per capita distributions of tribal property. Existing tribal mechanisms for determining membership in the tribal community were seen by federal policymakers as informal, and thus inadequate. Formal tribal membership rolls were thus prepared. Federal policy did not favor permitting non-Indians adopted into a tribe to acquire interests in property distributions. Nevertheless, some allotment-era laws did recognize that non-Indians could acquire property interests in the distribution of tribal property as part of allotment. *E.g.,* 25 U.S.C. § 181 (white man marrying Indian woman after Aug. 9, 1888, may not acquire any right in tribal property unless otherwise a member of any tribe or in the Five Civilized Tribes of Indian Territory); § 184 (children of Indian woman by blood and white man entitled to some rights and privileges to property of tribe to which member belonged). *Cf. Red Bird v. United States*, 203 U.S. 76

(1906). Additionally, some of the slave-holding Five Civilized Tribes were compelled by treaty to make their freedmen members of the tribe after the Civil War (*e.g.,* Treaty with Creeks, June 14, 1886, art. 2, 14 Stat. 785), and these freedmen, who amounted to almost twenty-three percent of the final rolls of the Five Civilized Tribes, were entitled to distributions of tribal property, as were the adopted white members who represented another three percent of the final rolls. *See generally* A. DEBO, AND STILL THE WATERS RUN 3-60 (1940).

These formal tribal rolls, influenced to a great extent by federal perceptions of individual property entitlements, have thus resulted in some anomalies. Enrolled members of an Indian tribe today, at least for purposes of receiving property distributions, can include some persons who are racially non-Indian, some who have very little Indian blood, and some who are racially Indian but who do not otherwise identify themselves as members of the Indian community. At the same time, persons who are both racially Indians and regarded as members of the tribal community can be excluded from tribal rolls.

Thus, the idea of federally defined tribal membership and enrollment of members is traceable to the exigent needs attendant to distributing tribal property and winding up the affairs of the tribe. The entire concept of enrollment in tribal membership may only represent a perverse holdover from the allotment era. Enrollment could be thought to envision the time when it would be necessary to ascertain tribal membership in order to distribute tribal property either as part of the final winding-up of tribal existence or as part of an ongoing effort to distribute tribal property or income such as the proceeds of claims judgments.

Often coexisting with this abstract concept of tribal membership is an actual tribal community composed of persons who are not all enrolled tribal members, but who nevertheless fully participate in the social, religious, and cultural life of the tribe if not its political and economic processes. Consider, for example, the facts in *Santa Clara Pueblo v. Martinez,* set forth and discussed in Chapter 3, sections C and D4. Plaintiff Julia Martinez was a full-blood member of the Santa Clara Pueblo and a lifelong resident of the Pueblo. Her husband was a full-blood Navajo. Their children were full-blood Indians but were not eligible for membership in either tribe since the Santa Clara Pueblo followed a patrilineal rule in the cases of mixed marriages and the Navajo Tribe followed a matrilineal rule. The children had lived all their lives on the Pueblo except for brief time spent away at school. They spoke and understood Tewa, the traditional and official language of the Pueblo. They observed Pueblo customs and accepted and were accepted into the traditional religious life of the Pueblo. In short, the Martinez children were full participants in the cultural and social life of the Santa Clara Pueblo, yet they could not enroll as members of the tribe under the 1939 tribal ordinance or otherwise hold public office or vote in tribal elections. In the event of their mother's death, the Martinez children had no right to remain on the reservation or to inherit their mother's home or possessory interests in tribal land. 436 U.S. at 111-12. Indeed, the court of appeals had described the following reason for the enactment of the tribal ordinance:

> The increase in mixed marriages produced concern about the enlarged demands for allocation of land and other tribal resources. The Pueblo's elders were apprehensive

that the population increase resulting from intermarriage would strain the Pueblo's finite resources.

540 F.2d at 1040.

Recognizing the limited purpose of formal rolls, many tribes have informal rolls, known as census or service rolls. Similarly, although some benefits may be granted by the federal government to enrolled members of federally recognized tribes only, many of the benefits accorded Indians under various statutes are available to Indians more broadly defined. As a result, the BIA often relies on informal rolls to determine who is an Indian entitled to receive federal services, as opposed to those entitled to receive distributions. See BIA Manual, Release 83-4, Part 8, *Enrollment*, § 8.5 (1959).

Unfortunately, the fact that the concept of membership need not always require formal enrollment in a federally recognized Indian tribe has eluded many courts and commentators. For example, the Supreme Court has recently begun to equate the term "Indian" with "tribal member," a trend discussed in greater length in Chapter 3, section D1 and in Chapter 4, section A2a. The way out of this complex problem is careful attention both to the language used in a particular federal law and the purpose for which the classification has been made, along with due deference to the basic right of Indian tribes as sovereigns to make their own membership determinations.

Federal statutes that refer to enrollment as a necessary prerequisite could be interpreted either to refer to formal or informal membership rolls. Certainly if the issue for which the determination is important involves internal affairs of the tribe, only the tribe should make this determination. *See Santa Clara Pueblo v. Martinez*, set forth and discussed in Chapter 3, sections C and D4. For a federal purpose that involves property rights, such as the distribution of judgment funds to the descendants of Indians deprived of their lands, the term will be interpreted as referring to formal enrollment in a federally approved roll, unless the law states otherwise. *See, e.g., Delaware Tribal Bus. Comm. v. Weeks*, 430 U.S. 73, 84-86 (1977). In short, when the concept is membership, the interpretation should hinge on whether the term is used as part of congressional power to control the property of Indian tribes, in which case the congressional definition will govern, or whether it is part of a statute designed to strengthen or protect tribal sovereignty, in which case the tribal definition must be ascendant.

Membership is not a *sine qua non* for many federal laws referring to Indians. Congress has often imposed a particular blood quantum requirement in addition to enrollment, or has dispensed with a requirement of formal enrollment altogether. See COHEN's HANDBOOK, *supra*, at 19-20. Before 1934, most federal statutes referring to Indians did not define the term. Court decisions interpreting the term for purposes of the federal criminal statutes have stressed the presence of the two factors outlined above. *See, e.g., Ex parte Pero*, 99 F.2d 28 (7th Cir. 1938); *Montana v. LaPier*, 790 P.2d 893 (1990).

For most statutory purposes it is not necessary for a person to be an enrolled member of a recognized tribe. The modern congressional trend is to define the term "Indian" broadly to include both formal and informal membership as well as requirements of a certain degree of Indian blood. Although formal enrollment is not necessary, enrollment is evidence of acceptance in the tribal community as a member and also the best evidence of blood quantum in those tribes (nearly all) setting a minimum blood quantum standard. This trend is especially apparent in those statutes in which Congress has extended benefits to Indian people in recognition of their relationship to tribes that have been both bene-fited and burdened by the historical relationship of tribes as political entities with the United States government.

The Indian Reorganization Act began this modern trend:

> The term "Indian" as used in [this Act] shall include all persons of Indian descent who are members of any recognized Indian tribe now under Federal jurisdiction, and all persons who are descendants of such members who were, on June 1, 1934, residing within the present boundaries of any Indian reservation, and shall further include all other persons of one-half or more Indian blood. For the purposes of [this Act,] Eskimos and other aboriginal peoples of Alaska shall be considered Indians.

25 U.S.C. § 479.

Recent statutes, such as the 1988 law creating a Department of Indian Education in the Department of Education, have taken into account the lack of a unitary definition of Indian by defining Indian as anyone "considered by the Secretary of the Interior to be an Indian for any purpose," a broad definition that permits many Indians who may not be formally enrolled to qualify for benefits. 25 U.S.C. § 5351(c).

The courts have historically been deferential to congressional determination of who is an Indian tribe or who is an Indian in recognition of Congress's broad power to regulate Indian affairs, which includes the power to determine which entities and people come within the purview of that power. This issue is discussed in greater depth in section B2 of this chapter and in Chapter 2, section B, note 3.

2. EQUAL PROTECTION AND SPECIAL LEGAL PROTECTIONS AFFORDED INDIANS AND INDIAN TRIBES

VIEIRA, RACIAL IMBALANCE, BLACK SEPARATISM AND PERMISSIBLE CLASSIFICATION BY RACE, 67 Michigan Law Review 1553, 1577-81 (1969)*

IV. Relations with Indian Tribes

Perhaps more applicable to present problems concerning the government's use of racial criteria is the historic differential treatment of Indians. Special restrictions have been placed on the freedom of Indians to alienate property, and the administration of criminal law in the Indian country has varied, depending on whether those involved in the offense were Indians.[123] In a few instances Indians have received preferential or compensatory treatment, a practice which may bear on the validity of some proposals to alleviate the consequences of prejudice against Negroes.

---

*Reprinted from 67 MICHIGAN LAW REVIEW 1553 (1969) with the permission of the author and The Michigan Law Review.

[123] For an extensive account of these issues, see U.S. Department of the Interior, Federal Indian Law (1966). See also Brown, The Indian Problem and the Law, 39 YALE L.J. 307 (1930); Cohen, Indian Rights and the Federal Courts, 24 MINN. L. REV. 144 (1940); Krieger, Principles of the Indian Law and the Act of June 18, 1934, 3 GEO. WASH. L. REV. 279 (1935).

The central question concerning the applicability of this body of law to other groups is whether or not the differential treatment of Indians is based on race. The late Felix Cohen argued vigorously that it is not. He emphasized that the relevant constitutional provisions[124] refer to Indian "tribes" and Indians "not taxed," and he urged that these are political designations which confer "no authority to govern Indians as a racial group." Under Cohen's view the special treatment of Indians can be explained by their allegiance to resident tribal nations, thereby making this line of precedents inapplicable to any other class, and enabling individual Indians to secure nondifferential treatment by severing their tribal ties. Support for his view is implicit in the principle of tribal self-government, which has a nonracial basis described by Chief Justice Marshall in a landmark case:[126]

> The Indian nations had always been considered as distinct, independent, political communities....
> ... The very fact of repeated treaties with them recognizes [their right of self-government]; and the settled doctrine of the law of nations is, that a weaker power does not surrender its independence — its right to self-government — by associating with a stronger, and taking its protection....
> The Cherokee Nation, then, is a distinct community.... The whole intercourse between the United States and this nation, is, by our Constitution and laws, vested in the government of the United States.

Similar support for Cohen's thesis is found in *Elk v. Wilkins*,[128] which relied on tribal rather than racial factors in holding that the fourteenth amendment does not confer citizenship on Indians born in the United States:

> Indians born within the territorial limits of the United States, members of, and owing immediate allegiance, to one of the Indian tribes (an alien, though dependent, power), although in a geographical sense born in the United States, are no more "born in the United States and subject to the jurisdiction thereof," within the meaning of the first section of the Fourteenth Amendment, than the children of subjects of any foreign government born within the domain of that government, or the children born within the United States, of ambassadors or other public ministers of foreign nations.

Nevertheless, although much federal Indian law can be explained on a racially neutral basis, some of it cannot. For example, Congress has at times removed restraints on alienation of property for mixed-blood Indians while retaining them for full-bloods. A classification in terms of the quantum of Indian blood is blatantly unrelated to tribal affiliation, and yet this statutory scheme was enforced by the Supreme Court in a series of cases.[130] Since restraints on freedom of alienation were designed "to protect the Indian against sharp practices," governmental action lifting the restraints for mixed-bloods and preserving them for full-bloods must reflect a legislative determination as to the capabilities of each group. Occasionally courts have explicitly endorsed

---

[124] The principal sources of federal authority over Indians are the commerce clause (U.S. Const. art. 1, § 8), and the powers to make treaties (U.S. Const. art. 2, § 2) and to regulate territories and possessions (U.S. Const. art. 4, § 3)....

[126] Worcester v. Georgia, 31 U.S. (6 Pet.) 515 (1832).

[128] 112 U.S. 94 (1884).

[130] United States v. Waller, 243 U.S. 452 (1917); United States v. First Nat'l Bank, 234 U.S. 245 (1914); Tiger v. Western Inv. Co., 221 U.S. 286 (1911). *See also* United States v. Ferguson, 247 U.S. 175 (1918) (administrative determination of blood quantum held final).

that determination,[132] but more often they have simply affirmed that "it was within the power of Congress to continue to restrict alienation by requiring, as to full-blood Indians, the consent of the Secretary of the Interior to a proposed alienation...."[133] In either event, racial generalizations were accepted in lieu of a precise classifying trait.

Racial considerations have similarly affected jurisdiction over crimes in the Indian country. Although federal criminal law extends generally to that territory, statutes have made it specifically inapplicable to offenses between Indians. In *United States v. Rogers*,[134] the Supreme Court construed an exemption from federal jurisdiction for crimes committed "by one Indian against the person or property of another Indian" to be based on the race of the parties rather than on tribal membership. In holding that a white defendant who had become a member of an Indian tribe through marriage was not exempted, the Court stated:

> [T]he exception is confined to those who by the usages and customs of the Indians are regarded as belonging to their race. It does not speak of members of a tribe, but the race generally — of the family of Indians; and it intended to leave them both, as regarded their own tribe, and other tribes also, to be governed by Indian usages and customs....
> ... Whatever obligations the prisoner may have taken upon himself by becoming a Cherokee by adoption, his responsibility to the laws of the United States remained unchanged and undiminished. He was still a white man, of the white race, and therefore not within the exception in the act of Congress.

Since federal, state, and tribal laws, and their administration are subject to wide variation, the *Rogers* interpretation placed a significant racial condition on the imposition of criminal sanctions in this area.[136]

A number of civil statutes bear similar overtones of race but have not been authoritatively construed. One provision states that a "white man, not otherwise a member of any tribe" acquires no right to tribal property by marriage.[137] The statute evidently does not operate against Indians or other nonwhites who are not members of any tribe. Federal law also provides that in all trials involving property disputes between an Indian and a white person "the burden of proof shall rest upon the white person, whenever the Indian shall make out a presumption of title in himself from the fact of previous possession or ownership."[138] Finally, Congress has directed that preferences be given to qualified Indians in filling vacancies for various positions in the Indian Office.[139] In

---

[132] The varying degrees of blood most naturally become the lines of demarcation between the different classes, because experience shows that generally speaking the greater percentage of Indian blood a given allottee has, the less capable he is by natural qualification and experience to manage his property...." United States v. Shock, 187 F. 862, 870 (1911).

[133] Tiger v. Western Inv. Co., 221 U.S. 286, 316 (1911).

[134] 45 U.S. (4 How.) 567 (1846).

[136] Under provisions presently in effect, jurisdiction over crimes in the Indian country continues to depend in some instances on whether both the defendant and the victim are Indians. 18 U.S.C. §§ 1152, 1153 (1964). [T]he current provisions, [however,] have been held by lower courts to have tribal, not racial, connotations. *E.g.,* State v. Williams, 13 Wash. 335, 43 P. 15 (1895).

[137] 25 U.S.C. § 181 (1964).

[138] 25 U.S.C. § 194 (1964).

[139] 25 U.S.C. §§ 44, 46, 472 (1964). These preferences were retained in explicit terms by the Civil Rights Act of 1964. 42 U.S.C. § 2000e-2 (i) (1964).

some cases the mandate for preferential hiring has been tied unmistakably to race rather than to tribal membership.[140]

It is not unlikely that many commentators will look upon the differential treatment of the Indian as a favorable precedent for utilizing racial classifications to remedy injustices to the Negro. Federal Indian law has classified by race,[141] and in many respects the law has been directed toward the protection of the disadvantaged minority. Some special treatment of the Indian might be explained by previous tribal relations, since those relations may have continuing detrimental effects which arguably the government should have power to neutralize. But that theory would not justify differential action based on quantum of Indian blood. Furthermore, the argument for preferential treatment of Negroes may legitimately urge that the residual effects of slavery, black codes, and segregation are no less debilitating than those of tribal isolation.

Yet despite those similarities, there are compelling reasons for courts to hesitate in adopting the analogy. First, it should be noted that the special status of Indians has rested in large part on the premise that they are a vulnerable people who, for their own protection, must be made wards of the national government. Inasmuch as this assumption often referred to the weakness of Indian persons rather than of Indian "nations," it reflects attitudes of white supremacy[142] that are plainly at odds with the past thirty years of race relations case law and hence provides a dubious basis for treating other minorities. Second, even if the analogy between the Negro and the Indian were apt, the history of United States-Indian relations is scarcely one which inspires imitation. Instead, that history might better serve "to warn us that the role of the Great White Father may be bitterly resented by those in his tutelage and that a guardian ordinarily prefers to postpone rather than to advance the day when his wards must face the rigors of freedom."[143] Third, a racial interpretation in this area places undue stress on a small portion of a large body of law. Although some cases involve classification by race, most of them are responsive to Mr. Cohen's formulation. And when race has had a decisive impact, that fact should invite skepticism over the merits of the decision rather than its easy application to another group. Finally, the value of these cases as constitutional precedent is greatly diluted by their peculiar surrounding circumstances. The events which led to the decisions, including treaties and physical conquests, have no parallel in the background of non-Indian groups; and since the cases antedate modern due process developments,[145] they did not face squarely the difficult questions inherent in racial classification.

---

[140]25 U.S.C. § 45 (1964) (preferences for "persons of Indian descent").

[141]This use of racial criteria cannot be explained and, hence, limited by the constitutional grants of power to regulate Indian affairs. [Racial considerations have] not been confined to implementing treaties with Indian nations, and may well be subject to the same restrictions for that purpose as for any other. Cf. Missouri v. Holland, 252 U.S. 416 (1920). Although federal control over United States possessions and over commerce with Indian tribes permits extensive regulation, this federal power should no more authorize racial distinctions than does the corresponding state power to regulate local commerce and local property.

[142]See note 132 supra.

[143]Bittker, The Case of the Checker-Board Ordinance: An Experiment in Race Relations, 71 YALE L.J. 1387, 1422 (1962).

[145]See, e.g., Palko v. Connecticut, 302 U.S. 319 (1937).

MORTON v. MANCARI

417 U.S. 535 (1974)

Mr. Justice BLACKMUN delivered the opinion of the Court.

The Indian Reorganization Act of 1934, also known as the Wheeler-Howard Act, 48 Stat. 984, 25 U.S.C. § 461 et seq., accords an employment preference for qualified Indians in the Bureau of Indian Affairs (BIA or Bureau). Appellees, non-Indian BIA employees, challenged this preference as contrary to the anti-discrimination provisions of the Equal Employment Opportunity Act of 1972, [and as a violation] of the Due Process Clause of the Fifth Amendment. A three-judge Federal District Court concluded that the Indian preference under the 1934 Act was impliedly repealed by the 1972 Act. [This Court] noted probable jurisdiction in order to examine the statutory and constitutional validity of this longstanding Indian preference....

I

Section 12 of the Indian Reorganization Act, 48 Stat. 986, 25 U.S.C. § 472, provides:

The Secretary of the Interior is directed to establish standards of health, age, character, experience, knowledge, and ability for Indians who may be appointed, without regard to civil-service laws, to the various positions maintained, now or hereafter, by the Indian Office, in the administration of functions or services affecting any Indian tribe. Such qualified Indians shall hereafter have the preference to appointment to vacancies in any such positions.

In June 1972, pursuant to this provision, the Commissioner of Indian Affairs, with the approval of the Secretary of the Interior, issued a directive (Personnel Management Letter No. 72-12) (App. 52) stating that the BIA's policy would be to grant a preference to qualified Indians not only, as before, in the initial hiring stage, but also in the situation where an Indian and a non-Indian, both already employed by the BIA, were competing for a promotion within the Bureau. The record indicates that this policy was implemented immediately.

Shortly thereafter, appellees, who are non-Indian employees of the BIA at Albuquerque, instituted this class action, on behalf of themselves and other non-Indian employees similarly situated, in the United States District Court for the District of New Mexico, claiming that the "so-called 'Indian Preference Statutes,'" [were repealed by Congress in] the 1972 Equal Employment Opportunity Act and deprived them of rights to property without due process of law, in violation of the Fifth Amendment. Named as defendants were the Secretary of the Interior, the Commissioner of Indian Affairs, and the BIA Directors for the Albuquerque and Navajo Area Offices. Appellees claimed that implementation and enforcement of the new preference policy "placed and will continue to place [appellees] at a distinct disadvantage in competing for promotion and training programs with Indian employees, all of which has and will continue to subject the [appellees] to discrimination and deny them equal employment opportunity."

[T]he District Court concluded that the Indian preference was implicitly repealed by § 11 of the Equal Employment Opportunity Act of 1972, Pub. L. 92-261, 86 Stat. 111, 42 U.S.C. § 2000e-16 (a) (1970 ed., Supp. II), proscribing

discrimination in most federal employment on the basis of race.[6] Having found
that Congress repealed the preference, it was unnecessary for the District Court
to pass on its constitutionality. The court permanently enjoined appellants
"from implementing any policy in the Bureau of Indian Affairs which would
hire, promote, or reassign any person in preference to another solely for the
reason that such person is an Indian." The execution and enforcement of the
judgment of the District Court was stayed by Mr. Justice Marshall on August 16,
1973, pending the disposition of this appeal.

II

The federal policy of according some hiring preference to Indians in the
Indian service dates at least as far back as 1834.[7] Since that time, Congress
repeatedly has enacted various preferences of the general type here at issue.
The purpose of these preferences, as variously expressed in the legislative history, has been to give Indians a greater participation in their own self-government;[9] to further the Government's trust obligation toward the Indian tribes;
and to reduce the negative effect of having non-Indians administer matters that
affect Indian tribal life.

The preference directly at issue here was enacted as an important part of the
sweeping Indian Reorganization Act of 1934. The overriding purpose of that
particular Act was to establish machinery whereby Indian tribes would be able
to assume a greater degree of self-government, both politically and economically. Congress was seeking to modify the then-existing situation whereby the
primarily non-Indian-staffed BIA had plenary control, for all practical purposes, over the lives and destinies of the federally recognized Indian tribes.
Initial congressional proposals would have diminished substantially the role of
the BIA by turning over to federally chartered self-governing Indian communities many of the functions normally performed by the Bureau. Committee

---

[6]Section 2000e-16 (a) reads:

All personnel actions affecting employees or applicants for employment (except with regard to
aliens employed outside the limits of the United States) in military departments as defined in
section 102 of Title 5, in executive agencies (other than the General Accounting Office) as
defined in section 105 of Title 5 (including employees and applicants for employment who are
paid from nonappropriated funds), in the United States Postal Service and the Postal Rate Commission, in those units of the Government of the District of Columbia having positions in the
competitive service, and in those units of the legislative and judicial branches of the Federal
Government having positions in the competitive service, and in the Library of Congress shall be
made free from any discrimination based on race, color, religion, sex, or national origin.

[7]Act of June 30, 1834, § 9, 4 Stat. 737, 25 U.S.C. § 45:

[I]n all cases of the appointments of interpreters or other persons employed for the benefit of
the Indians, a preference shall be given to persons of Indian descent, if such can be found, who
are properly qualified for the execution of the duties.
      ....

[9]Senator Wheeler, cosponsor of the 1934 Act, explained the need for a preference as follows:

We are setting up in the United States a civil service rule which prevents Indians from managing their own property. It is an entirely different service from anything else in the United States,
because these Indians own this property. It belongs to them. What the policy of this Government
is and what it should be is to teach these Indians to manage their own business and control their
own funds and to administer their own property, and the civil service has worked very poorly so
far as the Indian Service is concerned .... Hearings on S. 2755 and S. 3645 before the Senate
Committee on Indian Affairs, 73d Cong., 2d Sess., pt. 2, p. 256 (1934).

sentiment, however, ran against such a radical change in the role of the BIA. The solution ultimately adopted was to strengthen tribal government while continuing the active role of the BIA, with the understanding that the Bureau would be more responsive to the interests of the people it was created to serve.

One of the primary means by which self-government would be fostered and the Bureau made more responsive was to increase the participation of tribal Indians in the BIA operations.[15] In order to achieve this end, it was recognized that some kind of preference and exemption from otherwise prevailing civil service requirements was necessary.[16] Congressman Howard, the House sponsor, expressed the need for the preference:

> The Indians have not only been thus deprived of civic rights and powers, but they have been largely deprived of the opportunity to enter the more important positions in the service of the very bureau which manages their affairs. Theoretically, the Indians have the right to qualify for the Federal civil service. In actual practice there has been no adequate program of training to qualify Indians to compete in these examinations, especially for technical and higher positions; and even if there were such training, the Indians would have to compete under existing law, on equal terms with multitudes of white applicants.... The various services on the Indian reservations are actually local rather than Federal services and are comparable to local municipal and county services, since they are dealing with purely local Indian problems. It should be possible for Indians with the requisite vocational and professional training to enter the service of their own people without the necessity of competing with white applicants for these positions. This bill permits them to do so. 78 Cong. Rec. 11729 (1934).

Congress was well aware that the proposed preference would result in employment disadvantages within the BIA for non-Indians. Not only was this displacement unavoidable if room were to be made for Indians, but it was explicitly determined that gradual replacement of non-Indians with Indians within the Bureau was a desirable feature of the entire program for self-government. Since 1934, the BIA has implemented the preference with a fair degree of success. The percentage of Indians employed in the Bureau rose from 34% in 1934 to 57% in 1972. This reversed the former downward trend, [and this result] was due, clearly, to the presence of the 1934 Act. The Commissioner's extension of the preference in 1972 to promotions within the BIA was designed to bring more Indians into positions of responsibility and, in that regard, appears to be a logical extension of the congressional intent.

III

It is against this background that we encounter the first issue in the present case: whether the Indian preference was repealed by the Equal Employment

---

[15][Section 12] was intended to integrate the Indian into the government service connected with the administration of his affairs. Congress was anxious to promote economic and political self-determination for the Indian. *Mescalero Apache Tribe v. Hickel*, 432 F.2d, at 960 (footnote omitted).

[16]The bill admits qualified Indians to the position [*sic*] in their own service.

Thirty-four years ago, in 1900, the number of Indians holding regular positions in the Indian Service, in proportion to the total of positions, was greater than it is today.

The reason primarily is found in the application of the generalized civil service to the Indian Service, and the consequent exclusion of Indians from their own jobs. House Hearings 19 (memorandum dated Feb. 19, 1934, submitted by Commissioner Collier to the Senate and House Committees on Indian Affairs).

Opportunity Act of 1972. Title VII of the Civil Rights Act of 1964, 78 Stat. 253, was the first major piece of federal legislation prohibiting discrimination in *private* employment on the basis of "race, color, religion, sex, or national origin." 42 U.S.C. § 2000e-2 (a). Significantly, §§ 701 (b) and 703 (i) of that Act explicitly exempted from its coverage the preferential employment of Indians by Indian tribes or by industries located on or near Indian reservations. 42 U.S.C. §§ 2000e (b) and 2000e-2 (i).[19] This exemption reveals a clear congressional recognition, within the framework of Title VII, of the unique legal status of tribal and reservation-based activities. The Senate sponsor, Senator Humphrey, stated on the floor by way of explanation:

> [T]his exemption is consistent with the Federal Government's policy of encouraging Indian employment and with the special legal position of Indians. 110 Cong. Rec. 12723 (1964).

The 1964 Act did not specifically outlaw employment discrimination by the Federal Government. Yet the mechanism for enforcing longstanding Executive Orders forbidding Government discrimination had proved ineffective for the most part. In order to remedy this, Congress, by the 1972 Act, amended the 1964 Act and proscribed discrimination in most areas of federal employment. [Generally,] the substantive anti-discrimination law embraced in Title VII was carried over and applied to the Federal Government. [Nowhere] in the legislative history of the 1972 Act, however, is there any mention of Indian preference.

Appellees assert, and the District Court held, that since the 1972 Act proscribed racial discrimination in Government employment, the Act necessarily, albeit *sub silentio,* repealed the provision of the 1934 Act that called for the preference in the BIA of one racial group, Indians, over non-Indians.

[W]e conclude that Congress did not intend to repeal the Indian preference and that the District Court erred in holding that it was repealed.

First: There are the above-mentioned affirmative provisions in the 1964 Act excluding coverage of tribal employment and of preferential treatment by a business or enterprise on or near a reservation. 42 U.S.C. §§ 2000e (b) and 2000e-2 (i). [The] 1964 exemptions as to private employment indicate Congress' recognition of the longstanding federal policy of providing a unique legal status to Indians in matters concerning tribal or "on or near" reservation employment. The exemptions reveal a clear congressional sentiment that an Indian preference in the narrow context of tribal or reservation-related employment did not constitute racial discrimination of the [proscribed type].

Second: Three months after Congress passed the 1972 amendments, it enacted two *new* Indian preference laws. These were part of the Education Amendments of 1972, 86 Stat. 235, 20 U.S.C. §§ 887c (a) and (d), and § 1119a (1970 ed., Supp. II). The new laws explicitly require that Indians be given preference in Government programs for training teachers of Indian children. It

---

[19] Section 701 (b) excludes "an Indian Tribe" from the Act's definition of "employer." Section 703 (i) states:

> Nothing contained in this subchapter shall apply to any business or enterprise on or near an Indian reservation with respect to any publicly announced employment practice of such business or enterprise under which a preferential treatment is given to any individual because he is an Indian living on or near a reservation.

is improbable, to say the least, that the same Congress which affirmatively approved and enacted these additional and similar Indian preferences was, at the same time, condemning the BIA preference as racially discriminatory. In the total absence of any manifestation of supportive intent, we are loathe to imply this improbable result.

Third: Indian preferences, for many years, have been treated as exceptions to Executive Orders forbidding Government employment discrimination. The 1972 extension of the Civil Rights Act to Government employment is in large part merely a codification of prior anti-discrimination Executive Orders that had proved ineffective because of inadequate enforcement machinery. There certainly was no indication that the substantive proscription against discrimination was intended to be any broader than that which previously existed. By codifying the existing anti-discrimination provisions, and by providing enforcement machinery for them, there is no reason to presume that Congress affirmatively intended to erase the preferences that previously had co-existed with broad anti-discrimination provisions in Executive Orders.

Fourth: Appellees encounter head-on the "cardinal rule ... that repeals by implication are not favored." ...

This is a prototypical case where an adjudication of repeal by implication is not appropriate. The preference is a longstanding, important component of the Government's Indian program. The anti-discrimination provision, aimed at alleviating minority discrimination in employment, obviously is designed to deal with an entirely different and, indeed, opposite problem. Any perceived conflict is thus more apparent than real.

[In addition,] the Indian preference statute is a specific provision applying to a very specific situation. The 1972 Act, on the other hand, is of general application. Where there is no clear intention otherwise, a specific statute will not be controlled or nullified by a general one, regardless of the priority of enactment.

[Thus, we] hold that the District Court erred in ruling that the Indian preference was repealed by the 1972 Act.

IV

We still must decide whether, as the appellees contend, the preference constitutes invidious racial discrimination in violation of the Due Process Clause of the Fifth Amendment. *Bolling v. Sharpe,* 347 U.S. 497 (1954). The District Court, while pretermitting this issue, said: "[W]e could well hold that the statute must fail on constitutional grounds."

Resolution of the instant issue turns on the unique legal status of Indian tribes under federal law and upon the plenary power of Congress, based on a history of treaties and the assumption of a "guardian-ward" status, to legislate on behalf of federally recognized Indian tribes. The plenary power of Congress to deal with the special problems of Indians is drawn both explicitly and implicitly from the Constitution itself. Article I, § 8, cl. 3, provides Congress with the power to "regulate Commerce ... with the Indian Tribes," and thus, to this extent, singles Indians out as a proper subject for separate legislation. Article II, § 2, cl. 2, gives the President the power, by and with the advice and consent of the Senate, to make treaties. This has often been the source of the Government's power to deal with the Indian tribes. The Court has described the origin and nature of the special relationship:

> In the exercise of the war and treaty powers, the United States overcame the Indians and took possession of their lands, sometimes by force, leaving them an uneducated, helpless and dependent people, needing protection against the selfishness of others and their own improvidence. Of necessity, the United States assumed the duty of furnishing that protection, and with it the authority to do all that was required to perform that obligation and to prepare the Indians to take their place as independent, qualified members of the modern body politic.... *Board of County Comm'rs v. Seber,* 318 U.S. 705, 715 (1943).

See also *United States v. Kagama,* 118 U.S. 375, 383-384 (1886).

Literally every piece of legislation dealing with Indian tribes and reservations, and certainly all legislation dealing with the BIA, single[s] out for special treatment a constituency of tribal Indians living on or near reservations. If these laws, derived from historical relationships and explicitly designed to help only Indians, were deemed invidious racial discrimination, an entire Title of the United States Code (25 U.S.C.) would be effectively erased and the solemn commitment of the Government toward the Indians would be jeopardized. See *Simmons v. Eagle Seelatsee,* 244 F. Supp. 808, 814 n.13 (ED Wash. 1965), aff'd, 384 U.S. 209 (1966).

It is in this historical and legal context that the constitutional validity of the Indian preference is to be determined. As discussed above, Congress in 1934 determined that proper fulfillment of its trust required turning over to the Indians a greater control of their own destinies. The overly paternalistic approach of prior years had proved both exploitative and destructive of Indian interests. Congress was united in the belief that institutional changes were required. An important part of the Indian Reorganization Act was the preference provision here at issue.

Contrary to the characterization made by appellees, this preference does not constitute "racial discrimination." Indeed, it is not even a "racial" preference.[24] Rather, it is an employment criterion reasonably designed to further the cause of Indian self-government and to make the BIA more responsive to the needs of its constituent groups. It is directed to participation by the governed in the governing agency. The preference is similar in kind to the constitutional requirement that a United States Senator, when elected, be "an Inhabitant of that

---

[24] The preference is not directed towards a "racial" group consisting of "Indians"; instead, it applies only to members of "federally recognized" tribes. This operates to exclude many individuals who are racially to be classified as "Indians." In this sense, the preference is political rather than racial in nature. The eligibility criteria appear in 44 BIAM 335, 3.1:

.1 Policy — An Indian has preference in appointment in the Bureau. To be eligible for preference in appointment, promotion, and training, an individual must be one-fourth or more degree Indian blood and be a member of a Federally-recognized tribe. It is the policy for promotional consideration that where two or more candidates who meet the established qualification requirements are available for filling a vacancy, if one of them is an Indian, he shall be given preference in filling the vacancy. In accordance with the policy statement approved by the Secretary, the Commissioner may grant exceptions to this policy by approving the selection and appointment of non-Indians, when he considers it in the best interest of the Bureau.

This program does not restrict the right of management to fill positions by methods other than through promotion. Positions may be filled by transfers, reassignment, reinstatement, or initial appointment. App. 92.

State for which he shall be chosen," Art. I, § 3, cl. 3, or that a member of a city council reside within the city governed by the council. Congress has sought only to enable the BIA to draw more heavily from among the constituent group in staffing its projects, all of which, either directly or indirectly, affect the lives of tribal Indians. The preference, as applied, is granted to Indians not as a discrete racial group, but, rather, as members of quasi-sovereign tribal entities whose lives and activities are governed by the BIA in a unique fashion. See n.24, *supra*. In the sense that there is no other group of people favored in this manner, the legal status of the BIA is truly *sui generis*. Furthermore, the preference applies only to employment in the Indian service. The preference does not cover any other Government agency or activity, and we need not consider the obviously more difficult question that would be presented by a blanket exemption for Indians from all civil service examinations. Here, the preference is reasonably and directly related to a legitimate, nonracially based goal. This is the principal characteristic that generally is absent from proscribed forms of racial discrimination.

On numerous occasions this Court specifically has upheld legislation that singles out Indians for particular and special treatment. See, *e.g., Board of County Comm'rs v. Seber,* 318 U.S. 705 (1943) (federally granted tax immunity); *McClanahan v. Arizona State Tax Comm'n,* 411 U.S. 164 (1973) (same); *Simmons v. Eagle Seelatsee,* 384 U.S. 209 (1966), *aff'g* 244 F. Supp. 808 (ED Wash. 1965) (statutory definition of tribal membership, with resulting interest in trust estate); *Williams v. Lee,* 358 U.S. 217 (1959) (tribal courts and their jurisdiction over reservation affairs). Cf. *Morton v. Ruiz,* 415 U.S. 199 (1974) (federal welfare benefits for Indians "on or near" reservations). This unique legal status is of long standing, see *Cherokee Nation v. Georgia,* 5 Pet. 1 (1831); *Worcester v. Georgia,* 6 Pet. 515 (1832), and its sources are [varied and diverse]. As long as the special treatment can be tied rationally to the fulfillment of Congress' unique obligation toward the Indians, such legislative judgments will not be disturbed. Here, where the preference is reasonable and rationally designed to further Indian self-government, we cannot say that Congress' classification violates due process.

[*Reversed and remanded.*]

NOTES

1. Indian Preference After *Mancari*: Use of the Indian preference for reductions in force and reassignments within the Bureau of Indian Affairs and the Indian Health Service provoked some Congressional response. Under Pub. L. 96-135, § 2, 93 Stat. 1057, codified at 25 U.S.C. § 472a, both reductions in force and certain reassignments within the Bureau are exempted from the Indian preference. Furthermore, 25 U.S.C. § 472a(c)(1) authorizes any affected tribe to grant a waiver of Indian preference for employment. The same legislation also mandates the Office of Personnel Management to assist in placing non-Indian employees of the BIA and the Indian Health Service with other federal agencies.

The Indian Self-Determination and Educational Assistance Act of 1975 generally requires tribes that contracted with the federal government to assume management of federal programs to provide Indian preferences in both employment and the award of subgrants and subcontracts, 25 U.S.C. § 450e(b). Later legislation, however, exempted certain tribally operated Indian educational programs from Indian preference requirements where the tribal organization grants a written waiver of such laws. 25 U.S.C. § 2011(f).

In 1988, Congress created an Office of Indian Education in the Department of Education and directed the Secretary of the Department of Education to "give a preference to Indians in all personnel actions within the Office of Indian Education." 25 U.S.C. § 2641(c).

2. Political or Racial Classification? How sound is the suggestion offered in the *Mancari* opinion that the Indian employment preference is not a racial preference, but rather a "political" preference or "an employment criterion reasonably designed to further the cause of Indian self-government and to make the BIA more responsive to the needs of its constituent groups"? Does it further Indian self-government to assign a Navajo BIA employee to a program that services the Pine Ridge Sioux Reservation? While the Court notes that it is not a sufficient condition for the employment preference that an applicant be racially identifiable as an Indian, is not Indian racial ancestry a necessary condition for the preference? *Cf. Geduldig v. Aiello,* 417 U.S. 484 (1974) (exclusion of pregnant women from state disability insurance benefits did not constitute an impermissible gender classification since the distinction was based on pregnancy, not gender).

Recall that the Indian Reorganization Act of 1934, which created the employment preference at issue in *Mancari*, also contained, in section 19 its own definition of "Indian". 25 U.S.C. § 479. This definition provided that the term "Indian" would "include all persons of Indian descent who are members of any recognized Indian tribe now under Federal jurisdiction, and all persons who are descendants of such members who were, on June 1, 1934, residing within the present boundaries of any Indian reservation, and shall further include all persons of one-half or more Indian blood." The definition also specified that Eskimos and other aboriginal persons of Alaska should be considered Indians. In 1977, after *Mancari* was decided, the Bureau of Indian Affairs amended its regulations on qualifications for the Indian employment preference to conform with the statutory definition of Indian contained in the Indian Reorganization Act of 1934, 25 U.S.C. § 479 (1976). 43 Fed. Reg. 2393 (1978), establishing regulations that in amended form have been moved to 25 C.F.R. § 5.1. The present regulation essentially parallels the definition found in section 19 of the IRA. The definition of "Indian" in the Education Amendments of 1988 also essentially parallels the IRA definition. *See* 25 U.S.C. § 5351(4). Do these amendments render the Indian employment preference unconstitutional? Do they undermine the rationale offered in *Mancari* for the constitutionality of preferential treatment of Indians in Bureau employment practices?

The Justice Department has taken the position that the preference is unconstitutional because membership in a federally recognized tribe is no longer required to qualify for the preference in either the Interior Department or the newly created Office of Indian Education. The Department has also argued that any congressional granting of benefits to Indians who are not enrolled members of a federally recognized tribe must be treated as a racial classification subject to strict scrutiny. In 1990, Congress amended the Self-Determination Act to clarify that Indian preferences are given to Indians as defined in the Indian Reorganization Act. Act of May 24, 1990, Pub. L. 101-301, 104 Stat. 206, section 2(a)(6), *amending* 25 U.S.C. § 450i(m). In a statement accompanying the signing of the bill, President Bush expressed concern that "racial preferences, divorced from any requirement of tribal membership ... will not meet judicial scrutiny under the Constitution."

If this position were adopted by the Courts, what effect would such a construction have on congressional power to determine who is an Indian for purposes of federal power over Indian affairs expressed in the numerous classifications made in federal statutes?

3. Indians as a Constitutional Racial Classification: The Indian commerce clause contained in article 1, section 8, clause 3 of the Constitution expressly empowers Congress to "regulate Commerce ... with the Indian tribes." To what extent does this provision expressly authorize Congress to draw racial classifications in regulating Indian affairs? In *Simmons v. Eagle Seelatsee,* 244 F. Supp. 808, 814 (E.D. Wash. 1964) (three-judge panel), *aff'd,* 384 U.S. 209 (1966), the courts upheld a quarter-blood requirement for tribal membership against a constitutional challenge. The district court opinion commented: "[I]f legislation is to deal with Indians at all, the very reference to them implies the use of 'a criterion of race.' Indians can only be defined by their race." How close did the Supreme Court come in *Morton v. Mancari* or *United States v. Antelope, infra,* to adopting this rationale?

In *Metro Broadcasting, Inc. v. FCC,* 110 S. Ct. 2997 (1990), the Supreme Court deferred to the power of Congress to create preferences in upholding, by a 5-4 vote, minority racial preference policies adopted by the Federal Communications Commission. Congressional preferences must be treated differently, according to the Court:

> In *Fullilove v. Klutznick,* 448 U.S. 448 (1980), Chief Justice Burger, writing for himself and two other Justices, observed that although "[a] program that employs racial or ethnic criteria ... calls for close examination," when a program employing a benign racial classification is adopted by an administrative agency at the explicit direction of Congress, we are "bound to approach our task with appropriate deference to the Congress, a co-equal branch charged by the Constitution with the power to 'provide for the ... general Welfare of the United States' and 'to enforce, by appropriate legislation,' the equal protection guarantees of the Fourteenth Amendment." We explained that deference was appropriate in light of Congress' institutional competence as the national legislature, as well as Congress' powers under the Commerce Clause, the Spending Clause, and the Civil War Amendments.

Id. at 5057 (citations omitted).

In addition to providing a majority vote for this principle of deference, the Court decided for the first time that Congressional racial preferences need not be limited to remedying identified past discrimination, stating:

> We hold that benign race-conscious measures mandated by Congress — even if those measures are not "remedial" in the sense of being designed to compensate victims of past governmental or societal discrimination — are constitutionally permissible to the extent that they serve important governmental objectives within the power of Congress and are substantially related to achievement of those objectives.

Id.

If preferences for Indians as a class are held to be racial preferences, does *Metro Broadcasting* indicate that the Court will similarly defer to broad congressional power in Indian Affairs?

4. The Political Classification Rationale as a Limitation on Indian Policy and Rights: What potential does *Morton v. Mancari* have for limiting the possible scope of federal legislative protection for Indians? Although the Snyder Act, 25 U.S.C. § 13 (1976), authorizes the Bureau of Indian Affairs to provide various services and programs "for the benefit, care and assistance of the Indians throughout the United States," federal programs have generally been limited to Indians living on or near reservations. In *Morton v. Ruiz,* 415 U.S. 199 (1974), the Supreme Court struck down an administrative practice of limiting BIA general assistance benefits to Indians on reservations (or in areas serviced by the Bureau in Alaska and Oklahoma). The Papago plaintiffs lived fifteen miles from the Papago Reservation and had maintained close social, cultural, and political ties with the reservation. Noting that the Bureau had repeatedly sought appropriations to service Indians living on or near reservations and that the Bureau had not formally published any regulations reflecting the limitation, the Court declared the reservation limitation invalid. Since the holding in *Ruiz* is seemingly limited to Indians living on or near reservations who maintain close ties with their tribe, it is of little benefit to urban Indians who constitute nearly half of the nation's Native American population. *See also Lewis v. Weinberg,* No. 74-524-13 (D.N.M. Mar. 29, 1976) (Indian Public Health Service benefits). *See generally* Sclar, *Participation by Off Reservation Indians in Programs of the Bureau of Indian Affairs and in the Indian Health Services,* 33 MONT. L. REV. 191 (1972). Could Congress constitutionally extend Indian services and benefits to urban Indians? *Cf.* Indian Health Care Improvement Act of 1976, 25 U.S.C. § 1601 et seq. (extending educational assistance for health care professionals and alcoholism treatment programs to many urban Indians, including members of terminated or state-recognized tribes).

In *St. Paul Intertribal Hous. Bd. v. Reynolds,* 564 F. Supp. 1408, 1411 (D. Minn. 1983), the government argued that granting HUD subsidies to a state agency for low income rental units available to heads of households who were enrolled members of federally recognized tribes would violate Title VI of the Civil Rights Act of 1964 and Title VIII of the Civil Rights Act of 1968 because it constituted an impermissible racial preference. The government stressed that the project was far removed geographically from any Indian reservation and that the preference therefore had little, if anything, to do with the promotion of tribal self-government.

The district court rejected HUD's argument, stating that an Indian preference program is not racially discriminatory if "there is an expression of legislative intent to benefit Indians" as part of Congress's trust relationship. The court noted that the Housing Act of 1937 provides for funds for states and includes within the definition of "state" "Indian tribes, bands, and groups," 42 U.S.C. § 1437a(b)(6), and contains other provisions benefiting Indians. In addition, the court noted that the 1974 amendments to the Act set aside housing funds for low income Indian families "who are members of any Indian tribe, band, pueblo, group or community of Indians or Alaska natives which is recognized by the Federal Government," 42 U.S.C. § 1437c(c), without any limitation to on-reservation Indians. As a result, the court concluded that this statutory scheme was a manifestation of the federal-Indian trust responsibility and not a purely racial preference.

Another possible consequence of the *Morton* focus on the political, rather than racial, nature of the preference might be to limit the benefits that certain reservation Indians derive from their reservation residence. Thus, for example, the Supreme Court held in *Washington v. Confederated Tribes of the Colville Reservation,* 447 U.S. 134 (1980), discussed more extensively in Chapter 4, that only members of the governing tribe of a reservation were eligible for the exemption from state taxation for on-reservation transactions. Thus, members of other tribes, even if permanently residing on the reservation as a result of marriage or other family ties, were not entitled to the tax exemption.

Under many tribal codes and regulations promulgated by the Bureau of Indian Affairs, tribal courts exercise jurisdiction over all Indians found on their reservation irrespective of tribal membership. *See, e.g.,* 25 C.F.R. § 11.2. Similarly, the term "Indian," as used in the federal criminal jurisdiction statutes, has never required tribal membership. *See, e.g., United States v. Ives,* 504 F.2d 935, 953 (9th Cir. 1974), *vacated,* 421 U.S. 944 (1975), *cert. denied,* 429 U.S. 1103 (1976). *Ex parte Pero,* 99 F.2d 28, 30 (7th Cir. 1938). *See generally* Clinton, *Criminal Jurisdiction Over Indian Lands: A Journey Through a Jurisdictional Maze,* 18 ARIZ. L. REV. 503, 513-20 (1976).

In 1990 in the case of *Duro v. Reina,* set forth and discussed in Chapter 3, section D1, *infra,* the Court held that tribal courts do not have jurisdiction over nonmember Indians. Furthermore, in dicta the Court characterized congressional power as follows:

> That Indians are citizens does not alter the Federal Government's broad authority to legislate with respect to *enrolled* Indians as a class, whether to impose burdens or benefits.

Duro v. Reina, 110 S. Ct. 2053 (1990) (emphasis added).

Does the inclusion of the word "enrolled" suggest that the Court may restrict the power of Congress to enrolled members of federally recognized tribes?

UNITED STATES v. ANTELOPE

430 U.S. 641 (1977)

Mr. Chief Justice BURGER delivered the opinion of the Court.

The question presented by our grant of certiorari is whether, under the circumstances of this case, federal criminal statutes violate the Due Process Clause of the Fifth Amendment by subjecting individuals to federal prosecution by virtue of their status as Indians.

(1)

On the night of February 18, 1974, respondents, enrolled Coeur d'Alene Indians, broke into the home of Emma Johnson, an 81-year-old non-Indian, in Worley, Idaho; they robbed and killed Mrs. Johnson. Because the crimes were committed by enrolled Indians within the boundaries of the Coeur d'Alene Indian Reservation, respondents were subject to federal jurisdiction under the Major Crimes Act, 18 U.S.C. § 1153. They were, accordingly, indicted by a federal grand jury on charges of burglary, robbery, and murder....

(2)

In the United States Court of Appeals for the Ninth Circuit, respondents contended that their felony-murder convictions were unlawful as products of invidious racial discrimination. They argued that a non-Indian charged with precisely the same offense, namely the murder of another non-Indian within Indian country,[4] would have been subject to prosecution only under Idaho law,

---

[4][The United States Code] ostensibly extends federal jurisdiction to all crimes occurring in Indian country, except offenses subject to tribal jurisdiction. 18 U.S.C. § 1152. However, under *United States v. McBratney, supra,* and cases that followed, this Court construed § 1152 and its predecessors as not applying to crimes by non-Indians against other non-Indians. Thus, respon-

which in contrast to the federal murder statute, [contains no] felony-murder provision. To establish the crime of first-degree murder in the state court, therefore, Idaho would have had to prove premeditation and deliberation. No such elements were required under the felony-murder component of 18 U.S.C. § 1111.

[Such] disparity, so the Court of Appeals concluded, violated equal protection requirements implicit in the Due Process Clause of the Fifth Amendment. We granted the United States' petition for certiorari, 424 U.S. 907 (1976), and we reverse.

(3)

The decisions of this Court leave no doubt that federal legislation with respect to Indian tribes, although relating to Indians as such, is not based upon impermissible racial classifications. Quite the contrary, classifications expressly singling out Indian tribes as subjects of legislation are expressly provided for in the Constitution[6] and supported by the ensuing history of the Federal Government's relations with Indians.

> Indian tribes are unique aggregations possessing attributes of sovereignty over both their members and their territory, *Worcester v. Georgia,* 6 Pet. 515, 557 (1832); they are "a separate people" possessing "the power of regulating their internal and social relations...." *United States v. Mazurie,* 419 U.S. 544, 557 (1975).

Legislation with respect to these "unique aggregations" has repeatedly been sustained by this Court against claims of unlawful racial discrimination. In upholding a limited employment preference for Indians in the Bureau of Indian Affairs, we said in *Morton v. Mancari,* 417 U.S. 535, 552 (1974):

> Literally every piece of legislation dealing with Indian tribes and reservations ... single[s] out for special treatment a constituency of tribal Indians living on or near reservations. If these laws ... were deemed invidious racial discrimination, an entire Title of the United States Code (25 U.S.C.) would be effectively erased....

In light of that result, the Court unanimously concluded in *Mancari:*

> The preference, as applied, is granted to Indians not as a discrete racial group, but, rather, as members of quasi-sovereign tribal entities.... *Id.,* at 554.

Last Term, in *Fisher v. District Court,* 424 U.S. 382 (1976), we held that members of the Northern Cheyenne Tribe could be denied access to Montana state courts in connection with an adoption proceeding arising on their reservation. Unlike *Mancari,* the Indian plaintiffs in *Fisher* were being denied a benefit or privilege available to non-Indians; nevertheless, a unanimous Court dismissed the claim of racial discrimination:

> [W]e reject the argument that denying [the Indian plaintiffs] access to the Montana courts constitutes impermissible racial discrimination. The exclusive jurisdiction of the Tribal Court does not derive from the race of the plaintiff but rather from the quasi-sovereign status of the Northern Cheyenne Tribe under federal law. 424 U.S., at 390.

---

dents correctly argued that, had the perpetrators of the crimes been non-Indians, the courts of Idaho would have had jurisdiction over these charges.

[6] Article I, § 8, of the Constitution gives Congress power "[t]o regulate Commerce with foreign Nations, and among the several States, and with the Indian tribes."

Both *Mancari* and *Fisher* involved preferences or disabilities directly promoting Indian interests in self-government, whereas in the present case we are dealing, not with matters of tribal self-regulation, but with federal regulation of criminal conduct within Indian country implicating Indian interests. But the principles reaffirmed in *Mancari* and *Fisher* point more broadly to the conclusion that federal regulation of Indian affairs is not based upon impermissible classifications. Rather, such regulation is rooted in the unique status of Indians as "a separate people" with their own political institutions. Federal regulation of Indian tribes, therefore, is governance of once-sovereign political communities; it is not to be viewed as legislation of a *"racial"* group consisting of "Indians." *Morton v. Mancari, supra,* at 553 n.24. Indeed, respondents were not subjected to federal criminal jurisdiction because they are of the Indian race but because they were enrolled members of the Coeur d'Alene Tribe.[7]

We therefore conclude that the federal criminal statutes enforced here are based neither in whole nor in part upon impermissible racial classifications.

(4)

The challenged statutes do not otherwise violate equal protection. [Consequently,] only the disparity between federal and Idaho law [remains] as the basis for respondents' equal protection claim. Since Congress has undoubted constitutional power to prescribe a criminal code applicable in Indian country, [it makes no legal difference] that the federal scheme differs from a state criminal code otherwise applicable within the boundaries of the State of Idaho. Under our federal system, the National Government does not violate equal protection when its own body of law is evenhanded,[11] regardless of the laws of States with respect to the same subject matter.

The Federal Government treated respondents in the same manner as all other persons within federal jurisdiction, pursuant to a regulatory scheme that

---

[7] As was true in *Mancari,* federal jurisdiction under the Major Crimes Act does not apply to "many individuals who are racially to be classified as 'Indians.'" 417 U.S., at 553 n.24. Thus, the prosecution in this case offered proof that respondents were enrolled members of the Coeur d'Alene Tribe and thus not emancipated from tribal relations. Moreover, members of tribes whose official status has been terminated by congressional enactment are no longer subject, by virtue of their status, to federal criminal jurisdiction under the Major Crimes Act. *United States v. Heath,* 509 F.2d 16, 19 (9th Cir. 1974) ("While anthropologically a Klamath Indian even after the Termination Act obviously remains an Indian, his unique status *vis-à-vis* the Federal Government no longer exists"). In addition, as enrolled tribal members, respondents were subject to federal jurisdiction only because their crimes were committed within the confines of Indian country, as defined in 18 U.S.C. § 1151. Crimes occurring elsewhere would not be subject to exclusive federal jurisdiction. *Puyallup Tribe v. Department of Game,* 391 U.S. 392, 397 n.11 (1968).

It should be noted, however, that enrollment in an official tribe has not been held to be an absolute requirement for federal jurisdiction, at least where the Indian defendant lived on the reservation and "maintained tribal relations with the Indians thereon." *Ex parte Pero,* 99 F.2d 28, 30 (7th Cir. 1938). See also *United States v. Ives,* 504 F.2d 935, 953 (9th Cir. 1974) (dicta). Since respondents are enrolled tribal members, we are not called on to decide whether nonenrolled Indians are subject to 18 U.S.C. § 1153, and we therefore intimate no views on the matter.

[11] It should be noted, however, that this Court has consistently upheld federal regulations aimed *solely* at tribal Indians, as opposed to *all* persons subject to federal jurisdiction. See, *e.g., United States v. Holliday,* 3 Wall. 407, 417-418 (1866); *Perrin v. United States,* 232 U.S. 478, 482 (1914). See also *Rosebud Sioux Tribe v. Kneip,* [430 U.S.] at 613-615 n.47. Indeed, the Constitution itself provides support for legislation directed specifically at the Indian tribes. [This] Court noted in *Morton v. Mancari,* the Constitution therefore "singles Indians out as a proper subject for separate legislation." 417 U.S., at 552.

did not erect impermissible racial classifications; hence, no violation of the Due Process Clause infected respondents' convictions.

The judgment of the Court of Appeals is reversed, and the case is remanded for further proceedings consistent with this opinion.

Reversed and remanded.

NOTES

1. State Government, Equal Protection, and Indians: The relationship between the federal government, the states, and the tribes has raised a number of equal protection questions. *State ex rel. Adoption of Firecrow*, 167 Mont. 139, 536 P.2d 190 (1975), *rev'd sub nom. Fisher v. District Court*, 424 U.S. 382 (1976). *Fisher* reviewed the decision of the Montana Supreme Court in *Firecrow*, which held that Indian law doctrines that closed state courts to adoption matters involving tribal children and relegated such questions to tribal courts violated the equal protection clause of the state constitution, art. II, § 4, 1972 MONT. CONST. In *Fisher* the Supreme Court reversed and said:

> The exclusive jurisdiction of the Tribal Court does not derive from the race of the plaintiff but rather from the quasi-sovereign status of the Northern Cheyenne Tribe under federal law. Moreover, even if a jurisdictional holding occasionally results in denying an Indian plaintiff a forum in which a non-Indian has access, such disparate treatment of the Indian is justified because it is intended to benefit the class of which he is a member by furthering the congressional policy of Indian self-government.

Id. at 390-91 (citing *Morton v. Mancari*).

After the federal courts ordered the state conservation officials in the State of Washington to allocate approximately fifty percent of certain migratory fisheries in the Puget Sound and certain coastal areas to Indian fishers in order to enforce off-reservation fishing rights guaranteed the affected tribes by treaty (*see United States v. Washington*, 384 F. Supp. 312 (W.D. Wash. 1974), *aff'd*, 520 F.2d 676 (9th Cir. 1975), *cert. denied*, 423 U.S. 1086 (1976)), *vacated*, 443 U.S. 658 (1979), the state courts enjoined the relevant state agencies from complying with the federal court order, in part because they asserted that the order denied non-Indian fishermen equal protection of law. The Washington Supreme Court opinion asserted:

> Granted the equal protection clause of the Fourteenth Amendment does not mandate complete equality. But it cannot be seriously argued that an allocation of 50 percent of a natural resource of a state to a group of citizens comprising little more than .028 percent of the population does not deny such protection.

Washington State Commercial Passenger Fishing Vessel Ass'n v. Tollefson, 89 Wash. 2d 276, 571 P.2d 1373, 1376 (1977), *vacated*, 443 U.S. 658 (1980). *See also Puget Sound Gillnetters Ass'n v. Moos*, 88 Wash. 2d 677, 565 P.2d 1151 (1977), *vacated*, 443 U.S. 658 (1980), and *Purse Seine Vessel Owners Ass'n v. Moos*, 88 Wash. 2d 799, 567 P.2d 205 (1977). The United States Court of Appeals for the Ninth Circuit, noting that the enforcement of the earlier orders "has faced the most concerted official and private efforts to frustrate a decree of a federal court witnessed in this century" outside of the desegregation cases, expressly held that the enforcement of the Indian off-reservation fishing rights did not violate the equal protection clause of the fourteenth amendment. The court stated:

> The treaty fishers derive their rights from one of the cotenants, the tribes. The nontreaty fishers derive their rights from the other, the state as successor to the United

States. The population-head-count disparity is the unremarkable result of normal principles of property law applied to changing numbers within cotenant classes.

Puget Sound Gillnetters Ass'n v. United States Dist. Court, 573 F.2d 1123, 1128 (9th Cir. 1978).

In *Washington v. Washington State Com. Passenger Fishing Vessel Ass'n,* 443 U.S. 658 (1979), the Supreme Court summarily dismissed the constitutional challenge in a brief footnote:

> The simple answer to this argument is that this Court has already held that these treaties confer enforceable special benefits on signatory Indian tribes, ... and has repeatedly held that the peculiar semisovereign and constitutionally recognized status of Indians justifies special treatment on their behalves when rationally related to the Government's "unique obligation toward the Indians."

Id. at 673 n.20. While the United States Supreme Court summarily rejected the central thrust of the equal protection holding advanced by the Washington Supreme Court, the Court elsewhere in its opinion, while generally sustaining the federal court orders allocating to Indians the opportunity to take up to fifty percent of the salmon and steelhead fisheries, nevertheless seemed to contemplate reduction of Indian off-reservation fishing beyond that necessary "to provide the Indians with a livelihood — that is to say, a moderate standard of living." 443 U.S. at 686. Is this "moderate standard of living" limitation the product of either equal protection concepts or traditional property law?

In *Washington v. Confederated Bands & Tribes of the Yakima Nation,* 439 U.S. 463, 500-02 (1979), the Supreme Court briefly addressed the equal protection problems raised under the fourteenth amendment by *state* legislation singling out Indians for separate treatment. In its opinion the Court indicated:

> It is settled that "the unique legal status of Indian tribes under federal law" permits the Federal Government to enact legislation singling out tribal Indians, legislation that might otherwise be constitutionally offensive.... States do not enjoy this same unique relationship with Indians.

The Court went on to note, however, that the state legislation that it was reviewing was not enacted unilaterally by the state, but rather "was enacted in response to a federal measure [Public Law 280] explicitly designed to readjust the allocation of jurisdiction over Indians."

2. Egalitarian Attacks on Indian Policy: Despite the decisions in *Morton v. Mancari* and *United States v. Antelope* the political and legal debate over separate legal protections for Indians continues. In that debate the political, as well as the separate legal, concept of equal protection of laws has come to play a pivotal role. As suggested in the Pacific Northwest fishing dispute cases, the opponents of separate legal status for Indians have charged that it violates certain principles of equality and egalitarianism they claim are protected by the fourteenth amendment. In 1978 a federal bill was proposed, creatively entitled the "Native American Equal Opportunity Act," which was intended to abrogate all treaties entered into by the United States with Indian tribes, to eliminate all separate or special legal protections of Indians, and to terminate federal supervision over the property and members of Indian tribes. H.R. 13329, 95th Cong., 2d Sess. One of the major lobbying groups during the late 1970's fighting for the abrogation of the special legal status of Indians styled itself the Interstate Congress for Equal Rights and Responsibilities.

To what extent is the special legal status of Indians inconsistent with political principles of egalitarianism? Does the equal protection clause protect egalitarianism or only a more limited concept of equal opportunity? Has the American political process applied principles of egalitarianism to any other major questions of property ownership? To the extent that Indian rights, such as hunting and fishing rights, derive from property right guarantees made to the Indians in treaty or statute, does their legal protection really violate the equal protection clause? Could nonenforcement or abrogation of these property rights violate equal protection concepts? Might differential enforcement of Indian property rights raise as many equal protection problems as the existence of such rights?

3. Indian Preferences Granted by States: The State-owned and operated Museum of New Mexico in Santa Fe permits only Indians to sell hand-made goods in an Indian arts and crafts market under the portal of the Palace of the Governors, an historic structure under the control of the Board of Regents of the Museum. The Museum's mission was to present and preserve New Mexico's multicultural traditions. Although an informal rule limiting use of the portal to Indian artisans had been in effect since 1935, the Board of Regents adopted the following written policy in 1976:

> Whereas, the presence of Indian artists and craftsmen at the Palace of the Governors has been an integral part of history, tradition, and function of the Museum of New Mexico for many years;
> ... Now, Therefore, Be It Resolved By The Regents Of The Museum Of New Mexico that policy of the Museum with respect to the display and sale of merchandise on the grounds and areas of the Museum shall be as follows:
> 1. Other than during annually scheduled markets, no person nor group of persons will be permitted to display or sell merchandise on the grounds belonging to the Museum of New Mexico with the sole exception that the area directly under the portal in front of the Palace of the Governors may be used by Indians to display and sell arts and crafts produced by hand by Indian artists and craftsmen.

Non-Indian artisans argued that the policy, which all parties to the litigation, including the Indian artisan intervenors, agreed to be a preference for members of federally recognized Indian tribes, violated the equal protection clause of the fourteenth amendment. In *Livingston v. Ewing*, 455 F. Supp. 825 (D.N.M. 1978), *aff'd*, 601 F.2d 1100 (10th Cir. 1979), *cert. denied*, 444 U.S. 870 (1979), the district court held the preference was constitutional.

Most of the Indians who sold arts and crafts at the portal are members of the New Mexico Pueblos. According to the court, the Pueblo people "maintain their own native culture and remain unassimilated into the predominant American culture. They primarily speak their native languages and maintain strong ties with the traditional religious and social customs of their people." Moreover, the court stated that

> [i]t is undisputed that the viability and economic well-being of the Pueblos depends significantly upon the income which is produced by the sale of hand-made goods under the portal. Thus, there is a direct link between the portal program and the self-determination of these Indians. If the market were to be opened to all vendors, the Indians would gradually retreat from or evacuate the Portal, fearing conflicts with the non-Indian vendors. Conflicts between the plaintiff, Paul Livingston, and one or two of the Indians selling under the Portal have already occurred. The eventual outcome would probably be that the Pueblo Indians would be largely dependent upon welfare instead of their own work, and the quality and production of traditional arts and crafts might suffer.

Id. at 828.

On the other hand, the court noted that the plaintiffs had not established that their economic livelihood would suffer if they could not sell at the portal, because they could submit their hand-made jewelry to the Museum shop, which has no such preference. The court also noted that the Museum's primary purpose was to present the multicultural heritage of New Mexico in settings in which each culture could be displayed separately from the others because "comingling the cultures is less instructive because this fails to clarify the lines of historical development within each culture." *Id.* at 829. In this setting the Indian preference for sales under the portal reproduces an authentic traditional Indian market and is thus part of the Museum's exhibits. The court held that the preference was not a racial preference, citing both federal and state laws recognizing the special status of Indians, including the state constitution provision disclaiming state jurisdiction over Indian lands and a state law establishing a state agency to promote Indian arts and crafts. The court also relied on *Morton v. Mancari*, stating:

> The holding in [*Mancari*] makes clear that in any equal protection analysis dealing with Indians, the historical, legal and cultural context must be considered in determining whether an Indian preference constitutes invidious racial discrimination.
>
> The reasons for this approach are fairly obvious. Because the federal government and the State of New Mexico are committed to insure the political separateness and cultural survival of Indian tribes, and because Indians who live on or near a reservation are members of distinctive cultural communities which would be gradually destroyed if some protection were not given against forced assimilation, Indians have gained a unique status in the law which no other group, racial or otherwise, can claim. As a result, traditional equal protection analysis falls grossly short of dealing in a fair manner with the question of Indian preference, unless it takes these factors into account.

Id. at 831.

As a result, the court concluded that the preference, like the preference in *Mancari,* was political and not racial:

> The requirement that the sellers of Indian hand-made goods be Indian does not make the Museum's preference one based upon race. It is the only logical way the Museum could carry out its cultural selectivity and still serve the Museum's educational purposes. The Museum is not in the business of sponsoring an open market, and to maintain its own standards of authenticity and historical relevancy, the Museum could not allow for the sale of imitation crafts by non-indigenous craftsmen.

Id.

Since the court concluded that the preference was cultural and not racial, the court held the policy was rationally related to the legitimate state interests of preserving a unique cultural activity, enabling the Pueblos to survive as cultural and economic entities, educating the public by permitting it to interact with the traditional artisans, and promoting the important tourism industry in New Mexico. The court cited and relied on *New Orleans v. Dukes*, 427 U.S. 297, 303 (1976), in which the Supreme Court upheld a city ordinance barring new vendors from the historic French Quarter in New Orleans on the grounds that preferring existing vendors "enhanc[ed] the vital role of the French Quarter's tourist-oriented charm in the economy of New Orleans."

Can this preference be adequately justified on the same rationale offered by the Supreme Court in *Morton*? Does it make any difference that the classification seems less political and more racial, ethnic, or cultural? Should it make any difference that the classification was drawn by a state, which has no constitutionally granted power over Indian affairs, rather than by Congress, which expressly was granted authority to regulate Indian commerce? Recall that in the *Yakima* case, the Supreme Court said "States do not enjoy this same unique relationship [that the federal government has] with Indians." *See also Metro Broadcasting v. FCC*, discussed in note 3 after *Mancari, supra.*

3. INDIAN COUNTRY: THE GEOGRAPHIC LIMIT OF MOST FEDERAL INDIAN LAW

Since the inception of federal Indian law, efforts have been made to restrict the protected legal status of Indian tribes primarily to a defined geographic area. The long effort to demarcate jurisdictional boundaries for Indians dates back to the first treaties between the Indian tribes and the colonial authorities in the early seventeenth century. Use of the term "Indian country" to describe Indian enclaves dates at least to the Proclamation of 1763, by which the Crown tried to prevent unrestrained encroachment on Indian lands by designating the lands west of the crest of the Appalachians as Indian country protected from colonial settlement. Geographically based lines of demarcation for Indian country also were contained in the 1796, 1802, and 1834 Trade and Intercourse Acts. 1 Stat. 469, 2 Stat. 139, 4 Stat. 729. Another approach, in the 1834 Act, was essentially definition by creating a residue: Indian country was "that part of the United States west of the Mississippi" not within certain states, "to which Indian title has not been extinguished." *Bates v. Clark,* 95 U.S. 204 (1877). *But see* section 29 of the 1834 Act, 4 Stat. 734. With the westward expansion of non-Indian settlement, each of these lines became outmoded. Consequently, in the late nineteenth century, judicial decisions began to treat Indian country as a generic term encompassing land areas in which Indian autonomy was protected rather than an area subject to precise geographic description. *See, e.g., Ex parte Crow Dog,* 109 U.S. 556, 561-62 (1883).

Indian country has come to have important jurisdictional implications. Within Indian country tribal autonomy and self-government are generally fostered and state law enforcement is frequently precluded. The scope of some federal Indian statutes, such as the criminal jurisdictional provisions of 18 U.S.C. §§ 1152 and 1153, is expressly limited to Indian country. On the other hand, federal Indian law does not operate solely in Indian country. Some statutes operate anywhere in the United States. The federal statutory restraints against the alienation of Indian land, for example, have been held to apply to all tribally held land irrespective of whether the tribe is federally recognized or its land constitutes Indian country. *See Passamaquoddy Tribe v. Morton,* 528 F.2d 370 (1st Cir. 1975). Similarly, nineteenth century federal statutes proscribing the sale of liquor to Indians outside of Indian country frequently were sustained. *E.g., United States v. Holliday,* 70 U.S. (3 Wall.) 407 (1865); *United States v. Forty-Three Gallons of Whiskey,* 93 U.S. 188 (1876). More recently, Congress included within the coverage of the Indian Child Welfare Act of 1978, 25 U.S.C. § 1901 et seq., discussed in Chapter 4, child custody proceedings involving certain Indian children domiciled outside of Indian country. Thus, every statute must be carefully analyzed to determine the precise scope of its application. Nevertheless, despite these exceptions many important legal issues affecting Indians turn on whether the area in question constitutes Indian country.

Since 1948, the accepted definition of Indian country has been found in 18 U.S.C. § 1151 (1976):

Except as otherwise provided in sections 1154 and 1156 of this title, the term "Indian country," as used in this chapter, means (a) all land within the limits of any Indian reservation under the jurisdiction of the United States government, notwithstanding the issuance of any patent, and, including rights-of-way running through the reservation, (b) all dependent Indian communities within the borders of the United States whether within the original or subsequently acquired territory thereof, and whether within or without the limits of a state, and (c) all Indian allotments, the Indian titles to which have not been extinguished, including rights-of-way running through the same.

While this definition is contained in the federal criminal jurisdiction statutes, the Supreme Court has held that it "generally applies as well to questions of civil jurisdiction." *De Coteau v. District County Court,* 420 U.S. 425, 427 n.2 (1975). Thus, "Indian country" represents a term of art in Indian law, the meaning of which has important implications for jurisdiction and governance of the affected area.

CLINTON, CRIMINAL JURISDICTION OVER INDIAN LANDS: A JOURNEY THROUGH A JURISDICTIONAL MAZE, 18 Arizona Law Review 503, 507-13 (1976)*

The first clauses of sections 1151(a) and (b) merely restate prior law. Since the early definitions of Indian country were predicated in great part on aboriginal title, the removal of Indians to reservations in the 19th century prompted questions as to whether reservations created either by congressional act or Presidential proclamation were Indian country because they were not, in many instances, lands to which the tribe held aboriginal title. In *Donnelly v. United States*,[27] the Supreme Court rejected this distinction and specifically held that land set aside from the public domain by Executive order for use as an Indian reservation was Indian country. That portion of section 1151(a) which includes within the definition of Indian country "all land within the limits of any Indian reservation under the jurisdiction of the United States Government" is a direct outgrowth of *Donnelly.* Not all lands presently occupied by Indian tribes are the product of the federal reservation policy, however, and thus some Indian lands are not technically reservations. In *United States v. Sandoval*,[29] decided the same year as *Donnelly,* the Supreme Court held that the lands of the Pueblo Indians, which were not federally owned reservations, but rather consisted of communally owned lands held in fee simple, were nonetheless Indian country since they were occupied by "distinctly Indian communities" which were "dependent tribes" recognized and protected by the federal government. Section 1151(b) is a codification of *Sandoval.* The simple ownership of lands by a federally-recognized, dependent Indian tribe is sufficient to bring the lands so held within the ambit of the phrase "Indian country."

Section 1151(b) includes within the scope of Indian country all dependent Indian communities in the United States "whether within or without the limits of a state." Although the reasons for this language are not fully spelled out in the legislative history notes, its inclusion apparently is an effort to resolve a

---

*Copyright 1977 by the Arizona Board of Regents. Reprinted by permission.
[27] 228 U.S. 243 (1913). *See also* Pronovost v. United States, 232 U.S. 487 (1914) (The Flathead Indian Reservation within the State of Montana found to be Indian country).
[29] 231 U.S. 28 (1913).

conflict in Supreme Court decisions as to whether land located within the boundaries of a state, whose enabling act or constitution does not contain a disclaimer of state jurisdiction over Indian lands, is subject to state or federal jurisdiction. By enacting section 1151(b), Congress has put to rest any argument that Indian lands ceased being federal Indian enclaves when the state within which they are located was admitted to the Union without a disclaimer of jurisdiction.

A number of the clauses contained in section 1151 are designed to clarify the vestigial impact on jurisdictional arrangements of the General Allotment Act of 1887, and related programs. These programs altered the traditional communal ownership patterns for Indian lands by allotting and patenting specified parcels of land both within and without Indian reservations to individual Indians either in trust or in fee. For a time, these programs created problems of "checkerboard" jurisdiction within particular reservations, as provisions in these acts vested the states with jurisdiction over the allotted land. Moreover, since the Indian Reorganization Act of 1934 had indefinitely extended the trust period of lands still held under these allotment programs, many parcels of allotted land might have been left effectively in a checkerboard jurisdictional limbo. Although the courts had addressed many of the problems created by the allotment program, the provisions in section 1151 are an effort to codify the results of litigation and promulgate clear statutory solutions to other difficulties. Specifically, section 1151 resolved many of the jurisdictional problems created by allotment, by expressly including within the definition of Indian country all allotted and patented land located within the limits of an Indian reservation and all Indian allotments to which Indian title has not been extinguished, even if not located within a reservation.[37]

---

[37] The first important solution to the jurisdictional problems created by the allotment programs is found in section 1151(a), which includes within Indian country "all land within the limits of any Indian reservation under the jurisdiction of the United States Government, *notwithstanding the issuance of any patent.*" 18 U.S.C. § 1151(a) (1970) (emphasis added). This provision codifies prior case law holding that all land within the exterior boundaries of an Indian reservation remain Indian country despite the issuance of patents for parcels of land therein. *See* United States v. Celestine, 215 U.S. 278 (1909). *See generally* Beardslee v. United States, 387 F.2d 280 (8th Cir. 1967). Accordingly, section 1151(a) solves the potential problems of checkerboard jurisdiction within particular reservations created by the patenting of selected parcels therein. *See* Seymour v. Superintendent of Wash. State Penitentiary, 368 U.S. 351, 358 (1962). This checkerboard jurisdiction problem had so plagued law enforcement on Indian reservations in Kansas prior to the enactment of section 1151 that Congress sought to cure the problem by partially vesting criminal jurisdiction in the state. 18 U.S.C. § 3243 (1970)....

The second provision of section 1151 designed to cure residual jurisdictional problems left by the allotment program is the first clause of 1151(c), which brings within Indian country "all Indian allotments, the Indian titles to which have not been extinguished." 18 U.S.C. § 1151(c) (1970). This provision assures that all allotted lands within Indian reservations to which trust title was indefinitely extended by the Indian Reorganization Act of 1934 will be considered Indian country for purposes of the federal jurisdictional statutes. [More importantly,] 1151(c) contains no reference, unlike 1151(a), to a requirement that allotted land comprise property located within an established Indian reservation. The omission is deliberate. Section 1151(c) was intended to codify United States v. Pelican, 232 U.S. 442 (1914), where the Supreme Court held that allotted land within the Colville reservation which had been terminated as reservation land and placed in the public domain, was nevertheless Indian country, so long as an Indian held title to the allotted parcel. *Id.* at 449. Although *Pelican* strongly suggested that all allotted land to which Indian title had not been extinguished was Indian country, the pre-1948 case law in the state courts did not uniformly adhere to that principle.... *See also Ex parte* Wallace, 81 Okla. Crim. 176, 162 P.2d 205 (1945); State v. Shepard, 239 Wis. 345, 300 N.W. 905 (1941). The codification of *Pelican* in section 1151(c) appar-

[T]he definition of Indian country set forth in section 1151 [therefore] is quite expansive. Once a reservation has been established, or a dependent Indian community shown to exist, it will remain Indian country until terminated by Congress, irrespective of the nature of the land ownership. Moreover, even if individual allotted parcels of land are not located within the reservation, they may still constitute Indian country if the Indian title thereto has not been extinguished. A finding that the land on which a crime was committed is Indian country will generally result in exclusive tribal and federal jurisdiction, thereby excluding the exercise of state authority. Hence, the expansiveness of the definition of Indian country is important in preserving policies of tribal self-government and the protective federal trusteeship over Indians.

UNITED STATES v. JOHN
437 U.S. 634 (1978)

Mr. Justice BLACKMUN delivered the opinion of the Court.

These cases present issues concerning state and federal jurisdiction over certain crimes committed on lands within the area designated as a reservation for the Choctaw Indians residing in central Mississippi. More precisely, the questions presented are whether the lands are "Indian country," as that phrase is defined in 18 U.S.C. § 1151 (1976 ed.) and as it was used in the Major Crimes Act of 1885, being § 9 of the Act of March 3, 1885, 23 Stat. 385, later codified as 18 U.S.C. § 1153 (1970 ed.), and, if so, whether these federal statutes operate to preclude the exercise of state criminal jurisdiction over the offenses.

I

In October 1975, in the Southern District of Mississippi, Smith John was indicted by a federal grand jury for assault with intent to kill Artis Jenkins, in violation of 18 U.S.C. §§ 1153 and 113(a). He was tried before a jury and, on December 15, was convicted of the lesser included offense of simple assault. A sentence of 90 days in a local jail-type institution and a fine of $300 were

---

ently ends any dispute as to whether lands allotted from the public domain, from former Indian reservations, are Indian country. All such allotments fall within the statutory definition. *See* DeCoteau v. District County Court, 420 U.S. 425, 428 (1975); *In re* Carmen's Petition, 165 F. Supp. 942, 945-46 (N.D. Cal. 1958), *aff'd sub nom.* Dickson v. Carmen, 270 F.2d 809 (9th Cir. 1959), *cert. denied*, 361 U.S. 934 (1960).

Congress has specifically included rights-of-way running through any Indian reservation or allotment within its definition of Indian country. This clarified prior case law as to whether state highways or railroad rights-of-way running through a reservation constituted Indian land for jurisdictional purposes. *Compare* United States v. Soldana, 246 U.S. 530 (1918); *In re* Konaha, 131 F.2d 737 (7th Cir. 1942); *and* People ex rel. Schuyler v. Livingstone, 123 Misc. 605, 205 N.Y.S. 888 (Sup. Ct. 1924), *with* Clairmont v. United States, 225 U.S. 551 (1912); *and Ex parte* Tilden, 218 F. 920 (D. Idaho 1914). Since jurisdiction over reservations not affected by special congressional legislation [generally is] federal and tribal, the inclusion in the definition of highway rights-of-way restricts the authority of the state to enforce traffic and highway laws over such roads. *See* Ortiz-Barraza v. United States, 512 F.2d 1176, 1180 (9th Cir. 1975); *In re* Konaha, 131 F.2d 737 (7th Cir. 1942); State v. Warner, 71 N.M. 418, 379 P.2d 66 (1963); State v. Begay, 63 N.M. 409, 320 P.2d 1017 (1958). *See generally* Schantz v. White Lightning, 502 F.2d 67 (8th Cir. 1974) (North Dakota federal district court had no federal question or diversity jurisdiction over a tort claim arising out of an automobile accident on the Standing Rock Indian Reservation); Gourneau v. Smith, 207 N.W.2d 256 (N.D. 1973) (North Dakota state courts had no jurisdiction over a tort claim for an automobile accident occurring on highways within the Turtle Mountain Indian Reservation); *Enforcement of State Financial Responsibility Laws Within Indian Country*, 17 ARIZ. L. REV. 639, 831 (1975).

imposed. On appeal, the United States Court of Appeals for the Fifth Circuit, considering the issue on its own motion, [determined] that the District Court was without jurisdiction over the case because the lands designated as a reservation for the Choctaw Indians residing in Mississippi, and on which the offense took place, were not "Indian country," and that, therefore, § 1153 did not provide a basis for federal prosecution. 560 F.2d 1202, 1205-1206 (1977). The United States sought review [and certiorari was granted].

In April 1976, Smith John was indicted by a grand jury of Leake County, Mississippi, for aggravated assault upon the same Artis Jenkins, in violation of Miss. Code Ann. § 97-3-7(2) (Supp. 1977). The incident that was the subject of the state indictment was the same as that to which the federal indictment related. A motion to dismiss the charge on the ground the federal jurisdiction was exclusive was denied. John was tried before a jury in the Circuit Court of Leake County and, in May 1976, was convicted of the offense charged. He was sentenced to two years in the state penitentiary. On appeal, the Supreme Court of Mississippi, relying on its earlier decision in *Tubby v. State,* 327 So. 2d 272 (1976), and on the decision of the United States Court of Appeals for the Fifth Circuit in *United States v. State Tax Comm'n,* 505 F.2d 633 (1974), rehearing denied, 535 F.2d 300 (1976), rehearing en banc denied, 511 F.2d 469 (1976), held that the United States District Court had had no jurisdiction to prosecute Smith John, and that, therefore, his arguments against state court jurisdiction were without merit. 347 So. 2d 959 (1977). [The state court therefore found the state had jurisdiction and the Supreme Court granted review.]

II

There is no dispute that Smith John is a Choctaw Indian, and it is presumed by all that he is a descendant of the Choctaws who for hundreds of years made their homes in what is now central Mississippi. The story of these Indians, and of their brethren who left Mississippi to settle in what is now the State of Oklahoma, [is well known].

At the time of the Revolutionary War, these Indians occupied large areas of what is now the State of Mississippi. In the years just after the formation of our country, they entered into a treaty of friendship with the United States. Treaty at Hopewell, 7 Stat. 21 (1786). But the United States became anxious to secure the lands the Indians occupied in order to allow for westward expansion. The Choctaws, in an attempt to avoid what proved to be their fate, entered into a series of treaties gradually relinquishing their claims to these lands.

Despite these concessions, when Mississippi became a State on December 10, 1817, the Choctaws still retained claims, recognized by the Federal Government, to more than three quarters of the land within the State's boundaries. The popular pressure to make these lands available to non-Indian settlement, and the responsibility for these Indians felt by some in the Government, combined to shape a federal policy aimed at persuading the Choctaws to give up their lands in Mississippi completely and to remove to new lands in what for many years was known as the Indian Territory, now a part of Oklahoma and Arkansas. The first attempt to effectuate this policy, the Treaty at Doak's Stand, 7 Stat. 210 (1820), resulted in an exchange of more than five million acres. Because, however, of complications arising when it was discovered that much of the land promised the Indians already had been settled, most Choctaws remained in Mississippi. A delegation of Choctaws went to Washington, D. C., to untangle the situation and to negotiate yet another treaty. See 7 Stat. 234 (1825). Still, few Choctaws moved.

Only after the election of Andrew Jackson to the Presidency in 1828 did the federal efforts to persuade the Choctaws to leave Mississippi meet with some success. Even before Jackson himself had acted on behalf of the Federal Government, however, the State of Mississippi, grown impatient with federal policies, had taken steps to assert jurisdiction over the lands occupied by the Choctaws. In early 1829, legislation was enacted purporting to extend legal process into the Choctaw territory. 1824-1838 Miss. Gen. Laws 195 (Act of Feb. 4, 1829). In his first annual address to Congress on December 8, 1829, President Jackson made known his position on the Indian question and his support of immediate removal. [Thereafter], the Mississippi Legislature passed an act purporting to abolish the Choctaw government and to impose a fine upon anyone assuming the role of chief. The act also declared that the rights of white persons living within the State were to be enjoyed by the Indians, and the laws of the State were to be in effect throughout the territory they occupied. 1824-1838 Miss. Gen. Laws 207 (Act of Jan. 19, 1830).

In Washington, Congress debated whether the States had power to assert such jurisdiction and whether such assertions were wise. But the only message heard by the Choctaws in Mississippi was that the Federal Government no longer would stand between the States and the Indians. Appreciating these realities, the Choctaws again agreed to deal with the Federal Government. On September 27, 1830, the Treaty at Dancing Rabbit Creek, 7 Stat. 333, was signed.[8] It provided that the Choctaws would cede to the United States all lands still occupied by them east of the Mississippi, more than 10 million acres. They were to remove to lands west of the river, where they would remain perpetually free of federal or state control, by the fall of 1833. The Government would help plan and pay for this move. Each Choctaw "head of a family being desirous to remain and become a citizen of the States," [could] do so by signifying his intention within six months to the federal agent assigned to the area. Lands were to be reserved, at least 640 acres per household, to be held by the Indians in fee simple if they would remain upon the lands for five years. [Various other] lands were reserved to the various chiefs and to others already residing on improved lands. [Choctaws] who remained, however, were not to "lose the privilege of a Choctaw citizen," [a]lthough they were to receive no share of the annuity provided for those who chose to remove.

---

[8] Perhaps the best evidence of the circumstances surrounding this treaty lies in its very words. As signed by the Choctaws, it contained the following preamble:

> Whereas the General Assembly of the State of Mississippi has extended the laws of said State to persons and property within the chartered limits of the [Choctaw lands]; and the President of the United States has said that he cannot protect the Choctaw people from the operation of these laws: Now, therefore, that the Choctaw[s] may live under their own laws in peace with the United States and the State of Mississippi they have determined to sell their lands east of the Mississippi, and have accordingly agreed to the following articles of treaty.

The preamble was stricken from the treaty as ratified by the Senate. 7 Cong. Deb. 346-347 (1831).

The relations between the Federal Government and the Choctaws remaining in Mississippi did not end with the formal ratification of the Treaty at Dancing Rabbit Creek by the United States Senate in February 1831. 7 Cong. Rec. 3470. The account of the federal attempts to satisfy the obligations of the United States both to those who remained,[9] and to those who removed, is one best left to historians. It is enough to say here that the failure of these attempts, characterized by incompetence, if not corruption, proved an embarrassment and an intractable problem for the Federal Government for at least a century. *See, e.g., Chitto v. United States, supra.* It remained federal policy, however, to try to induce these Indians to leave Mississippi.

During the 1890's, the Federal Government became acutely aware of the fact that not all the Choctaws had left Mississippi. At that time federal policy toward the Indians favored the allotment of tribal holdings, including the Choctaw holdings in the Indian Territory, in order to make way for Oklahoma's statehood. The inclusion of the Choctaws then residing in Mississippi in the distribution of these holdings proved among the largest obstacles encountered during the allotment effort. But even during this era, when federal policy again supported the removal of the Mississippi Choctaws to join their brethren in the West, there was no doubt that there remained persons in Mississippi who were properly regarded both by the Congress and by the Executive Branch as Indians.

---

[9]*See generally, Chitto v. United States,* 138 F. Supp. 253, 133 Ct. Cl. 643, *cert. denied,* 352 U.S. 841 (1956); *Young, supra,* at 47-72; Riley, Choctaw Land Claims, 8 PUBLICATIONS OF THE MISSISSIPPI HISTORICAL SOCIETY 345 (1904).

It is generally acknowledged that, whether anxious to conceal the fact that far more Choctaws had remained in Mississippi than he had anticipated originally, or simply because he was disinterested in his job and generally dissolute, the agent in charge of the task refused to record the claims of those who elected to remain. *See, e.g., Coleman v. Doe,* 12 Miss. 40 (1844); *Chitto v. United States,* 138 F. Supp., at 257, 133 Ct. Cl., at 648-649. Speculators soon began pressing the cause of those who had been refused. Perhaps in large part due to their efforts, and the cloud created on the ceded lands as they were put up for sale without the proper recordation of Indian claims, Congress soon authorized investigation of the situation. *See* Am. State Papers, Public Lands, Volume 7, 448-525; H.R. Rep. No. 663, 24th Cong., 1st Sess. (1836).

Although one might wonder whether it was concern for the preservation of the claims for the Indians, or simply concern for the preservation of the claims, that motivated subsequent events, measures were taken to remedy the situation and to provide substitute lands for the Choctaws to replace those lands sold despite their attempt to file claims. One measure provided that the claimants would be issued scrip enabling them to claim substitute lands, but half the scrip was not to be delivered unless the claimants removed to territory west of the Mississippi. Act of August 23, 1842, 5 Stat. 513.

The administration of this statute was as unsuccessful as had been the administration of the original treaty. It appears that in practice, none of the scrip was delivered before removal, *Chitto v. United States,* 138 F. Supp., at 257, 133 Ct. Cl., at 649, and that Congress later established a fund to be paid in lieu of part of the scrip. 5 Stat. 777 (1845). After an attempt at settlement in 1852 proved unsuccessful, the United States and the Choctaws in Oklahoma in 1855 entered into still another treaty that provided that the Senate would make a determination of the amounts owing to the Choctaws generally for the failure of the United States to abide by its various treaty promises. Treaty of June 22, 1855, 11 Stat. 611. In March 1859, the Senate approved the general formula under which those amounts were to be calculated, Cong. Globe, 35th Cong., 2d Sess., 1691; S. Rep. No. 374, 35th Cong., 2d Sess., and the Secretary of the Interior, pursuant to this direction, computed the total to be almost $3 million. *See* House Exec. Doc. No. 82, 36th Cong., 1st Sess., *reprinted in* H.R. Rep. No. 251, 45th Cong., 2d Sess., 12 (1878). The War Between the States interrupted the payment of this Senate award, and, after the war, the Choctaws found themselves forced to prove their claims once again, this time in the federal courts. *See Choctaw Nation v. United States,* 119 U.S. 1 (1886), *rev'g* 21 Ct. Cl. 59.

It was not until 1916 that this federal recognition of the presence of Indians in Mississippi was manifested by other than attempts to secure their removal. The appropriations for the Bureau of Indian Affairs in that year included an item (for $1,000) to enable the Secretary of the Interior "to investigate the condition of the Indians living in Mississippi" and to report to Congress "as to their need for additional land and school facilities." 39 Stat. 138. *See* H.R. Doc. No. 1464, 64th Cong., 2d Sess. (1916). In March 1917, hearings were held in Union, Miss., by the House Committee on Investigation of the Indian Service, again exploring the desirability of providing federal services for these Indians. The efforts resulted in an inclusion in the general appropriation for the Bureau of Indian Affairs in 1918. This appropriation, passed only after debate in the House, 56 Cong. Rec. 1136-1140 (1918), included funds for the establishment of an agency with a physician, for the maintenance of schools, and for the purchase of land and farm equipment. Lands purchased through these appropriations were to be sold on contract to individuals in keeping with the general pattern of providing lands eventually to be held in fee by individual Indians, rather than held collectively. Further provisions for the Choctaws in Mississippi were made in similar appropriations in later years.

In the 1930s, the federal Indian policy had shifted back toward the preservation of Indian communities generally. This shift led to the enactment of the Indian Reorganization Act of 1934, 48 Stat. 984, and the discontinuance of the allotment program. The Choctaws in Mississippi were among the many groups who [supported that legislation.]

By this time, it had become obvious that the original method of land purchase authorized by the 1917 appropriations — by contract to a particular Indian purchaser — not only was inconsistent with the new federal policy of encouraging the preservation of Indian communities with commonly held lands, but also was not providing the Mississippi Choctaws with the benefits intended. [Thereafter in] 1939, Congress passed an Act providing essentially that title to all the lands previously purchased for the Mississippi Choctaws would be "in the United States in trust for such Choctaw Indians of one-half or more Indian blood, resident in Mississippi, as shall be designated by the Secretary of the Interior." 53 Stat. 851. In December 1944, the Assistant Secretary of the Department of the Interior officially proclaimed all the lands then purchased in aid of the Choctaws in Mississippi, totaling at that time more than 15,000 acres, to be a reservation. 9 Fed. Reg. 14907.

In April 1945, again as anticipated by the Indian Reorganization Act, § 16, 48 Stat. 987, 25 U.S.C. § 476 (1976 ed.), the Mississippi Band of Choctaw Indians adopted a constitution and bylaws; these were duly approved by the appropriate federal authorities in May 1945.

With this historical sketch as background, we turn to the jurisdictional issues presented by Smith John's case.

III

In order to determine whether there is *federal* jurisdiction over the offense with which Smith John was charged (alleged in the federal indictment to have been committed "on and within the Choctaw Indian Reservation and on land within the Indian country under the jurisdiction of the United States of America"), we first look to the terms of the statute upon which the United States relies, that is, the Major Crimes Act, 18 U.S.C. § 1153 (1970 ed.). This Act, as codified at the time of the alleged offense, provided: "Any Indian who commits ... assault with intent to kill ... within the Indian country, shall be subject to the same laws and penalties as all other persons committing any [such offense], within the exclusive jurisdiction of the United States." The definition of "Indian country" as used here and elsewhere in Chapter 53 of Title 18 is provided in § 1151. Both the Mississippi Court and the Court of Appeals concluded that the situs of the alleged offense did not constitute "Indian country," and that therefore § 1153 did not afford a basis for the prosecution of Smith John in federal court. We do not agree.

With certain exceptions not pertinent here, § 1151 includes within the term "Indian country" three categories of land. The first, with which we are here concerned, is "all land within the limits of any Indian reservation under the jurisdiction of the United States Government, notwithstanding the issuance of any patent." This language first appeared in the Code in 1948 as a part of the general revision of Title 18. The Reviser's notes indicate that this definition was based on several decisions of this Court interpreting the term as it was used in various criminal statutes relating to Indians. In one of these cases, *United States v. McGowan,* 302 U.S. 535 (1938), the Court held that the Reno Indian Colony, consisting of 28.38 acres within the State of Nevada, purchased out of federal funds appropriated in 1917 and 1926 and occupied by several hundred Indians theretofore scattered throughout Nevada, was "Indian country" for the purposes of what was then 25 U.S.C. § 247 (the predecessor of 18 U.S.C. § 3618 (1976 ed.)), providing for the forfeiture of a vehicle used to transport intoxicants into the Indian country. The Court noted that the "fundamental consideration of both Congress and the Department of the Interior in establishing this colony has been the protection of a dependent people." 302 U.S., at 538. The principal test applied was drawn from an earlier case, *United States v. Pelican,* 232 U.S. 442 (1914), and was whether the land in question "had been validly set apart for the use of the Indians as such, under the superintendence of the Government." 232 U.S., at 449.[18]

The Mississippi lands in question here were declared by Congress to be held in trust by the Federal Government for the benefit of the Mississippi Choctaw Indians who were at that time under federal supervision. There is no apparent reason why these lands, which had been purchased in previous years for the aid of those Indians, did not become a "reservation," at least for the purposes of federal criminal jurisdiction at that particular time. *See United States v. Celestine,* 215 U.S. 278, 285 (1909). But if there were any doubt about the matter in 1939 when, as hereinabove described, Congress declared that title to

---

[18]Some earlier cases had suggested a more technical and limited definition of "Indian country." *See, e.g., Bates v. Clark,* 95 U.S. 204 (1877). Throughout most of the 19th century, apparently the only statutory definition was that in § 1 of the Act of June 30, 1834, 4 Stat. 729. But this definition was dropped in the compilation of the Revised Statutes. *See Ex parte Crow Dog,* 109 U.S. 556 (1883). This Court was left with little choice but to continue to apply the principles established under the earlier statutory language and to develop them according to changing conditions. *See, e.g., Donnelly v. United States,* 228 U.S. 243 (1913). It is the more expansive scope of the term that was incorporated in the 1948 revision of Title 18.

lands previously purchased for the Mississippi Choctaws would be held in trust, the situation was completely clarified by the proclamation in 1944 of a reservation and the subsequent approval of the constitution and bylaws adopted by the Mississippi Band.

V

[Therefore, we] hold that § 1153 provides a proper basis for federal prosecution of the offense involved here, and that Mississippi has no power similarly to prosecute Smith John for that same offense. Accordingly, the judgment of the Supreme Court of Mississippi in No. 77-575 is reversed; further, the judgment of the United States Court of Appeals for the Fifth Circuit in No. 77-836 is reversed, and that case is remanded for further proceedings consistent with this opinion.

It is so ordered.

NOTES

1. **Indian Country in the Absence of a Treaty or Statute:** In the absence of the 1939 Act and the Proclamation of 1944, would the result have been the same in *United States v. John*? In *Youngbear v. Brewer,* 415 F. Supp. 807 (N.D. Iowa 1976), *aff'd,* 549 F.2d 74 (8th Cir. 1977) and *State v. Youngbear,* 229 N.W.2d 728 (Iowa 1975), *cert. denied,* 423 U.S. 1018 (1975), the courts held that the Sac and Fox Reservation in Iowa (commonly known as the Mesquakie Settlement) was Indian country despite the lack of any federal statute or order declaring the land to be a reservation. This settlement, like the Choctaw Reservation in Mississippi, was created when Indians either refused to remove or returned to lands ceded in removal treaties during the early nineteenth century. Originally, land was purchased with tribal funds under authority of a state statute in 1856 and held in trust for the Indians by state officials. A federal Indian agent was assigned to the settlement in 1865 and title to the land was conveyed by the state to the United States to be held in trust for the tribe in 1896. Similarly, the Eastern Band of the Cherokee Reservation in North Carolina was created by Indians who resisted removal during the early nineteenth century and has been treated as Indian country despite the absence of a specific statute or executive order proclaiming the Cherokee lands to be an Indian reservation. *See United States v. Lossiah,* 537 F.2d 1250 (4th Cir. 1976); *United States v. Hornbuckle,* 422 F.2d 391 (4th Cir. 1970); *United States v. Parton,* 132 F.2d 886 (4th Cir. 1943); *United States v. Wright,* 53 F.2d 300 (4th Cir. 1931), *cert. denied,* 285 U.S. 539 (1932). *Cf. State v. Ta-cha-na-tah,* 64 N.C. 614 (1870). Upon what basis could these lands be considered Indian country?

2. **Dependent Indian Communities:** The term "dependent Indian community" in section 1151(b) is derived from *Sandoval v. United States,* 231 U.S. 28 (1913), in which the Supreme Court applied the term to refer to the New Mexico pueblos — tribes that had long had relations with the federal government and for which agents had been appointed through the Indian Service. The term was further defined in *State v. Dana,* 404 A.2d 551 (Me. 1979), *cert. denied,* 444 U.S. 1098 (1980), in which the Maine Supreme Court considered whether the undisputed lands held by the Passamaquoddy Tribe in Maine constituted Indian country. These lands, like over 20 reservations along the east coast, were created by state authorities through treaties with the tribes that had not been approved by the federal government. Since these lands were not then

held or supervised by the United States they did not constitute an Indian reservation within the meaning of section 1151(a). Nevertheless, the court reasoned that they were lands held by a dependent Indian community within the meaning of section 1151(b) and thus constituted Indian country. The court rejected the state's suggestion that dependent Indian community status was limited to those tribes which had specifically been recognized as having a dependency relationship with the United States. The court said:

> It is true that the Court in *Sandoval* mentioned a prior "uniform course of action" by the federal government recognizing, and dealing with, the Pueblo Indians as "dependent," and that the very statute under attack was directed specifically to the Pueblo Indians and their lands. We cannot agree, however, that when Congress in 1948 spoke *generally* of "dependent Indian communities" as the object of its exercise of power, its intention was to incorporate *particular* factors which happened to be present in *Sandoval* as indispensable elements of the existence of a "dependent Indian community."
>
> In this regard, we reason as did the First Circuit Court of Appeals in *Passamaquoddy Tribe v. Morton,* [528 F.2d 370 (1st Cir. 1975)]. Congress has powers as to Indians that it may choose to exercise by acting either specifically or generally. By acting, in 1948, as to all "dependent Indian communities" situated anywhere in the United States, Congress acted *generally* to afford to each and every Indian community under its guardianship, and therefore dependent upon it, the protection that certain enumerated crimes committed within any such Indian community would be controlled by federal, instead of State, jurisdiction. In similar manner, Congress had acted *generally* as to "any ... tribe of Indians" when, by enacting the successive Indian Trade and Intercourse Acts, it subjected "any ... tribe of Indians" to its wardship, to be given the protection that Congress would be a special fiduciary guardian of the Indian lands.

The court found that since the general provisions of the restraint against alienation of Indian land, originally contained in the Trade and Intercourse Acts and currently codified at 25 U.S.C. § 177, applied to any and all Indian tribes, these statutes created a dependency relationship with each and every Indian tribe located within the United States irrespective of formal federal recognition or a course of dealings between the tribe and the United States government. *See also United States v. Levesque,* 681 F.2d 75 (1st Cir. 1982), *cert. denied,* 459 U.S. 1089 (1982) (Passamaquoddy Reservation also considered Indian country by federal court). Was the Maine Supreme Court correct that the statutory term "dependent Indian community" contained in section 1151(b) applied to any bona fide tribe over whose lands the United States was obligated under the Trade and Intercourse Acts to exercise a trusteeship? Would not *Dana* and *Levesque* suggest that any and all state-created reservations, including even reservations dating back to the early colonial period such as the Pamunkey Reservation in Virginia, now constitute Indian country within the meaning of section 1151? Is it clear that the Congress that enacted 18 U.S.C. § 1151(b) intended that provision to abrogate state-supervised reservations?

Since the crimes in *Dana* and *Levesque* occurred, the jurisdictional status of Passamaquoddy lands has been clarified by the Maine Indian Claims Settlement Act of 1980, Pub. L. No. 96-420, 94 Stat. 1785, which provides for concurrent tribal and state jurisdiction over lesser crimes and state jurisdiction over more serious crimes.

Dana also suggested that, as part of its determination whether the lands of an Indian community fell within section 1151(b), a court could decide as to a once *bona fide* but nonrecognized tribe whether the entity was still a tribe at the time of the crime. Is this a judicially workable procedure? What factors might be taken into account by the court? *Cf.* 25 C.F.R. pt. 54 (establishing an administrative procedure and criteria for federal recognition of unrecognized tribes).

In *United States v. South Dakota,* 665 F.2d 837 (8th Cir. 1981), *cert. denied,* 459 U.S. 823 (1982), the court considered the question of whether a tribally authorized housing development located near but outside of the reservation could be considered Indian country under 18 U.S.C. § 1151(b). The housing development was tribally owned and drew on federal Department of Housing and Urban Development funds. According to the court, resolution of the question centered on whether only the tribal lands, or the entire city in which they were located, should be considered a "community of reference" for purposes of determining whether or not the development was a dependent Indian community. The court ruled that the determination of Indian country status under section 1151(b) rested on whether (1) the United States retained title to the lands and authority to enact laws and regulations; (2) the nature of the area and the relationship of its inhabitants to Indian tribes and the federal government; and (3) the element of cohesiveness manifested by economic pursuits, common interests, or needs of the inhabitants. *See also United States v. McGowan,* 302 U.S. 535, 539 (1938); *United States v. Martine,* 442 F.2d 1022, 1023 (10th Cir. 1971); *Youngbear v. Brewer,* 415 F. Supp. 807, 809 (N.D. Iowa 1976), *aff'd,* 549 F.2d 74 (8th Cir. 1977). Using these criteria, the court held that the housing development constituted a dependent Indian community under section 1151(b). *See also United States v. Mound,* 477 F. Supp. 156 (D.S.D. 1979) (housing development established by tribe on land purchased by United States from allottees to be held in trust for tribe is dependent Indian community). *But see Weddell v. Meierhenry,* 636 F.2d 211 (8th Cir. 1980), *cert. denied,* 451 U.S. 941 (1981) (incorporated city of Wagner located within the boundaries of the original Yankton Sioux Reservation but outside of the diminished boundaries of that reservation did not constitute a dependent Indian community within the meaning of section 1151(b), even though both a BIA office and Public Health Service hospital were located within the community, since most of the property within the city was held in fee simple and most of the population was non-Indian). Should the racial make-up of a population and land ownership factors have an impact in determining whether a dependent Indian community exists? *See United States v. Morgan,* 614 F.2d 166, 170 (8th Cir. 1980) (requiring that "something [more than] mere density of population, [percentage of Indian inhabitants], and the history and background of area" be considered in making a determination). If a group of Indians is not living on a reservation and the land they occupy is not part of an allotment, do they constitute a dependent community? *See United States v. Martine,* 442 F.2d 1022, 1023 (10th Cir. 1971) (land outside the reservation purchased by tribe for occupancy by tribe members constitutes a dependent Indian community).

Another related, but converse, definitional problem is posed by 18 U.S.C. § 1154(c) which, for purposes of the federal liquor control laws, excludes from Indian country rights-of-way within a reservation and non-Indian fee patent land located in non-Indian communities within the reservation. Determining whether an area within the reservation constitutes a non-Indian community is not unlike attempting to determine whether a non-reservation area constitutes a dependent Indian community for purposes of section 1151(b). In *United States v. Mission Golf Course,* 548 F. Supp. 1177 (D.S.D. 1982), *aff'd sub nom. City of Mission v. United States,* 716 F.2d 907 (8th Cir. 1983), *cert. denied,* 464 U.S. 1041 (1984), the court held in a case seeking to apply the liquor control laws of the Rosebud Sioux Tribe to a golf course in Mission, South Dakota within the reservation that the land did not fall within the exemption in section 1154(c). Although there were no tribal or federal services located within the town of Mission, the character of the area around the city and golf course made both dependent Indian communities. The presence of Bureau of Indian Affairs property and an Indian Health Services dental clinic within the local high school complex in the town, the fact that a majority of the population of the county in which the town and golf course were located were Indian, joint provision of fire protection services by the city and the BIA, and the fact that a majority of the members of the golf course were Indians were among the factors the court considered in determining that both were dependent communities under section 1151(b). As a result the liquor control statute's exclusion of non-Indian communities did not apply.

3. Land Outside Reservations as Indian Country: Allotted Indian land still held in Indian trust title but located outside of Indian reservations is considered Indian country under the provisions of section 1151(c). Some of this land involves Indian allotments created out of the public domain for Indians overlooked during the allotment of their reservations. Some such land — for example, the land of the Eastern Navajo Agency — involves allotments created adjacent to, but outside of, the statutory boundaries of the reservation. Section 1151(c), however, has played a more important role with respect to Indian owned allotments that originally were within Indian reservations after the reservation was disestablished by Congress. In *DeCoteau v. District County Court,* 420 U.S. 425 (1975), for example, the Court held that Congress had disestablished the former Lake Traverse Reservation of the Sisseton-Wahpeton bands of the Sioux. Nevertheless, the Court carefully noted that since Indian owned allotments remained, "§ 1151(c) contemplates that isolated tracts of 'Indian country' may be scattered checkerboard fashion over a territory otherwise under state jurisdiction." 420 U.S. at 429 n.3.

4. Indian Country in Alaska and Oklahoma: The problem of the meaning of the "dependent Indian community" language of section 1151(b) remains very important in Alaska, because the Alaska Native Claims Settlement Act of 1971 (ANCSA) abolished the reservations of some native villages and authorized the native villages to incorporate under state law.

In addition, section 1151(c) continues to have enormous effect in Oklahoma, where many Indian allotments remain but various statutes and agreements terminated most reservations around the turn of the century. For a further discussion of the existence of Indian country in these two states, see Chapter 8, section A3 (Alaska) and section C (Oklahoma).

5. Determining the Boundaries of an Indian Reservation: Under the provisions of section 1151(a), whether land constitutes Indian country turns on whether it is located within the exterior boundaries of an Indian reservation. Thus, it is often important, as in *John,* to determine whether the land constitutes a reservation. Ascertaining the precise legal boundaries of an existing reservation may be equally significant. In many instances reservation boundaries have been changed since the treaty, statute, or executive order that first created the reservation. Additions may have been made to the land area owned by the tribe through purchase, statute, or executive order. Whether the acquisition of additional land enlarges the boundaries of the reservation so as to render the additional tracts Indian country often turns on the manner in which the land was acquired. For example, section 5 of the Indian Reorganization Act of 1934, 25 U.S.C. § 465 (1976), authorizes the Secretary of the Interior to acquire real property for Indians, including land located without existing reservations through purchase, exchange, gift, or assignment. Under section 7 of the Act, 25 U.S.C. § 467 (1976), the Secretary is authorized to proclaim any lands so acquired as new Indian reservations or as additions to existing reservations. In *Mescalero Apache Tribe v. Jones,* 411 U.S. 145 (1973), the Supreme Court considered the state tax status of a tribal ski enterprise operated on lands leased to the tribe by the United States from national forest lands adjacent to the reservation. The lands had been acquired under section 5 and had been leased rather than conveyed by actually transferring title in trust for the tribe because "it would have been meaningless for the United States, which already had title to the forest, to convey title to itself for the use of the Tribe." *Id.* at 155 n.11. Although no mention of this fact is made in the opinion, apparently no proclamation was ever issued under section 7 of the 1934 Act to cover the land so acquired. The Court treated the ski enterprise as a tribal activity conducted outside of the reservation, thereby upholding a nondiscriminatory state gross receipts tax on the tribal revenues from the enterprise. However, noting that section 5 of the 1934 Act expressly exempted real estate acquired under its provision from state and local taxation, the Court did hold that the state could not impose a use tax on certain fixtures purchased by the enterprise — a reminder that federal Indian statutes sometimes operate outside of Indian country. *Cf. Santa Rosa Band of Indians v. Kings County,* 532 F.2d 655 (9th Cir. 1975), *cert. denied,* 429 U.S. 1038 (1977) (land acquired under section 5 exempt from local building and zoning ordinances).

In addition to the difficulty of ascertaining whether additions to tribal land have enlarged the boundaries of a reservation, problems have frequently arisen as to whether the cession of Indian land to non-Indian purchasers has diminished the boundaries of the reservation. Under section 1151(a) all land within the exterior boundaries of any Indian reservation constitutes Indian country "notwithstanding the issuance of any patent ...." As noted in the excerpt from Professor Clinton's article, this provision was intended to partially resolve some of the jurisdictional ambiguities created by the allotment policy. The allotment policy had substantially opened Indian reservations to non-Indian settlement, and the Indian and non-Indian residential and ownership patterns were frequently heavily interspersed during the allotment period. Thus, on many modern reservations one finds substantial non-Indian land ownership and population. For example, in *Moe v. Confederated Salish & Kootenai Tribes,* 425 U.S. 463, 466 (1976), the Flathead Reservation was described as follows:

> Slightly over half of its 1.25 million acres is now owned in fee, by both Indians and non-Indians; most of the remaining half is held in trust by the United States for the Tribe. Approximately 50% of the Tribe's current membership of 5,749 reside on the reservation and in turn comprise 19% of the total reservation population. Embracing portions of four Montana counties — Lake, Sanders, Missoula, and Flathead — the present reservation was generally described by the District Court:
>
>> The Flathead Reservation is a well-developed agricultural area with farms, ranches and communities scattered throughout the inhabited portions of the Reservation. While some towns have predominantly Indian sectors, generally Indians and non-Indians live together in integrated communities. Banks, businesses and professions on the Reservation provide services to Indians and non-Indians alike.

Under section 1151(a) the mere sale of patented Indian land to non-Indians would not remove the land from Indian country. This provision was included in the 1948 statutory definition of Indian country in order to preclude the checkerboard jurisdictional arrangement that would otherwise exist if land held by non-Indians within the reservation were not considered Indian country. In

Seymour v. Superintendent, 368 U.S. 351, 358 (1962), the Court relied upon this Congressional intent to reject the suggestion that only Indian owned parcels within an allotted Indian reservation constituted Indian country. Speaking for a unanimous Court, Justice Black said:

> The State urges that we interpret the words "notwithstanding the issuance of any patent" to mean only notwithstanding the issuance of any patent to an Indian. But the State does not suggest, nor can we find, any adequate justification for such an interpretation. Quite the contrary, it seems to us that the strongest argument against the exclusion of patented lands from an Indian reservation applies with equal force to patents issued to non-Indians and Indians alike. For that argument rests upon the fact that where the existence or nonexistence of an Indian reservation, and therefore the existence or nonexistence of federal jurisdiction, depends upon the ownership of particular parcels of land, law enforcement officers operating in the area will find it necessary to search tract books in order to determine whether criminal jurisdiction over each particular offense, even though committed within the reservation, is in the State or Federal Government. Such an impractical pattern of checkerboard jurisdiction was avoided by the plain language of § 1151 and we see no justification for adopting an unwarranted construction of that language where the result would be merely to recreate confusion Congress specifically sought to avoid.

In order to apply section 1151(a), however, it is necessary to ascertain whether the land in question falls within the exterior boundaries of an Indian reservation. Can the boundaries of a reservation be diminished or the reservation extinguished to reflect changing social conditions? At what point and through what mechanism can this change legally occur?

SOLEM v. BARTLETT

465 U.S. 463 (1984)

Justice MARSHALL delivered the opinion of the Court.

On May 29, 1908, Congress authorized the Secretary of the Interior to open 1.6 million acres of the Cheyenne River Sioux Reservation for homesteading. Act of May 29, 1908, ch. 218, 35 Stat. 460 et seq. ("Act" or "Cheyenne River Act"). The question presented in this case is whether that Act of Congress diminished the boundaries of the Cheyenne River Sioux Reservation or simply permitted non-Indians to settle within existing Reservation boundaries.

I

In 1979, the State of South Dakota charged respondent John Bartlett, an enrolled member of the Cheyenne River Sioux Tribe, with attempted rape. Respondent pleaded guilty to the charge, and was sentenced to a ten-year term in the state penitentiary at Sioux Falls. After exhausting state remedies, respondent filed a pro se petition for a writ of habeas corpus in the United States District Court for the District of South Dakota. Respondent contended that the crime for which he had been convicted occurred within the Cheyenne River Sioux Reservation, established by Congress in the Act of March 2, 1889, ch. 405, § 4, 25 Stat. 889; that, although on May 29, 1908, Congress opened for settlement by non-Indians the portion of the Reservation on which respondent committed his crime, the opened portion nonetheless remained Indian country; and that the State therefore lacked criminal jurisdiction over respondent.[2]

Relying on previous decisions of the Eighth Circuit dealing with the Act of May 29, 1908,[3] the District Court accepted respondent's claim that the Act had not diminished the original Cheyenne River Sioux Reservation, and issued a writ of habeas corpus. On appeal, the Eighth Circuit, sitting en banc, affirmed, two judges dissenting. [Since] the Supreme Court of South Dakota has issued a pair of opinions offering a conflicting interpretation of the Act of May 29, 1908,[4] we granted certiorari [and] affirm.

II

In the latter half of the nineteenth century, large sections of the western States and Territories were set aside for Indian reservations. Towards the end of the century, however, Congress increasingly adhered to the view that the Indian tribes should abandon their nomadic lives on the communal reservations and settle into an agrarian economy on privately-owned parcels of land.[5] This shift was fueled in part by the belief that individualized farming would speed the Indians' assimilation into American society and in part by the continuing demand for new lands for the waves of homesteaders moving West.[6] As a result of these combined pressures, Congress passed a series of surplus land acts at the turn of the century to force Indians onto individual allotments carved out of reservations and to open up unallotted lands for non-Indian settlement. Initially, Congress legislated its Indian allotment program on a national scale,[7] but by the time of the Act of May 29, 1908, Congress was dealing with the surplus land question on a reservation-by-reservation basis, with each surplus land act employing its own statutory language, the product of a unique set of tribal negotiation and legislative compromise.

---

[2] 18 U.S.C. § 1153 provides: "Any Indian who commits against the person or property of another Indian or other person any of the following offenses, namely, ... assault with intent to commit rape ... within the Indian country, shall be subject to the same laws and penalties as all other persons committing any of the above offenses, within the exclusive jurisdiction of the United States." Within Indian country, State jurisdiction is limited to crimes by non-Indians against non-Indians, see New York ex rel. Ray v. Martin, 326 U.S. 496 (1946), and victimless crimes by non-Indians. Tribes exercise concurrent jurisdiction over certain minor crimes by Indians, 18 U.S.C. §§ 1152, 1153, unless a State has assumed jurisdiction under id., § 1162.

[3] United States v. Dupris, 612 F.2d 319 (1979), vacated and remanded on other grounds, 446 U.S. 980 (1980); United States v. Long Elk, 565 F.2d 1032 (1977); United States ex rel. Condon v. Erickson, 478 F.2d 684 (1973).

[4] See State v. Janis, 317 N.W.2d 133 (S.D. 1982); Stankey v. Waddell, 256 N.W.2d 117 (S.D. 1977).

[5] An account of the movement and its effect on the Cheyenne River Sioux Tribe appears in F. HOXIE, JURISDICTION ON THE CHEYENNE RIVER INDIAN RESERVATION: AN ANALYSIS OF THE CAUSES AND CONSEQUENCES OF THE ACT OF MAY 29, 1908, at 1-30 (undated manuscript) (hereinafter HOXIE), which was prepared for presentation in United States v. Dupris, supra, and incorporated into the record of this case. See also Note, Jurisdictional Confusion on the Cheyenne River Indian Reservation, 25 S.D.L. REV. 355 (1980).

[6] See FELIX S. COHEN'S HANDBOOK FOR FEDERAL INDIAN LAW 127-134 (1982 ed.) (hereinafter Cohen). The amount of surplus lands freed up by moving Indians onto individual allotments was considerable. For instance, in 1908, the 2,626 members of the Cheyenne River Sioux Tribe had over 2.8 million acres of reservation land, or over 1,000 acres per Tribal member. Under the allotment program, the average allotment per member was under 500 acres. See S. Rep. 439, 60th Cong., 1st Sess., 4 (1908); HOXIE 38, 40.

[7] See, e.g., General Allotment Act of 1887, c. 119, 24 Stat. 388 et seq.

The modern legacy of the surplus land acts has been a spate of jurisdictional disputes between State and Federal officials as to which sovereign has authority over lands that were opened by the acts and have since passed out of Indian ownership.[8] As a doctrinal matter, the States have jurisdiction over unalloted opened lands if the applicable surplus land act freed that land of its reservation status and thereby diminished the reservation boundaries. On the other hand, Federal, State, and Tribal authorities share jurisdiction over these lands if the relevant surplus land act did not diminish the existing Indian reservation because the entire opened area is Indian country under 18 U.S.C. § 1151(a). See nn. 1 and 2, *supra.*

Unfortunately, the surplus land acts themselves seldom detail whether opened lands retained reservation status or were divested of all Indian interests. When the surplus land acts were passed, the distinction seemed unimportant. The notion that reservation status of Indian lands might not be coextensive with Tribal ownership was unfamiliar at the turn of the century.

Indian lands were judicially defined to include only those lands in which the Indians held some form of property interest: trust lands, individual allotments, and, to a more limited degree, opened lands that had not yet been claimed by non-Indians. See *Bates v. Clark*, 95 U.S. 204 (1877); *Ash Sheep Co. v. United States*, 252 U.S. 159 (1920). Only in 1948 did Congress uncouple reservation status from Indian ownership, and statutorily define Indian country to include lands held in fee by non-Indians within reservation boundaries. See Act of June 25, 1948, ch. 645, § 1151, 62 Stat. 757 (codified at 18 U.S.C. § 1151).

Another reason why Congress did not concern itself with the effect of surplus land acts on reservation boundaries was the turn-of-the-century assumption that Indian reservations were a thing of the past. Consistent with prevailing wisdom, members of Congress voting on the surplus land acts believed to a man that within a short time — within a generation at most — the Indian tribes would enter traditional American society and the reservation system would cease to exist.[9] Given this expectation, Congress naturally failed to be meticulous in clarifying whether a particular piece of legislation formally sliced a certain parcel of land off one reservation.

Although the Congresses that passed the surplus land acts anticipated the imminent demise of the reservation and, in fact, passed the acts partially to facilitate the process, we have never been willing to extrapolate from this expectation a specific congressional purpose of diminishing reservations with the passage of every surplus land act. Rather, it is settled law that some surplus land acts diminished reservations, *see, e.g., Rosebud Sioux Tribe v. Kneip*, 430 U.S. 584 (1977); *DeCoteau v. District County Court*, 420 U.S. 425 (1975), and other

---

[8] Regardless of whether the original reservation was diminished, Federal and Tribal courts have exclusive jurisdiction over those portions of the opened lands that were and have remained Indian allotments. *See* 18 U.S.C. § 1151(c). In addition, opened lands that have been restored to reservation status by subsequent act of Congress, *see, e.g.*, Indian Reorganization Act of 1934, ch. 576, 48 Stat. 984 (codified at 25 U.S.C. 461 et seq. (1982)) (authorizing the return of opened lands to the original reservations), fall within the exclusive criminal jurisdiction of Federal and Tribal courts under 18 U.S.C. §§ 1152, 1153.

[9] *See Montana v. United States*, 450 U.S. 544, 559-560, n.9 (1981); Hoxie 1-20. Congress rejected the policy of allotment and surplus land sales in 1934. Indian Reorganization Act, 48 Stat. 984 et seq.

surplus land acts did not, *see, e.g., Mattz v. Arnett,* 412 U.S. 481 (1973); *Seymour v. Superintendent,* 368 U.S. 351 (1962). The effect of any given surplus land act depends on the language of the act and the circumstances underlying its passage.[10]

Between these extremes was the case of the Rosebud Sioux Reservation. In 1901, the Rosebud Sioux Tribe voted in favor of an agreement to cede a portion of their land in Gregory County to the United States in exchange for a sum certain. Three years later, Congress passed the Act of April 23, 1904, ch. 1484, 33 Stat. 254-258, which incorporated the agreement's cession language, but replaced sum-certain payment with a provision guaranteeing the Tribe only the proceeds from the sale of the opened lands. Over the following years, Congress passed two more surplus land acts involving Rosebud Reservation land into other counties; each of the subsequent acts authorized the sale and disposal of additional lands and promised the tribes the proceeds of the sales. See Act of March 2, 1907, ch. 2536, 34 Stat. 1230-1232; Act of May 30, 1910, ch. 260, 36 Stat. 448-452. Although none of the Rosebud Acts clearly severed the Tribe from its interest in the unallotted opened lands and even though the last two Acts were strikingly similar to the 1906 Act found not to have diminished the Colville Reservation in *Seymour v. Superintendent, supra,* this Court held that the circumstances surrounding the passage of the three Rosebud Acts unequivocally demonstrated that Congress meant for each Act to diminish the Rosebud Reservation. *Rosebud Sioux Tribe v. Kneip, supra.*

Our precedents in the area have established a fairly clean analytical structure for distinguishing those surplus land acts that diminished reservations from those acts that simply offered non-Indians the opportunity to purchase land within established reservation boundaries. The first and governing principle is that only Congress can divest a reservation of its land and diminish its boundaries. Once a block of land is set aside for an Indian Reservation and no matter what happens to the title of individual plots within the area, the entire block retains its reservation status until Congress explicitly indicates otherwise. *See United States v. Celestine,* 215 U.S. 278, 285 (1909).[11]

Diminishment, moreover, will not be lightly inferred. Our analysis of surplus land acts requires that Congress clearly evince an "intent to change boundaries" before diminishment will be found. *Rosebud v. Kneip, supra,* 430 U.S., at 615. The most probative evidence of congressional intent is the statutory language used to open the Indian lands. Explicit reference to cession or other language

---

[10] At one extreme, for example, the Act of March 3, 1891, ch. 543, 26 Stat. 1035 et seq., expressly stated that the Lake Traverse Indian Tribe agreed to "cede, sell, relinquish and convey" all interest in unallotted lands on the Lake Traverse Indian Reservation, and the Act further provided that the Tribe would receive full compensation in consideration for its loss. In *DeCoteau v. District County Court, supra,* we found that the Lake Traverse Act, with its express language of cession, diminished the Lake Traverse Indian Reservation. At the other extreme, the Act of March 22, 1906, ch. 1126, § 1, 34 Stat. 80, simply authorized the Secretary of Interior "to sell or dispose of" unallotted lands on a portion of the Colville Indian Reservation; under the Act, the Colville Tribe received whatever proceeds these sales generated, rather than a sum certain. *Id.,* § 9. 34 Stat., at 81. In *Seymour v. Superintendent,* [this Court] held that, because the Colville Act lacked an unconditional divestiture of Indian interest in the lands, the Act simply opened a portion of the Colville Reservation to non-Indian settlers and did not diminish the Reservation. *See also Mattz v. Arnett ....*

[11] At one time, it was thought that Indian consent was needed to diminish a reservation, but in *Lone Wolf v. Hitchcock,* 187 U.S. 553 (1903), this Court decided that Congress could diminish reservations unilaterally.

evidencing the present and total surrender of all tribal interests strongly suggests that Congress meant to divest from the reservation all unalloted opened lands. *DeCoteau v. District County Court, supra,* 420 U.S., at 444-445; *Seymour v. Superintendent, supra,* 368 U.S., at 355. When such language of cession is buttressed by an unconditional commitment from Congress to compensate the Indian tribe for its opened land, there is an almost insurmountable presumption that Congress meant for the tribe's reservation to be diminished. *See DeCoteau v. District County Court, supra,* 420 U.S., at 447-448.

As our opinion in *Rosebud Sioux Tribe* demonstrates, ... explicit language of cession and unconditional compensation are not prerequisites for a finding of diminishment. When events surrounding the passage of a surplus land act — particularly the manner in which the transaction was negotiated with the tribes involved and the tenor of legislative reports presented to Congress — unequivocally reveal a widely-held, contemporaneous understanding that the affected reservation would shrink as a result of the proposed legislation, we have been willing to infer that Congress shared the understanding that its action would diminish the reservation, notwithstanding the presence of statutory language that would otherwise suggest reservation boundaries remained unchanged. To a lesser extent, we have also looked to events that occurred after the passage of a surplus land act to decipher Congress's intentions. Congress's own treatment of the affected areas, particularly in the years immediately following the opening, has some evidentiary value, as does the manner in which the Bureau of Indian Affairs and local judicial authorities dealt with unalloted open lands. On a more pragmatic level, we have recognized that who actually moved onto opened reservation lands is also relevant to deciding whether a surplus land act diminished a reservation. Where non-Indian settlers flooded into the opened portion of a reservation and the area has long since lost its Indian character, we have acknowledged that de facto, if not de jure, diminishment may have occurred. *See Rosebud Sioux Tribe v. Kneip, supra,* at 588, n.3 and 604-605; *DeCoteau v. District County Court,* 429 U.S. at 428. In addition to the obvious practical advantages of acquiescing to de facto diminishment,[12] we look to the subsequent demographic history of opened lands as one additional clue as to what Congress expected would happen once land on a particular reservation was opened to non-Indian settlers.[13]

There are, of course, limits to how far we will go to decipher Congress's intention in any particular surplus land act. When both an act and its legislative history fail to provide substantial and compelling evidence of a congressional intention to diminish Indian lands, we are bound by our traditional solicitude for the Indian tribes to rule that diminishment did not take place and that the

---

[12] When an area is predominately populated by non-Indians with only a few surviving pockets of Indian allotments, finding that the land remains Indian country seriously burdens the administration of State and local governments. *See Rosebud Sioux Tribe v. Kneip, supra; DeCoteau v. District County Court, supra.* Conversely, problems of an imbalanced checkerboard jurisdiction arise if a largely Indian opened area is found to be outside Indian country. *See Seymour v. Superintendent*
....

[13] Resort to subsequent demographic history is, of course, an unorthodox and potentially unreliable method of statutory interpretation. However, in the area of surplus land acts, where various factors kept Congress from focusing on the diminishment issue, *see, supra,* at 1165, the technique is a necessary expedient.

old reservation boundaries survived the opening. *Mattz v. Arnett*, 412 U.S. 481, 505 (1973); *Seymour v. Superintendent*, 368 U.S. 351 (1962).

III

A

We now turn to apply these principles to the Act of May 29, 1908. We begin with the Act's operative language, which reads:

"[T]he Secretary of the Interior [hereby is authorized] and directed, as hereinafter provided, to sell and dispose of all that portion of the Cheyenne River and Standing Rock[14] Indian reservations in the States of South Dakota and North Dakota lying and being within the following described boundaries ....

"[F]rom the proceeds arising from the sale and disposition of the lands aforesaid, exclusive of the customary fees and commissions, there shall be deposited in the Treasury of the United States, to the credit of the Indians belonging and having tribal rights on the reservation aforesaid in the States of South Dakota and North Dakota the sums to which the respective tribes may be entitled ...."

Ch. 218, §§ 1, 6, 35 Stat. 460-461, 463. These provisions stand in sharp contrast to the explicit language of cession employed in the Lake Traverse and 1904 Rosebud Acts discussed in our opinions in DeCoteau and Rosebud Sioux Tribe. [Instead of] reciting an Indian agreement to "cede, sell, relinquish and convey" the opened lands, the Cheyenne River Act simply authorizes the Secretary to "sell and dispose" of certain lands. This reference to the sale of Indian lands, coupled with the creation of Indian accounts for proceeds, suggests that the Secretary of the Interior was simply being authorized to act as the Tribe's sales agent. Indeed, when faced with precisely the same language in *Seymour v. Superintendent*, [this Court] concluded that such provisions "did no more than to open the way for non-Indian settlers to own land on the reservation in a manner which the Federal Government, acting as guardian and trustee for the Indians, regarded as beneficial to the development of its wards."[15]

The balance of the Cheyenne River Act is largely consistent with the implication of the operative language that the Act opened but did not diminish the Cheyenne River Sioux Reservation. Nowhere else in the Act is there specific reference to the cession of Indian interests in the opened lands or any change in existing reservation boundaries. In fact, certain provisions of the Act strongly suggest that the unalloted opened lands would for the immediate future remain [an] integral part of the Cheyenne River Reservation. In § 1 of the Act, the Secretary was authorized to set aside portions of the opened lands "for agency, school, and religious purposes, to remain reserved as long as needed, and as long as agency, school, or religious institutions are maintained thereon for the

---

[14] As this language reveals, the Act dealt with land on two bordering Sioux reservations. Although for purposes of this case we are only concerned with the Act's effect on the Cheyenne River Reservation, nothing in the record leads us to suspect that Congress intended the Act to have a different effect on the Standing Rock Reservation.

[15] As Petitioner stresses, the operative language of the Cheyenne River Act is also similar to language in the 1907 and 1908 Rosebud Acts, which this Court held diminished the Rosebud Sioux Reservation. Our analysis of Rosebud acts, however, was strongly colored by the existence of a 1904 Rosebud act containing cession language "precisely suited" to disestablishment, and the admission of the Indians that the second two Rosebud acts must have diminished their reservation if the previous act did. [*Rosebud Sioux Tribe v. Kneip.*]

benefit of said Indians." 35 Stat. 461. It is difficult to imagine why Congress would have reserved lands for such purposes if it did not anticipate that the opened area would remain part of the reservation. This interpretation is supported by §2 of the Act, under which Cheyenne River Indians were given permission to continue to obtain individual allotments on the affected portion of the reservation before the land was officially opened to non-Indian settlers. [Further] in §2, Congress instructed the Geological Survey to examine the opened area for "lands bearing coal" and exempted those sections from allotment or disposal, the apparent purpose being to reserve those mineral resources for the whole tribe. *Id.*, at 462; see S. Rep. 439, 60th Cong., 1st Sess., 6 (1908).

This case is made more difficult, however, by the presence of some language in the Cheyenne River Act that indirectly supports petitioner's view that the Reservation was diminished. For instance, in a provision permitting Indians already holding allotment on the opened lands to obtain new allotments in the unopened territories, the Act refers to the unopened territories as "within the respective reservations thus diminished." C. 218, §2, 35 Stat. 461. Elsewhere, the Act permits tribal members to harvest timber on certain parts of the opened lands, but conditions the grant for "only as long as the lands remain part of the public domain." *Id.*, §9, 35 Stat. 464. On the assumption that Congress would refer to opened lands as being part of the public domain only if the lands had lost all vestiges of reservation status, petitioners and several amici point to the term "public domain" as well as the phrase "reservations thus diminished" as evidence that Congress understood the Cheyenne River Act to divest unalloted open lands of their reservation status. Undisputedly, the references to the opened areas as being in "the public domain" and the unopened areas as comprising "the reservation thus diminished" support petitioner's view that the Cheyenne River Act diminished the reservation. These isolated phrases, however, are hardly dispositive.[17] And, when balanced against the Cheyenne River Act's stated and limited goal of opening up reservation lands for sale to non-Indian settlers, these two phrases cannot carry the burden of establishing an express congressional purpose to diminish. Cf. *Mattz v. Arnett*, 412 U.S., at 497-499.[18] The Act of May 29, 1908, read as a whole, does not present an explicit expression of congressional intent to diminish the Cheyenne River Sioux Reservation.[19]

---

[17] There is also considerable doubt as to what Congress meant in using these phrases. In 1908, "diminished" was not yet a term of art in Indian law. When Congress spoke of the "reservation thus diminished," it may well have been referring to diminishment in common lands and not diminishment of reservation boundaries. *See United States ex rel. Condon v. Erickson*, 478 F.2d at 687. Similarly, even without diminishment, unallotted opened lands could be conceived of as being in the "public domain" inasmuch as they were available for settlement.

[18] Both the South Dakota Supreme Court and dissenting judges from the Eighth Circuit have found further support for diminishment in the so-called school lands provision and a subsequently enacted liquor prohibition for the opened lands. *Stankey v. Waddell*, 256 N.W.2d, at 121, 126; *United States v. Dupris*, 612 F.2d, at 334; *see* Act of May 29, 1908, ch. 218, §7, 35 Stat. 463 (school land provision); Act of Feb. 17, 1910, ch. 40, 36 Stat. 196-197 (liquor prohibition act). Although we credited similar provisions as supportive of our holding in *Rosebud Sioux Tribe v. Kneip*, [any] inferences from these provisions were obviously of secondary importance to our decision, see nn. 10 and 15, *supra*. Moreover, as independent evidence of a congressional intention to diminish, such evidence is suspect....

[19] Read as authorizing the Secretary to serve as the Tribe's sales agent, the Act fulfills Congress's original plan that the surplus lands of the Cheyenne River Sioux Reservation could be sold off once

B

The circumstances surrounding the passage of the Cheyenne River Act also fail to establish a clear congressional purpose to diminish the Reservation. In contrast to the Lake Traverse Act and 1904 Rosebud Act, the Cheyenne River Act did not begin with an agreement between the United States and the Indian Tribes, in which the Indians agreed to cede a portion of their territory to the Federal government. The Cheyenne River Act had its origins in "A bill to authorize the sale and disposition of a portion of the surplus and unalloted lands in the Cheyenne River and Standing Rock reservations," introduced by Senator Gamble of South Dakota on December 9, 1907. S. 1385, 60th Cong., 1st Sess. (1907). Once the bill was under consideration, the Secretary of the Interior dispatched an Inspector McLaughlin to the two affected Reservations to consult with the Tribes about the bills.

During his meeting with members of the Cheyenne River Tribe, Inspector McLaughlin admittedly spoke in terms of cession and the relinquishment of Indian interests in the opened territories. However, it is impossible to say that the Tribe agreed to the terms that presented. Due to bad weather during McLaughlin's visit, only 63 members of the Tribe attended his meeting. At the close of McLaughlin's presentation, the president of the Cheyenne River Business Council said that he would have to discuss the matter with the entire Tribe before he could respond to the proposed bill. McLaughlin agreed to delay submission of his report to Congress until he had received word from the Tribe, but, when the Tribe's vote had not reached Washington 14 days later, McLaughlin sent his report to Congress with the conclusion: "The general sentiment of the Indians in council with me at the agency was in favor of the relinquishment (of the opened lands.)" H.R. Rep. No. 1539, 60th Cong., 1st Sess., 7 (1908); see id., at 23-24, 28. McLaughlin, however, also informed Congress of the low attendance at his meeting with the Cheyenne River Tribe and acknowledged that he had never received formal approval from the Tribe. Id., at 8.

With a full report of Inspector McLaughlin's meeting with the Cheyenne River Tribe before it, Congress considered the Cheyenne River Act in April and May of 1908. In neither floor debates or legislative reports is there a clear statement that Congress interpreted Inspector McLaughlin's report to establish an agreement on the part of the Cheyenne River Indians to cede the opened areas.[21] Indeed, the most explicit statement of Congress's view of the Indian's position was: "The Indians upon both reservations are satisfied to have the surplus and unalloted lands disposed of under the provisions of the bill as amended." S. Rep. 439, 60th Cong., 1st Sess., 4 (1908), quoted in H.R. Rep. 1539, 60th Cong., 1st Sess., 3 (1908). For the most part, the legislative debate of the Cheyenne River Act centered on how much money the Indians would be paid for certain sections of the opened area that the United States was going to buy for school lands, and no mention was made of the Act's effect on the

---

members of the Tribe moved onto allotment lands. See Act of Mar. 2, 1889, ch. 405, § 12, 25 Stat. 892.

[21]One reason why Congress may not have interpreted the McLaughlin report as evidence of Tribal agreement to cede the land is that a delegation from the Tribe followed McLaughlin back to Washington to urge Congress not to pass the proposed legislation. See HOXIE 55-56. The particulars of the delegation's trip [are] not known.

reservation's boundaries or whether State or Federal officials would have jurisdiction over the opened areas. See 42 Cong. Rec. 4753-4755 (Apr. 15, 1908) (Senate debate); 42 Cong. Rec. 7003-7007 (May 26, 1908) (House debate).

To be sure, there are a few phrases scattered through the legislative history of the Cheyenne River Act that support petitioner's position. Both the Senate and House Reports refer to the "reduced reservation" and state that "lands reserved for the use of the Indians upon both reservations as diminished ... are ample ... for the present and future needs of the respective tribes." S. Rep. 439, *supra,* at 4, quoted and adopted in H.R. Rep. 1539, *supra,* at 3. However, it is unclear whether Congress was alluding to the reduction in Indian-owned lands that would occur once some of the opened lands were sold to settlers or to the reduction that a complete cession of tribal interests in the opened area would precipitate. See also n.17, *supra.* Without evidence that Congress understood itself to be entering into an agreement under which the Tribe committed itself to cede and relinquish all interests in unallotted opened lands, and in the absence of some clear statement of congressional intent to alter reservation boundaries, it is impossible to infer from a few isolated and ambiguous phrases a congressional purpose to diminish the Cheyenne River Sioux Reservation.

C

The subsequent treatment of the Cheyenne River Sioux Reservation by Congress, courts, and the Executive is so rife with contradictions and inconsistencies as to be of no help to either side. For instance, two years after the Cheyenne River Act, Congress passed a bill to sell a portion of the opened lands and called the area "surplus and unallotted lands in the Cheyenne River Indian Reservation," suggesting that the opened area was still part of the reservation. Act of June 23, 1910, ch. 369, 36 Stat. 602 (emphasis added). But, twelve years after that, Congress passed another piece of legislation referring to the opened lands as "the former" Cheyenne River Sioux Reservation and suggesting that the Reservation had been diminished. See Act of Apr. 25, 1922, ch. 140, 42 Stat. 499. Ample additional examples pointing in both directions leave one with the distinct impression that subsequent Congresses had no clear view whether the opened territories were or were not still part of the Cheyenne River Reservation. A similar state of confusion characterizes the Executive's treatment of the Cheyenne River Sioux Reservation's opened lands. Moreover, both parties have been able to cite instances in which State and Federal courts exerted criminal jurisdiction over the disputed area in the years following opening.[23] Neither sovereign dominated the jurisdictional history of the opened lands in the decades immediately following 1908.

What is clear, however, is what happened to the Cheyenne River Sioux Tribe after the Act of May 29, 1908, was passed. Most of the members of the Tribe

---

[23] According to one study, Federal, Tribal, and State courts shared jurisdiction over the opened areas in the decades following opening. HOXIE 100-128. Between 1910 and 1920, only two Indians were tried in state court for crimes committed on the opened lands. *Id.*, at 128. During this period, the Federal authorities were primarily responsible for Indian life on both opened and unopened portions of the reservation. In later years, however, the state courts came to assume that the opened areas fell within their general criminal jurisdiction. *See, e.g., State v. Barnes,* 81 S.D. 511, 137 N.W.2d 683 (1965). It was only in 1973 that the Eighth Circuit challenged this assumption in *United States ex rel. Condon v. Erickson, supra.*

obtained individual allotments on the lands opened by the Act. Because most of the tribe lived on the opened territories, tribal authorities and Bureau of Indian Affairs personnel took primary responsibility for policing and supplying social services to the opened lands during the years following 1908. The strong Tribal presence in the opened area has continued until the present day. Now roughly two-thirds of the Tribe's enrolled members live in the opened area. The seat of Tribal government is now located in a town in the opened area, where most important tribal activities take place.

Also clear is the historical fact that the opening of the Cheyenne River Sioux Reservation was a failure. Few homesteaders perfected claims on the lands, due perhaps in part to the price of the land but probably more importantly to the fact that the opened area was much less fertile than the lands in southern South Dakota opened by other surplus land acts.[26] As a result of [the] small number of homesteaders who settled on the opened lands and the high percentage of Tribal members who continue to live in the area, the population of the disputed area is now evenly divided between Indian and non-Indian residents. Under these circumstances, it is impossible to say that the opened areas of the Cheyenne River Sioux Reservation have lost their Indian character.

Neither the Act of May 29, 1908, the circumstances surrounding its passage, nor subsequent events clearly establish that the Act diminished the Cheyenne River Sioux Reservation. The presumption that Congress did not intend to diminish the Reservation therefore stands, and the judgment of the Eighth Circuit is

Affirmed.

NOTE: DETERMINING CONGRESSIONAL INTENT TO DIMINISH BOUNDARIES

While the result in *Solem* was not surprising, the unanimity of the Court's decision was somewhat startling in light of the divided case law that preceded the decision. In *United States v. Celestine*, 215 U.S. 278, 285 (1909), the Court held that the Tulalip Reservation in Washington remained Indian country notwithstanding the allotment of Tulalip land, including the land on which the crime in question occurred, to members of the tribe. Speaking for the Court, Justice Brewer wrote, "when Congress has once established a reservation all tracts included within it remain a reservation until separated therefrom by Congress." *Solem* is merely the most recent in a series of conflicting cases tracing the level of Congressional specificity required to support a finding of reservation diminishment or termination. Most of these cases involve interpreting the legal effect of allotment era statutes on the continued existence and the exterior boundaries of a reservation. As the *Solem* case suggests, however, the *immediate* impact of such allotment statutes and laws approving agreements with tribes on the continued existence or precise boundaries of the reservation

---

[26] During a debate on subsequent surplus land, Congressman Burke, a sponsor of the Cheyenne River Act, reported: "At the opening of the Cheyenne and the Standing Rock Reservations ... there were not sufficient people to begin to take anywhere near the land that was to be disposed of, and the reason they did not take it was the price of the land, which was undoubtedly too high." 49 Cong. Rec. 1106 (1913). According to the Government's estimates, only half of the opened lands ever passed out of Indian ownership....

was not then an immediately salient question since the allotment policy anticipated the ultimate dissolution of Indian reservations through the termination of
the trust restrictions on Indian land, 25 years after the policy entered into force.
Thus, the interpretive question posed in such cases constitutes a uniquely historical issue since the legal problem only emerged as a result of the legal persistence of Indian reservations after the allotment policy — an event neither assumed nor foreseen by the designers of the statutes in question. Consequently,
the more rigorously courts require the statutes authorizing the allotment of a
reservation or the opening of the reservation to non-Indian settlement to demonstrate a clear, unequivocal Congressional intent immediately to terminate or
diminish a reservation, the less likely the test will be satisfied.

In *Seymour v. Superintendent,* 368 U.S. 351 (1961), the Court held that the
south half of the Colville Indian Reservation in Washington neither had been
disestablished by a 1906 federal statute that approved the sale of mineral lands
and authorized non-Indian homesteading on surplus lands nor had the exterior
boundaries of the reservation been diminished by the law and the subsequent
Presidential proclamation implementing it. Contrasting the language of the
1906 statute with earlier language in an 1892 law that vacated and restored the
north half of the Colville Reservation to the public domain, Justice Black, speaking for the Court, said "[n]owhere in the 1906 Act is there to be found any
language similar to that in the 1892 Act expressly vacating the South Half of the
reservation and restoring the lands to the public domain." 368 U.S. at 355.
Justice Black also noted that this construction of the 1906 law had been adopted
by the Department of the Interior, the agency with primary responsibility over
Indian affairs.

In *Mattz v. Arnett,* 412 U.S. 481 (1973), the Court applied the *Seymour* case
to hold that the Klamath River Reservation in California remained Indian country, thereby exempting Indians from state statutes prohibiting gill net fishing.
Noting that the status of the reservation turned primarily on the effect of an
1892 Act of Congress opening the reservation to homesteading and non-Indian
settlement, Justice Blackmun, speaking for a unanimous Court, said:

> The respondent relies upon what he feels is significant language in the Act and
> upon references in the legislative history. He contends, "The fact that the lands were
> to be opened up for settlement and sale by homesteaders strongly militates against a
> continuation of such reservation status." ...
> We conclude, however, that this is a misreading of the effect of the allotment provi-
> sions in the 1892 Act. The meaning of those terms is to be ascertained from the
> overview of the earlier General Allotment Act of 1887, 24 Stat. 388. That Act permit-
> ted the President to make allotments of reservation lands to resident Indians and, with
> tribal consent, to sell surplus lands. Its policy was to continue the reservation system
> and the trust status of Indian lands, but to allot tracts to individual Indians for agricul-
> ture and grazing. When all the lands had been allotted and the trust expired, the
> reservation could be abolished. Unalloted lands were made available to non-Indians
> with the purpose, in part, of promoting interaction between the races and of encourag-
> ing Indians to adopt white ways. See § 6 of the General Allotment Act, 24 Stat. 390;
> United States Department of the Interior, Federal Indian Law 115-117, 127-129,
> 776-777 (1958). Under the 1887 Act, however, the President was not required to open
> reservation land for allotment; he merely had the discretion to do so.
> In view of the discretionary nature of this presidential power, Congress occasionally
> enacted special legislation in order to assure that a particular reservation was in fact
> opened to allotment. The 1892 Act was but one example of this. Its allotment provi-

sions, which do not differ materially from those of the General Allotment Act of 1887, and which in fact refer to the earlier Act, do not, alone, recite or even suggest that Congress intended thereby to terminate the Klamath River Reservation. See *Seymour v. Superintendent*, 368 U.S. 351, 357-358 (1962). Rather, allotment under the 1892 Act is completely consistent with continued reservation status. This Court unanimously observed, in an analogous setting in *Seymour, id.*, at 356, "The Act did no more [in this respect] than open the way for non-Indian settlers to own land on the reservation in a manner which the Federal Government, acting as guardian and trustee for the Indians, regarded as beneficial to the development of its wards." See *United States v. Celestine*, 215 U.S. 278 (1909); *United States v. Nice*, 241 U.S. 591 (1916). See also *Wilbur v. United States*, 281 U.S. 206 (1930); *Donnelly v. United States*, 228 U.S. 243 (1913).

Id. at 496-97. After an exhaustive review of the legislative history of the Act, Justice Blackmun concluded that the efforts to terminate the reservation that had been mounted in Congress had failed in favor of the new gradual process of allotment within a reservation framework. He also noted that Congress and the Department of the Interior had by their actions repeatedly recognized the continued existence of the reservation after 1892. Summarizing the test he thought appropriate in these diminishment cases, Justice Blackmun said:

> More significantly, throughout the period from 1871-1892 numerous bills were introduced which *expressly* provided for the termination of the reservation and did so in unequivocal terms. Congress was fully aware of the means by which termination could be effected. But clear termination language was not employed in the 1892 Act. This being so, we are not inclined to infer an intent to terminate the reservation. The Court stated in *United States v. Celestine*, 215 U.S., at 285, that "when Congress has once established a reservation all tracts included within it remain a part of the reservation until separated therefrom by Congress." A congressional determination to terminate must be expressed on the face of the Act or be clear from the surrounding circumstances and legislative history. See *Seymour v. Superintendent*, 368 U.S. 351 (1962); *United States v. Nice*, 241 U.S. 591 (1916).

Id. at 504-05.

Seymour and *Mattz* both seemed to suggest that a finding of reservation diminishment could only be supported either by an express and unequivocal Congressional statement or by a showing of an unequivocal Congressional intent to terminate the reservation. Since, as the *Solem* opinion suggests, Congress paid little heed to the question of the *immediate* impact of such statutes on continued reservation existence or on the boundaries of the reservation, erroneously believing that such questions eventually would vanish with the termination of the trust restrictions on allotted lands in such reservations, both cases suggested that findings of reservation diminishment or termination would be infrequent.

Both *Seymour* and *Mattz* involved reservations that had retained a distinctly Indian character notwithstanding the opening of the reservation to non-Indian settlement. In both cases, Indians were the dominant population group living on the reservation. The Court, however, was soon confronted with cases involving land within heavily alloted reservation areas in which Indians no longer made up the dominant population group.

In *DeCoteau v. District County Court*, 420 U.S. 425 (1975), the state questioned continued reservation status of the Lake Traverse Reservation of the Wahpeton and Sisseton bands of the Sioux established in 1867 in North Dakota.

The case involved both child custody proceedings and criminal cases that were consolidated for determination of the reservation status of the land in question. The causes of action in *DeCoteau* arose in part on non-Indian owned parcels with the reservation. Speaking for the Court, Justice Stewart described the reservation as encompassing 918,000 acres of land on which live 3,000 Indians and approximately 30,000 non-Indians. The Indians therefore constituted less than ten percent of the resident population. Only fifteen percent of the land area of the reservation was still held in restricted Indian trust allotments which were scattered in a random pattern throughout the 1867 reservation area. The state seemingly conceded that under 25 U.S.C. § 1151(c), the Indian owned parcels remained Indian country over which the state consequently lacked subject matter jurisdiction. The principle dispute centered on the status of non-Indian owned parcels within the 1867 reservation area. Justice Stewart, however, noted that in the child custody case it was stipulated that half of the conduct in question arose on the non-Indian owned parcels, while the remaining half occurred on Indian owned parcels within the 1867 reservation area. The opinion noted that "[i]n such a situation, there will obviously arise many practical and legal conflicts between state and federal jurisdiction with regard to the conduct of parties having mobility over the checkerboard territory. How these conflicts should be resolved is not before us." 420 U.S. at 429 n.3. In assessing whether the owned parcels not owned by Indians still constituted Indian country, the critical question was whether the Lake Traverse Reservation remained intact or whether it had been extinguished by an 1891 federal statute that ratified an 1889 Agreement with the tribe opening their reservation to allotment and non-Indian settlement on so-called surplus lands. Relying primarily on statements of tribal leaders suggesting a willingness to sell title to some of their land in exchange for resolution of a long overdue loyal scout claim reflected in transcripts and reports of the negotiations between leaders of the tribe and federal commissioners, Justice Stewart suggested that the surrounding circumstances indicated a clear intent to terminate the 1867 reservation agreed to by the tribe. Summarizing his holding and the principles on which it was based, he said:

> This Court does not lightly conclude that an Indian reservation has been terminated. "[W]hen Congress has once established a reservation all tracts included within it remain a part of the reservation until separated therefrom by Congress." *United States v. Celestine,* 215 U.S. 278, 285. The congressional intent must be clear, to overcome "the general rule that '[d]oubtful expressions are to be resolved in favor of the weak and defenseless people who are the wards of the nation, dependent upon its protection and good faith.'" *McClanahan v. Arizona State Tax Comm'n,* 411 U.S. 164, 174, quoting *Carpenter v. Shaw,* 280 U.S. 363, 367. Accordingly, the Court requires that the "congressional determination to terminate ... be expressed on the face of the Act or be clear from the surrounding circumstances and legislative history." *Mattz v. Arnett,* 412 U.S., at 505. See also *Seymour v. Superintendent,* 368 U.S. 351, and *United States v. Nice,* 241 U.S. 591. In particular, we have stressed that reservation status may survive the mere opening of a reservation to settlement, even when the moneys paid for the land by the settlers are placed in trust by the Government for the Indians' benefit. *Mattz v. Arnett, supra,* and *Seymour v. Superintendent, supra.*
> But in this case, "the face of the Act," and its "surrounding circumstances" and "legislative history," all point unmistakably to the conclusion that the Lake Traverse Reservation was terminated in 1891. The negotiations leading to the 1889 Agreement show plainly that the Indians were willing to convey to the Government, for a sum

certain, all of their interest in all of their unalloted lands. The Agreement's language, adopted by majority vote of the tribe, was precisely suited to this purpose:

> The Sisseton and Wahpeton bands of Dakota or Sioux Indians hereby cede, sell, relinquish, and convey to the United States all their claim, right, title, and interest in and to all the unalloted lands within the limits of the reservation set apart to said bands of Indians as aforesaid remaining after the allotments and additional allotments provided for in article four of this agreement shall have been made.

This language is virtually indistinguishable from that used in the other sum-certain, cession agreements ratified by Congress in the same 1891 Act. [That] the lands ceded in the other agreements were returned to the public domain, stripped of reservation status, can hardly be questioned, and every party here acknowledges as much. The sponsors of the legislation stated repeatedly that the ratified agreements would return the ceded lands to the "public domain." ... Cf. *Mattz v. Arnett,* 412 U.S., at 504 n.22.

It is true that the Sisseton-Wahpeton Agreement was unique in providing for cession of all, rather than simply a major portion of, the affected tribe's unalloted lands. But, as the historical circumstances make clear, this was not because the tribe wished to retain its former reservation, undiminished, but rather because the tribe and the Government were satisfied that retention of allotments would provide an adequate fulcrum for tribal affairs. In such a situation, exclusive tribal and federal jurisdiction is limited to the retained allotments. 18 U.S.C. § 1151 (c). See *United States v. Pelican,* 232 U.S. 442. With the benefit of hindsight, it may be argued that the tribe and the Government would have been better advised to have carved out a diminished reservation, instead of or in addition to the retained allotments. But we cannot rewrite the 1889 Agreement and the 1891 statute. For the courts to reinstate the *entire* reservation, on the theory that retention of mere allotments was ill-advised, would carry us well beyond the rule by which legal ambiguities are resolved to the benefit of the Indians. We give this rule the broadest possible scope, but it remains at base a canon for construing the complex treaties, statutes, and contracts which define the status of Indian tribes. A canon of construction is not a license to disregard clear expressions of tribal and congressional intent.

420 U.S. at 444-47. Thus, Justice Stewart concluded that "[i]n the present case ... the surrounding circumstances are fully consistent with an intent to terminate the reservation and inconsistent with any other purpose." 420 U.S. at 448. Three justices dissented, led by Justice Douglas. Justice Douglas noted the practical impediment to effective and efficient governance of the 1867 reservation area created by the Court's decision and protested:

> If South Dakota has its way, the Federal Government and the tribal government have no jurisdiction when an act takes place in a homesteaded spot in the checkerboard; and South Dakota has no say over acts committed on "trust" lands. But where in fact did the jurisdictional act occur? Jurisdiction dependent on the "tract book" promises to be uncertain and hectic. Many acts are ambulatory. In a given case, who will move — the State, the tribe, or the Federal Government? The contest promises to be unseemly, the only beneficiaries being those who benefit from confusion and uncertainty. Without state interference, Indians violating the law within the reservation would be subject only to tribal jurisdiction, which puts the responsibility where the Federal Government can supervise it. Checkerboard jurisdiction cripples the United States in fulfilling its fiduciary responsibilities of guardianship and protection of Indians. It is the end of tribal authority for it introduces such an element of uncertainty as to what agency has jurisdiction as to make modest tribal leaders abdicate and aggressive ones undertake the losing battle against superior state authority. As Mr. Justice Miller stated nearly 100 years ago concerning the importance of exclusive federal jurisdiction over acts committed by Indians within the boundaries of a reservation: "They owe no allegiance to the States, and receive from them no protection. Because of the local ill feeling, the

people of the States where they are found are often their deadliest enemies." *United States v. Kagama,* 118 U.S. 375, 384 (1886).

420 U.S., at 467-68 (Douglas, J., dissenting).

In *Rosebud Sioux Tribe v. Kneip,* 430 U.S. 584 (1977), the Court was asked to consider whether three separate unilateral Acts of Congress (two of which partially implemented prior agreements negotiated with the tribe that had been signed by a majority of the adult tribal males but had failed to secure approval of the three-quarters extraordinary majority required by prior treaty) had diminished portions of the boundaries of the Rosebud Sioux Reservation located within three counties in South Dakota. As in *Seymour, Mattz,* and *DeCoteau,* these statutes had been enacted during the allotment period and had ceded and opened unalloted portions of the Rosebud Sioux Reservation to non-Indian settlement. After an extensive review of the background and legislative history of the first statute, the Court concluded by divided vote that the natural construction was to read a congressional intent to disestablish the affected portions of the Rosebud Sioux Reservation. Rejecting the tribe's argument, predicated in part on *DeCoteau,* that any such cession required tribal consent, Justice Rehnquist said that Congress had simply unilaterally implemented the prior agreement of cession that had failed for want of the extraordinary majority. Rehnquist's opinion also rejected the tribe's efforts to distinguish *DeCoteau* due to the lack of payment of a sum certain in the statutes affecting the Rosebud Sioux lands. Justice Rehnquist said:

> We noted in *DeCoteau v. District County Court,* 420 U.S. 425 (1975), the fact that Congress had there ratified a sale for a sum certain. These two facts — Indian consent and a sum certain payment — aided us in determining that congressional intent was to terminate the Reservation. But as the Court of Appeals in the instant case recognized, "[t]he determination of disestablishment ... rests upon congressional intent, as to which the method of payment, whether lump-sum or otherwise, is but one of many factors to be considered." ... *DeCoteau* rested upon precisely such a determination, and neither the sum certain nor the consent was considered dispositive one way or the other. The statutory language discussed in *DeCoteau* is similar to the language of the 1904 Act. While the 1904 Act, to be sure, lacks a sum certain payment as well as approval by three-fourths of the adult male Indians, it, in common with *DeCoteau,* starts from the form of an agreement, which was fully explained to the Rosebud Tribe both in 1901 and in 1904.

Id. at 548 n.20. The opinion also noted, that while the subsequent jurisdictional history of the affected area was not entirely clear, the state had long exercised jurisdiction over the area and that the land in question was over 90% non-Indian. In the *Rosebud Sioux Tribe* opinion Justice Rehnquist purported to apply the test suggested in *Mattz* that "[a] congressional determination to terminate [an Indian reservation] must be expressed on the face of the Act or be clear from the surrounding circumstances and legislative history." 430 U.S. at 586. Justice Marshall protested for a three-member group of dissenters that the majority's approach clouded the jurisdiction, reservation status, and property rights of the Rosebud Sioux and a large number of other tribes that had statutes with similar language.

Was the *Seymour-Mattz* test rigorously applied in *DeCoteau* or *Rosebud Sioux Tribe?* Were differences in *contemporary* demographic profiles of the reservations, including particularly the current percentage of Indian population, influencing the outcomes of cases in which the legal test called solely for a historical inquiry? Should current demography play a role in the resolution of such questions? Does the opinion in the *Solem* case resolve any perceived inconsistency between reliance on contemporary demography and reliance on historical background to resolve these important questions of reservation termination and diminishment?

Recall that the Court in *Seymour* suggested that Congress sought to avoid checkerboard jurisdiction patterns when it expressly included all land within the exterior boundaries of an Indian reservation "notwithstanding the issuance of any patent." Does the approach to questions of reservation diminishment or termination reflected in *Solem* take adequate account of this stated Congressional policy?

C. THE UNEVEN HISTORY OF FEDERAL INDIAN POLICY: POLITICS, ASSIMILATION, AND AUTONOMY

Federal Indian law necessarily is a reflection of the policies Congress has from time to time adopted to deal with Indian affairs. The objectives of those policies have not always been consistent either within any given period or over a broader time perspective. Furthermore, shifting federal objectives and the oscillation of federal policy often have created situations that complicate and frustrate efforts to achieve later policy objectives. Thus, any attempt to understand federal Indian law must be grounded in a full appreciation of the history of federal Indian policy.

In the introduction to *Felix S. Cohen's Handbook of Federal Indian Law* (1942), then-solicitor of the Department of the Interior Nathan R. Margold wrote:

Federal Indian law is a subject that cannot be understood if the historical dimension of existing law is ignored. As I have elsewhere observed, the groups of human beings with whom Federal Indian law is immediately concerned have undergone, in the century and a half of our national existence, changes in living habits, institutions, needs and aspirations far greater than the changes that separate from our own age the ages for which Hammurabi, Moses, Lycurgus, or Justinian legislated. Telescoped into a century and a half, one may find changes in social, political, and property relations which stretch over more than 30 centuries of European civilization. The toughness of law which keeps it from changing as rapidly as social conditions change in our national life is, of course, much more serious where the rate of social change is 20 times as rapid. Thus, if the laws governing Indian affairs are viewed as lawyers generally view existing law, without reference to the varying times in which particular provisions are enacted, the body of the law thus viewed is a mystifying collection of inconsistencies and anachronisms. To recognize the different dates at which various provisions were enacted is the first step towards order and sanity in this field.

Not only is it important to recognize the temporal "depth" of existing legislation, it is also important to appreciate the past existence of legislation which has, technically, ceased to exist. For there is a very real sense in which it can be said that no provision of law is ever completely wiped out. This is particularly true in the field of Indian law. At every session of the Supreme Court, there arise cases in which the validity of a present claim depends upon the question: "What was the law on such and such a point in some earlier period?" Laws long repealed have served to create legal rights which endure and which can be understood only by reference to the repealed legislation. Thus, in seeking a complete answer to various questions of Indian law, one finds that he cannot rest with a collection of laws "still in force," but must constantly recur to legislation that has been repealed, amended, or superseded.

Id. at xxvii-xxviii.

The study of the history of federal Indian policy is a subject that could easily fill several volumes. A number of excellent sources exist on the history of federal Indian policy generally or on the experience of particular periods. *See, e.g.*, F. PRUCHA, THE GREAT FATHER (1984); F. COHEN, HANDBOOK OF FEDERAL INDIAN LAW ch. 2 (1982); S. TYLER, A HISTORY OF INDIAN POLICY (1973); S. TYLER, INDIAN AFFAIRS: A STUDY OF THE CHANGES IN POLICY OF THE UNITED STATES TOWARD INDIANS (1964); S. TYLER, INDIAN AFFAIRS: A WORK PAPER ON TERMINATION (1964); F. PRUCHA, AMERICAN INDIAN POLICY IN THE FORMATIVE YEARS (1962); F. PRUCHA, AMERICAN INDIAN POLICY IN CRISIS: CHRISTIAN REFORMERS AND THE INDIANS, 1865-1900 (1964); F. HOXIE, A FINAL PROMISE: THE CAMPAIGN TO ASSIMILATE THE INDIANS, 1880-1920 (1984); W. MOHR, FEDERAL INDIAN RELATIONS, 1774-1778 (1933); G. HARMON, SIXTY YEARS OF INDIAN AFFAIRS (1941); A. DEBO, A HISTORY OF THE INDIANS OF THE UNITED STATES (1970); G. FOREMAN, ADVANCING THE FRONTIER, 1830-1860 (1953); G. FOREMAN, INDIAN REMOVAL: THE EMIGRATION OF THE FIVE CIVILIZED TRIBES OF INDIANS (1932); J. KINNEY, A CONTINENT LOST — A CIVILIZATION WON (1937); O. PEAKE, HISTORY OF THE UNITED STATES INDIAN FACTORY SYSTEM, 1795-1822 (1954); W. WASHBURN, THE INDIAN IN AMERICA (1975); A. GIBSON, THE AMERICAN INDIAN: PREHISTORY TO THE PRESENT (1980). For excellent general bibliographies see F. PRUCHA, A BIBLIOGRAPHICAL GUIDE TO THE HISTORY OF INDIAN-WHITE RELATIONS IN THE UNITED STATES (1977); F. PRUCHA, UNITED STATES INDIAN POLICY: A CRITICAL BIBLIOGRAPHY (1977); F. PRUCHA, INDIAN-WHITE RELATIONS IN THE UNITED STATES: A BIBLIOGRAPHY OF WORKS PUBLISHED 1975-1980 (1982).

The following material is presented to provide a sufficient introduction to the history of federal Indian policy to facilitate understanding of modern federal Indian law. In reviewing this material consider the roles the federal government has played over time as a buffer of the Indian tribes against the states. Consider how the objectives of federal Indian policy have changed over time. For each period in question, assess whether the goals of federal policy were designed to promote Native American assimilation into the broader society or to protect Indian autonomy from the American society. Finally, assess how the changes in federal Indian policy over time have complicated the resolution of legal questions in the field of Indian law.

The Colonial Period (1492-1776)

The European nations that colonized America generally operated on the presumption that discovery vested certain rights to acquire land in the sovereign of the discovering nation. This theory, however, recognized the Indian right of occupancy to land held from time immemorial and merely limited the Indians' right to dispose of their lands to whomever they chose. Thus, the fact of discovery was seen as vesting certain preemption rights in the discovering nation as compared with other European countries and the subjects of the discovering power, but discovery did not extinguish the Indian right of occupancy.

The doctrines of the rights of discovery and the protection of aboriginal possession were profoundly shaped by papers presented by Franciscus de Vitoria in Spain in 1532. In response to those in Spain who then argued that the natives inhabiting the Americas were not Christian (and, according to some, not human) and therefore had no legitimate property rights in the lands that they occupied, Vitoria urged that "aborigines undoubtedly had true dominion in both public and private matters, just like Christians and that neither their princes nor private persons could be despoiled of their property on the ground of their not being true owners." F. VICTORIA, DE INDIS ET DE IURE BELLI RELECTIONES 128 (E. Nys ed., J. Bate trans. 1917). For Vitoria, the European nations could legitimately exercise power over the Indians or acquire their property only as a result of conquest in a "just" war or as a result of voluntary cession and agreement by the Indians. *See generally* Cohen, *The Spanish Origin of Indian Rights in the Law of the United States*, 31 GEO. L.J. 1 (1942). Felix Cohen later wrote of the influence of Vitoria's ideas:

> The Emperors of Spain and their subordinate administrators, like many able administrators since, did not consistently carry out Fra Vitoria's legal advice. They did, however, adopt many laws and issue many charters recognizing and guaranteeing the rights of Indian communities, and the theory of Indian title put forward by Vitoria came to be generally accepted by writers on international law of the sixteenth, seventeenth, and eighteenth centuries who were cited as authorities in early federal litigation on Indian property rights.
>
> The idea that land should be acquired from Indians by treaty involved three assumptions: (1) That both parties to the treaty are sovereign powers; (2) that the Indian tribe has a transferable title, of some sort, to the land in question; and (3) that the acquisition of Indian lands could not safely be left to individual colonists but must be controlled as a governmental monopoly. These three principles are embodied in the "New Project of Freedoms and Exemptions," drafted about 1630 for the guidance of officials of the Dutch West India Co., which declares:
>
>> The Patroons of New Netherland, shall be bound to purchase from the Lords Sachems in New Netherland, the soil where they propose to plant their Colonies, and shall acquire such right thereunto as they will agree for with the said Sachems.
>
> The Dutch viewpoint was shared by some of the early English settlers. In the spring of 1636, Roger Williams, who insisted that the right of the natives to the soil could not be abrogated by an English patent, founded the Rhode Island Plantations. This was the territory inhabited by the Narragansetts and for which Williams had treated.
>
> From time to time other British colonies became parties to treaties with the Indians. Unauthorized treating for the purchase of Indian land by individual colonists was prohibited in Rhode Island as early as 1651. By the middle of the eighteenth century, eight other colonies had laws forbidding such purchase unless approved by the constituted authorities. The effect of such laws was to eliminate conflicts of land titles that otherwise resulted from overlapping grants by individual Indians or tribes, to protect the Indians, in some measure, against fraud, and to center in the colonial governments a valuable monopoly.
>
> With the outbreak of the French and Indian War the problem of dealing with the natives which had been left largely to the individual colonies was temporarily returned to the control of the mother country. Later, treaties with the Indians were again negotiated by the colonies.
>
> On several occasions the Crown indicated its belief in the sanctity of treaty obligations. Some of the treaties contained definite stipulations regarding land tenure.

F. COHEN, HANDBOOK OF FEDERAL INDIAN LAW 47 (1942).

In the British colonies the crown set general policies but the management of Indian policies generally was left to the separate colonies. Some of the colonies, such as Massachusetts Bay, Virginia, and Connecticut, pursued policies of land expropriation followed by conquest when the Indians resisted. Thus, Indian wars in 1622 in Virginia and in 1675 in Virginia and New England resulted in a decimation and subjugation of some of the tribes of the eastern seaboard in the affected colonies. *See generally* F. JENNINGS, THE INVASION OF AMERICA (1975). By contrast, New York dealt with the Five Nations Iroquois Confederation through diplomatic means and treaty. Similarly, in the Southeast, Georgia treated with the Creeks and the Carolinas and Virginia dealt with the Cherokees as separate sovereign polities, using trade and diplomacy to manage relations with the affected tribes. Nevertheless, Indian dissatisfaction over land frauds, unauthorized encroachment by non-Indian settlers, and improprieties in the Indian trade produced periodic disruptions in Indian affairs. French and Spanish traders also fueled such disruptions and sought trade advantages, as well as military and diplomatic alliances for themselves. *See generally* A. TRELEASE, INDIAN AFFAIRS IN COLONIAL NEW YORK: THE SEVENTEENTH CENTURY (1960); G. NAMMACK, FRAUD, POLITICS AND THE DISPOSSESSION OF THE INDIANS (1969); J. REID, A BETTER KIND OF HATCHET (1976).

During the colonial period most colonies tried extensively to regulate Indian trade and land cessions. The colonial authorities were torn, however, between the conflicting demands posed by the profits to be made from Indian trade and lands on the one hand and the need to placate and pacify the Indians on the other. As a result, the separate management of Indian affairs by the colonies proved uneven, inconsistent and unsuccessful.

When certain Indian tribes either threatened to remain neutral or sided with the French during a series of French and Indian wars in the middle of the eighteenth century, the stage was set for a structural change in the management of Indian affairs. The colonial authorities led by Benjamin Franklin proposed a union of colonies at the Albany Congress of 1754. This proposed union was principally designed to assure centralized control over Indian affairs. Beginning in 1755 the Crown, acting independently, started to centralize the management of Indian affairs through the appointment of Indian agents directly responsible to London. The Proclamation of 1763 forbade further cessions of Indian land in the Indian territory roughly westward of the crest of the Appalachians. It also centralized in the Crown the process of licensing and approving all Indian land cessions eastward of that line, thereby revoking the earlier authority exercised by the colonies over this subject. And in 1764 the Crown proposed a plan for

> the regulation of Indian Affairs both commercial and political throughout all North America, upon one general system, under the direction of Officers appointed by the Crown, so as to set aside all local interfering of particular Provinces, which has been one great cause of the distracted state of Indian Affairs in general.

The plan was never formally approved, only partially implemented, and finally abandoned in 1768. The cost of centralized control was seen by the British government as outweighing the perceived benefits. *See generally* Clinton, *The Proclamation of 1763: Colonial Prelude to Two Centuries of Federal-State Con-*

flict Over the Management of Indian Affairs, 69 BOSTON U.L. REV. 329 (1989); F. JENNINGS, EMPIRE OF FORTUNE: CROWNS, COLONIES & TRIBES IN THE SEVEN YEARS WAR IN AMERICA (1988); F. JENNINGS, THE AMBIGUOUS IROQUOIS EMPIRE (1984); F. PRUCHA, AMERICAN INDIAN POLICY IN THE FORMATIVE YEARS 5-25 (1962); Clinton, *Book Review*, 47 U. CHI. L. REV. 846, 850-54 (1980).

The Confederation Period (1776-1789)

During the Revolution the principal objective of United States Indian policy was to secure the neutrality of the Indian tribes. This policy produced one of the first treaties between the United States and the Indians — the Treaty with the Delaware, Sept. 17, 1778, 7 Stat. 13. Among other things this treaty guaranteed the territorial integrity of the Delaware Nation and expressly contemplated the possibility that the United States might invite the Delaware Nation to form a state and join the Confederation with other tribes allied to the national government. This treaty also provided that the punishment of crimes by citizens of either party to the prejudice of the other would be "by judges or juries of both parties, as near as can be to the laws, customs and usages of the contracting parties and natural justice." *Id.* at art. IV.

In 1781 the nation approved the Articles of Confederation in which article IX vested the Continental Congress with "the sole and exclusive right and power of ... regulating the trade and managing all affairs with Indians not members of any of the states; provided, that the legislative right of any state within its own limits be not infringed or violated ...." This ambiguous commitment of Indian affairs power to national government — hedged, as it was, with two clauses purporting to reserve some ill-defined, residual state authority over Indian affairs — plagued the national government during the pre-Constitution period.

After the Revolution, the federal government sought to manage Indian relations and enter into treaties establishing boundary lines with various tribes. However, it met with resistance from certain states, particularly New York, North Carolina, and Georgia. Thus, for example, state officials in New York disrupted the negotiations of federal officials that led to the Treaty with the Six Nations, Oct. 22, 1784, 7 Stat. 15 (often called the Treaty of Fort Stanwix). State officials later negotiated treaties with the Six Nations that were inconsistent with the boundary lines established in the Treaty of Fort Stanwix. This latter fact accounts for certain modern land claims cases. North Carolina protested that federal treaty negotiations at Hopewell that produced the Treaty with the Cherokees, Nov. 28, 1785, 7 Stat. 18, violated its legislative rights since the treaty sought to guarantee Cherokee occupancy of lands within the state of North Carolina and to provide that "the Cherokees [were] under the protection of the United States, and of no other sovereign whatsoever." *Id.* at art. III. When the Continental Congress sought to guarantee Indian occupancy of land against encroachment of white settlers, it could secure approval only for a proclamation restraining alienation of Indian lands "without the limits or jurisdiction of any particular state." 25 JOURNALS OF THE CONTINENTAL CONGRESS 602 (1783).

The conflict between national and state governments over the management of Indian affairs came to a head when Georgia negotiated certain state treaties involving substantial lands with a rump delegation of the Creeks after national treaty commissioners had refused to deal with the group, deeming it unrepresentative of the Creek Nation. This action on the part of the State of Georgia spawned an Indian war on the eve of the convening of the Constitutional Convention in 1787. When Georgia requested the assistance of the Continental Congress, a committee appointed to look into the matter reported:

> An avaricious disposition in some of our people to acquire large tracts of land and often by unfair means, appears to be the principal source of difficulties with the Indians. [The members of this] committee conceive that it has been long the opinion of the country, supported by Justice and humanity, that the Indians have just claims to all lands occupied by and not fairly purchased from them. [Therefore] it cannot be supposed, the state has the powers [to make war with Indians or buy land from them] without making [the Indian affairs clause of article IX] useless and [thus] no particular state can have an exclusive interest in the management of Affairs with any of the tribes, except in some uncommon cases.

33 JOURNALS OF THE CONTINENTAL CONGRESS 457-59 (1787).

The Trade and Intercourse Act Era (1789-1835)

The adoption of the Constitution ushered in a new era in the national management of Indian affairs. Specifically, the Indian commerce clause of article 1, section 8, clause 3, authorized Congress to regulate "Commerce ... with the Indian Tribes" and enumerated the Indian tribes with two other sovereign entities, "foreign Nations" and "the several States." Article 1, section 2, also excluded "Indians not taxed" from the enumeration of state citizens for purposes of congressional apportionment, thereby suggesting that they were not part of the polity. In *The Federalist* No. 42, Madison wrote of the advantages of the Indian commerce clause over the articles:

> The regulation of commerce with the Indian tribes is very properly unfettered from two limitations in the articles of confederation, which render the provision obscure and contradictory. The power is there restrained to Indians, not members of any of the States, and is not to violate or infringe the legislative right of any State within its own limits. What description of Indians are to be deemed members of a State, is not yet settled, and has been a question of frequent perplexity and contention in the federal Councils. And how the trade with Indians, though not members of a State, yet residing within its legislative jurisdiction, can be regulated by an external authority, without so far intruding on the internal rights of legislation, is absolutely incomprehensible.

The first Congress acted promptly to assert the national government's exclusive control over Indian affairs by enacting the Trade and Intercourse Act of 1790, ch. 33, 1 Stat. 137. The breadth of congressional assertion of authority is indicated by the restraint on alienation of Indian lands contained in section 4 of the Act (now codified as amended at 25 U.S.C. § 177):

> That no sale of lands made by any Indians, or any nation or tribe of Indians within the United States, shall be valid to any person or persons, *or to any state*, whether having the right of preemption to such lands or not, unless the same shall be made and duly executed at some public treaty, held under the authority of the United States.

Id. (emphasis supplied). When compared with the limited Proclamation of 1783, which only restrained alienation of Indian lands "without the limits or jurisdiction of any particular State," the Trade and Intercourse Act of 1790 represented a new effort to place the exclusive management of trade, diplomatic relations, and land cessions involving the Indians exclusively in the hands of the federal government. This effort was, however, sometimes resisted by the states, and the constitutional tension created during this period is responsible for some of the modern claims of eastern tribes to possessory interests in land in several eastern states. *See generally* Clinton & Hotopp, *Judicial Enforcement of the Federal Restraints on Alienation of Indian Land: The Origins of the Eastern Land Claims*, 31 ME. L. REV. 17 (1979); O'Toole & Tureen, *State Power and the Passamaquoddy Tribe: A Gross National Hypocrisy?*, 23 ME. L. REV. 1 (1971).

The Trade and Intercourse Act of 1790 was by its terms temporary and was later succeeded by new temporary statutes in 1793, 1796, and 1799 and later by permanent Trade and Intercourse Acts in 1802 and 1834. Additionally, supplemental legislation was enacted in 1817 and 1822. Professor Francis Prucha in his excellent work on this period, AMERICAN INDIAN POLICY IN THE FORMATIVE YEARS (Harvard University Press 1962)* summarizes the policies reflected in these statutes as follows:

> For the management of these Indian affairs the United States by the 1830's had determined a set of principles which became the standard base lines of American Indian policy. The fundamental elements of the federal program were the following:
>
> (1) Protection of Indian rights to their land by setting definite boundaries for the Indian Country, restricting the whites from entering the area except under certain controls, and removing illegal intruders.
>
> (2) Control of the disposition of Indian lands by denying the right of private individuals or local governments to acquire land from the Indians by purchase or by any other means.
>
> (3) Regulation of the Indian trade by determining the conditions under which individuals might engage in the trade, prohibiting certain classes of traders, and actually entering into the trade itself.
>
> (4) Control of the liquor traffic by regulating the flow of intoxicating liquor into the Indian Country and then prohibiting it altogether.
>
> (5) Provision for the punishment of crimes committed by members of one race against the other and compensation for damages suffered by one group at the hands of the other, in order to remove the occasions for private retaliation which led to frontier hostilities.
>
> (6) Promotion of civilization and education among the Indians, in the hope that they might be absorbed into the general stream of American society.
>
> This Indian policy of the government was expressed in the formal treaties made with the Indian tribes, but it took shape primarily in a series of federal laws "to regulate trade and intercourse with the Indian tribes, and to preserve peace on the frontier." The first of these laws was passed in 1790, the final and enduring one in 1834. In them appeared the legislative statement of the decisions made by the United States as it was feeling its way toward satisfactory solutions to the problems resulting from the presence of uncultured tribesmen in the path of aggressive and land-hungry whites. On occasion, too, special programs such as the system of government trading factories were established in separate, but related, laws.
>
> The goal of American statesmen was the orderly advance of the frontier. To maintain the desired order and tranquility it was necessary to place restrictions on the contacts between the whites and the Indians. The intercourse acts were thus restrictive and prohibitory in nature — aimed largely at restraining the actions of the whites and providing justice to the Indians as the means of preventing hostility. But if the goal was an *orderly* advance, it was nevertheless *advance* of the frontier, and in the process of reconciling the two elements, conflict and injustice were often the result.

Id. at 2-3.

---

*Copyright © 1962 by the President and Fellows of Harvard College. Reprinted by permission.

As Prucha's work suggests, federal treaties with the Indians also were negotiated during this period and the treaty-making process continued until 1871. The federal statutes governing Indian affairs during this era principally set forth general federal policies that were implemented with specific tribes by treaty. Additionally, the Trade and Intercourse Acts regulated non-Indians who traded with or committed offenses against the Indians.

At least until 1817 federal statutes did not specifically apply to individual Indians in Indian country.* However in that year Congress passed the first statute providing for the exercise of federal criminal jurisdiction over tribal Indians who committed serious crimes against non-Indians in Indian country. Act of Mar. 3, 1817, ch. 92, 3 Stat. 383. This Act was later modified in 1834 and 1854 and forms the basis of the statute now codified at 18 U.S.C. § 1152. *See generally* Clinton, *Development of Criminal Jurisdiction over Indian Lands: The Historical Perspective*, 17 ARIZ. L. REV. 951 (1975).

Unlike the restraint against alienation of Indian lands, the trade licensing, liquor control, criminal, and certain other provisions of the Trade and Intercourse Acts applied only in "Indian country." Considerable effort was made in the treaties of the time to establish clear lines of demarcation separating protected Indian country enclaves from other lands claimed by the states. *See, e.g.,* Treaty with the Cherokees, July 2, 1791, 7 Stat. 39; Treaty with the Creek, Aug. 7, 1790, 7 Stat. 35. Beginning in 1796 the Trade and Intercourse Act codified the Indian country lines established by these various treaties, but the lines were continually changing as new treaties with United States ceded more Indian land. The statutory revisions were only partially able to keep up with the process of treaty making. *See generally* F. COHEN, HANDBOOK OF FEDERAL INDIAN LAW ch. 1 (1982 ed.); Clinton & Hotopp, *supra,* at 30-36, n.71.

During this period, Congress extensively managed the trade with Indian tribes. During most of the early nineteenth century until 1822 that regulation involved the establishment of federally sanctioned monopolies under the so-called factory system to handle trade with the Indians. *See* O. PEAKE, HISTORY OF THE UNITED STATES INDIAN FACTORY SYSTEM, 1795-1822 (1954).

The Removal Period (1835-1861)

The governments of the states became increasingly dissatisfied with the continued existence of Indian tribal enclaves within their boundaries. As early as 1802 the State of Georgia had ceded to the United States certain lands it formerly claimed in exchange for a promise to promptly extinguish Indian title and remove the Indians from the state. Until the War of 1812 the federal government did little to further the removal of the Indians, in part because the Indian tribes, particularly those on the western frontiers, held an important balance of power on the North American continent. Therefore, placating Native American tribes and preventing their alliance with the English against the

---

*Indians who left their territory and committed crimes against non-Indians on lands over which the states or territories exercised jurisdiction were apparently subject to state or territorial law. The 1796 Trade and Intercourse Act explicitly provides for the apprehension and arrest of such Indians in Indian country. Act of May 19, 1796, ch. 30, § 14, 1 Stat. 472-73.

American interests remained the dominant theme in federal Indian policy. The outcome of the War of 1812, however, ended this threat and set the stage for removal of the Indians.

The removal process began slowly at first with the federal government encouraging Indian tribes voluntarily to remove westward, ultimately accepting their agreements to do so by treaty. Thus, in the Treaty with the Cherokee, July 8, 1817, 7 Stat. 156, the federal government accepted a cession of land from some of the leaders of the lower Cherokee towns so that the Indians could remove westward of the Mississippi River to public lands on the Arkansas and White rivers. The leaders of the lower towns purportedly agreed to the removal in order "to continue the hunter life, and also [because of] the scarcity of game where they then lived." *Id.* at Preamble. The remaining Cherokees "proposed to begin the establishment of fixed laws and a regular government ...." *Id.* This treaty created a schism in the Cherokee Nation between "western Cherokee" who moved westward and the bulk of the tribe who remained to defend their ancestral homelands.

Efforts to secure voluntary removal continued throughout the 1820's but met with only limited success. *See, e.g.,* Treaty with the Choctaws, Oct. 18, 1820, 7 Stat. 210; Treaty with the Creeks, Feb. 12, 1825, 7 Stat. 237; Treaty with the Creeks, Jan. 24, 1826, 7 Stat. 286; Treaty with the Western Cherokee, May 6, 1828, 7 Stat. 311; Treaties with the Delawares, Aug. 3, 1829, and Sept. 24, 1829, 7 Stat. 326, 327; Treaty with the Choctaw, Sept. 27, 1830, 7 Stat. 333, 340.

Toward the end of the 1820's matters reached crisis proportions. In 1827 the Cherokee Nation, making good on its earlier treaty promise, organized a tribal constitution loosely patterned on the federal constitution and asserted sovereignty over its lands. Almost simultaneously gold was discovered in Cherokee country and non-Indian settlement pressures on the Cherokee lands increased. In 1828 the presidential election of Andrew Jackson, an ardent supporter of Indian removal, galvanized the states to take action. In 1828 and 1829 Georgia passed two statutes appropriating most of the lands of the Cherokee Nation, extending state law to these areas, and providing that all laws, ordinances, or regulations of the Cherokee Nation were null and void. These acts also outlawed the Cherokee tribal government and required that all white persons residing in the Cherokee nation secure a license from the governor and take an oath of allegiance to the state. Other statutes in 1830 also rendered Creek and Cherokee Indians incompetent to testify in cases in which a white person was a party. Similar statutes were enacted for the Creeks and Choctaws in Alabama and Mississippi and the Cherokees in Tennessee. As discussed earlier in this chapter, the Cherokees tried to resist these state statutes through federal court litigation. *See Cherokee Nation v. Georgia,* 30 U.S. (5 Pet.) 1 (1831); *Worcester v. Georgia,* 31 U.S. (6 Pet.) 515 (1832). In *Worcester* the Georgia laws were declared unconstitutional and the sovereignty of the Cherokees was reaffirmed. *See generally* Burke, *The Cherokee Cases: A Study in Law, Politics and Morality,* 21 Stan. L. Rev. 499 (1969) *and* Swindler, *Politics as Law: The Cherokee Cases,* 3 Am. Indian L. Rev. 7 (1975).

Despite this litigation victory, the Cherokees, like most of the other tribes in the southeastern states, were removed from the states and resettled on the west side of the Mississippi River in the Indian Territory, now eastern Oklahoma.

E.g., Act of May 28, 1830, 4 Stat. 411; Treaty with the Cherokee, Dec. 29, 1835, 7 Stat. 478; Treaty with the Chickasaw, May 24, 1834, 7 Stat. 450; Treaty with the Creeks, Feb. 14, 1833, 7 Stat. 417; Treaty with the Shawnee, Aug. 8, 1831, 7 Stat. 355; Treaty with the Choctaw, Sept. 27, 1830, 7 Stat. 333. *See generally* G. FOREMAN, INDIAN REMOVAL (1932); F. PRUCHA, *supra*, at 212-49; G. FOREMAN, THE FIVE CIVILIZED TRIBES (1934).

Thereafter until at least 1861 a central theme in federal Indian policy was the removal of the tribes beyond state boundary lines, often as a prelude to the admission of new states into the Union. *See, e.g.*, Treaty with the Sac and Fox Indians, Oct. 11, 1842, 7 Stat. 596. The political and jurisdictional importance of this process is captured in the guarantee made in Article 4 of the Treaty with the Creek and Seminole Tribes, Aug. 7, 1856, 11 Stat. 699:

> [N]o State or Territory shall ever pass laws for the government of the Creek and Seminole tribes of Indians, and [none of the tracts] of [Indian] country defined [in] the agreement shall ever be embraced or included within, or annexed to, any Territory or State, nor shall either, or any part of either, ever be erected into a Territory without the full and free consent of the legislative authority of the tribe owning the same.

Removal was not confined to the tribes of the southeastern states. The general policy was to remove all tribal Indians from lands within states or territorial boundaries. Thus, tribes were removed from the Midwest and the Pacific Northwest to the Indian Territory. In many cases, as in the case of certain New York tribes, the plans made for tribal removal were never fully implemented. *E.g.*, Treaty with the Tonawanda Band of the Seneca Indians, Nov. 5, 1857, 11 Stat. 735, 12 Stat. 991; Treaty with the New York Indians, Jan. 15, 1838, 7 Stat. 550. *See also* Treaty with the Menominee, May 12, 1854, 10 Stat. 1064; Treaty with the Menominee, Oct. 18, 1848, 9 Stat. 952.

The Reservation Policy (1861-1887)

Like the prior effort at establishing clear lines of demarcation for Indian country under the Trade and Intercourse Acts, the removal policy was hampered by the speed of westward expansion of non-Indian settlement. It was also impeded by the limited remaining unoccupied areas outside of the states and territories for removal of Indian tribes. Once westward settlement leap-frogged the Indian Territory to California, the effort to remove Indian tribes from the states was doomed. Thus, in California during the early 1850's, federal agents experimented with the creation of smaller reservations within the state. Treaties were negotiated with California tribes during this period and several reservations were established. However, the Senate refused to ratify these treaties, in part because they departed from the declared removal policy of clearing resident Native American tribes from the states.

Despite this inauspicious beginning, the reservation policy rapidly was adopted for other states and territories west of the Mississippi River. Thus, a number of treaties in the 1850's explicitly reserved land for permanent tribal occupancy. *E.g.*, Treaty with the Kansas, Oct. 5, 1859, 12 Stat. 1111; Treaty with the Winnebago, Apr. 15, 1859, 12 Stat. 1101; Treaty with the Menominee, May 12, 1854, 10 Stat. 1064. The first clear congressional recognition that such reservations were intended as permanent jurisdictional enclaves within the states is found in the Enabling Act for the Kansas Territory. This Act, which authorized the formation of the state of Kansas, explicitly stated that the establishment of the state would not be construed to extend state jurisdiction over Indians of the Kansas territory or to impair the rights of Indians on their property in the territory. Act of Jan. 29, 1861, ch. 20, § 1, 12 Stat. 127. *See generally* Clinton, *Development of Criminal Jurisdiction over Indian Lands: The Historical Perspective*, 17 ARIZ. L. REV. 951, 960-61 (1975). This disclaimer of jurisdiction established a pattern, and the enabling acts and constitutions of many states admitted to the Union after 1861 therefore contain such disclaimers of jurisdiction. *See, e.g.,* Act of July 7, 1958, Pub. L. No. 85-508, § 4, 72 Stat. 339 (Alaska); Act of June 20, 1910, ch. 310, §§ 2, 20, 36 Stat. 558-59, 569-70 (Arizona and New Mexico); Act of June 16, 1906, ch. 3335, §§ 1, 7, 34 Stat. 267, 272 (Oklahoma); Act of Feb. 22, 1889, ch. 180, § 4, 25 Stat. 677 (North Dakota, South Dakota, Montana and Washington).

The reservation policy was implemented throughout the remainder of the nineteenth century. Most of the famous Indian wars of the last half of the century, including General Custer's Last Stand at the Little Big Horn, were caused by federal military efforts to force Indian tribes onto reservations or forcibly to keep them there. Thus, the reservation was not only a means of keeping non-Indian settlers off Indian lands; during the late nineteenth century, it also was a device to keep the Indians forcibly fenced within geographic and political lines of demarcation. *See generally* D. BROWN, BURY MY HEART AT WOUNDED KNEE (1971).

Throughout this period, the Indian tribes of the Indian Territory — as well as certain other tribes east of the frontier like the Menominees, the Eastern Band of the Cherokees in North Carolina, or the New York Indians — were at peace and engaged in the work of improving their tribal institutions and their social and economic condition. *See generally* R. STRICKLAND, FIRE AND THE SPIRITS (1975); A. DEBO, THE RISE AND FALL OF THE CHOCTAW REPUBLIC (1934).

The Allotment Period and Forced Assimilation (1871-1934)

The period from 1871 to 1887 represented a transition period in federal Indian policy. While implementation of the reservation policy continued during this period, various indicia signaled significant structural changes in federal Indian policy. First, in 1871 the Congress ended formal treaty making with the Indian tribes. The Appropriations Act of Mar. 3, 1871, ch. 120, 16 Stat. 544, 566, codified at 25 U.S.C. § 71, provided:

> [N]o Indian nation or tribe within the territory of the United States shall be acknowledged or recognized as an independent nation, tribe, or power with whom the United States may contract by treaty: *Provided further,* That nothing herein contained shall be construed to invalidate or impair the obligation of any treaty heretofore lawfully made and ratified with any such Indian nation or tribe.

This Act grew out of a long-standing dispute between the Senate and the House of Representatives over control of Indian affairs. *See generally* F. HOXIE, THE FINAL PROMISE: THE CAMPAIGN TO ASSIMILATE THE INDIANS, 1880-1920 (1984); F. COHEN, HANDBOOK OF FEDERAL INDIAN LAW 27-28 (1982). The House of Representatives, dissatisfied with the preeminent role in Indian affairs that the

treaty ratification process gave to the Senate, had cut off funds for treaty negotiations as early as 1867. *See* Act of Mar. 29, 1867, ch. 13, § 6, 15 Stat. 9. *See also*
Act of Apr. 10, 1869, ch. 16, § 5, 16 Stat. 40. After 1871 agreements with Indian
tribes continued to be negotiated into the early twentieth century, but they were
approved by statutory enactment. *E.g.,* Act of Mar. 1, 1901, ch. 675, 31 Stat. 848
(Cherokees); Act of July 10, 1882, ch. 284, 22 Stat. 157 (Crows). In addition to
ending treaty making, section 3 of the Act of Mar. 3, 1871, also required that
contracts involving the payment of funds for services relative to Indian lands or
claims against the United States had to be approved by the Commissioner of
Indian Affairs and the Secretary of the Interior. *See also* Act of May 21, 1872,
ch. 177, 17 Stat. 136.

Stunned by the 1883 Supreme Court decision in *Ex parte Crow Dog,* discussed earlier in this chapter, Congress appended a section to the Appropriations Act of Mar. 3, 1885, ch. 341, 23 Stat. 362, 385, providing for the exercise
of federal court jurisdiction over seven major crimes committed by Indians on
Indian reservations in the states or territories against the person or property of
an "Indian or other person." This statute provided federal court jurisdiction for
the first time over intratribal affairs. Such matters had previously been left
exclusively to tribal authorities. The Federal Major Crimes Act has been
amended and expanded to cover sixteen enumerated crimes and presently is
codified at 18 U.S.C. § 1153.

Another departure in federal Indian policy was brought about by the Dawes
General Allotment Act of 1887, ch. 119, 24 Stat. 388, codified as amended at 25
U.S.C. § 331 et seq. As early as the Treaty with the Oto and Missouri, Mar. 15,
1854, 10 Stat. 1038, the federal government had experimented with a policy of
allotting tribally held lands into separate lots or parcels that were assigned to
tribal members for a permanent home and to encourage agricultural pursuits.
The roots of such allotment experiments can be traced even further back,
however. In some of the colonies prior to the Revolution, earlier experiments
had been undertaken which broke up large communally held tribal land estates
in favor of ownership in severalty by tribal members. The idea behind the
nineteenth century federal allotment policy was to lure the nomadic hunting
tribes away from their communal village existence and to encourage a sedentary, rural agricultural life on separate allotments. *See also* Treaty with the
Omaha, Mar. 16, 1854, 10 Stat. 1043; Treaty with the Shawnee, May 10, 1854,
10 Stat. 1053; Treaty with the Sacs and Foxes of Missouri, May 18, 1854, 10
Stat. 1074; Treaty with the Kickapoo, May 18, 1854, 10 Stat. 1078. All of these
early efforts involved voluntary tribal consent to the allotment process. While
the Civil War and Reconstruction temporarily interrupted the implementation
of the allotment policy, the Congress returned to allotment as a model for
federal Indian policy in the 1887 statute. This time, however, Congress contemplated forcing the Indians to accept allotment and coupled its allotment policy
with provisions that contemplated the ultimate dissolution of the Indian tribe
and its reservation.

As summarized in D. Otis, *History of the Allotment Policy, Hearings on H.R. 7902 Before the House Committee on Indian Affairs,* 73d Cong., 2d Sess., pt. 9, at 428 (1934),* the chief provisions of the General Allotment Act of 1887 were:

(1) a grant of 160 acres to each family head, of 80 acres to each single person over 18 years of age and to each orphan under 18, and of 40 acres to each other single person under eighteen;

(2) a patent in fee to be issued to every allottee but to be held in trust by the Government for 25 years, during which time the land could not be alienated or encumbered;

(3) a period of 4 years to be allowed the Indians in which they should make their selections after allotment should be applied to any tribe — failure of the Indians to do so should result in selection for them at the order of the Secretary of the Interior;

(4) citizenship to be conferred upon allottees and upon any other Indians who had abandoned their tribes and adopted "the habits of civilized life."

Like the Trade and Intercourse Acts and the Removal Act, which preceded it, the General Allotment Act of 1887 only stated and authorized a general policy. Implementation of the policy was left to individual negotiations with the affected tribe and the discretion of the executive. Thus, allotment was not implemented on all reservations, and even on reservations on which it was implemented, the degree of penetration of the policy into the traditional tribal land holding arrangements varied considerably. Consequently, the remaining modern effects of the allotment policy are very uneven across Indian country. Some tribes, like the Hopi and New Mexico pueblos and most of the tribes east of the Mississippi, were untouched by allotment. The land base of many other tribes, however, was ravaged by allotment, and the checkerboard land ownership patterns produced by the policy made rational land management and governance much more difficult.

Section 6 of the Dawes General Allotment Act, codified as amended at 25 U.S.C. § 349, contemplated that the Indian allottees would be subjected to state law and jurisdiction at the expiration of the restraint on alienation or, as later amended, the completion of the allotment program on any particular reservation. Section 5 of the Act also contemplated that "surplus" land, not needed for the fixed-acreage allotments to tribal members, would be ceded to the federal government for compensation through negotiations with the tribe. Such lands were thereafter opened to non-Indian settlement under the public lands program. Thus, Indian reservations were opened to non-Indian settlement for the first time.

Allotment was supported by those in Congress who favored opening Indian lands to non-Indian development. It was also supported by many Indian agents and Indian rights associations throughout the country. The support of the program by eastern Indian rights advocates was evident at the Lake Mohonk Conference in 1889. These Indian rights supporters sought to protect the Indian in his land holding. The feeling was that an Indian holding a patent from the federal government, restricted against alienation, enjoyed greater security for his land tenure than the protection afforded by tribal possession. Additionally, the program held forth the vision that the Indian would acquire the bene-

---

*From *The Dawes Act and the Allotment of Indian Lands,* by D. S. Otis. New edition copyright 1973 by the University of Oklahoma Press. Reprinted by permission.

fits of civilization through the pursuit of sedentary agricultural life and would, therefore, abandon his "uncivilized," nomadic, hunting tribal culture. Of course, these paradigm extremes rarely existed in practice. Despite the fact that agriculture already formed an important ingredient of many tribal cultures, Congress approved the allotment program, over significant tribal opposition, based on these cultural stereotypes.

Senator Teller warned the Senate that within thirty or forty years the Indians would be dispossessed of their lands and would curse those who professedly spoke in their defense. The Creeks, Choctaws, and Cherokees warned that a change from communal title to individual title would concentrate ownership of Indian land, within a few years, in the hands of a few persons. Despite these predictions the allotment program authorized by the General Allotment Act was implemented by a series of agreements and statutes specifying the allotment process and ceding surplus lands on particular reservations. *See generally* KINNEY, A CONTINENT LOST — A CIVILIZATION WON (1937).

While the 1887 Act restrained alienation of allotted land for a twenty-five-year period, later legislation authorized the Secretary of the Interior to shorten this period, to make sales of allotted land, to approve the issuance of a patent upon the death of the allottee, or to otherwise remove the restraints on alienation and authorize sale on a finding that the Indian allottee was competent to manage his own affairs. *E.g.,* Act of May 29, 1908, ch. 216, 35 Stat. 444, codified at 25 U.S.C. § 404; Act of Mar. 1, 1907, ch. 2285, 34 Stat. 1018, codified at 25 U.S.C. § 405; Act of May 27, 1902, § 7, ch. 888, 32 Stat. 275, codified at 25 U.S.C. § 379. The Act of Mar. 2, 1907, ch. 2523, 34 Stat. 1221, codified at 25 U.S.C. §§ 119, 121, applied the allotment concept to tribal trust funds, authorizing the allotment of pro rata shares in tribal trust funds to Indians deemed competent to manage their own affairs. *See also* Act of May 25, 1918, ch. 86, § 25, 40 Stat. 561, codified at 25 U.S.C. § 162, repealed by Act of June 24, 1938, ch. 648, § 2, 52 Stat. 1037. Other statutes authorized allottees to dispose of their restricted property by will, requiring secretarial approval for such distributions, and provided a plan for the administration of allottees' estates. Act of June 25, 1910, ch. 431, 36 Stat. 855, codified in various sections of 25 U.S.C.

The individualization of Indian land tenure caused by allotment required provisions for the productive use of property where the allottee was unable to work the allotment. Thus, the Act of Feb. 28, 1891, ch. 383, 26 Stat. 794, authorized the leasing of allotted land whenever the Secretary found that the allottee by reason of age or other disability was unable to personally occupy and improve the allotment. The same statute also authorized the leasing of tribal lands under authority of the tribal council, subject to approval of the Secretary of the Interior. This Act began the surface leasing program for Indian lands. It was later supplemented by a host of statutes governing leasing of tribal and allotted lands both for surface occupancy and for mineral, oil, and gas development. *See* 25 U.S.C. § 415; Act of May 11, 1938, ch. 198, 52 Stat. 347, codified at 25 U.S.C. §§ 396a-396g; Act of Mar. 3, 1927, ch. 299, 44 Stat. 1347, codified at 25 U.S.C. §§ 398a-398d; Act of May 29, 1924, ch. 210, 43 Stat. 244, codified at 25 U.S.C. § 398. Most such later leasing legislation was not restricted to allotted lands held by minors or incompetents. Ultimately, the surface and mineral leasing programs expanded to cover the remaining tribally held lands.

Act of May 11, 1938, ch. 198, 52 Stat. 347, codified at 25 U.S.C. §§ 396a-396g; Act of Mar. 3, 1927, ch. 299, 44 Stat. 1347, codified as amended at 25 U.S.C. §§ 398a-398e; Act of July 3, 1926, ch. 787, 44 Stat. 894, codified as amended at 25 U.S.C. § 402a; Act of May 29, 1924, ch. 210, 43 Stat. 244, codified at 25 U.S.C. § 398; Act of June 30, 1919, ch. 4, 41 Stat. 31, codified as amended at 25 U.S.C. § 399. Other federal legislation enacted during this period authorized for the first time the sale of timber on Indian lands. Act of June 25, 1910, ch. 431, 36 Stat. 857, codified as amended at 25 U.S.C. §§ 406-07; Act of June 7, 1897, ch. 3, 30 Stat. 90, codified at 25 U.S.C. § 197; Act of Feb. 16, 1889, ch. 172, 25 Stat. 673, codified at 25 U.S.C. § 196. Collectively, these leasing and timber statutes of the allotment period partially restored to the American marketplace the Indian real estate interests that the restraints on alienation contained in the early Trade and Intercourse Acts had removed from market dealings.

As originally adopted, the General Allotment Act of 1887 did not apply to the tribes of the Indian Territory. Later legislation extended the act or special allotment provisions to these tribes and suspended the laws of the tribal governments in the Indian Territory as a prelude to the admission of the state of Oklahoma into the Union. See Act of Apr. 26, 1906, ch. 1876, 34 Stat. 137; Act of July 1, 1902, ch. 1375, 32 Stat. 716; Act of July 1, 1902, ch. 1362, 32 Stat. 641; Act of July 1, 1902, ch. 1361, 32 Stat. 636; Act of June 28, 1898, ch. 517, 30 Stat. 495; Act of Mar. 1, 1901, ch. 676, 31 Stat. 861. See also Cherokee Nation v. Hitchcock, 187 U.S. 294 (1902); Stephens v. Cherokee Nation, 174 U.S. 445 (1899). See generally F. COHEN, HANDBOOK OF FEDERAL INDIAN LAW ch. 14 (1982 ed.); A. DEBO, AND STILL THE WATERS RUN (1972).

During the allotment period the federal government also implemented a number of other policies designed to assimilate Indians forcibly and destroy their culture and tribal institutions. See generally H. FRITZ, THE MOVEMENT FOR INDIAN ASSIMILATION: 1860-1890 (1963); A. DEBO, A HISTORY OF THE INDIANS OF THE UNITED STATES 299-331 (1970). The most dramatic of these efforts involved the formation by the Indian Service of the Bureau Police and the Courts of Indian Offenses. These institutions were created under federal regulations never explicitly authorized by statute. They involved the employment by the Service of Indian tribal members to serve as police officers and judges for their reservations, thereby creating an alternative power structure to the traditional forms of governance followed by the tribe. The Code of Indian Offenses, the regulations implemented by the Bureau Police and the Courts of Indian Offenses, initially proscribed not only serious criminal behavior but also many traditional Indian cultural and religious practices, including destruction of an Indian's personal property at death, tribal dances, and the payment of compensation to a woman's family when she is married. See generally W. HAGAN, INDIAN POLICE AND JUDGES (1966). At the height of this program, in 1900, Courts of Indian Offenses were established on two-thirds of the Indian reservations. The effort to enforce the prohibition on tribal dances against the Sioux in order to suppress the Ghost Dance, a messianic native religious movement, produced the "Wounded Knee Massacre" in 1890 in which 146 Indians were killed by the Seventh Cavalry. See A. DEBO, A HISTORY OF THE INDIANS OF THE UNITED STATES 290-94 (1970).

Another product of this assimilationist era of federal Indian policy was the Act of June 2, 1924, ch. 233, 43 Stat. 253, which conferred United States citizenship on "all noncitizen Indians born within the territorial limits of the United States." This Act simplified a plethora of provisions in the General Allotment Act and various special allotment statutes and treaties that originally contemplated that Indian allottees would become citizens upon the completion of the allotment process or the expiration of the restraints on alienation.

As Senator Teller predicted in 1887, the implementation of the allotment policy did result in the dispossession of the Indians. During the period from 1887 to 1934, Indian land holdings were reduced by two-thirds, from 138 million acres to 48 million acres. Most of the land was lost when it was declared "surplus" (i.e., not needed for fixed acreage allotments to tribal members) and later opened to non-Indian settlement under the homesteading laws. Some of the Indian landbase, however, fell out of federal trust restraints after the 25-year restrictions on alienation expired or when the land was taken, sometimes illegally, at state forced tax sales or in mortgage foreclosure proceedings.

The Indian Reorganization Act Period (1934-1940)

If the General Allotment Act was the predominant piece of legislation representing the public attitude in the late nineteenth and early twentieth centuries, then the Indian Reorganization Act of 1934 (Wheeler-Howard Act), ch. 576, 48 Stat. 984, codified at 25 U.S.C. §§ 461-479, provides an important clue to the ripening consciousness of the twentieth century. By 1934, there was a sense that something very serious was wrong with the direction of federal policy based on the General Allotment Act and the principles that undergirded it. There was chaos where it had been implemented and uncertainty where it had not taken hold.

In 1928 the famous Meriam Report was issued, summarizing the failure of the federal policies followed since the late nineteenth century. The report, entitled "Problems of Indian Administration," scored the loss of land from Indian ownership that occurred partly as a consequence of implementing the General Allotment Act philosophy and called for many of the reforms that reached fruition in the Indian Reorganization Act. Federal policy generally, as expressed in the National Industrial Recovery Act, seemed to rely on the strengthening of private corporate institutions. Federal Indian policy reflected this trend. As the nineteenth century dream of homesteading as a general solution to economic problems faded, confidence in allotment as a technique for providing a secure economic basis for Indian families also diminished.

President Franklin Roosevelt's appointment of John Collier as Commissioner of Indian Affairs marked the emergence of a very different kind of consciousness, and a different way of using the land to produce what at the time was considered to be the road to civilization. *See Readjustment of Indian Affairs, Hearings on H.R. 7902 Before the House Committee on Indian Affairs,* 73d Cong., 2d Sess. (1934). Collier had a vision of new Native American governments emerging to take control of the destiny of Indian communities, thereby displacing the heavy hand of the Indian Service which, to Collier's thinking, had been responsible for the debacle of the allotment policy and which thereby had gained too large a role in the daily governance of Indian affairs. Collier's thinking put him at odds with both his own agency and with more conservative elements of Congress. He was therefore only able to get portions of his programs enacted into law in the form of the Indian Reorganization Act of 1934 (IRA). Cursory review of the provisions of the IRA reveals, however, that it marked a major departure from the Indian policies of the previous half-century.

Section 1 of the IRA, 25 U.S.C. § 461, ended further allotment by providing "No land of any Indian reservation, created or set apart by treaty or agreement with the Indians [shall] be allotted in severalty to any Indian." Section 2 of the Act indefinitely extended the existing periods of trust restrictions on Indian allotted land where such restrictions had not already expired. 25 U.S.C. § 462. Later legislation in 1948, however, did permit the Secretary of the Interior to authorize the issuance of patents in fee and the conveyance of Indian allotments on application of the Indian owners, thereby selectively removing the restrictions. Act of May 14, 1948, c. 293, 62 Stat. 236, codified at 25 U.S.C. § 483. In order to rebuild the tribal landbase and make the remaining Indian lands more compact and governable, sections 4 and 5 of the IRA authorized the Secretary of the Interior to exchange lands of equal value and to acquire lands by gift or purchase at a cost of two million dollars a year (an authorization that has never been fully implemented). 25 U.S.C. §§ 464-465. Under section 7 of the Act, 25 U.S.C. § 467, the Secretary was authorized to proclaim any new lands so acquired as additions to existing reservations or as new reservations, provided that the "lands added to existing reservations shall be designated for the exclusive use of Indians entitled by enrollment or by tribal membership to residence at such reservations." In order to facilitate the long-term productive management of Indian forests, section 6 of the IRA directed the Secretary to make rules for the operation of Indian forestry units "on the principle of sustained-yield management," rather than clear cutting, and to restrict the grazing of livestock on Indian grazing units to the estimated carrying capacity of such ranges. 25 U.S.C. § 466. Recognizing the impairment of economic development created by the inability of Indian tribes to mortgage their land, their most important asset, the IRA authorized grants for the creation of Indian business corporations or other business entities and established a revolving loan fund authorized, but not appropriated, at twenty million dollars. 25 U.S.C. §§ 469-470. It also established educational grants and created an Indian preference for all positions in the Indian Office. 25 U.S.C. §§ 471-472. By far the most important provisions of the IRA, however, were sections 16-18 of the Act, which authorized the Secretary to approve constitutions and corporate charters for Indian tribes seeking to organize under its provisions. 25 U.S.C. §§ 476-478. These provisions were the heart of Collier's plan to displace the Indian Service with new indigenous tribal governments, reviving the sense of tribal self-government and control of their own destinies of which the Indian tribes had been robbed by the allotment policy. Section 16 of the Act, 25 U.S.C. § 476, provided:

Organization of Indian tribes; constitution and bylaws; special election.

Any Indian tribe, or tribes, residing on the same reservation, shall have the right to organize for its common welfare, and may adopt an appropriate constitution and bylaws, which shall become effective when ratified by a majority vote of the adult members of the tribe, or of the adult Indians residing on such reservation, as the case may be, at a special election authorized and called by the Secretary of the Interior under such rules and regulations as he may prescribe. Such constitution and bylaws, when ratified as aforesaid and approved by the Secretary of the Interior, shall be revocable by an election open to the same voters and conducted in the same manner as hereinabove provided. Amendments to the constitution and bylaws may be ratified and approved by the Secretary in the same manner as the original constitution and bylaws.

In addition to all powers vested in any Indian tribe or tribal council by existing law, the constitution adopted by said tribe shall also vest in such tribe or its tribal council the following rights and powers: To employ legal counsel, the choice of counsel and fixing of fees to be subject to the approval of the Secretary of the Interior; to prevent the sale, disposition, lease, or encumbrance of tribal lands, interests in lands, or other tribal assets without the consent of the tribe; and to negotiate with the Federal, State, and local Governments. The Secretary of the Interior shall advise such tribe or its tribal council of all appropriation estimates or Federal projects for the benefit of the tribe prior to the submission of such estimates to the Bureau of the Budget and the Congress.

Reflecting the duality between the public and private sectors in non-Indian American society, section 17 of the Act, 25 U.S.C. § 477, also authorized the Secretary to recognize charters of incorporation of tribal business corporations, a separation of governmental and business functions of the tribal community that was and remains alien to most tribes. Consistent with the democratic traditions of American society, section 18 of the IRA called for an election at which a majority of the adult members of the tribe would vote to take advantage of its provisions. 25 U.S.C. § 478. While this provision probably was originally intended only for purposes of the provisions of the Act dealing with the formation of constitutions and by-laws for tribal governments and charters of incorporation for tribal business entities, through a quirk of ill-considered draftsmanship this section applied to the entirety of the Act, including the provisions ending the allotment policy. Finally, in order to define those eligible for the benefits provided under the Act, including the Indian preference for employment with the Indian Service, section 19 of the Act, 25 U.S.C. § 479, contained a comprehensive definition of the term "Indian" which was in part keyed to tribal membership requirements established by the tribes themselves:

> The term "Indian" as used in [the IRA] shall include all persons of Indian descent who are members of any recognized Indian tribe now under Federal jurisdiction, and all persons who are descendents of such members who were, on June 1, 1934, residing within the present boundaries of any Indian reservation, and shall further include all other persons of one-half or more Indian blood. For the purposes of said sections, Eskimos and other aboriginal peoples of Alaska shall be considered Indians.

This section also defined an adult Indian eligible to vote in the elections provided for in section 18 as one who has attained the age of 21 years. The Act of June 15, 1935, ch. 260, 49 Stat. 378, codified at 25 U.S.C. §§ 478a-478b, amended the IRA to provide that only a majority of those actually voting in an IRA election, rather than an absolute majority of the entire adult tribal membership rolls, was needed to approve acceptance of the IRA. A total of 258 tribal elections were held in which 181 tribes then comprising 129,750 Indians accepted the Act and 77 tribes encompassing 86,365 Indians rejected it (including the 45,000 member Navajo nation). Another fourteen groups did not hold elections to exclude themselves. Within twelve years after the adoption of the Act, 161 tribal constitutions and 131 tribal corporate charters had been drafted and approved under the provisions of the IRA. For tribes that voted to exclude themselves from the coverage of the Act, all provisions of the Act, including those extending the trust periods on allotments, were not applicable. Such extensions, however, have been made by subsequent executive order. *See* Gilbert & Taylor, *Indian Land Questions,* 8 Ariz. L. Rev. 102, 113 (1967). *See generally* 25 C.F.R. app. (1980) (collecting relevant executive orders). The Navajo tribe was later reorganized under the Navajo Rehabilitation Act of 1950, ch. 92, 64 Stat. 44.

Since the provisions of section 16 of the IRA regarding tribal reorganization applied to "any Indian tribe, or tribes, residing on the same reservation," they were inapplicable to most of the tribes in Oklahoma whose reservations had been extinguished near the turn of the century. As a result, Congress enacted the Oklahoma Indian Welfare Act of 1936, ch. 831, 49 Stat. 1967, codified at 25 U.S.C. § 501 et seq., which authorized the Oklahoma tribes to organize for their common welfare and to adopt business charters like the IRA tribes. Like the IRA, the Oklahoma Act also authorized the Secretary to acquire real property interests in trust for the tribes.

During the Depression Indian tribes also benefitted greatly from New Deal programs of general application that were aimed at economic rehabilitation. These programs caused a significant infusion of new resources and funds into Indian reservations. This fact ironically made the Depression years some of the most prosperous times reservation Indians had known. *See* A. Debo, A History of Indians in the United States 342-48 (1970). The effects of the IRA on tribal sovereignty are discussed further in Chapter 3, section B1.

The Termination Era (1940-1962)

The explicit ideological nature of the Indian Reorganization Act provoked considerable debate, much of it after passage of the law. Hearings began during the 1940's which signaled a potential shift away from the protection of Indian autonomy sought by the IRA, even before the Act was fully implemented. The indictment levelled against the IRA is evident from the following excerpt from Hearings on S. 2103 Before the Committee on Indian Affairs, H.R. 76th Cong., 3d Sess. (1940):

A summary of the evidence in various forms brought to the attention of your committee seems to reveal the following: ...

2. Witnesses supporting the bills for repeal of the act were unanimous in their statements that [the Indians] were high pressured into accepting the act and adopting the constitutions and charters under authority of the act; that all local agency officials and Indians employed on work-relief projects were ordered to campaign actively for the act and that, under threat of losing their positions, they did so campaign; that officials of the Washington office of the Indian Bureau and Indians from other reservations were brought into local areas to campaign and that Indians both from outside and within the local areas were paid a salary and traveling expenses for campaigning; that the Civil Service Commission has held that it cannot take action against Bureau employees who campaigned in these various elections because of authority conferred upon the Secretary of the Interior under the so-called Wheeler-Howard Act; that meetings were held with the Indians and they were promised practically unlimited

credit to borrow money for industrial and agricultural purposes, for home, education, and other purposes; that Indians were promised self-government and lands which were to be purchased by the United States Government; that the elections had not been carried out by secret ballot as provided for in the act; and that in all the campaigns and the conduct of the elections, the press, the radio, the franking privilege of the Indian Bureau, Government cars, gas and oil, publications, and other Government facilities were freely used....

6. That individual rights of inheritance, private ownership of property, and private enterprise are being discouraged and destroyed by reason of some provisions of the act itself and the administration of the act.

7. That all efforts tend to force the Indians back into a primitive state; that tribal ceremonials, native costumes and customs, and languages are being both encouraged and promoted in the administration of this act; that the educational program of the Bureau of Indian Affairs has been revised to accomplish this purpose in place of the regular school courses in white schools.

8. That the act is not administered in such a manner as to provide the self-government which was promised to the Indians, but provides for more mandatory power for the Secretary of the Interior, and the program under the act has destroyed the self-governing rights which had previously been enjoyed. The constitutions prepared by the Indian Bureau officials for adoption by the Indians were so filled with the impositions of the Department that there was little room for the ideas of the Indians, yet the constitutions were supposed to be Indian made. They provide for the reference of everything of importance to the Secretary of the Interior.

9. That generally the officers elected by the Indians when organizations are set up by virtue of the provisions of the so-called Wheeler-Howard Act, are, or become, employed by some Government agency supervised by the Indian Bureau, or some other governmental function, and in the selection of lands and in the extension of credits, many of such tribal officers have secured advantages through their positions and in some cases advantages have been secured through fraud and malfeasance.

10. That the Indians were told that the act provided a means of repeal if they did not like it, yet not a tribe has yet been allowed to vote on repeal though some of them have presented petition after petition. In reply to such petitions they are told to revise their constitutions and that if they could not, they might vote on repeal.

11. That chaotic conditions prevail, due either to the administration of the act or to legal complications which resulted from the application of the act to certain tribes, that individual initiative of the Indians is being destroyed, that no progress is being made; that conditions generally are worse, and great unhappiness, confusion, and despair among the Indians have resulted.

Arguments advanced against the Wheeler-Howard Act in general, can be summarized as follows:

1. Acceptance of the act changed the status of the Indians from that of involuntary wardship to voluntary wardship.

2. The act provides for continued wardship of the Indians and gives the Secretary of the Interior increased authority.

3. The act is contrary to the established policy of the Congress of the United States to eventually grant the full rights of citizenship to the Indians.

4. The act provides for only one form of government for the Indians, viz, a communal government, with all property, real and personal, held in common; and it compels the Indians to live in communities segregated from the rest of American citizens.

5. The act itself and the administration of the act violates the rights of citizenship which the Indians have won through long years of efforts.

6. That the Indians prefer to be under the jurisdiction of the laws of the respective States where they reside.

Conclusion

Fundamentally the so-called Wheeler-Howard Act attempts to set up a state or a nation within a nation which is contrary to the intents and purposes of the American

Republic. No doubt but that the Indians should be helped and given every assistance possible but in no way should they be set up as a governing power within the United States of America. They shall be permitted to have a part in their own affairs as to government in the same way as any domestic organization exists within a State or Commonwealth but not to be independent or apart therefrom.

While the Indian Reorganization Act of 1934 survived such legislative attacks, these hearings inaugurated a new and very different era in Indian relations begun during the 1940's. During this period the notion of tribal sovereignty and the separate jurisdictional status of the reservations again came under attack. The legislative output of this decade was, however, relatively modest. Various statutes were enacted throughout the decade subjecting certain specific tribes or tribes in designated states to state jurisdiction. *See* Act of Oct. 5, 1949, ch. 604, 63 Stat. 705 (civil and criminal jurisdiction over the Agua Caliente Reservation in California); Act of June 30, 1948, ch. 759, 62 Stat. 1161 (Sac and Fox Reservation in Iowa); Act of May 31, 1946, ch. 279, 60 Stat. 229 (Devils Lake Reservation in North Dakota); Act of June 8, 1940, ch. 276, 54 Stat. 249, codified at 18 U.S.C. § 3243 (all reservations in Kansas). *See generally Youngbear v. Brewer,* 415 F. Supp. 807 (N.D. Iowa 1976), *aff'd,* 549 F.2d 74 (8th Cir. 1977); *State v. Lohnes,* 69 N.W.2d 508 (N.D. 1955). The most pervasive of these statutes were enacted in 1948 and 1952 and granted criminal and civil jurisdiction, respectively, to the state of New York over all reservations within the state. Act of Sept. 13, 1950, ch. 947, § 1, 64 Stat. 845, codified at 25 U.S.C. § 233; Act of July 2, 1948, ch. 809, 62 Stat. 1224, codified at 25 U.S.C. § 232. *See generally People v. Edwards,* 64 N.Y.2d 658, 474 N.E.2d 612, 485 N.Y.S.2d 252 (1984); *George v. Tax Appeals Tribunal,* 548 N.Y.S.2d 66 (App. Div. 1989); *Deloronde v. New York State Tax Comm'n,* 142 A.D.2d 90, 535 N.Y.S.2d 209 (1988); *New York v. Anderson,* 137 A.D.2d 259, 529 N.Y.S.2d 917 (1988); *Oneida Indian Nation of New York v. Burr,* 132 A.D.2d 402, 522 N.Y.S.2d 742 (1987).

In 1949 the Hoover Commission, a commission appointed to review executive branch reorganization, issued a report on Indian affairs. The report called for the total assimilation of the Indians "into the mass of the population as full, tax-paying citizens." COMMISSION ON ORGANIZATION OF THE EXECUTIVE BRANCH OF GOVERNMENT: INDIAN AFFAIRS: A REPORT TO CONGRESS 77-80 (1949). The report began a momentum toward a policy of federal termination that culminated in the 1950's, reaching its peak in 1953. In that year Congress passed House Concurrent Resolution 108 on August 1, 1953. HCR 108 provided:

Whereas it is the policy of Congress, as rapidly as possible to make the Indians within the territorial limits of the United States subject to the same laws and entitled to the same privileges and responsibilities as are applicable to other citizens of the United States, and to grant them all the rights and prerogatives pertaining to American citizenship; and

Resolved by the House of Representatives (the Senate Concurring), That it is declared to be the sense of Congress that, at the earliest possible time, all of the Indian tribes and the individual members thereof located within the States of California, Florida, New York, and Texas, and all of the following named Indian tribes and individual members thereof, should be freed from Federal supervision and control and from all disabilities and limitations specially applicable to Indians: The Flathead Tribe of Montana, the Klamath Tribe of Oregon, the Menominee Tribe of Wisconsin, the Potowatamie Tribe of Kansas and Nebraska, and those members of the Chippewa Tribe who are on the Turtle Mountain Reservation, North Dakota. It is further declared to be the sense of Congress that the Secretary of the Interior should examine all existing legislation dealing with such Indians, and treaties between the Government of the United States and each such tribe, and report to Congress at the earliest practicable date, but not later than January 1, 1954, his recommendations for such legislation as, in his judgment, may be necessary to accomplish the purposes of this resolution.

The Congress thereafter set about providing in separate statutes for the winding up of the affairs of various designated tribes and for their termination from federal supervision, from eligibility for federal benefits, and from coverage under federal Indian laws. At the end of this process the terminated tribes were to be fully subjected to state authority. *E.g.,* Act of Aug. 13, 1954, ch. 732, 68 Stat. 718, codified at 25 U.S.C. § 564 et seq. (Klamath); Act of June 17, 1954, ch. 303, 68 Stat. 250 (Menominee); Act of Aug. 13, 1954, ch. 733, 68 Stat. 724, codified at 25 U.S.C. § 691 et seq. (tribes of Western Oregon).

In each case the termination statute mandated the preparation of a termination plan that frequently took some time. Thus, the last termination plan, that of the Ponca, did not take effect until 1966. All other affected tribes were terminated by 1962. In all, approximately 109 tribes and bands were terminated. Over 1,362,155 acres of reservation land were affected, as were 11,466 tribal members. It has been estimated that 3% of all federally managed Indians and 3.2% of the total trust land were involved in these termination statutes. *See generally* Wilkinson & Biggs, *The Evolution of the Termination Policy,* 5 Am. Indian L. Rev. 139 (1977); Herzberg, *The Menominee Indians: Termination to Restoration,* 5 Am. Indian L. Rev. 143 (1978); Felsanthal & Preloznik, *The Menominee Struggle to Maintain Their Tribal Assets and Protect Their Treaty Rights Following Termination,* 51 N.D.L. Rev. 53 (1974).

During the termination period Congress also adopted a statute, commonly known as Public Law 280, which operated for affected reservations to transfer the jurisdiction over crimes and civil causes of action previously exercised by federal and tribal courts to state authorities. Act of August 15, 1953, ch. 505, 67 Stat. 588, codified in part at 18 U.S.C. § 1162 and 28 U.S.C. § 1360. This statute was essentially a halfway measure short of termination for tribes not yet ready for or objecting to complete termination of federal supervision. As originally enacted it mandatorily transferred jurisdiction to the states over all reservations in California, Minnesota (except the Red Lake Reservation), Nebraska, Oregon (except the Warm Springs Reservation), and Wisconsin (except the Menominee Reservation). It also authorized all other states to assume voluntarily complete or partial civil and criminal jurisdiction over other Indian reservations within the states. Alaska was later added to the list of states affected by the mandatory provisions of the Act when it was admitted to statehood. This important statute is discussed in greater detail in Chapter 4, section C1.

As part of the programs of the 1950's aimed at Indian assimilation, the Bureau of Indian Affairs set up a relocation program to encourage and assist reservation Indians to move to the cities. Once relocated, however, the BIA's responsibility for the urban Indian ceased. This program greatly contributed to the growth of urban Indian communities in Los Angeles, Minneapolis, Seattle, Chicago, Phoenix, and elsewhere after World War II.

The Self-Determination Era (1962-Present)

While many of the termination plans took effect in the early 1960's, this decade witnessed few new departures in federal Indian policy. On the other hand, during this period it was clear that the support for termination had waned. It was a period for regrouping and rethinking in the arena of Indian affairs. President Kennedy promised the Indians that "[t]here would be no change in treaty or contractual relationships without the consent of the tribes concerned. No steps would be taken to impair the cultural heritage of any group. [There also] would be protection for the Indian land lease ...." Kennedy's Secretary of the Interior, Stewart L. Udall, said of HCR 108 that it had "died with the 83rd Congress and is of no legal effect at the present time." A. DEBO, A HISTORY OF THE INDIANS OF THE UNITED STATES 405 (1970).

During the 1960's the long-unresolved problems of the Alaskan natives and their aboriginal claims to substantial portions of the state surfaced. Secretary of the Interior Udall ordered a halt to state selections of the public domain under the Alaska Statehood Act and all other dispositions of federal land until Congress could resolve the Alaskan native claims to the affected property. *Id.* at 383-404. This action, coupled with the requirement of the nation for a pipeline from Prudhoe Bay, galvanized a bargaining process between the affected interests that led to the enactment of the Alaska Native Claims Settlement Act of 1971 ("ANCSA"), Pub. L. No. 92-203, 85 Stat. 688, codified at 43 U.S.C. § 1601 et seq.

ANCSA awarded the Alaskan natives fee title to over forty million acres of land, federal payments of $462.5 million over an eleven-year period, and a royalty of two percent to a ceiling of $500 million on mineral development in Alaska in exchange for the extinguishment of their aboriginal claims to land in the state. The Act also organized the Alaskan natives into thirteen regional corporations, incorporated under state law, and various village corporations. It implemented the settlement "without establishing any permanent racially defined institutions, rights, privileges, or obligations, without creating a reservation system or lengthy wardship or trusteeship, and without adding to the categories of property and institutions engaging special tax privileges ...." 43 U.S.C. § 1601(b).

The 1960's were a period of often turbulent revitalization of tribal entities and improvement of conditions on Indian reservations. The Indian tribes benefited from many of the War on Poverty programs of the Johnson administration and new policy initiatives were frequently undertaken at the tribal level. *See generally* A. DEBO, A HISTORY OF THE INDIANS OF THE UNITED STATES 405-22 (1970). *See also* Address by President Lyndon Johnson to Congress, "The Forgotten American" (Mar. 6, 1968), reprinted in PUBLIC PAPERS OF THE PRESIDENTS 1968-1969, at 335 (1970).

Two important pieces of Indian legislation were passed during the 1960's. In the Act of Oct. 10, 1966, Pub. L. No. 89-635, § 1, 80 Stat. 880, codified at 28 U.S.C. § 1362, Congress authorized any Indian tribe or land with a governing body duly recognized by the Secretary of the Interior to file suit in federal district court without reference to amount in controversy for cases arising under the Constitution, law, and treaties of the United States. By this simple statute Congress placed the general capacity of an Indian tribe to sue on a clear statutory footing and thereby set the stage for the commencement during the 1970's of many cases brought by tribes involving land, hunting and fishing rights, and other claims that previously had been overlooked or not aggressively enforced by the federal government. Second, in 1968 Congress enacted the Indian Civil Rights Act of 1968, Pub. L. No. 90-284, 82 Stat. 77, codified in part at 25 U.S.C. § 1301 et seq. This legislation was the culmination of nearly a decade of Senate hearings on the civil rights of Indians. Among other things, the Act: (1) required all Indian tribes in exercising their self-governing powers to observe and protect most, but not all, of the guarantees of the Bill of Rights, the fourteenth amendment, and Article 1, section 10 of the Constitution; (2) amended Public Law 280 to require tribal consent for all future state acquisitions of jurisdiction over an Indian reservation; (3) authorized the federal courts to exercise habeas corpus jurisdiction to review tribal convictions; (4) provided for state-initiated retrocession to the federal government of jurisdiction previously acquired by the states under Public Law 280; and (5) mandated the preparation of a model code governing courts of Indian offenses and the revision and updating of *Felix Cohen's Handbook of Federal Indian Law** and other collections of primary Indian resource materials. The Indian Civil Rights Act is discussed in further detail in Chapter 3, section C.

In 1970 President Nixon served notice in a message to Congress that he intended to steer a policy course designed to strengthen tribal sovereignty, transfer control of Indian programs from federal to tribal governments, restore and protect the Indian land base, and forever declare an end to involuntary tribal termination. Message from the President of the United States Transmitting Recommendations for Indian Policy, H.R. Doc. No. 363, 91st Cong., 2d Sess. (1970). This message represented the single strongest statement to date by the federal government supporting the strengthening of tribal sovereignty and control while advocating protection of the Indian land base and resources. The statement also advocated the encouragement of economic development of Indian lands, particularly the facilitation of leasing of Indian resources. The potential inconsistency between the tribal sovereignty and control over the Indian reservation and the impacts caused by extensive leasing of Indian lands for non-Indian controlled economic development was not noted, although this tension became a major theme in Indian economic development during the decade.

The Nixon message set the legislative agenda for Congress in the field of Indian affairs for the entire decade. It thus ushered in one of the most productive periods for the enactment of statutes affecting Indian tribes. Some of this legislation affected only particular tribes. For example, the Menominee Tribe of Minnesota, the Siletz tribe of Oregon, the Wyandotte, Peoria, Ottawa, and Modoc Tribes of Oklahoma, and others were restored to federal recognition and supervision in 1973, 1977, and 1978, respectively, after having been terminated by legislation in the 1950's. Pub. L. 95-281, 92 Stat. 246, codified at 25 U.S.C. § 861 et seq. (Wyandotte, Peoria, Ottawa, and Modoc Tribes); Siletz Indian Tribe Restoration Act, Pub. L. No. 95-195, 91 Stat. 1415, codified at 25 U.S.C. § 711 et seq.; Menominee Restoration Act, Pub. L. No. 93-197, 87 Stat. 770, codified at 25 U.S.C. § 903 et seq. The pathbreaking Alaska Native Claims Settlement Act was passed, as already noted, in 1971.

---

*After considerable delay by the Department of the Interior a group of academics and practicing attorneys ultimately revised this classic Indian law treatise. *See* F. COHEN, HANDBOOK OF FEDERAL INDIAN LAW (1982 ed.).

Indian title to submarginal lands first allocated to tribal use under various New Deal programs of the 1930's was perfected by the Act of Oct. 17, 1975, Pub. L. No. 94-114, 89 Stat. 577, codified at 25 U.S.C. § 459 et seq. The Taos Pueblo was restored to ownership of Blue Lake, a sacred spot in tribal culture. Act of Dec. 15, 1970, Pub. L. No. 91-550, 84 Stat. 1437.

In the category of Indian laws of general application, the two most important pieces of legislation to emerge during the decade were the Indian Self-Determination and Education Assistance Act of 1975, Pub. L. No. 93-638, 88 Stat. 2203 (codified at 25 U.S.C. § 450a and elsewhere in titles 25, 42, and 50, U.S.C. app.), and the Indian Child Welfare Act of 1978, Pub. L. No. 95-608, 92 Stat. 3069, (codified at 25 U.S.C. § 1901 et seq.). The Indian Self-Determination Act was aimed at strengthening tribal governmental control over federally funded programs for Indians, including programs for educational assistance to local school districts. The heart of the statute is contained in two parallel provisions, 25 U.S.C. §§ 450f and 450g, authorizing the Secretary of the Interior and the Secretary of Health, Education, and Welfare (now Health and Human Services), under whose auspices the Indian Health Service and certain Indian educational programs were administered, to contract with Indian tribes for the formation, implementation, and administration of federally funded Indian programs. Other provisions of the 1975 Act, together with the Indian Education Act of 1972, Pub. L. No. 92-318, tit. IV, 86 Stat. 339 (codified at 20 U.S.C. § 3385), sought to increase Indian political control over federal programs of assistance for Indian education to public school systems.

The Indian Child Welfare Act of 1978 was designed to maximize tribal jurisdiction and to reduce the exercise of state jurisdiction in child custody or adoption proceedings involving Indian children who were tribal members or eligible for membership in a tribe. It also provided rigorous standards limiting state court intervention in such cases and requiring state authorities to attempt to place an Indian child needing placement in the home of an extended family member, the home of a tribal member, a tribal group home, or an Indian home before the child could be placed with a non-Indian family. The Act further provided for tribal intervention in such state custody proceedings and authorized federally funded programs to support tribal efforts to supervise and provide facilities for tribal children in need of placements.

In addition to these laws, the 1970's brought new federal legislation to strengthen and reorganize a federal revolving loan fund for Indian economic development and to provide federal loan guarantees for private-sector loans to support such development (25 U.S.C. § 1451 et seq.), to improve Indian health care services (25 U.S.C. § 1601 et seq.), to improve and increase tribal input into education programs of the BIA (25 U.S.C. § 2001 et seq.), and to establish and fund tribally controlled community colleges (25 U.S.C. § 1801 et seq.).

This rash of legislation — together with very visible Indian litigation initiatives and successes over fishing rights in the Pacific Northwest and the Great Lakes, water rights in the West, and tribal claims to land in the Northeast — generated some non-Indian resentment and new political efforts to alter federal Indian policy. The lack of consensus on the policy issue first emerged when the American Indian Policy Review Commission, established by Congress in 1975 (25 U.S.C. § 174), delivered its final report to Congress on May 17, 1977. AMER-

ICAN INDIAN POLICY REVIEW COMMISSION, FINAL REPORT (1977). This report generally recommended a continuation of the federal policy of protecting and strengthening tribal governments as permanent governmental units in the federal system. It disparaged assimilationist policies and proposals and called for reevaluation of the federal commitment to over 132 terminated and nonrecognized Indian tribes. The report called for increased financial support for tribal economic development and social and economic programs for tribal members. This strong reaffirmation for a policy of federal protection of Indian self-determination, while approved by the other members of the Commission, was criticized by Congressman Lloyd Meeds of Washington, the Vice-Chairman of the Commission and the former Chairman of the House Indian Affairs Subcommittee. He dissented, arguing that the Commission had given too broad a scope to the concept of tribal government, fearing that tribal governments would "hold sway over the lives and fortunes of many who have no representation in the governing body which makes decisions affecting their lives." *Id.* at 611.

After 1977, the political momentum for a fundamental change in the direction of federal Indian policy became intense. Organized political groups, like Montanans Opposed to Discrimination and the Interstate Congress for Equal Rights and Responsibilities, unsuccessfully lobbied Congress to extinguish Indian rights and force Indian assimilation. Others in Congress sought to go beyond Congressman Meeds's call for a limited reevaluation of Indian law and policy. In 1977 H.R.J. Res. 1 was proposed to limit Indian treaty hunting and fishing rights. Then Congressman Cunningham of Washington introduced H.R. 13329, 95th Cong., 2d Sess. (1978), Orwellianly entitled the Native Americans Equal Opportunity Act. If enacted, this bill would have, *inter alia,* directed the President within one year to abrogate all treaties entered into by the United States with Indians, terminated federal supervision over the property and rights of all Indian tribes, fully subjected all Indians to state jurisdiction, compelled Indian tribes to distribute certain tribal assets on a per capita basis to their members, eliminated the restraints on alienation and tax immunities enjoyed by tribal lands, and abrogated treaty-protected Indian hunting and fishing rights. While none of these bills was approved by Congress, the future of federal Indian policy remains in flux. *See generally* Clinton, *Isolated in Their Own Country: A Defense of Federal Protection of Indian Autonomy and Self-Government,* 33 STAN. L. REV. 979 (1981); Wilkinson, *Shall the Islands Be Preserved?,* 41 AM. W. 32 (1979).

The 1980's marked an important transitional period both for federal Indian policy and for tribal self-sufficiency. Increasing focus on general federal budget deficits resulted in persistent, and often unsuccessful, executive efforts during President Reagan's administration to reduce the funding of many federal programs targeted for Indians, to merge such specialized federal Indian programs into more general, often state administered, social services and benefits programs, or to eliminate federal funding altogether. Such trends were most evident in proposals to curtail funding for Indian housing programs and other proposals to radically alter the administrative structure and funding for the provision of medical services previously provided through the Indian Health Service. Since many of the tribes had assumed some responsibility under the

Indian Self-Determination Act of 1976 for the administration of many of the federally funded programs, some suggested that these trends represented a new age of creeping termination through the cessation of federal funding.

The federal budget reductions in Indian service programs and the simultaneous growth and strengthening of many tribal governments during the 1980's increasing directed focus on tribal economic development and self-sufficiency during the decade. In 1983, President Reagan issued a Statement on Indian Policy in which the federal protection of Indian tribal self-government was reaffirmed and Indian tribes were called upon to assume a greater fiscal role in providing governmental services and programs to tribal members through economic development and taxation. The statement indicated that "[i]t is important to the concept of self-government that tribes reduce their dependence on Federal funds by providing a greater percentage of the cost of their self-government." 1 PUBLIC PAPERS OF THE PRESIDENTS OF THE UNITED STATES: RONALD REAGAN, 1983, at 96, 97 (1984). The policy statement called for extensive economic development of reservation economies to support such fiscal tribal self-sufficiency. As part of this statement, President Reagan announced the formation of a Commission on Indian Reservation Economies. This commission issued its final report in November, 1984. Presidential Commission on Indian Reservation Economies, REPORT AND RECOMMENDATIONS TO THE PRESIDENT OF THE UNITED STATES (1984). While the report called for the formal rejection of the termination policy by repeal of the termination resolution which initiated the policy in 1953, it also contained many features that some tribal leaders viewed as a return to the thinking that produced the assimilationist allotment and termination policies. Chief among these features was a call for the privatization of reservation economies by removing the control of reservation economic development programs from tribal governments and enterprises and through the development of Indian reservation land by privately owned Indian corporations, partnerships, and sole proprietorships. The report was seriously criticized by many tribal governmental leaders and has not directly resulted in any successful legislative changes.

The major Indian legislation enacted during the 1980's also generally reflected the prominent focus on economic development of Indian reservations during this period. In the Indian Tribal Government Tax Status Act of 1982, Pub. L. 97-473, 96 Stat. 2608, partially codified at 26 U.S.C. § 7871, Indian tribes were extended many of the tax advantages that were already enjoyed by state and local governments, including deductibility for charitable contributions for tribal government, various federal tax exemptions, and limited authority to issue tax exempt tribal bonds. The Indian Mineral Development Act of 1982, Pub. L. 97-382, codified at 25 U.S.C. §§ 2101-2108, authorized the Secretary of the Interior to approve various types of mineral development agreements involving Indian tribes and their lands, including joint ventures and operating, production sharing, and service agreements, thereby freeing Indian mineral development from the primary reliance on the leasing of Indian mineral resources to non-Indian development firms that had marked the preceding laws. The Indian Land Consolidation Act of 1982, Pub. L. 97-459, 96 Stat. 2517, codified at 25 U.S.C. §§ 2201-2211, sought to remedy some of the vestigial effects of allotment by authorizing tribes to establish plans for land consolidation on heavily allotted, checkerboarded reservations, by affording tribes some control over the descent and distribution of allotted land, and by providing an escheat mechanism, the initial version of which was later declared unconstitutional, by which small, unproductive interests in allotted land might escheat to the tribe. The Indian Gaming Regulatory Act of 1988, Pub. L. 100-497, 102 Stat. 2467, created the Indian Gaming Commission to regulate the emerging Indian gaming operations that became a substantial source of tribal revenues during the 1980's.

NOTE: HISTORY, FEDERAL INDIAN POLICY, AND STATUTORY INTERPRETATION

The rate of change in federal Indian policy objectives has accelerated greatly in the last half-century. The period of allotment gave way to renewed protection of tribal autonomy in the Indian Reorganization Act of 1934. Federal protection of Indian tribal self-government, however, was quickly replaced by efforts to assimilate Indians into the social and legal mainstream of American society during the 1940's and 1950's. These efforts included enactment of Public Law 280 and a host of statutes terminating federal supervision over certain Indian tribes. Termination soon yielded in the late 1960's and the 1970's to renewed efforts to foster Indian tribal government and autonomy, including the Indian Self-Determination and Educational Assistance Act of 1975 and the Indian Child Welfare Act of 1978. As one federal policy gave way to another, statutes enacted during a prior period generally were not repealed. Rather, litigation regarding statutes enacted under a subsequently discarded Indian policy continued to crop up in the courts. How should the courts respond to such legal questions? Should they enforce the intent of the Congress that enacted the statute and ignore the subsequent shift in federal Indian policy or should they attempt to construe the statute in light of the subsequent changes in congressional policy?

This question repeatedly has arisen in construing Public Law 280 since most litigation over this termination-era statute has arisen after termination was abandoned in favor of renewed federal efforts to foster tribal autonomy. In *Bryan v. Itasca County*, 426 U.S. 373 (1976), set forth and discussed in Chapter 4, a unanimous Supreme Court narrowly construed the scope of civil jurisdiction committed to the states under Public Law 280, relying in part on congressional statements made in 1968 when the jurisdictional allocation schemes created by Public Law 280 were modified, consistently with then-prevailing federal policy of fostering tribal self-determination, to require tribal consent as a condition of further state assumptions of jurisdiction. *Cf. Menominee Tribe v. United States*, 391 U.S. 404 (1968). By contrast, in *Washington v. Confederated Bands & Tribes of Yakima Indian Nation*, 439 U.S. 463, 488 (1979), another case construing aspects of Public Law 280 also set forth and discussed in more detail in Chapter 4, the Court relied instead exclusively on the intent of the framers of the act: "Public Law 280 was the first jurisdictional bill of general applicability ever to be enacted by Congress. [It also was] without question reflective of the general assimilationist policy followed by Congress from the early 1950's through the late 1960's." *Id.* at 488. While the Court noted that later congressional actions might be inconsistent with its construction, it paid them no heed in construing the statute. Which approach represents a sounder effort at statutory construction? Does the approach proposed in *Bryan* obfuscate the original intent of the framers of the legislation? Will the methodology advanced by the Court in *Confederated Bands & Tribes of Yakima Indian Nation* frustrate current congressional Indian policy? What role should a court assume in this context? The complexity of such legal questions, together with the oscillation of federal policy objectives in the field of Indian affairs, helps account for the intricacy of a number of issues in federal Indian law.

D. AN INTERNATIONAL RESPONSE TO THE RIGHTS OF INDIGENOUS PEOPLES: A BROADER PERSPECTIVE

While in-depth consideration of the international protections of the rights of indigenous peoples and the comparative national responses to the problem is left to a later chapter, placing the protection of the rights of indigenous peoples in an international perspective highlights the global dimensions of federal Indian law. Accordingly, the 1989 International Labour Organisation Convention Concerning Indigenous and Tribal Peoples in Independent Countries, the major recent international convention directly addressing the rights of indigenous peoples, is presented here to provide an international policy benchmark against which to measure the federal Indian policies set forth in the remainder of the book. Since the United States is *not* signatory to the Convention, the Convention is not *legally* binding on the federal government. Rather, the Convention and its proposed amendments are suggestive of world public opinion on the treatment of indigenous populations.

THE CONVENTION CONCERNING INDIGENOUS AND TRIBAL PEOPLES IN INDEPENDENT COUNTRIES, 1989

The General Conference of the International Labour Organisation,

Having been convened at Geneva by the Governing Body of the International Labour Office, and having met in its 76th Session on 7 June 1989, and

Noting the international standards contained in the Indigenous and Tribal Populations Convention and Recommendation, 1957, and

Recalling the terms of the Universal Declaration of Human Rights, the International Covenant on Economic, Social and Cultural Rights, the International Covenant on Civil and Political Rights, and the many international instruments on the prevention of discrimination, and

Considering that the developments which have taken place in international law since 1957, as well as developments in the situation of indigenous and tribal peoples in all regions of the world, have made it appropriate to adopt new international standards on the subject with a view to removing the assimilationist orientation of the earlier standards, and

Recognising the aspirations of these peoples to exercise control over their own institutions, ways of life and economic development and to maintain and develop their identities, languages and religions, within the framework of the States in which they live, and

Noting that in many parts of the world these peoples are unable to enjoy their fundamental human rights to the same degree as the rest of the population of the States within which they live, and that their laws, values, customs and perspectives have often been eroded, and

Calling attention to the distinctive contributions of indigenous and tribal peoples to the cultural diversity and social and ecological harmony of humankind and to international co-operation and understanding, and

Noting that the following provisions have been framed with the co-operation of the United Nations, the Food and Agriculture Organisation of the United Nations, the United Nations Educational, Scientific and Cultural Organisation and the World Health Organisation, as well as of the Inter-American Indian Institute, at appropriate levels and in their respective fields, and that it is proposed to continue this co-operation in promoting and securing the application of these provisions, and

Having determined that these proposals shall take the form of an international Convention revising the Indigenous and Tribal Populations Convention, 1957;

adopts this ____ day of June of the year one thousand nine hundred and eighty-nine the following Convention, which may be cited as the Indigenous and Tribal Peoples Convention, 1989:

PART I. GENERAL POLICY

Article I

1. This Convention applies to:

(a) tribal peoples in independent countries whose social, cultural and economic conditions distinguish them from other sections of the national community, and whose status is regulated wholly or partially by their own customs or traditions or by special laws or regulations;

(b) peoples in independent countries who are regarded as indigenous on account of their descent from the populations which inhabited the country, or a geographical region to which the country belongs, at the time of conquest or colonisation or the establishment of present state boundaries and who, irrespective of their legal status, retain some or all of their own social, economic, cultural and political institutions.

2. Self-identification as indigenous or tribal shall be regarded as a fundamental criterion for determining the groups to which the provisions of this Convention apply.

3. The use of the term "peoples" in this Convention shall not be construed as having any implications as regards the rights which may attach to the term under international law.

Article 2

1. Governments shall have the responsibility for developing, with the participation of the peoples concerned, co-ordinated and systematic action to protect the rights of these peoples and to guarantee respect for their integrity.

2. Such action shall include measures for:

(a) ensuring that members of these peoples benefit on an equal footing from the rights and opportunities which national laws and regulations grant to other members of the population;

(b) promoting the full realisation of the social, economic and cultural rights of these peoples with respect for their social and cultural identity, their customs and traditions and their institutions;

(c) assisting the members of the peoples concerned to eliminate socio-economic gaps that may exist between indigenous and other members of the national community, in a manner compatible with their aspirations and ways of life.

Article 3

1. Indigenous and tribal peoples shall enjoy the full measure of human rights and fundamental freedoms without hindrance or discrimination. The provisions of the Convention shall be applied without discrimination to male and female members of these peoples.

2. No form of force or coercion shall be used in violation of the human rights and fundamental freedoms of the peoples concerned, including the rights contained in this Convention.

Article 4

1. Special measures shall be adopted as appropriate for safeguarding the persons, institutions, property, labour, cultures and environment of the peoples concerned.

2. Such special measures shall not be contrary to the freely-expressed wishes of the peoples concerned.

3. Enjoyment of the general rights of citizenship, without discrimination, shall not be prejudiced in any way by such special measures.

Article 5

In applying the provisions of this Convention:

(a) the social, cultural, religious and spiritual values and practices of these peoples shall be recognised and protected, and due account shall be taken of the nature of the problems which face them both as groups and as individuals;

(b) the integrity of the values, practices and institutions of these peoples shall be respected;

(c) policies aimed at mitigating the difficulties experienced by these peoples in facing new conditions of life and work shall be adopted, with the participation and co-operation of the peoples affected.

Article 6

1. In applying the provisions of this Convention, governments shall:

(a) consult the peoples concerned, through appropriate procedures and in particular through their representative institutions, whenever consideration is being given to legislative or administrative measures which may affect them directly;

(b) establish means by which these peoples can freely participate, to at least the same extent as other sectors of the population, at all levels of decision-making in elective institutions and administrative and other bodies responsible for policies and programmes which concern them;

(c) establish means for the full development of these peoples' own institutions and initiatives, and in appropriate cases provide the resources necessary for this purpose.

2. The consultations carried out in application of this Convention shall be undertaken, in good faith and in a form appropriate to the circumstances, with the objective of achieving agreement or consent to the proposed measures.

Article 7

1. The peoples concerned shall have the right to decide their own priorities for the process of development as it affects their lives, beliefs, institutions and spiritual well-being and the lands they occupy or otherwise use, and to exercise control, to the extent possible, over their own economic, social and cultural development. In addition, they shall participate in the formulation, implementation and evaluation of plans and programmes for national and regional development which may affect them directly.

2. The improvement of the conditions of life and work and levels of health and education of the peoples concerned, with their participation and co-operation, shall be a matter of priority in plans for the overall economic development of areas they inhabit. Special projects for development of the areas in question shall also be so designed as to promote such improvement.

3. Governments shall ensure that, whenever appropriate, studies are carried out, in co-operation with the peoples concerned, to assess the social, spiritual, cultural and environmental impact on them of planned development activities. The results of these studies shall be considered as fundamental criteria for the implementation of these activities.

4. Governments shall take measures, in co-operation with the peoples concerned, to protect and preserve the environment of the territories they inhabit.

Article 8

1. In applying national laws and regulations to the peoples concerned, due regard shall be had to their customs or customary laws.

2. These peoples shall have the right to retain their own customs and institutions, where these are not incompatible with fundamental rights defined by the national legal system and with internationally recognised human rights. Procedures shall be established, whenever necessary, to resolve conflicts which may arise in the application of this principle.

3. The application of paragraphs 1 and 2 of this Article shall not prevent members of these peoples from exercising the rights granted to all citizens and from assuming the corresponding duties.

Article 9

1. To the extent compatible with the national legal system and internationally recognised human rights, the methods customarily practised by the peoples

concerned for dealing with offenses committed by their members shall be respected.

2. The customs of these peoples in regard to penal matters shall be taken into consideration by the authorities and courts dealing with such cases.

Article 10

1. In imposing penalties laid down by general law on members of these peoples account shall be taken of their economic, social and cultural characteristics.

2. Preference shall be given to methods of punishment other than confinement in prison.

Article 11

The exaction from members of the peoples concerned of compulsory personal services in any form, whether paid or unpaid, shall be prohibited and punishable by law, except in cases prescribed by law for all citizens.

Article 12

The peoples concerned shall be safeguarded against the abuse of their rights and shall be able to take legal proceedings, either individually or through their representative bodies, for the effective protection of these rights. Measures shall be taken to ensure that members of these peoples can understand and be understood in legal proceedings, where necessary through the provision of interpretation or by other effective means.

PART II. LAND

Article 13

1. In applying the provisions of this Part of the Convention governments shall respect the special importance for the cultures and spiritual values of the peoples concerned of their relationship with the lands or territories, or both as applicable, which they occupy or otherwise use, and in particular the collective aspects of this relationship.

2. The use of the term "lands" in Articles 15 and 16 shall include the concept of territories, which covers the total environment of the areas which the peoples concerned occupy or otherwise use.

Article 14

1. The rights of ownership and possession of the peoples concerned over the lands which they traditionally occupy shall be recognised. In addition, measures shall be taken in appropriate cases to safeguard the right of the peoples concerned to use lands not exclusively occupied by them, but to which they have traditionally had access for their subsistence and traditional activities. Particular attention shall be paid to the situation of nomadic peoples and shifting cultivators in this respect.

2. Governments shall take steps as necessary to identify the lands which the peoples concerned traditionally occupy, and to guarantee effective protection of their rights of ownership and possession.

3. Adequate procedures shall be established within the national legal system to resolve land claims by the peoples concerned.

Article 15

1. The rights of the peoples concerned to the natural resources pertaining to their lands shall be specially safeguarded. These rights include the right of these peoples to participate in the use, management and conservation of these resources.

2. In cases in which the State retains the ownership of mineral or sub-surface resources or rights to other resources pertaining to lands, governments shall establish or maintain procedures through which they shall consult these peoples, with a view to ascertaining whether and to what degree their interests would be prejudiced, before undertaking or permitting any programmes for the exploration or exploitation of such resources pertaining to their lands. The peoples concerned shall wherever possible participate in the benefits of such activities, and shall receive fair compensation for any damages which they may sustain as a result of such activities.

Article 16

1. Subject to the following paragraphs of this Article, the peoples concerned shall not be removed from the lands which they occupy.

2. Where the relocation of these peoples is considered necessary as an exceptional measure, such relocation shall take place only with their free and informed consent. Where their consent cannot be obtained, such relocation shall take place only following appropriate procedures established by national laws and regulations, including public inquiries where appropriate, which provide the opportunity for effective representation of the peoples concerned.

3. Whenever possible, these peoples shall have the right to return to their traditional lands, as soon as the grounds for relocation cease to exist.

4. When such return is not possible, as determined by agreement or, in the absence of such agreement, through appropriate procedures, these peoples shall be provided in all possible cases with lands of quality and legal status at least equal to that of the lands previously occupied by them, suitable to provide for their present needs and future development. Where the peoples concerned express a preference for compensation in money or in kind, they shall be so compensated under appropriate guarantees.

5. Persons thus relocated shall be fully compensated for any resulting loss or injury.

Article 17

1. Procedures established by the peoples concerned for the transmission of land rights among members of these peoples shall be respected.

2. The peoples concerned shall be consulted whenever consideration is being given to their capacity to alienate their lands or otherwise transmit their rights outside their own community.

3. Persons not belonging to these peoples shall be prevented from taking advantage of their customs or of lack of understanding of the laws on the part of their members to secure the ownership, possession or use of land belonging to them.

Article 18

Adequate penalties shall be established by law for unauthorised intrusion upon, or use of, the lands of the peoples concerned, and governments shall take measures to prevent such offences.

Article 19

National agrarian programmes shall secure to the peoples concerned treatment equivalent to that accorded to other sectors of the population with regard to:

(a) the provision of more land for these peoples when they have not the area necessary for providing the essentials of a normal existence, or for any possible increase in their numbers;

(b) the provision of the means required to promote the development of the lands which these peoples already possess.

PART III. RECRUITMENT AND CONDITIONS OF EMPLOYMENT
Article 20

1. Governments shall, within the framework of national laws and regulations, in co-operation with the peoples concerned, adopt special measures to ensure the effective protection with regard to recruitment and conditions of employment of workers belonging to these peoples, to the extent that they are not effectively protected by laws applicable to workers in general.

2. Governments shall do everything possible to prevent any discrimination between workers belonging to the peoples concerned and other workers, in particular as regards:

(a) admission to employment, including skilled employment, as well as measures for promotion and advancement;

(b) equal remuneration for work of equal value;

(c) medical and social assistance, occupational safety and health, all social security benefits and any other occupationally related benefits, and housing;

(d) the right of association and freedom for all lawful trade union activities, and the right to conclude collective agreements with employers or employers' organisations.

3. The measures taken shall include measures to ensure:

(a) that workers belonging to the peoples concerned, including seasonal, casual and migrant workers in agricultural and other employment, as well as those employed by labour contractors, enjoy the protection afforded by national law and practice to other such workers in the same sectors, and that they are fully informed of their rights under labour legislation and of the means of redress available to them;

(b) that workers belonging to these peoples are not subjected to working conditions hazardous to their health, in particular through exposure to pesticides or other toxic substances;

(c) that workers belonging to these peoples are not subjected to coercive recruitment systems, including bonded labour and other forms of debt servitude;

(d) that workers belonging to these peoples enjoy equal opportunities and equal treatment in employment for men and women, and protection from sexual harassment.

4. Particular attention shall be paid to the establishment of adequate labour inspection services in areas where workers belonging to the peoples concerned undertake wage employment, in order to ensure compliance with the provisions of this Part of this Convention.

PART IV. VOCATIONAL TRAINING, HANDICRAFTS AND RURAL INDUSTRIES

Article 21

Members of the peoples concerned shall enjoy opportunities at least equal to those of other citizens in respect of vocational training measures.

Article 22

1. Measures shall be taken to promote the voluntary participation of members of the peoples concerned in vocational training programmes of general application.

2. Whenever existing programmes of vocational training of general application do not meet the special needs of the peoples concerned, governments shall, with the participation of these peoples, ensure the provision of special training programmes and facilities.

3. Any special training programmes shall be based on the economic environment, social and cultural conditions and practical needs of the peoples concerned. Any studies made in this connection shall be carried out in co-operation with these peoples, who shall be consulted on the organisation and operation of such programmes. Where feasible, these peoples shall progressively assume responsibility for the organisation and operation of such special training programmes, if they so decide.

Article 23

1. Handicrafts, rural and community-based industries, and subsistence economy and traditional activities of the peoples concerned, such as hunting, fishing, trapping and gathering, shall be recognised as important factors in the maintenance of their cultures and in their economic self-reliance and development. Governments shall, with the participation of these people and whenever appropriate, ensure that these activities are strengthened and promoted.

2. Upon the request of the peoples concerned, appropriate technical and financial assistance shall be provided wherever possible, taking into account the traditional technologies and cultural characteristics of these peoples, as well as the importance of sustainable and equitable development.

PART V. SOCIAL SECURITY AND HEALTH
Article 24

Social security schemes shall be extended progressively to cover the peoples concerned, and applied without discrimination against them.

Article 25

1. Governments shall ensure that adequate health services are made available to the peoples concerned, or shall provide them with resources to allow them to design and deliver such services under their own responsibility and control, so that they may enjoy the highest attainable standard of physical and mental health.

2. Health services shall, to the extent possible, be community-based. These services shall be planned and administered in co-operation with the peoples concerned and take into account their economic, geographic, social and cultural conditions as well as their traditional preventive care, healing practices and medicines.

3. The health care system shall give preference to the training and employment of local community health workers, and focus on primary health care while maintaining strong links with other levels of health care services.

4. The provision of such health services shall be co-ordinated with other social, economic and cultural measures in the country.

PART VI. EDUCATION AND MEANS OF COMMUNICATION
Article 26

Measures shall be taken to ensure that members of the peoples concerned have the opportunity to acquire education at all levels on at least an equal footing with the rest of the national community.

Article 27

1. Education programmes and services for the peoples concerned shall be developed and implemented in co-operation with them to address their special needs, and shall incorporate their histories, their knowledge and technologies, their value systems and their further social, economic and cultural aspirations.

2. The competent authority shall ensure the training of members of these peoples and their involvement in the formulation and implementation of education programmes, with a view to the progressive transfer of responsibility for the conduct of these programmes to these peoples as appropriate.

3. In addition, governments shall recognise the right of these peoples to establish their own educational institutions and facilities, provided that such institutions meet minimum standards established by the competent authority in

consultation with these peoples. Appropriate resources shall be provided for this purpose.

Article 28

1. Children belonging to the peoples concerned shall, wherever practicable, be taught to read and write in their own indigenous language or in the language most commonly used by the group to which they belong. When this is not practicable, the competent authorities shall undertake consultations with these peoples with a view to the adoption of measures to achieve this objective.

2. Adequate measures shall be taken to ensure that these peoples have the opportunity to attain fluency in the national language or in one of the official languages of the country.

3. Measures shall be taken to preserve and promote the development and practice of the indigenous languages of the peoples concerned.

Article 29

The imparting of general knowledge and skills that will help children belonging to the peoples concerned to participate fully and on an equal footing in their own community and in the national community shall be an aim of education for these peoples.

Article 30

1. Governments shall adopt measures appropriate to the traditions and cultures of the peoples concerned, to make known to them their rights and duties, especially in regard to labour, economic opportunities, education and health matters, social welfare and their rights deriving from this Convention.

2. If necessary, this shall be done by means of written translations and through the use of mass communications in the languages of these peoples.

Article 31

Educational measures shall be taken among all sections of the national community, and particularly among those that are in most direct contact with the peoples concerned, with the object of eliminating prejudices that they may harbour in respect of these peoples. To this end, efforts shall be made to ensure that history textbooks and other educational materials provide a fair, accurate and informative portrayal of the societies and cultures of these peoples.

PART VII. CONTACTS AND CO-OPERATION ACROSS BORDERS

Article 32

Governments shall take appropriate measures, including by means of international agreements, to facilitate contacts and co-operation between indigenous and tribal peoples across borders, including activities in the economic, social, cultural, spiritual and environmental fields.

PART VIII. ADMINISTRATION
Article 33

1. The governmental authority responsible for the matters covered in this Convention shall ensure that agencies or other appropriate mechanisms exist to administer the programmes affecting the peoples concerned, and shall ensure that they have the means necessary for the proper fulfillment of the functions assigned to them.

2. These programmes shall include:

(a) the planning, co-ordination, execution and evaluation, in co-operation with the peoples concerned, of the measures provided for in this Convention;

(b) the proposing of legislative and other measures to the competent authorities and supervision of the application of the measures taken, in co-operation with the peoples concerned.

PART IX. GENERAL PROVISIONS
Article 34

The nature and scope of the measures to be taken to give effect to this Convention shall be determined in a flexible manner, having regard to the conditions characteristic of each country.

Article 35

The application of the provisions of this Convention shall not adversely affect rights and benefits of the peoples concerned pursuant to other Conventions and Recommendations, international instruments, treaties, or national laws, awards, custom or agreements.

NOTES

1. ILO Convention No. 107: The 1989 International Labour Organization Convention on Indigenous and Tribal Peoples represents the most direct international statement on the rights of indigenous peoples. As reflected in article 36, this Convention revises an earlier 1957 convention, commonly known as International Labour Organization Convention 107. Indigenous groups had mixed reactions to the earlier convention since it represented an odd mixture of assimilationist policies and statements purporting to protect the rights of indigenous peoples to separate sovereignty and land rights. In Barsh, *Revision of ILO Convention No. 107*, 81 Am. J. Int'l Law 756 (1987),* the author describes the evolution of the two conventions:

> Emerging from the same pan-American "indigenist" movement that produced the Inter-American Indian Institute,[4] Convention No. 107 was [intended to address the growing isolation and marginalization] of Indian groups in the wake of national development, which its drafters conceived of as a product of racism and racial discrimination.[5] Hence, it urged states to ensure that indigenous and tribal peoples participate in

---

*Copyright © 1987 American Journal of International Law and Russel Barsh. Reprinted with permission of the copyright holders.

[4]*See* Barsh, *The IX Inter-American Indian Congress*, 80 AJIL 682 (1986).

[5]G. Bennett, Aboriginal Rights in International Law (Occasional Paper No. 37 of the Royal Anthropological Institute of Great Britain and Ireland, 1978); Swepston & Plant, *International*

and benefit from development, rather than being merely displaced by projects. It also promoted their inclusion in education and other public benefits, without adverse discrimination. Sharing decision-making power with these "less advanced" groups, however was taken no farther than "collaboration" with their leaders, and respect for their customs was encouraged only to the extent compatible with "the objectives of integration programmes."[6]

On the crucial issue of land rights, the original Convention did relatively little to restrict state power. Indigenous groups' "ownership, collective or individual, over the lands which [they] traditionally occupy" was recognized,[7] but so, too, was states' power to resettle communities "in the interest of national economic development."[8] Convention No. 107's chief safeguard against the widespread destruction of indigenous communities was the requirement that states provide displaced peoples with substitute lands of "at least equal [quality,] suitable to provide for their present needs and future development."[9] The impossibility of so doing in industrializing, heavily populated states was ignored.

Although the major initiative for the Convention came from the Americas, it also attracted the interest of several African and Asian states. They regarded their analogous problems, however, as "tribal" rather than "indigenous"; hence, the Convention was drafted carefully to include "tribal populations" "whose social and economic conditions are at a less advanced stage than ... other sections of the national community, and whose status is regulated wholly or partially by their own customs or traditions or by special laws or regulations";[10] as well as those "which are regarded as indigenous on account of their descent from the populations which inhabited the country ... at the time of conquest or colonisation and which ... live more in conformity with the social, economic and cultural institutions of that time than with [national] institutions."[11] That is, the Convention has as its objects "tribal" groups that were segregated culturally or legally from national society, whether or not this had arisen from the historical circumstances of colonization.

The Need for Change

The meeting of experts had little difficulty agreeing with S. K. Jain, Deputy Director of the International Labour Office, that "the world has changed since Convention 107 was adopted." As Kombo Ntonga Booke of Zaire's national trade union association put it, "the Convention has been overtaken by events," especially decolonization. Even Mexico's Fernando Yllanes Ramos, a draftsman of the original text, could say that "it would be mad for any State to ratify Convention 107 now when it is out of date." In fact, there had been no new ratifications since 1971.[12]

Not only was the Convention outmoded, but the peoples it was designed to protect were being subjected, in the words of Deputy Director Jain, to "unprecedented pressures which threaten their cultural identity and even their very existence." Viewed by many states as merely "an obstacle to development" or as a security risk along sensitive

---

standards and the protection of the land rights of indigenous and tribal populations, INTERNATIONAL LABOUR REV., No. 1, 1985, at 91; Barsh, *Indigenous North America and Contemporary International Law*[,] 62 OR. L. REV. 73, 81-84 (1983).

[6] *See especially* Arts. 5, 7(2) and 13(1) of the Convention [No. 107].

[7] *Id.*, Art. 11.

[8] *Id.*, Art. 12(1).

[9] *Id.*, Art. 12(2).

[10] *Id.*, Art. 1(a).

[11] *Id.*, Art. 1(b). Compare the working definitions prepared by the UN Centre for Human Rights, in UN Doc. E/CN.4/Sub.2/AC.4/1983/CRP.2 ("Ideas for the definition of indigenous populations from the international point of view").

[12] After the meeting of experts, Iraq ratified the Convention. Previously, it had been ratified by 14 Latin American states (Argentina, Bolivia, Brazil, Colombia, Costa Rica, Cuba, the Dominican Republic, Ecuador, El Salvador, Haiti, Mexico, Panama, Paraguay and Peru); 6 African states (Angola, Egypt, Ghana, Guinea-Bissau, Malawi and Tunisia); 4 states in Asia (Bangladesh, India, Pakistan and the Syrian Arab Republic); and 2 in Western Europe (Belgium and Portugal). On the basis of the criteria in the World Bank's study, *supra* note 3, it is estimated that these states (not including Iraq) administer some 100 million indigenous and tribal people.

frontiers, added the director of the Office's International Labour Standards Department, T. Sidibe, indigenous peoples were "losing their land at an accelerated pace." Newly independent states' preoccupation with "asserting their own unity," Yllanes Ramos observed, was contributing to increasingly polarized and potentially violent situations. Dr. Juan Ossio Acuna of Peru's Indian Institute agreed: to avoid conflict, "States *must* recognize the demands put forward by these groups."

Indeed, "the growth of indigenous organizations" over the past 10 years, Sidibe stressed, had become "a significant factor" in the reassessment of the Convention. "The Convention is mistrusted by those it is intended to protect," admitted Deputy Director Jain; in Dr. Ossio's view, this should not be underestimated in an age when "indigenous groups are winning attention internationally." "Unless we achieve the support of indigenous peoples," noted Guy Adam of the Canadian Labour Congress, "any revised Convention will be a dead letter." The ILO should thus be working "*with* the people," observed P.O. Molosi, of Botswana's Ministry of Local Government, "not *for* the people."

These comments underscored the low level of indigenous representation at the meeting of experts,[13] as Norway's Einar Hogetveit remarked. Nevertheless, it was a "precedent," according to Sidibe, that nongovernmental organizations were participating at all in a meeting of this kind. "The real experts are the indigenous peoples themselves," said Hayden Burgess of the World Council of Indigenous Peoples. Chairman Rudolfo Stavenhagen of the College of Mexico agreed: "We should ask why the indigenous organizations do not have the right to participate when we are considering [their] rights"; for "[i]f we are to move towards full participation, we should start right here." In fact, as the meeting progressed, there was little objection to including indigenous "observers" fully in the debate.

Integration Versus Self-Determination

As stated in its Preamble, the original Convention aimed at "facilitating" indigenous populations' "progressive integration into their respective national communities." The meaning and propriety of "integration" preoccupied the meeting of experts from the start. "There has been a consistent worldwide movement away from the notion of integrationism," observed Sidibe, as governments become "increasingly willing" to recognize indigenous "self-determination" and these peoples' "right to make their own decisions about the extent to which they should be integrated." Although "integration" originally had been proposed "without any malice, to ensure the survival of these communities," added Yllanes Ramos, it came to be associated with "destruction and absorption," or even, in the words of UNESCO's observer, Pierre Conde, "ethnocide [which] is a gross violation of human rights."[14]

All of the experts agreed with William Gray of Australia's Department of Aboriginal Affairs that indigenous peoples should enjoy the right "to retain their unique identity." Where they disagreed was over the extent to which power sharing would be necessary to make this right effective. Some experts spoke in terms of *participation* in existing institutions, such as Gray and Molosi.[15] Most, however, joined the call of the World Council of Indigenous Peoples for "*control* over their social and economic conditions." Conde, for example, spoke of the "right to [have] democratically constituted assemblies of their own choice."

---

[13] Representatives of two NGOs, the World Council of Indigenous Peoples and Survival International, were invited to serve as experts. in addition, there were "observers" from several indigenous NGOs in consultative status with ECOSOC (the Four Directions Council, the Consejo Indio de Sud America, the National Aboriginal and Islander Legal Service Secretariat), as well as several nonstatus indigenous organizations from Australia and India, and nonindigenous NGOs with expertise in this field.

[14] In the multiethnic, multitribal and entirely indigenous states of Africa, observed Djibrilla Diaroumeye of Niger, "who is going to integrate whom?"

[15] Dr. Ossio of Peru, arguing that cultural diversity should never be extinguished "in the name of equality," referred to the right to "take a more active part in national life," and to "more equality among groups" within the national political system.

Although UN Assistant Secretary-General Kurt Herndl and Ted Webster of the World Health Organization, among others, emphasized the *right to self-determination*, there was some resistance to including it in a revised convention, particularly among experts representing employers' organizations.[16] "The object of our group is to make [the revision] more relevant but also likely to be widely acceptable," warned Martin Freeman of Canada. Molosi similarly advocated "a balance between what is absolutely desirable and what is workable." On the other hand, Hogetveit argued that while the presence of the term "self-determination" might discourage ratification, it should be used out of respect for the wishes of indigenous peoples. He and Gray proposed defining self-determination, for the purposes of the revision, as "internal," following the advice of the Martinez Cobo report.[17] "Self-determination will be the only way we will tackle the problem," according to Molosi, but he suggested using a substitute or ellipsis. "The exact word may not be necessary."

2. Ratification of the Conventions: While Convention 169 only recently was promulgated and has not yet entered into force, the earlier Convention 107 had been ratified by twenty-seven nations, including many Latin American nations of Central and South America. The United States never joined Convention 107. Were the United States government giving serious consideration to ratifying Convention 169, would you advise it to do so? As you explore the materials in this book, consider the extent to which the United States adheres to the principles advanced in the Convention. What changes in federal Indian law, if any, would be required should the United States ratify the Convention?

3. Status of Indigenous Peoples in International Law: The promotion of self-determination for indigenous peoples presents a great problem in international law. Until the relatively recent emergence of an international human rights movement, the internal affairs of nations historically had not been subject to control or comment by the international community. Nevertheless, in the interest of human rights, the international community has attempted to advance the cause of self-determination for indigenous populations. Article 1 of the International Covenant on Economic, Social and Cultural Rights, adopted by the United Nations General Assembly in 1966, guarantees, "all peoples" the right of self-determination and the right to freely pursue their economic, social, and cultural development. Article 27 of the International Covenant on Civil and Political Rights, also adopted by the United Nations General Assembly in 1966, provides:

> In those States in which ethnic, religious or linguistic minorities exist, persons belonging to such minorities shall not be denied the right, in community with other members of their group, to enjoy their own culture, to profess and practise their own religion, or to use their own language.

In 1978 the President submitted each of these conventions to the Senate for ratification. Message from the President of the United States Transmitting Four Treaties Pertaining to Human Rights, Sen. Doc., Executives C, D, E, and F, 95th Cong., 2d Sess. (1978). Article V(c) of the Convention against Discrimination in Education, sponsored by the United Nations Educational, Scientific and Cultural Organization (UNESCO) provides:

---

[16] "In Brazil the self-determination of indigenous populations is not acceptable," argued Dr. Jose Antunes de Carvalho of that country's National Confederation of Industry, because "they cannot survive without the protection of the public authorities; but this does not rule out consultation."

[17] Study of the Problem of Discrimination Against Indigenous Populations, Final Part, UN Doc. E/CN.4/Sub.2/1983/21/Add.8, paras. 580-81.

[I]t is essential to recognize the right of national minorities to carry on their own educational activities, including the maintenance of schools and, depending on the educational policy of each State, the use of teaching in their own language.

In addition to these guarantees of cultural autonomy, a growing body of international law protects the political rights and aspirations of national minorities to autonomy and self-determination. *See, e.g.,* United Nations Declaration on Friendly Relations and Cooperation, adopted by the United Nations General Assembly in 1970 and Helsinki Final Act, Principle VIII, adopted at the Helsinki Conference on Security and Cooperation in Europe in 1975. *See generally* Cassese, *The Helsinki Declaration and Self-Determination* in HUMAN RIGHTS IN INTERNATIONAL LAW AND THE HELSINKI ACCORD 83 (T. Buergenthal ed. 1977). More recently, a United Nations Working Group on Indigenous Populations has been preparing a Draft Universal Declaration on Indigenous Rights. These and other international guarantees of rights for indigenous peoples are discussed in more detail in Chapter 9, section B.

What, if anything, do the ILO Conventions on Indigenous and Tribal Peoples suggest about the claims of some Indian leaders that their tribes are entitled to recognition among the family of nations in the international arena? *See, e.g.,* Lyons, *When You Talk About Client Relationships, You Are Talking About the Future of Nations,* in NATIONAL LAWYERS GUILD COMMITTEE ON NATIVE AMERICAN STRUGGLES, RETHINKING INDIAN LAW iv (1982). During the early colonial period, while tribes were not necessarily considered part of the family of civilized European nations, they were considered within the protections of international law then animated by natural law principles. *E.g.,* F. VICTORIA, DE INDIS ET DE IURE BELLI RELECTIONES (E. Nys ed., J. Bate trans. 1917). As a more positivist, state-oriented vision of international law emerged during the late seventeenth and eighteenth centuries, the treatment of indigenous peoples by colonial powers increasingly was seen as a matter of domestic, rather than international, protections. *See generally* Anaya, *Rights of Indigenous Peoples in International Law: Historical and Contemporary Perspectives,* 1989 HARV. INDIAN L. SYMP. Thus, in the *Cayuga Claims Case (Great Britain ex rel. Cayuga Indians in Canada v. United States),* Nielson Rep. 203, 307 (1927), an international arbitration panel, which included the eminent American legal theorist, Roscoe Pound, concluded that an Indian tribe was "not a legal unit in international law." *Id.* at 309. The arbitration tribunal based its conclusion primarily on an analysis of the domestic law of the United States on the status of Indian tribes. *But see* Fairbanks, *The Cheyenne and Their Law: A Positivist Inquiry,* 32 ARK. L. REV. 403 (1978) (arguing for sovereign state recognition of Indian tribes). More recently, the post-World War II focus on international protections of human rights and human dignity has again brought the treatment of indigenous peoples within the ambit of international law protections, as reflected by the ILO conventions. As you review the materials in this book consider whether United States policy is compatible with international guarantees of the type contained in the 1989 ILO Convention. To what extent does the international community deal with the same problems as those faced by the United States in regard to indigenous populations? If the United States should ratify any of the conventions outlined above, what changes would be required in the nation's approach to Indian questions? For other views on the level of international legal protections for and the international status of Indian tribes, see Clinebell & Thomson, *Sovereignty and Self-Determination: The Rights of Native Americans Under International Law,* 27 BUFFALO L. REV. 669 (1978); Alfredsson, *International Law, International Organizations, and Indigenous Peoples,* 36 J.

INT'L AFF. 113, 113-15 (Spring/Summer 1982); Barsh, *Current Developments: Indigenous Peoples: An Emerging Object of International Law,* 80 AM. J. INT'L L. 369-73; 377-85 (1986); Clinebell, *The Proper Status of Native Nations Under International Law* in NATIONAL LAWYERS GUILD COMMITTEE ON NATIVE AMERICAN STRUGGLES 131 (1982).

Chapter 2

FEDERAL POWER IN THE COMPETITION FOR CONTROL OF INDIAN COUNTRY

The protected status of American Indians is often articulated in terms of sovereignty and jurisdiction. Three governments have long struggled for control over transactions and events occurring on Indian lands — the federal government, the tribes, and the states. Any effort to understand Indian law must begin with an appreciation of the claims that each of these three competitors brings to the task of control of affairs in Indian country and end with some understanding of the shifting way in which they cooperate and conflict in defining and implementing law on Indian lands.

This chapter is devoted to the role of the federal government in this delicate regime. Chapter 3 will explore the powers of the tribe and Chapter 4 the scope and legitimacy of state authority in Indian country.

This chapter begins with an exploration of the constitutional sources and scope of congressional power over Indians and Indian tribes. Because much of this congressional power has been delegated to a powerful agency, the Bureau of Indian Affairs, the chapter then considers the role of the Bureau in regulating Indian Affairs. The chapter then turns its focus toward limitations on federal power over Indians, beginning with limitations anchored in specific constitutional guarantees. Next the chapter explores the canons of treaty and statutory construction that have been used to limit the reach of federal power indirectly through interpretations that favor Indians. The final limitation explored is the trust relationship, which has been a major device used to limit administrative power in the last 20 years.

In no other area has federal authority in Indian affairs been exercised as pervasively as in criminal jurisdiction. The chapter thus concludes by exploring the federal statutes structuring criminal jurisdiction over Indian lands.

A. THE SOURCES OF FEDERAL POWER OVER INDIAN AFFAIRS

1. THE MARSHALL COURT'S INTERPRETATION

WORCESTER v. GEORGIA

31 U.S. (6 Pet.) 515 (1832)

[This case, in which Chief Justice Marshall expounded on the sovereign status of Indian tribes and the constitutional sources of federal power over Indian tribes is reprinted *supra* page 18.]

NOTES

1. **The Constitutional Framework:** The Constitution refers to Indians three times, in the two apportionment clauses and in the commerce clause. Article 1,

section 2, clause 3 and section 2 of the fourteenth amendment exclude "Indians not taxed" for purposes of calculating the representation apportioned to each state in the House of Representatives. Indians are subject to taxation today; thus, these clauses have not had any legal or practical effect for some time. *See generally* 57 I.D. 195 (Solicitor's Opinion on interpretation of "Indians not taxed" provisions).

The more significant reference to Indians is contained in the Indian commerce clause. U.S. Const., art. I, § 8, cl. 3. This clause provides, "The Congress shall have Power ... To regulate Commerce ... with the Indian Tribes." The Indian commerce clause derives from Article IX of the Articles of Confederation, which granted Congress "the sole and exclusive right and power of ... regulating the trade and managing all affairs with the Indians, not members of any of the States, provided that the legislative right of any State within its own limits be not infringed or violated." Article IX and its proviso attempted to strike a balance between federal and state power by giving the federal government power over tribes, with states retaining control over assimilated Indians living within their borders. The article's language and purpose created chronic questions over which Indians could legitimately be considered "members" of the states and thus subject to the legitimate scope of the legislative rights of the states. A 1787 report of a special committee of the Continental Congress (discussed in *Worcester*) concluded the drafters of Article IX had intended Congressional power over tribal Indians to be paramount. Nevertheless, state claims to sole power to regulate "their" Indians caused an Indian war on the very eve of the Constitutional Convention. *See* 33 J. Cont. Cong. 458-59; *see also* Clinton, Book Review, 47 U. Chi. L. Rev. 846, 856 n.50 (1980). In commenting on the Indian commerce clause in number 42 of the *Federalist Papers*, James Madison criticized article IX as "obscure and contradictory." He added:

> [W]hat description of Indians are to be deemed members of a state is not yet settled, and has been a question of frequent perplexity and contention in the federal councils. And how the trade with Indians, though not members of a State, yet residing within its legislative jurisdiction can be regulated by an external authority, without so far intruding on the internal rights of legislation, is absolutely incomprehensible.

What light, if any, does the text and history of Article IX shed on the role the framers envisioned for Indian tribes in the constitutional system? What scope should be given the term "commerce" in the clause? Should it be construed to include, as did the Indian affairs clause of the Articles, "regulating the trade and managing all affairs with the Indians" or should it be limited to regulation of the economic intercourse with the Indian tribes? Assuming that the broad sweep of the Indian affairs clause of the Articles of Confederation supplies a meaning for the term "commerce ... with the Indian tribes," does the grant of power to regulate trade and manage affairs *with* the Indians include the power to regulate the affairs *of* the Indian tribes? How did Justice Marshall answer this question in *Worcester*?

2. Indian Treaties as a Source of Federal Power: Note Chief Justice Marshall's reliance on the treaty, war, and other foreign affairs powers of Articles I and II as, together with the commerce clause, "comprehend[ing] all that is required for the regulation of our intercourse with the Indians." *Worcester*, 31 U.S. (6 Pet.) 515, 559 (1832). Indian tribes were regarded as sovereign nations at the time the Constitution was written. Thus, treaties served as a primary method of adjusting relations between the federal government and Indian tribes from the Pre-Revolutionary War period until treaties with the Indian tribes were abandoned as a method of regulating Indian affairs in 1871. *See* 25 U.S.C. § 71 (1976); *see generally* F. Cohen, Handbook of Federal Indian Law

62-70 (1982) (examples of typical treaty provisions). The treaty-making authority no longer plays an on-going role in the arsenal of federal powers over Indian
matters. It is, nevertheless, accepted constitutional law that a treaty "may endow
Congress with a source of legislative authority independent of the powers enumerated in Article 1 (although, of course, still limited by the Constitution's
explicit constraints on federal action)." L. TRIBE, AMERICAN CONSTITUTIONAL
LAW 227 (2d ed. 1988). *See generally Missouri v. Holland*, 252 U.S. 416 (1920).

To what extent do the treaties with the Indian tribes still constitute independent sources of federal authority? For example, in Article I of the Treaty of
Fort Sully, Oct. 28, 1865, 14 Stat. 747, the Oglala Band of Sioux "acknowledge[d] themselves to be subject to the exclusive jurisdiction and authority of
the United States ...." Similarly, in *Worcester*, Justice Marshall analyzed Article
IX of the Treaty of Hopewell, Jan. 3, 1786, 7 Stat. 21, in which the Cherokees
agreed that "the United States in Congress assembled, shall have the sole and
exclusive right of regulating the trade with the Indians, and managing all their
affairs in such manner as they think proper." Do these clauses, and others like
them, constitute independent grants of authority to Congress to regulate Indian
affairs in areas otherwise not cognizable under the Indian commerce clause?
See, e.g., Ex parte Crow Dog, 109 U.S. 556, 567 (1883) (suggestion in dicta that
a treaty could of its own force operate to extend beyond statutory limits the
scope of criminal jurisdiction of the federal courts over Indian country). How
did Justice Marshall interpret the clause just quoted?

2. NINETEENTH CENTURY PRECEDENTS: THE PLENARY POWER ERA

UNITED STATES v. KAGAMA

118 U.S. 375 (1886)

[In 1883 the United States Supreme Court decided *Ex parte Crow Dog*, 109
U.S. 556, holding that the federal courts had no jurisdiction to try an Indian for
an intratribal murder occurring on an Indian reservation. Until 1871 the relations between the United States and the Indian tribes had been governed principally by treaties, and neither the treaties with the affected tribe nor the statutes
implementing them purported to vest the federal courts with jurisdiction over
such crimes. Justice Matthews noted that the policy of the government had
uniformly been that crimes "by Indians against each other were left to be dealt
with by each Tribe for itself, according to its local customs."

The *Crow Dog* decision caused an outcry of protest in Congress. In order to
remedy the perceived jurisdictional defect, Congress in 1885 enacted the first
Federal Major Crimes Act, 23 Stat. 385, quoted below.

The *Kagama* case tested the constitutionality of this statute. The case arose
when the accused, an Indian, demurred to an indictment charging him with the
murder of another Indian on the Hoopa Valley Indian Reservation in the State
of California. The circuit and district judges divided on the demurrer, and the
issue was certified to the Supreme Court.]

Mr. Justice MILLER delivered the opinion of the Court.
[The Major Crimes Act states:]

§ 9. That immediately upon and after the date of the passage of this act all Indians
committing against the person or property of another Indian or other person any of

the following crimes, namely, murder, manslaughter, rape, assault with intent to kill, arson, burglary and larceny, within any Territory of the United States, and either within or without the Indian reservation, shall be subject therefor to the laws of said Territory relating to said crimes, and shall be tried therefor in the same courts and in the same manner, and shall be subject to the same penalties, as are all other persons charged with the commission of the said crimes, respectively; and the said courts are hereby given jurisdiction in all such cases; and all such Indians committing any of the above crimes against the person or property of another Indian or other person, within the boundaries of any State of the United States, and within the limits of any Indian reservation, shall be subject to the same laws, tried in the same courts and in the same manner, and subject to the same penalties, as are all other persons committing any of the above crimes within the exclusive jurisdiction of the United States. 23 Stat. ch. 341, 362; § 9, 385.

[T]he offence charged in this indictment was committed within a State and not within a Territory, [but] the considerations which are necessary to a solution of the problem in regard to the one must in a large degree affect the other.

The Constitution of the United States is almost silent in regard to the relations of the government which was established by it to the numerous tribes of Indians within its borders.

In declaring the basis on which representation in the lower branch of the Congress and direct taxation should be apportioned, it was fixed that it should be according to numbers, *excluding Indians not taxed,* which, of course, excluded nearly all of that race, but which meant that if there were such within a State as were taxed to support the government, they should be counted for representation, and in the computation for direct taxes levied by the United States. This expression, excluding Indians not taxed, is found in the XIVth amendment, where it deals with the same subject under the new conditions produced by the emancipation of the slaves. Neither of these shed much light on the power of Congress over the Indians in their existence as tribes, distinct from the ordinary citizens of a State or Territory.

The mention of Indians in the Constitution which has received most attention is that found in the clause which gives Congress "power to regulate commerce with foreign nations and among the several States, and with the Indian tribes."

This clause is relied on in the argument in the present case, the proposition being that the statute under consideration is a regulation of commerce with the Indian tribes. But we think it would be a very strained construction of this clause, that a system of criminal laws for Indians living peaceably in their reservations, which left out the entire code of trade and intercourse laws justly enacted under that provision, and established punishments for the common-law crimes of murder, manslaughter, arson, burglary, larceny, and the like, without any reference to their relation to any kind of commerce, was authorized by the grant of power to regulate commerce with the Indian tribes. While we are not able to see, in either of these clauses of the Constitution and its amendments, any delegation of power to enact a code of criminal law for the punishment of the worst class of crimes known to civilized life when committed by Indians, there is a suggestion in the manner in which the Indian tribes are introduced into that clause, which may have a bearing on the subject before us. The commerce with foreign nations is distinctly stated as submitted to the control of Congress. Were the Indian tribes foreign nations? If so, they came within the

first of the three classes of commerce mentioned, and did not need to be re-
peated as Indian tribes. Were they nations, in the minds of the framers of the
Constitution? If so, the natural phrase would have been "foreign nations and
Indian nations," or, in the terseness of language uniformly used by the framers
of the instrument, it would naturally have been "foreign and Indian nations."
And so in [Cherokee Nation v. Georgia, supra Chapter 1,] brought in the
Supreme Court of the United States, under the declaration that the judicial
power extends to suits between a State and foreign States, and giving to the
Supreme Court original jurisdiction where a State is a party, it was conceded
that Georgia as a State came within the clause, but held that the Cherokees were
not a State or nation within the meaning of the Constitution, so as to be able to
maintain the suit.

But these Indians are within the geographical limits of the United States. The
soil and the people within these limits are under the political control of the
Government of the United States, or of the States of the Union. There exist
within the broad domain of sovereignty but these two. There may be cities,
counties, and other organized bodies with limited legislative functions, but they
are all derived from, or exist in, subordination to one or the other of these. The
territorial governments owe all their powers to the statutes of the United States
conferring on them the powers which they exercise, and which are liable to be
withdrawn, modified, or repealed at any time by Congress. What authority the
State governments may have to enact criminal laws for the Indians will be
presently considered. But this power of Congress to organize territorial governments, and make laws for their inhabitants, arises not so much from the clause
in the Constitution in regard to disposing of and making rules and regulations
concerning the Territory and other property of the United States, as from the
ownership of the country in which the Territories are, and the right of exclusive
sovereignty which must exist in the National Government, and can be found
nowhere else.

[The Hoopa Valley reservation] is land bought by the United States from
Mexico by the treaty of Guadaloupe Hidalgo, and the whole of California, with
the allegiance of its inhabitants, many of whom were Indians, was transferred
by that treaty to the United States.

The relation of the Indian tribes living within the borders of the United
States, both before and since the Revolution, to the people of the United States
has always been an anomalous one and of a complex character.

[Indians] were, and always have been, regarded as having a semi-independent
position when they preserved their tribal relations; not as States, not as nations,
not as possessed of the full attributes of sovereignty, but as a separate people,
with the power of regulating their internal and social relations, and thus far not
brought under the laws of the Union or of the State within whose limits they
resided.

Perhaps the best statement of their position is found in the two opinions of
this court by Chief Justice Marshall in [Cherokee Nation v. Georgia] and
[Worcester v. Georgia]. In the first of the above cases it was held that these
tribes were neither States nor nations, had only some of the attributes of sovereignty, and could not be so far recognized in that capacity as to sustain a suit in

the Supreme Court of the United States. In the second case it was said that they were not subject to the jurisdiction asserted over them by the State of Georgia, which, because they were within its limits, where they had been for ages, had attempted to extend her laws and the jurisdiction of her courts over them.

In the opinions in these cases they are spoken of as "wards of the nation," "pupils," as local dependent communities. In this spirit the United States has conducted its relations to them from its organization to this time. But, after an experience of a hundred years of the treaty-making system of government, Congress has determined upon a new departure — to govern them by acts of Congress. This is seen in the act of March 3, 1871, embodied in § 2079 of the Revised Statutes:

> No Indian nation or tribe, within the territory of the United States shall be acknowledged or recognized as an independent nation, tribe, or power, with whom the United States may contract by treaty; but no obligation of any treaty lawfully made and ratified with any such Indian nation or tribe prior to March third, eighteen hundred and seventy one, shall be hereby invalidated or impaired.

The case of Crow Dog, 109 U.S. 556, in which an agreement with the Sioux Indians, ratified by an act of Congress, was supposed to extend over them the laws of the United States and the jurisdiction of its courts, covering murder and other grave crimes, shows the purpose of Congress in this new departure. The decision in that case admits that if the intention of Congress had been to punish, by the United States courts, the murder of one Indian by another, the law would have been valid. But the court could not see, in the agreement with the Indians sanctioned by Congress, a purpose to repeal § 2146 of the Revised Statutes, which expressly excludes from that jurisdiction the case of a crime committed by one Indian against another in the Indian country. The passage of the act now under consideration was designed to remove that objection, and to go further by including such crimes on reservations lying within a State.

Is this latter fact a fatal objection to the law? [Does federal] authority extend to this case?

It seems to us that this is within the competency of Congress. These Indian tribes are the wards of the nation. They are communities dependent on the United States. Dependent largely for their daily food. Dependent for their political rights. They owe no allegiance to the States, and receive from them no protection. Because of the local ill feeling, the people of the States where they are found are often their deadliest enemies. From their very weakness and helplessness, so largely due to the course of dealing of the Federal Government with them and the treaties in which it has been promised, there arises the duty of protection, and with it the power. This has always been recognized by the Executive and by Congress, and by this court, whenever the question has arisen [in past cases such as Worcester v. Georgia].

The power of the General Government over these remnants of a race once powerful, now weak and diminished in numbers, is necessary to their protection, as well as to the safety of those among whom they dwell. It must exist in that government, because it never has existed anywhere else, because the theatre of its exercise is within the geographical limits of the United States, because it has never been denied, and because it alone can enforce its laws on all the tribes.

[The law is constitutional; thus the district court has jurisdiction.]

LONE WOLF v. HITCHCOCK

187 U.S. 553 (1903)

[Lone Wolf and other members of the Kiowa, Comanche, and Apache tribes brought a class suit seeking declaratory and injunctive relief to prevent the Secretary of the Interior from implementing a statute directing the sale of over 2 million acres of "surplus" Indian land (land not needed for allotment to tribal members) ceded by the tribes to the federal government. The cession resulted from an agreement signed by three-fourths of the adult males of the tribes as required by prior treaties. Tribal members claimed that signatures had been obtained by fraud and concealment and that, therefore, the agreement had not been approved by the requisite three-quarters majority. Nevertheless Congress enacted the statute, which differed from the agreement in a number of respects. The plaintiffs claimed the statute was invalid because it violated the treaty requirement of approval by an extraordinary majority and because it took their property without due process of law. When relief was denied, this appeal followed.]

Mr. Justice WHITE [delivered the opinion of the Court].
[The Treaty of Medicine Lodge, 15 Stat. 581, article 12] reads as follows:

Article 12. No treaty for the cession of any portion or part of the reservation herein described, which may be held in common, shall be of any validity or force as against the said Indians, unless executed and signed by at least three fourths of all the adult male Indians occupying the same, and no cession by the tribe shall be understood or construed in such manner as to deprive, without his consent, any individual member of the tribe of his rights to any tract of land selected by him as provided in article III (VI) of this treaty.

The appellants base their right to relief on the proposition that by the effect of the article just quoted the confederated tribes of Kiowas, Comanches and Apaches were vested with an interest in the lands held in common within the reservation, which interest could not be divested by Congress in any other mode than that specified in the said twelfth article, and that as a result of the said stipulation the interest of the Indians in the common lands fell within the protection of the Fifth Amendment to the Constitution of the United States, and such interest — indirectly at least — came under the control of the judicial branch of the government. We are unable to yield our assent to this view.

The contention in effect ignores the status of the contracting Indians and the relation of dependency they bore and continue to bear towards the government of the United States. To uphold the claim would be to adjudge that the indirect operation of the treaty was to materially limit and qualify the controlling authority of Congress in respect to the care and protection of the Indians, and to deprive Congress, in a possible emergency, when the necessity might be urgent for a partition and disposal of the tribal lands, of all power to act, if the assent of the Indians could not be obtained.

Now, it is true that in decisions of this court, the Indian right of occupancy of tribal lands, whether declared in a treaty or otherwise created, has been stated to be sacred, or, as sometimes expressed, as sacred as the fee of the United

States in the same lands. [*E.g., Johnson v. McIntosh; Cherokee Nation v. Georgia; Worcester v. Georgia.*] But in none of these cases was there involved a controversy between Indians and the government respecting the power of Congress to administer the property of the Indians. [These cases involved third parties who traced title to Indians. Only the United States has the power to interfere with Indian occupancy.] "It is to be presumed that in this matter the United States would be governed by such considerations of justice as would control a Christian people in their treatment of an ignorant and dependent race." [*Beecher v. Wetherby,* 95 U.S. 517, 525 (1877).]

Plenary authority over the tribal relations of the Indians has been exercised by Congress from the beginning, and the power has always been deemed a political one, not subject to be controlled by the judicial department of the government. Until the year 1871 the policy was pursued of dealing with the Indian tribes by means of treaties, and, of course, a moral obligation rested upon Congress to act in good faith in performing the stipulations entered into on its behalf. But, as with treaties made with foreign nations, *Chinese Exclusion Case,* 130 U.S. 581, 600, the legislative power might pass laws in conflict with treaties made with the Indians.

The power exists to abrogate the provisions of an Indian treaty, though presumably such power will be exercised only when circumstances arise which will not only justify the government in disregarding the stipulations of the treaty, but may demand, in the interest of the country and the Indians themselves, that it should do so. When, therefore, treaties were entered into between the United States and a tribe of Indians it was never doubted that the *power* to abrogate existed in Congress, and that in a contingency such power might be availed of from considerations of governmental policy, particularly if consistent with perfect good faith towards the Indians. In [*Kagama,*] speaking of the Indians, the court said:

> The power of the general government over these remnants of a race once powerful, now weak and diminished in numbers, is necessary to their protection, as well as to the safety of those among whom they dwell. It must exist in that government, because it never has existed anywhere else, because the theatre of its exercise is within the geographical limits of the United States, because it has never been denied, and because it alone can enforce its laws on all the tribes.

That Indians who had not been fully emancipated from the control and protection of the United States are subject, at least so far as the tribal lands were concerned, to be controlled by direct legislation of Congress, is also declared in *Choctaw Nation v. United States,* 119 U.S. 1, 27, and *Stephens v. Cherokee Nation,* 174 U.S. 445, 483.

In view of the legislative power possessed by Congress over treaties with the Indians and Indian tribal property, we may not specially consider the contentions pressed upon our notice that the signing by the Indians of the agreement of October 6, 1892, was obtained by fraudulent misrepresentations and concealment, that the requisite three fourths of adult male Indians had not signed, as required by the twelfth article of the treaty of 1867, and that the treaty as signed had been amended by Congress without submitting such amendments to the action of the Indians, since all these matters, in any event, were solely within the domain of the legislative authority and its action is conclusive upon the courts.

The act of June 6, 1900, which is complained of in the bill, was enacted at a time when the tribal relations between the confederated tribes of Kiowas, Comanches and Apaches still existed, and that statute and the statutes supplementary thereto dealt with the disposition of tribal property and purported to give an adequate consideration for the surplus lands not allotted among the Indians or reserved for their benefit. Indeed, the controversy which this case presents is concluded by the decision in *Cherokee Nation v. Hitchcock*, 187 U.S. 294, decided at this term, where it was held that full administrative power was possessed by Congress over Indian tribal property. In effect, the action of Congress now complained of was but an exercise of such power, a mere change in the form of investment of Indian tribal property, the property of those who, as we have held, were in substantial effect the wards of the government. We must presume that Congress acted in perfect good faith in the dealings with the Indians of which complaint is made, and that the legislative branch of the government exercised its best judgment in the premises. In any event, as Congress possessed full power in the matter, the judiciary cannot question or inquire into the motives which prompted the enactment of this legislation. If injury was occasioned, which we do not wish to be understood as implying, by the use made by Congress of its power, relief must be sought by an appeal to that body for redress and not to the courts. The legislation in question was constitutional, and the demurrer to the bill was therefore rightly sustained.

[*Affirmed.*]

UNITED STATES v. SANDOVAL

231 U.S. 28 (1913)

Mr. Justice VAN DEVANTER delivered the opinion of the Court.

This is a criminal prosecution for introducing [liquor] into Indian country, [the Santa Clara Pueblo. The district court dismissed the indictment, holding the underlying statute unconstitutional because it encroached on the state's police power.]

The question to be considered, then, is, whether the status of the Pueblo Indians and their lands is such that Congress competently can prohibit the introduction of intoxicating liquor into those lands notwithstanding the admission of New Mexico to statehood.

There are as many as twenty Indian pueblos scattered over the State, having an aggregate population of over 8,000. The lands belonging to the several pueblos vary in quantity, but usually embrace about 17,000 acres, held in communal, fee simple ownership under grants from the King of Spain made during the Spanish sovereignty and confirmed by Congress since the acquisition of that territory by the United States. As respects six of the pueblos, one being the Santa Clara, adjacent public lands have been reserved by executive orders for the use and occupancy of the Indians.

The people of the pueblos, although sedentary rather than nomadic in their inclinations, and disposed to peace and industry, are nevertheless Indians in race, customs, and domestic government. Always living in separate and isolated communities, adhering to primitive modes of life, largely influenced by superstition and fetishism, and chiefly governed according to the crude customs inherited from their ancestors, they are essentially a simple, uninformed and inferior people. Upon the termination of the Spanish sovereignty they were given enlarged political and civil rights by Mexico, but it remains an open question whether they have become citizens of the United States. Be this as it may, they have been regarded and treated by the United States as requiring special consideration and protection, like other Indian communities. Thus, public moneys have been expended in presenting them with farming implements and utensils, and in their civilization and instruction; agents and superintendents have been provided to guard their interests; central training schools and day schools at the pueblos have been established and maintained for the education of their children; dams and irrigation works have been constructed to encourage and enable them to cultivate their lands and sustain themselves; public lands, as before indicated, have been reserved for their use and occupancy where their own lands were deemed inadequate; a special attorney has been employed since 1898, at an annual cost of $2,000, to represent them and maintain their rights; and when latterly the Territory undertook to tax their lands and other property, Congress forbade such taxation, [in a statute stating their lands and other property "shall be free and exempt from taxation of any sort whatsoever ... until Congress shall otherwise provide." 33 Stat. 1048, 1069, c. 1479.]

[T]he reports of the superintendents charged with guarding their interests show that they are dependent upon the fostering care and protection of the Government, like reservation Indians in general; that, although industrially superior, they are intellectually and morally inferior to many of them; and that they are easy victims to the evils and debasing influence of intoxicants. [Examples follow:]

Santa Fe, 1905: "Until the old customs and Indian practices are broken among this people we cannot hope for a great amount of progress. The secret dance, from which all whites are excluded is perhaps one of the greatest evils. What goes on at this time I will not attempt to say, but I firmly believe that it is little less than a ribald system of debauchery."

[Under the Spanish] the Indians of the pueblos were treated as wards requiring special protection, were subjected to restraints and official supervision in the alienation of their property, and were the beneficiaries of a law [prohibiting the sale of wine to them.] After the Mexican succession they were elevated to citizenship and civil rights not before enjoyed, but whether the prior tutelage and restrictions were wholly terminated has been the subject of differing opinions.

[I]t is not necessary to dwell specially upon the legal status of this people under either Spanish or Mexican rule, for whether Indian communities within the limits of the United States may be subjected to its guardianship and protection as dependent wards turns upon other considerations. Not only does the Constitution expressly authorize Congress to regulate commerce with the Indian tribes, but long continued legislative and executive usage and an unbroken current of judicial decisions have attributed to the United States as a superior and civilized nation the power and the duty of exercising a fostering care and protection over all dependent Indian communities within its borders, whether within its original territory or territory subsequently acquired, and whether within or without the limits of a State. As was said by this court in [*Kagama*]:

"The power of the General Government over these remnants of a race once powerful, now weak and diminished in numbers, is necessary to their protection, as well as to the safety of those among whom they dwell. It must exist in that government, because it never has existed anywhere else, because the theatre of its exercise is within the geographical limits of the United States, because it has never been denied, and because it alone can enforce its laws on all the tribes." In *Tiger v. Western Investment Co.,* 221 U.S. 286, 315, prior decisions were carefully reviewed and it was further said: "Taking these decisions together, it may be taken as the settled doctrine of this court that Congress, in pursuance of the long-established policy of the Government, has a right to determine for itself when the guardianship which has been maintained over the Indian shall cease. It is for that body, and not for the courts, to determine when the true interests of the Indian require his release from such condition of tutelage."

Of course, it is not meant by this that Congress may bring a community or body of people within the range of this power by arbitrarily calling them an Indian tribe, but only that in respect of distinctly Indian communities the questions whether, to what extent, and for what time they shall be recognized and dealt with as dependent tribes requiring the guardianship and protection of the United States are to be determined by Congress, and not by the courts.

As before indicated, by an uniform course of action beginning as early as 1854 and continued up to the present time, the legislative and executive branches of the Government have regarded and treated the Pueblos of New Mexico as dependent communities entitled to its aid and protection, like other Indian tribes, and, considering their Indian lineage, isolated and communal life, primitive customs and limited civilization, this assertion of guardianship over them cannot be said to be arbitrary but must be regarded as both authorized and controlling.

[The defendant argues that the legislation cannot be applied to the Pueblos because they are citizens.] As before stated, whether they are citizens is an open question, and we need not determine it now, because citizenship is not in itself an obstacle to the exercise by Congress of its power to enact laws for the benefit and protection of tribal Indians as a dependent people.

It also is said that such legislation cannot be made to include the lands of the Pueblos, because the Indians have a fee simple title. It is true that the Indians of each pueblo do have such a title to all the lands connected therewith, excepting such as are occupied under executive orders, but it is a communal title, no individual owning any separate tract. In other words, the lands are public lands of the pueblo, and so the situation is essentially the same as it was with the Five Civilized Tribes, whose lands, although owned in fee under patents from the United States, were adjudged subject to the legislation of Congress enacted in the exercise of the Government's guardianship over those tribes and their affairs.

[Because it is] a legitimate exercise of [federal] power, the legislation in question does not encroach upon the police power of the State or disturb the principle of equality among the States.

[*Reversed.*]

NOTES

1. Extra-constitutional Power? According to a study by Professor Newton:

"In seeking to justify this assertion of federal power, however, the Court [in *Kagama*] had, through its earlier decisions, painted itself into a corner. In the first place, congressional power to regulate activities within the territories [using the property clause of Article IV, sec. 2] could not be invoked, because the land was within the state of California. Nor could the power to regulate Indian commerce be used, since at that time, the Court required a direct nexus with commerce to sustain federal laws regulating interstate and Indian commerce. The power to enact a criminal code applicable within the states, although fairly well-established today, was beyond the grant of power to regulate commerce with Indian tribes in 1885. Finally, the congressional power to effectuate treaties with Indian tribes was similarly inapplicable, since no treaty was involved."

Newton, *Federal Power Over Indians: Its Sources, Scope, and Limitations,* 132 U. PA. L. REV. 195, 213-14 (1984).* What power did the Court invoke and on what provision of the Constitution did the Court base this power?

If the answer involves a power created by the federal trusteeship over Indian affairs and the dependent status of the Indian tribes, can the decisions in *Kagama* and *Lone Wolf* be reconciled with accepted constitutional doctrines regarding the source and scope of federal authority? In *M'Culloch v. Maryland,* 17 U.S. (4 Wheat.) 316 (1819), Chief Justice Marshall said: "Let the end be legitimate, let it be within the scope of the constitution, and all means which are appropriate, which are plainly adopted to that end, which are not prohibited, but consistent with the letter and spirit of the constitution, are constitutional." Is the exercise of federal trusteeship power over Indian tribes a legitimate "end" within the scope of the Constitution, as Marshall used that term?

2. Plenary Power: Since the nineteenth century, the Court has often repeated the doctrine that the federal government possesses plenary power to regulate Indian affairs. *See, e.g., Stephens v. Cherokee Nation,* 174 U.S. 445, 484-86, 491 (1899) (upholding constitutionality of laws allotting tribal land of the Five Civilized Tribes and abolishing tribal courts); *Perrin v. United States,* 232 U.S. 478, 482 (1914) (liquor regulation); *United States v. Ramsey,* 271 U.S. 467, 471 (1926) (same).

What does the term "plenary power" mean? In the context of the interstate commerce clause, Chief Justice Marshall described the nature of plenary power as follows:

This power, like all others vested in Congress is complete in itself, may be exercised to its utmost extent, and acknowledges no limitations, other than are prescribed in the constitution. These are expressed in plain terms .... If, as has always been understood, the sovereignty of Congress, though limited to specified objects, is *plenary as to those objects,* the power over commerce with foreign nations, and among the several states, is vested in Congress as absolutely as it would be in a single government, having in its constitution the same restrictions on the exercise of the power as are found in the constitution of the United States.

Gibbons v. Ogden, 22 U.S. (9 Wheat.) 1, 196-97 (1824) (emphasis added).

Does *Kagama, Lone Wolf,* or *Sandoval* invoke the concept of plenary power in the same fashion suggested by Chief Justice Marshall in *Gibbons?* What is the difference? In addition to connoting the supremacy of federal over state law, the term has also been used to refer to exclusive power (such as the exclusive

---

power of the Senate to ratify treaties) and, finally, to refer somewhat vaguely to some sort of unlimited power: either unlimited as to the objectives Congress may pursue (such as using the Commerce Power to bar race discrimination) or unlimited by other textual provisions of the Constitution. *See generally* Engdahl, *State and Federal Power over Federal Property*, 18 Ariz. L. Rev. 283, 363-66 (1976). Does *Kagama, Sandoval,* or *Lone Wolf* invoke congressional power in any of these ways? Do any of these interpretations of the term raise constitutional questions? Does the source of the grant of power over Indian affairs to Congress in any way affect the scope of federal authority? Should it? *See, e.g., Mathews v. Diaz*, 426 U.S. 67, 81-82 (1976) ("narrow standard of review of decisions made by the Congress or the President in the area of immigration and naturalization"); cf. *Korematsu v. United States*, 323 U.S. 214, 217 (1944) (interning Japanese during World War II pursuant to war powers held not to violate equal protection clause). Finally, even if the Constitution quite clearly grants Congress the power to do something, like breaching a treaty by enacting a later inconsistent statute, does the exercise of this power necessarily carry no consequences? *See, e.g., Diggs v. Shultz*, 470 F.2d 461 (D.C. Cir. 1972) (Byrd amendment, permitting U.S. to import chrome to Southern Rhodesia in violation of a U.N. Security Council resolution constitutional under the last-in-time rule, but at the same time a breach of international law.) See also section C, *infra.*

3. A Doctrine Rooted in Prejudice? "The narrow question decided in the *Sandoval* case was that the dependent status of the Pueblo Indians was such that Congress could expressly prohibit the introduction of intoxicating liquors into their lands under its power "[t]o regulate Commerce ... with the Indian Tribes." *Mountain States Tel. & Tel. Co. v. Pueblo of Santa Ana*, 472 U.S. 237, 242 (1985) (Stevens, J.) If this was the narrow question, why was it necessary to discuss the Pueblo Indians' cultural practices and religious beliefs?

One author has commented:

> The undisguised contempt for the native culture was unrelieved by an open-minded assessment in any of the principal cases studied. Rather, the Indians were described as semi-barbarous, savage, primitive, degraded, and ignorant. The relationship between the federal government and the Indian was frequently termed as one between a superior and inferior. The white race was called more intelligent and highly developed. There was no question but that a higher civilization was thought to be justly replacing that of a passing race whose time was over and whose existence could no longer be justified. The very weakness of the Indians in resisting the tide seemed to be one of their greatest moral shortcomings, but not as serious as the Indian communal tradition. To the white observer, the lack of proprietary interest generally displayed by tribal members was repulsive and backward. Removing the "herd" instinct was deemed by some to be the key to civilizing the Indian.

Carter, *Race and Power Politics as Aspects of Federal Guardianship Over American Indians: Land-Related Cases, 1887-1924*, 4 Am. Indian L. Rev. 197, 227 (1976).* Many other commentators have also been struck by the openly ethnocentric tone of the opinions of the Plenary Power Era, see, e.g., R. Berkhofer, Jr., The White Man's Indian (1978); Note, *Constitutional Law: Congressional Plenary Power Over Indian Affairs — A Doctrine Rooted in Prejudice*, 10 Am. Indian L. Rev. 117 (1982); as well as recent judicial opinions, Williams, *Documents of Barbarism: The Contemporary Legacy of European*

Racism and Colonialism in the Narrative Traditions of Federal Indian Law, 31 ARIZ. L. REV. 237 (1989).

4. The Role of the Political Question Doctrine: In *Lone Wolf* the Court seemed to suggest that the exercise of federal authority in the field of Indian affairs constituted a political question not cognizable by the judiciary: "as Congress possessed full power in the matter, the judiciary cannot question or inquire into the motives which prompted the enactment of this legislation. If injury was occasioned, which we do not wish to be understood as implying, by the use made by Congress of its power, relief must be sought by appeal to that body for redress and not to the courts." *Lone Wolf,* 187 U.S. at 568; *see also United States v. Santa Fe Pac. R.R.,* 314 U.S. 339, 347 (1941); *Cherokee Tobacco,* 78 U.S. (11 Wall.) 616, 621 (1871) (statutory abrogation of treaty); *United States v. Holliday,* 70 U.S. (3 Wall.) 407 (1866). What does this statement mean? Does it necessarily mean the judiciary can never call Congress to account when power over Indians is challenged? *Lone Wolf* was an action brought by Lone Wolf on his own behalf and on behalf of many members of the affected tribes, challenging the method by which congressional agents obtained consent for an allotment treaty from tribal members. The plaintiffs sought an injunction against the operation of a federal statute carrying the agreement into effect. Congress maintained the signatures were legitimate. Despite the Court's broad language, could it be saying only that equity had no remedy, because the tribal members had a claim at law? *See* Henkin, *Is There a "Political Question" Doctrine?,* 85 YALE L.J. 597, 606, 622 (1976). Does *Sandoval* itself suggest any limits on congressional power to declare a group an Indian tribe and thus subject to federal Indian law?

What is the continued vitality of the plenary power and political question doctrines in twentieth century Indian law? These issues are explored in the following cases.

3. TWENTIETH CENTURY REFINEMENTS

UNITED STATES v. JOHN

437 U.S. 634 (1978)

Mr. Justice BLACKMUN delivered the opinion of the Court.

[A number of Choctaw Indians remained in Mississippi despite federal attempts to effect their removal to Oklahoma. In the portion of this case reprinted in Chapter 1, the Court held that land the government acquired for the Mississippi Choctaws was "Indian country" within the meaning of the Major Crimes Act, 18 U.S.C. § 1153, because the lands had been purchased in trust for them at the direction of Congress. In the section printed below, the court addressed the issue of congressional power to bring the modern Choctaws within the reach of federal Indian law.]

IV

Mississippi appears to concede, that if § 1153 provides a basis for the [federal] prosecution of Smith John for the offense charged, the State has no similar jurisdiction. This concession, based on the assumption that § 1153 ordinarily is pre-emptive of state jurisdiction when it applies, seems to us to be correct. It was a necessary premise of at least one of our earlier decisions.

The State argues, however, that the Federal Government has no power to produce this result. It suggests that since 1830 the Choctaws residing in Mississippi have become fully assimilated into the political and social life of the State, and that the Federal Government long ago abandoned its supervisory authority over these Indians. Because of this abandonment, and the long lapse in the federal recognition of a tribal organization in Mississippi, the power given Congress "[t]o regulate Commerce ... with the Indian Tribes," Const. Art. I, § 8, cl. 3, cannot provide a basis for federal jurisdiction. To recognize the Choctaws in Mississippi as Indians over which special federal power may be exercised would be anomalous and arbitrary.

We assume for purposes of argument, as does the United States, that there have been times when Mississippi's jurisdiction over the Choctaws and their lands went unchallenged. But, particularly in view of the elaborate history, recounted above, of relations between the Mississippi Choctaws and the United States, we do not agree that Congress and the Executive Branch have less power to deal with the affairs of the Mississippi Choctaws than with the affairs of other Indian groups. Neither the fact that the Choctaws in Mississippi are merely a remnant of a larger group of Indians, long ago removed from Mississippi, nor the fact that federal supervision over them has not been continuous, destroys the federal power to deal with them. *United States v. Wright,* 53 F.2d 300 [4th Cir. 1931].

The State also argues that the Federal Government may not deal specially with the Indians within the State's boundaries because to do so would be inconsistent with the Treaty at Dancing Rabbit Creek. This argument may seem to be a cruel joke to those familiar with the history of the execution of that treaty, and of the treaties that renegotiated claims arising from it. And even if that treaty were the only source regarding the status of these Indians in federal law, we see nothing in it inconsistent with the continued federal supervision of them under the Commerce Clause. It is true that this treaty anticipated that each of those electing to remain in Mississippi would become "a citizen of the States," but the extension of citizenship status to Indians does not, in itself, end the powers given Congress to deal with them.

DELAWARE TRIBAL BUSINESS COMMITTEE v. WEEKS

430 U.S. 73 (1977)

Mr. Justice BRENNAN delivered the opinion of the Court.

[The Delaware Indians had become geographically and politically divided into four present-day groups, called the Cherokee, Absentee, Munsee, and Kansas Delawares. The Cherokee and Absentee Delawares were both federally recognized Indian tribes. The Kansas Delawares had elected to take individual parcels of land in Kansas in 1866; their descendants are not members of a federally recognized tribe. At issue was the distribution of an Indian Claims Commission judgment awarded to the modern day descendants of members of the historic Delaware Nation. The congressional distribution scheme awarded 90% of the judgment to be distributed per capita solely to the Cherokee and Absentee Delawares, with the rest to go into the tribal treasuries of the two tribes. As a result, the Kansas Delawares received nothing. Weeks brought an action on behalf of all the Kansas Delawares alleging that the exclusion of the Kansas Delawares denied them equal protection of the laws.]

II

Appellants differ on the issue of whether this suit presents a nonjusticiable political question because of Congress' pervasive authority, rooted in the Constitution, to control tribal property. Stated in other words, they differ on the issue of whether congressional exercise of control over tribal property is final and not subject to judicial scrutiny, since the power over distribution of tribal property has "been committed by the Constitution" to the Congress, *Baker v. Carr,* 369 U.S. 186, 211 (1962), and since "[the] nonjusticiability of a political question is primarily a function of the separation of powers," *id.,* at 210. Appellants Cherokee and Absentee Delawares, citing [*Lone Wolf v. Hitchcock*], argue that Congress' distribution plan reflects a congressional determination not subject to scrutiny by the Judicial Branch, and that the District Court therefore erred in reaching the merits of this action. Appellant Secretary of the Interior, on the other hand, submits that the plenary power of Congress in matters of Indian affairs "does not mean that all federal legislation concerning Indians is ... immune from judicial scrutiny or that claims, such as those presented by [appellees], are not justiciable." [Brief for Appellants.] We agree with the Secretary of the Interior.

The statement in *Lone Wolf* that the power of Congress "has always been deemed a political one, not subject to be controlled by the judicial department of the government," however pertinent to the question then before the Court of congressional power to abrogate treaties, has not deterred this Court, particularly in this day, from scrutinizing Indian legislation to determine whether it violates the equal protection component of the Fifth Amendment. *See, e.g.,* [*Morton v. Mancari*]. "The power of Congress over Indian affairs may be of a plenary nature; but it is not absolute." *United States v. Alcea Band of Tillamooks,* 329 U.S. 40 (1946) (plurality opinion).

The question is therefore what judicial review of Pub. L. 92-456 is appropriate in light of the broad congressional power to prescribe the distribution of property of the Indian tribes. The general rule emerging from our decisions ordinarily requires the judiciary to defer to congressional determination of what is the best or most efficient use for which tribal funds should be employed. *Sizemore v. Brady,* 235 U.S. 441, 449 (1914). Thus, Congress may choose to differentiate among groups of Indians in the same tribe in making a distribution, *Simmons v. Seelatsee,* 384 U.S. 209 (1966), or on the other hand to expand a class of tribal beneficiaries entitled to share in royalties from tribal lands, *United States v. Jim,* [409 U.S. 80 (1972)], or to devote to tribal use mineral rights under allotments that otherwise would have gone to individual allottees, *Northern Cheyenne Tribe v. Hollowbreast,* 425 U.S. 649 (1976). The standard of review most recently expressed is that the legislative judgment should not be disturbed "as long as the special treatment can be tied rationally to the fulfillment of Congress' unique obligation toward the Indians ...." [*Morton v. Mancari, supra* Chapter 1.]

IV

We are persuaded on the record before us that Congress' omission of [Kansas Delawares] was "tied rationally to the fulfillment of Congress' unique obligation toward the Indians."

First, the Kansas Delawares are not a recognized tribal entity, but are simply individual Indians with no vested rights in any tribal property. Public Law 92-456 distributes tribal rather than individually owned property, for the funds were appropriated to pay an award redressing the breach of a treaty with a tribal entity, the Delaware Nation. [The tribal entity brought the claim before the Indian Claims Commission, and the judgment was designed to compensate the tribe.] As tribal property, the appropriated funds were subject to the exercise by Congress of its traditional broad authority over the management and distribution of lands and property held by recognized tribes, an authority "drawn both explicitly and implicitly from the Constitution itself." *Morton v. Mancari, supra,* at 551-52.

[The Kansas Delawares' ancestors] severed their relations with the tribe when they elected under [a] treaty to become United States citizens entitled to participate in tribal assets only to the extent of their "just proportion ... of the cash value of the credits of said tribe ... *then* held in trust by the United States." (Emphasis supplied.) We cannot say that the decision of Congress to exclude [them] and to distribute the appropriated funds only to members of or persons closely affiliated with the Cherokee and Absentee Delaware Tribes, was not "tied rationally to the fulfillment of Congress' unique obligation toward the Indians."

[The] conclusion that the exclusion of the Kansas Delawares from distribution under Pub. L. 92-456 does not offend the Due Process Clause of the Fifth Amendment of course does not preclude Congress from revising the distribution scheme to include the Kansas Delawares. The distribution authorized by Pub. L. 92-456 has not yet occurred, and Congress has the power to revise its original allocation. *United States v. Jim,* 409 U.S., at 82-83.

Reversed.

NOTES

1. Repudiation of Trusteeship as a Separate Source of Power: In *McClanahan v. Arizona State Tax Comm'n,* 411 U.S. 164, 172 n.7 (1973), the Court stated "[t]he source of federal authority over Indian matters has been the subject of some confusion, but it is now generally recognized that the power derives from federal responsibility for regulating commerce with Indian tribes and for treaty making." Assuming this dicta to be sound as a matter of constitutional doctrine, is it consistent with the full range of decisions based on plenary congressional power over Indian affairs?

2. Plenary Power and the Political Question Doctrine: In *Weeks* the Court appeared to repudiate the notion that the political question doctrine could bar consideration of the merits of a tribal property claim. Nevertheless, in the appeal of the Sioux Nation's claim for damages for the taking of the Black Hills, see *infra* Chapter 5, section B2, the government argued that Congress's power to take tribal property should be subjected only to minimal scrutiny by the Courts. Brief for the United States at 57-59 & n.49, *United States v. Sioux*

Nation, 448 U.S. 371 (1980). In rejecting that argument the Court distinguished *Lone Wolf* by saying: "[T]he [*Lone Wolf*] Court's conclusive presumption of congressional good faith was based in large measure on the idea that relations between this Nation and the Indian tribes are a political matter, not amenable to judicial review. That view, of course, has long since been discredited in taking cases, and was expressly laid to rest in [*Weeks*]."

3. Congressional Power to Recognize Tribes: Assuming the Indian commerce clause is the source of the power recognized in *John,* upon which groups can Congress visit this awesome power? Is there any limit on what group could be dealt with as an Indian tribe within the meaning of the Constitution? In *Baker v. Carr,* 369 U.S. 186, 215-17 (1962), the Supreme Court noted that the Court had long deferred to the political departments in determining whether Indians are recognized as a tribe because this issue "reflects familiar attributes of political questions." Nevertheless, citing *Sandoval,* the Court added: "Able to discern what is 'distinctly Indian,' the courts will strike down any heedless extension of that label. They will not stand impotent before an obvious instance of a manifestly unauthorized exercise of power." In the 1988 amendments to the Elementary and Secondary Education Act of 1965, 20 U.S.C. § 2701 *et seq.,* Congress included Title IV, "Education for Native Hawaiians." The findings accompanying that title declared: "Congress has the power to specially legislate for the benefit of Native Hawaiians." Act of Apr. 28, 1988, Pub. L. No. 100-237, § 4001, 102 Stat. 130, 358 (1988), codified at 20 U.S.C. § 4901. According to the Senate Select Committee on Indian Affairs Report accompanying the bill, congressional power to provide services to Native Hawaiians as a class is derived from its general trust relationship to all Indian tribes "constitutionally assigned to the Federal Government" by cases like *Worcester.* In concluding that Congress can provide services to Native Hawaiians, the Report states:

> While a number of legal arguments can be constructed to address the question of whether Native Hawaiians are legally the same as Indians; these formulations do not clearly address the underlying issue. When Congress has determined that a trust relationship exists for an "indigenous group" within its political boundaries, Congress has the authority and the power to determine the perimeters of the social service aspect of that relationship.

S. REP. No. 100-36, 100th Cong., 1st Sess. 6-7 (1987). Does this basis for power pose any constitutional problems? Would it be simpler to base this legislation on the Indian commerce clause? Is the term "Indian tribes" synonymous with indigenous peoples? The special problem of Native Hawaiians is explored in greater depth in Chapter 8.

4. *Weeks* and Judicial Deference: Although the Court did reach the merits in *Weeks,* was its analysis of the merits of the equal protection claim unduly deferential to congressional power? The decision upheld an act that distributed an Indian claims award to the Delaware Indians in a fashion that excluded from participation a group of Delawares known as the "Kansas Delawares." The majority noted the ancestors of the Kansas Delawares had severed their relations with the tribe when, under an 1866 treaty, they had elected to become United States citizens entitled only to participate in tribal assets to the extent of their pro-rata proportion *then* held in trust by the United States. Thus, the Court found the distinction "tied rationally to the fulfillment of Congress' unique obligation toward the Indians" and dismissed the due process challenge to the exclusion. Justice Stevens's dissent pointed out that although this distinction may be rational, it was not a distinction drawn by Congress. In fact, the legislative record indicated Congress's leaving the Kansas Delawares out of the distribution was nothing more than a legislative oversight. He thus would have invalidated the law as violating "the due process of lawmaking." *Weeks*, 430 U.S. at 97-98 (Stevens, J., dissenting).

5. Recent Invocations of Plenary Power: In *McClanahan* and other modern cases, the court has been careful to base its decision on enumerated powers. Nevertheless it continues to invoke the plenary power doctrine, albeit in dicta, often citing either *Kagama* or *Lone Wolf. See, e.g., United States v. Wheeler*, in which Justice Stewart said:

> Indian tribes are, of course, no longer "possessed of the full attributes of sovereignty" .... Their incorporation within the territory of the United States, and their acceptance of its protection necessarily divested them of some aspects of the sovereignty which they had previously exercised. By specific treaty provision they yielded up other sovereign power; by statute, in the exercise of its plenary control, Congress has removed still others.

435 U.S. 313, 323 (1978). Similarly, in *Santa Clara Pueblo v. Martinez*, 436 U.S. 49, 56 (1978), Justice Marshall wrote, "Congress has plenary authority to limit, modify or eliminate the powers of local self-government which the tribes otherwise possess." What is the utility of such concepts as plenary power and political question in the twentieth century? Does the invocation of these concepts in recent cases do nothing more than signal the Court's intent to continue its historic deference toward congressional policymaking in Indian affairs?

6. The Role of the Court in Making Law: As the previous cases illustrate, congressional power to act in Indian affairs is settled law, rarely questioned today. Not all federal laws affecting Indians can be traced to statutes, however. Since the days of *Johnson v. McIntosh* and *Worcester v. Georgia*, the Court has played an activist role by creating federal common law defining and sometimes delimiting tribal rights and powers. *Compare, e.g., National Farmers Union Ins. Cos. v. Crow Tribe*, 471 U.S. 845 (1985) (federal common law defines the outer boundaries of Indian tribal power over non-Indians) *with, e.g., County of Oneida v. Oneida Indian Nation*, 470 U.S. 226, 231-32 (1985) (federal common law creates cause of action to challenge land sales to states). What is the source and scope of the Court's authority to make federal common law? Indian law is one of several enclaves of federal common law. Professor Martha Field argues that the only limit on the court's power to create federal common law is the requirement that "the court must point to a federal enactment, constitutional or statutory, that it interprets as authorizing the federal common law rule." Field, *Sources of Law: The Scope of Federal Common Law*, 99 Harv. L. Rev. 881, 887, 927 (1986). In many fields of law where federal common law is frequently enunciated, courts are careful to point to statutory authority and explain their task as filling in the interstices of a complex regulatory scheme. *See, e.g., Textile Workers Union v. Lincoln Mills*, 353 U.S. 448 (1957). In some Indian law cases, however, the courts do not invoke a statutory or constitutional enactment. Nevertheless, Professor Field argues that Indian law fits within her limitation because Indian law is based on treaties, both those between the Indians and the United States and between the United States and Great Britain. *See* Field, *supra*, at 948-49. Relying on *Worcester v. Georgia*, she argues that Indian law fits a category in which "courts sometimes fail to address authority for federal common law simply because the existence of such authority is well-established." *Id.* at 948. As you encounter cases involving assertions of federal common law, ask whether you agree with this characterization.

B. ALLOCATION OF FEDERAL AUTHORITY: THE PERVASIVE INFLUENCE OF THE DEPARTMENT OF THE INTERIOR AND THE BUREAU OF INDIAN AFFAIRS

Administrative agencies play a major role in Indian law. Congress has delegated power to many federal agencies to affect Indian tribal and individual concerns. The Indian Health Service and the Administration for Native Americans in the Department of Health and Human Services, the Office of Indian Education in the Department of Education, and the Indian Housing program of the Department of Housing and Urban Development are important federal programs. But the most extensive as well as the broadest delegations of power have been to the Department of the Interior and are often exercised by the Bureau of Indian Affairs. The cases that follow introduce you to the pervasive influence of the Department of the Interior in the daily lives of Indian tribes and Indian peoples.

RAINBOW v. YOUNG

161 F. 835 (8th Cir. 1908)

Van Devanter, Circuit Judge.

[The superintendent of the Winnebago Indian Reservation issued an order requiring bill collectors to remain away from the reservation on the day lease moneys were to be distributed. A collector who violated the order was arrested and removed from the reservation by BIA Agency police. The collector then prevailed upon state authorities to arrest the Agency officers. The district court denied the Agency officers a writ of habeas corpus on the ground that there was no statutory authority for the order of the superintendent removing the collector from the reservation.]

Of the questions discussed by counsel, we deem it necessary to here notice the single one of the commissioner's authority to give the direction which was disregarded by Mr. Sloan and in the orderly execution of which he was removed from the reservation. While the members of the Winnebago tribe have received allotments in severalty and have become citizens of the United States and of the state of Nebraska, their tribal relation has not been terminated. They are not permitted to alienate, mortgage, or lease their allotments without the sanction of the Secretary of the Interior. Their lease moneys are collected and disbursed by officers of the United States; [t]heir lands and some at least of their other property are not taxable; and the United States maintains a reservation, an agency, and a training school for their benefit. In short, they are regarded as being in some respects still in a state of dependency and tutelage which entitles them to the care and protection of the national government; and when they shall be let out of that state is for Congress alone to determine. Besides, the reservation from which Mr. Sloan was removed is the property of the United States, is set apart and used as a tribal reservation, and in respect of it the United States has the rights of an individual proprietor, and can maintain its possession and deal with intruders in like manner as can an individual in respect of his own property. With these observations, we turn to the statutes bearing upon the authority of the Commissioner of Indian Affairs, [which provide:]

Sec. 441 [now 25 U.S.C. § 1]. The Secretary of the Interior is charged with the supervision of public business relating to the following subjects: ... Third, The Indians.

Sec. 463 [now 25 U.S.C. § 2]. The Commissioner of Indian Affairs shall, under the direction of the Secretary of the Interior, and agreeably to such regulations as the President may prescribe, have the management of all Indian affairs, and of all matters arising out of Indian relations.

Sec. 2058 [now repealed]. Each Indian agent shall, within his agency, manage and superintend the intercourse with the Indians agreeably to law; and execute and perform such regulations and duties, not inconsistent with law, as may be prescribed by the President, the Secretary of the Interior, the Commissioner of Indian Affairs, or the Superintendent of Indian Affairs.

"Sec. 2149 [now repealed]. The Commissioner of Indian Affairs is authorized and required, with the approval of the Secretary of the Interior, to remove from any tribal reservation any person being thereon without authority of law or whose presence within the limits of the reservation may, in the judgment of the commissioner, be detrimental to the peace and welfare of the Indians: and may employ for the purpose such force as may be necessary to enable the agent to effect the removal of such person.

And in Act March 3, 1903, c. 994, 32 Stat. 982, is the following:

That the Commissioner of Indian Affairs, with the approval of the Secretary of the Interior, may devolve the duties of any Indian agency or any part thereof upon the superintendent of the Indian training school located at such agency whenever in his judgment such superintendent can properly perform the duties of such agency.

No other statute imposes any limitation applicable here upon the exercise of the authority so given to the commissioner, and upon this record it cannot reasonably be doubted that the commissioner, in giving to the superintendent the direction before named, acted with the approval of the Secretary of the Interior.

[The] very general language of the statutes makes it quite plain that the authority conferred upon the Commissioner of Indian Affairs was intended to be sufficiently comprehensive to enable him, agreeably to the laws of Congress and to the supervision of the President and the Secretary of the Interior, to manage all Indian affairs, and all matters arising out of Indian relations, with a just regard, not merely to the rights and welfare of the public, but also to the rights and welfare of the Indians, and to the duty of care and protection owing to them by reason of their state of dependency and tutelage. And, while there is no specific provision relating to the exclusion of collectors from Indian agencies at times when payments are being made to the Indians, it does not follow that the commissioner is without authority to exclude them; for by section 2149 he is both authorized and required, with the approval of the Secretary of the Interior, to remove from any tribal reservation "any person" whose presence therein may, in his judgment, be detrimental to the peace and welfare of the Indians. This applies alike to all persons whose presence may be thus detrimental, and commits the decision of that question to the commissioner. Of course, it is necessary to the adequate protection of the Indians and to the orderly conduct of reservation affairs that some such authority should be vested in someone, and it is in keeping with other legislation relating to the Indians that it should be vested in the commissioner. *United States ex rel. West v. Hitchcock,* [205 U.S. 80 (1907)]. There is no provision for a re-examination by the courts of the question of fact so committed to him for decision, and, considering the nature of the question, the plenary power of Congress in the matter, and the obvious difficulties in the way of such a re-examination, we think it is intended that there shall be none.

[*Reversed*].

UNITED STATES v. CLAPOX

35 F. 575 (D.C. Or. 1888)

[This opinion, upholding the Secretary's power pursuant to a treaty and statutes to create the Court of Indian Offenses on the Umatilla Indian Reservation, is reprinted *supra* page 38.]

UNITED STATES v. EBERHARDT

789 F.2d 1354 (9th Cir. 1986)

POOLE, Circuit Judge.

In these cases the United States appeals district court orders that dismissed criminal prosecutions charging appellees with unlawful sale of anadromous fish caught within the Hoopa Valley Indian Reservation. Appellees were accused of violating regulations promulgated by the Department of Interior (Interior) that prohibit commercial fishing by Indians on that part of the Klamath River flowing through the Reservation. The district courts held that the regulations are invalid as an unauthorized modification of the Indians' reserved tribal right to fish for commercial purposes. Because we find that the statutory provisions authorizing Interior to manage Indian affairs permit the regulation of fishing on the Hoopa Valley Reservation, we reverse and remand for further proceedings.

I

Appellees are members of the Yurok Indian Tribe who, along with the Hoopa Indians, occupy the Hoopa Valley Reservation in California's Del Norte and Humboldt counties. Appellees were charged under section 3(a) of the Lacey Act Amendments of 1981, 16 U.S.C. § 3372(a) (1982), which makes it unlawful to sell fish taken in violation of any law or regulation of the United States or the law of any state. The regulation at issue here is contained in 25 C.F.R. § 250.8(d)-(f) (1985), and prohibits commercial fishing for anadromous fish on the Hoopa Valley Reservation, but permits fishing for subsistence and ceremonial purposes.

[T]he Indians have federally reserved commercial fishing rights based on the statutes authorizing creation of the reservation. The government claimed, however, that those rights are not absolute and that the ban on commercial fishing was justified as a temporary conservation measure. [The defendants] argued that the regulations prohibiting commercial fishing on the reservation were invalid as an unauthorized *modification or abrogation* of their right to take Klamath River fish.

[In March, 1985, the magistrate dismissed the informations, holding] that Interior was without authority to promulgate regulations that abrogated federally reserved tribal fishing rights. The magistrate also held that even if Interior were authorized to regulate fishing, the regulations as written were arbitrary, not necessary to achieve a conservation purpose, and discriminatory. [The district court affirmed the dismissal.]

III

The issue before us is whether the informations and indictment were subject to dismissal because Interior lacks authority to impose a moratorium on commercial fishing on the Klamath River by Indians of the Hoopa Valley Reservation. The validity of the moratorium depends on whether Congress has given Interior express or implied statutory authority to regulate Indian fishing.

[The Interior Department ban was part of a comprehensive plan adopted] pursuant to its responsibilities as trustee to preserve and protect Indian resources, and [was] designed "to allow for the exercise of Indian fishing rights consistent with conservation of the resource." 44 Fed. Reg. 17144 (1979). The regulations aim at promoting equal access to the Klamath River fishery resource by all Indians of the Reservation, and at assuring adequate spawning escapement.

At oral argument, appellees conceded that Interior has general authority to regulate Indian fishing. They challenge none of the other regulatory provisions. Appellees claim only that Congress has not authorized the abrogation of reserved tribal rights effected by the ban on commercial fishing.

Interior's authority for issuing the Hoopa Valley Reservation fishing regulations arises from the statutory delegation of powers contained in 25 U.S.C. §§ 2, 9 (1982).[7] These provisions generally authorize the Executive to manage Indian affairs but do not expressly authorize Indian fishing regulation. However, ever since these statutes were enacted in the 1830's, they have served as the source of Interior's plenary administrative authority in discharging the federal government's trust obligations to Indians. We conclude that these statutory provisions give Interior sufficient authority to promulgate the Indian fishing regulations at issue here and consequently, we reject appellees' argument that the regulations are invalid in the absence of specific legislation giving Interior authority to regulate Indian fishing.

Appellees rely on *Village of Kake v. Egan,* 369 U.S. 60 (1962), in which the Supreme Court noted that the authority conferred under 25 U.S.C. §§ 2, 9, does not give Interior "a general power to make rules governing Indian conduct." 369 U.S. at 63. [*Village of Kake* involved nonreservation Indians. More-

---

[7] 25 U.S.C. § 2 provides:

The Commissioner of Indian Affairs shall, under the direction of the Secretary of the Interior, and agreeably to such regulations as the President may prescribe, have the management of all Indian affairs and of all matters arising out of Indian relations.

25 U.S.C. § 9 provides:

The President may prescribe such regulations as he may think fit for carrying into effect the various provisions of any act relating to Indian affairs, and for the settlement of the accounts of Indian affairs....

over, in *Village of Kake* the] Court emphasized that the cited statutes gave Interior the power to regulate the exercise of existing rights, not to grant new rights, and that none of the Indians affected belonged to a reservation, which might have given Interior authority to permit Indian fishing contrary to state law.

[T]hese cases involve regulations managing the rights of reservation Indians fishing on their reservation. The regulations here do not grant Hoopa Valley Reservation Indians fishing rights; these rights were granted by Congress when it authorized the President to create the Reservation for Indian purposes. More-over, contrary to the district court's conclusion, Interior invokes the general trust statutes only as constituting authority to enact regulations to protect and conserve the fishery resource for the benefit of Indians, not as power to abro-gate reserved tribal rights.

We hold that the general trust statutes in Title 25 do furnish Interior with broad authority to supervise and manage Indian affairs and property commen-surate with the trust obligations of the United States.

Since its decision in *Village of Kake*, the Supreme Court has acknowledged Interior's authority to issue fishing regulations under the "general Indian powers" conferred by 25 U.S.C. §§ 2, 9. *Washington v. Washington State Com-mercial Passenger Fishing Vessel Association*, 443 U.S. 658, 691 (1979). Con-gress must be assumed to have given Interior reasonable power to discharge its broad responsibilities for the management of Indian affairs effectively. There-fore, we hold that Interior has authority under 25 U.S.C. §§ 2, 9, to regulate Indian fishing on the Hoopa Valley Reservation consistent with its obligations to manage and conserve Indian resources.

[*Reversed and remanded.*]

NOTES

1. **Broad delegations of power:** The broad delegations of power to the Presi-dent and Commissioner of Indian Affairs (now the Assistant Secretary of Inte-rior for Indian Affairs), now contained in 25 U.S.C. §§ 2 and 9, are given an expansive reading in each of the above cases. Are there limits to what can be held to be "management of all Indian affairs" in either the grant of power to Congress to regulate commerce with the Indian tribes or in individual rights guarantees of the Constitution? For instance, would a contemporary court be as deferential to a directive barring participation in a religious rite such as a sun dance, as Judge Deady was to the Secretary's rules regarding adultery in *Clapox*? *Eberhardt* represents a contemporary broad statement regarding sec-retarial power. Does the court recognize any legal or prudential limit on the secretary's power to regulate fishing on a reservation? Consider the statutes at issue in *Eberhardt* from an administrative law standpoint. Are they statutes that authorize independent policymaking or do they primarily authorize rulemaking for implementing policies promulgated by Congress? Is the court's interpreta-tion of these statutes consonant with administrative law principles?

In any of the above cases, did a narrower basis for the authority exist, either articulated, or implicit? A careful reading of other cases sometimes cited for the proposition that the Secretary's authority is nearly limitless often reveals the courts actually relied on specific statutes firmly grounded in federal control over Indian trade or Indian trust property. *See, e.g., United States ex rel. West v. Hitchcock*, 205 U.S. 80 (1907) (agreement with tribe that Secretary of the Interior had power to determine membership of tribe for purposes of receiving allotments from ceded land); *see also Parker v. Richard*, 250 U.S. 235 (1919) (upholding Interior regulation promulgated pursuant to federal law permitting leasing under rules to be fashioned by Secretary reserving discretion to Secretary to determine whether re-leasing oil and gas royalties held in trust was in best interest of Indian lessor or his heirs); *United States v. Birdsall*, 233 U.S. 223 (1914) (Sec. 2 authorized Commissioner of Indian Affairs to advise President whether to grant clemency for defendant convicted of violating federal statutes barring selling liquor in Indian country; therefore, attempted bribe of commissioner constituted a federal crime as an attempt to get the commissioner to do an act in violation of his official duty).

2. The Bureau of Indian Affairs: The Bureau of Indian Affairs began as part of the War Department in 1824. In 1849 Congress transferred the Bureau to the Department of the Interior. Since 1977, an Assistant Secretary of the Interior for Indian Affairs has headed the BIA. Previously, a Commissioner of Indian Affairs headed the BIA and reported, usually through an assistant secretary, to the Secretary of the Interior. Its annual budget is approximately one billion dollars. Staff of Senate Select Comm. on Indian Affairs, 100th Cong., 1st Sess., Budget Views and Estimates for Fiscal Year 1988, at 6 (Comm. Print 1987). As the Department's authorization for managing Indian affairs is broad, so is the Bureau's. This scheme is probably a product of the fact that day-to-day formulation of Indian policy was frequently left to the Indian Service (the Bureau's predecessor) during the first 150 years of national Indian policy and the Service, consequently, came to be a policy organ unto itself. Congress only mapped out in the broadest possible terms the purposes and objectives of national Indian policy; the Service was left to create programs and initiate action to implement those and other policy objectives.

Today, Bureau programs are authorized principally by the Snyder Act, first enacted in 1921:

The Bureau of Indian Affairs, under the supervision of the Secretary of the Interior, shall direct, supervise, and expend such moneys as Congress may from time to time appropriate, for the benefit, care, and assistance of the Indians throughout the United States for the following purposes:

General support and civilization, including education.

For relief of distress and conservation of health.

For industrial assistance and advancement and general administration of Indian property.

For extension, improvement, operation, and maintenance of existing Indian irrigation systems and for development of water supplies.

For the enlargement, extension, improvement, and repair of the buildings and grounds of existing plants and projects.

For the employment of inspectors, supervisors, superintendents, clerks, field matrons, farmers, physicians, Indian police, Indian judges, and other employees.

For the suppression of traffic in intoxicating liquor and deleterious drugs.

For the purchase of horse-drawn and motor-propelled passenger-carrying vehicles for official use.

And for general and incidental expenses in connection with the administration of Indian affairs.

25 U.S.C. § 13.

According to a 1976 study of the Bureau, commissioned for the American Indian Policy Review Commission, the Bureau "employs from 13,000 to 18,000 permanent and temporary employees and provides services under 33 program titles, all of which are specifically targeted at providing services to Indian tribes and their members." American Indian Policy Review Commission, Final Report 266 (1976). The Policy Review Commission study also pointed out the Bureau has been one of the most studied and criticized administrative agencies: at least 75 studies over the last 25 years have pointed out its many flaws, frequently calling for it to be abolished. Most recently, a Special Committee of the Senate Select Committee on Indian Affairs flatly stated: "In every area it touches, the BIA is plagued by mismanagement." Special Committee on Investigations of the Senate Select Committee on Indian Affairs, Final Report 8 (1989). Although the Committee did not recommend abolishing the Bureau, it called for an end to paternalism and a transfer of federal assets and annual appropriations to tribes who chose to execute formal agreements with the government. *Id.* at 17.

Essentially, five major criticisms have been voiced through the years: (1) Unconcern for or even hostility to tribal input on such vital issues as budget and management of resources; (2) Concentration of power in Area Offices that too often become fiefdoms for petty bureaucrats exercising too much control over reservation affairs and prevent communication between tribes and Washington policymakers; (3) Fundamental conflicts between the BIA's role as trustee of Indian land and money and administrator of federal services; (4) Ineffectiveness of the BIA in representing Indian interests to the Secretary of the Interior when Indian interests conflict with other interests of the Department, such as land management and reclamation; and (5) mismanagement and excessive management in general.

The Indian people, too, have joined in frequent criticism of the Bureau, although they often oppose attempts to dissolve or radically reorganize the Bureau, for several reasons. First, although the Bureau's employee costs are high, it remains the single largest employer of Indian people because of Indian preference in hiring. Second, dissolution or radical reorganization plans remind them of the hated termination period. Third, they fear diluting BIA power might deny them any voice in Washington. As a frequent critic of the BIA has said: "Tribal governments ... equate their own survival with the survival of the Bureau." Barsh, *The BIA Reorganization Follies of 1978: A Lesson in Bureaucratic Self-Defense,* 7 Am. Indian L. Rev. 1, 5 (1979); *see also* Our Brother's Keeper: The Indian in White America 112-39 (E. Cahn & D. Hearne, eds. 1970). Despite the criticism and the frequent attempts at reorganization, the Bureau endures. As another chronicler of Bureau politics has stated:

> The Bureau of Indian Affairs has always had a militant disinclination toward change. It is like Mother Nature, it can be probed, occupied, undermined, or incinerated, but its essence always seems to remain immutable, its form determined more by the composite debris of passing careers than by directed action. Any efforts to encourage basic change become the feckless hobbies of frustrated men.

Nickeson, *The Structure of the Bureau of Indian Affairs,* 40 Law & Contemp. Probs. 61, 61 (1976).

3. Courts of Indian Offenses Since *Clapox*: The Courts of Indian Offenses were originally established to further the assimilationist goals of the late nineteenth century. Nevertheless, these courts (usually called "CFR" courts because the regulations governing the courts can be found in 25 C.F.R. part 11) are still in effect on some 20 reservations that have not created their own tribal courts. Would the same arguments used in *Clapox* suffice to uphold the constitutionality of CFR courts today? A rare modern challenge to the constitutional basis of the Courts of Indian Offenses occurred in *Tillett v. Hodel*, 730 F. Supp. 381 (W.D. Okla. 1990). When the Kiowa tribe obtained an injunction against a tribal member ordering her to cease representing herself as an agent of the tribe, the defendant argued the injunction was invalid because the Department of the Interior lacked congressional authority to establish the courts. While noting the broad reading given the Snyder Act in *United States v. Clapox*, the court also based its conclusion regarding the Secretary's power on later enactments by Congress that made explicit reference to their existence, including the Indian Civil Rights Act and statutes providing for training of CFR court judges as well as the funding and the creation of a model code for the courts. Are these later actions of Congress sufficient to establish the authority of these CFR courts?

4. The Secretary's Approval Powers — A Unique Aspect of Pervasive Federal Involvement in Indian Affairs: Many statutes give the Secretary of the Interior specific power to approve transactions involving Indian trust property and even tribal constitutions. Specific sources exist for most aspects of the approval power. There is the power to approve contracts with tribes, 25 U.S.C. § 81, including attorney contracts, 25 U.S.C. § 81a, leases, 25 U.S.C. § 415, and tribal constitutions, 25 U.S.C. § 476. In fact, the Secretary may exercise broad supervision over tribal lands and assets, 25 U.S.C. § 464. Because many tribal constitutions contain provisions requiring the tribe to submit laws to the Secretary for approval, secretarial authority over day-to-day lawmaking on the reservation can be considerable. This aspect of the approval powers is discussed in greater depth in Chapter 3, section B2. How broadly should these various grants of power be read? Consider the following provision regarding contracts:

§ 81. Contracts with Indian tribes or Indians

No agreement shall be made by any person with any tribe of Indians, or individual Indians not citizens of the United States, for the payment or delivery of any money or other thing of value, in present or in prospective, or for the granting or procuring any privilege to him, or any other person in consideration of services for said Indians relative to their lands, or to any claims growing out of, or in reference to, annuities, installments, or other moneys, claims, demands, or thing, under laws or treaties with the United States, or official acts of any officers thereof, or in any way connected with or due from the United States, unless such contract or agreement be executed and approved as follows:

First. Such agreement shall be in writing, and a duplicate of it delivered to each party.

Second. It shall bear the approval of the Secretary of the Interior and the Commissioner of Indian Affairs indorsed upon it.

Third. It shall contain the names of all parties in interest, their residence and occupation; and if made with a tribe, by their tribal authorities, the scope of authority and the reason for exercising that authority, shall be given specifically.

Fourth. It shall state the time when and the place where made, the particular purpose for which made, the special thing or things to be done under it, and, if for the collection of money, the basis of the claim, the source from which it is to be collected, the disposition to be made of it when collected, the amount or rate per centum of the fee in all cases; and if any contingent matter or condition constitutes a part of the contract or agreement, it shall be specifically set forth.

Fifth. It shall have a fixed limited time to run, which shall be distinctly stated.

All contracts or agreements made in violation of this section shall be null and void, and all money or other thing of value paid to any person by any Indian or tribe, or any one else, for or on his or their behalf, on account of such services, in excess of the amount approved by the Commissioner and Secretary for such services, may be recovered by suit in the name of the United States in any court of the United States, regardless of the amount in controversy; and one-half thereof shall be paid to the person suing for the same, and the other half shall be paid into the Treasury for the use of the Indian or tribe by or for whom it was so paid.

In *United States ex rel. Buxbom v. Naegele*, 10 Indian L. Rep. 3099 (C.D. Cal., June 23, 1983), a district court held that a competitor of a billboard company could sue to void a contract between the Morongo Band of Mission Indians and a rival company to erect billboards on the reservation. The plaintiff argued that section 81 applied to all contracts between Indians and non-Indians not approved by the Secretary of the Interior. The tribe argued that section 81 applied only to contracts relating to Indian lands held in trust by the U.S. or obligating funds received from the federal government. The district court adopted the plaintiff's interpretation and invalidated a contract under which the tribe had netted $250,000. As a result the plaintiff was eligible to receive the statutory penalty of one-half the contract price. The court decried this result, but stated:

The language of section 81 is clear, and the court must assume that Congress meant what it said. Accordingly, the agreement between Naegele and the band must be set aside and plaintiff's motion for summary judgment must be granted. This decision is reached with considerable reluctance, since the heart of this action is really an unfair competition dispute between Buxbom and Naegele. The court cannot believe that Congress intended that section 81 be used by a business competitor to void the contract of his rival with an Indian tribe, especially when the latter was both represented by counsel and derived substantial benefits from the contract.

Id. at 3100.

In most cases construing 25 U.S.C. § 81, at issue in *Buxbom*, the tribe has requested the Secretary to disapprove a contract or at least has not contested the disapproval. *See, e.g., A.K. Mgt. Co. v. San Manuel Band of Mission Indians*, 789 F.2d 785 (9th Cir. 1986) (Band's cancellation of unapproved contract with management company for bingo enterprise upheld; band had no duty to seek approval); *Udall v. Littell*, 366 F.2d 668 (D.C. Cir. 1966), *cert. denied*, 385 U.S. 1007 (1967) (Secretary has power to cancel contract between attorney and Indian tribe upon discovery that attorney is using legal staff for unauthorized purposes).

In *Buxbom*, the Court relied on *Green v. Menominee Tribe*, 233 U.S. 558 (1914), as settling the issue that section 81 applies to all contracts irrespective of the source of money. In that case a supplier made an oral agreement with a tribe and its Indian agent by which it advanced money to the tribe for a logging enterprise. Proceeds from the enterprise were to be used to pay back the advance and were, in fact, paid by the tribe to the Indian agent who did not reimburse the supplier. When the supplier sued the tribe, the Court dismissed because there was no evidence the original oral contract had ever been approved. Do you see any basis to distinguish this case from *Buxbom*? The other case relied on by the court in *Buxbom* contains broad language regarding the scope of section 81, but held that section 81 does not apply to corporations formed by tribes under state law. *Inecon Agricorp. v. Tribal Farms, Inc.,* 656 F.2d 498 (9th Cir. 1981).

Not surprisingly, *Buxbom* has not been followed. Between the decision and the appeal, the Secretary retroactively approved the contract. On appeal the Ninth Circuit upheld the retroactive approval without reaching the questions regarding the scope of section 81 decided in the lower court. *United States ex rel. Buxbom v. Naegele Outdoor Adv. Co.,* 739 F.2d 473 (9th Cir. 1984), *cert. denied,* 469 U.S. 1109 (1985). *See generally Sac & Fox Tribe v. Apex Constr. Co.,* 757 F.2d 221 (10th Cir.), *cert. denied,* 474 U.S. 850 (1985) (§ 81 only applies to contracts obligating tribal trust money); *Wisconsin Winnebago Bus. Comm. v. Koberstein,* 762 F.2d 613, 617-19 (7th Cir. 1985) (Section 81 only applies to contracts relative to Indian land or obligating trust money or property). *See also United States ex rel. Shakopee-Mdewakanton Sioux Community v. Pan Am. Mgt. Co.,* set forth and discussed in Chapter 7, sections C4 and 5.

In sum, most statutes requiring approval involve transactions affecting tribal or individual Indian land restricted from alienation and protected from taxation. Are actions taken pursuant to these statutes more securely based on delegated constitutional power over Indians? In the absence of a such a statute could the Secretary rely on his broad power to manage Indian affairs to disapprove tribal regulatory transactions (for instance, a zoning ordinance) or consensual transactions (for instance, an agreement not involving tribal trust land or money)?

C. LIMITATIONS ON FEDERAL AUTHORITY

While *Sandoval* and *Baker v. Carr* both suggested that the Indian commerce clause itself may provide some limitations on the scope of plenary federal authority over Indian affairs, that promise remains unfulfilled. Nevertheless, there are other limits on federal power. First, the express provisions of the Bill of Rights have been applied to protect Indian individual and tribal rights from governmental action with varying degrees of success. As illustrated by the material in Chapter 1, tribes and individuals have invoked the first amendment's guarantee of free exercise of religion. This section of Chapter 2 first focuses on other constitutional provisions, such as invocation of equal protection and due process principles to challenge government action that burdens rather than benefits Indians. In addition, courts have applied the fifth amendment takings clause to award just compensation and even to invalidate federal action depriving individual tribal members of property rights in certain circumstances. Because takings clause jurisprudence requires an understanding of the property rights protected, these issues are only noted in this chapter, with a fuller analysis postponed until Chapter 5.

In addition to constitutional limitations on federal power, significant restraints have also been imposed as a result of the development of certain maxims of federal treaty and statutory interpretation designed in part to discharge the federal trusteeship over Indian affairs. These maxims also frequently avoid the necessity of deciding difficult constitutional questions. Accordingly, these important doctrines of statutory and treaty construction will be examined.

Finally, courts have imposed substantial limitations on federal power by discerning enforceable obligations to Indian tribes in the federal-Indian trust relationship. Thus, this focus on limitations ends by examining the source and scope of the trust relationship, its use as a basis for claims against the government for mismanagement of tribal resources and its limitations as a vehicle for protecting Indian rights.

1. CONSTITUTIONAL LIMITATIONS

MORTON v. MANCARI

417 U.S. 535 (1974)

[In this case, the Court distinguished legislation favoring Indian tribal members as political and not racial and therefore not subject to strict scrutiny. It thus upheld the Indian preference provision of the Indian Reorganization Act, because it was "tied rationally to the fulfillment of Congress' unique obligations toward the Indians." It is reprinted *supra* Chapter 1, page 91.]

WASHINGTON v. CONFEDERATED BANDS & TRIBES OF THE YAKIMA INDIAN NATION

439 U.S. 463 (1979)

Mr. Justice STEWART delivered the opinion of the Court.

In this case we are called upon to resolve a dispute between the State of Washington and the Yakima Indian Nation over the validity of the State's exercise of jurisdiction on the Yakima Reservation. In 1963 the Washington Legislature obligated the State to assume civil and criminal jurisdiction over Indians and Indian territory within the State, subject only to the condition that in all but eight subject-matter areas jurisdiction would not extend to Indians on trust or restricted lands without the request of the Indian tribe affected. Ch. 36, 1963 Washington Laws.[1]

---

[1] The statute, codified as R.C.W.A. 37.12.010, provides:

Assumption of criminal and civil jurisdiction by state. The State of Washington hereby obligates and binds itself to assume criminal and civil jurisdiction over Indians and Indian territory, reservations, country, and lands within this state in accordance with the consent of the United States given by the act of August 15, 1953 (Public Law 280, 83rd Congress, 1st Session), but such assumption of jurisdiction shall not apply to Indians when on their tribal lands or allotted lands within an established Indian reservation and held in trust by the United States or subject to a restriction against alienation imposed by the United States, unless the provisions of R.C.W.A. 37.12.021 (tribal consent) have been invoked, except for the following:

(1) Compulsory school attendance;
(2) Public assistance;
(3) Domestic relations;
(4) Mental illness;
(5) Juvenile delinquency;
(6) Adoption proceedings;
(7) Dependent children; and
(8) Operation of motor vehicles upon the public streets, alleys, roads and highways; Provided further, That Indian tribes that petitioned for, were granted and became subject to state jurisdiction pursuant to this chapter on or before March 13, 1963 shall remain subject to state civil and criminal jurisdiction as if chapter 36, Laws of 1963 had not been enacted.

The statute will be referred to in this opinion as Chapter 36.

The Yakima Nation did not make such a request. State authority over Indians within the Yakima Reservation was thus made by Chapter 36 to depend on the title status of the property on which the offense or transaction occurred and upon the nature of the subject-matter.

The Yakima Nation brought this action in a federal district court challenging the statutory and constitutional validity of the State's partial assertion of jurisdiction on its Reservation. The Tribe contended that the federal statute upon which the State based its authority to assume jurisdiction over the Reservation, Public Law 83-280, imposed certain procedural requirements, with which the State had not complied, — most notably, a requirement that Washington first amend its own constitution — and that in any event Pub. L. 280 did not authorize the State to assert only partial jurisdiction within an Indian Reservation. Finally, the Tribe contended that Chapter 36, even if authorized by Congress, violated the Equal Protection and Due Process guarantees of the Fourteenth Amendment.*

The District Court rejected both the statutory and constitutional claims and entered judgment for the State. On appeal, the contention that Washington's assumption of only partial jurisdiction was not authorized by Congress was rejected by the Court of Appeals for the Ninth Circuit, sitting en banc. The en banc court then referred the case to the original panel for consideration of the remaining issues. *Confederated Bands & Tribes of the Yakima Indian Nation v. Washington*, 550 F.2d 443 *(Yakima I)*. The three-judge panel, confining itself to consideration of the constitutional validity of Chapter 36, concluded that the "checkerboard" jurisdictional system it produced was without any rational foundation and therefore violative of the Equal Protection Clause of the Fourteenth Amendment. Finding no basis upon which to sever the offending portion of the legislation, the appellate court declared Chapter 36 unconstitutional in its entirety, and reversed the judgment of the District Court. *Confederated Bands & Tribes of the Yakima Indian Nation v. Washington*, 552 F.2d 1332 *(Yakima II)*.

The State then brought an appeal to this Court. In noting probable jurisdiction of the appeal, we requested the parties to address the issue whether the partial geographic and subject-matter jurisdiction ordained by Chapter 36 is authorized by federal law, as well as the Equal Protection Clause issue.[5]

---

*Public Law 280, mandating some states and authorizing others to assume criminal and civil jurisdiction over Indian reservations within their borders, is treated in the discussion of Termination Era legislation in Chapter 1, section C and covered extensively in Chapter 4, section C1, where the portions of the opinion interpreting Public Law 280 are set forth and discussed. — Eds.

[5]The three-judge appellate court's equal protection decision was based upon the disparity created by Chapter 36 in making criminal jurisdiction over Indians depend upon whether the alleged offense occurred on fee or nonfee land. 552 F.2d 1332, 1334-1335. The court found this criterion for the exercise of state criminal jurisdiction facially unconstitutional. The appellate court found it unnecessary, therefore, to reach the Tribe's contention that the eight statutory categories of subject-matter jurisdiction are vague or its further contention that the *application* of Chapter 36 deprived it of equal protection of the laws. 552 F.2d, at 1334.... The Tribe contends that Chapter 36 is void for failure to meet the standards of definiteness required by the Due Process Clause of the Fourteenth Amendment, asserting that the eight subject-matter categories over which the State has extended full jurisdiction are too vague to give tribal members adequate notice of what conduct is punishable under state law. This challenge is without merit. As the District Court observed, Chapter 36 creates no new criminal offenses but merely extends jurisdiction over certain classes of offenses defined elsewhere in state law. If those offenses are not sufficiently defined, individual tribal members may defend against any prosecutions under them at the time such prosecutions are brought. See *Younger v. Harris*, [401 U.S. 37.] The eight subject-matter areas are themselves defined with

I

The Confederated Bands and Tribes of the Yakima Indian Nation comprise 14 originally distinct Indian tribes that joined together in the middle of the 19th century for the purposes of their relationships with the United States. [Their] reservation [in southeastern Washington contains] 1,387,505 acres of land, of which some 80% is held in trust by the United States for the Yakima Nation or individual members of the tribe. The remaining parcels of land are held in fee by Indian and non-Indian owners. [Much of the land is heavily forested and sparsely populated. Three incorporated townships lie within the boundaries of the reservation. The inhabited portions of the reservation display a checker-board pattern.] The land held in fee is scattered throughout the Reservation, but most of it is concentrated in the northeastern portion close to the Yakima River and within the three towns of Toppenish, Wapato, and Harrah. Of the 25,000 permanent residents of the Reservation, 3,074 are members of the Yakima Nation, and tribal members live in all of the inhabited areas of the reservation. In the three towns — where over half of the non-Indian population resides — members of the Tribe are substantially outnumbered by non-Indian residents occupying fee land.

[The state] law at issue in this litigation [was enacted in 1963.] The most significant feature of the new statute was its provision for the extension of at least some jurisdiction over all Indian lands within the State, whether or not the affected tribe gave its consent. Full criminal and civil jurisdiction to the extent permitted by Pub. L. 280 was extended to all fee lands in every Indian reservation and to trust and allotted lands therein when non-Indians were involved. Except for eight categories of law, however, state jurisdiction was not extended to Indians on allotted and trust lands unless the affected tribe so requested. The eight jurisdictional categories of state law that were thus extended to all parts of every Indian reservation were in the areas of compulsory school attendance, public assistance, domestic relations, mental illness, juvenile delinquency, adoption proceedings, dependent children, and motor vehicles.

The Yakima Indian Nation did not request the full measure of jurisdiction made possible by Chapter 36, and the Yakima Reservation thus became subject to the system of jurisdiction outlined at the outset of this opinion.[19] This litigation followed.

II

The Yakima Nation relies on three separate and independent grounds in asserting that Chapter 36 is invalid. First, it argues that under the terms of Pub. L. 280 [which authorized the state to extend jurisdiction over Indian reservations] Washington was not authorized to enact Chapter 36 until the state consti-

---

reasonable clarity in language no less precise than that commonly accepted in federal jurisdictional statutes in the same field. The District Court's ruling that Chapter 36 is not void for vagueness under the Due Process Clause of the Fourteenth Amendment was therefore correct.

[19] Those tribes that had consented to state jurisdiction under the 1957 law remained fully subject to such jurisdiction. Wash. Rev. Code § 37.12.010 (1976). Since 1963 only one tribe, the Colville, has requested the extension of full state jurisdiction. 1 National American Indian Court Judges at 77-81. The Yakima Nation, ever since 1952 when its representatives objected before a congressional committee to a predecessor of Pub. L. 280, has consistently contested the wisdom and the legality of attempts by the State to exercise jurisdiction over its Reservation lands.

tution had been amended by "the people" so as to eliminate its [disclaimer of] state authority over Indian lands. Second, it contends that Pub. L. 280 does not authorize a State to extend only partial jurisdiction over an Indian reservation. Finally, it asserts that Chapter 36, even if authorized by Pub. L. 280, violates the Fourteenth Amendment of the Constitution. We turn now to consideration of each of these arguments.

[The portion of the Court's opinion in which it held that Public Law 280 does not require the state of Washington to amend its constitution before exercising jurisdiction and holding that Public Law 280 did authorize the state's extension of partial jurisdiction over Indian reservations is discussed in Chapter 4, section C1, dealing with state claims to power over Indians. The Court then addressed the constitutionality of the statute.]

V

Having concluded that Chapter 36 violates neither the procedural nor the substantive terms of Pub. L. 280, we turn, finally, to the question whether the "checkerboard" pattern of jurisdiction applicable on the reservations of nonconsenting tribes is on its face invalid under the Equal Protection Clause of the Fourteenth Amendment. The Court of Appeals for the Ninth Circuit concluded that it is, reasoning that the land-title classification is too bizarre to meet "any formulation of the rational basis test." The Tribe advances several different lines of argument in defense of this ruling.

First, it argues that the classifications implicit in Chapter 36 are racial classifications, "suspect" under the test enunciated in *McLaughlin v. Florida,* 379 U.S. 184, and that they cannot stand unless justified by a compelling state interest. Second, it argues that its interest in self-government is a fundamental right, and that Chapter 36 — as a law abridging this right — is presumptively invalid. Finally, the Tribe argues that Chapter 36 is invalid even if reviewed under the more traditional equal protection criteria articulated in such cases as *Massachusetts Bd. of Retirement v. Murgia,* [427 U.S. at 314].

We agree with the Court of Appeals to the extent that its opinion rejects the first two of these arguments and reflects a judgment that Chapter 36 must be sustained against an Equal Protection Clause attack if the classifications it employs "rationally further the purpose identified by the State." *Massachusetts Bd. of Retirement v. Murgia, supra.* It is settled that "the unique legal status of Indian tribes under federal law" permits the Federal Government to enact legislation singling out tribal Indians, legislation that might otherwise be constitutionally offensive. [*Morton v. Mancari.*] States do not enjoy this same unique relationship with Indians, but Chapter 36 is not simply another state law. It was enacted in response to a federal measure explicitly designed to readjust the allocation of jurisdiction over Indians. The jurisdiction permitted under Chapter 36 is, as we have found, within the scope of the authorization of Pub. L. 280. And many of the classifications made by Chapter 36 are also made by Pub. L. 280. Indeed, classifications based on tribal status and land tenure inhere in many of the decisions of this Court involving jurisdictional controversies between tribal Indians and the States, see, *e.g., United States v. McBratney,* 104 U.S. 621. For these reasons, we find the argument that such classifications are "suspect" an untenable one. The contention that Chapter 36 abridges a "funda-mental right" is also untenable. It is well established that Congress, in the exer-cise of its plenary power over Indian affairs, may restrict the retained sovereign powers of the Indian tribes. See, *e.g., United States v. Wheeler,* 435 U.S. 313. In enacting Chapter 36, Washington was legislating under explicit authority granted by Congress in the exercise of that federal power.

The question that remains, then, is whether the lines drawn by Chapter 36 fail to meet conventional Equal Protection Clause criteria, as the Court of Ap-peals held. Under those criteria, legislative classifications are valid unless they bear no rational relationship to the State's objectives. State legislation "does not violate the Equal Protection Clause merely because the classifications [it makes] are imperfect." *Dandridge v. Williams,* 397 U.S. 471, 491. Under these stan-dards we have no difficulty in concluding that Chapter 36 does not offend the Equal Protection Clause.

The lines the State has drawn may well be difficult to administer. But they are no more or less so than many of the classifications that pervade the law of Indian jurisdiction. Chapter 36 is fairly calculated to further the State's interest in providing protection to non-Indian citizens living within the boundaries of a reservation while at the same time allowing scope for tribal self-government on trust or restricted lands. The land-tenure classification made by the State is neither an irrational nor arbitrary means of identifying those areas within a reservation in which tribal members have the greatest interest in being free of state police power. Indeed, many of the rules developed in this Court's decisions in cases accommodating the sovereign rights of the tribes with those of the States are strikingly similar. In short, checkerboard jurisdiction is not novel in Indian law, and does not, as such, violate the Constitution.

[*Reversed.*]

EMPLOYMENT DIVISION, DEPARTMENT OF HUMAN RESOURCES OF OREGON v. SMITH

110 S. Ct. 1595 (1990)

[This case, holding that the free exercise clause of the first amendment does not require an exception from a state criminal law for the sacramental use of peyote by members of the Native American Church, is reprinted *supra* Chapter 1, page 46.]

NOTES

1. The "Tied-Rationally" Standard of Review: In *Mancari* the Court first used what has become known as the "tied-rationally" standard of review. *See* F. COHEN, HANDBOOK OF FEDERAL INDIAN LAW 221 (1982 ed.). Does this standard "put some teeth" into judicial review of congressional actions affecting Indians? *See* Gunther, *The Supreme Court, 1971 Term — Foreword: In Search of Evolving Doctrine on a Changing Court: A Model for a Newer Equal Protec-tion,* 86 HARV. L. REV. 1 (1972). One could argue that the standard applies only to legislation favoring Indians (and thus carrying out Congress's unique obliga-tions) or to legislation affecting Indians only as members of a political group and not a racial group. Certainly both factors were present in *Mancari.* Were both also present in *Weeks, supra* section A? *See* Comment, *Federal Plenary*

Power in Indian Affairs After Weeks and Sioux Nation, 131 U. PA. L. REV. 235, 260 (1982) (legislation clearly unfavorable to tribal interests should be subjected to less lenient scrutiny). Although the Court has invoked the "tied-rationally" standard in other cases involving Indian preferences, it has chosen to avoid it in cases imposing burdens on Indians. In *United States v. Antelope,* Chapter 1, *supra,* the Court flatly stated that all legislation dealing with Indians had a legitimate purpose — to govern Indian tribes — and would be upheld if not invidiously motivated or irrational. 430 U.S. 641, 645 (1977). On a spectrum ranging from very deferential to stricter scrutiny, how would you characterize the standard of review the Court used in *Yakima?*

2. **Indian Tribal Rights and Constitutional Guarantees of Individual Freedom:** The egalitarian principles of the equal protection clause and the individual freedoms accorded protection as fundamental rights under the due process clause do not provide a helpful framework when the question is protecting *tribal* rights, as both *Mancari* and *Yakima* illustrate. Equal protection and due process principles are designed to protect the individual from the community and not a community's right to govern itself free from a larger community (the majority). The constitutional guarantee of free exercise of religion, however, can be invoked to protect community as well as individual values by protecting a "traditional way of life [involving] deep religious conviction, shared by an organized group, and intimately related to daily living." *Wisconsin v. Yoder,* 406 U.S. 205, 216 (1972). To what extent can tribes rely on religious freedom arguments after *Employment Division v. Smith?*

The only analog in the Constitution that could be applied to Indian tribes, is the protection of states' rights from abuse by the majority in the federal system. The analogy is not that helpful, however. States' rights has been the banner first for slavery and then segregation. Moreover, the Court's attempts to fashion a limitation on congressional power from tenth amendment principles in order to protect state sovereignty was short-lived. *National League of Cities v. Usery,* 426 U.S. 833 (1976), *overruled, Garcia v. San Antonio Metro. Transit Auth.,* 469 U.S. 528 (1985). Nevertheless, significant structural provisions adequate to protect state sovereignty remain in the Constitution. In fact, this was one of the rationales for overruling *League of Cities.* The majority stated:

> [T]he composition of the Federal Government was designed in large part to protect the states from overreaching by Congress. The Framers thus gave the States a role in the Selection both of the Executive and the Legislative Branches of the Federal Government. The States were vested with indirect influence over the House of Representatives and the Presidency by their control of electoral qualifications and their role in presidential elections. They were given more direct influence in the Senate, where each State received equal representation and each Senator was to be selected by the legislature of his state. The significance attached to the States' equal representation in the Senate is underscored by the prohibition of any constitutional amendment divesting a State of equal representation without the State's consent. In short, the Framers chose to rely on a federal system in which special restraints on federal power over the States inhered principally in the workings of the National Government itself, rather than in discrete limitation on the objects of federal authority. State sovereign interests, then, are more properly protected by procedural safeguards inherent in the structure of the federal system than by judicially created limitations on federal power.

Garcia, 469 U.S. at 550-51. In light of the lack of any structural protection for Indian tribes in the Constitution, and their resulting lack of representation in the political process, which is magnified by their being the quintessential "discrete and insular" minority, should courts scrutinize federal action burdening Indian tribes more carefully? *See United States v. Carolene Prods. Co.,* 304 U.S.

144, 152-53 n.4 (1938); *see also* Newton, *Federal Power Over Indians: Its Sources, Scope and Limitations,* 132 U. Pa. L. Rev. 195, 241-47 (1984) (evaluating arguments for heightened scrutiny of legislation affecting Indian tribes).

Finally, traditional notions of what constitutes a compensable claim have posed insuperable barriers to recovery of compensation under the fifth amendment takings clause for harm to tribal culture, religion, or sovereignty. The major problem is that the fifth amendment protects economic harm to vested property rights, capable of measurement by money damages. *Cf. Ft. Sill Apache Tribe v. United States,* 477 F.2d 1360 (Ct. Cl. 1973).

3. Compensation for Taking Property: The Court has extended the fifth amendment's proscription against taking private property for public use without just compensation to Indian tribal and individual land. The Court indicated its willingness to extend fifth amendment protection to individual Indian property rights as early as 1912. In *Choate v. Trapp,* 224 U.S. 665 (1912), the Court held that the fifth amendment prevented the abrogation of a statutorily vested tax immunity of allotted Indian land without compensation. Justice Lamar's opinion for the Court said:

> There have been comparatively few cases which discuss the legislative power over private property held by the Indians. But those few all recognize that he is not excepted from the protection guaranteed by the Constitution. His private rights are secured and enforced to the same extent and in the same way as other residents or citizens of the United States.
>
> His right of private property is not subject to impairment by legislative action, even while he is, as a member of a tribe and subject to the guardianship of the United States as to his political and personal status.... But there was no intimation that the power of wardship conferred authority on Congress to lessen any of the rights of property which had been vested in the individual Indian by prior laws or contracts. Such rights are protected from repeal by the provisions of the Fifth Amendment.

Choate presented a fairly unusual situation in which the tribe had ratified an agreement consenting to allotment of tribal land held in fee simple title on condition that the land remain immune from taxation. Questions whether the unusual nature of the agreement in *Choate* limited its application to other allotted land were answered in 1987 in *Hodel v. Irving,* 481 U.S. 704 (1987), excerpted in Chapter 5, section E. The Court invalidated section 207 of the Indian Land Consolidation Act, Pub. L. 97-459, 96 Stat. 2517, 2519, which prevented individual allottees from passing on small undivided interests in allotted land to their heirs by providing that such interests would automatically escheat to the tribe. As a result, it seems clear the Court is prepared to treat all individual allotted land as a compensable property right.

Tribal land was treated as public property during the Plenary Power Era. *See, e.g., Stephens v. Cherokee Nation,* 174 U.S. 445, 488 (1899) ("the lands and moneys of these tribes are public lands and public moneys."). In the twentieth century the Court has held that tribal property recognized by treaty or statute as belonging to the tribe is a compensable property right, however. *See Sioux Tribe v. United States,* 448 U.S. 371 (1980), *infra* in Chapter 5, section B2.

2. INTERPRETIVE LIMITATIONS

UNITED STATES v. WINNEBAGO TRIBE

542 F.2d 1002 (8th Cir. 1976)

Heaney, Circuit Judge.

The United States, through the Army Corps of Engineers, brought suit to acquire by eminent domain certain lands for use in the Oxbow Recreation

Lakes, Snyder-Winnebago Complex, Missouri River Recreation Lakes Project....

I

We consider first whether the United States has the authority to take the Tribal lands by eminent domain.

It is undisputed that by the Treaty of March 8, 1865, the United States agreed "to set apart for the occupation and future home of the Winnebago Indians, forever," the Tribal lands at issue. Those lands are held in trust by the United States. It is also undisputed that Congress has the power to abrogate the Treaty to permit the taking of the Tribal lands by eminent domain. The Tribe contends that Congress has not exercised that power. We agree.

[Under the Supreme Court's precedents, treaties] will not be deemed to have been abrogated or modified absent a clear expression of congressional purpose, for "'the intention to abrogate or modify a treaty is not to be lightly imputed to the Congress.'"[5] *Menominee Tribe v. United States,* [391 U.S. 404, 413 (1968)]. *Accord, United States v. White,* 508 F.2d 453 (8th Cir. 1974). The United States' reliance upon *Federal Power Com. v. Tuscarora Indian Nation,* [362 U.S. 99 (1960)], for a contrary canon of construction, *i.e.,* that the general statutes of the United States apply to Indians and non-Indians alike, is misplaced. Contrary to the facts presented here, the Indian lands taken in *Tuscarora* were not held in trust by the United States and were not reserved by treaty. As we stated in *United States v. White, supra* at 455, the general rule of *Tuscarora* does not apply when the interest sought to be affected is reserved to the Indians by treaty. At issue in *White* was the question of whether a member of the Red Lake Band of Chippewa Indians could be prosecuted for shooting at a bald eagle within the confines of the reservation in the face of treaty rights that reserved to the Chippewa the right to hunt and fish on the ceded lands. *White* is controlling authority. Nothing in *Tuscarora* sanctions the taking of treaty lands without express congressional authorization.

The only evidence of congressional intent, argued by the parties as relevant, is a letter, dated December 31, 1943, of Major General E. Reybold, Chief of Engineers, to the Chairman of the House Committee on Flood Control made in connection with the Flood Control Act of 1944, 58 Stat. 887, and portions of the hearings before the Senate and House Committees on Appropriations. No reference is made to committee reports or statutory language.

The letter of Major General E. Reybold evinces an awareness that the acquisition of Indian lands would be necessary for the development of the Missouri

---

[5]The requirement of specific congressional intent to abrogate treaty rights is not impractical. The case cited by the United States, *United States v. Crance,* 341 F.2d 161 (8th Cir.), *cert. denied,* 382 U.S. 815, 86 S. Ct. 36, 15 L. Ed. 2d 63 (1965), is inapposite. The specific authorization necessary to abrogate the Treaty need not delineate the land to be taken by metes and bounds.

By letter to this Court, the United States Department of the Interior takes a position contrary to that asserted here by the Army Corps of Engineers and in support of the Tribe. It agrees that the intent to abrogate treaty rights must be clearly manifested by Congress and is of the opinion that the relevant statute and legislative history fail to meet that standard.

River Basin. But no mention is made of the Oxbow Lakes, Snyder-Winnebago Complex or the Treaty of 1865 with the Winnebago Indians. Moreover, the letter can be interpreted as contemplating the acquisition of Indian lands only with the approval of the Indians affected and the Secretary of the Interior. This doubtful expression of congressional intent must be resolved in favor of the Tribe. [*Bryan v. Itasca County,* 426 U.S. 373, (1976)]; *McClanahan v. Arizona Tax Commission,* [411 U.S. at 174]. Indeed, the interpretation that favors the Tribe is consistent with the later enactments of Congress that specifically authorized the taking of Indian lands.

The portions of the hearings before the Appropriation Committees of the Congress relied upon by the United States evince a general awareness that lands would be acquired for the development of the Oxbow Lakes, Snyder-Winnebago Complex specifically. No reference is made to the fact that lands held in trust by the United States and secured to the Tribe by the Treaty of 1865 would be or could be affected by the project. The concern of the committeemen focused on the allocation of the costs between the federal and state governments. These references to the Oxbow Lakes, Snyder-Winnebago Complex made during the appropriation hearings do not indicate the clear intent of the Congress to abrogate the Treaty. The United States, through the Army Corps of Engineers, was without authority to take the Tribal lands at issue by eminent domain.

[*Affirmed in part, reversed in part, and remanded.*]

UNITED STATES v. DION

476 U.S. 734 (1986)

Justice MARSHALL delivered the opinion of the Court.

Respondent Dwight Dion, Sr., a member of the Yankton Sioux Tribe, was convicted of shooting four bald eagles on the Yankton Sioux reservation in South Dakota in violation of the Endangered Species Act, 87 Stat. 884, as amended, 16 U.S.C. § 1531 et seq. (1982 ed. and Supp. II). The District Court dismissed before trial a charge of shooting a golden eagle in violation of the Bald Eagle Protection Act, 54 Stat. 250, 16 U.S.C. § 668 et seq. (Eagle Protection Act). Dion was also convicted of selling carcasses and parts of eagles and other birds in violation of the Eagle Protection Act and the Migratory Bird Treaty Act, 40 Stat. 755, as amended, 16 U.S.C. § 703 et seq. The Court of Appeals for the Eighth Circuit affirmed all of Dion's convictions except those for shooting bald eagles in violation of the Endangered Species Act. As to those, it stated that Dion could be convicted only upon a jury determination that the birds were killed for commercial purposes. It also affirmed the District Court's dismissal of the charge of shooting a golden eagle in violation of the Eagle Protection Act. We granted certiorari, and we now reverse the judgment of the Court of Appeals insofar as it reversed Dion's convictions under the Endangered Species Act and affirmed the dismissal of the charge against him under the Eagle Protection Act.

I

The Eagle Protection Act by its terms prohibits the hunting of the bald or golden eagle anywhere within the United States, except pursuant to a permit issued by the Secretary of the Interior. The Endangered Species Act imposes an equally stringent ban on the hunting of the bald eagle. The Court of Appeals for the Eighth Circuit, however, sitting en banc, held that members of the Yankton Sioux Tribe have a treaty right to hunt bald and golden eagles within the Yankton reservation for noncommercial purposes. It further held that the Eagle Protection Act and Endangered Species Act did not abrogate this treaty right. It therefore directed that Dion's convictions for shooting bald eagles be vacated, since neither the District Court nor the jury made any explicit finding whether the killings were for commercial or noncommercial purposes.[3]

[In the Treaty with the Yancton Sioux, Apr. 19, 1858, 11 Stat. 743,] the Yankton ceded to the United States all but 400,000 acres of the land then held by the tribe. The treaty bound the Yanktons to remove to, and settle on, their reserve land within one year. The United States in turn agreed to guarantee the Yanktons quiet and undisturbed possession of their reserved land, and to pay to the Yanktons, or expend for their benefit, various moneys in the years to come. The area thus reserved for the tribe was a legally constituted Indian reservation. The treaty did not place any restriction on the Yanktons' hunting rights on their reserved land.

All parties to this litigation agree that the treaty rights reserved by the Yankton included the exclusive right to hunt and fish on their land. As a general rule, Indians enjoy exclusive treaty rights to hunt and fish on lands reserved to them, unless the rights were clearly relinquished by treaty or have been modified by Congress. F. Cohen, Handbook of Federal Indian Law 449 (1982 ed.) (hereinafter Cohen). These rights need not be expressly mentioned in the treaty. See Menominee Tribe v. United States, 391 U.S. 404 (1968). Those treaty rights, however, little avail Dion if, as the Solicitor General argues, they were subsequently abrogated by Congress. We find that they were.

II

It is long settled that "the provisions of an act of Congress, passed in the exercise of its constitutional authority, ... if clear and explicit, must be upheld by courts, even in contravention of express stipulations in an earlier treaty" with a foreign power. Fong Yue Ting v. United States, 149 U.S. 698, 720 (1893). This Court applied that rule to congressional abrogation of Indian treaties in

---

[3]On remand from the en banc court, an Eighth Circuit panel rejected a religious freedom claim raised by Dion. Dion does not pursue that claim here, and accordingly we do not consider it. A statement made by the panel in rejecting that claim, though, casts some doubt on whether the issue of whether Dion had a treaty right to kill eagles for noncommercial purposes is squarely before us. The panel stated: "The record reveals that Dion, Sr. was killing eagles and other protected birds for commercial gain...." 762 F.2d 674, 680 (1980). Notwithstanding its statement that Dion's killings were for commercial gain, apparently inconsistent with the en banc court's refusal to pass on that issue, it issued a judgment vacating Dion's convictions for shooting bald eagles "pursuant to the opinion of this Court en banc." Id., at 694.

We find that this case properly presents the issue whether killing eagles for noncommercial purposes is outside the scope of the Eagle Protection Act and the Endangered Species Act. The Eighth Circuit panel did not disturb the en banc court's holding that Dion cannot be convicted absent a jury determination of whether the killings were for a commercial purpose, and vacated his convictions for shooting bald eagles because the jury made no such finding. The Solicitor General argues that Dion's convictions should have been affirmed whether the killings were for commercial or noncommercial purposes. The correctness of the holding below that killing for noncommercial purposes is not punishable, therefore, is squarely before us.

[*Lone Wolf v. Hitchcock*]. Congress, the Court concluded, has the power "to abrogate the provisions of an Indian treaty, though presumably such power will be exercised only when circumstances arise which will not only justify the government in disregarding the stipulation of the treaty, but may demand, in the interest of the country and the Indians themselves, that it should do so."

We have required that Congress' intention to abrogate Indian treaty rights be clear and plain. "Absent explicit statutory language, we have been extremely reluctant to find congressional abrogation of treaty rights...." *Washington v. Fishing Vessel Ass'n,* 443 U.S. 658, 690 (1979). We do not construe statutes as abrogating treaty rights in "a backhanded way," *Menominee Tribe v. United States,* 391 U.S. 404, 412 (1968); in the absence of explicit statement, "'the intention to abrogate or modify a treaty is not to be lightly imputed to the Congress.'" *Id.,* at 413. Indian treaty rights are too fundamental to be easily cast aside.

We have enunciated, however, different standards over the years for determining how such a clear and plain intent must be demonstrated. In some cases, we have required that Congress make "express declaration" of its intent to abrogate treaty rights. See *Leavenworth, Lawrence, & Galveston R. Co. v. United States,* 92 U.S. 733, 741-742 (1876); see also Wilkinson & Volkman [63 CALIF. L. REV. at] 627-630, 645-659. In other cases, we have looked to the statute's "'legislative history'" and "'surrounding circumstances'" as well as to "'the face of the Act.'" *Rosebud Sioux Tribe v. Kneip,* 430 U.S. 584 587 (1977), quoting *Mattz v. Arnett,* 412 U.S. 481, 505 (1973). Explicit statement by Congress is preferable for the purpose of ensuring legislative accountability for the abrogation of treaty rights. We have not rigidly interpreted that preference, however, as a per se rule; where the evidence of congressional intent to abrogate is sufficiently compelling, "the weight of authority indicates that such an intent can also be found by reviewing court from clear and reliable evidence in the legislative history of a statute." Cohen [at] 223. What is essential is clear evidence that Congress actually considered the conflict between its intended action on the one hand and Indian treaty rights on the other, and chose to resolve that conflict by abrogating the treaty.

A

The Eagle Protection Act renders it a federal crime to "take, possess, sell, purchase, barter, offer to sell, purchase or barter, transport, export or import, at any time or in any manner any bald eagle commonly known as the American eagle or any golden eagle, alive or dead, or any part, nest, or egg thereof." 16 U.S.C. § 668(a). The prohibition is "sweepingly framed"; the enumeration of forbidden acts is "exhaustive and careful." *Andrus v. Allard,* 444 U.S. 51, 56 (1979). The Act, however, authorizes the Secretary of the Interior to permit the taking, possession, and transportation of eagles "for the religious purposes of Indian Tribes," and for certain other narrow purposes, upon a determination that such taking, possession or transportation is compatible with the preservation of the bald eagle or the golden eagle.

Congressional intent to abrogate Indian treaty rights to hunt bald and golden eagles is certainly strongly suggested on the face of the Eagle Protection Act.

The provision allowing taking of eagles under permit for the religious purposes of Indian tribes is difficult to explain except as a reflection of an understanding that the statute otherwise bans the taking of eagles by Indians, a recognition that such a prohibition would cause hardship for the Indians, and a decision that [the] problem should be resolved not by exempting Indians from the coverage of the statute, but by authorizing the Secretary to issue permits to Indians where appropriate.

The legislative history of the statute supports that view. The Eagle Protection Act was originally passed in 1940, and did not contain any explicit reference to Indians. Its prohibitions related only to bald eagles; it cast no shadow on hunting of the more plentiful golden eagle. In 1962, however, Congress considered amendments to the Eagle Protection Act extending its ban to the golden eagle as well. As originally drafted by the staff of the Subcommittee on Fisheries and Wildlife Conservation of the House Committee on Merchant Marine and Fisheries, the amendments simply would have added the words "or any golden eagle" at two places in the Act where prohibitions relating to the bald eagle were described.

Before the start of hearings on the bill, however, the Subcommittee received a letter from Assistant Secretary of the Interior Frank Briggs on behalf of the Interior Department. The Interior Department supported the proposed bill. It noted, however, the following concern [quoting from Assistant Secretary Brigg's letter regarding the golden eagle's importance]: "[I]n enabling many Indian tribes, particularly those in the Southwest, to continue ancient customs and ceremonies that are of deep religious or emotional significance to them," [and concluding: "In the circumstances, it is evident that the Indians are deeply interested in the preservation of both the golden and the bald eagle. If enacted, the bill should therefore permit the Secretary of the Interior, by regulation, to allow the use of eagles for religious purposes by Indian tribes."].

The House Committee reported out the bill. In setting out the need for the legislation, it explained in part:

> Certain feathers of the golden eagle are important in religious ceremonies of some Indian tribes and a large number of the birds are killed to obtain these feathers, as well as to provide souvenirs for tourists in the Indian country. In addition, they are actively hunted by bounty hunters in Texas and some other States. As a result of these activities if steps are not taken as contemplated in this legislation, there is grave danger that the golden eagle will completely disappear. H.R. Rep. No. 1450, 87th Cong., 2d Sess., 2 (1962).

The Committee also reprinted Assistant Secretary Briggs' letter in its Report, and adopted an exception for Indian religious use drafted by the Interior Department. The bill as reported out of the House Committee thus made three major changes in the law, along with other more technical ones. It extended the law's ban to golden eagles. It provided that the Secretary may exempt, by permit, takings of bald or golden eagles "for the religious purposes of Indian tribes." And it added a final proviso: "Provided, That bald eagles may not be taken for any purpose unless, prior to such taking, a permit to do so is procured from the Secretary of the Interior." The bill, as amended, passed the House and was reported to the Senate Committee on Commerce.

At the Senate hearings, representatives of the Interior Department reiterated their position that, because "the golden eagle is an important part of the ceremonies and religion of many Indian tribes," the Secretary should be authorized to allow the use of eagles for religious purposes by Indian tribes. The Senate Committee agreed, and passed the House bill with an additional amendment allowing the Secretary to authorize permits for the taking of golden eagles that were preying on livestock. That Committee again reprinted Assistant Secretary Briggs' letter, S. Rep. No. 1986, 87th Cong., 2d Sess., 5-7 (1962), and summarized the bill as follows: "The resolution as hereby reported would bring the golden eagle under the 1940 act, allow their taking under permit for the religious use of the various Indian tribes (their feathers are an important part of Indian religious rituals) and upon request of a Governor of any State, be taken for the protection of livestock and game." The bill passed the Senate, and was concurred in by the House, with little further discussion.

It seems plain to us, upon reading the legislative history as a whole, that Congress in 1962 believed that it was abrogating the rights of Indians to take eagles. Indeed, the House Report cited the demand for eagle feathers for Indian religious ceremonies as one of the threats to the continued survival of the golden eagle that necessitated passage of the bill. Congress expressly chose to set in place a regime in which the Secretary of the Interior had control over Indian hunting, rather than one in which Indian on-reservation hunting was unrestricted. Congress thus considered the special cultural and religious interests of Indians, balanced those needs against the conservation purposes of the statute, and provided a specific, narrow exception that delineated the extent to which Indians would be permitted to hunt the bald and golden eagle.

Respondent argues that the 1962 Congress did not in fact view the Eagle Protection Act as restricting Indian on-reservation hunting. He points to an internal Interior Department memorandum circulated in 1962 stating with little analysis, that the Eagle Protection Act did not apply within Indian reservations. Memorandum from Assistant Solicitor Vaughn, Branch of Fish and Wildlife, Office of the Solicitor to the Director, Bureau of Sport Fisheries and Wildlife, April 26, 1962. We have no reason to believe that Congress was aware of the contents of the Vaughn memorandum. More importantly, however, we find respondent's contention that the 1962 Congress did not understand the Act to ban all Indian hunting of eagles simply irreconcilable with the statute on its face.

Respondent argues, and the Eighth Circuit agreed, that the provision of the statute granting permit authority is not necessarily inconsistent with an intention that Indians would have unrestricted ability to hunt eagles while on reservations. Respondent construes that provision to allow the Secretary to issue permits to non-Indians to hunt eagles "for Indian religious purposes," and supports this interpretation by pointing out testimony during the hearings to the effect that large-scale eagle bounty hunters sometimes sold eagle feathers to Indian tribes. We do not find respondent's argument credible. Congress could have felt such a provision necessary only if it believed that Indians, if left free to hunt eagles on reservations, would nonetheless be unable to satisfy their own needs and would be forced to call on non-Indians to hunt on their behalf. Yet there is nothing in the legislative history that even remotely supports that patronizing and strained view. Indeed, the Interior Department immediately after the passage of the 1962 amendments adopted regulations authorizing permits only to "individual Indians who are authentic, bona fide practitioners of such religion." 28 Fed. Reg. 976 (1963).[8]

Congress' 1962 action, we conclude, reflected an unmistakable and explicit legislative policy choice that Indian hunting of the bald or golden eagle, except pursuant to permit, is inconsistent with the need to preserve those species. We therefore read the statute as having abrogated that treaty right.

B

Dion also asserts a treaty right to take bald eagles as a defense to his Endangered Species Act prosecution. He argues that evidence that Congress intended to abrogate treaty rights when it passed the Endangered Species Act is considerably more slim than that relating to the Eagle Protection Act. The Endangered Species Act and its legislative history, he points out, are to a great extent silent regarding Indian hunting rights. In this case, however, we need not resolve the question of whether the Congress in the Endangered Species Act abrogated Indian treaty rights. We conclude that Dion's asserted treaty defense is barred in any event.

Dion asserts that he is immune from Endangered Species Act prosecution because he possesses a treaty right to hunt and kill bald eagles. We have held, however, that Congress in passing and amending the Eagle Protection Act divested Dion of his treaty right to hunt bald eagles. He therefore has no treaty right to hunt bald eagles that he can assert as a defense to an Endangered Species Act charge.

We do not hold that when Congress passed and amended the Eagle Protection Act, it stripped away Indian treaty protection for conduct not expressly prohibited by that statute. But the Eagle Protection Act and the Endangered Species Act, in relevant part, prohibit exactly the same conduct, and for the same reasons. Dion here asserts a treaty right to engage in precisely the conduct that Congress, overriding Indian treaty rights, made criminal in the Eagle Protection Act. Dion's treaty shield for that conduct, we hold, was removed by that statute, and Congress' failure to discuss that shield in the context of the Endangered Species Act did not revive that Treaty right.

It would not promote sensible law to hold that while Dion possesses no rights derived from the 1858 treaty that bar his prosecution under the Eagle Protection Act for killing bald eagles, he nonetheless possesses a right to hunt bald eagles, derived from that same treaty, that bars his Endangered Species Act prosecution for the same conduct. Even if Congress did not address Indian treaty rights in the Endangered Species Act sufficiently expressly to effect a valid abrogation, therefore, respondent can assert no treaty defense to a prosecution under the Act for a taking already explicitly prohibited under the Eagle Protection Act.

---

[8] Respondent's argument that Congress in amending the Eagle Protection meant to benefit nontreaty tribes is also flawed. Indian reservations created by statute, agreement, or executive order normally carry with them the same implicit hunting rights as those created by treaty. See Cohen [at] 224; *Antoine v. Washington,* 420 U.S. 194 (1975).

III

We hold that the Court of Appeals erred in recognizing Dion's treaty defense to his Eagle Protection Act and Endangered Species Act prosecutions. For the reasons stated in n. 3, *supra*, we do not pass on the claim raised by *amici* that the Eagle Protection Act, if read to abrogate Indian treaty rights, invades religious freedom. Cf. *United States v. Abeyta*, 632 F. Supp. 1301 (NM 1986). Nor do we address respondent's argument, raised for the first time in this Court, that the Statutes under which he was convicted do not authorize separate convictions for taking and for selling the same birds.

[*Reversed and remanded.*]

NOTES

1. Tests Used to Determine Whether a Later Statute Abrogates a Treaty: Treaties executed over one hundred years ago are still in effect and serve as important sources of rights. *See, e.g., Tsosie v. United States,* 825 F.2d 393 (Fed. Cir. 1987) (treaty promising reimbursement for wrongs committed by "bad men among the whites," is still in effect; therefore Navajo member permitted to sue for damage caused by lab technician posing as doctor who conducted an intimate medical examination). Nevertheless, like treaties with foreign nations, Indian treaties can be abrogated by a later inconsistent statute under the last-in-time rule. *Cherokee Tobacco,* 78 U.S. (11 Wall.) 616, 621 (1871) (Indian treaties accorded no higher sanctity than treaties with foreign nations). The courts have consistently treated the relevant judicial inquiry as a search for clearly expressed congressional intent to abrogate the treaty. *See, e.g., Rosebud Sioux Tribe v. Kneip,* 430 U.S. 584, 586 (1977). Unfortunately, the reported decisions have been remarkably inconsistent in the tests employed to determine intent and the rigor with which the chosen test is applied. Some cases, like the *Winnebago Tribe* case, apply the doctrine rigorously, scouring both the face of the affected statute and the legislative history for clear and unambiguous indications of an intent to modify Indian rights. *See, e.g., Seymour v. Superintendent,* 368 U.S. 351 (1962), *Mattz v. Arnett,* 412 U.S. 481 (1973).

Both the Eighth Circuit in *Winnebago Tribe* and the Supreme Court in *Dion* quoted and relied on *Menominee Tribe v. United States.* The case, which is set forth and discussed in Chapter 6, section A1, is a textbook example of judicial solicitude toward treaty rights. The Supreme Court held that the statute terminating the Menominee Reservation was not sufficiently explicit to terminate hunting and fishing rights or to subject them to state jurisdiction, despite language stating that after termination "the laws of the several States shall apply to the tribe and its members." The Court relied on evidence in the legislative record that the purpose of termination was to end the federal-Indian trust relationship, the absence of any evidence that Congress intended to affect property rights, and on other contemporaneous legislation indicating a policy to preserve hunting and fishing rights.

On the other hand, some cases, while adhering to the principle, find evidence of a specific congressional intent to modify Indian rights on a substantially more ambiguous record. *See, e.g., Rosebud Sioux Tribe v. Kneip,* 430 U.S. 584 (1977), *De Coteau v. District County Court,* 420 U.S. 425 (1975). For example, in two cases involving condemnation of land held by the Seneca for the Allegheny Reservoir Project the Court of Appeals for the District of Columbia Circuit found a congressional intent to abrogate the Indian title on very slim evidence. In *Seneca Nation of Indians v. Brucker,* 262 F.2d 27 (D.C. Cir. 1958), *cert. denied,* 360 U.S. 909 (1959) (*Seneca I*), the tribe vainly attempted to enjoin construction of the Kinzua dam that would flood 10,000 acres of its treaty land to create the Allegheny Reservoir. Although the evidence is clear that Congress knew that Seneca land would be flooded, there was no evidence that Congress was aware that the flooding violated the Treaty of Nov. 11, 1794, 7 Stat. 4, the oldest treaty still in effect between the United States and an Indian tribe. The court of appeals reasoned that the requisite intent was present, because the legislators "knew (1) that the Seneca lands would be flooded, (2) that the Seneca Nation was unwilling to relinquish any of its rights in the lands, and (3) that the lands could be taken by eminent domain." 262 F.2d at 28. Having lost the battle to prevent construction of the dam, the Senecas returned to court to challenge a condemnation of a strip of land through the remaining 2,300 acres for a four-lane, limited access highway to service the reservoir. The only evidence of congressional intent was contained in a brief reference in the Senate Report, S. REP. No. 609, 85th Cong., 1st Sess. 26 (1957):

> The Corps of Engineers has indicated a willingness to accept flowage easements over land owned by the Seneca Indians, in order that the reservation may be kept intact. The committee desires that the Corps of Engineers cooperate to the maximum extent practicable with the Seneca Indians, in order to minimize the effect of the Allegheny River Reservoir on the Indian lands. It is recognized that if the Seneca Indian Nation elects to grant easements for this purpose, they will control the reservoir area within the boundaries of their reservation, and that recreational benefits will inure to the Seneca Nation as a result of the development of this project. The committee recognizes that this procedure may not be entirely satisfactory to all the Seneca Indians, but also realizes that they have rights in the courts if they insist on determining the issues involved in the courts.

Nevertheless, the court of appeals had no trouble finding authorization in the original reservoir project, because the "replacement or relocation of existing highways unquestionably is a part of the reservation project." *Seneca Nation of Indians v. United States,* 338 F.2d 55, 56 (2d Cir. 1964), *cert. denied,* 380 U.S. 952 (1965) (*Seneca II*). *See generally* A. Josephy, Jr., *Cornplanter, Can You Swim,* in NOW THAT THE BUFFALO'S GONE: A STUDY OF TODAY'S AMERICAN INDIANS, at 127 (1982) (history of the land and the dam construction).

Where does *Dion* fit into this spectrum? The Court rejected requiring a clear statement on the face of a statute expressly abrogating Indian property rights as advocated by some commentators. *See* Wilkinson & Volkman, *Judicial Review of Indian Treaty Abrogation,* 63 CALIF. L. REV. 601 (1975). In place of this bright-line test, the Court adopted a flexible standard, stressing that "what is essential is clear evidence that Congress actually considered the conflict between its intended action on the one hand and Indian treaty rights on the other, and chose to resolve that conflict by abrogating the treaty." Although the legislative record contained ample evidence that Congress knew the Bald Eagle Protection Act would affect the strong interests of some Indian tribes in taking eagles for religious and cultural purposes, what evidence indicates Congress knew that treaties existed protecting these interests for some tribes like the Yankton Sioux Tribe? Does the distinction matter? Would a court conscientiously trying to follow the approach taken in *Dion* reach the same result as the courts in the *Seneca* cases, discussed above? Does the approach taken by the Court provide a mechanism to permit a sensitive weighing of all factors indicating intent or give too little weight to the Indian treaty or property rights?

2. The Endangered Species Act After *Dion*: Why did the Supreme Court fail to reach the question whether the Endangered Species Act abrogated Indian treaty rights to hunt for bald and golden eagles? In *United States v. Billie*, 667 F. Supp. 1485 (S.D. Fla. 1987), the district court reached this question in a case in which a Seminole tribal chairman was charged with violating the Endangered Species Act by taking a Florida panther, a species so endangered that there was testimony that only 20 to 50 remained.

The district court applied the test from *Dion* that there must be "clear evidence that Congress actually considered the conflict between its intended action on the one hand and Indian treaty rights on the other, and chose to resolve that conflict by abrogating" the Indian rights. *Id.* at 1492 (quoting *United States v. Dion*, 476 U.S. 734, 740 (1986)). The court found this evidence to be present. To begin with, the court focused on the face of the act: the statute represented a comprehensive scheme and on its face applied to all persons, presumably including Indians. The face of the act contained very few exceptions, with the only exception applying to native peoples being a narrow exemption for hunting for subsistence purposes for Alaskan natives. Next, the court turned to the legislative history, specifically relying on Senate and House hearings on two bills that had *not* passed the year before the ESA was enacted, both containing broader exemptions for Indians hunting for religious purposes.

In a hearing on one of the bills, Interior testified in favor of permitting Indians an exemption closely monitored by the Secretary for cultural and survival purposes. Another bill contained a provision expressly extinguishing Indian treaty rights. In testifying on the second bill, an Interior representative stated that Indians should not be able to exercise treaty rights to extinguish imperiled species. Finally, the same official suggested that Congress would have to make a clear statement if it intended to abrogate Indian hunting rights. Again, the two bills did not pass, but because the bill that eventually did pass came out of the same committees and contained no exemptions for Indians, but only a narrow exemption for Native Alaskans for subsistence, the court stated "the court believes that Congress would have also circumscribed non-Alaskan Indians' rights had it intended to preserve them." As a result, the court concluded: "Congress must have known that the limited Alaskan exemption would be interpreted to show congressional intent not to exempt other Indians." *Id.* at 1491. Is this test sufficient to meet the standard articulated in *Dion*? Could the history be read as indicating more a concern that if Congress abrogated treaty rights compensation might have to be paid and a decision to waffle on the issue by not saying anything about treaty rights and leaving the issue up to the courts?

In *Billie*, the court also rejected the defendant's free exercise of religion claim on the grounds that the use of panther parts by medicine men had not been demonstrated to be sufficiently essential to the practice of the Seminole's traditional religion.

3. Constitutional Limitations on Treaty Abrogation — The Just Compensation Clause: The rights guaranteed Indians by treaty and statute were often secured in exchange for large cessions of land or other rights by the Indians. Since many of the treaty and statutory rights guaranteed to Indians involved vested property rights for which just compensation must be paid under the fifth amendment should the national government abrogate the right, the requirement of a clear and congressional intent to infringe such rights avoids construction of federal statutes in a fashion that would impose unintended financial liabilities on the federal government. In *Menominee Tribe v. United States*, 391

U.S. 404 (1968), discussed in note 1, *supra*, the Court employed such a construction, saying:

> We find it difficult to believe that Congress, without explicit statement, would subject the United States to a claim for compensation by destroying property rights conferred by treaty, particularly when Congress was purporting by the Termination Act to settle the Government's financial obligations toward the Indians.

Id. at 413 (footnotes omitted).

Does the *Dion* holding that the Eagle Protection Act abrogated completely Indian treaty hunting rights give the defendant a claim in the Court of Claims for a taking of property? If so, how could a court measure the value of the property right?

4. Constitutional Limitations on Treaty Abrogation — The Free Exercise Clause: Recall that the Court did not reach the question whether the Eagle Protection Act infringed on Dion's right to practice his religion freely in violation of the first amendment. In a case decided the same year, but shortly before *Dion* was decided, the district court for the district of New Mexico reached that question and reversed the defendant's conviction. *United States v. Abeyta*, 632 F. Supp. 1301 (D.N.M. 1986).

Abeyta, a member of the Isleta Pueblo, had been convicted of shooting a golden eagle for use in religious ceremonies of his secret religious society, the Katsina Society. The court first held that the Eagle Protection Act did not abrogate the defendant's treaty right to hunt for golden eagles for religious purposes. In *Abeyta*, the defendant claimed rights to hunt under the Treaty of Guadalupe Hidalgo guaranteeing all Mexican citizens, including the Pueblos, "the free enjoyment of their liberty and property." The Treaty also contained an explicit promise of religious freedom, providing that the citizens of Mexico would be "secured in the free exercise of their religion without restriction." If a judge were to apply the principles articulated in *Dion* to these same facts, would he have to hold that the Eagle Protection Act also abrogated any treaty promises of religious freedom?

In the alternative, the court held that even if the defendant did not have a treaty right to hunt eagles, the government's punishing of him for taking an eagle, an act of religious conviction, violated his free exercise rights. As the court described the role of the eagle in Pueblo religions:

> In its ritual and reverent use of eagles and their feathers in religious ceremony, the Katsina Society is indistinguishable from myriad pueblo religious fellowships. The central tenets of ancient Indian religious faith are shared among New Mexico's pueblos and, of all birds, the eagle holds an exalted position in all pueblo religious societies. The use of their feathers, particularly from the tail and wings, is indispensable to the ceremonies of the Katsina Society and other pueblo ritual.

Id. at 1303.

The court held that the government's interest in protecting the golden eagle was not compelling, since there was testimony that the golden eagle was no longer endangered. Even if the purpose were regarded as compelling, the Court held the Eagle Protection Act's provisions for Indians to obtain eagle parts and feathers through the Secretary of the Interior was not the least restrictive means of achieving the laudable end of conserving the species. The court described the procedures for obtaining eagles as follows:

> Abeyta did not avail himself of the procedures established by the Secretary to procure feathers for ceremonial purposes. In any event, it would not have been fruitful for him to have done so. The federal eagle depository established and operated by the Fish and

Wildlife Service does not effectively fulfill the pueblos' need for eagle feathers for ceremonial use. The life span of the golden eagle is 15 to 20 years. Each breeding pair, of which there are currently approximately 150 in New Mexico, produces an average of one young per year. Few golden eagles die of natural causes each year and, although some die of unnatural causes such as trapping, poisoning, electrocution, shootings, collision with power lines, and loss of habitat, there are nevertheless insufficient carcasses to meet the religious needs of the pueblo societies. Thus, the depository takes 18 months to two years to fill requests from the pueblos for carcasses, tail feathers, and full sets of wing feathers for ceremonial use. As of August, 1985 there were 527 pending applications for eagle feathers or parts, nationwide. Of these, 55 percent, or 274, were pending in Fish and Wildlife Service Region II which comprises New Mexico, Arizona, Texas, and Oklahoma. Four of these pending applications were from members of Isleta Pueblo. It is clear that the depository does not provide applicants with fresh feathers annually for the solstice ceremonies. Despite the shortage, federal authorities have never issued a permit to kill a golden eagle for Indian religious purposes in New Mexico or anywhere else.

Id. at 1303-04.

Could the court reach the same result after *Employment Division v. Smith*?

5. The Importance of the Indian Treaty Right: In *Winnebago*, the tribal interest was the preservation of its very land base from flooding to provide the public with a recreation area. In *Dion* and some of the other conservation cases, the treaty right seeking protection involved hunting for purposes other than subsistence. In fact, in some of the conservation cases, the Indian defendant claimed the treaty permitted hunting for commercial sale of an endangered species or claimed a right for religious use to take an animal that all agree is practically extinct. *See United States v. Billie*, 667 F. Supp. 1485 (S.D. Fla. 1987), discussed in note 2, *supra*. Does judicial assessment of the importance of the treaty right at stake affect the rigor with which a test for treaty abrogation is either articulated or applied? Despite the articulation of various tests, has the Court in fact begun to balance the treaty right against the federal interest? Accepting for the sake of argument that the federal interest in conservation is exceptionally strong, should not the Court have asked whether the persistence and application of Indian reserved hunting rights to such species *alone* have endangered the survival of the species protected by the statutes?

6. Taking Versus Regulation: In Coggins & Modrcin, *Native American Indians and Federal Wildlife Law*, 31 STAN. L. REV. 375, 415-19 (1979)* the authors suggest that reviewing courts should shift their focus. At present, courts first determine whether or not a later law has abrogated a treaty. If so, the abrogation completely terminates the right. Under this all or nothing approach fairly slim evidence of congressional intent can result in the total loss of the treaty right. Instead, they argue, courts should adopt a distinction made in eminent domain law between a taking, entitling the owner to just compensation, and a regulation, in which the owner can still use his land, albeit to a limited extent, where compensation is not required. A refocus would ask first whether the statute was intended to apply to Indian treaty rights and then whether the statute modified rather than abrogated completely the right. In place of the tests discussed in the cases above, the authors urge courts to adopt the following methodology:

> To achieve a rational balancing, it is necessary first to find that Indians are within the
> definition of "persons" bound by the new laws. Courts should hold that the federal

___

*Copyright 1975 and 1979 by the Board of Trustees of the Leland Stanford Junior University. Reprinted by permission.

wildlife statutes have a dual effect: They override or modify treaty rights to the extent necessary for conservation of the species; and they impose upon federal officials an affirmative duty, in the nature of a trustee's responsibility, of implementing the statutes so that any benefits to be derived from the taking of protected species go first to treaty Indians.

Would such a distinction strike a better balance between protecting Indian treaty rights and protecting conservation? The authors believe it would, because the treaty right could be regulated as reasonably necessary to effectuate the conservation goal, but could be restored, and even given a preferential position when, for instance, danger to the species lessened.

7. Canons of Treaty Construction Favoring Indian Rights: While the preceding materials focus primarily on abrogation of Indian treaty rights, similar principles often govern construction of treaties and agreements affecting Indians when abrogation per se is not at issue. In construing treaties and agreements, courts have relied on several maxims: "[W]e will construe a treaty with the Indians as 'that unlettered people' understood it, and 'as justice and reason demand in all cases where power is exerted by the strong over those to whom they owe care and protection,' and counterpoise the inequality 'by the superior justice which looks only to the substance of the right without regard to technical rules.'" *United States v. Winans*, 198 U.S. 371, 380-81 (1905); *accord Choctaw Nation v. Oklahoma*, 397 U.S. 620, 631 (1970); *Tulee v. Washington*, 315 U.S. 681, 684-85 (1942) *United States v. Shoshone Tribe*, 304 U.S. 111, 116 (1938); "Doubtful expressions are to be resolved in favor of the weak and defenseless people who are wards of the nation, dependent upon its protection and good faith." *Carpenter v. Shaw*, 280 U.S. 363, 367 (1930); *accord Winters v. United States*, 207 U.S. 564, 576-77 (1908); "[A] treaty was not a grant of rights to the Indians, but a grant of rights from them — a reservation of those not granted." *Washington v. Washington State Com. Passenger Fishing Vessel Ass'n*, 443 U.S. 658, 680 (1979); *accord United States v. Winans*, 198 U.S. 371, 381 (1905).

8. Limiting the Applicability of General Federal Statutes: One area in which the question of a clear and specific congressional intent frequently arises involves whether general federal statutes expressing national policy automatically apply in Indian country. The cases in this area tend to be confusing because courts and litigants fail to analyze whether the application of the federal statute infringes upon a specific right guaranteed to Indians by treaty, statute, or otherwise. Thus it can appear that Indians are claiming an exemption from the federal law merely because they are Indians or the law is sought to be applied in Indian country. The origin of this confusion is traceable to the decision in *Federal Power Comm'n v. Tuscarora Indian Nation*, 362 U.S. 99 (1960). In affirming the right of utilities, acting under license from the Federal Power Commission, to condemn lands held by the Tuscarora tribe for a power project, the Supreme Court majority stated bluntly "general Acts of Congress apply to Indians as well as to others in the absence of a clear expression to the contrary." *Id.* at 120. Nevertheless, the decision turned on unique facts. The Federal Power Act, 16 U.S.C. § 797(e) (1982), placed some restrictions on the condemnation of reservation lands. The Tuscarora Nation held title to its lands in fee simple. Moreover, the lands were not technically denominated a reservation under the definition of reservation included in the Federal Power Act. Thus, the Court concluded that the statute's specific protections for reservation land did not apply, and treated the Tuscarora Tribe like other fee simple property owners whose property can be condemned for public works projects. Later cases analyzing *Tuscarora* have stressed the absence of a treaty promise to give the tribe any greater rights than normal property owners and the legislative history of the Power Act indicating that all Indian-owned property was not intended to be automatically immune from its provisions. *See Escondido Mut. Water Co. v. La Jolla Band of Mission Indians,* 466 U.S. 765, 787 (1984) (plain language of Federal Power Act requires Federal Power Commission to accept reasonable conditions imposed by Secretary of the Interior to protect reservations, but only as to projects physically located within reservation boundaries) (Federal Power Act applied because no treaty right was at issue and specific federal legislation, the Mission Indian Relief Act, did not create special Indian rights that were immune from the general eminent domain power).

The statement in *Tuscarora* that general laws do apply remains good law, but only as a statement of a general rule serving as a starting point for analysis. As stated above, courts first look for infringement on specific Indian rights. Where such Indian rights are involved, courts require a clear and specific congressional intent to limit such rights in the general federal statute or its legislative history. *See, e.g., EEOC v. Cherokee Nation,* 871 F.2d 937 (10th Cir. 1989) (Age Discrimination in Employment Act does not apply to Indian tribes); *Donovan v. Navajo Forest Prods. Indus.,* 692 F.2d 709 (10th Cir. 1982) (applying Occupational Safety and Health Act to tribal business would violate treaty promises of self-government); *Fort Apache Timber Co.,* 226 N.L.R.B. 503 (1976) (National Labor Relations Act does not authorize a collective bargaining election where tribe is employer).

In the absence of such rights, the general rule becomes applicable. *See, e.g., United States v. Farris,* 624 F.2d 890, 893-94 (9th Cir. 1980), *cert. denied,* 449 U.S. 1111 (1981) (upholding federal prosecution under Organized Crime Control Act of Indians operating on-reservation casino attended by substantial numbers of non-Indians) (collecting exceptions); *Donovan v. Coeur d'Alene Tribal Farm,* 751 F.2d 1113 (9th Cir. 1985) (Occupational Safety & Health Act applies to commercial activities carried on by tribal farm; no treaty and no interference with right of tribe to internal self-government); *Confederated Tribes of Warm Springs Reservation v. Kurtz,* 691 F.2d 878 (9th Cir. 1982), *cert. denied,* 460 U.S. 1040 (1983) (treaty silent on federal tax, thus general federal excise tax applies to tribal sawmill); *Navajo Tribe v. NLRB,* 288 F.2d 162 (D.C. Cir.), *cert. denied,* 366 U.S. 928 (1961) (National Labor Relations Act applied to non-Indian employers employing Indians on reservation).

Finally, although the specific right involved is usually traced to a treaty or statute, executive agreements and federal common law can also be sources of specific Indian rights. For example, in note 8 in *Dion* the Supreme Court stressed that Indian reservations created by executive order "normally carry with them the same implicit hunting rights as those created by treaty." *See also Cramer v. United States,* 261 U.S. 219, 225 (1923) (statutory grant to railroad construed as not automatically extinguishing aboriginal property rights derived from and protected by common law); *Cf. Donovan v. Coeur d'Alene Tribal Farm, supra* (general rule does not apply to federal laws interfering with purely internal tribal self government, even though not guaranteed by treaty) (dicta); *United States v. Billie,* 667 F. Supp. 1485 (S.D. Fla. 1987) (abrogation test of *Dion* applied to determine whether Endangered Species Act abrogated traditional hunting rights on an executive order reservation).

9. Canons of Statutory Construction: Once a determination has been made that a particular statute affects Indian tribes or individuals, courts have invoked canons of construction favoring creation and preservation of tribal rights. One rationale for such canons in the area of interpreting treaties and agreements is to redress unequal bargaining power. By parity of reasoning, the Court applied the canon requiring interpretation of doubtful expressions in favor of the Indians to cases involving interpretation of statutes ratifying agreements between the government and Indian tribes. *See, e.g., Choate v. Trapp,* 224 U.S. 665, 675-76, 78 (1912), *citing Jones v. Meehan,* 175 U.S. 1 (1899); *see also Antoine v. Washington,* 420 U.S. 194, 199-200 (1975) (statute ratifying agreement) (collecting cases). The Court began to recognize that other policies justify special care in interpreting statutes as well. As the Court stated in a recent case: "The canons of construction applicable in Indian law are rooted in the unique trust relationship between the United States and the Indians." *County of Oneida v. Oneida Indian Nation,* 470 U.S. 226, 247 (1985). Thus, the Court began to extend the rule requiring resolution of ambiguities in favor of Indian interest to statutes dealing with Indian matters. *See Mattz v. Arnett,* 412 U.S. 481, 504-05 (1973) (clear statutory language needed to terminate reservation status); *Squire v. Capoeman,* 351 U.S. 1, 6-7 (1956) (tax exemption). In addition, the Court has interpreted federal laws so as to minimize infringement on inherent tribal sovereignty, by "tread[ing] lightly in the absence of clear indications of legislative intent." *Santa Clara Pueblo v. Martinez,* 436 U.S. 49, 60 (1978). Finally, the presence of the same factors may call for construction of federal regulations as well as statutes to protect tribal interests. *Jicarilla Apache Tribe v. Andrus,* 687 F.2d 1324 (10th Cir. 1982) (Secretary violated BIA regulations in notice procedures for oil and gas leases; any doubt in interpretation of regulations should be resolved in favor of the tribe).

Nevertheless, a maxim of statutory construction can only go so far in winning a case. The interpretive process is a dynamic one, not governed by only one factor, or even by one overarching theory. *See* Eskridge & Frickey, *Statutory Interpretation as Practical Reasoning,* 42 STAN. L. REV. 321 (1990). The canon simply may not apply. For example, a canon favoring Indian rights gives no guidance in cases in which "the contesting parties are an Indian tribe and a class of individuals consisting primarily of tribal members." *Northern Cheyenne Tribe v. Hollowbreast,* 425 U.S. 649, 655 n.7 (1976). Moreover, competing canons of statutory construction requiring strict construction in favor of some other interest may outweigh or obscure the possibility of application of a canon favoring Indian tribes. *See, e.g., Montana v. United States,* 450 U.S. 544 (1981) (treaty language not strong enough to overcome presumption in favor of state ownership of beds of navigable water); *United States v. Mitchell,* 445 U.S. 535, 538 (1980) (traditional rule requiring strict construction against waiver of federal sovereign immunity applied to defeat jurisdiction in the Court of Claims for claim against the United States); *Andrus v. Glover Constr. Co.,* 446 U.S. 608, 618 (1980) (repeal by implication traditionally disfavored; therefore, law regarding promoting products of Indian industry held not explicit enough to repeal earlier procurement laws requiring competitive bidding on highway projects).

In addition, the canon of construction favoring Indian tribes may not overcome statutory language that is unambiguous. *See, e.g., Amoco Prod. Co. v. Village of Gambell,* 480 U.S. 531, 555 (1987) (no ambiguity, therefore special canons not applicable). Indeed, this important threshold question, whether statutory language is sufficiently ambiguous to require resolution by application of a canon favoring Indian tribes, is often hotly debated between the majority and dissent. For example, in *South Carolina v. Catawba Indian Tribe,* Justice Stevens, writing for the majority applied a general canon, the plain meaning rule, stating: "The canon of construction regarding the resolution of ambiguities in favor of Indians, however, does not permit reliance on ambiguities that do not exist; nor does it permit disregard of the clearly expressed intent of Congress." 476 U.S. 498, 506 (1986). In a footnote the Court cited many cases making the same point. *Id.* at n.16. Mr. Justice Blackmun's dissent collected an equally imposing list of competing cases. *Id.* at 520, 526, and stated: "the distinction smacks of the kind of semantic trap that this Court consistently has attempted to avoid when construing ... statutes ostensibly passed for the benefit of Indians." *Id.* at 527. As Eskridge and Frickey note, the Court has displayed this tendency to oversimplify the factors involved in interpretation in other areas of the law as well: "Too often the Court's statutory interpretations ignore opposing arguments or treat them in a dismissive, mechanical fashion, typically in footnotes, and too rarely do they engage in an open dialogue that notes the virtues of various positions and explains why one of them is preferable." Eskridge & Frickey, *supra* at 371. As the result of the majority's dismissal of the canons favoring Indian tribes, the Catawba Tribe lost its claim to a 225-acre tract of land in South Carolina.

Admittedly, competing policy concerns may cause different justices to emphasize different interpretive philosophies, or the Court may weigh other interpretive factors more heavily than the substantive, but fairly abstract, command of a canon. Nevertheless, *Catawba Tribe* and other recent cases arguably support the view that the Court has become less willing to apply canons favoring Indians. *See, e.g., Rice v. Rehner*, 463 U.S. 713, 724-25 (1983) (canon protecting tribal self-government rights applies only to aspects of sovereignty exercised traditionally by Indians and not to assertions of power in modern settings; liquor control). Finally, in *Mountain States Tel. & Tel. Co. v. Pueblo of Santa Ana*, 472 U.S. 237 (1985), the majority invoked several traditional canons of construction in resolving a difficult statutory issue adverse to the Pueblo's property interests without once mentioning any canons favoring Indian interests. This handful of cases may not be sufficient to indicate repudiation of canons favoring Indian tribes. Nevertheless, Judge Canby recently stated "future statutory construction [may] tilt less towards the interests of the Indians and the tribes than it has in the past." Canby, *The Status of Indian Tribes in American Law Today*, 62 WASH. L. REV. 1, 21 (1987).

Nevertheless, statutory interpretation engaged in with sensitivity toward the underlying policies of Indian law can yield results that protect tribal interests. For example, the Court in recent years has regarded post-enactment factors as relevant in questions of congressional intent. Although this approach has sometimes trumped a canon favoring Indians, *see Rosebud Sioux Tribe v. Kneip*, 430 U.S. 584 (1977), discussed in Chapter 1, section B, it can be a powerful mechanism to take into account policy changes since the enactment of a statute.

In *Bryan v. Itasca County*, 426 U.S. 373, 392 (1976), Minnesota argued that a provision of Public Law 280, granting it

> jurisdiction over civil causes of action between Indians or to which Indians are parties which arise in the areas of Indian country listed ... to the same extent that such State ... has jurisdiction over other civil causes of action, and those civil laws of such State ... that are of general application to private persons or private property shall have the same force and effect within such Indian country as they have elsewhere within the State ....

authorized the state to impose its tax laws on Indians living on reservations. Certainly, the language of the statute supported a very strong argument that the provision should be read as granting the state the authority to impose its civil regulatory laws upon Indians on reservations. Moreover, an interpretation consonant with federal policy at the time the statute was enacted would have bolstered the conclusion that it granted jurisdiction to tax. Nevertheless, the Court interpreted the statutory language as a choice of law provision and not a provision granting civil, regulatory jurisdiction. According to Eskridge and Frickey:

> *Bryan* is a useful illustration of the way in which evolutive considerations are often the decisive ones in statutory interpretation. On the face of the statute, Minnesota probably had the better argument. There was apparently nothing very specific in the legislative history, but if the enacting Congress had been asked about the *Bryan* issue while it was considering Public Law 280, one would guess that the answer would have supported Minnesota as well. Indeed, it would be difficult to find a Congress in this century that seemed more animated by the desire to destroy tribal sovereignty. For in addition to enacting Public Law 280, the 1953 Congress adopted a concurrent resolution that created the federal policy of terminating the unique federal legal status — and thus the sovereignty — of Native American tribes. A legal-process purpose inquiry might also support Minnesota, since the purpose of Public Law 280 was to extend state authority over certain tribal Indians. These legislative intentions and purpose, however, became obsolete within about five years. By the time *Bryan* made its way to the Supreme Court, the firmly established federal policy was to promote tribal sovereignty.

Eskridge & Frickey, *supra*, at 374-75.* For a comprehensive treatment of interpretive issues in Indian law, see Frickey, *Congressional Intent, Practical Reasoning, and the Dynamic Nature of Federal Indian Law*, 78 CALIF. L. REV. 1139 (1990).

3. LIMITING ADMINISTRATIVE POWER — THE FEDERAL TRUSTEESHIP OVER INDIAN AFFAIRS

a. The Development of a Cause of Action for Breach of Trust

CHEROKEE NATION v. GEORGIA

30 U.S. (5 Pet.) 1 (1831)

[Chief Justice Marshall's analogy of the relationship between Indian tribes and the federal government as like that of a guardian to its ward is often cited as the source of the theory that has become known as the federal-Indian trust relationship. The full case is reprinted *supra* Chapter 1, page 8.]

CHAMBERS, JUDICIAL ENFORCEMENT OF THE FEDERAL TRUST RESPONSIBILITY TO INDIANS, 27 Stanford Law Review 1213, 1213-48 (1975)**

It is generally accepted that the United States owes fiduciary duties to American Indians, but the meaning and extent of these duties have seldom been analyzed. The fiduciary relationship itself has been variously characterized — as "resembling" a guardianship, as a guardian-ward relationship, as a fiduciary or special relationship, or as a trust responsibility. The characterization of this

---

duty, however, is not nearly as important as determining its scope and analyzing its possible enforceability.

I. *Origins and Nature of the Trust Relationship*

A. *The Birth of the Trust Doctrine*

1. *Cherokee Nation v. Georgia*

Although the concept of a federal trust responsibility to Indians has been acknowledged at various times by Congress and the executive, the notion evolved judicially. The first Supreme Court decisions to formulate the trust responsibility doctrine involved the applicability of Georgia statutes to persons residing on Cherokee Indian lands within that state. These lands were secured to the Cherokees by federal treaties, and the central issue in the cases concerned the relationship between the United States and the Indians established by these treaties.

The first case, *Cherokee Nation v. Georgia,* was decided in 1831. Marshall noted also that the treaties with the Cherokees acknowledge some dependency upon the United States. He observed that Indian tribes, rather than being foreign states, "may, more correctly, perhaps, be denominated domestic dependent nations in a state of pupilage," and concluded that "[t]heir relation to the United States resembles that of a ward to his guardian."...

2. *Worcester v. Georgia*

The second Cherokee case, *Worcester v. Georgia,* decided in 1832, involved an appeal by two non-Indian missionaries residing on Cherokee lands from a conviction in Georgia state courts for violating some of the statutes challenged in *Cherokee Nation.* Speaking for the Court, Chief Justice Marshall held the state statutes unlawful under the supremacy clause and construed the treaties and the Indian Trade and Intercourse Acts as protecting the Indians' status as distinct political communities "having territorial boundaries, within which their authority [of self-government] is exclusive ...." Marshall also emphasized that the Indians' right to "all the lands within those territorial boundaries ... is not only acknowledged, but guaranteed by the United States."...

3. *The Meaning of the Cherokee Cases*

An overriding legal consequence of Marshall's guardianship concept was to integrate Indian occupancy and ownership of land into the system of American land tenure. A treaty was in essence a land transaction whereby the tribe ceded some lands in return for federal protection and sovereign recognition of Indian occupancy of the retained lands. By concluding treaties with and submitting to the protection of the United States, the tribe acknowledged that it was a sort of federal vassal or loyal subject. A guardian-ward relationship can thus be seen as a natural incident of such land tenure; since Indians were not citizens, the guardianship concept provided a way in which their ownership of real property could be acknowledged and protected.

The Marshallian guardianship or trust responsibility can also be viewed as an expansive protection of the tribe's status as a self-governing entity as well as its property rights. The federal guarantee recognizes a sort of "protectorate" status in the tribes, securing to them the power of managing their internal affairs in an autonomous manner except for a congressional power to regulate trade. Moreover, tribal autonomy is supported by a federal duty to protect the tribe's land and resource base.

Two ambiguities, however, remain in the Marshallian guardianship doctrine. The first is whether the trust relationship exists independently as a legal doctrine or is only a consequence of specific federal treaties and statutes. Secondly, it is unclear whether Marshall intended fiduciary duties to be directly enforceable against federal, as well as state, officials in such a manner as to prevent modification of the terms of the trust by either the executive or the legislative branch.

The independent legal doctrine question. It is possible to view the trust relationship delineated in the Cherokee cases as a consequence of specific federal preemption of state laws, with the "trust relationship" being merely a descriptive status arising out of the treaties and statutes. Thus, the exact trust relationship might vary from tribe to tribe, depending on the operative treaties....

Analyzed as an aspect of preemption, the Marshallian trust responsibility seems principally directed toward confirming federal, as opposed to state, control over management and disposition of lands ceded by the Indians rather than toward preserving tribal autonomy as against the federal trustee. Prior to, and sometimes after, the adoption of the Constitution, states had regulated and claimed the power to conclude treaties with Indian tribes within their boundaries. The southern states in particular remained hostile to various federal treaties that limited their westward expansion. It may have been this claim toward which Marshall's doctrine was primarily directed.

A different view of the Marshallian trust concept which places greater emphasis on tribal autonomy than upon federal preemption is also logically consistent with the two Cherokee opinions. Marshall could be read as holding that the Indian tribes, prior to discovery and colonization of their lands, were vested with "inherent" powers of sovereignty. The executive and legislative practice of concluding and ratifying treaties with the tribes could be seen simply as recognition of that status by the United States. Since the tribes inhabit the lands within the federal boundaries, however, they are not "foreign" sovereigns, but domestic ones entitled to federal protection and support, as well as to maintaining some governmental power and independence. Under this concept, the trust relationship is not so much created by the treaties as it is implicitly recognized by them.

Enforceability against federal officials. The Cherokee cases did not involve suits against federal officials, and the extent to which the Marshall Court intended fiduciary duties to be enforceable against federal officials is unclear. Strict adherence to fiduciary duties, such as the duty of exclusive loyalty and its corollary prohibition against misappropriating trust assets to the trustee's own use, could have precluded further cession of Indian territory. On the other hand, the Marshallian trust responsibility could conceivably be viewed simply as imposing a federal duty to safeguard Indian lands against intrusions by the states or private persons without federal approval. The guardianship would, under this approach, be consistent with recognition of a paramount federal power to control the flow of persons into Indian country and the pace and terms of future Indian land cessions. The trust responsibility, so limited, might simply require that future dealings with Indian tribes effecting land cessions be for fair value and made in good faith, while acknowledging an exclusively federal power to make such a transaction....

C. *The Trust Responsibility as Applied to the Executive Branch*

Lone Wolf and *Kagama* do not address executive power to take or adversely affect Indian property, and cases subsequent to them have placed tighter fiduciary restrictions on the power of executive officials over Indian property than those imposed on Congress. In several cases beginning in 1919 federal courts have exercised their general jurisdiction to enforce some limitations on federal executive action based exclusively on the trust responsibility.

In *Lane v. Pueblo of Santa Rosa*,[79] the Supreme Court enjoined the Secretary of the Interior from disposing of tribal lands under the general public land laws. The Court held that the plenary power of Congress described in *Lone Wolf* to regulate Indian lands for the benefit and protection of its wards "certainly ... would not justify ... treating the lands of the Indians as public lands of the United States, and disposing of the same under the Public Land Laws." That, the Court observed, "would not be an exercise of the guardianship, but an act of confiscation."[80]

Shortly after *Lane*, in *Cramer v. United States*,[81] the Court voided a federal land patent that 19 years earlier had conveyed lands occupied by Indians to a railway. The Indians' occupancy of the lands was not protected by any treaty, executive order, or statute, but the Court placed heavy emphasis on the trust responsibility and national policy protecting Indian land occupancy as a basis for relief. The Court held the trust responsibility limited the general statutory authority of these federal officials to issue land patents.

Lane and *Cramer* were filed in courts of general jurisdiction which awarded equitable relief. A subsequent case to elaborate on the Court's observations in *Lane* was *United States v. Creek Nation*.[85] In this action, the Supreme Court affirmed a money damage award by the Court of Claims to the Creeks for the taking of lands which had been excluded from their reservation and later sold to non-Indians following an incorrect federal survey of reservation boundaries. The result of these cases was a clear application of the trust responsibility to the executive without the plenary power to change the duty similar to that residing in Congress....

This doctrine would seem to have far-reaching significance, for it suggests an affirmative federal duty, especially by the Department of the Interior, to protect Indian trust property from injury by other federal projects — unless, of course, Congress had, pursuant to *Lone Wolf*, specifically authorized the injury and directed the payment of compensation. The suggested principle is that the trust relationship, independent of any express treaty or statutory provision, consti-

---

[79]249 U.S. 110 (1919).
[80]*Id.* at 113.
[81]261 U.S. 219 (1923).
[85]295 U.S. 103 (1935)....

tutes a general limitation on the authority of executive officials to act in a manner which adversely affects Indian trust property.

Such a principle would stretch beyond any direct implications of the Chero-kee case holdings, although it is not necessarily inconsistent with Marshall's analysis of the status of Indian tribes. Nor is the proposed doctrine directly incompatible with the *Kagama-Lone Wolf* cases, for those decisions deal with the power of Congress. The effect of the decisions, however, is a striking dispar-ity between the trust responsibility as it operates with respect to Congress and as it pertains to executive officials.

II. *Seeking Equitable Relief Against Executive Officials for Breach of Trust*

Ultimately, the desirability of recognizing a cause of action for equitable relief against federal executive officials turns on whether legal remedies — that is, money damages in the Indian Claims Commission or Court of Claims — pro-vide an adequate protection for Indian property rights. Moreover, as a technical matter it must be decided whether Congress has consented to such suits against executive officials.

A. *Availability of the Equitable Remedy in Light of the Adequacy of the Legal Remedy*

1. *The Need for Equitable Relief*

Allowing Indian claimants a right simply to money damages in the Indian Claims Commission or Court of Claims would be of some value in the protec-tion of Indian resources because federal interference with Indian property rights would be deterred somewhat by the possibility of having to pay money damages for breaches of trust. Precluding equitable relief, however, would rec-ognize a de facto executive power to condemn Indian resources without the specific consent of Congress. Admittedly, equitable relief against executive ac-tion would appear to afford greater protection to Indian property rights than to other private property rights....

The counterargument favoring specific performance of the federal trust re-sponsibility relies upon a connection between a resource base and the goal of maintaining a separate Indian culture as a distinct political community. If prop-erty is exchanged for money, the culture is more likely to lose its underlying environment. The purpose of the trusteeship guarantee as perceived by Chief Justice Marshall accordingly may not be realized.

The underlying purposes of the trust responsibility thus are probably deter-minative of the proper extent of judicial review. If it is a short-term "guardian-ship" designed to last until the wards become competent — *i.e.,* acclimated to the ways of the dominant culture and/or assimilated into it — then specific performance of trust obligations seems less important and property can be more readily transmuted into money. Even if the trust relationship were seen as permanent, its purposes could be limited to providing financial support for Indians and to ensuring that their lands and resources were not sold for an unconscionable consideration; in this event, judicial remedies limited to money damages for breach of trust would again seem adequate. A more expansive reading of the trust relationship, however, would suggest that the preservation of the trust corpus in a particular form — land and natural resources instead of money — is itself a critical value. If, as the Cherokee cases suggest, a chief objective of the trust responsibility is to protect tribal status as self-governing entities, executive extinguishment of the tribal land base diminishes the territory over which tribal authority is exercised and thereby imperils fulfillment of the guarantee of tribal political and cultural autonomy. If this is the correct interpretation of the trust responsibility, equitable relief in appropriate cases seems essential. Such relief is particularly vital to accommodate the conflicts between Indian trustee responsibilities and competing government projects that affect countless federal agencies.

2. *The Scope of Judicial Review*

The appropriate scope of such judicial review remains unclear. In some cases, a judicial assessment of whether the trustee had adhered to his fiduciary obligations and acted in the "best interests" of his Indian wards is relatively simple....

Judicial review in an action seeking equitable relief seems clearly appropriate to ascertain the basis for the Secretary's decision, given the possible presence of divided loyalty, and to determine whether the decision is consistent with the Secretary's fiduciary duties to his Indian beneficiaries. However, once a plausible argument is offered by the Secretary that the project is in the Indians' best interests, it is not clear how closely the court should scrutinize the basis for the Secretary's determination. A reviewing court will probably sustain the Secretary's determination without further inquiry so long as it was a reasonable one for a fiduciary. But such a standard should be applied with a careful awareness of the possible conflict-of-interest which may operate in the circumstances of the particular case....

IV. *Conclusion*

[T]he enduring teaching of the Cherokee cases is their perception of the underlying purposes of the trust relationship. Construing the early treaties as territorial arrangements among sovereign entities, Marshall correctly discerned that the basic guarantee of the United States was the territorial and governmental integrity of the tribes....

It is premature to ... announce the existence of a cause of action for breach of trust.... The trend, however, seems to be a sound one given the purposes of the trust responsibility emphasized by Marshall — the federal guarantee of the tribe's self-governing status. Given this objective, the property-related fiduciary standards appear to be an appropriate and probably necessary means toward achieving the end. Tribal autonomy will almost certainly be frustrated unless the option to continue a separate existence on a territorially secure reservation is protected, and legal remedies alone offer little protection.

CHEYENNE-ARAPAHO TRIBES v. UNITED STATES

512 F.2d 1390 (Ct. Cl. 1975)

DAVIS, Judge.

These consolidated cases, before us on cross-motions for summary judgment as to liability, challenge the Government's performance of its fiduciary duties as trustee of funds belonging to various Indian tribes. The suits are brought on behalf of a number of tribes either for themselves or as representatives of large or aboriginal groups, but for the purpose of these motions the parties have agreed that two tribes for each suit will be considered representative "test plaintiffs." No. 342-70 challenges the Government's management of judgment funds in the Treasury belonging to plaintiffs Southern Ute Tribe and Southern Ute Tribe as representative of the Confederated Bands of Ute Indians. No. 343-70 challenges defendant's conduct with respect to other trust funds of plaintiffs Southern Ute Tribe and Hoopa Valley Tribe.

Both petitions allege that defendant breached its fiduciary duties in the care of plaintiffs' funds by not making the funds productive (by not investing moneys ready for investment and also by delay in making funds available for investment), by not maximizing the productivity of funds, and by using the funds to its own benefit and to the detriment of the tribes. It is clear from past opinions of this court and of the Supreme Court, and from the actions of both Congress and the Executive Branch, that funds appropriated to Indians to satisfy judgments of the Indian Claims Commission or of this court, as well as funds produced by tribal activities, are, when kept in the Treasury, held in trust for the Indians. [B]ecause the United States in effect imposes trust status on the Indian funds, our jurisdiction [is] broad enough to cover the types of claims made here.

Test plaintiff Southern Ute Tribe is (or was during the relevant period) the beneficial owner of two judgment fund accounts, a proceeds of labor account, a fourth principal account and five interest accounts held in the Treasury. The balances in the accounts at times totaled several million dollars. Even larger amounts were held in the accounts of the Consolidated Ute Tribes, represented here by the Southern Utes. The Hoopa Valley Tribe was the owner of a proceeds of labor account, the balance of which never fell below $1,000,000 from July 1964 to early 1970, and which at times held as much as $3,000,000, and an interest account to which interest on the proceeds of labor account was credited.

When Congress, in the exercise of its power over the Indians, determined by statute and by treaty to hold funds due the tribes in trust rather than immediately distributing them to the Indians, it also developed a series of investment policies for those funds. We are not faced here with a claim that Congress breached its trust duties under the Constitution or treaties. Rather, plaintiffs urge that the Bureau of Indian Affairs has not properly used the tools Congress provided in order to meet the Government's fiduciary obligation.

The statutory scheme is that Indian trust funds deposited in the Treasury are to earn interest at the rate provided in the appropriate treaty or appropriations bill, and that if no interest rate is specified, the funds are to earn four percent simple interest per year. 25 U.S.C. §§ 161a, 161b (1970). In *Menominee Tribe of Indians v. United States,* 97 Ct. Cl. 158, 163-65 (1942), the court held that this provision prohibited the Treasury from paying interest on the interest earned by funds on deposit. Accordingly, the various interest funds owned by plaintiffs, when held in the Treasury, are totally unproductive. Defendant has in fact paid four percent simple interest on plaintiffs' other funds, and if this were the limit of the Government's power, plaintiffs' claim, which does not attack the statutes, would have to fail.

However, holding the money in the Treasury is only one of defendant's statutory alternatives. Until 1880, tribal funds, rather than being deposited in the Treasury, were required by law to be invested, usually at a minimum rate of return of 5%. *See* Act of January 9, 1837, ch. 1, 5 Stat. 135, R.S. § 2096; Act of September 11, 1841, ch. 25, 5 Stat. 465, R.S. § 3659. Because of defaults on some bonds in which the Secretary of Interior had invested and due to declining interest rates, Congress provided by the Act of April 1, 1880, ch. 41, 21 Stat. 70, for the holding of moneys in the Treasury and payment of interest as an alternative to investment when the Secretary of Interior "is of the opinion that the best interests of the Indians will be promoted by such deposits, in lieu of investments." Interest on Indian trust funds, where no rate was specified by the law or treaty setting up the fund, was set at four percent by the Act of Feb. 12, 1929, ch. 178, 45 Stat. 1164. In 1918, Congress clarified and limited the Secretary's power to invest rather than hold Indian funds by providing that the Secretary could withdraw Indian funds from the Treasury and place them in banks where such banks paid a higher rate of interest than the Treasury was obligated to give, and he could also invest the funds "for the best interest of the Indians" in "any public-debt obligations of the United States and in any bonds, notes, or other obligations which are unconditionally guaranteed as to both interest and principal by the United States." [25 U.S.C. § 162a.]

It is therefore legally possible, depending on the state of the market, for the Secretary, by investing rather than holding Indian funds, to provide the Indians with more than 4 percent simple interest. Because the investments are required by statute to be either heavily collateralized (in the case of bank deposits) or guaranteed by the Government, safety is not an issue. Moreover, because of the existence of a secondary market in many of the permitted investments (*e.g.* Treasury bills, Federal Home Loan Bank Board notes, Federal Intermediate Credit Bank notes, etc.), sudden requirements for cash do not present major obstacles to these types of investments. The four percent attainable by retaining the funds in the Treasury is, as another court has stated, a floor rather than a ceiling. *Manchester Band of Pomo Indians, Inc. v. United States,* 363 F. Supp. 1238, 1243-44 (N.D. Cal. 1973).

The fiduciary duty which the United States undertook with respect to these funds includes the "obligation to maximize the trust income by prudent investment," and the trustee has the burden of proof to justify less than a maximum return. *See Blankenship v. Boyle,* 329 F. Supp. 1089, 1096 (D.D.C. 1971). *See also* Restatement of Trusts 2d § 181 (1959). A corollary duty is the responsibility to keep informed so that when a previously proper investment becomes improper, perhaps because of the opportunity for better (and equally safe) investment elsewhere, funds can be reinvested. While the trustee has a reasonable time in which to make the initial investment or to reinvest, he becomes liable for a breach of trust if that reasonable time is exceeded. Restatement of Trusts 2d §§ 231 and comm. *b,* 181 and comm. *c* (1959).

[The case must be returned to the trial judge for further proceedings to determine the extent of liability.]

In assessing the return available outside of the Treasury, both in the earlier segment of the period and later, the trial judge should take into account the availability of eligible investments through the secondary markets as well as directly from the issuer. He will, in addition, have to decide the length of time within which it would have been reasonable for defendant to make funds available for investment, to make actual investments, and to reinvest where appropriate. As to funds which were invested, but at rates less than those found by the trial judge to be the maximum available, the trial judge will have to determine whether defendant breached its duties by not making a switch in investments which would have been made by "a man of ordinary prudence ... in dealing with his own property." Restatement of Trusts 2d § 174 (1959).

There are, as already indicated, several points on which we can now rule definitively. [T]he Government was duty bound to make the maximum productive investment unless and until specifically told not to do so by a tribe and until defendant also made an independent judgment that the tribe's request was in its own best interest. We find no evidence in the present record of such requests in the case of any of the test plaintiffs.

[In addition,] on those funds which defendant in effect borrowed from plaintiffs by retaining them in the Treasury, we hold defendant to a strict standard of fiduciary duty — if eligible investments were available at higher yields, defendant will be liable to plaintiffs for the difference between what interest defendant paid for the funds and the maximum the funds could have legally and practically earned if properly invested outside.

[Further,] we find that, except possibly for the earliest period, there were in fact, at all relevant times, proper sources of investment outside the Treasury which would have yielded higher returns than 4%.

[Last] is the problem of the interest accounts on which no interest was paid at all. [Because] defendant had available at all relevant times outside investments which would have yielded some substantial return, we hold that the government is liable for lost profits on these interest accounts.

[*Remanded.*]

UNITED STATES v. MITCHELL

463 U.S. 206 (1983)

Justice MARSHALL delivered the opinion of the Court.

The principal question in this case is whether the United States is accountable in money damages for alleged breaches of trust in connection with its management of forest resources on allotted lands of the Quinault Indian Reservation.

I

A

In the 1850's, the United States undertook a policy of removing Indian tribes from large areas of the Pacific Northwest in order to facilitate the settlement of non-Indians. [In the Treaty of Olympia] the Indians ceded to the United States a vast tract of land on the Olympic Peninsula in the State of Washington, and the United States agreed to set aside a reservation for the Indians.

[S]ince the coastal tribes drew their subsistence almost entirely from the water, [it was recommended they] be collected on a reservation suitable for their fishing needs. Acting on this suggestion, President Grant issued an Executive Order on November 4, 1873, designating about 200,000 acres along the Washington coast as an Indian reservation. The vast bulk of this land consisted of rain forest covered with huge, coniferous trees.

In 1905 the Federal Government began to allot the Quinault Reservation in trust to individual Indians under the [General Allotment Act and] the Quinault Allotment Act of Mar. 4, 1911, ch. 246, 36 Stat. 1345. [T]he entire Reservation had been divided into 2,340 trust allotments, most of which were 80 acres of heavily timbered land [by 1935]. About a third of the Reservation has since gone out of trust, but the bulk of the land has remained in trust status.

The forest resources on the allotted lands have long been managed by the Department of the Interior, which exercises "comprehensive" control over the harvesting of Indian timber. The Secretary of the Interior has broad statutory authority over the sale of timber on reservations. See 25 U.S.C. §§ 406, 407. Sales of timber "shall be based upon a consideration of the needs and best interests of the Indian owner and his heirs," § 406(a), and the proceeds from such sales are to be used for the benefit of the Indians or transferred to the Indian owner, §§ 406(a), 407. Congress has directed the Secretary to adhere to principles of sustained-yield forestry on all Indian forest lands under his supervision. 25 U.S.C. § 466. Under these statutes, the Secretary has promulgated detailed regulations governing the management of Indian timber. 25 CFR pt. 163 (1983). The Secretary is authorized to deduct an administrative fee for his services from the timber revenues paid to Indian allottees. 25 U.S.C. §§ 406(a), 413.

B

The respondents are 1,465 individuals owning interests in allotments on the Quinault Reservation, an unincorporated association of Quinault Reservation allottees, and the Quinault Tribe, which now holds some portions of the allotted lands. In 1971 respondents [sued in the Court of Claims seeking damages for] mismanagement of timberlands on the Quinault Reservation. More specifically, respondents claimed that the Government (1) failed to obtain a fair market value for timber sold; (2) failed to manage timber on a sustained-yield basis; (3) failed to obtain any payment at all for some merchantable timber; (4) failed to develop a proper system of roads and easements for timber operations and exacted improper charges from allottees for maintenance of roads; (5) failed to pay any interest on certain funds from timber sales held by the Government and paid insufficient interest on other funds; and (6) exacted excessive administrative fees from allottees. Respondents assert that the alleged misconduct constitutes a breach of the fiduciary duty owed them by the United States as trustee under various statutes.

[When the United States moved to dismiss for lack of jurisdiction over these breach of trust claims, the Court of Claims] denied the motion, holding that the General Allotment Act created a fiduciary duty on the United States' part to manage the timber resources properly and thereby provided the necessary authority for recovery of damages against the United States. In *United States v. Mitchell*, 445 U.S. 535 (1980), this Court reversed the ruling of the Court of Claims, stating that the General Allotment Act "created only a limited trust relationship between the United States and the allottee that does not impose any duty upon the Government to manage timber resources." We concluded that "[a]ny right of the respondents to recover money damages for Government mismanagement of timber resources must be found in some source other than [the General Allotment] Act." Since the Court of Claims had not considered respondents' assertion that other statutes render the United States answerable in money damages for the alleged mismanagement in this case, we remanded the case for consideration of these alternative grounds for liability.

On remand, the Court of Claims once again held the United States subject to suit for money damages on most of respondents' claims. [664 F.2d 265 (1981).] The court ruled that [other statutes] imposed fiduciary duties upon the United States in its management of forested allotted lands. The court concluded that the statutes and regulations implicitly required compensation for damages sustained as a result of the Government's breach of its duties. Thus, the court held that respondents could proceed on their claims.

Because the decision of the Court of Claims raises issues of substantial importance concerning the liability of the United States,[7] we granted the Government's petition for certiorari [and] affirm.

II

Respondents have invoked the jurisdiction of the Court of Claims under the Tucker Act, 28 U.S.C. § 1491, and its counterpart for claims brought by Indian tribes, 28 U.S.C. § 1505, known as the Indian Tucker Act. The Tucker Act states in pertinent part:

> The Court of Claims shall have jurisdiction to render judgment upon any claim against the United States founded either upon the Constitution, or any Act of Congress, or any regulation of any executive department or implied contract with the United States, or for liquidated or unliquidated damages in cases not sounding in tort.

It is axiomatic that the United States may not be sued without its consent and that the existence of consent is a prerequisite for jurisdiction. [W]e conclude that by giving the Court of Claims jurisdiction over specified types of claims against the United States, the Tucker Act constitutes a waiver of sovereign immunity with respect to those claims.

[The Court reviewed the history of the Tucker Act, concluding that its purpose was to permit persons the right to sue the government. The Court also concluded that the Indian Tucker Act, conferring jurisdiction on the Court of Claims to hear tribal claims "of a character which would be cognizable in the Court of Claims if the claimant were not an Indian tribe," had "a similar history."] For decades this Court consistently interpreted the Tucker Act as having provided the consent of the United States to be sued *eo nomine* for the classes of claims described in the Act. These decisions confirm the unambiguous thrust of the history of the Act.

---

[7] The Government has informed us that the damages claimed in this suit alone may amount to $100 million. Pet. for Cert. 24.

In *United States v. Testan,* 424 U.S. 392, 398, 400 (1976), and in *United States v. Mitchell,* 445 U.S., at 538, this Court employed language suggesting that the Tucker Act does not effect a waiver of sovereign immunity. Such language was not necessary to the decision in either case. Without in any way questioning the result in either case, we conclude that this isolated language should be disregarded. If a claim falls within the terms of the Tucker Act, the United States has presumptively consented to suit.

B

It nonetheless remains true that the Tucker Act "'does not create any substantive right enforceable against the United States for money damages.'" [*United States v. Testan.*] A substantive right must be found in some other source of law, such as "the Constitution, or any Act of Congress, or any regulation of an executive department." 28 U.S.C. § 1491. [The claim must be for money damages against the United States and the claimant must prove that the law relied upon "can fairly be interpreted as mandating compensation by the Federal Government for the damage sustained." *Eastport S.S. Corp. v. United States,* 372 F.2d 1002, 1009 (Ct. Cl. 1967).] In [*Mitchell I*] this Court concluded that the General Allotment Act [providing that the government hold the land "in trust" for the allottees] creates only a limited trust relationship [preventing] improvident alienation of the allotted lands and assur[ing] their immunity from state taxation.

[In conclusion] a court need not find a separate waiver of sovereign immunity in the substantive provision, [although] in determining the general scope of the Tucker Act, this Court has not lightly inferred the United States' consent to suit.

In this case, however, there is simply no question that the Tucker Act provides the United States' consent to suit for claims founded upon statutes or regulations that create substantive rights to money damages. If a claim falls within this category, the existence of a waiver of sovereign immunity is clear. The question in this case is thus analytically distinct: whether the statutes or regulations at issue can be interpreted as requiring compensation.

III

Respondents have based their money claims against the United States on various Acts of Congress and executive department regulations. We begin by describing these sources of substantive law. We then examine whether they can fairly be interpreted as mandating compensation for damages sustained as a result of a breach of the duties they impose.

A

The Secretary of the Interior's pervasive role in the sales of timber from Indian lands began with the Act of June 25, 1910 [as amended 25 U.S.C. §§ 406, 407.] The 1910 Act empowered the Secretary to sell timber on unallotted lands and apply the proceeds of the sales for the benefit of the Indians, § 7, and authorized the Secretary to consent to sales by allottees, with the proceeds to be paid to the allottees or disposed of for their benefit, § 8. Congress thus sought to provide for harvesting timber "in such a manner as to conserve the interests of the people on the reservations, namely, the Indians." From the outset, the Interior Department recognized its obligation to supervise the cutting of Indian timber. In 1911, the Department's Office of Indian Affairs promulgated detailed regulations [addressing] virtually every aspect of forest management, including the size of sales, contract procedures, advertisements and methods of billing, deposits and bonding requirements, administrative fee deductions, procedures for sales by minors, allowable heights of stumps, tree marking and scaling rules, base and top diameters of trees for cutting, and the percentage of trees to be left as a seed source. The regulations applied to allotted as well as tribal lands, and the Secretary's approval of timber sales on allotted lands was explicitly conditioned upon compliance with the regulations.

Over time, deficiencies in the Interior Department's performance of its responsibilities became apparent. [Thus] Congress expressly directed that the Interior Department manage Indian forest resources "on the principle of sustained-yield management." [25 U.S.C. § 466.]

Regulations promulgated under the Act [were] designed to assure that the Indians receive "'the benefit of whatever profit [the forest] is capable of yielding.'" *White Mountain Apache Tribe v. Bracker*, 448 U.S., at 149 (quoting 25 C.F.R § 141.3(a)(3) (1979)).

In 1964 [amendments directed the Secretary to] consider "the needs and best interests of the Indian owner and his heirs." 25 U.S.C. § 406(a). In performing this duty, the Secretary was specifically required to take into account: ["the need for maintaining the productive capacity of the land for the benefit of the owner and his heirs," the "highest and best use of the land," and "the present and future financial needs of the owner and his heirs"].

[In sum, the] Department of the Interior — through the Bureau of Indian Affairs — "exercises literally daily supervision over the harvesting and management of tribal timber," [*White Mountain Apache Tribe v. Bracker.*] Virtually every stage of the process is under federal control.

B

In [*Mitchell I* the Court held that the General Allotment Act] could not be read "as establishing that the United States has a fiduciary responsibility for management of allotted forest lands." In contrast to the bare trust created by the General Allotment Act, the statutes and regulations now before us clearly give the Federal Government full responsibility to manage Indian resources and land for the benefit of the Indians. They thereby establish a fiduciary relationship and define the contours of the United States' fiduciary responsibilities.

The language of these statutory and regulatory provisions directly supports the existence of a fiduciary relationship. For example, § 8 of the 1910 Act, as amended, expressly mandates that sales of timber from Indian trust lands be based upon the Secretary's consideration of "the needs and best interests of the Indian owner and his heirs" and that proceeds from such sales be paid to owners "or disposed of for their benefit." 25 U.S.C. § 406(a). Similarly, even in its earliest regulations, the Government recognized its duties in "managing the Indian forests so as to obtain the greatest revenue for the Indians consistent with a proper protection and improvement of the forests." U.S. Office of Indian

Affairs, Regulations and Instructions for Officers in Charge of Forests on Indian Reservations 4 (1911). Thus, the Government has "expressed a firm desire that the Tribe should retain the benefits derived from the harvesting and sale of reservation timber." [*White Mountain Apache Tribe v. Bracker.*]

Moreover, a fiduciary relationship necessarily arises when the Government assumes such elaborate control over forests and property belonging to Indians. All of the necessary elements of a common-law trust are present: a trustee (the United States), a beneficiary (the Indian allottees), and a trust corpus (Indian timber, lands, and funds).[30] "[W]here the Federal Government takes on or has control or supervision over tribal monies or properties, the fiduciary relationship normally exists with respect to such monies or properties (unless Congress has provided otherwise) even though nothing is said expressly in the authorizing or underlying statute (or other fundamental document) about a trust fund, or a trust or fiduciary connection." [*Navajo Tribe v. United States*, 624 F.2d 981, 987 (Ct. Cl. 1980).]

Our construction of these statutes and regulations is reinforced by the undisputed existence of a general trust relationship between the United States and the Indian people. This Court has previously emphasized "the distinctive obligation of trust incumbent upon the Government in its dealings with these dependent and sometimes exploited people." *Seminole Nation v. United States*, 316 U.S. 286, 296 (1942).

Because the statutes and regulations at issue in this case clearly establish fiduciary obligations of the Government in the management and operation of Indian lands and resources, they can fairly be interpreted as mandating compensation by the Federal Government for damages sustained. Given the existence of a trust relationship, it naturally follows that the Government should be liable in damages for the breach of its fiduciary duties. It is well established that a trustee is accountable in damages for breaches of trust. See Restatement (Second) of Trusts §§ 205-212 (1959); G. Bogert, Law of Trusts and Trustees § 862 (2d ed. 1965); 3 A. Scott, Law of Trusts § 205 (3d ed. 1967). This Court and several other federal courts have consistently recognized that the existence of a trust relationship between the United States and an Indian or Indian tribe includes as a fundamental incident the right of an injured beneficiary to sue the trustee for damages resulting from a breach of the trust.

The recognition of a damages remedy also furthers the purposes of the statutes and regulations [to] generate proceeds for the Indians. It would be anomalous to conclude that these enactments create a right to the value of certain resources when the Secretary lives up to his duties, but no right to the value of the resources if the Secretary's duties are not performed. "Absent a retrospective damages remedy, there would be little to deter federal officials from violating their trust duties, at least until the allottees managed to obtain a judicial decree against future breaches of trust." [Justice White's dissent from *Mitchell I.*]

The Government contends that violations of duties imposed by the various statutes may be cured by actions for declaratory, injunctive, or mandamus relief against the Secretary. [P]rospective equitable remedies are totally inadequate.

---

[30]See Restatement (Second) of Trusts § 2, Comment h, p. 10 (1959).

[T]he Indian allottees are in no position to monitor federal management of their lands on a consistent basis. Many are poorly educated, most are absentee owners, and many do not even know the exact physical location of their allotments. Indeed, it was the very recognition of the inability of the Indians to oversee their interests that led to federal management in the first place. A trusteeship would mean little if the beneficiaries were required to supervise the day-to-day management of their estate by their trustee or else be precluded from recovery for mismanagement.

In addition, by the time Government mismanagement becomes apparent, the damage to Indian resources may be so severe that a prospective remedy may be next to worthless. For example, if timber on an allotment has been destroyed through Government mismanagement, it will take many years for nature to restore the timber.

[T]he statutes and regulations at issue here can fairly be interpreted as mandating compensation by the Federal Government for violations of its fiduciary responsibilities in the management of Indian property. The Court of Claims therefore has jurisdiction over respondents' claims for alleged breaches of trusts.

[*Affirmed.*]

Justice POWELL, with whom Justice REHNQUIST and Justice O'CONNOR join, dissenting.

Today [the Court] has effectively reversed the presumption that absent "affirmative statutory authority," the United States has not consented to be sued for damages. It has substituted a contrary presumption, applicable to the conduct of the United States in Indian affairs, that the United States has consented to be sued for statutory violations and other departures from the rules that govern private fiduciaries. I dissent from the Court's departure from long-settled principles.

I

The Court does not — and clearly cannot — contend that any of the statutes standing alone reflects the necessary legislative authorization of a damages remedy. None of the statutes contains any "provision ... that expressly makes the United States liable" for [mismanagement] or grants a right of action "with specificity." [*Testan.*] Indeed, nothing in the timber-sales statutes addresses in any respect the institution of damages actions against the United States. Nor is there any indication in the legislative history [indicating congressional intent to consent to damages actions for mismanagement].

The Court for the most part rests its decision on the implausible proposition that statutes that do not in terms create a right to payment of money nonetheless may support a damages action against the United States.

The Court defends its departure from our precedents on the ground that the statutes and regulations upon which respondents rely need not be "construed in the manner appropriate to waivers of sovereign immunity." The Court in effect is overruling *Mitchell I sub silentio.*

II

[The Court's] conclusion rests on two dubious assumptions. First, the Court decides that the statutes create or recognize fiduciary duties. It then reasons that because a private express trust normally imports a right to recover damages for breach, and because injunctive relief is perceived to be inadequate, Congress necessarily must have authorized recovery of damages for failure to perform the statutory duties properly. The relevancy of the first conclusion is questionable, and the other departs from our precedents, chiefly *Testan* and *Mitchell I.*

The Court simply asserts that the statutes here "clearly establish fiduciary obligations." [According to Judge Nichols in the Court of Claims]: "The federal power over Indian lands is so different in nature and origin from that of a private trustee ... that caution is taught in using the mere label of a trust plus a reading of *Scott on Trusts* to impose liability on claims where assent is not unequivocally expressed." [664 F.2d 265,] at 283.[8] The trusteeships to which the Court has referred in the past have manifested more the view that pervasive control over Indian life is such a high attribute of federal sovereignty that States cannot infringe upon that control. The Court today turns this shield into a sword.

[I]t is clear that "[n]othing on the face" of any of the statutes at issue, or in their legislative histories, "fairly [can] be interpreted as mandating compensation" for the conduct alleged by respondents. [T]he Court concludes that the mere existence of a trust of some kind necessarily establishes that Congress has consented to a recovery of damages. In effect we are told to accept on faith the existence of a damages cause of action: "Given the existence of a trust relationship, it naturally follows that the Government should be liable in damages for the breach of its fiduciary duties." [T]he Court is influenced by its view that an injunctive remedy is inadequate to redress the violations alleged. [It is the nature] of sovereign immunity that unconsented claims for money damages are barred. The fact that damages cannot be recovered without the sovereign's consent hardly supports the conclusion that consent has been given. Yet this, in substance, is the Court's reasoning. If it is saying that a remedy is necessary to redress every injury sustained, the doctrine of sovereign immunity will have been drained of all meaning. Moreover, "many of the federal statutes ... that

---

[8] "There are a number of widely varying relationships which more or less closely resemble trusts, but which are not trusts, although the term 'trust' is sometimes used loosely to cover such relationships. It is important to differentiate trusts from these other relationships, since many of the rules applicable to trusts are not applicable to them." Restatement (Second) of Trusts § 4, Introductory Note, p. 15 (1959). For example, the Court often has described the fiduciary relationship between the United States and Indians as one between a guardian and a ward. But "[a] guardianship is not a trust." Restatement (Second) of Trusts § 7. There is no explanation, however, why the Court chooses one analogy and not another. The choice appears to be influenced by the fact that "[t]he duties of a trustee are more intensive than the duties of some other fiduciaries." *Id.*, § 2, Comment b.

[T]wo persons and a parcel of real property, without more, do not create a trust. Rather, "[a] trust ... arises as a result of a manifestation of an intention to create it." Restatement (Second) of Trusts § 2. This is the element that is missing in this case, and the Court does not, and cannot, find that Congress has manifested its intent to make the statutory duties upon which respondents rely trust duties.

Indeed, given the language of the statute at issue in *Mitchell I*, the case for finding that Congress intended to impose fiduciary obligations on the United States was much stronger there than it is here. [In Justice White's dissent in *Mitchell I*, he cited *Scott on Trusts*, which] specifically discusses the General Allotment Act as an example of the United States acting as a trustee. Furthermore, a trustee can "reserv[e] powers with respect to the administration of the trust." Restatement (Second) of Trusts § 37. Unless the United States agrees to be held liable in damage, even the existence of a trust does not necessarily establish that the Government has surrendered its immunity from damages.

expressly provide money damages as a remedy against the United States in carefully limited circumstances would be rendered superfluous." [*Testan.*]

NOTES

1. The Two Sides of the Trust Relationship: The trust relationship has been the source of two opposing visions, one emphasizing federal power, the other emphasizing federal responsibility. During the Plenary Power era the relationship served as a justification for broad assertions of power against the will of the Indian people. Has this aspect of the trust relationship disappeared with the enlightenment of recent cases or can these seemingly diametrically opposed visions of the federal-Indian relationship coexist? If so, how can the disparate lines of cases be reconciled, or what vision of the government-Indian relationship can better balance the competing interests of federal power and Indian rights?

Professor Milner Ball characterized the problem in the following way:

> The likely origin of the trust doctrine is not Marshall's notion of wardship but the later ethnocentrism that also produced the notions of superiority and unrestrained power. For example, in the 1877 case of *Beecher v. Wetherby* the Court announced its presumption that, in dealings with tribes, "the United States would be governed by such considerations of justice as would control a Christian people in their treatment of an ignorant and dependent race."[290] The "semi-barbarous condition" of Indians was expected some day to "give place to the higher civilization of our race."[291] Later, in *Kagama*, when the Court upheld the extension of federal criminal law to reservations, it did so because of alleged tribal weaknesses and helplessness.[292] Still later, when *Lone Wolf* held Congress could take Indian property in violation of treaty obligation, it did so because of a supposed congressional duty of "care and protection of the Indians."[293] ... This uninspiring heritage gave rise to the trust doctrine.

Ball, *Constitution, Courts, Indian Tribes*, 1987 A.B.F. Res. J. 1, 63.

After discussing recent cases, including *Mitchell*, in which tribes have been able to bring breach of trust claims against the executive, Professor Ball makes this observation:

> [T]here is a fundamental threat to [tribes] in the theory itself even when trust litigation is successful. To bring suit on the trust requires acceptance of the premises of the trust — that the United States is a trustee for the tribes and can legitimately claim such power over them and their resources. Positive employment of the trust by tribes may mean indirectly embracing the degrading ethnocentrism that supports the theory. Reliance upon the trust may also divert tribes from developing other concepts and from insisting upon the right to manage their own resources.

Id. at 65. Nevertheless, Professor Ball does concede that the trust theory has some utility:

> It is of advantage to tribes in recovering for federal executive abuse in mismanaging tribal land and money. It has sometimes been a moral referent for congressional actions and judicial decisions as well as judicial canons of construction.

Id. Do the advantages outweigh the disadvantages?

2. Marshall's Vision of the Trust Relationship: Chief Justice Marshall's opinion in *Cherokee Nation* is the origin in the Supreme Court of the notion of

---

[290] 95 U.S. (5 Otto) 517, 525 (1877).
[291] *Id.* at 291 [other citations omitted].
[292] 118 U.S. at 383-84.
[293] 187 U.S. at 564-65.

the federal trusteeship over Indian affairs. Before exploring the manner in which that trusteeship principle has been invoked since 1831, it is useful to consider what Marshall had in mind when he described the Indian tribes as "in a state of pupilage [whose] relation to the United States resembles that of a ward to his guardian." Did Marshall contemplate the federal trusteeship over Indian affairs as an independent source of federal authority over Indian affairs, as it was apparently invoked during the Plenary Power era? Why, then, did he describe the Indian commerce clause as "[i]ntending to give the whole power of managing those [Indian] affairs to the government about to be instituted"? On the other hand, did Marshall intend the trusteeship to limit the exercise of federal authority over Indian affairs? In other words, was Marshall's description of the guardian-ward relationship between the federal government and the Indian tribes conceived to create enforceable fiduciary obligations between the parties? If so, toward what end did Chief Justice Marshall conceive that the federal trust responsibility was created? *See also* Young, *Indian Tribal Sovereignty and American Fiduciary Undertakings,* 8 WHITTIER L. REV. 825 (1987) (arguing that the Marshallian view of the trust relationship is better grounded in principles of guardianship and international law, while the *Kagama* view of the trust relationship is grounded in racism and undercut by cases like *Weeks* extending constitutional protections to Indians).

Fiduciary relationships are generally created to protect the ward or beneficiary in a described fashion and to marshal trust assets toward a designated objective. From whom did the Indian tribes need protection? Moreover, to create a trust, "a manifestation of an intention to create it" is necessary in the common law. RESTATEMENT (SECOND) OF TRUSTS § 2 (1959). Whose intent is relevant? Finally, if the relationship envisioned by Justice Marshall created enforceable legal rights and obligations, what is the significance of the last paragraph of the opinion in *Cherokee Nation*? By what agency could such legal rights and obligations be enforced?

3. The Emergence of Breach of Trust as a Cause of Action: As the Chambers excerpt indicates, the emergence of a cause of action for breach of trust is a relatively recent phenomenon, one traceable in part to the enormous influence of the article itself. Before the Indian Claims Commission Act was enacted in 1946, Indian tribes did not have access to the Court of Claims to sue the government without first obtaining a special jurisdictional act from Congress. A number of decisions based on these special jurisdictional statutes had awarded damages for breach of trust in the 1940's. *See, e.g., Menominee Tribe v. United States,* 101 Ct. Cl. 10 (1944) (special act instructed court to apply same standards applicable to a private trustee in determining whether United States liable for mismanaging resources); *Seminole Nation v. United States,* 316 U.S. 286 (1942) (government's disbursement of treaty annuity payments at the request of the tribe to the tribal treasurer and creditors of the tribe when the government had reason to know that tribal officials were misappropriating tribal funds breached the government's fiduciary obligations to the Indians). In addition, tribes had successfully brought some claims for mismanagement of resources before the Indian Claims Commission under provisions permitting adjudication of claims based on statutes and treaties. Nevertheless, the Commission was a specialized tribunal designed to clear up ancient claims once and for all; its jurisdiction extended solely to claims arising before 1946. Even favorable breach of trust decisions in that forum had little precedential value in courts of general jurisdiction. As a result, one question at the time Chambers wrote was to what extent a court of general jurisdiction, like a federal court exercising federal question jurisdiction, would entertain a cause of action against the government for breach of trust. A second question seemed less problematic at the time Chambers wrote, perhaps because of the special act cases of the 1940's: to what extent the Court of Claims would recognize such a claim for money damages.

4. The Practical Impact of the Existence of a Claim for Breach of Trust on Management of Indian Property and Money: Surely the most important factor for the majority in *Mitchell II* was the necessity for a money damages remedy to ensure careful management of Indian property and money by creating a powerful deterrent to mismanagement, which has been a continuing problem for Indian people. *Manchester Band of Pomo Indians v. United States*, 363 F. Supp. 1238 (N.D. Cal. 1973), relied on by the Court of Claims, illustrates the state of management at the time. In *Manchester Band*, the district court imposed liability on the federal government for failure to maximize return on money held in trust by the federal government derived from a tribal dairy enterprise and from leases of tribal land. Not only had the federal government failed to invest the tribal trust funds in authorized securities but it had repeatedly failed to pay the statutory interest rate on the funds and in one instance had neglected for two and a half years to deposit a receipt to the credit of the tribe. The decision in *Cheyenne-Arapaho* had aleady resulted in greatly improved management of the some $1.7 billion the government holds in trust for Indian tribes. After *Mitchell II*, the government can no longer question whether its duties to manage trust funds prudently are remediable by a claim for money damages.

Although management of funds has improved, management of tribal property continues to cause concern. In December, 1987, for example, the Senate Select Committee on Indian Affairs became concerned about stories of widespread mismanagment of mineral resources. As a result, the Committee created a Special Subcommittee on Investigations to investigate abuses. Its report, issued in 1989, noted that the Department of Interior's Mineral Management Service has become increasingly professional in its management of resources, by creating computerized accounting and auditing. Nevertheless, the report found much to criticize in the Department's management of mineral resources. For example, the Committee reported that oil companies had been stealing oil from Indian lands:

> The Committee found that simple "smash-and-grab" theft — stealing entire tankfuls of crude oil by force — rarely occurs; but sophisticated and premeditated theft by mismeasuring and fraudulently reporting the amount of oil purchases has been the practice for many years of the largest purchaser of Indian oil in the United States and others. The Department of the Interior and its relevant agencies, charged with stewardship of federal and Indian land, have knowingly allowed this widespread oil theft to go undetected for decades, at the direct expense of Indian owners.

SPECIAL COMMITTEE ON INVESTIGATIONS OF THE SELECT COMMITTEE ON INDIAN AFFAIRS, UNITED STATES SENATE, FINAL REPORT AND LEGISLATIVE RECOMMENDATIONS 105, S. REP. 101-216, 101st Cong., 1st Sess. (1989).

5. Mismanagement Claims: Compare the opinions in *Cheyenne-Arapaho* and *Mitchell II* focusing on the following questions:

(a) *Source of the Claim:* What was the source of the claim in *Cheyenne-Arapaho* and *Mitchell II*? How do the two courts differ in assessing the Indians' basis for bringing a claim? Before the two opinions in *Mitchell*, courts were somewhat cavalier in pinpointing the source of the trust relationship. A study by Professor Newton identified "[o]wnership of Indian land, the helplessness of Indian tribes in the face of a superior culture, higher law, the entire course of dealings between the government and Indian tribes, treaties, and 'hundreds of cases and ... a bulging volume of the U.S. States Code'" as having been cited as sources. Newton, *Enforcing the Federal-Indian Trust Relationship After Mitchell*, 31 CATH. U.L. REV. 635, 637-38 (1982) (quoting *White v. Califano*, 581 F.2d 697, 698 (8th Cir. 1978) (other citations omitted). Note that the Tucker Act, the basis of jurisdiction in the Court of Claims (and concurrent jurisdiction in the federal district courts for claims involving less than $10,000), permits suits for claims "founded ... upon ... any Act of Congress." 28 U.S.C. § 1346(a)(2). What must a statute say in order to create a claim? Can the federal common law serve as the origin for such a claim after *Mitchell II*?

   (b) *Waiver of Sovereign Immunity:* What is necessary to establish a waiver of sovereign immunity? Three years before *Mitchell II* the Supreme Court held the General Allotment Act did not create a claim against the government for breach of trust involving mismanagement of property, stating the Tucker Act did not waive sovereign immunity for a statutory claim. *United States v. Mitchell*, 445 U.S. 535 (1980). Thus a claimant had to present two jurisdictional prerequisites — a statutory claim and a statutory waiver of sovereign immunity. Since waivers of sovereign immunity are disfavored, the court strictly construed the Allotment Act, holding it did not create a claim for timber mismanagement, much less provide a basis for waiving sovereign immunity. For this reason, the rules of liberal construction of statutes affecting Indians did not come into play. The Supreme Court's earlier decision was criticized as departing from established law regarding Court of Claims jurisdiction in general and creating nearly insurmountable obstacles for future Indian breach of trust claims in particular. *See, e.g.*, Hughes, *Can the Trustee Be Sued for Its Breach? The Sad Saga of United States v. Mitchell*, 26 S. DAK. L. REV. 447 (1982). How does the Court's approach in *Mitchell II* differ? Is the Court's approach in *Mitchell I* or *Mitchell II* more consonant with the Court's treatment of sovereign immunity in suits for money damages in non-Indian law cases? *See, e.g., United States v. Testan*, 424 U.S. 392 (1976). Which approach is more consistent with congressional intent? For an analysis of the factors influencing the outcome in *Mitchell II*, see Frickey, *Congressional Intent, Practical Reasoning, and the Dynamic Nature of Federal Indian Law*, 78 CALIF. L. REV. 1139 (1990).

   When the claim is brought in federal district court invoking federal question jurisdiction and seeking declaratory or injunctive rather than monetary relief, sovereign immunity is not a bar, because the Administrative Procedure Act, 5 U.S.C. § 702, waives immunity. *See, e.g., Assiniboine & Sioux Tribes v. Board of Oil & Gas Conserv.*, 792 F.2d 782, 793 (9th Cir. 1986) (APA waives immunity in federal question claims whether the source of the claim is statutory or nonstatutory).

   (c) *Duties of the Trustee — Scope of the Claim:* In *Mitchell II,* the Court held only that the Claims Court had jurisdiction over the breach of trust claim. Thus, a question not yet resolved by the Court is the method of interpreting the statutory scheme to determine the scope of the government's statutory duties. How did the Court of Claims in *Cheyenne-Arapaho* make this determination? In other words, did it look solely to the statutes as fixing the appropriate duties? What role did the common law play? The court held that 25 U.S.C. § 161a, which authorizes payment of 4% simple interest on funds "upon which interest is not otherwise authorized by law," set only a minimum rate of return, "a floor rather than a ceiling." The statutes do permit 4% simple interest per annum to be paid. What role did 25 U.S.C. § 162(a) play in the court's analysis? In 1984, section 161a was amended to provide that *all* Indian trust funds in the Treasury shall be invested by the Secretary of the Treasury, at the request of the Secretary of the Interior, in public debt securities with maturities suitable to the needs of the fund involved, as determined by the Secretary of the Interior, and bearing interest at rates determined by the Secretary of the Treasury, taking into consideration current market yields on outstanding marketable obligations of the United States of comparable maturities.

How might this statute change the analysis if the Secretary decided to invest all Indian funds in public debt securities, which yield the lowest rates of any investment? Does the statute represent a congressional declaration that the Secretary has discretion to make such a decision, even though such a decision could violate the prudent investor rule if taken by a private trustee? *See Hearing on S. 1999 and S. 2000 Before the Senate Select Comm. on Indian Affairs,* 98th Cong., 2d Sess. (1984).

Although the Supreme Court did not resolve the ultimate question regarding the breach of trust claims in *Mitchell II,* what signal, if any, did it give regarding the extent to which it will be willing to fill the interstices of the statutory language by looking to common law trust principles? The Court did distinguish between the general trust created by the Allotment Act and one creating full fiduciary obligations. In the Court of Claims the first kind of trust is more precisely called a "limited trust" to denote that the duties are limited to those fulfilling the specific purpose of the statute. As *Mitchell I* made clear, the distinction impinges upon the courts' discretion to determine the scope of trust duties. In *Cape Fox Corp. v. United States,* 4 Cl. Ct. 223, 232 (1983), the court explained: "Where Congress intended and recognized only a limited trust relationship[,] fiduciary obligations applicable to private trustees are not imposed upon the Government.... The substantive right to money need not be explicitly stated but the obligation for money compensation must be clear and strong." On the other hand, where statutes, regulations and elaborate control of a tribal resource create a "full fiduciary obligation," as in *Mitchell II,* the Court of Claims may be more willing to look to common law trust principles to determine the duties of the trustee. *Cf. Gila River Pima-Maricopa Indian Community v. United States,* 9 Cl. Ct. 660, 677-78 (1986) (once elaborate control of trust resource(s) establishes full fiduciary relationship, private trust law standards determine liability for breach of fair and honorable dealings provision of Indian Claims Commission Act).

6. Conflicting Interpretations of *Mitchell II*'s Mandate: Two recent cases involving the extent of the Secretary's duty to compute value for the purpose of maximizing the royalties collected under oil and gas leases rely on the dictates of *Mitchell II.* Nevertheless, the opinions illustrate differing judicial philosophies toward defining the scope of the Secretary's duties in a breach of trust case. The Court of Appeals for the Tenth Circuit relied on *Mitchell II* to hold that the Mineral Leasing Act, 25 U.S.C. §§ 396a-g, and federal leasing regulations were part of a comprehensive statutory scheme covering oil and gas management and thus were sufficient to establish a general fiduciary relationship and create a claim for mismanagement. Having determined that a claim existed, the court further held that the Secretary had a duty to maximize royalty income, which he breached in several respects, including adopting a method of calculation of royalties permitted by the applicable regulations but not sufficient to maximize royalty income. As a result, the Secretary was ordered to employ dual accounting to ensure that the royalty charged would secure the fairest return for the tribe. *Jicarilla Apache Tribe v. Supron Energy Corp.,* 782 F.2d 855 (10th Cir. 1986) (en banc) (per curiam), *rev'g* 728 F.2d 1555 (10th Cir. 1984) (panel), *cert.*

denied sub nom. Southern Union Co. v. Jicarilla Apache Tribe, 479 U.S. 970 (1986).

A panel of the full court had construed the statutes and regulations narrowly, agreeing with the government that the applicable regulations gave the Secretary discretion to adopt the particular method of accounting. Judge Seymour dissented, stating:

> In my view, however, the most significant error the majority makes is its employment of administrative law analysis without considering what role, if any, the Secretary's fiduciary duty should play in a court's examination of his administrative action. [T]he Secretary's actions in a situation like this are constrained by principles of Indian trust obligations as well as by principles of administrative law.

728 F.2d at 1566-67. In short, Judge Seymour argued that the court should go beyond the wording of the statutes and regulations. In overturning the panel, the full court adopted Judge Seymour's opinion.

In *Pawnee v. United States,* 830 F.2d 187 (Fed. Cir. 1987), *cert. denied,* 108 S. Ct. 2014 (1988), the Federal Circuit Court of Appeals agreed with the Tenth Circuit that the statutes and regulations governing oil and gas leasing created a general trust relationship, *id.* at 191, *citing Jicarilla Apache Tribe v. Supron, supra,* but took a narrower view of the scope of the Secretary's *duties.* At issue was 25 U.S.C. § 396, permitting individual allottees to enter into oil and gas leases with the Secretary's approval. The court held that the Secretary had not breached any duties, because the applicable regulations did not require him to use any other method to calculate royalties. Since the plaintiffs had not challenged the regulations themselves, the court dismissed for failure to state a claim, stating: "The scope and extent of the fiduciary relationship, with respect to this particular matter, is established by the regulation and leases." *Id.* at 192.

The two cases can be distinguished on several grounds. In *Jicarilla Apache,* the tribe based its claim on federal question jurisdiction and sought only declaratory relief against the government. As note 6 in section A3 above pointed out, federal question jurisdiction can be based on federal common law. Thus the need to anchor the claim in a statute was not jurisdictionally mandated as it would be in a claims case. *See also Red Lake Band of Chippewa Indians v. Barlow,* 834 F.2d 1393, 1399-1400 & n.7 (8th Cir. 1987) (although statute required trust fund to be used only for sawmill, liberal construction of statutory scheme and trust obligations permitted court to order another disposition because original intent could not be fulfilled, as sawmill was no longer operating). Second, the court in *Pawnee* merely dismissed a claim because the tribe had failed to challenge the regulations themselves; thus the opinion arguably says nothing regarding the result if the tribe had challenged the regulations. Third, the Indian Mineral Leasing Act, 25 U.S.C. §§ 396a-g (1982) is more comprehensive than the statute at issue in *Pawnee.* Nevertheless, it is significant that while both courts agreed that the statutory scheme created a comprehensive trust relationship regarding management of oil and gas resources, the Federal Circuit's dismissal of the claim because the tribe had not challenged the regulations themselves reads much like the Tenth Circuit panel decision and may signal a propensity to give great weight to discretionary language in assessing whether the Secretary has carried out his duties. For example, the Federal Circuit opinion employed a very narrow reading of the applicable regulations, quoting language in *Mitchell II* stating the statutes and regulations "define the contours of the United States' fiduciary responsibilities." *Pawnee,* 830 F.2d at 100, *quoting Mitchell II,* 463 U.S. at 224.

In short, both the panel decision in *Jicarilla Apache* and the majority opinion in *Pawnee* share a willingness to treat the issue of the scope of the Secretary's duties as resolvable by administrative law rather than Indian law principles, in contrast to the approach of the en banc opinion in *Jicarilla Apache*. Certainly federal courts exercising equitable jurisdiction have ample basis to turn to the common law of trusts to fill in the interstices of the Secretary's trust obligations. Nevertheless, whether in fact a court will do so depends in part on the relevant court's philosophy toward imposing common law rather than statutory obligations on the government. As more cases delineating the scope of the trust relationship accrue, a consensus can be expected to develop.

7. Breach of Duty of Loyalty: In *Navajo Tribe v. United States,* 364 F.2d 320 (Ct. Cl. 1966), the Court of Claims held the federal government liable for usurpation of an oil and gas lease held by a private corporation on lands in the Navajo Reservation. Oil and gas exploration had indicated the presence of helium-bearing gas within the lease area. When the corporation decided to surrender the lease, the Bureau of Mines, interested in helium production for the war effort during World War II, took an assignment of the lease without notifying the tribe of the lessee's desire to surrender the lease. The court held that the failure to inform the tribe of the lessor's desire to surrender the lease before the effective date of the assignment constituted the usurpation of a tribal business opportunity by the trustee, the federal government, since the tribe might have availed itself profitably of the opportunity to exploit its helium resource. The court analogized the government's action to "that of a fiduciary who learns of an opportunity, prevents the beneficiary from getting it, and seizes it for himself. *Id.* at 324 (citing *Ottawa Tribe v. United States,* 166 Ct. Cl. 373, 380 (1964), *cert. denied,* 379 U.S. 929 (1966). This case indicates a common problem of the federal trust administration of Indian natural resources — the conflict of interest between the government's need to further national goals and its fiduciary obligations to the Indians. This problem is especially acute in the Interior Department where the Secretary must often accommodate the competing interests of Bureaus like Land Management and Water Reclamation with Indian Affairs.

b. The Special Problem of Conflicts of Interest Within Government Departments

PYRAMID LAKE PAIUTE TRIBE v. MORTON

354 F. Supp. 252 (D.D.C. 1972)

GESELL, District Judge.

This is an action by [an] Indian tribe challenging a regulation issued by the Secretary of the Interior. The tribe claims that the regulation should be set aside as arbitrary, capricious, and an abuse of the Secretary's authority, and invokes applicable provisions of the Administrative Procedure Act, 5 U.S.C. § 706. A declaration of rights and affirmative injunctive relief is also sought on the ground the Secretary has unlawfully withheld and unreasonably delayed required actions, 5 U.S.C. § 706(1).

[The Court has jurisdiction to review the regulation, 43 C.F.R. § 418, under the Administrative Procedure Act.] [The regulation] is designed to implement pre-existing general regulations by establishing the basis on which water will be provided during the succeeding twelve months to the Truckee-Carson Irrigation District, which is located in Churchill County, Nevada, some 50 miles east of Reno. The Tribe contends that the regulation delivers more water to the District than required by applicable court decrees and statutes, and improperly diverts water that otherwise would flow into nearby Pyramid Lake located on the Tribe's reservation.

This Lake has been the Tribe's principal source of livelihood. Members of the Tribe have always lived on its shores and have fished its waters for food. Following directives of the Department of Interior in 1859, which were confirmed by Executive Order signed by President Grant in 1874, the Lake, together with land surrounding the Lake and the immediate valley of the Truckee River which feeds into the Lake, have been reserved for the Tribe and set aside from the public domain. The area has been consistently recognized as the Tribe's aboriginal home.

Recently, the United States, by original petition in the Supreme Court of the United States, filed September, 1972, claims the right to use of sufficient water of the Truckee River for the benefit of the Tribe to fulfill the purposes for which the Indian Reservation was created, "including the maintenance and preservation of Pyramid Lake and the maintenance of the lower reaches of the Truckee as a natural spawning ground for fish and other purposes beneficial to and satisfying the needs" of the Tribe. *United States v. States of Nevada and California,* (No. 59 Original, October Term 1972), complaint at 14.

[I]rrigation for farming and other uses within the District are accommodated through some 600 miles of main water ditches and drains and the water is ultimately parcelled out through 1,500 delivery points. The water fed into this system comes from the Carson River following storage in Lahontan Reservoir and by diversion of water from the Truckee River at Derby Dam where it passes through the Truckee Canal to be stored in the Lahontan Reservoir for subsequent or simultaneous release. The Secretary entered into a contract with the District in 1926 and this contract is still in effect.

As the map so clearly shows, any water diverted from the Truckee at Derby Dam for the District is thereby prevented in substantial measure from flowing further north into Pyramid Lake. The Lake is a unique natural resource of almost incomparable beauty. It has no outflow, and as a desert lake depends largely on Truckee River inflow to make up for evaporation and other losses. It is approximately five miles wide and twenty-five miles long and now has a maximum depth of 335 feet. Although the Lake has risen a few feet in recent years, it has dropped more than 70 feet since 1906. A flow of 385,000 acre feet of water per year from the Truckee River into the Lake is required merely to maintain its present level. The decreased level and inflow have had the effect of making fish native to the Lake endangered protected species, and have unsettled the erosion and salinity balance of the Lake to a point where the continued utility of the Lake as a useful body of water is at hazard.[2]

The regulation under attack is the most recent of a series of regulations issued from year to year since 1967 pursuant to general policies established by the Secretary. The Tribe contends that the Secretary's action is an arbitrary abuse of discretion in that the Secretary has ignored his own guidelines and

---

[2] Native fish which naturally spawn in the Truckee can no longer do this and the Lake must be stocked at least until 1974 when construction to permit the fish again to pass into the river for spawning is to be completed.

failed to fulfill his trust responsibilities to the Tribe by illegally and unnecessarily diverting water from Pyramid Lake.

The focus of the inquiry has been to determine whether the 378,000 acre feet of water which the regulation contemplates will be diverted from the Truckee River at Derby Dam may be justified on a rational basis. This determination must be made in the light of three major factors which necessarily control the Secretary's action: namely, the Secretary's contract with the District, certain applicable court decrees, and his trust responsibilities to the Tribe. The Secretary and the Tribe are in substantial agreement that these are the factors to be weighed. The issue, therefore, comes down to whether or not the Secretary's resolution of conflicting demands created by these factors was effectuated arbitrarily rather than in the sound exercise of discretion.

The Court has carefully reviewed the processes by which the Secretary arrived at the disputed regulation. The Secretary had before him various written recommendations from interested agencies and experts, including responsible expert studies presented by the Tribe. There was a wide variation in these recommendations suggesting diversion of water in varying amounts ranging from 287,000 acre feet to 396,000 acre feet. All purported to be made on the basis of guidelines and policies previously set by the Secretary. After reviewing these written submissions, the Secretary conferred with the Assistant Secretary for Water and Power Resources (with authority over the Bureau of Reclamation) and the Assistant Secretary for Public Land Management (with authority over Indian Affairs) and made what one of these Assistants characterized as a "judgment call." It is affirmatively stated that the Secretary did not accept the recommendation of any particular person or group. The record, therefore, is completely devoid of any explanation or indication of the factors or computations which he took into account in arriving at the diversion figure of 378,000 acre feet. [T]here is no way of knowing the basis on which his conclusions rested. [Thus] the government has failed to meet its burden of establishing that this decision was anything but arbitrary.

Furthermore, while the Secretary's good faith is not in question, his approach to the difficult problem confronting him misconceived the legal requirements that should have governed his action. A "judgment call" was simply not legally permissible. The Secretary's duty was not to determine a basis for allocating water between the District and the Tribe in a manner that hopefully everyone could live with for the year ahead. This suit was pending and the Tribe had asserted well-founded rights. The burden rested on the Secretary to justify any diversion of water from the Tribe with precision. It was not his function to attempt an accommodation.

In order to fulfill his fiduciary duty, the Secretary must insure, to the extent of his power, that all water not obligated by court decree or contract with the District goes to Pyramid Lake.[4] The United States, acting through the Secretary of Interior, "has charged itself with moral obligations of the highest responsibility and trust. Its conduct, as disclosed in the acts of those who represent it in dealings with the Indians, should therefore be judged by the most exacting

---

[4]The Secretary's own regulations recognize his trustee obligations. 43 C.F.R. §§ 418.1(b) and 418.3(a) (1972).

fiduciary standards." *Seminole Nation v. United States,* [316 U.S. 286, 297, (1942)]; *Navajo Tribe of Indians v. United States,* [364 F.2d 320 (Ct. Cl. 1966)].

The vast body of case law which recognizes this trustee obligation is amply complemented by the detailed statutory scheme for Indian affairs set forth in Title 25 of the United States Code.[5] Undertakings with the Indians are to be liberally construed to the benefit of the Indians, and the duty of the Secretary to do so is particularly apparent. It is not enough to assert the water and fishing rights of the Tribe by filing a suit in the United States Supreme Court.

The Secretary was obliged to formulate a closely developed regulation that would preserve water for the Tribe. He was further obliged to assert his statutory and contractual authority to the fullest extent possible to accomplish this result. Difficult as this process would be, and troublesome as the repercussions of his actions might be, the Secretary was required to resolve the conflicting claims in a precise manner that would indicate the weight given each interest before him. Possible difficulties ahead could not simply be blunted by a "judgment call" calculated to placate temporarily conflicting claims to precious water. The Secretary's action is therefore doubly defective and irrational because it fails to demonstrate an adequate recognition of his fiduciary duty to the Tribe. This also is an abuse of discretion and not in accordance with law.

The record before the Court clearly establishes the underlying defects and arbitrary nature of the challenged regulation. The Secretary erred in two significant respects. First, he disregarded interrelated court decrees, and, second, he failed to exercise his authority to prevent unnecessary waste within the District. The effect of this is to deprive the Tribe of water without legal justification.

Two decrees of the United States District Court for the District of Nevada, known as the *Orr Water Ditch* and *Alpine* decrees, govern the amounts and conditions under which water shall be available for beneficial uses in the District. Maximums of roughly 4.5 acre feet and 2.92 acre feet measured at farm headgates are provided in the *Orr* and *Alpine* decrees, respectively. Approximately 60-75 percent of the water needed to serve the District's 60,000 acres of land is covered by the *Alpine* decree, and the remaining needed water is covered by the *Orr* decree. The parties and this Court of course recognize that neither the Secretary nor this Court can adopt or require a regulation that would infringe upon these decrees, and their interpretation and application is, in a number of respects, uncertain. Nonetheless, regardless of ambiguities and inconsistencies, as the Secretary himself recognized in his own guidelines and regulations, 43 C.F.R. § 418.3 (1972), he was required to take both decrees into account. The evidence demonstrates conclusively that the Secretary formulated the regulation by totally ignoring the Alpine decree and must have reached his calculations by relying solely on larger quantities provided by the *Orr Water Ditch* decree.

In addition, the evidence conclusively showed that the regulation is wholly inadequate to prevent waste within the District, causing substantial and wholly unnecessary diversion of water from the Truckee River to the obvious detriment of the Tribe. It was amply demonstrated that water could be conserved for Pyramid Lake without offending existing decrees or contractual rights of

---

[5] *See, e.g.,* 25 U.S.C. §§ 174 and 476; *see* 43 U.S.C. § 614c.

the District through better management which would prevent unnecessary waste. The amount of exposed water can be reduced to limit evaporation. Better management will lessen seepage and overflow; users can be assessed for water taken; techniques exist for measuring water more efficiently at headgates; land not entitled to water under the decrees and contract with the District can be prevented from taking the water; and by the mere employment of a few individuals the system can be so policed that it will function on a basis consistent with modern water control practices. All of this can be accomplished in spite of the fact that the District has an antiquated system. Failure to take appropriate steps, under the circumstances, by the regulation constitutes agency action unlawfully withheld and unreasonably delayed when viewed in the light of the Secretary's trust responsibilities to the Tribe, 5 U.S.C. § 706(1).

Under the contract between the Secretary and the District the Secretary has the right to require the District to conduct its affairs in a non-wasteful manner but no such action was taken or is contemplated in the regulation. [Thus,] the regulation is arbitrary, capricious, an abuse of discretion and not in accordance with law.

[The Secretary is ordered to submit an amended regulation for approval.]

NOTE

The *Pyramid Lake Paiute Tribe* case only involved the unappropriated waters on the Truckee River flowage that were subject to administrative allocation. The case did not and could not attack the water that had been allocated in 1944 to other users along the flowage by the final decree in the *Orr Ditch* litigation. The problems that the Pyramid Lake Paiutes were having in maintaining the fisheries and other water-based resources of Pyramid Lake could not, however, be solved by the *Pyramid Lake Paiute Tribe* decree alone. The tribe needed to unsettle the prior decree if they were to maintain the level of Pyramid Lake adequately and to sustain its fisheries.

Accordingly, the United States and the tribe both later filed suit in federal district court in Nevada, seeking to overturn the *Orr Ditch* decree. After the district court dismissed the action, the Ninth Circuit affirmed the decision as to all prior and subsequent users of water along the flowage and their successors in interest, but reversed as to the major defendant, the Truckee-Carson Irrigation District (which had contracted with the United States to operate the Newlands Reclamation Project). *United States v. Truckee-Carson Irrig. Dist.*, 649 F.2d 1286 (9th Cir. 1981), *amended*, 666 F.2d 351 (1982). The Supreme Court granted certiorari and issued the following opinion.

NEVADA v. UNITED STATES

463 U.S. 110 (1983)

Justice REHNQUIST delivered the opinion of the Court.

In 1913 the United States sued to adjudicate water rights to the Truckee River for the benefit of the Pyramid Lake Indian Reservation and the planned Newlands Reclamation Project. Thirty-one years later, in 1944, the United States District Court for the District of Nevada entered a final decree in the case pursuant to a settlement agreement. In 1973 the United States filed the present action in the same court on behalf of the Pyramid Lake Indian Reservation seeking additional water rights to the Truckee River. The issue thus presented is whether the Government may partially undo the 1944 decree, or whether principles of res judicata prevent it, and the intervenor Pyramid Lake Paiute Tribe, from litigating this claim on the merits.

I

Nevada has, on the average, less precipitation than any other State in the Union. [T]he Truckee River, one of the three principal rivers flowing through west central Nevada, [flows] into Pyramid Lake, which has no outlet.

[I]n early 1844, Pyramid Lake was some 50 miles long and 12 miles wide. Since that time the surface area of the lake has been reduced by about 20,000 acres. [Created by President Grant in 1874, the] Reservation includes Pyramid Lake, and land surrounding it, the lower reaches of the Truckee River, and the bottom land alongside the lower Truckee.

[The Reclamation Act of 1902, 32 Stat. 388,] directed the Secretary of the Interior to withdraw from public entry arid lands in specified Western States, reclaim the lands through irrigation projects, and then to restore the lands to entry pursuant to the homestead laws and certain conditions imposed by the Act itself. Accordingly, the Secretary withdrew from the public domain approximately 200,000 acres in western Nevada, which ultimately became the Newlands Reclamation Project.

[The Newlands Project diverted water] from the Truckee River to the Carson River by constructing the Derby Diversion Dam on the Truckee River, and constructing the Truckee Canal through which the diverted waters would be transported to the Carson River. [The] Lahontan Dam [and] Lahontan Reservoir [were created for storage]. The combined waters of the Truckee and Carson Rivers impounded in Lahontan Reservoir are distributed for irrigation and related uses on downstream lands by means of lateral canals within the Newlands Reclamation Project.

Before the works contemplated by the Project went into operation, a number of private landowners had established rights to water in the Truckee River under Nevada law. The Government also asserted on behalf of the Indians of the Pyramid Lake Indian Reservation a reserved right under the so-called "implied-reservation-of-water" doctrine set forth in *Winters v. United States*, 207 U.S. 564 (1908). [In 1913 the] United States [instituted] what became known as the *Orr Ditch* litigation. The Government, for the benefit of both the Project and the Pyramid Lake Reservation, asserted a claim to 10,000 cubic feet of water per second for the Project and a claim to 500 cubic feet per second for the Reservation. The complaint named as defendants all water users on the Truckee River in Nevada. The Government expressly sought a final decree quieting title to the rights of all parties.

[A] Special Master issued a report and proposed decree in July 1924 [awarding] the Reservation an 1859 priority date in the Truckee River for 58.7 second-feet and 12,412 acre-feet annually of water to irrigate 3,130 acres of Reservation lands. The Project was awarded a 1902 priority date for 1,500 cubic feet per second to irrigate, to the extent the amount would allow,[3] 32,800 acres of land within the Newlands Reclamation Project. In February 1926 the District Court entered a temporary restraining order declaring the water rights as proposed by the Special Master. "One of the primary purposes" for entering a temporary order was to allow for an experimental period during which modifications of the declared rights could be made if necessary. Not until almost 10 years later, in the midst of a prolonged drought, was interest stimulated in concluding the *Orr Ditch* litigation. Settlement negotiations were commenced in 1934 by the principal organizational defendants in the case, [and] the representatives of the Project and the Reservation. The United States still acted on behalf of the Reservation's interests, but the Project was now under the management of the Truckee-Carson Irrigation District (TCID). The defendants and TCID proposed an agreement along the lines of the temporary restraining order. The United States objected, demanding an increase in the Reservation's water rights to allow for the irrigation of an additional 2,745 acres of Reservation land. After some resistance, the Government's demand was accepted and a settlement agreement was signed on July 1, 1935. The District Court entered a final decree adopting the agreement on September 8, 1944. No appeal was taken. Thus, 31 years after its inception the *Orr Ditch* litigation came to a close.

[In] 1973, the Government instituted [this action] seeking additional rights to the Truckee River for the Pyramid Lake Indian Reservation; the Pyramid Lake Paiute Tribe was permitted to intervene in support of the United States. The Government named as defendants all persons presently claiming water rights to the Truckee River and its tributaries in Nevada. The defendants include the defendants in the *Orr Ditch* litigation and their successors, approximately 3,800 individual farmers that own land in the Newlands Reclamation Project, and TCID. The District Court certified the Project farmers as a class and directed TCID to represent their interests.

[The government argues] that *Orr Ditch* determined only the Reservation's right to "water for irrigation," not the claim now being asserted for "sufficient waters of the Truckee River ... [for] the maintenance and preservation of Pyramid Lake, [and for] the maintenance of the lower reaches of the Truckee River as a natural spawning ground for fish." The complaint further averred that in establishing the Reservation the United States had intended that the Pyramid Lake fishery be maintained. Since the additional water now being claimed is allegedly necessary for that purpose, the Government alleged that the Executive Order creating the Reservation must have impliedly reserved a right to this water.[7]

The defendants below asserted res judicata as an affirmative defense. [T]he District Court sustained the defense and dismissed the complaint in its entirety.

---

[3] Notwithstanding the Project's 1902 priority, it was awarded far less water than the Government had claimed. [According to the Court of Appeals:] "there has never been irrigated more than about 65,000 acres of land in the Project."

[7] Between 1920 and 1940 the surface area of Pyramid Lake was reduced by about 20,000 acres. The decline [prevented the fish] from reaching their spawning grounds in the Truckee River, resulting in the near extinction of [the] species. [Efforts to restore the fish include fish] hatcheries operated by both the State of Nevada and the United States [and] the Marble Bluff Dam and Fishway [which] enabl[e] the fish to [reach] their spawning grounds in the Truckee. Both the District Court and Court of Appeals observed that "these restoration efforts 'appear to justify optimism for eventual success.'"

[T]he District Court first determined that all of the parties in this action were parties, or in privity with parties, in the *Orr Ditch* case. [According to the court, the Government intended] "to assert as large a water right as possible for the Indian reservation" [in the *Orr Ditch* litigation]. [The District Court explained]:

> The plaintiff and the Tribe may not litigate several different types of water use claims, all arising under the Winters doctrine and all derived from the same water source in a piece-meal fashion. There was but one cause of action in equity to quiet title in plaintiff and the Tribe based upon the Winters reserved right theory.

[T]he Court of Appeals found that the *Orr Ditch* decree did not conclude the dispute between the Tribe and the owners of Newlands Project lands. The court said that litigants are not to be bound by a prior judgment unless they were adversaries under the earlier pleadings or unless the specific issue in dispute was actually litigated in the earlier case and the court found that neither exception applied here.

The Court of Appeals conceded that "[a] strict adversity requirement does not necessarily fit the realities of water adjudications." Nevertheless, the court found that since neither the Tribe nor the Project landowners were parties in *Orr Ditch* but instead were both represented by the United States, and since their interests may have conflicted in that proceeding, the court would not find that the Government had intended to bind these nonparties inter se absent a specific statement of adversity in the pleadings. We granted certiorari in the cases challenging the Court of Appeals' decision, and we now affirm in part and reverse in part.

II

The Government [argues]: "The court of appeals has simply permitted a reallocation of the water decreed in *Orr Ditch* to a single party — the United States — from reclamation uses to a Reservation use with an earlier priority. The doctrine of res judicata does not bar a single party from reallocating its water in this fashion ...." We are bound to say that the Government's position, if accepted, would do away with half a century of decided case law relating to the Reclamation Act of 1902 and water rights in the public domain of the West. [The Court then summarized the history of the Reclamation Act, quoting extensively from *Ickes v. Fox,* 300 U.S. 82 (1937), holding that projects built under the Reclamation Act did not vest water rights in the government. According to *Ickes:*] "Appropriation was made not for the use of the government, but, under the Reclamation Act, for the use of the land owners; and by the terms of the law and of the contract already referred to, the water-rights became the property of the land owners, wholly distinct from the property right of the government in the irrigation works. [I]t long has been established law that the right to the use of water can be acquired only by prior appropriation for a beneficial use; and that such right when thus obtained is a property right, which, when acquired for irrigation, becomes, by state law and here by express provision of the Reclamation Act as well, part and parcel of the land upon which it is applied."

The law of Nevada, in common with most other Western States, requires for the perfection of a water right for agricultural purposes that the water must be beneficially used by actual application on the land. Such a right is appurtenant to the land on which it is used.

In the light of these cases, we conclude that the Government is completely mistaken if it believes that the water rights confirmed to it by the *Orr Ditch* decree in 1944 for use in irrigating lands within the Newlands Reclamation Project were like so many bushels of wheat, to be bartered, sold, or shifted about as the Government might see fit. Once these lands were acquired by settlers in the Project, the Government's "ownership" of the water rights was at most nominal; the beneficial interest in the rights confirmed to the Government resided in the owners of the land within the Project to which these water rights became appurtenant upon the application of Project water to the land. [T]he law of the relevant State and the contracts entered into by the landowners and the United States make this point very clear.

The Government's brief is replete with references to its fiduciary obligation to the Pyramid Lake Paiute Tribe of Indians, as it properly should be. But the Government seems wholly to ignore in the same brief the obligations that necessarily devolve upon it from having mere title to water rights for the Newlands Project, when the beneficial ownership of these water rights resides elsewhere.

Both the briefs of the parties and the opinion of the Court of Appeals focus their analysis of res judicata on provisions relating to the relationship between private trustees and fiduciaries, especially those governing a breach of duty by the fiduciary to the beneficiary. While these undoubtedly provide useful analogies in cases such as these, they cannot be regarded as finally dispositive of the issues. This Court has long recognized "the distinctive obligation of trust incumbent upon the Government" in its dealings with Indian tribes, see, e.g., *Seminole Nation v. United States*, 316 U.S. 286, 296 (1942). These concerns have been traditionally focused on the Bureau of Indian Affairs within the Department of the Interior. *Poafpybitty v. Skelly Oil Co.*, 390 U.S. 365, 374 (1968). See 25 U.S.C. § 1.

But Congress in its wisdom, when it enacted the Reclamation Act of 1902, required the Secretary of the Interior to assume substantial obligations with respect to the reclamation of arid lands in the western part of the United States. Additionally, in § 26 of the Act of Apr. 21, 1904, 33 Stat. 225, Congress provided for the inclusion of irrigable lands of the Pyramid Lake Indian Reservation within the Newlands Project, and further authorized the Secretary, after allotting five acres of such land to each Indian belonging to the Reservation, to reclaim and dispose of the remainder of the irrigable Reservation land to settlers under the Reclamation Act.

Today, particularly from our vantage point nearly half a century after the enactment the Indian Reorganization Act, it may well appear that Congress was requiring the Secretary of the Interior to carry water on at least two shoulders when it delegated to him both the responsibility for the supervision of the Indian tribes and the commencement of reclamation projects in areas adjacent to reservation lands. But Congress chose to do this, and it is simply unrealistic to suggest that the Government may not perform its obligation to represent Indian tribes in litigation when Congress has obliged it to represent other interests as well. In this regard, the Government cannot follow the fastidious standards of a private fiduciary, who would breach his duties to his single beneficiary solely by representing potentially conflicting interests without the beneficiary's consent. The Government does not "compromise" its obligation to one interest that Congress obliges it to represent by the mere fact that it simultaneously performs another task for another interest that Congress has obligated it by statute to do.

With these observations in mind, we turn to the principles of res judicata that we think are involved in this case.

III

[The doctrine of res judicata] "is essential to the maintenance of social order; for, the aid of judicial tribunals would not be invoked for the vindication of rights of person and property, if ... conclusiveness did not attend the judgments of such tribunals." *Southern Pacific R. Co. v. United States*, 168 U.S. 1, 49 (1897).[10] [W]hen a final judgment has been entered on the merits of a case, "[i]t is a finality as to the claim or demand in controversy, concluding parties and those in privity with them, not only as to every matter which was offered and received to sustain or defeat the claim or demand, but as to any other admissible matter which might have been offered for that purpose." *Cromwell v. County of Sac*, 94 U.S. 351, 352 (1877). The final "judgment puts an end to the cause of action, which cannot again be brought into litigation between the parties upon any ground whatever." *Commissioner v. Sunnen*, 333 U.S. 591, 597 (1948). *See Chicot County Drainage District v. Baxter State Bank*, 308 U.S. 371, 375, 378 (1940).

To determine the applicability of res judicata to the facts before us, we must decide first if the "cause of action" which the Government now seeks to assert is the "same cause of action" that was asserted in *Orr Ditch*; we must then decide whether the parties in the instant proceeding are identical to or in privity with the parties in *Orr Ditch*. We address these questions in turn.

A

Definitions of what constitutes the "same cause of action" have not remained static over time. Compare Restatement of Judgments § 61 (1942) with Restatement (Second) of Judgments § 24 (1982). We find it unnecessary in these cases to parse any minute differences which these differing tests might produce, because whatever standard may be applied the only conclusion allowed by the record in the *Orr Ditch* case is that the Government was given an opportunity to litigate the Reservation's entire water rights to the Truckee, and that the Government intended to take advantage of that opportunity.

[The Court compared the *Orr Ditch* decree and the complaint in the present case, concluding that both "show[ed] the Government's intention to assert in *Orr Ditch* the Reservation's full water rights."]

---

[10] The policies advanced by the doctrine of res judicata perhaps are at their zenith in cases concerning real property, land and water. [Q]uiet title actions for the adjudication of water rights, such as the *Orr Ditch* suit, [are] distinctively equipped to serve these policies because "[they enable] the court of equity to acquire jurisdiction of all the rights involved and also of all the owners of those rights, and thus settle and permanently adjudicate in a single proceeding all the rights, or claims to rights, of all the claimants to the water taken from a common source of supply." 3 C. Kinney, Law of Irrigation and Water Rights § 1535, p. 2764 (2d ed. 1912).

B

[W]e must next determine which of the parties before us are bound by the earlier decree. As stated earlier, the general rule is that a prior judgment will bar the "parties" to the earlier lawsuit, "and those in privity with them," from relitigating the cause of action. *Cromwell v. County of Sac*, 94 U.S., at 352.

There is no doubt but that the United States was a party to the *Orr Ditch* proceeding, acting as a representative for the Reservation's interests and the interests of the Newlands Project, and cannot relitigate the Reservation's "implied-reservation-of-water" rights with those who can use the *Orr Ditch* decree as a defense. We also hold that the Tribe, whose interests were represented in *Orr Ditch* by the United States, can be bound by the *Orr Ditch* decree.[14] This Court left little room for an argument to the contrary in *Heckman v. United States*, 224 U.S. 413 (1912), where it plainly said that "it could not, consistently with any principle, be tolerated that, after the United States on behalf of its wards had invoked the jurisdiction of its courts ... these wards should themselves be permitted to relitigate the question." *Id.*, at 446. See also Restatement (Second) of Judgments § 41(1)(d) (1982). We reaffirm that principle now.[15]

---

[14] We, of course, do not pass judgment on the quality of representation that the Tribe received. In 1951 the Tribe sued the Government before the Indian Claims Commission for damages, basing its claim of liability on the Tribe's receipt of less water for the fishery than it was entitled to. *Northern Paiute Tribe v. United States*, 30 Ind. Cl. Comm'n 210 (1973). In a settlement the Tribe was given $8 million in return for its waiver of further liability on the part of the United States.

[15] This Court held in *Hansberry v. Lee*, 311 U.S. 32, 44 (1940), that persons vicariously represented in a class action could not be bound by a judgment in the case where the representative parties had interests that impermissibly conflicted with those of persons represented. See also Restatement (Second) of Judgments § 42(1)(d) (1982). The Tribe seeks to take advantage of this ruling, arguing that the Government's primary interest in *Orr Ditch* was to obtain water rights for the Newlands Reclamation Project and that by definition any water rights given to the Tribe would conflict with that interest. We reject this contention.

We have already said that the Government stands in a different position than a private fiduciary where Congress has decreed that the Government must represent more than one interest. When the Government performs such duties it does not by that reason alone compromise its obligation to any of the interests involved.

[Once the Justice Department decided to get involved in the *Orr Ditch* suit a] Special Assistant United States Attorney assigned to the matter was apparently the first to recognize that the Government should in the same suit seek to establish the water rights to the Pyramid Lake Indian Reservation. [He] advanced the view that "[t]hese Indian reservation water rights are important and should be established to the fullest extent because they are senior and superior to most if not all the other rights on the river."

[At the same time the Commissioner of Indian Affairs was notified] that an assertion of the Reservation's rights should be included in *Orr Ditch*. The claim was advanced accordingly and thereafter the Bureau of Indian Affairs was kept aware of the *Orr Ditch* proceedings; during the settlement negotiations the BIA directly participated. The BIA is the agency of the Federal Government "charged with fulfilling the trust obligations of the United States" to Indians, *Poafpybitty v. Skelly Oil Co.*, 390 U.S. 365, 374 (1968), and there is nothing in the record of this case to indicate that any official outside of the BIA attempted to influence the BIA's decisions in a manner inconsistent with these obligations. The record suggests that the BIA alone may have made the decision not to press claims for a fishery water right, for reasons which hindsight may render questionable, but which did not involve other interests represented by the Government. For instance, in a 1926 letter to a federal official on the Pyramid Lake Reservation, the Commissioner of Indian Affairs explained:

"We feel that the Indians would be wise to assume that Truckee River water will be used practically as far as it can be for irrigation, and that the thing for the Indians to do is, if possible, instead of trying to stop such development to direct it so that it will inure to their benefit.

We then turn to the issue of which defendants in the present litigation can use the *Orr Ditch* decree against the Government and the Tribe. There is no dispute but that the *Orr Ditch* defendants were parties to the earlier decree and that they and their successors can rely on the decree. The Court of Appeals so held, and we affirm.

The Court of Appeals reached a different conclusion concerning TCID and the Project farmers that it now represents. The Court of Appeals conceded that the Project's interests, like the Reservation's interests, were presented in *Orr Ditch* by the United States and thus that TCID, like the Tribe, stands with respect to that litigation in privity with the United States. The court further stated, however, that "[a]s a general matter, a judgment does not conclude parties who were not adversaries under the pleadings," and that in "representative litigation we should be especially careful not to infer adversity between interests represented by a single litigant." Since the pleadings in *Orr Ditch* did not specifically allege adversity between the claims asserted on behalf of the Newlands Project and those asserted on behalf of the Reservation, the Court of Appeals ruled that the decree did not conclude the dispute between them. [A]s the Court of Appeals noted:

> "A strict adversity requirement does not necessarily fit the realities of water adjudications. All parties' water rights are interdependent. Stability in water rights therefore requires that all parties be bound in all combinations. Further, in many water adjudications there is no actual controversy between the parties; the proceedings may serve primarily an administrative purpose." 649 F.2d, at 1309.

We agree with these observations of the Court of Appeals. That court felt, however, that these factors did not control these cases because the "Tribe and

---

"... [I]f their ultimate welfare depends in part on their being able to hold their own in a civilized world ... they should look forward to a different means of livelihood, in part at least, from their ancestral one, of fishing and hunting. They should expect not only to farm their allotments but also to do other sorts of work and have other ways of making a living."

Furthermore, the District Court found that during the pendency of the *Orr Ditch* proceedings "a serious and reasonable doubt existed as to whether any *Winters* reserved water right could be claimed at all for an executive order Indian reservation."

In pressing for a different conclusion, the Tribe relies primarily on a finding by the District Court that it was the intention of the Government in *Orr Ditch* "to assert as large a water right as possible for the Indian reservation, and to do everything possible to protect the fish for the benefit of the Indians and the white population insofar as it was 'consistent with the larger interests involved in the propositions having to do with the reclamation of thousands of acres of arid and now useless land for the benefit of the country as a whole.'" The Tribe's focus on this ambiguous finding, however, has not blinded us to the District Court's specific finding on the alleged conflict.

"[T]here was a foreseeable conflict of purposes created by the Congress within the Interior Department and as between the Bureau of Reclamation on the one hand in asserting large water rights for its reclamation projects and the Bureau of Indian Affairs on the other in the performance of its obligations to protect the rights and interests of the Indians on the Pyramid Lake Paiute Indian Reservation. [T]his conflict of purposes was apparent prior to and during the *Orr Ditch* proceedings and was resolved within the executive department of government by top-level executive officers acting within the scope of their Congressionally-delegated duties and authority and were political and policy decisions of those officials charged with that responsibility, which decisions resulted in the extinguishment of the alleged fishery purposes water right.... The government lawyers in *Orr Ditch,* both departmental, agency and bureaus, as well as those charged with the responsibility for the actual conduct of the litigation, are not chargeable with an impermissible conflict of purpose or interest in carrying out the decisions and directions of their superiors in the executive department of government ...." The District Court's finding reflects the nature of a democratic government that is charged with more than one responsibility; it does not describe conduct that would deprive the United States of the authority to conduct litigation on behalf of diverse interests.

the Project were neither parties nor co-parties, however. They were non-parties who were represented simultaneously by the same government attorneys." [*Id.*] We disagree with the Court of Appeals as to the consequence of this fact.

It has been held that the successors in interest of parties who are not adversaries in a stream adjudication nevertheless are bound by a decree establishing priority of rights in the stream. [The] rule seems to be generally applied in stream adjudications in the Western States, where these actions play a critical role in determining the allocation of scarce water rights, and where each water rights claim by its "very nature raise[s] issues inter se as to all such parties for the determination of one claim necessarily affects the amount available for the other claims." *Marlett v. Prosser*, [179 P. 141, 142 (1919)].

In these cases, as we have noted, the Government as a single entity brought the action seeking a determination both of the Tribe's reserved rights and of the water rights necessary for the irrigation of land within the Newlands Project. But it separately pleaded the interests of both the Project and the Reservation. During the settlement negotiations the interests of the Project, and presumably of the landowners to whom the water rights actually accrued, were represented by the newly formed TCID and the interests of the Reservation were represented by the Bureau of Indian Affairs. The settlement agreement was signed by the Government and by TCID. It would seem that at this stage of the litigation the interests of the Tribe and TCID were sufficiently adverse for the latter to oppose the Bureau's claim for additional water rights for the Reservation during the settlement negotiations.

The Court of Appeals held, however, that "in representative litigation we should be especially careful not to infer adversity between interests represented by a single litigant," 649 F.2d, at 1309, analogizing the Government's position to that of a trustee under the traditional law of trusts. But as we have indicated previously, we do not believe that this analogy from the world of private law may be bodily transposed to the present situation.

The Court of Appeals went on to conclude: "By representing the Tribe and the Project against the *Orr Ditch* defendants, the government compromised its duty of undivided loyalty to the Tribe. See Restatement (Second) of Trusts, *supra*, § 170, & Comments p, q, r." *Id.*, at 1310. This section of the Restatement (Second) of Trusts (1959) is entitled "Duty of Loyalty," and states that: "(1) the trustee is under a duty to the beneficiary to administer the trust solely in the interest of the beneficiary." Comments p, q, and r deal respectively with "[c]ompetition with the beneficiary," "[a]ction in the interest of a third person," and "[d]uty of trustee under separate trusts."

As we previously intimated, we think the Court of Appeals' reasoning here runs aground because the Government is simply not in the position of a private litigant or a private party under traditional rules of common law or statute. [I]n the very area of the law with which we deal in these cases, this Court said in *Heckman v. United States*, 224 U.S., at 444-445:

> There can be no more complete representation than that on the part of the United States in acting on behalf of these dependents — whom Congress, with respect to the restricted lands, has not yet released from tutelage. Its effacacy [sic] does not depend on the Indian's acquiescence. It does not rest upon convention, nor is it circumscribed by rules which govern private relations. It is a representation which traces its source to

the plenary control of Congress in legislating for the protection of the Indians under its care, and it recognizes no limitations that are inconsistent with the discharge of the national duty.

These cases, we believe, point the way to the correct resolution of the instant cases. The United States undoubtedly owes a strong fiduciary duty to its Indian wards. See [*Seminole Nation*]; *Shoshone Tribe v. United States*, 299 U.S. 476, 497-498 (1937). It may be that where only a relationship between the Government and the tribe is involved, the law respecting obligations between a trustee and a beneficiary in private litigation will in many, if not all, respects adequately describe the duty of the United States. But where Congress has imposed upon the United States, in addition to its duty to represent Indian tribes, a duty to obtain water rights for reclamation projects, and has even authorized the inclusion of reservation lands within a project, the analogy of a faithless private fiduciary cannot be controlling for purposes of evaluating the authority of the United States to represent different interests.

At least by 1926, when TCID came into being, and very likely long before, when conveyances of the public domain to settlers within the Reclamation Project necessarily carried with them the beneficial right to appropriate water reserved to the Government for this purpose, third parties entered into the picture. The legal relationships were no longer simply those between the United States and the Paiute Tribe, but also those between the United States, TCID, and the several thousand settlers within the Project who put the Project water to beneficial use. We find it unnecessary to decide whether there would be adversity of interests between the Tribe, on the one hand, and the settlers and TCID, on the other, if the issue were to be governed by private law respecting trusts. We hold that under the circumstances described above, the interests of the Tribe and the Project landowners were sufficiently adverse so that both are now bound by the final decree entered in the *Orr Ditch* suit.

[I]n the final analysis we agree with the Court of Appeals that [the defendants who appropriated water afterwards] can use the *Orr Ditch* decree against the plaintiffs below. [E]xceptions to the res judicata mutuality [of estoppel] requirement have been found necessary, and we believe that such an exception is required in these cases. [E]ven though quiet title actions are in personam actions, water adjudications are more in the nature of in rem proceedings. Nonparties such as the subsequent appropriators in these cases have relied just as much on the *Orr Ditch* decree in participating in the development of western Nevada as have the parties of that case. We agree with the Court of Appeals that under "these circumstances it would be manifestly unjust ... not to permit subsequent appropriators" to hold the Reservation to the claims it made in *Orr Ditch*; "[a]ny other conclusion would make it impossible ever finally to quantify a reserved water right." 649 F.2d, at 1309.[16]

---

[16] The Tribe makes the argument that even if res judicata would otherwise apply, it cannot be used in these cases because to do so would deny the Tribe procedural due process. The Tribe argues that in *Orr Ditch* they were given neither the notice required by *Mullane v. Central Hanover Bank & Trust Co.*, 339 U.S. 306 (1950), nor the full and fair opportunity to be heard required by *Hansberry v. Lee*, 311 U.S. 32 (1940), and *Logan v. Zimmerman Brush Co.*, 455 U.S. 422 (1982). *Mullane*, which involved a final accounting between a trustee and beneficiaries, is of course inapposite. *Hansberry* was based upon an impermissible conflict in a class action between the representatives of the class and certain class members; we have already said that such a conflict did not exist in

IV

In conclusion we affirm the Court of Appeals' finding that the cause of action asserted below and the cause of action asserted in *Orr Ditch* are one and the same. We also affirm the Court of Appeals' finding that the *Orr Ditch* decree concluded the controversy on this cause of action between, on the one hand, the *Orr Ditch* defendants, their successors in interest, and subsequent appropriators of the Truckee River, and, on the other hand, the United States and the Tribe. We reverse the Court of Appeals, however, with respect to its finding concerning TCID, and the Project farmers it represents, and hold instead that the *Orr Ditch* decree also ended the dispute raised between these parties and the plaintiffs below.

[*Affirmed in part, reversed in part.*]

Justice BRENNAN, concurring.

The mere existence of a formal "conflict of interest" does not deprive the United States of authority to represent Indians in litigation, and therefore to bind them as well. If, however, the United States actually causes harm through a breach of its trust obligations the Indians should have a remedy against it. I join the Court's opinion on the understanding that it reaffirms that the Pyramid Lake Paiute Tribe has a remedy against the United States for the breach of duty that the United States has admitted. [See note 16.]

In the final analysis, our decision today is that thousands of small farmers in northwestern Nevada can rely on specific promises made to their forebears two and three generations ago, and solemnized in a judicial decree, despite strong claims on the part of the Pyramid Lake Paiutes. Here, as elsewhere in the West, [water] is insufficient to satisfy all claims. In the face of such fundamental natural limitations, the rule of law cannot avert large measures of loss, destruction, and profound disappointment, no matter how scrupulously evenhanded are the law's doctrines and administration. Yet the law can and should fix responsibility for loss and destruction that should have been avoided, and it can and should require that those whose rights are appropriated for the benefit of others receive appropriate compensation.*

NOTES

1. The Recurring Proposal for an Independent Trust Counsel: In 1973, President Nixon recommended that Congress establish an Indian Trust Coun-

---

these cases and that in any event this litigation is governed by different rules than those that apply in private representative litigation. *Logan* did not involve a fiduciary relationship, and like *Mullane*, was a suit where the complaining party would be left without recourse. In these cases, the Tribe, through the Government as their representative, was given adequate notice and a full and fair opportunity to be heard. If in carrying out their role as representative, the Government violated its obligations to the Tribe, then the Tribe's remedy is against the Government, not against third parties. As we have noted earlier, the Tribe has already taken advantage of that remedy.

*[O]ne of the purposes for establishment of the Pyramid Lake Reservation was "to provide the Indians with access to Pyramid Lake ... in order that they might obtain their sustenance, at least in part, from these historic fisheries." As a consequence, the Tribe retains a *Winters* right, at least in theory, to water to maintain the fishery, a right which today's ruling does not question. To some extent it may be possible to satisfy the Tribe's claims consistent with the *Orr Ditch* decree — for instance, through judicious management of the Derby Dam and Lahontan Reservoir, improvement of the quality of the Newlands Project irrigation works, application of heretofore unappropriated floodwaters, or invocation of the decree's provisions for restricting diversions in excess of those allowed by the decree.

sel Authority independent of both the Department of the Interior and the Department of Justice. The trust counsel would have had the authority to bring suit against federal agencies as well as states and private parties in the name of the United States as trustee. In explaining the rationale for creating an independent counsel, the President stated:

> The United States Government acts as a legal trustee for the land and water rights of American Indians. These rights are often of critical economic importance to the Indian people; frequently they are also the subject of extensive legal dispute. In many of these legal confrontations, the Federal government is faced with an inherent conflict of interest. The Secretary of the Interior and the Attorney General must at the same time advance *both* the *national* interest in the use of land and water rights *and* the *private* interests of Indians in land which the government holds as trustee.
>
> Every trustee has a legal obligation to advance the interests of the beneficiaries of the trust without reservation and with the highest degree of diligence and skill. Under present conditions, it is often difficult for the Department of the Interior and the Department of Justice to fulfill this obligation. No self-respecting law firm would ever allow itself to represent two opposing clients in one dispute; yet the Federal government has frequently found itself in precisely that position. There is considerable evidence that the Indians are the losers when such situations arise. More than that, the credibility of the Federal government is damaged whenever it appears that such a conflict of interest exists.

Message from the President of the United States Transmitting Recommendations for Indian Policy, H.R. Doc. 363, 91st Cong., 2d Sess. (1970). Although President Nixon's suggestion was well-received in Indian country, it was never implemented.

In 1990, a bill was introduced in the Senate to create a Trust Counsel for Indian Assets in the Department of the Interior. S. 2451, 101st Cong., 2d Sess. The trust counsel would be charged with creating standards to guide federal agencies in trust questions and providing an independent administrative review of all federal agency actions that affect Indian trust assets. Although the trust counsel would not be empowered to bring suit in the name of the United States, the trust counsel would have the power to investigate complaints that any agency of the United States "has violated, or plans to conduct an activity which would violate" the government's obligation to protect trust assets. Upon a determination that an actual or potential violation existed, the bill requires the trust counsel to submit a report both to the head of the agency involved and to Congress. If the trust counsel were to submit such a report and the agency head or Congress were to ignore it, would such a report be sufficient to establish that a breach of trust had occurred in subsequent litigation between the tribe and government? On the other hand, does the bill's failure to give the trust counsel authority to bring suit undercut the effectiveness of the counsel?

2. Concern for Potential Conflicts in Refusing to Order the Government to Represent Tribes: Breach of trust cases involving alleged mismanagement of property have secured the strongest victories for Indian tribes. Cases not involving actual control over property but rather inaction by the government have presented greater problems, especially when competing policy interests existed within the federal government. For instance, since 1893, a federal statute has provided: "In all States and Territories where there are reservations or allotted Indians the [United States Attorney] shall represent them in all suits of law and in equity." 25 U.S.C. § 175. Despite the mandatory language of the statute as codified, courts reviewing the issue have relied on language of discretion in the session laws from which the codification was taken, Act of Mar. 3, 1893, ch. 209, Sec. 1, 27 Stat. 631, to hold Congress did not intend to create an enforceable obligation to represent tribes attempting to preserve property rights. In many of these cases the courts were influenced by the fact that ordering the United States to represent the tribe would place the government in a conflict of interest. *See, e.g., Black Spotted Horse v. Else*, 767 F.2d 516 (8th Cir. 1985) (no duty to represent federal prisoner in suit against prison); *Rincon Band of Mission Indians v. Escondido Mut. Water Co.*, 459 F.2d 1082, 1085 (9th Cir. 1972) (contrary decision would force the United States to take an opposite position than one taken in another pending case to which it was a party); *Siniscal v. United States*, 208 F.2d 406, 410 (9th Cir. 1953), *cert. denied*, 348 U.S. 818 (1954) (government would be on opposite sides of same case, creating a conflict of interest).

3. Enforcing the Trust After *Nevada*: Does *Nevada* overrule *Pyramid Lake sub silentio*? If not, does *Nevada* undercut the cases permitting application of fiduciary standards derived from the common law to the executive department? How does the Court reconcile the cases? Not surprisingly the metaphor used by the majority in *Nevada*, that the government may be required to "carry water on at least two shoulders" has been invoked by the lower courts. In *Navajo Tribe v. United States*, 9 Cl. Ct. 227 (1985), the tribe claimed mismanagement damages caused by the government's failure to collect rental payments on uranium mining leases and for failing to require filling of uranium mines to minimize damages to tribal members from exposure to the uranium tailings that are a byproduct of the mining process. Although these two claims were based on the government's failure to exercise care in managing resources being exploited by third parties, the tribe also argued the government had breached its duty of loyalty. The tribe claimed that the government engaged in self-dealing when it failed to charge an agency created as part of the Manhattan Project, a government project, for exploring Navajo land for uranium needed to develop the atomic bomb. The court dismissed the tailings claim as time-barred, but did hold the government accountable for failing to collect rents and royalties from third persons. In evaluating the self-dealing claim, however, the court relied on *Nevada*, quoting the above passage in denying recovery. No statutes or regulations spoke to the issue of permits or permission from landowners and, in fact, the government sought no permission. The court conceded that such an action by a private trustee would constitute self-dealing and thus be a breach of the duty of loyalty, but held that *Nevada* governed the outcome, because "[t]he defendant was presented with its fiduciary obligation to the Indians and its obligation to promote the interests of national defense." *Id.* at 252. Is this a correct reading of *Nevada*? Or was the court influenced by other factors? The exploration had caused no actual harm to the land, because there had been no drilling or other harmful activity. Furthermore once uranium was found the tribe benefited from the royalties.

4. Conflicts of Interest in Representing Indian Tribes After *Nevada*: Does *Nevada* stand for the proposition that there can be no breach of duty when the government represents both an Indian tribe and an agency like the Bureau of Reclamation? In *White Mountain Apache Tribe v. Hodel*, 784 F.2d 921 (9th Cir. 1986), the tribe sought a declaratory judgment that the United States was not able to represent both the tribe and the Bureau of Land Management adequately in a water right adjudication in state court. In denying the requested relief, the court relied on *Nevada* for the proposition that merely representing both clients did not per se create a conflict of interest justifying departure from settled principles of res judicata. On the other hand, if in a given case, a tribe has evidence of actual malfeasance on the government's part in its representation of a tribe, the tribe could press a claim for breach of trust. Thus, the court recommended the tribe intervene in the state court proceeding and appeal an adverse decision if caused by the government's misrepresentation.

A Tenth Circuit decision has given a similarly narrow reading to *Nevada*. In *Sanguine, Ltd. v. United States Dep't of Interior,* an oil company sued the United States, challenging a rule requiring renegotiation of oil and gas leases on Indian lands. Shortly after suit was filed, the United States and the plaintiff agreed the rule was void and the trial court issued a consent decree to that effect. Subsequently, the court permitted the tribe to intervene, because the government, by settling the case only 33 days after the suit was filed, violated its duty as trustee. 736 F.2d 1416 (10th Cir. 1984). In a later decision the court held that implicit in the decision to let the tribe intervene was the decision that the tribe could relitigate the issue settled in the consent decree. *Id.,* 798 F.2d 389 (10th Cir. 1986), *cert. denied,* 479 U.S. 1054 (1987). The court distinguished *Nevada* as a case in which the United States had adequately represented the tribe.

5. Water Law and Res Judicata: What bearing does the fact that *Nevada* is a water case have on the court's application of the values embedded in the principles of res judicata? Would the same factors be present in land cases? *See, e.g., Bear v. United States,* 810 F.2d 153 (8th Cir. 1987) (res judicata bars relitigating title to accreted land even though settlement between tribe and state in earlier condemnation proceeding was void because not approved by Secretary of Interior); *Mashpee Tribe v. Watt,* 707 F.2d 23, 24 (1st Cir. 1983) ("Indian land claims are not entitled to a special exemption from [res judicata] principles") (attempted relitigation of Nonintercourse Act claim). *See generally* Florio, *Water Rights: Enforcing the Federal-Indian Trust After Nevada v. United States,* 13 AM. INDIAN L. REV. 79 (1987). The policies underlying water and land resource claims are explored in greater depth in Chapters 5 and 6.

6. The Limits of the Trust Relationship: As the excerpted cases illustrate, the trust principle has an important role to play in protecting tribal land, natural resources, and assets. The existence of a claim for money damages can act as a powerful deterrent to mismanagement. In addition, tribes can invoke the jurisdiction of the federal courts to obtain injunctive and declaratory relief to prevent continued mismanagement and to impose strictures derived from the rigorous standards of private trust law. Private trust law standards may not be fully applicable in the *Nevada* situation, however, although private trust law may still apply in cases of actual self-dealing. *Cf. Navajo Tribe v. United States,* 364 F.2d 320 (Ct. Cl. 1966).

Like any legal theory, the trust principle can only be extended so far, however. The extent to which the principle can be applied even to the executive branch without a clear statutory basis was discussed in the notes following *Mitchell II, supra.* In addition, trust principles may state only a moral obligation in the case of Congress. When the Menominee Tribe sued in the Court of Claims for breach of trust because of termination of their reservation, the Court held that sovereign immunity barred the claim, because it was not based on the Constitution or on a breach of a statute. *Menominee Tribe v. United States,* 607 F.2d 1335 (Ct. Cl. 1979), *cert. denied,* 445 U.S. 950 (1980). If a claim for damages existed, how could a court assess damages? In *Fort Sill Apache Tribe v. United States,* 477 F.2d 1360, 1366 (Ct. Cl. 1973), the Court of Claims held that the government was not accountable in damages for wrongfully imprisoning the entire Chiracahua Apache Tribe for 27 years. Absent specific language in a statute, the court stated, the trust relationship could not be extended to "intangible factors of tribal well-being, cultural advancement, and maintenance of tribal form and structure." For a critical comment on the *Fort Sill Apache* decision, see Note, 20 WAYNE L. REV. 1097 (1974).

Fort Sill Apache was based on the Fair and Honorable Dealings Clause of the Indian Claims Commission, popularly referred to as "clause 5." Indian Claims Commission Act, 60 Stat. 1049, 1050, § (2)(5). Despite the broad language used in that clause ("claims based upon fair and honorable dealings that are not recognized by any existing rule of law or equity") and some legislative history indicating congressional intent to permit Indian tribes to bring every sort of past grievance to the Commission, even those raising more moral than legal issues, the Commission interpreted the clause rather narrowly as requiring a breach of an affirmative duty to act created by statute, treaty, or other agreement. In *Gila River Pima-Maricopa Indian Community v. United States,* 427 F.2d 1194, (Ct. Cl.), *cert. denied,* 400 U.S. 819 (1970), the tribe sought damages for failure to provide education or medical services for the tribe, alleging that the duty to provide for the tribe arose when the government "undertook to, and did, subjugate the petitioner under wardship to a stagnation of self-expression ... [and] bridled petitioner into cultural impotency." *Id.* at 1195 (quoting petitioner's brief). The court denied the relief because of the absence of any specific duty to act.

The Indian Claims Commission, discussed in further detail in Chapter 5, section B4, *infra,* has been criticized for taking a narrow view of its jurisdictional mandate. According to Nancy Lurie, narrow constructions like that in *Fort Sill*

> put a very fine point on the language of the act and moved the preparation of cases in the direction of simple, quantifiable issues .... The Fort Sill case not only eliminated the need for the commission to wrestle with compensating for cruel and unusual punishment and other intangibles implied in the exceedingly broad grounds for suit in the act, but also eliminated grievances with which many tribes were directly familiar, knowing exactly how they had been cheated, and for which they sought justice.

Lurie, *Epilogue,* in IRREDEEMABLE AMERICA: THE INDIAN'S ESTATE AND LAND CLAIMS 363, 372 (I. Sutton ed. 1985).*

Would the same arguments necessarily control if a tribe sought declaratory or injunctive relief to prevent Congress from proceeding with a termination or other action destructive of a tribe's cultural or political identity? A recent comment argues that the best and most moral use of the trust relationship doctrine would be to protect tribes' right "to enough political autonomy to enable them to chart their own economic, social, and cultural development." Note, *Rethinking the Trust Doctrine in Federal Indian Law,* 98 HARV. L. REV. 422, 436 (1984).

LIMITING ADMINISTRATIVE POWER: A BROADER PERSPECTIVE

As you have seen, the Constitution, statutory interpretation, and the trust relationship can all be used to limit the vast power the BIA exercises over Indian affairs. In addition, courts have employed other devices to limit the intrusion of the BIA into tribal affairs. As discussed above, the Secretary has the power to approve many tribes' ordinances. If the Secretary's approval constituted federal action, the underlying transaction would be subjected to constitutional and statutory provisions requiring governmental action as a prerequisite.

For example, in *Davis v. Morton*, 469 F.2d 593 (10th Cir. 1972), set forth and discussed in Chapter 7, section C1a, the Tenth Circuit held that the secretarial approval of and involvement in the leasing of Indian land constituted "major Federal actions" within the meaning of § 102(2) of the National Environmental Protection Act, 42 U.S.C. § 4332(2), thereby requiring the preparation of an environmental impact study prior to the approval of the lease by the Bureau of Indian Affairs. In response to the argument that the Secretary was merely approving a lease negotiated by the tribe on land held in trust for the Indians, the court said:

> The fact that Indian lands are held in trust does not take it out of NEPA's jurisdiction .... All public lands of the United States are held by it in trust for the people of the United States .... To accept appellees' contention would preclude all federal lands from NEPA jurisdiction, something clearly not intended by Congress in passing the Act.

The District of Columbia Circuit did not read as much into the approval power in a case raising a constitutional question. In *Oliver v. Udall*, 306 F.2d 819 (D.C. Cir. 1962), *cert. denied*, 372 U.S. 908 (1963), individual tribal members challenged, on first amendment religious freedom grounds, a tribal code ban on peyote that had been adopted by the Navajo Council and approved by the Secretary of the Interior. The Court of Appeals for the District of Columbia Circuit declined the invitation to treat this secretarial approval as governmental action, however. Rather, the court viewed the Secretary's action as one of confirmation only, because he had approved only what the Tribal Council was already entitled to do. Characterizing the approval as abstinence from the assertion of positive power by the federal government, the court thus interpreted the power as merely a pro forma exercise of federal authority not subject to judicial review on constitutional grounds. Such cases may indicate a judicial willingness to limit the Secretary's power to approve tribal ordinances to determining whether the proposed tribal actions are within the tribe's jurisdiction. Chapter 3 contains a more comprehensive discussion of the Secretary's power to approve tribal ordinances and constitutions.

In addition, tribes often invoke the Administrative Procedure Act (APA), 5 U.S.C. §§ 701-706, to invalidate agency action harming Indian property or tribal self-government. *See, e.g., Navajo Tribe v. United States Dep't of Interior,* 667 F. Supp. 747 (D.N.M. 1987) (failure to follow department's own procedures violated APA); *Joint Tribal Council of Passamaquoddy Tribe v. Morton,* 388 F. Supp. 649 (D. Me.), *aff'd,* 528 F.2d 370 (1st Cir. 1975) (the federal government's refusal to initiate litigation on behalf of a tribe is reviewable under the Administrative Procedure Act where the refusal was predicated upon an error of law).

More frequently, courts will protect tribal property and self-government by employing a mixture of the above devices. Such an analysis usually begins by interpreting the applicable statutes cited as a basis for administrative power by applying canons of liberal construction. Next, in determining whether the Secretary's action was reasonable or "arbitrary and capricious," the standard of review employed under the Administrative Procedure Act, the reviewing court often stresses the importance of the Interior Department's guardianship role. Such an analysis can be a powerful tool to protect Indian interests, although it may deviate from strict principles of administrative law. A classic example is *Morton v. Ruiz,* 415 U.S. 199 (1974), in which the Supreme Court invoked the requirements of the Administrative Procedure Act to hold that a regulation limiting availability for the general assistance program to Indians living on a reservation was invalid because it had not been published in the Federal Register or in the Code of Federal Regulations. Although the decision sparked a harsh comment from the leading expert on administrative law, see Davis, *Administrative Law Surprises in the Ruiz Case,* 75 Colum. L. Rev. 823 (1975), the requirement that regulations affecting Indian peoples must be published has become part of the administrative law of Indian law. Similarly, in *Tooahnippah v. Hickel,* 397 U.S. 598 (1970), the Supreme Court held that the decision of the Regional Solicitor, acting for the Secretary of the Interior, in disapproving an Indian decedent's will was subject to judicial review under the Administrative Procedure Act. Furthermore, the Court held that in exercising the secretarial power to grant or withhold approval of an Indian's will under 25 U.S.C. § 373, the Secretary had no power to deny approval to a will that reflected a rational testamentary scheme based on an administrative concept of equity. Last, note that in *Pyramid Lake Paiute Tribe v. Morton,* 354 F. Supp. 252 (D.D.C. 1972), *supra,* the Court's conclusion that the Secretary of the Interior could not allocate water between competing agencies by means of a "judgment call" led to the conclusion that the allocation of water was arbitrary and capricious and thus violated the APA.

D. THE EXERCISE OF FEDERAL AUTHORITY: CRIMINAL JURISDICTION

Areas where the exercise of federal authority has been pervasive, such as criminal jurisdiction, illustrate how federal Indian policy has changed over time. One of the earliest and most far-reaching federal regulatory intrusions into Indian country has been in the area of federal criminal jurisdiction. In this section, we consider the extent to which the statutory and case law in this area executes the underlying purposes of federal Indian law. Does the exercise of federal authority further the federal government's trust obligations to the Indians? Is the exercise of federal power justified in terms of the reasons for the special legal protection of the Indians? To what extent is federal Indian policy in these areas consistent with the terms and spirit of the ILO Convention on Indigenous and Tribal Peoples discussed in Chapter 1, section D?

NOTES

1. **Tribal Self-Government and Criminal Jurisdiction:** As evidenced in *Ex parte Crow Dog,* 109 U.S. 556 (1883), discussed in Chapter 1, section A2, there was a long-standing federal policy of permitting tribal self-government and punishment of intratribal offenses. This policy was expressly guaranteed in a number of treaties with the Indian tribes. *See, e.g.,* Treaty with the Cherokees, July 19, 1866, art. XIII, 14 Stat. 803 ("the judicial tribunals of the [Cherokee] nation shall be allowed to retain exclusive jurisdiction in all civil and criminal cases arising within their country in which members of the nation, by nativity or adoption, shall be the only parties, or where the cause of action shall arise in the

Cherokee nation"). Indeed, the Creek and Seminole tribes were so concerned about jurisdictional matters that they secured a guarantee assuring that their lands would never become part of or subject to the jurisdiction of any state or federal territory. Treaty with the Creeks and Seminoles, Aug. 7, 1856, art. IV, 11 Stat. 700. *See also* Treaty with the Pottawatomies, Feb. 27, 1867, art. III, 15 Stat. 532. *See generally* Clinton, *Development of Criminal Jurisdiction over Indian Lands: The Historical Perspective*, 17 ARIZ. L. REV. 951, 956-57 (1975); Indian Civil Rights Task Force, Development of Tripartite Jurisdiction in Indian Country, 22 KAN. L. REV. 351, 353-66 (1974). The *Crow Dog* decision provoked the first major congressional deviation from the longstanding federal policy of furthering tribal sovereignty. In 1885, in direct response to *Crow Dog*, Congress enacted the Federal Major Crimes Act. *See* Clinton, *supra*, at 462-64. This Act, the constitutionality of which was upheld in *United States v. Kagama, supra* section A2, extended federal criminal jurisdiction for the first time to cover seven enumerated crimes committed by Indians in Indian country against the person or property of "another Indian or other person." In reviewing the materials that follow consider the extent to which this federal incursion on tribal self-government has expanded.

2. **Preemption of Tribal Authority by Federal Jurisdiction:** As the opinion in the *Crow Dog* case hints, the murder involved was the result of a blood feud, a traditional mechanism of social control among some Indian tribes prior to European contact and well into the nineteenth century. *E.g.*, J. REID, A LAW OF BLOOD 73-92 (1970). To what extent did the adoption of the Federal Major Crimes Act preempt tribal power over the crimes enumerated in the Act? Was the Act preemptive irrespective of whether the tribe exercised social control through traditional communal norms, such as the blood feud, or, rather, had adopted Anglo-American forms of law and court structure? The legislative history of the Act suggests that it was not intended to be preemptive of tribal authority. While there are critical remarks about the tribal custom of the blood feud in the legislative debates and a statement by the sponsor of the Act that "the law of the tribe, … is just no law at all," 16 CONG. REC. 934 (1885), the Act should be read in light of the fact that Congress had rejected a similar bill in 1874 because it conflicted with the exercise of tribal jurisdiction:

> The Indians, while their tribal relations subsist, generally maintain law, customs, and usages of their own for the punishment of offenses. They have no knowledge of the laws of the United States, and the attempt to enforce their own ordinances might bring them in direct conflict with existing statutes and subject them to prosecution for their violations.

S. REP. No. 367, 43d Cong., 1st Sess. (1874), quoted in F. COHEN, HANDBOOK OF FEDERAL INDIAN LAW 147 n.222 (1942). The original bill proposed in 1885 had provided that Indians committing any of the enumerated offenses "shall be tried therefor in the same courts and in the same manner *and not otherwise*" (emphasis added). The bill was amended to strike the italicized phrase, the sponsor of the amendment explaining:

> The effect of this modification will be to give the courts of the United States concurrent jurisdiction with the Indian courts in the Indian country. But if these words be not struck out, all jurisdiction of these offenses will be taken from the existing tribunals of the Indian country. I think it sufficient that the courts of the United States should have concurrent jurisdiction in these cases.

16 CONG. REC. 934 (1885).

Despite this legislative history, the lower federal courts quickly read the adoption of the Federal Major Crimes Act as preempting tribal authority. *United States v. Whaley*, 37 F. 145 (C.C.S.D. Cal. 1888); *cf. United States v. Cardish*, 145 F. 242, 246 (E.D. Wis. 1906). In *Whaley* the court found four tribal Indians guilty of the manslaughter of an Indian medicine man, suspected of poisoning twenty of his Indian patients, despite the fact that the four were merely carrying out a directive of the tribal council to kill the medicine man for his mistreatment of tribal members. The court did find, however:

> While the offense committed by the defendants would, if committed by a white man, have of course been murder, it may be, in view of the Indian nature, their customs, superstition, and ignorance, that in the circumstances attending the killing of the doctor there was wanting the malice that is essential to constitute the crime of murder. It was that view that prompted the district attorney to say that he could not contend for a verdict of guilty of murder, and to consent to the withdrawal of the plea of not guilty, and to the entry of a plea of guilty of manslaughter. And since justice should be tempered with mercy, perhaps the court may be justified, in imposing sentence, in being moved by the same considerations, and in inflicting a punishment which, under ordinary circumstances, would be considered far too light for so atrocious a crime.

37 F. at 146. Was *Whaley* correctly decided? Would it have been decided differently had the tribal death sentence originated from an Anglo-American type tribal court employing a written criminal code rather than from a traditional tribal council employing known and accepted, but unwritten, community norms? In *Talton v. Mayes*, 163 U.S. 376 (1896), the Supreme Court sustained the murder conviction of an Indian imposed by the courts of the Cherokee Nation, which, as a result of a long evolution, were patterned after Anglo-American models and employed a written criminal code. *See generally* R. STRICKLAND, FIRE AND SPIRITS (1975). While the opinion in *Talton* never cites the Federal Major Crimes Act and there is some question whether the Act applied in the Indian Territory where the Cherokee courts were located, the decision in that case may indicate the concurrent jurisdiction of tribal courts over Major Crimes Act offenses, at least where tribal institutions are structured along Anglo-American, rather than traditional Indian, models.

Since *Whaley*, federal courts have sometimes suggested in dicta that the Federal Major Crimes Act preempts tribal court jurisdiction over serious crimes committed by tribal members. *E.g., Sam v. United States*, 385 F.2d 213 (10th Cir. 1967); *Glover v. United States*, 219 F. Supp. 19 (D. Mont. 1963); *Iron Crow v. Ogallala Sioux Tribe*, 129 F. Supp. 15, 18 (D.S.D. 1955), *aff'd*, 231 F.2d 89 (8th Cir. 1956). In *Oliphant v. Suquamish Indian Tribe*, 435 U.S. 191, 203 n.14 (1978), Mr. Justice Rehnquist commented:

> The Major Crimes Act provides that Indians committing any of the enumerated offenses "shall be subject to the same laws and penalties as all other persons committing any of the above offenses, *within the exclusive jurisdiction of the United States*." (Emphasis added.) While the question has never been directly addressed by this Court, Courts of Appeals have read this language to exclude tribal jurisdiction over the Indian offender. *See, e.g., Sam v. United States*, 385 F.2d 213, 214 (CA10 1967); *Felicia v. United States*, 495 F.2d 353, 354 (CA8 1974). We have no reason to decide today whether jurisdiction under the Major Crimes Act is exclusive....
> ... The issue of exclusive jurisdiction over major crimes was mooted for all practical purposes by the passage of the Indian Civil Rights Act of 1968 which limits the punishment that can be imposed by Indian tribal courts to a term of 6 months or a fine of $500.

In 1986, Congress amended 25 U.S.C. § 1302(7) to permit tribal courts to impose sentences of up to one year and fines up to $5000. This increase in the permissible penalties may encourage tribes to take concurrent jurisdiction over more Major Crime Act offenses. For example, many tribes regularly prosecuted theft even though larceny was a Major Crimes Act offense until 1984 when Congress substituted felony theft for larceny in the Major Crimes Act. Tribal prosecution of Federal Major Crimes Act offenses sometimes has been sparked by the fact that federal prosecutors routinely decline to prosecute such offenses, especially the less serious offenses listed in the Act. Was the adoption of the Federal Major Crimes Act in the late nineteenth century intended to undermine tribal self-government or to supplement and complement tribal sovereignty? As particular tribal courts modernize along Anglo-American legal patterns, should the Federal Major Crimes Act remain in force?

CLINTON, CRIMINAL JURISDICTION OVER INDIAN LANDS: A JOURNEY THROUGH A JURISDICTIONAL MAZE, 18 Arizona Law Review 503, 520-52 (1976)*

D. The Jurisdictional Statutes

Federal criminal jurisdiction over Indian lands is governed by three types of statutes. First, statutes creating federal crimes applicable to the nation as a whole are also applicable to Indian lands. Second, statutes which proscribe specified conduct occurring on Indian lands create a federal crime with one of the material elements being the occurrence of the crime in Indian country. The third type of criminal statute affecting Indian lands specifically purports to structure the jurisdictional patterns for prosecution of certain crimes occurring thereon. The most pervasive and important of these statutes are, of course, sections 1152, 1153, and 3242 of title 18. However, other federal statutes, codified and uncodified, are also important in shaping the jurisdictional patterns. Sections 1152, 1153, and 3242 are the statutes of general applicability which structure the federal jurisdiction over most Indian reservations. This section will consequently deal primarily with these provisions.

1. Section 1152: The Interracial Crime Provision

Section 1152 is the successor of the first general federal jurisdictional statutes enacted for Indian lands. These early statutes were enacted as jurisdictional implementations of treaties which prescribed limited federal control over the lands reserved for the Indians. The Indian tribes, in negotiating treaties with the federal government, generally reserved tribal sovereignty and jurisdiction over intratribal matters. This pattern of Indian internal self-government was respected in all of the federal jurisdictional statutes until 1885. Section 1152 reflects the limited goals of the early jurisdictional statutes, stating:

> Except as otherwise expressly provided by law, the general laws of the United States as to the punishment of offenses committed in any place within the sole and exclusive jurisdiction of the United States, except the District of Columbia, shall extend to the Indian country.
> This section shall not extend to offenses committed by one Indian against the person or property of another Indian, nor to any Indian committing any offense in the Indian

---

*Copyright 1977 by the Arizona Board of Regents. Reprinted by permission.

country who has been punished by the local law of the tribe, or to any case where, by treaty stipulations, the exclusive jurisdiction over such offenses is or may be secured to the Indian tribes respectively.

The actual statutory crimes covered by section 1152 are relatively easy to describe. The first paragraph extends to Indian country the body of criminal law applied "within the sole and exclusive jurisdiction of the United States, except the District of Columbia"; that is, the body of federally defined crimes which Congress has established for other federal enclaves, such as national parks and military installations, as well as for admiralty and maritime law. Insofar as these crimes are promulgated, and their punishment prescribed by federal statute, the coverage of section 1152 is ascertainable from the United States Code.

Although the first paragraph of section 1152 appears to broadly grant complete and exclusive federal jurisdiction over Indian country,[94] the coverage of section 1152 is far more limited than the language suggests. Indeed, the major complications in ascertaining the jurisdiction conferred by section 1152 emerge from the numerous situations excepted from coverage. The second paragraph of the section contains a number of important exceptions. First, section 1152 exempts "offenses committed by one Indian against the person or property of another Indian." Intra-Indian crimes are not covered by section 1152, in furtherance of the treaty policy affording the Indian nations a measure of tribal self-government. This policy was undermined substantially in 1885, however, with the enactment of the Federal Major Crimes Act.

Second, excluded from the federal jurisdiction of section 1152 are crimes committed on Indian lands between non-Indians. This exception is not based on any language contained in section 1152 but rather is a judicially created exception. Its roots are found in a trilogy of Supreme Court decisions spanning 65 years: *United States v. McBratney*,[97] *Draper v. United States*,[98] and *New York ex rel. Ray v. Martin*.[99] In each case, the Supreme Court found that proper jurisdiction for a crime committed on Indian lands between non-Indians was in the state courts rather than the federal forum which the language of section 1152 seemingly provided. The Court paid scant attention to the language of section 1152, relying instead on the inherent jurisdiction exercised by the states over Indian lands within their borders as a consequence of their

---

[94] The language used in section 1152 suggests that federal jurisdiction is exclusive, and consequently the state courts have no jurisdiction over described crimes. A few older cases, particularly in the state courts, have construed the "sole and exclusive jurisdiction" phrase in the first paragraph of section 1152 to define the limitations on federal jurisdiction rather than an exclusion of state courts from hearing these matters.... The prevailing rule today is that the federal jurisdiction conferred by sections 1152 and 1153 is exclusive; where one of these sections applies, the state has no jurisdiction.

[97] 104 U.S. 621 (1881). McBratney was convicted of murder after trial in the federal court for the district of Colorado. The crime occurred within the Ute Reservation, which lies wholly within the boundaries of the State of Colorado. Both McBratney and the victim were white. McBratney successfully moved to overturn the judgment for want of jurisdiction....

[98] 164 U.S. 240 (1896). Draper was convicted of murder in federal court, the crime alleged to have been committed on the Crow Indian Reservation, within the boundaries of Montana. Both Draper and the deceased were Negroes. Addressing the issue of jurisdiction, the Court reaffirmed *McBratney* ....

[99] 326 U.S. 496 (1946). In *Martin*, the Supreme Court upheld the state court conviction of a non-Indian for murder of a non-Indian within the confines of the Allegany Reservation. *Id.* at 498-99.

admission to the Union without an express disclaimer of jurisdiction. Although the logic of this argument would apply equally well to interracial or even intra-Indian crimes committed on Indian lands, the Supreme Court has applied the *McBratney* analysis only to crimes committed on Indian lands between non-Indians. Indeed, dicta in later cases suggests that the rationale in *McBratney* and *Draper* has little to do with state sovereignty. Rather, the cases suggest that the non-ward status of the accused and the victim divests the federal government of any interest in prosecution despite the occurrence of the crime in Indian country.[102] Accordingly, *McBratney* and its progeny are expressly limited in application to crimes between non-Indians on Indian lands. While the analysis of the *McBratney* trilogy is certainly open to question, it appears to be too well entrenched to be overruled. The *McBratney* principle thus creates a judicial exception to section 1152 for crimes on Indian lands involving both a non-Indian accused and victim.

The combined impact of the *McBratney* trilogy and the express intra-Indian crime exclusion indicates that section 1152 jurisdiction is limited to interracial crimes, crimes in which an Indian is involved either as the defendant or the accused. One problem not confronted in the cases is how section 1152 is to be construed with reference to a crime involving multiple defendants or multiple victims.

[Another problem posed by section 1152 is] the so-called victimless crime. Since the jurisdiction granted by section 1152 has been construed to turn on the racial characterization of the accused and victim, victimless crimes do not fit neatly into the jurisdictional pattern established therein. Few cases have expressly discussed the victimless crime problem under section 1152. The only United States Supreme Court decisions on point appear to be *In re Mayfield* and *United States v. Quiver*. In *Mayfield* the Court held there was no federal

---

[102]United States v. Ramsey, 271 U.S. 467, 469 (1926); Donnelly v. United States, 228 U.S. 243, 271-72 (1913). In *Ramsey*, two white men were charged with murdering a fullblood Osage Indian upon a reservation. Discussing the issue of federal court jurisdiction, the Court stated:

> The authority of the United States under § 2145 to punish crimes occurring within the State of Oklahoma, not committed by or against Indians, was ended by the grant of statehood. [citing *McBratney* and *Draper*] But authority in respect of crimes committed by or against Indians continued after the admission of the state as it was before ... in virtue of the long-settled rule that such Indians are wards of the nation in respect of whom there is devolved upon the Federal Government "the duty of protection, and with it the power." ... The guardianship of the United States over the Osage Indians has not been abandoned; they are still the wards of the nation ... and it rests with Congress alone to determine when that relationship shall cease.

271 U.S. at 469.

In *Donnelly*, the defendant, a white man, was charged for a crime committed within the Hoopa Valley Reservation. Utilizing the logic of *McBratney*, he argued that when California was admitted to the Union, it received authority to punish crimes committed within its borders, even on land set aside for Indian reservations. Rejecting this argument, the Court stated:

> Upon full consideration we are satisfied that offenses committed by or against Indians are not within the principle of the *McBratney* and *Draper* Cases. This was in effect held, as to crimes committed *by* the Indians, in the *Kagama* Case, ... where the constitutionality of the second branch of § 9 of the act of March 3, 1885, ... was sustained upon the ground that the Indian tribes are the wards of the nation. This same reason applies — perhaps *a fortiori* — with respect to crimes committed by white men against the persons or property of the Indian tribes while occupying reservations set apart for the very purpose of segregating them from the whites and others not of Indian blood.

Id. at 271-72 (citations omitted).

criminal jurisdiction under the predecessor of section 1152 for the crime of adultery when committed by an Indian. Although Mayfield, a Cherokee, committed the adulterous act with a white woman, the Court nevertheless held that the jurisdiction for the crime was exclusively tribal, as a result of treaty and statutory provisions reserving exclusive jurisdiction in the Cherokee Nation for crimes in which members of that tribe were the only parties. Thus, the Court seemingly held that where an Indian was prosecuted for a consensual crime like adultery, the crime could not be considered interracial in character, even when the consenting party was a non-Indian. In *Quiver*, the Court reaffirmed the principle of *Mayfield* in a case involving adultery between two Indians. If the *Mayfield-Quiver* approach to victimless and consensual crime is applied consistently, it suggests that section 1152 has no application to such crimes. *Mayfield* and *Quiver* treat the accused as the sole party to a consensual or victimless crime. Since section 1152 only confers jurisdiction over bilateral interracial crimes, it has no application to consensual crimes under a *Mayfield-Quiver* analysis. If the crime is committed by an Indian, the jurisdiction is federal if the crime is enumerated within the grant of jurisdiction provided in section 1153, or exclusively tribal if not set forth therein. On the other hand, if the accused is a non-Indian, consistent application of *Mayfield* and *Quiver* would suggest that the jurisdiction would be exclusively vested in the state courts under the *McBratney* trilogy.

Of course, extending the concept of a consensual crime too far under this analysis could do serious harm to the protective function that federal jurisdiction is designed to play under the Indian trusteeship theory. For example, a white accused of the statutory rape of a 14-year-old Indian girl should be tried in federal court even if the accused can demonstrate that the girl "consented." The statute defining statutory rape is obviously designed to protect young children and deems them incapable of consent. Furthermore, the federal jurisdiction over the crime in question is designed to protect Indians. In essence, the policies underlying federal jurisdiction suggest that the jurisdiction over this hypothetical case should be federal despite the allegation of the victim's consent. Accordingly, the consensual or victimless crime exception to section 1152 jurisdiction must be applied carefully to assure that the exception does not run afoul of the very policies which resulted in the grant of federal jurisdiction in section 1152.

The final exception to the federal jurisdiction conferred in section 1152 is the last clause of the statute, exempting from federal jurisdiction "any case where, by treaty stipulations, the exclusive jurisdiction over such offenses is or may be secured to the Indian tribes respectively."[126] Since section 1152 jurisdiction covers interracial crimes, the "treaty" exception applies only to tribal jurisdiction conferred by treaty over interracial crimes.[127] Furthermore, since no treaty has

---

[126] This exception was designed as a savings clause to preserve contrary treaty arrangements from statutory abrogation. It dates back to 1817 when the first predecessor of section 1152 was enacted. Act of Mar. 3, 1817, ch. XCII, § 2, 3 Stat. 383.

[127] The section 1152 treaty exception does not preserve treaty provisions which provided for jurisdictional structures inconsistent with the federal jurisdiction conferred by the Federal Major Crimes Act. *See* 18 U.S.C.A. § 1153 (Supp. Pamphlet 1976). Thus, section 1153 supercedes any contrary prior treaty provision such as that found in the Treaty with the Cherokees, July 19, 1866, art. 13, 14 Stat. 799. *See generally* United States v. Consolidated Wounded Knee Cases, 389 F.

specified tribal jurisdiction for crimes committed by Indians against whites, the sole application of this treaty-savings clause is to jurisdictional structures conferring tribal jurisdiction over non-Indians who commit crimes on Indian land. Only nine treaties of this type, affecting 17 tribes, and covering non-Indian settlers on Indian land, were signed, all before the turn of the 19th century.[128] Although the leading commentator on Indian law, without reference to these specific treaties, concluded that none of the treaties which arguably fall within the treaty clause exception remain operative,[129] the clauses described above were clearly abrogated by later treaties for only 8 of the 17 affected tribes. Treaties with six of the other tribes contain ambiguous provisions which can be read as abrogating either the tribal jurisdiction over non-Indians previously granted, or the prior treaty itself. For the remaining three tribes, no subsequent treaty can be found abrogating the jurisdiction previously granted to them to try whites who "settle" upon lands owned by the tribe. [F]or most tribes that clause will have little operative relevance, since the treaties after 1800 generally failed to mention tribal court jurisdiction over non-Indians in any fashion.

2. The Assimilative Crimes Act and Indian Land

While it is historically questionable that Congress ever intended to incorporate and apply state law to Indian lands through the Assimilative Crimes Act,[134] it is now well settled that this Act applies to Indian country. In *Williams v. United States*,[135] the Supreme Court assumed that the Assimilative Crimes Act applied to Indian lands, as a result of the incorporation of federal enclave law for Indian country through the predecessor of section 1152. *Williams* indicates, however, that adoption of state law takes place only where no federally defined crime covering the Act exists. Thus, the state definition of a crime cannot be substituted under the Act in place of an applicable federal definition of the crime. Ascertaining the extent to which the Assimilative Crimes Act applies is complex because of the limited fashion in which it is incorporated for Indian lands. In order to understand the application of the Act to Indian lands, both

---

Supp. 235, 243 (D. Neb. 1975); Wilkinson & Volkman, *Judicial Review of Indian Treaty Abrogation: "As Long as Water Flows, or Grass Grows Upon the Earth" — How Long a Time Is That?*, 63 CALIF. L. REV. 601 (1975).

[128]These provisions typically read as follows:

If any citizen of the United States, or other person not being an Indian, shall attempt to settle on any of the lands allotted to the Wiandot and Delaware nations in this treaty, except on the lands reserved to the United States in the preceding article, such person shall forfeit the protection of the United States, and the Indians may punish him as they please.

[*E.g.*], Treaty with the Wyandots, Delawares, Chippawas, and Ottawas, Jan. 21, 1785, art. V, 7 Stat. 16 ....

[129]F. COHEN, *supra* note 23, at 365. *See also* Criminal Jurisdiction of Indian Tribes over Non-Indians, 77 I.D. 113, 115 (1970).

[134]

Whoever within or upon any of the places now existing or hereafter reserved or acquired as provided in section 7 of this title, is guilty of any act or omission which, although not made punishable by any enactment of Congress, would be punishable if committed or omitted within the jurisdiction of the State, Territory, Possession, or District in which such place is situated, by the laws thereof in force at the time of such act or omission, shall be guilty of a like offense and subject to a like punishment....

[135]327 U.S. 711 (1946).

the types of crimes incorporated under it and the limited situations in which it will be applied on Indian lands will be examined.

The Assimilative Crimes Act basically incorporates lesser state crimes into the federal criminal code and applies those state crimes to federal enclaves, including Indian lands, located within the states. The Act fills gaps in the coverage of the federal criminal code. The lesser state crimes adopted under it have been held to cover minor misdemeanors, including traffic offenses and game law violations. The Act thus adopts the state definition of lesser crimes for prosecutions in the federal courts arising out of certain criminal events on Indian lands. As a corollary, the states are granted certain criminal legislative powers over Indian reservations located within their boundaries which they would otherwise not have. The incorporation of state law under the Act is dynamic and ongoing; the Act incorporates any state law "in force at the time of such act or omission" which is not defined by federal statute.

Of greater complexity than ascertaining the crimes incorporated under the Assimilative Crimes Act is the problem of determining the situations in which it is applicable to Indian lands. The Act is applicable to Indian lands because it is incorporated into section 1152 as part of "the general laws of the United States as to the punishment of offenses committed in any place within the sole and exclusive jurisdiction of the United States." In short, Assimilative Crimes Act jurisdiction on Indian lands is a type of double derivative jurisdiction. State law is incorporated into the federal code under it for special maritime and territorial areas and the law applicable to the special maritime and territorial areas is incorporated into and applied to Indian lands under section 1152. The direct application of the Act to Indian country is limited to those situations covered by section 1152. Thus, it will not apply to a crime between non-Indians committed on Indian land, or to intra-Indian crimes. Therefore, the Act is only applicable to Indian lands for an interracial crime.[148]

A further problem is posed by victimless or consensual crimes, many of which will be lesser crimes defined by state rather than federal law. Consistent application of the *Mayfield-Quiver* doctrine requires that consensual or victimless crimes not be incorporated under the derivative jurisdiction of the Assimilative Crimes Act and section 1152. However, in *United States v. Sosseur*,[150] the Seventh Circuit upheld the application of a Wisconsin anti-gambling statute to an Indian who operated slot machines in Indian country under tribal license.[151]

---

[148] One further problem with ascertaining the extent of the Assimilative Crimes Act jurisdiction is posed by the question of whether the Act can ever be applied to an Indian defendant even for an interracial crime. While this problem is more fully explored in the next section, see text & notes 158-69 *infra*, it should be noted here that several good legal arguments support the view that federal prosecution of Indians must occur exclusively under 18 U.S.C.A. § 1153 (Supp. Pamphlet 1976), into which the Assimilative Crimes Act is not incorporated. Cf. Henry v. United States, 432 F.2d 114 (9th Cir. 1970), *modified,* 434 F.2d 1283 (9th Cir.), *cert. denied,* 400 U.S. 1011 (1971). While United States v. Butler, 541 F.2d 730 (8th Cir. 1976); United States v. Sosseur, 181 F.2d 873 (7th Cir. 1950); and United States v. Burland, 441 F.2d 1199 (9th Cir. 1971), clearly involve Federal Assimilative Crimes Act prosecutions of Indians, none of these address the fundamental questions posed by the overlap of the coverage of sections 1152 and 1153 which are vital to the resolution of the question whether the Act can be used to prosecute an Indian defendant for a crime occurring in Indian country.

[150] 181 F.2d 873 (7th Cir. 1950).

[151] *Id.* at 874-75. The court accepted the contention that jurisdiction existed under section 1152. It found that the crime was not literally "committed by one Indian against the person or property of

The implications of *Sosseur* are troubling. Victimless or consensual crime statutes enacted by the states generally involve legislation of morals in one sense or another. To allow the states, through the Act, to make moral judgments for the tribes, undermines the purpose for continuing reservation policy — permitting the Indian tribes to maintain their own separate, evolving, cultural traditions and government. The result in *Sosseur,* insofar as it applies to victimless or consensual crimes, is an aberration in terms of Indian policy.

3. *The Federal Major Crimes Act: Jurisdiction Over Indian Defendants*

The Federal Major Crimes Act was first enacted in 1885 to provide for federal jurisdiction over intra-Indian offenses. The Act represented the first significant intrusion into the federal policy theretofore followed of affording the Indian tribes virtually complete self-government and jurisdiction over internal matters. Section 1153 now states:

> [(a) Any Indian who commits against the person or property of another Indian or other person any of the following offenses, namely, murder, manslaughter, kidnapping, maiming, a felony under chapter 109A, incest, assault with intent to commit murder, assault with a dangerous weapon, assault resulting in serious bodily injury, arson, burglary, robbery, and a felony under section 661 of this title within the Indian country, shall be subject to the same law and penalties as all other persons committing any of the above offenses, within the exclusive jurisdiction of the United States.
>
> (b) Any offense referred to in subsection (a) of this section that is not defined and punished by Federal law in force within the exclusive jurisdiction of the United States shall be defined and punished in accordance with the laws of the State in which such offense was committed as are in force at the time of such offense. — Eds.]

Today, the Federal Major Crimes Act is the major federal jurisdictional statute for offenses committed by Indians on Indian lands. Like the jurisdiction afforded under section 1152, the federal jurisdiction conferred by section 1153 is exclusive of state jurisdiction. By its terms the Act provides a federal forum for the trial of 14 enumerated crimes when committed on Indian land by an Indian. Unlike the jurisdiction conferred in section 1152, federal jurisdiction over offenses committed by Indians on Indian lands governed by section 1153 is not dependent on the race of the victim. The language of section 1153 covers Indian offenses against the person or property of "another Indian or other person."

Of course, insofar as section 1153 covers offenses committed by an Indian against the person or property of a non-Indian, it overlaps the jurisdiction

---

another Indian" as required by the intra-Indian crime exception of that section. In giving a technical, literal reading to section 1152, the Seventh Circuit may have been in error. First, the court ignored the fact that the Supreme Court had rejected such a narrow reading of a predecessor of section 1152 when it decided *Ex parte* Mayfield, 141 U.S. 107 (1891), and United States v. Quiver, 241 U.S. 602 (1916).... Second, the Seventh Circuit's approach to the intra-Indian crime exception ignores the purpose of that provision.... The early federal jurisdictional statutes included the intra-Indian crime exception to effectuate treaties and the federal policy that Indian tribes will be left to govern themselves in intratribal matters. Indeed, in *Sosseur,* the tribal council had licensed the accused to operate slot machines and other gambling devices on the reservation. 181 F.2d at 874. Although the gambling facilities were frequented by tourists, it can hardly be said they were the "victims" of the defendant's gambling operations. In giving a literal reading to the language of the intra-Indian crime exception, the court ignored, and indeed undermined, the purpose of that clause to further Indian self-government over internal matters occurring on Indian lands. *Cf.* United States v. Blackfeet Tribe of Blackfeet Indian Reservation, 369 F. Supp. 562 (D. Mont. 1973).

conferred by section 1152. As a result of the 1976 amendments to section 1153, contained in the Indian Crimes Act of 1976, which adopted federal definitions of rape, assault with intent to commit rape, and assault resulting in serious bodily injury, this overlap poses few continuing problems. Aside from the mechanical problem of determining which statute to cite in the indictment,[160] the only continuing practical uncertainty created by the overlap of sections 1152 and 1153 for crimes committed by Indians in Indian country against the person or property of non-Indians revolves around the applicability of the Assimilative Crimes Act to such crimes. If a prosecution for such a crime can be brought under section 1152, this Act will be fully applicable and will incorporate a substantial body of state law defining lesser crimes. On the other hand, if such prosecutions of Indian offenders must be brought exclusively under section 1153, then the only state-defined crimes under which a federal district court can prosecute an Indian are the crimes of burglary and incest, which are enumerated in section 1153. Jurisdiction over all other lesser crimes would be preserved for tribal courts. While this question is surely close, several arguments support the latter approach to the problems created by the overlap between sections 1152 and 1153.

First, in at least one case that has thus far noted the problem, the court seems to suggest that section 1153 rather than section 1152 is the applicable statute for crimes committed on Indian lands by Indians against the person or property of

---

[160] *See* Henry v. United States, 432 F.2d 114 (9th Cir. 1970), *modified*, 434 F.2d 1283 (9th Cir.), *cert. denied*, 400 U.S. 1011 (1971) (holding that Indian defendants should be prosecuted under section 1153 rather than section 1152).

The overlap in jurisdiction between sections 1152 and 1153 was created by the inclusion of the phrase "or other person" in the Federal Major Crimes Act's description of the victim of the crime. Act of Mar. 3, 1885, ch. 341, § 9, 23 Stat. 385. The initial reason for the inclusion of this language in the Act is unclear from the legislative history. The Act was proposed in the House as a floor amendment to an Indian appropriations bill. The amendment as originally proposed only covered intra-Indian crimes. During the debate, the following colloquy occurred which resulted in the modification of the amendment:

MR. BUDD: Why not insert in the amendment after the words "another Indian," the words "or any other person?"

MR. CUTCHEON: Indians are already capable of being convicted and punished for a crime committed upon any other person than an Indian.

MR. BUDD: But it is not done.

MR. CUTCHEON: If, however, an Indian commits a crime against an Indian on an Indian reservation there is now no law to punish the offense except, as I have said, the law of the tribe, which is just no law at all.

MR. ELLIS: The language suggested by the gentleman from California [Mr. Budd] will not hurt the amendment.

MR. CUTCHEON: I have no objection to the amendment at all, and will accept it as a modification. I think this provision ought to be inserted in this bill; otherwise I fear it will not become law during this Congress.

16 Cong. Rec. 934 (1885). Obviously, this colloquy raises more questions than it answers. Representative Cutcheon was clearly aware that the predecessor of section 1152 already covered interracial crimes committed by Indians, and thought inclusion of the phrase "or any other person" was unnecessary. On the other hand, Representative Budd was clearly dissatisfied with the results achieved under the forerunner of section 1152 and wanted such crimes prosecuted under the statute which became the Federal Major Crimes Act. However, the crucial question of whether the Federal Major Crimes Act should constitute the exclusive statute under which Indian offenders could be federally prosecuted for crimes committed against non-Indians is unanswered by this legislative history.

non-Indians. Second, the legislative history of the recent amendments to section 1153 appears to accept the view that section 1153 is the applicable jurisdictional statute for any federal crime committed by an Indian. The Indian Crimes Act of 1976 itself suggests that the only state-defined crimes which will be applied to Indians in federal courts are burglary and incest; the normal maxims of statutory construction should suggest that section 1153 would control over section 1152. Third, applying section 1153 rather than section 1152 to crimes committed by Indians against non-Indians limits state legislative control over Indian lands in favor of tribal control and self-government — a result which is more consistent with modern federal Indian policy and Supreme Court decisions....

The operation of section 1153 is also very much dependent on a parallel provision of federal law. Under section 3242 of title 18, all persons tried under section 1153 are to be tried "in the same courts, and in the same manner, as are all other persons committing any of the above crimes within the exclusive jurisdiction of the United States." Section 3242 clearly affects many procedural matters. Furthermore, the requirement of section 3242 that section 1153 crimes be tried in the same manner as other federal offenses has recently taken on a substantive role. The crimes enumerated in section 1153 are exclusive in that a federal district court only has jurisdiction to entertain charges against Indians which are brought for one of the 14 specified crimes. Although federal jurisdiction only runs to charges brought for one of the 14 enumerated offenses, this jurisdiction includes the power to convict and sentence Indians for lesser-included offenses under the Federal Major Crimes Act. This conclusion is primarily derived from section 3242 and *Keeble v. United States*.[174]

In *Keeble*, an Indian defendant was charged with the fatal assault of another Indian on the reservation of the Crow Creek Sioux. Although assault resulting in serious bodily injury was an enumerated section 1153 offense, and is now a federally defined crime, at the time *Keeble* was decided, section 1153 incorporated the state law definition of the crime. The defendant requested a jury instruction on simple assault, a lesser-included offense; the trial court denied the request since simple assault was not one of the enumerated offenses contained in section 1153. The Eighth Circuit affirmed; the Supreme Court reversed. Although both statutory and due process arguments were pressed upon the Court, the decision rested on the language of section 3242, which requires Indian offenses heard under section 1153 to be tried in the same manner as other offenses within the exclusive jurisdiction of the United States. Since a non-Indian tried under section 1152 for the same crime would be entitled to the lesser-included offense instruction which Keeble was refused, the Court concluded that refusal of the requested instruction deprived Keeble of his right under section 3242 to be tried in the same manner as other persons committing like crimes.

Although *Keeble* mandated the issuance of a lesser-included offense instruction, "*Keeble* did not explicitly hold that jurisdiction for a conviction of and punishment for the lesser included offense existed in the federal court." In *Felicia v. United States*,[181] the Court of Appeals for the Eighth Circuit rejected

---

[174]412 U.S. 205 (1973).
[181]495 F.2d 353 (8th Cir.), *cert. denied*, 419 U.S. 849 (1974).

the argument that *Keeble* did not allow the district court to exercise jurisdiction to sentence for a lesser-included offense. Otherwise, the court stated, the lesser-included offense instruction would be "an exercise in futility." Although *Felicia* is consistent with *Keeble*'s command that a section 1153 prosecution be tried under section 3242 in the same manner as a section 1152 prosecution, a contrary result would, as one commentator has suggested, certainly be less intrusive on Indian tribal court jurisdiction.

The impact of *Keeble* on practice under section 1153 is far from clear. At least three Justices suggested that only crimes defined by federal statute, like the assault involved in *Keeble*, are part of the lesser-included offense jurisdiction granted to the federal courts under section 1153.[184] On Indian policy grounds this view is appealing because of the adverse impact on tribal court jurisdiction an expansive reading of *Keeble* forbodes. On the other hand, there is a certain lack of logic to limiting *Keeble* solely to lesser-included crimes defined by federal statute. The offense actually charged in *Keeble*, assault resulting in serious bodily injury, was defined by state law under the pre-1968 version of section 1153. To hold that only a federally defined offense can be a lesser-included offense to a state defined crime seems anomalous. Moreover, limiting lesser-included offense instructions to federally defined crimes is inconsistent with the rationale in *Keeble*. Since the Court relied on section 3242 to assure that Indians were not denied the benefits which were available to non-Indians charged with the same offense, the equality demanded by the *Keeble* holding suggests that a lesser-included offense instruction should be available even when the lesser offense is not federally defined. Since the Assimilative Crimes Act applies to prosecutions of non-Indians brought under section 1152, lesser-included offense instructions on state defined crimes will always be available in such prosecutions. Arguably, section 3242 and the *Keeble* equality principle demand the same for Indian defendants.

If the lesser offense is not defined by federal statute, there are several alternative ways to determine its definition and punishment. There is the law of the state in which the offense was committed, tribal law and order codes, or the Code of Indian Tribal Offenses. Several arguments can be made that state law governs the definition of lesser-included offenses in most instances. First, for those crimes defined by state law under the express language of section 1153 — burglary and incest — the adoption of state law arguably incorporates lesser-included offenses. Second, as *Keeble* requires equality of treatment between section 1152 and section 1153 prosecutions, state definition of lesser-included crimes under section 1153 comports with the effect of the Assimilative Crimes

---

[184] Keeble v. United States, 412 U.S. 205, 215-17 (1973) (Stewart, Powell & Rehnquist, JJ., dissenting):

It is a commonplace that federal courts are courts of limited jurisdiction, and that there are no common law offenses against the United States. "The legislative authority of the Union must first make an act a crime, affix a punishment to it, and declare the Court that shall have jurisdiction of the offense." ... "It is axiomatic that statutes creating and defining crimes cannot be extended by intendment, and that no act, however wrongful, can be punished under such a statute unless clearly within its terms." ... And it is also clear that simple assault by an Indian on an Indian reservation, the purported "lesser included offense" in this case, comes within no federal jurisdictional statute.

Id. at 215-16 (citations omitted)....

Act under section 1152. Third, the new paragraph in section 1153, adopting state law for any enumerated crime not defined by federal law, may apply to lesser-included offenses.[191]

An equally plausible argument can be made, however, that state definitions should be rejected in favor of the tribal law and order codes or the Code of Indian Tribal Offenses. First, adoption of tribal law will do less damage to the Indian tribal interests by furthering self-government and preventing an expansion of state legislative control over Indian law enforcement problems. Second, tribal law and order codes and the Code of Indian Offenses are directed toward Indian problems specifically, making them more palatable than the general state criminal codes. Adoption of tribal law in section 1153 prosecutions is not without difficulty, however. Tribal codes are often not readily available to the federal district courts, and reported decisions under either the tribal codes or the Code of Indian Offenses are virtually nonexistent. Moreover, under the Indian Civil Rights Act of 1968, tribal court jurisdiction is limited to punishments of no greater than 6 months imprisonment or a fine of 500 dollars or both. Courts will be forced, provided the *Keeble* rationale is extended to allow federal jurisdiction over non-federal lesser-included offenses under section 1153, to grapple with these varying interests and decide under which law these crimes should be defined.

Further questions are posed by *Keeble* for section 1153 jurisdiction. Although *Keeble* indicates that federal prosecutors cannot initiate prosecutions for crimes not specifically enumerated in section 1153, the impact of *Keeble* on procedure after the initiation of a section 1153 prosecution is unresolved. For example, the Court raised, but did not resolve, the issue whether the government could request and secure a lesser-included offense instruction in such a prosecution. Another issue unresolved by *Keeble* is the district court's authority in a section 1153 prosecution to inquire whether an indictment charging the violation of one of the 14 enumerated crimes is really a facade to facilitate the creation of federal jurisdiction over a lesser charge. Yet another problem posed by *Keeble* is whether a district court has jurisdiction to accept a bargained plea of guilty to a lesser-included offense.

Plea bargaining apparently became common practice in section 1153 prosecutions after *Keeble*. If the plea bargain is entered into after the prosecution is commenced, the *Keeble* requirement that section 1153 Indian defendants be treated in the same manner as non-Indians prosecuted under section 1152

---

[191]The amended version of section 1153 contains a paragraph which states that any other offense included in section 1153 which is not defined and punished by federal law shall be defined and punished in accordance with the state law in force at the time of such offense. Indian Crimes Act of 1976, Pub. L. No. 94-297, § 2, 90 Stat. 585. The provision seems to be an overly cautious reaction to Acunia v. United States, 404 F.2d 140 (9th Cir. 1968), which held, under the pre-1968 version of section 1153, that the crime of incest could not be prosecuted under the Major Crimes Act. Incest was not defined federally and at that time no provision of the Major Crimes Act expressly incorporated state definitions of that crime. As all offenses enumerated in section 1153 except incest and burglary are now defined by federal law, and state law is expressly adopted for incest and burglary prosecutions, the newly added last paragraph serves no apparent purpose, unless it is a prospective protective device or a vehicle for defining lesser-included offenses. It is important to note, however, that this new provision only refers to the "above offenses" enunciated in section 1153. Thus, this new provision neither expressly covers the lesser-included crime problem created by *Keeble* nor does it incorporate the Assimilative Crimes Act into section 1153 jurisdiction.

apparently mandates federal jurisdiction to accept the plea. However, if the accused and the prosecutor agree on a guilty plea to a lesser offense before the formal charge under section 1153 is lodged, the timing suggests that the indictment on the greater charge is a facade or sham to expand jurisdiction beyond that conferred by section 1153. Of course, the language of section 3242 only commands that Indians prosecuted under section 1153 "be tried ... in the same manner, as are all other persons committing any of the above crimes within the exclusive jurisdiction of the United States." Read narrowly, the word "tried" may not cover the entry of a guilty plea. In any event, federal judges must assure themselves of the factual basis for a guilty plea, including determining that jurisdictional requisites are met. Federal judges are best advised to inquire into the timing of the plea negotiations in order to assure both that they have jurisdiction under section 1153, and to build a record for later collateral attacks on the conviction. This inquiry would further protect the interests of the Indian tribes by assuring that section 1153 does not unnecessarily divest the tribal courts of jurisdiction....

5. Exceptions to the Federal Statutory Scheme

The federal jurisdictional scheme set forth in the statutory provisions already discussed establishes the criminal jurisdiction framework for many reservations. However, Congress has altered this jurisdictional scheme for some tribes by special legislation. In some instances, the relationship of the special legislation to the general statutory scheme is expressly stated by Congress; however, a number of ambiguities still remain. The two most important exceptions to the general jurisdictional arrangement arise out of federal Indian policy enunciated during the 1950's, as exemplified by Public Law 280 and the tribal termination acts.

Public Law 280 worked a major change in the criminal jurisdictional scheme, by requiring six states — Alaska, California, Minnesota, Nebraska, Oregon, and Wisconsin — to assume complete criminal and civil jurisdiction over most of the reservations located within their boundaries.[221] The Act also provided that within the affected reservations in these "mandatory" states, federal jurisdiction over crimes described in sections 1152 and 1153 would not apply. Congress avoided concurrent federal-state jurisdiction, apparently because of the potential multiple prosecution implications which otherwise might ensue.

Public Law 280 not only compelled six states to assume jurisdiction, it also permitted the assumption of Indian jurisdiction by any other states that desired to do so. The Act gave congressional consent to the assumption by the states of criminal and civil jurisdiction "by affirmative legislative action," and furthermore gave congressional consent to the amendment of state constitutions which contained disclaimers of jurisdiction over Indian lands, presumably a necessary predicate to the assumption of jurisdiction. As originally enacted, Public Law 280 required no tribal consent for a state's discretionary assumption of jurisdiction. A number of states assumed such jurisdiction despite contrary desires on the part of resident Indian tribes. However, Public Law 280 was amended by

---

[221] Act of Aug. 15, 1953, ch. 505, § 2, 67 Stat. 588 (now codified at 18 U.S.C. § 1162(a) (1970)). [Alaska was added to the original list of five states in 1958.]

the Indian Civil Rights Act of 1968 to prospectively require tribal consent, and to allow retrocession of jurisdiction undertaken by either mandatory or discretionary states pursuant to Public Law 280. No tribe has formally consented to the extension of state criminal jurisdiction over its lands. Five states — Nebraska, Nevada, Minnesota, Washington, and Wisconsin — have retroceded some of the criminal jurisdiction they assumed under Public Law 280.

The effect of the voluntary assumption of state jurisdiction under Public Law 280 on the federal jurisdiction conferred by sections 1152 and 1153 is unclear. Arguably, the state jurisdiction conferred is exclusive. First, in enacting Public Law 280, Congress did not expressly preserve federal jurisdiction. Second, because of the potential multiple prosecution aspects of concurrent jurisdiction and its concomitant fifth amendment implications, Congress has rather consistently frowned on concurrent state-federal jurisdictional arrangements for Indian lands. Most important, section 7 of Public Law 280 originally indicated that jurisdiction could be assumed by states "not having jurisdiction with respect to criminal offenses ... *as provided for in this Act.*" Since section 2 of the Act expressly negated continued operation of sections 1152 and 1153 in the mandatory states, the implication of the language of section 7 would suggest that the jurisdictional opportunities afforded discretionary states under section 7 included the same exclusive state jurisdictional structure provided for the mandatory states. While section 7 was later technically repealed and section 1321 of title 25 substituted in its place, the alteration of language in section 1321 was not designed to change the jurisdictional outcome. Rather, like its predecessor, section 1321 appears to afford the state the opportunity, now only with tribal consent, to assume complete criminal jurisdiction over Indian lands exclusive of any assertion of federal jurisdiction under sections 1152 and 1153.

The termination acts also significantly changed the operation of sections 1152 and 1153. The acts commonly provided that upon completion of the termination process "all statutes of the United States that affect Indians or Indian tribes because of their Indian status shall be inapplicable to them, and the laws of the several states shall apply to them in the same manner they apply to other persons or citizens within their jurisdiction." The acts clearly indicate that the termination process included the elimination of federal criminal jurisdiction formerly exercised over the terminated Indian lands under sections 1152 and 1153.

A number of statutes enacted during the forties also created exceptions to the exclusive federal jurisdictional scheme described above.[239] The scope of some of these statutes is confusing. Three statutes passed during the forties covered all Indian reservations in Kansas, the Sac and Fox Indian Reservation in Iowa, and the Devil's Lake Reservation in North Dakota. These acts were virtually identical in language and purported to grant the affected states criminal juris-

---

[239] For example, in the Act of July 2, 1948, ch. 809, 62 Stat. 1224 (codified at 25 U.S.C. § 232 (1970)), Congress granted the State of New York complete jurisdiction over all Indian lands within the state, apparently exclusive of any federal jurisdiction. Hunting and fishing rights, guaranteed to the New York Indians by custom, agreement, or treaty, were not affected by the Act. Similarly, Congress granted California complete and exclusive criminal jurisdiction over the Agua Caliente Reservation of Mission Indians. Act of Oct. 5, 1949, ch. 604, 63 Stat. 705. The Reservation land, however, was exempted from alienation, encumbrance, or state taxation. *See also* 18 U.S.C. § 1162(b) (1970).

diction over offenses committed on Indian lands. However, each statute contained a proviso stating that the grant of jurisdiction to the states "shall not deprive the courts of the United States of jurisdiction over offenses defined by the laws of the United States committed by or against Indians on Indian reservations." As the federal jurisdiction which such a statute reserved traditionally was exclusive, the issue arose regarding the scope of the jurisdiction conferred on the states through these three acts. In *Youngbear v. Brewer,* a federal district court construed the proviso contained in the Iowa Act to reserve exclusive jurisdiction to the federal courts over section 1153 crimes. The jurisdiction conferred on the state was only jurisdiction over lesser crimes not enumerated in section 1153 or defined by other federal statutes. This result was compelled by the legislative history of the acts, the maxims of statutory construction concerning laws affecting Indians, and the potential multiple prosecution problems which would be created by a contrary construction.

Other isolated, idiosyncratic exceptions to the general federal statutory scheme can also be found. In summary, although sections 1152, 1153, and 3242 set forth a general jurisdictional scheme for Indian lands, a number of exceptions to that scheme exist, not found in the language of those statutes. Accordingly, close attention must be paid to Public Law 280, the Indian Civil Rights Act, special congressional statutes, and idiosyncratic decisions for any particular reservation over which jurisdiction is at issue.

NOTES

1. Placing the Indian Jurisdiction Statutes in Perspective: With the exceptions of crimes committed in the exercise of treaty or other tribally guaranteed off-reservation rights, special federal and tribal criminal jurisdiction over Indians generally is geographically limited to Indian country. The federal criminal jurisdictional statutes affecting Indians are specifically limited to Indian country and do not govern crimes committed by Indians outside of Indian country. Such crimes may be prosecuted by state and federal authorities in the same manner as crimes committed by non-Indians. Should Indian tribes or the federal courts be given greater authority over crimes committed by tribal members off their reservation?

While often resisted by Indian people as an assault on their sovereignty, the federal courts generally hold that federal crimes of nationwide application may be enforced with equal force in Indian country in the absence of a more specific conflict with guaranteed treaty or other Indian rights. Thus, crimes such as mail fraud, securities fraud, and assaults on various federal officials in performance of their duties apply directly to Indians and others in Indian country without resort to the jurisdictional provisions of 18 U.S.C. §§ 1152-1153. *E.g., United States v. Camp,* 541 F.2d 737 (8th Cir. 1976); *Stone v. United States,* 506 F.2d 561 (8th Cir. 1974); *Walks On Top v. United States,* 372 F.2d 422 (9th Cir.), *cert. denied,* 389 U.S. 879 (1967).

Where the general federal criminal statute impairs treaty or other tribal rights, closer scrutiny must be given to determine whether Congress in enacting the general statute clearly and specifically recognized the existence of the conflicting Indian right and indicated an intent to abrogate it. *E.g., United States v. Dion,* excerpted in section C2, *supra.* Thus, the significance of sections 1152 and 1153 lies not in facilitating federal prosecution of federal crimes of general nationwide application, but, rather, in delineating the respective federal and tribal criminal jurisdiction over crimes that *outside* of Indian country would be handled by state authorities. The tradition of preemption of state authority in Indian country and the existence of these federal jurisdictional statutes clearly preempt state criminal jurisdiction over both crimes included within these provisions and over lesser intra-Indian crimes not covered by the Federal Major Crimes Act which are left exclusively to tribal jurisdiction.

2. Assimilative Crimes Act and the Organized Crime Control Act in Indian Country: In *United States v. Marcyes*, 557 F.2d 1361, 1365 n.1 (9th Cir. 1977), the court considered and rejected some of Professor Clinton's arguments against the application of the Assimilative Crimes Act in Indian country. The court said:

> Amicus argues that *Williams v. United States*, 327 U.S. 711, 66 S. Ct. 778, 90 L. Ed. 962 (1946) did not decide the question of whether the A.C.A. is applicable to Indian country. We disagree. In *Williams* the petitioner, a married white man, was convicted of having had sexual intercourse, within an Indian reservation, with an unmarried Indian girl who was over the age of 16 but under 18 years of age. This act was made punishable under the laws of the State of Arizona and was incorporated as a federal crime under the provisions of 18 U.S.C. § 468 (the predecessor to 18 U.S.C. § 13). The Supreme Court's initial statement was "[t]his case turns upon the applicability of the Assimilative Crimes Act ...." Since it was undisputed that the act took place within an Indian reservation, the threshold question necessarily decided was whether the A.C.A. even applied to Indian country. Amicus' argument that the court merely assumed its applicability without deciding the question is belied by the court's own words. The court stated:

>> It is not disputed that this Indian reservation is "reserved or acquired for the use of the United States, and under the exclusive or concurrent jurisdiction thereof," or that it is "Indian country" within the meaning of Rev. Stat. § 2145. [the predecessor to 18 U.S.C. § 1152]. This means that many sections of the Federal Criminal Code *apply to the reservation, including not only the Assimilative Crimes Act ....* 327 U.S. at 713, 66 S. Ct. at 779 (emphasis added).

> We would also note that the *Williams* court's ultimate decision, that the A.C.A. did not apply to the particular crime charged because the precise acts were made penal by Federal law and therefore the State's laws could not be incorporated, would never have been reached had the court felt that the A.C.A. did not apply to any crime committed upon Indian lands. Our own review of the language of 18 U.S.C. § 13 and 18 U.S.C. § 1152 convinces us that the district court was correct in holding that the A.C.A., by its own terms and through § 1152, is applicable to Indian country.

Did the court pay sufficient attention to the statutory construction problem posed by the overlap of 18 U.S.C. §§ 1152 and 1153? *Marcyes* affirmed the federal convictions of several Indians under the Assimilative Crimes Act for selling fireworks on the Puyallup Reservation in East Tacoma, Washington, in violation of the laws of the state of Washington. Was this result consistent with *United States v. Quiver* and *Ex parte Mayfield* (discussed in Professor Clinton's article), neither of which was cited in the *Marcyes* opinion? The *Marcyes* opinion also held that the Assimilative Crimes Act does not incorporate state regulatory crimes and make them applicable to Indian country. Rather, the Act only incorporates conduct which the state absolutely forbids to its citizens, such as the sale of fireworks, not conduct which it permits, but extensively regulates.

On the other hand, the Final Report of the American Indian Policy Review Commission stated:

> It has been a continuous tenet of Federal-Indian policy to leave tribes free to govern themselves under their own code of laws within the Indian country. The wholesale

adoption of State laws onto reservations by way of the Assimilative Crimes Act runs completely counter to that long standing Federal policy. It is the tribe, not the State or the Federal Government, which should determine whether Indian stick games may be played within the reservation, whether bingo games will be sanctioned, whether fire-crackers may be sold within the reservation. It may well be that Congress would want to control certain activities of a more substantial nature, but this should be done by specific legislation and only after a showing that the tribes themselves have failed to pass regulatory laws.

American Indian Policy Review Commission, Final Report 198 (1977).

Closely related to the question of the applicability of the Assimilative Crimes Act in Indian country is the issue of whether section 803(a) of the Organized Crime Control Act of 1970, codified at 18 U.S.C. § 1955, applies in Indian country. This section makes gambling a federal crime where such gambling "is a violation of the law of a State or political subdivision in which it is conducted" if five or more persons are involved and the gambling has been in continuous operation for more than thirty days or has a gross revenue of $2,000 in any single day. The Ninth Circuit held in *United States v. Farris*, 624 F.2d 890 (9th Cir. 1980), *cert. denied sub nom. Baker v. United States*, 449 U.S. 1111 (1981), that the gambling provisions of the Act applied to Indians in Indian country when state law prohibits gambling businesses, as Washington law did. Thus, the court found that the actions of the defendants in *Farris* were a "violation of the law of the state" for purposes of section 1955 even though it recognized that Washington had no subject matter jurisdiction to enforce its gambling laws against tribal members on the Puyallup Reservation.

The *Farris* court suggested that the gambling laws of the state of Washington could have been enforced by the United States against members of the Puyallup tribe on their reservation even in the absence of section 1955, through the Assimilative Crimes Act, 18 U.S.C. § 13. The holding of *United States v. Marcyes*, that the *prohibitory*, but not regulatory, criminal laws of the state of Washington may be enforced by the federal government on the Puyallup Reservation was reaffirmed by the court.

The distinction between prohibitory criminal laws and regulatory statutes to which criminal sanctions are appended drawn in *Marcyes* and *Farris* is consistent with the same distinction drawn by the courts in Public Law 280 cases involving the application in state courts of state law to Indians for offenses committed on their reservations. Since *Bryan v. Itasca County*, 426 U.S. 373 (1976), indicated that Public Law 280 does not grant *civil regulatory* jurisdiction, but merely private adjudicatory authority to state courts in civil cases, courts sometimes examine whether a state statute sought to be enforced against Indians in Indian country is "criminal/prohibitory" or actually "civil/regulatory," even where penal sanctions are imposed for violation of the law. In *California v. Cabazon Band of Mission Indians*, set forth below, the Court concluded that California's bingo statute regulated, rather than prohibited, bingo, in spite of the attached criminal sanctions and was preempted by federal law. Therefore, the Court held that the state lacked jurisdiction to enforce the bingo statute in Indian country. While these cases were Public Law 280 cases involving *state* jurisdiction to prosecute Indians in Indian country, they may be instructive in delineating the basis of a *federal* prosecution under the Assimilative Crimes Act and the gambling provisions of the Organized Crime Control Act of 1970, which adopt only state prohibitory criminal laws, not regulatory or licensing statutes to which penal sanctions have been appended.

PROBLEMS

One of the best ways to master the complex federal statutory pattern governing criminal jurisdiction over Indian lands is to establish an analytical framework and then work through a number of hypothetical problems.

In areas of Indian country not governed by Public Law 280 or some other specific statutory transfer of criminal jurisdiction to the states, the jurisdictional pattern will be governed by the crime charged, the locus of the crime, and the status of the parties. *See* Vollman, *Criminal Jurisdiction in Indian Country: Tribal Sovereignty and Defendants' Rights in Conflict*, 22 KAN. L. REV. 387 (1974). In analyzing any jurisdictional question, it is worthwhile to approach the inquiry in an orderly fashion. The first question that should be asked is whether the crime in question is a federal crime of nationwide application, such as assault on a federal officer in the performance of duties, or, rather, constitutes an *enclave* crime, such as murder, rape, or theft, that normally would be prosecuted by state authorities but is handled by federal or tribal authorities in Indian country. If the crime is a federal crime of nationwide application, federal jurisdiction exists irrespective of the locus of the crime or the status of the parties *unless the prosecution for the crime would interfere with Indian treaty or other rights.* If any conflicting Indian rights exist, a careful statutory analysis must be made as to whether Congress clearly and specifically intended to abrogate preexisting Indian rights when it enacted the federal criminal statute in question.

If the crime in question, however, constitutes an *enclave* crime a more complicated analysis is required. In the case of an enclave crime, the second logical question to ask is whether the locus of the crime is in Indian country. The legal concept of Indian country is explored at some length in Chapter 1. For enclave crimes occurring outside of Indian country the state generally will have jurisdiction irrespective of the status of the parties unless state prosecution of Indians for the crime will interfere with treaty or other guarantees of off-reservation rights. For enclave or other crimes occurring in Indian country, however, the state will *not* have jurisdiction unless *both* the accused and the victim were non-Indians. State jurisdiction over enclave crimes in Indian country involving only non-Indians is sanctioned by the controversial *McBratney* decision discussed in Professor Clinton's article. For enclave crimes occurring in Indian country, careful inquiry must be made regarding the status of the parties. The status of the parties will determine not only the existence of state jurisdiction in a *McBratney* situation, but also which of the two federal jurisdictional statutes applies, a question with considerable significance.

The problem of who constitutes an Indian for purposes of the criminal jurisdiction statutes involves considerable uncertainty. Historically, the statutes regarded an Indian as anyone who ethnologically had Indian ancestry and was culturally identifiable as an Indian. *E.g., Ex parte Pero*, 99 F.2d 28, 30 (7th Cir. 1938); *United States v. Ives*, 504 F.2d 935, 953 (9th Cir. 1974). In a footnote in *United States v. Antelope*, 430 U.S. 641, 646-47 n.7 (1977), Chief Justice Burger noted that tribal enrollment "has not been held be an absolute requirement for federal jurisdiction, at least where the Indian defendant lived on the reservation and 'maintained tribal relations with the Indians thereon.'" He also indicated that the Court was not required to decide that question in *Antelope* and therefore intimated no views on the matter. This cryptic remark casts doubt on the precise scope of the term "Indian" used in sections 1152 and 1153 for jurisdictional purposes. Historically, the classification clearly had been an ethnological racial classification. The Court's recent efforts in fifth amendment equal protection cases to characterize Indian law as involving political, rather than racial, classifications may push the court to the position that nonmember Indians are not Indians within the meaning of the criminal jurisdiction provisions. *E.g., United States v. Antelope, supra; Morton v. Mancari,* 417 U.S. 535 (1974). Any such unfortunate decision, however, would leave many persons of Indian ancestry who reside on Indian reservations subject to state criminal jurisdiction for the first time simply because they do not qualify for membership under tribal constitutions or enrollment ordinances, even though they are regarded as Indians by both the tribal community in which they live and by the surrounding non-Indian country. In the context of tribal jurisdiction the Supreme Court has held that tribes may not exercise criminal jurisdiction over nonmembers, *Duro v. Reina,* 110 S. Ct. 2053 (1990), set forth and discussed in Chapter 3, section D1, *infra.* At the same time, the Court noted that Congress can use broader categories for the purposes of federal jurisdiction.

In *United States v. Kagama,* 118 U.S. 375 (1886), the Court justified federal jurisdiction over the Indian crimes covered by the Federal Major Crimes Act in part on the basis of the potential prejudice of local juries against Indians. Justice Miller stated, "[b]ecause of local ill feeling, the people of the States where they are found are often their deadliest enemies." Is prejudice or hostility toward Indians accused of crime, especially those who reside on reservations, likely to be any less just because they are not enrolled members of any tribe? Notwithstanding potential prejudice, Indians of *terminated* tribes apparently are considered non-Indians for purposes of sections 1152 and 1153. *Compare United States v. Heath,* 509 F.2d 16, 19 (9th Cir. 1974) ("While anthropologically a Klamath Indian even after the Termination Act obviously remains an Indian, his unique status *vis-à-vis* the Federal Government no longer exists.") *with St. Cloud v. United States,* 702 F. Supp. 1456 (D.S.D. 1988) (Indian from terminated tribe constitutes an Indian under 18 U.S.C. § 1153 for purposes of crime committed on the reservation of a non-terminated tribe).

If the crime in question is interracial, i.e., committed by a non-Indian against the person or property of an Indian, or committed by an Indian against the person or property of a non-Indian, the crime is governed by the General Crimes Act, 18 U.S.C. § 1152. In that case, prosecution would be proper under federal law for any federally defined enclave crime contained in the United States Code, and prosecution would also be possible under the Assimilative Crimes Act, 18 U.S.C. § 13, and the General Crimes Act in *federal* court for any state prohibitory crime not otherwise covered by a federally defined offense. If the accused is an Indian, however, she may not be prosecuted in federal court under the General Crimes Act if already punished for the same offense under the laws of the tribe. If the enclave crime in question is intra-Indian, rather than intra-racial, federal prosecution is possible only under the Federal Major Crimes Act, 18 U.S.C. § 1153. That Act covers seventeen enumerated felonies. If the crime constitutes one of the enumerated crimes, federal jurisdiction exists. If not, the jurisdiction lies exclusively with the tribe. Note that, for intra-Indian crimes, adoption of state law under the Assimilative Crimes Act is not possible. In order to preserve exclusive tribal jurisdiction over lesser intra-Indian crimes, section 1153(b) expressly limits adoption of state law to offenses listed in section 1153(a) which are not defined and punished by federal law. The Assimilative Crimes Act only applies in Indian country through the General Crimes Act, 18 U.S.C. § 1152, and therefore only applies to the interracial crimes to which that section applies.

In order to apply these principles consider the following problems. In evaluating these problems also consider whether the result is consistent with the underlying reasons for a separate federal Indian policy.

Problem No. 1. Albert Rodgers, an enrolled member of the Cherokee Nation, and John Smith, a non-Indian, are suspected of the murder of Harvey Doe, a non-Indian, on a restricted Indian trust allotment within the former boundaries of the now extinguished reservation of the Cherokee Nation in eastern Oklahoma. Which courts have jurisdiction to try Rodgers or Smith for murder? Explain.

Problem No. 2. Joan Bear, an enrolled member of the Tohono O'Odham Indian Tribe, and John Doe, a non-Indian, are suspected of the murder of Ms. Bear's Indian husband, Jim Bear, on the Tohono O'Odham Reservation in southern Arizona. Which courts have jurisdiction to try Bear and Doe for murder? Explain.

Problem No. 3. Harvey MacDonald, an enrolled member of the Navajo Tribe, and Harold Carr, a non-Indian, are alleged to have conspired to pass a bad check to the Indian owner and operator of a store at Window Rock, Arizona, on the Navajo Reservation. No provision in Title 18 of the United States Criminal Code defines or punishes the forgery of a private check on an Indian reservation or other federal enclave. Which courts have authority to try MacDonald or Carr for forgery? Explain. Would the result in this problem be changed if the owner and operator of the store to whom the check was negotiated was a non-Indian? Explain.

Problem No. 4. Raymond White, a Chippewa Indian, is alleged to have embezzled funds from the non-Indian-owned corporation for which he worked as a bookkeeper on the Red Lake Reservation in Minnesota. While 18 U.S.C. § 1163 prohibits embezzlement from tribal governments or other tribal enterprises, no provision of the United States Code defines and punishes private embezzlements occurring in Indian country or other federal enclaves. In which courts could White be tried for embezzlement? Explain. Might the result in Problem No. 4 be altered if the corporation for which White worked was wholly owned by an Indian? Explain.

Problem No. 5. Harvey Roberts, a member of the Sac and Fox Tribe of Oklahoma, allegedly killed a non-Indian while driving a motor vehicle under the influence of alcohol on the Red Lake Chippewa Reservation in Minnesota. In which courts could Roberts be tried for manslaughter? In which courts could he be convicted of driving while under the influence of alcohol? Would your answers be different if the victim were a member of the Red Lake Chippewa Tribe?

CALIFORNIA v. CABAZON BAND OF MISSION INDIANS

480 U.S. 202 (1987)

Justice WHITE delivered the opinion of the Court.

The Cabazon and Morongo Bands of Mission Indians, federally recognized Indian tribes, occupy reservations in Riverside County, California. Each Band, pursuant to an ordinance approved by the Secretary of the Interior, conducts bingo games on its reservation. The Cabazon Band has also opened a card club at which draw poker and other card games are played. The games are open to the public and are played predominantly by non-Indians coming onto the reservations. The games are a major source of employment for tribal members, and the profits are the Tribes' sole source of income. The State of California seeks to apply to the two Tribes Cal. Penal Code Ann. § 326.5 (West Supp. 1987). That statute does not entirely prohibit the playing of bingo but permits it when the games are operated and staffed by members of designated charitable organizations who may not be paid for their services. Profits must be kept in special accounts and used only for charitable purposes; prizes may not exceed $250 per game. Asserting that the bingo games on the two reservations violated each of these restrictions, California insisted that the Tribes comply with state law.[3] Riverside County also sought to apply its local Ordinance No. 558 regulating bingo, as well as its Ordinance No. 331, prohibiting the playing of draw poker and the other card games.

The Tribes sued the county in Federal District Court seeking a declaratory judgment that the county had no authority to apply its ordinances inside the reservations and an injunction against their enforcement. The State intervened, the facts were stipulated and the District Court granted the Tribes' motion for summary judgment, holding that neither the State nor the county had any authority to enforce its gambling laws within the reservations. The Court of Appeals for the Ninth Circuit affirmed [and this appeal followed].

I

The Court has consistently recognized that Indian tribes retain "attributes of sovereignty over both their members and their territory," *United States v. Mazurie*, 419 U.S. 544 (1975), and that "tribal sovereignty is dependent on, and subordinate to, only the Federal Government, not the States," *Washington v. Confederated Tribes of the Colville Indian Reservation*, 447 U.S. 134, 154 (1980). It is clear, however, that state laws may be applied to tribal Indians on their reservations if Congress has expressly so provided. Here, the State insists that Congress has twice given its express consent: first in Pub. L. 280 in 1953, 67 Stat. 588, as amended, 18 U.S.C. § 1162, 28 U.S.C. § 1360 (1982 ed. and Supp. III), and second in the Organized Crime Control Act in 1970, 84 Stat. 937, 18 U.S.C. § 1955. We disagree in both respects.

In Pub. L. 280, Congress expressly granted six States, including California, jurisdiction over specified areas of Indian country within the States and provided for the assumption of jurisdiction by other States. In § 2, California was granted broad criminal jurisdiction over offenses committed by or against Indians within all Indian country within the State. Section 4's grant of civil jurisdiction was more limited. In *Bryan v. Itasca County*, 426 U.S. 373 (1976), [reprinted in Chapter 4, section C1, *infra*] we interpreted § 4 to grant states

[3] The Tribes admit that their games violate the provision governing staffing and the provision setting a limit on jackpots. They dispute the State's assertion that they do not maintain separate funds for the bingo operations. At oral argument, counsel for the State asserted, contrary to the position taken in the merits brief and contrary to the stipulated facts in this case, App. 65, p. 24, 82-83, p. 15, that the Tribes are among the charitable organizations authorized to sponsor bingo games under the statute. It is therefore unclear whether the State intends to put the tribal bingo enterprises out of business or only to impose on them the staffing, jackpot limit, and separate fund requirements. The tribal bingo enterprises are apparently consistent with other provisions of the statute: minors are not allowed to participate, the games are conducted in buildings owned by the Tribes on tribal property, the games are open to the public, and persons must be physically present to participate.

jurisdiction over private civil litigation involving reservation Indians in state court, but not to grant general civil regulatory authority. We held, therefore, that Minnesota could not apply its personal property tax within the reservation. [Consequently,] when a State seeks to enforce a law within an Indian reservation under the authority of Pub. L. 280, it must be determined whether the law is criminal in nature, and thus fully applicable to the reservation under § 2, or civil in nature, and applicable only as it may be relevant to private civil litigation in state court. The Minnesota personal property tax at issue in *Bryan* was unquestionably civil in nature. The California bingo statute is not so easily categorized. California law permits bingo games to be conducted only by charitable and other specified organizations, and then only by their members who may not receive any wage or profit for doing so; prizes are limited and receipts are to be segregated and used only for charitable purposes. Violation of any of these provisions is a misdemeanor. California insists that these are criminal laws which Pub. L. 280 permits it to enforce on the reservations.

Following its earlier decision in *Barona Group of the Capitan Grande Band of Mission Indians, San Diego County, Cal. v. Duffy*, 694 F.2d 1185 (9th Cir. 1982), *cert. denied*, 461 U.S. 929 (1983), which also involved the applicability of § 326.5 of the California Penal Code to Indian reservations, the Court of Appeals rejected this submission. 783 F.2d, at 901-903. In *Barona*, applying what it thought to be the civil/criminal dichotomy drawn in *Bryan v. Itasca County*, the Court of Appeals drew a distinction between state "criminal/prohibitory" laws and state "civil/regulatory" laws: if the intent of a state law is generally to prohibit certain conduct, it falls within Pub. L. 280's grant of criminal jurisdiction, but if the state law generally permits the conduct at issue, subject to regulation, it must be classified as civil/regulatory and Pub. L. 280 does not authorize its enforcement on an Indian reservation. The shorthand test is whether the conduct at issue violates the State's public policy. Inquiring into the nature of § 326.5, the Court of Appeals held that it was regulatory rather than prohibitory. This was the analysis employed, with similar results, by the Court of Appeals for the Fifth Circuit in *Seminole Tribe of Florida v. Butterworth*, 658 F.2d 310 (1981), *cert. denied*, 455 U.S. 1020 (1982), which the Ninth Circuit found persuasive.

We are persuaded that the prohibitory/regulatory distinction is consistent with *Bryan*'s construction of Pub. L. 280. It is not a bright-line rule, however; and as the Ninth Circuit itself observed, an argument of some weight may be made that the bingo statute is prohibitory rather than regulatory. But in the present case, the court reexamined the state law and reaffirmed its holding in *Barona*, and we are reluctant to disagree with that court's view of the nature and intent of the state law at issue here.

There is surely a fair basis for its conclusion. California does not prohibit all forms of gambling. California itself operates a state lottery, and daily encourages its citizens to participate in this state-run gambling. California also permits parimutuel horse-race betting. Although certain enumerated gambling games are prohibited under Cal. Penal Code Ann. § 330 (West Supp. 1987), games not enumerated, including the card games played in the Cabazon card club, are permissible. The Tribes assert that more than 400 card rooms similar to the Cabazon card club flourish in California, and the State does not dispute this fact. Also, as the Court of Appeals noted, bingo is legally sponsored by many different organizations and is widely played in California. There is no effort to forbid the playing of bingo by any member of the public over the age of 18. Indeed, the permitted bingo games must be open to the general public. Nor is there any limit on the number of games which eligible organizations may operate, the receipts which they may obtain from the games, the number of games which a participant may play, or the amount of money which a participant may spend, either per game or in total. In light of the fact that California permits a substantial amount of gambling activity, including bingo, and actually promotes gambling through its state lottery, we must conclude that California regulates rather than prohibits gambling in general and bingo in particular.[10]

California argues, however, that high stakes, *unregulated* bingo, the conduct which attracts organized crime, is a misdemeanor in California and may be prohibited on Indian reservations. But that an otherwise regulatory law is enforceable by criminal as well as civil means does not necessarily convert it into a criminal law within the meaning of Pub. L. 280. Otherwise, the distinction between § 2 and § 4 of that law could easily be avoided and total assimilation permitted. This view, adopted here and by the Fifth Circuit in the *Butterworth* case, we find persuasive. Accordingly, we conclude that Pub. L. 280 does not authorize California to enforce Cal. Penal Code Ann. § 326.5 (West Supp. 1987) within the Cabazon and Morongo Reservations.

California and Riverside County also argue that the Organized Crime Control Act (OCCA) authorizes the application of their gambling laws to the tribal bingo enterprises. The OCCA makes certain violations of state and local gambling laws violations of federal law. The Court of Appeals rejected appellants' argument, relying on its earlier decisions in *United States v. Farris*, 624 F.2d 890 (9th Cir. 1980), *cert. denied*, 449 U.S. 1111 (1981), and *Barona Group of the Capitan Grande Band of Mission Indians, San Diego County, Cal. v. Duffy*, 694 F.2d 1185 (9th Cir. 1982). 783 F.2d, at 903. The court explained that whether a tribal activity is "a violation of the law of a state" within the meaning of OCCA depends on whether it violates the "public policy" of the State, the same test for application of state law under Pub. L. 280, and similarly concluded that bingo is not contrary to the public policy of California.[13]

The Court of Appeals for the Sixth Circuit has rejected this view. *United States v. Dakota*, 796 F.2d 186 (1986).[14] Since the OCCA standard is simply whether the gambling business is being operated in "violation of the law of a State," there is no basis for the regulatory/prohibitory distinction that it agreed is suitable in construing and applying Pub. L. 280. 796 F.2d, at 188. And because enforcement of OCCA is an exercise of federal rather than state author-

---

[10] Nothing in this opinion suggests that cockfighting, tattoo parlors, nude dancing, and prostitution are permissible on Indian reservations within California. [S]tate laws governing an activity must be examined in detail before they can be characterized as regulatory or prohibitory....

[13] In *Farris*, in contrast, the court had concluded that a gambling business, featuring blackjack, poker, and dice, operated by tribal members on the Puyallup Reservation violated the public policy of Washington; the United States, therefore, could enforce OCCA against the Indians.

[14] In *Dakota*, the United States sought a declaratory judgment that a gambling business, also featuring the playing of blackjack, poker, and dice, operated by two members of the Keweenaw Bay Indian Community on land controlled by the community, and under a license issued by the community, violated OCCA. The Court of Appeals held that the gambling business violated Michigan law and OCCA.

ity, there is no danger of state encroachment on Indian tribal sovereignty. *Ibid.* This latter observation exposes the flaw in appellants' reliance on OCCA. That enactment is indeed a federal law that, among other things, defines certain federal crimes over which the district courts have exclusive jurisdiction. There is nothing in OCCA indicating that the States are to have any part in enforcing federal crimes or are authorized to make arrests on Indian reservations that in the absence of OCCA they could not effect. We are not informed of any federal efforts to employ OCCA to prosecute the playing of bingo on Indian reservations, although there are more than 100 such enterprises currently in operation, many of which have been in existence for several years, for the most part with the encouragement of the Federal Government.[16] Whether or not, then, the Sixth Circuit is right and the Ninth Circuit wrong about the coverage of OCCA, a matter that we do not decide, there is no warrant for California to make arrests on reservations and thus, through OCCA, enforce its gambling laws against Indian tribes.

II

Because the state and county laws at issue here are imposed directly on the Tribes that operate the games, and are not expressly permitted by Congress, the Tribes argue that the judgment below should be affirmed without more. They rely on the statement in *McClanahan v. Arizona State Tax Comm'n*, 411 U.S. 164, 170-171 (1973), that "'(s)tate laws generally are not applicable to tribal Indians on an Indian reservation except where Congress has expressly provided that State laws shall apply'" (quoting U.S. Dept. of the Interior, Federal Indian Law 845 (1958)). Our cases, however, have not established an inflexible per se rule precluding state jurisdiction over tribes and tribal members in the absence of express congressional consent. "(U)nder certain circumstances a State may validly assert authority over the activities of nonmembers on a reservation, and … in exceptional circumstances a State may assert jurisdiction over the on-reservation activities of tribal members." *New Mexico v. Mescalero Apache Tribe*, 462 U.S. 324, 331-332 (1983) (footnotes omitted). Both *Moe v. Confederated Salish and Kootenai Tribes*, 425 U.S. 463 (1976), and *Washington v. Confederated Tribes of the Colville Indian Reservation*, 447 U.S. 134 (1980), are illustrative. In those decisions we held that, in the absence of express congressional permission, a State could require tribal smokeshops on Indian reservations to collect state sales tax from their non-Indian customers. Both cases involved nonmembers entering and purchasing tobacco products on the reservations involved. The State's interest in assuring the collection of sales taxes from non-Indians enjoying the off-reservation services of the State was sufficient to warrant the minimal burden imposed on the tribal smokeshop operators.

---

[16]See S. Rep. No. 99-493, p. 2 (1986). Federal law enforcement officers have the capability to respond to violations of OCCA on Indian reservations, as is apparent from *Farris* and *Dakota*. This is not a situation where the unavailability of a federal officer at a particular moment would likely result in nonenforcement. OCCA is directed at large scale gambling enterprises. If state officers discover a gambling business unknown to federal authorities while performing their duties authorized by Pub. L. 280, there should be ample time for them to inform federal authorities, who would then determine whether investigation or other enforcement action was appropriate. A federal police officer is assigned by the Department of the Interior to patrol the Indian reservations in southern California. App. to Brief for Appellees 1d-7d.

This case also involves a state burden on tribal Indians in the context of their dealings with non-Indians since the question is whether the State may prevent the Tribes from making available high stakes bingo games to non-Indians coming from outside the reservations. Decision in this case turns on whether state authority is pre-empted by the operation of federal law; and "[s]tate jurisdiction is pre-empted ... if it interferes or is incompatible with federal and tribal interests reflected in federal law, unless the state interests at stake are sufficient to justify the assertion of state authority." *Mescalero*, 462 U.S., at 333, 334. The inquiry is to proceed in light of traditional notions of Indian sovereignty and the congressional goal of Indian self-government, including its "overriding goal" of encouraging tribal self-sufficiency and economic development.

These are important federal interests. They were reaffirmed by the President's 1983 Statement on Indian Policy. More specifically, the Department of the Interior, which has the primary responsibility for carrying out the Federal Government's trust obligations to Indian tribes, has sought to implement these policies by promoting tribal bingo enterprises. Under the Indian Financing Act of 1974, 25 U.S.C. § 1451 et seq. (1982 ed. and Supp. III), the Secretary of the Interior has made grants and has guaranteed loans for the purpose of constructing bingo facilities. See S. Rep. No. 99-493, p. 5 (1986); *Mashantucket Pequot Tribe v. McGuigan*, 626 F. Supp. 245, 246 (Conn. 1986). The Department of Housing and Urban Development and the Department of Health and Human Services have also provided financial assistance to develop tribal gaming enterprises. See S. Rep. No. 99-493, *supra*, at 5. Here, the Secretary of the Interior has approved tribal ordinances establishing and regulating the gaming activities involved. See H.R. Rep. No. 99-488, p. 10 (1986). The Secretary has also exercised his authority to review tribal bingo management contracts under 25 U.S.C. § 81, and has issued detailed guidelines governing that review. App. to Motion to Dismiss Appeal or Affirm Judgment, 63a-70a.

These policies and actions, which demonstrate the Government's approval and active promotion of tribal bingo enterprises, are of particular relevance in this case. The Cabazon and Morongo Reservations contain no natural resources which can be exploited. The tribal games at present provide the sole source of revenues for the operation of the tribal governments and the provision of tribal services. They are also the major sources of employment on the reservations. Self-determination and economic development are not within reach if the Tribes cannot raise revenues and provide employment for their members. The Tribes' interests obviously parallel the federal interests. California seeks to diminish the weight of these seemingly important tribal interests by asserting that the Tribes are merely marketing an exemption from state gambling laws. In *Washington v. Confederated Tribes of the Colville Indian Reservation*, 447 U.S., at 155, we held that the State could tax cigarettes sold by tribal smokeshops to non-Indians, even though it would eliminate their competitive advantage and substantially reduce revenues used to provide tribal services, because the Tribes had no right "to market an exemption from state taxation to persons who would normally do their business elsewhere." We stated that "(i)t is painfully apparent that the value marketed by the smokeshops to persons coming from outside is not generated on the reservations by activities in which the Tribes have a significant interest." *Ibid*. Here, however, the Tribes are not merely importing a product onto the reservations for immediate resale to non-Indians. They have built modern facilities which provide recreational opportunities and ancillary services to their patrons, who do not simply drive onto the reservations, make purchases and depart, but spend extended periods of time there enjoying the services the Tribes provide. The Tribes have strong incentive to provide comfortable, clean and attractive facilities and well-run games in order to increase attendance at the games.[23] The tribal bingo enterprises are similar to the resort complex, featuring hunting and fishing, that the Mescalero Apache Tribe operates on its reservation through the "concerted and sustained" management of reservation land and wildlife resources. *New Mexico v. Mescalero Apache Tribe*, 462 U.S., at 341. The Mescalero project generates funds for essential tribal services and provides employment for tribal members. We there rejected the notion that the tribe is merely marketing an exemption from state hunting and fishing regulations and concluded that New Mexico could not regulate on-reservation fishing and hunting by non-Indians. *Ibid.* Similarly, the Cabazon and Morongo Bands are generating value on the reservations through activities in which they have a substantial interest....

The sole interest asserted by the State to justify the imposition of its bingo laws on the Tribes is in preventing the infiltration of the tribal games by organized crime. To the extent that the State seeks to prevent any and all bingo games from being played on tribal lands while permitting regulated, off-reservation games, this asserted interest is irrelevant and the state and county laws are pre-empted. See n.3, *supra*. Even to the extent that the State and county seek to regulate short of prohibition, the laws are pre-empted. The State insists that the high stakes offered at tribal games are attractive to organized crime, whereas the controlled games authorized under California law are not. This is surely a legitimate concern, but we are unconvinced that it is sufficient to escape the pre-emptive force of federal and tribal interests apparent in this case. California does not allege any present criminal involvement in the Cabazon and Morongo enterprises [and] the prevailing federal policy continues to support these tribal enterprises, including those of the Tribes involved in this case.

We conclude that the State's interest in preventing the infiltration of the tribal bingo enterprises by organized crime does not justify state regulation of the tribal bingo enterprises in light of the compelling federal and tribal interests supporting them. State regulation would impermissibly infringe on tribal government, and this conclusion applies equally to the county's attempted regulation of the Cabazon card club. We therefore affirm the judgment of the Court of Appeals and remand the case for further proceedings consistent with this opinion.

It is so ordered.

---

[23] An agent of the California Bureau of Investigation visited the Cabazon bingo parlor as part of an investigation of tribal bingo enterprises. The agent described the clientele as follows:

"In attendance for the Monday evening bingo session were about 300 players.... On row 5, on the front left side were a middle-aged latin couple, who were later joined by two young latin males. These men had to have the game explained to them. The middle table was shared with a senior citizen couple. The aisle table had 2 elderly women, 1 in a wheelchair, and a middle-aged woman.... A goodly portion of the crowd were retired age to senior citizens." App. 176.

We are unwilling to assume that these patrons would be indifferent to the services offered by the Tribes.

Justice STEVENS, with whom Justice O'CONNOR and Justice SCALIA join, dissenting.

Unless and until Congress exempts Indian-managed gambling from state law and subjects it to federal supervision, I believe that a State may enforce its laws prohibiting high-stakes gambling on Indian reservations within its borders. Congress has not pre-empted California's prohibition against high-stakes bingo games and the Secretary of the Interior plainly has no authority to do so. While gambling provides needed employment and income for Indian tribes, these benefits do not. in my opinion, justify tribal operation of currently unlawful commercial activities. Accepting the majority's reasoning would require exemptions for cock fighting, tattoo parlors, nude dancing, houses of prostitution, and other illegal but profitable enterprises. As the law now stands, I believe tribal entrepreneurs, like others who might derive profits from catering to non-Indian customers, must obey applicable state laws.

In my opinion the plain language of Pub. L. 280 authorizes California to enforce its prohibition against commercial gambling on Indian reservations....

NOTE ON INDIAN GAMING

As federal financing for Indian governmental programs diminished during the 1980's, Indian tribal governments sought new revenue with which to fund desperately needed governmental programs. For tribes without mineral or other significant resources or tax basis, gaming activities became a very important new source of revenue over the last decade. Until the Court's decision in *Cabazon*, however, the stability of this revenue source remained in doubt since exact parameters of Indian gaming activities often ultimately turned on court decisions. Beginning with the *Seminole Tribe* case cited in the *Cabazon* opinion, the federal courts generally sustained Indian bingo activities, although, as reflected in *United States v. Dakota*, 796 F.2d 186 (6th Cir. 1986), they were less sympathetic to other forms of Indian sponsored gambling. Like *Cabazon*, many of these cases turned on the scope of state jurisdiction over Indian sponsored gaming activities in Indian country. Separate from that question, there remained the question of whether the Assimilative Crimes Act, 18 U.S.C. § 13, and the Organized Crime Control Act, 18 U.S.C. § 1955, proscribed such activities by adopting state gaming laws as federal law applicable in Indian country. While *Cabazon* clearly resolved the issues of state jurisdiction, its holding on questions of the applicability of such federal statutes was less clear.

Indian gaming stirred considerable controversy, including fears of competition with other non-Indian gaming operations and state lotteries and expressed, but unproven, concerns about organized crime infiltration. Furthermore, the *Cabazon* case failed to fully resolve the legality of such gaming activities under the Federal Organized Crime Control Act, discussed in the case. As a result of such political controversy and the *Cabazon* decision, Congress in 1988 enacted the Indian Gaming Regulatory Act, Pub. L. No. 100-497, 100 Stat. 2467 (codified at 25 U.S.C. §§ 2701-2721). This very complex legislation divides gaming in Indian country into three classes. Class I gaming includes social games for prizes of minimal value or traditional forms of Indian gaming engaged in as part of Indian ceremonies and celebrations. Class II games include all forms of bingo (including bingo aided by electronic, computer, or other technological aids) for prizes and any card games played in conformity with state law. For this purpose, bingo includes any game in which the holder of a card covers numbers or designations when objects similarly numbered or designated are drawn or electronically determined, including pull-tabs, lotto, punch boards, tip jars, instant bingo, and other similar games "if played in the same location." Banking card games, such as blackjack or baccarat, and electronic representations of other games of chance or slot machines are explicitly excluded from class II games.

The legislation also contains a grandfather provision for certain nonconforming games that actually were operated in Michigan, the Dakotas, and Washington, prior to the effective date of legislation. Class III gaming includes all other forms of gaming. The legislation establishes a three-member National Indian Gaming Commission. The chairman is appointed by the President with the advice and consent of the Senate, while the other two members are appointed by the Secretary of the Interior. The Commission monitors, inspects, and otherwise oversees class II gaming sponsored by Indians in Indian country. Under the Act, class I gaming is exclusively within the jurisdiction of the tribal government, while class III gaming is legal only where legal under both state and tribal law and state-tribal compact authorized under the Act. For class II gaming, section 11(b) of the Act mandates tribal operation under a tribal ordinance meeting certain extensive, detailed licensing, revenue management, auditing, and contract requirements overseen by the National Indian Gaming Commission. Part of the licensing process involves background checks by the Commission on primary management officials and key employees to exclude "any person whose activities, criminal record, if any, or reputation, habits and associations pose a threat to the public interest or to the effective regulation of gaming, or create or enhance the dangers of unsuitable, unfair, or illegal practices or methods and activities in the conduct of gaming." The section also contains a nonconforming use provision for individual Indian-owned class II games operating on September 1, 1986 so long as not less than sixty percent of the net revenues of such games is income to the Indian tribe.

The Commission may issue a certificate of self-regulation to tribal games that have operated for three years, including at least one year after the effective date of the Act, in conformity with certain detailed management, accounting, and auditing requirements of the Act. Section 12 of the Act also requires approval of the chairman of the Commission for any management contract for a tribal gaming operation and provides standards for such approval; section 13 provides a procedure for review of existing management contracts and ordinances. Section 20 of the Act regulates and significantly limits gaming on lands acquired by a tribe after the effective date of the Act. For most tribes, such gaming may take place only if the lands are within or contiguous to the boundaries of the reservation on the date of the Act or if the tribe had no reservation at that time. Special provision is made for tribes of Oklahoma and others whose reservations were terminated, so long as the land acquired for gaming is within the boundaries of the tribe's former reservation. These limitations, however, do not apply where the Secretary determines after consultation with the tribe, officials of surrounding tribes, and state and local officials that permitting gaming on newly acquired land "would be in the best interest of the Indian tribe and its members, and would not be detrimental to the surrounding community, but only if the Governor of the State in which the gaming activity is to be conducted concurs in the Secretary's determination" or the land is part of the settlement of a land claim or part of the creation of a new reservation for a tribe or restoration of the tribe to federal supervision. The Act also adds the following provision to Title 18 of the United States Code:

§ 1166. Gambling in Indian country

(a) Subject to subsection (c), for purposes of Federal law, all State laws pertaining to the licensing, regulation, or prohibition of gambling, including but not limited to criminal sanctions applicable thereto, shall apply in Indian country in the same manner and to the same extent as such laws apply elsewhere in the State.

(b) Whoever in Indian country is guilty of any act or omission involving gambling, whether or not conducted or sanctioned by an Indian tribe, which, although not made punishable by any enactment of Congress, would be punishable if committed or omitted within the jurisdiction of the State in which the act or omission occurred, under the laws governing the licensing, regulation, or prohibition of gambling in force at the time of such act or omission, shall be guilty of a like offense and subject to a like punishment.

(c) For the purpose of this section, the term "gambling" does not include —

(1) class I gaming or class II gaming regulated by the Indian Gaming Regulatory Act, or

(2) class III gaming conducted under a Tribal-State compact approved by the Secretary of the Interior under section 11(d)(8) of the Indian Gaming Regulatory Act that is in effect.

(d) The United States shall have exclusive jurisdiction over criminal prosecutions of violations of State gambling laws that are made applicable under this section to Indian country, unless an Indian tribe pursuant to a Tribal-State compact approved by the Secretary of the Interior under section 11(d)(8) of the Indian Gaming Regulatory Act, or under any other provision of Federal law, has consented to the transfer to the State of criminal jurisdiction with respect to gambling on the lands of the Indian tribe.

§ 1167. Theft from gaming establishments on Indian lands

(a) Whoever abstracts, purloins, willfully misapplies, or takes and carries away with intent to steal, any money, funds, or other property of a value of $1,000 or less belonging to an establishment operated by or for or licensed by an Indian tribe pursuant to an ordinance or resolution approved by the National Indian Gaming Commission shall be fined not more than $100,000 or be imprisoned for not more than one year, or both.

(b) Whoever abstracts, purloins, willfully misapplies, or takes and carries away with intent to steal, any money, funds, or other property of a value in excess of $1,000 belonging to a gaming establishment operated by or for or licensed by an Indian tribe pursuant to an ordinance or resolution approved by the National Indian Gaming Commission shall be fined not more than $250,000, or imprisoned for not more than ten years, or both.

§ 1168. Theft by officers or employees of gaming establishments on Indian lands

(a) Whoever, being an officer, employee, or individual licensee of a gaming establishment operated by or for or licensed by an Indian tribe pursuant to an ordinance or resolution approved by the National Indian Gaming Commission, embezzles, abstracts, purloins, willfully misapplies, or takes and carries away with intent to steal, any moneys, funds, assets, or other property of such establishment of a value of $1,000 or less shall be fined not more than $250,000 and be imprisoned for not more than five years, or both;

(b) Whoever, being an officer, employee, or individual licensee of a gaming establishment operated by or for or licensed by an Indian tribe pursuant to an ordinance or
resolution approved by the National Indian Gaming Commission, embezzles, abstracts,
purloins, willfully misapplies, or takes and carries away with intent to steal, any
moneys, funds, assets, or other property of such establishment of a value in excess of
$1,000 shall be fined not more than $1,000,000 or imprisoned for not more than
twenty years, or both.

UNITED STATES v. WHEELER

435 U.S. 313 (1978)

Mr. Justice STEWART delivered the opinion of the Court.

The question presented in this case is whether the Double Jeopardy Clause of
the Fifth Amendment bars the prosecution of an Indian in a federal district
court under the Major Crimes Act, 18 U.S.C. § 1153, when he has previously
been convicted in a tribal court of a lesser included offense arising out of the
same incident.

I

On October 16, 1974, the respondent, a member of the Navajo Tribe, was
arrested by a tribal police officer at the Bureau of Indian Affairs High School in
Many Farms, Ariz., on the Navajo Indian Reservation. He was taken to the
tribal jail in Chinle, Ariz., and charged with disorderly conduct, in violation of
§ 17-351 of the Navajo Tribal Code. On October 18, two days after his arrest,
the respondent pleaded guilty to disorderly conduct and a further charge of
contributing to the delinquency of a minor, in violation of § 17-321 of the
Navajo Tribal Code. He was sentenced to 15 days in jail or a fine of $30 on the
first charge and to 60 days in jail (to be served concurrently with the other jail
term) or a fine of $120 on the second.

Over a year later, on November 19, 1975, an indictment charging the respondent with statutory rape was returned by a grand jury in the United States
District Court for the District of Arizona. The respondent moved to dismiss this
indictment, claiming that since the tribal offense of contributing to the delinquency of a minor was a lesser included offense of statutory rape, the proceedings that had taken place in the Tribal Court barred a subsequent federal
prosecution. See *Brown v. Ohio*, 432 U.S. 161. The District Court, rejecting the
prosecutor's argument that "there is not an identity of sovereignties between the
Navajo Tribal Courts and the courts of the United States," dismissed the indictment. The Court of Appeals for the Ninth Circuit affirmed the judgment of
dismissal, concluding that since "Indian tribal courts and United States district
courts are not arms of separate sovereigns," the Double Jeopardy Clause barred
the respondent's trial. We granted certiorari to resolve an intercircuit conflict.

II

In *Bartkus v. Illinois*, 359 U.S. 121, and *Abbate v. United States*, 359 U.S.
187, this Court reaffirmed the well-established principle that a federal prosecution does not bar a subsequent state prosecution of the same person for the
same acts, and a state prosecution does not bar a federal one. The basis for this
doctrine is that prosecutions under the laws of separate sovereigns do not, in

the language of the Fifth Amendment, "subject [the defendant] for the same offence to be twice put in jeopardy" ....

III

It is undisputed that Indian tribes have power to enforce their criminal laws against tribe members. Although physically within the territory of the United States and subject to ultimate federal control, they nonetheless remain "a separate people, with the power of regulating their internal and social relations." *United States v. Kagama,* [118 U.S. 375,] at 381-382; *Cherokee Nation v. Georgia,* 5 Pet. 1, 16. Their right of internal self-government includes the right to prescribe laws applicable to tribe members and to enforce those laws by criminal sanctions. [T]he controlling question in this case is the source of this power to punish tribal offenders: Is it a part of inherent tribal sovereignty, or an aspect of the sovereignty of the Federal Government which has been delegated to the tribes by Congress?

A

The powers of Indian tribes are, in general, *"inherent powers of a limited sovereignty which has never been extinguished."* F. Cohen, Handbook of Federal Indian Law 122 (1941) (emphasis in original). Before the coming of the Europeans, the tribes were self-governing sovereign political communities. See *McClanahan v. Arizona State Tax Comm'n,* 411 U.S. 164, 172. Like all sovereign bodies, they then had the inherent power to prescribe laws for their members and to punish infractions of those laws.

Indian tribes are, of course, no longer "possessed of the full attributes of sovereignty." *United States v. Kagama, supra,* at 381. Their incorporation within the territory of the United States, and their acceptance of its protection, necessarily divested them of some aspects of the sovereignty which they had previously exercised. By specific treaty provision they yielded up other sovereign powers; by statute, in the exercise of its plenary control, Congress has removed still others.

But our cases recognize that the Indian tribes have not given up their full sovereignty. We have recently said that "Indian tribes are unique aggregations possessing attributes of sovereignty over both their members and their territory.... [They] are a good deal more than 'private, voluntary organizations.'" *United States v. Mazurie,* 419 U.S. 544, 557; [*see also Cherokee Nation v. Georgia*]. The sovereignty that the Indian tribes retain is of a unique and limited character. It exists only at the sufferance of Congress and is subject to complete defeasance. But until Congress acts, the tribes retain their existing sovereign powers. In sum, Indian tribes still possess those aspects of sovereignty not withdrawn by treaty or statute, or by implication as a necessary result of their dependent status. See *Oliphant v. Suquamish Indian Tribe,* [435 U.S., at] 191.

B

It is evident that the sovereign power to punish tribal offenders has never been given up by the Navajo Tribe and that tribal exercise of that power today is therefore the continued exercise of retained tribal sovereignty. Although both of the treaties executed by the Tribe with the United States provided for punishment by the United States of Navajos who commit crimes against non-Indians, nothing in either of them deprived the Tribe of its *own* jurisdiction to charge, try and punish members of the Tribe for violations of tribal law. On the contrary, we have said that "[i]mplicit in these treaty terms ... was the understanding that the internal affairs of the Indians remained exclusively within the jurisdiction of whatever tribal government existed." *Williams v. Lee*, 358 U.S. 217, 221-222.

Similarly, statutes establishing federal criminal jurisdiction over crimes involving Indians have recognized an Indian tribe's jurisdiction over its members. The first Indian Trade and Intercourse Act, Act of July 22, 1790, § 5, 1 Stat. 138, provided only that the Federal Government would punish offenses committed *against* Indians by "any citizen or inhabitant of the United States"; it did not mention crimes committed *by* Indians. In 1817 federal criminal jurisdiction was extended to crimes committed within the Indian country by "any Indian, or other person or persons," but "any offense committed by one Indian against another, within any Indian boundary" was excluded. Act of March 3, 1817, ch. 92, 3 Stat. 383. In the Indian Trade and Intercourse Act of 1834, § 25, 4 Stat. 733, Congress enacted the direct progenitor of the General Crimes Act, now 18 U.S.C. § 1152, which makes federal enclave criminal law generally applicable to crimes in "Indian country." In this statute Congress carried forward the intra-Indian offense exception because "the tribes have exclusive jurisdiction" of such offenses and "we can [not] with any justice or propriety extend our laws to" them. H.R. Rep. No. 474, 23d Cong., 1st Sess., 13 (1834). And in 1854 Congress expressly recognized the jurisdiction of tribal courts when it added another exception to the General Crimes Act, providing that federal courts would not try an Indian "who has been punished by the local law of the Tribe." Act of March 27, 1854, § 3, 10 Stat. 270.[22] Thus, far from depriving Indian tribes of their sovereign power to punish offenses against tribal law by members of a tribe, Congress has repeatedly recognized that power and declined to disturb it.

Moreover, the sovereign power of a tribe to prosecute its members for tribal offenses clearly does not fall within that part of sovereignty which the Indians implicitly lost by virtue of their dependent status. The areas in which such implicit divestiture of sovereignty has been held to have occurred are those involving the relations between an Indian tribe and nonmembers of the tribe. Thus, Indian tribes can no longer freely alienate to non-Indians the land they occupy. *Oneida Indian Nation v. County of Oneida*, 414 U.S. 661, 667-668; *Johnson v. M'Intosh*, 8 Wheat. 543, 574. They cannot enter into direct commercial or governmental relations with foreign nations. *Worcester v. Georgia*, 6 Pet. 515, 559; *Cherokee Nation v. Georgia*, 5 Pet., at 17-18; *Fletcher v. Peck*, 6

---

[22] This statute is not applicable to the present case. The Major Crimes Act, under which the instant prosecution was brought, was enacted in 1885. Act of March 3, 1885, § 9, 23 Stat. 385. It does not contain any exception for Indians punished under tribal law. We need not decide whether this "carefully limited intrusion of federal power into the otherwise exclusive jurisdiction of the Indian tribes to punish Indians for crimes committed on Indian land," *United States v. Antelope*, 430 U.S. 641, 643 n.1, deprives a tribal court of jurisdiction over the enumerated offenses, since the crimes to which the respondent pleaded guilty in the Navajo Tribal Court are not among those enumerated in the Major Crimes Act. Cf. *Oliphant v. Suquamish Indian Tribe*, [435 U.S.,] at n.14.

Cranch 87, 147 (concurring opinion of Mr. Justice Johnson). And, as we have recently held, they cannot try nonmembers in tribal courts. *Oliphant v. Suquamish Indian Tribe,* [435 U.S., at] 191.

These limitations rest on the fact that the dependent status of Indian tribes within our territorial jurisdiction is necessarily inconsistent with their freedom independently to determine their external relations. But the powers of self-government, including the power to prescribe and enforce internal criminal laws, are of a different type. They involve only the relations among members of a tribe. Thus, they are not such powers as would necessarily be lost by virtue of a tribe's dependent status. "[T]he settled doctrine of the law of nations is, that a weaker power does not surrender its independence — its right to self government, by associating with a stronger, and taking its protection." *Worcester v. Georgia, supra,* at 560-561.

C

That the Navajo Tribe's power to punish offenses against tribal law committed by its members is an aspect of its retained sovereignty is further supported by the absence of any federal grant of such power. If Navajo self-government were merely the exercise of delegated federal sovereignty, such a delegation should logically appear somewhere. But no provision in the relevant treaties or statutes confers the right of self-government in general, or the power to punish crimes in particular, upon the Tribe.

It is true that in the exercise of the powers of self-government, as in all other matters, the Navajo Tribe, like all Indian tribes, remains subject to ultimate federal control. Thus, before the Navajo Tribal Council created the present Tribal Code and Tribal Courts,[25] the Bureau of Indian Affairs established a Code of Indian Tribal Offenses and a Court of Indian Offenses for the reservation. See 25 CFR Part 11 (1977); cf. 25 U.S.C. § 1311.[26] Pursuant to federal regulations, the present Tribal Code was approved by the Secretary of the Interior before becoming effective. See 25 CFR § 11.1 (e) (1977). Moreover, the Indian Reorganization Act of 1934, § 16, 48 Stat. 987, 25 U.S.C § 476, and the Act of April 19, 1950, § 6, 64 Stat. 46, 25 U.S.C. § 636, each authorized the Tribe to adopt a constitution for self-government. And the Indian Civil Rights Act of 1968, 82 Stat. 77, 25 U.S.C. § 1302, made most of the provisions of the Bill of Rights applicable to the Indian tribes and limited the punishment tribal courts could impose to imprisonment for six months, or a fine of $500, or both.

But none of these laws *created* the Indians' power to govern themselves and their right to punish crimes committed by tribal offenders. Indeed, the Wheeler-Howard Act and the Navajo-Hopi Rehabilitation Act both recognized that Indian tribes already had such power under "existing law." See Powers of

[25] The Tribal Courts were established in 1958, and the law and order provisions of the Tribal Code in 1959, by resolution of the Navajo Tribal Council. See Titles 7 and 17 of the Navajo Tribal Code; *Oliver v. Udall,* 113 U.S. App. D.C. 212, 306 F.2d 819.

[26] Such Courts of Indian Offenses, or "CFR Courts," still exist on approximately 30 reservations "in which traditional agencies for the enforcement of tribal law and custom have broken down [and] no adequate substitute has been provided." 25 CFR § 11.1 (b) (1977). We need not decide today whether such a court is an arm of the Federal Government or, like the Navajo Tribal Court, derives its powers from the inherent sovereignty of the tribe.

Indian Tribes, 55 I.D. 14 (1934). That Congress has in certain ways regulated the manner and extent of the tribal power of self-government does not mean that Congress is the source of that power.

In sum, the power to punish offenses against tribal law committed by Tribe members, which was part of the Navajos' primeval sovereignty, has never been taken away from them, either explicitly or implicitly, and is attributable in no way to any delegation to them of federal authority. It follows that when the Navajo Tribe exercises this power, it does so as part of its retained sovereignty and not as an arm of the Federal Government.

D

The conclusion that an Indian tribe's power to punish tribal offenders is part of its own retained sovereignty is clearly reflected in a case decided by this Court more than 80 years ago, *Talton v. Mayes*, 163 U.S. 376. [Its relevance] to the present case is clear. The Court there held that when an Indian tribe criminally punishes a tribe member for violating tribal law, the tribe acts as an independent sovereign, and not as an arm of the Federal Government. Since tribal and federal prosecutions are brought by separate sovereigns, they are not "for the same offence," and the Double Jeopardy Clause thus does not bar one when the other has occurred.

IV

[T]ribal courts are important mechanisms for protecting significant tribal interests. Federal pre-emption of a tribe's jurisdiction to punish its members for infractions of tribal law would detract substantially from tribal self-government, just as federal pre-emption of state criminal jurisdiction would trench upon important state interests. Thus, just as in *Bartkus* and *Abbate*, there are persuasive reasons to reject the respondent's argument that we should arbitrarily ignore the settled "dual sovereignty" concept as it applies to successive tribal and federal prosecutions.

Accordingly, the judgment of the Court of Appeals is reversed, and the case is remanded for further proceedings consistent with this opinion.

NOTE

While the double jeopardy guarantee affords no constitutional protection against multiple trials and punishments in federal and tribal courts, 18 U.S.C. § 1152 does except from its coverage "any Indian committing any offense in the Indian country who has been punished by the local law of the tribe." This clause provides limited protection for Indians from multiple punishment by both tribal and federal courts. *United States v. La Plant*, 156 F. Supp. 660 (D. Mont. 1957). However, a prior acquittal in a tribal court will not preclude subsequent federal prosecution. It should be noted that 18 U.S.C. § 1153 contains no similar exception.

Chapter 3

TRIBAL GOVERNMENTAL AUTHORITY

The bulk of federal Indian law is devoted to protection of Indian tribal self-government and the Indian land-base upon which the exercise of tribal sovereignty is dependent. This chapter is devoted to the scope and operation of the sovereign powers of the Indian tribes. In reviewing these materials, consider the purpose of tribal self-government. Is the purpose only to preserve Indian cultures and religious traditions? If so, would the need for self-government lessen as a particular tribe becomes less unique? Or, are there other reasons to protect tribal sovereignty? Does the preservation of legal autonomy further goals other than preservation of existing separate traditions, such as the freedom of a group to determine its own political as well as social destiny? Are the various purposes for preserving tribal sovereignty furthered by the governmental structures established under federal Indian law and the scope of tribal powers? Is the system of tribal government recognized by the federal law consistent with Indian objectives and culture? What groups should tribal powers properly reach — Indians, enrolled members, members of the community, only those who have certain relationships with the tribe, or everyone within the boundaries of the reservation? Finally, do the restrictions on the reach of tribal authority render tribal self-governance unworkable in practice?

A. TRIBAL GOVERNMENTS IN THE UNITED STATES LEGAL SYSTEM

1. BASIC PRINCIPLES

TALTON v. MAYES

163 U.S. 376 (1896)

[Talton was indicted and convicted of murder in the tribal courts of the Cherokee Nation. Under then applicable Cherokee law, the grand jury which indicted Talton consisted of only five persons. Talton sought a writ of habeas corpus in federal district court and the judge refused to discharge the petitioner from custody. Talton appealed to the Supreme Court.]

Mr. Justice WHITE delivered the opinion of the court.

Appellant and the person he was charged with having murdered were both Cherokee Indians, and the crime was committed within the Cherokee territory.

To bring himself within the statute, the appellant asserts, 1st, that the grand jury, consisting only of five persons, was not a grand jury within the contemplation of the Fifth Amendment to the Constitution, which it is asserted is operative upon the Cherokee nation in the exercise of its legislative authority as to purely local matters; 2d, that the indictment by a grand jury thus constituted was not due process of law within the intendment of the Fourteenth Amendment. [We must consider] the relation of the Cherokee nation to the United States, and of the operation of the constitutional provisions relied on upon the purely local legislation of that nation.

By treaties and statutes of the United States the right of the Cherokee nation to exist as an autonomous body, subject always to the paramount authority of the United States, has been recognized. And from this fact there has consequently been conceded to exist in that nation power to make laws defining offences and providing for the trial and punishment of those who violate them when the offences are committed by one member of the tribe against another one of its members within the territory of the nation.

Thus, by the fifth article of the treaty of 1835, 7 Stat. 478, 481, it is provided:

> The United States hereby covenant and agree that the lands ceded to the Cherokee nation in the foregoing article shall, in no future time without their consent, be included within the territorial limits or jurisdiction of any State or Territory. But they shall secure to the Cherokee nation the right by their national councils to make and carry into effect all such laws as they may deem necessary for the government and protection of the persons and property within their own country belonging to their people or such persons as have connected themselves with them: Provided always that they shall not be inconsistent with the Constitution of the United States and such acts of Congress as have been or may be passed regulating trade and intercourse with the Indians; and also, that they shall not be considered as extending to such citizens and army of the United States as may travel or reside in the Indian country by permission according to the laws and regulations established by the government of the same.

This guarantee of self government was reaffirmed in the treaty of 1868, 14 Stat. 799, 803, the thirteenth article of which reads as follows:

> Article XIII. The Cherokees also agree that a court or courts may be established by the United States in said territory, with such jurisdiction and organized in such manner as may be prescribed by law: *Provided,* That the judicial tribunals of the nation shall be allowed to retain exclusive jurisdiction in all civil and criminal cases arising within their country in which members of the nation, by nativity or adoption, shall be the only parties, or where the cause of action shall arise in the Cherokee nation, except as otherwise provided in this treaty.

[The crime of murder of one Cherokee Indian by another] within the jurisdiction of the Cherokee nation is, therefore, clearly not an offence against the United States, but an offence against the local laws of the Cherokee nation. Necessarily, the statutes of the United States which provide for an indictment by a grand jury, and the number of persons who shall constitute such a body, have no application, for such statutes relate only, if not otherwise specially provided, to grand juries empanelled for the courts of and under the laws of the United States.

The question, therefore, is, does the Fifth Amendment to the Constitution apply to the local legislation of the Cherokee nation so as to require all prosecutions for offences committed against the laws of that nation to be initiated by a grand jury organized in accordance with the provisions of that amendment. The solution of this question involves an inquiry as to the nature and origin of the power of local government exercised by the Cherokee nation and recognized to exist in it by the treaties and statutes above referred to. Since the case of *Barron v. Baltimore,* 7 Pet. 243, it has been settled that the Fifth Amendment to the Constitution of the United States is a limitation only upon the powers of the

General Government, that is, that the amendment operates solely on the Constitution itself by qualifying the powers of the National Government which the Constitution called into being.

[The answer] depends upon whether the powers of local government exercised by the Cherokee nation are Federal powers created by and springing from the Constitution of the United States, and hence controlled by the Fifth Amendment to that Constitution, or whether they are local powers not created by the Constitution, although subject to its general provisions and the paramount authority of Congress. The repeated adjudications of this court have long since answered the former question in the negative. [*E.g., The Cherokee Cases.*]

True it is that in many adjudications of this court the fact has been fully recognized, that although possessed of these attributes of local self government, when exercising their tribal functions, all such rights are subject to the supreme legislative authority of the United States. *Cherokee Nation v. Kansas Railway Co.,* 135 U.S. 641, where the cases are fully reviewed. But the existence of the right in Congress to regulate the manner in which the local powers of the Cherokee nation shall be exercised does not render such local powers Federal powers arising from and created by the Constitution of the United States. It follows that as the powers of local self government enjoyed by the Cherokee nation existed prior to the Constitution, they are not operated upon by the Fifth Amendment, which, as we have said, had for its sole object to control the powers conferred by the Constitution on the National Government. The fact that the Indian tribes are subject to the dominant authority of Congress, and that their powers of local self government are also operated upon and restrained by the general provisions of the Constitution of the United States, completely answers the argument of inconvenience which was pressed in the discussion at bar. The claim that the finding of an indictment by a grand jury of less than thirteen violates the due process clause of the Fourteenth Amendment is conclusively answered by *Hurtado v. California,* 110 U.S. 516, and *McNulty v. California,* 149 U.S. 645. [T]he determination of what was the existing law of the Cherokee nation as to the constitution of the grand jury, were solely matters within the jurisdiction of the courts of that nation, and the decision of such a question in itself necessarily involves no infraction of the Constitution of the United States. [*Affirmed.*]

Mr. Justice HARLAN dissented.

UNITED STATES v. MAZURIE

419 U.S. 544 (1975)

[The defendants were convicted under 18 U.S.C. § 1154 for introducing alcoholic beverages into Indian country. Under 18 U.S.C. § 1161 the proscriptions of § 1154 do not apply to any act or transaction in conformity with the laws of the state "and with an ordinance duly adopted by the tribe having jurisdiction over such area of Indian country, certified by the Secretary of the Interior, and published in the Federal Register."

[The Mazuries owned and operated the Blue Bull bar on fee patent land within the Wind River Reservation in Wyoming that had passed out of Indian trust title as a result of the allotment policy. Until 1971 the tribe had authorized any liquor sale made on the reservation in accordance with state law and the Mazuries had operated the Blue Bull under state license. In 1971 the Wind River Tribes adopted a new tribal ordinance requiring both tribal and state licenses for retail liquor outlets within the reservation. The Mazuries applied for and were denied a tribal liquor license but nevertheless continued to operate the Blue Bull. The tribe had denied the license after hearing the testimony of witnesses who complained of singing and shooting at late hours, disturbances of elderly residents of a nearby housing development, and unauthorized entry of Indian minors into the bar.]

Mr. Justice REHNQUIST delivered the opinion of the Court.

III

The Court of Appeals expressed doubt that "the Government has the power to regulate a business on the land it granted in fee without restrictions." 487 F.2d, at 18. Because that Court went on to hold that even if Congress did possess such power, it could not be delegated to an Indian tribe, that Court did not find it necessary to resolve the issue of congressional power. We do, however, reach the issue, because we hereinafter conclude that federal authority was properly delegated to the Indian tribes. We conclude that federal authority is adequate, even though the lands were held in fee by non-Indians, and even though the persons regulated were non-Indians.

Article I, § 8, of the Constitution gives Congress power "[t]o regulate Commerce with foreign Nations, and among the several States, and with the Indian Tribes." This Court has repeatedly held that this clause affords Congress the power to prohibit or regulate the sale of alcoholic beverages to tribal Indians, wherever situated, and to prohibit or regulate the introduction of alcoholic beverages into Indian country. [*E.g.*,] *United States v. Holliday,* 3 Wall. 407, 417-418.

[N]either the Constitution nor our previous cases leave any room for doubt that Congress possesses the authority to regulate the distribution of alcoholic beverages by establishments such as the Blue Bull.

IV

The Court of Appeals said, however, that even if Congress possessed authority to regulate the Blue Bull, it could not delegate such authority to the Indian tribes. The court reasoned as follows:

> The tribal members are citizens of the United States. It is difficult to see how such an association of citizens could exercise any degree of governmental authority or sovereignty over other citizens who do not belong, and who cannot participate in any way in the tribal organization. The situation is in no way comparable to a city, county, or special district under state laws. There cannot be such a separate "nation" of United States citizens within the boundaries of the United States which has any authority, other than as landowners, over individuals who are excluded as members....
>
> The purported delegation of authority to the tribal officials contained in 18 U.S.C. § 1161 is therefore invalid. Congress cannot delegate its authority to a private, voluntary organization, which is obviously not a governmental agency, to regulate a business on privately owned lands, no matter where located. It is obvious that the authority of

Congress under the Constitution to regulate commerce with Indian Tribes is broad, but it cannot encompass the relationships here concerned. 487 F.2d, at 19.

This Court has recognized limits on the authority of Congress to delegate its legislative power. *Panama Refining Co. v. Ryan,* 293 U.S. 388 (1935). Those limitations are, however, less stringent in cases where the entity exercising the delegated authority itself possesses independent authority over the subject matter. *United States v. Curtiss-Wright Export Corp.,* 299 U.S. 304, 319-322 (1936). Thus it is an important aspect of this case that Indian tribes are unique aggregations possessing attributes of sovereignty over both their members and their territory, *Worcester v. Georgia,* 6 Pet. 515, 557 (1832); they are "a separate people" possessing "the power of regulating their internal and social relations...." [*Kagama;*] *McClanahan v. Arizona State Tax Comm'n,* 411 U.S. 164, 173 (1973).

Cases such as [*Worcester* and *Kagama*] surely establish the proposition that Indian tribes within "Indian country" are a good deal more than "private, voluntary organizations," and they thus undermine the rationale of the Court of Appeals' decision. These same cases, in addition make clear that when Congress delegated its authority to control the introduction of alcoholic beverages into Indian country, it did so to entities which possess a certain degree of independent authority over matters that affect the internal and social relations of tribal life. Clearly the distribution and use of intoxicants is just such a matter. We need not decide whether this independent authority is itself sufficient for the Tribes to impose Ordinance No. 26. It is necessary only to state that the independent tribal authority is quite sufficient to protect Congress' decision to vest in tribal councils this portion of its own authority "to regulate Commerce ... with the Indian tribes." Cf. [*Curtiss-Wright, supra*].

The fact that the Mazuries could not become members of the tribe, and therefore could not participate in the tribal government, does not alter our conclusion. This claim, that because respondents are non-Indians Congress could not subject them to the authority of the Tribal Council with respect to the sale of liquor,[12] is answered by this Court's opinion in *Williams v. Lee,* 358 U.S. 217 (1959). In holding that the authority of tribal courts could extend over non-Indians, insofar as concerned their transactions on a reservation with Indians, we stated:

> It is immaterial that respondent is not an Indian. He was on the Reservation and the transaction with an Indian took place there. [Citations omitted.] The cases in this Court have consistently guarded the authority of Indian governments over their reser-

---

[12] Respondents attempt to bolster this claim with the argument that "the basic rights and principles of equal protection and due process [are] currently not available to non-Indians within the tribal councils." Brief for Respondents 24. However, respondents make no claim that the tribal decision to deny them a license constituted a denial of equal protection or that it resulted from a hearing which lacked due process. Whether and to what extent the Fifth Amendment would be available to correct arbitrary or discriminatory tribal exercise of its delegated federal authority must therefore await decision in a case in which the issue is squarely presented and appropriately briefed. This observation is also applicable with regard to 25 U.S.C. § 1302(8), which provides that, "[n]o Indian tribe in exercising powers of self-government shall ... deny to any person within its jurisdiction the equal protection of its laws or deprive any person of liberty or property without due process of law." Quite apart from these potential sources of protection against arbitrary tribal action, such protection is to some extent assured by § 1161's requirement that delegated authority be exercised pursuant to a tribal ordinance which itself has been approved by the Secretary of the Interior.

vations. Congress recognized this authority in the Navajos in the Treaty of 1868, and has done so ever since. If this power is to be taken away from them, it is for Congress to do it. [*Lone Wolf v. Hitchcock.*]

For the foregoing reasons the judgment of the Court of Appeals must be reversed, and the convictions of respondents reinstated.
Reversed.

NOTES

1. The Source of Tribal Authority: One commentator has quoted the portion of *Talton* referring to the treaties and statutes recognizing Cherokee sovereignty as conclusively establishing that "[t]he Cherokees' right to self-government had its origin in federal treaties and statutes." Martone, *American Indian Tribal Self-Government in the Federal System: Inherent Right or Congressional License?*, 51 NOTRE DAME L. REV. 600, 624 (1976). How can this conclusion be correct in light of the Court's holding in *Talton*? If the federal government is the source of tribal authority, then tribal action would be governmental action and thus subject to the fifth amendment. If, on the other hand, tribal authority is not derived from the federal government, what is its source? If the answer is international law, why can tribes not make treaties with foreign nations or cede tribal land to foreign nations? Professor Stephen Young explains the legal position of Indian tribes this way:

> [T]he world of distinctly self-authenticating sources of power supervised by the federal courts is tripartite. The commonly accepted bilateral division between federal and state sovereignties is, in fact, only part of the legal galaxy in which we live. Indian tribes are also self-authenticating, because their will and integrity were created by and are sustained by no source other than their own internal beliefs and arrangements. Neither state nor federal governments ever put the breath of communal life into them. "Indian tribes 'within Indian country' are a good deal more than 'private, voluntary organizations ....'"

Young, *Indian Tribal Sovereignty and American Fiduciary Undertakings*, 8 WHITTIER L. REV. 825, 827 (1987) (quoting Mazurie, supra).*

2. Treaty Recognition of Inherent Tribal Authority: Many early treaties between the United States and Indian tribes did recognize inherent tribal authority to govern tribal members, and sometimes nonmembers. Several early treaties recognized the legal and political control of the Indians over their own territory. For example, article VI of the Treaty with the Wyandots, Delawares, Shawanoes, Ottawas, Chippewas, Putawatimes, Miamis, Eel-river, Weea's, Kickapoos, Piankashaws, and Kaskaskias, Aug. 3, 1795, 7 Stat. 49, 52 proclaimed:

> If any citizen of the United States, or any other white person or persons, shall presume to settle upon the lands now relinquished by the United States, such citizen or other person shall be out of the protection of the United States; and the Indian tribe, on whose land the settlement shall be made, may drive off the settler, or punish him in such manner as they shall think fit; and because such settlements made without the consent of the United States, will be injurious to them as well as to the Indians, the United States shall be at liberty to break them up, and remove and punish the settlers as they shall think proper, and so effect that protection of the Indian lands herein before stipulated.

---

*Copyright © 1987 Whittier Law Review and Stephen Young. Reprinted with permission of the copyright holders.

Similar language appears in many other treaties. *See, e.g.,* Treaty with the Shawnees, Jan. 31, 1786, art. VII, 7 Stat. 26, 27 (nonmembers "shall forfeit the protection of the United States and the [tribe] may punish [them] as they please"). Provisions for the exercise of tribal authority over non-Indians disappeared from the treaties negotiated in the nineteenth century. *See generally* Clinton, *Development of Criminal Jurisdiction Over Indian Lands: The Historical Perspective,* 17 ARIZ. L. REV. 951, 955 (1975). Nevertheless, various provisions appearing in the nineteenth-century treaties guarantee continuing tribal legal autonomy over tribal members. For example, article IV of the Treaty with Creeks and Seminoles, Aug. 7, 1856, 11 Stat. 699, 700 provided:

> [N]o State or Territory shall ever pass laws for the government of the Creek and Seminole tribes of Indians, and that no portion of either of the tracts of [their] country ... shall ever be embraced or included within, or annexed to, any Territory or State, nor shall either, or any part of either, ever be erected into a Territory without the full and free consent of the legislative authority of the tribe owning the same.

Treaties with the Choctaws, Chickasaws, Creeks, and Seminoles also expressly recognized the tribes' "unrestricted right of self-government, and full jurisdiction over persons and property, within their respective limits; excepting, however, all white persons, ... who are not by adoption or otherwise, members of either ... tribe." *E.g.,* Treaty with Creeks and Seminoles, Aug. 7, 1856, art. XV, 11 Stat. 699, 703-04.

3. Statutory Treatment of Tribes as States — The Indian Tribal Governmental Tax Act of 1982: The Indian Tribal Governmental Tax Status Act of 1982, Pub. L. No. 97-473 (codified as amended at 26 U.S.C. § 7871 and scattered sections of 26 U.S.C.), treats Indian tribes like states and local governments for certain federal tax purposes. The IRS has ruled that tribes are not taxable entities. Thus, tribal income, including commercial or business revenues of a tribe, is not subject to federal taxation. Before the 1982 Act, however, the IRS did tax interest paid on tribal governmental debt obligations but not on state governmental debt obligations. The IRS has justified such refusals to grant specific exemptions on a strict reading of the term "state" in the Revenue Code. By providing that "[a]n Indian tribal government shall be treated as a state" in interpreting the Revenue Code for certain purposes in which states are entitled to benefits and exemptions, the Tribal Tax Status Act was designed to provide cost efficient benefits under the Internal Revenue Code. One of the salutary effects of the Act is that tribes can now issue tax exempt debt obligations.

The law does not put tribes on an equal footing with states in all respects under the Tax Code, however. For example, tribes may only issue tax-free bonds to raise money for "essential governmental function[s]." 26 U.S.C. § 7871(c)(1). For a comprehensive contemporary analysis of the legislative history and the effect of the law on economic development, see Williams, *Small Steps on the Long Road to Self-Sufficiency for Indian Nations: The Indian Tribal Governmental Tax Status Act of 1982,* 22 HARV. J. LEGIS. 335 (1985). For an analysis of the effect of the Tax Reform Act of 1986 on the Tribal Tax Status Act, see Note, *The Tribal Tax Status Act and the Tax Reform Act of 1986 — Current Effect on Indian Tribal Economic Development,* 32 S. DAK. L. REV. 602 (1987).

4. Tribal Governments and Individual Liberties: Most limitations on the exercise of governmental power contained in the United States Constitution, such as the Bill of Rights, apply only to actions of federal or state governments. *Barron v. Baltimore,* 32 U.S. (7 Pet.) 243 (1833); *Civil Rights Cases,* 109 U.S. 3 (1883). Indian tribal governments derive their authority from neither federal nor state sources. Thus, since *Talton,* courts have held that tribal government action is not subject to these constitutional guarantees or to federal civil rights laws designed to enforce them. For instance, in *Native American Church v. Navajo Tribal Council,* 272 F.2d 131, 134-35 (10th Cir. 1959), the Tenth Circuit held that the first amendment's religious guarantees did not apply to the Navajo tribal government's proscription on the sale, use, or possession of peyote. The court said:

> [Indian tribes] have a status higher than that of states. They are subordinate and dependent nations possessed of all powers as such only to the extent that they have expressly been required to surrender them by the superior sovereign, the United States.... No provision in the Constitution makes the First Amendment applicable to Indian nations nor is there any law of Congress doing so.

See also Barona Group of Capitan Grande Band of Mission Indians v. American Mgt. & Amusement, Inc., 840 F.2d 1394 (9th Cir. 1987) (voiding of bingo management contract not reviewable under just compensation clause); *Barta v. Oglala Sioux Tribe,* 259 F.2d 553 (8th Cir. 1958), *cert. denied,* 358 U.S. 932 (1959) (tribal tax applied to non-Indian lessees of tribal land not reviewable under 5th or 14th amendments); *Seneca Constitutional Rights Org. v. George,* 348 F. Supp. 51 (W.D.N.Y. 1972) (tribal exercise of regulatory powers not state action as required by 42 U.S.C. § 1983 because tribe not an instrumentality of the state); *Glover v. United States,* 219 F. Supp. 19 (D.Mont. 1963) (tribal court proceedings not reviewable under due process clause) (collecting cases).

Of course, constitutional constraints of general nationwide application (i.e., not limited solely to federal or state action), such as the thirteenth amendment's proscription of slavery, apply fully to Indian tribes. *United States v. Choctaw Nation,* 38 Ct. Cl. 558 (1903), *aff'd,* 193 U.S. 115 (1904); *In re Sah Quah,* 31 F. 327 (D. Alaska 1886). Civil Rights statutes based on such provisions have also been applied to Indian tribes. *See Evans v. McKay,* 869 F.2d 1341 (9th Cir. 1989) (allegations of overt acts and racial remarks by members of the Blackfeet Tribe acting in their official capacities sufficient to withstand motion to dismiss claim based on 42 U.S.C. § 1981).

5. Federal and Tribal Action Intertwined as Governmental Action: Frequently, the federal government is intimately intertwined with tribal affairs. Thus, difficult questions sometimes arise as to whether the action under attack on constitutional grounds is tribal or federal. The problem is particularly acute for Courts of Indian Offenses. Established during the late nineteenth century drive to assimilate Indians, these courts were designed to break down traditional tribal structures by counterpoising an Anglo-American modeled judicial system that could in turn create a new, progressive power structure. *See generally* W. HAGAN, INDIAN POLICE AND JUDGES 104-25 (1966). CFR courts, so called because they are governed by federal regulations set forth at 25 C.F.R. pt. 11, continue to exist on approximately 20 reservations. Under these regulations the Commissioner of Indian Affairs appoints tribal judges, who must be tribal members, subject to confirmation by a two-thirds vote of the tribal council. 25 C.F.R. § 11.3(b). A tribe may replace its CFR court. Under section 11.1(d), a tribe may at any time adopt a law and order code and establish a tribal court pursuant to its constitution and bylaws. Thus, the Courts of Indian Offenses operate in Indian country largely at the sufferance of the tribes. In light of this structure, are such courts arms of the federal government or of the tribes? In *Colliflower v. Garland,* 342 F.2d 369 (9th Cir. 1965), the court of appeals held that the Court of Indian Offenses for the Fort Belknap Reservation was an arm of the federal government and subject to fifth amendment due process requirements, including the right to counsel, confrontation, fair hearing, and sufficient cause.

In *Mazurie* the Court relied in part on Indian tribes' inherent sovereignty in sustaining a broad congressional delegation against a delegation doctrine attack. If a given tribal action is viewed as delegated, even in part, would this delegation necessarily convert tribal action into governmental action? For instance, under the Indian Self-Determination Act of 1975, 25 U.S.C. §§ 450-450n, the Secretary of the Interior and the Secretary of Health and Human Services are authorized to contract with Indian tribes to assume the control and management of certain federally funded programs previously operated under the aegis of the Bureau of Indian Affairs or the Indian Health Service. Many tribes have contracted with the BIA to operate former CFR courts with federal funds. When operating such programs, are the tribes subject directly to all constitutional restraints, including Bill of Rights guarantees? What implications does footnote 12 of the *Mazurie* opinion have for tribal operation of such federally funded programs?

6. Secretarial Approval as Governmental Action: Does the statutory requirement for Secretarial approval or the approval itself transform the tribal action under attack on constitutional grounds into federal action? In *Cheyenne River Sioux Tribe v. Andrus,* 566 F.2d 1085 (8th Cir. 1977), *cert. denied,* 439 U.S. 820 (1978), the Eighth Circuit invalidated a tribal constitutional requirement limiting the franchise to members over 21 years of age, as applied to elections held to amend the tribal constitution. The court relied on section 16 of the Indian Reorganization Act of 1934, 25 U.S.C. § 476, which authorizes the Secretary of the Interior to ratify and approve amendments to tribal constitutions and bylaws after ratification "by a majority vote of the adult members of the tribe." The court concluded that this language placed the Secretary "in a regulatory position over these processes" and such elections were "Secretarial elections" governed by the twenty-sixth amendment.

A broad reading of the Secretary of the Interior's approval power would transform all tribal actions subject to approval into federal action. The District of Columbia Circuit refused to give the approval power such a broad reading, however. In *Oliver v. Udall,* 306 F.2d 819 (D.C. Cir. 1962), *cert. denied,* 372 U.S. 908 (1963), the court held that the exercise of secretarial power in approving the Navajo tribal ordinances banning peyote was not federal action subject to first amendment attack because "[t]he Secretary had simply recognized the valid governing authority of the Tribal Council." *Id.* at 823. In contrast, the Tenth Circuit held that the fact of secretarial approval of and involvement in the leasing of Indian land was sufficient to constitute "major Federal action" within the meaning of § 102(2) of the National Environmental Protection Act, 42 U.S.C. § 4332(2), thereby requiring the preparation of an environmental impact study prior to the approval of the lease by the Bureau of Indian Affairs. *Davis v. Morton,* 469 F.2d 593 (10th Cir. 1972). In response to the argument that the Secretary was merely approving a lease negotiated by the tribe on land held in trust for the Indians, the court said:

> The fact Indian lands are held in trust does not take it out of NEPA's jurisdiction.... All public lands of the United States are held by it in trust for the people of the United States. To accept appellees' contention would preclude all federal lands from NEPA jurisdiction, something clearly not intended by Congress in passing the Act.

Id. at 597 (citations omitted). Can *Davis* be reconciled with *Oliver?*

7. Cohen's Synthesis of the Doctrine of Inherent Sovereignty: In the 1942 edition of the *Handbook of Federal Indian Law,* Felix S. Cohen advanced a synthesis of the existing law regarding tribal sovereignty. This synthesis distinguished between external sovereignty, the authority to deal with other nations in a government-to-government relationship, and internal sovereignty, the authority to deal with internal affairs. As to external sovereignty, he conceded that the United States had arrogated this power by assuming control over Indian affairs. Thus, Indian tribes had no authority to make treaties with foreign nations or sell their tribal land to anyone other than the United States government. As to internal sovereignty, on the other hand, Cohen argued that "[p]erhaps the most basic principle of all Indian law, supported by a host of decisions ... is the principal that *those powers which are lawfully vested in an Indian tribe are not, in general, delegated powers granted by express acts of Congress, but rather inherent powers of a limited sovereignty which has never been extinguished.*" (Emphasis in original.) Thus, under Cohen's vision a question of internal sovereignty must be analyzed by starting with the proposition that the tribe had the power, a proposition that could then only be controverted by a treaty or statute explicitly taking away tribal power to deal with a particular matter. As a result, "[w]hat is not expressly limited remains within the domain of tribal sovereignty." F. COHEN, HANDBOOK OF FEDERAL INDIAN LAW 122 (1942 ed.).

What remains of this theory after the following case?

OLIPHANT v. SUQUAMISH INDIAN TRIBE

435 U.S. 191 (1978)

Mr. Justice REHNQUIST delivered the opinion of the Court.

[As a result of] the 1855 Treaty of Point Elliott, 12 Stat. 927, the Suquamish Indian Tribe relinquished all rights that it might have had in the lands of the State of Washington and agreed to settle on a 7,276-acre reservation near Port Madison, Wash. Located on Puget Sound across from the city of Seattle, the Port Madison Reservation is a checkerboard of tribal community land, allotted Indian lands, property held in fee simple by non-Indians, and various roads and public highways maintained by Kitsap County.[1]

The Suquamish Indians are governed by a tribal government which in 1973 adopted a Law and Order Code. The Code, which covers a variety of offenses from theft to rape, purports to extend the Tribe's criminal jurisdiction over both Indians and non-Indians.[2] Proceedings are held in the Suquamish Indian

---

[1] According to the District Court's findings of fact, "the Port Madison Indian Reservation consists of approximately 7,276 acres of which approximately 63% thereof is owned in fee simple absolute by non-Indians and the remaining 37% is Indian-owned lands subject to the trust status of the United States, consisting mostly of unimproved acreage upon which no persons reside. Residing on the reservation is an estimated population of approximately 2,928 non-Indians living in 976 dwelling units. There lives on the reservation approximately 50 members of the Suquamish Indian Tribe. Within the reservation are numerous public highways of the State of Washington, public schools, public utilities and other facilities in which neither the Suquamish Indian Tribe nor the United States has any ownership or interest."

The Suquamish Indian Tribe, unlike many other Indian tribes, did not consent to non-Indian homesteading of unallotted or "surplus" lands within their reservation pursuant to 25 U.S.C. § 348 and 43 U.S.C. §§ 1195-1197. Instead, the substantial non-Indian population on the Port Madison Reservation is primarily the result of the sale of Indian allotments to non-Indians by the Secretary of the Interior [and] of the lifting of various trust restrictions which has enabled individual Indians to sell their allotments. See 25 U.S.C. §§ 349, 392.

[2] Notices were placed in prominent places at the entrances to the Port Madison Reservation informing the public that entry onto the reservation would be deemed implied consent to the criminal jurisdiction of the Suquamish tribal court.

Provisional Court. Pursuant to the Indian Civil Rights Act of 1968, 25 U.S.C. § 1302, defendants are entitled to many of the due process protections accorded to defendants in federal or state criminal proceedings. However, the guarantees are not identical. Non-Indians, for example, are excluded from Suquamish tribal court juries.[4]

Both petitioners are non-Indian residents of the Port Madison Reservation. Petitioner Mark David Oliphant was arrested by tribal authorities during the Suquamish's annual Chief Seattle Days celebration and charged with assaulting a tribal officer and resisting arrest. After arraignment before the tribal court, Oliphant was released on his own recognizance. Petitioner Daniel B. Belgarde was arrested by tribal authorities after an alleged high-speed race along the Reservation highways that only ended when Belgarde collided with a tribal police vehicle. Belgarde posted bail and was released. Six days later he was arraigned and charged under the tribal code with "recklessly endangering another person" and injuring tribal property. Tribal court proceedings against both petitioners have been stayed pending a decision in this case.

Both petitioners applied for a writ of habeas corpus to the United States District Court for the Western District of Washington [arguing] that the Suquamish Indian Provisional Court does not have criminal jurisdiction over non-Indians. [T]he District Court denied the petitions [and] the Court of Appeals for the Ninth Circuit affirmed the denial of habeas corpus in the case of petitioner Oliphant. We granted certiorari to decide whether Indian tribal courts have criminal jurisdiction over non-Indians. We decide that they do not.

I

Respondents do not contend that their exercise of criminal jurisdiction over non-Indians stems from affirmative congressional authorization or treaty provision.[6] Instead, respondents urge that such jurisdiction flows automatically from the "Tribe's retained inherent powers of government over the Port Madison

---

[4] The Indian Civil Rights Act of 1968 provides for "a trial by jury of not less than six persons," 25 U.S.C. § 1302(10), but the tribal court is not explicitly prohibited from excluding non-Indians from the jury even where a non-Indian is being tried. In 1977, the Suquamish Tribe amended its Law and Order Code to provide that only Suquamish tribal members shall serve as jurors in tribal court.

[6] Respondents do contend that Congress has "confirmed" the power of Indian tribes to try and punish non-Indians through the Indian Reorganization Act of 1934, 25 U.S.C. § 476, and the Indian Civil Rights Act of 1968, 25 U.S.C. § 1302. Neither Act, however, addresses, let alone "confirms," tribal criminal jurisdiction over non-Indians. The Indian Reorganization Act merely gives each Indian Tribe the right "to organize for its common welfare" and to "adopt an appropriate constitution and bylaws." With certain specific additions not relevant here, the tribal council is to have such powers as are vested "by existing law." The Indian Civil Rights Act merely extends to "any person" within the tribe's jurisdiction certain enumerated guarantees of the Bill of Rights of the Federal Constitution.

As respondents note, an earlier version of the Indian Civil Rights Act extended its guarantees only to "American Indians," rather than to "any person." The purpose of the later modification was to extend the Act's guarantees to "all persons who may be subject to the jurisdiction of tribal governments, whether Indians or non-Indians." Summary Report on the Constitutional Rights of American Indians, Subcomm. on Const. Rights of the Senate Judiciary Comm., 89th Cong., 2d Sess., at 10 (1966). But this change was certainly not intended to give Indian tribes criminal jurisdiction over non-Indians. Nor can it be read to "confirm" respondents' argument that Indian tribes have inherent criminal jurisdiction over non-Indians. Instead, the modification merely demonstrates Congress' desire to extend the Act's guarantees to non-Indians if and where they come under a tribe's criminal or civil jurisdiction by either treaty provision or act of Congress.

Indian Reservation." Seizing on language in our opinions describing Indian tribes as "quasi-sovereign entities," [*Morton v. Mancari*], the Court of Appeals agreed and held that Indian tribes, "though conquered and dependent, retain those powers of autonomous states that are neither inconsistent with their status nor expressly terminated by Congress." According to the Court of Appeals, criminal jurisdiction over anyone committing an offense on the reservation is a "sine qua non" of such powers.

The Suquamish Indian Tribe does not stand alone today in its assumption of criminal jurisdiction over non-Indians. Of the 127 reservation court systems that currently exercise criminal jurisdiction in the United States, 33 purport to extend that jurisdiction to non-Indians. Twelve other Indian tribes have enacted ordinances which would permit the assumption of criminal jurisdiction over non-Indians. Like the Suquamish these tribes claim authority to try non-Indians not on the basis of congressional statute or treaty provision but by reason of their retained national sovereignty.

The effort by Indian tribal courts to exercise criminal jurisdiction over non-Indians, however, is a relatively new phenomenon. And where the effort has been made in the past, it has been held that the jurisdiction did not exist. Until the middle of this century, few Indian tribes maintained any semblance of a formal court system. Offenses by one Indian against another were usually handled by social and religious pressure and not by formal judicial processes; emphasis was on restitution rather than on punishment. In 1834 the Commissioner of Indian Affairs described the then status of Indian criminal systems: "With the exception of two or three tribes, who have within a few years past attempted to establish some few laws and regulations amongst themselves, the Indian tribes are without laws, and the chiefs without much authority to exercise any restraint." H.R. Rep. No. 474, 23d Cong., 1st Sess., at 91 (1834).

It is therefore not surprising to find no specific discussion of the problem before us in the volumes of United States Reports. But the problem did not lie entirely dormant for two centuries. A few tribes during the 19th century did have formal criminal systems. From the earliest treaties with these tribes, it was apparently assumed that the tribes did not have criminal jurisdiction over non-Indians absent a congressional statute or treaty provision to that effect. For example, the 1830 Treaty with the Choctaw Indian Tribe, which had one of the most sophisticated of tribal structures, guaranteed to the Tribe "the jurisdiction and government of all the persons and property that may be within their limits." [7 Stat. 333, Art. IV] Despite the broad terms of this governmental guarantee, however, the Choctaws at the conclusion of this treaty provision "express *a wish* that Congress *may grant* to the Choctaws the right of punishing by their own laws any white man who shall come into their nation, and infringe any of their national regulations."[8] Such a request for affirmative congressio-

---

[8] The history of Indian treaties in the United States is consistent with the principle that Indian tribes may not assume criminal jurisdiction over non-Indians without the permission of Congress. The earliest treaties typically expressly provided that "any citizen of the United States, who shall do an injury to any Indian of the [tribal] nation, or to any other Indian or Indians residing in their towns, and under their protection, shall be punished according to the laws of the United States." *See, e.g.,* Treaty with the Shawnees, Art. III, 7 Stat. 26 (1786). While, as elaborated further below, these provisions were not necessary to remove criminal jurisdiction over non-Indians from the Indian tribes, they would naturally have served an important function in the developing stage of

nal authority is inconsistent with respondents' belief that criminal jurisdiction over non-Indians is inherent in tribal sovereignty. Faced by attempts of the Choctaw Tribe to try non-Indian offenders in the early-1800's, the United States Attorneys General also concluded that the Choctaws did not have criminal jurisdiction over non-Indians absent congressional authority. *See* 2 Opinions of the Attorney General 693 (1834); 7 Opinions of the Attorney General 174 (1855). According to the Attorney General in 1834, tribal criminal jurisdiction over non-Indians is *inter alia* inconsistent with treaty provisions recognizing the sovereignty of the United States over the territory assigned to the Indian nation and the dependence of the Indians on the United States.

At least one court has previously considered the power of Indian courts to try non-Indians and it also held against jurisdiction. In *Ex parte Kenyon,* 14 Fed. Cas. 7,720, p. 353 (W.D. Ark. 1878), Judge Isaac C. Parker, who as District Court Judge for the Western District of Arkansas was constantly exposed to the legal relationships between Indians and non-Indians, held that to give an Indian tribal court "jurisdiction of the person of an offender, such offender must be an Indian." *Id.,* at 355. The conclusion of Judge Parker was reaffirmed only recently in a 1970 Opinion of the Solicitor of the Department of the Interior. *See* 77 I.D. 113 (1970).[11]

While Congress was concerned almost from its beginning with the special problems of law enforcement on the Indian reservations, it did not initially address itself to the problem of tribal jurisdiction over non-Indians. For the reasons previously stated, there was little reason to be concerned with assertions of tribal court jurisdiction over non-Indians because of the absence of formal tribal judicial systems. Instead, Congress' concern was with providing effective protection for the Indians "from the violence of the lawless part of our frontier inhabitants." Seventh Annual Address of President George Washington, I Mes-

---

United States-Indian relations by clarifying jurisdictional limits of the Indian tribes. The same treaties generally provided that "[i]f any citizen of the United States ... shall attempt to settle on any of the lands hereby allotted to the Indians to live and hunt on, such person shall forfeit the protection of the United States of America, and the Indians may punish him or not as they please." *See, e.g.,* Treaty with the Choctaws, Art. IV, 7 Stat. 21 (1786). Far from representing a recognition of any inherent Indian criminal jurisdiction over non-Indians settling on tribal lands, these provisions were instead intended as a means of discouraging non-Indian settlements on Indian territory, in contravention of treaty provisions to the contrary. *See* 5 Annals of Congress 903-904 (April 9, 1796). Later treaties dropped this provision and provided instead that non-Indian settlers would be removed by the United States upon complaint being lodged by the tribe. *See, e.g.,* Treaty with the Sacs and Foxes, 7 Stat. 84 (1804).

As the relationship between Indian tribes and the United States developed through the passage of time, specific provisions for the punishment of non-Indians by the United States, rather than by the tribes, slowly disappeared from the treaties....

Only one treaty signed by the United States has ever provided for any form of tribal criminal jurisdiction over non-Indians (other than in the illegal settler context noted above). The first treaty signed by the United States with an Indian tribe, the 1778 Treaty with the Delawares, provided that neither party to the treaty could "proceed to the infliction of punishments on the citizens of the other, otherwise than by securing the offender or offenders by imprisonment, or any other competent means, till a fair and impartial trial can be had by judges or juries *of both parties,* as near as can be to the laws, customs and usages of the contracting parties and natural justice: *The mode of such trials to be hereafter fixed by the wise men of the United States in Congress assembled,* with the assistance of ... deputies of the Delaware nation ... ." Treaty with the Delawares, Art. IV, 7 Stat. 14 (1778) (emphasis added). While providing for Delaware participation in the trial of non-Indians, this treaty section established that non-Indians could only be tried under the auspices of the United States and in a manner fixed by the Continental Congress.

[11]The 1970 Opinion of the Solicitor was withdrawn in 1974 but has not been replaced. No reason was given for the withdrawal.

sages and Papers of the Presidents, 1789-1897, at 181, 185 (1897, J. Richardson, ed.). Without such protection, it was felt that "all the exertions of the Government to prevent destructive retaliations by the Indians will prove fruitless and all our present agreeable prospects illusory." *Ibid.* Beginning with the Trade and Intercourse Act of 1790, 1 Stat. 137, therefore, Congress assumed federal jurisdiction over offenses by non-Indians against Indians which "would be punishable by the laws of [the] state or district ... if the offense had been committed against a citizen or white inhabitant thereof." In 1817, Congress went one step further and extended federal enclave law to the Indian country; the only exception was for "any offense committed by one Indian against another." 3 Stat. 383, as amended, 18 U.S.C. § 1152.

It was in 1834 that Congress was first directly faced with the prospect of Indians trying non-Indians. In the Western Territory Bill, Congress proposed to create an Indian territory beyond the western-directed destination of the settlers; the territory was to be governed by a confederation of Indian tribes and was expected ultimately to become a State of the Union. While the Bill would have created a political territory with broad governing powers, Congress was careful not to give the tribes of the territory criminal jurisdiction over United States officials and citizens traveling through the area. The reasons were quite practical:

> Officers, and persons in the service of the United States, and persons required to reside in the Indian country by treaty stipulations, must necessarily be placed under the protection, and subject to the laws of the United States. To persons merely travelling in the Indian country the same protection is extended. The want of fixed laws, of competent tribunals of justice, which must for some time continue in the Indian country, absolutely requires for the peace of both sides that this protection be extended. H.R. Rep. No. 474, 23d Cong., 1st Sess., at 18 (1834).

Congress' concern over criminal jurisdiction in this proposed Indian Territory contrasts markedly with its total failure to address criminal jurisdiction over non-Indians on other reservations, which frequently bordered non-Indian settlements. The contrast suggests that Congress shared the view of the Executive Branch and lower federal courts that Indian tribal courts were without jurisdiction to try non-Indians.

This unspoken assumption was also evident in other congressional actions during the 19th century. In 1854, for example, Congress amended the Trade and Intercourse Act to proscribe the prosecution in federal court of an Indian who has already been tried in tribal court. 10 Stat. 270, as amended, 18 U.S.C. § 1152. No similar provision, such as would have been required by parallel logic if tribal courts had jurisdiction over non-Indians, was enacted barring retrial of non-Indians. Similarly, in the Major Crimes Act of 1885, Congress placed under the jurisdiction of federal courts Indian offenders who commit certain specified major offenses. 23 Stat. 385, as amended, 18 U.S.C. § 1153. If tribal courts may try non-Indians, however, as respondents contend, those tribal courts are free to try non-Indians even for such major offenses as Congress may well have given the federal courts *exclusive* jurisdiction to try members of their own tribe committing the exact same offenses.[14]

---

[14] The Major Crimes Act provides that Indians committing any of the enumerated offenses "shall be subject to the same laws and penalties as all other persons committing any of the above offenses,

[A 1960 report expressly confirmed the Senate's] assumption that Indian tribal courts are without inherent jurisdiction to try non-Indians, and must depend on the Federal Government for protection from intruders. In considering a statute that would prohibit unauthorized entry upon Indian land for the purpose of hunting or fishing, the Senate Report noted that

> The problem confronting Indian tribes with sizable reservations is that the United States provides no protection against trespassers comparable to the protection it gives to Federal property as exemplified by title 18, United States Code, section 1863 [trespass on national forest lands]. Indian property owners should have the same protection as other property owners. For example, a private hunting club may keep non-members off its game lands or it may issue a permit for a fee. One who comes on such lands without permission may be prosecuted under State law but a non-Indian trespasser on an Indian reservation enjoys immunity. *This is by reason of the fact that Indian tribal law is enforceable against Indians only; not against non-Indians.*
>
> ....
>
> *Non-Indians are not subject to the jurisdiction of Indian courts and cannot be tried in Indian courts on trespass charges.* Further, there are no Federal laws which can be invoked against trespassers.
>
> ....
>
> The committee has considered this bill and believes that the legislation is meritorious. The legislation will give to the Indian tribes and to individual Indian owners certain rights that now exist as to others, and fills a gap in the present law for the protection of their property. S. Rep. No. 1686, 86th Cong., 2d Sess., 2-3 (1960) (emphasis added).

II

While not conclusive on the issue before us, the commonly shared presumption of Congress, the Executive Branch, and lower federal courts that tribal courts do not have the power to try non-Indians carries considerable weight. [Indian law is based primarily on treaties and statutes.] These instruments, which beyond their actual text form the backdrop for the intricate web of judicially made Indian law, cannot be interpreted in isolation but must be read in light of the common notions of the day and the assumptions of those who drafted them. *Ibid.*

While in isolation the Treaty of Point Elliott, 12 Stat. 927 (1855), would appear to be silent as to tribal criminal jurisdiction over non-Indians, the addition of historical perspective casts substantial doubt upon the existence of such jurisdiction. In the Ninth Article, for example, the Suquamish "acknowledge their dependence on the Government of the United States." As Chief Justice Marshall explained in *Worcester v. Georgia*, 6 Pet. 515, 551-552, 554, 8 L. Ed. 483 (1832), such an acknowledgement is not a mere abstract recognition of the United States' sovereignty. "The Indian nations were, from their situation, necessarily dependent on [the United States] for their protection from lawless and injurious intrusions into their country." *Id.*, at 555. By acknowledging their dependence on the United States, in the Treaty of Point Elliott, the Suquamish were in all probability recognizing that the United States would arrest and try

---

within the exclusive jurisdiction of the United States." While the question has never been directly addressed by this Court, Courts of Appeals have read this language to exclude tribal jurisdiction over the Indian offender. See, *e.g., Sam v. United States*, 385 F.2d 213, 214 (CA10 1967); *Felicia v. United States*, 495 F.2d 353, 354 (CA8 1974). We have no reason to decide today whether jurisdiction under the Major Crimes Act is exclusive.

non-Indian intruders who came within their reservation. Other provisions of
the Treaty also point to the absence of tribal jurisdiction. Thus the tribe
"agree[s] not to shelter or conceal offenders against the laws of the United
States, but to deliver them up to the authorities for trial." Read in conjunction
with 18 U.S.C. § 1152, which extends federal enclave law to non-Indian offenses
on Indian reservations, this provision implies that the Suquamish are to
promptly deliver up any non-Indian offender, rather than try and punish him
themselves.

By themselves, these treaty provisions would probably not be sufficient to
remove criminal jurisdiction over non-Indians if the Tribe otherwise retained
such jurisdiction. But an examination of our earlier precedents satisfies us that,
even ignoring treaty provisions and congressional policy, Indians do not have
criminal jurisdiction over non-Indians absent affirmative delegation of such
power by Congress. Indian tribes do retain elements of "quasi-sovereign" authority after ceding their lands to the United States and announcing their dependence on the Federal Government. See *The Cherokee Nation v. Georgia*, 5
Peters 1, 15, 8 L. Ed. 25 (1831). But the tribes' retained powers are not such that
they are limited only by specific restrictions in treaties or congressional enactments. As the Court of Appeals recognized[,] Indian tribes are proscribed from
exercising both those powers of autonomous states that are expressly terminated by Congress *and* those powers *"inconsistent with their status."* 544 F.2d,
at 1009.

Indian reservations are "a part of the territory of the United States." *United
States v. Rogers,* 4 How. 567, 571 (1846). Indian tribes "hold and occupy [the
reservations] with the assent of the United States, and under their authority."
Id., at 572. Upon incorporation into the territory of the United States, the
Indian tribes thereby come under the territorial sovereignty of the United
States and their exercise of separate power is constrained so as not to conflict
with the interests of this overriding sovereignty. "[T]heir rights to complete
sovereignty, as independent nations, [are] necessarily diminished." *Johnson v.
M'Intosh,* 8 Wheat. 543, 574 (1823).

We have already described some of the inherent limitations on tribal powers
that stem from their incorporation into the United States. In *Johnson v.
M'Intosh, supra,* we noted that the Indian tribes' "power to dispose of the soil at
their own will, to whomever they pleased," was inherently lost to the overriding
sovereignty of the United States. And in *The Cherokee Nation v. Georgia,
supra,* the Chief Justice observed that since Indian tribes are "completely under
the sovereignty and dominion of the United States, ... any attempt [by foreign
nations] to acquire their lands, or to form a political connexion with them,
would be considered by all as an invasion of our territory, and an act of hostility."

[In] submitting to the overriding sovereignty of the United States, Indian
tribes therefore necessarily give up their power to try non-Indian citizens of the
United States except in a manner acceptable to Congress. This principle would
have been obvious a century ago when most Indian tribes were characterized by
a "want of fixed laws [and] of competent tribunals of justice." H.R. Rep. No.
474, 23d Cong., 1st Sess., at 18 (1834). It should be no less obvious today, even

though present day Indian tribal courts embody dramatic advances over their historical antecedents.

In *Ex parte Crow Dog*, 109 U.S. 556 (1883), the Court was faced with almost the inverse of the issue before us here — whether, prior to the passage of the Major Crimes Act, federal courts had jurisdiction to try Indians who had offended against fellow Indians on reservation land. In concluding that criminal jurisdiction was exclusively in the tribe, it found particular guidance in the "nature and circumstances of the case." The United States was seeking to extend United States

> law, by argument and inference only, ... over aliens and strangers; over the members of a community separated by race [and] tradition, ... from the authority and power which seeks to impose upon them the restraints of an external and unknown code ... ; which judges them by a standard made by others and not for them .... It tries them, not by their peers, nor by the customs of their people, nor the law of their land, but by ... a different race, according to the law of a social state of which they have an imperfect conception .... *Id.,* at 571.

These considerations, applied here to the non-Indian rather than Indian offender, speak equally strongly against the validity of respondents' contention that Indian tribes, although fully subordinated to the sovereignty of the United States, retain the power to try non-Indians according to their own customs and procedure.

As previously noted, Congress extended the jurisdiction of federal courts, in the Trade and Intercourse Act of 1790, to offenses committed by non-Indians against Indians within Indian Country. In doing so, Congress was careful to extend to the non-Indian offender the basic criminal rights that would attach in non-Indian related cases. Under respondents' theory, however, Indian tribes would have been free to try the same non-Indians without these careful proceedings unless Congress affirmatively legislated to the contrary. Such an exercise of jurisdiction over non-Indian citizens of the United States would belie the tribes' forfeiture of full sovereignty in return for the protection of the United States.

In summary, respondents' position ignores that

> Indians are within the geographical limits of the United States. The soil and people within these limits are under the political control of the Government of the United States, or of the States of the Union. There exist in the broad domain of sovereignty but these two. There may be cities, counties, and other organized bodies with limited legislative functions, but they ... exist in subordination to one or the other of these. *United States v. Kagama,* 118 U.S. 375, 379 (1886).

We recognize that some Indian tribal court systems have become increasingly sophisticated and resemble in many respects their state counterparts. We also acknowledge that with the passage of the Indian Civil Rights Act of 1968, which extends certain basic procedural rights to *anyone* tried in Indian tribal court, many of the dangers that might have accompanied the exercise by tribal courts of criminal jurisdiction over non-Indians only a few decades ago have disappeared. Finally, we are not unaware of the prevalence of non-Indian crime on today's reservations which the tribes forcefully argue requires the ability to try non-Indians. But these are considerations for Congress to weigh in deciding whether Indian tribes should finally be authorized to try non-Indians. They have little relevance to the principles which lead us to conclude that Indian tribes do not have inherent jurisdiction to try and punish non-Indians. The judgments below are therefore reversed.

Reversed.

Mr. Justice BRENNAN took no part in the consideration or decision of these cases.

Mr. Justice MARSHALL, with whom THE CHIEF JUSTICE joins, dissenting.

I agree with the court below that the "power to preserve order on the reservation ... is a sine qua non of the sovereignty that the Suquamish originally possessed." 544 F.2d 1007, 1009 (CA9 1976). In the absence of affirmative withdrawal by treaty or statute, I am of the view that Indian tribes enjoy as a necessary aspect of their retained sovereignty the right to try and punish all persons who commit offenses against tribal law within the reservation. Accordingly, I dissent.

NOTES

1. The Judicial Role in Making Indian Policy: Some critics have argued that Felix Cohen's rule on inherent tribal sovereignty unduly narrowed tribal sovereignty by accepting federal power to divest it. *See, e.g.,* R. BARSH & J.Y. HENDERSON, THE ROAD: AMERICAN INDIAN TRIBES AND POLITICAL LIBERTY, 59-60 (1980); Ball, *Constitution, Court, Indian Tribes,* 1987 AM. B. FOUND. RES. J. 1, 43-44. Nevertheless, most accepted his formula as a proper accommodation of the competing interests of federal power and tribal sovereignty. The rule favored retention of tribal power, especially when coupled with the requirement that federal statutes be read carefully to preserve tribal sovereignty. What then is the basis for the *Oliphant* opinion? What is the source of the power the Court has exercised in fashioning the *Oliphant* rule? Is *Oliphant* an example of judicial restraint or of judicial activism? If the Court is merely interpreting the will of Congress, which alone possesses plenary power over Indian tribes, what do you think of the Court's method of statutory interpretation? *See* Collins, *Implied Limitations on the Jurisdiction of Indian Tribes,* 54 WASH. L. REV. 479, 490-99 (1979).

Justice Rehnquist relies on Justice Marshall's earlier statements that Indian tribes did not have the power to enter into treaties with foreign nations or alienate their land freely without federal consent. As Judge Canby has pointed out, the rule that tribes lost their external sovereignty arose from their dependent status on the national government, which has a trust relationship to Indian tribes. In contrast, Canby notes, "[i]t is not appropriate, however, to limit tribal power because of the tribe's dependent status when the power is lost to a state, upon whom the tribe is not dependent." Canby, *The Status of Indian Tribes in American Law Today,* 62 WASH. L. REV. 1, 18 n.57 (1987). What is the answer to this criticism?

2. Criminal Jurisdiction Over Non-Indians in Indian Country Before Oliphant: The *Oliphant* decision was extraordinarily unpopular in Indian country. As the opinion indicates, at least thirty tribes had been asserting criminal jurisdiction over non-Indians at the time the case was decided, many of them relying on statutes that deemed entry onto the reservation as an implied consent to the exercise of criminal jurisdiction by the tribe. Such tribes had posted conspicuous signs at entry points to their reservations informing those who entered of the effect of such statutes. Before the decision in *Oliphant,* those statutes seemingly had an arguable theoretical justification as applied to outsiders entering the reservation, although it would certainly have been harder to justify the theory as applied to non-Indian residents of the reservation, like Oliphant and Belgarde. Could the rule of *Oliphant* be avoided by excluding a non-Indian committing an offense against the tribe rather than by exercising criminal jurisdiction? See section D3, *infra*.

3. The Use of History and Method of Interpretation in *Oliphant*: In his opinion Justice Rehnquist makes substantial use of history to find an implied diminishment of the inherent sovereignty of Indian tribes over non-Indians. Is his reading of the historical background and its relevance an accurate one? Note that in footnote 8 he concedes that some of the early treaties contained language authorizing the tribes to punish non-Indian citizens of the United States who illegally settled in Indian country. He refuses, however, to treat these provisions as recognitions of the inherent sovereignty of the tribes over non-Indians in their midst, viewing them, rather, as apparent federal grants of authority to the tribes designed to prevent illegal settlement in Indian country. Yet, when he discusses in the same footnote other provisions that recognized federal authority over non-Indians who committed crimes in Indian country, he indicates that those provisions were "not necessary," since they merely restated the lack of inherent tribal criminal authority over non-Indians. Are not these provisions just as susceptible of a reading that the tribes had inherent criminal jurisdiction over all persons, Indian or non-Indian, within their lands and that specific treaty provisions were necessary to assure that the federal government at least had concurrent jurisdiction over citizens of the United States in order to protect them, where appropriate, from less developed tribal criminal processes of the late eighteenth and early nineteenth centuries? Which reading of the documents best comports with the actual behavior of the Indian tribes and the federal government on the then unsettled frontier? Would a relatively independent frontier Indian tribe in the late eighteenth or early nineteenth centuries have readily turned a non-Indian offender over to federal authorities based merely on the federal claim of lack of inherent tribal jurisdiction over the accused? Might these treaty provisions be more consistent with a view that most limitations on inherent tribal domestic, as opposed to diplomatic and international, authority must be textual and expressly approved by Congress? Contrast Justice Rehnquist's dissent in *United States v. Sioux Nation*, 448 U.S. 371, 437 (1980) in which he criticized what he characterized as revisionist history in the majority opinion and chided his fellow justices for overlooking that "in a Court opinion, as a historical and not a legal matter, both settler and Indian are entitled to the benefit of the Biblical adjuration: 'Judge not, that ye be not judged.'"

Is the historical evidence that Justice Rehnquist marshals very relevant to the question at issue? Most of the sources on which Justice Rehnquist relies, including the adoption of the predecessor of 18 U.S.C. § 1152, and the Western Territory Bill, arose before most Indian tribes had any type of formal court structure or written laws. Even though the Choctaw did have a formal court system at the time of the Choctaw treaty cited by the Court, in practice the system was still rudimentary. Insofar as these examples indicate a federal reluctance to relegate non-Indians to tribal justice, that reluctance may have been predicated on the tribal application of their traditional, unwritten control practices to non-Indians. The other treaties referred to by Justice Rehnquist provide even less support for his position. Promising to turn offenders over to the United States could just as well be read, in light of the principles of treaty construction covered in Chapter 2, as applying to extradition of fugitives from United States justice. Some of the evidence Justice Rehnquist cites, such as *Ex parte Kenyon* and the 1960 legislation, does support his argument. Should the Court have taken greater account of the impact of modernization of tribal court procedures and later congressional action apparently reinforcing tribal courts, such as the Indian Civil Rights Act, discussed in section C, *infra*?

4. **The Factual Setting of *Oliphant*:** The *Oliphant* case was in many ways one of the worst possible fact situations that could have reached the Court raising the issue of tribal jurisdiction over non-Indians. The reservation was heavily allotted, as reflected by footnote 1 of the opinion, with Indians comprising far less than one percent of the resident population of the reservation. The persons accused of crimes in the tribal courts were residents of the reservation living on fee patent land no longer held in Indian trust title. Might the result in the case have been any different had the issue arisen on an unallotted, isolated reservation like that of the Hopi Tribe in Arizona? Could a case involving non-Indian outsiders who entered the reservation bent on disrupting tribal activities have yielded a different result? In the face of the *Oliphant* opinion is there any room to argue that its holding does not apply to unallotted or isolated Indian reservations that remain substantially Indian-held or to non-Indians who are outsiders, as opposed to residents, and who enter the reservation? Can or should the type of reservation and the number of non-Indians living there affect the rules of Indian law? *See* Clinton, *Reservation Specificity and Indian Adjudication: An Essay on the Importance of Limited Contextualism in Indian Law*, 8 HAMLINE L. REV. 543 (1985). *See also* INDIAN RESERVATION SPECIAL MAGISTRATE: HEARING ON S. 1177 BEFORE THE SENATE SELECT COMMITTEE ON INDIAN AFFAIRS, 99th Cong., 2d Sess. 167-68 (1986) (Statement of Gerald Anton, President of the Salt River Pima-Maricopa Indian Community relating the tribe's agreement with city, county, and state officials to pursue a federal law specific to the needs of that reservation, which lies within the Phoenix metropolitan area.).

5. **Law Enforcement on the Reservation After *Oliphant*:** Since *Oliphant*, a non-Indian who commits a crime against an Indian victim must be tried in federal court (unless a federal statute, such as Public Law 280, has granted the state jurisdiction over crimes occurring on reservations). Unfortunately, the federal system is not geared towards prosecution of non-major crimes, most of which are misdemeanors. Funds for prosecution of federal crimes are finite, requiring busy prosecutors to allocate their resources as best they can. As a result, crimes like assaults and burglaries are simply not prosecuted, which creates grave problems for tribes attempting to police their reservation without the power to exercise criminal jurisdiction over non-Indians. Moreover, the distance between the federal courts and reservations can add to the problem. For example, the nearest federal courts and prosecutors to the Fort Peck Reservation in Montana are in Billings and Great Falls, over 250 miles from the reservation. Several bills designed to increase the number of federal prosecutors and place federal magistrates in Indian country have been unsuccessful, partly because of Indian opposition to the addition of another layer of federal law enforcement in Indian Country in place of a solution that would strengthen tribal authority. See S. 2832, 96th Cong., 2d Sess. (1980); S. 1177, 99th Cong., 2d Sess. (1986).

6. **Application of *Oliphant* to Nonmember Indians:** The Court phrased its opinion in *Oliphant* with reference to the application of tribal criminal jurisdiction to *non-Indians*. What is the Court's rationale for removing non-Indians from tribal criminal jurisdiction? In other words, if tribal court systems are

unfair, why did the Court permit tribes to exercise criminal jurisdiction over anyone? If non-Indians are entitled to special protection from Indian tribes, does the same rationale apply to nonmember Indians? For the answer, see *Duro v. Reina*, section D1, *infra*.

MONTANA v. UNITED STATES

450 U.S. 544 (1981)

[By a tribal regulation, the Crow Tribe of Montana prohibited hunting and fishing within its reservation by anyone who was not a member of the Tribe. Relying on its ownership of the bed of the Big Horn River, on treaties which created its reservation, and on its inherent power as a sovereign, the Tribe claimed authority to prohibit hunting and fishing by nonmembers of the Tribe even on lands within the reservation owned by them in fee simple. Montana, however, continued to assert its authority to regulate hunting and fishing by non-Indians within the reservation. The First Treaty of Fort Laramie of 1851, in which the signatory tribes acknowledged various designated lands as their respective territories, specified that, by making the treaty, the tribes did not "surrender the privilege of hunting, fishing, or passing over" any of the lands in dispute. In 1868, the Second Treaty of Fort Laramie established the Crow reservation, including land through which the Big Horn River flows, and provided that the reservation "shall be set apart for the absolute and undisturbed use and occupation" of the Tribe, and that no non-Indians except Government agents "shall ever be permitted to pass over, settle upon, or reside in" the reservation. To resolve the conflict between the Tribe and the State, the United States, proceeding in its own right and as fiduciary for the Tribe, filed an action seeking a declaratory judgment quieting title to the riverbed in the United States as trustee for the Tribe and establishing that the Tribe and the United States have sole authority to regulate hunting and fishing within the reservation, and an injunction requiring Montana to secure the Tribe's permission before issuing hunting or fishing licenses for use within the reservation. The District Court denied relief, but the Court of Appeals reversed. It held that the bed and banks of the river were held by the United States in trust for the Tribe; that the Tribe could regulate hunting and fishing within the reservation by nonmembers, except for hunting and fishing on fee lands by resident nonmember owners of those lands; and that nonmembers permitted by the Tribe to hunt or fish within the reservation remained subject to Montana's fish and game laws.

The Supreme Court opinion first addressed the ownership issue and held that title to the bed of the Big Horn River passed to Montana upon its admission into the Union, the United States not having conveyed beneficial ownership of the riverbed to the Crow Tribe by the treaties of 1851 or 1868. The Court held that as a general principle, the federal government holds lands under navigable waters in trust for future States, to be granted to such States when they enter the Union, and there is a strong presumption against conveyance of such lands by the United States. The 1851 treaty failed to overcome this presumption, since it did not by its terms formally convey any land to the Indians at all. And whatever property rights the 1868 treaty created, its language is not strong enough to overcome the presumption against the sovereign's conveyance of the riverbed. Cf. *United States v. Holt State Bank,* 270 U.S. 49. Moreover, the Court said that the situation of the Crow Indians at the time of the treaties presented no "public exigency" which would have required Congress to depart from its policy of reserving ownership of beds under navigable waters for the future States. By applying for the first time the general presumptive rule that the federal government holds title to navigable waters for future states to an Indian reservation created prior to statehood, the Supreme Court opinion abandoned on this issue the usual rules that Indian treaties are to be construed liberally in favor of the Indians and that Indian treaties are to be read as grants from, rather than to, the Indians.

Having addressed the ownership question, Justice Stewart's opinion for the majority then turned to the jurisdictional question in a context in which the State of Montana was found to own the beds of the streams in the reservation over which the Crow Tribe purported to assert exclusive jurisdiction. Furthermore, the major dispute in the case centered on fishing and the Court had found that the State of Montana effectively owned the entirety of the fish habitat.]

III

Though the parties in this case have raised broad questions about the power of the Tribe to regulate hunting and fishing by non-Indians on the reservation, the regulatory issue before us is a narrow one. The Court of Appeals held that the Tribe may prohibit nonmembers from hunting or fishing on land belonging to the Tribe or held by the United States in trust for the Tribe, and with this holding we can readily agree. We also agree with the Court of Appeals that if the Tribe permits nonmembers to fish or hunt on such lands, it may condition their entry by charging a fee or establishing bag and creel limits. What remains is the question of the power of the Tribe to regulate non-Indian fishing and hunting on reservation land owned in fee by nonmembers of the Tribe. The Court of Appeals held that, with respect to fee-patented lands, the Tribe may regulate, but may not prohibit, hunting and fishing by nonmember resident owners or by those, such as tenants or employees, whose occupancy is authorized by the owners. The court further held that the Tribe may totally prohibit hunting and fishing on lands within the reservation owned by non-Indians who do not occupy that land.

The Court of Appeals found two sources for this tribal regulatory power: the Crow treaties, "augmented" by 18 U.S.C. § 1165, and "inherent" Indian sovereignty. We believe that neither source supports the court's conclusion.

A

The purposes of the 1851 Treaty were to assure safe passage for settlers across the lands of various Indian tribes; to compensate the Tribes for the loss of buffalo, other game animals, timber and forage; to delineate tribal boundaries; to promote intertribal peace; and to establish a way of identifying Indians who committed depredations against non-Indians. As noted earlier, the treaty did not even create a reservation, although it did designate tribal lands. See *Crow Tribe v. United States,* 284 F.2d 361, 364, 366, 368 (Ct. Cl.). Only Article

5 of that treaty referred to hunting and fishing, and it merely provided that the eight signatory tribes "do not surrender the privilege of hunting, fishing, or passing over any of the tracts of country heretofore described." [11 Stat. 749.][6] The treaty nowhere suggested that Congress intended to grant authority to the Crow Tribe to regulate hunting and fishing by nonmembers on nonmember lands. Indeed, the Court of Appeals acknowledged that after the treaty was signed non-Indians, as well as members of other Indian tribes, undoubtedly hunted and fished within the treaty-designated territory of the Crows.

The 1868 Fort Laramie Treaty, 15 Stat. 649, reduced the size of the Crow territory designated by the 1851 Treaty. Article II of the Treaty established a reservation for the Crow Tribe, and provided that it be "set apart for the *absolute and undisturbed use and occupation* of the Indians herein named, and for such other friendly tribes or individual Indians as from time to time they may be willing, with the consent of the United States, to admit amongst them ...," (emphasis added) and that "the United States now solemnly agrees that no persons, except those herein designated and authorized so to do ... shall ever be permitted to pass over, settle upon, or reside in the territory described in this article for the use of said Indians...." The treaty, therefore, obligated the United States to prohibit most non-Indians from residing on or passing through reservation lands used and occupied by the Tribe, and, thereby, arguably conferred upon the Tribe the authority to control fishing and hunting on those lands. But that authority could only extend to land on which the Tribe exercises "absolute and undisturbed use and occupation." And it is clear that the quantity of such land was substantially reduced by the allotment and alienation of tribal lands as a result of the passage of the [General Allotment Act] and the Crow Allotment Act of 1920, 41 Stat. 751. If the 1868 Treaty created tribal power to restrict or prohibit non-Indian hunting and fishing on the reservation, that power cannot apply to lands held in fee by non-Indians.[9]

In *Puyallup Tribe v. Washington Game Dep't*, 433 U.S. 165 (1977) (*Puyallup III*), the relevant treaty included language virtually identical to that in the 1868

[6] The complaint in this case did not allege that non-Indian hunting and fishing on reservation lands has impaired this privilege.

[9] [N]othing in the Allotment Acts supports the view of the Court of Appeals that the Tribe could nevertheless bar hunting and fishing by nonresident fee owners. The policy of the Acts was the eventual assimilation of the Indian population, *Organized Village of Kake v. Egan*, 369 U.S. 60, 72, and the "gradual extinction of Indian reservations and Indian titles." *Draper v. United States*, 164 U.S. 240, 246. The Secretary of the Interior and the Commissioner of Indian Affairs repeatedly emphasized that the allotment policy was designed to eventually eliminate tribal relations. [T]hroughout the Congressional debates on the subject of allotment, it was assumed that the "civilization" of the Indian population was to be accomplished, in part, by the dissolution of tribal relations.

[Nothing] in the legislative history [suggests] that Congress intended that the non-Indians who would settle upon alienated allotted lands would be subject to tribal regulatory authority. Indeed, throughout the congressional debates, allotment of Indian land was consistently equated with the dissolution of tribal affairs and jurisdiction....

[Thus] Congress [did not] intend that non-Indians purchasing allotted lands would become subject to tribal jurisdiction when an avowed purpose of the allotment policy was the ultimate destruction of tribal government. And it is hardly likely that Congress could have imagined that the purpose of peaceful assimilation could be advanced if feeholders could be excluded from fishing or hunting on their acquired property.

The policy of allotment and sale of surplus reservation land was, of course, repudiated in 1934 by the Indian Reorganization Act, 48 Stat. 984 (current version at 25 U.S.C. § 461 et seq.). But what is relevant in this case is the effect of the land alienation occasioned by that policy on Indian treaty rights tied to Indian use and occupation of reservation land.

Treaty of Fort Laramie. The Puyallup Reservation was to be "set apart, and, so far as necessary, surveyed and marked out for their exclusive use ... [and no] white man [was to] be permitted to reside upon the same without permission of the tribe ...." See *id.*, at 174. The Puyallup Tribe argued that those words amounted to a grant of authority to fish free of state interference. But this Court rejected that argument, finding, in part, that it "clashe[d] with the subsequent history of the reservation ... ," *ibid.*, notably two Acts of Congress under which the Puyallups alienated, in fee simple, the great majority of the lands in the reservation, including all the land abutting the Puyallup River. Thus, "[n]either the Tribe nor its members continue to hold Puyallup River fishing grounds for their 'exclusive use.'" *Ibid. Puyallup III* indicates, therefore, that treaty rights with respect to reservation lands must be read in light of the subsequent alienation of those lands. Accordingly, the language of the 1868 Treaty provides no support for tribal authority to regulate hunting and fishing on land owned by non-Indians....

B

[T]he Court of Appeals also identified the power [to regulate non-Indian hunting and fishing on non-Indian lands] as an incident of the inherent sovereignty of the Tribe over the entire Crow reservation. But "inherent sovereignty" is not so broad as to support the application of Resolution No. 74-05 to non-Indian lands.

This Court most recently reviewed the principles of inherent sovereignty in *United States v. Wheeler,* 435 U.S. 313. In that case, noting that Indian tribes are "unique aggregations possessing attributes of sovereignty over both their members and their territory," *id.,* at 323, the Court upheld the power of a tribe to punish tribal members who violate tribal criminal laws. But the Court was careful to note that, through their original incorporation into the United States as well as through specific treaties and statutes, the Indian tribes have lost many of the attributes of sovereignty. The Court distinguished between those inherent powers retained by the tribes and those divested:

> The areas in which such implicit divestiture of sovereignty has been held to have occurred are those involving *the relations between an Indian tribe and nonmembers of the tribe....*
> These limitations rest on the fact that the dependent status of Indian tribes within our territorial jurisdiction is necessarily inconsistent with their freedom independently *to determine their external relations.* But the powers of self-government, including the power to prescribe and enforce internal criminal laws, are of a different type. They involve *only the relations among members of a tribe.* Thus, they are not such powers as would necessarily be lost by virtue of a tribe's dependent status. *Ibid.* (Emphasis added.)

Thus, in addition to the power to punish tribal offenders, the Indian tribes retain their inherent power to determine tribal membership, to regulate domestic relations among members, and to prescribe rules of inheritance for members. But exercise of tribal power beyond what is necessary to protect tribal self-government or to control internal relations is inconsistent with the dependent status of the tribes, and so cannot survive without express congressional delegation. Since regulation of hunting and fishing by nonmembers of a tribe on lands no longer owned by the tribe bears no clear relationship to tribal self-government or internal relations,[13] the general principles of retained inherent sovereignty did not authorize the Crow Tribe to adopt Resolution No. 74-05.

The Court recently applied these general principles in *Oliphant v. Suquamish Indian Tribe.* [Although] *Oliphant* only determined inherent tribal authority in criminal matters,[14] the principles on which it relied support the general proposition that the inherent sovereign powers of an Indian tribe do not extend to the activities of nonmembers of the tribe. To be sure, Indian tribes retain inherent sovereign power to exercise some forms of civil jurisdiction over non-Indians on their reservations, even on non-Indian fee lands. A tribe may regulate, through taxation, licensing, or other means, the activities of nonmembers who enter consensual relationships with the tribe or its members, through commercial dealing, contracts, leases, or other arrangements. [*E.g.,*] *Williams v. Lee,* 358 U.S. 217, 223. A tribe may also retain inherent power to exercise civil authority over the conduct of non-Indians on fee lands within its reservation when that conduct threatens or has some direct effect on the political integrity, the economic security, or the health or welfare of the tribe.

No such circumstances, however, are involved in this case. Non-Indian hunters and fishermen on non-Indian fee land do not enter any agreements or dealings with the Crow Tribe so as to subject themselves to tribal civil jurisdiction. And nothing in this case suggests that such non-Indian hunting and fishing so threaten the Tribe's political or economic security as to justify tribal regulation. The complaint in the District Court did not allege that non-Indian hunting and fishing on fee lands imperil the subsistence or welfare of the Tribe.[16] Furthermore, the District Court made express findings, left unaltered by the Court of Appeals, that the Crow Tribe has traditionally accommodated itself to the State's "near exclusive" regulation of hunting and fishing on fee lands within the reservation. And the District Court found that Montana's statutory and regulatory scheme does not prevent the Crow Tribe from limiting or forbidding non-Indian hunting and fishing on lands still owned by or held in trust for the Tribe or its members.

[*Reversed and remanded.*]

Justice BLACKMUN, with whom Justice BRENNAN and Justice MARSHALL join, dissenting in part.

Only two years ago, this Court reaffirmed that the terms of a treaty between the United States and an Indian tribe must be construed "'in the sense in which

---

[13] Any argument that Resolution No. 74-05 is necessary to Crow tribal self-government is refuted by the findings of the District Court that the State of Montana has traditionally exercised "near exclusive" jurisdiction over hunting and fishing on fee lands within the reservation, and that the parties to this case had accommodated themselves to the state regulation. The Court of Appeals left these findings unaltered and indeed implicitly reaffirmed them, adding that the record reveals no attempts by the Tribe at the time of the Crow Allotment Act to forbid non-Indian hunting and fishing on reservation lands.

[14] By denying the Suquamish Tribe criminal jurisdiction over non-Indians, however, the *Oliphant* case would seriously restrict the ability of a tribe to enforce any purported regulation of non-Indian hunters and fishermen....

[16] Similarly, the complaint did not allege that the State has abdicated or abused its responsibility for protecting and managing wildlife, has established its season, bag, or creel limits in such a way as to impair the Crow Indians' treaty rights to fish or hunt, or has imposed less stringent hunting and fishing regulations within the reservation than in other parts of the State. *Cf. United States v. Washington,* 384 F. Supp. 312, 410-411 (W.D. Wash.), aff'd, 520 F.2d 676 (CA9).

they would naturally be understood by the Indians.'" *Washington v. Fishing Vessel Assn.,* 443 U.S. 658, 676 (1979), quoting from *Jones v. Meehan,* 175 U.S. 1, 11 (1899). In holding today that the bed of the Big Horn River passed to the State of Montana upon its admission to the Union, the Court disregards this settled rule of statutory construction. Because I believe that the United States intended, and the Crow Nation understood, that the bed of the Big Horn was to belong to the Crow Indians, I dissent from so much of the Court's opinion as holds otherwise.[1]

NOTES

1. *Montana*'s **Effect on Non-Allotted Reservations:** Broad language in the *Montana* opinion could be read to refer generally to all assertions of tribal power over non-Indians, even on tribally owned reservation land. A few weeks after *Montana* was decided, the Supreme Court summarily vacated a Tenth Circuit decision and remanded it "for further consideration in light of *Montana v. United States.*" *New Mexico v. Mescalero Apache Tribe,* 450 U.S. 544 (1981), *remanding* 630 F.2d 724 (10th Cir. 1980). The Court of Appeals had held that the tribe's exemplary record of wildlife management justified the district court's order declaring that the tribe could regulate non-Indian hunting and fishing on its reservation and that the State of New Mexico could not apply or enforce its hunting and fishing laws against any person, Indian or non-Indian, within the boundaries of the reservation. In contrast to the Crow Reservation, where 28% of the reservation land was owned by non-Indians, the Mescalero Apache Reservation had never been allotted or otherwise opened to non-Indian settlement. In fact, non-Indians owned less than 4% of the reservation land. Upon reconsideration, the Tenth Circuit reinstated its prior opinion. *Id.,* 677 F.2d 55 (10th Cir. 1982). The Supreme Court affirmed in a unanimous opinion, stating "[o]ur decision in [*Montana*] does not resolve this question. Unlike this case, *Montana* concerned lands located within the reservation but *not* owned by the tribe or its members." *New Mexico v. Mescalero Apache Tribe,* 462 U.S. 324 (1983).

Despite the narrow reading given in *Mescalero Apache,* some courts have interpreted *Montana* broadly. *See, e.g., Superior Oil Co. v. United States,* 798 F.2d 529 (10th Cir. 1986) (*Montana* applies to regulation of oil and gas lessees by Navajo tribe). As you read the following materials evaluate the extent to which courts have limited *Montana* to exercises of jurisdiction over fee land within reservation boundaries.

2. **Domestic Dependent Nation Status as a Limitation on Tribal Power:** What guidance do *Oliphant* and *Montana* offer for determining in what other settings tribes will be held to have lost power to regulate non-Indians because of their dependent status? According to one commentator: "*Montana* shows the potential open-endedness of the Court's new willingness to find limitations of tribal power arising from the tribe's domestic dependent status. *Montana* comes very close to placing the burden on the tribe of showing why its self-government interests are affected sufficiently to support the regulation." Canby, *The Status of Indian Tribes in American Law Today,* 62 Wash. L. Rev. 1, 16 (1987).

3. **The Role of Tradition:** In *Montana* itself, the Court refused to permit the Crow Tribe to regulate the fishing and hunting in part because the tribe had

---

[1] I agree with the Court's resolution of the question of the power of the Tribe to regulate non-Indian fishing and hunting on reservation land owned in fee by nonmembers of the Tribe. I note only that nothing in the Court's disposition of that issue is inconsistent with the conclusion that the bed of the Big Horn River belongs to the Crow Indians....

traditionally acquiesced in state regulation of hunting and fishing on the fee lands. In a case upholding California's power to require an Indian trader to get a state license, the Supreme Court weighed heavily in favor of state regulation the fact that tribes had not traditionally regulated liquor trade. Although that case, *Rice v. Rehner,* set forth and discussed in Chapter 4, section A2, involved the reach of state power and not tribal power, if the Court were to adopt a balancing of interests approach to questions of tribal power over non-Indians, would a focus on tradition prevent tribes that had developed new enterprises from exercising power over non-Indians?

2. SOVEREIGN PERQUISITES: IMMUNITY FROM SUIT AND RECOGNITION OF JUDGMENTS

The federal government, states, and most foreign countries have adopted the doctrine of sovereign immunity, which immunizes the government from suit without its consent. *See Kawananakoa v. Polyblank,* 205 U.S. 349 (1907) (Holmes, J.) (rationale for doctrine). Constitutional law requires state courts to honor federal sovereign immunity and the federal courts must honor the states' sovereign immunity. An obvious justification for the doctrine is to protect the public fisc from treasury-draining lawsuits. In addition, however, modern adherents of the doctrine argue that suits against the government interfere with its day-to-day operations, both directly when suits seek equitable and injunctive relief and indirectly by requiring reallocation of the resources needed to defend such suits. Nevertheless, concern for the administration of justice to the individual has been viewed as outweighing the governmental interests, especially when the wrong complained of would be actionable if committed by a private person. The retreat from the doctrine has taken many forms. States and the federal government have waived sovereign immunity for many kinds of suits. In addition, state courts have begun to find implicit waivers of state immunity, often relying on a distinction between proprietary and governmental activities. This same distinction has been adopted by the states and the federal courts in cases involving foreign country defendants. Finally, the Supreme Court has held that the state courts are under no constitutional compulsion to recognize the sovereign immunity of sister states. *See Nevada v. Hall,* 440 U.S. 410 (1979). As a matter of domestic choice of law, however, most states recognize the immunity of sister states and foreign countries. One rationale for recognizing sister state and foreign country sovereign immunity is the very practical one of encouraging other governments to reciprocate when the forum's citizens litigate in foreign courts. Indian tribes are neither states nor arms of the federal government. What light do the cases that follow shed on the sovereign status of Indian tribes?

a. Sovereign Immunity

BOTTOMLY v. PASSAMAQUODDY TRIBE

599 F.2d 1061 (1st Cir. 1979)

COFFIN, Chief Judge.

This is a diversity action brought by an attorney against the Passamaquoddy Tribe and three of its former tribal governors to recover on a contingency contract for attorney's fees. [The district court dismissed for lack of jurisdiction and this appeal followed.]

II. *Tribal Sovereign Immunity*

As the Supreme Court, in *Santa Clara Pueblo v. Martinez,* 436 U.S. 49, 58 (1978), recently noted: "Indian Tribes have long been recognized as possessing the common-law immunity from suit traditionally enjoyed by sovereign powers."

[The court rejected the state's argument that only federally recognized Indian tribes are entitled to assert sovereign immunity from suit.] We are cited to, and our research has uncovered, no case which *conditions* the invocation of sovereign immunity on the factors emphasized by the state or appellant: formal federal recognition of the particular tribe by treaty or statute, a prolonged course of dealing between the tribe and the federal government, geographic location, the tribe's warlike nature, the absence of state protection of a tribe or the continued full exercise of a tribe's sovereign powers.

The absence of authority is not surprising, for the analysis urged by appellant and the state seems to us to fundamentally misconceive basic principles of federal Indian law. In effect, their approach would condition the exercise of an aspect of sovereignty on a showing that it had been granted to the tribe by the federal government, either by explicit recognition or implicitly through a course of dealing. As the Supreme Court recently explained, however, the proper analysis is just the reverse:

> The powers of Indian tribes are, in general, *"inherent powers of a limited sovereignty which has never extinguished."* F. Cohen, Handbook of Federal Indian Law 122 (1945) (emphasis in original) ....
>
> Indian tribes are, of course, no longer "possessed of the full attributes of sovereignty." ... Their incorporation within the territory of the United States, and their acceptance of its protection, necessarily divested them of some aspects of the sovereignty which they had previously exercised. By specific treaty provision they yielded up other sovereign powers; by statute, in the exercise of its plenary control, Congress has removed still others.
>
> But our cases recognize that the Indian tribes have not given up their full sovereignty.... The sovereignty that the Indian tribes retain is of a unique and limited character. It exists only at the sufferance of Congress and is subject to complete defeasance. But until Congress acts, the tribes retain their existing sovereign powers. *In sum, Indian tribes still possess those aspects of sovereignty not withdrawn by treaty or statute, or by implication as a necessary result of their dependent status....* United States v. Wheeler, 435 U.S. 313, 322-23 (1978) (emphasis added).

It is uncontroverted that one aspect of a tribe's sovereignty is its immunity from suit. Accordingly, the only remaining questions are whether Congress has divested the Tribe of its sovereign immunity or whether it has been lost "by implication as a necessary result of [its] dependent status." [*United States v. Wheeler.*]

It is clear that Congress has taken no action to deprive the Passamaquoddy Indians of their inherent immunity from suit. Surely its inattention would not suffice. And while the Court has found an "implicit divestiture of [a tribe's] sovereignty," [*United States v. Wheeler,*] in a number of areas such as free alienation of Indian land to non-Indians, *Oneida Indian Nation v. County of*

Oneida, 414 U.S. at 661, 667-68 (1974), and trial of non-members of a tribe in tribal courts, *Oliphant v. Suquamish Indian Tribe,* 435 U.S. 191, 195 (1978), the contrary must be the case here. The mere passage of time with its erosion of the full exercise of the sovereign powers of a tribal organization cannot constitute such an implicit divestiture. As the Court has held, "[t]he public policy which exempted the dependent as well as the dominant sovereignties from suit without consent continues this immunity even after dissolution of the tribal government. These Indian Nations are exempt from suit without Congressional authorization." *United States v. United States Fidelity & Guaranty Co.,* [309 U.S. 506, 512 (1940).]

Within this framework of analysis, we fail to see how the state's extensive involvement with the Tribe, *see Joint Tribal Council of the Passamaquoddy Tribe v. Morton, supra,* 528 F.2d at 374, can deprive the Tribe of its immunity from suit. [In conclusion,] the doctrine of sovereign immunity bars the instant suit against the Tribe. [The lower court was also correct] in dismissing the case as against the representatives of the Tribe. As the court properly found, the complaint in its original form and as amended, gave no suggestion that this was a suit against these persons for actions taken in their individual capacities. Instead, they were sued as having acted "for and on behalf of the tribe," and "[t]o say that this tribe is exempt from civil suit on its contracts and yet compel its principal chief[s] by judicial process, to take funds from its treasury, and turn them over to the court to be applied in discharge of its contracts is to destroy in practice the very exemption which at outset is conceded as legal right." *Adams v. Murphy,* [165 F. 304, 308 (8th Cir. 1908)].
Affirmed.

NOTES

1. **Continuing Justifications for Tribal Sovereign Immunity:** At least one member of the Court has wondered aloud whether a broad view of tribal sovereign immunity continues to be valid. In *Puyallup Tribe v. Department of Game,* 433 U.S. 165, 179 (1977), Justice Blackmun stated: "I am of the view that the doctrine may well merit re-examination in an appropriate case." What might be such an appropriate case? The New Mexico Supreme Court recently held that the state is not compelled to honor a tribe's sovereign immunity in the state's courts. *Padilla v. Pueblo of Acoma,* 107 N.M. 174, 754 P.2d 845 (1988), *cert. denied,* 109 S. Ct. 1767 (1989). If the doctrine is a doctrine of federal as well as tribal law, can such a result be justified? For a criticism, see Note, 102 HARV. L. REV. 556 (1988).

In *Padilla,* the state court also focused on the fact that the tribe was carrying on a business activity off the reservation. A recent Note recommends that courts restrict the availability of the doctrine of sovereign immunity. For example, the author recommends such a judicial abrogation in a case in which tribes have acted as proprietors operating a commercial activity, especially when that activity occurs off-reservation and injures non-Indians. Note, *Tribal Sovereign Immunity: Searching for Sensible Limits,* 88 COLUM. L. REV. 173 (1988). The author argues for this approach by comparing the justifications advanced for tribal immunity to those supporting state and foreign country immunity, discussed in the introduction to these materials. Would such an approach be consistent with the doctrine's requirement of an explicit congressional or tribal waiver? *See Morgan v. Colorado River Indian Tribe,* 103 Ariz. 425, 428, 443 P.2d 421, 424 (1968) ("Congress alone must determine the extent [of] immunities.... The fact that the Colorado Indian tribe was engaged in a proprietary function is immaterial."). Is such a distinction between proprietary and government activities workable in the case of Indian tribes? *See also United Nuclear Corp. v. Clark,* 584 F. Supp. 107 (D.D.C. 1984) (commercial activity exception, if it exists, does not apply to leasing nonrenewable resources). Recall that one reason given by the Court for abandoning a state sovereignty limitation on the reach of congressional power was the fact that *National League of Cities v. Usery,* 426 U.S. 833 (1976) and its progeny required courts to make similar distinctions. *Garcia v. San Antonio Metro. Transit Auth.,* 469 U.S. 528, 537-47 (1985).

In contrast, another Note argues that the justifications for restricting the sovereign immunity of other sovereigns do not extend to restricting tribal sovereign immunity, because of the limited revenue base of Indian tribes compared to states and the importance of building and maintaining tribal assets in order to provide for economic security and protect political autonomy. Note, *In Defense of Tribal Sovereign Immunity,* 95 HARV. L. REV. 1058, 1072-74 (1982). The issue of tribal sovereign immunity comes up often in the context of tribal economic development. See Chapter 7, section C5 for a fuller discussion of the issue in that context.

2. Circumventing Tribal Sovereign Immunity: To what extent can the sovereign immunity of tribes be circumvented by suing tribal officers? *See, e.g., Santa Clara Pueblo v. Martinez,* 436 U.S. 49, 59 (1978) (tribal officer not immune). The eleventh amendment bars suits against states in federal courts. To determine whether a particular suit falls within the scope of this constitutional immunity, courts look to the relief requested from the state officer. *Compare Ex parte Young,* 209 U.S. 123 (1908) (request for injunctive relief and contempt against state attorney general not a suit against the state proscribed by eleventh amendment) *with Edelman v. Jordan,* 415 U.S. 651 (1974) (compensatory damages or "equitable restitution" payable out of state treasury in suit against state officer precluded by eleventh amendment while prospective injunctive relief not precluded despite need for state financing to comply with order). Claims for injunctive relief enjoy no automatic exception from sovereign immunity, however. In each case, the question depends on whether the relief requested would require the tribe to act. *Cf. In re Ayers,* 123 U.S. 443 (1887) (action against state officer under impairment of contract theory barred by eleventh amendment where the object was "by injunction, indirectly, to compel the specific performance of the contract"). As *Bottomly* illustrates, these principles have been applied to tribal officers as well.

Tribal members are subject to suit, however. In *Puyallup Tribe v. Department of Game,* 433 U.S. 165 (1977), the Court sustained a sovereign immunity claim by the tribe in an off-reservation fishing rights case but noted that individual members of the tribe could be sued even though they exercised tribal rights to fish.

3. Who Can Waive Tribal Sovereign Immunity? In *Puyallup Tribe v. Department of Game,* 433 U.S. 165, 173 (1977), the Supreme Court held the tribe immune because the Court could find no evidence that "either the Tribe or Congress has waived its claim of immunity." One year later, in *Santa Clara Pueblo v. Martinez,* 436 U.S. 49, 58 (1978), the Court stated:

> Indian tribes have long been recognized as possessing the common-law immunity from suit traditionally enjoyed by sovereign powers. This aspect of tribal sovereignty,

like all others, is subject to the superior and plenary control of Congress. But "without congressional authorization," the "Indian Nations are exempt from suit." [quoting] *United States v. United States Fidelity & Guaranty Co.*, [309 U.S. 506, 512 (1940)].
It is settled that a waiver of sovereign immunity "'cannot be implied but must be unequivocally expressed.'" [quoting] *United States v. Testan*, [424 U.S. 392, 399 (1976)].

Does the quoted passage from *Martinez* undercut the earlier statement that tribes themselves have the power to waive sovereign immunity on their own initiative? If so, would such a disability result from the federal trust relationship? For an argument that such a disability would be inconsistent with the current policy favoring self-determination, see *United States v. Oregon*, 657 F.2d 1009 (9th Cir. 1981); *accord Wichita & Affiliated Tribes v. Hodel*, 788 F.2d 765, 772 (D.C. Cir. 1986) (collecting cases from four circuits agreeing that tribes can waive sovereign immunity).

On the other hand, if Congress can waive tribal sovereign immunity, as the Court seems to say, what is the basis for this congressional power? The answer depends on one's vision of the source of tribal sovereign immunity. If tribal immunity is only derived from the tribe's relationship with the United States, so that the tribe shares in the federal government's immunity, then Congress would be able to waive tribal immunity and at the same time tribes might be disabled from waiving it on their own. If, in contrast, tribal sovereign immunity is derived from the tribe's status as a sovereign entity, entitled thereby to the protection of the common law doctrine, there would be no doubt that the tribe could waive it. Moreover, if Congress could also waive tribal immunity, it would have to do so by abrogating tribal sovereignty. Which position did the First Circuit take in *Bottomly*?

4. Waiver of Sovereign Immunity by the Tribe: Even if sovereign immunity is seen as arising from the tribe's sovereign status, there may be some limits on a tribe's ability to waive immunity. *See* 25 U.S.C. § 81. In *Native Village of Eyak v. GC Contractors*, 658 P.2d 756 (Alaska 1983), the court stated that the Village had inherent sovereignty to waive immunity by a contract that did not require secretarial approval, because it did not "relate to Indian land." Nevertheless, the Alaska Supreme Court found a waiver on rather dubious grounds, as being implicit in a contractual provision submitting disputes to arbitration. *Accord Val/Del, Inc. v. Superior Court*, 145 Ariz. 558, 703 P.2d 502 (App.), *cert. denied*, 474 U.S. 920 (1985). In contrast, other courts have required a clearer statement to find a tribal waiver. The Ninth Circuit held that a contractual arbitration clause submitting disputes to the American Arbitration Association was not sufficiently clear to waive sovereign immunity in a judicial proceeding, because "such a reading of the arbitration clause runs counter to not only the strong presumption against tribal waivers of immunity, but also generally accepted principles governing the interpretation of contractual arbitration provisions." *Pan American Co. v. Sycuan Band of Mission Indians*, 884 F.2d 416 (9th Cir. 1989). *See also Atkinson v. Haldane*, 569 P.2d 151 (Alaska 1977) (fact that tribe had liability insurance was not sufficient to establish waiver because insurance was designed to protect tribe from a judicial finding against sovereign immunity). These cases apply the same principles of strict construction disfavoring waivers applicable in sovereign immunity cases generally. As with state or federal sovereign immunity, tribal waivers may be limited to certain kinds of cases, such as breach of contract actions, or certain kinds of relief (declaratory rather than damages), or even to the assets upon which a judgment can be executed. For example, in *Namekagon Dev. Co. v. Bois Forte Reservation*

Hous. Auth., 517 F.2d 508 (8th Cir. 1975), a suit brought by a developer against a tribe, the court found the tribe had waived sovereign immunity for breach of contract but not for execution of judgment against tribal funds, except those funds received from the government to pay contractual obligations to the developer.

Tribes organized under the Indian Reorganization Act may have provisions in tribal charters organized under section 17 of the IRA, authorizing them to sue and be sued. Some courts have held that such provisions constitute a sufficiently unequivocal, express congressional authorization to sue. *Martinez v. Southern Ute Tribe,* 150 Colo. 504, 374 P.2d 691 (1962) (sue and be sued clause in charter a complete waiver of all tribal immunity). The better view, however, is that sue and be sued clauses apply only to actions of the tribe in its section 17 corporate capacity and not in its section 16 governmental capacity. *See, e.g., Ramey Constr. Co. v. Apache Tribe,* 673 F.2d 315, 320 (10th Cir. 1982) (sue and be sued clause in charter did not apply to tribe as a constitutional entity) (suit by general contractor for breach of contract barred by sovereign immunity); *Boe v. Ft. Belknap Indian Community,* 455 F. Supp. 462, 463-64 (D. Mont. 1978), *aff'd,* 642 F.2d 276 (9th Cir. 1981) (same) (suit by tribal member in political dispute); *S. Unique, Ltd. v. Gila River Pima-Maricopa Indian Community,* 138 Ariz. 378, 674 P.2d 1376 (App. 1983) (upholding charter qualification of consent as limited to corporate assets only). To complicate matters, Indian tribes often do not distinguish between operations undertaken pursuant to a corporate charter that may have a sue and be sued clause and commercial activities undertaken by the tribe. *See* Pommersheim & Pechota, *Tribal Immunity, Tribal Courts, and the Federal System: Emerging Contours and Frontiers,* 32 S. Dak. L. Rev. 553, 558-61 (1986).

Appearance by the tribe as plaintiff in federal court does not waive sovereign immunity for cross-claims or counterclaims. *See, e.g., Citizens Band of Potawatomi Indian Tribe v. Oklahoma Tax Comm'n,* 888 F.2d 1303 (10th Cir. 1989), *cert. granted,* 111 S. Ct. 37 (1990); *Squaxin Island Tribe v. Washington,* 781 F.2d 715, at 723 & n.11 (9th Cir. 1986) (immunity barred counterclaim by defendant); *Wichita & Affiliated Tribes v. Hodel,* 788 F.2d 765 (D.C. Cir. 1986) (immunity barred cross-claim); *cf. United States v. United States Fid. & Guar. Co.,* 309 U.S. 506, 513 (1940) (United States suing for tribe not subject to cross-claims without explicit consent).

Tribes may waive sovereign immunity in tribal courts as long as trust property is not involved. As more civil cases are brought in tribal courts, some tribes, such as the Menominee Tribe, are enacting statutes waiving immunity in tribal court. Some tribal courts have held that sovereign immunity does not bar an action for declaratory and injunctive relief. *See, e.g., Gonzales v. Allen,* 16 Indian L. Rep. 6048 (Sho.-Ban. Tr. Ct. 1989). For a thorough analysis of tribal law on sovereign immunity, see Johnson & Madden, *Sovereign Immunity in Indian Tribal Law,* 12 Am. Indian L. Rev. 153 (1984).

5. Waiver of Tribal Sovereign Immunity by Congress: If Congress can waive tribal sovereign immunity, as the quotation from *Martinez* in note 3, *supra,* seems to indicate, statutory language purporting to waive tribal sovereign immunity should be strictly construed against finding a waiver. Nevertheless, this principle is not always honored. For example, in *Blue Legs v. BIA,* 867 F.2d 1094 (8th Cir. 1989), the court of appeals held that the Resource Conservation and Recovery Act of 1976, 42 U.S.C. § 6901 et seq., waived tribal sovereign immunity in federal court, because it explicitly provided for a civil action to be brought in district court against any person, specifically including Indian tribes within the definition of municipalities which were in turn specifically included within the definition of persons. Although the statutory language at issue in *Blue Legs* clearly granted jurisdiction, it was silent on the issue of tribal sovereign immunity. Both the canon of construction disfavoring waivers, relied on in the excerpt from *Martinez*, quoted in note 3, *supra*, and the canons favoring Indian sovereignty discussed in Chapter 2, section C2, should cause courts to be reluctant to find a congressional waiver of tribal sovereign immunity when the statute is ambiguous.

A case illustrating greater judicial sensitivity toward tribal sovereign immunity involved Public Law 638, the Indian Self-Determination Act, 25 U.S.C.A. §§ 450-450n (1983 & Supp. 1987), which permits tribes to enter into contracts with the federal government to supply services to the tribes. (These contracts are called "638 contracts" after the Public Law number.) As amended in 1988, section 450(c) of the Act requires the Secretary to obtain insurance for tribes carrying out 638 contracts, but requires the insurance carrier to explicitly waive any defenses to an ensuing lawsuit based on tribal sovereign immunity. Can this provision be read as demonstrating congressional intent to waive tribal immunity in a suit against the tribe? In *Evans v. McKay*, 869 F.2d 1341 (9th Cir. 1989), the Ninth Circuit gave this provision a very narrow reading, holding that section 450f(c) only precludes the *insurer* from raising tribal sovereign immunity. In addition, the court relied on 25 U.S.C. § 450n, which states that "[n]othing in this Act shall be construed as (1) affecting modifying, diminishing, or otherwise impairing the sovereign immunity from suit enjoyed by an Indian tribe."

The tribe cannot assert its tribal immunity against the United States, however. *See United States v. Red Lake Band of Chippewa Indians*, 827 F.2d 380, 382 (8th Cir. 1987), *cert. denied*, 485 U.S. 935 (1988) ("It is an inherent implication of superior power exercised by the United States over Indian tribes that a tribe may not interpose its sovereign immunity against the United States.") (Collecting cases).

b. Full Faith and Credit or Comity For Tribal Laws and Judgments

SHEPPARD v. SHEPPARD

104 Idaho 1, 655 P.2d 895 (1982)

[In a divorce proceeding brought by a non-Indian against his wife, an Indian, the husband argued that he should not have to pay child support for a child adopted by the couple in tribal court while they lived on the Ft. Hall Reservation, because the tribal court adoption was void. A state magistrate agreed with the husband and refused to award child support for any but the couple's three natural children. The district court reversed on this issue, and this appeal followed.]

SHEPARD, J.

II. *The Adoption*

We turn [next] to the validity of the adoption. The magistrate found that the adoption proceedings before the tribal court did not conform to the procedural requirements of the tribal code and held the adoption void. The district court reversed that portion of the magistrate's decision, holding that substantial compliance with tribal procedural requirements had been satisfied and George Sheppard was estopped to challenge the decree. We affirm, however, on other grounds, [because] we find the question of the tribal court jurisdiction to be dispositive. That issue was argued before and considered by the district court.

In effect George Sheppard attempts to mount a collateral attack on the tribal court decree of adoption. A final judgment entered by a court of competent jurisdiction is presumed valid and therefore the party asserting the invalidity of the judgment must carry the burden of proof sufficient to overcome the presumption. [*E.g., Clear v. Marvin*, 86 Idaho 87, 92, 383 P.2d 346, 349 (1963).] Tribal court decrees, while not precisely equivalent to decrees of the courts of sister states, are nevertheless entitled to full faith and credit. The full faith and credit clause of the United States Constitution provides that each state shall give full faith and credit to the "judicial proceedings of every other state" and that Congress may pass general laws to implement this clause. U.S. Const. art 4, § 1. In response, Congress passed 28 U.S.C. § 1738, which states in pertinent part:

> "Such ... judicial proceedings ... shall have the same full faith and credit in every court within the United States and its Territories and Possessions as they have by law or usage in the courts of such State, Territory or Possession from which they are taken."

The issue, then, is whether Indian tribes are, for the purpose of 28 U.S.C. § 1738, either "Territories" or "Possessions."

In the case of *United States ex rel. Mackey v. Cox*, 59 U.S. (18 How.) 100 (1856), a Cherokee probate court had granted letters of administration on the estate of a deceased tribal member and it was held that the federal courts of the District of Columbia were required to recognize those letters of administration as valid. The Court also stated, in discussing the differences between Indian territories and territories organized to eventually achieve statehood, that:

> "This, however, is no reason why the laws and proceedings of the Cherokee territory, so far as relates to rights claimed under them, should not be placed upon the same footing as other territories in the Union. It is not a foreign but a *domestic territory*, — a territory which originated under our constitution and laws." *Id.* at 103 (emphasis added).

More recently, the Supreme Court has indicated, citing *Cox* with approval, that full faith and credit analysis is appropriately applied to tribal courts. *Santa Clara Pueblo v. Martinez*, 436 U.S. 49, 65-66 n.21 (1978). Consequently, we agree with those courts which have found the phrase "Territories and Possessions" broad enough to include Indian tribes, at least as they are presently constituted under the laws of the United States. [*E.g., Jim v. CIT Financial Services*, 87 N.M. 362, 533 P.2d 751 (1975); *In re Adoption of Buehl*, 87 Wash. 2d 649, 555 P.2d 1334 (1976).] *See generally*, Ragsdale, *Problems in the Application of Full Faith and Credit for Indian Tribes*, 7 N.M.L. Rev. 133 (1977); Comment, *Conflicts Between State and Tribal Law: The Application of Full Faith and Credit Legislation to Indian Tribes*, 1981 Ariz. St. L.J. 801 (1981). We believe that this holding will facilitate better relations between the courts of this state and the various tribal courts within Idaho.[2]

---

[2] It has come to the attention of this Court that, in an action related to this case, the Shoshone-Bannock appellate court, in reversing the tribal trial court, held that it was not required to give full

One ground for successfully challenging the judgments of the courts of another state is to show that the court lacked subject matter jurisdiction. Full faith and credit is not to be accorded a decree of a court which lacked subject matter jurisdiction. George Sheppard asserts that the tribal court had no jurisdiction to approve the adoption of an Indian child by a husband and wife, one of whom is Indian and the other non-Indian. [Because George Sheppard failed to carry his burden of proving tribal law at the time of the adoption decree, there is] no proof that the asserted procedural defects rise to the level of jurisdictional defects.

Lower courts may take judicial note of the law of another state. *White v. White*, 94 Idaho 26, 480 P.2d 872 (1971). In *White*, judicial notice was allowed because "[m]odern communications have put the statutory compilations of other states within easy access of Idaho's courts." *Id.*, 94 Idaho at 30, 480 P.2d 872. Unfortunately, there is not the same "easy access" to the various compilations of the laws of the Shoshone-Bannock Tribes, and hence the policy behind the decision in *White* is not present in the instant case.

The order of the district court holding George Sheppard responsible for the adoptive child, Michael, is affirmed, as is the remand to the magistrate court for a determination of the proper amount of child support.

MEXICAN v. CIRCLE BEAR

370 N.W.2d 737 (S.D. 1985)

WOLLMAN, Justice.

This is an appeal from a judgment of the circuit court quashing a temporary restraining order and releasing the body of Charles Mexican, deceased, to his sisters, Irene Circle Bear and Sarah Mexican. We reverse and remand with directions to give recognition to the order of the Cheyenne River Tribal Court.

Charles Mexican and Mabel Mexican (for convenience we will refer to decedent and the parties by their first names) were married on March 17, 1955. Mabel is an enrolled member of the Cheyenne River Sioux Tribe of South Dakota; Charles was an enrolled member of the Oglala Sioux Tribe of South Dakota. Irene and Sarah are enrolled members of the Oglala Sioux Tribe.

Charles and Mabel were long-time residents of Red Scaffold, South Dakota, which is located [on] the Cheyenne River Sioux Reservation. Charles served as a medicine man for the Sioux Nation. He became ill in late 1984 and [died in the Sioux Sanitarium Hospital in Rapid City, South Dakota] on March 14, 1985. During his period of hospitalization in Rapid City, Charles was not visited by Mabel, which caused him to feel estranged from and unhappy with her. During his period of hospitalization Charles executed a will that purported to disinherit Mabel.

---

faith and credit to the decrees of Idaho state courts. In part this decision was based on the belief that state courts did not accord tribal courts full faith and credit. As we have shown, some state courts including this one, do. Secondly, the tribal court failed to acknowledge 28 U.S.C. § 1738, which requires "*every court within the United States*" to give full faith and credit to decrees of state courts (emphasis added). Along with this opinion extends the hope of a good working relationship between state and tribal courts, and we hope, therefore, that the Shoshone-Bannock courts will reconsider the application of full faith and credit in their proceedings. Indeed the commentators unanimously agree that tribal courts must afford other states full faith and credit. Ragsdale, *supra*, at 141; Comment, *supra*, at 818.

Prior to January 8, 1985, Charles' directions to Mabel were that he wished to be buried with his mother at Bridger, South Dakota. During his period of hospitalization, however, Charles expressed his desire that he be buried either with his deceased father at Rockyford, located within the boundaries of the Pine Ridge Indian Reservation, or in Rapid City, or in such place as designated by his son, John Mexican. Charles further stated that he did not want to be buried at Red Scaffold, South Dakota, and that he wanted his sisters to make arrangements for the disposal and burial of his body.

Upon learning of Charles' death and of his sisters' plans to bury him in Rapid City, Mabel obtained from the Cheyenne River Sioux Tribal Court on March 15, 1985, an ex parte order enjoining Irene and Sarah from burying Charles' body and directing those having physical custody of the body to turn it over to Mabel. Upon learning that [the] Funeral Home, which had custody of the body, would not honor the tribal court order, Mabel applied to the circuit court on March 16 for a temporary restraining order and order to show cause why Irene and Sarah and the funeral home should not be permanently enjoined from interfering with her rights and duties under state law to dispose of her husband's body. The trial court issued a restraining order and order to show cause. A hearing on the order to show cause was held in Rapid City on March 18. Irene and Sarah moved to continue the circuit court proceedings until the Cheyenne River Sioux Tribal Court had been given a chance to hold a hearing on the order that it had issued on March 15.

On March 19 a hearing was held in the Cheyenne River Sioux Tribal Court, at which Irene and Sarah, together with John Mexican and one of Irene's daughters, testified in support of Irene and Sarah's contentions that Charles and Mabel were estranged at the time of Charles' death and that Charles had directed that he be buried at a place other than on the Cheyenne River Reservation. Counsel for Irene and Sarah stated during the course of the hearing that "our claim is a tribal custom and usage, that's our claim to the body of Charles Mexican." Again, in arguing his clients' position at the conclusion of the hearing, counsel stated:

> [I]t would appear that the court could take judicial notice whatever the court considers tribal custom to be because I think that's a controlling matter here. I don't think the State law has really anything to do with it.... We feel that since the court has taken the matter over we're moving the court to vacate its Order of March 15, 1985. That the court indicate in an Order where it considers the tribal custom to be and that particular order would be a very great use by Judge Konenkamp who now has to make the final decision concerning this matter in Rapid City. But, I do know that he wants to know. He wants the tribal custom and usage of the tribe to be taken into consideration when he makes his decision. I think that's the way he's going to go. The State law might provide for white people. I do feel that he's not bound just like we're [sic] bound to accept state law. Most of the Judges are looking to give full faith and credit to tribal court orders and I think that's a good development. I think they're really looking to us to give them some advice in this matter that they know little or nothing about.

At the conclusion of the hearing, the tribal judge entered oral findings from the bench, reduced to writing and filed on March 20, and awarded custody of Charles' body to Mabel.

Among other things, the tribal court judge found that the customs of both the Oglala Sioux Tribe and the Cheyenne River Sioux Tribe are that upon the death of a married person the surviving spouse, absent any showing that the parties were separated at the time of death, has the duty to bury the deceased spouse and the right to custody of the body for the limited purpose of burial. The tribal court found that Charles and Mabel were not separated at the time of Charles' death. The tribal court also found that the will that Charles had executed on March 11, 1985, contained no direction regarding his wishes for the disposition of his body upon his death.

On March 20, 1985, a further hearing was held before the circuit court in Rapid City. The trial court was made aware of the tribal court judge's findings of fact and order. At the close of the hearing, the circuit court quashed its March 16 temporary restraining order and entered a judgment awarding the custody of Charles' body to Irene and Sarah. This appeal followed. The trial court stayed its judgment pending our decision on appeal.

SDCL 34-26-1 provides:

> Every person has the right to direct the manner in which his body or any part thereof shall be disposed of after his death, and to direct the manner in which any part of his body which becomes separated therefrom during his lifetime shall be disposed of. The provisions ... of §§ 34-26-14 to 34-26-19, inclusive, do not apply where such person has given directions for the disposal of his body or any part thereof inconsistent with those provisions.

SDCL 34-26-14 provides in part: "The person charged by law with the duty of burying the body of a deceased person is entitled to the custody of such body for the purpose of burying it ...."

SDCL 34-26-16 provides in part:

> The duty of burying the body of a deceased person ... devolves upon the persons hereinafter specified:
> (1) If the decedent was married the duty of burial devolves upon the husband or wife;
>
> ....

Although there is no property right as such in a dead body, the right to bury a dead body has been recognized by the courts as a quasi-property right. *See, e.g.,* 22 Am. Jur. 2d *Dead Bodies* § 4 (1965); 25A C.J.S. *Dead Bodies* § 2 (1966). The importance of the interest of the living in the bodies of the dead had been characterized as follows:

> "We can imagine no clearer or dearer right in the gamut of civil liberty and security than to bury our dead in peace and unobstructed; none more sacred to the individual, nor more important of preservation and protection from the point of view of public welfare and decency ...."

Scarpaci v. Milwaukee County, 96 Wis. 2d 663, [672] (1980) (quoting *Koerber v. Patek,* 123 Wis. 453 (1905)). It is with a recognition of and an appreciation for the highly personal nature of the right to arrange for the burial of the body of a deceased family member that we approach the resolution of the issue before us.

[The wife argued that comity required the circuit court to recognize the tribal court order.]

The doctrine of comity has been defined as follows:

> The extent to which the law of one nation, as put in force within its territory, whether by executive order, by legislative act, or by judicial decree, shall be allowed to

operate within the dominion of another nation, depends upon what our greatest jurists have been content to call "the comity of nations." Although the phrase has been often criticised, no satisfactory substitute has been suggested.

"Comity," in the legal sense, is neither a matter of absolute obligation on the one hand, nor of mere courtesy and good will upon the other. But it is the recognition which one nation allows within its territory to the legislative, executive, or judicial acts of another nation, having due regard both to international duty and convenience, and to the rights of its own citizens or of other persons who are under the protection of its laws.

Hilton v. Guyot, 159 U.S. 113, 163 (1894).

The *Hilton* Court went on to specify the circumstances that must exist as a condition precedent to the application of the doctrine of comity:

[W]e are satisfied that where there has been opportunity for a full and fair trial abroad before a court of competent jurisdiction, conducting the trial upon regular proceedings, after due citation or voluntary appearance of the defendant, and under a system of jurisprudence likely to secure an impartial administration of justice between the citizens of its own country and those of other countries, and there is nothing to show either prejudice in the court or in the system of laws under which it was sitting, or fraud in procuring the judgment, or any other special reason why the comity of this nation should not allow it full effect, the merits of the case should not, in an action brought in this country upon the judgment, be tried afresh, as on a new trial or an appeal, upon the mere assertion of the party that the judgment was erroneous in law or in fact. 159 U.S. at 202-03.

The *Hilton* conditions have been paraphrased as follows:

(1) the foreign court actually had jurisdiction over both the subject matter and the parties; (2) the decree was not obtained fraudulently; (3) the decree was rendered by a system of law reasonably assuring the requisites of an impartial administration of justice — due notice and a hearing; and (4) the judgment did not contravene the public policy of the jurisdiction in which it is relied upon.

In re Marriage of Red Fox, 23 Or. App. 393, [398] (1975).

This court has long recognized and applied the doctrine of comity. *See [e.g.,] Emerson-Brantingham Implement Co. v. Ainslie,* 38 S.D. 472 (1917).

Tribal governments are unique in the federal system. They derive their powers of government from their inherent sovereignty and not by delegation from the federal government. [*United States v. Wheeler,* 435 U.S. 313 (1978). Indian tribes exist as sovereign entities with powers of self-government. *See, e.g., Merrion v. Jicarilla Apache Tribe,* 455 U.S. 130 (1982). This retained sovereign power may, of course, be divested by Congress. *See, e.g., National Farmers Union Insurance Companies v. Crow Tribe,* [471 U.S. 845] (1985).

One of the attributes of tribal sovereignty is the power to adjudicate private civil disputes. As the United States Supreme Court stated in [*Santa Clara Pueblo v. Martinez,* 436 U.S. 49, 65 (1978)], "Tribal courts have repeatedly been recognized as appropriate forums for the exclusive adjudication of disputes affecting important personal and property interests of both Indians and non-Indians." 436 U.S. at 65.

We join with those courts that have held that tribal court orders should be recognized in state courts under the principle of comity. *Allen v. Industrial Commission,* 92 Ariz. 357 (1962); *Begay v. Miller,* 70 Ariz. 380 (1950); *Wippert v. Blackfeet Tribe,* 654 P.2d 512 (Mont. 1982); *In re Marriage of Limpy,* 636

P.2d 266 (Mont. 1981); *State v. District Court,* 187 Mont. 209 (1980); *In re Marriage of Red Fox, supra.*

In reaching this conclusion, we of necessity hold that the prerequisites to the application of the doctrine of comity as expressed in *Hilton v. Guyot, supra,* have been met.

With respect to the matter of jurisdiction, it is clear beyond peradventure that Irene and Sarah voluntarily submitted to the jurisdiction of the Cheyenne River Tribal Court by litigating the merits of the conflicting claims regarding the custody of Charles' body.

Counsel for Irene and Sarah forthrightly acknowledged during oral argument before this court that his clients were not contending that the March 20 tribal court order was obtained fraudulently.

The order was rendered by a court that gave the competing parties adequate opportunity to present evidence on their conflicting claims. Based upon our review of the transcript of the March 19, 1985, hearing and the findings of fact, conclusions of law, and order entered following the hearing, we are satisfied that the parties were afforded an impartial hearing that satisfied the requirements of due process. True, the March 15, 1985, order was entered ex parte, but that was merely in the nature of a temporary order, as was the circuit court order of March 16.

There remains the question whether the fact that tribal custom with respect to custody of a dead body is different from South Dakota law on the subject is reason enough to deny comity to the tribal court order. In *Knittle [v. Ellenbusch,* 38 S.D. 22 (1916)], the court was faced with the contention that it should not apply the law of a foreign state to the detriment of a citizen of South Dakota when there was no South Dakota law that would require the same result. [The court in *Knittle* stated that] "if comity is so restricted that a substantive law of the state of the contract will be disregarded whenever the state of the forum does not have the same law, the doctrine of comity becomes a farce."

[Thus, we] conclude that the fact that tribal custom is different from state law in that the right of a surviving spouse to the custody of the body of the deceased spouse for the purpose of burial takes precedence over the deceased spouse's express burial wishes is not reason enough to deny effect to an order based upon that custom. We would be hard pressed to say that the state legislature could not constitutionally repeal SDCL 34-26-1. Given the diversity of decisions regarding the right to custody of a dead body for burial purposes, *see generally* Annot. 54 A.L.R. 3rd 1027 (1973), we would be guilty of parochialism if we were to hold that tribal custom regarding that right is so abhorrent to the policy expressed in state law that it may not be given effect. Accordingly, we hold that recognition and enforcement of the tribal court order of March 20, 1985, would not contravene the public policy of this state.

[*Reversed and remanded.*]

HENDERSON, JUSTICE (concurring in result).

Out of courtesy and respect to the tribal judge's order, and as a willingness to grant a privilege, and not as a matter of right, but out of deference and good will, on behalf of the highest Court of this state, I would apply the principle of judicial comity to the tribal judge's order of March 20, 1985, which awarded the custody of Charles Mexican's body to his wife, Mabel Mexican. I do not recognize that the principle of the comity of nations should be here applied; and, hereby, I ascribe to the belief, in law, that there is a distinction between judicial comity and comity of nations. Comity is begotten from the womb of mutual respect and is not a child of obligation. We must live in mutual respect with our Indian brothers who serve on the trial courts of the various Indian reservations in South Dakota. They, in return, should likewise extend unto our courts reciprocating courtesy and respect.

[The tribal court judge's] bench decision of March 19, 1985, reduced to writing and filed on March 20, 1985, gives us a deep insight into [the role of tribal custom:]

> I will now rule for Mabel Mexican on this issue here simply based on tradition and custom, but I do want to leave this word with all of you, being relatives. This is a sad time indeed for all of you no matter which side you are on. You must bring yourself to understand that to come together to respect the memory of a medicine man you must put your feelings aside and no matter where he will be buried come to that funeral. You've all expressed your desires. You've all expressed that you loved him. That's what you need to do — don't let the white man's law or any other law tear you apart. If you respect custom and tradition, then respect our tradition and come, all of you. That I will leave with you. This Court now stands adjourned.

[W]ithin a state, we are addressing comity in a more limited geographic and conceptual scope. Perhaps the Sioux Tribe was, in the vernacular of the tribal judge, historically recognized by its own people as the "Great Sioux Nation," [but we] have but one nation, indivisible, and it is called the United States of America. Therefore, I am willing to give unto the judicial decision of this tribal judge all due deference and respect, as I have heretofore set forth, but not out of any recognition that the "Sioux Nation" is an independent nation within the United States of America. The Constitution of the United States of America established but one nation....

NOTES

1. Full Faith and Credit or Comity: There are two theories justifying the recognition of tribal court laws and judgments. The majority opinion in *Mexican* relies on the doctrine of comity, the doctrine generally applicable to recognition of the judgments and laws of foreign nations. Does the adoption of this theory at least implicitly recognize the sovereign status of Indian tribes? Is this the reason Justice Henderson's concurring opinion distinguishes between "judicial comity and comity of nations"? The Idaho Supreme Court adopted the second theory in *Sheppard*: that the full faith and credit clause of the Constitution and its implementing legislation, 28 U.S.C. § 1738, requiring "every court within the United States" to recognize "Acts, records, and judicial proceedings" of any "State, Territory or Possession" mandates state recognition of tribal court judgments. What is the rationale for interpreting the statute to cover Indian tribal court judgments? As the court noted in *Sheppard*, some language in an opinion written by Justice Thurgood Marshall seems to favor this approach. In a footnote, the Court stated "Judgments of tribal courts, as to matters properly within their jurisdiction, have been regarded in some circumstances as entitled to full faith and credit in other courts." *Santa Clara Pueblo v. Martinez,* 436 U.S. 49, 65 n.21 (1978) (citing *Mackey v. Coxe,* 59 U.S. 100 (1855)).

Which approach should be applied to recognition of tribal court judgments in state or federal courts? Professor Clinton argues that the reasoning of *Mackey v. Coxe*, discussed in the *Sheppard* case, and the present status of Indian tribes favor full faith and credit over the comity principle:

> While the early treatment of Indian tribes as domestic dependent nations outside the federal union arguably might once have made the comity model of intergovernmental cooperation appropriate, the subsequent *de facto* incorporation of Indian tribes into the federal union should significantly alter the extent of the enforceable legal obligation that state and federal courts have to recognize tribal laws and judgments.

Clinton, *Tribal Courts and the Federal Union*, 26 WILLAMETTE L. REV. 841, 906 (1990). If full faith and credit requires state courts to recognize tribal court judgments, must a tribal court in turn recognize state court judgments because the tribal court is a "court within the United States" within the meaning of 28 U.S.C. § 1738? If section 1738 is read as compelling states and federal courts to enforce tribal court judgments, a refusal to enforce a tribal court judgment would be an appealable federal question. If the same principles were applied to a tribal court's refusal to enforce a state court judgment, what problems might be foreseen in protecting the autonomy of tribal governments? Professor Ragsdale has pointed out that tribal courts may frequently legitimately refuse to enforce state court judgments in cases in which the state court lacked subject matter jurisdiction because of federal prohibitions based on preemption and infringement on tribal sovereignty. (These principles are covered in Chapter 4, section A2.) He has suggested a federal statute permitting federal court review in order to mitigate the tribal-state tensions that might result from frequent tribal court refusal to enforce state court judgments. Ragsdale, *Problems in the Application of Full Faith and Credit for Indian Tribes*, 7 N.M.L. REV. 133, 145-52. For an argument that neither the Constitution nor section 1738 can be read as including Indian tribes, see Vetter, *Of Tribal Courts and "Territories": Is Full Faith and Credit Required?*, 23 CAL. W.L. REV. 219 (1987). Another commentator has called for legislation extending full faith and credit to tribes, but only after tribes have taken steps to improve their judicial systems and Congress has created a new federal Indian court of appeals. Note, *Recognition of Tribal Decisions in State Courts*, 37 STAN. L. REV. 1397 (1985). What would be the basis of congressional power to enact such legislation?

2. Acts and Judicial Proceedings: The doctrine of full faith and credit applies to recognition and application of foreign *laws*, the choice of law issue, as well as to recognition of foreign judgments. In *Jim v. CIT Financial Servs. Corp.*, 87 N.M. 362, 533 P.2d 751 (1975), New Mexico gave full faith and credit to a Navajo tribal law. In contrast, Arizona in *Brown v. Babbitt Ford, Inc.*, 117 Ariz. 192, 571 P.2d 689 (Ct. App. 1977) held that the doctrine of comity governed the question whether the same Navajo ordinance at issue in *Jim* was entitled to enforcement. Does full faith and credit have more compulsive force in choice of law questions or in recognition of foreign judgments? *See Allstate Ins. Co. v. Hague*, 449 U.S. 302 (1981). For an analysis of both *Jim* and *Brown*, see Comment, *Conflicts Between State and Tribal Law: The Application of Full Faith and Credit Legislation to Indian Tribes*, 1981 ARIZ. ST. L.J. 801.

3. Federal Statutes Requiring Recognition of Tribal Law or Judgments: In addition to section 1738, Congress has on occasion directly confronted the issue of the full faith and credit due to tribal actions. In Public Law 280, Congress specifically provided authorized states covered by the act to recognize tribal law (but apparently not judgments) if not inconsistent with state law:

> Any tribal ordinance or custom heretofore or hereafter adopted by an Indian tribe,

band, or community in the exercise of any authority which it may possess shall, if not inconsistent with any applicable civil law of the State, be given full force and effect in the determination of civil causes of action pursuant to this section.

28 U.S.C. § 1360(c). *See also* 25 U.S.C. § 1322(c). More recently, in the Indian Child Welfare Act of 1978, § 101(d), Congress provided:

> The United States, every State, every territory or possession of the United States, and every Indian tribe shall give full faith and credit to the public acts, records, and judicial proceedings of any Indian tribe applicable to Indian child custody proceedings to the same extent that such entities give full faith and credit to the public acts, records, and judicial proceedings of any other entity.

25 U.S.C. § 1911(d)

See also Maine Indian Claims Settlement Act, 25 U.S.C. § 1725 ("The Passamaquoddy Tribe, the Penobscot Nation, and the State of Maine shall give full faith and credit to the judicial proceedings of each other."). Does the enactment of these laws indicate Congress does not believe that section 1738 applies to tribal laws and judgments? Is 28 U.S.C. § 1360(c) or 25 U.S.C. § 1911(d) more deferential to tribal laws? The Indian Child Welfare Act is covered in detail in Chapter 4, section C2.

3. A CONTRARY VIEW

SEPARATE DISSENTING VIEWS OF CONGRESSMAN LLOYD MEEDS, in American Indian Policy Review Commission, Final Report 573-83 (1977)

Sovereignty — Tribal Self-Government or Territorial Government?

The fundamental error of this report is that it perceives the American Indian tribe as a body politic in the nature of a sovereign as that word is used to describe the United States and the States, rather than as a body politic which the United States, through its sovereign power, permits to govern itself and order its *internal* affairs, but not the affairs of others. The report seeks to convert a political notion into a legal doctrine. In order to demythologize the notion of American Indian tribal sovereignty, it is essential to briefly describe American federalism.

In our Federal system, as ordained and established by the United States Constitution, there are but two sovereign entities: the United States and the States. This is obvious not only from an examination of the Constitution, its structure, and its amendments, but also from the express language of the 10th amendment which provides:

> The powers not delegated to the United States by the Constitution, nor prohibited by it to the states, are reserved to the States respectively, or to the people.

And, under the 14th amendment, all citizens of the United States who are residents of a particular State are also citizens of that State.

The Commission report (especially chapters 3 and 5), would have us believe that there is a third source of sovereign and governmental power in the United States. It argues that American Indian tribes have the characteristics of sovereignty over the lands they occupy analogous to the kind of sovereignty possessed by the United States and the States. The report describes Indian tribes as governmental units in the territorial sense. This fundamental error infects the balance of the report in a way which is contrary to American federalism and unacceptable to the United States, the States, and non-Indian citizens.

The blunt fact of the matter is that American Indian tribes are not a third set of governments in the American federal system. They are not sovereigns. The Congress of the United States has permitted them to be self-governing entities but not entities which would govern others. American Indian tribal self-government has meant that the Congress permits Indian tribes to make their own laws and be ruled by them. The erroneous view adopted by the Commission's report is that American Indian tribal self-government is territorial in nature. On the contrary, American Indian tribal self-government is purposive. The Congress has permitted Indian tribes to govern themselves for the purpose of maintaining tribal integrity and identity. But this does not mean that the Congress has permitted them to exercise general governmental powers over the lands they occupy. This is the crucial distinction which the Commission report fails to make. The Commission has failed to deal with the ultimate legal issue, which is the very subject of its charter.

In addition, the Commission has failed to make the distinction between the power of American Indian tribes to govern themselves on the lands they occupy, and their proprietary interest in those lands.... [A]s landowners, American Indian tribes have the same power over their lands as do other private landowners. This would include the power to exclude or to sue for trespass damages. But landowners do not have governmental powers over the land they own. Land ownership, alone, is insufficient to rise to governmental powers....

Indian reservations exist within the boundaries of the States and within the United States.... American Indian tribal self-government comes into play because the Congress, in exercising its powers under article I, § 8(3), of the United States Constitution, has, in general, insulated reservation Indians from State governmental power. In order to promote the preservation of their distinctive cultures and values, the Congress had decided that some American Indians should be allowed to make their own laws and be ruled by them. This does not mean that the Congress allows American Indian tribes to govern their reservations in the same way in which a State governs within its boundaries. A tribe's power is limited to governing the internal affairs of its members....

The doctrine of inherent tribal sovereignty, adopted by the majority report, ignores the historical reality that American Indian tribes lost their sovereignty through discovery, conquest, cession, treaties, statutes, and history. An international tribunal, Cayuga Indian Claims (*Great Britain v. United States*), 20 Am. J. Int'l L. 574, 577 (1926) (American and British Claims Arbitration Tribunal) and the United States Supreme Court, *Johnson v. M'Intosh*, 21 U.S. (8 Wheat.) 543, 574 (1823) and *Cherokee Nation v. Georgia*, 30 U.S. (5 Pet.) 1, 17 (1831), have applied these well-settled international law doctrines to extinguish American Indian tribal sovereignty. Hence, to the extent American Indian tribes are permitted to exist as political units at all, it is by virtue of the laws of the United States and not any inherent right to government, either of themselves or of others....

It is clear that nothing in the United States Constitution guarantees to Indian tribes sovereignty or prerogatives of any sort, let alone their continued existence....

Tribal government, no doubt, had one purpose when Indians were neither citizens of the United States nor of the State in which they lived. See, *Elk v. Wilkins*, 112 U.S. 94, 5 S. Ct. 41 (1884). But all non-citizen Indians were made citizens of the United States by the Act of June 2, 1924, ch. 233, 43 Stat. 253, 8 U.S.C. § 1401(a)(2). And, under the 14th amendment to the United States Constitution, citizens of the United States are citizens of the State wherein they reside. American Indians, therefore, are citizens of the state in which they reside and the United States. They cannot now claim that their tribal entity gives to them a source of governmental power in an extra-constitutional sense....

In *Cherokee Nation v. Georgia, supra*, 30 U.S. (5 Pet.) 1 (1831), the Court instructed us ... that tribes were not foreign nations under the Constitution. *Id.* at 18, 20. The Court described Indian tribes as "domestic dependent nations." *Id.* at 17. This was no doubt true in 1831. As the Court made clear, tribal Indians were "aliens, not owing allegiance to the United States." *Id.* at 16. And, compare the separate concurring opinions of Mr. Justice Johnson and Mr. Justice Baldwin with the dissenting opinion of Mr. Justice Thompson. The former denied tribal sovereignty while the latter affirmed it. I make these references to show that the issue of tribal sovereignty is one of long standing controversy. The majority would have us believe that the notion of tribal sovereignty is not an issue at all but a well settled legal doctrine....

By 1886, conditions had changed such that the Supreme Court would say:

> Indians are within the geographical limits of the United States. The soil and the people within the limits are under the political control of the Government of the United States or of the States of the Union. *There exist within [the] broad domain of sovereignty but these two. United States v. Kagama*, 118 U.S. 375, 379 (1886). [Emphasis added.]

[T]he Court's premise [in *Kagama*] was that sovereignty exists only in the United States and the States. Since the State had no jurisdiction, the United States had to have it....

If the Supreme Court instructed us in 1886 that "[t]here exist within the broad domain of sovereignty but these two [the United States and the States]," how can the majority of this Commission conclude that Indian tribal sovereignty exists in the territorial sense rather than in the more limited sense of congressionally licensed self-government over its own members and its internal affairs? Objectivity should have required this Commission to state that the issue of tribal sovereignty, though long settled against Indian claims, should be reopened by the Congress and report the various arguments on both sides, making whatever recommendations it deemed appropriate. The Congress could then either accept or reject recommendations as a matter of policy. The Commission, in essense [sic], is making political recommendations under the guise of legal doctrine. This Commission uses the word "sovereignty" as it is politically used by Indian tribes "without regard to the fact that as applied to Indian tribes 'sovereign' means no more than 'within the will of Congress.'" *United States v. Blackfeet Tribe*, 364 F. Supp. 192, 195 (D. Mont. 1973). Indeed, by 1901, the Supreme Court would tell us that "[t]he North American Indians do not and never have constituted 'nations' ...." *Montoya v. United States*, 180 U.S. 261, 21 S. Ct. 358 (1901)....

Another major case relied on by the Commission to support its theory is *United States v. Mazurie*, 419 U.S. 544 (1975). But it is clear that this case does not support inherent tribal sovereignty. On the contrary, the case merely held that (1) Congress has the power to regulate the sale of alcoholic beverages in Indian country under article I, § 8 of the Constitution, and that (2) Indian tribes are entities with some independent authority over matters that affect the internal and social relations of tribal life such that Congress could constitutionally delegate its own authority to the tribe. The Court specifically said "[w]e need not decide whether this independent authority [the tribe's] is itself sufficient for the tribes to impose Ordinance No. 26 [requiring retail liquor outlets within Indian country, including those on non-Indian land, to obtain a tribal license]." Despite this language, the Commission report says of *Mazurie* "it appeared that the tribe could exercise such regulatory power without benefit of Federal law on the basis of its own inherent sovereignty." [Commission report, ch. 5, part B at 156.] So much for objectivity. Unless words are infinitely elastic, the Court's opinion in *Mazurie* simply cannot be pressed into the meaning the majority report attributes to it. Similar misstatements of law abound in the report.

The Commission report neglects to mention that there is not a single case of the United States Supreme Court which has ever held that tribes possess inherent tribal sovereignty such that in the absence of congressional delegation they could assert governmental power (1) over nonmembers of the tribe, and (2) exclude State jurisdiction. The exclusion of State jurisdiction over reservation Indians has from *Worcester* to this day been based on Federal preemption. And, tribal jurisdiction over non-Indians, as in *Mazurie, supra,* and *Morris v. Hitchcock*, 194 U.S. 384 (1904), has been based on specific congressional delegation, not on general notions of tribal power....

My point is this. To the extent tribal Indians exercise powers of self-government in these United States, they do so because Congress permits it. Tribes exercise powers of self-government as Federal licensees, because and as long as Congress thinks it wise. More than a tribe's *external* attributes of sovereignty have been extinguished. The Commission draws a distinction between the extinguishment of external attributes of sovereignty, which it concedes the United States has done, and internal attributes of sovereignty, which it alleges the United States has never done. It is my position that the one goes with the other. American Indian tribal governments have only those powers granted them by the Congress.

Those powers have over and again been labeled self-government and not sovereignty. It is one thing for the Congress to permit tribal Indians to govern themselves and not be subject to Federal constitutional limitations and general Federal supervision. It is quite another thing for Congress to permit Indian tribes to function as general governmental entities not subject to Federal constitutional limitations or general Federal supervision. The position adopted by the Commission would have Indian tribes exercising powers which the United States itself cannot exercise because of constitutional limitations.

[T]he Commission has missed the opportunity to address some of the major issues arising out of American Indian law and policy. What does it mean to be a citizen of a State and yet be immune to its law? What is the basis for asserting that reservation Indians shall have representation in State government, but without taxation? On the other hand, what is the basis for asserting that non-Indian residents of Indian country shall not be represented in tribal government, yet be subject to tribal law, courts, and taxation? Is this obvious dual standard bothersome? And, if not, why not? What does it mean for a reservation to be within the boundaries of a State? ...

Who Did the Reserving?

In support of its argument that Indian tribes by treaty have retained to themselves inherent powers of self-government, the Commission relies upon *United States v. Winans*, 198 U.S. 371, 25 S. Ct. 662 (1905). It is true that there is dictum in that case to the effect that the treaty in that case "was not a grant of rights to the Indians, but a grant of right from them — a reservation of those not granted." 25 S. Ct. at 664.... The treaties vary. The reservations vary. Many Indians now exist on reservations which have no relationship to ancestral or aboriginal homes. Hence, it is clear that in these instances the United States reserved the land for Indians....

I make the remarks because, in my view, it is wholly erroneous to adopt, as this Commission has, the position that tribal Indians have reserved to themselves all rights not specifically extinguished by treaty. Generalizations, such as this one, are neither accurate nor helpful in seeking to define the powers of the United States, the States, and the Indians. It may be, as in *Winans*, that the relationship between the United States and a particular Indian tribe was one of arm's-length bargaining such that it could be said that a tribe actually reserved rights to itself. On the other hand, the relationship between the United States and other tribes was characterized by war and destruction. When these relationships culminated in peace treaties, it is simplistic, to say the least, to assert that the Indians reserved anything to themselves. It is clear that in most instances, the United States as the victorious party, dictated the terms of the treaty and reserved for the Indians various parcels of land.

So, as I have rejected the broad assertion of inherent tribal sovereignty, I also reject the broad assertion that tribal Indians have reserved to themselves inherent rights to self-government and property rights. Generalizations such as these have no place in law, and must yield to a judicious consideration of relevant treaties, statutes, State enabling legislation, history, and contemporary fact.

But the nature and scope of tribal self-government is too important to be left to case by case adjudication. I recommend that Congress enact comprehensive legislation which clearly defines the nature and scope of tribal self-government and makes it clear that the governmental powers granted tribes by the Congress are limited to the government of members and their internal affairs, and are not general governmental powers.

NOTE

Have Congressman Meeds's arguments against inherent tribal sovereignty stood the test of time? Certainly the Court's opinion in *Oliphant* reached a result he favored — that tribal courts have no criminal jurisdiction over non-Indians. Moreover, *Oliphant* created an exception to the rule that tribal sovereignty over internal affairs could only be lost through express congressional action. Nevertheless, did *Oliphant* reject the doctrine of inherent sovereignty completely as Congressman Meeds urged? If not, how have Congressman Meeds's arguments fared since *Oliphant*? As you read the rest of the chapter focus in particular on the following points. First, has his argument that tribes should have no governing power beyond what is necessary to maintain tribal integrity and identity gained any inroads on the Court? Second, Congressman Meeds would remove all power over non-Indians, even for activities undertaken on the reservation, to what is necessary for tribes to exercise their interests as property owners. Note in particular, Justice Stevens's theory that tribal sovereignty is based on tribal powers to exclude nonmembers from tribal land in *Merrion v. Jicarilla Apache Tribe, infra*, and *Brendale v. Confederated Tribes of the Yakima Indian Nation*, section D5b, *infra*. After you read these cases, ask yourself whether Justice Stevens's theory is as restrictive as Congressman Meeds's theory.

B. MODERN TRIBAL GOVERNMENTS

1. THE INDIAN REORGANIZATION ACT

COMMENT, TRIBAL SELF-GOVERNMENT AND THE INDIAN REORGANIZATION ACT OF 1934, 70 Michigan Law Review 955, 961-66, 972-74, 982 (1972)*

II. *The Indian Reorganization Act of 1934*

A. *Brief Legislative History*

The Wheeler-Howard Bill, as the originally proposed legislation was known, was entitled an act "[t]o grant to Indians living under Federal tutelage the freedom to organize for purposes of local self-government and economic enterprise." The bill represented a significant change in the approach to Indian legislation. Although the original Wheeler-Howard Bill was greatly restructured in the final version that became the IRA, some knowledge of its provisions is useful.

Title I of the Wheeler-Howard Bill, "Indian Self-Government," was the heart of the proposed legislation. In it were set forth the broad principles of self-government and the specific policy goal that "those functions of government now exercised over Indian reservations by the Federal Government through the Department of Interior and the Office of Indian Affairs shall be gradually relinquished and transferred to the Indians of such reservations ...."

The vehicle contemplated for realization of this goal was organization "for municipal and other purposes." Title I provided for issuance of charters "granting to the ... community group any or all of such powers of government and such privileges of corporate organization and economic activity, hereinafter enumerated, as may seem fitting" in light of a particular group's experience. Some mandatory charter requirements were imposed, such as a provision delineating membership criteria. In addition, optional powers were listed, among which was the power

> [t]o organize and act as a Federal municipal corporation, to establish a form of government, to adopt and thereafter to amend a constitution, and to promulgate and enforce

---

ordinances ... and [to exercise] any other functions customarily exercised by local
governments.

The term "constitution" was not used elsewhere in the bill. Unlike the final Act,
which contemplates adoption of a constitution as the principal organizational
method, the original bill was centered around the concept of the municipal-type
corporate charter. The remainder of Title I established procedures for adopting a charter and enumerated the powers and duties of chartered tribes and of
the Secretary of Interior and the Commissioner of Indian Affairs.

Title IV established a federal court of Indian affairs. This court would have
taken over original jurisdiction from the district courts in certain matters such
as crimes against the United States committed on a reservation and commercial
disputes between a tribe and outsiders. Furthermore, the court would have
appellate jurisdiction over the tribal courts in those cases in which it would have
original jurisdiction. All mention of these special courts was eliminated from the
final Act, primarily because the committee members and Indians disagreed,
with each other and among themselves, whether they would be a boon or a
hindrance to tribal sovereignty....

B. *The Act's Objectives: An Analytical Look Behind the Scenes*

The thrust of the IRA can be gathered from its operative provisions. Every
section in some way affects tribal self-government, although obviously not all
are equally relevant to this discussion.

Section 1 of the IRA ended the policy of allotment: "No land of any Indian
reservation ... shall be allotted in severalty to any Indian."[59] This provision,
while not going directly to self-government, was a key factor in making it possible; it alone assures the Act's historical significance.

Section 4 related to alienation. In general, it prohibited any transfer of Indian
land or shares in the assets of tribal corporations otherwise than to the tribe,
except that the Secretary could authorize voluntary exchanges of such lands or
interests of equal value when it would be "expedient and beneficial for or
compatible with the proper consolidation of Indian lands."[60] This provision
has had the desirable effect of further strengthening the tribal land base and
tribal control over it....

Section 18 provided that the Act would not apply to any reservation wherein
a majority of the adult Indians voted against its application at a special election
to be held within one year after the Act's approval.[65] This section marked a
significant change in approach to Indian legislation. Formerly, legislation had
been either special, applying by its terms to only one tribe or group of tribes, or
general, applying to all Indians without consideration of tribal differences.
Through section 18, the IRA became a type of enabling act, giving each tribe
the opportunity to determine for itself whether it wanted to come under the
Act. There was, however, a major flaw in the approach: a tribe could hold the

[59] 25 U.S.C. § 461 (1970).
[60] 25 U.S.C. § 464 (1970).
[65] 25 U.S.C. § 478 (1970). The time for holding elections was extended another year by Act of
June 15, 1935, ch. 260, § 2, 49 Stat. 378.

election only once. If it voted against application, it did not have the option of later reconsideration.

The essence of the IRA lay in those provisions relating directly to tribal organization, *viz.*, sections 16 and 17. The former provided:

> Any Indian tribe, or tribes, residing on the same reservation, shall have the right to organize for its common welfare, and may adopt an appropriate constitution and by-laws .... [Procedure is then established for ratification by members and approval by the Secretary of Interior.]
>
> In addition to all powers vested in any tribe or tribal council by existing law, the constitution adopted by said tribe shall also vest in such tribe or its tribal council the following rights and powers: To employ legal counsel, the choice of counsel and fixing of fees to be subject to the approval of the Secretary of the Interior; to prevent the sale, disposition, lease, or encumbrance of tribal lands, interests in lands, or other tribal assets without the consent of the tribe; and to negotiate with the Federal, State, and local governments....[69]

Section 17 first provided for issuance of a charter of incorporation to a tribe and established procedures for petition and ratification. It continued:

> Such charter may convey to the incorporated tribe the power to purchase, take by gift, or bequest, or otherwise, own, hold, manage, operate, and dispose of property of every description, real and personal, including the power to purchase restricted Indian lands and to issue in exchange therefor interests in corporate property, and such further powers as may be incidental to the conduct of corporate business, not inconsistent with law; but no authority shall be granted to sell, mortgage, or lease for a period exceeding ten years any of the land included in the limits of the reservation. Any charter so issued shall not be revoked or surrendered except by Act of Congress.

The purpose of adopting a charter is different than that of adopting a constitution, the charter being oriented more toward business than toward governmental organization.

Perhaps the prime objective of the IRA, which was crucial to any effective establishment of self-government, was elimination of the "absolutist" executive discretion previously exercised by the Interior Department and the Office of Indian Affairs. During the hearings, Commissioner of Indian Affairs John Collier presented to the House Committee examples which revealed the vastness of this discretionary power. Not only had administrative power grown beyond control, but its exercise and the effects of its exercise also changed from year to year, depending on the attitude or whim of a given commissioner. Further, this discretionary power was also exercised by local agency superintendents, a situation that led Senator Wheeler to refer to the local agent as "a czar." So all-encompassing was this power that "the Department [had] absolute discretionary powers over all organized expressions of the Indians.... [T]ribal councils exist[ed] by [the Department's] sufferance and [had] no authority except as ... granted by the Department." Consequently, the IRA sought to eliminate this boundless discretion or at least place a damper on its exercise. "This bill ... seeks

---

[69] 25 U.S.C. § 476 (1970). The reasons for the rather unusual juxtaposition of the terms "constitution" and "by-laws" are obscure. All tribes that adopted constitutions pursuant to the IRA also appear to have adopted by-laws. These by-laws may be unnecessary, since, for the most part, they contain governmental provisions that easily could have been written into the constitutions. *See, e.g.,* By-Laws of the Stockbridge Munsee Community of Wisconsin, in Charters, Constitutions and By-Laws of Indian Tribes of North America, pt. II, at 112-13 (G. Fay ed. 1967).

to get away from the bureaucratic control of the Indian Department, and it seeks further to give the Indians the control of their own affairs ....."

D. *Experience Under the IRA*

During the two-year period within which tribes could accept or reject the IRA, 258 elections were held. In these elections, 181 tribes (129,750 Indians) accepted the Act and 77 tribes (86,365 Indians, including 45,000 Navajos) rejected it. The IRA also applies to 14 groups of Indians who did not hold elections to exclude themselves. Within 12 years, 161 constitutions and 131 corporate charters had been adopted pursuant to the IRA. The experience of these tribes has been as varied as the tribes themselves. It is difficult to determine whether this experience has on the whole been beneficial. Such a judgment would depend on a great variety of factors, including previous political and organizational experience, available resources, and abilities of tribal leaders. For this reason, it would be unrealistic to pronounce a single judgment on the efficacy of the Act. Indeed, the diversity of experience suggests the presence of a minor paradox: the IRA seems to have led directly to both advances and reverses in tribal development.

The constitutions and charters themselves vary considerably, especially with respect to the forms of government adopted, "ranging from ancient and primitive forms in tribes where such forms have been perpetuated, to models based on progressive white communities." Likewise, the powers vested in the tribes through these documents "vary in accordance with the circumstances, experience, and resources of the tribe." On the other hand, there are provisions which appear in most constitutions in nearly identical terms. Most governments established under the IRA, unlike federal and state governments, have no provision for the separation of powers. The governing body is the tribal council, and in many instances it acts in a legislative as well as executive capacity. The council members, acting either in their capacity as elected political officials or as directors of the tribal corporation, also manage the common resources of the tribe. While it is often assumed that such a unification of powers is undesirable, most tribes have operated well under a unified system.

The law and order codes adopted by the various tribes reveal much about their approach to government. Tribes or other self-governing Indian groups generally have adopted codes, although some instead use regulations promulgated for that purpose by the Secretary of Interior. The character of these codes differs profoundly from that of state penal codes. Tribal codes typically delineate forty or fifty offenses, whereas state codes, exclusive of local ordinances, often list hundreds or even thousands of offenses. The tribal codes generally do not contain the catch-all provisions, such as vagrancy and conspiracy, so common in state codes. Punishment under tribal codes has traditionally been much less severe, seldom exceeding imprisonment for six months even for such offenses as kidnapping. In fact, except for stating a maximum penalty, tribal penal codes often leave wide discretion in the tribal court to adjust penalties to circumstances of both the offense and the offender. The form of punishment traditionally has not been imprisonment but rather forced labor for the benefit of the victim or the tribe. Finally, the tribal codes are generally available to the members and are widely read and discussed....

To be sure, the IRA has not worked perfectly. One major shortcoming has been the Act's inability to fulfill the promise of shifting to Indians the control of Indian Affairs. The reasons for this failure are diverse, although a major factor has been bureaucratic attitude. As one report noted:

> The [IRA] illustrates how a law intended to strengthen tribal governments and to give the people responsible business experience through making their own decisions has in fact actually increased federal control over them .... [E]very constitution adopted under the statute requires the Secretary of the Interior to review nearly all ordinances in various categories, notably those which define and punish offenses. Similarly, every [IRA] charter subjects to such approval almost the entire amount that a tribe can spend or make contracts for....
>
> This refusal to allow Indians to learn by trial and error may have had warrant in the 1930's at the time the first constitutions were adopted, for most tribes then had little knowledge of how to conduct a modern government and transact business in corporate form. Indeed, the corporate charters provided that the controls could be removed as the tribe gained experience, but in most instances the restraints still remain, continuing to be imposed when new charters are adopted.
>
> This policy probably stems from the widespread belief among the [Bureau of Indian Affairs] staff that as "guardian" or "trustee," the Bureau itself must make the vital decisions.... [This idea] will continue to hamper tribal self-development until legislation or strong executive direction dispels the doubts of Bureau employees.[152]

The corporate form of organization lends itself to use in tribal development, since it is "tribal" in its very nature. Incorporation creates a recognizable legal entity around which to focus community goals, be they making money or providing services to members. Moreover, these goals are more easily effected by the use of the corporate form. Prior discussion has emphasized the unique flexibility of the IRA. This feature should be capitalized upon, and tribes originally voting against application of the Act should be permitted to reconsider. Moreover, forceful removal of much administrative discretionary power may be necessary to allow proper development....

IV. *Conclusion*

The parallel between tribalism and incorporation has been suggested. It is not unreasonable to suggest therefore that the Indians' long history of tribalism as a way of life makes corporate organization a particularly appropriate means of modern Indian development. The experiences discussed above show that the corporate form is indeed amenable to Indian ways of business operation. It is also very possible that continued use of corporate organization will facilitate a greater cross-cultural understanding in our society.[205] Tribes and other Indian groups can thus absorb the corporation, whether chartered under the IRA or state law, as a useful tool for accomplishment of the desired ends.

---

[152] [COMMISSION ON THE RIGHTS, LIBERTIES, AND RESPONSIBILITIES OF THE AMERICAN INDIAN, THE INDIAN, AMERICA'S UNFINISHED BUSINESS] 34-35 [W. Brophy & S. Aberle ed. 1966)].

[205] "In the corporate structure, formal and informal, Indian tribalism has its greatest parallels and it is through this means that Indians believe that modern society and Indian tribes will finally reach a cultural truce." V. Deloria, [Custer Died for Your Sins: An Indian Manifesto] 224-25 [(Avon ed. 1969).]

BARSH, ANOTHER LOOK AT REORGANIZATION: WHEN WILL TRIBES HAVE A CHOICE, Indian Truth, No. 247, Oct. 1982, at 4-5, 10-12*

It is simplistic to defend reorganized tribal councils on the grounds that they are elected by the people. What is the alternative? Tribes cannot amend or replace their federal constitutions without the consent of the Secretary of the Interior. There is little likelihood of a tribal council simply shutting itself down in defiance if it results in automatic cancellation of the federal safety-net programs that prop more than 90% of tribes' economies. And the Indian Bureau has done a pretty good job of convincing tribes that tampering with the Reorganization structure will result in termination. Until tribes are given a real choice, that they do the best they can with the only choice they've had means little. Whether they feel Reorganization is better than some other form of self-government, tribes must see to their self-preservation by trying to fill council seats with men and women of integrity who will do all they can to act in the best interests of their constituents, and not humble themselves to federal administrators.

Rather than presume to know what is best for tribes, it is time this nation made a serious effort to give them a full, free, and unrestricted choice — true self-determination in the sense of international law. I don't believe the 1934 Indian Reorganization Act offered such a choice for the reasons that follow, and I consider the credibility of this country, as well as the tribes, depends on whether we have the courage to make that effort today....

Everyone knows that the 1934 Indian Reorganization Act suspended the policy of allotting reservations, opening "surplus" lands to homesteaders, and selling off inherited lands that cost tribes half their territory between 1890 and 1930. That was the Indian Bureau's strongest argument for the legislation, which became a personal crusade for Indian Commissioner John Collier. But the other side of the law was the establishment of constitutional tribal governments under the supervision of the Department of the Interior. Collier never told Congress that most large reservations already had sui generis councils, many of them survivals from the last century, nor that on some reservations there already had been contests between councils organized by the Indian Service to rubber stamp federal programs.

Many tribes fought Reorganization bitterly, arguing that it would be used to destroy the newly re-emerging councils and place community self-government where it had lingered in the 1880s and 1890s under federal administrative control. Collier dismissed these arguments as misinformed, assuring Congress that the Bureau would not interfere with Reorganized councils. He even hired a number of anthropologists, purportedly to help tribes design new political systems compatible with their cultural values and traditions. Congress took the bait, but in 1944 Assistant Interior Solicitor Charlotte Westwood admitted to an investigating committee that she had found an incredibly high degree of standardization among the new tribal constitutions, rendering them for all practical

purposes "nothing more than new Indian Office regulations."[1] Collier continued to insist that "no two are alike."...

The Measure of Indian Dissent

To ward off evidence of widespread Indian dissatisfaction with his draft
Reorganization bill, Collier kicked off a nationwide "road show" to mobilize
support. In April, 1934, he told Congress that 139,824 Indians were in favor of
Reorganization and 12,364 opposed, based on an "official vote" conducted on
the reservations.[2] It was scarcely a reliable figure, however. Different means of
assessing tribes' wishes were combined haphazardly. On 28 reservations the
Bureau asked for a vote of the existing tribal council organized and operated
under Bureau control — essentially asking Bureau employees to vote for a
Bureau project. Eight tribes were evaluated by taking straw polls at conferences
and meetings held by the Bureau to inform Indians about the draft legislation.
In three instances the Bureau accepted a single petition from individual tribal
members as evidence of approval or disapproval, and in two, Bureau tabulators
simply asked the Superintendent what he thought the tribe wanted. Only five
reservations actually conducted public referenda. Two tribes listed as approving
Reorganization actually told Bureau staff it was fine for other Indians as long as
it didn't apply to them.

If a tribe "approved" Reorganization, even by a slim majority election or vote
of council, its entire population was listed as favoring the draft legislation in
reports made to Congress. At Lac Courte Oreille, for instance, there were 500
eligible voters, and 310 signed a petition supporting Reorganization — 62 percent. Congress was told that all 1,538 Lac Courte Oreille supported the bill.

Tribal criticism continued, and Congress tactfully amended the bill in
markup to provide that its terms would "not apply to any reservation wherein a
majority of the adult Indians, voting at a special election duly called by the
Secretary of the Interior, shall vote against its application."[3] A plebiscite should
have settled any doubts that Indians got what they wanted. Unfortunately Collier's zeal resulted in irregularities that seriously impugn the significance of the
hundreds of special referendum elections held in 1934 and 1935.

From the outset there were conflicting interpretations of the law. At the 1934
hearings, Collier and the committees seemed to agree that Reorganization could
be rejected by a majority of those adults actually voting. Collier subsequently
advised the tribes that rejection of the Act required a majority of [all eligible
voters,] a considerably tougher standard. Interior Solicitor Nathan Margold
supported Collier's reading of the Act's admittedly vague language, relying
entirely on the placement of a single comma ("majority of the adult Indians,
voting") which had appeared mysteriously during a markup session and for
which, at a later investigative hearing, no one would admit responsibility.[5]

[1]Senate Report No. 1031, 78th Congress, 2nd Session (1944), page 5.

[2]"Hearings, 'To Grant Indians Freedom to Organize,'" Senate Committee on Indian Affairs,
73rd Congress, 2nd Session (1934), pages 103-105.

[3]Section 18, Act of June 18, 1934, 48 Stat. 988, as amended 25 U.S.C. 478.

[5]"Hearings, 'Indian Conditions and Affairs,'" 74th Congress, 1st Session (1935), pages 24, 51,
76-104; "Hearings, 'Yankton Tribe — Amend Wheeler-Howard Act,'" House Committee on Indian
Affairs, 76th Congress, 1st Session (1939).

More than a hundred referenda were held before Congress intervened. In 86 the Act was approved by an average two-thirds majority of the votes actually cast. The tabulated vote rejected the Act by a comparable margin on 31 reservations, but on 17 of these the act was nevertheless officially "approved" because more eligibles stayed home than voted. Eligibility lists were prepared by the Bureau based on census rolls and discretionary judgments of which individuals, if no longer actually living on the reservation, were still keeping some sort of relationship with the place.[6] Obviously any number of persons with little or no real interest in the reservations could be listed as eligible, and by simply not voting, out of indifference, ignorance or because their whereabouts were unknown and they were never notified, influence the fate of reservation residents....

Stories like this prompted House oversight hearings in 1935. Commissioner Collier insisted to incredulous committee members that he had always advocated the majority-eligible rule.[8] Nothing in the Act could possibly hurt Indians, he insisted, so it should apply to every reservation unless there was overwhelming resistance. "Congress should think seriously," he warned, "before allowing even a majority of Indians to shut out other individuals from the enjoyment of money and other opportunities" offered by Reorganization.[9] Indians should be grateful they were allowed to vote at all — it was an "extraordinary privilege."[10]

The Act cleverly conditioned eligibility for new individual benefits such as educational loans, business credit, and preferential federal employment on the outcome of referenda. The whole New Deal social welfare program for Indians was held for ransom against tribes' approval of Reorganization. This was the carrot of the carrot-and-stick. The stick was a provision that restrictions on the taxation and alienability of Indian lands would terminate in one year for reservations that voted against the Act.[11] ...

The message to Indians was plain: vote for Reorganization and you will be rewarded with money and jobs; vote against it, and you will lose your lands and homes, and the Bureau will do nothing to stop it. Tribes had no option of saying we want to keep our homes and communities, but we don't want the Bureau's "new and improved" colonialism. For all practical purposes, Indian voters in the 1934-1935 referenda faced a choice between continued arbitrary colonialism and a modified form of colonialism with improved welfare benefits and, temporarily, somewhat greater land security. The conservative American Indian Foundation, a forerunner of the National Congress of American Indians, likened the referenda to one-party elections in Hitler's Germany: you can vote for or against the inevitable.[13]

Congress was sufficiently concerned about tribes' ability to opt out of Reorganization, however, to change the election rules retroactively. Under [an] amendment the Act could be rejected by a *majority of those voting*, provided at least

---

[6]"Hearings, 'Indian Conditions and Affairs,'" *op. cit.*, pages 105, 108.

[8]*Ibid.*, page 106.

[9]*Ibid.*, pages 46-47, 111.

[10]*Ibid.*, page 22.

[11]Section 2, Act of June 18, 1934, as amended by Section 3, Act of June 15, 1935, 49 Stat. 378. 25 U.S.C. 462.

[13]["Hearings, 'Indian Conditions and Affairs,'" *op. cit.*, page] 20.

30 percent of eligible voters went to the polls.[14] The amendment also gave the Bureau until mid-1936 to complete the referendum process. Under the original rules the Act could be rejected only if at least 51 percent of all eligible actually voted against it. Under the new formula, the Act could be accepted or rejected by as few as 16 percent of the voters.

Given the options, it's remarkable any tribes mustered the votes to defeat Reorganization at the polls. Nationwide the Indian Bureau conducted a total of 259 referenda before and after the 1935 rule change.[15] Of these, 243 attracted the 30 percent of eligible voters needed for validation. Reorganization won 166 (64%) of the validated referenda. More than half of the "no" votes were in California.... Across the country, in referenda drawing 20 or more voters, 38,178 voted for Reorganization (61%) and 24,016 against.

This doesn't tell the whole story, however. In 54 communities where the Act was accepted, less than half of the eligibles actually voted for it, and on 5 reservations, less than one-fourth. It was possible, then, in many cases, that a minority of tribal members supported Reorganization, and won at the polls because opponents were unwilling or unable to vote. From a strict legal viewpoint the nonvoters had only themselves to blame for the results — assuming they stayed away out of indifference or on principle, and out of indifference or on principle, and not because of lack of notice or opportunity. From a practical perspective, nonetheless, building new institutions on minority constituencies is asking for trouble. In this respect the words of Joseph Bruner, president of the American Indian Federation, were prophetic when he told Congress in 1935 the voting had "sharpened the lines of old disputes and quarrels" on the reservations, with the Bureau's pet Indian leaders telling opponents they "will get nothing in the future."[16] ...

Contemporary International Norms

The United Nations Charter, interpretive resolutions, and the International Covenants on Human Rights, signed by President Carter in 1977, guarantee the right of all peoples to "self-determination." Self-determination is defined by the United Nations as peoples' right "freely to determine their political status, and to pursue their economic, social and cultural development."[17] Options for the exercise of self-determination, according to Resolution 1541(XV), 10 December 1960, include "emergence as a sovereign independent State, free association with an independent State, or integration with an independent State" — in other words, full independence, some kind of federal union or confederation, or political assimilation....

Let's Settle the Issue

The referenda were held in the 1930s, to be sure, but the United States is trying to defend their validity in the 1980s to a world that has grown up a great

---

[14] Act of June 15, 1935, 49 Stat. 378, 25 U.S.C. 478a.

[15] "Hearings, 'Wheeler-Howard Act — Exempt Certain Indians,'" House Committee on Indian Affairs, 76th Congress, 3rd Session (1940), pages 390-94. One tribe refused to vote, and for two others there are no records of the results, if any, of the balloting.

[16] "Hearings, 'Indian Conditions and Affairs,'" op. cit., page 74.

[17] Charter Article 1(2); Article 1 of each Covenant, G.A. Res. 2200A(XXI), 16 December 1966, Presidential signature 13 Weekly Compilation of Presidential Documents 1488 (1977) ....

deal, and learned a lot about colonialism in the intervening years. It is appropriate to challenge Washington — and Reorganized tribal councils — to resubmit the options to the people, complying faithfully with U.N. norms. This means, first and foremost, that full independence and free association are included as alternatives — together with incorporation into existing states of the Union.[23] It also means that Washington would have to agree in advance to respect the will of the indigenous electorate scrupulously and, for the first time in a century, absolutely renounce its pretense of "plenary power" to create, alter or abolish tribal governments at will — unless, of course, native people choose freely to re-delegate such a power to Congress.

The most interesting option would be what most of the tribes seem to have thought they were agreeing to in their treaties in the first place: free association as a "protectorate" in the sense of international law. The territorial security and political freedom of a protected state is guaranteed, militarily, by its protector in exchange for trade concessions, accommodation of military bases, coordination of foreign policy, or other arrangements of mutual convenience. The protector may act as the protected state's broker or agent in foreign affairs if so agreed, but it may not intrude in domestic policy except in accordance with explicit delegations of power by treaty.

If Reorganization has really been such a success and has the confidence of the Indian people, Washington has little to fear from a proper plebiscite. The status quo will be returned at the polls. If the fervent non-Indian promoters of "equal rights and responsibilities" are correct that Indians should be, and want to be just like everyone else, they will get their way in spite of the big, bad federal Indian bureaucracy they accuse of perpetuating Indian dependency. And if the spiritual revival on the reservations is real, traditional forms of government may at last be restored. At least we can stop arguing about what Indians want, and ask them.

NOTE

Other accounts of the enactment of the IRA appear in W. KELLY, INDIAN AFFAIRS AND THE INDIAN REORGANIZATION ACT (1953); Krieger, *Principles of the Indian Law and the Act of June 18, 1934,* 3 GEO. WASH. L. REV. 279 (1935). Both sides of the political spectrum have found fault with the IRA. The right criticized it as New Deal collectivist legislation. *See, e.g., Hearings on S. 2103 Before the Committee on Indian Affairs, House of Representatives,* 76th Cong., 3d Sess. (1940). In fact, John Collier was accused of socialist tendencies. *See* S. TYLER, A HISTORY OF INDIAN POLICY 136 (1973). In contrast, the left saw it as thinly disguised colonialism. Nevertheless, others have defended it as laying the foundation for rebuilding Indian tribal governments after years of domination by the federal government. In addition to the author of the excerpted Comment, see, e.g., V. DELORIA & C. LYTLE, AMERICAN INDIANS, AMERICAN JUSTICE 101; Tyler, *supra,* at 134-36. Are Professor Barsh's objections to the IRA substantive, procedural, or both? What solution does he advocate? Seventy-

---

[23] Full Independence is not conditioned on the size of the territory or people — the Lakota Sioux and Navajo reservations are considerably larger than the new insular republics in the Caribbean and Pacific, most of which are also Members of the United Nations (e.g., Vanuatu, Nauru, Antigua). Nor is being surrounded by another state necessarily a problem — Lesotho is an independent state and a U.N. Member, although it is completely landlocked by South Africa.

seven tribes, including the Navajo Tribe, rejected the provisions of the Act. What were seen as the benefits and the drawbacks of the IRA when it was enacted? As you will see in Chapter 8, section A2, Alaskan Native villages, most of which are not incorporated, have begun to see incorporation under the IRA as a mechanism to reassert tribal sovereignty. Do IRA tribes have more or less ability to govern themselves? As you read the rest of this chapter, ask to what extent the decisions recognizing inherent tribal sovereignty turn on whether or not the particular tribe is incorporated under the IRA.

2. THE SECRETARY'S POWER TO APPROVE CONSTITUTIONS AND LAWS

1. *Source and Scope:* Both Professor Barsh, a vocal opponent of the IRA, and the writer of the *Michigan Law Review* Comment criticize the IRA for leaving too much power with the Secretary of the Interior. The Secretary's role in approving constitutions and laws has been a focal point of tribal complaints since the passage of the Act. In 1988, the IRA was amended to address these concerns. In order to evaluate the effectiveness of these amendments, it is necessary to consider the criticisms lodged against the approval power. These criticisms have focused on the pervasiveness of this power and on the lack of standards imposed upon its exercise.

Section 16 of the Act required Secretarial approval for tribal constitutions. The Secretary exercised this power to ensure that tribal governmental structures fit the dominant culture's norms of what constituted appropriate government as well as to ensure that the regulatory duties of the Bureau would remain in force, as the following January 9, 1936, memorandum on the proposed constitution of the Puyallup Tribe illustrates. Note also the concern to ensure a tribal government that can work efficiently with the federal bureaucracy. (Memorandum of January 9, 1936). The Puyallup Constitution, said the Solicitor:

Confers very large powers over tribal affairs and individual conduct on a small council of five members .... There is no provision in this constitution for general meetings ... or for the submission to a referendum.

It seems to me that this set-up is very likely to produce a council that is not truly representative of the reservation. If this should happen the Department would find itself in conflict either with the Indians of the reservation or with the council, with no way provided for ironing out differences between the council and the members of the tribe. This danger is likely to be serious since experience shows that one of the most serious weaknesses of Indian tribal government in the past has been the susceptibility of tribal authorities to improper outside influences in connection with the disposition of tribal property. Setting up a small body of five individuals with power to act in matters affecting tribal property without any consultation or review by the tribe at large, and granting to these five individuals three years' tenure of office without possibility of recall or removal except by a vote of four out of five of the council members themselves, all has the effect, I am afraid, of making the tribe and its property easy prey for hunters....

... In addition to the foregoing criticisms the suggested structure of local government is undemocratic and defective, I think, in that it permits a minority of two members in the council of five to obstruct any action at all, without any possible recourse, merely by absenting themselves from a meeting. I would suggest that the provision requiring the presence of four members of the council for the transaction of business be replaced by the more usual provision recognizing a majority of the members as a quorum.

The foregoing impediments to a satisfactory relationship between the Department and the Puyallup Indians are aggravated by the provision that the council of five, with whom all departmental business must be transacted, is to meet regularly only four times a year. Many activities of the department in the future will have to be submitted to this council for comment or for approval and the three months' delay between council meetings will very definitely slow up the work of the Department in handling various pressing matters. On the large Sioux reservations, where it is difficult for representatives of scattered communities to come together and where most of the activities of the Indians along lines of self-government will be within the separate communities, quarterly meetings may be quite satisfactory. It is dangerous, I think, to transfer such a provision to a small unified reservation such as Puyallup. At least the Indians should be warned of the magnitude of the tasks they are undertaking and advised that this business can be transacted more efficiently, with fewer complaints, if the period between regular meetings is shortened.

What are the greatest concerns to the writer — the needs of the Puyallup tribe in light of its unique culture or the expectations and needs of the federal government?

Since most tribes were unfamiliar with the format of a constitution, the Secretary provided nearly identical draft constitutions to the tribes asking for help. These "boilerplate" constitutions in turn contained provisions requiring Secretarial approval of tribal laws and regulations. The constitutions typically included "a veto power over such tribal actions as the assessment of dues, fees, and taxes against nonmembers, the removal of nonmembers from the Indian community, the control of private land sales by members, the enactment of criminal and civil codes, and the appointment of guardians for minors and incompetents." Kelly, *Indian Adjustment and the History of Indian Affairs,* 10 ARIZ. L. REV. 559, 568 (1968). Some have contended that the Secretary was obliged to make sure that certain tribal actions would be subject to federal review. See Memorandum of the Solicitor to the Commissioner of Indian Affairs, *Proposed Constitution for Navajo Tribe,* June 21, 1954. On the other hand, the prevalence of tribal constitutional provisions including authority for Secretarial approval or review of tribal ordinances was attacked in the SUMMARY REPORT OF HEARINGS AND INVESTIGATIONS BY THE SUBCOMMITTEE ON CONSTITUTIONAL RIGHTS, SENATE COMMITTEE ON THE JUDICIARY, 88th Cong., 2d Sess. 1-4 (1964):

> Although the Secretary's power to approve tribal ordinances and resolutions might be authorized by Federal law, regulation, and by provision in a tribe's constitution or charter, the subcommittee in its research and consultations with officials in the Bureau of Indian Affairs, has failed to uncover any Federal statute which specifically requires secretarial approval of tribal ordinances.
>
> The most clearly defined authority for secretarial approval of tribal ordinances is contained in the tribal constitutions. A typical example is the constitution of the Oglala Sioux Tribe of the Pine Ridge Reservation in South Dakota, which provides that the tribal council shall exercise, subject to review or approval by the Secretary of the Interior, the following powers:
>
>> To appropriate for public purposes of the tribe any available tribal council funds....
>>
>> To levy taxes upon members of the Oglala Sioux Tribe and to levy taxes or license fees upon nonmembers doing business within the reservation....
>>
>> To exclude from the restricted lands of the Pine Ridge Reservation persons not legally entitled to reside therein.

To promulgate and enforce ordinances governing the conduct of members of the Oglala Sioux Tribe, and providing for the maintenance of law and order and the administration of justice by establishing a reservation court and defining its duties and powers....

To purchase, under condemnation proceedings in courts of competent jurisdiction, land or other property needed for public purposes....

To protect and preserve the property, wildlife, and natural resources — gases, oils, and other minerals, etc., of the tribe, and to regulate the conduct of trade and the use and disposition of property upon the reservation....

To regulate the inheritance of property, real and personal, other than allotted lands, within the territory of the Pine Ridge Reservation.

To provide for the appointment of guardians for minors and mental incompetents.[9]

If endorsement of the Secretary is not obtained, the ordinance is unenforceable. Moreover, in those cases in which the ordinance is not approved, the tribe has no authority to which it can appeal the Secretary's decision. This general approval power of the Secretary, the subcommittee has found, frustrates responsible tribal self-government.

In its 1976 report, The American Indian Policy Review Commission also criticized the use of the Approval Power:

It is ironic that this Act, which was intended to strengthen the governments of Indian tribes, is now generally regarded by the Indian people as an impediment to their governmental functions. The Act itself presents certain problems since it requires that the constitutions and bylaws adopted by tribes pursuant to the Act be ratified and approved by the Secretary. But, more significantly, much of the authority of the Secretary to pass upon the validity of tribal enactments stems from provisions of constitutions which tribes adopted pursuant to the Act. These provisions, taken from a "model" constitution drafted by the BIA after passage of the 1934 Act, commonly provide that the laws adopted by the tribe shall not take effect until such laws have been reviewed and approved by the Secretary.

This review process has been generally condemned as perpetuating a paternalistic relationship between the Department of the Interior and the tribes. Paternalism aside, it has also impeded tribes in their efforts to assert authority within reservation boundaries through the simple expedient of a Secretarial veto of tribal ordinances which he conceives as being beyond the power of a tribe. Thus, for years, the Department denied that tribes could exercise any jurisdiction over non-Indians even though there was no clear statute and no judicial decision to affirm the Department's position. The efforts of the Colville Tribe to impose a water use code within the boundaries of their reservation was thwarted by the refusal of the Secretary to approve their proposed code. In a most extraordinary case, the Coeur d'Alene Tribe was denied permission to enact a code provision regulating the playing of an Indian stick game within their reservation even though a Federal court had held that the playing of the game was not within the purview of Federal law. In this case, Departmental veto of the tribal ordinance was instigated at the request of the Department of Justice.

American Indian Policy Review Commission, Final Report, 188-89 (1977).

Recall the materials in Chapter 2, section B, *supra*. In deciding whether to approve, is it inappropriate for the Secretary to employ a balancing test that takes into account the interests of both the tribe and the surrounding community? What of a balancing test that includes consideration of other federal governmental interests (including those of non-Indian Bureaus within the Depart-

---

[9]Constitution and By-Laws of the Oglala Sioux Tribe of Pine Ridge Reservation, S.D., article IV, Powers of the Council, pp. 3-4.

ment of the Interior)? *See, e.g., Cheyenne River Sioux Tribe v. Andrus,* 566 F.2d 1085 (8th Cir. 1977) (26th amendment requires extending the right to vote in tribal elections to 18-year-olds). In *Moapa Band of Paiute Indians v. United States Dep't of Interior,* 747 F.2d 563 (9th Cir. 1984), the Secretary had disapproved an ordinance permitting houses of prostitution on a Nevada reservation because of a federal policy discouraging prostitution. Should the existence of a general federal policy be sufficient? In holding that the Secretary's action was permissible, the Ninth Circuit relied on this policy, but in addition stressed a provision in the tribal constitution permitting the Secretary to rescind tribal ordinances "for any cause." *Id.* at 565-66.

Not all constitutions delegate such broad powers to the Secretary, however. Some tribes, such as the Blackfeet, do not provide in their constitutions for secretarial review of law and order ordinances. In addition, tribes have begun to amend their constitutions to repeal those provisions requiring Secretarial approval, as the next section indicates. Moreover, numerous corporate charters promulgated pursuant to section 17 of the IRA contain a provision for the "termination of supervisory powers." In both instances, however, Secretarial approval is required. May the Secretary properly disapprove amendments and charters if they remove the Secretary's review authority?

2. *Secretarial Delay in Calling Elections as a Method of Imposing Standards:* Tribes attempting to organize and write new constitutions or amend their existing constitutions have encountered another method by which the Secretary seeks to ensure the constitutions will contain standards deemed appropriate. Section 16 requires the Secretary to call a tribal election to ratify the constitution. The Secretary has argued this provision grants authority to approve a draft constitution *before* the election is held on the theory that such pre-election clearance is necessary to prevent a tribe from ratifying and adopting provisions that the Secretary would then have to veto, thus requiring another expensive and time-consuming election.

In *Coyote Valley Band of Pomo Indians v. United States,* 639 F. Supp. 165 (E.D. Cal. 1986), three tribes argued that this procedure was not authorized by the IRA and was thus arbitrary and capricious in violation of the Administrative Procedure Act and also a breach of the Secretary's trust relationship. The tribes complained that some elections had been delayed for up to four years. As tribes in the process of organizing under the IRA for the first time, they were not eligible for BIA services until after the election. Moreover, the tribes complained that the Secretary did not publish any standards for constitutions. The district court held that these procedures were not authorized by the IRA and thus violated the APA. The court also held that the Secretary had a mandatory duty to call elections within a reasonable time after request by a tribe. The court rejected the Secretary's argument that pre-clearance was necessary to prevent delay and extra expense, stating:

> It is unlikely that a tribe would go to the trouble of requesting a secretarial election on a constitution which it knows is destined for disapproval — unless it *firmly* believes that the provisions found objectionable by the Secretary are valid and lawful.

Id. at 173. The court urged the Secretary to publish the standards the Department used in order to help the tribes determine which provisions the Secretary might find objectionable, explaining:

Once a tribe goes through this review process and makes a final request for an election, however, it will presumably have a document which *it* considers appropriate for the Secretary's approval. If the Secretary has expressed specific objections to certain constitutional provisions during the review period and the tribe nevertheless refuses to adopt the suggested modifications, the fight for approval will be carried on after the election, over a document which has been ratified by the tribe.

Under the current challenged procedure, defendants can delay the tribal reorganization process *indefinitely* simply by holding the draft constitution hostage and requiring modifications to be made prior to releasing it for elections. Such an approach may operate to stultify the initiative shown by tribal leaders in moving toward reorganization and to discourage all of those who have inevitably expended much time and effort in the preparation of the tribe's governing document. It would be an understatement to say that defendants' current procedure is antithetical both to the spirit of the IRA and to traditional notions of meaningful self-government. Thus, it is defendants' interpretation of the statute which would lead to "unjust or absurd" consequences.

Id.

3. *The 1988 Amendments to the IRA:* In 1988, Congress amended the IRA partly in response to the *Coyote Valley* litigation. The amendments make clear that the Secretary has no discretion to delay elections. The Secretary must call a ratifying election within 180 days of a request by a tribe seeking to organize or to revoke an existing constitution. The time limit for elections to amend an existing constitution is only 90 days. 25 U.S.C.A. § 476(c)(1) (Supp. 1989). During that period the Secretary must provide the tribe with technical assistance if requested. The Secretary must also review the constitution during this period to determine if any provisions are "contrary to applicable laws." 25 U.S.C. § 476(c)(2). Nevertheless, if the Secretary finds a provision objectionable, he cannot delay the election. He must give the tribe at least 30 days' notice that he objects and state the grounds in writing. *Id.*, § 476(c)(3). The intent of this provision appears to be to let the tribe and the Secretary resolve their differences during this period. Once a tribe ratifies its constitution, the Secretary must act within 45 days and may only disapprove a constitution upon a finding "that the proposed constitution, and bylaws or any amendments are contrary to applicable laws." Moreover, the amendment provides that Secretarial *inaction* will have the effect of approving the constitution. *Id.*, § 476(d).

The amendments do not set standards for the Secretary to use in basing his decision whether to approve a constitution. Instead, the amendments refer only to "applicable laws." The amendments also state: "Actions to enforce the provisions of this section may be brought in the appropriate federal district court." *Id.* The Senate Report indicates an intent to permit challenges *before* an election is held and without further exhaustion of administrative remedies: "The tribe also has the right to challenge *any* finding made by the Secretary as to the legality of a proposed tribal document in the appropriate Federal court." S. REP. No. 577, 100th Cong., 2d Sess. 2 (1988), *reprinted in* 1988 U.S. CODE CONG. & ADMIN. NEWS 3908, 3909. This threat of litigation may compel the Secretary to use more care in the future to ground disapproval on specific statutory and constitutional authorities instead of vague statements of policy.

Recent statements by the BIA to Congress indicate that the current administration is moving in this direction. For example, the Secretary did not oppose enactment of the legislation. On the contrary, the Secretary suggested an amendment that would have eliminated the need for Secretarial approval of constitutions, bylaws and the choice of counsel and fixing of fees. The Secretary cited the current administration's policy in favor of tribal self-government in support of this proposal. S. Rep. No. 577, *supra*, at 34-37.

A final change will permit more tribes to organize under the IRA. The original law provided that "[any] Indian tribe, or tribes, residing on the same reservation" could choose to organize. IRA § 16, Pub. L. No. 48-383, 48 Stat. 987, 1111 (1934). In contrast, the amendment permits "[a]ny Indian tribe" to organize. 25 U.S.C.A. § 476 (Supp. 1989). As a result, tribes without a land base will be able to organize. What are the implications of this provision? The reach of tribal powers is limited to activities taking place within a reservation. Nevertheless, a tribe organizing under the IRA can benefit from provisions of that act permitting the Secretary to take land in trust for the benefit of a recognized tribe. 25 U.S.C.A. § 465 (Supp. 1989). The Secretary also objected to this provision on the ground that the law regarding the reach of tribal power by a tribe without a land base is too speculative. S. Rep. No. 577, 100th Cong., 2d Sess. 35 (1988).

4. *Non-IRA Tribal Governments:* The Secretary claims power under 25 U.S.C. § 2 to approve the constitutions of tribes that rejected the Indian Reorganization Act. *See* S. Rep. No. 577, *supra*, at 35 (1988). These constitutions too, sometimes contain provisions requiring Secretarial review of ordinances. Must a tribe have such a document? The Navajo Tribe does not have a written constitution; nevertheless it submitted its severance tax ordinance to the Secretary for approval. Why? Was this a necessary step or one the tribe judged to be politically astute since the ordinance applied to non-Indian oil and gas lessees and was thus bound to be challenged? In response to the Navajo Tribe, the Secretary stated he had no authority to approve or disapprove the tribal ordinance. When the challenge reached the Supreme Court, the Court held that approval was not necessary. *See Kerr-McGee v. Navajo Tribe,* section D5, *infra.*

3. TRIBAL CONSTITUTIONS

Most of the 1930's constitutions were exactly the same. For examples of typical boilerplate constitutions, see COLORADO STATE COLLEGE, MUSEUM OF ANTHROPOLOGY, CHARTERS, CONSTITUTIONS, AND BY-LAWS OF THE INDIAN TRIBES OF NORTH AMERICA (Occasional Publications on Anthropology, Enthnology Series) (G. Fay ed. 1967). The Hopi Constitution contains some boilerplate — for example, the list of powers typical of that period (see Article VI). Note that approval is not required for all ordinances, however, in contrast to the Oglala Sioux Constitution quoted in the Senate committee report above. In addition, the rest of the Constitution was drafted to accommodate the somewhat theocratic organization of the Hopi Tribe, in which the Kikmongwi, traditional religious leaders, have a great deal of authority. *See generally* Ragsdale, *The Institutions, Laws and Values of the Hopi Indians: A Stable State Society*, 55 U. Mo. K.C. L. Rev. 335 (1987). The process of adoption of the constitution is described in F. WATERS, BOOK OF THE HOPI 314-17 (1963). How well do you think this accommodation works? In particular, the following section on the federal nature of the Tribe reflects deep-seated difficulties.

THE HOPI CONSTITUTION

Article III — Organization

Section 1. The Hopi Tribe is a union of self-governing villages sharing common interests and working for the common welfare of all. It consists of the following recognized villages: [First Mesa (consolidated villages of Walpi, Shitchumovi, and Tewa); Mishongnovi, Sipaulavi, Shungopavi, Oraibi, Kyakotsmovi, Bakabi, Hotevilla, and Moenkopi.]

Sec. 2. The following powers which the Tribe now has under existing law or which have been given by the Act of June 18, 1934, (48 Stat. 984) and acts amendatory thereof or supplemental thereto, are reserved to the individual villages:

(a) To appoint guardians for orphan children and incompetent members.

(b) To adjust family disputes and regulate family relations of members of the villages.

(c) To regulate the inheritance of property of the members of the villages.

(d) To assign farming land, subject to the provisions of Article VII.

Sec. 3. Each village shall decide for itself how it shall be organized. Until a village shall decide to organize in another manner, it shall be considered as being under the traditional Hopi organization, and the Kikmongwi of such village shall be recognized as its leader.

Sec. 4. Any village which does not possess the traditional Hopi self-government, or which wishes to make a change in that government or add something to it, may adopt a village Constitution in the following manner: A Constitution, consistent with this Constitution and By-laws, shall be drawn up, and made known to all the voting members of such village, and a copy shall be given to the Superintendent of the Hopi jurisdiction. Upon the request of the Kikmongwi of such village, or of 25% of the voting members thereof, for an election on such Constitution, the Superintendent shall make sure that all members have had ample opportunity to study the proposed Constitution. He shall then call a special meeting of the voting members of such village, for the purpose of voting on the adoption of the proposed Constitution, and shall see that there is a fair vote. If at such referendum, not less than half of the voting members of the village cast their votes, and if a majority of those voting accepts the proposed Constitution, it shall then become the Constitution of that village, and only officials chosen according to its provisions shall be recognized.

The village Constitution shall clearly say how the Council representatives and other village officials shall be chosen, as well as the official who shall perform the duties placed upon the Kikmongwi in this Constitution. Such village Constitution may be amended or abolished in the same manner as provided for its adoption.

Article IV — The Tribal Council

Section 1. The Hopi Tribal Council shall consist of a chairman, vice-chairman, and representatives from the various villages. The number of representatives from each village shall be determined according to its population, as follows: villages of 50 to 250 population, one representative; villages of 251 to 500 population, two representatives; villages of 501 to 750 population, three representatives; villages of over 750 population, four representatives....

Sec. 2. The term of office of the representatives shall be two years, except that at the first election or choosing of representatives following the adoption of this section, approximately one-half of the representatives shall serve for a term of one year. The determination as to which representative shall serve for one year shall be made by the tribal council and announced to each village Kickmongwi or Governor on or before the first day of October 1969. Representatives may serve any number of terms in succession or otherwise.

Sec. 3. Each representative must be a member of the village which he represents. He must be twenty-five years or more of age, and must have lived in the Hopi jurisdiction for not less than two years before taking office, and must be able to speak the Hopi language fluently.

Sec. 4. Each village shall decide for itself how it shall choose its representatives, subject to the provisions of section 5. Representatives shall be recognized by the Council only if they are certified by the Kikmongwi of their respective villages. Certifications may be made in writing or in person.

Sec. 5. One representative of the village of Moenkopi shall be selected from the Lower District, and certified by the Kikmongwi of Moenkopi, and one representative shall be selected by the Upper District, and certified by the official whom that District may appoint, or who may be specified in a village Constitution adopted under the provisions of Article III, section 4. This section may be repealed, with the consent of the Tribal Council, by vote of a two-thirds majority at a meeting of the voting members of Moenkopi village called and held subject to the provisions of Article III, section 4.

Sec. 6. No business shall be done unless at least a majority of the members are present.

Sec. 7. The chairman and vice-chairman shall be elected by secret ballot by all members of the Hopi Tribe. The tribal council shall choose from its own members or from other members of the tribe, a secretary, treasurer, sergeant-at-arms and interpreters and such other officers and committees as it may determine necessary, subject to the provisions of the By-laws, Article I.

Sec. 8. All members of the Hopi Tribe twenty-one years of age or over shall be qualified to vote in any election or referendum, other than village elections and referendums under such rules and regulations as may be prescribed by the Hopi Tribal Council and approved by the Secretary of the Interior.

Sec. 9. The chairman and vice-chairman shall each serve for a term of four years. Candidates for the offices of chairman and vice-chairman shall be members of the Hopi Tribe, twenty-five years of age or older and must be able to speak the Hopi language fluently. Each candidate for either of said offices must also have lived on the Hopi Reservation for not less than two years immediately preceding his announcement of such candidacy.

Sec. 10. Candidates for the offices of chairman and vice-chairman may declare their candidacy by filing with the tribal secretary or tribal chairman or vice-chairman a petition signed by at least ten adult members of the tribe at least 15 days before the date set for the election. It shall be the duty of the secretary to post the names of the qualified candidates for both the primary and final elections in a public place in each village at least ten days prior to the election....

Article VI — Powers of the Tribal Council

Section 1. The Hopi Tribal Council shall have the following powers which the Tribe now has under existing law or which have been given to the Tribe by the Act of June 18, 1934. The Tribal Council shall exercise these powers subject to the terms of this Constitution and to the Constitution and Statutes of the United States.

(a) To represent and speak for the Hopi Tribe in all matters for the welfare of the Tribe, and to negotiate with the Federal, State, and local governments, and with the councils or governments of other tribes.

(b) To employ lawyers, the choice of lawyers and fixing of fees to be subject to the approval of the Secretary of the Interior.

(c) To prevent the sale, disposition, lease or encumbrance of tribal lands, or other tribal property.

(d) To advise with the Secretary of the Interior and other governmental agencies upon all appropriation estimates for Federal projects for the benefit of the Tribe, before the submission of such estimates to the Bureau of the Budget or to Congress.

(e) To raise and take care of a tribal council fund by accepting grants or gifts from any person, State, or the United States Government, or by charging persons doing business within the Reservation reasonable license fees, subject to the approval of the Secretary of the Interior.

(f) To use such tribal council fund for the welfare of the Tribe, and for salaries or authorized expenses of tribal officers. All payments from the tribal council fund shall be a matter of public record at all times.

(g) To make ordinances, subject to the approval of the Secretary of the Interior, to protect the peace and welfare of the Tribe, and to set up courts for the settlement of claims and disputes, and for the trial and punishment of Indians within the jurisdiction charged with offenses against such ordinances.

(h) To act as a court to hear and settle claims or disputes between villages in the manner provided in Article VIII.

(i) To provide by ordinance, subject to the approval of the Secretary of the Interior, for removal or exclusion from the jurisdiction of any non-members whose presence may be harmful to the members of the Tribe.

(j) To regulate the activities of voluntary cooperative associations of members of the Tribe for business purposes.

(k) To protect the arts, crafts, traditions, and ceremonies of the Hopi Indians.

(l) To delegate any of the powers of the council to committees or officers, keeping the right to review any action taken.

(m) To request a charter of incorporation to be issued as provided in the Act of June 18, 1934.

(n) To adopt resolutions providing the way in which the Tribal Council itself shall do its business.

Sec. 2. Any resolution or ordinance which, by the terms of this Constitution, is subject to review by the Secretary of the Interior, shall be given to the Superintendent of the jurisdiction, who shall, within ten days thereafter, approve or disapprove the same.

If the Superintendent shall approve any ordinance or resolution, it shall thereupon become effective, but the Superintendent shall send a copy of the same, bearing his endorsement, to the Secretary of the Interior, who may, within ninety days from the date of enactment, veto said ordinance or resolution for any reason by notifying the Tribal Council of his decision.

If the Superintendent shall refuse to approve any ordinance or resolution submitted to him, within ten days after enactment, he shall report his reasons to the Tribal Council. If the Tribal Council thinks these reasons are not sufficient, it may, by a majority vote, refer the ordinance or resolution to the Secretary of the Interior, who may, within ninety days from the date of its enactment, approve the same in writing, whereupon the said ordinance or resolution shall become effective.

Sec. 3. The Hopi Tribal Council may exercise such further powers as may in the future be delegated to it by the members of the Tribe or by the Secretary of the Interior, or any other duly authorized official or agency of the State or Federal Government.

Sec. 4. Any rights and powers which the Hopi Tribe of Indians now has, but which are not expressly mentioned in this Constitution, shall not be lost or limited by this article, but may be exercised by the members of the Hopi Tribe of Indians through the adoption of appropriate by-laws and constitutional amendments.

NOTES

1. **Federal Constitutional and Hopi Values:** Article IV of the Hopi Constitution would present constitutional problems under the equal protection clause and the religion clauses (free exercise and establishment) were it in a state constitution. As to equal protection, the Hopi Constitution provides that the tribal council will consist of representatives from each of the villages with the number allotted to each village only roughly related to population. (Villages of 50-200 inhabitants have one representative, for instance). The Constitution makes a two-year residency a prerequisite and requires fluency in the Hopi language. As to the religion clauses, the Council cannot recognize a member unless he is certified by the Kikmongwi of the respective village. The Kikmongwi also assert considerable control of the membership process. For example, a nonmember seeking adoption into the tribe may apply to the Kikmongwi of the village for acceptance. The Kikmongwi may accept him "[a]ccording to the way of doing established in the village." Article II, section 2.

2. **Tribal Powers:** As stated above, Article VI of the Hopi Constitution contains a fairly typical boilerplate powers provision. Note that Section 1 confers on the tribe "powers which the Tribe now has under existing law or which have been given to the Tribe by the [IRA]," tracking the language in the IRA, which confirmed "all powers vested in any Indian tribe or tribal council by existing law," 25 U.S.C. § 476, before reciting specific exercises of tribal power. What does this language say about the extent of tribal inherent powers in the minds of policymakers at the time the IRA was enacted? Which of the powers are inherent? Which are delegated? If powers like the power "[t]o employ lawyers" (Hopi Constitution, Art. VI, Section 1(b)) and "[t]o make ordinances, subject to the approval of the Secretary of the Interior" (Section 1(g)), were delegated by the Act, what was the extent of inherent tribal authority before the IRA?

Most likely the drafters of the IRA chose this somewhat ambiguous language deliberately to avoid disagreements that might undercut majority support for the legislation. By referring generally to all inherent and delegated powers followed by a list of specifics, the drafters could sidestep debate on the full extent of tribal inherent sovereignty. This same cautious drafting was incorporated into the list of powers of most boilerplate constitutions. Recently, tribes have begun to amend their constitutions to assert the breadth of tribal power more explicitly. See the note that follows.

3. Remedies for Intratribal Constitutional Conflicts: Some members of the Hopi tribe have claimed that the tribal council is not operating in a fashion which accords appropriate power to the villages and the Kikmongwi. Do they have recourse to the federal courts? To the Secretary of the Interior? Note that the Hopi Constitution provides for Secretarial approval of some tribal ordinances. Must the Secretary withhold approval of these ordinances if the council membership is not Kikmongwi-certified?

The IRA constitution of the Hopi Tribe was severely tested when the Hopi Tribal Council, with the approval of the Secretary of the Interior, entered into a twenty-million-dollar coal lease with Peabody Coal. The lease authorized the strip mining of Black Mesa, an area sacred to the traditional Hopi religion. The Hopi traditionalists had boycotted the IRA election and most tribal elections since the adoption of the constitution on religious grounds; and the non-traditionalists had gained control of the tribal council and entered into the contested lease. The Kikmongwi filed suit in federal court, alleging that the strip mining of Black Mesa was a sacrilege, a desecration, and contrary to every principle of Hopi culture, life, and religion. Ultimately, the traditionalists were unable to secure a federal court adjudication on the merits. The doctrine of tribal sovereign immunity prevented the plaintiffs from joining the tribe as a defendant; thus, the suit was dismissed for failure to join an indispensable party. *Lomayaktewa v. Hathaway*, 520 F.2d 1324 (9th Cir. 1975), *cert. denied sub nom. Susenkewa v. Kleppe*, 425 U.S. 903 (1976). Could any provisions have been added to the Hopi Constitution that would have prevented this dispute? Does the origin of the dispute lie in the IRA or the constitution drafted under it, or rather was the problem one of implementation of the tribal constitution?

Is the concept of tribal government offered in the IRA antithetical to traditional tribal methods of governance, as some traditional Indian bodies have charged? The Hopi traditionals took their case to the United Nations, arguing that the government's control over the IRA council and the coal lease executed "at the bidding of the United States" denied them the fundamental right to self-determination guaranteed by international law. According to the petition:

> The United States established such an I.R.A. council and "constitutional" system in a concerted effort to supplant the traditional Hopi government with what can fairly be described as a "puppet regime." ... created in 1936 by means of a sham referendum orchestrated by the Bureau of Indian Affairs. The Hopi Tribal Council's Constitution and By-laws give the U.S. Secretary of the Interior absolute veto power over all of the Council's actions.

"Violations of the Human Rights of the Hopi People by the United States of America," Communication to the United Nations Commission on Human Rights and Sub-Commission on Prevention of Discrimination and Protection of Minorities, March 11, 1980, *reprinted in* National Lawyers Guild, Committee on Native American Studies, *Rethinking Indian Law* 141, at 163 (1982). If members of a tribe split into factions with one group advocating cultural and economic change and another group advocating maintenance of traditional ways, what standards can be used to determine which side is correct? For example, if a new vote were ordered on the Hopi reservation, what would prevent traditionalists from refusing to vote in that election as well? If they constitute a minority of the people on the reservation, would giving them an opportunity to vote do any good? Most important, *what body* should define and administer the appropriate standards? *See Kavena v. Hopi Tribal Court,* section D2, *infra.*

NOTE: CONSTITUTION-MAKING — RECENT EXAMPLES

The process of drafting or amending constitutions and charters of the Indian tribes continues. Indeed, the increased economic development potential on reservations has imposed a need for increased certainty in government. Furthermore, tribal government needs to keep pace with the complexities of governing expanding populations by modernizing governing structures, managing growing bureaucracies, and keeping pace with the expanding rights and obligations of tribal government under federal Indian law.

Two modern constitutions by IRA tribes illustrate attempts to break away from the old boilerplate constitutions. One is the constitution adopted by the Menominee Tribe of Wisconsin under the Menominee Restoration Act, 25 U.S.C. §§ 903-903f. The second constitution was adopted in 1986 by the Tohono O'Odham Nation of Arizona (formerly known as the Papago Tribe). Each asserts broad tribal inherent powers over persons and land within the reservations' geographic boundaries, including land added in the future. Each also asserts jurisdiction beyond reservation boundaries; the Tohono O'Odham Nation over its members only, while the Menominee Tribe asserts jurisdiction over "any persons, subjects, or real property which are, or may hereafter be, included within the jurisdiction of the Tribe under any law of the United States or of the Tribe." Menominee Constitution, Art. I; Tohono O'Odham Nation Constitution, Art. I. Absent from each is the stingy enumeration of tribal powers found in the boilerplate of article VI of the Hopi Constitution and in most IRA constitutions, although both contain the provisions on legislative authority required to be included in tribal constitutions by section 16 of the IRA. Menominee Constitution, Art. III; Tohono O'Odham Nation Constitution, Art. VI.

Both constitutions provide for an appointed judiciary and appellate review. In each, however, judges are appointed for a term and not for life. Menominee judges may be removed only by a 7/9 vote of the entire legislature, however, making their tenure more secure, while Tohono O'Odham judges serve for a 6-year term. Nevertheless, each guarantees the independence of the judiciary and provides for judicial review of tribal legislative acts. Menominee Constitution, Art. III, § 3 ("separate and equal branches" with the Supreme Court "the final and supreme interpreter of this Constitution"); Tohono O'Odham Constitution, Art. VIII § 10 (power to interpret and "declare the laws ... void if such laws are not in agreement with this constitution"). Both constitutions contain detailed provisions regarding regulation of land use and preservation of tribal property. Both also contain an itemization of personal rights similar to those set forth in the Indian Civil Rights Act, section C, *infra* and provide for initiatives and referenda, as well as popular recall of tribal officials.

Marked differences do exist between the two constitutions, however. The Menominee Constitution provides for at-large elections of the 9-person legislature in which all tribal members may vote and, like most tribal constitutions, contains no provision for a separate executive branch. In contrast, the Tohono O'Odham Constitution provides for district elections with votes apportioned by population so that each district is entitled to as many votes as there are members of the tribe in the district, divided by ten. More significant, the Tohono O'Odham Constitution provides for three branches of government. The Executive's domestic powers are similar to those in the United States Constitution, including the veto power and power to appoint department heads. Tohono O'Odham Constitution, Arts. IV, VII.

Notably absent in either constitution is any provision authorizing or requiring approval by the Secretary of the Interior or other federal officials for tribal legislation or actions other than the transfer, encumbrance, or leasing of tribal land. Even as to these actions, the Tohono O'Odham Constitution states that approval is necessary "only to the extent and for so long as such approval is expressly required by federal statutes." Tohono O'Odham Constitution, Art. VI, § 2.

4. THE ROLE OF OTHER SOCIAL CONTROL MECHANISMS IN TRIBAL GOVERNANCE

To outsiders, tribal councils are the most visible power structure in Indian Country. But it would be a mistake to assume that they are the only social control mechanisms on reservations. Religious organizations, age and kinship groups, and social clubs may all exert independent pressure on tribal members' conduct. In turn, a tribal member's standing in the community and participation in these cultural social control mechanisms is often an important factor in his or her getting elected to political office, as the following excerpt from Loretta Fowler's study of the Arapahoe Tribe of the Wind River Reservation illustrates.

FOWLER, WIND RIVER RESERVATION POLITICAL PROCESS: AN ANALYSIS OF THE SYMBOLS OF CONSENSUS, 5 American Ethnologist 748-69 (1978)*

The Cultural Context of Arapahoes Politics

Conveyed from one generation of Arapahoe to another, the advice of the chief Sharp Nose as he lay dying in 1901 was: "my friends I am dying of my battle wounds. Watch out for our children and yourselves. Stay together, and as the Arapahoe has always been, since the beginning, beware of the stranger and his strange ways." ... In situations that involve choices among Business Council candidates or, for that matter, choices about the nature of relations with neighbors and kin, individuals seek to affirm their cultural identity as Arapahoe. Arapahoe recognize that cultural identity is expressed in various ways and that some individuals conform to the ideal of being "really Arapahoe" more closely

---

*Reproduced by permission of the American Anthropological Association and Loretta Fowler from American Ethnologist 5:4, November 1978. Not for further reproduction.

than others. Such distinctions are central to choices made in voting for council-men.

To Be "Really Arapahoe"

Arapahoe cultural identity is complicated by the fact that the legal definition of an Arapahoe Indian is different from the cultural one; these two categories do not correspond directly ....

To be legally Arapahoe is not necessarily to be "really" Arapahoe. Being "really" Arapahoe in the eyes of one's peers involves the public demonstration of loyalty to the Arapahoe community, whence participation in networks of social, economic, and political reciprocity is assured. A "real" Arapahoe behaves so as to convey to others the qualities of "generosity" and ability to "get along with the people." In contrast, people who do not participate in club and ceremonial activities, nor help others who do so, are labeled "stingy" or "greedy" or "out for themselves" and are seen as being outside the sociopolitical system. Those who achieve some measure of personal success must work to keep a low profile, and persons who earn a good salary are expected to give conspicuous and generous financial aid to relatives and friends....

In short, in the political context one indicates that one is "really" Arapahoe by demonstrating to others that one is a loyal participant in the sharing network and that one knows and accepts one's proper place in society. This place is assigned by consensus of the Arapahoe community, in part according to a conceptual framework that can be documented for Arapahoe as early as the mid-nineteenth century.[13]

"Elders," the "Younger Generation," and "Young People"

Leadership as well as kinship groupings are seen by Arapahoes as corresponding to broad age categories ....

In the "elder" or "old people" category are placed Arapahoe individuals at least sixty years of age. They are viewed as having the greatest amount of wisdom, their opinion is required on most tribal matters of any importance, and they control the ceremonial life of the tribe. It is not that "elders" have the most power, but rather that their judgments, when given, tend to be most respected. They exert a tempering influence on the "younger generation," although they may not actually try to control behavior.... Persons in their mid-forties to late fifties are the "younger generation." Those in this category are thought to be more skilled in dealing with white society but not particularly wise. A third age category, "young people," is used by Arapahoes to refer to persons over the age of about forty. They are characterized by Arapahoes as not fully mature.

Leadership groupings — ceremonial offices, the Business Council, and sodalities — are all associated by Arapahoes with age categories, and are

---

[13] The organization of age-graded societies (at whose head were the tribal priests), which governed Arapahoe during times of the year when the camp encompassed most of the tribe, is discussed in Lowie 1916, Dorsey 1903, and Kroeber 1902-1907. By the first decade of this century, the societies no longer were operative, but the age-grading principle found resilience in peer-oriented sodalities that crosscut kinship ties. Today, the Entertainment Committee of elders draws members equally from both settlements, whereas most clubs exist as Ethete and Lower Arapahoe groups.

thought of as composed predominately of either "elders" or "the younger generation."

Only those of advanced years can have authority in the spiritual realm, and Arapahoes call these leaders Ceremonial Elders. The Elders include the Keeper of the Pipe, who directs the ritual associated with the tribal medicine bundle of which he is custodian, and the Four Old Men: the Sun Dance Chief, who directs the annual Sun Dance Lodge, and three other Medicine Men who cure and help direct aspects of various religious rituals. Other Ceremonial Elders are the Keeper of the Drum, who has custody of the tribal drum ("Drum Number One," as Arapahoes call it) used in all important tribal ceremonies, and the Eagles who know the religious songs and (with their female assistants) sing seated at Drum Number One. These persons, who are selected by all the Elders as a group, hold their positions for life.

The Business Council members are "younger generation" persons, who are thought to have shown experience and level-headedness somewhat beyond their years. Business Council members themselves exhibit deference to the "elders" and may consult them on important proposed innovations even though these proposals may be a matter for Business Council decision alone.

The sodalities, "clubs" or "committees," as they are called by Arapahoes[,] are also categorized as composed of either "elders" or "the younger generation." The Entertainment Committee is not strictly a sodality, in that members are elected at the same time as the Business Councilmen and like them serve a term of two years. This group oversees the activities of all the clubs and ranks second to the Business Council in secular authority. It is thought that most members of the Entertainment Committee should be "elders" because special knowledge of Arapahoe dance and song is needed and because committee members oversee the use of tribal funds allocated to the clubs. The Ethete Memorial Club, responsible for many aspects of funeral ritual, is composed primarily of "elders." Several other clubs have members in their late forties to late fifties and are labeled "younger generation clubs." ...

The Ceremonial Elders exert a controlling influence on the actions of councilmen and on Arapahoes in general through a compelling set of symbols that surround these ritual offices. Four Old Men is a metaphor that recalls the four corners of the universe and the supernatural power associated therewith. Suggestive of the special tie between the four Arapahoe priests and the Man Above (Creator), the title Four Old Men inspires awe and respect. Eagles are seen as messengers, transitory between heaven and earth, carrying prayers to the Man Above. This explains the importance of eagle plumage in Sun Dance regalia, and similarly of the label "Eagles" for the old men who sing religious song as prayers on behalf of the people.

Thus, in the political context, the intervention of the Four Old Men is particularly effective. For example, when accidents or deaths directly affect councilmen or sodality leaders, the opinion of the Ceremonial Elders as to whether or not these misfortunes are connected with failure to conform to the ideals of leadership is highly respected. More specifically councilmen are periodically honored by the Eagles with a Chief's Song. At these occasions, during tribal gatherings, the councilman walks solemnly around the Eagles, who are singing at the Drum in the center of the circle of spectators. The councilman's family is then obligated to "give-away," and equally important, the councilman is duly impressed that his office is a sacred obligation to serve the interests of the tribe as a whole and to respect the judgment of the elders who have so honored him.

Moreover, religious leaders serve to resolve social conflict in general. Men who participate in the annual Sun Dance have ceremonial advisors, called "grandfathers." Such a man must not be a relative of his "grandson." The bond between them obligates each to aid the other, precludes quarrels between the two, and prevents one from criticizing the other. Relatives of a man who behaves badly call upon the "grandfather" to correct him.

The "younger generation" also manipulates a set of symbols associated with the realm of leadership assigned to persons in this age group. "Younger generation" males today are acknowledged as more capable in dealing with whites than are "elders." More at ease speaking English, these men are acknowledged by the Indian community as more educated in the way of the wider society. Councilmen work to enhance this reputation. A council position is almost always preceded by Legion participation, and councilmen continue this involvement after election. As Legion members they carry the flag during the Arapahoe National Anthem and serve as a military honor guard at funerals of veterans. These kinds of activity impress spectators with the leaders' success in the white man's army as well as their ability to cope with the pressures of the wider society. The councilmen also publicly state that one of their primary aims is to use their skills to "help the old people." They are particularly generous in making grants to elders and conspicuous in appearing at federally funded projects that aid the elderly.

One young man, laying the groundwork for his future entry into tribal politics, made a particularly effective speech to a tribal gathering that illustrates the way these symbols surrounding age categories and the associated leadership roles can be manipulated. The man's family had just sponsored a give-away to announce his success in college. In his speech, he talked of the long winter months spent in his grandmother's log house, listening to her stories and watching her work. He said he respected his grandmother for her wisdom and ceremonial knowledge, and one day when he was sitting beside his grandmother and worrying about what it would be like to go to school, she said, "quick! There's nih?oooo, step on him!" A little brown spider was crawling across the floor and he stepped on it, which pleased his grandmother. The man finished the story and vowed to the crowd to use his educational attainments for the benefit of the Arapahoe people. Many individuals in the crowd commented on the merits of the story for several minutes afterward. The word for "spider" in the Arapahoe language is nih?oooo, but nih?oooo is also the word for white man. This young man had chosen his story carefully. By his story, he symbolically linked educational success, resistance to the demoralizing experiences in Indian-white contacts and commitment to Arapahoe culture and society. And he also affirmed his respect for elders by recounting his grandmother's great influence on his life.

The extent and nature of authority is viewed to be highly circumscribed in all spheres. As one Arapahoe man put it, "there is no one outstanding person on the reservation. If there is a certain function, the person in charge is sort of a boss — the president or chairman." In reference to how one goes about making a request or accomplishing something, another man explained: "Arapahoes have no influential people; it depends on what you want to do." Moreover, particular clubs are viewed as most influential at certain seasons: the Pow Wow Committees are most active during the summer, the Legions in the fall, the Christmas Clubs in winter, the Memorial Clubs in spring.

The activities and authority of each leadership grouping are clearly compartmentalized. Ceremonial Elders conduct religious rituals, and the Business Council is intermediary between Arapahoes and outsiders as well as administrator of tribal funds. Councilmen do not serve as officers in sodalities while they are on the council. The clubs are responsible for perpetuating nonsacred celebrations (such as social dances), for protecting financial resources over which they have control, and for helping the needy, especially families who have lost a relative through death. The Legions conduct military funerals and represent military accomplishments of the Arapahoes in tribal rituals. The Auxiliaries (female relatives of Legion members) aid the Legions and other clubs, primarily by cooking the food consumed during tribal ceremonies. The Christmas Clubs sponsor and organize the five-day winter dance and feast and give money and gifts to the people at that time. The Pow Wow Committees plan and organize intertribal gatherings during the summer....

The conceptual distinction between groups whose authority is in the sacred and groups whose authority is in the secular realm has particularly important repercussions in political process. During the last two generations, no individual has been a ceremonial leader and a councilman simultaneously. And men of the "younger generation" tend to apprentice themselves to one or the other of these leadership groups. By their absence at General Council meetings (or their reserve), Ceremonial Elders appear aloof from secular affairs. Yet it is this remoteness that buttresses their impact on secular leaders and enables them to exert informal sanctions to curb dissent and self-aggrandizement. The lack of direct involvement insulates them from the criticism councilmen face if they are unsuccessful in some aspect of tribal business, and the exclusion of councilmen from the ceremonial hierarchy intensifies the effectiveness of supernatural sanctions....

NOTE: TRIBAL GOVERNMENTS

Not surprisingly, with 291 Indian reservations and more than 487 identifiable Indian tribal communities, generalizations about tribal governments are dangerous, and may tell more about the generalizer than about the Indians. *See generally,* R. BERKHOFER, JR., THE WHITE MAN'S INDIAN (1978) (images of what is an Indian through the centuries used to justify often racist policies). Some tribes enjoy a stable community, with relatively little dissension. Others experience internal strife. Some tribes, like the Suquamish Tribe in Washington govern territories inhabited by many more non-Indians than Indians; others, like the Navajo, govern territories in which only a handful of non-Indians live. Some tribal court systems seem well run and efficient; others manifest serious problems. Some tribes are rich in resources, like the Crow Tribe; others make up for lack of natural resources by ingenuity, like the Cabazon Band of Mission Indians, who operate a lucrative bingo hall on their desert reservation, located conveniently to Los Angeles. More important, Indian tribes have widely divergent cultural backgrounds: their art, their myths, their religions, their law-ways differ radically from group to group. For example, in an omitted portion of her study Professor Fowler notes that Plains Indians, who have similar backgrounds in many respects, differ in the importance they attach to group and individual values.

Nevertheless, federal statutory and case law often treat all Indian tribes as the same. Under the IRA *all* tribes are urged to incorporate and adopt constitutions, in order to exercise sovereign powers. According to the Supreme Court, *no* tribe has the power to exercise criminal jurisdiction over any non-Indian. Should Congress and the Court take more care to refer to "tribally specific contexts" in answering questions regarding tribal sovereignty, especially jurisdictional questions? *See* Clinton, *Reservation Specificity and Indian Adjudication: An Essay on the Importance of Limited Contextualism in Indian Law,* 8 HAMLINE L. REV. 543, 545 (1985). Professor Clinton suggests that in cases in which contextualism is important, courts should begin to "carefully limit the reach of their holdings so as to avoid deciding the question for a reservation context not presented by the pending case, and ... attempt to frame the rationale for their dispositions in ways that take account of reservation context, and encourage those who later litigate such questions on other reservations to make a record that fully presents the reservation setting and contextual problems in each case." *Id.* at 593.

Perhaps one reason "reservation contextualism" has not been the order of the day is the difficulty in ascertaining accurately conditions on so many reservations. As Professor Fowler's study demonstrates, studies by ethnologists and anthropologists of modern-day tribal cultures can place an event that might be the source of (or solution to) a legal problem for the tribe in its appropriate social and cultural context. A study by Mary Shepardson, for example, explaining how the Navajo Tribal Council grew in importance as a tribal institution, while written in 1963, helps illuminate recent struggles between the Tribal Council and the Chairman and explain the important role of traditional Navajos in the political life of the Navajo people. Shepardson, *Navajo Ways in Government,* Memoir 96, American Anthropology Ass'n. Thus, an attorney representing a tribe could well benefit by searching for such sources, both to understand how the tribal culture might impact on his or her relationship with the tribal client, but also to put the legal issues in context.

C. THE INDIAN CIVIL RIGHTS ACT OF 1968: A FEDERAL STATUTORY RESTRAINT ON TRIBAL GOVERNMENTAL AUTHORITY

The Indian Civil Rights Act of 1968 (ICRA), Pub. L. No. 90-284, 82 Stat. 77, was the first major federal legislation regarding the operation of tribal government since 1934. Title II of the ICRA, codified as amended at 25 U.S.C. §§ 1301-1303, applied many, but not all, provisions of the Bill of Rights to Indian tribes.

1301. Definitions*

For purposes of this subchapter, the term —

(1) "Indian tribe" means any tribe, band, or other group of Indians subject to the jurisdiction of the United States and recognized as possessing powers of self-government;

(2) "powers of self-government" means and includes all governmental powers possessed by an Indian tribe, executive, legislative, and judicial, and all offices, bodies, and tribunals by and through which they are executed, including courts of Indian offenses; and

(3) "Indian court" means any Indian tribal court or court of Indian offense.

1302. Constitutional rights

No Indian tribe in exercising powers of self-government shall —

(1) make or enforce any law prohibiting the free exercise of religion, or abridging the freedom of speech, or of the press, or the right of the people peaceably to assemble and to petition for a redress of grievances;

(2) violate the right of the people to be secure in their persons, houses, papers, and effects against unreasonable search and seizures, nor issue warrants, but upon probable cause, supported by oath or affirmation, and particularly describing the place to be searched and the person or thing to be seized;

(3) subject any person for the same offense to be twice put in jeopardy;

(4) compel any person in any criminal case to be a witness against himself;

(5) take any private property for a public use without just compensation;

(6) deny to any person in a criminal proceeding the right to a speedy and public trial, to be informed of the nature and cause of the accusation, to be confronted with the witnesses against him, to have compulsory process for obtaining witnesses in his favor, and at his own expense to have the assistance of counsel for his defense;

(7) require excessive bail, impose excessive fines, inflict cruel and unusual punishments, and in no event impose for conviction of any one offense any penalty or punishment greater than imprisonment for a term of one year or a fine of $5000 or both [as amended, 1986 — Eds.];

(8) deny to any person within its jurisdiction the equal protection of its laws or deprive any person of liberty or property without due process of law;

(9) pass any bill of attainder or ex post facto law; or

(10) deny to any person accused of an offense punishable by imprisonment the right, upon request, to a trial by jury of not less than six persons.

1303. Habeas corpus

The privilege of the writ of habeas corpus shall be available to any person, in a court of the United States, to test the legality of his detention by order of an Indian tribe.

NOTE: BACKGROUND AND EARLY IMPLEMENTATION OF THE INDIAN CIVIL RIGHTS ACT

Talton v. Mayes and its progeny caused Senator Sam Ervin of North Carolina (a state with a large Indian population) to question whether Indians and non-Indians needed protection from abuses by tribal government. Seven years of hearings by the Senate Judiciary Subcommittee on Constitutional Rights led by Senator Ervin resulted in the "Indian Civil Rights Act." *See generally* Burnett,

---

*In 1990 the definition section was amended. Defense Appropriations Act for FY 91, Pub. L. No. 101-938, § 8077(b)-(d) (1990). Since the effect of the amendments lapses September 31, 1991, they are excerpted and discussed after *Duro v. Reina,* to which they were addressed. See note 5 after that case in Section D1, *infra.* — Eds.

An Historical Analysis of the 1968 "Indian Civil Rights" Act, 9 HARV. J. ON
LEGIS. 557 (1972); Comment, *The Indian Bill of Rights and the Constitutional
Status of Tribal Governments,* 82 HARV. L. REV. 1343 (1969). During the hearings, tribal reaction ranged from lukewarm acceptance to outright opposition.
Some tribal representatives protested that the Act was unnecessary. Others
argued it would impose rigid Anglo-American legal constraints on informal
tribal court systems. The Pueblos in the Southwest adamantly opposed the
ICRA, arguing that it would fundamentally alter their traditional theocratic way
of life. According to Burnett: "American Indian tribes were many and various,
and each had its unique problems; they were not equally prepared or willing to
accommodate themselves to the structures of the Constitution." Burnett, *supra,*
at 590.

Immediately after enactment of the Act, the federal courts began to take
jurisdiction over cases challenging the decisions of tribal councils and courts
under the provisions of the Act, finding jurisdiction under 28 U.S.C. § 1331
(general federal question), 1343 (civil rights), or 1361 (mandamus). Many decisions required exhaustion of tribal remedies before seeking federal review. *See,
e.g., O'Neal v. Cheyenne River Sioux Tribe,* 482 F.2d 1140 (8th Cir. 1973). In
the many cases decided during this era, courts applied the due process, equal
protection, and even the bill of attainder clauses to intrude substantially into
tribal decisionmaking. *See, e.g., Wounded Head v. Tribal Council of Oglala
Sioux Tribe,* 507 F.2d 1079 (8th Cir. 1975) (election procedures); *Brown v.
United States,* 486 F.2d 658 (8th Cir. 1973) (tribal apportionment); *Johnson v.
Lower Elwha Tribal Community,* 484 F.2d 200 (9th Cir. 1973) (due process
complaints in tribal land assignments); *Slattery v. Arapaho Tribal Council,* 453
F.2d 278 (10th Cir. 1971) (tribal membership criteria); *Dodge v. Nakai,* 298 F.
Supp. 26 (D. Ariz. 1969) (legislative exclusion of legal services lawyer from
reservation a bill of attainder). In all of these cases courts assumed both that the
ICRA created a claim to sue a tribe that violated any of its provisions and that
the ICRA waived tribal sovereign immunity from suit. The next case put an end
to those assumptions.

SANTA CLARA PUEBLO v. MARTINEZ

436 U.S. 49 (1978)

Mr. Justice MARSHALL delivered the opinion of the Court.

This case requires us to decide whether a federal court may pass on the
validity of an Indian tribe's ordinance denying membership to the children of
certain female tribal members.

Petitioner Santa Clara Pueblo is an Indian tribe that has been in existence for
over 600 years. Respondents, a female member of the tribe and her daughter,
brought suit in federal court against the tribe and its Governor, petitioner
Lucario Padilla, seeking declaratory and injunctive relief against enforcement
of a tribal ordinance denying membership in the tribe to children of female
members who marry outside the tribe, while extending membership to children
of male members who marry outside the tribe. Respondents claimed that this
rule discriminates on the basis of both sex and ancestry in violation of Title I of
[ICRA], which provides in relevant part that "[n]o Indian tribe in exercising

powers of self-government shall … deny to any person within its jurisdiction the equal protection of its laws." *Id.*, § 1302(8).

Title I of the ICRA does not expressly authorize the bringing of civil actions for declaratory or injunctive relief to enforce its substantive provisions. The threshold issue in this case is thus whether the Act may be interpreted to impliedly authorize such actions, against a tribe or its officers, in the federal courts. For the reasons set forth below, we hold that the Act cannot be so read.

I

Respondent Julia Martinez is a full-blooded member of the Santa Clara Pueblo, and resides on the Santa Clara Reservation in Northern New Mexico. In 1941 she married a Navajo Indian with whom she has since had several children, including respondent Audrey Martinez. Two years before this marriage, the Pueblo passed the membership ordinance here at issue, which bars admission of the Martinez children to the tribe because their father is not a Santa Claran.[2] Although the children were raised on the reservation and continue to reside there now that they are adults, as a result of their exclusion from membership they may not vote in tribal elections or hold secular office in the tribe; moreover, they have no right to remain on the reservation in the event of their mother's death, or to inherit their mother's home or her possessory interests in the communal lands.

After unsuccessful efforts to persuade the tribe to change the membership rule, respondents filed this lawsuit in the United States District Court for the District of New Mexico, on behalf of themselves and others similarly situated. Petitioners moved to dismiss the complaint on the ground that the court lacked jurisdiction to decide intratribal controversies affecting matters of tribal self-government and sovereignty. The District Court rejected petitioners' contention, finding that jurisdiction was conferred by 28 U.S.C. § 1343 (4) and 25 U.S.C. § 1302 (8). The court apparently concluded, first, that the substantive provisions of Title I impliedly authorized civil actions for declaratory and injunctive relief, and second, that the tribe was not immune from such suit. Accordingly, the motion to dismiss was denied.

Following a full trial, the District Court found for petitioners on the merits. While acknowledging the relatively recent origin of the disputed rule, the District Court nevertheless found it to reflect traditional values of patriarchy still significant in tribal life. The court recognized the vital importance of respon-

---

[2] The ordinance, enacted by the Santa Clara Pueblo Council pursuant to its legislative authority under the Constitution of the Pueblo, establishes the following membership rules:

1. All children born of marriages between members of the Santa Clara Pueblo shall be members of the Santa Clara Pueblo.

2. That children born of marriages between male members of the Santa Clara Pueblo and non-members shall be members of the Santa Clara Pueblo.

3. Children born of marriages between female members of the Santa Clara Pueblo and non-members shall not be members of the Santa Clara Pueblo.

4. Persons shall not be naturalized as members of the Santa Clara Pueblo under any circumstances.

Respondents challenged only subparagraphs (2) and (3). By virtue of subparagraph (4), Julia Martinez' husband is precluded from joining the Pueblo and thereby assuring the children's membership pursuant to subparagraph (1).

dents' interests,[5] but also determined that membership rules were "no more or less than a mechanism of social ... self-definition," and as such were basic to the tribe's survival as a cultural and economic entity. In sustaining the ordinance's validity under the "equal protection clause" of the ICRA, 25 U.S.C. § 1302 (8), the District Court concluded that the balance to be struck between these competing interests was better left to the judgment of the Pueblo:

> "[T]he equal protection guarantee of the Indian Civil Rights Act should not be construed in a manner which would require or authorize this Court to determine which traditional values will promote cultural survival and should therefore be preserved ....
> Such a determination should be made by the people of Santa Clara; not only because they can best decide what values are important, but also because they must live with the decision every day....
> "... To abrogate tribal decisions, particularly in the delicate area of membership, for whatever 'good' reasons, is to destroy cultural identity under the guise of saving it." 402 F. Supp., at 18-19.

On respondents' appeal, the Court of Appeals for the Tenth Circuit upheld the District Court's determination [on the issue of jurisdiction, but not] on the merits. While recognizing that standards of analysis developed under the Fourteenth Amendment's Equal Protection Clause were not necessarily controlling in the interpretation of this statute, the Court of Appeals apparently concluded that because the classification was one based upon sex it was presumptively invidious and could be sustained only if justified by a compelling tribal interest. Because of the ordinance's recent vintage, and because in the court's view the rule did not rationally identify those persons who were emotionally and culturally Santa Clarans, the court held that the tribe's interest in the ordinance was not substantial enough to justify its discriminatory effect. *Ibid.*

We granted certiorari [and] now reverse.

II

Indian tribes are "distinct, independent political communities, retaining their original natural rights" in matters of local self-government. [*Worcester v. Georgia; Mazurie*]; F. Cohen, Handbook of Federal Indian Law 122-123 (1941). Although no longer "possessed of the full attributes of sovereignty," they remain a "separate people, with the power of regulating their internal and social relations." *United States v. Kagama,* 118 U.S. 375, 381-382 (1886). They have power to make their own substantive law in internal matters, see *Roff v. Burney,* 168 U.S. 218 (1897) (membership); *Jones v. Meehan,* 175 U.S. 1, 29 (1899) (inheritance rules); *United States v. Quiver,* 241 U.S. 602 (1916) (domestic relations), and to enforce that law in their own forums, see, *e.g., Williams v. Lee,* 358 U.S. 217 (1959).

As separate sovereigns pre-existing the Constitution, tribes have historically been regarded as unconstrained by those constitutional provisions framed specifically as limitations on federal or state authority. Thus, in [*Talton v. Mayes,*] this Court held that the Fifth Amendment did not "operat[e] upon" "the powers of local self-government enjoyed" by the tribes. In ensuing years the lower

---

[5] The court found that "Audrey Martinez and many other children similarly situated have been brought up on the Pueblo, speak the Tewa language, participate in its life, and are, culturally, for all practical purposes, Santa Claran Indians." 402 F. Supp., at 18.

federal courts have extended the holding of *Talton* to other provisions of the Bill of Rights, as well as to the Fourteenth Amendment.

As the Court in *Talton* recognized, however, Congress has plenary authority to limit, modify or eliminate the powers of local self-government which the tribes otherwise possess. 163 U.S., at 384. Title I of ICRA, 25 U.S.C. §§ 1301-1303, represents an exercise of that authority. In 25 U.S.C. § 1302, Congress acted to modify the effect of *Talton* and its progeny by imposing certain restrictions upon tribal governments similar, but not identical, to those contained in the Bill of Rights and the Fourteenth Amendment. In 25 U.S.C. § 1303, the only remedial provision expressly supplied by Congress, the "privilege of the writ of habeas corpus" is made "available to any person, in a court of the United States, to test the legality of his detention by order of an Indian tribe." ...

III

Indian tribes have long been recognized as possessing the common-law immunity from suit traditionally enjoyed by sovereign powers. This aspect of tribal sovereignty, like all others, is subject to the superior and plenary control of Congress. But "without congressional authorization," the "Indian Nations are exempt from suit." *United States v. United States Fidelity & Guaranty Co.,* [309 U.S. 506, 512 (1940)].

It is settled that a waiver of sovereign immunity "'cannot be implied but must be unequivocally expressed.'" *United States v. Testan,* 424 U.S. 392, 399 (1976), quoting *United States v. King,* 395 U.S. 1, 4 (1969). Nothing on the face of Title I of the ICRA purports to subject tribes to the jurisdiction of the federal courts in civil actions for injunctive or declaratory relief. Moreover, since the respondent in a habeas corpus action is the individual custodian of the prisoner, see, e.g., 28 U.S.C. § 2243, the provisions of § 1303 can hardly be read as a general waiver of the tribe's sovereign immunity. In the absence here of any unequivocal expression of contrary legislative intent, we conclude that suits against the tribe under the ICRA are barred by its sovereign immunity from suit.

IV

As an officer of the Pueblo, petitioner Lucario Padilla is not protected by the tribe's immunity from suit. See *Puyallup Tribe, Inc. v. Washington Dept. of Game, supra,* 433 U.S., at 171-172; cf. *Ex parte Young,* 209 U.S. 123 (1908). We must therefore determine whether the cause of action for declaratory and injunctive relief asserted here by respondents, though not expressly authorized by the statute, is nonetheless implicit in its terms.

In addressing this inquiry, we must bear in mind that providing a federal forum for issues arising under § 1302 constitutes an interference with tribal autonomy and self-government beyond that created by the change in substantive law itself. Even in matters involving commercial and domestic relations, we have recognized that "subject[ing] a dispute arising on the reservation among reservation Indians to a forum other than the one they have established for themselves," *Fisher v. District Court,* 424 U.S. 382, 387-388 (1976), may "undermine the authority of the tribal court ... and hence ... infringe on the right of the Indians to govern themselves." *Williams v. Lee, supra,* 358 U.S., at 223. *A fortiori,* resolution in a foreign forum of intratribal disputes of a more "public" character, such as the one in this case, cannot help but unsettle a tribal government's ability to maintain authority. Although Congress clearly has power to authorize civil actions against tribal officers, and has done so with respect to habeas corpus relief in § 1303, a proper respect both for tribal sovereignty itself and for the plenary authority of Congress in this area cautions that we tread lightly in the absence of clear indications of legislative intent. Cf. *Antoine v. Washington,* 420 U.S. 194, 199-200 (1975); *Choate v. Trapp,* 224 U.S. 665, 675 (1912).

With these considerations of "Indian sovereignty ... [as] a backdrop against which the applicable ... federal statut[e] must be read," *McClanahan v. Arizona State Tax Commission,* 411 U.S. 164, 172 (1973), we turn now to those factors of more general relevance in determining whether a cause of action is implicit in a statute not expressly providing one. See *Cort v. Ash,* 422 U.S. 66 (1975). We note at the outset that a central purpose of the ICRA and in particular of Title I was to "secur[e] for the American Indian the broad constitutional rights afforded to other Americans," and thereby to "protect individual Indians from arbitrary and unjust actions of tribal governments." S. Rep. No. 841, 90th Cong., 1st Sess., 5-6 (1967). There is thus no doubt that respondents, American Indians living on the Santa Clara reservation, are among the class for whose especial benefit this legislation was enacted. Moreover, we have frequently recognized the propriety of inferring a federal cause of action for the enforcement of civil rights, even when Congress has spoken in purely declarative terms. See, *e.g., Jones v. Alfred H. Mayer Co.,* 392 U.S. 409, 414 n.13 (1968). These precedents, however, are simply not dispositive here. Not only are we unpersuaded that a judicially sanctioned intrusion into tribal sovereignty is required to fulfill the purposes of the ICRA, but to the contrary, the structure of the statutory scheme and the legislative history of Title I suggest that Congress' failure to provide remedies other than habeas corpus was a deliberate one.

A

Two distinct and competing purposes are manifest in the provisions of the ICRA: In addition to its objective of strengthening the position of individual tribal members vis-à-vis the tribe, Congress also intended to promote the well-established federal "policy of furthering Indian self-government." *Morton v. Mancari,* 417 U.S. 535, 551 (1974). This commitment to the goal of tribal self-determination is demonstrated by the provisions of Title I itself. Section 1302, rather than providing in wholesale fashion for the extension of constitutional requirements to tribal governments, as had been initially proposed, selectively incorporated and in some instances modified the safeguards of the Bill of Rights to fit the unique political, cultural, and economic needs of tribal governments. [F]or example, the statute does not prohibit the establishment of religion, nor does it require jury trials in civil cases, or appointment of counsel for indigents in criminal cases, cf. *Argersinger v. Hamlin,* 407 U.S. 2 (1972).[14]

---

[14]The provisions of § 1302 ... differ in language and in substance in many other respects from those contained in the constitutional provisions on which they were modeled. The provisions of the

[When] Congress seeks to promote dual objectives in a single statute, courts must be more than usually hesitant to infer from its silence a cause of action that, while serving one legislative purpose, will disserve the other. Creation of a federal cause of action for the enforcement of rights created in Title I, however useful it might be in securing compliance with § 1302, plainly would be at odds with the congressional goal of protecting tribal self-government. Not only would it undermine the authority of tribal forums, ... but it would also impose serious financial burdens on already "financially disadvantaged" tribes. Subcommittee on Constitutional Rights, Senate Judiciary Committee, Constitutional Rights of the American Indian: Summary Report of Hearings and Investigations Pursuant to S. Res. 194, 89th Cong., 2d Sess., 12 (Comm. Print 1966) (hereinafter cited as Summary Report).

Moreover, contrary to the reasoning of the court below, implication of a federal remedy in addition to habeas corpus is not plainly required to give effect to Congress' objective of extending constitutional norms to tribal self-government. Tribal forums are available to vindicate rights created by the ICRA, and § 1302 has the substantial and intended effect of changing the law which these forums are obliged to apply. Tribal courts have repeatedly been recognized as appropriate forums for the exclusive adjudication of disputes affecting important personal and property interests of both Indians and non-Indians. See, e.g., Fisher v. District Court, 424 U.S. 382 (1976); Williams v. Lee, 358 U.S. 217 (1959). See also Ex parte Crow Dog, 109 U.S. 556 (1883). Nonjudicial tribal institutions have also been recognized as competent law-applying bodies. See [Mazurie].[22] Under these circumstances, we are reluctant to disturb the balance between the dual statutory objectives which Congress apparently struck in providing only for habeas corpus relief.

B

Our reluctance is strongly reinforced by the specific legislative history underlying 25 U.S.C. § 1303. This history, extending over more than three years, indicates that Congress' provision for habeas corpus relief, and nothing more, reflected a considered accommodation of the competing goals of "preventing injustices perpetrated by tribal governments, on the one hand, and, on the other, avoiding undue or precipitous interference in the affairs of the Indian people." Summary Report, supra, at 11.

Second and Third Amendments, in addition to those of the Seventh Amendment, were omitted entirely. The provision here at issue, § 1302(8), differs from the constitutional Equal Protection Clause in that it guarantees "the equal protection of its [the tribe's] laws," rather than of "the laws." Moreover, § 1302(7), which prohibits cruel or unusual punishments and excessive bails, sets an absolute limit of six months imprisonment and a $500 fine on penalties which a tribe may impose. Finally, while most of the guarantees of the Fifth Amendment were extended to tribal actions, it is interesting to note that § 1302 does not require tribal criminal prosecutions to be initiated by grand jury indictment, which was the requirement of the Fifth Amendment specifically at issue and found inapplicable to tribes in Talton v. Mayes....

[22] By the terms of its Constitution, adopted in 1935 and approved by the Secretary of the Interior in accordance with the Indian Reorganization Act of 1934, 25 U.S.C. § 476, judicial authority in the Santa Clara Pueblo is vested in its tribal council.

Many tribal constitutions adopted pursuant to [the IRA], though not that of the Santa Clara Pueblo, include provisions requiring that tribal ordinances not be given effect until the Department of Interior gives its approval. In these instances, persons aggrieved by tribal laws may, in addition to pursuing tribal remedies, be able to seek relief from the Department of the Interior.

In settling on habeas corpus as the exclusive means for federal-court review of tribal criminal proceedings, Congress opted for a less intrusive review mechanism than had been initially proposed. Originally, the legislation would have authorized *de novo* review in federal court of all convictions obtained in tribal courts. At hearings held on the proposed legislation in 1965, however, it became clear that even those in agreement with the general thrust of the review provision — to provide some form of judicial review of criminal proceedings in tribal courts — believed that *de novo* review would impose unmanageable financial burdens on tribal governments and needlessly displace tribal courts. [Thus, a]fter considering numerous alternatives for review of tribal convictions, Congress apparently decided that review by way of habeas corpus would adequately protect the individual interests at stake while avoiding unnecessary intrusions on tribal governments.

[In light of] this history, it is highly unlikely that Congress would have intended a private cause of action for injunctive and declaratory relief to be available in the federal courts to secure enforcement of § 1302. Although the only committee report on the ICRA in its final form, S. Rep. No. 841, 90th Cong., 1st Sess. (1967), sheds little additional light on this question, it would hardly support a contrary conclusion. Indeed, its description of the purpose of Title I, as well as the floor debates on the bill, indicates that the ICRA was generally understood [as limiting judicial review to the habeas corpus mechanism under § 1303].

V

As the bill's chief sponsor, Senator Ervin, commented in urging its passage, the ICRA "should not be considered as the final solution to the many serious constitutional problems confronting the American Indian." 113 Cong. Rec. 13473 (1967). Although Congress explored the extent to which tribes were adhering to constitutional norms in both civil and criminal contexts, its legislative investigation revealed that the most serious abuses of tribal power had occurred in the administration of criminal justice. [Because] of this finding, and given Congress' desire not to intrude needlessly on tribal self-government, it is not surprising that Congress chose at this stage to provide for federal review only [by means of habeas corpus.][32]

As we have repeatedly emphasized, Congress' authority over Indian matters is extraordinarily broad, and the role of courts in adjusting relations between and among tribes and their members correspondingly restrained. See *Lone Wolf v. Hitchcock,* 187 U.S. 553, 565 (1903). Congress retains authority expressly to authorize civil actions for injunctive or other relief to redress violations of § 1302, in the event that the tribes themselves prove deficient in applying and enforcing its substantive provisions. But unless and until Congress makes clear its intention to permit the additional intrusion on tribal sovereignty that adjudication of such actions in a federal forum would represent, we are

---

[32] A tribe's right to define its own membership for tribal purposes has long been recognized as central to its existence as an independent political community. *See Roff v. Burney,* 168 U.S. 218 (1897); *Cherokee Intermarriage Cases,* 203 U.S. 76 (1906). Given the often vast gulf between tribal traditions and those with which federal courts are more intimately familiar, the judiciary should not rush to create causes of action that would intrude on these delicate matters.

constrained to find that § 1302 does not impliedly authorize actions for declaratory or injunctive relief against either the tribe or its officers.

[*Reversed.*]

Mr. Justice BLACKMUN took no part in the consideration or decision of this case.

Mr. Justice WHITE, dissenting.

The declared purpose of the [ICRA] is "to insure that the American Indian is afforded the broad constitutional rights secured to other Americans." S. Rep. No. 841, 90th Cong., 1st Sess., 6 (1967) (hereinafter Senate Report). The Court today, by denying a federal forum to Indians who allege that their rights under the ICRA have been denied by their tribes, substantially undermines the goal of the ICRA and in particular frustrates Title I's purpose [to protect Indians from arbitrary actions by their governments].

Many tribal constitutions adopted pursuant to 25 U.S.C. § 476, though not that of the Santa Clara Pueblo, include provisions requiring that tribal ordinances not be given effect until the Department of Interior gives its approval. See I American Indian Policy Review Commission, *supra,* at 187-188; 1961 Hearings (Pt. I), *supra,* at 95. In these instances, persons aggrieved by tribal laws may, in addition to pursuing tribal remedies, be able to seek relief from the Department of Interior.

DRY CREEK LODGE, INC. v. ARAPAHOE & SHOSHONE TRIBES

623 F.2d 682 (10th Cir.), *cert. denied,* 449 U.S. 1118 (1981)

SETH, Chief Judge.

The case originally came to this court upon a dismissal of plaintiffs' complaint for damages for lack of jurisdiction. [After we reversed, the case was tried on the merits on remand.] The jury returned a verdict for plaintiffs against the defendant Tribes only, judgment was entered, and costs were assessed against the Tribes. On motion by defendant Tribes the trial court granted a new trial on the ground that the jury did not properly handle the issue of damages.

Before the case was retried the Supreme Court handed down [*Santa Clara Pueblo v. Martinez*]. The trial court thereupon dismissed the action on the theory that Santa Clara had decided the issue of jurisdiction. The plaintiffs have taken this appeal.

The facts are, of course, the same as on the original appeal, and the case is again before us following a dismissal for lack of jurisdiction.

The facts are set out in our previous opinion but some restatement appears to be useful. Plaintiffs' land is within the exterior boundaries of the Wind River Reservation of the Shoshone and Arapahoe Indians in Wyoming. The reservation is large and the town of Riverton and other settlements are within its boundaries. Many more non-Indians than Indians live within the boundaries. There are a large number of patented tracts owned in fee by non-Indians not including the property in Riverton. The reservation boundaries have changed substantially from time to time.

The lands of plaintiff corporation were patented to a predecessor in title in 1924. There was a small road providing access from the land of Dry Creek Lodge to the principal highway. This had been used by plaintiffs and other persons for access to the fee land and other lands for a period of some eighty years.

Plaintiffs Cook, who are non-Indians, had owned the 160-acre tract for about ten years and had lived there. They decided to build a guest lodge for hunting, and consulted the superintendent of the reservation about the matter. He advised them that projects of that type were encouraged to provide employment. He also stated that there would be no access problem. A license to plaintiffs Cook was issued for the business. The individuals then formed Dry Creek Lodge, Inc. to build the facilities. This was done with a SBA loan. The lodge was completed and opened, but the next day the Tribes closed the road at the request of a nearby Indian family, the Bonatsies. The access road had crossed an allotment belonging to this family. Apparently the plaintiffs have lost the property by foreclosure. The access road was closed in 1974.

The Tribes have a Joint Business Council which is composed of the Business Councils of each Tribe. These Councils are the legislative, executive and judicial bodies for the Tribes. The Tribal Business Councils are elected by members of each Tribe. The record contains the minutes of several meetings of the Joint Council relative to closing the business and the access road. The Council directed that access to the Dry Creek Lodge be prevented by the federal officers, and the Bonatsies were apparently to erect the barricade. With the road blocked the persons on the Dry Creek land could not get out and were for all practical purposes confined there until a federal court issued a temporary restraining order. Thereafter the plaintiffs sought a remedy with the tribal court, but were refused access to it. The judge indicated he could not incur the displeasure of the Council and that consent of the Council would be needed. 25 C.F.R. § 11.22. The consent was not given. The state court cases were apparently removed to the federal court. In the federal court the defendants urged that there was no remedy — no jurisdiction. The defendants again assert there is no remedy in the federal court by reason of the *Santa Clara* case. The Tribal Business Council, according to the minutes, directed that the differences between the Bonatsie family and the plaintiffs should be settled by self-help, and this was done. The plaintiffs, however, did not respond in the same way. The defendants argue here, as they did in the trial court, that the plaintiffs have no remedy. There is no forum where the dispute can be resolved and the personal and property rights asserted by plaintiffs be considered.

[In *Santa Clara* the Supreme Court essentially directed the aggrieved tribal members to seek] the remedies available to them in their own tribal courts and from the officials they had elected. Much emphasis was placed in the opinion on the availability of tribal courts and, of course, on the intratribal nature of the problem sought to be resolved. With the reliance on the internal relief available the Court in *Santa Clara* places the limitations on the Indian Civil Rights Act as a source of a remedy. But in the absence of such other relief or remedy the reason for the limitations disappears.

The reason for the limitations and the references to tribal immunity also disappear when the issue relates to a matter outside of internal tribal affairs and when it concerns an issue with a non-Indian.

It is obvious that the plaintiffs in this appeal have no remedy within the tribal machinery nor with the tribal officials in whose election they cannot participate.

The record demonstrates that plaintiffs sought a forum within the Tribes to consider the issue. They sought a state remedy and sought a remedy in the federal courts. The limitations and restrictions present in *Santa Clara* should not be applied. There has to be a forum where the dispute can be settled.

The plaintiffs alleged that their personal and property rights under the Constitution had been violated by the defendants. A jury so found and awarded damages. There must exist a remedy for parties in the position of plaintiffs to have the dispute resolved in an orderly manner. To hold that they have access to no court is to hold that they have constitutional rights but have no remedy. The self-help which was suggested to shut down plaintiffs' "business," according to the Council minutes, and which was carried out with the help of the federal police, does not appear to be a suitable device to determine constitutional rights.

[*Reversed and remanded.*]

HOLLOWAY, Circuit Judge, dissenting:

I respectfully dissent.

To me this is a most disturbing case because of the result I feel compelled to reach. The jury found a violation of the plaintiffs' civil rights recognized by § 1302 of the Indian Civil Rights Act, under most distressing circumstances. And yet it seems we must say that the doors are closed against any orderly redress for the wrongs. State and federal courts are barred by the immunity doctrine from hearing the claims and access was denied to the tribal court, as the majority opinion points out. Nevertheless, I must reluctantly agree with the trial court's conclusion that the *Santa Clara* opinion compels dismissal as to the sole remaining defendants, the tribes....

NOTES

1. **The Impact of *Santa Clara Pueblo***: *Santa Clara Pueblo* brought a halt to federal courts' ability to review tribal governmental decisions, at least temporarily. After the case, two formidable barriers face a litigant attempting to get federal review of tribal decisions: tribal sovereign immunity and the need for a federal claim. *Santa Clara Pueblo* put teeth into the doctrine of sovereign immunity, applying the same strict standard to statutes purporting to waive tribal immunity as it does to statutes waiving federal sovereign immunity: waivers cannot be implied, but must be express. But even in cases in which a waiver is present (or can be circumvented), the Court held the ICRA simply did not create a claim cognizable in federal court, except for habeas corpus. If the ICRA does not create any claim in federal court, what forum is available to redress violations of civil rights? Must a tribe provide a traditional court system to adjudicate such disputes? Many tribes do not provide for a clear separation of powers between the judiciary and the legislative branch or provide for judicial review of tribal council actions. May a tribal council properly decide ICRA disputes?

2. **The 1986 Amendments to the ICRA:** The version of the ICRA referred to in *Martinez* prevented tribes from imposing more than 6 months in jail or $500 in fines, or both. In 1986 Congress increased the length of imprisonment to one year and the fine to $5000. The Anti-Drug Abuse Act of 1986, Pub. L. No. 99-570, § 4217, 100 Stat. 3207, 3207-146 (1986).

3. **The *Dry Creek* Exception:** Shortly after *Santa Clara Pueblo* was decided, Alvin Ziontz commented: "If tribal governments fail, however, to deal responsi-

bly with ICRA problems, *Martinez* will only have resulted in a reprieve, and there will be calls for Congress to amend the Indian Civil Rights Act so as to empower federal courts to review tribal action." Ziontz, *After Martinez: Indian Civil Rights Under Tribal Government,* 12 U.C. DAVIS L. REV. 1, 26 (1979) (footnote omitted). Is the approach in *Dry Creek Lodge* consistent with the Court's decision in *Santa Clara Pueblo v. Martinez?* What rationale did the Tenth Circuit provide to explain taking jurisdiction of the claim in *Dry Creek?* Did the Court adequately explain the basis for waiving sovereign immunity from suit? Had the Arapahoe and Shoshone Tribes provided a forum to Dry Creek Lodge, Inc., to litigate its claims under the ICRA, would the case have been decided in the same manner? *White v. Pueblo of San Juan,* 728 F.2d 1307, 1312 (10th Cir. 1984) (*Dry Creek* distinguished because plaintiff in *White* had not sought a remedy in tribal forum open to him); *Trans-Canada Enters. v. Muckleshoot Indian Tribe,* 634 F.2d 474 (9th Cir. 1980) (no remedy in federal court, because tribal forum available). Can *Dry Creek Lodge* be explained or justified on the grounds that non-Indians are not represented in tribal governments and will not be adequately protected in tribal forums? Does the ICRA provide adequate protection for them in tribal forums? If so, should the federal courts exercise jurisdiction over the ICRA claims of non-Indians? If not, should the tribal governments be able to exercise any form of jurisdiction over non-Indians? Were the Martinez children involved in *Santa Clara Pueblo* adequately represented in or protected by the processes of tribal government?

Dry Creek has been rejected by the Ninth Circuit, *R.J. Williams v. Ft. Belknap Hous. Auth.,* 719 F.2d 979, 981 (9th Cir. 1983) (*Dry Creek* analysis foreclosed by *Martinez*), and limited by the Tenth Circuit. *See, e.g., Ramey Constr. Co. v. Apache Tribe,* 673 F.2d 315, 319 n.4 (10th Cir. 1982) (*Dry Creek* based on "particularly egregious allegations of personal restraint and deprivation of personal rights"). When these egregious situations occur, however, courts may well be willing to take jurisdiction. *See generally* Gover & Laurence, *Avoiding Santa Clara Pueblo v. Martinez: The Litigation in Federal Court of Civil Actions Under the Indian Civil Rights Act,* 8 HAMLINE L. REV. 497, 499-515 (1985).

4. The Membership Rule in *Martinez*: Although control over who is included in a group is essential to a group's identity, should a federal norm of nonsubordination of women have been given greater weight in *Martinez?* Would or should the answer depend on whether the rule was a traditional tribal rule or a rule adopted in response to perceived explicit or implicit federal pressure? The federal government intervenes to impose federal norms on Indian tribes in some situations, such as in the drafting of constitutions or vetoing of tribal laws. In a recent article Professor Judith Resnick cites these examples as well as the Indian Civil Rights Act habeas corpus provision, the Hatch Bill, and the Tenth Circuit's decision in *Little Horn State Bank,* discussed *infra* section D, as examples of federal intervention to protect federal norms. According to Professor Resnick: "One explanation of *Santa Clara Pueblo* is, in general, that Indian tribes' treatment of their members is not of central concern to federal law, and, in particular, that membership rules that subordinate women do not threaten federal norms (either because federal law tolerates women holding lesser status than men or because federal law has labeled the issue one of 'private' ordering and non-normative.") Resnick, *Dependent Sovereigns: Indian Tribes, States, and the Federal Courts,* 56 U. CHI. L. REV. 671, 755 (1989). Does the conclusion that such a rule subordinates women necessarily reflect a Eurocentric conception of gender roles? A recent essay warns Anglo feminists against imposing their own views on Indian women: "One of the dangers we face as feminists is believing that we are capable of constructing a universal set of truths that will benefit all women." Goldsmith, *Individual v. Collective Rights: The Indian Child Welfare Act,* 13 HARV. WOMEN's L.J. 1 (1990). Tribal women in Canada have challenged gender-based membership rules before the Canadian Supreme Court and in international tribunals. See Chapter 9, section B2.

5. The Continuing Influence of *Martinez*: *Martinez* questions arise whenever anyone, Indian or non-Indian, challenges tribal authority. The next section of this chapter focuses on the exercise of tribal authority. Note how frequently *Martinez* and *Oliphant* are raised and the ways in which the applicable courts, federal and tribal, resolve these questions.

Two kinds of situations most frequently raise *Martinez* issues: the first is continuing assertions by non-Indian defendants in civil matters that tribal courts have violated their constitutional or statutory rights under the ICRA. For example, the Court in *Martinez* cited *Ex parte Young,* 209 U.S. 123 (1908), the leading case establishing that sovereign immunity is no defense to a suit against an official enforcing an unconstitutional law. Can this reference be read to require tribal courts to waive sovereign immunity in a case in which a tribal official enforces an ordinance that could violate the ICRA and permit federal court review of a tribal decision not to waive immunity? For an argument against this position, see Gover & Laurence, *Avoiding Santa Clara Pueblo v. Martinez: The Litigation in Federal Court of Civil Actions Under the ICRA,* 8 HAMLINE L. REV. 497, 503-05. Does *Martinez* leave any other doors open for assertion of such claims against the tribe? The second situation arises when tribal members with complaints about unfairness in the tribal political process attempt to invoke federal court jurisdiction to gain a hearing on their claims of mistreatment. Does *Martinez* leave any avenues to the federal courts open to these plaintiffs?

D. THE EXERCISE OF TRIBAL GOVERNMENTAL AUTHORITY

ZIONTZ, AFTER MARTINEZ: INDIAN CIVIL RIGHTS UNDER TRIBAL GOVERNMENT, 12 U.C. Davis Law Review 1, 10-33 (1979)*

II. *ICRA Enforcement Under Tribal Government*

After *Martinez,* a fundamental problem with tribal enforcement of the ICRA still remains: which governmental entity will decide the legality of the acts of the tribal council? Because of the political and constitutional position of the tribal courts and council in tribal government, it may not be feasible for tribal courts to exercise the traditional American power of judicial review over council action. A functional analysis of tribal courts and tribal councils strongly suggests that in most cases judicial review is inappropriate — at least for the present. The attempt of the Navajo courts to exercise that power and the internal governmental strife which ensued is examined as a case study illustrating the general problem.

A. *Judicial Review in the American and Tribal Contexts*

[Within] tribal court systems, sharp contrasts are immediately apparent. Most tribal courts owe their existence to the tribe's legislative bodies. Rather than

*Originally printed in 12 U.C. Davis L. Rev. 1 (1979). Reprinted by permission.

providing for coequal branches, tribal constitutions generally assign the central
role in tribal government to the tribal council. Tribal courts are, for the most
part, the creatures of ordinances enacted by the tribal council. Consequently, a
different relationship exists between the legislature and judiciary in Indian and
American governments. Historically, the role of tribal courts in tribal government has been quite limited. Furthermore, few tribal judges have had any
formal training in law. This seriously undermines the respect of tribal members
and other agencies of tribal government for the tribal courts. Tribal courts,
therefore, do not enjoy the general presumption accorded American judges
that their decisions are the product of a learned and impartial application of
systematic principles to the case before them.

Tribal councils are generally the central repositories of power on the reservation. Most tribal constitutions delegate to the tribal council the power to manage
the economic affairs of the tribe, provide for law and order and the general
welfare of the tribe. Councils function as legislative bodies and frequently as
executive and quasi-judicial bodies dealing with individual requests and complaints of members as well as public issues. In addition to their political function, councils function in the business and economic sphere in the same manner
as a corporate board of directors: planning, authorizing contracts and expenditures and setting policies. The council usually has power to hire and fire key
tribal employees, such as the executive director or business manager, department heads and tribal judges. The council frequently establishes committees,
usually headed by a council member, to oversee specific programs and projects
in such areas of land and forestry management, finance, leasing, adoption,
election procedures, law and order, hunting and fishing, and the like. The
council thus has control over a great deal of employment and appointment to
tribal governmental positions.

As a practical political matter, moreover, tribal councils tend to be intolerant
of any action of other organs of tribal government which appears to challenge
their authority. They usually regard themselves as representing the tribe and
being the voice of the tribe. For most purposes, the council is the government....

In 1934 Congress passed the Indian Reorganization Act (IRA) to provide a
framework for tribes to reestablish their governmental status. Many tribes
adopted tribal constitutions under the Act. For the most part, the Interior
Department drafted these constitutions. They generally provided for a council
elected by tribal membership, which would exercise primary governing authority. They also provided for establishment of a tribal court system and judicial
codes *if* the *council* so provided by ordinance. By 1935, most tribes had functioning tribal courts or Courts of Indian Offenses.

Thus, at their inception, the tribal courts were subordinate to the tribal councils which created them. More recently, tribal courts on some reservations have
established a degree of judicial independence. Nonetheless, while support for
tribal courts is increasing they are still considered a subordinate arm of tribal
government on a substantial proportion of the reservations. For example in a
1977 survey, it was found that tribal judges were appointed by the tribal council
on 64 reservations and elected by the membership at large only on 19 reserva-

tions. Moreover, many tribal courts report that it is not uncommon for political influence to be brought to bear upon them.

In 1977 there were federally-recognized tribal court systems on 127 reservations. In 1970 Indian judges formed the National American Indian Court Judges Association, whose function has been to organize judicial education programs for Indian court judges throughout the country and attempt to achieve greater separation of powers between the judicial and executive branches of Indian governments. About 200 tribal judges participated in regional seminars, taught by lawyers, judges and law professors, using case books and other publications specially prepared for Indian courts.

Tribal courts, however, continue to function primarily to mete out punishment to misdemeanants. In a 1977 survey, most tribal courts reported that civil matters comprised less than ten percent of their caseload. The vast majority of these cases involved domestic relations and juvenile cases, with the balance comprised of contract, property and personal injury cases. Unfortunately, most tribal judges have had little training in substantive and procedural civil law and feel ill-equipped to handle these cases.

While tribal courts have acquired substantial familiarity with criminal due process concepts, they have had little experience with the body of constitutional law applicable to individual liberties in the civil context of the first, fifth and fourteenth amendments. This is not to say that tribal judges have no understanding of these matters, for no doubt many do. But most tribal judges will have great difficulty applying American constitutional analysis to the actions of the tribal councils. They will need substantial training, at least equivalent to what they have received in the area of criminal law....

III. *Preservation of Tribal Autonomy*

[In a preceding section, the author recounted a conflict between the Navajo Tribal Council and the Court which began in 1978 when the tribal court asserted jurisdiction to determine the legality of the tribal council's actions in appropriating tribal funds to pay for a private attorney for Peter McDonald, the tribal chairman, who had been indicted for misuse of tribal funds. Soon after the court asserted its supremacy, the council enacted a law stripping the tribal courts of jurisdiction over council actions. Later that same year, the council created a new institution, the Supreme Judicial Council, comprised of three judges and five tribal council members with sole authority to decide questions regarding the legality of tribal council actions.]

A. *Congressional Power and Improving Tribal Response to the ICRA*

Martinez brought to an end federal court review of tribal governmental action. If tribal governments fail, however, to deal responsibly with ICRA problems, *Martinez* will only have resulted in a reprieve and there will be calls for Congress to amend the Indian Civil Rights Act so as to empower federal courts to review tribal action.

Tribal councils can take steps to improve the handling of ICRA complaints, so as to avoid internal strife and external pressure. Given the lack of federal court review, it seems likely tribal courts will be placed under increasing pressure to decide whether council action violated the ICRA. While some tribal courts may disclaim any power to make such decisions, others, like the Navajo Tribal Courts, will not be so reticent. Thus, in order to provide effective redress of ICRA complaints and retain ICRA jurisdiction, tribes should determine in advance the tribal court's authority rather than place burdens and risks on tribal judges. The alternatives available to tribal councils range from affirming broad tribal court authority to decide all questions of propriety of tribal action, to prohibiting courts from deciding any such questions.[128] ...

Finally, tribal councils may desire to entrust the process of judicial review to courts in whose special competency they and their members may have some confidence. They can consider the establishment of a special constitutional court, such as the Navajo Judicial Supreme Council, or they may wish to improve the structure of their appellate court system. There is no reason why tribes cannot design an appellate court system utilizing intertribal judicial arrangements so as to insure maximum impartiality.…

The Indian Civil Rights Act does not necessarily mandate judicial review. In *Howlett v. Salish and Kootenai Tribes,* [529 F.2d 233 (1976)] the Ninth Circuit ruled that the ICRA does not preclude the Indians from vesting the power to interpret the tribal constitution in the tribal council rather than in a tribal court. Moreover, *Martinez* makes it clear that the tribal council may well be an appropriate forum in which to decide ICRA issues.

There is still another reason why tribal councils may not see the wisdom of deferring to the judgment of tribal courts. At the present stage of development, the expertise of tribal judges in noncriminal constitutional law is not demonstrably superior to council members. In fact, the reverse may be the case. Furthermore, the tribal council usually has better access to legal advice than the tribal judge. Tribal councils are accustomed to dealing directly with tribal attorneys and requesting their assistance and advice in the drafting of ordinances, or in the undertaking of official action. Tribal judges often seek advice from the very same sources. There is no reason then, why the tribal council cannot make decisions as responsibly as tribal courts. Moreover, it is necessary to remember that there is nothing sacrosanct about judicial review as the sole means of determining legality of legislative action, particularly under the circumstances of Indian tribal societies in America today.

B. *Department of the Interior Review of ICRA Complaints*

Martinez seems to have raised the possibility that there will be increased interference with tribal autonomy by the Interior Department. It would be ironic if the effect of *Martinez* was to end federal court intervention in tribal

---

[128] For instance, the constitution for the Pueblo of Isleta, art. IX, § 5, declares that the Isleta Pueblo Tribal Court "shall determine the constitutionality of enactments of the [Isleta Pueblo] Council submitted to the court for review. *Id. cited in* [American Indian Lawyer Training Program, Indian Self-Determination and the Role of Tribal Courts] at 37 nn.5, 6. The Oglala Sioux Tribal Council, on the other hand, enacted a resolution which prohibits the tribal court from entertaining any action or suit against the Tribe, its agencies or officials unless the plaintiff has first exhausted his administrative remedies by filing his complaint with the Tribal Executive Committee. Oglala Sioux Resolution No. 76-03 (Sept. 16, 1977) (cited in Pine Ridge Village Council v. Trimble, 5 Indian Law Rep. § M, 6, 7).

government, only to have it replaced by Interior Department intervention. Yet, recent actions of the Interior Department indicate this result.

Shortly after the *Martinez* decision, an Interior Department official stated that the lack of a federal court remedy would impel the Secretary of the Interior to assume greater responsibility over tribal members' complaints against the action of tribal government. Specifically, the official asserted that if an action of the tribe or its officers is found violative of the tribal constitution, the Department may take what it deems to be appropriate action. This may include withholding approval of tribal budgets, restricting the flow of Bureau of Indian Affairs (BIA) funds to tribal programs, and withdrawing recognition of tribal governments or officials....

In March, 1978, the Fort Belknap Community Court invalidated the results of a tribal election on the ground that one of the candidates did not meet the Tribe's constitutional qualifications. [*Plumage v. Fort Belknap Election Board*, 5 Indian L. Rep. § L, at 7 (1978).] The Billings Area Director recognized the tribal court's ruling as valid and binding. The aggrieved parties appealed the Area Director's action to the Secretary.[141]

On August 23, 1978, the Assistant Secretary issued a written decision upholding the tribal court.[142] He took pains to point out that the Department had no alternative but to scrutinize the decision of the Fort Belknap court once an appeal had been taken from the Area Director's determination to recognize that court's ruling. His decision emphasized that "the Department of the Interior *is not* a judicial appeal level above tribal judicial forums empowered to sustain or reverse decisions of those forums." But, he declared that the Department views tribal constitutions and law and order codes as contracts with the Interior Department and concluded: "We cannot be bound or compelled to recognize any tribal action which may be in violation of those agreements."

In making this claim, however, the Assistant Secretary may have placed the Interior Department in precisely the position he earlier disclaimed. While the opinion went to great lengths to affirm the tribal court's authority to exercise judicial review, it also reserved for the Department the right to decide whether the tribal court's interpretation was arbitrary or unreasonable. Thus, although the Department would give great weight to the decision of the tribal court, it would not accept any interpretation "so arbitrary or unreasonable that its application would constitute a violation of the right to due process or equal protection."

Applying this standard, the Assistant Secretary upheld the tribal court's ruling in the *Plumage* case. Thus, the Assistant Secretary now claims administrative authority to review and ultimately determine the constitutionality of the action of tribal governments. This promises to open up an entirely new field of ICRA administrative review, for it is certain that determined litigants will resort to the Interior Department and its appellate process. In light of the importance of this potential for interference with tribal self-government, the Department of

[141] 25 C.F.R. Pt. 2 authorizes appeals from administrative actions to the Commissioner of the BIA, and to the Board of Indian Appeals. This Board is also authorized to conduct appeals and make decisions for the Secretary. 43 C.F.R. Pt. 4.

[142] Assistant Secretary's opinion, reported in 5 Indian L. Rep. § H at 17 (Aug. 23, 1978).

the Interior's rationale for intervention in tribal government deserves closer examination.

In the past, the Department of Interior has relied on the broad statutory authority contained in 25 U.S.C. § 2 to justify intervention in tribal affairs. This statute provides that the Commissioner of Indian Affairs shall "have the management of all Indian affairs and of all matters arising out of Indian relations" under Secretarial regulations. The Secretary has construed this section to give a broad charter to do almost anything deemed advisable in the management of Indian Affairs. That section, originally enacted in 1832, was followed by a major policy change in 1934 with the enactment of the Indian Reorganization Act. One of the principal features of the IRA provided for establishment of tribal organizations and was expressly intended to eliminate the broad authority which the Interior Department had exercised over tribes. The original bill retained broad governmental powers to review and even veto tribal actions, but these provisions were ultimately discarded....

The Interior Department now appears to claim precisely that authority which it sought and Congress denied in 1934 and 1968. Regardless of the Department's rationale, there is no statutory support for the authority claimed by the Department. Moreover, such a claim directly contravenes congressional policy. In similar circumstances, the Supreme Court has struck down claims of executive authority.

Admittedly, the Secretary is faced with a dilemma. On the one hand, direct review of complaints of violations of the ICRA and tribal constitutions should be precluded by virtue of congressional rejection of such authority. Conversely, the Secretary legitimately may be concerned about placing the federal government in complicity with illegal conduct. The fact remains, however, that Congress explicitly chose not to vest the Department with the power of administrative review. Instead, the Congress deferred to the sovereignty of tribal governments and the Interior Department should respect that decision....

The Secretary must bear in mind that *Martinez* was a mandate for tribal self government, not for the substitution of administrative review for judicial review....

1. TRIBAL JUDICIAL JURISDICTION

DURO v. REINA

110 S. Ct. 2053 (1990)

KENNEDY, J.

We address in this case whether an Indian tribe may assert criminal jurisdiction over a defendant who is an Indian but not a tribal member. We hold that the retained sovereignty of the tribe as a political and social organization to govern its own affairs does not include the authority to impose criminal sanctions against a citizen outside its own membership.

I

The events giving rise to this jurisdictional dispute occurred on the Salt River Indian Reservation [in Arizona, which is] the home of the Salt River Pima-

Maricopa Indian Community, a recognized Tribe with an enrolled membership. The petitioner in this case, Albert Duro, is an enrolled member of another Indian Tribe, the Torres-Martinez Band of Cahuilla Mission Indians. Petitioner is not eligible for membership in the Pima-Maricopa Tribe. As a nonmember, he is not entitled to vote in Pima-Maricopa elections, to hold tribal office, or to serve on tribal juries.

Petitioner has lived most of his life in his native State of California, outside any Indian reservation. Between March and June 1984, he resided on the Salt River Reservation with a Pima-Maricopa woman friend. He worked for the PiCopa Construction Company, which is owned by the Tribe.

On June 15, 1984, petitioner allegedly shot and killed a 14-year-old boy within the Salt River Reservation boundaries. The victim was a member of the Gila River Indian Tribe of Arizona, a separate Tribe that occupies a separate reservation. [Duro was charged with murder in violation of the Major Crimes Act, 18 U.S.C. § 1153, but the indictment was later dismissed.][1]

Petitioner [was turned over to the tribal police,] was taken to stand trial in the Pima-Maricopa Indian Community Court [and] charged with the illegal firing of a weapon on the Reservation. [Petitioner sought a writ of habeas corpus after the tribal court denied his motion to dismiss for lack of jurisdiction.]

[After the] District Court granted the writ, [a] divided panel of the Court of Appeals for the Ninth Circuit reversed [and this appeal followed.]

II

[In *United States v. Wheeler*, 435 U.S. 313 (1978), we found] that jurisdiction over a Navajo defendant by a Navajo court was part of retained tribal sovereignty, not a delegation of authority from the Federal Government. [The] analysis of tribal power was directed to the tribes' status as limited sovereigns, necessarily subject to the overriding authority of the United States, yet retaining necessary powers of internal self-governance. We recognized that the "sovereignty that the Indian tribes retain is of a unique and limited character." *Id.*, at 323.

A basic attribute of full territorial sovereignty is the power to enforce laws against all who come within the sovereign's territory, whether citizens or aliens. *Oliphant* recognized that the tribes can no longer be described as sovereigns in this sense. Rather, as our discussion in *Wheeler* reveals, the retained sovereignty of the tribes is that needed to control their own internal relations, and to preserve their own unique customs and social order. The power of a tribe to

---

[1] Jurisdiction in "Indian country," which is defined in 18 U.S.C. § 1151, is governed by a complex patchwork of federal, state, and tribal law. [The Court's discussion of 18 U.S.C. §§ 1152-1153 is omitted. See Chapter 2, section D — Eds.]

For Indian country crimes involving only non-Indians, longstanding precedents of this Court hold that state courts have exclusive jurisdiction despite the terms of § 1152. Certain States may also assume jurisdiction over Indian country crime with the consent of the affected Tribe pursuant to Public Law 280 [see Chapter 4, section C1 — Eds.].

The final source of criminal jurisdiction in Indian country is the retained sovereignty of the tribes themselves. It is undisputed that the tribes retain jurisdiction over their members, subject to the question of exclusive jurisdiction under § 1153 mentioned above. See [*United States v. Wheeler*]. The extent of tribal jurisdiction over nonmembers is at issue here. For a scholarly discussion of Indian country jurisdiction, see Clinton, Criminal Jurisdiction Over Indian Lands: A Journey Through a Jurisdictional Maze, 18 Ariz. L. Rev. 505 (1976).

prescribe and enforce rules of conduct for its own members "does not fall within that part of sovereignty which the Indians implicitly lost by virtue of their dependent status. The areas in which such implicit divestiture of sovereignty has been held to have occurred are those involving the relations between an Indian tribe and nonmembers of the tribe."

[The] finding that the tribal prosecution of the defendant in *Wheeler* was by a sovereign other than the United States rested on the premise that the prosecution was a part of the tribe's *internal* self-governance. Had the prosecution been a manifestation of external relations between the Tribe and outsiders, such power would have been inconsistent with the tribe's dependent status, and could only have come to the Tribe by delegation from Congress, subject to the constraints of the Constitution.

The distinction between members and nonmembers and its relation to self-governance is recognized in other areas of Indian law. Exemption from state taxation for residents of a reservation, for example, is determined by tribal membership, not by reference to Indians as a general class. We have held that States may not impose certain taxes on transactions of tribal members on the reservation because this would interfere with internal governance and self-determination. But this rationale does not apply to taxation of nonmembers, even where they are Indians:

"Nor would the imposition of Washington's tax on these purchasers contravene the principle of tribal self-government, for the simple reasons that nonmembers are not constituents of the governing Tribe. For most practical purposes they stand on the same footing as non-Indians resident on the reservation. There is no evidence that nonmembers have a say in tribal affairs or significantly share in tribal disbursements." *Washington v. Confederated Tribes of Colville Indian Reservation*, 447 U.S. 134, 161 (1980).

Similarly, in [*Montana v. United States*], we held that the Crow Tribe could regulate hunting and fishing by nonmembers on land held by the Tribe or held in trust for the Tribe by the United States. But this power could not extend to nonmembers' activities on land they held in fee. Again we relied upon the view of tribal sovereignty set forth in *Oliphant*:

"Though *Oliphant* only determined inherent tribal authority in criminal matters, the principles on which it relied support the general proposition that the inherent sovereign powers of an Indian tribe do not extend to the activities of nonmembers of the tribe." 450 U.S., at 565 (footnote omitted).

It is true that our decisions recognize broader retained tribal powers outside the criminal context. Tribal courts, for example, resolve civil disputes involving nonmembers, including non-Indians. *See, e.g.,* [*Santa Clara Pueblo v. Martinez;*] *Williams v. Lee*, 358 U.S. 217, 223 (1959). Civil authority may also be present in areas such as zoning where the exercise of tribal authority is vital to the maintenance of tribal integrity and self-determination. *See, e.g., Brendale v. Confederated Tribes and Bands of Yakima Indian Nation*, [109 S. Ct. 2994 (1989)]. As distinct from criminal prosecution, this civil authority typically involves situations arising from property ownership within the reservation or "consensual relationships with the tribe or its members, through commercial dealing, contracts, leases, or other arrangements." [*Montana v. United States.*] The exercise of criminal jurisdiction subjects a person not only to the adjudicatory power of the tribunal, but also to the prosecuting power of the tribe, and involves a far more direct intrusion on personal liberties.

The tribes are, to be sure, "a good deal more than 'private voluntary organizations,'" and are aptly described as "unique aggregations possessing attributes of sovereignty over both their members and their territory." [*United States v. Mazurie.*] In the area of criminal enforcement, however, tribal power does not extend beyond internal relations among members. Petitioner is not a member of the Pima-Maricopa Tribe, and is not now eligible to become one. Neither he nor other members of his Tribe may vote, hold office, or serve on a jury under Pima-Maricopa authority. For purposes of criminal jurisdiction, petitioner's relations with this Tribe are the same as the non-Indian's in *Oliphant.* We hold that the Tribe's powers over him are subject to the same limitations.

III

[A] review of history [is] somewhat less illuminating than in *Oliphant,* but tends to support the conclusion we reach. Early evidence concerning tribal jurisdiction over nonmembers is lacking because "[u]ntil the middle of this century, few Indian tribes maintained any semblance of a formal court system. Offenses by one Indian against another were usually handled by social and religious pressure and not by formal judicial processes; emphasis was on restitution rather than punishment." [*Oliphant* at 197.] Cases challenging the jurisdiction of modern tribal courts are few, perhaps because "most parties acquiesce to tribal jurisdiction" where it is asserted. See National American Indian Court Judges Association, Indian Courts and the Future 48 (1978). We have no occasion in this case to address the effect of a formal acquiescence to tribal jurisdiction that might be made, for example, in return for a tribe's agreement not to exercise its power to exclude an offender from tribal lands.

Respondents rely for their historical argument upon evidence that definitions of "Indian" in federal statutes and programs apply to all Indians without respect to membership in a particular tribe. For example, the federal jurisdictional statutes applicable to Indian country use the general term "Indian." In construing [an 1834 statute using the term] this Court stated that it "does not speak to members of a tribe, but of the race generally — of the family of Indians." *United States v. Rogers,* 4 How. 567, 573 (1846). Respondents also emphasize that Courts of Indian Offenses, which were established by regulation in 1883 by the Department of the Interior and continue to operate today on reservations without tribal courts, possess jurisdiction over *all* Indian offenders within the relevant reservation. See 25 CFR § 11.2(a) (1989).

This evidence does not stand for the proposition respondents advance. Congressional and administrative provisions such as those cited above reflect the Government's treatment of Indians as a single large class with respect to *federal* jurisdiction and programs. Those references are not dispositive of a question of *tribal* power to treat Indians by the same broad classification. [F]or the novel and disputed issue in the case before us, the statutes reflect at most the tendency of past Indian policy to treat Indians as an undifferentiated class. The historical record prior to the creation of modern tribal courts shows little federal attention to the individual tribes' powers as between themselves or over one another's members. Scholars who do find treaties or other sources illuminating have only [been] divided in their conclusions.

The brief history of the tribal courts themselves provides somewhat clearer guidance. The tribal courts were established under the auspices of the [IRA,] which allowed the expression of retained tribal sovereignty by authorizing creation of new tribal governments, constitutions, and courts. The new tribal courts supplanted the federal Courts of Indian Offenses operated by the Bureau of Indian Affairs. Significantly, new law and order codes were required to be approved by the Secretary of the Interior. See 25 U.S.C. § 476. The opinions of the Solicitor of the Department of the Interior on the new tribal codes leave unquestioned the authority of the tribe over its members.

Evidence on criminal jurisdiction over nonmembers is less clear, but on balance supports the view that inherent tribal jurisdiction extends to tribe members only. [Early opinions by the Solicitor were divided; two] later opinions, however, give a strong indication that the new tribal courts were not understood to possess power over nonmembers. One mentions only adoption of nonmembers into the tribe or receipt of delegated authority as means of acquiring jurisdiction over nonmember Indians. 1 Op. Sol. 849 (Aug. 26, 1938). A final opinion states more forcefully that the only means by which a tribe could deal with interloping nonmember Indians were removal of the offenders from the reservation or acceptance of delegated authority. 1 Op. Sol. 872 (Feb. 17, 1939).

These opinions provide the most specific historical evidence on the question before us and, we think, support our conclusion. Taken together with the general history preceding the creation of modern tribal courts, they indicate that the tribal courts embody only the powers of *internal* self-governance we have described. We are not persuaded that external criminal jurisdiction is an accepted part of the courts' function.

IV

Whatever might be said of the historical record, we must view it in light of petitioner's status as a citizen of the United States. Many Indians became citizens during the era of allotment and tribal termination around the turn of the century, and all were made citizens in 1924. That Indians are citizens does not alter the Federal Government's broad authority to legislate with respect to enrolled Indians as a class, whether to impose burdens or benefits. See *United States v. Antelope*, 430 U.S. 641 (1977); *Morton v. Mancari*, 417 U.S. 535 (1974). In the absence of such legislation, however, Indians like other citizens are embraced within our Nation's "great solicitude that its citizens be protected ... from unwarranted intrusions on their personal liberty." [*Oliphant* at 210.]

Criminal trial and punishment is so serious an intrusion on personal liberty that its exercise over non-Indian citizens was a power necessarily surrendered by the tribes in their submission to the overriding sovereignty of the United States. We hesitate to adopt a view of tribal sovereignty that would single out another group of citizens, nonmember Indians, for trial by political bodies that do not include them. As full citizens, Indians share in the territorial and political sovereignty of the United States. The retained sovereignty of the tribe is but a recognition of certain additional authority the tribes maintain over Indians who consent to be tribal members. Indians like all other citizens share allegiance to the overriding sovereign, the United States. A tribe's additional authority comes from the consent of its members, and so in the criminal sphere membership marks the bounds of tribal authority.

The special nature of the tribunals at issue makes a focus on consent and the protections of citizenship most appropriate. While modern tribal courts include many familiar features of the judicial process, they are influenced by the unique customs, languages, and usages of the tribes they serve. Tribal courts are often "subordinate to the political branches of tribal governments," and their legal methods may depend on "unspoken practices and norms." Cohen 334-335. It is significant that the Bill of Rights does not apply to Indian tribal governments. [*Talton v. Mayes.*] The Indian Civil Rights Act provides some statutory guarantees of fair procedure, but these guarantees are not equivalent to their constitutional counterparts. There is, for example, no right under the Act to appointed counsel for those unable to afford a lawyer.

Our cases suggest constitutional limitations even on the ability of Congress to subject American citizens to criminal proceedings before a tribunal that does not provide constitutional protections as a matter of right. Cf. *Reid v. Covert,* 354 U.S. 1 (1957). We have approved delegation to an Indian tribe of the authority to promulgate rules that may be enforced by criminal sanction in *federal* court, [*United States v. Mazurie,*] but no delegation of authority to a tribe has to date included the power to punish nonmembers in *tribal* court. We decline to produce such a result through recognition of inherent tribal authority.

Tribal authority over members, who are also citizens, is not subject to these objections. Retained criminal jurisdiction over members is accepted by our precedents and justified by the voluntary character of tribal membership and the concomitant right of participation in a tribal government, the authority of which rests on consent. This principle finds support in our cases decided under provisions that predate the present federal jurisdictional statutes. We held in *United States v. Rogers,* 4 How. 567 (1846), that a non-Indian could not, through his adoption into the Cherokee Tribe, bring himself within the federal definition of "Indian" for purposes of an exemption to a federal jurisdictional provision. But we recognized that a non-Indian could, by adoption, "become entitled to certain privileges in the tribe, and make himself amenable to their laws and usages." *Id.,* at 573.

With respect to such internal laws and usages, the tribes are left with broad freedom not enjoyed by any other governmental authority in this county. *See, e.g.,* [*Santa Clara Pueblo v. Martinez*]. This is all the more reason to reject an extension of tribal authority over those who have not given the consent of the governed that provides a fundamental basis for power within our constitutional system.

The United States suggests that Pima-Maricopa tribal jurisdiction is appropriate because petitioner's enrollment in the Torres-Martinez Band of Cahuilla Mission Indians "is a sufficient indication of his self-identification as an Indian, with traditional Indian cultural values, to make it reasonable to subject him to the tribal court system, which ... implements traditional Indian values and customs." Brief for United States as *Amicus Curiae* 27. But the tribes are not mere fungible groups of homogenous persons among whom any Indian would feel at home. On the contrary, wide variations in customs, art, language, and physical characteristics separate the tribes, and their history has been marked by both intertribal alliances and animosities. Petitioner's general status as an Indian says little about his consent to the exercise of authority over him by a particular tribe.

The Court of Appeals sought to address some of these concerns by adopting a "contacts" test to determine which nonmember Indians might be subject to tribal jurisdiction. But the rationale of the test would apply to non-Indians on the reservation as readily as to Indian nonmembers. Many non-Indians reside on reservations, and have close ties to tribes through marriage or long employment. Indeed, the population of non-Indians on reservations generally is greater than the population of all Indians, both members and nonmembers, and non-Indians make up some 35% of the Salt River Reservation population. The contacts approach is little more than a variation of the argument that any person who enters an Indian community should be deemed to have given implied consent to tribal criminal jurisdiction over him. We have rejected this approach for non-Indians. It is a logical consequence of that decision that nonmembers, who share relevant jurisdictional characteristics of non-Indians, should share the same jurisdictional status.

V

Respondents and *amici* contend that without tribal jurisdiction over minor offenses committed by nonmember Indians, no authority will have jurisdiction over such offenders. They assert that unless we affirm jurisdiction in this case, the tribes will lack important power to preserve order on the reservation, and nonmember Indians will be able to violate the law with impunity. Although the jurisdiction at stake here is over relatively minor crime, we recognize that protection of the community from disturbances of the peace and other misdemeanors is a most serious matter. But this same interest in tribal law enforcement is applicable to non-Indian reservation residents, whose numbers are often greater. It was argued in *Oliphant* that the absence of tribal jurisdiction over non-Indians would leave a practical, if not legal, void in reservation law enforcement. The argument that only tribal jurisdiction could meet the need for effective law enforcement did not provide a basis for finding jurisdiction in *Oliphant;* neither is it sufficient here.

For felonies such as the murder alleged in this case at the outset, federal jurisdiction is in place under the Major Crimes Act, 18 U.S.C. § 1153. The tribes also possess their traditional and undisputed power to exclude persons whom they deem to be undesirable from tribal lands. Tribal law enforcement authorities have the power to restrain those who disturb public order on the reservation, and if necessary, to eject them. Where jurisdiction to try and punish an offender rests outside the tribe, tribal officers may exercise their power to detain the offender and transport him to the proper authorities.

Respondents' major objection to this last point is that, in the circumstances presented here, there may not be any lawful authority to punish the nonmember Indian. State authorities may lack the power, resources, or inclination to deal with reservation crime. Arizona, for example, specifically disclaims jurisdiction over Indian country crimes. Ariz. Const., Art. 20, para. 4. And federal authority over minor crime, otherwise provided by the Indian Country Crimes Act, 18 U.S.C. § 1152, may be lacking altogether in the case of crime committed by a nonmember Indian against another Indian, since § 1152 states that general federal jurisdiction over Indian country crime "shall not extend to offenses committed by one Indian against the person or property of another Indian."

Our decision today does not imply endorsement of the theory of a jurisdictional void presented by respondents and the court below. States may, with the consent of the tribes, assist in maintaining order on the reservation by punishing minor crime. Congress has provided a mechanism by which the States now without jurisdiction in Indian country may assume criminal jurisdiction through Public Law 280, see n. 1, *supra*. Our decision here also does not address the ability of neighboring tribal governments that share law enforcement concerns to enter into reciprocal agreements giving each jurisdiction over the other's members. As to federal jurisdiction under § 1152, both academic commentators and the dissenting judge below have suggested that the statute could be construed to cover the conduct here. Others have disagreed. That statute is not before us and we express no views on the question.

If the present jurisdictional scheme proves insufficient to meet the practical needs of reservation law enforcement, then the proper body to address the problem is Congress, which has the ultimate authority over Indian affairs. We cannot, however, accept these arguments of policy as a basis for finding tribal jurisdiction that is inconsistent with precedent, history, and the equal treatment of Native American citizens.

[*Reversed.*]

Justice BRENNAN with whom Justice MARSHALL joins, dissenting.

The Court today holds that an Indian tribal court has no power to exercise criminal jurisdiction over a defendant who is an Indian but not a tribal member. The Court concedes that Indian tribes never expressly relinquished such power. Instead, the Court maintains that tribes *implicitly* surrendered the power to enforce their criminal laws against nonmember Indians when the tribes became dependent on the Federal Government. Because I do not share such a parsimonious view of the sovereignty retained by Indian tribes, I respectfully dissent.

I

The powers of Indian tribes are "'*inherent powers of a limited sovereignty which has never been extinguished.*'" [*United States v. Wheeler*] (emphasis in original). When the tribes were incorporated into the territory of the United States [as] "domestic dependent nations," [they became] implicitly divested of powers to have external relations because they are *necessarily* inconsistent with the overriding interest of the greater sovereign.

By contrast, we have recognized that tribes did not "surrender [their] independence — [the] right to self-government, by associating with a stronger [power], and taking its protection." [*Worcester v. Georgia*.] [*Oliphant*] held that tribes did not have the power to exercise criminal jurisdiction over *non-Indians* because such power was inconsistent with the overriding national interest. But it does not follow that because tribes lost their power to exercise criminal jurisdiction over non-Indians, they also lost their power to enforce criminal laws against Indians who are not members of their tribe.

A

[The majority] today appears to read *Oliphant* as holding that the exercise of criminal jurisdiction over anyone but members of the tribe is inconsistent with the tribes' dependent status.[1] [To the contrary,] *Oliphant* was based on an analysis of Congress' actions *with respect to non-Indians*. The Court first considered the "commonly shared presumption of Congress, the Executive Branch, and lower federal courts that tribal courts do not have the power to try non-Indians." *Id.*, at 206. Then the Court declared that the power to punish non-Indians was inconsistent with the tribes' dependent status, for such power conflicted with the overriding interest of the Federal Government in protecting its citizens against "unwarranted intrusions" on their liberty. "By submitting to the overriding sovereignty of the United States, Indian tribes therefore necessarily [gave] up their power to try *non-Indian* citizens of the United States except in a manner acceptable to Congress." *Id.*, at 210 (emphasis added).

[The *Oliphant* court] relied on [the federal criminal] statutory background to conclude that the exercise of tribal jurisdiction over non-Indians was inconsistent with the tribes' dependent status, for from the early days Congress had provided for federal jurisdiction over crimes involving non-Indians. Thus, from these affirmative enactments, it could be inferred that the tribes were tacitly divested of jurisdiction over non-Indians. But applying the same reasoning, the opposite result obtains with respect to tribal jurisdiction over nonmember Indians. From the very start, Congress has consistently exempted Indian-against-Indian crimes from the reach of federal or state power.... The appropriate inference to be drawn from this series of statutes excluding Indian-against-Indian crimes from federal jurisdiction is that tribes retained power over those crimes involving only Indians. See *Wheeler*, 435 U.S., at 324-326.

The Court acknowledges that these enactments support the inference that tribes retained power over *members* but concludes that no such inference can be drawn about tribal power over nonmembers. The Court finds irrelevant the fact that we have long held that the term "Indian" in these statutes does not differentiate between members and *nonmembers* of a tribe. Rather, the Court concludes that the federal definition of "Indian" is relevant only to *federal* jurisdiction and is "not dispositive of a question of *tribal* power." But this conclusion is at odds with the analysis in *Oliphant* in which the congressional enactments served as evidence of a "commonly shared presumption" that tribes had ceded their power over non-Indians. Similarly, these enactments reflect the

---

[1][T]he Court's citation to [*Montana v. United States*] for the "'general proposition that the inherent sovereign powers of an Indian tribe do not extend to the activities of nonmembers of the tribe,'" is also inapposite [because] *Montana* [affirmed] that tribes have, as a matter of inherent sovereignty, power over nonmembers when their conduct "threatens or has some direct effect on the political integrity, the economic stability, or the health or welfare of the tribe." *Id.*, at 566. The Court today provides no explanation for why the exercise of criminal jurisdiction over a nonmember who commits a crime on property held by the tribe "involves different concerns," such that tribes were implicitly divested of that power.

congressional presumption that tribes had power over all disputes between Indians regardless of tribal membership.

[T]he Court today creates a jurisdictional void in which neither federal nor tribal jurisdiction exists over non-member Indians who commit minor crimes against another Indian.[3] [The fact it is unlikely] that Congress intended to create a jurisdictional void in which *no* sovereign has the power to prosecute an entire class of crimes should inform our understanding of the assumptions about tribal power upon which Congress legislated. Since the scheme created by Congress did not differentiate between members and nonmember Indians, it is logical to conclude that Congress did not assume that the power retained by tribes was limited to member Indians.

B

The Court also concludes that because Indians are now citizens of the United States, the exercise of criminal jurisdiction over a nonmember of the tribe is inconsistent with the tribe's dependent status.... The touchstone in determining the extent to which citizens can be subject to the jurisdiction of Indian tribes, therefore, is whether such jurisdiction is acceptable to Congress. In *Oliphant*, federal statutes made clear that the prosecution of non-Indians in tribal courts is *not* acceptable to Congress. By contrast, the same statutes reflect the view that the prosecution of all Indians in tribal courts is acceptable to Congress.

[In addition,] we have not required consent to tribal jurisdiction or participation in tribal government as a prerequisite to the exercise of civil jurisdiction by a tribe, and the Court does not explain why such a prerequisite is uniquely salient in the criminal context. Nor have we ever held that participation in the political process is a prerequisite to the exercise of criminal jurisdiction by a sovereign. If such were the case, a State could not prosecute nonresidents, and this country could not prosecute aliens who violate our laws. The commission of a crime on the reservation is all the "consent" that is necessary to allow the tribe to exercise criminal jurisdiction over the nonmember Indian.

Finally, the Court's "consent" theory is inconsistent with the underlying premise of Indian law, namely, that Congress has plenary control over Indian affairs. Congress presumably could pass a statute affirmatively granting Indian tribes the right to prosecute anyone who committed a crime on the reservation — Indian or non-Indian — unconstrained by the fact that neither of these groups

---

[3] Because of the Indian-against-Indian exception in 18 U.S.C. § 1152, federal courts have no jurisdiction over such crimes. In addition, it has long been accepted that States do not have power to exercise criminal jurisdiction over crimes involving Indians on the reservation. See [*Worcester v. Georgia*]. In 1953, however, Congress enacted [Public Law 280,] which allows named States to assume jurisdiction over all crimes within Indian country. In [the ICRA] Congress modified Pub. L. 280 to require the affected tribe to consent to a State's assumption of jurisdiction. Arizona has not accepted jurisdiction over crimes occurring on Indian reservations. Thus, under the Court's holding today, the tribe, Federal Government and the State each lack jurisdiction to prosecute the crime involved in this case.

The Court erroneously equates the jurisdictional void that resulted from the holding in *Oliphant* with the void created by the opinion today. Since federal courts have jurisdiction over crimes involving non-Indians, any "void" resulting from the holding in *Oliphant* would have been caused by the discretionary decision of the Federal Government not to exercise its already-extablished jurisdiction. Such a "practical" void, is a far cry from the "legal" void created today, in which no sovereign has the power to prosecute an entire class of crimes.

participate in tribal government. It is therefore unclear why the exercise of power retained by the tribes — power not divested by Congress — is subject to such a constraint.

More understandable is the Court's concern that nonmembers may suffer discrimination in tribal courts because such courts are "influenced by the unique customs, languages, and usages of the tribes they serve."

But [the ICRA] addressed this problem [by] extend[ing] most of the Bill of Rights to any person tried by a tribal court. In addition, the ICRA provides the remedy of habeas corpus to challenge the legality of any detention order by a tribe. The equal protection provision requires that nonmembers not be subject to discriminatory treatment in the tribal courts. In addition, the due process clause ensures that each individual is tried in a fundamentally fair proceeding.

II

This country has pursued contradictory policies with respect to the Indians. Since the passage of the [IRA] however, Congress has followed a policy of promoting the independence and self-government of the various tribes. The Court's decision today not only ignores the assumptions on which Congress originally legislated with respect to the jurisdiction over Indian crimes, but also stands in direct conflict with current congressional policy. I respectfully dissent.

NOTES

1. Classes of Indians Affected by *Duro*: Note there are three classes of Indians on most reservations, only two of which are enrolled: enrolled members of the reservation's own tribe and enrolled members of other tribes, such as BIA and IHS employees. The last class is comprised of Indians who are treated as members of the community but are either not eligible for enrollment because, like the *Martinez* children, they do not meet the tribe's enrollment criteria or refuse to enroll, because they are traditionals who object to the IRA government, as in the case of Hopi traditionals. This last class can be large. For example, 25% of the defendants in criminal cases in 1989 on the Ft. Belknap reservation in Montana were nonmembers and 31% of the defendants on the Wind River reservation in Montana were also nonmembers. How would the decision in *Duro* affect each of these categories? How will the decision affect tribes' abilities to keep the peace both on a day-to-day basis and during the summer when thousands of Indians from many tribes congregate on various reservations for powwows? For an explanation of the factors resulting in the numbers of nonmember Indians on present-day Indian reservations, see *Miller v. Crow Creek Sioux Tribe*, 12 Indian L. Rep. 6008 (Intertr. Ct. App., Mar. 22, 1984), in which the Northern Plains Intertribal Court of Appeals upheld tribal court jurisdiction over a Sioux from one tribe prosecuted for malicious mischief in a tribal court of another Sioux tribe.

2. Jurisdiction in Indian Country: As noted after *Oliphant*, leaving non-Indian defendants to the federal criminal justice system has created problems of law enforcement, not the least of which is that federal prosecutors do not have the resources or the inclination to prosecute minor crimes. To what extent will the rule of *Duro* exacerbate these problems? What courts will have jurisdiction over nonmember Indian defendants after *Duro*? As the Court points out, crimes by nonmembers classified as major crimes will be under the exclusive authority of the United States. But what about misdemeanors and other felonies not listed as one of the 14 major crimes? Carefully evaluate the government's argument that there will be a jurisdictional void in these cases. Does the Court adequately deal with this issue? If a state does not have a jurisdictional disclaimer in its constitution, as is the case in Arizona, would a state necessarily have jurisdiction over these offenses after *Duro*? If not, could a tribe agree with a state to consent to a narrow assumption of state criminal jurisdiction over nonmember defendants only relying on Public Law 280? *See Washington v. Confederated Bands & Tribes of the Yakima Indian Nation*, discussed in Chapter 4, section C1.

3. Federal Power After *Duro*: Note that the Court suggests that Congress may continue to treat Indians as a single large class with respect to *federal* jurisdiction. At the same time, the Court also states: "[T]hat Indians are citizens does not allow the Federal Government broad authority to legislate with respect to *enrolled Indians as a class*, whether to impose burdens or benefits." (Emphasis added.) Does this latter statement accompanied by a citation to *Mancari* suggest the Court may begin to limit congressional power to enrolled Indians? *Cf. Armell v. Prairie Band of Potawatomi Indians*, 194 Ill. App. 3d 31, 550 N.E.2d 1060, *cert. denied*, 111 S. Ct. 345 (1990) (upholding power of Congress to legislate for nonreservation Indian children). If so, would such a limitation comport either with the Court's customary deference to congressional power over Indians or with constitutional jurisprudence in other areas of congressional power?

4. Possible Tribal Responses to *Duro*: Evaluate the suggestions the Court makes regarding ways in which tribes might deal with law enforcement problems after *Duro*. Which seem feasible? For example, when and how might a tribe obtain consent to jurisdiction without raising questions regarding coercion? Is exclusion from the reservation a workable solution, when so many of the offenders are married to members? How could an exclusion order be enforced? *See Crow Creek Sioux Tribe v. Buum*, section 3, *infra*. What are the strengths and weaknesses of the Court's suggestion that intertribal compacts might be a solution?

Although not suggested by the Court, except indirectly by the Court's reference to exclusion, might the law enforcement problems created by *Duro* cause tribes to develop creative civil alternatives to fines and incarcerations, such as orders to undergo alcohol or drug treatment, orders to undergo counselling for a child in need of supervision, etc?

5. Congressional Responses to *Duro*: Congress's initial response was a 1990 rider to the Defense Appropriations Act amending the definition sections of the Indian Civil Rights Act. To the definition of "powers of self-government" the amendment added: "means the inherent power of Indian Tribes, hereby recognized and affirmed, to excercise criminal jurisdiction over all Indians." Defense Appropriations Act for FY 91, Pub. L. No. 101-938, § 8077(b)-(d), (1990) (amending 25 U.S.C. § 1301(2) (1983).

The amendment also added a definition of the term "Indian," heretofore not defined in the ICRA:

> Indian means any person who would be subject to the jurisdiction of the United States as an Indian under section 1153, title 18, United States Code if that person were to commit an offense listed in that section in Indian country to which that section applies.

Id., § 8077(c) (amending 25 U.S.C. § 1301(4)).

What is the effect of this law? Can an amendment to a definition section of a statute made through an appropriations rider create substantive rights? Is the amendment intended to create or reaffirm rights? Why might the difference be important? Does this affirmation of tribal inherent power necessarily require the imposition of the Bill of Rights and other constitutional provisions, such as those requiring an independent federal judiciary, on tribal courts?

The conference committee report accompanying the bill also reaffirmed congressional power to set policy in the field of Indian law in no uncertain terms:

> Throughout the history of this country, the Congress has never questioned the power of tribal courts to excercise misdemeanor jurisdiction over non-tribal member Indians in the same manner that such courts exercise misdemeanor jurisdiction over tribal members. Instead, the Congress has recognized that tribal governments afford a broad array of rights and privileges to non-tribal members. Non-tribal member Indians own property on Indian reservations, their children attend tribal schools, their families receive health care from tribal hospitals and clinics. Federally-administered programs and services are provided to Indian people because of their status as Indians without regard to whether their tribal membership is the same as their reservation residence. The issue of who is an Indian for purposes of Federal law is well-settled as a function of two hundred years of Constitutional and case law and Federal statutes.

A final provision of the rider states:

> The effects of [the above provisions] as those subsections affect the criminal misdemeanor jurisdiction of tribal courts over non-member Indians shall have no effect after September 30, 1991.

Id., § 8077(d).

What does this provision mean? According to the Conference Committee Report, this "sunset" provision was added to permit the relevant congressional committees "to work with the Indian nations, the Departments of Interior and Justice, and the states, to develop more comprehensive legislation within the coming year to clarify the intent of the Congress on the issue of tribal power to exercise criminal misdemeanor jurisdiction over Indians." H. Rep. 101-938, 101st Cong., 2d Sess. (1990).

For an analysis of this unusual law, see Deloria & Newton, *Criminal Jurisdiction over Nonmember Indians,* 38 Fed. Bar News & J. No. 2 (March 1991).

6. BIA Responses to *Duro*: In a 1988 precursor to the Supreme Court's opinion in *Duro*, the United States Court of Appeals for the Eighth Circuit held that tribes did not have criminal jurisdiction over nonmembers. *Greywater v. Joshua*, 846 F.2d 486 (8th Cir. 1988). As a result, tribes in the Eighth Circuit have had two years' experience in which to respond. During that period, the BIA appointed existing tribal courts and judges to function as CFR courts and judges for cases involving nonmembers only. Recall that CFR courts exercise power delegated by the Secretary of the Interior and do have jurisdiction over nonmember Indians under the regulations promulgated by the Secretary. The BIA has proposed this same solution since *Duro* was decided, although tribal officials have not been very enthusiastic. What legal and political issues does this proposal raise? *See Tillett v. Hodel,* 730 F. Supp. 381 (W.D. Okla. 1990), discussed in Chapter 2, section B. *See also* note 5 after *United States v. Mazurie* in this chapter.

7. The Purpose of Tribal Sovereignty: Is the Court's reaffirmation of the fact that tribes are more than private voluntary organizations convincing? If tribes are different from social clubs, why does the Court stress that the purpose of tribal sovereignty is to "control their own internal relations, and to preserve their own unique customs and social order"? If these are the only purposes of tribal sovereignty, can the same purposes not be accomplished by private groups, such as the Elks or a garden club? Is the answer that tribe's retain considerable power over nonmembers and non-Indians in civil matters?

NATIONAL FARMERS UNION INSURANCE COS. v. CROW TRIBE

471 U.S. 845 (1985)

Justice STEVENS delivered the opinion of the Court.

[An Indian student injured by a motorcycle in the parking lot of a state school on the Crow Indian reservation sued the state school district in tribal court for $153,000: $3,000 for medical expenses and $150,000 for pain and suffering. Although process was served by Dexter Falls Down on the Chairman of the School Board, Wesley Falls Down, the school board chairman did not notify National, the school district's insurer. National only learned of the suit after default judgment was entered in the tribal court on October 29, 1982. National and the school district then sought relief in the federal district court. On November 3, 1982, the district court granted the insurance company and the school district a temporary restraining order in response to National's allegations that an application for a writ of execution was pending in tribal court. Finding the court had federal question jurisdiction, the district court later granted a permanent injunction on the ground that the tribal court lacked subject matter jurisdiction over the dispute.]

[A divided panel of the Ninth Circuit Court of Appeals reversed (736 F.2d 1320 (1984)), holding there was no ground for the district court to exercise jurisdiction over the matter.]

[T]he majority concluded that the District Court's exercise of jurisdiction could not be supported on any constitutional, statutory, or common-law ground. One judge [concurred in the result because he believed] that the petitioners had a duty to exhaust their Tribal Court remedies before invoking the jurisdiction of a federal court, and therefore concurred in the judgment directing that the complaint be dismissed.[4]

I

Section 1331 of the Judicial Code provides that a federal district court "shall have original jurisdiction of all civil actions arising under the Constitution, laws, or treaties of the United States." It is well settled that [f]ederal common law as

---

[4] After the District Court's injunction was vacated, tribal officials issued a writ of execution on August 1, 1984, and seized computer terminals, other computer equipment, and a truck from the School District. A sale of the property was scheduled for August 22, 1984. On that date, the School District appeared in the Tribal Court, attempting to enjoin the sale and to set aside the default judgment. The Tribal Court [agreed to postpone the sale pending a full hearing on the default judgment issue]. Petitioners also proceeded before the Court of Appeals, which denied an emergency motion to recall the mandate on August 20, 1984. The next day Justice REHNQUIST granted the petitioners' application for a temporary stay. On September 10, 1984, he continued the stay pending disposition of the petitioners' petition for certiorari. 469 U.S. 1032 (1984). On September 19, the Tribal Court entered an order postponing a ruling on the motion to set aside the default judgment until after final review by this Court. Subsequently, the Court of Appeals stayed all proceedings in the District Court. On April 24, 1985, Justice REHNQUIST denied an application to "dissolve" the Court of Appeals' stay.

articulated in rules that are fashioned by court decisions are "laws" as that term is used in § 1331. [Nevertheless it was] necessary [for petitioners] to assert a claim "arising under" federal law. [The right petitioners assert] — a right to be protected against an unlawful exercise of Tribal Court judicial power — has its source in federal law because federal law defines the outer boundaries of an Indian tribe's power over non-Indians.

As we have often noted, Indian tribes occupy a unique status under our law. At one time they exercised virtually unlimited power over their own members as well as those who were permitted to join their communities. Today, however, the power of the Federal Government over the Indian tribes is plenary. Federal law, implemented by statute, by treaty, by administrative regulations, and by judicial decisions, provides significant protection for the individual, territorial, and political rights of the Indian tribes. The tribes also retain some of the inherent powers of the self-governing political communities that were formed long before Europeans first settled in North America.

This Court has frequently been required to decide questions concerning the extent to which Indian tribes have retained the power to regulate the affairs of non-Indians. [T]he governing rule of decision has been provided by federal law. [W]hether an Indian tribe retains the power to compel a non-Indian property owner to submit to the civil jurisdiction of a tribal court is [a question] that must be answered by reference to federal law and is a "federal question" under § 1331. [Since] petitioners contend that federal law has divested the Tribe of this aspect of sovereignty, it is federal law on which they rely as a basis for the asserted right of freedom from Tribal Court interference. They have, therefore, filed an action "arising under" federal law within the meaning of § 1331. The District Court correctly concluded that a federal court may determine under § 1331 whether a tribal court has exceeded the lawful limits of its jurisdiction.

II

Respondents contend that, even though the District Court's jurisdiction was properly invoked under § 1331, the Court of Appeals was correct in ordering that the complaint be dismissed because the petitioners failed to exhaust their remedies in the tribal judicial system. They further assert that the underlying tort action "has turned into a procedural and jurisdictional nightmare" because petitioners did not pursue their readily available Tribal Court remedies. Petitioners, in response, relying in part on *Oliphant v. Suquamish Indian Tribe,* 435 U.S. 191 (1978), assert that resort to exhaustion as a matter of comity "is manifestly inappropriate."

In *Oliphant* we held that the Suquamish Indian Tribal Court did not have criminal jurisdiction to try and to punish non-Indians for offenses committed on the reservation. That holding adopted the reasoning of early opinions of two United States Attorneys General, and concluded that federal legislation conferring jurisdiction on the federal courts to try non-Indians for offenses committed in Indian Country had implicitly pre-empted tribal jurisdiction. We wrote:

"While Congress never expressly forbade Indian tribes to impose criminal penalties on non-Indians, we now make express our implicit conclusion of nearly a century ago that Congress consistently believed this to be the necessary result of its repeated legislative actions."

If we were to apply the *Oliphant* rule here, it is plain that any exhaustion requirement would be completely foreclosed because federal courts would always be the only forums for civil actions against non-Indians. For several reasons, however, the reasoning of *Oliphant* does not apply to this case. First, although Congress' decision to extend the criminal jurisdiction of the federal courts to offenses committed by non-Indians against Indians within Indian Country supported the holding in *Oliphant,* there is no comparable legislation granting the federal courts jurisdiction over civil disputes between Indians and non-Indians that arise on an Indian reservation. Moreover, the opinion of one Attorney General on which we relied in *Oliphant,* specifically noted the difference between civil and criminal jurisdiction. Speaking of civil jurisdiction, Attorney General Cushing wrote:

"But there is no provision of treaty, and no statute, which takes away from the Choctaws jurisdiction of a case like this, a question of property strictly internal to the Choctaw nation; nor is there any written law which confers jurisdiction of such a case in any court of the United States.

"The conclusion seems to me irresistible, not that such questions are justiciable nowhere, but that they remain subject to the local jurisdiction of the Choctaws.

"Now, it is admitted on all hands ... that Congress has 'paramount right' to legislate in regard to this question, in all its relations. *It has legislated, in so far as it saw fit, by taking jurisdiction in criminal matters, and omitting to take jurisdiction in civil matters.... By all possible rules of construction the inference is clear that jurisdiction is left to the Choctaws themselves of civil controversies arising strictly within the Choctaw Nation.*"

7 Op. Atty. Gen. 175, 179-181 (1855) (emphasis added).

Thus, we conclude that the answer to the question whether a tribal court has the power to exercise civil subject-matter jurisdiction over non-Indians in a case of this kind is not automatically foreclosed, as an extension of *Oliphant* would require. Rather, the existence and extent of a tribal court's jurisdiction will require a careful examination of tribal sovereignty, the extent to which that sovereignty has been altered, divested, or diminished, as well as a detailed study of relevant statutes, Executive Branch policy as embodied in treaties and elsewhere, and administrative or judicial decisions.

We believe that examination should be conducted in the first instance in the Tribal Court itself. Our cases have often recognized that Congress is committed to a policy of supporting tribal self-government and self-determination. That policy favors a rule that will provide the forum whose jurisdiction is being challenged the first opportunity to evaluate the factual and legal bases for the challenge.[21] Moreover the orderly administration of justice in the federal court will be served by allowing a full record to be developed in the Tribal Court before either the merits or any question concerning appropriate relief is ad-

[21] We do not suggest that exhaustion would be required where an assertion of tribal jurisdiction "is motivated by a desire to harass or is conducted in bad faith," cf. *Juidice v. Vail,* 430 U.S. 327, 338 (1977), or where the action is patently violative of express jurisdictional prohibitions, or where exhaustion would be futile because of the lack of an adequate opportunity to challenge the court's jurisdiction.

dressed.[22] The risks of the kind of "procedural nightmare" that has allegedly developed in this case will be minimized if the federal court stays its hand until after the Tribal Court has had a full opportunity to determine its own jurisdiction and to rectify any errors it may have made. Exhaustion of tribal court remedies, moreover, will encourage tribal courts to explain to the parties the precise basis for accepting jurisdiction, and will also provide other courts with the benefit of their expertise in such matters in the event of further judicial review.

III

Our conclusions that § 1331 encompasses the federal question whether a tribal court has exceeded the lawful limits of its jurisdiction, and that exhaustion is required before such a claim may be entertained by a federal court, require that we reverse the judgment of the Court of Appeals. Until petitioners have exhausted the remedies available to them in the Tribal Court system, n. 4, *supra*, it would be premature for a federal court to consider any relief. Whether the federal action should be dismissed, or merely held in abeyance pending the development of further Tribal Court proceedings, is a question that should be addressed in the first instance by the District Court.

[*Reversed and remanded*].

NOTES

1. **Tribal Judicial Jurisdiction Over Members:** Although Congress has legislated some limitations, discussed in Chapter 2, tribal courts retain and exercise considerable criminal jurisdiction over their own members. Tribes also retain civil jurisdiction over matters involving tribal members. Moreover, the Court has recognized the importance of this civil jurisdiction by interpreting federal laws carefully as not infringing on tribal court jurisdiction over civil matters. *See, e.g., Bryan v. Itasca County*, 426 U.S. 373 (1976) (Public Law 280 language applying civil laws of the states to Indian reservations operates only as a choice of law provision and does not deprive tribal courts of civil jurisdiction over tribal members). Many of these controversies, like *Bryan, supra*, arise in the context of competition between state and tribal courts, covered in greater detail in Chapter 4. *See, e.g., Fisher v. District Court*, 424 U.S. 382 (1976) (Tribal court, not state court, has exclusive jurisdiction over adoption proceeding involving tribal members arising on the reservation.).

2. **Enforcing the Indian Civil Rights Act in Tribal Courts:** Tribal courts have become more experienced in applying the principles of Anglo-American law embodied in the Indian Civil Rights Act since the time of the Zientz article. Although abuses of civil rights have been reported, tribal court opinions, at least those reported in the Indian Law Reporter, illustrate that many tribal judges conscientiously interpret the Indian Civil Rights Act. *See, e.g., Laurence v. Southern Puget Sound Inter-Tribal Hous. Auth.*, 14 Indian L. Rep. 6011 (Suquamish Tribal Ct. 1987) (reinstatement of benefits to tribal employee termi-

---

[22] Four days after receiving notice of the default judgment, petitioners requested that the District Court enter an injunction. Crow Tribal Court Rule of Civil Procedure 17(d) provides that a party in a default [action] may move to set aside the default judgment at any time within 30 days. Petitioners did not utilize this legal remedy. It is a fundamental principle of long standing that a request for an injunction will not be granted as long as an adequate remedy at law is available.

nated without due process); *In re K.D.M.*, 12 Indian L. Rep. 6002 (Chy. R. Sx. Ct. App. 1984) (lower court custody ruling vacated because of inadequate notice); *United States v. Meyers*, 12 Indian L. Rep. 6008 (Intertribal Ct. App. 1984) (indictment dismissed because slow paperwork in prosecutor's office denied defendant a speedy trial).

Sovereign immunity remains a barrier in tribal courts, however, at least for tribal members suing for money damages. *See, e.g., TBI Contrs., Inc. v. Navajo Tribe*, 16 Indian L. Rep. 6017 (Nav. Sup. Ct. 1988). Nevertheless, tribal courts have frequently held that the Indian Civil Rights Act waives sovereign immunity for claims not seeking money damages. *See generally* Taylor, *Modern Practice in the Indian Courts*, 10 U. PUGET SOUND L. REV. 231 (1987).

3. *Iowa Mutual Insurance Co. v. LaPlante*: Although *National Farmers Union* recognized that Section 1331 could be invoked to bring a federal common law claim based on *Oliphant* alleging that a tribal court has no power to adjudicate a certain kind of claim involving non-Indians, it also closed off easy access to the federal courts to challenge every such assertion by imposing an exhaustion requirement. Another class of *Martinez*-avoiding claims existed, however, albeit a smaller class. Non-Indian defendants residing in a different state from that in which the reservation was located (usually businesses incorporated in other states), began to invoke diversity jurisdiction, 28 U.S.C. § 1332, to secure federal jurisdiction. In 1986, the Court applied the principle of *National Farmers Union* to these cases. *Iowa Mut. Ins. Co. v. LaPlante*, 480 U.S. 9 (1987). An Indian employee injured on an Indian-owned ranch on the Blackfoot Indian Reservation sued Iowa Mutual for bad faith refusal to settle. Iowa Mutual's motion to dismiss for lack of in personam and subject matter jurisdiction was dismissed by the tribal court. The tribal code permitted appeal of the jurisdictional issues, but only after the case was decided on the merits. Before the tribal court case was concluded, however, the insurance company filed a declaratory judgment action in federal court, invoking diversity jurisdiction and seeking a declaration that the policy did not cover the employee's injuries, because the injury occurred outside the scope of his employment.

The district court dismissed the complaint for lack of subject matter jurisdiction, relying on *National Farmers Union* as requiring exhaustion of tribal remedies before diversity jurisdiction could be entertained. The Supreme Court agreed that *National Farmers Union* provided the governing principle. Despite the seemingly mandatory nature of the court's diversity jurisdiction, the Court was reluctant to "read the general grant of diversity jurisdiction to have implemented such a significant intrusion on tribal sovereignty," especially since Indians were not citizens able to invoke diversity jurisdiction at the time the statute was first enacted in 1789. *Id.* at 17. Nevertheless, the Court did not agree that dismissal for lack of subject matter jurisdiction was the appropriate response. It thus remanded the case to the Ninth Circuit, leaving that court to decide whether a stay "pending further Tribal Court proceedings or dismiss[al] under the prudential rule announced in *National Farmers Union*" was more appropriate. *Id.* at 20, n.14. Although such an approach will permit federal court intervention after the tribal court proceeding, the intervention, like that in *National Farmers Union*, will reach only the question whether the tribe's jurisdiction has been divested under the *Oliphant* principle. "Unless a federal court determines that a Tribal Court lacked jurisdiction, however, proper deference to the tribal court system precludes relitigation of issues raised by the LaPlantes' bad faith claim and resolved in the Tribal Courts." *Id.* at 19. In the words of one commentator, "*LaPlante*'s sweeping conclusion of nonjurisdictional nonreviewability

grants potentially enormous authority to tribal courts acting within their jurisdiction in civil cases." Arrow, *Contemporary Tensions in Constitutional Indian
Law*, 12 OKLA. CITY U.L. REV. 469, 491 (1987).

4. Application to Indian Plaintiffs: The Ninth Circuit has applied the principles of deference to tribal courts to prevent an Indian *plaintiff* from invoking
diversity jurisdiction to sue a non-Indian defendant for a breach of contract
claim arising on the reservation. *Wellman v. Chevron, U.S.A., Inc.*, 815 F.2d
577 (9th Cir. 1987). Whether it is the plaintiff or the defendant who is a non-
Indian, the court reasoned that the material issue for purposes of *National
Farmers* and *Iowa Mutual* was whether the dispute arose on the reservation. *Id.*
at 579.

5. Federal Court Jurisdiction Over Challenges to Tribal Court Authority:
What is the importance of the holding of *National Farmers Union* and *Iowa
Mutual*? Why did the Court refuse to extend the rationale of *Oliphant* to civil
jurisdiction in tribal court? Can any non-Indian now challenge tribal court
jurisdiction as inconsistent with the tribe's dependent status? Can any nonmember challenge tribal court civil jurisdiction on the same grounds after *Duro*? If
the same situation that arose in *Dry Creek Lodge* arose again and you represented the tribe, what advice would you give the tribe? Do *National Farmers
Union* and *Iowa Mutual* seem to indicate the Court will review the question of
tribal court jurisdiction on a case-by-case basis, a subject matter-by-subject matter basis, or a reservation-by-reservation basis? If on a case-by-case basis, has the
Court in effect provided for appeal from tribal court of all civil actions involving
non-Indians and perhaps nonmembers as well?

6. Exhausting Tribal Remedies: The Court in *National Farmers Union* used
the term "exhaustion" of tribal court remedies. Since then, cases by non-Indians
challenging tribal authority have routinely been stayed pending further tribal
court proceedings or dismissed under the exhaustion rule of *National Farmers
Union. See, e.g., Northwest South Dakota Prod. Credit Ass'n v. Smith*, 784 F.2d
323 (8th Cir. 1986) (foreclosure of mortgage on individually owned Indian land
within reservation must be attempted first in tribal court); *A & A Concrete, Inc.
v. White Mountain Apache Tribe*, 781 F.2d 1411 (9th Cir.), *cert. denied*, 476
U.S. 1117 (1986) (contract claim must be presented first in tribal court).

In administrative law, the requirement of exhaustion of administrative remedies is subject to exceptions, however. In *National Farmers Union*, the Court
indicated that these exceptions can be raised in federal court challenges to tribal
court jurisdiction as well, when the tribal court's taking jurisdiction is designed
to harass or is motivated by bad faith, "or where the action is patently violative
of express jurisdictional prohibitions, or where exhaustion would be futile because of the lack of adequate opportunity to challenge the court's jurisdiction."
National Farmers Union, supra, n.21. If a tribal code provision apparently bars
non-Indians from suing in tribal court, as some do, could an aggrieved non-
Indian take his claim directly to federal court? *Cf. DeMent v. Oglala Sioux
Tribal Court*, 874 F.2d 510 (8th Cir. 1989) (non-Indian tribal court defendant
in child custody case could not challenge tribal court authority on ground that
tribal code only applies to non-Indians who consent to jurisdiction; he must first
exhaust the jurisdictional argument in tribal court).

If the federal court determines that the tribal court has dismissed the case
because the tribal court had no subject matter jurisdiction over the controversy
or because no tribal law governs the outcome, can or should a federal court
retain the case? *See* Pommersheim, *The Crucible of Sovereignty: Analyzing
Issues of Tribal Jurisdiction*, 31 ARIZ. L. REV. 329, 347-55 (1989). May a federal

court make an independent determination that a tribe does not have civil jurisdiction over a particular kind of case and that as a result exhaustion would be
futile? In *Sheesley's Plumbing & Heating Co.*, 84 Bankr. 638 (D.S.D. 1988), the
tribal housing authority contracted with the plaintiff to build a housing project.
When the contractor defaulted on the contract, the tribal housing authority
attempted to call in a letter of credit from a local bank. At this point the plaintiff
filed bankruptcy. Although the tribe insisted the issue of tribal court jurisdiction
should be argued first in tribal court, the district court, disagreed, stating:

> The "exhaustion rule" announced in *Crow Tribe* and reaffirmed in *LaPlante* is inap-
> plicable to the present facts. Despite the strong language in *LaPlante* indicating that
> tribal courts have unlimited civil jurisdiction, this jurisdiction does not extend to bank-
> ruptcy proceedings. Jurisdiction of tribal courts is unlimited only in relation to matters
> of Indian self-government. Requiring tribal courts to perform as bankruptcy courts by
> requiring the tribal court to administer a debtor's estate would not promote self-gov-
> ernment among the Indian tribes, even assuming that a body of "bankruptcy" law
> existed in tribal court. Thus, Indian tribal courts have neither exclusive nor concurrent
> jurisdiction to hear bankruptcy proceedings. Because application of the exhaustion
> rule to cases filed in bankruptcy could not serve the interests of comity or judicial
> economy and would be an exercise in futility, the Court holds that the exhaustion rule
> of *Crow Tribe* and *LaPlante* does not apply to an adversary proceeding in bankruptcy.

Id. at 640-41.

In a recent case, a district court issued an injunction barring enforcement of a
tribal court order, giving only lip service to *National Farmers* and opting instead
to rely on the *Dry Creek Lodge* "egregious circumstances" exception of the
Tenth Circuit. *Little Horn State Bank v. Crow Tribal Court*, 690 F. Supp. 919
(D. Mont. 1988). A bank had sought the aid of a tribal court to enforce a state
court default judgment for foreclosure of a forklift purchased by a reservation
plaintiff. For reasons not apparent in the opinion, the tribal court took no
action for two years. Ten days after the plaintiff managed to repossess the
forklift, the tribal court issued an ex parte decree ordering the plaintiff to
return the forklift to the tribal court's impoundment yard. The defendant in
the tribal court then attempted to enforce the tribal court order in state court,
again without giving notice to the bank. The bank, still trying to invoke the
appropriate tribal court procedures, filed a motion to set aside the enforcement
of the tribal court order and a request for a hearing. At that point the tribal
judge told the plaintiff's attorney that the court would neither schedule a hearing nor receive any motions from the bank. The bank then brought an action
against the tribal court in federal district court, arguing that the tribal court's
actions violated the ICRA and was outside the tribe's powers.

Despite *National Farmers Union* and *Iowa Mutual*, the district court held that
the ICRA was the "most compelling basis for jurisdiction." *Id.* at 921. The court
cited *Dry Creek* as providing the correct rule for decision in a case in which one
of the parties was not an Indian, the underlying dispute is not an intratribal
dispute, and there are no other adequate remedies. The court cited *National
Farmers Union* as a case requiring federal courts to give respect to tribal courts,
stating: "This court, in keeping with its obligation to uphold the law will honor
that directive." *Id.* at 923. Nevertheless, the court then added: "[I]t has become
extremely difficult to do so in the face of such decidedly egregious facts as are
presented herein." *Id.* The court took the opportunity to give the tribal court a
stern lecture, ending with: "If the Crow Tribe wishes to earn the respect and
cooperation of its non-Indian neighbors, it must do more to engender that

respect and cooperation, not abuse those neighbors who attempt to work within its system." *Id.* at 924-25.

Although the court's reasoning did not strictly follow *National Farmers Union* and *Iowa Insurance*, the plaintiff also invoked 28 U.S.C. § 1331 as a basis for jurisdiction. Given the tribal court's treatment of the bank's attempts to use tribal procedures, the district court could have held that the plaintiff had exhausted tribal remedies and thus considered the question whether continued exercise of civil jurisdiction over nonmembers was inconsistent with the Crow Tribe's status.

A rather serious clash of federal and tribal court power was averted when the parties apparently settled. *Little Horn State Bank v. Crow Tribal Court*, 16 Indian L. Rep. 3075 (D. Mont., Feb. 27, 1989) (dismissed with prejudice pursuant to stipulation of the parties).

Not all tribal courts treat non-Indian plaintiffs so harshly. In *General Motors Acceptance Corp. v. Bitah*, 16 Indian L. Rep. 6002 (Nav. Sup. Ct. 1988), the Navajo Supreme Court held in favor of the non-Indian corporate plaintiff in a repossession action, rejecting the reservation defendant's claims of fraud and misrepresentation. *Accord Ducheneaux v. First Fed. Sav. & Loan Ass'n*, 16 Indian L. Rep. 6147 (Chy. R. Sx. Ct. App. 1989) (Although non-Indian plaintiff must get consent to sue Indian defendant in tribal court, consent clause in retail sales contract provided basis for remedy of foreclosure in tribal court.).

Several courts have invoked the exceptions mentioned in footnote 21 of *National Farmers Union. See, e.g., Superior Oil Co. v. United States*, 798 F.2d 1324 (10th Cir. 1986) (remand for a determination of whether Navajo Tribe acted in bad faith in withholding consent for seismic permits in order to let oil and gas lease expire to permit renegotiation); *Weeks Constr., Inc. v. Oglala Sioux Hous. Auth.*, 797 F.2d 668 (8th Cir. 1986) (after exhaustion case); *Heinert v. Oglala Sioux Tribe*, 14 Indian L. Rep. 3033 (D.S.D. Mar. 14, 1985) (flagrant violation of tribe's own ordinance barring jurisdiction over non-Indians who had not consented to suit made further exhaustion unnecessary).

7. Determining Whether the Tribal Court Retains Jurisdiction: Once a party has exhausted tribal court remedies, what factors should influence the outcome of the jurisdictional question? In *FMC v. Shoshone-Bannock Tribes*, 905 F.2d 1311 (9th Cir. 1990), the Ninth Circuit Court of Appeals reversed the district court's determination that a tribe did not have jurisdiction to enforce in tribal court a Tribal Employment Rights Ordinance against a non-Indian owned company operating a phosphorus plant on the reservation. The court held that to show appropriate deference under *National Farmers* the district court should have applied a clearly erroneous standard to a tribal court's finding of fact, although its *de novo* review of the tribal court's resolution of *federal* legal questions was appropriate. On the merits, the Ninth Circuit also reversed the district court, agreeing with the tribal court that under *Montana v. United States*, which provided the appropriate rule, the tribe retained its power to regulate employment practices because the company had entered into a consensual relationship with the tribe. Finally, the court remanded to the tribal court to give the company an opportunity to challenge the ordinance in tribal court under the Indian Civil Rights Act. If the tribal court rules against the company on the ICRA question, can the district court review its ruling?

8. The Intersection of *Martinez* and *National Farmers*: The plaintiff reached federal court in *National Farmers Union* by challenging tribal power to adjudicate disputes with non-Indians instead of making a claim based on the ICRA. By upping the ante, the plaintiff removed the case from the purview of

Martinez and the ICRA to the realm of *Oliphant* and the question whether the tribe's adjudicatory jurisdiction over non-Indians was inconsistent with its dependent status.

In their comprehensive yet entertaining article, Gover and Laurence call this theory "the *Oliphant* spin-off." They have cautioned that *National Farmers Union* may permit a non-Indian whose claim is really an Indian Civil Rights Claim to avoid the *Martinez* holding by arguing that the tribal court has lost its power to adjudicate disputes involving non-Indians by necessary implication from the particular tribe's status. Gover & Laurence, *Avoiding Santa Clara Pueblo v. Martinez: The Litigation in Federal Court of Civil Actions Under the Indian Civil Rights Act*, 8 HAMLINE L. REV. 497 (1985). Nevertheless, all agree that *National Farmers Union* and *Iowa Mutual* will make it harder to challenge tribal court authority. According to Professor Pommersheim:

> Before *Santa Clara Pueblo*, *National Farmers Union*, and *Iowa Mutual*, it was relatively easy to circumvent tribal courts. The notions of a direct federal cause of action under the Indian Civil Rights Act, federal question jurisdiction, and diversity jurisdiction permitted a significant bulk of civil causes of action arising on the reservation to be brought directly in federal courts, without any concern for the tribal forum. As a result, there was little federal concern for what occurred in tribal courts. There was also scant interest in the question of federal review and in the overall relationship of tribal courts to the federal system. But when direct access to federal courts was sharply curtailed, there was a concomitant growth of tribal court litigation and a renewed litigant and federal interest in prescribing the boundaries of tribal authority.

Pommersheim, *The Crucible of Sovereignty: Analyzing Issues of Tribal Jurisdiction*, 31 ARIZ. L. REV. 329, 360-61 (1989) (footnotes omitted).*

9. Lawyers on the Reservation: Separate tribal governments and courts presumably exist to preserve and protect the cultural, religious, legal, and political autonomy of Indian tribes. Generally, the cultural values of Indian tribes are cooperative and communal rather than competitive and adversarial. When licensed legal practitioners venture into tribal affairs they not infrequently bring with them their training in the adversary system. To what extent is that training incompatible with Indian tribal values and government? Is the Indian Civil Rights Act of 1968 compatible with these values?

When non-Indian attorneys become involved in tribal proceedings, they clearly need to be sensitive to tribal values. But should they abandon their normal zealous representation of their clients in favor of cooperative arrangements with the tribe? In an article written at the beginning of the Indian law revolution, when legal services attorneys began to serve Indian reservations, Dean Price identified some of the problems that would challenge an Anglo poverty lawyer on a reservation, especially relating to issues of economic development. Price, *Lawyers on the Reservation: Some Implications for the Legal Profession*, 1969 LAW & SOC. ORDER (now ARIZ. ST. L.J.) 161. Sensitivity to the tribal cultural context is even more important if the non-Indian attorney is representing a member in a civil rights suit. In a recent article, Michael Taylor, an attorney who has practiced law in many tribal courts, has this to say about the relationship of non-Indian attorneys to tribal clients in such cases:

> In order to effectively represent an individual plaintiff with a claim for violation of civil rights against a tribal agency or official in an Indian court, a non-Indian lawyer

must learn about the tribal culture, customs, and law that are the basis of the tribal concept of civil rights. This is especially important when the client is an Indian. The Indian client usually wants to remain an effective and respected part of reservation society, whether his lawsuit is won or lost, and this result may be compromised if the goal of the lawsuit is not somewhat consistent with the tribal understanding of personal rights.

Just as American concepts of fairness and civil rights are a product of a unique history and culture, so too are American Indian concepts derived from a unique history and culture. The differences between the two cultures sometimes result in variances in the answers given to the same question. The Indian civil rights advocate cannot assume that an argument neatly reasoned from the federal cases will prevail in an Indian court, or more importantly, that winning a judgment based on concepts of civil rights not accepted by the Indian community will solve the problems of a client or a community.[121] A stiff money judgment or injunction may not resolve the issue where the tribal culture puts little value in either. Simply put, Indian judges and juries respond more readily to concepts and solutions that they can agree will work to solve a problem within the reservation society.

Taylor, *Modern Practice in the Indian Courts*, 10 U. PUGET SOUND L. REV. 232, 255-56 (1987).* Frank Pommersheim, who practiced law for ten years on the Rosebud Sioux reservation, has also explored these themes. See especially, Pommersheim, *The Reservation as Place: A South Dakota Essay*, 34 S. DAK. L. REV. 246 (1989).

RECENT CHALLENGES TO TRIBAL COURT SYSTEMS

In 1986 the United States Civil Rights Commission embarked upon an investigation into tribal court systems, sparked by a series of articles in the *Washington Post* about abuses in tribal courts on the Pine Ridge Reservation. To date the Commission has held five hearings. Those hearings held near reservations (in Rapid City, South Dakota, in Portland, Oregon and in Flagstaff, Arizona) focused on complaints regarding enforcement of civil rights on the reservations. One hearing was held in Washington, D.C., focusing on the BIA's role in enforcement of civil rights on the reservation.

At the Washington hearing, Chairman Pendleton stated the investigation was focusing on both "particular" and "systemic" problems in ICRA enforcement. The Chairman distinguished between the two by explaining that particular problems could be cured by providing more money and training to tribal courts, while systemic problems could not. Examples of particular problems included firing of tribal prosecutors for disagreeing with the councils and inadequate recordkeeping. Two "systemic" problems concerned the Commission the most: (1) lack of separation of powers insulating tribal judges from retaliation from the council and (2) reliance by tribal councils on sovereign immunity as a defense to ICRA actions, even when the actions sought declarative and injunctive

---

[121] *See e.g., Othole v. Wesley and the Zuni Tribal Police Department*, 4 CLEARINGHOUSE REVIEW No. 5 at 492 (Zuni Tribal Ct. June 6, 1980) (Teenaged girl, wearing pajamas when arrested, was incarcerated overnight in a padded cell with an intoxicated adult male prisoner. Charges against her were dismissed. A small money judgment was obtained, the officer responsible was required to publish a public apology, and the tribal police agreed to undergo training in arrest, search, seizure, and civil rights).

*Copyright © 1987 University of Puget Sound Law Review and Michael Taylor. Reprinted with permission of the copyright holders.

relief. United States Commission on Civil Rights, Enforcement of the Indian Civil Rights Act: Hearing Held in Washington, D.C., Jan. 28, 1988, at 2-3.

In addition, in the Washington hearing the Commission sought to determine whether the BIA had responded to footnote 22 of *Martinez* by using its power to approve constitutions to ensure tribal compliance with the Indian Civil Rights Act.

Shortly after the Commission began its investigation, Senator Hatch introduced S. 2747 to amend the Indian Civil Rights Act. In pertinent part, the bill provided:

(a) Federal district courts shall have jurisdiction of civil rights actions alleging a failure to comply with rights secured by this Act. Sovereign immunity shall not constitute a defense to such an action.

(b) Any aggrieved individual, following the exhaustion of such tribal remedies as may be both timely and reasonable under the circumstances, or the Attorney General on behalf of the United States, may initiate an action in federal district court for declaratory, injunctive or other equitable relief against an Indian tribe, tribal organization, or official thereof, alleging failure to comply with rights secured by this Act.

(c) In any civil action brought by an aggrieved individual, or by the Attorney General, the federal district court shall adopt the findings of fact of the tribal court, if such findings have been made, unless the district court determines that:

(1) the tribal court was not fully independent from the tribal legislative or executive authority;

(2) the tribal court was not authorized to or did not finally determine matters of law and fact;

(3) the tribal court permitted those subject to the Act, on issues of declaratory, injunctive or other equitable relief, to interpose a defense of immunity;

(4) the tribal court failed to resolve the merits of the factual dispute;

(5) the tribal court employed a factfinding procedure not adequate to afford a full and fair hearing;

(6) the tribal court did not adequately develop material facts;

(7) the tribal court failed to provide a full, fair and adequate hearing; or

(8) the factual determinations of the tribal court are not fairly supported by the record,

in which event the district court shall conduct a *de novo* review of the allegations contained in the complaint.

(d) In any civil action brought under this Act the federal court shall, whenever a question of tribal law is at issue, accord due deference to the interpretation of the tribal court of tribal laws and customs.

S. 2747, 100th Cong., 2d Sess., 134 CONG. REC. S. 11,656 (1988).

No action was taken on the bill in the 100th Congress. Senator Hatch reintroduced the bill in the 101st Congress in March, 1989. S. 517, 101st Cong., 1st Sess., 135 CONG. REC. S. 2,190 (1989).

The combination of the Hatch Bill and the Commission's investigation greatly concerned tribal leaders. They complained that the Commission began the investigation with the conclusion that ICRA was not working, and sought out a few reservations experiencing particularly intense and long-running political difficulties and particular cases that would reinforce preconceived ideas that tribes should not have separate court systems. (For example, Judge Elbridge Coochise expressed concern at one hearing regarding a letter that Commissioner Allen had sent to Suzann Harjo, executive director of the National Conference of American Indians, advocating the repeal of the Indian Civil Rights

Act and the return of Indian tribes to the mainstream.) United States Commission on Civil Rights, Enforcement of the Indian Civil Rights Act: Hearing Held in Portland, Oregon on March 31, 1988 at 54. *See also* United States Commission on Civil Rights, Enforcement of the Indian Civil Rights Act: Hearing Held in Washington, D.C., Jan. 28, 1988, at 35 ("there is no room for a form of government other than Federal, State, or local") (statement of Commissioner Allen).

Concerned that the Commission was planning to recommend that *Martinez* be legislatively overturned, the Senate Select Committee on Indian Affairs held its own hearing in 1988 to take testimony from tribal leaders and Indian law scholars on the state of tribal court systems. TRIBAL COURT SYSTEMS AND INDIAN CIVIL RIGHTS ACT, 100th Cong., 2d Sess. (1988). The testimony in the Senate hearing was more favorable to Indian tribes. Witnesses in both hearings did agree about one thing, however — that the lack of federal funding for education and training is a primary factor affecting civil rights enforcement in Indian Country. Many witnesses also agreed that some avenue of appeal to the federal system is appropriate.

A fair evaluation of the Commission's work cannot be undertaken until it has issued its final recommendations. Nevertheless, it cannot be denied that some of the witnesses related stories that, if true, reveal abuses of power on some Indian reservations. In contrast, other witnesses' testimony, if true, demonstrated that other reservations are making considerable progress toward enforcing the ICRA.

Assume you are a tribal attorney asked to analyze the Hatch Bill. What will the bill accomplish? Does it overturn *Martinez*? In other words, if the bill were enacted would the situation return completely to the pre-*Martinez* wholesale review by federal courts? What, if any, protection does the bill afford tribal sovereignty? As a counterpoint to the Hatch Bill, which is the kind of bill many tribal leaders fear will be recommended by the Commission, consider the following draft written (although not recommended) by Professor Clinton:

§ 1260 Tribal Forums

Final judgments or decrees rendered in cases or controversies by the courts or other forums of Indian tribes with a governing body duly recognized by the Secretary of the Interior may be reviewed by the Supreme Court as follows:

....

(3) By writ of certiorari, where the validity of a treaty or statute of the United States is drawn in question or where the validity of a statute, ordinance, resolution or other legislative act of an Indian tribe with a governing body duly recognized by the Secretary of the Interior is drawn in question on the ground of its being repugnant to the Constitution or the provisions of the Indian Civil Rights, 25 U.S.C. § 1301-03, protecting the rights of persons against tribal governments; where is drawn in question the validity of the applications of a statute, ordinance, resolution or other legislative act of an Indian tribe with a governing body duly recognized by the Secretary of the Interior on the ground of its being repugnant to the Constitution or the provisions of the Indian Civil Rights, 25 U.S.C. § 1301-03, protecting the rights of persons against tribal governments and the decision is in favor of its validity; or where any right, title privilege, or immunity is specifically set up or claimed under the Constitution, treaties, or statutes of, or commission held or authority exercised under, the United States.

This proposal would protect tribal sovereignty by treating tribes the same as states. It limits review to certiorari jurisdiction by the Supreme Court, which is discretionary, and permits review of final judgments only. Professor Clinton argued that such a proposal would enable tribes to remain "the front line of defense" against ICRA violations by tribal officials, "thereby respecting the dignity of Indian tribal sovereignty, protected in *Martinez*." United States Commission on Civil Rights, Enforcement of the Indian Civil Rights Act: Hearing Held in Washington, D.C., Jan. 28, 1988, at 283. Nevertheless, the proposal is an abrogation of tribal sovereignty that would be applied to all tribes no matter how strong their civil rights record may be. For this reason, Professor Clinton believed that such a proposal is "the *most* that should be done at the present time to afford a federal judicial remedy for civil violations of the ICRA, if any such remedy is thought to be needed." *Id.*

Assume that you have been asked by the tribe to draft a bill that would accord deference to tribal sovereignty, yet provide for some limited federal court review. As a pragmatist, you might also think about what tribes could extract from Congress in return for giving up a measure of sovereignty. In addition, you might try to draft a law that would have a mechanism to treat each tribe individually. Once you draft your bill, discuss it with the class focusing both on the bill's political acceptance in Indian Country and in the national legislature.

2. TRIBAL POWER TO CONTROL THE POLITICAL PROCESS

RUNS AFTER v. UNITED STATES

766 F.2d 347 (8th Cir. 1984)

McMILLIAN, Circuit Judge.

These appeals [challenge] the validity of two tribal resolutions. [In 1972] the Cheyenne River Sioux Reservation was reapportioned from fifteen into six election districts for purposes of the election of Tribal Council representatives. See *Brown v. Cheyenne River Sioux Tribal Council*, 486 F.2d 658 (8th Cir 1973). In June 1981 a resolution was presented to the Tribal Council to reapportion the reservation into thirteen election districts. That resolution was not adopted by the Tribal Council. Later a petition to reapportion the reservation into thirteen election districts was circulated and signed by the required number of eligible voters. A majority of the voters approved reapportionment in a referendum election held in December 1981. However, the Tribal Council refused to acknowledge or implement the results of the referendum election. In May 1982 an action was filed in tribal court to enforce the reapportionment of the reservation. In June 1982 the tribal court upheld the reapportionment and ordered all future tribal elections to be held in thirteen reapportioned election districts.

The next day, however, the Tribal Council terminated the tribal court judge, allegedly because of the decision enforcing the reapportionment, rescinded the tribal court order directing elections to be held in thirteen election districts, and appointed a new tribal court judge. In July 1982 the new tribal court judge held that the resolution was invalid because the referendum election was invalid. In August 1982 a Tribal Council primary election was held using six election districts. Also in August 1982 one of the appellants, then Tribal Council member Joan LeBeau, wrote to the Bureau of Indian Affairs (BIA) to request a BIA investigation of the legality of the August 1982 primary election because it had not been conducted in thirteen reapportioned election districts. It appears that no action was taken by the BIA and in September 1982 the general election was held using six election districts.

[In 1983 several tribal members, including] Joan LeBeau, and an organization of Cheyenne River Sioux tribal members called the "Committee to Save Our Constitution" [filed a complaint in federal district court against the United States, the Department of the Interior, the BIA, and several individual government officials.] The complaint alleged that the defendants erred in recognizing the Tribal Council elected in 1982 because the election had been improperly conducted in six election districts and also sought judicial review of the BIA's final decision to refuse to intervene in the 1982 tribal election dispute. In April 1983 the BIA recognized the Tribal Council elected in the 1982 election. The district court [held] that the BIA's final decision recognizing the Tribal Council elected in 1982 from six election districts was correct because it followed the July 1982 decision of the tribal court. The district court judgment was not appealed.

In 1984 several of the named appellants in the present appeals were dissatisfied with the manner in which the Tribal Council had been conducting tribal affairs and decided to seek election to the Tribal Council. Five of the named appellants, Joan LeBeau, Gib LeBeau, Bertha Chasing Hawk, Grady Claymore, and Walter Woods, filed nominating petitions and were certified as eligible candidates by their respective district council election boards. These five appellants ran in the June 1984 primary election; four (Joan LeBeau, Gib LeBeau, Bertha Chasing Hawk, and Grady Claymore) received sufficient votes to run in the September 1984 general election and were so notified by the Tribal Election Board. Appellant Walter Woods barely lost in the primary election.

However, on July 12, 1984, the Tribal Council passed the two resolutions at issue in these appeals. In Resolution No. 190-84-CR the Tribal Council "forever barred" appellants Gib LeBeau, Joan LeBeau and Walter Woods from holding appointed or elected tribal office because of alleged "past misconduct in office." A second resolution, passed without identifying numbers, disqualified appellants Bertha Chasing Hawk and Grady Claymore from running in the September 1984 general election because of alleged non-residency in the district each sought to represent. As a result of these resolutions, four appellants were precluded from running in the September 1984 general election, and appellant Walter Woods, who would have been eligible to run in the general election following their disqualifications, was also precluded from running in the September 1984 general election.

In late August 1984 appellants [filed this suit seeking] to enjoin BIA recognition of and BIA distribution of federal and tribal funds to the 1984 Tribal Council; and to compel the holding of a valid general election in which the names of appellants Gib LeBeau, Bertha Chasing Hawk, and Grady Claymore would be included on the ballot. The complaint named as defendants the eight Tribal Council members who had voted in favor of the July 12 Tribal Council resolutions, the United States, [and various Interior Department officials].

The complaint alleged federal question jurisdiction under 28 U.S.C. §§ 1331, 1343, the Administrative Procedure Act, 5 U.S.C. § 701 et seq. (APA), and the 1871 Civil Rights Act, 42 U.S.C. §§ 1985, 1986. Appellants alleged that the tribal defendants violated 42 U.S.C. § 1985 and that the federal defendants knew the Tribal Council resolutions were invalid and had the authority to take appropriate action but failed to do so in violation of 42 U.S.C. § 1986. In particular, appellants alleged that the tribal defendants conspired to bar some of the appellants from holding tribal office in violation of 42 U.S.C. § 1985(1), that the tribal defendants conspired to bar some of the appellants from holding tribal office in retaliation for their earlier involvement in the Committee to Save Our Constitution action in violation of 42 U.S.C. § 1985(2), that the tribal defendants conspired to deny appellants the right to run for tribal office and to vote for qualified candidates in violation of the right to equal protection in violation of 42 U.S.C. § 1985(3), and that the federal defendants failed to take any action to prevent the tribal defendants from violating appellants' rights in violation of 42 U.S.C. § 1986.

The district court denied the motion for preliminary injunctive relief, [characterizing] appellants' complaint against the tribal defendants as an intratribal election dispute within the exclusive jurisdiction of the tribal court. The district court order denying preliminary injunctive relief was then appealed to this court. [F]or purposes of appeal we will assume that the Tribal Council resolutions in question are invalid. This is evidently the position of the BIA. [A letter from the BIA to the tribal council in October, 1984 advised the tribe it would] refuse to recognize the members of the Tribal Council elected from Districts 5 and 6, but the BIA would recognize actions taken by the Tribal Council when there were sufficient members present, excluding members from Districts 5 and 6, to constitute a quorum as specified in the tribal constitution.

[First] we must resolve the problem of subject matter jurisdiction. [F]ederal district courts do have subject matter jurisdiction under 28 U.S.C. § 1331 to review, pursuant to the APA, the BIA action. [Nevertheless,] appellants have not yet exhausted administrative remedies. [A]ppellants have filed an administrative appeal with the Department of the Interior seeking review of the BIA's refusal to require new elections in Districts 5 and 6. [T]he record [does not clearly indicate] whether any BIA administrative action has been taken and, if so, whether any administrative appeal is pending with respect to the Tribal Council resolutions "forever barring" appellant Walter Woods from tribal office and disqualifying Bertha Chasing Hawk and Grady Claymore for non-residency.

[T]he district court acted within its discretion in requiring appellants to exhaust administrative remedies. The governmental interest in requiring exhaustion are particularly strong in the present case. It cannot be denied that the BIA has special expertise and extensive experience in dealing with Indian affairs. The interest of the BIA and its parent Department of Interior in administrative autonomy also supports requiring exhaustion of administrative remedies. Moreover, as more fully explained below, the somewhat anomalous and complex relationship between the quasi-sovereign Indian tribes and the federal government also supports, in general, requiring appellants to initially seek an administrative solution through the BIA and the Department of Interior.

For these reasons, we affirm the district court's dismissal of the claim against the federal defendants for judicial review of the BIA's decision to refuse to require new elections [for failure to exhaust administrative remedies]. Next, to the extent that appellants' complaint can be characterized as one seeking federal judicial review of the two Tribal Council resolutions at issue, a characterization with which appellants do not agree, the district court correctly dismissed the complaint for lack of jurisdiction. Appellants essentially argue that the Tribal Council resolutions [were] politically motivated because appellants opposed the manner in which the Tribal Council was conducting tribal affairs, particularly the handling of tribal funds. Appellants alleged that the tribal council resolutions were clearly inconsistent with the tribal constitution, bylaws and election ordinance. Such an action would necessarily require the district court to interpret the tribal constitution and tribal law.

We believe the district court correctly held that resolution of such disputes involving questions of interpretation of the tribal constitution and tribal law is not within the jurisdiction of the district court. Appellants may seek review in tribal court or pursue alternative, political remedies.

[I]n *Santa Clara Pueblo v. Martinez,* 436 U.S. at 72, the Supreme Court held that the ICRA does not impliedly authorize actions for declaratory or injunctive relief against either the tribes or tribal officers. The Court noted that "Congress considered and rejected proposals for federal review of alleged violations of the Act arising in a civil context." *Id.* at 67. The Court concluded that "[c]reation of a federal cause of action for enforcement of the rights created in Title I [of the ICRA], however useful it might be in securing compliance with [the ICRA], plainly would be at odds with the congressional goal of protecting tribal self-government," *id.* at 64, "would undermine the authority of tribal forums," *id.,* and "would also impose serious financial burdens on already 'financially disadvantaged' tribes." *Id.*

For these reasons, despite the substantive guarantees of certain constitutional rights contained in the ICRA, "the only federal relief available under the Indian Civil Rights Act is a writ of habeas corpus," *Goodface v. Grassrope,* 708 F.2d at 338 n.4, and "[t]hus, actions seeking other sorts of relief for tribal deprivations of rights must be resolved through tribal forums." *Id.* But cf. *Santa Clara Pueblo v. Martinez,* 436 U.S. at 72-83 (White, J., dissenting) (would find implied federal cause of action in ICRA; given congressional concern about deprivation of individual Indians' rights by tribal authorities, improbable that Congress desired enforcement of rights to be left to very tribal authorities alleged to have violated them). We next turn to appellants' claims under 42 U.S.C. § 1985. The basis of federal jurisdiction for violations of 42 U.S.C. § 1985 is 28 U.S.C. § 1343. For the reasons discussed below, we hold appellants have failed to state a claim under 42 U.S.C. §§ 1985(1), (2) or (3), and affirm the district court's dismissal.

Appellants alleged that the tribal defendants, as members of the Tribal Council, by voting in favor of the two Tribal Council resolutions at issue, conspired to prevent by force, intimidation or threat their election to the Tribal Council, a position which appellants assert is an "office, trust or place of confidence under the United States," in violation of 42 U.S.C. § 1985(1). Appellants argue that Tribal Council members occupy a position of "confidence under the United

States" because Indian affairs are intimately supervised by the United States and because of the fiduciary relationship that exists between the United States and the Indian tribes. Appellants also alleged that the tribal defendants, as members of the Tribal Council, by voting in favor of the two Tribal Council resolutions at issue, conspired to injure appellants by preventing their election to the Tribal Council in retaliation for appellants' participation in the earlier Committee to Save Our Constitution lawsuit in federal court in violation of 42 U.S.C. § 1985(2). Appellants also alleged that the tribal defendants, all members of the Tribal Council, by voting in favor of the two Tribal Council resolutions at issue, conspired to deprive appellants of the "equal protection of the laws, or of equal privileges and immunities under the law," by barring or disqualifying appellants from tribal office on the basis of political opposition in violation of 42 U.S.C. § 1985(3). See *Means v. Wilson,* 522 F.2d 833, 839-40 (8th Cir. 1975) (holding that 42 U.S.C. § 1985(3) protects the right to vote in tribal elections against interference from private conspiracies and that political dissidents constituted a class for purposes of 42 U.S.C. 1985(3)), *cert. denied,* 424 U.S. 958 (1976). But cf. *Spotted Eagle v. Blackfeet Tribe,* 301 F. Supp. 85, 88 (D. Mont. 1969) (limited applicability of § 1985 in tribal context).

We need not consider whether the *Means v. Wilson* holding that 42 U.S.C. § 1985(3) prohibits political discrimination has been implicitly limited by *United Brotherhood of Carpenters v. Scott,* 463 U.S. 825 (1983), in which the Supreme Court held that § 1985(3) did not reach "conspiracies motivated by economic or commercial animus" and found "difficult the question whether § 1985(3) provided a remedy for every concerted effort by one political group to nullify the influence of or do other injury to a competing group by use of otherwise unlawful means," because appellants have failed to adequately allege a conspiracy. The tribal defendants are all members of the Tribal Council, the governing body of the tribe, who acted, in passing the two Tribal Council resolutions at issue, in their official capacities as tribal council members. The Tribal Council as an entity or governmental body cannot conspire with itself.

Moreover, individual members of the Tribal Council, acting in their official capacity as tribal council members, cannot conspire when they act together with other tribal council members in taking official action on behalf of the Tribal Council. "[T]here is no conspiracy if the conspiratorial conduct challenged is essentially a single act by a single corporation acting exclusively through its own directors, officers, and employees, each acting within the scope of his [or her] employment." *Herrmann v. Moore,* 576 F.2d 453, 459 (2d Cir.) (acting against law school and 38 individuals affiliated with the law school, including the dean and university trustees), *cert. denied,* 439 U.S. 1003 (1978). [The court distinguishes] *Means v. Wilson,* 522 F.2d at 840, [because] "the only possible adequate allegation of a conspiracy under 42 U.S.C. § 1985(3)" involved the tribal council president who was alleged to have conspired with other private individuals. By comparison, in the present case the allegations of conspiracy involve only tribal council members.

In addition, we believe that the individual members of the Tribal Council would enjoy absolute legislative immunity from liability under 42 U.S.C. § 1985 for official actions taken when acting in a legislative capacity.

Because appellants' claims against the federal defendants under 42 U.S.C. § 1986 are dependent upon their 42 U.S.C. § 1985 claims against the tribal defendants, which we have concluded failed to state a claim upon which relief could be granted, appellants' § 1986 claim must fail as well.

[*Affirmed.*]

LeCOMPTE v. JEWETT

12 Indian L. Rep. 6025
(Cheyenne River Sioux Ct. App., May 30, 1985)

Before GARRETT, GONZALEZ, GREAVES, Appellate Judges.
PER CURIAM.

Amended Memorandum Opinion

Appellant, Quentin LeCompte, initiated this action by filing a complaint in the tribal court on April 5, 1985. LeCompte filed a motion for a temporary restraining order with his complaint. The tribal court granted the temporary restraining order which provided that "the Defendants be restrained from taking any further action regarding [the] election which will be held on April 16, 1985." On April 11, 1985, however, the tribal court dissolved the temporary restraining order. This appeal followed.

The Cheyenne River Sioux Tribe [is organized under the IRA]. The constitution and bylaws provides for representation on the tribal council, the governing body created by the constitution, and the election of council representatives. *See* tribal constitution art. II; tribal bylaws art. II.

Article III, section 7 of the constitution provides that "[the] tribal council shall have supervision and authority over all subsequent elections as provided through by-laws or resolutions hereafter enacted." Pursuant to this authority, [the Council enacted] Ordinance No. 14 to govern the tribal primary election held on June 4, 1984, and the subsequent general election.[1]

Appellant, Quentin LeCompte, qualified as a candidate for District No. 6 under Ordinance No. 14. In the primary election, LeCompte came in fourth out of a total of 10 candidates.

Prior to the September 4, 1984 general election, however, the Cheyenne River Sioux Tribal Council enacted Resolution No. 190-84-CR [disqualifying] one of the top vote-getters in the primary election held in District No. 6, *viz:* Joan LeBeau.

At the September 4, 1984 general election, Quentin LeCompte won over Manson Garreau. The Cheyenne River Tribal Election Board certified LeCompte as the winner and he subsequently took his oath of office and was seated as the official representative from District No. 6.

Joan LeBeau [filed suit in federal court against] the United States, [BIA officials], and tribal council representatives [seeking] to enjoin the September 4, 1984 general election [claiming a violation of] civil rights. The district court denied the motion for injunctive relief on the basis that the court lacked subject

---

[1] Article III, section 4 mandates that tribal council representatives shall be elected at a general election held every two years on the first Tuesday after the first Monday in the month of September.

matter jurisdiction. [*See Runs After v. United States.*] They then appealed to the United States Court of Appeals for the Eighth Circuit.

While the appeal was pending before the Eighth Circuit Court of Appeals, the parties entered into a tentative agreement whereby the tribal appellees agreed to rescind Resolution No. 190-84-CR and authorize a new general election in Districts 6 and 5.[4] Based on the tribal council's action, the tribal election board scheduled a new general election for Districts 5 and 6 for Tuesday, April 16, 1985. It is this election that LeCompte seeks to enjoin.

There are two issues which must be decided in this appeal: (1) Did the tribal court err in holding that the doctrine of sovereign immunity bars Quentin LeCompte from seeking injunctive relief against the tribal election board to enjoin them from conducting the general election scheduled for District 7 on May 16, 1985 and (2) did the tribal court err in holding that the tribal election board has authority to schedule the May 16, 1985 general election for District No. 6 at its discretion?

A Sovereign Immunity

Indian tribes, like the Cheyenne River Sioux Tribe[,] possess attributes of sovereignty with attendant powers. [*Santa Clara Pueblo v. Martinez.*] Among the attributes of sovereignty possessed by Indian tribes is "the common-law immunity from suit traditionally enjoyed by sovereign powers." [*Santa Clara Pueblo v. Martinez* held] that nothing in the Indian Civil Rights Act of 1968, subjects tribes to the jurisdiction of the federal courts in civil actions for injunctive or declaratory relief. [*Martinez* stated:] "Tribal courts have repeatedly been recognized as appropriate forums for the exclusive adjudication of disputes affecting important personal property interests of both Indians and non-Indians."

In their brief, appellees argue that section 1-8-4 of the Law and Order Code of the Cheyenne River Sioux Tribe (hereinafter tribal code) grants absolute immunity from suit to appellees. We disagree. We expressly hold that the 1968 Indian Civil Right Act waives such immunity.

Section 1-8-4 provides:

Sec. 1-8-4. Sovereign Immunity

Except as required by federal law, or the Constitution and By-Laws of the Cheyenne River Sioux Tribe, or specifically waived by a resolution or ordinance of the Tribal Council specifically referring to such, the Cheyenne River Sioux Tribe shall be immune from suit in any civil action, and its officers and employees immune from suit for any liability arising from the performance of their official duties. [Emphasis supplied.]

The Court in *Santa Clara Pueblo v. Martinez, supra,* did not decide the issue of whether the 1968 Civil Rights Act waived tribal sovereign immunity in tribal courts in suits for injunctive and declaratory relief. We hold that both the 1968

---

[4] In a post-argument memorandum counsel for Quentin LeCompte informed the court that an agreement between the parties was never executed and negotiations to reach a settlement have now broken down. This court, nevertheless, is bound by the council's action rescinding Resolution No. 190-84-CR.

Indian Civil Rights Act and the Constitution of the Cheyenne River Sioux Tribe waived such sovereign immunity in tribal court.[7]

[Congress] intended that aggrieved parties should have access to a tribal forum.[8] [C]ounsel for appellees [argued] that, absent tribal court jurisdiction Quentin LeCompte would have no judicial remedy available. We cannot conceive that Congress enacted the 1968 Indian Civil Rights Act for the protection of individual liberties but did not intend that individuals would have no remedy available in tribal court.

As a matter of tribal law, we also find that the Indian people of the Cheyenne River Indian Reservation intended that the people should have a right to a tribal judicial forum to judicially review actions of the tribal council. Counsel for appellees argues, however, that no separation of powers exists between the tribal council and tribal court. We find this argument unpersuasive.

In the case of *Marbury v. Madison,* the Court found that "it is emphatically the province and duty of the judicial department to say what the law is" and went on to hold that the Constitution is the fundamental and paramount law of the nation and "any act of the legislature repugnant to the constitution is void." This principle applies to the tribal court and mandates a duty to review actions of the tribal council which are repugnant to the tribal constitution. [In the bylaws, the Indian people] intended the term "between Indians" to mean "between Indian parties" which included the tribe, tribal entities and tribal officials acting in their official capacities.

We also hold [that] appellant [has] an implied remedy directly under the tribal constitution to seek judicial review of the tribal council's actions absent a statutory remedy.

We accordingly reverse the tribal court and hold that sovereign immunity does not bar suits for injunctive and declaratory relief against appellees.

B. *The Authority of the Cheyenne River Election Board to Conduct the May 16, 1985 Election*

Quentin LeCompte argues that general elections can only be held "every two years on the first Tuesday after the first Monday in the month of September," i.e., September 4, 1984, and that the only exception for election of new councilmen to fill vacancies is by "resignation, recall, impeachment or death." *See* article IV, section 13 of the tribal constitution.

[T]he Tribal constitution applies only to situations where a primary and general election is conducted properly in the first place. In these instances, a candidate obtains a vested property right to his office and cannot be replaced except upon "resignation, recall, impeachment or death." This is not the case here.

---

[7] It is clear that the tribe enjoys complete sovereign immunity in tribal court in all actions for *monetary damages* under section 1-8-4, however. Moreover, we find nothing in the 1968 Indian Civil Rights Act or tribal constitution that authorizes actions for monetary damages in tribal court.

[8] At oral argument, counsel for appellees argued that the *Martinez* case does not require a tribal judicial tribunal as an exclusive forum. We are aware that the Court in *Martinez* stated that "[n]onjudicial tribal institutions have also been recognized as competent law-applying bodies." The Cheyenne River Sioux people, however, authorized the tribal council to establish a tribal court on the reservation under article V of the tribal bylaws and the tribal council under this authority adopted a westernized court system. *See* Tribal Code, Title I, chapter 2, § 1-2-1 *et seq.* Thus it is the intent of the tribal council that the tribal courts should have the exclusive authority to settle legal disputes.

In this case, the tribal council has admitted by its rescission of Resolution No. 190-84-CR that the rights of Joan LeBeau, one of LeCompte's competitors, were violated. The tribal council is the sole judge of the qualifications of its own members, article II, section(c) of tribal bylaws; section 2(b)(4) of Ordinance No. 14, and has now made a decision that Joan LeBeau must be allowed to run for the position of councilwoman for District No. 6. Joan LeBeau's right to due process and equal protection of the laws under the 1968 Indian Civil Rights Act, 25 U.S.C. § 1302(8), would be violated if a new election is not held.

Hence, the election board has a duty to schedule a new general election for Districts No. 5 and 6 at the earliest date possible and has reasonably set that date as May 16, 1985. Accordingly, this court affirms the tribal court holding that the tribal election board can schedule a new tribal election.

Although the parties did not raise this issue, this court notes that the tribal council approved a motion to *strike* the names of Bertha Chasing Hawk, [and] Grady Claymore, from the ballots of the May 16, 1985 general election. [T]here appears to be no apparent justification for the tribal council to strike the names of Chasing Hawk and Claymore from the election ballots once they are certified by the election board. These candidates must therefore be accorded the same treatment as other certified candidates who are being allowed to run for office in the May 16, 1985 general election in districts No. 5 and 6.[11]

[*Reversed in part and affirmed in part.*]

KAVENA v. HOPI INDIAN TRIBAL COURT

16 Indian L. Rep. 6063 (Mar. 21, 1989)

[According to the Hopi Constitution, reprinted above in section B, each village can decide whether to retain its traditional government under the leadership of the Kikmongwi. The constitution provides mechanisms for a village to adopt a new constitution. If requested by the Kikmongwi of the village or 25% of the voting members, the Superintendent (a BIA official) must publicize the proposed changes and call for a referendum election. See Article IV, § 4.

[A group of First Mesa residents, the Peoples Rights Committee (PRC) presented a proposed constitution and requested an election. The Superintendent determined that the petitioners represented 25% of the voters by comparing the number of valid signatures, 269, to the number of people who had been registered to vote in the last tribal chairman election, 705. He then scheduled a special election.

[A second group of First Mesa residents, Walpi Hopi Sovereign Rights Committee (SRC) tried to block the election, arguing that a list of *village* residents registered to vote in the last *tribal* election was not an accurate roll of village members eligible to vote in a village election, that an accurate roll could only come from the Kikmongwi of the Village, who is in charge of determining

---

[11] Both the District No. 6 council and the tribal election board certified Claymore as a candidate. The tribal council, without notifying Claymore or affording him an opportunity to be heard, disqualified him as a candidate. See July 12, 1984 minutes of the Cheyenne River Sioux Tribal Council, pp. 123-26. Since the tribal council, pursuant to section 3 of the tribal bylaws, delegated the authority to certify candidates to the tribal election board by adoption of Ordinance No. 14, section 2(d), the election board and not the tribal council had final authority to determine the qualifications of Claymore.

village membership under the constitution, and that such a list, when obtained would contain more than 1000 voters, thus rendering the petition for a new constitution invalid for lack of the requisite 25% of the voters.

The tribal court ordered a stay of the election for 90 days, because the voting list was invalid and because insufficient time had been given village residents to study the proposed constitution. The court also ordered the SRC to draft proposed guidelines to determine voter qualifications and election procedures. The SRC filed the guidelines with the court and included a village voter membership list supplied by the Kikmongwi with 1305 names. At that point the SRC asked the tribal court to issue a final order enjoining the election. The lower court refused, stating it would stay its hand until after the election was held. The SRC then sought an extraordinary writ in the Hopi Appellate Court.]

PER CURIAM.

IV. *Reasons for the Stay of the November 14 Election*

In granting our stay of the November 14 election we stated our intention to issue an opinion in due course setting forth our reasons for issuing that stay and giving directions to the tribal court regarding further proceedings in *Kavena v. Hamilton*. That opinion is as follows:

The Constitution of the Hopi Tribe provides the only method by which a village which is under the traditional Hopi organization may adopt a different form of village government. A decision by a village to adopt a new form of government is a decision with extremely important potential consequences for the village, its members and residents, and the entire Hopi Tribe. It is essential, therefore, that the procedures provided by the Hopi Constitution be strictly followed.

These procedures, however, were not adequately followed in this case. The most fundamental defect in the procedures that were used here concerns the BIA superintendent's determination of whether enough voting members of the village had petitioned to ask for a village referendum election.

The method prescribed by the Hopi Constitution for changing the form of village government is the adoption, through such an election, of a village constitution. Such an election is to be held only if either the Kikmongwi of the village or "25% of the voting members thereof" request that an election be conducted. In this case the PRC submitted a petition to the superintendent of the Hopi jurisdiction asking that a referendum election be held. That petition contained 269 valid signatures.

The superintendent correctly decided that, in determining whether this petition was sufficient, it would be necessary to ascertain the total number of voting members of First Mesa village. The superintendent sought to find this number, however, by asking the Hopi Tribal Council for a list of the First Mesa residents who were registered to vote in the last election for tribal chairman and vice-chairman. Despite explicit contrary advice given by the tribal chairman, the superintendent used this list as the basis of First Mesa village voting members.

The superintendent's use of this list was an incorrect implementation of the procedures provided by the Hopi Constitution. Hopi village membership for purposes of ascertaining those eligible to vote in a referendum on a proposed village constitution is a special concept that is not equivalent to residence in the village at the time of a tribal election. Village membership in a village, such as First Mesa, with the traditional Hopi organization, is a concept with much deeper meaning than mere physical presence or residence. Such membership involves the maintenance of religious and cultural ties and relationships with the village and its ceremonies. Many village members, for example, do not reside in the village of their membership. This can occur for a number of reasons, including the Hopi matrilineal tradition pursuant to which a husband will reside in the village of his wife's membership while retaining membership in his mother's village. Hopis may also reside off the reservation at their place of employment, while retaining membership in the village of their birth. Conversely, some of those who do physically reside in a traditional Hopi village may not be village members, often because they are members of other villages.

The proper procedure for the superintendent to use in determining who are the voting members of a village is for him to ask the Kikmongwi of that village to provide a list of the voting membership. The Kikmongwi is explicitly recognized in the Hopi Constitution as the leader of a village that is still under a traditional form of organization. The Kikmongwi, moreover, has an explicit constitutional role to play in admitting individuals to village and tribal membership.

After receiving an initial list of voting village members from the Kikmongwi, the superintendent should make that list known to those who might wish to seek its modification. As Chief Judge Ames properly held below, challenges to the Kikmongwi's list of village members may be based on the Hopi Constitution and By-Laws, other Hopi laws, or the Indian Civil Rights Act. The proper legal forum for resolution of such challenges is the Hopi Tribal Court.

In this case, Chief Judge Ames correctly held that the list of village members for referendum voting purposes should have been based on a list supplied by the Kikmongwi. We believe, however, that the decision of whether a sufficient percentage (25 percent) of the voting members of a village had signed the election petition should then have been made before the election was held. An election on so fundamental a matter as whether the traditional form of Hopi village organization should be abandoned is a major event in the history of a Hopi village and in the lives of many village members. A matter of such importance and potential disruptive effect should not go forward unless it is clear that the preconditions required by the Hopi Constitution have been met. It would also be extremely unfortunate to hold an election on a matter of such importance to the daily lives of village residents and then to place the outcome in doubt for a protracted period while legal proceedings took place. This is especially true if the "results" of the challenged election were announced or became known.

In addition to the fact that the adequacy of the referendum petition was not properly determined prior to the election, there were other important defects in the procedures leading up to the scheduled November 14 election....

Our determination to stay the November 14 First Mesa election was made in light of all of these defects in the procedure that was followed. In view of the fundamental nature of these defects, any future referendum election to change the form of government of First Mesa Village should not be called unless the procedures provided by the Hopi Constitution are newly initiated and followed, starting with the first step of those procedures — the submission of the proposed village constitution to the superintendent at the same time as it is made known to all voting members of the village. We note further that, for these purposes, it may be necessary for those proposing a village constitution to obtain a list of voting village members from the Kikmongwi at the outset of their efforts, so that those not residing in the village can be informed of the proposal from the beginning.

Having stayed the November 14, 1988 election, we now order that, upon proper motion by counsel, the tribal court should further grant their request for an order permanently enjoining that election and should grant all appropriate relief consistent with this opinion.

NOTES

1. Effect of *Martinez* on Federal Court Jurisdiction over Internal Political Disputes: Before *Martinez*, federal courts routinely asserted jurisdiction under the Civil Rights Act over intratribal political disputes. *See, e.g., Rosebud Sioux Tribe v. Driving Hawk*, 534 F.2d 98 (8th Cir. 1976) (election dispute); *Means v. Wilson*, 522 F.2d 833 (8th Cir. 1975), *cert. denied*, 424 U.S. 958 (1976) (applying equal protection clause principle of "one man-one vote" to Sioux tribal election); *Howlett v. Salish & Kootenai Tribes*, 529 F.2d 233 (9th Cir. 1976) (upholding tribal residency requirement because of compelling governmental purpose). Since 1976, however, federal courts have left the resolution of such disputes to the tribe, *see, e.g., Black Hills Sioux Nation Treaty Council v. Stevens*, 16 Indian L. Rep. 2131 (8th Cir. 1989) (suit dismissed as dealing with a political struggle to be resolved by the tribal court), albeit somewhat grudgingly in certain cases where it appeared the complainant had no remedy for what looked like a particularly egregious misuse of power. For example, in *Shortbull v. Looking Elk*, 677 F.2d 645 (8th Cir.), *cert. denied*, 459 U.S. 907 (1982), a tribal court judge interpreting two tribal ordinances ordered the election board to permit a non-enrolled member of the tribe to run for president. Tribal officials who did not comply were then held in contempt, at which point the tribal Executive Committee removed the judge and substituted another judge who interpreted the tribal ordinances as preventing Shortbull from seeking office. In denying jurisdiction over the dispute, the court felt constrained to state:

> We must, however, express serious concern that Shortbull's rights under § 1302 of the Indian Civil Rights Act (ICRA) may never be vindicated. Shortbull alleges that the tribal court, Chief Judge Red Shirt, ruled that he was entitled to run in the primary election because of the Tribal Council's January 24 resolution. It appears that because of this ruling, Judge Red Shirt was removed from office and was replaced by a judge more sympathetic to the Tribal Executive Committee, who quashed Judge Red Shirt's orders. Such actions raise serious questions under the Indian Civil Rights Act, but because the Supreme Court determined in *Martinez* that there is no private right of action under the ICRA, Shortbull has no remedy....
>
> We are thus presented with a situation in which Shortbull has no remedy within the tribal machinery nor with the tribal officials in whose election he cannot participate unless and until Congress provides otherwise. We question whether such a result is justified on the grounds of maintaining tribal autonomy and self-government: it frustrates the ICRA's purpose of "protect[ing] individual Indians from arbitrary and

unjust actions of tribal governments," and in this case it renders the rights provided by the ICRA meaningless. [*Martinez*] at 73, 83 (citations omitted) (White, J., dissenting).

2. Aftermath of the Cheyenne River Election Dispute: Is the risk of misuse of power sufficiently grave that Congress should authorize federal court supervision of Indian tribal elections? *Runs After* arose out of political turmoil on the Cheyenne River Sioux Reservation. The Civil Rights Commission heard testimony from the plaintiffs in South Dakota in 1986. Enforcement of the Indian Civil Rights Act: Hearing Before the United States Commission on Civil Rights at Rapid City, South Dakota, July 31-August 1, 26, 1986) 136-47 (Testimony of Joan LeBeau). Certainly, a reading of the Eighth Circuit case could lead a fairminded person to decry the tribe's actions. Nevertheless, the tribal appellate court opinion, never referred to by the Eighth Circuit, indicates the council had rescinded the resolution and scheduled a new general election. Although subsequent actions delayed the election, the plaintiffs in *Runs After* were elected. Judge Mario Gonzalez, who sits on the Cheyenne River Sioux Tribe Appellate Court, characterized the outcome as follows:

> There are individuals who were involved in that particular case, like Joan LeBeau, and we expressly held that her rights were violated under the Civil Rights Act, and she couldn't get such a remedy in the Federal courts or anywhere else. But in our court she got it. She was subject to a council resolution barring her from ever running for tribal office again. The council rescinded that action. Our court affirmed that her rights were violated. And she is sitting on the council now.

Id. at 247-48 (Testimony of Mario Gonzalez at hearing held on August 21, 1986).

3. Tribal Court Resolution of Internal Disputes: As *Kavena* illustrates, tribal courts can be effective guardians of tribal constitutional provisions. In *Chapoose v. Ute Indian Tribe*, 13 Indian L. Rep. 6023 (Ute Tribal Ct. 1986), the tribal judge courageously overturned a tribal business committee action on an enrollment matter, citing *Marbury v. Madison*. The court invalidated a tribal ordinance withdrawing jurisdiction from the tribal court as violating due process of law because it denied an impartial forum to persons seeking enrollment. In fact, this decision goes farther in protecting civil rights against legislative infringement than the federal constitution, at least as some interpret the Supreme Court's decision in *Ex parte McCardle*, 74 U.S. (7 Wall.) 506 (1869). The court then held the business committee in contempt of court for failing to comply with an earlier stipulation to enroll the children.

In a recent case, the Southern Ute Tribal Court held that, absent any tribal statute barring it from taking jurisdiction of a case alleging Indian Civil Rights Act and tribal statutory violations in the handling of a recall election, it had the power to do so. *Committee for Better Tribal Gov't v. Southern Ute Election Bd.*, 17 Indian L. Rep. 6095 (S. Ute Tr. Ct., Aug. 13, 1990). The court noted that the tribal code provision establishing the court charged the court "to administer justice equally and fairly in conformance with the Constitution of the Southern Ute Indian Tribe ... and to protect the rights, property, and welfare of all people within its jurisdiction." *Id.*, at 6096 (citing Southern Ute Indian Tribal Code, section 1-3-107 (1989 ed.)). The court also noted that the tribal code required tribal judges to take oaths to support the Constitution, laws, and treaties of the tribe. Although the court then held that some of the claims were barred by sovereign immunity, it held that the due process claims alleging that the election board had acted beyond the scope of its powers was fairly within the ultra vires exception to the doctrine. *See also Sekaquaptewa v. Hopi Tribal*

Election Bd., 13 Indian L. Rep. 6009 (Hopi Tr. Ct., Jan. 31, 1986) (invalidating tribal ordinance to the extent it could be interpreted as prohibiting eligible voters of the Hopi Tribe from voting in election for tribal chairman) (Abinanti, J., Chief Magistrate of Hoopa Valley Indian Reservation Court of Indian Offenses, sitting by special appointment as Hopi Judge Pro-Tem.); *Conroy v. Bear Runner*, 16 Indian L. Rep. 6037 (Oglala Tr. Ct. App., Feb. 3, 1984) (Occupation Tax Ordinance violated tribal constitution because not put to referendum; enforcement discriminatory and violative of ICRA equal protection clause).

4. BIA Involvement in Tribal Elections: In testimony before the Civil Rights Commission, Professor Clinton took the following position on the role of the BIA in ensuring tribal compliance with ICRA:

[The BIA] has a role, albeit a quite limited role, to play in the enforcement of the Indian Civil Rights Act. That role, however, is primarily one of education, funding, support, and diplomacy, backed ultimately by the power to recommend temporary cessation of the government-to-government relations with offending tribal governments until civil rights abuses have been corrected. The power vested in the BIA should not and does not provide legal remedies in individual cases other than those involving the exercise of approval powers expressly delegated to the Secretary of the Interior by federal statutory law or tribal constitutions. Any effort to enlarge the role of the BIA in enforcing the ICRA beyond that described here would clearly run afoul of treaty protected promises of tribal self-government, the well established principle of tribal sovereignty, Congressional policy and mandate contained in the Indian Reorganization Act and related statutes, and [the] general thrust announced in federal Indian policy of fostering and supporting Indian tribal self-government by respecting the government-to-government relations between federal and tribal institutions.

Statement of Robert N. Clinton, in Enforcement of the Indian Civil Rights Act, Hearing Before the United States Commission on Civil Rights, Washington, D.C., Jan. 28, 1988, 283-96.

Note that Professor Clinton's position is both more restrained and more activist than the Bureau's current policy. His position on the use of the approval power is more restrained: he argues that the Bureau should carefully confine its exercise of the approval power to those situations in which the approval is statutorily mandated or delegated by a tribal constitution. Even then, he argues, the Bureau must rely on statutory standards such as the ICRA itself instead of its own notions of good government. As the materials in Chapter 2, section B, and in section B2 of this chapter, indicate, the Bureau has at times taken a broader view of its approval powers. Professor Clinton also argues that the Bureau can and should use its authority to recognize tribal governments to encourage them to comply with the ICRA. Although the Bureau does not engage in such a monitoring function at present, Professor Clinton argues that an increased role, if performed with the same sensitivity toward tribal governments as is used when foreign governments are involved, would strike an appropriate balance between respecting tribal sovereignty and protecting human rights on the reservation. What are the strengths and weaknesses of his position regarding the appropriate role for the BIA?

3. TRIBAL POWER TO CONTROL ENTRY

CROW CREEK SIOUX TRIBE v. BUUM

10 Indian L. Rep. 6031 (Intertr. Ct. App., Apr. 1, 1983)

GREGORY, Appellate Judge (pro tem.).

This appeal stems from two judgments entered by the Honorable Melvin W. Joseph, Tribal Judge at the Crow Creek Sioux Tribal Court. The initial judgment entered July 20, 1982 ordered the defendant-appellant, Roger Buum, a non-Indian, be excluded from the boundaries of the Crow Creek Sioux Reservation for a period of one year. The second judgment entered August 17, 1982 found appellant, Roger Buum, hereafter referred to as "appellant," in contempt of the judgment dated July 20, 1982. The tribal judge ordered that the appellant be imprisoned for 10 days and pay a fine of $50.

Factual Basis for the Appeal

On July 20, 1982, the Honorable Melvin W. Joseph, Crow Creek Tribal Court Judge, entered a judgment on a civil complaint [that] had been filed by Ft. Thompson Police Captain, Norman V. Taylor, with the Crow Creek Sioux Tribal Court on July 16, 1982. The complaint alleged the appellant was a "public nuisance." A summons was served on the appellant on July 16, 1982 requiring appellant to answer the complaint on July 20, 1982. For one reason or another, appellant did not appear at the hearing on time. Appellant further did not appear within an extended period of time granted by the tribal court judge. As a result, a judgment was entered against the appellant ordering him excluded from the lands of the Crow Creek Sioux Tribal Reservation for an initial period of one year. Judge Joseph further ordered that the judgment could be reviewed annually. Appellant was served with a copy of the judgment on July 20, 1982.

On August 16, 1982, appellant was arrested and lodged in the Ft. Thompson jail for being in violation of the July 20, 1982 exclusion order. The following day, August 17, 1982, appellant was brought before Judge Melvin W. Joseph. Judge Joseph found the appellant in contempt. As a result, the Judge sentenced appellant to 10 days in the Ft. Thompson jail and fined the appellant $50. The appellant was thereafter imprisoned under a judgment captioned as civil. Appellant was given a stay of execution of his sentence pending the appeal to the Intertribal Court of Appeals. Appellant was released August 18, 1982. Further facts as necessary and where relevant will be referred to in conjunction with legal arguments addressed.

Issue I:

Does the Crow Creek Sioux Tribal Council and Crow Creek Sioux Tribal Court Have the Authority to Exclude an Individual, Specifically a Non-Indian Individual, From the Lands of the Crow Creek Sioux Tribal Reservation?

The Crow Creek Tribal Constitution specifically authorizes exclusion of a person from the Crow Creek Reservation. Article VI, section 1(n) states:

> The Council of the Crow Creek Reservation shall exercise the following powers subject to any limitations imposed by statutes or the Constitution of the United States and subject further to all express restrictions upon such powers contained in this constitution and the attached bylaws. (a) ... (m). (n) to exclude from the restricted lands of the Crow Creek Reservation persons not legally entitled to reside therein under the ordinances which shall be subject to the approval of the Commissioner of Indian Affairs.

The ordinances referred to in the Crow Creek Constitution need only be passed, approved and implemented in a lawful manner, with necessary government approval and be sufficient to meet any constitutional requirements test applied against the ordinance. The ordinance need not be specifically labelled as an exclusion ordinance since the remedy involved is the more likely exclusion power and speaks for itself.

The question then becomes whether the power of the Crow Creek Sioux Tribal Council has been delegated to the Crow Creek Sioux Tribal Court. The establishment of the Crow Creek Sioux Tribal Court was reaffirmed by section 02-01-01. In section 02-01-01(1), the tribal court was given jurisdiction "in all actions at law and in equity." Subsection 6 specifically states, "In all cases now or hereafter provided by law granting jurisdiction to the Crow Creek Sioux Tribal Court," the tribal court has jurisdiction.

Both the respondent and appellant agree that the Crow Creek Sioux Tribal Council has the inherent right to exclude member Indians and non-member Indians from the reservation. Respondent asserts that the Crow Creek Tribal Council and the Crow Creek Tribal Court have the inherent power to exclude persons not entitled to reside therein from the Crow Creek Sioux Reservation. Appellant concurs with respondent's position so far as what the Crow Creek Sioux Tribal Constitution expressly allows. *See* Crow Creek Sioux Tribal Constitution, Article VI, § 1(n). The appellant, upon questioning from the appellate bench, stated in paraphrased terms that the appellant was not arguing an extension of [*Oliphant v. Suquamish Indian Tribe*] to include civil action within the parameters of the *Oliphant* decision.

If, then, the action of the respondent was indeed civil, the general power and authority to exclude a non-Indian from its lands has historically existed and exists today. There is nothing to indicate that the Crow Creek Sioux Tribe or its proper delegate, the Crow Creek Sioux Tribal Court, has given away, been divested of, or expressly limited its right to oust non-Indians from its lands.

Non-members who lawfully enter tribal lands remain subject to the tribe's power to exclude them. This power necessarily includes the lesser power to place conditions on entry, on continued presence, or on reservation conduct, such as tax on business activities conducted on the reservation. When a tribe grants a non-Indian the right to be on Indian land, the tribe agrees not to exercise its ultimate power to oust the non-Indian as long as the non-Indian complies with the initial conditions of entry. However, it does not follow that the lawful property right to be on Indian land also immunizes the non-Indian from the tribe's exercise of its lesser included power to tax or to place other conditions on the non-Indians conduct or continued presence on the reservation. [See also *Barta v. Oglala Sioux Tribe of Pine Ridge Reservation*, 259 F.2d 553 (CA 8, 1958).] A non-member who enters the jurisdiction of the tribe remains subject to the risk that the tribe will later exercise it sovereign power.

Merrion v. Jicarilla Apache Tribe et al., 102 S. Ct. 894, 903 (1982).

Issue II.
Can the Appellant Be Adjudged a Public Nuisance and Thereafter Be Excluded From the Crow Creek Sioux Reservations as a Matter of Remedy or Relief?

The Crow Creek Sioux Tribal Code sets forth in section 07-07-01 the definition of a nuisance. [The tribal code defines a nuisance as] "unlawfully doing an act, or omitting to perform a duty, which act or omission either: 1. Annoys, injures, or endangers the comfort, repose, health or safety of others ... 4. In any way renders other persons insecure in life, or in the use of property." [Nuisances are classified as public or private, a public nuisance being defined as one that] "affects the entire community or neighborhood, or any considerable number of persons. [All] other nuisances are private." [Nuisances may be remedied by either a civil action or abatement. Either a public body or officer or a private person can bring an action to abate a nuisance.] "In all such actions the nuisance may be enjoined or ordered abated, and damages recovered in addition."

A common sense reading of section 07-07-01 indicates that a nuisance may indeed be a person. [Therefore,] the tribal court was justified in finding that appellant violated section 07-07-01(1) and (4). Appellant's actions constituted a public nuisance [as well. Under these] ordinances [the tribe] had the option to abate the nuisance by civil action. Pursuant to the Crow Creek Sioux Tribal Code, "In all such actions the nuisance may be enjoined or ordered abated, and damages recovered in addition."

Therefore, it is established that the Crow Creek Tribal Court is certainly possessed with an inherent and expressed power to exclude Indians and non-Indians from reservation lands. [Without the power to protect its people, the] Indian would then be virtually enslaved to the impunities of the non-Indian on Indian land and among Indian people. Even the convenient historical perspective used to support *Oliphant, supra*, may not be stretched this far. *Merrion, supra*, makes that clear. Therefore, the appellant being adjudged a public nuisance could thereafter be lawfully excluded from the lands of the reservations as a lawful remedy.

Issue III:
Does the Crow Creek Sioux Tribal Court Have the Authority to Impose a Civil Judgment on a Non-Indian When Said Judgment May Include a Fine and Term of Imprisonment?

The foregoing pages of this opinion make clear that, indeed, the Crow Creek Sioux Tribal Court had the authority to impose a civil judgment on a non-Indian. The better question becomes what determines and distinguishes a civil judgment from a criminal action against a non-Indian. Generally, the mere fact of a fine and jail sentence will not in and of itself determine the action to be a criminal procedure. We must look further to distinguish in what situation a judgment which includes a fine and incarceration in jail is civil and when criminal.

South Dakota statutory law and case law provide an example of civil contempt versus criminal contempt. In South Dakota, statutory contempt is a class one misdemeanor. The bases for that statutory contempt are found in SDCL § 16-15-1 et seq.

[In sum, t]he general distinction then between criminal and civil contempt is basically twofold. (1) In a civil contempt proceeding, the judge or hearing officer is specifically attempting to make the individual comply with a civil order. Unconditional punishment is a characteristic of criminal contempt. (2) A civil contempt procedure should allow for remissions or suspension of fine and confinement upon performance or purging of the contempt as the court may decide to incorporate it therein. The procedure should allow the court or tribunal to make any such remissions or suspension by supplemental order, judgment or decree as it may seem warranted. [W]here proper procedure is established, and proper authority granted, the Crow Creek Sioux Tribal Court could indeed impose a civil judgment on a non-Indian. That judgment may well include a fine and imprisonment.

Issue IV:
Was the Contempt Adjudged in the Case on Appeal Civil or Criminal in Nature?

The court must now address the factual situation as it relates to the Crow Creek Sioux Tribal contempt statute and its procedure. The Crow Creek Tribal Code, section 04-09-01 sets forth reasons for a contempt charge.

The remaining sections, 04-09-02, 04-09-03, 04-09-04, and 04-09-05, resemble contempt provisions found in SDCL § 23A-38-1 *et seq.*, a criminal procedure chapter. [T]here is and has been for some time a fine line between civil contempt and criminal contempt. Sometimes a criminal contempt charge may occur or arise out of a civil action. Nevertheless, there are means to determine the differences. [The problem] is that the Crow Creek Sioux Tribal Code does not provide for findings of fact and conclusions of law. It further does not provide for a purging from civil contempt. The respondent would have this court determine the contempt charge and procedure to be civil, since it is named as such. The appellant would have us determine that the contempt charge was criminal in nature based on its application. The naming of an action as civil is insufficient to conclusively determine that the procedure is civil. [*See, e.g., Stake v. Bullis*, 315 N.W.2d 485 (S.D. 1982).]

Respondent would have this court determine that the entire procedure was criminal in nature. All the facts of the case do not totally determine that to be true. Appellant's attorney in well written form and sound oral argument sets forth those elements of due process which must be afforded an individual under criminal procedure. The necessity of making that determination is addressed [next].

Issue V:
What Rights Must Be Afforded to the Appellant Under Tribal or Federal Law?

This court [decides that under] either criminal or civil contempt charges and the appropriate procedure, certain elements are lacking. Since a criminal contempt charge and actions taken as a result of that charge would not apply to a non-Indian individual in a tribal court, this court need not address due process rights and requirements. That issue is mooted by present federal law as interpreted by the United States Supreme Court. *See Oliphant, supra.* If, as the respondent contends, the contempt charge and proceeding was in fact civil in nature and procedure, this court must reverse the judgment of the tribal court.

In order for the Crow Creek Sioux Tribe and its Tribal Court to properly implement [a] civil contempt proceeding which, indeed, may exclude a non-

Indian individual from the lands of the Crow Creek Sioux Tribe, certain elements, items and safeguards must be implemented. A civil contempt proceeding should be conducted under trial procedure as with any other civil action. A civil contempt may, indeed, arise for the violation of an injunctional order abating a public nuisance. However, due process would require that in any prosecution of the civil contempt, the accused should be advised of the charges, have a reasonable opportunity to meet them by way defense or explanation and, if the accused individual requests, the right to call witnesses to give testimony relevant either to the issue of complete exculpation or in extenuation of the defense and in mitigation of the penalty to be imposed.

So, too, the existence of four elements of civil contempt must exist and be stated in findings of fact and conclusions of law. (1) Existence of an order; (2) knowledge of that order; (3) ability to comply with the order; and (4) willful and contumacious disobedience of the order. Given the informality, lack of funds, and oral tradition of the Lakota and Dakota people, any findings of fact and conclusions of law upon which an order or judgment is based may be orally read into a record. The record would be deemed sufficient if the findings and conclusions are clear and are preserved for appeal.

For sake of example, this court suggests that the Crow Creek Sioux Tribal Council and Court review the provisions of SDCL § 21-34. This chapter deals with the administrative process enforced under contempt powers. In no way is this court stating that the tribal court has no power to proceed under a civil contempt statute or that only an administrative body can proceed with a civil contempt proceeding. The South Dakota statutory cite is only suggested to give example of (1) the power of the court to compel obedience and punish violation; (2) the ability of the individual to purge himself from contempt of court; (3) the power of the court to make such emission or supplemental order; and (4) the power and authority of the tribal court to continue to enforce the original order from which the contempt arose.

The Crow Creek Tribal Constitution and Code, having an insufficient civil contempt statute and procedure, the appellant's conviction must be reversed. This court is not afraid to say that this appellant has escaped through a loophole in the law and with the assistance of competent counsel. However, the Crow Creek Sioux Tribal Council will most certainly pass resolutions complying with the order of this court. The power and authority of the Crow Creek Sioux Tribal Court is not diminished. The court is not admonished.

But for the technical procedure involved, the court was well within its power. Should the appellant decide to continue his activities when a proper civil contempt statute and procedure is in place, it is almost certain he will find no place to escape. If the tribe must give up non-Indians to non-Indian officials for violation of criminal offenses, then just as certainly a tribe has the right to exclude non-Indians from their land in order to preserve their land, their restricted sovereignty and the protection of its people. Even the United States Supreme Court refuses to strip that continuing pre-United States of America right from Indian people.

NOTES

1. **Treaty Promises Regarding Exclusion:** Many early treaties expressly protected the tribe's right to exclude persons from the reservation. *See, e.g.,* Treaty

with the Navajo Tribe of 1868, 15 Stat. 667, § 2 ("no persons except those ... authorized [by the government or the tribe] shall ever be permitted to pass over, settle upon, or reside in, the territory described in this article"). A treaty is not necessary, however, because the power is inherent. *See also Quechan Tribe v. Rowe*, 531 F.2d 408, 410 (9th Cir. 1976) (inherent power).

2. The Power to Exclude Nonmembers: In *Hardin v. White Mountain Apache Tribe*, 779 F.2d 476 (9th Cir. 1985), the Ninth Circuit held that a tribe's power to exclude nonmembers had not been implicitly divested after *Oliphant*. The tribe excluded a nonmember lessee permanently from the reservation after his conviction in federal court for concealing stolen property. In its opinion, the court relied on the same statements regarding power to exclude from *Merrion v. Jicarilla Apache Tribe, infra* section 5a, that the Intertribal Court of Appeals cited in the principal case. Nevertheless, the Ninth Circuit took pains to explain that its opinion was very narrow. In particular, the Ninth Circuit stressed that Mr. Hardin had been convicted of a federal crime. The Court stated:

> Although Hardin attempts to characterize his exclusion as punitive in nature, retribution cannot be the goal of an ordinance that is triggered by a nonmember's crimes against an entirely separate, external state or federal sovereign. The United States has already imposed its own punishment for the nonmember's crime. The intent of the tribal ordinance is merely to remove a person who "threatens or has some direct effect on the ... health or welfare of the tribe," [*Montana v. United States*], 450 U.S. at 566 — a permissible civil regulation of the Tribe's internal order.

779 F.2d at 478-79. Under this reasoning, could a tribe exclude a nonmember who had not been prosecuted for violating a state, federal, or tribal criminal law? What are the prerequisites to exclusion as a remedy for a violation of tribal civil law? Assuming that the tribe accorded the excluded person due process consonant with the ICRA, should such power be found to be implicitly divested? Of course, many tribes' treaties contain promises protecting the right of exclusion, as discussed above. Recall that *Oliphant* relied on the argument that the common assumption of the day was that there was no criminal jurisdiction over non-Indians. The linchpin of that conclusion was the absence of treaty promises guaranteeing the right to exercise criminal jurisdiction over non-Indians. A tribe without a treaty could thus argue that the prevalence of treaty promises regarding exclusion supports the assumption that tribes have retained the right to exclude.

The power to exclude nonmembers does not extend to nonmembers who own fee land within the boundaries of the reservation. *See Brendale v. Confederated Tribes & Bands of the Yakima Indian Reservation, infra*, section 5b.

3. The Power to Exclude Members: Does a tribe have the power to exclude members from the reservation? An excluded tribal member would have rights to due process enforceable in those tribal courts that have waived sovereign immunity for suits for equitable relief. Could such a person also seek redress in the federal courts? If so, on what theory could he or she rely? One argument might be as follows: The establishing of reservations for many tribes in the nineteenth century expressed a federal policy that reservations must be open to all tribal members. Thus, an excluded member could argue that the tribe's right to exclude had been implicitly divested because it is inconsistent with overriding federal policies. On the other hand, although the early treaties dealing with exclusion referred only to non-Indians, the parties may have assumed that the power to exclude members was so obvious it needed no stating. Moreover, the right to exclude members from the community is surely an inherent right of sovereign nations for which more concrete evidence of divestment should be required than the implicit divestiture rule of *Oliphant*, a rule applying so far only to tribal relations with nonmembers.

4. Exclusion Cases in Federal Forums Before *Martinez*: Before *Martinez*, federal courts entertained cases challenging exclusions brought by members and nonmembers. *See, e.g., Solomon v. LaRose*, 335 F. Supp. 715 (D. Neb. 1971) (exclusion of tribal members violated due process). In a well-known case, *Dodge v. Nakai*, 298 F. Supp. 26, 31-32 (D. Ariz. 1969), a district court overturned an order excluding a nonmember. Theodore Mitchell was the Executive Director of DNA, a legal services program financed by the Office of Economic Opportunity to serve the people of the Navajo Reservation. Mitchell had angered some members of the tribal leadership, because he established a policy permitting DNA to take cases brought by individual Navajos against tribal agencies. At a meeting between the Tribal Council's Advisory Committee and BIA representatives, Ms. Annie Wauneka, a member of the Advisory Committee, asked whether the recently enacted Indian Civil Rights Act would prevent a tribe from excluding someone from the reservation. When asked whether she had anyone in particular in mind, Ms. Wauneka answered no. At this point, several people laughed. All agree that the "loudest and most noticeable laughter" came from Mitchell. Ms. Wauneka reprimanded him and the meeting went on. *Id.* at 31.

The next day, when the meeting reconvened, Mrs. Wauneka approached Mr. Mitchell and asked him whether he was going to laugh again. He began to apologize, but she hit him several times and ordered him to leave. The following day, the Advisory Committee passed a resolution barring Mr. Mitchell from the reservation. The tribe argued that "Mitchell's laugh was in the nature of a guffaw, full of ridicule and scorn for the Advisory Committee, and so obnoxious as to provoke the assault by Mrs. Wauneka." *Id.* The court stated "No one would deny that a laugh similar to the one described by defendants is reprehensible, and that the laughing party is to be properly disapproved." *Id.* at 32. Nevertheless, the court held the exclusion violated the Indian Civil Rights Act, because: "it is difficult to construe the action of the Advisory Committee as being based upon anything other than a personal dislike for the conduct of Mitchell, conduct in the form of laughter that was deemed to be disrespectful to members of the Advisory Committee. Invocation of the drastic power of exclusion for this reason is wholly unreasonable." *Id.*

Was the court in *Dodge v. Nakai* sensitive to the constitutional and cultural differences in Indian tribal government? In an article criticizing the case, Alvin Ziontz commented:

> There were a number of critical factors influencing the court. One factor was that the subject of the exclusion was a lawyer whose exclusion might deprive Navajo tribal members of his needed legal services. A second concern of the court was that his exclusion was not based on grounds stated in the tribal code. The court expressed its apprehension that if the tribe could deal with Mr. Mitchell in a manner which the court considered arbitrary, many other white persons living on the reservations would also be subject to such action.
>
> But the aspect of the case which appears to be most significant in terms of ethnocentric judgments is the decision of the court that exclusion of Mitchell because of his laughter was unreasonable. The court rejected the contention of the defendants that Mitchell's laughter was opprobrious because it was an expression of ridicule and scorn for members of the council. The court insisted upon treating the matter simply as a question of disorderly conduct at a meeting.

Ziontz, *In Defense of Tribal Sovereignty: An Analysis of Judicial Error in Construction of the Indian Civil Rights Act,* 20 S.D.L. REV. 1, 50 (1975).* *But cf.* De Raismes, *The Indian Civil Rights Act of 1968 and the Pursuit of Responsible Tribal Self-Government,* 20 S.D.L. REV. 59 (1975).

5. Excluding Agents of the Federal Government: In *United States v. White Mountain Apache Tribe,* 784 F.2d 917 (9th Cir.), *cert. denied sub nom. White Mountain Apache Tribe v. Hodel,* 479 U.S. 1006 (1986), the Ninth Circuit Court of Appeals overturned a tribal court order enjoining United State agents from entering the reservation, holding that the power to exclude cannot be used against United States agents conducting official business on the reservation. What is the rationale for such a determination?

4. CONTROL OVER ENROLLMENT

"A tribe's right to define its own membership for tribal purposes has long been recognized as central to its existence as an independent political community." *Santa Clara Pueblo v. Martinez,* 436 U.S. 49, 72 n.32 (1978). *Martinez* closed the doors of the federal courts to suits challenging tribal enrollment decisions, at least when such challenges were based on the Indian Civil Rights Act. Long before the passage of the 1968 Civil Rights Act or *Martinez,* however, courts often stated that the determination of tribal membership was a uniquely internal matter over which they had no jurisdiction. *See, e.g., Patterson v. Council of Seneca Nation,* 245 N.Y. 433, 157 N.E. 734 (1927); *Red Bird v. United States (Cherokee Intermarriage Cases),* 203 U.S. 76 (1906) (upholding Cherokee National Council rule limiting property rights of whites and Indians of other tribes who had been accepted into the community following marriage to tribal members); *Martinez v. Southern Ute Tribe,* 249 F.2d 915 (10th Cir. 1957) (denying jurisdiction over challenge by a previously enrolled member of the tribe denied membership in a newly created tribal corporation that was the transferee of tribal property).

Currently, disputes frequently concern membership as a means to obtain property rights, especially where tribal assets take the form of desert land in Palm Springs or oil in Oklahoma. But there are more traditional interests in membership, such as political and social association on the reservation, education in Indian schools, and religion. Some tribes do not allow those who do not live on the reservation, or who marry non-Indians, to retain existing claims on tribal property and deny such Indians the opportunity to claim tribal assets for their children. Limiting membership and property sharing is accomplished in three ways: by blood quantum, by patrilineal or matrilineal descent rules, and by residency requirements. *See* COLORADO STATE COLLEGE, MUSEUM OF ANTHROPOLOGY, CHARTERS, CONSTITUTIONS, AND BY-LAWS OF THE INDIAN TRIBES OF NORTH AMERICA (Occasional Publications on Anthropology, Enthnology Series) (G. Fay ed., 1967). Many tribes seek to limit political participation to those of the immediate Indian community. Can tribes limit political rights to a class smaller than that eligible for property rights? The Eighth Circuit Court of Appeals upheld a Crow Creek Sioux Tribal rule requiring tribal council members to be one-half or more Indian blood, stating: "[T]he tribe has a sufficient cultural interest in setting a higher blood quantum requirement to hold office than for mere membership in the tribe if it so desires." *Daly v. United States,* 483 F.2d 700 (8th Cir. 1973). The court analogized the requirement to the United States Constitution's restriction of the presidency to citizens born in the United States. *See also Shortbull v. Looking Elk,* 677 F.2d 645 (8th Cir. 1982) (dismissing for lack of jurisdiction an Oglala Sioux Tribal ordinance preventing non-enrolled tribal members from running for tribal president); *Day v. Hopi Election Bd.,* 16 Indian L. Rep. 6057 (Hopi Tr. Ct., Feb. 29, 1988, July 18, 1989) (upholding election board disqualification of candidate for vice-chairman who did not demonstrate fluency in Hopi as required by the constitution).

Congress has the power to determine tribal membership, at least when tribal rolls are to be prepared for the purpose of determining rights to tribal property. *See, e.g., United States ex rel. West v. Hitchcock,* 205 U.S. 80 (1907) (agreement with tribe authorizing Secretary to determine membership for purposes of receiving allotments from ceded land); *Stephens v. Cherokee Nation,* 174 U.S. 445 (1899) (membership for purposes of sharing in distribution of funds); *Simmons v. Eagle Seelatsee,* 244 F. Supp. 808 (E.D. Wash. 1965), *aff'd,* 384 U.S. 209 (1966) (membership for purposes of taking restricted land by will or by inheritance). A peculiar instance of federal control of membership involved slaves held in various tribes during the Civil War. *See generally* A. ABEL, THE SLAVEHOLDING INDIANS (1915). Partly out of retribution caused by Indian sympathy for the Confederacy, the United States, by treaty, compelled adoption of important provisions that guaranteed former slaves the right to share in tribal property. *See, e.g.,* Treaty of March 21, 1866, with the Seminole Nation, art. 2, 14 Stat. 756. This heavy federal hand was curiously absent, however, when the Indian Nations, under the Oklahoma Welfare Act (1936) (Oklahoma version of the Indian Reorganization Act), were authorized to alter membership qualifications. The adoption of provisions limiting membership to persons of Indian blood was upheld by the Solicitor. See Memo. Sol. I.D. October 1, 1941 cited in F. COHEN, FEDERAL INDIAN LAW (1958) at 582.

Federal statutory membership provisions can still be reviewed by the federal courts despite *Martinez. See Santa Clara Pueblo v. Martinez, supra,* n.32.

5. TRIBAL TAXING AND REGULATORY AUTHORITY

a. The Power to Tax

MERRION v. JICARILLA APACHE TRIBE

455 U.S. 130 (1982)

Mr. Justice MARSHALL delivered the opinion of the Court.

Pursuant to long-term leases with the Jicarilla Apache Tribe, petitioners, 21 lessees, extract and produce oil and gas from the Tribe's reservation lands. In these two consolidated cases, petitioners challenge an ordinance enacted by the Tribe imposing a severance tax on "any oil and natural gas severed, saved and removed from Tribal lands." *See* Oil and Gas Severance Tax No. 77-0-02, App. 38. We granted certiorari to determine whether the Tribe has the authority to impose this tax, and, if so, whether the tax imposed by the Tribe violates the Commerce Clause.

I

The Jicarilla Apache Tribe resides on a reservation in northwestern New Mexico. Established by Executive Order in 1887, the reservation [is inhabited by approximately 2,100 individuals and] contains 742,315 acres, all of which are held as tribal trust property. [T]he Tribe's sovereign power is not affected by the manner in which its reservation was created. The Tribe is organized under the [Indian Reorganization Act. The Tribe's Constitution has been revised and approved by the Secretary of the Interior and contains a provision requiring tribal ordinances to be approved by the Secretary.]

To develop tribal lands, the Tribe has executed mineral leases encompassing some 69% of the reservation land. Beginning in 1953, the petitioners entered into leases with the Tribe. The Commissioner of Indian Affairs, on behalf of the Secretary, approved these leases, as required by the Act of May 11, 1938, ch. 198, 52 Stat. 347, 25 U.S.C. §§ 396a-396g (1938 Act). In exchange for a cash bonus, royalties, and rents, the typical lease grants the lessee "the exclusive right and privilege to drill for, mine, extract, remove, and dispose of all the oil and natural gas deposits in or under" the leased land for as long as the minerals are produced in paying quantities. Petitioners may use oil and gas in developing the lease without incurring the royalty. In addition, the Tribe reserves the rights to use gas without charge for any of its buildings on the leased land, and to take its royalties in kind. Petitioners' activities on the leased land have been subject to taxes imposed by the State of New Mexico on oil and gas severance and on oil and gas production equipment. *See* Act of Mar. 3, 1927, ch. 299, § 3, 44 Stat. 1347, 25 U.S.C. § 398c (permitting state taxation of mineral production on Indian reservations) (1927 Act).

Pursuant to its Revised Constitution, the Tribal Council adopted an ordinance imposing a severance tax on oil and gas production on tribal land. The ordinance was approved by the Secretary, through the Acting Director of the Bureau of Indian Affairs, on December 23, 1976. The tax applies to "any oil and natural gas severed, saved and removed from Tribal lands ...." The tax is assessed at the wellhead at $0.05 per million BTU's of gas produced and $0.29 per barrel of crude oil or condensate produced on the reservation, and it is due at the time of severance. Oil and gas consumed by the lessees to develop their leases or received by the Tribe as in-kind royalty payments are exempted from the tax.

In two separate actions, petitioners sought to enjoin enforcement of the tax by either the tribal authorities or the Secretary. The United States District Court for the District of New Mexico consolidated the cases, granted other lessees leave to intervene, and permanently enjoined enforcement of the tax. The District Court ruled that the Tribe lacked the authority to impose the tax, that only state and local authorities had the power to tax oil and gas production on Indian reservations, and that the tax violated the Commerce Clause.

The United States Court of Appeals for the Tenth Circuit, sitting en banc, reversed [reasoning] that the taxing power is an inherent attribute of tribal sovereignty that has not been divested by any treaty or Act of Congress, including the 1927 Act, 25 U.S.C. § 398c. The court also found no Commerce Clause violation. We granted certiorari, and we now affirm the decision of the Court of Appeals.

II

Petitioners argue, and the dissent agrees, that an Indian tribe's authority to tax non-Indians who do business on the reservation stems exclusively from its power to exclude such persons from tribal lands. Because the Tribe did not initially condition the leases upon the payment of a severance tax, petitioners assert that the Tribe is without authority to impose such a tax at a later time. We disagree with the premise that the power to tax derives only from the power to exclude. Even if that premise is accepted, however, we disagree with the conclusion that the Tribe lacks the power to impose the severance tax.

A

In *Washington v. Confederated Tribes of the Colville Indian Reservation*, [447 U.S. 134 (1980)] (Colville), we addressed the Indian tribes' authority to impose taxes on non-Indians doing business on the reservation. We held that "[t]he power to tax transactions occurring on trust lands and significantly involving a tribe or its members is a fundamental attribute of sovereignty which the tribes retain unless divested of it by federal law or necessary implication of their dependent status." *Id.*, at 152. The power to tax is an essential attribute of Indian sovereignty because it is a necessary instrument of self-government and territorial management. This power enables a tribal government to raise revenues for its essential services. The power does not derive solely from the Indian tribe's power to exclude non-Indians from tribal lands. Instead, it derives from the tribe's general authority, as sovereign, to control economic activity within its jurisdiction, and to defray the cost of providing governmental services by requiring contributions from persons or enterprises engaged in economic activities within that jurisdiction. See, *e.g., Gibbons v. Ogden,* [9 Wheat. 1, 199] (1824).

The petitioners avail themselves of the "substantial privilege of carrying on business" on the reservation. They benefit from the provision of police protection and other governmental services, as well as from "'the advantages of a civilized society'" that are assured by the existence of tribal government. Numerous other governmental entities levy a general revenue tax similar to that imposed by the Jicarilla Tribe when they provide comparable services. Under these circumstances, there is nothing exceptional in requiring petitioners to contribute through taxes to the general cost of tribal government.[5]

As we observed in *Colville, supra,* the tribe's interest in levying taxes on nonmembers to raise "revenues for essential governmental programs ... is strongest when the revenues are derived from value generated on the reservation by activities involving the Tribes and when the taxpayer is the recipient of

---

[5] Through various Acts governing Indian tribes, Congress has expressed the purpose of "fostering tribal self-government." *Colville,* 447 U.S., at 155. We agree with Judge McKay's observation that "[i]t simply does not make sense to expect the tribes to carry out municipal functions approved and mandated by Congress without being able to exercise at least minimal taxing powers, whether they take the form of real estate taxes, leasehold taxes or severance taxes." (McKay, J., concurring).

tribal services." 447 U.S., at 156-157. This surely is the case here. The mere fact that the government imposing the tax also enjoys rents and royalties as the lessor of the mineral lands does not undermine the government's authority to impose the tax. The royalty payments from the mineral leases are paid to the Tribe in its role as partner in petitioners' commercial venture. The severance tax, in contrast, is petitioners' contribution "to the general cost of providing governmental services." State governments commonly receive both royalty payments and severance taxes from lessees of mineral lands within their borders.

Viewing the taxing power of Indian tribes as an essential instrument of self-government and territorial management has been a shared assumption of all three branches of the Federal Government. In *Colville,* the Court relied in part on a 1934 opinion of the Solicitor for the Department of the Interior. In this opinion, the Solicitor recognized that, in the absence of congressional action to the contrary, the tribes' sovereign power to tax "'may be exercised over members of the tribe and over nonmembers, so far as such nonmembers may accept privileges of trade, residence, etc., to which taxes may be attached as conditions.'" 447 U.S., at 153 (quoting *Powers of Indian Tribes,* 55 I.D. 14, 46 (1934)). Congress has [also] acknowledged that the tribal power to tax is one of the tools necessary to self-government and territorial control. As early as 1879, the Senate Judiciary Committee acknowledged the validity of a tax imposed by the Chickasaw Nation on non-Indians legitimately within its territory. [T]he views of the three federal branches of government, as well as general principles of taxation, confirm that Indian tribes enjoy authority to finance their governmental services through taxation of non-Indians who benefit from those services. Indeed, the conception of Indian sovereignty that this Court has consistently reaffirmed permits no other conclusion. As we observed in [*United States v. Mazurie,*] "Indian tribes within 'Indian country' are a good deal more than 'private, voluntary organizations.'" They "are unique aggregations possessing attributes of sovereignty over both their members and their territory." Adhering to this understanding, we conclude that the Tribe's authority to tax non-Indians who conduct business on the reservation does not simply derive from the Tribe's power to exclude such persons, but is an inherent power necessary to tribal self-government and territorial management.

Of course, the Tribe's authority to tax nonmembers is subject to constraints not imposed on other governmental entities: the Federal Government can take away this power, and the Tribe must obtain the approval of the Secretary before any tax on nonmembers can take effect. These additional constraints minimize potential concern that Indian tribes will exercise the power to tax in an unfair or unprincipled manner, and ensure that any exercise of the tribal power to tax will be consistent with national policies.

We are not persuaded by the dissent's attempt to limit an Indian tribe's authority to tax non-Indians by asserting that its only source is the tribe's power to exclude such persons from tribal lands. Limiting the tribes' authority to tax in this manner contradicts the conception that Indian tribes are domestic, dependent nations, as well as the common understanding that the sovereign taxing power is a tool for raising revenue necessary to cover the costs of government.

Nor are we persuaded by the dissent that three early decisions upholding tribal power to tax nonmembers support this limitation. [T]here is a significant territorial component to tribal power: a tribe has no authority over a nonmember until the nonmember enters tribal lands or conducts business with the tribe. However, we do not believe that this territorial component to Indian taxing power, which is discussed in these early cases, means that the tribal authority to tax derives solely from the tribe's power to exclude nonmembers from tribal lands.

[Of the three decisions discussed by the dissent,] the decision in *Buster v. Wright* actually undermines the theory that the tribes' taxing authority derives solely from the power to exclude non-Indians from tribal lands. Under this theory, a non-Indian who establishes lawful presence in Indian territory could avoid paying a tribal tax by claiming that no residual portion of the power to exclude supports the tax. This result was explicitly rejected in *Buster v. Wright*. In *Buster*, deeds to individual lots in Indian territory had been granted to non-Indian residents, and cities and towns had been incorporated. As a result, Congress had expressly prohibited the Tribe from removing these non-Indian residents. Even though the ownership of land and the creation of local governments by non-Indians established their legitimate presence on Indian land, the court held that the Tribe retained its power to tax. The court concluded that "[n]either the United States, nor a state, nor any other sovereignty loses the power to govern the people within its borders by the existence of towns and cities therein endowed with the usual powers of municipalities, *nor by the ownership nor occupancy of the land within its territorial jurisdiction by citizens or foreigners.*" 135 F., at 952 (emphasis added). This result confirms that the Tribe's authority to tax derives not from its power to exclude, but from its power to govern and to raise revenues to pay for the costs of government.

We choose not to embrace a new restriction on the extent of the tribal authority to tax, which is based on a questionable interpretation of three early cases. Instead, based on the views of each of the federal branches, general principles of taxation, and the conception of Indian tribes as domestic, dependent nations, we conclude that the Tribe has the authority to impose a severance tax on the mining activities of petitioners as part of its power to govern and to pay for the costs of self-government.

B

Alternatively, if we accept the argument, advanced by petitioners and the dissent, that the Tribe's authority to tax derives solely from its power to exclude non-Indians from the reservation, we conclude that the Tribe has the authority to impose the severance tax challenged here. Nonmembers who lawfully enter tribal lands remain subject to the tribe's *power* to exclude them. This power necessarily includes the lesser power to place conditions on entry, on continued presence, or on reservation conduct, such as a tax on business activities conducted on the reservation. When a tribe grants a non-Indian the right to be on Indian land, the tribe agrees not to exercise its *ultimate* power to oust the non-Indian as long as the non-Indian complies with the initial conditions of entry. However, it does not follow that the lawful property right to be on Indian land also immunizes the non-Indian from the tribe's exercise of its lesser-included power to tax or to place other conditions on the non-Indian's conduct or continued presence on the reservation. A nonmember who enters the jurisdiction of the tribe remains subject to the risk that the tribe will later exercise its sovereign power. The fact that the tribe chooses not to exercise its power to tax when it initially grants a non-Indian entry onto the reservation does not permanently divest the tribe of its authority to impose such a tax.[10]

Petitioners argue that their leaseholds entitle them to enter the reservation and exempt them from further exercises of the Tribe's sovereign authority. Similarly, the dissent asserts that the Tribe has lost the power to tax petitioners' mining activities because it has leased to them the use of the mineral lands and such rights of access to the reservation as might be necessary to enjoy the leases. [T]his conclusion is not compelled by linking the taxing power to the power to exclude. Instead, it is based on additional assumptions and confusions about the consequences of the commercial arrangement between petitioners and the Tribe.

Most important, petitioners and the dissent confuse the Tribe's role as commercial partner with its role as sovereign. This confusion relegates the powers of sovereignty to the bargaining process undertaken in each of the sovereign's commercial agreements. It is one thing to find that the Tribe has agreed to sell the right to use the land and take from it valuable minerals; it is quite another to find that the Tribe has abandoned its sovereign powers simply because it has not expressly reserved them through a contract.

Confusing these two results denigrates Indian sovereignty. Indeed, the dissent apparently views the tribal power to exclude, as well as the derivative authority to tax, as merely the power possessed by any individual landowner or any social group to attach conditions, including a "tax" or fee, to the entry by a stranger onto private land or into the social group, and not as a sovereign power. The dissent does pay lipservice to the established views that Indian tribes retain those fundamental attributes of sovereignty, including the power to tax transactions that occur on tribal lands, which have not been divested by Congress or by necessary implication of the tribe's dependent status, [*Colville*] and that tribes "are a good deal more than 'private, voluntary organizations.'" [*Mazurie*.] However, in arguing that the Tribe somehow "lost" its power to tax petitioners by not including a taxing provision in the original leases or otherwise notifying petitioners that the Tribe retained and might later exercise its sovereign right to tax them, the dissent attaches little significance to the sovereign nature of the tribal authority to tax, and it obviously views tribal authority as little more than a landowner's contractual right. [S]overeignty is not conditioned on the assent of a nonmember; to the contrary, the nonmember's presence and conduct on Indian lands are conditioned by the limitations the tribe may choose to impose.

Viewed in this light, the absence of a reference to the tax in the leases themselves hardly impairs the Tribe's authority to impose the tax. Contractual arrangements remain subject to subsequent legislation by the presiding sovereign. Even where the contract at issue requires payment of a royalty for a license or

---

[10] Here, the leases extend for as long as minerals are produced in paying quantities, in other words, until the resources are depleted. Thus, under the dissent's approach, the Tribe would never have the power to tax petitioners regardless of the financial burden to the Tribe of providing and maintaining governmental services for the benefit of petitioners.

franchise issued by the governmental entity, the government's power to tax remains unless it "has been specifically surrendered in terms which admit of no other reasonable interpretation." *St. Louis v. United R. Co.,* 210 U.S. 266, 280 (1908).

[Petitioners do not claim] that petitioners' leases contain the clear and unmistakable surrender of taxing power required for its extinction. We could find a waiver of the Tribe's taxing power only if we inferred it from silence in the leases. To presume that a sovereign forever waives the right to exercise one of its sovereign powers unless it expressly reserves the right to exercise that power in a commercial agreement turns the concept of sovereignty on its head, and we do not adopt this analysis.

C

The Tribe has the inherent power to impose the severance tax on petitioners, whether this power derives from the Tribe's power of self-government or from its power to exclude. Because Congress may limit tribal sovereignty, we now review petitioners' argument that Congress, when it enacted two federal Acts governing Indians and various pieces of federal energy legislation, deprived the Tribe of its authority to impose the severance tax.

In *Colville,* we concluded that the "widely held understanding within the Federal Government has always been that *federal law to date has not worked a divestiture of Indian taxing power.*" 447 U.S., at 152 (emphasis added). Moreover, we noted that "[n]o federal statute cited to us shows any congressional departure from this view." *Id.,* at 153. Likewise, petitioners can cite to no statute that specifically divests the Tribe of its power to impose the severance tax on their mining activities. Instead, petitioners argue that Congress *implicitly* took away this power when it enacted the Acts and various pieces of legislation on which petitioners rely. Before reviewing this argument, we reiterate here our admonition in *Santa Clara Pueblo v. Martinez,* 436 U.S. 49, 60 (1978): "a proper respect both for tribal sovereignty itself and for the plenary authority of Congress in this area cautions that we tread lightly in the absence of clear indications of legislative intent."

[In the statutes cited by petitioners we] find no "clear indications" that Congress has implicitly deprived the Tribe of its power to impose the severance tax. In any event, if there were ambiguity on this point, the doubt would benefit the Tribe, for "[a]mbiguities in federal law have been construed generously in order to comport with ... traditional notions of sovereignty and with the federal policy of encouraging tribal independence." *White Mountain Apache Tribe v. Bracker,* 448 U.S. 136, 143-144 (1980). Accordingly, we find that the Federal Government has not divested the Tribe of its inherent authority to tax mining activities on its land, whether this authority derives from the Tribe's power of self-government or from its power to exclude....

IV

In *Worcester v. Georgia,* Chief Justice Marshall observed that Indian tribes had "always been considered as distinct, independent political communities, retaining their original natural rights." Although the tribes are subject to the authority of the Federal Government, the "weaker power does not surrender its independence — its right to self-government, by associating with a stronger, and taking its protection." *Id.,* at 561. Adhering to this understanding, we conclude that the Tribe did not surrender its authority to tax the mining activities of petitioners, whether this authority is deemed to arise from the Tribe's inherent power of self-government or from its inherent power to exclude nonmembers. Therefore, the Tribe may enforce its severance tax unless and until Congress divests this power, an action that Congress has not taken to date. Finally, the severance tax imposed by the Tribe cannot be invalidated on the ground that it violates the "negative implications" of the Commerce Clause.

 Affirmed.

Justice STEVENS, with whom THE CHIEF JUSTICE and Justice REHNQUIST join, dissenting.

II

The powers possessed by Indian tribes stem from three sources: federal statutes, treaties, and the tribe's inherent sovereignty. [There are no statutes or treaties on point.] Therefore, if the severance tax is valid, it must be as an exercise of the Tribe's inherent sovereignty. [Although] Indian tribes possess broad powers of self-governance over tribal members, [they] do not possess the same attributes of sovereignty that the Federal Government and the several States enjoy. In determining the extent of the sovereign powers that the tribes retained in submitting to the authority of the United States, this Court has recognized a fundamental distinction between the right of the tribes to govern their own internal affairs and the right to exercise powers affecting nonmembers of the tribe.

 The Court has been careful to protect the tribes from interference with tribal control over their own members. [Nevertheless, in] sharp contrast to the tribes' broad powers over their own members, tribal powers over nonmembers have always been narrowly confined. The Court has emphasized that "exercise of tribal power beyond what is necessary to protect tribal self-government or to control internal relations is inconsistent with the dependent status of the tribes, and so cannot survive without express congressional delegation." *Montana v. United States,* 450 U.S. 544, 564.

 [Tribal] authority to enact legislation affecting nonmembers is therefore of a different character than their broad power to control internal tribal affairs. This difference is consistent with the fundamental principle that "[i]n this Nation each sovereign governs only with the consent of the governed." *Nevada v. Hall,* 440 U.S. 410, 426. Since nonmembers are excluded from participation in tribal government, the powers that may be exercised over them are appropriately limited. Certainly, tribal authority over nonmembers — including the power to tax — is not unprecedented. An examination of cases that have upheld this power, however, demonstrates that the power to impose such a tax derives solely from the tribes' power to exclude nonmembers entirely from territory that has been reserved for the tribe. This "power to exclude" logically has been held to include the lesser power to attach conditions on a right of entry granted by the tribe to a nonmember to engage in particular activities within the reservation.

IV

[The Tribe granted petitioners the authority] to extract oil and gas from reservation lands. The Tribe now seeks to change retroactively the conditions of that authority. These petitioners happen to be prosperous oil companies. Moreover, it may be sound policy to find additional sources of revenue to better the economic conditions of many Indian tribes. If this retroactive imposition of a tax on oil companies is permissible, however, an Indian tribe may with equal legitimacy contract with outsiders for the construction of a school or a hospital, or for the rendition of medical or technical services, and then — after the contract is partially performed — change the terms of the bargain by imposing a gross receipts tax on the outsider. If the Court is willing to ignore the risk of such unfair treatment of a local contractor or a local doctor because the Secretary of the Interior has the power to veto a tribal tax, it must equate the unbridled discretion of a political appointee with the protection afforded by rules of law. That equation is unacceptable to me. Neither wealth, political opportunity, nor past transgressions can justify denying any person the protection of the law.

KERR-McGEE CORP. v. NAVAJO TRIBE

471 U.S. 195 (1985)

Chief Justice BURGER delivered the opinion of the Court.

We granted certiorari to decide whether the Navajo Tribe of Indians may tax business activities conducted on its land without first obtaining the approval of the Secretary of the Interior.

I

In 1978, the Navajo Tribal Council, the governing body of the Navajo Tribe of Indians, enacted two ordinances imposing taxes known as the Possessory Interest Tax and the Business Activity Tax. The Possessory Interest Tax is measured by the value of leasehold interests in tribal lands; the tax rate is 3% of the value of those interests. The Business Activity Tax is assessed on receipts from the sale of property produced or extracted within the Navajo nation, and from the sale of services within the Nation; a tax rate of 5% is applied after subtracting a standard deduction and specified expenses. The tax laws apply to both Navajo and non-Indian businesses, with dissatisfied taxpayers enjoying the right of appeal to the Navajo Tax Commission and the Navajo Court of Appeals.

The Navajo Tribe, uncertain whether federal approval was required, submitted the two tax laws to the Bureau of Indian Affairs of the Department of the Interior. The Bureau informed the Tribe that no federal statute or regulation required the Department of the Interior to approve or disapprove the taxes.

Before any taxes were collected, petitioner, a substantial mineral lessee on the Navajo Reservation, brought this action seeking to invalidate the taxes. Petitioner claimed in the United States District Court for the District of Arizona that the Navajo taxes were invalid without approval of the Secretary of the Interior. The District Court agreed and permanently enjoined the Tribe from enforcing its tax laws against petitioner.

The United States Court of Appeals for the Ninth Circuit reversed. Relying on *Southland Royalty Co. v. Navajo Tribe of Indians,* 715 F.2d 486 (CA10 1983), it held that no federal statute or principle of law mandated Secretarial approval.

We granted certiorari [and] affirm.

II

In [*Merrion v. Jicarilla Apache Tribe,*] we held that the "power to tax is an essential attribute of Indian sovereignty because it is a necessary instrument of self-government and territorial management." Congress, of course, may erect "checkpoints that must be cleared before a tribal tax can take effect." The issue in this case is whether Congress has enacted legislation requiring Secretarial approval of Navajo tax laws.

Petitioner suggests that the Indian Reorganization Act is such a law. Section 16 of the IRA authorizes any tribe on a reservation to adopt a constitution and bylaws, subject to the approval of the Secretary of the Interior. 25 U.S.C. § 476. The Act, however, does not provide that a tribal constitution must condition the power to tax on Secretarial approval. Indeed, the terms of the IRA do not govern tribes, like the Navajo, which declined to accept its provisions. 25 U.S.C. § 478.

Many tribal constitutions written under the IRA in the 1930's called for Secretarial approval of tax laws affecting non-Indians. See, e.g., Constitution and Bylaws of the Rosebud Sioux Tribe of South Dakota, Art. 4, § 1(h) (1935). But there were exceptions to this practice. For example, the 1937 Constitution and By-laws of the Saginaw Chippewa Indian Tribe of Michigan authorized the Tribal Council, without Secretarial approval, to "create and maintain a tribal council fund by ... levying taxes or assessments against members or non-members." Art. 4, § 1(g). Thus the most that can be said about this period of constitution writing is that the Bureau of Indian Affairs, in assisting the drafting of tribal constitutions, had a policy of including provisions for Secretarial approval; but that policy was not mandated by Congress.

Nor do we agree that Congress intended to recognize as legitimate only those tribal taxes authorized by constitutions written under the IRA. Long before the IRA was enacted, the Senate Judiciary Committee acknowledged the validity of a tax imposed by the Chickasaw Nation on non-Indians. *See* S. Rep. No. 698, 45th Cong., 3d Sess., 1-2 (1879). And in 1934, the Solicitor of the Department of the Interior published a formal opinion stating that a tribe possesses "the power of taxation [which] may be exercised over members of the tribe and over nonmembers." *Powers of Indian Tribes,* 55 I.D. 14, 46. The 73rd Congress, in passing the IRA to advance tribal self-government, *see Williams v. Lee,* 358 U.S. 217, 220 (1959), did nothing to limit the established, pre-existing power of the Navajos to levy taxes.

Some tribes that adopted constitutions in the early years of the IRA may be dependent on the Government in a way that the Navajos are not. However, such tribes are free, with the backing of the Interior Department, to amend their constitutions to remove the requirement of Secretarial approval. *See, e.g.,* Revised Constitution and Bylaws of the Mississippi Band of Choctaw Indians, Art. 8, § 1(r) (1975).

Petitioner also argues that the Indian Mineral Leasing Act of 1938, 52 Stat. 347, 25 U.S.C. § 396a et seq., requires Secretarial approval of Navajo tax laws. Sections 1 through 3 of the 1938 Act establish procedures for leasing oil and gas interests on tribal lands. And § 4 provides that "[a]ll operations under any oil, gas, or other mineral lease issued pursuant to the [Act] shall be subject to the rules and regulations promulgated by the Secretary of the Interior." 25 U.S.C. § 396d. Under this grant of authority, the Secretary has issued comprehensive regulations governing the operation of oil and gas leases. *See* 25 CFR pt. 211 (1984). The Secretary, however, does not demand that tribal laws taxing mineral production be submitted for his approval.

Petitioner contends that the Secretary's decision not to review such tax laws is inconsistent with the statute. In *Merrion*, we emphasized the difference between a tribe's "role as commercial partner," and its "role as sovereign." The tribe acts as a commercial partner when it agrees to sell the right to the use of its land for mineral production, but the tribe acts as a sovereign when it imposes a tax on economic activities within its jurisdiction. Plainly Congress, in passing § 4 of the 1938 Act, could make this same distinction.

Even assuming that the Secretary could review tribal laws taxing mineral production, it does not follow that he must do so. We are not inclined to impose upon the Secretary a duty that he has determined is not needed to satisfy the 1938 Act's basic purpose — to maximize tribal revenues from reservation lands. *See* S. Rep. No. 985, 75th Cong., 1st Sess., 2-3 (1937). Thus, in light of our obligation to "tread lightly in the absence of clear indications of legislative intent," [*Santa Clara Pueblo v. Martinez,*] we will not interpret a grant of authority to regulate leasing operations as a command to the Secretary to review every tribal tax relating to mineral production.

[T]he Federal Government is "firmly committed to the goal of promoting tribal self-government." [*New Mexico v. Mescalero Apache Tribe,* 462 U.S. 324, 334-335 (1983).] The power to tax members and non-Indians alike is surely an essential attribute of such self-government; the Navajos can gain independence from the Federal Government only by financing their own police force, schools, and social programs.

III

The Navajo government has been called "probably the most elaborate" among tribes. H.R. Rep. No. 78, 91st Cong., 1st Sess., 8 (1969). The legitimacy of the Navajo Tribal Council, the freely elected governing body of the Navajos, is beyond question.[4] We agree with the Court of Appeals that neither Congress nor the Navajos have found it necessary to subject the Tribal Council's tax laws to review by the Secretary of the Interior.

[*Affirmed.*]

---

[4] The Tribal Council has 88 members who are elected every four years. There are approximately 79,000 registered tribal voters, and 69% of these persons voted in the last tribal election in 1982.

NOTES

1. Taxation as a Source of Revenue: What are the practical limits of taxation of non-Indians doing business on a reservation as a source of tribal revenue? For instance, a low sales tax could attract off-reservation consumers to reservation retailers. In *Washington v. Confederated Tribes of the Colville Indian Reservation*, 447 U.S. 134 (1980), the Supreme Court held that a tribal tax on cigarettes purchased at a reservation smokeshop did not preempt the state from taxing the sales made to nonmembers of the tribe. The tribe's low tax had attracted many non-Indian purchasers seeking to avoid Washington's higher sales tax. As a consequence the tax raised considerable revenue. The Court's holding destroyed the tribe's tax advantage. In both *Merrion* and *Kerr-McGee*, the Court noted the states involved taxed the same activity. What businesses other than oil companies during a time of shortage would voluntarily subject themselves to taxation by both the tribe and the state? *See, e.g., Burlington N.R.R. v. Ft. Peck Tribal Exec. Bd.*, 701 F. Supp. 1493 (D. Mont. 1988) (upholding 3% tribal utility tax on railroad right of way on reservation land). Would the answer depend on the reasonableness of the tribal tax rate? In *Cotton Petr. Corp. v. New Mexico*, 109 S. Ct. 1698 (1989), an oil company argued that tribal taxation preempted state taxation or that in the alternative tribes should be treated as states for purposes of apportioning state and tribal taxes as required by the Interstate Commerce Clause. The Court rejected both arguments. See Chapter 4, section A2b, *infra*.

2. BIA Approval of Tribal Regulations: In *Merrion*, the Court stressed the federal involvement in the tax because the tribal ordinance had been approved by the BIA. Despite the strong language in the case regarding taxation as an inherent right, some wondered whether federal approval was a necessary prerequisite. *Kerr-McGee* put this notion to rest, at least for tribes that did not adopt the Indian Reorganization Act or who chose to amend their constitutions to do away with the "boilerplate" requirement of Secretarial approval for all ordinances. What then, is to prevent a tribe from exacting onerous taxes on those who do business with the tribe?

3. Competing Views of Tribal Power in *Merrion*: How do the majority and dissent's views on tribal sovereignty differ? The majority accepts as an alternative argument that the power to tax is derived from the power to exclude. Does this alternative argument reduce tribal sovereignty in any way? Justice Stevens's dissenting opinion takes a different position on tribal sovereignty, does it not? Justice Stevens's statement that tribes "became part of the United States" so that they "yielded their status as independent nations" posits a voluntary incorporation of tribes into the United States. Is this statement accurate? Moreover, Justice Stevens states that the power to exclude was "granted" to tribes. Is such a statement consistent with the doctrine of inherent sovereignty? The dissenting opinion apparently continues to recognize inherent sovereignty over tribal members. The dissenting justices give tribal power over nonmembers greater scrutiny because of a concern that nonmembers do not have access to the tribal political process. In footnote 4 of *United States v. Carolene Prods.*, 304 U.S. 144, 152-53 n.4 (1938), Justice Stone advanced the theory that defects in the majoritarian process may justify heightened judicial scrutiny of certain laws. Two examples cited in this famous footnote were legislation directly restricting the political process and legislation directed against racial and religious minorities. As to minorities, Justice Stone expressed the concern that "prejudice against discrete and insular minorities may be a special condition, which tends seriously to curtail the operation of those political processes ordinarily to be relied upon to protect minorities." Others have expanded upon this theme, most notably John Hart Ely. *See generally* J.H. ELY, DEMOCRACY AND DISTRUST: A THEORY OF JUDICIAL REVIEW (1980). Should this doctrine be applied to Indian tribes to justify restricting tribal actions that affect nonmembers? For a thoughtful study concluding that the Court's concern for representational integrity coupled with its distrust of tribes has caused the Court to give too little weight to tribal interests, see *The Most Dangerous Branch: An Institutional Approach to Understanding the Role of the Judiciary in American Indian Jurisdictional Determinations*, 1986 WIS. L. REV. 989.

Finally, the majority criticizes the dissent as denigrating tribal sovereignty by according tribes rights only as landowners and not as sovereigns, at least when nonmembers are involved. Do you agree? This theme has become predominant in the area of regulatory jurisdiction, as the next section illustrates.

b. The Power to Regulate Land Use

BRENDALE v. CONFEDERATED TRIBES & BANDS OF THE YAKIMA INDIAN NATION

109 S. Ct. 2994 (June 29, 1989)

[The Confederated Tribes and Bands of the Yakima Indian Nation occupy a reservation in Southeastern Washington of approximately 1.3 million acres. As a result of allotment, 20% of the reservation is now owned in fee by nonmembers of the Nation. Most of the fee lands are within three incorporated townships in the northeastern portion of the reservation. The rest of the fee lands are dispersed throughout the reservation, thus creating the typical checkerboard pattern.

[The western portion of the reservation is known as the closed area, and is primarily forested. The remaining one-third portion of the reservation is used for agricultural, dairy, and residential purposes and is known as the open area. Access to the closed area by the general public is restricted. Of the approximately 740,000 acres of land in the closed area lying within Yakima County, only 25,000 acres are fee land. The tribe has required these nonmember fee owners to get permits to use their land within the closed area until recently; at present the fee owners have access to their property. In contrast to the closed area, fee land comprises almost one-half of the open area.

[Both the Yakima Nation and the County have zoning ordinances covering the fee land within the reservation. The County's ordinance applies only to fee land, and not to trust land. The County has zoned the closed area as forest watershed, a designation that permits cabins, general stores, small motels, restaurants and bars to be built. The tribal zoning ordinance would not permit any such structures to be built within the area. The County designates the open area as general rural, which permits larger lots than does the Yakima Nation ordinance.

[Philip Brendale inherited a 160-acre lot from his mother that had descended from a great aunt, who had been a member of the tribe. Brendale is not a member of the tribe. The County gave Brendale permission to divide his land into 4 parcels. He then sought County permission to subdivide a twenty-acre parcel into ten 2-acre lots to be sold for cabin sites. This use would not be permitted under the tribal zoning law. When the County issued a Declaration of

Non-Significance indicating that an environmental impact statement (EIS) was not necessary, the tribe appealed to the Yakima County Board of Commissioners, arguing that the County had no power to zone the land and that an EIS was necessary in any event. The Commissioners ordered the County to prepare an EIS.

[Stanley Wilkinson is a non-Indian who owns a 40-acre plot in the open area near the northern boundary of the reservation on land overlooking the Yakima airport. Wilkinson sought permission from the County to subdivide his land into 20 lots for single family homes, a use that would not conform to the Yakima Nation ordinance which designated the land as agricultural. Again the County issued a Declaration of Non-Significance, and again the nation challenged both the county's authority to zone and the lack of an EIS. The Commissioners upheld the county planning department on both grounds.

[The Yakima Nation then filed suit in the district court seeking a declaratory judgment that the Yakima Nation had exclusive authority to zone all the land within the reservation and an injunction against further exercise of zoning authority by the county. The district court held that the Nation had exclusive authority to zone the Brendale but not the Wilkinson property. The district court found that the Brendale development would have a substantial detrimental effect on the area by damaging water quality, and disrupting wildlife habitats, for instance. In addition, the court relied on the presence of important religious and cultural sites in the area and the fact that timber harvesting in the area was an important source of income for the tribe. The court found that these same factors were not present in the open area, however. As a result, the court also held that the County was preempted from zoning the closed area, but not the open area. The Ninth Circuit reversed as to the open area, holding that the Nation's authority to zone was exclusive within the entire reservation. The Ninth Circuit reasoned that the essence of zoning ordinances is "to protect against the damage caused by uncontrolled development, which can affect all of the residents and land of the reservation." *Confederated Tribes & Bands of the Yakima Indian Nation v. Whiteside*, 828 F.2d 529, 534 (9th Cir. 1987). Without the ability to enforce a comprehensive zoning plan, the health and welfare of the tribe would be directly affected. Thus, under *Montana v. United States*, the tribe must be able to zone throughout the reservation.

[Brendale and Wilkinson petitioned for certiorari regarding their property; the County petitioned regarding the Wilkinson property only. Justice White, joined by the Chief Justice and Justices Scalia and Kennedy, announced the judgment of the Court regarding the property located in the open area. The justices in the plurality dissented regarding the closed area property. Justice Stevens, joined by Justice O'Connor, issued an opinion announcing the judgment of the Court as to the property located in the closed area and concurring in the judgment as to the open area property. Justice Blackmun, joined by Justices Brennan and Marshall, concurred in the judgment as to the closed area, but dissented as to the open area.

[Justice White first examined the Yakima Nation's 1855 treaty. He concluded that the treaty's promises that the tribe would have exclusive use of the land and authority to exclude non-Indians from the land had been abrogated by allotment of the land under the General Allotment Act. *Montana*, involving very similar treaty language, had settled this question. Moreover, *Montana* also answered the tribe's contention that the Indian Reorganization Act had repudiated the allotment policy and thus reinstated the tribe's right to exclusive use. The IRA only repudiated the policy, it did not restore the fee land to the tribe's exclusive use. Justice White then noted that Justice Stevens had conceded that the Allotment Act abrogated tribal power to exclude nonmembers from fee lands, yet had found a tribal power to define the character of the tribal community based on the power to exclude. Justice White argued that *Montana* contradicts Justice Stevens's position, because *Montana* rejected the argument that tribes have any power to exclude nonmembers or that there is any power derived from the power to exclude that gives tribes the right to regulate the activities of nonmembers. Finally, Justice White criticized Justice Stevens's approach as an unworkable invitation to further litigation because it is based on the percentage of fee lands within an area of the reservation. The plurality opinion then turned to the issue of inherent sovereignty.]

II B

An Indian tribe's treaty power to exclude nonmembers of the tribe from its lands is not the only source of Indian regulatory authority. In [*Merrion v. Jicarilla Apache Tribe*], the Court held that tribes have inherent sovereignty independent of that authority arising from their power to exclude. Prior to the settlement of the New World, Indian tribes were "self-governing sovereign political communities," [*United States v. Wheeler*], and they still retain some "elements of 'quasi-sovereign' authority after ceding their lands to the United States and announcing their dependence on the Federal Government," [*Oliphant*]. Thus, an Indian tribe generally retains sovereignty by way of tribal self-government and control over other aspects of its internal affairs.

A tribe's inherent sovereignty, however, is divested to the extent it is inconsistent with the tribe's dependent status, that is, to the extent it involves a tribe's "external relations." [*Wheeler.*] Those cases in which the Court has found a tribe's sovereignty divested generally are those "involving the relations between an Indian tribe and nonmembers of the tribe." *Ibid.* [*Montana*] recognized the general principle that the "exercise of tribal power beyond what is necessary to protect tribal self-government or to control internal relations is inconsistent with the dependent status of the tribes, and so cannot survive without express congressional delegation." Because regulation of hunting and fishing on fee lands owned by nonmembers of the Tribe did not bear any "clear relationship to tribal self-government or internal relations," this general principle precluded extension of tribal jurisdiction to the fee lands at issue.

The Yakima Nation contends that the Court's insistence in *Montana* on an express congressional delegation of tribal power over nonmembers is inconsistent with language in *Washington v. Confederated Tribes of the Colville Indian Reservation*, 447 U. S. 134, 153 (1980), that tribal powers are divested by implication only when "the exercise of tribal sovereignty would be inconsistent with the overriding interests of the National Government." We do not see this language as inconsistent with *Montana*. As the opinion in *Colville* made clear, that case involved "[t]he power to tax transactions occurring on trust lands and significantly involving a tribe or its members." *Id.*, at 152. It did not involve the regulation of fee lands, as did *Montana*. Moreover, the Court in *Montana* itself reconciled the two cases, citing *Colville* as an example of the sort of "consensual relationship" that might even support tribal authority over nonmembers on fee lands.[10]

[No one contends] that Congress has expressly delegated to the Yakima Nation the power to zone fee lands of nonmembers of the Tribe. Therefore under the general principle enunciated in *Montana*, the Yakima Nation has no authority to impose its zoning ordinance on the fee lands owned by petitioners Brendale and Wilkinson.

C

Our inquiry does not end here because the opinion in *Montana* noted two "exceptions" to its general principle. First, "[a] tribe may regulate, through taxation, licensing, or other means, the activities of nonmembers who enter consensual relationships with the tribe or its members, through commercial dealing, contracts, leases, or other arrangements." Second, "[a] tribe may also retain inherent power to exercise civil authority over the conduct of non-Indians on fee lands within its reservation when that conduct threatens or has some direct effect on the political integrity, the economic security, or the health or welfare of the tribe."

The parties agree that the first *Montana* exception does not apply in this case. [Instead, the Tribe] contends that the Tribe has authority to zone under the second *Montana* exception. We disagree.

Initially, we reject as overbroad the Ninth Circuit's categorical acceptance of tribal zoning authority over lands within reservation boundaries. We find it significant that the so-called second *Montana* exception is prefaced by the word "may" — "[a] tribe *may* also retain inherent power to exercise civil authority over the conduct of non-Indians on fee lands within its reservation." (emphasis added.) This indicates to us that a tribe's authority need not extend to all conduct that "threatens or has some direct effect on the political integrity, the economic security, or the health or welfare of the tribe," but instead depends on the circumstances. The Ninth Circuit, however, transformed this indication that there may be other cases in which a tribe has an interest in activities of nonmembers on fee land into a rule describing every case in which a tribe has such an interest. Indeed, the Ninth Circuit equated an Indian tribe's retained sovereignty with a local government's police power, which is contrary to *Montana* itself.

It is also evident that literal application of the second exception would make little sense in the circumstances of this case. To hold that the tribe has authority to zone fee land when the activity on that land has the specified effect on Indian properties would mean that the authority would last only so long as the threat-

---

[10] The Yakima Nation's reliance on statements about retained tribal sovereignty in *National Farmers Union Ins. Co. v. Crow Tribe*, and *Iowa Mutual Ins. Co. v. LaPlante*, is likewise misplaced. In neither of those cases did the Court decide whether the Indian tribe had authority over the nonmembers involved. Instead, the Court established an exhaustion rule, allowing the tribal courts initially to determine whether they have jurisdiction, and left open the possibility that the exercise of jurisdiction could be later challenged in federal court.

ening use continued. If it ceased, zoning power would revert to the county. Under the District Court's interpretation of *Montana*, not only would regulatory authority depend in the first instance on a factual inquiry into how a tribe's interests are affected by a particular use of fee land, but as circumstances changed over time, so, too, would the authority to zone. Conceivably, in a case like this, zoning authority could vest variously in the county and the tribe, switching back and forth between the two, depending on what uses the county permitted on the fee land at issue. Uncertainty of this kind would not further the interests of either the tribe or the county government and would be chaotic for landowners.[12]

Montana should therefore not be understood to vest zoning authority in the tribe when fee land is used in certain ways. The governing principle is that the tribe has no authority itself, by way of tribal ordinance or actions in the tribal courts, to regulate the use of fee land. The inquiry thus becomes whether and to what extent the tribe has a protectable interest in what activities are taking place on fee land within the reservation and, if it has such an interest, how it may be protected. Of course, under ordinary law, neighbors often have a protectable interest in what is occurring on adjoining property and may seek relief in an appropriate forum, judicial or otherwise. *Montana* suggests that in the special circumstances of checkerboard ownership of lands within a reservation, the tribe has an interest under federal law, defined in terms of the impact of the challenged uses on the political integrity, economic security, or the health or welfare of the tribe. But, as we have indicated above, that interest does not entitle the tribe to complain or obtain relief against every use of fee land that has some adverse effect on the tribe. The impact must be demonstrably serious and must imperil the political integrity, economic security or the health and welfare of the tribe. This standard will sufficiently protect Indian tribes while at the same time avoiding undue interference with state sovereignty and providing the certainty needed by property owners.

Since the tribes' protectable interest is one arising under federal law, the Supremacy Clause requires state and local governments, including Yakima County zoning authorities, to recognize and respect that interest in the course of their activities. The Tribe in this case, as it should have, first appeared in the county zoning proceedings, but its submission should have been, not that the county was without zoning authority over fee land within the Reservation, but that its tribal interests were imperiled. [G]iven that the county has jurisdiction to zone fee lands on the Reservation and would be enjoinable only if it failed to respect the rights of the Tribe under federal law, the proper course for the District Court in the Brendale phase of this case would have been to stay its hand until the zoning proceedings had been completed. At that time, a judgment could be made as to whether the uses that were actually authorized on Brendale's property imperiled the political integrity, the economic security, or

---

[12] Justice BLACKMUN asserts that his position, that "the general and longer-term advantages of comprehensive land management" justify tribal zoning of fee land, avoids this uncertainty. But this broad position would also authorize the Yakima Nation to zone all fee land within reservation boundaries, including that within the incorporated towns of Toppenish, Wapato, and Harrah. Although Justice BLACKMUN purports to avoid this "difficult question," there appears to be no principled basis on which to exclude the incorporated towns from the Tribe's zoning authority without leading to the very uncertainty Justice BLACKMUN attempts to dismiss as hypothetical.

the health or welfare of the Tribe. If due regard is given to the Tribe's protectable interest at all stages of the proceedings, we have every confidence that the nightmarish consequences predicted by Justice BLACKMUN, will be avoided. Of course if practice proves otherwise, Congress can take appropriate action.

III

The District Court found that Yakima County's exercise of zoning power over the Wilkinson property would have no direct effect on the Tribe and would not threaten the Tribe's political integrity, economic security, or health and welfare. [Based on these findings,] I would reverse the judgment of the Ninth Circuit as to the Wilkinson property.

The Brendale property presents a different situation. At the time the Tribe filed its suit, the County had agreed with the Tribe that an EIS was required before Brendale's development could go forward. The zoning proceedings had thus not been concluded, and the District Court's judgment was that the county had no power to go forward. That judgment was infirm under the approach outlined in this opinion. The zoning proceedings should have been allowed to conclude and it may be that those proceedings would adequately recognize tribal interests and make unnecessary further action in the District Court. If it were otherwise, the District Court could then decide whether the uses the State permits on the Brendale property would do serious injury to and clearly imperil the protectable tribal interests identified in this opinion. This part of the case in my view should therefore be returned to District Court. A majority of this Court, however, disagrees with this conclusion.

Accordingly, since with respect to the Wilkinson property, Justice STEVENS and Justice O'CONNOR agree that the judgment of the Court of Appeals in Nos. 87-1697 and 87-1711 should be reversed, that is the judgment of the Court in those cases. With respect to the Brendale property, I would vacate the judgment of the Court of Appeals and remand the case to the Court of Appeals with instructions to vacate the judgment of the District Court and to remand the case to that Court for further proceedings. Because the Court instead affirms the judgment of the Court of Appeals in No. 87-1622, I dissent as to that case.

Justice STEVENS, joined by Justice O'CONNOR, delivered an opinion announcing the judgment of the Court [regarding the Brendale property] and concurring in the judgment [regarding the Wilkinson property].

The United States has granted to many Indian tribes, including the Yakima Nation — "a power unknown to any other sovereignty in this Nation: a power to exclude nonmembers entirely from territory reserved for the tribe." [Merrion] (Stevens, J., dissenting). That power necessarily must include the lesser power to regulate land use in the interest of protecting the tribal community. Thus, the proper resolution of these cases depends on the extent to which the Tribe's virtually absolute power to exclude has been either diminished by federal statute or voluntarily surrendered by the Tribe itself. The facts of record, which are summarized in Justice WHITE's opinion, dictate a different answer as to the two tracts of land at issue.

I

[Tribal power] to exclude nonmembers from a defined geographical area obviously includes the lesser power to define the character of that area. In *New Mexico v. Mescalero Apache Tribe*, 462 U.S. 324 (1983), a unanimous Court recognized that "[a] tribe's power to exclude nonmembers entirely or to condition their presence on the reservation is ... well established." Likewise, in *Merrion*, the Court [also relied on the power to exclude as including the "lesser-included power ... to place ... conditions on the non-Indian's conduct or continued presence on the reservation"]. It is difficult to imagine a power that follows more forcefully from the power to exclude than the power to require that nonmembers, as a condition of entry, not disturb the traditional character of the reserved area.

At one time, the Yakima Nation's power to exclude nonmembers from its reservation was near-absolute. This power derived from [the tribe's inherent sovereignty and the 1855 Treaty]. [A]s of 1859, the Tribe's power to exclude was firmly established. The power to regulate land use ran parallel to the power to exclude. Just as the Tribe had authority to limit absolutely access to the Reservation, so it could also limit access to persons whose activities would conform to the Tribe's general plan for land use.

The Indian General Allotment Act of 1887 (Dawes Act), however, to some extent reworked fundamental notions of Indian sovereignty. [I]n 1934, the Indian Reorganization Act repudiated the allotment policy. In the interim, however, large portions of reservation lands were conveyed to nonmembers such as petitioners Wilkinson and Brendale.

The Dawes Act did not itself transfer any regulatory power from the Tribe to any state or local governmental authority. Nonetheless, by providing for the allotment and ultimate alienation of reservation land, the Act in some respects diminished tribal authority. As we recognized in [Montana, a] statute that authorizes the sale of a parcel of land in a reservation must implicitly grant the purchaser access to that property. In addition, to the extent that large portions of reservation land were sold in fee, such that the Tribe could no longer determine the essential character of the region by setting conditions on entry to those parcels, the Tribe's legitimate interest in land use regulation was also diminished. Although it is inconceivable that Congress would have intended that the sale of a few lots would divest the Tribe of the power to determine the character of the tribal community, it is equally improbable that Congress envisioned that the Tribe would retain its interest in regulating the use of vast ranges of land sold in fee to nonmembers who lack any voice in setting tribal policy.

Since the Dawes Act provided that individual allotments would be held in trust by the United States for members of the Tribe for a period of at least 25 years, it is evident that the tribal authority over land use within the Reservation remained undiminished during that period and at least until actual transfers of land to nonmembers began to occur. [A]s early as 1954 the Tribe had divided its Reservation into two parts, which the parties and the District Court consistently described as the "closed area" and the "open area," and the tribe continues to maintain the closed area as a separate community. That division, which was made many years before either petitioner Brendale or petitioner Wilkinson acquired title to reservation land, is of critical importance and requires a different disposition of their respective cases.[2]

II

[The Tribal] Council in a 1954 resolution declared "that the open range and forested area of the Yakima Indian Reservation is to *remain* closed to the general public" to protect the area's "grazing, forest, and wildlife resources." Resolution of Yakima Tribal Council (Aug. 4, 1954) (emphasis supplied). Under the 1954 resolution, entry into this area was "restricted to enrolled members of the Yakima Tribe, official agency employees, person with bona fide property or business interests," close relatives of enrolled members, members of certain other tribes, and certain permittees. In addition, the resolution provided that "[e]ntry into closed areas is forbidden all persons while under the influence of liquor."

[O]nly 25,000 acres [of the 807,000-acre closed area] are owned in fee. For the most part this area consists of forests, which provide the major source of income to the Tribe. Virtually all of the fee land is owned by lumber companies whose operations are subject to regulation by the Bureau of Indian Affairs (BIA). Excluding [this] land, the remaining fee land constitutes less than one percent of the closed area. There are no permanent inhabitants of the Yakima County portion of the closed area. One state-maintained highway traverses a portion of the area and several roads maintained by the BIA provide access to the closed area's interior. Apparently, however, the county does not maintain any roads in this portion of the reservation.

The Tribe operates a "courtesy permit system" that allows selected groups of visitors access to the closed area. [The Tribe] enforce[s] the courtesy permit system by monitoring ingress and egress at four guard stations and by patrolling the interior of the closed area.

Until recently the BIA supported the Tribe's policy of denying entry into the closed area by restricting use of BIA roads to members of the Tribe and a narrowly defined class of permittees. [I]n 1988 the BIA ultimately decided to allow the public to use BIA roads because they had been constructed with public funds. Contrary to the suggestion in Justice WHITE's opinion, however, the fact that nonmembers may now drive on these roads does not change the basic character of the closed area or undermine the Tribe's historic and consistent interest in preserving the pristine character of this vast, uninhabited portion of its Reservation.

[The District Court found that Brendale's] proposal would have a number of adverse environmental consequences and that the only interest that Yakima County possessed in overseeing the use of the Brendale property was that of "providing regulatory functions to its taxpaying citizens." The county did not appeal from the District Court's decision holding that the Tribe has the exclusive authority to regulate land use in the closed area.[3]

---

[2] The labels "closed area" and "open area" are, of course, irrelevant to my analysis. What is important is that the Tribe has maintained a defined area in which only a very small percentage of the land is held in fee and another defined area in which approximately half of the land is held in fee.

[3] Because the county did not appeal, we are not presented with the question whether the county might possess concurrent zoning jurisdiction over the closed area. The possibility that the county

Although the logging operations, the construction of BIA roads, and the transfer of ownership of a relatively insignificant amount of land in the closed area unquestionably has diminished the Tribe's power to exclude non-Indians from that portion of its Reservation, this does not justify the conclusion that the Tribe has surrendered its historic right to regulate land use in the restricted portion of the Reservation. By maintaining the power to exclude nonmembers from entering all but a small portion of the closed area, the Tribe has preserved the power to define the essential character of that area.

[Thus, the question becomes] whether the Tribe has authority to prevent the few individuals who own portions of the closed area in fee from undermining its general plan to preserve the character of this unique resource by developing their isolated parcels without regard to an otherwise common scheme. More simply, the question is whether the owners of the small amount of fee land may bring a pig into the parlor. In my opinion, just as Congress could not possibly have intended in enacting the Dawes Act that tribes would maintain the power to exclude bona fide purchasers of reservation land from that property, it could not have intended that tribes would lose control over the character of their reservations upon the sale of a few, relatively small parcels of land. Neither proposition is explicit in the Dawes Act, yet both appear necessary to a reasonable operation of the allotment process. [T]he Tribe's power to zone is like an equitable servitude; the burden of complying with the Tribe's zoning rules runs with the land without regard to how a particular estate is transferred. Cf. R. Cunningham, W. Stoebuck, & D. Whitman, Law of Property §§ 8.22-8.32, pp. 485-506 (1984) (hereinafter Cunningham). Indeed, there is strong authority for the proposition that equitable servitudes fall within the same family of property law as easements. See C. Clark, Real Covenants and Other Interests Which "Run with Land" 174-175 (1947); Pound, The Progress of the Law, 1918-1919, Equity, 33 Harv. L. Rev. 813 (1920). There is no basis for concluding that the allotted property carried the benefit of one type of "servitude" and not the burden of the other.

[N]otwithstanding the transfer of a small percentage of allotted land the Tribe retains its legitimate interest in the preservation of the character of the reservation. The Tribe's power to control the use of discrete, fee parcels of the land is simply incidental to its power to preserve the character of what remains almost entirely a region reserved for the exclusive benefit of the Tribe.

Nor does the Court's decision in [*Montana*] require a different result. First, the *Montana* case involved a discriminatory land use regulation. [In this case,] it is Brendale who seeks a special, privileged status. Second, in the *Montana* case we were careful to point out that the conduct of the non-Indians on their fee lands posed no threat to the welfare of the Tribe. In sharp contrast, in this case the District Court expressly found that Brendale's

> "planned development of recreational housing places critical assets of the Closed Area in jeopardy.... [O]f paramount concern to this court is the threat to the Closed Area's cultural and spiritual values. To allow development in this unique and undeveloped area would drastically diminish those intangible values. That in turn would undoubt-

---

might have jurisdiction to prohibit certain land uses in the closed area does not suggest that the Tribe lacks similar authority. This sort of concurrent jurisdiction, if it does exist, is simply a product of the unique overlapping of governmental authority that characterizes much of our Indian-law jurisprudence. See, *e.g., Cotton Petroleum Corp. v. New Mexico*, [109 S. Ct. 1698] (1989).

edly negatively affect the general health and welfare of the Yakima Nation and its members. This court must conclude therefore that the Yakima Nation may regulate the use that Brendale makes of his fee land within the Reservation's Closed Area." 617 F. Supp., at 744.

Finally, in holding in the *Montana* case that the Tribe could not regulate non-Indian fishing and hunting on fee land within the reservation, we stressed that the State of Montana, and not the Tribe, stocked the river with fish and provided a portion of the game found on the reservation. In addition, we held that the State owned the bed of the Big Horn River and thus rejected the Tribe's contention that it was entitled to regulate fishing and duck hunting in the river based on its purported ownership interest. No such state or county interest is asserted in this case.

In my view, the fact that a very small proportion of the closed area is owned in fee does not deprive the Tribe of the right to ensure that this area maintains its unadulterated character. This is particularly so in a case such as this in which the zoning rule at issue is neutrally applied, is necessary to protect the welfare of the Tribe, and does not interfere with any significant state or county interest. Although application of the pre-emption analysis advocated by Justice WHITE provides some assurance that the Reservation will not be overrun by various uses inconsistent with important tribal interests, it does not provide a means by which the Tribe can continue to define the character of the restricted area. The incremental shifts in the texture and quality of the surrounding environment occasioned by discrete land-use decisions within an expansive territory are not readily monitored or regulated by considering "whether the uses that were actually authorized on [the relevant] property imperiled the political integrity, the economic security, or the health or welfare of the Tribe."

I therefore agree with Justice BLACKMUN that the Tribe may zone the Brendale property. The judgment of the Court of Appeals is accordingly affirmed in No. 87-1622.

III

The authority of the Tribe to enact and enforce zoning ordinances applicable in the open area — where petitioner Wilkinson's property is located — requires a different analysis. Although the Tribe originally had the power to exclude non-Indians from the entire Reservation, the "subsequent alienation" of about half of the property in the open area has produced an integrated community that is not economically or culturally delimited by reservation boundaries. Because the Tribe no longer has the power to exclude nonmembers from a large portion of this area, it also lacks the power to define the essential character of the territory. As a result, the Tribe's interest in preventing inconsistent uses is dramatically curtailed. For this reason, I agree with Justice WHITE that the Tribe lacks authority to regulate the use of Wilkinson's property. So long as the land is not used in a manner that is pre-empted by federal law, the Tribe has no special claim to relief. It, of course, retains authority to regulate the use of trust land, and the county does not contend otherwise.

Unlike the closed area, the Tribe makes no attempt to control access to the open area. In this respect, the District Court found that "access to the area is not limited by the Yakima Nation and non-tribal members move freely throughout the area." The county has constructed and maintained 187 miles of road, all of which are equally accessible to reservation residents and the general public. Although the Tribe has asserted that it has the authority to regulate land use in the three incorporated towns, it has never attempted to do so. [The open area has been developed, while the closed area remains wilderness. Moreover, tribal members comprise only 20 percent of the open area's population. While both Indians and non-Indians can vote in County elections, only tribal members can vote in tribal elections. The County also provides social services to all, while] services provided by the Tribe — although theoretically available to all residents — are in practice generally used only by members of the Tribe. Furthermore, the District Court found that the county has a substantial interest in regulating land use in the open area — and in particular in protecting "the county's valuable agricultural land" — and that the open area lacks "a unique religious or spiritual significance to the members of the Yakima Nation."

[Since] a large percentage of the land in the open area is owned in fee [or leased] by nonmembers, [the Tribe] would have been unable [by exercising its power to exclude nonmembers] to establish the essential character of the region. In such circumstances, allowing a nonmember to use his or her land in a manner that might not be approved by the Tribal Council does not upset an otherwise coherent scheme of land use. [T]o the extent the open area has lost its character as an exclusive tribal resource, and has become, as a practical matter, an integrated portion of the county, the Tribe has also lost any claim to an interest analogous to an equitable servitude. Under the "change of neighborhood" doctrine, an equitable servitude lapses when the restriction, as applied to "the general vicinity and not merely a few parcels," has "become outmoded," has "lost its usefulness," or has become "'inequitable' to enforce." Cunningham § 8.20, pp. 482-483. See also Restatement of Property § 564 (1944). Because the open area no longer maintains the character of a unique tribal asset and because the Tribe accordingly lacks a substantial interest in governing land use, the power to zone has "become outmoded."

I therefore agree with Justice WHITE's conclusion that the Tribe lacks authority to zone the Wilkinson property.

IV

My conclusion that the dramatically different facts of these two cases should produce different results is subject to the obvious criticism that it does not identify a bright-line rule. The primary responsibility for line-drawing, however, is vested in the legislature. Moreover, line-drawing is inherent in the continuum that exists between those reservations that still maintain their status as distinct social structures and those that have become integrated in other local polities. [I]t would be fundamentally unfair to deny appropriate relief to either party in this case, which involves no difficulty in discerning the proper line, simply because a future case may be more difficult.

Accordingly, in No. 87-1622, the judgment of the Court of Appeals is affirmed. I concur in the judgment in Nos. 87-1697 and 87-1711, reversing the judgment of the Court of Appeals.

Justice BLACKMUN, with whom Justice BRENNAN and Justice MARSHALL join, concurring in the judgment in No. 87-1622 and dissenting in Nos. 87-1697 and 87-1711.

The Court's combined judgment in these consolidated cases — splitting tribal zoning authority over non-Indian fee lands between the so-called "open" and "closed" areas of the Yakima Indian Reservation — is Solomonic in appearance only. This compromise result arises from two distinct approaches to tribal sovereignty, each of which is inconsistent with this Court's past decisions and undermines the Federal Government's longstanding commitment to the promotion of tribal autonomy. Because the Court's judgment that the tribe does not have zoning authority over non-Indian fee lands in the "open" area of its reservation is wrong, in my view, as a matter of law and fashions a patently unworkable legal rule, I dissent in Nos. 87-1697 and 87-1711. Because Justice STEVENS' opinion reaches the right result for the wrong reason with respect to the Tribe's authority to zone non-Indian fee lands in the closed portion of the Reservation, I concur in the judgment [regarding the Brendale property].

I

[W]ith what seems to me to be no more than a perfunctory discussion of this Court's decisions both before and after *Montana*, Justice WHITE's opinion reads that case as establishing a general rule, modified only by two narrow exceptions, that Indian tribes have no authority over the activities of non-Indians on their reservations absent express congressional delegation.

Applying this rule, Justice WHITE further suggests that *Montana*'s "second exception" [does not permit] an Indian tribe to make rational and comprehensive land-use decisions for its reservation. Such a holding would guarantee that adjoining reservation lands would be subject to inconsistent and potentially incompatible zoning policies, and for all practical purposes would strip tribes of the power to protect the integrity of *trust* lands over which they enjoy unquestioned and exclusive authority.

[It is clear] *Montana* must be read to recognize the inherent authority of tribes to exercise civil jurisdiction over non-Indian activities on tribal reservations where those activities, as they do in the case of land use, implicate a significant tribal interest.

[O]nly once prior to *Montana* (and never thereafter) has [this Court] found an additional sovereign power to have been relinquished upon incorporation. [In *Oliphant*] we concluded that inherent criminal jurisdiction over non-Indians is inconsistent with the dependent status of the tribes. But our [later] decision in *Colville* [established] that nothing in *Oliphant* negates our historical understanding that the tribes retain substantial *civil* jurisdiction over non-Indians. [S]ubsequent to *Montana* [we] have reaffirmed this view: [holding] without equivocation that tribal civil jurisdiction over non-Indians on reservation lands is not an aspect of tribal sovereignty necessarily divested by reason of the tribes' incorporation with the dominant society. [*Merrion*.] And in *Iowa Mutual Ins. Co. v. LaPlante*, 480 U.S. 9 (1987), we noted: "Tribal authority over the activities of non-Indians on reservation lands is an important part of tribal sovereignty. Civil jurisdiction over such activities presumptively lies in the tribal courts unless affirmatively limited by a specific treaty provision or federal stat-ute."[5] These cases, like their predecessors, clearly recognize that tribal civil jurisdiction over non-Indians on reservation lands is consistent with the depen-dent status of the tribes.

[Given this background, the Court has read *Montana* too broadly.] Although the Court's opinion reads as a restatement, not as a revision, of existing doc-trine, it contains language flatly inconsistent with its prior decisions defining the scope of inherent tribal jurisdiction. [O]f critical importance for deciding the instant case, the *Montana* presumption has found no place in our subsequent decisions discussing inherent sovereignty.

But to recognize that *Montana* strangely reversed the otherwise consistent presumption in favor of inherent tribal sovereignty over reservation lands is not to excise the decision from our jurisprudence. Despite the reversed presump-tion, the plain language of *Montana* itself expressly preserves substantial tribal authority over non-Indian activity on reservations, including fee lands, and, more particularly, may sensibly be read as recognizing inherent tribal authority to zone fee lands.

[D]espite *Montana*'s reversal of the usual presumption in favor of inherent sovereignty over reservation activity, the decision reasonably may be read, and, in my view, should be read, to recognize that tribes may regulate the on-reserva-tion conduct of non-Indians whenever a significant tribal interest is threatened or directly affected. So construed, *Montana* fits with relative ease into the con-stellation of this Court's sovereignty jurisprudence.

Under this approach, once the tribe's valid regulatory interest is established, the nature of land ownership does not diminish the tribe's inherent power to regulate in the area. [There is no] power more central to "the economic secu-rity, or the health or welfare of the tribe," than the power to zone. [The] power of local governments to control land use is especially vital to Indians, who enjoy a unique historical and cultural connection to the land. And how can anyone doubt that a tribe's inability to zone substantial tracts of fee land within its own reservation — tracts that are inextricably intermingled with reservation trust lands — would destroy the tribe's ability to engage in the systematic and coordi-nated utilization of land that is the very essence of zoning authority? See N. Williams, American Land Planning Law § 1.08 (1988). [I]f *Montana* is to fit at all within this Court's Indian sovereignty jurisprudence, zoning authority — even over fee lands — must fall within the scope of tribal jurisdiction under *Montana*.

A finding of inherent zoning authority here would in no way conflict with *Montana*'s actual holding. [T]he critical difficulty in *Montana* was the tribe's failure even to allege that the non-Indians whose fishing and hunting it sought to regulate were in any measure affecting "[t]he political integrity, the economic security, or the health or welfare of the tribe."

---

[5] Justice WHITE would read *Iowa Mutual Ins. Co.* as not reaching the question whether tribal courts have civil jurisdiction over non-Indians, and dismisses the case as establishing no more than "an exhaustion rule" permitting tribal courts to determine their jurisdiction, or lack thereof, in the first instance. [Although] *Iowa Mutual* does reaffirm the exhaustion rule established in *National Farmers Union* [it] also stands for the proposition that civil jurisdiction over non-Indians *is* a recognized part of inherent tribal sovereignty and exists "unless affirmatively limited by a specific treaty provision or federal statute." 480 U.S., at 18.

Justice WHITE's opinion rejects this reading of *Montana* for several reasons, none of which withstands scrutiny. [He] suggests that applying *Montana*'s language literally to the problem of zoning fee lands would create the peculiar, and untenable, situation of having zoning authority vary over time between the tribe and the State depending on what effect a proposed land use might have on the tribe. This hypothetical problem is entirely of Justice WHITE's own creation. *Montana*'s literal language does not require, as he claims, a parcel-by-parcel, use-by-use determination whether a proposed use of fee land will threaten the political integrity, economic security, or health or welfare of the tribe. The threat to the tribe does not derive solely from the proposed uses of specific parcels of fee lands (which admittedly would vary over time and place). The threat stems from the loss of the general and longer-term advantages of comprehensive land management.

[The] opinion fashions a newfangled federal nuisance-type cause of action by which the tribe may bring suit in federal court to enjoin a particular proposed land use that seriously imperils the political integrity, economic security, or health or welfare of the tribe. While resort to this proposed cause of action may ultimately prevent blatantly abusive non-Indian uses of reservation lands, the opportunity to engage in protracted litigation over every proposed land use that conflicts with tribal interests does nothing to recognize the tribe's legitimate sovereign right to regulate the lands within its reservation, with the view to the long-term, active management of land use that is the very difference between zoning and case-by-case nuisance litigation.

[A] majority of the Court with respect to the "open" area, [has] established a regime that guarantees that neither the State nor the tribe will be able to establish a comprehensive zoning plan. Although under the majority's rule landowners may be certain as to which zoning authority controls the use of their land, adjoining parcels of land throughout the "open" area of the reservation (and throughout the entire reservation under Justice WHITE's theory) will be zoned by different zoning authorities with competing and perhaps inconsistent land-use priorities. This, in practice, will be nothing short of a nightmare, nullifying the efforts of both sovereigns to segregate incompatible land uses and exacerbating the already considerable tensions that exist between local and tribal governments in many parts of the Nation about the best use of reservation lands.

[I]t is my view that under all of this Court's inherent sovereignty decisions, including *Montana*, tribes retain the power to zone non-Indian fee lands on the reservation. [A]t the expense of long-recognized tribal rights, many of our precedents, and 150 years of federal policy, Justice WHITE's opinion replaces sovereignty with a form of legal tokenism: the opportunity to sue in court has replaced the opportunity to exercise sovereign authority. This substitution is without sound basis in law, and without practical value.

While Justice WHITE's opinion misreads the Court's decisions defining the limits of inherent tribal sovereignty, Justice STEVENS' opinion disregards those decisions altogether. By grounding the tribe's authority to zone non-Indian fee lands exclusively in its power to exclude non-Indians from the reservation, and by refusing even to consider whether the Tribe's inherent authority might support the zoning of non-Indian fee lands in the "open area," Justice STEVENS' opinion appears implicitly to conclude that tribes have no inherent authority over non-Indians on reservation lands. As is evident from my discussion of Justice WHITE's opinion, this conclusion stands in flat contradiction to every relevant Indian sovereignty case that this Court has decided.

Justice STEVENS' opinion also is at odds with this Court's reservation disestablishment decisions. [See Chapter 1, section B3 — Eds.] Justice STEVENS distinguishes between the "open" and "closed" areas of the Reservation on the ground that Congress, in enacting the Dawes Act, could not have intended for tribes to maintain zoning authority over non-Indian fee lands where, as in the "open area" of the Yakima Reservation, the allotment of reservation lands "has produced an integrated community that is not economically or culturally delimited by reservation boundaries." I fail to see how this distinction can be squared with this Court's decisions specifically rejecting arguments that those reservation areas where the Dawes Act has resulted in substantial non-Indian land ownership should be treated differently for jurisdictional purposes from those areas where tribal holdings predominate. See, e.g., Seymour [v. Superintendent], 368 U.S., [351], 357-359 [(1962)]. And I do not see how Justice STEVENS' theory can be squared with the unequivocal holdings of our cases that the Dawes Act did not diminish the reservation status of reservation lands alienated to non-Indian owners even where that part of the reservation had "lost its [Indian] identity." See, e.g., Mattz [v. Arnett], 412 U.S. [481,] 484-485 [(1973)].

[T]o the extent that Justice STEVENS' opinion discusses the characteristics of a reservation area where the Tribe possesses authority to zone because it has preserved the "essential character of the reservation," these characteristics betray a stereotyped and almost patronizing view of Indians and reservation life. The opinion describes the "closed area" of the Yakima Reservation as "pristine," and emphasizes that it is spiritually significant to the tribe and yields natural foods and medicines. The opinion then contrasts this unadulterated portion of the reservation with the "open area," which is "marked by 'residential and commercial developmen[t].'" In my view, even under Justice STEVENS' analysis, it must not be the case that tribes can retain the "essential character" of their reservations (necessary to the exercise of zoning authority), only if they forgo economic development and maintain those reservations according to a single, perhaps quaint, view of what is characteristically "Indian" today.

[In conclusion, o]ur past decision and common sense compel a finding that the tribe has zoning authority over all the lands within its reservation....

NOTES

1. Tribal Regulatory Jurisdiction After *Brendale*: Can any coherent land use management scheme be enforced on a heavily-allotted Indian reservation after *Brendale* by either the County or the tribe? Justice White's opinion would deny the tribe the right to zone any fee land whether in the open or closed areas of the reservation. What, if any, protection does his opinion give to the tribe involved? As to the closed area, Justice White's position did not carry a majority. Justice Stevens would permit the tribe to zone the closed area. How does Justice Stevens's view of tribal sovereignty differ from Justice White's? Note that both Justice Stevens and Justice White refer to property concepts in discussing tribal power. Has tribal power, at least in the area of land use planning, been denigrated to an equitable servitude? Would Justice Stevens recognize any inherent power over non-Indians that did not derive from the power to exclude?

Since a majority of the Court did not agree on the reasoning, how can a tribe determine whether it will be able to zone fee land? The opinion written by Justice Stevens with Justice O'Connor concurring will provide the crucial determining factor, because Justices White, Rehnquist, Scalia, and Kennedy oppose tribal zoning of any fee land, while the three dissenting justices would permit all zoning of fee land. What guidance does that opinion give? Justice Stevens bases tribal power on the power to exclude nonmembers from trust land. He argues that if there is sufficient trust land within an area so that if the tribe exercised its power to exclude nonmembers from that land it could define the character of the community, then the tribe should be able to zone the fee land as well as the trust land. If the percentage of fee land alone is determinative, would you advise a tribe to attempt to define a closed area with less fee land? Justice Stevens also considered the character of the area. In *Brendale*, the open area had been fairly well developed, with three incorporated townships. The area also abutted the border of the reservation near the Yakima municipal airport. If fee land were scattered more evenly throughout an entire reservation, would Justice Stevens find the tribe had more or less power to regulate land use?

2. Implications of *Brendale* for Regulation of Nonmembers: Does *Brendale* threaten taxation of nonmembers doing business on the reservation or regulation of nonmembers engaging in other activities on trust lands? Justice White's opinion distinguished *Washington v. Confederated Tribes of the Colville Indian Reservation*, 447 U.S. 134 (1980), which upheld a cigarette tax imposed on nonmembers, on the basis that *Colville* involved activities that were both consensual and occurring on trust lands. Thus, at the very least, the *Montana* exception for consensual activities continues to be valid. The second *Montana* exception is surely on shakier grounds after *Brendale*, however. As the dissent points out, if one considers land use planning as a whole, it seems obvious that comprehensive land use controls are essential to maintain a community's political integrity. Justice White's opinion did not look at the entire subject of land use, however, but refocused the inquiry instead on whether a particular proposed land use might threaten the tribe's political integrity, economic security, or health and welfare. Having recast the inquiry from the general to the particular, Justice White then argued that tribal power cannot vary depending on particular usage, because it would vary continually over time, depending on changing circumstances. Is this a logical argument? In recent years the Environmental Protection Agency has treated tribes the same as states for purposes of enforcing various environmental laws. After *Brendale*, the EPA can still continue this practice, but must it?

E. THE ROLE OF DISTINCTIVE TRIBAL GOVERNMENTS IN THE TWENTY-FIRST CENTURY

BRAKEL, AMERICAN INDIAN TRIBAL COURTS: THE COST OF SEPARATE JUSTICE 99-103 (American Bar Foundation, 1978)*

Cultural Survival Versus Cultural Demise

Persons who favor the continued operation of the tribal courts often associate the survival of the courts with the survival of tribal culture in general, and vice-versa. The demise of the courts, they say, would spell the demise of Indian culture. While it appears to be logical and has an immediate appeal, this either-or, all-or-nothing stance should be considered more closely.

It is implied that if one does not support one tribal institution one is anti-Indian, that if one does not recognize a total political-cultural autonomy for the Indians one must favor a total melting-pot assimilation. All claims of separate autonomy are regarded as natural; any movement toward integration is regarded as imposed and artificial. Such an extreme position is not helpful in discussing Indian affairs and problems in general or in assessing the workability of the tribal courts.

Whatever historical or moral arguments one may muster to the contrary, whatever ancient doctrines of "residual" sovereignty or present-day claims to white reparations may exist, it appears anomalous in the latter part of the twentieth century that one small ethnic group should be separated from the judicial system that extends to all other citizens of the United States. The burden of persuasion for separatist ideas should fall on the proponents of separatism. In the case for separate tribal courts, instead of advancing the usual political and mystical arguments, proponents should show that the courts have concrete operational advantages.

The present performance of the tribal courts can hardly be said to indicate the vitality of Indian tribal culture. Terminating their operation does not mean the end of Indian culture, realistically defined. Finally, in contrast with tribal leaders or spokesmen, the average reservation resident has little interest in seeing the tribal court system maintained or expanded.

Indian Courts Versus Indian Culture

In both conception and operation, the tribal courts are little more than pale copies of the white system. All remedies to their operational problems are directed toward making them better copies. This leaves only "localism" as a justification for their existence — that is, the desire for and convenience of locally controlled institutions. Local control, however, must be exercised responsibly: there must be mechanisms to check abuse of power and to promote optimum use of talent. In my view, official authority would be best utilized and personal power on the reservations would be best checked within the normal integrated setting of, and with the mechanisms available under, state and county jurisdiction. In twentieth-century America, the integrated approach is the only realistic

---

and the only acceptable approach (for Indians as well as non-Indians). Integration into the larger judicial system does not necessarily threaten the preservation of the elements of Indian culture that are capable of being preserved or the revival of those that are worthy of being revived any more than the perpetuation of a dependent and often inauthentic tribalism would guarantee them.

Even the most favored of the tribal courts are burdened by inexperienced and unprofessional judges, administrative and procedural irregularity, substantively inadequate fact finding, and insufficient exploration of the legal content or social implications of cases. To these, one must add the problems of perceived partiality toward particular political or social factions and, in the less favored courts, perhaps the reality of discrimination, in addition, or the outright abdication of juridical responsibilities. Even on the more "progressive" reservations, public confidence in the tribal courts is at best meager. Efforts to improve the courts are toward making them more like white courts or, worse, like a stereotype of white courts.... What relation do these practices have to Indian tribal culture?

It requires no great leap of logic to arrive at the view that all this is a roundabout way of achieving what can be achieved more directly through the "solution" of integration. That is not to say that extending state and county jurisdiction to the reservations would be without trauma or without the need for special formulas to assure Indian participation and representation; many Indians have negative perceptions of white justice; white officials are entrenched in most law-enforcement positions; and the Indians are at a great educational disadvantage. Nevertheless, integration is the only approach with real promise: it is inevitable in the long run, and it is not necessarily out of tune with the current trends (as opposed to the rhetoric) in Indian life and culture. The model of Indian justice for the 1970s and the future is not the Dakota, Montana, or even the Arizona (Navajo) one, but rather the Oklahoma model.

All steps taken to preserve the tribal courts or the reservation system can only be rearguard actions. The reservations, with their courts and other institutions, are destined to disappear in time. The only question is, When? The true motivations behind, and justification for, Indian separatism are psychological. As in the black movement in this country, separatist rhetoric may be useful in restoring a sense of personal (or "cultural," if one insists) identity and worth to the members of an ethnic minority that has a history of being suppressed, exploited, and kept dependent. That is its total role....

Indian Courts Versus the Indian People

It is difficult to ascertain what the Indian people want. Many of them are quite cynical about reservation life and reservation institutions, including the tribal courts. On the other hand, they are ignorant of or equally cynical about, if not fearful of, the alternatives. The Indians who have had some experience in the outside world and with white institutions usually express mixed feelings about their experiences. The current emphasis on "Indianness" and autonomy only complicates the picture for them. Those who have had no experience with white institutions also are influenced by the prevailing separatist rhetoric.

Few would argue the point that the reservation people should be left to choose for themselves. If they are to choose, however, they must be informed of the facts; and the misconceptions about the differences between Indian and non-Indian life and practices must be dispelled....

Efforts to improve the tribal courts with robes, money, new courtrooms, and more training programs are only band-aid measures, as are efforts to improve reservation conditions with more welfare money, food stamps, motels, resorts, oil and gas leases, and Washington, D.C., lawyers. The alternative of integrating the tribal judicial system with state and county institutions has many advantages. By definition, it would eliminate the Kafkaesque confusion among tribal, state, and federal courts and other agencies. At the same time, the Indian people would be no less free to be "Indian," "rural," "traditional," or "bound to the land or community" or to choose whatever life-style and values they may want. By the same token, the many Indians who want to embark on ("acculturated") professional careers would probably have a better chance to succeed and a better setting in which to use their professional skills. Today, Indians who want professional careers often fail at both realizing their ambitions and maintaining a satisfactory contact with the reservation....

POMMERSHEIM, THE CONTEXTUAL LEGITIMACY OF ADJUDICATION IN TRIBAL COURTS AND THE ROLE OF THE TRIBAL BAR AS AN INTERPRETIVE COMMUNITY: AN ESSAY, 18 New Mexico Law Review 49, 59-62 (1988)*

IV. *The Contextual Legitimacy of Adjudication in Tribal Courts*

The title of this essay suggests the importance of two critical terms, namely "contextual legitimacy" and "interpretive community" as key canons in helping to understand the nature and quality of adjudication in tribal courts. Each term will be defined and examined and then brought to bear in the tribal court context.

The concept of contextual legitimacy represents a particular gloss on the fundamental concepts of formal legitimacy. In the United States legal system, this demand for (formal) legitimacy has traditionally rested on the pristine view that judges should decide cases in accordance with the law. Most conventionally and simply stated, this has meant that any judicial decision must logically follow from the authoritative legal rule or rules, and not, for example, from personal or other values which are not validated by the law.[63] This classic formulation has been seriously criticized as inadequate to explain the relationship of judicial adjudication to the larger legal and political system of which it is a part. Further criticism argues that the legal and political system cannot be adequately understood apart from its social, historical, and cultural context.

It is this notion of contextual legitimacy that looks to the social, historical, and cultural setting of judicial adjudication that produces a most fruitful framework for examining tribal courts and tribal court adjudication. Tribal courts need to

---

*Copyright © 1988 New Mexico Law Review and Frank Pommersheim. Reprinted with permission of the copyright holders.

[63]S. BURTON, AN INTRODUCTION TO LAW AND LEGAL REASONING 169 (1985). This section of the essay draws substantially on the analytical framework set forth in this appealing work.

be viewed within this wide focus in order to better understand what social and cultural values are actually becoming embedded in these young systems. This is necessary to avoid a sterile analysis that looks to a narrow consideration about the application of rules of law unhinged from the larger concerns of tribal integrity and culture.

The concept of "contextual legitimacy" is a post-formalist view that suggests the meaning of legitimacy shifts from a concern for antecedent legitimating foundations, such as the logical application of rules of law, to a demand for a legal and political system which on the whole enjoys and merits the allegiance of the people. The propriety and integrity of adjudication therefore depends on their contribution to the legitimacy of the legal and political system in its social, historical, and cultural context.

Contextual legitimacy in this view has two interrelated components, namely the obligation and the desire to abide by the law within a legal and political system that merits people's fidelity and affirmation. Whether this obligation is generally recognized by the people is a question of social fact. Whether the desire exists to abide by the law is more a normative question. Yet neither aspect taken alone is sufficient to establish contextual legitimacy, and the two together imply a tension between the search for a more orderly and just society and the requirements of a constitutional democracy.

Although much of this undoubtedly sounds arcane, I believe it has significant import in examining tribal court systems. One of the dilemmas that permeates tribal courts is this whole notion of legitimacy. Certainly there are (or have been) identifiable segments of most tribes that refuse to consider tribal courts legitimate. In this regard, many tribal courts are vilified as "white men's" creations flowing from the IRA and an entire federal history directed to assimilation. The courts are seen as instruments of outside forces and values that are not traditional and therefore not legitimate.

On the other hand, there are segments of most tribal populations (and local non-Indian populations) who view tribal courts as illegitimate because they fall, or appear to fall, far below recognized state and federal standards in such matters ranging from the institutional separation of powers to the provision of civil due process and enforcement of judgments. These combined forces often threaten the viability of tribal courts as legitimate justice rendering mechanisms.

Legitimacy becomes illegitimacy when large numbers of people in fact cease to recognize an obligation to abide by law or judicial decisions with which they disagree. This is further aggravated in the tribal context when the tribal government, itself, may refuse to abide by tribal court decisions or submit to tribal court jurisdiction. Needless to say, real claims of illegitimacy have been made throughout United States legal history, ranging from the colonial claim of illegitimacy under the continued rule of the British crown to the large scale civil disobedience of segregationist laws in the South during the 1960's. Nevertheless, these wrenching claims have been weathered with the assistance of large doses of modification and reform.

It has been suggested that the normative aspect of contextual legitimacy depends on whether the system as a whole adequately contributes to a more orderly and just society in light of contemporary circumstances and evolving notions of justice. Such a view does not deny the importance of change and reform but holds that such claims do not challenge the legitimacy of the system as a whole. It is here, I believe, that tribal courts find themselves most delicately placed. The increase in the bona fide legitimacy of tribal courts is (and has been) inextricably bound to their amenability to change and reform that increases the net perception of the development of a more orderly and just system and society. This enhanced perception has actively drawn from both streams — traditional and progressive — of discontent.

What then, one might ask, are some examples of this growing legitimacy of tribal courts? Numerous examples exist and include such things as the increase of law trained Indian people within many systems, tribal and constitutional code revision, the nascent development of traditional and customary law, and the continued recognition of tribal courts by the United States Supreme Court as viable and important forums for resolution of reservation based claims involving both Indians and non-Indians.

A recent vivid example demonstrating the growth and development of legitimacy involves the following experience. During a recent visit to the Rosebud Sioux Tribal Court, Associate Judge Sherman Marshall, who is a law trained, bilingual member of the Rosebud Sioux Tribe, addressed students of my Indian law class. In the course of his presentation, Justice Marshall stated several times that he believed it was part of his job (but obviously not in his job description) to travel to the twenty tribal communities scattered over the most rural parts of the reservation to discuss what the tribal court was and what it was doing. Mr. Marshall understood full well that the success and legitimacy of the court depends, in significant part, on the understanding and support of community people — many of whom know little about tribal court or have had negative and dispiriting experiences with it. Legitimacy, at the grass roots level, is not a given, but rather the bedrock of much necessary but unappreciated toil. It is not only the message but also the messenger. It is important to note that a young, law-educated tribal member who is bilingual and bicultural is an emblematic figure, poised between two worlds, bringing the best message of both.

A second experience from the field trip provides an important example about the nature of legitimacy in the framework of the hearing of an actual case. In this instance, Justice Marshall was hearing a small claims matter between a grandmother and her daughter concerning the alleged failure of the daughter to pay the grandmother for taking care of her children.[72] Both parties were tribal members and were unrepresented as is the norm in both tribal and state claims proceedings.

Mr. Marshall requested the plaintiff to tell her story. She began and went on for sometime in a seemingly long and circular narrative. Mr. Marshall spoke to her several times briefly in Lakota, the tribal language of the Rosebud Sioux. She answered in Lakota and went on mixing English and Lakota. When she finally finished, he asked several direct questions necessary to making appropri-

---

[72] The roots of this dispute are more cultural than financial. The plaintiff indicated that she had brought this action not so much for the alleged money owed but to seek redress for the (cultural) wrong she suffered. As an elder and grandmother she felt an important cultural rule was violated when her daughter came and simply removed her children who were staying with the grandmother without obtaining the grandmother's endorsement and consent for their return. The nature of the dispute raises significant questions about whether there is or should be some other non-legal, but culturally consonant way, to mediate the conflict.

ate findings of fact. He then proceeded in the exact same manner to address and listen to the defendant. He concluded by informing the parties that he needed additional documentation and after he received it, he would make a prompt decision.

It was readily apparent that an unusual rapport was established between the judge and the parties. They could speak without interruption (a cultural prerogative of elders) and in their first language. Contextual legitimacy was palpable; yet the entire case and its hearing raised ongoing questions about the nature of legitimacy in tribal settings.

The process of striving for legitimacy is far from over and must continue as a dynamic force in Indian country. Many questions remain, including: those involving the development of traditional and customary law, the separation of powers, authentic appeal, and the enforcement of individual civil rights within the tribal context. In particular, the example cited above illustrates the need to discover the best possible means for resolving disputes that are primarily cultural, rather than strictly legal, in nature. Yet, as always, the core of legitimacy rests with the people themselves. Without their support and understanding, there can be little hope for continued advancement and growth.

TSO, TOM, C.J., THE PROCESS OF DECISION MAKING IN TRIBAL COURTS, 31 Arizona Law Review 225-36 (1989)*

The Navajo Court System

... Anglo judicial systems now pay a great deal of attention to alternative forms of dispute resolution. Before 1868 the Navajos settled disputes by mediation. Today our Peacemaker Courts are studied by many people and governments.[3] Anglo justice systems are now interested in compensating victims of crime and searching for ways to deal with criminal offenders other than imprisonment. Before 1868 the Navajos did this. Now Anglo courts recognize the concept of joint custody of children and the role of the extended family in the rearing of children. Navajos have always understood these concepts. We could have taught the Anglos these things one hundred and fifty years ago.

Today the Navajo courts are structured very much like those in the state and federal courts. We have seven judicial districts. The district courts are courts of general civil jurisdiction and of limited criminal jurisdiction. Civil jurisdiction extends to all persons residing within the Navajo Nation or who cause an act to

---

*Chief Justice, Supreme Court of the Navajo Nation. Copyright © 1989 by the Arizona Board of Regents. Reprinted by permission.

[3] In 1982, the judges of the Navajo courts implemented a new court system that was designed to integrate traditional Navajo dispute resolution methods with traditional Anglo-American judicial methods. Called the Peacemaker Court, it uses the traditional legal processes of mediation and arbitration to arrive at reasonable solutions to disputes while protecting the interests of the disputants.

The establishment of the Peacemaker Court represents a blending of the old with the new, with an eye towards accommodating needs that were simply not being met by the existing system. Recourse to the Peacemaker Court is voluntary; however, once the parties consent, the court has authority to enforce attendance through subpoena power. The court also has authority to compel the participation of any other person involved in the dispute. The activities of the Peacemaker Court are coordinated by and through the district courts. See Zion, The Navajo Peacemaker Court: Deference to the Old and Accommodation of the New, 11 Am. Indian L. Rev. 89-109 (1983).

occur within the nation.[4] The limitations on criminal jurisdiction are determined by the nature of the offense, the penalty to be imposed, where the crime occurred, and the status and residency of the individual charged with an offense. Each district also has a children's court, which hears all matters concerning children except for custody, child support and visitation disputes arising from divorce proceedings, and probate matters.

The second tier of the Navajo court system is the Navajo Nation Supreme Court, composed of three justices. The Supreme Court hears appeals from final lower court decisions and from certain final administrative orders. The Supreme Court abolished trial de novo at the appellate level and now only hears issues of law raised in the lower court record. In addition, the Peacemaker Courts, established in each judicial district, use traditional mediation processes and are supported by the district courts' supervision and enforcement of the agreements reached through mediation.

The tribal government is rapidly developing an extensive network of administrative bodies with quasi-judicial functions. The final decisions of bodies such as the Tax Commission and Board of Election Supervisors are appealable directly to the Navajo Supreme Court. Recourse from the decisions of other administrative bodies is sought through an original action in the trial court. All opinions of the Navajo Supreme Court, and some of the opinions of the district courts are published in the Navajo Reporter. Additionally, the Navajo courts have established rules of procedure for criminal, civil, probate and appellate matters.

The Selection of Judges

Navajo judges and justices are chosen through a process designed to insulate them from politics. When a judge is to be selected, interested persons submit applications to the Judiciary Committee of the Navajo Tribal Council. The Judiciary Committee screens the applicants and draws up a list of the most highly qualified people according to the qualifications set forth in the Navajo Tribal Code.[7] This list is then sent to the Tribal Chairman who appoints a judge from the list for a two year probationary period. Each appointment must be confirmed by the Tribal Council. During the probationary period, the judge receives training from carefully selected judicial education establishments which offer a quality legal-judicial education. There are currently two such establishments: the National Judicial College in Reno, Nevada and the National Indian Justice Center in Petaluma, California. The Navajo Nation Bar Association, the Judiciary Committee and the Chief Justice all evaluate the probationary judge.

If the probationary judge receives an adequate performance evaluation and satisfactorily completes his or her course of training, the Chief Justice and the Judiciary Committee recommend the judge for permanent appointment. This permanent appointment must be confirmed by the Tribal Council. Thereafter, the judge remains in office until retirement or removal under procedures established in the Tribal Code.[8] Permanent judges continue to be evaluated each year and receive training in areas where the evaluations show that knowledge

---

[4] Navajo Trib. Code tit. 7, § 253 (Cum. Supp. 1984-1985).
[7] Navajo Trib. Code tit. 7, § 354 (Cum. Supp. 1984-1985).
[8] Id. at §§ 352-353.

and skills are lacking. Through its careful selection process, its vigorous educational programs and its thorough evaluation procedures, the Navajo Nation maintains a high standard for it judiciary.

Substantive and Procedural Law in the Navajo Tribal Court System

Representation in Court

All parties may represent themselves in the courts. If a party chooses to be represented by counsel, a member of the Navajo Nation Bar Association must be chosen. Membership in the Navajo Nation Bar Association requires passing the Navajo bar examination, which is given twice a year. Both law school graduates and those who have not been to law school may practice in tribal courts. The practitioners who have not been to law school are called advocates and must complete either a certified Navajo Bar Training Course or serve an apprenticeship.

The contribution of the advocates to the Navajo court system is beyond measure. Both our language and our traditions make Anglo court systems strange to us. In traditional Navajo culture the concept of a disinterested, unbiased decisionmaker was unknown. Concepts of fairness and social harmony are basic to us; however, we achieve fairness and harmony in a manner different from the Anglo world. For the Navajo people, dispute settlement required the participation of the community elders and all those who either knew the parties or were familiar with the history of the problem. Everyone was permitted to speak. Private discussions with an elder who could resolve a problem was also acceptable. It was difficult for Navajos to participate in a system where fairness required the judge to have no prior knowledge of the case, and where who can speak and what they can say are closely regulated. The advocates helped the Navajos through this process, and the advocates continue to be an important link between the two cultures.

The Applicable Law

The law the Navajo courts must use consists of any applicable federal laws, tribal laws and customs. The structure of our courts is based upon the Anglo court system, but generally the law we apply is our own. When the Navajo Tribal Courts were established in 1959, the Navajo Nation did not have extensive laws of its own, and there were no reported opinions to guide the judges in the decision-making process. In 1959, the Navajo Tribal Code required the courts to apply the applicable laws of the United States, authorized regulations of the Interior Department, and any ordinances or customs of the Tribe not prohibited by such federal laws. Any matters not covered by tribal or federal law had to be decided by the law of the state in which the case arose. As the Navajo Nation encompasses land in three states, this sometimes led to confusion and the application of different laws in different parts of the reservation.

In 1985, the Tribal Code sections regarding applicable law were amended. Now, the courts are required to apply the appropriate law of the United States and laws or customs of the Navajo Nation that are not prohibited by federal law.[10] If the matter is not covered by tribal or federal law, the courts may look to any state laws and decisions for guidance,[11] or Navajo courts may fashion their own remedies.[12] The Navajo Nation Supreme Court makes the ultimate decisions on these issues, thereby developing an internal body of law. As a result, many of the briefs filed in that court and many of the opinions issued by it cite only Navajo cases.

It is easy to understand that the Navajo Tribal Code contains the written law of the Navajo Nation, and that this law is available to anyone.... Our common law is comprised of customs and long-used ways of doing things. It also includes court decisions recognizing and enforcing the customs or filling in the gaps in the written law. The common law of the Navajo Nation, then, consists of both customary law and court decisions. In a case decided in 1987, the Navajo Nation Supreme Court observed that:

> Because established Navajo customs and traditions have the force of law, this court agrees with the Window Rock District Court in announcing its preference for the term "Navajo Common Law" rather than "custom," as that term properly emphasizes the fact that Navajo custom and tradition is law, and more accurately reflects the similarity in the treatment of custom between Navajo and English common law.[13]

Decision Making in Tribal Courts

The Navajo Nation Supreme Court through case decisions is developing rules for pleading and proving Navajo common law.

The Integrity and Independence of the Decisionmakers

Once a court makes a decision, that decision is subject to change only through judicial processes. No other part of the tribal government has the authority to overrule that decision. The basis of the concept of a separate and independent judiciary is found in both Navajo common law and in the Tribal Code. The Tribal Code establishes the Judicial Branch as a separate branch of government.[14] The integrity of court decisions, however, has its basis in the respect given to the peacemakers as leaders who helped settle community disputes. In a case decided in 1978, the Navajo Supreme Court ruled that the respect given the peacemakers extends to the courts because Navajos have

> a traditional abiding respect for the impartial adjudicatory process. When all have been heard and the decision is made, it is respected. This has been the Navajo way since before the time of the present judicial system. The Navajo People did not learn this principle from the white man. They have carried it ... through history.... Those appointed by the People to resolve their disputes were and are unquestioned in their power to do so. Whereas once the clan was the primary forum (and still is a powerful and respected instrument of justice), now the People through their Council have delegated the ultimate responsibility for this to their courts.[15]

[10] Navajo Trib. Code tit. 7, § 204(a) (Cum. Supp. 1984-1985).
[11] Id. at § 204(c).
[12] Id. at § 204(b).
[13] In re Estate of Belone, 5 Navajo Rptr. 161, 165 (1987).
[14] Navajo Trib. Code tit. 7, § 201 (Cum. Supp. 1984-1985).
[15] Halona v. MacDonald, 1 Navajo Rptr. 189, 205-06 (1978).

The Old and the New Way

A close look at the Navajo Tribal Government would reveal many characteristics that appear to be Anglo in nature. Actually, many concepts have their roots in our ancient heritage. Others are foreign to our culture but have been accommodated in such a way that they have become acceptable and useful to us. Ironically, the Navajo, whose governmental structure and operation are perhaps most like those of the Anglo world amongst United States Indian tribes, is the tribe that has no constitution. The Anglo world places much value on the written word and there is a tendency to believe that if things are not written down, they do not exist.

Navajos have survived since before the time of Columbus as a separate and distinct people. What holds us together is a strong set of values and customs, not words on paper. I am speaking of a sense of community so strong that, before the federal government imposed its system on us, we had no need to lock up wrongdoers. If a person injured another or disrupted the peace of the community, he was talked to, and often ceremonies were performed to restore him to harmony with his world. There were usually no repeat offenders. Only those who have been subjected to a Navajo "talking" session can understand why this worked.[16]

Today we have police, prosecutors, jails, and written laws and procedures. I am convinced that our Anglo-based system of law enforcement is no more effective than the ways we traditionally handled law enforcement problems. Our present system certainly requires more money, more facilities, more resources and more manpower. But we have this system now, and it works as well as those of our brother and sister jurisdictions. My point is that the Anglo world has said to tribes, "Be like us. Have the same laws and institutions we have. When you have these things perhaps we will leave you alone." Yet what the Anglo world has offered, at least as far as Navajos are concerned, is either something we already had or something that works no better than what we had.

The popular concept of tolerance in America is based upon its image as a melting pot, where everyone blends together to form an indistinguishable mixture. This is fine for people who come to this country and want to jump into the pot. The melting pot can, however, become a good place to hide people. When differences cause discomfort or problems, it can make everyone the same. The real measure of tolerance and respect for tribes may well be how successfully the outside world can coexist with tribes. We are part of the total environment of America and at least as important as the snail darter or the California condor. What a tragedy if fifty years from now a news commentator should report on how the government has set aside a preserve in the desert where nine Indians are being saved from extinction and how it is hoped they will reproduce in captivity.

As economic development plans progress, the Navajo Nation Courts are likely to face a wide range of issues. The jurisdiction statutes of the Navajo Nation provide that the tribal courts have jurisdiction over all civil causes of action

---

[16] *See* M. Shepardson & B. Hamond, The Navajo Mountain Community 128-56 (1970) for a discussion of social control methods among the Navajo. For a description of traditional legal practices among other tribes, see K. Llewellen & E. Hoebel, The Cheyenne Way (1941).

where the defendant resides within the Navajo Indian Country or, regardless of residence, has caused an action to occur within the territorial jurisdiction of the Navajo Nation.[17] Future litigation involving the land and resources of the Navajo Nation will no doubt challenge tribal court jurisdiction. In light of the decisions in *National Farmers Union Insurance Cos. v. Crow Tribe of Indians*[18] and in *Iowa Mutual Insurance Co. v. LaPlante*,[19] however, these questions will be decided in the Navajo Nation Courts.

Beyond the jurisdictional issues, questions of what law will be applied in civil disputes are likely to arise. Whether federal law will attach in a specific case will depend on the facts. In cases where federal law does not apply, tribal common law and statutes will be used. The Navajo Uniform Commercial Code, Navajo Nation Corporation Code, Water Code, and Mining Code are examples of statutory provisions enacted to regulate on-reservation business ventures and the use of natural resources.

Non-Indians may have concerns about the impact of tradition and custom on case decisions. Navajo custom and tradition are unlikely to call for law entirely different from that expected in Anglo courts. They are more likely to supply additional factors to consider in an already familiar context. For example, the Anglo system is familiar with the concept of valuation and payment of the taking of land. Compensation for the loss of use to the surface user of land is an accepted concept in both Anglo and Navajo law. The difference will be in the valuation. Land that may appear to have little value to a non-Indian may be very valuable to a Navajo. It may have spiritual or historical value that has little to do with the income it can produce. The difficulty will be in assigning a dollar figure to values that have no measure in the market. This is not an impossible task. It is done every day in tort cases where damages are assessed for intangible harms like pain and suffering, intentional infliction of emotional distress, and loss of companionship.

Navajo courts will differ in the emphasis we place on the traditional relationship between Navajos and nature. We refer to the earth and sky as Mother Earth and Father Sky. These are not catchy titles; they represent our understanding of our place. The earth and sky are our relatives. Nature communicates with us through the wind and the water and the whispering pines. Our traditional prayers include prayers for the plants, the animals, the water and the trees. A Navajo prayer is like a plant. The stem or the backbone of the prayer is always beauty. By this beauty we mean harmony. Beauty brings peace and understanding. It brings youngsters who are mentally and physically healthy and it brings long life. Beauty is people living peacefully with each other and with nature.

Just like our natural mother, our Mother Earth provides for us. It is not wrong to accept the things we need from the earth. It is wrong to treat the earth with disrespect. It is wrong if we fail to protect and defend the earth. It would

---

[17] Navajo Trib. Code tit. 7, § 253 (Cum. Supp. 1984-1985). The definition of Navajo Indian Country is consistent with the federal definition ....

[18] 471 U.S. 845 (1985).

[19] 480 U.S. 9 (1987). The Court held that exhaustion of tribal court remedies, required in determinations of federal question jurisdiction under National Farmers Union, is also required in determination of diversity of citizenship jurisdiction. ...

be wrong for us to rob our natural mother of her valuable jewelry and to go away and leave her to take care of herself. It is just as wrong for us to rob Mother Earth of what is valuable and leave her unprotected and defenseless. If people can understand that the Navajo regard nature and the things in nature as relatives, then they will easily see that nature and the Navajos depend upon each other. Understanding this relationship is essential to understanding traditional Navajo concepts which may be applied in cases concerning natural resources and the environment.

We Navajos find it difficult to separate our lives into fragments or parts. Our ceremonies are religious, medical, social, and psychological. The seasons tell us how to live and what ceremonies to have. The earth gives us our food, the dyes for our rugs and the necessities for our ceremonies. These may be seen as everyday things. Today, the earth gives us income and jobs from mining, from oil, and from the forests. Water and earth combine to give Navajo Agricultural Products, Inc. the ability to produce large amounts of food for the Navajo people. Snow and rain and proper runoff from the mountains give us lakes for fishing. These may be seen as commercial things.

We cannot separate our needs and our relationships in the same fashion. This is why our laws and judicial interpretations must accommodate both of these things. For example, our tribal law requires that persons who want to harvest or remove anything from the forests have a permit. An exception is made, however, for persons who need to gather plants and forest products for ceremonial purposes. In a recent Navajo Supreme Court probate case,[21] the court held that any further division of the land would defeat the agricultural purposes of the land. Under Navajo common law, the parcel went to the heir who was best able to use the land for agricultural purposes. The other heirs were given set-offs in other items of the decedent's property. This case illustrates the Navajo Tribal Court system's ability to accommodate traditional values.

Conclusion

I have tried to give you a brief overview of the judicial decision-making process in the Navajo tribal courts, and to indicate some of the ways we attempt to accommodate the best from two cultures so that the Navajo Nation may proceed to develop within a framework that is familiar to us. We, the people, are a natural resource. Our culture and our history are natural resources. We are so related to the earth and the sky that we cannot be separated without harm. The protection and defense of both must be preserved. On the other hand, the dominant society views things in terms of separateness, of compartmentalization. For this reason, the Navajo Nation is best able to make the laws and decisions regarding our own preservation and development.

I have spoken of the Navajo experience, but I believe that much of what I have said applies to all Indian tribes. Understanding the challenges facing tribes is the first step toward meeting them. The process of making judicial decisions in the Navajo Nation reflects our response to these challenges.

NOTES

1. Brakel's Study: Clearly Samuel Brakel concluded that there should be no place for separate tribal court systems. What are some of his criticisms? Brakel's

---

[21]In re Estate of Wauneka, 13 Indian L. Rep. 6049 (1986).

study of tribal court systems was criticized for, among other things, comparing tribal judiciary systems to big city systems instead of the courts of rural areas such as justice of the peace courts they most resemble, and generally reflecting a Eurocentric bias. For a discussion and debate on Brakel's thesis compare Brakel, *American Indian Tribal Courts: Separate? "Yes," Equal? "Probably Not,"* 62 A.B.A.J. 1002 (1976) with Collins, Johnson & Perkins, *American Indian Courts and Tribal Self-Government,* 63 A.B.A.J. 808 (1977).

Do Judge Tso's description of the Navajo court system and Professor Pommersheim's reflections, based on ten years of practicing law on the Rosebud Sioux reservation, on the role of the tribal bar, seem to reflect courts that are "pale copies of the white system," held together by "band-aid measures"? Would it not be better to compare the progress made in tribal courts since the enactment of the ICRA toward protecting individual rights, for example, to the progress made in state courts in the much longer period from the beginning of the nineteenth century until the late twentieth century? More fundamentally, do you agree with Mr. Brakel that "[t]he reservations, with their courts and other institutions, are *destined* to disappear in time" (emphasis added)? Is this prediction of the imminent demise of tribes as separate peoples, made many times since the founding of the nation, any more likely to come true in the twenty-first century than it did in the eighteenth, nineteenth, and twentieth centuries? For recent efforts to defend federal protection of tribal self-government and autonomy, see C. Wilkinson, American Indians, Time, and the Law (1987); Deloria & Lytle, American Indians, American Justice (1983); Clinton, *Isolated in Their Own Country: A Defense of Federal Protection of Indian Sovereignty and Autonomy,* 33 Stan. L. Rev. 979 (1981).

2. Recent Developments on the Navajo Reservation: The Navajo Supreme Court faced a serious threat to its integrity shortly after Judge Tso's article was written. In 1989, the Navajo Tribal Council relieved its chairman, Peter MacDonald, from office, putting him on administrative leave with pay pending investigation into charges of serious misconduct that surfaced during an investigation by a Senate committee. *See* Special Comm. on Investigations of the Senate Select Comm. on Indian Affairs, Final Report and Legislative Recommendations, S. Rep. No. 216, 101st Cong., 1st Sess. 181-98 (1989). The powerful chairman first attempted to circumvent the procedures by appointing new judges from among his sympathizers and also recalling to the bench removed or retired judges. He also refused to accept the Chief Justice and Judiciary Committee's recommendation that Judge Robert Yazzie, a probationary judge, be given a permanent appointment. The Chairman's letter declining to appoint the judge came one hour after Judge Yazzie had ruled against the Chairman's claim that sovereign immunity barred the Council's action. Judge Yazzie promptly certified questions to the Supreme Court regarding the Chairman's and the Council's respective powers. In *In re Certified Questions I, Navajo Nation v. MacDonald,* 16 Indian L. Rep. 6098 (Nav. Sup. Ct. 1989) (per curiam), the Supreme Court held that the relevant tribal code procedures for appointing and recalling judges do not permit such actions, but instead clearly circumscribe the Chairman's role in the appointment and retention of judges.

In a subsequent opinion, the Navajo Supreme Court stated that Navajo law makes the Council superior to the Chairman, who exercises only delegated authority:

> After reviewing the history of the relationship between the council and the Chairman and Vice Chairman we conclude all authority of the offices of Chairman and Vice Chairman are derived from the council. The powers are incumbent in the offices to be

exercised by those people elected by the Navajo people to these two offices. The powers are there to be exercised in the best interests of the Navajo people.

There is nothing in either the history of the present Navajo government or in the tribal code to support the argument that the source of the Chairman's and Vice Chairman's governmental authority is the voting public. In addition, there is nothing to support the argument that the offices of Chairman and Vice Chairman are independent and separate from the Navajo Tribal Council. They all live in the same hogan and need each other to function.

The Navajo Tribal Council clearly has authority to withdraw, limit, or supervise the exercise of power it gives to the offices of Chairman and Vice Chairman. The power to create an office and delegate authority to that office includes the power to abolish, withdraw, limit, or supervise exercise of those powers by the office holder. The Navajo Tribal Council can prevent a Chairman or Vice Chairman from exercising certain powers it has delegated to the offices of Chairman and Vice Chairman and the council can specify how those powers can be exercised. The latter has frequently been done by the council as shown by the history of the Navajo government.

Public officials serving in the Navajo government, no matter what position they hold, are trustees of the Navajo people. These government officials occupy a fiduciary relationship to the Navajo people. The Navajo people have placed a high degree of trust in these officials, therefore, Navajo government officials owe an undivided duty to the Navajo people to serve the best interests of the Navajo people.

All Navajo government officials are obligated to exercise the powers of their offices honestly, faithfully, legally, ethically, and to the best of their abilities, in a way which is beyond suspicion of irregularities. In short, these officials are obligated to perform primarily in the best interests of the Navajo people. The Navajo people do not expect their officials to exercise powers corruptly or use powers for personal gain or profit. In fact, 2 Nav. T.C. § 1001 places a duty on the Chairman to "represent the Tribe in negotiations with governmental and private agencies and meet with many off-reservation organizations and groups in order to create favorable public opinion and good will toward the Navajo Tribe."

The Navajo traditional concept of fiduciary trust of a leader (naat'aanii) is just as relevant here. After the epic battles were fought by the Hero Twins, the Navajo people set on the path of becoming a strong nations. It became necessary to select naat'aaniis by a consensus of the people.

A naat'aanii was not a powerful politician nor was he a mighty chief. A naat'aanii was chosen based upon his ability to help the people survive and whatever authority he had was based upon that ability and the trust placed in him by the people. If a naat'aanii lost the trust of his people, the people simply ceased to follow him or even listen to his words. The naat'aanii indeed was expected to be honest, faithful and truthful in dealing with his people.

The Court stated that the Council could only take such actions on certain grounds:

The Navajo Tribal Council can place a Chairman or Vice Chairman on administrative leave with pay if they have reasonable grounds to believe that the official seriously breached his fiduciary trust to the Navajo people and if the leave will be in the best interests of the Navajo Nation. Leave which is in the best interests of the tribe will serve to protect the tribe against conduct which threatens or has some direct effect on the property and resources of the tribe, or the political integrity, economic security or health, safety, and welfare of the tribe.

Finally, the Court gave guidance on appropriate due process for placing the Chairman on leave and also adopted various tests from federal law for the district court to apply to assess the Chairman's argument that placing him on administrative leave was a bill of attainder in violation of the ICRA, noting somewhat slyly "A bill of attainder is apparently unknown to traditional Navajo culture." *Id.* at 6093. *In re Certified Questions II: Navajo Nation v. MacDonald*, 16 Indian L. Rep. 6086 (Nav. Sup. Ct. 1989) (per curiam).

Chapter 4

STATE CLAIMS TO POWER OVER INDIANS AND INDIAN COUNTRY

One of the clearest and most persistent themes involving Indian sovereignty has been the continuous struggle by the states to assert greater control over Indian reservations, either at the expense of the federal or tribal governments. The pace of the struggle, the form that it takes, and the forum in which the struggle occurs have changed over time. Some have asserted that states could determine unilaterally at what point it was appropriate for certain state laws to be applied in Indian country. Others have argued that it is a decision to be reached by the United States Congress. Views have varied on the extent to which the consent of the tribe must be obtained before a new level of authority can be interposed.

This chapter reviews the repeated efforts by state governments to extend their power and standards over Indian country within their borders. It is a process that has been influenced by economic, moral, and jurisprudential considerations, probably in that order. From a process perspective, the roles of court, legislature, and the Department of the Interior must be examined.

The modern federal policy of protecting Indian tribal sovereignty and autonomy fundamentally represents a federal effort to exempt Indians and their lands from the reach of state law and authority. Why this should be the case is often less than evident. Is the exercise of state sovereignty over tribal lands and peoples necessarily inconsistent with the continued existence of tribal Indian societies as separate semi-sovereign political entities? If so, cannot the same thing be said of the coexistence of federal authority and tribal power in Indian country? Is there something about the differences between the operation of federal and state authority in Indian country that makes the exercise of the latter less compatible with the continued existence of separate Indian tribal societies, cultures, and governments?

As these questions suggest, the history of federal Indian policy has been motivated by a strongly held feeling on the part of both Indians and non-Indians that the exercise of state authority over Indians and Indian reservations was incompatible with continued separate tribal identity. In treaties with various eastern tribes that had previously experienced the influx of non-Indian settlers and the assertion of state law over Indian land prior to removal, the United States sometimes agreed at the insistence of the Indians that, as in the case of the Creek and Seminole tribes, "no State or Territory shall ever pass laws for the government of the Creek or Seminole tribes of Indians, and that no portion of either of the tracts of [Indian] country defined [in] the agreement shall ever be embraced or included within, or annexed to, any Territory or State, nor shall either, or any part of either, ever be erected into a Territory without the full and free consent of the legislative authority of the tribe owning the same."

Treaty with the Creek and Seminole Tribes, Aug. 7, 1856, art. 4, 11 Stat. 699. Obviously, such treaty provisions, most of which were contained in the treaties with tribes removed to the Indian territory, were breached when Oklahoma became a state. Similarly, when federal Indian policy sought to break up and disestablish tribal cultures and sovereign authority, Congress acted to accomplish that result by the extension of state sovereignty. Thus section 6 of the General Allotment Act of 1887 provided that, upon the completion of the allotment process, both the civil and criminal laws of the state or territory in which the allottee resided would be applicable to him. *See generally* 61 I.D. 298, 303 (1954); 58 I.D. 455 (1943). More recently, the legislation of the 1950's contained express provisions that stated that upon termination of tribal entities and the federal trust status of land "the laws of the several States shall apply to them [members of the terminated tribe] in the same manner they apply to the other persons or citizens within their jurisdiction." 25 U.S.C. § 980 (concerning termination of federal supervision of the Ponca Tribe).

In 1887, in its opinion in the *Kagama* case set forth and discussed in Chapter 2, the Supreme Court offered the following justification for excluding state control over Indian affairs and authority over Indians and their lands: "They owe no allegiance to the States, and receive from them no protection. Because of the local ill feeling, the people of the States where they are found are often their deadliest enemies." Is that justification equally viable today? Do other policy objectives adequately support the long-standing congressional decision to exclude state authority over Indians in Indian country?

Judicial determinations of the division of power and the extent of state power have often occurred without adequate legislative guidance. And when the Congress has sought to guide, its ambivalence as to the appropriate answer has often increased the confusion. Once there has been a substantial congressional effort to define the manner by which power can be transferred from the federal government to the state — and the procedure which states must follow in taking the power — the judicial role changes. The major congressional effort to achieve these goals occurred in Public Law 280, and the Indian Child Welfare Act of 1978. Many of the state and federal decisions in this chapter interpret the manner in which states attempted to cope with Public Law 280. Because of the structure of Public Law 280, there are subtle complications. As will be seen, some states had increased power thrust upon them; the others had the choice (without Indian concurrence prior to 1968) to assume the federal gift. The latter states have varied in their responses. As a consequence, some jurisdictions will be clumsily referred to as "Public Law 280 states" and others as "non-Public Law 280 states." But because each state has a different pattern of taking jurisdiction, local legislation must be examined. Finally, as section A indicates, judicial tests for state power overlapped in ways not congruent with the tests set down by Congress. On occasion, states which have not taken power under Public Law 280 or equivalents have found means of extending state law nonetheless.

A. JUDICIAL APPROACHES TO INHERENT STATE AUTHORITY IN INDIAN COUNTRY

1. THE FORMATIVE PERIOD

CLINTON, REVIEW, 47 University of Chicago Law Review 846, 851-57 (1980)*

During the colonial period, differences over the management of Indian affairs and the legal status of the tribes plagued the English authorities in America. The Crown generally adhered to the view that, as separate peoples, the Indians were politically and legally autonomous within their territory until they voluntarily ceded their land to the Crown or were conquered in a just war, a view suggested by both international law and English common law.

By contrast, the colonies were divided in their approach to the management of Indian affairs. In New England and Virginia, the colonists claimed the right to appropriate uncultivated land of the Indians as vacant waste, a claim that frequently led to armed Indian response. Although the Crown occasionally intervened to protect the Indians from such claims, the management of Indian affairs was left principally to colonial authorities until the mid-seventeenth century. Virginia, Connecticut, and the Massachusetts Bay Colony therefore were able to subjugate rapidly many eastern tribes. These colonies also claimed authority to govern and manage the affairs of the dependent tribes. The colonial authorities in New York, however, more often dealt with the mighty Six Nation Confederacy of the Iroquois through diplomatic means befitting a separate sovereign people. Similarly, the Carolinas and, later, Virginia treated the Cherokees as a separate and autonomous state. The important case of *Mohegan Indians v. Governor of Connecticut*, heard through royal commissions and in the Privy Council between 1703 and 1773, attempted to resolve the legal status of Indian tribes. While the fundamental issue in the *Mohegan Indians* case involved a land dispute between the tribe and the colony, among the other issues presented was the legal status of the Indian tribes. Repeatedly throughout the proceedings the colonial authorities challenged the jurisdiction of the royal commissions and the Privy Council, claiming that the Indians were subject to colonial authority and law and that the dispute should be resolved by colonial courts. In each instance the colonial claim was rejected and jurisdiction sustained. In 1743 the Court of Commissioners explained its assertion of jurisdiction:

> The Indians, though living amongst the king's subjects in these countries, are a separate and distinct people from them, they are treated as such, they have a policy of their own, they make peace and war with any nation of Indian when they think fit, without controul from the English.

In affirming the autonomous and sovereign status of the Indian tribes, the *Mohegan Indians* case was the precursor by almost a century of the strong reaffirmation of Indian tribal sovereignty in *Worcester v. Georgia*.

While English law could proclaim the autonomous sovereign status of Indian tribes, the Crown was unable to protect Indian rights so long as the manage-

---

*Copyright 1980 by The University of Chicago. Reprinted by permission.

ment of Indian affairs lay principally with colonial authorities. Land frauds, inattention to the protection of the Indians from encroachment by white settlers, and fear of English intentions and expansion led many Indian tribes, particularly the Six Nations, to remain neutral or even side with the French during King George's War. Efforts by colonial authorities to enlist Indian support for the English demonstrated the disunity and ineptitude of the colonial management of Indian affairs. Thus in 1751 a member of the Council of the Colony of New York, noting that "the preservation of the whole continent depends upon a proper regulation of the Six Nations," recommended that the management of Indian affairs be taken away from the colonial commissioners in Albany and placed under the direction of a single superintendent of Indian affairs. The greatest impetus for a structural change in the management of Indian affairs occurred when a Mohawk leader threatened, at a conference during the summer of 1753, to break the chain of friendship that allied the Six Nations to the Colony of New York, as a result of a list of complaints over land frauds and illegal encroachments by whites against the Indians. This development set the stage for the famous Albany Congress of 1754 which proposed a Union of the Colonies that would have the power to "hold or direct all Indian Treaties in which the general interest or welfare of the Colonys may be concerned," to "make peace or declare War with the Indian Nations," to "make such Laws as they judge necessary for the regulating all Indian Trade," and to regulate the purchase of land from the Indians, at least outside of colonial boundaries.

Almost simultaneously, the English government acted to centralize the management of Indian affairs in officials directly responsible to the Crown. This centralization lasted until 1768 and included the appointment of superintendents for the management of Indian affairs in the northern and southern colonies, the Proclamation of 1763 which was designed to halt white encroachments on Indian territory and to introduce Crown control over Indian land cessions, and a plan formulated in 1764, but never fully approved or implemented, for

> the regulation of Indian Affairs both commercial and political throughout all North America, upon one general system, under the direction of Officers appointed by the Crown, so as to sett [sic] aside all local interfering of particular Provinces, which has been one great cause of the distracted state of Indian Affairs in general.

Ironically, the very success of the earlier policies of central management of Indian affairs in allying the Indians (particularly the Six Nations) with the English side had helped eliminate the French as a potential ally of the Indians during the French and Indian War, and so had rendered the benefits of the 1764 plan unworthy of the costs involved. The plan therefore was abandoned in 1768 in favor of a partial and unsuccessful return to decentralized colonial management of Indian affairs.

The newly independent United States thus was presented with two important unresolved problems concerning Indian affairs: the need to establish a centralized management of Indian matters and the need to determine the legal status of the tribes. The immediate response of the nation was as ambivalent and unsatisfactory as the colonial attitude had been. While the early treaties between the Continental Congress and the Indian tribes guaranteed the tribes legal and political autonomy, the national government was unable to convince recalcitrant states both of the need for national management of Indian affairs and of the existence of the political autonomy of the Indian tribes from state or even national control. The language in article IX of the Articles of Confederation reflects the lack of resolution of these issues by granting to the Continental Congress "the sole and exclusive [authority of] regulating the trade and managing all affairs with Indians not members of any of the states; provided, that the legislative right of any state within its own limits be not infringed or violated." How this ambiguous and internally inconsistent grant of Indian-affairs power to the national government was supposed to work was, as Madison put it, "incomprehensible."

The impossibility of successful management by the national government during the Articles of Confederation period was evident in several areas. Perhaps the greatest failure involved Indian land rights. States often claimed both the right of preemption — the right to acquire Indian land upon its voluntary cession or abandonment or through conquest — and the power to enter into treaties with the tribes to extinguish the Indians' claims to land, thereby frustrating and sometimes actively interfering with efforts by the national government to negotiate treaties. For example, federal treaty negotiations with the Six Nations were physically disrupted by New York authorities who claimed the exclusive right to treat with those Indians. North Carolina and Georgia protested to Congress regarding the national government's interference with their domestic affairs when the Continental Congress approved the Treaty of Hopewell, guaranteeing the territorial integrity of the Cherokee Nation.

The Continental Congress could do little to control the states in this regard. In 1783, when it tried to protect Indian lands from encroachment by white settlers, it was able to secure approval only for a proclamation forbidding the cession or grant of Indian lands "without the limits or jurisdiction of any particular state," absent the express consent of Congress. Tribes within a state thus were unprotected. When Georgia, whose unilateral treaty making spawned an Indian war on the eve of the convening of the Constitutional Convention, sought the national government's assistance, a committee of the Continental Congress summarized the national government's frustration:

> An avaricious disposition in some of our people to acquire large tracts of land and often by unfair means, appears to be the principal source of difficulties with the Indians. [This] committee conceive that it has been long the opinion of the country, supported by justice and humanity, that the Indians have just claims to all lands occupied by and not fairly purchased from them. [Furthermore, it] cannot be supposed, the state has the powers [to make war with Indians or buy land from them] without making [the Indian affairs clause of article IX] useless. [N]o particular state can have an exclusive interest in the management of Affairs with any of the tribes, except in some uncommon cases.

The framers of the Constitution were aware of the failures of the Articles and of the need to deal with these two previously unresolved issues in the field of Indian affairs. On June 19, 1787, Madison requested the Constitutional Convention to consider whether a plan offered by the New Jersey delegation would remedy the deficiencies of the Articles:

> Will it prevent encroachments on the Federal authority? A tendency to such encroachments has been sufficiently exemplified among ourselves, as well as in every other confederated republic. [As a result of] the Federal Articles, transactions with the Indians appertain to Congress, yet in several instances the States have entered into treaties and wars with them.

In adopting the "Indians not taxed" language in the Constitution, the framers thus showed that they rejected the notion, partially recognized in article IX of the Articles of Confederation, that some Indian tribes were subject to both state and federal control. Their exclusion from the enumeration for apportionment purposes reflects their autonomous political status.

More importantly, the Constitution vested exclusive authority to regulate commerce "with the Indian Tribes" in the Congress, freeing the grant of federal power over Indian affairs from the ambiguous and counterproductive reservation of state authority that had plagued the Indian affairs clause of article IX. The Indian commerce clause also recognized the sovereign status of the tribes by including them in the same clause with "foreign Nations" and "the several States." In *The Federalist*, [No. 42,] Madison wrote of the advantages of the Indian commerce clause over its counterpart in the Articles:

> The regulation of commerce with the Indian tribes is very properly unfettered from two limitations in the articles of confederation, which render the provision obscure and contradictory. The power is there restrained to Indians, not members of any of the States, and is not to violate or infringe the legislative right of any State within its own limits. What description of Indians are to be deemed members of a State, is not yet settled, and has been a question of frequent perplexity and contention in the federal Councils. And how the trade with Indians, though not members of a State, yet residing within its legislative jurisdiction, can be regulated by an external authority, without so far intruding on the internal rights of legislation, is absolutely incomprehensible.

WORCESTER v. GEORGIA

31 U.S. (6 Pet.) 515 (1832)

[The Court held that Georgia could not criminally prosecute and convict several white missionaries to the Cherokees, including Samuel A. Worcester, for violating an 1830 law enacted by the legislature of the state of Georgia that required any person residing within the Cherokee Nation to have a license or permit from the Georgia governor and to take an oath of loyalty. Georgia law also purported to annex the Cherokee Nation to the state, extend state law over the Cherokees, and disqualify Indians from testifying in state court. The Court held that the state laws violated the Indian commerce clause, the federal treaties with the Cherokee protecting their lands and political autonomy, and the Trade and Intercourse Acts, and therefore were preempted by federal law. The text of this opinion is set forth in Chapter 1, page 18.]

NOTES

1. **The Analytical Underpinnings of *Worcester*:** The strong preference for the exercise of federal authority, rather than state power, in the field of Indian affairs established in the Proclamation of 1763 and the history of the Indian commerce clause continued for most of the late eighteenth and nineteenth

centuries. Note that Justice Marshall stated three separate grounds, each of which is sufficient by itself to preempt state authority. First, the Court held that the State of Georgia wholly lacked any inherent sovereignty over Indians or Indian country because the framers of the Constitution had exclusively vested the Indian affairs power in the federal government. This approach suggests that whatever state jurisdiction exists in Indian country must be based on federal statutory delegation of authority under the Indian commerce clause. Second, the Court held that treaties recognizing the Cherokee Nation's political autonomy and setting land aside for the Cherokee reservation preempted state authority. This second approach suggests a broad preemptive force for treaties (and later statutes and executive orders) that recognize tribal autonomy; this broad preemption analysis is known as "Indian country preemption." Third, the Court held that specific federal statutes, in this case the Trade and Intercourse Acts, preempted the Georgia laws. Under this last form of preemption, specific statutes, regulations, or treaties are read broadly in light of federal policy toward Indians to preempt state regulation. Of the three potential methods of analyzing questions of state interference first employed in *Worcester*, the negative implications of the Indian commerce clause, Indian country preemption, and statutory preemption, which is most fully supported by the history of the Indian commerce clause? For more information on the importance of the Proclamation of 1763 in shaping American legal thought about Indian political status and the central versus local management of Indian affairs, see Clinton, *The Proclamation of 1763: Colonial Prelude to Two Centuries of Federal-State Conflict Over the Management of Indian Affairs*, 69 B.U.L. REV. 329 (1989).

2. State Jurisdiction When No Indian Interests Are Involved: Nineteenth-century legal developments did not, however, completely bear out the broadest possible readings of *Worcester*. Where no Indian interest whatsoever was involved, some late nineteenth and early twentieth century cases suggested the existence of some limited state sovereignty in Indian country. As already noted in Chapter 2, for example, the Court in *United States v. McBratney*, 104 U.S. 621 (1881), and *Draper v. United States*, 164 U.S. 240 (1896), held that state courts, rather than federal or tribal courts, had the jurisdiction to try non-Indians who committed crimes against the person or property of other non-Indians in Indian country. Similarly, in *Utah & Northern Ry. v. Fisher*, 116 U.S. 28 (1885), the Court held that the lands and property of the Utah and Northern Railway situated within the limits of the Fort Hall Indian Reservation were subject to territorial, and inferentially to state, taxation. The Court noted that "[t]he authority of the Territory may rightfully extend to all matters not interfering with that [treaty-guaranteed] protection [of Indian autonomy and self-government]." 116 U.S. at 31.

On the other hand, where any Indian interest existed, the early cases consistently held that state jurisdiction was lacking. In *The New York Indians*, 72 U.S. (5 Wall.) 761 (1866), and *The Kansas Indians*, 72 U.S. (5 Wall.) 737 (1866), the Court held that Indians were immune from state taxation, even if their land was allotted or they were scheduled for removal. In *The Kansas Indians*, the Court said:

> If the tribal organization of the Shawnees is preserved intact, and recognized by the political department of the government as existing[,] then they are a "people distinct from others" capable of making treaties, separated from the jurisdiction of Kansas, and to be governed exclusively by the government of the Union. If under the control of Congress, from necessity there can be no divided authority.

Id. at 755. And in *Harkness v. Hyde,* 98 U.S. 476 (1878), and *Langford v. Monteith,* 102 U.S. 145 (1880), the Court held that the civil process of state and territorial courts did not reach into Indian country even with respect to non-Indian defendants, at least where the cause of action arose on an Indian reservation. Dicta in *Langford* purported to limit the holding in *Harkness,* however, only to those reservations for which there was an explicit treaty or statutory disclaimer of state or territorial jurisdiction.

3. State Jurisdictional Disclaimers and the Equal Footing Doctrine: The dicta in *Langford, supra,* raises a very confusing and, apparently, now moribund line of cases involving state disclaimers of jurisdiction. As the removal policy was winding down, the pace at which states were being settled, formed, and admitted to the union began to outstrip the speed with which the federal government could remove tribes from the states prior to statehood. Thus, beginning with the admission of Wisconsin and Kansas, Congress began to insist that *some* states disclaim authority and jurisdiction over lingering vestiges of Indian country by including such disclaimers in the enabling or statehood legislation or by requiring the affected states to include such irrevocable disclaimers in their state constitutions. For example, article XXI, § 2 of the New Mexico Constitution contains a specific disclaimer

> to all lands lying within said boundaries owned or held by any Indian or Indian tribes, the right or title to which shall have been acquired through the United States, [and that] until the title of such Indian or Indian tribes shall have been extinguished the same shall be and remain subject to the disposition and under the absolute jurisdiction and control of the Congress of the United States.

See also § 4 of the Alaska Statehood Act, 72 Stat. 339 (1958); Montana, 25 Stat. 676, 677 (1889); Utah, 28 Stat. 107, 108 (1894); and New Mexico, 36 Stat. 557, 558-77 (1910). *See also* Wyoming Const., 1890, art. 21, § 26 and Idaho Const., 1890, art. 21, § 19.

The state disclaimers soon took on an historical significance beyond their initial intent. Seemingly ignoring the lessons of *Worcester,* the Supreme Court in a few instances suggested that negative implications could be drawn from the lack of such a disclaimer. For example, the *McBratney* decision was based in part on the lack of such a disclaimer in the Colorado Constitution. Similarly, in *Ward v. Race Horse,* 163 U.S. 504 (1896), the Court held that treaty rights of the Shoshone-Bannock to hunt and fish on unoccupied lands of the federal government were displaced or abrogated in Wyoming when the state entered the union on an equal footing with other states and without such a disclaimer. Ironically, this doctrine meant that with reference to Indian affairs states had some residual sovereignty and were on an equal footing unless Congress chose to place them in an unequal position through a disclaimer. Since the doctrine made little constitutional or legal sense, it has hardly affected state jurisdiction in the twentieth century. Indeed, adherence to this doctrine would mean that Congress could not recognize a tribe, create a new reservation, or otherwise create Indian country after statehood in a state that did not have a constitutional disclaimer involving the tribe in question. Without express reference to such disclaimers, the Court seemingly rejected this argument in *United States v. John,* 437 U.S. 634 (1978), set forth and discussed in Chapters 1 and 2. Thus, these old disclaimer and equal footing cases must be distinguished away, a process that has involved considerable ingenuity. As discussed in Chapter 2, the

McBratney case has come to be thought about as a case involving criminal jurisdiction over a crime by a non-Indian against the person or property of another non-Indian in Indian country, an approach which limits the case to its facts and ignores its rationale. *Ward* has come to stand for the proposition that states sometimes can regulate *off-reservation* hunting and fishing rights. *See Organized Village of Kake v. Egan*, 369 U.S. 60, 67-69 (1962) ("The disclaimer of right and title by the state was [for] proprietary rather than governmental interest" and citing *Ward*, "[e]ven where reserved by federal treaties, off-reservation hunting and fishing rights have been subject to state regulation.").

4. The Modern Era: Beyond these somewhat confused decisions, the Supreme Court did not return in a substantial manner to the problem of inherent state authority over Indians in Indian country until 1959. In the interim, allotment and termination policies had focused attention on unsuccessful legislative solutions to these jurisdictional questions. Thus, as recently as 1945, Justice Black could proclaim, "The policy of leaving Indians free from state jurisdiction and control is deeply rooted in the Nation's history." *Rice v. Olson*, 324 U.S. 786, 789 (1945). In 1981, Professor Clinton summarized the long-standing rule still prevailing as late as 1959 as follows: "[I]n the absence of clear and specific congressional authorization state law had no force in Indian country except in those cases where no Indian was involved and no Indian interest affected." Clinton, *State Power Over Indian Reservations: A Critical Comment on Burger Court Doctrine*, 26 S.D.L. Rev. 434, [438] (1981).

Before turning to the modern responses of the courts to the scope of inherent state authority in Indian country, it is important to separate a number of analytical questions. First, unlike criminal jurisdiction, where most of the issues of jurisdiction in Indian country are resolved by a reasonably clear set of federal statutes specifically addressed to jurisdiction, discussed in Chapter 2, which preempt most state jurisdiction, there are no generally applicable federal statutes for issues of civil jurisdiction. Thus many, but not all, issues of state civil jurisdiction, whether adjudicatory jurisdiction or state legislative taxing and regulatory authority, are primarily resolved by analyzing the inherent reach of state authority and the preemptive implications of statutes and treaties that may not deal expressly with jurisdiction. Second, while this chapter and the cases cited not infrequently treat the topic of "civil jurisdiction" as a monolithic category to which the same or analogous rules ought to apply, it is important to note that there are subcategories of questions subsumed within this general category of authority. For example, analytically there is a discernible distinction between the legislative authority of the state, e.g., the power to regulate or tax, in Indian country and the civil adjudicatory jurisdiction of the state courts to resolve private disputes. Should the same rules or principles apply to the resolution of a question of the reach of a state's taxing authority in Indian country that would be applied to determine the scope of state court subject matter jurisdiction? Even within the issue of the scope of civil adjudicatory jurisdiction of state courts in Indian country, there are separate issues. State courts might be limited in their subject matter jurisdiction over Indian country, i.e., the power to entertain certain kinds of disputes involving Indians or arising in Indian country, or they may be limited in their jurisdiction in Indian country over persons and property, i.e., the reach of their compulsory court processes over persons or property located in Indian country irrespective of the nature of the underlying claim. Should the same principles be applied to resolve these separate questions of subject matter jurisdiction and jurisdiction over persons and property? Do the courts in fact draw these distinctions? Finally, if the jurisdictional patterns largely excluding state law from operating in Indian country are to be altered, which body has been charged by the Constitution with the power to so undermine tribal sovereignty, Congress or the Court?

2. THE MODERN PREEMPTION ERA

a. Preemption in the Absence of Federal Regulatory Action

WILLIAMS v. LEE

358 U.S. 217 (1959)

Mr. Justice BLACK delivered the opinion of the Court.

Respondent, who is not an Indian, operates a general store in Arizona on the Navajo Indian Reservation under a license required by federal statute.[1] He brought this action in the Superior Court of Arizona against petitioners, a Navajo Indian and his wife who live on the Reservation, to collect for goods sold them there on credit. Over petitioners' motion to dismiss on the ground that jurisdiction lay in the tribal court rather than in the state court, judgment was entered in favor of respondent. The Supreme Court of Arizona affirmed, holding that since no Act of Congress expressly forbids their doing so Arizona courts are free to exercise jurisdiction over civil suits by non-Indians against Indians though the action arises on an Indian reservation. Because this was a doubtful determination of the important question of state power over Indian affairs, [certiorari was granted].

Despite bitter criticism and the defiance of Georgia which refused to obey this Court's mandate in *Worcester* the broad principles of that decision came to be accepted as law. Over the years this Court has modified these principles in cases where essential tribal relations were not involved and where the rights of Indians would not be jeopardized, but the basic policy of *Worcester* has remained. Thus, suits by Indians against outsiders in state courts have been sanctioned. [*E.g.,*] *Felix v. Patrick*, 145 U.S. 317, 332. And state courts have been allowed to try non-Indians who committed crimes against each other on a reservation. *E.g., New York ex rel. Ray v. Martin*, 326 U.S. 496. But if the crime was by or against an Indian, tribal jurisdiction or that expressly conferred on other courts by Congress has remained exclusive. *Donnelly v. United States*, 228 U.S. 243, 269-272; *Williams v. United States*, 327 U.S. 711. Essentially, absent governing Acts of Congress, the question has always been whether the state action infringed on the right of reservation Indians to make their own laws and be ruled by them. *Cf. Utah & Northern Railway v. Fisher*, 116 U.S. 28.

---

[1]31 Stat. 1066, as amended, 32 Stat. 1009, 25 U.S.C. § 262, provides:

Any person desiring to trade with the Indians on any Indian reservation shall, upon establishing the fact, to the satisfaction of the Commissioner of Indian Affairs, that he is a proper person to engage in such trade, be permitted to do so under such rules and regulations as the Commissioner of Indian Affairs may prescribe for the protection of said Indians.

Congress has also acted consistently upon the assumption that the States have no power to regulate the affairs of Indians on a reservation. To assure adequate government of the Indian tribes it enacted comprehensive statutes in 1834 regulating trade with Indians and organizing a Department of Indian Affairs. 4 Stat. 729, 735. Not satisfied solely with centralized government of Indians, it encouraged tribal governments and courts to become stronger and more highly organized. *E.g.,* [the IRA.] Congress has followed a policy calculated eventually to make all Indians full-fledged participants in American society. This policy contemplates criminal and civil jurisdiction over Indians by any State ready to assume the burdens that go with it as soon as the educational and economic status of the Indians permits the change without disadvantage to them. See H.R. Rep. No. 848, 83d Cong., 1st Sess. 3, 6, 7 (1953). Significantly, when Congress has wished the States to exercise this power it has expressly granted them the jurisdiction which *Worcester v. Georgia* had denied.[6]

No departure from the policies which have been applied to other Indians is apparent in the relationship between the United States and the Navajos. On June 1, 1868, a treaty was signed between General William T. Sherman, for the United States, and numerous chiefs and headmen of the "Navajo nation or tribe of Indians."[7] At the time this document was signed the Navajos were an exiled people, forced by the United States to live crowded together on a small piece of land on the Pecos River in eastern New Mexico, some 300 miles east of the area they had occupied before the coming of the white man. In return for their promises to keep peace, this treaty "set apart" for "their permanent home" a portion of what had been their native country, and provided that no one, except United States Government personnel, was to enter the reserved area. Implicit in these treaty terms, as it was in the treaties with the Cherokees involved in *Worcester v. Georgia*, was the understanding that the internal affairs of the Indians remained exclusively within the jurisdiction of whatever tribal government existed. Since then, Congress and the Bureau of Indian Affairs have assisted in strenghtening the Navajo tribal government and its courts. See the Navajo-Hopi Rehabilitation Act of 1950, § 6, 64 Stat. 46, 25 U.S.C. § 636. The Tribe itself has in recent years greatly improved its legal system through increased expenditures and better-trained personnel. Today the Navajo Courts of Indian Offenses exercise broad criminal and civil jurisdiction which covers suits by outsiders against Indian defendants. No Federal Act has given state courts jurisdiction over such controversies.[9] In a general statute Congress did express

---

[6]*See, e.g.,* 62 Stat. 1224, 64 Stat. 845, 25 U.S.C. §§ 232, 233 (1952) (granting broad civil and criminal jurisdiction to New York); 18 U.S.C. § 1162, 28 U.S.C. § 1360 (granting broad civil and criminal jurisdiction to California, Minnesota, Nebraska, Oregon, and Wisconsin). The series of statutes granting extensive jurisdiction over Oklahoma Indians to state courts are discussed in Cohen, [Handbook of Federal Indian Law] at 985-1051.

[7]15 Stat. 667. In 16 Stat. 566 (1871), Congress declared that no Indian tribe or nation within the United States should thereafter be recognized as an independent power with whom the United States could execute a treaty but provided that this should not impair the obligations of any treaty previously ratified. Thus the 1868 treaty with the Navajos survived this Act.

[9]In the 1949 Navajo-Hopi Rehabilitation Bill, S. 1407, 81st Cong., 1st Sess., setting up a 10-year program of capital and other improvements on the Reservation, Congress provided for concurrent state, federal and tribal jurisdiction. President Truman vetoed the bill because he felt that subjecting the Navajo and Hopi to state jurisdiction was undesirable in view of their illiteracy, poverty and primitive social concepts. He was also impressed by the fact that the Indians vigorously opposed the

its willingness to have any State assume jurisdiction over reservation Indians if the State Legislature or the people vote affirmatively to accept such responsibility. To date, Arizona has not accepted jurisdiction, possibly because the people of the State anticipate that the burdens accompanying such power might be considerable.

There can be no doubt that to allow the exercise of state jurisdiction here would undermine the authority of the tribal courts over Reservation affairs and hence would infringe on the right of the Indians to govern themselves. It is immaterial that respondent is not an Indian. He was on the Reservation and the transaction with an Indian took place there. The cases in this Court have consistently guarded the authority of Indian governments over their reservations. Congress recognized this authority in the Navajos in the Treaty of 1868, and has done so ever since. If this power is to be taken away from them, it is for Congress to do it. [*Lone Wolf v. Hitchcock.*]

Reversed.

NOTES

1. The Rationale of *Williams*: Does Justice Black's opinion draw a sharp line between those occasions when the state can and when it cannot assume jurisdiction? The principle derived is one which could cause extraordinary debate: When does state jurisdiction "undermine the authority of the tribal courts over Reservation affairs and [therefore] infringe on the right of the Indians to govern themselves"? Upon what legal theory did the exclusion of state authority in *Williams* rest? Was state power limited merely because of the existence of tribal sovereignty? Would the result in the case have been the same had the Navajo not been a tribe recognized by the federal government in treaty and statute as possessing tribal self-governing authority? Was federal law, then, preemptive of state jurisdiction? If so, was the preemptive federal law (1) the Indian commerce clause, (2) the treaties or statutes recognizing tribal self-government, (3) Public Law 280, or (4) some combination of the foregoing? What practical difference does it make as to which source of federal law is seen as preemptive?

2. The Infringement Test: A Sword for State Power or a Shield for the Tribes? Some state courts initially regarded the negative implications of the *Williams v. Lee* infringement test as an invitation to extend state jurisdiction to many situations in Indian country that they did not think involved tribal self-government. *See, e.g., McClanahan v. State Tax Comm'n*, 14 Ariz. App. 452, 484 P.2d 221 (1971), *rev'd*, 411 U.S. 164 (1974). By contrast, some federal courts regarded the test as an important shield of tribal sovereignty against the intrusions of state authority. *Arizona ex rel. Merrill v. Turtle*, 413 F.2d 683 (9th Cir. 1969), *cert. denied*, 396 U.S. 1003 (1970), finding no state extradition authority over Indian accused discovered on Navajo Reservation and wanted for a crime in other state, represents a good example of such use of the infringement test. The fact that the implications of *Williams* for state jurisdiction initially were often decided in state courts had some impact on the substantive results reached.

3. Infringement Test and Nonmembers: Of what significance to the decision in *Williams* is the fact that a non-Indian is involved in the adjudication? Would the result and rationale have been the same if a Navajo, or for that matter a

bill. 95 Cong. Rec. 14784-14785. After the objectionable features of the bill were deleted it was passed again and became law. 64 Stat. 44, 25 U.S.C. §§ 631-640.

Cheyenne, had been the plaintiff in the case? Notice, however, that the non-Indian is a *plaintiff* in the *Williams* action. Had the non-Indian trader been sued by a Navajo consumer for breach of warranty in the Arizona state courts, would the result be the same? Consider Justice Black's statement that "suits by Indians against outsiders in state courts have been sanctioned." Can that statement be reconciled with the general rationale in *Williams* and the infringement test in particular? *See, e.g., Paiz v. Hughes,* 76 N.M. 562, 417 P.2d 51 (1966) ("Permitting the [Indian] plaintiffs in these cases to prosecute their claims [against non-Indian defendants] for personal injuries and alleged wrongful death, in the New Mexico courts, will not affect the rights of the Jicarilla-Apache Indians to make their own laws and be ruled by them, will not affect their tribal relations, and will not affect the rights of the Federal Government."). Can this result be reconciled with tribal sovereignty? Should an individual tribal member be permitted to waive the authority of the tribe over the subject matter of the suit? Is tribal self-government an individual or a group right?

4. Indian Plaintiffs, State Courts, and the Strange Saga of the *Three Tribes* Cases: The dicta in *Williams* regarding Indian plaintiffs suing non-Indian defendants in state court played a very important role in *Three Affiliated Tribes of the Fort Berthold Reservation v. Wold Eng'g, P.C.,* 467 U.S. 138 (1984) (*Three Tribes I*) and *Three Affiliated Tribes of the Fort Berthold Reservation v. Wold Eng'g, P.C.,* 476 U.S. 877 (1986) (*Three Tribes II*). In these cases, the tribe sued the defendant's engineering firm in North Dakota state courts for breach of contract and negligence in conjunction with the defendant's work on a tribal water project. Pursuant to Public Law 280, North Dakota, after amending the disclaimer of jurisdiction in its constitution, enacted an assumption of state civil jurisdiction statute that read as follows:

> In accordance with the provisions of Public Law 280 [and the amended] North Dakota constitution, jurisdiction of the state of North Dakota shall be extended over all civil causes of action which arise on an Indian reservation *upon acceptance by Indian citizens in a manner provided by this chapter.* Upon acceptance the jurisdiction of the state shall be to the same extent that the state has jurisdiction over other civil causes of action, and those civil laws of this state that are of general application to private property shall have the same force and effect within such Indian reservation or Indian country as they have elsewhere within this state.

N.D. Cent. Code § 27-19-01 (1974) (emphasis supplied). North Dakota interpreted this provision as requiring any Indian plaintiff to consent to state jurisdiction for all purposes. The Fort Berthold Tribe declined to do so, in part to protect its tribal sovereign immunity, and the state courts dismissed the action, apparently assuming that, in the absence of full compliance with Public Law 280 and the state legislation thereunder, the state had no authority to hear the suit. In *Three Tribes I* the Court considered the question of whether either federal preemption doctrines or Public Law 280 precluded the North Dakota state courts from hearing the tribal claim as a matter of *federal* law. The Court found that neither Public Law 280 nor the preemptive infringement test of *Williams v. Lee* precluded the exercise of such authority:

> [W]e fail to see how the exercise of state-court jurisdiction in this case would interfere with the right of tribal Indians to govern themselves under their own laws. To be sure, the full breadth of state-court jurisdiction recognized in *Vermillion* cannot be squared with principles of tribal autonomy; to the extent that *Vermillion* [a North Dakota case interpreting the above-quoted statute] permitted North Dakota state courts to exercise jurisdiction over claims by non-Indians against Indians or over claims between Indians, it intruded impermissibly on tribal self-governance. See *Fisher v. District Court,*

424 U.S. 382 (1976); *Williams v. Lee, supra*. This Court, however, repeatedly has approved the exercise of jurisdiction by state courts over claims by Indians against non-Indians, even when those claims arose in Indian country. See *McClanahan v. Arizona State Tax Comm'n*, 411 U.S., at 173 (dictum); *Poafpybitty v. Skelly Oil Co.*, 390 U.S. 365 (1968); *Williams v. Lee*, 358 U.S., at 219 (dictum); *United States v. Candelaria*, 271 U.S. 432, 444 (1926); *Felix v. Patrick*, 145 U.S. 317, 332 (1892); *Fellows v. Blacksmith*, 19 How. 366 (1857). The interests implicated in such cases are very different from those present in *Williams v. Lee*, where a non-Indian sued an Indian in state court for debts incurred in Indian country, or in *Fisher v. District Court*, where this Court held that a tribal court had exclusive jurisdiction over an adoption proceeding in which all parties were tribal Indians residing on a reservation. As a general matter, tribal self-government is not impeded when a State allows an Indian to enter its courts on equal terms with other persons to seek relief against a non-Indian concerning a claim arising in Indian country. *The exercise of state jurisdiction is particularly compatible with tribal autonomy when, as here, the suit is brought by the tribe itself and the tribal court lacked jurisdiction over the claim at the time the suit was instituted.*

Id. at 148-49 (emphasis supplied). Since erroneous assumptions about the state court power under *federal* law to entertain the tribe's claim contributed to the outcome, the Court remanded the case to the North Dakota Supreme Court to decide whether North Dakota law, including the requirement of full consent to jurisdiction, precluded the exercise of state court jurisdiction. After the North Dakota Supreme Court ruled that, as a matter of *state* law, the North Dakota statute required the tribe to waive its sovereign immunity and consent to litigate any claim in suits to which it is a party in state court before it could make use of the state courts for this dispute, the case came back to the United States Supreme Court in *Three Tribes II*. Consent to jurisdiction was important, in part because of counterclaims that the defendant may have had against the plaintiff tribe. In *Three Tribes II*, which is set forth and discussed in more detail below in section 2b, the Court held that both Public Law 280 and the federal protections of tribal sovereignty preempted state law and prevented South Dakota from conditioning access to its courts on waivers of sovereign immunity or an open-ended consent to state jurisdiction. The Supreme Court therefore remanded the case to state court.

    6. Subject Matter Jurisdiction or Jurisdiction Over the Person of the Defendant: Is the result in *Williams v. Lee* predicated upon a lack of subject matter jurisdiction over the controversy, upon the lack of jurisdiction over the person of the defendant in the state court, or some other principle? If the sale of the goods in *Williams* had occurred outside of the Navajo Reservation in Flagstaff, Arizona, for example, would the courts of the state of Arizona lack subject matter jurisdiction over the controversy? If the state courts have subject matter jurisdiction over the case, does that mean that state officials may enter the Reservation and lawfully serve process on an Indian defendant domiciled there? As discussed above, in two nineteenth-century cases, *Harkness v. Hyde*, 98 U.S. 476 (1878), and *Langford v. Monteith*, 102 U.S. 145 (1880), the Supreme Court seemed to suggest that Indian reservations were jurisdictional enclaves outside of the reach of process issuing from the courts of the state or federal territory in which they were located. The breadth of that holding is clouded, however, since the *Langford* opinion contained dicta suggesting the now discredited approach that this special jurisdictional enclave status was dependent upon the existence of explicit treaty or statutory language applicable to the particular reservation that expressly disclaimed such state or territorial jurisdiction. Unfortunately, the Supreme Court has not returned to the issue to clarify it.

In default of a definitive Supreme Court decision, the courts are split on the question of exercise of jurisdiction over the person of an individual located in Indian country. *Compare Francisco v. State*, 113 Ariz. 427, 556 P.2d 1 (1976) ("based on the reasoning in *McClanahan* [and *Williams v. Lee*] that the Executive Order [setting aside the Papago Reservation] would preclude the extension of state law to Indians on the reservation, including the laws which effectuate the authority in the Sheriff to serve process") *with State Sec., Inc. v. Anderson*, 84 N.M. 629, 506 P.2d 786 (1973) ("State jurisdiction does not eliminate Indian jurisdiction, it exists concurrently with it. There is no interference with Indian self-government."). Should it make any difference whether the person upon whom state process is served in Indian country is a member of the tribe or, for that matter, even an Indian? Does it make any difference whether process is served by a state official, by a private process server, or by mail? Given the expansion of concepts of jurisdiction beyond territorial boundaries under *International Shoe Co. v. Washington*, 326 U.S. 310 (1945), cannot states that are frequently confronted with this problem, like Arizona or New Mexico, eliminate whatever legal impediment exists by enacting long-arm type statutes authorizing service by mail on persons domiciled on Indian reservations? For an excellent article setting forth proposals to use long-arm statutes to solve problems of jurisdiction over persons and property in Indian country, see Canby, *Civil Jurisdiction and the Indian Reservation*, 1973 UTAH L. REV. 206. If states may secure jurisdiction over persons located in Indian country by simply enacting a long-arm statute, why should they not be authorized to secure process more directly by sending a state sheriff onto the reservation to serve process personally on the defendant?

An important corollary of the problem of jurisdiction is the question of power to enforce court judgments, e.g., the power to levy on property. Does a state court have such enforcement authority merely because the court has jurisdiction over the subject matter of the controversy and has jurisdiction over the person of an Indian defendant if the property is located within the state, albeit on an Indian reservation? To put that question in the concrete, assume that in *Williams* the goods had been purchased in Flagstaff, Arizona, and that the defendant had been served with state court process in Flagstaff when she returned to plaintiff's store to complain about the appliance. May the state courts directly enforce any judgment awarded to the plaintiff on the defendant's property located on the Navajo reservation? In *Joe v. Marcum*, 621 F.2d 358 (10th Cir. 1980), the Tenth Circuit held in a similar context that state courts could not garnish the wages of an Indian earned on the reservation to enforce a valid state court default judgment. Applying, among other things, the test of *Williams v. Lee* the court said:

> Garnishment proceedings are indeed ancillary proceedings in the sense that they are in aid of a judgment previously obtained. However, such are independent proceedings in the sense that they are against the judgment debtor's employer, to attach wages held by the employer and due the judgment debtor. The subject matter of the present garnishment proceedings is money held by Utah International and due Joe. Utah International was served on the reservation. The garnishment *res* is located on the reservation and represents wages due for services rendered by Joe to Utah International on the reservation. Under such circumstances, to uphold the present garnishment would thwart the Navajo policy which does not permit garnishment of wages.

Id. at 362-63. *See also Annis v. Dewey County Bank*, 335 F. Supp. 133 (D.S.D. 1971). By contrast, in *Little Horn State Bank v. Stops*, 170 Mont. 510, 555 P.2d 211 (1976), *cert. denied*, 431 U.S. 924 (1977), the court reached the opposite result, explaining, "It had been a long standing doctrine that any court having jurisdiction to render a judgment also has the power to enforce that judgment through any order or writ necessary to carry its judgment into effect." Is that statement accurate?

McCLANAHAN v. ARIZONA STATE TAX COMMISSION

411 U.S. 164 (1973)

Mr. Justice MARSHALL delivered the opinion of the Court.

This case requires us once again to reconcile the plenary power of the States over residents within their borders with the semi-autonomous status of Indians living on tribal reservations. In this instance, the problem arises in the context of Arizona's efforts to impose its personal income tax on a reservation Indian whose entire income derives from reservation sources [only].

I

Appellant is an enrolled member of the Navajo tribe who lives on that portion of the Navajo Reservation located within the State of Arizona. Her complaint alleges that all her income earned during 1967 was derived from within the Navajo Reservation. Pursuant to Ariz. Rev. Stat. Ann. § 43-188 (f) (Supp. 1972-1973), $16.20 was withheld from her wages for that year to cover her state income tax liability. At the conclusion of the tax year, appellant filed a protest against the collection of any taxes on her income and a claim for a refund of the entire amount withheld from her wages. When no action was taken on her claim, she instituted this action in Arizona Superior Court on behalf of herself and those similarly situated, demanding a return of the money withheld and a declaration that the state tax was unlawful as applied to reservation Indians.

The trial court dismissed the action for failure to state a claim, and the Arizona Court of Appeals affirmed. Citing this Court's decision in [*Williams v. Lee,*] the Court of Appeals held that the test "is not whether the Arizona state income tax infringes on plaintiff's rights as an individual Navajo Indian, but whether such a tax infringes on the rights of the Navajo tribe of Indians to be self-governing." The court thus distinguished cases dealing with state taxes on Indian real property on the ground that these taxes, unlike the personal income tax, infringed tribal autonomy.

[Because] an individual income tax did not interfere with tribal self-government, it followed that appellant had failed to state a claim. The Arizona Supreme Court denied a petition for review of this decision, and the case came here on appeal.

II

It may be helpful to begin our discussion of the law applicable to this complex area with a brief statement of what this case does not involve. We are not here dealing with Indians who have left or never inhabited reservations set aside for their exclusive use or who do not possess the usual accoutrements of tribal self-government. *See, e.g., Organized Village of Kake v. Egan,* [369 U.S. 60 (1962)]. Nor are we concerned with exertions of state sovereignty over non-Indians who undertake activity on Indian reservations. *See,* [*e.g., Thomas v. Gay,* 169 U.S. 264 (1898)]. Nor, finally, is this a case where the State seeks to reach activity undertaken by reservation Indians on nonreservation lands. *See, e.g., Mescalero Apache Tribe v. Jones,* [411 U.S. 145 (1973)]. Rather, this case involves the narrow question whether the State may tax a reservation Indian for income earned exclusively on the reservation.

The principles governing the resolution of this question are not new. On the contrary, "[t]he policy of leaving Indians free from state jurisdiction and control is deeply rooted in the Nation's history." *Rice v. Olson,* 324 U.S. 786, 789 (1945). This policy was first articulated by this Court 141 years ago when Mr. Chief Justice Marshall held that Indian nations were "distinct political communities, having territorial boundaries, within which their authority is exclusive, and having a right to all the lands within those boundaries, which is not only acknowledged, but guarantied by the United States." [*Worcester v. Georgia.*] It followed from this concept of Indian reservations as separate, although dependent nations, that state law could have no role to play within the reservation boundaries.

> The Cherokee nation ... is a distinct community, occupying its own territory, with boundaries accurately described, in which the laws of Georgia can have no force, and which the citizens of Georgia have no right to enter, but with the assent of the Cherokees themselves, or in conformity with treaties, and with the acts of Congress. The whole intercourse between the United States and this nation, is, by our Constitution and laws, vested in the government of the United States. *Id.,* at 561.

Although *Worcester* on its facts dealt with a State's efforts to extend its criminal jurisdiction to reservation lands, the rationale of the case plainly extended to state taxation within the reservation as well. Thus, in *The Kansas Indians,* 5 Wall. 737 (1867), the Court unambiguously rejected state efforts to [tax real property of reservation Indians].

This is not to say that the Indian sovereignty doctrine, with its concomitant jurisdictional limit on the reach of state law, has remained static during the 141 years since *Worcester* was decided. Not surprisingly, the doctrine has undergone considerable evolution in response to changed circumstances. As noted above, the doctrine has not been rigidly applied in cases where Indians have left the reservation and become assimilated into the general community. *See, e.g., Oklahoma Tax Comm'n v. United States,* 319 U.S. 598 (1943). Similarly, notions of Indian sovereignty have been adjusted to take account of the State's legitimate interests in regulating the affairs of non-Indians. [*See, e.g., New York ex rel. Ray v. Martin,* 326 U.S. 496 (1946).] This line of cases was summarized in this Court's landmark decision in *Williams v. Lee:*

> Over the years this Court has modified [the *Worcester* principle] in cases where essential tribal relations were not involved and where the rights of Indians would not be jeopardized .... Thus, suits by Indians against outsiders in state courts have been sanctioned.... And state courts have been allowed to try non-Indians who committed crimes against each other on a reservation.... But if the crime was by or against an Indian, tribal jurisdiction or that expressly conferred on other courts by Congress has remained exclusive.... Essentially, absent governing Acts of Congress, the question has

always been whether the state action infringed on the right of reservation Indians to make their own laws and be ruled by them.

Id., at 219-220 (footnote omitted).

Finally, the trend has been away from the idea of inherent Indian sovereignty as a bar to state jurisdiction and toward reliance on federal preemption.[7] The modern cases thus tend to avoid reliance on platonic notions of Indian sovereignty and to look instead to the applicable treaties and statutes which define the limits of state power. *Compare, e.g., United States v. Kagama,* 118 U.S. 375 (1886), with *Kennerly v. District Court,* 400 U.S. 423 (1971).[8]

The Indian sovereignty doctrine is relevant, then, not because it provides a definitive resolution of the issues in this suit, but because it provides a backdrop against which the applicable treaties and federal statutes must be read. It must always be remembered that the various Indian tribes were once independent and sovereign nations, and that their claim to sovereignty long predates that of our own Government. Indians today are American citizens. They have the right to vote, to use state courts, and they receive some state services.[12] But it is nonetheless still true, as it was in the last century, that

> [t]he relation of the Indian tribes living within the borders of the United States ... [is] an anomalous one and of a complex character.... They were, and always have been, regarded as having a semi-independent position when they preserved their tribal relations; not as States, not as nations, not as possessed of the full attributes of sovereignty, but as a separate people, with the power of regulating their internal and social relations, and thus far not brought under the laws of the Union or of the State within whose limits they resided. [*United States v. Kagama.*]

III

When the relevant treaty and statutes are read with this tradition of sovereignty in mind, we think it clear that Arizona has exceeded its lawful authority by attempting to tax appellant. The beginning of our analysis must be with the treaty which the United States Government entered with the Navajo Nation in 1868. The agreement provided, in relevant part, that a prescribed reservation would be set aside "for the use and occupation of the Navajo tribe of Indians" and that "no persons except those herein so authorized to do, and except such officers, soldiers, agents, and employees of the government, or of the Indians, as may be authorized to enter upon Indian reservations in discharge of duties

---

[7] The source of federal authority over Indian matters has been the subject of some confusion, but it is now generally recognized that the power derives from federal responsibility for regulating commerce with Indian tribes and for treaty making.

[8] The extent of federal preemption and residual Indian sovereignty in the total absence of federal treaty obligations or legislation is therefore now something of a moot question. Cf. *Organized Village of Kake v. Egan,* 369 U.S. 60, 62 (1962); Federal Indian Law 846. The question is generally of little more than theoretical importance, however, since in almost all cases federal treaties and statutes define the boundaries of federal and state jurisdiction.

[12] The court below pointed out that Arizona was expending tax monies for education and welfare within the confines of the Navajo Reservation. It should be noted, however, that the Federal Government defrays 80% of Arizona's ordinary social security payments to reservation Indians, see 25 U.S.C. § 639, and has authorized the expenditure of more than $88 million for rehabilitation programs for Navajos and Hopis living on reservations. See also 25 U.S.C. §§ 13, 309, 309a. Moreover, "[c]onferring rights and privileges on these Indians cannot affect their situation, which can only be changed by treaty stipulation, or a voluntary abandonment of their tribal organization." *The Kansas Indians,* 5 Wall., at 757.

imposed by law, or the orders of the President, shall ever be permitted to pass over, settle upon, or reside in, the territory described in this article." 15 Stat. 668.

The treaty nowhere explicitly states that the Navajos were to be free from state law or exempt from state taxes. But the document is not to be read as an ordinary contract agreed upon by parties dealing at arm's length with equal bargaining positions. We have had occasion in the past to describe the circumstances under which the agreement was reached. [See *Williams v. Lee.*]

It is circumstances such as these which have led this Court in interpreting Indian treaties, to adopt the general rule that "[d]oubtful expressions are to be resolved in favor of the weak and defenseless people who are the wards of the nation, dependent upon its protection and good faith." *Carpenter v. Shaw*, 280 U.S. 363, 367 (1930). When this canon of construction is taken together with the tradition of Indian independence described above, it cannot be doubted that the reservation of certain lands for the exclusive use and occupancy of the Navajos and the exclusion of non-Navajos from the prescribed area was meant to establish the lands as within the exclusive sovereignty of the Navajos under general federal supervision. It is thus unsurprising that this Court has interpreted the Navajo treaty to preclude extension of state law — including state tax law — to Indians on the Navajo Reservation. See *Warren Trading Post Co. v. Arizona Tax Comm'n*, 380 U.S., at 687, 690; [*Williams v. Lee*].

Moreover, since the signing of the Navajo treaty, Congress has consistently acted upon the assumption that the States lacked jurisdiction over Navajos living on the reservation. Thus, when Arizona entered the Union, its entry was expressly conditioned on the promise that the State would "forever disclaim all right and title to ... all lands lying within said boundaries owned or held by any Indian or Indian tribes, the right or title to which shall have been acquired through or from the United States or any prior sovereignty, and that until the title of such Indian or Indian tribes shall have been extinguished the same shall be and remain subject to the disposition and under the absolute jurisdiction and control of the Congress of the United States." Arizona Enabling Act, 36 Stat. 569.

Nor is the Arizona Enabling Act silent on the specific question of tax immunity. The Act expressly provides that "nothing herein, or in the ordinance herein provided for, shall preclude the said State from taxing as other lands and other property are taxed any lands and other property *outside of an Indian reservation* owned or held by any Indian." *Id.*, at 570 (emphasis added). It is true, of course, that exemptions from tax laws should, as a general rule, be clearly expressed. But we have in the past construed language far more ambiguous than this as providing a tax exemption for Indians. *See, e.g., Squire v. Capoeman*, 351 U.S. 1, 6 (1956), and we see no reason to give this language an especially crabbed or restrictive meaning.[15]

---

[15] There is nothing in *Organized Village of Kake v. Egan*, 369 U.S. 60 (1962), to the contrary. In *Egan*, we held that "'absolute' federal jurisdiction is not invariably exclusive jurisdiction," and that this language in federal legislation did not preclude the exercise of residual state authority. See *id.*, at 68. But that holding came in the context of a decision concerning the fishing rights of *nonreservation* Indians. See *id.*, at 62. It did not purport to provide guidelines for the exercise of state authority in areas set aside by treaty for the exclusive use and control of Indians.

Indeed, Congress' intent to maintain the tax-exempt status of reservation Indians is especially clear in light of the Buck Act, 4 U.S.C. § 105 *et seq.*, which provides comprehensive federal guidance for state taxation of those living within federal areas. Section 106 (a) grants to the States general authority to impose an income tax on residents of federal areas, but § 109 expressly provides that "[n]othing in sections 105 and 106 of this title shall be deemed to authorize the levy or collection of any tax on or from any Indian not otherwise taxed." To be sure, the language of the statute itself does not make clear whether the reference to "any Indian not otherwise taxed" was intended to apply to reservation Indians earning their income on the reservation. But the legislative history makes plain that this proviso was meant to except reservation Indians from coverage of the Buck Act, see S. Rep. No. 1625, 76th Cong., 3d Sess., 2, 4 (1940); 84 Cong. Rec. 10685, and this Court has so interpreted it. *See Warren Trading Post Co. v. Arizona Tax Comm'n,* 380 U.S., at 691 n.18. While the Buck Act itself cannot be read as an affirmative grant of tax-exempt status to reservation Indians, it should be obvious that Congress would not have jealously protected the immunity of reservation Indians from state income taxes had it thought that the States had residual power to impose such taxes in any event. Similarly, narrower statutes authorizing States to assert tax jurisdiction over reservations in special situations are explicable only if Congress assumed that the States lacked the power to impose the taxes without special authorization.

Finally, it should be noted that Congress has now provided a method whereby States may assume jurisdiction over reservation Indians. [Public Law 280] grants the consent of the United States to States wishing to assume criminal and civil jurisdiction over reservation Indians, and confers upon the States the right to disregard enabling acts which limit their authority over such Indians. But the Act expressly provides that the State must act "with the consent of the tribe occupying the particular Indian country," 25 U.S.C. § 1322 (a),[17] and must "appropriately [amend its] constitution or statutes." 25 U.S.C. § 1324. Once again, the Act cannot be read as expressly conferring tax immunity upon Indians. But we cannot believe that Congress would have required the consent of the Indians affected and the amendment of those state constitutions which prohibit the assumption of jurisdiction if the States were free to accomplish the same goal unilaterally by simple legislative enactment.

Arizona, of course, has neither amended its constitution to permit taxation of the Navajos nor secured the consent of the Indians affected. Indeed, a startling aspect of this case is that appellee apparently concedes that, in the absence of compliance with [Public Law 280] the Arizona courts can exercise neither civil nor criminal jurisdiction over reservation Indians. But the appellee nowhere

---

[17] [Public Law 280] delegated civil and criminal jurisdiction over Indian reservations to certain States, although not to Arizona. The original Act also provided a means whereby other States could assume jurisdiction over Indian reservations without the consent of the tribe affected. However, in 1968, Congress passed the Indian Civil Rights Act which changed the prior procedure to require the consent of the Indians involved before a State was permitted to assume jurisdiction. 25 U.S.C. § 1322 (a). Thus, had it wished to do so, Arizona could have unilaterally assumed jurisdiction over its portion of the Navajo Reservation at any point during the 15 years between 1953 and 1968. But although the State did pass narrow legislation purporting to require the enforcement of air and water pollution standards within reservations, Ariz. Rev. Stat. Ann. §§ 36-1801, 36-1865 (Supp. 1972), it declined to assume full responsibility for the Indians during the period when it had the opportunity to do so.

explains how, without such jurisdiction, the [State may either impose or collect its tax].

IV

When Arizona's contentions are measured against these statutory imperatives, they are simply untenable. The State relies primarily upon language in *Williams v. Lee* stating that the test for determining the validity of state action is "whether [it] infringed on the right of reservation Indians to make their own laws and be ruled by them." Since Arizona has attempted to tax individual Indians and not the tribe or reservation as such, it argues that it has not infringed on Indian rights of self-government.

In fact, we are far from convinced that when a State imposes taxes upon reservation members without their consent, its action can be reconciled with tribal self-determination. But even if the State's premise were accepted, we reject the suggestion that the *Williams* test was meant to apply in this situation. It must be remembered that cases applying the *Williams* test have dealt principally with situations involving non-Indians. In these situations, both the tribe and the State could fairly claim an interest in asserting their respective jurisdictions. The *Williams* test was designed to resolve this conflict by providing that the State could protect its interest up to the point where tribal self-government would be affected.

The problem posed by this case is completely different. Since appellant is an Indian and since her income is derived wholly from reservation sources, her activity is totally within the sphere which the relevant treaty and statutes leave for the Federal Government and for the Indians themselves. Appellee cites us to no cases holding that this legislation may be ignored simply because tribal self-government has not been infringed.[20]

[Here], appellant's rights as a reservation Indian were violated when the State collected a tax from her which it had no jurisdiction to impose. Accordingly, the judgment of the court below must be
Reversed.

NOTES

1. The Rationale of *McClanahan*: What did Justice Marshall mean when he said that "[t]he Indian sovereignty doctrine [of *Worcester*] is relevant, then, not because it provides a definitive resolution of the issues in this suit, but because it provides a backdrop against which the applicable treaties and federal statutes must be read"? What aspect, if any, in *Worcester* was Marshall calling the "Indian sovereignty doctrine"? Can the seeds of the *McClanahan* opinion itself be directly traced to *Worcester*? What portions of the *Worcester* opinion parallel *McClanahan*: (1) the treatment of the impact of the Indian commerce clause on state power, (2) the *Worcester* reliance on the Treaty of Hopewell, or (3) the emphasis on the federal license held by Worcester and his codefendants under the Trade and Intercourse Acts? In the statement quoted above, was Marshall stating anything more than a preference for statutory or treaty preemption as a logical first inquiry and a preferred ground of decision? *Cf.* Note, *Preemption*

---

[20] *Organized Village of Kake v. Egan*, 369 U.S. 60 (1962), is not such a case. See n.15, *supra*.

as a Preferential Ground: A New Canon of Construction, 12 STAN. L. REV. 208 (1959). Compare the treatment given this issue in *Moe v. Confederated Salish & Kootenai Tribes*, 425 U.S. 463, 481 n.17 (1976), with the Court's response to the same question in *Washington v. Confederated Tribes of the Colville Reservation*, 447 U.S. 134 (1980).

In *McClanahan* Justice Marshall treated the issue of taxing (and, presumably, regulatory) legislative authority of the state under the same tests he would apply to civil adjudicatory jurisdiction because Arizona "nowhere explains how, without such [adjudicatory] jurisdiction, the State tax may either be imposed or collected." Is that explanation a sufficient reason for applying the same doctrinal approach to the question of state jurisdiction in diverse factual situations? For example, in *Arizona ex rel. Merrill v. Turtle*, 413 F.2d 683 (9th Cir. 1969), *cert. denied*, 396 U.S. 1003 (1970), the Ninth Circuit held that the state of Arizona lacked power to extradite a Cheyenne Indian wanted in Oklahoma on a criminal charge when the Indian was found on the Navajo Reservation within the state of Arizona. Noting that the Navajo extradition statute only authorized extradition to the three states in which the reservation was located (Arizona, New Mexico, and Utah), the court of appeals applied the *Williams v. Lee* infringement test and held that the power of extradition could not be shared by the Navajo tribal government and the state of Arizona without infringing upon the right of reservation Indians to make their own laws and be governed by them. *Contrast State ex rel. Old Elk v. District Court*, 552 P.2d 1394 (Mont.), *appeal dismissed*, 429 U.S. 1030 (1976) (no infringement where no tribal extradition ordinance). In *Whyte v. District Court*, 140 Colo. 334, 346 P.2d 1012 (1959), *cert. denied*, 363 U.S. 829 (1960), the court held that state courts lacked subject matter jurisdiction over a divorce action between two Indians domiciled on an Indian reservation based on an application of the *Williams* test. *Contrast Bad Horse v. Bad Horse*, 163 Mont. 445, 517 P.2d 893, *cert. denied*, 419 U.S. 847 (1974) (state had jurisdiction to enter divorce decree for Indians domiciled on reservation where marriage contracted off reservation). In *Schantz v. White Lightning*, 231 N.W.2d 812 (N.D. 1975), the court found state subject matter jurisdiction over an automobile accident case brought by the non-Indian passenger and driver of one car against the Indian driver of the second car arising out of an accident on the Standing Rock Sioux Reservation preempted by federal Indian law. *See also Gourneau v. Smith*, 207 N.W.2d 256 (N.D. 1973). The decision in *Schantz* is even more striking because (1) the suit in the state court was really to recover from the State Unsatisfied Judgment Fund established by state law, and the Attorney General of North Dakota, as counsel for the Fund, was urging the lack of his own state's subject matter jurisdiction; (2) in *Schantz v. White Lightning*, 502 F.2d 67 (8th Cir. 1974), the federal courts already had held that litigation over the same automobile accident could not be entertained in federal court absent satisfaction of all jurisdictional requisites for diversity jurisdiction; and (3) the Standing Rock Sioux Tribal Court was limited in its subject matter jurisdiction over cases in which non-Indians were parties to claims not exceeding $300 amount in controversy. Similarly, in *Wauneka v. Campbell*, 22 Ariz. App. 287, 526 P.2d 1085 (1974), the court held that the Arizona Motor Vehicle Safety Responsibility Act — which requires that after an accident a driver post a bond or show other evidence of financial responsibility, such as insurance, upon threat of loss of the driver's Arizona driver's license — could not be validly applied to automobile accidents between Indians on the Navajo Reservation despite the existence of a provision in the Navajo Tribal Code requiring every person operating a motor vehicle on the Navajo Reservation to "be the holder of a valid driver's license issued by the state in which such individual resides." Should the same test of jurisdiction be applied in all of these various types of cases? Are the sovereignty concerns they voice all substantially similar?

2. *Erie*, Diversity Jurisdiction, and Claims Arising in Indian Country: The Eighth Circuit's observation in *White Lightning* that diversity was lacking poses an interesting question about the jurisdiction of a federal court to hear a diversity case arising in Indian country over which state court jurisdiction was lacking. The question of whether a federal court may entertain on diversity jurisdiction grounds a suit involving Indians that could not be brought in a state court due to lack of subject matter jurisdiction is an interesting issue in light of *Erie R.R. v. Tompkins*, 304 U.S. 64 (1938), and its progeny. For some time the circuits have been split on the issue. *Compare, e.g., Hot Oil Servs. v. Hall*, 366 F.2d 295 (9th Cir. 1966) (no federal jurisdiction), *with Poitra v. Demarrias*, 502 F.2d 23 (8th Cir. 1974), *cert. denied*, 421 U.S. 934 (1975) (sustaining diversity jurisdiction). *See generally* Kutner, *Can Federal Courts Remain Open When State Courts Are Closed? Erie R. Co. v. Tompkins on the Indian Reservation*, 52 N.D.L. Rev. 647 (1976). In *Iowa Mut. Ins. Co. v. LaPlante*, 481 U.S. 1027 (1987), discussed in Chapter 3, section D1, the Court had the opportunity to resolve the conflict but did not directly address the question. Rather, the Court merely held that before any diversity action could be brought the plaintiff must exhaust available tribal remedies. While this holding might suggest the existence of federal jurisdiction to entertain the claim *after exhaustion*, the case does not directly so hold and therefore does not definitively resolve the split in the circuits on this question. In addition to the *Erie* question of whether federal courts can exercise diversity of citizenship jurisdiction over a case in which state subject matter jurisdiction is preempted, important choice-of-law questions are posed should the federal courts retain jurisdiction over such claims. While the general guarantees of tribal sovereignty protected by federal preemption doctrines suggest that tribal, rather than state, law should be applied to such cases, the Rules of Decision Act, 28 U.S.C. § 1652, provides that "[t]he laws of the several *states*, except where the Constitution or treaties of the United States or Acts of Congress otherwise require or provide, shall be regarded as the rules of decision in civil actions in the courts of the United States, *in cases where they apply*." (Emphasis added.) Could it be argued that the preemptive doctrines create a situation where state law should not be applied to such cases since they involve situations to which state law cannot generally apply? But does the Rules of Decision Act authorize the federal court to apply tribal law in such diversity cases? Is any such explicit statutory authorization required as a prerequisite for choosing to apply tribal law?

3. Continued Vitality of the Infringement Test: How convincing was the statement in *McClanahan* purporting to limit the *Williams v. Lee* infringement test to "cases [that] dealt principally with situations involving non-Indians"? In *Fisher v. District Court*, 424 U.S. 382 (1976), the Court applied the *Williams* test to resolve the question of whether state courts had jurisdiction to entertain neglect and dependency proceedings or adoption cases involving Indian children domiciled on the Northern Cheyenne Reservation. The Court said in a per curiam opinion:

> In litigation between Indians and non-Indians arising out of conduct on an Indian reservation, resolution of conflicts between jurisdiction of state and tribal courts has depended, absent a governing Act of Congress, on "whether the state action infringed on the right of reservation Indians to make their own laws and be ruled by them."

Williams v. Lee. [Because] this litigation involves only Indians, at least the same standard must be met before the state courts may exercise jurisdiction.

424 U.S. at 386. Thus, the Court found that "[s]tate-court jurisdiction plainly would interfere with the powers of self-government conferred upon the Northern Cheyenne Tribe and exercised through the Tribal Court." *Id.* at 387. In its conclusion, the Court referred to the self-governing procedures of the tribe under the IRA and stated that state-court "jurisdiction has now been preempted." *Id.* at 390.

In light of *McClanahan*, may the *Williams v. Lee* infringement test be used as a mechanism for justifying the exercise of state sovereignty over Indians? Can it be used to justify state authority over non-Indians in Indian country?

WASHINGTON v. CONFEDERATED TRIBES OF THE COLVILLE RESERVATION

447 U.S. 134 (1980)

Mr. Justice WHITE delivered the opinion of the Court.

In recent Terms we have more than once addressed the intricate problem of state taxation of matters involving Indian tribes and their members. *Moe v. Salish & Kootenai Tribes,* 425 U.S. 463 (1976); *McClanahan v. Arizona State Tax Comm'n,* 411 U.S. 164 (1973); *Mescalero Apache Tribe v. Jones,* 411 U.S. 145 (1973). We return to that vexing area in the present cases. Although a variety of questions are presented, perhaps the most significant is whether an Indian tribe ousts a State from any power to tax on-reservation purchases by nonmembers of the tribe by imposing its own tax on the transaction or by otherwise earning revenues from the tribal business. A three-judge District Court held for the Tribes. We affirm in part and reverse in part.

I

[The Confederated Tribes of Colville, Makah and Lummi and the United States on behalf of the Yakima tribe, filed separate cases that were consolidated,] contend[ing] that the State's cigarette and tobacco products taxes[1] could not lawfully be applied to sales by on-reservation tobacco outlets. They sought declaratory judgments to that effect, as well as injunctions barring the State from taking any measures to enforce the challenged taxes. In particular, the plaintiffs sought to enjoin the State from seizing as contraband untaxed cigarettes destined for delivery to their reservations. In the *Colville* case, the Tribes also challenged the State's assumption of civil and criminal jurisdiction over their reservations and, by amended pleadings, attacked the application of the State's vehicle excise taxes to Indian-owned vehicles. The *Yakima* case did not present these latter issues, but it did make a broad attack on the application of the State's general retail sales tax to on-reservation transactions.

[Both cases were tried] on Mar. 28, 1977, and the three-judge court entered its consolidated decision on Feb. 22, 1978. The court concluded (1) that it had

---

[1]The state tobacco products tax, which is imposed on cigars and pipe tobacco pursuant to Wash. Rev. Code § 82.26 (1976), is not before us. The District Court concluded that that tax fell upon the Indian sellers and not upon the non-Indian purchasers. The State did not appeal from this holding, and all parties agree that in consequence the tobacco products tax may not be imposed on sales by tribal dealers.

jurisdiction as a three-judge court to consider the issues presented; (2) that the state cigarette tax could not be applied to on-reservation transactions because it was pre-empted by the tribal taxing ordinances and constituted an impermissible interference with tribal self-government; (3) that the state retail sales tax could not be applied to tribal cigarette sales, but could be applied to sales of other goods to non-Indians; (4) that the State could not impose certain record-keeping requirements in connection with various tax-exempt sales; (5) that the State could not impose its vehicle excise taxes upon vehicles owned by the Tribes and their members, and (6) that the State's assumption of civil and criminal jurisdiction over the Makah and Lummi Tribes was unconstitutional. The court enjoined enforcement of the statutes it had struck down, and the State moved unsuccessfully for a new trial [and this appeal followed].

We begin by sketching the relevant factual background, which is not seriously in dispute. Thereafter, we explore the jurisdictional questions previously postponed and then turn to the merits.

II

The State of Washington levies a cigarette excise tax of $1.60 per carton, on the "sale, use, consumption, handling, possession or distribution" of cigarettes within the State. Wash. Rev. Code § 82.24.020 (1976). The tax is enforced with tax stamps; and dealers are required to sell only cigarettes to which such stamps have been affixed. § 82.24.030. Indian tribes are permitted to possess unstamped cigarettes for purposes of resale to members of the tribe, but are required by regulation to collect the tax with respect to sales to nonmembers. § 82.24.260; Wash. Admin. Code § 458-20-192 (1977). The District Court found, on the basis of its examination of state authorities, that the legal incidence of the tax is on the purchaser in transactions between an Indian seller and a non-Indian buyer.

The State has sought to enforce its cigarette tax by seizing as contraband unstamped cigarettes bound for various tribal reservations. It claims that it is entitled to make such seizures whenever the cigarettes are destined to be sold to non-Indians without affixation of stamps or collection of the tax.

Washington also imposes a sales tax on sales of personal property, including cigarettes. Wash. Rev. Code § 82.08.020 (1976). This tax, which was 5% during the relevant period, is collected from the purchaser by the retailer. § 82.08.050. It does not apply to on-reservation sales to reservation Indians. Wash. Admin. Code § 458-20-192 (1977).

The state motor vehicle excise tax is imposed on "the privilege of using in the state any motor vehicle." Wash. Rev. Code § 82.44.020 (1976). The tax is assessed annually, and during the relevant period the amount was two percent of the fair market value of the vehicle in question. In addition, the State imposes an annual tax in the amount of one percent of fair market value on the privilege of using campers and trailers in the State. § 82.50.400.

Each of the Tribes involved in this litigation is recognized by the United States as a sovereign Indian tribe. Each is governed by a business or tribal council approved by the Secretary of the Interior....

The Colville, Lummi, and Makah Tribes have nearly identical cigarette sales and taxing schemes. Each Tribe has enacted ordinances pursuant to which it has authorized one or more on-reservation tobacco outlets. These ordinances have been approved by the Secretary of the Interior; and the dealer at each tobacco outlet is a federally licensed Indian trader. All three Tribes use federally restricted tribal funds to purchase cigarettes from out-of-state dealers. The Tribes distribute the cigarettes to the tobacco outlets and collect from the operators of those outlets both the wholesale distribution price and a tax of 40 to 50 cents per carton. The cigarettes remain the property of the Tribe until sale. The taxing ordinances specify that the tax is to be passed on to the ultimate consumer of the cigarettes. From 1972 through 1976, the Colville Tribe realized approximately $266,000 from its cigarette tax; the Lummi Tribe realized $54,000 and the Makah Tribe realized $13,000.

While the Colville, Lummi, and Makah Tribes function as retailers, retaining possession of the cigarettes until their sale to consumers, the Yakima Tribe acts as a wholesaler. It purchases cigarettes from out-of-state dealers and then sells them to its licensed retailers. The Tribe receives a markup over the wholesale price from those retailers as well as a tax of 22.5 cents per carton. There is no requirement that this tax be added to the selling price. In 1975, the Yakima Tribe derived $278,000 from its cigarette business.

Indian tobacco dealers make a large majority of their sales to non-Indians — residents of nearby communities who journey to the reservation especially to take advantage of the claimed tribal exemption from the state cigarette and sales taxes. The purchaser saves more than a dollar on each carton, and that makes the trip worthwhile. All parties agree that if the State were able to tax sales by Indian smokeshops and eliminate that one-dollar saving the stream of non-Indian bargain hunters would dry up. In short, the Indian retailer's business is to a substantial degree dependent upon his tax-exempt status, and if he loses that status his sales will fall off sharply.

III

We first address our jurisdiction to hear the State's appeal. Two attacks are made upon that jurisdiction, one grounded in the intricacies of the now-repealed statute governing three-judge district courts and the other having to do with the timing of the State's appeal.

[The provisions of section 2281 do not require] a three-judge court where a constitutional challenge to a state statute is grounded only in the Supremacy Clause. [Furthermore] § 2281 is not brought into play by constitutional claims that are "insubstantial."

[The plaintiffs had claimed that the] state taxes were unconstitutional under the Indian Commerce Clause as well as the Supremacy Clause. [There is] language in footnote 17 [of] Moe v. Salish & Kootenai Tribes, 425 U.S. 463, 481, n.17 (1976) [suggesting] that the insubstantiality of Commerce Clause claims such as those before us flows from Mescalero Apache Tribe v. Jones, 411 U.S. 145 (1973), and McClanahan v. Arizona State Tax Comm'n, — both of which were decided before the present suits were filed.[22] [T]he United States reads too much into [the language of these decisions]. Neither *Mescalero* nor *McClanahan* "inescapably render[s] the [Tribes' Commerce Clause] claims frivolous" because neither holds that that clause is wholly without force in situations like the present. And even footnote 17 merely rejects the stark and rather unhelpful notion that the Commerce Clause provides an "*automatic* exemptio[n] 'as a matter of constitutional law'" in such cases. (Emphasis added.) It does not take that clause entirely out of play in the field of state regulation of Indian affairs....

IV

A

In [*Moe*] we considered a state taxing scheme remarkably similar to the cigarette and sales taxes at issue in the present cases. Montana there sought to impose a cigarette tax on sales by smokeshops operated by tribal members and located on leased trust lands within the reservation, and sought to require the smokeshop operators to collect the tax. We upheld the tax, insofar as sales to non-Indians were concerned, because its legal incidence fell on the non-Indian purchaser. Hence, "the competitive advantage which the Indian seller doing business on tribal land enjoys over all other cigarette retailers, within and without the reservation, is dependent on the extent to which the non-Indian purchaser is willing to flout *his* legal obligation to pay the tax." (Emphasis in original.) We upheld the collection requirement, as applied to purchases by non-Indians, on the ground that it was a "minimal burden" designed to aid the State in collecting an otherwise valid tax.

Moe establishes several principles relevant to the present cases. The State may sometimes impose a nondiscriminatory tax on non-Indian customers of Indian retailers doing business on the reservation. Such a tax may be valid even if it seriously disadvantages or eliminates the Indian retailer's business with non-Indians.[27] And the State may impose at least "minimal" burdens on the Indian retailer to aid in enforcing and collecting the tax. There is no automatic bar, therefore, to Washington's extending its tax and collection and recordkeeping requirements onto the reservation in the present cases.

Although it narrows the issues in the present cases, *Moe* does not definitively resolve several important questions. First, unlike in *Moe*, each of the Tribes

---

[22] Footnote 17 in its entirety reads as follows:

"It is thus clear that the basis for the invalidity of these taxing measures, which we have found to be inconsistent with existing federal statutes, is the Supremacy Clause, and not any automatic exemptions 'as a matter of constitutional law' either under the Commerce Clause or the intergovernmental-immunity doctrine as laid down originally in *M'Culloch v. Maryland*, 4 Wheat. 316 (1819). If so, then the basis for convening a three-judge court in this type of case has effectively disappeared, for this Court has expressly held that attacks on state statutes raising only Supremacy Clause invalidity do not fall within the scope of 28 U.S.C. § 2281. *Swift & Co. v. Wickham*, 382 U.S. 111 (1965). Here, however, the District Court properly convened a § 2281 court, because at the outset the Tribe's attack asserted unconstitutionality of these statutes under the Commerce Clause, a not insubstantial claim since *Mescalero* and *McClanahan* had not yet been decided. See *Goosby v. Osser*, 409 U.S. 512 (1973)." 425 U.S., at 481.

[27] The United States reads *Moe* too parsimoniously in asserting its inapplicability to cases, such as the present ones, in which the economic impact on tribal retailers is particularly severe. *Moe* makes clear that the Tribes have no vested right to a certain volume of sales to non-Indians, or indeed to any such sales at all.

imposes its own tax on cigarette sales, and obtains further revenues by participating in the cigarette enterprise at the wholesale or retail level. Second, Washington requires the Indian retailer to keep detailed records of exempt and
nonexempt sales in addition to simply precollecting the tax. *Moe* expressed no
opinion regarding the "complicated problems" of enforcement that distinctions
between exempt and nonexempt purchasers might entail. Third, *Moe* left unresolved the question of whether a State can tax purchases by on-reservation
Indians not members of the governing tribe, as Washington seeks to do in the
present cases. Finally, unlike in *Moe*[,] Washington has seized and threatens to
continue seizing, shipments of unstamped cigarettes en route to the reservations
from wholesalers outside the State. We address each of these questions.[28]

B

[*Oliphant* posed no barrier to the tribal taxation of non-Indians. Because they
have exercised this power to tax, the tribes further] contend that their involvement in the operation and taxation of cigarette marketing on the reservation
ousts the State from any power to exact its sales and cigarette taxes from nonmembers purchasing cigarettes at tribal smokeshops. The primary argument is
economic. It is asserted that smokeshop cigarette sales generate substantial revenues for the Tribes which they expend for essential governmental services,
including programs to combat severe poverty and underdevelopment at the
reservations. Most cigarette purchasers are outsiders attracted on to the reservations by the bargain prices the smokeshops charge by virtue of their claimed
exemption from state taxation. If the State is permitted to impose its taxes, the
Tribes will no longer enjoy any competitive advantage vis-à-vis businesses in
surrounding areas. Indeed, because the Tribes themselves impose a tax on the
transaction, if the state tax is also collected the price charged will necessarily be
higher and the Tribes will be placed at a competitive *disadvantage* as compared
to businesses elsewhere. Tribal smokeshops will lose a large percentage of their
cigarette sales and the Tribes will forfeit substantial revenues. Because of this
economic impact, it is argued, the state taxes are (1) pre-empted by federal
statutes regulating Indian affairs; (2) inconsistent with the principle of tribal
self-government; and (3) invalid under "negative implications" of the Indian
Commerce Clause.

It is painfully apparent that the value marketed by the smokeshops to persons
coming from outside is not generated on the reservations by activities in which
the Tribes have a significant interest. Cf. *Moe v. Salish & Kootenai Tribes;
McClanahan v. Arizona State Tax Comm'n.* What the smokeshops offer these
customers, and what is not available elsewhere, is solely an exemption from state
taxation. The Tribes assert the power to create such exemptions by imposing
their own taxes or otherwise earning revenues by participating in the reservation enterprises. If this assertion were accepted, the Tribes could impose a
nominal tax and open chains of discount stores at reservation borders, selling

---

[28] The incidence of the Colville, Lummi, and Makah taxes falls on the cigarette purchaser, since
the tribal ordinances specify that the tax is to be passed on to the ultimate consumer. The Yakima
ordinance, in contrast, does not require that the tax be added to the selling price, and the incidence
of the Yakima tax therefore does not fall on the purchaser. The State's challenge is directed only at
the Colville, Lummi, and Makah taxes.

goods of all descriptions at deep discounts and drawing customers from surrounding areas. We do not believe that principles of federal Indian law,
whether stated in terms of pre-emption, tribal self-government, or otherwise,
authorize Indian tribes thus to market an exemption from state taxation to
persons who would normally do their business elsewhere.

The federal statutes cited to us, even when given the broadest reading to
which they are fairly susceptible, cannot be said to pre-empt Washington's sales
and cigarette taxes. The [IRA], the Indian Financing Act of 1974, and the
Indian Self-Determination and Education Assistance Act of 1975, evidence to
varying degrees a congressional concern with fostering tribal self-government
and economic development, but none goes so far as to grant tribal enterprises
selling goods to nonmembers an artificial competitive advantage over all other
businesses in a State. The Indian traders statutes, 25 U.S.C. §§ 261 et seq.,
incorporate a congressional desire comprehensively to regulate businesses selling goods to reservation Indians for cash or exchange, see *Warren Trading Post
v. Arizona Tax Comm'n*, 380 U.S. 685 (1965), but no similar intent is evident
with respect to sales by Indians to nonmembers of the Tribe. [A]lthough the
Tribes themselves could perhaps pre-empt state taxation through the exercise
of properly delegated federal power to do so, cf. *Fisher v. District Court*, 424
U.S. 382, 390 (1976) (per curiam); [*United States v. Mazurie,*] we do not infer
from the mere fact of federal approval of the Indian taxing ordinances, or from
the fact that the Tribes exercise congressionally sanctioned powers of self-government, that Congress has delegated the far-reaching authority to pre-empt
valid state sales and cigarette taxes otherwise collectible from nonmembers of
the Tribe.

Washington does not infringe the right of reservation Indians to "make their
own laws and be ruled by them," [*Williams v. Lee*], merely because the result of
imposing its taxes will be to deprive the Tribes of revenues which they currently
are receiving. The principle of tribal self-government, grounded in notions of
inherent sovereignty and in congressional policies, seeks an accommodation
between the interests of the Tribes and the Federal Government, on the one
hand, and those of the State, on the other. [*McClanahan.*] While the Tribes do
have an interest in raising revenues for essential governmental programs, that
interest is strongest when the revenues are derived from value generated on the
reservation by activities involving the Tribes and when the taxpayer is the recipient of tribal services. The State also has a legitimate governmental interest in
raising revenues, and that interest is likewise strongest when the tax is directed
at off-reservation value and when the taxpayer is the recipient of state services.
As we have already noted, Washington's taxes are reasonably designed to prevent the Tribes from marketing their tax exemption to nonmembers who do
not receive significant tribal services and who would otherwise purchase their
cigarettes outside the reservations.

It can no longer be seriously argued that the Indian Commerce Clause, of its
own force, automatically bars all state taxation of matters significantly touching
the political and economic interests of the Tribes. See *Moe v. Salish & Kootenai
Tribes*, n.17. That clause may have a more limited role to play in preventing
undue discrimination against, or burdens on, Indian commerce. But Washington's taxes are applied in a nondiscriminatory manner to all transactions within

the State. And although the result of these taxes will be to lessen or eliminate tribal commerce with nonmembers, that market existed in the first place only because of a claimed exemption from these very taxes. The taxes under consideration do not burden commerce that would exist on the reservations without respect to the tax exemption.

We cannot fault the State for not giving credit on the amount of tribal taxes paid. It is argued that if a credit is not given, the tribal retailers will actually be placed at a competitive disadvantage, as compared to retailers elsewhere, due to the overlapping impact of tribal and state taxation. While this argument is not without force, we find that the Tribes have failed to demonstrate that business at the smokeshops would be significantly reduced by a state tax without a credit as compared to a state tax with a credit. With a credit, prices at the smokeshops would presumably be roughly the same as those off the reservation, assuming that the Indian enterprises are operated at an efficiency similar to that of businesses elsewhere; without a credit, prices at smokeshops would exceed those off the reservation by the amount of the tribal taxes, about 40 to 50 cents per carton for the Lummi, Makah, and Colville Tribes, and 22.5 cents per carton for the Yakima Tribe. It is evident that even if credit were given, the bulk of the smokeshops' present business would still be eliminated, since nonresidents of the reservation could purchase cigarettes at the same price and with greater convenience nearer their homes and would have no incentive to travel to the smokeshops for bargain purchases as they do [at present].

A second asserted ground for the invalidity of the state taxes is that they somehow conflict with the Tribes' cigarette ordinances and thereby are subject to pre-emption or contravene the principle of tribal self-government. This argument need not detain us. There is no direct conflict between the state and tribal schemes, since each government is free to impose its taxes without ousting the other. Although taxes can be used for distributive or regulatory purposes, as well as for raising revenue, we see no nonrevenue purposes to the tribal taxes at issue in these cases, and, as already noted, we perceive no intent on the part of Congress to authorize the Tribes to pre-empt otherwise valid state taxes. Other provisions of the tribal ordinances do comprehensively regulate the marketing of cigarettes by the tribal enterprises; but the State does not interfere with the Tribes' power to regulate tribal enterprises when it simply imposes its tax on sales to nonmembers. Hence, we perceive no conflict between state and tribal law warranting invalidation of the State's taxes.

C

We recognized in *Moe* that if a State's tax is valid, the State may impose at least minimal burdens on Indian businesses to aid in collecting and enforcing that tax. The simple collection burden imposed by Washington's cigarette tax on tribal smokeshops is legally indistinguishable from the collection burden upheld in *Moe*, and we therefore hold that the State may validly require the tribal smokeshops to affix tax stamps purchased from the State to individual packages of cigarettes prior to the time of sale to nonmembers of the Tribe.

The state sales tax scheme requires smokeshop operators to keep detailed records of both taxable and nontaxable transactions. The operator must record the number and dollar volume of taxable sales to nonmembers of the Tribe. With respect to nontaxable sales, the operator must record and retain for state inspection the names of all Indian purchasers, their tribal affiliations, the Indian reservations within which sales are made, and the dollar amount and dates of sales. In addition, unless the Indian purchaser is personally known to the operator he must present a tribal identification card....

Contrary to the District Court, we find the State's recordkeeping requirements valid *in toto*. The Tribes, and not the State as the District Court supposed, bear the burden of showing that the recordkeeping requirements which they are challenging are invalid. The District Court made the factual finding, which we accept, that there was no evidence of record on this question. Applying the correct burden of proof to the District Court's finding, we hold that the Tribes have failed to demonstrate that the State's recordkeeping requirements for exempt sales are not reasonably necessary as a means of preventing fraudulent transactions.

D

The State asserts the power to apply its sales and cigarette taxes to Indians resident on the reservation but not enrolled in the [Tribe imposing the taxes]. Federal statutes, even given the broadest reading to which they are reasonably susceptible, cannot be said to pre-empt Washington's power to impose its taxes on Indians not members of the Tribe. We do not so read the Major Crimes Act, which at most provides for federal-court jurisdiction over crimes committed by Indians on another Tribe's reservation. Similarly, the mere fact that nonmembers resident on the reservation come within the definition of "Indian" for purposes of the [IRA] does not demonstrate a congressional intent to exempt such Indians from state taxation.

Nor would the imposition of Washington's tax on these purchasers contravene the principle of tribal self-government, for the simple reason that nonmembers are not constituents of the governing Tribe. For most practical purposes those Indians stand on the same footing as non-Indians resident on the reservation. There is no evidence that nonmembers have a say in tribal affairs or significantly share in tribal disbursements. We find, therefore, that the State's interest in taxing these purchasers outweighs any tribal interest that may exist in preventing the State from imposing its taxes.

E

Finally, the State contends that it has the power to seize unstamped cigarettes as contraband if the Tribes do not cooperate in collecting the State's taxes....

We find that Washington's interest in enforcing its valid taxes is sufficient to justify these seizures. Although the cigarettes in transit are as yet exempt from state taxation, they are not immune from seizure when the Tribes, as here, have refused to fulfill collection and remittance obligations which the State has validly imposed. It is significant that these seizures take place outside the reservation, in locations where state power over Indian affairs is considerably more expansive than it is within reservation boundaries. Cf. *Mescalero Apache Tribe v. Jones*, 411 U.S. 145 (1973). By seizing cigarettes en route to the reservation, the State polices against wholesale evasion of its own valid taxes without unnecessarily intruding on core tribal interests.

[T]he judgments of the District Court are

Reversed in part and affirmed in part.

Mr. Justice BRENNAN, with whom Mr. Justice MARSHALL joins, concurring in part and dissenting in part.

[T]he State of Washington's cigarette taxing scheme should be invalidated both because it undermines the Tribes' sovereign authority to regulate and tax the distribution of cigarettes on trust lands and because it conflicts with tribal activities and functions that have been expressly approved by the Federal Government....

The Court draws support for its result from the suggestion that a decision invalidating these taxes would give the Tribes carte blanche to establish vast tax exempt shopping centers dealing in every imaginable good. I think these fears are substantially overdrawn. *Moe* made clear that Indians do not have an absolute entitlement to achieve some particular sales volume by passing their tax-exempt status to non-Indian customers, and I do not question that conclusion today. I would simply hold that the State may not impose a tax that forces the Tribes to choose between federally sanctioned goals and places their goods at an actual competitive disadvantage. Nothing in such a holding would emasculate state taxing authority or bring the specter of enormous tribal tax havens closer to reality. On the contrary, I am confident that the State could devise a taxing scheme without the flaws which mar the present one....

Mr. Justice STEWART, concurring in part and dissenting in part.

[W]hen a State and an Indian Tribe tax in a functionally identical manner the same on-reservation sales to nontribal members, it is my view that congressional policy conjoined with the Indian Commerce Clause requires the State to credit against its own tax the amount of the Tribe's tax. This solution fully effectuates the State's goal of assuring that its citizens who are not tribal members do not cash in on the exemption from state taxation that the Tribe and its members enjoy. On the other hand, it permits the Tribe to share with the State in the tax revenues from cigarette sales, without at the same time placing the Tribe's federally encouraged enterprises at a competitive disadvantage compared to similarly situated off-reservation businesses....

Mr. Justice REHNQUIST, concurring and dissenting.

Since early in the last century, this Court has been struggling to develop a coherent doctrine by which to measure with some predictability the scope of Indian immunity from state taxation. In recent years, it appeared such a doctrine was well on its way to being established. I write separately to underscore what I think the contours of that doctrine are because I am convinced that a well-defined body of principles is essential in order to end the need for case-by-case litigation which has plagued this area of the law for a number of years. That doctrine, I had thought, was at bottom a preemption analysis based on the principle that Indian immunities are dependent upon congressional intent, at least absent discriminatory state action prohibited by the Indian Commerce Clause. I see no need for this Court to balance the state and tribal interests in enacting particular forms of taxation in order to determine their validity. Absent discrimination, the question is only one of congressional intent. Either Congress intended to pre-empt the state taxing authority or it did not. Balancing of interests is not the appropriate gauge for determining validity since it is that very balancing which we have reserved to Congress. I concur in the Court's conclusion, however, that the cigarette tax is valid because Congress has not pre-empted state authority to impose the tax....

NOTES

1. The Indian Commerce Clause, Preemption, and State Authority: The *Colville* decision indicates the full complexity of the modern judicial doctrine that has evolved to resolve questions of state power over Indian affairs in the absence of clear acts of Congress allocating jurisdiction. Full appreciation of the subtleties of the modern doctrine can best be achieved by juxtaposing the *McClanahan, Moe,* and *Colville* decisions with the position of Chief Justice Marshall in *Worcester v. Georgia*, on the one hand, and with the position of Justice Rehnquist in *Colville*, on the other hand.

In *Worcester* Chief Justice Marshall had said that the state statute purporting to exercise authority over Worcester and other non-Indian missionaries in the Cherokee Nation was unconstitutional, in part because it "interfere[d] forcibly with the relations established between the United States and the Cherokee nation, the regulation of which, according to the settled principles of our constitution, are *committed exclusively* to the government of the Union." On the other hand, the negative implications of the Indian commerce clause appeared to play no role whatsoever in Justice Rehnquist's analysis of state power except possibly to prohibit discriminatory state legislation, leaving the entire question of state authority to the vagaries of Congressional preemption doctrines. Indeed, one important subtext of the *Colville* opinion is whether the Court's earlier *Moe* decision had overturned *Worcester's* reliance on the Indian commerce clause to preclude the exercise of state jurisdiction. In both *Moe* and *Colville* the essence of the state taxation of the cigarettes sold by the Indian smokeshops fell on commerce between Indians and non-Indians — the very core of the subject matter Chief Justice Marshall found in *Worcester* was committed to *exclusive* federal authority. In contrast to Justice Rehnquist, the majority in *Colville* rejected the demise of the dormant Indian commerce clause analysis. They described the current dormant Indian commerce clause doctrine as follows: "That clause may have a more limited role to play in preventing undue discrimination against, or burdens on, Indian commerce." In light of the history of the Indian commerce clause and Chief Justice Marshall's use of it in *Worcester*, could it not be said that even the majority's "limited role" approach considerably understates the constitutionally intended force of the doctrine? Even if one accepts this "limited role" analysis, did the Court arrive at the correct conclusion? While it is reasonably easy to see why the Washington taxes in *Colville* or the Montana taxes in *Moe* were not discriminatory, could it not be said that they impose undue "burdens" on Indian commerce? How can this statement in *Colville* be reconciled with the comment in *Williams v. Lee* that "essentially, absent governing Acts of Congress, the question has always been whether the state action infringed on the right of reservation Indians to make their own laws and be ruled by them." Which case relegated the doctrine of the negative implications of the Indian commerce clause to a relatively minor role in the judicial solution to state power issues in Indian country: *Williams, McClanahan, Moe,* or *Colville?*

In *Worcester* Chief Justice Marshall also relied on the preemptive effect of the federal promises of tribal sovereignty and self-government that he inferred from the terms of the Treaty of Hopewell. The argument seemed to be that the federal policy of recognizing an Indian tribe and protecting its homeland and legal autonomy wholly preempted state power in Indian country, even over *non-Indian* missionaries such as Worcester. Are *Williams* and *McClanahan* consistent with that approach? Are *Moe* and *Colville* consistent with this theme from *Worcester? Moe* assumed without discussion that states had inherent authority to tax *non-Indians* in Indian country and *Colville* expands that assumption even to resident non-member Indians. From what source does the state derive this authority? Justice Rehnquist's position in this area is most interesting. In a section of the opinion omitted from the excerpt, he stated: "Absent discrimination, the question is only one of congressional intent. Either Congress intended to preempt the state taxing authority or it did not. Balancing of interests is not the appropriate gauge for determining validity since it is that very balancing which we have reserved to Congress." Elsewhere in his opinion, he indicated that, at least in the taxing area, such statutory preemption is not to be found by implication, but "must be provided [by Congress] in 'plain words.'" 447 U.S. at 180. How does Justice Rehnquist's approach to treaty and statutory preemption differ in the Indian affairs area from that of the majority in *McClanahan* and *Colville?* Is the Rehnquist approach followed by the Court when the issue is state power over tribal members in Indian country? Is it followed when the question is state power in Indian country over non-Indians or over Indians who are not tribal members? In light of *Worcester* and *Williams,* should not the same doctrinal test control the issue of state power over either tribal members or nonmembers in Indian country?

The opinions in *Moe* and *Colville* would seem to suggest that state authority to tax cigarette sales to non-Indians and nonmember Indians derived primarily from the fact that the legal incidence of the tax, that is the formal transaction upon which the tax fell, was the purchase by the non-Indian. In *California State Bd. of Equalization v. Chemehuevi Tribe,* 474 U.S. 9 (1985), a tribal smokeshop sought to distinguish *Moe* and *Colville* on the ground that the structure of the California cigarette tax imposed the legal incidence of the tax on the Indian retailer of the cigarettes without any requirement that the tax be passed through to the ultimate consumer. In a brief *per curiam* opinion, the Court rejected the argument, stating:

> None of our cases has suggested that an express statement that the tax is to be passed on to the ultimate purchaser is necessary before a State may require a tribe to collect cigarette taxes from non-Indian purchasers and remit the amounts of such tax to the State. Nor do our cases suggest that the only test for whether the legal incidence of such a tax falls on purchasers is whether the taxing statute contains an express "pass on and collect" provision.

Id. at 11. The Court ultimately rejected the premise of the tribe's argument and concluded that the legal incidence of the California cigarette tax actually fell on the consumer. Does *Chemehuevi* suggest that permitting state taxation or regulation of transactions involving non-Indians or nonmembers in Indian country only starts a slippery analytical slope that inevitably leads to some state taxation or regulation of *Indians* in Indian country in contravention of *Worcester* and *McClanahan,* not to mention the intent of the framers of the Indian commerce clause? In *Moe,* the Court sustained a state requirement that forced Indian retailers to *precollect* the tax and keep records, and in *Colville* the Court broadened the record-keeping obligations and sustained cigarette stamp requirements as a precollection device. Ostensibly, the Court sustained these devices as *means* toward the end of collecting the tax on sales to non-Indians and nonmembers. Are not these regulations, however, a substantial expansion of state power over Indians in Indian country, albeit through a doctrinal "back door"?

Despite the rulings in *Moe, Colville,* and *Chemehuevi,* the Tenth Circuit granted an injunction against the enforcement of state cigarette taxes on cigarettes sold at a tribally owned store. *Citizens Band of Potawatomi Indian Tribe v. Oklahoma Tax Comm'n,* 888 F.2d 1303 (10th Cir. 1989), *cert. granted,* 111 S. Ct. 37 (1990). Noting that the store was located on tribally owned trust land and was therefore located in Indian country, the court rejected the state's argument that there was no Indian country in Oklahoma. Thus, since the store was located in Indian country, the Tenth Circuit concluded that Oklahoma lacked any jurisdiction to tax even sales to nonmembers. The court purported to distinguish *Colville* and other cigarette tax cases on the ground that these cases arose on Public Law 280 reservations, whereas Oklahoma had disclaimed jurisdiction over Indian lands on entering the union and had never assumed any jurisdiction under Public Law 280. Can *Moe, Colville,* and *Chemehuevi* be so easily distinguished? Did Public Law 280 play any role in the *Colville* decision? On the other hand, might not the Tenth Circuit's assumption that states have no inherent power in Indian country better comport with the history and traditions of federal Indian policy than the decisions in these cases?

The Court's Indian country preemption analysis can be best understood when juxtaposed against federal statutory preemption analysis used in other non-Indian law contexts. *See generally* L. TRIBE, AMERICAN CONSTITUTIONAL LAW 479-528 (2d ed. 1988). While it is clear under the supremacy clause that an exercise of state power that directly conflicts with a federal statute or that could pose a serious threat of conflicting enforcement efforts is preempted by federal law, *Williams, McClanahan, Moe,* and *Colville* cannot readily be explained on this branch of the preemption analysis since state law did not conflict with any clear federal statutory or treaty provision. Rather, it was the *implied* federal protection of tribal self-government derived from federal treaties and statutes recognizing the Indian reservation and protecting its autonomy that was preemptive in these cases. *Contrast, e.g., Jones v. Rath Packing Co.,* 430 U.S. 519 (1977); *City of Burbank v. Lockheed Air Term., Inc.,* 411 U.S. 624 (1973). Indeed, it is precisely this lack of a clear and express preemptive statutory or treaty provision that provoked Justice Rehnquist's comments in *Colville.* In light of the history of the Indian commerce clause and the historic lack of state authority in Indian country, should the courts absolutely require the existence of a clear and specific federal law that preempts state authority merely because such clear statutory conflict is frequently required to find preemption in other fields?

On the other hand, federal preemption of state law can occur where the federal regulation is either so pervasive or involves a field of such dominant national concern that the federal statutory action has "occupied the field" to the exclusion of even consistent state laws. *E.g., Ray v. Atlantic Richfield Co.,* 435 U.S. 151 (1978); *Rice v. Sante Fe Elev. Corp.,* 331 U.S. 218 (1947). In the *Rice* case Justice Douglas stated:

The question in each case is what the purpose of Congress was.

[Thus] we start with the assumption that the historic police powers of the States were not to be superceded by the Federal Act unless that was the clear and manifest purpose of Congress. Such a purpose may be evidenced in several ways. The scheme of federal regulation may be so pervasive as to make reasonable the inference that Congress left no room for the States to supplement it. Or the Act of Congress may touch a field in which the federal interest is so dominant that the federal system will be assumed to preclude enforcement of state laws on the same subject. Likewise, the object sought to be obtained by the federal law and the character of obligations imposed by it may reveal the same purpose. Or the state policy may produce a result inconsistent with the objective of the federal statute. It is often a perplexing question whether Congress has precluded a state action or by the choice of selective regulatory measures has left the police power of the States undisturbed except as the state and federal regulations collide.

331 U.S. at 230-31 (citations omitted). Do any of these categories adequately explain the results in the foregoing cases? Is there indeed a pervasive regulatory statute or treaty in each of these foregoing cases? Even if one is willing to read the *implied* protections of tribal sovereignty derived from treaty or statute as a federal occupation of the geographic "field" of Indian country, difficult problems remain. If federal regulations, or at least protections of the legal autonomy of Indian country, are either so pervasive or so infused with a dominant national interest, how can one explain the inherent state power over non-Indians and over Indians who are not tribal members which is recognized in *Moe* and *Colville*? Of course, in each case it may be necessary to determine the outer boundaries of the field that Congress has occupied. However, is there any justification for drawing the boundary line in the Indian affairs field in a fashion that results in federal preemption of matters involving tribal members in Indian country but excludes from the preemptive effect of federal law in Indian country state regulations or taxing of non-Indians or even Indians who are not tribal members? Can this result be reconciled with *Worcester* or *Williams v. Lee*?

This discussion of the preemption doctrine, of course, suggests that the analysis in a particular case might be altered if a pervasive federal regulatory scheme in fact existed and the proponents of preemption were, therefore, not relying solely on the implied federal policy of protecting Indian sovereignty. It is to this problem that the next section is devoted.

For a general review of the preemption doctrine in the field of Indian affairs, see Laurence, *The Indian Commerce Clause*, 23 ARIZ. L. REV. 203 (1981); McCoy, *The Doctrine of Tribal Sovereignty: Accommodating Tribal, State and Federal Interests*, 13 HARV. C.R.-C.L. L. REV. 357 (1978); Werhan, *The Sovereignty of Indian Tribes: A Reaffirmation and Strengthening in the 1970's*, 54 NOTRE DAME LAW. 5 (1978); Mettler, *A Unified Theory of Indian Tribal Sovereignty*, 30 HASTINGS L.J. 89 (1978).

2. State Authority Over Nonmember Indians: The decision in *Colville* to exclude Indians who were not members of the affected tribes from the preemptive effect of federal law and thereby to authorize state taxation of their purchases in Indian country was certainly novel. *Contrast Arizona ex rel. Merrill v. Turtle*, 413 F.2d 683 (9th Cir. 1969), *cert. denied*, 396 U.S. 1003 (1970) (state of Arizona lacked authority to extradite to Oklahoma a Cheyenne Indian who resided on the Navajo reservation with his Navajo wife since the exercise of such power would infringe on tribal government and interfere with the Navajo extradition procedures). As indicated in earlier discussions of the membership distinction in Chapter 1, section B1b and in the notes following *Duro v. Reina* in Chapter 3, section D1, one can reasonably question the support for and origins of such differential treatment of Indians. Note that the exclusion of nonmembers from the federal preemption analysis seemingly applies to all Indians who are not members of the governing tribe. Thus, even Indians who are members of a recognized Indian tribe must pay the state taxes if they are not members of the tribe governing the reservation where the sale took place. Is this result a logical outgrowth of *Morton v. Mancari*, which sustained the Indian employment preference for BIA hiring and advancement on the ground that it was a rational political preference related to self-government rather than a racial classification? Under the BIA employment preference, a member of the Navajo tribe would still receive employment preference over a non-Indian for a BIA position involving work with the Red Lake Chippewa in Minnesota.

Under the rule of *Colville*, however, this same Navajo would *not* be immune from state taxation for on-reservation transactions if he married a Santa Clara woman and lived for the rest of his life on the Santa Clara Pueblo. Moreover, the children of this union, if ineligible for enrollment as Santa Clarans, would also have to pay state taxes even if they spoke Tewa and otherwise fully participated in the cultural and social life of the Pueblo, like the Martinez children in *Santa Clara Pueblo v. Martinez, supra* Chapter 3, section C. Is there any sufficient justification for subjecting them to state taxation while exempting Julia Martinez? On the other hand, a member of the Santa Clara Pueblo who lived in Phoenix, Arizona, for example, but returned periodically to the reservation, seemingly would be exempt from state taxation for on-reservation transactions despite nonresidency. Note also that the Court's holding in *Colville* was not merely addressed to Indians who are temporarily and casually on a reservation other than their own. It is specifically addressed to "Indians who are *resident* on the reservation but not enrolled in the governing Tribe" (emphasis supplied). Did the Court fully appreciate the complexities of the tribal community in its ruling?

3. **Sovereign Immunity, State Regulation, and Enforcement Limitations:** The tribal ordinances of the Colville, Makah, and Lummi tribes at issue in *Colville* all made these tribes the retailers of the cigarettes and the tribes retained ownership of the cigarettes until they were sold. In light of this feature of the tribal scheme, how can the state of Washington enforce the recordkeeping requirements that the Court sustained? Recall that Indian tribes generally have sovereign immunity. In the *McClanahan* decision, the inability of the state to enforce its purported tax was one of the factors to which the Court pointed to indicate that the state lacked taxing power. Justice Marshall wrote, "[The state] nowhere explains how, without such jursidiction, the State's tax may either be imposed or collected." Did the Court pay sufficient attention to this problem in its *Colville* opinion? Is the power of the state of Washington to seize unstamped cigarettes that are destined for the tribe outside the reservation, which the Court sustained in *Colville*, a sufficient enforcement mechanism? Does the state have any other enforcement powers available to it?

4. **Transaction Occurring Both On- and Off-Reservation:** As the discussion of *Mescalero Apache Tribe v. Jones*, 411 U.S. 145 (1973), *infra*, indicates, states generally have full power over Indians for off-reservation conduct. Does *Colville* hold that where a state purports to tax Indians for conduct occurring both on- and off-reservation that it must always prorate the tax to the extent of the off-reservation conduct? Is that approach equally applicable to the problem of regulation? How, if at all, would such an approach be applied to the issues of jurisdiction over litigation involving a series of transactions (e.g., the negotiation of the sale of securities) some of which occurred off-reservation?

5. **State Authority Over Non-Indian Owned Land in Indian Country:** Did the *Colville* opinion presage the Supreme Court's decision a year later in *Mon-*

tana v. United States, 450 U.S. 544 (1981), set forth and discussed in Chapter 3, section A1? *Montana* held that tribes could not regulate and states could control nonmember activities on non-Indian owned land in Indian country, at least where the transaction involved no consensual relations with the tribe and the political integrity, economic security, or health and welfare of the tribe was not at stake. Did *Oliphant, Moe, Colville,* and *Montana* signal a movement by the Court away from *Worcester, Williams,* and *McClanahan* as guideposts for the scope of tribal and state sovereignty in Indian country? What factors seem to be motivating the Court?

b. The Effect of Federal Regulation on State Jurisdiction

In *Worcester* Chief Justice Marshall based his opinion, in part, on the clear inconsistency between the Federal Trade and Intercourse Acts and the intrusive Georgia legislation. The exercise of federal authority over Indian affairs may have preemptive effects on state power. Such federal law might be of two types. First, the federal law might explicitly allocate jurisdiction between the competing governments. Public Law 280 and the Indian Child Welfare Act of 1978 will be analyzed at length at the end of this chapter as examples of this type of jurisdictional allocation. Second, the federal law may seek to regulate or tax the conduct of persons in Indian country. This section considers the preemptive effect of such substantive, seemingly nonjurisdictional, statutes.

CENTRAL MACHINERY CO. v. ARIZONA STATE TAX COMMISSION

448 U.S. 160 (1980)

Mr. Justice MARSHALL delivered the opinion of the Court.

This case presents the question whether a State may tax the sale of farm machinery to an Indian tribe when the sale took place on an Indian reservation and was made by a corporation that did not reside on the reservation and was not licensed to trade with Indians.

[Below] the Superior Court for Maricopa County held that the State had no jurisdiction to tax the transaction, and accordingly it ordered a refund. The Supreme Court of Arizona reversed. *State v. Central Machinery Co.*, 121 Ariz. 183, 589 P.2d 426 (1978).[2]

We noted probable jurisdiction, 444 U.S. 882 (1979), and now reverse.

In 1790, Congress passed a statute regulating the licensing of Indian traders. Act of July 22, 1790, ch. 33, 1 Stat. 137. Ever since that time, the Federal Government has comprehensively regulated trade with Indians to prevent "fraud and imposition" upon them. H. R. Rep. No. 474, 23d Cong., 1st Sess., 11 (1834) (committee report with respect to Indian Trade and Intercourse Act of 1834, ch. 161, 4 Stat. 729). In the current regulatory scheme, the Commissioner of Indian Affairs has "the sole power and authority to appoint traders to the Indian tribes and to make ... rules and regulations ... specifying the kind and quantity of goods and the prices at which such goods shall be sold to the Indians." 25 U.S.C. § 261. All persons desiring to trade with Indians are subject to the Commissioner's authority. 25 U.S.C. § 262. The President is authorized to prohibit the introduction of any article into Indian land. 25 U.S.C. § 263. Penal-

---

[2] It is stipulated that appellant will pay over any tax refund to Gila River Farms.

ties are provided for unlicensed trading, introduction of goods, or residence on a reservation for the purpose of trade. 25 U.S.C. § 264. The Commissioner has promulgated detailed regulations to implement these statutes. 25 C.F.R. Part 251 [now 25 C.F.R. 140 (1982)].

In *Warren Trading Post Co. v. Arizona Tax Comm'n*, 380 U.S. 685, the Court unanimously held that these "apparently all-inclusive regulations and the statutes authorizing them," *id.*, at 690, prohibited the State of Arizona from imposing precisely the same tax as is at issue in the present case on the operator of a federally licensed retail trading post located on [the Navajo reservation.]

There are only two distinctions between *Warren Trading Post, supra,* and the present case: appellant is not a licensed Indian trader, and it does not have a permanent place of business on the reservation. The Supreme Court of Arizona concluded that these distinctions indicated that federal law did not bar imposing the transaction privilege tax on appellant. We disagree.

The contract of sale involved in the present case was executed on the Gila River Reservation, and delivery and payment were effected there. Under the Indian trader statutes, 25 U.S.C. §§ 261-264, this transaction is plainly subject to federal regulation. It is irrelevant that appellant is not a licensed Indian trader. Indeed, the transaction falls squarely within the language of 25 U.S.C. § 264, which makes it a criminal offense for "[a]ny person ... to introduce goods, or to trade" without a license in the Indian country, or on any Indian reservation." It is the existence of the Indian trader statutes, then, and not their administration, that pre-empts the field of transactions with Indians occurring on reservations.[4]

Nor is it relevant that appellant did not maintain a permanent place of business on the reservation. The Indian trader statutes and their implementing regulations apply no less to a nonresident person who sells goods to Indians on a reservation than they do to a resident trader....

Since the transaction in the present case is governed by the Indian trader statutes, federal law pre-empts the asserted state tax. As we held in *Warren Trading Post, supra,* 380 U.S., at 691, n.18, by enacting these statutes Congress "has undertaken to regulate reservation trading in such a comprehensive way that there is no room for the States to legislate on the subject." It may be that in light of modern conditions the State of Arizona should be allowed to tax transactions such as the one involved in this case. Until Congress repeals or amends the Indian trader statutes, however, we must give them "a sweep as broad as [their] language," *United States v. Price*, 383 U.S. 787, 801 (1966), and interpret them in light of the intent of the Congress that enacted them, see *Wilson v. Omaha Indian Tribe*, 442 U.S. 653, 666 (1979); *Oliphant v. Suquamish Indian Tribe*, 435 U.S. 191, 206 (1978).

[*Reversed.*]

Mr. Justice STEWART, with whom Mr. Justice POWELL, Mr. Justice REHNQUIST, and Mr. Justice STEVENS join, dissenting.

---

[4] In any event, it should be recognized that the transaction at issue in this case was subjected to comprehensive federal regulation. Although appellant was not licensed to engage in trading with Indians, the Bureau of Indian Affairs had approved both the contract of sale for the tractors in question and the tribal budget, which allocated money for the purchase of this machinery.

The question before us is whether the appellant is immune from a state tax imposed on the proceeds of the sale by it of farm machinery to an Indian tribe. The Court concludes that an affirmative answer is required by the rationale of *Warren Trading Post Co. v. Arizona Tax Comm'n*, 380 U.S. 685, a case that is similar in some respects to this one. While I agree that *Warren Trading Post, supra*, states the relevant legal principles, I cannot agree that those principles lead to the result reached by the Court in this case. Accordingly, I dissent.

[T]he rationale of the decision in *Warren Trading Post, supra*, was not so simple [because the case rested on two grounds]. First, as the Court today reiterates, a tax on the gross income of a licensed trader residing on the reservation could "disturb and disarrange the statutory plan Congress set up in order to protect Indians against prices deemed unfair or unreasonable," *id.*, 380 U.S., at 691. Second, the Court saw in that case no governmental justification to support the State's "put[ting] financial burdens on [the trader] or the Indians with whom it deals in addition to those Congress or the tribes have prescribed," *ibid.* Because Congress for nearly a century had "left the Indians ... free to run the reservation and its affairs without state control," Arizona had been "automatically relieved ... of all burdens for carrying on those same responsibilities," *id.*, at 690. That being so, the Court did not "believe that Congress intended to leave to the State the privilege of levying this tax," *id.*, at 691.

Neither of these considerations is present here. First, although the appellant was obliged to obtain federal approval of the sale transaction in this case, see 25 U.S.C. §§ 262 and 264, it was not subjected to the much more comprehensive regulation that governs licensed traders engaged in a continuous course of dealing with reservation Indians. See 25 C.F.R. Part 251....

Second, the Court inexplicably ignores the State's wholly legitimate purpose in taxing the appellant, a corporation that does business within the State at large and presumably derives substantial benefits from the services provided by the State at taxpayer's expense. Aside from entering the reservation to solicit and execute the contract of sale and to receive payment, circumstances that are certain to characterize all sales to reservation Indians after today's decision, the appellant conducts its affairs in all respects like any other business to which the State's nondiscriminatory tax concededly applies. Thus, quite unlike the circumstances in *Warren Trading Post, supra*, the State in this case has not been relieved of all duties or responsibilities respecting the business it would tax. Yet, despite the settled teaching of the Court's decisions in this area that every relevant state interest is to be given weight, see *Washington v. Confederated Tribes, supra; McClanahan v. Arizona State Tax Comm'n*, 411 U.S. 164, 171; cf. *White Mountain Apache Tribe v. Bracker*, 448 U.S. 136, the Court does not even consider the State's valid governmental justification for taxing the transaction here involved.

It is important to recognize the limits inherent in the principles of federal preemption on which the *Warren Trading Post* decision rests. Those limits make necessary in every case such as this a careful inquiry into pertinent federal, tribal, and state interests, without which a rational accommodation of those interests is not possible. Had such an inquiry been made in this case, I am convinced the Court could not have concluded that Arizona's exercise of the sovereign power to tax its non-Indian citizens had been pre-empted by federal law.

WHITE MOUNTAIN APACHE TRIBE v. BRACKER

448 U.S. 136 (1980)

[Pursuant to a contract with an organization of petitioner White Mountain Apache Tribe, petitioner Pinetop Logging Co. (Pinetop), a non-Indian enterprise authorized to do business in Arizona, felled tribal timber on the Fort Apache Reservation and transported it to the tribal organization's sawmill. Pinetop's activities were performed solely on the reservation. Respondents, state agencies and members thereof, sought to impose on Pinetop Arizona's motor carrier license tax, which is assessed on the basis of the carrier's gross receipts, and its use fuel tax, which is assessed on the basis of diesel fuel used to propel a motor vehicle on any highway within the State. Pinetop paid the taxes under protest and then brought suit in state court, asserting that under federal law the taxes could not lawfully be imposed on logging activities conducted exclusively within the reservation or on hauling activities on Bureau of Indian Affairs (BIA) and tribal roads. The trial court awarded summary judgment to respondents, and the Arizona Court of Appeals affirmed in pertinent part rejecting petitioners' preemption claim.]

[Mr. Justice MARSHALL.]

II

Congress has broad power to regulate tribal affairs under the Indian Commerce Clause, Art. 1, § 8, cl. 3. This congressional authority and the "semi-independent position" of Indian tribes have given rise to two independent but related barriers to the assertion of state regulatory authority over tribal reservations and members. First, the exercise of such authority may be pre-empted by federal law. See, e.g., Warren Trading Post Co. v. Arizona Tax Comm'n, 380 U.S. 685 (1965); [McClanahan.] Second, it may unlawfully infringe "on the right of reservation Indians to make their own laws and be ruled by them." [Williams v. Lee.] See also Washington v. Yakima Indian Nation, 439 U.S. 463, 470 (1979); Fisher v. District Court, 424 U.S. 382 (1976) (per curiam); Kennerly v. District Court of Montana, 400 U.S. 423 (1971). The two barriers are independent because either, standing alone, can be a sufficient basis for holding state law inapplicable to activity undertaken on the reservation or by tribal members. They are related, however, in two important ways. The right of tribal self-government is ultimately dependent on and subject to the broad power of Congress. Even so, traditional notions of Indian self-government are so deeply engrained in our jurisprudence that they have provided an important "backdrop," [McClanahan,] against which vague or ambiguous federal enactments must always be measured.

The unique historical origins of tribal sovereignty make it generally unhelpful to apply to federal enactments regulating Indian tribes those standards of pre-emption that have emerged in other areas of the law. Tribal reservations are not States, and the differences in the form and nature of their sovereignty make it treacherous to import to one notions of pre-emption that are properly applied to the other. The tradition of Indian sovereignty over the reservation and tribal members must inform the determination whether the exercise of state authority has been pre-empted by operation of federal law. *Moe v. Salish & Kootenai Tribes,* [425 U.S., at] 475. As we have repeatedly recognized, this tradition is reflected and encouraged in a number of congressional enactments demonstrating a firm federal policy of promoting tribal self-sufficiency and economic development. Ambiguities in federal law have been construed generously in order to comport with these traditional notions of sovereignty and with the federal policy of encouraging tribal independence. See [*McClanahan*]. We have thus rejected the proposition that in order to find a particular state law to have been preempted by operation of federal law, an express congressional statement to that effect is required.[11] *Warren Trading Post Co. v. Arizona State Tax Comm'n, supra.* At the same time any applicable regulatory interest of the State must be given weight, [*McClanahan*] and "automatic exemptions 'as a matter of constitutional law'" are unusual. *Moe v. Salish & Kootenai Tribes, supra,* 425 U.S., at 481, n.17.

When on-reservation conduct involving only Indians is at issue, state law is generally inapplicable, for the State's regulatory interest is likely to be minimal and the federal interest in encouraging tribal self-government is at its strongest. More difficult questions arise where, as here, a State asserts authority over the conduct of non-Indians engaging in activity on the reservation. In such cases we have examined the language of the relevant federal treaties and statutes in terms of both the broad policies that underlie them and the notions of sovereignty that have developed from historical traditions of tribal independence. This inquiry is not dependent on mechanical or absolute conceptions of State or tribal sovereignty, but has called for a particularized inquiry into the nature of the State, Federal, and tribal interests at stake, an inquiry designed to determine whether, in the specific context, the exercise of state authority would violate federal law. Compare *Warren Trading Post Co. v. Arizona State Tax Comm'n, supra,* and *Williams v. Lee, supra,* with *Moe v. Salish & Kootenai Tribes, supra,* and *Thomas v. Gay,* 169 U.S. 264 (1898). Cf. [*McClanahan;*] *Mescalero Apache Tribe v. Jones, supra,* 411 U.S., at 148.

III

With these principles in mind, we turn to the respondents' claim that they may, consistent with federal law, impose the contested motor vehicle license and use fuel taxes on the logging and hauling operations of petitioner Pinetop. At the outset we observe that the Federal Government's regulation of the harvesting of Indian timber is comprehensive. That regulation takes the form of Acts of Congress, detailed regulations promulgated by the Secretary of the Interior, and day-to-day supervision by the Bureau of Indian Affairs. Under 25 U.S.C. §§ 405-407, the Secretary of the Interior is granted broad authority over the sale of timber on the reservation. Timber on Indian land may be sold only with the

---

[11] In the case of "Indians going beyond reservation boundaries," however, "a nondiscriminatory state law" is generally applicable in the absence of "express federal law to the contrary." *Mescalero Apache Tribe v. Jones, supra* at 148-149.

consent of the Secretary, and the proceeds from any such sales, less administrative expenses incurred by the Federal Government, are to be used for the benefit of the Indians or transferred to the Indian owner. Sales of timber must "be based upon a consideration of the needs and best interests of the Indian owner and his heirs." 25 U.S.C. § 406. The statute specifies the factors which the Secretary must consider in making that determination. In order to assure the continued productivity of timber-producing land on tribal reservations, timber on unallotted lands "may be sold in accordance with the principles of sustained yield." 25 U.S.C. § 407. The Secretary is granted power to determine the disposition of the proceeds from timber sales. He is authorized to promulgate regulations for the operation and management of Indian forestry units. 25 U.S.C. § 466.

Acting pursuant to this authority, the Secretary has promulgated a detailed set of regulations to govern the harvesting and sale of tribal timber. Among the stated objectives of the regulations is the "development of Indian forests by the Indian people for the purpose of promoting self-sustaining communities, to the end that the Indians may receive from their own property not only the stumpage value, but also the benefit of whatever profit it is capable of yielding and whatever labor the Indians are qualified to perform." 25 C.F.R. § 141.3(a)(3) [Part 141 of 25 C.F.R. is now 25 C.F.R. Part 163 (1982)]. The regulations cover a wide variety of matters: for example, they restrict clear-cutting, § 141.5; establish comprehensive guidelines for the sale of timber, § 141.7; regulate the advertising of timber sales, §§ 141.8-141.9; specify the manner in which bids may be accepted and rejected, § 141.11; describe the circumstances in which contracts may be entered into, §§ 141.12-141.13; require the approval of all contracts by the Secretary, § 141.13; call for timber cutting permits to be approved by the Secretary, § 141.19; specify fire protective measures, § 141.21; and provide a board of administrative appeals, § 141.23. Tribes are expressly authorized to establish commercial enterprises for the harvesting and logging of tribal timber. § 141.6.

Under these regulations, the Bureau of Indian Affairs exercises literally daily supervision over the harvesting and management of tribal timber. In the present case, contracts between FATCO and Pinetop must be approved by the Bureau; indeed, the record shows that some of those contracts were drafted by employees of the Federal Government. Bureau employees regulate the cutting, hauling, and marking of timber by FATCO and Pinetop. The Bureau decides such matters as how much timber will be cut, which trees will be felled, which roads are to be used, which hauling equipment Pinetop should employ, the speeds at which logging equipment may travel, and the width, length, height, and weight of loads.

The Secretary has also promulgated detailed regulations governing the roads developed by the Bureau of Indian Affairs. 25 C.F.R. Part 162 [now 25 C.F.R. Part 170 (1982)]. Bureau roads are open to "[f]ree public use." § 162.8. Their administration and maintenance are funded by the Federal Government, with contributions from the Indian tribes. §§ 162.6-162.6a. On the Fort Apache Reservation the Forestry Department of the Bureau has required FATCO and its contractors, including Pinetop, to repair and maintain existing Bureau and tribal roads and in some cases to construct new logging roads. Substantial sums have been spent for these purposes. In its federally approved contract with FATCO, Pinetop has agreed to construct new roads and to repair existing ones. A high percentage of Pinetop's receipts are expended for those purposes, and it has maintained separate personnel and equipment to carry out a variety of tasks relating to road maintenance.

In these circumstances we agree with petitioners that the federal regulatory scheme is so pervasive as to preclude the additional burdens sought to be imposed in this case. Respondents seek to apply their motor vehicle license and use fuel taxes on Pinetop for operations that are conducted solely on Bureau and tribal roads within the reservation.[14] There is no room for these taxes in the comprehensive federal regulatory scheme. In a variety of ways, the assessment of state taxes would obstruct federal policies. And equally important, respondents have been unable to identify any regulatory function or service performed by the State that would justify the assessment of taxes for activities on Bureau and tribal roads within the reservation.

At the most general level, the taxes would threaten the overriding federal objective of guaranteeing Indians that they will "receive ... the benefit of whatever profit [the forest] is capable of yielding...." 25 C.F.R. § 141.3(a)(3). Underlying the federal regulatory program rests a policy of assuring that the profits derived from timber sales will inure to the benefit of the Tribe, subject only to administrative expenses incurred by the Federal Government. That objective is part of the general federal policy of encouraging tribes "to revitalize their self-government" and to assume control over their "business and economic affairs." *Mescalero Apache Tribe v. Jones, supra,* 411 U.S., at 151. The imposition of the taxes at issue would undermine that policy in a context in which the Federal Government has undertaken to regulate the most minute details of timber production and expressed a firm desire that the Tribes should retain the benefits derived from the harvesting and sale of reservation timber.

In addition, the taxes would undermine the Secretary's ability to make the wide range of determinations committed to his authority concerning the setting of fees and rates with respect to the harvesting and sale of tribal timber. The Secretary reviews and approves the terms of the Tribe's agreements with its contractors, sets fees for services rendered to the tribe by the Federal Government, and determines stumpage rates for timber to be paid to the Tribe. Most notably in reviewing or writing the terms of the contracts between FATCO and its contractors, federal agents must predict the amount and determine the proper allocation of all business expenses, including fuel costs. The assessment of state taxes would throw additional factors into the federal calculus, reducing tribal revenues and diminishing the profitability of the enterprise for potential contractors.

---

[14] In oral argument counsel for respondents appeared to concede that the asserted state taxes could not lawfully be applied to tribal roads and was unwilling to defend the contrary conclusion of the court below, which made no distinction between Bureau and tribal roads under state and federal law. Tr. of Oral Arg., at 34-37. Contrary to respondents' position throughout the litigation and in their brief in this Court, counsel limited his argument to a contention that the taxes could be asserted on the roads of the Bureau of Indian Affairs. *Ibid.* For purposes of federal pre-emption, however, we see no basis, and respondents point to none, for distinguishing between roads maintained by the Tribe and roads maintained by the Bureau of Indian Affairs.

Finally, the imposition of state taxes would adversely affect the Tribe's ability to comply with the sustained-yield management policies imposed by federal law. Substantial expenditures are paid out by the Federal Government, the Tribe, and its contractors in order to undertake a wide variety of measures to ensure the continued productivity of the forest. These measures include reforestation, fire control, wildlife promotion, road improvement, safety inspections, and general policing of the forest. The expenditures are largely paid for out of tribal revenues, which are in turn derived almost exclusively from the sale of timber. The imposition of state taxes on FATCO's contractors would effectively diminish the amount of those revenues and thus leave the Tribe and its contractors with reduced sums with which to pay out federally required expenses.

As noted above, this is not a case in which the State seeks to assess taxes in return for governmental functions it performs for those on whom the taxes fall. Nor have respondents been able to identify a legitimate regulatory interest served by the taxes they seek to impose. They refer to a general desire to raise revenue, but we are unable to discern a responsibility or service that justifies the assertion of taxes imposed for on-reservation operations conducted solely on tribal and Bureau of Indian Affairs roads. Pinetop's business in Arizona is conducted solely on the Fort Apache Reservation. Though at least the use fuel tax purports to "compensat[e] the state for the use of its highways," Ariz. Rev. Stat. Ann. § 28-1552, no such compensatory purpose is present here. The roads at issue have been built, maintained, and policed exclusively by the Federal Government, the Tribe, and its contractors. We do not believe that respondents' generalized interest in raising revenue is in this context sufficient to permit its proposed intrusion into the federal regulatory scheme with respect to the harvesting and sale of tribal timber.

Respondents' argument is reduced to a claim that they may assess taxes on non-Indians engaged in commerce on the reservation whenever there is no express congressional statement to the contrary. That is simply not the law. In a number of cases we have held that state authority over non-Indians acting on tribal reservations is pre-empted even though Congress has offered no explicit statement on the subject. See *Warren Trading Post, supra; Williams v. Lee, supra; Kennerly v. District Court of Montana, supra.* The Court has repeatedly emphasized that there is a significant geographical component to tribal sovereignty, a component which remains highly relevant to the pre-emption inquiry; though the reservation boundary is not absolute, it remains an important factor to weigh in determining whether state authority has exceeded the permissible limits. "'The cases in this Court have consistently guarded the authority of Indian governments over their reservations.'" *United States v. Mazurie, supra,* 419 U.S., at 558, quoting *Williams v. Lee,* 358 U.S. 217, 223 (1959). Moreover, it is undisputed that the economic burden of the asserted taxes will ultimately fall on the Tribe.[15] Where, as here, the Federal Government has undertaken comprehensive regulation of the harvesting and sale of tribal timber, where a num-

---

[15]Of course, the fact that the economic burden of the tax falls on the Tribe does not by itself mean that the tax is pre-empted, as *Moe v. Salish & Kootenai Tribes,* 425 U.S. 463 (1976), makes clear. Our decision today is based on the pre-emptive effect of the comprehensive federal regulatory scheme, which, like that in *Warren Trading Post Co. v. Arizona Tax Comm'n, supra,* leaves no room for the additional burdens sought to be imposed by state law.

ber of the policies underlying the federal regulatory scheme are threatened by the taxes respondents seek to impose, and where respondents are unable to justify the taxes except in terms of a generalized interest in raising revenue, we believe that the proposed exercise of state authority is impermissible.[16]

Both the reasoning and result in this case follow naturally from our unanimous decision in *Warren Trading Post Co. v. Arizona Tax Comm'n, supra....* The present case, we conclude, is in all relevant respects indistinguishable from *Warren Trading Post.*

[*Reversed.*]

Mr. Justice STEVENS, with whom Mr. Justice STEWART and Mr. Justice REHNQUIST join, dissenting.

[Given the posture of this case] I think the most appropriate disposition would be to vacate the judgment of the Arizona Court of Appeals and remand for further consideration in light of the concessions made on behalf of the State in this Court. As the Court and Mr. Justice Powell point out, it is difficult to see why those concessions are not an acknowledgement that the State has no authority to tax the use of roads in which it has no interest....

Even assuming, however, that the state courts would uphold the imposition of taxes based on the use of BIA roads, despite their similarities with private and tribal roads, I would not find those taxes to be pre-empted by federal law. In *Warren Trading Post v. Arizona Tax Commission*, 380 U.S. 685, the Court held that state taxation of a non-Indian doing business with a tribe on the reservation was pre-empted because the taxes threatened to "disturb and disarrange" a pervasive scheme of federal regulation and because there was no governmental interest on the State's part in imposing such a burden. See [*Central Machinery Co.*] (Stewart, J., dissenting). In this case we may assume *arguendo* that the second factor relied upon in *Warren Trading Post* is present. As a result, Pinetop may well have a right to be free from taxation as a matter of due process or equal protection.[7] But I cannot agree that it has a right to be free from taxation because of its business relationship with the petitioner tribe.

As the Court points out, the Federal Government has imposed a detailed scheme of regulation on the tribal logging business. Thus, among other things, the BIA approves and sometimes drafts contracts between the tribe and non-Indian logging companies such as Pinetop and requires the tribe and its contractors to follow its dictates as to where to cut, haul and mark timber, and as to which roads to construct and repair.

---

[16] Respondents also contend that the taxes are authorized by the Buck Act, 4 U.S.C. § 105 *et seq.*, and the Hayden-Cartwright Act, 4 U.S.C. § 104. In *Warren Trading Post Co. v. Arizona State Tax Comm'n, supra*, [380 U.S., at] 691, n.18 (1965), we squarely held that the Buck Act did not apply to Indian reservations, and respondents present no sufficient reason for us to depart from that holding. We agree with petitioners that the Hayden-Cartwright Act, which authorizes state taxes "on United States military or other reservations," was not designed to overcome the otherwise preemptive effect of federal regulation of tribal timber. We need not reach the more general question whether the Hayden-Cartwright Act applies to Indian reservations at all.

[7] The Due Process Clause may prohibit a State from imposing a tax on the use of completely private roads if the tax is designed to reimburse it for use of state-owned roads. Or it may be that once the State has decided to exempt private roads from its taxing system, it is also required, as a matter of equal protection, to exempt other types of roads that are identical to private roads in all relevant respects.

[T]he Court's prediction of massive interference with federal forest-management programs seems overdrawn, to say the least. The logging operations involved in this case produced a profit of $1,508,713 for the Indian tribal enterprise in 1973. As noted above, the maximum annual taxes Pinetop would be required to pay would be $5,000-$6,000 or less than 1% of the total annual profits. Given the State's concession in this Court that the use of certain roads should not have been taxed as a matter of state law, the actual taxes Pinetop would be required to pay would probably be considerably less. It is difficult to believe that these relatively trivial taxes could impose an economic burden that would threaten to "obstruct federal policies."

Under these circumstances I find the Court's reliance on the indirect financial burden imposed on the Indian tribe by state taxation of its contractors disturbing. As a general rule, a tax is not invalid simply because a nonexempt taxpayer may be expected to pass all or part of the cost of the tax through to a person who is exempt from tax....

Mr. Justice POWELL, dissenting and concurring.

I write separately because I would distinguish [*Central Machinery Co.*] [and] *White Mountain Apache Tribe v. Bracker*. [I concur with the Court] that a non-Indian contractor continuously engaged in logging upon a reservation is subject to such pervasive federal regulation as to bring into play the pre-emption doctrine of *Warren Trading Post Co. v. Arizona Tax Comm'n*, 380 U.S. 685 (1965). But *Warren Trading Post* simply does not apply to routine state taxation of a non-Indian corporation that makes a single sale to reservation Indians. I therefore join the Court's opinion in *White Mountain Apache Tribe*, but I dissent from its decision in *Central Machinery*.

I

Central Machinery

Warren Trading Post held that Arizona could not levy its transaction privilege tax against a company regularly engaged in retail trading with the Indians upon a reservation. The company operated under a federal license, and it was subject to the federal regulatory scheme authorized by 25 U.S.C. §§ 261-264. "These apparently all-inclusive regulations," the Court concluded, "show that Congress has taken the business of Indian trading on reservations so fully in hand that no room remains for state laws imposing additional burdens upon traders." 380 U.S., at 690.

The Court today is too much persuaded by the superficial similarity between *Warren Trading Post* and *Central Machinery*. The Court mistakenly concludes that a company having no license to trade with the Indians and no place of business within a reservation is engaged in "the business of Indian trading on reservations...." *Ibid.* Although "any person" desiring to sell goods to Indians inside a reservation must secure federal approval, see 25 U.S.C. §§ 262, 264, the federal regulations — and the facts of this case — show that a person who makes a single approved sale need not become a fully regulated Indian trader. Even itinerant peddlers who engage in a pattern of selling within a reservation are merely "considered as traders" for purposes of the licensing requirement. 25 C.F.R. § 251.9(b). "The business of a licensed trader," in fact, "must be managed by the bonded principal, who must habitually reside upon the reservation...." 25 C.F.R. § 251.14.[1] Since *Warren Trading Post* involved a resident trader subject to the complete range of federal regulation, the Court had no occasion to consider whether federal regulation also pre-empts state taxation of a seller who enters a reservation to make a single transaction.

Our most recent cases undermine the notion that 25 U.S.C. §§ 261-264 occupy the field so as to pre-empt all state regulation affecting licensed Indian traders. The unanimous Court in *Moe v. Salish and Kootenai Tribes*, 425 U.S. 463, 481-483 (1976), concluded that a State could require tribal retailers to prepay a tax validly imposed on non-Indian customers. Rejecting an argument based on *Warren Trading Post*, the Court concluded that federal laws "passed to protect and guard [the Indians] only affect the operation, within the [reservation], of such state laws as conflict with the federal enactments.' " 425 U.S., at 483 quoting *United States v. McGowan*, 302 U.S. 535, 539 (1938). In [*Colville*,] the Court holds that a State can require licensed traders to keep detailed tax records of their sales to both Indians and non-Indians.

Finally, unlike taxes imposed upon an Indian trader engaged in a continuous course of dealing within the reservation, the tax assessed against *Central Machinery* does not "to a substantial extent frustrate the evident congressional purpose of ensuring that no burden shall be imposed upon Indian traders for trading with Indians except as authorized by Acts of Congress or by valid regulations promulgated under those Acts." ...

II

White Mountain Apache Tribe

White Mountain Apache Tribe presents a different situation. Petitioner Pinetop Logging Co. operates solely and continuously upon an Indian reservation under its contract with a tribal enterprise. Pinetop's daily operations are controlled by a comprehensive federal regulatory scheme designed to assure the Indian tribes the greatest possible return from their timber. Federal officials direct Pinetop's hauling operations down to such details as choice of equipment, selection of routes, speeds of travel, and dimensions of the loads. Pinetop does all of the hauling at issue in this case over roads constructed, maintained, and regulated by the White Mountain Apache Tribe and the Bureau of Indian Affairs. The Bureau requires the Tribe and its contractors to repair existing roads and to construct new roads necessary for sustained logging. Pinetop exhausts a large percentage of its gross income in performing these contractual obligations.

Since the Federal Government, the Tribe, and its contractors are solely responsible for the roads that Pinetop uses, I "cannot believe that Congress intended to leave to the State the privilege of levying" road use taxes upon Pinetop's operations. See *Warren Trading Post, supra*, at 691. The State has no interest in raising revenues from the use of Indian roads that cost it nothing and

---

[1] The regulation dealing with itinerant peddlers was promulgated after the decision in *Warren Trading Post*. See 30 Fed. Reg. 8267 (1965). Thus, the regulations before the Court in *Warren Trading Post* required all licensed Indian traders to conduct their businesses under the management of a habitual resident upon the reservation. 25 C.F.R. § 251.14 (1958).

over which it exercises no control. See [*Colville*]. The addition of these taxes to the road construction and repair expenses that Pinetop already bears also would interfere with the federal scheme for maintaining roads essential to successful Indian timbering. See 380 U.S., at 691. The Tribe or its contractors would pay twice for use of the same roads. This double exaction could force federal officials to reallocate work from non-Indian contractors to the tribal enterprise itself or to make costly concessions to the contractors. I therefore join the Court in concluding that this case "is in all relevant respects indistinguishable from *Warren Trading Post.*"

NEW MEXICO v. MESCALERO APACHE TRIBE

462 U.S. 324 (1983)

Justice MARSHALL, delivered the opinion of the Court.

We are called upon to decide in this case whether a State may restrict an Indian Tribe's regulation of hunting and fishing on its reservation. With extensive federal assistance and supervision, the Mescalero Apache Tribe has established a comprehensive scheme for managing the reservation's fish and wildlife resources. Federally approved tribal ordinances regulate in detail the conditions under which both members of the Tribe and nonmembers may hunt and fish. New Mexico seeks to apply its own laws to hunting and fishing by nonmembers on the reservation. We hold that this application of New Mexico's hunting and fishing laws is pre-empted by the operation of federal law.

I

The Mescalero Apache Tribe (Tribe) resides on a reservation located within Otero County in south central New Mexico. The reservation, which represents only a small portion of the aboriginal Mescalero domain, was created by a succession of Executive Orders promulgated in the 1870's and 1880's. The present reservation comprises more than 460,000 acres, of which the Tribe owns all but 193.85 acres. Approximately 2,000 members of the Tribe reside on the reservation, along with 179 non-Indians, including resident federal employees of the [BIA] and the [IHS].

The Tribe is organized under the [IRA. Its Constitution] requires the Tribal Council

"[t]o protect and preserve the property, wildlife and natural resources of the tribe, and to regulate the conduct of trade and the use and disposition of tribal property upon the reservation, providing that any ordinance directly affecting non-members of the tribe shall be subject to review by the Secretary of Interior." App. 53a.

The Constitution further provides that the Council shall

"adopt and approve plans of operation to govern the conduct of any business or industry that will further the economic well-being of the members of the tribe, and to undertake activity of any nature whatsoever, not inconsistent with Federal law or with this constitution, designed for the social or economic improvement of the Mescalero Apache people, ... subject to review by the Secretary of the Interior." *Ibid.*

Anticipating a decline in the sale of lumber which has been the largest income-producing activity within the reservation, the Tribe has recently committed substantial time and resources to the development of other sources of income. The Tribe has constructed a resort complex financed principally by federal funds,[3] and has undertaken a substantial development of the reservation's hunting and fishing resources. These efforts provide employment opportunities for members of the Tribe, and the sale of hunting and fishing licenses and related services generates income which is used to maintain the tribal government and provide services to Tribe members.[4]

Development of the reservation's fish and wildlife resources has involved a sustained, cooperative effort by the Tribe and the Federal Government. Indeed, the reservation's fishing resources are wholly attributable to these recent efforts. Using federal funds, the Tribe has established eight artificial lakes which, together with the reservation's streams, are stocked by the Bureau of Sport Fisheries and Wildlife of the United States Fish and Wildlife Service, Department of the Interior, which operates a federal hatchery located on the reservation. None of the waters are stocked by the State.[5] The United States has also contributed substantially to the creation of the reservation's game resources. Prior to 1966 there were only 13 elk in the vicinity of the reservation. In 1966 and 1967 the National Park Service donated a herd of 162 elk which was released on the reservation. Through its management and range development the Tribe has dramatically increased the elk population, which by 1977 numbered approximately 1,200. New Mexico has not contributed significantly to the development of the elk herd or the other game on the reservation, which includes antelope, bear, and deer.

The Tribe and the Federal Government jointly conduct a comprehensive fish and management program. Pursuant to its Constitution and to an agreement with the Bureau of Sport Fisheries and Wildlife,[8] the Tribal Council adopts hunting and fishing ordinances each year. The tribal ordinances, which establish bag limits and seasons and provide for licensing of hunting and fishing, are subject to approval by the Secretary under the Tribal Constitution and have been so approved. The Tribal Council adopts the game ordinances on the basis of recommendations submitted by a Bureau of Indian Affairs' range conservationist who is assisted by full-time conservation officers employed by the Tribe. The recommendations are made in light of the conservation needs of the reservation, which are determined on the basis of annual game counts and surveys. Through the Bureau of Sport Fisheries and Wildlife, the Secretary also deter-

---

[3] Financing for the complex, the Inn of the Mountain Gods, came principally from the Economic Development Administration (EDA), an agency of the United States Department of Commerce, and other federal sources. In addition, the Tribe obtained a $6 million loan from the Bank of New Mexico, 90% of which was guaranteed by the Secretary of the Interior under the Indian Financing Act of 1974, 25 U.S.C. § 1451 et seq. (1976 ed. and Supp. V), and 10% of which was guaranteed by trial funds. Certain additional facilities at the Inn were completely funded by the EDA as public works projects, and other facilities received 50% funding from the EDA....

[4] Income from the sale of hunting and fishing licenses, "package hunts" which combine hunting and fishing with use of the facilities at the Inn, and campground and picnicking permits totalled $269,140 in 1976 and $271,520 in 1977. The vast majority of the nonmember hunters and fishermen on the reservation are not residents of the State of New Mexico.

[5] The State has not stocked any waters on the reservation since 1976.

[8] That agreement, which provides for the stocking of the reservation's artificial lakes by the Bureau, obligates the Tribe to "designate those waters of the Reservation which shall be open to public fishing" and to "establish regulations for the conservation of the fishery resources." App. 71a.

mines the stocking of the reservation's waters based upon periodic surveys of the reservation.

Numerous conflicts exist between state and tribal hunting regulations. For instance, tribal seasons and bag limits for both hunting and fishing often do not coincide with those imposed by the State. The Tribe permits a hunter to kill both a buck and a doe; the State permits only buck to be killed. Unlike the State, the Tribe permits a person to purchase an elk license in two consecutive years. Moreover, since 1977, the Tribe's ordinances have specified that state hunting and fishing licenses are not required for Indians or non-Indians who hunt or fish on the reservation.[10] The New Mexico Department of Game and Fish has enforced the State's regulations by arresting non-Indian hunters for illegal possession of game killed on the reservation in accordance with tribal ordinances but not in accordance with state hunting regulations.

In 1977 the Tribe filed suit against the State and the Director of its Game and Fish Department in the United States District Court for the District of New Mexico, seeking to prevent the State from regulating on-reservation hunting or fishing by members or nonmembers. On August 2, 1978, the District Court ruled in favor of the Tribe and granted declaratory and injunctive relief against the enforcement of the State's hunting and fishing laws against any person for hunting and fishing activities conducted on the reservation. The United States Court of Appeals for the Tenth Circuit affirmed. Following New Mexico's petition for a writ of certiorari, this Court vacated the Tenth Circuit's judgment, and remanded the case for reconsideration in light of *Montana v. United States*, 450 U.S. 544 (1981). On remand, the Court of Appeals adhered to its earlier decision. We granted *certiorari* [and] now affirm.

II

New Mexico concedes that on the reservation the Tribe exercises exclusive jurisdiction over hunting and fishing by members of the Tribe and may also regulate the hunting and fishing by nonmembers. New Mexico contends, however, that it may exercise concurrent jurisdiction over nonmembers and that therefore its regulations governing hunting and fishing throughout the State should also apply to hunting and fishing by nonmembers on the reservation. Although New Mexico does not claim that it can require the Tribe to permit nonmembers to hunt and fish on the reservation, it claims that, once the Tribe chooses to permit hunting and fishing by nonmembers, such hunting and fishing is subject to any state-imposed conditions. Under this view the State would be free to impose conditions more restrictive than the Tribe's own regulations, including an outright prohibition. The question in this case is whether the State may so restrict the Tribe's exercise of its authority.

Our decision in *Montana v. United States, supra,* does not resolve this question. Unlike this case, *Montana* concerned lands located within the reservation but not owned by the Tribe or its members. We held that the Crow Tribe could not as a general matter regulate hunting and fishing on those lands.[12] But as to

---

[10] Prior to 1977 the Tribe consented to the application to the reservation of the State's hunting and fishing regulations.

[12] Even so, the Court acknowledged that "Indian tribes retain inherent sovereign power to exercise some forms of civil jurisdiction over non-Indians on their reservations, even on non-Indian fee

"land belonging to the Tribe or held by the United States in trust for the Tribe," we "readily agree[d]" that a Tribe may "prohibit nonmembers from hunting or fishing ... [or] condition their entry by charging a fee or establish bag and creel limits." *Id.*, at 557. We had no occasion to decide whether a Tribe may only exercise this authority in a manner permitted by a State.

On numerous occasions this Court has considered the question whether a State may assert authority over a reservation. The decision in [*Worcester v. Georgia*] reflected the view that Indian tribes were wholly distinct nations within whose boundaries "the laws of [a State] can have no force." We long ago departed from the "conceptual clarity of Mr. Chief Justice Marshall's view in *Worcester,*" *Mescalero Apache Tribe v. Jones*, 411 U.S. 145, 148 (1973), and have acknowledged certain limitations on tribal sovereignty. For instance, we have held that Indian tribes have been implicitly divested of their sovereignty in certain respects by virtue of their dependent status, that under certain circumstances a State may validly assert authority over the activities of nonmembers on a reservation, and that in exceptional circumstances a State may assert jurisdiction over the on-reservation activities of tribal members.

Nevertheless, in demarcating the respective spheres of state and tribal authority over Indian reservations, we have continued to stress that Indian tribes are unique aggregations possessing "'attributes of sovereignty over both their members and their territory,'" [*Bracker,*] quoting *United States v. Mazurie*, 419 U.S. 544, 557 (1975). Because of their sovereign status, tribes and their reservation lands are insulated in some respects by a "historic immunity from state and local control," *Mescalero Apache Tribe v. Jones, supra*, at 152, and tribes retain any aspect of their historical sovereignty not "inconsistent with the overriding interests of the National Government." [*Colville.*]

The sovereignty retained by tribes includes "the power of regulating their internal and social relations," [*United States v. Kagama*]. A tribe's power to prescribe the conduct of tribal members has never been doubted, and our cases establish that "'absent governing Acts of Congress,'" a State may not act in a manner that "'infringed on the right of reservation Indians to make their own laws and be ruled by them.'" [*McClanahan,*] quoting [*Williams v. Lee*].

A tribe's power to exclude nonmembers entirely or to condition their presence on the reservation is equally well established. See, *e.g., Montana v. United States*, 450 U.S. 544 (1981); *Merrion v. Jicarilla Apache Tribe*, 455 U.S. 130 (1982). Whether a State may also assert its authority over the on-reservation activities of nonmembers raises "[m]ore difficult questions," *Bracker, supra*, at 144. While under some circumstances a State may exercise concurrent jurisdiction over non-Indians acting on tribal reservations, see, *e.g.,* [*Colville;*] *Moe v. Salish & Kootenai Tribes*, 425 U.S. 463 (1976), such authority may be asserted only if not pre-empted by the operation of federal law. [*E.g., Ramah Navajo School Bd., Inc. v. Bureau of Revenue of New Mexico*, 458 U.S. 832 (1982).]

In *Bracker* we reviewed our prior decisions concerning tribal and state authority over Indian reservations and extracted certain principles governing the

lands." 450 U.S., at 565. The Court stressed that in *Montana* the pleadings "did not allege that non-Indian hunting and fishing on [non-Indian] reservation lands [had] impaired [the Tribe's reserved hunting and fishing privileges]," *id.*, at 558, n. 6, or "that non-Indian hunting and fishing on fee lands imperil the subsistence or welfare of the Tribe," *id.*, at 566, and that the existing record failed to suggested "that such non-Indian hunting and fishing ... threaten the Tribe's political or economic security." *Ibid.*

determination whether federal law pre-empts the assertion of state authority over nonmembers on a reservation. We stated that that determination does not depend "on mechanical or absolute conceptions of state or tribal sovereignty, but call[s] for a particularized inquiry into the nature of the state, federal, and tribal interests at stake." 448 U.S., at 145.

We also emphasized the special sense in which the doctrine of pre-emption is applied in this context. Although a State will certainly be without jurisdiction if its authority is pre-empted under familiar principles of pre-emption, we cautioned that our prior cases did not limit pre-emption of state laws affecting Indian tribes to only those circumstances. "The unique historical origins of tribal sovereignty" and the federal commitment to tribal self-sufficiency and self-determination make it "treacherous to import ... notions of pre-emption that are properly applied to ... other [contexts]." *Bracker, supra*, at 143. By resting pre-emption analysis principally on a consideration of the nature of the competing interests at stake, our cases have rejected a narrow focus on congressional intent to pre-empt state law as the sole touchstone. They have also rejected the proposition that pre-emption requires "'an express congressional statement to that effect.'" *Bracker, supra*, at 144. State jurisdiction is pre-empted by the operation of federal law if it interferes or is incompatible with federal and tribal interests reflected in federal law, unless the state interests at stake are sufficient to justify the assertion of state authority. *Bracker, supra*, at 145. See also *Ramah Navajo School Bd., supra*, at 845, quoting *Hines v. Davidowitz*, 312 U.S. 52, 67 (1941).[16]

Certain broad considerations guide our assessment of the federal and tribal interests. The traditional notions of Indian sovereignty provide a crucial "backdrop," *Bracker, supra*, at 143, citing *McClanahan, supra*, at 172, against which any assertion of state authority must be assessed. Moreover, both the tribes and the Federal Government are firmly committed to the goal of promoting tribal self-government, a goal embodied in numerous federal statutes.[17] We have stressed that Congress' objective of furthering tribal self-government encompasses far more than encouraging tribal management of disputes between members, but includes Congress' overriding goal of encouraging "tribal self-sufficiency and economic development." *Bracker*, 448 U.S., at 143 (footnote omit-

---

[16] The exercise of state authority may also be barred by an independent barrier — inherent tribal sovereignty — if it "unlawfully infringe[s] 'on the right of reservation Indians to make their own laws and be ruled by them.'" *White Mountain Apache Tribe v. Bracker*, 448 U.S. 136, 142 (1980), quoting *Williams v. Lee*, 358 U.S. 217, 220 (1959).

[17] For example, the Indian Financing Act of 1974, 25 U.S.C. § 1451 et seq. (1976 ed. and Supp. V), states: "It is hereby declared to be the policy of Congress ... to help develop and utilize Indian resources, both physical and human, to a point where the Indians will fully exercise responsibility for the utilization and management of their own resources and where they will enjoy a standard of living from their own productive efforts comparable to that enjoyed by non-Indians in neighboring communities." § 1451. Similar policies underlie the Indian Self-Determination and Education Assistance Act of 1975, 25 U.S.C. § 450 et seq., as well as the Indian Reorganization Act of 1934, 25 U.S.C. § 461 et seq. (1976 ed. and Supp. V), pursuant to which the Mescalero Apache Tribe adopted its Constitution. The "intent and purpose of the Reorganization Act was 'to rehabilitate the Indian's economic life and to give him a chance to develop the initiative destroyed by a century of oppression and paternalism.'" *Mescalero Apache Tribe v. Jones*, 411 U.S. 145, 152 (1973), quoting H.R. Rep. No. 1804, 73d Cong., 2d Sess., 6 (1934). The Indian Civil Rights Act of 1968, 25 U.S.C. § 1301 et seq., likewise reflects Congress' intent "to promote the well-established federal 'policy of furthering Indian self-government.'" *Santa Clara Pueblo v. Martinez*, 436 U.S. 49, 62 (1978), quoting *Morton v. Mancari*, 417 U.S. 535, 551 (1974).

ted). In part as a necessary implication of this broad federal commitment, we have held that tribes have the power to manage the use of their territory and resources by both members and nonmembers,[18] to undertake and regulate economic activity within the reservation, *Merrion*, 455 U.S., at 137, and to defray the cost of governmental services by levying taxes. *Ibid.* Thus, when a tribe undertakes an enterprise under the authority of federal law, an assertion of state authority must be viewed against any interference with the successful accomplishment of the federal purpose. See generally [*Bracker*;] *Ramah Navajo School Bd.*, 458 U.S., at 845, quoting *Hines v. Davidowitz, supra*, at 67 (state authority precluded when it "'stands as an obstacle to the accomplishment of the full purposes and objectives of Congress'").

Our prior decisions also guide our assessment of the state interest asserted to justify state jurisdiction over a reservation. The exercise of state authority which imposes additional burdens on a tribal enterprise must ordinarily be justified by functions or services performed by the State in connection with the on-reservation activity. *Ramah Navajo School Bd., supra*, at 843, and n.7; [*Bracker*; *Central Machinery*] (Powell, J., dissenting). Thus a State seeking to impose a tax on a transaction between a tribe and nonmembers must point to more than its general interest in raising revenues. See, e.g., [*Warren Trading Post; Bracker; Ramah Navajo School Bd.*]. See also [*Colville*], 447 U.S., at 157 ("governmental interest in raising revenues is ... strongest when the tax is directed at off-reservation value and when the taxpayer is the recipient of state services"); *Moe*, 425 U.S., at 481-483 (State may require tribal shops to collect state cigarette tax from nonmember purchasers). A State's regulatory interest will be particularly substantial if the State can point to off-reservation effects that necessitate state intervention. Cf. *Puyallup Tribe v. Washington Game Dept.*, 433 U.S. 165 (1977).

III

With these principles in mind, we turn to New Mexico's claim that it may superimpose its own hunting and fishing regulations on the Mescalero Apache Tribe's regulatory scheme.

A

It is beyond doubt that the Mescalero Apache Tribe lawfully exercises substantial control over the lands and resources of its reservation, including its wildlife. As noted [above], and as conceded by New Mexico,[19] the sovereignty retained by the Tribe under the Treaty of 1852 includes its right to regulate the

---

[18] Our cases have recognized that tribal sovereignty contains a "significant geographical component." *Bracker, supra*, at 151. Thus the off-reservation activities of Indians are generally subject to the prescriptions of a "nondiscriminatory state law" in the absence of "express federal law to the contrary." *Mescalero Apache Tribe v. Jones, supra*, at 148-149.

[19] New Mexico concedes that the Tribe originally relied on wildlife for subsistence, that tribal members freely took fish and game in ancestral territory, and that the Treaty of July 1, 1852, 10 Stat. 979, between the Tribe and the United States confirmed the Tribe's rights regarding hunting and fishing on the small portion of the aboriginal Mescalero domain that was eventually set apart as the Tribe's reservation. See also *United States v. Winans*, 198 U.S. 371, 381 (1905) (recognizing that hunting and fishing "were not much less necessary to the existence of the Indians than the atmosphere they breathed").

use of its resources by members as well as nonmembers. In *Montana v. United States*, we specifically recognized that tribes in general retain this authority.

Moreover, this aspect of tribal sovereignty has been expressly confirmed by numerous federal statutes.[20] Pub. L. 280 specifically confirms the power of tribes to regulate on-reservation hunting and fishing. 67 Stat. 588, 18 U.S.C. § 1162(b); see also 25 U.S.C. § 1321(b). This authority is afforded the protection of the federal criminal law by 18 U.S.C. § 1165, which makes it a violation of federal law to enter Indian land to hunt, trap, or fish without the consent of the tribe. See *Montana v. United States*, 450 U.S., at 562.[21] The 1981 Amendments to the Lacey Act, 16 U.S.C. § 3371 et seq. (1976 ed., Supp. V), further accord tribal hunting and fishing regulations the force of federal law by making it a federal offense "to import, export, transport, sell, receive, acquire, or purchase any fish or wildlife ... taken or possessed in violation of any ... Indian tribal law." § 3372(a)(1).

B

Several considerations strongly support the Court of Appeals' conclusion that the Tribe's authority to regulate hunting and fishing pre-empts state jurisdiction. It is important to emphasize that concurrent jurisdiction would effectively nullify the Tribe's authority to control hunting and fishing on the reservation. Concurrent jurisdiction would empower New Mexico wholly to supplant tribal regulations. The State would be able to dictate the terms on which nonmembers are permitted to utilize the reservation's resources. The Tribe would thus exercise its authority over the reservation only at the sufferance of the State. The tribal authority to regulate hunting and fishing by nonmembers, which has been repeatedly confirmed by federal treaties and laws and which we explicitly recognized in [*Montana*], would have a rather hollow ring if tribal authority amounted to no more than this.

Furthermore, the exercise of concurrent state jurisdiction in this case would completely "disturb and disarrange," *Warren Trading Post Co. v. Arizona Tax Comm'n, supra*, at 691, the comprehensive scheme of federal and tribal management established pursuant to federal law. As described [in *Warren*], federal law requires the Secretary to review each of the Tribe's hunting and fishing ordinances. Those ordinances are based on the recommendations made by a federal range conservationist employed by the Bureau of Indian Affairs. Moreover, the Bureau of Sport Fisheries and Wildlife stocks the reservation's waters based on its own determinations concerning the availability of fish, biological requirements, and the fishing pressure created by on-reservation fishing.[23]

---

[20] The Tribe's authority was also confirmed more generally by the Indian Reorganization Act of 1934, 25 U.S.C. § 476, which reaffirms "all powers vested in any Indian tribe or tribal council by existing law."

[21] The provision of Pub. L. 280 granting States criminal jurisdiction over Indian reservations under certain conditions provides that States are not thereby authorized to

"deprive any Indian or any Indian tribe, band, or community of any right, privilege, or immunity afforded under Federal treaty, agreement, or statute with respect to hunting, trapping, or fishing *or the control, licensing or regulation thereof*." 18 U.S.C. § 1162(b) (emphasis added). The same language is contained in 25 U.S.C. § 1321(b).

[23] In addition, as noted earlier, the Federal Government played a substantial role in the development of the Tribe's resources.

Concurrent state jurisdiction would supplant this regulatory scheme with an inconsistent dual system: members would be governed by tribal ordinances, while nonmembers would be regulated by general state hunting and fishing laws. This could severely hinder the ability of the Tribe to conduct a sound management program. Tribal ordinances reflect the specific needs of the reservation by establishing the optimal level of hunting and fishing that should occur, not simply a maximum level that should not be exceeded. State laws in contrast are based on considerations not necessarily relevant to, and possibly hostile to, the needs of the reservation. For instance, the ordinance permitting a hunter to kill a buck and a doe was designed to curb excessive growth of the deer population on the reservation. Enforcement of the state regulation permitting only buck to be killed would frustrate that objective. Similarly, by determining the tribal hunting seasons, bag limits, and permit availability, the Tribe regulates the duration and intensity of hunting. These determinations take into account numerous factors, including the game capacity of the terrain, the range utilization of the game animals, and the availability of tribal personnel to monitor the hunts. Permitting the State to enforce different restrictions simply because they have been determined to be appropriate for the State as a whole imposed on the Tribe the possibly insurmountable task of ensuring that the patchwork application of state and tribal regulations remains consistent with sound management of the reservation's resources.

Federal law commits to the Secretary and the Tribal Council the responsibility to manage the reservation's resources. It is most unlikely that Congress would have authorized, and the Secretary would have established, financed, and participated in tribal management if it were true that New Mexico was free to nullify the entire arrangement.[24] Requiring tribal ordinances to yield whenever state law is more restrictive would seriously "undermine the Secretary's [and the Tribe's] ability to make the wide range of determinations committed to [their] authority." *Bracker*, 448 U.S., at 149.

The assertion of concurrent jurisdiction by New Mexico not only would threaten to disrupt the federal and tribal regulatory scheme, but would also threaten Congress' overriding objective of encouraging tribal self-government and economic development. The Tribe has engaged in a concerted and sustained undertaking to develop and manage the reservation's wildlife and land resources specifically for the benefit of its members. The project generates funds for essential tribal services and provides employment for members who reside on the reservation. This case is thus far removed from those situations, such as on-reservation sales outlets which market to nonmembers goods not manufactured by the tribe or its members, in which the tribal contribution to an enterprise is de minimis. See [*Colville*].[26] The tribal enterprise in this case

---

[24] The Secretary assumed precisely the opposite is true — that state jurisdiction is pre-empted — when he approved a tribal ordinance which provided that nonmembers hunting and fishing on the reservation need not obtain state licenses. That assumption is also embodied in an agreement between the Tribe and the Department of the Interior's Bureau of Sport Fisheries and Wildlife, [that] openly acknowledges that tribal regulations need not agree with state laws. The agreement provides that "[i]nsofar as possible said regulations shall be in agreement with State regulations." App. 71a. (Emphasis added.)

[26] In [*Colville*] the Court held that the sales of tribal smokeshops which sold cigarettes to nonmembers were subject to the state sales and cigarette taxes. The Court relied on the fact that the

clearly involves "value generated on the reservation by activities involving the Trib[e]." *Id.*, at 156-157. The disruptive effect that would result from the assertion of concurrent jurisdiction by New Mexico would plainly "'stan[d] as an obstacle to the accomplishment of the full purposes and objectives of Congress,'" *Ramah Navajo School Bd.*, 458 U.S., at 845, quoting *Hines v. Davidowitz*, 312 U.S., at 67.

C

The State has failed to "identify the regulatory function or service ... that would justify" the assertion of concurrent regulatory authority. *Bracker, supra*, at 148. The hunting and fishing permitted by the Tribe occur entirely on the reservation. The fish and wildlife resources are either native to the reservation or were created by the joint efforts of the Tribe and the Federal Government. New Mexico does not contribute in any significant respect to the maintenance of these resources, and can point to no other "governmental functions it provides," *Ramah Navajo School Bd., supra*, at 843, in connection with hunting and fishing on the reservation by nonmembers that would justify the assertion of its authority.

The State also cannot point to any off-reservation effects that warrant state intervention. Some species of game never leave tribal lands, and the State points to no specific interest concerning those that occasionally do. Unlike *Puyallup Tribe v. Washington Game Dept.*, this is not a case in which a treaty expressly subjects a tribe's hunting and fishing rights to the common rights of nonmembers and in which a State's interest in conserving a scarce, common supply justifies state intervention. 433 U.S., at 174, 175-177. The State concedes that the Tribe's management has "not had an adverse impact on fish and wildlife outside the Reservation." App. to Brief in Opposition 35a....

IV

In this case the governing body of an Indian Tribe, working closely with the Federal Government and under the authority of federal law, has exercised its lawful authority to develop and manage the reservation's resources for the benefit of its members. The exercise of concurrent jurisdiction by the State would effectively nullify the Tribe's unquestioned authority to regulate the use of its resources by members and nonmembers, interfere with the comprehensive tribal regulatory scheme, and threaten Congress' firm commitment to the encouragement of tribal self-sufficiency and economic development. Given the strong interests favoring exclusive tribal jurisdiction and the absence of state interests which justify the assertion of concurrent authority, we conclude that the application of the State's hunting and fishing laws to the reservation is preempted.

[*Affirmed*].

NOTES

1. The Importance of Federal Indian Law Preemption Doctrines: Notions of preemption derived from the supremacy clause of article IV of the Constitu-

---

tribal smokeshops were not marketing "value generated on the reservation," but instead were seeking merely to market a "tax exemption to nonmembers who do not receive significant tribal services."

tion resolve many jurisdictional disputes involving states' claims to authority in Indian country. Since cases like *Moe* and *Colville* suggest that states have some inherent authority over non-Indians in Indian country, preemption doctrines are particularly critical where, as in the three preceding cases, non-Indians are involved in business dealings with Indians either as suppliers or as customers. While the framers of the Constitution probably intended the Indian commerce clause to deprive states of any claims to authority over such transactions, the modern caselaw has not sustained that role for dormant Indian commerce clause claims. Rather, as suggested in *Colville*, the modern role of dormant Indian commerce clause doctrine is to prevent states from discriminating against or placing undue burdens upon such Indian commerce. By default, the primary role of structuring state power in this area therefore has fallen to statutory preemption doctrines of the type exemplified in the preceding cases.

While the courts use the term preemption as if it referred to a single doctrine, actually a broad range of approaches recently has been lumped together under this general rubric. For example, in *Central Machinery* and in the *Warren Trading Post* case upon which it relies, one critical regulatory statute, the Federal Licensed Trader Act, Act of July 22, 1790, ch. 33, 1 Stat. 137, codified as amended at 25 U.S.C. § 261, preempted state authority to tax the transactions of even off-reservation non-Indian vendors subject to the regulatory regime of the Act, even if they had failed to comply with the Act by securing the required licenses. By contrast, in *White Mountain Apache*, *Mescalero Apache*, and the *Cabazon* case, set forth in Chapter 2, section D and discussed further below, the complex patterns of factors suggesting federal administrative support for or supervision of various Indian activities preempted the application of state law.

The preemption principles of *White Mountain Apache Tribe* were reaffirmed in *Ramah Navajo School Bd., Inc. v. Bureau of Revenue*, 458 U.S. 832 (1982). In *Ramah* the Supreme Court held that New Mexico's attempt to impose a gross receipts tax on a non-Indian construction company involved in the construction of a school for Indian children on the Navajo Reservation was preempted by federal law. The Navajo tribal organization had contracted with the BIA for the construction of the new school, and the tribe then subcontracted, subject to BIA approval, with the non-Indian construction company that did business both on and off the reservation. The Court relied on several congressional statutes that authorized the BIA to provide for Indian education, both on and off the reservation, including the Snyder Act, 25 U.S.C. § 13, the Johnson-O'Malley Act, 25 U.S.C. § 452 et seq., the Navajo-Hopi Rehabilitation Act, 25 U.S.C. § 631 et seq., and the Indian Self-Determination and Education Assistance Act, 25 U.S.C. § 450 et seq. The Court noted that federal education policies had recently shifted toward encouraging Indian-controlled educational institutions on the reservation, reflected in the Indian Self-Determination and Education Assistance Act of 1975. Pursuant to these statutes, the Secretary of the Interior had promulgated regulations now found in 25 C.F.R. pt. 274, for "school construction for previously private schools now controlled and operated by tribes." *Id.* at 840-41 *quoting* 25 C.F.R. § 274.1 (1981). The Court held that the burden of the state tax, "although nominally falling on the non-Indian contractor, necessarily impedes the clearly expressed federal interest in promoting the 'quality and quantity' of educational opportunities for Indians for depleting the funds available for the construction of Indian schools." *Id.* at 842.

In his dissent in *Ramah*, Justice Rehnquist objected that the majority was more concerned with the extent of economic burden on the tribe than with the preemptive effect of federal regulations. He claimed that the regulatory scheme relied upon in *Ramah* to demonstrate comprehensive and pervasive federal regulation of the subject matter amounted to little more than a grant application process, detailing procedures by which tribes may apply for federal funds in order to carry out school construction.

Is it clear that the asserted state tax in this case would obstruct the federal policy, particularly if the cost of construction is assumed to include various applicable taxes? Although the economic burden of the state-imposed gross receipts tax was held to fall on the tribe in *Ramah*, the tribe was paying for the construction of the school through congressional appropriations earmarked for that purpose. In *United States v. New Mexico*, 455 U.S. 720 (1982), decided the same term as *Ramah*, the Court held in a non-Indian context that New Mexico could impose its gross receipts, sales, and compensating use taxes on private contractors that conduct business with the federal government and that "immunity may not be conferred simply because the tax has an effect on the United States, or even because the federal government shoulders the entire economic burden of the levy." Are these principles of inter-governmental tax immunity relevant to the Indian preemption analysis? Does *Ramah* suggest that where a tribe is acting to effect congressionally expressed policies, any state tax whose economic burden ultimately falls on the tribe, irrespective of the legal incidence of the tax, will be preempted?

RICE v. REHNER

463 U.S. 713 (1983)

Justice O'CONNOR delivered the opinion of the Court.

The question presented by this case is whether the State of California may require a federally licensed Indian trader, who operates a general store on an Indian reservation, to obtain a state liquor license in order to sell liquor for off-premises consumption. Because we find that Congress has delegated authority to the States as well as to the Indian tribes to regulate the use and distribution of alcoholic beverages in Indian country, we reverse the judgment of the Court of Appeals for the Ninth Circuit.

I

The respondent Rehner is a federally licensed Indian trader[2] who operates a general store on the Pala Reservation in San Diego, California. The Pala Tribe had adopted a tribal ordinance permitting the sale of liquor on the reservation providing that the sales conformed to state law, and this ordinance was approved by the Secretary of the Interior. See 25 Fed. Reg. 3343 (1960). Rehner then sought from the State an exemption from its law requiring a state license for retail sale of distilled spirits for off-premises consumption.[3] When she was refused an exemption, Rehner filed suit seeking a declaratory judgment that

---

[2] There is some confusion among the parties and amici as to whether the court below held that the tribes had exclusive jurisdiction over the licensing and distribution of liquor on reservations irrespective of the identity of the vendor. Although we acknowledge that the decision below is somewhat ambiguous in this respect, we construe the opinion as applying only to vendors, like Rehner, who are members of the governing tribe.

[3] The California licensing scheme is found in Cal. Bus. & Prof. Code Ann. §§ 23000 et seq. (West).

she did not need a license from the State, and an order directing that liquor wholesalers could sell to her. The District Court granted the State's motion to dismiss, ruling that Rehner was required to have a state license under [a federal law][4] [and this appeal followed].

II

The decisions of this Court concerning the principles to be applied in determining whether state regulation of activities in Indian country is preempted have not been static. In [*Worcester v. Georgia*], Chief Justice Marshall wrote that an Indian reservation "is a distinct community, occupying its own territory, with boundaries accurately described, in which ... [state laws] can have no force ...." Despite this early statement emphasizing the importance of tribal self-government, "Congress has to a substantial degree opened the doors of reservations to state laws, in marked contrast to what prevailed in the time of Chief Justice Marshall," *Organized Village of Kake v. Egan*, 369 U.S. 60, 74 (1962). "[E]ven on reservations, state laws may be applied unless such application would interfere with reservation self-government or would impair a right granted or reserved by federal law." *Mescalero Apache Tribe v. Jones*, 411 U.S. 145, 148 (1973) (hereafter *Mescalero Apache Tribe*).

Although "[f]ederal treaties and statutes have been consistently construed to reserve the right of self-government to the tribes," Cohen's Handbook of Federal Indian Law 273 (1982) [hereafter Cohen], [this Court has more recently] employed a pre-emption analysis that is informed by historical notions of tribal sovereignty, rather than determined by them. "[C]ongressional authority and the 'semi-independent position' of Indian tribes ... [are] ... two independent but related barriers to the assertion of state regulatory authority over tribal reservations and members." *Bracker, supra*, 448 U.S., at 142. Although "[t]he right of tribal self-government is ultimately dependent on and subject to the broad power of Congress," *id.*, at 143, we still employ the tradition of Indian sovereignty as a "backdrop against which the applicable treaties and federal statutes must be read" in our pre-emption analysis. *McClanahan, supra*, 411 U.S., at 172. We do not necessarily require that Congress explicitly pre-empt assertion of state authority insofar as Indians on reservations are concerned, but we have recognized that "any applicable regulatory interest of the State must be given weight" and "'automatic exemptions "as a matter of constitutional law"'" are unusual." *Bracker, supra*, 448 U.S., at 144 (quoting *Moe v. Salish & Kootenai Tribes*, 425 U.S. 463, 481, n.17 (1976)).

The role of tribal sovereignty in pre-emption analysis varies in accordance with the particular "notions of sovereignty that have developed from historical traditions of tribal independence." *Bracker, supra*, 448 U.S., at 145. These traditions themselves reflect the "accommodation between the interests of the

---

[4][18 U.S.C.] Section 1161 provides:

"The provisions of sections 1154, 1156, 3113, 3488, and 3618, of this title, shall not apply within any area that is not Indian country, nor to any act or transaction within any area of Indian country provided such act or transaction is in conformity both with the laws of the State in which such act or transaction occurs and with an ordinance duly adopted by the tribe having jurisdiction over such area of Indian country, certified by the Secretary of the Interior, and published in the Federal Register."

Tribes and the Federal Government, on the one hand, and those of the State, on the other." [*Colville*.] However, it must be remembered that "tribal sovereignty is dependent on, and subordinate to, only the Federal Government, not the States." *Id.*, at 154. "The sovereignty that the Indian tribes retain is of a unique and limited character. It exists only at the sufferance of Congress and *is subject to complete defeasance*." *United States v. Wheeler*, 435 U.S. 313, 323 (1978) (emphasis added). *See also Confederated Tribes, supra*, 447 U.S., at 178-179 (opinion of REHNQUIST, J.).

When we determine that tradition has recognized a sovereign immunity in favor of the Indians in some respect, then we usually are reluctant to infer that Congress has authorized the assertion of state authority in that respect "'except where Congress has expressly provided that State laws shall apply.'" *McClanahan, supra*, 411 U.S., at 171 (quoting U.S. Dept. of the Interior, Federal Indian Law 845 (1958) (hereafter Indian Law)). Repeal by implication of an established tradition of immunity or self-governance is disfavored. *Bryan v. Itasca County*, 426 U.S. 373, at 392. If, however, we do not find such a tradition, or if we determine that the balance of state, federal, and tribal interests so requires, our pre-emption analysis may accord less weight to the "backdrop" of tribal sovereignty.

A

We first determine the nature of the "backdrop" of tribal sovereignty that will inform our pre-emption analysis. The "backdrop" in this case concerns the licensing and distribution of alcoholic beverages, and we must determine whether there is a tradition of tribal sovereign immunity that may be repealed only by an explicit directive from Congress.

We begin by noting that [t]o the extent that Rehner seeks to sell to non-Indians, or to Indians who are not members of the tribe with jurisdiction over the reservation on which the sale occurred, the decisions of this Court have already foreclosed Rehner's argument that the licensing requirements infringe upon tribal sovereignty.

If there is any interest in tribal sovereignty implicated by imposition of California's alcoholic beverage regulation, it exists only insofar as the State attempts to regulate Rehner's sale of liquor to other members of the Pala Tribe on the Pala reservation. The only interest that Rehner advances in this regard is that freedom to regulate alcoholic beverages is important to Indian self-governance. To the extent California limits the absolute number of licenses that it distributes, state regulation may effectively preclude this aspect of self-governance. Rehner relies on our statement in *United States v. Mazurie*, 419 U.S. 544, 557 (1975), that the distribution and use of intoxicants is a "matte[r] that affect[s] the internal and social relations of tribal life."

Rehner's reliance on *Mazurie* as establishing tribal sovereignty in the area of liquor licensing and distribution is misplaced. In *Mazurie*, we held that "independent tribal authority is quite sufficient to protect Congress' decision to vest in tribal councils this portion of [*Congress'*] *own authority*" to regulate commerce with the Indians. *Ibid.* (emphasis added). We expressly declined to base our holding on whether "independent [tribal] authority *is itself* sufficient for the tribes to impose" their own liquor regulations. *Ibid.* (emphasis added).

The reason that we declined is apparent in the light of the history of federal control of liquor in this context, which must be characterized as "one of the most comprehensive [federal] activities in Indian affairs ...." Cohen, at 307. Unlike the authority to tax certain transactions on reservations that we have characterized as "a fundamental attribute of sovereignty which the tribes retain unless divested of it by federal law or necessary implication of their dependent status," [*Colville*] at 152, tradition simply has not recognized a sovereign immunity or inherent authority in favor of liquor regulation by Indians. The colonists regulated Indian liquor trading before this Nation was formed, and Congress exercised its authority over these transactions as early as 1802. Congress imposed complete prohibition by 1832, and these prohibitions are still in effect subject to suspension conditioned on compliance with state law and tribal ordinance.

Although in Indian matters, Congress usually acts "upon the assumption that the States have no power to regulate the affairs of Indians on a reservation," *Williams v. Lee*, 358 U.S. 217, 220 (1959), that assumption would be unwarranted in the narrow context of the regulation of liquor. In addition to the congressional divestment of tribal self-government in this area, the States have also been permitted, and even required, to impose regulations related to liquor transactions. As a condition of entry into the United States, Arizona, New Mexico, and Oklahoma were required by Congress to enact prohibitions against the sale of liquor to Indians and introduction of liquor into Indian country.[9] Several states, including California, pursuant to state police power, long prohibited liquor transactions with Indians. These state prohibitions indicate that "'absolute' federal jurisdiction is not invariably exclusive jurisdiction." *Kake Village, supra*, 369 U.S., at 68. Indeed, we have recognized expressly that "[t]he federal prohibition against taking intoxicants into this Indian colony does not deprive the State of Nevada of its sovereignty over the area in question. The Federal Government does not assert exclusive jurisdiction within the colony. Enactments of the Federal Government passed to protect and guard its Indian wards only affect the operation, within the colony, of such state laws *as conflict with the federal enactments*." *United States v. McGowan*, 302 U.S. 535, 539 (1938) (footnote omitted) (emphasis added).

This historical tradition of concurrent state and federal jurisdiction over the use and distribution of alcoholic beverages in Indian country is justified by the relevant state interests involved. Rehner's distribution of liquor has a significant impact beyond the limits of the Pala Reservation. The State has an unquestionable interest in the liquor traffic that occurs within its borders, and this interest is independent of the authority conferred on the States by the Twenty-first Amendment. *Crowley v. Christensen*, 137 U.S. 86, 91 (1890). Liquor sold by Rehner to other Pala tribal members or to non-members can easily find its way out of the reservation and into the hands of those whom, for whatever reason, the State does not wish to possess alcoholic beverages, or to possess them

---

[9]See Ariz. Const., art. 20, § 3 (prohibition removed in 1954); N.M. Const., art. 21, § 1 (prohibition removed in 1953); Okla. Const., art. 1, § 7 (prohibition removed in 1959).

through a distribution network over which the State has no control. This particular "spillover" effect is qualitatively different from any "spillover" effects of income taxes or taxes on cigarettes. "A State's regulatory interest will be particularly substantial if the State can point to off-reservation effects that necessitate State intervention." *New Mexico v. Mescalero Apache Tribe*, 462 U.S. 324, 336 (1983).

There can be no doubt that Congress has divested the Indians of any inherent power to regulate in this area. In the area of liquor regulation, we find no "congressional enactments demonstrating a firm federal policy of promoting tribal self-sufficiency and economic development." *Bracker, supra*, 448 U.S., at 143 (footnote omitted). With respect to the regulation of liquor transactions, as opposed to the state income taxation involved in *McClanahan*, Indians cannot be said to "possess the usual accoutrements of tribal self-government." *McClanahan, supra*, 411 U.S., at 167-168.

The court below erred in thinking that there was some single notion of tribal sovereignty that served to direct any preemption analysis involving Indians. Because we find that there is no tradition of sovereign immunity that favors the Indians in this respect, and because we must consider that the activity in which Rehner seeks to engage potentially has a substantial impact beyond the reservation, we may accord little if any weight to any asserted interest in tribal sovereignty in this case.

B

We must next determine whether the State authority to license the sale of liquor is pre-empted by federal law. [Below, the court] held that § 1161 preempted state regulation of licensing and distribution, and that the reference to state law in § 1161 was not sufficiently explicit to permit application of the state licensing law.

We disagree with both aspects of the court's analysis. As we explained in II A above, the tribes have long ago been divested of any inherent self-government over liquor regulation by both the explicit command of Congress and "as a necessary implication of their dependent status." [Furthermore, Congress] has also historically permitted concurrent state regulation through the imposition of criminal penalties on those who supply Indians with liquor, or who introduce liquor into Indian country. Therefore, this is not a case in which we apply a presumption of a lack of state authority.

The presumption of preemption derives from the rule against construing legislation to repeal by implication some aspect of tribal self-government. See *Bryan v. Itasca County*, 426 U.S. 373, 391-392 (1976); *Morton v. Mancari*, 417 U.S. 535, 549-551 (1974). Because there is no aspect of exclusive tribal self-government that requires the deference reflected in our requirement that Congress expressly provide for the application of state law, we have only to determine whether application of the state licensing laws would "impair a right granted or reserved by federal law." [By enacting section 1161] Congress authorized, rather than pre-empted, state regulation over Indian liquor transactions.

[A review of the legislative history indicates] that Congress viewed § 1161 as abolishing federal prohibition, and as legalizing Indian liquor transactions as long as those transactions conformed both with tribal ordinance and state law. It is also clear that Congress contemplated that its absolute but not exclusive power to regulate Indian liquor transactions would be delegated to the tribes themselves, and to the States, which historically shared concurrent jurisdiction with the federal government in this area. Early administrative practice and our prior decision in *United States v. Mazurie, supra*, confirm this understanding of § 1161.

[The Ninth Circuit and Rehner both] believed that § 1161 was merely an exemption from *federal* criminal liability, and affirmatively empowered neither Indian tribes nor the State to regulate liquor transactions. [*Mazurie*] rejected this argument with respect to Indian tribes, and there is no reason to accept it with respect to the State. In *Mazurie* we held that in enacting § 1161 Congress intended to *delegate* to the tribes a portion of its authority over liquor transactions on reservations. Since we found this delegation on the basis of the statutory language requiring that liquor transactions conform "*both* with the laws of the State ... and with an ordinance duly adopted" by the governing tribe (emphasis added), we would ignore the plain language of the statute if we failed to find this same delegation in favor of the States.[14] The thrust of Rehner's argument, and the primary focus of the court below, is that state authority in this area is preempted because such authority requires an express statement by Congress in the light of the canon of construction that we quoted in *McClanahan*: "'State laws generally are not applicable to tribal Indians on an Indian reservation except where Congress has expressly provided that State laws shall apply.'" 411 U.S., at 170-171 (quoting Indian Law, at 845). As we have established above, because of the lack of a tradition of self-government in the area of liquor regulation, it is not necessary that Congress indicate expressly that the State has jurisdiction to regulate the licensing and distribution of alcohol.[15]

Even if this canon of construction were applicable to this case, our result would be the same. The canon is quoted from the 1958 edition of the Federal Indian Law, published by the Dept. of the Interior. See Indian Law, at 845. In that same volume, the Solicitor of the Interior assumed that § 1161 would result in state prosecutions for failing to have a state license. See *id.*, at 382-383. Whatever Congress had to do to provide "expressly" for the application of state law, the Solicitor obviously believed that Congress had done it in § 1161. Indeed, even in *McClanahan*, we suggested that § 1161 satisfied the canon of

---

[14] Indeed, given the history of concurrent state jurisdiction and the tradition of complete prohibition imposed on the Indians, the delegation to the States is more readily apparent than the delegation to the tribes.

[15] This canon is based, in part, on the notion that we normally resolve any doubt in a pre-emption analysis in favor of the Indians because of their status as "wards of the nation." *McClanahan v. Arizona State Tax Commission*, 411 U.S. 164, 174 (1973) (quoting *Carpenter v. Shaw*, 280 U.S. 363, 367 (1930)). Even if this canon properly informed a pre-emption analysis that involved a historic tradition of federal and state regulation, its application in the context of liquor licensing and distribution would be problematic. Liquor trade has been regulated among the Indians largely due to early attempts by the tribes themselves to seek assistance in controlling Indian access to liquor. See Talk delivered by Little Turtle to President Thomas Jefferson on January 4, 1802, reprinted in IV American State Papers, Indian Affairs, Vol. I, Class II, at 655 (1802). In many respects, the concerns about liquor expressed by the tribes were responsible for the development of the dependent status of the tribes. When the substance to be regulated is that primarily responsible for "dependent" status, it makes no sense to say that the historical position of Indians as federal "wards" militates in favor of giving exclusive control over licensing and distribution to the tribes.

construction requiring that Congress expressly provide for application of state law. In discussing statutes that did satisfy the canon, we cited § 1161 and stated that "state liquor laws may be applicable within reservations." 411 U.S., at 177, n.16. More important, we have consistently refused to apply such a canon of construction when application would be tantamount to a formalistic disregard of congressional intent. "We give this rule [resolving ambiguities in favor of Indians] the broadest possible scope, but it remains at base a canon for construing the complex treaties, statutes, and contracts which define the status of Indian tribes. A canon of construction is not a license to disregard clear expressions of tribal and congressional intent." *DeCoteau v. District County Court*, 420 U.S. 425, 447 (1975). See also *Andrus v. Glover Construction Co.*, 446 U.S. 608, 619 (1980). In the present case, congressional intent is clear from the face of the statute and its legislative history.

[In conclusion,] § 1161 was intended to remove federal discrimination that resulted from the imposition of liquor prohibition on Native Americans. Congress was well aware that the Indians never enjoyed a tradition of tribal self-government insofar as liquor transactions were concerned. Congress was also aware that the States exercised concurrent authority insofar as prohibiting liquor transactions with Indians was concerned. By enacting § 1161, Congress intended to delegate a portion of its authority to the tribes as well as to the States, so as to fill the void that would be created by the absence of the discriminatory federal prohibition. Congress did not intend to make tribal members "super citizens" who could trade in a traditionally regulated substance free from all but self-imposed regulations. See 678 F.2d, at 1352 (Goodwin, J., dissenting). Rather, we believe that in enacting § 1161, Congress intended to recognize that Native Americans are not "weak and defenseless," and are capable of making personal decisions about alcohol consumption without special assistance from the Federal Government. Application of the state licensing scheme does not "impair a right granted or reserved by federal law." *Kake Village, supra*, 369 U.S., at 75. On the contrary, such application of state law is "specifically authorized by ... Congress ... and [does] not interfere with federal policies concerning the reservations." *Warren Trading Post Co. v. Arizona Tax Commission*, 380 U.S. 685, 687, n.3 (1965).

[*Reversed and Remanded.*]

Justice BLACKMUN, with whom Justice BRENNAN and Justice MARSHALL join, dissenting.

The Court today holds that a State may prevent a federally licensed Indian trader from selling liquor on an Indian reservation, or may condition the trader's right to sell liquor upon payment of a substantial license fee. Because I believe the State lacks authority to require a license, I dissent. Since 1790, see Act of July 22, 1790, 1 Stat. 137, the Federal Government has regulated trade with the Indians and has required persons engaging in such trade to obtain a federal license. Existing law provides: "The Commissioner of Indian Affairs shall have the *sole* power and authority to appoint traders to the Indian tribes and to make such rules and regulations as he may deem just and proper specifying the kind and quantity of goods and the prices at which such goods shall be sold to the Indians." Act of Aug. 15, 1876, ch. 289, § 5, 19 Stat. 200, 25 U.S.C. § 261 (emphasis added).

A person wishing to trade with the Indians is "permitted to do so under such rules and regulations as the Commissioner of Indian Affairs may prescribe," once he has established "to the satisfaction of the Commissioner ... that he is a proper person to engage in such trade." Act of Mar. 3, 1901, ch. 832, § 1, 31 Stat. 1066, as amended by the Act of Mar. 3, 1903, ch. 994, § 10, 32 Stat. 1009, 25 U.S.C. § 262.

Pursuant to this statutory authority, the Commissioner of Indian Affairs has promulgated detailed regulations governing the licensing and conduct of Indian traders. [T]he Court [has] stated that these statutes and regulations "would seem in themselves sufficient to show that Congress has taken the business of Indian trading on reservations so fully in hand that no room remains for state laws imposing additional burdens upon traders." [*Warren Trading Post.*] The Court held that a State could not levy a gross proceeds tax upon the income of a licensed Indian trader, reasoning that imposition of the tax "would to a substantial extent frustrate the evident congressional purpose of ensuring that no burden shall be imposed upon Indian traders ... except as authorized by Acts of Congress or by valid regulations promulgated under those Acts. This state tax on gross income would put financial burdens on [the trader] or the Indians with whom it deals in addition to those Congress or the tribes have prescribed, and could thereby disturb and disarrange the statutory plan Congress set up...." *Id.*, at 691....

The Court does not explain how it reconciles California's liquor licensing requirement with federal law governing Indian traders. Instead, the Court appears to rest its conclusion on three propositions. First, the Court asserts that "tradition simply has not recognized a sovereign immunity or inherent authority in favor of liquor regulation by Indians." Second, the Court finds a "historical tradition of concurrent state and federal jurisdiction over the use and distribution of alcoholic beverages in Indian country." Third, the Court concludes that Congress "authorized ... state regulation over Indian liquor transactions" by enacting 18 U.S.C. § 1161. None of these propositions supports the Court's conclusion.

The Court gives far too much weight to the fact that Indian tribes historically have not exercised regulatory authority over sales of liquor. In prior preemption cases, the Court's focus properly and consistently has been on the reach and comprehensiveness of applicable federal law, colored by the recognition that "traditional notions of Indian self-government are so deeply engrained in our jurisprudence that they have provided an important 'backdrop' ... against which vague or ambiguous federal enactments must always be measured." [*Bracker*] quoting [*McClanahan*]. The Court's analysis has never turned on whether the particular area being regulated is one traditionally within the tribe's control. In *Ramah Navajo School Board, Inc. v. Bureau of Revenue*, 458 U.S. 832 (1982), for example, the Court held that comprehensive and pervasive federal regulation of Indian schools precluded the imposition of a state tax on construction of such a school. The Court did not find it relevant that federal policy had not "encourag[ed] the development of Indian-controlled institutions" until the early 1970's, *id.*, at 840, or that the school in question was "the first independent Indian school in modern times," *id.*, at 834. In *Moe v. Salish & Kootenai Tribes*, 425 U.S. 463 (1976), the Court held that a State could not require the operator of an on-reservation "smoke shop" to obtain a state cigarette retailer's license; the Court did not inquire whether tribal Indians traditionally had exercised regulatory authority over cigarette sales. And in *Mescalero Apache Tribe v. Jones*, 411 U.S. 145 (1973), the Court concluded that a State could not impose a use tax on personalty installed in ski lifts at a tribal resort, yet it could scarcely be argued that the construction of ski resorts is a matter with which Indian tribes historically have been concerned.

It is hardly surprising, given the once-prevalent view of Indians as a dependent people in need of constant federal protection and supervision, that tribal authority until recent times has not extended to areas such as education, cigarette retailing, and development of resorts. State authority has been pre-empted in these areas not because they fall within the tribes' historic powers, but rather because federal policy favors leaving Indians free from state control, and because federal law is sufficiently comprehensive to bar the States' exercise of authority. And "[c]ontrol of liquor has historically been one of the most comprehensive federal activities in Indian affairs." F. Cohen, Handbook of Federal Indian Law 307 (1982 ed.). Federal regulation began in 1802, Act of Mar. 30, 1802, § 21, 2 Stat. 146, and sales of liquor to Indians or in Indian country were absolutely prohibited by federal law until 1953. See 18 U.S.C. §§ 1154, 1156.

In light of this absolute prohibition, the Court's reliance in this case upon what it perceives as a "historical tradition of concurrent state and federal jurisdiction over the use and distribution of alcoholic beverages in Indian country," is disingenuous at best. The Court correctly notes that States were permitted, and in some instances required, to enforce these federal prohibitions through their own criminal laws. But the sources cited by the Court do not even suggest that the States had independent authority to decide who might sell liquor in Indian country, or to impose regulations in addition to those found in federal law.

The only possible source of State authority to regulate liquor sales, and the source upon which the Court ultimately relies, is 18 U.S.C. § 1161. This statute provides that various federal criminal prohibitions against the sale of liquor in Indian country shall not apply to sales "in conformity both with the laws of the State ... and with an ordinance duly adopted by the tribe having jurisdiction over [the] area ...." Section 1161 operates as "local-option legislation allowing Indian tribes, with the approval of the Secretary of the Interior, to regulate the introduction of liquor into Indian country, so long as state law [is] not violated." *United States v. Mazurie*, 419 U.S. 544, 547 (1975). As is demonstrated by the Court's review of the legislative history, and indeed by the language of the statute itself, § 1161 ensures that sales of liquor that would be contrary to state law remain prohibited by federal statute. If a State is altogether "dry," Indian country within that State must be "dry" as well. If a State bans liquor sales to minors or liquor sales on Sundays, sales to minors and Sunday sales also are forbidden in the Indian country. Section 1161, in other words, as the Court has said in the past, "permit[s] application of state liquor law *standards* within an

Indian reservation." *Warren Trading Post Co.* v. *Arizona Tax Comm'n*, 380 U.S., at 687, n.3 (emphasis added).[16] ...

[In conclusion, the] Court obviously argues to a result that it strongly feels is desirable and good. But that, however strong the feelings may be, is activism in which this Court should not indulge. I therefore dissent.

CALIFORNIA v. CABAZON BAND OF MISSION INDIANS

480 U.S. 202 (1987)

[The *Cabazon* case found that state bingo and other regulatory gaming laws could not be applied to Indian activities in Indian country in part because loans and grants from the Department of the Interior and the Department of Housing and Urban Development demonstrated the federal government's approval and active promotion of Indian bingo activities. The *Cabazon* decision is set forth in Chapter 2, page 296.]

NOTE: THE SIGNIFICANCE OF *RICE* AND *CABAZON*

In light of the existence of a congressional statute in *Rice*, should not the decision have turned on the Court's interpretation of the legislative purposes of the statute? Of what relevance is the history of liquor regulation in Indian country or the lack of any tribal tradition of controlling liquor in light of the pervasive federal regulation that previously existed in this area? The Court's preoccupation with such questions and the peripheral role that the somewhat ambiguous legislative history of section 1161 played in *Rice* suggested that the Court might use the *Rice* rationale to enlarge state authority over Indians in Indian country, even in the absence of controlling federal legislation. If a tribe traditionally had not regulated an area, whether air pollution, toxic wastes, zoning, or gaming, states might argue that, absent any history of tribal governance of the field, the federal preemption of state authority in the area should be reduced or found lacking. In light of *Cabazon*, it appears that *Rice* will not play this role. While gaming was common in Indian tribes, extensive tribal regulation of Indian gaming operations serving both non-Indian and Indian clients was historically unknown. Furthermore, just like the liquor regulations involved in *Rice*, the gaming operations were said to have externalities off the reservation. Nevertheless, in *Cabazon*, the Court did not rely on the analysis in *Rice* and, instead, suggested that the state gaming laws were preempted by federal law. The *Cabazon* case therefore suggests that some of the more expansive dicta regarding state authority in *Rice* should be read skeptically.

A further problem with the *Rice* analysis is the manner in which it locks Indian tribes into *historical* conceptions of their sovereignty and precludes Indian polities from evolving to meet the new demands of modern tribal societies. Indian tribes, like all societies and governments, are continually evolving as they cope with new and changing internal and external demands. *Cf.* F. COHEN,

---

[16] Since California exercises general criminal jurisdiction over Indian country pursuant to § 2 of Pub. L. 280, 67 Stat. 588, 18 U.S.C. § 1162, it may enforce directly any substantive criminal provisions governing liquor sales on Indian reservations. For example, it is a misdemeanor under California law to sell or furnish liquor to a minor, Cal. Bus. & Prof. Code Ann. § 25658 (West 1964); this provision is as applicable in Indian country as elsewhere.

HANDBOOK OF FEDERAL INDIAN LAW 288 (1942 ed.) (cautioning against a menagerie theory of Indian property rights that denied Indians ownership because they merely roamed over their property). Near extinction of the buffalo herds, loss of vital hunting or fishing areas, and other changes forced Indian tribes to adapt their cultural practices to new circumstances. Does Justice O'Connor's opinion in *Rice v. Rehner* fall prey to a menagerie theory of Indian law that treats Indian reservations as historic human zoos? Does this approach risk curtailing tribal sovereignty in ways that preordain tribal failures for want of authority in coping with new and changing tribal problems?

COTTON PETROLEUM CORP. v. NEW MEXICO

490 U.S. 163 (1989)

Justice STEVENS delivered the opinion of the Court.

This case is a sequel to *Merrion v. Jicarilla Apache Tribe*, 455 U.S. 130 (1982),* in which we held that the Jicarilla Apache Tribe (Tribe) has the power to impose a severance tax on the production of oil and gas by non-Indian lessees of wells located on the Tribe's reservation. We must now decide whether the State of New Mexico can continue to impose its severance taxes on the same production of oil and gas.

I

All 742,135 acres of the Jicarilla Apache Reservation are located in northwestern New Mexico [on a reservation created by executive order].

The Tribe, which consists of approximately 2500 enrolled members, is organized under the [IRA]. The Indian Mineral Leasing Act of 1938 grants the Tribe authority, subject to the approval of the Secretary of the Interior (Secretary), to execute mineral leases. 52 Stat. 347, 25 U.S.C. § 396a et seq. Since at least as early as 1953, the Tribe has been leasing reservation lands to non-members for the production of oil and gas. [Such mineral leases currently] encompass a substantial portion of the reservation and constitute the primary source of the Tribe's general operating revenues. In 1969, the Secretary approved an amendment to the Tribe's Constitution authorizing it to enact ordinances, subject to his approval, imposing taxes on non-members doing business in the reservation. The Tribe enacted such an ordinance in 1976, imposing a severance tax on "any oil and natural gas severed, saved and removed from Tribal lands." Oil and Gas Severance Tax, Ordinance No. 77-0-02, Jicarilla Apache Tribal Code, Tit. II, ch. 1 (1978) (Equity) (hereinafter J.A.T.C.). [The Secretary of the Interior approved the ordinance in 1976] and in 1982 this Court upheld the Tribe's power to impose a severance tax on pre-existing as well as future leases. See *Merrion*. Subsequently, the Tribe enacted a privilege tax, which the Secretary also approved. See Oil and Gas Privilege Tax, Ordinance No. 85-0-434 (1985), J.A.T.C. Tit. II, ch. 2.[2]

---

*[*Merrion* is set forth and discussed in Chapter 3, section D5 — Eds.]

[2] Effective January 1, 1988, the Tribe added a third tax, which is based on the value of possessory interests — including leasehold interests — held by taxpayers on the reservation. [Since] Cotton does not seek refund of state taxes paid after the possessory interest tax took effect, and because this tax was not enacted until after the New Mexico Court of Appeals issued its decision, we leave it to the side for purposes of our decision.

In 1976, Cotton Petroleum Corporation (Cotton), a non-Indian company in the business of extracting and marketing oil and gas, acquired five leases covering approximately 15,000 acres of the reservation. There were then 15 operating wells on the leased acreage and Cotton has since drilled another 50 wells. The leases were issued by the Tribe and the United States under the authority of the Indian Mineral Leasing Act of 1938. Pursuant to the terms of the leases, Cotton pays the Tribe a rent of $125 per acre, plus a royalty of 12½ percent of the value of its production. In addition, Cotton pays the Tribe's oil and gas severance and privilege taxes, which amount to approximately six percent of the value of its production. Thus, Cotton's aggregate payment to the Tribe includes an acreage rent in excess of one million dollars, plus royalties and taxes amounting to about 18½ percent of its production.

Prior to 1982, Cotton paid, without objection, five different oil and gas production taxes to the State of New Mexico. The state taxes amount to about eight percent of the value of Cotton's production. The same eight percent is collected from producers throughout the State. Thus, on wells outside the reservation, the total tax burden is only eight percent, while Cotton's reservation wells are taxed at a total rate of 14 percent (eight percent by the State and six percent by the Tribe). No state tax is imposed on the royalties received by the Tribe.

At the end of our opinion in *Merrion*, 455 U.S., at 158-159, n.26, we added a footnote rejecting the taxpayer's argument that the tribal tax was invalid as a "multiple tax burden on interstate commerce" because imposed on the same activity already taxed by the State. One of the reasons the argument failed was that the taxpayer had made no attempt to show that the Tribe was "seek[ing] to seize more tax revenues than would be fairly related to the services provided by the Tribe." *Ibid*. After making that point, the footnote suggested that the state tax might be invalid under the Commerce Clause if in excess of what "the *State's* contact with the activity would justify."[5] *Ibid*. (emphasis in original).

In 1982, Cotton paid its state taxes under protest and then brought an action in state court challenging the taxes under the Indian Commerce, Interstate

---

[5]The entire footnote reads as follows:

"Petitioners contend that because New Mexico may tax the same mining activity at full value, the Indian tax imposes a multiple tax burden on interstate commerce in violation of the Commerce Clause. The multiple taxation issue arises where two or more taxing jurisdictions point to some contact with an enterprise to support a tax on the entire value of its multi-state activities, which is more than the contact would justify. *E.g., Standard Oil Co. v. Peck*, 342 U.S. 382, 384-385 (1952). This Court has required an apportionment of the tax based on the portion of the activity properly viewed as occurring within each relevant State. *See, e.g., Exxon Corp. v. Wisconsin Dep't of Revenue*, 447 U.S. 207, 219 (1980); *Washington Revenue Dep't v. Association of Washington Stevedoring Cos.*, 435 U.S. 734, 746, and n.16 (1978).

"This rule has no bearing here, however, for there can be no claim that the Tribe seeks to tax any more of petitioners' mining activity than the portion occurring within tribal jurisdiction. Indeed, petitioners do not even argue that the Tribe is seeking to seize more tax revenues than would be fairly related to the services provided by the Tribe.... In the absence of such an assertion, and when the activity taxed by the Tribe occurs entirely on tribal lands, the multiple taxation issue would arise only if a *State* attempted to levy a tax on the same activity, which is more than the *State's* contact with the activity would justify. In such a circumstance, any challenge asserting that tribal and state taxes create a multiple burden on interstate commerce should be directed at the state tax, which, in the absence of congressional ratification, might be invalidated under the Commerce Clause. These cases, of course, do not involve a challenge to state taxation, and we intimate no opinion on the possibility of such a challenge." 455 U.S., at 158-159, n.26 (emphasis in the original).

Commerce, Due Process and Supremacy Clauses of the Federal Constitution. Relying on the *Merrion* footnote, Cotton contended that state taxes imposed on reservation activity are only valid if related to actual expenditures by the State in relation to the activity being taxed. In support of this theory, Cotton presented evidence at trial tending to prove that the amount of tax it paid to the State far exceeded the value of services that the State provided to it and that the taxes paid by all non-member oil producers far exceeded the value of services provided to the reservation as a whole.[6] Cotton did not, however, attempt to prove that the state taxes imposed any burden on the Tribe.

After trial, the Tribe sought, and was granted, leave to file a brief *amicus curiae.*

[T]he New Mexico district court issued a decision upholding the state taxes. [It] found that "New Mexico provides substantial services to both the Jicarilla Tribe and Cotton"[7] and concluded that the State had a valid interest in imposing taxes on non-Indians on the reservation. After squarely rejecting Cotton's theory of the case, the court stated that "[t]he theory of public finance does not require expenditures equal to revenues." ...

The New Mexico Court of Appeals affirmed. [Participating as *amicus curiae,* the Tribe] urged a different approach to the case. Unlike Cotton, the Tribe argued that the state taxes could not withstand traditional pre-emption analysis. The Tribe conceded that state laws, to the extent they do not interfere with tribal self-government, may control the conduct of non-Indians on the reservation. It maintained, however, that the taxes at issue interfered with its ability to raise taxes and thus with its right to self-government. The Court of Appeals rejected this argument because the record contained no evidence of any adverse impact on the Tribe and, indeed, indicated that the Tribe could impose even higher taxes than it had without adverse effect.[9]

The New Mexico Supreme Court granted, but then quashed, a writ of certiorari. We then noted probable jurisdiction and invited the parties to brief and argue the following additional question:

"Does the Commerce Clause require that an Indian Tribe be treated as a State for purposes of determining whether a state tax on nontribal activities conducted on an

---

[6] Cotton's evidence tended to prove that for the tax years 1981-1985 it paid New Mexico $2,298,953, while only receiving the equivalent of $89,384 in services to its operations in return. Cotton's evidence further suggested that over the same period the State received total tax revenues of $47,483,306 from the on-reservation, non-member oil and gas producers, while only providing $10,704,748 in services to the reservation as a whole.

[7] The district court found that New Mexico spends approximately three million dollars per year in providing on-reservation services to Cotton and the Tribe. [The court also] found that New Mexico does not discriminate against the Tribe or its members in providing state services; indeed, the State spends as much or more per capita on members of the Tribe than on non-members. The court further found that New Mexico provides services on the reservation not provided by either the Tribal or Federal governments, and provides additional services off the reservation that benefit the reservation and members of the Tribe.

Finally, the court found that the State regulates the spacing and mechanical integrity of wells located both on and off the reservation.

[9] The Court of Appeals noted that Cotton, and not the Tribe, paid the taxes at issue; that "[t]he record contains no evidence of an impact [on] tribal sovereignty"; that Cotton drilled twelve new wells while subject to both the state and tribal taxes and "shows no signs of disrupting production because of the tax burden"; and that at trial "[t]he Tribe's own consultant indicated that the Tribe could charge an even higher tax despite the state taxes imposed on Cotton." 106 N.M., at 522, 745 P.2d, at 1175.

Indian Reservation must be apportioned to account for taxes imposed on those same activities by the Indian Tribe?"

We now affirm the judgment of the New Mexico Court of Appeals.

II

This Court's approach to the question whether a State may tax on-reservation oil production by non-Indian lessees has varied over the course of the past century. At one time, such a tax was held invalid unless expressly authorized by Congress; more recently, such taxes have been upheld unless expressly or impliedly prohibited by Congress. The changed approach to these taxes is one aspect of the evolution of the doctrine of intergovernmental tax immunity that we recently discussed in detail in *South Carolina v. Baker*, 485 U.S. [505] (1988).

During the first third of this century, this Court frequently invalidated state taxes that arguably imposed an indirect economic burden on the Federal Government or its instrumentalities by application of the "intergovernmental immunity" doctrine. [I]n 1922, the Court applied the intergovernmental immunity doctrine to invalidate a state tax on income derived by a non-Indian lessee from the sale of his interest in oil produced on Indian land. See *Gillespie v. Oklahoma*, 257 U.S. 501 (1922). Consistently with the view of intergovernmental immunity that then prevailed, the Court stated that "a tax upon such profits is a direct hamper upon the effort of the United States to make the best terms that it can for its wards." *Id.*, at 506 (citing *Weston v. Charleston*, 2 Pet. 449, 468 (1829)). The same reasoning was used to invalidate a variety of other state taxes imposed on non-Indian lessees at that time.[10]

Shortly after reaching its zenith in the *Gillespie* decision, the doctrine of intergovernmental tax immunity started a long path in decline and has now been "thoroughly repudiated" by modern case law. [I]n *Helvering v. Mountain Producers Corp.*, 303 U.S. 376, 386-387 (1938), the Court squarely overruled *Gillespie*. Thus, after *Mountain Producers Corp.* was decided, oil and gas lessees operating on Indian reservations were subject to nondiscriminatory state taxation as long as Congress did not act affirmatively to pre-empt the state taxes. See also *Oklahoma Tax Comm'n v. Texas Co.*, 336 U.S. 342 (1949).

In sum, it is well-settled that, absent express congressional authorization, a State cannot tax the United States directly. See *McCulloch v. Maryland*, 4 Wheat. 316 (1819). It is also clear that the tax immunity of the United States is shared by the Indian tribes for whose benefit the United States holds reservation lands in trust. See *Montana v. Blackfeet Tribe of Indians*, 471 U.S. 759, 764 (1985). Under current doctrine, however, a State can impose a nondiscriminatory tax on private parties with whom the United States or an Indian tribe does business, even though the financial burden of the tax may fall on the United States or tribe. [While] a lessee's oil production on Indian lands is therefore not "automatically exempt from state taxation," Congress does, of course, retain the power to grant such immunity. *Mescalero Apache Tribe v. Jones*, 411 U.S. 145,

---

[10] The Court [has] held that non-Indian mineral lessees were exempt from state occupation and privilege taxes, exempt from state taxes on the value of their leasehold, exempt from state gross production taxes, and exempt from state ad valorem taxes in some circumstances.

150 (1973). Whether such immunity shall be granted is a question that "is essentially legislative in character." *Texas Co., supra*, at 365-366.

The question for us to decide is whether Congress has acted to grant the Tribe such immunity, either expressly or by plain implication. In addition, we must consider Cotton's argument that the "multiple burden" imposed by the state and tribal taxes is unconstitutional.

III

[W]e have applied a flexible pre-emption analysis sensitive to the particular facts and legislation involved. Each case "requires a particularized examination of the relevant state, federal, and tribal interests." *Ramah Navajo School Bd., Inc. v. Bureau of Revenue of New Mexico*, 458 U.S. 832, 838 (1982). Moreover, in examining the pre-emptive force of the relevant federal legislation, we are cognizant of both the broad policies that underlie the legislation and the history of tribal independence in the field at issue. It bears emphasis that although congressional silence no longer entails a broad-based immunity from taxation for private parties doing business with Indian tribes, federal pre-emption is not limited to cases in which Congress has expressly — as compared to impliedly — pre-empted the state activity. Finally, we note that although state interests must be given weight and courts should be careful not to make legislative decisions in the absence of congressional action, ambiguities in federal law are, as a rule, resolved in favor of tribal independence.

Against this background, Cotton argues that the New Mexico taxes are pre-empted by the "federal laws and policies which protect tribal self-government and strengthen impoverished reservation economies." Most significantly, Cotton contends that the Indian Mineral Leasing Act of 1938, 52 Stat. 347, 25 U.S.C. § 396a et seq. (1938 Act), exhibits a strong federal interest in guaranteeing Indian tribes the maximum return on their oil and gas leases. Moreover, Cotton maintains that the Federal and Tribal Governments, acting pursuant to the 1938 Act, its accompanying regulations, and the Jicarilla Apache Tribal Code, exercise comprehensive regulatory control over Cotton's on-reservation activity. Cotton describes New Mexico's responsibilities, in contrast, as "significantly limited." Thus, weighing the respective state, federal and tribal interests, Cotton concludes that the New Mexico taxes unduly interfere with the federal interest in promoting tribal economic self-sufficiency and are not justified by an adequate state interest. We disagree.

The 1938 Act neither expressly permits state taxation nor expressly precludes it, but rather simply provides that "unallotted lands within any Indian reservation or lands owned by any tribe ... may, with the approval of the Secretary of the Interior, be leased for mining purposes, by authority of the tribal council ..., for terms not to exceed ten years and as long thereafter as minerals are produced in paying quantities." 25 U.S.C. § 396a. The Senate and House Reports that accompanied the Act, moreover — even when considered in their broadest possible terms — shed little light on congressional intent concerning state taxation of oil and gas produced on leased lands. See S. Rep. No. 985, 75th Cong., 1st Sess. (1937); H.R. Rep. No. 1872, 75th Cong., 3d Sess. (1938). Both Reports reflect that the proposed legislation was suggested by the Secretary and considered by the appropriate committees, which recommended that it pass without amendment. Beyond this procedural summary, the Reports simply rely on the Secretary's letter of transmittal to describe the purpose of the Act. That letter provides that the legislation was intended, in light of the disarray of federal law in the area, "to obtain uniformity so far as practicable of the law relating to the leasing of tribal lands for mining purposes," and, in particular, was designed to "bring all mineral leasing matters in harmony with the Indian Reorganization Act" of 1934. *Id.*, at 1, 3; S. Rep. No. 985, *supra*, at 2, 3. In addition, the letter contains the following passage:

> "*It is not believed that the present law is adequate to give the Indians the greatest return from their property.* As stated, present law provides for locating and taking mineral leases in the same manner as mining locations are made on the public lands of the United States; but there are disadvantages in following this procedure on Indian lands that are not present in applying for a claim on the public domain. For instance, on the public domain the discoverer of a mineral deposit gets extralateral rights and can follow the ore beyond the side lines indefinitely, while on the Indian lands under the act of June 30, 1919, he is limited to the confines of the survey markers not to exceed 600 feet by 1,500 feet in any one claim. The draft of the bill herewith would permit the obtaining of sufficient acreage to remove the necessity for extralateral rights with all of its attending controversies." *Id.*, at 2; H.R. Rep. No. 1872, *supra*, at 2 (emphasis supplied).

Relying on the first sentence in this paragraph, Cotton argues that the 1938 Act embodies a broad congressional policy of maximizing revenues for Indian tribes. [T]he proposition that, in authorizing mineral leases, Congress sought to provide Indian tribes with a profitable source of revenue [certainly is not remarkable]. It is however quite remarkable, indeed unfathomable in our view, to suggest that Congress intended to remove all state imposed obstacles to profitability by attaching to the Senate and House Reports a letter from the Secretary that happened to include the phrase "the greatest return from their property." Read in the broadest terms possible, the relevant paragraph suggests that Congress sought to remove "disadvantages in [leasing mineral rights] on Indian lands that are not present in applying for a claim on the public domain." S. Rep. No. 985, *supra*, at 2; H.R. Rep. No. 1872, *supra*, at 2. By 1938, however, it was established that oil and gas lessees of public lands were subject to state taxation. See *Mid-Northern Oil Co. v. Walker*, 268 U.S. 45 (1925). It is thus apparent that Congress was not concerned with state taxation, but with matters such as the unavailability of extralateral mineral rights on Indian land. Nor do we read the *Blackfeet* footnote, 471 U.S., at 767, n.5, to give the Secretary's words greater effect. We think it clear that the footnote simply stands for the proposition that the Act's purpose of creating a source of revenue for Indian tribes provides evidence that Congress did not intend to authorize direct state taxation of Indian royalties.

We thus agree that a purpose of the 1938 Act is to provide Indian tribes with badly needed revenue, but find no evidence for the further supposition that Congress intended to remove all barriers to profit maximization. The Secretary's letter of transmittal, even when read permissively for broad policy goals and even when read to resolve ambiguities in favor of tribal independence, supports no more.

Our review of the legislation that preceded the 1938 Act provides no additional support for Cotton's expansive view of the Act's purpose. This history is relevant in that it supplies both the legislative background against which Congress enacted the 1938 Act and the relevant "backdrop" of tribal independence. Congress first authorized mineral leasing on Indian lands in 1891. See Act of Feb. 28, 1891, § 3, 26 Stat. 795, 25 U.S.C. § 397 (1891 Act). That legislation, which empowered tribes to enter into grazing and mining leases, only applied to lands "occupied by Indians who have bought and paid for the same," and was thus interpreted to be inapplicable to Executive Order reservations. Mineral leasing on reservations created by Executive Order — like the Jicarilla Apache reservation — was not authorized until almost four decades later. After years of debate concerning whether Indians had any right to share in royalties derived from oil and gas leases in Executive Order reservations,[12] Congress finally enacted legislation in 1927 that authorized such leases. See Indian Oil Act of 1927, 44 Stat. (part 2) 1347, 25 U.S.C. § 398a (1927 Act).

While both the 1891 and 1927 Acts were in effect, *Gillespie* was the prevailing law and, under its expansive view of inter-governmental tax immunity, States were powerless to impose severance taxes on oil produced on Indian reservations unless Congress expressly waived that immunity. Just two years after *Gillespie* was decided, Congress took such express action and authorized state taxation of oil and gas production in Treaty reservations. See Indian Oil Leasing Act of 1924, 43 Stat. 244, current version at 25 U.S.C. § 398. See also *British-American Oil Producing Co. v. Board of Equalization, supra* (applying 1924 Act to uphold state tax imposed on the production of oil and gas in the Blackfeet Indian Reservation). More significantly for purposes of this case, when Congress first authorized oil and gas leasing on Executive Order reservations in the 1927 Act, it expressly waived immunity from state taxation of oil and gas lessees operating in those reservations. See Indian Oil Act of 1927, 44 Stat. (part 2) 1347, 25 U.S.C. § 398c. Thus, at least as to Executive Order reservations, state taxation of non-member oil and gas lessees was the norm from the very start. There is, accordingly, simply no history of tribal indepen-

---

[12]This history is recounted in L. Kelly, The Navajo Indians and Federal Indian Policy 48-103 (1968) (hereinafter Kelly).

Of particular significance, in 1922, the Secretary took the position that Executive Order reservations "are without question lands 'owned by the United States,'" and thus subject to leasing under the Mineral Lands Leasing Act of 1920, 41 Stat. 450, 30 U.S.C. § 189. Harrison, 49 L.D. 139, 144. As such, the Executive Order tribes had no right to share in royalties derived from oil and gas leases. Two years later, then-Attorney General Stone rendered an opinion concluding that the Mineral Lands Leasing Act did not apply to Executive Order reservations. 34 Op. Atty. Gen. 171, 181. This decision made clear that new federal legislation would be required to open Executive Order reservations to oil and gas leasing. For the next few years, a number of legislative solutions were proposed and considered. For example, in 1926, Representative Carl Hayden introduced legislation that would have provided for Executive Order reservation leasing in accordance with the Indian Oil Leasing Act of 1924, 43 Stat. 244, but which, in lieu of permitting a state production tax, would have given to the relevant State 37½ percent of the royalties, rent, and bonuses received by the tribe. This payment was to be used for building and maintaining roads on the reservation or to support public schools attended by Indian children. A bill introduced in the Senate would have attached no qualification to how the State might spend its 37½ percent share. Finally, Congress settled on the terms of the Indian Oil Act of 1927, which authorized oil and gas leasing in Executive Order reservations and allowed States to tax "any lessee upon lands within Executive order Indian reservations in the same manner as such taxes are otherwise levied and collected." 44 Stat. (part 2) 1347, 25 U.S.C. § 398c.

dence from state taxation of these lessees to form a "backdrop" against which the 1938 Act must be read.

We are also unconvinced that the contrast between the 1927 Act's express waiver of immunity and the 1938 Act's silence on the subject suggests that Congress intended to repeal the waiver in the 1938 Act and thus to diametrically change course by implicitly barring state taxation. The general repealer clause contained in the 1938 Act provides that "[a]ll Act[s] or parts of Act[s] inconsistent herewith are hereby repealed." 52 Stat. 348. Although one might infer from this clause that all preceding, nonconflicting legislation in the area, like the 1927 Act's waiver provision, is implicitly incorporated, we need not go so far to simply conclude that the 1938 Act's omission demonstrates no congressional purpose to close the door to state taxation. Moreover, the contrast between the 1927 and 1938 Acts is easily explained by the contemporaneous history of the doctrine of intergovernmental tax immunity. In 1927, *Gillespie* prevailed, and States were only permitted to tax lessees of Indian lands if Congress expressly so provided. By the time the 1938 Act was enacted, however, *Gillespie* had been overruled and replaced by the modern rule permitting such taxes absent congressional disapproval.[13] Thus, Congress' approaches to both the 1927 and 1938 Acts were fully consistent with an intent to permit state taxation of non-member lessees.[14]

Cotton nonetheless maintains that our decisions in [*Bracker*] and *Ramah Navajo School Bd., Inc. v. Bureau of Revenue of New Mexico,* 458 U.S. 832 (1982), compel the conclusion that the New Mexico taxes are pre-empted by federal law. In pressing this argument, Cotton ignores the admonition included in both of those decisions that the relevant pre-emption test is a flexible one sensitive to the particular state, federal, and tribal interests involved.

---

[13] Although *Gillespie* was not explicitly overruled until 1938 in *Helvering v. Mountain Producers Corp.,* 308 U.S. 376, the holding in that case was plainly foreshadowed by the development of the law in this area during the preceding decade. The fact that the text of the 1938 Act had been drafted before our decision in *Mountain Producers* was actually handed down does not, therefore, have the significance that the dissent ascribes to it.

[14] Our decision in *Montana v. Blackfeet Tribe of Indians,* 471 U.S. 759 (1985), is not to the contrary. In that case we considered the distinct question of whether the 1938 Act, through incorporation of the 1927 Act, expressly authorized direct taxation of Indian royalties. In concluding that it did not, we made clear that our holding turned on the rule that Indian tribes, like the Federal Government itself, are exempt from direct state taxation and that this exemption is "lifted only when Congress has made its intention to do so unmistakably clear." *Id.,* at 765. We stressed that the 1938 Act "contains no explicit consent to state taxation," and that the reverse implication of the general repealer clause that the 1927 waiver might be incorporated "does not satisfy the requirement that Congress clearly consent to state taxation." *Id.,* at 766-767. Our conclusion that the 1938 Act does not expressly authorize direct taxation of Indian tribes does not entail the further step that the Act impliedly prohibits taxation of non-members doing business on a reservation.

Nor can a congressional intent to pre-empt state taxation be found in the Indian Reorganization Act of 1964, 48 Stat. 964, 25 U.S.C. § 461 et seq., the Indian Financing Act of 1974, 38 Stat. 77, 25 U.S.C. § 1451 et seq., or the Indian Self-Determination Act of 1975, 88 Stat. 2208, 25 U.S.C. § 450 et seq. Although these statutes "evidence to varying degrees a congressional concern with fostering tribal self-government and economic development," *Washington v. Confederated Tribes of Colville Indian Reservation,* 447 U.S. 134, 155 (1980), they no more express a congressional intent to preempt state taxation of oil and gas lessees than does the 1938 Act. More instructive is the Crude Oil Windfall Profit Tax Act of 1980, 94 Stat. 229, 26 U.S.C. § 4985 et seq. In imposing the Windfall Profits Tax, Congress expressly exempted certain Indian producers, see 26 U.S.C. § 4994(d), but decided not to exempt "oil received by non-Indian lessees of tribal interests." See S. Rep. No. 96-394, p. 61 (1979). See also H.R. Conf. Rep. No. 96-817, p. 108 (1980). If Congress was of the view that taxing non-Indian lessees would interfere with the goal of promoting tribal economic self-sufficiency, it seems unlikely that it would have imposed this additional tax on those lessees.

The factual findings of the New Mexico district court clearly distinguish this case from both *Bracker* and *Ramah Navajo School Bd.* After conducting a trial, that court found that "New Mexico provides substantial services to both the Jicarilla Tribe and Cotton," costing the State approximately three million dollars per year. Indeed, Cotton concedes that from 1981 through 1985 New Mexico provided its operations with services costing $89,384, but argues that the cost of these services is disproportionate to the $2,298,953 in taxes the State collected from Cotton. Neither *Bracker*, nor *Ramah Navajo School Bd.*, however, imposes such a proportionality requirement on the States.[15] Rather, both cases involved complete abdication or noninvolvement of the State in the on-reservation activity. The present case is also unlike *Bracker*, and *Ramah Navajo School Bd.*, in that the district court found that "[n]o economic burden falls on the tribe by virtue of the state taxes," and that the Tribe could, in fact, increase its taxes without adversely affecting on-reservation oil and gas development. Finally, the district court found that the State regulates the spacing and mechanical integrity of wells located on the reservation. Thus, although the federal and tribal regulations in this case are extensive,[16] they are not exclusive, as were the regulations in *Bracker* and *Ramah Navajo School Bd.*

We thus conclude that federal law, even when given the most generous construction, does not pre-empt New Mexico's oil and gas severance taxes. This is not a case in which the State has had nothing to do with the on-reservation activity, save tax it. Nor is this a case in which an unusually large state tax has imposed a substantial burden on the Tribe.[17] It is, of course, reasonable to

---

[15] Nor are we inclined to do so today. Not only would such a proportionality requirement create nightmarish administrative burdens, but it would also be antithetical to the traditional notion that taxation is not premised on a strict quid pro quo relationship between the taxpayer and the tax collector. See *Carmichael v. Southern Coal & Coke Co.*, 301 U.S. 495, 521-523 (1987).

[16] The federal regulations provide, inter alia, that tribal leases may only be offered for sale pursuant to specified standards governing notice and bidding, 25 CFR § 211.3(a) (1988), that the Secretary reserves "the right to reject all bids when in his judgment the interests of the Indians will be best served by so doing," § 211.3(b), that corporate bidders must submit detailed information concerning their officers, directors, shareholders, and finances, § 211.5, that no single lease for oil and gas may exceed 2,560 acres, § 211.9, and that a primary lease may not exceed 10 years, § 211.10. The regulations also address the manner of payment and amount of rents and royalties, §§ 211.12, 211.13(a), and provide for Interior Department inspection of lessees' premises and records, § 211.18. Other federal regulations address the spacing, drilling, and plugging of wells, and impose reporting requirements concerning production and environmental protection. See 43 CFR §§ 3160.0-1 — 3186.4 (1987).

The Tribe imposes further regulations, including a requirement that anyone seeking to conduct oil and gas operations in the reservation must obtain a permit from the Tribal Oil and Gas Administration, J.A.T.C., Tit. 18, ch. 1, § 3, must post a bond, § 4(B), must open covered premises for inspection, § 5(C)(2), and must comply with the Tribe's environmental protection ordinance, § 6(A)(3).

[17] We therefore have no occasion to reexamine our summary affirmance of the Court of Appeals for the Ninth Circuit's conclusion that Montana's unique severance and gross proceeds taxes may not be imposed on coal mined on Crow tribal property. See *Montana v. Crow Tribe of Indians*, 484 U.S. 997 (1988), summarily aff'g 819 F.2d 895 (1987). In that case, as the Ninth Circuit noted, the state taxes had a negative effect on the marketability of coal produced in *Montana.* See *id.*, at 900. Moreover, as the Solicitor General stated in urging that we affirm the judgment of the Court of Appeals, the Montana taxes at issue were "extraordinarily high." Motion to Affirm for United States, O.T. 1987, No. 87-343, p. 12. According to the Crow Tribe's expert, the combined effective rate of the Montana taxes was 32.9 percent, "more than twice that of any other state's coal taxes." 819 F.2d, at 899, n.2. See also Justice BLACKMUN 's discussion of the "enormous revenues" generated by the Montana severance tax in *Commonwealth Edison Co. v. Montana*, 453 U.S. 609, 641-642 (1981) (BLACKMUN, J., dissenting).

infer that the New Mexico taxes have at least a marginal effect on the demand for on-reservation leases, the value to the Tribe of those leases, and the ability of the Tribe to increase its tax rate. Any impairment to the federal policy favoring the exploitation of on-reservation oil and gas resources by Indian tribes that might be caused by these effects, however, is simply too indirect and too insubstantial to support Cotton's claim of pre-emption. To find pre-emption of state taxation in such indirect burdens on this broad congressional purpose, absent some special factor such as those present in *Bracker* and *Ramah Navajo School Bd.*, would be to return to the pre-1937 doctrine of intergovernmental tax immunity.[18] Any adverse effect on the Tribe's finances caused by the taxation of a private party contracting with the Tribe would be ground to strike the state tax. Absent more explicit guidance from Congress, we decline to return to this long-discarded and thoroughly repudiated doctrine.

IV

Cotton also argues that New Mexico's severance taxes — "insofar as they are imposed without allocation or apportionment on top of Jicarilla Apache tribal taxes" — impose "an unlawful multiple tax burden on interstate commerce." In support of this argument, Cotton relies on three facts: (1) that the State and the Tribe tax the same activity; (2) that the total tax burden on Cotton is higher than the burden on its off-reservation competitors who pay no tribal tax; and (3) that the state taxes generate revenues that far exceed the value of the services it provides on the reservation.

As we pointed out in the *Merrion* footnote, see n.5, *supra*, a multiple taxation issue may arise when more than one State attempts to tax the same activity. If a unitary business derives income from several States, each State may only tax the portion of that income that is attributable to activity within its borders. See, e.g., *Exxon Corp. v. Wisconsin Department of Revenue*, 447 U.S. 207 (1980). Thus, in such a case, an apportionment formula is necessary in order to identify the scope of the taxpayer's business that is within the taxing jurisdiction of each State. In this case, however, all of Cotton's leases are located entirely within the borders of the State of New Mexico and also within the borders of the Jicarilla Apache reservation. Indeed, they are also within the borders of the United States. There are, therefore, three different governmental entities, each of which has taxing jurisdiction over all of the non-Indian wells. Cf. [*Colville*] (Indian tribe did not oust State of power to impose cigarette tax on on-reservation sales to non-Indian customers by imposing its own tax on transaction). The federal sovereign has the undoubted power to prohibit taxation of the Tribe's lessees by the Tribe, by the State, or by both, but since it has not exercised that power, concurrent taxing jurisdiction over all of Cotton's on-reservation leases exists. Cf. *Commonwealth Edison Co. v. Montana*, 453 U.S., at 617 (noting that because the taxed activity took place exclusively within Montana — although much of it on federal lands within the State — no nexus or apportionment

---

[18] It is important to keep in mind that the primary burden of the state taxation falls on the non-Indian taxpayers. Amicus curiae briefs supporting the position of Cotton Petroleum Corp. in this case have been filed by [twelve oil companies]. Apparently all of those oil companies correctly interpreted the import of the 1988 Act until a seed of doubt was [sown] by our footnote in *Merrion*.

problem existed). Unless and until Congress provides otherwise, each of the other two sovereigns has taxing jurisdiction over all of Cotton's leases.

It is, of course, true that the total taxes paid by Cotton are higher than those paid by off-reservation producers. But neither the State nor the Tribe imposes a discriminatory tax. The burdensome consequence is entirely attributable to the fact that the leases are located in an area where two governmental entities share jurisdiction. As we noted in *Merrion*, the tribal tax does "not treat minerals transported away from the reservation differently than it treats minerals that might be sold on the reservation." 455 U.S., at 157-158. Similarly, the New Mexico taxes are administered in an even-handed manner and are imposed at a uniform rate throughout the State — both on and off the reservation.

Cotton's most persuasive argument is based on the evidence that tax payments by reservation lessees far exceed the value of services provided by the State to the lessees, or more generally, to the reservation as a whole. There are, however, two sufficient reasons for rejecting this argument. First, the relevant services provided by the State include those that are available to the lessees and the members of the Tribe off the reservation as well as on it. The intangible value of citizenship in an organized society is not easily measured in dollars and cents; moreover, the district court found that the actual per capita state expenditures for Jicarilla members are equal to or greater than the per capita expenditures for non-Indian citizens. Second, there is no constitutional requirement that the benefits received from a taxing authority by an ordinary commercial taxpayer — or by those living in the community where the taxpayer is located — must equal the amount of its tax obligations.

[I]n effect, [Cotton] asks us to divest New Mexico of its normal latitude because its taxes have "some connection" to commerce with the Tribe. The connection, however, is by no means close enough. There is simply no evidence in the record that the tax has had an adverse effect on the Tribe's ability to attract oil and gas lessees. It is, of course, reasonable to infer that the existence of the state tax imposes some limit on the profitability of Indian oil and gas leases — just as it no doubt imposes a limit on the profitability of off-reservation leasing arrangements — but that is precisely the same indirect burden that we rejected as a basis for granting non-Indian contractors an immunity from the state taxation in *Helvering v. Mountain Producers Corp.*, 303 U.S. 376 (1938), *Oklahoma Tax Comm'n v. United States*, 319 U.S. 598 (1943), *Oklahoma Tax Comm'n v. Texas Co.*, 336 U.S. 342 (1949), [*Moe*,] and [*Colville*].

V

In our order noting probable jurisdiction we invited the parties to address the question whether the Tribe should be treated as a State for the purpose of determining whether New Mexico's taxes must be apportioned. All of the Indian tribes that have filed amicus curiae briefs addressing this question — including the Jicarilla Apache Tribe — have uniformly taken the position that Indian tribes are not States within the meaning of the Commerce Clause. This position is supported by the text of the Clause itself. Article I, § 8, cl. 3, provides the "Congress shall have the power ... To regulate Commerce with foreign Nations, and among the several States, and with the Indian Tribes." Thus, the

Commerce Clause draws a clear distinction between "States" and "Indian Tribes." As Chief Justice Marshall observed in [*Cherokee Nation*]: "The objects to which the power of regulating commerce might be directed, are divided into three distinct classes — foreign nations, the several states, and Indian Tribes. When forming this article, the convention considered them as entirely distinct." In fact, the language of the Clause no more admits of treating Indian tribes as States than of treating foreign nations as States.

It is also well-established that the Interstate Commerce and Indian Commerce Clauses have very different applications. In particular, while the Interstate Commerce Clause is concerned with maintaining free trade among the States even in the absence of implementing federal legislation, see *McLeod v. J.E. Dilworth Co.*, 322 U.S. 327, 330 (1944); *Pike v. Bruce Church, Inc.*, 397 U.S. 137 (1970), the central function of the Indian Commerce Clause is to provide Congress with plenary power to legislate in the field of Indian affairs, see *Morton v. Mancari*, 417 U.S. 535, 551-552 (1974); F. Cohen, Handbook of Federal Indian Law 207-208, and nn.2, 3 and 9-11 (1982). The extensive case law that has developed under the Interstate Commerce Clause, moreover, is premised on a structural understanding of the unique role of the States in our constitutional system that is not readily imported to cases involving the Indian Commerce Clause. Most notably, as our discussion of Cotton's "multiple taxation" argument demonstrates, the fact that States and tribes have concurrent jurisdiction over the same territory makes it inappropriate to apply Commerce Clause doctrine developed in the context of commerce "among" States with mutually exclusive territorial jurisdiction to trade "with" Indian tribes.

Accordingly, we have no occasion to modify our comment on this question in the *Bracker* case:

> "Tribal reservations are not States, and the differences in the form and nature of their sovereignty make it treacherous to import to one notions of pre-emption that are properly applied to the other." 448 U.S., at 143.

[*Affirmed.*]

Justice BLACKMUN, with whom Justice BRENNAN and Justice MARSHALL join, dissenting.

Although the Jicarilla Apache Tribe is not a party to the appeal, this case centrally concerns "the boundaries between state regulatory authority and [the Tribe's] self-government." [*Bracker*]. The basic principles that define those boundaries are well established. The Court today, while faithfully reciting these principles, is less faithful in their application.

Pre-emption is essentially a matter of congressional intent. In this case, our goal should be to determine whether the State's taxation of Cotton Petroleum's reservation oil production is consistent with federal Indian policy as expressed in relevant statutes and regulations. First and foremost, we must look to the statutory scheme Congress has established to govern the activity the State seeks to tax in order to see whether the statute itself expresses Congress' views on the question of state taxation. As the discussion in Part I below reveals, the statute most relevant to this case makes clear that Congress intended to foreclose the kind of tax New Mexico has imposed. Second, we must consider other indications of whether federal policy permits the tax in question. Part II below demonstrates that, under established principles, state taxation is pre-empted by federal and tribal interests in this case. Because the record is more than adequate to demonstrate the pre-emptive force of federal and tribal interests, I dissent.[1]

I

The most relevant statute is the Indian Mineral Leasing Act of 1938, pursuant to which the Jicarilla Apache entered into mineral leases with appellant Cotton Petroleum. The 1938 Act is silent on the question of state taxation. But, as interpreted by this Court in *Montana v. Blackfeet Tribe*, the silence of the 1938 Act is eloquent and argues forcefully against the result reached by the majority....

The argument that the 1938 congressional silence regarding lessee taxation is consistent with an intent to permit such taxation cannot, for two reasons, withstand close scrutiny. First, even if the majority is correct in seeking the meaning of Congress' silence in changes in this Court's intergovernmental tax immunity jurisprudence, the facts defeat the majority's theory. Second, and fundamentally, the majority's court-centered approach fails to give due weight to a far more significant intervening event: the major change in federal Indian policy embodied in the Indian Reorganization Act of 1934.

The case which overruled Justice Holmes' opinion for the Court in *Gillespie* was *Helvering v. Mountain Producers Corp.*, 303 U.S. 376 (1938). *Mountain Producers* was decided on March 7, 1938. The majority, indeed, is correct that the 1938 Act was enacted on May 11, 1938, after that case was decided. But a review of the history of the 1938 Act reveals that it had assumed final form well before this Court's March 7, 1938, decision in *Mountain Producers*. The majority's chronology thus is somewhat misleading, at least if the realities of the legislative process are to have any relevance to the analysis of legislative intent.

[A]lthough the majority is technically correct that the 1938 Act did not become law until after the announcement of this Court's decision in *Mountain Producers*, the legislation was formulated, considered by the House and Senate committees, referred out of the committees without amendment, and passed by the Senate, all before *Mountain Producers* on March 7, 1938, changed the law of intergovernmental tax immunity. Up until that point, the clear meaning of the statute, as our decision in *Montana* makes clear, is that the State lacked power to impose the tax at issue in this case. There is no evidence that the change in the law wrought by *Mountain Producers* was brought to the attention of the House. It defies historical sense to make *Mountain Producers* the centerpiece of the interpretation of a statute which reached final form before *Mountain Producers* was decided.

The Court in *Montana* put forward a more sensible explanation of the absence of state taxation authority in the 1938 Act. As the relevant House and

---

[1] The Court today addresses, in addition to pre-emption, the question whether the Interstsate Commerce Clause applies to problems of multiple state and Indian taxation. I agree with the majority's comclusion in Part V of its opinion that an Indian tribe is not to be equated with a State for purposes of the Interstate Commerce Clause. It would seem to follow that the Clause has no application to this case. I thus see no purpose in the majority's detailed application of Interstate Commerce Clause analysis in Part IV of its opinion.

Senate Reports explain, the 1938 Act was crafted, proposed, and enacted in light of the recently enacted Indian Reorganization Act. The IRA worked a fundamental change in federal Indian law marked by two principal goals: "to rehabilitate the Indian's economic life and to give him a chance to develop the initiative destroyed by a century of oppression and paternalism.'" *Mescalero Apache Tribe v. Jones*, 411 U.S. 145, 152 (1973), quoting H.R. Rep. No. 1804, 73d Cong., 2d Sess., 6 (1934).

The majority's observation, ante, at 17, that "[t]here is ... no history of tribal independence from state taxation of these lessees to form a 'backdrop' against which the 1938 Act must be read" cannot be dispositive. The IRA, enacted only a few years before the 1938 Act, is itself sufficient "backdrop" to inform our interpretation, for the IRA marked the rejection of all the assumptions upon which prior statutes providing for state taxation of reservation mineral production had been based. [T]he IRA embodied an approach to tribal independence which would be undone by limiting Indian tribes to those powers they had been permitted to exercise in the past.... It would be entirely consistent with the spirit of the IRA for the Department [of the Interior], and for Congress, to have done away with the express authorization of state taxation in order to leave room for Indians to operate in the sphere of taxation unimpeded by the States. That Indians had never before asserted the right to freedom from state taxation was simply a product of the unfortunate state of affairs that the IRA sought to remedy.

In sum, we are given to choose between two possible interpretations of the silence of the 1938 Act. One, adopted by the majority, focuses on the change in this Court's intergovernmental immunity doctrine which took place at the very end of the process leading to the 1938 Act. The other focuses on a fundamental change in congressional Indian policy which took place shortly before the process began, and was expressly noted as its motivating force. The latter interpretation is clearly the more compelling. I must conclude that, contrary to the majority's view, the silence of the 1938 Act is not consistent with a congressional intent that non-Indian lessees of Indian mineral lands shall be subject to state taxation for their on-reservation activities.[7] This conclusion does not constitute, as the majority says, a "return to [the] long-discarded and thoroughly repudiated doctrine" of constitutional intergovernmental tax immunity. Rather, it reflects a fuller understanding of the policies underlying federal Indian law in the mid to late-1930s and continuing, in relevant part, into the present time.

II

Even if we did not have such direct evidence of Congress' intent to preclude state taxation of non-Indian oil production on Indian lands, that conclusion would be amply supported by a routine application of the traditional tools of Indian pre-emption analysis....

---

[7]Even if the silence of the 1938 Act simply were held to be ambiguous, our precedents consistently have required that ambiguities in statutes affecting tribal interests be resolved in favor of Indian independence. *Ramah Navajo School Board, Inc. v. Bureau of Revenue*, 458 U.S. 832, 838 (1982); *White Mountain Apache Tribe v. Bracker*, 448 U.S. 136, 143-144 (1980). That canon of interpretation would require rejecting the conclusion the majority reaches here.

Federal regulation of leasing of Indian oil lands "is both comprehensive and pervasive." *Ramah,* 458 U.S., at 839. Provisions of the 1938 Act regulate all stages of the process of oil and gas leasing and production on Indian reservations. The auction or bidding process through which leases are acquired is supervised by the Department of the Interior. 25 U.S.C. § 396b. Successful lessees must furnish a bond to secure compliance with lease terms, § 396c, and each lessee's operations are in all respects subject to federal rules and regulations, § 396d. Longstanding regulations promulgated pursuant to the 1938 Act govern the minute details of the bidding process, 25 CFR § 211.3 (1988), and give the Secretary of the Interior the power to reject bids that are not in the best interest of the Indian lessor, § 211.9, [and that govern] the term of each lease, §§ 211.13 and 211.16. Turning to the regulation of the lessee's operations, federal law controls when operations may start, § 211.20, and federal supervisory personnel are empowered to ensure the conservation of resources and prevention of waste, §§ 211.19-211.21. Additional restrictions are placed on lessees by the Federal Oil and Gas Royalty Management Act of 1982, 96 Stat. 2447, 30 U.S.C. §§ 1701 et seq., which further safeguards tribal interests by imposing additional inspection, collection, auditing security, and conservation requirements on lessees.

In addition, the Jicarilla Apache, as expressly authorized by their Constitution, have enacted regulations of their own to supplement federal guidelines, and have created a tribal Oil and Gas Administration to exercise tribal authority in this area.[8] See Jicarilla Apache Tribal Code, Tit. 18, ch. 1, §§ 1-7 (1987) and their Revised Constitution, Art. XI, § 1(a)(3). Indeed, just as we earlier found of the Mescalero Apache: "The ... Tribe has engaged in a concerted and sustained undertaking to develop and manage the reservation's ... resources specifically for the benefit of its members." *New Mexico v. Mescalero Apache Tribe,* 462 U.S. 324, 341 (1983).

The majority acknowledges that federal and tribal regulations in this case are extensive. But because the District Court found that the State regulates spacing and the mechanical integrity of wells, and that federal and tribal regulations are therefore not "exclusive," the majority concludes without further ado that there is sufficient state activity to support the State's claimed authority to tax.[9] The majority's reliance on the proposition that "[t]his is not a case in which the State has had nothing to do with the on-reservation activity, save tax it," reflects a mechanical and absolutist approach to the delicate issue of pre-emption that this Court expressly has repudiated. *White Mountain Apache.* "[C]omplete abdication or noninvolvement" has never been the applicable standard.

Just as the majority errs by adopting a standard of "exclusivity," it places undue significance on the fact that the State made some expenditures that benefited Cotton Petroleum's on-reservation activities. Concededly, the State did spend some money on the reservation for purposes directly and indirectly

---

[8]Tribal regulation is expressly contemplated by regulations promulgated under the 1938 Act, which specify that certain statutory and regulatory provisions "may be superseded by the provisions" of tribal law enacted pursuant to the IRA. 25 CFR § 211.29 (1988).

[9]The manner in which a State exercises a regulatory role in the area of well spacing indeed underscores the comprehensiveness of federal law in this area: state law applies not of its own force, but only if its application is approved by the Bureau of Land Management. Furthermore, additional federal spacing requirements apply to Indian lands. See 43 CFR §§ 3162.3-1(a) and (b) (1987).

related to oil and gas production. It is clear on this record, however, that the infrastructure which supports oil and gas production on the Jicarilla Apache reservation is provided almost completely by the federal and tribal governments rather than by the State. Indeed, the majority appears to accept the fact that the state taxes are vastly disproportionate, as well it must: $89,384 in services, as compared with $2,293,953 in taxes, speaks for itself.[11] But the majority deems this fact legally irrelevant in order to avoid imposing a "proportionality require-ment" that would be inconsistent with the notion that taxation is not based on a *quid pro quo*. That notion, drawn from Due Process and Commerce Clause analysis, is inapposite in the pre-emption context. Pre-emption analysis calls for a close consideration of conflicting interests and of their potential impact on one another. Under the majority's analysis, insignificant state expenditures, reflect-ing minimal state interests, are sufficient to support state interference with significant federal and tribal interests. The exclusion of all sense of proportion has led to a result that is antithetical to the concerns that animate our Indian pre-emption jurisprudence.

Finally, the majority sorely underestimates the degree to which state taxation of oil and gas production adversely affects the interests of the Jicarilla Apache. Assuming that the Tribe continues to tax oil and gas production at present levels, on-reservation taxes will remain 75% higher (14% as opposed to 8% of gross value) than off-reservation taxes within the State. The state trial court was not disturbed by this fact: it found that Cotton Petroleum had plans to dig new wells, and took that to be proof positive that the taxes imposed by the State did not deter drilling. But the court failed to recognize that Cotton Petroleum's new wells were infield (or "infill") wells, drilled between existing producing wells to increase the efficiency of drainage on lands already leased. An infill well is essentially a no-risk proposition, in that there is little doubt that the well will be productive. Therefore, Cotton Petroleum's willingness to drill infill wells does not reflect its willingness to develop new lands. Federal and tribal interests legitimately include long-term planning for development of lease revenues on new lands, where there is greater economic risk, and a greater probability that difference in tax rates will have an adverse effect on a producer's willingness to drill new wells and on the competitiveness of Jicarilla leases. "[B]oth the rate at which mining companies acquire Indian land leases and the rate at which they develop them are dependent on the future balance between the deterrents to and the advantages of Indian land leasing. Where the balance will be struck cannot be predicted, for there are simply too many variables involved." Federal Trade Commission, Staff Report on Mineral Leasing on Indian Lands 48 (1975) (FTC Report). Dual state and tribal taxation inevitably affects that balance.

In weighing the effect of state taxation on tribal interests, logic dictates that it is necessary not only to consider the size of the tax, but also the importance of

---

[11]The distribution of responsibility is even clearly reflected in the relevant oil-and-gas-related expenditures during the 5-year period at issue in this case: federal expenditures were $1,206,800; tribal expenditures were $736,358; the State spent, at most, $89,384. In any event, it is clear from this Court's rejection of the Montana severance tax at issue in *Montana v. Crow Tribe*, 484 U.S. 997 (1988), that the mere fact that the State has made some expenditures that benefit the taxed activities is not sufficient to avoid a finding of pre-emption. See Motion to Affirm filed by the United States in *Montana v. Crow Tribe*, O.T. 1987, No. 87-343, p. 21 (Montana spent $500,000 to pay 25% of the cost of a road used by employees and suppliers of a mine).

the taxed activity to the tribal economy. See *California v. Cabazon Band of Mission Indians*, 480 U.S. 202, 218 (1987) (noting, in invalidating state regulation of tribal bingo operations, that bingo games constituted the sole source of tribal income). In this case, too, it is undisputed that oil and gas production is the Jicarilla Apache economy — a common pattern in reservations with substantial oil and gas reserves.

Furthermore, where, as here, the Tribe has made the decision to tax oil and gas producers, the long-term impact of state taxation on the Tribe's freedom of action in the sphere of taxation must also be considered. Tribal taxation has been widely perceived as necessary to protect Indian interests. The fact that the Jicarilla Apache have seen fit to impose their own taxes renders the threat to tribal interests which is always inherent in state taxation all the more apparent.[14] The market can bear only so much taxation, and it is inevitable that a point will be reached at which the State's taxes will impose a ceiling on tribal tax revenues. That the Jicarilla Apache have not yet raised their taxes to a level at which the combined effect of tribal and state taxation has been proved to diminish tribal revenues cannot be dispositive. Our decisions have never required a case-specific showing that state taxation in fact has deterred tribal activity; the potential for conflict is sufficient.

The majority observes that this is not "a case in which an unusually large state tax has imposed a substantial burden on the Tribe, " and deems the tribal interest "indirect and ... insubstantial." But the majority does not explain why interferences with federal policy of only the dramatic magnitude of the tax at issue in *Montana v. Crow Tribe of Indians*, 484 U.S. 997 (1988), meet the pre-emption threshold. In *Warren Trading Post Co. v. Arizona Tax Comm'n*, 380 U.S. 685, 691 (1965), the Court rejected a 2% tax on the gross proceeds of a non-Indian trader on an Indian reservation because it put "financial burdens on [the trader] or the Indians ... in addition to those Congress or the tribes have prescribed, and could thereby disturb and disarrange the statutory plan Congress set up in order to protect Indians." Indeed, the dissenters in *White Mountain Apache* characterized the less-than-1% tax struck down in that case as "relatively trivial" and "unlikely to have a serious adverse impact on the tribal business," 448 U.S., at 159 (dissenting opinion of STEVENS, J.). That the tax burden was held sufficient to support a finding of pre-emption in *White Mountain Apache* and *Warren Trading Post* undermines the majority's position here....

I respectfully dissent.

NOTES

Does *Cotton Petroleum* signal a rejuvenation of the *Rice v. Rehner* preemption analysis? Does the Court's focus on the lack of any historical tradition of

---

[14]Although this Court ruled in [*Colville*] that the mere fact of Indian taxation does not oust a State's power to tax, this Court clearly relied in *Colville* on the fact that value generated by the activity there at issue (smokeshops) was not developed on the reservation by activities in which the Tribe has an interest. We observed in *Colville* that the Tribe was basically importing goods and marketing its tax immunity. *Id.*, at 155. That is not so here. Indeed, our decision in *Colville* expressly left open the possibility that "the Tribe themselves could perhaps pre-empt state taxation through the exercise of properly delegated federal power to do so." *Id.*, at 156.

tribal severance taxes resemble *Rice*'s expansion of state authority based on the lack of any historical tradition of tribal regulation of the field?

The majority opinion in *Cotton Petroleum* relies heavily on the demise of the intergovernmental immunity doctrine and its significance for the problem of tax exemption. In light of the fact that Cotton Petroleum is a private corporate entity rather than a governmental body, what is the significance, if any, of the intergovernmental tax immunity doctrine to the disposition of the case? Note that the state of New Mexico had not and, under the *Blackfeet* case discussed in *Cotton Petroleum*, could not tax the *tribal* royalties from oil and gas or mineral development in Indian country. In light of *Blackfeet* is not the Court's invocation of the intergovernmental immunity doctrine somewhat misplaced?

Might *Cotton Petroleum* stand for the proposition that state taxation, and maybe regulation, of non-Indian enterprises leasing Indian land and resources can be sustained unless it has a *direct* effect on the tribe? If so, has the Court adopted the same direct/indirect effects tests for the Indian preemption doctrine that it rejected in favor of a more pragmatic test a half-century ago in the Court's dormant commerce clause cases? *Compare Buck v. Kuykendall*, 267 U.S. 307 (1925) (direct/indirect effects test) *with Southern Pac. Co. v. Arizona*, 325 U.S. 761 (1945) (rejection of direct/indirect effects test in favor of practical assessment of "the nature and extent of the burden" of the state regulation and a balancing of state interests against freedom of interstate commerce). In 1988 the Supreme Court summarily affirmed a Ninth Circuit decision holding two Montana taxes with an effective rate of 32.9% of the value of coal mined by non-Indian producers on tribal land preempted. *Montana v. Crow Tribe*, 484 U.S. 997 (1988), aff'g *Crow Tribe v. Montana*, 819 F.2d 895 (9th Cir. 1987). How can *Cotton Petroleum* and *Montana v. Crow Tribe* be reconciled? Does either the majority or the dissent provide any insights into this question?

Recall that the Indian commerce clause originally was adopted to prevent state frustration of federal efforts to protect Indian lands and resources. In light of that history, how can one justify the Court's willingness to permit multiple taxation and burdens on the development of Indian resources which make such development *more* expensive in Indian country within the state than outside of Indian country? Why does not such a tax pattern constitute a discriminatory pattern of taxation? Is not the tax apportionment doctrine of the interstate commerce clause precisely designed to prevent such discrimination against commerce?

In *Hoopa Valley Tribe v. Nevins*, 881 F.2d 657 (9th Cir. 1989), the Ninth Circuit distinguished *Cotton Petroleum Corp. v. New Mexico* and held that federal law preempted assessment of a state timber yield tax. The Hoopa Valley Indian Reservation consists of over 80,000 acres of commercial timber land. Remoteness of the reservation limits tribal employment opportunities and therefore the tribe relies primarily on timber-related revenues for its economic well-being. In an effort to promote timber management, conservation and production, the state of California adopted a timber yield tax. Cal. Rev. & Tax Code §§ 38101-38908. The tax is assessed judging the value of the timber when it is harvested and is imposed on the first non-exempt entity procuring ownership of the timber. The Hoopa Valley Tribe filed suit challenging the application of the tax to private companies. The district court held "that the exercise of state authority in assessing the timber yield tax against companies which purchase Tribal timber ... is preempted by the pervasive federal regulation of Indian timber and is thus in violation of federal law." *Hoopa Valley Tribe v. Nevins*, 590 F. Supp. 198, 203 (N.D. Cal. 1984). Affirming the district court's determination, the Ninth Circuit carefully distinguished the factual situation from *Cotton Petroleum*. The court noted that, in *Cotton Petroleum*, New Mexico "regulated the oil and gas activities affected by the tax" and that the "New Mexico tax primarily burdened non-Indian taxpayers." *Hoopa*, 881 F.2d at 660. In contrast, the Ninth Circuit noted that "California plays no role in the Hoopa Valley Tribe's timber activities" and "the burden of the tax concededly falls on the tribe." *Id.* (making reference to the district court opinion). Although the state provided a variety of services to residents of the reservation, because those services were not related to timber activities, the court was unpersuaded by the state's argument that the tax serves any legitimate state interests of raising revenues for services provided. *Id.* at 660-61.

THREE AFFILIATED TRIBES OF THE FORT BERTHOLD RESERVATION v. WOLD ENGINEERING

476 U.S. 877 (1986)

Justice O'CONNOR delivered the opinion of the Court.

Petitioner, Three Affiliated Tribes of the Fort Berthold Reservation, sought to sue respondent, Wold Engineering, P.C., in state court for negligence and breach of contract. The North Dakota Supreme Court held that Chapter 27-19 of the North Dakota Century Code (1974) disclaimed the unconditional state court civil jurisdiction North Dakota had previously extended [under *Vermillion v. Spotted Elk*, 85 N.W.2d 432 (1957),] to tribal Indians suing non-Indians in state court. It ruled that under Chapter 27-19, petitioner could not avail itself of state court jurisdiction unless it consented to waive its sovereign immunity and to have any civil disputes in state court to which it is a party adjudicated under state law. The question presented is whether Chapter 27-19, as construed by the North Dakota Supreme Court, is repugnant to the Federal Constitution or is pre-empted by federal Indian law.

I

This is the second time this Court has been called upon to address this jurisdictional controversy. See *Three Affiliated Tribes v. Wold Engineering (Three Tribes I)*, 467 U.S. 138 (1984). Because the facts and procedural history of the litigation were set forth in some detail in *Three Tribes I*, our present recitation will be brief.

Historically, Indian territories were generally deemed beyond the legislative and judicial jurisdiction of the state governments. See *id.*, at 142. This restriction was reflected in the federal statute which admitted North Dakota to the union, Enabling Act of Feb. 22, 1889, § 4, cl. 2, 25 Stat. 677, and was embodied in the form of jurisdictional disclaimers in North Dakota's original Constitution. See N.D. Const., Art. XVI, § 203, cl. 2 (1889). The pre-existing federal restrictions on state jurisdiction over Indian country were largely eliminated, however, in 1953 with Congress' enactment of [Public Law 280]. Pub. L. 280 gave federal consent to the assumption of state civil and criminal jurisdiction over Indian country and provided the procedures by which such an assumption could be made. As originally enacted, Pub. L. 280 did not require the States to obtain the consent of affected Indian tribes before assuming jurisdiction over them, but Title IV of the Civil Rights Act of 1968 amended Pub. L. 280 to require that all subsequent assertions of jurisdiction be preceded by tribal consent. Pub. L. 90-284, §§ 401, 402, 406, 82 Stat. 78-80, codified at 25 U.S.C. §§ 1321, 1322, 1326.

[A]s this Court in *Three Tribes I* affirmed, North Dakota's recognition of jurisdiction [in *Vermillion*] over the claims of Indian plaintiffs against non-Indian defendants was lawful because such jurisdiction did not interfere with the right of tribal Indians to govern themselves and was not subject to Pub. L. 280's procedural requirements since the jurisdiction was lawfully assumed prior to that enactment.

In 1958, North Dakota amended its Constitution to authorize its legislature to provide by statute for the acceptance of jurisdiction over Indian country, see N.D. Const., Art. XIII, § 1, cl. 2, and in 1963, the North Dakota legislature enacted Chapter 27-19. That Chapter provides, in pertinent part:

> In accordance with the provisions of Public Law 280 ... and [the amended] North Dakota constitution, jurisdiction of the state of North Dakota shall be extended over all civil claims for relief which arise on an Indian reservation upon acceptance by Indian citizens in a manner provided by this chapter. Upon acceptance the jurisdiction of the state is to the same extent that the state has jurisdiction over other civil claims for relief, and those civil laws of this state that are of general application to private property have the same force and effect within such Indian reservation or Indian country as they have elsewhere within this state. N.D. Cent. Code § 27-19-01 (Supp. 1985).

In subsequent cases, the North Dakota Supreme Court read this provision to "completely disclaim" the state jurisdiction recognized in *Vermillion* in cases in which the defendant was an Indian, absent tribal consent to jurisdiction as provided by statute. See, e.g., *In re Whiteshield*, 124 N.W.2d 694 (1963). However, until the instant suit, the court never squarely held that Chapter 27-19 also disclaimed the jurisdiction *Vermillion* lawfully recognized over cases in which an Indian sued a non-Indian in state court for a claim arising in Indian country. See *Three Tribes I*, 467 U.S., at 144-145.

Petitioner filed the instant suit against respondent in state court for negligence and breach of contract in connection with respondent's construction of a water-supply system on petitioner's reservation. At the time the suit was filed, petitioner's tribal court did not have jurisdiction over such claims. After counterclaiming for petitioner's alleged failure to make payments on the system, respondent moved to dismiss petitioner's complaint, arguing that the state court had no jurisdiction because petitioner has never consented to state court jurisdiction over the Fort Berthold Reservation under Chapter 27-19.

[In *Three Tribes I* we held] that federal law did not preclude the state court from asserting jurisdiction over petitioner's claim. In particular, we ruled that Pub. L. 280 neither required nor authorized North Dakota to disclaim the jurisdiction it had lawfully exercised over the claims of Indian plaintiffs against non-Indian defendants prior to the enactment of Pub. L. 280. See *Three Tribes I*, 467 U.S., at 150. Because the North Dakota Supreme Court's interpretation of Chapter 27-19 and its accompanying constitutional analysis appeared to rest on a possible misunderstanding of Pub. L. 280, this Court vacated the judgment and remanded the case to allow the North Dakota court to reconsider the jurisdictional questions in light of the proper interpretation of the governing federal statute.

On remand, the North Dakota Supreme Court held that Chapter 27-19 terminated any residuary jurisdiction that may have existed over claims arising in Indian country brought by tribal Indians against non-Indians in state court. It further held that state law barred petitioner from maintaining its suit in state court absent its waiver of its sovereign immunity in accordance with the statutory procedures. Finally, the court rejected petitioner's due process and equal protection challenges. It stated that petitioner had not been denied a due process right to access to the courts by action of the state, reasoning that it was the Indian people who had deprived themselves of access to state jurisdiction in declining to avail themselves of the State's jurisdictional offer by waiving their sovereign immunity. The North Dakota court then ruled that the jurisdictional disclaimer did not violate the Equal Protection Clause because, by virtue of the consent provision, "[t]he statute does not treat [the Tribe] less than equal, it treats them more than equal." *Id.*, at 107.

We granted certiorari to examine petitioner's claims that Chapter 27-19 violates the Federal Constitution and is pre-empted by federal Indian law.

[Since] we believe that the North Dakota law is pre-empted insofar as it is applied to disclaim pre-existing jurisdiction over suits by tribal plaintiffs against non-Indians for which there is no other forum, absent the Tribe's waiver of its sovereign immunity and consent to the application of state civil law in all cases to which it is a party, we reverse.

II

[The *Bracker*] pre-emption inquiry yields the conclusion that the legislative plan embodied in Pub. L. 280 forecloses North Dakota from disclaiming jurisdiction over petitioner's suit, and further, that the state interest advanced by the North Dakota jurisdictional scheme in this context is overshadowed by long-standing federal and tribal interests.

A

Pub. L. 280 represents the primary expression of federal policy governing the assumption by States of civil and criminal jurisdiction over the Indian Nations. The Act was the result of "comprehensive and detailed congressional scrutiny," *Kennerly v. District Court of Montana*, 400 U.S. 423, 424, n.1, 427 (1971), and was intended to replace the ad hoc regulation of state jurisdiction over Indian country with general legislation, providing "for all affected States to come within its terms." S. Rep. No. 699, 83d Cong., 1st Sess., 5 (1953), U.S. Code Cong. & Admin. News 1953, pp. 2409, 2412. In examining the effect of comprehensive legislation governing Indian matters such as this, "our cases have rejected a narrow focus on congressional intent to pre-empt state law as the sole touchstone. They have also rejected the proposition that pre-emption requires 'an express congressional statement to that effect.'" *New Mexico v. Mescalero Apache Tribe, supra*, 462 U.S., at 334 (quoting *White Mountain Apache Tribe v. Bracker, supra*, 448 U.S., at 144) (footnote omitted). Rather, we have found that where a detailed federal regulatory scheme exists and where its general thrust will be impaired by incompatible state action, that state action, without more, may be ruled pre-empted by federal law. See, e.g., *Warren Trading Post Co. v. Arizona Tax Comm'n*, 380 U.S. 685 (1965).

Given the comprehensiveness of the federal regulation in this area of Indian law, our conclusion in *Three Tribes I* that Congress generally intended to authorize the assumption, not the disclaimer, of state jurisdiction over Indian country is persuasive evidence that the instant disclaimer conflicts with the federal scheme. But we need not rest upon this conclusion alone, for Congress' specific treatment of the retrocession of previously assumed jurisdiction permits no doubt that North Dakota's disclaimer is inconsistent with the requirements of Pub. L. 280.

As originally enacted, Pub. L. 280 plainly contemplated that, if States chose to extend state court jurisdiction over causes of action arising in Indian country, they would be required to honor that commitment, for the Act made no provision for States to return any jurisdiction to the United States. Congress' failure to provide for the retrocession of jurisdiction assumed by the States is fully consistent with the purposes underlying Pub. L. 280: promoting the gradual assimilation of Indians into the dominant American culture and easing the fiscal and administrative burden borne by the Federal Government by virtue of its control over Indian affairs. Were States permitted to, at their option and at any time, retrocede all or part of the jurisdiction they had assumed and to leave Indians with no recourse for civil wrongs, the congressional plan of gradual but steady assimilation could be disrupted and the divestment of federal dominance nullified.

When Congress subsequently revisited the question of retrocession in the 1968 Amendments, it provided that "[t]he United States is authorized to accept a retrocession by any State," 25 U.S.C. § 1323(a), but it specifically limited this authorization to the retrocession of jurisdiction assumed under Pub. L. 280 pursuant to the original 1953 version of the statute. This retrocession provision apparently was added in response to Indian dissatisfaction with Pub. L. 280. In light of this congressional purpose, the fact that Congress did not provide for retrocession of jurisdiction lawfully assumed prior to the enactment of Pub. L. 280 or of jurisdiction assumed after 1968 cannot be attributed to mere oversight or inadvertence. Since Congress was motivated by a desire to shield the Indians from unwanted extensions of jurisdiction over them, there was no need to provide for retrocession in those circumstances because the previously assumed jurisdiction over Indian country was only lawful to the extent that it was consistent with Indian tribal sovereignty and self-government, see, e.g., *Williams v. Lee*, 358 U.S. 217 (1959), and the jurisdiction assumed after 1968 could be secured only upon the receipt of tribal consent. See 25 U.S.C. § 1321.

North Dakota may not, and indeed has not attempted to, rely on § 1323(a) as authority for its disclaimer of jurisdiction over claims such as petitioner's because it did not assume such jurisdiction under any of the provisions specified in § 1323(a), nor has the United States accepted the retrocession. We have previously enforced the procedural requirements and the jurisdictional provisions of Pub. L. 280 quite stringently, consistent with our understanding that the jurisdictional scheme embodied in that Act was the product of a wide-ranging and detailed congressional study. Accordingly, we conclude that since North Dakota's disclaimer is not authorized by § 1323(a), it is barred by that section.

In sum, because Pub. L. 280 was designed to extend the jurisdiction of the States over Indian country and to encourage state assumption of such jurisdiction, and because Congress specifically considered the issue of retrocession but did not provide for disclaimers of jurisdiction lawfully acquired other than under Pub. L. 280 prior to 1968, we must conclude that such disclaimers cannot be reconciled with the congressional plan embodied in Pub. L. 280 and thus are pre-empted by it.

B

Our consideration of the State's interest in disclaiming the pre-existing, unconditional jurisdiction extended to tribal Indians suing non-Indian defendants, and in replacing it with an extension of jurisdiction conditioned on the Tribe's waiver of its sovereign immunity and its agreement to the application of state law in all suits to which it is a party, reinforces our conclusion that Chapter 27-19 is inconsistent with federal law. Simply put, the state interest, as presently implemented, is unduly burdensome on the federal and tribal interests.

As the North Dakota Supreme Court explained, Chapter 27-19 was originally designed as a unilateral assumption of jurisdiction over Indian country, which was intended to provide a means of enforcing contracts between Indians and non-Indians and a tribunal for trying tort actions, family law matters, and "many [other] types of actions too numerous to mention." 364 N.W.2d, at 102, and n.5. The North Dakota legislature added the consent provision to Chapter 27-19 as a compromise to "accommodate the will of the Indian people." *Id.*, at 103. Those Indians who opposed the assertion of state jurisdiction against them would not be subjected to it absent consent, but neither would they be permitted to enjoy state jurisdiction as plaintiffs absent consent to suit as defendants. Certainly, the State's interest in requiring that all its citizens bear equally the burdens and the benefits of access to the courts is readily understandable. But here, federal interests exist which override this state interest.

The federal interest in ensuring that all citizens have access to the courts is obviously a weighty one. [Decisions in this Court and many state courts] have long recognized that Indians share this interest in access to the courts, and that tribal autonomy and self-government are not impeded when a State allows an Indian to enter its court to seek relief against a non-Indian concerning a claim arising in Indian country. North Dakota conditions the Tribe's access to the courts on its waiver of its tribal sovereign immunity and agreement to the application of state civil law in all state court civil actions to which it is or may be a party. These conditions apply regardless of whether, as here, the Tribe has no other effective means of securing relief for civil wrongs. As the State concedes, even if the Tribe were to have access to tribal court to resolve civil controversies with non-Indians, it would be unable to enforce those judgments in state court; thus, the Tribe cannot be said to have a meaningful alternative to state adjudication by way of access to other tribunals in such cases. Respondent argues that the Tribe is not truly deprived of access to the courts by the North Dakota jurisdictional scheme because the Tribe could have unrestricted access to the State's courts by "merely" consenting to the statutory conditions. We conclude, however, that those statutory conditions may be met only at an unacceptably high price to tribal sovereignty and thus operate to effectively bar the Tribe from the courts.

The North Dakota jurisdictional scheme requires the Tribe to accept a potentially severe intrusion on the Indians' ability to govern themselves according to their own laws in order to regain their access to the state courts. The statute provides that "[t]he civil jurisdiction herein accepted and assumed [upon Indian consent] shall include but shall not be limited to the determination of parentage of children, termination of parental rights, commitments by county courts, guardianship, marriage contracts, and obligations for the support of spouse, children, or other dependents." N.D. Cent. Code § 27-19-08 (Supp. 1985). Although these subjects clearly encompass areas of traditional tribal control, the North Dakota statute contemplates that state civil law will control in these areas. Respondent argues that Chapter 27-19 safeguards tribal self-government by also providing that any tribal ordinance or custom "shall, if not inconsistent with the applicable civil law of this state, be given full force and effect in the determination of civil claims for relief pursuant to this section." § 27-19-09. This provision plainly provides that state law will generally control, however, and will merely be supplemented by nonconflicting Indian ordinances or customs, even in cases that arise on the reservation, that involve only Indians, and that concern subjects which are within the jurisdiction of the tribal court.

This result simply cannot be reconciled with Congress' jealous regard for Indian self-governance. [The North Dakota statute's] requirement that the Tribe consent to suit in *all* civil causes of action before it may again gain access to state court as a plaintiff also serves to defeat the Tribe's federally conferred immunity from suit. The common law sovereign immunity possessed by the Tribe is a necessary corollary to Indian sovereignty and self-governance. [I]n the absence of federal authorization, tribal immunity, like all aspects of tribal sovereignty, is privileged from diminution by the States.

To be sure, not all conditions imposed on access to state courts which potentially affect tribal immunity, and thus tribal self-government, are objectionable. For instance, even petitioner concedes that its tribal immunity does not extend to protection from the normal processes of the state court in which it has filed suit. See Tr. of Oral Arg. 7, 10-11 ("The Three Affiliated Tribes believe it would be proper in the interest of justice that they would be subject to discovery proceedings and to proceedings that would insure a fair trial to the non-Indian defendants"). Petitioner also concedes that a non-Indian defendant may assert a counterclaim arising out of the same transaction or occurrence that is the subject of the principal suit as a setoff or recoupment. It is clear, however, that the extent of the waiver presently required by Chapter 27-19 is unduly intrusive on the Indian's common law sovereign immunity, and thus on its ability to govern itself according to its own laws. By requiring that the Tribe open itself up to the coercive jurisdiction of state courts for all matters occurring on the reservation, the statute invites a potentially severe impairment of the authority of the tribal government, its courts, and its laws.

Pub. L. 280 certainly does not constitute a "governing Act of Congress" which validates this type of interference with tribal immunity and self-government.

[T]he 1968 Amendments to Pub. L. 280 pointedly illustrate the continuing congressional concern over tribal sovereignty. The impetus for the addition of a consent requirement in the 1968 Amendments was congressional dissatisfaction with the involuntary extension of state jurisdiction over Indians who did not feel they were ready to accept such jurisdiction, or who felt threatened by it.

[T]he State's interest is overly broad and overly intrusive when examined against the backdrop of the federal and tribal interests implicated in this case. See *Rice v. Rehner*, 463 U.S., at 719. The perceived inequity of permitting the Tribe to recover from a non-Indian for civil wrongs in instances where a non-Indian allegedly may not recover against the Tribe simply must be accepted in view of the overriding federal and tribal interests in these circumstances, much in the same way that the perceived inequity of permitting the United States or North Dakota to sue in cases where they could not be sued as defendants because of their sovereign immunity also must be accepted. Our examination of the state, tribal, and federal interests implicated in this case, then, reinforces our conclusion that North Dakota's disclaimer of jurisdiction over suits such as this cannot be reconciled with the congressional plan embodied in Pub. L. 280.

The judgment of the North Dakota Supreme Court is reversed and remanded for further proceedings not inconsistent with this opinion

It is so ordered.

Justice REHNQUIST, with whom Justice BRENNAN and Justice STEVENS join, dissenting.

North Dakota law provides that in order for an Indian tribe such as petitioner to avail itself of the jurisdiction of North Dakota courts as a plaintiff, it must also accept the jurisdiction of those courts when it is properly named as a defendant in them. This Court holds that such a rule — which would commend itself to most people as eminently fair — is pre-empted by federal law.... I think there is nothing in Pub. L. 280 nor in federal Indian policy that prohibits North Dakota from applying its statute in the manner in which it did in this case, and I therefore dissent from the Court's contrary conclusion.

NOTE: THE PREEMPTIVE EFFECT OF PUBLIC LAW 280

After some experimentation during the 1940's with specific legislation for named reservations, e.g., 18 U.S.C. § 3243 (Kansas) and 25 U.S.C. §§ 232, 233 (New York), Congress passed Public Law 280 in 1953 both to provide state criminal and civil jurisdiction over Indian country in certain named mandatory states and to further provide a mechanism by which any other state not having such jurisdiction could voluntarily remove any impediments to assuming such jurisdiction, such as state constitutional disclaimers of jurisdiction, and could assume such authority by express legislative enactment. This original authority for voluntary assumption of jurisdiction was amended in 1968 to thereafter require tribal consent through a tribal referendum and to provide a mechanism for state-initiated retrocession to the federal government of authority assumed under Public Law 280. 25 U.S.C. § 1321. While detailed consideration of the actual contours of Public Law 280 jurisdiction is postponed until later in this chapter, *Three Tribes II* requires consideration of the preemptive force of this legislation.

In light of the existence of Congressional legislation providing a mechanism for the assumption of jurisdiction over Indian country, one reasonably might question how states could exercise any jurisdiction in Indian country without strict compliance with the procedures set forth in the legislation. Initially, some decisions suggested that Public Law 280 procedures were preemptive and that state failure to assume jurisdiction under Public Law 280 precluded any state jurisdiction. For example, the Supreme Court opinions in *Williams v. Lee*, involving a non-Indian trader in Indian country, and *McClanahan*, involving a Navajo taxpayer, both note that the failure of Arizona to enact any legislation outside of the environmental arena under Public Law 280 contributed to a finding that state authority was preempted. In *Kennerly v. District Court of Montana*, 400 U.S. 423 (1971), the Court held that, notwithstanding a 1967 Blackfeet tribal council resolution suggesting that state courts could exercise jurisdiction concurrent with tribal courts over suits involving tribal members, Montana state courts lacked jurisdiction over a debt action commenced against two resident members of the Blackfeet Indian Tribe where the cause of action arose on the Blackfeet Reservation. The *per curiam* opinion for the Court noted that before the 1968 amendments Public Law 280 "conditioned the assumption of state jurisdiction on 'affirmative legislative action' by the State; the Act made no provision whatsoever for tribal consent, either as a necessary or sufficient condition to the assumption of state jurisdiction." The Court further rejected the argument that the 1968 tribal consent amendments might retroactively validate the assumption of state authority, since under the amendment the tribal consent "must be manifested by majority vote of the enrolled Indians within the affected area of Indian country." The Court therefore concluded that "[l]egislative action by the Tribal Council does not comport with the explicit requirements of the Act." *Id.* at 429.

These early indications that Public Law 280 represented the exclusive means by which states could secure jurisdiction gradually faded as cases like *Moe*, *Colville*, and *Montana v. United States* (set forth in Chapter 3), without significant reference to Public Law 280, suggested that states had considerable inherent authority over non-Indians in Indian country and had limited, indirect authority to require Indians to conform to state laws as a means of facilitating enforcement of legitimate state laws taxing or regulating non-Indians in Indian country. Precisely why Public Law 280 was not preemptive in such situations is difficult to imagine, particularly since the Court thereafter paid scant attention to the question. Perhaps the Court concluded that the preemptive scope of the legislation was strictly limited by statutory provisions that conferred jurisdiction in criminal cases "over offenses committed by or against Indians [within] Indian country," 18 U.S.C. § 1162, and "over civil causes of action between Indians or to which Indians are parties which arise [within] Indian country," 28 U.S.C. § 1360. Whatever the explanation, the Court thereafter virtually ignored the preemptive implications of Public Law 280 until *Three Tribes I* and *II*.

B. STATE AUTHORITY OVER INDIANS AND INDIAN PROPERTY OUTSIDE OF INDIAN COUNTRY

MESCALERO APACHE TRIBE v. JONES

411 U.S. 145 (1973)

Mr. Justice WHITE delivered the opinion of the Court.

The Mescalero Apache Tribe operates a ski resort in the State of New Mexico, on land located outside the boundaries of the Tribe's reservation. The State has asserted the right to impose a tax on the gross receipts of the ski resort and a use tax on certain personalty purchased out of State and used in connection with the resort. Whether paramount federal law permits these taxes to be levied is the issue presented by this case.

The home of the Mescalero Apache Tribe is on reservation lands in Lincoln and Otero Counties in New Mexico. The Sierra Blanca Ski Enterprises, owned and operated by the Tribe, is adjacent to the reservation and was developed under the auspices of the [IRA]. After a feasibility study by the Bureau of Indian Affairs, equipment and construction money was provided by a loan from the Federal Government under § 10 of the Act, 25 U.S.C. § 470, and the necessary land was leased from the United States Forest Service for a term of 30 years. The ski area borders on the Tribe's reservation but, with the exception of some cross-country ski trails, no part of the enterprise, its buildings, or equipment is located within the existing boundaries of the reservation....

I

At the outset, we reject — as did the state court — the broad assertion that the Federal Government has exclusive jurisdiction over the Tribe for all purposes and that the State is therefore prohibited from enforcing its revenue laws against any tribal enterprise "[w]hether the enterprise is located on or off tribal land." Generalizations on this subject have become particularly treacherous. The conceptual clarity of Mr. Chief Justice Marshall's view in [*Worcester v. Georgia*] has given way to more individualized treatment of particular treaties and specific federal statutes, including statehood enabling legislation, as they, taken together, affect the respective rights of States, Indians, and the Federal Government. [I]n the special area of state taxation, absent cession of jurisdiction or other federal statutes permitting it, there has been no satisfactory authority for taxing Indian reservation lands or Indian income from activities carried on within the boundaries of the reservation, and [*McClanahan*] lays to rest any doubt in this respect by holding that such taxation is not permissible absent congressional consent.

But tribal activities conducted outside the reservation present different considerations. "State authority over Indians is yet more extensive over activities ... not on any reservation." *Organized Village of Kake*, [369 U.S. 60,] at 75. Absent express federal law to the contrary, Indians going beyond reservation boundaries have generally been held subject to nondiscriminatory state law otherwise applicable to all citizens of the State. [*E.g.*], *Puyallup Tribe v. Department of Game*, 391 U.S. 392, 398 (1968); *Tulee v. Washington*, 315 U.S. 681, 683 (1942); *Ward v. Race Horse*, 163 U.S. 504 (1896). That principle is as relevant to a State's tax laws as it is to state criminal laws, see *Ward v. Race Horse, supra*, at 516, and applies as much to tribal ski resorts as it does to fishing enterprises. See *Organized Village of Kake, supra*.

The Enabling Act for New Mexico, 36 Stat. 557, reflects the distinction between on- and off-reservation activities. Section 2 of the Act provides that the people of the State disclaim "all right and title" to lands "owned or held by any

Indian or Indian tribes the right or title to which shall have been acquired through or from the United States ... and that ... the same shall be and remain subject to the disposition and under the absolute jurisdiction and control of the Congress of the United States." But the Act expressly provides, with respect to taxation, that "nothing herein ... shall preclude the said State from taxing, as other lands and other property are taxed, any lands and other property outside of an Indian reservation owned or held by any Indian, save and except such lands as have been granted ... or as may be granted or confirmed to any Indian or Indians under any Act of Congress, but ... all such lands shall be exempt from taxation by said State [only] so long and to such extent as Congress has prescribed or may hereafter prescribe." It is thus clear that in terms of general power New Mexico retained the right to tax, unless Congress forbade it, all Indian land and Indian activities located or occurring "outside of an Indian reservation."

We also reject the broad claim that the [IRA] rendered the Tribe's off-reservation ski resort a federal instrumentality constitutionally immune from state taxes of all sorts. *M'Culloch v. Maryland*, 4 Wheat. 316 (1819). The intergovernmental-immunity doctrine was once much in vogue in a variety of contexts and, with respect to Indian affairs, was consistently held to bar a state tax on the lessees of, or the product or income from, restricted lands of tribes or individual Indians. The theory was that a federal instrumentality was involved and that the tax would interfere with the Government's realizing the maximum return for its wards. This approach did not survive; its rise and decline in Indian affairs is described and reflected in *Helvering v. Mountain Producers Corp.*, 303 U.S. 376 (1938); *Oklahoma Tax Comm'n v. United States*, 319 U.S. 598 (1943); and *Oklahoma Tax Comm'n v. Texas Co.*, 336 U.S. 342 (1949), where the Court cut to the bone the proposition that restricted Indian lands and the proceeds from them were — as a matter of constitutional law — automatically exempt from state taxation. Rather, the Court held that Congress has the power "to immunize these lessees from the taxes we think the Constitution permits Oklahoma to impose in the absence of such action" and that "[t]he question whether immunity shall be extended in situations like these is essentially legislative in character." *Oklahoma Tax Comm'n v. Texas Co., supra*, at 365-366.

The [IRA] neither requires nor counsels us to recognize this tribal business venture as a federal instrumentality. Congress itself felt it necessary to address the immunity question and to provide tax immunity to the extent it deemed desirable. There is, therefore, no statutory invitation to consider projects undertaken pursuant to the Act as federal instrumentalities generally and automatically immune from state taxation. Unquestionably, the Act reflected a new policy of the Federal Government and aimed to put a halt to the loss of tribal lands through allotment. It gave the Secretary of the Interior power to create new reservations, and tribes were encouraged to revitalize their self-government through the adoption of constitutions and bylaws and through the creation of chartered corporations, with power to conduct the business and economic affairs of the tribe. As was true in the case before us, a tribe taking advantage of the Act might generate substantial revenues for the education and the social and economic welfare of its people. So viewed, an enterprise such as the ski resort in this case serves a federal function with respect to the Government's role in Indian affairs. But the "mere fact that property is used, among others, by the United States as an instrument for effecting its purpose does not relieve it from state taxation." *Choctaw, Oklahoma & Gulf R. Co. v. Mackey*, 256 U.S. 531, 536 (1921).

The intent and purpose of the Reorganization Act was "to rehabilitate the Indian's economic life and to give him a chance to develop the initiative destroyed by a century of oppression and paternalism." H.R. Rep. No. 1804, 73d Cong., 2d Sess., 6 (1934). See also S. Rep. No. 1080, 73d Cong., 2d Sess., 1 (1934). [The IRA] did not strip Indian tribes and their reservation lands of their historic immunity from state and local control. But, in the context of the [IRA,] we think it unrealistic to conclude that Congress conceived of off-reservation tribal enterprises "virtually as an arm of the Government." *Department of Employment v. United States*, 385 U.S. 355, 359-360 (1966). On the contrary, the aim was to disentangle the tribes from the official bureaucracy.... We accordingly decline the invitation to resurrect the expansive version of the intergovernmental-immunity doctrine that has been so consistently rejected in modern times.

II

The Tribe's broad claims of tax immunity must therefore be rejected. But there remains to be considered the scope of the immunity specifically afforded by [IRA § 5], 25 U.S.C. § 465.

A

Section 465 provides, in part, that "any lands or rights acquired" pursuant to any provision of the Act "shall be taken in the name of the United States in trust for the Indian tribe or individual Indian for which the land is acquired, and such lands or rights shall be exempt from State and local taxation.[11] On its face, the statute exempts land and rights in land, not income derived from its use. It is true that a statutory tax exemption for "lands" may, in light of its context and purposes, be construed to support an exemption for taxation on income derived from the land. See *Squire v. Capoeman*, 351 U.S. 1 (1956). But, absent clear statutory guidance, courts ordinarily will not imply tax exemptions and will not exempt off-reservation income from tax simply because the land from which it is derived, or its other source, is itself exempt from tax.

> This Court has repeatedly said that tax exemptions are not granted by implication.... It has applied that rule to taxing acts affecting Indians as to all others.... If Congress intends to prevent the State of Oklahoma from levying a general non-discriminatory estate tax applying alike to all its citizens, it should say so in plain words. Such a conclusion cannot rest on dubious inferences.

---

[11] The ski resort land was not technically "acquired" "in trust for the Indian tribe." But, as the Solicitor General has pointed out, "it would have been meaningless for the United States, which already had title to the forest, to convey title to itself for the use of the Tribe." Brief for the United States as *amicus curiae* 13. We think the lease arrangement here in question was sufficient to bring the Tribe's interest in the land within the immunity afforded by § 465. It should perhaps be noted that the Tribe has not suggested that it is immune from taxation by virtue of its status as a lessee of land owned by the Federal Government.

Oklahoma Tax Comm'n v. United States, 319 U.S., at 606-607. [On its face] therefore, there is no reason to hold that [§ 465] forbids income as well as property taxes. Nor does the legislative history support any other conclusion. As we have noted, several explicit provisions encompassing a broad tax immunity for chartered Indian communities were dropped from the bills that preceded the Wheeler-Howard bill. Similarly, the predecessor to the exemption embodied in § 465 dealt only with lands acquired for new reservations or for additions to existing reservations. 1934 House Hearings 11. Here, the rights and land were acquired by the Tribe beyond its reservation borders for the purpose of carrying on a business enterprise as anticipated by §§ 476 and 477 of the Act. These provisions were designed to encourage tribal enterprises "to enter the white world on a footing of equal competition." 78 Cong. Rec. 11732. In this context, we will not imply an expansive immunity from ordinary income taxes that businesses throughout the State are subject to. We therefore hold that the exemption in § 465 does not encompass or bar the collection of New Mexico's nondiscriminatory gross receipts tax and that the Tribe's ski resort is subject to that tax.

B

We reach a different conclusion with respect to the compensating use tax imposed on the personalty installed in the construction of the ski lifts. According to the Stipulation of Facts, that personal property has been "permanently attached to the realty." In view of § 465, these permanent improvements on the Tribe's tax-exempt land would certainly be immune from the State's ad valorem property tax. See *United States v. Rickert*, 188 U.S. 432, 441-443 (1903). We think the same immunity extends to the compensating use tax on the property. The jurisdictional basis for use taxes is the use of the property in the State. See *Henneford v. Silas Mason Co.*, 300 U.S. 577 (1937). It has long been recognized that "use" is among the "bundle of privileges that make up property or ownership" of property and, in this sense at least, a tax upon "use" is a tax upon the property itself. This is not to say that use taxes are for all purposes to be deemed simple ad valorem property taxes. See, *e.g.*, *United States v. Detroit*, 355 U.S. 466 (1958), and its companion cases; *Sullivan v. United States*, 395 U.S. 169 (1969). But use of permanent improvements upon land is so intimately connected with use of the land itself that an explicit provision relieving the latter of state tax burdens must be construed to encompass an exemption for the former.... The judgment of the Court of Appeals is

Affirmed in part and reversed in part.

Mr. Justice DOUGLAS, with whom Mr. Justice BRENNAN and Mr. Justice STEWART concur, dissenting in part.

The power of Congress granted by Art. I, § 8 "[t]o regulate Commerce ... with the Indian Tribes" is an exceedingly broad one. In the liquor cases the Court held that it reached acts even off Indian reservations in areas normally subject to the police power of the States. *Perrin v. United States*, 232 U.S. 478. The power gained breadth by reason of historic experiences that induced Congress to treat Indians as wards of the Nation. The laws enacted by Congress varied from decade to decade.

The present Act, 48 Stat. 984, 25 U.S.C. § 461 *et seq.*, was enacted in 1934 with various purposes in mind, the ones most relevant being, first, "[t]o permit Indian tribes to equip themselves with the devices of modern business organization, through forming themselves into business corporations," and second, "[t]o establish a system of financial credit for Indians." S. Rep. No. 1080, 73d Cong., 2d Sess., 1....

The Court makes much of the fact that the ski enterprise is not on the reservation. But that seems irrelevant to me by reason of § 5 of the [IRA], 25 U.S.C. § 465. While the lease of Forest Service lands was not technically "acquired ... in trust for the Indian tribe," the Court concedes that the lease arrangement was sufficient to bring the Tribe's interest in the land within the immunity afforded by § 465. And so the question respecting income taxes comes down to whether these taxes are within the scope of "such lands or rights" as used in § 5....

The 1934 Act obviously is an effort by Congress to extend its control to Indian economic activities outside the reservation for the benefit of its Indian wards. The philosophy permeating the present Act was articulated by Mr. Chief Justice Marshall in [*Worcester*]:

> From the commencement of our government, Congress has passed acts to regulate trade and intercourse with the Indians; which treat them as nations, respect their rights, and manifest a firm purpose to afford that protection which treaties stipulate.

As noted in *Warren Trading Post v. Tax Comm'n*, 380 U.S. 685, most tax immunities of Indians have related to activities in reservations. But, as we stated in that case, the fact that the activities occurred on a reservation was not the controlling reason, "but rather because Congress in the exercise of its power granted in Art. I, § 8, has undertaken to regulate reservation trading in such a comprehensive way that there is no room for the States to legislate on the subject." *Id.*, at 691 n.18....

NOTES

1. The Boundary of On-Reservation Activity: As a statement of general principle *Mescalero Apache* is correct in suggesting that historically Indians, and now Indian tribes, are usually subject to state authority for various conduct, including crimes, occurring off the reservation. Ever since the Trade and Intercourse Acts many (but not all) preemptive federal statutes have applied only to Indian country, leaving to state authorities the management of affairs outside of Indian country. *Contrast Passamaquoddy Tribe v. Morton*, 528 F.2d 370 (1st Cir. 1975) (federal statutory restraints on alienation of Indian land apply to all tribal land within the United States irrespective of lack of federal recognition of the tribe).

The more interesting question is whether the Court was correct in treating the Sierra Blanca Ski Enterprises as an off-reservation enterprise when it was located on land adjacent to the tribal reservation leased to it by the United States Forest Service in order (according to footnote 11) to avoid the meaningless gesture of having "the United States, which already had title to the forest, ... convey title to itself for the use of the Tribe." Had the land in fact been conveyed rather than leased would it not have become part of the tribal estate and thereby part of the reservation? The answer to that question is more complex than first appears. While not noted in the *Mescalero Apache* opinion, section 7 of the Indian Reorganization Act, 25 U.S.C. § 467, authorizes

[t]he Secretary of the Interior ... to proclaim new Indian reservations on lands acquired pursuant to any authority conferred [by the Indian Reorganization Act], or to add such lands to existing reservations. *Provided*, That lands added to existing reservations shall be designated for the exclusive use of Indians entitled by enrollment or by tribal membership to residence at such reservations.

Apparently, no such proclamation had been issued over the leased lands involved in *Mescalero Apache*, in part because the Secretary has been extremely reluctant to invoke the authority conferred by section 7 and has issued such proclamations only rarely. In light of the proviso in section 7 could a proclamation have been issued adding the leased lands to the Mescalero Apache's Reservation? Does the lack of a proclamation under section 7 of the IRA help explain why the Court treated the Sierra Blanca Ski Enterprises as an off-reservation business?

Failure to issue a section 7 proclamation has not prevented other courts from treating land acquired under section 5 of the Indian Reorganization Act, 25 U.S.C. § 465, as part of the tribal reservation and therefore as Indian country. For example, in *Santa Rosa Band of Indians v. Kings County*, 532 F.2d 655 (9th Cir. 1975), the court held that land acquired under section 5 of the Indian Reorganization Act, 25 U.S.C. § 465, for use as part of a housing project for members of the Santa Rosa Band was exempt from local zoning and building ordinances despite the apparent lack of any proclamation under section 7. As to the status of the lands the court merely stated:

The language used in § 465 must be read against [the judicially created doctrines involving the status of Indian trust property], which provides the implicit substance of what the language signifies. We are confident that when Congress in 1934 authorized the Secretary to purchase and hold title to lands for the purpose of providing land for Indians, it understood and intended such lands to be held in the legal manner and condition in which trust lands were held under applicable court decisions — free of state regulations.

532 F.2d at 666. Can this statement be justified in light of the lack of any proclamation under section 7, a fact the court failed to note?

What, if anything, does the *Mescalero Apache* decision have to say about state power over tribal or allotted lands or matters occurring thereon in the diminished portions of the Rosebud Sioux Reservation or in the former Lake Traverse Reservation? *Cf. Rosebud Sioux Tribe v. Kneip*, 430 U.S. 584 (1977), and *DeCoteau v. District Court*, 420 U.S. 425 (1975), both discussed in Chapter 1, section B3.

2. *Kake v. Egan* and Federal Authority to Preempt State Jurisdiction Over Off-Reservation Matters: In *Organized Village of Kake v. Egan*, 369 U.S. 60 (1962), the Supreme Court held that the state of Alaska's authority to apply its anti-fish-trap conservation laws to members of two native villages was not preempted by federal law or policy even though the federal government had authorized use of the traps. The Secretary of the Interior had relied on the White Act, a conservation statute, and the general provisions of the Snyder Act as providing authority for the regulation permitting the traps. The Court held that the statutory authority was not sufficiently specific to preempt the contrary state law. Unfortunately, Justice Frankfurter's opinion contained some very broad language regarding the reach of state law both on and off Indian reservations. First, the language in the opinion intimated that the presumption is in favor of state jurisdiction absent specific preemptive statutes even for activity occurring on Indian reservations. But *Kake* was a case involving state jurisdiction where there was no reservation at all. The existence of a reservation is critical in determining the scope of state jurisdiction. *Metlakatla Indian Community v. Egan*, 369 U.S. 45 (1962), decided the same day as *Kake*, held that the federal government, rather than the state of Alaska, had jurisdiction over the use of traps in the Metlakatla Indian Community, a federally recognized reservation created by statute. The extent to which *Kake* has added to judicial confusion is a tribute to the power of a scholarly opinion, even where that scholarship is faulty. Note that in *McClanahan*, the Court took pains to distinguish *Kake*, in footnotes 8, 15, and 20. In footnote 15, for example, the Court stressed that *Kake* was a case involving *non-reservation* Indians (emphasis in original).

Second, the Court asserted that states have full authority to regulate all Indian activity off of reservations, even activity exercising aboriginal rights:

> [S]tate regulation of off-reservation fishing certainly does not impinge on treaty-protected reservation self-government, the factor found decisive in *Williams v. Lee*. Nor have appellants any fishing rights derived from federal laws. This Court has never held that States lack power to regulate the exercise of aboriginal Indian rights, such as claimed here, or of those based on occupancy. Because of the migratory habits of salmon, fish traps at Kake and Angoon are not merely local matters.

Id. at 75-76. Is such a broad statement consistent with the history and purposes of the Indian Commerce Clause? If the relationship between tribes and states is solely a matter of federal law, should not federal law control the extent to which states may affect aboriginal rights? Were many of the tribes affected by the Indian commerce clause federally recognized by treaty at the time that the Constitution was drafted in 1787? What does this language from *Kake* indicate about the propriety of the Maine state court decision in *State v. Dana*, discussed in Chapter 1, holding that criminal jurisdiction over the then federally unrecognized Passamaquoddy Reservation in Maine nevertheless was exclusively federal and tribal since the state-created and recognized reservation constituted Indian country as a dependent Indian community under 18 U.S.C. § 1151(b)? Is *Kake* limited to the peculiar problems of the aboriginal rights of Alaskan natives prior to the enactment of the Alaskan Native Claims Settlement Act of 1971? If so, why were those claims treated differently? Does *Kake* have any application to tribes in the east coast which are not federally recognized but trace their title to land from aboriginal sources or from colonial grants and treaties? In a recent case reported in the *New York Times*, the Vermont Supreme Court upheld a lower court ruling that Abenaki Indians fishing on aboriginal land the title to which had never been extinguished were free from state fish and game regulations, because aboriginal rights are federal rights not normally subject to state regulation. "Vermont Justices Say Indians May Fish Without Licenses," N.Y. Times, Aug. 6, 1990, § B, at 8, col. 5.

Although it is true that Indians are generally subject to state authority for transactions occurring off reservations, federal authority under the Indian commerce clause does reach off reservation so that the actual exercises of that power in statute or treaty may nevertheless have preemptive effects on state authority. The narrow holding in *Kake* is merely that the statutory authority was not sufficiently precise to preempt state authority. Consider, for example, the treatment of the taxability of the materials used in the ski lift in *Mescalero Apache*. Does the statutory preemption doctrine operate with the same strength and in the same manner for off-reservation activities as for on-reservation matters? What differences, if any, exist in these two contexts? Did the Court in

Mescalero Apache treat the tax exemption language in § 465 in the same manner as the disclaimer of jurisdiction involved in *McClanahan,* decided the same day?

For another example of off-reservation preemption of state authority, consider the materials on off-reservation hunting and fishing rights in Chapter 6.

C. CONGRESSIONAL ALLOCATION OF JURISDICTION

1. PUBLIC LAW 280

As noted earlier, judicially created jurisdictional allocations have operated only in the absence of affirmative congressional jurisdictional allocations in Indian country. Congress has addressed the jurisdictional allocation problem in laws of general application in four major contexts. First, as discussed in Chapter 2, the criminal jurisdiction statutes, including 18 U.S.C. §§ 1151-1153, allocate law enforcement authority among federal, tribal, and state governments. Second, Public Law 280, enacted in 1953, and significantly amended in 1968, authorized certain states to assume a more significant power role in Indian country. Third, in the Indian Child Welfare Act of 1978, 25 U.S.C. § 1901 et seq., Congress sought to assure a more significant tribal role in adjudications affecting the custody and adoption of Indian children. Fourth, other statutes, like the liquor control laws discussed above in *Rice v. Rehner,* adopt certain state regulatory or taxing laws for Indian country. *See generally In re Colwash,* 57 Wash. 2d 196, 356 P.2d 994 (1960); *State ex rel. Adams v. Superior Court of Okanogan Juvenile Court Session,* 57 Wash. 2d 181, 356 P.2d 985 (1960). In addition to statutes of general application, Congress has sometimes enacted statutes reallocating jurisdiction on a state or reservation-specific basis. *See, e.g.,* 18 U.S.C. § 3243 (criminal jurisdiction in Kansas); 25 U.S.C. §§ 232-233 (civil and criminal jurisdiction in New York).

Once enacted, such jurisdictional allocation statutes focus judicial attention on questions related to the procedures and substantive content intended by the framers of the legislation. The next two sections are devoted to these questions in the context of Public Law 280 and the Indian Child Welfare Act.

PUBLIC LAW 280, Act of Aug. 15, 1953, ch. 505, 67 Stat. 588-90 (Selected Provisions)

§ 1162. State jurisdiction over offenses committed by or against Indians in the Indian country

(a) Each of the States listed in the following table shall have jurisdiction over offenses committed by or against Indians in the areas of Indian country listed opposite the name of the State to the same extent that such State has jurisdiction over offenses committed elsewhere within the State, and the criminal laws of such State shall have the same force and effect within such Indian country as they have elsewhere within the State:

State of	Indian country affected*
California	All Indian country within the State

---

*Alaska was added to the list of mandatory Public Law 280 states contained in both 18 U.S.C. § 1162 (criminal jurisdiction) and 28 U.S.C. § 1360 (civil jurisdiction) by the Act of Aug. 8, 1958,

State of	Indian country affected
Minnesota	All Indian country within the State, except the Red Lake Reservation
Nebraska	All Indian country within the State
Oregon	All Indian country within the State, except the Warm Springs Reservation
Wisconsin	All Indian country within the State, except the Menominee Reservation

(b) Nothing in this section shall authorize the alienation, encumbrance, or taxation of any real or personal property, including water rights, belonging to any Indian or any Indian tribe, band, or community that is held in trust by the United States or is subject to a restriction against alienation imposed by the United States; or shall authorize regulation of the use of such property in a manner inconsistent with any Federal treaty, agreement, or statute or with any regulation made pursuant thereto; or shall deprive any Indian or any Indian tribe, band, or community of any right, privilege or immunity afforded under Federal treaty, agreement, or statute with respect to hunting, trapping, or fishing or the control, licensing, or regulation thereof.

(c) The provisions of [18 U.S.C. §§ 1152 and 1153] shall not be applicable within the areas of Indian country listed in subsection (a) of this section....

Sec. 4. Title 28, United States Code, is hereby amended by inserting in chapter 85 thereof immediately after section 1359 a new section, to be designated as section 1360, as follows:

§ 1360. State civil jurisdiction in actions to which Indians are parties

(a) Each of the States listed in the following table shall have jurisdiction over civil causes of action between Indians or to which Indians are parties which arise in the areas of Indian country listed opposite the name of the State to the same extent that such State has jurisdiction over other civil causes of action, and those civil laws of such State that are of general application to private persons or private property shall have the same force and effect within such Indian country as they have elsewhere within the State:

State of	Indian country affected
California	All Indian country within the State
Minnesota	All Indian country within the State, except the Red Lake Reservation
Nebraska	All Indian country within the State

Pub. L. 85-615, 72 Stat. 545, in connection with its admission to the Union. In 1954 the Menominee Reservation in Wisconsin was made a Public Law 280 reservation, as part of its termination process, by the deletion of the exception contained in the original Act. Wisconsin has since retroceded to the federal government jurisdiction over the Menominee Reservation under the provisions of 25 U.S.C. § 1323, as has Nebraska over the Winnebago and Omaha Reservations. [Eds.]

State of	Indian country affected
Oregon	All Indian country within the State, except the Warm Springs Reservation
Wisconsin	All Indian country within the State, except the Menominee Reservation

(b) Nothing in this section shall authorize the alienation, encumbrance, or taxation of any real or personal property, including water rights, belonging to any Indian or any Indian tribe, band, or community that is held in trust by the United States or is subject to a restriction against alienation imposed by the United States; or shall authorize regulation of the use of such property in a manner inconsistent with any Federal treaty, agreement, or statute or with any regulation made pursuant thereto; or shall confer jurisdiction upon the State to adjudicate, in probate proceedings or otherwise, the ownership or right to possession of such property or any interest therein.

(c) Any tribal ordinance or custom heretofore or hereafter adopted by an Indian tribe, band, or community in the exercise of any authority which it may possess shall, if not inconsistent with any applicable civil law of the State, be given full force and effect in the determination of civil causes of action pursuant to this section....

Sec. 6. Notwithstanding the provisions of any Enabling Act for the admission of a State, the consent of the United States is hereby given to the people of any State to amend, where necessary, their State constitution or existing statutes, as the case may be, to remove any legal impediment to the assumption of civil and criminal jurisdiction in accordance with the provisions of this Act: *Provided*, That the provisions of this Act shall not become effective with respect to such assumption of jurisdiction by any such State until the people thereof have appropriately amended their State constitution or statutes as the case may be.

Sec. 7. The consent of the United States is hereby given to any other State not having jurisdiction with respect to criminal offenses or civil causes of action, or with respect to both, as provided for in this Act, to assume jurisdiction at such time and in such manner as the people of the State shall, by affirmative legislative action, obligate and bind the State to assumption thereof.

TITLE IV OF PUBLIC LAW 90-284, 82 Stat. 78 (1968), 25 U.S.C. §§ 1321-1326 (Selected Provisions)

§ 1321. Assumption by State of criminal jurisdiction — Consent of United States; force and effect of criminal laws

(a) The consent of the United States is hereby given to any State not having jurisdiction over criminal offenses committed by or against Indians in the areas of Indian country situated within such State to assume, with the consent of the Indian tribe occupying the particular Indian country or part thereof which could be affected by such assumption, such measure of jurisdiction over any or all of such offenses committed within such Indian country or any part thereof as may be determined by such State to the same extent that such State has jurisdiction over any such offense committed elsewhere within the State, and the criminal laws of such State shall have the same force and effect within such Indian country or part thereof as they have elsewhere within that State.

Alienation, encumbrance, taxation, and use of property; hunting, trapping, or fishing

(b) Nothing in this section shall authorize the alienation, encumbrance, or taxation of any real or personal property, including water rights, belonging to any Indian or any Indian tribe, band, or community that is held in trust by the United States or is subject to a restriction against alienation imposed by the United States; or shall authorize regulation of the use of such property in a manner inconsistent with any Federal treaty, agreement, or statute or with any regulation made pursuant thereto; or shall deprive any Indian or any Indian tribe, band, or community of any right, privilege, or immunity afforded under Federal treaty, agreement, or statute with respect to hunting, trapping, or fishing or the control, licensing, or regulation thereof....

§ 1322. Assumption by State of civil jurisdiction — Consent of United States; force and effect of civil laws

(a) The consent of the United States is hereby given to any State not having jurisdiction over civil causes of action between Indians or to which Indians are parties which arise in the areas of Indian country situated within such State to assume, with the consent of the tribe occupying the particular Indian country or part thereof which would be affected by such assumption, such measure of jurisdiction over any or all such civil causes of action arising within such Indian country or any part thereof as may be determined by such State to the same extent that such State has jurisdiction over other civil causes of action, and those civil laws of such State that are of general application to private persons or private property shall have the same force and effect within such Indian country or part thereof as they have elsewhere within that State.

Alienation, encumbrance, taxation, use, and probate of property

(b) Nothing in this section shall authorize the alienation, encumbrance, or taxation of any real or personal property, including water rights, belonging to any Indian or any Indian tribe, band, or community that is held in trust by the United States or is subject to a restriction against alienation imposed by the United States; or shall authorize regulation of the use of such property in a manner inconsistent with any Federal treaty, agreement, or statute, or with any regulation made pursuant thereto; or shall confer jurisdiction upon the State to adjudicate, in probate proceedings or otherwise, the ownership or right to possession of such property or any interest therein.

Force and effect of tribal ordinances or customs

(c) Any tribal ordinance or custom heretofore or hereafter adopted by an Indian tribe, band, or community in the exercise of any authority which it may possess shall, if not inconsistent with any applicable civil law of the State, be given full force and effect in the determination of civil causes of action pursuant to this section....

§ 1323. Retrocession of jurisdiction by State

(a) The United States is authorized to accept a retrocession by any State of all or any measure of the criminal or civil jurisdiction, or both, acquired by such State pursuant to the provisions of section 1162 of Title 18, section 1360 of Title 28, or section 7 of the Act of August 15, 1953 (67 Stat. 588), as it was in effect prior to its repeal by subsection (b) of this section.

(b) Section 7 of the Act of August 15, 1953 (67 Stat. 588), is hereby repealed, but such repeal shall not affect any cession of jurisdiction made pursuant to such section prior to its repeal....

§ 1324. Amendment of State constitutions or statutes to remove legal impediment; effective date

Notwithstanding the provisions of any enabling Act for the admission of a State, the consent of the United States is hereby given to the people of any State to amend, where necessary, their State constitution or existing statutes, as the case may be, to remove any legal impediment to the assumption of civil or criminal jurisdiction in accordance with the provisions of this subchapter. The provisions of this subchapter shall not become effective with respect to such assumption of jurisdiction by any such State until the people thereof have appropriately amended their State constitution or statutes, as the case may be....

§ 1326. Special election

State jurisdiction acquired pursuant to this subchapter with respect to criminal offenses or civil causes of action, or with respect to both, shall be applicable in Indian country only where the enrolled Indians within the affected area of such Indian country accept such jurisdiction by a majority vote of the adult Indians voting at a special election held for that purpose. The Secretary of the Interior shall call such special election under such rules and regulations as he may prescribe, when requested to do so by the tribal council or other governing body, or by 20 per centum of such enrolled adults.

GOLDBERG, PUBLIC LAW 280: THE LIMITS OF STATE JURISDICTION OVER RESERVATION INDIANS, 22 U.C.L.A. Law Review 535, 537-47, 549-52, 558-59 (1975)*

Passed in 1953, PL-280[10] was an attempt at compromise between wholly abandoning the Indians to the states and maintaining them as federally pro-

---

*Copyright 1975 by the Regents of the University of California. Reprinted by permission.

[10] Act of Aug. 15, 1953, ch. 505, 67 Stat. 588-90 (now codified as amended in scattered sections of 18, 28 U.S.C.).Act of June 8, 1940, ch. 276, 54 Stat. 249 (criminal jurisdiction to Kansas); Act of May 31, 1946, ch. 279, 60 Stat. 229 (criminal jurisdiction to North Dakota over the Devils Lake Reservation); Act of June 30, 1948, ch. 759, 62 Stat. 1161 (criminal jurisdiction to Iowa over the Sac and Fox Reservations); Act of July 2, 1948, ch. 809, 62 Stat. 1224 (criminal jurisdiction to New York) (codified at 25 U.S.C. § 232 (1970)); Act of Oct. 5, 1949, ch. 604, 63 Stat. 705 (civil and criminal

tected wards, subject only to federal or tribal jurisdiction. The statute originally transferred to five willing states and offered all others, civil and criminal jurisdiction over reservation Indians regardless of the Indians' preference for continued autonomy. PL-280 did not, however, terminate the trust status of reservation lands.

From the outset, PL-280 left both the Indians and the states dissatisfied, the Indians because they did not want state jurisdiction thrust upon them against their will, the states because they resented the remaining federal protection which seemed to deprive them of the ability to finance their newly acquired powers. Predictably, disagreement between the Indians and the states erupted over the scope of jurisdiction offered by PL-280 and the means by which transfers of jurisdiction were to be effected. Among the matters in dispute were whether states assuming jurisdiction under PL-280 acquired the power to tax and zone on Indian reservations, and whether states asserting PL-280 jurisdiction had satisfied the procedural prerequisites for doing so.

Recent social, economic, and political developments have made the Indians and states especially anxious that their respective interpretations of PL-280 prevail. The expansion of metropolitan areas near Indian reservations has increased the states' interest in regulating and exploiting residential and recreational development on trust land. States have been notably desirous of acquiring pollution and subdivision control. The discovery of substantial energy resources on reservations, and consequent industrial development, have spurred similar state interest in regulating and taxing those activities. At the same time, tribal governments have been receiving encouragement from the federal government to develop tribal enterprises and strengthen their administrative apparatus, increasing their interest in freedom from state power. Finally, growing demands on the part of Indians that they receive their share of state services and their share of representation in state legislatures have produced concomitant demands on the part of the states that Indians submit to state jurisdiction.

The jurisdictional stakes are considerably higher today than they were when PL-280 was enacted; at the same time federal Indian policy is more devoted to fulfilling federal responsibility for Indians and building effective tribal governments. Broadly speaking, the model for federal Indian policy seems to be changing from one favoring state power with minimum protection for Indian interests to one favoring tribal autonomy with minimum protection for state interests. Nevertheless, since PL-280 is the most direct evidence of congressional intent with respect to state jurisdiction, the debate over the scope of state power on Indian reservations must contend with policy choices Congress made when PL-280 was enacted. Amendments to the Act adopted in 1968 did, however, bring PL-280 more in conformity with current policy by rendering all *future* assertions of state jurisdiction under the Act subject to the affected Indians' consent, and authorizing states to return jurisdiction to the federal government. But controversies persist over jurisdiction claimed by the states prior to [the 1968 amendments].

---

jurisdiction to California over Agua Caliente Reservation); Act of Sept. 13, 1950, ch. 947, 64 Stat. 845 (civil jurisdiction to New York).

II. *Legislative Background*

PL-280 differed from earlier relinquishments of federal Indian jurisdiction in that it authorized every state to assume jurisdiction at any time in the future. Previous transfers had been limited to some or all the reservations in a single state,[20] and had followed consultation with the individual state and affected tribes by the Bureau of Indian Affairs (hereinafter referred to as B.I.A.). Although PL-280 itself had begun as an attempt to confer jurisdiction on California only, by the time it was reported out of the Senate, the prevailing view was that "any legislation in [the] area should be on a general basis, making provision for all affected States to come within its terms …." The Senate Report of the bill in committee suggests why Congress was concerned with effectuating a general transfer of jurisdiction after years of an ad hoc policy which had involved careful evaluation in each case from the point of view of both Indians and the states. The Report indicates the foremost concern of Congress at the time of enacting of PL-280 was lawlessness on the reservations and the accompanying threat to Anglos living nearby. In 1953, responsibility for law enforcement on the reservations was irrationally fractionated. If a non-Indian committed a crime against another non-Indian or a crime without an apparent victim, such as gambling or drunk driving, only state authorities could prosecute him under state law. But if either the offender or victim was Indian, the federal government had exclusive jurisdiction to prosecute, applying state law in federal court under the Assimilative Crimes Act. Finally, if offender and victim were both Indians, the federal government had exclusive jurisdiction if the offense was one of the "Ten Major Crimes;" otherwise, tribal courts had exclusive jurisdiction. Since federal law enforcement was typically neither well-financed nor vigorous, and tribal courts often lacked the resources and skills to be effective, the result, described by House Indian Affairs Subcommittee member Wesley D'Ewart, of Montana, was "[t]he complete breakdown of law and order on many of the Indian reservations …." Throughout the hearings of PL-280 and its predecessor bills in the previous Congress, Representative D'Ewart repeatedly voiced "[t]he desire of all law abiding citizens living on or near Indian reservations for law and order." The primary law enforcement thrust of PL-280 is further evidenced by the fact that several predecessor bills offered the states criminal jurisdiction only, and PL-280 itself exempted several reservations completely from state jurisdiction solely because they had legal systems and organizations "functioning in a reasonably satisfactory manner."

Of course, conferring jurisdiction on the states was not the only available solution to the very real law enforcement problem. [Conferring state] criminal jurisdiction was preferred to other alternatives however, because it was the cheapest solution; Congress was interested in saving money as well as bringing law and order to the reservations.

---

[20] Act of June 8, 1940, ch. 276, 54 Stat. 249 (criminal jurisdiction to Kansas); Act of May 31, 1946, ch. 279, 60 Stat. 229 (criminal jurisdiction to North Dakota over the Devils Lake Reservation); Act of June 30, 1948, ch. 759, 62 Stat. 1161 (criminal jurisdiction to Iowa over the Sac and Fox Reservations); Act of July 2, 1948, ch. 809, 62 Stat. 1224 (criminal jurisdiction to New York) (codified at 25 U.S.C. § 232 (1970)); Act of Oct. 5, 1949, ch. 604, 63 Stat. 705 (civil and criminal jurisdiction to California over Agua Caliente Reservation); Act of Sept. 13, 1950, ch. 947, 64 Stat. 845 (civil jurisdiction to New York).

There is much less evidence of the congressional rationale for conferring civil jurisdiction on the states, and much less factual support for that decision. State civil jurisdiction over reservation Indians was believed to have been somewhat more extensive than state criminal jurisdiction, though typically, state courts were powerless to resolve claims against reservation Indians arising on the reservation. Since federal law governed many important civil relations involving Indians, the B.I.A., charged with administering these laws, played a considerable governing role on the reservations. In this context, the Senate Report on PL-280 declared that the Indians "have reached a stage of acculturation and development that makes desirable extension of State civil jurisdiction ...." The implication of this and similar statements was that Indians were just as socially advanced as other state citizens, and should therefore be released from second-class citizenship as well as the paternalistic supervision of the B.I.A.

Considering the absence of any significant investigation of the Indians' stage of social development prior to the broad delegation of jurisdiction to every state by PL-280, it seems unlikely that Congress knew or cared about the Indians' readiness for state jurisdiction. Furthermore, it is difficult to reconcile this theme of advanced acculturation with the prevailing notion that state criminal jurisdiction was necessary because the Indians were disorderly and incapable of self-government. Most likely, civil jurisdiction was an afterthought in a measure aimed primarily at bringing law and order to the reservations, added because it comported with the pro-assimilationist drift of federal policy, and because it was convenient and cheap.

The choice Congress made in PL-280 did not wholly satisfy either the tribes or the states. The source of the Indians' displeasure was the absence of a provision for tribal consent prior to state assumption of jurisdiction. The states, on the other hand, were unhappy about the absence of a provision either granting federal subsidies to states that accepted jurisdiction or removing reservation lands from tax-exempt trust status. These aspects of the law have generated efforts directed at Congress, the state legislatures, and the courts to mold or remold PL-280 to suit [the preferences of the Indians or the states].

III. *Objections to PL-280*

A. *Controversy Over Indian Consent*

Indian antagonism to PL-280 has stemmed almost entirely from its initial unilateral imposition of state law. Congress omitted a tribal consent requirement from PL-280 for the same reasons it abandoned its policy of conferring jurisdiction state by state after consultation with the affected tribes. In both instances, concern about bringing law and order to the reservations at reduced federal expense dictated immediate transfers of jurisdiction to the states. Thus, when Congressperson D'Ewart inserted a tribal consent provision in one of the predecessor bills to PL-280 in order to obtain the support of the tribes in his state, B.I.A. Commissioner Dillon S. Meyer stated:

[I]t might be possible to pass a referendum in some of the reservations against action by the State, where they have a completely inadequate law and order code and completely inadequate court system and completely inadequate policing system, and we would recommend if we found that situation that they be included anyhow.

Indian opposition to the absence of a tribal consent provision in PL-280 was initially based on the principle of tribal sovereignty. The departure from past practice of consulting with the Indians prior to transferring jurisdiction was considered a deliberate slight.

Another reason for opposition was the fear that state jurisdiction would in practice operate to the disadvantage of the Indians. The Indians in many instances preferred federal to state jurisdiction because the B.I.A., for all its faults, at least perceived the Indians as its special responsibility and concern. Many Indians feared that their people would be discriminated against in state courts and given longer sentences simply because they were Indians; that state law enforcement officials would ignore crimes when Indians were the victims but act vigorously when a white was harmed; and that many of their elders were not sufficiently fluent in the language and customs of white America to enable them to cope with state jurisdiction. They disliked the ousting of their functioning tribal courts and law-making bodies and feared that the state institutions taking their place would be neither sufficiently sensitive to Indian traditions nor adequately staffed and financed. The latter fear was especially warranted in view of PL-280's failure to provide a tax base or subsidies to the states to support their newly acquired law enforcement obligations.

Between 1953 and 1968, a wide variety of influential persons and organizations urged Congress to add an Indian consent provision to PL-280. Some states, however, did not wait for Congress to act. Instead, they undertook by themselves to accommodate the Indians' desire to determine when and how state jurisdiction should be assumed. Since the 1968 amendments (adding Indian consent provisions) to PL-280 did not affect prior assertions of jurisdiction under the Act, the nature and validity of these efforts retain importance.

The five, later six, states that were granted PL-280 jurisdiction immediately and irrevocably (mandatory states) lacked the flexibility to condition their jurisdiction on Indian consent. By virtue of language in PL-280 any jurisdiction other than state jurisdiction on the reservations was henceforth invalid, except as provided in the Act. While Congress had consulted with these states prior to passage of PL-280 in order to ascertain their desire for such jurisdiction, and had exempted certain reservations in these states at the Indians' request, it had not authorized the mandatory states to create further exemptions in response to Indian wishes. In contrast, the states merely authorized to assume jurisdiction at their discretion (optional states) could take the Indians' wishes into account before asserting their power, and many did so, either formally or informally. For some states, this recognition of Indian sovereignty was spontaneous; in others, it was formed by the bitter experience of states such as Wyoming,[56] South Dakota,[57] Washington,[58] and New Mexico, in which the Indians had

---

[56] In a state referendum in 1964, Wyoming rejected an attempt to amend its constitution to empower the legislature to accept PL-280 jurisdiction. The sponsor of the measure had not bothered to consult with the Indians prior to introducing [the bill].

[57] In 1964, after the South Dakota legislature had enacted a measure unilaterally extending state jurisdiction to the reservations, the Indians instituted a referendum, bombarded the voters of the state with publicity and literature opposing the measure, and secured the law's defeat. Dep't of Indian Affairs, State of Montana, Tribal Governments and Law and Order 19-20 (1968) [hereinafter cited as Tribal Governments].

[58] Washington's first attempt to accept PL-280 jurisdiction met with strong Indian opposition and was defeated. Thereafter, in 1957, a bill was passed with the support of the Indians which permitted

waged vigorous and successful battles against bills and constitutional amendments imposing state jurisdiction unilaterally. Although Arizona[60] and Iowa[61] simply asserted jurisdiction without seeking concurrence of the affected Indians, and Idaho and Washington ignored Indian preferences as to some subject matters,[62] Florida first solicited the consent of the Seminole tribe, Nevada consulted with every tribe in the state prior to assuming jurisdiction, and Idaho,[65] Montana,[66] North Dakota,[67] South Dakota,[68] and Washington[69] established some form of Indian consent procedure despite the absence of a requirement in PL-280.

[In the Indian Civil Rights Act of 1968], Congress eliminated the need for self-imposed limits on state jurisdiction in the future by establishing a tribal consent provision in PL-280 itself. Congress provided in the Civil Rights Act of 1968 that henceforth no state could acquire PL-280 jurisdiction over the objections of the affected Indians. Furthermore, in an action which most legislators believed did no more than make explicit existing law, the 1968 Act declared that state jurisdiction could be acquired one tribe at a time, so long as a majority of the adult enrolled members of the tribe expressed their consent in a special election. Finally, in a more controversial action, it allowed acceptance of jurisdiction over some subject matters, but not others.[81]

This change in PL-280 is significant evidence of a shift in federal Indian policy from the pro-assimilationist orientation of the 1950's to a greater concern for strengthening tribal institutions and encouraging economic development on reservations. Interestingly, the opposition to tribal consent was not couched in law and order language this time. Rather, the opponents stressed the need for state control of economic development on the reservations, a need which has precipitated much conflict over PL-280 in recent years, especially in the Southwest. Later actions by Congress indicate a willingness to permit enclaves of tribal sovereignty within a state, despite the parade of horribles described by state officials, so long as the federal government maintained control over tribal decisions which might seriously endanger state interests.

The significance of the addition of a tribal consent provision to PL-280 lies not only in its recognition of the principle of Indian self-determination, but also in its new conception of the role of state jurisdiction on reservations. The tribal

---

Washington to assume jurisdiction only after a tribe had requested that it do so. See Civil Rights Report, *supra* note 50, at 145. The Indians were partially defeated on the tribal consent issue in 1963, however, when jurisdiction was extended unilaterally to some subject matters. Wash. Rev. Code §§ 37.12.010-.060 (Supp. 1971).

[60] Ariz. Rev. Stat. Ann. §§ 36-1801, 36-1856 (Supp. 1973) (water pollution control).

[61] Iowa Code Ann. §§ 1.12-.15 (Supp. 1974). Iowa extended its civil jurisdiction over the Sac and Fox Reservations, which were already subject to state criminal jurisdiction.

[62] Idaho Code § 67-5101 (1973); Wash. Rev. Code §§ 37.12.010—.060 (Supp. 1971).

[65] Idaho Code § 67-5102 (1973).

[66] Mont. Rev. Code Ann. §§ 83-802, 83-806 (1966). For a discussion of the considerations that influenced Montana's decision to include a tribal consent provision, refer to Dep't of Indian Affairs, State of Montana, A Study of Problems Arising from the Transfer of Law & Order Jurisdiction on Indian Reservations to the State of Montana 11 (1961).

[67] N.D. Cent. Code § 27-19-02 (1974).

[68] S.D. Compiled Laws Ann. § 1-1-13 (1967). The law provides for state jurisdiction unless within three months the tribe rejects it in a referendum held at [the expense of the tribe].

[69] Wash. Rev. Code § 37.12.021 (Supp. 1971).

[81] 25 U.S.C. § 1321(a) (1970) provides that states may assume criminal jurisdiction "over any or all ... offenses"; 25 U.S.C. § 1322(a) (1970) provides that states may assume civil jurisdiction over "any or all ... civil causes of action arising within ... Indian country ...."

consent provision transformed PL-280 from a law which justified state jurisdiction on law enforcement, budgetary, and assimilationist grounds to one which justified state jurisdiction as a means of providing services to Indian communities. Among the strongest arguments in favor of the 1968 Act's amendment was that the institution of state jurisdiction under PL-280, far from improving reservation law and order and elevating Indians from second-class citizenship, had subjected them to discriminatory treatment in the courts, as well as discrimination in the provision of state services. Once tribal consent became a prerequisite to state jurisdiction, and jurisdiction could be acquired one subject matter at a time, the way was opened for tribes and states to negotiate for the extension of state jurisdiction in those situations where it was to their mutual advantage.

The beneficial impact of the 1968 amendments to PL-280 should not be overemphasized, however. The Indian consent provision was not made retroactive, and thus earlier assumptions of state jurisdiction over Indian objections were not affected. Moreover, it did not enable Indians who had consented to state jurisdiction under a state-initiated consent provision to reconsider their decisions.

B. Controversy Over Financing State Jurisdiction

The absence of an Indian consent provision in PL-280 reflected insensitivity to the interests of the Indians; the absence of federal subsidies to PL-280 states demonstrated similar insensitivity to the dilemma of states handed jurisdiction but simultaneously denied the means to finance it. This financial dilemma derives from a basic inconsistency in federal policy. On the one hand, Congress wished to satisfy state demands for improved law and order on the reservation; on the other hand, Congress was itself unwilling to pay for such improvements or to enable the states to do so by lifting the tax-exempt status of Indian trust lands.[87]

The failure to resolve this inconsistency had disastrous consequences for states acquiring PL-280 jurisdiction. Local governments acquiring jurisdiction were required to hire more police, more judges, more prison guards, more probation and parole officers, and more juvenile aid officers, and to build new police stations, courthouses, and jails. It could have been predicted that a state which undertook law enforcement on the reservation as vigorously as elsewhere in the state would incur higher expenses than the federal government, even

---

[87] This inconsistency was exposed during the hearings on PL-280 when Congressperson Young of Nevada confronted counsel for the B.I.A., Harry Sellery, with the questionable value of offering the states jurisdiction but denying them the power to tax Indian property as the means of financing it. Counsel responded that if federal financial assistance were made available to fill the gap,

there [would] be some tendency ... for the Indian to be thought of and perhaps to think of himself because of the financial assistance which comes from the Federal Government as still somewhat a member of a race or group which is set apart from other citizens of the State. And it is desired to give him and the other citizens of the State the feeling of a conviction that he is in the same status and has access to the same services, including the courts, as other citizens of the State who are not Indians.

Hearings Transcript I, *supra* note 22, at 8. When counsel was reminded that differentiation between Indians and non-Indians would be *increased* by the failure to provide federal financial aid, since the Indians would enjoy a unique exemption from state property taxes, he replied curtly: "The Department [of the Interior] has recommended, nevertheless, that no financial assistance be afforded to the States." *Id.* at 9.

allowing for the greater expense of operating a federal as opposed to a municipal court. The new resources available to the states under PL-280 such as fines
and court costs were clearly inadequate; estimates based on federal experience
indicated such funds would cover only about 10 percent of all newly-acquired
law enforcement expenses. The mandatory PL-280 states were hardest hit; they
could not avoid the economic consequences of federal withdrawal from the
reservations by refusing jurisdiction under the Act.

Financial hardship for the states translated into inadequate law enforcement
for the reservations. The most notable failure among the mandatory states was
Nebraska, where the Omaha and Winnebago reservations were left without any
law enforcement at all once federal officers withdrew [from providing such
services].

C. *Retrocession*

Had PL-280 originally contained a provision permitting the states and the
tribes to demand the return or "retrocession" of state PL-280 jurisdiction to the
federal government, much of the dissatisfaction with the Act would have been
avoided, though federal dissatisfaction might have been greater. Retrocession
would have allowed both states and tribes to experiment with state jurisdiction,
the states to determine whether it was too costly, the tribes to determine
whether it fairly met their needs. In addition, retrocession would have permitted jurisdictional arrangements to reflect changed circumstances. If a tribe subject to PL-280 jurisdiction developed new economic resources, or a new generation of tribal members wished to establish strong tribal governing institutions,
the state could be required to relinquish jurisdiction.

Notwithstanding these potential benefits from retrocession, the device received little attention during the debates over PL-280 and its predecessor bills,
and no recognition in the statute itself. The failure to include a means by which
states could effect retrocession is perhaps attributable to a congressional wish to
rid the federal government forever of its costly supervisory responsibilities on
the reservations. The omission of a provision allowing Indians to demand retrocession is undoubtedly explained by the very law and order and pro-
assimilationist impulses that accounted for the absence of an Indian consent
provision.

Eventually, however, Congress extended the advantages of retrocession to the
states, although not to the Indians. By 1968, the states' financial difficulties with
PL-280 had become so apparent that relief was provided in the form of a
section of the 1968 Civil Rights Act enabling any state which had previously
assumed jurisdiction under PL-280 to offer the return of all or any measure of
its jurisdiction to the federal government by sending a resolution to the Secretary of the Interior. The Secretary could accept or reject the retrocession in his
discretion.[112] Under this provision, the Indians could not participate in the

---

[112] 25 U.S.C. § 1323 (1970). Why this opportunity was not extended to states acquiring jurisdiction *after* 1968 is somewhat unclear, since both optional and mandatory states were authorized to
return jurisdiction accepted before 1968. A possible ground for distinction is that the 1968 Act, by
expressly authorizing partial assumptions of jurisdiction, rendered retrocession less financially im-
perative for the states. In addition, Congress may have felt that states should not be as free to

retrocession decision, although they might attempt to do so informally through appeals directly to the Secretary.

The absence of an Indian veto over state-initiated retrocession was undesirable from the Indians' point of view because the states could decide to retrocede only part of their PL-280 jurisdiction, and might use that power to relieve themselves of the most costly forms of jurisdiction while retaining those most offensive to the Indians. Perhaps Congress believed that the Secretary's veto power over a state's proposed retrocession would make a tribal veto unnecessary in those situations where a state's partial retrocession seriously disadvantaged the Indians, or where the Indians actually preferred to retain complete state jurisdiction.

A more glaring omission was the failure to create any mechanism by which Indians could initiate and *force* retrocession on an unwilling state which had acquired jurisdiction. It is difficult to justify this omission on assimilationist grounds or on the ground of the inadequacy of tribal law enforcement facilities because other language in the 1968 Act required tribal consent before any initial extension of state jurisdiction, regardless of the quality of law enforcement machinery on the reservation. Perhaps objections to allowing tribal-initiated retrocession derived from concern that the tribes would seek to retrocede less than all the jurisdiction the state had initially assumed, under circumstances where the state was unwilling to exercise only the remainder. Or perhaps Congress felt that reservations which had already been subjected to PL-280 jurisdiction were so weakened as to be incapable of resuming self-government.

BRYAN v. ITASCA COUNTY
426 U.S. 373 (1976)

Mr. Justice BRENNAN delivered the opinion of the Court.

This case presents the question reserved in [*McClanahan*]: whether the grant of civil jurisdiction to the States conferred by § 4 of [Public Law 280] 28 U.S.C. § 1360, is a congressional grant of power to the States to tax reservation Indians except insofar as taxation is expressly excluded by the terms of the statute.

Petitioner Russell Bryan, an enrolled member of the Minnesota Chippewa Tribe, resides in a mobile home on land held in trust by the United States for the Chippewa Tribe on the Leech Lake Reservation in Minnesota. In June 1972, petitioner received notices from the auditor of respondent Itasca County, Minn., that he had been assessed personal property tax liability on the mobile home totaling $147.95. Thereafter, in September 1972, petitioner brought this suit in the Minnesota District Court seeking a declaratory judgment that the State and county were without authority to levy such a tax on personal property of a reservation Indian on the reservation and that imposition of such a tax was contrary to federal law. The Minnesota District Court [upheld the tax, the] Minnesota Supreme Court affirmed, [w]e granted certiorari, and now reverse.

I

[This Court's decisions in] *McClanahan* and *Moe* preclude any authority in respondent county to levy a personal property tax upon petitioner's mobile

retrocede jurisdiction acquired after Indian consent which the 1968 Act's amendments of PL-280 required before jurisdiction could be acquired.

home in the absence of congressional consent. Our task therefore is to determine whether § 4 of Pub. L. 280, 28 U.S.C. § 1360, constitutes such consent. [Section 1360] does not in terms provide that the tax laws of a State are among "civil laws ... of general application to private persons or private property." The Minnesota Supreme Court concluded, however, that they were, finding in § 4(b) of the statute a negative implication of inclusion in § 4(a) of a general power to tax.... The Minnesota Supreme Court reasoned that "unless paragraph (a) is interpreted as a general grant of the power to tax, then the exceptions contained in paragraph (b) are limitations on a nonexistent power." 303 Minn., at 402, 228 N.W.2d, at 253. Therefore, the state court held: "Public Law 280 is a clear grant of the power to tax." *Id.* at 406, 228 N.W.2d at 256. We disagree. That conclusion is foreclosed by the legislative history of Pub. L. 280 and the application of canons of construction applicable to congressional statutes claimed to terminate Indian immunities.

II

The primary concern of Congress in enacting Pub. L. 280 that emerges from its sparse legislative history was with the problem of lawlessness on certain Indian reservations, and the absence of adequate tribal institutions for law enforcement. See Goldberg, Public Law 280: The Limits of State Jurisdiction over Reservation Indians, 22 U.C.L.A. L. Rev. 535, 541-542 (1975). The House Report states:

> These States lack jurisdiction to prosecute Indians for most offenses committed on Indian reservations or other Indian country, with limited exceptions....
> As a practical matter, the enforcement of law and order among the Indians in the Indian country has been left largely to the Indian groups themselves. In many States, tribes are not adequately organized to perform that function; consequently, there has been created a hiatus in law-enforcement authority that could best be remedied by conferring criminal jurisdiction on States indicating an ability and willingness to accept such responsibility. H.R. Rep. No. 848, 83d Cong., 1st Sess., 5-6 (1953).

Thus, provision for state criminal jurisdiction over offenses committed by or against Indians on the reservations was the central focus of Pub. L. 280 and is embodied in § 2 of the Act, 18 U.S.C. § 1162.

In marked contrast in the legislative history is the virtual absence of expression of congressional policy or intent respecting § 4's grant of civil jurisdiction to the States. Of special significance for our purposes, however, is the total absence of mention or discussion regarding a congressional intent to confer upon the States an authority to tax Indians or Indian property on reservations. Neither the Committee Reports nor the floor discussion in either House mentions such authority. This omission has significance in the application of the canons of construction applicable to statutes affecting Indian immunities, as some mention would normally be expected if such a sweeping change in the status of tribal government and reservation Indians had been contemplated [by the Congress].

Piecing together as best we can the sparse legislative history of § 4, subsection (a) seems to have been primarily intended to redress the lack of adequate Indian forums for resolving private legal disputes between reservation Indians, and between Indians and other private citizens, by permitting the courts of the

States to decide such disputes; this is definitely the import of the statutory wording conferring upon a State "jurisdiction over civil causes of action between Indians or to which Indians are parties which arise in ... Indian country ... to the same extent that such State ... has jurisdiction over other civil causes of action." With this as the primary focus of § 4(a), the wording that follows in § 4(a) — "and those civil laws of such State ... that are of general application to private persons or private property shall have the same force and effect within such Indian country as they have elsewhere within the State" — authorizes application by the state courts of their rules of decision to decide such disputes. Cf. 28 U.S.C. § 1652. This construction finds support in the consistent and uncontradicted references in the legislative history to "permitting" "*State courts to adjudicate* civil controversies" arising on Indian reservations, H.R. Rep. No. 848, pp. 5, 6 (emphasis added), and the absence of anything remotely resembling an intention to confer general state civil regulatory control over Indian reservations. In short, the consistent and exclusive use of the terms "civil causes of action," "aris[ing] on," "civil laws ... of general application to private persons or private property," and "adjudicat[ion]," in both the Act and its legislative history virtually compels our conclusion that the primary intent of § 4 was to grant jurisdiction over private civil litigation involving reservation Indians in state court.

[This] construction is also more consistent with Title IV of the Civil Rights Act of 1968, 82 Stat. 78, 25 U.S.C. §§ 1321-1326. Title IV repeals § 7 of Pub. L. 280 and requires tribal consent as a condition to further state assumptions of the jurisdiction provided in 18 U.S.C. § 1162 and 28 U.S.C. § 1360. Section 402 of Title IV, 25 U.S.C. § 1322, tracks the language of § 4 of Pub. L. 280. Section 406 of Title IV, 25 U.S.C. § 1326, which provides for Indian consent, refers to "State jurisdiction acquired pursuant to this subchapter with respect to criminal offenses or civil causes of action ...." It is true, of course, that the primary interpretation of § 4 must have reference to the legislative history of the Congress that enacted it rather than to the history of Acts of a later Congress. Nevertheless, Title IV of the 1968 Act is intimately related to § 4, as it provides the method for further state assumptions of the jurisdiction conferred by § 4, and we previously have construed the effect of legislation affecting reservation Indians in light of "intervening" legislative enactments. *Moe v. Salish & Kootenai Tribes*, 425 U.S., at 472-475. It would be difficult to suppose that Congress in 1968 intended the meaning of § 4 to vary depending upon the time and method by which particular States acquired jurisdiction. And certainly the legislative history of Title IV makes it difficult to construe § 4 jurisdiction acquired pursuant to Title IV as extending general state civil regulatory authority, including taxing power, to govern Indian reservations. Senator Ervin, who offered and principally sponsored Title IV, see *Kennerly v. District Court of Montana, supra*, at 429 n.5, referred to § 1360 civil jurisdiction as follows:

> Certain representatives of municipalities have charged that the repeal of [§ 7 of] Public Law 280 would hamper air and water pollution controls and provide a haven for undesirable, unrestricted business establishments within tribal land borders. Not only does this assertion show the lack of faith that certain cities have in the ability and desire of Indian tribes to better themselves and their environment, but, *most importantly, it is irrelevant, since Public Law 280 relates primarily to the application of state civil and criminal law in court proceedings*, and has no bearing on programs set up by

the States to assist economic and environmental development in Indian territory. (Emphasis added.) Hearing before the Subcommittee on Indian Affairs of the House Committee on Interior and Insular Affairs, No. 90-23, 90th Cong., 2d Sess., 136 (1968).

III

Other considerations also support our construction. Today's congressional policy toward reservation Indians may less clearly than in 1953 favor their assimilation, but Pub. L. 280 was plainly not meant to effect total assimilation. Public L. 280 was only one of many types of assimilationist legislation under active consideration in 1953. H.R. Rep. No. 848, pp. 3-5; *Santa Rosa Band of Indians v. Kings County*, 532 F.2d 655, 662 (CA9 1975). And nothing in its legislative history remotely suggests that Congress meant the Act's extension of civil jurisdiction to the States should result in the undermining or destruction of such tribal governments as did exist and a conversion of the affected tribes into little more than "'private, voluntary organizations,'" *United States v. Mazurie*, 419 U.S. 544, 557 (1975) — a possible result if tribal governments and reservation Indians were subordinated to the full panoply of civil regulatory powers, including taxation, of state and local governments. The Act itself refutes such an inference: there is notably absent any conferral of state jurisdiction over the tribes themselves, and § 4(c), 28 U.S.C. § 1360(c), providing for the "full force and effect" of any tribal ordinances or customs "heretofore or hereafter adopted by an Indian tribe ... if not inconsistent with any applicable civil law of the State," contemplates the continuing vitality of tribal government.

Moreover, the same Congress that enacted Pub. L. 280 also enacted several termination Acts — legislation which is cogent proof that Congress knew well how to express its intent directly when that intent was to subject reservation Indians to the full sweep of state laws and state taxation. These termination enactments provide expressly for subjecting distributed property "and any income derived therefrom by the individual, corporation, or other legal entity ... to the same taxes, State and Federal, as in the case of non-Indians," 25 U.S.C. §§ 564j, 749, 898, and provide that "all statutes of the United States which affect Indians because of their status as Indians shall no longer be applicable to the members of the tribe, and the laws of the several States shall apply to the tribe and its members in the same manner as they apply to other citizens or persons within their jurisdiction." 25 U.S.C. §§ 564q, 757, 899; cf. 25 U.S.C. § 726. These contemporaneous termination Acts are *in pari materia* with Pub. L. 280. *Menominee Tribe v. United States*, 391 U.S., at 411. Reading this express language respecting state taxation and application of the full range of state laws to tribal members of these contemporaneous termination Acts, the negative inference is that Congress did not mean in § 4(a) to subject reservation Indians to state taxation. Thus, rather than inferring a negative implication of a grant of general taxing power in § 4(a) from the exclusion of certain taxation in § 4(b), we conclude that construing Pub. L. 280 *in pari materia* with these Acts shows that if Congress in enacting Pub. L. 280 had intended to confer upon the States general civil regulatory powers, including taxation, over reservation Indians, it would have expressly said so.

IV

Additionally, we note that § 4(b), excluding "taxation of any real or personal property ... belonging to any Indian or any Indian tribe ... that is held in trust by the United States or is subject to a restriction against alienation imposed by the United States," is not obviously the narrow exclusion of state taxation that the Minnesota Supreme Court read it to be. On its face the statute is not clear whether the exclusion is applicable only to taxes levied directly on the trust property specifically, or whether it also excludes taxation on activities taking place in conjunction with such property and income deriving from its use. And even if read narrowly to apply only to taxation levied against trust property directly, § 4(b) certainly does not expressly authorize all other state taxation of reservation Indians.

Moreover, the express prohibition of any "alienation, encumbrance, or taxation" of any trust property can be read as prohibiting state courts, acquiring jurisdiction over civil controversies involving reservation Indians pursuant to § 4, from applying state laws or enforcing judgments in ways that would effectively result in the "alienation, encumbrance, or taxation" of trust property. Indeed, any other reading of this provision of § 4(b) is difficult to square with the identical prohibition contained in § 2(b) of the Act, which applies the same restrictions upon States exercising criminal jurisdiction over reservation Indians. It would simply make no sense to infer from the identical language of § 2(b) a general power in § 2(a) to tax Indians in all other respects since § 2(a) deals only with criminal jurisdiction.

Indeed, § 4(b) in its entirety may be read as simply a reaffirmation of the existing reservation Indian-Federal Government relationship in all respects save the conferral of state-court jurisdiction to adjudicate private civil causes of action involving Indians....

Finally, in construing this "admittedly ambiguous" statute, *Board of Comm'rs v. Seber*, 318 U.S., at 713, we must be guided by that "eminently sound and vital canon," *Northern Cheyenne Tribe v. Hollowbreast*, 425 U.S. 649, 655 n.7 (1976), that "statutes passed for the benefit of dependent Indian tribes ... are to be liberally construed, doubtful expressions being resolved in favor of the Indians." *Alaska Pacific Fisheries v. United States*, 248 U.S. 78, 89 (1918). See *Choate v. Trapp*, 224 U.S. 665, 675 (1912); *Antoine v. Washington*, 420 U.S. 194, 199-200 (1975). This principle of statutory construction has particular force in the face of claims that ambiguous statutes abolish by implication Indian tax immunities. *McClanahan v. Arizona State Tax Comm'n*, 411 U.S., at 174; *Squire v. Capoeman*, 351 U.S. 1, 6-7 (1956); *Carpenter v. Shaw*, 280 U.S. 363, 366-367 (1930). "This is so because ... Indians stand in a special relation to the federal government from which the states are excluded unless the Congress has manifested a clear purpose to terminate [a tax] immunity and allow states to treat Indians as part of the general community." *Oklahoma Tax Comm'n v. United States*, 319 U.S. 598, 613-614 (1943) (Murphy, J., dissenting). What we recently said of a claim that Congress had terminated an Indian reservation by means of an ambiguous statute is equally applicable here to the respondent's claim that § 4(a) of Pub. L. 280 is a clear grant of power to tax, and hence a termination of traditional Indian immunity from state taxation:

Congress was fully aware of the means by which termination could be effected. But clear termination language was not employed in the ... Act. This being so, we are not inclined to infer an intent to terminate .... A congressional determination to terminate must be expressed on the face of the Act or be clear from the surrounding circumstances and legislative history. *Mattz v. Arnett*, 412 U.S. 481, 504-505 (1973).

[*Reversed.*]

NOTES

1. **Assumption of Jurisdiction by Option States — *Washington v. Yakima Tribe*:** In 1979, the Supreme Court decided a case interpreting the provisions of Public Law 280 governing the procedures necessary for option states to assume jurisdiction and the extent to which option states could limit their assumption of jurisdiction. In *Washington v. Confederated Bands & Tribes of the Yakima Indian Nation*, 439 U.S. 463 (1979), the tribes raised constitutional as well as statutory objections to Washington's assumption of jurisdiction. The portion of the case stating the facts and containing the Court's analysis of the constitutional issues is reprinted in Chapter 2, section C1. The tribes' statutory arguments, however, were of equal if not greater importance. In 1963, the State of Washington assumed only partial jurisdiction over Indian reservations within the state:

> The State of Washington hereby obligates and binds itself to assume criminal and civil jurisdiction over Indians and Indian territory, reservations, country, and lands within this state in accordance with the consent of the United States given by the act of August 15, 1953 (Public Law 280, 83rd Congress, 1st Session), but such assumption of jurisdiction shall not apply to Indians when on their tribal lands or allotted lands within an established Indian reservation and held in trust by the United States or subject to a restriction against alienation imposed by the United States, unless the provisions of R.C.W.A. 37.12.021 (tribal consent) have been invoked, except for the following:
>
> (1) Compulsory school attendance;
> (2) Public assistance;
> (3) Domestic relations;
> (4) Mental illness;
> (5) Juvenile delinquency;
> (6) Adoption proceedings;
> (7) Dependent children; and
> (8) Operation of motor vehicles upon the public streets, alleys, roads and highways;

Provided further, That Indian tribes that petitioned for, were granted and became subject to state jurisdiction pursuant to this chapter on or before March 13, 1963 shall remain subject to state civil and criminal jurisdiction as if chapter 36, Laws of 1963 had not been enacted.

Chapter 36, 1963 Washington Laws, R.C.W.A. § 37.12.010.

The Yakima tribes made two statutory challenges. First, they relied on section 7 of Public Law 280, authorizing states which had entered the Union under Enabling Acts that required them to insert disclaimers over Indian lands in their constitutions to amend the constitutions where necessary to provide for assumption of jurisdiction. That provision, which is reprinted above, contained a proviso, stating:

> "*Provided*, That the provisions of this Act shall not become effective with respect to such assumption of jurisdiction by any such State until the people thereof have appropriately amended their State constitution or statutes as the case may be.

The tribe argued that section 7 required states with disclaimers to amend their constitutions. Since Washington had not amended its constitution to remove Article XXVI, which disclaimed state authority, its assumption of jurisdiction violated the statute. Second, the tribe argued that Public Law 280 authorized states only to assume the full range of jurisdiction permitted by the statute. As a result, the partial jurisdiction assumed by the state was invalid. Finally, the tribe argued that the state's action, if authorized by Public Law 280, violated the equal protection and due process clauses of the United States Constitution.

The Court rejected both statutory arguments. The Court noted an earlier opinion, *Kennerly v. District Court of Montana*, 400 U.S. 423, 427 (1971), requiring states to follow the procedural provisions of Public Law 280 strictly. In addition, the Court stated that the language of section 6 was "delphic" and quoted the canon of construction relied on in *Bryan* — that ambiguities in legislation affecting tribal sovereignty be construed in favor of Indians. Nevertheless, the Court held that the proviso of section 7 did not require states to amend their constitutions, but only gave the federal government's consent, which was necessary to remove the impediment created by the Enabling Acts prohibiting states to assume jurisdiction. If a state's own internal law did not require amending the state constitution, federal law did not require it. As to the earlier precedent, the Court noted:

> [T]hose principles will not stretch so far as to permit us to find a federal requirement affecting the manner in which the States are to modify their organic legislation on the basis of materials that are essentially speculative.

Yakima, 439 U.S. at 484. In addition, the Court stressed that although Public Law 280 should not be construed as a termination statute, it certainly reflected the assimilationist policy at the time it was enacted and should be interpreted in light of the legislative history indicating that Congress intended to facilitate a transfer of jurisdiction to the states.

The Court also rejected the argument that Public Law 280 required the so-called "option" states to assume the full jurisdiction over Indian reservations imposed on the mandatory states. The Court concluded that although the legislation was not clear on this point, Congress must have intended to treat the mandatory and option states differently, because Congress had consulted the mandatory states, but not the option states. The Court concluded that Congress would not have intended to force the option states, which had very little contact with Indians in the past, to choose between assuming the full panoply of Public Law 280 jurisdiction or none at all. Again, interpreting the statute in light of Public Law 280's goal of facilitating transfer of jurisdiction to the states, the Court concluded that "[i]t is clear that the all-or-nothing approach suggested by the Tribe would impede even the most responsible and sensitive jurisdictional arrangements designed by the States." *Id.* at 497. Is the Court's interpretation of the statute consistent with the approach the Court took in *Bryan* and *Kennerly?*

In *Rosebud Sioux Tribe v. South Dakota*, 900 F.2d 1164 (8th Cir. 1990), the court distinguished *Yakima* and held, contrary to an earlier South Dakota Supreme Court decision, that South Dakota had not under Public Law 280 validly secured any criminal or civil jurisdiction over highways running through Indian country. In 1961 the South Dakota legislature had enacted legislation that purported to accept civil and criminal jurisdiction over Indian lands conditioned on satisfactory federal reimbursement arrangements proclaimed effective by the governor. While the required reimbursements and executive proclamation never occurred prior to the amendment of Public Law 280 in 1968 to require tribal consent, the language of the legislation seemed to exempt the criminal and civil jurisdiction over highways in Indian country from the proclamation requirement. The South Dakota Supreme Court, however, invalidated the 1961 legislation, holding that the state assumption of highway jurisdiction did not effectively remove the state constitutional disclaimer of jurisdiction. The *Hankins* court believed, contrary to the later decision in *Yakima*, that Public Law 280 required such state constitutional disclaimers to be amended prior to assuming state jurisdiction. *In re Hankins*, 30 S.D. 435, 125 N.W.2d 839 (1964). Thereafter, South Dakota stopped exercising authority over highways running through the reservations for a period of time. After the Court's decision in *Yakima*, however, the state of South Dakota sought to rejuvenate its 1961 legislative claim to highway jurisdiction and secured a decision from the state supreme court overruling *Hankins* and concluding that the 1968 tribal consent amendments did not apply since its validation of jurisdiction related back to the passage of the statute in 1961. *State v. Ohihan*, 427 N.W.2d 365 (S.D. 1988). Recognizing that jurisdiction over highways may be the only area where the exercise of authority may come close to being self-financing, the Eighth Circuit distinguished *Yakima*. It held that South Dakota's single issue assumption of jurisdiction was not responsive to the concerns about lawlessness that led to passage of Public Law 280 and that the 1961 statute reflected a refusal to accept the burdens of jurisdiction, as required by Public Law 280. The court therefore found that South Dakota had not validly assumed jurisdiction over highways within Indian country prior to the 1968 tribal consent amendments.

2. Civil Adjudicatory, Regulatory, and Taxing Jurisdiction: Before *Bryan*, the courts found two types of limitations on the exercise of state power. First, the language in 28 U.S.C. § 1360(a) authorizing the state authorities to apply only the "civil laws of such State ... that are of general application" was thought to exclude local ordinances such as zoning and building codes since they are not of statewide, i.e., "general," application. *Santa Rosa Band of Indians v. Kings County*, 532 F.2d 655 (9th Cir. 1975), *cert. denied*, 429 U.S. 1038 (1977); *Snohomish County v. Seattle Disposal Co.*, 70 Wash. 2d 668, 425 P.2d 22, *cert. denied*, 389 U.S. 1016 (1967). *But see Rincon Band of Mission Indians v. County of San Diego*, 324 F. Supp. 371 (S.D. Cal. 1971), *rev'd on other grounds*, 495 F.2d 1 (9th Cir.), *cert. denied*, 419 U.S. 1008 (1974); *Agua Caliente Tribal Council v. City of Palm Springs*, 347 F. Supp. 42 (C.D. Cal. 1972). Second, the courts read expansively the restrictions on jurisdiction contained in § 1360(b). Thus, for example, the court in the *Santa Rosa* case said:

> Relying on the canon of construction applied in favor of Indians, the Court has ruled in different contexts that the word "encumbrance" is to be broadly construed and is not limited to a burden which hinders alienation of the fee ... , rather focussing on the effect the challenged state action would have on the value, use and enjoyment of the land. Following the Court's lead, and resolving, as we must, doubts in favor of the Indians, we think that the word as used here may reasonably be interpreted to deny the state the power to apply zoning regulations to trust property.

532 F.2d at 667. Did *Bryan* diminish the significance of these decisions? Compare the *Segundo* case that follows.

The *Bryan* decision excluding state taxing and regulatory laws from the civil jurisdiction assumed by states under Public Law 280 was critical to the Court's decision in *California v. Cabazon Band of Mission Indians*, 408 U.S. 202, 210 (1987), set forth in Chapter 2, section D, holding that state law did not restrict the gaming activities of a federal Indian tribe in California, a mandatory Public Law 280 state. The Court adopted a civil-regulatory criminal-prohibitory dichotomy that lower federal courts had developed based on the *Bryan* rationale. Congress passed the Indian Gaming Regulatory Act, 25 U.S.C. § 2701 et seq., discussed in Chapter 2, section D, in response to *Cabazon*. That legislation subjected certain non-bingo-like gaming, described as class III games, in part to state legal regulation. In *Lac Du Flambeau Band of Lake Superior Chippewa Indians v. Wisconsin*, 743 F. Supp. 645 (W.D. Wis. 1990), the court held that neither Public Law 280 nor the Indian Gaming Regulatory Act authorized the state of Wisconsin to enforce its criminal laws prohibiting class III gaming against two casinos which engaged or intended to engage in class III gaming operated by different Chippewa bands in Indian country in Wisconsin. Insofar as Public Law 280 was concerned, the court relied on *Cabazon* and *Bryan* and held that the state civil and criminal jurisdiction assumed by Wisconsin did not reach gaming since Wisconsin had amended its constitution to permit lotteries, which the court found, contrary to some state interpretations, to be an inclusive term of reference for any gaming. Thus, gaming was regulated rather than prohibited in Wisconsin, and under *Cabazon* and *Bryan*, Wisconsin lacked authority to enforce such regulatory criminal limitations. Since the Indian Gaming Regulatory Act, which subjected certain Indian class III gaming to state regulatory laws, provided for federal, rather than state, prosecution under 18 U.S.C. § 1166, it provided the state no further authority for the enforcement of state gaming laws in state courts.

SEGUNDO v. CITY OF RANCHO MIRAGE
813 F.2d 1387 (9th Cir. 1987)

LOVELL, District Judge:

Appellants, members of the Agua Caliente Band of Cahuilla Indians and their non-Indian lessee, appeal an adverse judgment by the District Court upholding rent control ordinances enacted by the Appellee cities of Rancho Mirage and Cathedral City and applied to allotted lands of the Indian Appellants. The central issue on appeal is whether local rent control ordinances may be applied to a mobile home park operated by a non-Indian entity on Indian land held in trust by the United States.

Facts

Appellants are Indian allottees of several parcels of land located within the Agua Caliente Reservation, situated near Palm Springs, California. In 1968, with approval of the Secretary of the Interior, Appellants entered into a 65-year lease with Palm Springs Mobile Country Club for the construction and operation of a mobile home park on the allotments. Now known as De Anza Palm Springs Mobile Country Club, the park lies partially within the limits of Rancho Mirage and partially within the limits of Cathedral City.

Under the lease, De Anza pays Appellant allottees a guaranteed minimum annual rental plus 15% of the gross receipts from the subleasing of mobile home spaces plus a percentage of receipts from other business activities operated on the premises.

On May 4, 1982, the City of Rancho Mirage enacted a local ordinance establishing a Mobile Home Fair Practices Commission and imposing maximum rent increase limits upon all mobile home parks located within the City. A similar ordinance was approved by Cathedral City on March 18, 1983. The two ordinances are substantially identical and, in pertinent part, limit annual rent increases in mobile home parks to 75 percent of the increase in the applicable Consumer Price Index for the year preceding the rent increase. Park owners may apply to the respective Commissions for a "hardship" increase.

Following Appellees' attempts to enforce the ordinances against De Anza, Appellants filed complaints for declaratory and injunctive relief and for monetary damages, seeking a ruling that the subject ordinances could not be applied to allotted lands held in trust by the United States, and that the cities be permanently enjoined from attempting to enforce the ordinances against the allottees and their lessee De Anza. After a consolidated bench trial, the District Court entered findings of fact and conclusions of law, finding the ordinances to be valid exercises of the cities' police powers, regulating only relations between non-Indians and having no significant impact on the allottees.

Appellants contend that the District Court erred in failing to find invalid the application of the ordinances to the De Anza park, in failing to find a violation of 42 U.S.C. § 1983, in ruling that the trust patents under which the allottees hold their land would expire in October 1986, and in relying solely upon the testimony of Appellees' single expert witness in reaching its determination.

Discussion

The dispositive issue in this case is whether the ordinances are valid under either Public Law 280 or federal common law [dealing with preemption in Indian country].

B. Expiration of the Trust Patents

The District Court ruled that the trust patents under which the allottees hold their lands would expire on October 11, 1986; thus, the court reasoned, once the patents expired and the allottees became subject to all laws of the State of California, the rent control ordinances would apply to the De Anza mobile home park regardless of Appellants' status as tribal members. 25 U.S.C. § 349.

The trust patents were issued October 12, 1961, for a period of 25 years. See 25 U.S.C. § 348. The District Court failed to recognize, however, that the Secretary of the Interior, on July 20, 1983, extended the trust period to January 1, 1989. 25 C.F.R. app. 1 (1986) (text at 48 Fed. Reg. 34,026 (1983)).[3] The trust status clearly having been extended, the District Court's ruling was in error.

C. Public Law 280

Under Public Law 280 (P.L. 280), state laws "of general application" were extended into Indian Country, to be applied with "the same force and effect ... as they have elsewhere within the State." Although its language is broad, P.L. 280 has been narrowly interpreted to confer state jurisdiction over private civil litigation involving reservation Indians, and does not constitute a grant of general civil regulatory authority. [E.g., Bryan.]

---

[3] Testimony was also presented indicating that, regardless of the location of the allotments, all trust or restrictive periods on allotments expiring on a given date generally have been extended by a single Executive order issued annually. See also 25 C.F.R. app. 1 at 779 (1986).

This court has refused to extend P.L. 280 jurisdiction to local governments. *Santa Rosa Band of Indians v. Kings County*, 532 F.2d 655, 661 (9th Cir. 1975), *cert. denied*, 429 U.S. 1038 (1976). Accord *United States v. County of Humboldt*, 615 F.2d 1260 (9th Cir. 1980). We held in *Santa Rosa* that Congress' apparent intent in enacting P.L. 280 was to "make the tribal government over the reservation more or less the *equivalent* of the county or local government in other areas within the state, empowered ... to regulate matters of local concern within the area of its jurisdiction." *Santa Rosa*, 532 F.2d at 663 (emphasis added). On this basis, and in view of the present federal policy to foster tribal self-government and economic self-development, we concluded that P.L. 280 subjected Indian Country to only the civil laws of the state, and not to local regulation. *Id.* at 661, 664.

Under *Santa Rosa* and *Bryan*, it is clear that P.L. 280 cannot serve as the jurisdictional basis for application of the subject ordinances within Indian country.

D. *Federal Common Law*

In the development of federal Indian law, the Supreme Court long ago departed from the "view that 'the laws of [a State] can have no force' within reservation boundaries." See *White Mountain Apache Tribe v. Bracker*, 448 U.S. 136, 141 (1980) (quoting *Worcester v. Georgia*, 6 Pet. 515, 560 (1832)). Nevertheless, the Court continues to recognize inherent "attributes of sovereignty [in Indian tribes] over both their members and their territory." 448 U.S. at 142; see also *New Mexico v. Mescalero Apache Tribe*, 462 U.S. 324, 332 (1983).

State laws may be applied to Indian reservations unless such application would impair a right granted or reserved by federal law or would infringe upon the right of reservation Indians to make their own laws and be ruled by them. *Rice v. Rehner*, 463 U.S. 713, 718 (1983). These principles constitute two independent but related barriers to the exercise of state jurisdiction, since either can be a sufficient basis for holding state law inapplicable. *Bracker*, 448 U.S. at 143. The trend has been to rely more on federal preemption, using notions of Indian self-government as a "'backdrop' against which any assertion of state authority must be assessed." *Mescalero Apache*, 462 U.S. at 334 (quoting *Bracker*, 448 U.S. at 143).

State law is generally inapplicable when concerned solely with on-reservation conduct involving Indians. See *Bracker*, 448 U.S. at 144; *Santa Rosa*, 532 F.2d at 658. Where the State asserts authority over the conduct of non-Indians engaging in activity on the reservation, the court must undertake

> a particularized inquiry into the nature of the state, federal, and tribal interests at stake, an inquiry designed to determine whether, in the specific context, the exercise of state authority would violate federal law. *Bracker*, 448 U.S. at 145.

Appellants assert that federal statutes and extensive regulation of leasing by the Secretary of the Interior preempt application of the ordinances to the De Anza park.

Leasing of Indian lands, whether tribally or individually owned, is authorized by 25 U.S.C. § 415(a). Such lands may be leased by the Indian owners with the approval of the Secretary of the Interior. *Id*. Section 415 limits the period of all leases so granted to a term of 25 years, except leases on certain reservations, including the Agua Caliente Reservation, which may be for a term of not to exceed 99 years. It further provides that "all leases and renewals shall be made under such terms and regulations as may be prescribed by the Secretary of the Interior." Several factors are specified which must be considered by the Secretary prior to approval of any lease or extension of an existing lease. *Id*.

Regulations have been promulgated under section 415, requiring certain lease provision[s], setting limits on duration, establishing requirements for subleasing, and providing other restrictions. 25 C.F.R. Part 162 (1986). In part, the regulations prohibit the Secretary from approving a lease at less than the fair annual rental, unless in his judgment such action would be in the best interests of the landowners. 25 C.F.R. § 162.5(b) (1986). The regulations require the lease to be limited to the "minimum duration, commensurate with the purpose of the lease, that will allow the highest economic return to the owner consistent with prudent management and conservation practices," and additionally require periodic review of the equities involved. 25 C.F.R. § 162.8 (1986). Any adjustments of rental resulting from such review must be made with the written concurrence of the owners and the approval of the Secretary. *Id*.

In addition to the specific provisions regarding leasing of Indian lands, 25 C.F.R. § 1.4 provides that unless specifically adopted by the Secretary, none of the laws, ordinances, codes, resolutions, rules or other regulations of any State or political subdivision thereof limiting, zoning or otherwise governing, regulating, or controlling the use or development of any real or personal property, ... shall be applicable to any such property leased from ... any Indian or Indian tribe ... that is held in trust by the United States ....

Pursuant to 25 C.F.R. § 1.4(b), the Secretary has adopted and made applicable all laws of the State of California regulating or controlling the use or development of property held in trust by the United States for an Indian or Indian tribe and located within the State of California. 30 Fed. Reg. 8722 (1965). The Secretary expressly excluded the laws, ordinances and other regulations of the various counties and cities within the State, concluding that such local laws would be considered separately. *Id*. The Secretary has not adopted or applied the subject ordinances of the Cities of Rancho Mirage and Cathedral City.[5]

Appellees argue that the federal statutes authorizing the leasing of trust lands and the regulations governing such leasing do not constitute a comprehensive regulatory scheme with preemptive effect on state and local laws. We cannot agree.

---

[5] The Tribe has entered into an agreement with Cathedral City, extending the City's land use controls to trust lands within the City limits. By the terms of the contract, the Tribe agreed to (1) adopt by ordinance all existing Cathedral City land use controls, and (2) designate the City as its agent for enforcement of Tribal land use controls on trust lands within the City limits. The City agreed to allow appeals from any final land use decision by the City to the Tribal council, for the purpose of preserving Tribal control over reservation land use.

The contract expressly provides that it in no way limits the authority and duty of the Department of the Interior and Bureau of Indian affairs to negotiate and administer existing and future leases of trust lands. Appellants and the Tribe, as amicus, assert that this provision in the contract was intended to prevent any local attempt to regulate the use of leased trust lands, and did not authorize application of the City's rent control ordinances to appellants' allotted lands. Appellees have not suggested that the contract applies to the ordinances in question.

In *White Mountain Apache Tribe v. Bracker, supra,* the Supreme Court found that comprehensive federal regulation of Indian timber harvesting pre-empted application of Arizona's tax laws to a non-Indian logging company operating entirely on [Indian owned lands].

The Court subsequently held that federal law preempted a state tax imposed on the gross receipts of a non-Indian construction company from a tribal school board for the construction of a school for Indian children on the reservation. *Ramah Navajo School Board, Inc. v. Bureau of Revenue of New Mexico,* 458 U.S. 832, 846-47 (1982). Relying on congressional enactments empowering the BIA to provide for Indian education and the "comprehensive regulations" promulgated thereunder, the Court found no substantive distinction from *White Mountain,* and held the state tax inapplicable. *Id.,* 458 U.S. at 839-42.

A similar result was reached in *New Mexico v. Mescalero Apache Tribe,* in which the Court held that New Mexico could not enforce its hunting and fishing regulations within the [exterior boundaries of an Indian reservation].

The Court's seeming departure from the *White Mountain* line of cases came in *Rice v. Rehner,* where it permitted California to require Indian traders to obtain a state liquor license to sell liquor for off-premises consumption. 463 U.S. at 733-34. Applying the *White Mountain* analysis, the Court found no federal preemption of liquor regulation by the states. *Id.* at 734. The Court principally relied upon the "historical tradition of concurrent state and federal jurisdiction over the use and distribution of alcoholic beverages in Indian country," combined with the specific language of 18 U.S.C. § 1161, which repudiated the federal prohibition against liquor transactions with Indians so long as such transactions conformed with the laws of the State. *Id.* at 724, 733. In fact, the court reasoned that section 1161 withdrew prior federal preemption of liquor regulation and conferred such authority on the states, concurrently with the tribes. *Id.* at 726.

Applying *White Mountain* and its progeny to the facts of this case, we conclude that application of the rent control ordinances at issue is preempted by federal law.

The statutory and regulatory scheme present in this case is substantially similar to those involved in *White Mountain, Ramah,* and *Mescalero Apache.* The Secretary is required to undertake detailed consideration of the lease provisions to determine whether the lease furthers the best interests of the Indian owner. See 25 U.S.C. § 415(a); 25 C.F.R. § 162.5. The overriding federal interest is to obtain the "highest economic return to the owner consistent with prudent management and conservation practices." 25 C.F.R. § 162.8. Although daily supervision is not required, major revisions in the lease arrangement, such as subleases or assignments and rental adjustments, require Secretarial approval. See 25 C.F.R. §§ 162.8, 162.12. See also *Central Machinery Co. v. Arizona State Tax Comm'n,* 448 U.S. 160, 165 n.4 (1980). More important[,] the regulations expressly provide that local ordinances limiting or in any way regulating the use or development of property may not be applied to lands held in trust by the United States. 25 C.F.R. § 1.4.[6]

---

[6] Section 1.4 was upheld by this court as a valid exercise of the Secretary's rulemaking authority in *Santa Rosa.* See 532 F.2d at 665.

Unlike *Rice v. Rehner*, the United States has enacted no law conferring jurisdiction in this area upon the states or their political subdivisions. On the contrary, the regulatory scheme surrounding leasing of Indian lands leaves "no room" for application of the ordinances at issue.

It is beyond question that land use regulation is within the Tribe's legitimate sovereign authority over its lands. See *Cardin v. De La Cruz*, 671 F.2d 363 (9th Cir.), *cert. denied*, 459 U.S. 967 (1982); *Montana v. United States*, 450 U.S. 544 (1981). *Accord Knight v. Shoshone and Arapahoe Indian Tribes of the Wind River Reservation*, 670 F.2d 900 (10th Cir. 1982). The Tribe's concern with land use and development is evidenced by its contract with Cathedral City and the ordinance enacted in conjunction therewith.[7] Although tribal rent control ordinances have not been enacted, failure of the Tribe to legislate does not constitute a relinquishment of its authority to do so. See generally *Merrion v. Jicarilla Apache Tribe*, 455 U.S. 130, 145 (1982) ("A nonmember who enters the jurisdiction of the tribe remains subject to the risk that the tribe will later exercise its sovereign power.").

To permit concurrent jurisdiction by Appellees in this area "not only would threaten to disrupt the federal and tribal regulatory scheme, but would also threaten Congress' overriding objective of encouraging tribal self-government and economic development." *Mescalero Apache*, 462 U.S. at 341. Unlike the field of taxation, where the laws of both the State and Tribe may be enforced simultaneously, *Washington v. Confederated Tribes of the Colville Indian Reservation*, 447 U.S. 134, 158 (1980), the cities' rent control ordinances would necessarily preclude enforcement of a conflicting ordinance enacted by the Tribe, and would "effectively nullify" the Tribe's authority to regulate the use of its lands. 462 U.S. at 343-44. The cities' interest in providing affordable housing to its citizens who choose to live within the boundaries of the reservation cannot overcome the interests of the Tribe in being able to make its own laws in this important area and to be governed by them. See *Cabazon Band of Mission Indians v. County of Riverside*, 783 F.2d 900 (9th Cir. 1986), *aff'd*, 55 U.S.L.W. 4225 (U.S. Feb. 25, 1987).

Viewing the "backdrop" of tribal sovereignty in conjunction with the comprehensive regulatory scheme governing leases of Indian land, we conclude that the rent control ordinances adopted by the Appellee cities are preempted by federal law.

Conclusion

Following recent Supreme Court precedent in the area of federal preemption, and applying the backdrop of tribal sovereignty, we conclude that application of the ordinances adopted by the cities of Rancho Mirage and Cathedral City to the mobile home park situated on allotted lands held by the United States in trust for the Appellants is preempted by federal law.

[*Reversed and remanded* for the lower court to enter a permanent injunction against enforcement of the ordinances.]

---

[7]Ordinance No. 10 of the Agua Caliente Band of Cahuilla Indians, adopted by the Tribal Council January 24, 1984. A similar arrangement apparently exists with the City of Palm Springs, and the Tribe is continuing negotiations with the City of Rancho Mirage.

NOTE ON STATE TAXING AND REGULATORY AUTHORITY
UNDER PUBLIC LAW 280

Bryan made it reasonably clear that Public Law 280 conferred no state taxing or regulatory authority on states which acquired Public Law 280 jurisdiction. Rather, the civil authority states acquired under Public Law 280 was limited to adjudicating civil causes of action between private parties. Since the adjudication of civil controversies generally involves the application of a body of legal rules that regulate the conduct of private parties toward one another, the precise dividing line under Public Law 280 between prohibited state regulatory efforts and permitted adjudication sometimes remains obscure. For example, in *State ex rel. Dept. of Human Servs. v. Whitebreast*, 409 N.W.2d 460 (Iowa 1987), the Court ruled that the State of Iowa lacked subject matter jurisdiction under Public Law 280 to sue a Mesquakie Indian father in state court for recovery of child support payments made by the state to his child who lived on the Sac and Fox Reservation in Iowa (the Mesquakie Settlement). The state argued that jurisdiction existed under Public Law 280 since the Department of Human Services merely stood in the shoes of the mother or other legal guardian seeking to collect payments in what otherwise would have been a private dispute absent the assignment of the right to recover to the state in exchange for public assistance payments. The father, on the other hand, successfully resisted, claiming that since the State of Iowa sought recovery *for the state* of public monies paid out for a public program, the suit sought to recover funds in the nature of a tax which was precluded under Public Law 280 and *Bryan*. The Iowa Supreme Court agreed that since the exaction was for public benefit, the suit in essence sought to enforce a collection in the nature of a tax which was prevented by *Bryan*. Thus, the court ruled that the exclusive jurisdiction to entertain the state's claim lay with the Sac and Fox Tribe in Iowa, notwithstanding Public Law 280. The father also argued, however, that even if one accepted the notion that suit did not involve a tax, the efforts of the state to impose *state*, rather than tribal, child support laws through such litigation-imposed state regulatory law through Public Law 280, a result he claimed was similarly rejected by *Bryan*. He specifically noted that state family law and the support obligations attendant thereto was centered around the nuclear family model and took no account of the traditional Indian extended family. The Iowa Supreme Court rejected that contention, suggesting that the application of such state family concepts to truly private litigation involving Indians in Indian country would not offend *Bryan*. Is the distinction between state civil laws and regulatory statutes a viable one? Are not regulatory statutes public refinements of ancient torts? If a state court could apply, for example, common law nuisance doctrine, does it make sense to bar the use of environmental protection statutes?

In *Confederated Tribes & Bands of the Yakima Indian Nation v. Whiteside*, 828 F.2d 529 (9th Cir. 1987), *aff'd in part & rev'd in part sub nom. Brendale v. Confederated Tribes & Bands of the Yakima Indian Nation*, 109 S. Ct. 2994 (1989), the Ninth Circuit reaffirmed the principles set forth in the *Segundo* case. The *Whiteside* decision involved consolidated cases questioning the authority of state and local officials to enforce zoning and related building codes to both closed and open portions of the Yakima reservation. While the bulk of the Ninth Circuit opinion focused on questions of inherent tribal and state authority in Indian country, the Supreme Court summarily dismissed the argument that Public Law 280 granted states authority to apply such laws in Indian country. The opinion merely stated, "Public Law 280 grants state courts jurisdiction over civil litigation involving reservation Indians, but does not intrude upon tribal regulatory authority. [Since] zoning is clearly regulatory, Public Law 280 does not affect Yakima's authority to zone." *Id.* at 532. In the Supreme Court, as in the Ninth Circuit, none of the opinions in *Brendale* relied on Public Law 280. Most of the opinions in *Brendale* focused instead on tribal sovereignty. The full *Brendale* opinion is set forth and discussed in Chapter 3, section D5b.

Public Law 280 also extended state criminal jurisdiction to many reservations. As noted, in *Segundo* the Supreme Court held that *Cabazon Band of Mission Indians v. County of Riverside* clearly found that the regulatory/prohibitory crimes distinction derived from *Bryan* by many lower federal courts represented a correct interpretation of both the criminal jurisdiction provisions of Public Law 280 and, apparently, the Organized Crime Control Act. As developed more fully in Chapter 2, this interpretation of Public Law 280 facilitated the development of thriving and lucrative Indian gaming enterprises in Indian country at precisely the time when federal support for Indian tribal programs was shrinking. This modern development began when the Fifth Circuit, relying on *Bryan*, held in *Seminole Tribe v. Butterworth*, 658 F.2d 310 (5th Cir. 1981), that Florida's bingo laws could not be enforced against the operation of highly profitable bingo halls by the Seminole Tribe. Florida statutes authorized bingo games operated by certain religious, charitable, and civic groups so long as the entire proceeds from the game were used by the organizations for charity. Thus, the court classified the Florida statute as "civil/regulatory," rather than "criminal/prohibitory," and therefore found that *Bryan* precluded enforcement. The court distinguished *United States v. Marcyes*, 557 F.2d 1361 (9th Cir. 1977) (Washington fireworks laws apply to Indians in Indian country under the Assimilative and General Crimes Acts, 18 U.S.C. §§ 13, 1152), on the grounds that the bingo games, unlike fireworks, were regulated rather than banned by the state. The court also expressly rejected an argument based on *Colville*, discussed earlier in this chapter, that a distinction had to be drawn between Indian and non-Indian players. It said, "In the present case the only regulation is directed at the Indian operators of the bingo hall, not its non-Indian bingo players." 658 F.2d at 317 n.9. One member of the panel dissented, noting that "it is because such activity is prohibited by Florida that this business was started and is successful." 658 F.2d at 317. *See also Barona Group of Capitan Grande Band of Mission Indians v. Duffy*, 694 F.2d 1185 (9th Cir. 1982), *cert. denied*, 461 U.S. 929 (1983); *Oneida Tribe v. Wisconsin*, 518 F. Supp. 712 (W.D. Wis. 1981) (same result).

On reservations subject to Public Law 280 jurisdictional transfers, what jurisdiction does the tribe retain? *Bryan*'s reliance on section 1360(c) might suggest that tribes retain whatever judicial and legislative jurisdiction they had prior to the enactment of Public Law 280. Since section 1360(c) refers only to the laws and customs of the tribe, might it be argued that their authority was limited under Public Law 280 merely to legislative authority and then only if not inconsistent with state law? May a Public Law 280 tribe choose to recognize, protect, and provide a forum for the redress of a cause of action not recognized by state statutory or common law? May it at least legislatively create the cause of action, leaving the redress of the claim to state forums? A number of tribes, such as the Omaha Tribe in Nebraska, have without legal challenge provided tribal forums for the adjudication of civil disputes even while subject to state civil Public Law 280 jurisdiction.

Compare the significance attached by the Court to the legislative history of the 1968 amendments in interpreting Public Law 280 in the *Yakima* and *Bryan* opinions. In *Bryan* the Court relies heavily on the 1968 legislative history to bolster its interpretation of the 1953 statute, while in *Yakima* the opinion rejects contrary evidence found in the 1968 legislative history as irrelevant to the interpretation of a statute enacted in 1953. In construing statutes, how should courts deal with subsequent shifts in legislative policy that do not directly repeal or amend prior statutes? Which is the preferable approach, *Yakima* or *Bryan*? Which approach is more consistent with majoritarian democracy?

2. INDIAN CHILD WELFARE ACT OF 1978

INDIAN CHILD WELFARE ACT OF 1978, Pub. L. 95-608, 25 U.S.C. § 1901 et seq.

§ 1901. Congressional findings

Recognizing the special relationship between the United States and the Indian tribes and their members and the Federal responsibility to Indian people, the Congress finds —

(1) that clause 3, section 8, article I of the United States Constitution provides that "The Congress shall have Power ... To regulate Commerce ... with Indian tribes" and, through this and other constitutional authority, Congress has plenary power over Indian affairs;

(2) that Congress, through statutes, treaties, and the general course of dealing with Indian tribes, has assumed the responsibility for the protection and preservation of Indian tribes and their resources;

(3) that there is no resource that is more vital to the continued existence and integrity of Indian tribes than their children and that the United States has a direct interest, as trustee, in protecting Indian children who are members of or are eligible for membership in an Indian tribe;

(4) that an alarmingly high percentage of Indian families are broken up by the removal, often unwarranted, of their children from them by nontribal public and private agencies and that an alarmingly high percentage of such children are placed in non-Indian foster and adoptive homes and institutions; and

(5) that the States, exercising their recognized jurisdiction over Indian child custody proceedings through administrative and judicial bodies, have often failed to recognize the essential tribal relations of Indian people and the cultural and social standards prevailing in Indian communities and families.

§ 1902. Congressional declaration of policy

The Congress hereby declares that it is the policy of this Nation to protect the best interests of Indian children and to promote the stability and security of

Indian tribes and families by the establishment of minimum Federal standards for the removal of Indian children from their families and the placement of such children in foster or adoptive homes which will reflect the unique values of Indian culture, and by providing for assistance to Indian tribes in the operation of child and family service programs.

§ 1903. Definitions

For the purposes of this chapter, except as may be specifically provided otherwise, the term —

(1) "child custody proceeding" shall mean and include —

(i) "foster care placement" which shall mean any action removing an Indian child from its parent or Indian custodian for temporary placement in a foster home or institution or the home of a guardian or conservator where the parent or Indian custodian cannot have the child returned upon demand, but where parental rights have not been terminated;

(ii) "termination of parental rights" which shall mean any action resulting in the termination of the parent-child relationship;

(iii) "preadoptive placement" which shall mean the temporary placement of an Indian child in a foster home or institution after the termination of parental rights, but prior to or in lieu of adoptive placement; and

(iv) "adoptive placement" which shall mean the permanent placement of an Indian child for adoption, including any action resulting in a final decree of adoption. Such term or terms shall not include a placement based upon an act which, if committed by an adult, would be deemed a crime or upon an award, in a divorce proceeding, of custody to one of the parents.

(2) "extended family member" shall be as defined by the law or custom of the Indian child's tribe or, in the absence of such law or custom, shall be a person who has reached the age of eighteen and who is the Indian child's grandparent, aunt or uncle, brother or sister, brother-in-law or sister-in-law, niece or nephew, first or second cousin, or stepparent;

(3) "Indian" means any person who is a member of an Indian tribe, or who is an Alaska Native and a member of a Regional Corporation as defined in section 1606 of Title 43;

(4) "Indian child" means any unmarried person who is under age eighteen and is either (a) a member of an Indian tribe or (b) is eligible for membership in an Indian tribe and is the biological child of a member of an Indian tribe;

(5) "Indian child's tribe" means (a) the Indian tribe in which an Indian child is a member or eligible for membership or (b), in the case of an Indian child who is a member of or eligible for membership in more than one tribe, the Indian tribe with which the Indian child has the more significant contacts;

(6) "Indian custodian" means any Indian person who has legal custody of an Indian child under tribal law or custom or under State law or to whom temporary physical care, custody, and control has been transferred by the parent of such child;

(7) "Indian organization" means any group, association, partnership, corporation, or other legal entity owned or controlled by Indians, or a majority of whose members are Indians;

(8) "Indian tribe" means any Indian tribe, band, nation, or other organized group or community of Indians recognized as eligible for the services provided to Indians by the Secretary because of their status as Indians, including any Alaska Native village as defined in section 1602(c) of Title 43;

(9) "parent" means any biological parent or parents of an Indian child or any Indian person who has lawfully adopted an Indian child, including adoptions under tribal law or custom. It does not include the unwed father where paternity has not been acknowledged or established;

(10) "reservation" means Indian country as defined in section 1151 of Title 18 and any lands, not covered under such section, title to which is either held by the United States in trust for the benefit of any Indian tribe or individual or held by any Indian tribe or individual subject to a restriction by the United States against alienation;

(11) "Secretary" means the Secretary of the Interior; and

(12) "tribal court" means a court with jurisdiction over child custody proceedings and which is either a Court of Indian Offenses, a court established and operated under the code or custom of an Indian tribe, or any other administrative body of a tribe which is vested with authority over child custody proceedings.....

Subchapter I — Child Custody Proceedings

§ 1911. Indian tribe jurisdiction over Indian child custody proceedings — Exclusive jurisdiction

(a) An Indian tribe shall have jurisdiction exclusive as to any State over any child custody proceeding involving an Indian child who resides or is domiciled within the reservation of such tribe, except where such jurisdiction is otherwise vested in the State by existing Federal law. Where an Indian child is a ward of a tribal court, the Indian tribe shall retain exclusive jurisdiction, notwithstanding the residence or domicile of the child.

Transfer of proceedings; declination by tribal court

(b) In any State court proceeding for the foster care placement of, or termination of parental rights to, an Indian child not domiciled or residing within the reservation of the Indian child's tribe, the court, in the absence of good cause to the contrary, shall transfer such proceeding to the jurisdiction of the tribe, absent objection by either parent, upon the petition of either parent or the Indian custodian or the Indian child's tribe: *Provided*, That such transfer shall be subject to declination by the tribal court of such tribe.

State court proceedings; intervention

(c) In any State court proceeding for the foster care placement of, or termination of parental rights to, an Indian child, the Indian custodian of the child and the Indian child's tribe shall have a right to intervene at any point in the proceeding.

Full faith and credit to public acts, records, and judicial proceedings of Indian tribes

(d) The United States, every State, every territory or possession of the United States, and every Indian tribe shall give full faith and credit to the public acts, records, and judicial proceedings of any Indian tribe applicable to Indian child custody proceedings to the same extent that such entities give full faith and credit to the public acts, records, and judicial proceedings of any other entity.

§ 1912. Pending court proceedings — Notice; time for commencement of proceedings; additional time for preparation

(a) In any involuntary proceeding in a State court, where the court knows or has reason to know that an Indian child is involved, the party seeking the foster care placement of, or termination of parental rights to, an Indian child shall notify the parent or Indian custodian and the Indian child's tribe, by registered mail with return receipt requested, of the pending proceedings and of their right of intervention. If the identity or location of the parent or Indian custodian and the tribe cannot be determined, such notice shall be given to the Secretary in like manner, who shall have fifteen days after receipt to provide the requisite notice to the parent or Indian custodian and the tribe. No foster care placement or termination of parental rights proceeding shall be held until at least ten days after receipt of notice by the parent or Indian custodian and the tribe or the Secretary: *Provided*, That the parent or Indian custodian or the tribe shall, upon request, be granted up to twenty additional days to prepare for such proceeding.

Appointment of counsel

(b) In any case in which the court determines indigency, the parent or Indian custodian shall have the right to court-appointed counsel in any removal, placement, or termination proceeding. The court may, in its discretion, appoint counsel for the child upon a finding that such appointment is in the best interest of the child. Where State law makes no provision for appointment of counsel in such proceedings, the court shall promptly notify the Secretary upon appointment of counsel, and the Secretary, upon certification of the presiding judge, shall pay reasonable fees and expenses out of funds which may be appropriated pursuant to section 13 of this title.

Examination of reports or other documents

(c) Each party to a foster care placement or termination of parental rights proceeding under State law involving an Indian child shall have the right to examine all reports or other documents filed with the court upon which any decision with respect to such action may be based.

Remedial services and rehabilitative programs; preventive measures

(d) Any party seeking to effect a foster care placement of, or termination of parental rights to, an Indian child under State law shall satisfy the court that active efforts have been made to provide remedial services and rehabilitative programs designed to prevent the breakup of the Indian family and that these efforts have proved unsuccessful.

Foster care placement orders; evidence; determination of damage to child

(e) No foster care placement may be ordered in such proceeding in the absence of a determination, supported by clear and convincing evidence, including testimony of qualified expert witnesses, that the continued custody of the child by the parent or Indian custodian is likely to result in serious emotional or physical damage to the child.

Parental rights termination orders; evidence; determination of damage to child

(f) No termination of parental rights may be ordered in such proceeding in the absence of a determination, supported by evidence beyond a reasonable doubt, including testimony of qualified expert witnesses, that the continued custody of the child by the parent or Indian custodian is likely to result in serious emotional or physical damage to the child.

§ 1913. Parental rights, voluntary termination — Consent; record; certification matters; invalid consents

(a) Where any parent or Indian custodian voluntarily consents to a foster care placement or to termination of parental rights, such consent shall not be valid unless executed in writing and recorded before a judge of a court of competent jurisdiction and accompanied by the presiding judge's certificate that the terms and consequences of the consent were fully explained in detail and were fully understood by the parent or Indian custodian. The court shall also certify that either the parent or Indian custodian fully understood the explanation in English or that it was interpreted into a language that the parent or Indian custodian understood. Any consent given prior to, or within ten days after, birth of the Indian child shall not be valid.

Foster care placement; withdrawal of consent

(b) Any parent or Indian custodian may withdraw consent to a foster care placement under State law at any time and, upon such withdrawal, the child shall be returned to the parent or Indian custodian.

Voluntary termination of parental rights or adoptive placement; withdrawal of consent; return of custody

(c) In any voluntary proceeding for termination of parental rights to, or adoptive placement of, an Indian child, the consent of the parent may be withdrawn for any reason at any time prior to the entry of a final decree of termination or adoption, as the case may be, and the child shall be returned to the parent.

Collateral attack; vacation of decree and return of custody; limitations

(d) After the entry of a final decree of adoption of an Indian child in any State court, the parent may withdraw consent thereto upon the grounds that consent was obtained through fraud or duress and may petition the court to vacate such decree. Upon a finding that such consent was obtained through fraud or duress, the court shall vacate such decree and return the child to the parent. No adoption which has been effective for at least two years may be invalidated under the provisions of this subsection unless otherwise permitted under State law.

§ 1914. Petition to court of competent jurisdiction to invalidate action upon showing of certain violations

Any Indian child who is the subject of any action for foster care placement or termination of parental rights under State law, any parent or Indian custodian from whose custody such child was removed, and the Indian child's tribe may petition any court of competent jurisdiction to invalidate such action upon a showing that such action violated any provision of sections 1911, 1912, and 1913 of this title.

§ 1915. Placement of Indian children — Adoptive placements; preferences

(a) In any adoptive placement of an Indian child under State law, a preference shall be given, in the absence of good cause to the contrary, to a placement with (1) a member of the child's extended family; (2) other members of the Indian child's tribe; or (3) other Indian families.

Foster care or preadoptive placements; criteria; preferences

(b) Any child accepted for foster care or preadoptive placement shall be placed in the least restrictive setting which most approximates a family and in which his special needs, if any, may be met. The child shall also be placed within reasonable proximity to his or her home, taking into account any special needs of the child. In any foster care or preadoptive placement, a preference shall be given, in the absence of good cause to the contrary, to a placement with —

(i) a member of the Indian child's extended family;

(ii) a foster home licensed, approved, or specified by the Indian child's tribe;

(iii) an Indian foster home licensed or approved by an authorized non-Indian licensing authority; or

(iv) an institution for children approved by an Indian tribe or operated by an Indian organization which has a program suitable to meet the Indian child's needs.

Tribal resolution for different order of preference; personal preference considered; anonymity in application of preferences

(c) In the case of a placement under subsection (a) or (b) of this section, if the Indian child's tribe shall establish a different order of preference by resolution, the agency or court effecting the placement shall follow such order so long as the placement is the least restrictive setting appropriate to the particular needs of the child, as provided in subsection (b) of this section. Where appropriate, the preference of the Indian child or parent shall be considered: *Provided,*

That where a consenting parent evidences a desire for anonymity, the court or agency shall give weight to such desire in applying the preferences.

Social and cultural standards applicable

(d) The standards to be applied in meeting the preference requirements of this section shall be the prevailing social and cultural standards of the Indian community in which the parent or extended family resides or with which the parent or extended family members maintain social and cultural ties.

Record of placement; availability

(e) A record of each such placement, under State law, of an Indian child shall be maintained by the State in which the placement was made, evidencing the efforts to comply with the order of preference specified in this section. Such record shall be made available at any time upon the request of the Secretary or the Indian child's tribe.

§ 1916. Return of custody — Petition; best interests of child

(a) Notwithstanding State law to the contrary, whenever a final decree of adoption of an Indian child has been vacated or set aside or the adoptive parents voluntarily consent to the termination of their parental rights to the child, a biological parent or prior Indian custodian may petition for return of custody and the court shall grant such petition unless there is a showing, in a proceeding subject to the provisions of section 1912 of this title, that such return of custody is not in the best interests of the child.

Removal from foster care home; placement procedure

(b) Whenever an Indian child is removed from a foster care home or institution for the purpose of further foster care, preadoptive, or adoptive placement, such placement shall be in accordance with the provisions of this chapter, except in the case where an Indian child is being returned to the parent or Indian custodian from whose custody the child was originally removed.

§ 1918. Reassumption jurisdiction over child custody proceedings — Petition; suitable plan; approval by Secretary

(a) Any Indian tribe which became subject to State jurisdiction pursuant to the provisions of the Act of August 15, 1953 (67 Stat. 588), as amended by subchapter III of chapter 15 of this title, or pursuant to any other Federal law, may reassume jurisdiction over child custody proceedings. Before any Indian tribe may reassume jurisdiction over Indian child custody proceedings, such tribe shall present to the Secretary for approval a petition to reassume such jurisdiction which includes a suitable plan to exercise such jurisdiction.

Criteria applicable to consideration by Secretary; partial retrocession

(b) (1) In considering the petition and feasibility of the plan of a tribe under subsection (a) of this section, the Secretary may consider, among other things:

(i) whether or not the tribe maintains a membership roll or alternative provision for clearly identifying the persons who will be affected by the reassumption of jurisdiction by the tribe;

(ii) the size of the reservation or former reservation area which will be affected by retrocession and reassumption of jurisdiction by the tribe;

(iii) the population base of the tribe, or distribution of the population in homogeneous communities or geographic areas; and

(iv) the feasibility of the plan in cases of multitribal occupation of a single reservation or geographic area.

(2) In those cases where the Secretary determines that the jurisdictional provisions of section 1911(a) of this title are not feasible, he is authorized to accept partial retrocession which will enable tribes to exercise referral jurisdiction as provided in section 1911(b) of this title, or, where appropriate, will allow them to exercise exclusive jurisdiction as provided in section 1911(a) of this title over limited community or geographic areas without regard for the reservation status of the area affected.

Approval of petition; publication in Federal Register; notice; reassumption period; correction of causes for disapproval

(c) If the Secretary approves any petition under subsection (a) of this section, the Secretary shall publish notice of such approval in the Federal Register and shall notify the affected State or States of such approval. The Indian tribe concerned shall reassume jurisdiction sixty days after publication in the Federal Register of notice of approval. If the Secretary disapproves any petition under subsection (a) of this section, the Secretary shall provide such technical assistance as may be necessary to enable the tribe to correct any deficiency which the Secretary identified as a cause for disapproval.

Pending actions or proceedings unaffected

(d) Assumption of jurisdiction under this section shall not affect any action or proceeding over which a court has already assumed jurisdiction, except as may be provided pursuant to any agreement under section 1919 of this title.

§ 1919. Agreements between States and Indian tribes — Subject coverage

(a) States and Indian tribes are authorized to enter into agreements with each other respecting care and custody of Indian children and jurisdiction over child custody proceedings, including agreements which may provide for orderly transfer of jurisdiction on a case-by-case basis and agreements which provide for concurrent jurisdiction between States and Indian tribes.

Revocation; notice; actions or proceedings unaffected

(b) Such agreements may be revoked by either party upon one hundred and eighty days' written notice to the other party. Such revocation shall not affect any action or proceeding over which a court has already assumed jurisdiction, unless the agreement provides otherwise.

§ 1920. Improper removal of child from custody; declination of jurisdiction; forthwith return of child: danger exception

Where any petitioner in an Indian child custody proceeding before a State court has improperly removed the child from custody of the parent or Indian custodian or has improperly retained custody after a visit or other temporary relinquishment of custody, the court shall decline jurisdiction over such petition and shall forthwith return the child to his parent or Indian custodian unless returning the child to his parent or custodian would subject the child to a substantial and immediate danger or threat of such danger.

§ 1921. Higher State or Federal standard applicable to protect rights of parent or Indian custodian of Indian child

In any case where State or Federal law applicable to a child custody proceeding under State or Federal law provides a higher standard of protection to the rights of the parent or Indian custodian of an Indian child than the rights provided under this subchapter, the State or Federal court shall apply the State or Federal standard.

§ 1922. Emergency removal or placement of child; termination; appropriate action

Nothing in this subchapter shall be construed to prevent the emergency removal of an Indian child who is a resident of or is domiciled on a reservation, but temporarily located off the reservation, from his parent or Indian custodian or the emergency placement of such child in a foster home or institution, under applicable State law, in order to prevent imminent physical danger or harm to the child. The State authority, official, or agency involved shall insure that the emergency removal or placement terminates immediately when such removal or placement is no longer necessary to prevent imminent physical damage or harm to the child and shall expeditiously initiate a child custody proceeding subject to the provisions of this subchapter, transfer the child to the jurisdiction of the appropriate Indian tribe, or restore the child to the parent or Indian custodian, as may be appropriate....

25 C.F.R PART 23 — INDIAN CHILD WELFARE ACT

Subpart A — Purpose, Definitions, and Policy

§ 23.1 Purpose.

The purpose of the regulations in this Part is to govern the provision of administration and funding of the Indian Child Welfare Act of 1978 (Pub. L. 95-608, 92 Stat. 3069, 25 U.S.C. 1901-1952).

§ 23.2 Definitions.

(a) "Act" means the Indian Child Welfare Act, Pub. L. 95-608 (92 Stat. 3073), 25 U.S.C. 1901 et seq.

(b) "Child custody proceeding," which shall mean and include:

(1) "Foster care placement" — any action removing an Indian child from its parent or Indian custodian for temporary placement in a foster home or institution or the home of a guardian or conservator where the parent or Indian custodian cannot have the child returned upon demand, but where parental rights have not been terminated;

(2) "Termination of parental rights" — an action resulting in the termination of the parent-child relationship;

(3) "Preadoptive placement" — the temporary placement of an Indian child in a foster home or institution after the termination of parental rights, but prior to or in lieu of adoptive placement; and

(4) "Adoptive placement" — the permanent placement of an Indian child for adoption, including any action resulting in a final decree of adoption.

(5) Such term or terms shall not include a placement based upon an act which, if committed by an adult, would be deemed a crime in the jurisdiction where the act occurred or upon an award, in a divorce proceeding, of custody to one of the parents. It does include status offenses, such as truancy, incorrigibility etc.

(c) "Extended family member" shall be as defined by the law or custom of the Indian child's tribe or, in the absence of such law or custom, shall be a person who has reached the age of eighteen and who is the Indian child's grandparent, aunt or uncle, brother or sister, brother-in-law or sister-in-law, niece or nephew, first or second cousin, or stepparent.

(d) "Indian" means:

(1) Jurisdictional Purposes: For purposes of matters related to child custody proceedings any person who is a member of an Indian tribe, or who is an Alaska Native and a member of a Regional Corporation as defined in section 7 or the Alaska Native Claims Settlement Act (85 Stat. 688, 689).

(2) Service eligibility for on or "near" reservation Children and Family Service Programs. For purposes of Indian child and family service programs under section 201 of the Indian Child Welfare Act (92 Stat. 3075), any person who is a member, or a one-fourth degree or more blood quantum descendant of a member of any Indian tribe.

(3) Service eligibility for off-reservation Children and Family Service Programs: For the purpose of Indian child and family programs under section 202 of the Indian Child Welfare Act (92 Stat. 3073) any person who is a member of a tribe, band, or other organized group of Indians, including those tribes, bands, or groups terminated since 1940 and those recognized now or in the future by the state in which they reside, or who is a descendent, in the first or second degree, of any such member, or is an Eskimo or Aleut or other Alaska Native, or is considered by the Secretary of the Interior to be an Indian for any purpose, or is determined to be an Indian under regulations promulgated by the Secretary of Health, Education, and Welfare. Membership status is to be determined by the tribal law, ordinance, or custom.

(e) "Indian child" means any unmarried person who is under age eighteen and is either (1) a member of an Indian tribe, or (2) is eligible for membership in an Indian tribe and is the biological child of a member of an Indian tribe.

(f) " Indian child's tribe" means (1) the Indian tribe in which an Indian child is a member or is eligible for membership or (2) in the case of an Indian child who is a member of or is eligible for membership in more than one tribe, the Indian tribe with which the Indian child has the more significant contacts. (Refer to Guidelines for State Courts — Indian Child Custody Proceedings.)

(g) "Indian custodian" means any Indian person(s) who has legal custody of an Indian child under tribal law or custom or under state law or to whom temporary physical care, custody, and control has been transferred by the parent of such child.

(h) "Indian organization" means any group, association, partnership, corporation, or other legal entity owned or controlled by Indians, or a majority of whose members are Indians.

(i) "Indian tribe" means any Indian tribe, band, nation or other organized group or community of Indians recognized as eligible for the services provided to Indians by the Secretary because of their status as Indians, including any Alaska Native village as defined in section 3(c) of the Alaska Native Claims Settlement Act (85 Stat. 688, 689), as amended.

(j) "Parent" means any biological parent or parents of an Indian child or any Indian person who has lawfully adopted an Indian child, including adoptions under tribal law or custom. It does not include the unwed father where paternity has not been acknowledged or established.

(k) "Reservation" means Indian country as defined in section 1151 of Title 18, United States Code, and any lands not covered under such section, title to which is either held by the United States in trust for the benefit of any Indian tribe or individual subject to a restriction by the United States against alienation.

(l) "State Court" means any agent or agency of a State including the District of Columbia or any territory or possession of the United States or any political subdivisions empowered by law to terminate parental rights or to make foster care placements, preadoptive placements, or adoptive placements.

(m) "Tribal court" means a court with jurisdiction over child custody proceedings and which is either a court of Indian Offenses, a court established and operated under the code or custom of an Indian tribe, or any other administrative body of a tribe which is vested with authority over child custody proceedings.

(n) Multi-service Indian center means an off-reservation social service center having an established social service delivery program; or, if located in an officially designated "near" reservation area, a social service center serving a clientele of varied tribal affiliations, but with no more than one-half of its clientele from the tribe which requested designation of the "near" reservation area.

(o) For other applicable definitions refer to 25 CFR 20.1 and 271.2.

§ 23.3 Policy.

The policy of the Act and of these regulations is to protect Indian children from arbitrary removal from their families and tribal affiliations by establishing procedures to insure that measures to prevent the breakup of Indian families are followed in child custody proceedings. This will insure protection of the best interests of Indian children and Indian families by providing assistance and funding to Indian tribes and Indian organizations in the operation of child and family service programs which reflect the unique values of Indian culture and promote the stability and security of Indian families. In administering the grant authority for Indian Child and Family Programs it shall be Bureau policy to emphasize the design and funding of programs to promote the stability of Indian families.

§ 23.4 Information collection.

The information collection requirements contained in § 23.28 are those necessary to comply with the application requirements of Office of Management and Budget (OMB) Circular No. A-102. The Standard Form 424 and attachments prescribed by such circular are approved by OMB under 44 U.S.C. 3501 et seq. and assigned approval number 0348-0006. Section 23.24 describes the types of information that would satisfy the application requirements of Circular A-102 for this grant program. Information necessary for an application for Federal assistance will be submitted on Standard Form 424 which may be obtained with application materials in accordance with 25 CFR 23.23. This information is being collected for the purpose of applying for Federal assistance. The information will be used in selecting the recipients and determining the amount of the Indian Child Welfare Act grant awards. The obligation to respond is a requirement to obtain the benefits.

Subpart B — Notice of Involuntary Child Custody Proceedings and Payment for Appointed Counsel

§ 23.11 Notice.

(a) If the identity or location of the parents, Indian custodians or the Indian child's tribe cannot be determined, notice of the pendency of any involuntary child custody proceeding involving an Indian child in a state court shall be sent by registered mail with return receipt requested to the appropriate address listed in paragraph (b) of this section [of the regional area directors of the BIA].

(c) Notice shall include the following information if known:

(1) Name of the Indian child, birthdate, birthplace,

(2) Indian child's tribal affiliation,

(3) Names of Indian child's parents or Indian custodians, including birthdate, birthplace, and mother's maiden name, and

(4) A copy of the petition, complaint or other document by which the proceeding was initiated.

(d) Upon receipt of the notice, the Bureau shall make a diligent effort to locate and notify the Indian child's tribe and the Indian child's parents or Indian custodians. Such notice may be by registered mail with return receipt requested or by personal service and shall include the information provided under paragraph (c) of this section in addition to the following:

(1) A statement of the right of the biological parents, Indian custodians and the Indian tribe to intervene in the proceedings.

(2) A statement that if the parent(s) or Indian custodian(s) is unable to afford counsel, counsel will be appointed to represent them.

(3) A statement of the right of the parents, the Indian custodians and the child's tribe to have, upon request, up to twenty additional days to prepare for the proceedings.

(4) The location, mailing address and telephone number of the court.

(5) A statement of the right of the parents, Indian custodians and the Indian child's tribe to petition the court for transfer of the proceeding to the child's tribal court, and their right to refuse to permit the case to be transferred.

(6) A statement of the potential legal consequences of the proceedings on the future custodial and parental rights of the parents or Indian custodians.

(7) A statement that, since child custody proceedings are usually conducted on a confidential basis, tribal officials should keep confidential the information contained in the notice concerning the particular proceeding and not reveal it to anyone who does not need the information in order to exercise the tribe's rights under the Act.

(e) The Bureau shall have ten days, after receipt of the notice from the persons initiating the proceedings, to notify the child's tribe and parents or Indian custodians and send a copy of the notice to the court. If within the ten-day time period the Bureau is unable to verify that the child is in fact an Indian, or meets the criteria of an Indian child as defined in section (4) of the Act, or is unable to locate the parents or Indian custodians, the Bureau shall so inform the court prior to initiation of the proceedings and state how much more time, if any, it will need to complete the search. The Bureau shall complete its search efforts even if those efforts cannot be completed before the child custody proceeding begins.

(f) Upon request from a potential participant in an anticipated Indian child custody proceeding, the Bureau shall attempt to identify and locate the Indian child's tribe, parents or Indian custodians for the person making the request.

§ 23.12 Designated tribal agent for service of notice.

Any Indian tribe entitled to notice may designate by resolution, or by such other form as the tribal constitution or current practice requires, an agent for service of such notice other than the tribal chairman and send a copy of the designation to the Secretary. The Secretary shall publish the name and address of the designated agent in the *Federal Register* on an annual basis. A current listing of such agents will be maintained by the Secretary and will be available through the Area Offices.

§ 23.13 Payment for appointed counsel in state Indian child custody proceedings.

(a) When a state court appoints counsel for an indigent party in an Indian child custody proceeding, for which the appointment of counsel is not authorized under state law, the court shall send written notice of the appointment to the Bureau of Indian Affairs Area office designated for that state in § 23.11 of this part. The notice shall include the following:

(1) Name, address and telephone number of attorney who has been appointed.

(2) Name and address of client for whom counsel is appointed.

(3) Relationship of client to child.

(4) Name of Indian child's tribe.

(5) Copy of the petition or complaint.

(6) Certification by the court that state law makes no provision for appointment of counsel in such proceedings.

(7) Certification by the court that the client is indigent.

(b) The Area Director shall certify that the client is eligible to have his or her appointed counsel compensated by the Bureau of Indian Affairs unless:

(1) The litigation does not involve a child custody proceeding as defined in 25 U.S.C. 1903(1);

(2) The child who is the subject of the litigation is not an Indian child as defined in 25 U.S.C. 1903(4);

(3) The client is neither the Indian child who is the subject of the litigation, the Indian child's parent as defined in 25 U.S.C. 1903(9), or the child's Indian custodian as defined in 25 U.S.C. 1903(6);

(4) State law provides for appointment of counsel in such proceedings;

(5) The notice of the Area Director of appointment of counsel is incomplete; or

(6) No funds are available for such payments.

(c) No later than 10 days after receipt of the notice of appointment of counsel, the Area Director shall notify the court, the client and the attorney in writing whether the client has been certified as eligible to have his or her attorney fees and expenses paid by the Bureau of Indian Affairs. In the event that certification is denied, the notice shall include written reasons for that decision together with a statement that the Area Director's decision may be appealed to the Commissioner of Indian Affairs under the provisions of the 25 CFR Part 2.

(d) When determining attorney fees and expenses the court shall:

(1) Determine the amount of payments due appointed counsel by the same procedures and criteria it uses in determining the fees and expenses to be paid appointed counsel in juvenile delinquency proceedings.

(2) Submit approved vouchers to the Area Director who certified eligibility for Bureau payment together with the court's certification that the amount requested is reasonable under the state standards and considering the work actually performed in light of the criteria that apply in determining fees and expenses for appointed counsel in juvenile delinquency proceedings.

(e) The Area Director shall authorize the payment of attorney fees and expenses in the amount requested in the voucher approved by the court unless:

(1) The court has abused its discretion under state law in determining the amount of the fees and expenses; or

(2) The client has not been previously certified as eligible under paragraph (c) of this section; or

(3) The voucher is submitted later than ninety (90) days after completion of the legal action involving a client certified as eligible for payment of legal fees under paragraph (b) of this section.

(f) No later than 15 days after receipt of a payment voucher the Area Director shall send written notice to the court, the client and the attorney stating the amount of payment, if any, that has been authorized. If the payment has been denied or the amount authorized is less than the amount requested in the voucher approved by the court, the notice shall include a written statement of the reasons for the decision together with a statement that the decision of the

Area Director may be appealed to the Commissioner under the procedures of 25 CFR Part 2.

(g) Failure of the Area Director to meet the deadlines specified in paragraphs (c) and (f) of this section may be treated as a denial for purposes of appeal under paragraph (f) of this section.

MATTER OF GUARDIANSHIP OF D.L.L. & C.L.L.

291 N.W.2d 278 (S.D. 1980)

DUNN, Justice.

Petitioner appeals from the order of dismissal of the proceedings and the denial of her petition for letters of guardianship. We affirm.

Appellees R.L. and K.L. (parents of D.L.L. and C.L.L.) are residents of the Lower Brule Sioux Indian Reservation and have five children. Each member of the family is a member of the Lower Brule Sioux Tribe. Petitioner operates the House of Shalom, a group foster home, in Presho, South Dakota.

In the late summer of 1976, Mr. L. was informed that an ulcer on his right foot would necessitate amputation of the leg at the hip. An informal arrangement was made to the effect that his two oldest children — D.L.L. and C.L.L. — would stay at petitioner's foster home during the 1976-77 school year. On November 26, 1976, the Lower Brule Sioux Tribal Court entered an order giving temporary custody of the four oldest children to petitioner at her foster home during the aforementioned school year. Petitioner and the parents were in agreement on this matter, and Mr. L. signed a document that stated that this arrangement was desired. Mr. L. anticipated a lengthy hospitalization at this time, and testimony in the lower court indicates that this factor was the prime motivation behind the grant of temporary custody. Petitioner desired the court to facilitate obtaining Bureau of Indian Affairs funds for the children's support.

When the court order expired, Mr. L. remained hospitalized and Mrs. L. was temporarily in California. Petitioner obtained another temporary custody order on June 27, 1977. The two younger children, however, returned to their home in Lower Brule during the summer without an authorizing court order. Mr. L. returned in late summer. On September 29, 1977, Mr. and Mrs. L. obtained a release order that terminated the temporary placement of the two younger children and returned them to their parents' custody. In this same release order, the Tribal Court provided for weekend visitations between the parents and their two older children, D.L.L. and C.L.L.

After some problems concerning alcohol consumption occurred during one of these visitation periods, petitioner obtained a Tribal Court order restricting visitation and requiring an order each time a visitation period was desired.

On March 9, 1979, petitioner informed the Tribal Court that D.L.L. was pregnant. Petitioner contends that the pregnancy was the result of an alleged rape by an unidentified party and that the rape occurred during a visitation period at Lower Brule during the Fourth of July holiday in 1978. Based upon the date of the birth of the child, the parents dispute that the alleged rape occurred during the July visitation. On March 16, 1979, the Tribal Court entered an order approving a visitation for the coming weekend. Petitioner did not obey the order. On March 22, the Tribal Court ordered that the children be returned to Lower Brule to reside in their parents' home until further order of the court. This order was not obeyed, and petitioner commenced the guardianship action that forms the basis of this appeal.

The trial court's dismissal of this action was based upon existing case law and the Indian Child Welfare Act of 1978. Petitioner contends that the 1978 Act unconstitutionally ceded the jurisdiction of South Dakota to the United States. It is true that a long line of United States Supreme Court cases, beginning with *Barber v. Barber*, 62 U.S. 582 (1859), holds that states have exclusive jurisdiction in domestic relations cases. Nevertheless, Congress has seen fit to exercise its legislative will over Indian tribes and their members based upon Art. I, § 8, of the United States Constitution, which states: "The Congress shall have Power ... [t]o regulate Commerce with foreign Nations, and among the several States, and with the Indian Tribes." This section of the Constitution has been used many times as the basis of federal authority over Indian matters. *McClanahan v. Arizona Tax Commission*, 411 U.S. 164 (1973).

The Tenth Amendment, which reserves all nondelegated powers to the states or the people, has not been violated by the 1978 Act. The plenary power of Congress to legislate with respect to Indians is a deep-seated one. Such legislation does not infringe upon the Tenth Amendment as long as the legislative power is not exercised arbitrarily. No evidence has been introduced in support of an allegation of arbitrariness of the 1978 Act.

Likewise, petitioner's claim that the 1978 Act violates Article XXII of the South Dakota Constitution is unfounded. The United States has plenary power under the United States Constitution to govern tribal Indians. This power does not derive from a conveyance by South Dakota, and petitioner's claim that Article XXII reserves jurisdiction to the state whenever an Indian is off the reservation is incorrect. The proper inquiry is whether the actions of the state would infringe on the right of reservation Indians to make and be governed by their own laws. *Williams v. Lee*, 358 U.S. 217 (1959); *Utah & Northern R. Co. v. Fisher*, 116 U.S. 28 (1885). Even when a tribal member is off the reservation, tribal courts provide the appropriate forum for settlement of disputes over personal and property interests of Indians that arise out of tribal relationships. *Fisher v. District Court*, 424 U.S. 382 (1976); *Williams v. Lee, supra*. Indian relations are of an anomalous and complex character, and tribal courts are better able than other forums to evaluate questions of Indian traditions. *Santa Clara Pueblo v. Martinez*, 436 U.S. 49 (1978); *United States v. Quiver*, 241 U.S. 602 (1916). To justify the application of a state law affecting these relations there must be some clear provision to that effect. *Quiver*, 241 U.S. at 606. It follows that when tribes have the power to make their own substantive law in internal matters they also have the power to enforce those laws in their own forums.

The fact that the children in this case spent some time off the reservation is not determinative of the proper forum. Even though a member of an Indian tribe may be outside the territorial boundaries of the reservation, the tribal government may regulate the absent member's affairs involving questions of membership, *Roff v. Burney*, 168 U.S. 218 (1897), and questions of domestic relations, *United States v. Quiver, supra*. The locus of the act of a member is not conclusive. Rather, the test is a broader one, hinging on whether the matter demands exercise of the tribe's responsibility of self-government. *Williams v. Lee*, 358 U.S. 217 (1959); *Littell v. Nakai*, 344 F.2d 486 (9th Cir. 1965). There can be no greater threat to essential tribal relations and to the tribal power of self-government than to interfere in questions of custody of tribal members.

Petitioner argues that D.L.L. and C.L.L. are being denied equal protection and due process in violation of the Fifth Amendment. She claims that the denial of access to state court was based upon "invidious racial discrimination." This is incorrect. The denial of access to state court was based solely upon the political status of the parents and children and the quasi-sovereign nature of the tribe. This is a discriminatory classification which is not prohibited by the United States Constitution. *Fisher v. District Court*, 424 U.S. 382 (1976).

Petitioner argues that this dispute arises under § 101(b) of the 1978 Act as opposed to § 101(a). She contends that the Tribal Court is divested of jurisdiction under § 101(b) because the state court proceeding was commenced within 180 days of the enactment of the 1978 Act. Section 113 of the Act explicitly provides that the 180-day limitation does not apply to § 101(a).

Section 101(a) states that an Indian tribe shall have exclusive jurisdiction

as to any State over any child custody proceeding involving an Indian child who resides or is domiciled within the reservation of such tribe ... Where an Indian child is a ward of a tribal court, the Indian tribe shall retain exclusive jurisdiction, notwithstanding the residence or domicile of the child.

We find that these children were wards of the Tribal Court prior to the state court action. The Tribal Court acted upon a written request of the father to have the children placed in the temporary custody of the Tribal Court. This, in turn, enabled the Tribal Court to place the children with petitioner. It is not required that the court order specifically use the words "ward of the court" in order to effectuate such a status. *In re Jennings*, 68 Ill. 2d 125, 11 Ill. Dec. 256, 368 N.E.2d 864 (1977). This order was of a continuing nature, not final when issued, and could be changed at an unspecified time in the future. The person to whom the order is referenced is a ward of the court. *In re Wolfe*, 91 Ohio L. Abst. 167, 187 N.E.2d 658 (1962). The only legal rights of the petitioner vis-à-vis the children were those outlined by the Tribal Court.

Furthermore, the children remained residents and domiciliaries of the reservation. The domicile of a minor child is the domicile of the parents until legally changed....

Finally, the reservation residency and domicile of the children was not lost by any supposed abandonment or emancipation on the part of the parents. There was no express mutual agreement by the parents granting emancipation. Emancipation can be implied "when there has been complete abandonment of parental responsibility and control, and the child is actually obtaining support by other means...." SDCL 25-5-19. In this case, the father foresaw a lengthy, expensive hospitalization and agreed, for the welfare of the children, to grant petitioner temporary custody. There is no evidence of "complete abandonment of parental responsibility and control." Likewise, there has been no desertion here. An involuntary, temporary inability to assume a parental role is not abandonment. *In re Adoption of Christofferson*, 89 S.D. 287, 232 N.W.2d 832 (1975). The personal health problems of the parents, whether physical or alcohol-related, do not show intent to abandon. If these problems of the parents are adversely affecting the welfare of the children, the proper forum for relief is the Tribal Court.

[*Affirmed.*]

NOTES ON THE CONSTITUTIONALITY OF THE INDIAN CHILD WELFARE ACT

The constitutional questions raised in the foregoing case were debated with even greater vigor by Congress in the legislative history of the Indian Child Welfare Act (ICWA). In letters to the congressional committee, Assistant Attorney General (now Judge) Patricia M. Wald raised questions regarding the constitutionality of the bill. First, the Department of Justice questioned whether the broad definition of "Indian child" contained in the proposed legislation might constitute invidious racial discrimination in violation of the fifth amendment. Second, the Department of Justice questioned whether such pervasive federal legislation in an area of traditional state concern, like child welfare and custody, might violate the tenth amendment. Finally, the Department of Justice challenged the constitutionality of authorizing Indian tribes to exercise jurisdiction over children domiciled off the reservation and over nonmember children domiciled on or off reservation, stating:

> An eligible Indian who has chosen, for whatever reasons, not to enroll in a tribe would be in a position to argue that depriving him of access to the State courts on matters related to family life would be invidious. Such an Indian presumably has, under the first amendment, the same right of association as do all citizens, and indeed would appear to be in no different situation from a non-Indian living on reservation who ... would have access to State courts. The only difference between them would, in fact, be the racial characteristics of the former.

H. Rep. No. 95-1386, 95th Cong., 2d Sess. 37 (1978). In another letter, the Department stated:

> [W]e are not convinced that Congress' power to control the incidents of such litigation involving nonreservation Indian children and parents pursuant to the Indian commerce clause is sufficient to override the significant State interest in regulating the procedure to be followed by its courts in exercising State jurisdiction over what is a traditionally state matter. It seems to us that the Federal interest in the off-reservation context is so attenuated that the 10th Amendment and general principles of federalism preclude the wholesale invasion of State power contemplated by section 102 [25 U.S.C. § 1912].

Id. at 40.

In response to these concerns, some changes were made in the proposed legislation. To what extent does the text of the ICWA resolve these questions? The congressional reports responded to some of these concerns by noting that the committees disagreed with the constitutional assessments offered by the Department of Justice. *Id.* at 12. Thus, the House report offered an extensive brief to support the constitutionality of the ICWA, the major outlines of which are evident in the preamble to the statute. First, responding to the concern that the definition of Indian child might constitute invidious racial discrimination because it included persons who are not enrolled tribal members, the report noted that the definition of "Indians" contained in section 19 of the IRA also was not limited to tribal members and, yet, was approved in *Morton v. Mancari*, set forth and discussed in Chapter 1, section B2. The report noted that a number of cases decided in the wake of federal efforts to wind up the affairs of the Oklahoma tribes at the turn of the century had sustained the power of Congress to disregard tribal membership rolls and make its own judgments about entitlements to per capita distributions. *See, e.g., Stephens v. Cherokee Nation*, 174 U.S. 445 (1899); *Sizemore v. Brady*, 235 U.S. 441 (1914). *See also* F. COHEN, HANDBOOK OF FEDERAL INDIAN LAW 45 n.10 (1942). Thus, the report argued,

> [T]he constitutional and plenary power of Congress over Indians and Indian tribes and affairs cannot be made to hinge upon the cranking into operation of a mechanical [enrollment] process established under tribal law, particularly with respect to Indian children who, because of their minority, cannot make a reasoned decision about their tribal and Indian identity.

Id. at 17.

Second, insofar as the tenth amendment was concerned, the report took the position that so long as the ICWA constituted an appropriate exercise of the plenary power of Congress over Indian affairs, the supremacy clause of article VI, clause 2 of the Constitution required inconsistent state policies to yield. Relying on *Wakefield v. Little Light*, 276 Md. 333, 347 A.2d 228 (1975), and *Wisconsin Potowatomies of Hannahville Indian Community v. Houston*, 393 F. Supp. 719 (W.D. Mich. 1973), the report noted that "a tribe's children are vital to its integrity and future. Since the United States has the responsibility to protect the integrity of the tribes, we can say with the *Kagama* court, '... there arises the duty of protection, and with it the power.'" *Id.* at 15. The legislative history of the ICWA further indicated that Indian children were being placed in foster care or adopted at alarming rates, often because social workers did not understand Indian extended family child-rearing practices or because poverty was equated with neglect. *See* Hearings on S. 1214 Before the Senate Select Comm. on Indian Affairs, 95th Cong., 1st Sess., 538-40 (1977). Indeed, it was estimated during the Congressional inquiry that somewhere between a quarter and a third of all Indian children had been removed from their Indian homes. It should also be noted that the Supreme Court's decision in *Garcia v. San Antonio Metro. Transit Auth.*, 469 U.S. 105 (1985) (federalism limitations of the tenth amendment are enforced by political, rather than judicial, branches of the federal government), decided long after the enactment of the Indian Child Welfare Act, puts to rest any lingering potential tenth amendment challenges to this legislation.

Finally, the report responded to the Department of Justice's concern about the exercise of tribal jurisdiction over Indian children domiciled off reservation by pointing out that the scope of congressional power is not limited to the Indian reservation. *Citing United States v. Holliday*, 70 U.S. 407 (1865), *and Perrin v. United States*, 232 U.S. 478 (1914), the report pointed out that congressional power derives from "the presence of the Indians and their status as wards of the Government" and reached such tribal Indians whether on or off an Indian reservation. *Id.* at 15.

Does the House report adequately respond to the concerns of the Department of Justice? Does the foregoing case give proper weight to the constitutional issues involved? The equal protection issue was more fully analyzed and resolved in favor of the Act's constitutionality in *Armell v. Prairie Band of Potawatomi Indians*, 194 Ill. App. 3d 31, 550 N.E.2d 1060, *cert. denied*, 111 S. Ct. 345 (1990).

Note that under section 1915(a) the preferences for placement of Indian children covered by the act is initially to a member of the child's extended family, but thereafter to "(2) other members of the Indian child's tribe; or (3) other Indian families." Can the third preference be justified on the basis of the political classification rationale of *Morton v. Mancari*, set forth and discussed in Chapter 1? If not, does that observation suggest a problem with the *Morton* rationale or, rather, does it suggest the unconstitutionality of this statutory preference? Notice that similar distinctions are made throughout the Act, including the foster care placement provisions of section 1915(b).

MISSISSIPPI BAND OF CHOCTAW INDIANS v. HOLYFIELD

490 U.S. 30 (1989)

Justice BRENNAN delivered the opinion of the Court.

This appeal requires us to construe the provisions of the Indian Child Welfare Act that establish exclusive tribal jurisdiction over child custody proceedings involving Indian children domiciled on the tribe's reservation.

I

A

The Indian Child Welfare Act of 1978 (ICWA), 92 Stat. 3069, 25 U.S.C. §§ 1901-1963, was the product of rising concern in the mid-1970's over the consequences to Indian children, Indian families, and Indian tribes of abusive child welfare practices that resulted in the separation of large numbers of Indian children from their families and tribes through adoption or foster care placement, usually in non-Indian homes. Senate oversight hearings in 1974 yielded numerous examples, statistical data, and expert testimony documenting what one witness called "the wholesale removal of Indian children from their homes, ... the most tragic aspect of Indian life today." Indian Child Welfare Program, Hearings before the Subcommittee on Indian Affairs of the Senate Committee on Interior and Insular Affairs, 93d Cong., 2d Sess., 3 (hereinafter 1974 Hearings) (statement of William Byler). Studies undertaken by the Association on American Indian Affairs in 1969 and 1974, and presented in the Senate hearings, showed that 25 to 35 percent of all Indian children had been separated from their families and placed in adoptive families, foster care, or institutions. *Id.*, at 15; see also H. R. Rep. No. 95-1386, p. 9 (1978) (hereinafter House Report). Adoptive placements counted significantly in this total: in the State of Minnesota, for example, one in eight Indian children under the age of 18 was in an adoptive home, and during the year 1971-1972 nearly one in every four infants under one year of age was placed for adoption. The adoption rate of Indian children was eight times that of non-Indian children. Approximately 90% of the Indian placements were in non-Indian homes. 1974 Hearings, at 75-83. A number of witnesses also testified to the serious adjustment problems encountered by such children during adolescence,[1] as well as the impact of the adoptions on Indian parents and the tribes themselves. See generally 1974 Hearings.

Further hearings, covering much the same ground, were held during 1977 and 1978 on the bill that became the ICWA.[2] While much of the testimony again focused on the harm to Indian parents and their children who were involuntarily separated by decisions of local welfare authorities, there was also considerable emphasis on the impact on the tribes themselves of the massive removal of their children. For example, Mr. Calvin Isaac, Tribal Chief of the Mississippi Band of Choctaw Indians and representative of the National Tribal Chairmen's Association, testified as follows:

> "Culturally, the chances of Indian survival are significantly reduced if our children, the only real means for the transmission of the tribal heritage, are to be raised in non-Indian homes and denied exposure to the ways of their People. Furthermore, these practices seriously undercut the tribes' ability to continue as self-governing communities. Probably in no area is it more important that tribal sovereignty be respected than in an area as socially and culturally determinative as family relationships." 1978 Hearings, at 193. See also *id.*, at 62.[3]

Chief Isaac also summarized succinctly what numerous witnesses saw as the principal reason for the high rates of removal of Indian children:

> "One of the most serious failings of the present system is that Indian children are removed from the custody of their natural parents by nontribal government authorities who have no basis for intelligently evaluating the cultural and social premises underlying Indian home life and childrearing. Many of the individuals who decide the fate of our children are at best ignorant of our cultural values, and at worst contemptful of the Indian way and convinced that removal, usually to a non-Indian household or institution, can only benefit an Indian child." *Id.*, at 191-192.[4]

---

[1] For example, Dr. Joseph Westermeyer, a University of Minnesota social psychiatrist, testified about his research with Indian adolescents who experience difficulty coping in white society, despite the fact that they had been raised in a purely white environment: "[T]hey were raised with a white cultural and social identity. They are raised in a white home. They attended predominantly white schools, and in almost all cases, attended a church that was predominantly white, and really came to understand very little about Indian culture, Indian behavior, and had virtually no viable Indian identity. They can recall such things as seeing cowboys and Indians on TV and feeling that Indians were a historical figure but were not a viable contemporary social group.

"Then during adolescence, they found that society was not to grant them the white identity that they had. They began to find this out in a number of ways. For example, a universal experience was that when they began to date white children, the parents of the white youngsters were against this, and there were pressures among white children from the parents not to date these Indian children....

"The other experience was derogatory name calling in relation to their racial identity ....

"[T]hey were finding that society was putting on them an identity which they didn't possess and taking from them an identity that they did possess." 1974 Hearings, at 46.

[2] Hearing on S. 1214 before the Senate Select Committee on Indian Affairs, 95th Cong., 1st Sess. (1977) (hereinafter 1977 Hearings); Hearings on S. 1214 before the Subcommittee on Indian Affairs and Public Lands of the House Committee on Interior and Insular Affairs, 95th Cong., 2d Sess. (1978) (hereinafter 1978 Hearings).

[3] These sentiments were shared by the ICWA's principal sponsor in the House, Rep. Morris Udall, see 124 Cong. Rec. 38102 (1978) ("Indian tribes and Indian people are being drained of their children and, as a result, their future as a tribe and a people is being placed in jeopardy"), and its minority sponsor, Rep. Robert Lagomarsino, see *ibid.* ("This bill is directed at conditions which ... threaten ... the future of American Indian tribes....").

[4] One of the particular points of concern was the failure of non-Indian child welfare workers to understand the role of the extended family in Indian society. The House Report on the ICWA noted: "An Indian child may have scores of, perhaps more than a hundred, relatives who are

The congressional findings that were incorporated into the ICWA reflect these sentiments. The Congress found:

"(3) that there is no resource that is more vital to the continued existence and integrity of Indian tribes than their children ... ;
"(4) that an alarmingly high percentage of Indian families are broken up by the removal, often unwarranted, of their children from them by nontribal public and private agencies and that an alarmingly high percentage of such children are placed in non-Indian foster and adoptive homes and institutions; and
"(5) that the States, exercising their recognized jurisdiction over Indian child custody proceedings through administrative and judicial bodies, have often failed to recognize the essential tribal relations of Indian people and the cultural and social standards prevailing in Indian communities and families." 25 U.S.C. § 1901.

At the heart of the ICWA are its provisions concerning jurisdiction over Indian child custody proceedings. Section 1911 lays out a dual jurisdictional scheme. Section 1911(a) establishes exclusive jurisdiction in the tribal courts for proceedings concerning an Indian child "who resides or is domiciled within the reservation of such tribe," as well as for wards of tribal courts regardless of domicile. Section 1911(b), on the other hand, creates concurrent but presumptively tribal jurisdiction in the case of children not domiciled on the reservation: on petition of either parent or the tribe, state-court proceedings for foster care placement or termination of parental rights are to be transferred to the tribal court, except in cases of "good cause," objection by either parent, or declination of jurisdiction by the tribal court.

Various other provisions of ICWA Title I set procedural and substantive standards for those child custody proceedings that do take place in state court. The procedural safeguards include requirements concerning notice and appointment of counsel; parental and tribal rights of intervention and petition for invalidation of illegal proceedings; procedures governing voluntary consent to termination of parental rights; and a full faith and credit obligation in respect to tribal court decisions. See §§ 1901-1914. The most important substantive requirement imposed on state courts is that of § 1915(a), which, absent "good cause" to the contrary, mandates that adoptive placements be made preferentially with (1) members of the child's extended family, (2) other members of the same tribe, or (3) other Indian families.

The ICWA thus, in the words of the House Report accompanying it, "seeks to protect the rights of the Indian child as an Indian and the rights of the Indian community and tribe in retaining its children in its society." House Report, at 23. It does so by establishing "a Federal policy that, where possible, an Indian child should remain in the Indian community," ibid., and by making sure that Indian child welfare determinations are not based on "a white, middle-class

---

counted as close, responsible members of the family. Many social workers, untutored in the ways of Indian family life or assuming them to be socially irresponsible, consider leaving the child with persons outside the nuclear family as neglect and thus as grounds for terminating parental rights." House Report, at 10. At the conclusion of the 1974 Senate hearings, Senator Abourezk noted the role that such extended families played in the care of children: "We've had testimony here that in Indian communities throughout the Nation there is no such thing as an abandoned child because when a child does have a need for parents for one reason or another, a relative or a friend will take that child in. It's the extended family concept." 1974 Hearing 473. See also *Wisconsin Potowatomies of Hannahville Indian Community v. Houston*, 398 F. Supp. 719 (W.D. Mich. 1973) (discussing custom of extended family and tribe assuming responsibility for care of orphaned children).

standard which, in many cases, forecloses placement with [an] Indian family."
Id., at 24.[6]

Beyond its jurisdictional and other provisions concerning child custody proceedings, the ICWA also created, in its Title II, a program of grants to Indian
tribes and organizations to aid in the establishment of child welfare programs.
See 25 U.S.C. §§ 1981-1984.

B

This case involves the status of twin babies, known for our purposes as B. B.
and G. B., who were born out of wedlock on December 29, 1985. Their mother,
J. B., and father, W. J., were both enrolled members of appellant Mississippi
Band of Choctaw Indians (Tribe), and were residents and domiciliaries of the
Choctaw Reservation in Neshoba County, Mississippi. J. B. gave birth to the
twins in Gulfport, Harrison County, Mississippi, some 200 miles from the reservation. On January 10, 1986, J. B. executed a consent-to-adoption form before
the Chancery Court of Harrison County. Record 8-10.[7] W. J. signed a similar
form.[8] On January 16, appellees Orrey and Vivian Holyfield filed a petition
for adoption in the same court, *id.*, at 1-5, and the chancellor issued a Final
Decree of Adoption on January 28. *Id.*, at 13-14.[10] Despite the court's apparent
awareness of the ICWA,[11] the adoption decree contained no reference to it,
nor to the infants' Indian background.

Two months later the Tribe moved in the Chancery Court to vacate the
adoption decree on the ground that under the ICWA exclusive jurisdiction was
vested in the tribal court. *Id.*, at 15-18.[12] On July 14, 1986, the court overruled
the motion, holding that the Tribe "never obtained exclusive jurisdiction over

---

[6] The quoted passages are from the House Report's discussion of § 1915, in which the ICWA
attempts to accomplish these aims, in regard to nondomiciliaries of the reservation, through the
establishment of standards for state-court proceedings. In regard to reservation domiciliaries, these
goals are pursued through the establishment of exclusive tribal jurisdiction under § 1911(a).

[7] Section 1913(a) of the ICWA requires that any voluntary consent to termination of parental
rights be executed in writing and recorded before a judge of a "court of competent jurisdiction,"
who must certify that the terms and consequences of the consent were fully explained and understood. Section 1913(a) also provides that any consent given prior to birth or within 10 days thereafter is invalid. In this case the mother's consent was given 12 days after the birth. See also n.26, *infra.*

[8] W. J.'s consent to adoption was signed before a notary public in Neshoba County on January 11,
1986. Record 11-12. Only on June 3, 1986, however — well after the decree of adoption had been
entered and after the Tribe had filed suit to vacate the decree — did the chancellor of the Chancery
Court certify that W. J. had appeared before him in Harrison County to execute the consent to
adoption. *Id.*, at 12-A.

[10] Mississippi adoption law provides for a 6-month waiting period between interlocutory and final
decrees of adoption, but grants the chancellor discretionary authority to waive that requirement and
immediately enter a final decree of adoption. See Miss. Code Ann. § 93-17-13 (1972). The chancellor did so here, Record 14, with the result that the final decree of adoption was entered less than
one month after the babies' birth.

[11] The chancellor's certificates that the parents had appeared before him to consent to the adoption recited that "the Consent and Waiver was given in full compliance with Section 103(a) of Public
Law 95-608" (i.e., 25 U.S.C. § 1913(a)). Record 10, 12-A.

[12] The ICWA specifically confers standing on the Indian child's tribe to participate in child
custody adjudications. Section 1914 authorizes the tribe (as well as the child and its parents) to
petition a court to invalidate any foster care placement or termination of parental rights under state
law "upon a showing that such action violated any provision of sections 1911, 1912, and 1913" of the
ICWA. See also § 1911(c) (Indian child's tribe may intervene at any point in state-court proceedings
for foster care placement or termination of parental rights). "Termination of parental rights" is
defined in § 1908(1)(ii) as "any action resulting in the termination of the parent-child relationship."

the children involved herein ...." The court's one-page opinion relied on two facts in reaching that conclusion. The court noted first that the twins' mother "went to some efforts to see that they were born outside the confines of the Choctaw Indian Reservation" and that the parents had promptly arranged for the adoption by the Holyfields. Second, the court stated: "At no time from the birth of these children to the present date have either of them resided on or physically been on the Choctaw Indian Reservation." *Id.*, at 78.

The Supreme Court of Mississippi affirmed. 511 So. 2d 918 (1987). It rejected the Tribe's arguments that the state court lacked jurisdiction and that it, in any event, had not applied the standards laid out in the ICWA. The court recognized that the jurisdictional question turned on whether the twins were domiciled on the Choctaw Reservation. It answered that question as follows:

> "At no point in time can it be said the twins resided on or were domiciled within the territory set aside for the reservation. Appellant's argument that living within the womb of their mother qualifies the children's residency on the reservation may be lauded for its creativity; however, apparently it is unsupported by any law within this state, and will not be addressed at this time due to the far-reaching legal ramifications that would occur were we to follow such a complicated tangential course." *Id.*, at 921.

The court distinguished Mississippi cases that appeared to establish the principle that "the domicile of minor children follows that of the parents," *ibid.*; see *Boyle v. Griffin*, 84 Miss. 41, 36 So. 141 (1904); *Stubbs v. Stubbs*, 211 So. 2d 821 (Miss. 1968); see also *In re Guardianship of Watson*, 317 So. 2d 30 (Miss. 1975). It noted that "the Indian twins ... were voluntarily surrendered and legally abandoned by the natural parents to the adoptive parents, and it is undisputed that the parents went to some efforts to prevent the children from being placed on the reservation as the mother arranged for their birth and adoption in Gulfport Memorial Hospital, Harrison County, Mississippi," 511 So. 2d, at 921. Therefore, the court said, the twins' domicile was in Harrison County and the state court properly exercised jurisdiction over the adoption proceedings. Indeed, the court appears to have concluded that, for this reason, none of the provisions of the ICWA was applicable. *Ibid.* ("these proceedings ... actually escape applicable federal law on Indian Child Welfare"). In any case, it rejected the Tribe's contention that the requirements of the ICWA applicable in state courts had not been followed: "[T]he judge did conform and strictly adhere to the minimum federal standards governing adoption of Indian children with respect to parental consent, notice, service of process, etc." *Ibid.*[13]

Because of the centrality of the exclusive tribal jurisdiction provision to the overall scheme of the ICWA, as well as the conflict between this decision of the

---

[13] The lower court may well have fulfilled the applicable ICWA procedural requirements. But see n.8, *supra*, and n.26, *infra*. It clearly did not, however, comply with or even take cognizance of the substantive mandate of § 1915(a): "In any adoptive placement of an Indian child under State law, a preference shall be given, in the absence of good cause to the contrary, to a placement with (1) a member of the child's extended family; (2) other members of the Indian child's tribe; or (3) other Indian families" (emphasis added). Section 1915(e), moreover, requires the court to maintain records "evidencing the efforts to comply with the order of preference specified in this section." Notwithstanding the Tribe's argument below that § 1915 had been violated, see Brief for Appellant 20-22 and Appellant's Brief in Support of Petition for Rehearing 11-12 in No. 57,659 (Miss. Sup. Ct.), the Mississippi Supreme Court made no reference to it, merely stating in conclusory fashion that the "minimum federal standards" had been met. 511 So. 2d 918, 921 (1987).

Mississippi Supreme Court and those of several other state courts,[14] we granted plenary review [and now reverse].

II

Tribal jurisdiction over Indian child custody proceedings is not a novelty of the ICWA. Indeed, some of the ICWA's jurisdictional provisions have a strong basis in pre-ICWA case law in the federal and state courts. See, e.g., *Fisher v. District Court*, 424 U.S. 382 (1976) (per curiam) (tribal court had exclusive jurisdiction over adoption proceeding where all parties were tribal members and reservation residents); *Wisconsin Potowatomies of Hannahville Indian Community v. Houston*, 393 F. Supp. 719 (WD Mich. 1973) (tribal court had exclusive jurisdiction over custody of Indian children found to have been domiciled on reservation); *Wakefield v. Little Light*, 276 Md. 333, 347 A.2d 228 (1975) (same); *In re Adoption of Buehl*, 87 Wash. 2d 649, 555 P.2d 1334 (1976) (state court lacked jurisdiction over custody of Indiana children placed in off-reservation foster care by tribal court order); see also *In re Lelah-puc-ka-chee*, 98 F. 429 (ND Iowa 1899) (state court lacked jurisdiction to appoint guardian for Indian child living on reservation). In enacting the ICWA Congress confirmed that, in child custody proceedings involving Indian children domiciled on the reservation, tribal jurisdiction was exclusive as to the States.

The state-court proceeding at issue here was a "child custody proceeding." That term is defined to include any "'adoptive placement' which shall mean the permanent placement of an Indian child for adoption, including any action resulting in a final decree of adoption." 25 U.S.C. § 1903(1)(iv). Moreover, the twins were "Indian children." See 25 U.S.C. § 1903(4). The sole issue in this case is, as the Supreme Court of Mississippi recognized, whether the twins were "domiciled" on the reservation.[16]

Section 1911(a) does not apply "where such jurisdiction is otherwise vested in the State by existing Federal law." This proviso would appear to refer to Pub. L. 280, 67 Stat. 588, as amended, which allows States under certain conditions to assume civil and criminal jurisdiction on the reservations. ICWA § 1918 permits a tribe in that situation to reassume jurisdiction over child custody proceedings upon petition to the Secretary of the Interior. The State of Mississippi has never asserted jurisdiction over the Choctaw Reservation under Public Law 280. See F. Cohen, Handbook of Federal Indian Law 362-363, and nn.122-125 (1982); cf. *United States v. John*, 437 U.S. 634 (1978).

A

The meaning of "domicile" in the ICWA is, of course, a matter of Congress' intent. The ICWA itself does not define it. The initial question we must confront is whether there is any reason to believe that Congress intended the ICWA definition of "domicile" to be a matter of state law. While the meaning of

---

[14]See, e.g., *In re Adoption of Halloway*, 732 P.2d 962 (Utah 1986); *In re Adoption of Baby Child*, 102 N.M. 735, 700 P.2d 198 (App. 1985); *In re Appeal in Pima County Juvenile Action No. S-903*, 130 Ariz. 202, 635 P.2d 187 (App. 1981), cert. denied sub nom. *Catholic Social Services of Tucson v. P. C.*, 455 U.S. 1007 (1982).

[16]"Reservation" is defined quite broadly for purposes of the ICWA. See 25 U.S.C. § 1903(10). There is no dispute that the Choctaw Reservation falls within the definition.

a federal statute is necessarily a federal question in the sense that its construction remains subject to this Court's supervision, [nevertheless] Congress sometimes intends that a statutory term be given content by the application of state law. [We start] with the general assumption that "in the absence of a plain indication to the contrary, ... Congress when it enacts a statute is not making the application of the federal act dependent on state law." [One important] reason for this rule of construction is that federal statutes are generally intended to have uniform nationwide application. [Thus], the cases in which we have found that Congress intended a state-law definition of a statutory term have often been those where uniformity clearly was not intended. [Another] reason for the presumption against the application of state law is the danger that "the federal program would be impaired if state law were to control." [Thus], "we look to the purpose of the statute to ascertain what is intended." ...

First, and most fundamentally, the purpose of the ICWA gives no reason to believe that Congress intended to rely on state law for the definition of a critical term; quite the contrary. It is clear from the very text of the ICWA, not to mention its legislative history and the hearings that led to its enactment, that Congress was concerned with the rights of Indian families and Indian communities vis-à-vis state authorities.[17] More specifically, its purpose was, in part, to make clear that in certain situations the state courts did not have jurisdiction over child custody proceedings. Indeed, the congressional findings that are a part of the statute demonstrate that Congress perceived the States and their courts as partly responsible for the problem it intended to correct. See 25 U.S.C. § 1901(5) (state "judicial bodies ... have often failed to recognize the essential tribal relations of Indian people and the cultural and social standards prevailing in Indian communities and families").[18] Under these circumstances it is most improbable that Congress would have intended to leave the scope of the statute's key jurisdictional provision subject to definition by state courts as a matter of state law.

Second, Congress could hardly have intended the lack of nationwide uniformity that would result from state-law definitions of domicile. An example will illustrate. In a case quite similar to this one, the New Mexico state courts found exclusive jurisdiction in the tribal court pursuant to § 1911(a), because the illegitimate child took the reservation domicile of its mother at birth — notwithstanding that the child was placed in the custody of adoptive parents two days after its off-reservation birth and the mother executed a consent to adoption ten days later. In re Adoption of Baby Child, 102 N.M. 735, 737-738, 700 P.2d 198,

---

[17]This conclusion is inescapable from a reading of the entire statute, the main effect of which is to curtail state authority. See especially §§ 1901, 1911, 1912, 1913, 1914, 1915, 1916, 1918.

[18]See also 124 Cong. Rec. 38103 (1978) (letter from Rep. Morris K. Udall to Assistant Attorney General Patricia M. Wald) ("state courts and agencies and their procedures share a large part of the responsibility" for crisis threatening "the future and integrity of Indian tribes and Indian families"); House Report, at 19 ("contributing to this problem has been the failure of State officials, agencies, and procedures to take into account the special problems and circumstances of Indian families and the legitimate interest of the Indian tribe in preserving and protecting the Indian family as the wellspring of its own future"). See also In re Adoption of Halloway, 732 P.2d, at 969 (Utah state court "quite frankly might be expected to be more receptive than a tribal court to [Indian child's] placement with non-Indian adoptive parents. Yet this receptivity of the non-Indian forum to non-Indian placement of an Indian child is precisely one of the evils at which the ICWA was aimed").

200-201 (App. 1985).[19] Had that mother traveled to Mississippi to give birth, rather than to Albuquerque, a different result would have obtained if state-law definitions of domicile applied. The same, presumably, would be true if the child had been transported to Mississippi for adoption after her off-reservation birth in New Mexico. While the child's custody proceeding would have been subject to exclusive tribal jurisdiction in her home State, her mother, prospective adoptive parents, or an adoption intermediary could have obtained an adoption decree in state court merely by transporting her across state lines.[20] Even if we could conceive of a federal statute under which the rules of domicile (and thus of jurisdiction) applied differently to different Indian children, a statute under which different rules apply from time to time to the same child, simply as a result of her transport from one State to another, cannot be what Congress had in mind.

We therefore think it beyond dispute that Congress intended a uniform federal law of domicile for the ICWA.[22]

B

It remains to give content to the term "domicile" in the circumstances of the present case. The holding of the Supreme Court of Mississippi that the twin babies were not domiciled on the Choctaw Reservation appears to have rested on two findings of fact by the trial court: (1) that they had never been physically present there, and (2) that they were "voluntarily surrendered" by their parents. 511 So. 2d, at 921; see Record 78. The question before us, therefore, is whether under the ICWA definition of "domicile" such facts suffice to render the twins nondomiciliaries of the reservation.

We have often stated that in the absence of a statutory definition we "start with the assumption that the legislative purpose is expressed by the ordinary meaning of the words used." [Therefore, we] look both to the generally accepted meaning of the term "domicile" and to the purpose of the statute.

That we are dealing with a uniform federal rather than a state definition does not, of course, prevent us from drawing on general state-law principles to determine "the ordinary meaning of the words used." Well-settled state law can inform our understanding of what Congress had in mind when it employed a term it did not define. Accordingly, we find it helpful to borrow established

---

[19] Some details of the *Baby Child* case are taken from the briefs in *Pino v. District Court*, O.T. 1984, No. 84-248. That appeal was dismissed under this Court's Rule 58, 472 U.S. 1001 (1985), following the appellant's successful collateral attack, in the case cited in the text, on the judgment from which appeal had been taken.

[20] Nor is it inconceivable that a State might apply its law of domicile in such a manner as to render inapplicable § 1911(a) even to a child who had lived several years on the reservation but was removed from it for the purpose of adoption. Even in the less extreme case, a state-law definition of domicile would likely spur the development of an adoption brokerage business. Indian children, whose parents consented (with or without financial inducement) to give them up, could be transported for adoption to States like Mississippi where the law of domicile permitted the proceedings to take place in state court.

[22] We note also the likelihood that, had Congress intended a state-law definition of domicile, it would have said so. Where Congress did intend that ICWA terms be defined by reference to other than federal law, it stated this explicitly. See § 1903(2) ("extended family member" defined by reference to tribal law or custom); § 1903(6) ("Indian custodian" defined by reference to tribal law or custom and to state law).

common-law principles of domicile to the extent that they are not inconsistent with the objectives of the congressional scheme.

"Domicile" is, of course, a concept widely used in both federal and state courts for jurisdiction and conflict-of-laws purposes, and its meaning is generally un- controverted. See generally Restatement §§ 11-23; R. Leflar, L. McDougal, & R. Felix, American Conflicts Law 17-38 (4th ed. 1986); R. Weintraub, Commen- tary on the Conflict of Laws 12-24 (2d ed. 1980). "Domicile" is not necessarily synonymous with "residence. [O]ne can reside in one place but be domiciled in another. [D]omicile is established [for adults] by physical presence in a place in connection with a certain state of mind concerning one's intent to remain there. *Texas v. Florida*, 306 U.S. 398, 424 (1939). One acquires a "domicile of origin" at birth, and that domicile continues until a new one (a "domicile of choice") is acquired. [Because] most minors are legally incapable of forming the requisite intent to establish a domicile, their domicile is determined by that of their parents. *Yarborough v. Yarborough*, 290 U.S. 202, 211 (1933). In the case of an illegitimate child, that has traditionally meant the domicile of its mother. [Based on] these principles, it is entirely logical that "[o]n occasion, a child's domicile of origin will be in a place where the child has never been." Restatement § 14, Comment *b*.

It is undisputed in this case that the domicile of the mother (as well as the father) has been, at all relevant times, on the Choctaw Reservation. [Therefore], it is clear that at their birth the twin babies were also domiciled on the reserva- tion, even though they themselves had never been there. The statement of the Supreme Court of Mississippi that "[a]t no point in time can it be said the twins ... were domiciled within the territory set aside for the reservation," 511 So. 2d, at 921, may be a correct statement of that State's law of domicile, but it is inconsistent with generally accepted doctrine in this country and cannot be what Congress had in mind when it used the term in the ICWA.

Nor can the result be any different simply because the twins were "voluntarily surrendered" by their mother. Tribal jurisdiction under § 1911(a) was not meant to be defeated by the actions of individual members of the tribe, for Congress was concerned not solely about the interests of Indian children and families, but also about the impact on the tribes themselves of the large numbers of Indian children adopted by non-Indians. See 25 U.S.C. §§ 1901(3) ("there is no resource that is more vital to the continued existence and integrity of Indian tribes than their children"), 1902 ("promote the stability and security of Indian tribes"). The numerous prerogatives accorded the tribes through the ICWA's substantive provisions, e.g., §§ 1911(a) (exclusive jurisdiction over reservation domiciliaries), 1911(b) (presumptive jurisdiction over nondomiciliaries), 1911(c) (right of intervention), 1912(a) (notice), 1914 (right to petition for invalidation of state-court action), 1915(c) (right to alter presumptive placement priorities applicable to state-court actions), 1915(e) (right to obtain records), 1919 (au- thority to conclude agreements with States), must, accordingly, be seen as a means of protecting not only the interest of individual Indian children and families, but also of the tribes themselves.

In addition, it is clear that Congress' concern over the placement of Indian children in non-Indian homes was based in part on evidence of the detrimental impact on the children themselves of such placements outside their culture.[24] Congress determined to subject such placements to the ICWA's jurisdictional and other provisions, even in cases where the parents consented to an adoption, because of concerns going beyond the wishes of individual parents. As the 1977 Final Report of the congressionally established American Indian Policy Review Commission stated, in summarizing these two concerns, "[r]emoval of Indian children from their cultural setting seriously impacts a long-term tribal survival and has damaging social and psychological impact on many individual Indian children." Senate Report, at 52.[25]

These congressional objectives make clear that a rule of domicile that would permit individual Indian parents to defeat the ICWA's jurisdictional scheme is inconsistent with what Congress intended.[26] See *In re Adoption of Child of Indian Heritage*, 111 N.J. 155, 168-171, 543 A.2d 925, 931-933 (1988). The

---

[24] In large part the concerns that emerged during the congressional hearings on the ICWA were based on studies showing recurring developmental problems encountered during adolescence by Indian children raised in a white environment. See n.1, *supra*. See also 1977 Hearings, at 114 (statement of American Academy of Child Psychiatry); S. Rep. No. 95-597, p. 43 (1977) (hereinafter Senate Report). More generally, placements in non-Indian homes were seen as "depriving the child of his or her tribal and cultural heritage." *Id.*, at 45; see also 124 Cong. Rec. 38102-38103 (1978) (remarks of Rep. Lagomarsino). The Senate Report on the ICWA incorporates the testimony in this sense of Louis La Rose, chairman of the Winnebago Tribe, before the American Indian Policy Review Commission:

> "I think the cruelest trick that the white man has ever done to Indian children is to take them into adoption courts, erase all of their records and send them off to some nebulous family that has a value system that is A-1 in the State of Nebraska and that child reaches 16 or 17, he is a little brown child residing in a white community and he goes back to the reservation and he has absolutely no idea who his relatives are, and they effectively make him a non-person and I think ... they destroy him." Senate Report, at 43.

Thus, the conclusion seems justified that, as one state court has put it, "[t]he Act is based on the fundamental assumption that it is in the Indian child's best interest that its relationship to the tribe be protected." *In re Appeal in Pima County Juvenile Action No. S-903*, 130 Ariz., at 204, 635 P.2d, at 189.

[25] While the statute itself makes clear that Congress intended the ICWA to reach voluntary as well as involuntary removal of Indian children, the same conclusion can also be drawn from the ICWA's legislative history. For example, the House Report contains the following expression of Congress' concern with both aspects of the problem:

> "One of the effects of our national paternalism has been to so alienate some Indian [parents] from their society that they abandon their children at hospitals or to welfare departments rather than entrust them to the care of relatives in the extended family. Another expression of it is the involuntary, arbitrary, and unwarranted separation of families." House Report, at 12.

[26] The Bureau of Indian Affairs pointed out, in issuing nonbinding ICWA guidelines for the state courts, that the terms "residence" and "domicile" "are well defined under existing state law. There is no indication that these state law definitions tend to undermine in any way the purposes of the Act." 44 Fed. Reg. 67584, 67585 (1979). The clear implication is that state law that did tend to undermine the ICWA's purpose could not be taken to express Congress' intent. There is some authority for the proposition that abandonment can effectuate a change in the child's domicile, *In re Adoption of Halloway*, 732 P.2d, at 967, although this may not be the majority rule. See Restatement § 22, Comment *e* (abandoned child generally retains the domicile of the last-abandoning parent). In any case, as will be seen below, the Supreme Court of Utah declined in the *Halloway* case to apply Utah abandonment law to defeat the purpose of the ICWA. Similarly, the conclusory statement of the Supreme Court of Mississippi that the twin babies had been "legally abandoned," 511 So. 2d, at 921, cannot be determinative of ICWA jurisdiction.

There is also another reason for reaching this conclusion. The predicate for the state court's abandonment finding was the parents' consent to termination of their parental rights, recorded before a judge of the state Chancery Court. ICWA § 1913(a) requires, however, that such a consent be recorded before "a judge of a court of competent jurisdiction." See n.7, *supra*. In the case of reservation-domiciled children, that could be only the tribal court. The children therefore could not be made nondomiciliaries of the reservation through any such state-court consent.

appellees in this case argue strenuously that the twins' mother went to great lengths to give birth off the reservation so that her children could be adopted by the Holyfields. But that was precisely part of Congress' concern. Permitting individual members of the tribe to avoid tribal exclusive jurisdiction by the simple expedient of giving birth off the reservation would, to a large extent, nullify the purpose the ICWA was intended to accomplish.[27] The Supreme Court of Utah expressed this well in its scholarly and sensitive opinion in what has become a leading case on the ICWA:

> "To the extent that [state] abandonment law operates to permit [the child's] mother to change [the child's] domicile as part of a scheme to facilitate his adoption by non-Indians while she remains a domiciliary of the reservation, it conflicts with and undermines the operative scheme established by subsections [1911(a)] and [1913(a)] to deal with children of domiciliaries of the reservation and weakens considerably the tribe's ability to assert its interest in its children. The protection of this tribal interest is at the core of the ICWA, which recognizes that the tribe has an interest in the child which is distinct from but on a parity with the interest of the parents. This relationship between Indian tribes and Indian children domiciled on the reservation finds no parallel in other ethnic cultures found in the United States. It is a relationship that many non-Indians find difficult to understand and that non-Indian courts are slow to recognize. It is precisely in recognition of this relationship, however, that the ICWA designates the tribal court as the exclusive forum for the determination of custody and adoption matters for reservation-domiciled Indian children, and the preferred forum for non-domiciliary Indian children. [State] abandonment law cannot be used to frustrate the federal legislative judgment expressed in the ICWA that the interests of the tribe in custodial decisions made with respect to Indian children are as entitled to respect as the interests of the parents." *In re Adoption of Halloway*, 732 P.2d 962, 969-970 (1986).

We agree with the Supreme Court of Utah that the law of domicile Congress used in the ICWA cannot be one that permits individual reservation-domiciled tribal members to defeat the tribe's exclusive jurisdiction by the simple expedient of giving birth and placing the child for adoption off the reservation. Since, for purposes of the ICWA, the twin babies in this case were domiciled on the reservation when adoption proceedings were begun, the Choctaw tribal court possessed exclusive jurisdiction pursuant to 25 U.S.C. § 1911(a). The Chancery Court of Harrison County was, accordingly, without jurisdiction to enter a decree of adoption; under ICWA § 1914 its decree of January 28, 1986, must be vacated.

III

We are not unaware that over three years have passed since the twin babies were born and placed in the Holyfield home, and that a court deciding their fate today is not writing on a blank slate in the same way it would have in

---

[27] It appears, in fact, that all Choctaw women give birth off the reservation because of the lack of appropriate obstetric facilities there. See Juris. Statement 4, n.2. In most cases, of course, the mother and child return to the reservation after the birth, and this would presumably be sufficient to make the child a reservation domiciliary even under the Mississippi court's theory. Application of the Mississippi domicile rule would, however, permit state authorities to avoid the tribal court's exclusive § 1911(a) jurisdiction by removing a newborn from an allegedly unfit mother while in the hospital, and seeking to terminate her parental rights in state court.

January 1986. Three years' development of family ties cannot be undone, and a separation at this point would doubtless cause considerable pain.

Whatever feelings we might have as to where the twins should live, however, it is not for us to decide that question. We have been asked to decide the legal question of who should make the custody determination concerning these children — not what the outcome of that determination should be. The law places that decision in the hands of the Choctaw tribal court. Had the mandate of the ICWA been followed in 1986, of course, much potential anguish might have been avoided, and in any case the law cannot be applied so as automatically to "reward those who obtain custody, whether lawfully or otherwise, and maintain it during any ensuing (and protracted) litigation." *Halloway, supra*, at 972. It is not ours to say whether the trauma that might result from removing these children from their adoptive family should outweigh the interest of the Tribe — and perhaps the children themselves — in having them raised as part of the Choctaw community.[28] Rather, "we must defer to the experience, wisdom, and compassion of the [Choctaw] tribal courts to fashion an appropriate remedy." *Ibid*.

The judgment of the Supreme Court of Mississippi is reversed and the case remanded for further proceedings not inconsistent with this opinion.

It is so ordered.

Justice STEVENS, with whom The CHIEF JUSTICE and Justice KENNEDY join, dissenting.

The parents of these twin babies unquestionably expressed their intention to have the state court exercise jurisdiction over them. J. B. gave birth to the twins at a hospital 200 miles from the reservation, even though a closer hospital was available. Both parents gave their written advance consent to the adoption and, when the adoption was later challenged by the Tribe, they reaffirmed their desire that the Holyfields adopt the two children. As the Mississippi Supreme Court found, "the parents went to some efforts to prevent the children from being placed on the reservation as the mother arranged for their birth and adoption in Gulfport Memorial Hospital, Harrison County, Mississippi." 511 So. 2d 918, 921 (1987). Indeed, both parents appear before us today, urging that Vivian Holyfield be allowed to retain custody of B. B. and G. B.

Because J. B.'s domicile is on the reservation and the children are eligible for membership in the Tribe, the Court today closes the state courthouse door to her. I agree with the Court that Congress intended a uniform federal law of domicile for the Indian Child Welfare Act of 1978 (ICWA), 92 Stat. 3069, 25 U.S.C. §§ 1901-1963, and that domicile should be defined with reference to the objectives of the congressional scheme. [However], I cannot [accept] the cramped definition the Court gives that term. To preclude parents domiciled on a reservation from deliberately invoking the adoption procedures of state court, the Court gives "domicile" a meaning that Congress could not have intended and distorts the delicate balance between individual rights and group rights recognized by the ICWA....

---

[28] We were assured at oral argument that the Choctaw court has the authority under the tribal code to permit adoption by the present adoptive family, should it see fit to do so. Tr. of Oral Arg. 17.

While the Act's substantive and procedural provisions effect a major change in state child custody proceedings, its jurisdictional provision is designed primarily to preserve tribal sovereignty over the domestic relations of tribe members and to confirm a developing line of cases which held that the tribe's exclusive jurisdiction could not be defeated by the temporary presence of an Indian child off the reservation. The legislative history indicates that Congress did not intend "to oust the States of their traditional jurisdiction over Indian children falling within their geographic limits." House Report, at 19; Wamser, Child Welfare Under the Indian Child Welfare Act of 1978: A New Mexico Focus, 10 N.M.L. Rev. 413, 416 (1980). The apparent intent of Congress was to overrule such decisions as that in *In re Cantrell*, 159 Mont. 66, 495 P.2d 179 (1972), in which the State placed an Indian child, who had lived on a reservation with his mother, in a foster home only three days after he left the reservation to accompany his father on a trip. Jones, Indian Child Welfare: A Jurisdictional Approach, 21 Ariz. L. Rev. 1123, 1129 (1979). Congress specifically approved a series of cases in which the state courts declined jurisdiction over Indian children who were wards of the tribal court, *In re Adoption of Buehl*, 87 Wash. 2d 649, 555 P.2d 1334 (1976); *Wakefield v. Little Light*, 276 Md. 333, 347 A.2d 228 (1975), or whose parents were temporarily residing off the reservation, *Wisconsin Potowatomies of Hannahville Indian Community v. Houston*, 393 F. Supp. 719 (WD Mich. 1973), but exercised jurisdiction over Indian children who had never lived on a reservation and whose Indian parents were not then residing on a reservation. *In re Greybull*, 23 Ore. App. 674, 543 P.2d 1079 (1975); see House Report, at 21.[6] It did not express any disapproval of decisions such as that of the United States Court of Appeals for the Ninth Circuit in *United States ex rel. Cobell v. Cobell*, 503 F.2d 790 (1974), *cert. denied*, 421 U.S. 999 (1975), which indicated that a Montana state court could exercise jurisdiction over an Indian child custody dispute because the parents "by voluntarily invoking the state court's jurisdiction for divorce purposes, ... clearly submitted the question of their children's custody to the judgment of the Montana state courts." 503 F.2d at 795 (emphasis deleted).

The Report of the American Indian Policy Review Commission, an early proponent of the ICWA, makes clear the limited purposes that the term "domicile" was intended to serve: "Domicile is a legal concept that does not depend exclusively on one's physical location at any one given moment in time, rather it is based on the apparent intention of permanent residency. Many Indian families move back and forth from a reservation dwelling to border communities or even to distant communities, depending on employment and educational opportunities .... In these situations, where family ties to the reservation are strong, but the child is temporarily off the reservation, a fairly strong legal

---

[6]None of the cases cited approvingly by Congress involved a deliberate abandonment. In *Wakefield v. Little Light*, 276 Md. 333, 347 A.2d 228 (1975), the court upheld exclusive tribal jurisdiction where it was clear that there was no abandonment. In *Wisconsin Potowatomies of Hannahville Indian Community v. Houston*, 393 F. Supp. 719 (WD Mich. 1973), there was no abandonment, the children had lived on the reservation and were members of the Indian Tribe, and the children's clothing and toys were at a home on the reservation that continued to be available to them. Finally, in *In re Adoption of Buehl*, 87 Wash. 2d 649, 555 P.2d 1334 (1976), the child was a ward of the tribal court and an enrolled member of the Tribe.

argument can be made for tribal court jurisdiction." Report on Federal, State, and Tribal Jurisdiction 86 (Comm. Print 1976).[7]

Although parents of Indian children are shielded from the exercise of state jurisdiction when they are temporarily off the reservation, the Act also reflects a recognition that allowing the tribe to defeat the parents' deliberate choice of jurisdiction would be conducive neither to the best interests of the child nor to the stability and security of Indian tribes and families. Section 1911(b), providing for the exercise of concurrent jurisdiction by state and tribal courts when the Indian child is not domiciled on the reservation, gives the Indian parents a veto to prevent the transfer of a state court action to tribal court.[8] "By allowing the Indian parents to 'choose' the forum that will decide whether to sever the parent-child relationship, Congress promotes the security of Indian families by allowing the Indian parents to defend in the court system that most reflects the parents' familial standards." Jones, 21 Ariz. L. Rev., at 1141. As Mr. Calvin Isaac, Tribal Chief of the Mississippi Band of Choctaw Indians stated in testimony to the House Subcommittee on Indian Affairs and Public Lands with respect to a different provision: "The ultimate responsibility for child welfare rests with the parents and we would not support legislation which interfered with that basic relationship." Hearings on S. 1214 before the Subcommittee on Indian Affairs and Public Lands of the House Committee on Interior and Insular Affairs, 95th Cong., 2d Sess., 62 (1978).[9]

Although the specific suggestion made by the Department of Justice was not in fact implemented, it is noteworthy that there is nothing in the legislative history to suggest that the recommended change was in any way inconsistent with any of the purposes of the statute.

---

[7] In a letter to the House of Representatives, the Department of Justice explained its understanding that the provision was addressed to the involuntary termination of parental rights in tribal members by state agencies unaware of exclusive tribal jurisdiction:

"As you may be aware, the courts have consistently recognized that tribal governments have exclusive jurisdiction over the domestic relationships of tribal members located on reservations, unless a State has assumed concurrent jurisdiction pursuant to Federal legislation such as Public Law 88-280. It is our understanding that this legal principle is often ignored by local welfare organizations and foster homes in cases where they believe Indian children have been neglected, and that S. 1214 is designed to remedy this, and to define Indian rights in such cases." House Report, at 35.

[8] The explanation of this subsection in the House Committee Report reads as follows:

"Subsection (b) directs a State court having jurisdiction over an Indian child custody proceeding to transfer such proceeding, absent good cause to the contrary, to the appropriate tribal court upon the petition of the parents or the Indian tribe. Either parent is given the right to veto such transfer. The subsection is intended to permit a State court to apply a modified doctrine of forum non conveniens, in appropriate cases, to insure that the rights of the child as an Indian, the Indian parents or custodian, and the tribe are fully protected." Id., at 21.

In commenting on the provision, the Department of Justice suggested that the section should be clarified to make it perfectly clear that a state court need not surrender jurisdiction of a child custody proceeding if the Indian parent objected. The Department of Justice letter stated:

"Section 101(b) should be amended to prohibit clearly the transfer of a child placement proceeding to a tribal court when any parent or child over the age of 12 objects to the transfer." Id., at 32.

[9] Chief Isaac elsewhere expressed a similar concern for the rights of parents with reference to another provision. See Hearing, supra n.1, at 158 (Statement of Calvin Isaac on behalf of National Tribal Chairmen's Association) ("We believe the tribe should receive notice in all such cases but where the child is neither a resident nor domiciliary of the reservation intervention should require the consent of the natural parents or the blood relative in whose custody the child has been left by the natural parents. It seems there is a great potential in the provisions of section 101(c) for infringing parental wishes and rights").

If J. B. and W. J. had established a domicile off the reservation, the state courts would have been required to give effect to their choice of jurisdiction; there should not be a different result when the parents have not changed their own domicile, but have expressed an unequivocal intent to establish a domicile for their children off the reservation. The law of abandonment, as enunciated by the Mississippi Supreme Court in this case, does not defeat, but serves the purposes of the Act. An abandonment occurs when a parent deserts a child and places the child with another with an intent to relinquish all parental rights and obligations. Restatement (Second) of Conflict of Laws § 22, Comment *e* (1971) (hereinafter Restatement); *In re Adoption of Halloway*, 732 P.2d 962, 966 (Utah 1986). If a child is abandoned by his mother, he takes on the domicile of his father; if the child is abandoned by his father, he takes on the domicile of his mother. Restatement § 22, Comment *e*; 25 Am. Jur. 2d, Domicil § 69 (1966). If the child is abandoned by both parents, he takes on the domicile of a person other than the parents who stands in loco parentis to him. *In re Adoption of Halloway, supra*, at 966; ... cf. *In re Guardianship of D. L. L. and C. L. L.*, 291 N.W.2d 278, 282 (S.D. 1980).[10] To be effective, the intent to abandon or the actual physical abandonment must be shown by clear and convincing evidence. *In re Adoption of Halloway, supra*, at 966; *C. S. v. Smith*, 483 S.W.2d 790, 793 (Mo. App. 1972).[11]

When an Indian child is temporarily off the reservation, but has not been abandoned to a person off the reservation, the tribe has an interest in exclusive jurisdiction. The ICWA expresses the intent that exclusive tribal jurisdiction is not so frail that it should be defeated as soon as the Indian child steps off the reservation. Similarly, when the child is abandoned by one parent to a person off the reservation, the tribe and the other parent domiciled on the reservation may still have an interest in the exercise of exclusive jurisdiction. That interest is protected by the rule that a child abandoned by one parent takes on the domicile of the other. But when an Indian child is deliberately abandoned by both parents to a person off the reservation, no purpose of the ICWA is served by closing the state courthouse door to them. The interests of the parents, the Indian child, and the tribe in preventing the unwarranted removal of Indian children from their families and from the reservation are protected by the Act's substantive and procedural provisions. In addition, if both parents have intentionally invoked the jurisdiction of the state court in an action involving a non-

---

[10] The authority of a State to exercise jurisdiction over a child in a child custody dispute when the child is physically present in a State and has been abandoned is also recognized by federal statute. See Parental Kidnapping Prevention Act of 1980, 94 Stat. 3569, 28 U.S.C. § 1738A(c)(2); see also Uniform Child Custody Jurisdiction Act, 9 U.L.A. § 3 (1988).

[11] The Court suggests that there could be no legally effective abandonment because the parents consented to termination of their parental rights before a judge of the state court and not a tribal court judge. *Ante*, at 20 n.26. That suggestion ignores the findings of the State Supreme Court that the natural parents did virtually everything they could do to abandon the children to persons outside the reservation: "[T]he Indian twins have never resided outside of Harrison County, Mississippi, and were voluntarily surrendered and legally abandoned by the natural parents to the adoptive parents, and it is undisputed that the parents went to some efforts to prevent the children from being placed on the reservation as the mother arranged for their birth and adoption in Gulfport Memorial Hospital, Harrison County, Mississippi." 511 So. 2d 918, 921 (Miss. 1987). In any event, even a consent to adoption that does not meet statutory requirements may be effective to constitute an abandonment and change the minor's domicile. See *Wilson v. Pierce*, 14 Utah 2d 317, 321, 383 P.2d 925, 927 (1963); H. Clark, Law of Domestic Relations in the United States 633 (1968).

Indian, no interest in tribal self-governance is implicated. See *McClanahan v. Arizona State Tax Comm'n*, 411 U.S. 164, 173 (1973); *Williams v. Lee*, 358 U.S. 217, 219-220 (1959); *Felix v. Patrick*, 145 U.S. 317, 332 (1892).

The interpretation of domicile adopted by the Court requires the custodian of an Indian child who is off the reservation to haul the child to a potentially distant tribal court unfamiliar with the child's present living conditions and best interests. Moreover, it renders any custody decision made by a state court forever suspect, susceptible to challenge at any time as void for having been entered in the absence of jurisdiction.[12] Finally, it forces parents of Indian children who desire to invoke state court jurisdiction to establish a domicile off the reservation. Only if the custodial parent has the wealth and ability to establish a domicile off the reservation will the parent be able use the processes of state court. I fail to see how such a requirement serves the paramount congressional purpose of "promot[ing] the stability and security of Indian tribes and families." 25 U.S.C. § 1902.

The Court concludes its opinion with the observation that whatever anguish is suffered by the Indian children, their natural parents, and their adoptive parents because of its decision today is a result of their failure to initially follow the provisions of the ICWA. *Ante,* at 18. By holding that parents who are domiciled on the reservation cannot voluntarily avail themselves of the adoption procedures of state court and that all such proceedings will be void for lack of jurisdiction, however, the Court establishes a rule of law that is virtually certain to ensure that similar anguish will be suffered by other families in the future. Because that result is not mandated by the language of the ICWA and is contrary to its purposes, I respectfully dissent.

NOTES

1. The Focus of the Indian Child Welfare Act: The Indian Child Welfare Act of 1978 contemplates that two different courts might encounter Indian child custody proceedings — tribal or state courts. As the *Holyfield* case and the widely publicized *Halloway* case, cited therein, dramatically demonstrate, tribal courts generally have *exclusive* jurisdiction over Indian child custody proceedings involving children domiciled on the reservation who are members of or eligible for membership in the tribe. By contrast, state courts will have jurisdiction over Indian children in a number of situations. First, if an Indian child is

---

[12] The facts of *In re Adoption of Halloway*, 732 P.2d 962 (Utah 1986), which the Court cites approvingly, *ante,* at 21-22, vividly illustrate the problem. In that case, the mother, a member of an Indian Tribe in New Mexico, voluntarily abandoned an Indian child to the custody of the child's maternal aunt off the Reservation with the knowledge that the child would be placed for adoption in Utah. The mother learned of the adoption two weeks after the child left the Reservation and did not object and, two months later, she executed a consent to adoption. Nevertheless, some two years after the petition for adoption was filed, the Indian Tribe intervened in the proceeding and set aside the adoption. The Tribe argued successfully that regardless of whether the Indian parent consented to it, the adoption was void because she resided on the Reservation and thus the tribal court had exclusive jurisdiction. Although the decision in *Halloway,* and the Court's approving reference to it, may be colored somewhat by the fact that the mother in that case withdrew her consent (a fact which would entitle her to relief even if there were only concurrent jurisdiction, see 25 U.S.C. § 1913(c)), the rule set forth by the majority contains no such limitation. As the Tribe acknowledged at oral argument, any adoption of an Indian child effected through a state court will be susceptible of challenge by the Indian tribe no matter how old the child and how long it has lived with its adoptive parents. Tr. of Oral Arg. 15.

neither a tribal member nor eligible for membership, because of the definition of the statutory term "Indian child" found in 25 U.S.C. § 1903(4) the case is simply not covered by the Act. Second, as the *Holyfield* opinion notes, section 1911(a) specifically exempts from exclusive tribal jurisdiction over Indian children domiciled in Indian country those situations "where such jurisdiction is otherwise vested in the State by existing Federal law." As the Court notes, this exception probably has primary reference to jurisdiction over Indians in Indian country that states assumed under Public Law 280. Furthermore, section 1918 provides a *tribally-initiated* process by which such state jurisdiction over Indian children domiciled on reservation may be retroceded to the federal government so that the tribal courts may assume exclusive jurisdiction. Note that on Public Law 280 reservations, nothing in the Act prevents tribes from exercising *concurrent* jurisdiction over Indian child custody proceedings, and state courts could defer to such tribal jurisdiction as a matter of comity, although they would not be required to do so by the Act. Third, section 1911(b) contemplates state jurisdiction over Indian children domiciled off reservation if either parent objects to a transfer to tribal court or if the state court finds "good cause" not to transfer to tribal court. In light of *Holyfield*, it would appear that the question of what constitutes "good cause" involves a federal law question requiring a uniform federal rule and subject to review by the Supreme Court.

Note that *tribal* court Indian child custody proceedings generally are not governed by most of the procedural and substantive provisions of the Act. Thus, for example, when the Mississippi Choctaw tribal court entertains a child custody proceeding involving the twins whose adoption was at issue in *Holyfield*, the tribal court will *not* be bound by the placement preferences of section 1915(a). Rather, the issue will be completely governed by tribal law. Other than the coverage definitions and jurisdictional provisions found in sections 1903 and 1911, most of the procedural and substantive provisions of the Act apply only to child custody proceedings heard in a state court under state law. To test whether you clearly understand the focus and operation of the Act, consider what options a tribe on a Public Law 280 reservation has to affect the process and outcome of foster care and adoption proceedings involving tribal children when those proceedings are conducted in state courts. For example, can the tribe alter the placement preferences of section 1915(a) and (b)? What other options does the tribe have in these contexts?

2. Operation of the Indian Child Welfare Act:

a. Domicile: As *Holyfield* demonstrates, domicile is critical to the Indian Child Welfare Act since it represents the primary dividing line between exclusive tribal jurisdiction and potential concurrent state authority. In *Holyfield*, the Court relied heavily on the definition of domicile developed in the highly publicized case of *Matter of Adoption of Halloway*, 732 P.2d 962 (Utah 1986). *Halloway* involved an Indian child who lived on a reservation for almost three years, six months spent with his natural mother and the remainder with his grandmother. A maternal aunt removed the child from the reservation with his mother's consent. The record indicated that the natural mother believed that the child would be placed in temporary foster care, although she had discussed adoption as an option with the aunt prior to the removal. Two weeks later the mother learned of the proposed adoption of the child by a non-white family. After another two months the natural mother executed a consent for adoption in a Utah district court. The adoptive family immediately filed a petition for adoption and upon the court's order notified the Navajo Nation of the adoption proceeding five months later. Two years after the petition was filed, the Navajo

Nation intervened in the adoption proceeding. The aunt testified that she did not want the child placed in an Indian home and removed him from the reservation for that purpose. The trial court decided that the child's domicile was in Utah and not on the reservation. In addition, the court held that the time the child spent with the adoptive parents satisfied the good cause requirement of 1911(b) to preclude transfer of jurisdiction over a child domiciled off reservation from state court to the tribal court. The Utah Supreme Court reversed, finding that if state law were applicable, the trial court correctly determined that the domicile had changed. Jeremiah's mother had abandoned him, and under Utah law the domicile of an illegitimate child is that of the mother even when the child and mother are separated, unless the mother abandons the child. In the case of abandonment the child assumes the domicile of the person who is acting parent at the time of abandonment. Nevertheless, the Court ruled that federal, rather than state, definitions of domicile controlled since federal law preempts state law in cases of conflict. The Utah Supreme Court stated:

> There certainly is nothing in the ICWA or its legislative history to suggest that state law controls if, in application, its subtleties bring it into conflict with the ICWA in ways that Congress apparently did not foresee. Under general supremacy principles, state law cannot be permitted to operate "as an obstacle to the accomplishment and execution of the full purposes and objectives of Congress" (quoting *Hines v. Davidowitz*, 312 U.S. 52, 67-68).

Id. at 967.

In *B.R.T. v. Executive Dir. of Soc. Servs. Bd. of N.D.*, 391 N.W.2d 594 (N.D. 1986), an Indian mother sought to have the action terminating her parental rights invalidated because the action violated the ICWA. Specifically, she asserted that the juvenile court lacked jurisdiction because she and the child were domiciliaries of the Standing Rock Sioux Reservation. The court found that her petition for termination of parental rights stated her domicile as Bismark, which was undisputed in juvenile court. Furthermore, she initially objected to the tribe having jurisdiction, notice, or a right to intervene. The court concluded that on this record, the juvenile court properly could ascertain that the mother was not domiciled at the reservation and thus assume jurisdiction. Does *Holyfield* permit the Indian mother to defeat exclusive tribal jurisdiction through such pleadings?

b. Disruption of Existing Indian Families: In *Matter of Adoption of T.R.M.*, 525 N.E.2d 298 (Ind. 1988), *cert. denied*, 109 S. Ct. 2072 (1989), the court found abandonment by an Indian mother who was not domiciled on a reservation. The mother lived off the reservation and consented to the adoption of her unborn child. When the child was born, the mother notified the proposed adoptive parents who where good friends of the mother to come and take the child. The parents returned to Indiana with the child who then was seven days old. At the time of this case the child was seven. In justifying its decision, the court stated that in this particular case the purposes of the ICWA would not be served by tribal jurisdiction because the adoption proceeding did not constitute a "breakup of the Indian family."

In *Claymore v. Serr*, 405 N.W.2d 650 (S.D. 1987), a non-Indian mother commenced adoption proceedings to have her child adopted by her new husband. The child's Indian biological father heard of the proposed adoption proceedings and sought declaratory judgment concerning his paternity, child support, visitation rights, and a permanent restraining order against further adoption proceedings. The biological father and mother continued a sporadic relationship after the birth of the child and prior to the mother's marriage. The father never provided any substantial support of the child or the mother. The trial court terminated the biological father's parental rights and gave permission for the adoption. The South Dakota Supreme Court affirmed the refusal to refer the case to the Cheyenne River Sioux Tribal Court on the basis of either sections 1911(a) or (b). Relying on the trial court's findings, it determined that there was no existing Indian family and the purposes of ICWA in preventing the breakup of Indian families therefore would not be served by tribal court jurisdiction. The court said that in order to accomplish the act's purpose, the jurisdictional provisions require a finding that the child subject to the custody proceeding is a member of an existing Indian family. Is this approach justified by the language or purposes of the Indian Child Welfare Act? *See also Matter of Adoption of Baby Boy L.*, 231 Kan. 199, 643 P.2d 168 (1982); *Miller v. Miller*, 703 S.W.2d 609 (Mo. App. 1986); *but see In re Custody of S.B.R.*, 43 Wash. App. 622, 719 P.2d 154 (1986) (criticizing *Baby Boy L.* as creating an unjustified exception to the statutory scheme of the ICWA).

In re Adoption of a Child of Indian Heritage, 111 N.J. 155, 543 A.2d 925 (1988), held that the ICWA applies to illegitimate Indian children voluntarily relinquished to a non-Indian family shortly after birth. Can this result be reconciled with the analysis of *Baby Boy L.? See generally* Comment, *The Indian Child Welfare Act of 1978: Does It Apply to the Adoption of an Illegitimate Indian Child?*, 38 CATH. U.L. REV. 511 (1989).

c. Notice: Notice to the parents and the tribe of the pendency of an Indian child custody proceeding and of the right to intervene constitutes a critical feature of the ICWA. In *Matter of Adoption of a Child of Indian Heritage*, 543 A.2d 925 (N.J. 1988), a putative Indian father and members of his extended family sought to have the adoption of his child vacated because he did not receive notice of the proceedings as provided by the Act. In determining the applicability of the ICWA, the court noted that the Act applied even when an unwed mother voluntarily gave up her child and there was no breakup of an existing Indian family. Criticizing cases like *Baby Boy L.*, the opinion noted, "[W]e disagree with this interpretation of the Act because it posits as a determinative jurisdictional test the voluntariness of the conduct of the mother. The Act itself does not suggest this factor as a jurisdictional test of the Act's coverage, although it is unquestionably relevant in the Act's application." *Id.* at 932. The court found, however, that since the putative father had not established or acknowledged his paternity prior to the termination of his parental rights under either New Jersey law or the ICWA, he is not entitled to notice. The court relied on the fact that the ICWA definition of parents specifically excludes an "unwed father where paternity has not been acknowledged or established." 25 U.S.C. § 1903(9).

In *Havens v. Henning*, 418 N.W.2d 311 (S.D. 1988), an order terminating the parental rights of a mother was reversed because the state trial court failed to provide proper notice to either of the respective tribes in which the mother and father were enrolled. Although the notice sent to the mother's tribe informed the tribe of the impending termination of the mother's parental rights, it did not inform the tribe of its right to intervene, and there was no record of the notice being sent by registered mail, as required by the Act. The court found that at a minimum the notice must comply with the standards of 25 U.S.C. § 1912(a), but better practice would be to follow the more detailed guidelines set forth in the federal regulations, 25 C.F.R. § 23.11. The same court in *Matter of B.J.E.*, 422 N.W.2d 597 (S.D. 1988), affirmed a termination of parental rights, stating that proper notice was given. At the time of the filing of the petition, the mother had three children, although she was pregnant at the time with a fourth child. The state agency filing the petition was unaware of the pregnancy. The notice of the petition sent to the tribe therefore only listed the names of the three children. The state later requested that the unborn child be added to the petition and a certified-mail copy was sent to the tribe. An amended petition was filed again after the child's birth, where he was specifically named, but there is no record that notice of the filing of this amended petition was sent to the tribe. A notice of final dispositional hearing, however, was sent in which the fourth child was named. The court found that although the amended petition naming the fourth child was not sent to the tribe, the fact that there were records showing that several documents were sent to the tribe naming the child was evidence of sufficient notice.

d. Placement Preferences Under the ICWA: In *Matter of J.R.S.*, 690 P.2d 10 (Alaska 1984), the court reversed and remanded the adoption proceedings of an Indian child by non-Indian foster parents because the trial court had denied tribal intervention in the parental termination proceedings and in the adoption proceedings. The state court interpreted the Act as contemplating these proceedings to be separate and distinguishable. While not objecting to the denial of tribal intervention on the termination proceedings, the court saw the denial of tribal intervention in the adoption proceedings as a fatal flaw. The court found that permitting the parties at the adoption placement proceeding to set aside the ICWA placement preferences denied the tribe, the most fervent defender of those preferences, the right to intervene and was thus contrary to the purpose of the Act. Although section 1911(c) does not explicitly provide for tribal intervention in adoption placement, as opposed to the proceedings for foster care placement or termination of parental rights, the court found that foster care placement and termination proceedings as defined in section 1903(1) of the Act encompass adoptive placement. Since terminating parental rights and adoptive placement are two different procedures under state law, the court found that tribal intervention during the placement stage was necessary to preserve tribal interests and the purpose of the ICWA.

In *Matter of M.E.M.*, 725 P.2d 212 (Mont. 1986), the court determined that the ICWA adoptive placement preferences gave the aunt of an Indian child sufficient "interest" to intervene under the Montana Rules of Civil Procedure. The court noted that the aunt is an "extended family member" under section 1915(a), that her interests were generated by that placement preference, and that none of the parties in the adoption proceeding would represent her interests.

e. Appointment of Counsel: The provision for appointment of counsel in section 1912(b) was briefly noted by Justice Blackmun, dissenting in *Lassiter v. Department of Soc. Servs.*, 452 U.S. 18, 39-40 n.5 (1981) (holding that failure to appoint counsel for indigent parents in proceedings for termination of parental rights in cases on which no criminal charges could be based did not deprive the parents of due process of law).

f. Public Law 280 and the ICWA: In *Native Village of Venetie I.R.A. Council v. Alaska*, 687 F. Supp. 1380 (D. Alaska 1988), a tribal court sought to compel full faith and credit under the ICWA for tribal court adoption decrees. The state court had said that the Act does not apply to tribes in Alaska because of the Public Law 280 exception carved out in section 1911(a). The court noted that it is possible for tribes in Public Law 280 states to get exclusive jurisdiction under the ICWA through the approval of the Department of the Interior by means of a retrocession process. The tribal courts in this case had not done so. The tribal courts argued that they still retained concurrent jurisdiction because of tribal sovereignty. The court after a lengthy discourse on the principles of tribal sovereignty stated that federal law can totally remove and abolish tribal sovereignty and had done so in the Public Law 280 states. Is that an accurate interpretation of either Public Law 280 or the ICWA? This case is more fully discussed in Chapter 8, section A3, note 2.

g. Federally Assisted Foster Care Programs: In *Native Village of Stevens v. Smith*, 770 F.2d 1486 (9th Cir. 1985), *cert. denied*, 475 U.S. 1121 (1986), an Alaskan Native village sought a declaratory judgment that tribal-approved foster homes are the same as state-approved foster homes for purposes of federally assisted foster care placement programs administered by the State of Alaska. In section 1931(b), the ICWA provides that "[f]or purposes of qualifying for assistance under a federally assisted program, licensing or approval of foster or adoptive homes or institutions by an Indian tribe shall be deemed equivalent to licensing or approval by a State." Nevertheless, the circuit court affirmed the trial court's summary dismissal of the village's action. While acknowledging that tribal and state foster homes are substantially equivalent, the court found that foster care placements ordered by tribal courts did not meet the qualifications for funding of this particular program. The funding act requires that the state or public agency receiving funding must have an agreement for funding. The tribal foster home does not have such an agreement with the state and the state refuses to negotiate one. The court also found that section 1919(a) of the ICWA authorizes agreements between tribes and states on such questions, but does not *require* them. The Ninth Circuit opinion did not find that any language in the ICWA or the Aid to Families with Dependent Children program required states to involuntarily enter into agreements with tribes, nor did the court see any need to impose such a requirement.

3. The Effect of the Act on Indian Children from Interracial Marriages: Note that the coverage formula of the Act involves the questions of whether the child in question is a member of a tribe or eligible for membership in a tribe. Thus, as demonstrated in *In re Bulltail*, set forth below, where a child is covered by the Act exclusive jurisdiction may exist in tribal court even though a non-Indian parent objects. For a child of mixed Indian and non-Indian parentage who is an enrolled tribal member or eligible for membership, can non-Indian relatives qualify as members of the "extended family" under 25 U.S.C. § 1915(a)(i) or (b)(i)? Under section 1915 is it sufficient good cause for a state court to adopt placement alternatives other than those set forth in paragraphs (a) or (b) that the court considers such alternative placement "in the best interest of the child" in light of his or her non-Indian relatives? Should courts follow the approach of the *Baby Boy L.* case by holding that the ICWA is not implicated in a case involving a non-Indian parent since the state court decree would not result in the disruption of any existing *Indian* family? Would such an approach be consistent with the purposes of Act?

For surveys of the ICWA, see Barsh, *Indian Child Welfare Act of 1978: A Critical Analysis*, 31 HASTINGS L.J. 1287 (1980); Guerrero, *Indian Child Welfare Act of 1978: A Response to the Threat to Indian Culture Caused by Foster and Adoptive Placements of Indian Children*, 7 AM. INDIAN L. REV. 51 (1979); Wamser, *Child Welfare Under the Indian Child Welfare Act of 1978: A New Mexico Focus*, 10 N.M.L. REV. 413 (1980); Comment, *The Indian Child Welfare Act — Tribal Self-Determination Through Participation in Child Custody Proceedings*, 1979 WIS. L. REV. 1202; Note, *In re D.L.L. & C.L.L., Minors:*

Ruling on the Constitutionality of the Indian Child Welfare Act, 26 S.D.L. REV. 67 (1981).

IN RE BULLTAIL

1 Tribal Court Reporter A-42 (1978)

Agency, Crow Indian Reservation

WILKINSON, Chief Judge.

This matter comes before this Court upon the motion of Ciaran Wells, the natural mother of the above mentioned minor child to dismiss the guardianship petition in this Court on the grounds of lack of both personal and subject matter jurisdiction.

The facts of this case involve a minor child who is approximately one and a half years old (1½) and who is an enrolled member of the Crow Tribe. The child resided with his mother until December 3, 1978, when he was found by the paternal grandmother in a bar in Billings, Montana with the mother. Clara and Joe Bulltail, the paternal grandparents, are also enrolled members of the Crow Tribe with a permanent residence in Pryor, Montana. Clara Bulltail filed a petition for guardianship in this Court on December 6, 1978, alleging that the baby was neglected and citing various acts of neglect. That petition was withdrawn in favor of a petition by the natural father, Thomas Bulltail, which was filed in the Court on December 8, 1978. The child, the grandparents and the father are all within the boundaries of the Crow Indian Reservation. That petition alleged that the guardianship should be granted upon the following grounds, at paragraph 7:

> I am a legal parent of Thomas and his mother is a hopeless alcoholic, unfit mother and she has tried to commit suicide on November 27th. She is unstable and I fear for the child's life and safety in her present state of mind and condition.

The mother, Ciaran Wells, a non-member of the Crow Tribe filed a motion to dismiss these proceedings and appeared by and through her attorney in open court, Michael Akin of Montana Legal Services Association, to contest the jurisdiction of this Court based on personal and subject matter jurisdictions. The Bulltails appeared by and through their attorney, Urban J. Bear Don't Walk. Testimony and arguments were had on the motion and the respective parties were given an opportunity to adequately brief the question of jurisdiction.

This Court's jurisdiction has to be based as determined in part with regard to the applicable procedures set forth at Title 10 of the Crow Tribal Code passed and adopted by the Crow Tribal Council on July 8, 1975, at a duly called meeting of the Crow Tribal Council. The section contained at Section 10-130 states as follows:

Jurisdiction — Commencement of Proceedings

(1) The Crow Tribal Court, competent to decide child custody matters, has jurisdiction to make a child custody determination by initial or modification decree if:

(a) The Crow Indian Reservation:
  (i) Is the home of the child at the time of commencement of the proceedings; or
  (ii) Has been the child's home within six (6) months before commencement of proceeding and the child is absent from this home because of his removal or retention by the person claiming custody or for other reasons, and a parent or person acting as parent continues to live within the Crow Indian Reservation; or
(b) It is in the best interest of the child that a court of the Crow Tribe assume jurisdiction because:
  (i) The child and his parents or child and at least one (1) contestant have a significant connection with the Crow Tribe; and
  (ii) There is available within the Crow Indian Reservation substantial evidence concerning the child's present or future care, protection, training, and personal relationship; or
(c) The child is physically present within the Crow Indian Reservation and:
  (i) Has been abandoned; or
  (ii) It is necessary in an emergency to protect him because he has been subjected to or threatened with mistreatment or abuse or is neglected or dependent; or
(d)(i) No other state or tribe has jurisdiction under prerequisites substantially in accordance with sub-sections (1) (a), (1) (b), or (1) (c) of this section or another state or tribe has declined to exercise jurisdiction on the ground that the Crow Reservation is the more appropriate forum to determine custody of the child;
  (ii) It is in the best interest that the court assume jurisdiction.
(2) Except under subsections (1) (c) and (1) (d) of this section, physical presence in the Crow Reservation of the child or of the child and one of the contestants is not alone sufficient to confer jurisdiction on a court of the Crow Reservation to make a child custody determination.
(3) Physical presence of the child, while desirable, is not a prerequisite for jurisdiction to determine his custody.

On the 9th day of July, 1978, the Crow Tribal Council discarded the operative effect of Title 25, Code of Federal Regulations commonly referred to as a Court of Indian Offenses. The Crow Tribal Council enacted a comprehensive Tribal Code along with procedures for the Tribal Court system. The Crow Tribe now has its own Tribal Court System known as the Crow Tribal Court. Custody issues are an integral part of the new Tribal Code. See Chapter 10 above.

This court believes that it has jurisdiction under Section 10-130(1)(c)(ii) of the Tribal Code in that the child is physically present within the Crow Indian Reservation and the petition on file on its face alleges sufficient facts to show neglect for the purpose of this code section.

Also, this Court believes that it has jurisdiction under the prerequisite of 10-130 (1) (d) (ii) in that no other forum has jurisdiction of the minor child and it is in the best interest of the child to proceed to a hearing on the merits of this case by having this Court assume jurisdiction. This Court is aware by judicial notice that a habeas corpus act has been filed in state court on December 9,

1978. However, the grandparents, the father and the child appear to be beyond the personal jurisdiction of the state court. See *Martin v. Denver Juvenile Court*, 493 P.2d 1093 (Colo. 1972); *Francisco v. State of Arizona*, 556 P.2d 11 (1976). Also, there is no outstanding custody decree of another jurisdiction involved here. Also, the State of Montana and the Crow Tribe have no agreement similar to the one Montana has with other states, i.e. the Uniform Child Custody Act. Furthermore, an action for custody was initiated in this Court before any actions were begun in any other jurisdiction.

This Court has both personal and subject matter jurisdiction and believes a denial of that jurisdiction is not only legally incorrect but would also be adverse to the best interest of the child in determining who should be responsible for his future custody. Thus, jurisdiction can be invoked under this provision of the code as well.

This Court also believes its jurisdiction is based on the recently adopted Indian Child Welfare Act. On the 8th day of November, 1978, President Carter signed Public Law 95-608 commonly known as the Indian Child Welfare Act. For the reasons more fully explained herein, this Court has "exclusive" jurisdiction because of the passage of this act.

The Indian Child Welfare Act is a clear recognition by Congress of the Crow Tribe's *parens patriae* interest in Crow children. According to the customary law of the Crow Tribe, all children are wards of the Tribe all through their minority until they are eighteen years old. This Court is not unmindful that custody matters of enrolled Crow children have taken place throughout the courts of the United States. See *Wakefield v. Littlelight*, 276 Md. 333, 347 A.2d 228 (1975).

This Court is vested with "exclusive" jurisdiction under the Indian Child Welfare Act when the child either is domiciled or resides within the Crow Reservation. Section 101 (a). Such exclusive jurisdiction precludes actions in the state district courts. Those courts must give "full faith and credit" to the decrees of this Court.

The crux of this matter is that jurisdiction over custody matters is essentially an *in rem* proceeding. 42 Am Jur. 2d, Infants, §§ 33, 35, 40. It is true that various states have attempted to weaken this principle by enacting legislation such as the Uniform Child Custody Jurisdiction Act. Without such arrangements, however, that jurisdiction in which the child is found obtains *in rem* jurisdiction over the child. The State of Montana has not seen it in their interest to make like arrangements with the Crow Tribe. *Kennerly v. District Court*, 400 U.S. 423 (1971); *Fisher v. District Court*, 424 U.S. 382 (1976); *Crow Tribe v. Deernose*, 487 P.2d 1133 (1971).

In addition all persons who come before this Court will be extended the benefits of the Indian Civil Rights Act, 25 U.S.C. 1301 *et seq.*, when they litigate matters in the Crow Tribal Court. In the only case which has come before the U.S. Supreme Court, on the scope of the Indian Civil Rights Act, *Martinez v. Santa Clara Pueblo*, 46 U.S.L.W. 4412 (May 15, 1978) the Court directed that Tribal Courts have been the "traditional forums to resolve disputes" between Indians and non-Indians. See *Kennerly v. District Court, supra*, and *Williams v. Lee*, 358 U.S. 217 (1959). The protections of the Indian Civil Rights Act will be extended to Ciaran Wells, as well as all other litigants that come before this Court.

Because of the circumstances of this matter, though, Thomas Aaron Bulltail will be made a ward of the Crow Tribal Court and under the legal custody of this Court, but will reside with his natural father.

Chapter 5

CONCEPTS OF PROPERTY IN FEDERAL INDIAN LAW

This chapter deals with the transfer in occupancy and control over large parts of the continent from Indians to Europeans. It is concerned with what Honori has called "the restriction of ownership in the social interest and the relation between ownership and public administration," A. GUEST, OXFORD ESSAYS IN JURISPRUDENCE (1961). The historical material in the first section is important because it provides rich opportunities to discuss the law's capacity to justify ends deemed to benefit a dominant group at the expense of an oppressed group despite the stress on neutral principles in Anglo-Saxon jurisprudence derived from the belief that if principles respecting property and ownership are not universally applied, then the security of all property is somewhat lessened. Yet this Anglo-Saxon commitment to private property obviously yielded to the rapacity of the European settlers and the frontier expansionists. At the same time that the legal system developed rules of law justifying a great deal of this confiscation, the system also developed rules designed initially to protect the federal government's superior right to acquire property from the Indians but which later evolved into powerful tools to protect present Indian occupancy of land. In addition, another thread runs through Indian property law: Although the rules developed technically permit some confiscation to go uncompensated, legislators have frequently responded to public opinion by designing mechanisms to compensate Indian tribes for loss of land "as a matter of grace, not because of legal liability," *Tee-Hit-Ton Indians v. United States*, section B, *infra*.

After the historical section, this chapter turns first to rules justifying confiscation. One of the most powerful of these rules is the characterization of some Indian property as compensable and others as not compensable by the legal devices of "aboriginal" versus "recognized" title, a distinction that some argue leaves many reservations created by Executive Order on the "uncompensable" side of the line.

While there is valuable material in these decisions on the concept of ownership, the decisions do not engage in an Hohfeldian effort to determine the rudiments of property, which emphasizes that property must be defined wholly in terms of the relationship between persons, and between persons and government, rather than persons and a thing such as land. Thus, to say that X owns a piece of land tells very little; it is much more important to know the extent of X's rights and powers against other persons and X's immunity from certain actions by the government. Unfortunately, most efforts to define ownership or title merely list the incidents of ownership without any strong indication of their relative importance. The standard incidents of ownership include, in some measure, the right to possess, the right to manage, the right to the income, the right to the capital, and the right to transmit. This issue of intensity of the incidents of ownership is particularly clear in the history of Indian land tenure in the United States. While individuals or communities have had certain incidents of ownership, sometimes by custom or by treaty, or sometimes by statute and Executive Order, the preeminent incident has been the constant possibility of government intervention.

The chapter next turns to the claims process and its alternatives, offering insights into the way the judicial system can be manipulated to postpone effectively the application of a rule that is practically undesirable but jurisprudentially necessary, if principles of neutrality are to be honored. The claims cases illustrate dramatically how control of the remedy has influenced the meaningfulness of the right. They also illustrate some of the practical problems experienced by attorneys representing fairly large groups whose leadership and hence litigation strategy can be changed at the last stages of long-drawn out litigation. Finally, they offer an opportunity to consider the efficacy of various legislative mechanisms for resolving Indian claims.

After examining the issue of confiscation, the chapter turns to a more positive side of the federal-Indian relationship: the government's obligation to protect Indian possessory rights from third parties. In this section, common law rules as well as the Nonintercourse Act are examined and revealed to be powerful tools for protecting what remains of tribal property.

Because the issue of protection of artifacts and skeletal remains involves issues of title, issues of protection of possession, the failure of existing rules, and the desirability of a legislative solution, this issue is treated separately in the next section of the chapter.

The chapter ends by considering individual Indian property rights. This last section focuses on the important differences between individual and tribal property and the conflicts between them. It also provides an opportunity to examine whether the Supreme Court is more sensitive to individual Indian property rights because these rights resemble more closely the dominant culture's vision of property.

A. THE RIGHT OF THE DISCOVERER

JOHNSON v. M'INTOSH

21 U.S. (8 Wheat.) 543 (1823)

[In this case, Chief Justice Marshall held that as the successor to England, the original discoverer of the area in question, the United States had acquired the preemptive right to procure Indian land by purchase or conquest according to the Doctrine of Discovery. Thus, title obtained through a direct grant by an Indian tribe to a private individual could not prevail against title obtained by means of a patent of land acquired by the government from the same tribe. The opinion is reprinted in Chapter 1, page 2.]

ROYCE, INDIAN LAND CESSIONS IN THE UNITED STATES, 18
United States Bureau of Ethnology, pt. 2, 535-37, 548-57, 554-55 (1897)

It is doubtless true that the recognition of the Indian tribes as distinct nationalities, with which the Government could enter into solemn treaties, was a legal fiction which should be superseded by a more correct policy when possible. But necessity often makes laws, and in this instance forced the Government to what was, in its early days, probably the best possible policy in this respect, consistent with humanity, which it could have adopted.

A doubt has also been expressed as to whether the United States or any European power could, with perfect honesty and integrity, purchase lands of the natives under their care and protection. Bozman,[1] who expresses this doubt, bases it on the following considerations:

> First, it is not a clear proposition that savages can, for any consideration, enter into a contract obligatory upon them. They stand by the laws of nations, when trafficking with the civilized part of mankind, in the situation of infants, incapable of entering into contracts, especially for the sale of their country. Should this be denied, it may then be asserted that no monarch of a nation (that is, no sachem, chief, or headmen, or assemblage of sachems, etc.) has a power to transfer by sale the country, that is, the soil of the nation, over which they rule.

That the Indians of the United States have been and are still considered wards of the Government must be conceded. It also must be admitted that, as a general rule of law, wards cannot divest themselves of their title to land except through the decree of court or some properly authorized power. But in the case of the Indians the Government is both guardian and court, and as there is no higher authority to which application can be made, its decision must be final, otherwise no transfer of title would be possible, however advantageous it might be to the wards.

Bozman's theory seems to overlook the fact that Indians, except perhaps in a few isolated cases, never claimed individual or exclusive personal titles in fee to given and designated portions of the soil. What, therefore, is held in common may, it would seem, by the joint action of those interested, be transferred or alienated.

However, it is not our object at present to theorize as to what should or might have been done, but to state what was done in this respect, and thus to show on what policy the various territorial cessions and reservations mentioned in the present work are based.

The correct theory on this subject appears to be so clearly set forth by John Quincy Adams in his oration at the anniversary of the Sons of the Pilgrims, December 22, 1802, that his words are quoted, as follows:

> There are moralists who have questioned the right of Europeans to intrude upon the possessions of the aborigines in any case and under any limitations whatsoever. But have they maturely considered the whole subject? The Indian right of possession itself stands, with regard to the greatest part of the country, upon a questionable foundation. Their cultivated fields, their constructed habitations, a space of ample sufficiency for their subsistence, and whatever they had annexed to themselves by personal labor, was undoubtedly by the laws of nature theirs. But what is the right of a huntsman to the forest of a thousand miles over which he has accidentally ranged in quest of prey? Shall the liberal bounties of Providence to the race of man be monopolized by one of ten thousand for whom they were created? Shall the exuberant bosom of the common mother, amply adequate to the nourishment of millions, be claimed exclusively by a few hundreds of her offspring? Shall the lordly savage not only disdain the virtues and enjoyments of civilization himself, but shall he control the civilization of a world? Shall

---

[1] History of Maryland, p. 569. [Footnotes have been renumbered.]

he forbid the wilderness to blossom like the rose? Shall he forbid the oaks of the forest to fall before the ax of industry and rise again transformed into the habitations of ease and elegance? Shall he doom an immense region of the globe to perpetual desolation, and to hear the howlings of the tiger and the wolf silence forever the voice of human gladness? Shall the fields and the valleys which a beneficent God has framed to teem with the life of innumerable multitudes be condemned to everlasting barrenness? Shall the mighty rivers, poured out by the hands of nature as channels of communication between numerous nations, roll their waters in sullen silence and eternal solitude to the deep? Have hundreds of commodious harbors, a thousand leagues of coast, and a boundless ocean been spread in the front of this land, and shall every purpose of utility to which they could apply be prohibited by the tenant of the woods? No, generous philanthropists! Heaven has not been thus inconsistent in the works of its hands. Heaven has not thus placed at irreconcilable strife its moral laws with its physical creation.[2]

The French Policy

....

That no idea of purchasing or pretending to purchase the possessory right of the natives had been entertained by the French up to 1686, is evident from a passage in the letter of M. de Denonville to M. de Seignelay, May 8, 1686,[3] where he states:

The mode observed by the English with the Iroquois, when desirous to form an establishment in their neighborhood, has been, to make them presents for the purchase of the fee and property of the land they would occupy. What I consider most certain is, that whether we do so, or have war or peace with them, they will not suffer, except most unwillingly, the construction of a fort at Niagara.

That the war policy was the course adopted is a matter of history.

How, then, are we to account for the fact that the relations of the French with the Indians under their control were, as a general rule, more intimate and satisfactory to both parties than those of other nations? Parkman has remarked that "The power of the priest established, that of the temporal ruler was secure.... Spanish civilization crushed the Indian; English civilization scorned and neglected him; French civilization embraced and cherished him." Although this cannot be accepted as strictly correct in every respect, yet it is true that intimate, friendly relations existed between the French and their Indian subjects, which did not exist between the Spanish or English and the native population. However, this cannot be attributed to the legal enactments or defined policy of the French, but rather to their practical methods.

Instead of holding the natives at arm's length and treating them only as distinct and inferior people and quasi independent nations, the French policy was to make them one with their own people, at least in Canada....

The English Policy

In attempting to determine from history and the records the British policy in dealing with the Indians in regard to their possessory rights, the investigator is somewhat surprised to find (except so far as they relate to the Dominion of Canada and near the close of the government rule over the colonies) the data

---

[2] Report of the Commissioner of Indian Affairs for 1867, p. 143.

[3] New York Colonial Documents, vol. IX, p. 289.

are not only meager but mostly of a negative character. It must be understood, however, that this statement refers to the policy of the English government as distinct from the methods and policy of the different colonies, which will later be noticed.

The result of this investigation, so far as it relates to the possessions formerly held by Great Britain within the present limits of the United States, would seem to justify Parkman's statement that "English civilization scorned and neglected the Indian," at least so far as it relates to his possessory right. It is a significant fact that the Indian was entirely overlooked and ignored in most, if not all, of the original grants of territory to companies and colonists. Most of these grants and charters are as completely void of allusion to the native population as though the grantors believed the lands to be absolutely waste and uninhabited.

For example, the letters patent of James I to Sir Thomas Gage and others for "two several colonies," dated April 10, 1606, although granting away two vast areas of territory greater than England, inhabited by thousands of Indians, a fact of which the King had knowledge both officially and unofficially, do not contain therein the slightest allusion to them.

Was this a mere oversight? More than a hundred years had elapsed since the Cabots had visited the coast; Raleigh's attempted colonization twenty years before was well known, and the history of the discovery and conquest of Mexico had been proclaimed to all the civilized world. Still the omission might be considered a mere oversight but for the fact that his second charter (May 23, 1609), to "The Treasurer and Company of Adventurers and Planters of the City of London for the Colony of Virginia," and that of March 12, 1611-12, are equally silent on this important subject. It may be said, and no doubt truly, that the Crown merely granted away its title in the lands, its public domain, leaving the grantees to deal with the inhabitants as they might find most advantageous. Nevertheless this view will not afford an adequate excuse for the total disregard of the native occupants. The grants were to subjects, and the rights of sovereignty were retained.

The so-called "Great Patent of New England," granted "absolutely" to the "said council called the council established at Plymouth, etc.," the "aforesaid part of America, lying and being in breadth from forty degrees of northerly latitude from the equinoctial line, to forty-eight degrees of said northerly latitude inclusively, and in length of and within all the breadth aforesaid throughout the main land from sea to sea, together also with all the firm land, soils, grounds, havens, ports, rivers, waters, fishings, mines, and minerals," yet there is not the slightest intimation that any portion of this territory was occupied by natives. There is, however, a proviso that the grant is not to include any lands "actually possessed or inhabited by any other Christian prince or state," but the Indians are wholly ignored.

That the Indians were not wholly forgotten when the charter of Charles I, granting Maryland to Lord Baltimore, was penned, is evident from two or three statements therein. But none of these, nor anything contained in the charter, has any reference to the rights of these natives, or show any solicitude for their welfare or proper treatment. The first of these is a mere recognition of the fact that the territory is partly occupied by them: "A certain region, hereinafter described, in a country hitherto uncultivated, in the parts of America, and partly occupied by savages having no knowledge of the Divine Being." The next is that mentioning as the payment required "two Indian arrows of those parts to be delivered at the said castle of Windsor, every year on Tuesday in Easter week." The third is a mere mention of "savages" as among the enemies the colonists may have to encounter. The fourth and last allusion to the natives is in the twelfth section, which authorizes Lord Baltimore to collect troops and wage war on the "barbarians" and other enemies who may make incursion into the settlements, and "to pursue them even beyond the limits of their province," and "if God shall grant it, to vanquish and captivate them; and the captives to put to death, or according to their discretion, to save." The only allusion to the natives in William Penn's charter is the same as the latter in substance and almost the same in words....

It appears by a report of the Lords of Trade, read before the Council at the Court of Saint James, November 23, 1761, and approved, the King being present, that the government had at last been aroused to the necessity of paying regard to the Indians' rights, as shown by the following quotation therefrom:[4]

> That it is as unnecessary as it would be tedious to enter into a Detail of all the Causes of Complaint which, our Indian Allies had against us at the commencement of the troubles in America, and which not only induced them tho reluctantly to take up the Hatchet against us and desolate the Settlement on the Frontiers but encouraged our enemies to pursue those Measures which have involved us in a dangerous and critical war, it will be sufficient for the present purpose to observe that the primary cause of that discontent which produced these fatal Effects was the Cruelty and Injustice with which they had been treated with respect to their hunting grounds, in open violation of those solemn compacts by which they had yielded to us the Dominion, but not the property of those Lands. It was happy for us that we were early awakened to a proper sense of the Injustice and bad Policy of such a Conduct towards the Indians, and no sooner were those measures pursued which indicated a Disposition to do them all possible justice upon this head of Complaint than those hostilities which had produced such horrid scenes of devastation ceased, and the Six Nations and their Dependents became at once from the most inveterate Enemies our fast and faithfull Friends.

> ....

This condition of affairs was no doubt due largely to the lack of any settled and well-defined policy on the part of the government in its dealings with the Indians in regard to their lands. This subject, as hitherto stated, seems to have been relegated, at least to a large extent, to the colonists or grantees of the royal charters; and although complaints from the Indians, or from others in their behalf, were frequently made directly to governmental authorities, it does not appear that the latter were aroused thereby to the necessity of adopting some policy on this subject. It was not until the war with France and the expedition against Canada that the government felt compelled to deal directly with this subject.

---

[4] Colonial documents, number five, vol. VII, p. 473.

WILLIAMS, THE MEDIEVAL AND RENAISSANCE ORIGINS OF THE STATUS OF THE AMERICAN INDIAN IN WESTERN LEGAL THOUGHT, 57 Southern California Law Review 1, 68-85 (1983)*

B. *Franciscus de Victoria and the Law of Nations*

The most important and influential of [the] Spanish Humanist writers was Franciscus de Victoria, a Dominican scholar and the first Spanish thinker to systematically apply Thomistic natural law theory to the relations between states. His juridical system of a Law of Nations helped establish the foundations of modern international law and his works on Indian rights are widely recognized as the source of the basic legal principles of post-sixteenth century Spanish colonial administration.

His influence on the conception of the Indian and the tribe in Western legal thought, however, extends far beyond post-Reformation Europe and Spain. Even in the twentieth century United States, his work is recognized as originating "the pattern and creative principles that are the distinctive contribution of Spanish juristic thought to our Federal Indian law."[294] No understanding of the liberal conception of the legal status of the Indian and the tribe in Western thought is complete without an appreciation of the pivotal role played by Victoria in formulating that conception.

1. Victoria's *On the Indians Lately Discovered*

A frequent adviser to the Spanish Crown on numerous legal issues, Victoria, a Dominican, as was Aquinas, held the *prima* chair in theology at the University of Salamanca from 1526 until his death in 1546. Victoria's most important work on Indian rights is contained in a lecture he delivered at the University in 1532 entitled *On the Indians Lately Discovered*.

On the Indians Lately Discovered was the first work by a major Spanish Renaissance writer to embrace the Thomistic Humanist idea that there existed

a natural-law connection between all nations, and that this connection, while it did not issue in any authority exercised by the Whole over its parts, at any rate involved a system of mutual social rights and duties. From this point of view international law was conceived as a law binding *inter se* upon States which were still in a state of nature in virtue of their sovereignty, and binding upon them in exactly the same way as the pre-political Law of Nature had been binding upon individuals when they were living in a state of nature.[298]

In applying this Thomistic idea of a natural law connection between states to the Spanish conquest in the Americas, Victoria developed three basic arguments which later Humanist and Enlightenment theorists on international law adopted essentially intact as the accepted Law of Nations on Indian-European relations. These three arguments, examined in detail in this section, are that: (1) the inhabitants of the Indies possessed natural legal rights as free and rational men; (2) the Pope's grant to Spain of title to the Indies was "baseless" and could

---

*Copyright © 1983 by the Southern California Law Review and Robert A. Williams, Jr. Reprinted with permission of the copyright holders.

[294] Cohen, [*The Spanish Origin of Indian Rights in the Law of the United States*, 31 Geo. L.J. 1] at 1 [(1942)].

[298] 1 O. Gierke, Natural Law [and the Theory of Society — 1500-1800,] at 85 [(E. Barker trans. 1934)] (footnote omitted).

not affect the inherent rights of the Indian inhabitants; and (3) transgressions of the Law of Nations by the Indians might serve to justify Spain's conquest and hegemony of the Americas.

Together, these arguments based on natural law denied the legitimacy of the papal hierocratic foundations of Spain's New World empire. Moreover, they allowed Victoria to reformulate the basis of a possible Spanish title on more acceptable, secular Humanist foundations that still maintained the hierarchical orientation of the Spanish colonial system. Through Victoria's synthesis, the two core goals of Spanish imperial policy, assimilation and appropriation, were thus carried over into emerging continental international jurisprudence, but in a modern liberal, as opposed to medieval papal, ideological form.

Victoria divided his lecture, *On the Indians Lately Discovered,* into three sections. In section one, utilizing Roman concepts of natural law *ius gentium* Thomistic philosophy, canon law, and Holy Scripture, Victoria argued that the Indians of the Americas were rational beings, and therefore could claim the same natural rights possessed by virtue of their humanity which any Christian European might claim. By virtue of these natural rights, they "were true owners alike in public and in private law before the advent of the Spaniards among them."[303] The Indians, being possessed of this divinely inspired natural reason common to all men, fulfilled any and all requirements for true ownership of their possessions, and, according to Victoria, "just like Christians, ... neither their princes nor private persons could be despoiled of their property" without just cause.[304] ...

In essence, Victoria's argument was based on a purely "modern" notion "that certain basic rights inhere in men *as men,* not by reason of their race, creed, or color, but by reason of their humanity."[317] Victoria's Humanist argument on the legal equality of Indians and Europeans contained in section one of *On the Indians Lately Discovered* is regarded as his most enduring contribution to Western liberal Indian jurisprudence. Felix Cohen, the most influential twentieth century American legal scholar on Federal-Indian relations, calls Victoria's principle of racial equality between red men and white, "the first principle of ... Indian law"[319] in the United States.

Victoria's second major argument about Indian rights is contained in section two of *On the Indians Lately Discovered.* The most important point in this section is Victoria's assertion [that] "[t]he Pope has no temporal power over the Indian aborigines or over other unbelievers."[320] ...

Thus, section two's importance for Spanish colonial theory (and the Humanist program in general) was in its attempt to deny the legal validity of the *Requerimiento,* the papal hierocratically informed document relied on by Spain to justify Indian conquest. Under the *Requerimiento,* the inhabitants of the New World were "required" to "acknowledge the Church as the ruler and superior of the whole world, and the high priest called Pope, and in his name

---

[303] F. Victoria, [De Indis et de Iure Belli Relectiones] at 115 [(1917)].
[304] *Id.* at 128.
[317] Cohen, *supra* note [294], at 11-12 (emphasis in original).
[319] *Id.* at 11.
[320] F. Victoria, *supra* note [303], at 137.

the king and queen ... in his place, as superiors and lords and kings of these islands and this mainland."[324]

Under Spanish colonial law, failure on the part of the Indians to obey the terms of the *Requerimiento* provided sufficient cause for the Spanish conquistadores to confiscate Indian possessions and to make war upon them, "as vassals who do not obey and refuse to receive their lord."[325] ...

Victoria argued that the contentions to title contained in such documents as the *Requerimiento* were wholly "baseless" according to human, divine, and natural law.... Concluding his argument, Victoria claimed, "even if the barbarians refuse to recognize any lordship of the Pope, that furnishes no ground for making war on them and seizing their property."[330] As the Indians were free according to natural and divine law, no human law (such as the *Requerimiento*) whether issued by priest or king, could bind them without their consent. Such a law "would be void of effect, inasmuch as law presupposes jurisdiction.... [T]he law could not bind one who was not previously subject to it."[331] ...

2. Victoria's Law of Nations as Applied to the Indians of the New World

In the first two sections of *On the Indians Lately Discovered,* Victoria argued that the inhabitants of the Indies possessed inherent natural rights common to all rational men, and that these rights could not be violated by Spain merely on the grounds of a "baseless" papal grant of title....

In section three of *On the Indians Lately Discovered,* however, Victoria developed a third major argument respecting Indian rights.... The thrust of Victoria's argument in the third part of *On the Indians Lately Discovered* centered on his idealized notion of a Law of Nations "which either is natural law or is derived from natural law."[339] ... Presaging later liberal theorists on the consensual, legitimating origins of collective state coercion, Victoria, like Dante before him, postulated that the principles and rules of this Law of Nations, as determined by the majority of mankind, would unequivocally "have the force of law, even though the rest of mankind objected thereto."[344] ...

Victoria derived the binding rules and principles of the Law of Nations from a variety of sources, including Roman law, Holy Scripture, St. Augustine, antique classical writers, St. Thomas, and other authorities.... Victoria postulated the novel theory that certain basic duties were imposed by the Law of Nations upon the indigenous societies of the Americas.

The first duty imposed upon the Indians, according to Victoria was that of "natural society and fellowship."[352] Under this duty

[T]he Spaniards have a right to travel into the lands in question and to sojourn there, provided they do no harm to the natives, and the natives may not prevent them. Proof of this may in the first place be derived from the law of nations (*jus gentium*) .... For, ... it is reckoned among all nations inhumane to treat visitors and foreigners badly

[324] R. BERKHOFER, JR., [THE WHITE MAN'S INDIAN] at 123 [(1978)].
[325] *Id.* at 124.
[330] F. VICTORIA, *supra* note [303], at 137.
[331] *Id.* at 134.
[339] F. VICTORIA, *supra* note [303], at 151.
[344] *Id.* at 153.
[352] *Id.* at 151.

without some special cause, while on the other hand, it is humane and correct to treat visitors well.[353]

Significantly, no law promulgated by the Indians could avoid this natural law duty, for "if there were any human law which without any cause took away rights conferred by natural and divine law, it would be inhumane and unreasonable and consequently would not have the force of law."[354]

The second duty imposed upon the Indians by the Law of Nations according to Victoria was to allow free and open commerce.... According to Victoria, the Law of Nations mandated that the Indians permit the Spaniards to engage in free and open trade.

> The Spaniards may lawfully carry on trade among the native Indians, so long as they do no harm to their country, as, for instance, by importing thither wares which the natives lack and by exporting thence either gold or silver or other wares of which the natives have abundance. Neither may the native princes hinder their subjects from carrying on trade with the Spanish ....
> ... Also, the sovereign of the Indians is bound by the law of nature to love the Spaniards. Therefore the Indians may not causelessly prevent the Spaniards from making their profit where this can be done without injury to themselves.[356]

To Victoria, the right to engage in commerce and trade was one of the natural rights of man.... Victoria's third duty imposed upon the Indians under the Law of Nations was directed to the perceived nonacquisitive value structure of tribal culture. The Spaniards might justly appropriate Indian communally held and shared resources, Victoria argued, because

> [i]f there are among the Indians any things which are treated as common both to citizens and to strangers, the Indians may not prevent the Spaniards from a communication and participation in them. If, for example, other foreigners are allowed to dig for gold in the land of the community or in rivers, or to fish for pearls in the sea or in a river, the natives can not prevent the Spaniards from doing this, but they have the same right to do it as other[s] have, so long as the citizens and indigenous population are not hurt thereby.[359]

Another duty that natural law imposed upon the Indians was the obligation to permit "the propagation of Christianity."[360] Implicitly accepting the propriety of assimilating the Indian to European norms of ethics and morality, Victoria stated:

> Christians have a right to preach and declare the Gospel in barbarian lands.... [F]or if the Spaniards have a right to travel and trade among the Indians, they can teach the truth to those willing to hear them, especially as regards matters pertaining to salvation and happiness, much more than as regards matters pertaining to any human subject of instruction.... [B]ecause the natives would otherwise be outside the pale of salvation, if Christians were not allowed to go to them carrying the Gospel message.... *[B]ecause brotherly correction is required by the law of nature, just as brotherly love is. Since, then, the Indians are all not only in sin, but outside the pale of salvation, therefore, it concerns Christians to correct and direct them; nay, it seems that they are bound to do so ....* [L]astly, because they are our neighbors, as said above: "Now the Lord has laid a command on everyone concerning his neighbour" (*Ecclesiasticus* ch. 17). Therefore it

---

[353] *Id.*
[354] *Id.* at 152.
[356] *Id.* at 152-53.
[359] *Id.* at 153.
[360] *Id.* at 156.

concerns Christians to instruct those who are ignorant of these supremely vital matters.[361] ...

In section three of his lecture ... Victoria had truly broken new theoretical ground. He succeeded in providing a possible justification for Spanish hegemony in the New World that was based on secularly rationalized natural law premises. The Indians might be subjected to Spanish rule for denying the Spanish conquistadores free passage in their territory, preventing Spanish merchants from making their profit, refusing to share communally held wealth, or hindering the propagation of Christianity. Any of these actions by the Indians would constitute transgressions of the Law of Nations for which the Spaniards could wage a just war and assume all the rights of conquest. In Victoria's view, the Indian's consent to this Law of Nations was immaterial since the majority of the world's civilized states had already consented to the norms embodied in his codification of the Law of Nations. Consequently, despite their lack of knowledge or acceptance of the dictates of the Law of Nations, the Indians were nonetheless bound. As Victoria had stated in a previous lecture: "The world as a whole, being in a way one single State, has the power to create laws that are just and fitting for all persons, as are the rules of international law."[367]

In his lecture, *On the Indians Lately Discovered*, Victoria boldly cast aside the dubiously regarded papal hierocratic premises underlying Spain's hegemony in the New World. Henceforth, the justness of Spanish rule would be assessed according to the rationalized norms of universally obligatory natural law of international conduct: the Law of Nations. The development of a Thomistically informed concept of natural law enabled Victoria to free the Indian from his subservient status within the Church's hierarchical world view. Yet, this same Thomistic corpus and its universalized normative content paradoxically compelled Victoria to create a new basis upon which to justify the continuation of Spanish domination. Though the Indian was free according to natural law, that same law defined the conditions of his new-found liberty. To the Indian, this European idea of the nature of freedom must have appeared as alien and threatening as the demand which it inevitably entailed — that the Indian abandon his tribal culture and unquestioningly adopt the world view of his European masters.

NOTES

1. Justifications for Taking Indian Land: G. Nash, in The Image of the Indian in the Southern Colonial Mind 14 (1971) (unpublished manuscript), distinguishes between two justifications for taking Indian land: "To some extent the problem was resolved by arguing that the English did not intend to take the Indians' land but wanted only to share with them the resources of the New World where there was land enough for all.... A second and far more portentous way of resolving the problem of land possession was to deny the humanity of the Indians." For a period after the so-called massacres in 1622, the second justification was in ascendancy. Retribution controlled. *See also* F. JENNINGS, THE INVASION OF AMERICA (1975); Eisinger, *The Puritan's Justification for Taking the Land*, 84 ESSEX INST. HIST. COLLECTIONS 131 (1948); Caven, *Indian*

---

[361]*Id.* (emphasis added).
[367]J. SCOTT, [THE SPANISH CONCEPTION OF INTERNATIONAL LAW AND OF SANCTIONS] at 1 [(1934)].

Policy in Early Virginia, 1 Wm. & Mary Q. 3d Series, 65 (1944); Washburn, *The Moral and Legal Justifications for Dispossessing the Indians,* in Seventeenth Century America 15-32 (J. Smith ed. 1959). Reviews of the literature occur in W. Washburn & W. Fenton, American Indian and White Relations to 1830: Needs and Opportunities for Study (Williamsburg, 1957), and D. Sheehan, *Indian-White Relations in Early America,* A Review Essay, Third Series, 26 (1969), 267-85. Seminal is R. Pearce, The Savages of America: A Study of the Indian and the Idea of Civilization (Baltimore, 1953). A recent publication which explores Indian attitudes is D. Brown, Bury My Heart at Wounded Knee: An Indian History of the American West (1971). *See also* W. Washburn, Red Man's Land, White Man's Law (1972).

2. Justice Johnson's View of the Relation of Indian Tribes to Their Lands: In *Cherokee Nation v. Georgia,* 30 U.S. (5 Pet.) 1, 22 (1831), Justice Johnson indicated that the right of discovery fluctuated with the degree of sophistication of the government of the area. In the "populous and civilized nations beyond the Cape of Good Hope," discovery meant only exclusive right to trade. In America, however, there was only "a race of hunters connected in society by scarcely a semblance of organic government." Therefore, discovery meant absolute appropriation. Justice Johnson, who considered the issue a political question, also stated: "Where is the rule to stop? Must every petty kraal of Indians, designating themselves a tribe or nation, and having a few hundred acres ... be recognized as a state?" *Id.* at 25. How would Justice Marshall answer this question?

3. Incidents of the Tribal Right of Occupancy: Although *Johnson v. McIntosh* held the grant of land by the Indian tribe to be invalid, it was not because Indians had no right to alienate their land to non-Indians. The court explicitly stated that such grants could be valid under the internal law of the tribe. 21 U.S. (8 Wheat.) 543, at 593. Moreover, in a later case, the Court explained that grants by Indians to non-Indians could be valid if ratified by the sovereign. *Mitchel v. United States,* 34 U.S. (9 Pet.) 711, 758-59 (1835). One could argue that the right of occupancy could be viewed as a technique to preserve Indian territory as an island free of white intervention. Since the tribes and individual Indians were disabled under *Johnson* from alienating their land without federal approval, the integrity of the Indian holdings could be preserved. Note also that the decision is federalist in tone: the right of land status is a relationship between the federal government and the tribe. States are not permitted to draw the Indian lands under their sway without permission of the federal government.

Although *Johnson* has been frequently praised as a realistic accommodation of competing interests, recent critics have traced present-day American Indian law's bias against Indian tribalism back to *Johnson* and the European tradition that informed that opinion. *See, e.g.,* R. Barsh & J. Henderson, The Road: Indian Tribes and Political Liberty 45-49 (1980); Berman, *The Concept of Aboriginal Rights in the Early Legal History of the United States,* 27 Buffalo L. Rev. 637, 644 (1978) ("the reasoning of the case created a theory of conquest that stands as a centerpiece for the judicial diminution of native rights"); Williams, *The Algebra of Federal Indian Law: The Hard Trail of Decolonizing and Americanizing the White Man's Indian Jurisprudence,* 1986 Wis. L. Rev. 219, 252-58. According to Professor Williams:

> Marshall's famous opinion declaiming a superior status and right in European Nations "discovering" lands held by American Indian Nations had little to do with what the Western European-derived legal tradition might call the "Rule of Law." Rather, Indian

land rights and status were determined by an intense political conflict that sacrificed principles and the "Rule of Law" to interest and expediency."

Williams, *Jefferson, the Norman Yoke, and American Indian Lands*, 29 ARIZ. L. REV. 165, 166 (1987).*

For detailed treatments of the evolution of the concept of aboriginal title, see Newton, *At the Whim of the Sovereign: Aboriginal Title Reconsidered,* 31 HASTINGS L.J. 1215 (1980); Henderson, *Unraveling the Riddle of Aboriginal Title,* 5 AM. INDIAN L. REV. 75 (1977); Cohen, *Original Indian Title,* 32 MINN. L. REV. 28 (1947). For discussion of the law of aboriginal title in other common law jurisdictions, see Bennett, *Aboriginal Title in the Common Law: A Stony Path Through Feudal Doctrine,* 27 BUFFALO L. REV. 617 (1978); Smith, *Concept of Native Title,* 24 TORONTO L.J. 1 (1974); Mickenberg, *Aboriginal Rights in Canada and the United States,* 9 OSGOODE HALL L.J. 119 (1971). *See also* Chapter 9.

4. Extinguishment and Compensability: Although *Johnson v. McIntosh* made it clear that the government had the power to extinguish Indian title, it did not address the question whether the federal government would be required to pay just compensation for a confiscation of Indian land. Nevertheless, the Court referred to the Indians' "legal right" to the land in *Johnson*. In addition, other Marshall court opinions declared Indian title to be "sacred as the fee simple of the Whites." *See, e.g., Mitchel v. United States,* 34 U.S. (9 Pet.) 711, 746 (1835) (quoting *Cherokee Nation v. Georgia,* 30 U.S. (5 Pet.) 1, 48 (1831) (Baldwin, J., concurring). Such language certainly seems to refer to a property interest in the constitutional sense. Still, these cases involved disputes between Indians and non-Indian citizens or states. For other early judicial perceptions of the nature of Indian title, see *Barker v. Harvey,* 181 U.S. 481 (1901) (California); *United States v. Ritchie,* 58 U.S. (17 How.) 525 (1855) (California); *Choteau v. Molony,* 57 U.S. (16 How.) 203 (1853) (Iowa); and *Goodell v. Jackson,* 20 Johns. 698 (1823) (New York). It was not until the twentieth century that the Court was forced to address directly the issue of compensability.

B. PROTECTION AGAINST CONFISCATION

1. ABORIGINAL TITLE

TEE-HIT-TON INDIANS v. UNITED STATES

348 U.S. 272 (1955)

Mr. Justice REED delivered the opinion of the Court.

This case rests upon a claim under the Fifth Amendment by petitioner, an identifiable group of American Indians of between 60 and 70 individuals residing in Alaska, for compensation for a taking by the United States of certain timber from Alaskan lands allegedly belonging to the group.[1] The area claimed is said to contain over 350,000 acres of land and 150 square miles of water. The Tee-Hit-Tons, a clan of the Tlingit Tribe, brought this suit in the Court of Claims under 28 U.S.C. § 1505. The compensation claimed does not arise from any statutory direction to pay. Payment, if it can be compelled, must be based upon a constitutional right of the Indians to recover. This is not a case that is

---

*Copyright © 1987 by the Arizona Board of Regents and Robert A. Williams, Jr. Reprinted with permission of the copyright holders.

[1]A partial taking is compensable. (citations omitted).

connected with any phase of the policy of the Congress, continued throughout our history, to extinguish Indian title through negotiation rather than by force, and to grant payments from the public purse to needy descendants of exploited Indians. The legislation in support of that policy has received consistent interpretation from this Court in sympathy with its compassionate purpose.

[The Court of Claims found] that petitioner was an identifiable group of American Indians residing in Alaska; that its interest in the lands prior to purchase of Alaska by the United States in 1867 was "original Indian title" or "Indian right of occupancy." It was further held that if such original Indian title survived the Treaty of 1867, 15 Stat. 539, Arts. III and VI, by which Russia conveyed Alaska to the United States, such title was not sufficient basis to maintain this suit as there had been no recognition by Congress of any legal rights in petitioner to the land in question. The court said that no rights inured to plaintiff by virtue of legislation by Congress.

[The] petitioner claims a compensable interest [in land] located near and within the exterior lines of the Tongass National Forest. By Joint Resolution of August 8, 1947, 61 Stat. 920, the Secretary of Agriculture was authorized to contract for the sale of national forest timber located within this National Forest "notwithstanding any claim of possessory rights." The Resolution defines "possessory rights"[7] and provides for all receipts from the sale of timber to be maintained in a special account in the Treasury until the timber and land rights are finally determined. Section 3(b) of the Resolution provides:

> "Nothing in this resolution shall be construed as recognizing or denying the validity of any claims of possessory rights to lands or timber within the exterior boundaries of the Tongass National Forest.

The Secretary of Agriculture, on August 20, 1951, pursuant to this authority contracted for sale to a private company of all merchantable timber in the area claimed by petitioner. This is the sale of timber which petitioner alleges constitutes a compensable taking by the United States of a portion of its proprietary interest in the land.

The problem presented is the nature of the petitioner's interest in the land, if any. Petitioner claims a "full proprietary ownership" of the land; or, in the alternative, at least a "recognized" right to unrestricted possession, occupation and use. Either ownership or recognized possession, petitioner asserts, is compensable. If it has a fee simple interest in the entire tract, it has an interest in the timber and its sale is a partial taking of its right to "possess, use and dispose of it." *United States v. General Motors Corp.*, 323 U.S. 373, 378. It is petitioner's contention that its tribal predecessors have continually claimed, occupied and used the land from time immemorial; that when Russia took Alaska, the Tlingits had a well-developed social order which included a concept of property ownership; that Russia while it possessed Alaska in no manner interfered with their claim to the land; that Congress has by subsequent acts confirmed and recog-

---

[7]*Id.*, § 1: "That 'possessory rights' as used in this resolution shall mean all rights, if any should exist, which are based upon aboriginal occupancy or title, or upon section 8 of the Act of May 17, 1884 (23 Stat. 24), section 14 of the Act of March 3, 1891 (26 Stat. 1095), or section 27 of the Act of June 6, 1900 (31 Stat. 321), whether claimed by native tribes, native villages, native individuals, or other persons, and which have not been confirmed by patent or court decision or included within any reservation."

nized petitioner's right to occupy the land permanently and therefore the sale of the timber off such lands constitutes a taking *pro tanto* of its asserted rights in the area.

The Government denies that petitioner has any compensable interest. It asserts that the Tee-Hit-Tons' property interest, if any, is merely that of the right to the use of the land at the Government's will; that Congress has never recognized any legal interest of petitioner in the land and therefore without such recognition no compensation is due the petitioner for any taking by the United States.

I. *Recognition.* — The question of recognition may be disposed of shortly. Where the Congress by treaty or other agreement has declared that thereafter Indians were to hold the lands permanently, compensation must be paid for subsequent taking. The petitioner contends that Congress has sufficiently "recognized" its possessory rights in the land in question so as to make its interest compensable. Petitioner points specifically to two statutes to sustain this contention. The first is § 8 of the Organic Act for Alaska of May 17, 1884, 23 Stat. 24. The second is § 27 of the Act of June 6, 1900, which was to provide for a civil government for Alaska, 31 Stat. 321, 330. The Court of Appeals in the *Miller* case, *supra,* felt that these Acts constituted recognition of Indian ownership. 159 F.2d 997, 1002-1003.

We have carefully examined these statutes and the pertinent legislative history and find nothing to indicate any intention by Congress to grant to the Indians any permanent rights in the lands of Alaska occupied by them by permission of Congress. Rather, it clearly appears that what was intended was merely to retain the *status quo* until further congressional or judicial action was taken. There is no particular form for congressional recognition of Indian right of permanent occupancy. It may be established in a variety of ways but there must be the definite intention by congressional action or authority to accord legal rights, not merely permissive occupation. *Hynes v. Grimes Packing Co.,* 337 U.S. 86, 101.

This policy of Congress toward the Alaskan Indian lands was maintained and reflected by its expression in the Joint Resolution of 1947 under which the timber contracts were made.

II. *Indian Title.* — (a) The nature of aboriginal Indian interest in land and the various rights as between the Indians and the United States dependent on such interest are far from novel as concerns our Indian inhabitants. It is well settled that in all the States of the Union the tribes who inhabited the lands of the States held claim to such lands after the coming of the white man, under what is sometimes termed original Indian title or permission from the whites to occupy. That description means mere possession not specifically recognized as ownership by Congress. After conquest they were permitted to occupy portions of territory over which they had previously exercised "sovereignty," as we use that term. This is not a property right but amounts to a right of occupancy which the sovereign grants and protects against intrusion by third parties but which right of occupancy may be terminated and such lands fully disposed of by the sovereign itself without any legally enforceable obligation to compensate the Indians.

This position of the Indian has long been rationalized by the legal theory that discovery and conquest gave the conquerors sovereignty over and ownership of the lands thus obtained. 1 Wheaton's International Law, c. V. The great case of *Johnson v. McIntosh*, 8 Wheat. 543, denied the power of an Indian tribe to pass their right of occupancy to another. It confirmed the practice of two hundred years of American history "that discovery gave an exclusive right to extinguish the Indian title of occupancy, either by purchase or by conquest." 8 Wheat. at page 587.

[In another case,] *Beecher v. Wetherby*, 95 U.S. 517, a tract of land which Indians were then expressly permitted by the United States to occupy was granted to Wisconsin. In a controversy over timber, this Court held the Wisconsin title good.

"The grantee, it is true, would take only the naked fee, and could not disturb the occupancy of the Indians: that occupancy could only be interfered with or determined by the United States. It is to be presumed that in this matter the United States would be governed by such considerations of justice as would control a Christian people in their treatment of an ignorant and dependent race. Be that as it may, the propriety or justice of their action towards the Indians with respect to their lands is a question of governmental policy, and is not a matter open to discussion in a controversy between third parties, neither of whom derives title from the Indians. The right of the United States to dispose of the fee of lands occupied by them has always been recognized by this court from the foundation of the government." [*Id.* at] 525.

In 1941 a unanimous Court wrote, concerning Indian title, the following:

"Extinguishment of Indian title based on aboriginal possession is of course a different matter. The power of Congress in that regard is supreme. The manner, method and time of such extinguishment raise political, not justiciable, issues." *United States v. Santa Fe Pacific R. Co.*, 314 U.S. 339, 347.

No case in this Court has ever held that taking of Indian title or use by Congress required compensation. The American people have compassion for the descendants of those Indians who were deprived of their homes and hunting grounds by the drive of civilization. They seek to have the Indians share the benefits of our society as citizens of this Nation. Generous provision has been willingly made to allow tribes to recover for wrongs, as a matter of grace, not because of legal liability.

(b) There is one opinion in a case decided by this Court that contains language indicating that unrecognized Indian title might be compensable under the Constitution when taken by the United States. *United States v. Tillamooks,* 329 U.S. 40.

Recovery was allowed under a jurisdictional Act of 1935, 49 Stat. 801, that permitted payments to a few specific Indian tribes for "legal and equitable claims arising under or growing out of the original Indian title" to land, because of some unratified treaties negotiated with them and other tribes. The other tribes had already been compensated. Five years later this Court unanimously held that none of the former opinions in Vol. 329 of the United States Reports expressed the view that recovery was grounded on a taking under the Fifth Amendment. *United States v. Tillamooks,* 341 U.S. 48. Interest, payable on recovery for a taking under the Fifth Amendment, was denied.

Before the second *Tillamook* case, a decision was made on Alaskan Tlingit lands held by original Indian title. *Miller v. United States,* 159 F.2d 997. That opinion holds such a title compensable under the Fifth Amendment on reasoning drawn from the language of this Court's first *Tillamook* case. After the *Miller* decision, this Court had occasion to consider the holding of that case on Indian title in *Hynes v. Grimes Packing Co.,* 337 U.S. 86, 106, note 28. We there commented as to the first *Tillamook* case: "That opinion does not hold the Indian right of occupancy compensable without specific legislative direction to make payment." We further declared "we cannot express agreement with that [compensability of Indian title by the *Miller* case] conclusion."

[T]his Court in the second *Tillamook case,* 341 U.S. 48, held that the first case was not "grounded on a taking under the Fifth Amendment." Therefore no interest was due. This latter *Tillamook* decision by a unanimous Court supported the Court of Claims in its view of the law in this present case. We think it must be concluded that the recovery in the *Tillamook* case was based upon statutory direction to pay for the aboriginal title in the special jurisdictional act to equalize the Tillamooks with the neighboring tribes, rather than upon a holding that there had been a compensable taking under the Fifth Amendment.[18] This leaves unimpaired the rule derived from *Johnson v. McIntosh* that the taking by the United States of unrecognized Indian title is not compensable under the Fifth Amendment.

This is true, not because an Indian or an Indian tribe has no standing to sue or because the United States has not consented to be sued for the taking of original Indian title, but because Indian occupation of land without government recognition of ownership creates no rights against taking or extinction by the United States protected by the Fifth Amendment or any other principle of law.

(c) What has been heretofore set out deals largely with the Indians of the Plains and east of the Mississippi. The Tee-Hit-Tons urge, however, that their stage of civilization and their concept of ownership of property takes them out of the rule applicable to the Indians of the States. They assert that Russia never took their lands in the sense that European nations seized the rest of America.

---

[18] In *Cariqo v. Insular Government of the Philippine Islands,* 212 U.S. 449, this Court did uphold as valid a claim of land ownership in which tribal custom and tribal recognition of ownership played a part. Petitioner was an Igorot who asserted the right to register ownership of certain land although he had no document of title from the Spanish Government and no recognition of ownership had been extended by Spain or by the United States. The United States Government had taken possession of the land for a public use and disputed the fact that petitioner had any legally recognizable title.

The basis of the Court's decision, however, distinguishes it from applicability to the Tee-Hit-Ton claim. The Court relied chiefly upon the purpose of our acquisition of the Philippines as disclosed by the Organic Act of July 1, 1902, which was to administer property and rights "for the benefit of the inhabitants thereof." 32 Stat. 695. This purpose in acquisition and its effect on land held by the natives was distinguished from the settlement of the white race in the United States where "the dominant purpose of the whites in America was to occupy the land." 212 U.S., at 458. The Court further found that the Spanish law and exercise of Spanish sovereignty over the islands tended to support rather than defeat a prescriptive right. Since this was no communal claim to a vast uncultivated area, it was natural to apply the law of prescription rather than a rule of sovereign ownership or dominium. Cariqo's claim was to a 370-acre farm which his grandfather had fenced some fifty years before and was used by three generations as a pasture for livestock and some cultivation of vegetables and grain. The case bears closer analogy to the ordinary prescriptive rights situation rather than to a recognition by this Court of any aboriginal use and possession amounting to fee simple ownership.

The Court of Claims, however, saw no distinction between their use of the land and that of the Indians of the Eastern United States. That court had no evidence that the Russian handling of the Indian land problem differed from ours. The natives were left the use of the great part of their vast hunting and fishing territory but what Russia wanted for its use and that of its licensees, it took. The court's conclusion on this issue was based on strong evidence.

In considering the character of the Tee-Hit-Tons' use of the land, the Court of Claims had before it the testimony of a single witness who was offered by plaintiff. He stated that he was the chief of the Tee-Hit-Ton tribe. He qualified as an expert on the Tlingits, a group composed of numerous interconnected tribes including the Tee-Hit-Tons. His testimony showed that the Tee-Hit-Tons had become greatly reduced in numbers. Membership descends only through the female line. At the present time there are only a few women of childbearing age and a total membership of some 65.

The witness pointed out that their claim of ownership was based on possession and use. The use that was made of the controverted area was for the location in winter of villages in sheltered spots and in summer along fishing streams and/or bays. The ownership was not individual but tribal. As the witness stated, "Any member of the tribe may use any portion of the land that he wishes, and as long as he uses it that is his for his own enjoyment, and is not to be trespassed upon by anybody else, but the minute he stops using it then any other member of the tribe can come in and use that area."

When the Russians first came to the Tlingit territory, the most important of the chiefs moved the people to what is now the location of the town of Wrangell. Each tribe took a portion of Wrangell harbor and the chief gave permission to the Russians to build a house on the shore.

The witness learned the alleged boundaries of the Tee-Hit-Ton area from hunting and fishing with his uncle after his return from Carlisle Indian School about 1904. From the knowledge so obtained, he outlined in red on the map, which petitioner filed as an exhibit, the territory claimed by the Tee-Hit-Tons. Use by other tribal members is sketchily asserted. This is the same 350,000 acres claimed by the petition. On it he marked six places to show the Indians' use of the land: (1) his great uncle was buried here, (2) a town, (3) his uncle's house, (4) a town, (5) his mother's house, (6) smokehouse. He also pointed out the uses of this tract for fishing salmon and for hunting beaver, deer and mink.

The testimony further shows that while membership in the tribe and therefore ownership in the common property descended only through the female line, the various tribes of the Tlingits allowed one another to use their lands. Before power boats, the Indians would put their shelters for hunting and fishing away from villages. With the power boats, they used them as living quarters.

In addition to this verbal testimony, exhibits were introduced by both sides as to the land use. These exhibits are secondary authorities but they bear out the general proposition that land claims among the Tlingits, and likewise of their smaller group, the Tee-Hit-Tons, was wholly tribal. It was more a claim of sovereignty than of ownership. The articles presented to the Court of Claims by those who have studied and written of the tribal groups agree with the above testimony. There were scattered shelters and villages moved from place to place as game or fish became scarce. There was recognition of tribal rights to hunt and fish on certain general areas, with claims to that effect carved on totem poles. From all that was presented, the Court of Claims concluded, and we agree, that the Tee-Hit-Tons were in a hunting and fishing stage of civilization, with shelters fitted to their environment, and claims to rights to use identified territory for these activities as well as the gathering of wild products of the earth. We think this evidence introduced by both sides confirms the Court of Claims' conclusion that the petitioner's use of its lands was like the use of the nomadic tribes of the States Indians.[20]

The line of cases adjudicating Indian rights on American soil leads to the conclusion that Indian occupancy, not specifically recognized as ownership by action authorized by Congress, may be extinguished by the Government without compensation.[21] Every American schoolboy knows that the savage tribes of

---

[20] It is significant that even with the Pueblo Indians of the Mexican Land Sessions, despite their centuries-old sedentary agricultural and pastoral life, the United States found it proper to confirm to them a title in their lands. The area in which the Pueblos are located came under our sovereignty by the Treaty of Guadalupe Hidalgo, 9 Stat. 922, and the Gadsden Purchase Treaty of December 30, 1853, 10 Stat. 1031. The treaty of Guadalupe Hidalgo contained a guarantee by the United States to respect the property rights of Mexicans located within the territory acquired. Art. VIII, 9 Stat. 929. This provision was incorporated by reference into the Gadsden Treaty. Art. V, 10 Stat. 1035. The latter treaty also contained a provision that no grants of land within the ceded territory made after a certain date would be recognized or any grants "made previously [would] be respected or be considered as obligatory which have not been located and duly recorded in the archives of Mexico." Art. VI, 10 Stat. 1035. This provision was held to bar recognition of fee ownership in the Pueblo of Santa Rosa which claimed such by immemorial use and possession as well as by prescription against Spain and Mexico because they could produce no paper title to the lands. *Pueblo of Santa Rosa v. Fall,* 12 F.2d 332, 335, reversed on other grounds, 273 U.S. 315.

Disputes as to the Indian titles in the Pueblos and their position as wards required congressional action for settlement. See Brayer, Pueblo Indian Land Grants of the "Rio Abajo," New Mexico; Cohen, Handbook of Federal Indian Law, c. 20. These problems were put in the way of solution only by congressional recognition of the Pueblos' title to their land and the decisions of this Court as to their racial character as Indians, subject to necessary federal tutelage. 10 Stat. 308, Creation of Office of Surveyor-General of New Mexico to report area of bona fide holdings; Report of Secretary of the Interior, covering that of the Surveyor-General of New Mexico, S. Exec. Doc. No. 5, 34th Cong., 3d Sess. 174, 411; Confirmation of titles for approved Pueblo Land Claims, 11 Stat. 374; S. Doc. No. 1117, 57th Cong., 2d Sess. 581-582, Report of Secretary of Interior showing New Mexico Pueblos with confirmed titles.

Representative Sandidge, who reported the first Pueblo Confirmation Act to the House of Representatives, stated that the Pueblo claims, "although they are valid, are not held to be so by this Government, nor by any of its courts, until the claim shall have been acted on specifically. I will say, furthermore, that the whole land system of the Territory of New Mexico is held in abeyance until these private land claims shall have been acted on by Congress." Cong. Globe, 35th Cong., 1st Sess. 2090 (1858).

The position as Indians of the inhabitants of the Pueblos was considered in *United States v. Joseph,* 94 U.S. 614, and *United States v. Sandoval,* 231 U.S. 28.

For an interesting sidelight on the difficulties inherent in the problems, see Brayer, *supra,* p. 14, and *United States v. Ritchie,* 17 How. 525.

Thus it is seen that congressional action was deemed necessary to validate the ownership of the Pueblos whose claim was certainly founded upon stronger legal and historical basis than the Tlingits.

[21] The Departments of Interior, Agriculture and Justice agree with this conclusion. See Committee Print No. 12, Supplemental Reports dated January 11, 1954, on H.R. 1921, 83d Cong., 2d Sess.

Department of Interior: "That the Indian right of occupancy is not a property right in the accepted legal sense was clearly indicated when *United States v. Alcea Band of Tillamooks,* 341 U.S. 48 (1951), was reargued. The Supreme Court stated, in a per curiam decision, that the taking of lands to which Indians had a right of occupancy was not a taking within the meaning of the fifth amendment entitling the dispossessed to just compensation.

"Since possessory rights based solely upon aboriginal occupancy or use are thus of an unusual nature, subject to the whim of the sovereign owner of the land who can give good title to third

this continent were deprived of their ancestral ranges by force and that, even
when the Indians ceded millions of acres by treaty in return for blankets, food
and trinkets, it was not a sale but the conquerors' will that deprived them of
their land.

[Given] the history of Indian relations in this Nation, no other course would
meet the problem of the growth of the United States except to make congressional contributions for Indian lands rather than to subject the Government to an
obligation to pay the value when taken with interest to the date of payment. Our
conclusion does not uphold harshness as against tenderness toward the Indians,
but it leaves with Congress, where it belongs, the policy of Indian gratuities for
the termination of Indian occupancy of Government-owned land rather than
making compensation for its value a rigid constitutional principle.

Affirmed.

MR. JUSTICE DOUGLAS, with whom THE CHIEF JUSTICE and MR. JUSTICE
FRANKFURTER concur, dissenting.

The first Organic Act for Alaska became a law on May 17, 1884, 23 Stat. 24. It
contained a provision in § 8 which reads as follows:

> the Indians or other persons in said district shall not be disturbed in the possession of
> any lands actually in their use or occupation or now claimed by them but the terms
> under which such persons may acquire title to such lands is reserved for future legisla-
> tion by Congress: *And provided further,* That parties who have located mines or
> mineral privileges therein under the laws of the United States applicable to the public
> domain, or who have occupied and improved or exercised acts of ownership over such
> claims, shall not be disturbed therein, but shall be allowed to perfect their title to such
> claims by payment as aforesaid.

[The conclusion] seems clear that Congress in the 1884 Act recognized the
claims of these Indians to their Alaskan lands. What those lands were was not
known. Where they were located, what were their metes and bounds, were also
unknown. Senator Plumb thought they probably were small and restricted. But
all agreed that the Indians were to keep them, wherever they lay. It must be
remembered that the Congress was legislating about a Territory concerning
which little was known. No report was available showing the nature and extent
of any claims to the land. No Indian was present to point out his tribe's domain.
Therefore, Congress did the humane thing of saving to the Indians all rights
claimed; it let them keep what they had prior to the new Act. The future course
of action was made clear — conflicting claims would be reconciled and the
Indian lands would be put into reservations.

That purpose is wholly at war with the one now attributed to the Congress of
reserving for some future day the question whether the Indians were to have
any rights to the land.

There remains the question what kind of "title" the right of use and occupancy embraces. Some Indian rights concern fishing alone. See *Tulee v. Washington,* 315 U.S. 681. Others may include only hunting or grazing or other
limited uses. Whether the rights recognized in 1884 embraced rights to timber,
litigated here, has not been determined by the finders of fact. The case should
be remanded for those findings. It is sufficient now only to determine that

---

parties by extinguishing such rights, they cannot be regarded as clouds upon title in the ordinary
sense of the word...."

under the jurisdictional Act the Court of Claims is empowered to entertain the complaint by reason of the recognition afforded the Indian rights by the Act of 1884.

NEWTON, AT THE WHIM OF THE SOVEREIGN: ABORIGINAL TITLE RECONSIDERED, 31 Hastings Law Journal 1215, 1241-53 (1980)*

Extinguishment by Conquest

In holding in *Tee-Hit-Ton* that aboriginal title was not a compensable property interest under the fifth amendment, Justice Reed relied heavily on the doctrine of discovery cases, and in particular on *Johnson v. M'Intosh*. Unfortunately, the portion of the *Tee-Hit-Ton* opinion discussing these cases is poorly structured. The Court first quoted several lengthy passages from *Johnson,* followed with several assertions of fact regarding the case in controversy, and finished by purporting to state the obvious conclusion. Despite the Court's poor drafting, one can nevertheless discern a semblance of logic in the opinion. Initially, the Court noted that conquest was a legitimate means of extinguishing aboriginal title. Recognizing this, the Court went on to suggest that the government and its predecessors, as a matter of historical fact, had conquered the Indians, either through actual warfare or by forcing treaties on the Indians. Consequently, all aboriginal title had been extinguished before *Tee-Hit-Ton,* with the exception of the title Congress had chosen to grant back to the Indians.

The Court in *Tee-Hit-Ton* relied on *Johnson* to provide the cornerstone for converting the doctrine of discovery to this doctrine of conquest. Two passages from *Johnson* regarding extinguishment of Indian title by conquest were cited, including the statement that "[c]onquest gives a title which the Courts of the conqueror cannot deny, whatever the private and speculative opinions of individuals may be respecting the original justice of the claim which has been successfully asserted." The Court's reliance on these passages from *Johnson* was misplaced for several reasons. The only war relevant to the decision in *Johnson* was the war between France and England to settle England's claim to the land east of the Mississippi, including the land in controversy in the case. This war in no way affected the Indian tribes' interest in their land, as the opinion pointed out. Hence, the language was merely dicta.

The dicta in *Johnson* regarding extinguishment of Indian title by conquest does not support Justice Reed's conclusion that all Indian land had been conquered. Authorities differ on whether Justice Marshall actually recognized conquest as a valid method of extinguishment of Indian title under American law. Regardless of how the passages in *Johnson* are interpreted, however, it is evident that *Johnson* did *not* establish that all Indian title had been extinguished by conquest, for *Johnson* itself, as well as its progeny, recognized that purchase was the primary method of extinguishment of Indian title. Had discovery itself extinguished Indian title to land, most of the decisions in those cases would have been unnecessary.

---

*Copyright © 1980 Hastings College of the Law, reprinted with permission.

In addition, Justice Reed's use of the term "conquest" is itself questionable. Both at the time of *Johnson* and today, conquest has been a narrow concept with clearly defined effects on the conquered people. For example, conquest generally requires some sort of physical possession by force of arms. Thus, the conclusion that all Indian land has been conquered was as illogical as it was unprecedented. Even if Justice Reed meant only that the congressional resolution at issue in *Tee-Hit-Ton* was the functional equivalent of a declaration of war followed by conquest, such a conclusion was not warranted by either the language of the resolution or the rules of international law regarding conquest. Finally, even if the federal government's actions in the forty-eight contiguous states could have been interpreted as examples of the "conqueror's will," the Alaska natives had never fought a skirmish with either Russia or the United States, but instead welcomed newcomers to Alaska with open arms. To say that the Alaska natives were subjugated by conquest stretches the imagination too far. The only sovereign act that can be said to have conquered the Alaska native was the *Tee-Hit-Ton* opinion itself.

Extinguishment as a Political Question

In constructing the rule of *Tee-Hit-Ton,* Justice Reed asserted that the decision of Congress to recognize aboriginal title was not subject to judicial review. This conclusion logically followed from two unexpressed premises: first, that political questions, such as the decision to declare war, are not justiciable; and second, that extinguishment of Indian title is a purely political question. In support of the latter premise, the court placed critical reliance on language from two cases, *Beecher v. Wetherby*[183] and *United States ex rel. Hualpai Indians v. Santa Fe Pacific Railroad*[184] *(Walapai Tribe).*

Beecher involved a dispute over tribal land the United States granted to Wisconsin in 1848, before the tribe's aboriginal title had been extinguished. The United States Government subsequently attempted to cede the land back to the tribe, despite its prior grant of the land to Wisconsin. Both the plaintiff and defendant claimed title to lumber taken from the land, the plaintiff's claim based on a United States patent issued in 1872 and the defendant's claim based on the State's issuance of patents in 1865 and 1870. In holding only the grant by Wisconsin valid, the Court stated that "the propriety or justice of ... [the government's] action towards the Indians with respect to their lands is a question of governmental policy, and is not a matter open to discussion in a controversy between third parties, neither of whom derives title from the Indians."

The Court's position in *Beecher* was sound. Because many land titles can be traced to a period of Indian occupancy, judicial time and individual resources would be wasted if third parties were permitted to contest the sovereign's decision to extinguish the tribal right of occupancy. Additionally, there seems little justification in allowing a third party to contest the sovereign's decision with respect to a tribe if the tribe itself is an uninterested party. *Tee-Hit-Ton* was *not* a controversy between third parties, but a direct controversy between a native Alaska tribe and the government. Hence, what proved to be a compelling justifi-

---

[183]95 U.S. 517 (1877).
[184]314 U.S. 339 (1941).

cation in *Beecher* was wholly lacking under the facts of *Tee-Hit-Ton*. Indeed, contest between a tribe and the government regarding the consequences of congressional extinguishment or the government's liability seems to be precisely the sort of matter subject to judicial review....

Speculation on Tee-Hit-Ton: The Court's Motivation

The break from precedent in *Tee-Hit-Ton* cannot but help raise questions about the dramatic shift in the Court's attitude toward Indian rights. Justice Reed's characterization in *Tee-Hit-Ton* of the Indians as "savage tribes," having only "permission from the [W]hites to occupy," and thus entitled only to "gratuities" from the sovereign reflects a remarkably different view than Chief Justice Marshall's characterization in *Johnson* of the Indian tribes as sovereign nations made up of persons possessed of the same human rights as citizens of the discovering nations. There are several possible explanations for this shift of tone.

Realism

One possible explanation for the Court's departure from precedent in *Tee-Hit-Ton* is that earlier opinions deliberately misrepresented relations between the government and Indian tribes as generally amicable, at a time when the government's activities involved confrontations with Indians and confiscation of aboriginal land. Despite Chief Justice Marshall's direct exposure to such a confrontation in *Worcester,* one might claim he chose to romanticize the Indian tribes to create the appearance of fair dealings between the United States Government and the tribes. Justice Reed's view of history in *Tee-Hit-Ton* on the other hand, may be more accurate, representing a trend toward honesty on the part of the Court.

Even if true, this argument is unconvincing as either an explanation of or justification for the rule in *Tee-Hit-Ton*. As an explanation of the decision, it fails to account for Chief Justice Marshall's candid recognition that many people believed Indians had no right to their land because of their inferior culture, an argument made to the Court in the earlier case of *Fletcher v. Peck,* as well as by the defendant's attorney in *Johnson*. This belief may have explained to the Chief Justice why the European nations applied the doctrine of discovery, once confined to unoccupied land, to an inhabited country. It cannot justify, however, a rule of law that would deny any rights to the indigenous people....

To reject a rule of law establishing the rights of Indians to their land on the ground that the government frequently aided or encouraged the confiscation of Indian land is no more persuasive than the argument that because the government encouraged the perpetuation of second class status for Blacks, the rule of *Brown v. Board of Education,* establishing the equality of Blacks and Whites, is dishonest and therefore should be rejected.

Fiscal Considerations

A second, more plausible explanation for the Court's shift in tone is that the Court was faced with serious fiscal considerations. The rule in *Tee-Hit-Ton* may represent the Court's attempt to save the public treasury from having to

pay out what were perceived as nearly ruinous damage awards on claims pending before the Indian Claims Commission. By promulgating the rule in *Tee-
Hit-Ton*, the Court left Congress free to extinguish aboriginal title to Alaska,
where the land's wealth in resources was just becoming known, without incurring a duty to compensate the natives.

In *Tee-Hit-Ton*, the Court's concern with fiscal considerations was more
obvious than it had been in *Tillamooks II*, where the argument first had been
made. In *Tillamooks II*, the Government appended an exhibit to its brief that
listed all the claims filed with the newly-created Indian Claims Commission
prior to August 11, 1950, the cut-off date for claims arising before 1946. The
appendix was designed to demonstrate the potential liability of the United
States if all the land claims then pending were held to be takings under the fifth
amendment, thereby requiring an interest award. The resulting sum was over
$9,000,000,000, of which $8,000,000,000 was interest. Apparently the appendix
proved effective in *Tillamooks II*, convincing the three justices remaining on
the Court from the *Tillamooks I* majority, including Chief Justice Vinson, to
reverse the award of interest....

Ethnocentrism

Understanding American governmental policy toward Indian tribes during
the time of *Tee-Hit-Ton* affords some insight into the Court's willingness to
permit concerns of the public purse to enter its constitutional decisionmaking
process. The termination era of the 1950's was the second of two major eras in
which Congress attempted to terminate any special status conferred on Indian
tribes as separate sovereigns by steps designed to assimilate Indians into the
dominant culture. In 1954, Congress passed a resolution calling for the termination of federal trust responsibility over Indians. This goal was to be accomplished by extinguishing tribal land, paying individual tribal members for their
share, and allowing the states to exercise civil and criminal jurisdiction over the
Indian reservations within their borders. Congress hoped through legislation to
deprive the Indians of separate sovereignty and to subject them, and their land,
to the same state sovereignty as non-Indian state citizens.

The termination era, regarded as a low point in United States-Indian relations, did no more than reflect the dominant culture's belief in the superiority
of its culture. Americans, many of whom had been assimilated from diverse
cultures within one generation, generally were unwilling to accept the American
Indian tribes' failure to adapt after several hundred years. Policy makers reasoned that the more Indians were given any kind of special treatment, the less
likely they would be to adopt the ways of the dominant culture. Thus,
assimilationists were opposed to according Indians any special legal status.

Members of the Supreme Court were not immune from these concerns. Justices Jackson and Black expressed their qualms about Indian land claims litigation in a concurring opinion in *Northwestern Bands of Shoshone Indians v.
United States*.[208] They asserted that a moral duty alone was owed the Indian
tribes, because the Indians' predicament posed more sociological than legal

---

[208]324 U.S. 335, 354 (1945). (Jackson, J., concurring).

problems. To the two Justices, interpreting the old treaties was a futile task because the Indians had a different concept of land ownership:

> Ownership meant no more to them than to roam the land as a great common, and to possess and enjoy it in the same way that they possessed and enjoyed sunlight and the west wind and the feel of spring in the air. Acquisitiveness, which develops a law of real property, is an accomplishment only of the "civilized."

Accordingly, language assented to by the Indians in treaties may have had no meaning or significance to them.

Two aspects of these claims caused the Justices particular concern. First, they rejected the contention that a tribe of only 1,500 at the time of the treaty could have "owned" the 15,000,000 acres that were the subject of the Treaty of Box Elder. Second, they were disturbed that the wronged generation of Shoshones, "hav[ing] gone to the Happy Hunting Ground," would leave their present day descendants, who were already accorded special status, a windfall award. If the Indians had no sense of private property, the Justices concluded, why should the Court require the Government to give the Indians, "who needed 10,000 acres apiece to sustain themselves through hunting and nomadic living," the value of land measured "in terms of what was gained to our people, who sustain themselves in large numbers on few acres by greater efficiency and utilization?"[214]

This same ethnocentric tone was reflected in *Tee-Hit-Ton*. In the first paragraph of the opinion, Justice Reed pointed out that the case involved the claims of only sixty to seventy Indians to over 350,000 acres of land. Later in the opinion, in concluding that the Alaska natives' aboriginal rights were the same as those of the Indians of the lower forty-eight states, he repeated the figures, apparently in disbelief that such a small number of natives could claim to own so many acres just because they "moved from place to place as game or fish became scarce."

The two concerns expressed by Justices Black and Jackson in their concurrence in *Northwestern Bands* help explain the Court's reliance on fiscal considerations in *Tee-Hit-Ton*. The native Alaskans' claim of ownership to most of Alaska was based on the same nomadic land use pattern as the Tlingits' in *Tee-Hit-Ton*. Hence, it was obvious that the case would have a far greater impact than merely determining the value of the timber cut in the Tongass Forest. In addition, the Indian Claims Commission cases, often based on the same nomadic land use pattern, addressed the propriety of awarding money judgments to the descendants of the generation originally wronged. The *Tee-Hit-Ton* rule provided the court with a way to avoid sanctioning a land use pattern its members regarded as inferior, to give Congress a free hand to acquire Alaska, and to protect the Treasury from having to pay large money judgments to the "descendants of exploited Indians." Thus, deep-seated ethnocentric thinking, coupled with a concern for ruinous damage awards against the government, may well have motivated the Court in *Tee-Hit-Ton*.

---

[214] *Id.* Professor Cohen called this view of Indians' relationships to their lands the "menagerie theory" because it views the Indians as being more like animals foraging for food than human beings having a culture worthy of respect....

The previous analysis demonstrates several significant shortcomings with the Court's rationale in *Tee-Hit-Ton*. First, the decision, though purportedly based on the doctrine of discovery, succeeded in significantly limiting the protection that doctrine traditionally has afforded Indian-held aboriginal title. The distinction between recognized and aboriginal title relied on by the Court was derived from erroneous interpretations of precedent and was used to rationalize previous holdings by the Court in which the existence of such a distinction had never been acknowledged. By adopting the distinction, the Court not only made an unwarranted break from the prior deferential treatment of Indian title by the Court, but undermined what traditionally had been regarded as a form of ownership having the characteristics of a legal property right.

Second, the Court bolstered its conclusion through misplaced reliance on cases holding that determinations by Congress regarding aboriginal title were unreviewable under the political question doctrine. Analysis of these cases strongly draws into question the Court's use of the doctrine to shield Congress from liability. Moreover, the Court's reliance in *Tee-Hit-Ton* on the political question doctrine is even more suspect in light of recent decisions limiting considerably the scope of the doctrine.

Finally, analysis of the historical context of the case suggests that the result in *Tee-Hit-Ton* was precipitated by fiscal and political considerations. As a consequence, the traditional decisionmaking procedure of the Court was subverted, and the rights of Indians to their aboriginal lands were narrowed significantly.

CLINTON & HOTOPP, JUDICIAL ENFORCEMENT OF THE FEDERAL RESTRAINTS ON ALIENATION OF INDIAN LAND: THE ORIGINS OF THE EASTERN LAND CLAIMS, 31 Maine Law Review 17, 70-71 (1979)*

In order for an Indian tribe to establish aboriginal title, several elements must be present. First, the tribe must demonstrate exclusive use, occupancy, and possession of the lands in question.[275] Exclusive occupancy requires that the tribe have excluded or have the power to exclude others from the lands so occupied.[276] Temporary occupancy by friends or raiding by enemies does not destroy the exclusive occupancy required for aboriginal title, but a tribe permitting such temporary occupancy by allies or guests must first have established its exclusive use and occupancy of the territory for the requisite time period.[277] The occupancy need not be continuous, however. Thus, areas which were seasonally hunted or fished may still be claimed by aboriginal title so long as the area was occupied seasonally to the exclusion of other tribes.[278] Furthermore, tribes which jointly used certain areas can establish their joint Indian title to

---

*© 1979 by the University of Maine School of Law. Reprinted by permission.

[275] United States v. Santa Fe Pac. R.R., 314 U.S. 339 (1941); Tlingit & Haida Indians of Alaska v. United States, 389 F.2d 778 (Ct. Cl. 1968); United States v. Seminole Indians of Fla., 180 Ct. Cl. 375 (1967). *Cf.* Lummi Tribe of Indians v. United States, 181 Ct. Cl. 753 (1967).

[276] Confederated Tribes of the Umatilla Reserv. v. United States, 8 Ind. Cl. Comm'n 513, 552 (1960).

[277] Lummi Tribe v. United States, 5 Ind. Cl. Comm. 543, 552 (1957); Omaha Tribe v. United States, 4 Ind. Cl. Comm. 627, 649-50 (1957).

[278] Confederated Tribes of Warm Springs Reserv. v. United States, 177 Ct. Cl. 184, 194 (1966); Spokane Tribe of Indians v. United States, 163 Ct. Cl. 58 (1963).

such areas if their joint occupancy was exclusive of other claimants.[279] Second, exclusive use and occupancy must be from time immemorial or, at least for a very long time.[280] Accordingly, aboriginal title is not established at the moment a tribe first dominates a particular territory. Rather, the rights of aboriginal title must have time "to take root, transforming a conquered province into domestic territory."[281] Third, while aboriginal possession requires proof of lengthy occupancy, that occupancy may have commenced after the United States or a European colonial power acquired sovereignty over the land.[282] Thus, aboriginal title may be established after European colonization of North America had commenced. Fourth, the Indian tribe must not have voluntarily abandoned the territory which it claims.[283] Temporary dispossession following enemy raids is not abandonment unless the territory is not reoccupied.[284] Similarly, an Indian tribe does not relinquish aboriginal title by failing to resist white encroachment[285] or by being involuntarily forced onto a smaller reservation.[286]

To prove facts demonstrating aboriginal title, tribes may rely on the testimony of archaeologists, anthropologists, historians, and other scholars. However, the statutory allocation of the burden of proof contained in 25 U.S.C. § 194 may not aid the tribe in establishing aboriginal title since the statute by its terms only shifts the burden of proof to the non-Indian claimant after the Indians have shown presumption of title through prior possession.

NOTES

1. The Debate Over Compensability Before *Tee-Hit-Ton*: In *United States v. Alcea Band of Tillamooks,* 329 U.S. 40, 45 (1946), Chief Justice Vinson, in an opinion joined by three other justices (including Justice Frankfurter), held that a special jurisdictional act authorized recovery for the extinguishment of aboriginal title. The plurality opinion stated that the jurisdictional act merely "remove[d] the impediments of sovereign immunity and lapse of time .... No new right or cause of action is created." As to recovery of compensation, the opinion stated:

> Admitting the undoubted power of Congress to extinguish original Indian title compels no conclusion that compensation need not be paid. [T]aking original Indian title without compensation and without consent does not satisfy the "high standards for fair dealing" required of the United States in controlling Indian affairs. The Indians have more than a merely moral claim for compensation.

Id. at 47 (citations omitted). The plurality rejected the government's claimed distinction between recognized and aboriginal title, stating:

---

[279]Confederated Tribes of Warm Springs Reserv. v. United States, 177 Ct. Cl. 184 (1966).
[280]Sac and Fox Tribe of Indians v. United States, 315 F.2d 896, 903 (Ct. Cl. 1963).
[281]*Id.* at 905.
[282]Sac and Fox Tribe of Indians v. United States, 383 F.2d 991, 996-99 (Ct. Cl. 1967), *rev'g* Iowa Tribe v. United States, 6 Ind. Cl. Comm. 464, 501-02 (1958), *cert. denied,* 389 U.S. 900 (1967).
[283]Williams v. City of Chicago, 242 U.S. 434 (1917). *See also* Buttz v. Northern Pac. R.R., 119 U.S. 55 (1886); Shore v. Shell Petroleum Corp., 60 F.2d 1 (10th Cir.), *aff'g* 55 F.2d 696, *cert. denied,* 287 U.S. 656 (1932).
[284]New York Indians v. United States, 170 U.S. 1 (1898), *modified,* 170 U.S. 614 (1898), *appeal dismissed,* 173 U.S. 464 (1899); Caddo Tribe v. United States, 8 Ind. Cl. Comm. 354, 374 (1960); Omaha Tribe v. United States, 4 Ind. Cl. Comm. 627, 649-50 (1957).
[285]*See* Seminole Indians v. United States, 13 Ind. Cl. Comm. 326, 362-63 (1964).
[286]United States v. Santa Fe Pac. R.R., 314 U.S. 339 (1941); Holden v. Joy, 84 U.S. (17 Wall.) 211 (1872).

Furthermore, some cases speak of the unlimited power of Congress to deal with those Indian lands which are held by what petitioner would call "recognized" title, yet it cannot be doubted that, given the consent of the United States to be sued, recovery may be had for an involuntary, uncompensated taking of "recognized title." We think the same rule applicable to a taking of original Indian title. "Whether this tract ... was properly called a reservation ... or unceded Indian country, ... is a matter of little moment .... [T]he Indians' right of occupancy has always been held to be sacred; something not be taken from him except by his consent, and then upon such consideration as should be agreed upon." *Minnesota v. Hitchcock,* 185 U.S. 373, 388-89 (1902).

Id. at 51-52.

Justice Reed, joined by two other justices, dissented, stating:

This distinction between rights from recognized occupancy and from Indian title springs from the theory under which the European nations took possession of the lands of the American aborigines. This theory was that discovery by the Christian nations gave them sovereignty over and title to the lands discovered. *Johnson v. M'Intosh,* 8 Wheat. 543, 572-86; 1 Story, Commentaries on the Constitution (5th Ed.) § 152. While Indians were permitted to occupy these lands under their Indian title, the conquering nations asserted the right to extinguish that Indian title without legal responsibility to compensate the Indian for his loss. It is not for the courts of the conqueror to question the propriety or validity of such an assertion of power. Indians who continued to occupy their aboriginal homes, without definite recognition of their right to do so are like paleface squatters on public lands without compensable rights if they are evicted.

Id. at 58.

Justice Black merely concurred in the result in *Tillamooks I,* resting his brief opinion solely on the statute. In *United States v. Alcea Band of Tillamooks,* 341 U.S. 48 (1951), the Court explained the result in the first case as based solely on a construction of the jurisdictional statute, rather than the fifth amendment. Thus, interest on the judgment was not recoverable as it would have been had a constitutional taking been involved.

2. The Role of Conquest: Professor Newton views *Tee-Hit-Ton* as resting in part on Justice Reed's observation that "[e]very American schoolboy knows that the savage tribes of this continent were deprived of their ancestral ranges by force and that, even when the Indians ceded millions of acres by treaty in return for blankets, food and trinkets, it was not a sale but the conquerors' will that deprived them of their land." Was it prior conquest, as Justice Reed's comments might suggest or, rather, the 1947 Joint Resolution that represented the "conquest" that extinguished the Tee-Hit-Ton's original title? What difference does it make? If Justice Reed's comments are given their full scope, could aboriginal title enforceable against third parties exist anywhere in the United States today? See section C, *infra.*

3. Indian Concepts of Property: The lack of understanding of Indian tribe's concepts of property has helped to foster the ethnocentrist "menagerie theory." See Newton excerpt, *supra,* note 214. Interdisciplinary scholarship can do much to shed light on Indian property concepts. A recent article applying insights derived from anthropology and economic theory to traditional Indian property concepts concluded that the Kwakiutl Indians had "a well-developed system of exclusive property rights." Johnsen, *The Formation and Protection of Property Rights Among the Southern Kwakiutl Indians,* 15 J. LEGAL STUDIES 41, 66-67 (1986). Ironically, this system was reinforced by the institution of the potlatch, a ceremonial giving away of material goods condemned by outsiders as proof of the wastefulness of the Northwest Coast tribes who engaged in it. *Id.* at 46.

4. Extinguishment of Aboriginal Title: Congress has the power to extinguish aboriginal title "by treaty, by the sword, by purchase, by the exercise of complete dominion adverse to the right of occupancy, or otherwise." *United States ex rel. Hualpai Indians v. Santa Fe Pac. R.R.*, 314 U.S. 339, 347 (1941). Moreover, in determining whether title has been extinguished, the Court has stated that "extinguishment cannot be lightly implied in view of the avowed solicitude of the Federal Government for the welfare of its Indian wards." *Id.* at 354. *See generally* Annotation, *Proof and Extinguishment of Aboriginal Title to Indian Lands*, 41 A.L.R. Fed. 425 (1979).

Can title also be extinguished by abandonment in the face of encroachment of non-Indians? As Clinton & Hotopp indicate, the Indian Claims Commission early indicated such actions would not extinguish title. Nevertheless, the Court of Claims has alluded to the possibility that abandonment could be sufficient to extinguish aboriginal title in a proper case. *See, e.g., Wichita Indian Tribe v. United States*, 696 F.2d 1378 (Fed. Cir. 1983) (abandonment possible, but not proven).

5. Incidents of Title: As the *Tee-Hit-Ton* opinion itself suggests, aboriginal title extends to ownership of standing timber. It also extends to mineral assets on aboriginal land. *United States v. Northern Paiute Nation*, 393 F.2d 786 (Ct. Cl. 1968) (Distinction between aboriginal and recognized title is irrelevant to determination of fair market value under the Indian Claims Commission Act permitting compensation for a taking of aboriginal land.) How should hunting, fishing and water rights on non-treaty reservations be characterized? *Cf. Village of Gambell v. Hodel*, 869 F.2d 1273 (9th Cir. 1989) (Alaska Native Claims Settlement Act did not extinguish aboriginal rights to hunt and fish in the Outer Continental Shelf). Resource rights are treated in depth in Chapter 6.

2. RECOGNIZED TITLE

UNITED STATES v. KIOWA, COMANCHE & APACHE TRIBES

479 F.2d 1369 (Ct. Cl. 1973), *cert. denied sub nom.*
Wichita Indian Tribe v. United States, 416 U.S. 936 (1974)

NICHOLS, Judge.

[The Kiowa, Comanche, and Apache tribes filed a claim with the Indian Claims Commission seeking compensation for the loss of treaty recognized land in the Southwest.] The Appellee-Tribes filed a motion for summary judgment on the issue of recognized title on February 13, 1970. Before the Commission ruled, the Wichita Indian Tribe of Oklahoma and Affiliated Bands filed a motion for leave to intervene, originally claiming aboriginal title to the land in question and subsequently claiming recognized title under the Treaty of 1865. The Commission granted the motion for leave to intervene. Both Appellees — Kiowa, Comanche and Apache Tribes — and Appellant, United States, seek reversal of this Commission decision. It granted the motion for summary judgment and the United States appeals. We reverse on both issues.

[The Tribes'] claim of recognized title rests on the language of the Treaty of October 18, 1865, 14 Stat. 717, 718. Article II thereof reads:

Article II. The United States hereby agree that the district of country embraced within the following limits, or such portion of the same as may hereafter from time to time be designated by the President of the United States for that purpose, ... shall be and is hereby set apart for the absolute and undisturbed use and occupation of the tribes who are parties to this treaty, and of such other friendly tribes as have hereto-fore resided within said limits, or as they may from time to time agree to admit among them, and that no white person except officers, agents, and employés of the government shall go upon or settle within the country embraced within said limits, unless formally admitted and incorporated into some one of the tribes lawfully residing there, according to its laws and usages. The Indians parties hereto on their part expressly agree to remove to and accept as their permanent home the country embraced within said limits, whenever directed so to do by the President of the United States, in accordance with the provisions of this treaty, and that they will not go from said country for hunting or other purposes without the consent in writing of their agent or other authorized person, specifying the purpose for which such leave is granted, and such written consent in all cases shall be borne with them upon their excursions, as evidence that they are rightfully away from their reservation, and shall be respected by all officers, employés, and citizens of the United States, as their sufficient safeguard and protection against injury or damage in person or property, by any and all persons, whomsoever....

The land described in the above article constituted Royce Areas 510 and 511. The origin of the controversy in this case is the phrase "the district of country embraced within the following limits, or such portion of the same as may here-after from time to time be designated by the President of the United States for that purpose ...." The question of whether the 1865 Treaty recognized title in the Appellees gains particular import because in 1867 by another Treaty, 15 Stat. 581, the United States established a reservation for the Appellees which was comprised of only Royce Area 510, some 3,000,000 acres. Thus if title to both Royce Areas 510 and 511 was recognized in the 1865 Treaty the Appellees would have a claim to be compensated for the loss of Royce Area 511. The Commission, in an opinion signed by four commissioners, held that the Treaty recognized title to both Areas, but there was a dissent by Chairman Kuykendall.

[I]ntentions of the parties to an Indian Treaty need not be demonstrated by formal language. *Miami Tribe of Oklahoma v. United States,* 175 F. Supp. 926 (Ct. Cl. 1959). Therefore a court must take special care in interpreting such a Treaty so as to be able to understand what was intended. When a court en-deavors to interpret a Treaty between the United States and an Indian Tribe it is bound by the unambiguous words of that Treaty and cannot rewrite them. Where the words of the Treaty leave room for more than one interpretation the court is to interpret the Treaty in a manner not prejudicial to the Indians. [*Worcester v. Georgia.*] In interpreting the words of the Treaty, the proceed-ings leading up to the Treaty and the events which follow it should be examined if necessary in order to elucidate the intention of the recognizing party, the United States. Thus in order to reach a conclusion as to whether the 1865 Treaty recognized title to Royce Areas 510 and 511 one must first attempt to ascertain the intention of the parties from the language of the Treaty. As stated by Judge Madden in *The Miami Tribe of Oklahoma,* 175 F. Supp. at 940:

... By "recognition," the courts have meant that Congress intended to acknowledge, or if one prefers, to grant, to Indian tribes rights in land which were in addition to the Indians' traditional use and occupancy rights exercised only with the permission of the sovereign. Those additional rights may be sufficient to spell out fee simple title in the Indians if that is what Congress wished, or they may result in something less than fee simple title. The extent of those new and additional rights and the accompanying obligations of the sovereign and the tribe will usually be determined by the Congressional enactment, the treaty, or the agreement, conferring them....

The language of the 1865 Treaty indicates that the Areas granted were subject to redefinition and diminution at the will of the President. The Tribes were granted Royce Areas 510 and 511 "or such portion of the same as may hereafter from time to time be designated by the President of the United States for that purpose." It is true that the Treaty spoke of the land granted as the Indians permanent home; however, that does not detract from the fact that the *extent* of that grant was left to later determination. Therefore, without a demonstration of a contrary intention on the part of the United States the language of the 1865 Treaty would defeat the Appellees claim.

The Appellees point to a number of cases which hold that the language need not state formally that the United States intends to recognize title in order for recognition to be accomplished. In *Miami Tribe of Oklahoma,* for example, Judge Madden viewed the Tribe's right to occupy the land in question permanently or until they were disposed to sell it as tantamount to recognized title. In that case if the Indians chose to sell the land they could sell only to the United States, which Appellant urged diminished the nature of the title held. Judge Madden disposed of the Government's argument by noting 175 F. Supp. at pp. 936, 938, that:

> Where Congress has by treaty or statute conferred upon the Indians or acknowledged in the Indians the right to *permanently* occupy and use land, then the Indians have a right or title to that land which has been variously referred to in court decisions as "treaty title," "reservation title," "recognized title," and "acknowledged title" ....
> ... [A]n agreement to permit the Indians to occupy land permanently or until they were disposed to sell it to the United States seemed to the Commission, as it does to us, to be a clear indication of an intention on the part of the United States to recognize in the Indian treaty parties more than aboriginal use and occupancy title to the land in question.

In the *Miami Tribe of Oklahoma* case the nature of the grant was the question before the court while, in the case at bar, the Treaty demands that the court also deal with the question of the extent of the grant. Thus the analogy to *Miami Tribe of Oklahoma* is of little aid to the Appellees because we cannot hold that the 1865 Treaty recognized permanent title in the Appellee Tribes without first answering the question: recognized title to what? We are faced with the language of the Treaty which allegedly, "recognized" title to Royce Areas 510 and 511 "or such portion of the same as may hereafter from time to time be designated by the President of the United States for that purpose ...."

The court is aware that formal statements of recognition are not necessary in order that a Treaty be deemed to have recognized title in a particular Tribe. However, as stated in *Tee-Hit-Ton v. United States,* 348 U.S. 272 (1955), "there must be the definite intention by congressional action or authority to accord legal rights, not merely permissive occupation."

The court is also aware of those cases under which either the events surrounding the Treaty or action subsequent to the Treaty were deemed to have demonstrated the intention on the part of the United States to recognize title, notwithstanding the language of the Treaty.

The case closest to the one at bar in which Treaty language was seen as overturned by subsequent action is *Klamath & Moadoc Tribes v. United States,* 85 Ct. Cl. 451 (1937), *aff'd,* 304 U.S. 119 (1938). In that case the Tribe had entered into a Treaty in 1864 which permitted them to occupy certain territory "until otherwise directed by the President ...." Shortly thereafter a portion of the territory granted to the Tribe was mistakenly granted to the State of Oregon which in turn sold the land.

[The] limitation language [in *Klamath*] involved: "until otherwise directed by the President" did not expressly relate to the territorial extent of the grant, as the corresponding language does here. This court did not speculate, nor did it need to, as to what direction "otherwise" the President might have given. Apparently, by other Treaty provisions, he might have moved other Tribes on the same reservation, or perhaps, he might have put the Klamaths on some other reservation. In either event, suppose they thought of the grant as conveying specific property, there was nothing to suggest in the limitation language that they might be deprived of that property, or part thereof, without compensation. It was expressly spelled out that the location of other Tribes on the reservation would not forfeit any rights guaranteed to the Treaty parties. It was reasonable for this court to conclude, after non-exercise of the Presidential power over 40 years, that it had lapsed, and was no longer a factor in determining the extent of the Klamaths' property interest. The Government, too, had repeatedly since recognized the Klamaths as owners.

Here, on the other hand, the very language of the grant put the grantees on specific notice that the territorial extent of the grant was uncertain and yet to be determined. Instead of embracing a wide range of possibilities, the Presidential action was to focus on one thing only, the territorial extent. It does not seem that any reasonable grantee could have supposed he was getting a *permanent* grant of the entire tract. It is not suggested the Kiowas were so ignorant they actually misunderstood what they were getting, or could have done so. A long lapse of time might have allowed title to firm up to all the two Royce Areas, but no such lapse was allowed to occur. There was nothing to suggest that the President, if he acted, would deprive the Kiowas of anything, rather, he would for the first time define what it was they had, which until then they did not know. The Commission relied mistakenly on this *Klamath* case.

Appellees can point to no action on the part of the President or Congress consistent with the recognition of title. The subsequent Treaty of 1867 unequivocally recognized title to only Royce Area 510. Appellees point to language in Article XI of the 1867 Treaty where reference is made to "the old reservation as defined [in the Treaty of 1865]." Such language simply supports the allegation that some Area was reserved to the Tribes in 1865 but does not dispose of the question of what Area was reserved in view of the phrase permitting the President to set the bounds of the reservation at a later date. Appellees also point to Article XVI of the 1867 Treaty where the Tribes retained the right to hunt on the "lands formerly called theirs." However, in view of the fact that a similar provision was found in the 1865 Treaty it appears likely that this reference is to lands which the Tribes claimed by aboriginal title and not those allegedly recognized in the 1865 Treaty.

[N]egotiations leading to the Treaty of 1865 indicate that while it was intended that an Area be set aside for the Appellees, no agreement was reached as to the boundaries of that Area. In fact the Area described in the proceedings prior to the Treaty differs from that which was designated in either the 1865

Treaty or the 1867 Treaty. After the negotiation and before the ratification of the Treaty of 1865 the Commissioner of Indian Affairs, D. N. Cooley, writing to the Secretary of Interior stated in part:

> ... As to the treaty with the Kiowas and Comanches. It will be observed, in regard to this treaty, that it does not undertake to limit the Indians to any small reservation, but includes a very large district of country, comprising about 62,000 square miles, which they are to be allowed to have "absolute and undisturbed use and occupation," i.e.: the tribes treated with and "such as they may agree to admit among them." This vast region, thus set apart, *may be limited at the discretion of the President.* (Emphasis supplied.)

It thus appears from this contemporaneous interpretation that the United States did not intend to and did not recognize permanent title to the land in question in the 1865 Treaty.

In attempting to interpret the 1865 Treaty this court is faced with a Treaty which by its words does not recognize *permanent* possession of the lands in question. The words reveal an intent to grant something less than recognized title in the entire Area described. This apparent intent was not contradicted by the proceedings prior to the Treaty nor by interpretations of the Treaty following its signing but prior to its ratification. No action was taken by the United States inconsistent with the apparent intent of the Treaty.

[Nevertheless, it] does not follow that the Indians had nothing under the 1865 Treaty. They had a moral and equitable claim that the President's power to delimit boundaries be exercised in a manner fair and just to them, in light of their needs and in light of what they had given up; also in light of the lawful claims of Texas and of other Tribes. Thus, in *Citizen Band of Potawatomi Indians v. United States*, 391 F.2d 614, 622 (1967), *cert. denied*, 389 U.S. 957 (1968) we [stated]:

> A fair interpretation of the treaty is that the President would select the 144,000 acres in his capacity as "Great White Father" of the Indians as well as head of the United States government. A callous disregard of the interests of either would be an abuse of discretion....

[The] grant of Blackacre or such portion of Blackacre as the grantor might decide upon in his discretion would hardly be considered to convey a marketable title. It is only the peculiar mystique of Indian law that allows a question here. If the grantor of Blackacre stood to the grantee in the relationship of parent, guardian, or trustee, the grantee would have something, but he still could hardly describe himself as the owner of all Blackacre.

[*Reversed and remanded.*]

UNITED STATES v. SIOUX NATION

448 U.S. 371 (1980)

Mr. Justice BLACKMUN delivered the opinion of the Court.

This case concerns the Black Hills of South Dakota, the Great Sioux Reservation, and a colorful, and in many respects tragic, chapter in the history of the Nation's West. Although the litigation comes down to a claim of interest since 1877 on an award of over $17 million, it is necessary, in order to understand the controversy, to review at some length the chronology of the case and its factual setting.

I

For over a century now the Sioux Nation has claimed that the United States unlawfully abrogated the Fort Laramie Treaty of April 29, 1868, 15 Stat. 635, in Art. II of which the United States pledged that the Great Sioux Reservation, including the Black Hills, would be "set apart for the absolute and undisturbed use and occupation of the Indians herein named." *Id., at* 636. The Fort Laramie Treaty was concluded at the culmination of the Powder River War of 1866-1867, a series of military engagements in which the Sioux tribes, led by their great chief, Red Cloud, fought to protect the integrity of earlier-recognized treaty lands from the incursion of white settlers.

The Fort Laramie Treaty included several agreements central to the issues presented in this case. First, it established the Great Sioux Reservation, a tract of land bounded on the east by the Missouri River, on the south by the northern border of the State of Nebraska, on the north by the forty-sixth parallel of north latitude, and on the west by the one hundred and fourth meridian of west longitude, in addition to certain reservations already existing east of the Missouri. The United States "solemnly agree[d]" that no unauthorized persons "shall ever be permitted to pass over, settle upon, or reside in [this] territory."

Second, the United States permitted members of the Sioux tribes to select lands within the reservation for cultivation. In order to assist the Sioux in becoming civilized farmers, the Government promised to provide them with the necessary services and materials, and with subsistence rations for four years.

Third, in exchange for the benefits conferred by the treaty, the Sioux agreed to relinquish their rights under the Treaty of September 17, 1851, to occupy territories outside the reservation, while reserving their "right to hunt on any lands north of North Platte, and on the Republican Fork of the Smoky Hill river, so long as the buffalo may range thereon in such numbers as to justify the chase." The Indians also expressly agreed to withdraw all opposition to the building of railroads that did not pass over their reservation lands, not to engage in attacks on settlers, and to withdraw their opposition to the military posts and roads that had been established south of the North Platte River.

Fourth, Art. XII of the treaty provided:

> "No treaty for the cession of any portion or part of the reservation herein described which may be held in common shall be of any validity or force as against the said Indians, unless executed and signed by at least three fourths of all the adult male Indians, occupying or interested in the same."

The years following the treaty brought relative peace to the Dakotas, an era of tranquility that was disturbed, however, by renewed speculation that the Black Hills, which were included in the Great Sioux Reservation, contained vast quantities of gold and silver. In 1874 the Army planned and undertook an exploratory expedition into the Hills, both for the purpose of establishing a military outpost from which to control those Sioux who had not accepted the terms of the Fort Laramie Treaty, and for the purpose of investigating "the country about which dreamy stories have been told." D. Jackson, Custer's Gold

14 (1966) (quoting the 1874 annual report of Lieutenant General Philip H. Sheridan, as Commander of the Military Division of the Missouri, to the Secretary of War). Lieutenant Colonel George Armstrong Custer led the expedition of close to 1,000 soldiers and teamsters, and a substantial number of military and civilian aides. Custer's journey began at Fort Abraham Lincoln on the Missouri River on July 2, 1874. By the end of that month they had reached the Black Hills, and by mid-August had confirmed the presence of gold fields in that region. The discovery of gold was widely reported in newspapers across the country. Custer's florid descriptions of the mineral and timber resources of the Black Hills, and the land's suitability for grazing and cultivation, also received wide circulation, and had the effect of creating an intense popular demand for the "opening" of the Hills for settlement. The only obstacle to "progress" was the Fort Laramie Treaty that reserved occupancy of the Hills to the Sioux.

Having promised the Sioux that the Black Hills were reserved to them, the United States Army was placed in the position of having to threaten military force, and occasionally to use it, to prevent prospectors and settlers from trespassing on lands reserved to the Indians. For example, in September 1874, General Sheridan sent instructions to Brigadier General Alfred H. Terry, Commander of the Department of Dakota, at Saint Paul, directing him to use force to prevent companies of prospectors from trespassing on the Sioux reservation. At the same time, Sheridan let it be known that he would "give a cordial support to the settlement of the Black Hills," should Congress decide to "open up the country for settlement, by extinguishing the treaty rights of the Indians." App. 62-63. Sheridan's instructions were published in local newspapers. See id., at 63.

Eventually, however, the Executive Branch of the Government decided to abandon the Nation's treaty obligation to preserve the integrity of the Sioux territory. In a letter dated November 9, 1875, to Terry, Sheridan reported that he had met with President Grant, the Secretary of the Interior, and the Secretary of War, and that the President had decided that the military should make no further resistance to the occupation of the Black Hills by miners, "it being his belief that such resistance only increased their desire and complicated the troubles." Id., at 59. These orders were to be enforced "quietly," ibid., and the President's decision was to remain "confidential." Id., at 59-60 (letter from Sheridan to Sherman).

With the Army's withdrawal from its role as enforcer of the Fort Laramie Treaty, the influx of settlers into the Black Hills increased. The Government concluded that the only practical course was to secure to the citizens of the United States the right to mine the Black Hills for gold. Toward that end, the Secretary of the Interior, in the spring of 1875, appointed a commission to negotiate with the Sioux. The commission was headed by William B. Allison. The tribal leaders of the Sioux were aware of the mineral value of the Black Hills and refused to sell the land for a price less than $70 million. The commission offered the Indians an annual rental of $400,000, or payment of $6 million for absolute relinquishment of the Black Hills. The negotiations broke down.

In the winter of 1875-1876, many of the Sioux were hunting in the unceded territory north of the North Platte River, reserved to them for that purpose in the Fort Laramie Treaty. On December 6, 1875, for reasons that are not entirely clear, the Commissioner of Indian Affairs sent instructions to the Indian agents on the reservation to notify those hunters that if they did not return to the reservation agencies by January 31, 1876, they would be treated as "hostiles." Given the severity of the winter, compliance with these instructions was impossible. On February 1, the Secretary of the Interior nonetheless relinquished jurisdiction over all hostile Sioux, including those Indians exercising their treaty-protected hunting rights, to the War Department. The Army's campaign against the "hostiles" led to Setting Bull's notable victory over Custer's forces at the battle of the Little Big Horn on June 25. That victory, of course, was short-lived, and those Indians who surrendered to the Army were returned to the reservation, and deprived of their weapons and horses, leaving them completely dependent for survival on rations provided them by the Government.

In the meantime, Congress was becoming increasingly dissatisfied with the failure of the Sioux living on the reservation to become self-sufficient. The Sioux' entitlement to subsistence rations under the terms of the Fort Laramie Treaty had expired in 1872. Nonetheless, in each of the two following years, over $1 million was appropriated for feeding the Sioux. In August 1876, Congress enacted an appropriations bill providing that "hereafter there shall be no appropriation made for the subsistence" of the Sioux, unless they first relinquished their rights to the hunting grounds outside the reservation, ceded the Black Hills to the United States, and reached some accommodation with the Government that would be calculated to enable them to become self-supporting. Act of August 15, 1876, 19 Stat. 176, 192. Toward this end, Congress requested the President to appoint another commission to negotiate with the Sioux for the cession of the Black Hills.

This commission, headed by George Manypenny, arrived in the Sioux country in early September and commenced meetings with the head men of the various tribes. The members of the commission impressed upon the Indians that the United States no longer had any obligation to provide them with subsistence rations. The commissioners brought with them the text of a treaty that had been prepared in advance. The principal provisions of this treaty were that the Sioux would relinquish their rights to the Black Hills and other lands west of the one hundred and third meridian, and their rights to hunt in the unceded territories to the north, in exchange for subsistence rations for as long as they would be needed to ensure the Sioux' survival. In setting out to obtain the tribes' agreement to this treaty, the commission ignored the stipulation of the Fort Laramie Treaty that any cession of the lands contained within the Great Sioux Reservation would have to be joined in by three-fourths of the adult males. Instead, the treaty was presented just to Sioux chiefs and their leading men. It was signed by only 10% of the adult male Sioux population.[13]

Congress resolved the impasse by enacting the 1876 "agreement" into law as the Act of Feb. 28, 1877 (1877 Act), 19 Stat. 254. The Act had the effect of

---

[13] The commission's negotiations with the chiefs and head men is described by [D.] Robinson, [A History of the Dakota or Sioux Indians] at 439-42 [where he] states: "As will be readily understood, the making of a treaty was a forced put, so far as the Indians were concerned. Defeated, disarmed, dismounted, they were at the mercy of a superior power and there was no alternative but to accept the conditions imposed upon them. This they did with as good grace as possible under all of the conditions existing...."

abrogating the earlier Fort Laramie Treaty, and of implementing the terms of the Manypenny Commission's "agreement" with the Sioux leaders.[14]

The passage of the 1877 Act legitimized the settlers' invasion of the Black Hills, but throughout the years it has been regarded by the Sioux as a breach of this Nation's solemn obligation to reserve the Hills in perpetuity for occupation by the Indians...."

II

[Pursuant to a special statute enacted by Congress to permit the Sioux to relitigate their claim to compensation for the taking of the Black Hills free from a res judicata defense based on prior unsuccessful litigation of the same issue,] a majority of the Court of Claims, sitting en banc, in an opinion by Chief Judge Friedman, affirmed the Commission's holding that the 1877 Act effected a taking of the Black Hills and of rights-of-way across the reservation.[19] In doing so, the court applied the test it had earlier articulated in *Fort Berthold*, 390 F.2d, at 691, asking whether Congress had made "a good faith effort to give the Indians the full value of the land," in order to decide whether the 1877 Act had effected a taking or whether it had been a noncompensable act of congressional guardianship over tribal property. The court characterized the Act as a taking, an exercise of Congress' power of eminent domain over Indian property. It distinguished broad statements seemingly leading to a contrary result in *Lone Wolf v. Hitchcock*, 187 U.S. 553 (1903) inapplicable to a case involving a claim for just compensation.

The court thus held that the Sioux were entitled to an award of interest, at the annual rate of 5%, on the principal sum of $17.1 million, dating from 1877.

We granted the Government's petition for a writ of certiorari, in order to review the important constitutional questions presented by this case, questions not only of long-standing concern to the Sioux, but also of significant economic import to the Government....

---

[14] The 1877 Act "ratified and confirmed" the agreement reached by the Manypenny Commission with the Sioux tribes. 19 Stat. 254. It altered the boundaries of the Great Sioux Reservation by adding some 900,000 acres of land to the north, while carving out virtually all that portion of the reservation between the one hundred and third and one hundred and fourth meridians, including the Black Hills, an area of well over 7 million acres. The Indians also relinquished their rights to hunt in the unceded lands recognized by the Fort Laramie Treaty, and agreed that three wagon roads could be cut through their reservation. *Id.*, at 255.

In exchange, the Government reaffirmed its obligation to provide all annuities called for by the Fort Laramie Treaty, and "to provide all necessary aid to assist the said Indians in the work of civilization; to furnish to them schools and instruction in mechanical and agricultural arts, as provided for by the treaty of 1868." *Id.*, at 256. In addition, every individual was to receive fixed quantities of beef or bacon and flour, and other foodstuffs, in the discretion of the Commissioner of Indian Affairs, which "shall be continued until the Indians are able to support themselves." *Ibid.* The provision of rations was to be conditioned, however, on the attendance at school by Indian children, and on the labor of those who resided on lands suitable for farming. The Government also promised to assist the Sioux in finding markets for their crops and in obtaining employment in the performance of Government work on the reservation. *Ibid.*

Later congressional actions having the effect of further reducing the domain of the Great Sioux Reservation are described in *Rosebud Sioux Tribe v. Kneip*, 430 U.S. 584, 589 (1977).

[19] While affirming the Indian Claims Commission's determination that the acquisition of the Black Hills and the rights-of-way across the reservation constituted takings, the court reversed the Commission's determination that the mining of gold from the Black Hills by prospectors prior to 1877 also constituted a taking. The value of the gold, therefore, could not be considered as part of the principal on which interest would be paid to the Sioux.

IV

A

In reaching its conclusion that the 1877 Act effected a taking of the Black Hills for which just compensation was due the Sioux under the Fifth Amendment, the Court of Claims relied upon the "good faith effort" test developed in its earlier decision in *Three Tribes of Fort Berthold Reservation v. United States,* 390 F.2d 686 (1968). The *Fort Berthold* test had been designed to reconcile two lines of cases decided by this Court that seemingly were in conflict. The first line, exemplified by *Lone Wolf v. Hitchcock,* 187 U.S. 553 (1903), recognizes "that Congress possesse[s] a paramount power over the property of the Indians, by reason of its exercise of guardianship over their interests, and that such authority might be implied, even though opposed to the strict letter of a treaty with the Indians." *Id.,* at 565. The second line, exemplified by the more recent decision in *Shoshone Tribe v. United States,* 299 U.S. 476 (1937), concedes Congress' paramount power over Indian property, but holds, nonetheless, that "[t]he power does not extend so far as to enable the Government 'to give the tribal lands to others, or to appropriate them to its own purposes, without rendering, or assuming an obligation to render, just compensation.'" *Id.,* at 497 (quoting *United States v. Creek Nation,* 295 U.S. 103, 110 (1935)). In *Shoshone Tribe,* Mr. Justice Cardozo, in speaking for the Court, expressed the distinction between the conflicting principles in a characteristically pithy phrase: "Spoliation is not management." 299 U.S., at 498.

The *Fort Berthold* test distinguishes between cases in which one or the other principle is applicable:

> "It is obvious that Congress cannot simultaneously (1) act as trustee for the benefit of the Indians, exercising its plenary powers over the Indians and their property, as it thinks is in their best interests, and (2) exercise its sovereign power of eminent domain, taking the Indians' property within the meaning of the Fifth Amendment to the Constitution. In any given situation in which Congress has acted with regard to Indian people, it must have acted either in one capacity or the other. Congress can own two hats, but it cannot wear them both at the same time.
>
> "Some guideline must be established so that a court can identify in which capacity Congress is acting. The following guideline would best give recognition to the basic distinction between the two types of congressional action: Where Congress makes a good faith effort to give the Indians the full value of the land and thus merely transmutes the property from land to money, there is no taking. This is a mere substitution of assets or change of form and is a traditional function of a trustee." 390 F.2d, at 691.

Applying the *Fort Berthold* test to the facts of this case, the Court of Claims concluded that, in passing the 1877 Act, Congress had not made a good-faith effort to give the Sioux the full value of the Black Hills. The principal issue presented by this case is whether the legal standard applied by the Court of Claims was erroneous.[26]

---

[26] It should be recognized at the outset that the inquiry presented by this case is different from that confronted in the more typical of our recent "taking" decisions. *E.g., Kaiser Aetna v. United States,* 444 U.S. 164 (1979); *Penn Central Transp. Co. v. New York,* 438 U.S. 104 (1978). In those cases the Court has sought to "determin[e] when 'justice and fairness' require that economic injuries caused by public action be compensated by the Government, rather than remain disproportionately concentrated on a few persons." *Penn Central,* 438 U.S., at 124. Here, there is no doubt that the

B

The Government contends that the Court of Claims erred insofar as its holding that the 1877 Act effected a taking of the Black Hills was based on Congress' failure to indicate affirmatively that the consideration given the Sioux was of equivalent value to the property rights ceded to the Government. It argues that "the true rule is that Congress must be assumed to be acting within its plenary power to manage tribal assets if it reasonably can be concluded that the legislation was intended to promote the welfare of the tribe." Brief for United States 52. The Government derives support for this rule principally from this Court's decision in *Lone Wolf v. Hitchcock.*[27]

In the penultimate paragraph of the opinion, however, the Court in *Lone Wolf* went on to make some observations seemingly directed to the question whether the Act at issue might constitute a taking of Indian property without just compensation. The Court there stated:

> "The act of June 6, 1900, which is complained of in the bill, was enacted at a time when the tribal relations between the confederated tribes of Kiowas, Comanches, and Apaches still existed, and that statute and the statutes supplementary thereto dealt with the disposition of tribal property and purported to give an adequate consideration for the surplus lands not allotted among the Indians or reserved for their benefit. Indeed, the controversy which this case presents is concluded by the decision in *Cherokee Nation v. Hitchcock,* 187 U.S. 294, decided at this term, where it was held that full administrative power was possessed by Congress over Indian tribal property. In effect, the action of Congress now complained of was but an exercise of such power, a mere change in the form of investment of Indian tribal property, the property of those who, as we have held, were in substantial effect the wards of the government. *We must presume that Congress acted in perfect good faith in the dealings with the Indians of which complaint is made, and that the legislative branch of the government exercised its best judgment in the premises.* In any event, as Congress possessed full power in the matter, the judiciary cannot question or inquire into the motives which prompted the enactment of this legislation. If injury was occasioned, which we do not wish to be understood as implying, by the use made by Congress of its power, relief must be sought by an appeal to that body for redress and not to the courts. The legislation in question was constitutional." *Ibid.* (Emphasis supplied.)

The Government relies on the italicized sentence in the quotation above to support its view "that Congress must be assumed to be acting within its plenary power to manage tribal assets if it reasonably can be concluded that the legislation was intended to promote the welfare of the tribe." Several adjoining passages in the paragraph, however, lead us to doubt whether the *Lone Wolf* Court meant to state a general rule applicable to cases such as the one before us.

First, *Lone Wolf* presented a situation in which Congress "purported to give an adequate consideration" for the treaty lands taken from the Indians. In fact, the act at issue set aside for the Indians a sum certain of $2 million for surplus reservation lands surrendered to the United States. 31 Stat. 678; see 187 U.S., at

---

Black Hills were "taken" from the Sioux in a way that wholly deprived them of their property rights to that land. The question presented is whether Congress was acting under circumstances in which that "taking" implied an obligation to pay just compensation, or whether it was acting pursuant to its unique powers to manage and control tribal property as the guardian of Indian welfare, in which event the Just Compensation Clause would not apply.

[27] [The Tribe does] not claim that Congress was without power to take the Black Hills from them in contravention of the Fort Laramie Treaty of 1868. [It] claim[s] only that Congress could not do so inconsistently with the command of the Fifth Amendment: "nor shall private property be taken for public use, without just compensation."

555. In contrast, the background of the 1877 Act "reveals a situation where Congress did not 'purport' to provide 'adequate consideration,' nor was there any meaningful negotiation or arm's-length bargaining, nor did Congress consider it was paying a fair price." 601 F.2d, at 1176 (concurring opinion).

Second, given the provisions of the act at issue in *Lone Wolf*, the Court reasonably was able to conclude that "the action of Congress now complained of was but ... a mere change in the form of investment of Indian tribal property." Under the Act of June 6, 1900, each head of a family was to be allotted a tract of land within the reservation of not less than 320 acres, an additional 480,000 acres of grazing land were set aside for the use of the tribes in common, and $2 million was paid to the Indians for the remaining surplus. 31 Stat. 677-678. In contrast, the historical background to the opening of the Black Hills for settlement, and the terms of the 1877 Act itself, see Part I, *supra*, would not lead one to conclude that the Act effected "a mere change in the form of investment of Indian tribal property."

Third, it seems significant that the views of the Court in *Lone Wolf* were based, in part, on a holding that "Congress possessed full power in the matter." Earlier in the opinion the Court stated: "Plenary authority over the tribal relations of the Indians has been exercised by Congress from the beginning, and the power has always been deemed a political one, not subject to be controlled by the judicial department of the government." 187 U.S., at 565. Thus, it seems that the Court's conclusive presumption of congressional good faith was based in large measure on the idea that relations between this Nation and the Indian tribes are a political matter, not amenable to judicial review. That view, of course, has long since been discredited in taking cases, and was expressly laid to rest in *Delaware Tribal Business Comm. v. Weeks*, [430 U.S. 73, 84 (1977).]

Fourth, and following up on the political question holding, the *Lone Wolf* opinion suggests that where the exercise of congressional power results in injury to Indian rights, "relief must be sought by an appeal to that body for redress and not to the courts." Unlike *Lone Wolf*, this case is one in which the Sioux have sought redress from Congress, and the Legislative Branch has responded by referring the matter to the courts for resolution. Where Congress waives the Government's sovereign immunity, and expressly directs the courts to resolve a taking claim on the merits, there would appear to be far less reason to apply *Lone Wolf*'s principles of deference.

The foregoing considerations support our conclusion that the passage from *Lone Wolf* here relied upon by the Government has limited relevance to this case. More significantly, *Lone Wolf*'s presumption of congressional good faith has little to commend it as an enduring principle for deciding questions of the kind presented here. In every case where a taking of treaty-protected property is alleged,[29] a reviewing court must recognize that tribal lands are subject to Congress' power to control and manage the tribe's affairs. But the court must

---

[29] Of course, it has long been held that the taking by the United States of "unrecognized" or "aboriginal" Indian title is not compensable under the Fifth Amendment. *Tee-Hit-Ton Indians v. United States*, 348 U.S. 272, 285 (1955). The principles we set forth today are applicable only to instances in which "Congress by treaty or other agreement has declared that thereafter Indians were to hold the lands permanently." *Id.*, at 277. In such instances, "compensation must be paid for subsequent taking." *Id.*, at 277-278.

also be cognizant that "this power to control and manage [is] not absolute. While extending to all appropriate measures for protecting and advancing the tribe, it [is] subject to limitations inhering in ... a guardianship and to pertinent constitutional restrictions." *United States v. Creek Nation*, 295 U.S. 103 (1935).

As the Court of Claims recognized in its decision below, the question whether a particular measure was appropriate for protecting and advancing the tribe's interests, and therefore not subject to the constitutional command of the Just Compensation Clause, is factual in nature. The answer must be based on a consideration of all the evidence presented. We do not mean to imply that a reviewing court is to second-guess, from the perspective of hindsight, a legislative judgment that a particular measure would serve the best interests of the tribe. We do mean to require courts, in considering whether a particular congressional action was taken in pursuance of Congress' power to manage and control tribal lands for the Indians' welfare, to engage in a thoroughgoing and impartial examination of the historical record. A presumption of congressional good faith cannot serve to advance such an inquiry.

C

We turn to the question whether the Court of Claims' inquiry in this case was guided by an appropriate legal standard. We conclude that it was. In fact, we approve that court's formulation of the inquiry as setting a standard that ought to be emulated by courts faced with resolving future cases presenting the question at issue here:

> "In determining whether Congress has made a good faith effort to give the Indians the full value of their lands when the government acquired [them], we therefore look to the objective facts as revealed by Acts of Congress, congressional committee reports, statements submitted to Congress by government officials, reports of special commissions appointed by Congress to treat with the Indians, and similar evidence relating to the acquisition....
>
> "The 'good faith effort' and 'transmutation of property' concepts referred to in *Fort Berthold* are opposite sides of the same coin. They reflect the traditional rule that a trustee may change the form of trust assets as long as he fairly (or in good faith) attempts to provide his ward with property of equivalent value. If he does that, he cannot be faulted if hindsight should demonstrate a lack of precise equivalence. On the other hand, if a trustee (or the government in its dealings with the Indians) does not attempt to give the ward the fair equivalent of what he acquires from him, the trustee to that extent has taken rather than transmuted the property of the ward. In other words, an essential element of the inquiry under the *Fort Berthold* guideline is determining the adequacy of the consideration the government gave for the Indian lands it acquired. That inquiry cannot be avoided by the government's simple assertion that it acted in good faith in its dealings with the Indians."[30]

---

[30] An examination of this standard reveals that, contrary to the Government's assertion, the Court of Claims in this case did not base its finding of a taking solely on Congress' failure in 1877 to state affirmatively that the "assets" given the Sioux in exchange for the Black Hills were equivalent in value to the land surrendered. Rather, the court left open the possibility that, in an appropriate case, a mere assertion of congressional good faith in setting the terms of a forced surrender of treaty-protected lands could be overcome by objective indicia to the contrary. And, in like fashion, there may be instances in which the consideration provided the Indians for surrendered treaty lands was so patently adequate and fair that Congress' failure to state the obvious would not result in the finding of a compensable taking.

To the extent that the Court of Claims' standard, in this respect, departed from the original formulation of the *Fort Berthold* test, such a departure was warranted. The Court of Claims'

D

We next examine the factual findings made by the Court of Claims, which led it to the conclusion that the 1877 Act effected a taking. First, the Court found that "[t]he only item of 'consideration' that possibly could be viewed as showing an attempt by Congress to give the Sioux the 'full value' of the land the government took from them was the requirement to furnish them with rations until they became self-sufficient." This finding is fully supported by the record, and the Government does not seriously contend otherwise.[31]

Second, the court found, after engaging in an exhaustive review of the historical record, that neither the Manypenny Commission, nor the congressional committees that approved the 1877 Act, nor the individual legislators who spoke on its behalf on the floor of Congress, ever indicated a belief that the Government's obligation to provide the Sioux with rations constituted a fair equivalent for the value of the Black Hills and the additional property rights the Indians were forced to surrender. This finding is unchallenged by the Government.

A third finding lending some weight to the Court's legal conclusion was that the conditions placed by the Government on the Sioux' entitlement to rations "further show that the government's undertaking to furnish rations to the Indians until they could support themselves did not reflect a congressional decision that the value of the rations was the equivalent of the land the Indians were giving up, but instead was an attempt to coerce the Sioux into capitulating to congressional demands."

[T]he Court of Claims [also] rejected the Government's contention that the fact that it subsequently had spent at least $43 million on rations for the Sioux (over the course of three quarters of a century) established that the 1877 Act was an act of guardianship taken in the Sioux' best interest. The court concluded: "The critical inquiry is what Congress did — and how it viewed the obligation it was assuming — at the time it acquired the land, and not how much it ultimately cost the United States to fulfill the obligation." It found no basis for believing that Congress, in 1877, anticipated that it would take the Sioux such a lengthy period of time to become self-sufficient, or that the fulfillment of the Government's obligation to feed the Sioux would entail the large expenditures ultimately made on their behalf. We find no basis on which to question the legal standard applied by the Court of Claims, or the findings it reached, concerning Congress' decision to provide the Sioux with rations.

E

The aforementioned findings fully support the Court of Claims' conclusion that the 1877 Act appropriated the Black Hills "in circumstances which involved

---

present formulation of the test, which takes into account the adequacy of the consideration given, does little more than reaffirm the ancient principle that the determination of the measure of just compensation for a taking of private property "is a judicial, and not a legislative, question." *Monongahela Navigation Co. v. United States,* 148 U.S. 312, 327 (1893).

[31] The 1877 Act [*supra* n.14] purported to provide the Sioux with "all necessary aid to assist the said Indians in the work of civilization," and "to furnish to them schools and instruction in mechanical and agricultural arts, as provided for by the treaty of 1868." 19 Stat. 256. The Court of Claims correctly concluded that the first item "was so vague that it cannot be considered as constituting a meaningful or significant element of payment by the United States." As for the second, it "gave the Sioux nothing to which they were not already entitled [under the 1868 treaty]."

an implied undertaking by [the United States] to make just compensation to the tribe." *United States v. Creek Nation,* 295 U.S., at 111. We make only two additional observations about this case. First, dating at least from the decision in *Cherokee Nation v. Southern Kansas Railway Co.,* 135 U.S. 641, 657 (1890), this Court has recognized that Indian lands, to which a tribe holds recognized title, "are held subject to the authority of the general government to take them for such objects as are germane to the execution of the powers granted to it; provided only, that they are not taken without just compensation being made to the owner." In the same decision the Court emphasized that the owner of such lands "is entitled to reasonable, certain and adequate provision for obtaining compensation before his occupancy is disturbed." *Id.,* at 659. The Court of Claims gave effect to this principle when it held that the Government's uncertain and indefinite obligation to provide the Sioux with rations until they became self-sufficient did not constitute adequate consideration for the Black Hills.

Second, it seems readily apparent to us that the obligation to provide rations to the Sioux was undertaken in order to ensure them a means of surviving their transition from the nomadic life of the hunt to the agrarian lifestyle Congress had chosen for them. Those who have studied the Government's reservation policy during this period of our Nation's history agree. It is important to recognize that the 1877 Act, in addition to removing the Black Hills from the Great Sioux Reservation, also ceded the Sioux' hunting rights in a vast tract of land extending beyond the boundaries of that reservation. Under such circumstances, it is reasonable to conclude that Congress' undertaking of an obligation to provide rations for the Sioux was a *quid pro quo* for depriving them of their chosen way of life, and was not intended to compensate them for the taking of the Black Hills.

V

In sum, we conclude that the legal analysis and factual findings of the Court of Claims fully support its conclusion that the terms of the 1877 Act did not effect "a mere change in the form of investment of Indian tribal property." *Lone Wolf v. Hitchcock,* 187 U.S., at 568. Rather, the 1877 Act effected a taking of tribal property, property which had been set aside for the exclusive occupation of the Sioux by the Fort Laramie Treaty of 1868. That taking implied an obligation on the part of the Government to make just compensation to the Sioux Nation, and that obligation, including an award of interest, must now, at last, be paid.

[*Affirmed.*]

Mr. Justice REHNQUIST, dissenting.

III

Even if I could countenance the Court's decision to reach the merits of this case, I also think it has erred in rejecting the 1942 Court's interpretation of the facts. That Court rendered a very persuasive account of the congressional enactment. As the dissenting judges in the Court of Claims opinion under review pointedly stated, "The majority's view that the rations were not consideration for the Black Hills is untenable. What else was the money for?"

I think the Court today rejects that conclusion largely on the basis of a view of the settlement of the American West which is not universally shared. There was undoubtedly greed, cupidity, and other less-than-admirable tactics employed by the government during the Black Hills episode in the settlement of the West, but the Indians did not lack their share of villainy either. It seems to me quite unfair to judge by the light of "revisionist" historians or the mores of another era actions that were taken under pressure of time more than a century ago.

Different historians, not writing for the purpose of having their conclusions or observations inserted in the reports of congressional committees, have taken different positions than those expressed in some of the materials referred to in the Court's opinion. This is not unnatural, since history, no more than law, is an exact (or for that matter an inexact) science....

That there was tragedy, deception, barbarity, and virtually every other vice known to man in the 300-year history of the expansion of the original 13 colonies into a Nation which now embraces more than three million square miles and 50 States cannot be denied. But in a Court opinion, as a historical and not a legal matter, both settler and Indian are entitled to the benefit of the Biblical adjuration: "Judge not, that ye be not judged."

NOTES

1. Recognized Title Before *Tee-Hit-Ton*: Before *Tee-Hit-Ton* the courts did not distinguish between recognized and aboriginal title, often using the term "Indian title" to describe Indian land. *See, e.g., United States v. Shoshone Tribe,* 304 U.S. 111 (1938). When the term "recognized" was used, it was used to denote two different concepts. First, the term was used to determine whether a claim for taking of property was within the scope of the special jurisdictional act authorizing suit in the Court of Claims only for claims. In such cases, the term "recognized" was used in analyzing whether the treaty acknowledged rights to the land. *See, e.g., Northwestern Bands of Shoshone Indians v. United States,* 324 U.S. 335 (1945) (claim for taking 15 million acres did not arise from the Treaty of Box Elder). Second, the term was used to determine the boundaries of land ceded for an unconscionable consideration under the Indian Claims Commission Act. In such cases, a tribe that could prove an earlier treaty had acknowledged or recognized its boundaries could avoid having to prove actual aboriginal use and occupancy of the ceded territory. *See, e.g., Quapaw Tribe v. United States,* 1 Ind. Cl. Comm'n 474, 491 (1951), *aff'd,* 120 F. Supp. 283 (Ct. Cl. 1954). Should the term "recognition" in these earlier cases be read as having the same meaning as the term "recognition" in *Tee-Hit-Ton*?

2. Treaty Language Recognizing Title: According to *Tee-Hit-Ton*, recognition requires congressional action. Does the ratification of a treaty necessarily suffice to recognize title in the *Tee-Hit-Ton* sense? Treaties or statutes setting aside land as a permanent home for the Indians will generally vest the tribe with recognized Indian title. The question is ultimately one of congressional intent, requiring a careful analysis of both the language and history of the treaty or statute.

In *United States v. Kiowa, Comanche & Apache Tribes,* 479 F.2d 1369 (Ct. Cl. 1973), *cert. denied sub nom. Wichita Indian Tribe v. United States,* 416 U.S.

936 (1974), the Court of Claims rejected the tribes' claim that the following language recognized title:

> Article II. The United States hereby agree that the district of country embraced within the following limits, or such portion of the same as may hereafter from time to time be designated by the President of the United States for that purpose ... shall be and is hereby set apart for the absolute use and occupation of the tribes who are parties to the treaty ....

Treaty of October 18, 1865, 14 Stat. 717, 718. The Court of Claims held that the treaty gave the President discretion to alter the boundaries of the reservation and thus created no compensable interest, despite the fact that the treaty stated the land would be the permanent home of the tribes. The court distinguished *United States v. Klamath & Moadoc Tribes*, 304 U.S. 119 (1938), a case decided before *Tee-Hit-Ton*, in which compensation was awarded even though the treaty contained the phrase "until otherwise directed by the President" as a case in which the treaty language "was seen as overturned by subsequent action." *Kiowa*, 479 F.2d at 1374. *See also Strong v. United States*, 518 F.2d 556 (Ct. Cl.), *cert. denied*, 423 U.S. 1015 (1975); *Sac & Fox Tribe v. United States*, 315 F.2d 896 (Ct. Cl.), *cert. denied*, 375 U.S. 921 (1963). What accounts for such differences in the construction of the operative effects of a treaty or statute? What role, if any, should the maxims of statutory and treaty construction, discussed in Chapter 2, section C2, play in the resolution of recognition questions? In particular, what role, if any, should official actions taken after a treaty has been entered into influence the interpretation of treaty language regarding recognition?

3. Other Acts Recognizing Title: Indian tribes have also acquired land by purchase, as in the case of the Choctaw of Mississippi, or by grant from a prior sovereign. Since the *Tee-Hit-Ton* doctrine requires congressional action, statutes can serve to recognize title as well as treaties. The legislative creation of a land claim process permitting Indian claims to be made along with other claims deriving from the prior sovereign was treated as recognizing title in note 20 of *Tee-Hit-Ton*. *Cf. Zuni Indian Tribe v. United States*, 16 Cl. Ct. 670 (1989) (special act permitting adjudication of claims to land "held by aboriginal title ... acquired from the Tribe without payment of adequate compensation by the U.S.") (land taken by various acts or omissions of the U.S. between 1846 and 1876 was not recognized by the Treaty of Guadalupe Hidalgo or by the failure of the Surveyor-General to comply with a congressional mandate to identify land entitled to congressional protection). At times the government has returned land to an Indian tribe. A well-known example is the 1970 statute returned the sacred Blue Lake to the Pueblo de Taos reservation. Act of Dec. 15, 1970, Pub. L. No. 91-550, 84 Stat. 1437. The statute declared: "The lands held in trust pursuant to this section shall be a part of the Pueblo de Taos Reservation, and shall be administered under the laws and regulations applicable to other trust Indian lands." *Id.,* § 4(b). Is such language sufficient to create recognized title?

4. Incidents of Recognized Title: In two cases decided before *Tee-Hit-Ton* awarding compensation for a taking of Indian land, the Supreme Court held that the tribes were entitled to compensation for standing timber and minerals even if the tribes had not been exploiting the resources. *United States v. Klamath & Moadoc Tribes*, cited above, and its companion case, *United States v. Shoshone Tribe*, 304 U.S. 111 (1938). *See* Cohen, *Original Indian Title*, 32 MINN. L. REV. 28, 54-55 (1947). Why was the tribe denied the value of the gold taken by the miners in *Sioux Nation*? Whether or not such rights are compensable upon confiscation depends of course on whether they have been recognized in the *Tee-Hit-Ton* sense. Both *Klamath* and *Shoshone Tribe* are regarded as recognized title cases. See note 1, *supra.*

5. Tribal Property and the *Sioux Nation* Rule: Why is a special rule necessary to determine whether, in fact, a taking of recognized title has occurred? In the case of non-Indian property, physical invasion of property constitutes a compensable taking. *See, e.g., Loretto v. Teleprompter Manhattan CATV Corp.*, 458 U.S. 419 (1982). *Tee-Hit-Ton* established that recognized title is a protectable property interest, and the Court in *Sioux Nation* treated the Sioux Nation's title as recognized. The Court conceded that the agreement was invalid and that the 1877 statute breached the Treaty of Fort Laramie and legitimized the settlers' invasion of Sioux land. In fact, the Court conceded that the tribe's property had in fact been taken "in a way that wholly deprived [the Sioux] of their property rights to that land." See footnote 26. Section IV of the Court's opinion then distinguished *Lone Wolf*, which is set forth and discussed in Chapter 2, section A2, on several grounds, including that it was based on a now discredited notion that Indian property questions were political questions. The Court's major distinction, however, was based on reinterpreting *Lone Wolf* as a case alleging mismanagement, in which the government acting as a guardian transmuted the tribal property into money. Thus it became necessary to determine how to distinguish between the government's role when it acts as a guardian changing the form of tribal property as in *Lone Wolf*, and when it acts as a sovereign exercising its power of eminent domain. What is the rule the Court adopts to make this crucial determination? Is this rule easy to apply? Can the government avoid liability for a taking if it can demonstrate it has acted in good faith but negligently, by, for instance, grossly undervaluing the property? Should the question of whether property has been taken depend on such considerations? Professor Newton has argued that the appropriate test ought to be whether or not the tribe consented to the taking, instead of a test requiring a determination of whether the government has "fairly (or in good faith) attempt[ed] to provide his ward with property of equivalent value." Newton, *The Judicial Role in Fifth Amendment Takings of Indian Land: An Analysis of the Sioux Nation Rule*, 61 Or. L. Rev. 245 (1982).

Pre-judgment interest cannot be assessed for most claims against the government, including breach of trust claims. One exception is claims for just compensation under the takings clause. Does the fact that a successful constitutional claim would result in the payment of over a million dollars in interest while a breach of trust claim would not require payment of any interest affect the Court's adoption of the *Sioux Nation* rule rather than a more straightforward rule? *See* Friedman, *Interest on Indian Claims: Judicial Protection of the Fisc*, 5 Val. U.L. Rev. 26 (1970).

6. Other Exceptions to the Takings Clause: *Sioux Nation* represents one exception to the application of the takings clause, an exception that applies only to takings of Indian land. Other exceptions to the takings clause applying to all land apply to Indian land as well. For example, in a recent case, a tribe owned the riverbed underlying portions of the Arkansas River in Oklahoma in fee simple absolute. When the tribe sued for just compensation for damages caused to the riverbed by a federal project designed to widen the channel of the river to improve navigation, a unanimous court held that the commerce clause creates a navigational servitude in the United States.

"The proper exercise of this power is not an invasion of any private property rights in the stream or the lands underlying it, for the damage sustained does not result from taking property from riparian owners within the meaning of the Fifth Amendment but from the lawful exercise of a power to which the interests of riparian owners have always been subject."

United States v. Cherokee Nation, 480 U.S. 700 (1987) (quoting *United States v. Rands,* 389 U.S. 121, 123 (1967)). In *Cherokee Nation,* the tribe had received its land in fee simple from the government after moving from its aboriginal homeland. Should a contrary result follow if the tribe's land was aboriginal land predating the sovereignty of the United States?

3. EXECUTIVE ORDER RESERVATIONS

After Congress abandoned treaty-making in 1871, 25 U.S.C. § 71, the federal government nevertheless continued the process of land cessions and the allocation and protection of Indian tribal reserves. This process was sometimes accomplished by agreements with the Indian tribes that were ratified by statutory enactment, thereby generally recognizing the Indian title so protected. *See, e.g.,* Act of Feb. 28, 1877, ch. 72, 19 Stat. 254 (Sioux Nation, Northern Arapaho, and Cheyenne Indians). In addition, presidents also set aside over twenty-three million acres from the public domain by executive orders for the use and occupancy of the Indians until 1918-1919, when Congress declared an end to the practice. 25 U.S.C. § 211 (codification of 1918 Act prohibiting the creation of new reservations in New Mexico and Arizona "except by Act of Congress"); 43 U.S.C. § 150 (codification of 1919 Act stating: "No public lands of the United States shall be withdrawn by Executive Order, proclamation, or otherwise, for or as an Indian reservation except by act of Congress."). *See also* 25 U.S.C. § 398d (prohibiting changes in boundaries of executive order Indian reservations "except by Act of Congress").

Article IV, section 3, clause 2 of the Constitution provides "The Congress shall have Power to dispose of and make all needful Rules and Regulations respecting the Territory and other Property belonging to the United States." This provision raises a host of complex, interrelated, constitutionally based questions regarding executive order lands not affirmatively authorized or recognized by Congress. Included among the questions are:

(1) whether the President has the power to set aside portions of the public domain for the Indians without congressional authorization;

(2) whether the title acquired under a mere executive order is recognized or unrecognized; and

(3) whether the President, without participation by the Congress, may terminate and extinguish Indian land rights created by executive order.

SIOUX TRIBE v. UNITED STATES

316 U.S. 317 (1942)

Mr. Justice BYRNES delivered the opinion of the Court.

This is an action to recover compensation for some 5½ million acres of land allegedly taken from the petitioner tribe in 1879 and 1884. The suit was initiated under the Act of June 3, 1920, 41 Stat. 738, permitting petitioner to submit to the Court of Claims any claims arising from the asserted failure of the United States to pay money or property due, without regard to lapse of time or statutes of limitation. The Court of Claims denied recovery, 94 Ct. Cls. 150, and we brought the case here on certiorari.

The facts as found by the Court of Claims are as follows:

In 1868 the United States and the Sioux Tribe entered into the Fort Laramie Treaty (15 Stat. 635). By Article II of this treaty, a certain described territory, known as the Great Sioux Reservation and located in what is now South Dakota and Nebraska, was "set apart for the absolute and undisturbed use and occupation" of the Tribe. The United States promised that no persons, other than government officers and agents discharging their official duties, would be permitted "to pass over, settle upon, or reside in the territory described in this article, or in such territory as may be added to this reservation for the use of said Indians." For their part, the Indians relinquished "all claims or right in and to any portion of the United States or Territories, except such as is embraced within the limits aforesaid." No question arises in this case with respect to the lands specifically included within the Reservation by this treaty.

The eastern boundary of the Great Sioux Reservation, as constituted by the Ft. Laramie Treaty, was the low water mark on the east bank of the Missouri River. The large tract bordering upon and extending eastward from the east bank of the river remained a part of the public domain open to settlement and afforded easy access to the Reservation. As a result, great numbers of white men "infested" the region for the purpose of engaging in the liquor traffic. Anxiety over this development led the Commissioner of Indian Affairs, on January 8, 1875, to suggest to the Secretary of the Interior that he request the President to issue an executive order withdrawing from sale and setting apart for Indian purposes a certain large tract of the land along the eastern bank of the Missouri River. In the Commissioner's letter to the Secretary of the Interior, and in the latter's letter of January 9th to the President, the reason advanced for the proposed executive order was that it was "deemed necessary for the suppression of the liquor traffic with the Indians upon the Missouri River." On January 11, 1875, the President signed the suggested order.

[Three other small tracts of land were similarly later withdrawn from the public domain to suppress the liquor traffic.]

About two and a half years after the last of these four executive orders withdrawing lands from sale and setting them apart for the use of the Sioux, the Commissioner of Indian Affairs submitted to the Secretary of the Interior a report upon a suggestion that the orders be modified so as to permit the return of the lands to the public domain. The report, dated June 6, 1879, reviewed the problems arising from the liquor trade during the years following the Fort Laramie treaty, recalled that the purpose of the four executive orders of 1875 and 1876 had been to eliminate this traffic, observed that they had "to a great extent accomplished the object desired, viz: the prevention of the sale of whiskey to the Indians," and concluded that any change in the boundaries established by the executive orders would "give renewed life to this unlawful traffic, and be detrimental to the best interests of the Indians."

Three weeks later, however, upon reconsideration, the Commissioner informed the Secretary that, in his opinion, the lands included in the executive orders of 1875 and 1876 might be "restored to the public domain, and the interests of the Indians still be protected." [Consequently,] he recommended that the lands withdrawn from sale by the President in 1875 and 1876 be returned to the public domain, with the exception of three small tracts directly opposite the Cheyenne, Grand River, and Standing Rock agencies. On August 9, 1879, an executive order to this effect was promulgated and the land, with the exceptions indicated, was "restored to the public domain." Five years later, the Commissioner informed the Secretary that the Grand River Agency had ceased to exist and that the agents at Cheyenne and Standing Rock considered it no longer necessary to withhold the tracts opposite their agencies from the public domain "for the purpose for which they have thus far been retained." Consequently, an executive order was prepared and signed by the President on March 20, 1884, restoring these three small pieces of land to the public domain, "the same being no longer needed for the purpose for which they were withdrawn from sale and settlement."

One additional event remains to be noted. In the Indian Appropriation Act for 1877, approved August 15, 1876 (19 Stat. 176, 192), Congress provided:

> ... [H]ereafter there shall be no appropriation made for the subsistence of said Indians [i.e., the Sioux], unless they shall first agree to relinquish all right and claim to any country outside the boundaries of the permanent reservation established by the treaty of eighteen hundred and sixty-eight [the Fort Laramie treaty] for said Indians; and also so much of their said permanent reservation as lies west of the one hundred and third meridian of longitude [the western boundary set by the Fort Laramie treaty had been the 104th meridian], and shall also grant right of way over said reservation to the country thus ceded for wagon or other roads, from convenient and accessible points on the Missouri River ....

On September 26, 1876 — a date subsequent to the first three of the four executive orders setting apart additional lands for the use of the Sioux, but about two months prior to the last of those orders — the Sioux Tribe signed an agreement conforming to the conditions imposed by Congress in the Indian Appropriation Act and promised to "relinquish and cede to the United States all the territory lying outside the said reservation, as herein modified and described ...."

Petitioner's position is that the executive orders of 1875 and 1876 were effective to convey to the Tribe the same kind of interest in the lands affected as it had acquired in the lands covered by the Fort Laramie Treaty, that the executive orders of 1879 and 1884 restoring the lands to the public domain deprived petitioner of this interest, and that it is entitled to be compensated for the fair value of the lands as of 1879 and 1884.

[Art. IV, § 3] of the Constitution confers upon Congress exclusively "the power to dispose of and make all needful rules and regulations respecting the territory or other property belonging to the United States." Nevertheless, "from an early period in the history of the government it has been the practice of the President to order, from time to time, as the exigencies of the public service required, parcels of land belonging to the United States to be reserved from sale and set apart for public uses." *Grisar v. McDowell,* 6 Wall. 363, 381. As long ago as 1830, Congress revealed its awareness of this practice and acquiesced in it. By 1855 the President had begun to withdraw public lands from sale by executive order for the specific purpose of establishing Indian reservations. From that date until 1919, hundreds of reservations for Indian occupancy and for other purposes were created by executive order. Department of the Interior, *Executive Orders Relating to Indian Reservations, passim; United States v. Midwest Oil Co.,* 236 U.S. 459, 469-470. Although the validity of these orders was occasionally questioned, doubts were quieted in *United States v. Midwest Oil Co., supra.* In that case, it was squarely held that, even in the absence of express statutory authorization, it lay within the power of the President to withdraw lands from the public domain. Cf. *Mason v. United States,* 260 U.S. 545.

The Government therefore does not deny that the executive orders of 1875 and 1876 involved here were effective to withdraw the lands in question from the public domain. It contends, however, that this is not the issue presented by this case. It urges that, instead, we are called upon to determine whether the President had the power to bestow upon the Sioux Tribe an interest in these lands of such a character as to require compensation when the interest was extinguished by the executive orders of 1879 and 1884. Concededly, where lands have been reserved for the use and occupation of an Indian Tribe by the terms of a treaty or statute, the tribe must be compensated if the lands are subsequently taken from them. *Shoshone Tribe v. United States,* 299 U.S. 476; *United States v. Shoshone Tribe,* 304 U.S. 111; *United States v. Klamath Indians,* 304 U.S. 119. Since the Constitution places the authority to dispose of public lands exclusively in Congress, the executive's power to convey any interest in these lands must be traced to Congressional delegation of its authority. The basis of decision in *United States v. Midwest Oil Co.* was that, so far as the power to withdraw public lands from sale is concerned, such a delegation could be spelled out from long continued Congressional acquiescence in the executive practice. The answer to whether a similar delegation occurred with respect to the power to convey a compensable interest in these lands to the Indians must be found in the available evidence of what consequences were thought by the executive and Congress to flow from the establishment of executive order reservations.

It is significant that the executive department consistently indicated its understanding that the rights and interests which the Indians enjoyed in executive order reservations were different from and less than their rights and interests in treaty or statute reservations. The annual reports of the Commissioner of Indian Affairs during the years when reservations were frequently being established by executive order contain statements that the Indians had "no assurance for their occupation of these lands beyond the pleasure of the Executive," that they "are mere tenants at will, and possess no permanent rights to the lands upon which they are temporarily permitted to remain," and that those occupying land in executive order reservations "do not hold it by the same tenure with which Indians in other parts of the Indian Territory possess their reserves."

Although there are abundant signs that Congress was aware of the practice of establishing Indian reservations by executive order, there is little to indicate what it understood to be the kind of interest that the Indians obtained in these lands. However, in its report in 1892 upon a bill to restore to the public domain a portion of the Colville executive order reservation, the Senate Committee on Indian Affairs expressed the opinion that under the executive order "the Indians were given a license to occupy the lands described in it so long as it was the pleasure of the Government they should do so, and no right, title, or claim to such lands has vested in the Indians by virtue of this occupancy."

[T]he most striking proof of the belief shared by Congress and the Executive that the Indians were not entitled to compensation upon the abolition of an executive order reservation is the very absence of compensatory payments in such situations. It was a common practice, during the period in which reservations were created by executive order, for the President simply to terminate the existence of a reservation by cancelling or revoking the order establishing it. That is to say, the procedure followed in the case before us was typical. No compensation was made, and neither the Government nor the Indians suggested that it was due. It is true that on several of the many occasions when Congress itself abolished executive order reservations, it provided for a measure of compensation to the Indians. In the Act of July 1, 1892, restoring to the public domain a large portion of the Colville reservation, and in the Act of February 20, 1893, restoring a portion of the White Mountain Apache Indian Reservation, Congress directed that the proceeds from the sale of the lands be used for the benefit of the Indians. But both acts contained an explicit proviso: "That nothing herein contained shall be construed as recognizing title or ownership of said Indians to any part of said ... Reservation, whether that hereby restored to the public domain or that still reserved by the Government for their use and occupancy." Consequently, the granting of compensation must be regarded as an act of grace rather than a recognition of an obligation.

We conclude therefore that there was no express constitutional or statutory authorization for the conveyance of a compensable interest to petitioner by the four executive orders of 1875 and 1876, and that no implied Congressional delegation of the power to do so can be spelled out from the evidence of Congressional and executive understanding. The orders were effective to withdraw from sale the lands affected and to grant the use of the lands to the petitioner. But the interest which the Indians received was subject to termination at the will of either the executive or Congress and without obligation to the United States. The executive orders of 1879 and 1884 were simply an exercise of this power of termination, and the payment of compensation was not required.

Affirmed.

NOTES

1. The Nature of Executive Order Title: Does *Sioux Tribe* hold that all lands held solely under executive order are unrecognized for purposes of the fifth amendment and may be extinguished at the will of the Chief Executive or is its holding limited by the narrow and peculiar reasons for which the executive order lands were set aside in the case? In *Confederated Bands of Ute Indians v. United States,* 330 U.S. 169 (1947), the Court, relying on *Sioux Tribe,* held that lands set apart for the Utes by executive order in 1875 in an effort to resolve a boundary dispute created by an erroneous survey of the line established in an 1868 treaty were not recognized Indian property. Thus, such lands could be withdrawn without compensation by a subsequent 1882 executive order restoring the lands to the public domain in the aftermath of the so-called "Meeker massacre" perpetrated by the Utes. The Court stressed, "There is not one word in [any] Act showing a congressional purpose to convey the Executive Order lands, or any other lands, to the Indians." *Id.* at 177. Might the result in *Sioux Tribe* or *Confederated Bands of Ute Indians* be different if the executive orders creating the reservations had remained in force for longer periods of time?

Recall that in deciding a similar issue of congressional intent, whether a statute has diminished the boundaries of a reservation, the Court has recently begun to focus on such pragmatic concerns as how the land was treated in the years following enactment by both the general public and the executive as well as Congress. *Solem v. Bartlett,* 465 U.S. 463 (1984), set forth and discussed in Chapter 1, section B3. *See also United States v. Kiowa, Comanche & Apache Tribes,* 479 F.2d 1369 (Ct. Cl. 1973), discussed *supra* section B2 of this chapter, at note 2 following *Sioux Nation* (later actions established reservation intended as a permanent home). Could a tribe today point to presidential and congressional inaction as well as positive congressional actions, such as annual appropriations and the many statutes that treat tribes as rightful occupants or even owners of land as "recognizing a tribe as owners"? In other words, if in the more than 40 years since *Sioux Tribe* and *Confederated Utes* were decided the government has not followed a policy of terminating the existence of executive order reservations and has treated Indian tribes inhabiting those reservations the same as tribes inhabiting treaty reservations, can such a course of conduct influence the analysis regarding compensability, either by demonstrating sufficient congressional intent to protect existing reservations or by creating a reliance interest in the tribes that has risen to the status of a property interest? *Cf.* Singer, *The Reliance Interest in Property,* 40 STAN. L. REV. 611 (1988).

2. General Recognition of All Executive Order Reservations: It has been estimated that over two million acres of executive order land remained unrecognized by explicit statutory provision as of 1953. Note, *Tribal Property Interests in Executive-Order Reservations: A Compensable Indian Right,* 69 YALE L.J. 627, 629 n.14 (1960). Commentators have searched for a general federal law recognizing all executive order land. In *Sioux Tribe* the Court rejected the tribe's argument that Congress had demonstrated an intent to treat executive order lands as recognized Indian title lands in the General Allotment Act of 1887, ch. 119, § 1, 24 Stat. 389, codified as amended at 25 U.S.C. § 331, by expressly authorizing the allotment in severalty to tribal members of land located on reservations "created for [Indian] use, either by treaty stipulation or by virtue of an Act of Congress or Executive order." The Court stated:

> We think that the inclusion of executive order reservations meant no more than that Congress was willing that the lands within them should be allotted to individual Indians according to the procedure outlined. It did not amount to a recognition of tribal ownership of the lands prior to allotment. Since the lands involved in the case before us were never allotted — indeed, the executive orders of 1879 and 1884 terminated the reservation even before the Allotment Act was passed, — we think the Act has no bearing upon the issue presented.

Sioux Tribe, 316 U.S. at 330. Does the case completely foreclose an argument that the GAA recognized title at least to reservations that have been allotted?

Finally, a 1927 Act of Congress, enacted in response to litigation raising the question whether Indians claiming title to executive order lands were entitled to the royalties from mineral, oil and gas development of such lands, expressly authorized such mineral development and leasing for the benefit of the Indians. Act of Mar. 3, 1927, ch. 299, 44 Stat. 1347, §§ 1-3, codified at 25 U.S.C. §§ 398a-398e. At least one commentator has argued this Act is an intentional blanket recognition of unrecognized executive order lands by Congress. Note, *Tribal Property Interests in Executive Order Reservations: A Compensable*

Indian Right, 69 YALE L.J. 627, 631-39 (1960). *But see Sekaquaptewa v. MacDonald,* 448 F. Supp. 1183, 1192-93 (D. Ariz. 1978), *aff'd in part & rev'd in part,* 619 F.2d 801 (9th Cir.), *cert. denied,* 449 U.S. 1010 (1980) (explicitly rejecting the argument, but holding that the Navaho Boundary Act of 1934, ch. 521, 48 Stat. 960, recognized nine million acres of executive order land).

3. Recognition of Specific Executive Order Reservations: Some executive order reservations were created under the authority of a treaty or statute. *See, e.g.,* Act of Apr. 8, 1864, § 2, 13 Stat. 39, 40, providing "[T]here shall be set apart by the President, and at his discretion, not exceeding four tracts of land, within the limits of [California], to be retained by the United States for the purpose of Indian reservations, which shall be of suitable extent for the accommodation of the Indians of said state ...." In 1876, President Grant issued an executive order formally setting apart land in Northern California which has become part of the Hoopa Valley Reservation, declaring that the land "be and hereby is, withdrawn from public sale and set apart for Indian purposes, as one of the Indian reservations authorized to be set apart, in California, by act of Congress approved April 8, 1864." 1 C. KAPPLER, INDIAN AFFAIRS: LAWS & TREATIES 815 (1904). Could the Indians of that reservation argue that their land had been recognized? Other executive order lands were later recognized by subsequent acts of Congress. *See, e.g., Three Affiliated Tribes of the Ft. Berthold Reservation v. United States,* 390 F.2d 686 (Ct. Cl. 1968); *Sekaquaptewa v. MacDonald,* 448 F. Supp. 1183 (D. Ariz. 1978) (Navajo reservation).

4. Incidents of Unrecognized Executive Order Title: In recent years the Supreme Court has not distinguished between types of title when questions arise regarding what property rights attach to reservation status. In *United States v. Dion,* Chapter 2, section C2, *supra,* the Court dismissed a statutory interpretation argument that distinguished between treaty and nontreaty hunting rights, stating: "Indian reservations created by statute, agreement, or executive order normally carry with them the same implicit hunting rights as those created by treaty." *United States v. Dion,* 476 U.S. 734, 745 n.8 (1986). *See also, Winters v. United States,* 207 U.S. 564, 577 (1908) (water rights attach to executive order reservation). Again, the question of compensability for confiscation raises the issue of recognition.

5. The Navajo-Hopi Dispute Over Executive Order Land: An 1882 executive order reservation preserved certain aboriginal land for the Hopi "and such other Indians as the Secretary of the Interior may see fit to settle thereon." Executive Order of President Chester Arthur, December 16, 1882, *reprinted in Healing v. Jones,* 210 F. Supp. 125, 129 n.1 (D. Ariz. 1962). Both Navajos and Hopis lived in the area at the time. Through the years, many more Navajos began to settle there. When Hopi tribal leaders turned to Congress for aid, Congress enacted a law in 1958 authorizing suit to be brought settling title to the land. This jurisdictional act was held to have recognized the joint title of *both* tribes to most of the disputed area in *Healing v. Jones,* 174 F. Supp. 211 (D. Ariz. 1959), *aff'd,* 373 U.S. 758 (1963) (per curiam). Unfortunately, this decision only intensified the dispute. By 1974, 10,000 Navajos inhabited the Hopi land, and Congress enacted the Navajo and Hopi Relocation Act, Pub. L. No. 93-531, 88 Stat. 1712, codified as amended at 25 U.S.C. §§ 640d-640d-28, providing for a judicial partition of the disputed Joint Use Area and setting up a commission charged with devising a plan to relocate members of each tribe to their tribe's portion of the area. The Commission's work was to have been done by July 6, 1986, but many delays have occurred, including the resistance of a number of traditional Navajo Indians to relocation. The Navajo Tribe has been active in opposing relocation, while the Hopi Tribe has consistently favored relocation. Nevertheless, as Whitson has pointed out:

> There are at least two versions of the "Navajo-Hopi Land Dispute." Advocates of the more publicized version claim that Navajo and Hopi Indians are having a "range war" over land in the Joint Use Area (JUA) of the Hopi Reservation in Arizona.[11] They say that the United States set aside land for the Hopis in 1882 but that Navajos raided and encroached on the Hopi villages. A federal court found that each tribe had joint rights to most of the land and ordered the two to share the disputed land. However, Navajos continued to disregard Hopi land rights until the area of Hopi land use was completely surrounded by the Navajo. It became necessary for Congress and the courts to intervene again: a series of laws and court orders instituted a massive relocation program to transfer to the Hopi Tribe control over the land.
>
> The other version of the land dispute focuses more on the common ground between the two peoples and the problems created by decades of federal intrusion into tribal affairs.[14] Many Navajo and Hopi say they have no quarrel with one another and that federal intervention is inappropriate. They say that the land dispute is a sham, created by the federal government and sustained by federally-created tribal councils, attorneys employed by the United States government, and federal bureaucrats who neither represent nor protect the Indians' interests. They also say neither tribe has benefited from federal intervention and that the only gain is to the large financial interests that have moved in to profit from the relocation program. Many Navajo people, weary of the repeated U.S. government relocation programs carried out against their people for the last 100 years, refuse to leave.[16] In the meantime, the Hopi Kikmongwis (spiritual leaders) have taken the mutual concerns of the traditional Navajo and Hopi to the United Nations.[17]

Whitson, *A Policy Review of the Federal Government's Relocation of Navajo Indians Under P.L. 93-531 and P.L. 96-305,* 27 ARIZ. L. REV. 371, 373-74 (1985).* For a history of the dispute containing interviews with Hopi and Navajo traditionals, see A. PARLOW, CRY SACRED GROUND: BIG MOUNTAIN, USA (1988). A claim by 47 traditional Navajos that the relocation violated both first amendment free exercise rights and international law was rejected. *See Manybeads v. United States,* 730 F. Supp. 1515 (D. Ariz. 1989).

---

[11] This version of the history of the relocation policy is detailed in *Healing v. Jones (II),* 210 F. Supp. 125 (D. Ariz. 1962), aff'd, 373 U.S. 758 (1963) (per curiam). Most news coverage of the issue has focused on the "range war" theory. *See, e.g., In Arizona: A New "Long Walk?"* 115 TIME MAGAZINE 4 (June 30, 1980).

[14] For descriptions of this version, see J. KAMMER, THE SECOND LONG WALK (1981). *See also* Mander, *Kit Carson in a Three-Piece Suit,* 32 CO-EVOLUTION Q. 52-63 (Winter 1981).

[16] The Relocation Commission estimates that between 75 and 100 families may not apply for relocation assistance before the statutory deadline of July 7, 1986. *Department of the Interior and Related Agencies Appropriations for 1985: Hearings Before the Subcomm. on the Department of the Interior and Related Agencies before the House of Representatives' Committee on Appropriations,* 98th Cong., 2d Sess. 30 (March 22, 1984) (statement of Sandra L. Massetto, Vice-Chairperson, [Navajo Hopi Indian Relocation Commission]). This figure may not represent all of those who refuse to leave. The Navajo newspaper reports that a "grassroots" organization, Dine Against Relocation, opposes relocation and has about 700 members. Navajo Times, March 15, 1984, at 1, col. 1.

[17] *See generally,* S. TULLBERG, R. COULTER, & C. BERKEY, INDIAN LAW RESOURCE CENTER, VIOLATIONS OF THE HUMAN RIGHTS OF THE HOPI PEOPLE BY THE UNITED STATES OF AMERICA (March 11, 1980) (communicated to the United Nations Commission on Human Rights and Sub-Commission on Prevention of Discrimination and Protection of Minorities)....

4. THE CLAIMS PROCESS AND ALTERNATIVES

a. The Indian Claims Commission

Even if Congress is not constitutionally compelled to compensate tribes for the extinguishment of aboriginal title, it has rather consistently done so, usually paying compensation far in excess of the blankets, food, and trinkets suggested by Justice Reed in *Tee-Hit-Ton*. The early nineteenth century treaties of cession generally extinguished aboriginal title in exchange for recognition of diminished holding as a reservation or, during the removal period, for new lands solemnly guaranteed to the tribe and for substantial annuities. *See, e.g.,* Treaty with the Poncas, Mar. 12, 1858, 12 Stat. 997 (land ceded in exchange for, *inter alia,* a recognized reservation; annual annuities of $12,000 for five years, $10,000 thereafter for ten years, and $8,000 for the succeeding fifteen years; expenditures of $20,000 for removal and housing; $5,000 for education; the establishment of saw and grist mills and mechanics shops; the expenditure of up to $7,500 for assisting the Poncas in pursuing agricultural and mechanical pursuits; and $20,000 to adjust and settle the Poncas' outstanding debts). While there were certainly some instances in which tribes were deprived of their aboriginal homelands without compensation or with less than fair compensation, for example the Sioux Nation's loss of the Black Hills, Congress later sought to remedy such claims by special jurisdictional acts authorizing Indian tribes to pursue claims in the Court of Claims. Since such statutes constituted a waiver of the federal government's sovereign immunity, they were construed narrowly. For example, in *Northwestern Bands of Shoshone Indians v. United States,* 324 U.S. 335 (1945), the Court held that a special jurisdictional act authorizing suits for claims "arising under or growing out of the treaty [of Box Elder]" did not authorize a claim for a taking of the land, because the Court's construction of the treaty indicated that the treaty itself had not created any rights in the land. After dealing with Indian claims through 142 ad hoc jurisdictional statutes for nearly a century, the Congress in 1946 enacted the Indian Claims Commission Act of 1946, ch. 959, 60 Stat. 1049 [formerly codified at 25 U.S.C. §§ 70-70v-3]. The Act created a special Commission to hear Indian claims accruing before August 13, 1946. The Commission jurisdiction was defined in § 2 of the Act as follows:

> The Commission shall hear and determine the following claims against the United States on behalf of any Indian tribe, band, or other identifiable group of American Indians residing within the territorial limits of the United States or Alaska: (1) claims in law or equity arising under the Constitution, laws, treaties of the United States, and Executive orders of the President; (2) all other claims in law or equity, including those sounding in tort, with respect to which the claimant would have been entitled to sue in a court of the United States if the United States was subject to suit; (3) claims which would result if the treaties, contracts, and agreements between the claimant and the United States were revised on the ground of fraud, duress, unconscionable consideration, mutual or unilateral mistake, whether of law or fact, or any other ground cognizable by a court of equity; (4) claims arising from the taking by the United States, whether as the result of a treaty of cession or otherwise, of lands owned or occupied by the claimant without the payment for such lands of compensation agreed to by the claimant; and (5) claims based upon fair and honorable dealings that are not recognized by any existing rule of law or equity.

Id. § 2.

The Act established a jurisdictional cut-off point of five years from the date of enactment for all claims. The Act provided that claims accruing after 1946 could be presented to the Court of Claims. Additionally, the statute waived any otherwise applicable statutes of limitations and provided that laches could not be raised as a defense. Finally, the statute permitted the Commission to deduct from its awards certain offsets and counterclaims of the United States, excluding expenditures for goods, rations, or provisions, expended gratuitously for the benefit of Indians if it found that "the nature of the claim and the entire course of dealings and accounts between the United States and the claimant in good conscience warrants such actions ...." *Id.*

Originally given a ten-year life, the Commission had to be extended periodically because it was unable to complete the task of adjudicating the 375 claims filed with it in the time available. The Commission expired on September 31, 1978, and transferred the 102 remaining dockets to the Court of Claims. For a valuable survey of the Commission's work and an index to its decisions in the Reports of the Indian Claims Commission, see UNITED STATES INDIAN CLAIMS COMMISSION, FINAL REPORT (1978). For a comprehensive treatment of the ICC, see IRREDEEMABLE AMERICA: THE INDIANS' ESTATE AND LAND CLAIMS (I. Sutton ed. 1985). *See also* Barsh, *Indian Land Claims Policy in the United States,* 58 N.D.L. REV. 7 (1982); Vance, *The Congressional Mandate and the Indian Claims Commission,* 45 N.D.L. REV. 325 (1969).

Note that the list of claims cognizable in the Indian Claims Commission did not specifically distinguish between aboriginal and recognized title claims, although four of the categories could be used to make a claim for a taking of property: clause (1) for constitutional claims; clause (3) for claims permitting revision of treaties ceding land for unconscionable consideration; clause (4) for takings of property; and clause (5) for a breach of fair and honorable dealings.

Shortly after *Tee-Hit-Ton* was decided, the government argued that the above clauses only extended to claims involving recognized title land. In other words, that clause (4) only permitted compensation for a taking of recognized title land. As to clauses (3) and (5), the Court summarized the government's argument as follows:

> Government appellant does say, however, that when Congress used the term "treaties" in clause (3) it did not mean to include *all* treaties, but only certain ones, i.e., treaties relating to land held by the claimants under fee simple or reservation [recognized] title; and that when Congress used the word "dealings" in clause (5), it did not mean all dealings, but rather it meant to exclude from consideration any dealings relative to the claimant's Indian title land.

Otoe & Missouria Tribe of Indians v. United States, 131 F. Supp. 265, 275, (Ct. Cl.) *cert. denied,* 350 U.S. 848 (1955).

The Court of Claims rejected the argument, based on the plain language and legislative history of the Indian Claims Commission Act, thus establishing the Indian Claims Commission's jurisdiction to award compensation for the extinguishment of aboriginal Indian title. Such claims are not entitled to interest payments, however.

The Claims Commission's reports are a source of many valuable historical and anthropological insights into the dispossessing of Native Americans. Nevertheless, the Commission has not been without its critics. To begin with, the Commission failed to fulfill its mandate to establish an Investigative Division. Instead of a system where experts would advise and inform the Commission, the Commission adopted an adversary model and limited remedies to money damages. Moreover, the Commission adopted rules designed to minimize damage awards against the government. For instance, the Commission developed rules like the *Sioux Nation* rule that turned potential fifth amendment takings cases into treaty revision or breach of trust cases, thus avoiding judgments upon which interest would be due. *See generally* Friedman, *Interest on Indian Claims: Judicial Protection of the Fisc,* 5 Val. U.L. Rev. 26 (1970).

Was an Indian Claims Commission possible only at a time of affluence? Were there provisions built into the Indian Claims Commission Act that kept judgments low? Was the Commission merely a bow towards justice, existing only to satisfy soft-hearted people? Normally, a claims procedure is viewed as a technique for public expiation for various torts or breaches of contract. But how much sense does it make for judges, anthropologists, lawyers, and Congressmen to go through incredible contortions to determine what occurred one hundred years ago and base compensation on such a determination? Suspicions concerning the staleness of evidence, loss of information, hearsay, and the cost of litigation suggest that the claims procedure is extremely odd.

It may be, however, that there was another goal: the distribution of a large sum of money to a large number of Indians, either as individuals or as tribes, without any conditions on the use of the funds. The claims process can be viewed as a peculiar sort of economic development act, providing substantial financing for certain tribes. It is fairly clear that appropriations could be obtained much more easily using the rhetoric of obligation than the rhetoric of need, but the resulting system of distributing the money becomes weirdly twisted in the process. A related justification appears in *Pawnee Tribe v. United States,* 109 F. Supp. 860, 869 (Ct. Cl. 1953): "It was anticipated that with the settlement of these claims, many Indians would abandon their connection with the tribes and their dependence upon the United States." Thus, in some ways, the Claims legislation is part of the stream of termination bills, providing adequate financial resources to encourage alternative ways of living. Again, the peculiar form of deciding who gets how much money may make the claims process an unusual vehicle for achieving these goals. Also, the press of the "legal conscience," to use Cohen's term, may be more deeply felt at certain times in the nation's history. There is certainly a connection between the passage of the Claims Commission Act in 1946 and the world role the United States saw itself playing. Congressman Karl Mundt urged enactment of the bill on the following ground:

> In other words, if any Indian tribe can prove it has been unfairly and dishonorably dealt with by the United States it is entitled to recover. This ought to be an example for all the world to follow in its treatment of minorities.

92 Cong. Rec. A4923 (1946).

Finally, the Indian claims process occupies an interesting jurisprudential slot. The questions raised by judges are different from those asked in anthropological studies of the legal ways of a primitive culture, as in, for example,

Gluckman's study of Barotse jurisprudence or Adamson and Hoebel's study of Cheyenne law. The effort in the claims process to determine the relation between American Indians and the land was a political question for Congress; it did not partake of the scholarly neutrality that characterized social anthropological inquiry. And for the judges the question is how charitable Congress had decided to be. For a thoughtful criticism of the Commission by an ethnologist who was an expert witness in many ICC cases, see Lurie, *Epilogue,* in IRREDEEMABLE AMERICA: THE INDIANS' ESTATE AND LAND CLAIMS 363 (1985). Although the Indian Claims Commission is out of business, the following cases indicate some of the Commission's enduring legacy.

UNITED STATES v. DANN

470 U.S. 39 (1985)

Justice BRENNAN delivered the opinion of the Court.

The question presented in this case is whether the appropriation of funds into a Treasury account pursuant to 31 U.S.C. § 724a (1976 ed., Supp. V)[1] constitutes "payment" under § 22(a) of the Indian Claims Commission Act, 60 Stat. 1055, 25 U.S.C. § 70u(a) (1976 ed.).[2]

I

This case is an episode in a longstanding conflict between the United States and the Shoshone Tribe over title to lands in the western United States. In 1951 certain members of the Shoshone Tribe sought compensation for the loss of aboriginal title to lands located in California, Colorado, Idaho, Nevada, Utah, and Wyoming.[4] Eleven years later, the Indian Claims Commission entered an interlocutory order holding that the aboriginal title of the Western Shoshone had been extinguished in the latter part of the 19th century, *Shoshone Tribe v. United States,* 11 Ind. Cl. Comm'n 387, 416 (1962), and later awarded the Western Shoshone in excess of $26 million in compensation. *Western Shoshone Identifiable Group v. United States,* 40 Ind. Cl. Comm'n 318 (1977). The Court

---

[1] The statute provided:

"There are appropriated, out of any money in the Treasury not otherwise appropriated, such sums as may be necessary for the payment, not otherwise provided for, as certified by the Comptroller General, of final judgments, awards, and compromise settlements, which are payable in accordance with the terms of ... awards rendered by the Indian Claims Commission...."

[2] The statute provided:

"When the report of the Commission determining any claimant to be entitled to recover has been filed with Congress, such report shall have the effect of a final judgment of the Court of Claims, and there is authorized to be appropriated such sums as are necessary to pay the final determination of the Commission.

"The payment of any claim, after its determination in accordance with this Act, shall be a full discharge of the United States of all claims and demands touching any of the matters involved in the controversy."

The Indian Claims Commission was terminated on September 30, 1978, pursuant to 25 U.S.C. § 70v (1976 ed.).

[4] Section 2 of the Indian Claims Commission Act, 60 Stat. 1050, as amended, 25 U.S.C. § 70a (1976 ed.), authorized claims to be brought on behalf of "any Indian tribe, band, or other identifiable group of American Indians" for "claims arising from the taking by the United States, whether as the result of a treaty of cession or otherwise, of lands owned or occupied by the claimant without the payment for such lands of compensation agreed to by the claimant...."

of Claims affirmed this award. *Temoak Band of Western Shoshone Indians v. United States,* 593 F.2d 994 (Ct. Cl. 1979). On December 6, 1979, the Clerk of the Court of Claims certified the Commission's award to the General Accounting Office. Pursuant to 31 U.S.C. § 724a (1976 ed., Supp. V), this certification automatically appropriated the amount of the award and deposited it for the Tribe in an interest-bearing trust account in the Treasury of the United States.

Under 25 U.S.C. § 1402(a) and § 1403(a), the Secretary of the Interior is required, after consulting with the Tribe, to submit to Congress within a specified period of time a plan for the distribution of the fund. In this case, the Secretary has yet to submit a plan of distribution of the $26 million owing to the refusal of the Western Shoshone to cooperate in devising the plan. The fund apparently has now grown to $43 million.

In 1974, the United States brought an action in trespass against two sisters, Mary and Carrie Dann, members of an autonomous band of the Western Shoshone, alleging that the Danns, in grazing livestock without a permit from the United States, were acting in violation of regulations issued by the Secretary of the Interior under the authority of the Taylor Grazing Act, 43 U.S.C. § 315b. The 5,120 acres at issue in the suit are located in the northeast corner of Nevada. In response to the United States' suit, the Danns claimed that the land has been in the possession of their family from time immemorial and that their aboriginal title to the land precluded the Government from requiring grazing permits. The United States District Court for the District of Nevada rejected the Danns' argument and ruled that aboriginal title had been extinguished by the collateral-estoppel effect of the Indian Claims Commission's judgment in 1962. The Court of Appeals for the Ninth Circuit reversed and remanded, however, on the ground that "[w]hatever may have been the implicit assumptions of both the United States and the Shoshone Tribes during the litigation ... , the extinguishment question was not necessarily in issue, it was not actually litigated, and it has not been decided."

On remand, the District Court held that aboriginal title was extinguished when the final award of the Indian Claims Commission was certified for payment on December 6, 1979. On appeal, the Government defended the judgment of the District Court on the ground that the "full discharge" language of § 22(a) of the Indian Claims Commission Act, see n.2, *supra,* precluded the Danns from raising the defense of aboriginal title. Although Congress had not yet approved a plan for the distribution of the funds to the Western Shoshone, the United States maintained that the requirement of "payment" under § 22(a) was satisfied by the congressional appropriation of the $26 million award into the Treasury account. The Danns argued that until Congress approved a plan for the distribution of the money to the Tribe, "payment" was not satisfied.

The Court of Appeals held that "payment" had not occurred within the meaning of § 22(a) and reversed the District Court. The court reasoned that until a plan of distribution was adopted by the Congress, there remained "significant legal blocks in the way of delivery to the payee," and thus the "ordinary meaning" of payment was not satisfied. We granted certiorari to resolve the question of whether the certification of the award and appropriation under § 724a constitutes payment under § 22(a). We reverse.

II

The legislative purposes of the Indian Claims Commission Act and the principles of payment under the common law of trust as they have been applied to the context of relations between Native American communities and the United States require that we hold that "payment" occurs under § 22(a) when funds are placed by the United States into an account in the Treasury of the United States for the Tribe pursuant to 31 U.S.C. § 724a (1976 ed., Supp. V).

A

The Indian Claims Commission Act had two purposes. The "chief purpose of the [Act was] to dispose of the Indian claims problem with finality." H.R. Rep. No. 1466, 79th Cong., 1st Sess., 10 (1945). This purpose was effected by the language of § 22(a): "When the report of the Commission determining any claimant to be entitled to recover has been filed with Congress, such report shall have the effect of a final judgment of the Court of Claims ...." Section 22(a) also states that the "payment of any claim ... shall be a full discharge of the United States of all claims and demands touching any of the matters involved in the controversy." To hold, as the court below has, that payment does not occur until a final plan of distribution has been approved by Congress would frustrate the purpose of finality by postponing the preclusive effects of § 22(a) while subjecting the United States to continued liability for claims and demands that "touch" the matter previously litigated and resolved by the Indian Claims Commission.

The second purpose of the Indian Claims Commission Act was to transfer from Congress to the Indian Claims Commission the responsibility for determining the merits of native American claims. [Congressman Jackson, chairman of the House Committee on Indian Affairs noted during the floor debate] that the House was acting in response to a study by the Brookings Institution that had concluded that "there ought to be a prompt and final settlement of all claims between the Government and its Indian citizens, and that the best way to accomplish this purpose is to set up temporarily an Indian Claims Commission which will sift all these claims, subject to appropriate judicial review, and bring them to a conclusion once and for all." 92 Cong. Rec. 5312 (1946).

[L]anguage that Attorney General Clark asserted would give the decisions of the Indian Claims Commission the effect of a final judgment binding upon Congress [was deleted in the Senate version]. The Conference adopted the House version "in order to make perfectly clear the intention of both houses that the determinations of the Commission should, unless reversed [by the Court of Claims], have the same finality as judgments of the Court of Claims." H.R. Conf. Rep. No. 2693, 79th Cong., 2d Sess., 8 (1946). As enacted, the Indian Claims Commission Act explicitly incorporated this standard of finality in § 22(a).

The court below justified its decision on the ground that in making "payment" turn on the submission and approval of a final plan of distribution, Congress would have one last opportunity to review the merits of claims litigated before the Indian Claims Commission. This justification for delay obviously conflicts with the purpose of relieving Congress of the burden of having to resolve these claims.

B

[T]he Court of Appeals' interpretation is in conflict with the accepted legal uses of the word "payment" — uses we assume Congress intended to adopt when it enacted § 22(a). To accept the argument of the Court of Appeals would give the word "payment" a meaning that differs markedly from its common-law meaning, which has long been applied by this Court to the relations between Native American tribes and the United States.

The common law recognizes that payment may be satisfied despite the absence of actual possession of the funds by the creditor. Funds transferred from a debtor to an agent or trustee of the creditor constitute payment, and it is of no consequence that the creditor refuses to accept the funds from the agent or the agent misappropriates the funds. The rationale for this is that fiduciary obligations and the rules of agency so bind the trustee or agent to the creditor (*i.e.*, the beneficiary or principal) as to confer effective control of the funds upon the creditor.

The Court has applied these principles to relations between native American communities and the United States. In *Seminole Nation v. United States*, 316 U.S. 286 (1942), the United States was obligated by treaty to pay annual annuities to members of the Seminole Nation. Instead, the Government transferred the money to the Seminole General Council. Members of the Tribe argued that because the Seminole General Council had misappropriated the money, the Government had not satisfied its obligation to pay the individual members of the Tribe. In disposing of the case, the Court relied upon the rule that "a third party who pays money to a fiduciary for the benefit of the beneficiary, with knowledge that the fiduciary intends to misappropriate the money or otherwise be false to his trust, is a participant in the breach of trust and liable therefor to the beneficiary." *Id.*, at 296. The Court's holding was based on its recognition of the traditional rule that a debtor's payment to a fiduciary of the creditor satisfies the debt.

[T]he general rule in *Seminole Nation* is authority for our holding that the United States has made "payment" under § 22(a). The final award of the Indian Claims Commission placed the Government in a dual role with respect to the Tribe: the Government was at once a judgment debtor, owing $26 million to the Tribe, and a trustee for the Tribe responsible for ensuring that the money was put to productive use and ultimately distributed in a manner consistent with the best interests of the Tribe. In short, the Indian Claims Commission ordered the Government *qua* judgment debtor to pay $26 million to the Government *qua* trustee for the Tribe as the beneficiary. Once the money was deposited into the trust account, payment was effected.

[*Reversed and remanded.*]

PUEBLO OF SANTO DOMINGO v. UNITED STATES

647 F.2d 1087 (Ct. Cl. 1981),
cert. denied, 456 U.S. 1006 (1982)

KUNZIG, Judge, delivered the opinion of the court:

This is a petition originally filed with the Indian Claims Commission (ICC) in 1951 pursuant to the Indian Claims Commission Act [alleging] various trespasses by the federal Government on petitioner's alleged tribal lands. On October 29, 1969, attorneys for both sides filed a stipulation with ICC that the lands had in fact been taken and that the Government was liable for just compensation. This represented a significant change in the theory of the case. ICC thereafter determined the extent of the lands taken and the taking dates in a decision of May 9, 1973. 30 Ind. Cl. Comm. 234 (1973). This court then affirmed the holdings of ICC on this part of the case. [This] case, along with many others, was transferred to this court in an incomplete state upon the expiration of ICC's statutory life in 1978. No determination of the proper amount of compensation has yet been made.

This cause now comes before the court upon various motions and objections all of which center upon petitioner's request to withdraw from the stipulation of October 29, 1969. Petitioner contends that its *then* attorneys were not authorized to enter the stipulation and that, consequently, the stipulation should not be deemed to have binding effect. Our single response is that it is far too late in the day to make a motion of this nature.

The governing rules and principles are of the type we refer to as "hornbook law."

"An attorney employed for purposes of litigation has the general implied or apparent authority to enter into such stipulations or agreements, in connection with the conduct of the litigation, as appears to be necessary or expedient for the advancement of his client's interest or to accomplishment of the purpose for which the attorney was employed." 7A C.J.S. *Attorney and Client* § 205, at 341 (1980). "Such stipulations or agreements are binding on the client, without regard to the client's actual knowledge or consent." *Id.* at 341-342. "However, an attorney has no power to bind his client by an agreement or stipulation which he has not been expressly, impliedly, or apparently authorized to make." *Id.* at 342. *"[U]nless he has been specifically authorized to do so [i.e., not merely impliedly or apparently], an attorney may not by stipulation or agreement, surrender any substantial rights of his client...."* *Id.* (emphasis supplied). *"[T]here is a strong rebuttable presumption that the acts of an attorney are within the scope of his employment,* in the absence of a showing of the knowledge of the adverse party of restrictions thereon." *Id.,* § 172, at 258 (emphasis supplied). "There is a rebuttable presumption that an attorney has authority from his client to enter into a stipulation which may amount to a surrender of [his] client's rights, unless [the] adverse party as well as [the] court is aware that the attorney is acting in direct opposition to his client's instructions." *Id.* at 259 n.84.

Notwithstanding the foregoing limitations, "a client may be bound by a stipulation or agreement made by his attorney *without express authority"* where the client "fails to apply, seasonably, for relief from the stipulation." *Id.,* § 205, at 343 (emphasis supplied). The rationale presumably lies in the rule of agency that, "An affirmance of an unauthorized transaction can be inferred from a failure to repudiate it." Rest. (Second) of Agency § 94 (1958). Petitioner's attempt herein to withdraw from a stipulation entered nearly twelve years ago falls egregiously outside the permissible range of delay.

It has been said that, "Stipulations are looked upon with favor by the courts, since they tend to promote disposition of cases, simplification of issues and the saving of expense to litigants. The ends of justice are furthered by stipulations of settlement and the reluctance of courts to vitiate such agreements is founded in fundamental logic." [*In re Estate of Moss*, 248 N.E.2d 513, 516 (Ill. App. 1969).]

Procedurally, the pending motions are governed by Rule 152(b) of this court's rules of procedure. Rule 152(b) commands that the motion shall be made within a "reasonable time." We have stated that the Rule requires "diligence" upon the part of the moving party. *Andrade v. United States*, [485 F.2d 660, 664 (Ct. Cl. 1973)], *cert. denied sub nom. Pitt River Tribe v. United States*, 419 U.S. 831 (1974). Again, the conclusion is unavoidable that petitioner has tarried far too long. Time is now especially of the essence since Congress has expressed its desire that the special Indian claims litigation be wound up by having terminated the operations of the ICC in 1978.

All other arguments raised by petitioner, although not directly addressed in this opinion, have been considered and found to be without merit.

Accordingly, after consideration of the submissions of the parties, without oral argument of counsel, all of petitioner's interrelated motions and objections are denied. Defendant's objections are sustained. The case will go forward in the trial division in accordance with the stipulation of October 29, 1969, the ICC decision of May 9, 1973, and this court's affirming opinion of April 16, 1975.

NICHOLS, Judge, dissenting:

The court is denying the motions without oral argument or receipt of any testimony. I dissent, respectfully, because I do not think we should make a decision on the grounds given without the facts we do not have and which a trial judge could provide. I favor a remand to obtain those facts. The panel has such a useful set of assumptions it does not need facts.

The Indians, through new counsel, want to withdraw from a stipulation made for them in 1969 by former counsel, that specifies that the United States took (at an unstipulated date) the tracts involved in this litigation. They would revert to the theory stated in their original petition that defendant committed trespasses on their land but did not take it. After the stipulation the Commission, using the stipulation as a basis, determined the taking dates of the various tracts. [In the appeal] our panel did not have before it or consider whether any tract or tracts might in truth not have been taken at all.

That appeal was on an interlocutory order under 25 U.S.C. § 70s and no judgment was entered as a result of the affirmance, nor has there been one since. I assume, however, the decision is "law of the case" [and the] Indians may therefore reopen only if they can persuade the court that the decision "was clearly erroneous and works a manifest injustice." They say that they always wanted to limit claims to a trespass theory where possible and that their original counsel drafted the petition on that theory, yet in stipulating disregarded their express instructions. It is a seeming fact that many tribes have only belatedly recognized the pecuniary advantages of restricting their Indian Claims Commission taking claims to instances where a prior title extinguishment was unquestionable, whereas claimants in the earlier years of operations under the 1946 Act tended to try to maximize the extent of takings to maximize the cash thereby to be realized. This change threatens the early completion of our tasks under the Indian Claims Commission Act, and I share the panel's irritation towards it. But really belated changes in the thrust of the litigation are objectionable on equitable grounds which do not apply with equal force if that is what the tribe wanted all along. This distinction the panel cavalierly ignores. A mere self-serving statement of what Indians now say they always wanted would not be entitled to much weight, but here they proffer the original text of the petition and would show their original instructions to counsel and they may have a prima facie case. I would not take any of this on faith. I would permit the tribe to withdraw the stipulation and vacate the vol. 206 decision only on clear and convincing evidence that their original position was as alleged, that they communicated it to counsel in his instructions, that he violated the instructions without notice to them, and that they took timely action when they learned what he had done.

The Indians charge serious misconduct and conflict of interests on the part of their former counsel. Misconduct on the part of its trial bar is always a proper concern of a court and this is doubly true in the case of Indian litigants who are supposed to lack the capability to protect or perhaps even perceive their own interests vis-°-vis their counsel, and to monitor him where a conflict exists. The panel is not interested in finding out whether misconduct occurred. Presumably it knows by superrational intuition that the charges are unfounded. It is true that such charges have been a commonplace accompaniment of efforts to change the thrust of a tribal claim. Our Indian litigation bar is or perhaps was made up of upright persons and we have to make every reasonable presumption in their favor when misconduct charges lack specifics and are simply part of the thunder and lightning coming with a charge [sic] of front. Doubtless we must look for substantiation and specificity before we even investigate.

Unfortunately the machinery of the Indian Claims Commission Act is such as to generate conflicts of interest. One of many such situations is the one asserted here, *i.e.*, the attorney's interest, but not the tribe's is to effect a judicial sale, as it were, of tribal land at values of some historic past date, not of the present, to be set by the Commission, whether or not the Indians may in reality ever have had their title extinguished except by the ICC proceeding itself. One prediction I make with confidence, is that attorneys' conflicts of interests and the measures required to cope with them will loom larger in future litigation than they have in the past. [A] conflict long tacitly ignored in ICC cases is that the counsel's interest on the usual contingent fee basis turns only on the amount of award to be extracted from defendant; yet the tribe's interest is not only in the amount of the award, but also in minimizing what land title or claim thereto it has to give up, which may be substantial. Thus for example, a million dollar award may be better for counsel, but worse for the tribe, compared to a half million, if the former operates to extinguish Indian title to substantial tracts by virtue of 25 U.S.C. § 70u, while the latter does not. If the tribe thereby retains title to lands worth $500,000 or more, it gains by the smaller award. The Supreme Court in *United States v. Santa Fe Pacific Railroad*, 314 U.S. 339 (1941), sets forth the canon that received general lip service in ICC cases, that any alleged extinguishment of Indian title not the result of express congressional action "cannot be lightly implied." This was not always easy to implement where the Indians were expelled *de facto* but not *de jure*, and instances have occurred where awards were made and title extinguished by judgment where there was no expulsion even *de facto*. The tendency was to think if the Indians were alleging a tract was taken, no harm could follow from accepting their view. The right kind of Indian counsel are well aware of this kind of problem and are exceedingly careful their clients know of everything done, and have given well informed consent. I think Indians who allege attorney misconduct of this kind are entitled to have the fact at least mentioned in the decision throwing them out of court, are entitled to a hearing if they display a moderate amount of corroboration, and are entitled to corrective action, the law of the case rule notwithstanding, if they establish by clear and convincing evidence the misconduct actually occurred.

There is a remarkable parallel between the facts of this case and the instance in 1957 when new counsel saved the famous Sioux claim for the Black Hills taking when it was gasping on the ropes. On November 7, 1956, this court [upheld] an ICC decision denying the Black Hills claim, with others, in toto. [On] October 4, 1957, *i.e.*, almost a year later, new counsel filed a motion for rehearing to vacate the November 7, 1956, affirmance, and to remand to the ICC for a full and complete hearing and disposition on the merits. The motion relied on allegedly incompetent legal representation by [the Sioux Tribe's former attorney] resulting in the tribal claims being determined on the basis of a distorted and empty record. Specifically, they said [the attorney,] unknown to his clients —

(a) advised government counsel in secret he would drop certain claims,

(b) presented the claims that remained on an erroneous and untenable legal theory,

(c) urged a standard for measuring damages which the courts have always rejected,

(d) volunteered concessions contrary to fact,

(e) failed to conduct research, and

(f) did not prepare properly for trial.

The motion also faulted the ICC for not using its own investigative resources which, the movants said, were created in anticipation that the adversary system would not always protect the Indians. The movants said that in hearing the appeal, this court must have perceived that the Sioux were not competently represented.

The government opposition stated that the tribe continued [the attorney] as counsel after it could not but have observed his conduct at the trial, and for two years after the ensuing adverse ICC decision of April 5, 1954; the first expression of dissatisfaction by the tribe was almost a month after this court's decision of November 7, 1956. The government brief in opposition also cited a long array of decisions of this court in which defendant was not allowed to reopen cases lost because of the kind of counsel's error imputed to [the attorney].

It is easy to see what our present panel, with its incantation of "hornbook law," would have done with new counsel's egregious set of allegations and assertions, and how overwhelming it would have considered the government response to be.

This court as then constituted cannot be accused of reacting in haste or irritation. It withdrew its decision, though only after it had been published in F.

Supp., where it still may be read as an interesting relic. On November 5, 1958, it vacated its decision and remanded the case.

The order, signed by Chief Judge Marvin Jones, shows that the court did not undertake itself to pass on the sufficiency of the reasons assigned in the motion. The new counsel were not required to, and did not, supply affidavits or other documents in support. The order reads that the motion to vacate the judgment and to remand the case is granted to the extent the case is remanded for "a determination by the said Commission as to (1) whether the claimant Indians are entitled on the basis of statements made in support of the above motions to have the proof in this case reopened, and (2) if so, to receive the additional proof and … reconsider its prior decision in this matter." That is in essence the procedure I proposed here, that the panel rejected, *i.e.,* that our trier of fact should, subject of course to our review, pass on the sufficiency of statements made in support of the motion or motions.

The 1958 order was unpublished and apparently there was public confusion [regarding] what had happened to the case, though counsel knew it was back at the ICC. By a "summary of proceedings," 182 Ct. Cl. 912 (1968), we published a notice of what we had done 10 years before and where the case was. While this court did not spell out its reasons, it would appear by its actions to have taken into account the implicit major premise of the motion: that in the case of Indian litigants the ICC and this court were required not to visit on Indians the consequences of defective representation or attorney misconduct, which under the normal operation of the adversary system would be fatal to a claim. It was not necessary to spell this out to the judges of that day. This factor the panel here has wholly failed to take into account. There is somewhat of a presumption that Indian claimants are not competent to look after their own interests and the court must look after them. If the Pueblo of Santo Domingo is different, the panel has done nothing to establish the fact.

The Indians undertook to explain why they waited from 1969 to 1980 to complain about the stipulation. The panel by ignoring the explanation presumably holds it is inadequate, the function we assigned to the trier of fact in the *Sioux* case. I would have cautioned the Indians to make their explanation a good one. The panel rightly says that the motions are under our Rule 152 and the applicable standard in passing on such a motion is whether the party seeking relief has acted within a reasonable time, and that "diligence is required." *Andrade v. United States,* [*supra*], involved a compromise settlement the ICC approved, but which dissident Indians wished to attack. They had attacked it before the ICC. They wanted an appellate review of the approval decision before this court but they were inordinately dilatory in asking for it. [W]e had the full fact findings of the ICC [and] knew the dissidents had alleged to the ICC, years earlier, the same acts of attorney misconduct they charged here. Thus we needed no further fact finding. The case is certainly not authority, as it is used, for erecting a kind of irrebuttable presumption that a lapse of time, 11 years or any other, is so excessive that no fact finding is necessary and no explanation will be listened to.

I suppose I will be charged with being soft on Indian claims and with wishing to prolong Indian litigation. Neither is my intention. The panel refers to the desire of the Congress that the Indian claims litigation be wound up. The

Congress also desired that all litigable pre-1946 claims be disposed of under the 1946 Act, so it would not have to deal again with the importunities of Indian claimants, as before 1946 it had to do. If the panel decision stands, the Indians may, if they are sincere, decide to forgo the valuation phase of the case and allow their petition to be dismissed. The court cannot prevent their making that election, though it can dismiss with prejudice. We all know that a dismissal with prejudice means little in Indian litigation. Indians, like the Sioux, lose with prejudice over and over again, and still they return. When the Indians are back on the doorstep of Congress demanding further legislative relief, Congress may want to know why the ICC and ourselves have not heard the importunities of the Indians, found the facts, and decided what relief is appropriate on the basis of facts, not arbitrary irrebuttable presumptions. Thus I predict that the panel may well prolong Indian litigation more than my solution would have done. Frankly, I think it unlikely that pre-1946 Indian claims will be finally laid to rest in the lifetime of any present members of the court, say nothing of new ones coming along. The 1946 Act was not very successful as an appeaser of Indian discontent, or as a solution to their social problems, but as a breeder of costly and prolonged litigation, it has been a triumph beyond anyone's fondest hopes. I think the panel and I might allow one another credit for both desiring to lay this hydra-headed monster in its grave as soon as it can decently and lawfully be done. It is easier to start something like this than stop it, however. In this instance, I respectfully differ with the panel as to the means.

What we have here is a decision possibly within the court's discretionary power, for the guidelines on exercise of Rule 152 authority are few and not specific. Still the decision in its unwisdom is "an exercise of *raw* judicial power" in the deathless words of Justice White, dissenting in *Roe v. Wade,* 410 U.S. 113, 222 (1973). I emphasize the word "raw." To end with another quote, the prophet Job lamented: "Would that mine enemy had written a book." This court, like other courts, is not entirely without enemies, and I do not know anything we could say or do that would give them more satisfaction than the panel opinion herein.

NOTES

1. **History of the Western Shoshone Title Litigation:** In the *Dann* case, the Dann Band's title land was held to have been extinguished by an Indian Claims Commission proceeding to which the Dann Band was not a party, even though the Dann sisters had never abandoned their land. One commentator has described the origin of this type of problem as follows:

> [O]nce the representative of an identifiable group is recognized, this claimant group is the exclusive representative of all tribal descendants, even though not all of the competing interests are represented. This situation arises where Indians still occupy aboriginal land, and are therefore unlikely to file a claim with the ICC for lands to which they apparently still hold title. Members who were displaced by the government from a portion of the tribal land, however, had a monetary incentive to include the entire ancestral parcel in their claim. Furthermore, Indians still living on aboriginal land may not have had notice that a separate descendant group claimed the extinguishment of aboriginal title. Then, when the Indians occupying aboriginal land attempted to intervene in the ICC proceedings, they were usually denied the right because the proceedings were at an advanced stage.

Orlando, *Aboriginal Title Claims in the Indian Claims Commission: United States v. Dann and Its Due Process Implications,* 13 B.C. ENVTL. AFF. L. REV. 241, 261 (1986).*

The dry language of the Supreme Court's opinion in *United States v. Dann* obscures a long-fought battle by various bands of Western Shoshone Indians to obtain a court ruling that title to their land in Nevada had never been extinguished by a sovereign act. Complicating this effort was the fact that the Western Shoshone never constituted a monolithic Indian "tribe," as most non-Indians conceive of that concept. Instead, the Western Shoshone consisted of a loose confederation of autonomous groups bound together by cultural and clan affiliations. When the Temoak Bands of Western Shoshone, one of 22 Western Shoshone tribes, filed a claim for compensation for a taking of aboriginal title in the Indian Claims Commission, the Commission designated as plaintiff an entity called "the Western Shoshone Identifiable Group," constituted solely for the purpose of litigating the claim. In other words, this group, selected at meetings called by the Temoak Band's attorneys, did not serve any political function in the Western Shoshone Nation. The Indian Claims Commission held that the Western Shoshone lost their land "by gradual encroachment by whites, settlers and others, and the acquisition, disposition or taking of their lands by the United States for its own use and benefit ...." Because no single incident could be pinpointed as the taking date, the Commission concluded it could "not now definitely set the date of acquisition of these lands." *Shoshone Tribe v. United States,* 11 Ind. Cl. Comm'n 387, 416 (1962). In 1966, the Western Shoshone Identifiable Group, through its attorney, entered into a stipulation with the government setting a formal taking date in the nineteenth century in order to proceed to the valuation phase, which eventually resulted in the $26 million judgment discussed in the *Dann* case. *Western Shoshone Identifiable Group v. United States,* 29 Ind. Cl. Comm'n 5, 7 (1972) (decision and description of stipulation).

The problem was that most Western Shoshone people still lived on some 3 million acres of land to which they held unextinguished aboriginal title. It appears that the plaintiffs in the Indian Claims Commission proceeding sincerely believed that the taking date settled the issue only as to land no longer controlled by the Western Shoshone people. In the early 1970's, a group of Western Shoshones became concerned about the effect of the claims proceedings on their present title. They attempted to intervene in the Indian Claims Commission proceeding and obtain a stay of the judgment pending presentation of an amended claim to excise land presently occupied by Western Shoshone people from the compensation claim. The Court of Claims ultimately characterized this attempt as an intratribal conflict over litigation strategy and held that the intervention came too late. *Western Shoshone Legal Defense & Educ. Ass'n v. United States,* 531 F.2d 495 (Ct. Cl.), *cert. denied,* 429 U.S. 855 (1976).

Mary and Carrie Dann had been active in this attempt to escape the effects of the judgment. In 1974, the Dann sisters were cited for trespass by the government. In 1976, the Temoak Band discharged their attorney and decided to join the attempt to establish title to the unextinguished lands. In a letter to the Secretary of the Interior, the Band's Chairman explained why this seeming late shift in strategy had occurred:

There are many strange things about the way these lawyers have operated. They no longer report to us but to a "claims committee" which was elected by just a few Indians and has no rules or any way for the people to control them. These lawyers not only have refused to protect the title to the land we still have but have fought our people who have tried to do it themselves through the Western Shoshone Legal Defense and Education Association.

We have now fired these lawyers and are looking for a replacement."

Respondents' Appendix at R2-R3, *United States v. Dann,* 470 U.S. 39 (1985).

Again the commission turned down the request for a stay and issued its final award. 40 Ind. Cl. Comm'n 305 (1977), *aff'd, Temoak Band v. United States,* 593 F.2d 994 (Ct. Cl.), *cert. denied,* 444 U.S. 973 (1979). *See generally Western Shoshone Identifiable Group v. United States,* 652 F.2d 41, 48-49 (Ct. Cl. 1981) (history of the litigation in the context of requests for review of attorney fee award).

The Ninth Circuit held that the Danns were not precluded from relitigating the issue of title in their trespass case because it had not been fully litigated in the Indian Claims Commission proceeding. Furthermore, the Ninth Circuit held res judicata did not attach because Claims Commission judgment would not be final until Congress actually paid the money to the Western Shoshone people. *United States v. Dann,* 706 F.2d 919, 927 (9th Cir. 1983). Is there any claim the Danns can still assert after the Supreme Court decision? For the answer, see section E, note 1, *infra.*

2. **The Preclusive Effect of ICC Judgments:** Does the Court's opinion in *Dann* stand for the proposition that aboriginal title can be extinguished by encroachment or abandonment? On the issue of finality, since the money remained in the Treasury at the time of the opinion, what was the Court's theory of payment? How could the Danns be bound by a judgment to which they were never a party? In *Hansberry v. Lee,* 311 U.S. 32 (1940), the Court held that giving res judicata effect to class judgment in which potential claimants were not given notice or an opportunity to opt out violated due process. If, as the Court maintains, a major purpose of the Indian Claims Commission was to provide a forum to fully and finally litigate all remaining Indian land claims, why were there no procedures guaranteeing intervention by all interested parties? The Claims Commission early held it had no jurisdiction over individual Indian claims. Nothing in its rules prevented the Indian Claims Commission from permitting intervention for interested autonomous groups like the Dann Band. Congressional eagerness to resolve outstanding claims may have contributed to its legislative vision of all Indian tribes as cohesive groups having a central organization that could represent tribal wishes on litigation strategy. Nevertheless, in a case in which it was clear from the start that no such group existed, the Claims Court should have been more willing to permit intervention, in light of potential due process concerns. Does the Court in *Dann* address the due process issues? For a criticism of the Court's opinion, see Orlando, *Aboriginal Title Claims in the Indian Claims Commission: United States v. Dann and Its Due Process Implications,* 13 B.C. ENVTL. AFF. L. REV. 241 (1986).

3. **Election of Remedies:** The Indian Claims Commission early held that its jurisdiction was limited to granting money damages. *Osage Nation v. United States,* 1 Ind. Cl. Comm'n 54 (1948), *rev'd on other grounds,* 97 F. Supp. 381 (Ct. Cl.), *cert. denied,* 342 U.S. 896 (1951). Even before *Dann,* federal courts refused to take jurisdiction over attempts by tribes seeking to block distribution of ICC judgments in order to seek alternative remedies, holding that the Indian Claims Commission provided the exclusive forum for land claims. *See, e.g.,*

Oglala Sioux Tribe v. United States, 650 F.2d 140 (8th Cir. 1981), *cert. denied,* 455 U.S. 907 (1982) (the ICC was the exclusive forum for all Indian treaty claims); *Six Nations Confederacy v. Andrus,* 610 F.2d 996, 998 (D.C. Cir. 1979), *cert. denied,* 447 U.S. 922 (1980) (attempt to enjoin distribution of judgment funds to avoid finality).

This principle was extended even further in *Navajo Tribe v. New Mexico,* 809 F.2d 1455 (10th Cir. 1987). The tribe argued that President Teddy Roosevelt's action in restoring 1.9 million acres of tribal executive order land to the public domain was invalid because it violated a statute requiring that the land be allotted to Navajos before being restored. The tribe argued that all patents issued after restoration were invalid and sued private and public landowners as well as the United States as guardian, seeking declaratory relief as well as damages from the landowners for the use of the land. The Tenth Circuit dismissed the claim against the United States, relying on *Oglala Sioux, supra.* The tribe distinguished *Oglala Sioux* as a case in which compensation had been received for the land taken, while in this case no claim had been filed nor had any compensation been received. Since the Indian Claims Commission could only award damages for a taking of land, and since the tribe was seeking a declaration that it still possessed equitable title in the land, the tribe argued that its claim should be permitted to continue in the district court. The Tenth Circuit rejected this argument, relying on language in *Dann* that the purpose of the Claims Commission was to settle all Indian land claims. The Court held that one purpose of the Indian Claims Commission Act was to restrict tribes to money damages remedies, and thus work a judicial sale of land in order to prevent tribes from dispossessing third parties who currently occupied the land. As a result, the court held the tribe's claim was exclusively cognizable in the Indian Claims Commission. Since the claim accrued in the early twentieth century, the claim was thus time-barred. The Tenth Circuit also upheld the dismissal of the case as to all the other defendants on the grounds that the United States was an indispensable party.

4. Attorney-Client Relationships in Claims Cases: What was the basis of the tribe's argument that their attorney had a conflict of interest in *Pueblo of Santo Domingo?* If the argument is that the Indian Claims Commission Act virtually guaranteed attorneys representing the tribes a 10% fee, would such an argument provide a basis for overturning other Indian Claims Commission judgments? What was the majority's major concern in denying the motion? Did Judge Nichols's dissent adequately address these concerns? Note that in both principal cases stipulations figured prominently. In *Dann,* the attorney for the Western Shoshone Identifiable Group stipulated to the date of taking in order to permit the claim to proceed to the valuation phase. In *Santo Domingo,* the attorney stipulated that the lands had been taken, thus changing the theory of the case from a trespass claim under which the tribe would have an opportunity to establish its ownership of the land and claim damages for trespass. As of 1989, the Pueblo was still unsuccessfully attempting to get the stipulation overturned. *Pueblo of Santo Domingo v. United States,* 16 Cl. Ct. 139 (1988) (motion to reopen to amend stipulation based on newly discovered evidence held untimely). In each case the tribe or an element of a tribe also attempted to dismiss the tribal attorney (*Pueblo of Santo Domingo*) or at least establish that the attorney did not represent all the constituent elements of the tribe (*Dann*).

The entire claims process including the role of claims attorneys has been criticized in recent years. *See, e.g.,* V. DELORIA, JR., BEHIND THE TRAIL OF

CONCEPTS OF PROPERTY IN FEDERAL INDIAN LAW

BROKEN TREATIES 23-41 (1974); Price, *Lawyers on the Reservation: Some Implications for the Legal Profession,* 1969 ARIZ. ST. L.J. 161, 187-90. A particularly thoughtful assessment can be found in Lurie, *Epilogue,* in IRREDEEMABLE AMERICA: THE INDIANS ESTATE AND LAND CLAIMS 363 (I. Sutton ed. 1985). Nevertheless before the legal services and public interest law movements created organizations that represented tribes without charge, tribes had a great deal of difficulty securing legal help.

b. The Court of Claims

The Indian Claims Commission also provided that claims accruing after 1946 would be presented in the Court of Claims as follows:

> The United States Claims Court shall have jurisdiction of any claim against the United States accruing after August 13, 1946, in favor of any tribe, band, or other identifiable group of American Indians residing within the territorial limits of the United States or Alaska whenever such claim is one arising under the Constitution, laws or treaties of the United States, or Executive orders of the President, or is one which otherwise would be cognizable in the Court of Claims if the claimant were not an Indian tribe, band or group.

28 U.S.C. § 1505 (as amended). Under section 1505, are claims for the extinguishment of aboriginal title compensable if they accrue after August 13, 1946? What is the legal effect of this provision on executive order title? Could such a jurisdictional provision be read to have recognized title to all executive order reservations? If, on the other hand, the President has no power to create a compensable interest in land, could the government argue that a particular executive order did not create a claim within the meaning of section 1505? Would such an interpretation make the phrase regarding executive orders meaningless? *Cf. United States v. Mitchell,* 463 U.S. 206, 218-19 (1983) (Section 1505 did not create any new claims, but merely opened up the Court of Claims to Indian tribes on an equal footing with other citizens).

c. Legislative Resolution of Indian Tribal Claims

Congress has occasionally resolved disputes regarding the extent, duration and scope of Indian land tenure. These congressional actions take several forms. First, Congress has occasionally restored land to a tribe. Second, Congress has resolved claims to large areas of land in legislation often called settlement acts. The term is a misnomer, since the legislation has not always been based on a consensual transaction. For instance, the Alaska Native Claims Settlement Act was not based on a formal agreement with the Natives of Alaska, while the Maine Indian Tribes Settlement Act had the formal consent of the affected tribes. Finally, the Navajo and Hopi Relocation Act, discussed *supra* section B3, note 5, represents a unique legislative attempt to resolve intertribal Indian land conflict. Tribes in the west, where public land is plentiful, have been successful in getting more than 500,000 acres of their former land restored to them out of the public domain. *See* Barsh, *Indian Land Claims Policy in the United States,* 58 N.D.L. REV. 7, 73 & n.358 (1982) (collecting statutes). The return of the Blue Lake to the Taos Pueblo is perhaps the best-known example, but other tribes have also had modest amounts of land restored. *See* Martin, *From Judgment to*

Restoration: The Havasupai Land Claims Case, in IRREDEEMABLE AMERICA: THE INDIANS' ESTATE AND LAND CLAIMS 71 (1985) (return of 185,000 acres to reservation and grant of exclusive use for traditional purposes of 95,300 acres of National Forest). *See generally* Sutton, *Incident or Event? Land Restoration in the Claims Process,* in *id.,* at 211.

Claims settlements have taken many forms. For instance, the Pueblo Lands Act of 1924, 43 Stat. 636, which established an executive commission to adjudicate and confirm Pueblo title, is discussed in note 20 of the *Tee-Hit-Ton* case, *supra* section B1. For a recent Supreme Court discussion of this law, see *Mountain States Tel. & Tel. Co. v. Pueblo of Santa Ana,* 472 U.S. 237 (1985). Legislation of this type often establishes an executive commission or refers the land dispute to judicial resolution while simultaneously legislating a partial or complete standard for arbitration or adjudication of the dispute. See also the California Land Claims Act of 1851, 9 Stat. 631 (executive commission), discussed in Cramer, *supra,* at 181. *See generally* Flushman & Barbieri, *Aboriginal Title: The Special Case of California,* 17 PAC. L.J. 391 (1986) (arguing the Act extinguished all aboriginal title in California not confirmed by the executive commission).

In other cases such legislation may itself impose a settlement of the dispute. Two of the recently settled Eastern land claims illustrate some of the differing approaches. Each involved a statutory ratification of an agreement by the parties. In the Rhode Island Indian Claims Settlement Act, the Narragansett Tribe was awarded three and one-half million dollars and certain lands. 25 U.S.C. 1701-1706. The Rhode Island settlement authorized the Narragansett to incorporate as a state corporation and to hold their lands in corporate hands. The Act specifically provided that "the settlement lands shall be subject to the civil and criminal laws and jurisdiction of the State of Rhode Island." 25 U.S.C. § 1708. Furthermore, 25 U.S.C. § 1707(c) specifically authorized the corporation "to grant or otherwise convey (including any involuntary conveyance by means of eminent domain or condemnation proceedings) any easement for public or private purposes pursuant to the laws of the State of Rhode Island." That section also specified that the United States would have no further duties or liabilities to the Narragansetts, their corporation, or their lands other than implementing the settlement legislation. However, section 1707 also authorized the Secretary of the Interior to recognize the Narragansetts and provided that in the case of such recognition "the settlement lands may not be sold, granted, or otherwise conveyed or leased to anyone other than the Indian Corporation, and no such disposition of the settlement lands shall be of any validity in law or equity, unless the same is approved by the Secretary pursuant to regulations adopted by him for that purpose." *See also* Pub. L. No. 96-484, 94 Stat. 2365 (resolving claims of unrecognized Pamunkey Tribe of Virginia against a railroad for noncompliance with federal restraint on alienation of Indian land).

The statutes settling the claims by the Passamaquoddy, Penobscot, and Maliseet Indians to large portions of the state of Maine are considerably more complex. Maine Indian Claims Settlement Act of 1980, codified at 25 U.S.C. §§ 1721-1735. The federal legislation establishes two separate trust funds. The Maine Indian Claims Settlement Fund established by the federal legislation was authorized $27 million in appropriations, the income of which was to be divided evenly between the Passamaquoddy and Penobscot tribes. Additionally the federal legislation established a $54.5 million Maine Indian Claims Land Acquisition Fund, with $26.8 million allocated each to the Passamaquoddy and Penobscot tribes and $900,000 held in trust for the Houlton Band of the Maliseet Indians. Under the Act the existing holdings of the Passamaquoddy and Penobscot tribes together with the first 150,000 acres acquired for each tribe with funds from the Land Acquisition Fund were to be held by the United States in trust for the tribe. Smaller holdings were envisioned for the Maliseets. Land so held was subjected to the restraints against alienation normally applied to Indian lands and may be leased, timbered, or subjected to the acquisition of rights-of-way only in accordance with existing federal Indian law. 25 U.S.C. § 1724(g)(2) & (3). However, the Act specifically authorizes the Secretary to sell trust land "if at the time of sale the Secretary has entered into an option agreement or contract of sale to purchase other lands of approximate equal value." *Id.* § 1724(g)(3)(f). Both the federal legislation and the Maine Implementing Act authorize the state condemnation of Passamaquoddy, Penobscot, or Maliseet lands but require compensation in the form of substitute lands or require the reinvestment of the proceeds of such compensation in acreage within the unorganized or unincorporated areas of the state of Maine to add to the tribes' land bases. *Id.* § 1724(i).

Unlike the Alaska Native Claims Settlement Act and the Rhode Island Indian Claims Settlement Act, the Maine Indian Claims Settlement Act abandons the corporate model of settlement and adopts a modified and diminished sovereignty approach. Under the federal legislation the federal government disclaims criminal jurisdiction. *Id.* § 1725(c). The Act provides that upon its implementation the members of the affected tribes "shall be subject to the civil and criminal jurisdiction of the State, the laws of the State, and the civil and criminal jurisdiction of the courts of the State, to the same extent as any other person...." *Id.* § 1725(a). The Act also authorizes the affected tribes and other members to sue or be sued in both state and federal courts. The state legislation implementing the settlement provides for continuing sovereign immunity "when the respective tribe or nation is acting in its governmental capacity to the same extent as any municipality or like officers or employees thereof within the state." ME. REV. STAT. ANN. tit. 30, § 6206(2) (1980 Supp.).

The Maine Implementing Act specifically authorizes the tribe to exercise jurisdiction over lesser offenses, lesser juvenile crimes, civil actions arising on the reservation, Indian child custody matters, and other domestic relations matters, including marriage, divorce, and support. ME. REV. STAT. ANN. tit. 30, § 6209 (1980 Supp.). The Maine Implementing Act also recognizes the exclusive right of the tribes to enforce tribal law on the reservations and the concurrent power of state law enforcement agencies to enforce applicable state laws on the reservations. ME. REV. STAT. ANN. tit. 30, § 6210 (1980 Supp.). While the Maine Implementing Act expressly analogizes the Indian tribes to domestic municipalities for many purposes, it provides that the prosecution in tribal court for a criminal or juvenile offense over which one of the tribes has jurisdiction shall not bar or constitute collateral estoppel in a prosecution in state court arising out of the same conduct over which the state has jurisdiction. *Id.* § 6209(4) (1980 Supp.). Under the Maine Implementing Act the affected tribes are eligi-

ble for participation and entitled to receive whatever program benefits the state
provides to municipalities and tribal members are eligible for all benefits and
services provided to other persons in the state. *Id.* § 6211 (1980 Supp.).

While the trust funds established by the federal legislation are tax exempt, the
Maine Implementing Act calls for the affected tribes to:

> make payments in lieu of taxes on all real and personal property within their respec-
> tive Indian territory in an amount equal to that which would otherwise be imposed ...
> on such real and personal property provided, however, that any real or personal
> property within Indian territory used by either tribe or nation predominantly for
> governmental purposes shall be exempt from taxation to the same extent that such
> real or personal property owned by a municipality is exempt under the laws of the
> State.

Id. § 6208(2) (1980 Supp.).

The Maine settlement also recognizes the right of the affected tribes to regulate hunting, trapping, the taking of wildlife from Indian territory, and fishing
in small tribally owned ponds. However, it requires the tribes to establish and
maintain registration stations for accurate recording and reporting of wildlife
taken. Fishing in all rivers or streams in Indian territory or any pond over ten
acres is regulated by the state. However the Maine Implementing Act provides
that no state law, rule, or regulation may prevent tribal members from taking
fish within reservation boundaries "for their individual sustenance" unless the
state Commissioner of Inland Fisheries and Wildlife has reason to fear a significant depletion of fish outside of the boundaries of the reservation and has
notified the affected tribe and sought remedial legislation and the tribe has
failed to take satisfactory action. *Id.* § 6207 (1980 Supp.).

C. PROTECTION OF INDIAN POSSESSION

UNITED STATES ex rel. HUALPAI INDIANS v. SANTA FE PACIFIC RAILROAD CO.

314 U.S. 339 (1941)

Mr. Justice DOUGLAS delivered the opinion of the Court.

This is a suit brought by the United States, in its own right and as guardian of
the Indians of the Walapai (Hualpai) Tribe in Arizona (28 U.S.C. § 41(1), § 24
Judicial Code) to enjoin respondent from interfering with the possession and
occupancy by the Indians of certain land in northwestern Arizona. Respondent
claims full title to the lands in question under the grant to its predecessor, the
Atlantic and Pacific Railroad Co., provided for in the Act of July 27, 1866, 14
Stat. 292. The bill sought to establish that respondent's rights under the grant
of 1866 are subject to the Indians' right of occupancy both inside and outside
their present reservation which was established by the Executive Order of President Arthur, January 4, 1883. The bill consists of two causes of action — the
first relating to lands inside, and the second, to lands outside, that reservation.
The bill prayed, *inter alia,* that title be quieted and that respondent "account for
all rents, issues and profits derived from the leasing, renting or use of the lands
subject to said right of occupancy" by the Indians. Respondent moved to dismiss
on the ground that the facts alleged were "insufficient to constitute a valid cause
of action in equity." The District Court granted that motion [and the] Court of

Appeals affirmed. We granted the petition for certiorari because of the importance of the problems raised in the administration of the Indian laws and the land grants.

Sec. 2 of the Act of July 27, 1866, the Act under which respondent's title to the lands in question derived, provided: "The United States shall extinguish, as rapidly as may be consistent with public policy and the welfare of the Indians, and only by their voluntary cession, the Indian title to all lands falling under the operation of this act and acquired in the donation to the road named in the act."

Basic to the present causes of action is the theory that the lands in question were the ancestral home of the Walapais, that such occupancy constituted "Indian title" within the meaning of § 2 of the 1866 Act, which the United States agreed to extinguish, and that in absence of such extinguishment the grant to the railroad "conveyed the fee subject to this right of occupancy." *Buttz v. Northern Pacific Railroad,* 119 U.S. 55, 66. The Circuit Court of Appeals concluded that the United States had never recognized such possessory rights of Indians within the Mexican Cession[2] and that in absence of such recognition the Walapais had no such right good against grantees of the United States.

Occupancy necessary to establish aboriginal possession is a question of fact to be determined as any other question of fact. If it were established as a fact that the lands in question were, or were included in, the ancestral home of the Walapais in the sense that they constituted definable territory occupied exclusively by the Walapais (as distinguished from lands wandered over by many tribes), then the Walapais had "Indian title" which, unless extinguished, survived the railroad grant of 1866.

"Unquestionably it has been the policy of the Federal Government from the beginning to respect the Indian right of occupancy, which could only be interfered with or determined by the United States." *Cramer v. United States,* 261 U.S. 219, 227. This policy was first recognized in [*Johnson v. M'Intosh*] and has been repeatedly reaffirmed. [*E.g., Worcester v. Georgia.*] As stated in *Mitchel v. United States,* [9 Pet. 711,] 746, the Indian "right of occupancy is considered as sacred as the fee simple of the whites." Whatever may have been the rights of the Walapais under Spanish law, the *Cramer* case assumed that lands within the Mexican Cession were not excepted from the policy to respect Indian right of occupancy. Though the *Cramer* case involved the problem of individual Indian occupancy, this Court stated that such occupancy was not to be treated differently from "the original nomadic tribal occupancy." (p. 227.) Perhaps the assumption that aboriginal possession would be respected in the Mexican Cession was, like the generalizations in *Johnson v. M'Intosh, supra,* not necessary for the narrow holding of the case. But such generalizations have been so often and so long repeated as respects land under the prior sovereignty of the various European nations, including Spain, that, like other rules governing titles to property they should now be considered no longer open. Furthermore, treaties negotiated with Indian tribes, wholly or partially within the Mexican Cession, for delimitation of their occupancy rights or for the settlement and adjustment of their boundaries, constitute clear recognition that no different policy as respects aboriginal possession obtained in this area than in other areas. Certainly it

---

[2]See Treaty of Guadalupe Hidalgo, 9 Stat. 922.

would take plain and unambiguous action to deprive the Walapais of the benefits of that policy. For it was founded on the desire to maintain just and peaceable relations with Indians. The reasons for its application to other tribes are no
less apparent in case of the Walapais, a savage tribe which in early days caused
the military no end of trouble.

Nor is it true, as respondent urges, that a tribal claim to any particular lands
must be based upon a treaty, statute, or other formal government action. As
stated in the *Cramer* case, "The fact that such right of occupancy finds no
recognition in any statute or other formal governmental action is not conclusive." 261 U.S. at 229.

Extinguishment of Indian title based on aboriginal possession is of course a
different matter. The power of Congress in that regard is supreme. The manner, method and time of such extinguishment raise political, not justiciable,
issues. As stated by Chief Justice Marshall in *Johnson v. M'Intosh, supra,* p. 586,
"the exclusive right of the United States to extinguish" Indian title has never
been doubted. And whether it be done by treaty, by the sword, by purchase, by
the exercise of complete dominion adverse to the right of occupancy, or otherwise, its justness is not open to inquiry in the courts. If the right of occupancy of
the Walapais was not extinguished prior to the date of definite location of the
railroad in 1872, then the respondent's predecessor took the fee subject to the
encumbrance of Indian title. For on that date the title of respondent's predecessor attached as of July 27, 1866.

Certainly, prior to 1865 any right of occupancy of the Walapais to the lands in
question was not extinguished; nor was the policy of respecting such Indian title
changed. The Indian Trade and Intercourse Act of June 30, 1834, 4 Stat. 729,
was extended over "the Indian tribes in the Territories of New Mexico and
Utah" by § 7 of the Act of February 27, 1851, 9 Stat. 574, 587. The 1834 Act,
which derived from the Act of July 22, 1790, 1 Stat. 137, made it an offense to
drive stock to range or feed "on any land belonging to any Indian or Indian
tribe, without the consent of such tribe" (§ 9); gave the superintendent of Indian
affairs authority "to remove from the Indian country all persons found therein
contrary to law" (§ 10); made it unlawful to settle on "any lands belonging,
secured, or granted by treaty with the United States to any Indian tribe" (§ 11);
and made invalid any conveyance of lands "from any Indian nation or tribe of
Indians." (§ 12).

[In] the Act of March 3, 1865, 13 Stat. 541, 559, which provided:

> "All that part of the public domain in the Territory of Arizona, lying west of a direct
> line from Half-Way Bend to Corner Rock on the Colorado River, containing about
> seventy-five thousand acres of land, shall be set apart for an Indian reservation for the
> Indians of said river and its tributaries."

It is plain that the Indians referred to included the Walapais. The suggestion
for removing various Indian tribes in this area to a reservation apparently
originated with a former Indian agent, Superintendent Poston, who was a Territorial Representative in Congress in 1865. His explanation on the floor of the
House of the bill, which resulted in the creation of the 1865 reservation, indicates that he had called a council of the confederated tribes of the Colorado,
including the Walapais, and had told them that "they should abandon" their
lands and confine themselves to the place on the Colorado river which was later

proposed for a reservation. He entered into no agreement with them nor did he propose a treaty. He merely stated that if elected to Congress he would try to get Congress to provide for them. As stated by the Commissioner of Indian Affairs in 1864, "Assuming that the Indians have a right of some kind to the soil, Mr. Poston's arrangement proposes a compromise with [them]."

We search the public records in vain for any clear and plain indication that Congress in creating the Colorado River reservation was doing more than making an offer to the Indians, including the Walapais, which it was hoped would be accepted as a compromise of a troublesome question. We find no indication that Congress by creating that reservation intended to extinguish all of the rights which the Walapais had in their ancestral home. That Congress could have effected such an extinguishment is not doubted. But an extinguishment cannot be lightly implied in view of the avowed solicitude of the Federal Government for the welfare of its Indian wards. As stated in *Choate v. Trapp*, 224 U.S. 665, 675, the rule of construction recognized without exception for over a century has been that "doubtful expressions, instead of being resolved in favor of the United States, are to be resolved in favor of a weak and defenseless people, who are wards of the nation, and dependent wholly upon its protection and good faith." Nor was there any plain intent or agreement on the part of the Walapais to abandon their ancestral lands if Congress would create a reservation. Furthermore, the Walapais did not accept the offer which Congress had tendered. In 1874 they were, however, forcibly removed to the Colorado River reservation on order from the Indian Department. But they left it in a body the next year. And it was decided "to allow them to remain in their old range during good behavior." They did thereafter remain in their old country and engaged in no hostilities against the whites. No further attempt was made to force them onto the Colorado River reservation, even though Congress had made various appropriations to defray the costs of locating the Arizona Indians in permanent abodes, including the Colorado River reservation. On these facts we conclude that the creation of the Colorado River reservation was, so far as the Walapais were concerned, nothing more than an abortive attempt to solve a perplexing problem. Their forcible removal in 1874 was not pursuant to any mandate of Congress. It was a high-handed endeavor to wrest from these Indians lands which Congress had never declared forfeited.[13] No forfeiture can be predicated on an unauthorized attempt to effect a forcible settlement on the reservation, unless we are to be insensitive to the high standards for fair dealing in light of which laws dealing with Indian rights have long been read. Certainly,

---

[13] See Walapai Papers, [S. Doc. No. 273, 74th Cong., 2d Sess.,] p. 108. General Schofield reported on May 24, 1875, to the Adjutant General as follows:

"The Hualpai Indians have been our firm friends for many years, and our active allies whenever their services have been required against the hostile Apaches. In return for their fidelity they have been treated with great injustice and cruelty. They were forced to leave their homes in the mountains and go upon a reservation in the Colorado desert, where they have suffered from the extreme heat, to which they were unaccustomed, from disease, and from hunger."

"The injustice and bad faith shown by the government toward the Hualpais and the Indians which Gen'l. Crook had collected upon the Verde reservation are calculated to undo as far as possible the good work which Gen'l. Crook and his troops had accomplished with so much wisdom and gallantry. It is useless to attempt to disguise the fact that such treatment of the Indians is in violation of the just and humane policy prescribed by the President and a disgrace to any civilized country."

a forced abandonment of their ancestral home was not a "voluntary cession" within the meaning of § 2 of the Act of July 27, 1866.

The situation was, however, quite different in 1881. Between 1875 and that date there were rather continuous suggestions for settling the Walapais on some reservation. In 1881 the matter came to a head. A majority of the tribe, "in council assembled," asked an officer of the United States Army in that region "to aid them and represent to the proper authorities" the following proposal:

"They say that in the country, over which they used to roam so free, the white men have appropriated all the water; that large numbers of cattle have been introduced and have rapidly increased during the past year or two; that in many places the water is fenced in and locked up; and they are driven from all waters. They say that the Railroad is now coming, which will require more water, and will bring more men who will take up all the small springs remaining. They urge that the following reservation be set aside for them while there is still time; that the land can never be of any great use to the Whites; that there are no mineral deposits upon it, as it has been thoroughly prospected; that there is little or no arable land; that the water is in such small quantities, and the country is so rocky and void of grass, that it would not be available for stock raising. I am credibly informed, and from my observations believe, the above facts to be true. I, therefore, earnestly recommend that the hereafter described Reservation be, at as early a date as practicable, set aside for them."

Pursuant to that recommendation, the military reservation was constituted on July 8, 1881, subject to the approval of the President. The Executive Order creating the Walapai Indian Reservation was signed by President Arthur on January 4, 1883. There was an indication that the Indians were satisfied with the proposed reservation. A few of them thereafter lived on the reservation; many of them did not. While suggestions recurred for the creation of a new and different reservation, this one was not abandoned. For a long time it remained unsurveyed. Cattlemen used it for grazing, and for some years the Walapais received little benefit from it. But in view of all of the circumstances, we conclude that its creation at the request of the Walapais and its acceptance by them amounted to a relinquishment of any tribal claims to lands which they might have had outside that reservation and that relinquishment was tantamount to an extinguishment by "voluntary cession" within the meaning of § 2 of the Act of July 27, 1866. The lands were fast being populated. The Walapais saw their old domain being preempted. They wanted a reservation while there was still time to get one. That solution had long seemed desirable in view of recurring tensions between the settlers and the Walapais. [Given] this historical setting, it cannot now be fairly implied that tribal rights of the Walapais in lands outside the reservation were preserved. [Consequently,] acquiescence in that arrangement must be deemed to have been a relinquishment of tribal rights in lands outside the reservation and notoriously claimed by others.

On January 23, 1941, the date of the filing of this petition for certiorari, respondent quitclaimed to the United States [the lands it claimed under the 1866 Act] within the Walapai Indian Reservation. Since the decree below must stand as to the second cause of action and since by virtue of the quitclaim deeds the United States has received all the lands to which the first cause of action relates, the decree will not be reversed. It is apparent, however, that it must be modified so as to permit the accounting as respects lands in the first cause of action. It does not appear whether those lands were included in the ancestral home of the Walapais in the sense that they were in whole or in part occupied exclusively by them or whether they were lands wandered over by many tribes. As we have said, occupancy necessary to establish aboriginal possession is a question of fact. The United States is entitled to an accounting as respects any or all of the lands in the first cause of action which the Walapais did in fact occupy exclusively from time immemorial.[24] Such an accounting is not precluded by the Act of February 20, 1925, 43 Stat. 954, which authorized the Secretary of the Interior "to accept reconveyances to the Government of privately owned and State school lands and relinquishments of any valid filings, under the homestead laws, or of other valid claims within the Walapai Indian Reservation." The implication is that there may be some land within the reservation that is not subject to Indian occupancy. But that Act certainly cannot be taken as an extinguishment of any and all Indian title that did exist or as a repeal by implication of §2 of the Act of July 27, 1866, requiring such extinguishment by "voluntary cession." It was passed so that lands "retained for Indian purposes may be consolidated and held in a solid area so far as may be possible." Such statements by the Secretary of the Interior as that "title to the odd-numbered sections" was in the respondent do not estop the United States from maintaining this suit. For they could not deprive the Indians of their rights any more than could the unauthorized leases in *Cramer v. United States, supra.*

Hence, an accounting as respects such lands in the reservation which can be proved to have been occupied by the Walapais from time immemorial can be had. To the extent that the decree below precludes such proof and accounting, it will be modified. And as so modified, it is
Affirmed.

COUNTY OF ONEIDA v. ONEIDA INDIAN NATION

470 U.S. 226 (1985)

Justice POWELL delivered the opinion of the Court.*
These cases present the question whether three Tribes of the Oneida Indians may bring a suit for damages for the occupation and use of tribal land allegedly conveyed unlawfully in 1795.

I

The Oneida Indian Nation of New York, the Oneida Indian Nation of Wisconsin, and the Oneida of the Thames Band Council (the Oneidas) instituted this suit in 1970 against the Counties of Oneida and Madison, New York. The Oneidas alleged that their ancestors conveyed 100,000 acres to the State of New York under a 1795 agreement that violated the Trade and Intercourse Act of 1793 (Nonintercourse Act), 1 Stat. 329, and thus that the transaction was void. The Oneidas' complaint sought damages representing the fair rental value of

---

[24] In case of any lands in the reservation which were not part of the ancestral home of the Walapais and which had passed to the railroad under the 1866 Act, the railroad's title would antedate the creation of the reservation in 1883 and hence not be subject to the incumbrance of Indian title.

*THE CHIEF JUSTICE, Justice WHITE, and Justice REHNQUIST join only Part V of this opinion.

that part of the land presently owned and occupied by the Counties of Oneida and Madison, for the period January 1, 1968, through December 31, 1969.

The United States District Court for the Northern District of New York initially dismissed the action on the ground that the complaint failed to state a claim arising under the laws of the United States. The United States Court of Appeals for the Second Circuit affirmed. We then granted certiorari and reversed. *Oneida Indian Nation v. County of Oneida,* 414 U.S. 661 (1974) (*Oneida I*). We held unanimously that, at least for jurisdictional purposes, the Oneidas stated a claim for possession under federal law. The case was remanded for trial.

On remand, the District Court trifurcated trial of the issues. In the first phase, the court found the counties liable to the Oneidas for wrongful possession of their lands. In the second phase, it awarded the Oneidas damages in the amount of $16,694, plus interest, representing the fair rental value of the land in question for the 2-year period specified in the complaint. Finally, the District Court held that the State of New York, a third-party defendant brought into the case by the counties, must indemnify the counties for the damages owed to the Oneidas. The Court of Appeals affirmed the trial court's rulings with respect to liability and indemnification. It remanded, however, for further proceedings on the amount of damages. The counties and the State petitioned for review of these rulings. Recognizing the importance of the Court of Appeals' decision not only for the Oneidas, but potentially for many eastern Indian land claims, we granted certiorari, to determine whether an Indian tribe may have a live cause of action for a violation of its possessory rights that occurred 175 years ago. We hold that the Court of Appeals correctly so ruled.

II

The respondents in these cases are the direct descendants of members of the Oneida Indian Nation, one of the six nations of the Iroquois, the most powerful Indian Tribe in the Northeast at the time of the American Revolution. From time immemorial to shortly after the Revolution, the Oneidas inhabited what is now central New York State. Their aboriginal land was approximately six million acres, extending from the Pennsylvania border to the St. Lawrence River, from the shores of Lake Ontario to the western foothills of the Adirondack Mountains.

Although most of the Iroquois sided with the British, the Oneidas actively supported the colonists in the Revolution. This assistance prevented the Iroquois from asserting a united effort against the colonists, and thus the Oneidas' support was of considerable aid. After the War, the United States recognized the importance of the Oneidas' role, and in the Treaty of Fort Stanwix, 7 Stat. 15 (Oct. 22, 1784), the National Government promised that the Oneidas would be secure "in the possession of the lands on which they are settled." Within a short period of time, the United States twice reaffirmed this promise, in the Treaties of Fort Harmar, 7 Stat. 33 (Jan. 9, 1789), and of Canandaigua, 7 Stat. 44 (Nov. 11, 1794).[1]

---

[1] The Treaty of Fort Harmar stated that the Oneidas and the Tuscaroras were "again secured and confirmed in the possession of their respective lands." 7 Stat. 34. The Treaty of Canandaigua of

During this period, the State of New York came under increasingly heavy pressure to open the Oneidas' land for settlement. Consequently, in 1788, the State entered into a "treaty" with the Indians, in which it purchased the vast majority of the Oneidas' land. The Oneidas retained a reservation of about 300,000 acres, an area that, the parties stipulated below, included the land involved in this suit.

In 1790, at the urging of President Washington and Secretary of War Knox, Congress passed the first Indian Trade and Intercourse Act, ch. 33, 1 Stat. 137. The Act prohibited the conveyance of Indian land except where such conveyances were entered pursuant to the treaty power of the United States. In 1793, Congress passed a stronger, more detailed version of the Act, providing that "no purchase or grant of lands, or of any title or claim thereto, from any Indians or nation or tribe of Indians, within the bounds of the United States, shall be of any validity in law or equity, unless the same be made by a treaty or convention entered into pursuant to the constitution ... [and] in the presence, and with the approbation of the commissioner or commissioners of the United States" appointed to supervise such transactions. 1 Stat. 330, § 8. Unlike the 1790 version, the new statute included criminal penalties for violation of its terms.

Despite Congress' clear policy that no person or entity should purchase Indian land without the acquiescence of the Federal Government, in 1795 the State of New York began negotiations to buy the remainder of the Oneidas' land. When this fact came to the attention of Secretary of War Pickering, he warned Governor Clinton, and later Governor Jay, that New York was required by the Nonintercourse Act to request the appointment of federal commissioners to supervise any land transaction with the Oneidas. The State ignored these warnings, and in the summer of 1795 entered into an agreement with the Oneidas whereby they conveyed virtually all of their remaining land to the State for annual cash payments. It is this transaction that is the basis of the Oneidas' complaint in this case.

The District Court found that the 1795 conveyance did not comply with the requirements of the Nonintercourse Act. In particular, the court stated that "[t]he only finding permitted by the record ... is that no United States Commissioner or other official of the federal government was present at the ... transaction." The petitioners did not dispute this finding on appeal. Rather, they argued that the Oneidas did not have a federal common-law cause of action for this violation. Even if such an action once existed, they contended that the Nonintercourse Act pre-empted it, and that the Oneidas could not maintain a private cause of action for violations of the Act. Additionally, they maintained that any such cause of action was time-barred or nonjusticiable, that any cause of action under the 1793 Act had abated, and that the United States had ratified the conveyance. The Court of Appeals, with one judge dissenting, rejected these arguments. Petitioners renew these claims here; we also reject them and affirm the court's finding of liability.

1794 provided: "The United States acknowledge the lands reserved to the Oneida, Onondaga and Cayuga Nations, in their respective treaties with the state of New-York, and called their reservations, to be their property; and the United States will never claim the same, nor disturb them ... in the free use and enjoyment thereof: but the said reservations shall remain theirs, until they choose to sell the same to the people of the United States, who have the right to purchase." 7 Stat. 45.

III

At the outset, we are faced with petitioner counties' contention that the Oneidas have no right of action for the violation of the 1793 Act. Both the District Court and the Court of Appeals rejected this claim, finding that the Oneidas had the right to sue on two theories: first, a common-law right of action for unlawful possession; and second, an implied statutory cause of action under the Nonintercourse Act of 1793. We need not reach the latter question as we think the Indians' common-law right to sue is firmly established.

A

Federal Common Law

By the time of the Revolutionary War, several well-defined principles had been established governing the nature of a tribe's interest in its property and how those interests could be conveyed. It was accepted that Indian nations held "aboriginal title" to lands they had inhabited from time immemorial. See Cohen, *Original Indian Title*, 32 Minn. L. Rev. 28 (1947). The "doctrine of discovery" provided, however, that discovering nations held fee title to these lands, subject to the Indians' right of occupancy and use. As a consequence, no one could purchase Indian land or otherwise terminate aboriginal title without the consent of the sovereign. *See* Clinton & Hotopp, *Judicial Enforcement of the Federal Restraints on Alienation of Indian Land: The Origins of the Eastern Land Claims*, 31 Me. L. Rev. 17, 19-49 (1979).

With the adoption of the Constitution, Indian relations became the exclusive province of federal law. From the first Indian claims presented, this Court recognized the aboriginal rights of the Indians to their lands. The Court spoke of the "unquestioned right" of the Indians to the exclusive possession of their lands, [*Cherokee Nation*,] and stated that the Indians' right of occupancy is "as sacred as the fee simple of the whites." *Mitchel v. United States,* 9 Pet. 711, 746 (1835). This principle has been reaffirmed consistently. Thus, as we concluded in *Oneida I,* "the possessory right claimed [by the Oneidas] is a *federal* right to the lands at issue in this case." 414 U.S., at 671 (emphasis in original).

Numerous decisions of this Court prior to *Oneida I* recognized at least implicitly that Indians have a federal common-law right to sue to enforce their aboriginal land rights. [For example,] the Court held that Indians have a common-law right of action for an accounting of "all rents, issues and profits" against trespassers on their land. [*United States v. Santa Fe Pacific R. Co.*] [The] opinion in *Oneida I* implicitly assumed that the Oneidas could bring a common-law action to vindicate their aboriginal rights. [W]e noted that the Indians' right of occupancy need not be based on treaty, statute, or other formal Government action. We stated that "absent federal statutory guidance, the governing rule of decision would be fashioned by the federal court in the mode of the common law." *Id.* at 674.

In keeping with these well-established principles, we hold that the Oneidas can maintain this action for violation of their possessory rights based on federal common law.

B

Pre-emption

[Congressional action after the 1793 statute was enacted] and later versions of the Nonintercourse Act demonstrate that the Acts did not pre-empt common-law remedies. In 1822 Congress amended the 1802 version of the Act to provide that "in all trials about the right of property, in which Indians shall be party on one side and white persons on the other, the burden of proof shall rest upon the white person, in every case in which the Indian shall make out a presumption of title in himself from the fact of previous possession and ownership." § 4, 3 Stat. 683; see 25 U.S.C. § 194. Thus, Congress apparently contemplated suits by Indians asserting their property rights.

[I]n *Wilson v. Omaha Indian Tribe,* 442 U.S. 653 (1979), [this] Court construed the 1822 amendment to apply to suits brought by Indian tribes as well as individual Indians. Citing the very sections of the Act that petitioners contend pre-empt a common-law action by the Indians, the Court interpreted the amendment to be part of the overall "design" of the Nonintercourse Acts "to protect the rights of Indians to their properties." *Id.,* at 664.

We recognized in *Oneida I* that the Nonintercourse Acts simply "put in statutory form what was or came to be the accepted rule — that the extinguishment of Indian title required the consent of the United States." Nothing in the statutory formulation of this rule suggests that the Indians' right to pursue common-law remedies was thereby pre-empted. Accordingly, we hold that the Oneidas' right of action under federal common law was not pre-empted by the passage of the Nonintercourse Acts.

IV

Having determined that the Oneidas have a cause of action under federal common law, we address the question whether there are defenses available to the counties. We conclude that none has merit.

A

Statute of Limitations

There is no federal statute of limitations governing federal common-law actions by Indians to enforce property rights. In the absence of a controlling federal limitations period, the general rule is that a state limitations period for an analogous cause of action is borrowed and applied to the federal claim, provided that the application of the state statute would not be inconsistent with underlying federal policies.[13] We think the borrowing of a state limitations period in these cases would be inconsistent with federal policy. Indeed, on a number of occasions Congress has made this clear with respect to Indian land claims.

---

[13] Under the Supremacy Clause, state-law time bars, e.g., adverse possession and laches, do not apply of their own force to Indian land title claims. See *Ewert v. Bluejacket,* 259 U.S. 129, 137-138 (1922); *United States v. Ahtanum Irrigation District,* 236 F. 2d 321, 334 (CA9 1956), *cert. denied,* 352 U.S. 988 (1957).

In adopting the statute that gave jurisdiction over civil actions involving Indians to the New York courts, Congress included this proviso: "[N]othing herein contained shall be construed as conferring jurisdiction on the courts of the State of New York or making applicable the laws of the State of New York in civil actions involving Indian lands or claims with respect thereto which relate to transactions or events transpiring prior to September 13, 1952." 25 U.S.C. § 233. This proviso was added specifically to ensure that the New York statute of limitations would not apply to pre-1952 land claims. In *Oneida I,* we relied on the legislative history of 25 U.S.C. § 233 in concluding that Indian land claims were exclusively a matter of federal law. This history also reflects congressional policy against the application of state statutes of limitations in the context of Indian land claims.

Congress recently reaffirmed this policy in addressing the question of the appropriate statute of limitations for certain claims brought by the United States on behalf of Indians. Originally enacted in 1966, this statute provided a special limitations period of 6 years and 90 days for contract and tort suits for damages brought by the United States on behalf of Indians. 28 U.S.C. §§ 2415(a), (b). The statute stipulated that claims that accrued prior to its date of enactment, July 18, 1966, were deemed to have accrued on that date. § 2415(g). Section 2415(c) excluded from the limitations period all actions "to establish the title to, or right of possession of, real or personal property."

In 1972 and again in 1977, 1980, and 1982, as the statute of limitations was about to expire for pre-1966 claims, Congress extended the time within which the United States could bring suits on behalf of the Indians. The legislative history of the 1972, 1977, and 1980 amendments demonstrates that Congress did not intend § 2415 to apply to suits brought by the Indians themselves, and that it assumed that the Indians' right to sue was not otherwise subject to any statute of limitations. Both proponents and opponents of the amendments shared these views.

With the enactment of the 1982 amendments, Congress for the first time imposed a statute of limitations on certain tort and contract claims for damages brought by individual Indians and Indian tribes. These amendments, enacted as the Indian Claims Limitation Act of 1982, Pub. L. 97-394, 96 Stat. 1976, note following 28 U.S.C. § 2415, established a system for the final resolution of pre-1966 claims cognizable under §§ 2415(a) and (b). The Act directed the Secretary of the Interior to compile and publish in the Federal Register a list of all Indian claims to which the statute of limitations provided in 28 U.S.C. § 2415 applied. The Act also directed that the Secretary notify those Indians who may have an interest in any such claims. The Indians were then given an opportunity to submit additional claims; these were to be compiled and published on a second list. Actions for claims subject to the limitations periods of § 2415 that appeared on neither list were barred unless commenced within 60 days of the publication of the second list. If at any time the Secretary decides not to pursue a claim on one of the lists, "*any* right of action shall be barred unless the complaint is filed within one year after the date of publication [of the notice of the Secretary's decision] in the Federal Register." Pub. L. 97-394, 96 Stat. 1978, § 5(c) (emphasis added). Thus, § 5(c) implicitly imposed a 1-year statute of limitations within which the Indians must bring contract and tort claims that are covered by §§ 2415(a) and (b) and not listed by the Secretary. So long as a listed claim is neither acted upon nor formally rejected by the Secretary, it remains live.[15]

The legislative history of the successive amendments to § 2415 is replete with evidence of Congress' concern that the United States had failed to live up to its responsibilities as trustee for the Indians, and that the Department of the Interior had not acted with appropriate dispatch in meeting the deadlines provided by § 2415. E.g., Authorizing Indian Tribes to Bring Certain Actions on Behalf of their Members with Respect to Certain Legal Claims, and for Other Purposes, H.R. Rep. No. 97-954, p. 5 (1982). By providing a 1-year limitations period for claims that the Secretary decides not to pursue, Congress intended to give the Indians one last opportunity to file suits covered by §§ 2415(a) and (b) on their own behalf. Thus, we think the statutory framework adopted in 1982 presumes the existence of an Indian right of action not otherwise subject to any statute of limitations. It would be a violation of Congress' will were we to hold that a state statute of limitations period should be borrowed in these circumstances.

B

Laches

The dissent argues that we should apply the equitable doctrine of laches to hold that the Oneidas' claim is barred. Although it is far from clear that this defense is available in suits such as this one,[16] we do not reach this issue today. While petitioners argued at trial that the Oneidas were guilty of laches, the District Court ruled against them and they did not reassert this defense on appeal. As a result, the Court of Appeals did not rule on this claim, and we likewise decline to do so. [In Section IV-C, the Court held that language of formal repeal in the 1796 version of the Nonintercourse Act did not abate the cause of action.]

---

[15] The two lists were published in the Federal Register on March 31, 1983, and November 7, 1983, respectively. 48 Fed. Reg. 13698, 51204. The Oneidas' claims are on the first list compiled by the Secretary. *Id.,* at 13920. These claims would not be barred, however, even if they were not listed. The Oneidas commenced this suit in 1970 when no statute of limitations applied to claims brought by the Indians themselves. Additionally, if claims like the Oneidas', *i.e.,* damages actions that involve litigating the continued vitality of aboriginal title, are construed to be suits "to establish the title to, or right of possession of, real or personal property," they would be exempt from the statute of limitations of the Indian Claims Limitations Act of 1982. The Government agrees with this view. Brief for United States as *Amicus Curiae* 24-25.

[16] We note, as Justice STEVENS properly recognizes, that application of the equitable defense of laches in an action at law would be novel indeed. Moreover, the logic of the Court's holding in *Ewert v. Bluejacket,* 259 U.S. 129 (1922), seems applicable here: "the equitable doctrine of laches, developed and designed to protect good-faith transactions against those who have slept on their rights, with knowledge and ample opportunity to assert them, cannot properly have application to give vitality to a void deed and to bar the rights of Indian wards in lands subject to statutory restrictions." *Id.,* at 138. Additionally, this Court has indicated that extinguishment of Indian title requires a sovereign act. *See, e.g., Oneida I,* 414 U.S. 661, 670 (1974); *United States v. Candelaria,* 271 U.S. 432, 439 (1926), quoting *United States v. Sandoval,* 231 U.S. 28, 45-47 (1913). In these circumstances, it is questionable whether laches properly could be applied. Furthermore, the statutory restraint on alienation of Indian tribal land adopted by the Nonintercourse Act of 1793 is still the law. *See* 25 U.S.C. § 177. This fact not only distinguishes the cases relied upon by the dissent, but also suggests that, as with the borrowing of state statutes of limitations, the application of laches would appear to be inconsistent with established federal policy. Although the issue of laches is not before us, we add these observations in response to the dissent.

D

Ratification

We are similarly unpersuaded by petitioners' contention that the United States has ratified the unlawful 1795 conveyances. Petitioners base this argument on federally approved treaties in 1798 and 1802 in which the Oneidas ceded additional land to the State of New York.

[C]anons of construction applicable in Indian law are rooted in the unique trust relationship between the United States and the Indians. Thus, it is well established that treaties should be construed liberally in favor of the Indians. [This] Court has applied similar canons of construction in nontreaty matters. Most importantly, the Court has held that congressional intent to extinguish Indian title must be "plain and unambiguous," *United States v. Santa Fe Pacific R. Co.* at 346, and will not be "lightly implied," *id.* at 354. Relying on the strong policy of the United States "from the beginning to respect the Indian right of occupancy," *id.,* at 345 (citing *Cramer v. United States,* 261 U.S. 219, 227 (1923)), the Court concluded that it "[c]ertainly" would require "plain and unambiguous action to deprive the [Indians] of the benefits of that policy," *id.* at 346.

In view of these principles, the treaties relied upon by petitioners are not sufficient to show that the United States ratified New York's unlawful purchase of the Oneidas' land. The language cited by petitioners, a reference in the 1798 treaty to "the last purchase" and one in the 1802 treaty to "land heretofore ceded," far from demonstrates a plain and unambiguous intent to extinguish Indian title. There is no indication that either the Senate or the President intended by these references to ratify the 1795 conveyance.

E

Nonjusticiability

The claim also is made that the issue presented by the Oneidas' action is a nonjusticiable political question. The counties contend first that Art. 1, § 8, cl. 3, of the Constitution explicitly commits responsibility for Indian affairs to Congress. Moreover, they argue that Congress has given exclusive civil remedial authority to the Executive for cases such as this one, citing the Nonintercourse Acts and the 1794 Treaty of Canandaigua. Thus, they say this case falls within the political question doctrine because of "a textually demonstrable constitutional commitment of the issue to a coordinate political department." *Baker v. Carr,* 369 U.S. 186, 217 (1962). Additionally, the counties argue that the question is nonjusticiable because there is "an unusual need for unquestioning adherence to a political decision already made." *Ibid.* None of these claims is meritorious.

This Court has held specifically that Congress' plenary power in Indian affairs under Art. 1, § 8, cl. 3, does not mean that litigation involving such matters necessarily entails nonjusticiable political questions. [*E.g., Sioux Nation.*] If Congress' constitutional authority over Indian affairs does not render the Oneidas' claim nonjusticiable, *a fortiori*, Congress' delegation of authority to the President does not do so either.

We are also unpersuaded that petitioners have shown "an unusual need for unquestioning adherence to a political decision already made." *Baker v. Carr, supra,* at 217. The basis for their argument is the fact that in 1968, the Commissioner of Indian Affairs declined to bring an action on behalf of the Oneidas with respect to the claims asserted in these cases. The counties cite no cases in which analogous decisions provided the basis for nonjusticiability. Our cases suggest that such "unusual need" arises most of the time, if not always, in the area of foreign affairs. Nor do the counties offer convincing reasons for thinking that there is a need for "unquestioning adherence" to the Commissioner's decision. Indeed, the fact that the Secretary of the Interior has listed the Oneidas' claims under the § 2415 procedure suggests that the Commissioner's 1968 decision was not a decision on the merits of the Oneidas' claims. *See* n.15, *supra.*

VI

The decisions of this Court emphasize "Congress' unique obligation toward the Indians." *Morton v. Mancari,* 417 U.S. 535, 555 (1974). The Government, in an *amicus curiae* brief, urged the Court to affirm the Court of Appeals. The Government recognized, as we do, the potential consequences of affirmance. It was observed, however, that "Congress has enacted legislation to extinguish Indian title and claims related thereto in other eastern States, ... and it could be expected to do the same in New York should the occasion arise." See Rhode Island Indian Claims Settlement Act, 25 U.S.C. § 1701 *et seq.*; Maine Indian Claims Settlement Act, 25 U.S.C. § 1721 *et seq.* We agree that this litigation makes abundantly clear the necessity for congressional action.

One would have thought that claims dating back for more than a century and a half would have been barred long ago. As our opinion indicates, however, neither petitioners nor we have found any applicable statute of limitations or other relevant legal basis for holding that the Oneidas' claims are barred or otherwise have been satisfied. The judgment of the Court of Appeals is affirmed with respect to the finding of liability under federal common law,[27] and reversed with respect to the exercise of ancillary jurisdiction over the counties' cross-claim for indemnification. The cases are remanded to the Court of Appeals for further proceedings consistent with our decision.

Affirmed in part, reversed in part, and remanded.

Justice STEVENS, with whom THE CHIEF JUSTICE, Justice WHITE, and Justice REHNQUIST join, dissenting in No. 83-1065.*

In 1790, the President of the United States notified Cornplanter, the Chief of the Senecas, that federal law would securely protect Seneca lands from acquisition by any State or person:

---

[27] The question whether equitable considerations should limit the relief available to the present day Oneida Indians was not addressed by the Court of Appeals or presented to this Court by petitioners. Accordingly, we express no opinion as to whether other considerations may be relevant to the final disposition of this case should Congress not exercise its authority to resolve these far-reaching Indian claims.

*Justice Stevens concurred in the judgment that the federal court lacked ancillary jurisdiction over the counties' cross claims against the state.

"If ... you have any just cause of complaint against [a purchaser] and can make satisfactory proof thereof, the federal courts will be open to you for redress, as to all other persons." 4 American State Papers, Indian Affairs, Vol, 1, p. 142 (1832).

The elders of the Oneida Indian Nation received comparable notice of their capacity to maintain the federal claim that is at issue in this litigation. They made no attempt to assert the claim, and their successors in interest waited 175 years before bringing suit to avoid a 1795 conveyance that the Tribe freely made, for a valuable consideration. The absence of any evidence of deception, concealment, or interference with the Tribe's right to assert a claim, together with the societal interests that always underlie statutes of repose — particularly when title to real property is at stake — convince me that this claim is barred by the extraordinary passage of time. It is worthy of emphasis that this claim arose when George Washington was the President of the United States.

The Court refuses to apply any time bar to this claim, believing that to do so would be inconsistent with federal Indian policy. This Court, however, has always applied the equitable doctrine of laches when Indians or others have sought, in equity, to set aside conveyances made under a statutory or common-law incapacity to convey. Although this action is brought at law, in ejectment, there are sound reasons for recognizing that it is barred by similar principles.

In reaching a contrary conclusion, the Court relies on the legislative histories of a series of recent enactments. In my view, however, the Oneida were barred from avoiding their 1795 conveyance long before 1952, when Congress enacted the first statute that the Court relies on today. Neither that statute, nor any subsequent federal legislation, revived the Oneida's dormant claim....

WILSON v. OMAHA INDIAN TRIBE

442 U.S. 653 (1979)

Mr. Justice WHITE delivered the opinion of the Court.

At issue here is the ownership of a tract of land on the east bank of the Missouri River in Iowa. Respondent Omaha Indian Tribe, supported by the United States as trustee of the Tribe's reservation lands,[1] claims the tract as part of reservation lands created for it under an 1854 treaty. Petitioners, including the State of Iowa and several individuals, argue that past movements of the Missouri River washed away part of the reservation and the soil accreted to the Iowa side of the river, vesting title in them as riparian landowners.

Two principal issues are presented. First, we are faced with novel questions regarding the interpretation and scope of Rev. Stat. § 2126, as set forth in 25 U.S.C. § 194, a 145-year-old, but seldom used, statute that provides:

[1] In *Heckman v. United States*, 224 U.S. 413 (1912), the Court explained the source and nature of this trust relationship. In the exercise of its plenary authority over Indian affairs, Congress has the power to place restrictions on the alienation of Indian lands. Where it does so, it continues guardianship over Indian lands and "[d]uring the continuance of this guardianship, the right and duty of the Nation to enforce by all appropriate means the restrictions designed for the security of the Indians cannot be gainsaid.... A transfer of the [Indian land] is not simply a violation of the proprietary rights of the Indian. It violates the governmental rights of the United States." *Id.*, at 437-438. Accordingly, the United States is entitled to go into court as trustee to enforce Indian land rights. "It [is] not essential that it should have a pecuniary interest in the controversy." *Id.*, at 439. See also *Morrison v. Work*, 266 U.S. 481, 485 (1925); *Choate v. Trapp*, 224 U.S. 665, 678 (1912); F. Cohen, Handbook of Federal Indian Law 94-96 (1942).

In all trials about the right of property in which an Indian may be a party on one side, and a white person on the other, the burden of proof shall rest upon the white person, whenever the Indian shall make out a presumption of title in himself from the fact of previous possession or ownership.

Second, we must decide whether federal or state law determines whether the critical changes in the course of the Missouri River in this case were accretive or avulsive.

I

In 1854, the Omaha Indian Tribe ceded most of its aboriginal lands by treaty to the United States in exchange for money and assistance to enable the Tribe to cultivate its retained lands. Treaty of Mar. 16, 1854, 10 Stat. 1043; see *United States v. Omaha Indians,* 253 U.S. 275, 277-278 (1920). The retained lands proved unsatisfactory to the Tribe, and it exercised its option under the treaty to exchange those lands for a tract of 300,000 acres to be designated by the President and acceptable to the Tribe. The Blackbird Hills area, on the west bank of the Missouri, all of which was then part of the Territory of Nebraska, was selected. The eastern boundary of the reservation was fixed as the center of the main channel of the Missouri River, the thalweg. That land, as modified by a subsequent treaty and statutes, has remained the home of the Omaha Indian Tribe.

In 1867, a survey by T. H. Barrett of the General Land Office established that the reservation included a large peninsula jutting east toward the opposite, Iowa, side of the river, around which the river flowed in an oxbow curve known as Blackbird Bend. Over the next few decades, the river changed course several times, sometimes moving east, sometimes west.[6] Since 1927, the river has been west of its 1867 position, leaving most of the Barrett survey area on the Iowa side of the river, separated from the rest of the reservation

As the area, now on the Iowa side, dried out, Iowa residents settled on, improved, and farmed it. These non-Indian owners and their successors in title occupied the land for many years prior to April 2, 1975, when they were dispossessed by the Tribe, with the assistance of the Bureau of Indian Affairs.

Four lawsuits followed the seizure, three in federal court and one in state court. The Federal District Court for the Northern District of Iowa consolidated the three federal actions, severed claims to damages and lands outside the Barrett survey area, and issued a temporary injunction that permitted the Tribe to continue possession. The court then tried the case without a jury. At trial, the Government and Tribe argued that the river's movement had been avulsive, and therefore the change in location of the river had not affected the boundary of the reservation. Petitioners argued that the river had gradually eroded the reservation lands on the west bank of the river, and that the disputed land on

---

[6] In *Nebraska v. Iowa,* 143 U.S. 359 (1892), the Court decided a boundary dispute between the States of Nebraska and Iowa caused by the wanderings of the Missouri. "[T]he fickle Missouri River," however, "refused to be bound by the ... decree," Eriksson, The Boundaries of Iowa, 25 Iowa J. of Hist. and Pol. 163, 234 (1927); and in 1943 Nebraska and Iowa entered into a Compact fixing the boundary between the States independent of the river's location. Congress ratified the Compact in the Act of July 12, 1943, ch. 220, 57 Stat. 494. Since the time of the Compact, the Army Corps of Engineers has been largely successful in taming the river. See *Nebraska v. Iowa,* 406 U.S. 117, 119 (1972).

the east bank, in Iowa, had been formed by gradual accretion and belonged to the east-bank riparian owners. Both sides sought to quiet title in their names.

The District Court concluded that state rather than federal law should be the basis of decision. The court interpreted the Rules of Decision Act, 28 U.S.C. § 1652, as not requiring the application of federal law in land disputes, even though the United States and an Indian tribe were claimants, unless the Constitution, a treaty, or an Act of Congress specifically supplanted state law. The court found no indication in those sources that federal law was to govern. It then went on to conclude that 25 U.S.C. § 194 was not applicable to the case because it was impossible for the Tribe to make out a prima facie case that it possessed the disputed lands in the past without proving its case on the merits. Thus, § 194 had no significance because it was "inextricably entwined with the merits."

Applying Nebraska law, which places the burden of proof on the party seeking to quiet title, the court concluded that the key changes in the river had been accretive, and that the east-bank riparians, the petitioners, were thus the owners of the disputed area.[11]

The Court of Appeals reversed. It began by ruling that the District Court should have applied federal rather than state law [first, because] the boundary of the reservation was coincidental with an interstate boundary at the time the river moved [and second, because] the Court of Appeals construed our decision in *Oneida Indian Nation v. County of Oneida*, 414 U.S. 661, 677 (1974), as requiring the application of federal law because the Tribe asserted a right to reservation land based directly on the 1854 treaty and therefore arising under and protected by federal law.

The Court of Appeals also ruled that the District Court had erred by refusing to apply 25 U.S.C. § 194. Because the Tribe had proved that the 1854 treaty included the land area within the Barrett survey, it had made a sufficient showing of "previous possession or ownership" to invoke the statute and place the burden of proof on petitioners. Adopting the District Court's construction "would negate the application of the § 194 statutory burden upon a pleading that simply recites Indian land had been destroyed by the erosive action of a river."

[Next, the court] the law to the evidence and found that the evidence was in equipoise. Because § 194 placed the burden of proof on the non-Indians, however, the court ruled that judgment must be entered for the Tribe.

We granted separate petitions for certiorari filed by the State of Iowa and its Conservation Commission in No. 78-161 and by the individual petitioners in No. 78-160, but limited to the questions whether 25 U.S.C. § 194 is applicable in the circumstances of this litigation, in particular with respect to the State of Iowa, and whether federal or state law governs the substantive aspects of these

---

[11]Although the District Court hewed closely to Nebraska case law, it also observed that insofar as the relevant definitions of avulsion and accretion were concerned, there was no significant difference between Iowa and Nebraska law, except that under Iowa law accretion was presumed, which was not the case under Nebraska law. Because Nebraska law would not aid the defendants by a presumption of accretion, the Tribe was favored by the application of Nebraska law. The District Court was also of the view that the federal accretion-avulsion law was not substantially different. As we shall see, the Court of Appeals differed with the District Court in this respect.

cases. We are in partial, but serious, disagreement with the Court of Appeals, and vacate its judgment.

II

Petitioners challenge on several grounds the Court of Appeals' construction and application of § 194 to these cases. First, they argue that by its plain language the section does not apply when an Indian tribe, rather than one or more individual Indians, is the litigant. We think the argument is untenable. The provision first appeared in slightly different form in 1822, Act of May 6, 1822, 3 Stat. 683, as part of an Act amending the 1802 Indian Trade and Intercourse Act, Act of Mar. 30, 1802, 2 Stat. 139, which was one of a series of Acts originating in 1790 and designed to regulate trade and other forms of intercourse between the North American Indian tribes and non-Indians. Because of recurring trespass upon and illegal occupancy of Indian territory, a major purpose of these Acts as they developed was to protect the rights of Indians to their properties. Among other things, non-Indians were prohibited from settling on tribal properties, and the use of force was authorized to remove persons who violated these restrictions. The 1822 provision was part of this design; and with only slight change in wording, it was incorporated in the 1834 consolidation of the various statutes dealing with Indian affairs. Act of June 30, 1834, 4 Stat. 729. Section 22 of that Act is now 25 U.S.C. § 194, already set out in this opinion. Although the word "Indian" in the second line of § 22 of the 1834 Act replaced the word "Indians" in the 1822 provision, there is no indication that any change in meaning was intended; and none should be implied at this late date, particularly in light of 1 U.S.C. § 1, which provides that unless the context indicates otherwise, "words importing the singular include and apply to several persons, parties, or things."

Even construed as including the plural, however, it is urged that the word "Indians" does not literally include an Indian tribe, and that it is plain from other provisions of the Act that Congress intended to distinguish between Indian tribes and individual Indians. But as we see it, this proves too much. At the time of the enactment of the predecessors of § 194, Indian land ownership was primarily tribal ownership; aboriginal title, a possessory right, was recognized and was extinguishable only by agreement with the tribes with the consent of the United States. *Oneida Indian Nation v. County of Oneida,* 414 U.S., at 669-670. Typically, this was accomplished by treaty between the United States and the tribe, and typically the land reserved or otherwise set aside was held in trust by the United States for the tribe itself. "'Whatever title the Indians have is in the tribe, and not in the individuals, although held by the tribe for the common use and equal benefit of all the members.'" *United States v. Jim,* 409 U.S. 80, 82 (1972), quoting *Cherokee Nation v. Hitchcock,* 187 U.S. 294, 307 (1902). It is clear enough that, when enacted, Congress intended the 1822 and 1834 provisions to protect Indians from claims made by non-Indian squatters on their lands. To limit the force of these provisions to lands held by individual Indians would be to drain them of all significance, given the historical fact that at the time of the enactment virtually all Indian land was [held by tribes].

The second argument, presented in its most acute form by the State of Iowa, is that § 194 applies only where the Indians' antagonist is an individual white person and has no force at all where the adverse claimant is an artificial entity.[16] We cannot accept this broad submission. The word "person" for purposes of statutory construction, unless the context indicates to the contrary, is normally construed to include "corporations, companies, associations, firms, partnerships, societies, and joint stock companies, as well as individuals." 1 U.S.C. § 1. And in terms of the protective purposes of the Acts of which § 194 and its predecessors were a part, it would make little sense to construe the provision so that individuals, otherwise subject to its burdens, could escape its reach merely by incorporating and carrying on business as usual.

[Nevertheless, it] does not follow that the "white persons" to whom will be shifted the burden of proof in title litigation with Indians also include the sovereign States of the Union. [M]uch depends on the context, the subject matter, legislative history, and executive interpretation. The legislative history here is uninformative, and executive interpretation is unhelpful with respect to this dormant statute. But in terms of the purpose of the provision — that of preventing and providing remedies against non-Indian squatters on Indian lands — it is doubtful that Congress anticipated such threats from the States themselves or intended to handicap the States so as to offset the likelihood of unfair advantage. Indeed, the 1834 Act, which included § 22, the provision identical to the present § 194, was "intended to apply to the whole Indian country, as defined in the first section." H.R. Rep. No. 474, 23d Cong., 1st Sess., 10 (1834). Section 1 defined Indian country as being "all that part of the United States west of the Mississippi, and not within the states of Missouri and Louisiana, or the territory of Arkansas, and, also, that part of the United States east of the Mississippi River, and not within any state to which the Indian title has not been extinguished ...." 4 Stat. 729. Although this definition was discarded in the Revised Statutes, see Rev. Stat. § 5596, it is apparent that in adopting § 22 Congress had in mind only disputes arising in Indian country, disputes that would not arise in or involve any of the States.

Nor have we discovered anything since its passage or in connection with the definition of Indian country now contained in the Criminal Code, 18 U.S.C. § 1151, indicating that Congress intended the words "white person" in § 194 to include any of the original or any of the newly admitted States of the Union. We hesitate, therefore, to hold that the State of Iowa must necessarily be disadvantaged by § 194 when litigating title to the property to which it claims ownership, particularly where its opposition is an organized Indian tribe litigating with the help of the [government].

Petitioners also defend the refusal of the District Court to apply § 194 on the grounds that a precondition to applying it is proof of prior possession or title in the Indians and that this involves the merits of the issue on which this case turns — whether the changes in the river were avulsive or accretive. We think the

---

[16]Petitioners cite *United States v. Perryman,* 100 U.S. 235 (1880), as support for their position that § 194 must be construed literally to apply only to a "white person," or individual Caucasian. But that case dealt with another provision of the 1834 Nonintercourse Act, § 16, and there were distinct grounds in the legislative history indicating that the term "white person" as used in § 16 did not include a Negro. Whether *Perryman* would be followed today is a question we need not decide.

Court of Appeals had the better view of the statute in this regard. Section 194 is triggered once the Tribe makes out a prima facie case of prior possession or title to the particular *area* [causing controversy].

Petitioners also assert that even if § 194 is operative and even if the Tribe has made out its prima facie case, only the burden of going forward with the evidence, and not the burden of persuasion, is shifted to the State. Therefore they, the petitioners, should prevail if the evidence is in equipoise. The term "burden of proof" may well be an ambiguous term connoting either the burden of going forward with the evidence, the burden of persuasion, or both. But in view of the evident purpose of the statute and its use of the term "presumption" which the "white man" must overcome, we are in agreement with the two courts below that § 194 contemplates the non-Indian's shouldering the burden of persuasion as well as the burden of producing evidence once the tribe has made out its prima facie case of prior title or possession.

III

A

[In contrast to land titles merely derived from a federal grant, the] area within the survey was part of land to which the Omahas had held aboriginal title and which was reserved by the Tribe and designated by the United States as a reservation and the Tribe's permanent home. The United States continues to hold the reservation lands in trust for the Tribe and to recognize the Tribe pursuant to the Indian Reorganization Act of 1934, 48 Stat. 984, 25 U.S.C. § 461 *et seq.*

In these circumstances, where the Government has never parted with title and its interest in the property continues, the Indians' right to the property depends on federal law, "wholly apart from the application of state law principles which normally and separately protect a valid right of possession." *Oneida Indian Nation v. County of Oneida,* 414 U.S., at 677. It is rudimentary that "Indian title is a matter of federal law and can be extinguished only with federal consent" and that the termination of the protection that federal law, treaties, and statutes extend to Indian occupancy is "exclusively the province of federal law." *Id.,* at 670. Insofar as the applicable law is concerned, therefore, the claims of the Omahas are "clearly distinguishable from the claims of land grantees for whom the Federal Government has taken no such responsibility." *Id.,* at 684 (Rehnquist, J., concurring). This is not a case where the United States has patented or otherwise granted lands to private owners in a manner that terminates its interest and subjects the grantees' incidents of ownership to determination by the applicable state law. The issue here is whether the Tribe is no longer entitled to possession of an area that in the past was concededly part of the reservation as originally established. That question, under *Oneida,* is a matter for the federal law to decide.

B

Although we have determined that federal law ultimately controls the issue in this case, it is still true that "[c]ontroversies ... governed by federal law, do not inevitably require resort to uniform federal rules.... Whether to adopt state law or to fashion a nationwide federal rule is a matter of judicial policy 'dependent upon a variety of considerations always relevant to the nature of the specific governmental interests and to the effects upon them of applying state law.'" *United States v. Kimbell Foods, Inc.*, 440 U.S. 715, 727-728 (1979), quoting *United States v. Standard Oil Co.*, 332 U.S. 301, 310 (1947).[19] The Court of Appeals, noting the existence of a body of federal law necessarily developed by this Court in the course of adjudicating boundary disputes between States having their common border on a navigable stream, purported to find in those doctrines the legal standards to apply in deciding whether the changes in the course of the Missouri River involved in this case had been avulsive or accretive in nature.

The federal law applied in boundary cases, however, does not necessarily furnish the appropriate rules to govern this case. No dispute between Iowa and Nebraska as to their common border on or near the Missouri River is involved here. The location of that border on the ground was settled by Compact in 1943 and by further litigation in this Court, *Nebraska v. Iowa*, 406 U.S. 117 (1972). The federal interest in this respect has thus been satisfied, except to the extent that the Compact itself may bear upon a dispute such as this. *United States v. Kimbell Foods, Inc.*, *supra*, advises that at this juncture we should consider whether there is need for a nationally uniform body of law to apply in situations comparable to this, whether application of state law would frustrate federal policy or functions, and the impact a federal rule might have on existing relationships under state law. An application of these factors suggests to us that state law should be borrowed as the federal rule of decision here.

First, we perceive no need for a uniform national rule to determine whether changes in the course of a river affecting riparian land owned or possessed by the United States or by an Indian tribe have been avulsive or accretive.

[Moreover,] given equitable application of state law, there is little likelihood of injury to federal trust responsibilities or to tribal possessory interests. On some occasions, Indian tribes may lose some land because of the application of a particular state rule of accretion and avulsion, but it is as likely on other occasions that the tribe will stand to gain. The same would be the case under a federal rule, including the rule that the Court of Appeals announced in this case. The United States fears a hostile and unfavorable treatment at the hands of state law, but, as we have said, the legal issues are federal and the federal courts will have jurisdiction to hear them. *Oneida Indian Nation v. County of Oneida*, 414 U.S. 661 (1974). Adequate means are thus available to insure fair treatment of tribal and federal interests.

This is also an area in which the States have substantial interest in having their own law resolve controversies such as these. Private landowners rely on state real property law when purchasing real property, whether riparian land or not. There is considerable merit in not having the reasonable expectations of these

---

[19]Compare P. Bator, P. Mishkin, D. Shapiro, & H. Wechsler, Hart & Wechsler's The Federal Courts and the Federal System 768 (2d ed. 1973):

The federal "command" to incorporate state law may be a judicial rather than a legislative command; that is, it may be determined as a matter of choice of law, even in the absence of statutory command or implication, that, although federal law should "govern" a given question, state law furnishes an appropriate and convenient measure of the content of this federal law.

private landowners upset by the vagaries of being located adjacent to or across from Indian reservations or other property in which the United States has a substantial interest. Borrowing state law will also avoid arriving at one answer to the avulsive-accretion riddle in disputes involving Indians on one side and possibly quite different answers with respect to neighboring land where non-Indians are the disputants. Indeed, in this case several hundred acres of land within the Barrett survey are held in fee, and concededly are not Indian property. These tracts would not be governed by [a federal rule].

IV

In sum, the Court of Appeals was partially correct in ruling that § 194 was applicable in this case. By its terms, § 194 applies to the private petitioners but not to petitioner State of Iowa. We also agree with the Court of Appeals' conclusion that federal law governed the substantive aspects of the dispute, but find it in error for arriving at a federal standard, independent of state law, to determine whether there had been an avulsion or an accretion. Instead, the court should have incorporated the law of the State that otherwise would have been applicable which, as we have said, is the law of Nebraska. Of course, because of its view of the controlling law, the Court of Appeals did not consider whether the District Court had correctly interpreted Nebraska law and had properly applied it to the facts of this case.

[*Vacated and remanded.*]

Mr. Justice POWELL took no part in the consideration or decision of these cases.

Mr. Justice BLACKMUN with whom THE CHIEF JUSTICE joins, concurring.

I join the Court's opinion, but I write briefly to add a comment about my views as to the scope of 25 U.S.C. § 194.

Section 194 applies to a property dispute between an Indian and a "white person." The property dispute here is between Indians, on the one hand, and, on the other, nine individuals, two corporations, and the State of Iowa. See 575 F.2d 620, 622 (CA8 1978). The Court holds that "white person" includes an artificial entity and thus that § 194 applies in the dispute between the Omahas and the two corporate petitioners. Contrariwise, the Court holds that "white person" does not include a sovereign State, and thus that § 194 does not apply in the dispute between the Omahas and petitioner State of Iowa. The Court, however, does not expressly discuss § 194's applicability to the nine individual claimants [nor is there any evidence in the record regarding their race].

The Court seems to hold implicitly, therefore, that "white person" in § 194 includes any "non-Indian" individual. I would prefer to make this holding explicit. In my view, any other construction of § 194 would raise serious constitutional questions. To construe § 194 as applicable to disputes between Indians and Caucasians, but not to disputes between Indians and black or oriental individuals, would create an irrational racial classification highly questionable under the Fifth Amendment's equal protection guarantee. To avoid this result, § 194's reference to a "white person" must be read to mean any "non-Indian" individual or entity, and I so interpret the Court's holding today. To the extent that *Perryman* is inconsistent with this reading, I must regard that case as overruled *sub silentio.*

NOTES

1. Patents to Third Parties: An important test for the significance of Indian title came as the United States sought to encourage the spread of railroads across the continent. Often, the lands astride the right of way were Indian lands. In *Nadeau v. Union Pac. R.R.,* 253 U.S. 442 (1920), the Court upheld Congress's power to grant rights of way over trust land to a railroad in derogation of the tribal right of possession. Although cession of the fee as well as the tribal right of occupancy would not have required compensation, at least for rights of way across unrecognized Indian reservations, the government often provided for compensation without regard to the nature of the Indian land. The government would couple the prospective cession with the promise to extinguish the Indian title and to establish treaty commissions, thus preserving at least the appearance of legality. In addition to *Santa Fe Pacific Railroad* (usually known as *Walapai Tribe*,) see *Buttz v. Northern Pac. R.R.,* 119 U.S. 55, 66-71 (1886) (a well-stated and somewhat cynical picture of the process). In addition, if the railroad patent had an exceptions clause, the Supreme Court applied principles of liberal construction to interpret the exception as applying to Indian land. *See, e.g., Cramer v. United States,* 261 U.S. 219, 225 (1923) (exception for land "granted, sold, reserved ... other otherwise disposed of" held to except aboriginal land); *Leavenworth, L. & G.R.R. v. United States,* 92 U.S. 733, 746 (1876) (exception for land "reserved to the United States ... for any other purpose whatsoever" held to except reservation land). *Cf. Minnesota v. Hitchcock,* 185 U.S. 373, 391 (1902) (school land grant exception for land "sold or otherwise been disposed of" held to except reservation land). Often this result has been achieved by applying the canon stated in *Walapai Tribe, supra,* that "extinguishment cannot be lightly implied." Recent efforts by tribes to claim interference with tribal ownership rights by railroads operating rights of way through reservation lands have been successful. *See, e.g., United States v. Southern Pac. Transp. Co.,* 543 F.2d 676 ((9th Cir. 1976) (successful trespass claim against railroad; congressional grant to railroad of right of way not sufficient to grant land within boundaries of reservation); *Burlington N.R.R. v. Ft. Peck Tribal Exec. Bd.,* 701 F. Supp. 1493 (D. Mont. 1988) (tribal property tax based on tribal ownership upheld; congressional grant to railroad of right of way did not extinguish tribal interest in land).

2. The Nonintercourse Act: The Nonintercourse Act has been applied to *all* categories of Indian land, including land held in fee simple absolute by an Indian tribe. *See United States v. Candelaria,* 271 U.S. 432, 440-44 (1926) (Nonintercourse Act creates a guardianship authorizing the U.S. to sue on behalf of tribe to quiet title). The best-known application of this federal restraint on alienation in recent years has occurred in claims of eastern Indian tribes (including the Oneida, Cayuga, and Mohawk of New York; Catawba of South Carolina; Narragansett of Rhode Island; Western Pequot and Schaghticoke of Connecticut; and Mashpee of Massachusetts) to land on the East Coast. The lower courts had uniformly held that state defenses, such as statutes of limitations and laches, could not be advanced in the federal claims. What is the Supreme Court's reasoning for adopting this position in the *Oneida* case? Did the Supreme Court completely close the door to invoking the doctrine of laches? Is Justice Stevens's position logical? Sound? *See generally* Vollman, *A*

Survey of Eastern Indian Land Claims: 1970-1979, 31 Me. L. Rev. 5 (1979); O'Toole & Tureen, *State Power and the Passamaquoddy Tribe: "A Gross National Hypocrisy?",* 23 Me. L. Rev. 1 (1971); Note, *Oneida Indian Nation v. County of Oneida: Tribal Rights of Action and the Indian Trade and Intercourse Act,* 84 Colum. L. Rev. 1852, & 1861-62 n.70 (1984) (collecting cases). For a complete history of the Maine litigation, see P. Brodeur, Restitution (1985).

The Rhode Island and Maine claims have been settled, and several other claims are in the process of settlement. Many of the other claims have been completely or partially resolved, not always to the benefit of the Indian claimants. In *South Carolina v. Catawba Indian Tribe,* 476 U.S. 498 (1986), the Supreme Court held that the Catawba Division of Assets Act of 1959, 25 U.S.C. §§ 931-938, a Termination Era statute, expressly made all state laws, including state statutes of limitations, applicable to the Catawba Tribe. On remand, the Fourth Circuit held that the applicable state statute of limitations barred the claim. *Catawba Indian Tribe v. South Carolina,* 865 F.2d 1444 (4th Cir. 1989). In *Mashpee Tribe v. New Seabury Corp.,* 592 F.2d 575 (1st Cir.), *cert. denied,* 444 U.S. 866 (1979), the court affirmed the dismissal of the Mashpee land claim, because the jury had found the plaintiff was not an Indian tribe at certain relevant dates. The definition of tribe relied on was first set out in a 1901 case: "a body of Indians of the same or a similar race, united in a community under one leadership or government, and inhabiting a particular, though sometimes ill-defined, territory." *Montoya v. United States,* 180 U.S. 261, 266 (1901). *Cf. Mashpee Tribe v. Secretary of Interior,* 820 F.2d 480 (1st Cir. 1987) (refusal of request by Christiantown, Chappaquiddick, Herring Pond and Troy tribes to grant declaratory judgment that tribal status existed) (Mashpee Tribe barred by res judicata); *Cayuga Indian Nation v. Cuomo II,* 667 F. Supp. 938 (N.D.N.Y 1987) (*Mashpee* limited to cases brought by unrecognized tribes; federal recognition satisfies requirement of tribal status). For competing views regarding the application of the *Montoya* definition, see St. Clair & Lee, *Defense of Nonintercourse Act Claims: The Requirement of Tribal Existence,* 31 Me. L. Rev. 91 (1979); Note, *Tribal Status and the Indian Nonintercourse Act: An Alternative to the Montoya Definition of Tribe,* 29 Cath. U.L. Rev. 625 (1980).

The Oneida and the Cayuga tribes originally brought claims in the Indian Claims Commission for breach of fair and honorable dealings based on the loss of their lands to the states and private parties. The Oneida tribe withdrew its claim before final resolution. In contrast, the Cayuga tribe settled its claim for $70,000 in 1975. Would the principles of finality of the *Dann* case and the notion accepted by lower courts that the Claims Commission is the exclusive forum for resolution of land claims, discussed *supra* section B4, require dismissal of such a claim? For an answer, see *Cayuga Indian Nation v. Cuomo,* 667 F. Supp. 938, 946-48 (N.D.N.Y. 1987).

3. Preconstitutional Land Claims: The Oneida nation also brought a claim to 5 million acres in New York, naming a class of 60,000 defendants, arguing that two treaties with the state violated Article IX of the Articles of Confederation, pre-1790 federal treaties with the tribe, and the Continental Congress's Proclamation of 1783. These claims in part involve the construction of the provision of Article IX of the Articles of Confederation that gave the confederation Congress "the sole and exclusive right and power of Indians, not members of any of the States, provided that the legislative right of any State within its own limits be not infringed or violated." In *Oneida Indian Nation v. New York,* 860 F.2d 1145 (2d Cir. 1988), *cert. denied,* 110 S. Ct. 200 (1989), the Second

Circuit Court of Appeals upheld the validity of the state treaties, holding that the quoted language granted states the right to make treaties with Indians to purchase land during the pre-Constitutional period.

For other judicial discussions of the meaning of the Article IX language, see *United States v. Oneida Nation,* 576 F.2d 870 (Ct. Cl. 1978), *aff'g* 37 Ind. Cl. Comm'n 522 (1976) (holding federal government liable for breach of fair and honorable dealings clause of ICC act for failure to help Oneidas get fair price for pre-1790 cessions to state); *Seneca Nation v. United States,* 173 Ct. Cl. 917 (1965), *aff'g in part & rev'g in part* 12 Ind. Cl. Comm'n 755 (1963) (Article IX did not impose any obligation on federal government regarding land in original 13 states; thus, tribe had no claim cognizable in the ICC for pre-1790 sale). *See generally* Clinton & Hotopp, *Judicial Enforcement of the Federal Restraints on Alienation of Indian Land: The Origins of the Eastern Land Claims,* 31 ME. L. REV. 17, 19-29 (1979); Note, *Conundrums Along the Mohawk: Pre-constitutional Land Claims of the Oneida Indian Nation,* 11 REV. OF L. & SOC. CHANGE 473 (1982-83); Note, *State Sovereignty and Indian Land Claims: The Validity of New York's Treaties Prior to the Nonintercourse Act of 1790,* 31 SYRACUSE L. REV. 797 (1980).

4. Claims Against Third Parties Based on Aboriginal Title: Tribes holding aboriginal title are entitled to an accounting for third parties' trespasses on unextinguished land, even if they no longer inhabit the land. *See also United States v. Southern Pac. Transp. Co.,* 543 F.2d 676 (9th Cir. 1976) (declaring a railroad right of way invalid after 90 years). If Indians claiming lands by aboriginal possession have an enforceable right of occupancy against third parties under which damages or an accounting for trespass may be awarded, are the accrued damage claims protected by the fifth amendment taking clause even if the underlying aboriginal title is not? In short, can Congress not only extinguish aboriginal title at will but also retroactively extinguish accrued Indian rights against third parties based on violations of the Indian right of occupancy? For example, could Congress extinguish the Oneida's claim by retroactively ratifying the state treaties made in violation of the Nonintercourse Act?

In *United States v. Atlantic Richfield Co.,* 612 F.2d 1132, 1135-38 (9th Cir.), *cert. denied,* 449 U.S. 888 (1980), the Ninth Circuit held that the provisions of the Alaska Native Claims Settlement Act (ANCSA) extinguishing retroactively both aboriginal title and claims based on aboriginal title included claims against third parties for trespass and did not violate the due process clause. The Inupiat Community then brought suit in the Court of Claims for compensation, arguing that the statutory extinguishment of claims based on aboriginal title was a taking of vested property rights. The Court of Claims held that the claims did not represent a compensable property interest because if aboriginal title itself was not a compensable property interest, claims based on aboriginal title could not be protected either. *Inupiat Community of the Arctic Slope v. United States,* 680 F.2d 122 (Ct. Cl.), *cert. denied,* 459 U.S. 969 (1982).

Legislation settling Eastern land claims contains language retroactively extinguishing aboriginal title as of the date of the ratified transfer. The Maine Indian Claims Settlement Act, for instance, also provides that all claims "based on any interest in or right involving such land or natural resources, including but without limitation claims for trespass damages or claims for use and occupancy, shall be deemed extinguished as of the date of transfer." 25 U.S.C. § 1723(c). The existing settlements were true settlements, unlike the Alaska Native Claims Settlement Act, which was imposed upon the Native Alaskans. Could Congress decide to extinguish a Nonintercourse Act claim like the Oneida claim by retroactively validating the treaties with the state, because the tribe refused to settle out of court and determined to press its case for the return of its land and for trespass damages in federal court? If Congress decided to pay fair market value, at what date would the value be measured — the date of the original treaty or the date of the legislation? Could it do so without paying fair market value for the land? Would the legislation also require compensation for the trespass claims? In a memorandum to Judge Gunter, who had been asked by President Carter to help mediate the dispute, Professor Archibald Cox argued that such an action would violate the due process clause. Do you agree? *Cf.* Clinton & Hotopp, *Judicial Enforcement of the Federal Restraints on Alienation of Indian Land: The Origins of the Eastern Land Claims,* 31 ME. L. REV. 17, 80 (1979) (suggesting that extinguishment of trespass damages claims in the Eastern land cases would constitute a compensable taking); Newton, *At the Whim of the Sovereign: Aboriginal Title Reconsidered,* 31 HASTINGS L.J. 1215, 1267-84 (1980); Newton, *Federal Power Over Indians: Its Sources, Scope, and Limitations,* 132 U. PA. L. REV. 195, 257-61 (1984).

5. The Burden of Proof in Indian Land Claims: The importance of 25 U.S.C. § 194 to the disposition of Indian land claims is evident from the Eighth Circuit's handling of the *Omaha Tribe* case on remand. *Omaha Indian Tribe v. Wilson,* 614 F.2d 1153 (8th Cir.), *cert. denied,* 449 U.S. 825 (1980). Finding the evidence somewhat inconclusive to establish that the change in river course was gradual (accretive), rather than sudden or perceptible (avulsive), the court invoked § 194. Judge Lay wrote for the court:

> Evidence of river movement in the critical periods too often gives no more than a basis for an "educated guess" .... Particularly in light of the requirement that defendants, because of the presumption applicable under 25 U.S.C. § 194, succeed on the strength of their own case, and not any weakness in their opponents' claim to title, we conclude they failed to meet their burden of proof. As we stated previously, "the ultimate conclusion may not rest on mere guesswork."

Id. at 1161. The court therefore remanded the case to the trial court with directions to enter judgment quieting title to the trust lands at issue in favor of Indians against the adverse private claimants. As to the claims of the state of Iowa, however, involving approximately 700 acres, the court noted that § 194 did not apply. Eventually the lower court held that the tribe had failed to meet its burden of proof against the state that the change in river course was avulsive. Commenting on the three appeals in all at that time, the lower court stated: "The extensive history of this dispute indicates that it may die of old age before it can be successfully adjudicated." *United States v. Wilson,* 578 F. Supp. 1191, 1191 (N.D. Iowa), *aff'd in part & rev'd in part, Omaha Indian Tribe v. Jackson,* 854 F.2d 1089 (8th Cir. 1988), *cert. denied,* 109 S. Ct. 2429 (1989).

6. Conflicting State and Tribal Claims to Ownership of Riverbeds Within Reservations — *Montana v. United States*: According to the equal footing doctrine, the federal government holds land under navigable waterways in trust for the states to be granted to the states when they "enter the Union and assume sovereignty on an 'equal footing' with the established States." *Montana v. United States,* 450 U.S. 544, 551 (1981). The federal government has the power to grant such land before statehood, "in order to perform international obligations ... or to carry out other public purposes ... for which the United States hold the Territory." *Shively v. Bowlby,* 152 U.S. 1, 48 (1894). Nevertheless, courts are reluctant to read such grants as conveying the riverbed absent very explicit language. "A court ... must, therefore, begin with a strong presumption against conveyance by the United States." *Montana,* 450 U.S. at 552. In 1981, the Supreme Court applied this strict construction to the question whether the Second Treaty of Fort Laramie, a treaty which the Court stated recognized title to the Crow Reservation in the *Tee-Hit-Ton* sense, "conveyed beneficial ownership" of the riverbed of the Big Horn River, which crossed the Crow Reservation. *Id.* at 551. The treaty provided that land be "set apart for the absolute and undisturbed use and occupation" of the Indians. It further provided that "no persons [except those named in the treaty and agents of the U.S.] shall ever be permitted to pass over, settle upon, or reside in the territory described in this article...." Second Treaty of Fort Laramie of 1868, 15 Stat. 649, Art. 2. Despite this language, the Court held: "Whatever property rights the language of the 1868 treaty created, however, its language is not strong enough to overcome the presumption against the sovereign's conveyance of the riverbed." *Id.* at 554. The principal reason given by the court was the lack of explicit language in the treaty referring to ownership of the riverbed.

Treaties executed during the Removal Era granted Eastern tribes land in Indian Territory to induce them to relocate. In most treaties, however, like the Second Treaty of Fort Laramie, the tribe granted a portion of its aboriginal land to the United States, reserving land for the tribe. Thus, these treaties do not often contain the kind of explicit language of conveyance of the riverbed required by *Montana*. Moreover, canons of treaty construction, such as the canon requiring interpretation of treaty language as the Indians would have understood it, would seem to have called for a different result. See Chapter 2, section C2, *supra*. As Barsh and Henderson have stated: "When Indian treaties were negotiated a century ago there was no question that ... a metes and bounds description was sufficient to vest all territorial rights in the tribe. Since that was the practice at the time, it is not surprising that Indian treaties do not commonly identify enclosed waters. If it stands, the rule ... would work a retroactive confiscation of most tribes' submerged reservation lands." Barsh & Henderson, *Contrary Jurisprudence: Tribal Interests in Navigable Waterways Before and After Montana v. United States,* 56 WASH. L. REV. 627, 682 (1981).

One court has held that unextinguished aboriginal title to a riverbed takes precedence over any state claim on the theory that since the United States never acquired the full title, it had nothing to grant to the state at statehood. *United States v. Pend Oreille County Pub. Util. Dist. No. 1,* 585 F. Supp. 606 (E.D. Wash. 1984), *noted in* 16 ENVTL. L. REV. 163 (1985). The *Pend Oreille* case is of limited precedential authority, of course, especially since the court also held that an Indian Claims Commission settlement awarding the tribe compensation for the land along the river did not serve to extinguish title, relying on the later-discredited Ninth Circuit opinion in *United States v. Dann.* Nevertheless, could a similar argument be made in a case like *Montana,* where the cession involved the tribe's aboriginal land? When a treaty cedes aboriginal land and reserves land for the tribe, what is the legal effect of the reservation on the tribe's aboriginal title? Does the treaty extinguish *all* tribal aboriginal title, including title to its retained land, or does the treaty merely extinguish title to the ceded land while confirming the tribe's aboriginal title to the retained portion?

Loss of ownership of submerged land under navigable waters has wide-ranging implications for an Indian tribe. For example, in *Montana,* state ownership of the riverbed of the Big Horn River was held to weigh against tribal power to regulate fishing. Moreover, such land may contain minerals or may otherwise constitute a source of income. *See, e.g., United States v. Aam,* 14 Indian L. Rep. 3124 (W.D. Wash. 1987) (tidelands used for fishing and recreational uses); *Yankton Sioux Tribe v. South Dakota,* 796 F.2d 241 (8th Cir. 1986), *cert. de-*

nied, 483 U.S. 1005 (1987) (harvesting fireweed on dry lake bed). *See generally* Note, *Riverbed Ownership Law Metamorphosed into a Determinant of Tribal Regulatory Authority — Montana v. United States,* 1982 WIS. L. REV. 264.

D. PRESERVING TRIBAL RIGHTS IN ARTIFACTS AND HUMAN REMAINS

CHARRIER v. BELL

496 So. 2d 601 (La. App.), *cert. denied,*
498 So. 2d 753 (La. 1986)

PONDER, J.

Plaintiff appealed the trial court's judgment denying both his claim as owner of Indian artifacts and his request for compensation for his excavation work in uncovering those artifacts under the theory of unjust enrichment. We affirm.

Plaintiff is a former Corrections Officer at the Louisiana State Penitentiary in Angola, Louisiana, who describes himself as an "amateur archeologist." After researching colonial maps, records and texts, he concluded that Trudeau Plantation[1], near Angola, was the possible site of an ancient village of the Tunica Indians. He alleges that in 1967 he obtained the permission of Mr. Frank Hoshman, Sr., who he believed was the owner of Trudeau Plantation, to survey the property with a metal detector for possible burial locations. After locating and excavating approximately 30 to 40 burial plots, lying in a circular pattern, plaintiff notified Mr. Hoshman that he had located the Tunica village. Although the evidence is contradictory, plaintiff contends that it was at that time that Mr. Hoshman first advised that he was the caretaker, not the owner, of the property.

Plaintiff continued to excavate the area for the next three years until he had located and excavated approximately 150 burial sites, containing beads, European ceramics, stoneware, glass bottles; iron kettles, vessels and skillets; knives, muskets, gunflints, balls and shots; crucifixes, rings and bracelets; and native pottery. The excavated artifacts are estimated to weigh two to two and one-half tons.

In search of a buyer for the collection, plaintiff talked to Dr. Robert S. Neitzel of Louisiana State University, who, in turn, informed Dr. Jeffrey D. Brain of Harvard University. Dr. Brain, who was involved in a survey of archeology along the lower Mississippi River, viewed the artifacts and began discussions of their sale to the Peabody Museum of Harvard University. The discussions resulted in the lease of the artifacts to the Museum, where they were inventoried, catalogued and displayed.

Plaintiff initially informed Dr. Neitzel and Dr. Brain that he had found the artifacts in a cave in Mississippi, so as to conceal their source; later he did disclose the actual site of the find to Dr. Brain, who had expressed his concern over the title of the artifacts. Dr. Brain then obtained permission from the landowners to do further site testing and confirmed that it was the true source of the artifacts.

---

[1] Trudeau Plantation consists of approximately 150 acres located on a bluff in the southeast quadrant of the meeting of the Mississippi River and Tunica Bayou. Angola is on the other side of the bayou.

Confronted with the inability to sell the collection because he could not prove ownership, plaintiff filed suit against the six nonresident landowners of Trudeau Plantation, requesting declaratory relief confirming that he was the owner of the artifacts. Alternatively, plaintiff requested that he be awarded compensation under the theory of unjust enrichment for his time and expenses.

The State of Louisiana intervened in the proceeding on numerous grounds, including its duty to protect its citizens in the absence of the lawful heirs of the artifacts. In 1978, the State purchased Trudeau Plantation and the artifacts from the six landowners and agreed to defend, indemnify and hold the prior owners harmless from any and all actions.

In 1981 the Tunica and Biloxi Indians were recognized as an American Indian Tribe by the Bureau of Indian Affairs of the Department of the Interior. The Tunica-Biloxi Indians of Louisiana, Inc. intervened in the instant suit seeking title to the artifacts and the site of the burial ground. At the same time, the tribe removed the action to federal district court, where they also filed a parallel action seeking title to the artifacts. The federal district court, on September 8, 1982, remanded the matter to state court and stayed the parallel action. *Charrier v. Bell*, 547 F. Supp. 580 (M.D. La. 1982). The Tunicas then withdrew, without prejudice, their claim to the property where the artifacts were located and the State subordinated its claim of title or trust status over the artifacts in favor of the Tunicas.

The trial judge held that the Tunica-Biloxi Tribe is the lawful owner of the artifacts, finding that plaintiff was not entitled to the artifacts under La. C.C. art. 3423 as it read prior to amendment by Act No. 187 of 1982, which required discovery "by chance." The judge also found that plaintiff had no claim to the artifacts on the basis of abandonment under La. C.C. art. 3421, as it read prior to the amendment by Act No. 187 of 1982, because the legal concept of abandonment does not extend to burial goods.

The trial court also denied relief under the theory of unjust enrichment, finding that any impoverishment claimed by plaintiff was a result of his attempts "for his own gain" and that his presence and actions on the property of a third party placed him in a "precarious position, if not in legal bad faith."

The issues before this court are the adequacy of proof that the Tunica-Biloxi Indians are descendants of the inhabitants of Trudeau, the ownership of the artifacts, and the applicability of the theory of unjust enrichment.

Plaintiff first argues that the evidence that the members of the Tunica-Biloxi Indians of Louisiana, Inc., are legal descendants of the inhabitants of Trudeau Plantation was insufficient to entitle them to the artifacts. He asserts that federal recognition of the tribe "merely proves that the Tribe is the best representative of the Tunica Indians for purposes of receiving federal benefits," and points to evidence of intermixing by the Tunica tribe with other tribes.

The fact that members of other tribes are intermixed with the Tunicas does not negate or diminish the Tunicas' relationship to the historical tribe. Despite the fact that the Tunicas have not produced a perfect "chain of title" back to those buried at Trudeau Plantation, the tribe is an accumulation of the descendants of former Tunica Indians and has adequately satisfied the proof of descent. This is evident from the "Final Determination for Federal Acknowledgment of the Tunica-Biloxi Indian Tribe of Louisiana," *Fed. Reg.* Vol. 46, No.

143, p. 38411 (July 27, 1981), which specifically found that the "contemporary Tunica-Biloxi Indian Tribe is the successor of the historical Tunica, Ofa and Avoyel tribes, and part of the Biloxi tribe." The evidence supports the finding that at least some portion of the Tunica tribe resided at Trudeau Plantation from 1731-1764. No contrary evidence, other than that suggesting intermixing, was presented at the trial of this case. Plaintiff's argument is without merit.

Plaintiff next argues that the Indians abandoned the artifacts when they moved from Trudeau Plantation, and the artifacts became *res nullius* until found and reduced to possession by plaintiff who then became the owner.

Plaintiff contends that he has obtained ownership of the property through occupancy, which is a "mode of acquiring property by which a thing which belongs to nobody, becomes the property of the person who took possession of it, with the intention of acquiring a right of ownership upon it." La. C.C. art. 3412, prior to amendment by Act No. 187 of 1982.

One of the five methods of acquiring property by occupancy is "By finding (that is, by discovering precious stones on the sea shore, or things abandoned, or a treasure.)" La. C.C. art. 3414, prior to amendment by Act No. 187 of 1982. Plaintiff contends that the artifacts were abandoned by the Tunicas and that by finding them he became the owner.

Both sides presented extensive expert testimony on the history of the Tunica Indians, the French, English and Spanish occupation of the surrounding territory and the presence or absence of duress causing the Tunicas to abandon the Trudeau site.

However, the fact that the descendants or fellow tribesmen of the deceased Tunica Indians resolved, for some customary, religious or spiritual belief, to bury certain items along with the bodies of the deceased, does not result in a conclusion that the goods were abandoned. While the relinquishment of immediate possession may have been proved, an objective viewing of the circumstances and intent of the relinquishment does not result in a finding of abandonment. Objects may be buried with a decedent for any number of reasons. The relinquishment of possession normally serves some spiritual, moral, or religious purpose of the descendant/owner, but is not intended as a means of relinquishing ownership to a stranger. Plaintiff's argument carried to its logical conclusion would render a grave subject to despoliation either immediately after interment or definitely after removal of the descendants of the deceased from the neighborhood of the cemetery.

Although plaintiff has referred to the artifacts as *res nullius*, under French law, the source of Louisiana's occupancy law, that term refers specifically to such things as wild game and fish, which are originally without an owner. The term *res derelictae* refers to "things voluntarily abandoned by their owner with the intention to have them go to the first person taking possession." P. Esmein, *Aubry & Rau Droit Civil Francais*, Vol. II, 168, p. 46 (7th ed. 1966). Some examples of *res derelictae* given by *Aubry and Rau* include things left on public ways, in the cities or to be removed by garbage collectors.

The artifacts fall into the category of *res derelictae*, if subject to abandonment. The intent to abandon *res derelictae* must include the intent to let the first person who comes along acquire them. Obviously, such is not the case with burial goods.

French sources have generally held that human remains and burial goods located in cemeteries or burial grounds are not "treasure" under article 716 of the French Civil Code and thereby not subject to occupancy upon discovery. The reasoning has been that any contrary decision would lead to and promote commercial speculation and despoilment of burial grounds. The French commentator Demolombe noted the special treatment that should be given to burial goods, stating that such objects "have not been placed underground with the same intention which informs the deposit of what is called treasure, which in the latter case is, for a temporary period. Rather, they are an emplacement for a perpetual residence therein. 13 C. Demolombe, *Course de Code Napoleon* § 37, pp. 45-46 (2c ed. 1862).

The same reasoning that the French have used to treat burial goods applies in determining if such items can be abandoned. The intent in interring objects with the deceased is that they will remain there perpetually, and not that they are available for someone to recover and possess as owner.

For these reasons, we do not uphold the transfer of ownership to some unrelated third party who uncovers burial goods. The trial court concluded that La. C.C. art. 3421, as it read prior to passage of Act No. 187 of 1982, was not intended to require that objects buried with the dead were abandoned or that objects could be acquired by obtaining possession over the objections of the descendants. We agree with this conclusion.

The cases cited by plaintiff are distinguishable.

In *Touro Synagogue v. Goodwill Industries of New Orleans Area, Inc.*, 233 La. 26, 96 So. 2d 29 (1957), the court found that a cemetery had been abandoned for burial purposes and the owner had the right to sell the property; however, the court conditioned the sale on the disinterment and reinterment (in another cemetery) of the remains of the deceased.

[A finding] that Indians did not abandon the artifacts will [not] require the federal court to conclude that the Tunicas did not abandon the real property at Trudeau Plantation. [T]he question of the abandonment of the real property was excluded from the case. This opinion should not be interpreted as making any expression thereon.

Plaintiff next argues that he is entitled to recover a sum of money to compensate his services and expenses on the basis of an *actio de in rem verso* [unjust enrichment].

We first question whether there has been an enrichment. While the nonresident landowners were "enriched" by the sale of the property to the state, the ultimate owners of the artifacts presented substantial evidence that the excavation caused substantial upset over the ruin of "ancestral burial grounds," rather than any enrichment.

Even if the Indians have been enriched, plaintiff has failed to prove that he has sustained [impoverishment]. The *actio de in rem verso* [is] derived from the similar French action [and] is influenced greatly by French Civil Code articles from which our own are copied. The impoverishment element in French law is met only when the factual circumstances show that it was not a result of the plaintiff's own fault or negligence or was not undertaken at his own risk. Obviously the intent is to avoid awarding one who has helped another through his own negligence or fault or through action taken at his own risk. Plaintiff was acting possibly out of his own negligence, but more probably knowingly and at his own risk [because he knew he was on the property without the owner's consent]. Under these circumstances, plaintiff has not proven the type of impoverishment necessary for a claim of unjust enrichment.

Additionally, plaintiff has failed to show that any enrichment was unjustified, entitling him to an action to recover from the enriched party. [Under Louisiana law] descendants have a right to enjoin the disinterment of their deceased relatives, as well as to receive damages for the desecration involved. Such a right would be subverted if descendants were obliged to reimburse for the expenses of the excavation. [Thus, there] is a legal justification for any enrichment received by the Tribe and plaintiff is not entitled to invoke the equitable theory.
   [*Affirmed.*]

NOTES

1. Conflicts Between Archeologists and Indian Tribes: Indian concern to protect both land containing archeological sites and artifacts and remains taken from the land does not always coincide with the interests of archeologists. In fact, the two groups have reason to distrust each other. Tribes point to museum displays of skeletal remains as insensitive and unprecedented as far as any other racial group is concerned. They argue that many artifacts in museum hands are sacred; others are important links to their cultural past, which belong in tribal hands. They charge, for instance, that the Smithsonian Institution and other institutions in the U.S. currently control over 300,000 human remains of Native Americans. Unlike the remains of other Americans, no matter how ancient the remains might be, Indian remains are regarded as archeological resources, to be studied and displayed. Thus, tribes are reluctant to divulge any information on burial sites known to them on or off reservations. Archeologists on the other hand have recently become more concerned with preserving sites rather than taking artifacts out of sites for display in museums. They now fear that as development on Indian reservations increases, Indian tribes will fail to protect archeological sites, including burial sites. *See generally* Holt, *Archeological Preservation on Indian Lands: Conflicts and Dilemmas in Applying the National Historic Preservation Act,* 15 ENVTL. L. 413 (1985); Rosen, *The Excavation of American Indian Burial Sites: A Problem in Law and Professional Responsibility,* 82 AM. ANTHROPOLOGY 5 (1980); Winter, *Indian Heritage Preservation and Archaeologists,* 45 AM. ANTIQUITY 121 (1980).

2. Sites on Tribal Land: When third parties invade Indian land to treasure hunt, tribes should be able to protect their right to possession through trespass actions or other remedies, no matter what type of title is involved, as the preceding section of this chapter illustrates. Nevertheless, the complexities of the law regarding civil jurisdiction can create problems for a tribe trying to prevent someone from taking tribal artifacts. A tribal court can exercise civil jurisdiction over both members and nonmembers, subject to the possibility of divestment of jurisdiction over nonmembers under the principles stated in *National Farmers Union Ins. Cos. v. Crow Tribe,* 471 U.S. 845 (1985) and *Iowa Mut. Ins. Co. v. La Plante,* 480 U.S. 9 (1987). Can a tribe prevent a nonmember from excavating artifacts found on fee land within the boundaries of a "checkerboard" reservation?

A tribe without a tribal court system may be able to invoke the federal court's aid to prevent someone from taking away tribal artifacts. The Tlingit Indians of the Chilkat Indian Village have waged a long battle to keep four carved wooden posts and a carved screen called a "rain screen" under tribal control, which have been called "the finest example of Native art, either Tlingit or Tsimshian, in Alaska." *Chilkat Indian Village v. Johnson*, 870 F.2d 1469, 1471 (9th Cir. 1989) (quoting Emmons, *The Whale House of Chilkat*, in RAVEN'S BONES 81 (1982)). In 1976, the village enacted an ordinance prohibiting the removal of any artifacts without permission of the Tribal Council. A member of the tribe claimed she had inherited the artifacts under the Tlingit system of descent and distribution. When the tribe prevented her from removing them, her suit against the tribe in federal district court was dismissed because of sovereign immunity. *Johnson v. Chilkat Indian Village*, 457 F. Supp. 384 (D. Alaska 1978). In 1984, the rain screen and posts were removed and sold to an art dealer. When the tribe learned of the theft, the tribe sued both the thieves and the art dealer in district court, arguing that the defendants had violated both tribal and federal law. Although the Ninth Circuit upheld dismissal of the claim against the defendants who were members of the tribe, the court held that the tribe's claim to enforce its ordinance against the nonmember defendants was cognizable under 28 U.S.C. § 1331 as a claim based on federal common law protecting tribal sovereignty.

Federal law provides some protection for tribal lands from archeological excavation. The Archeological Resources Protection Act of 1979, 16 U.S.C. §§ 470aa-470*ll*, requires a federal permit for excavation on "Indian" lands and imposes a provision for tribal consent before a permit can be issued. *Id.* § 470cc. The law is problematic in several respects. First, the law only covers artifacts that are more than 100 years old. Thus, recent burial sites would not be covered. In addition, the definition of "Indian" lands does not include state or privately owned land within the boundaries of an Indian reservation. *Id.* § 470ee. This gap in coverage would have a detrimental effect on tribes with checkerboard reservations. Finally, the law provides that "any ... ultimate disposition ... shall be subject to the consent of the Indian or Indian tribe which owns or has jurisdiction over such lands." *Id.* § 479dd. This provision creates some ambiguity as to who actually owns the artifacts. *See* Suagee, *American Indian Religious Freedom and Cultural Resources Management: Protecting Mother Earth's Caretakers*, 10 AM. INDIAN L. REV. 1, 39 (1982). Nevertheless, tribes can exercise considerable control over the excavation of tribal artifacts. *See* Northey, *The Archeological Resources Protection Act of 1979: Protecting Prehistory for the Future*, 6 HARV. ENVTL. L. REV. 61, 74-76, 91-94 (1982).

3. Archeological Sites on Public Land: Can tribes prevent the destruction of archeological sites on public land? The Archeological Resources Protection Act of 1979, discussed above, also contains provisions protecting tribal artifacts and remains on public lands. The law declares these resources to be the property of the United States. 16 U.S.C. § 470cc(b)(3). Nevertheless, the law requires the public land manager to notify an Indian tribe when granting a permit on public land might harm "any religious or cultural site." *Id.* § 470cc(c). The law also mandates compliance with the American Indian Religious Freedom Act and requires consultation with Indian tribes in formulating regulations. Nevertheless, the law provides no assurances that tribal input can affect the outcome. Many burial sites and some archeological sites have religious significance. Tribes have invoked the free exercise clause of the first amendment as a basis to enjoin activity that would destroy or seriously damage religious sites, including burial sites. In *Lyng v. Northwest Indian Cem. Protective Ass'n*, 485 U.S. 439 (1988), discussed in Chapter 1, section A2, *supra*, the Court rejected such an argument, stating that even assuming the construction of a road would seriously impair the Indians ability to practice their religion, "the Constitution simply does not provide a principle that could justify upholding respondents' legal claims." *Id.* at 452. Nevertheless tribes may still be able to invoke the first amendment as requiring an easement to use public lands for religious purposes. The Court in *Lyng* was careful to leave open such a possibility, stating: "[t]he Constitution does not permit government to discriminate against religions that treat particular physical sites as sacred, and a law forbidding the Indian respondents from visiting the Chimney Rock area would raise a different set of constitutional questions." *Id.* at 453.

4. Sites on Private Land: As the principal case illustrates, ownership of artifacts excavated from private lands by or under the supervision of the landowner presents unique problems. What was the court's rationale for finding that the tribe owned the artifacts? If the private landowners had not sold their land to the state and the state had not subordinated its interest to the tribe, would the result be the same? Do owners of property always acquire all items buried in the soil? Could an argument be made that the tribe in ceding land to the United States never intended to cede burial sites contained in the ceded land? Can it be argued that the United States took the land with an obligation to protect burial sites?

Tribal-state agreements regarding repatriation and protection can be a very effective method to protect tribal artifacts and human remains. Beginning with Iowa in 1974, many states have enacted or are considering such measures. Wolinsky, *Unburying Indian Bones: Science vs. Spirituality,* 9 Am. C. Physicians Obs. 1 (1989). For example, California has enacted a provision preventing anyone from possessing "artifacts or human remains" taken from a "Native American grave or cairn" after January 1, 1984. Cal. Pub. Resources Code § 5097.99. The law also gives the California Native American Heritage Commission, five of whose members must be "elder, traditional people, or spiritual leaders of California Native American tribes nominated by Native American organizations, tribes, or groups within the state, *id.* § 5097.92, authority to mediate disputes and enforce the law.

In *People v. Van Horn,* 218 Cal. App. 3d 1378, 267 Cal. Rptr. 804 (1990), the state court upheld the statute in a case affirming an injunction against a California archaeologist who refused to return two metates (millstones) found in a site he excavated on private land while making a survey for the city of Vista, which was considering acquisition of the land. The defendant argued that the law was void for vagueness, violated the due process and equal protection clauses of the fourteenth amendment, and violated the establishment clause of the first amendment. In rejecting the defendant's arguments, the court described the statute as follows:

The legislative purpose of the 1982 additions is stated in a historical note following section 5097.94. The note recites:

(a) The Legislature finds as follows:

(1) Native American human burials and skeletal remains are subject to vandalism and inadvertent destruction at an increasing rate.

(2) State laws do not provide for the protection of these burials and remains from vandalism and destruction.

(3) There is no regular means at this time by which Native American descendents can make known their concerns regarding the treatment and disposition of Native American burials, skeletal remains, and items associated with Native American burials.

(b) The purpose of this act is:

(1) To provide protection to Native American human burials and skeletal remains from vandalism and inadvertent destruction.

(2) To provide a regular means by which Native American descendents can make known their concerns regarding the need for sensitive treatment and disposition of Native American burials, skeletal remains, and items associated with Native American burials.

Subdivisions (k) and (*l*) of section 5097.94 give the Commission the following additional powers and duties:

(k) To mediate, upon application of either of the parties, disputes arising between landowners and known descendents relating to the treatment and disposition of Native American human burials, skeletal remains, and items associated with Native American burials.

The agreements shall provide protection to Native American human burials and skeletal remains from vandalism and inadvertent destruction and provide for sensitive treatment and disposition of Native American burials, skeletal remains, and associated grave goods consistent with the planned use of, or the approved project on, the land.

(*l*) To assist interested landowners in developing agreements with appropriate Native American groups for treating or disposing, with appropriate dignity, of the human remains and any items associated with Native American burials."

Section 5097.98 recites:

(a) Whenever the commission receives notification of a discovery of Native American human remains from a county coroner pursuant to subdivision (c) of Section 7050.5 of the Health and Safety Code, it shall immediately notify those persons it believes to be most likely descended from the deceased Native American. The descendents may, with the permission of the owner of the land, or his or her authorized representative, inspect the site of the discovery of the Native American remains and may recommend to the owner or the person responsible for the excavation work means for treating or disposing, with appropriate dignity, of the human remains and any associated grave goods. The descendents shall complete their inspection and make their recommendation within 24 hours of their notification by the Native American Heritage Commission. The recommendation may include the scientific removal and nondestructive analysis of human remains and items associated with Native American burials.

(b) Whenever the commission is unable to identify a descendent, or the descendent identified fails to make a recommendation, or the landowner or his or her authorized representative rejects the recommendation of the descendent and the mediation provided for in subdivision (k) of Section 5097.94 fails to provide measures acceptable to the landowner, the landowner or his or her authorized representative shall reinter the human remains and items associated with Native American burials with appropriate dignity on the property in a location not subject to further subsurface disturbance.

Id. at 1393, 276 Cal. Rptr. at 819.

5. The Unique Problem of Indian Remains: Once skeletal remains have been disinterred and are in the hands of museums and universities, existing law does not hold out much hope for tribal leaders who want to have the remains reinterred. Nevertheless, tribal leaders have been successful in publicizing the situation and appealing to the strong cultural value among all groups of great respect for remains. An example of this respect is *Mexican v. Circle Bear*, 370 N.W.2d 737 (S.D. 1985), *supra* Chapter 3, section A2b, in which a state court recognized a tribal court judgment regarding the disposition of a dead body of a tribal member who died off the reservation, even though the tribal law reregarding control over the burial differed from state law. Stories, such as the one regarding a farmer who dug up an Indian cemetery and exhibited 146 skeletons as a roadside attraction, have begun to arouse public sympathy. Some 13 states have enacted legislation to protect all unmarked graves, including Indian graves, from desecration. Tribes in California have succeeded in persuading several counties to enact ordinances requiring reburial of remains unearthed at construction sites. In addition, private museums, such as the Field Museum in Chicago, have announced procedures for tribes to regain human remains. The Native American Rights Fund has taken an active role in the effort to protect remains and other artifacts, both in representing tribes such as the Tunica and in seeking more state legislation.

Several bills were introduced in the 100th Congress to identify, protect, and return skeletal remains, but none were enacted. Finally, in 1989, Congress enacted the National Museum of the American Indian Act, Pub. L. 101-185, 103 Stat. 1336 (1989), codified at 20 U.S.C.A. §§ 80q to 80q-15 (Supp. 1990). The statute provides for the creation of a new National Museum of the American Indian under the auspices of the Smithsonian Institution. In addition, the statute provides for repatriation of some of the Smithsonian's estimated 19,000 Indian remains. The law requires the Smithsonian to inventory and identify the origins of human remains and funerary objects under its control "in consultation and cooperation with traditional Indian religious leaders and government officials of Indian tribes ...." Section 11, 20 U.S.C.A. § 80q-9 (Supp. 1990). Original versions of the bill required only that the objects be identified; the version that was enacted, however, goes further and provides for the repatriation of some of the remains and artifacts:

> (c) *Return of Indian Human Remains and Associated Indian Funerary Objects.* — If any Indian human remains are identified by a preponderance of the evidence as those of a particular individual or as those of an individual culturally affiliated with a particular Indian tribe, the Secretary [of the Smithsonian], upon the request of the descendants of such individual or of the Indian tribe shall expeditiously return such remains (together with any associated funerary objects) to the descendants or tribe, as the case may be.

Id. § 13, 20 U.S.C.A. § 80q-9(c).

The law even provides for the return of funerary objects not associated with specific human remains, if the object can be identified, again by a preponderance of evidence, as coming from a particular burial site. A similar provision provides for the inventory and return of Native Hawaiian remains and funerary objects. *Id.* § 13, 20 U.S.C.A. § 80q-11.

Although the agreement was path-breaking, an ad hoc committee of Native Americans, anthropologists, and museum officials which has recently finished a one-year study of the problem mandated by Congress would go much further and include not merely human remains and funerary objects, but also sacred artifacts and artifacts that are part of the cultural or political patrimony of a tribe, thus broadening the class of artifacts that tribes may seek to repatriate. The committee has also recommended that *all* the nation's museums be required to inventory their collections of human remains and artifacts, identify modern tribes that have a cultural affiliation with the remains, consult with the tribe, and respect the tribe's wishes on disposition, repatriation or reburial of the artifacts and remains. Not surprisingly, the museum representatives on the committee dissented from these recommendations, arguing both for a narrower definition of what remains and artifacts can be claimed and for a stricter requirement of a direct connection between a modern tribe and the specific remains or artifacts. The committee's recommendations have been endorsed by Senators Inouye and McCain, the Chair and Vice-chair of the Senate Select

Committee on Indian Affairs, and they have announced their intention to use the recommendations as a basis for legislation.

E. INDIVIDUAL PROPERTY RIGHTS

CRAMER v. UNITED STATES

261 U.S. 219 (1923)

Mr. Justice SUTHERLAND delivered the opinion of the Court.

This appeal brings up for review a decree of the Circuit Court of Appeals, directing the cancellation of a land patent issued in 1904 by the United States to the defendant, the Central Pacific Railway Company.

[The United States brought suit] acting in behalf of three Indians, who, it was claimed, had occupied the lands continuously since before 1859. The Act of July 25, 1866, c. 242, 14 Stat. 239, granted to the predecessor of the defendant company a series of odd numbered sections of land, including those named, but excepted from the grant such lands as "shall be found to have been granted, sold, reserved, occupied by homestead settlers, pre-empted, or otherwise disposed of." [T]he District Court found for the plaintiff upon the issue of actual occupancy and entered a decree confirming the right of possession in the Indians, which, however, was confined to the land actually enclosed, being an irregular body of about 175 acres and which did not in terms cancel the patent.

[The District Court] found that as early as 1859 the Indians named lived with their parents upon the lands described and had resided there continuously ever since; that they had under fence between 150 and 175 acres in an irregularly shaped tract, running diagonally through the two sections, portions of which they had irrigated and cultivated; that they had constructed and maintained dwelling houses and divers outbuildings, and had actually resided upon the lands and improved them for the purpose of making for themselves homes....

The decree of the Circuit Court of Appeals agreed with that of the District Court generally but extended the right of possession to the whole of each of the legal subdivisions which was fenced and cultivated in part, and reversed the decree, with instructions to enter one cancelling the patent in respect of the entire 360 acres.

A reversal of this decree is now sought upon several grounds.

1. It is urged that the occupancy of land by individual Indians does not come within the exceptive provision of the grant.

Until the Act of March 3, 1875, c. 131, 18 Stat. 402, 420, extending the homestead privilege to Indians, the right of an individual Indian to acquire title to public lands by entry was not recognized. It cannot, therefore, be said that these lands were occupied by homestead settlers nor were they granted, sold or preëmpted, but the question remains, were they "reserved ... or otherwise disposed of?" Unquestionably it has been the policy of the Federal Government from the beginning to respect the Indian right of occupancy, which could only be interfered with or determined by the United States. *Beecher v. Wetherby,* 95 U.S. 517, 525; *Minnesota v. Hitchcock,* 185 U.S. 373, 385. It is true that this policy has had in view the original nomadic tribal occupancy, but it is likewise true that in its essential spirit it applies to individual Indian occupancy as well; and the reasons for maintaining it in the latter case would seem to be no less cogent, since such occupancy being of a fixed character lends support to another well understood policy, namely, that of inducing the Indian to forsake his wandering habits and adopt those of civilized life. That such individual occupancy is entitled to protection finds strong support in various rulings of the Interior Department, to which in land matters this Court has always given much weight. That department has exercised its authority by issuing instructions from time to time to its local officers to protect the holdings of non-reservation Indians against the efforts of white men to dispossess them.

[I]n apparent recognition of possible individual Indian possession, [Congress] has in several of the state enabling acts required the incoming State to disclaim all right and title to lands "owned or *held* by *any Indian* or Indian tribes." [*See, e.g.,*] 25 Stat. 676, c. 180, § 4, par. 2.

The action of these individual Indians in abandoning their nomadic habits and attaching themselves to a definite locality, reclaiming, cultivating and improving the soil and establishing fixed homes thereon was in harmony with the well understood desire of the Government which we have mentioned. To hold that by so doing they acquired no possessory rights to which the Government would accord protection, would be contrary to the whole spirit of the traditional American policy toward these dependent wards of the nation.

The fact that such right of occupancy finds no recognition in any statute or other formal governmental action is not conclusive. The right, under the circumstances here disclosed, flows from a settled governmental policy.

[T]he possession of the property in question by these Indians was within the policy and with the implied consent of the Government. That possession was definite and substantial in character and open to observation when the railroad grant was made, and we have no doubt falls within the clause of the grant excepting from its operation lands "reserved ... or otherwise disposed of."

2. It is insisted that any rights these Indians might otherwise have had are barred by the provisions of the Act of March 3, 1851, c. 41, 9 Stat. 631. This statute required every person claiming lands in California by virtue of any right or title derived from the Spanish or Mexican governments to present the same for settlement to a commission created by the act. There was a provision directing the commission to ascertain and report the tenure by which the mission lands were held and those held by civilized Indians, and other Indians described. The act plainly has no application. The Indians here concerned do not belong to any of the classes described therein and their claims were in no way derived from the Spanish or Mexican governments. Moreover, it does not appear that these Indians were occupying the lands in question when the act was passed.

Barker v. Harvey, 181 U.S. 481, does not support the defendants' contention. There the Indians whose claims were in dispute were Mission Indians claiming a right of occupancy derived from the Mexican Government. They had failed to present their claims to the Commission, and this, it was held, constituted an abandonment. The Indians here concerned have no such claim and are not shown to be within the terms of the Act of 1851 in any respect. It further appeared in that case that prior to the cession to the United States the Mexican authorities, upon examination, found that the Indians had abandoned the lands and thereupon made an absolute grant to the plaintiff's predecessors, and, this grant having been confirmed by the Commission, a patent for the lands had issued.

[Finally, the] Circuit Court of Appeals erred in holding that the right of the Indians extended to the entire area of each legal subdivision, irrespective of the inclosure, and we agree with the District Court in confining the right to the lands actually inclosed, including the whole of the northeast quarter of the southwest quarter of Section 13, the small portion thereof which had not been enclosed having been improved. The Court of Appeals, in support of its conclusion, relied upon *Quinby v. Conlan,* 104 U.S. 420. In that case Conlan had entered upon a quarter section of land, occupied a portion thereof, and declared his purpose to acquire a preemption right to the whole, and soon thereafter had filed his declaratory statement in legal form, claiming the whole as a pre-emptor. This Court sustained Conlan's claim as against Quinby, a subsequent settler. Here the claim for the Indians is based on occupancy alone, and the extent of it is clearly fixed by the inclosure, cultivation and improvements. The evidence does not disclose any act of dominion on their part over, or any claim or assertion of right to, any lands beyond the limits of their actual possessions as thus defined. Under the circumstances, their rights are confined to the limits of actual occupancy and cannot be extended constructively to other lands never possessed or claimed, simply because they form part of the same legal subdivisions. [The general rule is] that possession alone, without title or color of title confers no right beyond the limits of actual possession.

Certain other contentions of defendants we deem it unnecessary to review, although they have been carefully considered. Aside from that stated in the last paragraph we find no error, but for the reasons there given, the decree of the Circuit Court of Appeals is reversed and the cause remanded to the District Court, with instructions to amend its decree so as to cancel the patent in respect of the lands possessed by the Indians and, as so amended, that decree is affirmed.

Reversed.

HODEL v. IRVING

481 U.S. 704 (1987)

Justice O'CONNOR delivered the opinion of the Court.

The question presented is whether the original version of the "escheat" provision of the Indian Land Consolidation Act of 1983, Pub. L. 97-459, Tit. II, 96 Stat. 2519, effected a "taking" of appellees' decedents' property without just compensation.

I

Towards the end of the 19th century, Congress enacted a series of land Acts which divided the communal reservations of Indian tribes into individual allotments for Indians and unallotted lands for non-Indian settlement. This legislation seems to have been in part animated by a desire to force Indians to abandon their nomadic ways in order to "speed the Indians' assimilation into American society," *Solem v. Bartlett,* 465 U.S. 463, 466 (1984), and in part a result of pressure to free new lands for further white settlement. Two years after the enactment of the General Allotment Act of 1887, ch. 119, 24 Stat. 388, Congress adopted a specific statute authorizing the division of the Great Reservation of the Sioux Nation into separate reservations and the allotment of specific tracts of reservation land to individual Indians, conditioned on the consent of three-fourths of the adult male Sioux. Act of Mar. 2, 1889, ch. 405, 25 Stat. 888. Under the Act, each male Sioux head of household took 320 acres of land and most other individuals 160 acres. In order to protect the allottees from the improvident disposition of their lands to white settlers, the Sioux allotment statute provided that the allotted lands were to be held in trust by the United States. Until 1910 the lands of deceased allottees passed to their heirs "according to the laws of the State or Territory" where the land was located, and after 1910, allottees were permitted to dispose of their interests by will in accordance with regulations promulgated by the Secretary of the Interior. 25 U.S.C. § 373. Those regulations generally served to protect Indian ownership of the allotted lands.

The policy of allotment of Indian lands quickly proved disastrous for the Indians. Cash generated by land sales to whites was quickly dissipated and the Indians, rather than farming the land themselves, evolved into petty landlords, leasing their allotted lands to white ranchers and farmers and living off the meager rentals. The failure of the allotment program became even clearer as successive generations came to hold the allotted lands. 40-, 80-, and 160-acre parcels became splintered into multiple undivided interests in land, with some parcels having hundreds and many parcels having dozens of owners. Because the land was held in trust and often could not be alienated or partitioned the fractionation problem grew and grew over time.

A 1928 report commissioned by the Congress found the situation administratively unworkable and economically wasteful. L. Meriam, Institute for Government Research, The Problem of Indian Administration 40-41. Good, potentially productive, land was allowed to lie fallow, amidst great poverty, because of the difficulties of managing property held in this manner. In discussing the Indian Reorganization Act of 1934, Representative Howard said:

> "It is in the case of the inherited allotments, however, that the administrative costs become incredible.... On allotted reservations, numerous cases exist where the shares of each individual heir from lease money may be 1 cent a month. Or one heir may own minute fractional shares in 30 or 40 different allotments. The cost of leasing, bookkeeping, and distributing the proceeds in many cases far exceeds the total income. The Indians and the Indian Service personnel are thus trapped in a meaningless system of minute partition in which all thought of the possible use of land to satisfy human needs is lost in a mathematical haze of bookkeeping." 78 Cong. Rec. 11728 (1934) (remarks of Rep. Howard).

In 1934, in response to arguments such as these, the Congress acknowledged the failure of its policy and ended further allotment of Indian lands [by enacting the Indian Reorganization Act].

But the end of future allotment by itself could not prevent the further compounding of the existing problem caused by the passage of time. Ownership continued to fragment as succeeding generations came to hold the property, since, in the order of things, each property owner was apt to have more than one heir. In 1960, both the House and the Senate undertook comprehensive studies of the problem. These studies indicated that one-half of the approximately 12 million acres of allotted trust lands were held in fractionated ownership, with over three million acres held by more than six heirs to a parcel. Further hearings were held in 1966, but not until the Indian Land Consolidation Act of 1983 did the Congress take action to ameliorate the problem of fractionated ownership of Indian lands.

Section 207 of the Indian Land Consolidation Act — the escheat provision at issue in this case — provided:

> "No undivided fractional interest in any tract of trust or restricted land within a tribe's reservation or otherwise subjected to a tribe's jurisdiction shall descendent [sic] by intestacy or devise but shall escheat to that tribe if such interest represents 2 per centum or less of the total acreage in such tract and has earned to its owner less than $100 in the preceding year before it is due to escheat."

Congress made no provision for the payment of compensation to the owners of the interests covered by § 207. The statute was signed into law on January 12, 1983 and became effective immediately.

The three appellees — Mary Irving, Patrick Pumpkin Seed, and Eileen Bisonette — are enrolled members of the Oglala Sioux Tribe. They are, or represent, heirs or devisees of members of the Tribe who died in March, April and June 1983. Eileen Bisonette's decedent, Mary Poor Bear-Little Hoop Cross, purported to will all her property, including property subject to § 207, to her five minor children in whose name Bisonette claims the property. Chester Irving, Charles Leroy Pumpkin Seed, and Edgar Pumpkin Seed all died intestate. At the time of their deaths, the four decedents owned 41 fractional interests subject to the provisions of § 207. The Irving estate lost two interests whose value together was approximately $100; the Bureau of Indian Affairs placed total values of approximately $2,700 on the 26 escheatable interests in the Cross estate and $1,816 on the 13 escheatable interests in the Pumpkin Seed estates. But for § 207, this property would have passed, in the ordinary course, to appellees or those they represent.

Appellees filed suit in the United States District Court for the District of South Dakota, claiming that § 207 resulted in a taking of property without just compensation in violation of the Fifth Amendment. The District Court concluded that the statute was constitutional. It held that appellees had no vested interest in the property of the decedents prior to their deaths and that Congress had plenary authority to abolish the power of testamentary disposition of Indian property and to alter the rules of intestate succession.

The Court of Appeals for the Eighth Circuit reversed. Although it agreed that the appellees had no vested rights in the decedents' property, it concluded that their decedents had a right, derived from the original Sioux Allotment Statute, to control disposition of their property at death. The Court of Appeals held that the appellees had standing to invoke that right and that the taking of that right without compensation to decedents' estates violated the Fifth Amendment.[1]

---

[1]The Court of Appeals, without explanation, went on to "declare" that not only the original version of § 207, but also the amended version not before it, 25 U.S.C. § 2206 (1982 ed., Supp. III), unconstitutionally took property without compensation. Since none of the property which escheated

III

The Congress, acting pursuant to its broad authority to regulate the descent and devise of Indian trust lands, *Jeferson v. Fink,* 247 U.S. 288, 294 (1918), enacted § 207 as a means of ameliorating, over time, the problem of extreme fractionation of certain Indian lands. By forbidding the passing on at death of small, undivided interests in Indian lands, Congress hoped that future genera-tions of Indians would be able to make more productive use of the Indians' ancestral lands. We agree with the Government that encouraging the consolida-tion of Indian lands is a public purpose of high order. The fractionation prob-lem on Indian reservations is extraordinary and may call for dramatic action to encourage consolidation. The Sisseton-Wahpeton Sioux Tribe, appearing as amicus curiae in support of the United States, is a quintessential victim of fractionation. Forty-acre tracts on the Sisseton-Wahpeton Lake Traverse reser-vation, leasing for about $1,000 annually, are commonly subdivided into hun-dreds of undivided interests, many of which generate only pennies a year in rent. The average tract has 196 owners and the average owner undivided inter-ests in fourteen tracts. The administrative headache this represents can be fathomed by examining Tract 1305, [a 43-acre tract valued at $8,000, which] has 439 owners, one-third of whom receive less than $.05 in annual rent and two-thirds of whom receive less than $1. The largest interest holder receives $82.85 annually. The common denominator used to compute fractional inter-ests in the property is 3,394,923,840,000. The smallest heir receives $.01 every 177 years. If the tract were sold (assuming the 439 owners could agree) for its estimated $8,000 value, he would be entitled to $.000418. The administrative costs of handling this tract are estimated by the Bureau of Indian Affairs at $17,560 annually.

This Court has held that the Government has considerable latitude in regulat-ing property rights in ways that may adversely affect the owners. See *Keystone Bituminous Coal Assn. v. DeBenedictis,* 480 U.S. [470] (1987); *Penn Central Transportation Co. v. New York City,* 438 U.S. 104, 125-127 (1978); *Goldblatt v. Hempstead,* 369 U.S. 590, 592-593 (1962). The framework for examining the question of whether a regulation of property amounts to a taking requiring just compensation is firmly established and has been regularly and recently reaf-firmed. As THE CHIEF JUSTICE has written:

> "[T]his Court has generally 'been unable to develop any "set formula" for determin-ing when "justice and fairness" require that economic injuries caused by public action be compensated by the government, rather than remain disproportionately concen-trated on a few persons.' *Penn Central Transportation Co. v. New York City,* 438 U.S.], at 124. Rather, it has examined the 'taking' question by engaging in essentially ad hoc, factual inquiries that have identified several factors — such as the economic impact of the regulation, its interference with reasonable investment backed expecta-tions, and the character of the governmental action — that have particular signifi-cance. *Ibid.*" *Kaiser Aetna v. United States,* [444 U.S. 164,] at 175 [1979].

There is no question that the relative economic impact of § 207 upon the owners of these property rights can be substantial. Section 207 provides for the escheat of small undivided property interests that are unproductive during the

---

in this case did so pursuant to the amended version of the statute, this "declaration" is, at best, dicta. We express no opinion on the constitutionality of § 207 as amended.

year preceding the owner's death. Even if we accept the Government's assertion that the income generated by such parcels may be properly thought of as *de minimis*, their value may not be. While the Irving estate lost two interests whose value together was only approximately $100, the Bureau of Indian Affairs placed total values of approximately $2,700 and $1,816 on the escheatable interests in the Cross and Pumpkin Seed estates. These are not trivial sums. There are suggestions in the legislative history regarding the 1984 amendments to § 207 that the failure to "look back" more than one year at the income generated by the property had caused the escheat of potentially valuable timber and mineral interests. Of course, the whole of appellees' decedents' property interests were not taken by § 207. Appellees' decedents retained full beneficial use of the property during their lifetimes as well as the right to convey it *inter vivos*. There is no question, however, that the right to pass on valuable property to one's heirs is itself a valuable right. Depending on the age of the owner, much or most of the value of the parcel may inhere in this "remainder" interest.

The extent to which any of the appellees' decedents had "investment-backed expectations" in passing on the property is dubious. Though it is conceivable that some of these interests were purchased with the expectation that the owners might pass on the remainder to their heirs at death, the property has been held in trust for the Indians for 100 years and is overwhelmingly acquired by gift, descent, or devise. Because of the highly fractionated ownership, the property is generally held for lease rather than improved and used by the owners. None of the appellees here can point to any specific investment-backed expectations beyond the fact that their ancestors agreed to accept allotment only after ceding to the United States large parts of the original Great Sioux Reservation.

Also weighing weakly in favor of the statute is the fact that there is something of an "average reciprocity of advantage," *Pennsylvania Coal Co. v. Mahon,* 260 U.S. 393, 415 (1922), to the extent that owners of escheatable interests maintain a nexus to the Tribe. Consolidation of Indian lands in the Tribe benefits the members of the Tribe. All members do not own escheatable interests, nor do all owners belong to the Tribe. Nevertheless, there is substantial overlap between the two groups. The owners of escheatable interests often benefit from the escheat of others' fractional interests. Moreover, the whole benefit gained is greater than the sum of the burdens imposed since consolidated lands are more productive than fractionated lands.

If we were to stop our analysis at this point, we might well find § 207 constitutional. But the character of the Government regulation here is extraordinary. In *Kaiser Aetna v. United States,* 444 U.S., at 176, we emphasized that the regulation destroyed "one of the most essential sticks in the bundle of rights that are commonly characterized as property — the right to exclude others." Similarly, the regulation here amounts to virtually the abrogation of the right to pass on a certain type of property — the small undivided interest — to one's heirs. In one form or another, the right to pass on property — to one's family in particular — has been part of the Anglo-American legal system since feudal times. The fact that it may be possible for the owners of these interests to effectively control disposition upon death through complex *inter vivos* transactions such as revocable trusts, is simply not an adequate substitute for the rights taken, given the nature of the property. Even the United States concedes that total abrogation of the right to pass property is unprecedented and likely unconstitutional. Moreover, this statute effectively abolishes both descent and devise of these property interests even when the passing of the property to the heir might result in consolidation of property — as for instance when the heir already owns another undivided interest in the property. Compare 25 U.S.C. § 2206(b) (1982 ed., Supp. III). Since the escheatable interests are not, as the United States argues, necessarily *de minimis*, nor, as it also argues, does the availability of *inter vivos* transfer obviate the need for descent and devise, a *total* abrogation of these rights cannot be upheld. But cf. *Andrus v. Allard,* 444 U.S. 51 (1979) (upholding abrogation of the right to sell endangered eagles' parts as necessary to environmental protection regulatory scheme).

In holding that complete abolition of both the descent and devise of a particular class of property may be a taking, we reaffirm the continuing vitality of the long line of cases recognizing the States', and where appropriate, the United States', broad authority to adjust the rules governing the descent and devise of property without implicating the guarantees of the Just Compensation Clause. The difference in this case is the fact that both descent and devise are completely abolished; indeed they are abolished even in circumstances when the governmental purpose sought to be advanced, consolidation of ownership of Indian lands, does not conflict with the further descent of the property.

There is little doubt that the extreme fractionation of Indian lands is a serious public problem. It may well be appropriate for the United States to ameliorate fractionation by means of regulating the descent and devise of Indian lands. Surely it is permissible for the United States to prevent the owners of such interests from further subdividing them among future heirs on pain of escheat. It may be appropriate to minimize further compounding of the problem by abolishing the descent of such interests by rules of intestacy, thereby forcing the owners to formally designate an heir to prevent escheat to the Tribe. What is certainly not appropriate is to take the extraordinary step of abolishing both descent and devise of these property interests even when the passing of the property to the heir might result in consolidation of property. Accordingly, we find that this regulation, in the words of Justice Holmes, "goes too far." *Pennsylvania Coal Co. v. Mahon,* 260 U.S., at 415.

Affirmed.

Justice BRENNAN, with whom Justice MARSHALL and Justice BLACKMUN join, concurring.

I find nothing in today's opinion that would limit *Andrus v. Allard,* 444 U.S. 51 (1979) to its facts. Indeed, largely for reasons discussed by the Court of Appeals, I am of the view that the unique negotiations giving rise to the property rights and expectations at issue here make this case the unusual one. Accordingly, I join the opinion of the Court.

Justice SCALIA, with whom THE CHIEF JUSTICE and Justice POWELL join, concurring.

I join the opinion of the Court. I write separately to note that in my view the present statute, insofar as concerns the balance between rights taken and rights left untouched, is indistinguishable from the statute that was at issue in *Andrus v. Allard,* 444 U.S. 51 (1979). Because that comparison is determinative of whether there has been a taking, in finding a taking today our decision effectively limits *Allard* to its facts.

Justice STEVENS, with whom Justice WHITE joins, concurring in the judgment.

The Government has a legitimate interest in eliminating Indians' fractional holdings of real property. Legislating in pursuit of this interest, the Government might constitutionally have consolidated the fractional land interests affected by § 207 of the Indian Land Consolidation Act of 1983, in three ways: It might have purchased them; it might have condemned them for a public purpose and paid just compensation to their owners; or it might have left them untouched while conditioning their descent by intestacy or devise upon their consolidation by voluntary conveyances within a reasonable period of time....

Since Congress plainly did not authorize either purchase or condemnation and the payment of just compensation, the statute is valid only if Congress, in § 207, authorized the third alternative. In my opinion, therefore, the principal question in this case is whether § 207 represents a lawful exercise of the sovereign's prerogative to condition the retention of fee simple or other ownership interests upon the performance of a modest statutory duty within a reasonable period of time.

III

[T]he Secretary contends that § 207 falls within the permissible boundaries of legislation that may operate to limit or extinguish property rights. The Secretary places great emphasis on the minimal value of the property interests affected by § 207, the legitimacy of the governmental purpose in consolidating such interests, and the fact that the tribe, rather than the United States, is the beneficiary of the so-called "escheat." These points, considered in turn and as a whole, provide absolutely no basis for reversing the judgment of the Court of Appeals.

The value of a property interest does not provide a yardstick for measuring "the scope of the dual constitutional guarantees that there be no taking of property without just compensation, and no deprivation of property without the due process of law." *Texaco, Inc. v. Short,* 454 U.S. 516, 540-541 (1982) (BRENNAN, J., dissenting). The sovereign has no license to take private property without paying for it and without providing its owner with any opportunity to avoid or mitigate the consequences of the deprivation simply because the property is relatively inexpensive. *Loretto v. Teleprompter Manhattan CATV Corp.,* 458 U.S. 419, 436-437 and 438, n.16 (1982). The Fifth Amendment draws no distinction between grand larceny and petty larceny.

The legitimacy of the governmental purposes served by § 207 demonstrates that the statute is not arbitrary, see *Delaware Tribal Business Committee v. Weeks,* 430 U.S. 73 (1977), and that the alleged "taking" is for a valid "public use" within the meaning of the Fifth Amendment. Those facts, however, do not excuse or mitigate whatever obligation to pay just compensation arises when an otherwise constitutional enactment effects a taking of property. Nor does it lessen the importance of giving a property owner fair notice of a major change in the rules governing the disposition of his property.

The fact that § 207 provides for an "escheat" to the tribe rather than to the United States does not change the unwarned impact of the statute on an individual Indian who wants to leave his property to his children. The statute takes the disposition of decedent's fractional land interests out of the control of the decedent's will or the laws of intestate succession; whether the United States or the Tribe retains the property, the landowner's loss is the same. The designation of the Tribe as beneficiary is an essential feature, however, in two respects. Since the Tribe is the beneficiary, its own interests conflict with its duty to bring the workings of the statute to the attention of the property owner. In addition, the designation of the Tribe as beneficiary highlights the inappropriateness of the majority's takings analysis. The use of the term "escheat" in § 207 differs in a substantial way from the more familiar uses of that term. At common law the property of a person who died intestate and without lawful heirs would escheat to the sovereign; thus the doctrine provided a mechanism for determining ownership of what otherwise would have remained abandoned property. In contrast, under § 207 the statutory escheat supersedes the rights of claimants who would otherwise inherit the property; it allocates property between two contending parties.

Section 207 differs from more conventional escheats in another important way. It contains no provisions assuring that the property owner was given a fair opportunity to make suitable arrangements to avoid the operation of the statute. Legislation authorizing the escheat of unclaimed property, such as real estate, bank accounts, and other earmarked funds, typically provides as a condition precedent to the escheat an appropriate lapse of time and the provision of adequate notice to make sure that the property may fairly be treated as abandoned.[11] Similarly, interpleader proceedings in District Court provide procedural safeguards, including an opportunity to appear, for those whose rights will be affected by the judgment. See 28 U.S.C. § 1335; Federal Rule of Civil Procedure 22. The statute before us, in contrast, contained no such mechanism, apparently relying on the possibility that appellees' decedents would simply learn about the statute's consequences one way or another.

While § 207 therefore does not qualify as an escheat of the kind recognized at common law, it might be regarded as a statute imposing a duty on the owner of highly fractionated interests in allotted lands to consolidate his interests with those of other owners of similar interests. The method of enforcing such a duty is to treat its nonperformance during the owner's lifetime as an abandonment of the fractional interests. This release of dominion over the property might justify its escheat to the use of the sovereign.

----

[11] For example, the Government both provides a grace period and bears an affirmative responsibility to prevent escheat in the distribution of funds to which enrolled members of the Peoria Tribe are statutorily entitled [in] 25 U.S.C. § 1222. See 25 U.S.C. § 1226 (Any per capita share, whether payable to a living enrollee or to the heirs or legatees of a deceased enrollee, which the Secretary of the Interior is unable to deliver within two years after the date the check is issued ... shall revert to the Peoria Tribe").

State statutes governing abandoned property typically provide for a grace period and notice. See, e.g., N.Y. Aband. Prop. Law §§ 300-302 (McKinney 1944 and Supp. 1987) (property held by banking organizations); Ill. Rev. Stat., ch. 141, 102, 112 (1985) (property held by banking or financial organizations). Statutes governing the escheat of property of decedents intestate and without heirs also provide for notice and an opportunity for interested parties to assert their claims. See, e.g., Cal. Civ. Proc. Code Ann. §§ 1420, 1423 (West 1982); Tex. Prop. Code Ann. §§ 71.101-71.106 (1984 and Supp. 1987).

[A] statute providing for the lapse, escheat, or abandonment of private property cannot impose conditions on continued ownership that are unreasonable, either because they cost too much or because the statute does not allow property owners a reasonable opportunity to perform them and thereby to avoid the loss of their property....[12]

The Due Process Clause of the Fifth Amendment thus applies to § 207's determination of which acts and omissions may validly constitute an abandonment, just as the Takings Clause applies to whether the statutory escheat of property must be accompanied by the payment of just compensation.[13] It follows, I believe, that § 207 deprived decedents of due process of law by failing to provide an adequate "grace period" in which they could arrange for the consolidation of fractional interests in order to avoid abandonment. Because the statutory presumption of abandonment is invalid under the precise facts of this case, I do not reach the ground relied upon by the Court of Appeals — that the resulting escheat of abandoned property would effect a taking of private property for public use without just compensation.

[C]itizens "are presumptively charged with knowledge of the law," [but] that presumption may not apply when "the statute does not allow a sufficient 'grace period' to provide the persons affected by a change in the law with an adequate opportunity to become familiar with their obligations under it." [*Atkins v. Parker*, 472 U.S. 115, 130 (1985) (citing *Texaco, Inc.*, 454 U.S., at 532).] Unlike the foodstamp recipients in *Parker*, who received a grace period of over 90 days and individual notice of the substance of the new law, [*Id.*] at 130-131, the Indians affected by § 207 did not receive a reasonable grace period. Nothing in the record suggests that appellees' decedents received an adequate opportunity to put their affairs in order.[19]

The conclusion that Congress has failed to provide appellees' decedents with a reasonable opportunity for compliance implies no rejection of Congress' plenary authority over the affairs and the property of Indians. The Constitution vests Congress with plenary power "to deal with the special problems of Indians." [*Morton v. Mancari*, 417 U.S. 535, 551 (1974).] As the Secretary acknowledges, however, the Government's plenary power over the property of Indians "is subject to constitutional limitations." The Due Process Clause of the Fifth Amendment required Congress to afford reasonable notice and opportunity for compliance to Indians that § 207 would prevent fractional interests in land from descending by intestate or testate succession. In omitting any opportunity at all for owners of fractional interests to order their affairs in light of § 207, Congress has failed to afford the affected Indians the due process of law required by the Fifth Amendment.

---

[12][A]n Indian owner of a fractional interest cannot consolidate interests or collect $100 per annum from it without the willing participation of other parties.

[13] The Fifth Amendment to the Constitution provides that no person shall "be deprived of life, liberty, or property, without due process of law; nor shall private property be taken for public use, without just compensation."

[19] Nothing in the record contradicts the possibility that appellees themselves only became aware of the statute upon receiving notices that hearings had been scheduled for the week of October 24, 1983 to determine if their tribe had a right through escheat to any lands that might otherwise have passed to appellees. The notices were issued on October 4, 1983, after the death of appellees' decedents, and therefore afforded no opportunity for decedents to comply with § 207 or for appellees to advise their decedents of the possibility of escheat.

Accordingly, I concur in the judgment.

NOTE ON ALLOTTED LANDS

The history of the allotment policy has been treated elsewhere in this book. *See* Chapter 1, section 0. Although that policy has been repudiated, the problems of Indian land tenure caused by allotment remain. Allotment issues are complex and form a separate and specialized body of jurisprudence important to the field of Indian law beyond the scope of this book and its focus on the tribe. What follows is, thus, a brief summary of some of the ways the allotment policy continues to affect Indian tribes today. *See generally* F. COHEN, HANDBOOK OF FEDERAL INDIAN LAW ch. 11 (b) & (c) (1982 ed.).

The most important effect of the policy was the great loss of Indian land. During the allotment era the Indian land base shrank by nearly two-thirds, from 138 million acres held in trust for Indian tribes in 1887 to 48 million acres held for the benefit of Indians in 1934, when the Indian Reorganization Act withdrew the authority to allot Indian lands in severalty. 25 U.S.C. § 461. The legal processes by which land was transferred from Indian to non-Indian hands varied. First, the allotment policy and the implementing agreements specifically envisioned the ceding and subsequent sale to non-Indian settlers of "surplus" land, not needed for limited-acreage allotments to tribal members. Second, upon the expiration of the twenty-five-year restrictions against alienation, or the shortening of that period by the proper issuance of a certificate of competency to an allottee, sale of the land by the individual Indian holder was authorized. Significant land sales, including evidence of land frauds, occurred through the second method.

The Indian Reorganization Act of 1934, ended this second method of land loss. For tribes that approved the IRA, the law indefinitely extended the trust periods for allotted lands as to which the twenty-five-year period had not expired. 25 U.S.C. § 462. Executive orders extended other unexpired trust periods. 25 C.F.R. appendix (1988). Nevertheless, Congress did not completely end the practice of issuing patents in fee. In 1948, Congress authorized the Secretary of the Interior to remove the restraints on allotted land, issue patents in fee, and approve conveyances upon application of the Indian owners. 25 U.S.C. § 483. *See Sampson v. Andrus*, 483 F. Supp. 240 (D.S.D. 1980) (Section 483 permits Secretary to partition land upon request by one of two owners). *See also* 25 U.S.C. § 404; 25 U.S.C. § 405.

A third method of land loss continues today. Some land has been removed from restricted trust status by its descent and distribution to non-Indian legatees or heirs. The individualization of Indian land title brought about by the allotment policy required some procedures for the descent and distribution of Indian property upon the death of the allottee. Thus, 25 U.S.C. § 348 authorized the issuance of the patent to the allottee's "heirs" according to the laws of the state or territory where such land is located, and the Secretary of the Interior was further authorized under 25 U.S.C. § 373 to approve Indian wills for the descent and distribution of property of the allottee. To enforce these provisions, the Department of the Interior has become a land records office for individual claims to allotted land. Furthermore, the United States has set up an administrative probate system, independent of the probate systems of the states, for the administration of the estates of Indians holding restricted trust property. *See, e.g., Tooahnippah v. Hickel,* 397 U.S. 598 (1970) (Secretary of the Interior does not have unlimited discretion under 25 U.S.C. § 373 "to revoke or rewrite a will that reflects a rational testamentary scheme"). Provisions for the administrative probate of the estates of allottees holding restricted trust lands are found at 25 U.S.C. §§ 371-380.

The land tenure of allotted Indian lands differs from tribal land tenure in a number of other ways that can result in present-day land loss. For example, the holders of allotted lands may execute a mortgage or deed of trust to such lands and such lands are thereafter subject to foreclosure or sale under the mortgage or deed of trust in the manner provided by state law, 25 U.S.C. § 483a. The mortgagee may have to foreclose in tribal court, however. *See Northwest South Dakota Prod. Credit Ass'n v. Smith,* 784 F.2d 323 (8th Cir. 1986). In addition, 25 U.S.C. § 357 authorizes states to condemn allotted lands for any public purpose, but requires the state to pay compensation to the allottee. Such a condemnation action, however, must be prosecuted in federal court and the United States is an indispensable party to any such proceeding. *Minnesota v. United States,* 305 U.S. 382 (1939). Moreover, the state may not simply seize the land even if inverse condemnation is permissible under state law, but must invoke formal condemnation procedures. *United States v. Clarke,* 445 U.S. 253 (1980).

In sum, loss of allotted land continues today, although not nearly on the same scale as during the allotment era. In recent years allottees have begun to make claims for the return of allotted land lost through defective or invalid transfers of allotted Indian land. For background and description of these claims, see Peterson, *That So-Called Warranty Deed: Clouded Land Titles on the White Earth Indian Reservation in Minnesota,* 59 N.D.L. REV. 159 (1983) (Over 900 individual claims involving 90,000 acres); LaFave, *South Dakota's Forced Fee Indian Land Claims: Will Landowners Be Liable for Government's Wrongdoing?,* 30 S.D.L. REV. 59 (1984) (estimate of 9,500 forced fee claims affecting 1.5 to 2 million acres in Western U.S.). Claims against the United States, however, are governed by the applicable federal statute of limitations. *See United States v. Mottaz,* 476 U.S. 834 (1986) (12-year statute of limitations of Quiet Title Act, the exclusive means to challenge U.S. title, bars the claim). Concluding that the federal statute of limitations bars the forced fee claims, courts have also dismissed suits against states, counties, and individual parties, ruling that the U.S. was an indispensable party. *See, e.g., Nichols v. Rysavy,* 809 F.2d 1317 (8th Cir.), *cert. denied,* 484 U.S. 848 (1987); *Manypenny v. United States,* 125 F.R.D. 497 (D. Minn. 1989). In 1985 Congress enacted the White Earth Reservation Land Settlement Act to extinguish the forced fee claims on the White Earth Reservation and provide for a mechanism to obtain compensation in the amount of fair market value plus 5% interest. The law was upheld in *Littlewolf v. Lujan,* 877 F.2d 1058 (D.C. Cir. 1989) (even if law a taking, it provides a reasonable mechanism to obtain just compensation).

In addition to individualizing Indian land tenure, the allotment policy also had other long-term effects on Indian reservations. First, allotment opened Indian reservation enclaves to non-Indian settlement. Thus, it impaired the possibility of a purely geographically based concept of tribal sovereignty by interspersing non-Indian and Indian ownership, often in a checkerboard pattern. This result has spawned many of the jurisdictional issues already discussed above in Chapter 3.

For further discussion of the allotment policy and its history, see D. Otis, *History of the Allotment Policy,* in *Readjustment of Indian Affairs, Hearings on H.R. 7902 Before the Committee on Indian Affairs,* 73d Cong., 2d Sess., pt. 9, at 428 et seq. (1934); J. KINNEY, A CONTINENT LOST — A CIVILIZATION WON (1937); W. SEMPLE, OKLAHOMA INDIAN LAND TITLES ANNOTATED (1952).

IN RE ESTATE OF WAUNEKA

13 Indian L. Rep. 6049
(Nav. Sup. Ct., Mar. 7, 1986)

AUSTIN, Associate Justice.

Ben Wauneka Sr., administrator of the estate, appeals the denial of his claim against Dennis Williams for unauthorized use of estate farmland. Ben Wauneka Sr., as an heir, also appeals the judgment which distributed the farmland to the heirs in equal parcels.

Charley Nez Wauneka Sr., died intestate on January 10, 1979. There is no surviving spouse. In his final report and proposed distribution, Ben Wauneka Sr., the eldest son, proposed that the entire farmland consisting of 10.8 acres be awarded to him. Objections to the proposed distribution of the farmland were filed by the opposing heirs (Eunice Wauneka, Lucille W. Hunt, Charley Wauneka Jr.) and by Dennis Williams. Dennis Williams is not an heir. Opposing heirs are all children of the decedent.

Both objections alleged that Dennis Williams had purchased the farmland from the decedent. In an earlier *de novo* decision the court of appeals had rejected the purchase argument and ruled that the farmland was estate property. *Wauneka Sr. v. Williams,* A-CV-46-81. Opposing heirs subsequently amended their objection to request equal distribution of the farmland.

[Ben Wauneka, Sr., as the administrator of the estate can bring a claim against Dennis Williams for unauthorized use and occupancy of 10.8 acres of estate farmland. In *Wauneka, Sr. v. Williams,* A-CV-46-81, the court of appeals held that the farmland was estate property, but had permitted Williams to cut and take away the alfalfa growing at the date of the trial. That opinion held only that Williams's use and occupancy was legitimate for that one growing season, in order to avoid crop waste for the 1983 season.]

Ben Wauneka Sr., as an heir, first contends that the district court erred in distributing 10.8 acres of farmland to the heirs in equal parcels. Ben Wauneka Sr. argues that he should be awarded the entire farmland under the doctrine of equitable distribution. Alternatively, Ben Wauneka Sr. contends that the farmland as distributed by the district court is unequal on its face. He argues that the parcel awarded to him is undeveloped, contains the roughest area, and it does not have the grazing capacity nor the production potential as the other parcels. We hold for equitable distribution therefore we do not reach the merits on the second claim.

In *Wauneka v. Williams,* the court of appeals sitting *de novo* found that none of the parties, including the decedent, had a valid permit granting them the right to use and occupy the farmland. However, the court found that the decedent held the use rights to the land through a lifetime of continuous and exclusive use.

The land is substantially improved. It is fenced and at least 7.6 acres has been continuously used for growing alfalfa since 1969. The other 3.2 acres, denoted "not in use," is used primarily for pasturing cattle. A small creek, which we presume is used for irrigation, crosses the land lengthwise. The land was surveyed and plotted on a map by the Bureau of Indian Affairs in 1979. It is unclear why a permit was not issued.

The courts of the Navajo Nation have the authority to probate the unrestricted property of a decedent. 7 N.T.C. § 253(c). The question arises as to whether the property in this case falls into the category of unrestricted property. Restricted property, we believe, includes reservation land for which the Navajo Nation holds title for the common use and equal benefit of all tribal members. See *United States v. Jim,* 409 U.S. 80 (1972); *Mashpee Tribe v. Watt,* 542 F. Supp. 797 (D. Mass. 1982), *aff'd,* 707 F.2d 23 (1st Cir.), *cert. denied,* 104 S. Ct. 555 (1983). Unrestricted property includes property owned by individuals, and for which the Navajo Nation does not hold title for all tribal members.

Land use on the Navajo Reservation is unique and unlike private ownership of land off the reservation. While individual tribal members do not own land similar to off-reservation, there exists a possessory use interest in land which we recognize as customary usage. An individual normally confines his use and occupancy of land to an area traditionally inhabited by his ancestors. This is the customary use area concept.

The Navajo Tribal Council has recognized that customary usage is a property right for which compensation is available if diminished by the sovereign. 16 N.T.C. § 1402, CJA-18-60. In *Dennison v. Tucson Gas and Electric Company,* 1 Nav. R. 95 [2 Indian L. Rep. No. 4, p. 52] (1974), the court recognized customary usage as a property right protected by the Navajo Bill of Rights and the Indian Civil Rights Act, 25 U.S.C § 1301 *et seq.* (1968). Customary usage is therefore viewed as a property interest by the Navajo Nation.

Wauneka Sr. v. Williams found that the decedent exercised continuous and exclusive possessory use of the land during his lifetime. The decedent's use was never disrupted by either the sovereign, the Bureau of Indian Affairs, or other land users from the immediate area. It is clear then that the decedent possessed a recognized property interest in the farmland. The farmland is fenced and readily ascertainable. We hold that this customary use area and the improvements incident can pass as property under our laws of succession.

Under our rules, Navajo custom, if proven, controls the distribution of intestate property. Custom takes priority and even if it conflicts with our rules of probate. Nav. R. Probate Proc., Rule 10; See *Johnson v. Johnson,* 3 Nav. R. 9 (1980); *Apache v. Republic National Life Insurance,* 3 Nav. R. 250 (W.R.D.C. 1982).

Ben Wauneka Sr. argues that he proved custom in the Blue Canyon area at the trial *dc novo* through the undisputed testimony of a well-known medicineman. In his brief, Ben Wauneka Sr. states: "It is the custom in this area of the Navajo Nation for the eldest son to inherit land." Brief for appellant at 6.

However, a brief statement without further elaboration is not overly persuasive. We consider this custom as only one factor in our decision.

Customary law has been frequently used by our courts to determine allocation of property. The customary trust is an excellent device to use in property distribution cases involving permits and land. The customary trust is a unique Navajo innovation which requires the appointment of a trustee to hold the productive property for the benefit of the family unit. See *Matter of the Trust of Benally*, 1 Nav. R. 10 (1969); *Johnson v. Johnson*, 3 Nav. R. 9 (1980).

The customary trust is most efficient if there is cooperation and participation by all concerned. Those elements are unfortunately lacking in this case. The dissension among the heirs is counterproductive to any concept of a customary trust. The best interests of the heirs will not be served by a trust which would only be an impetus for further family discord. The Navajo Nation has long disapproved of fragmenting agricultural and grazing lands. While our statutes specifically address permitted lands, we believe the policy is equally applicable here. At 3 N.T.C. § 217 we are reminded that:

(a) Upon the death of an assignee his land use permit shall be transferred to his most logical heir as determined by the Tribal Court. The Court shall make every effort to assign the land as one unit or combine it with another. The Court should make every effort to keep the land assignment in one tract and not subdivide it.

The statutes governing inheritance of land associated with major irrigation projects and small irrigation projects contain the same language.

We adhere to the land policy of the Navajo Nation. We disfavor dividing up of small parcels of land. The practical effect of progressive fragmentation of land results in possession of even smaller parcels by an astronomical number of heirs. The proration of allotments is a prime example of problems with fragmentation we can do without on the Navajo Reservation.

Splitting 10.8 acres of customary use land in this case results in each heir possessing a little over two and one-half acres. Inevitably, progressive fragmentation decreases the usefulness of the land and the benefits derived from the land diminishes. An increase of squabbles over land use is apparent as customary users attempt to expand their use beyond their few acres. Our compliance with the Navajo land policy is made with the knowledge that opposing heirs have been awarded other equitable portions of the estate. Perhaps in the future, there will be situations which mandate contrary decisions, but we will not dwell on that here.

Every acre of land on the reservation not reserved for a special purpose is a part of someone's customary use area. Navajo history teaches us that land and livestock nourished our development as a nation. Today there are Navajo people who have devoted their entire lives to etching [sic] a living from the land. If left undisturbed these independent individuals will continue to sustain themselves from the land despite other people's need for a wage income.

It is undisputed that of all of the heirs Ben Wauneka Sr. holds the best position to make proper and beneficial use of the land. Ben Wauneka Sr. is unemployed, does not have use rights to any other land, and he makes his living solely from the land in question. Ben Wauneka Sr. possesses the necessary implements to operate and maintain the farmland. Ben Wauneka Sr. has lived near the farmland all his life and he has worked the land in the past. Ben

Wauneka Sr. needs the land to sustain his livelihood. We cannot say the same for the other heirs.

The opposing heirs have all expressed their intent to dispose of their parcels if awarded. Obviously the opposing heirs have no interest in farming the land. Each of the opposing heirs has been generously awarded other property of the estate. The opposing heirs are also either employed, live away from the land, or they do not possess the equipment to operate and maintain the land. The opposing heirs cannot complain that they were not well provided for.

Our decision to award Ben Wauneka Sr. this portion of the estate property is not inconsistent with our laws of property distribution. *Joe v. Joe*, 1 Nav. R. 320 (1978), dealt with the division of religious paraphernalia in a divorce action. There the court allowed both parties to be awarded sufficient paraphernalia to perform ceremonies. Both parties had the capability to put the items to proper use. We believe Ben Wauneka Sr. is the most suitable heir who can put the land to proper and beneficial use, therefore he is awarded the farmland.

The case will be remanded to the district court for a trial on the administrator's claim against Dennis Williams.

NOTES

1. The Effect of *Cramer* on Individual Aboriginal Title: What was the nature of the title protected in *Cramer*? Could it be asserted against the United States Government? In *United States v. Dann,* set forth and discussed above, section B4, the Court refused to address the question whether the Dann sisters held individual aboriginal title, because the courts below had not yet addressed it. Nevertheless, the Court stated: "We have recognized that individual aboriginal rights may exist in certain contexts," citing *Cramer.*

On remand, the Ninth Circuit Court of Appeals distinguished *Cramer* in limiting the Danns' claim for aboriginal title to the land they could prove they used and occupied before 1934, when the land in the area had been withdrawn from settlement by the government. In *Cramer* the Supreme Court had been influenced by the policy favoring settlement on public lands by Indians and others as well as by the policy to encourage nomadic Indians to settle in one place. The Ninth Circuit noted that neither one of these policies is in effect at present, as demonstrated by the withdrawing of public lands from entry and current laws strictly limiting the land available for homesteading or allotment by Indians. The Court did extend the principle of *Cramer* to include user rights, however. The court upheld the lower court's ruling that the Danns had acquired grazing rights, although limiting the rights to those acquired before the Taylor Grazing Act established the exclusive mechanism for acquiring such rights. *United States v. Dann*, 873 F.2d 1189 (9th Cir. 1989).

2. Confiscation of Allotments: Are individual allotments recognized as that term was used in the *Tee-Hit-Ton* case? Does the answer depend on whether the original tribal land had been recognized, as had the Great Sioux Reservation out of which the allotments in *Irving* were made? Does the answer depend on the language in the particular patent or the agreement or statute under which the allotment was made? In *Choate v. Trapp*, 224 U.S. 665 (1912), the Supreme Court held that the fifth amendment prevented the abrogation of a statutorily vested tax immunity of allotted Indian land without compensation. The Court read the statutes or agreements liberally as creating private property rights "vested in the individual Indian by prior laws and contracts." *Id.* at 678. The

Court stressed the consensual nature of the allotment of Choctaw and Chickasaw land in Oklahoma, especially the fact that the individuals agreed to give up their claim to tribal property in return for the patents. *Id.* at 669. "Upon delivery of the patent the agreement was executed, and the Indian was thereby vested with all the right conveyed by the patent," including the provision that the land would not be taxable to the original allottee for 21 years. *Id.* at 672. To reach the conclusion that a property right had vested, the Court relied on principles of liberal construction of statutes and agreements with Indian tribes. *Id.* at 675.

Choate can thus be read fairly narrowly. Other cases involving compensability of allotted lands gave Congress very broad power to alter allotment schemes without incurring liability. For example, in *Northern Cheyenne Tribe v. Hollowbreast,* 425 U.S. 649 (1976), the Court held that the Northern Cheyenne Allotment Act, Pub. L. No. 69-330, 44 Stat. 690 (1926), did not vest the allottees with subsurface mineral rights despite the following statement in the law:

> [A]t the expiration of fifty years from the date of the approval of this Act the coal or other minerals, including oil, gas, and other natural deposits of said allotments shall become the property of the respected allottees or their heirs: *Provided further,* That the unallotted lands of said tribe of Indians shall be held in common, subject to the control and management thereof as Congress may deem expedient for the benefit of said Indians.

Having concluded that the allottees had no vested property rights protected by the taking clause of the fifth amendment, the Court held that Congress could by subsequent statute terminate the promise of subsurface mineral rights to the allottees and reserve all subsurface rights in the allotted land "in perpetuity for the benefit of the tribe." Act of July 24, 1968, Pub. L. 90-424, 82 Stat. 424. The Court did not apply rules of liberal construction on the ground that such rules do not apply to intratribal disputes. 425 U.S., at 649 n.7. Significantly, the total coal reserves on the affected lands were conservatively estimated to have a value in excess of two billion dollars. *See also United States v. Jim,* 409 U.S. 80 (1972) (per curiam) (congressional enlargement of the statutorily defined class of Navajo Indians entitled to benefit from mineral leasing royalties derived from tribal lands did not constitute taking of vested property rights). Finally, it must be noted that the Indian Reorganization Act extended the trust period for all Indian allotments indefinitely, thus creating potential claims for compensation by individuals if allotted land were regarded as creating compensable property rights.

In short, when the tension between individual and tribal property rights has been caused by a government policy shift away from assimilation toward tribal government, and when protecting the individuals would either require the tribe or the government to pay millions of dollars, the Court has sought to uphold the government's action.

Although it would seem from the above cases that only a careful reading of the specific agreements and statutes providing for allotment on the affected reservation would reveal whether the allotted land was compensable, the Court in *Hodel* did not undertake such an inquiry. Does this omission indicate the Court is prepared to assume that all allotted land should be treated as private property? Or does it merely indicate the Court is willing to make that assumption about the Sioux Nation because the Great Sioux Reservation involved recognized title?

3. Special Rules for Indian Property? Note the majority's failure to cite any Indian takings cases. Does *Hodel* signal the Court's willingness, only a few terms after *Sioux Nation*, to apply the same standards to Indian and non-Indian takings cases? If so, is this a positive trend? In a mock opinion dissenting from the student-written majority for his course on Supreme Court Decision Making at the Harvard Law School, Professor Derrick Bell stated the counterargument rather forcefully:

> [The majority] in an untimely attack of self-righteousness, ignores the needs of Indian leaders, the intent of Congress, and the dictates of judicial restraint to do a kind of benighted justice to a few Indian heirs at the expense of the common good and — it must be said — common sense. Plagued by guilt, the Court, even in its attempted penance, rewards those Indians ready to sacrifice the custom and tradition of tribal community property for the dubious benefits of individual gain.
>
> [The majority] reaches deep into a carefully cached horde of first-year property principles to make impressively inappropriate arguments based on the difference between life estates and holdings in fee simple. For Indian leaders struggling for survival on that pitiful portion of their once vast holdings, this use of the common law to dash their Congressionally-endorsed plans may be less painful but is a no less permanent deprivation of their property interests than that effected at an earlier time by lawless force.
>
> Significantly, the Fifth Amendment was never effectively invoked when the lands of the Indian were being ripped off via a myriad of treaties and "land deals" so outrageously unfair as to shame the nation and this Court a century and more later. To invoke the takings clause now to bar a tribe from recovering that acreage which many of them are unable to purchase, is to add another ignominious chapter in the still-unfinished history of the greatest land theft the world has ever known.

Bell, Dissent to *Hodel v. Irving* (1987) (unpublished memorandum reprinted with permission of author). If, on the other hand, the same "benighted policies" Professor Bell condemns have been successful in instilling the value of individual ownership of land in allottees and thus given them a justified expectation of continued ownership, is it fair for Congress to sacrifice this individual interest without compensation in the interest of the tribe?

4. Amendment to the Lands Consolidation Act: The 1984 amendment to ILCA provides for escheat only if the interest is "incapable of earning $100 in any one of the 5 years from the date of decedent's death" in place of the provision looking back one year in the original version. 25 U.S.C.A. § 2206 (1989 Supp.). In addition, the amended act also gives non-Indian or non-member heirs the right to elect to receive a life tenancy in the property, with the remainder going to the tribe. *Id.* § 2205(1). Finally, the amended act also requires the tribe to compensate devisees if the decedent devised the land in a will. *Id.* § 2205(3). Do these provisions better withstand constitutional scrutiny in light of the Court's analysis in *Irving*? *See* Arrow, *Contemporary Tensions in Constitutional Indian Law*, 12 Okla. City L. Rev. 469, 497-504 (1987) (amendments probably constitutional).

5. Tribal Laws Regarding Individual Property: As *Wauneka* illustrates, it should not be assumed that lands held under tribal title do not involve individual occupancy and use. Most tribes have formal systems of land assignments, often set forth in their IRA constitution and bylaws, by which tribal land is assigned to individual tribal members for occupancy or other productive uses. *See, e.g.*, Constitution of the Sac & Fox Tribe of the Mississippi in Iowa, art. XI (1937). These tribal systems of land assignments differ from allotments in at least two significant respects. First, the title to tribal land subject to assignment is generally held by the United States in trust for the tribe. The land assignment therefore represents a permissive use, like a lease, for a fixed term or at will, rather than an actual ownership interest. This difference in the nature of the title acquired preserves to the tribe, as sovereign and owner of the beneficial interest, substantially more power to regulate and terminate the assignment. Thus, the tribe has greater power to orchestrate and control land use and allocation on tribal lands. Second, land assignments are governed by tribal law rather than the externally imposed standards of state and federal property law that govern allotments. This difference also preserves greater tribal control over land assignment and affords the tribe greater ability to infuse tribal values and community sentiment into land use decisions. Tribal decisions about land assignments are, however, subject to challenge in tribal court under the Indian Civil Rights Act, 25 U.S.C. § 1302.

Chapter 6

HUNTING, FISHING, AND WATER RIGHTS: THE OPERATION OF THE RESERVED RIGHTS DOCTRINE

When the federal government set aside lands for Indian reservations, it did far more than allocate the beneficial use of real estate. The demarcation of Indian country created jurisdictional lines that protected Indian peoples and, to a more limited extent, Indian culture from outside influences. As Chief Justice Marshall noted in *Johnson v. M'Intosh,* 21 U.S. (8 Wheat.) 543 (1823), traditional Indian cultures often were built in part on a hunter-gatherer tradition in which Indian people derived some of their subsistence and some of their commercial trade goods from the wildlife of the forests, from the fisheries of the rivers and lakes, and from other natural food resources, such as wild rice, that might be available in the tribe's traditional resource area. Federal Indian law long has recognized the importance of such food-gathering activities to traditional Indian cultures by treating land used seasonally as hunting, fishing, or food-gathering grounds as protected by aboriginal title. *See, e.g., Confederated Tribes of the Warm Springs Reservation v. United States,* 177 Ct. Cl. 184, 194 (1966); *Spokane Tribe of Indians v. United States,* 163 Ct. Cl. 58 (1963); *State v. Coffee,* 97 Idaho 905, 908, 556 P.2d 1185, 1188 (1976) ("[A]boriginal title was more than just a right to remain camped on the land. It was a right to continue, at least temporarily, a way of life. To the extent that hunting or fishing was an integral part of the Indian's way of life prior to the coming of the white man, it became a part of the way of life allowed to continue after establishment of the sovereign. Thus, hunting and fishing rights are part and parcel with aboriginal title."). Indeed, this tradition stretches back to a seventeenth century royal commission that criticized colonial expropriation of Indian hunting areas. Clinton, *The Proclamation of 1763: Colonial Prelude to Two Centuries of Federal-State Conflict Over the Management of Indian Affairs,* 69 B.U.L. REV. 329, 333 (1989).

Despite the stereotype painted in Chief Justice Marshall's opinions, Indian tribes were not merely hunter-gatherer societies. Most tribes at one point in their history engaged in significant agricultural pursuits. Indeed, the hunter-gatherer stereotype of Indian culture is rapidly dispelled when one recalls that it was the Indians who taught the European colonists how to grow many agricultural products that are now staples in North American and world cultures, including tobacco and corn. In order to engage in such agricultural pursuits, the Indian tribes were heavily reliant on water resources. Reliance on water was a comparatively small problem for the agricultural pursuits of the Creek and Cherokee towns in the water-rich southeastern United States. The Pueblos of the arid Southwest, however, also developed highly sophisticated flood plain or dry farming methods and their ancestors relied on complex irrigation systems to further their agricultural pursuits. Even the hunter-gatherer societies of the arid West, such as the Shoshones, or the buffalo hunters of the plains, like the Sioux and Cheyenne, relied heavily on water resources for subsistence and for processing their gathered food supplies.

If Indian peoples and societies were to be protected in the Indian reservations guaranteed to tribal communities, access to food resources and to water was essential. This chapter is devoted to analyzing the body of legal doctrine that has emerged surrounding the protection of Indian food-gathering activities and water rights. The chapter also explores another major theme in the history of Indian law — the competition between Indian and non-Indian for access to and control over scarce resources. When food and water resources were plentiful, the competition posed few legal problems because the two competing claimants could fully satisfy their needs without affecting one another or endangering the survival of the resources. The resources appeared unlimited. Beginning with the massive dislocation of native economies engendered by the Euro-American induced disappearance of the buffalo herds, the late nineteenth and twentieth centuries brought serious shortages of wildlife, fisheries, and other natural food supplies, caused by environmental destruction and over-intensive harvesting of the resources. The twentieth century also brought a scarcity of water resources created by urban development, irrigation projects, mining, and power projects in the arid West.

In times of shortage, law often steps in to sort out the competing demands for scarce resources and to try to prevent violent self-help remedies. In the field of Indian law, such decisions, like many others affecting Indian peoples, are complicated by the competition for jurisdiction and control between the federal government, the states, and the tribes. Indeed, resolution of the jurisdictional questions in some cases determines the allocation of the resource. As will be seen in the Pacific Northwest fishing dispute, discussed at the end of section A of this chapter, the long-term exercise of jurisdiction over Indian fishing by the states of Washington and Oregon resulted in allocating virtually all of the harvest of fisheries in the region to non-Indian commercial fishers despite treaty rights guaranteeing certain substantive fishing rights to the affected Indians. Recent intervention by the federal courts has produced a major reallocation of the resource in favor of the Indians.

This chapter pulls together themes of jurisdiction and property previously reviewed and indicates how they interact in the resolution of concrete disputes. The chapter presents two case studies of a much broader and long-term theme in the history of federal Indian policy — the role of law in resolving competing claims to resources held by Indians but needed or wanted for non-Indian economic development. Since the first colonists made the North American continent their home by displacing a resident Indian population, these competing claims have pervaded the history of contact between Indians and non-Indians. In the national courts, attempts to relieve this tension stretch back at least to the two early nineteenth-century decisions by the Supreme Court in *The Cherokee Cases*. Carefully appraise modern judicial resolutions to determine whether, or why, they provide any greater permanency than previous efforts.

This chapter also provides important insights into the manner in which treaties, statutes, or executive orders creating Indian land should be construed.

Many of the food-gathering and water rights covered in this chapter are the product of the so-called reserved rights doctrine. As briefly summarized in *United States v. Winans,* 198 U.S. 371, 381 (1905), this rule of construction provides that a "treaty was not a grant of rights to the Indians, but a grant of rights from them — a reservation of those not granted." In reviewing these materials consider what effect the historical perspective enshrined in this rule of construction has on Indian rights.

A. HUNTING, FISHING, AND FOOD-GATHERING RIGHTS

1. ON-RESERVATION RIGHTS

MENOMINEE TRIBE v. UNITED STATES

391 U.S. 404 (1968)

Mr. Justice DOUGLAS delivered the opinion of the Court.

The Menominee Tribe of Indians was granted a reservation in Wisconsin by the Treaty of Wolf River in 1854, 10 Stat. 1064. By this treaty the Menominees retroceded certain lands they had acquired under an earlier treaty and the United States confirmed to them the Wolf River Reservation "for a home, to be held as Indian lands are held." Nothing was said in the 1854 treaty about hunting and fishing rights. Yet we agree with the Court of Claims that the language "to be held as Indian lands are held" includes the right to fish and to hunt. The record shows that the lands covered by the Wolf River Treaty of 1854 were selected precisely because they had an abundance of game. See *Menominee Tribe v. United States,* 95 Ct. Cl. 232, 240-241 (1941). The essence of the Treaty of Wolf River was that the Indians were authorized to maintain on the new lands ceded to them as a reservation their way of life which included hunting and fishing.

What the precise nature and extent of those hunting and fishing rights were we need not at this time determine. For the issue tendered by the present decision of the Court of Claims, 179 Ct. Cl. 496, 388 F.2d 998, is whether those rights, whatever their precise extent, have been extinguished.

That issue arose because, beginning in 1962, Wisconsin took the position that the Menominees were subject to her hunting and fishing regulations. Wisconsin prosecuted three Menominees for violating those regulations and the Wisconsin Supreme Court held that the state regulations were valid, as the hunting and fishing rights of the Menominees had been abrogated by Congress in the Menominee Indian Termination Act of 1954. 68 Stat. 250, as amended, 25 U.S.C. §§ 891-902.

Thereupon the tribe brought suit in the Court of Claims against the United States to recover just compensation for the loss of those hunting and fishing rights. The Court of Claims by a divided vote held that the tribe possessed hunting and fishing rights under the Wolf River Treaty; but it held, contrary to the Wisconsin Supreme Court, that those rights were not abrogated by the Termination Act of 1954. We granted the petition for a writ of certiorari in order to resolve that conflict between the two courts. On oral argument both petitioner and respondent urged that the judgment of the Court of Claims be affirmed. The State of Wisconsin appeared as *amicus curiae* and argued that the judgment be reversed.

In 1953 Congress by concurrent resolution instructed the Secretary of the Interior to recommend legislation for the withdrawal of federal supervision over certain American Indian tribes, including the Menominees. Several bills were offered, one for the Menominee Tribe that expressly preserved hunting and fishing rights. But the one that became the Termination Act of 1954, *viz.*, H.R. 2828, did not mention hunting and fishing rights. Moreover, counsel for the Menominees spoke against the bill, arguing that its silence would by implication abolish those hunting and fishing rights. It is therefore argued that they were abolished by the Termination Act.

The purpose of the 1954 Act was by its terms "to provide for orderly termination of Federal supervision over the property and members" of the tribe. Under its provisions, the tribe was to formulate a plan for future control of tribal property and service functions theretofore conducted by the United States. On or before April 30, 1961, the Secretary was to transfer to a tribal corporation or to a trustee chosen by him all property real and personal held in trust for the tribe by the United States.

The Menominees submitted a plan, looking toward the creation of a county in Wisconsin out of the former reservation and the creation by the Indians of a Wisconsin corporation to hold other property of the tribe and its members. The Secretary of the Interior approved the plan with modifications; the Menominee Enterprises, Inc., was incorporated; [10] and numerous ancillary laws were passed by Wisconsin integrating the former reservation into its county system of government. The Termination Act provided that after the transfer by the Secretary of title to the property of the tribe, all federal supervision was to end and "the laws of the several States shall apply to the tribe and its members in the same manner as they apply to other citizens or persons within their jurisdiction."

It is therefore argued with force that the Termination Act of 1954, which became fully effective in 1961, submitted the hunting and fishing rights of the Indians to state regulation and control. We reach, however, the opposite conclusion. The same Congress that passed the Termination Act also passed Public Law 280, 67 Stat. 588, as amended, 18 U.S.C. § 1162. The latter came out of the same committees of the Senate and the House as did the Termination Act; and it was amended [11] in a way that is critical here only two months after the

---

[10] Wisconsin questions whether Menominee Enterprises, Inc., to which all tribal assets were conveyed pursuant to the termination plan (26 Fed. Reg. 3726), should be viewed as the successor entity to the tribe and the present holder of the hunting and fishing rights, and, if so, to what extent the corporation or the tribal members thereof can withhold or parcel out these rights.

The Menominees, on the other hand, claim the rights are held by Menominee Indian Tribe of Wisconsin, Inc., a tribal body organized in 1962....

The corporation adopted a resolution defining those persons entitled to exercise the hunting and fishing rights .... We believe it inappropriate, however, to resolve the question of who the beneficiaries of the hunting and fishing rights may be; and we expressly reserve decision on it. Neither it nor the nature of those rights nor the extent, if any, to which Wisconsin may regulate them has been fully briefed and argued by the parties either in the Court of Claims or in this Court, and the posture of the present litigation does not require their resolution.

[11] As originally enacted Public Law 280 exempted the Menominees from its provisions. The House Reports on Pub. L. 280 (H.R. 1063, 83d Cong., 1st Sess.) and on Pub. L. 661 (H.R. 9821, 83d Cong., 2d Sess.) indicate that the Menominees had specifically asked for exemption from the provisions of the bill that eventually became Pub. L. 280, on the ground that their tribal law and

Termination Act became law. As amended, Public Law 280 granted designated States, including Wisconsin, jurisdiction "over offenses committed by or against Indians in the areas of Indian country" named in the Act, which in the case of Wisconsin was described as "All Indian country within the State." But Public Law 280 went on to say that "Nothing in this section ... shall deprive any Indian or any Indian tribe, band, or community of any right, privilege, or immunity afforded under Federal treaty, agreement, or statute *with respect to hunting, trapping, or fishing* or the control, licensing, or regulation thereof." (Emphasis added.) That provision on its face contains no limitation; it protects any hunting, trapping, or fishing right granted by a federal treaty. Public Law 280, as amended, became the law in 1954, nearly seven years *before* the Termination Act became fully effective in 1961. In 1954, when Public Law 280 became effective, the Menominee Reservation was still "Indian country" within the meaning of Public Law 280.

Public Law 280 must therefore be considered *in pari materia* with the Termination Act. The two Acts read together mean to us that, although federal supervision of the tribe was to cease and all tribal property was to be transferred to new hands, the hunting and fishing rights granted or preserved by the Wolf River Treaty of 1854 survived the Termination Act of 1954....

We decline to construe the Termination Act as a backhanded way of abrogating the hunting and fishing rights of these Indians. While the power to abrogate those rights exists (see [*Lone Wolf v. Hitchcock*]) "the intention to abrogate or modify a treaty is not to be lightly imputed to the Congress." *Pigeon River Co. v. Cox Co.,* 291 U.S. 138, 160.

Our conclusion is buttressed by the remarks of the legislator chiefly responsible for guiding the Termination Act to enactment, Senator Watkins, who stated upon the occasion of the signing of the bill that it "in no way violates any treaty obligation with this tribe."

We find it difficult to believe that Congress, without explicit statement, would subject the United States to a claim for compensation by destroying property rights conferred by treaty, particularly when Congress was purporting by the Termination Act to settle the Government's financial obligations toward the Indians.[15]

[*Affirmed.*]

Mr. Justice MARSHALL took no part in the consideration or decision of this case.

Mr. Justice STEWART, with whom Mr. Justice BLACK joins, dissenting.

[The Menominee termination] statute is plain on its face: after termination the Menominees are fully subject to state laws just as other citizens are, and no

---

order program was functioning satisfactorily. Subsequently, the tribe reconsidered its position and sponsored H.R. 9821, amending Pub. L. 280 to extend its provisions to the Menominee Reservation. The Department of the Interior recommended favorable action on the proposed amendment, and the amendment was enacted into law on August 24, 1954 (68 Stat. 795), two months after the passage of the Menominee Termination Act.

[15] Compare the hearings on the Klamath Termination bill, which took place shortly before the Menominee bills were reached, in which Senator Watkins expressed the view that perhaps the Government should "buy out" the Indians' hunting and fishing rights rather than preserve them after termination. See Joint Hearings, Subcommittees of the Committees on Interior and Insular Affairs, 83d Cong., 2d Sess., Pt. 4, on S. 2745 and H.R. 7320, pp. 254-255.

exception is made for hunting and fishing laws. Nor does the legislative history contain any indication that Congress intended to say anything other than what the unqualified words of the statute express. In fact two bills which would have explicitly preserved hunting and fishing rights were rejected in favor of the bill ultimately adopted — a bill which was opposed by counsel for the Menominees because it failed to preserve their treaty rights.

The Court today holds that the Termination Act does not mean what it says. The Court's reason for reaching this remarkable result is that it finds "in pari materia" another statute which, I submit, has nothing whatever to do with this case.

[The Menominee Termination Act] by its very terms provides:

[A]ll statutes of the United States which affect Indians because of their status as Indians shall no longer be applicable to the members of the tribe .... 25 U.S.C. § 899.

Public Law 280 is such a statute. It has no application to the Menominees now that their reservation is gone.

The 1854 Treaty granted the Menominees special hunting and fishing rights. The 1954 Termination Act, by subjecting the Menominees without exception to state law, took away those rights. The Menominees are entitled to compensation.

I would reverse the judgment of the Court of Claims.

SAC & FOX TRIBE v. LICKLIDER

576 F.2d 145 (8th Cir.), *cert. denied*, 439 U.S. 955 (1978)

STEPHENSON, Circuit Judge.

This case presents the question of whether the state of Iowa has jurisdiction to regulate hunting, fishing and trapping by members of the Sac and Fox Tribe of the Mississippi in Iowa (Tribe) on a tract of land in Tama County, Iowa, occupied by the Tribe.

The Tribe presently resides on a 3,000 acre tract of land in Tama County, Iowa, which is held in trust by the United States for the use and benefit of the Tribe. In response to recent arrests of Tribe members by Iowa officials for violation of Iowa fish and game laws, the Tribe [challenged state authority. The district court held the state had jurisdiction and dismissed]. These appeals by the Tribe and the United States followed.

I

[T]he Sac and Fox Tribe ceded all its land west of the Mississippi River (which includes the present Tama tract in Iowa) to the United States [in 1842] and agreed to move to a reservation located in what is now the state of Kansas. The move was to be accomplished within three years after the treaty date. Many members of the Fox Tribe and some members of the Sac Tribe who agreed to move to the reservation in Kansas pursuant to the 1842 treaty became dissatisfied with the Kansas reservation and returned to Iowa. In 1856 the Iowa legislature consented to the continued residence of the Sac and Fox then in Iowa and urged the United States to pay these Indians their proportionate annuities under the various treaties with the Sac and Fox Tribe. 1854-1857 Iowa Laws ch.

30 (5th Extra Gen. Assembly). The Tribe purchased a small tract of land in 1857 and title was taken by the governor of Iowa in trust for the Indians.

In 1865 the federal government sent an Indian agent to Iowa to supervise the Tribe. In 1867 Congress approved the payment of the 1842 treaty annuities to the Tribe in Iowa "so long as they are peaceful and have the assent of the government of Iowa to reside in that State." Act of Mar. 2, 1867, ch. 173, 14 Stat. 492, 507 (1868). Additionally in 1867 another treaty was negotiated with the Sac and Fox Tribe which required each absent member to move onto the reservation in the Indian Territory or lose his right to funds arising under all treaties with the Sac and Fox. The Tribe in Iowa was specifically exempted from this requirement. Treaty of Oct. 14, 1868, 15 Stat. 495, 504 (1869).

Between 1856 and 1896, the Tribe acquired more land in Tama County with funds generated through the sale of pelts and horses, charitable contributions, and treaty annuities. By 1896, the governor of Iowa held the title to 2,720 acres of land in trust for the benefit of the Tribe. The Indian agent held the title to an additional 280 acres as trustee for the benefit of the Tribe.

In 1896 Iowa tendered exclusive jurisdiction over the Tribe and their lands held in trust for them to the United States, with the following exception:

> Nothing contained in this act shall be so construed as to prevent on any of the lands referred to in this act the service of any judicial process issued by or returnable to any court of this state or judge thereof, or to prevent such courts from exercising jurisdiction of crimes against the laws of Iowa committed thereon either by said Indians or others, or of such crimes committed by said Indians in any part of this state ....

1894-1897 Iowa Laws ch. 110 (26th Extra Gen. Assembly). The United States accepted this tender, stating in part:

> That the United States hereby accepts and assumes jurisdiction over the Sac and Fox Indians of Tama County, in the State of Iowa, and of their lands in said State, as tendered to the United States by the act of the legislature of said State passed on the sixteenth day of January, eighteen hundred and ninety-six, subject to the limitations therein contained ....

Act of June 10, 1896, ch. 398, 29 Stat. 321, 331 (1897).

In 1937 the Tribe adopted a constitution and bylaws pursuant to the [IRA]. In 1948, Congress conferred concurrent criminal jurisdiction on the state over offenses committed "by or against Indians on the Sac and Fox Indian Reservation" located in Iowa. Act of June 30, 1948, ch. 759, 62 Stat. 1161.[5] Finally in 1967, the Iowa Legislature acted to assume civil jurisdiction over actions involving Indians arising "within the Sac and Fox Indian settlement in Tama county" to the extent that such jurisdiction was available under the federal Act of Aug. 15, 1953, ch. 505, 67 Stat. 588, 589. See Iowa Code § 1.12.

---

[5] The Act of June 30, 1948, reads in pertinent part as follows:

That jurisdiction is hereby conferred on the State of Iowa over offenses committed by or against Indians on the Sac and Fox Indian Reservation in that State to the same extent as its courts have jurisdiction generally over offenses committed within said State outside of any Indian reservation: Provided, however, That nothing herein contained shall deprive the courts of the United States of jurisdiction over offenses defined by the laws of the United States committed by or against Indians on Indian reservations.

This court has recently interpreted this statute in *Youngbear v. Brewer*, 549 F.2d 74 (8th Cir. 1977), as preserving exclusive federal jurisdiction over offenses defined in 18 U.S.C. § 1153 (Federal Major Crimes Act), and as granting the state of Iowa jurisdiction over all other offenses.

II

[T]he Bureau of Indian Affairs has expended funds for the Tribe in the areas of social services, land management, employment assistance, health services, including water and sanitation, police services, and education [since 1897]. Finally, in the Act of June 30, 1948, Congress specifically referred to the Tama tract when it spoke of "offenses committed by or against Indians on the Sac and Fox Indian Reservation ...." (Emphasis added.)

[W]e are persuaded that the land located in Tama County and occupied by the Tribe constitutes an Indian reservation.

III

The resolution of the "reservation" question, however, does not terminate this court's inquiry. In our opinion we must further look to the applicable treaties and statutes to determine the limit of the state's power on the Tama reservation.

A state has initial authority to regulate the taking of fish and game by reason of its police power. *Geer v. Connecticut*, 161 U.S. 519 (1896). The federal government, however, may preempt state control over fish and game by executing a valid treaty. [Thus], "the state may enact and enforce no statute or regulation in conflict with treaties in force between the United States and the Indian nations." *United States v. State of Washington*, 520 F.2d 676, 684 (9th Cir. 1975), *cert. denied*, 423 U.S. 1086 (1976). In the instant case the issue is whether the federal government, through treaties and statutes, has preempted Iowa's regulation of the Tribe's hunting, fishing and trapping on the Tama reservation.

It is important to note at the outset that the relevant treaties and statutes are to be read with the tradition of Indian sovereignty in mind. [*McClanahan v. Arizona State Tax Comm'n.*]

In turning to the treaties and statutes before us, it must be remembered that although we have earlier stated that the Tama tract is in fact a reservation, we so held because of the various actions taken by the federal government in relation to the Tribe. It is abundantly clear that the reservation was not created by a specific treaty. Therefore, some of the maxims to be applied in the interpretation of treaties with Indian tribes are generally inapplicable here.

As stated earlier, the Treaty of Oct. 11, 1842, is unequivocal in that the confederated tribes of Sacs and Foxes ceded to the United States all the lands west of the Mississippi River in which they had any claim or title or interest. The treaty further called for the complete relocation of the confederated tribes to a reservation in what is now the state of Kansas. We are persuaded that by this treaty the confederated tribes relinquished their aboriginal rights to hunt and fish on the present Tama reservation.

The United States contends, however, that the Tribe's hunting, fishing and trapping rights were necessarily rejuvenated as a result of the subsequent creation of the Tama reservation. Congressional actions following the 1842 treaty convince us otherwise. For example, in 1867 Congress approved the payment of the 1842 treaty annuities to the Tribe "so long as they are peaceful and have the assent of the government of Iowa to reside in that State." Act of Mar. 2, 1867, ch. 173, 14 Stat. 492, 507 (1868). Although the scope of Iowa's control and jurisdiction over the Tribe are not clear from this language, it is apparent that at least in 1867 Congress contemplated some control by Iowa over the Tribe.

It is important that in 1896 Iowa tendered exclusive jurisdiction over the Tribe and their lands to the United States with the proviso that "[n]othing contained in this Act shall be so construed as ... to prevent such [Iowa] courts from exercising jurisdiction of crimes against the laws of Iowa committed [on the Tribe's land] ...." 1894-1897 Iowa Laws ch. 110 (26th Extra Gen. Assembly). The federal government accepted this tender of jurisdiction pursuant to the act of the Iowa legislature "subject to the limitations therein contained." Act of June 10, 1896, ch. 398, 29 Stat. 321, 331 (1897). In construing these two acts, a federal court has stated:

> [A]s it was clearly contemplated that these Indians would continue to reside as a tribe upon their lands in Tama county, and would be brought in some respects into contact with the people of Iowa, it was deemed wise and proper to reserve, for the protection of the latter, jurisdiction in certain particulars over the lands of the reservation, and jurisdiction to punish crimes against the people of Iowa; and these are the purposes of section 3 of the act, which reserves to the state ... jurisdiction in the courts of the state over crimes against the laws of Iowa committed on the reservation by Indians....
>
> ....
>
> The state of Iowa has the right to exercise its police powers for the protection of its own citizens, but it cannot regulate the affairs of the tribal Indians in their relations to each other, for in these relations the Indians are under the control and protection of the national government.

Peters v. Malin, supra, 111 F. at 253-54, 255.

A fair reading of the two acts leads us to the conclusion that in 1896 Congress consented to Iowa's jurisdiction over crimes committed on the Tama tract by members of the Tribe. Although the United States argues that violation of state fish and game laws are "victimless" crimes at most, we are constrained to find that nevertheless they are still crimes.[8]

Finally, we are convinced that this court's recent decision in *Youngbear v. Brewer, supra,* supports our holding in the instant case. In *Youngbear,* we affirmed the lower court's decision[9] that in the Act of June 30, 1948, Congress granted jurisdiction generally to the state of Iowa over crimes committed by or against Indians on the Tama reservation, with the exception of those crimes listed in 18 U.S.C. § 1153 (Federal Major Crimes Act). As to those crimes, the federal courts retained exclusive jurisdiction. Because a violation of Iowa's fish and game laws does not fall within the exception noted above, it follows that Congress has recognized Iowa's jurisdiction to enforce its fish and game laws on the Tama reservation.

The Tribe argues that *Menominee Tribe of Indians v. United States,* 391 U.S. 404 (1968), requires that statutes affecting jurisdiction over reservation Indians must specifically address hunting, fishing and trapping rights before they are affected. [In contrast to *Menominee Tribe,* in this] case Congress did not specifically exempt the Tribe's hunting, fishing and trapping rights from state jurisdiction as it did in respect to all Indian country within the state of Wisconsin in

---

[8] Violations of the Iowa fish and game laws can result, upon conviction or a plea of guilty, in a $100 fine or 30 days in jail. *See* Iowa Code §§ 109.32, 109.119.

[9] See *Youngbear v. Brewer,* 415 F. Supp. 807 (N.D. Iowa 1976).

18 U.S.C. § 1162. To the contrary, Congress, in the Act of June 30, 1948, has given the state of Iowa jurisdiction over crimes committed by Indians on the Tama reservation with the exception of the major crimes listed in 18 U.S.C. § 1153. As the Supreme Court's conclusion in *Menominee* was based largely on 18 U.S.C. § 1162, we do not find *Menominee* controlling.

In summary, we are persuaded that the federal government has created through its various actions, with the statutory consent and cooperation of the state of Iowa, a de facto reservation in Tama County, Iowa. The resolution of this issue, however, does not end our inquiry, for a state's power on a reservation is determined by the applicable treaties and statutes. Our reading of the 1842 treaty convinces us that the Tribe yielded up its aboriginal rights to hunt, fish and trap on the land. Furthermore, by statute, Congress acceded to Iowa's statutory withholding of jurisdiction over all crimes against the state, except those enumerated in the Federal Major Crimes Act. By its legislative actions, we are persuaded that Congress has recognized the state of Iowa's jurisdiction to enforce its fish and game laws on the reservation.

It is important to note that our decision today does not prevent the tribal members from hunting, fishing and trapping on the reservation. The tribal members, like other Iowa landowners, may in general hunt on their own land without purchasing a license, subject to laws governing seasons and limits. We only hold that the state may enforce its fish and game laws on the reservation in the same manner in which it enforces Iowa's fish and game laws against any Iowa landowner.

[*Affirmed.*]

NOTES

1. **The Basis of On-Reservation Food-Gathering Rights:** Indian tribes generally enjoy full hunting, fishing, and food-gathering rights on their own reservation. Thus, the courts uniformly hold that except where absolutely essential to the conservation of a species, state conservation and licensing laws have no application to tribal members hunting, fishing, or gathering food on their own reservation. *See, e.g., Mattz v. Arnett,* 412 U.S. 481 (1973); *Cheyenne-Arapaho Tribes v. Oklahoma,* 618 F.2d 665 (10th Cir. 1980); *Moore v. United States,* 157 F.2d 760 (9th Cir. 1946), *cert. denied,* 330 U.S. 827 (1947). The *Sac & Fox* case represents the only major exception to the uniform trend of recognizing Indian on-reservation food-gathering rights.

While the case law almost uniformly recognizes on-reservation Indian hunting and fishing rights, the cases are not as explicit in defining the origins, nature, and scope of such rights. In general, Indian hunting, fishing, and food-gathering rights often derive from aboriginal title, treaties, and agreements, statutes, and executive orders promulgated after the 1871 prohibition of further treaties with Indian tribes. The theoretical basis of the Indian on-reservation hunting and fishing rights nevertheless is somewhat mixed. *See generally* F. COHEN, HANDBOOK OF FEDERAL INDIAN LAW 442-46 (1982 ed.). Indian food-gathering rights are frequently preserved in treaties. Some treaties expressly provide for exclusive hunting and fishing rights. *See, e.g.,* Treaty with the Klamaths, Moadocs, and Yahooshin Band of Snakes, Oct. 14, 1864, art. 1, 16 Stat. 707, 708. Nevertheless, a treaty is "not a grant of rights to the Indians, but a grant of rights from them — a reservation of those not granted." *United*

States v. Winans, 198 U.S. 371, 381 (1905). Therefore, express provision for food-gathering rights in the treaty is not necessary to establish their existence. For example, the *Menominee Tribe* case found the creation of hunting and fishing rights in the Treaty of Wolf River despite the fact that the treaty never explicitly mentions such rights. Rather, the rights were created by merely recognizing that the tribal land would be "held as Indian lands are held." Thus, *Menominee Tribe* suggests that hunting, fishing, and food-gathering rights are property rights that derive from the very nature and purpose of tribal land tenure.

Because of communication and translation difficulties between Indians and non-Indians during most treaty negotiations, courts follow a general rule that language in treaties is to be construed in favor of the Indians. *See, e.g., Washington v. Washington State Com. Passenger Fishing Vessel Ass'n,* 443 U.S. 658 (1979). After 1871, Congress prohibited further treaties with Indian tribes. Consequently, agreements with the tribes were entered into under statute, executive order, or agreement later approved by statute. Courts have generally applied the same rules of liberal construction to such laws as are applied to treaties. *See, e.g., Antoine v. Washington,* 420 U.S. 194 (1975).

In *Menominee Tribe,* the Supreme Court treated such rights as property rights protected under the Treaty of Wolf River and not extinguished by the Menominee Termination Act. For example, referring to the tribal hunting and fishing rights guaranteed in the Treaty of Wolf River, the *Menominee* opinion noted: "We find it difficult to believe that Congress, without explicit statement, would subject the United States to a claim for compensation by destroying *property rights* conferred by treaty, particularly when Congress was purporting by the Termination Act to settle the Government's financial obligations toward the Indians." *Menominee Tribe* also suggested that Indian hunting and fishing rights are compensable property rights protected under the taking clause of the fifth amendment. With respect to this compensation issue, the origin of the hunting and fishing rights is significant. If the rights are based solely on aboriginal title, however, Indians generally would not be entitled to compensation based on the harsh rule of *Tee-Hit-Ton Indians v. United States,* 348 U.S. 272 (1955). If, on the other hand, such rights are based on a treaty or statute their abrogation gives rise to a claim for compensation. *See, e.g., Confederated Tribes v. United States,* 43 Indian Cl. Comm'n 505 (1978); *Shoshone Tribe v. United States,* 299 U.S. 476 (1937); *Whitefoot v. United States,* 293 F.2d 658, 659 (Ct. Cl. 1961), *cert. denied,* 369 U.S. 818 (1962). The *Sac & Fox* case also treats the Sac and Fox on-reservation food-gathering rights as a property right voluntarily ceded by the Sac and Fox in their 1842 removal treaty and not regained by their subsequent purchase of land within Iowa.

An additional legal theory, however, often may support on-reservation hunting and fishing rights — preemption of state regulatory and law enforcement authority. As discussed in Chapter 4, generally state regulatory laws, such as conservation laws, do not apply to tribal members in Indian country, and state governments often lack law enforcement authority in Indian country. Thus, absent some federal statutory authority for the enforcement of state conservation laws in Indian country, application of the usual rules of preemption applicable to Indians in Indian country would preclude enforcement of state conservation and licensing laws against tribal members for on-reservation activity. For example, the Eastern Band of the Cherokee Tribe has hunting and fishing rights on its reservation in North Carolina despite the fact that, like the Sac and Fox (Mesquakie) community in Iowa, its current reservation was created by the

process of federal recognition of a tribal community that remained in its aboriginal homeland on purchased land in violation of a removal treaty. *See Eastern
Band of Cherokee Indians v. North Carolina Wildlife Resources Comm'n,* 588
F.2d 75 (4th Cir. 1978), *cert. dismissed,* 446 U.S. 960 (1980). In light of the
subsequent federal recognition of the Sac and Fox Reservation in Iowa, why did
the state of Iowa have any jurisdiction to enforce its conservation laws on the
reservation? Did the 1948 statute transferring to the state of Iowa criminal
jurisdiction over lesser crimes committed on the reservation vest such jurisdiction in the state? The *Sac & Fox* opinion takes little account of this dimension of
on-reservation hunting and fishing rights, assuming that the authority granted
to the state of Iowa in the 1948 federal statutory grant of state criminal jurisdiction over Indians on the Sac and Fox Reservation fully resolved the problem.
Recall that this statute was a forerunner of Public Law 280 and compare 18
U.S.C. § 1162(c). *Cf. Bryan v. Itasca County,* 426 U.S. 373 (1976) (Public Law
280 conferred on the states civil adjudicatory jurisdiction but not legislative,
taxing, or regulatory authority). Yet, Public Law 280 explicitly disclaims criminal state authority over hunting and fishing rights. 18 U.S.C. § 1162(b). Additionally, under 25 U.S.C. § 1322(b) states have no civil jurisdiction in Public Law
280 states over hunting and fishing rights protected by federal treaty, agreement or previous statute. The California Attorney General has determined that
since there were no ratified treaties there is no operative limit in California. See
41 Op. Cal. Att'y Gen. 17 (Op. No. 227, 1963); 42 *Id.* 147 (Op. No. 90, 1963).
But see Donahue v. California Justice Ct., 15 Cal. App. 3d 557, 93 Cal. Rptr.
310, *cert. denied,* 404 U.S. 990 (1971) and *Elser v. Gill Net Number One,* 246
Cal. App. 2d 30, 54 Cal. Rptr. 568 (1st Dist. 1966). By contrast, the Wisconsin
Attorney General has taken a position more protective of Indian hunting rights.
56 Op. Wis. Att'y Gen. 11 (1967) (reversing a prior ruling).

For further review of the case law on Indian hunting and fishing rights, see
generally, e.g., Bean, *Off-Reservation Hunting and Fishing Rights: Scales Tip
in Favor of States and Sportsmen?,* 51 N.D.L. Rev. 11 (1974); Burnett, *Indian
Hunting, Fishing and Trapping Rights: The Record and the Controversy,* 7
Idaho L. Rev. 49 (1970); Hobbs, *Indian Hunting and Fishing Rights II,* 37
Geo. Wash. L. Rev. 1251 (1969); Johnson, *The States Versus Indian Off-Reservation Fishing: A United States Supreme Court Error,* 47 Wash. L. Rev. 207
(1972); Noble, *Tribal Powers to Regulate Hunting in Alaska,* 4 Alaska L. Rev.
223 (1987); Reynolds, *Indian Hunting and Fishing Rights: The Role of Tribal
Sovereignty and Preemption,* 62 N.C.L. Rev. 743 (1984); Schmidhauser, *The
Struggle for Cultural Survival: The Fishing Rights of the Treaty Tribes of the
Pacific Northwest,* 52 Notre Dame Law. 30 (1976); Comment, *Accommodation
of Indian Treaty Rights in an International Fishery: An International Problem
Begging for an International Solution,* 54 Wash. L. Rev. 403 (1979); Comment,
Regulation of Treaty Indian Fishing, 43 Wash. L. Rev. 670 (1968); Comment,
Indian Regulation of Non-Indian Hunting and Fishing, 1974 Wis. L. Rev. 499.

2. On-Reservation Food-Gathering Rights and Reservation Diminishment:
The rather uniform recognition of Indian on-reservation food-gathering rights
obviously places an important premium on determining whether the food-gathering activity occurred on-reservation or in Indian country. Thus, many on-
reservation hunting and fishing rights cases turn on questions of title to land or
its status as a reservation. *Compare, e.g., Mattz v. Arnett,* 412 U.S. 481 (1973),
with *Organized Village of Kake v. Egan,* 369 U.S. 60 (1962). In particular, many
recent hunting and fishing cases ultimately turn on the question of reservation
diminishment or termination discussed at greater length in Chapter 1, section

B3. *E.g., Lower Brule Sioux Tribe v. South Dakota,* 711 F.2d 809 (8th Cir. 1983), *cert denied,* 464 U.S. 1042 (1984); *White Earth Band of Chippewa Indians v. Alexander,* 683 F.2d 1129 (8th Cir. 1982).

A series of Minnesota cases involving the food-gathering rights of various bands of Chippewa Indians illustrates the importance of reservation status. In *Leech Lake Band of Chippewa Indians v. Herbst,* 334 F. Supp. 1001 (D. Minn. 1971), the Leech Lake Band sought the right to hunt, fish, and gather wild rice unhindered by state regulation on lands owned by county, state, and federal governments within the Leech Lake reservation boundaries. Although the band had ceded this land to the federal government under the Nelson Act of 1889 and a contemporaneous written agreement pursuant to the Act, Judge Devitt held that Congress had not intended reservation disestablishment with respect to the ceded lands. Following *Menominee,* Judge Devitt found no express congressional intent to abrogate the band's food-gathering rights on the ceded land; thus, state game laws were not applicable. In *United States v. Minnesota,* 466 F. Supp. 1382 (D. Minn. 1979), *aff'd sub nom. Red Lake Band of Chippewa Indians v. Minnesota,* 614 F.2d 1161 (8th Cir.), *cert. denied,* 449 U.S. 905 (1980), the Red Lake Band sought declaratory judgment that its members retained food-gathering rights free from state regulation on lands ceded to the federal government under virtually identical circumstances as found in *Herbst.* In this case, however, Judge Devitt asserted that hunting and fishing rights were mere incidents of Indian title, extinguished once such title was extinguished. Therefore, with respect to the ceded lands, *Menominee* did not control and the Red Lake Band's rights were subject to state regulation. Also compare *Minnesota v. Clark,* 282 N.W.2d 902 (Minn. 1979), *cert. denied,* 445 U.S. 904 (1980) (despite land cessions by the White Earth Band of Chippewa under the Nelson Act, their reservation was not disestablished; following *Menominee,* food-gathering rights were not abrogated) with *Minnesota v. Keezer,* 292 N.W.2d 714 (Minn. 1980), *cert. denied,* 450 U.S. 930 (1981) (relinquishment of title to Neds Lake area of Minnesota by the Sioux tribe eliminated any residual Chippewa hunting and fishing rights held pursuant to a treaty between the tribes).

As a general rule, the prior cession of Indian land by treaty, agreement, or statute extinguishes the preexisting hunting and fishing rights. In *Oregon Dep't of Fish & Wildlife v. Klamath Indian Tribe,* 473 U.S. 753 (1985), for example, the Court ruled that a 1901 agreement clarifying and diminishing the boundaries of the Klamath Reservation did not preserve the right to fish on ceded lands within the former boundaries of the reservation even though such land areas were covered by a 1864 treaty that had guaranteed "the exclusive right of taking fish in the streams and lakes" included in said reservation, and the 1901 agreement and its legislative history were absolutely silent on the question of abrogation of the preexisting fishing rights. Justice Stevens' opinion for the majority carefully canvassed the purposes and legislative history of the 1864 treaty and the 1901 agreement and concluded:

[E]ven though "legal ambiguities are resolved to the benefit of the Indians," [the] courts cannot ignore plain language that, viewed in historical context and given a "fair appraisal," [very] clearly runs counter to the tribes' later claims. Careful examination of the entire record in this case leaves us with the firm conviction that the exclusive right to hunt, fish, and gather roots, berries, and seeds on lands reserved to the Klamath Tribe by the 1864 Treaty was not intended to survive as a right to be free of state regulation in the ceded lands that were outside the reservation after the 1901 agreement.

Id. at 774. *See also Cheyenne-Arapaho Tribes of Oklahoma v. Oklahoma, supra; Red Lake Band of Chippewa Indians v. Minnesota, supra;* and *Minnesota v. Keezer, supra.* In *Kimball v. Callahan,* 493 F.2d 564 (9th Cir.), *cert. denied,* 419 U.S. 1019 (1974), however, the Court, relying on *Menominee Tribe,* held that withdrawing Klamath Indians retained rights to hunt and fish in the lands ceded to the federal government to implement the Klamath Termination Act. *See also United States v. Felter,* 752 F.2d 1505 (10th Cir. 1985).

3. Aboriginal Food-Gathering Rights: As previously noted, federal law recognizes and protects the aboriginal right to hunt and fish by treating lands to which the Indian tribes customarily resorted for food-gathering as subject to aboriginal title. Courts have generally required a showing of actual use and occupancy of the lands over an extended period of time to determine the existence of aboriginal title. *See Confederated Tribes v. United States,* 177 Ct. Cl. 184 (1966). Aboriginal title to the lands, however, is not necessary to the existence of aboriginal hunting and fishing rights. *See United States ex rel. Hualpai Indians v. Santa Fe Pac. R.R.,* 314 U.S. 339 (1941). As indicated in the *Sac & Fox* case, aboriginal hunting and fishing rights remain in the Indians unless granted to the United States by treaty, abandoned, or extinguished by statute. Without such extinguishment, the aboriginal rights may be exercised to the same extent as other non-reservation rights are under treaties, statutes, agreements, or executive orders. *See* COHEN, *supra,* at 443. *But cf. Organized Village of Kake v. Egan,* 369 U.S. 60 (1963) ("This Court has never held that States lack power to regulate the exercise of aboriginal Indian [fishing] rights, such as claimed here, or of those based on occupancy.").

4. Scope of Food-Gathering Rights: What is the property protected when courts protect Indian food-gathering rights? Is it the wild game that lives on or periodically migrates over Indian land? Does the right include the habitat for the wildlife resource? *See United States v. Washington,* 759 F.2d 1353 (9th Cir.) (*en banc*), *cert. denied,* 474 U.S. 994 (1985) (Indian treaty-guaranteed fishing rights construed not to include the right "to have the fishing habitat protected from man-made despoliation"). Why do the Indians' on-reservation hunting and fishing rights include the right to be free from state conservation (i.e., season and limits) laws, licensing fees, and reporting requirements? Do they include the right to be free from federal or tribal conservation or licensing requirements? *Cf.* 25 C.F.R. pt. 250 (1982) (regulations governing fishing by tribal members on the Hoopa Valley Indian Reservation in California).

One way to understand the meaning and source of Indian hunting and fishing rights is to assess how the court in the *Sac & Fox* case viewed such rights and to determine whether it correctly analyzed the issue. For the Eighth Circuit, Indian hunting and fishing rights were viewed as property rights that were ceded by the tribe to the federal government in the 1842 removal treaty and were not subsequently reestablished by the later creation of the reservation. How sound is that analysis of the problem? Consider the fact that prior to the Treaty of Wolf River of 1854, the Menominees had also signed a removal treaty that ceded their land and contemplated their ultimate removal from the state of Wisconsin. Treaty with the Menominee, Oct. 18, 1848, 95 Stat. 952. Also consider the fact that the Eastern Band of the Cherokee Tribe has hunting and fishing rights on its reservation in North Carolina despite the fact that it was created by the same gradual process of federal recognition of a tribal community that remained in its aboriginal homeland in violation of a removal treaty. See *Eastern Band of Cherokee Indians v. North Carolina Wildlife Resources Comm'n,* 588 F.2d 75 (4th Cir. 1978), *cert. dismissed,* 446 U.S. 960 (1980). In light of the subsequent federal recognition of the Sac and Fox Reservation in

Iowa, why did the state of Iowa have any jurisdiction to enforce its conservation laws on the reservation? Did the 1948 statute transferring to the state of Iowa criminal jurisdiction over lesser crimes committed on the reservation vest such jurisdiction in the state? Recall that this statute was a forerunner of Public Law 280 and compare 18 U.S.C. § 1162(c). *Cf. Bryan v. Itasca County,* set forth and discussed in Chapter 4. (Public Law 280 conferred on the states civil adjudicatory jurisdiction but not legislative, taxing, or regulatory authority.) On the other hand, if Indian on-reservation fishing rights are merely the incidental product of the jurisdictional arrangements for Indian country, why do they involve compensable property rights protected under the takings clause?

5. The Irrelevance of *Geer v. Connecticut* to Indian Food-Gathering: In the *Sac & Fox* case the Eighth Circuit began its analysis by citing *Geer v. Connecticut,* 161 U.S. 519 (1896), for the proposition that the state has "initial authority to regulate the taking of fish and game by reason of its police power." In *Geer* the Supreme Court sustained a prohibition on the killing of certain game birds for export from the state on two theories: (1) that the state owned its wild game and held it in trust for its people and (2) that the state police power included the power and duty "to preserve for its people a valuable food supply." Was *Geer* an appropriate starting point for the analysis of food-gathering rights on Indian land in the *Sac & Fox* case? After *Sac & Fox* was decided, the Supreme Court in *Hughes v. Oklahoma,* 441 U.S. 322 (1979), overruled *Geer* as "artificial and formalistic" and rejected "the 19th century legal function of state ownership." *See generally* Comment, *State Wildlife Regulation and the Commerce Clause: Fall of the State Ownership Doctrine,* 20 URB. L. ANN. 215 (1980).

6. Limitations on On-Reservation Food-Gathering Rights: While on-reservation hunting and fishing rights historically involved exemption of Indians exercising such rights from all state, but not tribal or federal, conservation regulations, some cases suggest that state regulation of such rights is permissible where necessary to the conservation of fish and game. *See Puyallup Tribe v. Department of Game,* 433 U.S. 165, 173-77 (1977), discussed below, and *United States v. Oregon,* 657 F.2d 1009, 1016 (9th Cir. 1981). *See also Puyallup Tribe v. Department of Game,* 391 U.S. 392, 402 n.14 (1968), discussed below (origin of the "necessary for the conservation of fish" standard in an off-reservation case). On reservations not covered by Public Law 280, however, it is unclear how, if at all, the state conservation officials could enforce such conservation measures against Indians exercising their on-reservation hunting and fishing rights. Even on Public Law 280 reservations, 18 U.S.C. § 1162(b) provides that "[n]othing in this section ... shall deprive any Indian or any Indian tribe, band, or community of any right, privilege, or immunity afforded under Federal treaty, agreement, or statute with respect to hunting, trapping, or fishing or the control, licensing, or regulation thereof."

7. Nonmember Food-Gathering in Indian Country: While tribal members generally enjoy on-reservation hunting and fishing rights, the situation with respect to non-Indians or nonmember Indians is substantially less clear, as the Supreme Court briefly noted in *Oliphant v. Suquamish Tribe,* 435 U.S. 191 (1978). In 1960, Congress enacted a statute now codified at 18 U.S.C. § 1165 to supplement or complement tribal enforcement of conservation and game licensing rules by providing for federal prosecution of non-Indians who illegally take game or fish in Indian country:

> Whoever, without lawful authority or permission, willfully and knowingly goes upon any lands that belong to any Indian or Indian tribe, band, or group and either are held

by the United States in trust or are subject to a restriction against alienation imposed by
the United States, or upon any lands of the United States that are reserved for Indian
use, for the purpose of hunting, trapping, or fishing thereon, or for the removal of
game, peltries, or fish therefrom, shall be fined not more than $200 or imprisoned not
more than ninety days, or both, and all game, fish, and peltries in his possession shall
be forfeited.

Under section 1165 the term "lands" includes waterways. *United States v.
Bouchard*, 464 F. Supp. 1316 (W.D. Wis. 1978), *rev'd sub nom. Lac Courte
Oreilles Band of Lake Superior Chippewa Indians v. Voigt*, 700 F.2d 341 (7th
Cir.), *cert. denied*, 464 U.S. 805 (1983); *United States v. Pollman*, 364 F. Supp.
995 (D. Mont. 1973). Section 1165 does not apply to tribal members who hunt
or fish in Indian country in violation of tribal ordinances even where the tribe
lacks any enforcement processes for effectuating its ordinances. *United States v.
Jackson*, 600 F.2d 1283 (9th Cir. 1979). The act therefore applies principally to
nonmembers. *United States v. Sanford*, 547 F.2d 1085 (9th Cir. 1976); *United
States v. Pollman, supra.*

Section 1165 undoubtedly authorizes Indian tribes to adopt laws and ordinances regulating hunting and fishing by nonmembers, including non-Indians,
in Indian country. Enforcement of such ordinances, at least for nonmembers,
is, however, left to the federal courts. *See generally* Comment, *Indian Regulation of Non-Indian Hunting and Fishing*, 1974 WIS. L. REV. 499. A further
important question involves whether section 1165 and tribal ordinances enacted
under it preempt state conservation authority in Indian country. Some early
state cases seemed to suggest that section 1165 and tribal ordinances were preemptive. *Donahue v. California Justice Court*, 15 Cal. App. 3d 557, 93 Cal.
Rptr. 310, *cert. denied*, 404 U.S. 990 (1971) (section 1165 preempts state jurisdiction to prevent a nonmember Indian from fishing with gill net on Hoopa
Valley Reservation).

8. Rights of Access and Indian Hunting and Fishing Rights: It has long
been recognized that Indian hunting and fishing rights often include rights of
access, in the nature of easements, to protect treaty-guaranteed access to customary fishing or hunting sites. *United States v. Winans*, 198 U.S. 371 (1905).
By contrast, in *Blake v. Arnett*, 663 F.2d 906 (9th Cir. 1981), the court held that
the patents secured by non-Indian owners of reservation land conveyed to them
after trust restrictions on Indian allotments expired were not encumbered by
any easement of access to the Klamath River to permit members of the Yurok
Tribe to exercise customary fishing rights. Even though the court recognized
that some of the land in *Winans* had never been part of any Indian reservation
and the land involved in the *Blake* case was within the Hoopa Valley Reservation, the court nevertheless distinguished *Winans*:

> Under *Winans*, patents did not cut off the fishing and hunting rights there involved,
> which were expressly reserved by treaty. Here whether we look at the Executive Order
> of 1885 that created the old Klamath River Reservation or to the Executive Order of
> 1891, which created the Hoopa Valley Reservation Extension, we find no such express
> reservation or creation of fishing or hunting rights. This may be because all of the
> reservation, when created, was riparian to the Klamath River, thus affording complete
> access for fishing by the reservation Indians to the lower twenty miles of the river. It
> probably did not occur to anyone to mention fishing rights. Similarly, the tribe occu-
> pied the reservation and could of course hunt upon it, so long as no action by the
> United States prevented it.

We conclude that Congress intended that the allotments and patents, granted under the Act of 1887, would grant an unencumbered title to the Indian allottees and their successors in interest, which would not be subject to any interest in the land that might be implied from the mere creation of the reservation.

NEW MEXICO v. MESCALERO APACHE TRIBE
462 U.S. 324 (1983)

[In *New Mexico v. Mescalero Apache Tribe* the Court held that tribal and federal wildlife programs preempted state authority to enforce state conservation licensing and take limits against nonmembers hunting on Indian lands within the Mescalero Apache Reservation. This opinion is set forth in Chapter 4, page 541.]

NOTE: REGULATION OF NON-INDIAN FOOD GATHERING

In *Montana v. United States,* 450 U.S. 544 (1981), set forth in Chapter 3, section A1, the Supreme Court held that state regulation of non-Indian hunting and fishing was permissible on fee land owned by non-Indians within the reservation. The Court did not, however, address the court of appeals' fourth holding that the state has the power to regulate hunting and fishing *anywhere* within the reservation by nonmembers of the tribe as long as those regulations have as their purpose the conservation and proper management of game and fish.

The Fourth Circuit also held that extensive federal participation in reservation wildlife development is itself an element indicating federal preemption. *See Eastern Band of Cherokee Indians v. North Carolina Wildlife Resources Comm'n,* 588 F.2d 75, 78 (4th Cir. 1978). In *Eastern Band,* the federal government and the tribe had developed the reservation fishing program with no state assistance. The court found that where the state plays no role in stocking reservation waters, it "has no perceivable interest in reservation fishing." *Compare Eastern Band* with *Confederated Tribes of the Colville Reservation v. Washington,* 591 F.2d 89 (9th Cir. 1979). In *Colville,* the tribe owned a resort on its reservation and encouraged non-Indian fishing in reservation waters that the U.S. Fish and Wildlife Service had stocked with fish. The tribe enacted ordinances requiring non-Indians to purchase a tribal fishing license but not a state license. State game officers subsequently entered the reservation and cited non-Indians for fishing without a state license. The court discussed preemption and found no congressional or tribal intent to preempt state regulation. Therefore, the court held that the state may require non-Indians to purchase state licenses to fish on the reservation and the state may impose regulations more restrictive than those applied by the tribes. Nevertheless, the court did not decide whether future tribal efforts designed to preempt the state would be consistent with congressional intent, nor whether such efforts, if consistent with congressional goals, would preempt state regulation.

UNITED STATES v. DION
474 U.S. 900 (1985)

[The *Dion* case holds that the Eagle Protection Act abrogates Indian treaty-guaranteed hunting rights to take bald and golden eagles except as permitted by the Act under a permit system for religious uses. The opinion in the case is set forth in Chapter 2, page 218.]

NOTE: FEDERAL AUTHORITY OVER INDIAN HUNTING AND FISHING RIGHTS

Dion indicates that Congress has the constitutional authority to abrogate unilaterally Indian food-gathering rights and may do so through a clear and specific legislative statement. The *Menominee Tribe* case, however, suggests that Congressional abrogation of Indian hunting and fishing rights renders the United States liable to a fifth amendment claim for just compensation since such food-gathering rights generally constitute a vested property right protected by the takings clause.

Instead of abrogation, can the federal government regulate or tax the exercise of Indian hunting and fishing rights? If Indian hunting and fishing rights guarantee an unlimited opportunity to gather food for subsistence, religious, commercial, and other purposes, subject only to those externally imposed regulations that are absolutely necessary to the conservation of the species, would not federal regulation or taxation of the exercise of such rights constitute a partial abrogation of the right, thereby subjecting the United States to liability for just compensation under the fifth amendment? On the other hand, if Indian food-gathering rights are not so expansive, precisely what is the scope and nature of the right?

Building on the potentially oppressive conception of plenary federal authority in the area of Indian affairs, the cases suggest considerable federal authority to regulate and therefore to partially limit guaranteed Indian hunting and fishing rights. In *Northern Arapahoe Tribe v. Hodel*, 808 F.2d 741 (10th Cir. 1987), the court sustained the authority of the Secretary of the Interior to issue interim game regulations for the Wind River Reservation to preserve the reservation game resources after the Shoshone Tribe and the Northern Arapahoe Tribe could not agree on a game code and after the Shoshone Tribe requested the Secretary to act to protect game resources. The court said:

> Congress has delegated to the Secretary broad authority to manage Indian affairs, see 25 U.S.C. § 2, and to promulgate regulations relating to Indians affairs, see *id.* at § 9. Sections 2 and 9, however, do not vest the Secretary with general regulatory authority. See *Organized Village of Kake v. Egan*, 369 U.S. 60, 63 (1962). Section 2 delegates the general management of Indian affairs and relations to the Secretary of the Interior and Commissioner of Indian Affairs. The language of section 9 vests authority "for carrying into effect the various provisions of any act relating to Indian affairs," 25 U.S.C. § 9. Given the language of the statute and the fact that hunting on the reservation has historically been a matter of tribal self-regulation, we are reluctant to hold that sections 2 and 9 by themselves could support the regulations. [H]owever, we conclude that sections 2 and 9 together with the Treaty [of July 3, 1868, 15 Stat. 673], construed in accordance with the special relationship between the United States and Indian tribes, provide the necessary authority for the Secretary to enact these regulations.

In particular, in justifying the interim federal game regulations the court stressed the Shoshone's request for regulation and the clear risk of endangerment or extinction to the large game resources of the reservation caused by the severity of winter snowstorms that had driven big game resources down to lower elevations where they were easy prey. Similarly, in *United States v. Eberhardt*, set forth and discussed in Chapter 2, section B, the court also relied on 25 U.S.C. §§ 2 and 9 to reverse a district court opinion invalidating federal fishing regulations prohibiting tribal members on the Hoopa Valley Reservation from engaging in commercial fishing for anadromous fish. Believing that the Department of the Interior had no lawful authority to unilaterally abrogate or modify Indian fishing rights where not essential to conservation, the district court had invalidated the regulations. The court of appeals reversed. Its opinion noted that "[o]nly Congress can modify or abrogate Indian tribal rights; it will be held to have done so only when its intention to do so has been made absolutely clear." Nevertheless, the appellate court concluded that the regulations were promulgated pursuant to the Department's rulemaking authority and therefore could be set aside under the relevant provision of the Administrative Procedure Act, 5 U.S.C. § 706(2)(A), only if they were arbitrary, capricious, an abuse of discretion, or otherwise not in accordance with the law. Finding that modification of Indian fishing rights was not alone a sufficient grounds to invalidate the federal regulations, the court remanded to the district court to determine whether the regulations were arbitrary or capricious.

The Lacey Act, 16 U.S.C. § 3372, makes it a federal criminal offense in Indian country "to import, export, transport, sell, receive, acquire, or purchase any fish or wildlife or plant taken or possessed in violation of any law, treaty, or regulation of the United States or in violation of any Indian tribal law." In *United States v. Sohappy*, 770 F.2d 816 (9th Cir. 1985), *cert. denied*, 477 U.S. 906 (1986), the court affirmed the convictions of David Sohappy and others for transporting, selling, or acquiring fish in violation of the Lacey Act. The court rejected the defendants' contention that the Lacey Act did not apply to Indian defendants who transported fish in violation of tribal law, arguing that the Act manifested Congress' general desire to protect wildlife for the general welfare. The court noted that "[g]iven Congress' goal of preserving wildlife, it is only reasonable to assume that Congress intended the Lacey Act to encompass everyone, including Indians." *Id.* at 821.

After repeated conflicts between the United States Internal Revenue Service and Native Americans exercising their hunting and fishing rights over the taxation of the proceeds of commercial food gathering, Congress passed subtitle E of the Technical and Miscellaneous Revenue Act of 1988, Pub. L. 100-647, 102 Stat. 3640-42, to resolve such questions. Basically, this legislation amends the United States Internal Revenue Code to clearly indicate that no income, business, social security, or like taxes are due from any tribal members or qualified Indian entity exercising "fishing rights secured as of March 17, 1988, by treaty between such tribe and the United States or by an Executive order or an act of Congress." The Act also indicates that distributions with respect to equity interests in qualified Indian entities are subject to similar rules so long as the distribution derives from income attributable to Indian fishing rights-related activity. The legislation also amends 25 U.S.C. § 71 to preempt state and local taxation of such activities to the same extent that they are immune from federal taxation.

2. OFF-RESERVATION FOOD-GATHERING RIGHTS

As a general rule, Indian conduct outside of Indian reservations is subject to nondiscriminatory state law otherwise applicable to all citizens of the state. *See*

Mescalero Apache Tribe v. Jones, 411 U.S. 145 (1973). Subject to constitutional and federal statutory restraints, protection of wildlife and regulation of hunting and fishing are within the police power of the states. *See Baldwin v. Fish & Game Comm'n,* 436 U.S. 371 (1978). Thus, the Supreme Court has never held that the states lack power to regulate the exercise of off-reservation hunting and fishing rights based on aboriginal title or occupancy. *Organized Village of Kake v. Egan,* 369 U.S. 60 (1962).

Indians sometimes have argued for the existence of off-reservation rights based on aboriginal claims or on substantially less than explicit treaty language. Where made, such claims have generally failed. *See, e.g., Minnesota v. Keezer,* 292 N.W.2d 714 (Minn. 1980). In *State v. Quigley,* 52 Wash. 2d 234, 324 P.2d 827 (1958), for example, the Washington Supreme Court held that once aboriginal rights to land are extinguished and the land passes into private ownership, aboriginal hunting rights are also extinguished. Thus, even though an Indian purchased land within his aboriginal hunting region, his right to hunt was subject to state regulation. In *State v. Coffee,* 97 Idaho 905, 556 P.2d 1185 (1976), the Idaho Supreme Court held that the Kootenai Indians did retain their aboriginal right to hunt on open and unclaimed lands despite congressional extinguishment of the tribe's right to the land. Nevertheless, the court held that the tribe did not retain aboriginal hunting rights on privately owned land and that state regulations would be applicable on such land. Tribes have sometimes claimed that outright cessions of land made in prior treaties did not include a cession of hunting and fishing rights because such rights were not explicitly mentioned. These claims have also been unsuccessful. *See, e.g., Red Lake Band of Chippewa Indians v. Minnesota,* 614 F.2d 1161 (8th Cir. 1980).

Off-reservation food-gathering rights therefore are created primarily by language guaranteeing off-reservation food-gathering activities or in some instances by the persistence of prior guarantees of on-reservation rights after the reservation in question was diminished or otherwise reduced in size by cession. The rule requiring express guarantees of such rights, of course, is the opposite of the liberal construction given to treaties to create on-reservation hunting and food-gathering rights. *See Menominee Tribe v. United States,* 391 U.S. 404 (1968). The approach nevertheless is consistent with the more grudging construction given to statutes affecting Indian off-reservation activities. *See Mescalero Apache Tribe v. Jones,* 411 U.S. 145 (1973).

The *Mescalero Apache Tribe* case did recognize that specific federal treaty or statutory provisions may preempt state jurisdiction outside of Indian country. A number of treaties in the Pacific Northwest and Great Lakes areas contain such explicit guarantees of off-reservation hunting or fishing rights. *See, e.g.,* Treaty with the Confederated Tribes and Bands of Indians Residing in Middle Oregon, June 25, 1855, 12 Stat. 963; Treaty with the Quinaielt and Quillehute, Jan. 22, 1856, and July 1, 1855, 12 Stat. 971. Typical of Pacific Northwest provisions is the following:

> The right of taking fish, at all usual and accustomed grounds and stations, is further secured to said Indians in common with all citizens of the Territory, and of erecting temporary houses for the purpose of curing, together with the privilege of hunting, gathering roots and berries, and pasturing their horses on open and unclaimed lands:

Provided, however, That they shall not take shellfish from any beds staked or cultivated by citizens ....

Treaty with Nisqually, Payallup and Other Tribes, Dec. 26, 1855, art. 3, 10 Stat.
1133 (commonly known as the Treaty of Medicine Creek). The 1836 Treaty
with the Ottawa and Chippewa provided: "The Indians stipulate for the right of
hunting on the lands ceded, with the other usual privileges of occupancy, until
the land is required for settlement." Treaty with the Ottawa and Chippewa,
Mar. 28, 1836, art. 13, 7 Stat. 491.

The extent of federal preemption of state regulation by an Indian treaty
turns on the intent of the parties as reflected in the language of the treaty and
the circumstances under which the treaty was negotiated. *See, e.g., Washington
v. Washington State Com. Passenger Fishing Vessel Ass'n,* 443 U.S. 658 (1979), set
forth below. Treaty or statutory provisions purporting to reserve such
off-reservation rights are subject to the rules requiring liberal construction of
Indian treaties in a manner that executes the Indian understanding of the
agreement, as the cases in this section will indicate. Even where off-reservation
rights are recognized, significant questions remain regarding the meaning, scope,
and extent of such rights and the power of the states, tribes, and the federal
government to regulate the exercise of such off-reservation rights.

UNITED STATES v. WINANS

198 U.S. 371 (1905)

Mr. Justice McKENNA delivered the opinion of the court.

This suit was brought to enjoin the respondents from obstructing certain
Indians of the Yakima Nation in the State of Washington from exercising fishing rights and privileges on the Columbia River in that State, claimed under the
provisions of the treaty between the United States and the Indians, made in
1859.

There is no substantial dispute of facts, or none that is important to our
inquiry.

The treaty is as follows:

....

The exclusive right of taking fish in all the streams where running through or
bordering said reservation, is further secured to said confederated tribes and bands of
Indians, as also the right of taking fish at all usual and accustomed places, in common
with citizens of the Territory, and of erecting temporary buildings for curing them;
together with the privilege of hunting, gathering roots and berries, and pasturing their
horses and cattle upon open and unclaimed land....

The respondents or their predecessors in title claim under patents of the
United States the lands bordering on the Columbia River and under grants
from the State of Washington to the shore land which, it is alleged, fronts on the
patented land. They also introduced in evidence licenses from the State to
maintain devices for taking fish, called fish wheels.

At the time the treaty was made the fishing places were part of the Indian
country, subject to the occupancy of the Indians, with all the rights such occupancy gave. The object of the treaty was to limit the occupancy to certain lands
and to define rights outside of them.

The pivot of the controversy is the construction of the second paragraph. Respondents contend that the words "the right of taking fish at all usual and accustomed places *in common* with the citizens of the Territory" confer only such rights as a white man would have under the conditions of ownership of the lands bordering on the river, and under the laws of the State, and, such being the rights conferred, the respondents further contend that they have the power to exclude the Indians from the river by reason of such ownership.

[W]e have said we will construe a treaty with the Indians as "that unlettered people" understood it, and "as justice and reason demand in all cases where power is exerted by the strong over those to whom they owe care and protection," and counterpoise the inequality "by the superior justice which looks only to the substance of the right without regard to technical rules." 119 U.S. 1; 175 U.S. 1. How the treaty in question was understood may be gathered from the circumstances.

The right to resort to the fishing places in controversy was a part of larger rights possessed by the Indians, upon the exercise of which there was not a shadow of impediment, and which were not much less necessary to the existence of the Indians than the atmosphere they breathed. New conditions came into existence, to which those rights had to be accommodated. Only a limitation of them, however, was necessary and intended, not a taking away. In other words, the treaty was not a grant of rights to the Indians, but a grant of rights from them — a reservation of those not granted. And the form of the instrument and its language was adapted to that purpose. Reservations were not of particular parcels of land, and could not be expressed in deeds as dealings between private individuals. The reservations were in large areas of territory and the negotiations were with the tribe. They reserved rights, however, to every individual Indian, as though named therein. They imposed a servitude upon every piece of land as though described therein. There was an exclusive right of fishing reserved within certain boundaries. There was a right outside of those boundaries reserved "in common with citizens of the Territory." As a mere right, it was not exclusive in the Indians. Citizens might share it, but the Indians were secured in its enjoyment by a special provision of means for its exercise. They were given "the right of taking fish at all usual and accustomed places," and the right "of erecting temporary buildings for curing them." The contingency of the future ownership of the lands, therefore, was foreseen and provided for — in other words, the Indians were given a right in the land — the right of crossing it to the river — the right to occupy it to the extent and for the purpose mentioned. No other conclusion would give effect to the treaty. And the right was intended to be continuing against the United States and its grantees as well as against the State and its grantees.

The respondents urge an argument based upon the different capacities of white men and Indians to devise and make use of instrumentalities to enjoy the common right. Counsel say: "The fishing right was in common, and aside from the right of the State to license fish wheels the wheel fishing is one of the civilized man's methods, as legitimate as the substitution of the modern combined harvester for the ancient sickle and flail." But the result does not follow that the Indians may be absolutely excluded. It needs no argument to show that the superiority of a combined harvester over the ancient sickle neither increased nor decreased rights to the use of land held in common. In the actual taking of fish white men may not be confined to a spear or crude net, but it does not follow that they may construct and use a device which gives them exclusive possession of the fishing places, as it is admitted a fish wheel does. Besides, the fish wheel is not relied on alone. Its monopoly is made complete by a license from the State. The argument based on the inferiority of the Indians is peculiar. If the Indians had not been inferior in capacity and power, what the treaty would have been, or that there would have been any treaty, would be hard to guess.

The construction of the treaty disposes of certain subsidiary contentions of respondents. The Land Department could grant no exemptions from its provisions. It makes no difference, therefore, that the patents issued by the Department are absolute in form. They are subject to the treaty as to the other laws of the land.

It is further contended that the rights conferred upon the Indians are subordinate to the powers acquired by the State upon its admission into the Union. In other words, it is contended that the State acquired, by its admission into the Union "upon an equal footing with the original States," the power to grant rights in or to dispose of the shore lands upon navigable streams, and such power is subject only to the paramount authority of Congress with regard to public navigation and commerce. The United States, therefore, it is contended, could neither grant nor retain rights in the shore or to the lands under water.

The elements of this contention and the answer to it are expressed in *Shively v. Bowlby,* 152 U.S. 1. It is unnecessary, and it would be difficult, to add anything to the reasoning of that case. The power and rights of the States in and over shore lands were carefully defined, but the power of the United States, while it held the country as a Territory, to create rights which would be binding on the States was also announced, opposing the dicta scattered through the cases, which seemed to assert a contrary view.

[E]xtinguishment of the Indian title, opening the land for settlement and preparing the way for future States, were appropriate to the objects for which the United States held the Territory. And surely it was within the competency of the Nation to secure to the Indians such a remnant of the great rights they possessed as "taking fish at all usual and accustomed places." Nor does it restrain the State unreasonably, if at all, in the regulation of the right. It only fixes in the land such easements as enables the right to be exercised.

The license from the State, which respondents plead to maintain a fishing wheel, gives no power to them to exclude the Indians, nor was it intended to give such power. It was the permission of the State to use a particular device. What rights the Indians had were not determined or limited. This was a matter for judicial determination regarding the rights of the Indians and rights of the respondents. And that there may be an adjustment and accommodation of them the Solicitor General concedes and points out the way. We think, however, that such adjustment and accommodation are more within the province of the Circuit Court in the first instance than of this court.

[*Reversed and remanded.*]

Mr. Justice WHITE dissents.

NOTES

1. History of Interpretation of Off-Reservation Hunting and Fishing Rights Treaty Guarantees: The decision in *Winans* represented the beginning of the evolution in the construction of the meaning and scope of off-reservation hunting and fishing rights. Prior to *Winans,* a divided Court had held in *Ward v. Race Horse,* 163 U.S. 504 (1896), that the right reserved to the Bannock Indians in an 1868 treaty "to hunt on unoccupied lands of the United States, so long as game may be found thereon" did not survive the admission of Wyoming to statehood. The Court majority argued that

> [t]o suppose that the words of the treaty intended to give to the Indian the right to enter into already established States and seek out every portion of unoccupied government land and there exercise the right of hunting, in violation of the municipal law, would be to presume that the treaty was so drawn as to frustrate the very object it had in view.

163 U.S. at 509. The Court noted that the treaty right was "temporary and precarious" because it was wholly dependent on retention of title to unoccupied lands by the federal government. Also citing *Geer v. Connecticut,* the Court argued that a contrary construction would frustrate the unquestioned power of a state to control and regulate the taking of game. Thus, the Court found that the 1868 treaty, if construed as the Indians argued, violated the so-called "equal footing" doctrine because Wyoming was admitted to the Union on an equal footing with all other states and was therefore entitled to regulate the taking of game throughout the state.

Winans clearly rejected the view that the equal footing doctrine limits the exercise of treaty-guaranteed off-reservation hunting and fishing rights. However, *Winans* left a legacy of confusion as to the nature and scope of such rights. Fundamentally, *Winans* involved the question of access to a usual and accustomed fishing station with which the defendants had interfered by the operation of their fish wheel. Thus, the most limited holding of *Winans* treats the off-reservation rights as merely a guarantee of access to fishing sites in the nature of an easement or encumbrance on the title of subsequent title holders. Such a construction guarantees the Indians neither specific rights in the fishery resource nor freedom from state regulation. Two aspects of *Winans* suggest, however, that the Court had in mind a broader construction of the off-reservation treaty rights. First, the Court noted that the fish wheel interfered with the movement of the fish upstream and therefore depleted the available resource. Second, the defendants' fish wheel was state licensed. Thus, the Court's ruling suggested that the Indians' treaty-guaranteed off-reservation fishing rights imposed some limits on the usually unquestioned power of the state to control and regulate the taking of game. The subsequent cases on off-reservation food gathering are best understood as representing an evolutionary effort to work out these ambiguities in *Winans.* As is often true in the long-term development of a path of cases, these cases include some false starts and dead ends. *Ward v. Race Horse* is one of those dead ends, but there were others.

The early cases after *Winans* seemed to stress in particular the access aspects of *Winans.* Either as a product of their facts or their holdings, the early cases treated off-reservation fishing rights primarily as a guarantee of access to traditional fisheries sites even when held in private hands — the "easement" view of the right. For example, in *Seufert Bros. v. United States,* 249 U.S. 194 (1919), the Court affirmed an injunction against a private company and its employees restraining them from interfering with the treaty-guaranteed fishing rights of the Yakima. The suit was brought by the United States to enforce the Indians' rights to establish fish wheels on sites adversely claimed by the defendant corporation. The Court construed the Yakima treaty rights as the Indians understood them, "that they had the right to resort to these fishing grounds and make use of them in common with other citizens of the United States ...." 249 U.S. at 198-99. Responding to the defendants' suggestion that the Indians in exercising their off-reservation rights were limited to the methods employed in primitive times, the district court had said, "I see no reason why Indians may not be permitted to advance in the arts and sciences as well as any other people, and, if they can catch their supply of food fish by a more scientific and expeditious method, there exists no good reason why they may not be permitted to do so." *United States ex rel. Williams v. Seufert Bros.,* 233 Fed. Rep. 579, 584 (D. Or. 1916).

In *New York ex rel. Kennedy v. Becker,* 241 U.S. 556 (1916), the Supreme Court indicated that the easement construction of off-reservation hunting rights might subsume their entire scope. This case involved the state prosecution of Seneca Indians for violation of state conservation laws when exercising rights reserved under a federally approved indenture to exercise "the privilege of fishing and hunting on the said tract of land hereby intended to be conveyed [by the federal indenture to private claimants]." According to the Court,

> It has frequently been said that treaties with the Indians should be construed in the sense in which the Indians understood them. But it is idle to suppose that there was any actual anticipation at the time the treaty was made of the conditions now existing to which the legislation in question was addressed. Adopted when game was plentiful — when the cultivation contemplated by the whites was not expected to interfere with its abundance — it can hardly be supposed that the thought of the Indians was concerned with the necessary exercise of inherent power under modern conditions for the preservation of wild life. But the existence of the sovereignty of the State was well understood, and this conception involved all that was necessarily implied in that sovereignty, whether fully appreciated or not. We do not think that it is a proper construction of the reservation in the conveyance to regard it as an attempt either to reserve sovereign prerogative or so to divide the inherent power of preservation as to make its competent exercise impossible.

241 U.S. at 563.

In 1942 the Court began to limit the sweeping dicta in *Kennedy* suggesting that Indian hunting and fishing rights were wholly subject to state control. In *Tulee v. Washington,* 315 U.S. 681 (1942), the Court held that the state of Washington could not impose a licensing fee for the exercise of the Yakimas' off-reservation treaty fishing rights. The Court said:

> [W]e are of the opinion that the state is without power to charge the Yakimas a fee for fishing. A stated purpose of the licensing act was to provide for "the support of the state government and its existing public institutions." Laws of Washington (1937) 529, 534. The license fees prescribed are regulatory as well as revenue producing. But it is clear that their regulatory purpose could be accomplished otherwise, that the imposition of license fees is not indispensable to the effectiveness of a state conservation program. Even though this method may be both convenient and, in its general impact, fair, it acts upon the Indians as a charge for exercising the very right their ancestors intended to reserve. We believe that such exaction of fees as a prerequisite to the enjoyment of fishing in the "usual and accustomed places" cannot be reconciled with a fair construction of the treaty. We therefore hold the state statute invalid as applied in this case.

315 U.S. at 685. *Tulee* clearly indicated, as *Winans* had previously suggested, that off-reservation treaty rights preempted the force of state conservation laws to some extent. It remained for later cases to work out the scope and contours of that preemption.

   2. **The *Puyallup* Cases and the Start of the Modern Litigation:** In *Puyallup Tribe v. Department of Game,* 391 U.S. 392 (1968) ("*Puyallup I*"), the Court was faced with suits by the state of Washington to secure a declaratory judgment that the Puyallup Tribe was subject to state conservation measures in the exercise of their off-reservation fishing rights and to enjoin the Nisqually Indians from using set nets and drift nets in violation of state law. The Court assumed that the off-reservation fishing rights of the affected tribes historically and presently had "commercial aspects" and said that Indian right "may, of course, not be qualified by the State, even though all Indians born in the United States are now citizens of the United States." 391 U.S. at 392. Nevertheless, the Court held that "the manner of fishing, the size of the take, the restriction of commercial fishing, and the like may be regulated by the state in the interest of conservation, provided that the regulation meets appropriate standards and does not discriminate against the Indians." *Id.* The Court described its appropriate standards by saying, "the power of the State was to be measured by whether it was "necessary for the conservation of fish."" 392 U.S. at 402 n.14. The Court remanded the case to the trial court for determination of the measures reasonable and necessary for conservation with the admonition that "the conservation issue must also cover the issue of equal protection implicit in the phrase 'in common with.'" 391 U.S. at 403. *See also Maison v. Confederated Tribes,* 314 F.2d 169 (9th Cir.), *cert. denied,* 375 U.S. 829 (1963); *Sohappy v. Smith,* 302 F. Supp. 899 (D. Or. 1969), *aff'd,* 529 F.2d 570 (9th Cir. 1976); *see also* Schmidhauser, *The Struggle for Cultural Survival: The Fishing Rights of the Treaty Tribes of the Pacific Northwest,* 52 NOTRE DAME LAW. 30 (1976); Comment, *State Power and Indian Treaty Right to Fish,* 59 CAL. L. REV. 485 (1971).

   Professor Ralph Johnson was severely critical of the *Puyallup I* decision, stating:

> Because agreements with the Indians are treaties, the Indians are not subject to state regulation unless the treaty so provides or unless Congress so legislates. The treaties with the Indians do not provide for state regulation and Congress has never authorized such regulation. Therefore, the Supreme Court should clearly hold that the states have no power to regulate Indian off-reservation fishing unless and until Congress expressly delegates the power to do so ....
>
> [T]he vagueness of the case law standards portends a continuing series of clashes between the Indians and the states, each seeking to carve out the broadest possible claim in this legal thicket. But the creation of adequate standards will not be an easy task.

Johnson, *The States Versus Indian Off-Reservation Fishing: A United States Supreme Court Error,* 47 WASH. L. REV. 207, 208-09 (1972).*

   Professor Johnson's prediction regarding the difficulty of working out the scope of state jurisdiction through adjudication proved correct, as *Puyallup I* engendered a flood of litigation in the Pacific Northwest during the last decade. In *Department of Game v. Puyallup Tribe,* 414 U.S. 44 (1973) ("*Puyallup II*"), the same litigation returned to the Court, this time to resolve the question of whether the state conservation authorities could prohibit all Indian net fishing

---

for steelhead trout in order to conserve the steelhead fish runs. The state authorities argued that after the allotment of steelhead caught by sport fishers, the remainder was necessary for spawning in order to replenish the run. The Court struck down the state regulations because they discriminated against Indian treaty fishers. "There is discrimination here because all Indian net fishing is banned and only hook-and-line fishing entirely preempted by non-Indians is allowed." 414 U.S. at 44. However, the Court cautioned:

> The aim is to accommodate the rights of Indians under the Treaty and the rights of other people.
> We do not imply that these fishing rights persist down to the very last steelhead in the river. Rights can be controlled by the need to conserve a species; and the time may come when the life of a steelhead is so precarious in a particular stream that all fishing should be banned until the species regains assurance of survival. The police power of the State is adequate to prevent the steelhead from following the fate of the passenger pigeon; and the Treaty does not give the Indians a federal right to pursue the last living steelhead until it enters their nets.

414 U.S. at 49. Justice White noted in a brief concurring opinion, joined by Chief Justice Burger and Justice Stewart, that the state of Washington through its hatchery program was responsible for a substantial proportion of the steelhead run in question. He then commented, "... the Treaty does not obligate the State of Washington to subsidize the Indian fishery with planted fish paid for by sports fishermen." 414 U.S. at 49.

The *Puyallup* litigation again returned to the Court in *Puyallup Tribe v. Department of Game*, 433 U.S. 165 (1977) ("*Puyallup III*"). *Puyallup III* involved the review of the state regulations governing Puyallup treaty fishing rights promulgated after the remand in *Puyallup II*. Before the state courts considered these regulations on remand, a crucial change in the facts of the case occurred. In *United States v. Washington*, 496 F.2d 620 (9th Cir.), *cert. denied*, 419 U.S. 1032 (1974), the Ninth Circuit Court of Appeals held that the Puyallup Reservation had not been extinguished. Under this ruling, the reservation boundaries thus included almost all of the area where the fishing in *Puyallup I* and *Puyallup II* had taken place. From the commencement of the Puyallup litigation in 1963, the state of Washington had conceded that it had no right to regulate fishing on the reservation. Nevertheless, the Washington Supreme Court both recognized the Ninth Circuit's decision and held that the state could regulate Indian fishing *off* and *on* the reservation. Thus, before the Supreme Court in *Puyallup III*, the tribe shifted its defense to one based on on-reservation rights.

The tribe claimed both sovereign immunity from suit and that its reservation still existed and included large sections of the city of Tacoma. On the sovereign immunity issue, the Court sustained the tribe's claim and therefore vacated that portion of the lower court order requiring the tribe to report the catch of its members each week. However, the Court treated the designation of the tribe as a surrogate for designating the various members of the tribe and permitted the case to proceed without any reference to potential indispensable party issues. The Court rejected the significance of the tribe's belated on-reservation fishing rights claim, noting that of the original 18,000-acre reservation the tribe retains only 22 acres none of which abutted the Puyallup River. Nevertheless, the Court stopped short of finding that the Puyallup Reservation had been disestablished. Rather, the Court said:

> The resource being regulated is indigenous to the Puyallup River. Virtually all adult steelhead in the river have returned after being spawned or planted by respondent

upstream from the boundaries of the original Puyallup Reservation, which encompass the lowest seven miles of the river. Though it would be decidedly unwise, if Puyallup treaty fishermen were allowed untrammeled on-reservation fishing rights, they could interdict completely the migratory fish run and "pursue the last living [Puyallup River] steelhead until it enters their nets." ... In practical effect, therefore, the petitioner is reasserting the right to exclusive control of the steelhead run that was unequivocally rejected in both *Puyallup I* and *Puyallup II*. At this stage of this protracted litigation, we are unwilling to re-examine those unanimous decisions or to render their holdings virtually meaningless. We therefore reject petitioner's claim to an exclusive right to take steelhead while passing through the reservation.

433 U.S. at 176-77. Finally, the Court reviewed the state standards and found that they met appropriate conservation standards in that "the court determined the number of steelhead in the river and how many could be taken without diminishing the number in future years; the court then allocated 45% of the annual natural steelhead run available for taking to the treaty fishermen's net fishery." 433 U.S. at 177. The Court withheld comment on the lower court's exclusion of hatchery fish from the calculation as not available to the Indians since this issue was not presented in the petition for certiorari.

Puyallup III indicates that questions of conservation and state regulation not infrequently mask the true underlying dispute: the allocation of the resource between Indians and non-Indians. Thus, in *United States v. Washington*, 384 F. Supp. 312 (W.D. Wash. 1974) (Boldt, J.), *aff'd*, 520 F.2d 676 (9th Cir. 1975), *cert. denied*, 423 U.S. 1086 (1976), the courts construed guarantees of off-reservation fishery rights to require that "[t]reaty Indians thus are to have the opportunity to take up to 50 percent of the available harvest at their traditional grounds." 520 F.2d at 683. This ruling spawned a major political and legal dispute in the Pacific Northwest. *See, e.g., Puget Sound Gillnetters Ass'n v. United States District Court*, 573 F.2d 1123 (9th Cir. 1978); *Washington State Com. Passenger Fishing Vessel Ass'n v. Tollefson*, 89 Wash. 2d 276, 571 P.2d 1373 (1977), *vacated*, 434 U.S. 658 (1979). *Purse Seine Vessel Owners Ass'n v. Moos*, 88 Wash. 2d 799, 567 P.2d 205 (1977). The political and legal conflict engendered by those cases ultimately led the Supreme Court to intervene.

WASHINGTON v. WASHINGTON STATE COMMERCIAL PASSENGER FISHING VESSEL ASSOCIATION

443 U.S. 658 (1979)

Mr. Justice STEVENS delivered the opinion of the Court.

To extinguish the last group of conflicting claims to lands lying west of the Cascade Mountains and north of the Columbia River in what is now the State of Washington, the United States entered into a series of treaties with Indian tribes in 1854 and 1855.[2] The Indians relinquished their interest in most of the territory in exchange for monetary payments. In addition, certain relatively small parcels of land were reserved for their exclusive use, and they were afforded other guarantees, including protection of their "right of taking fish at

---

[2] Treaty of Medicine Creek (10 Stat. 1132), the Treaty of Point Elliott (12 Stat. 927), the Treaty of Point No Point (12 Stat. 933), the Treaty of Neah Bay (12 Stat. 939), the Treaty with the Yakimas (12 Stat. 951), and the Treaty of Olympia (12 Stat. 971). The parties to the treaties and to this litigation include these Indian Tribes: Hoh; Lower Elwha Band of Clallam Indians; Lummi; Makah; Muckleshoot; Nisqually; Nooksack Tribe; Port Gamble Band of Clallam Indians; Puyallup; Quileute; Quinault; Sauk-Suiattle; Skokomish; Sqaxin Island; Stillaguamish; Suquamish; Swinomish; Tulalip; Upper Skagit; The Yakima Nation, 384 F. Supp. 312, 349; 459; F. Supp. 1028.

usual and accustomed grounds and stations ... in common with all citizens of the Territory."

The principal question presented by this litigation concerns the character of that treaty right to take fish. Various other issues are presented, but their disposition depends on the answer to the principal question. Before answering any of these questions, or even stating the issues with more precision, we shall briefly describe the anadromous fisheries of the Pacific Northwest, the treaty negotiations, and the principal components of the litigation complex that led us to grant these three related petitions for certiorari.

I

Anadromous fish hatch in fresh water, migrate to the ocean where they are reared and reach mature size, and eventually complete their life cycle by returning to the fresh-water place of their origin to spawn. Different species have different life cycles, some spending several years and travelling great distances in the ocean before returning to spawn and some even returning to spawn on more than one occasion before dying. The regular habits of these fish make their "runs" predictable; this predictability in turn makes it possible for both fishermen and regulators to forecast and to control the number of fish that will be caught or "harvested." Indeed, as the terminology associated with it suggests, the management of anadromous fisheries is in many ways more akin to the cultivation of "crops" — with its relatively high degree of predictability and productive stability, subject mainly to sudden changes in climatic patterns — than is the management of most other commercial and sports fisheries.

Regulation of the anadromous fisheries of the Northwest is nonetheless complicated by the different habits of the various species of salmon and trout involved, by the variety of methods of taking the fish, and by the fact that a run of fish may pass through a series of different jurisdictions. Another complexity arises from the fact that the State of Washington has attempted to reserve one species, steelhead trout, for sport fishing and therefore conferred regulatory jurisdiction over that species upon its Department of Game, whereas the various species of salmon are primarily harvested by commercial fishermen and are managed by the State's Department of Fisheries. Moreover, adequate regulation must not only take into account the potentially conflicting interests of sport and commercial fishermen, as well as those of Indian and nontreaty fishermen, but also must recognize that the fish runs may be harmed by harvesting either too many or too few of the fish returning to spawn.

The anadromous fish constitute a natural resource of great economic value to the State of Washington. Millions of salmon, with an average weight of from four or five to about 20 pounds, depending on the species, are harvested each year. Over 6,600 nontreaty fishermen and about 800 Indians make their livelihood by commercial fishing; moreover, some 280,000 individuals are licensed to engage in sport fishing in the State.

II

One hundred and twenty-five years ago when the relevant treaties were signed, anadromous fish were even more important to most of the population of western Washington than they are today. At that time, about three-fourths of the approximately 10,000 inhabitants of the area were Indians. Although in some respects the cultures of the different tribes varied — some bands of Indians, for example, had little or no tribal organization[5] while others, such as the Makah and the Yakima, were highly organized — all of them shared a vital and unifying dependence on anadromous fish.

Religious rites were intended to insure the continual return of the salmon and the trout; the seasonal and geographic variations in the runs of the different species determined the movements of the largely nomadic tribes. Fish constituted a major part of the Indian diet, was used for commercial purposes, and indeed was traded in substantial volume.[7] The Indians developed food preservation techniques that enabled them to store fish throughout the year and to transport it over great distances. They used a wide variety of methods to catch fish, including the precursors of all modern netting techniques. Their usual and accustomed fishing places were numerous and were scattered throughout the area, and included marine as well as fresh water areas.

All of the treaties were negotiated by Isaac Stevens, the first Governor and first Superintendent of Indian Affairs of the Washington territory, and a small group of advisors. Contemporaneous documents make it clear that these people recognized the vital importance of the fisheries to the Indians and wanted to protect them from the risk that non-Indian settlers might seek to monopolize their fisheries. There is no evidence of the precise understanding the Indians had of any of the specific English terms and phrases in the treaty. It is perfectly clear, however, that the Indians were vitally interested in protecting their right to take fish at usual and accustomed places, whether on or off the reservations, and that they were invited by the white negotiators to rely and in fact did rely heavily on the good faith of the United States to protect that right.

Referring to the negotiations with the Yakima Nation, by far the largest of the Indian tribes, the District Court found:

> At the treaty council the United States negotiators promised, and the Indians understood, that the Yakimas would forever be able to continue the same off-reservation food gathering and fishing practices as to time, place, method, species and extent as they had or were exercising. The Yakimas relied on these promises and they formed a

---

[5] Indeed, the record shows that the territorial officials who negotiated the treaties on behalf of the United States took the initiative in aggregating certain loose bands into designated tribes and even appointed many of the chiefs who signed the treaties.

[7] "At the time of the treaties, trade was carried on among the Indian groups throughout a wide geographic area. Fish was a basic element of the trade. There is some evidence that the volume of this intra-tribal trade was substantial, but it is not possible to compare it with the volume of present day commercial trading in salmon. Such trading was, however, important to the Indians at the time of the treaties. In addition to potlatching, which is a system of exchange between communities in a social context often typified by competitive gifting, there was a considerable amount of outright sale and trade beyond the local community and sometimes over great distances. In the decade immediately preceding the treaties, Indian fighting increased in order to accommodate increased demand for local non-Indian consumption and for export, as well as to provide money for purchase of introduced commodities and to obtain substitute non-Indian goods for native products which were no longer available because of the non-Indian movement into the area. Those involved in negotiating the treaties recognized the contribution that Indian fishermen made to the territorial economy because Indians caught most of the non-Indians' fish for them, plus clams and oysters." 384 F. Supp., at 351 (citations to record omitted). See also *id.,* at 364 (Makah Tribe "maintained from time immemorial a thriving economy based on commerce" in "marine resources").

material and basic part of the treaty and of the Indians' understanding of the meaning of the treaty. *Id.*, at 381 (record citations omitted).

See also *id.*, at 363 (similar finding regarding negotiations with the Makah tribe).

The Indians understood that non-Indians would also have the right to fish at their off-reservation fishing sites. But this was not understood as a significant limitation on their right to take fish. Because of the great abundance of fish and the limited population of the area, it simply was not contemplated that either party would interfere with the other's fishing rights. The parties accordingly did not see the need and did not intend to regulate the taking of fish by either Indians or non-Indians, nor was future regulation foreseen.

Indeed, for several decades after the treaties were signed, Indians continued to harvest most of the fish taken from the waters of Washington, and they moved freely about the territory and later the State in search of that resource. The size of the fishery source continued to obviate the need during the period to regulate the taking of fish by either Indians or non-Indians. Not until major economic developments in canning and processing occurred in the last few years of the 19th century did a significant non-Indian fishery develop. It was as a consequence of these developments, rather than of the treaty, that non-Indians began to dominate the fisheries and eventually to exclude most Indians from participating in it — a trend that was encouraged by the onset of often-discriminatory state regulation in the early decades of the 20th century.

In sum, it is fair to conclude that when the treaties were negotiated, neither party realized or intended that their agreement would determine whether, and if so how, a resource that had always been thought inexhaustible would be allocated between the native Indians and the incoming settlers when it later became scarce.

III

Unfortunately, that resource has now become scarce, and the meaning of the Indians' treaty right to take fish has accordingly become critical. The United States Court of Appeals for the Ninth Circuit and the Supreme Court of the State of Washington have issued conflicting decisions on its meaning. In addition, their holdings raise important ancillary questions that will appear from a brief review of this extensive litigation....

The District Court agreed with the parties who advocated an allocation to the Indians, and it essentially agreed with the United States as to what that allocation should be. It held that the Indians were then entitled to a 45% to 50% share of the harvestable fish that will at some point pass through recognized tribal fishing grounds in the case area.[16] The share was to be calculated on a river-by-

---

[16] The Solicitor General estimates that over half of the anadromous fish in the case area do *not* pass through such grounds and are exempt from the order. Brief for the United States, at 72-73. This estimate is consistent with the State's figures on the number of salmon caught in 1977, see JA 635-639, which indicate that the Indians caught only about 18% of the fish taken in the case area that year. Of course, the Indians claim that they were prevented from catching as many fish that year as they were entitled to under the District Court's order because of interference by non-Indian fishermen. But even if the 18% figure were increased by the amount of fish the Indians claim they should have caught, see Brief of Respondent Indian Tribes, at 72, n.273, the Indians' take would only amount to about 20% of the total number of fish taken in the case area.

river, run-by-run basis, subject to certain adjustments. Fish caught by Indians for ceremonial and subsistence purposes as well as fish caught within a reservation were excluded from the calculation of the tribes' share. In addition, in order to compensate for fish caught outside of the case area, *i.e.,* beyond the State's jurisdiction, the court made an "equitable adjustment" to increase the allocation to the Indians. The court left it to the individual tribes involved to agree among themselves on how best to divide the Indian share of runs that pass through the usual and accustomed grounds of more than one tribe, and it postponed until a later date the proper accounting for hatchery-bred fish. [T]he Court of Appeals for the Ninth Circuit affirmed, and we denied certiorari.

The injunction entered by the District Court required the Department of Fisheries ("Fisheries") to adopt regulations protecting the Indians' treaty rights. 384 F. Supp., at 416-417. After the new regulations were promulgated, however, they were immediately challenged by private citizens in suits commenced in the Washington state courts. The State Supreme Court, in two cases that are herein consolidated form in No. 77-983, ultimately held that Fisheries could not comply with the federal injunction. *Puget Sound Gillnetters Ass'n v. Moos,* 88 Wn. 2d 677, 565 P. 1151; *Fishing Vessel Ass'n v. Tollefson,* 89 Wn. 2d 276, 571 P.2d 1373.

As a matter of federal law, the state court first accepted the Game Department's and rejected the District Court's interpretation of the treaty and held that it did not give the Indians a right to a share of the fish runs, and second concluded that recognizing special rights for the Indians would violate the Equal Protection Clause of the Fourteenth Amendment. The opinions might also be read to hold, as a matter of state law, that Fisheries had no authority to issue the regulations because they had a purpose other than conservation of the resource. In this Court, however, the Attorney General of the State disclaims the adequacy and independence of the state law ground and argues that the state-law authority of Fisheries is dependent on the answers to the two federal-law questions discussed above. We defer to that interpretation, subject, of course, to later clarification by the State Supreme Court. Because we are also satisfied that the constitutional holding is without merit,[20] our review of the state court's judgment will be limited to the treaty issue.

When Fisheries was ordered by the state courts to abandon its attempt to promulgate and enforce regulations in compliance with the federal court's decree — and when the Game Department simply refused to comply — the District Court entered a series of orders enabling it, with the aid of the United States Attorney for the Western District of Washington and various federal law enforcement agencies, directly to supervise those aspects of the State's fisheries necessary to the preservation of treaty fishing rights. The District Court's power to take such direct action and, in doing so, to enjoin persons who were not parties to the proceeding was affirmed by the United States Court of Appeals

---

[20] The Washington Supreme Court held that the treaties would violate equal protection principles if they provided fishing rights to Indians that were not also available to non-Indians. The simplest answer to this argument is that this Court has already held that these treaties confer enforceable special benefits on signatory Indian tribes, *e.g., Tulee, supra; Winans, supra,* and has repeatedly held that the peculiar semisovereign and constitutionally recognized status of Indians justifies special treatment on their behalves when rationally related to the Government's "unique obligation toward the Indians." *Morton v. Mancari,* 417 U.S. 535, 555.

for the Ninth Circuit. That court, in a separate opinion, also held that regulations of the International Pacific Salmon Fisheries Commission posed no impediment to the District Court's interpretation of the treaty language and to its enforcement of that interpretation. Subsequently, the District Court entered an Enforcement Order regarding the salmon fisheries for the 1978 and subsequent seasons, which, prior to our issuance of a writ of certiorari to review the case, was pending on appeal in the Court of Appeals.

Because of the widespread defiance of the District Court's orders, this litigation has assumed unusual significance. We granted certiorari in the state and federal cases to interpret this important treaty provision and thereby to resolve the conflict between the state and federal courts regarding what, if any, right the Indians have to a share of the fish, to address the implications of international regulation of the fisheries in the area, and to remove any doubts about the federal court's power to enforce its orders.

IV

The treaties secure a "right of taking fish." The pertinent articles provide:

> The right of taking fish at usual and accustomed grounds and stations is further secured to said Indians in common with all citizens of the Territory, and of erecting temporary houses for the purpose of curing, together with the privilege of hunting and gathering roots and berries on open and unclaimed lands. *Provided, however,* That they shall not take shell-fish from any beds staked or cultivated by citizens.

At the time the treaties were executed there was a great abundance of fish and a relative scarcity of people. No one had any doubt about the Indians' capacity to take as many fish as they might need. Their right to take fish could therefore be adequately protected by guaranteeing them access to usual and accustomed fishing sites which could be — and which for decades after the treaties were signed were — comfortably shared with the incoming settlers.

Because the sparse contemporaneous written materials refer primarily to assuring access to fishing sites "in common with citizens of the Territory," the State of Washington and the commercial fishing associations, having all adopted the Game Department's original position, argue that it was merely access that the negotiators guaranteed....

A treaty, including one between the United States and an Indian tribe, is essentially a contract between two sovereign nations. *E.g.,* [*Lone Wolf v. Hitchcock*]. When the signatory nations have not been at war and neither is the vanquished, it is reasonable to assume that they negotiated as equals at arms length. There is no reason to doubt that this assumption applies to the treaty at issue here.

Accordingly, it is the intention of the parties, and not solely that of the superior side, that must control any attempt to interpret the treaties. When Indians are involved, this Court has long given special meaning to this rule. It has held that the United States, as the party with the presumptively superior negotiating skills and superior knowledge of the language in which the treaty is recorded, has a responsibility to avoid taking advantage of the other side. "[T]he treaty must therefore be construed, not according to the technical meaning of its words to learned lawyers, but in the sense in which they would naturally be understood by the Indians." *Jones v. Meehan,* 175 U.S. 1, 10. This rule, in fact, has thrice been explicitly relied on by the Court in broadly interpreting these very treaties in the Indians' favor.

Governor Stevens and his associates were well aware of the "sense" in which the Indians were likely to view assurances regarding their fishing rights. During the negotiations, the vital importance of the fish to the Indians was repeatedly emphasized by both sides, and the Governor's promises that the treaties would protect that source of food and commerce were crucial in obtaining the Indians' assent. It is absolutely clear, as Governor Stevens himself said, that neither he nor the Indians intended that the latter "should be excluded from their ancient fisheries," and it is accordingly inconceivable that either party deliberately agreed to authorize future settlers to crowd the Indians out of any meaningful use of their accustomed places to fish. That each individual Indian would share an "equal opportunity" with thousands of newly arrived individual settlers is totally foreign to the spirit of the negotiations. Such a "right," along with the $207,500 paid the Indians, would hardly have been sufficient to compensate them for the millions of acres they ceded to the Territory.

[W]e think greater importance should be given to the Indians' likely understanding of the other words in the treaty and especially the reference to the "right of *taking* fish" — a right that had no special meaning at common law but that must have had obvious significance to the tribes relinquishing a portion of their pre-existing rights to the United States in return for this promise. This language is particularly meaningful in context of anadromous fisheries — which were not the focus of the common law — because of the relative predictability of the "harvest." In this context, it makes sense to say that a party has a right to "take" — rather than merely the "opportunity" to try to catch — some of the large quantities of fish that will almost certainly be available at a given place at a given time. This interpretation is confirmed by additional language in the treaty. The fishing clause speaks of "securing" certain fishing rights, a term the Court has previously interpreted as synonymous with "reserving" rights previously exercised. Because the Indians had always exercised the right to meet their subsistence and commercial needs by taking fish from treaty area waters, they would be unlikely to perceive a "reservation" of that right as merely the chance, shared with millions of other citizens, occasionally to dip their nets into the territorial waters. Moreover, the phrasing of the clause quite clearly avoids placing each individual Indian on an equal footing with each individual citizen of the State. The referent of the "said Indians" who are to share the right of taking fish with "all citizens of the Territory" is not the individual Indians but the various signatory "tribes and bands of Indians" listed in the opening article of each treaty. Because it was the tribes that were given a right in common with non-Indian citizens, it is especially likely that a class right to a share of fish, rather than a personal right to attempt to land fish, was intended.

In our view, the purpose and language of the treaties are unambiguous; they secure the Indians' right to take a share of each run of fish that passes through tribal fishing areas. But our prior decisions provide an even more persuasive reason why this interpretation is not open to question. For notwithstanding the bitterness that this litigation has engendered, the principal issue involved is virtually a "matter decided" by our previous holdings.

The Court has interpreted the fishing clause in these treaties on six prior occasions. In all of these cases the Court placed a relatively broad gloss on the Indians' fishing rights and — more or less explicitly — rejected the State's "equal opportunity" approach; in the earliest and the three most recent cases, moreover, we adopted essentially the interpretation that the United States is reiterating here.

[The Court discussed its opinions in *Winans, Seufert Bros., Tulee* and the three *Puyallup* cases.]

Not only all six of our cases interpreting the relevant treaty language but all federal courts that have interpreted the treaties in recent times have reached the foregoing conclusions, see *Sohappy v. Smith,* 302 F. Supp. 899, 908, 911 (Ore. 1969) (citing cases), as did the Washington Supreme Court itself prior to the present litigation. *State v. Satiacum,* 50 Wn. 2d 513, 523-524, 414 P.2d 400 (1957). A like interpretation, moreover, has been followed by the Court with respect to hunting rights explicitly secured by treaty to Indians "in common with all other persons," *Antoine v. Washington,* 420 U.S. 94, 205-206, and to water rights that were merely implicitly secured to the Indians by treaties reserving land — treaties that the Court enforced by ordering an apportionment to the Indians of enough water to meet their subsistence and cultivation needs. *Arizona v. California,* 373 U.S. 564, 598-601, following *United States v. Powers,* 305 U.S. 527, 528-533; *Winters v. United States,* 207 U.S. 564, 576.

The purport of our cases is clear. Nontreaty fishermen may not rely on property law concepts, devices such as the fish wheel, license fees, or general regulations to deprive the Indians of a fair share of the relevant runs of anadromous fish in the case area. Nor may treaty fishermen rely on their exclusive right of access to the reservations to destroy the rights of other "citizens of the territory." Both sides have a right, secured by treaty, to take a fair share of the available fish. That, we think, is what the parties to the treaty intended when they secured to the Indians the right of taking fish in common with other citizens.

V

We also agree with the Government that an equitable measure of the common right should initially divide the harvestable portion of each run that passes through a "usual and accustomed" place into approximately equal treaty and non-treaty shares, and should then reduce the treaty share if tribal needs may be satisfied by a lesser amount. Although this method of dividing the resource, unlike the right to *some* division, is not mandated by our prior cases, it is consistent with the 45%-55% division arrived at by the Washington state courts, and affirmed by this Court, in *Puyallup III* with respect to the steelhead run on the Puyallup River. The trial court in the *Puyallup* litigation reached those figures essentially by starting with a 50% allocation based on the Indians' reliance on the fish for their livelihoods and then adjusting slightly downward due to other relevant factors. The District Court took a similar tack in this case, *i.e.,* by starting with a 50-50 division and adjusting slightly downward on the Indians' side when it became clear that they did not need a full 50%.

The division arrived at by the District Court is also consistent with our earlier decisions concerning Indian treaty rights to scarce natural resources. In those cases, after determining that at the time of the treaties the resource involved was necessary to the Indians' welfare, the Court typically ordered a trial judge or special master, in his discretion, to devise some apportionment that assured that the Indians' reasonable livelihood needs would be met. This is precisely what the District Court did here, except that it realized that some ceiling should be placed on the Indians' apportionment to prevent their needs from exhausting the entire resource and thereby frustrating the treaty right of "all other citizens of the Territory."

Thus, it first concluded that at the time the treaties were signed, the Indians, who comprised three-fourths of the territorial population, depended heavily on anadromous fish as a source of food, commerce, and cultural cohesion. Indeed, it found that the non-Indian population depended on Indians to catch the fish that the former consumed. Only then did it determine that the Indian's present-day subsistence and commercial needs should be met, subject, of course, to the 50% ceiling.

It bears repeating, however, that the 50% figure imposes a maximum but not a minimum allocation. As in *Arizona v. California* and its predecessor cases, the central principle here must be that Indian treaty rights to a natural resource that once was thoroughly and exclusively exploited by the Indians secures so much as, but not more than, is necessary to provide the Indians with a livelihood — that is to say, a moderate living. Accordingly, while the maximum possible allocation to the Indians is fixed at 50%,[27] the minimum is not; the latter will, upon proper submissions to the District Court, be modified in response to changing circumstances. If, for example, a tribe should dwindle to just a few members, or if it should find other sources of support that lead it to abandon its fisheries, a 45% or 50% allocation of an entire run that passes through its customary fishing grounds would be manifestly inappropriate because the livelihood of the tribe under those circumstances could not reasonably require an allotment of large number of fish.

Although the District Court's exercise of its discretion, as slightly modified by the Court of Appeals, is in most respects unobjectionable, we are not satisfied that all of the adjustments it made to its division are consistent with the preceding analysis.

The District Court determined that the fish taken by the Indians on their reservations should not be counted against their share. It based this determination on the fact that Indians have the exclusive right under the treaties to fish on their reservations. But this fact seems to us to have no greater significance than the fact that some nontreaty fishermen may have exclusive access to fishing

---

[27] Because the 50% figure is only a ceiling, it is not correct to characterize our holding "as guaranteeing the Indians a specified percentage" of the fish. See POWELL, J., dissenting.

The logic of the 50% ceiling is manifest. For an equal division — especially between parties who presumptively treated with each other as equals — is suggested, if not necessarily dictated, by the word "common" as it appears in the treaties. Since the days of Solomon, such a division has been accepted as a fair apportionment of a common asset, and Anglo-American common law has presumed that division when, as here, no other percentage is suggested by the language of the agreement or the surrounding circumstances. E.g., 2 American Law of Property § 6.5, at 19 (A. Casner ed. 1952); E. Hopkins, Handbook on the Law of Real Property § 209, at 336 (1896).

sites that are not "usual and accustomed" places. Shares in the fish runs should not be affected by the place where the fish are taken. Cf. *Puyallup III*, 433 U.S., at 173-177.[28] We therefore disagree with the District Court's exclusion of the Indians' on-reservation catch from their portion of the runs.[29]

This same rationale, however, validates the Court-of-Appeals-modified equitable adjustment for fish caught outside the jurisdiction of the State by nontreaty fishermen from the State of Washington. So long as they take fish from identifiable runs that are destined for traditional tribal fishing grounds, such persons may not rely on the location of their take to justify excluding it from their share....

On the other hand, as long as there are enough fish to satisfy the Indians' ceremonial and subsistence needs, we see no justification for the District Court's exclusion from the treaty share of fish caught for these purposes. We need not now decide whether priority for such uses would be required in a period of short supply in order to carry out the purposes of the treaty. See 384 F. Supp., at 343. For present purposes, we merely hold that the total catch — rather than the commercial catch — is the measure of each party's right.

Accordingly, any fish (1) taken in Washington waters or in United States waters off the coast of Washington and (2) taken from runs of fish that pass through the Indians' usual and accustomed fishing grounds and (3) taken by either members of the Indian tribes that are parties to this litigation, on the one hand, or by non-Indian citizens of Washington, on the other hand, shall count against that party's respective share of the fish.

VI

Regardless of the Indians' other fishing rights under the treaties, the State argues that an agreement between Canada and the United States pre-empts their rights with respect to the sockeye and pink salmon runs on the Fraser River.

In 1930 the United States and Canada agreed that the catch of Fraser River salmon should be equally divided between Canadian and American fishermen. Convention of May 26, 1930, 50 Stat. 1355, as amended by 8 U.S.T. 1058. To implement this agreement, the two governments established the International Pacific Salmon Fisheries Commission (IPSFC). Each year that Commission proposes regulations to govern the time, manner, and number of the catch by the fishermen of the two countries; those regulations become effective upon approval of both countries....

---

[28] This Court's decision in *Puyallup III*, which approved state regulation of on-reservation fishing in the interest of conservation, was issued after the District Court excluded the Indians' on-reservation take and the Court of Appeals affirmed. See 520 F.2d, at 690. There is substantial doubt in my mind that those courts would have decided the question as they did had *Puyallup III* been on the books.

[29] A like reasoning requires the fish taken by treaty fisherman off of the reservations and at locations other than "usual and accustomed" sites, to be counted as part of the Indians share. Of course, the District Court, in its discretion, may determine that so few fish fit into this, or any other, category (e.g., "take-home" fish caught by non-treaty commercial fishermen for personal use) that accounting for them individually is unnecessary, and that an estimated figure may be relied on in making the annual computation. Indeed, if the amount is truly *de minimis*, no accounting at all may be required.

First, we agree with the Court of Appeals that the Convention itself does not implicitly extinguish the Indians' treaty rights. Absent explicit statutory language, we have been extremely reluctant to find congressional abrogation of treaty rights, e.g., *Menominee Tribe v. United States*, 391 U.S. 404, and there is no reason to do so here. Indeed, the Canadian Government has long exempted Canadian Indians from regulations promulgated under the Convention and afforded them special fishing rights....

VII

In addition to their challenges to the District Court's basic construction of the treaties, and to the scope of its allocation of fish to treaty fishermen, the State and the commercial fishing associations have advanced two objections to various remedial orders entered by the District Court.[32] It is claimed that the District Court has ordered a state agency to take action that it has no authority to take as a matter of state law and that its own assumption of the authority to manage the fisheries in the State after the state agencies refused or were unable to do so was unlawful.

These objections are difficult to evaluate in view of the representations to this Court by the Attorney General of the State that definitive resolution of the basic federal question of construction of the treaties will both remove any state-law impediment to enforcement of the State's obligations under the treaties, and enable the State and its Fisheries to carry out those obligations. Once the state agencies comply, of course, there would be no issue relating to federal authority to order them to do so nor any need for the District Court to continue its own direct supervision of enforcement efforts.

The representations of the Attorney General are not binding on the courts and legislature of the State, although we assume they are authoritative within its executive branch. Moreover, the State continues to argue that the District Court

---

[32] The associations advance a third objection as well — that the District Court had no power to enjoin individual nontreaty fishermen, who were not parties to its decisions, from violating the allocations that it has ordered. The reason this issue has arisen is that state officials were either unwilling or unable to enforce the District Court's orders against nontreaty fishermen by way of state regulations and state-law enforcement efforts. Accordingly, nontreaty fishermen were openly violating Indian fishing rights, and, in order to give federal-law enforcement officials the power via contempt to end those violations, the District Court was forced to enjoin them. The commercial fishing organizations, on behalf of their individual members, argue that they should not be bound by these orders because they were not parties to (although the associations all did participate as *amici curiae* in) the proceedings that led to their issuance.

If all state officials stand by the Attorney General's representations that the State will implement the decision of this Court, this issue will be rendered moot because the District Court no longer will be forced to enforce its own decisions. Nonetheless the issue is still live since state implementation efforts are now at a standstill and the orders are still in effect. Accordingly, we must decide it.

In our view, the commercial fishing associations and their members are probably subject to injunction under either the rule that nonparties who interfere with the implementation of court orders establishing public rights may be enjoined, e.g., *United States v. Hall*, 472 F.2d 261 (CA5 1972), cited approvingly in *Golden State Bottling Co. v. NLRB*, 414 U.S. 168, 180, or the rule that a court possessed of the res in a proceeding in rem, such as one to apportion a fishery, may enjoin those who would interfere with that custody. See *Vendo Co. v. Lektro-Vend Corp.*, 433 U.S. 623, 641. But in any case, these individuals and groups are citizens of the State of Washington, which was a party to the relevant proceedings, and "they, in their public rights as citizens of the State, were represented by the State in those proceedings, and, like it, were bound by the judgment." *City of Tacoma v. Taxpayers*, 357 U.S. 320, 340-341. Moreover, a court clearly may order them to obey that judgment. See *Golden State Bottling, supra*, at 179-180....

exceeded its authority when it assumed control of the fisheries in the State, and the commercial fishing groups continue to argue that the District Court may not order the state agencies to comply with its orders when they have no state-law authority to do so. Accordingly, although adherence to the Attorney General's representations by the executive, legislative, and judicial officials in the State would moot these two issues, a brief discussion should foreclose the possibility that they will not be respected. State-law prohibition against compliance with the District Court's decree cannot survive the command of the Supremacy Clause of the United States Constitution. *Cooper v. Aaron,* 358 U.S. 1; *Abelman v. Booth,* 62 U.S. 506. It is also clear that Game and Fisheries, as parties to this litigation, may be ordered to prepare a set of rules that will implement the Court's interpretation of the rights of the parties even if state law withholds from them the power to do so. E.g., *North Carolina Board of Education v. Swann,* 402 U.S. 143; *Griffin v. County School Board,* 377 U.S. 218; *Tacoma v. Taxpayers of Tacoma,* 357 U.S. 320. Once again the answer to a question raised by this litigation is largely dictated by our *Puyallup* trilogy. There, this Court mandated that state officers make precisely the same type of allocation of fish as the District Court ordered in this case. See *Puyallup III,* 433 U.S., at 177.

Whether Game and Fisheries may be ordered actually to promulgate regulations having effect as a matter of state law may well be doubtful. But the District Court may prescind that problem by assuming direct supervision of the fisheries if state recalcitrance or state-law barriers should be continued. It is therefore absurd to argue as do the fishing associations, both that the state agencies may not be ordered to implement the decree and also that the District Court may not itself issue detailed remedial orders as a substitute for state supervision. The federal court unquestionably has the power to enter the various orders that state official and private parties have chosen to ignore, and even to displace local enforcement of those orders if necessary to remedy the violations of federal law found by the court. [E.g.], *Milliken v. Bradley,* 433 U.S. 267, 280-281, 290; *Swann v. Charlotte-Mecklenburg Board of Education,* 402 U.S. 1, 14. Even if those orders may have been erroneous in some respects, all parties have an unequivocal obligation to obey them while they remain in effect.

In short, we trust that the spirit of cooperation motivating the Attorney General's representation will be confirmed by the conduct of state officials. But if it is not, the District Court has the power to undertake the necessary remedial steps and to enlist the aid of the appropriate federal-law enforcement agents in carrying out those steps. Moreover, the comments by the Court of Appeals strongly imply that it is prepared to uphold the use of stern measures to require respect for federal court orders.[36]

The judgments of the Court of Appeals for the Ninth Circuit, the District Court for the Western District of Washington, and the Supreme Court of the State of Washington are vacated and the respective causes are remanded to

---

[36] "The state's extraordinary machinations in resisting the [1974] decree have forced the district court to take over a large share of the management of the state's fishery in order to enforce its decrees. Except for some desegregation cases [citations omitted], the district court has faced the most concerted official and private efforts to frustrate a decree of a federal court witnessed in this century. The challenged orders in this appeal must be reviewed by this court in the context of events forced by litigants who offered the court no reasonable choice." 573 F.2d., 1123, 1126 (CA 9 1978).

those courts for further proceedings not inconsistent with this opinion, except that the judgment in *United States v. Washington,* 573 F.2d 1118 (the International Fisheries case) is affirmed.

[Dissenting opinion of Mr. Justice POWELL, joined by Justices STEWART and REHNQUIST has been omitted.]

NOTES

1. Further Developments in the Pacific Northwest Fishing Litigation: The continuing sensitivity to the issues in the *Washington Fishing* case is revealed by an unusual modification by the Court of its opinion in the above case. Upon consideration of a motion by the state of Washington, footnote 16 of *Washington v. Washington State Com. Passenger Fishing Vessel Ass'n* was modified as follows:

> A factual dispute exists on the question of what percentage of the fish in the case area actually passes through Indian fishing areas and is therefore subject to the District Court's allocations. In the absence of any relevant findings by the courts below, we are unable to express any view on the matter.

444 U.S. 816 (1979). Was the modification necessary?

The Pacific Northwest litigation moved into a second phase, which involved Indian efforts to assert their off-reservation treaty rights to protect the fishery resource. In *United States v. Washington,* 506 F. Supp. 187 (W.D. Wash. 1980), the court held that hatchery fish should not be excluded from the Indian treaty allocation because "the State lacks an ownership interest in released hatchery fish ...." *Id.* at 202. The court also held "that implicitly incorporated in the treaties' fishery clause is the right to have the fishery habitat protected from man-made despoliation." *Id.* at 203. The Ninth Circuit, while affirming this decision as to the hatchery fish, reversed on the issue of protection from man-made pollution. *United States v. Washington,* 759 F.2d 1353 (9th Cir.), *cert. denied,* 474 U.S. 994 (1985).

The orders in the Pacific Northwest cases were subject to the continued monitoring and adjustment of the federal courts. For later efforts to adjust orders in various Pacific Northwest fishing cases in light of actual catch experience, see *United States v. Washington,* 774 F.2d 1470 (9th Cir.), *cert. denied sub nom. Quinault Indian Nation v. Washington,* 474 U.S. 1100 (1986); *United States v. Washington,* 761 F.2d 1404 (9th Cir. 1985); *United States v. Oregon,* 718 F.2d 299 (9th Cir. 1983); *United States v. Oregon,* 657 F.2d 1009 (9th Cir. 1982); *United States v. Oregon,* 699 F. Supp. 1456 (D. Or. 1988). Recently, the Pacific Northwest tribes have found themselves in competition with one another for the fisheries resource and the emphasis has moved from litigation to negotiation.

2. Off-Reservation Hunting Rights: While most of the cases in this section involve the exercise of off-reservation fishing rights, treaties and agreements also reserved off-reservation hunting and food-gathering rights to certain tribes. For example, in *Antoine v. Washington,* 420 U.S. 194 (1975), the Supreme Court held that Washington conservation laws were preempted in application to an Indian hunting on the north half of the former Colville Indian Reservation when the statute ceding the land provided "the right to hunt and fish in common with all other persons on lands not allotted to said Indians shall not be taken away or in anywise abridged." The Court disposed of the conservation issue by briefly noting: "The State of Washington has not argued, let alone established, that applying the ban on out-of-season hunting of deer by the Indians on the land in question is in any way necessary or even useful for the conservation of deer." 420 U.S. at 207.

3. Other Off-Reservation Food-Gathering Rights: Concurrent with the Pacific Northwest litigation, a similar series of cases arose in state and federal courts in Michigan. At issue in these cases was the application of state gill-net fishing regulations to Indians fishing under an 1836 treaty with the Chippewa and Ottawa tribes that guaranteed "the right of hunting the lands ceded, with the other usual privileges of occupancy, until the land is required for settlement." In *People v. LeBlanc*, 399 Mich. 31, 248 N.W.2d 199 (1976), the Michigan Supreme Court held that this language reserved off-reservation fishing rights for the tribes, but these rights were not exclusive and Indian fishers would be subject to state gill-net regulations under the rule in *Puyallup I*. Three years later, after extensive hearings on the historical circumstances surrounding the treaty negotiations, a federal district court rejected the *LeBlanc* construction of the treaty. Because the 1836 treaty did not contain the phrase "in common with," a crucial term of the Puyallup treaties, the District Court held that the state of Michigan had no power to regulate off-reservation fishing by Ottawa and Chippewa Indians in the Great Lakes region.

Before this ruling reached the Sixth Circuit Court of Appeals, the Department of the Interior issued regulations governing the exercise of off-reservation fishing rights. 25 C.F.R. pt. 256 (1980). On appeal, the Sixth Circuit remanded the case to determine whether these regulations preempted the force of state conservation laws over Indian treaty fishers. *United States v. Michigan*, 623 F.2d 448 (6th Cir. 1980). Before the district court could consider the case on remand, the Reagan Administration entered office and its new Secretary of the Interior announced his decision not to renew the federal regulations at issue. Despite eight years of the government's urgings to the contrary, the Secretary opined that *LeBlanc* accurately stated the law applicable to treaty fishing. In response to the state's emergency motion to set aside the remand and put in place state regulations to replace the lapsed federal regulations, the Sixth Circuit held that, indeed, *LeBlanc* did accurately state the rule of the case. *United States v. Michigan*, 653 F.2d 277 (6th Cir.), *cert. denied*, 454 U.S. 1124 (1981).

The Court of Appeals established several criteria for evaluation of the state fishing regulations. The court cautioned that, under *LeBlanc*, "any such state regulations restricting Indian fishing rights under the 1836 treaty, including gill-net fishing, (a) must be a necessary conservation measure, (b) must be the least restrictive alternative method available for preserving fisheries in the Great Lakes from irreparable harm, and (c) must not discriminatorily harm Indian fishing or favor other classes of fishermen." *Id.* at 279. Moreover, the Sixth Circuit held that "[o]nly upon a finding of necessity, irreparable harm and the absence of effective Indian tribal self-regulation should the District Court sanction and permit state regulation of gill net fishing." *Id.*

When the case finally reached the District Court on remand, the court held that the federal preemption issue was moot. Nevertheless, the court retained jurisdiction to determine whether any future attempts by the state to impose regulations on treaty fishers would meet the *LeBlanc* requirements. *United States v. Michigan*, 520 F. Supp. 207 (W.D. Mich. 1981).

LAC COURTE OREILLES BAND OF LAKE SUPERIOR CHIPPEWA INDIANS v. WISCONSIN

700 F.2d 341 (7th Cir. 1983)

PELL, Circuit Judge.

The principal case on this consolidated appeal, *Lac Courte Oreilles Band v.*

Voight (LCO) was an action for a declaratory judgment that a band of Lake Superior Chippewa Indians (LCO band) has retained treaty-reserved off-reservation hunting, fishing, trapping and gathering rights, collectively termed "usufructuary rights," in public lands in the northern third of Wisconsin and that such rights preclude State regulation. The defendants in *LCO* are primarily State officials who are being sued in both their individual and representative capacities. On cross-motions for summary judgment, the district court granted the defendants' motion, reasoning that the Indians' usufructuary rights were released or extinguished by the Treaty of September 30, 1854 (Treaty of 1854).[1] In reaching this conclusion, the district judge expressly rejected the State's contention that the usufructuary rights had been revoked by the Executive Order of February 6, 1850 (Removal Order of 1850).

United States v. Wisconsin & Sawyer County (Ben Ruby), which has been consolidated with *LCO* for purposes of appeal, similarly involved a determination by the district judge, on cross-motions for summary judgment, that the Removal Order of 1850 was invalid. The State has cross-appealed the district court's holding pertaining to the Removal Order of 1850 in both *LCO* and *Ben Ruby*.

The three principal issues presented by *LCO* and *Ben Ruby* are:

(1) what was the nature of the usufructuary rights enjoyed by the LCO band pursuant to the treaties of 1837 and 1842;

(2) whether those rights were extinguished by the Removal Order of 1850; and if not,

(3) whether those rights were released or extinguished by the Treaty of 1854.

I. Facts

Because one of the subsidiary issues in these cases is whether they were appropriate for resolution by summary judgment, a rather detailed recitation of the evidence before the district court is required.

The LCO band was one of many bands of Chippewa Indians who lived in areas of northern Wisconsin, the Upper Peninsula of Michigan, and northeastern Minnesota. Together with several other bands, the LCO band was referred to as "Lake Superior Chippewas." The Chippewa bands subsisted mainly by hunting, fishing, trapping, harvesting wild rice, making maple sugar, and engaging in various gathering activities.

During at least the first half of the nineteenth century, the policy of the federal Government was to buy Indian lands where white settlement was anticipated and to provide for removal of the Indians to lands farther west. This is called the "removal policy."

In 1837, Wisconsin Territorial Governor Henry Dodge was authorized to negotiate a treaty with the Chippewas for the purchase of land in northern Wisconsin, just south of the Lake Superior basin. On March 3, 1837, Congress appropriated $10,000 for "holding treaties with the various tribes of Indians east of the Mississippi River, for the cession of lands held by them ... and for

---

[1]Because of the district judge's conclusion that the Indians' usufructuary rights were released or extinguished in 1854, his disposition of *LCO* does not reach the issue of what regulations the State might impose on the Indians' usufructuary activities if those rights were still in force.

their removal west of the Mississippi." 5 Stat. 158, 161. On May 13, 1837, the Office of Indian Affairs wrote Treaty Commissioner Dodge concerning the Government's purposes in seeking a treaty at that time. The letter indicated that the land was valuable for its pine timber and that acquisition by the United States would open the territory for white settlement.

A treaty council was held. According to the notes of Verplanck Van Antwerp, secretary of the council, Commissioner Dodge told the assembled Indian chiefs in July 1837 that the Government wished to buy a portion of their land that was barren of game and not suited for agriculture. Dodge described the land sought as "abound[ing] in pine timber, for which their Great Father the President of the United States wished to buy it from them, for the use of his white children." The Indians responded that they wanted to be able to continue their gathering and hunting activities on the lands, that they wished annuities for sixty years, after which their grandchildren could negotiate for themselves, and that they desired provisions for the half-breeds and traders. Governor Dodge pointed out to the Indians that the "Great Father" never buys lands for a term of years, but that he would agree on behalf of the President to grant the Indians the "free use of the rivers, and the privilege of hunting upon the lands you are to sell to the United States during his pleasure."

The following day the Indians reiterated, through their spokesman Aish-ke-bo-gi-ko-she, that they wished to reserve the privilege of using the land for gathering, hunting, and fishing activities. They said that they could not live, deprived of these means of sustenance. Commissioner Dodge replied, in part: "I will make known to your Great Father, your request to be permitted to make sugar, on the lands; and you will be allowed, during his pleasure, to hunt and fish on them. It will probably be many years before your Great Father will want all these lands for the use of his White Children."

The Treaty of 1837, which was signed by a Lac Courte Oreilles chief, among others, embodied these understandings. Article 1 of that Treaty states that the Chippewas "cede to the United States all that tract of country" described in the article. The United States agreed to pay annuities to the Indians, to distribute money to the half-breeds, and to pay some Indian debts. Article 5 of the Treaty states:

> The privilege of hunting, fishing and gathering the wild rice, upon the lands, the rivers and the lakes included in the territory ceded, is guarantied to the Indians during the pleasure of the President of the United States.

In 1841, Congress appropriated $5,000 for the expenses of negotiating a treaty to extinguish Indian title to lands in Michigan, a portion of which was held by the Chippewa bands. In July 1842, Robert Stuart, Superintendent of the Michigan Indian Agency wrote to the Secretary of War. He stated that, subsequent to the 1841 appropriation, it had been learned that the mineral district Congress wished to acquire extended beyond northern Michigan into Wisconsin. He recommended purchase of the Wisconsin as well as the Michigan land, stating that "the main importance of immediately acquiring this territory, is owing to its supposed great mineral productivity." He noted that it would not be necessary to remove the Indians from the land until the land was required for white settlement. A month later, Stuart was appointed commissioner to negotiate the proposed treaty with the Chippewas. His instructions stressed the importance of gaining the mineral lands and acquiring control over the south shore of Lake Superior. He was told that general removal of the Indians from the territory would not occur for "considerable time."

Stuart reported the outcome of his negotiations with the Chippewas in an annual report to the Bureau of Indian Affairs dated October 28, 1841. He noted the importance of the mineral deposits on the land and indicated that the concluded treaty had arranged a sharing of annuities between the Lake Superior tribes and the Mississippi tribes. This sharing was necessary to end a feud that had developed between the tribes after the 1837 treaty.

The 1842 treaty included a cession of land north of that ceded in 1837. Article II of the Treaty of 1842 stated:

> The Indians stipulate for the right of hunting on the ceded territory, with the other usual privileges of occupancy, until required to remove by the President of the United States, and that the laws of the United States shall be continued in force, in respect to their trade and intercourse with the whites, until otherwise ordered by Congress.

The December 5, 1842, report on the treaty by the Commissioner of Indian Affairs to the Secretary of War stressed the importance of acquiring the minerals and of commanding the south shore of Lake Superior. A report by the Superintendent of the Wisconsin Indians to the Commissioner of Indian Affairs the following year noted that exclusive possession of the Lake Superior shore would be commercially important, especially as settlements and mineral trade expanded.

Copper mining along the south shore of Lake Superior, as well as white settlement on the ceded areas, increased greatly following the treaty. As early as 1846, the Commissioner of Indian Affairs again suggested that the Chippewas be removed to land set apart for them west of the Mississippi. The reports of the period indicate that the Commissioner envisioned "improvement of the Indian race" by decreasing their reliance on traditional activities such as hunting and fishing and by compelling them to "resort to agriculture and other pursuits of civilized life." The fact that whites were selling whiskey to the Indians was seen as another reason for removal.

During the summer of 1847, two Government agents attempted to secure Chippewa agreement to a plan of resettlement. They were unsuccessful. In 1847, the Commissioner of Indian Affairs again suggested that resettlement was desirable. His report did not mention conflicts between the Indians and whites. The LaPointe subagent was more specific. He recorded two incidents of violence between the Chippewas and white settlers. In one, an Indian was acquitted of a murder charge on the ground of self-defense. In the other, the investigating agent concluded that the whites were at fault. The Commissioner wrote:

> I fear, that in our accounts of outrages and crime, we have done the Chippewas, if no other tribe, injustice in many cases; for I find on comparing them with almost any civilized community of the same size, for four years, there will be found the smaller aggregate of crime on the part of the savage; and every crime of any magnitude which has been committed may be traced to the influence of the white man.

In his 1848 Report, the Commissioner noted that, although most other Wisconsin tribes had been removed, the Chippewas remained in Wisconsin. The

Commissioner stressed the desirability of "civilizing" the Indians by requiring them to settle on smaller grounds where they would have to rely on agriculture. No conflicts between Indians and whites were reported.

The 1849 Report of the Commissioner of Indian Affairs again repeated the reasons for removal stressed in earlier years. Additionally, he referred to white "citizens who suffer annoyance and loss from depredations." The report of the LaPointe subagent for 1849 had specifically addressed this problem and had concluded that the sale of whiskey by the whites to the Indians was causing the most difficulty. The subagent acknowledged that it was possible the Indians were punished for acts they committed whereas whites who committed similar acts went free.

In 1849, the Lake Superior Chippewas petitioned Congress for twenty-four sections of land at "LaCotore" and at "LaPoint." They indicated that they wanted the land for permanent cultivation and permanent homes. Further, in October of that year, the Legislative Assembly of the Minnesota Territory requested the President to remove the Chippewas to another unsettled area.

At the urging of the Commissioner of Indian Affairs and the Secretary of the Interior, the President issued an executive order on February 6, 1850. This Order stated in relevant part:

> The privileges granted temporarily to the Chippewa Indians of the Mississippi, by the fifth article of the treaty made with them on the 29th of July 1837 "of hunting, fishing and gathering the wild rice upon the lands, the rivers and the lakes included in the territory ceded" by the treaty to the United States, and the rights granted to the Chippewa Indians of the Mississippi and Lake Superior by the second article of the treaty with them of October 4th, 1842, of hunting on the territory which they ceded by that treaty, with the other usual privileges of occupancy until required to remove by the President of the United States, are hereby revoked and all of the said Indians remaining on the lands ceded as aforesaid, are required to remove to their unceded lands.

The Indians were surprised and dismayed by the order. Benjamin Armstrong, a trader who lived in Chippewa territory and reported in a book his experiences with the Indians wrote:

> No conversation that was held [during the 1842 treaty negotiations] gave the Indians an inkling or caused them to mistrust that they were ceding away their lands, but supposed that they were simply selling the pine and minerals, as they had in the treaty of 1837, and when they were told in 1849, to move on and thereby abandon their burying grounds — the dearest thing to an Indian known — they began to hold councils and to ask each as to how they had understood the treaties, and all understood them the same, that was: that they were never to be disturbed if they behaved themselves.

B. G. Armstrong, Early Life Among the Indians 12 (1892). Armstrong also reported that the Indians' attempts thereafter to learn of any depredations which could have been the cause of removal were unsuccessful. In short, the Indians believed they would not be removed unless they misbehaved and they found no evidence of misbehavior.

This understanding was repeated in a letter written to the white settlers in Minnesota by a Chippewa chief in 1850. He stated that the treaty commissioner had told the Indians in 1842 that they would not be removed for at least 20 years and probably never. The chief indicated that the treaty had been signed on the reliance that it was only the copper on the land that was sought by the United States. A letter written January 21, 1851, from the Secretary of the American Board of Commissioners for Foreign Missions informed the Commissioner of Indian Affairs that the Indians had been told they could remain where they were for an indefinite period, "except so far as they might be required to give place to miners"; and the Commissioner said to them: "You and I shall never see the day when your Great Father will ask you to remove." The Secretary indicated that, absent that promise, the treaty would never have been signed. The Secretary's version of the treaty was corroborated by several sources including C. Mendenhall, a miner who wrote to the Commissioner of Indian Affairs on January 6, 1851, W. W. Warren, a farmer who was employed by the Government to teach farming to the Indians, and Indian Agent Henry Gilbert in his 1853 report to the Commissioner of Indian Affairs.

A further effort to effect removal to the western lands was made in 1850 by changing the place for payment of the Chippewas' annuities from LaPointe to Sandy Lake in the Minnesota Territory. The trip resulted in the death of many Indians. The following February 1851, subagent Watrous suggested paying the annuities in early spring and late fall in the Minnesota Territory. He hoped that this would be more effective in inducing the Indians to stay at Sandy Lake. Watrous was subsequently appointed superintendent of removal.

On August 24, 1851, Indian Commissioner Lea of the Office of Indian Affairs advised Watrous by telegram to "Suspend action with reference to the removal of Lake Superior Chippewas for further orders." On September 5, 1851, Lea confirmed that the suspension had been ordered by the Secretary of the Interior, pending the President's decision as to whether the Indians would be permitted to remain on their lands.

Also in September 1851, Assistant Superintendent Boutwell reported to the Minnesota Territorial Governor concerning the problems encountered in trying to effect removal of the Chippewas. Boutwell reported that a compromise had been achieved concerning the place for payment of annuities and indicated that, despite the telegram suspending removal operations, "as the Indians are ready to go I shall start them."

On September 20, 1851, Watrous reported to the Territorial Governor that 900 Chippewas remained on the ceded lands. He expressed apprehension that those who had been removed would return. These observations were reported to the Commissioner of Indian Affairs in Superintendent Ramsey's annual report dated November 27, 1851.

In the meantime, Chippewa Chief Buffalo had written the Commissioner on November 6, 1851, complaining about the hardship caused by the removal attempts and particularly the designation of where the annuities were paid. He requested that all future payments be made at LaPointe.

The Indians were dissatisfied with the provisions given them during the winter of 1851. On April 5, 1852, a group of chiefs went to Washington to see the President. They were accompanied by Benjamin Armstrong who subsequently reported much that transpired. According to Armstrong, on June 12, 1852, Chief Buffalo dictated a memorial to President Fillmore. He again expressed his understandings that treaty annuities were to be paid at LaPointe and that the Indians were to be permitted to remain on their lands for "one hundred years to come." The Chief beseeched the President and his agents to honor the Treaty of 1842 as the Indians understood it. President Fillmore told the delegation that he would countermand the Removal Order of 1850 and that annuity payments would henceforth be made at LaPointe. He gave Chief Buffalo a written instrument explaining these promises. The delegation returned home. There is apparently no current record of the President's explicit contravention of the removal order.

There is some inconsistency in reports as to what transpired thereafter. Armstrong reported that the annuities for 1852 were paid at LaPointe, that the President's letter was explained to Chief Buffalo and that the chief also stated that there was yet one more treaty to be made with the President, "and that he hoped in making it they would be more careful and wise than they had heretofore been and reserve a part of their land for themselves and their children." Armstrong, *supra*, at 32.

In his October, 1852 report, however, Superintendent Ramsey reported that the Chippewas had been told there would be no further payment of annuities upon ceded land. Ramsey stated that limiting annuities to those Indians who had removed was the best way to further the removal goal.

Armstrong's report that the 1853 and 1854 annuity payments were made at LaPointe was corroborated by a report of Indian Agent Henry Gilbert. Gilbert reported that the Indians would "sooner submit to extermination than comply with [the Removal Order]." Further, he reported that the whites and Indians were living harmoniously.

In the annual report of the Office of Indian Affairs dated November 24, 1854, the Commissioner noted that some bands of Lake Superior Chippewa were still living on the lands ceded by the treaties of 1837 and 1842. He stated: "It has not, thus far, been found necessary or practicable to remove them." He observed that:

> [I]t may be necessary to permit them all [the Chippewas] to remain, in order to acquire a cession of the large tract of country they still own east of the Mississippi, which, on account of its great mineral resources, is an object of material importance to obtain. They would require but small reservations; and thus permanently settled, the efforts made for their improvement will be rendered more effectual.

The reservation idea was apparently acceptable to the white settlers of Wisconsin. In February, 1854, of that year the Wisconsin legislature sent a memorial to the President and Congress. This memorial noted that the "Chippewa Indians in the region of Lake Superior are a peaceable, quiet, and inoffensive people, rapidly improving in the arts and sciences; that they acquire their living by hunting, fishing, manufacturing maple sugar, and agricultural pursuits." The memorial requested the President to rescind the prior Removal Order and to guarantee the payment of annuities to the Indians at LaPointe. The memorial also requested laws to "encourage the permanent settlement of those Indians as shall adopt the habits of the citizens of the United States."

In a letter dated August 11, 1854, the Indian Affairs Commissioner directed agent Gilbert to attempt to reach a treaty with the Chippewas, extinguishing their title to lands in Minnesota and Wisconsin. Gilbert was authorized to reserve 748,000 acres for permanent homes of the Indians in areas which did not include mineral lands and which were out of the path of white settlement.

The Indians requested Armstrong to be the interpreter, expressing their conclusion that interpreters at other treaty negotiations had made mistakes. Armstrong recorded Chief Buffalo as saying, in part:

> We do not want to be deceived any more as we have in the past. We now understand that we are selling our lands as well as the timber and that the whole, with the exception of what we shall reserve, goes to the great father forever.

Armstrong, *supra*, at 38.

The Treaty of LaPointe was concluded September 30, 1854. It provided that the Lake Superior Chippewas living in Minnesota ceded their territory to the United States. These Minnesota bands were granted usufructuary rights on the ceded land pursuant to Article 11. Article 2 specified that the United States agreed to withhold from sale, for the use of the Chippewas, certain described tracts of land. One was set aside for the LCO band. The treaty provided that the boundaries would thereafter be fixed under the direction of the President. Other Articles of the treaty provided for annuity payments, provisions for half-breeds and traders, the provision of various hunting devices and ammunition to the Indians, a ban on spirituous liquors, and a promise that the Indians would not be removed from the homes permanently set apart for them.

Even after the reservation boundaries were settled, many Chippewa Indians continued to roam throughout the ceded area, engaging in their traditional pursuits.

II. *Standard of Review on Cross-Motions for Summary Judgment*

[On cross-motions for summary judgment we] apply the traditional standard that summary judgment will not lie unless, construing all inferences in favor of the party against whom the motion is made, no genuine issue of material fact exists. [O]nly inferences that follow reasonably from the evidence need be considered.

Relatively few aspects of this case turn on what could be characterized as factual questions. Relevant issues which might be so classified are: (1) the Indians' understanding of the qualifying language in the Treaties of 1837 and 1842, and (2) whether the Indians "misbehaved" prior to 1850. Rather than considering the appropriateness of summary judgment on these specific questions at this point in our discussion, we consider each issue, *infra*, applying the standard enunciated above.

III. *Canons of Construction Pertinent to Indian Law*

First, the Supreme Court has held that Indian treaties must be construed as the Indians understood them. In [*Worcester v. Georgia,*] the Court stated:

> The language used in treaties with the Indians should never be construed to their prejudice. If words be made use of, which are susceptible of a more extended meaning than their plain import, as connected with the tenor of the treaty, they should be considered as used only in the latter sense.... How the words of the treaty were understood by this unlettered people, rather than their critical meaning, should form the rule of construction.

In *Jones v. Meehan*, 175 U.S. 1, 11 (1899), the Court stated that a "treaty must therefore be construed, not according to the technical meaning of its words to learned lawyers, but in the sense in which they would naturally be understood by the Indians." The Supreme Court has applied this canon of construction because the Indians and the Government were not bargaining from positions of equal strength, *Choctaw Nation v. United States*, 119 U.S. 1, 28 (1886); the treaties were drawn up by representatives of the United States in a written language unfamiliar to the Indians, *Jones v. Meehan*, 175 U.S. 1, 10-11 (1899); the Indians' comprehension of treaty terms depended on interpreters employed by the Government, *id.*; and, finally, because the Indians were unfamiliar with the legal manner of expression, *id.* For all these reasons, Indian treaties must be construed as the Indians understood them.

A second — and related — rule of construction is that ambiguous words and phrases in Indian treaties have been resolved in favor of the Indians. *Arizona v. California*, 373 U.S. 546, 599-601 (1963); *Alaska Pacific Fisheries v. United States*, 248 U.S. 78, 89 (1918); *Winters v. United States*, 207 U.S. 564, 576-77 (1908). This rule is particularly applicable if the language of a treaty supports two inferences, one favoring the Indians and one the Government. As stated by the *Winters* Court:

> On account of their relations to the Government, it cannot be supposed that the Indians were alert to exclude by formal words every inference which might mitigate against or defeat the declared purpose of themselves and the Government even if it could be supposed that they had the intelligence to foresee the "double sense" which might some time be urged against them.

Taken together, these canons mandate that we adopt a liberal interpretation in favor of the Indians. We may consider the history of the treaty, the negotiations, and the parties' practical construction. Moreover, these same principles must be applied in construing an act of Congress that purports to extinguish treaty rights of the Indians. E.g., [*United States v. Michigan*]. Bearing these principles in mind, we turn to the major issues relevant to this appeal.

IV. *Nature of This Tribe's Usufructuary Rights*

The first principal issue relevant to the *LCO* appeal concerns the legal effect of the usufructuary rights enjoyed by the tribe pursuant to the Treaties of 1837 and 1842. These rights derive in part from Article 5 of the Treaty of 1837 which states:

> The Indians stipulate for the right of hunting on the ceded territory, with the other usual privileges of occupancy, until required to remove by the President of the United States.[6]

The Supreme Court precedent relating to Indians' rights has drawn a distinction between "aboriginal title" and "treaty-reserved title." [*Tee-Hit-Ton Indians*]; accord, *United States v. Sioux Nation*, 448 U.S. 371, 415 n.29 (1980). By analogy, aboriginal rights of use enjoy a different legal status than treaty-recognized rights of use. Compare *United States v. Santa Fe Pacific Railroad*, 314 U.S. 339, 358 (1941), with *Menominee Tribe v. United States*, 391 U.S. 404, 413

---

[6] Other courts have recognized that "the other usual privileges of occupancy" include the right to fish and engage in traditional gathering activities. E.g., *United States v. Michigan*, 471 F. Supp. 192 (W.D. Mich. 1979), aff'd in relevant part, 653 F.2d 277 (6th Cir.), *cert. denied*, 454 U.S. 1124 (1981); *People v. Le Blanc*, 399 Mich. 31, 248 N.W.2d 199 (1976). That proposition is not challenged by the defendants in this case.

(1968). For purposes of this appeal, the difference is significant in determining how explicit a subsequent Congressional enactment must be in order to abrogate the Indians' usufructuary rights.

The defendants in *LCO* have conceded that the tribe possessed treaty-recognized rights of use to the land ceded pursuant to the Treaties of 1837 and 1842. They suggest, however, that the qualifying treaty language pertaining to those rights eradicates any distinction from aboriginal rights for purposes of analysis.

A. *Aboriginal Title Versus Treaty-Recognized Title*

[A]brogation of treaty-recognized title requires an explicit statement by Congress or, at least, it must be clear from the circumstances and legislative history surrounding a Congressional act. *Mattz v. Arnett*, 412 U.S. 481, 505 (1973).

B. *Aboriginal and Treaty-Recognized Rights of Use*

1. *No Dependence on Right of Permanent Occupancy*

Both aboriginal and treaty-recognized title carry with them a right to use the land for the Indians' traditional subsistence activities of hunting, fishing, and gathering. Treaty-recognized rights of use, or usufructuary rights, do not necessarily require that the tribe have title to the land. For instance, [*Winans*] illustrates a treaty-recognized right that was not dependent on either the Indians' title or right to occupy permanently the land in which it was to be exercised....

2. *Degree of Explicitness Required to Abrogate Rights*

The primary relevance of the distinction between aboriginal rights of use and treaty-recognized usufructuary rights to the instant case lies in the degree of explicitness required to abrogate such rights. Reflecting the ease with which Congress may extinguish aboriginal title, the Supreme Court required only an implicit abrogation of off-reservation usufructuary rights in *United States v. Santa Fe Pacific Railroad*, 314 U.S. 339 (1941)....

By contrast, the abrogation of treaty-recognized rights, like the extinguishment of treaty-recognized title, appears to require something more explicit. The parties disagree as to precisely what is required. Both parties, however, recognize the importance of *Menominee Tribe v. United States*, 391 U.S. 404 (1968), to this inquiry.

[The *Menominee*] Court, upholding the Court of Claims, held that the Termination Act had not cancelled the Menominees' rights and that they could bring an injunctive suit against Wisconsin's disturbing their hunting and fishing rights. The Court concluded:

> We find it difficult to believe that Congress, *without explicit statement*, would subject the United States to a claim for compensation by destroying property rights conferred by treaty, particularly when Congress was purporting by the Termination Act to settle the Government's financial obligations towards the Indians.

391 U.S. at 413 (footnotes omitted) (emphasis added).

The defendants contend that *Menominee* permits an implicit abrogation of treaty-recognized rights so long as there is "supporting evidence that the parties to the later legislation intended and understood that the extinguishment of rights would result." The tribe, by contrast, asserts that only an explicit Congressional statement permits cancellation of rights consistent with *Menominee*. We have stated the facts of *Menominee* at some length because we find merit in the defendants' assertion that the factual situation in that case is quite different from the instant case.[8]

Mattz v. Arnett, 412 U.S. 481 (1973), a more recent Supreme Court case, is helpful in determining the scope of *Menominee*. In *Mattz*, the issue was whether the Act of June 17, 1892, should be read as an implicit termination of an Indian reservation that had been created by an earlier executive order. The Court held that the reservation was not terminated, stating: "A congressional determination to terminate must be expressed on the face of the Act or be clear from the surrounding circumstances and legislative history." *Id.* at 505 (citations omitted).

Although *Mattz* dealt with cancellation of treaty-recognized title rather than treaty-recognized usufructuary rights, we believe the distinction is irrelevant to the determination as to how explicit a subsequent Congressional Act must be in order to extinguish Indians' treaty-recognized rights. An abrogation of treaty-recognized rights subjects the United States to a claim for compensation, *Menominee*, 391 U.S. at 404, just as a rescission of treaty-recognized title does, *United States v. Sioux Nation*, 448 U.S. 371, 415 n.29 (1980). The *Menominee* Court found no explicit statement regarding cancellation of the tribe's hunting and fishing rights; further, it found such a termination inconsistent with the purpose of the Termination Act, 391 U.S. at 413, and with the Congressional intent evidenced by reading the Termination Act in pari materia with Public Law 280, *id.* at 410-11. We believe that the proper reading of *Menominee* is consistent with *Mattz*: a termination of treaty-recognized rights by subsequent legislation must be by explicit statement or must be clear from the surrounding circumstances or legislative history.

C. *Rights of the LCO Tribe Pursuant to the Treaties of 1837 and 1842*

1. *Implied Reservation*

Initially, we note that the tribe contends the Chippewas held treaty-recognized title to their lands pursuant to the Treaty of August 19, 1825, 7 Stat. 272 (Treaty of Prairie du Chien). They reason that this recognized title included the right to use the land for traditional pursuits and, that absent specific language in the Treaties of 1837 and 1842 extinguishing such rights, they were impliedly reserved to the Indians.

The state defendants assert that the Treaty of Prairie du Chien was not before the district court and should this court deem it relevant, a remand is essential. We do not believe a remand is mandated on that issue.

We need not rely on an implicit reservation of rights because the usufructuary rights of the LCO tribe were explicitly addressed in the Treaties of 1837 and 1842. [*Winans*,] on which the appellants correctly rely as involving treaty-recognized usufructuary rights, does not appear to depend on any treaty prior to that in which the cession of land and simultaneous reservation of usufructuary rights were made. Although the tribe may indeed be correct in stating both that

---

[8] We do not agree with the defendants' suggestion, however, that the fact *Menominee* involved rights pursuant to a treaty granting a reservation makes that case inapposite to the present appeal. The rights of use in that case were indeed originally tied to treaty-recognized title. Nonetheless, the usufructuary rights have independent significance.

the Treaty of Prairie du Chien conferred recognized title on the tribe, and that usufructuary rights were implicitly reserved in later treaties, this line of analysis is not essential to our disposition of this case.

2. *Explicit Reservation*

Even though the parties agree that there was an explicit reservation of usufructuary rights in the two treaties, they disagree as to the impact of the qualifying language in the treaties: the statement in the Treaty of 1837 that the enumerated rights are guaranteed "during the pleasure of the President of the United States" and the language in the 1842 treaty indicating that the stipulated rights would endure until the Indians were "required to remove by the President of the United States." The limiting language raised two questions. The first is whether these non-permanent usufructuary rights recognized by treaty can be abrogated by a less explicit showing of intent than permanent treaty-recognized rights. The second is the meaning of the qualifying language in the two relevant treaties. We discuss each in turn.

The defendants strenuously urge that because the LCO's treaty-reserved usufructuary rights were "temporary," they could be extinguished by implication. The defendants support the district judge's characterization of the recognized rights as analogous to "permissive occupation" and rely on language in *Minnesota Chippewa Tribe v. United States*, 315 F.2d 906, 911 (Ct. Cl. 1962), and [*Tee-Hit-Ton Indians*]. Essentially the defendants are arguing that non-permanent treaty-recognized rights are like aboriginal rights.

The term "permissive occupation" is more misleading than helpful in analyzing the case at bar. In [*Tee-Hit-Ton Indians,*] the Supreme Court employed the term in concluding that the rights of the Indian plaintiffs to Alaskan land were not legal rights and therefore no compensation was due for the taking of timber from those lands. The Court rejected the argument that treaty-recognized title had been conferred on the Indians by either of two Congressional Acts, noting that the intention of those acts had been to "retain the status quo until further congressional or judicial action was taken." The "status quo" was the Indians' aboriginal title.

In *Minnesota Chippewa Tribe v. United States*, 315 F.2d 906, 911 (Ct. Cl. 1963), the court's reference to "permissive occupation" was a direct quote from *Tee-Hit-Ton Indians*, and was relevant to the court's conclusion that the Indians indeed had recognized title to disputed land. As used in both *Tee-Hit-Ton Indians* and *Minnesota Chippewa Tribe*, "permissive occupation" is synonymous to aboriginal title.

The judge below first used the term "permissive occupation" in the *Ben Ruby* case, 464 F. Supp. at 1348, which was a quiet title action decided in the same opinion with the *LCO* case. He relied on *Mole Lake Band v. United States*, 139 F. Supp. 938 (Ct. Cl. 1956), *cert. denied*, 352 U.S. 892. In *Mole Lake*, the Court of Claims had found that the intention of the parties to the cession treaties of 1837 and 1842 was to pass title in the land to the United States and that the Indians were to have "only a revocable license to use the land until the President required them to vacate it." 139 F. Supp. at 940.

We concur with the general proposition that if the Indians' right of occupancy is temporary, their interest in the land is more similar to a "revocable license" than it is to "title." Even so, we do not think it necessarily follows that an expressly granted revocable license to use land confers no greater rights than "aboriginal title" which carries no legal right at all against the United States. Even in the context of the *Ben Ruby* case, therefore, the term "permissive occupation" would appear less than an exact statement of the rights enjoyed by the Indians.

The term "permissive occupation" is especially inapplicable, however, to the *LCO* case which involves the reservation of usufructuary rights rather than a claim of title. *Tee-Hit-Ton Indians, Ben Ruby, Minnesota Chippewa Tribe,* and *Mole Lake* all concerned questions of title. It is perfectly consistent with the basic tenets of property law that one may enjoy a right of use that is limited in duration. The fact that it is so limited makes it no less of a legal right.

We are not persuaded, therefore, that the rights of the LCO band pursuant to the Treaties of 1837 and 1842 were other than treaty-recognized rights of use which are of legal significance. Despite his use of the term "permissive occupation," the district judge apparently reached the same conclusion on this point. The fact that the rights enjoyed by the LCO band were legally enforceable against the United States compels the conclusion that they should not be extinguished by mere implication.

The second dispute between the parties concerns the meaning of the limiting language. "During the pleasure of the President" and "until required to remove by the President" would appear to confer unbridled discretion on the Government to extinguish the usufructuary rights. As the district court recognized, however, Indian treaties must ordinarily be construed as they were understood by the Indians. [E.g., *Worcester v. Georgia.*]

The judge below found that the Chippewas understood the treaties to mean that they enjoyed the use of their lands for an unlimited time unless they misbehaved by harassing white settlers. In reaching this conclusion, the district judge relied on the Indian's statements during the negotiations preceding the Treaty of 1837 indicating that they wished to continue hunting and fishing on the ceded lands and that they envisioned their grandchildren negotiating for further annuities in sixty-years time. He also noted that both Indians and non-Indians present at the 1842 treaty negotiations later wrote that the Indians had been assured they would not have to remove unless they misbehaved.

The defendants challenge Judge Doyle's conclusion as going beyond his "discretion" and argue that both treaties were made pursuant to the removal policy which contemplated placing the Indians on lands farther west. They also argue that Judge Doyle should not have relied on the writings of persons present at the negotiations because this is evidence of "low quality."

The difficulty with the defendants' argument is that it does not really address what the Indians believed the treaty to mean. The fact that the treaties were conceived pursuant to a policy of "removal" is not consistent with either the assertion that the treaties were unacceptable to the Indians unless modified by an oral understanding that allowed them to stay on the land so long as they did not harass white settlers or the Government's recognition that this concession was therefore essential. Further, whether those persons who wrote of their recollections provided only "low quality" evidence for a trial over a hundred years later is somewhat irrelevant given that it is the only evidence of the Indians' understanding of the treaty.

One further point must be made although it is not explicitly argued by the defendants. A finding as to the "intent" of the Indians is arguably a factual finding that is inappropriate to a disposition by summary judgment. Because this aspect of the case was decided adversely to the defendants, we construe all inferences in favor of the defendants in determining whether a genuine issue of material fact exists. [Since] the defendant's evidence on this point does not address what the Indians believed the treaty to mean but, rather, the motive of the Government in seeking the treaty, we conclude that no genuine issue of fact existed.

We concur therefore in the district judge's conclusion that the qualifying language in the two treaties did not confer the unlimited discretion on the Executive that it appears to; rather, it required that the Indians be denied their usufructuary privileges only if the Indians were instrumental in causing disturbances with white settlers.

D. *Analogous Precedent*

Two cases that involve a reservation of usufructuary rights by qualified treaty language support our conclusion that an abrogation of such rights should not be found without compelling evidence that such an extinguishment was intended. In both *United States v. Michigan*, 471 F. Supp. 192 (W.D. Mich. 1979), aff'd in relevant part, 653 F.2d 277 (6th Cir.), *cert. denied*, 454 U.S. 1124 (1981), and *People v. LeBlanc*, 399 Mich. 31, 248 N.W.2d 199 (1976), Chippewa bands claimed the right to fish, free from State regulation, in portions of the Great Lakes. Pursuant to the Treaty of 1836, 7 Stat. 495, the tribes had ceded lands to the United States. The treaty stated that: "The Indians stipulate for the right of hunting on the lands ceded, with the other usual privileges of occupancy, until the land is required for settlement."

After concluding the above-quoted language of Article XIII embraced the right to fish, both courts addressed the question whether the rights had been extinguished by subsequent settlement of the land. The *LeBlanc* court found that the qualifying language was included in the treaty in order to allow white settlement of the land. Because the Great Lakes themselves weren't required for settlement the fishing rights were not terminated. The Michigan court noted that the language of limitation was "ambiguous as to any definite period of Indian occupancy," 471 F. Supp. at 259, and relying on *LeBlanc*, concluded that the fishing rights were not terminated by operation of the language.

Both the *Michigan* and *LeBlanc* courts also rejected claims that the Treaty of 1855 had abrogated the treaty-recognized fishing rights....

The treaties relevant to the *Michigan* and *LeBlanc* cases are not identical to those before this court. We do not suggest that either *Michigan* or *LeBlanc* is dispositive of the instant controversy. It is important, however, that both the Michigan district court and the Supreme Court of that state found that "conditional" usufructuary rights could be abrogated only by an extremely strong showing that such was the intent of Congress. It is also significant that the courts were careful not to construe the language of limitation so as to prejudice the Indians.

The district court in *Michigan* concluded that the State had no power to regulate Indian fishing because of the recognized treaty rights. By contrast, the *LeBlanc* court found that certain State regulations would be permissible and carefully outlined the scope of such regulation.

The Sixth Circuit twice considered the *Michigan* case. The first time, the case was remanded for a determination whether federal regulations regarding gill-net fishing preempted the field. In the context of reaching that disposition, the Sixth Circuit stated:

> Although this Court has not finally decided the issue, it is inclined to view ... [that] in the absence of federal regulations occupying the field, the Supreme Court of Michigan in *People v. LeBlanc, supra,* has correctly stated that applicable standard governing state regulation of gill net fishing.

United States v. Michigan, 623 F.2d 448, 450 (6th Cir. 1980) (per curiam). It is clear that the aspect of the district court's disposition that was not wholly endorsed by the Sixth Circuit was the permissible scope of state regulation.

Because of Judge Doyle's conclusion that the LCO's treaty rights were extinguished in 1854, the permissible scope of regulation in the face of treaty-recognized rights was not decided below. It is not before this court on appeal. We fail to see what relevance the Sixth Circuit's favorable reference to the *LeBlanc* decision has to the instant controversy.

Concerning the issues in *Michigan* and *LeBlanc* that are relevant to this case, the *Michigan* district court and the state court reached the same conclusion: that treaty-recognized usufructuary rights are not to be found abrogated by implication and that the rights at issue in those cases were still viable. In its latest consideration of *Michigan*, the Sixth Circuit affirmed this view, stating: "The treaty-guaranteed fishing rights preserved to the Indians in the 1836 Treaty, including the aboriginal rights to engage in gill net fishing, continue to the present day as federally created and federally protected rights." *United States v. Michigan,* 653 F.2d 277, 279 (6th Cir.), *cert. denied,* 454 U.S. 1124 (1981).

E. Summary

A treaty is essentially a contract between two sovereign powers. [*Washington State Commercial Passenger Fishing Vessel Association.*] It is not surprising, therefore, that the rule we find emerging from prior cases dealing with Indian rights is a rather straightforward statement of contract law. If the Government explicitly promised the Indians a property interest in land, the Government would be subject to a claim for compensation if it breached the terms of the agreement. If the United States promised a tribe that it would enjoy certain rights either for a specified period or until a specified event or events occurred, those rights were legally enforceable by the Indians. When the period expired or the contemplated event or series of events occurred, the rights could be extinguished by the Government without liability.

If the *LCO* case involved a property interest that by its very nature contemplated permanence, such as title, the argument of the defendants would be more persuasive. What was given the Indians pursuant to the treaties of 1837 and 1842, however, was a right of use for a period, the duration of which was determined by the Indians' behavior.

If harassment of white settlers occurred, the Executive could extinguish the Indians' rights without the Government's incurring liability. If the Chippewas' rights were abrogated for any other reason, however, the Government would potentially be subject to a claim for compensation. An act of Congress should therefore be construed as extinguishing usufructuary rights only if the legislation expressly stated that such was the intent of Congress or if the legislative history and surrounding circumstances made clear that abrogation of treaty-recognized rights was intended by Congress.

V. *Removal Order of 1850*

A. *Standing of Defendants to Cross-Appeal*

The judge below held that neither the Removal Order of 1850 nor the Government's attempts forcefully to remove the Indians terminated the Chippewas' usufructuary rights. His reasoning, which was developed in the *Ben Ruby* portion of the combined opinion, was as follows: (1) the Treaties of 1837 and 1842 permitted removal only if the Indians harassed white settlers; (2) the record failed to disclose the kind of serious misbehavior that would have justified removal under the terms of the two treaties; (3) the Removal Order of 1850 was not authorized by the two earlier treaties and was therefore without legal effect because it was beyond the scope of the President's powers.

[We] assume, without so deciding, that the defendants are aggrieved parties who have standing to challenge the findings of the judge below as to the Removal Order....

[Neither *res judicata* nor principles of collateral estoppel bar relitigation of the question whether the 1850 Removal Order was valid.]

C. *Validity of 1850 Removal Order*

Congress has plenary authority over Indian affairs. E.g., *Warren Trading Post v. Arizona Tax Commission*, 380 U.S. 685 (1965). This power is rooted in the treaty power, U.S. Const. art. II, § 2, cl. 2, and the Indian commerce clause, *id.* at art. I, § 8, cl. 3. E.g., *White Mountain Apache Tribe v. Bracker*, 448 U.S. 136 (1980).

An executive order cannot exceed the scope of the authority delegated by Congress. [The President cannot] purport to implement a treaty by action which in fact exceeds the limits of that treaty.

[W]e concur with the district judge's conclusion that the Treaties of 1837 and 1842 authorized termination of the Chippewas' right to exercise their usufructuary privileges on ceded land only if the Indians misbehaved by harassing white settlers. The pivotal question relevant to the validity of the 1850 Removal Order is therefore whether the Indians had misbehaved.

This is arguably a question of fact. It was decided, in favor of the tribe, on a motion for summary judgment. Applying the standard set forth in Section II, *supra*, we can uphold the judgment below on this point only if, construing all inferences in favor of the defendants, there exists no genuine issue of material fact.

As early as 1846, the sale of whiskey to the Indians by white settlers was seen as a problem and a reason for removing the Indians. One could infer from this that Indian misbehavior existed; one could not reasonably conclude the white settlers were blameless for whatever incidents occurred.

Two incidents of Indian violence were reported by the LaPointe subagent in 1847. In one, the Indian was found to have acted in self-defense; in the other, a white was found to be at fault. In the same report that discussed these incidents, the subagent concluded that "every crime of any magnitude which has been committed may be traced to the influence of the white man." In 1848, no conflicts between Indians and whites were reported by the Commissioner of Indian Affairs.

The 1849 Report of the Commissioner and the report of the LaPointe sub-agent for the year 1849 discussed disturbances caused by the Chippewa. Again, the sale of whiskey was blamed and, additionally, the subagent suggested that the Indians were punished in situations where white settlers were not.

The question before the district court was whether the totality of these incidents created at least an inference that the 1850 Removal Order was a direct response to Indian misbehavior. In light of the fact that the Order of 1850 made no reference whatsoever to Indian disruptions and that the incidents themselves were relatively few in number and at least in part instigated by whites, we think Judge Doyle correctly concluded that no genuine issue of material fact existed as to whether those acts of misbehavior motivated the 1850 Removal Order.

Whatever policy or other reasons might have motivated the Removal Order, we concur in Judge Doyle's conclusion that the 1850 Order exceeded the scope of the 1837 and 1842 treaties and was therefore invalid.

VI. *Treaty of 1854*

As a preliminary matter, we note that the tribe contends the Treaty of 1854 was before the district court for only the limited purpose of demonstrating a shift in the Government's policy from removing the Indians to providing them reservations. The defendants, not surprisingly, disagree. Our review of the pleadings suggests that this would be a difficult question to resolve, primarily because both parties framed their contentions in the broadest possible language.

At oral argument, the tribe asserted that it believed the appeal could be resolved without remand on the subject of the 1854 treaty and that the Indians were urging a remand only as a secondary position. We believe that a resolution on the merits is possible and observe that it in no way prejudices the tribe.

Judge Doyle found that the Treaty of 1854, by which the Chippewa bands were granted reservations on portions of the land they had ceded to the Government in 1837 and 1842, extinguished the LCO's usufructuary rights on the remainder of the ceded land. As discussed in Section IV, *supra*, the Treaty of 1854 should be held to have abrogated these treaty-recognized rights only if the 1854 enactment expressly refers to termination of the usufructuary rights or if the circumstances and legislative history surrounding the treaty make clear that

Congress intended such an abrogation. See *Menominee Tribe v. United States*, 391 U.S. 401, 415 (1968). Because the Treaty of 1854 made no reference whatsoever to the usufructuary rights of the Chippewas who had previously ceded their territory to the United States, our analysis focuses on whether the circumstances surrounding the treaty compel the conclusion that termination of such rights was intended.

A. Relationship Between Occupancy and Usufructuary Rights

A fundamental aspect of Judge Doyle's reasoning regarding the Treaty of 1854 was his conclusion that the Treaties of 1837, 1842, and 1854 all evidence an intent to link occupancy with the exercise of usufructuary rights. Judge Doyle reasoned that because the 1854 treaty provided permanent homes for the LCO band on specified tracts, it withdrew any conditional right to establish such homes on non-reservation lands in the ceded territory. The court concluded that if the right to establish homes on the whole of the territory was lost, the right to hunt and fish thereon was similarly relinquished.

It should be noted that the district judge did not suggest that usufructuary rights are *always* tied to occupancy. Such a conclusion would be clearly inconsistent with precedent such as [*Winans*]. His conclusion was simply that the Treaty of 1854, read in pari materia with the earlier Treaties of 1837 and 1842, inextricably linked occupancy and usufructuary rights.

In so concluding, Judge Doyle relied on the statement by Chief Buffalo at the treaty negotiations that he now understood the "whole" of these non-reservation lands would go to the United States. The district court stated in *LCO* that this statement "indicates the Indian understanding that they were relinquishing any general claims they might have had to lands outside their reservations." 464 F. Supp. at 1359. The statement made by Chief Buffalo does not compel this conclusion. There is evidence that the Indians misunderstood the Treaties of 1837 and 1842 when those treaties were signed. Rather than recognizing that they were relinquishing title to their territory, the Chippewas then believed that they were merely granting the United States a right to the timber and minerals that were the primary impetus for Governmental interest in the land. Subsequently, the Indians came to understand that they had relinquished title to the territories. In this context, the statement by Chief Buffalo at the time of the 1854 treaty negotiations would appear to be a reference only to the Minnesota land that was to be ceded to the United States pursuant to the 1854 treaty. His words indicate that he understood the Indians were giving up title to that land. There is no justification for construing Chief Buffalo's remarks either as relating to the territories previously ceded or as a "general release" of all Indian claims and rights in those territories.

In addition to his reliance on Chief Buffalo's remarks, Judge Doyle found those aspects of the 1854 treaty pertaining to the Minnesota cession relevant when read in pari materia with the Treaties of 1837 and 1842.

B. In Pari Materia Analysis

The portions of the 1854 treaty relevant to this analysis are Articles 1, 2, and 11. Article 1 records a cession of the territory held by the Lake Superior

Chippewa residing in Minnesota to the United States. Article 2 grants reservations to, inter alia, the LCO band and the Minnesota Chippewas who ceded their land pursuant to Article 1. Article 11 states, in part: "And such of them as reside in the territory hereby ceded, shall have the right to hunt and fish therein, until otherwise ordered by the President." As a result of this provision, the Chippewas residing in Minnesota obtained treaty-recognized usufructuary rights on non-reservation lands.

The district judge and the defendants think Article 11 suggests that the LCO band, like other Chippewa bands which ceded land pursuant to the earlier treaties, was relinquishing its usufructuary rights in 1854. As stated by the district court: "Had the parties intended the 1854 treaty to continue to preserve those rights in the lands ceded in 1837 and 1842, it is reasonable to believe that they would have made it explicit in 1854." 464 F. Supp. at 1359. The district judge reached this conclusion because usufructuary rights were specifically recognized in Article 11.

We disagree. The Treaties of 1837, 1842, and 1854 are consistent in that each treaty includes both a cession of land and a reservation of usufructuary rights on the ceded land by those Indians relinquishing their territory. The LCO band had ceded its territory pursuant to the two earlier treaties in which its reservations of usufructuary rights were explicit. Omission of any reference to those rights in the 1854 treaty suggests that the LCO band believed their right to use ceded land for traditional pursuits to be secure and unaffected by the 1854 treaty.

We are not persuaded that either the remarks of Chief Buffalo or the absence of an explicit reservation of the LCO's usufructuary rights in the 1854 treaty compel the conclusion that occupancy and the usufructuary rights were understood by the Indians and the Government to be inextricably linked at the time of the 1854 treaty negotiations. We turn therefore to a somewhat different line of analysis relied on by Judge Doyle and urged by the defendants.

C. Relevance of the 1850 Removal Order

This line of analysis posits that the Indians relinquished their usufructuary rights on most of the land previously ceded in return for the Government's promise, in Article 11 of the Treaty of 1854, that they would not be removed from the land completely. That article, in a portion not quoted above, states that the "Indians shall not be required to remove from the homes hereby set apart for them."

This argument is not persuasive in light of considerable evidence in the record indicating the Indians believed both that the Government had abandoned its removal policy by 1854 and that they could be removed only for misbehavior.

First, the Indians had been told by President Fillmore that he would countermand the Removal Order and that the annuities would be paid at a location nearer their homes henceforth. There is evidence that the 1853 and 1854 annuities were indeed paid to the Indians at nearby LaPointe. It is reasonable to conclude that the Indians therefore believed the United States had abandoned efforts to resettle them in more western territory.

It is not necessary for this court to reach a legal conclusion as to whether President Fillmore had the power to or in fact did countermand the Removal Order. Similarly, it is not essential to decide that the Government had repudiated its "removal policy" and would henceforth pursue a "reservation policy." The defendants' argument turns on what the Indians believed as a result of the 1850 Removal Order. We conclude only that the evidence suggests the Chippewa believed precisely the opposite of what the defendants urge.

Second, as discussed *supra*, the Chippewas believe that they had been promised the right to remain on and use the ceded land unless they misbehaved. They hadn't misbehaved. They were surprised and deeply disturbed by the Removal Order. That Order was subsequently not enforced. These facts suggest that the Chippewa more likely understood that the Government had acknowledged their rights to be subject to extinguishment only upon misbehaving.

D. *Summary*

Nothing in the record compels the conclusion that the LCO band understood the Treaty of 1854 as abrogating their treaty-recognized usufructuary rights. Similarly, nothing compels the conclusion that the Government intended such an extinguishment.

Turning first to the Indian understanding of the treaty, the LCO band was heavily dependent on the exercise of their usufructuary activities throughout the ceded region at the time of the treaty negotiations. Even if some Indians contemplated turning to agriculture as a principal means of subsistence, there is no indication such a transition had been implemented to any extent at the time of the treaty. Second, the Indians in fact continued their hunting and fishing activities on the ceded territory long after their reservations were created pursuant to the 1854 treaty. Third, as discussed *supra*, the sequence of events following the attempted removal of the Chippewas in 1850 would logically have confirmed their belief that removal and extinguishment of usufructuary activities could be avoided if they did not harass white settlers. Fourth, as also discussed above, the inclusion in the 1854 treaty of a reservation of usufructuary rights by the Minnesota Chippewas suggests, in our view, that the LCO band believed their usufructuary rights to be secure and unaffected by the treaty.

As to the intentions of the Government, it is noteworthy that the Removal Order of 1850 referred specifically to the extinguishment of usufructuary rights as well as ordering removal of the Chippewas. This suggests that the Government knew the Indians did not understand the exercise of usufructuary rights to be dependent on their permanent occupancy of the land; further, it illustrates that the United States was well able to draft an explicit statement abrogating such rights. The Government's provision of guns and ammunition to the Indians pursuant to the 1854 treaty suggests that the United States did not envision the Indians abandoning their traditional pursuits.

The rationale employed by Judge Doyle and the arguments advanced by the defendants at best support the implied abrogation of the LCO band's usufructuary rights pursuant to the 1854 treaty. As developed at length in Section IV, *supra*, the extinguishment of treaty-recognized rights by subsequent Congressional act will be found only if it is clear that such a termination was intended. The evidence supporting relinquishment or abrogation in the instant case fails to meet that standard. We conclude therefore that the LCO band's usufructuary rights were neither terminated nor released by the 1854 treaty.

In resolving this case, the panel has construed the references to these historical documents as the tribe suggests: a demonstration that more evidence might be presented in support of the tribe's position regarding the 1854 treaty if a remand on that issue were required. As our disposition makes clear, no such remand is warranted. We have reached this conclusion without reference to the documents that are in controversy.

Conclusion

As to the collateral matters posed by this appeal, the tribe's motion to dismiss the defendants' cross-appeal in *Ben Ruby* and *LCO* is denied. The defendant's motion to strike the tribe's collateral estoppel argument and the tribe's references in their brief to documents not in the record are denied.

The LCO band enjoyed treaty-recognized usufructuary rights pursuant to the Treaties of 1837 and 1842. The Removal Order of 1850 did not abrogate those rights because the Order was invalid. These aspects of our holding are consistent with the conclusions reached by the judge below. We disagree with the district judge's conclusion that the Treaty of 1854 represented either a release or extinguishment of the LCO's usufructuary rights. At most, the structure of the treaty and the circumstances surrounding its enactment *imply* that such rights cannot, however, be abrogated by implication. The LCO's rights to use the ceded lands remain in force.

Having considered all the arguments urged by the parties, the district court's summary judgment in favor of the defendants as to the continued existence of the LCO's usufructuary rights is reversed. The exercise of these rights is limited to those portions of the ceded lands that are not privately owned. The case is remanded to the district judge with instructions to enter judgment for the LCO band on that aspect of the case and for further consideration as to the permissible scope of State regulation over the LCO's exercise of their usufructuary rights.

Reversed and remanded.

NOTES

For later developments in the on-going stormy and sometimes violent Wisconsin fishing litigation, see *Lac Courte Oreilles Band of Lake Superior Chippewa Indians v. Wisconsin,* 707 F. Supp. 1034 (W.D. Wis. 1989); *Lac Courte Oreilles Band of Lake Superior Chippewa Indians v. Wisconsin,* 686 F. Supp. 226 (W.D. Wis. 1988); *Lac Courte Oreilles Band of Lake Superior Chippewa Indians v. Wisconsin,* 668 F. Supp. 1233 (W.D. Wis. 1987); *Lac Courte Oreilles Band of Lake Superior Chippewa Indians v. Wisconsin,* 663 F. Supp. 682 (W.D. Wis. 1987); *Lac Courte Oreilles Band of Lake Superior Chippewa Indians v. Wisconsin,* 653 F. Supp. 1420 (W.D. Wis. 1987). *See also Wisconsin v. Baker,* 464 F. Supp. 1377 (W.D. Wis. 1978).

After the Seventh Circuit's opinion in *Lac Courte Oreilles Band,* the Supreme Court decided *Oregon Dep't of Fish & Wildlife v. Klamath Indian Tribe,* 473

U.S. 753 (1985), which took a somewhat looser approach to the effect of subsequent land cessions and the creation of reservations on prior treaty-guaranteed off-reservation hunting and fishing rights. Should the *Lac Courte Oreilles Band* result be reconsidered in light of the *Klamath* case? In analyzing this question, consider the role that res judicata and collateral estoppel should play in resolving this question. Both doctrines were relied upon heavily by the Supreme Court in *Nevada v. United States*, 463 U.S. 110 (1983), set forth in Chapter 2, section C3.

B. COMPETITION FOR CONTROL OF WATER

Indian water rights are to the late twentieth century what Indian land rights were to the nineteenth century. In the Southwest, water is in exceedingly short supply and the competition for it is intense. Yet, the extent of Indian title to most water in this area is indefinite. Many of the same utilitarian arguments made with respect to land in the nineteenth century have been applied to water in the last several decades. The question often becomes not who owns the water but how can it best be used: for the reservations and their relatively few inhabitants or for the industrial metropolises of the Southwest? Water rights are as critical for Indian well-being and development now as land rights were in the late nineteenth century. As with land, Congress has assumed enormous powers in the definition of Indian rights to water. And the pressures and techniques to encourage Indian consent to the modification of Indian water rights are strikingly reminiscent of the acquisitive practices of the non-Indian community during the nineteenth century.

In order to understand the nature of Indian water rights, a basic knowledge of western water is in order as background. Unlike water-rich eastern riparian states, in the western states the doctrine of "prior appropriation" controls. The prior appropriation doctrine holds that actual beneficial use of the water is the basis of the property right. The owner is entitled to take a specific quantity of water, deriving from his beneficial use, and such water user's priority to that amount of water dates from the time it was first applied to such beneficial uses. This scheme creates a temporal and quantitative ladder of priorities among competing water users. Just as important is the rule governing what happens in time of shortage. During shortages, the senior appropriator's right is satisfied *in full* before the junior appropriator obtains any of his share. The theory of Indian water rights is inconsistent with both these elements of western water law. As reflected in the *Winters* case, set forth below, the Indian right to the water does not depend on present use or priority but, rather, on future need. The seniority of the right usually is not measured by the date of first beneficial use of the right. Rather, Indian rights date from reservation creation.

Water rights are important to understand because of their relationship to the underlying philosophy of development of the land to which they apply. The western law of prior appropriation rests on basic and fundamental assumptions about the value of using, presently, a scarce and important resource. It is a harsh, pragmatic, pioneer doctrine that places a premium on development and has little regard for conservation. The assumptions underlying the Indian reserved rights doctrine, as will be seen, are far different. The seeming conflict between the two — an ideological and economic conflict — is reflected in F.

TRELEASE, FEDERAL-STATE RELATIONS IN WATER LAW (1971) and in the important water law study for which the Trelease report was a foundation, UNITED STATES NATIONAL WATER COMMISSION, WATER POLICIES FOR THE FUTURE, FINAL REPORT TO THE PRESIDENT AND TO THE CONGRESS OF THE UNITED STATES (1972). See also Ranquist, The Winters Doctrine and How It Grew: Federal Reservation of Rights to the Use of Water, 1975 B.Y.U.L. REV. 639.

WINTERS v. UNITED STATES

207 U.S. 564 (1908)

[After the United States obtained cessions of land from the Gros Ventre and Assiniboine Tribes, patents were issued to individuals who wished to establish farms upstream on the Milk River. Some years after those farmers had established diversion and irrigation works, the United States determined to build irrigation works for the Indian reservation to enable farming to take place there. The contest arose because the water available was insufficient to meet the needs both of the upstream farmers and the Indian reservation. Under western water law, the prior appropriation by the farmers of Milk River water for irrigation purposes should prevail, but it did not due to the nature of Indian water rights established in this opinion.]

Mr. Justice McKENNA delivered the opinion of the Court.

[This] case, as we view it, turns on the agreement of May, 1888, resulting in the creation of Fort Belknap Reservation. In the construction of this agreement there are certain elements to be considered that are prominent and significant. The reservation was a part of a very much larger tract which the Indians had the right to occupy and use and which was adequate for the habits and wants of a nomadic and uncivilized people. It was the policy of the Government, it was the desire of the Indians, to change those habits and to become a pastoral and civilized people. If they should become such the original tract was too extensive, but a smaller tract would be inadequate without a change of conditions. The lands were arid and, without irrigation, were practically valueless. And yet, it is contended, the means of irrigation were deliberately given up by the Indians and deliberately accepted by the Government. The lands ceded were, it is true, also arid; and some argument may be urged, and is urged, that with their cession there was the cession of the waters, without which they would be valueless, and "civilized communities could not be established thereon." And this, it is further contended, the Indians knew, and yet made no reservation of the waters. We realize that there is a conflict of implications, but that which makes for the retention of the waters is of greater force than that which makes for their cession. The Indians had command of the lands and the waters — command of all their beneficial use, whether kept for hunting, "and grazing roving herds of stock," or turned to agriculture and the arts of civilization. Did they give up all this? Did they reduce the area of their occupation and give up the waters which made it valuable or adequate? And, even regarding the allegation of the answer as true, that there are springs and streams on the reservation flowing about 2,900 inches of water, the inquiries are pertinent. If it were possible to believe affirmative answers, we might also believe that the Indians were awed by the power of the Government or deceived by its negotiators. Neither view is possible. The Government is asserting the rights of the Indians. But extremes need not be taken into account. By a rule of interpretation of agreements and treaties with the Indians, ambiguities occurring will be resolved from the standpoint of the Indians. And the rule should certainly be applied to determine between two inferences, one of which would support the purpose of the agreement and the other impair or defeat it. On account of their relations to the Government, it cannot be supposed that the Indians were alert to exclude by formal words every inference which might militate against or defeat the declared purpose of themselves and the Government, even if it could be supposed that they had the intelligence to foresee the "double sense" which might some time be urged against them.

Another contention of appellants is that if it be conceded that there was a reservation of the waters of Milk River by the agreement of 1888, yet the reservation was repealed by the admission of Montana into the Union, February 22, 1889, c. 180, 25 Stat. 676, "upon an equal footing with the original States." The language of counsel is that "any reservation in the agreement with the Indians, expressed or implied, whereby the waters of Milk River were not to be subject of appropriation by the citizens and inhabitants of said State, was repealed by the act of admission." But to establish the repeal counsel rely substantially upon the same argument that they advance against the intention of the agreement to reserve the waters. The power of the Government to reserve the waters and exempt them from appropriation under the state laws is not denied, and could not be. *The United States v. The Rio Grande Ditch & Irrigation Co.*, 174 U.S. 690, 702; *United States v. Winans*, 198 U.S. 371. That the Government did reserve them we have decided, and for a use which would be necessarily continued through years. This was done May 1, 1888, and it would be extreme to believe that within a year Congress destroyed the reservation and took from the Indians the consideration of their grant, leaving them a barren waste — took from them the means of continuing their old habits, yet did not leave them the power to change to new ones.

Appellants' argument upon the incidental repeal of the agreement by the admission of Montana into the Union and the power over the waters of Milk River which the State thereby acquired to dispose of them under its laws, is elaborate and able, but our construction of the agreement and its effect make it unnecessary to answer the argument in detail. For the same reason we have not discussed the doctrine of riparian rights urged by the Government.

[*Affirmed.*]

ARIZONA v. CALIFORNIA

373 U.S. 546 (1963)

Mr. Justice BLACK delivered the opinion of the Court.

[T]he United States has asserted claims to waters in the main [Colorado] river and in some of the tributaries for use on Indian Reservations, National Forests, Recreational and Wildlife Areas and other government lands and works. While the Master passed upon some of these claims, he declined to reach others, particularly those relating to tributaries. We approve his decision as to which claims required adjudication, and likewise we approve the decree he recommended for the government claims he did decide. We shall discuss only the claims of the United States on behalf of the Indian Reservations.

The Government, on behalf of five Indian Reservations in Arizona, California, and Nevada, asserted rights to water in the mainstream of the Colorado River.[97] The Colorado River Reservation, located partly in Arizona and partly in California, is the largest. It was originally created by an Act of Congress in 1865, but its area was later increased by Executive Order. Other reservations were created by Executive Orders and amendments to them, ranging in dates from 1870 to 1907. The Master found both as a matter of fact and law that when the United States created these reservations or added to them, it reserved not only land but also the use of enough water from the Colorado to irrigate the irrigable portions of the reserved lands. The aggregate quantity of water which the Master held was reserved for all the reservations is about 1,000,000 acre-feet, to be used on around 135,000 irrigable acres of land. Here, as before the Master, Arizona argues that the United States had no power to make a reservation of navigable waters after Arizona became a State; that navigable waters could not be reserved by Executive Orders; that the United States did not intend to reserve water for the Indian Reservations; that the amount of water reserved should be measured by the reasonably foreseeable needs of the Indians living on the reservation rather than by the number of irrigable acres; and, finally, that the judicial doctrine of equitable apportionment should be used to divide the water between the Indians and the other people in the State of Arizona.

The last argument is easily answered. The doctrine of equitable apportionment is a method of resolving water disputes between States. It was created by this Court in the exercise of its original jurisdiction over controversies in which States are parties. An Indian Reservation is not a State. And while Congress has sometimes left Indian Reservations considerable power to manage their own affairs, we are not convinced by Arizona's argument that each reservation is so much like a State that its rights to water should be determined by the doctrine of equitable apportionment. Moreover, even were we to treat an Indian Reservation like a State, equitable apportionment would still not control since, under our view, the Indian claims here are governed by the statutes and Executive Orders creating the reservations.

Arizona's contention that the Federal Government had no power, after Arizona became a State, to reserve waters for the use and benefit of federally reserved lands rests largely upon statements in *Pollard's Lessee v. Hagan,* 3 How. 212 (1845), and *Shively v. Bowlby,* 152 U.S. 1 (1894). Those cases and others that followed them gave rise to the doctrine that lands underlying navigable waters within territory acquired by the Government are held in trust for future States and that title to such lands is automatically vested in the States upon admission to the Union. But those cases involved only the shores of and lands beneath navigable waters. They do not determine the problem before us and cannot be accepted as limiting the broad powers of the United States to regulate navigable waters under the Commerce Clause and to regulate govern-

---

[97] The Reservations were Chemehuevi, Cocopah, Yuma, Colorado River and Fort Mohave.

ment lands under Art. IV, § 3, of the Constitution. We have no doubt about the power of the United States under these clauses to reserve water rights for its reservations and its property.

Arizona also argues that, in any event, water rights cannot be reserved by Executive Order. Some of the reservations of Indian lands here involved were made almost 100 years ago, and all of them were made over 45 years ago. In our view, these reservations, like those created directly by Congress, were not limited to land, but included waters as well. Congress and the Executive have ever since recognized these as Indian Reservations. Numerous appropriations, including appropriations for irrigation projects, have been made by Congress. They have been uniformly and universally treated as reservations by map makers, surveyors, and the public. We can give but short shrift at this late date to the argument that the reservations either of land or water are invalid because they were originally set apart by the Executive.[102]

Arizona also challenges the Master's holding as to the Indian Reservations on two other grounds; first, that there is a lack of evidence showing that the United States in establishing the reservations intended to reserve water for them; second, that even if water was meant to be reserved the Master has awarded too much water. We reject both of these contentions. Most of the land in these reservations is and always has been arid. If the water necessary to sustain life is to be had, it must come from the Colorado River or its tributaries. It can be said without overstatement that when the Indians were put on these reservations they were not considered to be located in the most desirable area of the Nation. It is impossible to believe that when Congress created the great Colorado River Indian Reservation and when the Executive Department of this Nation created the other reservations they were unaware that most of the lands were of the desert kind — hot, scorching sands — and that water from the river would be essential to the life of the Indian people and to the animals they hunted and the crops they raised. In the debate leading to approval of the first congressional appropriation for irrigation of the Colorado River Indian Reservation, the delegate from the Territory of Arizona made this statement:

> Irrigating canals are essential to the prosperity of these Indians. Without water there can be no production, no life; and all they ask of you is to give them a few agricultural implements to enable them to dig an irrigating canal by which their lands may be watered and their fields irrigated, so that they may enjoy the means of existence. You must provide these Indians with the means of subsistence or they will take by robbery from those who have. During the last year I have seen a number of these Indians starved to death for want of food. Cong. Globe, 38th Cong., 2d Sess. 1321 (1865).

[In *Winters* the Court] concluded that the Government, when it created that Indian Reservation, intended to deal fairly with the Indians by reserving for them the waters without which their lands would have been useless. *Winters* has been followed by this Court as recently as 1939 in *United States v. Powers*, 305 U.S. 527. We follow it now and agree that the United States did reserve the water rights for the Indians effective as of the time the Indian Reservations were created. This means, as the Master held, that these water rights, having

---

[102]See *United States v. Midwest Oil Co.*, 236 U.S. 459, 469-475 (1915); *Winters v. United States*, 207 U.S. 564 (1908).

vested before the Act became effective on June 25, 1929, are "present perfected rights" and as such are entitled to priority under the Act.

We also agree with the Master's conclusion as to the quantity of water intended to be reserved. He found that the water was intended to satisfy the future as well as the present needs of the Indian Reservations and ruled that enough water was reserved to irrigate all the practicably irrigable acreage on the reservations. Arizona, on the other hand, contends that the quantity of water reserved should be measured by the Indians' "reasonably foreseeable needs," which, in fact, means by the number of Indians. How many Indians there will be and what their future needs will be can only be guessed. We have concluded, as did the Master, that the only feasible and fair way by which reserved water for the reservations can be measured is irrigable acreage. The various acreages of irrigable land which the Master found to be on the different reservations we find to be reasonable....

NOTES

1. Meaning of the Reserved Rights Doctrine: The reserved rights doctrine has been interpreted in distinct ways with important differences in implication. As enunciated in the *Winters* case, the doctrine stands for the proposition that, on making a treaty with the United States government, the Indians *themselves* reserved for their own use sufficient water to make their reservations productive. Thus, "when the Indians made the treaty granting rights to the United States, they reserved the right to use the waters of Milk River, at least to an extent reasonably necessary to irrigate their lands. The right so reserved continues to exist against the United States and its grantees, as well as against the state and its grantees." *Winters v. United States,* 143 F. 740, 749 (9th Cir. 1906).

The second interpretation of the reserved rights doctrine holds that when the United States created the various Indian reservations, the United States reserved the necessary water from the adjacent rivers and streams for those reservations. Thus, in *Arizona v. California,* "[t]he Master found both as a matter of fact and law that when the United States created these reservations or added to them, it reserved not only land but also the use of enough water from the Colorado to irrigate the irrigable portions of the reserved lands." The Supreme Court went on to hold that "[w]e have no doubt about the power of the United States ... to reserve water rights for its reservations and its property." 373 U.S. at 598. Under this theory, the reservations for Indian use are much like federal reservations for other uses, such as national forests or parks. The *Winters* construction of the reserved rights doctrine gives greater recognition to tribal sovereignty and may suggest entitlement to a greater quantum of water. Under this interpretation, the reserved water rights may be seen as recognized property rights vested in the Indians, which may be defended against all comers, including the United States; therefore, the taking of such property is compensable. In *Arizona v. California (Arizona I),* 373 U.S. at 595-601, the Supreme Court seemed to adopt a public domain theory with respect to such land. When the federal government removes land from the public domain for federal uses — including Indian reservations — it has the power also to reserve sufficient water from the public domain for use on these lands. *See also Report of the Special Master* in *Arizona v. California,* 259 (1960): "In the *Winters* case the United States exercised its power to reserve water by treaty; but the power itself stems from the United States' property rights in the water, not from the treaty power." While the original *Winters* construction of the reserved rights doctrine is more compatible with vested Indian property rights in the reserved water, the second interpretation is more easily reconcilable with the protection of Indian water rights on reservations that were created not by treaty but by act of Congress or executive order.

Regardless of which construction is placed upon the reserved rights doctrine, however, it is clear that Indians on reservations — no matter how the reservation was created — have the right to use sufficient water from included and adjacent streams and rivers and groundwater to make those reservations productive, that the Indian water right is superior to all subsequently created state water rights, and that it is when created unquantified, albeit not unquantifiable. Reserved rights attach to reservations whether or not the instruments creating them mention water rights. Water rights were not mentioned in the treaty involved in the *Winters* case nor in the act of Congress and executive orders creating the Indian reservations involved in *Arizona v. California*. In both cases, the Supreme Court held that an implied reservation of water rights was made at the time the Indian reservations were created.

The right to control and have access to available water has been one of absolute necessity for Indians living on arid reservations. Without reserving existing water rights, these reservations would be useless. This point was recognized by the courts as early as 1905 when the Supreme Court held that certain rights necessary to the development of the reservation, such as fishing, hunting, and water, were reserved by the Indians rather than granted to the United States. *United States v. Winans,* section A2, *supra.*

2. Scope of Indian Water Rights: Both *Winters* and *Arizona v. California* (*Arizona I*) suggest that the scope of Indian water rights may be summarized as follows:

> a. State-created water rights in existence before the date the reservation was created are superior to the reserved right; those state-created water rights arising thereafter are subordinate.
>
> b. The reserved right, unlike state-created appropriative rights, does not depend upon diversion from the stream and application to beneficial use. The reserved right arises when the reservation is established even though the water right is not exercised for decades thereafter. In this respect the right is like a riparian right. In time of shortage, however, it is unlike a riparian right, for it does not share the available supply pro rata but rather takes its place on the priority schedule and receives water ahead of all rights of later date.
>
> c. The federal reserved right need not be created or exercised in accordance with state law. Not only does creation of the reserved right not depend on diversion of water and application of it to beneficial use, but the right does not depend upon a filing with the state water agency or upon recording of the claim and it is not subject to state laws on forfeiture and abandonment.
>
> d. The quantity of water to be enjoyed under a reserved right is measured by the quantity necessary to fulfill the purposes of the reservation, both at the present time and in the future.

Arizona v. California quantified this amount for the Indian reservations as the amount of water necessary to irrigate all the irrigable land on each reservation. This quantity represents for those reservations the amount of water they are entitled to for all time unless, of course, the reservations are enlarged by additional withdrawals. For the five Indian reservations and two wildlife refuges involved in that case, reserved water rights aggregated just under one million acre-feet in diversions. *Arizona v. California* (*Arizona II*), 376 U.S. 340 (1964).

See also Arizona v. California (Arizona III), 439 U.S. 419 (1979). *See generally* Meyers, *The Colorado River,* 19 STAN. L. REV. 1, 65-66 (1966).

3. Quantification Formulae: Debate has raged with particular energy over the formula for quantification of Indian reserved water rights. Though the Court in *Arizona v. California* adopted the practicably irrigable acreage standard under which the quantum of the reserved right can be fixed for reservations created primarily for agricultural uses by reference to the number of irrigable acres located on a reservation, one might ask the result if the reservation sees as its future another use — such as economic development — requiring a greater supply of water. In *United States v. Ahtanum Irrig. Dist.*, 330 F.2d 897, 915 (9th Cir. 1964), *cert. denied*, 381 U.S. 924 (1965), the Ninth Circuit held that the Yakima were entitled to exercise reserved rights to water "to the extent that the said water can be put to a beneficial use." But the Supreme Court, in its supplemental decree to *Arizona v. California (Arizona III)*, 439 U.S. 419 (1979), stated that while usage of adjudicated water rights by the lower Colorado tribes was not restricted to agricultural application, the quantity of water needed to supply consumptive use required for irrigation constituted the measure for determining the quantity of adjudicated rights. Also, the right to a particular quantity may mean more than just the amount needed for direct use. The reserved right may encompass a supply adequate to maintain the level of groundwater sources of springs on the reservation and the level of a lake. *See Cappaert v. United States*, 426 U.S. 128 (1976) (holding that federal reserved rights include groundwater). *Contra, In re General Adjudication of All Rights to Use Water in the Big Horn River Sys.*, 753 P.2d 76 (Wyo. 1988), *aff'd on equally divided vote*, 109 S. Ct. 863 (1989) (rejecting application of *Winters* doctrine to groundwater for lack of precedent, while recognizing that "[t]he logic which supports a reservation of surface water to fulfill the purpose of the reservation also supports reservation of groundwater). Further, if Indian reservation rights are elastic and expandable, other users of water cannot depend on fixed allocations for their needs. This clearly complicates multistate water planning. For competing views on the quantum of Indian reserved rights, compare Veeder, *Indian Prior and Paramount Rights to the Use of Water*, 16 ROCKY MT. MIN. L. INST. 631 (1971), with Bloom, *Indian "Paramount" Rights to Water Use*, 16 ROCKY MT. MIN. L. INST. 669 (1971).

Recall that in *Washington v. Washington State Passenger Fishing Vessel Ass'n*, Justice Steven's opinion for the Court relied on analogies to *Winters* and *Arizona v. California* in analyzing the appropriate accommodation of Indian and non-Indian allocation of the fisheries resources involved in that case. Thus, he described *Arizona v. California* as having authorized the court or a special master "to devise some apportionment that assured that the Indians' reasonable needs would be met." 443 U.S. at 685. He continued the analogy, stating:

> As in *Arizona v. California* and its predecessor cases, the central principle here must be that Indian treaty rights to a natural resource that once was thoroughly and exclusively exploited by the Indians secures so much as, but not more than, is necessary to provide the Indians with a livelihood — that is to say, a moderate living.

443 U.S. at 686. Does Justice Stewart's focus on the income and livelihood derived from a natural resource comport with the prior thrust of the Court decisions in *Winters* and *Arizona v. California* or does it herald a new departure and a potential novel approach to allocating or quantifying Indian water rights and other resources? In *Arizona v. California* were the present population of the reservation, the standard of living of tribal members, or the level of their income significant factors in the quantification calculations?

In the cases following *Winters,* courts struggled with the problem of reconciling the changing Indian need for water with the non-Indian need for a definite allocation to permit development of the off-reservation lands sharing the same watershed with the Indians. Thus, in *Conrad Inv. Co. v. United States,* 161 F. 829 (9th Cir. 1908), decided shortly after the Supreme Court decision in *Winters,* the court stated:

> It is further objected that the decree of the Circuit Court provides that, whenever the needs and requirements of the [Indian] complainant for the use of the waters of Birch Creek for irrigating and other useful purposes upon the reservation exceed the amount of water reserved by the decree for that purpose, the complainant may apply to the court for a modification of the decree. This is entirely in accord with complainant's rights as adjudged by the decree. Having determined that the Indians on the reservation have a paramount right to the waters of Birch Creek, it follows that the permission given to the defendant to have the excess over the amount of water specified in the decree should be subject to modification, should the conditions on the reservation at any time require such modification.

Id. at 835. In 1939 the Ninth Circuit reversed itself. In *United States v. Walker River Irrig. Dist.,* 104 F.2d 334 (9th Cir. 1939), the court permanently fixed that reservation's entitlement by making a determination of the population of the tribe over a period of seventy years, the number of acres cultivated, the quantity of water in the area, and the needs for domestic, stock-watering, and power-generating purposes.

In *United States v. Ahtanum Irrig. Dist.,* 236 F.2d 321 (9th Cir. 1956), *cert. denied,* 352 U.S. 988 (1957), the court rejected any notion that the amount of water reserved to an Indian reservation was to be measured by the Indians' needs at the time the reservation was created:

> It is plain from our decision in the *Conrad Inv. Co.* case ... that the paramount right of the Indians to the waters of Ahtanum Creek was not limited to use of the Indians at any given date but this right extended to the ultimate needs of the Indians as those needs and requirements should grow to keep pace with the development of Indian agriculture upon the reservation.

Id. at 327. *See also United States v. Ahtanum Irrig. Dist.,* 330 F.2d 897 (9th Cir. 1964), *cert. denied,* 381 U.S. 924 (1965). And, of course, *Arizona v. California* adopted as the most practical test the amount of water necessary to irrigate reservation land susceptible of irrigation.

In *United States v. New Mexico,* 438 U.S. 696 (1978), Justice Rehnquist, writing for the majority, stated that

> [w]hile many of the contours of what has come to be called the "implied-reservation-of-water doctrine" remains unspecified, the Court has repeatedly emphasized that Congress reserved "only that amount of water necessary to fulfill the purpose of the reservation, no more." *Cappaert,* 426 U.S., at 141. See *Arizona v. California,* 373 U.S., at 600, 601; *District Court for Eagle County,* 401 U.S., at 523. Each time this Court has applied the "implied-reservation-of-water doctrine," it has carefully examined both the asserted water right and the specific purposes for which the land was reserved, and concluded that without the water the purposes of the reservation would be entirely defeated.

438 U.S. at 700. The Court, in that case, addressed itself specifically to the extent of federal reserved water rights in national forests. It held that the federal reserved rights doctrine was limited to the original purposes for creation of such national forest lands, namely continuous timber supply and watershed conservation. Any expansion in the purposes for which national forests

were managed subsequent to the Forest Service Organic Act of 1897, which established the national forest system, had no effect and could not be used to maintain minimum instream flows in the forests to meet the newer needs such as the preservation of fish and wildlife and the protection of recreational and aesthetic values. The Court noted that such an expansion could cut deeply into the water used by state and private appropriators in a fully appropriated river. The relevance of the New Mexico decision to Indian reserved water rights lies in the idea of the specific purposes for which the land was reserved. Though the decision is limited in its application to non-Indian federal reservations, one may query whether the Court might some day consider whether recreational or aesthetic purposes were implied in a treaty's provisions dealing with tribal reserved water rights. In *United States v. Finch,* 548 F.2d 822 (9th Cir. 1976), *rev'd on other grounds,* 433 U.S. 676 (1977), the Ninth Circuit broadly interpreted the original purpose of an Indian reservation to include fishery management even though agriculture was the sole purpose mentioned at the reservation's creation in 1868.

One issue that has particularly plagued the quantification of Indian water rights is the frequent Indian demand to maintain minimum stream flows and lake levels to support tribal fisheries. *E.g., Pyramid Lake Paiute Tribe v. Morton,* 354 F. Supp. 252 (D.D.C. 1973), *rev'd,* 499 F.2d 1095 (D.C. Cir. 1974), *cert. denied,* 420 U.S. 962 (1975) (effort to maintain lake level of Pyramid Lake to preserve natural fishery spawning areas). In light of *Winters* and *New Mexico,* the recent cases raising such questions generally have focused attention on whether fishing and fishery preservation were within the original purposes for which the reservation was created. For example, in *Joint Bd. of Control of the Flathead, Mission & Jocko Irrig. Dists. v. United States,* 832 F.2d 1127 (9th Cir. 1987), *cert. denied,* 108 S. Ct. 1732 (1988), the court was asked to adjudicate a dispute between the Confederated Salish and Kootenai tribes and the local federal irrigation projects over the manner in which the Department of the Interior allocated its water. The court noted that at the time of the Treaty of Hell Gate of 1859, which established the Flathead Reservation, the tribes were heavily dependent on fishing and the treaty protected their prior aboriginal fishing rights. Thus, the court rejected the district court's conclusion that the Indians must share water rights needed to exercise their prior fishing rights with junior appropriators, such as the irrigation district. *See also United States v. Adair,* 723 F.2d 1394 (9th Cir. 1983), *cert. denied sub nom. Oregon v. United States,* 467 U.S. 1252 (1984); *Colville Confederated Tribes v. Walton,* 752 F.2d 397 (9th Cir. 1985), *cert. denied,* 475 U.S. 1010 (1986). By contrast, in *Wyoming v. Owl Creek Irrig. Dist. (In re General Adjudication of All Rights to Use Water in the Big Horn River Sys.),* 750 P.2d 681, 753 P.2d 76 (Wyo. 1988), *aff'd by equally divided vote,* 109 S. Ct. 863 (1989), the court held that the Shoshone and Arapahoe Tribes of the Wind River Reservation had no right to preserve minimum stream flow for fisheries. The court noted that the 1868 Treaty with the Shoshones and Bannacks which established the reservation sought to encourage only agriculture, while only mentioning other activities such as hunting, lumbering, and milling. The court held that even though the Tribes' evidence established that historically they were partially dependent on fish for their diet, they had not established sufficient evidence to be entitled to *any* water for fishery maintenance. The court distinguished other cases permitting such fisheries stream flow rights on the grounds that the tribes in question were "heavily, if not totally, dependent on fish for their livelihood." Even though the special master had concluded that at least some water should be awarded on a showing that tribes historically were partially dependent on fish, the Wyoming Supreme Court affirmed the district court's deletion of the award.

As economies on Indian reservations evolved away from agrarian activities and diversified, questions emerged as to whether reserved Indian water rights include water for activities such as mining, industrial, commercial, municipal, and domestic consumption. Recent cases have relied heavily on the theory of the *New Mexico* case which seems to limit the *measure* of federal, but not necessarily Indian, reserved rights to the purposes for which the federal reservation *originally* was created. One might distinguish Indian reserved water rights on the basis that, unlike the National Forest lands involved in *New Mexico* and most other federal reservations, Indian reservations were reserved for human habitation by Indian tribes which, like all other civilizations, evolve over time. While some have suggested that *New Mexico* does not directly apply to Indian reserved rights, *State ex rel. Greely v. Confederated Salish & Kootenai Tribes of the Flathead Reservation*, 712 P.2d 754, 766-67 (Mont. 1985); F. COHEN, HANDBOOK OF FEDERAL INDIAN LAW 583-84 (1982 ed.), many of the cases have looked to the *New Mexico* case for guidance on these questions. *E.g., United States v. Adair, supra,* at 1408. For example, in *Wyoming v. Owl Creek Irrig. Dist., supra,* the court rejected any water allocation for mineral and industrial uses. Even though the court conceded that the parties were fully aware of the valuable minerals that lay beneath the reservation when the treaty was signed that created the Reservation, the court found that there was no evidence that parties to the treaty originally created the Wind River Reservation for mineral or industrial purposes. Similarly, the court rejected any allocation of water for wildlife management or aesthetic uses since neither use fell within the original purposes for which the reservation was created. By contrast, the court noted that no separate allocation for municipal, domestic, livestock, and commercial uses was necessary since such allocations properly were included within the agricultural reserved water award. For the court, the practicably irrigable acreage standard established in *Arizona v. California (Arizona I)*, 373 U.S. at 601, specifically included the water necessary for agriculture and related purposes. Taken together, these cases indicate that the *Arizona v. California* practicably irrigable acreage standard for quantification represents an expansive concept which includes municipal, domestic, livestock, and commercial uses on Indian reservations intended primarily for agriculture. The cases also suggest that where a tribe proves that other uses, such as hunting and fishing, were originally intended when the reservation was established, the court may award water allocations beyond the practicably irrigable acreage standard.

Standards such as the practicably irrigable acreage standard do not control Indian *use* of their reserved water rights but, rather, merely quantify the *amount* of water to which Indians are entitled under the *Winters* doctrine. Thus, water allocated on this standard can be diverted for mining, industrial, or other purposes never originally contemplated in the treaty. The point of any such standard is that it limits the quantity of water to which the tribes have title under the *Winters* doctrine. By quantifying Indian reserved rights under such standards, the courts prevent the usually prior Indian reserved rights from expanding with technology and use and thereby posing a serious threat to the utility of the rights held by junior appropriators under state law.

The seeming conflict between non-Indian needs and Indian rights was the subject of scrutiny by the National Water Commission, a governmental entity created in 1968. Its 1973 Final Report states that "the future utilization of Indian rights on fully appropriated streams will divest prior uses initiated under state law ... and will impose economic hardship, amounting to disaster in some cases, on users with large investments made over long periods of time." *Final Report of the National Water Commission* at 477 (1973). The solution proposed is that at any time construction of a reservation water resource project impairs a pre-existing non-Indian right "valid under state law" and initiated prior to 1963, the United States should pay the non-Indian just compensation. The report realizes that such a law would make even more unlikely federal financing of water rights projects on Indian reservations since the cost would now include compensation to non-Indian users. The basis for the Commission's proposed recommendation is that non-Indian users could not have reasonably known, prior to 1963 (the date of the *Arizona v. California* decision), the extent of Indian rights. But what kind of a right did the non-Indians have? What were their reasonable expectations of the length of time they could use the water? Recall that the tribes probably did not have the funds for irrigation works and it could reasonably have appeared to the settlers that massive irrigation on the reservation was at least several decades away. Now a quantification and leasing arrangement is sought so that the water can be sold to others by the tribe or the United States. Should the fact that the United States has not adequately financed reservation water projects be a basis for legitimating non-Indian use? Should the non-Indian users have been on notice as a consequence of *Winters* that their own use was in constant jeopardy? Ironically, these non-Indian users often had been federally financed.

Assuming, as the National Water Commission does, that quantification of Indian water rights is a concept that makes sense and could be useful both to Indian and non-Indian claimants, what forum should quantify and inventory the Indians' water right? The trend seems to be toward including all claims to a river system in a state court proceeding, even where the claims arise out of a federal reservation. *See United States v. District Court for Eagle County,* 401 U.S. 520 (1971). But there is more than a touch of unfairness in the trend. The state courts and state administrative agencies have been generally hostile to the assertion of Indian rights — whether they are rights to land, to water, or to the assertion of Indian law-making power. The Commission's proposed recommendations would not require federal compliance with state rules or procedures inconsistent with federal rights, but this may be an unadministrable distinction. Furthermore, there would be an appeal to a federal forum, though critical facts would already have been "found" in an often adverse arena.

In the face of the uncertainties of existing water law and the substantial capital investment necessary to realize the economic benefit of reserved water rights, tribes may find themselves modifying their rights through other means of quantification in order to gain a measure of economic security. In the case of the Navajo Tribe, for example, there were two occasions when it found it desirable to bargain its unquantified reserved rights under *Winters* for other gains. In 1962, Congress confirmed a tribal determination providing for federal financing of the massive Navajo Indian Irrigation Project on the eastern portion of the reservation in exchange for a surrender of the Navajo priority to waters needed for the San Juan-Chama Diversion project to divert headwaters of the San Juan System into the Rio Grande River System that serves Albuquerque. In 1968, the tribe resolved to forebear from using Colorado River water on the western portion of the reservation in exchange for some monetary consideration and the promise of beneficial economic development, actions that made possible the construction of the Navajo Generating Station and the availability of the water needed by the Salt River Project to operate it.

There is some question of whether the information to which the tribe had access was sufficient to allow for an informed decision to compromise and whether the disparity in economic strength between the tribe and the non-Navajo interests that it negotiated with, such as the federal Bureau of Reclamation, Upper Colorado River Commission, Salt River Project, and New Mexico Interstate Stream Commission, resulted in an inequitable settlement. *See* Price & Weatherford, *Indian Water Rights in Theory and Practice: Navajo Experience in the Colorado River Basin,* 40 LAW & CONTEMP. PROBS. 97 (1976). *See also* DuMars & Ingram, *Congressional Quantification of Indian Reserved Water Rights: A Definitive Solution or a Mirage?* 20 NAT. RESOURCES J. 17 (1980) (raising questions concerning the competing values involved when the Navajos exchanged certain reserved rights upon receipt of federal projects).

The reasoning of *Winters* assumes a bargained arrangement where water was reserved for the prospering of the reserved lands. Is the *Winters* reasoning applicable in the context, say, of New Mexico pueblos where the land now held has been held from time immemorial and there has been no cession, treaty, or executive agreement establishing the pueblo? In *New Mexico v. Aamadt,* 537 F.2d 1102 (10th Cir. 1976), *cert. denied,* 429 U.S. 1121 (1977), the court held that when Congress confirmed the pueblos' title to their land in 1858, no reservation of either land or water was created for the Indians. Therefore, the later recognition of reserved water rights under *Winters* may not be applicable to the pueblos. Since *Winters* reasoning may not be applicable, should pueblo lands be bound by state rules governing appropriation of water? The court said no, stating that the federal government had not relinquished jurisdiction and control over the pueblos as trustee and guardian when it relinquished the fee title. *See* Note, *Water Law: Pueblo Indians' Water Rights,* 54 DEN. L.J. 302 (1977). The court indicated that the pueblos' claim to water was derived from their aboriginal rights, which are established by continuous and exclusive use of property over a long period of time and which were recognized by the United States under the Treaty of Guadalupe-Hidalgo to the extent recognized by the prior Spanish and Mexican sovereigns. *See* Merrill, *Aboriginal Water Rights,* 20 NAT. RESOURCES J. 45 (1980). Are the aboriginal water rights any less "paper" rights than the Navajo reserved rights? Also, will there be any less temptation to agree to extinguishment of potentially substantial, but possibly historically unverifiable, aboriginal rights for immediate monetary compensation or promises of economic assistance? For discussion of an analogous situation that resulted in the Alaska Native Claims Settlement Act, see Black, *Alaskan Native Claims,* 4 NAT. RESOURCES J. 223 (1971).

Besides the reserved right to a particular quantity of water, is there a right to a particular quality of water imbedded in the *Winters* doctrine? Off-reservation activities — whether agricultural, industrial, or silvicultural — can potentially affect the water quality on reservation, and thus may impact on Indian farm and fishery efforts. Assuming the existence of a reserved right, can it be satisfied by the delivery of nonpotable or overly saline water? Consider, for example, both the high salinity of the Colorado River by the time it approaches the Mexican border, and the presence of a portion of the Cocopah Indian Reservation on its bank in the southwestern corner of Arizona. *See* COLORADO RIVER BASIN SALINITY CONTROL FORUM, WATER QUALITY STANDARDS FOR SALINITY: COLORADO RIVER SYSTEM, PROPOSED REPORT ON 1981 REVIEW (July 9, 1981), tables 3-5; KLEINMAN & BROWN, COLORADO RIVER SALINITY: IMPACTS ON AGRICULTURAL, MUNICIPAL, AND INDUSTRIAL USERS, WATER AND POWER RESOURCES

SERVICES (Dec. 1981); FOREMAN, INDIAN WATER RIGHTS: A PUBLIC POLICY AND ADMINISTRATIVE MESS, appendix B at 158-61 (1981).

Should changed technology be taken into account in defining the scope of the reserved right? When the Navajo Reservation was created, most Colorado River water was inaccessible because its flow was so far below ground level. Enormous investment and the construction of Navajo Dam now make the water more readily available. Upstream and downstream uses (including the development of cities) may have been premised on a view of the Indian right based on the productivity of water diversion techniques at the time the reservation was created. Now, as a consequence of advances, there is a shift in water availability. Assuming that the Indian reserved right encompasses exploitation made possible by the development of superior technology, who should bear the increased cost of water for competing users? Should it be the taxpayers as a whole or the users themselves? Often, the only means of financing the expensive diversion works that increase the Indians' share of water is through congressional appropriations. But a Congressman might be loath to vote an appropriation that will lead to the permanent diversion of scarce water from powerful urban and rural constitutents to Indian users.

4. Modification or Abrogation of Indian Water Rights and the Taking Clause: What are the fifth amendment consequences of modifying Indian water rights? Do they have the status of aboriginal Indian title, and therefore, the fragile quality assigned by the Supreme Court in *Tee-Hit-Ton,* discussed in Chapter 5, where land held under such title was deemed not covered by the taking clause of the fifth amendment? Professor Meyers has argued that all water rights may not be compensable, though no definitive answer has yet been provided. Meyers, *The Colorado River,* 10 STAN. L. REV. 1, 47 (1966). *But see United States v. 5,677.94 Acres of Land,* 162 F. Supp. 108 (D. Mont. 1958). Under Professor Meyers's theory that the United States may assert its superior easement of navigation to condemn water rights, is it possible that some uses or diversions are not compensable but that others are? *See California v. United States,* 438 U.S. 615 (1978), *Dugan v. Rank,* 372 U.S. 609 (1963); and *International Paper Co. v. United States,* 282 U.S. 399 (1931) (all suggesting the compensability of water rights under the fifth amendment). In *United States v. Shoshone Tribe,* 304 U.S. 111 (1938), the Court held that the tribe's beneficial interest in the land of its reservation included the timber and minerals, so just compensation was due upon federal appropriation of the resources. Attention must be paid to the jurisdiction statute that establishes the grounds for recovery. The treaty with the Shoshone contained nothing to suggest that the United States intended to retain beneficial interest. Where a reservation is created by treaty or statute, the reserved water rights would seem to be as compensable as timber or minerals. The result might differ if the reservation was created by executive order and never afterward recognized by statute. *See Sioux Tribe v. United States,* 316 U.S. 317 (1942). The existing case law, including *Winters* and *Arizona v. California,* suggests that unlike aboriginal title, however, Indian water rights, once defined, are usually vested property rights and specifically enforceable.

F. COHEN, HANDBOOK OF FEDERAL INDIAN LAW 604 (1982 ed.) notes that "states may not regulate how reservation Indians utilize their reserved water rights. Regulatory jurisdiction over Indians resides exclusively with the federal government and tribes," citing *Bryan v. Itasca County,* 426 U.S. 373 (1976), among other cases for this proposition. In Justice Brennan's opinion for the majority in *Bryan,* he quotes prior cases to the effect that "'Congress has ...

acted consistently upon the assumption that the States have no power to regulate the affairs of Indians on a reservation,' *Williams v. Lee*, 358 U.S. 217, 220
(1959), and therefore 'State laws generally are not applicable to tribal Indians
on an Indian reservation except where Congress has expressly provided that
State laws shall apply.' *McClanahan v. Arizona State Tax Comm'n*, 411 U.S.
164, 170, 171 (1973) (quoting ... FEDERAL INDIAN LAW 845 (1958))." It is at least
conceivable that Congress could change the rules of the game and allow for
state regulation of on-reservation water use by Indians. If Congress did so,
would such legislation effectuate a compensable taking of Indian water rights?
See Menominee Tribe v. United States, 391 U.S. 404 (1968).

In *United States v. Cherokee Nation*, 480 U.S. 700 (1987), the Court relied on
the federal navigation servitude to deny the Cherokee Nation compensation for
federal interference with its ownership of the riverbed of the Arkansas River.
Specifically, the Tribe claimed that the construction of the McClellan-Kerr
Project by the Army Corps of Engineers was a taking of their interest in the
affected portions of the riverbed. The court held that the federal navigation
servitude applies to all riparian and other riverbed interests, even for the
unique situation of a privately owned stream, as the Cherokee characterized
their portion of the Arkansas River. The paramount navigation servitude held
by the United States therefore permitted the United States to interfere with the
Tribe's riverbed interests by constructing the McClellan-Kerr Project without
paying compensation to the Tribe. The *Cherokee Nation* case involved claimed
compensation for interference with the real property interests of the Tribe.
Should the navigation servitude apply with the same force to federal interferences with Indian *water* use? What if the federal appropriation of Indian water
rights is for non-navigation purposes?

In 25 U.S.C. § 357, provision is made for condemnation of Indian allotments
for any public purpose under the laws of the state or territory where they are
located. What are the possible ramifications of this statute on the reserved water
rights of diligent Indian allottees when the state plans a water project in an arid
area?

NEVADA v. UNITED STATES

463 U.S. 110 (1983)

[The opinion in the *Nevada* case holds that the doctrine of *res judicata* precluded reopening of a 1944 decree adjudicating water claims and quantifying
Indian reserved water rights along the Truckee River in Nevada and California.
The Pyramid Lake Paiute Tribe had claimed that the opinion should be reopened due to the federal government's conflict of interest since the United
States represented both the affected tribes and the competing reclamation
projects along the Truckee flowage. The Tribe needed more water than provided by the decree to maintain the lake levels of Pyramid Lake at levels sufficient to conserve fisheries and for other purposes. The Court noted that as a
trustee "the Government is simply not in the position of a private litigant or a
private party under traditional rules of common law or statute." Finding that
the Bureau of Indian Affairs separately advised on and made decisions about
the government's position in the litigation, the Court held that the Tribe's
interests were represented and the Tribe was therefore bound by the decree.
The opinion is set forth in Chapter 2, page 259.]

NOTE

The non-Indian need for quantification and stability of Indian water rights is evident from the *Nevada* decision and another case decided earlier the same Term of Court, *Arizona v. California* (*Arizona IV*), 460 U.S. 605 (1983). In *Arizona*, certain tribes, noting that a prior water decree was subject to "appropriate adjustment," sought to reopen a 1979 final water decree adjudicating rights in the Colorado River. Over three dissents, the Court, noting that "[c]ertainty of rights is particularly important with respect to water rights in the Western United States," 460 U.S. at 620, declined based on the doctrines of law of the case and *res judicata* to reopen the 1979 decree in order to recalculate the Indians practicably irrigable acreage (the water quantification test applied to Indian *Winters* rights in this case) to take account of lands omitted in error and developments in irrigation technology. Justice White's opinion for the Court observed:

> Recalculating the amount of practicably irrigable acreage runs directly counter to the strong interest in finality in this case. A major purpose of this litigation, from its inception to the present day, has been to provide the necessary assurance to States of the Southwest and to various private interests, of the amount of water they can anticipate to receive from the Colorado River system. "In the arid parts of the West ... claims to water for use on federal reservations vie with other public and private claims for the limited quantities to be found in the rivers and streams." *United States v. New Mexico,* 438 U.S. 696 (1978). If there is no surplus of water in the Colorado River, an increase in federal reserved water rights will require a "gallon-for-gallon reduction in the amount of water available for water-needy state and private appropriators." *Id.* at 705.

If water adjudications like those in *Nevada* and *Arizona* finally quantify and adjudicate Indian water rights irrespective of error or later technological developments, careful attention should be paid to the procedure by which adjudication and quantification of Indian water rights occurs. The next case, *Arizona v. San Carlos Apache Tribe,* and *Colorado River Water Conservation District,* discussed in the next opinion, address this question. Do they provide sufficient protections for Indian *Winters* rights?

ARIZONA v. SAN CARLOS APACHE TRIBE

463 U.S. 545 (1983)

Justice BRENNAN delivered the opinion of the Court.

These consolidated cases form a sequel to our decision in *Colorado River Water Conservation District v. United States,* 424 U.S. 800 (1976). That case held that (1) the McCarran Amendment, 66 Stat. 560, 43 U.S.C. § 666, which waived the sovereign immunity of the United States as to comprehensive state water rights adjudications,[1] provides state courts with jurisdiction to adjudicate

[1]The McCarran Amendment provides in relevant part:

"(a) Consent is hereby given to join the United States as a defendant in any suit (1) for the adjudication of rights to the use of water of a river system or other source, or (2) for the administration of such rights, where it appears that the United States is the owner of or is in the process of acquiring water rights by appropriation under State law, by purchase, by exchange, or otherwise, and the United States is a necessary party to such suit. The United States, when a party to any such suit, shall (1) be deemed to have waived any right to plead that the State laws are inapplicable or that the United States is not amenable thereto by reason of its sovereignty, and (2) shall be subject to the judgments, orders and decrees of the court having jurisdiction, and may

Indian water rights held in trust by the United States, and (2), in light of the clear federal policies underlying the McCarran Amendment, a water rights suit brought by the United States in federal court was properly dismissed in favor of a concurrent comprehensive adjudication reaching the same issues in Colorado state court. The questions in these cases are parallel: (1) What is the effect of the McCarran Amendment in those States which, unlike Colorado, were admitted to the Union subject to federal legislation that reserved "absolute jurisdiction and control" over Indian lands in the Congress of the United States? (2) If the courts of such States do have jurisdiction to adjudicate Indian water rights, should concurrent federal suits brought by Indian tribes, rather than by the United States, and raising only Indian claims, also be subject to dismissal under the doctrine of *Colorado River*?

I

Colorado River arose out of a suit brought by the Federal Government in the United States District Court for the District of Colorado seeking a declaration of its rights, and the rights of a number of Indian Tribes, to waters in certain rivers and their tributaries located in one of the drainage basins of the State of Colorado. In the suit, the Government asserted reserved rights, governed by federal law, as well as rights based on state law. Shortly after the federal suit was commenced, the United States was joined, pursuant to the McCarran Amendment, as a party in the ongoing state-court comprehensive water adjudication being conducted for the same drainage basin. The Federal District Court, on motion of certain of the defendants and intervenors, dismissed the federal suit, stating that the doctrine of abstention required deference to the state proceedings. The Court of Appeals reversed the District Court, and we in turn reversed the Court of Appeals.

We began our analysis in *Colorado River* by conceding that the District Court had jurisdiction over the federal suit under 28 U.S.C. § 1345, the general provision conferring district court jurisdiction over most civil actions brought by the Federal Government. We then examined whether the federal suit was nevertheless properly dismissed in view of the concurrent state-court proceedings. This part of the analysis began by considering "whether the McCarran Amendment provided consent to determine federal reserved rights held on behalf of Indians in state court," 424 U.S., at 809, since "given the claims for Indian water rights in [the federal suit], dismissal clearly would have been inappropriate if the state court had no jurisdiction to decide those claims." *Ibid.* We concluded:

> "Not only the Amendment's language, but also its underlying policy, dictates a construction including Indian rights in its provisions. [*United States v. District Court for Eagle County*, 401 U.S. 520 (1971),] rejected the conclusion that federal reserved rights in general were not reached by the Amendment for the reason that the Amendment '[deals] with an all-inclusive statute concerning "the adjudication of rights to the use of water of a river system."' *Id.*, at 524. This consideration applies as well to federal water rights reserved for Indian reservations." *Id.*, at 810.

In sum, considering the important federal interest in allowing all water rights on a river system to be adjudicated in a single comprehensive state proceeding,

---

obtain review thereof, in the same manner and to the same extent as a private individual under like circumstances ...."

and "bearing in mind the ubiquitous nature of Indian water rights in the Southwest," it was clear to us "that a construction of the Amendment excluding those rights from its coverage would enervate the Amendment's objective." *Id.*, at 811.

We buttressed this conclusion with an examination of the legislative history of the McCarran Amendment. We also noted:

> "Mere subjection of Indian rights to legal challenge in state court ... would no more imperil those rights than would a suit brought by the Government in district court for their declaration .... The Government has not abdicated any responsibility fully to defend Indian rights in state court, and Indian interests may be satisfactorily protected under regimes of state law. The Amendment in no way abridges any substantive claim on behalf of Indians under the doctrine of reserved rights. Moreover, as Eagle County said, 'questions [arising from the collision of private rights and reserved rights of the United States], including the volume and scope of particular reserved rights, are federal questions which, if preserved, can be reviewed [by the Supreme Court] after final judgment by the Colorado court.' 401 U.S., at 526." *Id.*, at 812-813 (citations omitted).

We then considered the dismissal itself. We found that the dismissal could not be supported under the doctrine of abstention in any of its forms, but that it was justified as an application of traditional principles of "'[w]ise judicial administration giving regard to conservation of judicial resources and comprehensive disposition of litigation.'" [A]lthough the federal courts had a "virtually unflagging obligation ... to exercise the jurisdiction given them," 424 U.S., at 817, there were certain very limited circumstances outside the abstention context in which dismissal was warranted in deference to a concurrent state-court suit. [W]e noted the comprehensive nature of the state proceedings and the considerable expertise and technical resources available in those proceedings. We concluded:

> "[A] number of factors clearly counsel against concurrent federal proceedings. The most important of these is the McCarran Amendment itself. The clear federal policy evinced by that legislation is the avoidance of piecemeal adjudication of water rights in a river system. This policy is akin to that underlying the rule requiring that jurisdiction be yielded to the court first acquiring control of property, for the concern in such instances is with avoiding the generation of additional litigation through permitting inconsistent dispositions of property. This concern is heightened with respect to water rights, the relationships among which are highly interdependent. Indeed, we have recognized that actions seeking the allocation of water essentially involve the disposition of property and are best conducted in unified proceedings. The consent to jurisdiction given by the McCarran Amendment bespeaks a policy that recognizes the availability of comprehensive state systems for adjudication of water rights as the means for achieving these goals." *Id.*, at 819 (citations omitted).

For these reasons, and others,[3] we affirmed the judgment of the District Court dismissing the federal complaint.

II

The two petitions considered here arise out of three separate consolidated appeals that were decided within three days of each other by the same panel of

---

[3] The other factors were the apparent absence at the time of dismissal of any proceedings in the District Court other than the filing of the complaint, the extensive involvement of state water rights in the suit, the 300-mile distance between the Federal District Court in Denver and the state tribunal, and the Government's apparent willingness to participate in other comprehensive water proceedings in the state courts.

the Court of Appeals for the Ninth Circuit. In each of the underlying cases, either the United States as trustee or certain Indian Tribes [including the Northern Cheyenne Tribe in Montana, the San Carlos Apache and Navajo Tribes in Arizona] on their own behalf, or both, asserted the right to have certain Indian water rights in Arizona or Montana adjudicated in federal court.

[The Enabling Acts under which both Montana and Arizona were admitted to statehood and the state constitutions contain disclaimers of jurisdiction over Indian property phrased in a substantially identical fashion. For example, in response to the requirements of the Montana Enabling Act, the Montana Constitution provided that the people of Montana

> agree and declare that they forever disclaim all right and title to ... all lands ... owned or held by any Indian or Indian tribes; and that until title thereto shall have been extinguished by the United States, the same shall be and remain subject to the disposition of the United States, and said Indian lands shall remain under the absolute jurisdiction and control of the Congress of the United States.

Enabling Act of Feb. 22, 1889, § 4, 25 Stat. 677 (North Dakota, South Dakota, Montana, and Washington); Mont. Const., Ordinance No. 1 (1895). In the Ninth Circuit, the tribes successfully claimed that these constitutional disclaimers disabled Arizona and Montana state courts from adjudicating Indian water claims, thereby seeking to distinguish *Colorado River*.]

We granted certiorari, 459 U.S. 821 (1982), in order to resolve a conflict among the Circuits regarding the role of federal and state courts in adjudicating Indian water rights.[9] We now reverse.

III

A

At the outset of our analysis, a number of propositions are clear. First, the federal courts had jurisdiction here to hear the suits brought both by the United States and the Indian Tribes. Second, it is also clear in these cases, as it was in *Colorado River*, that a dismissal or stay of the federal suits would have been improper if there was no jurisdiction in the concurrent state actions to adjudicate the claims at issue in the federal suits. Third, the parties here agree that the Court of Appeals erred in believing that, in the absence of state jurisdiction otherwise, Pub. L. 280 would have authorized the States to assume jurisdiction over the adjudication of Indian water rights. To the contrary, Pub. L. 280 specifically withheld from state courts jurisdiction to adjudicate ownership or right to possession "of any real or personal property, *including water rights*, belonging to any Indian or any Indian tribe, band, or community that is held in trust by the United States or is subject to a restriction against alienation imposed by the United States." 28 U.S.C. § 1360(b) (emphasis added). Thus, the presence or absence of jurisdiction must rise or fall without reference to whether the States have assumed jurisdiction under Pub. L. 280.

---

[9] In *Jicarilla Apache Tribe v. United States*, 601 F.2d 1116 (1979), the Court of Appeals for the Tenth Circuit held that the Enabling Act under which New Mexico was admitted to the Union (whose language is essentially the same as the Enabling Acts at issue in these cases) did not bar state jurisdiction over Indian water rights, and upheld the District Court's dismissal of a general water adjudication brought in federal court by the Jicarilla Apache Tribe.

Finally, it should be obvious that, to the extent that a claimed bar to state jurisdiction in these cases is premised on the respective State Constitutions, that is a question of state law over which the state courts have binding authority. Because, in each of these cases, the state courts have taken jurisdiction over the Indian water rights at issue here, we must assume, until informed otherwise, that — at least insofar as state law is concerned — such jurisdiction exists. We must therefore look, for our purposes, to the federal Enabling Acts and other federal legislation, in order to determine whether there is a federal bar to the assertion of state jurisdiction in these cases.

B

That we were not required in *Colorado River* to interpret the McCarran Amendment in light of any statehood Enabling Act was largely a matter of fortuity, for Colorado is one of the few Western States that were not admitted to the Union pursuant to an Enabling Act containing substantially the same language as is found in the Arizona and Montana Enabling Acts. Indeed, a substantial majority of Indian land — including most of the largest Indian reservations — lies in States subject to such Enabling Acts. Moreover, the reason that Colorado was not subject to such an Enabling Act, and Arizona and Montana were, has more to do with historical timing than with deliberate congressional selection. Colorado was admitted to the Union in 1876. In 1882, this Court held in *United States v. McBratney*, 104 U.S. 621, that the federal courts in Colorado had no criminal jurisdiction in a murder committed by one non-Indian against another on an Indian reservation, pointing out that the case did not concern "the punishment of crimes committed by or against Indians, the protection of the Indians in their improvements, or the regulation by Congress of the alienation and descent of property and the government and internal policy of the Indians." *Id.*, at 624. We also suggested, however, that the result might have been different if Congress had expressly reserved all criminal jurisdiction on Indian reservations when Colorado was admitted to the Union, pointing to a similar disclaimer contained in the legislation by which Kansas was admitted to statehood in 1861. Probably in response to the *McBratney* decision, Congress resumed the practice of including reservations in Enabling Acts, and did so in the case of virtually every State admitted after 1882.

Despite *McBratney* and *The Kansas Indians*, the presence or absence of specific jurisdictional disclaimers has rarely been dispositive in our consideration of state jurisdiction over Indian affairs or activities on Indian lands. In *Draper v. United States*, 164 U.S. 240 (1896), for example, this Court held that, despite the jurisdictional reservation in the Montana Enabling Act, a federal court still did not have jurisdiction over a crime committed on an Indian reservation by one non-Indian against another. We stated:

"As equality of statehood is the rule, the words relied on here to create an exception cannot be construed as doing so, if, by any reasonable meaning, they can be otherwise treated. The mere reservation of jurisdiction and control by the United States of 'Indian lands' does not of necessity signify a retention of jurisdiction in the United States to punish all offenses committed on such lands by others than Indians or against Indians." *Id.*, at 244-245.

Similarly, in *Organized Village of Kake v. Egan*, 369 U.S. 60 (1962), we held that a reservation in the Alaska Enabling Act did not deprive the State of the right to regulate Indian fishing licensed by the Department of the Interior, finding that the state regulation neither interfered with Indian self-government nor impaired any right granted or reserved by federal law. Conversely, *Worcester v. Georgia*, 6 Pet. 515 (1832), perhaps the most expansive declaration of Indian independence from state regulation ever uttered by this Court, pertained to one of the original 13 States, unbound by any Enabling Act whatsoever. See also, e.g., *The New York Indians*, 5 Wall. 761, 769-770 (1867) (reaching same conclusion as *The Kansas Indians, supra*, but without benefit of disclaimer). And our many recent decisions recognizing crucial limits on the power of the States to regulate Indian affairs have rarely either invoked reservations of jurisdiction contained in statehood Enabling Acts by anything more than a passing mention or distinguished between disclaimer States and nondisclaimer States.

In light of this history, the parties in these cases have engaged in a vigorous debate as to the exact meaning and significance of the Arizona and Montana Enabling Acts. We need not resolve that debate, however, nor need we resort to the more general doctrines that have developed to chart the limits of state authority over Indians, because we are convinced that, whatever limitation the Enabling Acts or federal policy may have originally placed on state-court jurisdiction over Indian water rights, those limitations were removed by the McCarran Amendment. Cf. *Washington v. Yakima Indian Nation*, 439 U.S., at 484-493. Congress clearly would have had the right to distinguish between disclaimer and nondisclaimer States in passing the McCarran Amendment. But the Amendment was designed to deal with a general problem arising out of the limitations that federal sovereign immunity placed on the ability of the States to adjudicate water rights, and nowhere in its text or legislative history do we find any indication that Congress intended the efficacy of the remedy to differ from one State to another. Moreover, we stated in *Colorado River* that "bearing in mind the ubiquitous nature of Indian water rights in the Southwest, it is clear that a construction of the Amendment excluding those rights from its coverage would enervate the Amendment's objective." 424 U.S., at 811. The "ubiquitous nature of Indian water rights" is most apparent in the very States to which Congress attached jurisdictional reservations. See *supra*, at 561. To declare now that our holding in *Colorado River* applies only to that minority of Indian water claims located in States without jurisdictional reservations would constitute a curious and unwarranted retreat from the rationale behind our previous holding, and would work the very mischief that our decision in *Colorado River* sought to avoid. We need not rely on the possibly overbroad statement in *Draper v. United States* that "equality of statehood is the rule," 164 U.S., at 244, in order to conclude that, in this context at least, "equality of statehood" is sensible, necessary, and, most important, consistent with the will of Congress.

IV

The second crucial issue in these cases is whether our analysis in *Colorado River* applies with full force to federal suits brought by Indian tribes, rather than by the United States, and seeking adjudication only of Indian water rights.[16] This question is not directly answered by *Colorado River*, because we specifically reserved in that case "[w]hether similar considerations would permit dismissal of a water suit brought by a private party in federal district court." 424 U.S., at 820, n.26. On reflection, however, we must agree with Justice STEVENS, who, in dissenting from our decision, wrote:

> "[T]he Federal Government surely has no lesser right of access to the federal forum than does a private [party], such as an Indian asserting his own claim. If this be so, today's holding will necessarily restrict the access to federal court of private plaintiffs asserting water rights claims in Colorado." *Id.*, at 827.

The United States and the various Indian respondents raise a series of arguments why dismissal or stay of the federal suit is not appropriate when it is brought by an Indian tribe and only seeks to adjudicate Indian rights. (1) Indian rights have traditionally been left free of interference from the States. (2) State courts may be inhospitable to Indian rights. (3) The McCarran Amendment, although it waived United States sovereign immunity in state comprehensive water adjudications, did not waive Indian sovereign immunity. It is therefore unfair to force Indian claimants to choose between waiving their sovereign immunity by intervening in the state proceedings and relying on the United States to represent their interests in state court, particularly in light of the frequent conflict of interest between Indian claims and other federal interests and the right of the Indians under 28 U.S.C. § 1362 to bring suit on their own behalf in federal court.[17] (4) Indian water rights claims are generally based on federal rather than state law. (5) Because Indian water claims are based on the doctrine of "reserved rights," and take priority over most water rights created by state law, they need not as a practical matter be adjudicated *inter sese* with other water rights, and could simply be incorporated into the comprehensive state decree at the conclusion of the state proceedings.

---

[16] As is apparent from our discussion of the facts, [some of suits here involved cases] brought by the United States. In light of our express holding in *Colorado River*, what we say here with regard to the suits brought by the Indians must apply *a fortiori* to the suits brought by the United States. In addition, some of the cases before us sought adjudication of all the rights to a particular water system, rather than merely Indian or other federal water rights, and it is argued that these suits avoid the "piecemeal adjudication of water rights" which we found in *Colorado River* to be inconsistent with federal policy. [Since] one of the best arguments in favor of retaining federal jurisdiction in Indian water cases is that Indian water rights can be adjudicated separately and then incorporated into the results of the comprehensive state proceedings, [the correct] analysis of the more ambitious federal suits at issue here must also follow *a fortiori* from our discussion in text. A comprehensive federal adjudication going on at the same time as a comprehensive state adjudication might not literally be "piecemeal." It is, however, duplicative, wasteful, inconsistent with the McCarran Amendment's policy of "recogniz[ing] the availability of comprehensive state systems for adjudication of water rights as the means for [conducting unified water rights proceedings]," 424 U.S., at 819, likely to "generat[e] ... additional litigation" as a result of "inconsistent dispositions of property," *ibid.*, and permeated with state-law issues entirely tangential to any conceivable federal interest....

[17] This argument, of course, suffers from the flaw that, although the McCarran Amendment did not waive the sovereign immunity of Indians as parties to state comprehensive water adjudications, it did (as we made quite clear in *Colorado River*) waive sovereign immunity with regard to the Indian rights at issue in those proceedings. Moreover, contrary to the submissions by certain of the parties, any judgment against the United States, as trustee for the Indians, would ordinarily be binding on the Indians. In addition, there is no indication in these cases that the state courts would deny the Indian parties leave to intervene to protect their interests. Thus, although the Indians have the right to refuse to intervene even if they believe that the United States is not adequately representing their interests, the practical value of that right in this context is dubious at best.

Each of these arguments has a good deal of force. We note, though, that very similar arguments were raised and rejected in *United States v. District Court for Eagle County*, 401 U.S. 520 (1971), and *Colorado River*. More important, all of these arguments founder on one crucial fact: If the state proceedings have jurisdiction over the Indian water rights at issue here, as appears to be the case, then concurrent federal proceedings are likely to be duplicative and wasteful, generating "additional litigation through permitting inconsistent dispositions of property." *Colorado River*, 424 U.S., at 819. Moreover, since a judgment by either court would ordinarily be *res judicata* in the other, the existence of such concurrent proceedings creates the serious potential for spawning an unseemly and destructive race to see which forum can resolve the same issues first — a race contrary to the entire spirit of the McCarran Amendment and prejudicial, to say the least, to the possibility of reasoned decisionmaking by either forum. The United States and many of the Indian Tribes recognize these concerns, but in responding to them they cast aside the sort of sound argument generally apparent in the rest of their submissions and rely instead on vague statements of faith and hope. The United States, for example, states that adjudicating Indian water rights in federal court, despite the existence of a comprehensive state proceeding, would not

> "entail any duplication or potential for inconsistent judgments. The federal court will quantify the Indian rights only if it is asked to do so before the State court has embarked on the task. And, of course, once the United States district court has indicated its determination to perform that limited role, *we assume* the State tribunal will turn its attention to the typically more complex business of adjudicating all other claims on the stream. *In the usual case*, the federal court will have completed its function earlier and its quantification of Indian water rights will simply be incorporated in the comprehensive State court decree." Brief for United States 30 (emphasis added).

Similarly, the Navajo Nation states:

> "There is no reasonably foreseeable danger that [the] federal action [brought by the Navajo] will duplicate or delay state proceedings or waste judicial resources. While the Navajo claim proceeds in federal court, the state court *can* move forward to assess, quantify, and rank the 58,000 state claims. The Navajo federal action will be concluded long before the state court has finished its task." Brief for Respondent Navajo Nation in No. 81-2147, p. 22 (emphasis added; footnote omitted).

The problem with these scenarios, however, is that they assume a cooperative attitude on the part of state courts, state legislatures, and state parties which is neither legally required nor realistically always to be expected. The state courts need not "turn their attention" to other matters if they are prompted by state parties to adjudicate the Indian claims first. Moreover, considering the specialized resources and experience of the state courts, it is not at all obvious that the federal actions "will be concluded long before" the state courts have issued at least preliminary judgments on the question of Indian water rights.

The McCarran Amendment, as interpreted in *Colorado River*, allows and encourages state courts to undertake the task of quantifying Indian water rights in the course of comprehensive water adjudications. Although adjudication of those rights in federal court instead might in the abstract be practical, and even wise, it will be neither practical nor wise as long as it creates the possibility of duplicative litigation, tension and controversy between the federal and state forums, hurried and pressured decisionmaking, and confusion over the disposition of property rights.

Colorado River, of course, does not require that a federal water suit must always be dismissed or stayed in deference to a concurrent and adequate comprehensive state adjudication. Certainly, the federal courts need not defer to the state proceedings if the state courts expressly agree to stay their own consideration of the issues raised in the federal action pending disposition of that action. Moreover, it may be in a particular case that, at the time a motion to dismiss is filed, the federal suit at issue is well enough along that its dismissal would itself constitute a waste of judicial resources and an invitation to duplicative effort. [W]e do not deny that, in a case in which the arguments for and against deference to the state adjudication were otherwise closely matched, the fact that a federal suit was brought by Indians on their own behalf and sought only to adjudicate Indian rights should be figured into the balance. But the most important consideration in *Colorado River*, and the most important consideration in any federal water suit concurrent to a comprehensive state proceeding, must be the "policy underlying the McCarran Amendment." [D]espite the strong arguments raised by the respondents, we cannot conclude that water rights suits brought by Indians and seeking adjudication only of Indian rights should be excepted from the application of that policy or from the general principles set out in *Colorado River*. In the cases before us, assuming that the state adjudications are adequate to quantify the rights at issue in the federal suits, and taking into account the McCarran Amendment policies we have just discussed, the expertise and administrative machinery available to the state courts, the infancy of the federal suits, the general judicial bias against piecemeal litigation, and the convenience to the parties, we must conclude that the District Courts were correct in deferring to the state proceedings.[21]

V

Nothing we say today should be understood to represent even the slightest retreat from the general proposition we expressed so recently in *New Mexico v. Mescalero Apache Tribe*, 462 U.S., at 332: "Because of their sovereign status, [Indian] tribes and their reservation lands are insulated in some respects by a 'historic immunity from state and local control,' *Mescalero Apache Tribe v. Jones*, [411 U.S. 145, 152 (1973)], and tribes retain any aspect of their historical sovereignty not 'inconsistent with the overriding interests of the National Government.' *Washington v. Confederated Tribes*, [447 U.S. 134, 153 (1980)]." Nor should we be understood to retreat from the general proposition, expressed in *Colorado River*, that federal courts have a "virtually unflagging obligation ... to exercise the jurisdiction given them." 424 U.S., at 817. But water rights adjudication is a virtually unique type of proceeding, and the McCarran Amendment

---

[21] We leave open for determination on remand as appropriate whether the proper course in such cases is a stay of the federal suit or dismissal without prejudice. See *Moses H. Cone Hospital*, 460 U.S., at 28 (reserving issue). In either event, resort to the federal forum should remain available if warranted by a significant change of circumstances, such as, for example, a decision by a state court that it does not have jurisdiction over some or all of these claims after all.

is a virtually unique federal statute, and we cannot in this context be guided by general propositions.

We also emphasize, as we did in *Colorado River*, that our decision in no way changes the substantive law by which Indian rights in state water adjudications must be judged. State courts, as much as federal courts, have a solemn obligation to follow federal law. Moreover, any state-court decision alleged to abridge Indian water rights protected by federal law can expect to receive, if brought for review before this Court, a particularized and exacting scrutiny commensurate with the powerful federal interest in safeguarding those rights from state encroachment.

The judgment of the Court of Appeals in each of these cases is reversed, and the cases are remanded for further proceedings consistent with this opinion.

So ordered.

Justice MARSHALL, dissenting.

In *Colorado River Water Conservation District v. United States*, 424 U.S. 800 (1976), this Court recognized a narrow rule of abstention governing controversies involving federal water rights. We stated that in light of "the virtually unflagging obligation of the federal courts to exercise the jurisdiction given them," *id.*, at 817, "[o]nly the clearest of justifications," *id.*, at 819, will warrant abstention in favor of a concurrent state proceeding. Substantially for the reasons set forth in Justice STEVENS' dissenting opinion, I believe that abstention is not appropriate in these cases. Unlike the federal suit in *Colorado River*, the suits here are brought by Indian Tribes on their own behalf. These cases thus implicate the strong congressional policy, embodied in 28 U.S.C. § 1362, of affording Indian tribes a federal forum. Since § 1362 reflects a congressional recognition of the "great hesitancy on the part of tribes to use State courts," S. Rep. No. 1507, 89th Cong., 2d Sess., 2 (1966), tribes which have sued under that provision should not lightly be remitted to asserting their rights in a state forum. Moreover, these cases also differ from *Colorado River* in that the exercise of federal jurisdiction here will not result in duplicative federal and state proceedings, since the District Court need only determine the water rights of the Tribes. I therefore cannot agree that this is one of those "exceptional" situations justifying abstention. 424 U.S., at 818.

Justice STEVENS, with whom Justice BLACKMUN joins, dissenting.

"Nothing in the McCarran Amendment or in its legislative history can be read as limiting the jurisdiction of the federal courts." *Colorado River Water Conservation District v. United States*, 424 U.S. 800, 821, n.2 (1976) (Stewart, J., dissenting). That Amendment is a waiver, not a command. It permits the United States to be joined as a defendant in state water rights adjudications; it does not purport to diminish the United States' right to litigate in a federal forum and it is totally silent on the subject of Indian tribes' rights to litigate anywhere. Yet today the majority somehow concludes that it commands the federal courts to defer to state-court water rights proceedings, even when Indian water rights are involved. Although it is customary for the Court to begin its analysis of questions of statutory construction by examining the text of the relevant statute, one may search in vain for any textual support for the Court's holding today.

> "Most of the land in these reservations is and always has been arid.... It can be said without overstatement that when the Indians were put on these reservations they were not considered to be located in the most desirable area of the Nation. It is impossible to believe that when Congress created the great Colorado River Indian Reservation and when the Executive Department of this Nation created the other reservations they were unaware that most of the lands were of the desert kind — hot, scorching sands — and that water from the river would be essential to the life of the Indian people and to the animals they hunted and the crops they raised." *Arizona v. California*, 373 U.S. 546, 598-599 (1963).

This Court has repeatedly recognized that the Government, when it created each Indian reservation, "intended to deal fairly with the Indians by reserving for them the waters without which their lands would have been useless." *Id.*, at 600. This doctrine, known as the *Winters* doctrine, is unquestionably a matter of federal, not state, law. Its underlying principles differ substantially from those applied by the States to allocate water among competing claimants. Unlike state-law claims based on prior appropriation, Indian reserved water rights are not based on actual beneficial use and are not forfeited if they are not used. Vested no later than the date each reservation was created, these Indian rights are superior in right to all subsequent appropriations under state law. Not all of the issues arising from the application of the *Winters* doctrine have been resolved, because in the past the scope of Indian reserved rights has infrequently been adjudicated. The important task of elaborating and clarifying these federal-law issues in the cases now before the Court, and in future cases, should be performed by federal rather than state courts whenever possible.

Federal adjudication of Indian water rights would not fragment an otherwise unified state-court proceeding. Since Indian reserved claims are wholly dissimilar to state-law water claims, and since their amount does not depend on the total volume of water available in the water source or on the quantity of competing claims, it will be necessary to conduct separate proceedings to determine these claims even if the adjudication takes place in state court. Subsequently the state court will incorporate these claims — like claims under state law or Federal Government claims that have been formally adjudicated in the past — into a single inclusive, binding decree for each water source. Thus, as Justice Stewart wrote in dissent in *Colorado River*: "Whether the virtually identical separate proceedings take place in a federal court or a state court, the adjudication of the claims will be neither more nor less 'piecemeal.' Essentially the same process will be followed in each instance." 424 U.S., at 825.

To justify virtual abandonment of Indian water rights claims to the state courts, the majority relies heavily on *Colorado River Water Conservation District*, which in turn discovered an affirmative policy of federal judicial abdication in the McCarran Amendment.[4] I continue to believe that *Colorado River*

---

[4]Although giving lip service to the balancing of factors set forth in *Colorado River*, the Court essentially gives decisive weight to one factor: the policy of unified water rights adjudication purportedly embodied in the McCarran Amendment. The Court's entire discussion of the applicability in these cases of the four *Colorado River* factors is found in a single vague sentence. It is worth noting, however, that the Court leaves open the possibility that Indian water claims will occasionally be heard in federal court.

read more into that Amendment than Congress intended, and cannot acquiesce in an extension of its reasoning. Although the Court's decision in *Colorado River* did, indeed, foreshadow today's holding, it did not involve an Indian tribe's attempt to litigate on its own behalf, 424 U.S., at 820, n.26. The majority today acknowledges that the question in these cases was "not directly answered," but in fact was "specifically reserved," in *Colorado River*.

Although in some respects Indian tribes' water claims are similar to other reserved federal water rights, different treatment is justified. States and their citizens may well be more antagonistic toward Indian reserved rights than other federal reserved rights, both because the former are potentially greater in quantity and because they provide few direct or indirect benefits to non-Indian residents. Indians have historically enjoyed a unique relationship with the Federal Government, reflecting the tribes' traditional sovereign status, their treaty-based right to federal protection, and their special economic problems. Recently the Court reaffirmed "'the distinctive obligation of trust incumbent upon the Government in its dealings with these dependent and sometimes exploited people.'" *United States v. Mitchell, ante,* at 225, quoting *Seminole Nation v. United States,* 316 U.S. 286, 296 (1942).

One important aspect of the special relationship is 28 U.S.C. § 1362, which embodies a federal promise that Indian tribes will be able to invoke the jurisdiction of federal courts to resolve matters in controversy arising under federal law. Congress thereby assured Indians a neutral federal forum — a guarantee whose importance should not be underestimated.[8] The Senate Report noted:

> "There is great hesitancy on the part of tribes to use State courts. This reluctance is founded partially on the traditional fear that tribes have had of the States in which their reservations are situated. Additionally, the Federal courts have more expertise in deciding questions involving treaties with the Federal Government, as well as interpreting the relevant body of Federal law that has developed over the years." S. Rep. No. 1507, 89th Cong., 2d Sess., 2 (1966).

Section 1362 also assured the tribes that they need not rely on the Federal Government to protect their interests, an important safeguard in light of the undeniable potential for conflicts of interest between Indian claims and other Federal Government claims.

Despite the silence of the McCarran Amendment regarding Indian tribal claims, and the clear promise of a federal forum embodied in § 1362, the Court holds that considerations of "wise judicial administration" require that Indian claims, governed by federal law, must be relegated to the state courts. It is clear to me that the words "wise judicial administration" have been wrenched com-

---

[8] The majority recognizes that there is "a good deal of force" to the assertion that "[s]tate courts may be inhospitable to Indian rights." Federal officials responsible for Indian affairs have consistently recognized the appropriateness of deciding Indian claims in federal, not state, courts. *See, e.g.,* H.R. Rep. No. 2040, 89th Cong., 2d Sess., 2 (1966) (describing position of Interior Department); National Water Comm'n, Water Policies for the Future, Final Report to the President and to the Congress of the United States 478-479 (1973). American Indian Policy Review Commission, Task Force Four, Report on Federal, State, and Tribal Jurisdiction 176 (Comm. Print 1976); American Indian Policy Review Commission, Final Report 333-334 (Comm. Print 1977).

Although the Court correctly observes that state courts, "as much as federal courts, have a solemn obligation to follow federal law," state judges, unlike federal judges, tend to be elected and hence to be more conscious of the prevailing views of the majority. Water rights adjudications, which will have a crucial impact on future economic development in the West, are likely to stimulate great public interest and concern.

pletely from their ordinary meaning. One of the Arizona proceedings, in which process has been served on approximately 58,000 known water claimants, illustrates the practical consequences of giving the state courts the initial responsibility for the adjudication of Indian water rights claims. Because this Court may not exercise appellate jurisdiction in state-court litigation until after a final judgment has been entered by the highest court of the State, no federal tribunal will be able to review any federal question in the case until the entire litigation has been concluded. The Court promises that "any state-court decision alleged to abridge Indian water rights protected by federal law can expect to receive, if brought for review before this Court, a particularized and exacting scrutiny commensurate with the powerful federal interest in safeguarding those rights from state encroachment." If a state court errs in interpreting the *Winters* doctrine or an Indian treaty, and this Court ultimately finds it necessary to correct that error, the entire comprehensive state-court water rights decree may require massive readjustment. If, however, the quantification of Indian rights were to be adjudicated in a separate federal proceeding — which presumably would be concluded long before the mammoth, conglomerate state adjudication comes to an end — the state judgment would rest on a solid foundation that this Court should never need to examine.

The Court acknowledges the logical force of these propositions, but sets them aside because the exercise of concurrent federal-court jurisdiction would create "the possibility of duplicative litigation, tension and controversy between the federal and state forums, hurried and pressured decisionmaking, and confusion over the disposition of property rights." These possibilities arise, as the Court candidly admits, from a pessimistic assessment of the likelihood that state courts, state legislatures, and state parties will assume a "cooperative attitude." In other words, the state courts might engage in an unseemly rush to judgment in order to give the Indians less water than they fear that the federal courts might provide. If state courts cannot be expected to adhere to orderly processes of decisionmaking because of their hostility to the Indians, the statutory right accorded to Indian tribes to litigate in a federal tribunal is even more important.

In my view, a federal court whose jurisdiction is invoked in a timely manner by an Indian tribe has a duty to determine the existence and extent of the tribe's reserved water rights under federal law. It is inappropriate to stay or dismiss such federal-court proceedings in order to allow determinations by state courts. In the cases before us today, complaints were timely filed in federal court by the Indian Tribes, before or shortly after the institution of state water adjudication proceedings; the state proceedings in Arizona and Montana remain at an early stage. The District Court should therefore grant the Tribes leave to amend the various complaints, where necessary, to seek adjudication of the scope and quantity of Indian reserved water rights and to eliminate other claims; the suits should then proceed in federal court....

NOTES

1. State Adjudication of Indian Water Rights: When state courts adjudicate Indian water rights under the McCarran Amendment and *Colorado River Water Conservation District* and *San Carlos Apache*, whose law governs issues regarding the priority, quantity, and use of Indian water rights? What problems, if any, does this system of adjudication pose? The Court stated in *Colorado River Water Conserv. Dist.*, 424 U.S. 800, 812-13 (1976), and in *United States v. District Court for Eagle County*, 401 U.S. 520, 525-26 (1971), that it stands ready to correct abuses in reserved water rights cases that are adjudicated

in state courts by exercising its certiorari jurisdiction. The efficacy of this solution may be doubted, however, particularly when the quantification of reserved
water rights is predicated on complex factual determinations. See *Wilson v.
Omaha Indian Tribe,* 442 U.S. 653, 673-74 (1979). F. COHEN, HANDBOOK OF
FEDERAL INDIAN LAW at 601-02 n.14 (1982 ed.). Thus, state court adjudication
of *Winters* rights, without a significant possibility of Supreme Court review,
presents non-Indian private appropriators and both local and state governments in water-scarce areas with the opportunity to have judges who may be
more responsive to local political pressures adjudicate such claims. *See* extract
of letter from Anthony Rogers to Senator Edward M. Kennedy (June 23, 1976),
reproduced in Nelson, *The* Winters *Doctrine: Seventy Years of Application of
"Reserved" Water Rights to Indian Reservations,* Arid Lands Resource Information Paper No. 9, n. 158 (University of Arizona 1977).

Where states use administrative, rather than judicial, processes to resolve
rights claims, at least one court surprisingly held that *Colorado River Water
Conservation District* and *San Carlos Apache* still apply to relegate the United
States and the tribes to state administrative tribunals, even where the adjudication sought an alteration of a prior *federal* court water decree. *United States v.
Walker River Irrig. Dist.,* 15 Indian L. Rep. 3083 (D. Nev. No. C-125-ECR,
decided May 17, 1988).

The *San Carlos Apache* case did not resolve the *state* law questions raised by
the disclaimers of jurisdictions. When the United States and tribes, however,
have suggested that under state law the constitutional disclaimers precluded
adjudication of Indian water rights, state courts generally rejected the suggestion. *United States v. Superior Court of Maricopa County,* 144 Ariz. 265, 697
P.2d 658 (1985); *State ex rel. Greely v. Confederated Salish & Kootenai Tribes of
the Flathead Reservation,* 218 Mont. 76, 712 P.2d 754 (1985). *See also Wyoming v.
Owl Creek Irrig. Dist. (In re General Adjudication of All Rights to Use Water in
the Big Horn River Sys.),* 750 P.2d 681, 753 P.2d 76 (Wyo. 1988), *aff'd by equally
divided vote sub nom. Wyoming v. United States,* 109 S. Ct. 863 (1989).

The United States and Indian tribes have long opposed state adjudication of
Indian *Winters* rights because of concerns that state tribunals and administrative agencies might not be fair, deliberative forums for the adjudication of such
claims. The *San Carlos Apache* and *Colorado River Water Conservation District*
cases suggest that the Supreme Court stands ready to correct any legal errors in
the application of federal water law. Is that protection sufficient? Can it protect
against or correct biased or erroneous findings of fact? The assumption that
state tribunals will provide less neutral adjudication obviously is not shared by
the Court. On what premises can such an assumption be justified? Does it make
any difference that state judges are elected or appointed, often with far less
judicial independence that federal judges are assured under article III, section
1 of the United States Constitution? Should the fact that state administrative
agencies often have little job security affect the adequacy of the forum? On the
other hand, in some cases the worst fears of tribal water advocates have not
always been realized in state court. For example, in *In re General Adjudication
of All Rights to Water in the Gila River Sys. & Source,* 15 Indian L. Rep. 5099
(Ariz. Super. Ct., Maricopa County, Nos. W-1, W-2, W-3, and W-4, decided
Sept. 9, 1988), the state court accepted most of the Indian positions. It held that
Indian *Winters* rights applied to both surface and groundwater sources and
rejected the efforts by adverse claimants to exclude their groundwater wells
from the stream adjudication.

While state courts may have jurisdiction to adjudicate and quantify Indian water rights, the special jurisdictional status of Indian country and the sovereign immunity of Indian tribes continue to pose significant barriers for states and others seeking information on water usage or seeking to monitor and enforce water law decrees. *See, e.g., Joint Bd. of Control of the Flathead, Mission & Jocko Irrig. Dists. v. Bureau of Indian Affairs,* 16 Indian L. Rep. 3001 (D. Mont. No. CV 87-217-BLG-JFB, decided Sept. 9, 1988) (information on water resources on the Flathead Indian Reservation exempt from disclosure under Freedom of Information Act).

2. Authority to Regulate Water Use in Indian Country: In Pelcyger, *Indian Water Rights: Some Emerging Frontiers,* 21 ROCKY MT. MIN. L. INST. 743, 769-70 (1976),* the author argued that:

> The tribe may have jurisdiction to regulate non-Indians' water uses even though some of the non-Indians' substantive rights may be governed by state law. A non-Indian's right to obtain water for land located within a reservation may be governed by substantive considerations found in state law, such as whether a surplus is found to exist, but the decision on whether or not those substantive considerations are met, that is whether there is, in fact, a surplus, may properly reside with the tribe to the exclusion of the state.

Recall that in *Oliphant v. Suquamish Indian Tribe,* set forth and discussed in Chapter 3, section A, the Supreme Court held that Indian tribal courts do not have inherent criminal jurisdiction to try and to punish non-Indians. Also recall that in *Merrion v. Jicarilla Apache Tribe,* also set forth in Chapter 3, section D5, the Court held that Indian tribes could tax non-Indian economic enterprises in Indian country, but that in *Confederated Tribes of the Colville Reservation v. Washington,* set forth in Chapter 4, section A2, the Court held that absent "clear manifestation" of congressional intent to preempt state regulation, or a showing that state regulation presented an obstacle to achieving federal policy, a state was not precluded from taxing non-Indian purchases of Indian commerce in Indian country. Considering these cases as well as *Colorado River* and *San Carlos* decisions, how much vitality is left of Pelcyger's argument? Does the *Brendale* decision rejecting tribal authority to zone non-Indian land on "open" portions of a reservation undermine the Pelcyger argument? *See Brendale v. Confederated Tribes and Bands of the Yakima Indian Nation,* set forth in Chapter 3, section D5. Might your analysis of these problems depend in part on the legal source and theory of non-Indian water rights in Indian country? In that connection, consider the materials that follow on rights derived from Indian allotments. Even prior to *Brendale,* the Ninth Circuit had rejected the Yakima Nation Water Code as invalid insofar as it purported to control use by non-Indians of excess waters on or passing through the Yakima Indian Reservation. *Holly v. Confederated Tribes & Bands of the Yakima Indian Nation,* 655 F. Supp. 557 (E.D. Wash. 1986), *aff'd sub nom. Holly v. Torus,* 812 F.2d 714 (9th Cir.), *cert. denied,* 484 U.S. 823 (1987). *See also United States v. Anderson,* 736 F.2d 1358 (9th Cir. 1984) (tribes cannot use criminal or quasi-criminal sanctions to regulate non-Indian use of excess water within their reservations).

---

*Pelcyger, Indian Water Rights: Some Emerging Frontiers, 21 Annual Rocky Mountain Mineral Law Institute 743 (1976), copyright 1976 by Matthew Bender and Co., Inc.

COLLINS, INDIAN ALLOTMENT WATER RIGHTS, 20 Land and Water Law Review 421 (1985)*

[Where one finds valuable Indian allotments and water], legal disputes have arisen over the federal water rights appurtenant to allotments. Although Congress has primary authority over the subject, it has provided only general legislative standards. The courts have been required to make most of the governing rules. They have recognized federal water rights appurtenant to Indian allotments, and at least some federal water rights have survived transfer of the allotments to non-Indian successors. Several questions remain unsettled.

Some of the uncertainty is part of the broader question of the general scope of federal Indian reservation water rights. Allotment water rights mostly derive from tribal rights, and allotment rights compete with the water rights that tribes retain. One issue is the proper measure of tribal water rights for irrigated agriculture, stock watering, domestic use, fisheries, and power generation. Another is whether tribes have federal water rights for other purposes, such as mining, manufacturing, or recreation.

Other allotment water rights questions arise from transfers, trust removal, and subjection to state law. There have been disputes over how much of a tribe's federal water right passed to allotment owners when allotments were made, and over how much of an allottee's water right survives termination of the federal trust over the allotment and transfer to non-Indians. The last question can also be posed as one of federalism because state law applies to most former allotments, and undeveloped allotment water rights conflict with state water law.

Unlike most other questions about Indian water rights, the unsettled allotment issues do not place Indians squarely at odds with non-Indians. Rather, current owners of allotments and former allotments are arrayed against competing users of scarce water supplies. Tribes, Indians, and non-Indians can appear on either side in a particular case....

The Effect of Tribal Land Transfers on Reservation Water Rights

The *Winters* Court's reasons to imply a reservation water right extend to any Indian reservation with recognized title that is dry enough to show need. The Supreme Court in *Arizona v. California* held that reservations set aside by unilateral action of Congress or the Executive have the same implied water right. At one time the extent of tribal lands was very great, but most of this land has long since passed out of tribal ownership. The greater part was ceded to the United States, much was allotted in trust to individual members of tribes, and the rest has been retained in tribal trust.

Winters water rights did not survive outright cessions to the United States. Most of the lands acquired from tribes were opened to disposition under the public land laws. Public lands statutes required grantees of the United States to obtain new water rights under state law.[42] These laws necessarily had the effect

---

*Copyright © Land and Water Review and Richard B. Collins. Reprinted with permission of the copyright holders.

[42]See California Oregon Power Co. v. Beaver Portland Cement Co., 295 U.S. 142, 162 (1935); United States v. Anderson, 736 F.2d at 1362-63. This rule has been followed even when government diversion works were conveyed with the patent. Nevada Ditch Co. v. Bennett, 30 Or. 59

of extinguishing federal reservation water rights when tribal ownership was unconditionally ceded to the United States.

In a few instances, lands acquired by the United States from Indian tribes were directly transferred to different federal reservations, such as national forests. In *United States v. Adair*, the government claimed that land transferred from an Indian reservation to a national forest and a wildlife refuge retained its reservation water right for purposes common to the Indian and successor reservations with a continuous priority dating from the founding of the Indian reservation.[43] The Ninth Circuit rejected that claim, but a similar claim was sustained in *United States v. City and County of Denver*.[45] The Colorado Supreme Court held that land transferred from national forest to national park use had a continuous water right for purposes common to the two reservations dating from the founding of the forest reserve. These cases may be distinguishable because the circumstances in *City and County of Denver* showed a continuous reservation purpose more clearly than did the circumstances in Adair. In any case, the amount of water needed for national forest purposes is small and the use is not consumptive, so the issue is a minor one.[46]

The Supreme Court has held that allottees of tribal land acquired the right to use a portion of their reservations' water right.[47] But the nature and extent of the right acquired by allottees has not been established, and a number of cases have raised questions about how the end of the federal trust affects allottees' federal water rights. These issues are reviewed in the remainder of this article.

The Allotment System

Allotment was a major federal policy to compel assimilation of tribal Indians. Beginning in 1854, most federal treaties recognizing tribal reservations gave individual Indians the right to obtain exclusive use of parcels of reservation land for agricultural self-support.[48] These treaty clauses were nominally consensual, but their prevalence and uniformity of wording strongly imply that they were essentially imposed on tribes. After 1871, allotment clauses continued to appear in agreements ratified by federal statute.[49] In 1887, Congress aban-

---

102-05, 45 P. 472, 484-85 (1896). See also Story v. Woolverton, 31 Mont. 346, 78 P. 589 (1904) (military reservation).

This rule does not apply to tribal cessions in trust conditioned on future sales. If these lands are later restored to tribes, the original *Winters* right remains. Big Horn Master's Report, *supra* note 31, at 35-44, 270; Big Horn Adjudication, *supra* note 31, No. 4993, slip op. at 23 (Wyo. Dist. Ct. May 10, 1983).

Parcels within Indian irrigation projects may also be an exception to this rule.

[43]723 F.2d 1394, 1417-19 (9th Cir. 1983), *cert. denied*, 104 S. Ct. 3536 (1984).

[45]656 P.2d 1, 30-31 (Colo. 1983).

[46]See United States v. New Mexico, 438 U.S. 696 (1978); United States v. City and County of Denver, 656 P.2d 1, 20-34 (Colo. 1983).

[47]United States v. Powers, 305 U.S. 527 (1939).

[48]See Felix S. Cohen, [Handbook of Federal Indian Law (1982 ed.)] at 613 [hereinafter Felix S. Cohen]. There were fifty-seven such treaties from 1854 until treaty-making ended in 1871. See 11 Cong. Rec. 1060 (1881) (listing all treaties providing for allotment).

All these treaty clauses entitled a tribal family to acquire exclusive use of a parcel of tribal land for agricultural purposes and authorized the President to protect improvements and allow some kind of succession on death. Some clauses expressly allowed patents to issue if the land was actually cultivated. *See, e.g.*, Treaty with the Eastern Band Shoshonees and Bannack, July 3, 1868, art. 6, 15 Stat. 673, 675; Treaty with the Oto and Missouri, Mar. 15, 1854, art. 6, 10 Stat. 1038, 1039.

[49]In 1871, Congress formally ended the making of treaties with Indian tribes. Act of Mar. 3, 1871, ch. 120, § 1, 16 Stat. 544, 566 (codified at 25 U.S.C. § 71 (1982)). The House of Representa-

doned the veneer of consent and passed the General Allotment Act authorizing the President to require that reservations be allotted.[50] Separate agreements and statutes for particular reservations carried out the General Allotment Act's mandate. Under one or more of these acts, most reservations were at least partially allotted.

Recognition of Allotment Water Rights

[The allotment] trust patents made no mention of water rights. Yet it is clear that Congress expected allottees in dry areas to have some right to irrigation water. Section 7 of the General Allotment Act states:

> In cases where the use of water for irrigation is necessary to render the lands within any Indian reservation available for agricultural purposes, the Secretary of the Interior is authorized to prescribe such rules and regulations as he may deem necessary to secure a just and equal distribution thereof among the Indians residing upon any such reservations; and no other appropriation or grant of water by any riparian proprietor shall be authorized or permitted to the damage of any other riparian proprietor.[63]

Section 7 is based on the concept that each allottee should have the use of the allotment's fair share of whatever irrigation water the reservation has, and it empowers the Secretary to assure allottees of their water shares.[64] But the Secretary's regulatory power has largely gone unexercised. We have no comprehensive administrative interpretation. Nor does section 7 tell us the source or extent of allottees' water rights.

Some of the special allotment acts for particular reservations adverted to irrigation.[66] These also show Congress' understanding that Indian allottees would have water for irrigation, but the statutes again do not make clear the source or extent of allotment water rights.

Several statutes authorized the Secretary to acquire developed irrigation water supplies for reservation Indians as consideration for granting irrigation companies water access and ditch easements on Indian trust lands.[67] Most of these laws said nothing about the nature of the water rights acquired by the Indians or those of the companies.

---

tives sought the statute because the House members objected to the Senate's exclusive role in treaty ratification. The government nevertheless continued to make formal agreements with Indian tribes that were ratified by statute. Felix S. Cohen, *supra* note 48, at 107, 127. For decades after 1871, these agreements were commonly called "treaties," even by Congress and the courts. See, e.g., *Winters*, 143 F. at 743 ("the treaty of May 1, 1888").

[50] Act of Feb. 8, 1887, ch. 119, 24 Stat. 388 (codified as amended in scattered sections of 25 U.S.C. §§ 331-381 (1982)). Similar bills had been debated since 1879. All those seriously considered had included a requirement of tribal consent, until it was removed during the final debate in the House. See 18 CONG. REC. 225 (1886); Felix S. Cohen, *supra* note 48, at 130-32.

[63] Ch. 119, § 7, 24 Stat. 390 (codified at 25 U.S.C. § 381 (1982)).

[64] See United States v. Powers, 16 F. Supp. 155, 159-60 (D. Mont. 1936), *aff'd in part, rev'd in part*, 94 F.2d 783 (9th Cir. 1938), aff'd, 305 U.S. 527 (1939). Section 7 was added to an allotment bill in 1884 in the same form as later enacted. The Senate Indian Affairs Committee drafted it. See 15 Cong. Rec. 2241 (1884). No committee report then or later explained it. It may have been added in response to a senator's objection during an earlier debate. See 11 Cong. Rec. 785 (1881) (statement of Sen. Morgan).

The reference to "riparian proprietor" may reflect the drafters' assumption that only riparian allotments would have water rights based on the common law of water rights in the eastern states. See Anderson v. Spear-Morgan Livestock Co., 107 Mont. 18, 27, 79 P.2d 667, 669 (1938) (dictum). Other courts have ignored this part of the statute.

[66] E.g., Act of May 30, 1908, ch. 237, 35 Stat. 558 (Ft. Peck Res.).

[67] E.g., Act of Feb. 15, 1897, ch. 228, § 8, 29 Stat. 527 (Gila River Res.); Act of July 23, 1894, ch. 152, § 2, 28 Stat. 118 (Yakima Res.).

Congress has regularly provided tribal and federal funds for construction and maintenance of water supply and irrigation works on Indian reservations. These appropriations statutes also lack any general definition of Indian water rights.

In the 1939 case of *United States v. Powers*, the Supreme Court reviewed what Congress and the Department of the Interior had done and held that allotments have an appurtenant right to the use of a share of the federal reservation water right.[70] But the case did not require the Court to specify the nature or extent of allottees' rights, and the Court did not volunteer a clear definition.[71]

An allottee's right to use a share of tribal water should be measured by the same criteria used to measure the tribe's reservation right. Each allotment's share should be determined by reasonable water needs for allotment purposes. Irrigation uses are limited to the water needed to irrigate the allotment's practicably irrigable acreage.

Retained tribal rights for other purposes could pose problems. If a tribe retains a reservation right to maintain a fishery or power site or to operate a mine, it may be difficult to apportion the available water between tribal and allotment rights. Tribes have legislative authority over their members in Indian country and have some authority over non-Indians. But allotment water rights are federal property interests protected against tribal as well as state infringement. Tribal authority to allocate water between allotted and tribal land has not been tested.

Trust Transfers of Allotments

Few trust allotments are now owned by original allottees. By the time the first allottees died or sold, most allotments remained undeveloped. It has consistently been assumed that trust transfers — mostly by intestate succession — implicitly include the allotment's water right. That is, the allotment heir has the same right as the original allottee to put to use a share of the reservation water right. This assumption seems plainly correct. The purposes of the federal allotment laws are the same for an Indian heir as for the ancestor. Also, the rule of most water law systems is that appurtenant water rights are implicitly transferred with the land unless the written conveyance or the circumstances show a contrary intent. There is nothing about trust transfer of allotments to justify a departure from this rule.

Some Indians acquired trust allotments from public lands rather than tribal common lands. Other allotments were acquired by purchase. When these allotments were set aside in trust, the reservation water right theory may have applied to reserve unappropriated water sufficient for allottees' reasonable

---

[70] 305 U.S. 527 (1939). See also United States v. Pierce, 235 F.2d 885, 891 n.6 (9th Cir. 1956).
[71] See *infra* text accompanying notes 132-47.

The federal water right acquired by allottees could have been limited to water actually put to use before allotment, but this would make little sense. Most allotments were undeveloped when made and there was no system for allottees to acquire new water rights. Hence, the allotment right was at least an inchoate right to put to use a share of the tribal reservation right, as the courts have held or assumed....

needs (including any water already in use on the allotment).[81] Neither public domain nor purchased allotments have yet appeared in reported water rights cases. If a reserved right is recognized, it would be subject to the rules applicable to allotments made out of tribal lands.

Water Rights of Leased Allotments

Federal statutes allow trust allotments to be leased for agricultural, mining, or other purposes. Mining leases may last until the minerals are commercially exhausted, and other leases may be made for long periods. The leasing laws do not refer to water rights, nor do any other statutes expressly authorize water rights to be leased with the land. But some allotment lease statutes expressly apply only to "irrigable land," implying that an appurtenant water right may be leased with the land. Another federal statute allows allotments within certain irrigation projects to be leased with water rights.[86] More importantly, in 1921 the Ninth Circuit held that a general agricultural lessee of a trust allotment may use the reservation water right appurtenant to it.[87] There are no other reported cases, but the decision seems to have been followed by the Interior Department and lease parties, even for mining leases.[88] The current statute governing most allotment surface leases expressly allows leases for the purpose of developing the land's "natural resources."[89] The lease term probably includes water rights.[90]

No federal statute allows allotment water rights to be leased for use on land other than the allotments to which the rights are appurtenant. Water is not considered a mineral for purposes of federal mineral leasing laws, so water rights cannot be severed from the land by leasing.

Water Rights of Former Allotments

As shown above, owners of trust allotments made out of tribal lands implicitly acquired shares of the tribe's federal reservation water right. These shares pass

---

[81] The general rule on federal conveyances of public lands is stated in California Oregon Power Co. v. Beaver Portland Cement Co., 295 U.S. 142 (1935). But federal policy always protected the Indians' possessory rights, a rule applied to individual Indians as well as tribes. See Cramer v. United States, 261 U.S. 219 (1923). Applied to water rights, this policy probably protects actual uses of water being made by Indians at the time a public domain allotment was patented.

[86] 25 U.S.C. § 390(1982) (San Carlos, Ft. Hall, Flathead, and Duck Valley Res.). See 25 C.F.R. § 162.13 (1984).

[87] Skeem v. United States, 273 F. 93 (9th Cir. 1921). The land had been leased under what is now 25 U.S.C. § 403 (1982).

[88] See United States v. Anderson, No. 3643, slip op. at 17-19 (E.D. Wash. Aug. 23, 1982), aff'd, 736 F.2d 1358 (9th Cir. 1984); Op. Solic. Dep't of Interior (Feb. 1, 1964), reprinted in 2 Opinions of the Solicitor of the Dep't of the Interior Relating to Indian Affairs 1930 (Gov't Printing Office 1978) (approving lease of reservation land with its irrigation water right for a resort development and housing); Mining Lease between Sentry Royalty Co. and the Navajo Tribe (June 6, 1966) (contract no. 14-20-0603-9910) (coal lease with right to pump groundwater for coal slurry pipeline). Use of the federal water right for nonagricultural purposes could be based on either recognition of such purposes or on transfer of an irrigation-defined right to a different use.

[89] 25 U.S.C. §§ 415-415d (1982).

[90] See S. Rep. No. 375, 84th Cong., 1st Sess. 3-4 (1955). The history does not specifically state that water rights were assumed to be included in the term "natural resources." But it refers to leases for irrigated agriculture and to farming leases calling for investment by the lessee, suggesting the assumption.

to trust transferees of original allottees, and the shares may be used by lessees of allotments. In these situations, allotments are continuously held in federal trust and remain federal Indian country. In all relevant respects, the property is subject only to federal law.

When allotments go out of federal trust, the protections and immunities of the federal allotment laws are removed. The land becomes subject to state or tribal law.[93] State and tribal law must recognize vested federal property rights, but neither the statutes governing removal of the federal trust nor the fee patents issued under those statutes explicitly refer to allotment water rights. The effects of trust removal and subjection to state law are left to the courts.

The courts have had difficulty deciding the effects of trust removal on federal water rights of former allotments and have had problems accommodating state law to federal rights. Some courts have held that no federal water rights survived removal of the federal trust, while others have held that non-Indian successors have federal rights similar to those of Indian allottees. Often cases have arisen many years after allotments went out of trust and were transferred to non-Indians. The courts have probably been influenced by the transferees' apparent reliance interests that have accrued during these years of delay.

Some courts have had difficulty because they have failed to recognize two important distinctions between classes of former allotments. First, former allotments within Indian irrigation or federal reclamation projects have a different history than other allotments. The nature of these projects and the statutes that govern them minimize problems of determining allotment water rights and of accommodating those rights to state water law.

The second distinction is between federal water rights that are developed and those that are undeveloped when non-project allotments go out of trust and are subjected to state law. Whatever part of their federal reservation water rights allottees put to use ought to be vested federal property rights that survive removal of the trust. This rule can be easily accommodated to western state water law because state water rights are based on developed uses of water.

When water rights of non-project allotments are undeveloped at the time they pass out of trust, arguments to limit or extinguish the rights are stronger. Undeveloped federal water rights conflict with state laws that limit water rights to amounts in beneficial use and that provide for forfeiture of water rights that are unused for extended periods. Policies of the federal allotment laws offer arguments against continuing protection of unused allotment water rights. It is not surprising that the courts have reached inconsistent results in adjudicating undeveloped water rights of former allotments.

---

[93] Outside Indian country, the federal trust title is the only general source of federal preemption. Its removal subjects the land and events on it to ordinary state jurisdiction. See 25 U.S.C. § 349 (1982); Felix S. Cohen, *supra* note 48, at 349-52, 380, 410-11. Within Indian country, removal of the federal trust title leaves the land subject to the general federal preemption protecting tribal self-government. On most matters, Indians and their property are subject to tribal rather than state jurisdiction. Tribal jurisdiction over allotments is then unfettered by the federal trust title. Non-Indians and their property in Indian country are subject to state jurisdiction when Indians are unaffected. Otherwise, they are subject to limited tribal jurisdiction. Mescalero Apache Tribe v. New Mexico, 103 S. Ct. 2378 (1983); See Felix S. Cohen, *supra* note 48, at 348-49.

Water Rights of Former Allotments Within Irrigation Projects

When the federal government bought land from Indian tribes, much of the money was kept in trust accounts in the Treasury subject to Congress' control. Congress "appropriated" these trust funds for various purposes it deemed beneficial to tribal owners, including development of reservation water supplies. Congress also appropriated federal funds for Indian reservation irrigation projects. Some were made reimbursable by tribes, others were gratuitous.

Most Indian irrigation projects were built to serve allotments.[95] Eventually Congress and the Bureau of Indian Affairs realized that it was inequitable to use tribal funds to build and maintain projects that benefited only some members, so Congress began to require reimbursement from the landowners served. Some allottees' capital reimbursement obligations were deferred until the end of the trust. Others were payable during the trust.

Before 1900, Indian reservation irrigation projects were managed locally by reservation superintendents. In that year, Congress provided for two Indian Service superintendents of irrigation. The central office grew into a separate irrigation division in the Bureau of Indian Affairs that became known as the Indian Irrigation Service. But the Indian irrigation bureaucracy was overshadowed by the powerful Reclamation Service of the Department of the Interior. Some Reclamation Service projects included Indian trust lands, and some Indian irrigation projects were built by the Reclamation Service and then turned over to the Indian Irrigation Service. As a result, Reclamation Act procedures became entangled with Indian irrigation project management.

Under the Reclamation Act, projects were built with federal funds to serve lands in project areas. Lands previously in private ownership were served, but much project land was public domain reserved under the Reclamation Act for project purposes. Reclamation projects acquired water rights in conformity with state or territorial law by purchase, exchange, or condemnation, or by new appropriations. Farms to be irrigated were sold to entrymen with project water rights, and buyers had to reimburse the federal government for the capital costs of construction and water rights acquisition. This scheme was applied to lands for which irrigation was only planned, as well as for lands already irrigated when sold. Reimbursement was to begin only after water was actually delivered. Payment was spread over many years, and the land was subject to a lien until final payment was made.

After 1902, parts of this scheme were imitated in Indian irrigation projects. Under the General Allotment Act, all tribal members were to be given allotments, and any remaining land could then be declared "surplus" and sold to the United States or opened to entry on the tribe's account. When "surplus" lands were within Indian irrigation projects, they were sold to entrymen with express project water rights as under the Reclamation Act.[102] When allotments within

---

[95] The exceptions were in the Southwest, where some tribes had established agricultural systems that were allowed to continue.

[102] See Act of May 30, 1908, ch. 237, § 2, 35 Stat. 558 (Ft. Peck Res.); Act of May 9, 1908, ch. 216, § 15, 35 Stat. 444, 448 (Flathead Res.); Act of Dec. 21, 1904, ch. 22, § 5, 33 Stat. 595, 598 (Yakima Res.); Act of Apr. 21, 1904, ch. 1402, §§ 25-26, 33 Stat. 189, 224 (Yuma, Colorado River & Pyramid Lake Res.). The latter Act expressly refers to the Reclamation Act, and the Fort Peck Act expressly

irrigation projects went out of trust and were sold under federal control, the United States advertised and sold them with explicit project water rights in the same manner.[103]

For these reasons, owners of former Indian allotments within irrigation or reclamation projects own project water rights. Rights were expressly conveyed to them, and they paid for them, albeit aided by the generous subsidies of these projects.

Prior to 1902, many managers of Indian reservation water projects appropriated water without complying with state or territorial law. But there was doubt about what was required, and there were instances when reservation superintendents at least filed notices of appropriation under state law. After 1902, the Reclamation Act had an influence. Four statutes required specific Indian irrigation projects to appropriate water under state laws.[106] The Indian Service decided that some other projects should make state filings for water rights already in use.[107] Then the first court decisions recognizing implied federal reservation water rights were handed down. Congress did not again require that Indian projects appropriate under state law, and state law filings for Indian irrigation projects became irregular.

Later, a few courts expressly recognized federal reservation rights of Indian trust lands in both Reclamation Service and Indian Service projects.[109] Other irrigation projects have probably relied on federal reservation water rights at least in part. The projects have seldom generated controversies that require decisions about reservation rights. All lands irrigated by a project are treated equally. Costs are allocated on a per-acre basis throughout the project, and water shortages are suffered ratably among project lands. And when projects actually irrigate Indian trust land or former allotments, few care whether the

refers to state law. The Yakima Act is discussed in Status Unit of the Wapato Irrigation Project, 53 Interior Dec. 622 (1932).

[103]See United States v. Heinrich, 12 F.2d 938, 940 (D. Mont. 1926), aff'd on other grounds, 16 F.2d 112 (9th Cir. 1926) (United States advertised project allotment for sale with "a perpetual water right"); Act of May 26, 1926, ch. 403, § 8, 44 Stat. 658, 660 (Crow Res.); Act of Mar. 3, 1921, ch. 135, § 6, 41 Stat. 1355, 1357 (Ft. Belknap Res.); Act of May 18, 1916, ch. 125, 39 Stat. 123, 140-42, 153-54 (Flathead, Ft. Peck, Blackfeet, Colville & Yakima Res.), construed in Patents in Fee, 45 Interior Dec. 600 (1917); Wind River Reservation — Repayment of Irrigation Construction Costs, 52 Interior Dec. 709 (1929); Cf., Scholder v. United States, 428 F.2d 1123, 1127-29 (9th Cir.), cert. denied, 400 U.S. 942 (1970).

[106]Act of May 30, 1908, ch. 237, § 2, 35 Stat. 558, 560 (Ft. Peck Res.); Act of Mar. 1, 1907, ch. 2285, 34 Stat. 1015, 1035 (Blackfeet Res.); Act of June 21, 1906, ch. 3504, 34 Stat. 375 (Uintah Res.); Act of Mar. 3, 1905, ch. 1452, art. III, 33 Stat. 1016, 1017, 1020 (Wind River Res.).

The Fort Peck and Blackfeet laws include provisions that would modify state water law in specific ways. In 1914, the Secretary reported to Congress on complications arising from the administration of these laws. See H.R. Doc. Nos. 1250, 1274, 63d Cong., 3d Sess. 1914) (Uintah and Wind River Res.). In the case of the Wind River Reservation, Wyoming's Congressman Mondell made great efforts to get the Indian Service to make state law filings. See 51 Cong. Rec. 3661, 3673 (1914) (Rep. Mondell).

[107]Irrigation projects have been built on the Crow Reservation in Montana since 1885. In April 1905, the Indian Service directed the reservation superintendent to file notices of appropriation under state law for water previously in use. Record at 497, United States v. Powers, 305 U.S. 527 (1939).

[109]See Nevada v. United States, 103 S. Ct. 2906 (1983) (reviewing 1944 decree according reservation priority date to reclamation project water right of Pyramid Lake Res.); United States v. Ahtanum Irr. Dist., 236 F.2d 321 (9th Cir. 1956), cert. denied, 352 U.S. 988 (1957); Big Horn Master's Report, supra note 31, at 328-29; Big Horn Adjudication, supra note 31, No. 4993, slip op. at 66-67 (Wyo. Dist. Ct. May 10, 1983).

original water rights were federal or state, or whether the rights have reservation priority dates or project priority dates.

Project allotment water rights that are federal in origin have survived trust removal and subjection to state law. This has occurred whether the project water rights were already developed or merely planned at the trust's end. In some cases transfers were authorized by explicit statutes. When the land was undeveloped, both the water right and the debt for reimbursement were deferred until water was actually delivered. The water right was not perfected until the debt was paid.

This explicit system was patterned after the Reclamation Act and is largely separate from the allotment laws governing non-project allotments. Therefore, the history of project allotments has little relevance to the question of disposition of federal water rights when non-project allotments go out of trust.

Effects of Trust Removal on Water Rights Developed by Allottees

Federal reservation water rights that Indian allottees put to use during the federal trust should be recognized as vested property rights that survive trust removal, subjection to state law, and conveyance to non-Indians. This protects allottees' investments in the land, and both buyers and sellers would reasonably expect this value to be transferred. In all states, developed water rights normally pass with land transfers, and removal of the federal trust should not counter this assumption. No substantial conflict with state law results because water put to use with a known priority date fits nicely into the prior appropriation system of the western states.

Not to allow developed water rights to survive trust removal would be contrary to the federal trust purpose of encouraging allottees to become self-sufficient farmers. Allottees wishing to develop their land using reservation water rights would be deterred from doing so if they would later be unable to enjoy or transfer the full value of developed water facilities. More fundamentally, failure to allow developed rights to survive removal of the trust and subjection to state law might be an unconstitutional taking.[113]

The Wyoming state courts have held that no federal reservation water rights survive the end of the federal trust and conveyance to non-Indians.[114] The

---

[113] Indian trust allotment ownership is protected by the fifth amendment. Choate v. Trapp, 224, U.S. 665 (1912). Whether denying the right to transfer a developed right would constitute a taking seems a close question. The courts have sustained broad congressional power over Indian trust property. E.g., Delaware Tribal Bus. Comm. v. Weeks, 430 U.S. 73 (1977). On the other hand, allottees were strongly encouraged by government agents to develop their land to fulfill the purpose of the allotment statutes. To strip the value of an allottee's investment at the trust's end would, at least in some situations, make a strong case for a taking.

[114] Merrill v. Bishop, 74 Wyo. 298, 287 P.2d 620 (1955); Big Horn Master's Report, *supra* note 31, at 44-55. Supplemental and Final Report of the Special Master, In re The General Adjudication of All Rights to Use Water in the Big Horn River System and All Other Sources, State of Wyoming, No. 4993, at 1-6 (Wyo. Dist. Ct. Jun. 1, 1984) [hereinafter cited as Supplemental Big Horn Master's Report]. The *Merrill* decision was arguably dictum on this point, but it was treated as a holding in the *Big Horn Adjudication*.

The *Big Horn* court also said that the state law priority date for former trust lands is the date of a state permit or the date the land went out of Indian ownership, whichever is earlier. Big Horn Adjudication, *supra* note 31, No. 4993, slip op. at 24, 63 (Wyo. Dist. Ct. May 10, 1983); *Id.*, No. 101-234, slip op. at 4-5, 15-16 (Wyo. Dist. Ct. Jun. 8, 1984). The latter standard is hard to understand. Possibly the court meant to refer to the project priority date for some of the land involved in the case. See *supra* text accompanying notes 100-10.

courts did not distinguish between water rights developed during the trust and those not yet developed at the trust's end, although it appears that some developed rights were in fact involved. To that extent, these cases were wrongly decided.

Only one court has distinguished developed water rights of former allotments from undeveloped rights. The United States District Court for the Eastern District of Washington, in *Colville Confederated Tribes v. Walton*, decided that state water law ought to apply fully and immediately after allotments go out of trust and are conveyed to non-Indians.[116] But the court sensed that it would be unfair to declare forfeiture of developed federal water rights based on the allottees' failure to comply with state water law. So the court attempted a compromise. It held that the developed water rights continued after the trust's end and conveyance to non-Indians, but the court took away the water rights' reservation priority date. The court awarded priority based on the dates of the allottees' first use while the land was still in trust. In other words, the court awarded the priority dates that the water rights would have had if state law had applied to the allottees during the trust.

This was an ill-considered solution. It immediately made the former allotments' water rights junior to those of the tribe and of other owners who had the reservation priority date. In cases when the reservation priority date is quite senior on the watershed and the dates of an allottee's actual water use are junior to intervening appropriators, the *Walton* court's ruling could destroy the value of an allottee's investment. By contrast, if an allottee's dates of use are relatively senior on the watershed and much better than a new priority under state law, the court's ruling would allow valuable water rights to outlive the trust and be transferred. This holding could have led to arbitrary results, but it was reversed on appeal and no other court has reached a like decision.

There may have been instances in which allotments went out of trust and were transferred to non-Indians at a time when allottees had begun water diversion works but had not yet actually diverted some or all of the water contemplated. To protect allottees' investments, successors should be allowed to perfect the rights initiated by allottees and should enjoy the reservation priority date.

The state law doctrine of relation back supports this view. All western state water law systems recognize a landowners right to a priority dating from the beginning of a water development project as long as the owner has given public notice of intent to develop. Landowners may transfer unperfected water rights and if their successors finish development with reasonable diligence, the priority of the perfected rights will relate back to the date the prior landowners gave notice.

When Indian allottees begin water development projects, state law does not require public notice of intent to develop because allottees' water rights are governed by federal law. Allottees can also obtain the early reservation priority

---

[116] 460 F. Supp. 1320, 1326-29 (E.D. Wash. 1978), rev'd 647 F.2d 42 (9th Cir. 1981), cert. denied 454 U.S. 1092 (1982). A Wyoming district court and special master relied on the *Walton* district court's decision on this point. Big Horn Master's Report, *supra* note 31, at 44-47, 271, 343; Big Horn Adjudication, *supra* note 31, No. 4993, slip op. at 21-24, 63 (Wyo. Dist. Ct. May 10, 1983); Supplemental Big Horn Master's Report, *supra* note 114, at 2-6.

date. In all other respects, recognition of allottees' rights to remove the trust and convey incompletely developed water rights subject to later perfection would merely put allottees on an equal footing with non-Indians who transfer similarly incomplete projects under state law.

If post-trust owners can perfect allotment water rights by completing developments begun by allottees, the successors must do so with reasonable diligence. They then have the same rights they would have acquired if the allottees had finished their projects during the trust, including reservation priority dates.

If courts recognize developed and partially developed allotment water rights as vested property rights that survive trust removal and transfer to non-Indians, state law must respect the rights when the land comes under state jurisdiction. States can require former allotment owners to file notice and otherwise adhere to state recording and water management laws. The water rights themselves will not present difficulties because the uses that define allotments' federal water rights are beneficial uses in every western state. Water rights based on beneficial use and with known priority dates can simply be integrated into state systems.

Effects of Trust Removal on Undeveloped Allotment Water Rights

Most former allotments were entirely undeveloped when taken out of trust. Consequently, most reported cases on water rights of former allotments have involved claims to federal reservation water rights that were not developed, in any sense described above, during the trust period. That is, during the trust allotment water rights had not been converted to project rights with the project serving the allotments, nor had the allottees developed or begun to develop their reservation water rights.

It is a difficult question whether undeveloped federal water rights ought to continue after allotments pass out of trust and come under state jurisdiction. Unlike developed rights, undeveloped federal water rights do not involve investments by allottees that ought to be protected. Undeveloped reservation rights also substantially conflict with state laws that require beneficial use of water.

Court Decisions Allowing Post-Trust Perfection of Undeveloped Federal Water Rights

The courts have rejected indefinite continuation of undeveloped federal water rights after removal of the federal trust and conveyance to non-Indians. But most decisions have allowed owners of former allotments to perfect as much of the undeveloped federal rights as they put to use with reasonable diligence after the trust ends.[126] As stated above, the Wyoming state courts

---

[126] United States v. Anderson, 736 F.2d 1358, 1362 (9th Cir. 1984); United States v. Adair, 723 F.2d at 1417; Colville Confederated Tribes v. Walton, 647 F.2d 42, 50-51 (9th Cir. 1981), cert. denied, 454 U.S. 1092 (1981); United States v. Powers, 16 F. Supp. 155, 153 (D. Mont. 1936), aff'd in part, rev'd in part, 94 F.2d 783 (9th Cir. 1938), aff'd, 305 U.S. 527 (1939); United States v. Hibner, 27 F.2d 909, 912 (D. Idaho 1928).

Two opinions of the Montana Supreme Court seem to say the successor has the same right as the allottee with no reasonable diligence requirement, but the court was following *Powers* and probably meant no broader right. Lewis v. Hanson, 124 Mont. 492, 496, 227 P.2d 70, 72 (1951) (dictum); Anderson v. Spear-Morgan Livestock Co., 107 Mont. 18, 27, 79 P.2d 667, 669 (1938) (dictum).

have disagreed and have held that all federal rights expire when the trust ends and the land is conveyed to non-Indians.

In *Colville Confederated Tribes v. Walton*, the Ninth Circuit sustained a former allotment owner's right to perfect undeveloped federal water rights with reasonable diligence.[128] The court reasoned that any other result would impair allottees' property rights, which may not be done without clear authority in federal law. This is the classic circular argument of property law. The allottee was able to transfer a property interest because the allottee had a property interest. One could as easily decide that an allottee's right to the undeveloped part of the reservation water right is a mere opportunity to perfect the right while the land remains in trust, an opportunity that serves the trust purpose and expires when the land becomes subject to state law.

Other Indian immunities from state law expire automatically with transfer out of trust. The most notable is immunity from state taxes. While the land is in trust, this immunity has been held to be a property interest of allottees. Yet allottees cannot transfer it. It is not obvious why the undeveloped water right — which can also be characterized as an Indian immunity from state law — should receive different treatment.

The most important precedent on allotment water rights is the Supreme Court's 1939 decision in *United States v. Powers*.[132] *Powers* involved water rights of former allotments, and the decision appears to support a post-trust right to perfect undeveloped federal water rights. But the case has been treated as inconclusive on the issue, even by courts that have sustained post-trust perfection.

Powers arose on the Crow Reservation in Montana. Beginning in 1885, the Interior Department used tribal funds to build irrigation works serving allotments on the reservation. Non-Indian buyers of Crow Reservation allotments outside the Indian irrigation projects diverted water in private ditches built after the government's diversions. In the drought year of 1934, there was not enough water to go around. The United States sued to enjoin upstream, non-Indian diverters, claiming that they had no right to any water on the reservation. The allotment purchasers' principal answer alleged that they had bought undeveloped allotments, then had irrigated them with reasonable diligence. They claimed that this entitled them to a "just and equal share" of the reservation water right.

The United States District Court for the District of Montana denied the government's claim and quieted title in the purchasers on the theory they had pleaded. The Ninth Circuit affirmed dismissal of the government's claim but vacated the district court's decree quieting title in the purchasers because all owners on the stream system were not parties. The Supreme Court affirmed and concluded: "The [United States has] shown no right to the injunction asked. We do not consider the extent or precise nature of respondents' rights in the waters. The present proceeding is not properly framed to that end."

Based on this conclusion, some commentators have argued that *Powers* did not determine whether allotment successors can acquire undeveloped federal

[128] *Walton*, 647 F.2d at 50-51.
[132] 305 U.S. 527 (1939).

water rights.[139] All that the Court decided was that the purchasers in *Powers* had some right to water, enough to defeat the government's attempt to enjoin their diversions. The purchasers' rights might have been based on water rights developed by the allottees during the trust, or they might have been based on state law.

State law may allocate whatever water is available after the reservation water right is satisfied.[140] Non-Indians who homesteaded "surplus" tribal land within reservations have been acquiring state water rights since the 1890s. A 1904 statute applicable only to the Crow Reservation had expressly authorized settlers to use reservation water supplies subject to the Indians' rights.[142] And a number of the *Powers* allotment purchasers — possibly all of them — had filed state law notices of appropriation.[143]

However, state water rights were not the basis of the *Powers* decision. Had they been, the Court would have had to determine whether the Indians' senior rights required abatement of the purchasers' diversions. Nor was the Court's opinion neutral on the question of the purchasers' federal water rights. The Court stated:

---

[139] See Dufford, Water for Non-Indians on the Reservation: Checkerboard Ownership and Checkerboard Jurisdiction, 15 Gonz. L. Rev. 95, 112-113 n.62 (1979); Getches, Water Rights on Indian Allotments, 26 S. Dak. L. Rev. 405, 423 (1981).

A related argument is that the theory of the United States as plaintiff in *Powers* would have denied the transfer of the reservation water right from the tribal beneficiary to allottees at the time trust allotments were first made. Neither the Court nor the parties focused on the question of a further transfer to successors when allotments went out of trust. Although this is true, the Court still had to recognize some defect in the Government's case against defendants, who were all successors. Nevertheless, this argument was accepted by the court in Colville Confederated Tribes v. Walton, 647 F.2d 42, 50 n.13 (9th Cir. 1981), cert. denied, 454 U.S. 1092 (1981). That court reached the same conclusion as *Powers*, but it did not view *Powers* as controlling.

In Merrill v. Bishop, 74 Wyo. 298, 307, 287 P.2d 620, 622 (1955), which involved the water rights of white owners of former allotments, the Wyoming Supreme Court cited *Powers* but said: "We do not find that case to have any particular bearing on the case at bar...." No reasons were stated.

[140] Cappaert v. United States, 426 U.S. 128, 141, 143-46 (1976); Conrad Investment Co. v. United States, 161 F. 829, 833-34 (9th Cir. 1908). Contra *Walton*, 647 F.2d at 52. But on this issue, *Walton* is limited to the rare cases where a stream system is entirely within an Indian reservation. *United States v. Anderson*, 736 F.2d 1359, 1365 (9th Cir. 1984).

[142] The Act of Apr. 27, 1904, ch. 1624, 33 Stat. 352, ratified and amended an agreement with the Crow Tribe ceding the northern part of its reservation to the United States. Congress unilaterally added a new Article VIII providing:

> Art. VIII. The right to take out water upon the diminished reservation subject to any prior claim of the Indians thereto by reason of previous appropriation, and the right to construct, maintain, and operate dams, flumes, and canals upon and across the said diminished reservation for the purpose of irrigating lands within any portion of the ceded tract are hereby granted, such rights to be exercised by persons, companies, or corporations under such rules, regulations, and requirements as may be prescribed by the Secretary of the Interior.

Id. at 359.

There are several citations to the 1904 Act in the *Powers* record, but none to this section. It did not directly apply, because defendants were not irrigators on "the ceded tract" but were within "the diminished reservation." It is contrary to the Government's theory as stated in the text. It is arguably contrary to the defendants' theory, because it seems to make the water rights of allotment successors in "the ceded tract" junior to the Indians.

[143] At the initial pleading stage, four defendants relied on claims of state law rights. Record at 117-33, *Powers*, 305 U.S. 527 (1939) (counterclaims of defendants Yates); *id.* at 147-52 (first counterclaim of defendants Dethlefsen). The other eleven who answered relied on claims of succession to federal rights. *Id.* at 59-101. After the pleading stage all defendants relied on federal rights claims. *Id.* at 229-52. But most of them placed in evidence state law notices of appropriation they had filed. *Id.* at 127-33, 489-91, 518-21. Since no party was basing its legal position on state law claims, the trial court did not determine their validity or extent.

Respondents maintain that under the Treaty of 1868 waters within the Reservation were reserved for the equal benefit of tribal members (*Winters v. United States*, 207 U.S. 564) and that when allotments of land were duly made for exclusive use and thereafter conveyed in fee, the right to use some portion of tribal waters essential for cultivation passed to the owners.

The respondents' claim to the extent stated is well founded.

Furthermore, the purchasers' pleadings asserted without contradiction that most of the water rights of the former allotments in *Powers* had been undeveloped when the land passed out of trust. Hence, the claim that the *Powers* Court held that undeveloped federal water rights survive trust removal is stronger than has been assumed.

There may be reasons for the Supreme Court to reconsider the question. No party in *Powers* was asserting state law. The Court had no perspective on the decision's effect on state law appropriators who diverted before the allotment purchasers but whose rights would be junior to the purchasers' federal rights.[146] Moreover, the government argued only that no federal water rights passed from the tribe to the allottees. There was no focus on the trust's end, conveyance to non-Indians, or the federal statutes governing these events. But a lower court would be justifiably reluctant to initiate a reexamination. A Supreme Court opinion like *Powers*, even if arguably dictum, casts a long shadow.

Arguments Against Post-Trust Perfection of Undeveloped Federal Rights

The decisions holding that undeveloped federal water rights of allotments may be perfected with reasonable diligence after the trust ends have been strongly criticized.[148] Critics argue that the continuing immunity from state water laws upheld in these decisions is not justified by the controlling federal statutes. The purpose of the allotment statutes is to assist Indian allottees to become self-sufficient agriculturalists. This purpose is rarely served by allowing non-Indian successors to acquire and perfect undeveloped federal reservation water rights.[149] The chance to get undeveloped water rights with an early priority date gives non-Indians a powerful incentive to induce Indians to sell undeveloped allotments. When this occurs, the federal purpose that allottees use the land to become self-sufficient is usually thwarted.

Critics of post-trust perfection also argue that non-Indian allotment successors did not expect to enjoy the undeveloped part of the allotments' federal water rights. They point out that non-Indian successors have usually sought to appropriate new water rights under state law. If purchasers did not expect to acquire undeveloped federal water rights, presumably they did not pay allottees

---

[146] The streams involved were not wholly within the Crow Reservation, although some off-reservation claims were in Wyoming, presenting an interstate complication. Record at 58, *Powers*, 305 U.S. 527 (1939).

[148] See D. Getches, Water Law in a Nutshell, 312-14 (1984); Dufford, *supra* note 139, at 101-21; Getches, *supra* note 139, at 420-23; Note, 17 Land & Water L. Rev. 155, 160-68 (1982); Note, Colville Confederated Tribes v. Walton: Indian Water Rights and Regulation in the Ninth Circuit, 43 Mont. L. Rev. 247, 259-63 (1982); Note, 58 Wash. L. Rev. 89, 95-100, 108-09 (1982).

[149] This assumes that the consideration received by allottees will not be reinvested in productive assets, an assumption borne out by past events. See Felix S. Cohen, *supra* note 48, at 136-38, 144.

for them. They receive a windfall if courts later decide that they own undeveloped rights.

One consequence of any federal water right surviving the end of the trust and transfer to non-Indians is that the amount of land sharing in the reservation water right with its early priority date remains large. Aggressive non-Indian owners then compete with the tribe and with remaining trust allottees.[151] In times of shortage, there may be less water for each owner than needed. This consequence is justified for water rights developed by allottees during the trust, but it is questionable for undeveloped rights in which allottees have made no investments.

Critics of post-trust perfection advocate that the undeveloped part of an allotment's federal water right should expire when the allotment is taken out of trust and subjected to state jurisdiction.[152] They contend that this rule is more consistent with the purposes of the governing federal statutes, it is favored by the usual federalism theory that federal preemption of state law should not outlast the federal purpose, and it would reduce disruption of western state water law. Moreover, this rule would avoid the complexities caused by the post-trust perfection rule that most courts follow because the courts' rule requires adjudication of allotment successors' due diligence in perfecting undeveloped federal rights.[153]

Arguments for Allowing Post-Trust Perfection

Proponents of post-trust perfection have several responses to these arguments. Post-trust perfection accords Indian allottees more to sell or give to their successors. The available evidence suggests that Indian sellers have benefited

---

[151]See Getches, *supra* note 139, at 425.

A factor that determines who are the opposing parties to a case is the disposition of the part of the undeveloped water right, if any, that does not survive removal of the trust and transfer to non-Indians. In any western state, the water would first become available to meet shortages for holders of existing rights with the same priority date (the reservation date), then to holders of junior rights, usually under state law. In a particular case, the gain may be enjoyed by a tribe, by other allottees or successors, by non-Indians claiming under state law, or even by later federal reservations. Another factor is the reacquisition in trust of former allotments, usually by tribes. In this circumstance, tribes benefit from transfer of undeveloped rights. United States v. Anderson, 736 F.2d 1358 (9th Cir. 1984).

[152][Such a] view was advocated by the United States in Colville Confederated Tribes v. Walton, 460 F. Supp. 1320, 1326-29 (E.D. Wash. 1978), rev'd, 647 F.2d 42 (9th Cir. 1981), cert. denied, 454 U.S. 1092 (1981). It was not accepted by either the district or appeals courts.

[153]An alternative rule would eliminate the undeveloped right upon transfer to non-Indians unless the parties intended a transfer. Intent would be presumed in the case of gratuitous transfers by descent or devise but would have to be proved in the case of purchases. that is, it would have to be shown that transfer of the undeveloped water right was contemplated and that the right was paid for. This view was advocated by the United States after remand and in light of the appellate opinion in *Walton.* Memorandum for the United States, May 5, 1982, Colville Confederated Tribes v. Walton, Nos. 3421, 3831 (E.D. Wash Aug. 31, 1983), rev'd, No. 83-4285 (9th Cir. Jan. 21, 1985). It was rejected by the district court based on law of the case. *Walton,* No. 84-3504, slip op. at 1-8. The United States did not appeal.

This theory seems doubtful for two reasons. First, it focuses on transfer rather than on application of state law. Second, when a property owner's intent to make a transfer is at issue, the question is whether the owner intended to transfer the interest or to retain it. Here, the proposed rule would extinguish a water right not intended to be transferred. The benefit would accrue to some third party appropriator usually unknown to the grantor. No grantor intends that result.

very little from this right, but future Indian sellers might and gratuitous transfers to heirs and devisees present a more sympathetic case.[154]

Proponents can also point out that the conflict between the post-trust perfection rule and state water law is relatively minor. If allotment rights must be perfected with reasonable diligence, then they are treated like projects governed by the state law doctrine of relation back. Some western states are in fact quite lenient in their definitions of reasonable diligence and allow a very long time to perfect.

Proponents of post-trust perfection can partially answer the argument about buyers' expectations. While it is true that most non-Indian successors filed for state law water rights after acquiring former allotments, these filings were not clearly inconsistent with successors' later claims to federal water rights. Doubt about federal rights may have led cautious buyers to file in case the federal rights were not upheld. The Indian Service itself made many state law filings prior to *Winters*. Some successors may have filed because it was the cheapest way to obtain cooperation of a district engineer or other state official hostile to federal rights. Also, owners of former allotments probably must comply with procedural state laws in order to retain and perfect federal water rights. In most western states they would have to file notices of appropriation. These arguments are undercut, however, by the fact that most allotment successors filed for new priority dates and did not claim reservation priority dates.

Post-Trust Perfection Should Be Upheld

If the courts were deciding the issue on a clean slate, a rule that an allotment's undeveloped federal water right expires when the allotment goes out of trust and becomes subject to state law is preferable because it is more faithful to the purposes of the governing federal statutes. This rule would not be inequitable because other Indian immunities from state law expire with the trust. Also, this rule would place buyers of former allotments on an equal footing with homesteaders of ceded reservation common land who acquired under the public land laws.

However, the issue is not a new one. Thousands of allotments have gone out of trust in the past. Some post-trust water uses have been continuous for very long periods. The resulting reliance interest is an important social value strongly reflected in the law of property.

Assessing the legitimate reliance interest of former allotment owners is complex, and there is evidence both for and against actual reliance.[159] One question already discussed is the inference to be drawn from the fact that most non-Indian buyers of former allotments filed for state water rights. This factor suggests that buyers did not rely on federal water rights, but it is inconclusive.

---

[154] Another affirmative policy argument is that to some degree the post-trust perfection rule will promote alienability of land. But a basic purpose of the federal scheme is to restrain alienability.

[159] Judging the reasonable expectations of non-Indians who have acquired property from Indians is a difficult challenge for courts because many non-Indians believed that Indians should yield all their resources to the "superior" whites. For example, in the *Winters* case, the courts found the idea that the non-Indian defendants could take all Milk River water and leave the Indians none to be unreasonable, but many politicians disagreed. See Hundley *supra* note 10, at 22, 27-28, 31-32, 36-37, 40-42. In other cases, the courts have bowed to the political will. See e.g., United States v. Ahtanum Irr. Dist., 236 F.2d 321 (9th Cir. 1956), cert. denied, 352 U.S. 988 (1957).

A related question is whether undeveloped federal water rights were reflected in allotment prices when allotments were conveyed out of trust. Limited evidence suggests that they were not. More information could be obtained by reviewing Bureau of Indian Affairs appraisal practices. All sales directly out of trust require appraisals.[161] But the appraisals are unlikely to be helpful for several reasons. First, at the time of early transfers, undeveloped water rights in some locations had no positive value, that is, water was not yet scarce enough to make undeveloped rights worth more than new appropriations. Second, the valuation of undeveloped rights is difficult and has been worked out in concrete terms only recently. It would be hard to fault a 1920 appraiser for ignoring a value he had no practical way to measure. Third, it is quite possible that the appraisals will show no valuation of undeveloped water rights either for transfers in trust or for transfers out of trust. If so, the appraisals would ignore the undeveloped right transfer during the trust, which no one has questioned.

The most important factor favoring a legitimate reliance interest is legal precedents. The first decision sustaining a post-trust right to perfect undeveloped federal water rights was reported in 1928.[163] It was followed in obiter dicta several times thereafter, it was not seriously challenged until the 1970s, and it was reaffirmed in several recent decisions.[164] There may have been reasonable reliance on these precedents by allotment buyers or others who bought from them.

Even if *Powers* is not controlling, when it is considered with the more explicit precedents, the chances are significant that owners of former allotments have reasonably relied on acquiring undeveloped federal water rights. This consideration should outweigh the policy reasons favoring expiration of undeveloped rights at the trust's end, and the courts should continue to sustain the right to post-trust perfection of federal water rights if developed with reasonable diligence.

When Undeveloped Federal Water Rights Are Lost

None of the federal court opinions expressly addressed the question of when the diligence requirement arises. It could arise at the trust's end, or perhaps there must also be subjection to state law or conveyance to non-Indians or both. If all three events have occurred, a court need not consider the issue.

Subjection of a former allotment to state law ought to be an event relevant to the reasonable diligence requirement. It is state law that requires beneficial use of water as a condition of water rights ownership. Therefore, when allotments

---

[161]See 25 C.F.R. § 152.24 (1984); 43 C.F.R. § 4.301 (1984). When a trust allotment is sold by the United States as grantor and trustee, there is an appraisal. When an allotment goes out of trust through a fee patent to an Indian allottee, heir, or devisee, there is usually no appraisal even if the patentee immediately sells the land.

[163]United States v. Hibner, 27 F.2d 909 (D. Idaho 1928).

[164]See *supra* note 126 and cases cited therein. See also Clyde, Indian Water Rights n.2; Waters and Water Rights § 145.1 (R. Clark ed. 1967); Felix S. Cohen, Handbook of Federal Indian Law 220 (Gov't Printing Office 1941) ("The *Powers* case compels the view that the right to use water is a right appurtenant to the land within the reservation, and that unless excluded it passes to each grantee in subsequent conveyances of allotted land."); Op. Solic. Dep't of Interior (Mar. 14, 1958), reprinted in 2 Opinions of the Solicitor of the Dep't of the Interior Relating to Indian Affairs 1829 (Gov't Printing Office 1978); Trelease, Indian Water Rights for Mineral Development, in Natural Resources Law on American Indian Lands 222, 231 (P. Maxfield ed. 1977).

outside Indian reservation boundaries go out of trust, the diligence requirement should be imposed even if Indian allottees retain ownership. Whether the
owners of former allotments are Indians or non-Indians, the land and its
owners are subject to state law for all relevant purposes.

Allotments within self-governing Indian reservations pose harder questions.
If Indian allottees retain ownership, the land and its owners remain immune
from state jurisdiction. Even if the land is conveyed to non-Indians, it does not
come under state jurisdiction for all purposes. In *Colville Confederated Tribes
v. Walton*, former allotments owned by non-Indians were located on a water
system entirely within a self-governing Indian reservation. The Colville Tribes
claimed exclusive jurisdiction over the water against the State of Washington,
and the Ninth Circuit sustained the claim. But the court required that the
undeveloped federal water right be put to use with reasonable diligence. The
court later held that the diligence requirement was a rule of federal law. State
law on reasonable diligence was considered only for "guidance." Therefore, the
court imposed this requirement either because of the trust's end or because of
the trust's end and conveyance to non-Indians. We cannot be sure which events
triggered the diligence requirement because the court did not discuss the
point.[169]

If the requirement of diligent perfection arises solely as a consequence of the
trust's end, it would apply to reservation Indian owners of former allotments as
well as to non-Indian owners. This would present troublesome questions in light
of the manner in which former allotments held by reservation Indians have
been treated. There was a period when the Bureau of Indian Affairs issued fee
patents to Indians without their consent and sometimes over their objections. At
other times, the Bureau required allotments to be taken out of trust simply to
make an inter vivos transfer to another Indian.[171] Even when Indians voluntarily took reservation allotments out of trust, the federal policy to assist reservation Indian self-sufficiency still applies to them. In this situation, it is contrary to
the allotment statutory scheme to end undeveloped water rights of former
allotments if the Indian owners do not put the water to use with reasonable
diligence.

An analogous question is posed by the Wyoming courts' expiration rule,
which is advocated by critics of post-trust perfection. Undeveloped federal
water rights might expire solely as a consequence of trust removal, or the courts
might also require that former allotments come under state jurisdiction, be
conveyed to non-Indians, or both. In the Big Horn River Adjudication, which
involved former allotments owned by reservation Indians, a Wyoming district
court held that the federal water rights of these parcels did not expire when
taken out of trust. For federal water rights to expire under the Wyoming rule,
the allotments must either be conveyed to non-Indians, or come under state

---

[169] The tribal jurisdiction question was decided differently when the water source flowed outside
a reservation as well as within, as is commonly the case. In United States v. Anderson, 736 F.2d
1358, 1363-66 (9th Cir. 1984), the court held that state jurisdiction then applies to reservation
allotments acquired by non-Indians.

[171] No statute generally authorizes inter vivos transfers. At the present time, the Bureau allows
them under statutes authorizing trust removal from grantors together with statutes allowing new
trust titles for grantees. See 25 C.F.R. § 151.3(b) (1984). For many years, some local Bureau officials
refused to allow new trust titles for grantees.

jurisdiction, or both. The Wyoming Court correctly refused to impose the state courts' expiration rule on former allotments still owned by reservation Indians.

Reasonable Diligence

As shown above, the majority rule allows allotment successors to perfect undeveloped federal water rights if done with reasonable diligence. Water rights that are partially developed by allottees during the trust present a compelling case for the same right. These rules require courts to decide how promptly allotment water rights must be perfected after allotments go out of trust.

Western state water law offers a possible standard in the relation back doctrine. Under that doctrine, a would-be appropriator may give notice of a planned diversion scheme or otherwise show the intent to appropriate. If the scheme is then pursued to completion within a reasonable time and with due diligence, the water right acquired has the priority date of the initial notice, rather than the later date of actual water diversion. If this doctrine is applied to former allotments, the owners (at least those who are subject to state law) would have to give notice promptly after the trust ends and then develop their diversion projects with reasonable diligence. Having done so, they would be rewarded with the early reservation priority dates. The first court to sustain post-trust perfection of undeveloped federal water rights on former allotments seemed to refer to state law on relation back.

Applied to undeveloped allotments, the relation back doctrine requires adjustment. When a would-be appropriator gives notice or forms an intent under state law, a specific diversion must already be proposed in order to make the notice meaningful. When an allotment goes out of trust and becomes subject to state law, there would have to be a reasonable planning time to formulate a project and give notice. But allotments are not large parcels, so this need not be long. States can propose standards appropriate to their laws.

The only reported case in which reasonable diligence in perfecting undeveloped federal water rights on former allotments has been adjudicated is *Colville Confederated Tribes v. Walton.*[177] The Ninth Circuit held that federal law controlled, but state law on reasonable diligence under the relation back doctrine would be examined for "guidance." The court then applied state law precedents to the facts and determined how much water had been put to use within a reasonable time after the allotments had gone out of trust.[179] The decision reversed a federal district court's astonishing conclusion that water

---

[177] *Walton*, No. 83-4285 (9th Cir. Jan. 21, 1985).

[179] *Id.* slip op. at 9-12. Since 1917, Washington has required an appropriator to obtain a permit before undertaking a water use, then to begin and complete construction within the time allowed by the state supervisor of water resources. Wash. Rev. Code §§ 90.03.250, -.320 (1962). In setting and extending time limits and assessing an applicant's diligence, the supervisor is to consider "the cost and magnitude of the project and the engineering and physical features to be encountered, and shall allow such time as shall be reasonable and just under the conditions then existing, ... having due regard to the good faith of the applicant and the public interests affected." *Id.* § 90.03.320.

This section seems to require that an allotment successor who is subject to state law get a state permit soon after the trust ends, to give notice to other users. The state law's diligence standard after a permit is obtained might be applied by analogy to determine how promptly the permit should be sought.

development begun more than twenty-three years after allotments went out of trust was undertaken with reasonable diligence.[180]

The Ninth Circuit's reference to state law for "guidance" appears to be an application of the rule that federal property law ordinarily adopts state law rules of decision. The court had already determined that the former allotments involved in the case were governed by tribal rather than state law, so this rule was arguably inappropriate. But the parties did not try to show that tribal law on the question would be any different from state law, so the court did not have to choose between conflicting laws.

Conclusion

Federal water rights of Indian allotments have been gradually defined by adjudication. It is settled that allotments out of tribal land have an appurtenant right to use a proportionate share of the reservation water right for agricultural purposes. If a reservation has a federal water right for other purposes as well, its relation to the agricultural water rights of allotments complicates both quantification of rights and management of stream systems.

Disposition of federal reservation water rights is less settled when allotments go out of trust, become subject to state law, and are acquired by non-Indians. Results have varied from the rights' elimination to their full continuation subject to a loose requirement that they be put to use within a reasonable time. In part this is because courts see widely differing circumstances, and most cases involve particular reliance claims based on events of many years before.

Whenever allottees have invested in water development, the federal water rights actually or partially developed should be vested property rights that are not affected by the end of the trust or conveyance to non-Indians. States should be able to impose only procedural requirements such as notice. Any other rule would at times unfairly destroy the value of allottees' investments.

A more difficult question is whether undeveloped federal reservation water rights may be perfected after the trust ends. The policies of governing federal statutes and principles of federalism favor expiration of any portion of the right that is wholly undeveloped when allotments go out of trust and become subject to state law. But most reviewing courts have sustained post-trust perfection of undeveloped rights if put to use with reasonable diligence after the trust ends. One of these decisions, *United States v. Powers*, was affirmed by the Supreme Court. Whether *Powers* is a controlling precedent on post-trust perfection of undeveloped federal rights has been disputed, but one can make a good argument that it is. Since almost all adjudications of allotment water rights have been in the federal courts of the Ninth Circuit, the scope of *Powers* is a crucial question for other courts. *Powers* is doubtful enough to justify its reexamination, but it is likely to be followed. If it is, the principal issue remaining for the

---

[180] Nos. 3421, 3831, slip op. at 2-7 (E.D. Wash. Aug. 31, 1983), rev'd, No. 83-4285, (9th Cir. Jan. 21, 1985). This proceeding followed the remand ordered in 647 F.2d 42 (9th Cir. 1981).

The court's August 31, 1983 opinion stated that the three allotments in question went out of trust and were acquired by non-Indian purchasers in 1921, 1923, and 1925. The Waltons acquired them by purchase in 1948. The district court awarded the Waltons a federal reservation water right to irrigate 104 acres, seventy-four acres of which were newly irrigated by the Waltons after 1948.

courts is to define the diligence required to perfect undeveloped federal water rights.

NOTES

1. Indian Allotments and Water Rights: Despite the importance of the question to the development of both Indian and non-Indian owned allotments and former allotments, the cases on the water rights associated with Indian allotments are not very definitive. As Professor Collins's article indicated, the Supreme Court's decision in *Powers* clearly indicated that Indian-held allotments took some portion of the *Winters* water rights held by the tribe prior to allotment and that their successors in interests, whether Indian or non-Indian, acquired some right to water. The precise nature and extent of those rights, however, remains the subject of considerable dispute, as the Collins article indicates. The quantification of such Indian rights, their impact on the tribal allocation, and their transferability to non-Indians when the land was alienated or passed out of trust remained substantially less clear despite the importance of these questions to the economic development of such lands.

For Indian owners of allotments, the rule seems to be that they hold a percentage of the prior tribal reserved water rights in a water system that is equal to the percentage that their practically irrigable acreage bears to the irrigable acreage contained in the reservation itself. The problem for their successors in interest is considerably more complex, as the Collins article indicates.

In *Colville Confederated Tribes v. Walton*, 647 F.2d 42 (9th Cir.), *cert. denied*, 454 U.S. 1092 (1981), the court held that a ratable share of the reserved tribal water rights of the Colville Tribes passed to allottees and that these rights could be and were conveyed to their non-Indian successors in interest subject to loss if not put to use "with reasonable diligence." *Id.* at 51. The published 1981 opinion followed a withdrawn 1980 opinion in which the court had held that a non-Indian purchaser of Indian allotted land acquired no reserved water rights. In a footnote to the withdrawn 1980 *Walton* opinion, the court had stated that this reading of *Powers* was erroneous, since the Supreme Court in *Powers* "expressly reserved the issue of transferability" by not considering the extent or precise nature of water rights of non-Indian successors to Indian allottees. The Ninth Circuit in the published 1981 *Walton* opinion, however, found in *Powers* a recognition that some sort of water right was appurtenant to and passed with an allotment when purchased by non-Indians. *See* footnote 13 of the *Walton* opinion. In a later opinion, *Colville Confederated Tribes v. Walton*, 752 F.2d 397 (9th Cir. 1985), *cert. denied*, 475 U.S. 1010 (1986), the court reviewed the water allocation awarded by the district court and reduced the award to the non-Indian owner since the court erred in permitting the perfection of reserved water rights by the reasonable diligence of *subsequent* non-Indian successors beyond the immediate successor in interest. The opinion noted:

> A careful reading [of the Court's earlier *Walton* opinion] leaves no doubt that the immediate grantee of the original allottee must exercise due diligence to perfect his or her inchoate right to the allottee's ratable share of reserved waters. This interpretation is supported by our reference to *Walton II* in subsequent cases. *See, e.g., United States v. Anderson*, 736 F.2d 1358, 1362 (9th Cir. 1984) ("use it or lose it"); *United States v. Adair*, 723 F.2d 1394, 1417 (9th Cir. 1983), *cert. denied*, 104 S. Ct. 3536 (1984). Once perfected, the water right must be "maintained by continued use [or] it is lost." *Walton II*, 647 F.2d at 51.
>
> The district court on remand was to "calculate the respective rights of the parties." *Id.* at 53. Calculating Walton's share required an investigation into the diligence with

which the *immediate* grantee from the Indian allottees appropriated water, and the extent to which successor grantees, up to and including Walton, continued to use the water thus appropriated. Otherwise, any remote purchaser could appropriate enough water to irrigate all irrigable acreage with a priority date as of the creation of the Reservation. The reasonable diligence requirement of *Walton II* would be meaningless.

In *United States ex rel. Ray v. Hibner,* 27 F.2d 909 (D. Idaho 1928), the United States sought an adjudication of the rights of Indians of the Fort Hall Reservation and their successors in interest to the waters of Toponce Creek. The Fort Bridger Treaty of 1869, which established the reservation, also granted twenty-two allotments to Indians occupying and cultivating land that was within the reservation. The treaty also stated that the water of streams within the allotments that was necessary for irrigation in land in actual cultivation was reserved for the Indian allottees. The court held that non-Indian successors to these allottees were entitled to reserved water rights "for the actual acreage that was under irrigation at the time title passed from the Indians, and such increased acreage as [the non-Indians] might with reasonable diligence place under irrigation, which would give ... , under the doctrine of relation, the same priority as owned by the Indians." 27 F.2d at 912. Since there was no forfeiture of water rights by failure to cultivate the allotments during a period of Indian ownership, the priority date was not that time at which the Indian allottee began to put the water to beneficial use, but rather the time of the creation of the reservation. Thus, the non-Indian successor's priority date would relate back to the date of the creation of the reservation and not just to the actual date of appropriation. While such a successor was not governed by the state law of prior appropriation with respect to priority date, the court did find that policy recognized in the development of arid lands such as those dealt with in the case required that the successor continue to put the water to beneficial use in order to preserve the rights to it. Also, the Court stated that "granting to the Indian lands the (reserved) right to ... water ... will not prohibit the next appropriator on the stream from using the water, when it is not diverted and used from the stream by the Indians and applied by them to a beneficial use ...."

In *United States v. Ahtanum Irrig. Dist.,* 236 F.2d 321 (1956), the Ninth Circuit appeared in dictum to take another view of the water rights of non-Indian purchasers of allotments. The court accepted the argument that certain of these successors in interest, who had failed for ten years to assert any rights to seventy-five percent of the waters of Ahtanum Creek, had yet maintained a vested interest in the waters of the Creek by virtue of their status as successors to the Indian allottees for whom the waters were reserved. This vested interest, it was claimed, was equal to the reserved rights of the original allottees. The court read *United States v. Powers,* 305 U.S. 527 (1939), to confirm the successor's claims to a pro rata share of reserved waters.

In a thoughtful article entitled *Water Rights on Indian Allotments,* 26 S.D.L. REV. 405 (1981), Professor David Getches argues that while the Supreme Court in *Powers* did recognize an Indian allottee's right to that part of the tribal water necessary for farming the allotment, there "is nothing in the General Allotment Act to suggest that Congress was dividing up and conveying tribal water rights in severalty as it did tribal lands." *Id.* at 416. If that is indeed the case, then the reserved water rights would continue to be owned by the tribe both after creation of allotments and conveyance of the fee patents to Indian allottees. Thus, no reserved rights would pass to non-Indian purchasers of allotments. Professor

Getches contends that because the goal of the Allotment Act was to integrate Indian allottees into mainstream society, ending their status as government wards and their dependence on the tribe, it followed that they would no longer receive the benefit of preferential treatment under the reserved water rights doctrine once the federal trust period had expired. The end of the trust period would free the allottee from restrictions on encumbrancing or disposing of the property, but it would also expose the property to taxes and local and state regulation. The state laws relative to the perfection and maintenance of water rights would be among those regulations applying to the allotments.

Clearly differing with his colleague Professor Collins, Getches argues that a pro rata reserved right for allottees would place them at an advantage over non-Indian homesteaders governed by the appropriative rights doctrine and over Indian allottees whose land was still in trust. Getches notes that a pro rata reserved right for allottees and their successors would even call into question the extent of the tribe's rights when water use for irrigation was subject to abatement due to scarcity. In the latter case, because the allottees would have reserved rights allowing for full pro rata shares, during droughts the tribal water requirements would be in conflict with allotment requirements without benefit of a hierarchy of dominant and subordinate water rights. Whereas non-Indian appropriators whose perfection of a water right was prior to the creation of a reservation would be senior to the right of the tribe, and non-Indian appropriators whose perfection was subsequent to the creation would be junior, tribal and allottee rights would be equal and thus difficult to adjudicate. Getches cautions that reserved rights could extend to potentially thousands of individuals, advising that the trust ownership of the tribal reserved water rights remain with the government even after the fee patents to land are conveyed to allottees.

Briefly summarized, the approach recommended in the Getches article for establishing the extent of the water rights of the patented allottees and their successors is the following:

> [The allottees recognized rights should be predicated on] appropriations based on actual use of irrigation water during the trust period. That is, to the extent the allottee has used the tribe's reserved rights for irrigation, rights should be recognized as included in the conveyance of the land from the federal government. The state would be required to honor the existence of the right, but from the time title was taken in fee, state requirements for maintaining the right would apply. This approach satisfies the inference that Congress intended *some* right to water to attach to allotments, without perverting the reserved rights doctrine and exacerbating the certainties that already exist. Treating them as if they were homesteaders rewards allottees who have actually made use of their land for agriculture as Congress intended. Yet they have security during the trust period and could depend on irrigation water from their tribe's reserved rights, with the Secretary [of the Interior] regulating supply to prevent any inequities in distribution.

Id. at 422.* Under Professor Getches' scheme the water rights acquired by allottees and their successors in interest after expiration of the trust period are ultimately credited against state, rather than tribal, water allocations.

Professor Getches criticizes the holding in both *Hibner* and the 1981 published *Walton* opinion, particularly the "due or reasonable diligence" element for the establishment of water rights for non-Indian purchasers of allotments. The perfection of reserved rights during a period of such diligence could result in the irrigation of an entire allotment by the enthusiastic purchaser who

* Reprinted by permission of David H. Getches, University of Colorado, School of Law, Boulder, and the South Dakota Law Review. Copyright © 1981.

achieves access to water that he or she might well never have if the individual
was a homesteader governed by the prior appropriations doctrine. Since the
value of such rights would be great to the non-Indian, there would be incentive
for him or her to buy allotments instead of homestead elsewhere, and there
would be pressure on the allottees to sell. Not only would the sale of allotments
eat into the tribe's water sources, but allottee would have no inducement to
increase the value of the allotment by developing its agricultural potential during the period of Indian ownership.

In *Wyoming v. Owl Creek Irrig. Dist. (In re General Adjudication of All
Rights to Use Water in the Big Horn River Sys.)*, 750 P.2d 681, 753 P.2d 76
(Wyo. 1988), *aff'd by equally divided vote sub nom. United States v. Wyoming*,
109 S. Ct. 863 (1989), the court appeared to accept Professor Collins's analysis
since it held that Indian allottees who held fee lands shared in the tribal reserved rights with a priority as of the date of the creation of the Wind River
Reservation, and it remanded the case to calculate the water rights of non-
Indian grantees of the allottees "with an 1868 priority date for the PIA [practi-
cably irrigable acreage] they can show were irrigated by their Indian predecessors or put under irrigation within a reasonable time thereafter." 753 P.2d at
113-14. The court also noted that any subsequent Indian or tribal purchaser
from such a non-Indian holder would have precisely the same rights on such
reacquired lands.

2. Leasing Indian Water Rights: Another issue relating to transferability of
Indian water rights raised in the Collins article is the question of whether a tribe
or restricted allottee may lease or sell water rights for off-reservation uses. This
issue is not tied strictly to conveyance of allotments to non-Indians. Aboriginal
title to land, it was said, was a right of use only and could not be alienated. Is the
same true of Indian water rights? Do they exist for the present and potential use
of the Indian owners only? Or can the rights be conveyed to others, even if
Indian lands are not sold? On the Colorado River Reservation, there is an active
program of leasing tribal agricultural lands, almost wholly to non-Indians, for
the purpose of taking advantage of the reservation's Colorado River allocation.
It is generally assumed that the rights are alienable. Both statutory and case law
have provided answers with regard to certain types of alienation, but interstices
in the law remain. In *Skeem v. United States*, 273 F. 93 (9th Cir. 1921), the
court held that the lease of allotments to non-Indians did not affect the tribal
water rights if the Indians chose not to maintain residency. The use of reserved
water rights by lessees, by virtue of continued Indian ownership of the allotments, still bore a relationship to the tribe. However, here both Indian land and
water were leased together. What benefits and disadvantages might be foreseen
if reserved water rights were leased for use off-reservation by non-Indians?
What would be the economic and cultural implications of turning these *Winter*
rights into clearly saleable commodities?

The National Water Commission, mentioned in a previous note, recommended that the governing body of an Indian tribe should have the right to
lease water appurtenant to a reservation at fair market value, and proposed that
the United States should have the obligation to buy such water when offered.
FINAL REPORT at 480. The virtue to the tribe of leasing reserved rights arises
from the possibility to realize income immediately and steadily. An example
may be helpful: Suppose a pueblo tribe along the Rio Grande has an unperfected reserved right to 15,000 acre-feet of water. At the present time, it has
only a modest irrigation program, and there is not the prospect of substantially
more irrigation in the near future. The tribe would benefit by being able to

lease the 15,000 acre-feet to the government (for about $300,000 per year). Reservations with a need for reliable income might favor an approach that would so reward them.

Some hazard to the tribe lies in the implications of severing the water right from the reservation. The economic use of unexploited assets may make sense but the effect on the future of the reservation may be substantial. Under the National Water Commission's set of proposals, it is clear that non-Indian users can begin to make investments based on the reliability of the supply of water. Vested economic interests will be established based on the Indian water. Where water rights are leased, it would be natural to ask whether the Indians could recapture the right for their own benefit at the expiration of the lease. The answer must be that there will be difficulties in effective recapturing, unless alternative supplies of water are developed during the lease period by the non-Indian users. This conclusion is based on two reasons. First, effective implementation and exploitation of reserved rights usually requires congressional appropriations for the massive investments necessary on the reservation. Funds needed for irrigation works, reservoirs, pumping facilities, and the like are unlikely to be provided by Congressmen with other constituents who will be adversely affected if the Indians can, themselves, exploit through sale or lease the water to which they are entitled. And the moral pressure to provide substantial funds for such irrigation works will be eased by the fact that the tribe is already exploiting its water through the mechanism of a lease. A likely result of adoption of the Water Commission's proposals is that the congressional appropriations for water-based economic development on Indian reservations would be adversely affected. Second, consistent with nineteenth-century judicial decisions, the United States Congress may have the power unilaterally to convert water resources permanently into cash, that is to open up the Indian water rights for non-Indian settlement. Under existing doctrine the trust responsibility is not legally violated because, as courts have put it, the trust *res* is merely converted from one form (water) to another (cash). As long as fair market value is obtained, the United States is not liable as a fiduciary.

In light of the discussion of quantification earlier in this chapter, leasing reserved rights, therefore, may be seen as appealing on two grounds: It provides an income source for the reservation and it provides more security to non-Indian water users in the West. However, it is troublesome for another much more complicated reason. Quantification and leasing are at war with the fundamental reasoning of the *Winters* decision and with the idea of development and growth by the Indian community on the reservation. Yet, in some instances, the sort of "progress" envisioned by *Winters* may be impossible or unwanted, and the substitution of income for a large portion of water rights may be welcome. It may be, however, that the cultural implications of the leasing of water and the implications of the leasing of land are not greatly different. *See* DuMars & Ingram, *Congressional Quantification of Indian Reserved Water Rights: A Definitive Solution or a Mirage,* 20 NAT. RESOURCES J. 17, 31-32 (1980); Comment, *Leasing Indian Water Off the Reservation: A Use Consistent with the Reservation Purpose,* 76 CALIF. L. REV. 179 (1988). *But see* Palma, *Considerations and Conclusions Concerning the Transferability of Indian Water Rights,* 20 NAT. RESOURCES J. at 92-96 (1980).

25 U.S.C. 177 (1976) provides that:

No purchase, grant, lease, or other conveyance of lands, or of any title or claim thereto, from any Indian nation or tribe of Indians, shall be of any validity in law or equity, unless the same be made by treaty or convention entered into pursuant to the Constitution.

To what extent are Indian water rights protected as by the federal restraint against alienation "of lands, or of any title or claim thereto ..." contained in 25 U.S.C. § 177? In *United States v. Ahtanum Irrig. Dist.*, 236 F.2d 321 (9th Cir. 1956), the court was confronted with the validity of a 1908 agreement which the Chief Engineer of the Indian Irrigation Service entered into with a large number of white users of water from Ahtanum Creek that bargained away valuable Indian water rights by quantifying the Indians' claim to twenty-five percent of the natural flow of the creek. The agreement was never specifically approved by Congress. The opinion of the Ninth Circuit made repeated references to section 177 and seemed to assume that the alienation of water rights required congressional approval. The court, however, sustained the 1908 agreement on the basis that Congress had explicitly authorized the Secretary of the Interior to "have the management of all Indian affairs, and of all matters arising out of Indian relations," 25 U.S.C. § 2, and that in conferring these powers upon the Secretary of the Interior Congress must have had it in mind that a part of the Secretary's task of supervisor and of management of Indian affairs would necessarily deal with certain relations between Indians on the one hand and their white neighbors on the other." 236 F.2d at 335.

In *United States v. Truckee-Carson Irrig. Dist.*, 5 Indian L. Rep. F-13 (D. Nev. No. R. 1987-JBA, filed Dec. 12, 1977), *rev'd on other grounds*, 649 F.2d 1286 (9th Cir. 1981), *rev'd*, 463 U.S. 110 (1983), the court confronted a similar question involving the power of the judiciary to adjudicate and alienate Indian water rights without congressional approval. Responding to the claim that under section 177 ownership of Indian water rights could only be altered by congressional legislation rather than adjudication, the district court held that a water law decree was not a "conveyance" within the meaning of section 177. The court also found federal approval by the fact that the United States appeared in the prior adjudication and therefore consented to the consequences of the litigation. Finally, considering whether water rights constituted "lands, or ... any title or claim thereto" within the meaning of section 177, the district court said:

Dealing with the second requirement, "of lands," the Tribe cites *North Side Canal Co. v. Twin Falls Canal Co.*, 12 F.2d 311 (D. of Idaho), in which the court stated:

"Land," in a statute of this general nature must necessarily be given a broad and comprehensive meaning. "Land," in such sense, includes water upon the land, and water claimed to be appropriated for use in the development, by irrigation, of the land.

The Tribe also cites *Holmes v. United States*, 53 F.2d 960 (9th Cir. 1931), in which the court stated:

The primary meaning of the word "land" at common law is "any ground, soil or earth whatsoever; as arable, meadows, pastures, woods, waters, marshes, furzes and heath." 2 Blackstone, Com. 18.

However, it could also be argued that since § 177 was derived from the Act of June 30, 1834, long before the concept of the *Winters* doctrine was recognized, that Congress was concerned with the typical situation wherein the backward, unschooled Indians were being taken advantage of by the white men in trading or selling their lands for inadequate prices. The concept that the Indians also were reserved sufficient water to go along with their lands was not conceived of until *Winters v. United States, supra,* which was decided in 1908.

Should tribes have any greater right to lease or otherwise alienate their water than they have to alienate their land?

Chapter 7

ECONOMIC DEVELOPMENT OF INDIAN LANDS: CONTROL OF RESOURCES AND CULTURAL DESTINY

Until the late nineteenth century, Indian lands were set aside for the exclusive use and occupancy of Indians. Reservations or other lines of political demarcation were designed to separate non-Indian and Indian societies and sought, often unsuccessfully, to keep the Indian and non-Indian economies and markets highly segregated. Trade had been licensed and regulated by the federal government even before the first Trade and Intercourse Act of 1790. Yet there was and is a lure and perhaps an inevitability to the concept of economic development of Indian reservations. From the outset of colonial settlement in the Americas, the question was hardly ever whether there would be an accommodation between Indian claims and the settler economy, but rather what kind of accommodation would take place. It may well be that economic relationships determine cultural, political, and legal realities. Trade imposes its own imperatives for change. That being the case, the notion of a separate tribal entity with its own separate culture, political sovereignty, and economy would be hard to maintain even in a period where the predominant relationship between the Indians and the settlers was one of exchange of goods and where the non-Indians did not seek to establish their own activities on Indian lands. But trade and intercourse with Indian communities was not confined to mere trade, no matter how restrictive a model for licensing non-Indian dealings with tribes and their members was established under federal law. Relationships between Euro-American settlers and Indians always involved a competition for land, military advantage, and other resources associated with economic progress.

In the nineteenth century, the theory was that economic needs of the settler community would be met by reducing the scope of Indian land occupancy, changing reservation boundaries, removal and other similar techniques. Indian communities would stay separate, but the American settler economy could grow. In the mid-twentieth century this ideology has changed. Changes in leasing statutes, new concepts of joint ventures, and other development methods have retained what may be the fiction of Indian ownership of resources while transferring the use, and frequently the primary economic benefits, of such resources to non-Indian hands. Fiction is the appropriate word to the extent that retention of control over the scope of resources is important to shaping the Indian tribe's cultural and political future. The Meriam Report in 1928 bemoaned the decline of tribally held lands as a consequence of the Dawes Act and other measures; similar impacts on tribal cultures and sovereignty may occur if key elements of tribal lands become committed to non-Indian use under lease terms as long as ninety-nine years. That is not to say that the economic consequences of leasing might not have immediate beneficial effects for the reservation; it is only to suggest that while leasing is superficially benign, it should not automatically be assumed that it is a superior mechanism for the disposition of Indian resources.

In previous chapters of this book, we have emphasized the jurisdictional aspects of the competition for resources. Ownership questions aside, the battle for control of such resources has frequently taken the legal form of jurisdictional disputes. What is the proper forum for the determination of Indian reserved water rights? What government can determine economic growth through the imposition of its own taxes? What government can shape and control activities on the reservation through its criminal law? What government ultimately determines how Indian land and resources shall be held and used? Repeatedly, we have seen how resolution or even the phrasing of these questions can have significant impacts on the continued political strength of Indian tribes and the maintenance of their cultural diversity.

In 1971 President Nixon, in his famous message to Congress outlining his new Indian policy, declared an end to involuntary termination of Indian tribes and proclaimed a policy of assuring that the Indian "can assume control of his own life without being separated involuntarily from the tribal group." Message from the President of the United States Transmitting Recommendations for Indian Policy, H.R. Doc. 91-363, 91st Cong., 2d Sess. 3 (1970). The President stated that "[s]elf-determination among the Indian people can and must be encouraged without the threat of eventual termination." *Id.* The President simultaneously proposed:

> I also urge that legislation be enacted which would permit any tribe which chooses to do so to enter into leases of its land for up to 99 years. Indian people now own over 50 million acres of land that are held in trust by the Federal government. In order to compete in attracting investment capital for commercial, industrial and recreational development of these lands, it is essential that the tribes be able to offer long-term leases. Long-term leasing is preferable to selling such property since it enables tribes to preserve the trust ownership of their reservation homelands. But existing law limits the length of time for which many tribes can enter into such leases. Moreover, when long-term leasing is allowed, it has been granted by Congress on a case-by-case basis, a policy which again reflects a deep-rooted pattern of paternalism. The twenty reservations which have already been given authority for long-term leasing have realized important benefits from that privilege and this opportunity should now be extended to all Indian tribes.

Id. at 8. How the goals of self-determination and protecting Indian tribal communities could be reconciled with long-term leasing or mineral development was never addressed in the President's message. However, this conflict became an important legal and political issue during the 1970's and 1980's.

One must wonder, however, at the impact on the Native American societies of the coincidence of the encouragement of economic development and the multiventured and seemingly nonpaternalistic movement toward self-determination. In the late nineteenth century, native lands were opened to settlement by treaty, congressional action, and other means. In the late twentieth century, the inclusion of Native American lands in the economy as a whole appears to be occurring as a consequence of many of the same economic and political forces but using different mechanisms. What appears enlightened now may, in retrospect, be subjected to criticism similar to the criticism that was directed at the

General Allotment Act, removal, and other federal policies. Self-determination describes a process by which tribal governments make decisions; it does not indicate what effect those decisions will have on the cultural and political future of the tribe.

The potential for economic development of Indian reservations depends, in great part, on the natural, human, and economic resources available on the reservation. On some reservations the only major resource is inexpensive Indian labor. On many other reservations, however, valuable land and natural resources spurs Indian and non-Indian interest in development. While the Indian tribes were often left during the nineteenth century with seemingly less valuable, nonproductive lands, later events, including the discovery of mineral resources or irrigation, have frequently made Indian land and resources highly prized in the latter part of the twentieth century. The extent of the value of these resources and the attitude of the federal government toward their management is briefly summarized in the following excerpt from AMERICAN INDIAN POLICY REVIEW COMMISSION, FINAL REPORT 305, 314, 324, 338-39 (1978):

Indian people have had to relinquish their lands and resources, giving way to the white man's needs. In 1887, there were almost 2 billion acres of land under Indian use. By 1924, this total had shrunk to 150 million acres; by 1975, to 50 million acres. This process was most dramatic during the early history of this country. But economic and social deprivation still continued. Too often, Indian timber, minerals, water, rich agriculture and grazing lands, are exploited through leases whose return is grossly unfair.

The administration of Federal programs and the execution of the trust responsibility of the U.S. Government should be directed toward establishing or reconstituting viable economies. Instead, a relationship of dependency has been allowed to grow between Indian people and the United States Government. A look at the Federal Indian budget demonstrates that the primary condition being fostered continues to be one of dependency.

Sixty percent of the Indian budget is committed to providing social-welfare services, which are generally available to all other Americans as well. Yet, only 9.5 percent of the budget is used for the execution of the trust responsibility of the United States to protect the remaining natural resources of Indians and further development of Indian country....

Agriculture

Indian lands and natural resources are located on over 200 reservations in 26 States and encompass in excess of 50 million acres. About 129 reservations have Indian populations of at least 200 and land of at least 1,000 acres.

Indian lands include: (1) 5.3 million acres of commercial forest land, which is about 1 percent of the Nation's commercial forest land and includes about 38 billion board-feet of timber, or 1½ percent of the Nation's total; (2) 44 million acres of rangeland, or about 5 percent of the Nation's total; (3) about 2.5 million acres of cropland, or 1 percent of the Nation's total.

According to 1975 BIA statistics, the gross value of agricultural products grown on Indian range and croplands amounted to $394 million. Of this amount, Indians received $123 million or less than one-third of the total value of range and farm products grown on Indian lands. Non-Indians, on the other hand, received $271 million or 69 percent of the total value of agricultural products produced on Indian lands....

Timber

Timber has the potential for being one of the most important Indian resources for development of reservation economies. Unlike mineral resources, timber is a renewable resource, and, therefore, can contribute indefinitely to tribal revenues. Excluding

Alaska, the total standing timber inventory in Indian country is estimated at 40 billion board-feet.

Indian forestry lands are the largest private holding of forested and commercial forest land in the United States. One-fourth of all Indian lands are forested, and 10 percent of all Indian lands are commercial forest lands. Timber contributes from 25 to 100 percent of tribal revenues for 57 reservations; more than 80 percent on 11 of these reservations. Income from stumpage (standing trees) alone for 1974 was $73 million.

Nevertheless, at present the potential yield of Indian timber lands is not being achieved. It is estimated that the $73 million derived from stumpage sales was 20% less than could have been obtained if harvesting had matched the annual allowable cut (AAC). In some areas harvesting on Indian lands was 65 to 75 percent below annual allowable cut. It is estimated that between 1970 and 1974 the dollar loss to tribes from insufficient logging was $25,486,767.

This problem is compounded by the fact that the BIA has failed to implement reforestation and precommercial thinning programs for many tribal forests. If the AAC is not adjusted for those tribal forests affected, it will inevitably (and soon) deplete the resource. Ironically, the BIA, by its inflexibility, fails in both respects by setting the AAC too low for some forests and too high for others....

Mineral Resources

In a report to the Senate Committee on Energy and Natural Resources (then Interior and Insular Affairs), March 31, 1976, the General Accounting Office (GAO) stated that Indian oil and gas reserves amount to approximately 3 percent of the United States total reserves. This was broken down into 40 reservations in 17 States. The estimate on oil reserves as of November 1973, was approximately 4.2 billion barrels with gas resources at about 17.5 trillion cubic feet. There was also an estimation of approximately 100-200 billion tons of identified coal reserves located on 33 reservations in 11 States. This was approximately 7-13 percent of the United States identified coal resources of 1.581 billion tons. In a report by the Federal Trade Commission that Indian lands have the potential of containing more than one-tenth of the United States currently minable coal reserves. A brief review of the relative importance of Indian minerals to production in the United States would also prove helpful. Data gathered from a USGS survey shows that production of coal on Indian lands in 1974 was 1.9 percent of all United States production which made up 35.8 percent of all production on Federal and Indian lands. The value of production of oil and gas on Indian lands was 4.4 percent of the total United States production. If off-shore leases are excluded, the production value rises to 13.6 percent of the total production value on all Federal and Indian lands. Aside from the major Indian energy resources, there are a variety of other minerals of considerable value on Indian lands. For example, phosphate production on Indian lands was 4.9 percent of the total United States production which amounted to 35.4 percent on Federal and Indian lands. In 1974, 100 percent of the Federal and Indian land uranium production was on Indian lands. It must be noted that of all mining on Federal and Indian lands, production from Indian held resources was 15.6 of the total.

While the AIPRC report would suggest that Indian country contains substantial untapped wealth, these figures must be placed in perspective. The natural resources available to Indian tribes are distributed unevenly. Some tribes, like the Navajo, Crow, or Northern Cheyenne, have mineral resources from which they are building tribal capital, while others have few, if any, available natural resources to exploit and little development potential for their barren reservations. Some tribes have deliberately withheld some of their resources from production because of the destruction of environmental and communal tribal values that widespread development might entail. Lack of development capital has frequently frustrated the Indian exploitation of their own resources and many Indian tribes fear, often with good reason, that non-Indian development will mean loss of control and sovereignty and a further transfer of land, resources, and wealth from Indian to non-Indian ownership. A morass of legal problems, including jurisdictional and ownership entanglements and BIA bureaucracy, has often frustrated economic development of Indian lands and resources. Some Indian land and resources also remain economically undeveloped due to geographic or technological inaccessability, sometimes caused by the lack of a supporting economic infrastructure because of the failure of the federal or state governments or the inability of tribal governments to provide certain needed services to Indian reservations, like roads, electricity, irrigation projects, and the like. For general surveys and bibliographic information about economic development of Indian country, see NATIONAL INDIAN LAW LIBRARY, BIBLIOGRAPHY ON INDIAN ECONOMIC DEVELOPMENT: AIDS FOR THE DEVELOPMENT OF ESSENTIAL LEGAL TOOLS FOR THE PROTECTION AND REGULATION OF COMMERCIAL ACTIVITIES ON INDIAN RESERVATIONS (2d ed. 1984); UNIVERSITY OF NEW MEXICO NATIVE AMERICAN STUDIES PROGRAM, ECONOMIC DEVELOPMENT IN AMERICAN INDIAN RESERVATIONS (1979); S. HABERFELD, R. POSNER, L. LEE & B. DEVAN, A SELF-HELP MANUAL FOR TRIBAL ECONOMIC DEVELOPMENT (1982); MINERAL DEVELOPMENT ON INDIAN LANDS (Rocky Mtn. Mineral L. Found. ed. 1989).

When questions of economic development of Indian country emerge, what are the appropriate roles for tribal choice, for federal direction or mandate, and for state initiatives? These questions have become quite compelling in Indian country. For much of the post-Depression era, Indian reservation economies have been bolstered by an infusion of federal program funds that support tribal governments, reservation infrastructures, and specific programs in Indian country. As federal program funds dwindled during the 1980's, tribes began to search for economic resources to bolster weak economies that were being further depleted by withdrawal of federal program support upon which they had come to rely. Tribes searched for new economic development strategies that varied from mineral and timber development, through industrialization, to bingo and resort operations and other forms of commericial enterprise. Such developments placed new strains on tribal communities and created new legal and technical challenges for tribal governments and Indian business enterprises. In the remainder of this chapter, examine some of the opportunities and problems created by such developments.

A. INTRODUCTORY PERSPECTIVES ON ECONOMIC DEVELOPMENT IN INDIAN COUNTRY

PRESIDENTIAL COMMISSION ON INDIAN RESERVATION ECONOMIES, REPORT AND RECOMMENDATIONS TO THE PRESIDENT OF THE UNITED STATES 21-57 (1984)

Introduction to the Recommendations

The Presidential Commission on Indian Reservation Economies proceeded upon the assumption that Indian reservation economies were an integral part of the national economy and not distinctly separate third world economies. In conducting its study on Indian reservation economies, therefore, it did not explicitly rely upon theories such as: traditional economic development theory of lesser developed countries, the Rostow linear stages model, the Harrod-Domar growth model, the Marxist neo-colonial dependence model, the false paradigm model, or even the Dualist model, as sources to explain Indian reservation underdevelopment. The Commission avoided presupposing a "model modernized society" as a standard for either approximation or comparison. Moreover, it did not believe that mail-order models or solutions, complete with their rates, routes and time-tables, would be sources for fertile recommendations. The Commission recognized that no Indian tribe or nation can simply import an Industrial Revolution from without, unpack it like a piece of machinery, and then set it in motion.

From the beginning, the Commission approached the problem of studying Indian reservation economic underdevelopment empirically and deductively. It sought to learn what the obstacles were that adversely affected competitive returns to land, labor and capital, as they were factored into an economic production function....

The processes of social and economic transformation necessary to make Indian reservations viable areas of economic growth will require whole-hearted commitment to change by all levels of government. The Federal-Indian relationship needs to mature beyond that of benign paternalism to that of a federalist partnership. Indian tribal governments need to exercise sovereign responsibility and to select development policies which make it possible for individual Indians to succeed in business. The recommendations which follow, however, recognize that the real motivating power of change must come from the Indian people and from their leadership. The direction and pace at which change proceeds should be determined, not by the federal government, but by the Indian people.

Development Framework: Introduction

The social and economic processes of transforming an economy encompass more than approaches to increasing per capita income, savings and investment ratios, or economic integration. An environmental framework favorable to economic development needs to be articulated. This is vital in order to break out of that process of circular and cumulative causation which sees low productivity leading to low incomes, low incomes leading to low levels of living, and low levels of living leading to low productivity.

The changes anticipated by the recommendations made in this section contemplate a new Federal-Indian relationship, no longer characterized by paternalism, but imbued with a sense of partnership between the United States and Indian tribal governments. A framework capable of supporting such a new partnership will require a reordering of the ways in which the United States and Indian tribes relate to each other, to new responsibilities, and to new challenges. A modernization of social and political arrangements is needed in order to create a basis from which social and economic self-sufficiency can be built.

There will always be resistance to constructing a social and political framework which is capable of providing incentives and opportunity, and which in parting from the old order, releases the considerable productive capabilities latent in Indian society. Economic development, without subsidy, can be successfully put together only within a new social and economic setting which entails a radical break with the past dependency on the federal government....

Modernization of Tribal Governments

[S]ocial and economic characteristics among the 487 Indian tribal governments vary widely, making the notion of model constitutions troublesome. In general, there are more non-Indians living within the borders of Indian reservations than there are Indian residents. Approximately 35% of all Indian reservations and Alaskan villages have fewer than 100 resident members. Less than 15% of all Indian reservations have 2,000 or more members. The high degree of social and economic integration within tribal borders imposes burdens on tribal government functioning. Land and resource ownership characteristics also vary widely. Of the $175 million dollars in royalties, rents and bonuses from mineral leases on Indian lands, the majority went to Council of Energy Resource Tribes which constitute fewer than 10% of the nation's Indian organization. In addition, the distribution of grazing lands, farm lands, irrigable lands, timber lands, fisheries and water resources are such that wealth is not evenly distributed among the Indian organizations.

In order to deal more effectively with the demands which de facto social and economic integration impose on tribal governments and in consideration of the substantial differences among Indian reservations and their tribal governments, Indian tribes need to modernize their systems of governance.

Generally speaking, Indian tribal governments are hindered in their pursuit of economic and business development by their antiquated or inappropriate political structures. Moreover, their failure to adhere to a constitutional principle separating executive, legislative and judicial powers has had a detrimental effect on governmental functioning. For example, the failure to establish a clear separation of powers between the tribal council and the tribal judiciary has resulted in political interference with tribal courts, weakening their independence, and raising doubts about fairness and the rule of law. Similarly, the penchant of tribal councils to operate by "resolution" rather than by "ordinance" has the effect of politicizing executive administration, particularly where the chairman-executive is also an elected member of the council. The overlap in authorities undermines stable functioning of tribal government.

[The Commission's recommendations to improve tribal government included that tribes provide for separation of powers among the executive, legislative, and judicial branches; insulation of business functions from political control and management by tribal governments; and strengthening of the rule of law on reservations by providing for appeal from tribal courts to the federal system.]

Reorganization of Government Support Systems

Bureau of Indian Affairs management of Indian trust resources creates numerous land, labor, and capital obstacles to Indian reservation economic development. In terms of land and resources, incompetent asset management undermines local initiative and raises costs to Indian tribes and businesses. In terms of labor, Bureau personnel are either under-qualified to manage their present responsibilities, or unable to provide expert technical assistance for business development. Moreover, education and training programs are so overcontrolled by the Bureau, that local control of Indian programs and schools is more rhetorical than factual. Training programs are not focused on private sector labor markets. They are generally not cost effective in terms of employment, and the training and counseling bureaucracy consumes more funds on itself than it contracts directly to tribes. In terms of capital, the Bureau's organizational structure, functioning, and operational deficiencies are such that the cost of doing business on Indian reservations is raised considerably when Indian business development is required to involve the BIA. Furthermore, business development is frequently deterred by BIA where its bureaucratic processes are required for approvals. Excessive regulation has compliance and control for its goals. A Byzantine system of overregulation actually deters investment by raising costs, creating uncertainty, and undermining local initiative. Exacerbating the development climate is the fact that BIA consumes more than two-thirds of its budget on itself, contracting only 27% of its programs to Indian tribes; leaving very little for investment purposes. Inadequate federal funding exists as an identified obstacle to Indian economic development because the system of delivering support to Indian tribes and Native groups is not designed to provide them with the kind of support they need. The system is designed for paternalistic control and it thrives on the failure of Indian tribes.

A reorganization of government systems which focuses on trust responsibility from the perspective of protection, rather than management, which provides a population-resource formula for block grants to tribes, and which acknowledges their rights to manage their own affairs, would provide the right kind of support. The last ten years of Bureau failure at Indian Self-Determination and Education Assistance Act contracting cannot be overcome by entrusting to the Bureau's bureaucracy, the responsibility of reforming itself. Bureau control over budget reallocations and the contract terms of P.L. 93-638 contracting has led to continued domination of tribal social and economic development. Such a governmental reorganization should also provide for continued government operation of programs and basic services where tribes do not wish to participate in block grants or in enhanced P.L. 93-638 contracting efforts.

Legislation creating a new federal agency for supporting Indian tribes and maintaining the federal trust responsibility should also possess the appropriate legal authorities for accessing resource information developed and maintained by other agencies within the federal government. The Bureau of Land Management and the Minerals Management Service are agencies whose authorities should be evaluated for possible transfer of land surveying and resource recordkeeping functions related to federal-Indian lands. A federal agency which provides financial support and trust protection services would reduce the federal presence in Indian affairs. It also would result in the transfer of most appropriated funds directly to tribes and Native groups, and would provide a protective umbrella for tribal government, by making accountability possible through local autonomy.

[The Commission's recommendations to improve federal government support systems included a National Commission on Indian Business Development created by Executive Order and operated from the White House. The Commission also urged the reform of trust assets management in several recommendations suggesting legislation to create an Indian trust services administration that would focus on protection rather than management of Indian resources, and administer block grants to those tribes electing to receive them and ISDEA contract and grant programs for tribes not choosing to receive block grants.]

Rationalization of Intergovernmental Authority

Concurrent legislative jurisdiction by state and local governments, with tribal governments, over non-Indian residents of Indian reservations, and over economic activity on reservations involving non-Indians, have produced significant litigation and jurisdictional conflicts. Disputes of this kind constitute a major source of obstacles to Indian reservation economic development. When businesses believe that there will be dual taxation if they locate on Indian reservations and do business there, they tend to locate along the outside border of a reservation. In spite of *White Mountain Apache Tribe v. Bracker*, 448 U.S. 160 (1980), denying the state's right to tax a non-Indian business entity doing business with an Indian tribe, there is still widespread ambiguity over the extent to which state taxing power may reach.

In order to minimize the adverse effects of dual taxation on economic activity and to avoid discouraging a partnership among non-Indians and Indians, legal persons residing or doing business within the boundaries of a reservation should not incur the burdens of supporting two sovereigns. Indians and non-Indians, at the discretion of a tribal referendum, should be able to accept the exclusive taxing authority and jurisdiction of an Indian tribe, to the extent that state authority may not also apply. Such acceptance of exclusive tribal taxing authority would also create a responsibility on the part of the tribe to provide necessary public services to all residents within its boundaries.

[The Commission recommended that legislation provide for referenda by which all] franchised voters residing within the exterior boundaries of a Federal-Indian reservation, may by majority vote, accept the exercise of exclusive tribal government taxation authority and responsibility for the provision of public services to all people; the effect of which referenda shall be to preempt state taxing jurisdiction; and that such legislation not limit the power of tribes to enter into local service agreements with other units of state or local government.

Capital Formation — Introduction

One of the major obstacles to Indian economic development is "access" to sources of capital by Indian individuals, Indian businesses and Indian tribes. The problem is one of getting capital to the right places. Risk aversion, however, influences the degree of that access. In determining risk, financial institutions must take rate of return on investment into account. Unfortunately, there are additional factors raising risk to investment on Indian reservations which are not found off of reservations. Major factors which raise risk or impose additional costs are:

— Trust status of Indian surface and subsurface resources
— Federal regulation and management of those resources
— Public sector management of business activity by Tribes

— State, local, tribal government concurrent regulation

The fact that Indian lands and resources are held in trust by the federal government means that they cannot be flexibly used as collateral for loans from financial institutions which require suitable security. Federal regulation and management of Indian lands and resources, primarily by the Bureau of Indian Affairs, imposes a complex framework of regulatory controls over resource decision making and resource use. These controls exist in treaties, executive orders and statutes and govern specific resources, such as: land, minerals, timber, water, fishing, etc. Since tribes are the major land and resource owners on Indian reservations, they are intimately involved in promoting business development activity. The problem is that the goals of tribal governments decapitalize their business by redirecting retained earnings toward support of tribal government rather than toward business expansion. Tribal governments often compete with individual Indians or Indian businesses rather than providing an environment conducive to their success. State and local governments frequently impose additional regulation and taxation of business activity on Indian reservations, in excess of the public services which they provide.

The Indian reservation environment is regulated and managed by the federal government; it is also regulated, managed, and taxed by state, local and tribal governments. The heavy degree of governmental involvement in business activity, whether it involves trust assets or not, creates an environment hostile to private sector development. The traditional response of the federal government has been to provide capital grant and loan guarantee programs because tribes have had difficulty in accessing private sector capital markets where weak security or additional costs increase risk. While federal capital programs may have provided a substitute capital market to alleviate the security problems which trust status creates, nothing has been done to alleviate the costs which excessive federal, state, local and tribal governments impose....

Preservation of the trust relationship is, however, the most important test by which Indian tribes measure Federal-Indian policy. Centuries of dishonor by the United States in fulfilling its duty of care and protection, as set forth in practically every Treaty, have instilled a fear in Indian tribes that is rational, to the extent that there have been historical takings of Indian lands, and irrational, to the extent that such a relationship does impair access to capital resources, thereby impeding efforts toward self-sufficiency.

The President's 1983 American Indian Affairs Policy Statement seeks to uphold the trust relationship. Consistent with the President's policy, his Commission on Indian Reservation Economies has considered numerous alternatives to improving the opportunities for capital formation, consistent with continued maintenance of the federal trust responsibility.

Private Ownership of Tribal Enterprises

In the United States, the private sector accounts for about 88% of the gross national product. Private sector capital is the basis for the production of goods and services and is indispensable to economic growth. It is the engine which supports public sector services. A free enterprise system is characterized by private ownership of the means of production and all other kinds of property, and by considerable individual freedom in pursuing economic activities for the sake of personal profit. Private property, individual freedom and the profit motive are basic attributes of the national economic system. By contrast, Indian reservations are characterized by government-run tribal businesses, utilizing tribally held property, and operated in many instances in a not-for-profit manner. In all capitalist systems, governments do play an economic role, but not to the same extent as tribal governments.

Private enterprise includes all economic activities that are independent of government control, or outside of the so-called public sector, that are carried on principally for profit. Also included are those nonprofit organizations which are directed at satisfying private needs, such as private hospitals and private schools. Private enterprise is owned individually, or by groups, as well as the self-employed.

The Private Sector Survey on Opportunities and Constraints, commissioned by the President's Commission on Indian Reservation Economies found that extensive tribal government management and involvement in business development activity contributed to the failure of tribal enterprises. Merely separating the corporate functions of tribal enterprises from interference by tribal government and employing competent management will not achieve a privatization of tribal enterprises capable of offering profit motivation, private property ownership, or individual freedom. Private ownership of tribal enterprises contemplates ownership of the means of production, private management, for-profit motivation and freedom for individual Indians or groups of Indians who have or share an interest in participating in business activity on an Indian reservation. Tribes could just as easily lease tribally held assets to their members as they presently do to nonmember businesses which use their resources. Existing businesses could be sold to tribal members, or ownership transferred by way of stock transfers, rather than per capita distributions of corporate retained earnings. Employee stock participation plans could also be offered. There is no one correct approach to privatizing tribal enterprises. There are, however, many possibilities for offering individual Indians incentives. There is no difference between a per capita payment from a tribal enterprise, a judgment fund, a mineral royalty or bonus, and a welfare distribution, where no opportunity exists for individual Indians to self-actualize or to succeed through individual effort.

Securities Regulation

[The Securities and Exchange Commission is a federal agency that] enforces a number of federal laws: the Securities Act of 1933, Public Utility Holding Company Act of 1935, Trust Indenture Act of 1939, Investment Advisers Act of 1940, Investment Company Act of 1940, and the Securities Act Amendments of 1975.

Securities and Exchange Commission statutes and regulations presently exempt states and local governments from registration under the 1934 Securities Act, thereby reducing, significantly, their costs in issuing securities and financing economic development. Since tribal governments are not specifically identified in the statute providing for exemption, Indian tribes will potentially incur higher costs for securities which they issue in private capital markets. Consistent with the President's policy statement recognizing Indian tribes as tribal governments, Indian tribes should be accorded the same treatment as that provided to states and local governments.

Indian Tax Status

Under the provisions of the Indian Tribal Governmental Tax Status Act of 1982, Indian tribal governments are accorded the same treatment as states or local political subdivisions of states, for purposes of certain sections of the Internal Revenue Code. The Tax Status Act accords tax-exempt treatment status to revenue bonds issued by Indian tribal governments, which are used to support basic infra-structure or community development construction. Industrial revenue bonds which are used to finance business development are not accorded the same treatment.

Industrial development bonds are tax-exempt bonds issued by local governments to attract industrial enterprises. The bond is for a plant nominally owned by the municipal government, but actually secured by the long-term lease of a firm that negotiates with the local government. The business, therefore, has the advantage of lower-cost borrowing on a tax-free bond, and the municipality gets a new industry. Manufacturers also use industrial revenue bonds for pollution control projects.

Industrial revenue bonds which can be used to help finance new businesses on reservations and encourage the development of local reservation industries are not now accorded tax-exempt status by the Internal Revenue Code. Although it is generally recognized that Indian tribes should be accorded similar status to that of states and local governments, the lack of federal exemption for interest paid on industrial revenue bonds places them in an inferior status. President Reagan's 1983 Indian Affairs Policy Statement seeks to treat Indian tribes as governments.

The ability to access pre-existing capital markets through industrial revenue bonds by offering tax-exempt status to interest paid on such bonds would provide tribes with an important means of attracting profitable business expansions and significantly enhance the potential for expanding local business activity.

Trust Fund Investment

[The current system of Bureau of Indian Affairs trust fund investment and management] effectively denies tribes the right to determine their own investment objectives, to choose between investing in a short-term highly liquid portfolio, or in a medium-term wealth maximization portfolio. It also fails to account properly for invested funds.

[The Commission recommended:] that the Bureau of Indian Affairs with tribal concurrence, contract as many of the trust fund's operational and management functions as possible, to private fund managers, subject to federal laws protecting trust fund assets and income, and realign those functions not contracted, into a more efficient and effective organization; [and] that tribes also be offered the freedom to choose between investing their funds in a privately contracted investment fund, or in local financial institutions, subject to federal laws protecting trust fund assets and income.

[The Commission recommended] that an independent Indian venture capital fund(s) be created which can provide loans and take equity positions in partnership with Indian businesses, and which is capitalized through private sector subscriptions, matched on a limited basis by funds previously used to support the Bureau of Indian Affairs' economic development activities.

[The Commission also recommended] that the Indian Finance Act be appropriately amended so that private financial institutions be permitted to contract for administrative functions as well as make loans, utilize guarantees, etc., subject to annual appropriations, revolving fund limitations, and fund management by the treasury department.

[The Commission further recommended] that the Indian loan guaranty fund be amended to provide for guarantees to underwriters of surety bonds, to a maximum extent of 50 percent, and that private underwriters rather than the Bureau of Indian Affairs be permitted to make the underwriting determination.

Business Development — Introduction

Role of Tribal Government

In order for successful business development to take place on Indian reservations there is a need for tribal development, investment, and implementation policies and strategies which are favorable to business development. A. Waterson summarized his experience in "Development Planning: Lessons of Experience," thus:

> The available evidence makes it clear that in countries with development plans, lack of adequate government support for the plans is the prime reason why most are never carried out. Conversely, the cardinal lesson that emerges from the planning experience of developing countries is that the sustained commitment of a politically stable government is the sine qua non for development. Where a country's political leadership makes development a central concern, the people can also be interested through a judicious use of economic incentives. And, although it is never easy to reform administrative and institutional inefficiency, commitment by political leaders is a necessary condition for reform; without it, reform is impossible.

Indian tribes need to rethink what their role should be in economic development. Instead of monopolizing reservation economic activity, the role of encouraging private sector development through tribal development, investment, and implementation policies and strategies, should be given serious consideration. Tribal leadership needs to act to improve the reservation business climate, to exercise sovereign immunity responsibly, and to link tribal public financing of infrastructure to business development activity....

Business Planning, Management, and Technical Assistance

Because business developments are extremely prone to failure in their early years, there is a definite need for tribal governments to be more hard-nosed in evaluating their ideas than they have been in the past.... A business orientation which focuses on local comparative advantages in relation to production of goods and services, and their markets, needs to be developed. Every Indian reservation has economic advantages to offer, whether or not they are possessed of abundant natural resources. To the extent that human capital is present, the productive employment of labor in the right business activity can be that advantage. A business planning process which seeks to build businesses that are profitable is indispensable to reservation economic development....

Private Indian Business Development Centers, which provide appropriate business management and business technical assistance in such areas as industrial engineering, production design, marketing, finance, etc., could provide no-nonsense sources of assistance. They could assist tribes to prepare business plans on products or services, market research and evaluation, pricing, sales and advertising plans, break-even analyses; assist on product, facilities, management, and organizational improvements; profit and loss forecasting; approaches to capitalization, etc. The provision of expert private-sector-located management and technical assistance, unlike that presently provided by the federal government, could provide the difference between success and failure.

Business planning, management, and technical assistance capabilities need to be acquired or created if Indian reservation economic development is to succeed....

Encouraging Private Initiative Through Private Business Associations

Tribal governments should not act in competition with private Indian, individuals or private business associations. For example, where the degree of fractionated land ownership is high, undivided interest holders could be encouraged to pool their interests in allotments, and by leasing tribal lands, engage in cooperative farming and ranching. Instead of receiving insignificant lease rental as they now do, they could benefit from employment and profits. With 60% of Indian lands leased to non-Indian owners, significant potential exists for innovative private business associations to engage in economic activity.

Moreover, tribes need not be the prime promoters of business activity. Indian business development corporations could be created to provide sources of equity or debt financing to private Indian individuals. They, rather than non-Indian lessees, could lease tribal resources and use them in business activity....

Labor Markets — Introduction

Economists classify markets in terms of their structure, that is, the number and size of economic buyers and sellers, the degree to which products differ from one another, and the ease with which new producers or suppliers can enter a market. The structure of the market determines the amount and kind of competition that will prevail and how prices will ultimately be set. Labor markets are those contacts between buyers and sellers for a given kind of labor. For the majority of jobs, such contacts occur in a relatively small geographic area, limited mainly by the distance people are willing to travel to work. For certain occupations, the labor market can be nationwide. In most cases however, the labor market area consists of a medium-sized or large urban center and the territory surrounding it. About 250 such areas in the United States are considered major labor market areas by the Labor Department's Bureau of Employment Security.

The traditional competitive free market model for labor is characterized by consumer sovereignty, individual utility and profit maximization, perfect competition and economic efficiency with very many "atomistic" producers and consumers, none of whom is large enough to influence prices or wages. The level of employment and the "wage rate" are determined simultaneously with all other prices and factor uses in the economy by the forces of supply and demand.

The problem with the traditional labor market model is that it is not very applicable to the realities of wage and employment determination on Indian reservations. Wage rates are typically not flexible downward since they are largely determined by "institutional" forces, including labor union pressures, legislated government salary scales, and corporate or business hiring practices. There are many more Indian laborers seeking employment at the going wage than there are jobs available. Involuntary unemployment and underemployment are pervasive.

The national labor movement experience is extended to Indian reservations through a host of federal labor laws which do benefit labor, but do not benefit Indian labor in economic activity located within Indian reservation boundaries. Since the structure of labor markets determines the degree of competition, and that structure benefits organized labor to the detriment of Indian labor, a more effective approach to stimulating local Indian labor markets would be to recognize the rights of Indian tribal governments to exercise their own governmental powers in the regulation of local, reservation based, labor markets. In 1980, there were 106,947 American Indians and Alaska Natives living on Indian reservations or other trust lands located in 27 states, 16-65 years old, who were unemployed and were actively seeking employment. A great many of these Indians were unable to work on construction, mining, and resource development projects located on their own reservations because of federal laws benefiting the importation of outside labor. Considering the small number of unemployed Indians nationally, relaxing the application of federal laws in favor of local tribal governmental regulation would not materially damage organized labor's hold on off-reservation labor markets.

The stereotype of "Indians who don't want to work," is challenged by the fact that federal laws benefiting non-Indian and non-local labor work against employment of Indians. There is a difference between not wanting to work, and being barred from working. [The Commission's recommendations to increase the opportunities for Indian employment included exemptions from the Davis-Bacon Act's requirement that federal contractors pay the prevailing wages in an area, permitting tribes to elect to exclude themselves from NLRB jurisdiction over collective bargaining insofar as it would impede tribal preference laws, and amending the Taft-Hartley Act to permit tribes the right-to-work option currently granted states.]

Development Incentives — Introduction

The potential market demand of federal procurement of goods and services from the private sector, which amounted to some $165 billion in FY 1983, and such preferential procurement instruments as already exist, would appear to offer large opportunities for Indian owned enterprises, both individually and tribally owned. However, testimony from the Commission's public hearings from around the country and analysis of the literature indicate that Indian tribes and firms are encountering difficulty in making federal contracting and procurement work for them in the same way that it is for other small and disadvantaged minority-owned firms, for small businesses, for firms in labor surplus areas, and for enterprises benefiting from mandatory procurement requirements for the Federal Prison Industries and the National Industries for the Blind and the Severely Handicapped.

In the obstacle analysis work of the Commission, the major federal capital obstacle to Indian economic development was identified as federal contract and procurement system weaknesses. The Bureau of Indian Affairs was cited for not effectively implementing its Buy-Indian Act authorities in its contracting and procurement activities and for being unduly restrictive in requiring Indian firms to be 100% owned and controlled by Indians. Note that the Small Business Act only requires 51% ownership for participation by disadvantaged minority businesses in SBA's assistance programs. The more restrictive requirement by BIA limits the ability of Indian firms to obtain capital and access to technical and management expertise by joint venturing with private investors.

The Defense Department was criticized for not implementing its discretionary Buy-Indian authorities, in place since Fiscal Year 1982, for purchases from qualified Indian suppliers of goods and services who could meet the quality, cost and delivery requirements dictated by the Department of Defense mission. The SBA was heavily criticized for its restrictiveness and procedural rigidities which favor minorities, but not Indian tribes or Indian enterprises, and for inconsistency and confusion among different district and regional offices as to the requirements of who is considered to be an Indian, whether tribal enterprises are eligible, how to handle the issue of federal, state or Indian tribal government charters for Indian enterprises, whether to allow non-Indians or non-disadvantaged but experienced businessmen on boards of directors for tribal enterprises, who to include in determining economic disadvantage of an entire tribe, and how "management of daily operations" was to be considered for a tribal enterprise with a salaried professional administrator. The Labor Surplus Areas Program (LSA), which allows federal agencies to set aside contracts for competition among firms which carry out more than 50 percent of the contract in labor surplus areas, was criticized because Indian reservations are not regarded as "civil jurisdictions" for LSA classification purposes....

[C]urrent federal contracting with Indian tribes and Indian firms comes to less than two-tenths of one percent of total federal procurement. This minimal amount includes the "638" contracts by the Bureau of Indian Affairs and the Indian Health Service, "Buy Indian" contracting by BIA and IHS, and SBA subcontracts with Indian 8(a) firms. If contracts with Indian firms could be increased each year by one-tenth of one percent of total government procurement, this would add some $200 million in new contracts for Indian enterprises. Such an increment each year would be minuscule in terms of federal procurement and would not present onerous burdens on any single federal agency. A one-tenth of one percent annual increment would be only a small portion of larger annual increases of total procurement so that no business would be taken away from any existing firms or minority or other disadvantaged groups. Such an increase could be easily absorbed by Indian enterprises.

A goal is suggested of a government-wide Indian procurement target of $1 billion over an initial five year period to be achieved through cumulative increments of $200 million per year, starting in FY 1985, as a means of stimulating private sector Indian business development and employment. This goal is consistent with the President's Executive Order 12432 on Minority Business Enterprises which established a $22 billion target in federal contract and subcontract awards to minority firms over the three year period of FY 1983 to FY 1985.

Based upon Bureau of Labor Statistics figures, it is estimated that yearly increments of $200 million in federal procurement contracts to Indian enterprises would result in some 9,000 new jobs within Indian firms and some 3,000 new jobs in businesses supplying parts, materials and services to these Indian firms. This direct and indirect employment impact is estimated to generate some $171 million per year in additional income to the economies of the Indian reservations and the surrounding local communities. It is also estimated that this would in turn generate $19 million additional revenue in federal income tax each year. Sustained increments over the initial five year period would translate by 1989 into 44,000 new jobs in Indian enterprises that year, 15,000 new jobs in surrounding communities, $855 million in resulting wage income, and $94 million in additional federal income tax. Revising or refining future five-year procurement targets should be determined by the proposed National Commission on Indian Business Development.

As a development incentive, the federal procurement opportunity would not require any new federal funds. It would draw upon the budgets of government agencies who already purchase goods and services from the private sector to carry out their government missions. It would not give money to Indians. It would improve the access by Indian firms to the federal marketplace and allow them the opportunity to earn their way. Indian individuals would benefit as would Indian tribes, the surrounding community, and the federal government from decreased welfare payments and increased federal income tax payments.

Each federal agency would be called upon to make use of existing procurement authorities and instruments in seeking to reach government-wide targets for Indian procurement of $1 billion over the initial five year period. Actions would include revision of E.O. 12432 consistent with the intent of the overall procurement recommendations. Other actions would include assigning oversight and reporting responsibility for Indian procurement within the network of the Offices of Small and Disadvantaged Business Utilization created by the Small Business Act, seeking equal access by Indian firms for participation in 8(a) contracting by the Small Business Administration, in small business set-aside contracting, in labor surplus area set-aside contracting, and others as appropriate. Further actions should include effective implementation of the Buy Indian authorities of the Department of Defense, Indian Health Service, and Bureau of Indian Affairs, as well as expanding the scope of the Acts.

The Small Business Administration and other agencies should recognize Indian individuals and tribal enterprises located on Indian reservations or trust lands which have been organized under federal or tribal laws, as well as those off-reservation Indian enterprises which have been organized under state charters. Such recognition is consistent with the President's government-to-government policy statement....

In addition to improving access by Indians to federal procurement opportunities, Enterprise Zones could be additional development incentives. Currently, Indian reservations have very little in the way of private sector economies. In order to assist economically depressed areas, the Administration has proposed the Enterprise Zone Employment and Development Act. This act would designate zones within which major tax incentives and regulatory relief could be offered to stimulate job creation, business growth and physical revitalization. Indian reservations should be an important part of this proposal.

NOTES

President Reagan appointed the Presidential Commission on Indian Reservation Economies in his American Indian Policy Statement issued January 24, 1983, mentioned in the final report of the Commission. This statement was issued shortly after then Secretary of the Interior James Watt made public comments about socialism on Indian reservations. Indian leaders were widely critical of these statements since they feared such criticisms echoed prior attacks on tribal collective ownership and management of Indian property that had been politically used to justify both the allotment policy of the late nineteenth century and the termination policy of the twentieth century. Although the Commission report contained a strongly worded recommendation that Congress repeal House Concurrent Resolution 108, which instituted the Termination Era, does the Commission report rejuvenate and defend the arguments historically advanced to justify termination?

The extensive focus of the Commission report on privatization of reservation economies attracted considerable critical comment and opposition. Tribal leaders extensively condemned the report and none of its proposals attracted sufficient support to secure enactment of remedial legislation. One commentator, noting that a majority of the Commission was composed of a hand-picked group of Indian tribal chairmen, business, and political leaders, suggested that the report proposed "altering the communal philosophy of shared benefits and maximum employment which lies at the heart of most tribal enterprises under tribal control." Williams, *The Algebra of Federal Indian Law: The Hard Trail of Decolonizing and Americanizing the White Man's Indian Jurisprudence*, 1986 WIS. L. REV. 219, 280-81 n.233. Thus, he argued that some Indians have become convinced that political and economic accommodation will only be achieved at the cost of sacrificing Indian visions of political and economic development that may be seen to be at odds with the national interest. *Id.* at 281.

In contrast to the report of the Presidential Commission on Indian Reservation Economies, seven years earlier, the congressionally created American Indian Policy Review Commission had recommended that economic development proceed on Indian reservations under tribal control and management. For example, the Commission recommended that

[t]he present laws be amended to insure *tribal control* of the development of Indian-owned natural resources, including water, coal, oil, uranium, gravel and clay, and other minerals. The laws, once amended, should be flexible enough to allow the tribes to determine for themselves the best form of organization which will enable them to control development and realize the maximum financial returns from the development of their natural resources.

AMERICAN INDIAN POLICY REVIEW COMMISSION, FINAL REPORT 347 (1977). Similarly, the Commission recommended that Congress enact legislation to assure that Small Business Administration funds and technical assistance be made available to "businesses which are chartered or operated by tribal governments." *Id.* at 362.

The separate political and jurisdictional structures in Indian country effectively remove most Indian land from the political control and regulation of state government in order to insure that tribal members can chart their own political destiny. Has the economic dependency of Indians on the free market economy which the reservation system produced inexorably forced the tribes away from tribal communal economic values and toward the individualism and competition of private enterprise? Is some tribal communal accommodation with free market approaches possible by treating the tribe as the corporate enterprise, just as national oil industries in Saudi Arabia and Mexico operate in the free global market? On the other hand, given that tribes, states, and even nations are no longer economically self-sufficient, can tribally owned and managed enterprises function competitively in a global economy increasingly dependent on privately owned multinational corporations? Can tribes continue what Professor Williams calls the "communal philosophy of shared benefits and maximum employment" in a highly competitive world driven by economic concerns of maximum efficiency and lowest cost?

B. VENTURE ENTERPRISES, CAPITAL FORMATION, AND INDIAN DEVELOPMENT

The manner in which a development transaction is structured may make a substantial difference on a number of issues. It may, among other things, affect immunity from state or local regulation, provide greater security and certainty for purposes of satisfying investors, or determine the level of tribal control of or benefit from the development transaction. In the last decades, as tribes have become more active in their participation in economic development, a greater array of potential models for economic development on the reservation have been proposed, and sometimes implemented. Simple leases, leases with operating interests, clauses which permit eventual tribal ownership of an enterprise, service contracts, and many more arrangements have been designed and adopted. To what extent, however, are such creative transaction structures limited by outmoded regulations, like the mineral or oil and gas leasing regulations, which often contain rigid, unidimensional provisions for development? Such questions often are critical since many tribes lack internal capital sources to finance development projects and must look to outside capital sources. Often such venture capital sources desire greater control over their investment than Indian tribes are willing to afford. The following materials discuss the economic, ideological, cultural, and legal concerns that are intermeshed in considering appropriate models for the development of natural resources.

1. TRIBAL DEVELOPMENT OF INDIAN RESOURCES

BARSH & HENDERSON, TRIBAL ADMINISTRATION OF NATURAL RESOURCE DEVELOPMENT, 52 North Dakota Law Review 307, 327-39 (1975)*

V. *Advantages of Tribal Ownership*

Tribal ownership and control of natural resource development is both a lawful and an economically preferable alternative to federal or tribal regulation of private enterprise. The demonstrated inefficiencies of federal administration have made it impossible for tribes to enjoy a satisfactory share of resource revenues. Tribal resources have served as little more than low-interest savings accounts, with the greater part of total revenue leaving the reservation as wages and profits to non-Indians. Simple solutions are not adequate to the task. Bidding up rents and royalties will increase income without stemming the outflow of wages and profits, if indeed it does not eliminate the principal existing attraction of reservation investment. Taxation would have the identical effect. Reorganizing the Bureau and disambiguating the law, together with a stronger tribal court system, may reduce significantly the costs of outside firms doing business on reservations and make it possible to bid up rents and royalties, but cash outflow will still continue.

One alternative is to invest tribal funds in secondary and tertiary industries in hopes of recapturing some of this outflow. Presumably if outside labor finds suitable opportunities to spend money on the reservation where they work, that is where they will spend it. Another possibility is to invest tribal funds in human capital development, minimizing the likelihood that primary industries on reservations will need to import labor. Quotas on employment of reservation citizens, if they can be negotiated without corresponding rent or royalty reductions, could also minimize the outflow of revenue due to wages. But neither possibility promises to have any effect on the revenue going to compensate outside investors.

Why shouldn't the tribes, as owners of reservation resources, also become capitalists and employers? One argument often heard is that tribes are incompetent to manage such large firms. But the same might be said of the directors of many private companies, who hire experts to analyze marketing and production problems. There is no reason why tribes cannot do likewise. There is also a feeling that the current arrangement (leasing) makes development "free." After all, the tribe contributes no capital, and in fact contributes only what it has always had without expense: its resources. Selling nonrenewable resources at anything less than the maximum possible return is hardly free. It is a loss of potential income. And if the underlying reason for this attitude is an assumption that tribes cannot accumulate the capital necessary to go into business, the answer is that they can borrow private capital in the same manner as private firms, and can, in addition, participate in some federal grant and loan programs.[93] As in any business, the only relevant consideration is whether the rate

---

*Copyright © 1976 by the North Dakota Law Review. Reprinted by permission.

[93] Tribal bonds might be tax-free if used solely for financing public services or public industries flowing directly into the tribal treasury. *See* McDaniel, Federal Income Taxation of Industrial

of return on capital invested in development will exceed the cost to the tribe of borrowing it.

There is finally a dark hint that tribal ownership is socialistic or un-American. This has a significant history all its own. From the beginning, Indians have been accused of a kind of primitive, dis-economical communism. Many early cases and observations seemed to indicate that this was the affliction from which the savages had to be saved. But rather than tribes becoming more capitalistic, America has become increasingly socialized. Many means of transportation are publicly owned and operated on a theory that they could not be adequately maintained by private capital, and other industries are publicly owned purely for purposes of revenue.

On the other hand, states derive more local benefit from a conventional business economy than tribes. In a diversified local economy, income recirculates. Wages from local firms return to other community enterprises as consumer spending and become wages again. Community capitalists also return income to local business in the form of consumer spending. But tribes generally have little in the way of retail or service industries; they are usually too small to support a diversified economy. Consequently reservation wages tend to be spent elsewhere, and reservation profits tend to be invested elsewhere.

Taxing reservation business profits at a rate high enough to compensate for this outflow of wages and profits might discourage businesses from locating on the reservation in the first place. An alternative is to keep profits in the local economy by maximizing reservation (individual and tribal) ownership. Tribal ownership can offset some of the obstacles of federal supervision and increase the profitability of some resources, relative to individual Indian ownership. It can also accomplish the redistributive objectives of state and federal regulation.

A. *Overcoming Obstacles*

If, as we argued above, federal supervision results in a discriminatorily high cost of doing business on reservation, then tribes may prove better able to overcome this obstacle (while it lasts) than individual Indian entrepreneurs. Tribal ownership may reduce the number of costly, duplicative transactions, lower the cost of credit, and increase the security of business property rights.

Federal supervision increases the number of steps in negotiation of reservation business arrangements. Each step adds delay and uncertainty. One way of minimizing this cost is by minimizing the number of transactions subject to Bureau review that will be necessary to develop a given resource fully. The more entrepreneurs have control of the reservation resource, the greater the number of transactions that inevitably will be involved in developing it fully.

Bonds: The Public Interest, 1 Urban Lawyer 157 (1969). Tribal bonds could of course, be secured by revenue rather than land. In addition tribes might invest their trust funds in resource industries. According to Sorkin, Indian Trust Funds, printed in 1969 Joint Comm. Print, pt. 2, *supra* note 1, at 452, these funds were invested at up to $6^{1}/4\%$ in 1968 by the Treasury Department. That was at about the prevailing rate of interest on government bonds in that year, and rather below the return on corporate bonds. Federal Reserve Bulletin A34 (April 1971). Sorkin attributes failure of tribes to invest these funds in their own industrialization to inexperience and the fear that they will lose revenue. It should be observed in light of the argument we are making, that a small loss in rate of return might be compensated for in new infrastructure, human capital development, and the relative efficiency of direct wage subsidies over administering the redistribution of investment income.

Therefore there will always be an economy of scale in consolidating a resource into a single tribal ownership.

In addition, a tribe can marshal more power to contest non-approval than its members. Falling back on its treasury, its power to tax, and its business income, the tribe is better able to retain counsel, lobby, and litigate. Tribal leaders have more political "clout" than individual Indians; their official capacity gives them more access to congressmen and the Executive office. The Bureau is more likely to exercise its veto powers over a number of private entrepreneurs than over a single tribal owner.

Because of its resources, taxing power, (albeit limited) ability to influence congressional grant and subsidy policy, and continuous corporate existence, a tribal owner offers better security for a potential commercial lender than an individual Indian. To be sure, tribes enjoy sovereign immunity, but they may waive it in particular cases. Waiver has been construed as consent to suit in state courts, but the tribe could expressly require that it be sued in its own courts, or that its own substantive law be applied. As long as the tribes' courts and law offer predictability comparable to state courts, even a waiver of immunity so limited would go far to minimize the costs of uncertainty in the enforcement of its contracts.

The principle offsetting factor is the susceptibility of tribes to the National Environmental Protection Act. Although tribes may be better able to overcome other problems of federal supervision than individual entrepreneurs, this problem applies to them alone. In the balance, its effect may be small. There is, in addition, a more persuasive reason for preferring tribal ownership in the resource area which would apply even in the absence of federal supervision: greater economic efficiency.

B. *Efficiency*

Under certain limited circumstances, the net revenue of a regulated firm may actually exceed the net revenue of private enterprise engaged in the same activities. The chief criteria are exclusion problems, infrastructure (or "public goods"), externalities, and fractional ownership....

[Generally a] regulated company has little incentive to cut costs when these can be recovered in the rate formula. Bureaucrats managing a public firm and drawing fixed incomes similarly have little incentive to cut costs or otherwise maximize profits.

These drawbacks are not applicable to tribal ownership. There is no substantial danger of monopoly pricing because the tribal firm must sell its product in a competitive, interstate market; only a negligible quantity of goods such as coal and oil would be saleable on the reservation. Futhermore, the bureaucrats in the tribal firm share in its profits because of the characteristic distribution of a part of tribal income in direct per capita payments. The small size of the tribe maximizes the incentive of profit sharing, and minimizes the risk that the tribal firm will be unresponsive to pressure from its citizens to cut costs to the extent that they rank among its consumers.

2. *Infrastructure*

The components of "infrastructure," such as transportation, communications, and power transmission, are characterized by steep initial costs and relatively low marginal costs. The fixed facilities (e.g., tracks, lines), once built, cost about the same to maintain regardless of how many persons use them. Moreover, their general social benefits, which can be thought of as economic articulation, are enjoyed by everyone in the community, not only those persons purchasing their services. It is therefore difficult if not impossible to obtain private financing for such a project — the investment is too great, the time until it shows a profit too long, and many if not most of its real benefits not recapturable as revenue.

Financing and operating infrastructure are frequently undertaken by local government. In the alternative, local government invests in and grants the subsidy of monopoly to a private firm, conditioned upon rate regulation. By either method, taxation and borrowing on public credit are essential sources of necessary capital. On reservations, raising capital for infrastructure creates a vicious circle. Tribes lack adequate tax bases without industry; indeed, for many of them primary industry is or will tend to be their principle source of revenue and the only security for their creditors. At the same time, the absence of suitable infrastructure can be expected to be a cost to reservation enterprises and thereby reduce tribal revenues.

It seems logical for tribes simultaneously to develop both infrastructure and resource production. By coordinating these two facets of development, tribes can channel resource revenue directly back into upgrading infrastructure and, accordingly, maximize future returns. Many facilities useful to private resource industries can be developed into multipurpose public utilities. If coal development, for example, requires telephones, rail lines, and roads, expanding these basic services to meet domestic needs will cost less than meeting the developer's and area needs in two independent and uncoordinated systems. The relatively small size or small number of towns on most reservations means that public and private utility needs can be served by vitually the same network.

3. Externalities

Many resource industries have a tendency to create "externalities" — costs external to the apparent book value of the enterprise. The most familiar externality is environmental damage. Because it may be insidious, thinly and widely spread, and tend to affect all persons whether or not they are consumers of the product, private action to remedy environmental damage is costly to mobilize and unlikely to be effective. The government may intervene, but even then often in vain, because the damage may be irreversible and not compensable. In that case, public control is the only practical solution.

Since the land base of most tribes is severely limited, environmental externalities may pose an unusually serious threat. The community can little afford to lose any potentially developable surface or water. It ought therefore to be entitled to resort to more radical means to preserve its territorial security.

4. Fractional Ownership

Finally, where a large portion of the reservation is individually owned in fractional shares, private development bears higher costs of accumulating adequate property than on state lands. Eminent domain could be justified as a cheap way of consolidating reservation property if exercised on behalf of a tribal enterprise rather than a private firm.

Any consideration of the costs of tribal resource economies must recognize that some resources, such as water, petroleum, and fisheries, not only cross ownership units within the reservation, but cross reservation boundaries into neighboring states. Consequently any attempt by a tribe to limit the rate of exploitation of these resources can be wholly frustrated by the failure of states to impose equal limits. The states could take advantage of tribes by exploiting what tribes conserve.

For example, the federal interest in preserving its own prerogatives with respect to water has resulted in a special analogy to the reserve rights doctrine. Under this rule a fixed quota is reserved for tribal purposes pursuant to some evaluation of future requirements. A quota cannot, however, be accurately preserved without some coordinate measuring and regulating agency. In past cases there has been an unfortunate tendency for the federal "trustee" of these reserve rights to defer regulation to the interested states.

The ordinary solution to this problem within the federal system is interstate compact. By establishing coordinate agencies with broad supervisory powers, the states have contrived to apportion their fugaceous resources to their mutual satisfaction, with some flexibility over time, and more comprehensively than private contracts can provide. No compact power has ever been recognized in tribes as such, although a number of tribes routinely contract for services from neighboring states, under the supervision of the Bureau.

In the absence of any explicit prohibition of tribal compact, it seems appropriate for tribes to be included within the meaning of the interstate compact clause. Any other interpretation would frustrate the purpose of that provision, which can be understood as authorizing regional economic and resource planning. The alternative of repeated tribe-state adjudication of respective rights in resources on the basis of "equitable apportionment," of which states avail themselves in the absence of compact, will always be defective for want of procedures for routine enforcement.

COMMENT, INDIAN COAL AUTHORITIES: THE CONCEPT OF FEDERAL PREEMPTION AND INDEPENDENT TRIBAL COAL DEVELOPMENT OF THE NORTHERN GREAT PLAINS, 53 North Dakota Law Review 469, 469-75 (1977)*

I. Introduction

The Indian tribes of the Northern Great Plains are confronted by full-scale coal development on their reservations. The tribes presently faced with this prospect are the Three Affiliated Tribes of the Ft. Berthold Reservation, the Northern Cheyenne and Crow Tribes, and the Affiliated Tribes of the Ft. Peck Reservation. The impact of this prospective development on the economic status of these Indian reservations has not yet been fully realized. Like Indians everywhere, these tribes suffer from inadequate education, massive unemployment, sub-standard housing and poor health care.

---

*Copyright © 1977 by the North Dakota Law Review. Reprinted by permission.

Federal statutes and regulations which control reservation mineral development address only one form of coal development, that of leasing. Congress and the Department of the Interior have encouraged the tribes of the Northern Great Plains to lease large tracts of reservation land for coal development. Although the federal leasing policy has benefited the tribes,[5] their interests have not always been well protected.[6] For instance, the Secretary of the Interior, in implementing government policy toward tribal coal development, has been faced with a conflict of interests in recent years. On the one hand, the Department of the Interior has the responsibility to guide the tribes in the use of their lands,[7] and on the other hand, it has the responsibility to promote the orderly and timely development of natural resources. In zealous attempts to promote development of reservation "black gold," the Secretary has largely ignored his responsibility to consider "cultural continuity, tribal survival, [and] the integrity of the land surface." This situation partly stems from the fact that the Department of the Interior has "no clear directive to follow" when conflicts in these responsibilities arise. Naturally, this conflict in the dual responsibilities of the Department of the Interior has affected its treatment of Indian coal leases.

As a result, the tribes have begun to take a closer look at their control over coal development. As a first step toward achieving greater control over coal development, the Northern Cheyenne and Crow Tribes have completed and the Three Affiliated Tribes of Ft. Berthold are in the process of obtaining invalidation of their coal leases and permits.[11] At the same time, the tribes are also considering alternatives to replace leasing that would effectively shift responsibility for mineral development from the federal government to the tribes. For the tribes, any feasible alternative must safeguard cultural and tribal unity

---

[5] Leasing has benefited the tribes by providing employment and ready income in the form of royalties. For example, the Sarpy Creek Mine on the Crow Reservation in Montana presently employs 65 members of the Crow Tribe. Statistics from Bureau of Indian Affairs, Billings Area Office, Billings, Mont. (1976). For a discussion of Indian mineral lease provisions concerning rents and royalties, see Leased and Lost, [5 Econ. Priorities Rep. at 33 (1974)].

[6] For example, in a Petition to Secretary of the Interior Rogers C. B. Morton on January 9, 1974, the Northern Cheyenne Tribe charged the Secretary with wholesale violations of federal regulations as applied to permits and leases covering 214,000 acres, the equivalent of approximately one-half of the reservation. Among the allegations were: failure to require an environmental impact statement as provided by 25 C.F.R. Part 177 (1974) [now 25 C.F.R. pt. 216 (1982)]; failure to provide a technical examination of prospective surface exploration and mining operations under 25 C.F.R. § 177.4(a) (1) (1974); and issuance of permits and leases in excess of the maximum acreage limitation as provided by 25 C.F.R. § 171.9(b) (1) (1974) [now 25 C.F.R. § 211.9(b)(1) (1982)].

[7] To facilitate leasing, the Secretary of the Interior has been delegated broad discretion by Congress as trustee of the Indian tribes. As an example of the Secretary's broad discretion section 2 of the Omnibus Tribal Leasing Act of May 11, 1938 grants to the Secretary ample authority to prescribe terms and conditions of lease sales, to reject all bids, and to accept less than the highest bid if he determines it to be in the best interest of the tribe. Omnibus Tribal Leasing Act of May 11, 1938, Pub. L. No. 75-506, ch. 198, § 2, 52 Stat. 347, (codified in 25 U.S.C. § 396(b) (1970)).

The Department of the Interior has stated: "'The principal goal of the Department in regard to the development of minerals on Indian land is to assist the Indian landowners in deriving the maximum economic benefits from their resources consistent with sound conservation practices and environmental protection.'"

[11] See Decision of the Secretary of the Interior, Thomas S. Kleppe, Relating to Crow Tribe v. Kleppe (Jan. 13, 1977): Decision of the Secretary of the Interior, Rogers C. B. Morton, on the Northern Cheyenne Petition (June 4, 1974); letter from Anson A. Baker, Superintendent of the Bureau of Indian Affairs for the Three Affiliated Tribes of the Ft. Berthold Reservation to Consolidation Coal Co. (Aug. 29, 1975) (on file with the North Dakota Law Review).

and utilize coal to increase the economic basis of the reservations. One alternative that the tribes are seriously considering is the creation of a tribal coal authority.[12]

II. *Definition of a Tribal Coal Authority*

It is important to discuss briefly the concept of a tribal coal authority in order to understand fully its functions and advantages over the traditional form of mineral leasing on the reservations. The following discussion will focus upon the governmental and corporate powers which might be possessed by a tribal coal authority and the possible implementation of these powers under a contract mining structure negotiated with a mining company for purposes of tribal coal development.[15]

A. *Governmental and Corporate Powers*

The concept of a tribal coal authority is patterned after the general model utilized in federal and state governments such as the Tennessee Valley Authority and the Port of New York Authority. A tribal coal authority would be a proprietorship possessing the characteristics of both a private corporation and a government agency. Although its functions may be different among the reservations, a tribal coal authority basically would include the following: perpetual corporate existence; the power to negotiate contracts; adoption of a corporate seal; the power to hold real and personal property; the capacity to sue and be sued; and the authority to employ its own personnel. As a quasi-political entity, a coal authority would be endowed with certain governmental powers. Among these powers would be the authority to construct tribal facilities for use in coal development, the capacity to provide police protection, and implementation of a reservation mineral inventory.[24]

Use of a tribal authority for coal development has distinct advantages over a government agency created for the same purpose. Governmental authorities are generally assigned a single responsibility when created and are delegated broad discretion over employment, salaries to be paid, and administrative organization, subject to general procedures promulgated in the enabling legislation. Separated from the rest of the government infra-structure, decision-making

---

[12] A tribe that chooses to adopt an independent approach to coal development undoubtedly will have to face a bureaucratic impasse. Within the Bureau of Indian Affairs there is generally

[a] lack of expertise ... in dealing with new forms of development; that is, if a tribe proposes anything outside the scope of the standard lease agreement, there is no one who can deal with it. Consequently, the burden of selling a new idea is always on the tribe which often lacks the experience, expertise and the dollars to fight the bureaucracy of agency, area and national offices. Since the likelihood of having the expertise needed is less at the lower levels, agency and area offices often act as stumbling blocks either out of fear of change or out of the lack of knowledge.

Americans for Indian Opportunity (AIO), A Question of Power: Indian Control of Indian Resource Development 8 (1976) (compiled from conference on Indian Tribes as Developing Nations held in Racine, Wis., Sept. 21-23, 1975) [hereinafter cited as AIO Report].

[15] Discussion of a coal authority will be based primarily on the concept to be utilized by the Crow Tribe, which enacted a resolution providing for creation of a coal authority in 1976 (resolution on file with the North Dakota Law Review).

[24] A reservation mineral authority could be undertaken by the tribal coal authority or the authority could be empowered to hire outside expertise for this purpose. *See generally* AIO Report *supra* note 12, at 24.

within the tribal coal authority would be centralized solely in the management of an elected or appointed board of directors, free from the "inflexible bureaucratic rules and procedures" applicable to other divisions of government. The adoption of a tribal authority would insulate the negotiation of business arrangements, so essential to coal development, from tribal politics. A stable policy toward coal development within the reservation is critical to the development of a viable long-term mining program for both the tribe and third parties who have contracted to mine or sell the coal.

B. *Service Contract Structure*

Because the tribes have limited management expertise and capacity, a tribal coal authority would undoubtedly have to negotiate a service contract with a mining company. Under this type of contract, a mining company would be hired to mine tribal coal for a fee based upon a fixed price per ton mined, a percentage of the profits, a fixed price with added incentives, or a combination of these methods of compensation. The company's contribution under a service contract would be its management capability over mining operations. Although these operations would be subject to the overall direction of the tribal coal authority, the basic duties of the company would probably include the following: an evaluation of coal reserves and the preparation of mining and economic feasibility plans for mine facilities; observance of applicable federal reclamation laws; operation and maintenance of mine facilities in a prudent manner;[34] the supply of all equipment, machinery and facilities as provided by the contract;[35] payment of North Dakota and Montana severance taxes, if applicable;[36] and the hiring and training of tribal members for positions in the mine work force.[37]

On the other hand, the service contract would require the tribal coal authority to do the following: cooperate in securing government exploration permits;[38] construct mine facilities and supply equipment; approve exploration, development, mining, reclamation and economic feasibility plans;[39] and inspect all

---

[34] Leasing provisions relating to efficient and prudent operations are presently included in all of the standard mineral lease forms of the Department of the Interior. *See, e.g.*, Ch. IV, § 3, Amended Coal Mining Lease, Tract 3, Sale 1, Westmoreland-Crow Lease (Nov. 24, 1974).

[35] The duty to supply equipment and facilities for coal development would be subject to negotiation. The tribe would have to decide whether to commit itself to this large capital investment or to compensate the company for investment in these assets.

[36] It is unclear to what extent a company that is engaged by a coal authority to mine Indian coal would be subject to state severance taxes. The authority to tax Indian coal that is leased for mining purposes is granted to the states by 25 U.S.C. § 398c (1970). This section speaks of leases only and may not be applicable to coal development undertaken by a tribal coal authority that employs a mining company under a service contract....

A resolution for a severance tax of 25% of the market price per ton of coal mined on the Crow Reservation was passed by the Tribal Council on Jan. 31, 1976 and approved by the Secretary of the Interior on Jan. 17, 1977. Information obtained from the Bureau of Indain Affairs, Billings Area Office, Billings, Mont. The issue of Montana's application of its severance tax to Crow coal reserves will probably be litigated in the near future.

[37] Preferential employment provisions are presently contained in most Indian mineral lease forms furnished by the Department of the Interior although they are not required by statute or federal regulations. *See* Bureau of Competition, Federal Trade Comm'n, Mineral Leasing Indian Lands 27 (Oct. 1975).

[38] *See* 25 C.F.R. § 171.27a (1976) [now 25 C.F.R. § 211.27a (1982)].

[39] Under a service mining contract such approval would be necessary for the tribal coal authority in order to maintain adequate control. *See generally* AIO Report, *supra* note 12, at 26.

mine facilities and reclamation activities. A tribal coal authority would retain the option of selling the coal directly to power companies or granting an exclusive right to sell the coal to the development company under the service contract. As another alternative, a tribal authority could hire a separate sales concern for this purpose. Under any of these options, a tribe may realize a significantly higher return than is presently derived from leasing.[42] The tribal coal authority may also be responsible for providing the capital necessary in coal development. The necessary long-term financing could be obtained from customers whose benefit would be a reduced sales price, or from lending institutions and federal programs.[43]

NOTE

To what extent would the formation of tribal development authorities of the type proposed in the preceding article resolve the taxing and jurisdictional questions raised in footnote 36 of the article? *Compare White Mountain Apache Tribe v. Bracker with Cotton Petr. Corp. v. New Mexico,* both set forth and discussed in Chapter 4. After the preceding articles were written, Congress enacted the Indian Mineral Development Act of 1982, Pub. L. 97-382, 96 Stat. 1938, 25 U.S.C. §§ 2101-2108. The statute, which is discussed in more detail below, provides statutory support for many of the non-lease tribal mineral, oil, and gas development alternatives, such as joint ventures, service and managerial contracts, and other agreements desired by tribes to secure larger control over development on their reservations.

2. JOINT VENTURES

EASTERN NAVAJO INDUSTRIES v. BUREAU OF REVENUES

89 N.M. 369, 552 P.2d 805 (1976)

HERNANDEZ, Judge.

[Eastern Navajo Industries is a New Mexico corporation. A majority (51%) of the corporation's stock is owned by Navajo Indians, the rest is owned by Taylor and McKinney, who, although having some Indian heritage, are not members of the Navajo tribe. Taylor, McKinney, and three Navajo Indians are officers of the corporation and served on its board of directors. The corporation's plant and offices are located on trust land outside the boundaries of the Navajo Indian Reservation. The corporation contracted with the Navajo Housing Authority, a tribal entity, to build housing on the Navajo reservation paid for by the Authority from federal housing funds it administered. When the New Mexico Bureau of Revenues assessed gross receipts tax on the corporation's revenues derived from building houses for the Authority designated for tribal members on trust land outside reservation boundaries, the corporation appealed.]

---

[42] Under most of the present coal leases, tribes receive a fixed royalty without regard to the quality or sulphur content of the coal mined or the optimum market price. Under a service contract, the tribe's return would be directly related to the market price per ton of coal mined. AIO Report, *supra* note 12, at 22.

[43] One federal source of funding that a tribe could utilize to obtain investment capital is the Indian Business Development Program. *See* 25 C.F.R. Part 80 (1976) [now 25 C.F.R. pt. 286 (1982)]. Over a long period of time, revenues could then be applied to decrease corporate debt, while the coal resources would provide collateral for expansion of the enterprise.

The taxpayer raised four points of error. We find the third dispositive of this appeal: III. "The State of New Mexico cannot impose or collect a gross receipts tax on taxpayer since such a tax is a severe burden upon and a hindrance to the self-government of the Navajo Tribe."

The position of the Bureau has two aspects. The Bureau argues that "[o]rganizing a modern business corporation, the character of which is determined by state law, is a departure from the ancestral customs and folkways of Indian people. Once that step has been taken, the participants have made the choice, for better or worse, to separate themselves, at least for purposes of the corporate activity, from those traditions." The second point argued by the Bureau is that "[n]othing in the record even arguably supports a conclusion that tribal self-government is being hindered. There is no conflict between the State of New Mexico assessing the gross receipts tax against Eastern Navajo and the Tribe's efforts to provide housing for its people." We do not agree.

Other facts important to our determination appear in the record. The corporation was formed at the instigation and under the auspices of the Navajo Tribal Council. Messrs. Taylor and McKinney were approached by members of the Chairman's Office of the Navajo Tribe and by the Eastern Navajo Agency, a division of the Bureau of Indian Affairs. The Eastern Navajo Agency assembled the 54 Indians necessary to comprise the 51% Indian shareholder majority. Mr. McKinney testified, "We had nothing to do as far as what Indian received any stock. These names were given to us and the amount of stock to be issued to each one of them by the Navajo Tribe and the Eastern Navajo Agency." These shareholders bought stock in the company with loans from the federal government under a program designed to facilitate Indian self-help. McKinney testified: "We had to qualify through the Federal Housing Administration as an Indian-owned organization, ... we have that certificate of qualification."

Further testimony established that the funds used by the Navajo Housing Authority to form the corporation were obtained from the Indian Business Development Fund. We take judicial notice of 25 C.F.R. § 80 (1971) [now 25 C.F.R. § 286], which sets out the provisions of the Indian Business Development Fund, as authorized by 25 U.S.C. § 13 (1970):

> 80.2 *Purpose and scope.* This part sets forth the regulations for the administration of the Indian Business Development Fund. The purpose of the fund is to stimulate Indian entrepreneurship and employment. This purpose is achieved by providing non-reimbursable, supplemental capital grants to establish profit-making Indian economic enterprises which will employ Indians.

> 80.12 *Indian groups.* Any group of eligible individual Indians which may legally engage in private enterprise may apply for a grant. *This includes Indian corporations organized under Federal or State law* and, if authorized to enter contracts on behalf of an Indian tribe, those organizations commonly known as "Tribal Enterprises," which are economic enterprises. However, for *Indian corporations,* fifty-one percent [51%] or more of the stock must be owned by eligible Indians or by an Indian tribe. [Emphasis ours.]

Under project requirements, these regulations provided:

> 80.41 *Eligibility requirements.* The project must satisfy all the following requirements to be eligible for consideration:

> (a) It is a profit-making enterprise which generates jobs for Indians.
> (b) It is owned or controlled by an *Indian group* or an individual Indian.

(c) It is located on a reservation or in the immediate vicinity ....

(d) It must have the potential to become a profitable operation within the total cost of establishing the business....

80.62 *Authority of Area Director.* Area Directors are authorized to determine eligibility of *Indian groups* not serviced by a single Superintendent, to receive their applications, and to recommend approval or disapproval of the application to the Commissioner [of Indian Affairs]. [Emphasis ours.]

Incorporation of this taxpayer is consistent with the method of incorporation sanctioned by Navajo tribal law for purposes of qualifying for tribal loans. Title 5, N.T.C. § 211, which states that the purpose of this subchapter of the Code is "to establish procedures to govern all future loans by the Tribe to members, cooperative and private corporations," defines a "private corporation" as a:

... corporation organized by a group of Tribal members, or by Tribal members and others, pursuant to the laws of the United States or of states within which the Navajo jurisdiction extends and wherein the business or undertaking is to be located. The majority of stock of such corporation must be owned by Tribal members.

Thus, federal regulations defining federal loan policy for Indian enterprises and the Navajo Tribal Code specifically authorize incorporation of an Indian commercial enterprise under state law without the corresponding loss of "Indianness" that is argued by the Bureau of Revenue in the instant case.

We also take judicial notice of the following sections of the Navajo Tribal Code covering regulation and control of businesses within the Navajo Nation and Community development.

The Code at Title 5, N.T.C. § 51 states:

The Navajo Tribal Council, in order to promote the further economic development of the Navajo People, and in order to clearly establish and exercise the Navajo Tribe's authority to regulate the conduct and operations of business within the Navajo Nation, hereby declares that the Navajo Tribe of Indians has the sole and exclusive authority to grant, deny, or withdraw the privilege of doing business within the Navajo Nation, except where such authority is withdrawn from the Navajo Tribe by the Constitution and applicable laws of the United States.

The Code at Title 6, N.T.C. § 354 states:

The [Navajo Housing] Authority shall be organized and operated for the purposes of: (1) Remedying in the areas subject to the jurisdiction of the Navajo Tribe unsafe and insanitary housing conditions, that are injurious to the public health, safety and morals; (2) Alleviating the acute shortage of decent, safe and sanitary dwellings for families of low income; and (3) Providing employment opportunities in areas subject to the jurisdiction of the Navajo Tribe through the reconstruction, improvement, extention, alteration or repair and operating of low-rent dwellings.

[A] corporation and its stockholders are separate entities [under] New Mexico [law] as well. However, it is also the law in New Mexico that a court is not always bound to regard the legal status of a corporation as an existence in itself regardless of its stockholders. [Nevertheless,] 25 C.F.R. § 80.12 explicitly requires consideration of the ethnicity of the stockholders of corporations who would qualify under its terms: "... for Indian corporations, fifty-one percent [51%] or more of the stock must be owned by eligible Indians or by an Indian tribe." Under this federal standard, taxpayer is an Indian corporation.

To disregard the Indian ethnicity of taxpayer's shareholders would be to fail to recognize the specific directives of the Indian Business Development Fund Act. That is to say we must look beyond the taxpayer's corporate form to the fact that 51% of its stock is owned by individual Navajo Indians. Consequently, there is no alternative but to view the assessment by the Bureau of Revenue as a tax upon Indians doing business upon an Indian land or reservation. And as we stated in *Hunt v. O'Cheskey*, 85 N.M. 381, 512 P.2d 954 (Ct. App. 1973):

> New Mexico's attempt to tax the gross receipts of an Indian whose business is carried on exclusively upon reservation land is an attempt to determine what business may be carried on within the reservation. Such an attempt is an attempt to interfere with Indian self-government.
>
> [Thus,] New Mexico does not have the authority to tax the privilege of an Indian to engage in business on an Indian reservation.

[The recent case of] *G. M. Shupe, Inc. v. Bureau of Revenue*, No. 2183, 89 N.M. 265, 550 P.2d 277 (1976), is readily distinguishable from the present case. The taxpayer in *Shupe* is a Washington corporation, qualified to do business in New Mexico. It is constructing a dam on the Nambe Pueblo under contract with the U.S. Department of the Interior, Bureau of Reclamation. The taxpayer presented the issue that the gross receipts tax was illegally imposed because taxpayer's activities were on Indian land. This court held that the tax was correctly assessed to this corporation for two reasons: (1) taxpayer corporation was not an Indian entity, and (2) the imposition of the tax does not infringe on Indian rights of self-government.

Our holding in the present case is the converse. Eastern Navajo Industries is an Indian entity, according to federal definition, so that the imposition of the gross receipts tax on this taxpayer constitutes an interference with Indian self-government.

The Commissioner was in error in his Decision and Order for the reasons stated above and consequently the assessment is annulled.

It is so ordered.

LOPEZ, J., concurs.

SUTIN, J., dissenting.

The majority opinion has adopted a principle of law unknown in American jurisprudence on Indian Law — that a domestic business corporation which services an Indian tribe is exempt from the provisions of the Gross Receipts Tax Act because the imposition of the tax is a severe burden on the self-government of an Indian tribe. I dissent....

NOTE

As the *Eastern Navajo Industries* case and report of the Presidential Commission on Indian Reservation Economies indicate, several federal agencies have established programs to support the development of Indian business enterprise. *See generally* BUREAU OF INDIAN AFFAIRS, FINANCIAL ASSISTANCE FOR INDIAN ECONOMIC DEVELOPMENT PROJECTS (1985). The Indian Financing Act of 1974, 25 U.S.C. §§ 1451-1543, established a $50 million revolving fund to set up various programs of federal-governmental loans and grants to Indian businesses, loan guarantees and insurance for loans from the private sector, and interest subsidies. *See also* 15 U.S.C. § 4726 (Export Enhancement Act of 1988 provides assistance to Indian organizations in the development of foreign markets for authentic American Indian arts and crafts); 25 U.S.C. § 450e (Indian Self-Determination and Education Assistance Act authorizes a preference in the award of subcontracts to Indian-owned economic enterprises for contracts entered into pursuant to the Act); 25 U.S.C. § 636 (Aid to Small Business Act of 1953 was amended in 1981 to empower the Administration to make loans to qualified small business concerns, including those owned by Indian Tribes); 25 C.F.R. pt. 256 (1982). In part, these programs constitute a recognition that the restraints against alienation of Indian lands prevent the tribes from securing investment capital by mortgaging their single most valuable assets, their lands and resources. However, the federal funding of these programs has not fully supplied the need for capital formation assistance. Indian tribes also are eligible for a variety of other governmental programs. *E.g., St. Paul Intertribal Hous. Bd. v. Reynolds*, 564 F. Supp. 1408, 1412 (D. Minn. 1983) (Department of Housing and Urban Development is not barred by equal protection clause or civil rights statutes from providing HUD program funds to programs approved under Minnesota Urban Indian Housing Act); *Anderson v. O'Brien*, 84 Wash. 2d 64, 524 P.2d 390 (1974) (Kalispel Tribe eligible for state funds under Washington Economic Assistance Act of 1972 to assist in construction of industrial park).

C. DEVELOPMENT IN INDIAN COUNTRY

As reflected in the introduction to this chapter, some Indian reservations contain significant natural resources, including oil and gas, coal and other valuable mineral resources, and timber. Other reservations are valuable for agricultural or range land. On some reservations, management of such resources is severely complicated by allotment and the checkerboarded ownership and fractionated heirship problems that it created. On other reservations, the land and resources may be held communally by the tribe, thereby simplifying the economic management of the resources. Tribal, federal, and individual decisions on how to capitalize on such valuable resources pose significant legal and political problems, chief among which is the form the transaction will take. This section is devoted to the federal legal and political regimes which govern and structure the forms of such transactions.

1. LEASING

The process of leasing Indian lands as the major means of exploiting Indian resources and securing revenue raises important questions about the role and duty of the Secretary of the Interior and the power of the tribe. We turn first to these questions because, without an understanding of the leasing process, it is difficult to understand the complexities involved in economic development of Indian reservations.

a. Surface Leasing and Policy Considerations Relative to Leasing

CHAMBERS & PRICE, REGULATING SOVEREIGNTY: SECRETARIAL DISCRETION AND THE LEASING OF INDIAN LANDS, 26 Stanford Law Review 1061, 1061-87 (1974)*

Indian trust land can be leased by its tribal or individual owner only after the Secretary of the Interior has approved the transaction. Surface leasing of Indian land is governed principally by 25 U.S.C. § 415; enacted in 1955, section 415 permits leasing for a wide range of purposes — "public, religious, educational, recreational, residential or business." The basis for the leasing statute and its requirement of approval by the Secretary is in part the commerce clause, which authorizes Congress "[t]o regulate Commerce ... with the Indian tribes." More broadly, statutes such as section 415, which wholly or partially restrain the alienation of Indian lands, have been sustained as exercises of the federal guardianship or trust responsibility to "protect" the Indians.[4] But while the trust responsibility serves as a source for the Secretary's approval power, it is unclear whether and to what extent it furnishes standards which limit his discretion in administrative exercise of that power.

The use of Indian land by non-Indian lessees is now very substantial. Indian trust land totals slightly over 50 million acres, of which about 7 million acres are leased to non-Indian farmers or are used under permit by non-Indian ranchers for grazing. Another 8 million acres are covered by mineral leases; while generally beyond the scope of this study, such leases may prevent surface use of the lands by Indians (for example, when the land is strip mined).

Between 1890 and 1955, lease terms were limited, by and large, to periods of 5 or 10 years;[8] although business leases were not formally prohibited, the effect was to discourage commercial development and use of Indian trust lands by non-Indians. Under section 415, the lease period may be up to 25 years, with an option to renew for another 25-year period. Subsequent to 1955, section 415 has been amended, and other statutes have been enacted, to extend 99-year leasing authority to 24 tribes.[9]

---

*Copyright © 1974 by the Board of Trustees of the Leland Stanford Junior University. Reprinted by permission.

[4] The constitutionality of the approval power, as a restraint on alienation of trust property, was sustained in Tiger v. Western Inv. Co., 221 U.S. 286 (1911)....

[8] Prior to 1891, the leasing of Indian land was formally prohibited by statute. Act of June 30, 1834, ch. 161, § 12, 4 Stat. 730 (codified at 25 U.S.C. § 177 (1970)). The Act of Feb. 28, 1891, ch. 383, § 3, 26 Stat. 795 (partly codified at 25 U.S.C. § 397 (1970)) was the first general Indian leasing statute. It, and most subsequent enactments until the 1955 Act, permitted only short-term leases.

[9] By amendments to § 415, 99-year leasing authority has been extended to the following tribes or reservations for the indicated purposes: Agua Caliente (resort hotel development), Navajo (business enterprises), Dania (shopping center and tourist development), Southern Ute (recreation). Fort Mojave (tourist-recreation development of the Colorado River), Pyramid Lake (lakeshore recreation-resort), Gila River (industrial, commercial, recreational, and residential developments), San Carlos Apache (recreation and industrial projects), Spokane (lakeshore development), Hualapai (tourism and recreation), Swinomish (residential development along Puget Sound), Cochiti, Zuni, Pojoaque, and Tesuque Pueblos (resort and residential developments), Tulalip (home site developments along Puget Sound), Yavapai-Prescott (apartment developments and commercial operations), Coeur D'Alene (resolution of heirship land problems, land consolidation program), Burns Paiute (no particular improvement contemplated), Kalispel (land consolidation program), Soboba (water supply system; residential and municipal community).

An important result of the 1955 Act and its progeny has been the growth of "business" leases. While these leases cover only 105,000 acres, far less than 1 percent of Indian country, their impact is significant in a number of ways. First, they are sometimes very productive of income. In fiscal year 1973, Indians derived nearly $28 million from nonmineral surface leases. Over one-quarter of that amount was derived from "business" leases on a relatively few reservations — two tribes derived more than $1 million from business leasing, while eight other tribes each netted more than $100,000. Second, extended leases of valuable reservation resources can be the cornerstone of a reservation economic development program. Leasing can now be a strategy whereby land — a major economic factor of production on most reservations — is conveyed for a term to non-Indians as an inducement to invest capital and to bring industries, jobs, or services to the reservation.

When lease terms were limited, it was rare that a particular lease had great cultural or political effects on the tribe. Surface leases were short-term, normally agricultural; [14] mistakes were reversible because the leases were not of great permanence. There was debate, particularly in the late 19th century, as to whether leasing rather than working the land was in the best interests of the individual Indian, and there could be some question about the quality of the bargain struck by the lessor. But the Secretary's concerns about the impact of leasing did not often go beyond those areas. This is no longer the case. The issues that come before the Secretary in the context of approval of long-term business leases are of enormous significance in terms of the lawmaking power of the tribe and its cultural and political future. Some leases may bring large numbers of non-Indians onto the reservation or may entice states to attempt to exercise regulatory and taxing powers over reservations. More than the landscape may be changed: an influx of non-Indians or state authority may interfere with tribal control over the reservation and continuation of tribal culture.

The Secretary has largely ignored these broader consequences of leasing. His principal view of Indian trust land is as a resource to be used singularly for the production of income in the form of lease revenues; that conception is embodied in the Secretary's regulations governing leases. A different approach to leasing and land management would be to emphasize the overall economic and social impact upon the tribe. A somewhat narrower version of this approach, emphasizing the jobs or services which would be produced or offered by the potential lessee, is the one embraced by the burgeoning economic development

---

In addition, 99-year leasing authority is conferred by 25 U.S.C. § 416 (1970) upon the Salt River and San Xavier reservations in Arizona; this statute is clearly designed to deal with residential leasing. The Colorado River Reservation also possesses 99-year leasing authority by the Act of Apr. 30, 1964, Pub. L. No. 88-302, 78 Stat. 188, amending Act of Sept. 5, 1962, Pub. L. No. 87-627, 76 Stat. 428 and Act of June 11, 1960, Pub. L. No. 85-506, 74 Stat. 199.

[14] Even now, agricultural leases and grazing permits are virtually all of short duration. Section 415 limits grazing leases to 10 years in duration, and the Secretary's regulations allow 10-year lease periods only for leases "which require substantial development or improvement of the land." 25 C.F.R. § 131.8(d) (1973) [now 25 C.F.R. § 162.8(d) (1982)]. Agricultural leases are restricted to "five years for dry-farming land or ten years for irrigable land," id. § 131.8(c), except for leases which require substantial improvements of the land to grow specialized crops — for such leases § 415 allows 25-year terms. Most grazing by non-Indians on Indian lands is done pursuant to revocable permits.

programs fostered and financed particularly during the last decade by the Interior Department and by other federal agencies.[17]

The two approaches are not necessarily antithetical, for an emphasis on jobs does not entirely depreciate the receipt of lease income, and the converse is also true. But a distinction can be made in the basic purposes and consequences of these two approaches. If reservation land is simply a source for income production, then it should be devoted to its "highest and best use" in order to maximize lease revenues. That is a conventional goal of trust management. If, on the other hand, reservation land has multiple purposes and should be utilized as a part of an overall resource development plan that has as its goal the economic and cultural viability of an Indian tribe, there would be trade-offs of various kinds which should be considered by the Secretary in exercising his approval power: between income and jobs, income and services, income and economic growth, income and conservation of an Indian culture on the land.

To illustrate the first approach, certain kinds of business leases are concerned almost exclusively with the land as a resource for income production. Palm Springs is a paradigm: the Agua Caliente Reservation in California has virtually disappeared pursuant to scores of long-term development leases, and in its place a thriving residential-resort community has been created which produces over $2 million per year in lease revenues for the tribal members. Another example of the use of leased land to provide income is provided by the two New

[17]The Bureau of Indian Affairs has established a "booster" division, its Division of Industrial Development and Tourism, to encourage commercial lessees to locate in Indian country. While the BIA Real Property Management Division reviews leases to ascertain the adequacy of the rental, the Industrial Development staff encourages leasing on (or near) the reservation to provide jobs. This Division also administers some manpower training funds for on-the-job training pursuant to 25 U.S.C. § 309 (1970) and two business loan programs — a revolving loan fund established by 25 U.S.C. § 470 (1970) and an Indian Business Development Fund.

The major incentives for economic development leasing come not from the Department of the Interior but from a number of grant and loan programs administered by other federal agencies. During the past 6 years, such agencies have expended over $150 million in grants and loans to further "economic development" on Indian reservations. These programs are heavily, but not exclusively, directed toward industrialization. The Economic Development Administration (EDA; formerly Area Redevelopment Administration) of the Department of Commerce, which has advanced nearly $100 million in grants and loans to Indian reservations, has concentrated its funds in the area of public works, including industrial parks, and business loans. EDA has financed the construction of over 25 industrial parks. Typically, EDA provides water, sewage, and road facilities in the industrial parks. The parks, as of the summer of 1971, had a total of 27 tenants providing 1,700 jobs for Indians. EDA has also advanced $36 million for recreation and tourism projects.

The Small Business Administration (SBA) has guaranteed a substantial number of loans to tribes for the purpose of constructing plants and other facilities on industrial parks. Typically, the tribe will lease the acreage of an industrial park to a local development corporation which obtains a bank loan guaranteed by SBA. SBA-guaranteed loans generally run for 20 to 25 years; SBA requires the lease term to be twice that of the loan. The manpower training programs of the Labor Department and the BIA complete the trilogy of federal grant-making programs which subsidize and encourage industrial development on reservations.

On the Gila River Reservation in Arizona, a combination of EDA, SBA, and manpower training programs has created 200 to 300 jobs for tribal members. Interestingly, however, a majority of the jobs in the industrial parks on the reservation are filled by non-Indian residents of adjacent communities. The number of tribal jobs could be increased, but many tribal members seem disinterested in the jobs, even with training features. The work is often found to be very boring and repetitive — assembly-line type of labor of the most unskilled variety. By contrast, a tribally owned farming enterprise at Gila River has hired approximately 100 Indians to work half the agriculturally leased land on the reservation. It may be that this concern coincides more with the history of the Pimas as a farming people.

Mexico pueblos, Cochiti and Tesuque, which have leased, on a percentage basis with a minimum ground rent, over 20 percent of their reservations for the construction of non-Indian residential communities.[20] Although construction of the communities may provide employment for tribal members, the prime benefit of these leases will be the lease income received. The pueblo leases have stirred great controversy within and without the Indian communities involved. There is concern with the commitment of Indian water resources to non-Indian uses,[21] with the problems posed for tribal government by the attempts of the state to assert its regulatory and taxing authority over the leased lands, with the disruption of traditional culture and life by threatened close proximity to a large non-Indian community, and with the possible involvement of unscrupulous promoters who may leave the tribes in a direct relationship with sublessees living on the land and with an obligation to administer the development and provide costly services to the community.[23]

Industrial leasing is more often connected with goals other than producing lease revenues: many plant sites are leased for minimal rental on the theory that the factory may produce jobs or provide goods and services on the reservation. But industrial leasing has also provoked considerable controversy, particularly concerning the development of immense fossil-fuel power plants and the strip mining of coal for these plants on the Navajo and Hopi Reservations. These power plants, designed to meet the needs of Tucson, Phoenix, Los Angeles, Albuquerque, and other southwestern metropolises, may create massive air pollution in portions of Indian country of the Southwest; moreover, leases permitting strip mining affect a part of the reservations sacred to Indian traditional religion.[24]

---

[20] Two reservations in California — Colorado River and Ft. Mojave — have also leased land to developers near the Colorado River. The Colorado River lease of 9,000 acres is only a few percent of its total land, while the Mojave leases cover over one-third of the reservation's 37,000-acre land area. The Cochiti lease covers approximately 6,000 of the 28,775 acres on that Pueblo while the Tesuque lease covers over 5,000 of 16,810 acres. See id. at 9, 75, 86-88.

[21] The pueblos have assigned a portion of their water rights to the developers. Indian water rights are valuable to the lessees because they carry a priority as of the date the reservation was established (usually in the 19th century) rather than the date the lease is made or the date appropriation of the water commences, see Winters v. United States, 207 U.S. 564 (1908). Moreover, the measure of the Indian water right is any water that can be put to beneficial use either now or in the future. There may be some question as to how future beneficial use is measured — whether it is limited to agricultural uses or irrigable acreage, or whether it can be used for any purpose. Compare United States v. Walker River Irrig. Dist., 104 F.2d 334, 340 (9th Cir. 1939), with Pyramid Lake Paiute Tribe v. Morton, 354 F. Supp. 252 (D.D.C. 1972). In any event, the Indian water right is not lost by nonuse and is thus distinct from other water rights in appropriative states. See Arizona v. California, 373 U.S. 546, 599-601 (1963); United States v. Ahtanum Irrig. Dist., 236 F.2d 321, 326 (9th Cir. 1956), cert. denied, 352 U.S. 988 (1957).

[23] Pursuant to the leases, the developer and (at Cochiti) a tribally chartered town substantially controlled by him are responsible for most municipal services. As a community is established, it may be that the chartered town will exercise taxing power over residents and be self-sustaining with respect to services. However, should this not occur and should the developer become bankrupt or be dissolved without acquisition by, or creation of, a successor corporation, it is possible that the tribe would become responsible for providing some of these services.

[24] Both these leases and the ones on the pueblos have given rise to litigation. E.g., Jicarilla Apache Tribe v. Morton, 471 F.2d 1275 (9th Cir. 1973); Davis v. Morton, 469 F.2d 593 (10th Cir. 1972); Lomayaktewa v. Morton, Civil No. 72-106 (D. Ariz. Feb. 15, 1973), appeal docketed, No. 73-2132, 9th Cir., Apr. 11, 1973; Sangre de Cristo Dev. Corp. v. City of Santa Fe, 84 N.M. 343, 503 P.2d 323 (1972), cert. denied, 411 U.S. 438 (1973). Plaintiffs in some of the cases have claimed, so far without success, that the Secretary breached his trust obligation by approving the leases. See Yazzie v.

The Secretary of the Interior's approval power presumably is conferred to invest in him authority to determine which leases are consistent with federal Indian policy and his trust responsibility to protect the interests of the beneficiaries. Yet the Secretary has provided little indication of what standards ought to be applied. Even for long-term business leases, the Secretary has followed essentially the same lease approval procedures as he did before section 415 was enacted; his procedures and concerns remain clerical and limited. Yet with the rise of these leases, it has become increasingly important to develop a coherent theory of the Secretary's trust duties and the purposes of his trusteeship. A virtually unconfined discretion now has potentially hazardous implications. Tribal self-government is endangered by the likelihood that the Secretary may have the authority and duty to disapprove leases desired by the tribe or its members. Unbounded discretion also creates the possibility of arbitrariness and uncertainty, two conditions that discourage development on reservation lands. Jurisdictional disputes flourish among state, tribal, and federal governments in part because the Secretary has failed to act decisively in proposing consistent or careful jurisdictional arrangements. These costs were barely tolerable when leasing was a less significant aspect of tribal political and economic development. But since 1955, the burdens of uncertainty have become aggravated as tribes themselves turn increasingly to major development projects and as the environmental and social implications of long-term leases have become far more pronounced.

In order to determine the appropriate standards for exercise of the Secretary's approval power, a judgment must be made as to which policy goals are to be furthered by his leasing supervision. If the goal of leasing is merely the production of income, the Secretary's function could be limited to ensuring that the tribe or individual beneficiary receives fair financial value for the lease. If other policies are of equal or greater importance, however, more could be required: for example, the Secretary could be viewed as having some trust responsibility to preserve a reservation land base, to protect the tribe's continued political existence and governmental self-sufficiency, to preserve the environment of the reservation, to encourage development of a viable economic and social structure on the reservation, to ensure equitable participation in the enterprise by the lessor, or to determine what law (state, tribal, or federal) should apply to disputes that arise from the lease enterprise. Perhaps the Secretary's trusteeship could even include an obligation to ensure that the lease is consistent with a broad, coherent rehabilitative strategy of the federal government.

These are not always exclusive or necessary considerations in the exercise of the approval power with regard to any particular lease. But there has been virtually no analysis of how the Secretary should resolve these often competing considerations. In the remainder of this Article, we offer a short review of the history of leasing policy, an analysis of the scope of the Secretary's trust duties, and certain recommendations for the future.

Morton, Civil No. 71-201 (D. Ariz. Jan. 15, 1973); Tewa Tesuque v. Morton, Civil No. 9630 (D.N.M. July 2, 1973), *appeal docketed*, No. 73-1817, 10th Cir., Sept. 4, 1973.

I. *History of Indian Leasing Policy*

A. *Nineteenth-Century Prohibitions on Leasing*

Pervasive authorized use of Indian lands by non-Indians is principally a 20th-century phenomenon.[26]

[The 1790 Trade and Intercourse Act] provided that "no sale of lands made by any Indians, or any nation or tribe of Indians within the United States shall be valid ... unless the same shall be made ... at some public treaty"; the prohibition on private leasing was explicitly confirmed in later enactments....

B. *Leasing and the Allotment Legislation*

A formal turning point in land tenure was the General Allotment Act of 1887. Allotments, basically an individuation of tenure, were intended to divide the common landholdings of the tribe among families. Usually, the lands allotted remained in trust with a future date set for the complete transfer of the land to nontrust status. The 1887 Act empowered the President unilaterally to create allotments on any reservation. Unallotted reservation lands were designated as surplus and thus available for sale, the proceeds to be credited to the Indians or expended for their benefit.

An underlying purpose of the 1887 Act was advancement of the Indians by "civilization": Indians were to be acculturated in the white tradition, individualism was to supplant communal ways, and farming was to be substituted for hunting. Another important role of allotment was to open reservation lands for sale to whites, a consequence of which was to weaken tribal government by depriving the tribe of land ownership and encouraging nonmembers of the tribe to enter the reservation.

This result was an intended one, for an objective of the Act was to assimilate Indians into the cultural mainstream. Under the allotment system, land was to be the prime civilizing tool, and reservation land tenure was molded to influence behavior, to teach the civilizing lesson, and to provide an atmosphere in which the Indians could learn settler traditions and adjust to settler culture. There were two immediate land tenure consequences. First, the tribal communal pattern by which Indian land was owned was forced to yield to a division of land with each family individually responsible for its limited acreage. Second, since farming required less land than hunting, lands not needed for individual allotment could be and were sold, and the proceeds used to finance Indian advancement (for example, by supplying schools at which white farmers could teach agriculture or vocational training).

---

[26]There is some evidence that unauthorized leases were concluded between tribes and private persons prior to the 1891 leasing statute. By the 1830's, substantial lands of the Seneca Nation had been leased without federal approval. *See* Gunther, Governmental Power and New York Indian Lands — A Reassessment of a Persistent Problem of Federal-State Relations, 8 Buffalo L. Rev. 1 (1958). These leases, apparently executed in the mistaken belief that the Trade and Intercourse Acts, *see* notes 30-36 *infra* and accompanying text, did not apply to New York, were ratified by statute in 1875. Act of Feb. 19, 1875, ch. 90, 18 Stat. (pt. III) 330, *as amended*, Act of Sept. 30, 1890, ch. 1132, 26 Stat. 558 (1890). There may also have been unauthorized leasing in the Indian Territory, which subsequently became the State of Oklahoma. *See* F. Cohen, Handbook of Federal Indian Law 327 n.441 (1971).

The civilizing purpose of the allotment legislation was to be achieved by having the allottee work the land himself. Leasing was seen as generally inconsistent with this purpose, though supporters of the Act ultimately pressed for leasing authority, apparently because they believed (as did some Indian agents in the field) that leasing would intersperse good white farmers throughout the reservation "who would as object lessons be of incalculable value in teaching the principles of farming." Advocates of allotment also supported leasing a part of the allotment so as to produce capital to cultivate the remainder of the allotted land. Moreover, a number of Indians on the reservations (such as unmarried women, the aged, and the young) were thought unable to farm their allotments profitably, so that these lands would otherwise lie in disuse.

The first general leasing statute, in 1891, permitted an Indian to rent his land only if he was unable to work it "by reason of age or other disability."[49] The lease term was limited to 3 years for farming and grazing and 10 years for mining. So grudging was the authority that the approval of the Secretary of the Interior himself was required for a lease. The Interior Department, in administering the 1891 Act, reported that "[a]gents are expressly directed that it is not intended to authorize the making of any lease by an allottee who possesses the necessary physical and mental qualifications to enable him to cultivate his allotment, either personally or by hired help."

In 1894, however, the annual Indian Appropriation Act increased the agricultural lease term to 5 years, allowed 10-year business and mining leases, and permitted leases by allottees who suffered from "inability" to work their land.[51] This Act also permitted leasing of unallotted surplus tribal lands. In 1894, some 295 leases of allotted lands were approved, in contrast to 4 and 2 in the previous 2 years.[52] Lease approvals increased to around 1,000 per year after 1895.[53] Congress vacillated for a time as to the appropriate leasing policy: in 1897, the annual appropriation act[54] reestablished the more restrictive criteria and terms of the 1891 Act, but in 1900 the 1894 statute was reenacted, and lease approvals in that year reached 2,500.

[49] Act of Feb. 28, 1891, ch. 383, § 3, 26 Stat. 795 (partly codified at 25 U.S.C. § 397 (1970)). "Age" referred to minors and those disabled by senility; "other disability" in the Act was interpreted by the Secretary to mean unmarried women, women whose husbands or sons were unable to work the land, and Indians with chronic illness or incurable physical or mental defects. Comm'r of Indian Affairs Ann. Rep. 476 (1893) [hereinafter cited as Annual Report with a year]; D. Otis, [The Dawes Act and the Allotment of Indian Lands] at 116-17.

[51] Act of Aug. 15, 1894, ch. 290, 28 Stat. 305 (1894). The Commissioner confessed himself unable to formulate a precise definition for this term, and permitted any allottee who was "for any reason unable to cultivate his lands" to lease them. Annual Report, supra note 49, at 421 (1894).

[52] D. Otis, supra note [49], at 118. Much of this leasing was in Oklahoma, where the Five Civilized Tribes had been given special authority to execute leases as early as 1882, cf. Act of Aug. 7, 1882, ch. 446, 22 Stat. 349; Act of Oct. 1, 1890, ch. 1252, 26 Stat. 640, and where some illicit leasing had also occurred, see United States v. Rogers, 23 F. 658, 665 (W.D. Ark. 1885); F. Cohen, supra note 26, at 327 n.441. Almost all the other leases reported were on the Crow Reservation in Montana (846,000 acres) and the Shoshone Reservation in Wyoming (383,691 acres). Some of the single leases covered over 100,000 acres. See Annual Report, supra note 49, at 33-37 (1894).

[53] See D. Otis, supra note [49], at 121. Eastern "friends of the Indian" became alarmed at the increase, and the Mohonk Conference in 1894 adopted a resolution that leasing laws "are widely resulting in dispossessing ignorant Indians of their property rights, without an adequate return, to their great disadvantage and the enriching of designing white men." Id. at 119; see generally F. Prucha, Americanizing the American Indians (1973).

[54] Act of June 7, 1897, ch. 3, 30 Stat. 85.

In 1904, the Commissioner of Indian Affairs adopted regulations to protect against indiscriminate leasing of allotments. However, in 1910 a more general leasing statute relaxed the strictures of the earlier acts, allowing leases, with secretarial approval, for farming and grazing of allotted and tribal lands without restriction except as to lease term (5 years, as in the 1891 Act).[59] In the two decades following the 1910 statute, large portions of reservations became leased to non-Indian farmers and ranchers, and the pattern of substantial short-term agricultural and grazing leases and permits that persists today in much of Indian country was established.[60] There were few significant statutory changes between 1910 and 1955. The permissible lease term was increased to 10 years for some farming leases.[61] In the Indian Reorganization Act of 1934, tribes which adopted charters empowering them to do so were allowed to conclude 10-year leases of tribal lands without secretarial approval.[62] Very few such charters have been approved, but since this was the maximum period permitted by law at the time, the 1934 Act represented a substantial paper transfer of federal power to the tribes, thus, in appearance, strengthening tribal government.

There were also some special enactments, prior to 1955, that authorized long-term leasing. In 1940, Congress authorized the leasing of lands on the Port Madison, Snohomish, and Tulalip Reservations in Washington for 25 years and one renewable 25-year term.[63] In 1946, 25-year leases for "religious, educational, recreational, business, or public purposes" were authorized for all Indian tribes and individual allottees or "association[s] of Indians" in the State of Washington.[64] And the Navajo and Hopi Rehabilitation Act of 1950 extended 25-

---

[59] The Commissioner's Report in 1911 indicates that 8.5 million acres of Indian lands were under lease or permit. Most of this leasing was still in Oklahoma, or on two reservations in Montana (Crow and Ft. Peck) and Arizona (San Carlos and Ft. Apache). There was leasing of 2.5 million acres of allotted lands; 1,432,000 of these acres were on reservations in Oklahoma. See Annual Report, *supra* note 49, at 216-21 tables 44 & 45 (1911). In 1913, there were nearly 14 million acres under lease or permit. Of these, 11 million acres were tribally owned, and 3 million acres were allotted. More than half the lease income ($2,707,441 of $4,396,151) was from leases in Oklahoma. See Annual Report, *supra* note 49, at 214-19 tables 48 & 49 (1913).

[60] By 1944, leasing patterns rather similar to the present time had been established. Almost 13 million acres were covered by agricultural leases and grazing permits. Eleven reservations accounted for two-thirds of this total, and all but one of these were in the Northwest or Great Plains: Crow (Mont.) (1,778,809 acres), Pine Ridge (S.D.) (980,738), Ft. Peck (Mont. & N.D.) (795,522), Rosebud (S.D.) (716,908), Klamath (Ore.) (664,895), Cheyenne River (S.D.) (640,597), Colville (Wash.) (622,487), Standing Rock (N.D.) (604,890), Blackfeet (Mont.) (596,960), Kiowa (Okla. & Tex.) (417,508), and Ft. Belknap (Mont.) (413,025). Annual Report, *supra* note 49, at 20-27 table VI (1944).

Since lease and permit figures are aggregated, we cannot compare these figures precisely with the present day. As to the reservations we visited, however, they seem strikingly similar in the case of Rosebud and Pine Ridge. In both cases, then as now, about three-quarters of the reservation is farmed or grazed by non-Indians. Cheyenne River is less heavily leased and under permit at present, due to vigorous tribal efforts to encourage Indian ranching.

[61] Act of May 18, 1916, ch. 125, § 1, 39 Stat. 128 (codified at 25 U.S.C. § 394 (1970)); Act of July 3, 1926, ch. 787, 44 Stat. 894 (codified at 25 U.S.C. § 402(a) (1970)). These statutes pertain only to agricultural leases of lands which are capable of irrigation. A statute enacted in 1921, Act of Mar. 3, 1921, ch. 119, § 1, 41 Stat. 1232 (codified at 25 U.S.C. § 393 (1970)), allows leases of allotted lands for farming and grazing purposes for any period allowed by the Secretary's regulations, subject to the approval of the reservation superintendent.

[62] Act of June 18, 1934, ch. 576, § 17, 48 Stat. 988 (codified at 25 U.S.C. § 477 (1970)).

[63] Act of Oct. 9, 1940, ch. 781, 54 Stat. 1057 (codified at 25 U.S.C. § 403(a) (1970)).

[64] Act of Aug. 9, 1946, ch. 929, § 1, 60 Stat. 962 (codified at 25 U.S.C. § 403b (1970)).

year (one-term renewable) leasing authority to those tribes and to tribal members holding allotments.[65]

C. *The 1955 Act*

The 1955 Act[66] was a major innovation in Indian land policy because it permitted all Indians for the first time to lease their land for up to 50 years, and for a broad variety of purposes — industrial, commercial, and residential among them. It is evident from the legislative history of the Act that its major purpose was to increase Indian income by opening Indian land to market forces and encouraging long-term leasing for commercial purposes. Congress was concerned that restricted lease periods had discouraged lessees from obtaining long-term construction financing and had thus foreclosed uses of land which required substantial investment....

II. *Possible Policy Goals of Leasing Supervision*

A. *The "Free Market" Approach — Abolition of the Approval Power*

One way to approach the appropriate policies to be served by the Secretary's approval power is to ask why there should be such federal supervision at all. Without the specific approval power, trust land could be leased at the discretion of the tribal or individual beneficial owner. Analytically, a "free market" approach has political and economic attractions, particularly as it pertains to tribal lands. Secretarial intervention could either be removed completely or retained simply to perform the most ministerial of functions — as a "recorder of land records," the Secretary could simply certify that the lessor does in fact own the leased lands. Tribal "self-determination" seems maximized by this approach, and economically, Indian resources would become fully subject to market forces. Resources would be more efficiently allocated in the national economy as a whole, and in theory at least, Indian income would likewise increase.

The removal of federal supervision over leasing of lands presupposes, however, that there is no purpose within the trust responsibility that justifies retaining the approval power. A proposal to abolish the approval power appears functionally equivalent to a termination of the trust responsibility over long-term leasing of Indian lands. In the mid-1950's, Congress enacted several bills terminating the federal trusteeship over particular tribes.

B. *Assuring that Fair Market Value Is Received*

The approval power as presently exercised requires that the Secretary scrutinize only the financial fairness of the transaction — a "fair market value" ap-

---

[65] Act of Apr. 19, 1950, ch. 92, § 5, 64 Stat. 46 (codified at 25 U.S.C. § 635(a) (1970)). In 1950, Congress also gave its consent to leases of certain lands by the Seneca Nation to the extent such leases "may be permitted by the laws of the State of New York." Act of Aug. 14, 1950, ch. 707, § 5, 64 Stat. 442. These lands were chiefly the non-Indian villages, such as Salamanca, which had been established on various Seneca lands in the 19th century, leases for which had been allowed by the Act of Feb. 19, 1875, ch. 90, §§ 1, 3-4, 18 Stat. (pt. III) 330, *as amended*, Act of Sept. 30, 1890, ch. 1132, 26 Stat. 558.

[66] Act of Aug. 9, 1955, Pub. L. No. 255, ch. 615, 69 Stat. 539 (codified at 25 U.S.C. § 415(a) (1970)).

proach. The Secretary's regulations provide as the chief prerequisite for approval that the lease shall be for "the present fair annual rental."[75] The internal manual used by BIA officials is more explicit: "The objective of the Bureau ... in approving leases or permits on trust or restricted land is to obtain for the Indian owners the maximum financial return from the land, consistent with sound land utilization principles."[76]

Limiting the lease approval process to a financial review with the exclusive purpose of protecting Indian lessors against their own improvidence is functionally analogous to a sort of termination. Such a narrow secretarial review may have been all that was intended by Congress; the 1955 act may represent consent by Congress to a transfer of Indian lands to non-Indians by lease rather than by sale (the general result under the termination acts).[77] The Secretary's

---

[75] 25 C.F.R. § 131.5(b) (1973) [now 25 C.F.R. § 162.5(b) (1982)]. The regulations contain a series of exceptions to the "fair annual rental" requirement. The most important of these is contained in § 131.5(b)(3), which provides that leases for less than the "fair annual rental" may be approved if the lease is in the Secretary's judgment "in the best interest of the landowners." This provision, adopted in 1961, appears to vest nearly boundless discretion in the Bureau to approve leases for a nominal rental if justified by noneconomic benefits to the lessor. It would seem to mandate the weighing of all sorts of social policies to decide if a below-market lease is justified. The Bureau has refrained from the exercise of such open discretion. The internal manual used by the BIA gives very limited scope to the "best interests" exception, stating that when it is not possible to lease land on the basis of its highest and best use for a term compatible with income maximization, "leases may be granted or approved for a term compatible with proper protection and preservation of the property at the highest rental that may be realized. While, generally, such leases should be limited to a term of one year, a longer term may in some cases be justified." BIA Manual pt. 54, § 5.3.

The regulations also provide that an allottee may lease land to a member of his family, and a tribe may lease land "for purposes of subsidization for the benefit of the tribe" and "for homesite purposes to tribal members provided the land is not commercial or industrial in character" at nominal rentals. 25 C.F.R. § 131.5(b)(2) (1973). Land may also be leased to "agencies of the Federal, State or local governments" at a nominal rental. Id. This exception creates something of a conflict of interest because the Secretary may be both lessee and trustee for the lessor of tribal land. For example, the BIA has established an "administrative reserve" on the Pine Ridge Reservation which, prior to 1960, included the entire village at Pine Ridge. The tribe received no rent for any land leased in this reserve. The small commercial shops in the village apparently paid rent to no one. The payment of less than fair value for government use of Indian land seems inappropriate, for payment of a market lease rental would be a desirable form of financial assistance to the tribe. Leasehold income from government offices might, in some cases, provide the core for financing of office building construction or similar developments.

[76] BIA Manual pt. 54, § 5.1. We have found no instance of a lease disapproval except for failure to achieve the fair annual rental standard or for violation of pertinent federal (or tribal, in one case) laws. Short-term agricultural and grazing leases are generally approved by the reservation BIA office. Longer leases are submitted to one of the 10 BIA area offices, which have been delegated authority to approve leases of up to 65 years. Id. pt. 10, § 3.3 (E)(1). Leases for longer than this term must be approved by the Commissioner of Indian Affairs, pursuant to authority delegated to him from the Secretary. Id. § 2.1. At each of these three tiers, the critical reviewing personnel are in the Real Property Management Division. On occasion, however, this Division may arrange for technical consultants from the U.S. Geological Service, or legal advice from the Field Solicitor or Regional Solicitor. The review process is designed chiefly to assure compliance with the regulations and the fair rental standard. Careful attention is given to the appraisal report where an appraisal has been made.

[77] Some of § 415's supporters in 1955 recognized a connection between long-term leasing and termination. Mr. Donald Belcher, Assistant Director of the Bureau of the Budget, echoed this theme in a letter to Senator Murray: "Removal of the anachronistic restrictions on Indian people is one phase of the administration's efforts to bring about the integration of our Indian populations and the eventual termination of the Federal responsibility over Indian affairs." S. Rep. No. 375, 84th Cong., in Sess. 6 (1955).

role in such a process would be merely to ensure that the compensation paid for the transfer is fair.[78]

It is not far-fetched to view the kinds of current residential development on the reservation — made possible by the 1955 Act — as a sort of termination, or a 20th-century equivalent to 19th-century negotiated reductions in Indian land. For value received, the tribe surrenders a significant portion of its land, irrevocably in effect, to the non-Indian community. It receives consideration for the transaction but so too, usually, did its 19th-century predecessors. Through the lease instrument — often for 99 years — the fiction of Indian retention is maintained, but the impact on the tribe is often inconsistent with the form. In this context, 99-year leases are tantamount to the sale of the fee. It may be possible to recapture a site from agricultural or even industrial users, but where discrete cohesive communities, indeed cities, are constructed, the likelihood that they could be dislodged is minimal. There is nothing to suggest that these lease-communities are planning for a terminable future.

There is an additional disadvantage to limiting the approval process to a financial scrutiny of the transaction. It assumes that the federal-Indian relationship is exclusively a "spendthrift" trust, the only purpose of which is to protect the Indian from his own incompetence. Particularly with respect to tribal leases, such a premise is both demeaning and empirically outdated in most cases. The "incompetent ward" justification for the approval power and for the underlying trust responsibility presumes that the federal trusteeship ceases when the trust beneficiary comes of age. But there may be a more enduring purpose behind the trusteeship. It could represent a federal guarantee that Indian tribes may exist as a "distinct political society" and may maintain a separate culture apart from the mainsteam. Thus, much of the criticism of the termination policy derives from the more basic rejection of federally induced assimilation that is its objective and from a fundamental commitment and adherence to the contrary premise that a separate culture for Indians is the underlying objective of the trust relationship, and that a reservation land base is necessary for such a culture to thrive, or even to subsist.

C. *Preservation of Indian Culture*

There are many themes to federal Indian policy, but one of them surely is the use of the reservation as a protective bastion for indigenous cultures. Although it has been fashionable at times to degrade this policy by referring to it as the "menagerie theory" or museum theory of federal Indian policy, preservation has historically been a principal goal of federal policy toward Indians. For example, much federal legislation, beginning with the first Trade and Intercourse Acts, has sought to control population mix by excluding or limiting non-Indian settlement on Indian lands. Treaties reserving lands to the Indians frequently excluded non-Indians from these areas except by federal permission. There has been the continuous understanding that a large proportion of white

---

[78] This conception of the Secretary's role was taken by Assistant Secretary Lewis in his comments on the 1955 act: "The Secretary of the Interior would merely be authorized to prescribe regulatory safeguards and to veto improvident transactions." H.R. Rep. No. 1093, 84th Cong., 1st Sess. 4 (1955).

settlers in Indian country could mean the destruction of the indigenous culture. In a sense, the pre-1955 statutory schemes which prohibited long term surface leases were designed to prevent this result.

One basis for the commitment to preserve the Indian culture and land base is rooted in the historical process of legal treaties and agreements by which the country was ceded by the Indian tribes to the United States. As payment for massive land cessions by the Indian tribes, those promissory bargains included a covenant by the United States to secure reservation lands and other resources to the Indians, generally forever. Fulfillment of this contractual bargain may entail a special status for Indian lands, even in perpetuity, and even if a particular generation of Indians waives the benefits of the bargain. Such a commitment may also be founded on a basic policy judgment that Indian culture itself is a positive value to be preserved, and that forced cultural assimilation becomes more likely without separate lands on which the culture can be nourished.

Defense of sale and leasing restrictions solely in terms of "preserving the Indian culture" against the onslaught of modernism may seem, in a large sense, somewhat of an illusion. No culture is static; it may therefore be contradictory to talk of "preserving" something which changes constantly and has already changed enormously as a consequence of interaction with the settler values. Yet, even if preservation is not a completely accurate description of the process, nevertheless by withholding the land from the market by limiting eligibility for residence to specified classes of persons (tribal members, for example), a culture is permitted to develop which is significantly different from the culture which would evolve under the free or fair market approaches to leasing. By restricting reservation land use to Indians except in limited circumstances (for example, certain types and terms of leases) a rationing system is arrived at which provides some protection for the Indian zone.

The approval power may exist, then, largely to safeguard the conditions regarded as essential to the continued cohesiveness of the tribe and its culture — if not to its static preservation. These would appear to include a sufficient land base and an opportunity to exercise some quantum of governmental authority. The trust responsibility could be read as placing the highest value on the federal guarantee of space, immune from state intervention, where an Indian society can be pursued. In this sense, the beneficial ownership of reservation land may be likened to a life estate. Each generation may be obliged to pass the land base on to the next, and the Secretary may function as a guardian for generations yet unborn so as to guarantee that the cultural homeland and heritage will not be diminished in size or value. Another analogy might be to a sort of guaranteed annual income. Ownership without a power of alienation tends to assure that a certain amount of income (both economic and social) will accrue to the Indians without the expenditure of additional public resources.

D. The "Rehabilitative" Approach

Related to — but going beyond — the preservation approach are what might be called the rehabilitative functions of the Secretary. Throughout the late 19th century, it was often stated that the Secretary's function was to prepare the Indians for life in the mainstream, that the reservation was in the nature of a school. Since rehabilitative strategies are tied to the use of land, much of the shifting policy with respect to reservations can be explained on this basis. The allotment acts, which involved massive land transfers to individual family units, had a rehabilitative purpose, as did the industrialization of the reservations in the 1960's.

The Secretary could, then, have far-reaching power to approve or disapprove leases (or even to initiate leases) depending upon whether the contemplated land uses further a particular rehabilitative strategy. Under this approach, the major purpose of the reservation is to establish a locus to carry out federal rehabilitative policy, and beneficial ownership by the tribal group is deemphasized. In this view, the Secretary, as trustee, has widespread authority to determine the purposes of the trust and implement those purposes. If the Secretary determines that the reservation should be worked by the Indians, then leasing would be prohibited. If it would be wise to have an intermingling of settlers and tribal members, then incursions would be tolerated. If the land should not be put up for sale because it cushions Indian adjustment to the harsh realities of modern life, then the government has the necessary power to prevent sales.

The rehabilitative approach is markedly less attractive than either the "free market" or the preservative approaches (even though it may be a better guide to history). The self-government aspects of reservation life become more of a fiction; to the extent it is allowed to function at all, the tribal government is expected to exercise minimal power. Its existence is tolerated temporarily as a sort of civics lesson to cushion the assimilation of tribal members into the dominant society and to better their preparation for mainstream responsibilities. Because strong tribal governments are essential to the continued economic, political, and social viability of Indian cultures, the deemphasis of tribal governments required by the rehabilitative approach is undesirable.

Furthermore, while the Secretary will necessarily have some discretion no matter what policies he attempts to implement under the rehabilitative approach such discretion is particularly broad. So pervasive a discretion is dangerous because the Secretary may be influenced by the needs and dictates of other non-Indian public projects and policies for which he is responsible within the Department of the Interior. The Secretary's administration of Indian lands may at times reflect those needs rather than Indian needs; a public official in his other capacities, the Secretary has often been tempted or required to evaluate lease bargains with reference to the "public interest" rather than with reference to his trust responsibilities.

III. *A Proposal for Limiting the Approval Power*

A basic flaw in federal Indian policy, as we have tried to indicate, is its shapelessness, its potential for arbitrariness and uncertainty attributable in large part to the vast discretion of the Secretary. During times of heavy-handed stewardship, as in the early 1900's, the discretion involved in the approval process resulted in tight control over the contour of tribal decisions. Then, and again in the early 1950's, the Secretary determined what were proper ordinances for the reservation; he even decided what were suitable religious experiences. Through manipulation of land use and through federal subsidies the Department of the

Interior intervened massively in the patterns of land use and the demography of the reservation. At present, with the mood of the country favoring tribal self-government, the Secretary's hand is not so obviously present. But there is a danger that federal intervention will again increase, especially as the land, water, and mineral resources of the reservation become more pressingly critical for the urban non-Indian metropolises of the Southwest. As a consequence, it is essential that there be a tighter understanding of the bounds of the Secretary's discretion and a clearer perception of suitable grounds for the invocation of the approval power.

We favor a combination of approaches — the "free market" approach for short-term leases of tribal lands and a more "preservative" approach for long-term leases, with retention of financial review for all leases of allotted lands. There are recognized dangers in the preservative approach; the remainder of this Part addresses the two major problems involved in attempting to use the approval power as a means to implement preservative policy goals. First, as discussed above, such use of the approval power may give too much discretion to the Secretary. Second, the Secretary is faced with the formidable task of allocating jurisdiction among federal, state, and tribal governments in a way that recognizes the legitimate jurisdictional claims of the first two while at the same time strengthening tribal self-government.

A. *Limiting the Secretary's Discretion*

1. *Abolition of the approval power for short-term leases*

In order to limit the Secretary's discretion, retraction of the approval power seems appropriate for short-term leases of tribal lands. Although this might be accomplished administratively by announcing that any tribal lease will be approved, legislation may be required. Analogous statutes have been enacted to transfer leasing authority from the Secretary to the tribe, with retention of the counseling function in the Secretary. For example, in 1970 Congress authorized the Tulalip Tribe to conclude leases of tribal lands for terms up to 30 years without Bureau approval. The Tribe was required to adopt regulations governing such leases prior to their execution, with the regulations to be approved by the Secretary. Congress, in enacting the Tulalip leasing statute, expressed confidence in the tribal organization and its powers of self-government. Administratively, the Bureau has treated the Navajo Tribe and some other tribes in much the same fashion. The Tulalips and Navajos are not unique in this respect; discretion to lease without secretarial approval could be more broadly vested in other tribes.

But where the approval power is eroded, the Secretary should be required, consistent with the trust obligation, to function as a counselor and advisor, supplying information to the lessor. The Secretary now performs valuable technical services as part of his administration of the approval power — appraising land values, collecting and distributing income, and providing environmental and other scientific studies and services. If his veto power were abolished but his counseling responsibilities were retained, particularly as they relate to preservation of a land base and tribal self-government, several functions of his trust responsibility might be balanced and reconciled. These would include encouraging self-government and preservation of Indian landownership, and securing some of the best aspects of the "free market" approach.

One function retained by the Secretary might also be to prepare an "impact statement" in advance of lease approval. Such a statement might include the lease impact on land preservation, depletion of the reservation's resources, employment, the need for associated planning, the continued adequacy of retained lands as a cultural homeland for the tribe, and the functioning of tribal self-government.

In his advisory capacity, the Secretary should also devote substantially more resources to making, and periodically updating, appraisals of lease transactions. In theory, the BIA currently does support its assessment of fair annual rental by appraising the land values and reasonable return of leased lands. However, appraisals of individual tracts or allotments to be leased for agricultural purposes are rare on many reservations. The Bureau's Appraisal Department employs fewer than 100 professional appraisers for all its central, area, and reservation superintendent offices. It is unable to satisfy all requests for appraisals of reservation land; in fact, it completes only about 60 percent of the requests actually made. Many realty officers, knowing of the backlog and delay in securing an appraisal, simply do not request one. At many reservations, the determination of fair annual rental for agricultural land appears to be set by "rule of thumb" techniques rather than by formal appraisals. At the Cheyenne River and Pine Ridge reservations in South Dakota, for example, the realty office determines "land values" of comparable land up for sale, and pegs its rentals at 5 percent of these values. The realty office at the Gila River Reservation in Arizona relies on its past experience and general knowledge of farming conditions and the real estate market to review agricultural leases. Such processes are necessarily subjective and may take insufficient account of the peculiarities of an individual unit or allotment. Experience on a number of reservations suggests that rents can be dramatically increased by instituting formal appraisals.[108]

2. *Retention of the approval power for long-term leases*

In implementing his preservative obligations, the Secretary has a responsibility to safeguard against lease dispositions that dramatically alter the character of the reservation as lands set aside for Indian occupancy, the practice of Indian

---

[108] For example, on the Rosebud Reservation in South Dakota, the BIA began appraising agricultural leaseholds in one area of the reservation several years ago. As a direct result, the average rent rose by 40%. But the BIA has only two appraisers to cover the entire Rosebud Reservation, and agricultural land has been appraised only in Tripp and Gregory counties in the eastern part of the reservation. In 1971, the Rosebud Tribal Council raised its tribal minimum to almost double the prior rate. The new tribal minimum was based upon an impressively detailed grazing study done by BIA appraisers in October 1970. This study found that the average rental rate on deeded lands within the reservation and on lands adjacent to the reservation was about $1.55 per acre. The report recommended that the BIA "stocking rate" (the rate which sets the number of cattle which may be grazed on a particular range unit) should be slightly changed, so that more cattle could graze on the land, and that the new tribal minimum be raised to $1.50 per acre (the difference being fence and water costs to the lessee). The prior rate had been $.80 per acre. Interview with BIA personnel, Rosebud Reservation, July 1971. Current studies of this sort should be done for other reservations. In a number of different areas, studies have shown substantial increases in rents after current appraisals are made. Interview with Donald Maynard, BIA Realty Specialist, in Washington, D.C., Mar. 15, 1974.

culture, and the exercise of tribal self-government. For this reason, there should be some retained secretarial approval power for tribal leases beyond a certain term of years, at least as an initial matter. Tribes could, of course, be given full powers of self-government, including even a power to dispose of tribal lands, and it may be that the Secretary should act simply as a counselor to these long-term transactions. But the dissolution of an Indian reservation, or even a part of it, is a decision which a tribe — which after all may be only the temporary majority of one generation — has historically not been permitted to make except with the consent of Congress. Adherence to such a decision on the part of a tribal majority may indeed be transient; members of several tribes terminated during the 1950's have requested resumption of the trust relationship, and bills have been proposed in Congress to accomplish that result.

Congress recognized the need for review of long-term leases in the Tulalip statute, which limited tribal leasing without the Secretary's approval only to leases of less than 30 years' duration. Without specifically endorsing that period, it is clear that different rules and different prescriptions could be fashioned for leases with long terms. We conclude that some Federal power to disapprove very long-term tribal leases should be retained in order to allow the Secretary to implement his preservative trusteeship duties.

An interpretation of the trusteeship which emphasizes land preservation would not require disapproval by the Secretary of all long-term leases conveying substantial amounts of trust land. The leases by the small Agua Caliente tribe in the Palm Springs community, for example, are exceedingly lucrative and produce large annual per capita distributions to tribal members, sufficient, some would say, to compensate for any cultural deprivation. But careful controls are desirable, for a culture once lost is irretrievable.

AMERICAN INDIAN POLICY REVIEW COMMISSION, FINAL REPORT 318-22 (1977)

Leasing

. . . .

In recent years, two steps have been taken to try to improve the Indian credit position. The Indian Finance Act of 1974[35] was enacted authorizing loans and providing grants for a number of purposes and the law governing the Farmers Home Administration loan program was amended to provide for loans to Indian tribes for acquisition of lands.[36] However, utilization of the revolving loan fund at BIA has not been effectively directed at resolution of the land question and the loan program of FMHA has serious impediments. More importantly, neither of these credit facilities has reached to the problem of excessive leasing of lands to non-Indians.

The leasing program has, in many instances, tied up tribal and individually owned trust land for years and today poses serious obstacles to tribal initiatives toward economic development and self-sufficiency. In its 1975 Land Use Inventory, the BIA estimated that Indian owned resources directly supported some

---

[35]25 U.S.C. sec. 1451 et seq.
[36]25 U.S.C. secs. 488-492.

120,000 jobs by both Indian and non-Indian. This amounts to 20 percent of the entire Indian service population recognized by the BIA. A long step toward self-sufficiency would be taken if all of these jobs were held by Indians — the owners of the resource.

There are numerous problems with the leasing program aside from its adverse impact on tribal initiative to develop their own agricultural enterprises. The most serious of these problems are the inequitable lease rates that are obtained....

Crow Competent Leasing

A competent lease is a 5- or 10-year lease of allotted agricultural land in which the rent is prepaid for the entire term of the lease. For a given piece of land, the first 5-year period was paid in a lump sum when the land first went into competent lease status. Subsequently, once a year the current lease is canceled and a new one written, with payment of rent for the last year of the new lease discounted to the present. December is the most usual time to cancel and rewrite the leases.

The BIA's role is recording of leases. As long as the allotment is owned by five or fewer people, a competent lease is valid. If an allottee or a group of owners wishes to regain control of its land, he must wait 5 or 10 years. For poor people, this can be a long wait. Further, for many of the leases, and particularly for rangeland, even after the 5-year period, there would be only one potential lessor. Many of the lessors are large operators who lease land from many Indians. Many own fee-patented land interspersed among Indian allotments which they lease.

In June 1975, 868,281 acres of 1,205,926 acres of allotted land were under competent lease. This is 72 percent of the allotted land.

Such leasing constitutes a partial alienation of allotted land. Competent leases can be used as collateral for loans, while trust land cannot. This feature depends upon the existence of an assignment clause in the lease. Since Indians use competent leases as collateral for loans, such leases provide a method of financing, without which, Indians might otherwise feel forced to sell their lands.

Land Leases on the Fort Hall Indian Reservation

Since 1973, a controversy has raged at Fort Hall over a finding by the Economic Research Associates of Los Angeles, consultants for the tribe's overall economic development plan, required by EDA. They found that Fort Hall Indians failed to get equitable income for all agricultural land leased to non-Indian tenants. Typical nonreservation leases in the Fort Hall area averaged 35 percent of gross crop value, while Fort Hall leases were equivalent to about 2.3 percent of gross crop value.

In response to this study and a tribal request for an investigation, GAO conducted an investigation and also found there was a large disparity in lease rates, particularly in irrigated reservation land. Irrigated reservation land was found to rent at an average of $15.36 compared to $75.41 for high quality irrigated nonreservation land. Dry farm acreage rentals were approximately equal for reservation/nonreservation lands, but a substantial disparity was also found to exist for pasture rental. These findings of GAO were softened, how-ever, by a finding that certain intangibles caused non-Indian lessors to be less willing to pay the same rent as for non-Indian land, but these intangibles were not fully identified.

In 1975, another firm, Farm Management Co., did another evaluation of leasing at Fort Hall. They calculated the value of cash leases for both high quality and average quality nonreservation land, thus taking into consideration the tangible costs raised by GAO, and compared them to the value of cash leases for the same quality land on the reservation.

[Because] potatoes are normally rotated every other year with a grain crop, the average cash rent [for nonreservation land] is $56-$70 on the better soils and $17-$24 on the sandier soils. After the first reports of ERA and GAO, the tribal council increased the standard rent per acre from an average of $15 to $35 an acre. However, this fixed fee allows the better lands to stay in farming at a bargain price while the poorer or marginal lands were abandoned because of lower yields, greater fertilizer expense and difficulty in irrigating this type of soil. Using standard lease rates for the entire reservation has caused the tribe to receive less rent than it should for better farmland and the poorer land is left idle.

In 1974, the Shoshone-Bannock Tribes at Fort Hall commissioned an addi-tional comprehensive study by an economist, Mr. Jack Peterson, under a HUD 701 planning grant. This study published in 1974, and updated in 1976, con-firms the continued inequitable leasing practices.

Leasing practices have provided Indian landowners with very substandard returns for the following reasons:

Fixed rate rentals on Indian land are substantially less
than on non-Indian land.
Indian fixed rate rentals are preferred over crop share
rental.
Indian lessors have no recourse when leases are violated.
Leases are for lengthy periods of time.
Lease regulations for proper conservation practices are
unenforceable.

What is the alternative to leasing? On several of the sample reservations, particularly Umatilla and Crow Creek, tribes have consolidated tracts of trust land and are farming it. This would solve a multitude of problems. First, effi-cient-size units could be created. Second, the tribe has better access to capital and technical assistance than do individuals. Third, returns are usually higher than leasing and are directly received by the tribe.

These criticisms related equally to farm and grazing lands. The lack of readily available capital and the lack of a sound policy directed toward land consolida-tion, acquisition, and termination of these present lease programs combine to thwart tribal development and economic self-sufficiency.

Credit and Technical Assistance

Aside from fractionated land ownership, the major obstacles to development of a viable Indian farm economy are inadequate credit and lack of necessary technical assistance.

The Indian farm operator has three major sources of credit: commercial banks, Farmers Home Administration, and the BIA Revolving Loan Fund. Both commercial banks and the FHA require acceptable collateral, and as GAO reported they were reluctant to accept Indian land as collateral because of its trust status. In reviewing new BIA revolving loans made during fiscal year 1975, it appears that the bulk of individual loans were made for purposes other than agriculture. Only 16 percent went for agriculture and livestock activities. (See table 5.)

Table 5. — Distribution by type of new BIA revolving loans to individuals, fiscal year 1975

Type of loans	Percent
Agriculture	15.9
Farming	8.4
Livestock	7.6
Business enterprise	22.7
Consumer credit	11.3
Education	0.4
Fisheries	1.3
Land	5.8
Housing	34.6
Refinancing	7.9
Total percent	99.9
Total	$15,315,532

Technical Assistance

The technical assistance and agricultural advisory services available to Indian farmers is supplied through a cooperative BIA/USDA effort. Under a memorandum of understanding between the Extension Service and the BIA, the Extension Service provides leadership and direct assistance to State extension services in planning, conducting, and evaluating extension programs in those States where the BIA has contracts with State extension services. Funds for this work are transferred directly from the BIA to the State extension services.

However, USDA officials have complained that the actual amount of technical assistance and advice provided to Indian operators has declined in recent years because the BIA is reluctant to seek increased appropriations. The BIA extension budget has remained small and virtually constant since 1971.

Table 6. — Extension Service BIA funds directed to State extension service

1971	$1,748,331
1972	1,877,232
1973	1,732,737
1974	1,695,020
1975	1,709,633

Source: USDA.

The nature of fiscal funding makes job security uncertain for extension agents. This affects the quality of personnel that work in the program. For most, it is a temporary job. USDA would prefer direct appropriations. This would increase the level of funding and promote job security. Ultimately, the funds should be given directly to the tribe so that they may contract with those who will supply the best technical [expertise].

DAVIS v. MORTON

469 F.2d 593 (10th Cir. 1972)

HILL, Circuit Judge.

This is an appeal from the United States District Court for the District of New Mexico for dismissing appellants' action against the United States government. Appellants allege the government failed to follow the provisions of the National Environmental Policy Act (NEPA), 42 U.S.C. § 4321 et seq., and of 25 U.S.C. § 415 before approving a 99-year lease on the Tesuque Indian Reservation in Santa Fe County, New Mexico.

The facts are simple and uncontroverted. On April 17, 1970, a 99-year lease of restricted Indian lands was executed by the Pueblo of Tesuque (Pueblo), as lessor, and Sangre de Cristo Development Company, Inc. (Sangre), a New Mexico corporation, as lessee. The agreement granted Sangre a lease on a 1300-acre tract of land called "Tract 1" and granted lease options on four other tracts, thereby subjecting approximately 5400 acres to the lease. The purpose of the lease is to develop the property for residential, recreational and commercial purposes. Ultimately a small city is planned with a population of approximately 15,000 inhabitants.

On May 24, 1970, appellee Walter O. Olson, Area Supervisor for the New Mexico District of the Bureau of Indian Affairs of the Department of the Interior, approved the lease agreement pursuant to 25 U.S.C. § 415. Olson's authority was granted to him by appellee Lewis R. Bruce, Commissioner of Indian Affairs in the Department of the Interior, and by appellee Rogers C. B. Morton, Secretary of the Interior of the United States. Appellants charged that appellees were without authority to grant the lease since no environmental impact study was conducted prior to approval of the lease as required by NEPA, 42 U.S.C. § 4332 (2)(C).[1] They further asserted that appellees violated 25 U.S.C. § 415(a) by approving the lease on Indian lands without first being assured that certain statutory mandates had been met.

Two issues are presented on appeal. First, does the Secretary's authority to ratify or reject leases relating to Indian lands constitute major federal action? Second, does 25 U.S.C. § 415, as amended, have any effect on a lease signed

---

[1] The Congress authorizes and directs that, to the fullest extent possible: ... (2) all agencies of the Federal Government shall — ... (C) include in every recommendation or report on proposals for legislation and other major Federal actions significantly affecting the quality of the human environment, a detailed statement by the responsible official on — (i) the environmental impact of the proposed action, (ii) any adverse environmental effects which cannot be avoided should the proposal be implemented, (iii) alternatives to the proposed action, (iv) the relationship between local short-term uses of man's environment and the maintenance and enhancement of long-term productivity, and (v) any irreversible and irretrievable commitments of resources which would be involved in the proposed action should it be implemented....

before the amendment's enactment date? As we answer the first issue in the affirmative, it will be unnecessary to discuss the retroactive effect of § 415.

Appellees' primary thesis is that although the contractual relationship between Sangre and the Pueblo is a lease, it is not a federal lease and therefore does not constitute major federal action. The United States did not initiate the lease, was not a party, possessed no interest in either the lease or the development, did not participate financially or benefit from the lease in any way. Before federal action will constitute major federal action under the mandates of NEPA, the government must initiate, participate in or benefit from the project.

We feel the government's interpretation of NEPA is too constrained for our court to adopt. Title 42 U.S.C. § 4331 (b) states:

[I]t is the continuing responsibility of the Federal Government to use all practicable means, consistent with other essential considerations of national policy, to ... (2) assure for all Americans safe, healthful, productive, and esthetically and culturally pleasing surroundings; (3) attain the widest range of beneficial uses of the environment without degradation, risk to health or safety, or other undesirable and unintended consequences; (4) preserve important historic, cultural, and natural aspects of our national heritage, and maintain, wherever possible, an environment which supports diversity and variety of individual choice; ....

[Taking into account both the language of the Act and its legislative history], there is little doubt that Congress intended all agencies under their authority to follow the substantive and procedural mandates of NEPA.

The problem boils down to whether granting leases on Indian lands constitutes major federal action as required in NEPA § 102(2) (C). Upon review of the lease and relevant case law, we feel the lower court erred in holding the lease did not constitute major federal action. The lease refers to the United States government countless times. All notices and approvals must be made by the Pueblo and the United States. The Secretary is required to give written approval before encumbrances can be made on the leased land. The lease protects the United States government against damage or injury to people or property on the leased premises. Certainly the fact the United States government might be held liable for injury or damages incurred on the Indian land unless the lease provides otherwise makes the government more than an impartial, disinterested party to the contract between Pueblo and Sangre.

[W]here a federal license or permit is involved, or where Congress possesses and has utilized its plenary power of regulation under the interstate commerce clause or other constitutional authority, federal approval constitutes major federal action. [Appellees, however,] argue the government is operating in a different capacity when dealing with Indian lands. It is the appellees' contention that Indian lands, such as those of the Pueblo, are held in trust by the government for the Indians. Therefore, the appellees should approve the lease if it is advantageous to the beneficiaries of the trust.

Appellees also charge that Congress did not intend to enmesh the discretionary execution of these fiduciary duties in the procedural and bureaucratic web that NEPA § 102(2) (C) imposes. To impose this burden on private Indian land places the Indians at an economic and competitive disadvantage, and subjects their property to judicial challenge by non-Indian competitors laboring under no such environmental restriction.

It is interesting to note that appellees proffer no case law to support their arguments. The fact Indian lands are held in trust does not take it out of NEPA's jurisdiction. Cf. *Federal Power Comm'n v. Tuscarora*, 362 U.S. 99, 116, 80 S. Ct. 543, 4 L. Ed. 2d 584 (1960). All public lands of the United States are held by it in trust for the people of the United States. *Utah Power & Light v. United States*, 243 U.S. 389, 409, 37 S. Ct. 387, 61 L. Ed. 791 (1916). To accept appellees' contention would preclude all federal lands from NEPA jurisdiction, something clearly not intended by Congress in passing the Act.

Appellees' second contention that Congress did not intend to enmesh the discretionary execution of these fiduciary duties in the procedural and bureaucratic web imposed by NEPA § 102(2) (C) also falls on deaf ears. In *Calvert Cliffs' Coord. Comm. v. United States A. E. Comm'n, supra,* the court answered this problem by stating that "Section 102 duties are not inherently flexible.... Considerations of administrative difficulty, delay or economic cost will not suffice to strip the section of its fundamental importance." (449 F.2d p. 1115).

We conclude approving leases on federal lands constitutes major federal action and thus must be approved according to NEPA mandates. As our court had occasion to consider once before, this Act was intended to include all federal agencies, including the Bureau of Indian Affairs. See *National Helium Corporation v. Morton*, 455 F.2d 650 (10th Cir. 1971).

The lower court felt NEPA did not apply to Indian lands or otherwise the amendment to 25 U.S.C. § 415 would not have addressed the problem of environmental concerns. We do not draw that conclusion. NEPA is a very broad statute covering both substantive and procedural problems relating to the environment. The amendment to 25 U.S.C. § 415 deals primarily with the addition of Indian tribes to the group having long-term lease authority. Only briefly is the environmental problem discussed. The amendment only requires the Secretary to satisfy himself on the environmental issue; nowhere are any specific procedural guidelines set out as in NEPA. In *Calvert Cliffs' Coord. Comm. v. United States A. E. Comm'n, supra,* a similar problem arose. The court correctly determined that unless the obligations of another statute are clearly mutually exclusive with the mandates of NEPA, the specific requirements of NEPA will remain in force. The reasoning is applicable in the instant case. The general statement in § 415 in no way implies leases on Indian lands were not covered by NEPA. The amendment merely reaffirms congressional intent that environmental considerations are to play a factor in any Bureau of Indian Affairs decisions.

For the reasons stated above, we feel the lower court erred in dismissing appellants' request for a temporary and permanent injunction enjoining appellees from approving or acting on any submissions or approvals under the lease until the environmental impact of the project is studied and evaluated.

The judgment appealed from is reversed, and the case is remanded to the trial court with directions to grant the relief prayed for.

NOTES

1. Federal or Tribal Action? A discordant note as to the federal government's trusteeship responsibility is introduced by NEPA according to *Davis*. The trustee is obliged to consider the impact of a tribal decision on the environment of lands of nontribal people. *Compare* 25 U.S.C. § 415(e). When and how do we require such consideration of externalities when development on private lands is involved? Does *Davis* place special duties of environmental solicitude on Indian lands?

In *Oliver v. Udall*, 306 F.2d 819 (D.C. Cir. 1962), the court held that the secretarial approval of a tribal ordinance did not constitute a sufficient federal action to render the decision subject to first amendment challenge. Rather, according to the court, "the Secretary's approval of tribal action in 1959 was entirely in keeping with that abstinence from federal intervention in the internal affairs of an Indian tribe which the law clearly requires. The Secretary had simply recognized the valid governing authority of the Tribal Council." In approving a tribal lease does the Secretary do any more than "[recognize] the valid governing authority of the Tribal Council?" Can the *Davis* result be reconciled with *Oliver*? Can the difference in results be reconciled based solely on the externalities involved in a lease approval decision?

The National Environmental Protection Act is seemingly silent on its applicability to Indian country. In the face of such congressional silence, should the statute be read to apply to the leasing or development of Indian lands? *Compare Federal Power Comm'n v. Tuscarora Indian Nation*, 362 U.S. 99 (1960), with *United States v. White*, 508 F.2d 453 (8th Cir. 1974). Should it make any difference whether the development is being undertaken by the Indians or by non-Indian lessees? Should the approach to such issues be affected by whether the reservation's ownership of the land is based on treaty-guaranteed title or executive order? Other important environmental statutes, like the Clean Air Act, codified as amended at 42 U.S.C. § 7401 et seq., originally were wholly silent on their applicability to Indian reservations, but the regulations promulgated under such acts indicate how they apply to Indian lands and, sometimes, take account of the self-governing status of Indian tribes. *See, e.g.,* 40 C.F.R. § 52.21(c) (3) (v) (4) (1981); *Nance v. Environmental Protection Agency*, 645 F.2d 701 (9th Cir. 1981) (sustaining approval of an Indian tribe's redesignation of its reservation from Class II to Class I air quality standards, thereby severely restricting development of the reservation); *Oljato Chapter of Navajo Tribe v. Train*, 515 F.2d 654 (D.C. Cir. 1975) (unsuccessful Indian attack on EPA refusal to revise standard for performance of coal-fired power plants under Clean Air Act). Where federal environmental laws, like the Clean Air Act, make no mention of Indian tribes or Indian country, do they nevertheless implicitly authorize state regulation of Indian lands when they mandate federal approval of state enforcement criteria and a state plan but leave environmental enforcement responsibilities primarily to the state? While substantial arguments suggest that such statutes did not delegate such regulatory and adjudicatory authority to the states, the silence of the Congress on such questions leaves room for some doubt. Recognizing this problem, some of the more recent federal environmental protection legislation has directly addressed the problem of regulating environmental quality attendant to the development of Indian reservations. For example, the Surface Mining Control and Reclamation Act of 1977 (SMCRA), codified at 30 U.S.C. § 1201 et seq., specifically contemplates a different enforcement scheme for mining on Indian lands. While the act provides for eventual state enforcement under federally approved state plans after a temporary period of interim federal regulations and enforcement, the statute singles out Indian lands and subjects them to continued federal regulation and enforcement until the Secretary of the Interior can make recommendations and report proposed legislation to Congress that will "achieve the purpose of [SMCRA] and [recognize] the special jurisdictional status of these [Indian] lands." 30 U.S.C. § 1300. More recently, Congress has directly addressed the applicability of some environmental laws to Indian tribes. Pub. L. 99-499, 100 Stat. 1615, amending 42 U.S.C. § 9601(36) (authorizing Indian tribes to apply, like a state, to carry out enforcement roles under the Superfund legislation); Pub. L. 99-339, § 302(b)(1), 100 Stat. 666, amending 42 U.S.C. § 300f(10) (Safe Drinking Water Act); see also 33 U.S.C. § 1362(4) (Federal Water Pollution Control Act).

2. Secretarial Approval and Environmental Impact Statements — Environmental and Tribal Protections or Tools for Frustrating Indian Economic Development? The *Davis* case demonstrates how environmental protection statutes can be used to attempt to delay or frustrate tribal or federal development plans for Indian land. In the *Davis* case the decisions under attack were made by the tribal council. In light of the strong federal policy of protecting Indian self-government and avoiding federal court intrusions on tribal decisions, as reflected in *Santa Clara Pueblo v. Martinez, supra* Chapter 3, section C, is such a use of federal environmental statutes appropriate? Can it be justified by the overriding federal concern for protecting environmental values? Does your view of the appropriateness of the application of federal environmental laws to Indian lands change when the tribal government invokes such laws, as in *Nance v. Environmental Protection Agency, supra*, to protect its members from the developmental goals of non-Indians and, sometimes, other agencies of the federal government? Even when the tribal government seeks to invoke such federal environmental legislation, there may be some long-term costs to tribal sovereignty. For example, the reclassification of the Northern Cheyenne Reservation as a Class I air quality area sought by the Northern Cheyenne governing body will prevent future tribal governments, as well as non-Indian lessees, from significantly developing the Northern Cheyenne Reservation. The redesignation thus delimits future uses of reservation land that may be supported by transient majorities of the Northern Cheyenne tribe. While federal environmental statutes, in this instance, no doubt added stability to the land management process, was such redesignation an appropriate intrusion of the federal government on the vagaries of local tribal control?

One unfortunate consequence of the secretarial approval and NEPA impact statement requirements set forth in *Davis* is that third parties sometimes can challenge, and therefore sometimes delay implementation of, federal action approving tribal development plans. In *Ringsred v. City of Duluth*, 828 F.2d 1305 (8th Cir. 1987), disaffected members of the Duluth community filed suit to prevent construction of a parking ramp in downtown Duluth as part of a larger bingo project proposed jointly by the Fond du Lac Band of Lake Superior Chippewa and the City of Duluth with the approval of the Secretary of the Interior. While the court doubted that an outsider to the deal had any standing to challenge secretarial approval under the provisions of 25 U.S.C. § 81, the Eighth Circuit entertained and rejected the outside challenger's NEPA challenge.

Requirements of secretarial approval of surface and other leases also complicate the problem of reacting to breaches of lease agreements. Under 25 C.F.R. § 162.14, a lessee in violation or default of lease provisions can be served with a 10-day notice to show cause why the lease should not be cancelled, but such notice can be served only "[u]pon a showing satisfactory to the Secretary that there has been [such] a violation." Thus, secretarial lease approval requirements are leveraged by regulations into requirements for approval of cancellations. In *Yavapai-Prescott Indian Tribe v. Watt*, 707 F.2d 1072 (9th Cir. 1983), the Ninth

Circuit ruled that tribes could not unilaterally cancel surface leases approved by the Secretary under the authority of 25 U.S.C. § 415 without involving the Secretary in the cancellation process as required by the regulations. *See also United States v. Karlen*, 645 F.2d 635 (8th Cir. 1981); *Anderson v. Cumming*, 659 F.2d 1087 (9th Cir. 1981); *Sessions, Inc. v. Morton*, 384 F. Supp. 694 (C.D. Cal. 1972) (reviews of federal lease cancellations).

Secretarial approval requirements do not always frustrate the desires of tribal communities, however. In *Seva Resorts, Inc. v. Hodel*, 876 F.2d 1394 (9th Cir. 1989), the Ninth Circuit sustained the refusal of the Secretary to sign certain lease and concession agreements for the development of a marina complex on adjacent Indian and federal land at Antelope Point in the Glen Canyon National Recreation Area. After the tribe had negotiated the agreements, tribal authorities became quite concerned about their relationship with Seva, the developer, fearing that Seva might not have the capital or expertise to complete the contemplated $30 million project and that the Navajo Nation might be forced to invest additional funds in an undercapitalized project. Furthermore, Navajo officials questioned whether the tribe should not receive some consideration for the exclusive rights it granted and the value of the land on which the project would be constructed. The Navajo voiced these concerns to the National Park Service and thereafter the Secretary refused to approve the project. The Ninth Circuit sustained the Secretary's refusal to approve the project both under his authority to approve Indian surface leases delegated in 25 U.S.C. § 415 and under his authority to approve concessions projects on federal lands delegated in the Concessions Policies Act of 1965, 16 U.S.C. § 20 et seq.

b. Mineral Leasing

The history of mineral leasing and oil and gas development on Indian reservations has a more subtle side than the history of leasing of surface resources. In terms of the "civilizing" function of a reservation, we have seen that there was specific thought given to the way in which the allotment and leasing of land would serve federal goals for individual and tribal development. These goals may have been disputable, but at least there were goals by which the performance under the leases could be evaluated. When it comes to mineral leasing, it is as if there is not a clear conviction on the part of the federal government that mineral development is related to the future direction of the tribes. How land was held, what kind of farming took place, what size parcels were worked, the relationship of Indian to non-Indian parcels were all factors considered and consciously manipulated in the surface leasing and development policies. All of these factors had obvious impacts on the evolution of affected tribes. The manner in which oil and gas, uranium, or coal is extracted from the ground has, however, received far less attention and has been treated by the federal government as far less connected with the cultural evolution and destiny of the affected tribes.

As a consequence, federal policy appears more coercive with respect to the leasing of Indian oil and gas and mineral resources. In some instances, the Navajo Tribe constituting a good example, the very inception and structure of modern tribal government was tied to the need of the federal government for an entity that could provide certainty of title to the companies seeking to develop petroleum resources on the reservation. Elsewhere, there were occasions, as in Oklahoma in the twentieth century, where the Secretary intervened in the composition of tribal council membership to assure a government that was favorably disposed to efficiently leasing on-reservation resources.

As in the area of water rights, the sophistication and expertise available over the last century to lessees of energy resources long outstripped, at least until recently, the expertise available to the tribes and their BIA advisers. In the 1950's, as newly developing countries around the world engaged in new and innovative energy transactions that returned far greater value to the lessors, the tribal leases began to look even more rigid and unproductive to the tribes. As reflected by the following materials, pressure began building for a review of federal patterns with respect to the leasing and development of Indian resources.

AMERICAN INDIAN POLICY REVIEW COMMISSION, FINAL REPORT 338-47 (1977)

Mineral Resources

There has been a considerable amount of criticism about the leasing practices of Indian mineral resources. A majority of the criticism is aimed at the manner in which the Federal Government manages these resources. Well-documented arguments have been made which point out that the development of the non-Indian community has been, in many cases, paid for by the Indians through their resources. Much has been said about the source of the problem. The effort here is to point out the difficulties and recommend a set of policies to design and correct these unfortunate circumstances. It would be helpful to briefly discuss some important data on the amount of resources we are referring to.

In a report to the Senate Committee on Energy and Natural Resources (then Interior and Insular Affairs), March 31, 1976, the General Accounting Office (GAO) stated that Indian oil and gas reserves amount to approximately 3 percent of the United States total reserves. This was broken down into 40 reservations in 17 States. The estimate on oil reserves as of November 1973, was approximately 4.2 billion barrels with gas resources at about 17.5 trillion cubic feet. There was also an estimation of approximately 100-200 billion tons of identified coal reserves located on 33 reservations in 11 States. This was approximately 7-13 percent of the United States identified coal resources of 1.581 billion tons. In a report by the Federal Trade Commission [it was stated] that Indian lands have the potential of containing more than one-tenth of the United States currently minable coal reserves. A brief review of the relative importance of Indian minerals to production in the United States would also prove helpful. Data gathered from a USGS survey shows that production of coal on Indian lands in 1974 was 1.9 percent of all United States production which made up 35.8 percent of all production on Federal and Indian lands. The value of production of oil and gas on Indian lands was 4.4 percent of the total United States production. If off-shore leases are excluded, the production value rises to 13.6 percent of the total production value on all Federal and Indian lands. Aside from the major Indian energy resources, there are a variety of other minerals of considerable value on Indian lands. For example, phosphate production on Indian lands was 4.9 percent of the total United States production which amounted to 35.4 percent on Federal and Indian lands. In 1974, 100 percent of the Federal and Indian land uranium production was on Indian lands. It must be noted that of all mining on Federal and Indian lands, production from Indian held resources was 15.6 [percent] of the total.

Inequitable Mineral Leases

The present policies on the leasing of Indian resources leave tribes with inequitable agreements. These agreements ensure that revenues received from mineral resources are only a fraction of what they should be. Measured by international standards, the leases negotiated on behalf of Indians are among the poorest agreements ever made.

Deficiencies in Contracts

One of the major deficiencies in Indian lease agreements is that royalty rates are usually too low and fixed in dollars per unit of production of the resources which, of course, ignores increases in value rather than percentage of value, which increases income as minerals increase in value. In four out of the five Navajo coal leases consummated between 1957 and 1968, the royalty was fixed between $0.15-$0.375 a ton. Since then, the average value per ton of coal rose from $4.67 (1968) to $18.75 (1975). There is no simple way to change these inequitable terms because there are no adjustment clauses in the leases, and the leases are for 10 years "and as long hereafter as minerals are produced in paying quantities." The royalty is arguably fixed for the life of the deposit. Some tribes have attempted to negotiate royalty rates in spite of the BIA written leases. The Crow Tribe was successful in forcing the rate of coal from the originally offered 11 cents per ton to 17.5 cents per ton. As a general principle, in a time of inflation, a fixed price contract for any commodity is a poor contract. Even if the relative price of a commodity does not rise in relation to all other goods over time, the general rise in the price level will hurt tribes with fixed rates per ton rather than percentages of value. In a review of 15 coal leases from 3 tribes, 12 had fixed royalty rates while only 3 had royalty rates based on the selling price of the coal. Although USGS, in 1971, changed its policy of calculating royalties based in fixed amounts per ton to percent of selling price, they approved royalty rates for leases at 17.5 cents per ton without recommending percentage royalty rates.

Coal Lease Acreage Limitation

In reviewing 15 leases, it was discovered that 10 were in excess of the 2,560-acre limitation mandated by 25 CFR § 171.9(b) [now 25 C.F.R. § 211.9(b) (1982)] and § 172.13 [now 25 C.F.R. § 212.13 (1982)]. Decisions on size of leases must be determined by the tribes. It is noted that for coal development to be profitable the size of the lease has to be greater than 2,560 acres. It appears that a review of the acre limitation must be done.

Enforcement of Provision of Contracts

The BIA and USGS are charged with the responsibilities of enforcing Indian mineral lease provisions. There is considerable documentation that such enforcement is not taking place. There has been a failure to require full compliance with information provisions of exploration permits. The USGS has the responsibility of performing gas and oil well site inspections for lease compliance. The inspections include drilling, producing, abandonment, and meter proving inspections. It has been found that only a very small percentage of required inspections is being carried out.

It has been found that significant amounts of royalty payments were being received late. In fact, of the survey that was performed, only one tribe was properly enforcing its lease provisions adequately....

The loss to the tribes is significant. For example, in a review of 20 producing oil and gas leases done over a 14-month period on one reservation, it was revealed that over $270,000 in royalty payments were 1 to 11 months late. If the 1.5 percent late charge provision were enforced, it would mean that the tribe would receive an additional $6,000. That $270,000 invested for 1 year at a conservative 6 percent rate would have produced $16,200 additional income to the tribe.

Enforcement of contracts requires reviews and audits of lessees. These requirements are not being performed. USGS regulations require lessees to submit reports which include reports of operations listing various actions. These reports, for the most part, are not being submitted. Many post audits are not being performed. In one area of the review, only 5 percent of the past audits were being performed. The benefits of such audits are significant. In that same area, over a 2-year period, an additional $798,000 was collected through such audits. The functions of reviewing and auditing require auditors and reviewers, which requires funds to be expended. In view of the fact that significant benefits can be received with adequate reviews and audits, it would be appropriate to put greater effort in this area.

Enforcement of lease provisions for hiring are to a large extent not done. The reason is that the tribes and the BIA are unable to determine the effectiveness of Indian preference in hiring provisions. Only in a few cases were there procedures which required the lessee to report on their employment of Indians in the Indian community. If procedures were established for enforcement of preference provisions, the tribes and BIA would better be able to determine the effectiveness of such provisions. Indeed, where such procedures were established, there was substantial Indian employment in the minerals industry, as was the case on the Navajo Nation where enforcement procedures had been established. In that situation of the 1,313 people who were employed in the coal industry, 712 were Indian. The total annual earnings, in that situation, were approximated at $8.2 million. In other cases, because accurate figures on the number of people employed were not available, it was not possible to determine the number of Indians employed in the mineral industry; however, indications were that Indian employment in the industry was minimal.

Enforcement of Provisions for Reclamation

The tribes, BIA, State and local agencies, and USGS are all involved in reclamation activities on Indian lands. Monitoring of reclamation on Indian lands activities is the responsibility of USGS. The responsibilities of USGS in this area are not outlined in the CFR, although they are discussed in various sections. There are no formal agreements among the different organizations to coordinate these activities. The result is that each organization is operating independently.

Environmental Controls Are Too Weak

Indians are unable to prevent environmental degradation resulting from development except through the very cumbersome mechanism of the National Environmental Protection Act. NEPA's main contribution is to cause delay. A tribe may wish to control the form of development rather than to delay it; yet, without the opportunity to bargain effectively, the tribe cannot impose the controls it wants or extract a higher royalty in return for not imposing the controls. It may be too early to know how much strength tribes can put in codes controlling development, particularly on leases which already have been signed.

The Duration of Leases Is Too Long

Nearly all can be indefinitely extended if production is occurring. The provisions for redetermining the rental rates are usually weak. The extension provision results from the Omnibus Mineral Leasing Act of May 11, 1938 (25 U.S.C. § 396 a-f), which states that minerals may be leased "... for a term not to exceed ten years and as long thereafter as minerals are produced in paying quantities." The limit of 10 years is contradicted by the possible indefinite extension of time. Long-lived leases accentuate the low price problem identified earlier. In a time of general inflation, a fixed-price-per-ton payment can become a very small share of the total income from a particular mineral production activity. For percentage royalties, should the usual landowner's share drift upward over a time, a tribe with a long lease would lose relative to those with short term leases.

Long term leasing problems can be avoided if terms could be renegotiated periodically. Some leases contain provisions enabling the Secretary of Interior to redetermine royalty rates and other provisions of a lease every 10 years. But such leases rarely contain a method by which a tribe can force such Secretarial action by not defining the reasons which require redetermination of lease terms.

Demographic Changes Can Cause Some Adverse Social Problems

Mineral development invariably increases the population of non-Indians on or near a reservation, creating political difficulties for the tribal government and cultural problems for the Indians. Tribes wish to be able to reach a reasonable accommodation with the non-Indians who move in, but are unable to do so if they cannot set controls which are widely known from the very arrival of the new residents. An alternative in some cases is for Indians to provide the labor for developing the minerals. Although training may entail some costs, the tribe could exchange rental receipts for training opportunities if it could bargain effectively. If they could choose, some tribes might wish to impose environmental controls and workplace controls which lower the monetary return, while other tribes may prefer to maximize the monetary return. Unfortunately, tribes now receive low monetary return without any of the other controls either.

Most of the problem areas identified earlier come about because of the weak beginning position of tribes in relation to the potential resource developers.

Reasons for Inequitable Lease Arrangements

Trosper analyzed the reasons underlying these inequitable leases. The reasons are numerous. First, neither the Indian people nor BIA officials possess adequate information on the size of deposits, the costs of exploration, costs of production, and market prices. The BIA has never carried out a complete topographic or geologic mapping of tribal lands. BIA does not have the expertise. The United States Geological Service (USGS) is supposed to advise the BIA; however, funds to do the work have never been appropriated to permit this to be done. Thus, it is impossible for tribes to put a value on their resources. Second, the BIA does not employ personnel with the skills necessary to undertake negotiations even if the data was available. For example, the BIA Navajo Area Office does not employ a geologist or mining engineer, nor is there a procedure for BIA personnel to exchange information with other BIA officials who are conducting similar negotiations. BIA in Washington opposes such exchange of information saying that "... tribes may believe that what has been obtained on one reservation could be obtained on their reservation without giving consideration to differing circumstances ... also it would be difficult and expensive to establish a system."

Third, bargaining power in lease negotiations is reduced because of inordinately long capricious delays in the approval process. For example, in January, 1973, the Navajo Nation sent out 25 invitations for uranium exploration. By January, 1974, they had determined that Exxon had made the best offer and entered into a flexible agreement. According to the agreement, after a deposit is found, the Navajos can choose whether they want to receive a negotiated royalty or a 49 percent working interest. The Navajo Nation requested Secretarial approval of the agreement. In turn, on April 2, 1974, the Commissioner of Indian affairs requested the Navajo area director to undertake an environmental impact statement which was finally initiated in January, 1976. Meanwhile, on March 10, 1975, an Assistant Secretary of the Interior determined that there was no reason for the Secretary not to approve the lease agreement. But this determination had no immediate impact. For the lease was not approved until January, 1977. The 3-year delay cost the Navajos $1,642,500 in unpaid interest.

Fourth, tribal bargaining power is weakened by State taxation of non-Indian mineral developers. State taxes on mineral production (severance and sales taxes) fall upon the owners rather than the developers of the resources. The developer passes along his taxes to the owners in the form of lower royalties. The developer does this by including State taxation when he calculates his expected profit. The larger the tax, the smaller the royalty. Most often, taxes exceed royalties. For example, on the Crow Reservation, the Montana State tax revenue received from a private minining operation amounted to $3,988,424 for the period of July 1975 to March 1976. During the same period, the tribe's royalties were $1,270,530. A State tax, upon mineral developers, is, in fact, a tax upon Indians. Indians do not both tax and receive royalties. Usually, they just receive royalties. The difference between the two is important from a company's point of view.

Depending upon how Federal tax laws treat tribal taxation, it might be possible for a company to deduct a tax from its Federal tax rather than from its before-tax income.

To illustrate this, consider a $500,000 annual royalty charge. A company deducts it and pays taxes on the remaining profits — for example — at a 40 percent rate. Converting the royalty to a tax means that before-tax income would rise by the $500,000; the company would pay 40 percent of this, or $200,000, in increased taxes. But the company now deducts the tribal tax of $500,000 from its now higher Federal tax. The result is that the company's total after-tax income rises by $300,000. The company would prefer paying a tax rather than a royalty, and a tribe could bargain for a higher cash return from taxation than from rental.

Fifth, Indian tribes and Indian individuals, as tribal members, continue to have difficulty obtaining credit. Access to credit would improve the threat by Indians to perform development themselves rather than in conjunction with outside developers. With the very large capital requirements of some mineral development methods, this constraint may not be relevant; even if tribes were as able as anyone to get credit, they could not finance a large coal development. Even the energy corporations enter consortiums and use Government guarantees to assemble the required financial backing. Access to credit would enable a tribe to hold out during a negotiation by decreasing its need for cash from a lease. Access to capital could also improve access to information.

Finally, the tribe's bargaining position is weakened by the fact that mineral revenues constitute an important source of tribal income. For example, in 1975, 70 percent of Navajo tribal revenue was generated from mineral leases. Thus, the Navajo tribal government is not in a position to cancel leases, or even refuse to negotiate new leases if it wants to maintain its administrative and service functions. Thus, fiscal necessity dictates the rate of resource exploitation.

New Forms of Agreements

Until the early 1960's, most Third World Countries were in a similar position to Indian tribes. Unlike Indian tribes, however, they have been able to shift the balance of power and in doing so have secured a larger share of mineral income. Their increased leverage derives from their newly asserted sovereignty; from the growing political awareness of their citizens; from the entrance of new transnational corporations; and lastly, from the threat that they will develop their resources themselves. Third World Countries were able to switch from fixed royalties to royalties based on a percentage of value of the exploited resource, supplemented by income taxes on the company profits. They have also been experimenting with new forms of agreements such as joint ventures, production-sharing, and service contracts. Under a joint venture, the country shares expenses and profits rather than receiving a royalty. Under production-sharing or service contract, the foreign firms obtain no ownership interest, and the resource owner is able to retain control. In production-sharing agreements, the country and the firm share output in predetermined proportions. Under a service contract, the country merely purchases services from the firm reimbursing it for actual costs. Additional payment to the firm based on profits, in some cases, is given to encourage efficiency.

Indian tribes have not been able to enter joint ventures because of the capital required. However, there are indications that energy companies are willing to go into joint ventures with tribes for development of their mineral resources. Participation agreements may be very attractive to tribes, but a tribe going into 50-50 partnership should take precautions to insure that their participation is not superficial in nature, and they assure that they have an effective role in management decisions within the operating company. The experience of developing nations in joint ventures where the mineral companies pay all exploration and development costs has been that the companies usually demand that the government not tax production. Some of these countries were surprised to learn that they had shorted themselves of potential earnings by giving up their tax right. This is usually true where the ratio of loan capital to equity is relatively low and most of the money goes to repayment of debts. One very important factor is access to information about the operation of production and the technical know-how to interpret all of the technical data that came with such responsibilities. There are two problems which are central to joint management control. One is making sure that the tribal managers get all the necessary data to make the best decisions and the other is in trying to decide which issues they should direct their efforts to.

One tribe, the Blackfeet, has entered into a service contract where the contractor has no ownership or equitable interest in the lands or minerals produced nor a leasehold interest in the mineral estate. All production is owned by the tribe. The contractor owns the equipment, and advances funds for exploration and production — receiving repayment from the production. The tribe receives a one-sixth royalty and 50 percent net profits after the contractor has recouped his costs. The contractor receives the other 50 percent.

At the same time, while joint ventures, production-sharing and service contracts would allow more Indian control over resource development, they might not always increase resource returns. The potential benefits from these agreements are subject to more risk than are the returns from a royalty agreement. For example, under a joint venture, the tribe risks losing its equity capital if no discovery is made or if substitutes are developed. And while production-sharing or service contracts are not subject to this, these agreements yield higher revenues only if carefully monitored. The Blackfeet Tribe will have to verify the actual amount produced, the actual costs incurred, and the selling price. Thus, these new agreements require the use of scarce tribal capital and technical skill and knowledge.

It should be emphasized that service contracts have one important advantage over royalty agreements and joint venture and that is the non-Indian firm acquires no taxable interest in Indian land or minerals.

Tribal Goals and Mineral Development

Mineral development can provide improved opportunities for progress toward self-sufficiency where agreements allow fuller participation through increased jobs and income, expansion of local markets, and improvements of the infrastructure. But, at the same time, tribes must be allowed to control the unwanted side effects. Environmental degradation and the rapid influx of non-Indians to the Indian community can negatively affect undesirable outcomes. Tribal governments must be free to balance benefits and costs and choose the rate of mineral development which will support their aspirations.

Tribes have been unable to develop their own resources as a result of:

1. lack of control over the resources;
2. lack of technological expertise and skilled labor; and
3. lack of capital.

The BIA has seldom attempted to assist the tribes in tribal development of their mineral and petrochemical resources. Rather, its involvement in resource exploitation has consisted largely of arranging leases of Indian land including the mineral contents to major petrochemical and mining companies at questionable rates.

Indian people are losing valuable non-renewable resources to corporate developers. The return to Indian individuals and tribes is minimal. The most valuable development asset of many tribes is being wasted for them.

Tribal goals of self-sufficiency, income, jobs, and environmental protection are the fundamental priorities which should be addressed in any decisions about use of resources.

NOTE: MINERAL AND OIL & GAS LEASING

Some, but not all, of the deficiencies noted in the federal mineral leasing programs are attributable to the out-dated statutes and regulations under which the leasing program is run. For example, the leasing statutes provide that the duration of mineral leases shall be "for a term not to exceed ten years *and as long thereafter as minerals are produced* in *paying quantities.*" 25 U.S.C. §§ 396a, 398, 398a (emphasis added). Significantly, section 2 of the General Mineral Leasing Act, 25 U.S.C. § 396b, provides that "the foregoing provisions shall in no manner restrict the right of tribes organized or incorporated under [sections 16 and 17 of the Indian Reorganization Act], to lease lands for mining purposes as therein provided and in accordance with the provisions of any constitution and charter adopted by any Indian tribe ...." The leasing statutes nowhere define the durational phrase "as long thereafter as minerals are produced in paying quantities."

The old regulations adopted in 1957 to regulate mining were not very helpful. 25 C.F.R. pts. 211 (leasing of tribal lands for mining), 212 (leasing of allotted lands for mining), 213 (leasing of restricted lands of Five Civilized Tribes for mining), 214 (leasing of Osage Reservation lands for mining except oil and gas), 215 (lead and zinc operations and mining on the Quapaw Agency), 227 (oil and gas development of Wind River Reservation) (1982). *See also* 25 C.F.R. pts. 216 (surface exploration, mining, and reclamation of lands), 226 (oil and gas leasing of Osage Reservation) (1982). For the most part these regulations deal with bidding and royalty payment procedures. They do not generally regulate operations by mineral developers except for the provisions of 25

C.F.R. §§ 216.100-216.114, adopted in 1977, dealing with surface reclamation in coal mining operations. These regulations do not define the durational terms of the lease more precisely than the statute. 25 C.F.R. § 211.10. While these regulations require secretarial approval for all leases, they set forth no standards suggesting how the approval discretion will be exercised. Under 25 U.S.C. § 396b and 25 C.F.R. § 211.2 (1982), mineral leases may be negotiated by the tribe but oil and gas leases must be advertised for bid unless the Commissioner grants the Indian owners written permission to negotiate a lease. Under the regulations, oil, gas and mineral leases other than coal are limited to 2,560 acres. Coal leases are ordinarily limited to this acreage but the Commissioner may approve a larger lease if "in the interest of the lessor and ... necessary to permit the establishment or construction of thermal power plants or other industrial facilities on or near the reservation." 25 C.F.R. § 211.9 (1982). Neither the leasing statutes nor the regulations require the employment or training of Indians in the development operations on leased lands, although lease forms used by the BIA since 1957 provide:

> The lessee shall employ Indians, giving priority to lessor and other members of its tribe in all positions for which they are qualified and available and shall pay the prevailing wage rates for similiar services in the area. The lessee shall do everything practicable to employ qualified Indians, giving priority to the lessor and other members of its tribe and their equipment in the hauling of all materials under this lease, insofar as the lessee does not use its own equipment for that purpose. Lessee agrees to make special efforts to work Indians, giving priority to the lessor or other members of its tribe into skilled, technical, and other higher jobs in connection with the lessee's operations under this lease.

For a sourcebook on mineral leasing on Indian lands, see INSTITUTE ON MINERAL DEVELOPMENT ON INDIAN LANDS (Rocky Mtn. Mineral L. Found. 1990).

Various proposals have been made to amend or modify the mineral development regulations. 45 Fed. Reg. 53,164-53,180 (1980), 42 Fed. Reg. 46,352-46,367, 18,083-18,099 (1977). None of the proposed major revisions of the regulations were ever adopted. The most recent proposal, 45 Fed. Reg. 53,164-53,180 (1980), addresses some of the problems raised in the Indian Policy Review Commission Report. These proposals would have modified the leasing regulations then found at 25 C.F.R. pts. 171-77 and now set forth in 25 C.F.R. pts. 211-16 (1982). For example, section 171.5(b) of the proposed regulations defines "paying quantities" in the phrase "as long thereafter as minerals are produced in paying quantities" to mean: "That quantity of recovered minerals which produces during the fiscal year of the contract a profit to the operator over and above the total cost of: Extraction (exclusive of exploration), processing (including benefication), and handling to the point of sale; all salaries and employee expenses incident to such extraction, processing, and handling; and business licenses, repairs of equipment, and transportation." Written evidence demonstrating such facts must be made available at the end of the lease term and at the end of each fiscal year thereafter. The 1980 proposal also precluded voluntary suspension of operations for more than thirty days without the express written consent of the Superintendent unless production is rendered impossible by an act of God or "some other cause clearly beyond the operator's control." Section 171.6 of the proposed regulations also purports to structure the exercise of secretarial discretion as follows:

§ 171.6 Approval of contracts.

(a) A prospecting contract or a mining contract shall be approved by the Superintendent if he/she determines in writing that the following conditions are met:

(1) The contract provides a fair and reasonable remuneration to the Indian mineral owner;

(2) The contract does not have adverse cultural or environmental consequences to the Indian lands and community affected sufficient to outweigh its benefits to the Indian mineral owner, and

(3) The contract complies with the requirements of this part, Part 177 of this title, of other applicable regulations, the provisions of applicable federal law, and applicable tribal law where not inconsistent with federal law.

Such determinations must also be made prior to the award of any contract pursuant to § 171.4(c) of this part.

(b) The determination required by subsection (a) of this section shall be based on the written findings required by § 171.7(a) of this part and § 177.4 of Part 177 of this title.

(c) "Fair and reasonable remuneration" within the meaning of paragraph (a)(1) of this section means a return on the Indian-owned minerals:

(1) not less than that received by non-Indian mineral owners in comparable contemporary contractual arrangements for the development of similar minerals,

(2) not less than that received by the Federal Government in comparable contemporary contractual arrangements for the development of similar federally-owned minerals, and

(3) not less than the minimum rental and royalty payments which would be applicable to those minerals were they federally-owned.

A determination of what constitutes a comparable contemporary contractual arrangement is within the sound discretion of the Commissioner.

Section 171.7 of the 1980 proposal would have required the preparation of a written economic assessment of each contract with the assistance of the mining supervisor. This assessment was structured to include inquiry into the proposed lessee's ability to perform diligently, adequacy of royalties considering the history and economics of the mineral industry, availability of water needed for production operations, maximization of return, adequacy of payment and enforcement clauses, compactness of area to be mined and notice to all owners or potential claimants of the property. The proposed regulations also provided for more intensive monitoring of lease compliance. Additionally, section 177.4 required the preparation of an environmental impact statement for each lease that includes the following:

(b) Such assessment shall examine the prospective effects of the proposed operation upon the environment and the local Indian culture, and shall specifically consider:

(1) The prevention and control of flooding, erosion, and earth slides;

(2) The effect of the operation on the quality and flow of water and watercourses in the affected area;

(3) The effect on air quality;

(4) The need for reclamation of the affected area by revegetation, replacement of soil, or other means;

(5) Land uses both before and after operations;

(6) The protection of fish and wildlife and their habitat;

(7) Measures designed to guarantee health and safety;

(8) The effect on resources of historical, scenic, archeological, and ethnological value;

(9) The impact on the local Indian population, with particular reference to:

(i) The possible dislocation of people from their homes or occupations;

(ii) The influx of non-Indians into the Indian community, and its effect on the local cost of living, tribal government, housing, educational services, police protection, transportation and communication facilities, health care, and intercultural relationships;

(iii) Noise and esthetics; and

(iv) Threats to vegetation, wildlife, and natural or other monuments which play an important role in local Indian culture or religion; and

(10) Any other potentially adverse effects on the environment.

Such an assessment shall be prepared in accordance with regulations promulgated by the Council on Environmental Quality, 40 CFR 1508.9, and the Environmental Quality Handbook, 30 BLAM Supplement 1. When it is recognized prior to the preparation of the assessment that a complete environmental impact statement needs to be prepared prior to approval of the contract, preparation of that environmental impact statement may be regarded as satisfying the requirements of this section. Prior to contract approval, the environmental assessment shall be made specifically available to the Indian mineral owner and to the governing body of the local Indian tribe, and shall also be made available for public review at the Bureau office having jurisdiction over the proposed contract.

(c) In order to make a determination of the effect of the contract on prehistoric, historic, architectural, archeological, cultural, and scientific resources, in compliance with the National Historic Preservation Act, 16 U.S.C. § 470 et seq., Executive Order 11593 (May 1971), and regulations promulgated thereunder, 36 CFR Parts 60, 63, and 800, and the Archeological and Historic Preservation Act, 16 U.S.C. 469a-1 et seq., the Superintendent shall, prior to approval of a contract, perform surveys of the cultural resources so as to evaluate and make a determination of the effect of the exploration and mining activities on properties which are listed in the National Register of Historic Places, 16 U.S.C. § 470a, or are eligible for listing in the National Register. If the surveys indicate that properties listed in or eligible for listing in the National Register will be affected, the Superintendent shall seek the comment of the Advisory Council on Historic Preservation pursuant to 36 CFR Part 800. If the mineral development will have an adverse effect on such properties, the Superintendent shall ensure that the properties will either be avoided, the effects mitigated or the data preserved.

Why do you suppose final regulations implementing these proposals were never promulgated?

DECISION OF THE SECRETARY OF THE INTERIOR RELATING TO *CROW TRIBE v. KLEPPE*

4 Indian Law Reporter I-1 (1977)

I have before me the record of a lawsuit filed by the Crow Tribe of Indians against the Secretary of the Interior and the Commissioner of Indian Affairs in their official capacities, and against Shell Oil Company, Inc., American Metals Climax (AMAX), Inc., Peabody Coal Company, Inc., and Gulf Oil Company, Inc. The Crow Tribe alleges, among other things, that coal leases held by Shell and AMAX, and exclusive lease options held by Gulf and Peabody, are invalid because they were issued and approved in violation of applicable laws and regulations of this Department. The complaint also alleges that the Department of the Interior through the Bureau of Indian Affairs has breached its fiduciary responsibility to the Crow Tribe by approving the challenged leases and permits.

The Office of the Solicitor and the staff of the Commissioner of Indian Affairs have reviewed this record thoroughly, and the results of that review have convinced me that an all-out defense of these charges on their merits would be inconsistent with previous, important administrative decisions of this Department. I have, therefore, decided to announce to the parties in this litigation the results of that Departmental review. Both the tribe and the companies involved have repeatedly expressed their interest in coal development on the Crow Reservation, and I hope by my decision today to encourage the tribe and the companies to expedite a resolution of these difficult issues in a more cooperative forum in order that the development, which all parties desire, may proceed in an orderly manner, consistent with the nation's policy of Indian self-determination through tribal self-government, and consistent with this Department's trust responsibility to the Crow Tribe of Indians.

The Crow Tribe challenges the lawfulness of the Department's approval of coal leases and prospecting permits (with exclusive options to lease) to these four companies in three separate coal sales on the Crow Reservation. After careful research and consideration, the Department has determined that the salient facts are as follows:

First Coal Sale

Bids for coal prospecting permits on four tracts of land were opened on April 2, 1968. Tracts numbered 2 and 3 received no bids. Shell Oil Company's bid of $1,101,000.27 was accepted on tract number 4 which consisted of 82,724.91 acres for a bonus payment of $12.967 per acre. In addition, Peabody Coal Company's bid of $87,844.16 was accepted for tract number 1 which consisted of 86,121.73 acres for a bonus payment of $1.015 per acre. Both permits contained exclusive options to lease at 17.5 cents per ton royalty.

Shell's permit was renewed for two additional years on July 21, 1969, with an additional bonus payment of $1.00 per acre, and on June 8, 1972, the Billings Acre Director of the Bureau of Indian Affairs approved a coal mining lease to Shell covering 30,247 acres of the permitted lands.

With respect to this Shell lease, number 14-20-0252-3849, for 30,247 acres, I have determined that the record contains no clear evidence of an explicit waiver of the acreage limitation contained in 25 CFR, § 171.9 [now 25 C.F.R. § 211.9 (1982)]. Therefore, I direct Shell Oil Company and the Crow Tribe to conform this lease to 2,560 acres or less, or clearly to demonstrate the need to waive this limitation.

With respect to this lease, I have determined that Departmental approval thereof is a major Federal action significantly affecting the quality of the human environment; therefore, no further administrative action will be taken until the Department has completed an Environmental Impact Statement, as required by law.

The Peabody permit, number 14-20-0252-3417, was extended for two years on June 19, 1970, and approved by the Bureau of Indian Affairs on September 28, 1970, for an additional bonus payment of $1.00 per acre. On June 2, 1972,

Peabody notified the Crow Tribe of its desire to go to lease on 11,000 acres of the permitted lands. The tribe and Peabody entered into negotiations on terms and conditions of the lease. These negotiations were never concluded and, eventually, were suspended indefinitely pending preparation by the Department of an Environmental Impact Statement.

With respect to Peabody's permit and request for a lease of 11,000 acres, I have determined that the Area Director is correct in his decision that the terms of the permit do not support a request for a lease in excess of 2,560 acres. Any larger lease must be negotiated with the tribe, subject to the approval of the Area Director.

I have determined that approval of a coal mining lease under this permit would be a major Federal action significantly affecting the quality of the human environment; therefore, no such lease will be approved until the Department has completed an Environmental Impact Statement, as required by law.

Second Coal Sale

Bids for coal prospecting permits on ten tracts of land were opened on August 13, 1969. No bids were received on tracts 1 through 6. Gulf Mineral Resources Company (to which Gulf Oil Corporation is the successor) was the successful bidder on tracts 7 through 10. Subsequently, Gulf was issued coal prospecting permits totaling 73,293.87 acres for bonus payments totaling $259,780.00. Tract number 7 consisted of more than 20,000 acres; number 8 of more than 14,000 acres; number 9 of more than 21,000 acres; and number 10 of more than 17,000 acres.

In late 1971 and early 1972, all four of these prospecting permits ... were extended for an additional two years. In late 1973, Gulf requested a single lease covering virtually all the permitted lands. Gulf was then advised by the Bureau of Indian Affairs that no action could be taken on this request until an environmental impact statement was completed.

I have determined that the BIA was correct in asserting that the law requires completion of an Environmental Impact Statement before any action can be taken on Gulf's request for a lease under these permits. No administrative action will be taken until such a statement has been prepared, as required by law.

With respect to each of Gulf's permits and its request for a lease, I have determined that the Area Director is correct in his decision that the terms of the permits do not support a request for leases in excess of 2,560 acres. Any larger lease must be negotiated with the tribe, subject to the approval of the Area Director.

Third Coal Sale

Bids were opened on September 16, 1970, for coal prospecting permits on 10 tracts of land, only four of which received any bids. The only one which is at issue here is tract number 5 from this sale, which consisted of 16,167 acres and which, following an oral auction after the sealed bids were opened, eventually went to AMAX for a bonus payment of $251,000.00, or $15.33 per acre. This permit was approved by the BIA on October 13, 1970, and on February 15, 1973, the BIA approved a coal mining lease to AMAX of 14,236.81 acres.

With respect to this lease, ... I have determined that the record contains no clear evidence of an explicit waiver of the acreage limitation contained in 25 CFR, § 171.9 [25 C.F.R. § 211.9 (1982)]. Therefore, I direct AMAX and the Crow Tribe to conform this lease to 2,560 acres or less, or clearly to demonstrate the need to waive this limitation.

With respect to this AMAX lease, I have determined that Departmental approval thereof is a major Federal action significantly affecting the quality of the human environment; therefore, no further administrative action will be taken until the Department has completed an Environmental Impact Statement, as required by law.

Conclusion

The decisions I am announcing today reflect only the results of this Department's view of the transactions challenged in this litigation, and I hope they will result in a discontinuance of that litigation. I have made no attempt to come to a legal conclusion regarding many of the legal questions raised by the Crow Tribe in its complaint.

Several facts are clear, however. First, none of the parties to this litigation is accomplishing its objectives at present, and I hope by my decision today to break this impasse. Second, I recognize, as have my predecessors, that I am charged with administering the nation's responsibility to the Crow Tribe of Indians, and that is a duty I take no less solemnly than any of the others of this high office. Third, I have decided that I cannot justify the expenditure of hundreds of thousands of dollars of the taxpayers' money to complete the Environmental Impact Statements I have determined to be necessary until the tribe and the companies involved have come to agreement over the basic legality of their contractual arrangements and I am confident that all applicable laws and Departmental regulations have been complied with or, in the case of the regulations mentioned herein, properly and explicitly waived.

The decisions I am announcing today are based upon a careful and thorough review of the records of the challenged transactions and the depositions, memoranda, and litigation reports which have been generated by this litigation. These determinations are consistent with the important June 4, 1974, decision of then-Secretary Morton in acting on a petition submitted by the Northern Cheyenne Tribe and raising similar issues arising from similar circumstances.

Secretary Morton's decision seems to have been a wise and prudent one, and I see no reason to tamper with it. Therefore, I am offering to the Crow Tribe and to the companies here involved the same assurance that was there offered to the Northern Cheyenne Tribe and its lessees and permittees, namely, that the terms and conditions upon which coal development may proceed on the Crow Reservation will require their joint support and agreement prior to any further approval by me.

I hope that, in light of my decision today, the Crow Tribe and the companies involved in this litigation will attempt at once to resolve their differences in a more cooperative forum in order that the development, in which all parties have expressed repeated interest, may proceed in an orderly manner.

The resources of this Department will be available to provide any assistance within our capabilities and authority. And I am hereby instructing the Commissioner of Indian Affairs to be particularly alert to ensure that further administrative efforts are conducted with scrupulous regard to all applicable laws and regulations.

NOTE

The Crow leasing dispute, and the similar, earlier effort by the Northern Cheyenne, involved the fortuitous existence of the excess acreage factor that permitted the renegotiation of the leases. What was really concerning the Crows was, among other things, the compensation negotiated for coal under older leases signed before inflation in energy prices. To what extent should tribes be permitted to reopen such agreements? What responsibility should the tribe have for its own prior approval of the lease, whether or not such approval occurred with significant advice from its trustee, the federal government? If economic development is to take place, and if there is to be substantial capital investment by outside investors such as banks, co-venturers, or lessees, there necessarily must be some security of contract. How should such security be balanced against the power of the tribe or the Secretary to reexamine or reopen a transaction as result of later changes in economic factors or even a subsequent change in the political balance or outlook of a tribe?

2. MINERAL DEVELOPMENT WITHOUT LEASING

INDIAN MINERAL DEVELOPMENT ACT OF 1982, P.L. 97-382, 96 Stat. 1938, 25 U.S.C. §§ 2101-2108

§ 2101. Definitions

For the purposes of this Act, the term

(1) "Indian" means any individual Indian or Alaska Native who owns land or interests in land the title to which is held in trust by the United States or is subject to a restriction against alienation imposed by the United States;

(2) "Indian tribe" means any Indian tribe, band, nation, pueblo, community, rancheria, colony, or other group which owns land or interests in land title to which is held in trust by the United States or is subject to a restriction against alienation imposed by the United States; and

(3) "Secretary" means the Secretary of the Interior.

§ 2102. Tribal Minerals Agreement; authorization

(a) Any Indian tribe, subject to the approval of the Secretary and any limitation or provision contained in its constitution or charter, may enter into any joint venture, operating, production sharing, service, managerial, lease or other agreement, or any amendment, supplement or other modification of such agreement (hereinafter referred to as a "Minerals Agreement") providing for the exploration for, or extraction, processing, or other development of, oil, gas, uranium, coal, geothermal, or other energy or nonenergy mineral resources (hereinafter referred to as "mineral resources") in which such Indian tribe owns a beneficial or restricted interest, or providing for the sale or other disposition of the production or products of such mineral resources.

(b) Any Indian owning a beneficial or restricted interest in mineral resources may include such resources in a tribal Minerals Agreement subject to the concurrence of the parties and a finding by the Secretary that such participation is in the best interest of the Indian.

§ 2103. Evaluation and approval or disapproval of Minerals Agreement by Secretary

(a) The Secretary shall approve or disapprove any Minerals Agreement submitted to him for approval within (1) one hundred and eighty days after submission or (2) sixty days after compliance, if required, with section 102(2)(C) of the National Environmental Policy Act of 1969 (42 U.S.C. 4332(2)(C)), or any other requirement of Federal law, whichever is later. Any party to such an agreement may enforce the provisions of this subsection pursuant to section 1361 of title 28, United States Code.

(b) In approving or disapproving a Minerals Agreement, the Secretary shall determine if it is in the best interest of the Indian tribe or of any individual Indian who may be party to such agreement and shall consider, among other things, the potential economic return to the tribe; the potential environmental, social, and cultural effects on the tribe; and provisions for resolving disputes that may arise between the parties to the agreement: *Provided*, That the Secretary shall not be required to prepare any study regarding environmental, socioeconomic, or cultural effects of the implementation of a Minerals Agreement apart from that which may be required under section 102(2)(C) of the National Environmental Policy Act of 1969 (42 U.S.C. 4332(2)(C)).

(c) Not later than thirty days prior to formal approval or disapproval of any Minerals Agreement, the Secretary shall provide written findings forming the basis of his intent to approve or disapprove such agreement to the affected Indian tribe. Notwithstanding any other law, such findings and all projections, studies, data or other information possessed by the Department of the Interior regarding the terms and conditions of the Minerals Agreement, the financial return to the Indian parties thereto, or the extent, nature, value or disposition of the Indian mineral resources, or the production, products or proceeds thereof, shall be held by the Department of the Interior as privileged proprietary information of the affected Indian or Indian tribe.

(d) The authority to disapprove agreements under this section may only be delegated to the Assistant Secretary of the Interior for Indian Affairs. The decision of the Secretary or, where authority is delegated, of the Assistant Secretary of the Interior for Indian Affairs, to disapprove a Minerals Agreement shall be deemed a final agency action. The district courts of the United States shall have jurisdiction to review the Secretary's disapproval action and shall determine the matter de novo. The burden is on the Secretary to sustain his action.

(e) Where the Secretary has approved a Minerals Agreement in compliance with the provisions of this Act and any other applicable provision of law, the

United States shall not be liable for losses sustained by a tribe or individual Indian under such agreement: *Provided,* That the Secretary shall continue to have a trust obligation to ensure that the rights of a tribe or individual Indian are protected in the event of a violation of the terms of any Minerals Agreement by any other party to such agreement: *Provided further,* That nothing in this Act shall absolve the United States from any responsibility to Indians, including those which derive from the trust relationship and from any treaties, Executive orders, or agreement between the United States and any Indian tribe.

§ 2104. Review of existing agreement

(a) [The] Secretary shall review within ninety days of enactment of this Act [enacted Dec. 22, 1982], any existing Minerals Agreement, which does not purport to be a lease, entered into by any Indian tribe and approved by the Secretary after January 1, 1975, but prior to enactment of this Act, to determine if such agreement complies with the purposes of this Act. Such review shall be limited to the terms of the agreement and shall not address questions of the parties' compliance therewith. The Secretary shall notify the affected tribe and other parties to the agreement of any modifications necessary to bring an agreement into compliance with the purposes of this Act. The tribe and other parties to such agreement shall within ninety days after notice make such modifications. If such modifications are not made within ninety days, the provisions of this Act may not be used as a defense in any proceeding challenging the validity of the agreement.

(b) The review required by subsection (a) of this section may be performed prior to the promulgaton of regulations required under section 8 of this Act and shall not be considered a Federal action within the meaning of that term in section 102(2)(C) of the National Environmental Protection Act of 1969 (42 U.S.C. 4332(2)(C)).

§ 2105. Application of and to 25 U.S.C. §§ 396a et seq. and other laws

Nothing in this Act shall affect, nor shall any Minerals Agreement approved pursuant to this Act be subject to or limited by, the Act of May 11, 1938 (52 Stat. 347; 25 U.S.C. 396a et seq.), as amended, or any other law authorizing the development or disposition of the mineral resources of an Indian or Indian tribe.

§ 2106. Advice, assistance, and information to be furnished by the Secretary upon request during negotiation of Minerals Agreement

In carrying out the obligations of the United States, the Secretary shall ensure that upon the request of an Indian tribe or individual Indian and to the extent of his available resources, such tribe or individual Indian shall have available advice, assistance, and information during the negotiation of a Minerals Agreement. The Secretary may fulfill this responsibility either directly through the use of Federal officials and resources or indirectly by providing financial assistance to the Indian tribe or individual Indian to secure independent assistance.

§ 2107. Rules and regulations; consultation with Indian organizations and tribes having mineral development expertise

Within one hundred and eighty days of the date of enactment of this Act [enacted Dec. 22, 1982], the Secretary of the Interior shall promulgate rules and regulations to facilitate implementation of this Act [25 U.S.C. §§ 2101 et seq.]. The Secretary shall, to the extent practicable, consult with national and regional Indian organizations and tribes with expertise in mineral development both in the initial formulation of rules and regulations and any future revision or amendment of such rules and regulations. Where there is pending before the Secretary for his approval a Minerals Agreement of the type authorized by section 3 of this Act [25 U.S.C. § 2102] which was submitted prior to the enactment of this Act [enacted Dec. 22, 1982], the Secretary shall evaluate and approve or disapprove such agreement based upon section 4 of this Act [25 U.S.C. § 2103], but shall not withhold or delay such approval or disapproval on the grounds that the rules and regulations implementing this Act [25 U.S.C. §§ 2101 et seq.] have not been promulgated.

§ 2108. Prior mineral development rights preserved

Nothing in this Act shall impair any right of an Indian tribe organized under section 16 or 17 of the Act of June 18, 1934 (48 Stat. 987), as amended [25 U.S.C. § 476 or 477], to develop their mineral resources as may be provided in any constitution or charter adopted by such tribe pursuant to that Act.

NOTE

Does the Indian Mineral Development Act of 1982 adequately address some of the problems with leasing of Indian minerals that were raised by the American Indian Policy Commission Final Report and preceeding law review articles? How are those problems resolved by this legislation?

3. TIMBER DEVELOPMENT

WHITE MOUNTAIN APACHE TRIBE v. BRACKER

448 U.S. 136 (1980)

[The *White Mountain Apache Tribe* case held that the State of Arizona could not apply certain motor vehicle fuel and road use taxes to the operations of a non-Indian trucking firm that contracted to haul timber for tribal timber operations on the White Mountain Apache Reservation. The opinion is set forth and discussed at greater length in Chapter 4, page 533. In particular, refer to the section of the opinion describing the history and scope of the federal statutes and regulations governing timber operations in Indian country.]

NOTE: INDIAN TIMBER MANAGEMENT

In *United States v. Mitchell*, 445 U.S. 535 (1980), cited in note 12 of *White Mountain Apache Tribe*, the Court held that the General Allotment Act of 1887 did not impose any trust responsibility on the federal government to manage the timber held by individual Indian allottees. The Court held that the reference to trust restrictions in the General Allotment Act merely created a limited trust, stating:

> [the] events surrounding and following the passage of the General Allotment Act indicate that the Act should not be read as authorizing, much less requiring, the Government to manage timber resources for the benefit of the allottees. In 1874, this Court determined that Indians held only a right of occupancy, and not title, to Indian lands, and therefore that they could cut timber for purposes of clearing the land, but not for the primary purpose of marketing the timber. *United States v. Cook,* 19 Wall. 591. In 1889, two years after the General Allotment Act was enacted, the Attorney General determined that the rule of *United States v. Cook, supra,* applied to allotted as well as unallotted lands, unless a statute explicitly provided to the contrary. 19 Op. Atty. Gen. 232. Congress ratified the Attorney General's opinion by enacting a provision authorizing the sale of dead timber on Indian allotments and reservations, but forbidding the sale of live timber. Act of Feb. 16, 1889, ch. 172, 25 Stat. 673. See also *Pine River Logging Co. v. United States,* 186 U.S. 279 (1902).
>
> As time passed, Congress occasionally passed legislation authorizing the harvesting and sale of timber on specific reservations. See, e.g., ch. 1350, 34 Stat. 91 (1906) (Jicarilla Apache Reservation). In 1910, Congress reversed its general policy. It empowered the Secretary of the Interior to sell timber on unallotted lands and apply the proceeds of the sales, less administrative expenses, to the benefit of the Indians. Ch. 431, § 7, 36 Stat. 857, as amended, 25 U.S.C. § 407. The Secretary was also authorized to consent to the sale of timber by any owner of any Indian land "held under a trust or other patent containing restrictions on alienations." *Id.,* § 8, as amended, 25 U.S.C. § 406(a). The Secretary was directed to pay the proceeds of these sales, less administrative expenses, to the "owner" of the allotted lands. *Ibid.* Congress subsequently enacted other legislation directing the Secretary on how to manage Indian timber resources [25 U.S.C. § 466].

While *Mitchell I* decided that the General Allotment Act had not imposed on the federal government any fiduciary responsibility for the management of Indian timber resources or forest lands because commercial Indian timber sales were not contemplated at the time the statute was enacted, the case did not decide whether the later enacted statutes described above imposed such requirements. After the Court of Claims decided that they did, a divided Supreme Court affirmed that decision in *United States v. Mitchell,* 463 U.S. 206 (1983) (*Mitchell II*), set forth in Chapter 2, section C3. The Court held that since the federal government assumed elaborate control over Indian forests and timber operations under these later statutes and the regulations promulgated thereunder, all elements of a classic trust were present. *See also Navajo Tribe v. United States,* 9 Cl. Ct. 336 (1986). The trust doctrine implications of both of these cases is considered in more depth in Chapter 2.

The federal timber sale statutes referred to in *White Mountain Apache Tribe* and *Mitchell I* have been amended several times, most recently in 1988. They currently read as follows:

§ 406. Sale of timber lands held under trust

(a) Deductions for administrative expenses; standards guiding sales. The timber on any Indian land held under a trust or other patent containing restrictions on alienations may be sold by the owner or owners with the consent of the Secretary of the Interior, and the proceeds from such sales, after deductions for administrative expenses to the extent permissible under the Act of February 14, 1920, as amended (25 U.S.C. 413), shall be paid to the owner or owners or disposed of for their benefit under regulations to be prescribed by the Secretary of the Interior. It is the intention of Congress that a deduction for administrative expenses may be made in any case unless the deduction would violate a treaty obligation or amount to a taking of private property for public use without just compensation in violation of the fifth amendment to the Constitution. Sales of timber under this subsection shall be based upon a consideration of the needs and best interests of the Indian owner and his heirs. The Secretary shall take into consideration, among other things, (1) the state of growth of the timber and the need for maintaining the productive capacity of the land for the benefit of the owner and his heirs, (2) the highest and best use of the land, including the advisability and practicality of devoting it to other uses for the benefit of the owner and his heirs, and (3) the present and future financial needs of the owner and his heirs.

(b) Undivided interests. Upon the request of the owners of a majority Indian interest in land in which any undivided interest is held under a trust or other patent containing restrictions on alienations, the Secretary of the Interior is authorized to sell all undivided Indian trust or restricted interests in any part of the timber on such land.

(c) Unrestricted interests. Upon the request of the owner of an undivided but unrestricted interest in land in which there are trust or restricted Indian interests, the Secretary of the Interior is authorized to include such unrestricted interest in a sale of the trust or restricted Indian interests in timber sold pursuant to this section, and to perform any functions required of him by the contract of sale for both the restricted and the unrestricted interests, including the collection and disbursement of payments for timber and the deduction from such payments of sums in lieu of administrative expenses.

(d) Representation of minors and others. For the purposes of this Act, the Secretary of the Interior is authorized to represent any Indian owner (1) who is a minor, (2) who has been adjudicated non compos mentis, (3) whose ownership interest in a decedent's estate has not been determined, or (4) who cannot be located by the Secretary after a reasonable and diligent search and the giving of notice by publication.

(e) Emergency sales. The timber on any Indian land held under a trust or other patent containing restrictions on alienations may be sold by the Secretary of the Interior without the consent of the owners when in his judgment such action is necessary to prevent loss of values resulting from fire, insects, disease, windthrow, or other natural catastrophes.

(f) Change in status without affecting contractual obligations. A change from a trust or restricted status to an unrestricted status of any interest in timber that has been sold pursuant to this section shall not affect the obligations of the Secretary of the Interior under any contract of sale that is in effect at the time such change in status occurs.

§ 407. Sale of timber on unallotted lands

Under regulations prescribed by the Secretary of the Interior, the timber on unallotted trust land in Indian reservations or on other land held in trust for tribes may be sold in accordance with the principles of sustained-yield management or to convert the land to a more desirable use. After deduction, if any, for administrative expenses under the Act of February 14, 1920 (41 Stat. 415; 25 U.S.C. § 413), the proceeds of the sale shall be used —

(1) as determined by the governing bodies of the tribes concerned and approved by the Secretary, or

(2) in the absence of such a governing body, as determined by the Secretary for the tribe concerned.

§ 407d. Charges for special services to purchasers of timber

The Secretary of the Interior is authorized to charge purchasers of timber on Indian lands that are held by the United States in trust, or that are subject to restrictions against alienation or encumbrance imposed by the United States, for special services requested by the purchasers in connection with scaling, timber marking, or other activities under the contract of purchase that are in addition to the services otherwise provided by the Secretary, and the proceeds derived therefrom shall be deposited to the credit of the appropriation from which the special services were or will be provided.

§ 466. Indian forestry units; rules and regulations

The Secretary of the Interior is directed to make rules and regulations for the operation and management of Indian forestry units on the principle of sustained-yield management, to restrict the number of livestock grazed on Indian range units to the estimated carrying capacity of such ranges, and to promulgate such other rules and regulations as may be necessary to protect the range from deterioration, to prevent soil erosion, to assure full utilization of the range, and like purposes.

Indian timber operations managed by the Bureau of Indian Affairs are further governed by the timber regulations found in 25 C.F.R. Part 163. The sale of lumber produced from tribal timber operations on trust land is governed by 25 C.F.R. Part 164, and special timber regulations exist for some reservations. *E.g.,* 25 C.F.R. Part 165 (Red Lake). For a survey of the special problems of timber operations on lands in Alaska subject to the Alaska Native Claims Settlement Act, see *City of Angoon v. Hodel,* 803 F.2d 1016 (9th Cir. 1986).

4. INDIAN GAMING

While some reservations have extensive mineral, oil and gas, or timber resources, many reservations lack natural resources that can be exploited in the interest of economic development. Furthermore, many tribes resist the natural and human environmental degradation attendant to extensive exploitation of such natural resources. Quite logically, as federal program funds began to dwindle during the 1980's, many tribes looked around for a new souce of tribal revenue. Since many tribal members lived at or near the poverty line, extensive reliance on internal taxation to support tribal programs was futile. Thus, revenue sources had to be found that would bring new income or a new tax base onto the reservation without increasing the tax burdens already borne by tribal members. Municipalities often attempt to shift some of their tax obligations in this fashion by adopting hotel and motel taxes which are paid by transient guests coming into the city, rather than by local residents. The tribes sought precisely the same type of shifting of financial tax burdens by developing economic enterprises that would bring outside income and capital onto the reservation which could be further developed both commercially and through the imposition of tribal taxes. Initially, tribes sought to capitalize on their tax immunities by developing commercial enterprises, such as tribal smokeshops, that could sell items heavily taxed by the states, like cigarettes or gasoline, below the price paid for such items off reservation. While many tribes still engage in such activities, federal litigation involving the immunity from state taxation of such sales to non-Indians often frustrated this general effort at economic development in Indian country. *California State Bd. of Equalization v. Chemehuevi Indian Tribe,* 474 U.S. 9 (1985); *Washington v. Confederated Tribes of the Colville Indian Reservation,* 447 U.S. 134 (1980); *Moe v. Confederated Salish & Kootenai Tribes,* 425 U.S. 463 (1976). In the *Colville* case the Court explained the basis of its decision by noting that "[i]t is painfully apparent that the value marketed by the smokeshops to persons coming from the outside is not generated on the reservation by activities in which the Tribes have a significant inter-cst." 447 U.S. at 155. By contrast, more recent efforts to develop Indian bingo and other Indian gaming operations involve tribally generated commercial activity and have been sustained, first by the Courts, and later by Congress in the Indian Gaming Regulatory Act, Pub. L. 100-497, 100 Stat. 497, discussed in the notes that follow.

CALIFORNIA v. CABAZON BAND OF MISSION INDIANS

480 U.S. 202 (1986)

[The edited text of the *Cabazon* decision is set forth in Chapter 2, page 296. The case sustains the power of the tribe to operate a bingo operation free from state regulation, adopting a prohibitory/regulatory distinction as the line of demarcation that separates the legitimate authority to enforce state laws in Indian country under both the criminal provisions of Public Law 280, 18 U.S.C. § 1162, and the federal Organized Crime Control Act, 18 U.S.C. § 1955. The Court specifically distinguished the *Colville* decision, noting that "the Tribes are not merely importing a product onto the reservations for immediate resale to non-Indians. They have built modern facilities which provide recreational opportunities and ancillary services to their patrons, who do not simply drive onto the reservations, make purchases and depart, but spend extended periods of time there enjoying the services the Tribes provide." 480 U.S. at 219.]

UNITED STATES ex rel. SHAKOPEE MDEWAKANTON SIOUX COMMUNITY v. PAN AMERICAN MANAGEMENT CO.

616 F. Supp. 1200 (D. Minn. 1985), *appeal dismissed*, 789 F.2d 632 (8th Cir. 1986)

MURPHY, District Judge.

MEMORANDUM OPINION AND ORDER

These related cases arise out of a dispute over the management agreements for bingo facilities operating on tribal trust lands of the Shakopee Mdewakanton Sioux Community (Community) near Prior Lake, Minnesota.

[The Mdewakanton Sioux Community] is a federally recognized Indian tribe which has adopted and operates under a Constitution approved by the Secretary of the Interior pursuant to the provisions of the [IRA]. It is a small Indian community occupying less than 300 acres of tribal land.

On April 10, 1982, defendant New England Entertainment Co. (New England) signed a management agreement with the Community to develop and run a bingo operation on tribal lands.[3] The agreement was negotiated over a three day period. Although Department of the Interior and Bureau of Indian Affairs (BIA) officials were consulted about the agreement, they did not formally approve or reject it at that time. Counsel for New England who negotiated the contract states that the BIA officials present at the negotiating session represented that the agreement did not require BIA approval and that it was the government's position that 25 U.S.C. § 81 did not apply to contracts of this

---

[3] In 1980, the Community had adopted a resolution authorizing the Community Chairman, Norman Crooks, to take all steps necessary to bring a bingo operation to the reservation.

type.[4] Mariana Shulstad participated in the negotiations in her role as the First Assistant Field Solicitor for the United States Department of the Interior. She states that it was her opinion at the time that, under applicable law, neither she nor the representatives of the BIA had any authority to approve or disapprove the contract. Norman Crooks who signed the agreement as chairman of the community states that he also believed at the time, based on the representations of the government officials, that no approval of the contract was necessary. The agreement specifically notes at the outset that the Community is an organized and federally recognized Indian community. The agreement contains a legal description of the property located on tribal trust land and allows the management company to record the agreement "in any Public Records." The opening section of the agreement states that the Community is the owner of the described property which it seeks to develop to enhance its economic self-sufficiency and self-government. The Community is also said to be "desirous of vesting in [the management company] the exclusive right and obligation to finance, construct, improve, develop, manage, operate, and maintain the property in conformance with the terms and conditions of this Management Agreement."

Under the terms of the agreement, the management company was engaged for a term of 15 years "to finance and/or assist the Community in obtaining financing, to construct, improve, develop, manage, operate and maintain the property as a facility for the conduct of bingo games and to create other revenue producing activities upon said property as mutually agreed upon." Furthermore, the Community:

> specifically warrants and represents to [the management company] that Community shall not act in any way whatsoever, either directly or indirectly, to cause this Management Agreement to be altered, amended, modified, cancelled, terminated and/or attempt to assign or transfer this Management Agreement or any right to or interest in said Agreement, without consent of the [management company]. Further, Community warrants and represents it shall take all actions necessary to insure that the Management Agreement shall remain in good standing at all times.

Two provisions specifically limit liens or encumbrances on the property. In the section where the management company is given responsibility to supervise the completion of all the construction and development, the agreement provides that [i]n no case shall liens or encumbrances attach to the land or structures thereon, which shall at all times remain the property of the Community." Later in the agreement a provision specifically binding the Community states that the:

> Community hereby specifically warrants and represents to [the management company] that Community shall not act in any way whatsoever, either directly or indirectly to cause any party to become an encumbrancer of the property subject to this Agreement without the prior written consent of [the management company] except as provided in this Agreement.

---

[4] Apparently, counsel for New England was previously aware that the BIA did not approve management agreements for bingo halls, but "it was his practice to meet with the [BIA] to get its tacit approval of any management agreement, although there was no necessity for it." Affidavit of Barry E. Rosenthal P4.

In return for providing the duties contained in the management agreement, New England was to receive "forty-five percent (45%) of the net operating profits for each fiscal year resulting from and in connection with any business activities upon the property." Initially, however, 100% of the net operating profits was to be applied to retire the debt incurred in constructing and developing the facilities. The management company also has the right to compel the Community to enter into a new management agreement under the same terms and conditions if the Community elects to establish any other bingo activities on other property on its Reservation during the 15 year period of the current agreement.

The bingo operation has operated at a large profit since commencing business and is the major source of revenue and jobs to the Community. The initial debt was repaid within the first year of operation. To date the Community has received approximately $3,321,000 in profit distributions. The parties managing the operations have received approximately $2,685,000 in management fees.

In 1982 New England assigned its interests in the agreement to New England/Pan American Entertainment Company. In 1983 New England/Pan American Entertainment Company assigned its interests to Little Six. Norman Crooks, then chairman of the Community, signed a consent to each of these assignments on behalf of the Community. On July 8, 1983 Little Six executed a new management agreement for the bingo operation. That agreement was also signed by Norman Crooks in his capacity as chairman of the Community. The terms of this agreement are essentially identical to the earlier contract with the addition of a provision for arbitration. The assignments and the new agreement were not submitted to the BIA for approval.

In July 20, 1984 defendant Fritz, Deputy Assistant Secretary-Indian Affairs, issued a memorandum to all BIA area directors indicating that where tribes requested approval of their management contracts, the department should undertake to review them. The memorandum included instructions to be observed in reviewing tribal bingo management contracts. The memorandum noted that given the department's uncertain authority to promulgate regulations of this nature, and the time it would take to do so, there was no intention to issue regulations at that time. The memorandum states that the instructions were being issued because of the recent decisions of two federal courts holding that 25 U.S.C. § 81 renders tribal bingo management contracts invalid unless they are approved pursuant to that section. The memorandum also noted that it was Fritz's view and that of the Solicitor's Office that these decisions were erroneous.

On October 9, 1984, Little Six executed a separate management agreement to develop and manage a new bingo lounge in the Community Cultural Center. As with the other agreements, Norman Crooks signed the agreement in his capacity as chairman of the Community. The terms of the agreement are essentially identical to those in the earlier agreements.

Following the issuance of the July 20, 1984 memorandum by Fritz, Mariana Shulstad recommended to Norman Crooks, as chairman of the Community, that the Community request BIA approval of the bingo management agreements for the bingo lounge and the bingo hall or palace. On October 19, 1984,

Crooks wrote the BIA and requested official approval of the bingo lounge agreement and of the 1983 management agreement for the bingo hall.

On December 22, 1984 Crooks was removed as chairman of the Community. Shortly thereafter an investigation into the bingo operations was authorized by the Community which ultimately led to its filing a complaint on February 8, 1985. Little Six in turn filed an action in state court which was then removed to federal court and consolidated with the prior pending action.[5]

On March 5, 1985 the Community filed a motion for summary judgment seeking to have the bingo management agreements held null and void pursuant to 25 U.S.C. §§ 81 and 415. The motion was withdrawn, however, after the BIA area director issued an opinion on March 8, 1985 approving the 1983 bingo management agreement and disapproving the 1984 bingo lounge management agreement. Both the Community and Little Six appealed the decision within the Department of the Interior: the Community appealing the approval of the 1983 management agreement and Little Six appealing the disapproval of the 1984 bingo lounge management agreement. The Community noted that it would be premature for the court to rule on the validity of the contracts under 25 U.S.C. § 81 until the administrative appeals were decided and the Department of the Interior had made a final administrative determination.

On June 17, 1985 Fritz issued his decision on the cross-appeals. The area director's disapproval of the bingo lounge contract was affirmed, while the approval of the bingo hall contract was reversed. Both contracts were thus disapproved. By letter dated June 20, 1985 the Community renewed its motion for summary judgment, stating that since final administrative action had been taken, the motion was ripe for determination. [D]efendants filed a cross-motion for partial summary judgment seeking dismissal of all named defendants with the exception of Little Six. [Thereafter,] Little Six filed a motion for a stay of all proceedings in the action brought by the Community pending final disposition of Little Six's challenge to the Secretary's decision.

[The parties agreed] that there are no genuine issues of material fact that would prevent a decision on the merits. Little Six and the government requested and received permission to submit additional briefings on certain issues; those submissions were received by the court on July 22, 1985 which time the matters were taken under advisement.

Discussion

A. *Little Six v. Hodel*

[In addition to a number of jurisdictional, administrative procedure, and constitutional arguments, all resolved against it,] Little Six also attacks the merits of the Secretary's decision, arguing that the record reveals no rational basis for the decision and thus is arbitrary and capricious. The government

---

[5] The court has issued several orders relating to the Community's initial motion for a preliminary injunction and actions taken by Little Six and the Community in response to the BIA Area Director's disapproval of the bingo lounge agreement and approval of the 1983 bingo hall agreement. For purposes of these motions, that background and the court's previous memoranda opinions need not be detailed again. On April 17, 1985 the court ordered Little Six to provide the Community with its share of the March net operating profits for the bingo hall. On that same date the court also appointed Thomas A. Keller, III, Esq. as special master.

contends that the decision is not only rational, but is the clearly correct decision based on the record.

[In rejecting the 1983 bingo agreement, the Secretary found that,] considering all the factors discussed in his order, the agreement was not in the best interests of the tribe. The Secretary noted that the failure of the agreement to comply with certain principles addressed in instructions 2, 4, and 18 of the July 20, 1984 memorandum "is a fairly clear indication that the contract is not in the Community's best interest." The Secretary also considered evidence of interference by Little Six in tribal governmental affairs. Finally, he noted that the Community's opposition to the management agreement is "entitled to great weight ... in light of the well-established federal policy recognizing a government-to-government relation with the tribes and favoring tribal self-determination."

The court concludes that the agency has articulated, and there exists, a rational basis for the decision. For the reasons already stated, the Deputy-Secretary's use of the instructions was permissible. Little Six's vehement argument against application of the instructions is meritless because, with or without the written instructions, the Deputy-Secretary acting in his trust capacity for Indian lands, must seek the best interests of the Indian tribe. The Secretary brings to bear on the review process his experience and expertise, and the instructions are merely a formal recitation of the decisionmaking process that the agency employs with or without such instructions. The Secretary's finding that the contract should not be approved, because of its 15 year term with no provision for renegotiation of the 45% management fee, has a rational basis. This finding was based not on a technical violation of an instruction, but rather because, in the Secretary's judgment, there is "serious potential for unfairness to tribes in long-term inflexible management contracts." Contrary to Little Six's assertions, the Secretary did consider the economics and risks underlying this type of business venture, but concluded that "[a]lthough a high fee might be justified at the outset of a contract to offset risks taken by the management company, such justification would not normally be expected to continue throughout a contract period of several years duration," here, 15 years.[13]

The Secretary also gave great weight to the Community's opposition to the agreement, and that factor in and of itself may be a sufficient basis for the Secretary to conclude the contracts were not in the best interest of the tribe. See *Ho-Chunk Management Corp. v. Fritz,* [618 F. Supp. 616] (W.D. Wis. 1985) (Shabaz, J.). Coupled with the other noted grounds for disapproval, it is evident that a proper review and judgment was made by the Secretary and his disapproval of the contracts was not arbitrary or capricious.[14]

---

[13] Little Six asserts that because of the involvement of a department attorney in the initial contract negotiations where these terms were agreed upon, it should be assumed that the contract would have been approved by the Secretary if it had been submitted for review in 1983. It is undisputed that the department attorney had no authority to approve or disapprove the contract, however; the power to review lay first with the Area Director and ultimately with the Deputy Assistant Secretary — Indian Affairs. The Secretary's application of the best interest standard provides reason to believe that the same conclusions would have been reached at an earlier review, however.

[14] [According to the government,] Little Six has challenged only the decision disapproving the 1983 management agreement. The complaint filed by Little Six seeks in part to have the June 17, 1985 decision of the Deputy Assistant Secretary declared null and void. Thus, the language of the

B. *United States of America ex rel. Shakopee Mdewakanton Sioux Community v. Pan American Management Company, et al.*

Before the court are cross-motions for summary judgment and defendants' motion for a stay. A motion for summary judgment may be granted if the pleadings and affidavits show that "there is no genuine issue as to any material fact and that the moving party is entitled to judgment as a matter of law." Fed. R. Civ. P. 56(c). In passing upon a motion for summary judgment, the court is required to view the facts in the light most favorable to the party opposing the motion and to give that party the benefit of all reasonable inferences to be drawn from the underlying facts disclosed in pleadings and affidavits.

[The Tribal Community's] motion for summary judgment seeks to have the bingo hall and bingo lounge management contracts declared null and void under 25 U.S.C. § 81. Section 81 provides in relevant part[:]

> No agreement shall be made by any person with any tribe of Indians, or individual Indians not citizens of the United States, for the payment or delivery of any money or other thing of value, in present or in prospective, or for the granting or procuring any privilege to him, or any other person in consideration of services for said Indians relative to their lands, or to any claims growing out of, or in reference to, annuities, installments, or other moneys, claims, demands, or thing, under laws or treaties with the United States, or official acts of any officers thereof, or in any way connected with or due from the United States, unless such contract or agreement be executed and approved as follows:
>
> ....
>
> Second. It shall bear the approval of the Secretary of the Interior and the Commissioner of Indian Affairs indorsed upon it.
>
> ....
>
> All contracts or agreements made in violation of this section shall be null and void.

The bingo management agreements for the hall and the lounge have both been disapproved by the Deputy Assistant Secretary of Interior-Indian Affairs, thus if § 81 is applicable to the agreements they are void.

Little Six argues that § 81 only applies to contracts between tribes and attorneys or claims-agents relating to lobbying the government. It argues that this interpretation is supported by the case law, legislative history, and administrative interpretation. It reads statutory language so that the portion of § 81 covering "services for said Indians relative to their lands" is limited by the subsequent language "under the laws and treaties of the United States." The Community argues on the other hand that the plain language of the statute, legislative history, and subsequent interpretations by the courts and the agency support application of § 81 to all contracts "relative to" Indian lands.

"The starting point in every case involving construction of a statute is the language itself." *Ernst & Ernst v. Hochfelder*, 425 U.S. 185, 197 (1976). Section 81 is drafted broadly to encompass any agreement made by "any person" involving payment in consideration "of services for ... Indians relative to their lands or to any claims growing out of, or in reference to, annuities, installments, or other monies, claims demands, or thing, under laws or treaties with the United States, or official acts of any officers thereof, or in any way connected

---

complaint and requested relief encompasses both the decision to disapprove the 1983 and to disapprove the 1984 agreement. The Secretary's decision on the 1984 agreement, as well as the 1983 agreement, should be upheld on the present record.

with or due from the United States." The plain meaning of the statute is that its provisions apply either to agreements relative to their lands, "or" alternatively, to claims by the tribes growing out of the listed events and arising "under laws or treaties with the United States." *See* F. Cohen, Handbook of Federal Indian Law 281. Little Six asserts that this last phrase should be construed to be a limitation upon the first type of agreements, those relative to Indian lands, as well as upon claims growing out of annuities and other demands. The statute does not support such a narrow construction, however. The broad language "relative to their lands" evidences the intent of Congress to cover almost all land transactions in Indian property. See *Central Machinery Co. v. Arizona State Tax Comm'n*, 48 U.S. 160, 166 (1980) ("Until Congress repeals or amends the Indian ... statutes ... we must give them "a sweep as broad as their language" and interpret them in light of the Congress that enacted them." (Indian trader statutes)); *Wisconsin Winnebago Business Committee v. Koberstein & Ho-Chunk Management*, 762 F.2d 613 (7th Cir. May 29, 1985). The language "relative to their lands" is clear and complete and stands apart from the alternative language which follows the word "or." Interpreting it to stand independent of the subsequent clauses is consistent with the broad introductory language. In contrast, the subsequent language of "any claims ... or other monies, claims, demands, or thing," is not self-contained or specifically defined and is clearly modified by the provision "under laws or treaties." Interpreting § 81 to apply to all contracts relative to Indian land is also consistent with the longstanding policy of regulating all transactions in Indian land, which predates this country's formation as an independent nation. *Id.*; F. Cohen, Handbook of [Federal] Indian Law 508-09 (1982).

This interpretation of § 81 is supported both by recent case law and by earlier decisions. In *Wisconsin Winnebago Business Committee*, the Seventh Circuit in reviewing the applicability of § 81 to an almost identical bingo management agreement held that it was obvious from the language of the statute that it was intended to cover almost all land transactions in Indian property.[17] *Wisconsin Winnebago Business Committee*; see also *Flandreau Indian Management Co. v. Flandreau Santee Sioux Tribe*, Civ. 84-4055 (D.S.D. April 11, 1984) (Jones, J.). In *Green v. Menominee Tribe*, 233 U.S. 558 (1914), the Supreme Court held that an oral contract between an Indian tribe and a trader for supplies to be used in logging Indian land "was so clearly within the text of the statute that it suffices to direct attention to such text without going further. But if it be conceded for argument's sake that there is ambiguity involved in determining from the text whether the statute is applicable, we are of the opinion that the case as made is so within the spirit of the statute and so exemplifies the wrong which it was intended to prevent and the evils which it was intended to remedy as to dispel any doubt otherwise engendered." *Id.* at 569. Little Six puts forth alternative interpretations of the *Green* decision, but the court finds the language to be

---

[17] In *Sac and Fox Tribe v. Apex Constr. Co., Inc.*, 757 F.2d 221 (10th Cir. 1985), the court held it need not decide if § 81 governed the construction contract at issue because it found the statute not applicable to Economic Development Administration grant monies. The district court has held that § 81 was not applicable because the statute's purpose is "to protect Indian people from dissipating their lands through agreements for imaginary services costing exorbitant amounts." *Id.* at 222. To the extent the district court's reasoning in *Sac and Fox Tribe* might differ with that in *Winnebago* and in this action, it is rejected.

straightforward. *Green* supports the proposition that the plain meaning of § 81 compels its application to contracts relative to Indian lands.

Where the language of a statute is sufficiently clear in its context, it controls without resort to the more tangential aid of legislative history. [Thus, the] language of § 81 placed within the context of federal oversight of Indian land is controlling and conclusive. The court has nevertheless reviewed the parties' extensive analysis of the legislative history and administrative interpretations. Unquestionably, these materials can give rise to conflicting interpretations. Careful consideration of the parties' arguments and the legislative history against the backdrop of the statutory language and federal policy of regulating Indian land transactions leads the court to conclude that § 81 was intended to be applicable to contracts for services relative to Indian lands.

There is no dispute that the main impetus behind the enactment of § 81 was the fraud and abuse being inflicted upon Indian tribes by attorneys and claim agents allegedly representing their interests before the federal government. *See, e.g.*, Cong. Globe, 41st Cong. 3d Sess. 1483-87. The overriding evil which Congress sought to address and protect the Indians from was "improvident and unconscionable contracts." *In re Sanborn*, 148 U.S. 222, 227 (1893). The contractual relations with attorneys and claims agents were foremost on Congress' mind because they provided many sordid examples of the exploitation of Indians by nonIndians. Yet, Congress also considered and debated whether the provision totally prohibited Indians from making contracts and noted in several places the expansive and alternative nature of the language adopted. *See* Cong. Globe, 41st Cong., 3d Sess. 1486 (Section 81 "would prevent such contracts ... in any matter relating to the land or annuities that they hold or derive from the United States") (Section 81 is limited to such agreements or services as are made or rendered relative to the lands of the Indians or to any claim against annuities from or treaties with the United States.").

The debates indicate that Congress intended the broad language incorporated in § 81 and that the language should be given its full meaning. The application of § 81 to contracts relative to Indian lands is drawn from the literal language of the statute and, furthermore, is fully consistent with Congress' concern for the protection of Indians from nonIndians.[18] [*Wisconsin Winnebago Business Committee*.]

The court next must turn to whether the bingo management agreements are "agreement[s] ... relative to [Indian] land." A careful review of the management agreements shows them to be inextricably tied up in the property rights flowing from the establishment of the bingo operations on tribal trust lands. The very existence of the bingo operations arises from the Indian tribe's sovereignty over tribal trust lands which makes state gaming laws inapplicable to games on reservations. See *Wisconsin Winnebago Business Committee*, [at 616] n.3. This is the very reason why bingo can be profitably offered by the Community. But for its land, state law would not permit it.[19] The agreements give the management

---

[18] The parties each argue and dissect the varied interpretations given § 81 by the Department of the Interior. The administrative treatment is for the most part not contemporaneous with the passage of § 81 and is inconclusive at best.

[19] It is obviously not the case that every contract with Indian tribes would require § 81 approval. Little Six's argument that application of § 81 here would lead to this result is simply incorrect. The

company the absolute right to control the construction, development, maintenance, and operation of the property. The legal description of the tribal property encompassed by the agreement is specifically included in an appendix to the agreement. The agreement also extends to any other bingo facilities established on tribal trust lands during the lifetime of the contract. Little Six is given the right to record the agreements "in any Public Records" and the Community is prohibited from directly or indirectly causing "any party to become an encumbrancer of the property subject to this Agreement without the prior written consent of [Little Six]."

In *Wisconsin Winnebago Business Committee* virtually identical contractual language was held to be "relative to Indian land" under § 81. This court finds the reasoning of that case persuasive and holds that the agreements' numerous ties with the land makes them "relative to [Indian] lands." If there is any doubt in the applicability of § 81 it is resolved by several canons of statutory construction rooted in the "unique trust relationship between the United States and the Indians." *Oneida County v. Oneida Indians*, 105 S. Ct. 1245, 1258 (1985). Thus, statutes "passed for the benefit of dependent Indian tribes ... are to be liberally construed, doubtful expressions being resolved in favor of the Indians." *Bryan v. Itasca County*, 426 U.S. 373, 392 (1976) (quoting *Alaska Pacific Fisheries v. United States*, 248 U.S. 78, 89 (1918); see also *McClanahan v. Arizona Tax Commission*, 411 U.S. 164, 174 (1973). Furthermore, ambiguous provisions are to be interpreted to the Indian tribe's benefit. *Montana v. Blackfeet Tribe of Indians*, 105 S. Ct. 2399, 2403-04 (1985).

Little Six raises the defense of estoppel and asserts that application of § 81 to the agreements would be violative of the ex post facto clause and unconstitutionally vague. For the reasons stated previously the Community is not estopped to assert § 81, and the statute's application is not an ex post facto violation. See also *Green v. Menominee Tribe*, 233 U.S. 558, 570-71 (1914) (no estoppel). Section 81 is also not unconstitutionally vague under the due process clause of the Fifth Amendment. Its literal language conveyed sufficiently definite warnings for parties contracting with Indian tribes when measured by common understanding or practice.

[Therefore, the] court has carefully considered the statutory provisions and the undisputed language of the agreements at issue and finds that even when evaluating the facts in the light most favorable to Little Six, the plaintiff is entitled to judgment as a matter of law declaring the management agreements null and void under 25 U.S.C. § 81.

In sum, the court finds that in *Little Six Enterprises v. Hodel*, Civ. 4-85-888, the defendants are entitled to summary judgment on all counts and the action should be dismissed with prejudice. In *United States of America ex rel. Shakopee Mdewakanton Sioux Community*, Civ. 4-85-231, the court finds that all defendants other than Little Six should be dismissed. The court also finds that the Community is entitled to partial summary judgment because as a matter of law the bingo management agreements are null and void under § 81.

[The court granted the motion of the Tribe for partial summary judgment and declared the management agreements between Little Six Enterprises and

---

bingo management agreements contain numerous provisions, as stated above, that specifically implicate Indian lands in the performance of the contracts and relate Little Six services to the land. Furthermore, the very existence of this type of operation is wholly dependent on the Indian land.

the Shakopee Mdewakanton Sioux Community for the bingo hall and bingo lounge null and void.]

ENTERPRISE MANAGEMENT CONSULTANTS, INC. v. UNITED STATES ex rel. HODEL

883 F.2d 890 (10th Cir. 1989)

Before LOGAN, McWILLIAMS, and SEYMOUR, Circuit Judges.

SEYMOUR, Circuit Judge.

Enterprise Management Consultants, Inc. (EMCI) brought this suit against the Citizen Band Potawatomi Tribe of Oklahoma (Tribe) and officials of the United States Department of Interior. The district court granted the Tribe's motion to dismiss on the basis of sovereign immunity, but denied the Tribe's motion for sanctions under Fed. R. Civ. P. 11. The court also concluded that it had no jurisdiction over the suit against the federal officials. See *Enterprise Management Consultants, Inc. v. United States*, 685 F. Supp. 221 (W.D. Okla. 1988). We affirm.

I

This litigation is one of several interrelated disputes between EMCI and the Tribe arising from two bingo management contracts that were not approved by the Secretary of the Interior and the Commissioner of Indian Affairs as required by 25 U.S.C. § 81 (1982). A detailed recitation of the events which generated this appeal is set out in our opinion filed this day in *United States ex rel. Citizen Band Potawatomi Indian Tribe of Oklahoma v. Enterprise Management Consultants, Inc.*, 883 F.2d 886 (10th Cir. 1989) (*Citizen Band*). Briefly stated, in *Citizen Band* the Tribe sued EMCI for a declaration that the unapproved contracts were void under section 81. The district court in that action ordered the 1985 contract submitted for consideration by the appropriate federal officials. When they refused to approve it, EMCI sought agency review of the decision, which was then affirmed on administrative appeal. EMCI filed the instant suit seeking judicial review of the administrative action. The trial court in *Citizen Band* stayed determination of the merits in that case pending the outcome of these proceedings, and in the meantime enjoined the Tribe from interfering with EMCI's operation of the bingo games. The propriety of that injunction is the subject of the *Citizen Band* opinion issued today.

In the present suit, EMCI seeks injunctive relief prohibiting all defendants from enforcing disapproval of the contract, mandamus relief requiring the federal defendants to approve the contract, and declaratory relief stating that section 81 does not apply to the contract, that the Bureau of Indian Affairs (BIA) abused its discretion in disapproving the contract, and that both the Tribe and the BIA are estopped from enforcing this disapproval.

II

The district court ruled that EMCI's suit against the Tribe is barred by sovereign immunity. This doctrine, "which recognizes the sovereignty of Indian tribes and seeks to preserve their autonomy, protects tribes from suits in federal and state courts." *Wichita & Affiliated Tribes of Oklahoma v. Hodel*, 788 F.2d 765, 771 (D.C. Cir. 1986). The Supreme Court has unequivocally stated that Indian tribes possess "the common-law immunity from suit traditionally enjoyed by sovereign powers." *Santa Clara Pueblo v. Martinez*, 436 U.S. 49, 58 (1978). Although this immunity is subject to Congressional control, "'without congressional authorization,' the 'Indian Nations are exempt from suit.'" *Id.* (citation omitted). Moreover, "[i]t is settled that a waiver of sovereign immunity 'cannot be implied but must be unequivocally expressed.'" *Id.* (citations omitted).

The Tribe has not consented to be sued in this action. The only ground offered by EMCI to support its argument that the Tribe is nevertheless amenable to suit is our decision in *Dry Creek Lodge, Inc. v. Arapahoe & Shoshone Tribes*, 623 F.2d 682 (10th Cir. 1980). The majority in *Dry Creek Lodge* articulated an exception to the doctrine of sovereign immunity set out in *Santa Clara Pueblo*, basing its decision on three factors: an alleged violation of the Indian Civil Rights Act, the denial of a tribal forum, and a conflict involving a matter outside internal tribal affairs. Because *Dry Creek Lodge* created an exception to traditional tribal immunity arising from highly unusual circumstances, later opinions of this circuit indicate that it must be narrowly construed. *See White v. Pueblo of San Juan*, 728 F.2d 1307, 1312-13 (10th Cir. 1984) ("Necessarily the *Dry Creek* opinion must be regarded as requiring narrow interpretation in order to not come into conflict with the decision of the Supreme Court in *Santa Clara*."); *Ramey Const. Co. v. The Apache Tribe of the Mescalero Reservation*, 673 F.2d 315, 319 n.4 (10th Cir. 1982) (*Dry Creek Lodge* "involved particularly egregious allegations of personal restraint and deprivation of personal rights"). The dispositive factors in *Dry Creek Lodge* are absent here. We therefore affirm the dismissal of the Tribe on the basis of its sovereign immunity from suit.

III

The district court held that it had no jurisdiction over the federal officials both because EMCI lacked standing to protest their actions under section 81, and because the action of federal officials under section 81 is committed to agency discretion and therefore is not judicially reviewable. We do not reach these issues because we conclude that the action should be dismissed for lack of an indispensable party.

The indispensable party issue was not raised in the trial court or by the parties on appeal. However, courts and commentators generally agree that this issue is not waivable, and that a reviewing court has "an independent duty to raise it sua sponte." [*Wichita & Affiliated Tribes*, 788 F.2d at 772 n.6.][2]

---

[2][T]he advisory committee notes to the 1966 amendment to Rule 12(h) state:

"It is to be noted that while the defenses specified in subdivision (h)(1) are subject to waiver as there provided, *the more substantial defenses of* failure to state a claim upon which relief can be granted, *failure to join a party indispensable under Rule 19,* and failure to state a legal defense to a claim (see Rule 12(b)(6), (7), (f)), as well as the defense of lack of jurisdiction over the subject matter (see Rule 12(b)(1)), *are expressly preserved against waiver by amended subdivision (h)(2)* and (3)." Fed. R. Civ. P. 12(h) advisory committee's note (emphasis added).

[Here, plaintiff] EMCI seeks to obtain the validation of a contract with the Tribe which the Tribe, in a separate action, has brought suit to have declared void. The Tribe's interest in the validity of this contract, to which it is a party, would be directly affected by the relief EMCI seeks. Rule 19(a) thus requires joinder of the Tribe because it is a "person claim[ing] an interest relating to the subject of the action and is so situated that the disposition of the action in his absence may ... as a practical matter impair or impede his ability to protect that interest."

We must therefore determine whether, under Rule 19(b), the Tribe is an indispensable party so that the action cannot in equity and good conscience proceed in its absence. In so doing, we are guided by our decision in *Jicarilla Apache Tribe v. Hodel*, 821 F.2d 537 (10th Cir. 1987), which considered the issue in the context of closely analogous facts. After the Tribe brought suit in that case to cancel oil and gas leases, the lessees sued the United States to preserve their interest in the same leases. The district court dismissed the lessees' action "in part because the Tribe was an essential party to the litigation but was immune from suit." *Id.* at 539. We affirmed, stating that "'[n]o procedural principle is more deeply imbedded in the common law than that, in an action to set aside a lease or a contract, all parties who may be affected by the determination of the action are indispensable.'" *Id.* at 540 (quoting *Lomayaktewa v. Hathaway*, 520 F.2d 1324, 1325 (9th Cir. 1975), *cert. denied*, 425 U.S. 903 (1976)). The holding in *Jicarilla Apache Tribe* is equally applicable in this case.

In addition to the effect this action would have on the Tribe's interest in the contract, the suit would also effectively abrogate the Tribe's sovereign immunity by adjudicating its interest in that contract without consent. *Id.* at 540-41. Although some courts have considered whether under Rule 19(b) the United States as a party may adequately represent a tribe's legal position in litigation by virtue of its fiduciary duty to that tribe, see, e.g., *Wichita & Affiliated Tribes*, 788 F.2d at 774-75, the Tribe's interest here in its sovereign right not to have its legal duties judicially determined without consent is an interest which the United States' presence in this suit cannot protect. This case is therefore distinguishable from those in which the United States initiates suit on behalf of a tribe and adequately represents the tribe's interest as a plaintiff, see, e.g., *Heckman v. United States*, 224 U.S. 413 (1912), a situation which does not implicate the tribe's right not to be sued without consent. When, as here, a necessary party under Rule 19(a) is immune from suit, "there is very little room for balancing of other factors" set out in Rule 19(b), because immunity "'may be viewed as one of those interests "compelling by themselves."'" *Wichita & Affiliated Tribes*, 788 F.2d at 777 n.13 (quoting 3A Moore's Federal Practice (Para) 19.15, at 19-266 n.6 (1984)); see also 7 C. Wright, A. Miller & M. Kane, Federal Practice & Procedure § 1617 (1986).

We recognize that the Supreme Court requires a court addressing the issue for the first time on appeal to view the Rule 19 factors entirely from an appellate perspective, considering a victorious plaintiff's interest in preserving his judgment, the defendant's failure to assert his interest, the interest of the outsider, and the interest of the courts and society in judicial efficiency. [In the instant case,] plaintiff EMCI lost on the merits in the trial court and thus can assert no interest in the judgment. Moreover, while the United States and the courts may have an interest in preserving this judgment, we believe that their interests are outweighed by the Tribe's interest in maintaining its sovereign immunity, a right as compelling at the appellate level as it is when raised in the trial court. "The dismissal of this suit is mandated by the policy of tribal immunity. This is not a case where some procedural defect such as venue precludes litigation of the case. Rather, the dismissal turns on the fact that society has consciously opted to shield Indian tribes from suit without congressional or tribal consent." *Wichita & Affiliated Tribes*, 788 F.2d at 777. This action must be dismissed for lack of an indispensable party.

IV

Finally, we address the district court's denial of the Tribe's request to award Rule 11 sanctions against EMCI for suing it without consent in violation of its clear right to sovereign immunity. "Rule 11 requires sanctions against attorneys who file signed pleadings, motions or other papers in district court which are not well grounded in fact, are not warranted by existing law or a good faith argument for its extension, or are filed for an improper purpose." *Adamson v. Bowen*, 855 F.2d 668, 672 (10th Cir. 1988). The imposition of such sanctions is committed to the trial court's discretion. The majority of the panel, Judges Logan and McWilliams, has concluded that the trial court did not abuse its discretion in denying Rule 11 sanctions against EMCI. Similarly, it declines to impose sanctions for filing a frivolous appeal, as requested by the Tribe.[5]
[*Affirmed.*]

NOTE: THE INDIAN GAMING REGULATORY ACT OF 1988

In response to the development of Indian gaming activities, to the *Cabazon* decision, and to decisions like the *Shakopee* cases holding that 25 U.S.C. § 81 governed Indian gaming management contracts, Congress enacted the Indian

---

[5] I would reverse the trial court's refusal to grant Rule 11 sanctions, and I therefore respectfully dissent from this portion of the opinion. The only discussion by the court concerning the denial of sanctions does not support its decision. Indeed, the court recognized that "nothing presented ... here obviates the principle of the Tribe's nonamenability to a suit like this." Rec., vol. II, at 11. The court further stated that although it thought EMCI had behaved prudently in filing the instant suit, it disagreed with EMCI's decision to include the Tribe, stating that it did not "believe [it] would have filed a complaint of such comprehensiveness other than just a direct appeal of the [administrative] decision." *Id.*

While I will rarely second-guess a district court's decision not to apply Rule 11 sanctions, [here] the clarity of law and the circumstances of this litigation convince me that there was no objectively reasonable basis for naming the Tribe as a defendant in the complaint. At the time EMCI filed the instant suit, *Santa Clara Pueblo* had made clear that Indian tribes are not amenable to suit absent their consent or that of Congress. Moreover, this circuit's decisions by then left no room for an argument that the exception in *Dry Creek Lodge* could be extended beyond the highly unusual facts of that case. See *White*, 728 F.2d at 1312-13; *Ramey*, 673 F.2d at 319 n.4. Our decision in *Jicarilla Apache Tribe* had also made clear that a Tribe under the circumstances here is immune from suit. See 821 F.2d at 539-41. I am particularly persuaded by the fact that in the related litigation where EMCI is the defendant, EMCI asserted in its counterclaim allegations similar to those it presses against the Tribe here. The Tribe raised the defense of sovereign immunity, and the district court in that litigation dismissed the counterclaims on that basis, all before EMCI sued the Tribe in this action.

For the same reasons, I would grant the Tribe's motion for damages and costs for EMCI's filing of a frivolous appeal. See Fed. R. App. P. 35; *Braley v. Campbell*, 832 F.2d 1504, 1510-11 (10th Cir. 1987) (en banc).

Gaming Regulatory Act of 1988, Pub. L. 100-497. 100 Stat. 497. The regulatory content of this legislation is discussed in greater detail in Chapter 2, section D. To review, however, this legislation basically sets up three classes of Indian gaming. Class 1 gaming includes "social games solely for prizes of minimal value or traditional forms of Indian gaming engaged in by individuals as part of, or in connection with, tribal ceremonies or celebrations." Class II gaming basically includes bingo, lotto, pull-tabs, or other games similar to bingo. Class III gaming includes all other forms of gambling. Under the Act, tribes have exclusive jurisdiction over class I gaming, and class II gaming remains subject to tribal jurisdiction, albeit under the supervision of and pursuant to minimal standards established by the Indian Gaming Commission established by the Act. Class III gaming can be conducted by tribes in Indian country only pursuant to both a tribal ordinance meeting certain minimum standards *and* pursuant to a tribal-state compact entered into with a state that permits other organizations, entities, and persons to engage in such forms of gaming. Most Indian gaming operations must be tribally owned with revenues supporting tribal operations. Provisions exist for gaming on newly acquired lands and there are certain exceptions provided for non-conforming games. *See generally United States v. Sisseton-Wahpeton Sioux Tribe*, 897 F.2d 358 (8th Cir. 1990); *United States v. Burns*, 725 F. Supp. 116 (N.D.N.Y. 1989).

As reflected in both the *Citizen Band* and *Shakopee* cases, in the early days of Indian gaming, many tribes entered into gaming management contracts with outside firms, some of whom provided some venture capital, but who often took large portions of the profits and left the tribe with sizable debts. As reflected in those opinions, before enactment of the Indian Gaming Regulatory Act many tribes successfully invoked the approval requirements of 25 U.S.C. § 81 to void such disadvantageous agreements by arguing that under that statute such contracts required approval of the Secretary of the Interior, even though until 1984 the Secretary did not review such agreements. *See also United States ex rel. Citizens Band of the Potawatomi Indian Tribe v. Enterprise Mgt. Consultants*, 883 F.2d 886 (10th Cir. 1989); *Barona Group of the Capitan Grande Band of Mission Indians v. American Mgt. & Amusement, Inc.*, 840 F.2d 1394 (9th Cir. 1988); *A.K. Mgt. Co. v. San Manuel Band of Mission Indians*, 789 F.2d 785 (9th Cir. 1986). The Indian Gaming Regulatory Act adopts a new statutory regime to deal with such management contracts, delegating to the Commission the approval power over gaming management contracts theretofore exercised by the Secretary of the Interior under section 81. Reflecting the broad authority delegated in the presidentially appointed Chairman of the Commission, sections 12 and 13 of the Act, set forth below, provide minimum standards for such contracts and require review by the Chairman and the Commission of all existing contracts.

Management Contracts

SEC. 12. (a)(1) Subject to the approval of the Chairman, an Indian tribe may enter into a management contract for the operation and management of a class II gaming activity that the Indian tribe may engage in under section 11(b)(1), but, before approving such contract, the Chairman shall require and obtain the following information:

(A) the name, address, and other additional pertinent background information on each person or entity (including individuals comprising such entity) having a direct financial interest in, or management responsibility for, such contract, and, in the case of a corporation, those individuals who serve on the board of directors of such corporation and each of its stockholders who hold (directly or indirectly) 10 percent or more of its issued and outstanding stock;

(B) a description of any previous experience that each person listed pursuant to subparagraph (A) has had with other gaming contracts with Indian tribes or with the gaming industry generally, including specifically the name and address of any licensing or regulatory agency with which such person has had a contract relating to gaming; and

(C) a complete financial statement of each person listed pursuant to subparagraph (A).

(2) Any person listed pursuant to paragraph (1)(A) shall be required to respond to such written or oral questions that the Chairman may propound in accordance with his responsibilities under this section.

(3) For purposes of this Act, any reference to the management contract described in paragraph (1) shall be considered to include all collateral agreements to such contract that relate to the gaming activity.

(b) The Chairman may approve any management contract entered into pursuant to this section only if he determines that it provides at least —

(1) for adequate accounting procedures that are maintained, and for verifiable financial reports that are prepared, by or for the tribal governing body on a monthly basis;

(2) for access to the daily operations of the gaming to appropriate tribal officials who shall also have a right to verify the daily gross revenues and income made from any such tribal gaming activity;

(3) for a minimum guaranteed payment to the Indian tribe that has preference over the retirement of development and construction costs;

(4) for an agreed ceiling for the repayment of development and construction costs;

(5) for a contract term not to exceed five years, except that, upon the request of an Indian tribe, the Chairman may authorize a contract term that exceeds five years but does not exceed seven years if the Chairman is satisfied that the capital investment required, and the income projections, for the particular gaming activity require the additional time; and

(6) for grounds and mechanisms for terminating such contract, but actual contract termination shall not require the approval of the Commission.

(c)(1) The Chairman may approve a management contract providing for a fee based upon a percentage of the net revenues of a tribal gaming activity if the Chairman determines that such percentage fee is reasonable in light of surrounding circumstances. Except as otherwise provided in this subsection, such fee shall not exceed 30 percent of the net revenues.

(2) Upon the request of an Indian tribe, the Chairman may approve a management contract providing for a fee based upon a percentage of the net revenues of a tribal gaming activity that exceeds 30 percent but not 40 percent of the net revenues if the Chairman is satisfied that the capital investment required, and income projections, for such tribal gaming activity require the additional fee requested by the Indian tribe.

(d) By no later than the date that is 180 days after the date on which a management contract is submitted to the Chairman for approval, the Chairman shall approve or disapprove such contract on its merits. The Chairman may extend the 180-day period by not more than 90 days if the Chairman notifies the Indian tribe in writing of the reason for the extension. The Indian tribe may bring an action in a United States district court to compel action by the Chairman if a contract has not been approved or disapproved within the period required by this subsection.

(e) The Chairman shall not approve any contract if the Chairman determines that —

(1) any person listed pursuant to subsection (a)(1)(A) of this section —

(A) is an elected member of the governing body of the Indian tribe which is the party to the management contract;

(B) has been or subsequently is convicted of any felony or gaming offense;

(C) has knowingly and willfully provided materially important false statements or information to the Commission or the Indian tribe pursuant to this Act or has refused to respond to questions propounded pursuant to subsection (a)(2); or

(D) has been determined to be a person whose prior activities, criminal record if any, or reputation, habits, and associations pose a threat to the public interest or to the effective regulation and control of gaming, or create or enhance the dangers of unsuitable, unfair, or illegal practices, methods, and activities in the conduct of gaming or the carrying on of the business and financial arrangements incidental thereto;

(2) the management contractor has, or has attempted to, unduly interfere or influence for its gain or advantage any decision or process of tribal government relating to the gaming activity;

(3) the management contractor has deliberately or substantially failed to comply with the terms of the management contract or the tribal gaming ordinance or resolution adopted and approved pursuant to this Act; or

(4) a trustee, exercising the skill and diligence that a trustee is commonly held to, would not approve the contract.

(f) The Chairman, after notice and hearing, shall have the authority to require appropriate contract modifications or may void any contract if he subsequently determines that any of the provisions of this section have been violated.

(g) No management contract for the operation and management of a gaming activity regulated by this Act shall transfer or, in any other manner, convey any interest in land or other real property, unless specific statutory authority exists and unless clearly specified in writing in said contract.

(h) The authority of the Secretary under section 2103 of the Revised Statutes (25 U.S.C. 81), relating to management contracts regulated pursuant to this Act, is hereby transferred to the Commission.

(i) The Commission shall require a potential contractor to pay a fee to cover the cost of the investigation necessary to reach a determination required in subsection (e) of this section.

Review of Existing Ordinances and Contracts

SEC. 13. (a) As soon as practicable after the organization of the Commission, the Chairman shall notify each Indian tribe or management contractor who, prior to the enactment of this Act, adopted an ordinance or resolution authorizing class II gaming or class III gaming or entered into a management contract, that such ordinance, resolution, or contract, including all collateral agreements relating to the gaming activity, must be submitted for his review within 60 days of such notification. Any activity conducted under such ordinance, resolution, contract, or agreement shall be valid under this Act, or any amendment made by this Act, unless disapproved under this section.

(b)(1) By no later than the date that is 90 days after the date on which an ordinance or resolution authorizing class II gaming or class III gaming is submitted to the Chairman pursuant to subsection (a), the Chairman shall review such ordinance or resolution to determine if it conforms to the requirements of section 11(b) of this Act.

(2) If the Chairman determines that an ordinance or resolution submitted under subsection (a) conforms to the requirements of section 11(b), the Chairman shall approve it.

(3) If the Chairman determines that an ordinance or resolution submitted under subsection (a) does not conform to the requirements of section 11(b), the Chairman shall provide written notification of necessary modifications to the Indian tribe which shall have not more than 120 days to bring such ordinance or resolution into compliance.

(c)(1) Within 180 days after the submission of a management contract, including all collateral agreements, pursuant to subsection (a), the Chairman shall subject such contract to the requirements and process of section 12.

(2) If the Chairman determines that a management contract submitted under subsection (a), and the management contractor under such contract, meet the requirements of section 12, the Chairman shall approve the management contract.

(3) If the Chairman determines that a contract submitted under subsection (a), or the management contractor under a contract submitted under subsection (a), does not meet the requirements of section 12, the Chairman shall provide written notification to the parties to such contract of necessary modifications and the parties shall have not more than 120 days to come into compliance. If a management contract has been approved by the Secretary prior to the date of enactment of this Act, the parties shall have not more than 180 days after notification of necessary modifications to come into compliance.

Insofar as these provision operate to invalidate preexisting Indian gaming management contracts, do they violate due process or taking limitations of the fifth amendment? Does it make any difference that most such preexisting contracts theretofore were subject to the requirements of 25 U.S.C. § 81 and had never been approved as a result of the policy of the Secretary prior to 1984 not to review or approve such contracts? Consider the fact that section 81 explicitly provides that contracts made in violation of its provisions "shall be null and void." Do the provisions for cure of defects within 180 days if the Chairman determines that preexisting contracts are not in compliance with section 12 standards ameliorate any constitutional difficulty with the Act? Note that subsequent disenchantment of the tribal government with the contract management firm does not constitute a grounds for disapproval of a preexisting contract under section 12. Cf. *United States v. Burns*, 725 F. Supp. at 127-28 (N.D.N.Y. 1989) (discussing certain other constitutional problems with the Indian Gaming Regulatory Act).

5. SPECIAL CONTRACTUAL PROBLEMS OF DOING BUSINESS WITH INDIAN TRIBES

The *Shakopee* and *Citizens Band* cases in the preceding section highlight two very important contractual problems that must be considered in doing business with Indian tribes — (1) requirements of Secretarial approval for certain contracts, leases, and other agreements and (2) the sovereign immunity of the tribe and its trustee, the United States.

As already noted, oil and gas, mineral, and surface leases for tribal or allotted Indian lands must be approved by the Secretary of the Interior pursuant to the statutory authorizations discussed earlier in this chapter. Similarly, *Shakopee* highlights the fact that under 25 U.S.C. § 81 other types of contracts involving Indian tribes need Secretarial approval as prerequisite to contractual validity. Section 81 applies to contracts with tribes "relative to their lands, or to any claims growing out of, or in reference to, annuities, installments, or other moneys, claims, demands, or thing, under laws or treaties with the United States, or official acts of any officers thereof, or in any way connected with or due from the United States." Section 81 not only requires that such contracts be in writing and approved by the Secretary of the Interior, it also contains other requirements as to the form of the contract, including that the contract shall contain the names, residence, occupation, and authority of all parties in interest to the contract and requires that the contract run only for a "limited time" distinctly stated in the contract. Further implementing section 81, 25 U.S.C.

§ 84 restricts assignments of contracts subject to the approval requirements of section 81 unless the Secretary approves them and names, residences, and occupations of such assignees be entered on the contract. Similarly, 25 U.S.C. § 85 requires prior approval for any contract with any Indian relating to tribal funds or property held in trust by the United States. In *Inecon Agricorp. v. Tribal Farms, Inc.*, 656 F.2d 498 (9th Cir. 1981), the Ninth Circuit ruled that section 81 does not apply to contracts entered into by subordinate economic business enterprises organized by the tribes where the tribal role under the agreement is a very limited one.

In addition to bingo management contracts and other agreements affecting or otherwise relative to Indian lands, section 81 and other similar statutes require approval of the Secretary of the Interior for tribal attorney contracts. *See also* 25 U.S.C. §§ 81a-81b, 82, 82a. After delay in approval of attorney fee contracts became a considerable problem, particularly in cases seeking approval of contracts involving claims against the United States, Congress amended these provisions for attorney fee contract approval in the Indian Civil Rights Act of 1968, Pub. L. 90-284, Title VI, § 601, 82 Stat. 80, codified at 25 U.S.C. § 1331. Under 25 U.S.C. § 1331 any application for approval of any attorney fee contract made by an Indian or Indian tribe or group is deemed approved if it is neither granted nor denied within 90 days following the application.

The problem of tribal sovereign immunity, particularly when combined with procedural requirements of joining indispensable parties in litigation, frequently constitutes a formidable barrier to the enforcement of business contracts entered into with tribes and tribal groups, as reflected by the next case.

McCLENDON v. UNITED STATES

885 F.2d 627 (9th Cir. 1989)

FLETCHER, Circuit Judge:

[Gilbert and Bernadine McClendon and Norman and Connie McDanel (collectively, "McClendon") brought an action in the United States District Court against the United States and the Colorado Indian River Tribal Council ("Tribe"), alleging that the Tribe breached the terms of a lease agreement. The lease agreement had been entered into to settle a title dispute after the United States had initiated ejectment litigation on behalf of the Tribe against the Clarks, the McClendons' predecessor in interest, over title to the disputed property. The settlement agreement gave the United States title to the property in trust for the Tribe while granting the Clarks a long-term lease on the property at a favorable rental. In 1984, the Clarks assigned a portion of their leasehold interest to McClendon. Following this assignment, McClendon signed a business lease with the Tribe governing this property. The terms of this 1984 lease were basically identical to the terms of the earlier Clark lease. McClendon then applied for, and received from the Tribe, various permits to construct a mobile home park. According to McClendon, during the course of construction the Tribe withdrew the previously issued permits and demanded submission of new development plans. McClendon also alleges that during the course of review of the new plans, the Tribe sought to increase the rent fixed by the lease, and to compel McClendon to abandon the mobile home project.

[McClendon then brought this action, seeking damages, a declaration that the Tribe's actions constitute a breach of the lease agreement, and injunctive relief. The district court dismissed the action for lack of subject matter jurisdiction on the basis of tribal sovereign immunity. It rejected McClendon's argument that sovereign immunity was waived through participation in the stipulated judgment entered into in settlement of the Clark lawsuit. It also noted that the stipulated judgment and accompanying findings contained no express reservation of district court jurisdiction over the lease, and that there is in these documents no reference of any sort to the Clark lease. Finally, the court found that the lease, itself, contains no waiver of sovereign immunity and that, in fact, the Clark lease documents were drafted specifically to avoid such waiver. McClendon filed a timely notice of appeal. The district court dismissed the action for lack of subject matter jurisdiction.]

II. *Jurisdiction Over the Tribe*

A. *Tribal Sovereign Immunity*

Because they are sovereign entities, Indian tribes are immune from unconsented suit in state or federal court. [e.g.,] *Santa Clara Pueblo v. Martinez*, 436 U.S. 49, 58 (1978). Indian tribes can waive their sovereign immunity. A waiver may not be implied, but must be expressed unequivocally. The issue of tribal sovereign immunity is jurisdictional in nature. [E.g., *Puyallup Tribe, Inc. v. Washington Dep't of Game*, 433 U.S. 165, 172 (1977)].

Initiation of a lawsuit necessarily establishes consent to the court's adjudication of the merits of that particular controversy. By initiating the 1972 action, the Tribe accepted the risk that it would be bound by an adverse determination of ownership of the disputed land. However, the "terms of [a sovereign's] consent to be sued in any court define that court's jurisdiction to entertain the suit." *Jicarilla Apache Tribe v. Hodel*, 821 F.2d 537, 539 (10th Cir. 1987) (quoting *United States v. Testan*, 424 U.S. 392, 399 (1976)). Thus, a tribe's waiver of sovereign immunity may be limited to the issues necessary to decide the action brought by the tribe; the waiver is not necessarily broad enough to encompass related matters, even if those matters arise from the same set of underlying facts.

Jicarilla Tribe is instructive in this regard. The Jicarilla Tribe brought suit to cancel certain oil and gas leases on reservation lands awarded by the Department of the Interior. While that suit was pending, Dome Petroleum Corporation brought an independent action seeking to pay adjusted bonuses to preserve its interest in certain of these leases. The district court dismissed Dome's suit for lack of jurisdiction over the Jicarilla Tribe, and the court of appeals affirmed, noting:

> Although the Tribe's filing of the Jicarilla litigation may have waived its immunity with regard to Dome's intervention in that suit, we cannot construe the act of filing that suit as a sufficiently unequivocal expression of waiver in subsequent actions relating to the same leases .... Waiver of immunity in the present action was not one of the terms of the Tribe's initial suit; it therefore cannot be made a party to this subsequent litigation.

Jicarilla Tribe, 821 F.2d at 539-40 (emphasis added). Thus, *Jicarilla Tribe* indicates that tribal initiation of litigation alone does not establish waiver with respect to related matters. The dispute over the lease agreement in this case is no more closely linked with the Tribe's underlying suit than was Dome's action to the Jicarilla Tribe's lease cancellation suit.

Similarly, we consistently have held that a tribe's participation in litigation does not constitute consent to counterclaims asserted by the defendants in those actions. See, e.g., *Squaxin Indian Tribe v. Washington*, 781 F.2d 715, 723 (9th Cir. 1986) (neither tribe's initiation of suit for injunctive relief, nor tribe's continued sale of liquor while preliminary injunction in force, constituted waiver of sovereign immunity with respect to state's counterclaim for taxes allegedly due); *Chemehuevi*, 757 F.2d at 1053 (tribe's initiation of a suit for declaratory and injunctive relief against enforcement of California's cigarette tax as applied to tribal sales to non-Indian purchasers did not constitute waiver of the tribe's sovereign immunity with respect to California's counterclaim for taxes allegedly due). But see *United States v. Oregon*, 657 F.2d at 1014-16 (tribe's intervention to establish fishing rights constituted consent to district court's jurisdiction to issue and modify equitable decree which encompassed the tribe's rights). These cases are consistent with the conclusion in *Jicarilla Tribe* that a tribe's consent to suit through initiation of litigation may be limited in scope.

McClendon argues that the 1972 suit constituted a waiver of immunity against actions to enforce the terms of the lease agreement. McClendon relies particularly upon the rationale of *United States v. Oregon*, 657 F.2d at 1009, in which we held that an Indian tribe had manifested its consent to suit by intervening as a plaintiff in a suit brought by the United States against Oregon to establish the fishing rights of Indian tribes occupying the Columbia River basin.[2] In that case, the district court ruled in favor of the plaintiffs on the merits. As part of the equitable remedy fashioned by the court, it established a procedure for promulgating future fishing regulations, and retained jurisdiction to expedite enforcement of its decree.

Eleven years after initial judgment was entered, the state of Washington applied to the district court for an injunction against tribal fishing of spring chinook. The court granted the injunction and the Tribe appealed, contending, inter alia, that Washington's suit was barred by sovereign immunity. This court rejected that argument, affirming the district court.

First, we noted that the initial action was analogous to an action in rem, with the fishery constructively in possession of the court. We stated that "[b]y seeking equity, this Tribe assumed the risk that any equitable judgment secured could be modified if warranted by changed circumstances." *Id*. at 1015. We then concluded:

> Here, Washington alleged that the very resource sought to be protected, the anadromous fishery, was in jeopardy. Since the existence of the salmon was inextricably linked to the res in the court's constructive custody, the court was empowered to enjoin interference with that custody.

Id. at 1016.

---

[2] We also held in *United States v. Oregon* that the Tribe explicitly agreed to submit disputes over the management of the fishery to the U.S. District Court. 657 F.2d at 1016. However, this second rationale clearly was independent of the first. *Id*. at 1014. Thus, *United States v. Oregon* must be viewed as establishing that Indian tribes may, in certain circumstances, consent to suit by participation in litigation.

The rationale of *United States v. Oregon* does not extend to this case. The 1972 action merely sought a declaration of land ownership. Unlike the initial action in *United States v. Oregon*, no ongoing equitable remedy was necessary; there was no res over which the district court had to maintain control in order to do equity. By initiating the 1972 action, the Tribe merely consented to the court's jurisdiction to decide ownership of the land in question. The initiation of the suit, in itself, does not manifest broad consent to suit over collateral issues arising out of the settlement of the litigation, such as interpretation or enforcement of the lease agreement. See *Jicarilla Tribe*, 821 F.2d at 539-40. We conclude that disputes over interpretation of the 1984 lease agreement are collateral disputes, and are not so inextricably linked with the 1972 suit that initiation of the latter, in itself, constitutes consent to suit over the former.

McClendon argues that allowing the Tribe to sue without exposing itself to suit for subsequent related matters is unfair. However, as the Supreme Court has noted, "[t]he perceived inequity of permitting the Tribe to recover from a non-Indian for civil wrongs in instances where a non-Indian allegedly may not recover against the Tribe simply must be accepted in view of the overriding federal and tribal interests in these circumstances." *Three Affiliated Tribes v. Wold Eng'g*, 476 U.S. 877, 893 (1986). Moreover, "[t]ribes and persons dealing with them long have known how to waive sovereign immunity when they so wish." *American Indian Agric. Credit Consortium, Inc. v. Standing Rock Sioux Tribe*, 780 F.2d 1374, 1379 (8th Cir. 1985). McClendon could have negotiated a term in the lease agreement governing consent to suit. Given that courts consistently have required express and unequivocal waiver of sovereign immunity, if McClendon failed to negotiate such a waiver, considerations of equity are not in McClendon's favor.

Although we hold that initiation of the 1972 Clark litigation does not, in itself, constitute waiver of sovereign immunity with respect to this action, our inquiry does not end there. We must also determine whether the Tribe consented to this suit in the settlement documents filed with the district court, the Clark lease, or the McClendon lease. We conclude that nothing in any of these documents manifests the Tribe's consent to suit over disputes involving interpretation of the lease provisions.

Nothing in the settlement documents presented to the district court indicates an intent to waive sovereign immunity with respect to any further disputes arising between the Tribe and the Clarks or their successors-in-interest. Moreover, the leases themselves contain no provision governing sovereign immunity or consent to suit. Thus, the second rationale for finding waiver of sovereign immunity in *United States v. Oregon*, 657 F.2d at 1016, also has no application to this case.[5]

---

[5] The settlement agreement in that case contained a clause stating that

[i]n the event that significant management problems arise from this agreement that cannot be resolved by mutual agreement, the parties agree to submit the issues to federal court for determination. In any event, the Court shall retain jurisdiction over the case of *U.S. v. Oregon*, Civil 68-513 (D.C. Or.)

Id. at 1016 (emphasis added). As we noted earlier, such a provision could have been negotiated in this case, but it was not.

Not only are the relevant documents in this case silent with respect to the Tribe's consent to suit, but the Tribe presented evidence to the district court indicating that certain language in an early draft of the Clark lease which could possibly have been read as a waiver of sovereign immunity was deleted from the lease. After the Tribe's attorneys discovered this language, it was removed, and the redrafted language was incorporated into the lease executed by the Clarks and the Tribe. Thus, as the district court noted, the possibility of waiver of sovereign immunity was expressly contemplated, and rejected, by the Tribe. There was no consent to suit over the terms of the Clark lease, or the later McClendon lease....

III. *Jurisdiction Over the United States*

McClendon sued the United States as well as the Tribe. Although we have determined that there is no jurisdiction over the Tribe, we must decide whether this action can be maintained against the United States alone. We hold that it cannot. Because the Tribe is a party to the lease agreement sought to be enforced, it is an indispensable party under Fed. R. Civ. P. 19. See *Lomayaktewa v. Hathaway*, 520 F.2d 1324, 1325-26 (9th Cir. 1975), *cert. denied*, 425 U.S. 903 (1976); see also *Jicarilla Tribe*, 821 F.2d at 540. Any judgment in favor of McClendon will adversely affect the Tribe's interests, and because the relief sought by McClendon relates to the activities of the Tribe, any relief obtained in the Tribe's absence would be inadequate. McClendon's action must be dismissed in its entirety.

IV. *Conclusion*

The initiation of the 1972 suit against the Clarks does not, in itself, constitute waiver of the Tribe's sovereign immunity against this action to enforce the terms of a lease, even though the lease was entered into as a result of an agreement to settle the earlier suit. The Tribe did not manifest unequivocal consent to suit in the settlement documents, the Clark lease, or the McClendon lease. Thus, McClendon's action against the Tribe is barred by sovereign immunity. The Tribe is an indispensable party under Rule 19, so the action cannot be maintained solely against the United States. The district court's judgment is *Affirmed.*

NOTE: TRIBAL SOVEREIGN IMMUNITY AND BUSINESS AGREEMENTS

The combined impact of the doctrines of sovereign immunity and the indispensable party doctrine evident in *McClendon* poses a common problem for the judicial enforcement of business documents involving Indian lands and Indian tribes where the parties have not thoroughly considered these questions beforehand. *E.g., Enterprise Mgt. Consultants, Inc. v. United States ex rel. Hodel*, 883 F.2d 890 (10th Cir. 1989) *and Jicarilla Apache Tribe v. Hodel*, 821 F.2d 537 (10th Cir. 1987). Some special problems with the doctrine of tribal sovereign immunity recently were noted by Justice White, dissenting from the denial of review in *Pueblo of Acoma v. Padilla*, 109 S. Ct. 1767 (1989):

Respondent Frank Padilla, a roofing consultant, filed suit in New Mexico state court alleging a breach of contract by petitioner Pueblo of Acoma, doing business as Sky City Contractors. Petitioner had hired respondent to supervise Sky City's installation of roofs on two building projects located off the Acoma Indian Reservation. The New Mexico Supreme Court held that petitioner was not protected from suit by tribal sovereign immunity. According to the New Mexico Court, a State's "exercise of jurisdiction over a sovereign Indian tribe for off-reservation conduct is solely a matter of comity." App. to Pet. for Cert. 10 (citing *Nevada v. Hall*, 440 U.S. 410 (1979)). Because the State of New Mexico allows breach of contract actions to be brought against itself, the Court reasoned, such actions were allowable against Indian tribes as well.

This decision conflicts with decisions of the Arizona courts applying tribal sovereign immunity to off-reservation activities. In *Morgan v. Colorado River Indian Tribe*, 103 Ariz. 425, 427-428, 443 P.2d 421, 423-424 (1968), the Arizona Supreme Court held that the Colorado River Indian Tribe was immune from suit for an accident at the Blue Water Marina Park, a tribal enterprise located outside the boundaries of its reservation. The Court did not treat the question as one of comity; indeed, the Court noted that under identical circumstances the State of Arizona would be liable. *Id.*, at 428, n.1, 443 P.2d, at 424, n.1. See also *S. Unique, Ltd. v. Gila River Pima-Maricopa Indian Community*, 138 Ariz. 378, 380-381, 674 P.2d 1376, 1378-1379 (App. 1983) (breach of contract action arising out of business transaction initiated off reservation). The doctrine of tribal sovereign immunity, as applied by the Arizona courts, extends not only to an Indian tribe but also to a "subordinate economic organization" of the tribe. *White Mountain Apache Indian Tribe v. Shelley*, 107 Ariz. 4, 6-7, 480 P.2d 654, 656-657 (1971); *Smith Plumbing Co. v. Aetna Casualty & Surety Co.*, 149 Ariz. 524, 532, 720 P.2d 499, 507, *cert. denied*, 479 U.S. 987 (1986). The New Mexico Supreme Court expressly recognized that Sky City Contractors was a subordinate economic organization of petitioner, App. to Pet. for Cert. 8 (citing *White Mountain Apache, supra*), yet nevertheless held that it was not immune from suit.

An opportunity to resolve this conflict was presented by our grant of certiorari in *Oklahoma Tax Comm'n v. Graham*, 109 S. Ct. 52 (1988), although we ultimately decided the case on other grounds. In that case, two questions were before us: whether the case had been properly removed to federal court and whether tribal sovereign immunity barred an action to collect taxes "on commercial activities conducted by an Indian tribe on off-reservation lands." We held that the case had not been properly removed, and as a result did not need to reach the sovereign immunity question. The present case provides an opportunity to resolve the issue we did not reach in *Graham* and thereby to resolve the conflict among the state courts.

I would grant the petition for certiorari and resolve the question on which we previously granted certiorari but did not decide.

As discussed in Justice White's dissent, efforts to structure contractual relationships to provide for off-reservation contractual performance, if possible, or to use subordinate economic organizations are two common contractual means employed, short of a blanket waiver, to ameliorate the consequences of tribal sovereign immunity for parties who contract with tribal operations. *Compare Namekagon Dev. Co. v. Bois Forte Reservation Hous. Auth.*, 517 F.2d 508 (8th Cir. 1975) (subordinate tribal housing authority set up under a tribal ordinance that authorized the housing authority "to sue or be sued in its corporate name" could be sued by a housing contractor where the source of funds for payment was federal HUD program funds) *with Padilla v. Pueblo of Acoma*, 107 N.M. 174, 754 P.2d 845 (1988), *cert. denied*, 109 S. Ct. 1767 (1989) (tribal sovereign immunity extended to Sky City Contractors, a subordinate economic enterprise of the Pueblo of Acoma, for contractual claims). *See also R.C. Hedreen Co. v. Crow Tribal Hous. Auth.*, 521 F. Supp. 599 (D. Mont. 1981). Another common contractual approach to resolving sovereign immunity concerns involves the posting of a performance bond by the tribe, thereby insuring tribal payment or other performance. In *White Mountain Apache Tribe v. Smith Plumbing Co.*, 856 F.2d 1301 (9th Cir. 1988), the court sustained the authority of state courts to entertain an action to enforce such a performance bond against a non-Indian insurer, so long as the only funds or assets affected by the judgment were those of the non-Indian insurer. Another common method of anticipating such sovereign immunity concerns involves arbitration clauses. Arbritration agreements, like all other contracts, however, sometimes must be judicially enforced. Consider the efficacy of arbitration agreements in avoiding tribal sovereign immunity defenses in light of the case that follows.

STOCK WEST, INC. v. CONFEDERATED TRIBES OF THE COLVILLE RESERVATION

873 F.2d 1221 (9th Cir. 1989)

TANG, Circuit Judge:

Stock West, Inc. contracted with two Colville tribal entities to construct and later manage a sawmill on the Colville reservation. The tribe claimed that Stock West failed to perform its contractual duties and brought an action in tribal court. Stock West filed a demand for arbitration in tribal court pursuant to terms of the contracts. The tribal court ruled that it had jurisdiction, and ruled also that since the validity of the arbitration clauses was in doubt, the court would decide the underlying contract dispute rather than have the matter submitted to arbitration. [In *Confederated Tribes of Colville Reservation v. Stock West, Inc.*, 15 Indian L. Rep. 6019 (Colville Trib. Ct. 1988), the court ruled that the contracts in question had not been approved by the Secretary of the Interior as required by 25 U.S.C. § 81.] A February 1989 trial date has been set.

Stock West then filed an action in district court to compel arbitration and to enjoin the tribal court proceedings. The district court ruled that it had diversity jurisdiction to compel arbitration, but that it would not exercise its jurisdiction and instead would dismiss the case on the grounds of comity. On appeal, Stock West challenges the dismissal and the refusal to compel arbitration, and the tribe cross-appeals challenging the ruling that the district court had jurisdiction.

I. *Factual Background*

A. *Background to Contracts*

In November and December 1983, members of the Stock family met with representatives of the Confederated Tribes of the Colville Reservation to discuss the possibility of building a sawmill on the reservation. The meetings took place both at the Stocks' office in Oregon and on the reservation in Washington. A Professional Services Agreement ("PSA") signed by James Stock and a tribal representative on January 20, 1984, provided that "Stockwest" was to provide business and marketing plans concerning the proposed sawmill to the tribe. According to paragraph 11 of the PSA:

> [a]ll disputes over the subject matter of this agreement or performance thereof will proceed to final resolution in Colville Tribal Courts and be controlled and bound by the laws of the Colville Confederated Tribes.

B. *The Contracts: The CMA and the MMA*

The two major contracts at issue in this case are the Construction Management Agreement ("CMA") and the Management and Marketing Agreement

("MMA"). These contracts were signed on July 23, 1984 by James Stock on behalf of Stock West, and a tribal representative on behalf of Colville Tribal Enterprise Corporation ("CTEC") and Colville Indian Precision Pine Company ("CIPP").[3] These contracts were signed on the reservation.

Under the CMA, Stock West was to manage and supervise all facets of the construction of the sawmill. Stock West maintained an office at CIPP headquarters on the reservation. The construction itself was not to be performed by Stock West, but rather by tribal employees or contractors. Actual construction of the sawmill started in approximately August 1984 and was substantially completed by February 1986.

Under the MMA, Stock West was to provide management and marketing services once the sawmill was in operation. To perform these contractual obligations, James Stock was made a director and president of CIPP. Stock West also opened a sales office in Portland, Oregon and served as a selling agent of CIPP.

For the purposes of the present controversy, the most relevant provisions of the contracts are the sections dealing with arbitration,[4] choice of law,[5] and waiver of sovereign immunity.[6] But unlike the PSA, neither the CMA nor the MMA include a provision vesting jurisdiction in tribal court.

II. *Procedural Background*

A. *Tribal Court Proceedings*

According to the tribe, Stock West failed to perform its contractual duties. Around July 15, 1986, the tribal parties served on Stock West a Notice of Default.[7] Stock West filed a response on July 28, 1986 in which it did not answer the tribe's claims of default but instead filed a demand for arbitration and selected an arbitrator as per the terms of the contracts. The tribe refused to

---

[3] CTEC was an entity separate from the tribal Business Council and was created to deal with the building of the sawmill. CIPP was organized as a wholly owned subsidiary of CTEC to own and operate the sawmill after completion. Both CTEC and CIPP were organized and chartered pursuant to tribal law.

[4] The CMA (Section 6) and the MMA (Section 12) have identical arbitration clauses which provide in part that:

[a]ll claims disputes and other matters in question between the parties arising out of or relating to this agreement or the breach thereof shall be decided in accordance with the following procedure. Either party may demand arbitration and appoint an arbitrator, and the other party shall appoint a second arbitrator within thirty (30) days after being notified in writing of the appointment of the first arbitrator. The two arbitrators shall select a third, and the decision of the three arbitrators or a majority of them shall be final and binding on both parties.... This provision shall be specifically enforceable.... The award rendered by the arbitrators shall be final, and judgment may be rendered upon it in accordance with applicable law in any court having jurisdiction thereof.

[5] The CMA (Section 14b) indicates that "[t]he validity, meaning, enforceability and effect of this agreement, and the rights and liabilities of the parties hereto, shall be determined in accordance with the laws of Washington." The MMA (Section 20.2), with identical language, provides that Oregon law is to apply.

[6] Both the CMA (Section 11) and the MMA (Section 18) provide that "CIPP and CTEC hereby expressly waive their sovereign immunity from suit or action in a court of competent jurisdiction by Stock West for all matters arising out of or relating to this agreement."

[7] Section 7.1 of the CMA and Section 14.1 of the MMA ("Default by Stock West") allow CTEC or CIPP to terminate the contract in the event of Stock West's default. Default is defined to include the failure of Stock West to perform any contractual duty.

agree to arbitration and refused to pay Stock West sums that Stock West says was owed.

On July 30, 1986, the tribe filed for (a) declaratory and injunctive relief, (b) recoupment of money paid and damages, and (c) a temporary restraining order (TRO). The tribal court issued the TRO. An amended complaint was filed on March 4, 1987.

On August 7, 1986, Stock West filed a Special Appearance in tribal court and entered into a Stipulated Joint Motion for Continuance on the hearing for the preliminary injunction. On August 22, 1986, the tribal court entered a preliminary injunction restraining Stock West from interfering with operations at the mill and requiring the tribe to post a bond.

On August 17, 1987, after full briefing and oral argument, the tribal court ruled in a published decision that it had jurisdiction over the defendants. *Confederated Tribes of the Colville Reservation v. Stock West*, 14 Ind. L. Rep. 6025 (Colville Tribal Ct. 1987).

Stock West then filed motions to dismiss the tribe's action and to compel arbitration under the terms of the contracts and the federal Arbitration Act. 9 U.S.C. §§ 1-4. Again after full briefing and oral argument, the tribal court denied these motions on May 2, 1988, ruling that the CMA and MMA were void for lack of Bureau of Indian Affairs (BIA) approval[8] and that the tribe's claims are thus a matter for the court, not an arbitrator, to resolve. *Confederated Tribes of the Colville Reservation v. Stock West*, 15 Ind. L. Rep. 6019 (Colville Tribal Ct. 1988).

On July 25, 1988, the tribal court entered a pretrial order setting discovery deadlines. A trial date was set for February 13, 1989.

B. *District Court Proceedings*

On April 7, 1987, Stock West filed an action in federal district court to compel arbitration under the terms of the CMA and the MMA and to enjoin the tribal parties from pursuing the matter in tribal court. After a hearing, the district court granted the tribe's motion to dismiss.[9] Although the district court found that it had diversity jurisdiction under 28 U.S.C. § 1332, it dismissed Stock West's action, ruling that out of a sense of comity this Court should abstain in favor of Tribal Court jurisdiction, which [Stock West] concedes is concurrent.

Stock West now brings this appeal, challenging the district court's dismissal of its action and refusal to compel arbitration. The tribe cross-appeals, challenging the district court's determination that it had jurisdiction to compel arbitration.

---

[8]According to 25 U.S.C. § 81, [n]o agreement shall be made by any person with any tribe of Indians ... for the payment or delivery of any money or other thing of value, ... unless such agreement ... shall bear the approval of the Secretary of the Interior and the Commissioner of Indian Affairs indorsed upon it." Both the CMA and the MMA make reference to 25 U.S.C. § 81. Section 14 of the CMA indicates compliance with other provisions of 25 U.S.C. § 81 and the MMA includes a provision to be signed by the BIA. But no BIA approval was ever obtained for the contracts. *Confederated Tribes of the Colville Reservation v. Stock West*, 15 Ind. L. Rep. 6019 (Colville Tribal Ct. 1988).

[9]Originally, the defendants in the federal action were the tribe itself, the tribal business council, CTEC, and CIPP. At the time of the district court's dismissal order, only CTEC and CIPP remained as defendants.

Does Federal Subject Matter Jurisdiction Exist?

In considering the jurisdiction questions, it should be remembered that "[i]t is a fundamental principle that federal courts are courts of limited jurisdiction." A federal court is presumed to lack jurisdiction in a particular case unless the contrary affirmatively appears [in the federal jurisdictional statutes].

A. Federal Question Jurisdiction Under 28 U.S.C. § 1331

It is clear that with respect to the underlying substantive dispute, the tribe is correct in declaring that no federal question jurisdiction exists in this case.

[Plaintiff] Stock West's reliance on the Arbitration Act, 9 U.S.C. §§ 1-4, is insufficient to confer federal question jurisdiction. *General Atomic Co. v. United Nuclear Corp.*, 655 F.2d 968 (9th Cir. 1981), *cert. denied*, 455 U.S. 948 (1982).

In addition, federal question jurisdiction does not exist merely because an Indian tribe is a party or the case involves a contract with an Indian tribe.[11] "Otherwise the federal courts might become a small claims court for all such disputes." *Gila River Indian Community v. Henningson, Durham & Richardson*, 626 F.2d 708, 715 (9th Cir. 1980), *cert. denied*, 451 U.S. 911 (1981).[12]

B. Diversity Jurisdiction Under 28 U.S.C. § 1332

In considering whether federal diversity jurisdiction exists, aside from issues of exhaustion and comity, the wording of 28 U.S.C. § 1332 must be considered, which provides in relevant part that

> [t]he district courts shall have original jurisdiction of all civil actions where the matter in controversy exceeds the sum or value of $10,000, exclusive of interest and costs, and is between (1) citizens of different States; (2) citizens of a State and citizens or subjects of a foreign state ....

28 U.S.C. § 1332(a).

1. *Citizenship of Tribal Parties.* Regarding the citizenship of the tribal parties for the purposes of diversity jurisdiction, first, it is perhaps clear that an Indian tribe is not a foreign state. *Cherokee Nation v. Georgia*, 30 U.S. (5 Pet.) 1, 20 (1831). Thus, diversity jurisdiction must depend upon the tribal parties, CTEC and CIPP, being a resident of the state in whose borders the reservation is located, in this case, Washington. There is authority for the proposition that for purposes of diversity jurisdiction, an Indian corporation is a citizen of the state in whose borders the reservation is located [*See, e.g.,*] *R.J. Williams Co. v. Fort Belknap Hous. Auth.*, 719 F.2d 979, 982 n.2 (9th Cir. 1983), *cert. denied*, 472 U.S. 1016 (1985) (tribal housing authority considered Montana citizen for diversity purposes); [*see also*] W. Canby, American Indian Law 151 (1981) (For diversity purposes, "Indians are citizens of the states where they reside.").

---

[11] "Stock West argues that since the tribe waived its sovereign immunity in both the CMA (Section 11) and in the MMA (Section 18), the federal courts thus have jurisdiction. This argument is weak. Mere consent to be sued does not confer jurisdiction on any particular court. *Weeks Constr., Inc. v. Oglala Sioux Hous. Auth.*, 797 F.2d 668 (8th Cir. 1986).

[12] Nevertheless, as discussed below, the issue of whether the tribal court has jurisdiction is a federal question that a federal court may consider after tribal court remedies have been exhausted.

2. *Citizenship of Stock West.* Since the amount in controversy exceeds $10,000, the remaining question is whether Stock West is also a Washington citizen, in which case diversity would be defeated. For the purposes of diversity jurisdiction, a corporation is a citizen of any state in which it is incorporated and of the state where it has its principal place of business. 28 U.S.C. § 1332(c). In *Co-Efficient Energy Sys. v. CSL Indus., Inc.*, 812 F.2d 556 (9th Cir. 1987), for example, a corporation incorporated in Nevada but with a principal place of business in California sued California defendants. The court ruled that as per 28 U.S.C. § 1332(c), no diversity jurisdiction existed and that the case was properly dismissed. Similarly, in the instant case, the tribe argues that although Stock West was incorporated in Oregon, its sole place of business was in Washington and thus it should be considered a Washington citizen for diversity purposes.

We presume that the factual basis for the district court's finding of diversity jurisdiction was that the tribal parties were citizens of Washington and that Stock West was a citizen of Oregon. We defer to the district court on this factual issue and find that the parties are of diverse citizenship.

3. *Diversity Jurisdiction.* Given the existence of diversity of citizenship between the parties and at least $10,000 in controversy, the next question is whether the district court necessarily had diversity jurisdiction under 28 U.S.C. § 1332 considering the presence of tribal parties.

> The diversity jurisdiction of federal courts is more limited in Indian country than it is elsewhere. The limitation arises from the fact that federal courts in diversity cases sit as alternatives to the state courts and apply state law. In that capacity, they have the same potential of interfering with tribal self-government that the state courts do.

W. Canby, American Indian Law 151-52 (1981).

According to *R.J. Williams Co. v. Fort Belknap Hous. Auth.*, 719 F.2d 979, 982 (9th Cir. 1983), in order for a federal court to have diversity jurisdiction, "the courts of the state in which the federal court sits must be able to entertain the action." See also *Hot Oil Serv., Inc. v. Hall*, 366 F.2d 295, 297 (9th Cir. 1966) ("In our case, the District Court could not have had diversity jurisdiction unless the state court would also have had subject-matter jurisdiction."). Following this reasoning, because the Washington state courts would arguably not have jurisdiction to hear the instant case under the holding of *Williams v. Lee*, 358 U.S. 217 (1959), no diversity jurisdiction would exist.

The vitality of the reasoning set forth in *R.J. Williams*, *Hot Oil*, and *Woods*, however, is now dubious in light of the Supreme Court's opinion in *Iowa Mutual Ins. Co. v. LaPlante*, 480 U.S. 9 (1987), which involved diversity of citizenship between Indian and non-Indian parties, and presumably an amount in controversy exceeding $10,000. The federal District Court in *Iowa Mutual*, citing *Woods*, noted that since the Montana state courts lacked jurisdiction over the suit, it also lacked subject matter jurisdiction and dismissed the case. 480 U.S. 13. We affirmed in an unpublished opinion. 774 F.2d 1174 (9th Cir. 1985). The Supreme Court held in favor of deferral to the tribal courts, but ruled that we "should not have affirmed the District Court's dismissal for lack of subject-matter jurisdiction." 480 U.S. 19-20. Therefore, a federal court may have diversity jurisdiction under 28 U.S.C. § 1332 with tribal parties even if the state courts would not have jurisdiction. We thus hold that the district court below correctly held in favor of diversity jurisdiction. The tribe's cross-appeal is denied.

IV. *Did the District Court Err in Not Exercising Its Jurisdiction and in Dismissing the Case on the Grounds of Comity?*

Having found subject matter jurisdiction, the next question is whether the district court should have exercised its jurisdiction or deferred to the tribal court. We analyze this question in a two-step process, first by considering whether the tribal court has jurisdiction, and second by considering the public policies underlying the principle of comity in this context.

A. *Does the Tribal Court Have Jurisdiction?*

Once all tribal remedies are exhausted and the tribal courts finally decide that tribal jurisdiction exists, then the district court can decide the question of tribal jurisdiction. This determination is in itself a "federal question" which federal courts have jurisdiction to review under 28 U.S.C. § 1331. *National Farmers Union Ins. Co. v. Crow Tribe of Indians*, 471 U.S. 845, 852 (1985). Thus, in the instant case, if tribal remedies were exhausted on the jurisdiction issue, the district court would have jurisdiction under 28 U.S.C. § 1331 to review the tribal court's finding of jurisdiction. By deferring to the tribal court proceedings because of comity, the district court was essentially ruling that the tribal court has jurisdiction to hear the case. We have jurisdiction to review this decision under 28 U.S.C. § 1291.

The Colville Tribal Law and Order Code, § 1.9.01, provides for a three-judge tribal Appellate Court "to hear appeals from final judgments, sentences, and other final orders of the Trial Court." Presumably, the Colville Appellate Court could review the trial court's findings as to tribal jurisdiction in the instant case, though not necessarily on an interlocutory basis. Therefore, under *National Farmers*, the federal courts should not even make a ruling on tribal court jurisdiction in this case until tribal remedies are exhausted. We could dismiss on this basis alone.

Assuming, arguendo, that the federal courts could decide the tribal jurisdiction question, the tribal courts have jurisdiction to hear this case, even if the jurisdiction is concurrent with the federal judiciary. "Although the criminal jurisdiction of the tribal courts is subject to substantial federal limitation, their civil jurisdiction is not similarly restricted." *Iowa Mutual*, 480 U.S. at 13 (citation omitted).

There is no simple test for determining whether tribal court jurisdiction exists. The Court in National Farmers concluded that

> the answer to the question whether a tribal court has the power to exercise civil subject-matter jurisdiction over non-Indians ... is not automatically foreclosed.... Rather, the existence and extent of a tribal court's jurisdiction will require a careful examination of tribal sovereignty, the extent to which that sovereignty has been altered, divested, or diminished, as well as a detailed study of relevant statutes, Executive Branch policy as embodied in treaties and elsewhere, and administrative or judicial decisions.

471 U.S. at 855-56.

Also, the Court in *Iowa Mutual* noted that civil jurisdiction over the activities of non-Indians on reservation lands "presumptively lies in the tribal courts unless affirmatively limited by a specific treaty provision or federal statute." 480 U.S. at 18. The court went on to point out that in matters concerning reservation affairs, "tribal courts are best qualified to interpret and apply tribal law." *Id.* at 16.

In the instant case, it seems clear that the tribal court has jurisdiction. The dispute arises out of the reservation and concerns tribal resources, and there are apparently no treaties or statutes[16] that would limit tribal court jurisdiction in this case. In addition, Colville tribal law explicitly provides for jurisdiction in cases like this.[17]

As an additional issue, the tribe claims that the question of tribal jurisdiction is moot because Stock West had consented to tribal jurisdiction. The tribe cites the case of *Cowan v. Rosebud Sioux Tribe*, 404 F. Supp. 1338 (D.S.D. 1975) to support this argument. But the *Cowan* case merely stands for the proposition that personal jurisdiction may be waived by contract. On the other hand, a party cannot waive by consent or contract a court's lack of subject matter jurisdiction. Thus, even if the consent of Stock West was adequate to confer personal jurisdiction onto the tribal court, the question of whether the tribal court has subject matter jurisdiction over the case would still not be resolved.

B. *Was the District Court's Deferral to the Tribal Court on the Grounds of Comity Appropriate?*

Because abstention involves the discretionary exercise of a court's equity powers, it is reviewed only for an abuse of discretion.

[The Supreme Court's decision in the] *Iowa Mutual* case, 480 U.S. 9 (1987), is directly relevant to this issue. In *Iowa Mutual*, LaPlante, a Blackfeet Indian, sued Iowa Mutual, an Iowa corporation, in Blackfeet Tribal Court for damages resulting from a truck accident on the reservation. The Blackfeet reservation is located within the borders of Montana. The tribal court ruled that it had jurisdiction to hear the case. Iowa Mutual, asserting diversity jurisdiction, then brought an action in federal court against LaPlante seeking declaratory relief. The district court dismissed the case for lack of subject matter jurisdiction and we affirmed. 774 F.2d 1174 (9th Cir. 1985). The Supreme Court reversed, ruling that the district court should not have dismissed but should have either (a) retained jurisdiction and stayed any action pending the tribal courts' resolution of the jurisdiction question, or (b) prudentially dismissed the case in favor of the tribal court proceedings. *Iowa Mutual*, 480 U.S. at 19-20. The Court, reiterating the holding of *National Farmers*, 471 U.S. at 856, that exhaustion of

[16] Stock West argues that the strong federal policy favoring arbitration, such as embodied in the Arbitration Act, 9 U.S.C. § 2, should overcome the policy of comity in favor of the tribal court. But Stock West does not argue that the Arbitration Act deprives the tribal court of jurisdiction. Furthermore, particularly since the validity of the arbitration clauses in the contracts [is itself] in dispute, Stock West's argument that the federal courts should not defer to the tribal court is weak.

[17] "The jurisdiction of the Tribal Court and the effective area of this Code shall include all territory within the Reservation boundaries, and the lands outside the boundaries of the Reservation held in trust by the United States for Tribal members of the Tribes, and it shall be over all persons therein...." Colville Law and Order Code § 1.3.01. The Code further provides that tribal jurisdiction is to be concurrent with "any valid" federal or state jurisdiction. § 1.3.02.

tribal remedies is a prerequisite to a federal action, held that since Iowa Mutual had not fully exhausted tribal remedies by appealing to the Blackfeet Tribal Appeals Court, the federal action should not proceed. *Iowa Mutual*, 480 U.S. at 19.

Also, in *Wellman v. Chevron U.S.A., Inc.*, 815 F.2d 577 (9th Cir. 1987), a Blackfeet Indian contractor brought a diversity action for breach of contract against a non-Indian corporation involving work that was to have been performed on tribal lands. The district court dismissed for lack of subject matter jurisdiction. Citing *Iowa Mutual*, we found that "[t]he ruling was correct though based on the wrong reason. The dismissal should have been based upon comity, rather than lack of subject matter jurisdiction." *Wellman*, 815 F.2d at 578; *see also Littell v. Nakai*, 344 F.2d 486, 489 (9th Cir. 1965) (even though the litigation "falls within the letter of the diversity statute, we believe that the basic principle of diversity jurisdiction requires reference of the suit to the Navajo Tribal Courts"), *cert. denied*, 382 U.S. 986 (1966).

Indeed, the existence of diversity jurisdiction does not preclude a federal court from deferring to tribal proceedings because of comity.

> [T]he diversity ... statute makes no reference to Indians and nothing in the legislative history suggests any intent to render inoperative the established federal policy promoting tribal self-government.

Iowa Mutual, 480 U.S. at 17.

Furthermore, the requirement for exhaustion can exist in the presence of federal jurisdiction. The Court in *Iowa Mutual* specifically noted that the requirement of exhaustion of tribal remedies does not deprive the federal courts of jurisdiction. 480 U.S. at 16 n.8.

It was proper for the district court to defer on the grounds of comity. The correctness of the district court's application of comity is supported by the facts that "Congress is committed to a policy of supporting tribal self-government and self-determination." *National Farmers*, 471 U.S. at 856 (footnote omitted), and that "[t]ribal authority over the activities of non-Indians on reservation lands is an important part of tribal sovereignty." *Iowa Mutual*, 480 U.S. at 18. Indeed, "[i]n diversity cases, ... unconditional access to the federal forum would place it in direct competition with the tribal courts, thereby impairing the latter's authority over reservation affairs." *Id.* at 16.

[*Affirmed.*]

D. TAXATION AND REGULATION OF INDIAN LEASED LAND: THE POTENTIAL FOR LOSS OF TRIBAL CONTROL

As amended in 1970, 25 U.S.C. § 415(a) requires the Secretary of the Interior *inter alia* to "satisfy himself [of] ... the availability of police and fire protection and other services; the availability of judicial forums for all criminal and civil causes arising on the leased land...." Significantly, the statutory requirement only calls for review of issues of adjudicatory jurisdiction when the more difficult questions involve the effect of leasing to non-Indian developers on tribal and state legislative taxing and regulatory authority. This section is devoted to a review of the effect of leasing of Indian land to non-Indian developers and other economic development activity on the adjudicatory and legislative powers of the tribal governments and the states. As a preliminary matter, it should be noted that the federal government has imposed taxes on the revenues or income derived by non-Indians from the development of Indian lands and its power to do so seems unquestionable. *See, e.g., Heiner v. Colonial Trust Co.,* 275 U.S. 232 (1927). *Contrast Squire v. Capoeman,* 351 U.S. 1 (1956) (sale of standing timber on allotted lands received by Indian owner not subject to capital gains tax); *Clark v. United States,* 587 F.2d 465 (10th Cir. 1978) (federal income taxes inapplicable to oil and gas bonuses and delivery rentals paid to noncompetent restricted members of Five Civilized Tribes on mineral development of restricted allotted land).

If we set aside for a moment the cultural aspects of development, it is clear that unless their rate of return provides adequate compensation, investors will seek some confidence and predictability in certain aspects of their investment. One of the most important issues confronting a potential developer is exposure to taxation. There are at least two parts to this issue: state taxation of non-Indian activities on Indian lands and tribal taxation of the same activities. The answers to such questions and the relationship of state and tribal taxing and regulatory authority will play an important role in the pace and strategy of non-Indian investment decisions on Indian lands.

This section will focus on questions of tribal and state power to tax and regulate the economic development of Indian lands. Since this section draws on questions of tribal and state authority covered in Chapters 3 and 4, it necessarily draws and elaborates on some of the cases set forth in those chapters.

1. STATE TAXATION OF NON-INDIAN DEVELOPMENT

One of the more important current issues involves state taxation of leases, personal property, and activities conducted on Indian lands by non-Indians. For Indians the issue involves key questions of sovereignty and control as well as competition for a great source of badly needed tribal revenue in some cases. States and counties see such conduct as opportunistic, seeking a tax haven and competitive advantage without any real relationships to the Indian cultural and political mission. Early Supreme Court decisions such as *Thomas v. Gay,* 169 U.S. 264 (1898) (unsuccessful challenge by non-Indian lessee of grazing land on Osage Reservation in the Oklahoma Territory to a territorial statute authorizing counties to levy property taxes on cattle and other personal property), supported the notion that states and municipalities could tax non-Indian developers on Indian land only when their taxes had no direct effect on Indians or their property:

> As to that portion of the argument which claims that, even if the Indians were not interested in any way in the property taxed, the territorial authorities would have no right to tax the property of others than Indians located upon these reservations, it is sufficient to cite the cases of *Utah & Northern Railway v. Fisher,* 116 U.S. 28, and *Maricopa & Phoenix Railroad v. Arizona,* 156 U.S. 347, in which it was held that the property of railway companies traversing Indian reservations are subject to taxation by the States and Territories in which such reservations are located.
>
> But it is urged that the Indians are directly and vitally interested in the property sought to be taxed, and that their rights of property and person are seriously affected by the legislation complained of: that the money contracted to be paid for the privilege

of grazing is paid to the Indians as a tribe, and is used and expended by them for their own purposes, and that if, by reason of this taxation, the conditions existing at the time the leases were executed were changed, or could be changed by the legislature of Oklahoma at its pleasure, the value of the lands for such purposes would fluctuate or be destroyed altogether according to such conditions.

But it is obvious that a tax put upon the cattle of the lessees is too remote and indirect to be deemed a tax upon the lands or privileges of the [Indians or their tribes].

[The argument] that such a tax on the cattle constitutes a tax on the lands within the reasoning in the case of *Pollock v. Farmers' Loan and Trust Co.,* 157 U.S. 429, is purely fanciful. The holding there was that a tax on rents derived from lands was substantially a tax on the lands. To make the present case a similar one the tax should have been levied on the rents received by the Indians, and not on the cattle belonging to third parties.

It is further contended that this tax law of the Territory of Oklahoma, in so far as it affects the Indian reservations, is in conflict with the constitutional power of Congress to regulate commerce with the Indian tribes. It is said to interfere with, or impose a servitude upon, a lawful commercial intercourse with the Indians, over which Congress has absolute control, and in the exercise of which control it has enacted the statute authorizing the leasing by the Indians of their unoccupied lands for grazing purposes.

The unlimited power of Congress to deal with the Indians, their property and commercial transactions, so long as they keep up their tribal organizations, may be conceded; but it is not perceived that local taxation, by a State or Territory, of property of others than Indians would be an interference with Congressional power. It was decided in *Utah & Northern Railway v. Fisher,* 116 U.S. 28, that the lands and railroad of a railway company within the limits of the Fort Hill Indian reservation in the Territory of Idaho was lawfully subject to territorial taxation, which might be enforced within the exterior boundaries of the reservation by proper process. The question was similarly decided in *Maricopa & Phoenix Railroad v. Arizona Territory,* 156 U.S. 347.

The taxes in question here were not imposed on the business of grazing, or on the rents received by the Indians, but on the cattle as property of the lessees, and, as we have heretofore said that as such a tax is too remote and indirect to be deemed a tax or burthen on interstate commerce, so is it too remote and indirect to be regarded as an interference with the legislative power of Congress.

The rule in *Thomas v. Gay* clearly derived from earlier cases authorizing states and territories to tax the value of non-Indian-owned railroad property located within Indian reservations. *Maricopa & P.R.R. v. Arizona,* 156 U.S. 347 (1895); *Utah & N. Ry. v. Fisher,* 116 U.S. 28 (1885). These cases authorized state and territorial taxation of non-Indians in Indian country only as to matters that did not interfere with the treaty protections of Indians. Thus, if state taxation of non-Indians adversely affected Indian interests, *Utah & N. Ry.* suggested that the exercise of state authority was precluded. Consequently, in *Gay* the Court carefully limited its holding to taxation of the cattle, rather than the leasehold or the underlying property, each of which might involve the interests of the Indian tribe. *See also Wagoner v. Evans,* 170 U.S. 588 (1898); *Truscott v. Hurlbut Land & Cattle Co.,* 73 Fed. 60 (9th Cir. 1896). Except for one district court case, the doctrine of *Thomas v. Gay* thus remained for most of this century a relatively narrow authorization for states to tax non-Indian property in Indian country where no Indian interest was involved. The only case expanding the rule of *Thomas v. Gay* in any significant fashion was *United States v. Erie County,* 31 F. Supp. 57 (W.D.N.Y. 1939). In *Erie County* the court held that leasehold interests in Indian land leased for a 99-year term by a non-Indian corporation could be taxed by the county so long as tribal Indians did not bear the ultimate liability for the tax. *Contrast United States v. City of Salamanca,* 31 F. Supp. 60 (W.D.N.Y. 1939) (Indian lands leased to tribal member not taxable).

Discovery of significant oil and gas resources in Oklahoma after the turn of the century produced a series of Supreme Court decisions on the taxability of leasehold interests, minerals, and revenues derived from restricted trust allotments in Oklahoma. However, these cases are *sui generis* to Oklahoma. Recall from Chapter 1 that the Curtis Act had suspended the Indian tribal governments and destroyed the Indian reservations of the former Indian Territory just after the turn of the century. The former tribal lands were all allotted under the General Allotment Act or specific agreements and statutes. Thus, the case law spawned by the oil boom in Oklahoma developed in an off-reservation context. Furthermore, most of the cases were decided prior to the adoption of 18 U.S.C. § 1151(c) in 1948, which declared that restricted Indian allotments to which Indian title had not been extinguished constituted Indian country. Thus, the body of case law developed for Oklahoma is not readily applicable to problems arising on Indian reservations.

Even though the Oklahoma reservations and tribal governments had been abolished, many of the early cases treated the minerals and revenues derived by non-Indian lessees from restricted trust allotments and the leaseholds themselves as tax exempt. In *Choctaw & G.R.R. v. Harrison,* 235 U.S. 292 (1914), the Court struck down an Oklahoma tax on the gross sales of coal dug by a non-Indian lessee from mines on lands of the Choctaw and Chickasaw Indians. The mines were operated pursuant to the Atoka Agreement with the tribes, which expressly contemplated coal exploitation of Indian land for the benefit of the Indians. Thus, the Court held that the state tax illegally taxed a federal instrumentality acting under congressional authorization. The federal instrumentality doctrine was later used to strike down state property taxes upon a non-Indian mineral leasehold interest on restricted Indian land in Oklahoma. *Indian Territory Illuminating Oil Co. v. Oklahoma,* 240 U.S. 522 (1916). The same rule was applied to invalidate state income taxes applied to the income of non-Indian mineral lessees of restricted Indian allotments, *Gillespie v. Oklahoma,* 257 U.S. 501 (1922), and to property taxes imposed on minerals or oil extracted from restricted Indian lands. *Jaybird Mining Co. v. Weir,* 271 U.S. 609 (1926); *Large Oil Co. v. Howard,* 248 U.S. 549 (1919); *Howard v. Gypsy Oil Co.,* 247 U.S. 503 (1918). *See also United States v. Rickert,* 188 U.S. 432 (1903).

In *Indian Territory Illuminating Oil Co. v. Board of Equalization,* 288 U.S. 325 (1933), the Court brought the expansion of tax immunities for non-Indian lessees of restricted Indian land in Oklahoma to a grinding halt. In that case the Court sustained the application of ad valorem property taxes to the owners of ore extracted from Indian lands after it had been removed from Indian lands and stored in the lessees' ore tanks. Responding to the federal instrumentality argument, the Court said "[t]he holding of the oil in question, which had been segregated and withdrawn from the restricted lands as petitioner's exclusive property, awaiting disposition at petitioner's pleasure, was for its sole advantage and cannot be said to be so identified with its operations as a governmental instrumentality as to entitle it to exemption from the general property taxes empowered by the State in return for the protection the State afforded." 288 U.S. at 328. In *Taber v. Indian Territory Illuminating Oil Co.,* 300 U.S. 1

(1937), the Court applied the same analysis to sustain a nondiscriminatory state ad valorem property tax on equipment used by a non-Indian lessee in oil and gas operations on restricted Indian allotments in Oklahoma. Finally in *Oklahoma Tax Comm'n v. Texas Co.*, 336 U.S. 342 (1949), the Court overruled many of its prior cases and held that the non-Indian lessee of mineral rights in restricted allotted lands in Oklahoma had no immunity from nondiscriminatory state gross production and excise taxes on ore produced from such Indian lands. The Court said, "Moreover, even if the status of respondents as federal instrumentalities ... were fully conceded, it seems difficult to imagine how any substantial interference with performing their functions as such in developing the leaseholds could be thought to flow from requiring them to pay the small tax Oklahoma exacts to satisfy their shares of state expense...." 336 U.S. at 351. *See also Phillips Petr. Co. v. Oklahoma Tax Comm'n*, 542 P.2d 1303 (Okla. 1975). Would the result be different if tribal governments had survived in Oklahoma and had sought to tax or regulate non-Indian mineral development?

The *sui generis* status of the Oklahoma cases is also evidenced by the fact that even restricted Indians could be taxed in Oklahoma where authorized by Congress. In *Oklahoma Tax Comm'n v. United States*, 319 U.S. 598 (1943), the Court found that a 1933 federal statute authorized the state to tax the transfer of estates of deceased members of the Five Civilized Tribes. In *Shaw v. Gibson-Zahniser Oil Corp.*, 276 U.S. 575 (1928), the Court held that a noncompetent Indian who used the oil and gas royalties on restricted trust lands to purchase more land that previously had been subject to state, county, and municipal taxation did not acquire a tax immunity in the purchased land even though it was taken in trust title held by the Secretary of the Interior. *See also Leading Fighter v. County of Gregory*, 230 N.W.2d 114 (S.D. 1975) (land purchased in Gregory County near Rosebud Sioux Reservation by Indian with proceeds of sale of restricted trust allotment not exempt from state taxation).

More recent cases have focused on concepts of inherent tribal authority and federal statutory preemption to resolve difficult questions of taxation, particularly taxation of oil and gas or mineral development in Indian country.

MERRION v. JICARILLA APACHE TRIBE

455 U.S. 130 (1982)

[An edited version of the *Merrion* decision is set forth in Chapter 3, page 449. In *Merrion* the Court sustained the inherent sovereignty of tribes to impose tribal severance taxes on non-Indian mineral development on leased Indian lands notwithstanding the lack of any express statement of tribal taxation in the mineral leases. The Court expressly reserved the question of whether the state might have authority to impose its severance taxes on non-Indian development of the same minerals.]

MONTANA v. BLACKFEET TRIBE

471 U.S. 759 (1985)

Justice POWELL delivered the opinion of the Court.

This case presents the question whether the State of Montana may tax the Blackfeet Tribe's royalty interests under oil and gas leases issued to non-Indian lessees pursuant to the Indian Mineral Leasing Act of 1938, ch. 198, 52 Stat. 347, 25 U.S.C. § 396a et seq. (1938 Act).

I

Respondent Blackfeet Tribe filed this suit in the United States District Court for the District of Montana challenging the application of several Montana taxes[1] to the Tribe's royalty interests in oil and gas produced under leases issued by the Tribe. The leases involved unallotted lands on the Tribe's reservation and were granted to non-Indian lessees in accordance with the 1938 Act. The taxes at issue were paid to the State by the lessees and then deducted by the lessees from the royalty payments made to the Tribe. The Blackfeet sought declaratory and injunctive relief against enforcement of the state tax statutes. The Tribe argued to the District Court that the 1938 Act did not authorize the State to tax tribal royalty interests and thus that the taxes were unlawful. The District Court rejected this claim and granted the State's motion for summary judgment. The court held that the state taxes were authorized by a 1924 statute, Act of May 29, 1924, ch. 210, 43 Stat. 244, 25 U.S.C. § 398 (1924 Act), and that the 1938 Act, under which the leases in question were issued, did not repeal this authorization. The District Court was not persuaded by a 1977 opinion of the Department of the Interior supporting the Blackfeet's position, noting that the Department previously had expressed contrary views, 507 F. Supp. 446, 451 (1981).

A panel of the United States Court of Appeals for the Ninth Circuit affirmed the District Court's decision. On rehearing en banc, the Court of Appeals reversed in part and remanded the case for further proceedings. The court held that the tax authorization in the 1924 Act was not repealed by the 1938 Act and thus remained in effect for leases executed pursuant to the 1924 Act. The court also held, however, that the 1938 Act did not incorporate the tax provision of the 1924 Act, and therefore that its authorization did not apply to leases executed after the enactment of the 1938 Act. The court reasoned that the taxing provision of the 1924 Act was inconsistent with the policies of the [IRA]. Since the 1938 Act was adopted specifically to harmonize Indian leasing laws with the IRA, Congress could not have intended the 1924 Act to apply to leases issued under the 1938 Act. The court remanded the case to the District Court to determine where the legal incidence of the taxes fell, and directed the court to consider whether, if the taxes fell on the oil and gas producers instead of the Indians, the taxes were pre-empted by federal law. We granted the State's petition for certiorari to resolve whether Montana may tax Indian royalty interests arising out of leases executed after the adoption of the 1938 Act [and] affirm the decision of the en banc Court of Appeals that it may not.

II

Congress first authorized mineral leasing of Indian lands in the Act of Feb. 28, 1891, 26 Stat. 795, 25 U.S.C. § 397 (1891 Act). The Act authorized leases for

---

[1]At issue are the taxes adopted in the following statutes: the Oil and Gas Severance Tax, Mont. Code Ann. § 15-36-101 et seq. (1983); Oil and Gas Net Proceeds, Mont. Code Ann. § 15-23-601 et seq. (1983); Oil and Gas Conservation, Mont. Code Ann. § 82-11-101 et seq. (1983); and the Resource Indemnity Trust Tax, Mont. Code Ann. § 15-38-101 et seq. (1983).

terms not to exceed 10 years on lands "bought and paid for" by the Indians. The 1891 Act was amended by the 1924 Act. The amendment provided in pertinent part:

"Unallotted land ... subject to lease for mining purposes for a period of ten years under section 397 ... may be leased ... by the Secretary of the Interior, with the consent of the [Indian] council ..., for oil and gas mining purposes for a period of not to exceed ten years, and as much longer as oil or gas shall be found in paying quantities, and the terms of any existing oil and gas mining lease may in like manner be amended by extending the term thereof for as long as oil or gas shall be found in paying quantities: *Provided*, That the production of oil and gas and other minerals on such lands may be taxed by the State in which said lands are located in all respects the same as production on unrestricted lands, and the Secretary of the Interior is authorized and directed to cause to be paid the tax so assessed against the royalty interests on said lands: *Provided*, however, That such tax shall not become a lien or charge of any kind or character against the land or the property of the Indian owner." Act of May 29, 1924, ch. 210, 43 Stat. 244, 25 U.S.C. § 398.

Montana relies on the first proviso in the 1924 Act in claiming the authority to tax the Blackfeet's royalty payments.

In 1938, Congress adopted comprehensive legislation in an effort to "obtain uniformity so far as practicable of the law relating to the leasing of tribal lands for mining purposes." S. Rep. No. 985, 75th Cong., 1st Sess., 2 (1937) (hereafter Senate Report). Like the 1924 Act, the 1938 Act permitted, subject to the approval of the Secretary of the Interior, mineral leasing of unallotted lands for a period not to exceed 10 years and as long thereafter as minerals in paying quantities were produced. The Act also detailed uniform leasing procedures designed to protect the Indians. See 25 U.S.C. §§ 396b-396g. The 1938 Act did not contain a provision authorizing state taxation; nor did it repeal specifically the authorization in the 1924 Act. A general repealer clause was provided in § 7 of the Act: "All Act [sic] or parts of Acts inconsistent herewith are hereby repealed." The question presented by this case is whether the 1924 Act's proviso that authorizes state taxation was repealed by the 1938 Act, or if left intact, applies to leases executed under the 1938 Act.

III

The Constitution vests the Federal Government with exclusive authority over relations with Indian tribes. As a corollary of this authority, and in recognition of the sovereignty retained by Indian tribes even after formation of the United States, Indian tribes and individuals generally are exempt from state taxation within their own territory. In *The Kansas Indians*, 5 Wall. 737 (1867), for example, the Court ruled that lands held by Indians in common as well as those held in severalty were exempt from state taxation. It explained that "[i]f the tribal organization ... is preserved intact, and recognized by the political department of the government as existing, then they are a 'people distinct from others,' ... separated from the jurisdiction of [the State], and to be governed exclusively by the government of the Union." *Id.*, at 755. Likewise, in *The New York Indians*, 5 Wall. 761 (1867), the Court characterized the State's attempt to tax Indian reservation land as extraordinary, an "illegal" exercise of state power, *id.*, at 770, and "an unwarrantable interference, inconsistent with the original title of the Indians, and offensive to their tribal relations," *id.*, at 771.

As the Government points out, this Court has never wavered from the views expressed in these cases. [*E.g., Bryan v. Itasca County,* 426 U.S. 373, 375-378, 392-393 (1976).]

In keeping with its plenary authority over Indian affairs, Congress can authorize the imposition of state taxes on Indian tribes and individual Indians. It has not done so often, and the Court consistently has held that it will find the Indians' exemption from state taxes lifted only when Congress has made its intention to do so unmistakably clear. *E.g., Bryan v. Itasca County, supra,* at 392-393; *Carpenter v. Shaw,* 280 U.S. 363, 366-367 (1930). The 1924 Act contains such an explicit authorization. As a result, in *British-American Oil Producing Co. v. Board of Equalization of Montana,* 299 U.S. 159 (1936), the Court held that the State of Montana could tax oil and gas produced under leases executed under the 1924 Act.[3]

The State urges us that the taxing authorization provided in the 1924 Act applies to leases executed under the 1938 Act as well. It argues that nothing in the 1938 Act is inconsistent with the 1924 taxing provision and thus that the provision was not repealed by the 1938 Act. It cites decisions of this Court that a clause repealing only inconsistent Acts "implies very strongly that there may be acts on the same subject which are not thereby repealed," and that such a clause indicates Congress' intent "to leave in force some portions of former acts relative to the same subject-matter." The State also notes that there is a strong presumption against repeals by implication, [particularly] an implied repeal of a specific statute by a general one, *Morton v. Mancari,* 417 U.S. 535, 550-551 (1974). Thus, in the State's view, sound principles of statutory construction lead to the conclusion that its taxing authority under the 1924 Act remains intact.

The State fails to appreciate, however, that the standard principles of statutory construction do not have their usual force in cases involving Indian law. As we said earlier this Term, "[t]he canons of construction applicable in Indian law are rooted in the unique trust relationship between the United States and the Indians." *Oneida County v. Oneida Indian Nation,* 470 U.S. 226, 247 (1985). Two such canons are directly applicable in this case: first, the States may tax Indians only when Congress has manifested clearly its consent to such taxation, e.g., *Bryan v. Itasca County, supra,* at 393; second, statutes are to be construed liberally in favor of the Indians, with ambiguous provisions interpreted to their benefit, e.g., *McClanahan v. Arizona State Tax Comm'n,* 411 U.S. 164, 174 (1973); *Choate v. Trapp,* 224 U.S. 665, 675 (1912).[4] When the 1924 and 1938 Acts are considered in light of these principles, it is clear that the 1924 Act does not authorize Montana to enforce its tax statutes with respect to leases issued under the 1938 Act.

IV

Nothing in either the text or legislative history of the 1938 Act suggests that Congress intended to permit States to tax tribal royalty income generated by

---

[3] In *British-American Oil Producing Co. v. Board of Equalization of Montana,* the Court interpreted the statutory leasing authority over lands "bought and paid for by the Indians" to include land reserved for the Indians in exchange for their cession or surrender of other lands or rights, as well as that acquired by Indians for money.

[4] Indeed, the Court has held that although tax exemptions generally are to be construed narrowly, in "the Government's dealings with the Indians the rule is exactly the contrary. The construction, instead of being strict, is liberal ...." *Choate v. Trapp,* 224 U.S., at 675.

leases issued pursuant to that Act. The statute contains no explicit consent to state taxation. Nor is there any indication that Congress intended to incorporate implicitly in the 1938 Act the taxing authority of the 1924 Act.[5] Contrary to the State's suggestion, under the applicable principles of statutory construction, the general repealer clause of the 1938 Act cannot be taken to incorporate consistent provisions of earlier laws. The clause surely does not satisfy the requirement that Congress clearly consent to state taxation. Nor would the State's interpretation satisfy the rule requiring that statutes be construed liberally in favor of the Indians.

Moreover, the language of the taxing provision of the 1924 Act belies any suggestion that it carries over to the 1938 Act.[6] The tax proviso in the 1924 Act states that "the production of oil and gas and other minerals on such lands may be taxed by the State in which said lands are located ...." 25 U.S.C. § 398. Even applying ordinary principles of statutory construction, "such lands" refers to "[u]nallotted land ... subject to lease for mining purposes ... under section 397 [the 1891 Act]." When the statute is "liberally construed ... in favor of the Indians," *Alaska Pacific Fisheries v. United States*, 248 U.S. 78, 89 (1918), it is clear that if the tax proviso survives at all, it reaches only those leases executed under the 1891 Act and its 1924 amendment.[7]

---

[5] In fact, the legislative history suggests that Congress intended to replace the 1924 Act's leasing scheme with that of the 1938 Act. As the Court of Appeals recognized, Congress had three major goals in adopting the 1938 Act: (i) to achieve "uniformity so far as practicable of the law relating to the leasing of tribal lands for mining purposes," Senate Report 2; H.R. Rep. No. 1872, 75th Cong., 3d Sess., 1 (1938); (ii) to "bring all mineral-leasing matters in harmony with the Indian Reorganization Act," Senate Report 3; H.R. Rep. No. 1872, *supra*, at 3; and (iii) to ensure that Indians receive "the greatest return from their property," Senate Report 2; H.R. Rep. No. 1872, *supra*, at 2. As the Court of Appeals suggested, these purposes would be undermined if the 1938 Act were interpreted to incorporate the taxation proviso of the 1924 Act. See 729 F.2d 1192, 1196-1198 (9th Cir. 1984).

[6] The Court of Appeals held that the 1938 Act did not repeal implicitly the 1924 consent to state taxation and thus that this consent continues in force with respect to leases issued under the 1924 or 1891 Acts Id., at 1200. Because the Blackfeet have not sought review on this question, we need not decide whether the Court of Appeals was correct. We assume for purposes of this case that the 1924 Act's authorization remains in effect for leases executed pursuant to that statute.

[7] We are likewise unpersuaded by the State's contention that we should defer to the administrative interpretation that the 1924 taxing proviso applies to leases executed under the 1938 Act. The State relies on opinions of the Department of the Interior in making this argument. As the Court of Appeals pointed out, however, the administrative record is not as strongly consistent as the State contends. *Id.*, at 1202-1203. The opinions issued prior to 1956 did not mention the 1938 Act or leases executed pursuant thereto. Thus, at best, they did not address the issue presented by this case, but simply assumed that the 1924 Act and this Court's decision in *British-American Oil Producing Co. v. Board of Equalization of Montana*, 299 U.S. 159 (1936), applied to leases executed under the 1938 Act. It was not until its 1956 opinion that the Department of the Interior considered the relationship between the 1938 and 1924 Acts. The Department then held that the taxing provision had not been repealed by the 1938 Act. This 1956 opinion was unpublished and did not analyze whether Congress had intended the 1924 Act's provision to apply to leases entered pursuant to the 1938 Act. A 1966 opinion relied on the 1956 opinion. In 1977, the Department reconsidered the issue carefully and in far greater detail than it had in 1956, and reversed its prior decision. *See* 729 F.2d, at 1202-1203. On this record, we cannot accept the premise of the State's argument for deference to agency interpretation, that is, that the Department had a consistent 40-year practice. This is particularly true where, as here, the language and purpose of the 1938 Act are — for the reasons set forth above — clearly to the contrary.

V

In the absence of clear congressional consent to taxation, we hold that the State may not tax Indian royalty income from leases issued pursuant to the 1938 Act. Accordingly, the judgment of the Court of Appeals is

Affirmed.

Justice WHITE, with whom Justice REHNQUIST and Justice STEVENS join, dissenting.

The question is whether the proviso to the Act of May 29, 1924, ch. 210, 43 Stat. 244, 25 U.S.C. § 398, authorizes a State to tax oil and gas production under leases entered into under the Indian Mineral Leasing Act of 1938, ch. 198, 52 Stat. 347, 25 U.S.C. §§ 396a-396g. In my view, the proviso constitutes a sufficiently explicit expression of congressional intent to permit such taxation.

[I also] consider it relevant, though not dispositive, that the suggestion that the 1924 Act does not authorize taxation of production on 1938 Act leases is contrary to the interpretation of both Acts that apparently prevailed in the Department of the Interior until 1977. Opinions issued by the Office of the Solicitor of the Interior in the years following the passage of the 1938 Act discussed the scope of state authority to tax under the proviso to the 1924 Act with no mention of the possibility that the 1938 Act had any effect on such authority. See 58 I.D. 535 (1943); Opinion of the Department of Interior, M-36246, Oct. 29, 1954, 2 Op. Solicitor of Dept. of Interior Relating to Indian Affairs 1917-1974, p. 1652 (1979); Opinion of the Department of Interior, M-36310, Oct. 13, 1955. In 1956, the Department issued an opinion explicitly concluding that the 1924 proviso applied to leases under the 1938 Act, and the Department reaffirmed this position in 1966. See Opinion of the Department of Interior, M-36345, May 4, 1956; Letter from Harry R. Anderson, Asst. Secretary of the Interior, Oct. 27, 1966, reprinted at App. to Pet. for Cert. 301. Not until 1977 did the Department change its view of the effect of the 1938 Act on the taxation authority contained in the proviso. This history admittedly does not conclusively establish what the Department's position was at the time of the passage of the 1938 Act and in the years immediately following. Still, it is significant that it was not until years after the passage of the 1938 Act that the Department first suggested that the 1924 proviso's explicit authorization of taxation did not extend to leases under the 1938 Act. Had Congress really intended to cut off the State's authority to tax mineral production on all leases entered into after 1938, it would seem odd that no one in the Interior Department was aware of this intention.

Because the proviso to the 1924 Act explicitly authorizes state taxation of mineral production on "such lands" as are concerned in this case, and because nothing in the language of the 1938 Act, its legislative history, its underlying policies, or its administrative construction suggests that the express language of the proviso should not govern this case, I would hold that the state taxes at issue here are authorized by federal law. I therefore dissent.

COTTON PETROLEUM CORP. v. NEW MEXICO

490 U.S. 163 (1989)

[An edited version of the *Cotton Petroleum* opinion is set forth in Chapter 4, page 561. In *Cotton Petroleum* the Court sustained the authority of states to impose severance taxes on non-Indian lessees who developed Indian mineral resources and held that state taxes were not preempted by the co-existence of tribal severance taxes on the same minerals. Furthermore, the Court rejected the notion that such multiple tax burdens were illegal in the absence of a showing that either the state or the tribe imposed a discriminatory tax. As the Court indicated, "[t]he burdensome consequence [of multiple tax burdens making total taxes paid by developers of Indian minerals higher than those paid by off-reservation producers] is entirely attributable to the fact that the leases are located in an area where two governmental entities share jurisdiction." 109 S. Ct. at 1714.]

NOTE: TAXATION OF INDIAN MINERAL DEVELOPMENT

Why was the Congressional policy against state taxation that the Court found in the 1938 Act which was dispositive in *Blackfeet* not also dispositive of the issue in *Cotton Petroleum*? In *Cotton Petroleum*, the Court paid little attention to either the 1938 Act or the *Blackfeet* decision. Can these two cases be reconciled? *See generally* F. COHEN, HANDBOOK OF FEDERAL INDIAN LAW ch. 7 (1982 ed.); Goldberg, *A Dynamic View of Tribal Jurisdiction to Tax Non-Indians*, 40 LAW & CONTEMP. PROBS. 166 (1976); Ames, *Tribal Taxation of Non-Indian Mineral Lessees, An Undefined Inherent Power*, 6 J. CONTEMP. L. 55 (1979); Note, *Balancing the Interests in Taxation of Non-Indian Activities on Indian Lands*, 64 IOWA L. REV. 2459 (1979); Comment, *Tribal Power to Tax Non-Indian Mineral Lessees*, 19 NAT. RESOURCES J. 969 (1979); Comment, *The Case for Exclusive Tribal Power to Tax Mineral Lessees of Indian Lands*, 124 U. PA. L. REV. 491 (1975); Comment, *Indian Taxation: Underlying Policies and Present Problems*, 59 COLO. L. REV. 1261 (1971).

In *Cotton Petroleum*, should the Court have considered whether the complex statutory and regulatory process for federal lease approval of non-Indian development of Indian lands preempts state taxing authority? *Compare White Mountain Apache Tribe v. Bracker*, 448 U.S. 136 (1980); *California v. Cabazon Band of Mission of Indians*, 480 U.S. 202 (1987).

WHITE MOUNTAIN APACHE TRIBE v. BRACKER
448 U.S. 136 (1980)

[An edited version of the decision in *White Mountain Apache* is set forth in Chapter 4, page 533. The Supreme Court held that Arizona could not impose its carrier use tax based on gross business receipts and its motor vehicle fuel taxes on the activities of a non-Indian firm that hauled lumber on the reservation under contract with a tribal timber operation. In finding that the state taxes were preempted, the Court relied heavily on the extensive federal regulation of tribal timber operations and federal regulation of tribal and BIA roads.]

FORT MOJAVE TRIBE v. SAN BERNARDINO COUNTY
543 F.2d 1253 (9th Cir. 1976), *cert. denied*,
430 U.S. 983 (1977)

SNEED, Circuit Judge:

This case requires us to determine whether a possessory interest tax may be imposed on non-Indian lessees of property held in trust by the United States Government for reservation Indians. Five years ago we held, in *Agua Caliente Band of Mission Indians v. County of Riverside*, 442 F.2d 1184 (9th Cir. 1971), *cert. denied*, 405 U.S. 933, (1972), that such a tax was valid. The trial judge in the instant case found *Agua Caliente* to be controlling. We continue to support the holding of that case. We consider it proper, however, to look closely at the specific status of the Fort Mojave Indians in deciding whether the rationale of the *Agua Caliente* case should be applied to this situation. Also, it is important to review this area of the law in the light of recent Supreme Court decisions concerning taxation by state and local governments affecting Indians.

I. *Factual Situation*

The Fort Mojave Tribe is organized under the provisions of the [IRA] (hereinafter called the "Act"), unlike the Agua Caliente Band. Thus the Fort Mojave Indians operate under a recognized system of self-government, with a constitution and a business charter which cannot be revoked or surrendered except by Act of Congress. All reservation land is held in trust for the Fort Mojave Tribe as a whole; no individual allotments were ever made under the General Allotment Act of 1887, 25 U.S.C. § 331 et seq.

The Fort Mojave Indians, as part of a plan for the economic development of their reservation, have entered into several 99-year leases with non-Indian lessees. The major development plans include a resort and housing project, as well as the possibility of building a major nuclear power plant. The reservation is located within three states, California, Nevada and Arizona. Since California is the only one of these three states that imposes a possessory interest tax,[1] development of the California section of the reservation may be slowed.[2] The Indians are opposing the California tax because they want to be able to make leasing decisions without regard to the state in which the property is located. The Indians also object to the California tax because they have their own possessory interest tax. They fear that this "double taxation" will further impede development....

---

[1]"Possessory interests" means the following:

    (a) Possession of, claim to, or right to the possession of land or improvements, except when coupled with ownership of the land or improvements in the same person.
    (b) Taxable improvements on tax-exempt land.

Cal. Rev. & Tax. Code § 107.

[2]The economic, as opposed to the legal, incidence of the tax sought to be imposed in this case is uncertain under certain assumptions with respect to the demand for the goods and services of the lessee the tax in question will fall entirely on the consumers of these goods and services. Under other assumptions with respect to such demand and with respect to the supply and demand for leasehold interests similar to that here being taxed, the tax in question will fall entirely on the lessee. Other assumptions with respect to these matters will place the burden on the Indians. Which assumptions correspond to the facts is unknown and probably not knowable. In this case, we proceed on the assumption that it is *possible* for the economic burden of the tax, in whole or in part, to fall on the Indians. We know not whether it is *probable* that it will do so.

III. *Analysis of Statutes*

A. *The Indian Reorganization Act*

The Indians' major argument is that their status as a self-governing tribe organized under the provisions of the Indian Reorganization Act precludes the imposition of this tax by the County of San Bernardino. Section 16 of the Act 25 U.S.C. § 476 provides that "the constitution adopted by said tribe shall also vest in such tribe or its tribal council the following rights and powers ... to prevent the sale, disposition, lease or encumbrance of tribal lands, interests in lands, or other tribal assets without the consent of the tribe." The Indians argue that the imposition of a possessory interest tax on the lessee encumbers their reversionary interest in the land. Alternatively, they argue that the lease itself is an "other asset" of the tribe which is encumbered if subject to taxation. We reject these arguments as going beyond the expressed Congressional intent in enacting the Act to further the achievement of economic independence for the Indians and the establishment of effective systems of tribal self-government. H.R. Rep. No. 1804, 73d Cong., 2d Sess, 6 (1934).

While the imposition of a possessory interest tax on the leasehold interest will have an economic effect on the Indian lessors, and perhaps, although not certainly, will reduce the amount of rent they will be able to collect the legal incidence of the tax clearly falls on the lessee. The lessor will never be personally liable for any delinquent taxes arising under this taxing statute. *Agua Caliente Band of Mission Indians v. County of Riverside, supra* at 1186. Cal. Rev. & Tax. Code, § 107. Under these circumstances, there cannot be a direct encumbrance on the lessor's reversionary interest. Similarly, the lease, apart from the lessor's reversionary interest, even if considered an asset of the tribe, is not directly encumbered simply because the amount of the tax is determined by the value of the leasehold. Whatever may be the scope of the indirect burden placed on the lessor's interest in this case, we hold that it is not sufficient to constitute an encumbrance of an "interest in land or other tribal asset."

Our conclusion is buttressed by the Supreme Court's decision in *Mescalero Apache Tribe v. Jones*, 411 U.S. 145, (1973). There the Court, relying on the statement that section 476 of the Act was designed to encourage tribal enterprises "to enter the white world on a footing of equal competition," 78 Cong. Rec. 11732, found that traditional tax immunities had neither been expanded nor reduced by the Act. *Mescalero, supra* at 153-54 n.9. Because the court would not imply tax exemptions absent clear statutory guidelines it upheld the imposition of a state tax on the gross receipts of a ski resort operated by the Mescaleros on land located outside the boundaries of their reservation. We follow that lead here and refuse to find that the Act created a tax exemption for non-Indian lessees of Indian land. Congress has given no clear indication that such a result was desired. When such a signal is given, the state and local governments must retreat.

B. *Pub. L. No. 280*

We turn to another relevant federal statute. California is one of the five states mandated by PL-280 to exercise both civil and criminal jurisdiction over the

Indian country within their borders. Thus, both the Agua Caliente Band and the Fort Mojave Tribe are subject to California jurisdiction. Section 4(b) of PL-280, 28 U.S.C. § 1360(b), specifically provides that the grant of civil jurisdiction precludes taxation of "any real or personal property ... belonging to any Indian or any Indian tribe." We interpreted that language in *Agua Caliente* as not forbidding the imposition of a possessory interest tax on the lessee of Indian property. *Agua Caliente, supra* at 1187.

[Therefore] neither the Act nor PL-280 evidences a Congressional intent to preclude the taxation that is being challenged here. However, we cannot say that PL-280 directly authorizes such taxation. *Bryan v. Itasca County, supra,* forecloses the possibility of such a statement by specifically holding that the PL-280 grant of civil jurisdiction only confers jurisdiction over civil causes of action involving Indians. It is not a general grant of regulatory and taxing power over Indians. This is not, however, fatal to the state's cause. Although *McClanahan, supra,* held that, in the absence of Congressional consent, states are preempted from taxing Indian reservation lands or Indian income from activities carried on within the boundaries of the reservation, the court specifically did not deal with "exertions of state sovereignty over non-Indians who undertake activity on Indian reservations." *McClanahan, supra* at 411 U.S. 168. When the state action is directed at non-Indians, with only indirect effects on Indians or Indian lands, it is necessary to reconcile the federal preemption rationale with the state's recognized authority to regulate its citizens. *McClanahan, supra* at 179. Reconciliation requires that state legislation primarily directed at non-Indian lessees of Indian land be considered as not automatically preempted by the federal government in the absence of specific authorization. See [e.g.,] *Thomas v. Gay,* 169 U.S. 264, 18 S. Ct. 340, 42 L. Ed. 740 (1898); *Utah & Northern R.R. v. Fisher,* 116 U.S. 28 (1885). To permit such non-Indians to enjoy the immunity designed for Indians requires, we believe, a stronger Congressional signal than a statute which neither precludes nor authorizes the taxation in question. This does not contravene the maxim that ambiguous statutes should be construed to benefit Indians. The maxim was never intended to authorize constructions which, on their face, benefit non-Indians handsomely and Indians only marginally, if at all.

C. *The* Williams *Test*

The final hurdle facing the county is the test formulated in *Williams v. Lee, supra,* to determine whether a statute not otherwise preempted is valid. [*Williams*] held that "absent governing Acts of Congress, the question has always been whether the state action infringed on the right of reservation Indians to make their own laws and be ruled by them." The Court in *McClanahan* specifically recognized that this test is principally applicable in situations involving non-Indians.

[As opposed to the facts in *Williams,* the] interference with Indian self-government in the instant case is much less serious. No Indian or Indian land is being subjected to direct state court process. The only effect of the tax on the Indians will be the indirect one of perhaps reducing the revenues they will receive from the leases as a result of their inability to market a tax exemption.

Such an indirect economic burden cannot be said to threaten the self-governing ability of the tribe.

The assertion that "double taxation," resulting from the imposition of a tax both by the county and the tribe, impairs the ability of the tribe to levy its tax is not persuasive. There is no improper double taxation here at all, for the taxes are being imposed by two different and distinct taxing authorities. The tribe faces the same problem as other taxing agencies confront when they seek to impose a tax in an area already taxed by another entity having taxing power. We hold that the uncertain economic burden here imposed on the tribe's ability to levy a tax does not interfere with their right of self-government.

Our holding is supported by the recent Supreme Court decision in *Moe v. Confederated Salish and Kootenai Tribes*, 425 U.S. 463 (1976) [upholding a tax even though the legal burden fell on the Indian seller]. In the instant case, there is no legal burden imposed on the Indian lessor at all. In both cases, the Indians incur the possibility of an economic loss. However, the court in *Moe* did not consider that a sufficient burden to invalidate the sales tax as applied to non-Indians making purchases on the reservation. Therefore, we do not find in the instant case a sufficient burden on the tribe's ability to govern itself to justify striking down California's possessory interest tax as applied to non-Indian lessees of Indian land.

IV. *Enforcement of the Tax as a Direct Encumbrance on the Land*

The Indians argued both in *Agua Caliente* and the instant case that the procedures available under state law to collect the tax could result in a direct cloud on their title and an unlawful encumbrance on Indian real property. The court in *Agua Caliente, supra* n.16, did not decide this question because it found that no attempt had yet been made to seize and sell any of the interests taxed and therefore the issue was not properly before the court. In the instant case the appellants give details of several situations in which notice of seizure was made and one case in which the sale was advertised before the lessee finally paid the tax. Nonetheless, there have been no completed tax sales and it is highly unlikely that any injuries to Indian rights will occur. The reasons for our confidence with respect to the future are two statutes, 25 U.S.C. § 415 and 25 U.S.C. § 476. The first requires the approval of the Secretary of the Interior of any lease of restricted Indian lands while the second explicitly gives the tribe the right to prevent the lease of tribal lands. We have no reason to believe these statutes will not be invoked to thwart tax sales contrary to the wishes of the Secretary and the Indians.

These statutes, designed to protect Indians, do not render the county power-less to enforce the tax here involved against the lessee. Even if his interest is treated by the assessors as "unsecured property," *i.e.*, property insufficient to secure the payment of the tax, California law permits the seizure and sale of personal property, improvements, and possessory interests of the assessee. Cal. Rev. & Tax. Code § 2951 (1974). California law also permits a direct suit to recover taxes against the owner of unsecured property against which taxes have been assessed. Cal. Rev. & Tax Code, section 3003. This case does not require us to trace out precisely the accommodations which the county and the lessee must make to protect the Indians in the event the lessee defaults in payment of the tax here being challenged. Enough has been said to indicate that we are confident these accommodations are both legal and feasible.

Therefore, the California possessory interest tax is valid as applied to the non-Indian lessees of land within the Fort Mojave Indian Reservation and the judgment of the district court is affirmed.

Affirmed.

NOTE

The *Fort Mojave* decision adopts an approach frequently taken by many courts that separates tribal activity on Indian lands from non-Indian economic development that merely takes place on such lands. This approach, in a sense, continues the historical trend of perceiving non-Indian activities taking place within the boundaries of the reservation as taking place within the boundaries of the state and subject to state jurisdiction. This trend is, however, somewhat inconsistent with the message of the *Worcester* case. Nevertheless, in this sense *Fort Mojave* is the lineal descendant of *Thomas v. Gay* and *McBratney*. The possessory interest tax is the device used to abstract non-Indian activity from the lands on which such activities take place. Does the Court's later decision in *White Mountain Apache* suggest that state taxation of non-Indian lessees and other non-Indians who contract with tribes in economic development projects often will be preempted if a comprehensive pattern of federal regulation can be demonstrated in the economic area which the state seeks to tax or which would be impeded by state taxation?

2. STATE REGULATION OF ECONOMIC DEVELOPMENT

BRENDALE v. CONFEDERATED TRIBES & BANDS OF THE YAKIMA INDIAN NATION

109 S. Ct. 2994 (1989)

[The *Brendale* case held that tribes could not apply their zoning laws to non-Indian-owned land in open areas of a reservation that were predominantly populated by non-Indians but could apply its zoning ordinances to non-Indian lands located in other areas of the reservation that generally were owned by the tribe or otherwise had maintained a distinctly Indian character. It is excerpted in Chapter 3, page 461.]

SNOHOMISH COUNTY v. SEATTLE DISPOSAL CO.

70 Wash. 2d 668, 425 P.2d 22 (1967) (en banc),
cert. denied, 389 U.S. 1016 (1967)

FINLEY, Chief Justice.

The defendant Seattle Disposal Company leased land known as Allotments 91 and 92 from the intervenor, the Tulalip Tribes, for the purpose of operating what is called a sanitary land-fill garbage and refuse disposal site. The lease was authorized by Ordinance No. 29 passed by the Tulalip Tribes, an Indian group organized as a federal corporation pursuant to the Indian Reorganization Act, 48 Stat. 988, 25 U.S.C. § 477.

Allotment 91 was purchased in 1960 in the name of the United States in trust for the Tulalip Tribes. The Tulalip Tribes purchased Allotment 92 at a Snohomish County Superior Court sale in November of 1963. Both parcels of land are located within the Tulalip Indian Reservation and within Snohomish County. Under Snohomish County Zoning Ordinance No. 7, as amended, a conditional use permit is required in order to carry on garbage disposal operations, except on lands exempt from county regulation. Neither Seattle Disposal nor the Tulalip Tribes ever applied for a permit to allow garbage operations on Allotments 91 and 92, and such a permit was never issued.

The plaintiff, Snohomish County, brought suit aginst Seattle Disposal, seeking an injunction to prevent Seattle Disposal from disposing of, or preparing to dispose of, garbage within the county without first procuring a conditional use permit. The Tulalip Tribes moved for leave to intervene, and the trial court granted permission to do so. Both Seattle Disposal and the Tulalip Tribes moved for summary judgment on the basis that the court lacked jurisdiction over the subject matter of the action. The trial court granted summary judgment in accordance with the motions on the grounds, among others, that the state and its governmental agencies have no jurisdiction over the use of the land in question, that the zoning ordinance if applied to Allotments 91 and 92 would constitute an encumbrance in violation of 28 U.S.C. § 1360 and RCW 37.12.060, and that the Tulalip Tribes have the power to the exclusion of the county or state to regulate the use of the land in question and have done so by Ordinance No. 29. The county has appealed [and argues] that Public Law 280 operated as an authorization for Washington to assume jurisdiction, and that ch. 240, Laws of 1957, as amended by ch. 36, Laws of 1963, now codified as RCW 37.12, acted as the consent of people, in terms of art. 26 of the Washington Constitution, to the assumption of civil and criminal jurisdiction over Indians and their lands within the state. This general proposition is clearly the law, and the Tulalip Tribe has voluntarily come within this grant of state jurisdiction. *State v. Paul*, 53 Wash. 2d 789, 337 P.2d 33 (1959). The county further recognizes the limitation on this assumption of jurisdiction, which appears in RCW 37.12.060 as taken from 28 U.S.C. § 1360, which reads as follows:

Chapter limited in application. *Nothing in this chapter shall authorize the alienation, encumbrance, or taxation of any real or personal property,* including water rights and tidelands, belonging to any Indian or any Indian tribe, band, or community *that is held in trust by the United States or is subject to a restriction against alienation imposed by the United States;* or shall authorize regulation of the use of such property in a manner inconsistent with any federal treaty, agreement, or statute or with any regulation made pursuant thereto .... (Italics ours.)

There is no question but that Allotment 91, title to which was taken in the name of the United States in trust for the Tulalip Indians, comes within the limitation expressed in RCW 37.12.060. The county argues, however, that Allotment 92 does not come within the terms of this limitation. We disagree. Allotment 92 was *sold* free and clear of all trusts or restraints against alienation, pursuant to 70 Stat. 290, 25 U.S.C. § 403a-1, at the judicial sale in the partition action of Snohomish County Superior Court Civil Cause No. 76503. However, the purchase of Allotment 92 by the Tulalip Tribes reimposed the requirement, under 54 Stat. 1057, 25 U.S.C. § 403a and 70 Stat. 290, 25 U.S.C. § 403a-2, that any long term lease or sale of this land be made only with the consent of the Secretary of the Interior. The necessity of the Secretary's approval constitutes a restriction against alienation imposed by the United States. See *La Motte v. United States*, 254 U.S. 570 (1921). Thus the limitation stated in RCW 37.12.060 and 28 U.S.C. § 1360, applies, and the state is without authority to encumber or tax either Allotment 92 or 91.

[We follow] the approach taken by the United States Supreme Court in *Squire v. Capoeman*, 351 U.S. 1 (1956). In that case the Court concluded that the words "charge or encumbrance," as they appear in the General Allotment Act of 1887, should be interpreted broadly, and any doubt should be resolved in favor of the Indians for whose benefit that legislation, as well as the legislation before us, was intended. We, therefore, hold that Snohomish County Zoning Ordinance No. 7, if construed to apply to Allotments 91 and 92, constitutes an encumbrance within the meaning of 28 U.S.C. § 1360, and RCW 37.12.060.

We find support for this result in an opinion by the Acting Solicitor for the Department of the Interior which concludes that the state in the exercise of its police power may not interfere by zoning ordinance with land held by the United States in trust for Indians. 58 I.D. 52 (1942). See, also, an opinion of the Washington Attorney General, AGO 59-60, No. 59 (1959), in which the same conclusion is reached. We find nothing in Public Law 280 or in other applicable federal law to indicate an intention to the contrary. Thus, we conclude that, even apart from the inclusion of zoning ordinances within the word encumbrance, the federal government has not intended to allow states or their governmental agencies to interfere with the use of restricted Indian lands by means of zoning ordinances.

The county also argues that since Seattle Disposal is a non-Indian organization it should not be able to benefit from the special rights or privileges granted to Indians. The Tulalip Indians are clearly authorized, subject to the regulation of the Secretary of the Interior, to make commercial leases for substantially unlimited purposes. See 54 Stat. 1057, 25 U.S.C. § 403a; 60 Stat. 962, 25 U.S.C. § 403b; and 69 Stat. 539, 25 U.S.C. § 415. Limitation on the use to which a lessee from the Tulalip Tribes can put Indian lands is limiting the Indian use. The county cannot indirectly accomplish federally prohibited interference with property that it could not accomplish directly. See AGO, No. 59 (1959); *Jordan v. O'Brien*, 70 S.D. 393, 18 N.W.2d 30 (1945); *United States v. County of Allegheny*, 322 U.S. 174 (1944).

The county also contends that to hold that the zoning ordinance does not apply to the lands in question and to allow Indian self-regulation would deny to the members of the Tulalip Tribes and to residents of adjoining lands the equal protection of the laws. This novel argument would find a denial of equal protection in each of the myriad cases of juxtaposed but different regulation by different sovereigns in our system of federalism. We have already determined that this state has no jurisdiction to control either directly or indirectly the use of the Indian lands in question. Where there is no jurisdiction, there can be no denial of equal protection.

We are aware of the Congressional intent to make Indians as nearly as possibly full and equal citizens. We are also aware of the intent, clearly expressed in 60 Stat. 962, 25 U.S.C. § 403b, and 69 Stat. 539, 25 U.S.C. § 415, to promote

Indian commercial activities. See, also, Kelly, The Economic Basis of Indian Life, 311 Annals of Am. Academy of Polit. and So. Science 71 (May 1957). That our decision today promotes the latter policy rather than the former is not the result of a judgment as to competing values, but rather a determination as to what to us clearly seems to be the applicable law. The state has, of course, been granted jurisdiction to inspect and regulate health, sanitation, and related matters on Indian tribal lands. 45 Stat. 1185, 25 U.S.C. § 231. In the matter of the regulation of the use of restricted Indian lands, however, the United States has conferred on the Indians a degree of immunity from regulation by state and local government, and only the United States can remove this immunity. Cf. *Dept. of Game v. Puyallup Tribe, Inc.*, 70 Wash. Dec. 2d 241, 422 P.2d 754 (1966).

[*Affirmed.*]

HALE, Judge (dissenting).

I dissent for three reasons: (1) Zoning laws, it seems to me, are not encumbrances on land but rather are an exercise of the police power to foster the public welfare, health and safety; (2) although Indian reservations may be partially immune from state regulations, this immunity ought not extend to activities which immediately and directly affect the citizenry at large; and (3) any immunity from the state's police regulations enjoyed by the Indians for activities on the reservation should not cover their non-Indian lessees or assigns. I believe, therefore, that neither Indians nor their lessees may operate a garbage dump on the reservation in violation of the zoning laws of [the county].

NOTE

In his dissent from the denial of review in the *Snohomish County* case Justice Douglas said:

> The Solicitor General, in a memorandum expressing the views of the United States, asserts that the decision below was correct because it accorded with an administrative regulation of the Department of the Interior. This regulation [4] provides that no local zoning ordinance shall be applicable to land leased from an Indian tribe where, as here, the land is held in trust by or is subjected to a restriction against alienation by the United States. The Supreme Court of Washington did not rely on this regulation,[5] and whether it is valid or unduly restricts the state authority conferred by Public Law

---

[4] 25 CFR § 1.4 provides:

(a) Except as provided in paragraph (b) of this section, none of the laws, ordinances, codes, resolutions, rules or other regulations of any State or political subdivision thereof limiting, zoning or otherwise governing, regulating, or controlling the use or development of any real or personal property, including water rights, shall be applicable to any such property leased from or held or used under agreement with and belonging to any Indian or Indian tribe, band, or community that is held in trust by the United States or is subject to a restriction against alienation imposed by the United States.

(b) The Secretary of the Interior or his authorized representative may in specific cases or in specific geographic areas adopt or make applicable to Indian lands all or any part of such laws, ordinances, codes, resolutions, rules or other regulations referred to in paragraph (a) of this section as he shall determine to be in the best interest of the Indian owner or owners in achieving the highest and best use of such property....

[5] The court below did rely on a 1942 decision of the Department of the Interior, 58 I.D. 52, holding that a Minnesota county could not apply a nonresidential zoning ordinance to certain Indian lands. But this decision was rendered before Public Law 280 was enacted.

280 and 25 U.S.C. § 231 is an important federal question this Court should decide. I would grant certiorari.

389 U.S. at 1029. Since the decision in *Bryan v. Itasca County,* discussed in Chapter 4, section C1, the Public Law 280 issue that Justice Douglas wanted addressed has been decided adversely to state jurisdiction. The question remains, however, whether 25 C.F.R. § 1.4 preempts the operation of all state and local laws regulating zoning, building, or other development restrictions where non-Indians develop Indian lands. Obviously, if section 1.4 is a valid regulation, it is preemptive. Some courts have questioned the statutory authority supporting the promulgation of section 1.4 and found it unauthorized. *E.g., Norvell v. Sangre de Cristo Dev. Co.,* 372 F. Supp. 348, 354-55 (D.N.M. 1974), *rev'd on juris. grounds,* 519 F.2d 370 (10th Cir. 1975). The *Sangre de Cristo* court considered and rejected the suggestion that the regulation could be justified under 25 U.S.C. §§ 2 and 9, which vest the Commission of Indian Affairs with the management of "all Indian affairs and of all matters arising out of Indian relations," and which authorize the President to proscribe "such regulations as he may think fit for carrying into effect the various provisions of any act relating to Indian affairs." The Court also considered but rejected the suggestion that 25 U.S.C. § 415 authorized the regulation. The basis for its view was that the amendment to section 415, which authorized the Secretary to consider jurisdictional issues, was not added until 1970, after the lease in question was approved and five years after section 1.4 was promulgated. Could the regulation be justified based on 25 U.S.C. § 231? *See also Rincon Band of Mission Indians v. County of San Diego,* 324 F. Supp. 371 (S.D. Cal. 1971), *rev'd,* 495 F.2d 1 (9th Cir. 1974), *cert. denied,* 419 U.S. 1008 (1974).

SEGUNDO v. CITY OF RANCHO MIRAGE

813 F.2d 1387 (9th Cir. 1987)

[An edited version of the *Segundo* opinion is set forth in Chapter 4, page 614. In *Segundo* the Ninth Circuit held that local mobile home rent control ordinances could not be applied to the individual Indian owners or non-Indian lessees of allotted lands on which the non-Indian developers operated a mobile home park. Relying on both *White Mountain Apache v. Bracker* and the provisions of 25 C.F.R. § 1.4, the court found that the municipal rent control ordinances were preempted by federal law.]

E. ECONOMIC DEVELOPMENT OF INDIAN COUNTRY IN PERSPECTIVE

Economic development strategies clearly have environmental and cultural impact on the lives of the Indian peoples whose reservations they touch. *E.g.,* P. RENO, MOTHER EARTH, FATHER SKY, AND ECONOMIC DEVELOPMENT: NAVAJO RESOURCES AND THEIR USE (1981). Some tribes have sought to minimize such adverse impacts by relying on communal economic activity and capitalizing on activities, such as salmon fishing and processing, that were traditional in their culture. *E.g.,* D. BOXBERGER, TO FISH IN COMMON: THE ETHNOHISTORY OF LUMMI INDIAN FISHING (1989). Consider the impact of the individualization development strategies suggested by the final report of the Presidential Commission on Indian Reservation Economies that began this chapter in light of the materials that follow and the remainder of this chapter. *See also* Swimmer, *A Blueprint for Economic Development in Indian Country*, 10 J. ENERGY L. & POLICY 13 (1989). What impact would they have on tribal culture, the reservation, and the continued vitality of tribal governments?

POMMERSHEIM, ECONOMIC DEVELOPMENT IN INDIAN COUNTRY: WHAT ARE THE QUESTIONS?, 12 American Indian Law Review 195 *passim* (1987)*

What Is the Context of Development?

In most scholarly writing on economic development in Indian country, broad generalizations are made with little sensitivity or attention given to tribes' past experiences, except in noting their general lack of success. Most tribes are clearly underdeveloped by almost any definition,[6] and the usual ways suggested to overcome underdevelopment are agricultural development,[7] community economic development,[8] and escape from the shackles of the "colonizer-oppressor."[9] Such standard approaches place the issue of economic development in a tidy framework that misapprehends the reality they seek to address. This initial misunderstanding of the economic situation fatally distorts any future development project, often in a manner that directly leads to failure. These standard approaches are only beneficial when they are employed with a proper understanding of the particular tribal and reservation context in which they are to apply.

The emphasis on tribal context is rooted in policy analysis concepts. The development problem is too often treated as a material entity, part of "a well structured world of unambiguous objectives, mutually exclusive choice, authoritative decision making and willing decision endurers."[10] Actually, there is a more intractable reality that "involves a staggering variety of people and organizations, all pulling, pushing and otherwise interacting with each other in pursuit of their various interests." The first task, then, is to turn this "mess" into a problem about which something constructive can be done. This is not easy, but it is a fundamental necessity.

It may be possible to untangle such "messes" by focusing on the tribal context of the people, their interactions, and the institutional settings in which these interactions take place. Considerable emphasis is placed on the various entities,

---

*Copyright © 1987 American Indian Law Review and Frank Pommersheim.

[6]"Underdeveloped" is most often used in the economic sense and is equated with extensive poverty and low productivity. "Development," on the other hand, is most often defined as a process whereby an economy's real national income increases over a long period of time. More apt, perhaps, is the formulation of economist John Kenneth Galbraith that development is providing people a release from the acculturation of poverty and providing them with some opportunity for upward mobility. Also note Professor Galbraith's own cautionary observation that one of the most compelling errors in social perception is the mistake in "believing that the advanced industrial countries, socialist and capitalist, are a guide and model for economic and social development of the new countries of the world." Galbraith, *Ideology and Agriculture*, Harper's Magazine, Feb. 1985, at 15.

[7]*See* Ickes, *Tribal Economic Independence — The Means to Achieve True Tribal Self-Determination*, 26 S.D.L. Rev. 494 (1981).

[8]*See* S. Haberfeld, R. Posner, L. Lee & B. Devan, A Self-Help Manual for Tribal Economic Development (1982).

[9]*See* B. Johansen & R. Maestas, Wasi'Chu: The Continuing Indian Wars (1979).

[10]B. Johnston & W. Clark, Redesigning Rural Development 11 (1982).

including, for example, political groups, families, and community organizations that mediate these interactions. Development efforts do not proceed with a clean slate. This on-going social reality permeates the design of any development effort because development policies "are not designed but redesigned as modifications of existing policies which in turn provide foundations for policies that will follow."

The assessment of past experience is therefore one element of focus. We cannot learn from past experiences, both successes and failures, until they are diagnosed and understood. This diagnosis is not always readily apparent. What went wrong with past development efforts? On the Rosebud Sioux Reservation, for example, what actually caused the demise of Rosebud Electronics, Lakota Products, the Sicangu Arts and Crafts Cooperative, and the persistent failures of the Rosebud Sioux Tribal Ranch? Were there failures of program design, capital resources, management expertise, marketing, and/or employee motivation? What about the forces of political devisiveness, social upheaval, and unfavorable macroeconomic forces? Successes need the same scrutiny. Why did something go right? In much of Indian country, available data from the past is extremely limited, but such retrospective efforts that are undertaken will be quite useful. These initial forays may be primitive methodologically, but the close examination of what evidence there is may yield valuable insights.

The past not only informs the social reality that influences the making of development policy, but it also affects individuals. Past experience with development projects often shapes personal commitment. For example, any reservation-based employment training project in South Dakota must consider that many eligible individuals will have been through three or four similar programs within the previous six or seven years, such as the federal Comprehensive Employment and Training Act (CETA),[13] Bureau of Indian Affairs (BIA) Employment Assistance,[14] Community Action Program (C.A.P.) Employment Training,[15] and South Dakota State Vocational and Technical Training.[16] As the ever-increasing unemployment rates on reservations confirm, these projects have all failed because they provided good skills training but no permanent employment or, as in the case of CETA, temporary jobs with no training. The end result is the same. When the program is over, including the individual stipend or subsidy involved, the individual is still unemployed. Such experience often withers both personal enthusiasm and the work ethic. These problems must be taken into account. They are not insurmountable, but if ignored invite the likelihood of future project failures.

Raking the coals of the past is central to any competent problem analysis. "The goal is to extract from past experience some enlightening perspectives from which to redesign [rural] development. By better understanding past experience, we hope better to profit from its successes and better to avoid its mistakes." Retrospection alone, however, is perilous; it does not carry us for-

---

[13] Comprehensive Employment and Training Act of 1973, repealed at 29 U.S.C. §§ 801-999 (1984).
[14] 25 U.S.C. § 13 (1983), 25 C.F.R. § 26.1-26.8 (1984).
[15] Economic Opportunity Act of 1964, as amended and partially repealed at 42 U.S.C. §§ 2701-2995d (1984).
[16] S.D. Codified Laws ch. 13-39 (1982).

ward with sufficient vision. It needs the complement of a conceptual framework for evaluating the likely long-term consequences of present actions, often referred to by business managers as "assessing the futurity." Of the small number of initially successful development projects, too many eventually fail because this conceptual analysis is missing. Many good projects end because they cannot be sustained. Their resources, including human and financial capital, are not properly integrated into the development equation and are often exhausted without possibility of replacement or renewal. "The assessment of futurities is an exercise in identifying option generating and option foreclosing actions, in articulating major tradeoffs and complementarities, and generally, in appreciating some of the long term implications inherent in policy choice." It is a process which seeks to thrust the lessons of the past into the future.

A strategic analysis for development also requires a method of weighing the nature and quality of present conditions for economic development in the tribal context. Such investigation and evaluation need not be cumbersome, longitudinal research. There are very real limits on the usefulness of any analysis beyond which there is only impotence and needless abstraction. The analysis must be, in economic parlance, "optimal," arraying time and resources in their most productive fashion given the nature of existing constraints. The goal is fruitful action, not extreme analytic nicety. Therefore, the most erudite or precise approach is not necessarily the best.

A reliable guideline here is simplicity. "In place of spurious pretense of comprehensive authority, we have found that analysis benefits from being 'as ruthlessly parsimonious and economical as possible while still retaining responsiveness to the management objectives and actions appropriate to the problem.'" The experts serve the analysis and not vice versa. The end product is a set of reliable questions whose answers form an agenda for action:

> We focus first on the most intensely felt needs of the policy endurers: What is wrong with the present situation? What specific evils are most in need of mitigation? What aspects of past policies require correction? We next turn to the specific actions or interventions which policy makers and implementors believe to be potentially feasible and desirable: What actually might be done? What resources are available? What political coalitions are needed and possible? Finally, we proceed to mobilize the small subset of expert knowledge or experience which is necessary to establish relationships between the implementors' action and the endurers' needs. To be sure, things are left out of such an analysis. Optimal prescriptions are not even aspired to; the modest hope is to find something merely better; with luck and cunning, the exercise has been known to produce insights and progress.

The goal is not to eliminate uncertainty but to more successfully contain and accommodate it. "In practiced terms, this means using the best analysis and knowledge that we can muster to help policy makers to see a little further ahead, to comprehend a few more interactions, and to avoid some of the truly disastrous and irreversible mistakes to which development is prone."[17] The goal is to minimize error and to maximize successful adaptation; to move forward to reduce the ravages of poverty and stasis.

What Are the Goals of Development?

The goals of development often appear self-evident, even facile. Development means economic growth, more jobs, a better standard of living. Yet the

---

[17] *Id.* at 35.

empirical results, particularly from the developing nations, are dismaying. Economic growth in certain segments of a society may actually further depress the income of the poorest class. Economic growth, ironically, may eliminate jobs for the poor. Untrammeled economic growth often increases, rather than decreases, income disparities. Significant economic growth, particularly in the rural areas, often simply does not occur. In many developing countries, these national experiences have been quite painful. As a result, there has been a substantial revision of development policy.

The most consistent articulation of this rethinking emphasizes four objectives: (1) self-sustaining, cumulative economic growth; (2) expanding employment; (3) reducing poverty; and (4) slowing population growth. These objectives are often dislodged in practice by competing interests with more political clout, or by powerful macroeconomic forces that are too pervasive and too powerful for localized projects to overcome. Therefore, in many cases, these four goals are unrealized. Nevertheless, they suggest a rich benchmark for measuring comparable efforts in Indian country.

The development literature about Indian country is not extensive. The most comprehensive economic development manual flatly asserts that "tribes have found it difficult deciding where to start and how to proceed in developing their economics. They have no appropriate economic development theories or practical guides that tribal leaders have found helpful."[24] The authors conclude that

> tribes can wait no longer for private initiative to play the pivotal role in reservation economic development. Tribal leadership must take the initiative. It must institute central economic planning at the tribal level which spells out a logical sequence of direct interventions designed to stimulate and support income and job generating activities on the reservation. Tribes must manage and nurture growth in their own reservations, by combining public sector and private sector involvement.

....

What Is the Dialectic of Goals?

Having considered the possible roles of tribal government in the development process, the overriding question remains: what are the specific objectives of development on the reservation? These objectives are most singularly identified in the word "jobs." This is not surprising given the devastating unemployment that exists on many reservations. Yet such a narrow and often unexamined focus is nearsighted. Reducing rampant unemployment must be a cornerstone concern, but ironically a blind commitment to jobs alone will not significantly alter unemployment rates, especially in the long run. Attacking unemployment takes more than jobs.

Other underlying elements, such as the sustainability of the venture, the wage and skill structure of the new jobs, and the nature of the unemployed population, must be examined in order to gauge the true impact of any proposed project. The CETA program is a textbook example. It purported to be a comprehensive employment training program designed to train individuals already in the workforce to upgrade their skills and enhance employability. This as-

---

[24]S. Haberfield, R. Posner, L. Lee & B. Devan, *supra* note 8, at 1-1.

sumed that there were jobs available and that the only thing many individuals needed was training. Yet on most reservations, particularly in South Dakota, this was not and is not the case. Jobs do not exist on the reservation and "training" peoples makes no real sense unless there is a component in the program that *creates* jobs. Job training per se cannot significantly reduce unemployment on the reservation.

The creation of new employment opportunities requires new economic endeavor and growth. These economic endeavors, however, must be sustainable; that is, they must reasonably address economic opportunity in such a way that they fulfill continuing needs and are completely and permanently integrated into the economy. For example, a company is willing to locate on the reservation because it has a contract with the tribe to build forty houses and to employ qualified local people. What is the likelihood that the company will stay on the reservation after it completes the contract? Is there enough construction activity on or near the reservation so that the company can be competitive and continue to perform its services? If not, the opportunity will be a one-shot deal, not to be rejected or scorned, but not to be confused with true economic development.

The creation of jobs also raises questions about the wage and skill levels of the new jobs. Is the skill requirement, whether entry level or advanced, within the reach of an appropriate number of the unemployed? Is the proposed wage and wage structure sufficient incentive to attract enough qualified workers? In economic terms, what do the supply and demand curves and resulting equilibrium wage look like?

[Further, the] final element drawn from the Third World comparison is population. Such discussions are often fraught with racial and cultural biases. Experts who proclaim the necessity of sharp reversals in personal, cultural, and philosophical beliefs are both insensitive and ethnocentric. In the reservation context, population questions are seldom asked; the most relevant would seem to be what level of development will sustain current and future generations in accordance with their material and cultural needs?

The braid of development has many strands: the rich interweave of sustainable economic growth, increased numbers of jobs, the alleviation of poverty, and concern for population suggests an innovative design that only the tribes and Indian people can refine and complete.

Development, Culture, and Meaning: The Deeper Questions

No discussion in this area is complete without a review of the deeper questions about the nature of exchange and the moral foundation of development and economic activity. Economic activity in Indian country is often characterized as a "must" with little attention paid to the implications for personal and cultural meaning, that aspect of life captured by the saying that "man does not live by bread alone."

Development activity is almost always completely premised on the assumed value of economic growth, increased income, and the cash nexus. Increased income augments purchasing power and the ability to get the material things one needs for one's self and one's family. This adds to the material well-being of both the individual and the community. Yet this kind of commodity exchange is not inevitable or exclusive, notwithstanding the overriding presumption to the contrary. It is this very presumption that disturbs many people in Indian country because it seems to mean a further walk down that non-Indian road that leads to assimilation and "civilization." In other words, to many Indians, it is to cultural ruin.

Traditional Western ideas of economic transfer recognize the possibility of creating some kind of bond in the exchange. Commodity exchange creates the most meager of connections. Traditional societies throughout the world have seen exchange in a much broader context. It is a context in which things are not bought and sold but are given as gifts according to special rules for exchange.[50] Bestowing these gifts not only creates economic bonds, it creates bonds of a psychological, social, and spiritual nature.

> If we take the synthetic power of gifts, which establish and maintain the bonds of affection between friends, lovers, and comrades, and if we add to these a circulation wider than a binary give-and-take, we shall soon derive society, or at least those societies — family, guild, fraternity, sorority, band, community — that cohere through faithfulness and gratitude. While gifts are marked by motion and momentum at the level of the individual, gift exchange at the level of the group offers equilibrium and coherence, a kind of anarchist stability. We can also say, to put the point conversely, that in a group that derives its cohesion from a circulation of gifts the conversion of gifts to commodities will have the effect of fragmenting the group, or even destroying it.[51]

This system, or the remnants thereof, is cause to reflect on the nature of exchange implicit in economic development theories.

> Many tribal groups circulate a large portion of their material wealth as gifts. Tribesmen are typically enjoined from buying and selling food, for example; even though there may be a strong sense of "mine and thine," food is always given as a gift and the transaction is governed by the ethics of gift exchange, not those of barter or cash purchase. Not surprisingly, people live differently who treat a portion of their wealth as a gift. To begin with, unlike the sale of a commodity, the giving of a gift tends to establish a relationship between the parties involved. Furthermore, when gifts circulate within a group, their commerce leaves a series of interconnected relationships in its wake, and a kind of decentralized cohesion emerges.

This perception of exchange is relevant in Indian country, at least on the reservations in South Dakota. All important events are characterized by the sharing of food, such as the traditional ceremonies, wakes, namings, and powwows, and even the visit of an Indian Law class to tribal court.[53]

This kind of exchange is further amplified by the traditional Lakota "give-away," which celebrates or commemorates births, marriages, graduations, namings, and deaths by the distribution of gifts such as horses, quilts, blankets, pots and pans, footlockers, and cigarettes to all present. The give-away creates bonds that are traceable to both exterior and invisible economies of the community and spirit.

---

[50] See generally M. Mauss, The Gift (1967).

[51] L. Hyde, The Gift 74-75 (1983).

[53] In the fall of 1984, I took my Indian Law class to visit the Rosebud Sioux Tribal Court. The court staff provided a special meal for the class at the courthouse. The vice-president of the tribe welcomed the class and said a traditional prayer over the meal. Many of the students found this an unexpected and powerful experience.

The give-away reflects a desire for cooperation and sharing to permeate the economic sphere. Although it may not achieve this goal completely on the reservation, its practice is more than mere nostalgia. It illustrates a profound ambivalence about the economic development ethos that values production and acquisition. There is something to be said for both materialistic and intangible economic systems. There is no easy answer to this dilemma for planners, but it is important to acknowledge the possibility of economic development that takes gift-giving or some variation of it as its model.

Such a development model must encounter the harsh realities of poverty and dependence, but the exchange of complementary efforts should enhance the chances for cross-fertilization and success in economic progress. Development may proceed along other than a monocultural path. So little is known about what actually works in the development field that a well-conceived plan that draws on the best of the old and the new, the indigenous and the imported, offers the best hope for advancement and accomplishment.

Development discussions are often couched in technical jargon from the fields of politics, economics, and technology that seems detached from the day-to-day lives of the people who are to be benefited. Development emphasizes economic growth and income enhancement as worthy means to defeat poverty. If life were that simple, it could be left at that. Unfortunately, individual and social life is not that tidy. Economic questions are inextricably entwined with social and moral questions. The organization of economic life in any society inevitably touches on the fundamental issue of cultural meaning. How does the pursuit of development affect communities and individuals at this level of meaning?

Much of this discussion is hidden in ideology. In the Third World, there is the ubiquitous clash between socialism and capitalism and their respective economic and political claims. In Indian country, the clash is less pronounced. Although there is no clear ideological opposition to the dominant theme of capitalist development, an undertow of opposition and resistance is present all the same. It is therefore instructive to examine some issues that development raises beyond the question of improving economic performance.

Development means substantial change and, as a general matter, that change can be continuous or discontinuous with an individual's personal and social past. Part of this change is institutional, but any change of such magnitude finally takes root in the individual at the level of consciousness and meaning. There is no doubt that capitalist development pushes individuality, the profit motive, and the accumulation of wealth. In contrast, traditional Lakota values involve the importance of the group, noneconomic bonds, and the sharing of wealth. This formulation is a typology that suggests the kind of tension that issues of development raise in Indian country. This is not meant to suggest a fixed reality but rather the end points of a continuum on which individuals and communities are arrayed at *different points* all along the continuum. It is not a simple question of one or the other, but rather many shades and blends of both. This is the complex, reality that development must confront.

There is, as always, no easy answer to this problem, but there are some signposts for guidance. Development work must concern itself with a "calculus of meaning" that realizes "all material development is, in the end, futile unless it serves to enhance the meanings by which human beings live. This is why it is so important to be careful about riding roughshod over traditional values and institutions." The calculus of meaning finds a necessary complement in the notion of "cognitive respect," which involves "a recognition that no outsider, including the outsider who possesses power, is in a position to 'know better' when it comes to the finalities of other people's lives." Economic planning and development can only be successful if there is an authentic commitment to understand history, culture, and individuals and communities at the grass-roots level.

Such an investment in time and dedication is generally not part of the development cost/benefit analysis, and it is also beyond what is provided by most experts and lending institutions. This shortcoming is rarely identified in the literature, which seldom concerns itself with deficits in the community of experts. Development involves reexamination and self-scrutiny by all participants in the development process, including those who do not engage regularly in professional soul-searching and who do not have to suffer the adverse consequences of their failure to do so.

The burdens of development may seem impossible to surmount, but they are not. Development is the paramount world issue in the latter part of the twentieth century, and this is no less true in Indian country. The questions of development often refer to complex historical, institutional, and cultural forces, but the *answers* lie with people.

> Ultimately, development is about neither numbers nor solutions; rather it is about people. Our bias for hope derives from our inclination to see people not only as the ends of development programs but also as the means for these programs' effective implementation.... [P]eople viewed as problem solving agents capable of acquiring increased competence and confidence, constitute a uniquely abundant and self-renewing resource. The very real prospect of exploiting this unique resource more broadly and effectively is among the most cogent and underrated justifications for hope.

In economic development planning, we must be guided, not by claims of theoretical perfection, but by a deep commitment to do the best we can in actual tribal situations. This is a commitment that is wisely tempered by compassion and humility.

THE BLACK MESA CRISIS (Traditional Life & Land League,[1] 1970)

The most destructive and dangerous method of mining coal is now being used to desecrate Black Mesa, Sacred Female Mountain to the Navajo Indians and sacred to the Hopi for a dozen centuries before the coming of the Euro-Americans. The white man is uncaringly defiling the religion of the indigenous North Americans, disrupting sacred places and holy mountains, and ignoring the desires and warnings of the Navajo and Hopi People. The strip-mining of Black Mesa is a blasphemy to the traditional Indians and a threat to all land and life, according to their religious leaders. This is being done to make "cheap" power for the white man's cities and to make way for the dying nova of Euro-American civilization.

---

[1]A voluntary organization interested in the cause of "traditional" Indians.

The ancient and still strong examples of the way man should live, and the way the Euro-Americans must learn to live, are threatened *directly* with extinction by the Black Mesa Project. The traditional Hopi and Navajo are living ways of life order, more stable and more at one with Nature than that of the Anglos. The nomadic Navajo and the agrarian-village culture of the Hopi are examples of traditional ways more-or-less intact, now fighting big business exploitation and governmental economic-cultural manipulation to remain so.

From the beginning the indigenous North Americans told the invading white man the Euro-American way of life was dangerous to all land and life on Earth. They were not heard — they were massacred. Now all that they have warned us of has come to pass: the waters we drink are poisoned, the air we breathe is poisoned, the food we eat is poisoned, our agricultural lands are dead and dying, the people in our cities have gone insane, and the whole of the cycle of life is being destroyed by the way we live....

Land and Life

The Hopi:

Excerpts from a letter to President Richard Nixon: "We, the True and Traditional religious leaders, recognized as such by the Hopi People, maintain full authority over all land and life contained within the Western Hemisphere. We are granted our stewardship by virtue of our instructions as to the meaning of Nature, Peace and Harmony as spoken to our People by Him, known to us as Massau'u, the Great Spirit, who long ago provided for us the sacred stone tablets which we preserve to this day. For many generations before the coming of the white man, and for many generations before the coming of the Navajo, the Hopi People have lived in that sacred place known to you as the Southwest and known to us to be the spiritual center of our continent. Those of us of the Hopi Nation who have followed the path of the Great Spirit without compromise have a message which we are committed, through our prophecy, to convey to you.

"The white man, through his insensitivity to the way of Nature, has desecrated the face of Mother Earth. The white man's advanced technological capacity has occurred as a result of his lack of regard for the spiritual path and for the way of all living things. The white man's desire for material possessions and power has blinded him to the pain he has caused Mother Earth by his quest for what he calls natural resources. All over the country, the waters have been tainted, the soil broken and defiled, the air polluted. Living creatures die from poisons left because of industry. And the path of the Great Spirit has become difficult to see by all men, even by many Indians who have chosen instead to follow the path of the white man.

"We have accepted the responsibility designated by our prophecy to tell you that all life will stop unless men come to know that every one must live in Peace, and in Harmony with Nature. Only those People who know the secrets of Nature, the Mother of us all, can overcome the possible destruction of all land and life.

"Today the sacred lands where the Hopi live are being desecrated by men who seek coal and water from our soil that they may create more power for the white man's cities. This must not be allowed to continue for if it does Mother Nature will react in such a way that almost all men will suffer the end of life as they now know it." This letter is signed for Chief Mina Lansa (Oraibi), Chief Claude Kawangyawma (Shungopavy), Chief Starlie Lomayaktowa (Mushongnovy), and Chief Dan Katchongva (Hotevilla) by Thomas Banyacya, interpreter.

The Navajo:

Beauty and Harmony are the heart of the Navajo Way of Life. This harmony comes from the eternal and natural balance of the Male Mountain (Lukachukai) and the Female Mountain (Black Mesa). The singers and traditional religious leaders have stated that if these mountains, the sources of harmony, are damaged, the Navajo Way will be destroyed. "I do not agree with this mining," said one Navajo. "See that hill? My father and grandfather said that is a holy place. Now what will happen to that holy place?"

"An old story," says a tribal leader. "Our water and our land resources will be drained, taken out of the reservation, and in exchange we get a handful of jobs and a small payoff. What will be left of our Way of Life?"

"This is not economic development. This is economic termination of the reservation," he says.

"Everyone talks of self-determination for the Indians," says another Navajo. "And what do they do? They offer us self-destruction. Of our resources and religion."

Chapter 8

SPECIAL PROTECTIONS OF RIGHTS OF CERTAIN NATIVE COMMUNITIES

While federal Indian law often approaches questions of Indian sovereignty and rights based on common patterns of protection and experience, in a very real sense every Native community represents a unique case posing special problems for federal Indian law. Each tribe has its own unique history and culture, each has had a different relationship with the United States government or the government of the state in which it exists, and each relies on different sources for the origin of its right to a tribal homeland. Some have had extensive treaty relations with the United States, others limited treaty contacts, and still others have been ignored by the federal government. The land of some tribes is protected by treaty, while others rely on statutes, executive orders, tribal or federal purchase, or even aboriginal title. Nevertheless, there are substantial commonalities to many of these patterns and the general principles of federal Indian law covered in other chapters therefore generally apply with full force to most federally recognized tribes in Indian country notwithstanding the variability of their history.

Even then, as we have already seen, federal statutory law sometimes deliberately creates variations from the general pattern of federal protections of Indian sovereignty and autonomy. For example, certain tribally specific statutes enacted during the 1940's transferred criminal jurisdiction to the states over the Kansas Reservations, the Mesquakie Settlement in Iowa, and the Devil's Lake Reservation in North Dakota; transferred both civil and criminal jurisdiction over the New York Reservations; and made special jurisdictional provisions for the Agua Caliente Reservation in California. These statutes proved to be a prelude to two other types of federal statute designed to vary the structure of protections for indigenous communities — Public Law 280 and the termination statutes of the 1950's. Finally, negotiated settlements of complex Indian claims, especially those recently negotiated, sometimes resulted in special alterations in common patterns of relationships between tribal governments and the states. *E.g.*, Maine Indian Claims Settlement Act of 1980, Pub. L. 96-420, 94 Stat. 1785, codified at 25 U.S.C. § 1721 *et seq.*; Rhode Island Claims Settlement Act of 1978, Pub. L. 95-395, 92 Stat. 813, codified at 25 U.S.C. § 1701 *et seq.*

Coverage of all of these varied patterns is impossible since the historical patterns are almost as varied as the number of tribes. Nevertheless, there are several particularly distinctive patterns of protection for certain Native communities that sufficiently depart from the common Native experience elsewhere in the United States to deserve special attention. This chapter focuses attention on the special historical experiences and legal protections of four such types of Native communities, the Native communities of Alaska, Native Hawaiians, the tribes of eastern Oklahoma, and terminated and non-recognized tribes.

A. ALASKAN NATIVES

American law has treated Alaskan Natives differently from tribes in the "Lower 48." At what point did this treatment begin and what was its justification? The Alaska Native Claims Settlement Act of 1971 ("ANCSA") took this differential treatment even further, devising a completely new system for Alaskan Natives. As you read the materials that follow, ask what the Alaska Natives gained from ANCSA and what they forfeited. What trade-offs of competing values were involved in the legislation and why were they imposed?

1. THE ALASKA NATIVE CLAIMS SETTLEMENT ACT IN THE 1970'S

LAZARUS & WEST, THE ALASKA NATIVE CLAIMS SETTLEMENT ACT: A FLAWED VICTORY, 40 Law & Contemporary Problems 132, 132-38 (1976)*

For the eighty thousand natives of Alaska (Indians, Eskimos and Aleuts), passage of the Alaska Native Claims Settlement Act of 1971 (ANCSA)[1] constituted a triumph over long-time governmental inertia. With increasing urgency, the natives had pressed their claims of aboriginal title to virtually all the 375 million acres of land within the state. While Congress proved nominally willing to preserve such claims,[3] almost a century had elapsed without action to confirm or extinguish them.[4] By 1969-1970, however, the rapidly escalating rate of economic development in Alaska, combined initially with pressure from a more sympathetic administration,[5] impelled a reluctant state and, subsequently, private industry to join the natives in seeking a comprehensive legislative determination of their land rights.[6] The Claims Act soon followed.

---

*Copyright © 1976 by Duke University School of Law. Reprinted by permission.

[1] Act of Dec. 18, 1971, Pub. L. No. 92-203.

[3] See Act of July 7, 1958, Pub. L. No. 85-508, 72 Stat. 339; Act of June 6, 1900, ch. 786, 31 Stat. 321; Act of May 14, 1898, ch. 299, 30 Stat. 409; Act of March 3, 1891, ch. 543, 26 Stat. 989; Act of May 17, 1884, ch. 53, § 8, 23 Stat. 24; Lazarus, Native Land Claims in Alaska, 7 Am. Indian 39 (1958).

[4] The Indian Claims Commission Act, which was enacted in 1946, has served as the principal legislative vehicle for settling the claims of Indians against the United States. See 25 U.S.C. § 70 (1970). This legislation, however, has not been utilized by Alaska Natives for the reasons noted by the House of Representatives in its report on the House version of the Claims Act:

> The Indian Claims Commission has not been available to the Natives in Alaska, in a practical sense, because the great bulk of the aboriginal titles claimed by the Natives have not been taken or extinguished by the United States. The United States has simply not acted.

H.R. Rep. No. 523, 92d Cong., 1st Sess. 4 (1971).

[5] In response to native requests, supported by such Indian-interest organizations as the Association on American Indian Affairs, Inc., Secretary of the Interior Stewart L. Udall in late 1966 imposed an informal and unannounced moratorium upon the patenting of lands selected by the state pursuant to section 6 of the Alaska Statehood Act. Act of July 7, 1958, Pub. L. No. 85-508, 72 Stat. 339. Before leaving office, Secretary Udall issued Public Land Order No. 4582, 34 Fed. Reg. 1025 (1969), formally withdrawing all unreserved public lands in Alaska from disposition pending a determination of native rights, and during the course of his confirmation hearings Secretary-designate Walter J. Hickel, former Governor of Alaska, agreed to honor the Udall "land freeze" for two years.

[6] See generally M. Berry, The Alaska Pipeline: The Politics of Oil and Native Land Claims (1975). The switch in the state's position from opposition to native land claims legislation and the subsequent change in industry attitudes from indifference to active support stemmed in substantial

The victory for the native cause achieved through ANCSA was overwhelming, both comparatively and absolutely. In June 1967, Secretary of the Interior Stewart L. Udall recommended to Congress a legislative settlement which included the grant of trust title in up to fifty thousand acres for each native village (a maximum of about ten million acres) and authorization for the Alaska Attorney General to sue for the value of any remaining native lands at 1867 prices. By July 1969, Secretary of the Interior Walter J. Hickel had raised the administration's suggested price for the extinguishment of native claims to $500 million and ownership of up to ten million acres. Under the Claims Act, the natives in fact will receive fee title to over forty million acres of land, payments from the United States Treasury of $462.5 million over an eleven year period, and a royalty of two per cent up to a ceiling of $500 million on mineral development in Alaska. This settlement provides far more money and leaves far more land in native ownership than any previous treaty, agreement, or statute for the extinguishment of aboriginal title in our nation's history.

In addition to funds and resources, however, the Claims Act presents the natives of Alaska with a unique challenge. Rejecting traditional federal-Indian relationships, Congress directed that the settlement be administered through corporations organized under state law, and defined the precise manner in which native funds and income from native property were to be allocated. Within this statutory framework, though, the natives retain relatively unfettered control over their assets, and are free from Bureau of Indian Affairs supervision.[11] ANCSA thus reflects a new departure in government dealings with Indians — a policy which places on the natives alone the crucial task of translating the immediate benefits of the settlement into permanent, socially and economically productive enterprises.

I

The Principal Provisions of the Claims Act

The Claims Act not only effected a comprehensive legislative settlement of all aboriginal land titles and claims, it also enabled Alaska to resume land selections under the Statehood Act, and removed a major legal obstacle to construction of the Alaska pipeline and a potential cloud upon the titles of all non-natives claiming rights to land in the state under federal law. What the natives received, or were required to do in return, is summarized below.

A. The Native Corporations

Pursuant to section 7(a) of the Claims Act, the Secretary of the Interior divided the State of Alaska into twelve geographic regions composed, as far as

---

part from native successes in the courts. Specifically, in Alaska v. Udall, 420 F.2d 938 (9th Cir. 1969), the Court of Appeals for the Ninth Circuit, in rejecting a state attack upon the validity of the land freeze, ruled that lands claimed by the natives could not be deemed, as a matter of law, "vacant, unappropriated, and unreserved" and thus subject to selection under the Statehood Act. In Native Village of Allakaket v. Hickel, Civil No. 706-70 (D.D.C., filed Oct. 18, 1972), the District Court for the District of Columbia enjoined construction of the Alaska pipeline across native lands.

[11] The settlement is to be effected "without establishing any permanent racially defined institutions, rights, privileges, or obligations, without creating a reservation system or lengthy wardship or trusteeship, and without adding to the categories of property and institutions enjoying special tax privileges ...." 43 U.S.C. § 1601(b).

practicable, of natives having a common heritage and sharing common interests. In order to qualify for benefits under ANCSA, the natives of a particular region first had to organize a Regional Corporation under the "business for profit" laws of the State of Alaska.[14] Section 7(g) of the Claims Act provides that each "Regional Corporation shall be authorized to issue such number of shares of common stock, divided into such classes of shares as may be specified in the articles of incorporation to reflect the provisions of this Act, as may be needed to issue one hundred shares of stock to each Native enrolled in the region ...." Until December 18, 1991, stock in the Regional Corporations is subject to a restriction upon alienation and carries voting rights only if the holder is a native.

Within each region, eligible native villages must also organize under state corporation laws before receiving benefits under the Act.[16] These Village Corporations are neither stockholders in nor subsidiaries of the Regional Corporations,[17] but the Claims Act nonetheless requires the Regional Corporations to supervise the redistribution to Village Corporations of monies received from the Alaska Native Fund and from timber and mineral resources, to withhold money until acceptable plans have been approved by the Regional Corporation for the use of distributable funds,[19] and to review and approve the articles of incorporation, including proposed amendments and annual budgets of the Village Corporations for a period of five years.[20]

B. *The Alaska Native Fund*

Section 6 of the Claims Act establishes in the United States Treasury an Alaska Native Fund into which money from two major sources is to be depos-

---

[14] 43 U.S.C. §§ 1606(d), 1607(a) (Supp. IV, 1974). Section 7(c) of ANCSA, 43 U.S.C. § 1606(c), provides that, "[i]f a majority of all eligible Natives eighteen years of age or older who are not permanent residents of Alaska elect ... to be enrolled in a thirteenth region ... the Secretary shall establish such a region for the benefit of the Natives who elected to be enrolled therein, and they may establish a Regional Corporation ...." The Secretary ruled that a majority of the adult natives who are nonresidents of Alaska did not elect to form a thirteenth region, but his determination has been overturned by a federal district court, and a thirteenth Regional Corporation was organized on January 1, 1976. Alaska Native Ass'n of Oregon v. Morton, Civil No. 2133-73; Alaska Fed'n of Natives Int'l v. Morton, Civil No. 2141-73 (D.D.C., filed Dec. 30, 1974). Moreover, the district court's decision was confirmed by the Act of January 2, 1976, Pub. L. No. 94-204, § 8, 89 Stat. 1145, 1149.

[16] *Id.* § 1607(a). At the present time all of the more than two hundred native villages in Alaska certified by the Secretary of the Interior as eligible for benefits under the Act have organized as business corporations pursuant to Alaska law.

[17] All of the stockholders of a Village Corporation also are stockholders of the Regional Corporation for their region, but only some of the stockholders of the Regional Corporation will be stockholders of any particular Village Corporation. Under the Claims Act, the Village Corporations do not own stock of the Regional Corporation, and the Regional Corporation does not own stock of the Village Corporations.

[19] A Regional Corporation may withhold money otherwise distributable to a Village Corporation

until the village has submitted a plan for the use of the money that is satisfactory to the Regional Corporation ... [and] may require a village plan to provide for joint ventures with other villages, and for joint financing of projects undertaken by the Regional Corporation that will benefit the region generally.

43 U.S.C. § 1606(l) (Supp. IV, 1974).

[20] *Id.* § 1607(b). This vesting of authority in one set of private corporations over the business, assets, and affairs of a second independent set of private corporations appears unprecedented in the annals of American legal history.

ited. The Fund is to receive federal appropriations in the total amount of $462,500,000 over an eleven year period beginning with the fiscal year 1972, the year during which the Act became effective. In addition, a share in the amount of two per cent of specified federal and state mineral revenues is to be paid into the Fund, without regard to any time limitations, until such payments reach $500 million.

Section 6(c) of the Claims Act provides that, after completion of a native roll by the Secretary, all money in the Fund "shall be distributed at the end of each three months of the fiscal year among the Regional Corporations organized pursuant to section 7 on the basis of the relative numbers of Natives enrolled in each region."[23] Pursuant to section 7(j) of ANCSA, however, during the first five years following enactment, not less than 10 per cent of all money received by the Regional Corporations from the Fund must be distributed among their stockholders and, in addition, not less than 45 per cent of such money during the first five year period and 50 per cent thereafter is to be distributed by the Regional Corporations to Village Corporations and to the class of regional stockholders who are not residents of native villages which have organized Village Corporations. Thus, ANCSA specifically mandates that initially at least 55 per cent, and subsequently at least 50 per cent, of all money distributed from the Fund to Regional Corporations shall be redistributed to their stockholders, to non-residents of villages, and to Village Corporations.

C. *Land Entitlement Under the Claims Act*

Pursuant to section 11(a) of the Act, the Secretary of the Interior has withdrawn over one hundred million acres of "public lands"[25] in Alaska "from all forms of appropriation under the public land laws, including the mining and mineral leasing laws, and from selection under the Alaska Statehood Act...." Village Corporations had the collective right, before December 18, 1974, to select up to twenty-two million acres from the lands so withdrawn, with the exact land entitlement of each village being dependent upon its population.[27] The difference between the acreage actually selected by Village Corporations

---

[23] *Id.* § 1605(c). The final roll was certified by the Secretary of the Interior on December 18, 1973, and the balance of the money then held in the Fund was distributed to the Regional Corporations immediately thereafter. Previously, the corporations had received small advances from the Fund pursuant to special congressional authorization in order to conduct necessary business activities. *See* Second Supplemental Appropriations Act of May 27, 1972, Pub. L. No. 92-306, 86 Stat. 163, 167; Interior Dep't Appropriations Act for the Fiscal Year Ending June 30, 1973, Pub. L. No. 92-369, 86 Stat. 508, 510. The roll was ordered reopened by the Act of January 2, 1976, *supra* note 14, to accommodate those natives who missed the filing deadline.

[25] "Public lands" are defined in section 3(e) of ANCSA as:

all Federal lands and interests therein in Alaska except: (1) the smallest practicable tract, as determined by the Secretary, enclosing land actually used in connection with the administration of any Federal installation, and (2) land selections of the State of Alaska which have been patented or tentatively approved under section 6(g) of the Alaska Statehood Act, as amended ... or identified for selection by the State prior to January 17, 1969.

Id. § 1609(e).

[27] *Id.* §§ 1611(a), 1615(a). In villages outside southeast Alaska, the Village Corporations are entitled to select a minimum of three townships (69.120 acres) for a population between twenty-five and ninety-nine and a maximum of seven townships (161.280 acres) for a population over 600. *Id.* § 1613(a). All villages in southeastern Alaska are limited to land selections of one township (23.040 acres), regardless of population. *Id.* § 1613(b).

and the authorized twenty-two million acres is to be allocated by the Secretary among eleven Regional Corporations (excluding southeastern Alaska) on the basis of the number of natives enrolled in each region, and then is to be reallocated by the Regional Corporations to the villages "on an equitable basis after considering historic use, subsistence needs, and population." The Village Corporations will receive a fee simple "patent to the surface estate in the lands selected," while the Secretary of the Interior is directed to "issue to the Regional Corporation for the region in which the lands are located a patent to the subsurface estate in such lands ...." The Act also provided that Regional Corporations could obtain title to an additional sixteen million acres of land selected prior to December 18, 1975 from withdrawn public lands.[31]

Although Regional Corporations will receive full title to their own land selections and a fee simple patent to the subsurface estate under lands selected by native villages, groups, and individuals, ANCSA further provides that these corporations will not enjoy the entire benefit of this property. Section 7(i) of the Claims Act requires that each Regional Corporation divide among all twelve Regional Corporations on an annual basis 70 per cent of the revenues derived from the timber resources and subsurface estate patented to it. Moreover, as in the case of the Fund, section 7(j) provides that, during the five years following enactment, not less than 10 per cent of all funds received by a Regional Corporation under section 7(i) must be distributed among its stockholders and, in addition, not less than 45 per cent of such revenues during the first five year period, and 50 per cent thereafter, shall be distributed by the Regional Corporation to Village Corporations established in its region, and to the class of its stockholders who are not residents of native villages having organized Village Corporations. Thus, ANCSA vests substantial real property interests in the Regional Corporation, but further dictates that each Regional Corporation must share its revenues from timber and subsurface resources with other Regional Corporations, Village Corporations, and certain stockholders.

---

[31] *Id.* § 1611(c). Sealaska Corporation, organized by the natives of southeastern Alaska, and the thirteenth Regional Corporation, which will be organized under section 7(c) of the Claims Act, *see* note 14 *supra*, are not entitled to make these section 12(c) selections. In addition, since eligibility for section 12(c) selections is determined on a land-loss formula, only six Regional Corporations actually so qualify.

In exercising rights under section 12(c), lands withdrawn pursuant to subsection 11(a)(1) must be selected before lands withdrawn pursuant to subsection 11(a)(3) may be selected, provided that "within the lands withdrawn by subsection 11(a)(1) the Regional Corporation may select only even numbered townships in even numbered ranges, and only odd numbered townships in odd numbered ranges." 43 U.S.C. § 1611(c) (Supp. IV, 1974). The purpose of this provision was to prevent native corporations in combination from controlling large, solid blocks of land.

Section 14(c) provides that "[i]mmediately after selection by a Regional Corporation, the Secretary shall convey to the Corporation title to the surface and/or the subsurface estates, as is appropriate, in the lands selected." *Id.* § 1613(e). As a practical matter, the Bureau of Land Management will not be able to complete the required survey of native land selections for decades, so the Secretary will have difficulty in issuing a patent promptly. In recognition of this fact, the land selection regulations provide for issuance of interim conveyances. 43 C.F.R. § 2650.0-5(h) (1974).

The Regional Corporations also possess a land entitlement under section 14(h) of ANCSA which is not to exceed two million acres, including the subsurface estate beneath lands patented to native groups and individuals. 43 U.S.C. § 1613(h) (Supp. IV, 1974).

PRICE, A MOMENT IN HISTORY: THE ALASKA NATIVE CLAIMS SETTLEMENT ACT, 8 U.C.L.A.-Alaska Law Review 89, 95-101 (1979)*

Where does the Alaska Native Claims Settlement Act fit in the history of Federal Indian policy? The hallmark of the legislation is the corporate nature of the structures created.

The spectacular aspect of the Claims Act is its embrace of this corporate ideology. If the General Allotment Act of 1887 had the small farmer as its ideal and goal for the Indian family, the Alaska legislation has the corporate shareholder as its model. The General Allotment Act was not successful; as a consequence of the delay by Bureau personnel and the reluctance of certain tribes, Indian allotments were limited to a marked, rather than a pervasive influence on Indian lands. Not so the Alaska Settlement Act. By legislative stroke, the Congress converted all Alaska Natives into members of the corporate world, receivers of annual reports, proxy statements, solicitations and balance sheets. The Native received a shotgun initiation into the American mainstream.

The ardor with which this original conversion has been received is testimony to its ideological force in our society. Village entities, for example, could, under the Act, organize as profit or non-profit corporations. Of the over 200 Village Corporations formed under the Act, not a single one initially filed papers as a nonprofit corporation notwithstanding tax and other benefits that might have resulted from the choice of the nonprofit form. It is possible that there was a lack of information on the choices available. But it is also possible that the persistence of the profit motif in the Act, in its justification and in the resultant planning meant that retention of the for-profit form was, itself, perceived as an aspect of maturity of development. The assets transferred by the bill, one billion dollars and 40 million acres of land, are for the most part transferred to the twelve regional corporations within Alaska. Each of the enrolled Natives holds 100 shares in the regional corporation. The corporations are incorporated under Alaska state laws and are administered in accordance with the state's corporation statutes.

Aside from the symbolic differences, there are, of course, quite important actual differences between the tribe as paradigm and the corporation as paradigm for the organization of indigenous people. The major distinction relates to governance. The essence of a tribe is its existence as a political entity. How much authority the tribe may have is often open to question. The tribe, amorphous, ill-defined, subject to competitive pressures by other governments, may have difficulty asserting power to zone, to tax, to define criminal conduct and assess penalties for violations. There may be ambiguities in the authority over non-Indians or non-members or members that are not within the political boundaries of the tribe. But the essence of a tribe is its legitimate claim to some political authority. By choosing the corporate form, Congress has negated this claim to political authority. A corporation is an owner of assets and a manager of assets. It has no authority over personal conduct or behavior, and, without specific statutory aids, has no governing power to control what kind of development or subsistence activity occurs within its sphere of influence.

The Native Corporations, as established, still retain some of the vestiges of governance. The very titles of the corporations, particularly the Village Corporations, imply some faint remnant of governance. In the Arctic Slope area, there has been formed an organized borough, with governing authority under state law, whose boundaries coincide with a virtually all-Native population, so that there is some symmetry between the Arctic Slope Native Corporation and a true political entity. At this stage, the perceptions of the Native Corporations include the feeling that they are quasi-governmental, and are concerned with *both* the future of the state and the fate of their stockholders in a way that is closer to political entities than it is to private corporations. Finally, through lobbying in Juneau and Washington and through their impact on the political process, the Native Corporations seek indirectly to have some of the effect of a government on the future of the state.

A second major conceptual difference between a tribe and a corporation as paradigm relates to immunity from state law. Since the end of the eighteenth century, one of the hallmarks of tribal status has been the immunity of tribal lands from the imposition of state law. In terms of land use, the central aspect of this immunity has been the lack of application of state and local property taxes and the absence of the authority to zone. There have been degrees of immunity that have existed as a consequence of legislation, of judicial decision or of random practices. But always, as part of the essence of the nature of a tribe, there has been the notion of immunity from state law.

The Native Corporations have limited immunity from state and local property taxation for a period of twenty years but only if their land is not leased to third parties or developed (there may be, as always, ambiguities in the application of that term). Otherwise their operations and their properties are conceptually as subject to state laws as any other corporate entity within the state. There will be modifications as the Corporations seek to interpose Indian Reorganization Act councils and as the state and federal governments provide special exemptions from taxation for subsistence purposes. But the essence of the distinction persists.

An exceedingly important, but ill-understood distinction between tribe and corporation as paradigm relates to the rights of the members against the central entity. A tribe is not only a political authority with governance powers, it also has extraordinary immunity from actions by members that may weaken the authority of the tribe. As a consequence of Supreme Court decisions interpreting the United States Constitution, it has been held that a tribe is neither a state nor an agent of the federal government for determining whether individuals have rights to be protected against tribal acts which would otherwise be declared discriminatory. Furthermore, the Indian Civil Rights Act, which was passed by Congress to establish certain rights of individual members against the tribe, has been held not to confer jurisdiction upon state or federal courts to determine whether a violation has occurred. Accordingly, a tribe may be able, free of federal judicial interference, to deprive individual members of the right to vote, to infringe upon their free speech rights, and to decide that elections to determine the makeup of the governing entity will be extremely rare.

Stockholders in the Native Corporation have much more piercing and effective rights against the governing entity of the corporation. Alaska Native Corporations are governed by Alaska state law and all the protections furnished to stockholders in non-Native Corporations apply.[38] As a consequence, the individual shareholder has rights to disclosure, to notice of Board meetings, to attend annual meetings and other similar rights. The capacity of the Board to modify such rights is governed by state law. More important, the shareholder, under Alaska state law, has specific remedies in state court if it is felt that an action was taken that violated a duty to the corporation. Proxy fights can be, and have been, waged. There may be frequent efforts to hold special meetings of the shareholders, empowered to displace the Board of Directors and enlist new management, except as limited under state law, particularly where there is cumulative voting. In terms of stability, this means that a Native Corporation management may have less assurance of its tenure than a politically established leadership of a tribe. This is particularly true because the Congress, by amendment to the Native Claims Settlement Act, removed Native proxy fights from the protection and stewardship of the Securities and Exchange Commission.[46]

There is a fourth difference between corporation as paradigm and tribe as paradigm that is of critical importance in understanding the distinction. Concomitant to a tribe's authority to govern is its power to act, particularly its power to serve the individual needs of its subjects. A tribe can determine that certain of its members should have low cost housing or special loan programs or individual health services all based on their needs for such programs and their incomes. It is not clear that a Native Corporation under Alaska law has that leeway. A corporation which used its revenues to help poor shareholders at the expense of wealthier ones might be open to a shareholder's action rather than to praise for progressive redistribution policies.

This constraint is of fundamental importance. There may be those who look to the Native Corporation to serve, in complex and creative ways, the needs of their shareholders. And it would be superb if they did so. But there is the fear, which may substantially affect the decisions of corporate officers, that business judgment rules will be brought to bear upon their actions. And groups of shareholders, anxious to obtain control, or at least obtain what they perceive to be fair, will attack conduct which is discriminatory, even beneficially so.

A fifth distinction between the tribe and the corporation relates to the power to dispose of property. To the extent that a tribe is a government, governmental considerations attach to its own decision to dispose of property held in common. To some extent, there is an attitudinal barrier to disposing of tribal property even if the tribe is legally permitted to do so. And, generally, absent specific Congressional consent, and then usually only with Secretarial approval,[48] there is a prohibition on the sale of tribal real property.

Under the Native Claims Settlement Act, one of the very specific achievements was the removal of any barrier against sale of corporate land.[49] No Secretarial approval is necessary. The land is held by the Native Corporation in fee simple so that the managers of the corporation can enter into whatever

---

[38] Alaska Stat., Title 10. *See* Brown v. Ward, 593 P.2d 247 (1979).
[46] Act of January 2, 1976, 43 U.S.C. § 1625, 89 Stat. 1147. State law provides standards similar to federal law. Brown v. Ward, *supra* note 38.
[48] 25 U.S.C. § 348.
[49] 43 U.S.C. § 1613.

transactions, consistent with corporate policy, they deem valid. For a period of ten years, Regional Corporations had the power to review the sale of land by Village Corporations within their[49a] Region. But the right of review did not automatically include any veto right; furthermore, it was not clear that the inclination of the Regions would be to frequently exercise its right of review.

Finally, there is the right to ongoing federal benefits. The Alaska Native Claims Settlement Act does not, by its own terms purport to sever Alaska Natives from any special federal programs. And there is no sign that, for the average shareholder, there is the kind of improvement in life that would suggest the lack of need for federal benevolence. That said, however, there is an aesthetic and constitutional sense in which the existence of tribes as paradigms, as compared to corporations, is more hospitable to the continued receipt of certain federal benefits. From an aesthetic perspective, there are undoubtedly those who think that Alaska Natives have now been given a dowry and sent off to succeed or fail. They are not like tribes where there is a continued federal interest in fostering self-government. From a constitutional sense, the question is whether benefits that are addressed specially to Natives are racial or tribal in basis. The most recent Supreme Court case,[50] dealing with employment preferences for Indians in the Bureau of Indian Affairs, seemed quite pointedly to rest on the Bureau's role in governing tribes. To the extent Natives are not part of self-governing entities, there may be challenges to their inclusion in Indian-specific programs.

The corporate structure and the financial responsibilities under the Act have another consequence. It must change the characteristics of leadership. This is certainly only a hypothesis, but the construct of values that were respected in the historic Native village will change. The corporate executives will be those who are willing to forego subsistence activities, to place a higher priority on board meetings than on salmon fishing, and to spend time talking to lawyers and financiers and bankers rather than the people of the villages. It is possible that there will develop a leadership cadre in the Native corporations that will become somewhat removed from the shareholders. The Native corporations, in this sense, will approximate other large businesses and that management will, more and more, be separated from ownership.

In a sense, the gospel of capitalism has gripped the leadership of the regional corporations just as in another day, another kind of gospel was introduced for its educative and assimilative influence. The profitmaking mandate has become a powerful vision, a powerful driving force.

I have concentrated on the Alaska Native Claims Settlement Act in terms of its reformist aspect, namely the imposition of the corporate imprint on Native life in the state. But there is the other theme in the history of Indian legislation that is important here as well: namely the theme of opening resources for non-aboriginal use and development. The Settlement Act fits within the traditional Indian policy because it quiets title to land in the state. While it reserves ten percent of the land for Native ownership, the legislation makes it clear that there is no continuing encumbrance on aboriginal title to the remainder of the

[49a] 43 U.S.C. § 1613(c) (5).
[50] Morton v. Mancari, 414 U.S. 1142 (1974).

land.[52] Furthermore, because of its lack of limitation on sale or lease of land, the legislation was essentially thought to open the land for development.

Passage of the Act was and still is looked at as a technique for placing large parts of the state in private hands. Perhaps out of stereotypical perceptions, the non-Native expectation seems to be that the lands involved will only be temporarily in Native ownership. The Act even more clearly unlocks much of the mineral wealth in Alaska. There would have been no Native Claims Settlement Act of the present magnitude had it not been for the intense interest of the oil companies in its passage.

The Native Claims Settlement Act is the clear descendant of the earliest American approaches to Indian policy. Native occupancy is undisturbed until there is pressure for Native lands.

There are many who hailed the Alaska Native Claims Settlement Act as a great departure in the history of the dealings between the settler population and the Indian minority. The Act may still prove to be a great step forward. But for now, the conclusion must be that the Act has its antecedents, and its relationship to the history of Indian law is clearer than its place outside that history.

NOTES

1. **ANCSA as a Treaty Substitute:** Professor Wilkinson has called ANCSA a "treaty substitute." C. WILKINSON, AMERICAN INDIANS, TIME AND THE LAW 8 (1987). In what respect does ANCSA resemble a treaty? What consequences would flow from labeling ANCSA a treaty substitute? Some have analogized ANCSA as more like a statutory imposition of an assimilationist policy. *See, e.g.,* Comment, *The Alaska Native Claims Settlement Act: An Illusion in the Quest for Native Self-Determination,* 66 OR. L. REV. 195, 211-14 (1987) (ANCSA very similar to allotment and termination legislation in effect if not in purpose).

2. **Continuing Trust Relationship After ANCSA:** Section 2(b) of the Settlement Act disavows any intent to create "a lengthy wardship or trusteeship, and [to add] to the categories of property and institutions enjoying special tax privileges or to the legislation establishing special relationships between the United States Government and the State of Alaska." 43 U.S.C. § 1601(b). What effect does or should the inclusion of this language have on the continuing existence of a trust relationship between the Alaska Natives and the United States? See Chapter 2, section C3. In *Cape Fox Corp. v. United States,* 456 F. Supp. 784, *rev'd on other grounds,* 646 F.2d 399 (9th Cir. 1981), the district court interpreted the quoted language as demonstrating that ANCSA did not create any trust relationship. Does this interpretation necessarily follow? If the reference to unwillingness to create any new relationships refers to the village and regional corporations created by ANCSA, does it necessarily apply to the relationship between the U.S. and existing IRA and traditional village governments? Later cases have applied trust principles in interpreting legislation providing for services to Natives. *See, e.g., Eric v. Secretary of HUD,* 464 F. Supp. 44, 49-50 (D. Alaska 1978) (Bartlett Act, providing for housing for Native Alaskans, enacted to fulfill trust responsibility to Natives; HUD accountable under trust principles.). In addition, the provision in Section 2(c) of the Act requiring the Secretary to review and make recommendations for future programs seems to indi-

---

[52] Alaska Claims Settlement Act, § 4. *See also,* United States v. Atlantic Richfield Company, 435 F. Supp. 1009 (D. Alas. 1977), where the U.S. District Court circumscribed tort claims arising before the act for territorial trespass.

cate that Congress envisioned some sort of special relationship to continue between Congress and Natives. For a discussion of the legislative history of section 2(b) and an argument that it should be narrowly interpreted, see D. CASE, ALASKAN NATIVES AND AMERICAN LAW 16-18 (1984).

Later statutes, such as the Indian Financing Act of 1974, the Indian Self-Determination Act, the Indian Health Care Improvement Act, and the Indian Child Welfare Act, make clear that Natives are within the ambit of federal legislation dealing generally with Indian tribes, and that a trust relationship therefore exists as to the subject of that legislation at the very minimum. The author of the comment excerpted above criticized the *Cape Fox* court's refusal to recognize a trust relationship between the government and Native corporations after ANCSA in light of these later statutes treating corporations as tribes for certain purposes. Stanford Comment, *supra*, at 248-53.

3. **Extinguishment of Aboriginal Title in Alaska:** Recall that in *Tee-Hit-Ton Indians v. United States*, discussed and excerpted in Chapter 5, section B1, the Supreme Court held that Alaskan Natives' claims based on aboriginal title could be extinguished without any more than a moral duty to pay compensation. Aboriginal title is protected against incursions by third parties, however, giving rise to the trespass claims pressed by Alaskan Natives when the state began to lease aboriginal land to oil companies. The major impetus for the Settlement Act from Congress's perspective was the need to extinguish the title and any claims based on aboriginal title. *See generally* M. BERRY, THE ALASKA PIPELINE: THE POLITICS OF OIL AND NATIVE LAND CLAIMS (1975). Section 4 of ANCSA contained broad language extinguishing property rights:

43 U.S.C. § 1603. Declaration of settlement

(a) *Aboriginal title extinguishment through prior land and water area conveyances.* All prior conveyances of public land and water areas in Alaska, or any interest therein, pursuant to Federal law, and all tentative approvals pursuant to section 6(g) of the Alaska Statehood Act, shall be regarded as an extinguishment of the aboriginal title thereto, if any.

(b) *Aboriginal title and claim extinguishment where based on use and occupancy; submerged lands underneath inland and offshore water areas and hunting or fishing rights included.* All aboriginal titles, if any, and claims of aboriginal title in Alaska based on use and occupancy, including submerged land underneath all water areas, both inland and offshore, and including any aboriginal hunting or fishing rights that may exist, are hereby extinguished.

(c) *Aboriginal claim extinguishment where based on right, title, use, or occupancy of land or water areas; domestic statute or treaty relating to use and occupancy; or foreign laws; pending claims.* All claims against the United States, the State, and all other persons that are based on claims of aboriginal right, title, use, or occupancy of land or water areas in Alaska, or that are based on any statute or treaty of the United States relating to Native use and occupancy, or that are based on the laws of any other nation, including any such claims that are pending before any Federal or state court or the Indian Claims Commission, are hereby extinguished.

Although a trial judge in the District Court for the District of Columbia stated concern that extinguishing preexisting claims based on aboriginal title would violate the due process clause of the fifth amendment, *Edwardsen v. Morton*, 369 F. Supp. 1359, 1364 (D.D.C. 1973), the Alaska federal court had no such problem, stating: "trespass claims based on unrecognized aboriginal title are not protected property interests and, therefore the Settlement Act's extinguishment of Native trespass claims against third parties presents no constitutional problems." *United States v. Atlantic Richfield Co.*, 435 F. Supp. 1009, 1029-30 (D.

Alaska 1977). Although the Ninth Circuit Court of Appeals affirmed the lower court, it did not reach the constitutional question because the suit involved only trespass claims against third parties and not a direct claim against the government. 612 F.2d 1132, (9th Cir. 1980). It was not until 1982 that the Court of Claims resolved the issue by rejecting the argument that compensation was due for the Settlement Act's taking of the preexisting trespass claims. *Inupiat Community of the Arctic Slope v. United States*, 680 F.2d 122 (Ct. Cl. 1982), *cert. denied*, 459 U.S. 969 (1982). The Court of Claims upheld congressional power to extinguish the claims based on aboriginal title as "a political decision not subject to judicial reexamination." *Id.* at 129.

   4. Early criticisms of ANCSA: Contemporary observers hailed the Settlement Act as a positive resolution of the land claims of Alaskan Natives. Nevertheless, these same observers expressed concern about the unusual form of the settlement. As Professor Price points out, the drafters of ANCSA deliberately decided to create a statute that would serve as a machine, driving the Natives in Alaska toward self-sufficiency and assimilation. Unaware that they, too, were trapped in their own cultural vision of what constituted self-sufficiency and success, the drafters sought to impose this vision on a largely rural people, most of whom, in 1971 as well as today, lived mainly by subsistence hunting and fishing. Thus, they rejected a reservation system and put in place a system of Native-run, for-profit corporations. Instead of land over which the Natives exercised some degree of governmental power, as is the case in the Lower 48, the law created the system of village and regional corporations described in the above excerpts making each Native alive at that time an instant shareholder. These corporations would be the training ground for Natives to gain the business expertise needed to develop the assets of the corporation and to live successfully in the modern world.

   Indeed, Dean Price's prediction about the development of a cadre of business-experienced Natives has come to pass. In addition, most agree that ANCSA has forced the state to take Native corporations seriously, thus giving Alaskan Natives much better political clout in the statehouse. In turn, Natives have become increasingly active in political issues that affect them, especially issues of subsistence hunting and fishing. Certainly a core of members with this expertise is essential for any indigenous group to be able to take control of its own economic and cultural development. On the other hand, corporations were a flawed vehicle for development for reasons stated above and in the following materials. To give a simple illustration, contrast stock held in a Native corporation with stock acquired as an investment in the normal way. An investor first accumulates surplus capital and then chooses to invest that capital in stock shares. In other words, the investor has decided at that point that she can afford the investment. Moreover, if the shareholder has chosen well, during the period of ownership the value of the shareholder's holdings can increase by payment of dividends or because the value of the stock itself goes up through trading on the market.

   A Native shareholder, on the other hand, did not obtain the stock in a classic exchange transaction, by freely exchanging surplus capital for shares. Instead, the stock was given in exchange for collectively owned land. Since the Native shareholder presumably has no surplus capital to begin with and may still be struggling to get by, the temptation to sell once restrictions are lifted is very hard, if not impossible, to resist.

   Concerns were also raised about the effect of ANCSA on existing Alaskan IRA and traditional tribal governments. Along with apprehensions that ANCSA may be inconsistent with the goal of ensuring the continued viability of Native communities as separate cultures in the modern world, commentators identified many other potential pitfalls in the complicated statute. *See, e.g.,* Branson, *Square Pegs in Round Holes: Alaska Native Claims Settlement Corporations Under Corporate Law,* 8 U.C.L.A.-Alaska L. Rev. 103 (1979); Price, Purtich & Gerber, *The Tax Exemption of Native Lands Under Section 21(d) of the Alaska Native Claims Settlement Act,* 6 U.C.L.A.-Alaska L. Rev. 1 (1976); Price, *Region-Village Relations Under the Alaska Native Claims Settlement Act,* 5 U.C.L.A.-Alaska L. Rev. 58 (1975).

Many criticized the alienability provisions of the act: In 1991 the shares of stock would become freely alienable and subject to federal securities laws. In addition, all land was to be subjected to state taxation 20 years after its conveyance to the corporations. Village land is designed to be used for subsistence. If the land continues to be used for subsistence, a village unable to pay its state taxes might lose its land. The Alaska National Interest Land Conservation Act (ANILCA), discussed in the next excerpt, instituted some mechanisms for protecting land used for subsistence; ANCSA has also been amended numerous times, most recently in 1987. The following excerpt and notes discuss the efficacy of ANILCA and the ANCSA amendments on these vital issues.

2. ALASKA IN THE 1990's

WALSH, SETTLING THE ALASKA NATIVE CLAIMS SETTLEMENT ACT, 38 Stanford Law Review 227, 232-42 (1985)*

C. *The Precarious Nature of Native Control Over ANCSA Corporations and Lands*

The history of [the allotment and termination] policies serves as a lesson to today's Alaska Natives. The cultural and economic problems that will face Alaska Natives in the coming years resemble those that resulted from termination policy and the Dawes Act. The United States is in danger of repeating in Alaska the mistakes and tragic consequences of past Native American policy.

Although ANCSA does not contain any significant direct restrictions on the transfer of ANCSA Native Lands, the Native corporations alone have the power to decide the disposition of ANCSA lands, which insulates those lands from nonNative control. This policy reflects the desire of Congress to allow Alaska Natives maximum control over their own destiny and the destiny of their land. ANCSA protects the Native corporations themselves during a twenty year "implementation period" by banning the sale or transfer of stock in ANCSA corporations.[35] The corporations also enjoy a near total exemption from the requirements of the major federal securities laws[36] as well as immunity from state and local property taxes on undeveloped land.[37] These special protections come to an end on December 18, 1991, when all old ANCSA corporate stock will vanish

---

[35] 43 U.S.C. § 1606(h)(1) (1982). Upon the death of a stockholder during this period, the stock passes to the heirs of that stockholder, whether Native or nonNative. *Id.* at § 1606(h)(2).

[36] *Id.* at § 1625.

[37] *Id.* at § 1620.

and the corporations will issue stock without alienation restrictions.[38] With the end of the implementation period, the danger that Native stockholders will lose control of the land by losing control of the corporations becomes substantial. Not only will impoverished Natives be easy marks for outside corporations looking to gain control of the Native corporations as an inexpensive way to gain control of ANCSA lands, but many especially impoverished Natives will lose their stock to creditors and welfare recoupment policies. And somewhat better-off Natives may sell their stock to meet day-to-day living expenses.[40] NonNative development interests will play off the immediate financial need of many Natives against the long term cultural and economic requirements of the Native people by making systematic stock purchases from individual Natives. As a Native resident of Stevens Village put it, "People who deal with money know how to hit people when they are weak. I know that sometimes I might be weak."[41]

At the same time that financial pressures will effectively be forcing individual Natives to sell their stock in Native corporations to nonNatives, the Native corporations will feel pressure to sell off their land. After 1991, those lands will begin to lose their immunity from state and local taxes.[42] While a number of the regional corporations and larger village corporations could probably meet some level of property taxation, many of the smaller village corporations will be unable to bear even a small tax burden on their large land holdings.[43] Most village corporations received only small initial financial grants under ANCSA, and are struggling desperately to stay afloat.[44] A 1975 amendment to ANCSA provides for one possible solution by allowing village corporations to merge with the more financially stable regional corporations.[45] Many village corporations, however, are reluctant to submerge their individual identities in a regional organization.[46] Villages traditionally have formed the nucleus of Alaska

---

[38] *Id.* at § 1606(h)(3)(A).

[40] Social scientists surveying Alaska Natives in 1983 concluded that some 40% would sell their ANCSA stock under pressure of financial need. [U.S. Dept of the Interior, ANCSA 1985 Study] at IV 32 to IV-97 [(Draft, June 29, 1984.) [hereinafter cited as Draft 1985 ANCSA Study]]. In addition to this "voluntary" alienation of stock, Natives are subject to various state statutes that might result in the attachment of stock for the satisfaction of welfare assistance or other debts to the state. Alaska Stat. §§ 47.23.120, 47.25.070, 47.25.220. 47.25.240, 47.25.580 (1984). Given that over one quarter of all Alaska Natives fall below the poverty line, see Draft ANCSA 1985 Study, *supra*, at IV-18 to IV-19, the state of Alaska stands to gain a significant interest in many Native corporations. Whether or not the state would actually enforce such claims or attempt to gain control of Native corporations is hard to judge; such policies would certainly create a political maelstrom.

[41] Tundra Times, Aug. 1, 1984, at 17 (statement of Al Stevens).

[42] 43 U.S.C. § 1620 (1982). In 1980, the Alaska National Interest Lands Conservation Act (ANILCA) extended certain exemptions from state and local taxes past the 1991 deadline. 94 Stat. 2371, 2434 (1980) (codified at 43 U.S.C. § 1620(d) (1982)).

[43] *See* Draft ANCSA 1985 Study, *supra* note 40, at V-12, V-107 to V-117 (summary of village corporation financial data showing precarious nature of village corporation resources).

[44] Village corporations have resorted to mergers and consolidations in order to remain solvent, shrinking the original 224 village corporations to the present figure of 172. One study has predicted that only 13 village corporations have a fair chance of survival. *Id.* at V-12.

[45] Pub. L. No. 94-204, § 6, 89 Stat. 1148 (1976) (codified at 43 U.S.C. § 1627 (1976)).

[46] *See, e.g., Village Input Sought,* Tundra Times, Nov. 7, 1984, at 6 (an example of the strength and importance of village structure to Alaska Native culture in the eyes of Alaska Natives). Many villagers have strong opinions about the "regionalization" of Alaska Native society. The 1984 Alaska Federation of Natives Convention in Anchorage saw village-region tension come to the surface of "unity" discussions. The perceived pro-development interests of the regional corporations drew fire from many Natives. As one Stevens Village shareholder commented, "Our economic identity is not

Native tribal organization; to force their amalgamation with the much larger regional corporations would do much to break down the local Native culture.[47] A Hobson's choice may face these villages: either the sale of their land or the retention of the land with a substantial restructuring of their way of life.

Thus, the end of ANCSA's implementation period in 1991 may spell disaster for the economic and cultural future of Alaska Natives. Not only may Native corporations fall into nonNative hands, but sudden property tax liability may force Native corporations to relinquish their lands on the tax auctioneer's block. Native Alaskans are increasingly aware of these dangers, however, and have already begun to search for ways to protect the integrity of the ANCSA settlement.

D. *Strategies for Native Control of ANCSA Corporations and Lands Under Present Law*

1. *The Alaska National Interest Lands Conservation Act*

In 1980, Congress enacted the Alaska National Interest Lands Conservation Act (ANILCA), which planned the use of the large federal land holdings in Alaska and amended ANCSA in several respects.[48] ANILCA gave Native corporations the power to limit voting rights to Native stockholders,[49] avoiding any equal protection problems that might have arisen had the corporations tried to limit voting rights on their own. The Act also allowed Native corporations to amend their bylaws to give the corporation the right to buy any stock offered for sale by a stockholder. The family of a Native who is about to sell his stock may also be given this "right of first refusal," though it is unclear whose right has priority in the case of conflict.[51] In addition, ANILCA established a "land bank" for undeveloped lands that offers a limited immunity from taxes if a landowner is willing to place a ten-year moratorium on development of the "banked" land and also agrees to manage the land in a manner consistent with federal management of adjoining or "directly affected" federal land.[52]

These provisions, while steps in the right direction, are insufficient safeguards of Native control over ANCSA corporations and lands. By failing to prohibit all nonNative purchases of ANCSA stock, ANILCA does not prevent the undermining of the cultural pride Natives have placed in the new corporations. A system allowing the profits of "Native" corporations to flow into the hands of nonNatives has an ironic flavor, even if the nonNative stockholders pay market price for their shares. That Congress itself has repeatedly recognized the distinctively ethnic, Native Alaskan character of the ANCSA corporations only makes the irony more striking.[54]

---

the same as the regional corporations. It is the fish, the game, the ducks, the trees!" *Id.* at 10. *See also* Draft ANCSA 1985 Study, *supra* note 40, at V-13 to -14.

[47] *See generally* D. Case, Alaska Natives and American Laws 333-62 (1984) (describing traditional and contemporary village settlement patterns of various Native Alaskan groups).

[48] Alaska National Interest Lands Conservation Act, Pub. L. No. 96-487, 94 Stat. 2371-2551 (1980) (codified at 16 U.S.C. §§ 3101-3233, 43 U.S.C. §§ 1606, 1631-1641 (1982)) [hereinafter cited as ANILCA].

[49] 43 U.S.C. § 1606(h)(3)(B)(i) (1982).

[51] 43 U.S.C. § 1606(h)(3)(B)(ii) (1982).

[52] *Id.* at § 1636.

[54] In several pieces of legislation, Congress has equated ANCSA corporations with traditional Native tribes for the purposes of administering benefits....

But more concrete problems arise as well. Though the Native stockholder voting limitation ameliorates the consequences of nonNatives buying significant percentages of ANCSA corporate stock, it is uncertain whether such a provision will be meaningful over any substantial length of time. If a Native corporation's stock rests primarily in nonNative hands, the Native directors of the corporation might feel constrained by the need to maintain stockholder confidence and move to accommodate the ideas and plans of the nonNative majority stockholders.[55] NonNative views on the use of ANCSA lands would substantially conflict with the Native subsistence hunting use presently protected by the Native corporations. Moreover, while the ANILCA right of first refusal may slow down nonNative takeovers, it by no means guarantees Native control. Many of the corporations teeter on the edge of insolvency and could not hope to buy out stockholders on an ad hoc basis, let alone in the case of a rush to sell stock. Nor are impoverished families likely to buy out stockholders, especially given the fact that they themselves may be forced to consider sale of their stock.[57]

Finally, although the protections offered by ANILCA's land bank system are significant, the conditions placed upon those protections may prevent Native corporations from taking full advantage of the program. The bank concept places tight restrictions on the use and transfer of land bank lands, requiring that a corporation agree to a ten-year moratorium on alienation and surrender management of the land to the U.S. government for that period. This second provision may be especially difficult to reconcile with Native use and control of ANCSA land. Federal management may limit subsistence hunting and fishing activities,[59] the primary value of the land to most Natives.

2. *Extension of the stock alienation ban by the Native corporations*

If the ANILCA stock protection provisions do not adequately protect Native corporations, perhaps the Native corporations could take action to protect

---

[55] Although the views of nonvoting stockholders would influence corporation directors to a significantly lesser degree than those of voting (i.e. Native) stockholders, nonvoting stockholders would not be left without a voice. A nonvoting stockholder could still bring a derivative action against the directors for breach of fiduciary duty, a threat that could not help but influence Native director decisionmaking. Native directors of an ANCSA corporation, even if elected by Native stockholders alone, would thus have to pay close attention to the opinions of nonNative stockholders. Of course, a restriction on corporate voting rights would tend to diminish the attractiveness of an ANCSA corporation to outside investors, reducing the likelihood of a corporation "ruled" by a minority of Natives.

[57] While Alaska Native income grew more rapidly in the seventies than did Alaska nonNative income, in 1980 the average income of Native families remained only 56% of that of nonNative families. Some 26% of Alaska's Native population still falls below the poverty line. [Draft ANCSA 1985 Study, *supra* note 40] at IV-18 to IV-19.

[59] While ANILCA's Title VIII, 16 U.S.C. § 3111 (1982), pledges the Department of the Interior to give priority to subsistence uses of public lands, that priority is not absolute. The Secretary has the discretion to restrict subsistence use of federal lands, 16 U.S.C. § 3126 (1982), and thus restrict subsistence use of Native corporation land placed in the ANILCA land bank. ANILCA limits this power to those cases where restrictions on subsistence are necessary for "public safety, administration or to assure the continued viability of a particular fish or wildlife population." 16 U.S.C. § 3126(b) (1982). These are circumstances under which Natives might well agree with the imposition of restrictions. At the same time, however, this discretionary authority eliminates Native control of subsistence management for Native corporation lands placed in the land bank. In case of disagreement over proper subsistence management of such land, the Secretary's decision would be final, not that of the erstwhile Native owners.

themselves by banning or restricting the transfer of stock. Under Alaska state law and the common law of corporations, however, even a closely held corporation cannot place unreasonable restrictions on the alienation of stock.[60] The courts would almost certainly strike down a total ban on the transfer of stock, or a partial ban along ethnic lines, as comprising such an unreasonable restraint.[61] The corporations themselves, it appears, cannot protect stock much beyond the protections provided in ANILCA....

ANCSA establishes a series of links between various Native corporations. The most important link for the purposes of land control is the relationship between village and regional corporations. Regional corporations own the subsurface rights to village corporation lands.[64] Village corporations receive a certain percentage of regional corporation profits.[65] The regional corporation may withhold these funds until the village submits a plan for the use of the funds approved by the regional corporation.[66] Although the exact legal meaning of these links has yet to be established, some possibilities are clear. If a regional corporation were to become controlled by nonNatives, for example, Native-controlled villages within that region might be forced, legally and financially, to comply with the regional corporation's land development plans. The regional corporation has the power to require that village corporations participate in joint ventures. It is easy to imagine the conflict that would result if a nonNative controlled regional corporation were to require a village corporation to contribute to a village land mineral development plan to which the village was completely opposed.

A maverick nonNative regional corporation might also force changes in operating procedures in other, still Native-controlled, regional corporations. ANCSA contains revenue sharing provisions whereby any profit culled from mineral or timber resources by a regional corporation flows in part to all twelve

---

[60] Closely held corporations have more discretion to impose alienation restrictions than do publicly held corporations. Annot., 69 A.L.R. 3d 1327, 1329 (1976). If a closely held corporation cannot ban transfer, neither can a publicly held corporation. While there is presently no Alaska case law on this issue, the law from state to state is fairly uniform. For cases finding "reasonable" alienation restraints valid, and indicating that a complete ban on stock alienation would be the paradigmatic "unreasonable" restraint, see Mason v. Mallard Tel. Co., 213 Iowa 1076, 240 N.W. 671 (1932); Longyear v. Hardman, 219 Mass. 405, 106 N.E. 1012 (1914); Wright v. Iredell Tel. Co., 182 N.C. 308, 108 S.E. 744 (1921); Farmers' M. & S. Co. v. Laun, 146 Wis. 252, 131 N.W. 366 (1911).

[61] Courts generally have found alienation bans "reasonable" where it has been shown that a particular corporation has sufficient need to restrict ownership so as to override the general legal bias against alienation restrictions. Annot., 69 A.L.R. 3d 1327, 1331-32 (1976). Native corporations might argue that their need is sufficient to justify a complete ban on alienation, but this line of reasoning almost certainly would fall in state court, given powerful common law doctrine against total bans on alienation. Id. See also 2 F. O'Neal, Close Corporations § 7.06 (2d ed. 1971). In addition, a corporation-imposed ban along racial or ethnic lines runs into significant equal protection difficulties....

The fact that the status of Native corporations as closely held corporations is not settled only adds to the confusion. Applying O'Neal's functional definition, the ANCSA corporations are "close," since their shares "are not generally traded in the securities markets." Id. at § 1.02. Whether this will continue to be the case after 1991 is hard to judge. If, however, one of the myriad other definitions of "close corporations" is applied, the Native corporations may not fall into this "close" category. See id. at §§ 1.01-.03. If this is the case, highly restrictive alienation measures will be even more unlikely to survive judicial scrutiny. See Annot., 69 A.L.R.3d 1327, 1329 (1976); see also Note, Close Corporations in Alaska, 7 UCLA-Alaska L. Rev. 123 (1977).

[64] 43 U.S.C. § 1613(f) (1982).

[65] Id. at § 1606(j).

[66] Id. at § 1606(l).

other regional corporations.[68] The Act does not clearly set out whether one regional corporation might sue another for incompetent management under this provision. If such a cause of action could be maintained, however, a nonNative-controlled corporation might force Native-controlled corporations to drop unprofitable land-use programs designed to benefit Native people.

3. Retribalization: Transfer of ANCSA lands to tribal governments

A primary Native concern in the development of a just and lasting land claims settlement is to vest land-control decisions in the hands of Native villages.[70] To the extent that village corporations are synonymous with the villages, ANCSA addresses this Native concern. As 1991 draws nearer, however, village council members and village corporate directors alike have begun to question the propriety of leaving village lands in the hands of business entities. Native leaders have begun to realize that the corporate form of control may not guarantee that the Native people of a village will decide on the use of ANCSA land.

If ANILCA stock protection provisions are not adequate to guarantee the continued Native control of the corporations, and the corporations are unable to guarantee Native control themselves, then perhaps Native land could be transferred from those corporations to Native tribal governments, thus ensuring Native control of ANCSA lands.[72] The Indian Reorganization Act of 1934 (IRA),[73] established the statutory basis for tribal government in the United States. Many IRA governments presently operate in Alaska, often side-by-side with traditional pre-IRA tribal governments and state municipal governments.[74] The IRA authorizes the Secretary of the Interior to obtain land to be held in trust for the IRA governments.[75] Transferring ANCSA land to these governments, effectively "retribalizing" those lands, would substantially eliminate any future concern over the control of Native land. Under a retribalization scheme, the United States would take ANCSA lands into trust, and hold them for the benefit of the Natives.[76] Such trust lands could not be alienated without the consent of the Secretary of the Interior,[77] and would be exempt from taxation.[78]

This retribalization plan, however, presents certain problems. For instance, the Secretary has discretion on whether to take lands into trust.[79] In 1979, the

---

[68] *Id.* § 1606(i).

[70] *See Village Input Sought*, Tundra Times, Nov. 7, 1984, at 6; *Berger Says People Understand ANCSA, 1991*, 3 Alaska Federation of Natives Newsletter, May/June 1984, at 9.

[72] *See* D. Case, *supra* note 47, at 377; Alaska Native News, May/June 1984, at 15 (summarizing AFN Resolution No. 83-07); Case, Summary of 1991 Related Issues in Alaska (unpublished manuscript, Jan. 21, 1983) (on file with Stanford Law Review); *see also* note 178 *infra* (discussing proposals made by a new report on Alaska Native life, Village Journey).

[73] Ch. 576, 48 Stat. 984 (1934) (codified as amended at 25 U.S.C. §§ 461-479 (1982)). Traditional tribal governments existed before the IRA and continue to exist after ANCSA....

[74] D. Case, *supra* note 47, at 375-78.

[75] 25 U.S.C. § 465 (1982).

[76] *See id.* at § 465; Draft ANCSA 1985 Study, *supra* note 40, at V-21. ANCSA corporate stock would not change hands, since the land is merely one asset of any given corporation. For a discussion of the problems arising from the transfer of major assets under Alaska corporate law, see notes 87-89 *infra* and accompanying text.

[77] 25 U.S.C. § 483 (1982).

[78] *Id.*, at § 465.

[79] *Id.* at §§ 465, 473(a).

Assistant Solicitor for Indian Affairs published an opinion which found that the language of ANCSA apparently intended to end the reservation system in Alaska and that an increase in the amount of Alaska land held in trust would thus constitute an abuse of the Secretary's discretion.[80] Whether an IRA tribal government might effectively avoid this potential roadblock simply by accepting ANCSA lands in fee is uncertain. If an IRA government accepts such lands, the lands might still be subject to taxation and possible auction by IRA government creditors.[81]

Another problem lies in the tension between the village and regional corporations. Although village corporations tend to support such land transfers, regional corporations are more hesitant.[82] The regional corporations own subsurface rights to all village lands;[83] retribalization without safeguards for reasonable development by the regional corporation would create a sore spot in village-region relations.[84] Without corporation support, transfer provisions are unlikely to succeed.[85] As Byron Mallott, President of Sealaska Regional Corporation pointed out during Alaska Native Review Commission hearings on the 1991 problem, "I wear two hats. And it often causes me conflict .... The land does not belong to Natives as Native land, but to the corporations, which have their own discipline and values sometimes far removed from the shareholders."[86]

State law poses yet another hurdle for the retribalization plan. ANCSA organized the Native corporations under state law, which requires the approval of two-thirds of the stockholders for the transfer of "major assets" of any corporation.[87] The corporation must buy the shares of any minority stockholders who so desire.[88] Before 1991, the Settlement Act prohibits the sale of stock, even to the corporation itself.[89] Thus, a single dissenting stockholder might be able to prevent the transfer prior to 1991, since ANCSA would bar the corporation from buying that stockholder's shares. And after the stock becomes freely alienable, any significant nonNative buy-in would make transfer of lands to an IRA government difficult. If many nonNatives own stock and demand to be bought out, the corporation might not be able to raise the capital necessary to do so.

---

[80] Case, *supra* note 72, at 19-20 (citing a 1979 unpublished opinion by Assistant Solicitor Thomas Fredericks).

[81] Ironically, land taken in fee by a non-IRA traditional tribal government may be protected from involuntary alienation to a greater extent than land taken in trust for an IRA government. Under the IRA, trust land may be alienated with the Secretary's approval, whereas 25 U.S.C. § 177 (1982) requires a treaty or statute to approve transfer of other lands from the ownership of traditional Indian organizations. *See* Case, *supra* note 72, at 19-20.

[82] *See Native Alaskans Fear Law Will Take Land, Traditions*, San Jose Mercury News, Nov. 4, 1985, at 1, 10a (statement of John Schaefer, President of Northwest Alaska Native Association, a regional corporation. "If I make a choice to protect our lands, it limits our ability to make money."); *AFN Convention Delegates Approve 1991 Package*, Tundra Times, Oct. 28, 1985, at 1, 16; Arctic Pol'y Rev., June 1984, at 12 (statement of Byron Mallot, President of Sealaska Corporation).

[83] 43 U.S.C. §§ 1613(e), 1613(f) (1982).

[84] *See* notes 64-69 *supra* and accompanying text (discussing the relationship between village and regional Native corporations).

[85] The Alaska Federation of Natives has passed a resolution favoring such provisions. Arctic Pol'y Rev., June 1984, at 10....

[86] Arctic Pol'y Rev., June 1984, at 12.

[87] Alaska Stat. §§ 10.05.438-10.05.441 (1985). *See* Case, *supra* note 72, at 24.

[88] Alaska Stat. §§ 10.05.447-10.05.462 (1985).

[89] 43 U.S.C. § 1606(h)(1) (1982).

All of these concerns illustrate the impracticality of the retribalization plan under present law. Despite the appeal of this approach to village corporations, therefore, other solutions to the Native land control problem may prove more productive.

In sum, ANCSA created a system of Native corporations to manage the land claims settlement and to provide for the future economic development of the Natives. Those corporations received the bulk of the compensation award and more importantly, title to Native land grants. For the first twenty years of their existence, the Native corporations enjoy special protection by the federal government. In late 1991 that protection expires. Native corporation stock becomes alienable, possibly resulting in nonNative control of the Native corporation and lands. Tax immunities for Native lands begin to disappear, opening the door to tax sales of ANCSA lands. Under ANCSA as presently written, it will be difficult to prevent Native corporations and lands from falling out of Native hands. The use of ANILCA provisions designed to shelter ANCSA Native corporations, the voluntary extension of stock alienation bans, and the transfer of ANCSA lands to village tribal governments offer inadequate hope of preventing that loss.

NOTES

1. The Alaska National Interest Conservation Act (ANILCA): Although ANCSA was designed in part to protect subsistence rights of Natives by such strategies as granting the surface land to village corporations, it did not go far enough because it did not deal with lands not owned by regional or village corporations. The Alaska National Interest Conservation Act (ANILCA) was enacted to protect subsistence rights of Natives and rural residents (most of whom are Natives) to public lands. *See generally* Conn & Garber, *State Enforcement of Alaska Native Tribal Law: The Congressional Mandate of the Alaska National Interest Lands Conservation Act,* 1989 HARV. IND. L. SYMPOSIUM 99.

Subsistence serves a vital function both culturally and economically for Alaskan Natives. *See generally* T. BERGER, VILLAGE JOURNEY: THE REPORT OF THE ALASKA NATIVE REVIEW COMMISSION 49-70 (1985). As David Case has explained: "[T]he very acts of hunting, fishing, and gathering, coupled with the seasonal cycle of these activities and the sharing and celebrations which accompany them are intricately woven into the fabric of their social, psychological and religious life." D. CASE, ALASKAN NATIVES AND AMERICAN LAWS 276 (1984). As for the economic aspect, subsistence is a necessity for many Natives. According to one commentator:

Studies have shown that 35% of Alaska's Natives obtain at least half of their food from subsistence activities. One study of the subsistence habits of the North Slope Inupiat Eskimos shows that 45% of Native households are estimated to obtain half or more of their food from subsistence. Eighty-seven percent of the population consumed subsistence food obtained by a member of the household, and 11%, mostly the elderly, consumed subsistence foods that were given to them by other members of the community. Thus, at least one study reveals that 98% of the Inupiat households on the North Slope obtain at least some of their food from subsistence activities.

Households rely on subsistence activities because the average Native family has a lower real income, a diminished opportunity for full-time employment, and a substantially higher cost of living than average American families. If subsistence resources decrease, more public assistance will be necessary to enable the Natives to survive. However, even if the assistance could be provided, it would not serve as an adequate

substitute for an entire way of life, and such payments would have to be accompanied
by intensive psychiatric and vocational programs.

Rinaldi, *Amoco Production v. Village of Gambell: The Limits to Federal Protec-*
tion of Native Alaskan Subsistence, 7 VA. J. NAT. RES. L. 147, 150-51 (1987).*

It is not surprising that Natives have long organized over subsistence issues.
As David Case has said: "For Alaska Natives, subsistence became a political and
cultural rallying cry some years before it became a law." Case, *Subsistence and*
Self-Determination: Can Alaska Natives Have a More "Effective Voice"?, 60 U.
COLO. L. REV. 1009, 1009 (1989). Natives have taken an active role in co-manag-
ing programs that protect subsistence hunting and fishing under ANILCA and
the Marine Mammal Protection Act (MMPA), 16 U.S.C. § 1361 *et seq.* For
example, Natives of the Arctic Slope, who depend on whaling for their livelihood, have created the Alaska Eskimo Whaling Commission which has in turn
entered into a cooperative agreement with the National Oceanic and Atmo-
spheric Administration to aid NOAA in enforcing international whaling agreements and the MMPA by monitoring disputes between Eskimo whalers and
setting and enforcing whaling quotas. For a description of the Whaling Commission, see Case, *supra*, 1026-35.

2. The Effect of *Amoco Production Co. v. Village of Gambell* on Subsis-
tence Rights in the Outer Continental Shelf: ANILCA was designed to protect
Natives' subsistence lifestyle. In particular, section 810 provides procedural protections designed to give Natives affected by any development on federal land
notice and an opportunity to be heard. 16 U.S.C. § 3120. More important, the
section permits development only upon a finding by the agency that the project
involves only that amount of public land needed for the agency's purpose. In
addition, the agency must take steps to reduce the impact of the activity on
subsistence uses.

Natives in Western Alaska sought to enjoin the U.S. from granting oil and gas
leases to areas in the Outer Continental Shelf (OCS) because they feared that a
spill would have drastic effects on the fisheries essential to many Alaskan Natives' livelihood (a fear that became a reality with the Exxon Valdez oil spill).
The Natives first argued that ANCSA's extinguishment provision, discussed
above, did not apply to the OCS, because the OCS was not "in Alaska" within
the meaning of that provision. Second, they argued that even if the native rights
in the OCS had been extinguished by ANCSA, the Secretary of the Interior had
failed to comply with the procedural and substantive provisions of ANILCA.
Because of the broad language of ANCSA section 4 the district court felt compelled to hold that ANCSA had extinguished aboriginal title in the OCS. Nevertheless, the court concluded that the Secretary had not complied with ANILCA.
As a result, a preliminary injunction was issued. The Court of Appeals upheld
the judgment, but the Supreme Court reversed. *In Amoco Production Co. v.*
Village of Gambell, 480 U.S. 531 (1987), the Supreme Court held that ANILCA
by its terms did not apply to the OCS, because the territorial reach of ANILCA,
"land situated in Alaska," ANILCA § 102, 16 U.S.C. § 3102(3), had a "precise
geographic/political meaning" that excluded the OCS. *Id.* at 547. For criticisms
of this aspect of the case, see Rinaldi, cited *supra* note 1 and Twitchell, *Amoco*
Production Co. v. Village of Gambell: Federal Subsistence Protection Ends at
Alaska's Borders, 18 ENVTL. L. 635 (1988). The court then vacated the question
of the scope of ANCSA § 4 and remanded the issue to the Court of Appeals.

Upon remand, the Court of Appeals reversed itself on the extinguishment issue, holding that although the Natives no longer had sovereignty over the OCS, Section 4 of ANCSA was not explicit enough to extinguish Native aboriginal title to the OCS in light of the Supreme Court's interpretation of the term "in Alaska" in ANILCA. *People of Village of Gambell v. Hodel*, 869 F.2d 1273 (9th Cir. 1989). In short, the court held that if ANILCA was not specific enough to extend protection to the OCS, ANCSA, containing the same geographical reference, was not specific enough to extinguish aboriginal title in the OCS. The court again remanded to the district court to determine whether the Outer Continental Shelf Act extinguished aboriginal subsistence rights. If not, the questions whether in fact the Natives possessed aboriginal subsistence rights in the OCS and whether the drilling interfered with those rights would have to be decided. The answers to these questions will have far-reaching impact on native subsistence rights.

3. The Special Problem of Afterborn Children: One of ANCSA's most unusual features is that only those Natives born on or before the effective date of the Act could share in its benefits. In contrast, settlement schemes involving payment of money to the tribe permit children born after the date of the settlement to share in the benefits. ANCSA thus created preferred family members by excluding "afterborn" children from receiving any shares of stock. As a result, these children could only acquire stock by inheritance. As families split into favored and disfavored groups, many began to call for remedial legislation to provide for these "afterborn children."

4. Insolvency of Native Corporations: As the excerpt indicates, corporate insolvency has been a serious problem since ANCSA. When Natives became instant corporate shareholders, they had not acquired the financial sophistication possessed by most shareholders who choose to place their money in the stock market. According to a recent article:

> All Native corporations under ANCSA were set up in a vacuum, without first developing entrepreneurial skills or capital wealth in the area served by the corporations. [Tanana Chiefs Conference, Inc., Interior Region Post-ANCSA Impact Analysis (Mar. 1983)] at 18. The difficulties of operating a small village corporation according to standard business principles are illustrated in an article published in *Alaska Industry Magazine*. The article points out that, in April 1978, over 79% of the village corporations were delinquent in their required filings with the State Division of Banking, Securities, and Corporations. Sanak Native Corporation, located on the Aleutian Chain, with 26 shareholders, spends twice its annual income on its required annual corporate audit. A Helping Hand for the Native Village Firms, *Alaska Industry Mag.*, July 1987.

Black, Bundy, Christianson & Christianson, *When Worlds Collide: Alaska Native Corporations and the Bankruptcy Code*, 6 ALASKA L. REV. 81 n.33 (1989).

Village corporations, especially, often operate marginal businesses to provide employment for members and spend a large share of money on social welfare programs, two business operations not normally undertaken by a well-managed mainstream business. Although the village corporations have suffered the worst, regional corporations have not been immune from financial difficulties. As of 1989 four corporations had filed for relief under the Bankruptcy Code. *Id.* at 73, 75 n.6 (naming Tigara, Bering Straits, Haida and the Thirteenth Regional Corporation). On the other hand, it is important to note that some of the Regional Corporations are flourishing, "operat[ing] diverse enterprises at a profit and play[ing] a major role in Alaska's economy." *Id.*, at 80 & n.30 (citing Cook Inlet's 1987 earnings of $120,300,017).

As with other legislation designed to assimilate indigenous peoples, such as the allotment policy, ANCSA has created expectations in those Natives, such as shareholders of the prosperous regional corporations, who have benefited from its provisions. Can ANCSA be reformed without defeating these expectations?

5. The Native Review Commission Report: In 1983, the Inuit Circumpolar Conference, an international organization of Eskimos from Alaska, Canada, and Greenland, asked Thomas R. Berger, former Justice of the British Columbia Supreme Court, to come to Alaska as head of the Native Review Commission and investigate the effect of ANCSA on the Native Alaskan people, especially the majority who still live in villages. Over a two-year period Justice Berger visited 62 villages and towns, holding village meetings and listening to testimony from Natives. In 1985, his report, *Village Journey*, was published. The following excerpt summarizes the Report's major recommendations.

THOMAS R. BERGER, VILLAGE JOURNEY: THE REPORT OF THE ALASKA NATIVE REVIEW COMMISSION 167-72 (1985)

Recommendations: Land

Since the land is now a corporate asset, the scope of possible recommendations is limited. It is not possible simply to urge that a law should be passed transferring the land from Native corporations to tribal governments. The land is, under the law, private property belonging to the corporations. My recommendations are, therefore, addressed to the Native shareholders in the corporations. Given congressional action, it will be possible for the Native people to unscramble the omelet.

I recommend that the shareholders of village corporations who are concerned that their land may be lost should transfer their land to tribal governments to keep the land in Native ownership. The matter is one of urgency in the villages, and it should be done at once. The tribal government would hold this land in fee simple, although some tribes may wish to place their land in trust with the federal government. In either case, the tribal government would be able to claim sovereign immunity with respect to the land. Congress should pass legislation to facilitate the transfer of land by the village corporations to tribal governments without regard for dissenters' rights. Where village corporations have merged, the lands formerly held by each village corporation should be transferred by the merged corporation to the appropriate tribal governments.

Tribal governments would exercise all of the functions of the corporations with respect to any further village-land selections and conveyances. Land should be turned over to tribal governments on condition that they admit to membership all of the original shareholders in the village corporation. Tribal governments have the power to determine their own membership, and Natives born after 1971 should be members of a tribe. This arrangement accommodates the children born after 1971; they should be included in the tribe by virtue of their being born into it.

Congress should enact legislation to clarify the village tribal governments' right to exercise a veto power over all subsurface development on village-owned ANCSA lands. Village corporations presently have such a right under Section 14(f) of ANCSA, but it is not clear that this right extends to all village corporation lands.

I recommend that the lands required by Section 14(c)(3) of ANCSA to be conveyed to state-chartered local governments or to the state in trust should be transferred to the tribal government. Unoccupied federal townsite lands in unincorporated communities or in communities that dissolve their municipalities should also be conveyed to the tribal governments. Unless those entitled were to waive their entitlements to fee land, the tribal government would be required to make the other conveyances under ANCSA Section 14(c) to protect the interests of residents and local businesses. The airport reconveyances required under Section 14(c)(4) should go to the tribal governments.

Recommendations: Village Corporations

Because my recommendations relate only to the land, they would leave the village corporations and the merged corporations with all their other business assets. If a village corporation has a thriving business or investments, nothing I have said would impair the corporation's right to continue to carry on its business, to make a profit, and to pay dividends to shareholders. In most cases, however, it seems likely that, without their land, the village corporations will be dissolved.

If a village corporation is already engaged in profitable activities based on land development, the land, after it is transferred to the tribal government, can be leased back to the corporation for business purposes. The tribal government would also have the option of chartering a tribal corporation to take over the operations of the village corporation.

If the village dissolves its corporation and transfers all of its assets to the tribal government, the tribal government should receive revenues otherwise due the village corporation under ANCSA Section 7(j).

Recommendations: Regional Corporations

I have concerned myself principally with the future of the villages, a concern that entails specific recommendations regarding the land that belongs to the village corporations. The regional corporations own the subsurface of the village lands and sixteen million acres of other land, much of which is checkerboarded with village lands. The regional corporations together have the right to select approximately one million acres of special-purpose lands, but they are of less importance to the villages. It is the village subsurface lands held by the regional corporations and the sixteen million acres adjacent to the village lands that are of concern to Native subsistence interests. If the regional corporation loses its lands, Native subsistence users would no longer have access to them; moreover, the new owner could use the lands in ways destructive to village interests.

Regional corporations should consider transferring the subsurface of village lands to the respective village tribal governments. If it were deemed advisable to keep the subsurface in some type of regional organization to continue the interlocking arrangement between regions and villages that Congress had in mind, an alternative would be to transfer the subsurface to a regional tribal government. If such an institution did not already exist, then the affected region would have to establish one, and this might require congressional action.

Regional corporations should also consider at least three options with respect to the sixteen million acres of wholly owned regional-corporation lands adjacent to the villages. First, they should consider transferring these lands to the villages to ensure unified village control of the greatest possible acreage. Second, the regional corporations should consider transferring these lands to regional tribal governments, perhaps in conjunction with the transfer of village corporation lands to village tribal governments, if it seemed important to maintain both village and regional land-owning institutions. Finally, the regional corporations should consider assigning subsistence easements to village or regional tribal governments. Regional corporations would then continue to own the lands, but use of the lands would be restricted to subsistence purposes. New owners of regional lands would have to honor the easement. Such easements would be similar to conservation easements, now familiar in the Lower 48, but might require amendments to state and federal law to ensure that regional corporations granting the easements would receive the same tax advantages afforded grantors of conservation easements.

None of these options appears to be exclusive of each other; they could be used singly or in combination, depending on the wishes of regional and village corporation shareholders. It should also be noted that these options could be implemented in a region where the village and regional corporations are merged. In such a region, all the shareholders participate in only one corporation, which owns all the interests in all the lands, so it would be easier then to decide which lands should be transferred to village ownership and which lands, if any, should be retained in regional control.

The establishment of regional tribal organizations, recognized as such under federal law, would also provide the regional corporations with the option of assigning non-real estate assets with a view to securing the advantages of tribal immunity. The regional tribalization of lands should also be considered from the standpoint of the at-large shareholders for whom the loss of these lands may be especially significant.

Recommendations: Self-Government

Tribal governments established in all of Alaska's Native villages should assert their Native sovereignty.

Pending and future applications by villages in Alaska for tribal constitutions and charters under the Indian Reorganization Act should be granted. The state should recognize tribal governments as appropriate local governments for all purposes under state law. These measures, important for Native self-rule, may entail the dissolution of some, but not all, of the state-chartered local governments in Native villages.

I do not recommend the general establishment of Native reservations in Alaska. Instead, tribal governments would hold the land in fee simple. But if there are villages that want their land taken in federal trust, this should be done.

I urge that all land subject to the jurisdiction of Native governments should be described as Indian Country or, as the case may be, Eskimo Country or Aleut Country. This phrase would accurately describe the situation, and it would release everyone from a vocabulary that now confines the discussion of alternatives.

Recommendations: Subsistence

I recommend that tribal governments should have exclusive jurisdiction over fish and wildlife on Native lands, whether owned by Native corporations or by tribal governments. On federal and state lands (ninety percent of Alaska's land area), Native governments in partnership with state and federal governments should exercise jurisdiction on all hunting, trapping, and gathering lands used by tribal members. On all Native lands, the Native peoples would have the exclusive right, as tribal members, to subsistence, subject to exclusive tribal jurisdiction.

Exclusive Native rights, although appropriate for Native-owned lands and waters, are not appropriate for state and federal lands and waters in Alaska, because Native peoples do not own these areas and their claims to them have been extinguished. A different regime is required here, one that would fully protect the Native peoples' interests. Rights of access on state and federal lands and waters and a share of the resources fully sufficient for Native subsistence must be guaranteed. Shared jurisdiction with the state and federal governments should be exercised so that Native hunting and fishing rights are not regulated except for conservation purposes. Native authorities should impose and enforce regulations before federal or state authorities intervene. The James Bay and Northern Quebec Agreement is perhaps the best model. The federal Marine Mammal Protection Act is an American example of a legal regime which intervenes in Native subsistence only when necessary.

The health and abundance of fish and wildlife depend on the quality of the environment throughout their range. Many species will migrate beyond Native-owned lands or lands used for Native subsistence within the state and federal domain. To ensure a continuing supply of subsistence resources for Alaska Natives, Congress must clearly establish a policy of protection for migratory species and provide for Native participation in the overseeing of that protection.

NOTES

1. Retribalization: The movement to transfer land to IRA governments, called the retribalization or sovereignty movement, faces two significant barriers. First, can the transfers take place without compensating dissenters' rights? If compensation is necessary, many corporations would not be able to make the transfers. Second, can the governments assert sovereign immunity from suit? If so, this immunity would protect the land from creditors even if the land were not held in trust. What conditions are necessary prerequisites to implement the Berger proposals regarding retribalization? Permitting corporations to buy out dissenting stockholders has little or no chance of success for most village corporations and the poorer regional corporations. To implement the recommendation regarding self-government, Berger proposed that Congress adopt provisions permitting Native corporations to retribalize free from the strictures of Alaska corporate law:

> Under Alaska state law, shareholders who object to the transfer of ANCSA land to a tribal government would have the right to be bought out at market value. Congress has

the power under the Commerce Clause to authorize retribalization of ANCSA land without regard to the rights of dissenting shareholders under Alaska state law. In 1973, Congress restored the Menominees' tribal government and extinguished the right of dissenting shareholders to be bought out. It has already exercised this power in Alaska in the 1976 legislation authorizing mergers of ANCSA corporations without regard to dissenters' rights. It will have to exercise it again to enable the villages to retain their land.

T. Berger, Village Journey, at 158-59. Not surprisingly, the issue of extinguishing dissenters' rights caused the most controversy. *See, e.g.*, Branson, *ANCSA and 1991: A Framework for Analysis*, 4 Alaska L. Rev. 197, 207 (1987) (criticizing the report's failure to take account of recent innovations in corporate law, such as restricting share transfers by setting a fixed option price, which would permit the corporation to buy back a Natives' shares at a price that could be far less than fair market price).

2. The "1991" Amendments: In 1987 Congress enacted legislation to address some of the issues that had become known as "1991 issues." Alaska Native Claims Settlement Act Amendments of 1987, Pub. L. No. 100-241, 101 Stat. 1788 (1987) (codified at 43 U.S.C. §§ 1601-1628). The legislative course was not smooth, with the Senate and House version differing on a major provision. Resolving this difference resulted in the loss of the provision and dissension among the two largest Native lobbying groups, the American Federation of Natives and the Alaskan Native Conference.

The Alaskan Federation of Natives originally proposed a list of eight amendments. In modified form, and with an important exception, Congress adopted seven of those amendments. The most important provision extends restrictions on alienation of the stock of most corporations unless the corporation by a majority vote of the shareholders opts to lift the restrictions. 43 U.S.C. § 1629c(b). Because an opt-out provision favors the status quo, an opt-in arrangement was made for the Natives of Bristol Bay. In that region the regional and village corporations must vote to *continue* the restrictions. *Id.* § 1629(d).

Another provision permits corporations to issue additional stock — settlement common stock — to provide for afterborn children and those who had been omitted from the rolls earlier. *Id.* § 1606(g)(1). Corporations may also issue additional shares of voting or non-voting stock in several classes: with restrictions against alienation, or shares to be held only by Natives and "entities established for the sole benefit of Natives." *Id.* § 1606(g)(2)(B). Corporations which choose to terminate restrictions against alienation can also limit voting rights to Natives. *Id.* § 1606(g)(3)(C). On the other hand, corporations can also issue voting stock to non-Natives if a majority of the shareholders desires to do so.

The corporations are permitted to overcome dissenters' rights, in certain situations. For example, a corporation voting on whether to continue restrictions need not, but can, provide for buy-back of dissenters' shares by enacting a contemporaneous resolution to that effect. *Id.* § 1229d(a). Requiring a majority vote on this issue provides some protection to dissenters in situations in which they command a majority or comprise a substantial minority capable of including other shareholders. Moreover, dissenters who comprise at least 25% are able to force a vote on matters such as lifting restrictions. Finally, continuing with the theme of different treatment for the Natives of Bristol Bay, the amendments require corporations in that region to compensate dissenters who vote unsuccessfully to terminate restrictions on alienation.

Recall that the Berger commission recommended permitting transfer of stock or land to tribal governments without regard for dissenters' rights. The original house bill contained a provision, called the qualified transferee entity (QTE) provision, leaving the question of compensation up to each corporation. Congressional concern for individual Natives' rights coupled with a concern that overriding dissenters' rights might be held to be a fifth amendment taking after *Hodel v. Irving*, 481 U.S. 704 (1987), set forth and discussed in Chapter 5, section E, resulted in the omission of this important provision as a last-minute compromise to obtain passage of the bill. In its place is the "settlement trust option" of new section 39, *id.* § 1269e. Under this provision, corporations "may convey assets (including stock or beneficial interests therein) to a Settlement Trust in accordance with the laws of the State ...." *Id.* § (a)(1)(A). Surface land conveyed to the trusts may not be alienated except to the settlor corporation. Subsurface land may not be conveyed, however, and the conveyances are subject to such state laws as those governing creditors' rights. Moreover, dissenters' rights are protected "if the rights of beneficiaries in the Settlement Trust receiving a conveyance are inalienable." *Id.* § (a)d(2)(A)-(B). Although the section prohibits Settlement Trusts from operating as businesses, nothing in the provision bars the Settlement Trusts from operating as governments.

The "1991" amendments also amend ANILCA to provide a greater protection for land used for subsistence: if a corporation does not develop, lease, or sell land, that land is made exempt from state and local property taxes, adverse possession, and other laws that execute creditor's rights, by, for example, permitting forced sales to satisfy judgments. ANILCA § 11 (codified at 43 U.S.C. § 1636(d).

This brief description merely highlights some of the more important provisions of this complex piece of legislation. An excellent report on the legislative history and a thorough analysis of the amendments has been written by a member of the Tlingit tribe who is also a shareholder in the Sealaska Regional Corporation and a law school graduate. London, *The "1991 Amendments" to the Alaska Native Claims Settlement Act: Protection for Native Lands?*, 8 STAN. ENVTL. L.J. 200 (1989).

3. SOVEREIGNTY

ANCSA revoked all reservations in Alaska except the Metlakatla reservation. ANCSA was silent, however, about the continuing status of existing IRA or traditional governments in Alaska. Alaska is also a Public Law 280 state, but that fact alone does not affect important areas of civil and regulatory tribal authority, as demonstrated in Chapter 4, section C1. There are two crucial preconditions to the exercise of sovereign status: a governmental organization and territory over which to exercise authority. Many governmental organizations exist in Alaska. According to David Case:

> There are two types of "Native" governments in Alaska, those which are chartered under State law and those recognized under federal law. The former are "Native" in fact only and do not have any legal status guaranteeing they will remain ethnically Native. Federally recognized governments, on the other hand, are exclusively Native either because of their inherently sovereign status or because of specific statutory or administrative recognition and support. There appear to be at least three types of federally recognized Native governments: 1) traditional governing councils, 2) IRA governing councils, and 3) the Tlingit and Haida Central Council.

D. Case, Alaska Natives and American Laws 372 (1984). Some ANCSA corporations also function in some ways like governments (rightly or wrongly). In addition, 120 ANCSA village corporations are also state-chartered municipalities. Finally, many of these same village corporations have either an IRA government or a traditional village council. In recent years, the IRA and traditional village councils have begun to exercise (or re-exercise) governmental power. Since the village and regional ANCSA corporations and not the governments own the land, however, what is the territory that can be used to measure the extent of village corporation power? A tribal government does not have to own land to exercise authority, but there must be some method of delineating territory under the tribe's authority. In the Lower 48 states this question is answered by an analysis of whether the tribe's area is Indian country, an issue discussed at length in Chapter 1, section B3. Indian country includes not only reservations, but "dependent Indian communities." According to the *Handbook of Federal Indian Law*, this phrase means "those tribal Indian communities under federal protection that did not originate in either a federal or tribal act of 'reserving' or were not specifically designated as a reservation." *Id.* 38 (1982 ed.).

This second precondition for the exercise of sovereign power has been the most controversial. Although the sovereignty or retribalization movement in Alaska provided a major impetus for the 1987 amendments to ANCSA, the drafters of the amendments took pains to take no stand on sovereignty issues, stating:

> Sec. 17 (a) No provision of this Act (the Alaska Native Claims Settlement Act Amendments of 1987), exercise of authority pursuant to this Act, or change made by, or pursuant to, this Act in the status of land shall be construed to validate or invalidate or in any way affect —
>
> (1) any assertion that a Native organization (including a federally recognized tribe, traditional Native council or Native council organized pursuant to the Act of June 18, 1934 [the IRA], as amended has or does not have governmental authority over lands (including management of, or regulation of the taking of, fish and wildlife) or persons within the boundaries of the State of Alaska, or
>
> (2) any assertion that Indian country (as defined by 18 U.S.C. 1151 or any other authority) exists or does not exist within the boundaries of the state of Alaska.

30 U.S.C. § 1601 note.

As a result, the issue of whether Native governments can exercise sovereign powers after ANCSA remains with the courts. Not surprisingly, the views taken by the Alaska state courts and the federal courts are different.

NATIVE VILLAGE OF STEVENS v. ALASKA MANAGEMENT & PLANNING

757 P.2d 32 (Alaska 1988)

Matthews, Justice.

This case arises out of a contract dispute between the Native Village of Stevens (Stevens Village) and Alaska Management & Planning (AMP). A jury returned a verdict for AMP, finding that Stevens Village had breached the contract. On appeal, Stevens Village raises three grounds on which it believes the verdict should be set aside. First, it claims that this suit is barred by the doctrine of sovereign immunity. Second, it contends that the contract violated government procurement regulations and was therefore unenforceable. Finally, it contends that the contract was a personal service contract containing no definite term of duration and was therefore terminable at the will of either party. We conclude that Stevens Village does not have sovereign immunity. We further conclude that the second ground Stevens Village raises is meritorious. However, AMP is nonetheless entitled to a quantum meruit recovery. Because we find the contract unenforceable we do not reach the third ground raised by Stevens Village. We therefore reverse and remand for a retrial on the issue of damages.

I. *Statement of the Case*

A. *Statement of Facts*

Stevens Village is an Alaska Native Village organized under the [IRA], located on the Yukon River in Interior Alaska. In 1982, Stevens Village received a federal Department of Housing and Urban Development (HUD) grant for $369,000 to be used to bring electricity to the village. The Tanana Chiefs Conference, Inc. (TCC) assisted Stevens Village in obtaining the HUD grant and hiring an engineering and management firm (Marks Engineering) to manage the electrification project.

AMP is a joint venture specializing in Alaskan bush village and community development projects. AMP is owned and operated by David Slaby and James Nims. On March 31, 1983, Stevens Village entered into a contract with AMP pursuant to which AMP would perform "planning and management services, and be established as Architect and Engineer of record for the community of Stevens Village." AMP was also to provide such services as grant writing, construction administration, budgeting, and construction progress evaluation. In May, 1983, the parties amended the agreement. AMP agreed to provide construction administration, expediting, engineering, and construction services on the electrification project in place of Marks Engineering. Under the original contract, AMP was to be compensated at seven percent of construction costs plus five percent of total costs for financial management services. Under the amendment to the agreement, relating solely to the electrification project, AMP was to receive $35 per hour plus expenses.

By letter dated December 2, 1983, Stevens Village terminated the contract with AMP. Stevens Village claims that HUD and the state had found problems with the electrification project's administration and the Village's relationship to AMP. Stevens Village also asserts that AMP failed to provide a status report requested by state officials and that it fired AMP for failing to perform its contractual obligations. AMP, on the other hand, claims that it was fired because Stevens Village learned it could get the same services free from TCC or the federal Public Health Service.

[When AMP sued the Village for breach of contract, the Village unsuccessfully invoked sovereign immunity. Rejecting the Village's motion to dismiss, the trial court held on the merits that the Village was liable for $38,891 for breach of contract.]

II. *Discussion*

A. *This Suit Is Not Barred by the Doctrine of Sovereign Immunity*

1. *Summary.*

American Indian tribes outside of Alaska have long been recognized as sovereign governmental entities immune from suit. [Nevertheless, w]e conclude that Stevens Village does not have sovereign immunity because it, like most native groups in Alaska, is not self-governing or in any meaningful sense sovereign. This conclusion is supported by the decisions of this court, *Atkinson v. Haldane*, 569 P.2d 151 (Alaska 1977) and *Metlakatla Indian Community, Annette Island Reservation v. Egan*, 362 P.2d 901 (Alaska 1961). Further, the history of the relationship between the federal government and Alaska Natives up to the passage of the Alaska Indian Reorganization Act, 49 Stat. 1250 (1936) indicates that Congress intended that most Alaska Native groups not be treated as sovereigns. Finally, neither the Alaska Indian Reorganization Act, nor subsequent Congressional acts have signaled a change from non-sovereign to sovereign status.

2. *Alaska Supreme Court cases.*

We addressed the question of sovereign immunity in *Atkinson v. Haldane*, 569 P.2d 151 (Alaska 1977). We noted that:

> [T]he tribal sovereignty of Indians was first recognized in *Worcester v. Georgia*, 31 U.S. (6 Pet.) 515, 557, 8 L. Ed. 483, 499 (1832), in which Chief Justice Marshall stated that the Indian nations were distinct political communities, having territorial boundaries, within which their authority is exclusive, and having a right to all the lands within those boundaries, which is not only acknowledged, but guaranteed by the United States.

569 P.2d at 157. After a review of many authorities, we concluded that judicial recognition of tribal sovereign immunity turned on whether Congress, or the executive branch of the federal government, had recognized the particular group in question as a tribe. 569 P.2d at 161-63.

In *Atkinson* we held that the Metlakatlans, located on the Annette Island Reservation, possessed tribal sovereign immunity. We noted that "[t]he interactions of the United States government and the Alaska Native peoples as a whole have been much different from those between the government and the tribes in the other states." *Id.* at 154. We observed that a general reservation system was never developed in Alaska and the federal government never attempted to enter into treaties with Alaska Natives. *Id.* However, we stated that the Metlakatlans were "an exception to the exception," *id.*, in that Congress had set up a reservation for them. "The Metlakatlans' reservation status sets them apart from other Alaska Natives, making them much more like the tribes of the other states." *Id.* at 154-55 (footnote omitted). Further, we noted that the Metlakatlans have "a strong central tribal organization unlike most Alaska Native groups." *Id.* at 155. We noted that in general, "[t]he Native villages and communities of Alaska were not organized on 'tribal' lines, and the village rather than the ethnological tribe has been the central unit of organization." *Id.* at 155 n.12.

We concluded our historical discussion in *Atkinson* as follows:

Thus, based on the foregoing, we conclude that the reservation status of the Metlakatla Indian Community sets them apart from other Alaska Natives and that the status of the Metlakatla Indian Community has always more closely resembled the status of the tribes in other states than the status of other Natives in Alaska.

569 P.2d at 156. Our emphasis on the differences between the Metlakatlans and the other Alaska Native groups suggests that other Alaska Native groups would not be afforded sovereign immunity.

In *Metlakatla Indian Community, Annette Island Reserve v. Egan*, 362 P.2d 901 (Alaska 1961), *rev'd in part*, 369 U.S. 45 (1962), we had occasion to review in detail the historical relationship between the federal government and Alaska Natives. The issue in *Metlakatla* was whether regulations issued by the Secretary of the Interior authorizing fish traps operated by the Indian communities of Metlakatla, Kake, and Angoon were valid. Alaska state law prohibited fish traps. We held that the Secretarial regulations were invalid as to all three communities.[3]

Our opinion made the following points which are germane to the present case. "The United States has never entered into any treaty or similar type agreement with any group of Indians in Alaska." *Id.* at 917. "None of the Indians of appellant communities have ever been exempt from taxation by the Territory or State of Alaska." *Id.* at 919. "Crimes committed by Indians in Alaska have always been punished by the territorial and state courts." *Id.* at 920. "There is not now and never has been an area of Alaska recognized as Indian country with one possible exception." *Id.*[4] "There are not now and never have been tribes of Indians in Alaska as that term is used in federal Indian law." *Id.* at 917-18. "No Indian tribe, independent nation or power has been recognized in Alaska." *Id.* at 920.

As noted, *Metlakatla* was reversed by the Supreme Court as to the community of Metlakatla and affirmed as to the communities of Kake and Angoon. Thus, the statement in *Metlakatla* that no tribes have been recognized in Alaska was inaccurate because the Metlakatlans have received Congressional recognition. In all other respects, however, the legal conclusions in *Metlakatla* are accurate.

---

[3]On appeal, the United States Supreme Court reversed our decision as to the community of Metlakatla, *Metlakatla Indian Community, Annette Island Reserves v. Egan*, 369 U.S. 45 (1962) and affirmed our decision as to the communities of Kake and Angoon, *Organized Village of Kake v. Egan*, 369 U.S. 60 (1962). The Secretarial power in *Metlakatla* was grounded on an 1891 act of Congress setting apart a reservation for the Metlakatlans, including waters surrounding the land reservation. The 1891 statute empowered the Secretary to govern the use of the Reservation by the Metlakatlans "under such rules and regulations as he might from time to time prescribe." 369 U.S. at 48. This authority was unique to Metlakatla. Thus, the Secretary's regulations were authorized as to Metlakatla, but not as to the native villages of Kake and Angoon.

[4]The exception noted by the *Metlakatla* court was the Moquawkie reserve recognized in *Petition of McCord*, 151 F. Supp. 132 (D. Alaska, 1957). The United States District Court for the District of Alaska, in an unpublished oral decision, *Native Village of Tyonek v. Puckett*, 82-369 Civil (Transcript of Oral Decision, December 3, 1986), has concluded that the Village of Tyonek located on the former Moquawkie Reserve has sovereign immunity, "based on Tyonek's history and the manner in which the federal government has dealt with Tyonek." *Id.* at 20. The history of Tyonek is unique among Alaska Villages, as recognized in *Petition of McCord*, 151 F. Supp. at 136, because Tyonek occupied an Executive Order Reservation at the time it adopted a constitution and by-laws under the Alaska Indian Reorganization Act, 49 Stat. 1250 (1936). *Village of Tyonek*, 82-369 Civil (Transcript) at 5.

3. *The history of the relationship between the United States Government and Alaska Natives, until the passage of the Alaska Indian Reorganization Act in 1936, indicates that Congress intended that most Alaska Native groups not be treated as sovereigns.*

Federal-Native relationships were examined in detail by a task force appointed to study the subject by the Governor of Alaska. The task force issued a report of impressive scholarship.[7] The conclusion of the Report, for the period from the Alaska purchase until passage of the Alaska Indian Reorganization Act, is as follows:

> The language of federal statutes applicable to Alaska, their interpretation by the Courts and their administration and enforcement by the army, the navy, the Secretary of the Interior, and the territorial legislature, and the contemporaneous views of the most knowledgeable Native then living in Alaska indicate that between 1867 and 1936 Congress intended Alaska Natives to be subject to federal and territorial laws generally applicable to all Alaska residents.

Report, *supra*, note 7, at 100 (footnote omitted).

The events set out in the report which support the conclusion that Congress intended that Alaska Native groups not be treated as sovereign include the following.

First. Soon after the Treaty of Cession, the United States District Court concluded that Alaska was not "Indian country" and thus the Indian Intercourse Act of 1834 did not apply in Alaska. *United States v. Seveloff,* 1 Alaska Fed. 64 (D. Ore. 1872). The court concluded:

> If Congress should think it desirable that this or any other provision of the Indian Intercourse Act should be in force in Alaska, it can so provide ....

In 1873, Congress responded to the *Seveloff* decision in a limited fashion. It extended only the sections of the Intercourse Act dealing with alcohol control. This implies that Congress did not intend the comprehensive protection which the Act was meant to afford to Indians to apply in Alaska....

Second. In 1884, Congress enacted the Alaska Organic Act, establishing for the first time a civil government for the District of Alaska. 23 Stat. 24 (1884). The Organic Act, with unusual economy, enacted an entire criminal and civil code for Alaska by adopting the laws of Oregon. The Report notes:

> Nothing in the language of the 1884 Act or its legislative history indicates that Congress intended any area of Alaska to be Indian country or that Alaska Natives in Native villages would not be subject to the civil and criminal laws of Oregon to the same extent as the white residents of the District.

Report, *supra* note 7, at 77.

Alaska Natives were held subject to the general civil and criminal laws of Oregon under the Organic Act, even though Alaska's second governor recommended in his report to Congress that the Act be amended so that Natives would be exempt from its provisions. In *Kie v. United States,* 1 Alaska Fed. 125 (1886), a Tlingit Indian who had killed his wife in a Tlingit village was held properly subject to prosecution under a provision of the Oregon Criminal Code

---

[7] Report of the Governor's Task Force on Federal-State-Tribal Relations (Feb. 14, 1986) (hereinafter Report).

which was applicable in Alaska rather than under the Federal Indian Major Crimes Act, 23 Stat. 362 (1885) which was applicable to homicides committed by one Indian against another Indian in Indian country.

In *In re Sah Quah*, 31 F. 327 (1886), a person who was a slave under Tlingit custom filed a habeas corpus petition alleging that his subjugation was illegal. His Tlingit master argued: "[T]hat Alaska is Indian country, and that they as inhabitants are subject to no law, save the usages and customs of Indians." *Id.* at 328. The court concluded that Alaska was not Indian country, except for the purpose of control of alcoholic beverages, and that the rule of *Ex Parte Crow Dog*, 109 U.S. 556 (1883) [did not apply in Alaska].

Third. In 1899, Congress enacted a detailed criminal code superseding the criminal laws of Oregon which had been [applied through the Organic Act]. Either the Indian Major Crimes Act, or tribal law, depending on the nature of the crime, and not the 1899 Alaska Criminal Code would apply to Natives within Native villages if Native villages were sovereign or located in "Indian country." However, Congress enacted a statute in 1909 which made it quite clear that the 1899 Criminal Code was to be applicable.

The 1909 Act empowered the Attorney General of the United States to appoint "any person employed in the Alaska School Service" as a special peace officer with authority "to arrest ... any Native of the District of Alaska charged with the violation of any provisions of the [1899] Criminal Code of Alaska." The only schools under the jurisdiction of the Alaska School Service were Native schools in Native villages. Report, *supra* note 7, at 89. "Therefore, it is obvious that Congress considered the criminal code of Alaska to be applicable to Indians not living in white communities." *United States v. Booth*, 161 F. Supp. 269 (Alaska 1958).

Fourth.

In 1900 the Congress replaced the Oregon Civil Code with a detailed Alaska Civil Code. 31 Stat. 321 (1900). Like the 1899 Alaska Criminal Code, nothing in the legislative history of the 1900 Alaska Civil Code indicates that the Congress intended to exempt Alaska Natives living in Native villages from the purview of the Civil Code.

Report, *supra* note 7, at 90 (footnote integrated into text).
Fifth.

In 1912, some 45 years after first asserting jurisdiction over Alaska, Congress established a territorial legislature to which it delegated a significant segment of its criminal and civil jurisdiction over the territory. Section 9 of the 1912 Act extended the legislature power of the territorial legislature "to all rightful subjects of legislation not inconsistent with the Constitution and laws of the United States." Section 9 then specifically exempted a list of subjects from the legislature's criminal and civil jurisdiction. Alaska Natives and Native villages were not included on the list and there is no evidence in the legislative history of the 1912 Act that Congress intended to limit the territorial legislature's civil and criminal jurisdiction over Alaska Natives living in Native villages.

The territorial legislature did enact laws governing Alaska Natives living in Native Villages. "One of the 1913 Legislature's first enactments was a statute which compelled Native children to attend Bureau of Education Schools and established the failure of a Native parent to sent his or her child to school as a criminal offense." The second territorial legislature in 1915 enacted a law authorizing Alaska Natives living in Native villages with forty or more residents to establish "a self-governing village organization for the purpose of governing certain local affairs ...." Ch. 11, § 1, SLA 1915. According to the Report:

> The 1915 Act is a contemporaneous expression of the territorial legislature's understanding that Congress had delegated the legislature's civil jurisdiction over the internal form and powers of self-government in Native villages and that the area within and surrounding such villages was not Indian country.

Report, *supra* note 7, at 94. Further, the territorial legislature levied and collected taxes from Alaska Natives living in Native villages to the same extent that it levied and collected taxes from other residents. E.g., Ch. 29, § 1, SLA 1919. Where Indians have sovereign powers, states and territories lack jurisdiction to tax them. F. Cohen, Handbook of Federal Indian Law 406 (1982); Report, *supra* note 7, at 97.

  4. *Neither the Alaska Indian Reorganization Act of 1936 nor subsequent Congressional legislation has granted or recognized sovereign status to Alaska Native groups.*

The Indian Reorganization Act (IRA) was designed to encourage Indians to "revitalize their self-government through the adoption of constitutions and by-laws and through the creation of chartered corporations, with power to conduct the business and economic affairs of the tribe." *Mescalero Apache Tribe v. Jones*, 411 U.S. 145, 151 (1973). Section 16 of the IRA empowers an Indian tribe, "or tribes residing on the same reservation" to adopt a constitution and by-laws subject to approval of the Secretary of the Interior. 25 U.S.C. § 476. Section 17 authorized the Secretary to issue charters of incorporation to tribes. 25 U.S.C. § 477.

When the IRA was initially passed in 1934, section 16 but not section 17 was applicable to Alaska. Since section 16 was limited to a tribe or tribes residing on a reservation and Alaska had few reservations, its applicability was quite limited. This was changed by the Alaska Indian Reorganization Act, 49 Stat. 1250 (1936), which in section 1 extended section 17 and some other sections of the IRA to Alaska with the following proviso:

> PROVIDED, That groups of Indians in Alaska not recognized prior to May 1, 1936 as bands or tribes, but having a common bond of occupation, or association, or residence within a well-defined neighborhood, community or rural district, may organize to adopt constitutions and by-laws and to receive charters of incorporation and federal loans under §§ 10, 16, and 17 ... of the [IRA].

Section 2 of the Act authorized the Secretary of the Interior to designate Indian reservations in Alaska and to withdraw public lands "actually occupied by Indians or Eskimos" for that purpose.

  The proviso language of section 1 of the Alaska Indian Reorganization Act "assumed that Alaska Natives were not members of federally recognized Indian tribes .... " Report, *supra* note 7, at 110-11.[18] It was thus an express Congressional statement applicable to most Native groups in Alaska that they had not been recognized as tribes.

---

[18] The House Committee on Indian Affairs said that this proviso "is necessary because of the peculiar nontribal organizations under which the Alaska Indians operate. They have no tribal organization as the term is understood generally." H. Rep. No. 2244, 74th Cong., 2d Sess. (1936).

The more controversial section 2 of the Act, which empowered the Secretary to create reservations in Alaska, was regarded by the Interior Department as necessary to protect economic rights of Alaska Natives. Report, *supra* note 7, at 109, 111. Reservations were also thought to be a necessary precondition to native communities' exercising local government powers under section 16 of the IRA. As Secretary Ickes stated in his letter to the House Committee on Indian Affairs accompanying the Bill: "[I]f native communities of Alaska are to set up systems of local government, it will be necessary to stipulate the geographical limits of their jurisdictions. Reservations set up by the Secretary of the Interior will accomplish this."[19]

Stevens Village does not have a reservation and, insofar as the record shows, never had one. It was organized under section 16 of the IRA and the proviso of section 1 of the Alaska IRA. However, consistent with the legislative history of the Alaska IRA, the constitution of Stevens Village does not give it general police power — the power to keep order — except on "any reserve set aside by the federal government for the village." Withholding the general police power was accomplished under Interior Department instructions which stated in part: "The power to prescribe ordinances for civil government, relating particularly to law and order, may extend only to such lands as may be held as an Indian reservation for the use of the community ...."[21]

Since Stevens Village was never granted a reservation, the power of local government has never been extended to it. In our view, the mere approval of a section 16 constitution for Stevens Village by the Secretary of the Interior, which itself withholds the power of local government to the Village, does not suffice to afford the Village tribal status for the purpose of application of the doctrine of tribal sovereign immunity.

In summary, the Alaska Indian Reorganization Act is important for two reasons. First, it expressly states that Native groups in Alaska have not been accorded tribal recognition. Second, it sets forth a means by which Native groups might achieve self-governing status. However, in the case of Stevens Village that status was not achieved.[22]

We see nothing in legislation passed subsequent to the Alaska Indian Reorganization Act which constitutes a recognition of tribal sovereign authority. To the contrary, passage of the Alaska Native Claims Settlement Act (ANCSA) evidences Congress's intent that non-reservation villages be largely subject to state law. The policy of ANCSA is expressed in section 2(b):

the settlement should be accomplished rapidly, with certainty, in conformity with the real economic and social needs of Natives, without litigation, with maximum participa-

---

[19] H. Rep. No. 2447, 74th Cong., 2d Sess. 3-5 (1936) (letter from Harold Ickes to Honorable Will Rogers), reprinted in Report, *supra* note 7, at 112.

[21] Dept. of Interior, Instructions for Organizations in Alaska Under the Reorganization Act of June 18, 1934 (48 Stat. 984) and the Alaska Act of May 1, 1936 (49 Stat. 1250) and the Amendments Thereto, Instruction I(a) (December 22, 1937), reprinted in Report, *supra* note 7, at 113.

[22] The parties briefed another IRA issue in this case: whether section 16 of the IRA, 25 U.S.C. § 476 (1982), prevents the execution against Stevens Village's assets without its consent. Entities organized under section 16 of the IRA are vested with the power "to prevent the sale, disposition, lease, or encumbrance of tribal lands, interests in lands, or other tribal assets without the consent of the tribe." However, this appeal is from a money judgment, not from an order characterizing assets as subject to execution. The question of what, if any, assets are available to satisfy the judgment should be raised in the trial court in a post-judgment proceeding.

tion by Natives in decisions affecting their rights and property, without establishing any permanent racially defined institutions, rights, privileges, or obligations, without creating a reservation system or lengthy wardship or trusteeship, and without adding to the categories of property and institutions enjoying special tax privileges or to the legislation establishing special relationships between the United States government and the State of Alaska ....

43 U.S.C. § 1601(b).

ANCSA grants fee simple title in Native lands to regional and village corporations which are organized under state law and which are to be treated as any other Alaska corporations, with temporary exceptions as to the alienability of stock. *Id.* §§ 1606, 1607 (1982). The funds paid under ANCSA are paid to the regional corporations. *Id.* § 1605. After a temporary period, ANCSA lands are subject to state and local taxation. *Id.* § 1620. ANCSA abolishes all reservations in Alaska except the Annette Island Reserve. *Id.* § 1618. ANCSA gives either state chartered municipalities or the state itself at least 1,280 acres of the land underlying each village. *Id.* § 1613. Significantly, this grant does not go to IRA corporations, which would have been logical recipients if they were meant to have a role in local government. Indeed, there is nothing in the legislative history of ANCSA which remotely suggests that IRA villages are to be recognized as having a government role.

5. *Conclusion.*

In a series of enactments following the Treaty of Cession and extending into the first third of this century, Congress had demonstrated its intent that Alaska Native communities not be accorded sovereign tribal status.

[The lower court erred in finding the contract enforceable even though it violated federal procurement regulations. The court accordingly remanded the case to the district court for a retrial on the issue of damages based on *quantum meruit.*]

Affirmed in part, remanded in part.

RABINOWITZ, Chief Justice, joined by COMPTON, Justice, dissenting.

I dissent from Part II.A. of the court's opinion which addresses the issue of sovereign immunity. In my view Congress has never stated with sufficient clarity an intent to waive the sovereign immunity of Alaska Native villages. While I agree that the federal government has never expressly recognized Alaska Native villages as tribes for purposes of sovereign immunity, it is firmly established that a historically sovereign tribe is immune from suit, even in the absence of federal recognition, until Congress or the tribe expressly waives its immunity. Accordingly, I would remand this case for a factual determination as to whether Stevens Village possesses the attributes of a sovereign Indian tribe that would entitle it to sovereign immunity.

I

The court holds that "Congress has demonstrated its intent that Alaska Native communities not be accorded sovereign tribal status," and that therefore "Stevens Village is not entitled to utilize the defense of tribal sovereign immunity." It is true that if Congress waived the Village's sovereign immunity, the

Village would be barred from utilizing this defense. "[T]ribal sovereignty ... is subject to the superior and plenary control of Congress." *Santa Clara Pueblo v. Martinez*, 436 U.S. 49, 58 (1978).

However, if Congress is to waive[2] a tribe's sovereign immunity, it must clearly express this intent: "It is settled that a waiver of sovereign immunity '*cannot be implied* but must be *unequivocally expressed.*'" *Id.* (emphasis added; citation omitted). Accordingly, the Ninth Circuit Court of Appeals has "rejected the contention that congressional enactments unrelated to immunity may implicitly grant authority to bring suit against Indian tribes." *Chemehuevi Indian Tribe v. California State Bd. of Equalization*, 757 F.2d 1047, 1053 (9th Cir.) (compulsory counterclaim requirement of Rule 13(a) of the Federal Rules of Civil Procedure held not to be waiver of tribal immunity), *rev'd on other grounds*, 474 U.S. 9 (1985).

This court has previously recognized these principles. In *Atkinson v. Haldane*, 569 P.2d 151, 167 (Alaska 1977), we stated: "[S]overeign immunity ... [is] waived only if it is clear from the unambiguous language of [the statute] and its legislative history that Congress intended such a waiver." In the case at bar, the court ignores these canons and infers a congressional waiver of immunity from a battery of enactments that do not address the issue of sovereign immunity.

The court first cites numerous pre-1936 enactments and judicial decisions suggesting that Native villages were at that time subject to state law and not considered "Indian country." None of these enactments, however, contained an express waiver of sovereign immunity. When Congress subjects an Indian tribe to state jurisdiction, it does not implicitly strip the tribe of its inherent sovereignty. For example, Public Law 280 explicitly granted to certain states, including Alaska, extensive civil and criminal jurisdiction over Indian tribes. Even this broad grant of jurisdiction, however, was not sufficient to waive sovereign immunity. The Supreme Court recently held: "We have never read Pub L 280 to constitute a waiver of tribal sovereign immunity, nor found Pub L 280 to represent an abandonment of the federal interest in guarding Indian self-governance." *Three Affiliated Tribes of the Fort Berthold Reservation v. Wold Engineering*, 476 U.S. 877 (1986). In short, state jurisdiction over an Indian tribe is not inconsistent with tribal sovereignty in general or with tribal sovereign immunity in particular. Thus, nothing in any of the pre-1936 enactments cited by the court constitutes a waiver of sovereign immunity.

The court next turns to the Indian Reorganization Act (IRA). The court cites no provision of the Act which remotely resembles a waiver of sovereign immunity. Indeed, it is somewhat perplexing even to infer a waiver from the provisions of the IRA. One of the clear purposes of the IRA was to revitalize tribal self-government, see, e.g., *Mescalero Apache Tribe v. Jones*, 411 U.S. 145, 151-52 (1973), and sovereign immunity "is a necessary corollary to Indian sov-

---

[2] The court's opinion does not explain whether Congress waived or discontinued the villages' sovereign immunity, or somehow declared that the immunity never existed. Whatever the case may be, any congressional expression of intent must meet the strict standard applied to waiver. Any lesser standard would run afoul of the settled principle that "statutes passed for the benefit of dependent Indian tribes ... are to be liberally construed, doubtful expressions being resolved in favor of the Indians." *Bryan v. Itasca County*, 426 U.S. 373, 392 (1976) (quoting *Alaska Pac. Fisheries v. United States*, 248 U.S. 78, 89 (1918)).

ereignty and self-governance." *Three Affiliated Tribes*, 90 L. Ed. 2d at 894. The United States Supreme Court has held that "[t]he Reorganization Act did not strip Indian tribes ... of their historic immunity from state and local control." *Mescalero Apache Tribe*, 411 U.S. at 152.[4] Although I agree with the court's conclusion that IRA incorporation alone does not constitute federal recognition of tribal status, I cannot agree that this Act, when combined with the previous enactments, somehow constitutes a waiver of sovereign immunity.

Similarly, in ANCSA, the final enactment considered by the court, Congress did not address immunity. The court does not cite a single provision of ANCSA that directly or indirectly suggests a waiver of sovereign immunity. Rather, the court infers this intent, an approach which is at odds with the rule that a waiver of immunity must be clearly expressed.

One of the provisions the court uses to bolster its waiver conclusion is the section that permits taxation of certain lands granted pursuant to ANCSA. 43 U.S.C.A. § 1620(d) (1986). In my view this section supports the opposite conclusion, because it is an excellent example of the type of clear expression Congress must make to waive an immunity, in this case tax immunity.

The court concludes that ANCSA "evidences Congress's intent that non-reservation villages be largely subject to state law." Even assuming that this is true, it does not deprive the villages of sovereign immunity. As discussed above in connection with the earlier enactments and Public Law 280, Congress does not necessarily waive the sovereign immunity of Indian tribes when it subjects them to some measure of state law.

In short, nothing in ANCSA, the IRA, or any of the earlier enactments approaches the type of express congressional statement that is necessary to waive sovereign immunity. Thus, if Stevens Village is a "tribe" under common law principles of tribal sovereign immunity, this court lacks jurisdiction to adjudicate the claim in the instant case.

II

The court also concludes that an Indian tribe may not avail itself of sovereign immunity in the absence of express recognition of tribal status by either Congress or the executive branch of the federal government. This argument has been considered and rejected by the federal courts, is inconsistent with the underlying basis of the doctrine of tribal sovereign immunity, and is not supported by our own decisions.[6]

---

[4] The court suggests that Alaska Native villages incorporated under IRA section 16 possess no governmental powers because they were never granted reservations. I disagree for two reasons. First, this argument nullifies the plain language of the Alaska amendment to the IRA, which on its face allows "groups of Indians in Alaska" to incorporate under section 16 without any mention of reservations. *See* 25 U.S.C.A. § 473a (1983).

Second, this argument would negate many constitutions approved under section 16, including that of Stevens Village, which explicitly grant powers of self-government even in the absence of a reservation....

[6] I agree with the court that IRA incorporation alone does not constitute federal recognition of tribal status for purposes of sovereign immunity, but my reasons are somewhat different.

As the court's opinion notes, the Alaska amendment to the IRA allowed any "group[] of Indians in Alaska" with a "common bond" to incorporate. 25 U.S.C.A. § 473a (1983). The "common bond" language is extremely broad. In fact, it is nearly identical to that in a previously-enacted statute providing for the organization of federal credit unions having nothing to do with Indians. 12

In support of its express federal recognition analysis, the court relies on *Atkinson v. Haldane*, 569 P.2d 151 (Alaska 1977). However, as we noted in *Atkinson*, sovereign immunity is a federal doctrine, and this court is bound under the supremacy clause to follow the holdings of the United States Supreme Court. [O]ur research has uncovered no case which *conditions* the invocation of sovereign immunity on the factors emphasized by the state or appellant: formal federal recognition of the particular tribe by treaty or statute, a prolonged course of dealing between the tribe and the federal government, geographic location, the tribe's warlike nature, the absence of state protection of a tribe or the continued full exercise of a tribe's sovereign powers.

The absence of authority is not surprising, for the analysis urged by appellant and the state seems to us to fundamentally misconceive basic principles of federal Indian law. In effect, their approach would condition the exercise of an aspect of sovereignty on a showing that it had been granted to the tribe by the federal government, either by explicit recognition or implicitly through a course of dealing. [T]he proper analysis is [that i]mmunity from suit is one attribute of sovereignty retained by Indian tribes, which are sovereign entities predating annexation by the United States. "It is as though the immunity which was theirs as sovereigns passed to the United States for their benefit, as their tribal properties did." *United States v. United States Fidelity & Guar. Co.*, 309 U.S. 506, 512-13 (1940).

Therefore, there is no need for the federal government expressly to recognize the sovereignty of a tribe for the tribe to retain most attributes of its sovereignty. As the Supreme Court explained just last year, "Because the Tribe retains all inherent attributes of sovereignty that have not been divested by the Federal Government, the proper inference from silence ... is that the sovereign power ... remains intact." *Iowa Mut. Ins. Co. v. LaPlante*, [480 U.S. 9] (1987) (quoting *Merrion v. Jicarilla Apache Tribe*, 455 U.S. 130, 149 n.14 (1982)).

In the instant case Congress has neither expressly recognized the Village as a tribe for purposes of sovereign immunity nor expressly waived the Village's immunity. Therefore, if the Village is in fact a historically sovereign tribe, this court is bound to honor its immunity from suit.

The court cites three Supreme Court cases pertaining to the subject of sovereign immunity: *Three Affiliated Tribes of the Fort Berthold Reservation v. Wold Engineering*; *Santa Clara Pueblo v. Martinez*; and *U.S. Fidelity*. In each of these cases there was apparently some federal recognition of the tribe. However, there is no indication that the Court relied on this fact in finding the tribes entitled to sovereign immunity. None of the three cases explicitly mentions federal recognition of tribal status in their respective discussions of sovereign immunity. To the contrary, the discussion in each suggests that the basis of immunity is historical sovereign status rather than any federal recognition.

It is true that the basis of the finding of tribal sovereign immunity in *Atkinson v. Haldane*, 569 P.2d 151 (Alaska 1977), was express federal recognition. How-

U.S.C.A. § 1759 (1980). Whether or not so intended by Congress, the expansive "common bond" language has resulted in reorganization under IRA section 16 of Alaska Native groups that clearly had no historical existence as tribal governmental units. For example, the Ketchikan Indian Corporation is organized under both IRA sections 16 and 17. Yet its members "are not descended from any particular Indian community, but are natives of differing groups who happen to live in Ketchikan." *Board of Equalization v. Alaska Native Bhd. and Sisterhood, Camp. No. 14*, 666 P.2d 1015, 1025 (Alaska 1983) (Rabinowitz, J., concurring). Therefore, it seems unlikely that Congress intended to recognize all IRA section 16 corporations as tribes for purposes of sovereign immunity.

ever, contrary to the implication of the court's opinion today, nothing in the *Atkinson* opinion suggests that this is the only way sovereign immunity can be established. Once Congress or the executive branch has recognized a tribe, the question is nonjusticiable, and there is no further need for the court to explore the historical basis for the finding of sovereignty. As we explained, "Once the executive branch has determined that the Metlakatla Indian Community is an Indian tribe, which is a nonjusticiable political question, the Community is entitled to all the benefits of tribal status." *Id.* at 163. Even in the absence of such recognition, however, we remain bound to honor the sovereignty of a historical Indian tribe. We recognized this implicitly in describing immunity from suit as a "retain[ed] ... vestige[]" of a formerly complete sovereignty. *Id.* at 160.

III

Having determined that the federal government has not expressly recognized Stevens Village as a tribe for purposes of sovereign immunity, I would remand the case to afford the Village the opportunity to make a factual showing as to its alleged tribal status.

It appears that no court has ever fashioned a definition of "tribe" specifically for purposes of determining sovereign immunity. Unfortunately, reference to definitions of "tribe" for other purposes does not necessarily provide a definitive answer in the sovereign immunity context....

In my view the BIA standards [set forth in 25 C.F.R. § 83.2] provide an appropriate test for determining whether an entity is a tribe for purposes of sovereign immunity. I am not unmindful of the fact that these factors were developed with the experiences and characteristics of Indians in the lower 48 states in mind. Therefore, I would view these factors merely as guidelines that may be tailored to accommodate the unique history and circumstances of Native groups in Alaska. Thus our trial courts should consider other factors that may be relevant in determining whether a particular Alaska Native group has proved its tribal status.[11]

AMP argues that Stevens Village did not meet its burden of proof because it did not present any evidence of its historical tribal status. The Village responds that it has "reams of documentation," but declined to present it in the trial court because AMP did not contest the Village's tribal status. The record is incomplete and does not clearly reveal the arguments that AMP made in the superior court. However, neither party could easily have anticipated the standards this court would adopt in proving tribal status. Given the importance of the issue presented, I would remand to provide Stevens Village with the opportunity to prove its historical tribal status under the standards set forth above.

---

[11] This view of the sovereignty of Native villages is consistent with a decided trend in federal legislation to treat Alaska Natives on an equal basis with Indians in the lower 48 states. See, e.g., Indian Self-Determination Act, 25 U.S.C.A. § 450b(b) (1983) (definition of tribe includes an Alaska Native village or regional or village corporation established pursuant to ANCSA); Indian Financing Act, 25 U.S.C.A. § 1452(c) (1983) (same); Indian Child Welfare Act, 25 U.S.C.A. § 1903(8) (1983) (definition of tribe includes Alaska Native villages as defined in 43 U.S.C. § 1602(c)); Indian Tribal Governmental Tax Status Act, 26 U.S.C.A. § 7701(a)(40)(A) (Supp. 1988) (definition of tribe includes Alaska Native entities whom the Secretary of the Interior deems to be exercising governmental functions).

IV

As stated earlier I agree with the court that there has never been any express federal recognition of Alaska Native villages as tribes for purposes of sovereign immunity. However, it is equally clear that Congress has never expressly denied sovereign immunity to these villages. The unfortunate but inescapable fact is that Congress has steadfastly avoided defining the extent and limits of Native sovereignty in Alaska. Illustrative of this fact are the recent "1991" amendments to ANCSA, in which Congress declared, "[N]o provision of this Act shall ... confer on, or deny to, any Native organization any degree of sovereign governmental authority over lands ... or persons in Alaska ...." Alaska Native Claims Settlement Act Amendments of 1987, Pub. L. No. 100-241, § 2(8)(B), 101 Stat. 1788, 1789 (1988). *See also id.* § 17(a), 101 Stat. 1814. The Senate Report on the bill stated:

> It is the Committee's clear intent that this bill leave parties in the sovereignty issue, in exactly the same status as if the amendments were not enacted.
> ... This is an issue which should be left to the courts in interpreting applicable law and [the] amendments should play no substantive or procedural role in such court decisions.

S. Rep. No. 201, 100th Cong., 1st Sess. 23 (1987).

Thus, it appears that Congress has chosen to abdicate to the courts on this issue. In the absence of any express federal recognition or waiver of sovereign immunity, this court is bound to follow the common law principles of tribal sovereign immunity announced by the Supreme Court. In my view the court's opinion fails to do this.

NOTES

1. Criticisms of *Native Village of Stevens*: On what basis did the majority conclude that Native villages in Alaska are "not self-governing or in any meaningful sense sovereign"? For example, of what relevance is the fact that the U.S. never entered into treaties with any Alaskan groups or that Alaska has criminal jurisdiction over Natives, or that Alaskan Natives never fought a war with the U.S.? Some states have criminal jurisdiction over Indians in the Lower 48 states; many tribes in the Lower 48 states did not enter into treaties with the United States as well. Are these factors relied on as undercutting tribal sovereignty in the Lower 48 states? Is the court's reliance on the Governor's Task Force justified? Is the Task Force's reliance on nineteenth century Indian country decisions by one judge, Matthew Deady, justified? Does Justice Rabinowitz's dissent argue that villages should be treated as tribes for all purposes? A recent article by Professor Sidney Harring tracing the history of the Tlingit people's relationship with the U.S. government, analyzed the Deady opinions and concluded:

> Judge Matthew Deady of the federal district court in Portland, with jurisdiction over Alaska until 1884, singlehandedly determined the legal status of Alaska natives with a series of rulings inconsistent with both existing federal Indian policy and with the actual intent of the Department of the Interior regarding the legal status of Alaska natives. None of Deady's rulings was ever appealed to the United States Supreme Court. No Alaska native had either the resources [or] sufficient confidence in American legal institutions to do so.

Harring, *The Incorporation of Alaskan Natives Under American Law: United States and Tlingit Sovereignty, 1867-1900*, 31 ARIZ. L. REV. 279, 326 (1989).* For an analysis and criticism of the *Stevens* opinion, see Kisken, *The Uncertain Legal Status of Alaska Natives After Native Village of Stevens v. Alaska Management & Planning: Exposing the Fallacious Distinctions Between Alaska Natives and Lower 48 Indians*, 31 ARIZ. L. REV. 405 (1989).

In *In re City of Nome*, 780 P.2d 363 (Alaska 1989), the Alaska Supreme Court held that land owned not in trust but in fee by the Nome Eskimo Community, a tribal government organized under the IRA, was exempt from foreclosure by the City of Nome for nonpayment of taxes by virtue of IRA § 16, which recognizes that IRA governments have power "to prevent the sale, disposition, lease, or encumbrance of tribal lands, interest in lands, or other tribal assets." Despite some evidence in the legislative history that the IRA provision was only concerned with the appropriation of Indian assets by the Secretary of the Interior, the state court gave section 16 an expansive interpretation in light of the IRA's purpose to promote tribal self-determination. "The broad terms in which [Congress] legislated indicate that it intended ... to stop erosion of the tribal land base in whatever form that erosion took." *City of Nome*, at 367. Noting that this argument had been expressly left open in *Village of Stevens*, *supra*, n.22, the Court reviewed the legislative history and concluded: "Regardless of whether NEC is a 'tribe' for other purposes, there can be little doubt that it is a 'tribe' for purposes of [section 16]." *Id.* at 365.

In *Doyle v. Native Village of Mekoryuk*, 17 Indian L. Rep. 5075 (Alaska Super. Ct., Mar. 16, 1990), a superior court granted a wholly Native-owned business operated by a Village summary judgment because of tribal sovereign immunity, relying on *City of Nome*. Was this reliance appropriate? The court also noted that *Village of Stevens* excepted tribes with reservation status and that the Village was located on Nunivak Island, an Executive Order reservation created in 1929. Would this fact have provided a surer footing for the court's holding in light of the Alaska Supreme Court precedent? *Cf. Harrison v. Alaska*, 791 P.2d 359 (Alaska App. 1990) (only exceptions to the general rule of *Stevens* denying Alaska Natives self-governing powers are Metlakatla Indian Community, the only reservation retained by ANCSA, and the community of Tyonek) (citing *Village of Stevens*, *supra*, n.4).

2. The Ninth Circuit Analysis: *Tyonek*, *Venetie*, and *Noatak*: The federal courts have addressed the important issues of sovereignty in several different contexts. In *Native Village of Tyonek v. Puckett*, 17 Indian L. Rep. 2002 (D. Alaska 1986) (unpublished), the district court held that a counterclaim against a tribal plaintiff was barred by sovereign immunity. The district court noted:

> Tribes have been held to possess this immunity even when they have not been officially recognized as Indian tribes by the federal government, when they have no prolonged course of dealing with federal or state governments, when they do not reside on reservations or in "Indian country," and "'even after dissolution of the[ir] tribal governments.'"

Id. at 2006, (quoting *Bottomly v. Passamaquoddy Tribe*, 599 F.2d 1061, 1065 & nn.5-6 (4th Cir. 1957)). The district court also referred to the village as having a unique status because it is located on a former Executive Order reservation. Although the Ninth Circuit affirmed this aspect of the decision, it did not further comment on the tribal sovereignty issue. *Village of Tyonek v. Puckett*,

890 F.2d 1054 (9th Cir. 1989), *cert. applied for*, 58 U.S.L.W. 3357 (Nov. 28, 1989).

The decision in *Alaska ex rel. Yukon Flats School Dist. v. Native Village of Venetie*, 856 F.2d 1384 (9th Cir. 1988), could also have far-reaching consequences. ANCSA revoked the reservation that had surrounded two villages, Venetie, an IRA village, and Arctic Village, a traditional village. Each village organized under ANCSA, but in 1978, the villages transferred title to the land to a joint governing body, the Native Village of Venetie Tribal Government. The tribal government imposed business taxes on non-Native contractors of the state constructing a public high school in Venetie. When the tribal government sued the state in tribal court to collect the tax, the state did not appear in tribal court, but instead challenged the tax in federal court. Obviously this case raises some of the most troublesome sovereignty questions in Indian law, involving as it does issues of tribal sovereign immunity, power over nonmembers, exhaustion of tribal remedies, and whether the ANCSA land transferred to the tribal government is Indian country. The district court reserved decision on the villages' sovereign immunity and exhaustion claims, but did grant a preliminary injunction against the tribal court proceedings.

The Ninth Circuit noted the importance of the issues raised in the case in upholding the preliminary injunction. The court stated that in balancing the harm to the state and the village the district court had been influenced by two arguments:

> First, [the district court] was persuaded that the other 200 native villages in Alaska would be prompted to engage in similar taxation which would create tremendous uncertainty and difficulty for the State and other businesses providing services to those villages. Second, it was persuaded that if appellees paid the alleged tax liability and litigated in the Native Court, the amount paid would be unavailable for reimbursement if appellees ultimately prevailed.
>
> The first argument is persuasive in light of the posture of this action and political realities in the State. We note, as did the parties and the district court, that this action presents a question of first impression. One amicus brief informs us of at least one similar action pending in the District of Alaska. See *Alyeska Pipeline Service Co. v. Kluti Kaah Native Village of Copper Center*, No. A87-201 Civil (D. Alaska). The other amicus brief informs us that it was filed on behalf of over 180 Native Alaskan Communities that "have a vital interest in the issues presented in this appeal." Thus, the district court was acknowledging obvious and substantial developments in the area of Native Alaskan taxation, and the high profile of this particular action. It is not unrealistic to conclude that a decision denying this preliminary injunction would add fuel to the engines of Native Alaskan taxation, have a chilling effect on potential contractors, and subject the State to a significant financial burden (as a result of either paying the future levies or litigating their validity).

Id. at 1389.

As to the likelihood of the state's success on the merits, the court concluded that the issues of whether the village constituted Indian country and whether the village could claim tribal sovereign immunity were too complex to be resolved at the initial stage of the litigation. The court gave the following guidance to aid the lower court to make the determination of tribal status:

> [B]efore we can conclude as to appellants' immunity from this action, we must determine whether Native Village or Venetie is a tribe for legal purposes.
>
> Contrary to appellants' contention, this court's decision in *Price v. State of Hawaii*, 764 F.2d 623 (9th Cir. 1985), *cert. denied*, 474 U.S. 1055 (1986), did not hold that organization under the IRA is conclusive evidence of tribal status. In *Price*, the court merely stated that tribal status would be arguable in the event of IRA organization. *Id.*

at 626. Also, amici have noted that the language of the IRA's Alaska amendment, 25 U.S.C. § 473(a), raises doubt as to whether IRA organization should be construed so conclusively in the case of Alaskan Natives. Furthermore, much uncertainty exists concerning the structure of Native Village, Venetie, and Arctic Village that may have an impact on the IRA analysis.

If the IRA does not settle the matter, the inquiry would shift to whether Native Village or Venetie has been otherwise recognized as a tribe by the federal government. See, e.g., *Price*, 764 F.2d at 626-28. Failing there, tribal status may still be based on conclusions drawn from careful scrutiny of various historical factors. See, e.g., *Mashpee Tribe v. New Seabury Corp.*, 592 F.2d 575, 582-88 (1st Cir.), *cert. denied*, 444 U.S. 866 (1979).

Once tribal status is determined, other considerations arise. The sovereign immunity that naturally flows from tribal sovereignty will not be effective if it has been divested by Congress or otherwise lost by implication. See *United States v. Wheeler*, 435 U.S. 313, 322-26 (1978); *Bottomly*, 599 F.2d at 1066. Nor will it be effective if it was waived during incorporation under the IRA. See W. Canby, American Indian Law 74-75 (1981). And even if the tribe and its instrumentalities are immune, the individual officers of the tribe will not be immune unless they were "acting in their representative capacity and within the scope of their authority." *Hardin v. White Mountain Apache Tribe*, 779 F.2d 476, 479 (9th Cir. 1985).

Id. at 1387.

Because the issue of tribal status had not yet been resolved, the court also did not decide whether the state must exhaust tribal court remedies under *National Farmers Union Insurance Cos. v. Crow Tribe* and *Iowa Insurance v. LaPlante*, discussed in Chapter 3, section D1, because that analysis depended on the status of the village.

In *Native Village of Noatak v. Hoffman*, 896 F.2d 1157 (9th Cir. 1990), Noatak Village, a village with an IRA government, and Circle Village, a village with a traditional government, protested the dilution of a state revenue sharing law. The state law originally provided for payment of $25,000 to Native village governments *not* incorporated as cities. When the state Department of Community and Regional Affairs decided to expand the benefitted class to other rural villages with a predominantly Native population, the Native villages argued that such an expansion diluted the funds and represented a departure from an acceptable political classification to a racial classification in violation of equal protection and various federal statutes.

Since the villages sought jurisdiction under 28 U.S.C. § 1362, the court had to determine whether section 1362 applied to Native villages, whether section 1362 implicitly waived the state's eleventh amendment immunity from suit, and whether the tribe had stated a claim under federal law. The court first determined that Alaskan Native villages qualify as tribes for purposes of § 1362. The court reasoned as follows:

> Are the Native Villages "tribes" which have been "duly recognized by the Secretary of the Interior?" The Native Villages represent bodies of Indians of the same race united in a community under a single government in a particular territory — Noatak at Bering Strait, Circle Village at Upper Yukon-Porcupine. They therefore meet the basic criteria to constitute Tribes. *Montoya v. United States*, 180 U.S. 261, 266 (1901).
>
> No statute expressly outlines how a tribe may become duly recognized for purposes of section 1362 jurisdiction. In *Price v. Hawaii*, 764 F.2d 623, 626 (9th Cir. 1985), *cert. denied*, 474 U.S. 1055 (1986),* this court left open the question whether formal organization or incorporation of a tribe followed by approval of the organization or incorporation by the Secretary of the Interior constituted being "duly recognized" for the

---

*This case is reprinted in section B of this chapter. — Eds.

purpose of the statute. We see no reason to suppose that the Secretary of the Interior needs to issue a special document conferring a right to sue under the statute. Noatak Village has a governing body approved by the Secretary. 25 U.S.C. § 476. It is therefore a tribe with a duly recognized governing body and qualifies for the benefits of section 1362. Cf. *Alaska v. Native Village of Venetie*, 856 F.2d 1384, 1387 (9th Cir. 1988) (uncertainty existed concerning structure of Alaska Indian villages involved; tribal status not resolved solely by reference to organization of tribe under Indian Reorganization Act).

Circle Village, like Noatak, is listed as a Native Village in the Alaska Native Claims Act, 43 U.S.C. § 1610(b)(1). The purpose of this Act was to make "a fair and just settlement of all claims by Natives and Native Groups of Alaska, based on aboriginal land claims." 43 U.S.C. § 1601(a). The Villages acknowledged by the Act were distinguished from ineligible villages "of a modern and urban character," where the majority of the residents were not natives. 43 U.S.C. § 1610(b)(2), (3). The Villages acknowledged by the Act were possessed of aboriginal land claims and became eligible for the benefits provided under the Act. The Act was congressional recognition of the Native Villages.

In addition, in three recently enacted statutes — the Indian Self-Determination Act, 25 U.S.C. § 450b(e); the Indian Financing Act, 25 U.S.C. § 1452(c); and the Indian Child Welfare Act, 25 U.S.C. § 1903(8) — Congress treated the Native Villages as Indian tribes. Arguably, Congress intended to confer recognition only for the particular purposes of each piece of legislation. See, e.g., *Native Village of Venetie*, 856 F.2d at 1387. But the nature and scope of the federal government's relationship with the Native Villages, as evidenced by these Acts, indicates that the recognition extends to legal claims. "[I]t is a settled principle of statutory construction that statutes passed for the benefit of dependent Indian tribes are to be liberally construed, with doubtful expressions being resolved in favor of the Indians." *Three Affiliated Tribes v. Wold Eng'g, P.C.*, 467 U.S. 138, 149 (1984).

It is true that section 1362 speaks of recognition by the Secretary of the Interior, not Congress, but the Secretary is only using power delegated by Congress. If Congress has recognized the tribe, *a fortiori* the tribe is entitled to recognition and is in fact recognized by the Secretary of the Interior. Consequently, Circle Village, as well as Noatak, qualifies under section 1362.

Id. at 1160.

Thus finding it necessary to reach the eleventh amendment issue, the court then held that section 1362 implicitly waived the state's immunity from suit by Indian tribes under the principles of federalism underlying the eleventh amendment, concluding:

> [T]here is no need for an explicit overriding of state immunity if the state in consenting to the Constitution has consented to being sued. The states did give consent to federal jurisdiction of Indian affairs. The Eleventh Amendment has not revoked the consent of the states, because neither in terms nor purpose does the amendment apply to Indian tribes. No other general immunity protects the state from suit by the tribes.

Id. at 1164-65.

This conclusion puts the Ninth Circuit in conflict with the contrary holding of the Eighth Circuit in *Standing Rock Sioux Indian Tribe v. Dorgan*, 505 F.2d 1135 (8th Cir. 1974), on this important issue, which affects all Indian tribes. On the merits, the court held that the tribe had stated a cognizable claim based on equal protection and on the allegation that the Commissioner's actions violated federal laws and policies in favor of self-government. The Supreme Court has granted certiorari, 59 U.S.L.W. 3243 (1990).

3. Stating a Federal Claim Based on the Limits of Tribal Sovereignty: Recall that the Supreme Court has held that the extent of tribal jurisdiction over nonmembers is a question of federal common law and thus implicates claims arising under the Constitution, laws and treaties of the United States for purposes of 28 U.S.C. § 1331. *National Farmers Union Insurance Cos. v. Crow Tribe*, set forth and discussed in Chapter 3, section D1. In both *National Farmers* and *Iowa Insurance*, a nonmember of the tribe sought federal jurisdiction over the tribe based on this principle. In two cases Native villages have invoked this principle to assert a federal claim over non-Indians. *Chilkat Indian Village v. Johnson*, 570 F.2d 1469 (9th Cir. 1989); *Native Village of Tyonek v. Puckett*, 890 F.2d 1054 (9th Cir. 1989). While basing the claim on federal common law may be appropriate for the non-Indian challenging tribal court jurisdiction, does not permitting the tribe to raise this issue anticipate a federal defense in violation of the well-pleaded complaint rule? *See Gully v. First Nat'l Bank*, 299 U.S. 109, 112-13 (1936). In *Chilkat Indian Village, supra*, which is noted in Chapter 5, section D, note 2, Judge Canby concluded that claims of jurisdiction over nonmembers did not anticipate a federal defense, stating: "the Village's allegations of sovereign power, as a matter of federal statute and 'reserved powers' (which could only be cognizable as a matter of federal common law), to apply its ordinance to Johnson and his corporation, bring this case within the rule of *Oneida Indian Nation v. County of Oneida*, 414 U.S. 661 (1974)." *Id.* at 1475. In contrast, the court concluded that the issue of whether a tribe could exercise jurisdiction over its own members remained purely a matter of internal tribal law. *See also Boe v. Fort Belknap Indian Community*, 642 F.2d 276 (9th Cir. 1981). Should the question regarding tribal power over nonmembers or non-Indians also initially be treated as a question of internal tribal law under the principles of *National Farmers Union* and *Iowa Insurance*? Even if the Ninth Circuit's analysis of this issue is correct, given the uncertain state of the federal law regarding tribal sovereignty, is it wise for a tribe to seek the aid of the federal courts in enforcing its ordinances against nonmembers? In *Village of Tyonek, supra*, the Tribe sued to enforce two tribal ordinances, one barring rental of housing units built with tribal funds to nonmembers and another barring nonmembers from the Village for longer than 24 consecutive hours. Do you see any problem with either of these ordinances?

B. NATIVE HAWAIIANS

SENATE SELECT COMMITTEE ON INDIAN AFFAIRS, IMPROVING THE EDUCATION STATUS OF NATIVE HAWAIIANS, Senate Report 100-36, 100th Cong., 1st Sess., 12-17 (1987)

The Historical Relationship

A review of the history of relations between Hawaiian Natives and the United States demonstrates that there are significant parallels to aspects of U.S.-Indian history and gives credence to the observations of the commentators and the Courts that a Federal-Native Hawaiian Relationship exists.

It is been estimated that approximately 300,000 native people occupied the "Sandwich Islands," as Hawaii was then called when Western society discovered them in 1778. The indigenous Hawaiians had a complex political and economic but self-sufficient system in existence at time of contact. The system has been compared to the feudal system of medieval Europe. Private property — fee simple title — did not exist. Land occupancy rights ran from greater lords to lesser lords to commoners; obligations ran in reverse order.[19] Major differences did exist: land use rights were personal and did not necessarily pass to heirs; and "commoners" were not tied to the specific lords or land and could move. Each island was autonomous until 1810 when Kamehameha I united the islands by conquest and negotiation.

Certain similarities to the Indian situation at the time of discovery are pertinent. Both populations were politically autonomous, and both populations were self-sufficient in their traditional economies and life styles. Neither population had a private property system; but they did however control most, and in some cases all, of the lands within their political boundaries.

All of these situations would change. The various ways that Indian lands have been alienated from Indian ownership [have] been documented in proceedings of the Indian Claims Commission, and other sources. Interestingly, treaties[,] which have become a major source of evidence in establishing a trust relationship, were often the instruments of land loss. The role of the United States in these transactions was fairly clear, it either directly obtained the Indian land or failed to protect the tribes in their land dealings.

The role of the United States in the Hawaiian loss of land was different in form than in the Indian situation but just as central. Treaties with the Native Hawaiian government were not generally land transactions but were means of assuring commercial access. The first treaty of peace and friendship proposed in 1826 was not ratified by the United States.[20] The first ratified treaty (1849)[21] dealt with friendship, commerce and navigation. A second treaty was entered into in 1875; dealing with commercial reciprocity.[22] A final treaty, also concerning commercial reciprocity was entered into in 1884.[23] Throughout the 19th century, it would be the American merchants along with American missionaries who under the auspices of "civilizing" a system they felt was culturally inferior to their own would intervene with the military support of the United States government in internal Hawaiian affairs. This active intervention first focused on access to Hawaiian commercial timber, then after the trees were depleted, switched to access to the land itself for the establishment of the plantation economy that would dominate Hawaii in the second half of the nineteenth century. This interference would find early expression in the western style constitution of 1840 and culminate in an insurrection against the Hawaiian monarchy.

During the first half of the 19th century, the merchants were supported by their respective Governments, (French, British and American) by the use of naval war ships.[24] In effect the Westerners, and eventually the United States, using the threat of military force reduced the Kingdom of Hawaii to the functional equivalent of a dependent sovereign — a suzerainty.

---

[19] N. Levy, *Native Hawaiian Land Rights*, 63 Cal. L. Rev. 848 (1975) provides an extensive discussion of these matters and is relied upon throughout this paper.

[20] Treaty with Hawaii on Commerce, Dec. 23, 1826, United States-Hawaii, 3 C. Bevans, Treaties and Other Internal Agreements of the United States, 1776-1949, at 861 (1971).

[21] Treaty with Hawaii on Friendship, Commerce and Navigation, Dec. 20, 1849, U.S.-Hawaii, 9 Stat. 977.

[22] Treaty with Hawaii on Commercial Reciprocity, Jan. 30, 1875, U.S.-Hawaii, 19 Stat. 625.

[23] Treaty with Hawaii on Commercial Reciprocity, Dec. 6, 1884, U.S.-Hawaii, 25 Stat. 1399.

[24] Levy, *supra*, n. 16 at 852.

The influence of the western powers was greatly felt in the land system:

> By 1845, the land tenure system could neither maintain itself in the face of a hostile foreign world or accommodate itself to the wishes of that world.[25]

A land Commission dominated by Westerners was appointed. It would oversee the "Great Mahele"; the end of the traditional Hawaiian land system and the substitution of a more western style system of fee ownership. Cohen points out that:

> By destroying the interlocking communal nature of land tenure its [the Great Mahele] effect was similar to allotment and termination acts on the mainland.

Land rights were concentrated in the hands of the very few. The King and the chiefs held title to 99 percent of all the lands. Many of the commoners who lived on the land were not permitted a realistic opportunity to obtain title to their lands. In a process not dissimilar to that which occurred with Indian lands after allotment, title to much of [the] land was soon transferred to non-Hawaiian ownership. Large plots of lands owned by royalty no longer had communal obligations attached and were therefore not productive without western capital or management systems. They were sold off at "distress prices" and fraud was not uncommon; ultimately a plantation economy with imported non-Hawaiian labor was firmly established. Small plots were also uneconomical and most were soon lost.

All commentaries seem to agree that in the second half of the 19th Century a small number of Westerners (2000) came to control most of the land in Hawaii:

> Native Hawaiians had been excluded from the mainstream of the economy; they had lost ownership of most privately held land and had been reduced to a minority of the inhabitants of the Kingdom.[26]

Control of land, however, was not enough. The Westerners who by the latter part of the nineteenth century were primarily Americans, sought political control. As noted previously the first Hawaiian constitution of 1840 was procured by western influence. The constitution of 1887, known as the "Bayonet Constitution" was forced on the Monarchy by armed merchants — American citizens. This constitution restricted the right to vote to those who paid taxes, including non-citizens. Native Hawaiians were disenfranchised and the American merchants obtained a virtual dictatorship.

At this point, although legally part of a foreign state, the American merchants felt that they were "part of the American system"; a view publicly echoed by U.S. Secretary of State Blaine. However, the imposition of the "McKinley tariff" on foreign sugar (including Hawaiian sugar) created a significant economic crisis. Sugar fell from $100 a ton to $60 a ton and property values collapsed in Hawaii.[27]

The last royal ruler of Hawaii, Queen Liliuokalani, came to the throne in 1892 and attempted to replace the "Bayonet constitution" with a new one that would have significantly eroded Western power. Foreigners were to be pre-

---

[25] *Ibid.*, at 853.

[26] Cohen, *supra*, n.8, at 800.

[27] S. Morrison and H.S. Commager, The Growth of the American Republic 5th Ed., Vol. 2 (1962).

cluded from obtaining citizenship or from voting. In January 1893, shortly before the new constitution was to go into effect, and while President Harrison, who favored annexation, was still in office, armed American merchants, aided by the U.S. minister in Hawaii, John L. Stevens, and marines from the U.S.S. Boston forced the Queen to relinquish her governmental authority.

A provisional government dominated by American merchants was established. This government immediately sought annexation by the United States. The goal of annexation, however, would take a few years. Assuming office shortly after the overthrow of the Queen, President Cleveland, supported by the Blount report[28] refused to support annexation.[29] The Blount report found that the overthrow of the Queen had been illegal; and recommended that she be restored to power. The Provisional government of Hawaii refused to follow Blount's recommendations and instead established the Republic of Hawaii. The Republic thereupon took over all crown and government lands without compensation.

Another report on the overthrow of the Queen and the propriety of annexation would be prepared by the Senate Foreign Relations Committee; it is known as the Morgan Report.[30] The Morgan Report approved the United States support of the merchants. It used a familiar theory ... determining Hawaii to be a dependent sovereignty of the United States, an analogous theory to that used in the landmark decisions that gave judicial recognition to the Federal-Indian relationship, *Worcester* and *Cherokee Nation*. The report stated:

> [I]t is a recognized fact that Hawaii has been all the time under a virtual suzerainty of the United States ... a de facto supremacy over the country.

A "suzerainty" was understood in International law to be the relationship that a more powerful sovereign has over a dependent one; the dependent sovereign was usually viewed as less "civilized" than the powerful sovereign.

After the Morgan Report, by a joint resolution of Congress the United States annexed Hawaii in 1898.[31] Cohen states that with annexation "Native Hawaiians become a dependent indigenous people of the United States."[32]

Native Hawaiian conditions which were stressed at the time of annexation continued to deteriorate. Indian conditions were at [the] same time also suffering from similar circumstances; loss of traditional life styles and food resources; loss of the native land base; and destruction of traditional modes of self-government. By the 1920's, reformers were concerned about the conditions of Native people. For Indians, the Red Cross survey of conditions, and the Meriam Commission report would result in a partial reversal of many of the policies of the 19th century.

---

[28] James Blount was the former Chairman of the House of Representatives Committee on Foreign Affairs, appointed as Special Commissioner to Hawaii. See Kuykendall, *The Hawaiian Kingdom, The Kalakaua Dynasty* (1967) for an in depth treatment of this era in Hawaiian affairs.

[29] President's Message Relating to the Hawaiian Islands, H.R. Exec. Doc. No. 47, 53rd Cong., 2d Sess., XIV-XV (1893).

[30] S. Rep. No. 227, 53rd Cong., 2d Sess. (1893).

[31] 30 Stat. 750 (1898).

[32] *Supra*, n.8, at 802.

For Hawaiian Natives the concern would focus in the Hawaiian Homes Commission Act.[33] The Act set aside 200,000 acres of land to be leased at nominal rates for 99 years to Native Hawaiians. Congress viewed the Hawaiian Homes Commission as a "plan for the rehabilitation of the Hawaiian Race." The bill was introduced by the nonvoting Delegate from Hawaii, J. K. Kalanianole, a member of the royal family of Hawaii, based on a plan developed by Senator Wise of the Legislative Commission of the Territory of Hawaii.

The Hawaiian Homes Commission Act also addressed another concern prevalent at the time. This was the concern of many of "growers" whose long term leases on their plantations were expiring, that under the homesteading laws applicable in the territories, much of "their land" could be lost to homesteading. These hundreds of thousands of agricultural acres were removed from the Homesteading provisions.

Hawaiians were thought to be a dying race, numbering a scant 22,500 in 1920. The House Committee Report[34] on the Homes Commission quotes from the hearing record to establish the cause of the problem it was attempting to remedy.

> Secretary [of the Interior] LANE. One thing that impressed me ... was the fact that the natives of the islands who are our wards, I should say, and for whom in a sense we are trustees, are falling off rapidly in numbers, and many of them are in poverty.
> ....
> Mr. MONAHAN. What caused this dying away of the race[?] ...
> Secretary LANE. ... It is always incident to the comings of civilization and we always carry disease germs with us to which these people are not immune ....

The Committee's response to any challenge to the bill's constitutionality as "unconstitutional class legislation" was to point out, among other arguments, that Congress had the authority to provide special benefits for unique groups such as "Indians, soldiers and sailors ...." This is the same argument in embryonic form, that the Supreme Court would later use in *Morton v. Mancari* to sustain special programs for Indians. The Hawaiian Homes Commission Act is universally viewed as Congress' recognition of the special relationship the United States has to Native Hawaiians.

When Hawaii became a state in 1959, the dominant Federal-Indian policy was then the termination of Indian Reservations and the transfer of much Federal administrative responsibility to States. It is therefore not surprising that the Hawaiian Homes Commission was made part of the responsibilities of the State of Hawaii upon Hawaii's admission to the union. Since the rights involved were Federal, Federal responsibility was retained. Any changes proposed by the State that could impair Hawaiian Native rights require Congressional consent, and the United States is the only party with specific standing to sue in Federal courts to enforce the provisions of the trust.[35]

Another important provision was also included in the Admission Act that demonstrated Congress' denotation of Native Hawaiians as a special beneficiary group. That provision required the State of Hawaii to utilize the income and proceeds from lands the United States ceded to Hawaii for the benefit of the

---

[33] 42 Stat. 108 (1921).
[34] H.R. Rep. No. 839, 66th Cong., 2d Sess. 4 (1920).
[35] P.L. 86-3, set out in full in 48 U.S.C. prec. sec. 491.

people of Hawaii, and specifically Native Hawaiians. Again the United States retained a supervisory trustee role.[36]

Since statehood Congress has periodically legislated for the benefit of Native Hawaiians.[37] It has not, however, comprehensively addressed Hawaiians Native issues. This situation is not entirely different from the Federal-Indian relationship, which also has not been comprehensively spelled out. Many of the Indian programs are premised on general statutory authority. The Executive branch has been allowed great latitude in defining the nature and scope of programs.[38] Absent an express direction from Congress, the agencies operating Federal programs have not included Hawaiian Natives. Although it is possible and administratively feasible to include Hawaiian Natives, given the broad discretion asserted by federal agencies, inclusion of the Hawaiian Native population in Federal programs by agency action is not very likely. Department of the Interior regulations on tribal recognition apply only in the continental United States and therefore exclude Hawaiians.[39] Furthermore much agency activity in the last decade has focused on reducing beneficiaries by narrowing eligibility criteria.

In many ways, native Hawaiian issues resemble those of Native Alaskans prior to the Alaskan Native Claims Settlement Act. In addressing the issue of whether "Eskimos" were "Indians" even though not of the same racial origin, courts have determined that the term "Indians" is not a racial classification but a term of art for the aboriginal peoples of America.[40] Alaskan Natives were sometimes included in Indian programs, although not always. Periodically programs were passed for Alaskan Natives that did not have Indian counterparts.[41] Alaskan Natives with several exceptions did not have reservations or trust lands. In addition to resolving Alaskan land claims, the Settlement Act provided for a comprehensive definition of Alaskan Natives, and the creation of a series of entities, including existing traditional Native villages, as the mechanisms for land holding as well as service delivery. These mechanisms have no counterpart in Indian affairs in the lower forty-eight states, but have become routine parts of the Federal-Alaskan Native relationship.

Many distinct issues, and many divergent views exist on the subject of Hawaiian Land Claims. Absent such a comprehensive approach to Hawaiian issues, as was provided for Alaskan Natives by the Alaskan Natives Claims Settlement Act, or some other comprehensive mechanism, Congress will determine on a by-case basis whether any particular program should be part of the Federal-Hawaiian relationship. As Cohen has stated "... there is no reason to doubt that Congress has power to legislate specifically for the benefit of Native Hawaiians."[42]

NOTE

In *Hawaii v. United States*, 676 F. Supp. 1024 (D. Haw. 1988), aff'd, 866 F.2d 313 (9th Cir. 1989), Hawaii brought an action to quiet title in its name on behalf

[36] 73 Stat. 4, sec. 5(f) (1959).
[37] See the discussion on pages 6-7.
[38] Morton v. Ruiz, 415 U.S. 199, 231 (1974) "the power of an administrative agency to administer a congressionally created and funded program necessarily requires the formulation of policy and the making of rules to fill any gap left implicitly or explicitly by Congress."
[39] 25 C.F.R. 54.2.
[40] Pence v. Kleppe, 529 F.2d 135 (9th Cir. 1976).
[41] For example the importation of Reindeer for benefit of Alaskan Natives, 25 U.S.C. sec. 500.
[42] *Supra*, n.8, at 803.

of the Hawaii Homes Commission to the Lualualei lands, purportedly ceded to the United States from Hawaii in 1898. The district court concluded that Hawaii's action was barred by the Quiet Title Act, 28 U.S.C. § 2409a, for failure to meet its twelve-year statute of limitations. The Quiet Title Act was the only way for a state to contest United States' interest in land. If the land is used or required for national defense purposes, the Quiet Title Act bars state action until that use or requirement ceases, provided "the State action was brought more than twelve years after the State knew or should have known of the claims of the United States." Actual notice is not required; all that is required is "reasonable awareness" that the United States claims "some interest" adverse to the plaintiff. The Lualualei lands are used and required by the United States for national defense purposes, including a naval radio transmitting facility and a naval ammunition depot. The court concluded that because the State of Hawaii had sufficient notice that the United States and the Department of the Navy claimed some interest adverse to Hawaii in the Lualualei lands for longer than twelve years before bringing suit, Hawaii's action was barred until the United States no longer used the lands for national defense purposes. The district court therefore granted defendants' motion for summary judgment. The district court's decision was affirmed by the Ninth Circuit. The Court of Appeals made it clear that any requirement of actual notice imposed by Hawaii common law was irrelevant when applying the Quiet Title Act, which only requires constructive notice for the running of the statute of limitations.

CONSTITUTION OF THE STATE OF HAWAII

Article XII. Hawaiian Affairs

Hawaiian Homes Commission Act

Section 1. Anything in this constitution to the contrary notwithstanding, the Hawaiian Homes Commission Act, 1920, enacted by the Congress, as the same has been or may be amended prior to the admission of the State, is hereby adopted as a law of the State, subject to amendment or repeal by the legislature; provided that if and to the extent that the United States shall so require, such law shall be subject to amendment or repeal only with the consent of the United States and in no other manner; provided further that if the United States shall have been provided or shall provide that particular provisions or types of provisions of such Act may be amended in the manner required for ordinary state legislation, such provisions or types of provisions may be so amended. The proceeds and income from Hawaiian home lands shall be used only in accordance with the terms and spirit of such Act. The legislature shall make sufficient sums available for the following purposes: (1) development of home, agriculture, farm and ranch lots; (2) home, agriculture, aquaculture, farm and ranch loans; (3) rehabilitation projects to include, but not limited to, educational, economic, political, social and cultural processes by which the general welfare and conditions of native Hawaiians are thereby improved; (4) the administration and operating budget of the department of Hawaiian home lands; in furtherance of (1), (2), (3) and (4) herein, by appropriating the same in the manner provided by law. Thirty percent of the state receipts derived from the leasing of cultivated sugarcane lands under any provision of law or from water licenses shall be transferred to the native Hawaiian rehabilitation fund, section

213 of the Hawaiian Homes Commission Act, 1920, for the purposes enumerated in that section. Thirty percent of the state receipts derived from the leasing of lands cultivated as sugarcane lands on the effective date of this section shall continue to be so transferred to the native Hawaiian rehabilitation fund whenever such lands are sold, developed, leased, utilized, transferred, set aside or otherwise disposed of for purposes other than the cultivation of sugarcane. There shall be no ceiling established for the aggregate amount transferred into the native Hawaiian rehabilitation fund.

Section 2. The State and its people do hereby accept, as a compact with the United States, or as conditions or trust provisions imposed by the United States, relating to the management and disposition of the Hawaiian home lands, the requirement that section 1 hereof be included in this constitution, in whole or in part, it being intended that the Act or acts of the Congress pertaining thereto shall be definitive of the extent and nature of such compact, conditions or trust provisions, as the case may be. The State and its people do further agree and declare that the spirit of the Hawaiian Homes Commission Act looking to the continuance of the Hawaiian homes projects for the further rehabilitation of the Hawaiian race shall be faithfully carried out.

Section 3. As a compact with the United States relating to the management and disposition of the Hawaiian home lands, the Hawaiian Homes Commission Act, 1920, as amended, shall be adopted as a provision of the constitution of this State, as provided in section 7, subsection (b), of the Admission Act, subject to amendment or repeal only with the consent of the United States, and in no other manner; provided that (1) sections 202, 213, 219, 220, 222, 224 and 225 and other provisions relating to administration, and paragraph (2) of section 204, sections 206 and 212 and other provisions relating to the powers and duties of officers other than those charged with the administration of such Act, may be amended in the constitution, or in the manner required for state legislation, but the Hawaiian home-loan fund, the Hawaiian home-operating fund and the Hawaiian home-development fund shall not be reduced or impaired by any such amendment, whether made in the constitution or in the manner required for state legislation, and the encumbrances authorized to be placed on Hawaiian home lands by officers other than those charged with the administration of such Act, shall not be increased, except with the consent of the United States; (2) that any amendment to increase the benefits to lessees of Hawaiian home lands may be made in the constitution, or in the manner required for state legislation, but the qualifications of lessees shall not be changed except with the consent of the United States; and (3) that all proceeds and income from the "available lands," as defined by such Act, shall be used only in carrying out the provisions of such Act.

Section 4. The lands granted to the State of Hawaii by Section 5(b) of the Admission Act and pursuant to Article XVI, Section 7, of the State Constitution, excluding therefrom lands defined as "available lands" by Section 203 of the Hawaiian Homes Commission Act, 1920, as amended, shall be held by the State as a public trust for native Hawaiians and the general public.

Section 5. There is hereby established an Office of Hawaiian Affairs. The Office of Hawaiian Affairs shall hold title to all the real and personal property now or hereafter set aside or conveyed to it which shall be held in trust for native Hawaiians and Hawaiians. There shall be a board of trustees for the Office of Hawaiian Affairs elected by qualified voters who are Hawaiians, as provided by law. The board members shall be Hawaiians. There shall be not less than nine members of the board of trustees; provided that each of the following Islands have one representative: Oahu, Kauai, Maui, Molokai and Hawaii. The board shall select a chairperson from its members.

Section 6. The board of trustees of the Office of Hawaiian Affairs shall exercise power as provided by law: to manage and administer the proceeds from the sale or other disposition of the lands, natural resources, minerals and income derived from whatever sources for native Hawaiians and Hawaiians, including all income and proceeds from that pro rata portion of the trust referred to in section 4 of this article for native Hawaiians; to formulate policy relating to affairs of native Hawaiians and Hawaiians; and to exercise control over real and personal property set aside by state, federal or private sources and transferred to the board for native Hawaiians and Hawaiians. The board shall have the power to exercise control over the Office of Hawaiian Affairs through its executive officer, the administrator of the Office of Hawaiian Affairs, who shall be appointed by the board.

Section 7. The State reaffirms and shall protect all rights, customarily and traditionally exercised for subsistence, cultural and religious purposes and possessed by ahupua'a tenants who are descendants of native Hawaiians who inhabited the Hawaiian Islands prior to 1778, subject to the right of the State to regulate such rights.

HAWAII REVISED STATUTES

Chapter 10. Office of Hawaiian Affairs

§ 10-1. Declaration of purpose.

(a) The people of the State of Hawaii and the United States of America as set forth and approved in the Admission Act, established a public trust which includes among other responsibilities, betterment of conditions for native Hawaiians. The people of the State of Hawaii reaffirmed their solemn trust obligation and responsibility to native Hawaiians and furthermore declared in the state constitution that there be an office of Hawaiian affairs to address the needs of the aboriginal class of people of Hawaii.

(b) It shall be the duty and responsibility of all state departments and instrumentalities of state government providing services and programs which affect native Hawaiians and Hawaiians to actively work toward the goals of this chapter and to cooperate with and assist wherever possible the office of Hawaiian affairs.

§ 10-2. Definitions.

In this chapter, if not inconsistent with the context:
"Administrator" means the administrator of the office of Hawaiian affairs;
"Beneficiary of the public trust entrusted upon the office" means native Hawaiians and Hawaiians;
"Board" means the board of trustees;

"Hawaiian" means any descendant of the aboriginal peoples inhabiting the Hawaiian islands which exercised sovereignty and subsisted in the Hawaiian Islands in 1778, and which peoples thereafter have continued to reside in Hawaii;

"Native Hawaiian" means any descendant of not less than one-half part of the races inhabiting the Hawaiian Islands previous to 1778, as defined by the Hawaiian Homes Commission Act, 1920, as amended; provided that the term identically refers to the descendants of such blood quantum of such aboriginal peoples which exercised sovereignty and subsisted in the Hawaiian Islands in 1778 and which peoples thereafter continued to reside in Hawaii;

"Office" means the office of Hawaiian affairs.

§ 10-3. Purpose of the office.

The purposes of the office of Hawaiian affairs include:

(1) The betterment of conditions of native Hawaiians. A pro rata portion of all the funds derived from the public land trust shall be funded in an amount to be determined by the legislature for this purpose, and shall be held and used solely as a public trust for the betterment of the conditions of native Hawaiians. For the purpose of this chapter, the public land trust shall be all proceeds and income from the sale, lease, or other disposition of lands ceded to the United States by the Republic of Hawaii under the joint resolution of annexation, approved July 7, 1898 (30 Stat. 750), or acquired in exchange for lands so ceded, and conveyed to the State of Hawaii by virtue of section 5(b) of the Act of March 18, 1959 (73 Stat. 4, the Admissions Act), (excluding therefrom lands and all proceeds and income from the sale, lease, or disposition of lands defined as "available lands" by section 203 of the Hawaiian Homes Commission Act, 1920, as amended), and all proceeds and income from the sale, lease, or other disposition of lands retained by the United States under sections 5(c) and 5(d) of the Act of March 18, 1959, later conveyed to the State under section 5(e);

(2) The betterment of conditions of Hawaiians;

(3) Serving as the principal public agency in this State responsible for the performance, development, and coordination of programs and activities relating to native Hawaiians and Hawaiians; except that the Hawaiian Homes Commission Act, 1920, as amended, shall be administered by the Hawaiian homes commission;

(4) Assessing the policies and practices of other agencies impacting on native Hawaiians and Hawaiians, and conducting advocacy efforts for native Hawaiians and Hawaiians;

(5) Applying for, receiving, and disbursing grants and donations from all sources for native Hawaiian and Hawaiian programs and services; and

(6) Serving as a receptacle for reparations.

§ 10-4. Office of Hawaiian affairs; established; general powers.

There shall be an office of Hawaiian affairs constituted as a body corporate which shall be a separate entity independent of the executive branch. The office, under the direction of the board of trustees, shall have the following general powers:

(1) To adopt, amend, and repeal bylaws governing the conduct of its business and the performance of the powers and duties granted to or imposed upon it by law;

(2) To acquire in any lawful manner any property, real, personal, or mixed, tangible or intangible, or any interest therein; to hold, maintain, use, and operate the same; and to sell, lease, or otherwise dispose of the same at such time, in such manner and to the extent necessary or appropriate to carry out its purpose;

(3) To determine the character of and the necessity for its obligations and expenditures, and the manner in which they shall be incurred, allowed, and paid, subject to provisions of law specifically applicable to the office of Hawaiian affairs;

(4) To enter into and perform such contracts, leases, cooperative agreements, or other transactions with any agency or instrumentality of the United States, or with the State, or with any political subdivision thereof, or with any person, firm, association, or corporation, as may be necessary in the conduct of its business and on such terms as it may deem appropriate;

(5) To execute, in accordance with its bylaws, all instruments necessary or appropriate in the exercise of any of its powers; and

(6) To take such actions as may be necessary or appropriate to carry out the powers conferred upon it by law.

§ 10-5. Board of trustees; powers and duties.

The board shall have the power in accordance with law to:

(1) Manage, invest, and administer the proceeds from the sale or other disposition of lands, natural resources, minerals, and income derived from whatever sources for native Hawaiians and Hawaiians, including all income and proceeds from that pro rata portion of the trust referred to in section 10-3, of this chapter;

(2) Exercise control over real and personal property set aside to the office by the State of Hawaii, the United States of America, or any private sources, and transferred to the office for native Hawaiians and Hawaiians;

(3) Collect, receive, deposit, withdraw, and invest money and property on behalf of the office;

(4) Formulate policy relating to the affairs of native Hawaiians and Hawaiians, provided that such policy shall not diminish or limit the benefits of native Hawaiians under Article XII, section 4, of the state Constitution;

(5) Otherwise act as a trustee as provided by law;

(6) Delegate to the administrator, its officers and employees such powers and duties as may be proper for the performance of the powers and duties vested in the board;

(7) Provide grants to public or private agencies for pilot projects, demonstrations, or both, where such projects or demonstrations fulfill criteria established by the board;

(8) Make available technical and financial assistance and advisory services to any agency or private organization for native Hawaiian and Hawaiian programs, and for other functions pertinent to the purposes of the office of Hawai-

ian affairs. Financial assistance may be rendered through contractual arrangements as may be agreed upon by the board and any such agency or organization; and

(9) Adopt and use a common seal by which all official acts shall be authenticated.

§ 10-6. General duties of the board.

(a) The general duties of the board shall be:

(1) To develop, implement, and continually update a comprehensive master plan for native Hawaiians and Hawaiians which shall include, but not be limited to, the following:

(A) Compilation of basic demographic data on native Hawaiians and Hawaiians;

(B) Identification of the physical, sociological, psychological, and economic needs of native Hawaiians and Hawaiians;

(C) Establishment of immediate and long-range goals pursuant to programs and services for native Hawaiians and Hawaiians;

(D) Establishment of priorities for program implementation and of alternatives for program implementation; and

(E) Organization of administrative and program structure, including the use of facilities and personnel;

(2) To assist in the development of state and county agency plans for native Hawaiian and Hawaiian programs and services;

(3) To maintain an inventory of federal, state, county, and private programs and services for Hawaiians and native Hawaiians and act as a clearinghouse and referral agency;

(4) To advise and inform federal, state, and county officials about native Hawaiian and Hawaiian programs, and coordinate federal, state, and county activities relating to native Hawaiians and Hawaiians;

(5) To conduct, encourage, and maintain research relating to native Hawaiians and Hawaiians;

(6) To develop and review models for comprehensive native Hawaiian and Hawaiian programs;

(7) To act as a clearinghouse for applications for federal or state assistance to carry out native Hawaiian or Hawaiian programs or projects;

(8) To apply for, accept and administer any federal funds made available or allotted under any federal act for native Hawaiians or Hawaiians; and

(9) To promote and assist the establishment of agencies to serve native Hawaiians and Hawaiians.

(b) The board shall have any powers which may be necessary for the full and effective performance and discharge of the duties imposed by this chapter, and which may be necessary to fully and completely effectuate the purposes of this chapter.

§ 10-7. Board of trustees.

The office of Hawaiian affairs shall be governed by a board to be officially known as the board of trustees, office of Hawaiian affairs. Members of the board shall be elected in accordance with chapter 13D, with reference to sections 11-15, 11-25, 12-5, 12-26, and vacancies shall be filled in accordance with section 17-7.

§ 10-10. Administrator; appointment, tenure, removal.

The board by a majority vote, shall appoint an administrator who shall serve without regard to the provisions of chapters 76 and 77 for a term to be determined by the board. The board, by a two-thirds vote of all members to which it is entitled, may remove the administrator for cause at any time.

§ 10-13. Appropriations; accounts; reports.

Moneys appropriated by the legislature for the office shall be payable by the director of finance, upon vouchers approved by the board, or by any officer elected or appointed by the board and authorized by the board to approve such vouchers on behalf of the board. All moneys received by or on behalf of the board shall be deposited with the director of finance and kept separate from moneys in the state treasury; except that any moneys received from the federal government or from private contributions shall be deposited and accounted for in accordance with conditions established by the agencies or persons from whom the moneys are received; and except that with the concurrence of the director of finance, moneys received from the federal government for research, training, and other related purposes of transitory nature, and moneys in trust or revolving funds administered by the office, shall be deposited in depositories other than the state treasury and shall be reported on to the state comptroller under section 40-81, and rules prescribed thereunder. Income derived from the sale of goods or services and income from lands and property as described in section 10-3, shall be credited to special or other funds; provided that upon the recommendation of the office, the comptroller shall establish such other separate accounts or special funds for other designated revenues as may be directed by the board or its authorized representative.

§ 10-13.5. Use of public land trust proceeds.

Twenty per cent of all funds derived from the public land trust, described in section 10-3, shall be expended by the office, as defined in section 10-2, for the purposes of this chapter.

§ 10-16. Suits.

(a) The office may sue and be sued in its corporate name. The State shall not be liable for any acts or omissions of the office, its officers, employees, and the members of the board of trustees, except as provided under subsection (b).

(b) In matters of tort, the office, its officers and employees, and the members of the board shall be subject to suit only in the manner provided for suits against the State under chapter 662.

(c) In matters of misapplication of funds and resources in breach of fiduciary duty, board members shall be subject to suit brought by any beneficiary of the public trust entrusted upon the office, either through the office of the attorney general or through private council.

(d) In matters involving other forms of remedies, the office, its officers and employees, and the members of the board shall be subject to suit as provided by any other provision of law and by the common law.

NOTE: THE CONSTITUTIONALITY OF THE OFFICE OF HAWAIIAN AFFAIRS

Since the constitutional and statutory provisions establishing the Office of Hawaiian Affairs (OHA) create a special legal status for Native Hawaiians and give descendants of Native Hawaiian special entitlements and benefits derived from income from certain trust lands, the constitutionality of such classifications was questioned in the process of its creation. In *Hoohuli v. Ariyoshi*, 631 F. Supp. 1153 (D. Haw. 1986), the district court rejected an equal protection challenge to legislative classifications of the Hawaii constitutional and statutory scheme protecting Native Hawaiians. The court rejected the notion that strict scrutiny applied to the plaintiffs' challenge since they only attacked the outer boundaries of the Hawaiian classification, i.e., a class including all descendants of an originally race-based class of Native Hawaiians, rather than the idea of a racial preference itself. Applying a rational basis standard, the district court held that the Hawaiian classification adopted by the state legislature merely paralleled and implemented the Native Hawaiian classifications previously drawn by Congress. The district court also rejected analogies to the equal protection decisions sustaining Indian classifications containing minimum blood quantum requirements which did not exist in the state definition of Native Hawaiian. The court found that Congress and states implementing Congressional decisions could classify Indians for purposes of entitlements or program benefits in any fashion they deem expedient. Indeed, the Court noted that in *Witt v. United States*, 681 F.2d 1144, 1148 (9th Cir. 1982), the Ninth Circuit had sustained a like classification for eligibility for allotments that only required an applicant to "trace an ancestor to the Dawes Commission rolls." More detailed arguments in favor of the constitutionality of the Hawaii legislative scheme are set forth in *Hawaii Attorney General's Opinion No. 80-8* and Van Dyke, *The Constitutionality of the Office of Hawaiian Affairs*, 7 U. HAWAII L. REV. 63 (1985). Central to many arguments in favor of the constitutionality of Native Hawaiian classifications drawn by the state of Hawaii was the notion that such classifications paralleled and implemented similar federal classifications for the purposes of many programs benefiting Indians, such as the Comprehensive Employment Training Act and the American Indian Religious Freedom Act.

While many of the statutory and constitutional provisions apply to Native Hawaiians of 50 percent or more Hawaiian blood, this classification continued to be quite controversial. The Hawaii legislature authorized OHA to conduct a referendum on the question of who should share in OHA's trust and entitlement programs among persons of Hawaiian ancestry. Of the 64,000 registered Native Hawaiians eligible to vote, 41 percent voted in an election conducted between December 5, 1989 and January 25, 1990. Of those voting, 79 percent voted in favor of rejecting the 50 percent requirement in preference for a unified definition of Native Hawaiian as anyone who can trace their ancestry to the native peoples who lived in Hawaii before the arrival of Captain James Cook in 1778. This expression of Native Hawaiian sentiment currently requires legislative action by the Hawaii legislature in the form of both constitutional amendment and statutory changes before it can be implemented by the OHA.

In Blondin, *A Case for Reparations for Native Hawaiians*, 16 HAWAII BAR J. 13, the author argues that the United States should treat Native Hawaiians like other Native Americans in light of their colonial history and their current conditions. The demoralizing and deteriorating effect of Western dominance on the Native Hawaiian is evidenced by social, economic and educational statistics. The Native Hawaiian is highly represented in the welfare rolls and overrepresented in Hawaii's penal institutions. Occupational statistics demonstrate that Hawaiians are concentrated in the lower levels of the state labor force and underrepresented in the professional fields. Education statistics point out that although 30% of the children in school are of Hawaiian ancestry, Native Hawaiians and part-Hawaiians constitute only 5% of graduating high school seniors and only 2.9% of those enrolled at the University of Hawaii's Manoa campus. *Id.* at 13 n.3. Can a rational explanation be advanced regarding the differences in federal policy involving Native Americans and Native Alaskans, on the one hand, and Native Hawaiians on the other?

There is little dispute that a public trust exists under federal and state law for the benefit of Native Hawaiians. There is considerably more dispute as to whether the federal government should assume a larger responsibility for the enforcement of that trust and whether the state has adequately managed its trust obligations under federal and state law. As the next several cases demonstrate, an important lingering problem is the judicial enforcement of these trust obligations. Hawaii statehood emerged as an issue during the termination era of federal Indian policy. Might that policy have influenced decisionmakers to provide for Hawaii to assume primary management of trust responsibilities for Native Hawaiians theretofore administered by the federal government? Just as the federal government has rethought termination and restored a number of terminated tribes, such as the Menominee in Wisconsin and the Siletz in Oregon, should the federal government reconsider its decision to vest primary trust management over Native Hawaiian affairs in the state government? In light of the existence of the federal-state compacts in the enabling and statehood acts and the Hawaii Constitution, can Congress reconsider its former decision?

PRICE v. HAWAII

764 F.2d 623 (9th Cir. 1985)

FARRIS, Circuit Judge:

A native Hawaiian tribal body seeks to compel the State of Hawaii to apply proceeds from a congressionally created land trust to finance the distribution of land for the benefit of native Hawaiians. The Hou Hawaiian tribe appeals the judgment of the U.S. District Court for Hawaii, Fong, J., which dismissed their complaint for lack of federal subject matter jurisdiction.

In 1920, Congress created the Hawaiian Home Lands Trust to provide lands for the use and benefit of native Hawaiian people of at least 50 percent native blood. The Home Lands Trust was incorporated into the Constitution of the State of Hawaii when Congress admitted the State into the Union in 1959.

Under section 5(f) of the Admission Act, the United States conveyed the bulk of its Hawaiian land holdings to the newly formed State, with the instruction that the lands and all property subsequently conveyed by the United States to the State be held by the State as a public trust. The lands which had already been reserved for disposition by the Hawaiian Homes Commission under the 1920 Act were included in the section 5(f) trust.

Proceeds from the section 5(f) trust are to be devoted to "one or more" of five statutory purposes, one of which is "for the betterment of the conditions of native Hawaiians." 73 Stat. 6. Section 5(f) places no other express limitations on the State's use of the trust fund proceeds.

The Hou Hawaiians sued in federal district court alleging that the State of Hawaii had breached its trust obligations to the United States and to the native Hawaiians by failing to expend any section 5(f) funds "for the betterment of the conditions of native Hawaiians." The Hou also alleged that the State was spending section 5(f) funds on "the maintenance of the State of Hawaii governmental structure," a purpose not authorized by the statute. The Hou requested an accounting of all section 5(f) lands; "just and fair" compensation for the State's prior neglect and a "just and fair portion" of future revenues produced by section 5(f) lands; and the use of the award to secure matching federal funds to implement the Hawaiian Homes Commission Act.

The district court granted the State's motion to dismiss, on the ground that our decision in *Keaukaha-Panaewa Community Association v. Hawaiian Homes Commission,* 588 F.2d 1216 (9th Cir. 1978), *cert. denied,* 444 U.S. 826 (1979) ("*Keaukaha I*"), compelled a finding that the district court lacked subject matter jurisdiction over the Hous' suit.

Following the dismissal, the United States Secretary of the Interior notified the Hou that it would not intervene in the action at this point. The district court subsequently denied the Hous' Motion for Reconsideration, rejecting the Hous' argument that *Keaukaha-Panaewa Community Association v. Hawaiian Homes Commission,* 739 F.2d 1467 (9th Cir. 1984) ("*Keaukaha II*"), affected the jurisdictional issue. The Hou timely [appealed].

I. *Do the Hou Qualify for § 1362 Jurisdiction?*

In both their Opening Brief and extensive supplemental briefing submitted at our request, the Hou [contend] that they are an "Indian tribe or band with a governing body duly recognized by the Secretary of the Interior," 28 U.S.C. § 1362, and hence may bring this suit under § 1362. Because neither the Hou nor their governing body have been "duly recognized" by the Secretary, they do not qualify for § 1362 jurisdiction even if we assume that they are an "Indian tribe or band."

A. *Statutes Governing Tribal Recognition*

No statute explicitly details the procedure by which a tribe may become "duly recognized by the Secretary" for purposes of establishing § 1362 jurisdiction. We note, however, that the Secretary must approve the organization or incorporation of a tribe. If the Hou had been formally organized or incorporated as a tribe, they could thus argue that they had been "duly recognized."

The statutes governing the formal organization and incorporation of an Indian tribe, see 25 U.S.C. §§ 476-477, explicitly do not apply to "any of the Territories, colonies, or insular possessions of the United States [except for] the Territory of Alaska." 25 U.S.C. § 473. In 1934, when § 473 was enacted, Hawaii was such a territory. Therefore, Congress did not originally intend the statutes governing the organization of new Indian tribes to apply to aboriginal groups in Hawaii.

Even if we assume that §§ 476-477 do apply to Hawaii today because it is now a State, the Hou have neither 1) adopted a constitution and bylaws ratified by majority vote of the adult members of the tribe and approved by the Secretary of the Interior, as required by § 476, nor 2) received a charter of incorporation, pursuant to § 477. Therefore, neither provision provides support for a claim of "recognition by the Secretary of the Interior."

B. *Regulations Governing Tribal Recognition*

Nor can the Hou claim "recognition" under the regulations by which the Interior Department's Bureau of Indian Affairs acknowledges tribal existence. See 25 C.F.R. Part 83 (1984). The regulations establish tribal existence as "a prerequisite to the protection, services and benefits from the Federal Government available to Indian tribes. Such acknowledgment shall also mean that the tribe is entitled to the immunities and privileges available to other federally acknowledged Indian tribes ...." 25 C.F.R. § 83.2. However, the regulations are explicitly limited to "only those American Indian groups indigenous to the continental United States ...." 25 C.F.R. § 83.3(a). The Hou Hawaiians acknowledge that they have not been "recognized" under these regulations.

C. *Factors for Determining Tribal Recognition*

Although no statute or regulation governs recognition of the Hou for purposes of establishing § 1362 jurisdiction, we conclude that the same factors which govern eligibility for federal benefits and "immunities and privileges," see 25 C.F.R. § 83.7, also [provide] some guidance for the jurisdictional inquiry. These factors, however, do not demonstrate that the Hou or their "governing body" have been "duly recognized" for § 1362 purposes.

1. *Historical continuity*

We first examine whether the group petitioning for recognition "has been identified from historical times until the present on a substantially continuous basis, as 'American Indian,' or 'aboriginal.'" 25 C.F.R. § 83.7(a). The importance of a tribe's longstanding existence is underscored by the regulations' exclusion of "[associations], organizations, corporations or groups of any character, formed in recent times," 25 C.F.R. § 83.3(c), from eligibility for Bureau of Indian Affairs benefits.

Although native Hawaiians *in general* may be able to assert a longstanding aboriginal history, the issue before us is whether the particular subgroup seeking recognition — the Hou Hawaiians — can establish that they are a longstanding aboriginal sovereign rather than a recently formed association. To allow any group of persons to "bootstrap" themselves into formal "tribal" status — simply because they are all members of a larger aboriginal ethnic body would be to ignore the concept of "tribe" as a distinct sovereignty set apart by historical and ethnological boundaries. *Cf.* F. Cohen, Handbook of Federal Indian Law 5 & n.17, 229 (1982). Because the Hou *ohana* was founded in 1974, it does not satisfy the historical requirement for tribal status implicit in § 83.7(a).

2. *Longstanding tribal political authority*

The BIA regulations also consider whether "the petitioner has maintained tribal political influence or other authority over its members as an autonomous entity throughout history until the present." 25 C.F.R. § 83.7(c). The Hous have alleged no facts indicating longstanding actual political authority over its members. To contrary effect, the Hou have submitted "Minutes of a General Meeting of the Elder Council" that indicate that their Chief and Elder Council were *first* elected on *January 27, 1985.* This recent election was apparently prompted by the Department of Health and Human Services' request that the Hou formalize their political trappings in order for them to obtain Health and Human Services' benefits.

3. *Other factors considered in BIA regulations*

The Hou have not alleged that "a substantial portion of the petitioning group inhabits a specific area or lives in a community viewed as American Indian and distinct from other populations in the area...." 25 C.F.R. § 83.7(b). Nor have they alleged that their members obey certain formal "procedures through which the group currently governs its affairs and its members." 25 C.F.R. § 83.7(d).

D. *Non-statutory Standards for Determining Tribal Recognition*

Apart from the BIA regulations, we are also guided by a 1974 letter from the Commissioner of Indian Affairs to the Chairman of the Senate Committee on Interior and Insular Affairs, in which the BIA reviewed its policies of recognizing Indian tribes over the previous twenty years. The letter describes five factors that the BIA used prior to the 1978 promulgation of the regulations discussed above, see 25 C.F.R. Part 83, in determining eligibility for BIA benefits.

The Hou fail to satisfy at least four of these five factors. The Hou 1) have not had treaty relations with the United States; 2) have not been denominated a tribe by act of Congress or Executive order; 3) have not been treated as a tribe by other Indian tribes;[1] and 4) have not demonstrated that the tribe exercises political authority over its members. It is unclear from the record whether the Hou share collective rights in tribal lands or funds, the fifth factor employed by the BIA.

---

[1] Although the Hou argue that they have been treated as a tribe by "the larger, federally recognized tribe of the Native Hawaiian people as a whole," the Hou have not shown that the Native Hawaiian people have themselves been "[d]uly recognized" as a tribe.

In summary, under both the BIA's current regulations for determining eligibility for federal benefits and "privileges and immunities," see 25 C.F.R. § 83.7, and the BIA's pre-regulation standard for recognizing a tribe, the Hou fail to demonstrate eligibility for recognition. In the absence of explicit governing statutes or regulations, we will not intrude on the traditionally executive or legislative prerogative of recognizing a tribe's existence. See *United States v. Sandoval*, 231 U.S. 28, 46 (1913) (recognition of tribe is "to be determined by Congress, and not by the courts"); *United States v. Holliday*, 70 U.S. (3 Wall.) 407, 419 (1865); F. Cohen, Handbook of Federal Indian Law 4-5 (1982). We therefore hold that the Hou do not qualify for § 1362 jurisdiction.

II. *Federal Question Jurisdiction*

The Hou also assert jurisdiction under 28 U.S.C. § 1331. "For this case to be within the purview of § 1331(a), a right or immunity created by the Constitution or laws of the United States must be an essential element of plaintiffs' claim."

We have recently held that § 5(f) of the Admission Act creates a federal "right" enforceable under 42 U.S.C. § 1983. *Keaukaha II*, 739 F.2d at 1472. The Act's trust obligation is "rooted in federal law, and power to enforce that obligation is contained in federal law, *see Keaukaha I*, 588 F.2d at 1218. Congress imposed the trust obligation as a condition of statehood and as a 'compact with the United States.' § 4, 73 Stat. 4." *Keaukaha II*, 739 F.2d at 1472. Under *Keaukaha II*, the Hou have properly invoked federal question jurisdiction.

The Hous' § 1331 jurisdiction alternatively rests on our holding in *Keaukaha II* that § 5(f) of the Admission Act imposes a trust obligation that constitutes a "compact with the United States." See 739 F.2d at 1472; but cf. *Keaukaha I*, 588 F.2d at 1227 n.12 (the Commission Act has not been incorporated as a federal-state compact). Unlike typical provisions of state law, this trust obligation is expressly protected from any amendments by the State legislature unless the United States has consented to those amendments. § 4, 73 Stat. 5; § 15, 73 Stat. 11. The terms of this federal-state compact, which has been recently reaffirmed by the Hawaii Supreme Court, see *Ahuna v. Department of Hawaiian Home Lands*, 64 Hawaii 327, 640 P.2d 1161, 1168 (1982), have been set forth in the plain language of the Hawaii State Constitution.

> "[A] case involving the construction of an *interstate* compact which requires a judicial determination of the nature and scope of obligations set forth therein 'arises' under the 'laws' of the United States within the meaning of § 1331(a)."

[The role of Congress] in the formation of a compact between the United States and a State is at least as great as Congress' role in approving a compact between two States. In addition, federal law is "an essential element" of a suit that charges a violation of a compact incorporating "the spirit of the Hawaiian Homes Commission Act looking to the continuance of the Hawaiian homes projects." Hawaii Const., art. XII, § 2; art. XII, § 4; art. XVI, § 7; see *Keaukaha II*, 739 F.2d at 1472. We therefore hold that the enforcement of the § 5(f) compact presents a federal question under 28 U.S.C. § 1331(a).

III. *Sovereign Immunity*

[The court held that the claims against the state and its agencies were barred by the eleventh amendment. The claims against Governor Ariyoshi seeking injunctive relief were not barred under the principle of *Ex parte Young.* The court then held that the Hou had standing to seek prospective injunctive relief against the Governor.]

V. *Implied Private Cause of Action*

We now consider whether the Hou may bring a private cause of action under the Admission Act.

Under the "co-plaintiff" doctrine, Indian tribes may claim a private cause of action when the United States is a trustee and is entitled to sue to protect the tribe's rights. See, e.g., *Keaukaha I,* 588 F.2d at 1224 n.7. But because the United States is not a formal trustee of the § 5(f) homelands trust, see *Keaukaha I,* 588 F.2d at 1224 n.7, and nothing in the legislative history or case interpretation indicates that Congress intended a different result for the § 5(f) ceded land trust at issue here, we hold that the Hou cannot claim a private cause of action under the "co-plaintiff" doctrine. *Id.*

Furthermore, our holding in *Keaukaha I* that individual Hawaiians do not have an implied cause of action under the Admission Act, see 588 F.2d at 1223-4, applies with equal force to bar the Hou Hawaiians from claiming a cause of action. Although the Hou are members of a "class for whose especial benefit the statute was enacted," [there is] nothing in the legislative history of the Admission Act indicat[ing] that Congress intended native Hawaiian groups, as distinguished from individual Hawaiians whose claims were rejected in *Keaukaha I,* to enjoy a private cause of action. "Indeed, the rare references in the Committee reports to enforcement of section 5's trust provisions refer exclusively to the public cause of action." *Keaukaha I,* 588 F.2d at 1223. Because the remaining two elements of the *Cort v. Ash* test — the general scheme of the Admission Act and the magnitude of the State's concern in this area — have also been decided by *Keaukaha I* in favor of the State, the Hou cannot claim an implied private cause of action. See *id.* at 1224.

VI *Conclusion*

The Hou have not established that they are "duly recognized by the Secretary of the Interior," and hence cannot claim jurisdiction under 28 U.S.C. § 1362. However, both the federal nature of the section 5(f) trust and the state-federal compact that led to its creation support general federal question jurisdiction under 28 U.S.C. § 1331. The Hou have also alleged an "injury-in-fact" sufficient to confer standing.

Because the State has not waived its sovereign immunity, we must dismiss the Hous' claims against all parties except George Ariyoshi in his capacity as governor. This claim against Ariyoshi, however, must be dismissed as well because the Hou cannot claim a private cause of action under the Admission Act.[3]

[*Affirmed.*]

NOTES

1. *Keaukaha I and II*: The *Price* decision relies heavily on the earlier Ninth Circuit decision in *Keaukaha-Panaewa Community v. Hawaiian Homes,* 739

---

[3]Because we lack jurisdiction to decide the case, we express no opinion on the merits of a suit to enforce the section 5(f) trust properly brought by the Department of the Interior.

F.2d 1467 (1984) (*Keaukaha II*). In *Keaukaha II* a group of Native Hawaiians brought suit under 42 U.S.C. § 1983 against the Hawaiian Homes Commission to remedy the loss of 25 acres of the Hawaiian Homes Commission Act lands. In holding that the Native Hawaiians had a federal cause of action under § 1983, the opinion for the Ninth Circuit stated, "While the management and disposition of the home lands was given over to the state of Hawaii with the incorporation of the Commission Act into the state constitution, the trust obligation is rooted in federal law, and power to enforce that obligation is contained in federal law." 739 F.2d at 1472. *Keaukaha II* cleared up some confusion that resulted from dicta in *Keaukaha I*, 588 F.2d 1216 (9th Cir. 1978). In *Keauhaha I*, the Ninth Circuit held that individual Native Hawaiians had no standing to sue in federal court under the Hawaiian Homes Commission Act and/or the Hawaiian Admissions Act. The court based its decision on the fact that the Admission Act expressly provided for the United States to sue on behalf of Native Hawaiians and therefore "no implied private right of action [existed] which would enable the native Hawaiians themselves to enforce the Act in federal court." *Keaukaha II* at 1470. Although recognizing that a trust for the benefit of Native Hawaiians had been established by these acts, the *Keaukaha I* court stated in dicta "[i]t is clear, however that for all practical purposes these benefits have lost their federal nature" 558 F.2d 1216. *Keaukaha I*, like *Price*, addressed only remedies, not the underlying rights of Native Hawaiians.

   2. **Trustees of Office of Hawaiian Affairs v. Yamashaki and State Enforcement of Public Trust Responsibilities:** State court efforts to judicially enforce public trust responsibilities for Native Hawaiians have met with little more success than federal ones. While the *Ahuna* case, set forth below, provides some limited trust enforcement of obligations that the state of Hawaii assumed at statehood that earlier were created under the Hawaii Home Lands Commission Act of 1920, more recent judicial efforts to enforce broader trust obligations have met with little success. For example, the constitutional and statutory restrictions assumed by Hawaii and set forth above require it to administer public lands in part for the benefit of Native Hawaiians. *E.g.*, HAWAII REV. STAT. § 10-3. Disputes as to the appropriate portion of funds to which Native Hawaiians were entitled led the Hawaii legislature in 1980 to adopt the provisions of § 10-13.5 of the Hawaii Revised Statutes allocating 20 percent of the revenues from public lands to be applied to benefit programs administered by the Office of Hawaiian Affairs. When disputes later emerged as to whether the OHA was entitled to a portion of funds derived from damages received from the state on account of illegal mining of sand on public lands and from income derived from sales, leases, and other alienations of lands surrounding harbors on all islands, from land on Sand Island, and from certain other public lands, the trustees of OHA sued to enforce their claim to the revenue. In *Trustees of Office of Hawaiian Affairs v. Yamasaki*, 737 P.2d 446 (Haw. 1987), the court ruled that these claims raised nonjusticiable policy questions, given the lack of judicially discoverable and manageable standards. The court reviewed the legislative history of the 1980 legislation and found that the reports noted "uncertainties with respect to the ceded lands comprising the trust res and the funds derived therefrom." *Id.* at 457. Thus, the court held that "[i]t would be encroaching on legislative turf [to resolve the controversy] because the seemingly clear language of HRS § 10-13.5 actually provides no 'judicially discoverable and manageable standards' for resolving the disputes and they cannot be decided without 'initial policy determination[s] of a kind clearly for nonjudicial determination.'" *Id.*

3. *Price v. Akaka*: In *Price v. Akaka*, 915 F.2d 469 (9th Cir. 1990), the court revisited Native Hawaiian claims to benefits provided for under the Admission Act. Native Hawaiian plaintiffs filed suit under 42 U.S.C. § 1983 for damages against the trustees of the Office of Hawaiian Affairs (OHA), contending that the defendants violated section 5(f) of the Admission Act by misappropriating public trust funds. Plaintiffs specifically asserted that (1) the trustees commingled trust funds with other OHA funds; (2) no funds were spent for the benefit of Native Hawaiians; and (3) the trustees used the funds for purposes not listed in section 5(f). The district court dismissed the action for both failure to state a claim and for lack of subject matter jurisdiction. The district court concluded that plaintiffs had no claim because the Admission Act does not require the actions that plaintiffs assert, i.e., that funds not be spent for purposes other than to benefit Native Hawaiians. In short, the district court decision seemed to permit Hawaii broad discretion in the expenditure of the trust fund once conveyed to OHA. The Court of Appeals, however, reversed. The court held that the plaintiffs had standing to bring their claim. The Ninth Circuit also rejected the district court's jurisdictional dismissal, perhaps clearing up any residual confusion over subject matter jurisdiction and actions brought under 42 U.S.C. § 1983. The court cited both *Keaukaha II* and *Price*, and confirmed that the Admission Act created federal rights that were enforceable under 42 U.S.C. § 1983. The court also concluded that, because Price was suing the trustees in their individual capacities rather than official capacities, the action was not barred by the eleventh amendment. More importantly, the Ninth Circuit rejected the notion that the mere payment of the trust funds under section 5(f) to the Office of Hawaiian Affairs did not remove the trust restrictions, thereby permitting OHA to expend the funds for non-listed purposes. Thus, the Ninth Circuit held that the trust restrictions apply to these funds even after they are received by OHA. The mere transfer to OHA did not constitute a final use or disposal of the funds. The Ninth Circuit therefore reversed the district court's dismissal and remanded the case for further proceedings.

In default of a judicial resolution of these questions, the Office of Hawaiian Affairs resorted to a much older form of dispute resolution involving indigenous peoples — negotiation — in this case with state officials led by Governor John Waihee. On February 8, 1990, the negotiating team announced an agreement embodied in two pending bills in the Hawaii legislature, HB 2896 and SB 3104. 7 Ka Wai Ola O Oha* No. 3 at 1 (March 1990). The agreement would clarify which lands comprise the public land trust subject to the provisions of § 10-13.5 and which types of revenues are subject to those provisions, and would set forth a process for establishing past-due amounts and a plan for repayment.

HOUGHTON, AN ARGUMENT FOR INDIAN STATUS FOR NATIVE HAWAIIANS — THE DISCOVERY OF A LOST TRIBE, 14 American Indian Law Review 1, 24-36 (1989)

Hawaiian Trust Lands: Ola ka lawai'a i kahi po'o manu.[173]

Native Hawaiians traditionally had a collective right in their lands and maintain their right in 200,000 acres of Hawaiian lands set aside for them by the

---

*Ka Wai Ola O Oha is the official newspaper of the Office of Hawaiian Affairs.

[173] Unlucky fishermen can still eat the head of their bait. Hawaiian proverb. This is a way of saying that one has not had good results.

United States Congress as the equivalent of a reservation. Both the historical developments surrounding the Hawaiian trust lands and the present status of those lands compel the conclusion that the Native Hawaiian people possess a collective right in tribal lands, and thus they satisfy the third consideration for determining tribal status.

The basis of the Hawaiian civilization was a complex system of land tenure[174] similar to the feudal system prevalent in Europe during the Middle Ages. This system was based on land divisions of the major Hawaiian Islands,[176] each of which contained one or more large constituent geographic divisions called *moku'aina*.[177] Each *moku'aina* was divided into large tracts of between 100 to 100,000 acres called *ahupua'a*. The boundaries of the *ahupua'a* generally followed natural land contours from a point on the summit of an inland mountain down to the ocean to form a wedge-shaped tract that included forest, agricultural, and coastal fishing lands.[180] As a result, the majority of *ahupua'a* were economically self-sufficient. Most *ahupua'a* were divided into smaller units called *'ili* and *'ili kupono*,[181] which in turn were subdivided into individual plots farmed by the general population, or *maka'ainana*.

A hierarchical social system paralleled this pattern of land division. Although the *maka'ainana* lived on their own plots of land, there was no concept of fee simple absolute ownership. Rather, all the lands in a particular *moku'aina* belonged solely to the high chief, the *ali'i 'ai moku*, who assigned the *ahupua'a* within his territory to his most important subchiefs or *ali'i 'ai ahupua'a*. These *ali'i* passed on the process of infeudation and parceled out the smaller *'ili* to lower-ranking chiefs called *konohiki*, who were responsible for land administration and general government.[186] In return for these land grants, each societal level supplied goods or services to the level immediately superior to it. In sum,

---

[174] For a detailed discussion of this land tenure system, see E. Handy, *supra* note 68, at 81-93 (1965); J. Hobbs, *supra* note 72; Levy, *supra* note 72, at 848; M. Kelly, "Changes in Land Tenure in Hawaii, 1778-1850" (June, 1956) (unpublished thesis in the University of Hawaii Library). For an explanation of Hawaiian land and property terms, see Territory v. Bishop Tr. Co., 41 Haw. 358, 361-62 (1956).

[176] Hawai'i, Maui, Lana'i, Moloka'i, O'ahu, Kaua'i, and Ni'ihau. This does not include the island of Kahoolawe, which was seldom populated except by an occasional fishing party, or the smaller islands of the chain, such as Kaula or Molokini, which were uninhabited.

[177] J. Chinen, The Great Mahele: Hawaii's Land Division of 1848, at 3 (1958). *See also* L. Cannelora, The Origin of Hawaiian Land Title and the Rights of Native Tenants (1974) (available from the Security Title Corp., 1001 Bishop Street, Suite 1200, Honolulu, Hawaii).

[180] *See* Kalipi v. Hawaiian Tr. Co., 66 Haw. 1, 656 P.2d 745, 749 (1982) (citing Boundaries of Pulehunui, 4 Haw. at 241). *See also* Palama v. Sheehan, 50 Haw. 298, 440 P.2d 95 (1968).

[181] For a description of the differences between the *ahupua'a, 'ili*, and *'ili kupono*, see Harris v. Carter, 6 Haw. 195, 206-07 (1877), where the Hawaii Supreme Court stated:

[E]rroneous opinions have sometimes prevailed as to what are "ahupuaas" and "ilis." An Ahupuaa has been called the "unit" of land in this country; but is by no means a measure of area, for Ahupuaas vary exceedingly as to size. Many Ahupuaas are divided into Ilis; other Ahupuaas have no Ilis in them.... There are two kinds of Ilis. One, the Ili of the Ahupuaa, [is] a mere subdivision of the Ahupuaa for the mere convenience of the chief holding the Ahupuaa.... The other class were the "ili Kupono." ... These were independent of the Ahupuaa [and the chief of the ili kupono was independent of the chief of the ahupuaa].

[186] E. Handy, *supra* note 68, at 38. *See* Brief of Hou Hawaiians as Amicus Curiae, *supra* note 72, at 6-7. Unlike the European serfs, however, Native Hawaiians were not bound to the land or any particular chief, but were free to move. Dep't of Budget and Finance, State of Hawaii, Land and Water Resource Management in Hawaii 148 (1979) (Jon Van Dyke, team leader) [hereinafter Land Management].

the government and landholdings were inextricably woven into the Native Hawaiian social fabric and formed the stylobate for the entire culture.

This system of feudal land tenure remained basically unchanged even when the first Hawaiian king, Kamehameha I (the Great), united all the islands into a single kingdom between 1794 and 1805. After his conquests, Kamehameha became the *ali'i 'ai moku* of the entire island chain and thus exercised supreme authority, as sole owner[188] and government, over all the lands of the kingdom. All Hawaiians held their lands at the King's pleasure; there were no inheritance rights and non-Hawaiians were excluded from holding land.[190]

Change eventually came, however, under pressure from Western influence after Kamehameha's death in 1819. Because of Hawaii's geographic position, it was becoming a principal trading center in the Pacific basin and a large number of whites settled on the Islands. The results closely paralleled those of Western contact with the Indians on the mainland. Increased settlement by whites caused the economy to change rapidly from one based on agriculture to one dependent on trade, and as the economy changed traditional Hawaiian culture changed with it. Under pressure from white settlers who wished to own land in fee simple, the King promulgated the Constitution of 1840 declaring that the land belonged collectively to the *ali'i*, and to the people, under the monarch's control.[192] Consequently, as whites began to acquire land under the new system, the traditional system began to collapse. Native population levels fell drastically and native land ownership fell with them.[193] In short, white settlement in areas populated by the native people had the same deleterious effects in Hawaii as on the mainland.[194]

These effects continued to intensify as more whites settled in the kingdom. Pressure from the growing number of westerners to make land available for

---

[188]*But see* United States v. Fullard-Leo, 331 U.S. 256, 266-69 (1947); Liliuokalani v. United States, 45 Ct. Cl. 418, 425 (1910). These mainland cases suggest that the Hawaiian kings did not own the land but held it in trust for the people. While this may have been the view later in the monarchy, see *infra* note 197 and accompanying text, cases from the Supreme Court of Hawaii suggest a different view under the first Kamehameha. *See, e.g.,* Hawaiian Comm'l & Sugar Co. v. Wailuku Sugar Co., 15 Haw. 675, 680 (1904) ("the King was the sole owner ... of the land and could do with [it] as he pleased").

[190]*Id.* at 7-8. As one voyager stated in 1818: "Europeans are not allowed to own land. They receive it on condition that after death it shall be returned to the king, and during their life time it is not transferable from one to another." 1 R. Kuykendall, Hawaiian Kingdom, *supra* note 69, at 60.

[192]Land, although "owned" by the king, in theory belonged to the *ali'i* and the people under them. The preamble stated: "Kamehameha I, was the founder of the Kingdom, and to him belonged all the land ... though it was not his own private property. It belonged to the chiefs, and the people in common, of whom Kamehameha I was the head, and had the management of the landed property." Haw. Const. of 1840, preamble, *reprinted in* Translation of the Constitution and Laws of the Hawaiian Islands Established in the Reign of Kamehameha III, at 11-13 (1842) [hereinafter Translation]; The Fundamental Law of Hawaii 3 (L. Thurston ed. 1904) [hereinafter L. Thurston].

[193]The following table illustrates the alarmingly rapid drop in the Native Hawaiian population:

Year	Population
1778	300,000
1832	130,313
1853	71,019
1860	67,084
1866	58,765
1872	51,531
1890	40,622

R. Kuykendall, Hawaii: A History, *supra* note 67, at 298.

[194]Compare the effects of the allotment period on the mainland tribes. *See generally*, D. Otis, The Dawes Act and Allotment of Indian Lands (1973).

development mounted on the government, and the result was the Great Mahele, the Great Division, of 1848.[195] In response to Western demands, King Kamehameha III divided the Hawaiian lands into private crown lands and government lands, the latter to be divided between the *ali'i* and the *maka'ainana*, thereby reaffirming the latter's collective right to the land. More than eight thousand Native Hawaiian commoners received small plots of land, called *kuleana*, within the *ahupua'a* in which they lived.[197] Legislation enacted immediately after the last *mahele* between the King and the *ali'i* allowed each native tenant or *hoa'aina* to apply for his own *kuleana*.[198] However, these land grants proved largely ineffective for several reasons. First, the act limited the land available for *kuleana* grants because it only allowed the *hoa'aina* to apply for a grant of land that they had actually cultivated[199] plus a small house lot of not less than a quarter of an acre. Second, a *hoa'aina* had to prove his claim before a Land Commission and pay the survey costs.[201] However, many *hoa'aina* were too poor to pay for the survey,[202] or lacked the sophistication necessary to prove their claims. Third, many *hoa'aina* refrained from applying for *kuleana* because they feared reprisals by their *ali'i* or by land agents. Finally, a later act of the legislature barred all *hoa'aina* claims not proven by 1854.[204] As a result, the majority of the native Hawaiian people was separated from the land. In addition, like the Indians on the mainland during the allotment period, many of those Native Hawaiians who were given land grants soon lost or sold the land because of their lack of understanding of a new and foreign land system or because of a need for money.[206] The increasing demands of white settlers thus brought about the swift destruction of the traditional native Hawaiian land system, and by 1852 thousands of acres of land were owned by a few

[195] Rules Adopted by Privy Council, Dec. 18, 1847, § 4, 4 Privy Council Record 1 (1847). *See* P. Vitorsek, J. Reiley & R. Rediske, Principles and Practices of Hawaiian Real Estate 1 (8th ed. 1981). "The term mahele means to divide or apportion.... [T]he Great Mahele of 1848 ... accomplished the division of the undivided interest in land between the King on one hand and the chiefs and konohikis on the other." McBryde Sugar Co. v. Robinson, 54 Haw. 174, 182 n.5, 504 P.2d 1330, 1336 n.5, (*McBryde I*), aff'd on reh., 55 Haw. 260, 517 P.2d 26 (1973), *appeal dismissed and cert. denied*, 417 U.S. 962, *and cert. denied*, 417 U.S. 976 (1974). For a detailed description of the Great Mahele, see J. Chinen, *supra* note 177.

[197] The Bishop Museum in Honolulu has determined the number to be 8,205. Levy, *supra* note 72, at 856 n.52.

[198] Act of Aug. 6, 1850, § 1, [1850] Haw. Laws 202, *reprinted in* 2 Revised Laws of Hawaii 1925, at 2141....

[199] Act of Dec. 21, 1849, § 6, [1850] Haw. Laws 202, *reprinted in* 2 Revised Laws of Hawaii 1925, at 2142.

[201] Act of Dec. 10, 1845, ch. 7, § 1, 2 (1847) Haw. Laws 107, *reprinted in* 2 Revised Laws of Hawaii 1925, at 2120. The Commission was charged with "the investigation and final ascertainment or rejection of all claims of private individuals, whether native or foreigners, to any landed property." *Id.*; Levy, *supra* note 72, at 853.

[202] The survey costs averaged less than $20. Brief of Hou Hawaiians as Amici Curiae, *supra* note 72, at 14.

[204] Act Relating to the Board of Commissioners to Quiet Land Titles, [1853] Haw. Laws 26, *reprinted in* 2 Revised Laws of Hawaii 1925, at 2145.

[206] *See, e.g.*, Kanakanui v. Leslie, 7 Haw. 223 (1888). Compare the effects on mainland Indians of the General Allotment Act, ch. 119, 24 Stat. 388 (1887) (codified in scattered sections of 25 U.S.C. (1982)). *See* D. Otis, *supra* note 194. Traditionally, the Native Hawaiians believed that no human could own land permanently. Like the mainland Indians, they believed that it belonged to the gods; the people were merely trustees who administered the land for the gods and the good of the community and could not sell or misuse it. Brief of Queen Liliukalani Tr. as Amicus Curiae, *supra* note 182, at 8-9; Breach of Trust, *supra* note 7, at 4.

whites while Native Hawaiians owned only a tiny fraction.[207] By 1896 Native Hawaiians, like mainland Indians, had become a landless minority in their own country.[208]

Furthermore, having asserted economic dominance over the kingdom by the late 1880s, the westerners turned to establish complete political control as well.[209] The principal white landowners founded the "Hawaiian League" in 1887 to increase their power at the expense of the monarchy. In consequence, the whites staged a coup d'etat on July 6, 1887, and forced the King to promulgate a new constitution, the "Bayonet Constitution" of 1887, supplanting the power of the King with that of the white landowners.[211] Nevertheless, the whites were dissatisfied with limited power and in 1893, with the help of the United States, they overthrew the Hawaiian government and replaced it with their own. The Republic of Hawaii was founded soon thereafter, and among its first official acts was the expropriation[213] of all crown lands without compensation to the Queen, Lili'uokalani.[214] The lands were immediately made available to westerners for purchase.

When Congress annexed Hawaii in 1898, the United States, without paying any compensation, took title to the crown and government lands expropriated from the Native Hawaiian people by the Republic.[215] In denying compensation to Queen Lili'uokalani or the Hawaiian people for the crown lands taken by the United States, the United States Court of Claims nevertheless recognized that Native Hawaiians had a collective right in the lands.[216] On July 9, 1921, Congress acknowledged an obligation to the indigenous people of Hawaii and their

---

[207] See Levy, supra note 72, at 860 n.80. By 1897, the white 9 percent of the population owned 67 percent of the taxable land; Hawaiians and part-Hawaiians, only 24 percent. A. Lind, An Island Community 57 (1938). In 1881, Native Americans owned more than 156 million acres of land. By 1934, they owned only 30 percent of that amount. F. Cohen, Handbook on Federal Indian Law 137-38 (Michie Co. ed. 1972); A. Josephy, The Indian Heritage of America 350-51 (1968) (Indians owned 138 million acres in 1887, which had fallen to 90 million acres by 1932).

[208] Report to the Joint Comm. on Hawaii, S. Doc. No. 151, 75th Cong., 3d Sess. 83 (1938); 1982 Handbook, supra note 2, at 800. Hawaiians and part-Hawaiians constituted a little under 35 percent of the population. A. Lind, Hawaii's People 27 (1967).

[209] See generally S. Stern, American Expansion in Hawaii 1842-1898 (1945).

[211] Compare Haw. Const. of 1864, art. XLV, reprinted in L. Thurston, supra note 192, at 174 (the upper legislature of the Hawaiian parliament was chosen by the king from the Hawaiian ali'i class) with Haw. Const. of 1887 art. LIX, reprinted in L. Thurston, supra, at 88-89 (the upper legislature was chosen by taxpayers, many of whom were white, from a field of candidates limited to wealthy landowners, the vast majority of whom were white). The king's absolute veto power was changed to a veto which could be overridden by a two-thirds vote of the legislature. Haw. Const. of 1887, reprinted in R. Lydecker, Roster Legislature of Hawaii 1841-1918, at 159 (1918). The overall voting power of Native Hawaiians was also greatly reduced. Under the requirements of the new constitution, only one-fourth of the native population was eligible to vote. G. Daws, Atlas of Hawaii 26-27 (1970).

[213] See Haw. Const. of 1894, art. XCV, [1895] Haw. Laws 118, reprinted in L. Thurston, supra note 192, at 237.

[214] See Liliuokalani, 45 Ct. Cl. 418.

[215] H. J. Res. 55, supra note 134, at § 1; Liliuokalani, 45 Ct. Cl. at 436;; 1982 Handbook, supra note 2, at 801, 804; Levy, supra note 72, at 863. See Note, Hawaii's Ceded Lands, 3 U. Haw. L. Rev. 101 (1981).

[216] Liliuokalani, 45 Ct. Cl. at 418:

The crown lands were the resourceful methods of income to sustain, in part at least, the dignity of the office to which they were inseparably attached. When the office ceased to exist they became as other lands of the Sovereignty and passed to the defendants as part and parcel of the public domain.

descendants by enacting the Hawaiian Homes Commission Act.[217] The Act established a land trust for the use and benefit of Native Hawaiians of about 200,000 out of the 2 million acres of public lands taken from the Native Hawaiian people.[218] The purpose of the trust, as proposed by the territorial legislature to Congress, was twofold: to recognize that the lands once belonging to the Kingdom of Hawai'i and now possessed by the United States were impressed with a trust relationship and belonged to the Native Hawaiian people,[219] and to provide an economic base for the improvement of the social and economic situation of that people.[220] Similarly, Congress was animated to restore some of Hawaii's lands to the Native Hawaiian people because "the Hawaiians were deprived of their lands without any say on their part." In fact, the chairman of the House Committee on Territories noted that the motivating factor behind the legislation was identical to that behind similar land trust legislation relating to the mainland Indian tribes "[b]ecause we came to this country and took their land away from them ... [a]nd if we can afford to [provide land trusts] for the Indians ... why can we not do the same for the Hawaiians?"[222] In short, as with legislation dealing with other aboriginal groups on the mainland recognized by Congress, the Hawaiian Homes Commission Act set aside in collective trust a portion of the aboriginal lands acquired by the United States,[223] with the idea of providing for the protection and rehabilitation of Native Hawaiians who, like the Indians on the mainland, had their lands taken from them by white settlers and eventually the United States government.

From 1921 to 1959 the land trust established by the Hawaiian Homes Commission Act was administered by the federal government. But when Hawaii was

---

[217] HHCA, *supra* note 140, at § 1. For a detailed discussion of both the land and the legal aspects of the program, *see generally* H. Dot, *supra* note 145; Legislative Research Bureau, State of Hawaii, Land Aspects of the Hawaiian Homes Program (1964) (Report No. 1b) (A. Spitz, author).

[218] The Act defines a Native Hawaiian as a person of 50 percent or more of "the blood of the races inhabiting the Hawaiian Islands previous to 1778." HHCA, *supra* note 140, at § 201(a)(7). On April 11, 1986, the House passed H.J. Res. 17 which, if passed by the Senate, would lower the blood quantum requirements for homestead eligibility to 25 percent for the surviving spouses and children of deceased leaseholders in order to allow them to continue living on their lands until the expiration of their leases. The bill was sponsored by Congressman Daniel Akaka (D-Haw.) and is opposed by many Native Hawaiians. *Hawaiian Homestead Rule Change*, Honolulu Advertiser, Apr. 12, 1986, at A3.

[219] Proposed Amendments to the Organic Act of the Territory of Hawaii, Hearings Before the House Comm. on the Territories, 66th Cong., 1st Sess. 32 (1920) [hereinafter Proposed Amendments — 1920]. The original Organic Act was the Act of Apr. 30, 1900, ch. 339, 31 Stat. 141 (set out in full at Haw. Rev. Stat. § 1-28).

[220] *See* Proposed Amendments — 1920, *supra* note 219, at 26, 38. In 1951, the Attorney General of Hawaii summarized the purpose of the Act as being: "to save the Native Hawaiian race from extinction by reason of its inability to meet successfully the economic and sociological changes brought about in the Islands." Legislative Auditor, State of Hawaii, Financial Audit of the Loan Funds of the Department of Hawaiian Home Lands 1979, at 4 (*citing* Haw. Att'y Gen. Op., Nov. 13, 1951).

[222] Proposed Amendments to the Organic Act of the Territory of Hawaii, Hearings on H.R. 7257 Before the House Comm. on the Territories, 67th Cong., 1st Sess. 141 (1921) [hereinafter Proposed Amendments — 1921]. It is interesting to note that despite the paternalistic rhetoric surrounding the debate on the Act, its principal proponents were the sugar cane barons who were worried about homesteaders occupying cultivated sugar fields. *See generally* M. Vause, "Hawaiian Homes Commission Act, 1920: History and Analysis" (June, 1962) unpublished thesis in the University of Hawaii Library).

[223] *Ahuna*, 64 Haw. 327, 640 P.2d 1161. While 200,000 acres of land were set aside, most of it was arid and of marginal agricultural value. Levy, *supra* note 72, at 865.

admitted to the Union, title to and administration of the trust was transferred to the state under section 5 of the Hawaii Admission Act[225] as a condition of statehood and adopted as state law.[227] In accordance with this transfer, section 5 of the Admission Act provided that:

> (b) the United States grants to the State of Hawaii, effective upon its admission into the Union, the United States' title ... to all lands defined as "available lands" by section 203 of the Hawaii Homes Commission Act, 1920, as amended ... (f) [t]he lands granted to the State of Hawaii by subsection (b) of this section ... together with the proceeds from the sale or other disposition of any such lands, shall be held by said State as a public trust.

The state in turn delegated its responsibility to the newly created Department of Hawaiian Home Lands, which was charged with administering the trust.[229] The functioning of the trust shows many similarities with Indian allotment lands on the mainland: Native Hawaiians lease homesteads, highly restricted in their alienability, for periods of ninety-nine years;[231] only heirs as enumerated in the Act may inherit;[232] and the land cannot be commercially mortgaged[233] or subleased.[234]

Despite the transfer of the management of the trust to the state of Hawaii, the United States, as trustee and original settlor of the trust, retained three powerful supervisory and enforcement controls to ensure the proper implementation of the trust.[235] First, if the Homelands Department concludes that lands not a part of the trust would better fulfill the Homes Commission Act's mandate, the Department can exchange those lands for others of equal value, but only with the approval of the U.S. Secretary of the Interior.[236] The Department of the Interior, the department charged with overseeing the government's relations with the Indian tribes, defines the relationship of the federal government to the trust as "[m]ore than merely ministerial .... [T]he United States can be said to have retained a role as trustee under the act while making the State the instrument for carrying out the trust."[237] Second, the federal government retains enforcement power over the trust.[238] The United States Department of Justice

---

[225] Act of Mar. 18, 1959, Pub. L. No. 86-3, 73 Stat. 4, as amended by Act of July 12, 1960, Pub. L. No. 86-624, § 41, 74 Stat. 422 (set out but not codified at 48 U.S.C. prec. §§ 491-724 (1982) (set out in full at Haw. Rev. Stat. §§ 1-78) [hereinafter Admission Act].

[227] Haw. Const. art. XII, § 1.

[229] Haw. Rev. Stat. § 26-17 (Supp. 1984).

[231] HHCA, *supra* note 140, at § 208(2).

[232] *Id.* § 209.

[233] *Id.* § 208(5).

[234] *Id.* A number of transactions resembling subleases made with various pineapple companies have, however, been approved by the state. *See* Legal Aspects of the Hawaiian Homes Program, *supra* note 145, at 14-16.

[235] For a general discussion of these powers, see Federal-State Task Force on the Hawaiian Homes Comm'n Act, Report to the United States Secretary of the Interior and the Governor of the State of Hawaii 18-24 (1983) [hereinafter Task Force Report].

[236] HHCA, *supra* note 140, at § 204(4); Admission Act, *supra* note 225, at § 4.

[237] Letter from Frederick N. Ferguson, Deputy Solicitor, U.S. Dep't of the Interior, to Philip Montez, Regional Director, Western Regional Office, United States Comm'n on Civil Rights (Aug. 27, 1979. *Contra* Keaukaha-Panaewa Community Ass'n v. Hawaiian Homes Comm'n, 588 F.2d 1216, 1224 n.7 (9th Cir. 1978), *cert. denied*, 444 U.S. 826 (1979). The Hawaii legislature recently considered a bill which, if passed, would allow Native Hawaiians to sue the state over the administration of the Hawaiian Homes Commission Act. *See* Honolulu Advertiser, Mar. 21, 1986, at A-16, col. 1.

[238] Admission Act, *supra* note 225, at § 5(f). Section 5(f) reads:

(f) such lands ... shall be managed and disposed of [by the State] for [the betterment of Native

has stated that this power gives it "exclusive litigation authority if suit were brought by the United States to enforce the trust."[239] Finally, the Congress has reserved the right to review and approve all substantive changes in the Act.[240]

A trust relationship between the United States and Native Hawaiians, similar to that of the United States and the mainland Indians, survived the transfer to the state of Hawaii of the management of the corpus of the trust. A trust relationship between the United States and an Indian tribe retains full force until Congress expressly repudiates it by contrary legislation, a repudiation that does not exist in the case of the Hawaiian Home Lands Trust. The United States has never sufficiently manifested withdrawal of its protection so as to sever completely the trust relationship. On the contrary, in retaining supervisory powers Congress has evinced an intent to continue that relationship. Similarly, the United States has not severed its trust relationship with some mainland tribes simply by having delegated a portion of its trust responsibilities to the states.[243] Thus, although the state of Hawaii has assumed the administration of the land trust, this assumption of responsibility for the Native Hawaiians' welfare is insufficient to abrogate the federal trusteeship.

Despite the dual responsibilities exercised over the trust by both the state of Hawaii and the federal government, more than sixty years after its inception the Hawaiian Homes program is a disappointing failure. Fewer than 15 percent of all Native Hawaiians have received homesteads under the program,[245] while some eight thousand applicants, wait, some as long as thirty years,[246] to be awarded lands. Out of the 200,000 acres of land originally set aside by Congress under the Act, only 27,000 acres have been distributed. About 17,000 acres have been inexplicably lost, and more than 16,000 acres have been withdrawn illegally by the state in contravention of the Act.[250] In fact, the state of Hawaii has neglected most of its responsibilities under the Act, and the state's actions

---

Hawaiians] and their use for any other object shall constitute a breach of trust for which suit may be brought by the United States.

[239] Letter from James W. Moorman, Assistant Attorney General, U.S. Dep't of Justice, to Philip Montez, Regional Director, Western Regional Office, United States Comm'n on Civil Rights (Aug. 13, 1979).

[240] Admission Act, *supra* note 225, at § 4.

[243] *Compare* Admission Act, *supra* note 225, §§ 4, 5(b) (delegation to state of power over Hawaiian home lands) *with* Act of Aug. 15, 1953, Pub. L. 83-280, 67 Stat. 588 (section 7 repealed and reenacted as amended, 1968) (codified as amended at 18 U.S.C. § 1162, 25 U.S.C. §§ 1321-1326, 28 U.S.C. §§ 1360, 1360 note (1982) ("Public Law 280") (delegation to several states of jurisdiction over mainland Indians). For a detailed discussion of Public Law 280, *see generally* Goldberg, *Public Law 280: The Limits of States' Jurisdiction Over Reservation Indians*, 22 U.C.L.A. L. Rev. 535 (1975).

[245] [1982-1983] Department of Hawaiian Home Lands Annual Report: Brief of Hou Hawaiians as Amici Curiae, *supra* note 72, at 29-30 n.11.

[246] Task Force Report, *supra* note 235, at 26. Some applicants were on the waiting list so long that they died before their names came up.

[250] Letter from James Watt, Secretary of the Dep't of the Interior, to George Ariyoshi, Governor of Hawaii, at 4 (Dec. 3, 1980) (*citing* United States Comm'n on Civil Rights, Opportunities for Native Hawaiians: Hawaiian Homelands 16 (1976)). Between statehood and 1978, the state of Hawaii had transferred by executive order 16,863 acres of HHCA lands to other state entities for use as airports, schools, parks, and reserves. *Id.* According to the Attorney General of Hawaii, the Governor's power to set aside public lands by executive order does not extend to HHCA lands and thus these transfers were illegal. Haw. Att'y Gen. Op. 75-3 (Mar. 31, 1975). *Accord*, HHCA, *supra* note 140, § 212 (Act provides that land not homesteaded may only be generally let).

have flown in the face of the state motto.[251] For example, the state on numerous occasions has exchanged trust lands for nontrust lands without first obtaining the permission of the Secretary of the Interior as required by law.[252] In addition, the state has diverted funds from the trust lands to pay for expenses unrelated to the trust[253] and leased land to non-Hawaiians for extremely low rental fees.[254] In the face of these breaches of trust on the part of the state, Native Hawaiians have brought numerous suits to enforce the provisions of the Act,[255] but have been unable to ameliorate the situation. The Hawaiian Home Lands Trust has thus been ineffective in returning Native Hawaiians to the lands set aside for them by Congress.

NOTE: FEDERAL RECOGNITION OF NATIVE HAWAIIANS

Although individual Native groups, such as the Hou, may not qualify for tribal status, Houghton's extensive survey of the history of Native Hawaiians before and after contact with Euro-Americans argues that Native Hawaiians as a whole do meet all five of the considerations listed in the *Handbook of Federal Indian Law* as influencing the decision whether a group constitutes a tribe (See Chapter 1, section B1. Why might Native Hawaiians seek greater federal recognition of their indigenous status and treatment more akin to that of the Indian tribes of the continental states? Congressional attention has been focused on this matter in recent years. Senate Report 100-36, which began this section, contains an elaborate defense of special federal legislative programs for Native Hawaiians, in that case in the area of education. The following summary of federal legislative action is taken from that report:

---

[251]The state motto is "*Ua mau ke ea o ka 'aina i ka pono*," which means "the life of the land is perpetuated in righteousness." Haw. Rev. Stat. § 5-9 (Supp. 1985).

[252]Letter from James Watt, *supra* note 250, at 2-3; Task Force Report, *supra* note 235, at 22. Section 204(4) of the HHCA, *supra* note 140, provides in part: "The Department of Hawaiian Home Lands may, with the permission of the Governor and the Secretary of the Interior ... exchange the title to available lands for lands publicly owned of an equal value." (Emphasis added.) As of 1980, only five of the numerous land exchanges had been submitted to the Department of the Interior for approval, the last one on March 16, 1967. Letter from James Watt, *supra* note 250, at 3. In addition, 1,700 acres of trust lands that had been surrendered had not been replaced, including lands that had been surrendered as early as 1962. Keaukaha-Panaewa Community Ass'n v. Hawaiian Homes Comm'n, No. CV 75-0260 (D. Haw. Sept. 9, 1976) (Finding of Fact 32), *rev'd on other grounds*, 588 F.2d 1216 (9th Cir. 1979), *cert. denied*, 444 U.S. 826 (1979).

[253]Legislative Auditor, State of Hawaii, Final Report of the Public Land Trust, Report to the Legislature of the State of Hawaii (Dec. 1986) (Report No. 86-17); Telephone interview with Kamuela Price, Federal-State Task Force on the Hawaiian Homes Commission Act, Apr. 12, 1986.

[254]Some land was leased to the United States Department of Defense for $1 per acre, and 16,000 acres were under lease to the Hawaiian Department of Land and Natural Resources for $5 per acre per year. Brief of Hou Hawaiians as Amici Curiae, *supra* note 72, at 29. Other lands have been leased to private concerns for equally low prices: 15,620 acres on Maui for $2 per acre per year, and 33,180 acres to the Parker cattle ranch on the island of Hawai'i for $3.85 per acre per year.

[255]*See, e.g.*, Price v. State, No. CV 84-2444 (D. Haw. 1984) (action to compel state to apply proceeds from trust lands to betterment of Native Hawaiians), *aff'd*, 764 F.2d 623 (9th Cir. 1985); *Keaukaha*, No. CV 75-0260 (challenging state use of trust lands for flood control project); Aki v. Beamer, No. CV 76-0144 (D. Haw. 1976) (challenging the validity of executive order setting aside trust lands as a park). *See* Letter from William Clark, Secretary of the U.S. Department of the Interior, to Kamuela Price, member of the Hou Hawaiians (May 8, 1984) (discussing suit by Hou concerning the proper administration of the HHCA).

2. The United States Congress Has Repeatedly Recognized the Special Status of Native Hawaiians and Has Included Native Hawaiians in Many Programs for Other Native Americans.

Among the congressional statutes singling out native Hawaiians for special treatment and preferences are the Hawaiian Homes Commission Act of 1920[149] and the Admissions Act of 1959.[150] After questions were raised in 1920 about the constitutionality of the Hawaiian Homes program, the federal solicitor of the Department of the Interior submitted an opinion arguing strongly in favor of its constitutionality. The opinion refers to congressional enactments that set aside lands for Indians[151] as precedents.[152] The House Committee on Territories agreed with this conclusion and stated that the legislation was based on "a reasonable and not an arbitrary classification" with "numerous congressional precedents for such legislation in previous enactments granting Indians [and other groups] special privileges in obtaining and using the public lands."[153]

In recent years, Congress has enacted additional statutes for the specific benefit of native Hawaiians. In 1980, Congress passed three statutes all identifying native Hawaiians as subjects of special federal attention:

a. The Native Hawaiian Education Study[154] states that "Congress declares its commitment to assist in providing the educational services and opportunities which Native Hawaiians need" and then establishes a seven-member Advisory Council to make recommendations to the Secretary of Education about how the Department of Education can better serve native Hawaiians.

b. Kalaupapa National Historical Park[155] establishes a national park at Kalaupapa on Molokai and provides employment preferences and training opportunities for Native Hawaiians (as well as qualified patients) for "positions established for the administration of the park."[156] The statute also establishes the Kalaupapa National Historical Park Advisory Commission of eleven members. Seven must be patients or former patients elected by the patient community and four are "appointed from recommendations submitted by the Governor of Hawaii, at least one of whom shall be a Native Hawaiian."[157]

c. The Native Hawaiians Study Commission Act[158] establishes a nine-member commission to "conduct a study of the culture, needs and concerns of the Native Hawaiians" and to prepare a report on this subject.[159] As used in this statute, "the term 'Native Hawaiian' means any individual whose ancestors were natives of the area which consisted of the Hawaiian Islands prior to 1778."

One recent federal action taken at the administrative level also recognizes the continuing federal responsibility for native Hawaiians. On January 21, 1983, United States Secretary of the Interior James G. Watt established the Federal-State Task Force on the Hawaiian Homes Commission Act, which prepared a report released in August,

---

[149] Act of July 9, 1921, 42 Stat. 108 (1921); see *supra* notes 36-42 and accompanying text.
[150] Pub. L. No. 86-3, 73 Stat. 4 (1959) (codified at 48 U.S.C. 491 (1976)); *see supra* notes 35 and 55 and accompanying text.
[151] Act of Feb. 28, 1891, ch. 383 § 1, 26 Stat. 794 (1910) (codified at 25 U.S.C. 331 (1982)).
[152] H. Doi, Legal Aspects of the Hawaiian Homes Program 43, Leg. Reference Bureau Rep. 1a (1964), *citing* Organic Act of the Territory of Hawaii: Hearings on Rehabilitation and Colonization of Hawaiians and Other Proposed Amendments and on the Proposed Transfer of the Buildings on the Federal Leprosy Investigation Station at Kalawao on the Island of Molokai Before the House Committee on Territories, 66th Cong., 2d Sess., 130-31 (1920).
[153] H.R. Rep. No. 839, 66th Cong., 2d Sess. (1920). This report discusses the rehabilitation of native Hawaiians.
[154] Pub. L. No. 96-374, § 1331, 94 Stat. 1499 (1980) (codified at 20 U.S.C. § 1221-1 (1982)).
[155] Pub. L. No. 96-565, tit. I, 94 Stat. 3321 (1980) (codified at 16 U.S.C. § 410jj (Supp. 1980)).
[156] *Id.* at § 107, 16 U.S.C. § 410jj-6 (1980).
[157] *Id.* at § 108(a), 16 U.S.C. § 410jj-7(a) (1980).
[158] Pub. L. No. 96-565, 94 Stat. 3324 (Supp. 1980) (codified at 42 U.S.C. § 2991 (1976)).
[159] *Id.* at § 303.

1983, "on ways to better effectuate the purposes of the Hawaiian Homes Commission Act." Three members of this Task Force were appointed by the Secretary of the Interior, and seven were appointed by the Governor of Hawaii. Funding and staffing were similarly shared.

In addition to these statutes and administrative actions recognizing the special political status of Native Hawaiians, Congress has specifically included native Hawaiians in a number of its recent enactments designed to benefit native Americans generally:

a. The Native American Programs Act of 1974[160] is designed "to promote the goal of economic and social self-sufficiency for American Indians, Hawaiian Natives and Alaskan Natives" by providing financial assistance to public and nonprofit agencies serving the native groups.[161] As used in this statute, "'Native Hawaiian' means any individual any of whose ancestors were natives of the area which consists of the Hawaiian Islands prior to 1778."[162] This program has provided funding for Alu Like, a non-profit organization designed to promote the economic development of native Hawaiians.

b. [The] American Indian Religious Freedom [Act][163] states that:

[I]t shall be the policy of the United States to protect and preserve for American Indians their inherent right of freedom to believe, express, and exercise the traditional religions of the American Indian, Eskimo, Aleut, and Native Hawaiians, including but not limited to access to sites, use and possession of sacred objects, and the freedom to worship through ceremonials and traditional rights.

The President is directed to implement this policy by working with the various federal departments. In this statute, the first time the words "American Indians" are used, they are used in the broad sense of applying to all native Americans.

c. The Native American Employment and Training Programs in the Comprehensive Employment and Training Act Amendments of 1978[164] states that "serious unemployment and economic disadvantage exist among members of ... Hawaiian native communities" and directs the Secretary of Labor to "arrange for programs to meet the employment and training needs of Hawaiian natives through such public agencies or private nonprofit organizations as the Secretary determines will best meet their needs."

d. The Drug Abuse Prevention, Treatment, and Rehabilitation Act[165] states that "Native Americans (including Native Hawaiians and Native American Pacific Islanders)" are to be given "special consideration" (along with other target groups) by the federal government for funding of programs to prevent, treat, and rehabilitate drug abusers.

e. The Comprehensive Alcohol Abuse and Alcoholism Prevention, Treatment, and Rehabilitation Act[166] states that the National Commission on Alcoholism and Other Alcohol-Related Problems should evaluate "the needs of special and underserved population groups, including American Indians, Alaskan Natives, Native Hawaiians, Native American Pacific Islanders ..." and that "Native Americans (including Native Hawaiians and Native American Pacific Islanders)" are to be given "special consideration" (along with other target groups) by the federal government for funding of programs to prevent, treat, and rehabilitate alcohol abusers.

AHUNA v. DEPARTMENT OF HAWAIIAN HOME LANDS

64 Haw. 327, 640 P.2d 1161 (1982)

RICHARDSON, Chief Justice.

This appeal seeks to determine whether an order filed on September 14,

---

[160] Pub. L. No. 93-644, 88 Stat. 2324 (1975) (codified at 42 U.S.C. § 2991 (1976)).
[161] *Id.* at §§ 802-03, 42 U.S.C. § 2991 a-b (1976).
[162] *Id.* at § 813(3), 42 U.S.C. § 2992 c(3) (1976).
[163] Pub. L. No. 95-341, 92 Stat. 469 (1978) (codified at 42 U.S.C. § 1996 (1978)).
[164] Pub. L. No. 95-524 § 302, 92 Stat. 1909 (1962) (codified at 29 U.S.C. § 872 (1978)).
[165] Pub. L. No. 98-24 § 5(a)(3), 97 Stat. 183 (1983) (codified at 21 U.S.C. § 1177 (1983)).
[166] Pub. L. No. 98-24 § 5(a)(2), 97 Stat. 183 (1983) (codified at 42 U.S.C. § 4577 (1983)).

1976, by Judge Kubota in the circuit court of the Third Circuit properly implemented a prior order filed on February 5, 1971 in the same case. Defendant-appellant Department of Hawaiian Home Lands specifically appeals from that portion of the 1976 order directing it, *inter alia*, to issue a lease to plaintiff-appellee Wallace Beck of the full ten acres in Lot 92 situated in the Panaewa Hawaiian homestead area on the island of Hawaii. Appellant contends it has complied fully with the 1971 order by awarding appellee a lease to approximately 6.5 acres of Lot 92. After examining the record and reviewing relevant legal and equitable precepts, we affirm the judgment of the court below because the prior order implicitly directed appellant to issue a lease to a ten-acre lot as close to appellee's present lot as possible or to show cause why such a lot could not be issued. Appellant neither issued such a lease nor adequately demonstrated why it was not possible to do so.

I

A

This action was initially filed on August 13, 1970, by a number of native Hawaiians[2] who were qualified under the Hawaiian Homes Commission Act, 1920, as amended, (hereafter HHCA)[3] to lease Hawaiian home lands for agricultural purposes at Panaewa, Hawaii. The action generally sought review under the Hawaii Administrative Procedure Act and a declaratory judgment that the policy of the Department of awarding agricultural lots at Panaewa on a permissive use basis contravened the HHCA and that the Department was obligated to issue leases to available agricultural tracts to all native Hawaiian applicants who were qualified to perform the conditions of the lease. The trial court dismissed the class action aspect of the complaint and the action was heard as an action on behalf of the named plaintiffs (appellee Beck being one of these named persons).

On February 5, 1971, Judge Menor issued a Decision and Order finding the use permit system practiced by appellant in violation of the HHCA.[4] In addition, the court fashioned specific relief for each of the plaintiffs in the order. In most cases, appellant was instructed either to award a lease of a specific lot to

---

[2]Section 201 of the Hawaiian Homes Commission Act defines "native Hawaiian" as "any descendant of not less than one-half part of the blood of the races inhabiting the Hawaiian Islands previous to 1778."

[3]Hawaiian Homes Commission Act, 1920; Act of July 9, 1921, c. 42, 42 Stat. 108, reprinted in 1 Haw. Rev. Stat. 146 (1976).

[4]With respect to the permissive use system, Judge Menor stated in his February 5, 1971 Order:

The use permit system apparently came about because of the high incidence of leasehold failures, not necessarily confined to the Panaewa Farm Lots subdivision. In this connection, the Court finds specifically that the Department was acting in good faith. The basic rationale of the system seems to be that the prospective leaseholder should first have to show the Department that he can in practice comply with the conditions of the lease before the lease is actually issued to him. While such a practice may have its merits, especially in view of the unwritten policy of the department to revoke a use permit only where a use permittee has absolutely done nothing towards improving and cultivating the premises after an extended period of time, and in the light of the tendency of younger generations of native Hawaiians (as well as other younger generations of Americans for that matter) to avoid farm work as much as possible, such a practice nevertheless is in conflict with the express provision of Section 205 that "[a]vailable lands shall be sold or leased only ... in the manner ... set out (in the Act)." There may conceivably be situations where by agreement of the parties a use permit may be authorized, but where, as here, a lease is applied for it shall, if

the individual plaintiff or to act upon the lease application of the plaintiff and explain any rejection of that application to the court. The court thus retained jurisdiction to insure the proper implementation of its [orders].

II

B

In awarding appellee 6.5 plus or minus acres of Lot 92, appellant failed to comply with the order to award appellee a lot as directed, but it nevertheless may justify the award if it can. But before we can address this question, we must first determine the extent of the burden imposed on appellant by the show cause provision.

It is generally acknowledged that the primary purpose of the HHCA was the rehabilitation of native Hawaiians. Senator John H. Wise, a member of the "Legislative Commission of the Territory (of Hawaii)," and one of the authors of the HHCA, described the law as a plan for the rehabilitation of the Hawaiian people.[10] In *In re Ainoa*, 60 Haw. 487, 591 P.2d 607 (1979), we recognized the purpose of the HHCA was to rehabilitate the native Hawaiians on lands given the status of Hawaiian home lands under section 204 of the HHCA. We further emphasized there that "(the) native Hawaiians are subjects of solicitude under the Act." 60 Haw. at 488, 591 P.2d at 608. This language indicates that we are aware of a high duty of care owed to native Hawaiians.

The legislative history at the inception of the HHCA strongly suggests that the federal government stood in a trusteeship capacity to the aboriginal people. Ex-Secretary of Interior Franklin K. Lane testified before the House Committee on the Territories:

> One thing that impressed me ... was the fact that the natives of the islands who are our wards, I should say, and for whom in a sense we are trustees, are falling off rapidly in numbers and many of them are in poverty. They never owned the lands of the islands. The land was owned by the King originally .... H.R. Rep. No. 839, 66th Cong., 2d Sess. 4 (1920).

The term "ward" connotes a notion of trusteeship. See generally *Cherokee Nation v. Georgia*, 30 U.S. (5 Pet.) 1 (1831). The Committee on the Territories described in part the general policy underlying the bill for the enactment of the HHCA in these words:

> Your committee is ... of the opinion that (1) the Hawaiian must be placed upon the land in order to insure his rehabilitation; (2) alienation of such land must, not only in

---

granted, be for a term of ninety-nine years (Section 208), subject, always to cancellation or revocation before the expiration of the term, upon such grounds as are in the Act specified.

[10] Senator Wise specifically stated:

The idea in trying to get the lands back to some of the Hawaiians is to rehabilitate them. I believe that we should get them on lands and let them own their own homes. I believe it would be easy to rehabilitate them. The people of New Zealand are increasing today because they have the lands to live on and are working out their own salvation." ... The Hawaiian people are a farming people and fishermen, out of door people, and when they were frozen out of their lands and driven into the cities they had to live in the cheapest places, tenements. That is one of the reasons why the Hawaiian people are dying. Now, the only way to save them, I contend, is to take them back to the lands and give them the mode of living that their ancestors were accustomed to and in that way rehabilitate them."

H.R. Rep. No. 839, 66th Cong., 2d Sess. 4 (1920).

the immediate future but also for many years to come, be made possible; (3) accessible water in adequate amounts must be provided for all tracts; (4) the Hawaiian must be financially aided until his farming operations are well underway. In framing such a program your committee is in a general way following the broad outlines of Senator Wise's plan. H.R. Rep. No. 839, 66th Cong., 2d Sess. 4 (1920).

The tenor of the foregoing statement by the committee also implies an intent to establish a trust relationship between the government and Hawaiian persons. The federal government ultimately responded to the plight of the native Hawaiians and enacted the HHCA, placing over 200,000 acres of land for the use and benefit of the native people under the aegis of the Hawaiian Homes Commission. See generally Levy, *Native Hawaiian Land Rights*, 63 Cal. L. Rev. 848 (1975). Finally, when we attained statehood in 1959, the State of Hawaii entered a compact with the United States to assume the management and disposition of the Hawaiian home lands and to adopt the HHCA as a provision of the State Constitution. Admission Act of March 18, 1959, Pub. L. No. 86-3, § 4, 73 Stat. 4, reprinted in 1 Haw. Rev. Stat. 78 (1976). The State and its people reaffirmed this compact by adding another provision to the Constitution whereby they accepted specific trust obligations relating to the management of the Hawaiian home lands imposed by the federal government [as a condition of statehood].

Thus from our review of the evolution of the HHCA and its impact on native Hawaiians, we conclude (1) that the federal government set aside certain public lands to be considered Hawaiian home lands to be utilized in the rehabilitation of native Hawaiians, thereby undertaking a trust obligation benefiting the aboriginal people; and (2) that the State of Hawaii assumed this fiduciary obligation upon being admitted into the Union as a state.

The Department of Hawaiian Home Lands, headed by the Hawaiian Homes Commission, received exclusive control of the Hawaiian home lands by section 204 of the HHCA. The HHCA further stated:

"The powers and duties of the governor and the board of land and natural resources, in respect to lands of the State, shall not extend to lands having the status of Hawaiian home lands, except as specifically provided in this title." HHCA, § 206.

We conclude from this history that the Hawaiian Homes Commission, which oversees the Department, is the specific state entity obliged to implement the fiduciary duty under the HHCA on behalf of eligible native Hawaiians. In dealing with eligible native Hawaiians collectively or individually, appellant must adhere to high fiduciary duties normally owed by a trustee to its beneficiaries. In light of the foregoing, we conclude that with respect to Judge Menor's order, the standard of conduct expected of appellant thereby was that befitting a trustee.

[In light of all] the circumstances surrounding the alleged breach of trust by the appellant, we are of an opinion that the actions of the trustees were unreasonable in this instance. As to the question of the trustees considering the interests of third parties, or non-beneficiaries, we think it impermissibly weighed the interests of certain third parties in withholding a portion of Lot 92.

The appellant argues that the trustee must deal impartially when there is more than one beneficiary, citing Restatement (Second) of Trust § 183 (1959).

We wholeheartedly concur. The trustees, however, have failed to sufficiently demonstrate that they considered the interests of all beneficiaries.

In testifying about the factors that the Commission considered in withholding the acreage from Lot 92, former Chairperson Billy Beamer testified:

> In viewing the Puainako Extension, *which is a benefit to all of the citizens of Hawaii*, and primarily, those on the Island of Hawaii, it is our responsibility, to look at the pluses and the minuses. And as to how much it is going *to cost the State* to detour or to deviate, versus the loss to the Hawaiian homestead land, or to the homesteader. In this instance, the decision was delayed, and we deliberated. The Commission approved of the Puainako Extension. And *our first consideration was the number of people that it would benefit* versus the inconvenience that it might cause, to a few. And could these inconveniences be countermanded or buffered or mitigated, by other kind (sic) of provisions. *Number two, the costs, which should be number one, to the taxpayer*, in detouring the road. And in this discussion, then, if we had committed to the County, a right of entry. And committed, in fact, and approved of the alignment, as proposed to the Department, it would be a lefthanded gift, to say to them that we approve of this alignment, and then, on the next hand, to award a lot that would cause them, unnecessary expense, to the taxpayer, by having to withdraw that lot, later, after improvements have been made.
>
> But we could avoid this expense, if we would eliminate that portion of the land, that may be effected [*sic*]. (Trans. Vol. III., pp. 30-31) (emphasis added).

This language clearly illustrates the consideration given by the trustees to the State and its taxpayers. Chairperson Beamer's statement fails to show that the commissioners considered the interests of the other native beneficiaries. The primary concern of the Commission, however, must be the administration of the HHCA on behalf of those eligible native Hawaiian beneficiaries.

Appellant contends that the Commission did indeed consider the interests of the Hawaiian beneficiaries, referring to the Commission Minutes of May 30, 1975, which reflect the Department Planning Director presented a study of the proposed Extension. The minutes indicate that the Extension would serve as the primary entrance to a future airport and that it would serve as a buffer between residential and industrial areas. One commissioner submitted that the people in the area were opposed to the highway. The report was then accepted by the Commission.

[Thus] we uphold Judge Kubota's implementation of Judge Menor's 1971 Order in every respect.

Affirmed.

C. TRIBES IN EASTERN OKLAHOMA (FORMERLY THE INDIAN TERRITORY)

HARJO v. KLEPPE

420 F. Supp. 1110 (D.D.C. 1976)

BRYANT, District Judge.

I. *Introduction*

This matter is now before the Court on the parties' cross-motions for summary judgment. The parties have stipulated that no genuine issues of material fact exist. Plaintiffs in this action seek declaratory and injunctive relief against the policy and practice of the Interior Department in recognizing and dealing with defendant Cox, Principal Chief of the Creek Nation, as the sole embodiment of the Creek tribal government, and in refusing to recognize, facilitate, or deal with a Creek National Council as a coordinate branch of the tribal government responsible for certain legislative and financial functions.

[Plaintiffs challenge] the legitimacy of Cox's authority to disburse tribal funds and enter into contracts on behalf of the Creek Nation without the approval of the Creek National Council. Specifically, the first cause of action alleges: (1) Article I of the 1867 Constitution of the Creek Nation lodges the lawmaking power of that Nation in the Creek Nation Council; (2) The Constitution of the Creek Nation places the financial affairs of the Nation exclusively under the control of the Creek National Council; (3) Congress, between 1866 and 1906 on several occasions, specifically recognized the Creek National Council as the ultimate repository of power within the Creek national government; (4) Under the terms of the Act of 1906, 34 Stat. 137, and the Treaties of 1856 and 1866 Congress imposed on defendants the duty to respect and follow the provisions of the Constitution of the Creek Nation; and (5) Federal defendants have approved the disbursement of tribal funds by defendant Cox on behalf of the Creek Nation and have paid federal funds to Cox contrary to the intent of Congress.

Defendants argue that ... (4) Various congressional acts have relieved the Creek Nation of sufficient authority that it has been rendered incompetent to handle the affairs of the tribe under the 1867 Constitution; (5) Congress was aware of the fact that the affairs of the Five Civilized Tribes (Creeks, Cherokees, Choctaws, Chickasaws, and Seminoles) were being administered by Principal Chiefs or Governors and therefore ratified this form of government when it enacted the Act of October 22, 1970, 84 Stat. 1091.

III. *The Merits*

The central issue to be resolved in this case is whether the tribal government of the Creek Nation has survived statutory dismemberment, and if so, whether the federal government is acting legally in recognizing the Principal Chief as the sole embodiment of that government. Phrased differently, the question is whether the federal government may permit funds belonging to the Creek Nation to be expended solely on the authority of the Principal Chief, or whether Creek and federal law require the participation of the Creek National Council in the tribe's financial decision-making. After extensive investigation and careful consideration, aided by the able written and oral presentations of counsel, the Court has arrived at the inescapable conclusion that despite the general intentions of the Congress of the late nineteenth and early twentieth centuries to ultimately terminate the tribal government of the Creeks, and despite an elaborate statutory scheme implementing numerous intermediate steps toward that end, the final dissolution of the Creek tribal government created by the Creek Constitution of 1867 was never statutorily accomplished, and indeed that government was instead explicitly perpetuated.

More than is sometimes the case, the legal analysis necessary to unravel the statutory tangle present here is inextricably bound up with the social, political, and economic history of the times from which the legislation emerged. While the Court can offer only the briefest of synopses in this opinion, it must be emphasized that an accurate perception of the matters discussed herein is heavily dependent upon at least a perusal of the sources cited in this opinion.[6]

As a result of the increasingly substantial expansionist pressures from the white population, the federal government in the 1820's adopted a policy of forcible removal of the culturally advanced Creeks from the southeastern United States. This policy, expressed in the Indian Removal Act of 1830, eventually resulted in the relocation of the Creek, Cherokee, Seminole, Choctaw and Chickasaw tribes to what is presently the state of Oklahoma. Among the rights granted to the Creeks by the Removal Treaty of March 24, 1832 was the right to perpetual self-government of their new lands. Because of their cultural and political sophistication relative to other Plains Indians, the Indians who had been removed from east of the Mississippi to the Oklahoma area became known as the Five Civilized Tribes. Prior to the Civil War, these tribes owned all of the present state of Oklahoma except the panhandle region.[10] As a penalty for their alliances with the Confederacy during the Civil War, the tribes were compelled to cede to the federal government the western half of their lands. The remaining lands occupied by the Five Civilized Tribes continued to be known as the Indian Territory. Two treaties were signed by the Creeks and the federal government during this period. In the treaty of August 7, 1856, 11 Stat. 699, Congress ratified once more a guarantee of Creek self-government. Article XV of that Treaty provided:

> "So far as may be compatible with the constitution of the United States, and the laws made in pursuance thereof, regulating trade and intercourse with the Indian tribes, the Creeks and Seminoles shall be secured in the unrestricted right of self-government, within their respective limits ...."

The treaty recognized the existence of a Creek Council, power of the Council to make laws, and authority of the Treasurer to receive and disburse funds. 11 Stat. 699, 700, 701, 702, 706.

The 1866 Treaty, 14 Stat. 785, specifically reaffirmed previous treaty obligations (including those of the 1856 treaty) not inconsistent with the new treaty. Article X of the treaty provided:

> "The Creeks agree to such legislation as Congress and the President of the United States may deem necessary for the better administration of justice and the protection of the rights of persons and property within the Indian territory. Provided, however, said legislation shall not in any manner interfere with or annul their present tribal organization, rights, laws, privileges and customs."

---

[6] The materials upon which the Court has chiefly relied with respect to the history of the periods involved in this case include the two books by Angie Debo, *And Still The Waters Run* and *The Road to Disappearance*, which appear to be the pre-eminent works in the field and which were used by the Court pursuant to the agreement of the parties; *University of California Publications in History*, Vol. 6: "The Formation Of The State Of Oklahoma," by Roy Gittinger (University of California Press, 1917) [hereinafter, "Gittinger"]; the *Congressional Record* for the periods during which the Acts of 1898, 1901, and 1906 were being debated; and the exhibits furnished by counsel and filed as part of the record in this case.

[10] For a history of the tribes during the pre-Civil War period, see Foreman, The Five Civilized Tribes, University of Oklahoma Press (1934).

The treaty ceded to the United States the western half of the Indian domain, about 3,250,560 acres, for $975,168, and was in general highly disadvantageous to the Creeks. A few days after ratification of the treaty by the U.S. Senate, Congress granted franchises to two railroads to cross the Indian Territory. The more important one of these for present purposes granted the right of way across the Territory from Kansas to Texas with alternate sections in a twenty-mile strip "whenever the Indian title shall be extinguished by treaty or otherwise … Provided, that said lands become a part of the public lands of the United States." This grant was to play an important role in the later enactment of a provision crucial to the outcome of this suit.

No further treaties were signed between the Creeks and the federal government. On October 12, 1867, the Creeks adopted a constitution and a code of laws for the "Muskogee Nation." The constitution was modeled on American federalism, with executive, legislative, and judicial branches. Legislative power was lodged in a National Council, a bi-cameral body in which each tribal town or "Talwa" was entitled to one delegate in the House of Kings and one in the House of Warriors, plus an additional delegate in the House of Warriors for every two hundred people. The members of the Council were elected for four year terms.

Executive power of the Creek Nation was delegated to the Principal Chief, elected by universal adult male suffrage for a term of four years. The constitution also provided for a Second Chief, similarly elected, to succeed the Principal Chief upon his death, resignation, or impeachment. The Principal Chief was given the power and responsibility *inter alia* to reprieve and pardon criminals, execute and enforce the laws, make an annual report to the National Council concerning the state of the nation, and approve or veto laws enacted and measures taken by the Council.

Article V of the constitution provides for a Treasurer of the Creek Nation, to be selected by the Council for a four year term, who is given the authority to receive funds and to "disburse the same as shall be provided by law." The Treasurer is to report at least yearly to the Council on the financial affairs of the nation. The constitution and laws provided that the National Council had initial responsibility for financial affairs, including making determinations as to the purposes for which Creek funds were to be spent. It also provided that the Principal Chief had the power of veto over such measures, a veto which could be overridden by a two-thirds vote of each House of the National Council. Once a spending measure received final approval, the Treasurer was to perform any necessary accounting and disbursing functions.[14]

The constitution also created a court system, whose jurisdiction was limited to Creek citizens. The nation was divided into six districts; each had a judge elected by the Council. The district court tried all criminal cases and minor civil cases, and trial by jury was provided. There was a Supreme Court of five justices chosen by the Council for four year terms, which tried all civil cases where the amount in controversy exceeded one hundred dollars.

---

[14] Constitution and Laws of the Muskogee Nation as compiled and codified by A. P. McKellop, Muskogee, Indian Territory (1893). The parties agree that this was in fact the distribution of authority and functions under the 1867 Constitution.

Generally speaking, the Creek Nation prospered during the final third of the nineteenth century. According to ancient Indian custom, all land was held by the tribe communally. Any citizen could cultivate as much land as he wanted, and when he ceased to work that land it reverted to the Nation. By 1890 however ranching had made serious inroads on the character of Creek country. Under various Creek laws, members of the tribe were able to obtain leases of land to be fenced in for grazing purposes; by 1896 about one-third of Creek lands were so held. Most of the land under lease was then sub-leased to cattle interests (often from Texas) at a large profit.

Also during this period the number of white persons living in the Indian Territory grew dramatically; numerous white towns appeared throughout the Territory. The white settlers were engaged in both farming and cattle raising, and despite the repeated pleas of the Creeks that the federal government remove the vast numbers of whites living illegally on Creek lands, the government failed to honor its obligations and the number of whites continued to grow. One of the recurrent problems in the relations between the Creeks and the whites at this time was the general absence of an adequate court system to deal with criminal and civil disputes. The Creek courts had no jurisdiction over whites, and federal courts in the area were created very slowly. Crime flourished, and the payment of debts was unenforceable. Finally, in 1895, federal courts with civil and criminal jurisdiction over United States citizens and over tribal citizens in mixed cases involving U.S. citizens were created for three judicial districts comprising the Indian Territory. The laws of Arkansas were designated to govern actions in these federal courts, in the absence of a federal statute. The authority of the tribal courts was further and fatally undermined two years later when, in the Appropriations Act of June 7, 1897, 30 Stat. 62, Congress extended the reach of the federal (and the incorporated Arkansas) law to cover all persons, including Indians, in the Territory, effective January 1, 1898.[20] The transition to federal law as the governing body of civil and criminal law was completed the following year by the Curtis Act, discussed below, which rendered tribal law unenforceable in the federal courts (§ 26) and, after allowing time for the completion of a portion of the cases then pending in the tribal courts, abolished the tribal courts and transferred the remaining cases to the federal courts (§ 28).

As might be expected, the white settlers were not happy with their inability to exercise any political control over the Indian Territory in which they lived, with their inability to get title to communally held Indian lands, and in general with the restrictions on their ability to mold their environment to their liking. As their numbers grew, so too did their demand that the communal tenure and tribal governments be abolished in favor of both individual tenure in which the lands could pass freely into white hands and the political reorganization of the Territory into a state. Proposals for forced allotment of Indian lands were not new; since the end of the Civil War many bills seeking the abolition of tribal tenure had been introduced into Congress. By 1890, when the Oklahoma Territory adjacent to the Indian Territory was opened and a territorial government

---

[20] It should be noted that Congress did not intend here to divest the National Council's power to legislate; indeed, the act specifically provided that such legislation was to be transmitted to the President after its enactment for his approval or veto.

created, the clamor for allotment had reached a new peak. All the federal agencies responsible for Indian affairs were advising Congress of the need to change the current system. The leading congressional proponent of allotment and assimilation was Senator Henry L. Dawes of Massachusetts. At his instance, the Congress in 1887 passed the Dawes Severalty Act, 24 Stat. 388, providing for allotments on Indian reservations with the remaining unalloted lands on those reservations to be purchased by the government and thrown open to homesteading. The Five Civilized Tribes were exempted from the Act's provisions, but regarded it as handwriting on the wall.

The next blow fell on March 3, 1893, when Congress created a commission to negotiate with the Five Tribes for the extinction of their communal titles and the eventual creation of a state. 27 Stat. 612, 645. The Commission was headed by Henry Dawes, who by then had retired from the Senate, and it became known as the Dawes Commission. During the next several years the Commission attempted to negotiate the dissolution of the tribes, but had minimal success; as a result they continued to report to Congress and to the public of what they regarded as the pressing need for dissolution of the tribes and allotment of the land. By 1895, the tribes still refused to deal with the Dawes Commission. In that year Congress responded by authorizing a survey of all the Indian land, and in 1896 directed the Commission to make a complete roll of the members of each tribe. Bills were also introduced in Congress each year calling for the forcible abolition of tribal status. In the 1897 Appropriations Act (30 Stat. 62), Congress began to force the issue by subjecting all laws passed by the National Council to Presidential veto, with the significant exceptions of resolutions of adjournment and acts relating to negotiations with the Dawes Commission. As a result of all this pressure, and apparently preferring a negotiated settlement to an imposed one, the tribes began to deal with the Commission. By 1898 all five tribes had drawn up compacts with the Commission, and the Seminole Agreement had even been ratified. It appeared likely, however, that the other agreements would not be ratified by the tribes' membership, and on June 28, 1898 Congress enacted the Curtis Act, which provided for forced allotments and the eventual termination of the tribal tenure without the Indians' consent. The Act incorporated the provisions of the tentative agreements with each of the four remaining tribes, providing that if the agreement with any tribe was ratified by the tribe the provisions of the agreement would substitute for the more drastic allotment provisions of the Act. The Creeks did in fact reject their agreement, and the Act went into effect in their country.

The Curtis Act, 30 Stat. 495, is the first of the four pieces of federal legislation critical to the resolution of this suit. In general, the Act provided for compulsory allotment of tribal lands to those determined by the Dawes Commission to be entitled to a place on the final rolls of the tribe (§ 11); ratified an 1895 decision of a federal territorial court that towns in the Territory had the right to establish municipal governments under sections of the Arkansas statutes placed in effect by the court act of 1890 (§ 14); made the civil law of the tribe unenforceable in the federal courts while abolishing the tribal courts (§§ 26, 28); and made various other provisions to facilitate the allotment process and assumption of control of the Territory by the increasingly numerous white settlers.

The feature of the Act most relevant to the question of continuing tribal governmental power is section 19, which provided:

"That no payment of any moneys on any account whatever shall hereafter be made by the United States to any of the tribal governments or to any officer thereof for disbursement, but payments of all sums to members of said tribes shall be made under direction of the Secretary of the Interior by an officer appointed by him; and per capita payments shall be made direct to each individual in lawful money of the United States, and the same shall not be liable to the payment of any previously contracted obligation."

While there is apparently no explanatory legislative history to assist in illuminating the ultimate purpose of this section, it is quite clear that Congress did not intend it as a limitation upon the constitutional power of the Creek government to allocate and spend tribal funds. It was, rather, a limited device intended to prevent any possible illegitimate diversion or embezzlement of the payments to be made to individual members of the tribes under the allotment programs and the general distribution of the value of tribal property rights.[29] If the section had any impact at all on the authority of Creek government, it was only to eliminate the function of the Treasurer in the actual disbursement of such moneys. This construction is confirmed by the very few judicial interpretations that section 19 has received. In *Seminole Nation v. United States,* 316 U.S. 286 (1942), the Supreme Court was faced with the question of whether certain payments which had been made by the U.S. government violated the section. The Court reasoned:

"The text of that section and its legislative history demonstrate that it prohibits only payments to tribal officers which are 'for disbursement' — i.e., payments to be distributed by them to members of the tribe. If the first clause of § 9 is construed as prohibiting all payments to the tribe or its officers, then the later clauses, providing only for payments to members and per capita payments, are inadequate to dispose of the problems raised by the first clause. For then no provision is made for the expenses of maintaining and conducting the tribal government, despite the fact that the Seminole tribal government was not only to continue after the Curtis Act but was in fact relieved of the necessity of securing Presidential approval of its legislation by an agreement ratified three days after the passage of that statute. See 30 Stat. 567, 569. Section 19, as originally introduced in the House, provided that payments of 'all expenses incurred in transacting their business' were to be made under the direction of the Secretary of the Interior. The deletion of this clause is persuasive that *Congress intended that tribal officers should retain the right to disburse their funds for expenses of their respective tribal governments. For these reasons we think § 19 prohibits payment by the Government to the tribal treasurer only when such payments are to be distributed by him to members of the tribe. It has no application to money earmarked for educational or tribal purposes, and money intended for any purpose the tribe may designate."* (Emphasis added.) 316 U.S. at 302-303.

The section received a similar construction in *Choctaw Nation v. United States,* 91 Ct. Cl. 320 (1940), *cert. denied,* 312 U.S. 695 (1941), where the Court held that

"... section 19 of the Curtis Act related only to moneys intended for disbursement per capita or for the purpose of carrying out agreements or acts of Congress concern-

---

[29] As a result of the incessant allegations by the Dawes Commission and other federal agencies of pervasive corruption and venality on the part of many tribal officials, there was a widespread perception in Congress that no tribal officials could be trusted to make these payments. For exam-

ing matters over which jurisdiction was taken from the tribal government and vested in the Secretary of the Interior when the authority of such tribal government was restricted and, as so limited, continued by ... subsequent acts of Congress .... We think the words 'all sums' as used in the second clause of the section relate to the same 'moneys' mentioned in the first. The words 'payments ... to members of said tribes' as used in the second clause has the same meaning as the word disbursement in the first clause. In other words, it appears that the restriction against payments intended for disbursement in the first clause is expressly carried over and rephrased in the second clause. For this reason we think the first clause was intended to change the method of 'making payments of all sums to members of said tribes'; and that the second clause was intended to supply a new method and directed that 'payments of all sums to members of said tribes shall be made under direction of the Secretary of the Interior by an officer appointed by him.'" 91 Ct. Cl. at 392.[32]

In summary, then, it is clear that with the passage of the Curtis Act, the territorial sovereignty of the Creek Nation had been seriously eroded. Territorial sovereignty, however, is not the issue in this case; the issue here is much narrower. The relevant question is whether or not the tribal government of the Creeks had been stripped of its power to deal with *tribal* affairs as such. While the tribe had clearly lost much of its authority in a territorial sense, or in the sense that a state has sovereignty, it is equally clear that the tribal government remained authoritative — in legal contemplation — as to matters of tribal organization and management, including control of tribal funds.

The provisions of the Curtis Act were so drastic from the Creek point of view that they soon consented to a new agreement to supersede the one contained in section 30 of that Act but rejected by the tribe. The new agreement was ratified by the tribe, and by the Congress in the Act of March 1, 1901, 31 Stat. 861. A number of the agreement's provisions bear on the issues before the Court. First, the agreement provided for the actual dissolution of the tribal government (§ 46) within about five years, by which time it was expected that the tribal affairs would have been wound up:

> "46. The tribal government of the Creek Nation shall not continue longer than March fourth, nineteen hundred and six, subject to such further legislation as Congress may deem proper."

The agreement recognized, however, that until such time as the Creek national government was in fact dissolved, it would continue to function under the

---

ples of the allegations and the perception, see *Stephens v. Cherokee Nation*, 174 U.S. 445, 450-460 (1899); *Seminole Nation v. United States*, 316 U.S. 286, 298-300, 304-305 (1942); Gittinger, *op. cit.*, pp. 189-190; for a contrasting view, see Debo, *And Still the Waters Run*, pp. 23-25.

[32] This holding must be taken as an overruling of the statement made earlier by the Court of Claims in *Creek Nation v. United States*, 78 Ct. Cl. 474, 489-490 (1933), that Congress intended *in* § *19* to invest the Secretary "with authority to disburse and expend the funds in such manner and for such purposes as would, in his judgment, satisfy the needs of the Creek Nation and promote the welfare and happiness of its citizens, subject to such limitations as Congress might subsequently impose," since the section cannot both grant the Secretary discretion to spend money as he judges best and at the same time relate solely to payments to tribal members. In any case, the earlier statement was conclusively overruled by the interpretation placed on § 19 by the Supreme Court in *Seminole Nation v. United States, supra.* The Court is unable to reconcile the passage quoted in the text immediately above (from 91 Ct. Cl. at 392) with the Court of Claims' earlier reliance in that case, *id.* at 376, on the language (quoted in this note) from the *Creek Nation* case, except to view that reliance as ? reading of the *Creek Nation* language as being based upon the effect of the Curtis Act as a whole, rather than solely upon § 19. In any event, this Court is bound in the instant case by the holding of the Supreme Court, which is in fact also the conclusion supported by the available historical evidence.

1867 Constitution, as modified by this act and prior agreements. Section 42 of the agreement recognized specifically the legislative and financial powers of the National Council, and continued the requirement that such legislation be subject to Presidential veto.[33] Moreover, it recognized that these functions were performed pursuant to the 1867 Creek Constitution in the requirement that the agreement be ratified by the National Council "as provided in the constitution of said nation." 31 Stat. 861.

The agreement and act did not place any further limits on the power of the National Council to make, and the principal chief to approve, decisions with respect to tribal finances. Like the Curtis Act, however, the agreement did provide for control of the Secretary of the Interior over disbursements and cash flow arising out of the implementation of the agreement. Section 31 provided that moneys payable to the tribe under the agreement were to be deposited to their credit in the U.S. Treasury, with an itemized monthly report going to the Principal Chief. Section 32 roughly corresponded to section 19 of the Curtis Act, and provided:

"32. All funds of the tribe, and all moneys accruing under the provisions of this agreement, when needed for the purposes of equalizing allotments or for any other purposes herein prescribed, shall be paid out under the direction of the Secretary of the Interior; and when required for per capita payments, if any, shall be paid out directly to each individual by a bonded officer of the United States, under direction of the Secretary of the Interior, without unnecessary delay."

By its terms, section 32 applied only to payments needed for equalization of allotments,[34] per capita payments, or for other expenditures arising from the agreement itself. Finally, the act and agreement explicitly reasserted the continuing authority of the National Council in controlling the use of any tribal funds not expended under the agreement:

"33. No funds belonging to said tribe shall hereafter be used or paid out for any purposes by any officer of the United States without consent of the tribe, expressly given through its national council, except as herein provided."

The agreement also interacted with the Creek government's executive branch in two primary ways. First, the act's allotment scheme provided for commissions to carry out the appraisal and allotment of land, and the sale of town lots. The

---

[33] "42. No act, ordinance, or resolution of the national council of the Creek Nation in any manner affecting the lands of the tribe, or of individuals after allotment, or the moneys or other property of the tribe, or of the citizens thereof, except appropriation for the necessary incidental and salaried expenses of the Creek government as herein limited, shall be of any validity until approved by the President of the United States. When any such act, ordinance, or resolution shall be passed by said council and approved by the principal chief, a true and correct copy thereof, duly certified, shall be immediately transmitted to the President, who shall, within thirty days after received by him, approve or disapprove the same. If disapproved, it shall be so indorsed and returned to the principal chief; if approved, the approval shall be indorsed thereon, and it shall be published in at least two newspapers having a bona fide circulation in the Creek Nation."

[34] Section 9 provided that after allotments had been made, any residual lands and any funds arising under the agreement should be used for equalizing the value of the allotments in the hands of the allottees. It also provided that other tribal funds should be used if funds provided for in the agreement proved insufficient. Among the funds made available under the agreement (§ 27) for equalization purposes were any treaty funds of the tribe, e.g., any funds remaining on deposit in the U.S. Treasury which belonged to the tribe by virtue of the Treaty of 1866. See Debo, *The Road to Disappearance*, p. 174; cf. *Choctaw Nation of Indians v. United States*, 318 U.S. 423 (1943); *Quick Bear v. Leupp*, 210 U.S. 50, 80 (1908).

Principal Chief was to appoint certain members of the commissions or committees, and if he failed or refused to do so the Secretary was directed to make the appointments (§§ 2 and 10). Secondly, the deeds conveying the individual allotments to members of the tribe were to be signed and delivered by the Principal Chief on forms provided by the Secretary. The conveyances were required to be approved by the Secretary before becoming final (§ 23). In sum, then, under the agreement the Creek government through its National Council retained its general authority for dealing with tribal affairs,[36] and for determining the purposes for which tribal funds would be spent, except to the extent those funds were needed for equalization of allotments or for other expenditures resulting from the act.[37]

During the next few years, the federal government continued to reorganize the Indian Territory in anticipation of imminent statehood. The enrollment and allotment process moved slowly ahead, and townsites were surveyed and towns created and organized. Throughout this period, the federal officials and agents dominated the lives of the Five Civilized Tribes, using their control over tribal disbursements and resources to ensure that the administration of the Territory during that time conformed to the preferences, values, and priorities of the Interior Department. As March 4, 1906 — the date set for the dissolution of the tribal governments — approached, however, much remained to be done. The Interior Department, which had taken over the allotment process upon the expiration of the Dawes Commission on June 10, 1905, was still in the process of disposing of much tribal property, and it was apparent that the affairs of the tribes could not be wound up by the date set for the final dissolution of the tribes. Indeed, there was still considerable resistance to the allotment program itself among the tribal members, particularly the fullbloods. The tribal rolls had not been completed, and there was considerable dispute over the question of whether allotments should carry restrictions on alienation. In order to finally address these and other issues, the Congress in early 1906 debated and enacted the "Five Tribes Act," 34 Stat. 137 (April 26, 1906); this act was the last to deal comprehensively with the affairs of the tribes.

Several sections of the Five Tribes Act are relevant to the scope of the surviving authority of the Creek national government and National Council. Section 2 continued the authority of the Secretary of the Interior to disburse Creek funds for the equalization of allotments, as provided by section 9 of the 1901 agreement. In order to ensure that the conveyance of allotments would not be interrupted by the refusal[40] of any Principal Chief to perform his duties (required

---

[36] Section 44 explicitly reconfirms the binding effect of prior treaties, except to the extent that they are inconsistent with the agreement. This of course includes treaties guaranteeing the Creeks the maximum self-government consistent with Congressional objectives. Treaty of 1856, 11 Stat. 699.

[37] The agreement was amended in 1902, 32 Stat. 500, 503, to require that the Secretary pay out per capita to all Creek citizens any tribal funds not needed for equalization of allotments, upon the final dissolution of the tribal government of the Creek Nation (§ 44).

[40] While Pleasant Porter, Principal Chief of the Creeks at the time of the passage of the act, had cooperated with federal authorities in this regard, it was possible in view of the remaining opposition to the dissolution of the tribes that a chief might be elected who would refuse to sign the deeds, thus halting the conveyance of allotments. Porter's predecessor, Isparhecher, was one such possibility. See Opler, "The Creek Indian Towns of Oklahoma in 1937," Papers in Anthropology, Vol. 13, No. 1, Spring 1972, pp. 46-49.

by section 23 of the 1901 agreement) of signing and delivering deeds, section 6 of the act provided:

"Sec. 6. That if the principal chief of the ... Creek ... tribe shall refuse or neglect to perform the duties devolving upon him, he may be removed from office by the President of the United States, or if any such executive become[s] permanently disabled, the office may be declared vacant by the President of the United States, who may fill any vacancy arising from *removal, disability* or *death* of the incumbent, by appointment of a citizen by blood of the tribe."

"If any such executive shall fail, refuse or neglect, for thirty days after notice that any instrument is ready for his signature, to appear at a place to be designated by the Secretary of the Interior and execute the same, such instrument may be approved by the Secretary of the Interior without such execution, and when so approved and recorded shall convey legal title, and such approval shall be conclusive evidence that such executive or chief refused or neglected after notice to execute such instrument ...." (Emphasis added.)

It is important to note that this section empowers the President to fill the office of principal chief in only three limited circumstances: the removal, disability, or death of the incumbent. It is quite clear from the circumstances in which the provision was enacted and from its legislative history that it was intended by the Congress simply to ensure that the office whose occupant was charged by statute with signing the allotment deeds would at all times be filled, and not to deprive the tribes of the right to continue electing their Principal Chiefs — under ordinary circumstances — as long as their tribal governments continued to exist.[41] Apart from the specified occurrences, the section provided no warrant or authority for Presidential appointment of a Principal Chief.[42]

---

[41] As originally drafted by the Department of the Interior, see Congressional Record, 59th Cong., 1st Sess., p. 1242 (Jan. 18, 1906), and approved by the House Committee, H. Rep't 183, 59th Cong., 1st Sess., p. 2, section 6 contemplated the continuance of the titular office of Principal Chief after the dissolution of the tribal government for the purpose of signing deeds and patents as required by the 1901 agreement. As reported to the House by the committee, the section would have provided in relevant part:

"Sec. 6. That the principal chiefs of the Choctaw, Cherokee, Creek, and Seminole tribes, and the governor of the Chickasaw tribe, recognized by the Secretary of the Interior at the time of the dissolution of the tribal governments, are hereby continued in office for the purpose of executing patents, deeds, and other conveyances affecting lands belonging to said tribes, respectively, and to represent the tribes in such matters as may be referred to them by the Secretary of the Interior...."

Congressional Record, *op. cit.*, p. 1250.

The section as drafted also contained the removal and appointment provisions appearing in the law finally enacted, in essentially the same form. As noted in the text below, it was decided during the debate of the bill not to dissolve the tribal governments, and § 28 was added to the bill to assure their continuance; this obviously necessitated a major change in the quoted draft provisions, and that change resulted in the final form of the section. Without the change in the intent of Congress, the tribal government of the Creeks would have been dissolved, and the President would have had the authority to perpetuate a nominal Principal Chief through the appointment authority, since the constitutional election process would have been eliminated in the dissolution of the tribal government and its underlying constitution. Because however the government was not to be dissolved, the Congress intended the appointment authority of the section to be used only when a vacancy arose in the Principal Chief's office resulting from removal, disability, or death of the incumbent (without timely replacement by tribal constitutional processes). The section was not intended therefore to have any impact on the normal constitutional process of election of the Creek Principal Chief as long as the constitutional tribal government continued to exist.

[42] Nor does the section provide the slightest support for the argument, made some years later by the Interior Department, that its real purpose and effect were to entirely supplant the Creek

The act also dealt in limited ways with the authority of the Creek Nation over its financial affairs. Section 10 in effect ratified the Secretary's earlier seizure of control over the tribal schools, directing that he run those schools until such time as either a Territorial or State school system was established which adequately provided for the education of Indian children. The section also limited the amount of tribal funds the Secretary could spend on the schools in any one year to that amount spent for the school year ending June 30, 1905.

Section 11 of the act provided as follows:

"Sec. 11. That all revenues of whatever character accruing to the ... tribes, whether before or after dissolution of the tribal governments, shall, after the approval hereof, be collected by an officer appointed by the Secretary of the Interior under rules and regulations to be prescribed by him; and he shall cause to be paid all lawful claims against said tribes which may have been contracted after July first, [1902], or for which warrants have been regularly issued, such payments to be made from any funds in the United States Treasury belonging to said tribes ... Provided, That all taxes accruing under tribal laws or regulation of the Secretary of the Interior shall be abolished from and after [Dec. 31, 1905], but this provision shall not prevent the collection after that date nor after the dissolution of the tribal government of all such taxes due up to and including [Dec. 31, 1905] ...."

The legislative history of this section indicates that it was intended to establish a mechanism to ensure the collection of revenues accruing to the tribes after the contemplated dissolution of the tribal governments, when there would be no tribal officer authorized to do so. The section had no effect on the tribes' authority to manage their financial affairs as long as the tribes were in existence; indeed, it implicitly confirmed that power by authorizing payment of tribal contracts and warrants. Also noteworthy is the recognition that until that time the tribes had retained the power of taxation; this provision, enacted at the urging of the white settlers in the Territory, does in effect modify the Creek constitution by abolishing the functions of the National Treasurer. That section 11 intended to make no further modification in the Creek government during the remaining period of its existence (originally expected by the bill's drafters to be relatively brief) is demonstrated by the second paragraph of the section, which requires any tribal officer or member in possession of tribal property to turn such property over to the Secretary upon *dissolution* of the tribal government.

Two other sections of the act, both in contemplation of the period after the dissolution of the tribal governments, affected Creek financial affairs. In section 24, Congress provided that any expenses incident to the establishment of public highways in the territory of any tribe be paid from tribal funds by the Secretary. Secondly, the act directed, in section 17, that after the financial affairs of any tribe had been wound up by the sale of any unallotted land or other property and the payment of any outstanding obligations, the Secretary should pay any remaining tribal funds to the members of the tribe on a per capita basis. This provision obviously presumed a prior dissolution of the tribe, since the tribal financial affairs could not be finally wound up until the tribe ceased to exist and

---

constitutional government and replace it with a "Principal Chief," serving at the pleasure of the President of the United States. As is clear from the legislative history discussed in note 41, *supra*, that result would only have been achieved by the Department had its original draft of section 6 survived the Congressional debates, which it did not. This legislative history makes quite clear that the combined effect of sections 6 and 28 as finally enacted was to continue indefinitely the Creek constitutional government and its underlying electoral processes.

function as such. In addition, the provision applied only to tribal assets involved in the allotment and division process; any assets accruing to the tribe at a later time would not appear to be within the ambit of the section. This construction is consistent with the fact that at the time the bill was drafted it was expected that the tribes would cease to exist as of March 4, 1906.

As Congress debated H.R. 5976 — which was to become the Five Tribes Act — in early 1906, it became apparent that it would be unable to complete legislative action on the bill before March 4th, the date set for tribal dissolution. There was great concern over the ramifications of tribal dissolution in the then-current state of affairs, particularly in regard to three problems. First, it was feared that if the tribal governments were dissolved without passage of the act, the tribal schools would cease to function. Secondly, in the absence of a Principal Chief the allotment process would be interrupted. Finally, it was feared that the dissolution of the tribes would cause the contingent grant of land made by the Congress immediately after the Treaty of 1866 to several railroad companies to vest in those companies by causing unallotted lands to become "public lands of the United States" upon the lapsing of tribal tenure. As a result, on March 2, 1906 Congress passed a joint resolution, 34 Stat. 822, extending the life of the tribes until the allotment and property distribution process had been completed, or until otherwise provided by Congress. Shortly thereafter, on April 26, the act itself became law, and it contained a provision which superseded the joint resolution. Section 28, added to the act (over the strenuous objections of the Secretary of the Interior) to avoid the problems posed by the dissolution of the tribes at that time, provided:

> "Sec. 28. That the tribal existence and present tribal governments of the Choctaw Chickasaw, Cherokee, Creek and Seminole tribes or nations are hereby continued in full force and effect for all purposes authorized by law, until otherwise provided by law, but the tribal council or legislature in any of said tribes or nations shall not be in session for a longer period than thirty days in any one year: *Provided*, That no act, ordinance, or resolution (except resolutions of adjournment) of the tribal council or legislature of any of said tribes or nations shall be of any validity until approved by the President of the United States: *Provided further*, That no contract involving the payment or expenditure of any money or affecting any property belonging to any of said tribes or nations made by them or any of them or by any officer thereof, shall be of any validity until approved by the President of the United States."

The legal effect of this provision was unmistakable: Congress had declined to terminate the tribal existence or dissolve the tribal governments, despite all of its earlier intentions to do so, and despite the fact that its failure to do so rendered some of the other provisions of the Five Tribes Act ineffective. While it was anticipated that the tribes would eventually be dissolved, the net effect of the act was to expressly preserve and ratify the then-existing authority of the tribal governments, while reiterating the necessity for Presidential approval of tribal legislation imposed earlier. That section 28 had the effect of continuing indefinitely the existence of the tribe has been confirmed by each court that has examined the question. The Supreme Court has explicitly held that the Creek Nation still exists, *Board of County Commissioners v. Seber*, 318 U.S. 705 (1943), *reh. den.*, 319 U.S. 782 (1943), and has described the effect of the act in these terms:

> "Congress at one time planned to terminate the existence of the Five Civilized Tribes in 1906, and the Act of 1906 was introduced into the House of Representatives with

the object of preserving Indian interests after tribal dissolution. In the course of discussion, Congress determined to continue the tribal existence, and the Act was amended to that effect before its passage."

Creek Nation v. United States, 318 U.S. 629, 638 (1943). Accord, *Creek Nation v. United States*, 78 Ct. Cl. 474, 493 (1933) ("While the ultimate dissolution of the tribal government was contemplated … its existence was continued, and thus the tribal government continued to exist and to function within the limits of its restricted jurisdiction and power during the period [through 1924]."); *Groundhog v. Keeler*, 442 F.2d 674 (CA 10, 1971).

Moreover, the Interior Department's later interpretations of this section as merely continuing in office the incumbent tribal officers while abolishing the Creek constitutional procedures for regularly filling those positions (and by logical implication therefore terminating the government itself when a sufficient number of those incumbents died or otherwise left office) is utterly untenable; such an interpretation conflicts with the legislative history and plain meaning of the section, see notes 41 and 42, *supra*. First, the March 2, 1906 joint resolution which initially extended the life of the tribal governments set as a termination date the completion of the distribution of the tribal estates. It would be illogical to assume (without any evidence whatever) that a provision which set a specific date for the total abolition of the tribal governments also *sub silentio* totally restructured those governments until that time; such a result would have been superfluous and would have served no discernible congressional purpose. And when even this termination date was removed from the extension section and replaced in section 28 of the final bill with provisions specifically allowing the functioning of that government, with certain specific limitations, the only reasonable conclusion to be reached is that — the final settlement of the tribal estates no longer appearing at all imminent — Congress concluded that the tribal governments should be continued into the indefinite future, with their functions limited by the proviso clauses of section 28. Secondly, the plain meaning of the words themselves point directly to that conclusion. It was the "present tribal governments" which were continued, not "incumbents" or "officers" or the like. This Court is also unaware of any instance in which the Congress has used the term "government" to mean particular individuals rather than the institution itself; given the connotations which have come to be associated with the term "government" in our political lexicon ("a government of laws, not of men"), a contrary meaning can hardly be imputed to the Congress. Nor is this conclusion undermined by the use of the adjective "present": that term is used to contrast the effect of § 28 with the situation which would have been occasioned by the failure to repeal the termination date. Moreover, accepted principles of statutory construction lead to the same conclusion. When Congress, enacting a provision specifically dealing with the continuing powers of an ongoing governing institution, reverses a determination to dissolve that institution but places express and particularized limitations on its activities, it cannot be taken to have intended to accomplish the drastically different result represented by viewing the provision as one continuing in office the incumbent officeholders and precluding their replacement through the normal processes of the institution, when those processes are wholly unmentioned in the legislation, directly or indirectly. For all these reasons, the Court can only conclude that the intent and effect of § 28 was to permit the Creek government to continue to operate under the 1867 constitution as modified by the various statutory limitations. In particular, the government remained competent to deal with tribal affairs relating to the distribution of the tribal estates and with other matters not relating to the allotment process.

During the period immediately following the approval of the Five Tribes Act, the Interior Department behaved as though it had been successful in its efforts to prevent the enactment of § 28 and the Congressional changes made in its draft of § 6. The available evidence[51] clearly reveals a pattern of action on the part of the Department and its Bureau Of Indian Affairs designed to prevent any tribal resistance to the Department's methods of administering those Indian affairs delegated to it by Congress. This attitude, which can only be characterized as bureaucratic imperialism, manifested itself in deliberate attempts to frustrate, debilitate, and generally prevent from functioning the tribal governments expressly preserved by § 28 of the Act.

In August 1907 the Creek National Council met for its usual session and passed a resolution calling the regular quadrennial election for Principal Chief and Second Chief. The attorney for the Creek Nation, who had been approved by and had heretofore worked closely with the Department, suggested that the Department advise the Principal Chief (Pleasant Porter, a leader of the faction resigned to cooperation with the Department in its effort to terminate the existence of the tribes) that what Congress really intended in the Five Tribes Act was to continue the present incumbents in office. Mott, the attorney, who was of course aware of the substantial body of sentiment in the tribe opposed to capitulation to the policy of tribal extinction, warned Commissioner of Indian Affairs Francis Leupp that if elections were held the result would be "bickering, confusion, and dissatisfaction," which would be "a source of annoyance and inconvenience to the Government." The Commissioner passed this advice on to the Secretary. Although the Commissioner apparently realized that the Creek National Council's resolution calling on the Principal Chief to call the election did not require approval of the department ("the resolution does not appear to require executive action"), he nevertheless suggests that the Chief be told that the Department "deems it inadvisable to take any action in the matter." The question was apparently referred by the Secretary to Assistant Attorney General George Woodruff, who naturally interpreted the Act as not restricting the tribe's power to hold its usual elections. This opinion was expressed in a letter to Chief Porter. In response to this advice, one of Assistant Attorney General Woodruff's subordinates, an attorney named Pollock who had been detailed to serve in the Department's Indian Territory field office at Muskogee, immediately wrote a letter back to Woodruff. In this letter he informed Woodruff that he himself had prepared an opinion holding that § 28 had continued "the form

---

[51] The primary source of evidence relevant to the events of this period, in addition to those sources already cited throughout this opinion, is the package of documents compiled by plaintiffs from the National Archives and the Federal Records Center in Suitland, Maryland, and submitted as exhibits to their Supplemental Memorandum In Support Of Motion For Summary Judgment, cited hereafter as "Pl. Mem. Exh."

of tribal government and not the personnel" in response to inquiries from the other four tribes. He relates that the Secretary had approved the opinion, but that after the intervention of Senator Curtis that approval was withdrawn.[55] The other four tribes were therefore advised that the Department had refused to express an opinion.[56] Pollock goes on to suggest that Woodruff had been unaware of the posture taken earlier by the Department with respect to the other four tribes, and he then recommends that the letter to Chief Porter be recalled and that Porter be advised that "the Department cannot offer any suggestions in the premises, or, perhaps better still, that there seems to be no necessity for such an election." In response to Woodruff's referral of Pollock's letter, Commissioner of Indian Affairs Leupp concedes to Woodruff that § 28 does appear to continue tribal offices rather than officers, but suggests that the Department should at any rate recognize the incumbents and give them "*de facto* standing." Events intervened however before the Department could act further when Chief Porter died suddenly a few days later. Seizing this opportunity to further frustrate the Creek constitutional government, Pollock immediately wired Leupp seeking prompt action. This wire vividly illustrates the true bases of the Department's actions during this period:

> "Anticipating effect death Chief Porter may have upon Snake faction [or] other recalcitrant Indians suggest importance department promptly appointing or recognizing his successor without specifically recognizing Creek law of succession. Same result would be accomplished by President appointing present second chief under section six [Five Tribes Act] thereby continuing present satisfactory administration which action we believe more expedient than a new election which would undoubtedly give strength to Snake movement."[58]

The Department accepted this advice and one day after the receipt of the telegram President Roosevelt appointed Moty Tiger, who as Second Chief of the Creek Nation would have succeeded to the office automatically under the Creek constitution, as Principal Chief. Thus the Department successfully preempted the constitutional processes of the tribe for its own purposes. While the use of the appointment power under these circumstances was of questionable legality, given the congressional intent that section 6 be used at the discretion of the President when necessary to allow allotment deeds to be signed, it nevertheless marked the beginning of the Department's usurpation of the power over selection of the Principal Chief of the Creek Nation. No Principal Chief was again to take office without federal appointment until 1971.[60]

Despite the Department's various attempts to undermine the functioning of the Creek government in 1906 and 1907, the Department continued to recognize the authority of the National Council over Creek funds, and the necessity for its approval before the Department could expend such funds for purposes

---

[55] Senator Curtis was of course the leading proponent of the tribal dissolution policies, had authored the Curtis Act, and had opposed the addition of § 28 to the Five Tribes Act.

[56] Taken as a whole, plaintiffs' exhibits strongly suggest the prevalence within the Department of a belief that if the law did not support the outcome sought by the Department, its objectives were nevertheless best served by refusing to divulge its interpretation and thereby maximizing the uncertainty with which tribal officials had to cope. Given the highly unsettled conditions of tribal affairs at the time, this expectation seems well-founded.

[58] [Among the Creek, the] Snake movement was the faction opposing tribal dissolution.

[60] The Presidential authority conferred by § 6 of the Five Tribes Act was delegated to the Secretary of the Interior by Executive Order No. 10250, 16 Federal Register 5358 (June 5, 1951).

not explicitly authorized by statute. The National Council had held a session subsequent to the appointment of Moty Tiger as Principal Chief, and in late November of 1907 the Department forwarded to the President for his approval (as required under § 28 of the Five Tribes Act) several pieces of legislation enacted by the National Council and approved by the Principal Chief. One of the Council's acts was "to provide for the continuation of the tribal government for the fiscal year ending December 4, 1908." The Secretary recommended the approval of the Council's appropriation of tribal funds for the operation of the government for the coming year. A few days later the Secretary also recommended approval of the Council's appropriation of funds to be paid to the Presbyterian Board of Home Missions, which ran the Nuyaka Creek Tribal Boarding School under contract with the tribe. The Board had made a claim against the tribe with the Secretary, and it is noteworthy that the Department had declined to pay the claim out of tribal funds without an express appropriation of the National Council. A few days later the Secretary recommended the approval of an act of the National Council abolishing the offices of National Auditor, Superintendent of Public Instruction, and Private Secretary to the Principal Chief, and creating the office of Executive Interpreter at an annual salary of $1500. And in early 1908, the Commissioner to the Five Civilized Tribes requested permission from the Secretary to pay a Creek general fund warrant, which he states is "properly drawn in accordance with the act of the Creek Council approved by the President," indicating the Department's continued recognition of the Council's authority over Creek funds and affairs. Nor did the Department seek to prevent the regular meeting of the Council in 1908. Subsequent to that meeting the Secretary recommended for Presidential approval an appropriation by the Council to pay the salary of the Executive Interpreter, the office created the previous year.

During this period there was a continued clamor from the white citizens of Oklahoma, which had achieved statehood on November 16, 1907 for Congress to finally wind up the affairs of the Five Tribes so that the development of the state could proceed unimpaired by the continuing rights of the Indians. In the Appropriations Acts of 1908 and 1909 (35 Stat. 70, 91; 35 Stat. 781, 804) the Secretary was directed to complete the work begun by the Dawes Commission by July 1, 1909 and 1910 respectively; because so much remained to be done, allotments in Creek lands continued at least until 1917, see 39 Stat. 969, 986, and the equalization program was still unfinished in 1921, see 41 Stat. 408, 426. Besides pushing the Department to finish the division of Creek lands, the Congress in the 1909 Appropriations Act attempted to complete the Creek equalization program by directing the Secretary to make equalization payments from Creek funds. Congress set eight hundred dollars as the basic value of each allotment, and stipulated that the equalization payments made under this provision should be regarded as conclusive settlement of all Creek equalization claims. The provision also recognized the continuing authority of the Creek government in fiscal and tribal matters, making approval of the National Council a condition precedent for these conclusive equalization payments. 35 Stat.

781, 805.[66] This special session of the National Council was held for six days beginning on April 19, 1909. Responding to widespread dissatisfaction with the low value set by Congress as the basis for equalization of allotments, the Council rejected the Congressional scheme. An appropriation act passed by the Council to cover certain expenses of the session was nevertheless approved by the President.

By late 1909 the Department had made considerable progress in demoralizing the Creek government. It had refused to permit elections to be held to fill vacancies on the Council, and had convinced Chief Moty Tiger that he could not call regular sessions of the Council without Department approval. Consistent with earlier and continuing BIA efforts to ensure that any Creek government be subservient to Bureau wishes, this marked the genesis of the strategy of dealing with the Principal Chief as though he were the sole repository of Creek governmental authority. As 1909 continued, however, the Council became concerned about the apparent subversion of its legal authority, and when Tiger failed to call the regular fall session of the Council, its members and other tribal leaders met in a rump session (which they termed the "Creek Convention") and passed a resolution demanding that the Council be convened. Tiger, who appears to have fulfilled the Department's expectation that he would be compliant with its wishes, simply referred the matter to the Commissioner to the Five Civilized Tribes. The Commissioner ultimately forwarded his response to the Secretary of the Interior, and that response illustrates the Bureau's developing attitude: in response to part of the Convention's resolution asserting that the Council had a legal right to meet and to represent Creek citizens, the Commissioner stated that if "there is any matter, however, which should be brought to the attention of Congress or the Department, *it could be done by the Principal Chief* in a communication or personally and the same would receive prompt attention." (Emphasis added.) After explaining why he considered it unnecessary for the Council to meet at that time, without commenting on the Creek claim that the Council was legally entitled to convene, the Commissioner recommended to the Secretary that he be authorized "to advise the Principal Chief that at any time when he deems it necessary he can submit a request for authority giving specific reasons therefor and the same will receive careful consideration." This situation continued for several years, with the Creek leaders and Council members calling for meetings of the Council and the Bureau assuming the authority for denying permission for such meetings to be held. In each case the leadership pointed to the continuing problems with and resistance to the allotment program, as well as the unsettled equalization issue, and asserted the right of the Council to deal with these problems (as well as others), and in each case the Bureau took the attitude that a meeting was unnecessary and that the Council need not deal with these matters.

One of the principal complaints made by the rump Creek Convention of 1909 was that "funds belonging to the Creek Nation are being disbursed without the knowledge or consent of the Creek Council, as provided for in the Agreement." The Bureau's response was to rationalize its expenditures as implicitly autho-

---

[66] The provision also authorized the Secretary to specify the duration of the special session of the Council which would be necessary to ratify the equalization scheme by limiting compensation to that length of time.

rized by the 1901 agreement and the Secretary's disbursement responsibility. This response typifies the attitude that had angered the tribe, a belief in the Bureau that it could charge off to tribal funds without the consent of the tribe any expenditure related in any way to the administration of Creek affairs. The Convention's complaint also reflects dissatisfaction with the actual administration of Creek financial transactions, which since the Curtis Act[,] had been so disorganized that it was impossible to distinguish between increments to and payments from tribal versus federal funds. When the Indian Territory first secured representation in Congress, a Cherokee citizen, Robert L. Owen, then a member of the U.S. Senate, managed to win passage for a resolution directing the Secretary of the Interior to prepare a statement of his administration of the Five Tribes' finances for the ten year period following the Curtis Act. This report was published in 1909, and it confirmed the accusations of the Indians that their funds were not being handled properly. Indeed, the Creeks were ultimately awarded more than $144,000 as a result of mishandling and illegal expenditures of their funds.[74] As a result of the obvious abuse by the Secretary of his control over tribal disbursements, the Oklahoma delegation in 1912 was able to secure the passage of a provision in the appropriation bill for that year restricting the Secretary's authority to make disbursements from tribal funds, except for certain limited purposes, without Congressional authorization. 37 Stat. 518, 531. This restriction was re-enacted in each appropriations bill thereafter, until 1922, when it was made permanent.

By 1914, Congress was again ready to deal with the issue of equalization of Creek allotments. In the appropriation act of that year, 38 Stat. 582, 598, 601, Congress again set the value of allotments at $800, and again called for a special session of the Creek National Council.[75] While the record is unclear as to what action the Council took with respect to the equalization provisions in the 1914 act, it appears not to have ratified the $800 value, holding out instead for a value of $1040 (the value set by the Creek Agreement of 1901) and in 1918 Congress directed that all but $150,000 of Creek Tribal funds be paid out per capita to members of the tribe for equalization purposes. 40 Stat. 561, 580. The 1914 session of the National Council also passed several other acts, one of which made it illegal for a member of the Council to consume alcoholic beverages. This act was transmitted by the Commissioner to the Five Tribes for his superiors, but was not transmitted to the President for approval apparently because of an expectation within the Department that the Council would not meet again.[76] The Council did meet again, however, in 1916. Although the Bureau had not authorized a meeting, Chief Tiger did call the Council into session in December of that year. One of the Council's principal actions at that session was the passage of a resolution requiring Chief Tiger to appoint a delegation to accompany him to Washington to consult with the Department. The resolution was transmitted to the Secretary's office, which responded that the resolution would not be submitted to the President for approval and that the session was

---

[74] *Creek Nation v. United States*, 78 Ct. Cl. 474 (1933).

[75] As was the case in 1909, the act also directed the Secretary to fix the length of the session and the reimbursement to be paid to the members attending the meeting.

[76] Pl. Mem. Exh. 19 notes that "no further action [on the act] necessary as last meeting of Creek National Council to be held."

unauthorized. In this response the Department stated that it had the authority
to prohibit Council meetings altogether by virtue of the provisions in the 1909
appropriation act, which allowed the Secretary to limit reimbursement of Council members for expenses for the 1909 special session to a fixed number of days.
This contention, which was apparently never raised either before this letter or
subsequently for at least fifteen years, is wholly without legal foundation. The
provision cited was clearly intended to deal only with the 1909 special session,
and the Department's assertion is belied by the legislative history of the 1909
act.[78] Moreover, even had the provision given the Secretary the general power
to determine whether or not to reimburse Council members for other meetings,
such a power would in no way have permitted him to forbid the Council to meet
at all. This response can only be viewed therefore as a further example of the
Department's failure to make a conscientious effort to adhere to the provisions
of law in dealing with the Five Tribes, a failure reflecting the belief that because
the tribes were unable to force the Department to recognize their legal rights
the Department could therefore proceed as it considered best. This pragmatic
approach succeeded in at least one respect: there is no further record of any
meeting of the Creek National Council after 1916.

Despite the efforts of the Department, however, the Creeks refused to abandon their tribal government and political life. When it became apparent that the
National Council could no longer have new members elected or convene in
regular session, the "Creek Convention" which had begun meeting around 1909
gained increased vitality and began to assume the former role of the Council.
Because the Creek tribal town structure remained strong, the Convention was
able to provide a forum for the discussion and resolution of Creek affairs quite
similar to that originally provided by the Council. In 1921 it was known as the
"Creek Mass Meeting," and by 1923 as the "Creek General Convention." A
majority of the tribal towns were apparently represented in its meetings, some
by National Council members and others by other newly elected representatives
of the towns (because no new election of National Council members had been
permitted, many were either old or dead by that time). The Convention continued to meet regularly and function for decades thereafter, and can effectively
be regarded as the successor in function to the National Council.

The surviving members of the National Council itself continued throughout
the 1920's to request permission for the Council to meet. Those requests were
denied for the usual reasons, and the Department also added that the restrictions on the Secretary's disbursements, originally enacted in 1912 and made
permanent subsequently, prevented his authorization of any Council session or
disbursements for reimbursement of expenses of members. The irony of this
suggestion is profound; here the Secretary twists a limitation enacted by Congress for the benefit of the tribes and as a result of his own gross mismanagement of tribal funds into a restriction instead on the tribes themselves. The
irony is magnified by the Secretary's own reversal of position a few years later

---

[78] Both the House and the Senate reports on the appropriation bills in 1909 state that the affairs
of the Five Tribes cannot be wound up in the immediate future, and that the committee intends to
address matters at issue with respect to the tribes in a bill later that session. The bill was therefore
not intended to make any such major changes with respect to the tribes. S. Rept. No. 1036, 60th
Cong., 2d Sess., at 8; H. Rept. No. 1897, 60th Cong., 2d Sess.

when, in defense of a suit by the Creeks to recover moneys illegally expended, he asserted his authority to make any disbursements related to tribal government. Indeed, the Court of Claims held in that suit that none of those restrictions limited use of tribal funds for expenses of the tribal governments, including those of council members. *Creek Nation v. United States*, 78 Ct. Cl. 474, 493-494. In short, the Department's assertion that no legal authority existed for a meeting of the Creek National Council was as unfounded in 1928 as it had been twenty years earlier.

The Creek Convention met regularly during the early 1930's, and on October 26, 1933 it passed a resolution calling upon the Commissioner of Indian Affairs to permit an election for the officers of Principal Chief and Second Chief. The new Commissioner, John Collier, was considerably more sympathetic than his predecessors to Indian desires for self-determination, and granted permission for the election to be held. The Convention met in June of 1934 and adopted rules and procedures for the election. Forty-two tribal towns participated in the election, and the winner, Roly Canard, was appointed Principal Chief by the President. During the subsequent four years (the constitutional period of office of a Principal Chief), the Convention and Chief functioned much as the Council and Chief had earlier, even forwarding to the Department resolutions for approval.

The assumption of office of the Roosevelt administration marked a temporary shift in federal Indian policy. Realizing that the prior allotment and assimilation policy had been a disaster, Secretary Ickes and Commissioner Collier secured the passage in 1934 of the Wheeler-Howard Act, 48 Stat. 984. The Supreme Court has described the Act as reflecting "a change in policy, the theory of which is that Indians can better meet the problems of modern life through corporate, group, or tribal action, rather than as assimilated individuals." *Board of County Commissioners v. Seber, supra* at 716, n. 20. The central provisions of the Act ended allotments in severalty, allowed the re-establishment of communal lands, and permitted the organization of tribal governments with control over tribal funds. As a result of the efforts of the Oklahoma delegation, however, these provisions were inapplicable to the Five Civilized Tribes. In 1936 Congress passed the Oklahoma Indian Welfare Act, 49 Stat. 1967, permitting Oklahoma Indians to take advantage of most of the provisions of the 1934 Wheeler-Howard Act. The Creek Nation has not — before the present time — attempted to organize under the provisions of the 1936 Act, and it is not at issue in this case.[87]

At the end of Chief Canard's customary four-year term, permission was again sought and obtained for an election to fill the office of Principal Chief. At the election of January 3, 1939, Alex Noon was elected to the post; he was subsequently appointed by the President. It appears from Secretary Ickes' letter to the President recommending the appointment that the Department had at this time begun to recognize the Creek Convention as the legislative body of the tribe; the Convention at this time was functioning much as the Council had

---

[87] The parties agree that the only relevance of the Act to the issues herein is that it provides an independent basis under which the Creek Nation could have organized subsequent to its passage; no contention is made that the Act had any effect on the status of the Creek National Government under existing law, nor does the Court find any such effect.

earlier. On January 27, 1944 the Creek General Convention met and, with twenty-four tribal towns represented by delegates, adopted a "Constitution and By-Laws." This "constitution," which had been years in drafting by Convention committees, essentially formalized the procedures which had evolved in the Convention for conducting the tribe's business. It made the Convention and the Principal Chief together the supreme governing authority of the tribe, with the delegates to the convention to be elected from the forty-four original tribal towns. A Business Committee was created to conduct the business of the tribe at the time when the Convention was not in session, subject to the Convention's direction. The Principal Chief was given the role of representing the tribe in any matters in which he was given authority to do so by law, by lawful regulations of the Interior Department, or by direction of the Convention. The constitution also provided that it was not to be construed in any way to alter, abridge, or otherwise jeopardize the rights and privileges of any member of the tribe. The constitution also changed the name of the supreme governing body (the former Convention and the Chief together) to the Creek Indian Council. The body was thereafter known more or less interchangeably as either the Creek Indian Council or as the Creek General Convention.

The 1944 Constitution, which in general represented a continuation of the Creek pattern of self-government that had evolved over the course of more than a century, was forwarded to the Department of the Interior by the Superintendent of the Five Civilized Tribes. He noted that the tribe was not attempting to organize under the Oklahoma Indian Welfare Act, but was rather creating a structure for conducting tribal affairs. The Superintendent also forwarded the Council's request for an appropriation of Creek funds for the expenses of the tribal government. In reply, the office of the Commissioner of Indian Affairs stated that no funds would be approved for a tribal organization which was not approved under the provisions of the Act, and pointed out that the new constitution could not be approved under the Act because the new governing document excluded the freedmen from membership in the tribe without having given them an opportunity to vote on that provision. The Bureau therefore did not act to make the funds available, and explicitly refused to give any official sanction to the new constitution. The Creeks however did not regard Departmental approval as such necessary for the adoption of the constitution, and therefore continued to operate the Creek Indian Council and Creek government pursuant to its provisions, without seeking further action by the Department. In 1945, the tribe again requested that tribal funds be made available for the operation of the Council, and the Bureau consented with the caveat that its consent not be construed as approval of the constitution. By the following year, the Bureau was prepared to state that "the Creek General Convention … has been recognized by this Office as having authority to speak for the tribe" and that the Convention "has acted as the official governing body of the Tribe" since 1924. The Creek General Convention or Indian Council continued to function under the format and procedures of the 1944 constitution through 1951, and during that period was recognized by the Department as the competent legislative authority of the tribe.

The vigor and liveliness of Creek political life, evident throughout the tribe's post-Revolutionary War history, did not abate with the Department's successful destruction of the Creek National Council during the first two decades of the twentieth century. As noted earlier, there were continual demands that the Council be convened and incessant debate about the unsettled state of tribal affairs. During the following three decades the venerable Creek tradition of political debate and factionalism was not cowed by adversity, as significant segments of the tribe rejected the policies of the Interior Department, the legitimacy of the General Convention, and the handling of tribal affairs by the Principal Chiefs and the Convention. One faction in fact continued to demand that the federal government honor its treaty and statutory obligations to the tribe, particularly with regard to tribal funds. Indeed, as late as 1946, Joseph Bruner, who had been elected to the old House of Kings in the National Council more than forty years earlier, wrote to the Secretary demanding that the Department cease its expenditure of tribal funds for the expenses of the General Convention, citing the original Creek Agreement and the Five Tribes Act. In response, the Department stated that it recognized the General Convention as the tribe's official governing body, despite the feelings of the tribal members associated with the Bruner faction. The response also cites the current appropriation act of the Department as authority for the expenditure of tribal funds for the Convention's expenses, under a provision allowing such expenditures for the expenses of tribal governing bodies, but fails to cite any legal authority for regarding the Convention as the Creeks' governing body. Ironically, this response reflects the same Bureau of Indian Affairs practice — deciding what policy was to be and only then "justifying" it by reference to the governing statutes — that was used earlier in the century to prevent a Creek legislature from functioning.

The factionalism that had been brewing throughout the 1940's came to a head after the election in 1950 of John Davis as Principal Chief, and his appointment to that position by the Secretary of the Interior. Davis was appointed on January 2, 1951, approximately six months early, due to the death of Chief Roly Canard shortly after Davis' election in October of 1950. Immediately upon taking office, Chief Davis declared that the credentials of the members of the newly-elected session of the Creek Indian Council or General Convention were improper or irregular, and thereafter refused to recognize that body as authoritative in any respect. Davis repudiated the 1944 constitution, and immediately appointed members of the various tribal towns as a new Creek Indian Council. As might be expected, Chief Davis' actions caused a furor in the tribe. The rival (elected) Council refused to accept his actions as legitimate, and continued to meet throughout Davis' first four-year term as Principal Chief. The Bureau of Indian Affairs, however, finding Davis and his Council to its liking, backed his actions, advising the many members of the tribe who attempted to have his actions nullified by the Bureau that since under section 6 of the Five Tribes Act the Principal Chief was the sole embodiment of tribal authority, Davis had the power to abolish the elective Creek Indian Council — which the Bureau regarded as merely advisory anyway — and replace it with an appointed Council to advise him. When members of the elected Council filed suit in the Okfuskee County District Court to set aside Chief Davis' actions, the court sustained the Bureau's position and refused to interfere with the functioning of Davis' Council, ruling instead that the elected Council was without authority over tribal affairs and that the Council appointed by Chief Davis had been recognized by the Bureau and was the official Creek council. This appointive council was then designated as the Creek Tribal Council, and the Bureau continued to deal with it instead of with the Creek Indian Council. The Creek Indian Council nevertheless continued to hold its regular sessions for the four-year terms of its members (ending in 1955), and apparently considered itself the representative primarily of the full-blood and restricted Creeks. Although the Court is without substantial information on this point, it appears that the Creek Indian Council as such ceased meeting at some point in the late 1950's. Since the appointment of the Creek Tribal Council by Chief Davis in the early 1950's, it appears that all the subsequent Councils have been appointed by the Principal Chiefs and have served in a progressively more advisory than legislative capacity with respect to the conduct of tribal affairs by the Principal Chief and the Bureau.

Despite the avalanche of criticism of Chief Davis' handling of tribal affairs, the Bureau continued to be pleased with his administration, and refused to undermine his position. The Bureau, which by the end of Davis' term in 1955 had once again reversed its policy and now favored termination of Indian tribes, had however begun to examine the possibility that the office of Principal Chief should be terminated or should be occupied on a part-time basis, and was also considering the possibility of eliminating any further elections of the Chiefs. As a result of this study and the prevailing philosophy of the Bureau at that time, the Bureau subsequently decided to appoint the Principal Chiefs without the benefit of any election by the tribe. Until 1970, therefore, the affairs of the Creeks were administered without even a token of democracy, and the Principal Chief was treated by the Bureau as being the sole embodiment of the Creek governmental authority. As is evident from the foregoing, the influence and control of the Bureau over the various incarnations of the Creek national government between 1920 and 1970 was exercised wholly without the benefit of any specific Congressional mandate. As such, it constitutes no support whatever for the defendants' position in this suit, and indeed the history of the period demonstrates the continued vitality and resilience of Creek political life and institutions, fatally undermining defendants' claim that the Creek political infrastructure is incapable of discharging the functions plaintiffs assert should be discharged by a Creek legislative institution.

The fourth and final piece of legislation critical to the resolution of plaintiffs' claims was enacted in 1970. The Act of October 22, 1970, 84 Stat. 1091, came at a time when federal Indian policy had once again reversed itself, this time in favor of tribal self-government. The Act provides:

> "*Be it enacted by the Senate and House of Representatives of the United States of America in Congress assembled,* That, notwithstanding any other provisions of law, the principal chiefs of the Cherokee, Choctaw, Creek, and Seminole Tribes of Oklahoma and the governor of the Chickasaw Tribe of Oklahoma shall be popularly selected by the respective tribes in accordance with procedures established by the officially recognized tribal spokesman and/or governing entity. Such established procedures shall be subject to approval by the Secretary of the Interior.
>
> "Sec. 2. The Secretary of the Interior or his representative is hereby authorized to assist, upon request, any of such officially recognized tribal spokesman and/or governing entity in the development and implementation of such procedures.

"Sec. 3. A principal officer selected pursuant to section 1 of this Act shall be duly recognized as the principal chief, or in the case of the Chickasaw Tribe, the governor, of that tribe.

"Sec. 4. Any principal officer currently holding office at the date of enactment of this Act shall continue to serve for a period not to exceed twelve months or until expiration of his most recent appointment, whichever is shorter, unless an earlier vacancy arises from resignation, disability, or death of the incumbent, in which case the office of principal chief or governor may be filled at the earliest possible date in accordance with section 1 of this Act.

"Sec. 5. Nothing in this Act shall prevent any such incumbent referred to in section 4 of this Act from being elected as a principal chief or governor."

The defendants concede that the Act makes no mention of the powers of the Principal Chiefs, and that its provisions do not explicitly alter the existing legal situation. The Department does argue, however, that the legislative history of the Act "shows that Congress was made aware of the fact that affairs of the Five Civilized Tribes were being administered by Principal Chiefs and a Governor," and that Congress therefore intended to abolish the underlying legal authority for a constitutional government and to ratify the present form of Creek tribal government.

The defendants' argument is logically and legally without foundation. First, it seems obvious that a bill whose purpose was to increase the autonomy and self-government of the tribe would hardly have done so by *sub silentio* dismantling an existing form of government which provided more self-government than the scheme allegedly to be substituted. Such an intent cannot be presumed without a clear indication in the legislative history. In construing the statute and its legislative history, two cardinal principles must be observed. First, in order to ratify an originally erroneous administrative interpretation of earlier legislation, Congress must give express consideration or make specific reference to the question at issue in the later legislation. [In the record there] must be some clear indication that Congress intended to alter an existing legal situation. Secondly, implied repeal is not a favored tenet of construction, and the court must try to give effect to earlier legislation which has not been expressly repealed. [T]his general presumption against implied repeal applies with special force where the established legal rights of Indians under federal legislation or treaties is involved. *Mattz v. Arnett*, 412 U.S. 481 (1972); *Choate v. Trapp*, 224 U.S. 665 (1912); *Jones v. Meehan*, 175 U.S. 1 (1899). The fact that Congress may have been "made aware of the fact that affairs of the Five Civilized Tribes were being administered by Principal Chiefs and a Governor," defendants' sole statutory interpretation argument, is therefore legally insufficient in the circumstances of this case to establish a repeal of the tribes' right to constitutional self-government in favor of a one-man elected monarchy.

Even beyond the impact of these canons of construction however is the legislative history itself, which clearly shows that Congress was unaware of any controversy or question with regard to the legal form of Creek tribal government, and in fact intended to deal only with the narrow issue of the method of selection of the Principal Chief. That legislative history shows moreover that the fundamental congressional judgment underlying the Act was a desire to facilitate tribal self-determination to the maximum extent possible. Of particular significance in this regard is the congressional decision to amend the bill, removing the original requirement that the Principal Chiefs or Governors be "elected," and replacing it with the term "popularly selected." As the House Committee explained, the members felt it "would be unwise to impose on the tribes by statute a mandatory requirement that the principal officers must be popularly elected. The choice of the method of selecting the principal officers should be left to the tribes themselves." H. Rep't. No. 91-1499, 91st Cong., 2d Sess. It seems obvious that the congressional attitude reflected by this explanation is wholly incompatible with the intention to actually limit the tribes' existing legal authority to determine their form of government which the defendants would have the Court imply into the Act. The purpose of the bill was rather, as the committee report puts it, simply "to permit the members of the Five Civilized Tribes of Oklahoma to select their own principal chiefs or governor." *Id.*

Finally, the House committee's own description of the legal situation to which the bill was addressed precludes any inference that it was intended to terminate the existence of or deal in any way with the legislative branch of the tribal governments. The committee's report described the situation as follows:

> "The Act of April 26, 1906 (34 Stat. 137) was intended to provide for a final disposition of the affairs of the Five Civilized Tribes. While the Act severely limited the authorities of the principal officers,[111] it recognized their continuing authority to dispose of tribal property. Section 6 of the act authorizes the President of the United States to remove these officers should they refuse to perform their duties under the act. The President is also authorized to fill any vacancy arising from removal, disability, or death by the appointment of a citizen by blood of the tribe. The President delegated his authority to the Secretary of the Interior in Executive Order No. 10250, dated June 5, 1951."

The Departmental report accompanying the committee report refers to the chiefs' functions in disposing of tribal property as "certain ministerial functions." It is clear therefore that the committee was only addressing itself to the impact of the 1906 Five Tribes Act upon the authority of the principal chiefs. The ministerial duties referred to are of course the signing and conveyance of allotment deeds. This partial description of the effect of the 1906 act does not even touch upon the effect of section 28 of that act on the role of the tribal legislatures, which were expressly preserved by that section. And since section 6 of the Five Tribes Act had no connection with the authority of the tribal legislatures, the House committee's reference to that section and to the act's impact on the role of the principal chiefs cannot be taken as dealing with the issue of the authority of tribal legislatures at all. For these reasons, the Court holds that the 1970 Act had no effect on the legal authority of the legislative branch of the Creek national government, and that under federal and Creek law the Creek national legislature retains the authority to make the initial decision controlling the expenditure of Creek funds for tribal purposes.

IV. *Conclusion*

The plaintiffs' claim in this case has been that the federal defendants, through their policies and practices, have acted illegally in recognizing the Prin-

---

[111] It appears to the Court that the term "principal officer" is used throughout the bill and report instead of simply "principal chief" because the chief of the Chickasaw tribe is known as "governor." The phrase "principal officers" has no relation whatever to the legislative branch of the tribal governments.

cipal Chief as the sole embodiment of the government in the Creek Nation, and that according to existing federal and Creek law tribal funds may not be disbursed by the federal defendants for general tribal purposes without the approval of the Creek national legislature. The federal defendants' responsive argument has been that either the Creek national government has, by Congressional action, been rendered incompetent to handle the tribe's financial decisionmaking, or in the alternative that Congress in enacting a 1970 law stripping the Interior Department of any power to appoint the Principal Chief of the tribe somehow impliedly abolished the entire federal and tribal legal scheme theretofore defining the form and scope of the tribal government.

The defendants' first argument has withstood neither logical, historical, nor legal analysis. If the Creek government had been rendered incapable of allocating its own funds, then the Interior Department would have been unable to implement or justify the policy which has in fact most recently been in force, i.e., recognition of the Principal Chief as the embodiment of Creek government responsible for and capable of making those decisions. By its very policies the Department demonstrates that a functioning and competent Creek government in fact continues to exist; the historical record demonstrates moreover that a competent legislative-executive government has persisted throughout more than half a century of the most adverse conditions imaginable. Indeed, plaintiffs do not challenge the Department's recognition that a functioning Creek government continues to exist, but rather contend that by law the Department may not confine its recognition of that government solely to one of its constituent institutions, the Principal Chief. Therefore the Department's argument that the Creek government has been rendered incompetent to handle Creek affairs is logically irreconcilable with its actual policies and practices, and must fall on that ground alone. However even had the defendants argued — as they have not in this Court, despite the use of such arguments by the Department over the course of the preceding seventy years — that Congress had somehow replaced the Creek constitutional form of government with an imposed government consisting of the Principal Chief, their position would have been legally and historically unsupportable. For such an argument to prevail, the Congress would have had to both terminate the authority of the Creek National Council to initially determine the tribal purposes for which Creek funds would be spent and also to invest the Principal Chief with that authority. Congress undoubtedly has the power to do any of those things, or to terminate the existence of the tribe entirely. However, because such an abolition of the Creek constitutional government would have been tantamount to a total repudiation of the tribe's right, solemnly guaranteed to it by treaty after treaty, to determine its own form of organization and government — and indeed a final repudiation of tribal sovereignty itself — familiar principles of statutory construction in general and of interpretation of federal Indian law in particular mandate that such congressional action be clear and explicit; where the statutes and their legislative histories fail to clearly establish such an intent, the Court may not supply one by judicial interpretation. As the Supreme Court recently noted, courts "are not obligated in ambiguous circumstances to strain to implement [an assimilationist] policy Congress has now rejected, particularly where to do so will interfere with the present congressional approach to what is after all, an ongoing relationship." *Bryan v. Itasca County*, 426 U.S. 373, at 388, n.14 (1976), citing with approval *Santa Rosa Band of Indians v. Kings County*, 532 F.2d 655 (C.A. 9, Nov. 3, 1975); the Court also goes on to indicate that present federal policy has returned to an intention to strengthen tribal self-government. *Id.*

This is not, in any event, a case of statutory ambiguity. As this Court's examination of the relevant statutes and history makes clear, not only did Congress not terminate the sovereign status of the tribe, it expressly reaffirmed that status. Nothing in the Acts of 1898, 1901, and 1906 or any other legislation abolished the Creek National Council or stripped it of its power to determine the uses to which tribal funds are to be put, except with respect to certain mandatory expenditures and uses connected with the allotment and equalization program, and with the abolition of the tribe's territorial jurisdiction in the process of organizing the Indian Territory for statehood. These limitations have long since become irrelevant to tribal affairs, leaving the elected legislature created by the 1867 constitution (and effectively re-established at least twice thereafter) the authoritative body for initial allocation of tribal funds. While Congress has limited the overall duration of legislative sessions in any one year, and has explicitly specified the procedures through which such legislative actions become final, it has equally explicitly recognized and preserved the authority of the national legislature and the basic form of government established by the 1867 constitution.

A necessary corollary to that conclusion is that Congress has not replaced that form of government with a government consisting exclusively of the Principal Chief. This conclusion is not only a logical necessity, but is also the only conclusion possible after an examination of the relevant statutes and history. None of those statutes had either the intent or the effect of investing the Principal Chief with the authority to determine the purposes to which tribal funds should be put; that he has now come to perform that function results wholly from the Interior Department-Bureau of Indian Affairs' determined use of its raw power over the tribe to bring about that result. And finally, for the reasons stated in the Court's earlier discussion of the issue, the Act of 1970 carried with it no congressional intent to abolish the existing legal situation and to replace it with government by Principal Chief alone.

In conclusion, plaintiffs have asked the Court to vindicate certain legal rights guaranteed them by solemn promises of the United States, given over the course of a century and a half. While the credibility of these promises has been gravely undermined by various federal actions, culminating in the abolition of the tribe's territorial sovereignty, the essence of those promises, that the tribe has the right to determine its own destiny, remains binding upon the United States, and federal policy in fact now recognizes self-determination as the guiding principle of Indian relations. Plaintiffs' claim is, at bottom, simply an assertion of their right to democratic self-government, a concept not wholly alien to American political thought. Plaintiffs have demonstrated a clear legal entitlement to have these rights vindicated, and the Court cannot honorably do otherwise.

V. *Relief*

Like most other aspects of this case, the fashioning of appropriate equitable relief is a complex matter. The premise from which the Court must begin is that the basic legal framework governing the management of Creek tribal affairs, financial and otherwise, is the Creek Constitution of 1867. As the foregoing discussion makes clear, under the 1867 Constitution and the relevant federal law, the expenditures of tribal funds which the federal defendants now make and permit to be made under the authority of the Principal Chief may not be legally made without the assent of a Creek national legislature. There is, however, no such legislature in existence today, nor has there been any such legislature as contemplated by the 1867 constitution since about 1916.[113] As a result, the Court must devise some mechanism for the restoration of legality to the administrative and disbursement operations of the federal defendants, which necessarily requires the re-establishment of a constitutional Creek government including a national legislature. At the same time, it would be highly anomalous in a case in which the underlying claim is one of self-determination for the Court to vindicate that right by simply mandating the creation of some particular sort of institution or government. It follows then that the re-creation of the constitutional Creek government should be accomplished by the Creeks themselves.

[The court discussed a proposed constitution being developed under Chief Cox's auspices. The Court noted that many of the provisions appeared to be the product of consensus among the varying factions, but that the proposed constitution deviated in three important respects from the traditional Creek government: 1) it did not provide for the traditional office of Second Chief; 2) the proposed legislature was unicameral rather than bicameral, and 3) election to the council would be from geographic districts instead of from the traditional tribal towns. In addition, the court concluded that even though the proposed constitution had been approved by the BIA it did not meet the formal requirements of the 1867 Constitution that any new constitution be approved by the national legislature. Since no such legislature existed the court devised a system in which the three major areas of remaining controversy could be submitted to tribal members themselves as the ultimate source of authority in a popular referendum. To implement the vote, the court created a five-person tribal commission with two persons to be selected by the plaintiffs, two by the Principal Chief, and one to be selected unanimously by the other four.]

The Court believes that the mechanism described herein can and will function with a minimum of difficulty and with considerable effectiveness. If the parties to this lawsuit, the members of the tribe, and the members of the commission can work together in a spirit of harmony and cooperation, the Court has no doubt that the political resourcefulness and resiliency exhibited for so long by the Creek Nation will finally enable the tribe to remove the uncertainty that has for so long dominated its political life and recapture the cherished self-determination that is its legal and moral right. The United States has given its word; the promise must be kept.

NOTES

1. Introduction: The *Harjo* case summarizes the structure and history of the Creek Nation after Congress sought to suspend the national government as part

---

[113] The present "Creek National Council" is neither elected pursuant to nor functions according to the 1867 constitution. It is essentially an advisory council evolved from Chief Davis' Tribal Council of the 1950's.

of the breakup of the Indian territory and the creation of the state of Oklahoma. The experiences of most of the Five Civilized Tribes (Cherokee, Choctaw, Creek, Chickasaw, and Seminole) and the Osage in eastern Oklahoma were similar, although important differences exist in the agreements and statutes implementing the allotment of the lands for these tribes. More importantly, in the later nineteenth and early twentieth century Congress saw these tribes as possessing important wealth and as being far along the road to civilization. It therefore sought to break up the reservations and, to a more limited extent, the tribal operations of these tribes in ways that surpassed the efforts undertaken at the same time outside eastern Oklahoma. Indeed, the tribes in the western sections of Oklahoma did not share the same experiences and their legal status and tribal operations are similar to tribes found outside of the state of Oklahoma. As a result, the tribes of eastern Oklahoma have had somewhat unique experiences. The following notes are primarily intended to briefly summarize some of the unique legal aspects generated by this special history. *See generally* Pipestem & Rice, *The Mythology of the Oklahoma Indians*, 6 AM. INDIAN L. REV. 259 (1978); Work, *The "Terminated" Five Tribes of Oklahoma: The Effect of Federal Legislation and Administrative Treatment on the Court of the Seminole Nation*, 6 AM. INDIAN L. REV. 81 (1978).

   2. Indian Country in Eastern Oklahoma: From statehood until 1978, it was often wrongly assumed that there was no Indian country for purposes of criminal jurisdiction in Oklahoma. The root of this false assumption was the decision in *Ex parte Nowabbi*, 61 P.2d 1139 (Okla. Crim. App. 1936). In *Nowabbi* the Oklahoma Court of Criminal Appeals found that Oklahoma allotments were not Indian country in which federal law would apply. Rather, the court held that the state of Oklahoma had criminal jurisdiction over allotments. The court reasoned that state law would apply in the absence of contrary provisions by Congress acting under authority of the Indian commerce clause. In *State v. Littlechief*, 573 P.2d 263 (Okla. 1978), the court considered the impact of the adoption of 18 U.S.C. § 1151 in 1948 and held that under the plain language of section 1151(c), Indian allotments held in trust by the United States were Indian country. Criminal jurisdiction over such lands therefore remained within the exclusive jurisdiction of the federal and tribal governments. The court reasoned that since Oklahoma had not assumed criminal jurisdiction under Public Law 280, the state could not exercise criminal jurisdiction over allotments. *See generally* Pipestem, *The Journey from Crow Dog to Little Chief: A Survey of Tribal Civil and Criminal Jurisdiction in Western Oklahoma*, 6 AM. INDIAN L. REV. 1 (1978).

   While the *Littlechief* case involved a tribe in western Oklahoma, its ruling is equally applicable to the lands of the former Indian Territory. The Oklahoma Court of Criminal Appeals revisited the issue of criminal jurisdiction of restricted allotments in the former Indian Territory in *State v. Burnett*, 671 P.2d 1165 (Okla. Crim. App. 1983). The court held that such restricted allotments constituted Indian country and dismissed state charges against several defendants arising out of a homicide on such lands. The defendants, with one exception, were Indians, charged with murdering an Osage on restricted Osage allotment land. The state argued that restrictions placed on allotments by the federal government only defined the status of the land, not the scope of state criminal jurisdiction. They sought to distinguish trust allotments from Indian restricted fee lands common among the Indian lands in the former Indian Territory. The court responded:

"Indian country," for our purposes, means "all Indian allotments, the Indian titles to which have not been extinguished, including rights-of-way running through the same." 18 U.S.C. § 1151(c) (1976). The Court, quoting from *United States v. Bowling*, [256 U.S. 484 (1921)], declared the essential identity of the two methods: [I]n one class as much as the other "the United States possesses a supervisory control over the land and may take appropriate measures to make sure that it inures to the sole use and benefit of the allottee and his heirs throughout the original or any extended period of restriction." In practical effect, the control of Congress, until the expiration of the trust or the restricted period, is the same. *United States v. Ramsey*, [271 U.S. at 471].

The State also suggests that *Ramsey* was decided at a time when the restrictions ran with the land, whereas the trend at present is to make the restrictions personal to the Indian, thus taking the present case out of § 1151(c). This is not well taken, for when Congress provided in Section 1151 that Indian country should include "all Indian allotments, the Indian titles to which have not been extinguished," it considered this description broad enough to encompass all Indian allotments while the title to same shall be held in trust by the Government, or while the same shall remain inalienable by the allottee without the consent of the United States. *In re Carmen's Petition*, 165 F. Supp. at 946. Under whatever theory, the land at issue was inalienable as a matter of federal law, and we find that it was Indian country. However, the State suggests that, even if the land is Indian country, it has validly assumed jurisdiction over such lands in this State [under Public Law 280].

Id. at 1167. Furthermore, Oklahoma had not taken any affirmative legislative action under Public Law 280 to acquire such criminal jurisdiction. Additionally, the state had made no attempt to repeal Article I, § 3 of the Constitution of the State of Oklahoma, which disclaimed state jurisdiction over Indian country. The state argued that Oklahoma had been exercising criminal jurisdiction over restricted allotments at least since 1936, and the Indians under Public Law 280 had consented by acquiescence to such jurisdiction. The court found this argument unpersuasive: "The states must 'manifes[t] by political action their willingness and ability to discharge their new responsibilities' in order to make effective the assumption of jurisdiction, [quoting *Kennerly v. District Court of Montana*, 400 U.S. 423 (1971);] and thus far, no one with the right and power to speak for and bind Oklahoma has done so." 671 P.2d at 1167. *Ex parte Nowabbi*, however, was not explicitly overruled until *State v. Klindt*, 782 P.2d 401 (Okla. Crim. App. 1989). In *Klindt* the court reviewed the history of judicial treatment of restricted fee patent lands since *Nowabbi* and concluded that later decisions had undermined the theory upon which that opinion was based and therefore overruled the precedent.

In *Citizens Band of Potawatomi Indian Tribe v. Oklahoma Tax Comm'n*, 888 F.2d 1303 (10th Cir. 1989), *cert. granted*, 111 S. Ct. 37 (1990), the Tenth Circuit held that the tribally owned lands of the Citizens Band of the Potawatomi, an Oklahoma tribe that was not part of the Five Civilized Tribes of eastern Oklahoma, constituted Indian country. The court expressly rejected Oklahoma's argument that there was no Indian country in Oklahoma, noting that "[i]t has long been the law that land purchased in a state by the federal government and held in trust for Indians is 'Indian country.'"

3. Tribal Courts: In 1982, the Muscogee (Creek) Nation passed an ordinance authorizing the Creek Tribal Court to enforce civil and criminal jurisdiction over tribal members. Subsequently the tribe sought funding from the Bureau of Indian Affairs for the Tribal Court and law enforcement program. The BIA denied the request for funds, maintaining that the Tribe had no power to establish tribal courts with civil and criminal jurisdiction. The tribe sued, seeking judicial review of the Bureau's decision. In *Muscogee (Creek) Nation v. Hodel*, 851 F.2d 1439 (D.C. Cir. 1988), the court again canvassed the history of the Creek Nation set forth in *Harjo* and held that authority to establish a tribal court system had not been extinguished by the Curtis Act or other special statutes applicable to the tribes of the former Indian Territory. The court found that the Curtis Act unequivocally abolished the then-existing tribal courts. A subsequent agreement with the Creeks also specifically provided that the agreement would not be construed as reviving the tribal courts. Paragraph 47 of an agreement ratified in the Act of March 1, 1901, 31 Stat. 861, provided that "[n]othing contained in this agreement shall be construed to revive or reestablish the Creek courts which have been abolished by former Acts of Congress." Furthermore, the Five Civilized Tribe Act, Act of April 26, 1906, 34 Stat. 137, did not revive the courts. The Muscogee Nation argued, however, that even if its courts were abolished by the Curtis Act and the subsequent agreement, the Oklahoma Indian Welfare Act of 1936 (OIWA), 49 Stat. 1967, codified at 25 U.S.C. §§ 503, repealed the earlier legislation and revived the Tribe's power to establish tribal courts. The crux of this issue was the meaning and effect of section 503 of the OIWA together with the general repealer clause contained in the legislation. Section 503 provides:

> Any recognized tribe or band of Indians residing in Oklahoma shall have the right to organize for its common welfare and to adopt a constitution and bylaws.

The corresponding provision of section 16 of the IRA affords such rights to any Indian tribe residing on the same reservation to adopt a constitution and bylaws to facilitate powers vested in it under *existing* law. The Department of the Interior argued that section 503, like the corresponding provisions of the IRA, limited the powers of the Oklahoma tribes to those powers vested by existing law, plus certain powers enumerated in the Indian Reorganization Act. The court rejected this interpretation.

> The IRA and the OIWA address the same subject, albeit for different tribes, and were enacted just two years apart. It is contrary to common sense as well as sound statutory construction to read the later, more general language to incorporate the precise limitations of the earlier statute. Where the words of a later statute differ from those of a previous one on the same or related subject, the Congress must have intended them to have a different meaning. [Had Congress] intended the tribal government provision to be identical to that in the IRA, it could have included a direct reference to the IRA in that provision as it did in the corporate charter provision. Indeed, Congress could have simply repealed the provisions of the IRA which exempted the Oklahoma tribes. It did neither. Therefore, it is necessary to examine the OIWA standing alone to determine if it repealed the abolition of Creek Tribal Courts.
> The OIWA clearly does not expressly repeal the abolition of the Tribal Courts. It contains no reference to the Curtis Act or the related legislation. It does, however, unlike the IRA, contain a general repealer clause. Act of June 26, 1936, 49 Stat. 1967, § 9 (codified at 25 U.S.C. § 509 (1983)). Therefore, any repeal would be by implication. Generally, repeal by implication is not favored.

Id. at 1444.

The OIWA confers the power to adopt a constitution. The regulations designed to implement both the IRA and the OIWA define constitution as "the written organizational framework of any tribe reorganized pursuant to a Federal statute for the exercise of governmental powers." 25 C.F.R. § 81.1(g). According to the court, this definition certainly encompasses the power to create courts with general civil and criminal jurisdiction. The OIWA was passed to "reorganize" the Oklahoma tribes. The court concluded that it "would be absurd to hold that isolated portions of the Curtis Act and the Creek Agreement survive even though the statutory context in which they appeared — allotment and assimilation — has been stripped away by the OIWA." *Id.* at 1445. The court held that unlike the IRA, "[i]f the intent of the OIWA was to give the Oklahoma tribes the same powers of self-government *exercised* by the IRA tribes, then the OIWA necessarily repealed the Curtis Act." *Id.* at 1446. Quoting from *United States v. Wheeler*, 435 U.S. at 332, the court said: "[T]ribal courts are important mechanisms for protecting significant tribal interests. Federal pre-emption of a tribe's jurisdiction to punish its own members for infractions of tribal law would detract substantially from tribal self-government ...." *Id.* Since the court recognized that the State of Oklahoma has no jurisdiction over Indians within the Creek Nation and the federal courts have jurisdiction only over major crimes committed by Indians within Indian country under the Federal Major Crimes Act, 18 U.S.C. § 1153, the court reasoned that to accept the construction of the OIWA advanced by the Department of the Interior would result in the creation of a jurisdictional "no man's land." Thus, the court sustained the authority of the Creek Nation to establish tribal courts to exercise jurisdiction over Indian country.

For a general discussion of the rejuvenation of tribal government in Oklahoma, see Chambers, *Oklahoma Indian Law — Cases of the Last Decade and Opportunities for the Next Decade*, 24 Tulsa L.J. 701 (1989).

4. Taxing and Regulatory Authority over Indians in the Former Indian Territory: In *Indian Country, U.S.A. v. Oklahoma ex rel. Okla. Tax Comm'n*, 829 F.2d 967 (10th Cir. 1987), the Tenth Circuit held that Oklahoma did not have authority to regulate and tax certain bingo and bingo-related activities conducted on treaty lands still held by the Creek Nation. In applying *California v. Cabazon Band of Mission Indians*, 480 U.S. 202 (1987), the court considered additional issues arising from the unique history of relations between the United States and the Five Civilized Tribes in the former Indian Territory. The court first concluded that the site of the bingo hall was considered Indian country and still retained reservation status within the meaning of 18 U.S.C. § 1151(a). The court rejected Oklahoma's argument that, upon admission to statehood, it acquired complete jurisdiction over all members of the Five Civilized Tribes and their lands within the former Indian Territory through a combination of federal legislation enacted prior to statehood, the language in the Oklahoma Enabling Act disclaiming a proprietary but not jurisdictional interest in Indian lands, and the fact that state courts succeeded the special United States court in the Indian Territory with respect to certain cases. Section 3 of the Oklahoma Enabling Act, 34 Stat. 270, provides:

> That the people inhabiting said proposed State do agree and declare that they forever disclaim all right and title in or to any unappropriated public lands lying within the boundaries to all lands lying within said limits owned or held by any Indian, tribe, or nation; and that until the title to any such public land shall have been extinguished by the United States, the same shall be and remain subject to the jurisdiction, disposal, and control of the United States.

Section 1 of the Oklahoma Enabling Act provided that "nothing contained in the said constitution shall be construed to limit or impair the rights of person or property pertaining to the Indians of said Territories (so long as such rights shall remain unextinguished) or to limit or affect the authority of the Government of the United States to make any law or regulation respecting such Indians, their lands, property, or other rights by treaties, agreement, law or otherwise, which it would have been competent to make if this Act had never been passed." Oklahoma Enabling Act, § 1, 34 Stat. at 267-68. The court said that the State's construction of the Oklahoma Enabling Act completely ignored the effect of section 1 of the act in which Congress explicitly preserved federal authority. The court reasoned:

> Section one is a general reservation of federal and tribal jurisdiction over "Indians, their lands, [and] property," except as extinguished by the tribes or the federal — not state — government.
>
> Sections one and three of the act, read *in pari materia,* cannot be read as a clear expression of congressional intent to disclaim federal or tribal jurisdiction over unallotted Creek tribal lands, such as those at issue in the present suit. Significantly, the enabling acts that the State attempts to distinguish from the Oklahoma Enabling Act contain no provision that parallels section one. See, e.g., Act of Feb. 22, 1889, 25 Stat. 676. The language of the Oklahoma act, read in its historical context, suggests that Congress intended to preserve its jurisdiction and authority over Indians and their lands in the new State of Oklahoma until it accomplished the eventual goal of terminating the tribal governments, assimilating the Indians, and dissolving completely the tribally-owned land base — events that never occurred and goals that Congress later expressly repudiated. The State has failed to cite any acts of Congress that clearly reveal an intent to divest the federal and tribal governments of jurisdiction over Creek tribal lands and to confer such authority on the State of Oklahoma.

Id. at 979.

The court then examined federal enactments prior to statehood, as well as Public Law 280, and concluded that there simply was no clear evidence that Congress intended to relinquish federal and tribal authority prior to extinguishing tribal title or dissolving the tribal government. The series of federal laws enacted prior to statehood and the Oklahoma Enabling Act therefore did not divest the federal government of authority over Creek tribal lands, did not abolish the Creek Nation's legislative and regulatory authority over such lands, and did not evince a clear intent by Congress to permit the state to assert jurisdiction.

On the issue of taxation, the court distinguished *Colville*:

> This case is markedly different. Here, the "product" is a form of entertainment that is wholly created, sold, and consumed within the boundaries of Creek Nation lands. Patrons do not travel onto Creek lands to play bingo in order to avoid sales taxes. The Tribe does not "market an exemption from state taxation to persons who would normally do their business elsewhere," *Colville*, 447 U.S. at 155, because high-stakes bingo is not generally available within the state.

Id. at 986.

In balancing tribal and state interests, the court found evidence that the overall economic effect of Creek Nation bingo on the state and local economy is positive. In contrast to the taxes in *Colville* and related cigarette cases, the state tax as applied to Creek Nation bingo was directed solely at on-reservation value. The Tribe had a very substantial interest in providing patrons well-run entertainment and attractive facilities. The imposition of a sales tax would burden the tribal enterprise by increasing the total cost of playing bingo and by imposing collection, remittance, and recordkeeping requirements. The state's interest, in contrast, was minimal.

> In the present case, the economic impact on the Tribe of adding the state sales tax onto the price of bingo games is perhaps more difficult to measure. That may often be the case, however, when a tribal enterprise acts as seller to non-member purchasers. In *Colville*, the state tax had a clearly adverse impact on the tribe because the tribe sought to generate revenues by imposing its own sales tax on private Indian retailers. Nevertheless, because the product was imported onto the reservation and the tribe did not have a substantial interest in the cigarette "smokeshops," the Court upheld the state

tax. When tribes develop their own tribally-owned enterprises, however, and create a product on the reservation, there is no need or incentive to impose a separate tribal tax because tribal revenues are generated in the form of profits from sales. Thus, the greater the tribal interest and involvement, the less chance for a direct conflict between state and tribal taxes, as in *Colville*.

Id. at 986-87 n.9.

5. Tribal Riverbed Lands: In *Choctaw Nation v. Oklahoma*, 397 U.S. 620 (1970), the Cherokee and Choctaw Nations of Oklahoma sued the state of Oklahoma and various corporations to which the state had leased oil and gas and other mineral rights. The tribes sought both to recover the royalties derived from the leases and to prevent future interference with its property rights, claiming that they had been since 1835 the absolute fee owner of certain land below the mean high water level of the Arkansas River. The district court held that land grants made to petitioners by the United States conveyed no rights to the bed of the navigable portion of the Arkansas River. The court thus held that title to the river bed remained in the United States until 1907, when it passed to the state upon Oklahoma's admission to the Union. On appeal, the United States Court of Appeals for the Tenth Circuit affirmed the judgment of the district court. The Nations appealed.

When it reviewed the lower court decisions, the Supreme Court recited the history of the Five Civilized Tribes set out in *Harjo* to begin its analysis, beginning with the 1785 Treaty of Hopewell with the Cherokees and the 1786 Treaty of Hopewell with the Choctaws. Both the Cherokees and Choctaws argued that they received title to the bed of the Arkansas River by treaty and patent from the United States. Because the land was not individually allotted or otherwise disposed of pursuant to the 1906 Act, title remained in petitioners or passed to the United States to be held in trust for them. Oklahoma disagreed, arguing that title remained in the United States, and passed to Oklahoma upon admission to the Union as an incident of statehood. A divided Supreme Court accepted the tribes' position:

> Together, petitioners were granted fee simple title to a vast tract of land through which the Arkansas River winds its course. The natural inference from those grants is that all the land within their metes and bounds was conveyed, including the banks and bed of rivers. To the extent that the documents speak to the question, they are consistent with and tend to confirm this natural reading. Certainly there was no express exclusion of the bed of the Arkansas River by the United States as there was to other land within the grants.
>
> As a practical matter, reservation of the riverbed would have meant that petitioners were not entitled to enter upon and take sand and gravel or other minerals from the shallow parts of the river or islands formed when the water was low. In many respects however, the Indians were promised virtually complete sovereignty over their new lands. See *Atlantic & Pacific R. Co. v. Mingus*, 165 U.S. 413, 435-436 (1897). We do not believe that petitioners would have considered that they could have been precluded from exercising these basic ownership rights to the river bed, and we think it very unlikely that the United States intended otherwise. Nor do we believe that the United States would intend that it rather than petitioners have title to the dry bed left from avulsive changes of the river's course, which as the District Court noted are common in this area. Indeed, the United States seems to have had no present interest in retaining title to the river bed at all; it had all it was concerned with in its navigational easement via the constitutional power over commerce. Cf. *Pollard v. Hagan*, 3 How. 212, 229 (1845).
>
> Finally, it must be remembered that the United States accompanied its grants to petitioners with the promise that "no part of the land granted to them shall ever be embraced in any Territory or State." In light of this promise, it is only by the purest of

legal fictions that there can be found even a semblance of an understanding (on which Oklahoma necessarily places its principal reliance), that the United States retained title in order to grant it to some future State.

397 U.S. at 634-35.

On remand, the Cherokees sued for an accounting for money received under the Oklahoma leases, for future rentals or royalties, and for an injunction against interference with the use of the bed. *Cherokee Nation v. Oklahoma*, 461 F.2d 674 (10th Cir. 1972). Oklahoma and its lessees argued that the Supreme Court did not decide present ownership of the riverbed, so the question was still open. Without present ownership, the Nations could not be entitled to the relief sought. The court of appeals rejected this argument. Oklahoma next argued that the Cherokee Nation was divested of sovereignty prior to Oklahoma's statehood, that the bed reverted to the United States, and that title passed to Oklahoma under the equal footing doctrine upon its admission to the Union in 1907. The court of appeals reasoned:

> We are not concerned with sovereignty, a political issue, but with land ownership. The question is not whether the Indians have sovereignty but whether the tribes are still in existence and capable of land ownership.
>
> We believe that this question is answered by the 1906 Act. Section 27 thereof provides that, upon dissolution of the tribes, lands belonging to them shall not become public lands nor the property of the United States but shall be held by the United States in trust for the Indians. 34 Stat. 148. Section 28 provides for the continuation of tribal existence and tribal government for all purposes authorized by law. *Ibid.*
>
> The Supreme Court has said that "when Congress has once established a [Indian] reservation, all tracts included within it remain a part of the reservation until separated therefrom by Congress." *Seymour v. Superintendent*, 368 U.S. 351, 359. There has been no separation here; the tribal governments still exist; and Oklahoma was admitted to the Union in 1907 upon compliance with the Enabling Act of June 16, 1906, 34 Stat. 267, which required a disclaimer of title to all lands owned "by any Indian or Indian tribes." *Ibid.* at 279. We adhere to the conclusion, which was implicit in our first decision, that the Indians have not divested themselves of the land in question. The claims of Oklahoma and its lessees must be rejected.

461 F.2d at 678.

Oklahoma and its lessees next argued that, if Oklahoma title fails, the Indians can recover only those damages allowable in a trespass action — stated otherwise, the mineral value, surface damage, and loss of use. The court reasoned that Oklahoma received money for leasing land which it did not own, contrary to the principle of unjust enrichment. The court also rejected the claim that Oklahoma must return the lease considerations:

> In our opinion Oklahoma has no right to retain the lease considerations. The right thereto lies between the lessees and the Indians. The lessees and Oklahoma made a mutual mistake of law. The documents determinative of title were all a matter of public record. We find nothing to suggest that Oklahoma engaged in conduct which misled or prejudiced the lessees. The trial court found, and we perceive nothing in the record to dispute the finding, that the lessees "got what they bargained for." The court decree protects the lessees against accountability to the Indians for actions taken under the leases. This includes damages for trespass. The lessees are not entitled to this protection plus return of the money which they paid for the leases. Whatever might be the situation if we were concerned only with the respective rights of Oklahoma and its lessees, we are confronted with the fact that the lessees have had the use of the land and have paid Oklahoma, not the rightful owner, therefor. If the lessees were awarded the return of the lease considerations which they have paid to Oklahoma, they would have received the use of the land for nothing and by the decree would be protected

against trespass claims by the real owners. Equity will not condone such a result. The lessees are not entitled to return of the lease considerations.

Id. at 680. The court ordered an accounting of bonuses, rentals, and royalties from the leases.

The court then considered dispute of ownership between the Choctaws and the Cherokees, both claiming ownership of that portion of the bed lying northerly of the main channel between the Canadian River and the state border. The court held it had no jurisdiction to determine a boundary dispute between Indian tribes without congressional action waiving immunity and consenting to suit.

In *United States v. Cherokee Nation of Oklahoma*, 480 U.S. 700 (1987), the Cherokee Nation of Oklahoma sued the United States for compensation for a taking under the fifth amendment based on damage to these riverbed interests caused by navigational improvements made by the federal government on the Arkansas River. The damage to sand and gravel deposits resulted from the McClellan-Kerr Project, approved by Congress in 1946, Act of July 24, 1946, ch. 595, 60 Stat. 634, 635-636, and designed to improve navigation by construction of a channel in the Arkansas River from its mouth at the Mississippi to Catoosa, Oklahoma.

The Cherokee Nation sought compensation but Congress refused to fund the claim after the Department of the Interior and the Army Corps of Engineers concluded that the United States' navigational servitude rendered it meritless. Congress did, however, provide the Cherokee Nation with the opportunity to seek judicial relief by conferring jurisdiction on the United States District Court for the Eastern District of Oklahoma to determine the claim. The district court granted summary judgment for the tribe, finding that a portion of the navigable Arkansas River was a private waterway belonging exclusively to the Cherokee Nation and the court of appeals affirmed, albeit adopting a balancing test. When the case reached the Supreme Court, the Court rejected the Cherokee's claim. The Court's opinion reasoned:

> We think the Court of Appeals erred in formulating a balancing test to evaluate this assertion of the navigational servitude. No such "balancing" is required where, as here, the interference with instream interests results from an exercise of the Government's power to regulate navigational uses of "the deep streams which penetrate our country in every direction." *Gibbons v. Ogden*, 9 Wheat. 1, 195 (1824). Though "this Court has never held that the navigational servitude creates a blanket exception to the Takings Clause whenever Congress exercises its Commerce Clause authority to promote navigation," *Kaiser Aetna v. United States*, 444 U.S. 164, 172 (1979), there can be no doubt that "[t]he Commerce Clause confers a unique position upon the Government in connection with navigable waters." *United States v. Rands*, 389 U.S. 121, 122 (1967). It gives to the Federal Government "a 'dominant servitude,'" *FPC v. Niagara Mohawk Power Corp.*, 347 U.S. 239, 249 (1954), which extends to the entire stream and the stream bed below ordinary high-water mark. The proper exercise of this power is not an invasion of any private property rights in the stream or the lands underlying it, for the damage sustained does not result from taking property from riparian owners within the meaning of the Fifth Amendment but from the lawful exercise of a power to which the interests of riparian owners have always been subject." *Rands, supra*, at 123.
>
> The application of these principles to interference with streambed interests has not depended on balancing this valid public purpose in light of the intended use of those interests by the owner. Thus, in *Lewis Blue Point Oyster Cultivation Co. v. Briggs*, 229 U.S. 82 (1913), the Court held that no taking occurred where dredging carried out under the direction of the United States destroyed oysters that had been cultivated on privately held lands under the waters of the Great South Bay in New York. The decision rested on the view that the dominant right of navigation "must include the

right to use the bed of the water for every purpose which is in aid of navigation." *Id.*, at 87. The Court did not rely on the particular use to which the private owners put the bed, but rather observed that their very title to the submerged lands "is acquired and held subject to the power of Congress to deepen the water over such lands or to use them for any structure which the interest of navigation, in its judgment, may require." *Id.*, at 88.

These well-established principles concerning the exercise of the United States' dominant servitude would, in the usual case, dictate that we reject respondent's "takings" claim. We do not understand respondent to argue otherwise[.] Instead, the Cherokee Nation asserts that its title to the Arkansas River bed is unique in scope and that interference with that interest requires just compensation. Respondent does not rely explicitly on any language of the relevant treaties, but rather on its reading of *Choctaw Nation v. Oklahoma,* 397 U.S. 620 (1970). We have noted that *Choctaw Nation* involved "very peculiar circumstances," *Montana v. United States,* 450 U.S., at 555, n.5, in that "the Indians were promised virtually complete sovereignty over their new lands." *Choctaw Nation, supra,* at 635. These circumstances allowed the claimants to overcome the strong presumption against conveyance of riverbed interests by the United States, designed to protect the interests of the States under the equal-footing doctrine. See *Montana v. United States, supra,* at 551-553; *Shively v. Bowlby,* 152 U.S. 1, 48-50 (1894). Respondent urges that these circumstances further indicate that the United States abandoned its navigational servitude in the area. Thus, in respondent's view, the treaties by which it gained fee simple title to the bed of the Arkansas River were such as to make the Arkansas River a "private stream, not intended as a public highway or artery of commerce." *Id.,* at 23.

We think that the decision in *Choctaw Nation* was quite generous to respondent, and we refuse to give a still more expansive and novel reading of respondent's property interests. There is certainly nothing in *Choctaw Nation* itself that suggests such a broad reading of the conveyance. To the contrary, the Court expressly noted that the United States had no interest in retaining title to the submerged lands because "it had all it was concerned with in its navigational easement via the constitutional power over commerce." *Choctaw Nation, supra,* at 635. The parties, including respondent here, clearly understood that the navigational servitude was dominant no matter how the question of riverbed ownership was resolved.

Any other conclusion would be wholly extraordinary, for we have repeatedly held that the navigational servitude applies to all holders of riparian and riverbed interests. [Since] the States themselves are subject to this servitude, we cannot conclude that respondent — though granted a degree of sovereignty over tribal lands — gained an exemption from the servitude simply because it received title to the riverbed interests. Such a waiver of sovereign authority will not be implied, but instead must be "'surrendered in unmistakable terms.'"

We also reject respondent's suggestion that the fiduciary obligations of the United States elevate the Government's actions into a taking. It is, of course, well established that the Government in its dealings with Indian tribal property acts in a fiduciary capacity. See *Seminole Nation v. United States,* 316 U.S. 286, 296-297 (1942). When it holds lands in trust on behalf of the tribes, the United States may not "give the tribal lands to others, or ... appropriate them to its own purposes, without rendering, or assuming an obligation to render, just compensation for them." *United States v. Creek Nation,* 295 U.S. 103, 110 (1935). These principles, however, do little to aid respondent's cause, for they do not create property rights where none would otherwise exist but rather presuppose that the United States has interfered with existing tribal property interests. As we have explained, the tribal interests at issue here simply do not include the right to be free from the navigational servitude, for exercise of the servitude is "not an invasion of any private property rights in the stream or the lands underlying it...." *United States v. Rands,* 389 U.S., at 123.

480 U.S. at 706-08.

The Muskogee City-County Port Authority constructed a wharf, cargo pier, and docking facility in the Arkansas River where it flows through Muskogee,

Oklahoma. After *Choctaw Nation*, the Cherokee Nation, as present owners of the river bed, challenged the legality of such construction without receiving tribal permission. *Cherokee Nation of Oklahoma v. Muskogee City-County Port Auth.*, 555 F. Supp. 1015 (E.D. Okla. 1983). The Port Authority argued that it had a right to build wharves and piers in the Arkansas River because it is a riparian landowner. The Cherokee Nation argued that riparian rights cannot apply to a privately owned navigable river, and the district court agreed.

> It is well settled that in the absence of a controlling local law otherwise limiting the rights of a riparian owner upon a navigable river, he has a property right, incident to his ownership of the bank, of access from the front of his land to the navigable part of the stream, and when not forbidden by public law may construct landings, wharves, or piers for this purpose. These riparian rights are created by state law rather than by federal law, and may vary from state to state. The Supreme Court of Oklahoma approved use of county funds to buy riparian land in order to construct wharves and piers in the Arkansas River at the Port of Catoosa in *Sublett v. City of Tulsa*, 405 P.2d 185 (Okla. 1965). Therefore, Oklahoma appears to follow the majority rule which gives a riparian owner the right to build wharves and piers in the shallow water of the shore of a navigable river.
>
> Since the riparian right which defendant relies on is created by state law, the question which must be asked is whether it is within the power of the State of Oklahoma to grant riparian rights on a navigable river which it does not own. This question is a difficult one, as the Arkansas River is the only navigable river which the United States Supreme Court has found to be owned by an entity other than a state, *Montana v. United States*, 450 U.S. 544, 555 [1981]. Because the State of Oklahoma does not own the bed of the Arkansas River as it flows through Muskogee, it is without power to grant riparian rights to the defendant Muskogee City-County Port Authority.

Id. at 1017.

For general discussions of the Oklahoma riverbed claims cases, see Comment, *Indian Water Rights: Giving With One Hand and Taking With the Other*, 6 PACE ENVTL. L. REV. 255 (1988); Note, *Indian Claims in the Bed of Oklahoma Watercourses*, 4 AM. INDIAN L. REV. 83 (1976).

6. Osage Headrights: One very valuable right held by some Oklahoma Indians involves the so-called Osage headrights, which ultimately derive significant income from mineral interests. In *West v. Oklahoma Tax Comm'n*, 334 U.S. 717 (1948), the Court held that Osage "headrights" were not exempt from state income taxation. The court summarized the nature and history of these headrights:

> It is essential at the outset to understand the history and nature of the arrangement whereby the United States holds in trust the properties involved in this case. See Cohen, Handbook of Federal Indian Law (1945) 446-455. In 1866, the United States and the Cherokee Nation of Indians executed a comprehensive treaty covering their various relationships. 14 Stat. 799. It was there agreed that the United States might settle friendly Indians in certain areas of Cherokee territory, including what is now Osage County, Oklahoma; these areas had previously been conveyed by the United States to the Cherokees. The treaty further provided that the areas in question were to be conveyed in fee simple to the tribes settled by the United States "to be held in common or by their members in severalty as the United States may decide."
>
> The Osage Indians subsequently moved to the Indian Territory and settled in what is now Osage County. In 1883, pursuant to the 1866 treaty, the Cherokees conveyed this area to the United States "in trust nevertheless and for the use and benefit of the said Osage and Kansas Indians." It is significant that fee simple title to the land was not conveyed at this time to the Osages; instead, the United States received that title as trustee for the Osages. Nor was any distinction here made between the land and the minerals thereunder, legal title to both being transferred to the United States.

On June 28, 1906, the Osage Allotment Act, providing for the distribution of Osage lands and properties, became effective. 34 Stat. 539. See *Levindale Lead Co. v. Coleman*, 241 U.S. 432. Provision was there made for the allotment to each tribal member of a 160-acre homestead, plus certain additional surplus lands. These allotted lands, said § 7, were to be set aside "for the sole use and benefit of the individual members of the tribe entitled thereto, or to their heirs, as herein provided." The homestead was to be inalienable and nontaxable for 25 years or during the life of the allottee. The surplus lands, however, were to be inalienable for 25 years and nontaxable for 3 years, except that the Secretary of the Interior might issue a certificate of competence to an adult, authorizing him to sell all of his surplus lands; upon the issuance of such a certificate, or upon the death of the allottee, the surplus lands were to become immediately taxable. § 2, Seventh; *Choteau v. Burnet*, 283 U.S. 691.

Section 3 of the Act stated that the minerals covered by these lands were to be reserved to the Osage Tribe for a period of 25 years and that mineral leases and royalties were to be approved by the United States. Section 4 then provided that all money due or to become due to the tribe was to be held in trust by the United States for 25 years[3]; but these funds were to be segregated and credited pro rata to the individual members or their heirs, with interest accruing and being payable quarterly to the members. Royalties from the mineral leases were to be placed in the Treasury of the United States to the credit of the tribal members and distributed to the individual members in the same manner and at the same time as interest payments on other moneys held in trust. In this connection, it should be noted that quarterly payments of interest and royalties became so large that Congress later limited the amount of payments that could be made to those without certificates of competence; provision was also made for investing the surplus in bonds, stocks, etc.[4]

According to § 5 of this 1906 statute, at the end of the 25-year trust period "the lands, mineral interests, and moneys, herein provided for and held in trust by the United States shall be the absolute property of the individual members of the Osage tribe, according to the role herein provided for, or their heirs, as herein provided, and deeds to said lands shall be issued to said members, or to their heirs, as herein provided, and said moneys shall be distributed to said members, or to their heirs, as herein provided, and said members shall have full control of said lands, moneys, and mineral interests, except as hereinbefore provided." It was also stated in § 2, Seventh, that the minerals upon the allotted lands "shall become the property of the individual owner of said land" at the expiration of 25 years, unless otherwise provided by Congress.

Moreover, § 6 provided that the lands, moneys and mineral interests of any deceased member of the Osage Tribe "shall descend to his or her legal heirs, according to the laws of the Territory of Oklahoma." Congress subsequently provided, in § 8 of the Act of April 18, 1912, 37 Stat. 86, 88, that any adult member of the tribe who was not mentally incompetent could by will dispose of "any or all of his estate, real, personal, or mixed, including trust funds, from which restrictions as to alienation have not been removed," in accordance with the laws of the State of Oklahoma. Such wills could not be probated, however, unless approved by the Secretary of the Interior before the death of the testator.

The 25-year trust period established by the 1906 statute has been extended several times by Congress, first to 1946 (41 Stat. 1249), then to 1958 (45 Stat. 1478), and

---

[3] The trust under which these funds were to be held was established in 1865 by treaty between the United States and the Great and Little Osage Indians, 14 Stat. 687. By the terms of this treaty, the proceeds of the sale of Osage lands in Kansas were to be placed in the United States Treasury to the credit of the tribe. Provisions for carrying out the terms of this treaty were made by Congress in 1880, 21 Stat. 291.

[4] By the Act of March 3, 1921, 41 Stat. 1249, Congress provided that so long as the income should be sufficient the adult Osage Indian without a certificate of competency should be paid $1,000 quarterly. See also Act of Feb. 27, 1925, 43 Stat. 1008. In the Act of June 24, 1938, 52 Stat. 1034, it was provided that where the restricted Osage had surplus funds in excess of $10,000 he was to be paid $1,000 quarterly, but if he had surplus funds of less than $10,000 he was to receive quarterly only his current income, not to exceed $1,000 quarterly.

finally to 1984 (52 Stat. 1034). The last extension provided that the "lands, moneys, and other properties now or hereafter held in trust or under the supervision of the United States for the Osage Tribe of Indians, the members thereof, or their heirs and assigns, shall continue subject to such trusts and supervision until January 1, 1984, unless otherwise provided by Act of Congress."

Application of the foregoing provisions to the estate in issue produces this picture: Legal title to the mineral interests, the funds and the securities constituting the corpus of the trust estate is in the United States as trustee. The United States received legal title to the mineral interests in 1883, when it took what is now Osage County from the Cherokees in trust for the Osages; and that title has not subsequently been transferred. Legal title to the various funds and securities adhered to the United States as the pertinent trusts were established and developed. Beneficial title to these properties was vested in the decedent and is now held by his sole heir, the appellant. The beneficiary at all times has been entitled to at least a limited amount of interest and royalties arising out of the corpus. And the beneficiary has a reversionary interest in the corpus, an interest that will materialize only when the legal title passes from the United States at the end of the trust period. But until that period ends, the beneficiary has no control over the corpus. See *Globe Indemnity Co. v. Bruce*, 81 F.2d 143, 150.

Id. at 719-23.

The court held that property held in trust by the United States is immune from any form of state taxation, unless Congress expressly consents to the imposition of such liability. The annual transfer of income from the headrights, rather than the trust property itself, was subject to Oklahoma state taxation. After the Court of Claims questioned the continued validity of *West* in light of recent trends in federal Indian law in *Mason v. Oklahoma*, 461 F.2d 1364 (Ct. Cl. 1972), the Supreme Court reaffirmed *West*: "The *West* decision has neither been overruled nor questioned in our subsequent cases. It is fully consistent with later developments and has been followed without protest for 24 years." *United States v. Mason*, 412 U.S. 391, 400 (1973) (rejecting breach of trust claim against the United States for paying Oklahoma estate taxes based on *West* decision). *See also Estate of Shelton v. Oklahoma*, 544 P.2d 495 (Okla. 1975) (following *West* and holding that Oklahoma Osage Indian headrights shall be included in a decedent's gross estate for inheritance tax purposes).

Like certain other forms of individual property created by allotment policies, Osage headrights sometimes passed into non-Indian ownership. In *Eckelt v. Herrel*, 783 P.2d 1 (Okla. 1982), the court held that the proceeds of "headrights" held by non-Indians were subject to attachment and sale by creditors.

[Plaintiff] contends the headrights themselves, owned by a non-Indian, are not exempt from state judicial process. Thus, if the headrights are not exempt, then neither are the proceeds.

The federal courts have held this to be true in certain circumstances. In *In re Irwin*, 60 Fed. 2d 495 (10th Cir. 1932), the Tenth Circuit Court of Appeals specifically held that "an Osage headright owned by a person not of Indian blood, passes to his trustee in bankruptcy. Any other conclusion would permit white persons to invest large sums in these headrights, and retain them against their creditors, contrary to the letter and spirit of the Bankruptcy Act." The court further explained the necessity of the approval of the Secretary of the Interior does not prevent a headright from passing to the trustee. Moreover, it explained the Act of April 12, 1924 (43 Stat. 94), provides that Osage headrights which are "vested in, determined, or adjudged to be the right or property of any person *not an Indian by blood may with the approval of the Secretary of the Interior and not otherwise be sold, assigned, and transferred* under such rules and regulations as the Secretary of the Interior may prescribe." The statutes confer no such right upon those of Indian blood. (Emphasis supplied.)

The reasoning in *In re Irwin* is still applicable. The 1984 legislation clearly indicates non-Indians are only prohibited from transferring headrights without approval of the Secretary of the Interior, and they must follow the proper procedures.[2]

Plaintiff further contends that even if the headrights themselves are not transferable, in this case, only the proceeds are involved.

In *Cook v. First National Bank of Pawhuska*, 145 Okla. 5, 291 P. 43 (1930) the Oklahoma Supreme [Court] held: "Proceeds from the sale of a headright owned by a non-Indian were subject to garnishment." In the case at bar, Plaintiff does not seek to attach the headrights. Neither did Defendant sell her headrights. The funds at issue were those proceeds paid to her by the federal government because of her ownership interest in the headright itself — proceeds she deposited and commingled with other funds in her bank account. Ownership of her headrights remains intact. Congressional intent evident in the 1984 act and all preceding enactments is preservation of the Osage Mineral Estate. See e.g., *Taylor v. Tayrien*, 51 F.2d 884 (10th Cir. 1931); *Taylor v. Jones*, 51 F.2d 892 (10th Cir. 1931); and *In re Irwin*. The role of the federal government is to protect the Indians. Thus, restrictions have attached to transfers by Indians. By requiring any non-Indian transfer to be subjected to an Indian right of first refusal, the 1984 act operates to insure Indians gain control over the minerals. Clearly, allowing a judgment creditor to garnish the proceeds from headrights does not violate the intent of the congressional restrictions. Such proceeds are subject to garnishment.

Id. at 2-3.

D. TERMINATED AND NONRECOGNIZED TRIBES

SOUTH CAROLINA v. CATAWBA INDIAN NATION

476 U.S. 498 (1985)

Justice STEVENS delivered the opinion of the Court.

At issue in this litigation is the right to possession of a "Tract of Land of Fifteen Miles square" described in a 1763 treaty between the King of England and the Catawba Head Men and Warriors.[1] The tract, comprising 144,000

---

[2] As affects non-Indians, the 1984 legislation, 25 U.S.C. § 331 Sec. 8. (a)(1) is essentially the same, except that any transfer of a headright owned by a non-Indian is subject to three rights of purchase:

Sec. 8. (a)(1) No headright owned by any person who is not of Indian blood may be sold, assigned, or transferred without the approval of the Secretary. Any sale of any interest in such headright (and any other transfer which divests such person of any right, title, or interest in such headright) shall be subject to the following rights of purchase:

(1) First right of purchase by the heirs in the first degree of the first Osage Indian to have acquired such headright under an allotment who are living and are Osage Indians, or, if they all be deceased, all heirs in the second through the fourth degree of such first Osage Indian to have acquired such headright under an allotment who are living and are Osage Indians, or, if they all be deceased, all heirs in the second through the fourth degree of such first Osage Indian who are living and are Osage Indians.

(2) Second right of purchase by any other Osage Indian for the benefit of any Osage Indian in his or her individual capacity.

(3) Third right of purchase by the Osage Tribal Council on behalf of the Osage Tribe of Indians.

[1] The 1763 Treaty of Fort Augusta was entered into by the Catawbas and British and colonial officials, and provides, in relevant part:

"And We the Catawba Head Men and Warriors in Confirmation of an Agreement heretofore entered into with the White People declare that we will remain satisfied with the Tract of Land of Fifteen Miles square a Survey of which by our consent and at our request has been already begun and the respective Governors and Superintendant on their Parts promise and engage that the aforesaid survey shall be compleated and that the Catawbas shall not in any respect be molested by any of the King's subjects within the said Lines but shall be indulged in the usual Manner of

acres and 225 square miles, is located near the northern border of South Carolina; some 27,000 persons now claim title to different parcels within the tract. The specific question presented to us is whether the State's statute of limitations applies to the Tribe's claim. The answer depends on an interpretation of a statute enacted by Congress in 1959 to authorize a division of Catawba tribal assets. See 25 U.S.C. §§ 931-938. We hold that the State's statute applies, but we do not reach the question whether it bars the Tribe's claim.

Simply stated, the Tribe[2] claims that it had undisputed ownership and possession of the land before the first Nonintercourse Act was passed by Congress in 1790; that the Nonintercourse Act prohibited any conveyance of tribal land without the consent of the United States; and that the United States never gave its consent to a conveyance of this land. Accordingly, the Tribe's purported conveyance to South Carolina in 1840 is null and void. Among the defenses asserted by petitioners is the contention that, even if the Tribe's claim was valid before passage and enactment of the Catawba Division of Assets Act, § 5 of the Act made the state statute of limitations applicable to the claim. Because that is the only contention that we review, it is not necessary to describe much of the historical material in the record.

I

In 1760 and 1763, the Tribe surrendered to Great Britain its aboriginal territory in what is now North and South Carolina in return for the right to settle permanently on the "Tract of Land of Fifteen Miles square" that is now at issue. For purposes of this summary judgment motion, it is not disputed that the Tribe retained title to the land when the Nonintercourse Acts were passed.

By 1840, the Tribe had leased most, if not all, of the land described in the 1763 treaty to white settlers. In 1840, the Tribe conveyed its interest in the "Tract of Land of Fifteen Miles square" to the State of South Carolina by entering into the "Treaty of Nation Ford." In that treaty, the State agreed, in return for the "Tract," to spend $5,000 to acquire a new reservation, to pay the Tribe $2,500 in advance, and to make nine annual payments of $1,500 in the ensuing years. In 1842, the State purchased a 630-acre tract as a new reservation for the Tribe, which then apparently had a membership of about 450 persons. This land is still held in trust for the Tribe by South Carolina.

The Tribe contends that the State did not perform its obligations under the treaty — it delayed the purchase of the new reservation for over 2½ years; it then spent only $2,000 instead of $5,000 to purchase the new land; and it was not actually "new" land because it was located within the original 144,000-acre tract. Still more importantly, as noted, the Tribe maintains that this entire transaction was void because the United States did not consent to the conveyance as required by the Nonintercourse Act.

At various times during the period between 1900 and 1943, leaders of the Tribe applied to the State for citizenship and for a "final settlement of all their

_____

hunting Elsewhere." XI Colonial Records of North Carolina 201-202 (1763), reprinted in App. 35.

[2] Respondent, Catawba Indian Tribe, Inc., is a nonprofit corporation organized under the laws of South Carolina in 1975. Like the District Court and the Court of Appeals, we assume that respondent is the successor in interest of the Catawba Indian Tribe of South Carolina. For convenience, we refer to respondent as the "Tribe" throughout this opinion.

claims against the State." Petitioners argue that these claims merely sought full performance of the State's obligations under the 1840 treaty, but, for purposes of our decision, we accept the Tribe's position that it was then asserting a claim under the Nonintercourse Acts and thus challenging the treaty itself. In any event, both state officials and representatives of the Federal Government took an interest in the plight of the Tribe.

In response to this concern, on December 14, 1943, the Tribe, the State, and the Office of Indian Affairs of the Department of the Interior entered into a Memorandum of Understanding which was intended to provide relief for the Tribe, but which did not require the Tribe to release its claims against the State. Pursuant to that agreement, the State purchased 3,434 acres of land at a cost of $70,000 and conveyed it to the United States to be held in trust for the Tribe. The Federal Government agreed to make annual contributions of available sums for the welfare of the Tribe and to assist the Tribe with education, medical benefits, and economic development. For its part, the Tribe agreed to conduct its affairs on the basis of the Federal Government's recommendations; it thereafter adopted a Constitution approved by the Secretary of the Interior pursuant to the [IRA].

In 1953, Congress decided to make a basic change in its policies concerning Indian affairs. The passage of House Concurrent Resolution 108 on August 1, 1953,[10] marked the beginning of the "termination era" — a period that continued into the mid-1960's, in which the Federal Government endeavored to terminate its supervisory responsibilities for Indian tribes.[11] Pursuant to that policy, the Federal Government identified the Catawba Tribe as a likely candidate for the withdrawal of federal services. Moreover, members of the Tribe desired an end to federal restrictions on alienation of their lands in order to facilitate financing for homes and farm operations. Accordingly, after discussions with representatives of the Bureau of Indian Affairs in which leaders of the Tribe were assured that any claim they had against the State would not be jeopardized by legislation terminating federal services, the Tribe adopted a resolution supporting such legislation and authorizing a distribution of tribal assets to the members of the Tribe.[14] After receiving advice that the Tribe supported legislation authorizing the disposal of the tribal assets and terminating federal responsibility for the Tribe and its individual members, Congress enacted the Catawba Indian Tribe Division of Assets Act, 73 Stat. 592, 25 U.S.C. §§ 931-938. The Act provides for the preparation of a tribal membership roll, § 931; the tribal council's designation of sites for church, park, playground, and cemetery purposes, § 933(b); and the division of remaining assets among the enrolled members of the Tribe, § 933(f). The Act also provides for the revocation of the

---

[10]That Resolution declared: "[I]t is the policy of Congress, as rapidly as possible, to make the Indians within the territorial limits of the United States subject to the same laws and entitled to the same privileges and responsibilities as are applicable to other citizens of the United States, to end their status as wards of the United States, and to grant them all of the rights and prerogatives pertaining to American citizenship." H.R. Con. Res. 108, 83d Cong., 1st Sess. (1953), 67 Stat. B132.

[11]According to one compilation, between 1954 and 1962, Congress passed 12 separate "Termination Acts," the 11th of which was the Catawba Act. See F. Prucha, The Great Father 1048 (1984)....

[14]The resolution adopted at the meeting of the Tribe on January 3, 1959, expressly noted that "nothing in this legislation shall affect the status of any claim against the State of South Carolina by the Catawba Tribe."

Tribe's Constitution and the termination of federal services for the Tribe, § 935. It explicitly states that state laws shall apply to members of the Tribe in the same manner that they apply to non-Indians. *Ibid.* Pursuant to that Act, the 3,434-acre reservation that had been acquired as a result of the 1943 Memorandum of Understanding was distributed to the members of the Tribe; the Secretary of the Interior revoked the Tribe's Constitution, effective July 1, 1962.

In 1980, the Tribe commenced this action seeking possession of the 225-square-mile tract and trespass damages for the period of its dispossession. All of the District Judges for the District of South Carolina recused themselves, and Judge Willson of the Western District of Pennsylvania was designated to try the case. After the development of a substantial record of uncontested facts, Judge Willson granted petitioners' motion for summary judgment. His order of dismissal was initially reversed by a panel of the Court of Appeals for the Fourth Circuit; sitting en banc, the full Court of Appeals adopted the panel's opinion. Because of the importance of the case, we requested the views of the Solicitor General of the United States and granted certiorari [and] now reverse.

II

Section 5 of the Catawba Act is central to this dispute. As currently codified, it provides:

> "The constitution of the tribe adopted pursuant to sections 461, 462, 463, 464, 465, 466 to 470, 471 to 473, 474, 475, 476 to 478, and 479 of this title shall be revoked by the Secretary. Thereafter, the tribe and its members shall not be entitled to any of the special services performed by the United States for Indians because of their status as Indians, all statutes of the United States that affect Indians because of their status as Indians shall be inapplicable to them, and the laws of the several States shall apply to them in the same manner they apply to other persons or citizens within their jurisdiction. Nothing in this subchapter, however, shall affect the status of such persons as citizens of the United States." 25 U.S.C. § 935.

This provision establishes two principles in unmistakably clear language. First, the special federal services and statutory protections for Indians are no longer applicable to the Catawba Tribe and its members. Second, state laws apply to the Catawba Tribe and its members in precisely the same fashion that they apply to others.

The Court of Appeals disagreed with this reading of the Act. For it concluded that the word "them" in the second sentence of § 5 could refer to the individual Indians who are members of the Tribe and not encompass the Tribe itself. Relying on the canon that doubtful expressions of legislative intent must be resolved in favor of the Indians, it thus held that the language in § 5 about the inapplicability of federal Indian statutes and the applicability of state laws did not reach the Tribe itself.

The canon of construction regarding the resolution of ambiguities in favor of Indians, however, does not permit reliance on ambiguities that do not exist; nor does it permit disregard of the clearly expressed intent of Congress.[16] It seems

---

[16]See *Oregon Dept. of Fish and Wildlife v. Klamath Indian Tribe*, 473 U.S. 753, 774 (1985) ("[E]ven though 'legal ambiguities are resolved to the benefit of the Indians,' *DeCoteau v. District County Court*, 420 U.S. 425, 447 (1975), courts cannot ignore plain language that, viewed in historical context and given a 'fair appraisal,' *Washington v. Washington Commercial Passenger*

clear to us that the antecedent of the words "them" and "their" in the second sentence of § 5 is the compound subject of the first clause in the sentence, namely, "the tribe and its members." To read the provision otherwise is to give it a contorted construction that abruptly divorces the first clause from the second and the third, and that conflicts with the central purpose and philosophy of the Termination Act. According the statutory language its ordinary meaning, moreover, is reinforced by the fact that the first sentence in the section provides for a revocation of the Tribe's Constitution. It would be most incongruous to preserve special protections for a tribe whose constitution has been revoked while withdrawing protection for individual members of that tribe.

Without special federal protection for the Tribe, the state statute of limitations should apply to its claim in this case. For it is well established that federal claims are subject to state statutes of limitations unless there is a federal statute of limitations or a conflict with federal policy. Although federal policy may preclude the ordinary applicability of a state statute of limitations for this type of action in the absence of a specific congressional enactment to the contrary, County of Oneida v. Oneida Indian Nation, 470 U.S. 226 (1985), the Catawba Act clearly suffices to reestablish the usual principle regarding the applicability of the state statute of limitations. In striking contrast to the situation in County of Oneida, the Catawba Act represents an explicit redefinition of the relationship between the Federal Government and the Catawbas; an intentional termination of the special federal protection for the Tribe and its members; and a plain statement that state law applies to the Catawbas as to all "other persons or citizens."

That the state statute of limitations applies as a consequence of terminating special federal protections is also supported by the significance we have accorded congressional action redefining the federal relationship with particular Indians. We have long recognized that, when Congress removes restraints on alienation by Indians, state laws are fully applicable to subsequent claims. Similarly, we have emphasized that Termination Acts subject members of the terminated tribe to "the full sweep of state laws and state taxation."[20] These principles reflect an understanding that congressional action to remove restraints on alienation and other federal protections represents a fundamental change in federal policy with respect to the Indians who are the subject of the particular legislation.

The Court of Appeals found support for its conclusion about the nonapplicability of the state statute of limitations in § 6 of the Catawba Act, which provides that nothing in the statute affects the rights of the Tribe under the laws of South Carolina.[21] The thrust of the Court of Appeals' reasoning was that, if a state law was inapplicable to the Tribe or its members before the effective date

---

Fishing Vessel Assn., 443 U.S. [658, 673 (1979)], clearly runs counter to a tribe's later claims"); Rice v. Rehner, 463 U.S. 713, 732 (1983) (canon of construction regarding certain Indian claims should not be applied "when application would be tantamount to a formalistic disregard of congressional intent"); Andrus v. Glover Construction Co., 446 U.S. 608, 618-619 (1980); DeCoteau v. District County Court, 420 U.S., at 447 ("A canon of construction is not a license to disregard clear expressions of tribal and congressional intent").

[20] Bryan v. Itasca County, 426 U.S. 373, 389 (1976)....

[21] As currently codified, § 6 provides:

"Nothing in this subchapter shall affect the rights, privileges, or obligations of the tribe and its members under the laws of South Carolina." 25 U.S.C. § 936.

of the Act, its application after the effective date necessarily violates § 6. But such a reading contradicts the plain meaning of § 5's reference to the applicability of state laws. In our view § 6 was merely intended to remove federal obstacles to the ordinary application of state law. Section 6 cannot be read to preserve, of its own force, a federal tribal immunity from otherwise applicable state law without defeating a basic purpose of the Act and negating explicit language in § 5. Most fundamentally, § 6 simply does not speak to the explicit redefinition of the federal relationship with the Catawbas that is the basis for the applicability of the state statute of limitations.

Finally, the Court of Appeals relied heavily on the assurance to the Tribe that the status of any claim against South Carolina would not be affected by the legislation. Even assuming that the legislative provisions are sufficiently ambiguous to warrant reliance on the legislative history, we believe that the Court of Appeals misconceived the import of this assurance. We do not accept petitioners' argument that the Catawba Act immediately extinguished any claim that the Tribe had before the statute became effective. Rather, we assume that the status of the claim remained exactly the same immediately before and immediately after the effective date of the Act, but that the Tribe thereafter had an obligation to proceed to assert its claim in a timely manner as would any other person or citizen within the State's jurisdiction. As a result, unlike the Court of Appeals, we perceive no contradiction between the applicability of the state statute of limitations and the assurance that the status of any state claims would not be affected by the Act.

We thus conclude that the explicit redefinition of the federal relationship reflected in the clear language of the Catawba Act requires the application of the state statute of limitations to the Tribe's claim.

III

The District Court held that respondent's claim is barred by the South Carolina statute of limitations. The Court of Appeals' construction of the 1959 federal statute made it unnecessary for that court to review the District Court's interpretation of state law. Because the Court of Appeals is in a better position to evaluate such an issue of state law than we are, we remand the case to that court for consideration of this issue.

It is so ordered.

JUSTICE BLACKMUN, with whom JUSTICE MARSHALL and JUSTICE O'CONNOR join, dissenting.

The Catawba Indian Tribe Division of Assets Act, 73 Stat. 592, 25 U.S.C. § 931 *et seq.*, was passed by Congress in 1959 to divide up the Tribe's federally supervised reservation so that individual Catawbas could sell or mortgage their allotments. The Court today concludes that the Act also had the incidental effect of applying a South Carolina statute of limitations to the Catawbas' pre-existing and longstanding claim to lands the State purported to purchase from the Tribe in 1840. I feel this interpretation cannot be reconciled with the language of the Act under this Court's traditional approach to statutes regulating Indian affairs. I therefore dissent.

I

Too often we neglect the past. Even more than other domains of law, "the intricacies and peculiarities of Indian law deman[d] an appreciation of history." Frankfurter, Foreword to A Jurisprudential Symposium in Memory of Felix S. Cohen, 9 Rutgers L. Rev. 355, 356 (1954).

Before the arrival of white settlers, the Catawba Indians occupied much of what is now North and South Carolina. In the 1760 Treaty of Pine Tree Hill, the Catawbas relinquished the bulk of their aboriginal territory to Great Britain in exchange for assurances that they would be allowed to live in peace on a small portion of that territory, a square of land 15 miles on each side (144,000 acres), which today surrounds and includes Rock Hill, S.C. Three years later, in the Treaty of Augusta, the Tribe again agreed to "remain satisfied with the Tract of Land of Fifteen Miles square," and the British once more promised that "the Catawba shall not in any respect be molested by any of the King's subjects within the said Lines." App. 35. It is the 144,000 acres reserved for the Catawbas in 1760 and again in 1763 — "a mere token of the[ir] once large domain" — that give rise to this litigation. See J. Brown, The Catawba Indians 8 (1966) (Brown).

[Ultimately by] the 1830's, however, nearly all of the 144,000 acres reserved for the Tribe in the Treaty of Augusta had been leased to non-Indians. This situation proved disastrous, because rents were "generally paid in old horses, old cows or bed quilts and clothes, at prices that the whites set on the articles taken." The Catawbas soon were reduced to "a state of starvation and distress," *ibid.*, and they ultimately gave in to repeated efforts by the State to purchase their land. In 1840, representatives of the Tribe and the State signed the Treaty of Nation Ford. Under this "treaty" — which the United States never joined or approved — the Catawbas relinquished all their land in exchange for two prom-ises. First, the State promised the sum of $16,000 in a series of resettlement payments. Second, the State pledged that it would purchase a new reservation "of the value of five thousand dollars," including 300 acres of "good arable lands fit for cultivation" in a thinly populated area of North or South Carolina satisfactory to the Indians. App. 38-39.[2]

[In the interim 146 years] that have passed since the Nation Ford agreement, the Catawbas repeatedly have pressed their claim to the 144,000 acres, which they feel were taken from them illegally. In the early 1900's, the Tribe peti-tioned both the Federal Government and the State of South Carolina for relief, arguing that the 1840 transfer was void because the United States had not approved it. The Commissioner of Indian Affairs advised the Catawbas in 1906 and again in 1909 that the Department of the Interior would not seek relief on their behalf. He explained that the Catawbas were "state Indians" for whom the

---

[2] According to Massey, the Indians "were driven to" this agreement "by being surrounded by white men, [who] cheat[ed] them out of their rights, and [by] partaking of the vices of the whites and but few of their virtues." Report to The Governor of South Carolina on the Catawba Indians 5 (1854), reprinted in 6 Record, Ex. 11. The "vices" to which Massey referred may have included the consumption of alcohol; the Catawbas later charged that state representatives negotiated the treaty by setting out a whiskey barrel and some tin cups and inviting the Indians to help themselves. This charge was reported to the Department of the Interior in a 1908 memorandum by Catawba tribal attorney Chester Howe. See Plaintiffs' Response to Defendants' Motion to Dismiss in No. 80-2050-6 (CA4) p. 23, n.30, citing Record Group 75, National Archives Central Files 1907-1939, BIA File No. 1753-1906.

United States had no responsibility, and, consequently, that the absence of such participation in the Treaty of Nation Ford did not void the transaction. In 1908, the South Carolina Attorney General reached the same conclusion, and advised the state legislature that the Tribe had no outstanding claim to any of the 144,000 acres. 1908 Op. S.C. Atty. Gen. 17, 18, 29-32. The Tribe nonetheless continued to press its claim to the land. A federal Indian agent visiting the Catawbas in December 1910, for example, was asked about the Tribe's prospects for recovering "their old reservation of 15 miles square"; he told them the Department of the Interior would not take their case into court. 6 Record, Ex. 21, pp. 11-12 (letter from C. Davis to Comm'r of Indian Affairs, Jan. 5, 1911).

[Therefore in 1958], after representatives from the Bureau of Indian Affairs suggested to the Catawbas that their financial difficulties could be alleviated by distributing the Tribe's federally supervised assets and ending federal restrictions on alienation, the Indians expressed concern about their claims against the State, but they were assured that the proposal would not jeopardize those claims. 6 Record, Ex. 53, pp. 7-8 (memorandum from program officer to Tribal Programs Branch Chief, Jan. 30, 1959) (quoted by the Court, ante, at 510, n.23). The Tribe then adopted a resolution calling on its Congressman, Robert Hemphill, to introduce and secure passage of legislation to remove restraints on alienation and to distribute tribal assets; the resolution specifically requested, however, that "nothing in this legislation shall affect the status of any claim against the State of South Carolina by the Catawba Tribe." App. 103.

Representative Hemphill asked the Bureau of Indian Affairs to draft legislation "to accomplish the desires set forth in the Resolution." He then presented the draft bill to the Catawbas and told them that it had been "drawn up to carry out the intent of the resolution." After a majority of the Tribe expressed approval, Representative Hemphill introduced the bill in Congress, explaining that the Tribe had given its consent. See 105 Cong. Rec. 5462 (1959). The result was the 1959 Division of Assets Act, which the Court today concludes may bar the Tribe from pursuing its claim to the lands reserved for it in 1760 and 1763.

In the 1970's, spurred by favorable legal rulings elsewhere in the country, Catawba leaders renewed their request to the Department of the Interior to seek relief for the Tribe. In 1977, the Solicitor of the Department concluded that the rebuffs given the Catawbas in 1906 and 1909 had been legally unjustified, and that the Tribe could establish a prima facie claim to the 144,000 acres. He further concluded that the Division of Assets Act operated prospectively only, and did not affect pre-existing rights. Accordingly, the Solicitor formally requested the Department of Justice to institute legal action on behalf of the Catawbas and to support the settlement discussions that the Tribe already had initiated with South Carolina officials. The litigation request was later withdrawn in an effort to emphasize that the Interior Department favored a negotiated settlement if at all possible, and settlement legislation backed by the Tribe was introduced in Congress. The legislative efforts apparently proved fruitless, and in October 1980 the Tribe filed this suit.

II

The Tribe's complaint asserts a right to possession of the reserved portion of its aboriginal territory under the Nonintercourse Act, the Federal Constitution, and the treaties of 1760 and 1763. These are federal claims, see *Oneida Indian Nation v. County of Oneida*, 414 U.S. 661, 666-678 (1974) (*Oneida I*), and the statute of limitations is thus a matter of federal law, see *County of Oneida v. Oneida Indian Nation*, 470 U.S. 226, 240-244 (1985) (*Oneida II*). Where, as here, Congress has not specified a statute of limitations, federal courts generally borrow the most closely analogous limitations period under state law, but only if application of the state limitations period would not frustrate federal policy.

[Since] I do not believe that Congress in 1959 expressed an unambiguous desire to encumber the Catawbas' claim to their 18th-century treaty lands, and because I agree with Justice Black that "[g]reat nations, like great men, should keep their word," *FPC v. Tuscarora Indian Nation*, 362 U.S. 99, 142 (1960) (dissenting opinion), I do not join the judgment of the Court.

MENOMINEE TRIBE v. UNITED STATES

391 U.S. 404 (1968)

[The *Menominee* case holds that notwithstanding similar language contained in the Menominee termination legislation subjecting members of the tribe to state law once the termination plan went into effect, the termination legislation did not make Menominees subject to state conservation laws, a result which would have interfered with or abrogated the treaty rights promised them in the Treaty of Wolf River of 1854. The canons of construction for treaties and statutes affecting Indians were very important to the Court's decision, as was the potential liability of the United States for a taking had the Court adopted a contrary construction of the termination legislation. Indeed, the *Menominee* decision involved an inverse condemnation suit brought by the tribe after state courts had ruled that Menominee hunting and fishing rights had been abrogated by the Menominee termination legislation. The Court rejected the taking claim since it found Menominee rights had not been abrogated. It is reprinted in Chapter 6, page 799.]

NOTE: TERMINATION LEGISLATION

Like many of the termination statutes, the Catawba termination statute was the product of the interaction of a general congressional policy reflected in House Concurrent Resolution 108, quoted in footnote 10 of the *Catawba* opinion, and a negotiation between federal agents and the tribe under which the tribe voted to accept the proposal with certain limitations. As reflected in footnote 14 of the opinion, the Catawba Nation agreed to the legislation only upon the express understanding that "nothing in this legislation shall affect the status of any claim against the State of South Carolina by the Catawba Tribe." Ever since the Supreme Court decision in *Worcester v. Georgia*, 31 U.S. (6 Pet.) 515 (1831), the Court has construed treaties and agreements with Indian tribes as the Indians would have understood them. Did the Court follow that approach in *Catawba*? In light of the language of section 6 of the termination legislation, upon which the Court of Appeals had relied, was the plain language textual approach of Justice Stevens' opinion even justified by the language of the statute? Reviewing the context of federal Indian law, Professor Rennard Strickland, paraphrasing Alexis de Tocqueville, noted that "it would be impossible to destroy men with more respect for the law." Strickland, *Genocide-at-Law: An Historic and Contemporary View of the Native American Experience*, 34 KAN. L. REV. 713, 719 (1986). Does the Court's opinion in *Catawba* merely represent a legal validation or apology for the type of fraud in treaty and other negotiations between Indians and the federal and state governments about which Indians have complained almost since contact with Euro-Americans? *See generally* Note, *Terminating Federal Protection with Plain Statements*, 72 IOWA L. REV. 1117 (1987).

Fortunately, as the *Menominee Tribe* decision reflects, the Supreme Court has not consistently followed the approach to interpreting termination legislation taken in *Catawba*. Greater respect historically has been paid by the federal judiciary to the canons of construction and to Indian understandings of the effect of relevant language. Likewise, in *Kimball v. Callahan*, 493 F.2d 564 (9th Cir.), *cert. denied*, 419 U.S. 1019 (1974), the Ninth Circuit relied on *Menominee Tribe* to hold that former members of the Klamath Tribe who withdrew from the tribe pursuant to an option afforded under the Klamath termination plan still had the right to hunt, trap, and fish within their ancestral Klamath Indian Reservation (now mostly contained in the Klamath National Forest) free of Oregon fish and game regulations, pursuant to the Treaty of October 14, 1864, 16 Stat. 707. The Ninth Circuit rejected efforts to distinguish *Menominee Tribe*:

> Defendants argue that *Menominee Tribe* is distinguishable because of significant differences between the Menominee and Klamath Termination Acts. True, unlike the Klamath Termination Act, the Menominee Act gave no option to the Menominee Indians to withdraw from the tribe and receive the money value of their interests in tribal property. Also, although title to the reservation changed hands in *Menominee Tribe*, the Menominees continued to occupy the same land before and after the Termination Act. The disputed land in this case, on the other hand, is no longer legally occupied by the Klamaths.
>
> While these are substantial points of distinction, we find nothing in the language of *Menominee Tribe* to indicate its reasoning does not transcend these distinctions.
>
> [Not only has Congress] failed to indicate clearly an intent to abrogate treaty rights; it in fact expressly preserved at least fishing rights on the former reservation. The Termination Act provides that "[n]othing [in the Act] shall abrogate any fishing rights or privileges of the tribe or the members thereof enjoyed under Federal treaty." 25 U.S.C. § 564m(b).
>
> [Because] the Act provides that nothing in it shall abrogate any treaty fishing rights, we conclude that a Klamath Indian possessing such rights on the former reservation at the time of its enactment retains them even though he relinquishes his tribal membership or the reservation shrinks pursuant to the Act. Otherwise, the Act would in fact have resulted in the abrogation of treaty rights.

Id. at 568-69.

In light of *Menominee*, would the Catawba Nation have a fifth amendment takings claim against the United States for extinguishing their land claim to the "Tract of Land of Fifteen Miles square"? Should it make any difference to that claim whether the actual extinguishment of the claim came as a direct result of the termination legislation or, rather, was merely the result of the running of the state statute of limitation without tribal action? In light of the Catawba tribe's understanding of the meaning of the termination legislation reflected in footnote 14, an understanding never clearly corrected by the federal government until the *Catawba* decision in 1985, does not the federal government share major responsibility for the extinguishment of the Catawba land claim? Would a ruling that no taking had occurred merely because the actual extinguishment of title was the product of Catawba inaction in the face of a state statute of limitation constitute another illustration of the type of genocide-at-law validation of improper federal action about which Professor Strickland complained?

As the *Catawba* case indicates, the termination statutes all contained a provision that stated that upon final termination

> members of the tribe shall not be entitled to any of the services performed by the United States for Indians because of their status as Indians and ... all statutes of the United States which affect Indians because of their status as Indians shall no longer be applicable to the members of the tribe, and the laws of the several States shall apply to the tribe and its members in the same manner as they apply to other citizens or persons within their jurisdiction.

See, e.g., 25 U.S.C. § 564q. Unlike similar language contained in section 6 of the General Allotment Act of 1887, codified as amended at 25 U.S.C. § 349, the language in the termination acts applied to all members of the tribe rather than applying personally to the allottees. Thus, where the state jurisdiction was not inconsistent with prior treaty guarantees, as it was in *Kimball* and *Menominee Tribe v. United States*, these provisions effectively transferred jurisdiction to the states. They did not, however, wholly abolish tribal authority over tribal members.

Applying the language of these provisions, the court in *United States v. Heath*, 509 F.2d 16 (9th Cir. 1974), held that for purposes of the federal Indian country jurisdiction statutes a terminated full-blood Klamath Indian who was accused of killing an Indian in Indian country must be treated as no longer an Indian for jurisdictional purposes. Thus, the accused was properly tried under 18 U.S.C. § 1152, rather than § 1153. Note that had the victim been a non-Indian, the logic of *Heath* would suggest that the jurisdiction lies with the state courts under *United States v. McBratney*, 104 U.S. 621 (1881); *Draper v. United States*, 164 U.S. 240 (1896); and *New York ex rel. Ray v. Martin*, 326 U.S. 496 (1946).

For surveys of the termination policy, see D. FIXICO, TERMINATION AND RELOCATION: FEDERAL INDIAN POLICY, 1945-60 (1986); F. PRUCHA, THE GREAT FATHER 1046-59 (1984); Wilkinson & Biggs, *The Evolution of the Termination Policy*, 5 AM. INDIAN L. REV. 137 (1977); Hertzberg, *The Menominee Indians: Termination to Restoration*, 6 AM. INDIAN L. REV. 143 (1978); Preloznik & Felsenthal, *The Menominee Struggle to Maintain Their Tribal Assets and Protect Their Treaty Rights Following Termination*, 51 N.D.L. REV. 53 (1975).

SENATE REPORT NO. 93-604, 93d Congress, 1st Session 1-3, 10-11 (1973)

The Menominee Tribe of Indians was aboriginally located on approximately 9½ million acres in what is now northern Wisconsin and upper Michigan. Through a series of treaties with the United States beginning in 1831, the Menominee ceded most of their original land to the United States in return for monetary compensation and various promises of support and protection. They were slowly pushed to the south and west onto their present 234,000 acre reservation in Wisconsin, situated about 50 miles west of Green Bay. The reservation guaranteed to the Menominee by treaty of 1848 (which also ceded a portion of their land for the use of the Stockbridge-Munsee Indians of New York) is characterized by lakes, streams, and forests with approximately 4,000 acres of water and 222,000 acres of timber.

By 1954, the Menominee tribe, as an entity, stood at the forefront of Indian tribes, in terms of economic, social, and cultural progress.

Their forests provided the main source of industry and income for the Menominee people. Their steadfast commitment to the policy of sustained-yield forestry had insured a continued harvest of some of the finest tracts of hardwood and pine timber in the country. The Menominee adopted the concept of sustained-yield management and began sawmill operations in Neopit, Wis., in order to retain their major natural resources for future generations.

For the past hundred years, the prevailing philosophy of the Menominee people was based on the strong desire to maintain their tribal lands, assets, and identity intact. They strongly resisted all attempts to allot their lands in severalty to the individual members under the Allotment Act, which has checker-boarded and divided many other Indian reservations. They maintained their tribal forest lands while much of Wisconsin was clear-cut for additional agricultural space. The land provided them with a tribal source of income, employment for its members, and a home for future generations.

Despite the heavy hand of Bureau of Indian Affairs paternalism, the tribe had made rapid progress in self-government and self-sufficiency. While the tribe had voted to accept the provisions of the Indian Reorganization Act of 1934, it continued to operate its tribal government under a constitution adopted in 1928.

In 1954, the tribe had over $10,000,000 on deposit in the U.S. Treasury, partially derived from judgments against the United States and partially derived from income from the forest industry. The tribe funded and operated its own hospital, schools, and community services. The responsibility of the sawmill operation was to provide employment for tribal members, and in addition to provide revenue to finance much of the cost of BIA services on the reservation. While individually the members of the tribe still ranked on or near the poverty level of income compared to a national scale, the tribal entity possessed a pride and dignity and a commitment to progress which had placed them at the forefront of Indian tribes....

By the act of June 18, 1954, as amended, the Congress provided that the termination of special Federal services and the grant to the Menominee Indians of full control over their affairs would be accomplished no later than April, 1961.

[The Menominee Termination Act provided that the Menominee Tribe should formulate and submit to the Secretary a plan for the future control of tribal property and of service functions conducted at that time by or under the supervision of the United States, including but not limited to services in the fields of health, education, welfare, credit, roads, and law and order. The resulting plan relied upon securing state legislation to furnish aid and protection to the Menominees in their new form of governance.

[To implement the Menominee plan, the State of Wisconsin created Menominee County and Town, whose boundaries are coterminous with the previously existing reservation. All of the social service functions which had been administered by the tribe and the Bureau of Indian Affairs were assumed by Menominee County and Town. Menominee Enterprises, Incorporated, which was also created by the State of Wisconsin, assumed the ownership of the land and assets that had been held in trust for the Menominee Tribe by the United States Government. Each person whose name appeared on the final tribal roll was given an income bond and 100 shares of stock in Menominee Enterprises, Incorporated, as evidence of his participation in the ownership of the land and assets that had been held by the United States.

[In order to help the Menominees solve the problems they faced after termination, significant Federal and State financial assistance have been made available including some $2 million provided under special authorizations contained in Public Law 87-432 (76 Stat. 53) and Public Law 89-653 (80 Stat. 903). Since termination, aid has amounted to approximately $20 million in State and Federal funds.

[In addition, the State of Wisconsin enacted special statutory provisions to attempt to alleviate certain organizational, administrative, and financial difficulties that were found to exist. A special Wisconsin legislative study group was set up to monitor progress and problems, and to make recommendations for legislative action that might be needed to correct the problems.

[Even with these special efforts, serious financial and other problems have plagued the Menominees since termination, and they and their institutions are now gravely threatened by insolvency and the loss of their land base. Menominee Enterprises, Inc., has already had to dispose of some land, its most valuable asset and one to which the Menominee people have a deep attachment, in order to meet its ongoing operational requirements and its tax liability obligation to Menominee County.

[To further complicate the financial problems besetting Menominee Enterprises, the sales of its products — primarily lumber produced at its saw mill — have been declining steadily from a high point of $4.1 million, with a profit of $744,000, in 1966. Even if this trend were to be reversed, rising costs for Menominee Enterprises, Inc., and in the lumber industry as a whole make a dramatic upswing in profits unlikely. It is apparent that the costs of running Menominee County will not be able to be met out of the profits of the saw mill, but most likely will be met by further sales of the land assets of the corporation. Dissipation of the land base will reduce the amount of land that is available for sustained management for forest products, thus jeopardizing the operation of the saw mill. The prognosis for the Menominees, then, is bleak: financial chaos or stopgap transfusions of increasing amounts of public moneys without any real chance of altering the downward spiral. Needless to say, the toll of this decline on the morale of the Menominees has been severe.]*

The plan adopted by the tribe provided for the incorporation of a profit corporation under Wisconsin State law, known as Menominee Enterprises, Inc.,

---

*The material in brackets is taken from a letter from John Kyle, Assistant Secretary of the Interior, to the Chairman of the Senate Committee on Interior and Insular Affairs that is set forth at the conclusion of the Senate Report.

to take title to the lands and assets of the tribe and to operate the tribal sawmill. One hundred shares of stock in the Corporation and one income bond was issued to each member of the tribe on the final roll. The stock was held and voted by an eleven-member Menominee Common Stock and Voting Trust elected by the membership.

This plan brought the Menominee people to the brink of economic, social and cultural disaster. The sawmill operation, which supported the tribe and most of the Federal services prior to termination, is now only marginally successful. Menominee Enterprises, Inc., saddled with a huge corporate indebtedness, a difficult management scheme, and high county and state taxation, is on the verge of bankruptcy. In order to meet its tax burden, pay interest on the income bonds, and continue to operate the mill on a marginal basis, the Corporation has had to sell portions of its land, which has had a traumatic effect on the tribe.

Only recently have the Menominee people been able to gain some measure of control of their own affairs from a corporate structure that has been dominated and controlled by non-Menominee persons. With a growing awareness of the state to which termination has brought them, the Menominee people have mounted a forceful effort to reimpose a Federal trust on their remaining lands and to restore special Federal services. Among those tribes that were subjected to the termination policy, the Menominee have uniquely retained intact most of their land base and have maintained a cohesive tribal identity and community.

Unless this bill is enacted, the dim future of the tribe is made clear in the concluding paragraph of an extensive report of the Bureau of Indian Affairs to the 93d Congress. The report states:

> The economic instability of MEI (Menominee Enterprises, Incorporated) combined with the elimination of public funds to the county make the situation perilous. Unless relief is made immediately available in the form of either a massive infusion of public funds or restoration, MEI will no longer be economically viable and Menominee County will go under.

NOTE: RESTORATION OF TERMINATED TRIBES

The problem of terminated tribes affords a unique window into several issues in Indian affairs. Included in the questions raised are the following issues: What is an Indian tribe and to what extent, if at all, is its sovereignty practically or theoretically dependent upon federal protection from state authority? To what extent do terminated tribes remain sovereign? To what extent are they exempted from state regulation and taxation? Does termination terminate and disband the tribe, or does it merely terminate the tribe's special eligibility for federal services and the federal preemption of state authority? While a tribal community may survive the termination process, what, if anything, is left of the tribal entity? In the Menominee case what legal form did the tribal entity have after termination? What consequences attend the extension of state authority to regulate, tax, and adjudicate to reservation Indians? Were the consequences experienced by the Menominee the inevitable result of the extension of state authority and the consequent diminution or complete loss of tribal sovereignty, or were they merely the avoidable results of inept management of the termination process? What were the economic consequences of subjecting tribal Indian resources to state taxation?

The experiences of the Menominee tribe under termination led to federal restoration of the tribe. Menominee Restoration Act of 1973, 25 U.S.C. § 903 et seq. As noted in the legislative report, restoration of the Menominee was somewhat simplified by the fact that the tribe had maintained its land base relatively intact. Even after passage of the Menominee Restoration Act, the state of Wisconsin ultimately retroceded criminal and civil jurisdiction to the federal government to restore the Menominee Tribe to a semblance of their pre-termination era status. 41 Fed. Reg. 8516 (1976).

Under the Siletz Indian Tribe Restoration Act of 1977, 25 U.S.C. § 711 et seq., the Siletz of Oregon were also restored to trust supervision. Their restoration was somewhat complicated by the lack of an intact land base. Thus, section 7 of the Act, 25 U.S.C. § 711e, provided for negotiations between the tribe and the Secretary of the Interior, with notification to and consultation with all appropriate state and local government officials in Oregon and other interested parties, to develop a plan for the establishment of such a reservation. Section 7 provides some interesting limitations on these negotiations:

Notification and consultation

(c) To assure that legitimate State and local interests are not prejudiced by the creation of a reservation for the tribe, the Secretary, in developing a plan under subsection (b) of this section for the establishment of a reservation, shall notify and consult with all appropriate officials of the State of Oregon, all appropriate local governmental officials in the State of Oregon and any other interested parties. Such consultation shall include the following subjects:

(1) the size and location of the reservation;
(2) the effect the establishment of the reservation would have on State and local tax revenues;
(3) the criminal and civil jurisdiction of the State of Oregon with respect to the reservation and persons on the reservation;
(4) hunting, fishing, and trapping rights of the tribe and members of the tribe, on the reservation;
(5) the provision of State and local services to the reservation and to the tribe and members of the tribe on the reservation; and
(6) the provision of Federal services to the reservation and to the tribe and members of the tribe and the provision of services by the tribe to members of the tribe.

Provisions of plan

(d) Any plan developed under this section for the establishment of a reservation for the tribe shall provide that —

(1) any real property transferred by the tribe or members of the tribe to the Secretary shall be taken in the name of the United States in trust for the benefit of the tribe and shall be the reservation for the tribe;
(2) the establishment of such a reservation will not grant or restore to the tribe or any member of the tribe any hunting, fishing, or trapping right of any nature, including any indirect or procedural right or advantage, on such reservation;
(3) the Secretary shall not accept any real property in trust for the benefit of the tribe or its members unless such real property is located within Lincoln County, State of Oregon;
(4) any real property taken in trust by the Secretary for the benefit of the tribe or its members shall be subject to all rights existing at the time such property is taken in trust, including liens, outstanding Federal, State, and local taxes, mortgages, out-

standing indebtedness of any kind, easements, and all other obligations, and shall be subject to foreclosure and sale in accordance with the laws of the State of Oregon;

(5) the transfer of any real property to the Secretary in trust for the benefit of the tribe or its members shall be exempt from all Federal, State, and local taxation, and all such real property shall, as of the date of such transfer, be exempt from Federal, State, and local taxation; and

(6) the State of Oregon shall have civil and criminal jurisdiction with respect to the reservation and persons on the reservation in accordance with section 1360 of Title 28 and section 1162 of Title 18.

Over the past twenty years, Congress has restored a number of terminated tribes to federal supervision. The provisions in each act vary with the demographic pattern of the Native community and tribe's ownership of a land base. *E.g.*, Act of Aug. 18, 1987, Pub. L. 100-89, Title II, 101 Stat. 670, codified at 25 U.S.C. 21§ 731 *et seq.* (Alabama and Coushatta Tribes); Act of October 17, 1984, Pub. L. 98-481, § 4, 98 Stat. 2251, codified at 25 U.S.C. § 714b (Confederated Tribes of Coos, Lower Umpqua, and Siuslaw Indians); Act of Nov. 22, 1983, Pub. L. 98-165, § 4, 97 Stat. 1064, codified at 25 U.S.C. § 713b (Confederated Tribes of the Grande Rondo Community of Oregon); Act of Dec. 29, 1982, Pub. L. 97-391, § 3, 96 Stat. 1960, codified at 25 U.S.C. § 712a (Cow Creek Band of Umpqua Tribe); Act of April 3, 1980, Pub. L. 96-227, 94 Stat. 317, codified at 25 U.S.C. § 761 *et seq.* (Paiute Tribes of Utah); Act of May 15, 1978, Pub. L. 95-281, 92 Stat. 246, codified at 25 U.S.C. § 861 *et seq.* (Wyandotte, Peoria, Ottawa, and Modoc Tribes of Oklahoma). *See generally* Note, *Terminating the Indian Termination Policy*, 35 STAN. L. REV. 1181 (1983).

PROCEDURES FOR ESTABLISHING THAT AN AMERICAN GROUP EXISTS AS AN INDIAN TRIBE

25 C.F.R. Part 83

§ 83.1 Definitions.

(a) "Secretary" means the Secretary of the Interior or his authorized representative.

(b) "Assistant Secretary" means the Assistant Secretary — Indian Affairs, or his authorized representative.

(c) "Department" means the Department of the Interior.

(d) "Bureau" means the Bureau of Indian Affairs.

(e) "Area Office" means the Bureau of Indian Affairs Area Office.

(f) "Indian tribe," also referred to herein as "tribe," means any Indian group within the continental United States that the Secretary of Interior acknowledges to be an Indian tribe.

(g) "Indian group" or "group" means any Indian aggregation within the continental United States that the Secretary of the Interior does not acknowledge to be an Indian tribe.

(h) "Petitioner" means any entity which has submitted a petition to the Secretary requesting acknowledgment that it is an Indian tribe.

(i) "Autonomous" means having a separate tribal council, internal process, or other organizational mechanism which the tribe has used as its own means of making tribal decisions independent of the control of any other Indian governing entity. Autonomous must be understood in the context of the Indian culture and social organization of that tribe.

(j) "Member of an Indian group" means an individual who is recognized by an Indian group as meeting its membership criteria and who consents to being listed as a member of that group.

(k) "Member of an Indian tribe" means an individual who meets the membership requirements of the tribe as set forth in its governing document or is recognized collectively by those persons comprising the tribal governing body, and has continuously maintained tribal relations with the tribe or is listed on the tribal rolls of that tribe as a member, if such rolls are kept.

(l) "Historically," "historical" or "history" means dating back to the earliest documented contact between the aboriginal tribe from which the petitioners descended and citizens or officials of the United States, colonial or territorial governments, or if relevant, citizens and officials of foreign governments from which the United States acquired territory.

(m) "Continuously" means extending from generation to generation throughout the tribe's history essentially without interruption.

(n) "Indigenous" means native to the continental United States in that at least part of the tribe's aboriginal range extended into what is now the continental United States.

(o) "Community" or "specific area" means any people living within such a reasonable proximity as to allow group interaction and a maintenance of tribal relations.

(p) "Other party" means any person or organization, other than the petitioner who submits comments or evidence in support of or in opposition to a petition.

§ 83.2 Purpose.

The purpose of this part is to establish a departmental procedure and policy for acknowledging that certain American Indian tribes exist. Such acknowledgment of tribal existence by the Department is a prerequisite to the protection, services, and benefits from the Federal Government available to Indian tribes. Such acknowledgment shall also mean that the tribe is entitled to the immunities and privileges available to other federally acknowledged Indian tribes by virtue of their status as Indian tribes as well as the responsibilities and obligations of such tribes. Acknowledgment shall subject the Indian tribe to the same authority of Congress and the United States to which other federally acknowledged tribes are subjected.

§ 83.3 Scope.

(a) This part is intended to cover only those American Indian groups indigenous to the continental United States which are ethnically and culturally identifiable, but which are not currently acknowledged as Indian tribes by the Department. It is intended to apply to groups which can establish a substantially continuous tribal existence and which have functioned as autonomous entities throughout history until the present.

(b) This part does not apply to Indian tribes, organized bands, pueblos or communities which are already acknowledged as such and are receiving services from the Bureau of Indian Affairs.

(c) This part is not intended to apply to associations, organizations, corporations or groups of any character, formed in recent times; provided that a group which meets the criteria in § 83.7(a)-(g) has recently incorporated or otherwise formalized its existing autonomous process will have no bearing on the Assistant Secretary's final decision.

(d) Nor is this part intended to apply to splinter groups, political factions, communities or groups of any character which separate from the main body of a tribe currently acknowledged as being an Indian tribe by the Department, unless it can be clearly established that the group has functioned throughout history until the present as an autonomous Indian tribal entity.

(e) Further, this part does not apply to groups which are, or the members of which are, subject to congressional legislation terminating or forbidding the Federal relationship.

§ 83.4 Who may file.

Any Indian group in the continental United States which believes it should be acknowledged as an Indian tribe, and can satisfy the criteria in § 83.7, may submit a petition requesting that the Secretary acknowledge the group's existence as an Indian tribe.

§ 83.5 Where to file.

A petition requesting the acknowledgment that an Indian group exists as an Indian tribe shall be filed with the Assistant Secretary — Indian Affairs, Department of the Interior, 18th and "C" Streets NW., Washington, D.C. 20245. Attention: Federal acknowledgment project.

§ 83.6 Duties of the Department.

(a) The Department shall assume the responsibility to contract, within a twelve-month period following the enactment of these regulations, all Indian groups known to the Department in the continental United States whose existence has not been previously acknowledged by the Department. Included specifically shall be those listed in chapter 11 of the American Indian Policy Review Commission final report, volume one, May 17, 1977. The Department shall inform all such groups of the opportunity to petition for an acknowledgment of tribal existence by the Federal Government.

(b) The Secretary shall publish in the *Federal Register* within 90 days after effective date of these regulations, a list of all Indian tribes which are recognized and receiving services from the Bureau of Indian Affairs. Such list shall be updated and published annually in the *Federal Register*.

(c) Within 90 days after the effective date of the final regulations, the Secretary will have available suggested guidelines for the format of petitions, including general suggestions and guidelines on where and how to research for required information. The Department's example of petition format, while preferable, shall not preclude the use of any other format.

(d) The Department shall, upon request, provide suggestions and advice to researchers representing a petitioner for their research into the petitioner's historical background and Indian identity. The Department shall not be responsible for the actual research on behalf of the petitioner.

§ 83.7 Form and content of the petition.

The petition may be in any readable form which clearly indicates that it is a petition requesting the Secretary to acknowledge tribal existence. All the criteria in paragraphs (a) through (g) of this section are mandatory in order for tribal existence to be acknowledged and must be included in the petition.

(a) A statement of facts establishing that the petitioner has been identified from historical times until the present on a substantially continuous basis, as "American Indian," or "aboriginal." A petitioner shall not fail to satisfy any criteria herein merely because of fluctuations of tribal activity during various years. Evidence to be relied upon in determining the group's substantially continuous Indian identity shall include one or more of the following:

(1) Repeated identification by Federal authorities;
(2) Longstanding relationships with State governments based on identification of the group as Indian;
(3) Repeated dealings with a county, parish, or other local government in a relationship based on the group's Indian identity;
(4) Identification as an Indian entity by records in courthouses, churches, or schools;
(5) Identification as an Indian entity by anthropologists, historians, or other scholars;
(6) Repeated identification as an Indian entity in newspapers and books;
(7) Repeated identification and dealings as an Indian entity with recognized Indian tribes or national Indian organizations.

(b) Evidence that a substantial portion of the petitioning group inhabits a specific area or lives in a community viewed as American Indian and distinct from other populations in the area, and that its members are descendants of an Indian tribe which historically inhabited a specific area.

(c) A statement of facts which establishes that the petitioner has maintained tribal political influence or other authority over its members as an autonomous entity throughout history until the present.

(d) A copy of the group's present governing document, or in the absence of a written document, a statement describing in full the membership criteria and the procedures through which the group currently governs its affairs and its members.

(e) A list of all known current members of the group and a copy of each available former list of members based on the tribe's own defined criteria. The membership must consist of individuals who have established, using evidence acceptable to the Secretary, descendancy from a tribe which existed historically or from historical tribes which combined and functioned as a single autonomous entity. Evidence acceptable to the Secretary of tribal membership for this purpose includes but is not limited to:

(1) Descendancy rolls prepared by the Secretary for the petitioner for purposes of distributing claims money, providing allotments, or other purposes;

(2) State, Federal, or tribal official records or evidence identifying present members or ancestors of present members as being an Indian descendant and a member of the petitioning group;

(3) Church, school, and other similar enrollment records indicating the person as being a member of the petitioning entity;

(4) Affidavits of recognition by tribal elders, leaders, or the tribal governing body, as being an Indian descendant of the tribe and a member of the petitioning entity;

(5) Other records or evidence identifying the person as a member of the petitioning entity.

(f) The membership of the petitioning group is composed principally of persons who are not members of any other North American Indian tribe.

(g) The petitioner is not, nor are its members, the subject of congressional legislation which has expressly terminated or forbidden the Federal relationship.

§ 83.8 Notice of receipt of petition.

(a) Within 30 days after receiving a petition, the Assistant Secretary shall send an acknowledgment of receipt, in writing, to the petitioner, and shall have published in the *Federal Register* a notice of such receipt including the name and location, and mailing address of the petitioner and other such information that will identify the entity submitting the petition and the date it was received. The notice shall also indicate where a copy of the petition may be examined.

(b) Groups with petitions on file with the Bureau on the effective date of these regulations shall be notified within 90 days from the effective date that their petition is on file. Notice of that fact, including the information required in paragraph (a) of this section, shall be published in the *Federal Register*. All petitions on file on the effective date will be returned to the petitioner with guidelines as specified in § 83.6(c) in order to give the petitioner an opportunity to review, revise, or supplement the petition. The return of the petition will not affect the priority established by the initial filing.

(c) The Assistant Secretary shall also notify, in writing, the Governor and attorney general of any State in which a petitioner resides.

(d) The Assistant Secretary shall also cause to be published the notice of receipt of the petition in a major newspaper of general circulation in the town or city nearest to the petitioner. The notice will include, in addition to the information in paragraph (a) of this section, notice of opportunity for other parties to submit factual or legal arguments in support of or in opposition to the petition. Such submissions shall be provided to the petitioner upon receipt by the Federal acknowledgment staff. The petitioner shall be provided an opportunity to respond to such submissions prior to a final determination regarding the petitioner's status.

§ 83.9 Processing the petition.

(a) Upon receipt of a petition, the Assistant Secretary shall cause a review to be conducted to determine whether the petitioner is entitled to be acknowledged as an Indian tribe. The review shall include consideration of the petition and supporting evidence, and the factual statements contained therein. The Assistant Secretary may also initiate other research by his staff, for any purpose relative to analyzing the petition and obtaining additional information about the petitioner's status, and may consider any evidence which may be submitted by other parties.

(b) Prior to actual consideration of the petition, the Assistant Secretary shall notify the petitioner of any obvious deficiencies, or significant omissions, that are apparent upon an initial review, and provide the petitioner with an opportunity to withdraw the petition for further work or to submit additional information or a clarification.

(c) Petitions shall be considered on a first come, first serve basis determined by the date of original filing with the Department. The Federal acknowledgment project staff shall establish a priority register including those petitions already pending before the Department.

(d) The petitioner and other parties submitting comments on the petition shall be notified when the petition comes under active consideration. They shall also be notified who is the primary Bureau staff member reviewing the petition, his backup, and supervisor. Such notice shall also include the office address and telephone number of the primary staff member.

(e) A petitioning group may, at its option and upon written request, withdraw its petition prior to publication by the Assistant Secretary of his finding in the *Federal Register* and, may if it so desires, file an entirely new petition. Such petitioners shall not lose their priority date by withdrawing and resubmitting their petitions later, provided the time periods in paragraph (f) of this section shall begin upon active consideration of the resubmitted petition.

(f) Within 1 year after notifying the petitioner that active consideration of the petition has begun, the Assistant Secretary shall publish his proposed findings in the *Federal Register*. The Assistant Secretary may extend that period up to an additional 180 days upon a showing of due cause to the petitioner. In addition to the proposed findings, the Assistant Secretary shall prepare a report which shall summarize the evidence for the proposed decision. Copies of such report shall be available for the petitioner and other parties upon written request.

(g) Upon publication of the proposed findings, any individual or organization wishing to challenge the proposed findings shall have a 120-day response period to present factual or legal arguments and evidence to rebut the evidence relied upon.

(h) After consideration of the written arguments and evidence rebutting the proposed findings, the Assistant Secretary shall make a determination regarding the petitioner's status, a summary of which shall be published in the *Federal Register* within 60 days form the expiration of the response period. The determination will become effective in 60 days from publication unless earlier withdrawn pursuant to § 83.10.

(i) The Assistant Secretary shall acknowledge the existence of the petitioner as an Indian tribe when it is determined that the group satisfies the criteria in § 83.7.

(j) The Assistant Secretary shall refuse to acknowledge that a petitioner is an Indian tribe if it fails to satisfy the criteria in § 83.7. In the event the Assistant Secretary refuses to acknowledge the eligibility of a petitioning group, he shall analyze and forward to the petitioner other options, if any, under which application for services and other benefits may be made.

§ 83.10 Reconsideration and final action.

(a) The Assistant Secretary's decision shall be final for the Department unless the Secretary requests him to reconsider within 60 days of such publication. If the Secretary recommends reconsideration, the Assistant Secretary shall consult with the Secretary, review his initial determination, and issue a reconsidered decision within 60 days which shall be final and effective upon publication.

(b) The Secretary in his consideration of the Assistant Secretary's decision may review any information available to him, whether formally part of the record or not; where reliance is placed on information not of record, such information shall be identified as to source and nature, and inserted in the record.

(c) The Secretary may request reconsideration of any decision by the Assistant Secretary but shall request reconsideration of any decision, which in his opinion:

(1) Would be changed by significant new evidence which he has received subsequent to the publication of the decision; or

(2) A substantial portion of the evidence relied on was unreliable or was of little probative value; or

(3) The petitioner's or the Bureau's research appears inadequate or incomplete in some material respect.

(d) Any notice which by the terms of these regulations must be published in the *Federal Register*, shall also be mailed to the petitioner, the Governors and attorney generals of the States involved, and to other parties which have commented on the proposed findings.

§ 83.11 Implementation of decisions.

(a) Upon final determination that the petitioner is an Indian tribe, the tribe shall be eligible for services and benefits from the Federal Government available to other federally recognized tribes and entitled to the privileges and immunities available to other federally recognized tribes by virtue of their status as Indian tribes with a government-to-government relationship to the United States as well as having the responsibilities and obligations of such tribes. Acknowledgment shall subject such Indian tribes to the same authority of Congress and the United States to which other federally acknowledged tribes are subject.

(b) While the newly recognized tribe shall be eligible for benefits and services, acknowledgment of tribal existence will not create an immediate entitlement to existing Bureau of Indian Affairs programs. Such programs shall become available upon appropriation of funds by Congress. Requests for appropriations shall follow a determination of the needs of the newly recognized tribe.

(c) Within 6 months after acknowledgment that the petitioner exists as an Indian tribe, the appropriate Area Office shall consult and develop in cooperation with the group, and forward to the Assistant Secretary, a determination of needs and a recommended budget required to serve the newly acknowledged tribe. The recommended budget will be considered along with other recommendations by the Assistant Secretary in the usual budget-request process.

NOTE: NONRECOGNIZED TRIBES

In 1977, prior to the adoption of these regulations, the Indian Policy Review Commission reported that of the more than 400 tribes within the nation's boundaries the BIA provided services to only 284. The Commission specifically identified 133 unrecognized tribal communities (excluding terminated tribes) encompassing almost 121,000 persons who were, thus, ineligible for federal services. Of these 133 communities, 27 of the tribes had some land holdings, over 37 had colonial treaties, over 32 were specifically mentioned in treaties with the United States, and over 30 were historically referred to in BIA records. AMERICAN INDIAN POLICY REVIEW COMMISSION, FINAL REPORT 461-75 (1977). For the landless tribal communities, will federal recognition bring any change in the scope of state authority?

The jurisdictional, service, and other problems of non-recognized tribes led to proposals for legislation, and finally in 1978, to these regulations providing a procedure by which such Indian communities could secure federal recognition. *See also Hearings on S. 2375 Before the Senate Select Comm. on Indian Affairs*, 95th Cong., 2d Sess. (1978). Several tribes have already established government-to-government relationships with the federal government under these recognition regulations. *E.g.*, 54 FED. REG. 51502 (1989) (San Juan Southern Paiute Tribe); 52 FED. REG. 4193 (Wampanoag Tribal Council of Gay Head, Inc.); 49 FED. REG. 24083 (1984) (Poarch Band of Creeks); 48 FED. REG. 6177 (1983) (Narragansett Indian Tribe of Rhode Island). The recognition process, however, has rejected several applications. *E.g.*, 53 FED. REG. 23694 (Machis Lower Alabama Creek Indian Tribe, Inc.); 52 FED. REG. 3709 (Samish Indian Tribe of Washington).

Perhaps one of the most complex and interesting current recognition problems involves the Lumbee Indians of North Carolina, a very large group of over 27,500 persons residing in and around Robeson, North Carolina. In 1956, during the termination era, this group sought recognition as Indians and Congress passed the Lumbee Act of 1956, Pub. L. 84-570, 70 Stat. 254. This statute merely provided that the group would be known as the Lumbee Indians of North Carolina but otherwise provided that they would continue to enjoy the same rights, privileges, and immunities as North Carolina citizens they theretofore enjoyed and should be subject to the same obligations and duties as other citizens. More importantly, in response to a recommendation from the Department of the Interior, the Act provided that "[n]othing in this Act shall make such Indians eligible for any services performed by the United States for Indians because of their status as Indians, and none of the statutes of the United States which affect Indians because of their status as Indians shall be applicable to the Lumbee Indians." Because of this last sentence there is some doubt that the administrative recognition process applies to the Lumbees since 25 C.F.R. § 83.7(g) expressly excludes from the administrative recognition process any terminated tribe or tribe that has been forbidden federal recognition. Nevertheless, in 1987 the Lumbees files a fully documented petition for federal acknowledgment. The Bureau of Indian Affairs has such a backlog of acknowledgment petitions that estimates suggest this one might not be considered until 1993. In response to both the uncertainty of coverage under the regulations and the time delay, Senate Bill 901 was introduced into the 100th Congress in 1989 to provide Congressional acknowledgment for the Lumbees and to make them eligible for federal services. The proposed legislation contains provisions reserving to North Carolina criminal jurisdiction and civil causes of action involving Lumbees occurring in the dependent Indian communities of the Lumbee Tribe. Similar legislation was introduced in the House of Representatives. Senate hearings have been held on the proposed legislation. *Senate Hearing 101-270*, 101st Cong., 2d Sess.

While tribes that do not currently have established government-to-government relationship with the federal government may be ineligible for many federal benefits, and some of the usual federal rules governing federally recognized Indian tribes may not apply to such communities, certain federal statutes and policies apply to all Indians, irrespective of federal recognition. For example, the federal restraint on alienation of Indian land contained in 25 U.S.C. § 177 applies to both federally recognized and unrecognized tribes. *E.g., Joint Tribal Council of Passamaquoddy Tribe v. Morton*, 528 F.2d 370 (1st Cir. 1975). Similarly, as the First Circuit held in *Bottomly v. Passamaquoddy Tribe*, 599 F.2d 1061 (1st Cir. 1979), set forth and discussed in Chapter 3, section A1a, federal common law doctrines of tribal sovereign immunity also apply to tribes which do not have governments recognized by the Secretary of the Interior. Similarly, when the Pamunkey Indians of Virginia, a tribe that had established a special trust relationship with the colony and later state of Virginia since the seventeenth century, sought to resolve a land claim, Congressional approval was required for the settlement in light of 25 U.S.C. § 177 notwithstanding their lack of federal acknowledgment. Pub. L. 96-44, 94 Stat. 2365 (1980). Thus, some doctrines of federal Indian law apply even to tribes indigenous to the United States that are not recognized by the Secretary of the Interior.

Chapter 9

OTHER RESPONSES TO CULTURAL PLURALISM: A BROADER PERSPECTIVE

According to Frances Svensson, "[the] confrontation between tribal populations and expanding states has been a phenomenon of every age and every continent." Svensson, *Comparative Ethnic Policy on the American and Russian Frontiers*, 36 J. INT'L AFF. 83, 83 (1982). This concluding chapter is designed to broaden the students' focus beyond domestic United States law to the internal law of other nations and international law. The comparative law section of this chapter examines the policies of other nations toward indigenous populations. The themes common in the discourse of aboriginal rights should be familiar to the student from the earlier chapters of this book, such as definitional problems, membership determinations, self-government, and the clash of separatism with the equality principle. The chapter first focuses on the experience of selected nations. Because the United States and British Commonwealth countries share a common heritage, Canada, New Zealand, and Australia are featured first. Courts in those countries frequently invoke the seminal opinions of Justice Marshall as well as recent United States decisions. Yet there are sharp contrasts in addition to the parallels in the treatment of the aboriginal peoples of those countries. Central and South America are also featured, for several reasons. American students have been sensitized by the environmental movement to issues such as massive deforestation of the rain forests that have had a devastating impact on Indians in the Amazon. Although the contrasts are more stark, there are parallels as well, such as a wardship system, in part owing to the Spanish influence on American Indian law. A final excerpt describes the system in South Africa.

The second section of the chapter then turns to international law. In recent years indigenous peoples have increasingly turned to international law as a forum both for publicizing their complaints about domestic laws and policies and to develop international standards that can be applied in domestic contexts. After an introduction providing a historical perspective on international law, the chapter turns to basic documents, such as the United Nations Charter and the Human Rights Covenants, including the Optional Protocol, and then to recent standard-setting activities: a reprise of ILO Convention No. 169, originally presented in Chapter 1, and the most recent Draft Declaration on the Rights of Indigenous Peoples of the Working Group on Indigenous Populations of the United Nations Economic and Social Council.

A. COMPARATIVE LAW: PROBLEMS AND PERSPECTIVES

SANDERS, ABORIGINAL RIGHTS IN CANADA: AN OVERVIEW, 2
Law & Anthropology 177-93 (Vienna 1987)*

The Populations

Indigenous peoples live in all parts of Canada. They are more evenly distributed, geographically, than the non-Indian populations, which are heavily concentrated near the southern borders of the country. These patterns of population distribution mean that the relative population of indigenous peoples varies tremendously from region to region. They are a majority in the Northeast Territories and about 25% of the population in the Yukon, the other northern territory. In parts of the eastern Arctic, northern Quebec and the northern interior of British Columbia, they are close to 100% of the population.

There are difficulties with exact figures for the indigenous populations. Since the middle of the 19th century the government has kept lists of "Indians" recognised as entitled to reside on Indian reserves. The lists, once established, were continued by criteria set out in the Indian Act, a national statute. The Indian Act imposed a single national system of patrilineal descent for determining membership of Indian bands, ignoring factors of race or culture. The Indian Act was amended in 1985 to permit Indian bands to develop their own criteria for band membership, a process currently underway in many Indian communities. The current numbers of Indians recognized under the Indian Act or Indian band membership codes would exceed 300,000.

The Indian Act membership system excluded many individuals who were racially and culturally Indian, and who became known as non-status Indians. The phenomenon does not parallel that of the non-recognized tribes in the United States. Non-status Indians are individuals who are excluded from particular Indian bands, while the bands themselves are recognized. Exclusion means that these individuals are not eligible to live on reserves and not eligible for federal government Indian programs which are provided to "status Indians." The Indian Act amendments of 1985 have resulted in the reinstatement of many individual non-status Indians into band membership and the assumption of control over membership criteria by bands themselves. These changes reduce both the numbers and political significance of non-status Indians in Canada.

The Indian peoples belong to 10 separate language groups. Cultural patterns vary greatly. These diverse societies were brought under a uniform national system of units recognized by the Indian Act. Most recognized bands have one or more "reserves" for their use. In most of Canada, the reserves were intended to be an agricultural land base for the Indian communities. Often reserves were not established in the non-agricultural northern areas. A variant reserve system was established on the west coast, where seasonal village sites and numerous fishing stations were made into reserves. The result is a pattern of multiple reserves per band, giving British Columbia more reserves that the rest of Canada.

The Inuit (with a population of over 15,000) live in the Northwest Territories, northern Quebec and northern Labrador. They are members of one language group which includes the Inuit in Greenland and Alaska. Their isolation meant that the Government developed little in the way of indigenous polity for them. They are excluded from the Indian Act. The policy of making treaties with Indian groups was never extended to their areas. No reserve system was established for them.

The Métis are a distinctive Canadian population. The prairie west was controlled by the great fur trading companies from 1670 to 1870. During this period agricultural settlers were excluded and a distinct mixed blood population developed. The classic "Métis" had a French fur-trader father and a Cree Indian mother. By the middle of the 19th century a distinct Métis political consciousness had developed.... In the 1930s Métis land policy was re-examined in Saskatchewan and Alberta. As a result there is a reserve system of eight Métis settlements under provincial law in northern Alberta. There is no agreement on the numbers of Métis in Canada or on their degree of distinctiveness or self-identification as Métis. On the prairies there are a number of Métis communities, but without any special legal recognition of their identity or land holdings.

The Constitution of 1867 gave the federal government jurisdiction over "Indians, and Lands reserved for the Indians." The term "Indian" for this purpose has been held to include "Inuit." The 1982 amendments to the Constitution have provisions which describe the Indians, Inuit and Métis as the "aboriginal peoples of Canada." Both before and after the amendments there has been legal debate as to whether "Métis" are under federal legislative jurisdiction.

The History of Dealings

Colonial Acquisition

British authority was not established by conquest. In general there was little open warfare between the Europeans and the Indian tribes, in marked contrast to the patterns of western expansion in the United States. It is a point of pride in Canada to assert that the Indian tribes had not been conquered (proving greater virtue to the north of the border than to the south).

British authority, in general, was not established by cession. The 18th century Indian treaties in Nova Scotia and New Brunswick did involve an Indian acceptance of British sovereignty, but in subsequent dealings the British simply assumed they had suzerainty or sovereignty over the tribes.... British authority was not based on a general denial of a pre-existing legal order (the basis for acquisition by "occupation and settlement"). Indian territorial rights were recognized in the Royal Proclamation of 1763 as pre-existing rights. Land cession treaties were signed for half the country. Elements of customary law were held to survive.

Canadian law contains no theory on the legal basis for British acquisition of the area. Slattery has described a national myth that North America was "juridically a vacant land" when European exploration and settlement began. Unlike Australia and New Zealand, that myth was never institutionalized into a doc-

trine of acquisition. Thus as Slattery concludes, Canada lacks any theory to
describe:

> ... when and how the native peoples of Canada were won to the allegiance of the
> crown and what effect this process had on their original land rights, customary laws,
> and systems of government.[5]

Treaties

Political relations with the tribes in Atlantic Canada were volatile because of
English-French rivalries and the American revolutionary war.... The French
did not sign treaties with the Indians of New France (now Southern Quebec).
The Indians in the area were migratory hunters with large traditional territories
and the French settlers used little land. As well, the French ingratiated themselves by allying with the local Indians against the Iroquois. Indian policy was
largely in the hands of the Church and the first reserves were established by
Roman Catholic orders .... In the Treaty of Paris of 1763 Quebec was transferred to Britain.

Indian policy in New England involved the systematic reliance on treaties to
gain territory and jurisdiction from Indian tribes. In the mid-18th century the
British centralized jurisdiction over Indian affairs, because of Indian unrest.
British policy faced a major challenge in 1763 when Chief Pontiac forged an
alliance of tribes .... The British response was a centralized scheme for North
America set out in the Royal Proclamation of 1763. The basic elements of the
Proclamation were:

> 1. An assertion of British authority over the "nations of tribes of Indians
> with whom we are connected and who live under our protection ...".
> 2. The recognition of Indian territorial rights to areas which had not al-
> ready been purchased from them.
> 3. The confirmation of a Crown monopoly on dealings with the Indians to
> obtain lands.
> 4. A description of the procedures for negotiating treaties with Indian
> tribes.
> 5. Temporary measures to stop western colonial settlement beyond a par-
> ticular line.

The Proclamation meant that the systematic treaty policy followed in New
England was to be continued.... The American revolution had no impact on
these developments. Treaty policies were pursued in the United States after the
revolution and in Canada after its formation in 1867. In 1860-70 the vast areas
draining into Hudson's Bay and the Arctic Ocean were added to Canada. The
national government began signing treaties in 1871 and continued signing
treaties with Indian tribes until the 1920s. Adhesions to existing treaties were
signed as late as the 1950s. Unlike the United States, where Congress ordered
the ending of Indian treaty-making in 1871, Canada has never declared an end
to treaty-making.

---

[5]B. Slattery, "The Hidden Constitution: Aboriginal Rights in Canada" in Bolt and Long (eds.),
The Quest for Justice (University of Toronto Press, Toronto, 1985) 114, 116.

In both the United States and Canada the historic treaty policy broke down in the last stages of national expansion. In the United States there are no treaties in California, Hawaii and Alaska. In Canada there are no treaties in British Columbia, the Yukon and the Inuit areas. As well the treaties with Indian tribes in the Northwest Territories were not fulfilled, and it has been established that the English texts do not reflect the Indian understanding of the arrangement.

Constitutional or Statutory Recognition

The Royal Proclamation of 1763 is the first major written constitutional document for Canada. While its exact legal status seems unclear, it is routine to say that it has the force of statute and that its Indian provisions have never been repealed.... The document did not give any legal status to Indian territorial rights, other than recognizing them as being in existence and as something to be acquired by the treaty process. The exact geographical application of the Proclamation has been the subject of a long and largely pointless debate in Canada. Clearly the framers were concerned about stopping European settlement west of the proclamation line, which for Canada meant southern Ontario (an area settled immediately after 1763). There is a reference to "proprietary governments" in the Proclamation, suggesting its application to the Hudson's Bay Company territories, though Canadian judicial decisions have denied such application. The geographical debate arose because the Judicial Committee of the Privy Council in 1887 ruled that Indian territorial rights were derived from the recognition in the Royal Proclamation. This clear misreading of the Proclamation has been rejected in more recent Canadian decisions, but the debate on geographical application has refused to die.[6]

The next significant constitutional provision came in 1867 with the creation of Canada as a federal state. The national government was given jurisdiction over "Indians, and Lands reserved for Indians" in s 91(24) of the Constitution (originally the British North America Act 1867 (UK)). It is generally accepted that the reason for national jurisdiction in 1867 was the protection of the Indians against local settlers, a theme articulated in both Britain and Upper Canada earlier in the 19th century.

The present land mass of Canada was put together in stages from 1867 to 1949. There are references to Indian rights in various constitutional documents over those years.... The end result is that constitutional provisions which involve the recognition of some substantive Indian rights exist for about half the land mass of Canada. Treaties also exist for about half the land mass of Canada, but the two geographical areas are not identical.

The Move Away from Recognition

In the mid-19th century the United States and Canada began exercising legislative jurisdiction over Indian issues. The prior patterns of dealings, based on treaties and consent, gave way to assumptions of sovereignty in the settler governments. The Indian Act began to take form in Canada, with provisions

---

[6]St. Catherines Milling Co. v. R. (1888) 14 AC 46; Calder v. Attorney General of British Columbia (1973) SC4 313.

governing band membership and local self-government. In the United States the Major Crimes Act 1886 and the General Allotment Act 1887 were upheld by the Courts though they were in breach of Indian treaties. These developments were consistent with the liberalism and positivism of the period. Tribes were no longer regarded as variant political communities, but as backward. The communal holdings of lands was seen as an anachronism, and measures to individualize titles occurred in the United States, Canada, Mexico, New Zealand, Japan and various parts of central and south America. Treaty making was ended by the United States Congress in 1871. New Zealand courts ruled that the Treaty of Waitangi of 1840 was a nullity, because the Maori had no system of law capable of being recognized....

British Columbia joined Canada in 1871. Fourteen treaties had been signed for small areas on Vancouver Island in the 1850s, but treaty making had been abandoned as official government policy. The Canadian government wanted to continue treaty making through to the coast, but was stopped by the opposition of the provincial government. After a number of disputes over the issue, the federal government abandoned the idea of treaties for the area. No treaties were signed in the Yukon or in the Inuit areas in the north....

Historians may have no difficulty in explaining the different policies followed at different times in Quebec, Ontario and British Columbia. But lawyers had problems. There seemed no legal theory which explained the patterns of dealings, except a theory that Indians had no legal rights. Treaties were political, not legal. We were dealing with policy not law....

The Move Back to Recognition

Canadian Indian policy largely slept through the 1930s, ignoring the innovations of the "Indian New Deal" in the United States. US policy, always more volatile, swung into termination in the 1950s, when Canada was gradually rediscovering its indigenous peoples. The ideological hostility to special status or collective rights that was manifested in the US termination policy simply did not find fertile ground in Canada, where limited patterns of French language rights and Catholic school rights were familiar and accepted. But if the French-Catholics made Canada more accepting of collective minority rights, Indian policy could also be affected by changes to French-English relations. The 1960s saw the rise of a strong French-Canadian nationalism.

Pierre Elliot Trudeau came to power in the late 1960s on a platform of no special status for Quebec. He applied the logic of his position to the only other holders of special status, the Indians. It was Trudeau's policy for French-Canada which led to his government's terminationist white paper on Indian policy in 1969. But the white paper was a dramatic departure from the general thrust of indigenous policy development in Canada in the post-war period. While there is support, particularly in some of the government bureaucracies, for the ending of Indian special status, that has not been an acceptable public stance for politicians at either the national or provincial levels. In this, Canada is markedly different from either the United States or Australia.

The move back to recognition came in slow stages. Indians gained political respect in both the United States and Canada because of their high enlistment rates in the Second World War.... Indian rights litigation began in the mid-1960s, with hunting and fishing cases. Initially the decisions were awful. The courts held that Indian treaty rights to hunt migratory birds had been ended implicitly (and probably unthinkingly) by general federal legislation. The Supreme Court of Canada tossed off that conclusion in one line, while devoting a number of pages to the question whether there had been adequate proof that the duck was wild. Quite properly, the judgement was the subject of a widely reprinted parody.[9]

In spite of the dismal judicial record, a major aboriginal title case from British Columbia went through the courts between 1969 and 1973. The case was *Calder v. Attorney General for British Columbia*. The Indians lost at trial. They lost on appeal. But their loss in the Supreme Court of Canada was technical, not substantive. Three judges ruled in favour of the Nishga Indians, saying that they retained ownership of their traditional territories. Three judges ruled that any Nishga rights had been ended by general colonial land legislation, enacted prior to 1871. The seventh judge ruled on a technical point and said nothing of the aboriginal title issue. The Indians had lost, but half the court had supported them on the aboriginal title issue. It was a startling decision. Jean Chretien, the Minister of Indian Affairs at the time, often referred to the Nishgas as having won the case. It had been a victory. The Supreme Court could not be trusted to uphold the status quo.

The timing of the judgement in the Nishga case was superb. It came at a time when there was a majority Liberal government in Ottawa, major Indian aboriginal title litigation in Quebec and the Northern Territories, and an extremely effective opposition critic on Indian affairs. Government policy shifted. In February, 1973, the national government agreed to open negotiations with the Indians in the Yukon to settle their aboriginal title claim. In August a broader policy was outlined. In September Morrow J. of the Supreme Court of the Northwest Territories ruled that the Dene Indians had established a prima facie case for aboriginal rights in the Mackenzie District, through which a major pipeline was being planned.[11] And in November Malouf J. of the Quebec Superior Court ordered a halt to the massive James Bay hydro-electric project on the basis of unextinguished Indian and Inuit aboriginal title.[12] Though the injunction was lifted one week later, pending a full hearing of an appeal, the initial order was too dramatic to be ignored....

Constitutional Amendment

While the issues of termination and land claims are familiar in other countries, the Canadian events connected with the "patriation" of the constitution are difficult for outsiders to comprehend. For particular political reasons, the Government of Canada decided in 1978 to attempt major amendments to the

---

[9] Sikyea v. R. (1964) SCR 642. [Eds. note: The parody, entitled Regina v. Ojibway, and often subtitled "Is a Pony Fortuitously Saddled With a Feather Pillow a Bird Within the Meaning of the Indian Act?", written by "Blue, J.," has been widely reprinted. See, e.g., 8 Crim. L.Q. 137 (1965).]
[11] Re Paulette and Register of Titles (No 2) (1974) 42 DLR (3d) 8.
[12] Kanatawat v. James Bay Development Corporation (unreported, 22 November 1973) (Quebec CA), reversing Quebec Superior Court (unreported, 15 November 1973). Leave to appeal to Supreme Court denied: (1975) 1 SCR 48.

Canadian constitution. The initiative was essentially a response to the issues of French-Canadian nationalism.... [T]he National Indian Brotherhood of Canada defined constitutional reform as an Indian issue, seeking (a) the recognition of aboriginal and treaty rights, (b) an Indian role in the constitutional reform process, and (c) the requirement of Indian consent to any constitutional amendment affecting Indian rights. The response of Canadian political leaders was accommodative. Indigenous rights were added to the list of agenda items.... In the fall of 1980, after a breakdown in federal-provincial negotiations, the federal Government dropped the provinces from the process, announcing that it would take its own constitutional proposals directly to Britain. This was a risky strategy, breaching normal rules of federal-provincial relations. Opposition was stronger than expected. By the beginning of 1981 the federal government was openly bargaining with interest groups and opposition parties in attempts to bolster support for its proposals.... The final provisions on indigenous people include three elements. Section 35 entrenches existing aboriginal and treaty rights. Section 25 protects indigenous rights against the general provisions of the Charter of Rights and Freedom. Section 37 redeems the promise of participation by providing for future First Minister's Conferences on aboriginal constitutional issues....

Recent Developments

Since the constitutional amendments of 1982, three First Minister's Conferences have been held at which representatives of four national indigenous organizations have publicly negotiated with the political leaders of Canada and the ten provinces. While certain constitutional amendments were agreed to at the first meeting in 1983, in general the major impact has come from the extensive media coverage including live television broadcasts....

Current Issues

Equality

In the past, Indian special status meant legal disabilities, though Indians were considered to be citizens. This second class citizenship was ended in stages in the years after the Second World War. The best known event was the extension of the vote in federal elections to Indians in 1960. 1960 was also the date of the enactment of the Canadian Bill of Rights, which included a guarantee of equality. Politicians of the period knew little about Indian issues and no discussion took place on possible conflict between the equality norm and the Indian Act. The courts gave no force to the Bill of Rights until the *Drybones* case challenged the special liquor sections of the Indian Act.[25] In question was a prohibition of public drunkenness with penalties slightly more serious than in the parallel prohibition for non-Indians. The Supreme Court struck down the Indian Act provision .... The next case challenged the complex rules for special status built around the reserve system. The Indian Act, which governs the reserve system, defined who was an Indian in order to allocate rights to reside on reserve lands. It was claimed that the Indian Act membership system dis-

---

[25] R. v. Drybones (1967) 64 DLR (3d) 260.

criminated on the basis of sex, by giving a wife and children the same status as the husband-father. An Indian woman who had lost status as a result of marriage to a non-Indian challenged the Indian Act system. The Supreme Court was unwilling to undercut the system of special status in the Indian Act and upheld the membership system.[26] The Court was unable to distinguish *Drybones* and unwilling to say that *Drybones* was wrong. The result was an unintelligible decision, but one which for the time being at least put an end to "equality" challenges to Indian special status....

Aboriginal Title

The issue of aboriginal rights and aboriginal title re-emerged in Canadian law and policies in the 1960s. Aboriginal title claims were rejected by the national Government in the white paper of 1969. Prime Minister Trudeau referred to such claims as historical claims.... At the time of his retirement, Trudeau was described in the media as having a strong personal interest in indigenous rights issues — a remarkable transformation....

The national government issued a short policy statement in August 1973, proposing the settlement of aboriginal title claims in major parts of the country through a process of negotiation.... The James Bay and Northern Quebec Agreements are long, complex documents, obviously drafted by lawyers and bureaucrats. However the agreements were approved by referenda in the Cree and Inuit villages. They have been implemented by a series of statutes, both at the national and provincial levels. They are comprehensive agreements, dealing with land, self-government, language and education. They have innovative provisions on the stabilization of the traditional hunting and trapping economy. They provide certain openings for locally controlled economic development. There have been problems in implementation, with Cree litigation against both the federal and provincial Governments. The federal Government acknowledged breach, and reached a settlement with the Cree. The disputes with the Province of Quebec are currently unresolved.

The second area of major concern in 1973 was the Northwest Territories, where Dene, Métis and Inuit claims posed possible obstacles to a natural gas pipeline, proposed to move United States natural gas from the north coast of Alaska to markets in the mid-western United States. The Canadian government appointed Justice Thomas Berger to head an inquiry into the pipeline proposal. Berger, in private practice, had acted for the Nishga Indians in the *Calder* case....

In the mid-1970s the Berger inquiry attracted national attention as it held community hearings throughout the Mackenzie District of the Northwest Territories. The end report was a visual and literary triumph.[29] ... The government realized that the Mackenzie valley pipeline scheme was lost and shifted to the alternate strategy of a route through the Yukon. A quick second inquiry gave cautious approval to that routing, but economic conditions were shifting. In the end no pipeline was built....

---

[26] Attorney General of Canada v. Lavell (1974) SCR 1349.
[29] T. Berger, Northern Frontier, Northern Homeland, The Report of The Mackenzie Valley Pipeline Inquiry (1977).

The third major area in the Government's mind in 1973 was British Columbia, the province with the longest history of Indian agitation on aboriginal title claims.... Indians were reluctant to re-litigate the *Calder* case. No major development projects forced the issue, for the general economic climate was deteriorating. The provincial government's strategy of saying as little as possible on the issue seemed to be succeeding. Then in 1985 the issue was back on the front pages of the newspapers. First the Gitksan Wet'suwet'en Tribal Council began an aboriginal title suit, claiming ownership and jurisdiction over their traditional lands. The statement of claim based the claim on both Canadian and international law. Separately a confrontation developed over the logging of Meares Island on the west coast of Vancouver Island. Indians and environmentalists obstructed loggers from one of the major forest companies. Indians got injunctions, with the result that logging ended pending determination of the aboriginal title issue.... Logging was stopped, for the moment at least, on Meares Island and Lyell Island. The province has restated its rejection of aboriginal title claims and will contest those claims in court.

The Treaties and Specific Claims

The exact legal character of Canadian Indian treaties has never been clear.... Under the British law applicable in Canada, treaties with foreign states were binding when signed by the executive. They did not require confirmation by Parliament. But they did not alter domestic law until implemented by legislation.... [I]n Canada as in New Zealand, there were no statutes specifically implementing the treaties.

Early litigation established that treaties were enforceable on the basis of contract law. While the Judicial Committee of the Privy Council explicitly avoided ruling that the treaties had no international law aspects, the only substantive holdings were enforcement of annuity promises as contractual obligations. The courts were faced with clear examples of government breach of treaty promises in the cases involving the Migratory Birds Convention Act in the 1960s. Those cases held that general federal legislation overrode treaty promises. The possibility of litigation for compensation for loss of rights was noted, but never pursued. No analysis of the nature of treaties occurs in the judgements, though they are clearly treated as domestic in character.

While the Government of Canada rejected aboriginal title claims in the White Paper of 1969, it accepted claims based on "lawful obligations," which could include claims based on treaties. This gave rise to the area of specific claims, as distinguished from the "comprehensive claims" which were based on unextinguished aboriginal title. The major activity has been a reconsideration of the adequacy of the reserve land base in Saskatchewan and British Columbia, within the logic of the treaties, or in the case of British Columbia, within the terms of federal-provincial commissions concerned with finalizing the reserve system in that province. The Saskatchewan treaty land entitlement program is supposed to be being copied for Manitoba, but no similar program as been hinted at for the other treaty areas of Alberta and Ontario. Instead, in those provinces there have been negotiations on the specific reserve land claims of individual bands, without a general framework at a regional or provincial level. The major innovation in Ontario is the Indian Commission of Ontario, a continuing body designed to facilitate negotiations between Indian groups and the federal and provincial governments on a range of issues, including specific claims.

The issue of the exact legal status of treaties was reopened in certain lower level court cases in the 1980s. Some judges were open to seeing the treaties as having an international law character. The supreme court of Canada in the *Simon* case said that they were not international law treaties, but were *sui generis*, a category unto themselves.[34] All we have is the assurance that the *sui generis* category is a legal category....

Self-government

Indian claims became more clearly political in the mid-1970s. In 1975 the Dene Declaration was issued in the Northwest Territories seeking recognition of the Dene as a nation and referring to the International process of decolonization. The National Indian Brotherhood spoke of the need to recognize Indian governments as an order of government within Canadian federalism. The Brotherhood reorganized as the Assembly of First Nations....

"Framework" legislation was introduced in June 1984, under which all Indian groups could negotiate some system of self-government. That legislation was widely criticized, but lapsed with the calling of the federal election. The new Minister of Indian Affairs rejected the idea of "framework" legislation, but without specific alternative proposals. The First Minister's Conference in the spring of 1985 represented a failure of the new Prime Minister to use his well-advertised negotiation skills to produce agreement on a constitutional provision of self-government. The government then turned to a case by case approach, in order to demonstrate some achievements in this area. The small, well organized Sechelt Indian band in British Columbia had pressed for special legislation for many years and had detailed proposals, drafted by their lawyer and approved by the band membership. They had been knocking on a closed door for over a decade: suddenly events made their impossible quest possible. The Sechelt Self-Government Act is now law. The legislation has been criticized by a number of other Indian groups. A number of other Indian communities are now seeking special legislation, but there is no policy statement by the Government as to how they intend to proceed. Undoubtedly the issue of self-government will again dominate the First Minister's Conference scheduled for the spring of 1987. That Conference is the last one scheduled to deal with aboriginal constitutional questions. It is unclear at the moment whether there will be a significant pressure for additional conferences.

GUERIN v. THE QUEEN

[1984] S.C.R. 335

DICKSON J.: The question is whether the appellants, the chief and councillors of the Musqueam Indian Band, suing on their own behalf and on behalf of all other members of the band, are entitled to recover damages from the federal Crown in respect of the leasing to a golf club of land on the Musqueam Indian

---

[34](1985) 24 DLR (4th) 390.

Reserve. Collier J., of the Trial Division of the Federal Court, declared that the Crown was in breach of trust. He assessed damages at $10,000,000. The Federal Court of Appeal allowed a Crown appeal, set aside the judgment of the Trial Division and dismissed the action.

I. *General*

Before adverting to the facts, reference should be made to several of the relevant sections of the *Indian Act*, R.S.C. 1952, c. 149, as amended. Section 18(1) provides in part that reserves shall be held by Her Majesty for the use of the respective Indian bands for which they were set apart. Generally, lands in a reserve shall not be sold, alienated, leased or otherwise disposed of until they have been surrendered to Her Majesty by the band for whose use and benefit in common the reserve was set apart (s. 37). A surrender may be absolute or qualified, conditional or unconditional (s. 38(2)). To be valid, a surrender must be made to Her Majesty, assented to by a majority of the electors of the band, and accepted by the Governor in Council (s. 39(1)).

The gist of the present action is a claim that the federal Crown was in breach of its trust obligations in respect of the leasing of approximately 162 acres of reserve land to the Shaughnessy Heights Golf Club of Vancouver. The band alleged that a number of the terms and conditions of the lease were different from those disclosed to them before the surrender vote and that some of the lease terms were not disclosed to them at all. The band also claimed failure on the part of the federal Crown to exercise the requisite degree of care and management as a trustee.

II. *The Facts*

The Crown does not attack the findings of fact made by the trial judge. The Crown simply says that on those facts no cause of action has been made out.

[In 1955, the Musqueam Indian Reserve contained 416.53 acres of valuable land in the City of Vancouver, British Columbia. Many parties were interested in acquiring land in the Reserve for development, including the Shaughnessy Heights Golf Club. Although the land could be sold for a much higher price to a developer, the government agreed to lease the land to the golf club. Under Canadian law, Band land can be leased or sold, but only by the government once the land has been formally surrendered to the government by the Band. The Band did surrender to the Queen in a formal document stating the land would be held "in trust to lease the same to such person or persons, and upon such terms as the Government of Canada may deem most conducive to our Welfare and that of our people." On January 22, 1958, the government signed a lease with the golf club.

[Although the Band knew about the plan to lease to the golf course and the original yearly rental, when the Band voted to agree to a surrender, the Band claimed and the lower court found, that the Band did not know about other terms which made the lease very favorable to the golf course. For example, the lease permitted the club to make the improvements necessary to build a country club on the land, but provided that the club could remove any improvements upon termination of the lease. In addition, the Band knew that the lease permitted renewals for up to 75 years with adjustments in price, but the Band did not know about a clause providing that the rent increases had to be based on the fair rental value of the land in an unimproved condition, which would greatly decrease the allowable rent increases, with a cap of 15% over the initial rental of $29,000 during the second renewal (from 1973 to 1988). Finally, the lease permitted the golf course, but not the Band, to cancel the lease at the end of each term with 6 months' notice. Finally, the Band initially believed the lease was for 10 year terms instead of 15 year terms. When told that the initial 15 year term could not be changed, the Band demanded that the renewal periods be limited to 10 year terms. Nevertheless, the lease signed by the government contained 15 year terms. Finally, the government did not give the Band a copy of the lease for 12 years.

[In light of these facts the trial judge found that the Band would not have agreed to the lease had it known the actual terms and held the government liable for breach of trust.]

III. Assessment at Trial and on Appeal of the Legal Effect of the Facts as Found

The plaintiffs based their case on breach of trust. They asserted that the federal Crown was a trustee of the surrendered lands. The trial judge agreed.

The Crown attempted to argue that if there was a trust it was, at best, a "political trust," enforceable only in Parliament and not a "true trust," enforceable in the courts.... The Crown then argued that if there were a legally enforceable trust its terms were those set out in the surrender document, permitting it to lease the 162 acres to anyone, for any purpose, and upon any terms which the Crown deemed most conducive to the welfare of the band. In the Crown's submission the surrender document imposed on it no obligation to lease to the golf club on the terms discussed at the surrender meeting; nor did it impose any duty on the Crown to obtain the approval of the band in respect of the terms of the lease ultimately entered into.

The trial judge rejected these submissions [finding the] Crown liable for breach of trust. In respect to damages ... the judge held that the measure of damages is the actual loss which the acts or omissions have caused to the trust estate, the plaintiffs being entitled to be placed in the same position so far as possible as if there had been no breach of trust. The judge proceeded on the basis that the band would not have agreed to the terms of the lease as signed and the club would not have agreed to a lease on the terms found by the judge to be the terms of the trust. Therefore it would have been possible for the band at some point to have leased the land for residential purposes on a 99-year leasehold basis on extremely favourable terms. In quantifying the award, the judge confessed to being unable to set out a precise rationale or approach, mathematical or otherwise. He said that the award was obviously a "global" figure: a considered reaction based on the evidence, the opinions, the arguments and, in the end, his own conclusions of fact. The judge assessed the plaintiffs' damages at $10,000,000.

The Federal Court of Appeal, speaking through Mr. Justice Le Dain, proceeded on the premise that the case presented on behalf of the band rested on the existence of a statutory trust in the private law sense based primarily on the terms of s 18(1) of the *Indian Act*. Section 18(1) reads:

18(1) Subject to the provisions of this Act, reserves shall be held by Her Majesty for the use and benefit of the respective bands for which they were set apart; and subject to this Act and to the terms of any treaty or surrender, the Governor in Council may determine whether any purpose for which lands in a reserve are used or are to be used is for the use and benefit of the band.

Le Dain J. scrutinized this section and concluded that it was not consistent with a "true trust" in the sense of an equitable obligation enforceable in a court of law. Especially telling, in his opinion, was the discretion vested by s 18(1) in the Governor in Council to determine whether a particular purpose to which reserve land is being put, or is proposed to be put, is "for the use and benefit of the band." In his view this discretion indicated it was for the government, not the courts, to determine what was for the use and benefit of the band. Such a discretion, in his opinion, was incompatible with an intention to impose an equitable obligation, enforceable in court, to deal with the land in a certain manner. Section 18(1) was therefore incapable of making the Crown a true trustee of those lands [at p. 469 D.L.R.]:

The extent to which the government assumes an administrative or management responsibility for the reserves of some positive scope is a matter of governmental discretion, not legal or equitable obligation. I am, therefore, of the opinion that s 18 of the *Indian Act* does not afford a basis for an action for breach of trust in the management or disposition of reserve lands.

Le Dain J. also rejected the alternative contention on behalf of the band that a trust was created by the terms of the surrender document, especially the words "in trust to lease the same," and that the Crown was in breach of that trust by its alleged failure to exercise ordinary skill and prudence in leasing the land ....

Having found no basis for the trust alleged, the Federal Court of Appeal allowed the Crown's appeal.

IV. *Fiduciary Relationship*

[T]he existence of an equitable obligation is the *sine qua non* for liability. Such an obligation is not, however, limited to relationships which can be strictly defined as "trusts." As will presently appear, it is my view that the Crown's obligations *vis-à-vis* the Indians cannot be defined as a trust. That does not, however, mean that the Crown owes no enforceable duty to the Indians in the way in which it deals with Indian land.

The fiduciary relationship between the Crown and the Indians has its roots in the concept of aboriginal, native or Indian title. The fact that Indian bands have a certain interest in lands does not, however, in itself give rise to a fiduciary relationship between the Indians and the Crown. The conclusion that the Crown is a fiduciary depends upon the further proposition that the Indian interest in the land is inalienable except upon surrender to the Crown.

An Indian band is prohibited from directly transferring its interest to a third party. Any sale or lease of land can only be carried out after a surrender has taken place, with the Crown then acting on the band's behalf. The Crown first took this responsibility upon itself in the Royal Proclamation of 1763 (R.S.C.

1970, App. II, No. 1). It is still recognized in the surrender provisions of the *Indian Act*. The surrender requirement, and the responsibility it entails, are the source of a distinct fiduciary obligation owed by the Crown to the Indians. In order to explore the character of this obligation, however, it is first necessary to consider the basis of aboriginal title and the nature of the interest in land which it represents.

(a) *The existence of Indian title*

In *Calder et al. v. A.G. B.C.*, [[1973] S.C.R. 313], this court recognized aboriginal title as a legal right derived from the Indian's historic occupation and possession of their tribal lands. With Judson and Hall JJ. writing the principal judgments, the court split three-three on the major issue of whether the Nishga Indians' aboriginal title to their ancient tribal territory had been extinguished by general land enactments in British Columbia. The court also split on the issue of whether the Royal Proclamation of 1763 was applicable to Indian lands in that province. Judson and Hall JJ. were in agreement, however, that aboriginal title existed in Canada (at least where it has not been extinguished by appropriate legislative action) independently of the Royal Proclamation of 1763....

The Royal Proclamation of 1763 reserved (at p. 127)

> ... under our Sovereignty, Protection, and Dominion, for the use of the said Indians, all the Lands and Territories not included within the Limits of Our said Three new Governments, or within the limits of the Territory granted to the Hudson's Bay Company, as also all the Lands and Territories lying to the Westward of the Sources of the Rivers which fall into the Sea from the West and North West as aforesaid.

In recognizing that the Proclamation is not the sole source of Indian title ... *Calder* is consistent with the position of Chief Justice Marshall in the leading American cases of [*Johnson v. M'Intosh* and *Worcester v. Georgia*].

The principle that a change in sovereignty over a particular territory does not in general affect the presumptive title of the inhabitants was approved by the Privy Council in *Amodu Tijani v. Secretary, Southern Nigeria*, [1921] 2 A.C. 399. That principle supports the assumption implicit in *Calder* that Indian title is an independent legal right which, although recognized by the Royal Proclamation of 1763, none the less predates it. For this reason the "political trust" cases concerned essentially the distribution of public funds or other property held by the government. In each case the party claiming to be beneficiary under a trust depended entirely on statute, ordinance or treaty as the basis for its claim to an interest in the funds in question. The situation of the Indians is entirely different. Their interest in their lands is a pre-existing legal right not created by Royal Proclamation, by s 18(1) of the *Indian Act*, or by any other executive order or legislative provision.

It does not matter, in my opinion, that the present case is concerned with the interest of an Indian band in a reserve rather that with unrecognized aboriginal title in traditional tribal lands. The Indian interest in the land is the same in both cases.... It is worth noting, however, that the reserve in question here was created out of the ancient tribal territory of the Musqueam band by the unilateral action of the Colony of British Columbia, prior to Confederation.

(b) *The nature of Indian title*

[T]here is no real conflict between the cases which characterize Indian title as a beneficial interest of some sort, and those which characterize it a personal, usufructuary right. Any apparent inconsistency derives from the fact that in describing what constitutes a unique interest in land the courts have almost inevitably found themselves applying a somewhat inappropriate terminology drawn from general property law. There is a core of truth in the way that each of the two lines of authority has described native title, but an appearance of conflict has none the less arisen because in neither case is the categorization quite accurate.

Indians have a legal right to occupy and possess certain lands, the ultimate title to which is [in] the Crown. While their interest does not, strictly speaking, amount to beneficial ownership, neither is its nature completely exhausted by the concept of a personal right. It is true that the *sui generis* interest which the Indians have in the land is personal in the sense that it cannot be transferred to a grantee, but it is also true, as will presently appear, that the interest gives rise upon surrender to a distinctive fiduciary obligation on the part of the Crown to deal with the land for the benefit of the surrendering Indians. These two aspects of Indian title go together, since the Crown's original purpose in declaring the Indians' interest to be inalienable otherwise than to the Crown was to facilitate the Crown's ability to represent the Indians in dealings with third parties. The nature of the Indians' interest is therefore best characterized by its general inalienability, coupled with the fact that the Crown is under an obligation to deal with the land on the Indians' behalf when the interest is surrendered. Any description of Indian title which goes beyond these two features is both unnecessary and potentially misleading.

(c) *The Crown's fiduciary obligation*

The concept of fiduciary obligation originated long ago in the notion of breach of confidence, one of the original heads of jurisdiction in chancery. In the present appeal its relevance is based on the requirement of a "surrender" before Indian land can be alienated.

The Royal Proclamation of 1763 provided that no private person could purchase from the Indians any lands that the Proclamation had reserved to them, and provided further that all purchases had to be by and in the name of the Crown, in a public assembly of the Indians held by the governor or commander-in chief of the colony in which the lands in question lay. [T]his policy with respect to the sale or transfer of the Indians' interest in land has been continuously maintained by the British Crown, by the governments of the colonies when they became responsible for the administration of Indian affairs, and, after 1867, by the federal government of Canada....

The purpose of this surrender requirement is clearly to interpose the Crown between the Indians and prospective purchasers or lessees of their land, so as to prevent the Indians from being exploited. This is made clear in the Royal Proclamation itself, which prefaces the provision making the Crown an intermediary with a declaration that "great Frauds and Abuses have been committed in purchasing Lands of the Indians, to the great Prejudice of our Interest and to the great Dissatisfaction of the said Indians...." Through the confirmation in the *Indian Act* of the historic responsibility which the Crown has undertaken, to act on behalf of the Indians so as to protect their interests in transactions with third parties, Parliament has conferred upon the Crown a discretion to decide for itself where the Indians' best interests really lie. This is the effect of s 18(1) of the Act.

This discretion on the part of the Crown, far from ousting, as the Crown contends, the jurisdiction of the courts to regulate the relationship between the Crown and the Indians, has the effect of transforming the Crown's obligation into a fiduciary one. [W]here by statute, agreement, or perhaps by unilateral undertaking, one party has an obligation to act for the benefit of another, and that obligation carries with it a discretionary power, the party thus empowered becomes a fiduciary. Equity will then supervise the relationship by holding him to the fiduciary's strict standard of conduct.

It is sometimes said that the nature of fiduciary relationships is both established and exhausted by the standard categories of agent, trustee, partner, director, and the like. I do not agree. It is the nature of the relationship, not the specific category of actor involved that gives rise to the fiduciary duty. The categories of fiduciary, like those of negligence, should not be considered closed.

It should be noted that fiduciary duties generally arise only with regard to obligations originating in a private law context. [T]he Indians' interest in land is an independent legal interest. It is not a creation of either the legislative or executive branches of government. The Crown's obligation to the Indians with respect to that interest is therefore not a public law duty. While it is not a private law duty in the strict sense either, it is none the less in the nature of private law duty. Therefore, in this *sui generis* relationship, it is not improper to regard the Crown as a fiduciary.

Section 18(1) of the *Indian Act* confers upon the Crown a broad discretion in dealing with surrendered land. In the present case, the document of surrender, set out in part earlier in these reasons, by which the Musqueam band surrendered the land at issue, confirms this discretion in the clause conveying the land to the Crown "in trust to lease ... upon such terms as the Government of Canada may deem most conducive to our Welfare and that of our people." When, as here, an Indian band surrenders its interest to the Crown, a fiduciary obligation takes hold to regulate the manner in which the Crown exercises its discretion in dealing with the land on the Indians' behalf.

I agree with Le Dain J. that before surrender the Crown does not hold the land in trust for the Indians. I also agree that the Crown's obligation does not somehow crystallize into a trust, express or implied, at the time of surrender. The law of trust is a highly developed, specialized branch of the law. An express trust requires a settlor, a beneficiary, a trust corpus, words of settlement, certainty of object and certainty of obligation. Not all of these elements are present here....

The Crown's fiduciary obligation to the Indians is therefore not a trust. To say as much is not to deny that the obligation is trust-like in character. As would be the case with a trust, the Crown must hold surrendered land for the use and benefit of the surrendering band. The obligation is thus subject to principles very similar to those which govern the law of trusts concerning, for example, the measure of damages for breach. The fiduciary relationship between the Crown and the Indians also bears a certain resemblance to agency, since the obligation can be characterized as a duty to act on behalf of the Indian bands who have surrendered lands, by negotiating for the sale or lease of the land to third parties. But just as the Crown is not a trustee for the Indians, neither is it their agent; not only does the Crown's authority to act on the band's behalf lack a basis in contract, but the band is not a party to the ultimate sale or lease, as it would be if it were the Crown's principal. I repeat, the fiduciary obligation which is owed to the Indians by the Crown is *sui generis*. Given the unique character both of the Indians' interest in land and of their historical relationship with the Crown, the fact that this is so should occasion no surprise.

The discretion which is the hallmark of any fiduciary relationship is capable of being considerably narrowed in a particular case. This is as true of the Crown's discretion *vis-à-vis* the Indians as it is of the discretion of trustees, agents, and other traditional categories of fiduciary. The *Indian Act* makes specific provision for such narrowing in ss. 18(1) and 38(2). A fiduciary obligation will not, of course, be eliminated by the imposition of conditions that have the effect of restricting the fiduciary's discretion. A failure to adhere to the imposed conditions will simply itself be a *prima facie* breach of the obligation. In the present case both the surrender and the Order in Council accepting the surrender referred to the Crown leasing the land on the band's behalf. Prior to the surrender the band had also been given to understand that a lease was to be entered into with the Shaughnessy Heights Golf Club upon certain terms, but this understanding was not incorporated into the surrender document itself. The effect of these so-called oral terms will be considered in the next section.

(d) *Breach of the fiduciary obligation*

[T]he Crown, in my view, was not empowered by the surrender document to ignore the oral terms which the band understood would be embodied in the lease. The oral representations form the backdrop against which the Crown's conduct in discharging its fiduciary obligation must be measured. They inform and confine the field of discretion within which the Crown was free to act. After the Crown's agents had induced the band to surrender its land on the understanding that the land would be leased on certain terms, it would be unconscionable to permit the Crown simply to ignore those terms. When the promised lease proved impossible to obtain, the Crown, instead of proceeding to lease the land on different, unfavourable terms, should have returned to the band to explain what had occurred and seek the band's counsel on how to proceed. The existence of such unconscionability is the key to a conclusion that the Crown breached its fiduciary duty. Equity will not countenance unconscionable behaviour in a fiduciary, whose duty is that of utmost loyalty to his principal.

While the existence of the fiduciary obligation which the Crown owes to the Indians is dependent on the nature of the surrender process, the standard of conduct which the obligation imports is both more general and more exacting than the terms of any particular surrender. In the present case the relevant aspect of the required standard of conduct is defined by a principle analogous to that which underlies the doctrine of promissory or equitable estoppel. The Crown cannot promise the band that it will obtain a lease of the latter's land on certain stated terms, thereby inducing the band to alter its legal position by surrendering the land, and then simply ignore that promise to the band's detriment.

In obtaining without consultation a much less valuable lease than that promised, the Crown breached the fiduciary obligation it owed the band. It must make good the loss suffered in consequence.

VII. *Measure of Damages*

In my opinion the quantum of damages is to be determined by analogy with the principles of trust law. Reviewing the record it seems apparent that the judge at trial considered all the relevant evidence. His judgment, as I read it, discloses no error in principle. I am content to adopt the quantum of damages awarded by the judge, rejecting, as he did, any claim for exemplary or punitive damages.

I would therefore allow the appeal, set aside the judgment in the Federal Court of Appeal and reinstate without variation the trial judge's award, with costs to the present appellants in all courts.

CONSTITUTION ACT, 1982

As amended by Constitutional Amendment Proclamation, 1983

(Selected Provisions)

Part I, *Canadian Charter of Rights and Freedoms.*

Sec. 25:

The guarantee in this Charter of certain rights and freedoms shall not be construed so as to abrogate or derogate from any aboriginal, treaty or other rights or freedoms that pertain to the aboriginal peoples of Canada including

(a) any rights or freedoms that have been recognized by the Royal Proclamation of October 7, 1763; and

(b) any rights or freedoms that now exist by way of land claims agreements or may be so acquired.

Part II, *Rights of the Aboriginal Peoples of Canada.*

Sec. 35:

(1) The existing aboriginal and treaty rights of the aboriginal peoples of Canada are hereby recognized and affirmed.

(2) In this Act, "aboriginal peoples of Canada" includes the Indian, Inuit and Métis peoples of Canada.

(3) For greater certainty, in subsection (1) "treaty rights" includes rights that now exist by way of land claims agreements or may be so acquired.

(4) Notwithstanding any other provision of this Act, the aboriginal and treaty rights referred to in subsection (1) are guaranteed equally to male and female persons.

NOTES

1. The Efficacy of the Political Process in the United States and Canada:
There are many similarities between United States and Canadian Indian law, as
the above excerpts indicate. In both countries, judges reverently trace legal
policy back to the seminal Marshall cases of *Johnson* and *Worcester*. There are
significant differences, however, not the least of which is explicit protection for
aboriginal and treaty rights in the Canadian constitution. What are some of the
factors explaining Sanders's point that protection of aboriginal rights is a popular political stance in Canada? As Sanders indicates, the publication of Justice
Berger's report on the proposed Northern Pipeline caused such a public outcry
that the project was cancelled. Justice Berger's recent report on the Alaska
Native Claims Settlement Act, *Village Journey*, calls for far-reaching modifications of that statute. See Chapter 8, section A2. Has its publication in the United
States had a similar impact? Sanders stresses that Canada did not engage in wars
with the Indian people as did the United States during its Western expansion.
Could this fact account for a different public perception of how native peoples
fit into the scheme of things in Canada? What role has the Quebec separatist
movement played in influencing the Canadian attitude toward diversity?

Canadian Indians comprise only 5% of the population overall. In the Northwest Territories, however, the Inuit people are a majority of those in the Northeast region, while Dene and Métis people comprise half of the population in the
Western Arctic area of the Northwest Territories. After first shunning the
territorial assembly, the native peoples of the Northwest Territories became
politically active, holding a majority of seats in the assembly and numerous
appointed administrative offices. As a result of their increased political clout,
Canada has agreed in principle to a division of the Northwest Territories into
separate political units that could eventually become provinces, as happened
with the provinces of Alberta and Saskatchewan, which had originally been part
of the Northwest Territories. The region north of the tree line inhabited by the
Inuit people would be called Nunavut, and the area claimed by the Dene and
Métis would be called Denendeh. A plebiscite held in the Northwest Territories
resulted in a majority vote in favor of the division. *See generally* Bayly, *Aboriginal Rights in Canada: The Northwest Territories*, 2 LAW & ANTHROPOLOGY 43,
46-48 (Vienna, 1987). As this book goes to press, this division has not become a
reality, however.

2. Tribal Self-Government in Canada: Both Canada and the United States
engaged in programs of forced assimilation in the late nineteenth and early
twentieth centuries, characterized by individualization of the land mass (by measures such as forced enfranchisement) and the growth of bureaucracies to administer Indian affairs. Canada has no analog to the Indian Reorganization Act,
however, which spurred the development of the modern governmental structures flourishing in the United States today. Another contributing factor is that
Canada broke large Indian tribes into very small bands (with an average of only
500 members) occupying small reserves, with separate tribal governments for
each band. These band councils exercise limited powers. For instance, the Minister has the power to disapprove by-laws. In addition, bands may only raise
money if they are certified as sufficiently advanced to do so. Even then, bands
have no power to tax nonmembers occupying reserve land. As the Sanders
excerpt demonstrates, since the 1970's the Canadian government has adopted a
policy of negotiating land claims settlements. These agreements, such as the
James Bay Agreement, have contained provisions guaranteeing a greater
amount of self-government. In recent years, the government has extended the

policy of negotiation to include agreements with specific Indian bands regarding self-government. At least one agreement, the Sechelt Self-Government Act of 1986, focused largely on the issue of self-government. For an analysis of recent agreements and their effect on self-government, see R. BARTLETT, SUBJUGATION, SELF-MANAGEMENT AND SELF-GOVERNMENT OF ABORIGINAL LANDS AND RESOURCES IN CANADA 6 (Institute of Intergovernmental Relations, Ontario, Canada 1986). Bartlett characterizes the current policy of Canada toward self-government as anticipating tribal governments as municipalities subject to the jurisdiction of the provinces. What are the benefits and flaws of such an arrangement?

3. Property Rights in Canada: Both Canada and the United States follow the Doctrine of Discovery, or at least that aspect of the doctrine permitting alienation of land only to the sovereign. Moreover, Canadian cases frequently cite, although they do not always follow, United States Indian law precedents. For instance, the *Calder* case, discussed by Sanders and in *Guerin*, fell short of adopting the *Tee-Hit-Ton* rule in Canada. Only three judges concluded that aboriginal title could be extinguished without compensation. The same three judges also concluded that aboriginal title could be extinguished by implication from general statements made by the Governor of British Columbia in proclamations and ordinances issued before the province became part of the Dominion and by an imperial act granting a railroad route across British Columbia linking it to the Dominion. Could such actions extinguish aboriginal title in the United States? In recent years, however, the Canadian high court has adopted a stricter standard for abrogation of property rights. In *Simon v. The Queen*, [1985] 2 S.C.R. 387, the Supreme Court held that "[g]iven the serious and far-reaching consequences of a finding that a treaty right has been extinguished, it seems appropriate to demand strict proof of the fact of extinguishment in each case where the issue arises." *Id.* at 405. The Court then cited Justice Douglas's opinion in *United States v. Santa Fe Pac. R.R.*, 314 U.S. 339, 354 (1941).

The lack of formal legal protection for their property has not prevented natives demanding protection of their land resources. A town's decision to expand a golf course that was part of aboriginal land claimed by Mohawks in Oka, Quebec, precipitated a 76-day armed standoff between the local Mohawk community, the Kanesatake band, the non-Indian residents of the town, and the Quebec government. Mohawks of a neighboring band closed the Mercier bridge into nearby Montreal, which intensified both the conflict and the amount of publicity given to the land claim. Although the Mohawk warriors surrendered to Canadian authorities on September 26, 1990, the planned expansion of the golf course has been cancelled, and the Natives are in the process of negotiating for the creation of a Reserve in the area. In addition, the action by the neighboring band, the Kahnawake band, demonstrated that the Canadian government's earlier division of tribes into smaller, more governable groups has not wholly succeeded in isolating native peoples from each other.

The highly publicized dispute at Oka has encouraged the Inuit and Cree of Quebec to make alliances with other indigenous groups in Canada and elsewhere to defend their food-gathering rights on the eastern shore of the Hudson Bay from being taken by the $6 billion Quebec hydroelectric project, which will flood an area the size of France. The project's developers, Hydro-Quebec, plan to generate $25 billion in exports of power to the United States. The Inuit and Cree people have linked up with environmentalist organizations, such as the Arctic-to-Amazonia Alliance and the Sierra Club to launch a publicity campaign aimed at educating people in the United States and Canada about the ecological damage that will result from such a massive project. For example, they sent an odeyak (half canoe and half kayak to symbolize the two native cultures) from Great Whale Village to New York City in time for 1990 Earth Day festivities. They also met with leaders of the Kayapo Indians from Brazil's rain forest, who recently succeeded in halting construction of a series of dams that would have flooded rain forest land, to discuss strategies for preserving their land. En route to New York City, the activists stopped in Montreal during a meeting of the Inter-Development Investment Bank, attracting more publicity and the public support of a prominent Brazilian legislator, Fabio Feldman. The Grand Council of the Cree have filed a suit in Canadian federal court to halt further work on the project pending a full environmental assessment (no environmental impact study had been made before earlier stages of the project.) In short, the Inuit and Cree people have been very successful to date in obtaining support for what has been termed the "major battle of the decade" for environmentalists and indigenous activists in Canada. *Cultural Survival Q.* 14(3), at 88 (1990).

4. Imposing Trust Duties on Government Officials: In *Guerin*, the Canadian government argued that any trust between Canadian natives and the Crown was merely a political trust and not a true trust. What is the distinction? How has the Supreme Court in the United States answered this argument? In 1979, a Canadian scholar criticized the Indian Act, and specifically Section 18, as follows:

> The provisions of the Indian Act clearly indicate the managerial prerogative of the Minister of Indian Affairs over reserves and band resources. The denial of self-government inflicted by such provisions is compounded by the denial of any legal remedy. Regarding reserves, section 18 (1) provides: "[S]ubject to this Act and to the terms of any treaty or surrender, the Governor in Council may determine whether any purpose for which lands in a reserve are used or are to be used is for the use and benefit of the band." A similar provision applies to Indian moneys. The provisions deny any action for breach of trust by the Minister. Thus the Indian Act classically seeks to confer on the Minister "power without responsibility" and necessarily imposes on band members responsibility for exercise of this power.

Bartlett, *The Indian Act of Canada*, 27 Buffalo L. Rev. 581, 603 (1978).*

Is this statement still accurate in light of *Guerin*? Contrast the opinion in *Guerin* with that in *Mitchell II, supra* Chapter 2, section C3. What is the source of the relationship? A treaty with the band? The surrender document? Would the same principles be applied if the government mismanaged reserve property occupied by a band instead of property leased to others? Did the high court turn to trust law, agency law, or some mixture of the two to determine the scope of the Crown's duties? How did the Court assess damages?

5. Special Preferences in Canadian Indian Law: How does Canadian law accommodate the competing values of equality for all citizens and the need for special preferences for native peoples? As Sanders indicates, challenges to Indian legislation based on the equality principle have had some success in Canada. Nevertheless, in *Attorney General v. Lavell*, [1974] S.C.R. 1349, discussed in the Sanders excerpt, the Supreme Court of Canada upheld the Indian Act's rigid patrilineal scheme for determining Indian status against a challenge that the provision violated the guarantee of freedom from gender discrimination in the 1960 Bill of Rights. Under the Indian Act, a woman who married a non-Indian male was automatically "enfranchised," meaning that she lost her Indian

---

*Copyright © 1978 Buffalo Law Review and Richard Bartlett. Reprinted with permission of the copyright holders.

status, including the right to live on reserve land. A man who married a non-Indian woman, on the other hand, retained his status. Moreover, the Indian Act imposed this patrilineal system on all Indian tribes within Canada whether or not the band itself traditionally had such a system.

In 1985 the Indian Act was amended, after a successful challenge to an international tribunal by an Indian woman who was enfranchised under the Indian Act. R.S.C. 1985 c. 27. The case, *In re Lovelace*, is reprinted in section B2, *infra*. The amendments repealed the provisions regarding automatic loss of status and further provided that membership decisions would in the future be controlled by the band. In addition, the amendments include provisions to enable women enfranchised by the Indian Act's discriminatory provisions to seek reinstatement. For an analysis, see R. BARTLETT, THE INDIAN ACT OF CANADA 11-15 (Native Law Centre, University of Saskatchewan 2d ed. 1988). If a band adopted a rigid patrilineal membership requirement, how would you analyze this action? Article 25 of the 1982 Constitution, printed above, is designed to except some aboriginal rights from scrutiny under other provisions of the Charter of Rights and Freedoms. If a band that traditionally did not exclude such women from membership were to adopt a patrilineal membership criterion for the express purpose of keeping down the membership rolls in order to conserve band resources, would such a provision be immune? What if the band's purpose was to conserve federal benefits? *See* Resnick, *Dependent Sovereigns: Indian Tribes, States, and the Federal Courts*, 56 U. CHI. L. REV. 671 (1989).

6. Métis and Non-status Indians: In the United States, terminated tribes and tribes that have never been recognized are placed outside the entire scheme of Indian law. In Canada, there are also large groups of native peoples who are outside the system. One group is comprised of non-status Indians, those who have become enfranchised by various assimilationist policies, often against their will. For many years educated Indians were automatically enfranchised, as were those who served in the military. Forced enfranchisement of Indian women who married non-Indians and unregistered Indians then constituted a major source of non-status Indians, as did the Indian Act's discriminatory provisions regarding illegitimate children (illegitimate sons but not daughters of Indian men could register; no illegitimate children of Indian women could register). It has been estimated that approximately 26,000 Indians were enfranchised after 1921.

The second group is comprised of Métis, a term applied to numerous mixed blood communities throughout Canada. The Métis in the Northwest Territories have been able to pursue land and self-government claims along with the Dene to whom they are related as Athabascans. In the rest of Canada, Métis have been treated differently, however. For example, a land grant system provided for individual grants to Métis with no restrictions against alienation. In addition, after 1930, the central government disavowed any obligations to the Métis, maintaining the provinces had sole authority to deal with them.

In Canada, non-status Indians and Métis have united in political organizations since the 1970's. They have not always been welcomed by band-based organizations and Inuit. As Morse and Groves have stated:

Marginal peoples ... face a paradoxical threat from periodic state efforts to clarify indigenous policy on a comprehensive scale. Finding a solution to the "Native question" — an exercise that almost all settler countries have periodically engaged in over the past century or more — invariably entails a reallocation of resources. This task speaks not only to the division of responsibility amongst authorities .... It also involves the reassertion or revision of the system for determining which groups and individuals are to be recognized as distinct from the broader society. This process often leads to new and newly rigid distinctions between peoples, in order to enhance state predictions of cost and the assignment of responsibility. In such periods of focused governmental decision-making, it becomes a matter of critical importance for marginal groups to have the new recognition system reflect their interests. This is a particular challenge for groups previously excluded, and for those whose current identities emerged from and are therefore associated with the old, imposed regime.

Morse & Groves, *Canada's Forgotten Peoples: The Aboriginal Rights of Métis and Non-Status Indians*, 2 Law & Anthropology 139, 140 (Vienna 1987).* The Morse and Groves study reviews and analyzes the effect of political developments such as the 1985 amendments to the Indian Act and the Constitution Act of 1982 on these groups.

7. The Effect of the "Patriation" of the Canadian Constitution on Aboriginal Rights: The Constitution Act of 1982 included the first constitutional Bill of Rights, the Charter of Rights and Freedoms. For background and analysis of the provisions in general, see Alexander, *The Canadian Charter of Rights & Freedoms in the Supreme Court of Canada*, 105 Can. L.Q. 561 (1989). What is the effect of the constitutional provisions excerpted above on Canadian aboriginal peoples? Is the notion of aboriginal rights restricted to customary laws and traditions existing at the time of contact or can it be interpreted to cover changing traditions? Does it refer to inherent self-government rights? To property rights? What does the term "existing" aboriginal rights mean? Existing in 1982 (and not arising later)? Existing because grounded in law separate from the Constitution Act? If the latter, then could it be argued that the Constitution Act itself does not recognize or create any legal rights? Finally, does the term "existing" indicate an intention to secure aboriginal rights against infringement by subsequent statutes or merely to continue the subordination to statutory law existing when the Constitution Act was enacted? One author has concluded that the Constitution Act does apply to rights created after its passage, does create legal rights in place of existing moral or political rights, and does place a protective barrier around aboriginal rights so that they cannot be automatically overridden by statute:

> These considerations suggest that sec. 35(1) erects a high barrier against statutory interference, one that can be surmounted only in emergencies, for pressing public need. So aboriginal and treaty rights are not, in ordinary circumstances, subject to statutory expropriation, even if generous monetary compensation is provided. What the Constitution Act, 1982 guarantees is the right itself, not its supposed monetary equivalent.

Slattery, *The Hidden Constitution: Aboriginal Rights in Canada*, 32 Am. J. Comp. L. 361, 384-85 (1984). For a different view, see Sanders, *The Rights of the Aboriginal Peoples of Canada*, 61 Can. B. Rev. 314, 331-32 (1983). Sanders has concluded that the constitution prevents any abrogation of aboriginal rights. He argues, for example, that imposing a land claims settlement would require a constitutional amendment. Furthermore, he argues that treaty rights can now only be extinguished or modified with the consent of the people.

8. The First Ministers' Conferences and the Meech Lake Accord of 1988: The Constitution Act of 1982 had called for a constitutional conference to be held the following year attended by the Prime Minister and the first ministers of

---

*Copyright © 1987 Verlag Verband der Wissenschaflichen Gesellschaften Österreichs, Robert Groves, and Bradford Morse. Reprinted by permission of the copyright holders.

each of the provinces to consider matters affecting aboriginal peoples. The 1983 First Ministers' Conference produced the constitutional amendments of 1983, which in turn called for two more constitutional conferences. The three constitutional conferences were attended by representatives of aboriginal peoples who openly negotiated with the government. Although only the first conference produced concrete results, the publicity generated in Canada by the televised conferences has done much to keep aboriginal rights in the public eye.

The 1984, 1985 and 1987 conferences focused on self-government. Unfortunately, the parties' positions on self-government remained too far apart to reach any accord. The government took the position that the Constitution Act of 1982 protected only existing recognized rights, and thus did not recognize any kind of inherent sovereignty. The government proposed an amendment that would commit provincial governments to establish institutions of aboriginal government and give constitutional recognition to agreements thus negotiated. In other words, the government's proposal would provide for a great deal of flexibility with many different models of self-government negotiated separately. Aboriginal representatives rejected this view of government as delegated from the provinces and the federal government; instead they argued for an amendment that would entrench inherent tribal sovereignty as an absolute right. Various middle grounds have been proposed but essentially the parties remain divided along these basic lines.

Debate on an aboriginal self-government amendment was overshadowed by the debate on bringing Quebec, which had refused to ratify the Constitutional Amendment in 1982, back into the constitutional system. As a result, Quebec did not participate in the First Ministers' Conferences. The government sought an accord to satisfy Quebec's concerns regarding its special identity in the federal system. On June 3, 1987, in the early hours of the morning, the First Ministers signed an accord at Meech Lake recognizing Quebec as "a distinct society" within Canada. The Meech Lake Accord also contained far-reaching provisions giving the provinces a greater voice in selecting judges of the Supreme Court and delegates to the Senate. Finally, the accord provided that all ten provinces must ratify the accord and any future constitutional amendment, instead of the seven provinces required in the past. As to aboriginal rights, the accord merely stated that "[n]othing in section 2 of the Constitution Act, 1867 affects section 25 or 27 of the Canadian Charter of Rights and Freedoms, section 35 of the Constitution Act, 1982 or class 24 of section 91 of the Constitution Act, 1867." 1987 Constitutional Accord, clause 16.

Because all ten provinces did not ratify the accord by June, 1990, it did not become effective. As might be imagined, the accord sparked quite a bit of controversy among various groups. Native groups objected to the failure to include anything on aboriginal self-government. More seriously, they objected to the requirement of ratification by all ten provinces, fearing that anti-native prejudice in one province could veto the creation of new native provinces in the Northwest Territories and the Yukon. *See* New Brunswick Aboriginal Peoples Council, Brief to the Select Committee on the 1987 Constitutional Accord, *reprinted in Forum: Meech Lake*, 38 U.N.B.L.J. 295 (1989).

McHUGH, THE CONSTITUTIONAL ROLE OF THE WAITANGI TRIBUNAL, New Zealand Law Journal 224(3) (July 1985)*

Over the past decade the laws affecting the Maori and their land have been the subject of intense scrutiny and debate. The recent White Paper on a Bill of Rights for New Zealand contains what is in many respects the culmination of this activity. The draft Bill of Rights provides that the treaty of Waitangi is to be part of the "supreme law" of the country and the rights recognized in the Treaty are given comprehensive, indeed total, protection from legislative and executive disruption. Article 26 of the draft Bill allows for a special reference to the Waitangi Tribunal when in any proceedings any question arises as to the consistency of some enactment, rule of law, act or policy with the Treaty. The Treaty is to be regarded "as always speaking and shall be applied to circumstances as they arise so that effect may be given to its spirit and true intent."

The possibility of the enactment of a Bill of Rights together with the pending extension of the Waitangi Tribunal's jurisdiction to include historic claims (Treaty of Waitangi Amendment Bill 1984, cl 3) undoubtedly means that the Tribunal's workload will increase significantly. This larger profile will bring the Tribunal more public attention, and with it controversy, than previously. Given the projected growth in importance of the Tribunal, it is important the legal community see this body as more than a creature of Parliament's social conscience. For too long New Zealand lawyers (taking with them most of the community) have seen Maori claims to customary or traditional rights in relation to land and fisheries as simply "moral" in nature. Once this *a priori* supposition is corrected, it can be seen that the Waitangi Tribunal performs an important constitutional function besides that of mere moral assuagement.

Recent work has seriously challenged the traditional position which New Zealand law has taken towards the question of Maori common law rights. The traditional view is that the Maori held no legally recognisable rights to their lands and fisheries after British annexation: to obtain any such status required some resuscitative legislation. In the absence of this statutory recognition (which local Courts were extremely loath to find), Maori property rights existed at the sufferance of the Crown. This traditional approach is an unsophisticated coupling of the feudal doctrine of tenures with Austinian legal philosophy. According to this, all property rights derive from some national grant by a sovereign and since Maori society lacked "sovereignty" (by Austinian criteria) it lacked property rights upon British annexation. This is the underlying equation in *Wi Parata v. The Bishop of Wellington* (1877) 3 NZ Jur (NS) SC 72.

The view is directly contradicted by the doctrine of aboriginal title, the name which has come to be given to the corpus of common law principles on the question of tribal land rights after British annexation. Whilst a familiar concept in North America, this doctrine has only recently been applied to the assessment of Maori rights under the Treaty of Waitangi. The doctrine was put in evidence before the Waitangi Tribunal hearing on the Kaituna River claim and extracted a sympathetic response (*Finding of the Waitangi Tribunal on the Kaituna Claim*

(1984) pp. 20-24). The Government has indicated its awareness of the implications of the doctrine in its White Paper on a Bill of Rights (p. 75).

The basis of the doctrine of aboriginal title is that the Crown acquired sovereignty over New Zealand, expressed in feudal terms blending *imperium* (the Crown's right to govern) and *dominium* (the Crown's position as paramount owner of all land within the colony). This *dominium*, irrespective of the common law mode of acquisition of the colony, was taken subject to pre-existing traditional property rights enjoyed by tribal peoples. This aboriginal title was expressed as a burden or qualification upon the Crown's ultimate title to land within its colonies. It has been held recently that this displacement of the beneficial interest of the Crown is "a qualification of the title of the Crown of such content and substance as to partake ... of the nature of a right of property" (*Guerin v. The Queen* (1982) 143 DLR (3 ed.) 416). The cases recognise that this common law title could be extinguished bilaterally through voluntary sale or relinquishment by the tribal owners, or unilaterally through the passage of expropriatory legislation such as the New Zealand Settlement Acts. The Crown enjoyed the sole capacity to quiet the native title, this was its much-vaunted "pre-emptive right," but held no prerogative power to extinguish that title unilaterally. This power was conferred by s 84 of the Native Land Act 1909 and its 1931 and 1953 successors.

This leaves the Treaty of Waitangi in a very simple position: it was no more than declaratory of rules which would have applied in any event. This was obvious to New Zealand lawyers during the 1840s. In *R. v. Symonds* (1847) NZPCC 387, 390, Chapman J observed that "in solemnly guaranteeing the native title, and in securing what is called the Crown's pre-emptive right, the Treaty of Waitangi ... does not assert either in doctrine or in practice any thing new or unsettled." This was an insight which years later was to elude the local judiciary....

For the most part the practical effect of the doctrine of aboriginal title upon Maori property rights is spent. The Maori customary or "territorial" title to most land in the country has long since been converted by the Native (now Maori) Land Court into Maori freehold land. In any event, s 155 of the Maori Affairs Act 1953, the latter day equivalent of s 84 of the Native Land Act 1909, prevents this territorial title being pleaded against the Crown and gives the Crown the *executive* power to declare such title extinguished. However "non-territorial" Maori rights appear to have been untouched by this process and of these rights traditional fishing rights will be the most important. To this extent the doctrine of aboriginal title has practical consequences in New Zealand. Of particular interest will be the question of the relationship of Maori fishing rights with the Land Transfer Act since it is clear that aboriginal rights are *not* prescriptive in character. It is to be expected this question will soon come before New Zealand Courts.

The common law doctrine of aboriginal title informs us that the Waitangi Tribunal is no mere sop for uneasy European consciences. It has the much more important task of not only moral but constitutional assuagement. Recent and prospective enlargements of the Tribunal's duties will only serve to underline this constitutional function.

In assessing the Tribunal's performance it is and will remain instructive to bear in mind overseas experiments and experience with aboriginal land claims mechanism.... It is interesting that the general experience in Anglo-American jurisdictions appears to have been that the adversary form of procedure is inherently unsuitable for such claims. Where specialist native land claims tribunals adopt the adversary model, each claim becomes reduced to an "all or nothing," win-or-lose equation which leaves little room for informal negotiation and compromise. This model accentuates the differences rather than the common ground between the Government and tribal claimants.

An example of the inadequacy of the adversary process can be seen in United States' Indian Claim Commission (1946-1978). Several years prior to the Commission's dissolution, its chairman was publicly critical of the adoption of the adversary model: It had "chosen to sit as a Court" and, as a result, the Congressional mandate had "been utterly frustrated" ((1969) 45 N. Dak. L.R. 323, 333). In Commonwealth jurisdictions a trend towards the same model was noticed by Colvin in 1981 (*Legal Process and the Resolution of Indian Claims* (1981)) with a consequential lack of success. This trend has continued in Australia.

The overseas experience indicates that native claims are best handled by negotiation, conciliation and settlement rather than adversary confrontation. In this respect it is heartening to note that the Waitangi Tribunal has "eschewed strict procedural rules" and has adopted an approach in harmony (to date) with Maori tradition and administrative fairness (*Kaituna Claim*, paras. 9.1 and 9.2). It may be that with its enlarged duties Court-like formality will start creeping into the Tribunal's deliberations, particularly with the increased susceptibility to judicial review which will inevitably result from a greater workload. This is a response of which the Tribunal will have to be aware....

It is equally plain, however, that the pure political process of unregulated negotiation (which previously has governed the Maori's historic claims) is also an unsatisfactory medium for the resolution of native claims. In Canada where this method obtains, the Indian and Inuit (Eskimo) people have recently complained to a House of Commons Special Committee (the "Penner Report") that the absence of any land claims body of law has stifled the progress of negotiations. The Iroquois representatives complained that upon a breakdown in negotiations "there is no way that we can arbitrate that situation" or coerce the Government back to the negotiating table (*Penner Report*, pp. 114-115). The Penner Committee recommended establishment of a "neutral party to facilitate the settlement" so that where a settlement cannot be reached, there should be access to a quasi-judicial process" (p. 115).

This might suggest, in the New Zealand context, that the Waitangi Tribunal be given coercive powers in cases where the Government indicates unwillingness to accept the recommendations (as initially was the case with the Motunui claim). It may be, though, that the constitutional entrenchment of the Treaty in a Bill of Rights will achieve something approaching this result: a claim that the Maori's constitutionally entrenched rights have been violated would be unlikely of success where the Tribunal has already delivered a contrary recommendation. In short, the Tribunal's recommendations will be a strong guideline to constitutionality under the Bill of Rights.

Nonetheless, it is clear that native land claims are viewed in North America as constitutional as well as moral problems. In large part this is due to reception of the doctrine of aboriginal title and, in the United States, the constitutional recognition of Indian treaties. It is interesting to note, as the White Paper on a Bill of Rights does, that Canada has recognised "existing aboriginal and treaty rights" in its Charter of Rights and Freedoms (Part II, art. 35). This is not to say that the results achieved have been greeted with uniform satisfaction. As legal philosophers would put it, native land claims present "polycentric" problems. There are too many insoluble aspects to such claims to expect any land claim mechanism, any procedure it adopts and any results it obtains, to be perfect. Nonetheless, it is important that the resolution of such claims is seen as compelled by constitutional as well as moral principle. Even if this approach does not help in the outcome, it stresses the importance of such claims. This correction of our *a priori* attitudes towards Maori rights will be salutary as the Waitangi Tribunal stands poised on the brink of a much larger role.

NOTES

1. The Constitutionalization of Aboriginal Rights in New Zealand: At present, the New Zealand constitution Bill of Rights, including the provisions dealing with the Maori-pakeha (settler) relationship discussed in the excerpt, remains in draft stage.

Note that McHugh, like Canadian scholars, comments favorably on the United States system as one in which Indian claims are regarded as constitutional and not just moral issues. To what extent do you agree with him? Would a declaration that the Treaty is supreme law in New Zealand, speaking to the future as well as the past, resolve the question of the extent to which Maori people have retained the right to govern themselves? Would it protect Maori land from confiscation or development?

2. Tribal Sovereignty in New Zealand: As the McHugh excerpt indicates, the Treaty of Waitangi is the seminal document invoked by both the pakeha community and the Maori people to justify their rights and prerogatives. Not surprisingly, interpretations of the treaty differ, especially on the issue of tribal sovereignty. In the English version, the Maori people acknowledge the sovereignty of the Crown and accept the rights and privileges of British subjects. Versions of the treaty signed by Maori representatives were written in Maori, however. In these versions, the treaty promised the Maori control and continued *rangatiratanga* over their lands, a Maori term connoting the exercise of sovereign powers. The term used to describe the power of the English Queen was *kawanatanga*, a word connoting less than supreme sovereignty. Kelsey, *Decolonization in the "First World" — Indigenous Peoples' Struggles for Justice and Self-Determination*, 5 WINDSOR Y.B. OF ACCESS TO JUST. 102, 105-17 (1985). The Treaty of Waitangi Act of 1975 recognizes that the English and Maori versions differ and authorizes the tribunal to resolve conflicts. The tribunal has acknowledged the Maori understanding of these two notions. If the Treaty of Waitangi is given constitutional status by the Bill of Rights, how can this Maori understanding be given effect? By an acknowledgment of inherent legal sovereignty? Or by a more modest delegation of power from the Crown?

Most Commonwealth courts have refused to accept the theory of inherent sovereignty of aboriginal peoples. In part, the reason is the influence of Austin's theory of indivisible sovereignty on English jurisprudence in the early twentieth century. Recognizing any quantum of sovereignty beyond the Crown was thus impossible, or so it seemed. In contrast, United States political theory was inspired by the Lockean notion of consent to be governed that contemplated both a legal and political (or popular) sovereignty. Founded as it was on a theory that sovereignty was divisible, the United States system could more easily accommodate a theory recognizing Indian tribes' retained sovereignty. *See* McHugh, *Maori Fishing Rights and the North American Indian*, 6 OTAGO L. REV. 62, 89 & n.6 (1985); McHugh, *Aboriginal Rights and Sovereignty: Commonwealth Developments*, 1988 NEW ZEALAND L.J. 57(7), 60-61.

3. Property Rights: The Treaty of Waitangi may not be held to have recognized any inherent sovereign powers of the Maori people, but most agree that the Treaty recognized aboriginal property rights. As in the United States, an early decision stating that the Maori property rights preceded and were not derived from the Treaty of Waitangi, *R. v. Symonds*, was followed by a decision, *Wi Parata v. The Bishop of Wellington*, stating that no property rights existed absent what McHugh calls "resuscitative legislation." In both countries twentieth century legislation has provided a mechanism to remedy eighteenth century confiscations of native land. The American Indian Claims Commission only granted monetary relief. What remedies can the Waitangi Tribunal grant? What are the strengths and weaknesses of each system? Do you agree with McHugh's criticisms of the adversary system in general as a mechanism for enforcing aboriginal rights? For a comprehensive analysis of Maori property rights, see McHugh, *Aboriginal Title in New Zealand Courts*, 2 CANTERBURY L. REV. 235 (1984).

The Treaty of Waitangi Tribunal has rendered some significant decisions affecting Maori land. For example, the tribunal recommended against permitting a synthetic fuels plant to discharge its waste near the aboriginal fishing grounds of the Te Atiawa Tribe of Taranaki. The fuel plant had complied with rigorous environmental restrictions and even survived a court challenge based on environmental concerns. Nevertheless, because the reefs and rivers in the claimed area were already significantly polluted, the tribunal recommended that another method be found to dispose of the plant's effluent. In addition, the tribunal also recommended that specific steps be taken to protect the fishing beds from further pollution by sewage or industrial waste. All the tribunal's recommendations were adopted. For more detail on this and other recent decisions involving development and planning, see Kelsey, *supra*; Kenderdine, *Statutory Separateness (2): The Treaty of Waitangi Act 1975 and the Planning Process*, 1985 NEW ZEALAND L.J. 300.

One author notes that recent cases indicate a new willingness by the judiciary to use the treaty as a source of a "trust-like" relationship between the government and the Maori. For example, in *Huakina Dev. Trust v. Waikato Valley Auth.*, [1987] 2 N.Z.L.R. 188, the Supreme Court referred to Maori spiritual beliefs protected by the treaty in interpreting an ambiguous law to benefit the Maori people. *See* Hastings, *New Zealand Practice with Particular Reference to the Treaty of Waitangi*, 38 INT'L & COMP. L.Q. 668 (1989). *See also* Tamihara, *To Take Maori: A Maori Perspective of Legislation and Its Interpretation with an Emphasis on Planning Law*, 5 AUCKLAND U.L. REV. 137 (1985).

NETTHEIM, AUSTRALIAN ABORIGINES AND THE LAW, 2 Law & Anthropology 371-84, 399-400 (Vienna 1987)*

Factual (Including Demographic) Background

There are two indigenous populations of Australia — the people from the Torres Strait Islands (which are part of the State of Queensland), and the larger group of people, known as Aboriginals, from the rest of Australia.... [T]he number of people identified as Aboriginal has grown in recent decades. The census of 1981 reported the overall figure as 159,897, comprising 144,665 Aboriginals and 15,232 Torres Strait Islanders. [M]ortality and life expectancy figures are conspicuously worse for Aboriginal people than for others.

Urban movement can lead to dispersal of Aboriginal families among non-Aboriginal communities, and this has been the deliberate policy of some agencies such as the NSW [New South Wales] Housing Commission. Or it can lead to concentration in "town camps" and the like. The most critical socio-economic problems beset the "fringe dwellers" of the "town camps" ....

There has also been a significant trend in the opposite direction in northern and central Australia, namely, a movement of small groups away from urban areas and larger settlements back to traditional lands. This is sometimes known as the "homelands" or "outstation" movement, and is perceived as a way of avoiding the problems of the larger communities and re-invigorating traditional values and life styles.

Many Aboriginals, of course, live in similar ways to the majority while still identifying themselves as Aboriginal.

Legal Identity and Membership

Aboriginals as a whole, or sub-groups of Aboriginals, as such, do not have any particular legal identity in Australian law. Aboriginals as individuals may have particular rights, entitlements or disabilities under the law. Land rights law, for example, will confer rights or entitlements on identifiable groups of Aboriginals such as "traditional owners" or members of or residents in Aboriginal communities. Aboriginal collectivities may gain legal identity under various Acts. Some legislation gives corporate status to Aboriginal Land Trusts, Aboriginal Land Councils, Aboriginal Community Councils, and other bodies.

Aboriginal bodies also avail themselves of general State or Territory law to become corporations or registered associations or co-operatives.... The Aboriginal Development Commission and the Department of Aboriginal Affairs require funded bodies to be incorporated under the Commonwealth Act or under State or Territory legislation.

In the past, national legislation had virtually nothing to say about Aboriginals because of two particular provisions in the Commonwealth Constitution:

51 The Parliament shall, subject to this Constitution, have power to make laws for the peace, order, and good government of the Commonwealth with respect to:

... (xxvi) The people of any race, other than the aboriginal race in any state, for whom it is deemed to be necessary to make special laws ....

---

127 In reckoning the numbers of the people of the Commonwealth, or of a State or other part of the Commonwealth aboriginal natives shall not be counted.

In a referendum for Constitutional amendment in 1967, s 127 was removed altogether, and s 51 (xxvi) was changed by deletion of the words "other than the aboriginal race in any State." But the Commonwealth Parliament had long had plenary power for the Northern Territory, and its laws for the Territory, in common with laws in the States, imposed a number of specific disabilities, entitlements and rights on Aboriginals in regard to such matters as access to alcohol, voting, freedom of movement, welfare, marriage and much else. Most of these provisions have now gone. But for the purpose of their operation Aboriginals were commonly defined by reference to such concepts as "full-blood," "half-caste," "quadroon" and so on. Fortunately, most of these definitions have also gone....

The Commonwealth Government some years ago adopted a three-part definition for the purposes of administering various programs of assistance. The definition has found its way into some legislation at federal and State level. The three elements are:

1. Aboriginal descent;
2. Self-identification as Aboriginal; and
3. Acceptance as Aboriginal by other Aboriginals.

[U]sage is not uniform. Some legislation uses the word "Aboriginal" without providing any definition at all or by providing a circular definition, such as that in the Aboriginal Land Rights (Northern Territory) Act 1976 (Cth) s 3(1).

"Aboriginal" means a person who is a member of the Aboriginal race of Australia.

A similar reference to "people of the Aboriginal race" was employed in the World Heritage Properties Conservation Act 1983 (Cth) s 8(1). The Act was passed by the Commonwealth Parliament in a successful attempt to block the construction of a hydro-electric dam in Tasmania's south-western wilderness. In the High Court in *Commonwealth v. Tasmania*[8] the Commonwealth argued that the Act was valid on the basis of several constitutional heads of power, including s 51(xxvi). The definition in the Act was held to be sufficient to accord with the reference to "race" in s 51(xxvi). Murphy J. said:

A broad reading of this power is that it authorizes any law for the benefit, physical and mental, of the people of the race for whom Parliament deems it necessary to pass special laws. Whatever technical meaning "race" might be given in other contexts, in the Australian Constitution it includes the Aborigines and Torres Strait Islanders and every subdivision of those peoples. To hold otherwise would be to make a mockery of the decision by the people to delete from s 51(26) the words "other than the aboriginal race in any State"; Constitution Alternation (Aboriginals) Act 1967 (Cth) which was manifestly done so that Parliament could legislate for the maintenance, protection and advancement of Aboriginal people.[9] ...

The three-part definition is more restrictive than a simple "descent" definition because all three elements need to be satisfied — the genealogical and the social (self-identification and community acceptance). On the other hand the

---

[8](1983) 46 ALR 625.
[9]*Id.*, 737.

presence (or absence) of the social elements may often be easier to establish as a matter of practice. The element of community acceptance involves reference to the Aboriginal people and gives them some degree of control in the matter. Likewise the definition recognizes the individual's right to decide whether to identify as Aboriginal.

Traditional Aboriginal societies place great emphasis on identification, kinship and genealogy, and members of those societies have a very clear idea of who they are and of their place in the world. Many other Aboriginal people may be less able to trace particular genealogies, but will be aware of their Aboriginal descent. Aboriginals who know of their descent, and identify as Aboriginal, are able to do so on a nation-wide basis; there are few of the characterisations that separate the indigenous peoples of Canada, for example, into sub-groups — Indian, Inuit, Metis; treaty or non-treaty; status or non-status, etc. There is some tendency for people who still have their "law" to be dismissive of "yellerfellers" from the south who have lost theirs. There are also the inevitable personal or organizational rivalries. But at the national, political level, Aboriginal people (with Torres Strait Islanders) have been able to establish a fair degree of identity and unity of purpose....

Legal Status of Group Members

As noted, Aboriginal people may have particular rights or entitlements under legislation. They may have particular rights or entitlements in regard to land or in regard to various forms of social or economic assistance. Few specific disabilities survive today in law (though many survive in practice, e.g. social discrimination). Aboriginal people are entitled to Australian citizenship on the same basis as other persons born in Australia....

Land Rights/Self Government/Natural Resources

Aboriginal law had its own rules on these matters.... From the time of first non-Aboriginal settlement in 1788 until the 1960s Aboriginal law on these matters was simply not recognized. At different times and in different parts of the country, British and colonial/state executive governments attempted, with limited success, to restrain non-Aboriginal settlement. Governments also set aside areas of "Crown land" as reserves for Aboriginal people, or gave freehold or leasehold interests to religious bodies to run as Aboriginal missions. As at January 1986, some 210,367 sq kms, representing 2.74% of Australia, were Aboriginal reserves or missions. In some places these areas coincided with land which the Aboriginal people regarded as their own; in other places they did not. The entire country and its resources were totally at the disposition of governments, and there was no formal recognition of Aboriginal self-government....

Land Rights

In the 1960s Aboriginal clans at Yirrkala on the Gove peninsula in the Northern Territory brought legal action to challenge the granting by the Commonwealth Government of bauxite leases to a mining company. Justice Blackburn of the Northern Territory Supreme Court held against them in *Milirrpum v.*

Nabalco Pty. Ltd.[17] There were several grounds for this conclusion, but the most significant was a ruling that Aboriginal title did not survive the acquisition of British sovereignty over Australia. The decision was not taken on appeal. The proposition that Anglo-Australian law does not recognize Aboriginal title is being challenged in *Mabo v. Queensland and the Commonwealth*, currently before the High Court.[18]

Since the 1960s, however, some Australian legislatures have recognized or granted land rights. In 1966 no Aboriginal Australian owned land by virtue of being Aboriginal. By January 1986 some 643,079 sq kms, representing 8.37% of the Australian land mass, were held by Aborigines in freehold.

The first step in this movement was in 1966. South Australia enacted an Aboriginal Land Trust Act which transferred title to Aboriginal reserves in the State to a state-wide Aboriginal body. The Trust then leased the land to local Aboriginal groups and communities and, generally, acted as landlord (under tight government supervision). This model was followed, with variations, in New South Wales, Victoria and Western Australia. Queensland retained the older system of government-owned and government-managed reserves until the mid-1980s. Tasmania had no Aboriginal reserves.

A reserve system also operated in the Northern Territory but it was in the Territory that the next major development occurred. In the aftermath of the Gove land rights case [*Milirrpum v. Nabalco*], the then federal Opposition pledged to recognize Aboriginal land rights in the Territory. When the Whitlam government won office in 1972 it commissioned Justice Woodward[*] to inquire how this goal might best be achieved. Woodward's recommendations[19] were substantially enacted by the Fraser Government as the Aboriginal Land Rights (Northern Territory) Act, 1976.

This Act provided for the direct transfer of existing reserves into the ownership of local (not Territory-wide) Aboriginal land trusts. It also made provision for a claims process in regard to "unalienated Crown land." If claimants can satisfy an Aboriginal Land Commissioner that the land is theirs under Aboriginal law, the Commissioner can recommend to the Minister that they receive "inalienable freehold" title under Australian law. As at January 1986, 458,100 sq kms, constituting 34.02% of the Northern Territory were held by Aboriginal people in freehold title. Much of this land is poor quality land in non-Aboriginal terms, which is why it has remained unalienated. It should also be noted that Aboriginal people represent some 64% of the Territory's non-urban population.

The Act establishes powerful organizations to perform management functions in regard to Aboriginal land and generally to represent traditional Aboriginal owners — the Northern Land Council, the Central Land Council and the smaller Tiwi Land Council. The Land Councils prepare and present land claims, and they represent Aboriginal owners in such matters as negotiation of

---

[17](1971) 17 FLR 141.

[18]See Australian Law Reform Commission Report 31, The Recognition of Aboriginal Customary Laws (AGPS, Canberra, 1986) (hereafter ALRC 31) vol 2, para. 901.

[*][Woodward had been counsel for the claimants in the *Gove* land rights case. — Eds.]

[19]Aboriginal Land Rights Commission (Commissioner: Justice E.A. Woodward), Second Report (AGPS, Canberra 1974).

mining and other resource development agreements. The Northern Territory legislature itself transferred ownership and land in the Coburg Peninsula to an Aboriginal Land Trust on condition that a National Park be established. Under Commonwealth auspices, Kakadu National Park and Uluru National Park are also under Aboriginal ownership....

An Aboriginal Land Fund Commission was established under separate legislation to purchase land for Aboriginal people on the open market anywhere in Australia. This function is now performed by an Aboriginal body, the Aboriginal Development Commission, which has a range of other functions in regard to housing, enterprise development and the like.

[T]he Pitjantjatjara Land Rights Act 1981 (SA) enacted after negotiations ... transferred inalienable freehold title to the former North-west reserve, comprising some 10% of the State's land area (102,630 sq kms) to a corporate body, Anangu Pitjantjatjaraku. All traditional owners are automatically members of the body corporate. The Maralinga Tjarutja Land Rights Act 1984 (SA) followed a similar pattern and transferred 50,000 sq kms to a corporate body. The corporate bodies under these two Acts not only hold title but also represent the traditional owners in negotiating access to lands, resource development agreements and so on....

Western Australia has been the scene of greatest contention in recent years. Paul Seaman QC published his report to the Government in September 1984, recommending transfer to local Aboriginal communities of reserve and mission land and also a land claims process.[25] However, considerable political opposition had developed in the meantime about any system of land rights that might give Aboriginal residents any significant control over mining. In March 1985 a land rights bill which was acceptable to the mining industry, pastoralists, and other vested interests was passed in the State's lower house but rejected in the opposition-controlled upper house.[26] The topic of land rights continued to be politically controversial through the State elections in February, 1986.

Self-Government

Aboriginal sovereignty over Australia has been denied in practice and in law.[27] In so far as the notion of self-government presupposes a land base, the concept can be examined in conjunction with land rights. It is, however, not always easy in the case of a community to disentangle powers of ownership from powers which may more appropriately be characterised as self-government.

The State-wide Aboriginal Land Trusts established in South Australia and in some other States are more properly described as agencies of proprietorship rather than of self-government. Even so, they were subject to tight government controls, particularly in Western Australia where the Trust did not even hold title but acted as an advisory body with some management functions.

Queensland never adopted the idea of an Aboriginal Lands Trust, but did develop on its reserves an elaborate system of Aboriginal or Islander Councils

[25] The Aboriginal Land Inquiry (Commissioner: P. Seaman QC) Report (Perth, WA Government Printer, 1984).
[26] Aboriginal Land Bill 1985 (WA).
[27] Coe v. Commonwealth (1978) 18 ALR 592; (1979) 24 ALR 118.

with a range of local government powers. There was also provision for Aboriginal and Islander Courts and Aboriginal and Islander police. These powers were exercised under close governmental control....

The Aboriginal Land Rights (Northern Territory) Act 1976 established Land Trusts to hold title but to perform no other function. Some resident communities have formed associations to manage revenues accruing to the communities from mining and other sources. But the major agencies of self-government in the Territory are the regional Land Councils — the Northern Land Council, the Central Land Council and the Tiwi Land Council. These Councils, made up of members from communities within their respective regions, have important management functions in regard to Aboriginal land. They prepare and present Aboriginal land claims, negotiate access to land and resource development agreements, and are the principal political agencies for dealing with governments (Commonwealth and Territory) and with other bodies....

Commonwealth Government Policies

The Commonwealth Parliament acquired power to pass laws with respect to Aboriginal people only in 1967 as a result of a constitutional amendment. In the 1970s Commonwealth Governments showed themselves to be more sensitive than State governments to Aboriginal claims and needs. Commonwealth Governments led the movement away from the philosophy of assimilation to a philosophy which would permit Aboriginal people to decide whether or not to assimilate and, if so, on what terms. This new approach required recognition of and respect for Aboriginal cultural identity.

In particular Commonwealth governments led the way to the new regime of land rights in the Northern Territory, and encouraged States to legislate along similar lines....

But the "backlash" referred to in Western Australia rapidly affected the Commonwealth Government as well. In February 1985 the Government published a discussion paper on its "Preferred National Land Rights Model." The model was denounced by Aboriginal organizations and also by the mining industry. [The model did not mention compensation at all and watered down previous government statements of principle.] It was proposed that the powers of Aboriginal land owners in the Northern Territory be reduced to conform to those in the model.[33] Thus, far from national legislation it seems that the Commonwealth will merely act to reduce the extent of land rights in the one jurisdiction, the Northern Territory, where federal legislation on the subject already exists....

Different Perceptions of Human Rights

The Australian Law Reform Commission in its reference on Aboriginal Customary Law had to grapple with the issue of possible disparity between Aboriginal and non-Aboriginal perceptions of human rights. The ALRC is bound by its statute, the Law Reform Commission Act 1973 (Cth), to see that its recommen-

---

[33] For the Government's stated policy, see Parl. Debs. (H. of R.) 18 March 1986, 1473-80. See also Aboriginal Land Rights (Northern Territory) Amendment Act 1986 (Cth).

dations conform to the International Covenant on Civil and Political Rights. It reported a number of potential problems with the following Articles of the Covenant:

Article 3, referring to "the equal right of men and women to the enjoyment of all the" Covenant rights — some have suggested that women occupy an inferior status, in some respects, in Aboriginal customary law.

Article 7, which forbids torture or cruel, inhuman or degrading treatment or punishment — some customary law punishments such as spearing through the thigh, might be thought to infringe Article 7.

Article 18's guarantee of freedom of religion may make little sense in Aboriginal law in which law is inseparable from religion.

Article 23(3) provides that no marriage shall be entered into without free and full consent of the intending spouses — Aboriginal law permits promised marriage.

The ALRC proposed that Australian law should not enforce promises to marry but should be available to provide protection from violence to those seeking protection.[68] A traditional marriage should not be recognised unless both parties had consented to it.[69] As to physical punishments under Aboriginal law which might be criminal offences under Australian law, the ALRC proposed legislation to the effect that Aboriginal customary law and tradition are to be taken into account by a partial defence (in homicide cases) but otherwise only in the sentencing of Aboriginal offenders.[70]

Discrimination and Equality Before the Law

The ALRC also addressed the question whether the special needs and problems of Aboriginal people can be reconciled with the values of non-discrimination and equality before the law. It concluded that provisions for the recognition of customary law will not be racially discriminatory, or involve a denial of equality before the law or equal protection, if such measures:

— are reasonable responses to the special needs of those Aboriginal people affected by the proposals;
— are generally accepted by them; and
— do not deprive individual Aboriginals of basic human rights, or of access to the general legal system and its institutions.[71]

The Commission distinguished the case of other ethnic groups that may have special needs, on the basis that the Aboriginals are the indigenous population and special measures are justified because of their history of dispersal and dispossession.

Land rights legislation is the primary area to date in which these considerations have been given legislative recognition. The justification of such recogni-

---

[68] ALRC 31, vol. 1 para. 249-53.
[69] Id., para. 262.
[70] Id., para. 453, 417, 522. For the Commission's general discussion of the human rights issues see generally id., ch. 9.
[71] Id., para. 158, 165 and see generally id., ch. 9.

tion was considered by the High Court in *Gerhardy v. Brown*.[72] Brown was charged with an offence under s 19 of the Pitjantjatjara Land Rights Act 1981 (SA) for being a non-Pitjantjatjara on Pitjantjatjara land without permit. In his defence he argued that s 19 was invalid as in conflict with s 9 of the Racial Discrimination Act 1975 (Cth). Millhouse J. of the SA Supreme Court accepted the argument.[73] On appeal, all members of the High Court held that s 19 of the State Act was saved by the force of s 8 of the Commonwealth Act. Section 8(1) exempts from the operation of the Act "special measures" to which Article 1(4) of the Convention applies. Article 1(4) reads:

> Special measures taken for the sole purpose of securing adequate advancement of certain racial or ethnic groups or individuals requiring such protection as may be necessary in order to ensure such groups or individuals equal enjoyment or exercise of human rights and fundamental freedoms shall not be deemed racial discrimination, provided, however, that such measures do not, as a consequence, lead to the maintenance of separate rights for different racial groups and that they shall not be continued after the objectives for which they were taken have been achieved.

But the future of land rights legislation is currently in doubt as the mining industry continues to mount expensive publicity campaigns against Aboriginal controls over mining activity. Such campaigns have fed a political backlash against the whole idea of Aboriginal land rights, and against the Aboriginal case generally. For the past twenty years a substantial proportion of Australian community has been ready to consider Aboriginal claims as presenting issues of justice, and to respond accordingly. At the present time it seems that fewer Australians are able to see the issues in these terms.

NOTES

1. Sovereignty: Australia never entered into treaties with Aboriginal peoples, for several reasons. First, there were no outright wars, although massacres by settlers and guerilla raids by Aboriginals did occur. Treaties marking the termination of hostilities were thus not necessary. Second, Australian settlers regarded Aboriginal people as sub-human compared to the North American Indians they viewed as more civilized and thus more deserving of being treated as sovereign entities. Third, there were no European competitors, and thus no need to obtain the kind of treaty pledges of loyalty the North American colonizers needed. *See* B.W. MORSE, ABORIGINAL SELF-GOVERNMENT IN AUSTRALIA AND CANADA 7-8 (Institute of Governmental Relations, Kingston, Ontario 1984). In the modern era, the closest Australia has come to a treaty has been the Pitjantjatjara Land Act, enacted to effectuate a land claims settlement. In 1981 the National Aboriginal Conference proposed that the Commonwealth enter into a compact, a Makarrata, with Aboriginal peoples. Such an action by the Commonwealth would require a constitutional amendment, however, adding to the difficulty of bringing about such a compact.

Nor does Australia recognize the doctrine of inherent sovereignty. Nettheim cites a 1979 case rejecting inherent sovereignty, *Coe v. Commonwealth of Australia*, [1979] 24 ALR 118. Nevertheless *Coe* will surely not be the last word on the issue, since the High Court dismissed the claim on procedural grounds. Coe, an Aboriginal lawyer and chair of the Aboriginal Legal Services, sought a de-

---

[72](1984) 57 ALR 472.
[73](1983) 49 ALR 169.

claratory judgment that Australia was not terra nullius (vacant land) at the time of white contact, and therefore the Crown never legitimately gained sovereignty or any property rights. Since the declaratory relief requested would effectively state that the Aboriginals owned all of Australia, it is not surprising that the court avoided addressing the merits. Judge Gibbs, with Judge Aickin concurring, would have held that Australian Aboriginals had no property and sovereignty rights at the time of contact. As to sovereignty, the justices stated that Aboriginal peoples had no executive, legislative, or judicial organs to exercise sovereignty and thus were never were sovereign. Judge Murphy, on the other hand, took a narrower view of the merits. He acknowledged that the settled colony principle is merely a "convenient falsehood," but argued that Crown sovereignty did not necessarily extinguish Aboriginal property rights. Since, however, three high court judges agreed that the Aboriginals did not retain sovereignty, it is doubtful that the doctrine of inherent sovereignty will take hold in Australia.

Australian Aboriginals do exercise a limited amount of sovereign powers created by general and specific legislation, as the Nettheim excerpt indicates.

2. Federal and Provincial Authority in the Australian Constitution: A major impediment to the development of unitary policy regarding tribal sovereignty is the fact that states have concurrent authority over Aboriginal affairs. As a consequence, reserves within the borders of states are owned by the states. As Nettheim indicates, the original Commonwealth constitution explicitly negated Commonwealth power over Aboriginal peoples. The 1959 amendment removing this impediment has encouraged the Commonwealth government to begin to set national policy. The High Court of Australia has upheld Commonwealth power to enact laws respecting Aboriginal peoples. *Commonwealth v. Tasmania*, 46 A.L.R. 625 (1983). According to Professor Hanks:

> The difficult question for the future is not whether the Commonwealth has the power to legislate to implement national policies in Aboriginal affairs but the choice of those national policies: will the Commonwealth continue the Australian tradition of imposing on the Aboriginal people policies and programs chosen by European-dominated institutions of government? Or will it establish structures and processes which ensure that national policies and programs are chosen by the Aboriginal people? Is the Commonwealth prepared to use its substantial powers in a way which responds to one of the most serious problems in Aboriginal society: powerlessness, the inability to influence (let alone control) the political decisions which impose on Aborigines inappropriate and counterproductive programs in such fundamental areas as health, housing, education and land use?

Hanks, *Aborigines and Government: The Developing Framework*, in ABORIGINES AND THE LAW 19, 37 (P. Hanks & B. Keon-Cohen eds. 1984).

3. The Equality Principle: Australia has ratified the Convention on the Elimination of All Forms of Racial Discrimination. In 1975, the Commonwealth enacted the Racial Discrimination Act to implement the Convention, specifically stating its intent to include the principles of freedom from racial discrimination in the enjoyment of property rights alone or with others guaranteed by the Convention and also specifically referencing Aboriginals and Torres Strait Islanders as intended beneficiaries of the Act. When Queensland enacted legislation declaring that the state owned all land occupied by the Miriam people of Murray Island (who are Torres Strait Aboriginals) and thus had the power to confiscate it without payment of compensation the Australian High Court held the provincial law void because it conflicted with the Commonwealth law. *Mabo v. Queensland*, [1988] 83 ALR 14. The Queensland government argued that the Murray Islanders had not been discriminated against based on race within the meaning of the Commonwealth law, because they had the same legal property rights as other persons in Australia. The majority of the High Court rejected this argument:

> Traditional rights are characteristically vested in members of the Miriam people; rights under Crown lands legislation are vested in grantees who may be of any race[,] colour or national or ethnic origin. However, it is not the source or history of legal rights which is material but their existence. It is the arbitrary deprivation of an existing legal right which constitutes an impairment of the human rights of a person in whom the existing legal right is vested.... By extinguishing the traditional legal rights characteristically vested in the Miriam people, the 1985 Act abrogated the immunity of the Miriam people from arbitrary deprivation of their legal rights in and over the Murray Islands. The Act thus impaired their human rights while leaving unimpaired the corresponding human rights of those whose rights in and over the Murray Islands did not take their origin from the laws and customs of the Miriam people.

Id. at 33. If the United States had been a signatory to the Convention could Indian people make a similar argument that uncompensated takings of aboriginal property violated the convention?

4. Property: Australia is the only former British colony that does not recognize aboriginal land rights. In *Milirrpum v. Nabalco*, the Gove Land Rights Case discussed by Nettheim, Judge Blackburn stated that title to Australia had not been gained by conquest but by settling an uninhabited land. Since Australia was thus *terra nullius*, no property rights existed in the Aboriginal peoples. Many commentators have criticized the opinion. In the words of Professor Richard Chisholm: "The system that was imposed and that remains today, was based on a lie, a legal fiction so gross that it is hard to believe — that when the white man came, Australia was uninhabited." Chisholm, *Aboriginal Law in Australia, The Law Reform Commission's Proposals for Recognition*, 10 U. Haw. L. Rev. 47, 47 (1988). *See also* Bartlett, *Aboriginal Land Claims at Common Law*, 15 U.W. Austl. L. Rev. 293 (1983); Chisholm & Hookey, *The Gove Land Rights Case: A Judicial Dispensation for the Taking of Aboriginal Lands in Australia?*, 5 Fed. L. Rev. 85 (1972); It can be argued, however, that the Gove Land Rights Case did not settle the law, because it represented the opinion of one judge, and was not appealed. Property issues were raised in *Coe*, but that case was decided on a procedural point.

Mabo v. Queensland, discussed by Nettheim, is expected to provide the authoritative answer from the High Court. The Court has yet to reach the merits, however. The 1988 decision discussed in the preceding note merely upheld the plaintiffs' demurrer to Queensland's defense that the state law resolved the case. Now that the state law has been invalidated, the question of the nature of the aboriginal rights of the plaintiffs is squarely before the court. For a recent argument that the power of extinguishment of aboriginal title should be limited to the Commonwealth government, see Blumm & Malbon, *Aboriginal Title, the Common Law and Federalism*, in The Emergence of Australian Law at 27 (1989).

It is not surprising that so many cases arise in Queensland. With the largest Aboriginal population, Queensland has the worst record of refusing to recognize aboriginal land rights. As one commentator has characterized it:

> Land has been set aside for indigenous people, but rights to occupy it are tenuous and have nothing to do with traditional ownership. Furthermore, the principle for determining location and size of reserved land has been that the land was of little value to Europeans. As reserve lands haver always been owned by the Crown, Aborigines have

never had any rights in nor been consulted over issues of excision, reduction, expansion or even cancellation of the reserves on which they reside.

Anderson, *Queensland Aborigines and Land Holding Legislation in Australia*, 3 LAW & ANTHROPOLOGY 71, 73 (Vienna 1988).* Since 1984 Queensland Aboriginals can receive land grants under state legislation and gain some land security. For example, an Act of Parliament is now required to alter the boundaries of granted land. Unfortunately, many of the smaller reserves, on which some 12,000 Aboriginals live, are not covered by the legislation. Moreover, the land granted has been of very poor quality. *Id.* at 78-80.

Even reserve land is entitled to no particular status. There is no surrender mechanism, as in Canada, requiring consent for sale or lease of reserve lands. In the past, states took reserve land without compensation and without notice. For example, 242,000 acres in Victoria have been removed from reserve lands since the late 1830's for private farming use as well as for state use with no compensation. MORSE, ABORIGINAL SELF-GOVERNMENT IN AUSTRALIA AND CANADA, *supra* at 33.

With no legal title to land, Aboriginals have been forced to negotiate with the Crown, Commonwealth, and states by appealing to moral and political values. As a consequence, courts have not played the role in the development of policy that they have in the United States. *Id.* at 36. The Northern Territory Act, discussed in the excerpt, is a notable example of successful negotiation by Aboriginal people and their supporters. For a report by the Aboriginal Land Commissioner on his experience in implementing this law, see Toohey, *Aboriginal Land*, 15 FED. L. REV. 159 (1985). Some states have followed suit with statutes providing mechanisms for Aboriginals to get a fee title to their land. For a useful canvassing of Commonwealth, territorial, and state land rights legislation, see McNamara, *Mineral Resources in Lands Owned by Australian Aborigines*, 7 J. ENERGY L. & POL'Y 1, 7-15 (1986); MORSE, ABORIGINAL SELF-GOVERNMENT IN AUSTRALIA AND CANADA, *supra* at 47-73. *See also* Leshy, *Indigenous Peoples, Land Claims, and Control of Mineral Development: Australian and U.S. Legal Systems Compared*, 8 U. NEW S. WALES L.J. 271 (1985).

5. Breach of Trust — The *Peinkinna* Case: In *Director of Aboriginal & Islanders Advancement v. Peinkinna* [1978] 17 ALR 129, the Aboriginal residents of the Aurukun reserve in Queensland sought declaratory and injunctive relief, arguing that a mining lease agreement was a breach of trust. The petitioners did not challenge the Director's authority to enter into the leases, but only the provision that 3% of the net profits of the mining leases would be paid to the Director in trust not merely for the 700 residents of the Aurukun reserve, but for *all* Aboriginal peoples of Queensland. The British Privy Council rejected this argument, holding that the Aborigines Act of 1972, § 30(2), authorized such an action by providing that the Director as trustee could participate in the profits of a mining lease "for the benefit of Aborigines resident on the reserve *or other Aborigines as the agreement provides*." (Emphasis added.) As a result, the Privy Council did not need to reach the question "whether the Director, as trustee of the reserve, is the trustee of a trust enforceable in equity." 17 ALR at 136. Nevertheless, the Privy Council did not reject the trust theory completely, stressing the explicit grant of authority of the state legislation. In fact, the Privy Council devoted some effort in its opinion to establishing that section 334 of the Queensland Land Acts 1962-1975 and various Orders in

Council reserving and setting apart the lands under the Land Acts in Aurukun might well be interpreted to make the Director a trustee of a public charitable trust of the land. *Id.* at 137-38. Even if this relationship existed, however, the Privy Council returned to the fact that the specific provision of the Aborigines Act authorized the action. The Privy Council also noted that it gave great weight to the argument that if a public charitable trust existed, only the Queen could enforce it as *parens patriae. Id.* at 139. Given the multiplicity of state and commonwealth statues dealing with Aboriginal property, Australian Aboriginals may turn again to arguments based on the trust theory, at least in cases in which the statutes are more ambiguous than the Aborigines Act provision at issue in *Peinkinna.*

PALLEMAERTS, DEVELOPMENT, CONSERVATION, AND INDIGENOUS RIGHTS IN BRAZIL, 8 Human Rights Quarterly 374 (August 1986)*

The Amazon Basin is the largest tropical moist forest area in the world. The greater part of the Amazon forest, over three-fifths of the basin's total area, lies in Brazil, covering 42 percent of that country's national territory. In 1970 the total indigenous population in Brazil numbered 120,000. The majority of the Indians of Brazil (61 percent) live in Amazonia in small, scattered tribal groups. They are largely dependent on the tropical forest for their cultural and economic survival.

Brazil's military rulers and economic elite view the Amazon forest as a vast "unoccupied" and "unproductive" frontier area which is to be "developed" and integrated into the national economy. Pursuing a policy which had been planned since the end of the 1940s, in the early 1970s the military government, with both the assistance of the World Bank, the Inter-American Development Bank, the United States Agency for International Development, and other international lending agencies, and the active participation of transnational corporations and national entrepreneurs, embarked on the "National Integration Plan" (*Plano de Integracao Nacional*) an ambitious program for the development of the Amazon region. The first step in this program was the building of thousands of miles of roads, including the famous Transamazonian Highway, to make the area accessible and to open it up for economic activities. A subsidiary aim of this road-building scheme was the resettlement of thousands of landless peasants from the poverty-stricken northeast, who were given small plots of land along the roads as a substitute for more drastic land reform. One hundred kilometer-wide strips of rainforest on either side of the entire Amazon road network, legally regarded as "vacant lands" (*terras devolutas*), were declared the property of the federal government by proclaiming them "areas indispensable for national development." These areas were later made available for commercial agricultural colonization projects. Although supposedly this was done "without prejudice to ... the rights of the [Indians]" numerous Indian tribes were dispossessed of their lands by this scheme. In 1970 President Medici stated official government policy as follows: "Men without land in the Northeast. Land without men in the Amazon."...

These "development" activities have been extremely destructive, both for the indigenous peoples of Amazonia, and for the ecological diversity and stability of the Amazonian forest ecosystem. Numerous Indian tribes have been dispossessed of their lands or exterminated by government agencies and private developers under the guise of "relocation" and "pacification." As one general unambiguously put it: "I am of the opinion, that an area as rich as this — with gold, uranium and diamonds — cannot afford the luxury of conserving half a dozen Indian tribes who are holding back the development of Brazil.."...

The Brazilian Civil Code defines Indians, legally known as *silvicolas* or "forest dwellers," as "relatively incapacitated" and subject to a special legal regime of tutelage. This regime is laid down in the Indian Statute, a law which, according to its own terms, "regulates the juridical situation of the Indians or forest dwellers." Thus Indians are legally minors under the guardianship of the Brazilian state. The tutelage is exercised by a federal government agency in charge of Indian affairs, known as the National Indian Foundation (*Fundaçao Nacional do Indio* — FUNAI). The consequences of the Indians' legal incapacity as regards land rights are twofold: Indians are legally incompetent to own land and cannot initiate legal proceedings in their own right to defend their precarious rights of "possession" and "usufruct" of the lands they inhabit.

FUNAI is presumed to represent and protect the interest of the indigenous communities subject to its guardianship. Indeed, the law provides that it is FUNAI's duty "to assume judicial or extrajudicial defense of the rights of the forest-dwellers." If, however, FUNAI in fact fails to fulfill its duty and to protect Indian rights against third parties or subordinates the interests of the Indians to the imperatives of the government's development policy, as is often the case, no legal recourse is available. Although the law stipulates that "the tribal groups or native community are legitimate parties for the defense of their rights in justice," they cannot themselves seek redress because only FUNAI can take legal proceedings on their behalf, an unlikely proposition if FUNAI is itself an accomplice of the infringement of the rights in question. It is a legal anomaly of FUNAI's guardianship that, unlike other forms of guardianship under the Civil Code, it is not subject to any judicial control.

The tutelage regime of the Indian Statute is inconsistent with the general principles of Brazilian law relating to guardianship in other respects as well. Indeed, the general rule is that in cases of "relative incapacity" the guardian's role is only to assist the ward in the free expression of his own will, not to act as a substitute for the ward. Yet the avowed policy of FUNAI is not to express and defend the interests of the Indians as defined by the Indians themselves, but rather to balance these interests against the "national interest" of the Brazilian state. As the president of FUNAI himself stated in 1980, "A FUNAI staff member should, more than anything, act as a judge between two cultures: that of the Whites and that of the Indians. When he begins to defend one side more than the other he becomes biased and, for this reason, undesirable.."...

Finally, it should be stressed that the primary aim of the government's policy with regard to indigenous peoples is to integrate them into the dominant society and its market economy. The assimilationist goal of Indian policy is expressly laid down in the Constitution of Brazil, which provides that "the Union shall have the power to legislate upon ... incorporation of forest-dwelling aborigines into the national community." It is further spelled out in the Indian Statute which speaks of "integrating them, progressively and harmoniously, in the national communion." Indian tribal groups are classified into three legal categories: "isolated," "integrating," i.e. "accepting certain practices and ways of life common to the other sectors of the national community, *of which they stand progressively more in need for their very subsistence*," and "integrated." Although the statute contains a number of references to the Indians' "free choice of their way of living and means of subsistence" and to the need to respect "their cultural values, traditions, usages and customs," these are little more than a thin veneer which scarcely conceals the overall thrust of the legislation toward a paternalistic and ethnocentric model of development....

ARVELO-JIMENEZ, THE POLITICAL STRUGGLE OF THE GUAYANA REGION'S INDIGENOUS PEOPLES, 36 Journal of International Affairs 43, 49-53 (Spring/Summer 1982)*

Economic and political interests are at the bottom of national expansion into Indian territories, taking outright some Indian land, increasingly encircling indigenous peoples' prospects for survival as distinct cultural segments within the Venezuelan nation state. Furthermore, *criollo* interests are asserted to be synonymous with the indigenous peoples' best interests and are subsumed into certain basic assumptions which inform current Amerindian Policy in Venezuela: 1) indigenous populations, it is asserted, should be drawn into permanent settlements so that education, health and other services can be more easily provided; 2) indigenous populations must produce cash crops in order to raise their own standards of living; 3) increased participation of indigenous populations in regional markets, in other words irreversible dependency on the market economy, should be induced through introduction of "modern" or "advanced" technologies — since 1972, together with collective land allocations, an agrarian development program has been introduced into indigenous economies (the operation of these new units of production of *Empresas Indigenas* is conditioned by the incorporation of new technologies and changes in the social relations of production); 4) indigenous populations live in areas whose natural resources are poorly understood or totally unknown by *criollo* society and therefore the state should create new reserves and parks that exclude any human habitation in order to protect untapped resources for the future generations of all Venezuelan citizens, and 5) indigenous populations live within strategic border regions and natural-resource areas and their lack of "national" identity poses a threat to national security; thus, the argument goes, the state must enforce strong military measures, since it is in the best interests of *all* Venezuelan citizens to have indigenous populations' mobility curbed and border areas under tight control....

The interests of the Venezuelan nation state and those of the indigenous peoples diverge over these issues. The roots of this divergence are old. They stem from the claim made by Venezuelan leaders since political independence that it is a one-nation, one-culture state. Since 1821, dominant *criollo* society has

---

been engaged in a broad effort to homogenize culturally distinct segments of its population in order to extend its hegemony over the entire area claimed as "national" territory.

The constitution acknowledges a de facto cultural heterogeneity still present within the boundaries of Venezuela; but this is interpreted as a transitory phenomenon. Article 77 states that the goal is to accomplish the gradual incorporation of indigenous peoples as *individual* Venezuelan citizens into the mainstream of national society. This fundamental premise, by which the *criollo* segment subdues culturally distinct groups and imposes its mode of incorporation into the Venezuelan society, pervades other legal as well as political and economic measures. Expressions of this restrictive process of political, cultural and economic domination can be observed in many spheres:

1. In the economic sphere it is increasingly impairing the viability of indigenous traditional economies:

a) In the Agrarian Reform Act, indigenous peoples' rights to communally held lands are recognized. However those rights are fundamentally undermined when these same people do not have a recognized collective juridical existence but rather only *individual* status as citizens. A land tenure policy by which collective titles are allocated to indigenous communities has been in effect since 1972. The land between communities however is appropriated by the state by defining it as "*baldios* " or wastelands, thus breaking up indigenous peoples' territorial land base.

b) Furthermore, through the National Security and Defense Act the state appropriates another vast strip of land by claiming it for reasons of national security, thus superseding other property rights.

c) Further alienation of large areas of Indian territories is accomplished by declaring them National Parks and Reserves and enforcing within them the National Plan for the Conservation of Nature.

d) All natural resources, renewable and nonrenewable, surface or sub-soil, belong to the state.

Implementation of the measures described in a), b), and c) has resulted in a drastic reduction of Indian territories and of the arable land available to the communities, and severely interfered with the viability of indigenous economies.... In addition, provision d) cut off indigenous peoples from any alternative economic program of development based on the exploitation of existing resources within their territories.

2. One example of political domination is the manipulation of indigenous peoples' image before public opinion, presenting them as peoples without a national identity, and hence their "logical" conversion into a problem of "national security." Hence, in the Sixth National Economic Plan, Priority Development Areas and Priority Rural Development Areas are delineated. Many are located along international borders in Indian territories and are defined as "unoccupied" or "empty" lands. The plans are designed to resolve the dual problems of regional development and geopolitical occupation of spaces inhabited by Indian peoples without national identity.

3. The following is an example of cultural domination. The constitution guarantees liberty of beliefs for all Venezuelan citizens, but, through agreements with missionary orders, the state sponsors de facto religious indoctrina-

tion by Christian missionaries among indigenous peoples, often in a compulsory fashion. When religious indoctrination is coupled with formal elementary education with "technical" training, it constitutes blatant violation of the constitutional right of liberty of beliefs by undermining traditional Indian belief- and value-systems.

The democratic regimes of the past twenty-two years have been characterized as ideologically pluralistic. However, according to politicians in the executive and legislative branches, the actions of Christian missionaries remain the most effective mechanism for keeping Indians from being influenced by dangerous "foreign" ideologies.

In short, the incorporation of indigenous peoples into the Venezuelan nation state is an issue not only because the social structure restricts their incorporation into an individual or uniform mode of incorporation, but also because they are deprived of the rights given to other citizens.

In Venezuela, the state is determined to put an end to cultural heterogeneity. In spite of this, Indians have some political maneuverability provided they are able to use their particular strengths and what might be seen as the fundamental weakness of the state....

NOTE, ETHNIC MINORITIES AND THE SANDINIST GOVERNMENT, Student Note, 36 Journal of International Affairs 155, 155-59 (1982) (John N. Burstein)*

[I]n January 1982, Nicaraguan army troops forced between 8,500 and 10,000 Miskitos to leave their villages along the Rio Coco, the river marking the border with Honduras. In many of the forty-odd settlements the soldiers had to burn houses to make the villagers leave, and to limit any advantages to troops on the other side of the border. The Miskitos were marched south through the roadless jungle to settlement sites about ... a four-day walk away. They since have been provided with land and all manner of public services as they construct permanent dwellings. In the previous two months, there had already been 60 deaths in the Rio Coco region. So, the Managua government justified its actions as protecting the Indians as their territory becomes a dangerous battleground between Sandinist troops and expatriate Nicaraguan counter-revolutionaries....

Geographically and socially, Nicaragua is divided into two parts, known as the Pacific and Atlantic Coasts. The former contains 90 percent of the population and the Pacific Coast people are homogeneously Mestizo in race, Spanish-speaking, and of broadly Spanish-American culture. The region is largely of a low mountainous terrain, and the country's largest cities and its industrial base are located there. The Atlantic Coast, extending from the eastern piedmont to the Caribbean coast, occupies 56 percent of the national territory; it closely corresponds to the two political "departments" of Zelaya and Rio San Juan.

There are some 30,000 Black Creoles, mostly concentrated around Bluefields (a port town), who speak English Creole and English. Native Indians are the largest population of the Atlantic Coast. The Miskito, numbering around

*Copyright © 1982. Published with permission of the Journal of International Affairs and the Trustees of Columbia University in the City of New York and John N. Burstein.

100,000, occupy the northern and central coastal and interior zones. The Sumo, some 5,000 people, reside within and to the south of the Miskito region. In addition, there are presently over 40,000 Spanish-speaking residents (called "Spaniards" locally) on the Atlantic Coast who are largely first and second generation immigrants from the Pacific side. They work either as merchants in the towns or homestead virgin lands in the interior.

The Atlantic Coast is thus not only racially, linguistically, and culturally different from the Pacific Coast, but contains within itself the distinct Indian, Creole and Hispanic ethnicities....

From 1749 to 1894 the Atlantic Coast was a British protectorate, officially fashioned into the "Mosquitia Kingdom" — with the Miskito "king" selected by the British colonists themselves.... North American influence in the region was enormous until the overthrow of the Somoza regime in 1979. Indeed, despite the military conquest of the Atlantic Coast and its incorporation into Nicaragua in 1894, a general attitude of rebelliousness to Managua rule [has been] a constant in the Nicaraguan national equation....

The Miskito Indians live primarily in villages of between five and one-hundred families; they farm, fish, hunt, gather and work as temporary laborers. They are semi-nomadic and maintain a syncretic culture and religion that merges traditional and Christian elements. The Rio Coco bisects the area in which the Miskito people live; and there are as many as 150,000 more Miskito in Honduras. Political leadership is officially in the hands of each village's "headman," a local arbiter and broker between the village and the Nicaraguan government; the headman is chosen by common consent between the villagers and the government's regional administrators....

There was very little participation on the part of the Atlantic Coast political and religious organizations in the two-year civil war ending in July 1979 with the overthrow of the Somoza dictatorship. Few revolutionaries either came from, or had much experience in, that part of the country. The Atlantic Coast was nevertheless important for the consolidation of the Sandinists' rule: there was the history of regional rebelliousness, the value of the area's natural resources and the Caribbean coast, and the danger from Somozista ex-National Guardsmen who took refuge in Honduras after losing the civil war.

Thus, immediately after the revolution, the Sandinists began a plan of major infrastructural investment for the incorporation of the Atlantic Coast....

In February 1980, the government established the Instituto Nicaraguense de la Costa Atlantica (INNICA), an official agency to coordinate all government activities in the region, principally around education, health and economic development. But from the outset, in carrying out any national programs the Nicaraguan revolutionaries have relied heavily on mass organizations, responsible to the Sandinist Front (the Frente Sandinista de Liberacion Nacional), and on government agencies. On the Atlantic Coast, the Sandinists initially hoped to disband the Southern Indigenous Creole Community (SICC) and the Alliance for the Progress of the Miskito and Sumo (ALPROMISO) — which were regionally specific and based on ethnicity — and replace them with the Sandinist mass organizations formed for peasants, wage earners, youth, women and so on.

SICC eventually was dissolved. But Sandinist Commander Daniel Ortega met with such resistance to his proposal in a November 1979 meeting with 450

ALPROMISO representatives that a compromise was reached. ALPROMISO was transformed into MISURASATA (Miskito, Sumo, Rama, Sandinista, Asla Takanka, or "Working Together"), which was to be the organ for revolutionary political mobilization on the Atlantic Coast.[8]

A "honeymoon" of real collaboration endured for the following year. MISURASATA had a seat on the forty-seven member State Council instituted on May 4, 1980. The government provided the Indian organization with offices and transportation on the Atlantic Coast and in Managua. The MISURASATA Executive Directorship, headed by Steadman Fagoth, enjoyed the confidence of the INNICA officials while Fagoth held the sway of a charismatic leader among the Miskitos.... In February 1981, the Sandinist-Indian alliance came apart when, just a few days before a scheduled mass meeting to treat the issue of Indian land demands, the top leadership of MISURASATA, and about thirty local Indian leaders, were jailed on the suspicion that an Atlantic Coast separatist movement was being planned. Resistance to the apprehensions in Prinzapolka resulted in the deaths of four Indians and four soldiers....

Fagoth fled to Honduras, accompanied by as many as 3000 Miskito followers. He officially joined forces shortly thereafter with counter-revolutionary organizations in Honduras.

[T]he role accorded to MISURASATA by the Sandinist government was, of course, reduced following these events.... Nevertheless, the position evolved by MISURASATA was fundamental to shaping Sandinist Atlantic Coast policy precisely because it served as a foil to which the government responded....

The fundamental issues concerning the Atlantic Coast natives may be classified under three general headings: natural resources, culture and language, and political participation.

Natural Resources: MISURASATA claims for the Indians and Creoles legal recognition of their territory, as defined both by historic land grants and by present residence, and which are frequently communally owned. This area amounts to 45,408 square kilometers, or 72 percent of the departments of Zelaya and Rio San Juan. The natives claim rights to subsoil resources and to those off the Caribbean coast, also.

Culture and Language: The ethnic minorities claim as their right the maintenance of their cultural traditions, including marriage, funeral, curing and other rites, and of their special forms of social organization. MISURASATA desires primary education and adult literacy programs in the minority languages of the Atlantic Coast, as well as the teaching of Spanish; the Indian organization proposes the creation of a special vice-ministry of education on the Atlantic Coast, which it would control.

Political Participation: MISURASATA leaders emphatically do not seek independence from Nicaragua for the Atlantic Coast. They ask for the special concession to the Indians, as the autochthonous inhabitants, of "self-determination" within their territorial boundaries, including the local control of municipal governments. As part of MISURASATA's "Plan 81," greater partici-

[8]Richard Adams, "*The Sandinistas and the Indians,*" Caribbean Review, Vol. 10, no. 1 (Winter 1981), p. 55.

pation in INNICA, and in the national government junta itself, is also solicited in the name of the Atlantic Coast people.

In short, these claims propose the existence of one integral people, with several regionally specific ethnic subunits, who collectively advocate territorial and cultural autonomy within a federalized state.

The revolutionary government has responded to these principles with considerable formal concordance along with actual government actions of a less complying nature.

Natural Resources: After taking power, the Sandinist government claimed for itself, of course, previously designated national lands — which included much of the Atlantic Coast — but it has also recognized the communal character of landholding of the Indians. The government has promised to pay "a part of earnings" from timber extracted from Indian communal lands to an unspecified recipient agency of the Atlantic Coast but Vice Minister of the Interior Luis Carrion declared it "impossible to concede" subsoil or marine resources of the region.[15]

Culture and Language: The Sandinista pursue a policy of social "integration" of the Atlantic Coast people, described by Carrion as, "to integrate without destroying, to integrate while respecting, to integrate while conserving the special, propitious contributions of the minorities."[16] The preservation of minority languages is guaranteed but only Spanish will be the official language of Nicaragua.[17] In May 1980, the government authorized bilingual education on the Atlantic Coast, beginning in 1981, for the first four years of primary school. While the adult literacy program was carried out in the minority languages, subsequent adult and primary education programs have since been conducted only in Spanish.

Political Participation: The Sandinists' primary concern is reflected in the first of the government's "Declaration of Principles concerning the Indian Communities of the Atlantic Coast" (August 12, 1981): "The Nicaraguan nation is territorially and politically one..."[20] In the same document the revolutionary government guarantees "the participation of the Atlantic Coast communities in social, economic and political affairs pertaining to the Coast and to the entire country." There is now, however, no significant participation of Atlantic Coast Indians or Creoles in either INNICA or the other government agencies working in the region; most Indian-initiated expression of political concerns appears to stem from the interaction between government representatives and villages, or the smaller subunits of the region.

In contrast, then, to MISURASATA's advocacy of regional autonomy for the Atlantic Coast within a federalized Nicaragua, the Sandinist government has proposed cultural plurality in the country while pursuing political and economic integration of the Atlantic through its gradually increasing participation in the

---

[15] Mario F. Espinoza, "*La Costa en las Unidad Nacional,*" Barricada International, September 2, 1981, p. 8.

[16] *Ibid.*

[17] GNR, "Declaracion de Principios de la Revolucion Popular Sandinista sobre las Comunidades Indigenas de la Costa Atlantica" (Managua, Nicaragua), August 12, 1981.

[20] [*Id.*]

Pacific Coast-centralized state and Sandinist Front institutions. The government's policy is, of course, a strategy to meet its major objectives, within the context of its restraints and capabilities....

NOTES

1. **Maintaining the Land Base:** Some generalizations can be made about the hundreds of Indian communities occupying areas in Central and South America. For instance, most governments formally recognize a right of primordial occupation of land. Nevertheless, a variety of other statutes and government policies undercut these formal statements. To begin with, most countries, like Nicaragua and Brazil, provide for national government ownership of all mineral and hydropower resources wherever found, including on Indian land. Nations with land in the Amazon, like Peru and Brazil, claim the forest areas, home of the forest-dwelling Indians, to be vacant land owned by the government. In order to secure title to this land, the forest-dwellers must seek recognition of their rights from the national government. Often the agency charged with making grants to Indians is also in charge of economic development. Consequently, land grant programs have moved slowly, often focusing more on certifying to non-Indians that land was *not* Indian land and thus available for development.

In addition, land reform measures such as those adopted in Brazil, Bolivia, Colombia, Ecuador, Panama, Paraguay, Peru, and Venezuela, also pose a threat to aboriginal property. Land reform often focuses on individualization of property, which is antithetical to indigenous peoples' conception of property as belonging to the collective. For example, a survey of Peruvian indigenous policy reported:

> On February 24, 1981, the Peruvian minister of agriculture met with a group of indigenous delegates from the lowlands who were concerned about the government's development plans. The minister told the group that the Indian Community structure was a kind of impenetrable enclosure imposed on the Indians by the Spanish and other foreigners. It acts as a barrier, he told them, which keeps out the benefits of the market economy. He assured the group that the current government would support individual land titles for those who prefer them as a means of breaking free of the Community.
>
> The implications are clear: from the minister's point of view, it is the Community structure, in both a legal and a sociological sense, and the Community land tenure which are responsible for Indian poverty and powerlessness. Clearly, in this sense, the Belaunde government represents a return to normalcy: a return to "normal" antagonistic relations between the state and the indigenous population in which the paramount issues are community and community land.

Smith, *Liberal Ideology and Indigenous Communities in Post-Independence Peru*, 36 J. INT'L AFF. 73, 75 (Spring/Summer 1982).*

Land reform is often designed to stimulate agricultural production, which in turn encourages further colonization of forest areas. Extinguishment of native title in favor of non-Indian interests can be accomplished in a number of ways. For instance, non-Indian encroachers can gain Indian land by prescription. Governments also provide for removal of tribal groups when necessary for national security or the national interest, often the building of hydroelectric plants or the development of mines. *See generally* Comment, *Land and the*

Forest-Dwelling South American Indian: The Role of National Law, 27 BUF-
FALO L. REV. 759 (1978) (written by J. Grasmick). As the Pallemaerts excerpt
illustrates, economic development of the Amazon area continues to pose a serious threat to the Indian land base and way of life. *See also* Gross, *The Indians
and the Brazilian Frontier,* 36 J. INT'L AFF. 1 (1982).

   2. Self Government and the Administration of Indian Policy: No Central or
South American country presently recognizes any inherent right of self-government for indigenous peoples. Most regard indigenous peoples as under the
protection of the national government. Before its new constitution, Brazil's
FUNAI represented one end of this spectrum: a strong central government
agency in charge of all activities affecting Indians, including representation in
court, approval of contracts of individual Indians, and land management and
development. Other countries' central organizations are less comprehensive. In
Mexico, for instance, the National Indigenist Institute (INI) has representatives
from all ministries and other groups dealing with indigenous peoples. It coordi-
nates and supervises activities of these groups, but does not directly administer
programs. Finally, in some countries, such as Colombia and Venezuela, much of
the administration of Indian policy is undertaken by missions. In Venezuela, for
instance, the national government contracts with missionary orders of the Catholic Church to administer programs directed at indigenous peoples. These contracts cover most of the indigenous areas in Venezuela. The contracts typically
delineate the mission's goal as aiding in settling and civilizing the peoples in the
area covered by the contract. To keep order, the missions have missionary
police. Furthermore, missions have the power to control entry into and exit out
of the areas; in fact, contracts typically bar the entry of Protestant missionaries.
In short, the missionary orders were regarded for a long time as the guardian of
the Indians instead of the government. Nevertheless in recent years, this notion
has begun to be repudiated. In Colombia, for instance, the Supreme Court held
that contracts delegating all civil, penal, and judicial authority to the Catholic
Church were invalid. Moreover, in Venezuela government officials have stated
that Indians are citizens with a right to vote and possess legal capacity. On
administration of Indian affairs generally, see Swepston, *The Indian in Latin
America: Approaches to Administration, Integration, and Protection,* 27 BUF-
FALO L. REV. 715 (1978). On Venezuela in particular, see Kuppe, *The Indigenous Peoples of Venezuela and the National Law,* 2 LAW & ANTHROPOLOGY 113
(Vienna 1987).

   3. The New Brazilian Constitution: As stated above, Brazil has often been
cited as having the most extreme form of guardianship. Indians were regarded
as being presumptively incapable of entering into contracts and performing
other legal acts. FUNAI, their guardian, administered every aspect of their legal
affairs. *See* Carneiro da Cunha, *Aboriginal Rights in Brazil,* 2 LAW & ANTHRO-
POLOGY 55 (Vienna 1987). The 1988 Brazilian constitution contains provisions
that will reduce FUNAI's role. The new Brazilian constitution provides that
interventions on Indian land, such as mining, cannot be authorized by the
executive, but only by the National Congress. The new constitution also contains several provisions that promise to provide greater protection to Indians. It
contains provisions recognizing the Indians' right to their cultures and languages. In addition, the new constitution for the first time permits Indians
access to the judicial system to litigate their claims. *See Indian Rights in the New
Brazilian Constitution,* in 13 CULTURAL SURVIVAL Q. 13(1) at 6 (1989).

   The most significant aspect of the new constitution is the provision protecting
original rights to land. According to Article 231, Paragraph 1:

Lands traditionally occupied by Indians are those inhabited by them permanently; those used for their productive activities; those indispensable for the preservation of the environmental resources necessary for their well being; and those lands necessary for their physical and cultural reproduction, according to their uses and customs and traditions.*

Although Indian minerals and water can still be exploited, the National Congress must first authorize any such exploitation. *See generally* Santilli, *Notes on the Constitutional Rights of the Brazilian Indians*, CULTURAL SURVIVAL Q. 13(1), at 13 (1989).

4. Destruction of Indian Peoples: The genocide that took place in the nineteenth century in the United States is occurring today in Central and South America. Many tribes have become extinct in the 20th century. Others are in imminent danger of extinction. For example, in 1980 the Fourth Russell Tribunal on the Rights of Indians in the Americas concluded that the Yanomanis of Brazil and Venezuela "face a high probability of genocide unless immediate protective action is taken." Kellman, *The Yanomanis: Their Battle for Survival*, 36 J. INT'L AFF. 15 (1982). Despite the grand language of the 1988 Brazilian constitution, destruction continues in that country. A recent report alleged that the thousands of miners who have entered Yanomani territory have been decimating the population by deliberate acts such as burning houses to drive Indians away and by introducing diseases that have been taking their toll on the population. *Roraima, Brazil: A Death Warning*, in CULTURAL SURVIVAL Q. 13(4), at 59. *See generally* Special Issue: *Central America and the Caribbean*, CULTURAL SURVIVAL Q. 13(3) 1989.

5. Indian Guerilla Movements: As encroachment on native land and violence toward Indians in Central and South America has increased, so has violent resistance by some native groups. Natives seek to preserve their way of life as well as their land; governments along the political spectrum often interfere with both, albeit for different reasons. Agrarian reform, a liberal agenda item, can be as threatening to the land base as the massive private economic development projects favored by conservatives. The natives' way of life may be offensive to the religious tradition of the dominant culture in a centrist or right-wing nation; it may threaten the cultural premises upon which a revolutionary government is based. As a result, guerilla movements have been formed in some countries. When these guerilla movements are located in border areas they pose an even greater threat to national security, especially for a government seeking to consolidate power and secure its borders in the face of internal and external challenges to its authority. Such governments will be reluctant to grant natives in border areas much autonomy. At the same time, their position as a threat gives these natives more clout in negotiations, as the Miskito Indians of Nicaragua have illustrated.

6. Recent Developments in Nicaragua: The people of the Atlantic Coast have made great gains in recent years. In 1987, the Nicaraguan government enacted Law No. 28, the Autonomy Statute, Estatuto de la Autonomia de las Regiones de la Costa Atlantica de Nicaragua, 238 La Gaceta 2833 (1987), which creates two autonomous regions in the Atlantic Coast, each to be governed by an elected regional council and further divided into municipalities. The regional governments function more as representatives of the central government and have only a consultative role in affecting national policy. Nevertheless, they

---

*Translated by Biorn Maybury-Lewis, reprinted in Santilli, *Notes on the Constitutional Rights of the Brazilian Indians*, CULTURAL SURVIVAL Q. 13(1), 13, 14 (1989).

do have power to set internal policies, such as policies governing indigenous land, although indigenous land is still subject to national development plans. Although long on rhetoric and short on specifics, the law still represents a first step toward recognizing indigenous rights in that country. Indigenous leaders continued to press for a treaty governing their relationship with the government in place of a statute. In February, 1988, YATAMA, the United Yapti Tasba Organizations, the indigenous group that has succeeded MISURASATA as the major organization representing the Atlantic Coast people, signed a preliminary accord with the government of Nicaragua, in which the government agreed that further negotiations should take place to recognize the land rights and political autonomy of the Atlantic Coast people. In September, 1989, the Sandinista government permitted YATAMA leaders to reenter Nicaragua with the right to travel freely and organize indigenous political parties. In early 1990, Violetta Chamorro was elected president of Nicaragua, defeating Daniel Ortega, the Sandinista president. Whether the new government will continue these negotiations remains to be seen.

BENNETT, THE POSITION OF CUSTOMARY LAW IN SOUTH AFRICA, 4 Law & Anthropology 27-28 (Vienna 1989)*

History of the Recognition of Customary Law

The attitude to recognition and enforcement of customary law has been determined by two dominant policies. When the British occupied the Cape Province, Roman-Dutch law was retained as the general law of the Colony (on the ground that it was a "civilized" system). No account was taken of other systems of law. The autochthonous Khoisan peoples, at the time of the British occupation, were few in number, dispersed over a wide area and their social and political institutions had disintegrated. Without the vigour of a living society to sustain it, there was no indigenous system of law to recognize [2] Apart from this the Cape administration saw its mission as one of "civilizing" the black population and so, when Kaffraria was annexed in the Eastern Cape, the government refused to recognize the customary law of the peoples living there.

In Natal, on the other hand, the policy of indirect rule was implemented to facilitate government of the large numbers of displaced people who flooded back into the Colony after the British annexation. With government support for chiefly authority, came recognition and application of customary law. In order to meet the criticism that the Natal administration was doing nothing to "civilize" its African population, an exemption procedure was provided whereby Africans could opt out of customary law if they satisfied certain requirements. In 1878 Zulu law was codified to facilitate the administration of justice (the Natal Code) and, despite many amendments, this Code remains in force.[6]

The Orange Free State never developed a coherent or sustained policy regarding customary law but, in Transvaal, in 1885, a policy similar to that of

---

[2] T.W. Bennett, The Application of Customary Law in Southern Africa: The Conflict of Personal Laws (1985) 40.

[6] By Proc. 2 of 1887, this was made binding in Zululand; it was revised in 1888, and made applicable in Natal in 1891 by Law 19. The Code has been revised again and the current form was promulgated by the executive in Proc. R195 of 1967.

Natal was adopted. Customary law was enforced provided that it was not inconsistent with the general principles of "civilization." The Transvaal courts (unlike their Natal counterparts) interpreted this formula to mean that customary forms of marriage and bridewealth transactions could not be enforced because both were deemed to be inherently uncivilized. By refusing to recognize norms which were fundamental to the structure of African society, the courts rendered the overall recognition of customary law "substantially ineffective."[9]

By 1910, the date of the Union, the diversity of approaches to customary law demanded serious reconsideration. In the Northern Cape (British Bechuanaland), chiefs had largely unfettered jurisdiction and regularly applied customary law. In Transkei chiefs' courts operated alongside magistrates' courts and both applied customary law except for certain important statutory modifications. In Natal there was a codified system of law and indirect rule. In the Cape customary law was not recognized at all and, in the Transvaal, the courts refused to countenance the fundamental institutions of African family life. "This chaotic state of affairs" prompted the Supreme Court to call for reform.

At the turn of the century, however, there were signs of profound social changes taking place. The tribal institutions that had formerly posed a threat to the security of the white conquest were finally extinguished in the Zulu rebellion. Africans now formed a sizable urban proletariat; many were educated and African political associations had emerged. The threat that these developments posed to white hegemony was met by a distinct shift in government policy: the revival of traditional, tribal institutions, including, of course, recognition and enforcement of customary law. In this way the energies of an increasingly competitive class of people who were beginning to challenge the whites on their own terms could be deflected. The merit of "tribalism" in the eyes of the government was that it promoted racial segregation and thus guaranteed continued white political and economic control of the country. It comes as no surprise then, to find that customary law is frequently identified with apartheid.

The multifaceted programme of apartheid was given its name and new impetus in 1948, when the Nationalist government came to power, but it had been evolving on the basis of a series of enactments passed long before. In 1913 the Native Land Act[10] prohibited Africans from buying or leasing land outside certain "scheduled" areas (which, at that time, comprised less than 8% of the area of the country). This restriction translated into statutory terms a recommendation of the South African Native Affairs Commission of 1903-5 that territorial segregation was necessary to safeguard the interests of whites. The Native Trust and Land Act of 1936[15] released more land for settlement of Africans. From the lands demarcated in these two Acts, the "reserves" (later "Bantustans" then "homelands" and now "national states") developed in the period after 1949. The vestiges of political competition were removed by the 1936 Representation of Natives Act. Prior to this, the Native Affairs Act of 1920 had provided for the formation of local councils in the reserves. Thus Africans were excluded from central government and allowed only local government along tribal lines in the reserves. What emerged was a division between African

---

[9] Meesadoosa v. Links 1915 TPD 357 at 361 ....
[10] Now called the Black Land Act.
[15] Now called the Development Trust and Land Act.

rural areas, where Africans were supposed to get on with their own development, and the white-controlled urban areas and farmlands which would form
the basis for the real economic and political life of the country.

Latterly the apartheid regime has been cloaked with the principle of self-
determination or free pursuit of cultural identity.[19] In reality this has meant a
sharp separation between the economically impoverished "national states" and
the ever-expanding industrial/urban complexes. Entry by Africans into the
urban areas has been restricted by influx control measures. Africans are considered necessary only as a labour force; able-bodied men are welcome for short
periods of time on a contract basis. The "national states" have become the
domain for women, children and the elderly.

NOTES

1. **Homelands and Reservations:** How would you answer the argument, frequently made, that the separatism many native peoples seek is similar to the
South African system of apartheid? *See* Berger, *Native Rights and Self-Determination*, 22 U.W. ONT. L. REV. 1, 13 (1984). For another review of the treatment of African people in South African law, see Olmesdahl, *Aboriginal Peoples and South African Law*, 3 LAW & ANTHROPOLOGY 277 (Vienna 1987).
Volume 4 of the *Journal of Law and Anthropology*, from which the Bennett
excerpt is taken, is devoted completely to the indigenous peoples of Southern,
Eastern, and Western Africa.

President de Klerk has announced that in early 1991 he will seek to repeal
both the Group Areas Act and the Lands Act, discussed in the principal excerpt,
thus ending segregation in South Africa. What are the implications of this
removal of formal barriers to ownership and occupation, if it occurs? President
de Klerk has voiced the opinion that free market forces will result in sorting out
any ownership issues that arise. Do you agree? If the more than 13% of the
country that is presently allocated to blacks in South Africa and held in trust by
the government is opened to the free market, what may become of the land?
Will blacks make claim to land presently owned by white farmers that was
dispossessed from them 200 years ago? Both the African National Congress and
the more radical Pan-Africanist Congress have called for redistribution of land.
Can such redistribution take place without compensation?

2. **Other National Responses:** The literature on issues affecting native peoples in other nations is rich and diverse. Space does not permit a complete
bibliography, but the following articles on nations not featured above may give
the interested student a place to begin her research. Lynch, *Native Title, Private
Right and Tribal Land Law: An Introductory Survey*, 57 PHILIPPINE L.J. 268
(1982); Weisbrot, *Papua New Guinea's Indigenous Jurisprudence and the Legacy of Colonialism*, 10 U. HAWAII L. REV. 1 (1988); Tamanaha, *The Role of
Custom and Traditional Leaders Under the Yap Constitution*, 10 U. HAWAII L.
REV. 81 (1988); Kulkarni, *Law, Tribal Communities, and Social Justice in India*,
3 LAW & ANTHROPOLOGY 1 (Vienna 1988). General sources include the recently
inaugurated *Yearbook on Law and Anthropology* published at the University of
Vienna. The *Cultural Survival Quarterly*, published in Cambridge, Massachu-

---

[19] Minister of Native Affairs, Native Policy of the Union of SA (issued by the State Information
Office in 1950 to the House of Assembly) 7. The statutory basis for this policy was the promotion of
Bantu (now Black) Self-Government Act 46 of 1959 which divided the African population into nine
ethnic units (now six), each to become "self-governing Black National units."

setts, covers many issues of interest to indigenous peoples. See, for example, Vol. 13, No. 3, "Central America and the Caribbean" (1989).

3. The Comparative Perspective: As the preceding materials demonstrate, many variables condition responses. Similarities between the two cultures can be significant. For instance, a collectivist state may be more tolerant of indigenous land holding patterns. *See* Svensson, *Comparative Ethnic Policy on the American and Russian Frontiers*, 36 J. INT'L AFF. 83 (1982). Such similarities can be manipulated by members of the dominant culture to integrate indigenous peoples. For example, the Jesuits among the Hurons in the Northeastern United States skillfully played on similarities between the two cultures and religions to convert a majority of the Huron population. This same contact destroyed the Huron confederacy, although this was not the intent of the missionary fathers. H.W. BOWDEN, AMERICAN INDIANS AND CHRISTIAN MISSIONS, 59-95 (1981).

When cultural differences are great and the dominant culture seizes upon these differences as evidence of racial and cultural inferiority, the dominant culture is more likely to take repressive measures designed to force integration. Ethnocentrism and racism played a central role in the early history of European contact with the Americas, see generally R. BERKHOFER, JR., THE WHITE MAN'S INDIAN (1978); Williams, *Documents of Barbarism: The Contemporary Legacy of European Racism and Colonialism in the Narrative Traditions of Federal Indian Law*, 31 ARIZ. L. REV. 237 (1989), as well as with parts of Africa, Asia, and Oceania colonized by European powers.

In addition to cultural differences, geographic isolation is a factor that often permits more policy room for indigenous peoples to continue their own ways. Moreover, when these indigenous peoples are located on a border, the dominant state may perceive a stronger need to take positive steps to secure their loyalty by giving them more autonomy. *See* Korn-Reidlinger, *The Tibeto-Burman Ethnic Group of the Baizu (Yunnan) in P.R. China's Law*, 2 LAW & ANTHROPOLOGY 255 (Vienna 1987). On the other hand, when the border state itself poses a threat to a politically fragmented state, repressive measures may result, as the Burstein excerpt illustrates. Nevertheless, such a situation may give the border people more of a bargaining chip, because alliance would permit the state to focus its energies on other external and internal threats to its existence.

Population density is also very important. When the indigenous peoples comprise a majority of the people in a contiguous area, it becomes more feasible to speak in terms of autonomy for the indigenous peoples, although the dominant culture may perceive the need to ensure that its members are not subject to the indigenous governments. In Canada, proportional representation of non-Indians in the state government has been discussed as necessary before granting statehood to Nunavut and Denendah. Similarly, in South Africa, most plans for granting full political rights to Blacks have included methods of guaranteeing some representation for the white minority. In the United States, also, there has been a movement to remove non-Indians from tribal criminal and civil jurisdiction. Of course the other side of this coin is that when the dominant culture perceives the need for the land occupied by the indigenous peoples, various mechanisms exist to wrest the land from native control.

Despite the rather bleak picture painted above, it must be noted that in almost every report on indigenous peoples from any country, stress is laid on the fact that the indigenous population has grown in the twentieth century. Moreover, indigenous peoples world-wide continue to seek to retain their cultural identity by various measures designed to permit them to retain a separate existence.

When existing law has failed, they have sought to educate the public and bring pressure to bear on legislatures, as the experiences in Canada and Australia illustrate. In the past 10 years indigenous peoples have joined together in an effort to obtain some recognition for their concerns in international law. This effort has produced a world-wide network between varied indigenous peoples who have begun to work together to put pressure on their individual states to produce change.

B. THE INTERNATIONAL RESPONSE

1. INTRODUCTION

S. JAMES ANAYA, THE RIGHTS OF INDIGENOUS PEOPLES AND INTERNATIONAL LAW IN HISTORICAL AND CONTEMPORARY PERSPECTIVE, 1989 Harvard Indian Law Symposium 191 (1990)*

The Native tribes of the American continents and other indigenous peoples similarly oppressed by the processes of colonialism have long sought to continue as distinct communities with historically based social, cultural and political attributes. Armed resistance, diplomacy and law have been used as instruments in this quest for survival. Through law indigenous peoples have asserted rights deriving from their status as the original occupants of invaded lands, and have sought to have those rights included within law's regulatory and legitimizing mechanisms.

Assertion of such rights of indigenous peoples ("*indigenous rights*") has included recourse to the domestic institutions of states that have grown up around indigenous communities. While often successful, indigenous rights proponents have encountered the limits of these institutions, which were founded to advance the collective interests of the encroaching societies. In the United States, for example, the courts have continued to recognize tribal rights of land and resource ownership as well as self-government; but they have done so only through the eyes of Western culture and then only at the sufferance of Congress, the most political branch of the federal government. And Congress has proven itself to be a receptive vehicle for the political forces adverse to those rights in ways that have inflicted deep scars on the integrity of Native communities. Even in the absence of Congressional action, the courts of this country have, over time, undermined Indian rights by various doctrinal means calculated to satisfy perceived needs of the dominant societal order.

The assertion of indigenous rights through domestic law is an effort to secure from *within* state structures adequate accommodation for the historical attributes of tribal communities. Faced with the limitations of domestic structures, indigenous groups have sought the same end from *outside* of them through recourse to international law and its presumptive authority to constrain the state.

Within the last several years indigenous groups from the Americas, Australia and other parts of the world have organized and joined in efforts to forge the protection of their asserted rights on the basis of international law. International law, like domestic law, however, is a mixed bag. On the one hand, early

---

international jurisprudence supporting indigenous rights and contemporary international human rights norms inspire[s] expectations among indigenous rights proponents. On the other hand, the discipline called international law, having originated in the European worldview of the late Middle Ages, developed into a state-centered system which has provided a veneer of legitimacy for states recognized by the international community as well as for the colonial patterns upon which many of them are based. Moreover, the system's traditional doctrine of state sovereignty, with its corollaries of territorial integrity, exclusive jurisdiction and non-intervention in domestic affairs, has hobbled the capacity of international law to affirm indigenous rights so unambiguously as to limit the action of states within their asserted spheres of control....

I. *The Early Affirmation of Indigenous Rights Within the Naturalist Frame*

Indigenous rights found support in the jurisprudence of the sixteenth and seventeenth centuries that traditionally is associated with the rise of modern international law. This jurisprudence, which included the works of Francisco de Vitoria (1480-1546) and Hugo Grotius (1583-1635), was rooted in perceptions of a universal normative order applying across all levels of humanity, independent of and higher than the positive law or decisions of temporal authority.

Conceptions about the source of the higher authority, characterized as natural or divine law, varied. For Vitoria and the other Spanish school theorists, God figured prominently and law merged with theology. Grotius, who is considered the most important of the "fathers of international law," moved toward a secular characterization of the law of nature, defining it as a "dictate of right reason" in conformity with morality and the social nature of human beings.[9]

Whatever the source of the perceived higher authority, it provided the jurisprudential grounds for theorists to conceive of and examine norms from a fundamentally humanist, moral perspective, and to withhold the imprimatur of *law* from the acts of earthly sovereigns if found to be against the perceived moral code. Further, the focus of the naturalist theorists went beyond the concerns of sovereigns to those of all levels of human interaction, although in varying degrees. In these respects, this jurisprudential framework resembles and gives inspiration to the modern human rights movement.

The view of a supra-state normative order applying across all levels of humanity had been encouraged by a politically complex medieval Europe, in which the king's realm had been but one among a maze of loyalties. The relationship of monarchs to large rural populations had been mediated from below by independent lords and sub-lords, while above were Pope and Emperor asserting universalist claims to which the king was theoretically subordinate. Against this backdrop of overlapping sovereigns, theologians and jurists did not hesitate to discern the contours of a universally binding natural or divine law.

Thus, in his ground breaking and influential lectures, *On the Indians Lately Discovered* (1532),[13] Vitoria boldly challenged the Spanish claims to Indian

---

[9] H. Grotius, [On the Law of War and Peace] 38-39 [(Classics of International Law ed. 1925) (2d. ed. 1946)]; *see* Lauterpacht, [*The Grotian Tradition in International Law*, 1946 British Y.B. Int'l. L. 1,] at 7.

[13] Published in F. Victoria, De Indis et de Ivre Belli Relectiones (Classics of International Law ed. 1917) (translation based on Boyer ed. 1557, Muñoz ed. 1565 & Simon ed. 1696) (using the Italian version of his name, "Francisci de Victoria.") [hereinafter De Indis.]

lands in the Western Hemisphere on the basis of natural and divine law precepts as informed by "Holy Scripture." Vitoria argued that the Indians of the Americas were the true owners of their lands, with "dominion in both public and private matters."[15] He held that neither imperial nor papal authority justified Spanish domination over the Indians, rejecting the view that the Emperor or Pope possessed lordship over the whole world. Moreover, Vitoria sustained that discovery of the Indians' lands alone could not confer title in the Spaniards "anymore than if it had been they who had discovered us."[17]

Vitoria also addressed the obligations of the Indians under the *jus gentium*, which he viewed as either "natural law or ... derived from natural law."[19] Under the *jus gentium*, according to Vitoria, Indians were bound to allow foreigners to travel to their lands, trade among them, and preach the gospel. In his related lecture, *On the Indians, or On the Law of War Made by the Spaniards on the Barbarians*,[21] Vitoria held that persistent interference by the Indians in efforts by the Spaniards to carry out these activities could lead to "just" war and conquest. Vitoria warned, however, against "imaginary causes of war."[22]

Vitoria's work, grounded in the European theocratic worldview, unquestionably was filled with cultural biases, and he provided enduring conceptual support for colonial patterns by his theory of just war. Nonetheless, as the late Felix Cohen observed, Vitoria's construct was one based on a premise of human equality.[24] Indians and non-Indians alike had rights, as well as duties. Like all others, Indians could have war waged against them for just cause; but in the absence of conquest following a just war, Indians could not be unilaterally dispossessed of their lands and their autonomous existence. The basic elements of this view were adopted by other prominent theorists of the period including Francisco, Suarez, Dominic Soto, Bartolome de las Casas, Balthasar Ayala and Alberico Gentilis.

Grotius followed in this vein.[26] But in keeping with his secularized construction of the governing law of nature, he removed the religious grounds for just war and conquest in his famous treatise *On the Law of War and Peace* (1625).[28] Further, Grotius affirmed that a necessary consequence of the natural law rights of *all* peoples, including "strangers to the true religion," was the ability to enter into treaty relationships:

> According to the law of nature this is no degree a matter of doubt. For the right to enter into treaties is so common to all men [sic] that it does not admit of a distinction arising from religion.[29]

Contemporary scholarship has established that these affirmations of indigenous rights by the early international law theorists were more than merely

---

[15] [*Id.*] at 127-128....

[17] *Id.* at 139.

[19] *Id.* at 151....

[21] Published in De Indis *supra* note 13.

[22] *Id.* at 156....

[24] F. Cohen, *The Spanish Origin of Indian Rights in the Law of the United States*, 31 Geo. L.J. 1, 11-12 (1942)....

[26] *See* H. Grotius, The Freedom of the Seas 13 (Carnegie Endowment for International Peace ed. 1916) (Elzevir ed. 1633) (citing Vitoria)....

[28] *See* On The Law of War and Peace, *supra* note [9], at 546-547.

[29] *Id.* at 397.

aspirational statements. Modern scholars have demonstrated that the early theorists' views came to be reflected in the declared policies of European political leaders (although these policies were not always followed) as well as in the subsequent centuries of treaty-making and consensual relations between the European powers and indigenous peoples.

II. *International Law in the Emerging Modern State System: Its Early Implications for Indigenous Rights*

The 1648 Treaty of Westphalia, which ended the Thirty Years War and the political hegemony asserted by the Catholic Church, ushered in the era of the independent territorial state. The emergence of the modern system of states engendered a revised framework for the developing conception of international law and its treatment of indigenous peoples.

This new framework finds its most notable formative expression in the writing of the Swiss diplomat Emmerich de Vattel (1714-1769). In his major work, *The Law of Nations or Principles of Natural Law* (1758),[32] Vattel helped consolidate the conception of international law as law concerned only with states. Against a backdrop of a system of European state-societies, each of which claimed autonomy, he defined the "*Law of Nations*" as "*the science of the rights which exist between Nations or states, and of the obligations corresponding to these rights.*"[33] Vattel adhered to the rhetoric of natural law, but he adopted the Hobbesian dichotomy of a "natural law of [individuals]" and a "natural law of States."[34] Vattel developed a complex construct of the natural law of states, to which he added the positive law of treaties and custom among states.

The transformation of the concept of the law of nature from a universal moral code for humankind into a dichotomy of natural rights of individuals and natural rights of states has been called "the most important intellectual development of the seventeenth century subsequent to Grotius."[36] The binary view of human reality reflected in the dichotomy has powerfully affected the entire tradition of Western liberal thought. The view acknowledges the rights of the individual on the one hand and the sovereignty of the total social collective on the other, but it is not alive to the rich variety of intermediate or alternative associational groupings actually found in human cultures, nor is it prepared to ascribe to such groupings any rights not reducible either to the liberties of the citizen or to the prerogatives of the state. Apparently for Vattel and others of his time the individual/state dichotomy adequately covered the spectrum of human concern, and it was possible to dissect the dichotomy and construct a legal regime focused only on states.

Vattel's construction of a discrete legal regime concerning only states — the *law of nations* — included the foundational principal that "Nations are free and independent from one another as men are by nature, [and accordingly] each Nation should be left to the peaceable enjoyment of that liberty which belongs

---

[32] E. de Vattel, The Law of Nations or the Principles of Natural Law (II Classics of International Law ed. 1916).
[33] *Id.* at 3.
[34] *Id.*, Preface, at 5a....
[36] [H.] Damerow, [A Critical Analysis of the Foundations of International Law] 29 [(1978)].

to it by its nature."[37] By this statement Vattel gave rise to the modern international law doctrine of sovereign equality and its corollaries of exclusive jurisdiction and nonintervention in domestic affairs. Unlike most exaltations of state sovereignty in modern international discourse, however, it is apparent Vattel did not view the state in isolation from its theoretical human underpinnings. Along the lines of Lockean social contract theory developed within the individual/state frame, Vattel viewed the state as an autonomous institution embodying civil society, consensually formed by individuals in their own interests of comfort and self-preservation. Thus,

> [t]he end of the natural society established among men in general is that they should mutually assist one another to advance their own perfection and that of their condition; and Nations, too, since they may be regarded as so many free persons living together in a state of nature, are bound mutually to advance this human society. Hence the end of the great society established by nature among all Nations is likewise that of mutual assistance in order to perfect themselves and their condition.[40]

For Vattel, therefore, the state was free and independent *as a result* of the natural law liberty of its human constituents, although conceived of in individualistic terms. And the state's attributes of exclusive jurisdiction and such were a means of maximizing the interests of individuals joined in social compact. But where would indigenous societies fit in the grand vision of civil society framed according to the individual/state perceptual dichotomy of rights? It would seem that to enjoy rights as distinct communities, particularly for the purposes of international law as framed by Vattel, they would have to be regarded as states.

Vattel defined states broadly to include all "political bodies, societies of men who have united together and combined their forces, in order to procure their mutual welfare and security...."[42] Furthermore, Vattel held that a state does not lose its sovereignty or independent status by placing itself under the protection of another as long as it retains its powers of self-government. But Vattel added, almost as if to beg the question, that once "a people ... has passed under the rule of another [it] is no longer a state, and does not come directly under the Law of Nations. Of this character were the Nations and the Kingdoms which the Romans subjected to their Empire."[44]

It is clear that Vattel believed at least some non-European aboriginal peoples qualified as states or nations (terms be used interchangeably) with rights as such. In forcefully bringing into question European expansionism in the Americas, Vattel remarked:

> Those ambitious Europeans States which attacked the American Nations and subjected them to their avaricious rule, in order, as they said, to civilize them, and have them instructed in the true religion — those usurpers, I say, justified themselves by a pretext equally unjust and ridiculous.[45]

Even Vattel's broad definition of the state, however, is conditioned by a basic prejudice in favor of political and social organization in the European mold. This European perspective is evident in Vattel's distinction between the "civi-

---

[37] *Id.* [at 8-9.]
[40] [Vattel, *supra* note 32,] at 6.
[42] [*Id.*] at 3.
[44] *Id.* at 12.
[45] *Id.* at 115-16.

lized Empires of Peru and Mexico" (no doubt referring to the Incas and the Aztecs) and the North American "peoples of those vast tracts of land [who] rather roamed over them than inhabited them."[46] As to the former, "conquest ... was a notorious usurpation, [while] the establishment of various colonies upon the continent of North America might, if done within limits, have been entirely lawful."[47] Vattel seemed to distinguish between forms of indigenous society on the basis of the supposed Lockean natural law duty to cultivate the soil which he accepted. Later theorists invoked and expounded on this distinction as a basis for denying indigenous peoples status as nations or states with rights in international law.

The question of whether American Indian tribes could qualify as states of international stature shaped the United States Supreme Court's early Indian law decisions. These decisions — which prominently made their way into the fabric of international law concerning indigenous rights — came half a century after Vattel's writing, at a time when the young country, founded on natural law visions of civil society, had yet to reconcile the anomalous existence of the Natives within its asserted boundaries. In *Worcester v. Georgia*, Chief Justice John Marshall writing for the Court made unambiguous his view that the Indian tribes, although physically within the boundaries of the United States, were nonetheless to be considered states of international stature. Citing Vattel, Marshall called the tribes "nations" and analogized them to the "'[t]ributary and feudatory states'" of Europe, which Vattel held to rank among sovereign states subject to the law of nations despite having assented to the protection of a stronger power.[51]

Accordingly, Marshall in this and other decisions he wrote for the Court determined the rights of Indians using conceptions clearly identifiable with the law of nations as grounded in the teachings of the early international law theorists. Marshall upheld the "original natural rights" of Indians over their lands, which they could not lose by discovery alone.[53] *Voluntary* cession and *actual* conquest, as with other nations on earth, were the basis upon which to gauge

---

[46] *Id.* at 38.

[47] *Id.*

[51] [31 U.S. (6 Pet.)] at 560-61. In a case decided the year before *Worcester*, Cherokee Nation v. Georgia, 30 U.S. (5 Pet.) 1 (1831), Marshall on behalf of the Court held that the Cherokee Nation did not qualify as a "foreign state" under the provision of the U.S. Constitution entitling such to invoke the Court's original jurisdiction. Marshall's holding rested on an interpretation of the meaning of the term "foreign state" as it is used in article III of the Constitution, in light of the Constitution's specific reference elsewhere to "Indian tribes" and the particular treaty relationship between the Cherokees and the United States. His statement that the Indian tribes could be denominated as "domestic dependent nations" was *not* based on a view of the tribes as having a status inherently inferior to the European or European-derived states, as many have suggested. Rather, that designation was based on his view that the Indians "acknowledge *themselves* in their treaties to be under the protection of the United States." *Id.* at 17 (emphasis added). Marshall declined to determine whether the Cherokee Nation was a foreign state for purposes other than the grant of original jurisdiction.

Wheaton, the Supreme Court reporter and friend of Marshall's, interpreted the Marshall decisions as upholding the international status of Indian nations in his classic treatise, Elements of International Law 50-51 (8th ed. 1866). At the same time, however, Wheaton excluded from among the subjects of international law "an unsettled horde of wandering savages not yet formed into civil society. The legal idea of a state necessarily implies that of the habitual obedience of its members to those persons in whom the superiority is vested, and of a fixed abode, and definite territory belonging to the people by whom it is occupied." *Id.* at 26.

[53] [*Id.*,] at 559.

whether an Indian Nation had been divested of its rights.[54] And in the absence of actual conquest, the protectorate of the United States over the tribes was a matter of treaty relationship, not unilateral imposition.

Over time, however, the federal government effectively asserted more and more authority over Indian tribes. Faced with the perceived limits of judicial competency to reverse the federal encroachments, the Supreme Court sustained them.[57] The Court, moreover, retreated from Marshall's adherence to the law of nations by reinterpreting his references to discovery and unaccomplished conquest[58] and by rejecting, implicitly if not explicitly, Marshall's assessment of the legal status of Indian nations.[59] To see tribes as "states" would always prove difficult for Western eyes.

III. The Positivists' International Law: A Tool for the Derogation of Indigenous Rights

The legal status of indigenous peoples and their rights suggested by Marshall likewise was not ultimately forthcoming in international law as it developed away from its natural law origins toward a model based on consensual relations among states. As the forces of colonization and empire consolidated indigenous lands within the hegemonic spheres of nineteenth century states, and as the difficulty of reconciling the rights of indigenous peoples with those forces became apparent, international legal discourse, as shaped by positivist theorists, abandoned indigenous rights. The major premises of the nineteenth and early

---

[54] See [id.], at 541-563; Cherokee Nation v. Georgia, 30 U.S. (5 Pet.) 1 (1831). In dictum in a case decided almost a decade before Worcester, Marshall suggested a willingness to diverge from the law of nations if necessary to uphold United States claims to Indian lands, but only, he further suggested, as a necessary result of the limits of domestic judicial competency:

> However extravagant the pretention of converting the discovery of an inhabited country into conquest may appear; if the principle has been asserted in the first instance, and afterwards sustained; if a country has been acquired and held under it; if the property of the great mass of the community originates in it, it becomes the law of the land, and cannot be questioned.... *However this restriction may be opposed to natural right, and to the usages of civilized nations, yet, if it be indispensable to that system under which the country has been settled, and be adapted to the actual conditions of the two people, it may, perhaps, be supported by reason, and certainly cannot be rejected by Courts of justice.*

Johnson v. M'Intosh, 21 U.S. (8 Wheat.) 543, 591-92 (1823) (emphasis added). This dictum has been much construed (and this writer would say misconstrued in light of Worcester) as a substantive endorsement of a doctrine of diminished Indian rights in favor of the European discoverer's power on the basis of discovery alone.

[57] See, e.g., United States v. Kagama, 118 U.S. (1886) (upholding Congressional power to legislate federal prosecution of crimes committed by Indians on reservations and thus infringe on internal tribal resolution of disputes); Lone Wolf v. Hitchcock, 187 U.S. 553 (1903) (affirming power of Congress unilaterally to abrogate Indian treaties); see generally C. Wilkinson, American Indians, Time and the Law 24-26 (1987) (identifying Kagama and Lone Wolf as progenitors of a jurisprudential trend away from the Marshall cases).

[58] See, e.g., Tee-Hit-Ton Indians v. United States, 348 U.S. 272, 279 (1954) ("This [diminished] position of the Indian has long been rationalized by the legal theory that discovery and conquest gave the conquerors sovereignty and ownership of the lands they obtained." [Citing Johnson v. McIntosh, 8 Wheat. 543.]

[59] In U.S. v. Rogers, 45 U.S. (4 How.) 567 (1846), Chief Justice Taney altogether reconstructed the history of Indian-European contact set forth by Marshall in Worcester. According to Taney,

> The native tribes who were found on this continent at the time of its discovery have never been acknowledged or treated as independent nations by European governments, nor regarded as the owners of the territories they respectively occupied.

45 U.S. at 571.

twentieth century positivist school ensured that international law would become a legitimizing force for colonization and empire rather than a liberating one for indigenous peoples.

The first of these major premises, which had been expressed by Vattel and reflected in Marshall's Supreme Court opinions, was that international law is concerned only with the rights and duties of states. A second and related premise, also derived from the previous framework as indicated by Vattel, was that international law upholds the sovereignty of states, which are presumed to be equal and independent, and thus guards the exercise of that sovereignty from outside interference. The positivist formulation, however, parted company with the view of Vattel and Marshall that natural law is part of international law. Accordingly, a third premise, which was at the core of the positivist school, was that international law is law *between* and not *above* states, and finds its theoretical basis in their *consent* as displayed by custom or treaty. The fourth premise was that the states that make international law and possess rights and duties under it are of a limited universe, and that universe for the positivist school did not include indigenous peoples outside the mold of European civilization.

These premises meant that Indian nations and other indigenous peoples, not qualifying as states, could not participate in the shaping of international law nor could they look to it to affirm the rights that had once been deemed to inhere in them by natural or divine law. States, on the other hand, both shaped the rules of international law and enjoyed rights under it independently of natural law considerations. It followed that states could create doctrine to affirm and perfect their claims over indigenous territories as a matter of international law without regard to the rights of the indigenous inhabitants. States could then treat the indigenous inhabitants according to domestic policies, shielded from uninvited outside scrutiny by international law itself. Principles of state sovereignty, originally conceived of a means of advancing human interests, would be the conceptual means of international law's complicity with inhumane forces.

Late nineteenth century theorists relied upon the positivist construct of international law in order to provide the imprimatur of *law* for conditions of dubious legitimacy. The construct was significant not only for upholding the territorial bases of the American states, but also for limiting the parameters of international concern over the ongoing colonization of the African and other non-European territories.

The British publicist John Westlake in his *Chapters on the Principles of International Law* (1894) provided one of the most complete expositions of the positivistic justification for the critical conceptual more of excluding indigeneous peoples from among the subjects of international law. Westlake distinguished between "civilized and uncivilized humanity" and viewed "international society" as limited to the civilized.[63] By making the European style government and sedentary lifestyle the test of "civilization," Westlake categorically excluded tribal peoples and their rights from international law. Westlake's rationale for imposing the requirement of European style government is extravagant and worth quoting at length:

---

[63] J. Westlake, [Chapters on Principles of International Law (1984)] at 136-38.

When people of the European race come into contact with American or African tribes, the prime necessity is a government under the protection of which the former may carry on the complex life to which they have been accustomed in their homes, which may prevent that life from being disturbed by contests by different European powers for supremacy on the same soil, and which may protect the natives in the enjoyment of a security and well-being at least not less than they enjoyed before the arrival of the strangers. Can the natives furnish such a government, or can it be looked for from the Europeans alone? In the answer to that question lies, for international law, the difference between civilisation and want of it.... The inflow of the white race cannot be stopped where there is land to cultivate, ore to be mined, commerce to be developed, sport to enjoy, curiosity to be satisfied. If any fanatical admirer of savage life argued that the whites ought to be kept out, he would only be driven to the same conclusion by another route, for a government on the spot would be necessary to keep them out. Accordingly, international law has to treat such natives as uncivilised.[65]

Westlake's rationalization was effectively an admission that international law was for the powerful. Not being among the "civilized" and powerful forces of colonization, indigenous peoples could not look to international law to thwart those forces. Indigenous peoples' rights had no place in the discourse. According to Westlake:

When again men like Victoria, Soto and Covarruvias maintained the cause of the American and African natives against the kings and peoples of Spain and Portugal, they were not so much impugning the title of their country as trying to influence its conduct, they were the worthy predecessors of those who now make among us the honorable claim to be "friends of the aborigines." Then and now such men occupy a field to which international law may be said to invite them by keeping itself within its limits. Even those who, in accordance with the modern tendency, make rights instead of law their starting point, can hardly avoid admitting that rights which are common to civilised and uncivilised humanity are not among those which it is a special function of international rights to develop and protect....

... This is true, and it does not mean that all rights are denied to such natives, but that the appreciation of their rights is left to the conscience of the state within whose recognized territorial sovereignty they are comprised, the rules of the international society existing only for the purposes of regulating the mutual conduct of its members.[66]

Through the early part of this century, the major international law publicists continued to repeat the view that indigenous peoples had no status or rights in international law. The later writings, however, apparently more confident of the view's acceptance, dispensed with the lengthy rationalization that Westlake devoted to it. Among these later writings was the 1924 edition of W.E. Hall's *A Treatise on International Law*, for which the exclusion was simply a necessary result of the positivist conception of international law as law by and for states grown out of European civilization:

It is scarcely necessary to point out that as international law is a product of the special civilization of modern Europe, and forms a highly artificial system of which the principles cannot be supposed to be understood or recognized by countries differently civilized, such states only can be presumed to be subject to it as are inheritors of that civilization.[67]

---

[65] [*Id.*] at 141-143.
[66] *Id.* at 136-138.
[67] W.E. Hall, A Treatise on International Law 47 (P. Higgins 8th ed. 1924)....

In the 1920 edition of the noted jurist Lassa Oppenheim's *International Law*, the basis for excluding indigenous peoples from among the subjects of international law was reduced to their subjective non-recognition by those within the so-called "Family of Nations." According to Oppenheim,

> As the basis of the Law of Nations is the common consent of the civilized States, statehood alone does not imply membership of the Family of Nations.... Through recognition only and exclusively a State becomes an International Person and a subject of International Law.[68]

Given the circularity of describing the members of the "Family of Nations" (the states with international personality) as those states recognized by the Family of Nations, Oppenheim was driven to provide a listing of them. Prominent among the privileged few were the "old Christian States of Western Europe" and "the body of Christian States which grew up outside Europe," including "the American States which arose out of colonies of European states." Oppenheim further included the two "non-Christian" states of Turkey and Japan, while excluding "such states as Persia, Siam, China, Abyssinia, and the like" because they had failed to "raise their civilization to the level of that of the Western" states.[71]

Inclusion of the American states within the "Family of Nations," of course, implied the exclusion of the American Indian tribes and similar indigenous peoples from any international status. But to eliminate whatever ambiguity remained, Oppenheim added expressly that the law of nations does not apply "to *organized wandering tribes*."[72]

Some positivist theorists of the period went beyond a merely contemporaneous exclusion of indigenous peoples from the subjects of international law. These theorists argued that the European states and their offspring within the Family of Nations *never had* considered the aboriginal peoples as capable of possessing rights on the international plane. The American jurist Charles Hyde, for example, explained that "[a]t the time of European explorations in the Western Hemisphere in the fifteenth and sixteenth centuries ... [s]tates were agreed that the native inhabitants possessed no rights of territorial control which the European explorer or his monarch was bound to respect."[73] Hyde accordingly concluded that "[t]he American Indians have never been regarded as constituting persons or States of international law."[74] Such bludgeoning of history is inconsistent with the early U.S. Supreme Court decisions affirming the international character of Indian nations and treaties, the 1975 World Court decision that lands inhabited by tribal peoples in the Western Sahara at the time of European contact were not then regarded as legally vacant,[76] and modern scholarship affirming the international character of the processes leading to the sixteenth and eighteenth century treaties with the natives of North America, Africa, and East Asia. The revisionism of the positivists was necessary,

---

[68] L. Oppenheim, International Law 134-35 (3d ed. 1920)....

[71] *Id.* at 34-35.

[72] *Id.* at 126.

[73] I C. Hyde, International Law Chiefly as Interpreted and Applied by the United States 163-64 (1922).

[74] *Id.* at 19.

[76] The Western Sahara Case, 1975 I.C.J. 12, 39.

however, in order to maintain a semblance of coherence in their vision of international law as law made *by* states and *for* states, exclusive of indigenous peoples and their rights.

With tribal peoples deemed incapable of enjoying status or rights in international law, international law was able to supply the rules governing the patterns of colonialization and ultimately legitimate the colonial order, without any consequences arising from the existence of aboriginal peoples. For international law purposes, indigenous lands prior to any colonial presence were considered legally unoccupied and accordingly cloaked in the legal jargon of *terra nullius* (vacant lands). Under this fiction, discovery could be employed as a means of upholding colonial claims to indigenous lands and bypassing any claim to possession by the natives in the "discovered" lands. In order to acquire indigenous lands, there was no longer any need to pretend conquest where war had not been waged, or to rely on the rules of war where it had. Likewise, the treaties with American tribes and other indigenous peoples could simply be ignored.

Any right of an indigenous community to govern itself in its lands, even if secured by treaty, as well as any right not to be conquered except in a "just war," was considered outside the competency of international law. Not having any basis in the collective will of the states that made international law, indigenous rights could not be considered part of international law. Instead, the positivistic international law doctrines of effective occupation of territory and recognition of such occupation by the "Family of Nations" actually provided the legal mechanism for the consolidation of territorial sovereignty over indigenous lands by the colonizing states.

The triumph of the positivists' treatment of indigenous rights is reflected in international tribunal decisions of the 1920's and 30's. In 1926 an international arbitration tribunal ruled that Great Britain could not maintain a claim for the "Cayuga Nation" as such, but only for the Cayuga Indians living in Canada on the basis of their British nationality.[83] In taking this position, the tribunal declared resolutely that an Indian "tribe is not a legal unit of international law." The Court cited Hyde, among others, for the proposition that Indians never *had* been considered subjects of international law.[85] And in the subsequent edition of his work, Hyde cited the Cayuga Indians decision to support that position.[86]

A second relevant international arbitration occurred in 1928 and involved competing claims to the Island of Palmas between the United States and the Netherlands.[87] The United States claim was derived from Spain, which had based its title primarily on prior discovery. The tribunal ruled in favor of the Netherlands because of its effective occupation and display of authority on the Island. The tribunal discussed various treaties the Dutch had entered into with native rulers but considered them only as "facts" relevant to the Netherland's assertion of sovereignty. The tribunal stated that such "*contracts between a*

---

[83] Cayuga Indians Case, VI R. Int'l Arb. Awards 173 (1926). The claim was based on obligations the latter had undertaken toward the Cayuga Indians in the 1814 Treaty between the U.S and Great Britain.

[85] *Id.* [at 176].

[86] I C. Hyde, International Law Chiefly as Interpreted and Applied by the United States 25, n.1 (2d ed. 1945).

[87] Island of Palmas Case, 2 R. Int'l Arb. Awards 831 (1928).

State ... and *native princes or chiefs of peoples* not recognized as members of the community of nations ... are not, in the international law sense, treaties or conventions capable of creating rights and obligations .... [89]

A third case concerned a 1933 ruling on the legal status of Eastern Greenland by the Permanent Court of International Justice.[90] Although acknowledging the indigenous Inuit ("Eskimo") population in Eastern Greenland, the court considered the question of its legal status as framed by the competing claims to sovereignty asserted by Norway and Denmark. Norway's assertion that parts of Greenland had been *terra nullius* at relevant times was trumped only by a finding that Denmark had effectively exercised sovereignty which had been recognized by others within the exclusive community of states. Neither the Inuit's presence nor their efforts at driving away Nordic settlers had any bearing on the territory's status. This case, like the *Island of Palmas Case*, illustrates the operation of the positivistic version of international law which affirmed colonial claims of sovereignty to the exclusion of indigenous rights.

International law's affirmation of state sovereignty over indigenous lands meant that the colonizing states and their offspring, guided at best by moral considerations, could shape policies concerning indigenous peoples to fit the dominant interests as matters only of domestic concern. The devastating and even genocidal results of such policies worldwide is no longer a matter of serious dispute. Assimilation, manipulation and even extermination have been the stuff of domestic policies concerning indigenous peoples, resulting in tremendous turmoil and human suffering. Indigenous peoples' asserted right to determine their own course in communion with the land that has been their life blood has been trampled upon.

The call for the re-emergence of indigenous rights in international law is a call for globally operative constraints against continuing forces that threaten the survival of indigenous communities and the institutions of human interaction they represent. But with what expectations of success can indigenous peoples now look to international law, which has been a tool for the genocidal patterns inflicted upon them?

IV. *Indigenous Rights in the Modern Era of Human Rights*

Today, just as the world order remains fundamentally state-centered, so too does international law. Positivistic assertions of state sovereignty and non-intervention remain alive as rhetorical tools with which to prop up the legacy of colonialism and to deny international stature to indigenous rights. Since the upheaval of the first and second world wars, however, international legal discourse has shifted from a strict positivist orientation to one in which visions of a peaceful world order have come to wield significant normative influence. Moreover, the processes of international law have become reflective of an increasingly interdependent world community interlinked by ever-improving communications technology and burgeoning international institutions. And these processes are increasingly influenced by non-state actors, including transnational corporations, liberation movements and international non-governmental orga-

---

[89] *Id.* [at 858] (emphasis in original).
[90] 1933 P.C.I.J. (ser. A/B) No. 53.

nizations. Accordingly, an influential trend in contemporary legal scholarship is to view international law as not simply reducible to the will of states as manifested by their custom or treaties. Leading publicists describe international law as a multifactoral process of *authoritative* and *controlling* decision operating across national frontiers, involving not only states but also relevant non-governmental actors, and existing at a minimum to maintain a peaceful world order.[94]

Within the contemporary processes of international law, visions of peace have resulted in a powerful discourse identified with the concept of human rights. This human rights discourse seeks to define international norms not by mere assessments of state conduct as in the positivist tradition, but rather by the prescriptive articulation of the expectations and values of the *human* constituents of the world community.[95] By directly addressing the concerns of human beings, this discourse seeks to expand the competency of international law over spheres previously reserved to the asserted sovereign prerogatives of states.

The modern discourse of human rights represents in significant measure the re-emergence of the classical era jurisprudential framework in which law was determined on the basis of visions of *what ought to be* rather than simply on the basis of *what is* and which contextualized the state as an instrument of humankind rather than as its master. Just as the historical naturalist framework of a perceived universal normative order provided a basis for enjoining sovereigns with regard to the treatment of indigenous peoples, particularly in its earlier version, the modern discourse of human rights provides [a] vehicle for efforts to have indigenous rights affirmed as a matter of contemporary international law.

The United Nations and other international organizations that emerged in the aftermath of the atrocities and suffering of the two world wars have been both a manifestation of and an impetus for the modern discourse of human rights in international law. In the multi-lateral treaties that are the constituent instruments of the major intergovernmental organizations, modern conceptions of human rights are included as guiding principles.

The U.N. Charter, most notably, establishes among that organization's purposes the promotion of "equal rights and self-determination of peoples," "respect for human rights and fundamental freedoms without distinction as to race, sex, language, or religion,"[97] and "conditions of economic and social progress and development."[98] Moreover, the U.N. members under the Charter "pledge themselves to take joint and separate action in cooperation with the Organization for the achievement" of these purposes.[99] At the same time, the

---

[94] *See, e.g.,* Lung-chu Chen, An Introduction to Contemporary International Law 3-4 (1989); B. Weston, R. Falk, & A. D'Amato, International Law and World Order: A Problem-Oriented Coursebook 14 (1980). For an extensive exposition of theoretical grounding of this view of international law, see McDougal, Laswell & Reisman, *Theories About International Jurisprudence: A Prologue to a Configurative Jurisprudence*, 8 Va. J. Int'l L. 188 (1968); *see also* C. Jenks, The Common Law of Mankind (1958); W. Friedman, The Changing Structure of International Law (1964).

[95] *See generally* Human Rights in the World Community: Issues and Action (R. Claude, B. Weston eds. 1989); New Directions in Human Rights (E. Lutz, H. Hannum, K. Burke eds. 1989); V. Van Dyke, Human Rights, Ethnicity, and Discrimination (1985).

[97] U.N. Charter, arts. 1.2, 1.3....

[98] U.N. Charter, art. 55.

[99] *Id.,* art. 56.

Charter yields to notions of state sovereignty by also including among its founding principles respect for the "territorial integrity" of member states and for
nonintervention in their domestic affairs.[100] Nonetheless, the statist conceptions are made to contend with the human rights objectives through the U.N.'s
deliberative processes. And these processes are influenced not only be reformist
tendencies among the organization's member states, but also by non-state actors,
including experts and non-governmental organizations, which are permitted to
participate in various (mostly non-voting) capacities.[101] The U.N. Secretariat,
which has significant powers of initiative, itself provides an important source of
non-state influence, particularly in matters of human rights.[102]

The humanitarian objectives of the U.N. and other major international organizations have been successfully deployed to develop human rights norms and
enforcement mechanisms, even while undermining the effect of sovereignty
principles. These processes suggest that principles of state sovereignty, still very
much alive in international law, are weakened to the extent they are considered
actually or potentially to endanger rather than complement human interests,
and that international law's competency over such interests will extend accordingly. The work of human rights advocates through international organizations
has led to an extensive body of norms aimed at protecting the individuals'
interests in physical integrity and security, non-discrimination, individual and
associational autonomy, and participatory democracy, and economic and social
well-being. These norms and accompanying oversight procedures, set forth in
multilateral treaties and other authoritative instruments such as U.N. General
Assembly resolutions, more or less regulate all states as to their own citizens.
Memories of the Nazi terrorist state, along with worldwide concern over a
continuing pattern of official action that is widely accepted as abusive of individual liberty interests, have left claims of exclusive domestic jurisdiction over such
interests with little force in today's international law.

The limits of sovereignty when confronted by a discourse of human rights
within international law's processes have been most dramatically manifest in the
U.N. practice [of] promoting the liberation of peoples from conditions of classical colonialism. The operative concept in that context has been self-determination, a concept articulated in the U.N. Charter and designated a right of "[a]ll
peoples" in the International Human Rights Covenants[106] promulgated
through the U.N. The concept of self-determination was included in a number
of General Assembly resolutions aimed specifically at decolonizing African and
Asian territories and setting in motion U.N. mechanisms toward that end.[107]

---

[100] *Id.*, arts. 2.4, 2.7.

[101] *See generally* Chiang, Pei-heng, Non-governmental Organizations at the United Nations:
Identity, Role, and Function (1981); P. Taylor, Nonstate Actors in International Politics (1984).

[102] *See generally* D. Bowett, The Law of International Institutions 87 (4th ed. 1982).

[106] International Covenant on Civil and Political Rights art. 1(1), *adopted* 16 Dec. 1966, *entered
into force*, 23 Mar. 1976, 999 U.N.T.S. 171; International Covenant on Economic, Social and
Cultural Rights art. 1(1), *adopted* 16 Dec. 1966, *entered into force*, 3 Jan. 1976, 993 U.N.T.S. 3.

[107] *See* United Nations Sub-Commission on Prevention of Discrimination and Protection of Minorities, The Right to Self-determination: Historical and Current Development on the Basis of
United Nations Instruments, U.N. Doc. E/CN.4/sub.2/404/Rev.1 at 33-36, 17-21 (1981) (Aureliu
Cristescu, Special Rapporteur). Besides adopting resolutions directed at specific colonial territories,
the U.N. adopted the important Declaration on the Granting of Independence to Colonial Coun-

U.N. practice has resulted in a preponderant view that self-determination means a legal right of independent statehood for territories under rule by overseas colonial powers, regardless of the doctrinal bases of territorial sovereignty claimed by the foreign powers over the territories.[108] Such colonialist sovereignty, ultimately considered by the relevant international actors to be repugnant to human interests, has given way to an internationally operative norm of human rights.

State sovereignty as an international law doctrine thus apparently is becoming one that functions only insofar as it approximates its original purpose of upholding *human* interests and maximizing the ends of *human* society. Vattel, as noted above, counseled in favor of a state's freedom from outside intervention but only under the view of the state as fulfilling collective human interests in comfort and self-preservation. In a global community that remains organized substantially by state jurisdictional boundaries, sovereignty principles continue, in some measure, to advance human interests in stability and autonomy. But to the degree attributes of sovereignty are deemed in modern international legal discourse to impede rather than further the realization of human values, those attributes are in effect suspended in favor of a corresponding measure of international legal competency.

Therefore, the task of establishing an international legal regime of indigenous rights which further encroaches upon the asserted sovereign prerogatives of states can be described as twofold: first, the substance of the rights must be articulated and promoted among the various relevant components of the world community; and secondly, the balance of human values involved must be demonstrated to justify whatever diminished deference to sovereignty principles that would result from incorporating the rights into international law. Within the last generation, indigenous peoples with increasing effectiveness have utilized available mechanisms of authoritative decisionmaking, including those of relevant international forums, to take on this task.[109] Today a number of nongovernmental organizations representing indigenous constituencies and other indigenous advocacy groups enjoy official consultative status with the United Nations Economic and Social Council, the parent body of the U.N.'s human rights organs.[110]

---

tries and Peoples, G.A. Res. 1514, 15 U.N. GAOR, Supp. (No. 16) at 66-67, U.N. Doc. A/4684 (1960).

[108] *See* U.N. Sub-Commission Study on Self-determination, *supra* note 107, at 21-24; M. Shaw, Title to Territory in Africa, 73-90 (1986). The International Court of Justice recognized the right to self-determination as the basis for the process of decolonization in the Namibia Case, 1971 I.C.J. 16, 31; and the Western Sahara Case, 1975 I.C.J. 12, 31-34. Juristic opinion affirming the right to self-determination generally has stated the right in broad terms, reflecting the language of U.N. instruments attaching the right to "all peoples." Beyond the context of classical colonialism, however, there is little agreement concerning the right's application. *See generally* L. Buchheit, Secession: The Legitimacy of Self-Determination 127-137 (1978) (analyzing divergent views on the asserted right of "secessionist self-determination"); U. Umuzorike, Self-Determination in International Law 177-203 (1972) (searching for the "content of self-determination").

[109] *See generally* Rethinking Indian Law 131-171 (National Lawyers Guild ed. 1982).

[110] These include Consejo Indio de Sud-America (CISA), Four Directions Council, Grand Council of the Crees (of Quebec), Indian Law Resource Center, Indigenous World Association, International Indian Treaty Council, International Organization of Indigenous Resources Development, Inuit Circumpolar Conference, National Aboriginal and Islander Legal Services Secretariat, National Indian Youth Council and World Council of Indigenous Peoples.

The demands for the protection of indigenous rights in international law have set in motion United Nations and related processes. In 1982, the Economic and Social Council established the Working Group on Indigenous Populations,[111] which reviews developments concerning indigenous peoples and is drafting a declaration on indigenous rights for consideration by the U.N. General Assembly. At its seventh session in August, 1989 the Working Group considered a second draft of the declaration.[112] The Working Group also has initiated a study on indigenous-state treaties and their contemporary significance.[113] In a further development, the International Labour Organization, a specialized agency of the U.N., adopted in June, 1989 its proposed Convention on Indigenous and Tribal Peoples (No. 169)[114] which immediately became open for ratification by states. The proposed Convention revises a 1957 I.L.O. Convention on the subject, the only previously existing international legal instrument specifically addressing indigenous rights but largely rejected by indigenous groups for its assimilationist characteristics.[115] Most recently, on November 18, 1989, the General Assembly of the Organization of American States resolved to "request the Inter-American Commission on Human Rights to prepare a juridical instrument relative to the rights of indigenous peoples, for adoption in 1992."[116]

All of these processes have involved indigenous rights advocates who, through a discourse drawing upon human rights concepts such as non-discrimination and self-determination, have progressively articulated and promoted a constellation of indigenous rights. The constellation includes rights of political, religious and cultural autonomy; control over education, ancestral lands and resources; treaty rights; and, moreover, the right of a self-defined indigenous community to determine the terms of its existence within the larger state-society.

These asserted rights, which contemplate the right-holders as historically-based indigenous communities rather than individuals or (inchoate) states, collide with the individual/state rights dichotomy which, having persisted in dominant conceptions of human society, has prevailed in the shaping of human

---

The author was general counsel to the National Indian Youth Council from 1985 through 1988 and represented the organization at the 1989 sessions of the U.N. Working Group on Indigenous Populations and at the 1989 International Labour Conference, discussed in text accompanying notes 126-131, *infra*.

[111]E.S.C. Res. 34, U.N. ESCOR Supp. (No. 1) at 26-27, U.N. Doc. E/1982/82 (1982).

[112]The first revised text of the draft Universal Declaration on the Rights of Indigenous Peoples, prepared by the Chairman-Rapporteur of the Working Group on Indigenous Populations, Ms. Erica-Irene Daes, appears in Report of the Working Group on Indigenous Populations on its seventh session Annex II, U.N. Doc. E/CN.4/sub.2/1989/36 (25 Aug. 1989) [hereinafter 1989 Working Group Report].

[113]The study was approved by the U.N. Economic and Social Council by its resolution 1988/134. *See* Report of the Working Group on Indigenous Populations on its sixth session at 25-29, U.N. Doc. E/CN.4/Sub.2/1988/24 (1988).

[114]Published in International Labour Conference, Report of the Committee on Convention 107 at 25/25-33, *Provisional Record*, No. 25, 76th Session, 1989 [hereinafter 1989 Report of Committee on Convention 107].

[115]*See* Berman, *The International Organization and Indigenous Peoples: Revision of I.L.O. Convention No. 107 at the 75th Session of the International Labour Conference, 1988*, 41 Int'l Comm. Jurists Rev. 48, 49 (1988)....

[116]The proposal for a new OAS legal instrument on indigenous rights is described in the *Annual Report of the Inter-American Commission on Human Rights, 1988-89* at 245-251, OEA/Ser.L/v/II.76, Doc 10 (September 18, 1989).

rights norms. The resulting conceptual difficulties, along with the significant challenges to notions of state sovereignty posed by the asserted rights, are evident in the seemingly endless debate over terminology within the U.N. and I.L.O. processes.

Indigenous groups insist on being identified as "peoples" rather than "populations" so as not to be reduced to simple aggregations of individuals. State governments resist the term "peoples" because of its association with the term "self-determination" (i.e. "All peoples have the right to self-determination") which in turn is associated with a right of independent statehood for overseas colonial territories. Indigenous peoples invoke a "right of self-determination" as an expression of their desire to continue as distinct communities free from oppression, but in virtually all instances deny aspirations to independent statehood. Indigenous rights advocates prefer the term "territories" over "lands" as more descriptive of their claims. Governments resist the term "territories" on the grounds that it implies sovereignty. And so on.

Although indigenous rights advocates have had but limited successes in the debate over terminology, the *concepts* they have promoted have been effectively communicated. The core idea of the right of self-defined indigenous communities to continue as distinct units of human interaction has taken root internationally, making any discussion of their assimilation into larger societies virtually obsolete among social science and legal experts and even government representatives. Further, the yielding of state sovereignty to a measure of international competency over the rights is increasingly indicated. Statist notions remain prevalent, yet there is notable movement toward realizing the evolving conceptions of indigenous rights through international law.

An example of this movement, and tension, is in the newly proposed I.L.O. Convention on Indigenous and Tribal Peoples. As an instrument adopted by the International Labour Conference with widespread support from the government delegates, the Convention on Indigenous and Tribal Peoples represents a measure of governmental consensus although not yet ratified or acceded to by any state.[126] The proposed Convention assumes state authority over indigenous peoples but at the same time carries the basic theme of the collective right of indigenous peoples to live and develop by their own designs as distinct communities. These dual tendencies co-exist rather comfortably in matters of religious and cultural autonomy and on surface ownership to lands indigenous peoples "traditionally occupy." As to subsurface resource and mineral ownership, which in many jurisdictions is retained by the state as to all lands, statist tendencies result in depriving indigenous interests status as "rights" in the Convention. Similarly, the language of the proposed Convention calls for respect of

---

[126] ILO Conventions are adopted by conferences of governmental, employer, and worker delegates, with government delegates comprising approximately half of the total number. A two-thirds majority of voting delegates is required for adoption. *See* Constitution of the International Labour Organization arts. 3(1), 19, 62 Stat. 3485, 4 Bevans 188, 15 U.N.T.S. 35. Having been adopted by the 1989 Labour Conference, the revised ILO Convention on indigenous peoples enters into force when two states have ratified it. R. Barsh has reported that at least six governments have expressed some interest in early ratification since the adoption of the Convention on June 20, 1989. *See* Barsh, *United Nations Report for Summer 1989*, in Sante' Mawi 'omi Wjit Mikmaq Foreign Affairs (7 Sept. 1989) (on file with author).

indigenous customary law and implementing institutions, but stops short of unambiguously enjoining the state in this regard.

Similar movement, and tension, are manifest in the work of the U.N. Working Group in its process of drafting a declaration on indigenous rights for adoption by the General Assembly. Although the precise legal significance of General Assembly rights declarations is a matter of some dispute, there is little question that they are in significant measure authoritative internationally.[133] Government comments directed at the development of an indigenous rights declaration generally express agreement with the five Working Group members, who are not government delegates but rather designated experts, on the basic thrust of upholding rights to guard the integrity of indigenous communities. Governments' jealousies of asserted sovereign prerogatives, however, continue to be manifest. Nonetheless the movement toward recognition of indigenous rights as a matter of international law is evident.

Perhaps most revealing of the movement is what states are appearing compelled to do in response to demands that extend into the international arena. Constitutional revisions to affirm indigenous rights in Brazil[136] and Canada,[137] an emerging invigorated federal policy of Indian "self-determination" in the U.S., legislation establishing regimes of indigenous autonomy in Nicaragua,[139]

[133] See generally Note, The Role of United Nations General Assembly Resolutions in Determining Principles of International Law in United States Courts, 1983 Duke L.J. 876.

[136] The new constitution of Brazil includes a specific chapter on Indian rights (Chapter VIII — On the Indians, of Title VIII — On the Social Order, articles 231 and 232). Under the new constitution, promulgated October 5, 1988, "Indians are entitled to the permanent ownership of the lands traditionally occupied by them including the exclusive fruition or enjoyment of existing soil resources, rivers and lakes." art. 231, para. 2. Provisions also are included concerning rights to mineral resources, native languages, culture and indigenous forms of social organization. See J. Gaiger Indigenous Rights in the 1988 Brazilian Constitution (manuscript on file with the author).

The Brazilian government quoted extensively from the constitutional provisions regarding indigenous rights in a report to the Working Group responding to criticism of its treatment of the Yanomani Indians, which report is included in U.N. Sub-Commission on Prevention of Discrimination and Protection of Minorities, Information Received from Governments, U.N. Doc. E/CN.4/Sub.2/AC.4/1989/2 at 7-9 (1989) [hereinafter Government Information Submitted to 1989 Working Group].

[137] The Canadian constitution was revised by the Constitution Act of 1982 to include, inter alia, a provision that "[t]he existing aboriginal and treaty rights of the aboriginal peoples of Canada are hereby recognized and affirmed." Article § 35(1). See generally Nakatsuru, A Constitutional Right of Indian Self-government, 43 U. Toronto Faculty L. Rev. 72, 80 (1985) ("Given the extensive public debate in political rhetoric about the significance of the section, it is unlikely the courts will disregard the remedial effects § 35(1) was intended to have."). In 1989 the Canadian government reported to the U.N. Working Group on its progress in negotiating land claims agreements with the native peoples of Canada. See Government information submitted to the 1989 Working Group, supra note 136, at 10-11; statement by the Observer Delegation of Canada (Review of Developments) before the U.N. Working Group on Indigenous Populations at its seventh session (July-August 1989) (on file with the author).

[139] After a surge of criticism internationally concerning the Nicaraguan government's treatment of the Indians of the isolated eastern region of the country, see, e.g., Inter-American Commission on Human Rights, Report on the Situation of Human Rights of a Segment of the Nicaraguan Population of Miskito Origin, OAS Doc. OEA/Ser.L/V/II.62, doc. 10 rev. 3 (1983), the Nicaraguan government entered into negotiations with Indian insurgents and adopted its Statute of Autonomy for the Atlantic Coast Regions of Nicaragua (Law No. 28, September 7, 1987). The statute, however, is much criticized by the Nicaraguan Indian organization, YATAMA, as well as by Indian advocacy groups worldwide, for not sufficiently meeting Indian aspirations. See generally T. MacDonald, The Moral Economy of the Miskito Indians: Local Roots of a Geopolitical Conflict, in Ethnicities and Nations: Processes of Inter-ethnic Relations in Latin America, Southeast Asia, and the Pacific 107 (R. Guidieri, F. Pellizzi & S. Tambiah eds. 1988).

the Philippines[140] and Bangladesh,[141] similar developments in Australia[142] and New Zealand[143] — all these, however imperfect, are manifestations of the *international* move toward the realizing of indigenous rights goals. In today's world, states' attempts to limit the words in written international legal instruments do not necessarily thwart the authority and control of norms that are thrust upon and exist in the conscience of the international community independently of those instruments.

Conclusion

The international processes and (re-)emerging norms of indigenous rights represent a dramatic manifestation of contemporary human rights discourse. These processes and norms unquestionably pose a challenge to widely held conceptions propping up asserted state prerogatives of control over matters of political and social organization beyond individual liberty interests. And because international law grew into a system that has incorporated such conceptions, these processes will continue to be fraught with tension. But as international law continues its shift *from* blind adherence to state prerogatives back *toward* concern for human beings in their diverse amalgamations, in the tradition of Vitoria and Grotius, and back *toward* remembering the state as an instrument of human society rather than its master, as instructed by Vattel; and as international law continues to shed its Eurocentric origins in favor of responding to the demands of a diverse world community; international law can hold out ever greater possibilities as a tool for indigenous peoples. No less important than the resulting norms of indigenous rights are the processes toward establishing those

[140] A representative of the Philippine government reported to the Working Group at its 1989 session on the "features of the Philippine Constitution providing for the creation of autonomous regions in both Muslim Mindanao and the Cordilleras" and on recent legislative initiatives to implement the constitutional provisions. Statement of the representative of the Philippine government before the U.N. Working Group on Indigenous Populations at its seventh session, 1989 at 2-3 (on file with the author).

[141] The government of Bangladesh reported to the 1989 session of the Working Group on the "adoption of three historic legislative bills by the Parliament of Bangladesh on 28 February, 1989, designed to set up three local elected and autonomous government councils ... with adequate power for the tribal people to run their own affairs and preserve their socio-cultural heritage and separate identity .... " U.N. Doc. E/CN.4/sub.2/AC.4/1989/2/Add.1 at 2 (1989).

[142] The government of Australia reported to the 1989 session of the U.N. Working Group on a resolution proposed by the Australian prime minister to parliament on the Aboriginal and Torres Strait Island people. Government Information Submitted to 1989 Working Group, *supra* note 136, at 3-6. The resolution affirmed "[t]he entitlement of aborigines and Torres Strait Islanders to self-management and self-determination subject to the constitution and the laws of the Commonwealth of Australia." *Id.* at 3. The resolution accompanied legislation for a commission to pursue indigenous self-determination goals. *Id.* at 5.

[143] There has been increasing recognition in New Zealand that the indigenous Maoris retain certain land and self-government rights which they possessed aboriginally and which are protected by the treaty of Waitangi in 1840. *See generally* Kenderdine, Statutory Separateness: Maori Issues in the Planning Process and the Social Responsibility of Industry, 1985 N.Z.L.J. 249; Mylonas-Widdal, *Aboriginal Fishing Rights in New Zealand*, 37 Int'l & Comp. L.Q. 386 (1988). At the 1989 session of the Working Group the Government of New Zealand reported that it "is presently evolving new measures to honor the principles of the Treaty of Waitangi and to restore and strengthen the operational base of Iwi (Maori tribes).... This restructuring is designed to give practical effect to the changes the Government considered necessary, following extensive consultation with Maoridom to give Maori people more say in their own destiny and in the development of the country as a whole." New Zealand statement under item 4 at the U.N. Working Group on Indigenous Populations, seventh session, 1989 at 1 (on file with the author).

norms in which indigenous peoples themselves — while regaining stature in international law — are playing a formidable part. In conjunction with continuing efforts in domestic forums, indigenous peoples can help shape a world order in which — in the words of the International Bill of Human Rights — "*All peoples* have the right to self-determination," and no less among them, indigenous peoples.

2. UNITED NATIONS CHARTER AND HUMAN RIGHTS COVENANTS

COMMENT, TOWARD CONSENT AND COOPERATION: RECONSIDERING THE POLITICAL STATUS OF INDIAN NATIONS, 22 Harvard Civil Rights-Civil Liberties Law Review 509, 589-602 (1987)*

A. *The Right to Self-Determination in Existing Sources of International Human Rights Law*

The right to self-determination is recognized in the United Nations Charter and the United Nations Human Rights Covenants, among other human rights instruments.[437] For indigenous groups, including Indian peoples, the exercise of the right to self-determination is essential to the transformation of their political status and their movement toward the goal of group empowerment. Whether the internationally defined right to self-determination applies to American Indians, however, depends on the breadth of the definition of "self-determination" and on the conception of Indian peoples in the international community; both are highly contested issues. It also depends on the extent to which the United States recognizes its international law obligations. Thus, forty years after the United Nations Charter was signed, the scope and applicability of the right to self-determination to American Indians remains unclear.

1. *The United Nations Charter*

The expression of self-determination for "peoples" marks the expansion of international concern "from nonagression among existing states to the liberation of colonies and emergence of new states."[442] The first article of the United Nations Charter states that one of the organization's primary purposes is "[t]o develop friendly relations among nations based on respect for the principle of equal rights and self-determination of peoples."[443] The colonial relationship between the United States and Indian nations fits within this general context. Therefore, the effort by Indian nations to achieve self-determination can be viewed as part of the larger, global struggle for national liberation from colonial

---

*Copyright © 1987 by the President and Fellows of Harvard College. Reprinted with permission of the Harvard Civil Rights-Civil Liberties Law Review.

[437] U.N. Charter arts. 1, 55, 56, and 73; International Covenant on Civil and Political Rights, [G.A. Res. 2200A, 21 U.N. GAOR Supp. (No. 16) at 49, U.N. Doc. A/6546 (1966)]; International Covenant on Economic, Social and Cultural Rights, G.A. Res. 2200A, 21 U.N. GAOR Supp. (No. 16) at 52, U.N. Doc. A/6546 (1966).

[442] Barsh, [*Indigenous North America and Contemporary International Law,* 62 Or. L. Rev. 73], at 80 (1983).

[443] U.N. Charter art. 1, ¶ 2.

regimes. From this perspective, human rights instruments developed by the United Nations and other international organizations are of particular relevance to Indian peoples. The United Nations' commitment to self-determination is further demonstrated in articles 55 and 56 of the Charter, which provide an affirmative foundation for the promotion of self-determination:

> Article 55. With a view to the creation of conditions of stability and well-being which are necessary for peaceful and friendly relations among nations based on respect for the principle of equal rights and self-determination of peoples, the United Nations shall promote: ...
>
> c. universal respect for, and observance of, human rights and fundamental freedoms for all without distinction as to race, sex, language, or religion.
>
> Article 56. All Members pledge themselves to take joint action in co-operation with the Organization for the achievement of the purposes set forth in Article 55.

These broad provisions outline the obligations of U.N. member nations. For example, in complaints to the United Nations Commission on Human Rights, Indian rights advocates have relied on the language of articles 1 and 55 of the Charter to support their claim that the United States is bound to recognize the Indian nations' right to self-determination.

Article 73 of the Charter, which concerns non-self-governing territories,[447] is also dedicated to popular self-determination, but its efficacy has been limited. It requires that: Members of the United Nations which have or assume responsibilities for the administration of territories whose peoples have not yet attained a full measure of self-government recognize the principle that the interests of the inhabitants are paramount, and accept as a sacred trust the obligation ... to develop self-government, to take due account of the political aspirations of the peoples, and to assist them in the progressive development of their free political institutions, according to the particular circumstance of each territory and its peoples and their varying stages of advancement.[448]

Several factors limit the usefulness of article 73 for Indian peoples. First, the provision indirectly legitimizes the negative aspects of the present "trust" relationship between the United States and Indian peoples by implying that subjugated peoples may not have reached a level of advancement enabling them to be fully self-governing. Second, the Charter allows the dominant society the discretion to "develop self-government" in colonized societies at any pace. The most severe impediment to the effectiveness of article 73 is the so-called "blue water thesis," an argument proposed in the U.N. General Assembly in the early 1950's for limiting the scope of the provision to territories that are geographically separated from the dominant society by an ocean. The debate focused on the conflict between freedom for subjugated peoples and concern for the territorial integrity of a nation. The "blue water" interpretation of article 73, advo-

---

[447] "Non-self-governing territory" is an international term for areas subject to the authority of another state. E. Osmanczyk, Encyclopedia of the United Nations and International Agreements 568 (1985).

[448] U.N. Charter art. 73. This decolonization provision, contained in Chapter XI of the Charter, replaced article 23 of the League of Nations Covenant. Under the League Covenant, the decolonization principle was applied to indigenous peoples within independent states. League of Nations Covenant art. 23. In the absence of contrary evidence, therefore, it is argued that the obligations in article 73 of the United Nations Charter were also intended to apply to all indigenous peoples. See G. Bennett, Aboriginal Rights in International Law 10-12 (1978).

cated largely by Latin American nations,[450] excludes most indigenous peoples from the rights outlined in the article, because they generally have been colonized within the borders of existing nations.

Other nations' representatives, however, most notably the 1953 Belgian U.N. delegation, have argued for a broad application of the Charter provision, criticizing the arbitrary distinction between overseas colonies and subjugated peoples within a nation's borders. According to the Belgian interpretation, a population may be geographically contiguous with a dominant society, but remain politically and culturally distinct, and therefore worthy of protection under article 73.

The controversy over the scope of this provision is unresolved. Subsequent United Nations instruments regarding decolonization and self-determination reveal a bias for the "blue water" interpretation. This bias has limited the potential role of article 73 in protecting indigenous rights and the applicable scope of the right to self-determination.

2. United Nations Declarations and the Definition of Self-Determination

The articles of the United Nations Charter establish self-determination as a motivating ideal in international human rights law. The meaning and application of that ideal have evolved in three declarations adopted by the United Nations General Assembly in 1960, 1965 and 1970, respectively.[454] While these declarations have no legally binding force, they interpret the broad language of the Charter and define the obligations of member nations more specifically, focusing primarily on a people's right to self-determination. The declarations also reflect the continuing debate over the "blue water thesis."

The 1960 Declaration on the Granting of Independence to Colonial Countries and Peoples condemned alien subjugation of peoples and called for the immediate transfer of all power to dependent peoples "in order to enable them to enjoy complete independence and freedom." This Declaration provides a broad and assertive definition of self-determination:

> The subjection of peoples to alien subjugation, domination, and exploitation constitutes a denial of fundamental human rights, is contrary to the Charter of the United Nations and is an impediment to the promotion of world peace and co-operation.

---

[450] In support of the "blue water" interpretation, Latin American states have argued that article 73 should apply only to overseas possessions, because "otherwise no state in the world would be immune from dismemberment." Barsh, *Indigenous North America and Contemporary International Law*, 62 Or. L. Rev. 73, 80, 85 (1983). "Latin American states argued that Indian groups in their countries, far from being 'non-self-governing,' were fully integrated politically. For example, the Ecuador delegation maintained that '[t]he Indian population of Ecuador formed an integral part of the nation.'" *Id.* (citing 7 U.N. GAOR C.4 (257th mtg.) at 55, U.N. Doc. A/2361 (1952)).

[454] Declaration on the Granting of Independence to Colonial Countries and Peoples, G.A. Res. 1514, 15 U.N. GAOR, Supp. (No. 16) at 66-67, U.N. Doc. A/4684 (1960).

Declaration on the Inadmissibility of Intervention in Domestic Affairs of States and the Protection of Their Independence and Sovereignty, G.A. Res. 2131, 20 U.N. GAOR, Supp. (No. 14) at 11-12, U.N. Doc. A/6014 (1965).

Declaration on Principles of International Law Concerning Friendly Relations and Cooperation Among States, G.A. Res. 2625, 25 U.N. GAOR Supp. (No. 28) at 121, U.N. Doc. A/8082 (1970).

A declaration in the U.N. system is a unanimously approved legal statement. E. Osmanczyk, *supra* note 447, at 194. While it has no binding force, a declaration's unanimous approval is evidence of its general acceptability. Embodying broad legal principles, U.N. declarations are often considered transitional steps toward the adoption of binding international conventions.

... All peoples have the right to self-determination; by virtue of that right they freely determine their political status and freely pursue their economic, social and cultural development.

This right to self-determination applies without regard to "political, economic, social or educational preparedness," [457] thereby overcoming any implication in article 73 that the subjugation of indigenous peoples may be justified by their state of "advancement."

The 1960 Declaration, however, also protects the territorial integrity of existing states:

Any attempt aimed at the partial or total disruption of the national unity and the territorial integrity of a country is incompatible with the purposes and principles of the Charter of the United Nations.

This constraint on the decolonization process is rooted in the "blue water thesis" interpretation of the Charter, thereby limiting decolonization to areas separated by ocean from administering states. This provision is inconsistent with the Declaration's emphasis on self-determination, since, in effect, it assumes that all populations within a given political boundary are legitimately subject to the rule of the politically dominant population. It may also prevent indigenous populations, who are "peoples" subject to "alien subjugation, domination, and exploitation," from exercising their right to self-determination under the Declaration.

Responding to controversy over the application of the 1960 Declaration and its territorial integrity provision, the United Nations General Assembly attempted to clarify the scope of self-determination five years later in the 1965 Declaration on the Inadmissibility of Intervention in Domestic Affairs of States and the Protection of Their Independence and Sovereignty. This instrument declares that:

All States shall respect the right of self-determination and independence of peoples and nations, to be freely exercised without any foreign pressure, and with absolute respect for human rights and fundamental freedoms. Consequently, all States shall contribute to the complete elimination of racial discrimination and colonialism in all its forms and manifestations.

Under this provision, all peoples — including indigenous peoples who may not be officially recognized as states — should be able to invoke the principle of territorial integrity to protect their right to self-determination. The concept of territorial integrity could therefore be turned around and used by an indigenous people to challenge external control by a dominant society. Guided by this Declaration, American Indian peoples can argue that since they are historically independent nations, federal intervention into their affairs violates the Declaration's requirement that all nations respect the right of self-determination of other peoples.

The General Assembly's third attempt to define self-determination and to reconcile decolonization and territorial integrity produced the 1970 Declaration on Principles of International Law Concerning Friendly Relations and Cooperation Among States, stating that:

---

[457][G.A. Res. 1514, *supra* note 454, at 67].

By virtue of the principles of equal rights and self-determination of peoples enshrined in the Charter of the United Nations, all peoples have the right freely to determine, without external interference, their political status and to pursue their economic, social and cultural development, and every State has the duty to respect this right in accordance with the provisions of the Charter.

In an attempt to diffuse the "blue water" controversy, the 1970 Declaration discourages any action that would impair the territorial integrity of "independent States conducting themselves in compliance with the principle of equal rights and self-determination of peoples ... and thus possessed of a government representing the whole people belonging to the territory." Under these terms, no state can assert the defense of territorial integrity if it has acquired land unlawfully or if a people is not politically integrated. These considerations prevent the United States from justifying control over Indian peoples based on national or territorial integrity.

The three United Nations declarations regarding decolonization have, in principle, broadened the scope of the right to self-determination, establishing it as a right of all peoples regardless of their political status or geographical location. Territorial integrity is not a compelling justification for a dominant society subjugating indigenous peoples who exist within the physical boundaries of another nation. Rather, the declarations support the claim of Indian peoples to the right to self-determination under international law.

3. Self-Determination for "Peoples": Article 1 of the International Covenants on Human Rights

The International Covenant on Civil and Political Rights and the International Covenant on Economic, Social and Cultural Rights are important sources of human rights law for American Indians. They transform the values embodied in the Universal Declaration of Human Rights[470] into binding legal norms. Together these instruments form the basis of contemporary human rights law. The General Assembly approved the covenants in 1966, and they became legally binding in 1976. As international treaties, the covenants are legally binding on all ratifying nations. President Carter signed the covenants in 1977 and submitted them to the Senate, but the United States has yet to formally ratify them. However, because some of the provisions have become part of customary international law, the covenants may still have binding force on the United States.[472]

The first article of each of those covenants secures the right to self-determination for all peoples, indicating the primary importance of this right in international law:

1. All peoples have the right to self-determination. By virtue of that right they freely determine their political status and freely pursue their economic, social and cultural development.

---

[470]G.A. Res. 217(A)III, Dec. 10, 1948, U.N. Doc. A/810, at 71.

[472]According to Bennett, the right to self-determination as expressed in the covenants, "has become an integral part of customary international law." G. Bennett, *supra* note 448, at 51. In general, the existence and definition of a customary norm are determined by international consensus. For evidence of custom, courts frequently rely on convention, state actions and statements, decisions by the International Court of Justice and national courts, general principles of law, writing by publicists on international law, and other documents such as United Nations resolutions and studies. *See* A. D'Amato, The Concept of Custom in International Law 44 (1971).

This is a bold and expansive statement of self-determination, but whether it, in principle, extends the right to American Indians is a controversial question. The answer depends on whether Indians are "peoples" under international law.

No definitive formulation of the term "people" exists in international law. As illustrated by the three U.N. declarations discussed above, it might not be possible to formulate a single definition of self-determination since any attempt encounters complex political conflicts. On one hand, some existing states fear that a broad definition of peoples entitled to self-determination would encourage secessionist movements, threatening their territorial integrity. On the other hand, the right to self-determination as embodied in the covenants is a "right of all peoples whether or not they have attained independence and the status of a State," and therefore should be applied broadly. The far-reaching political implications of the concept of a people, then, complicate any effort to formulate a generally accepted and universally applicable definition.

Within the context of the international right to self-determination, however, the term "people" has been analyzed on several occasions. The following discussion examines three authoritative definitions. The definition of a "people" cited most often is found in a decision of the International Court of Justice,[478] which employed the following language:

> a group of persons living in a given country or locality, having a race, religion, language and traditions of their own and united by this identity of race, religion, language and tradition, in a sentiment of solidarity, with a view to preserving their traditions, maintaining their form of worship, insuring the instruction and upbringing of their children in accordance with the spirit and traditions of their race and rendering mutual assistance to each other.

A second definition employing various elements that have emerged from discussion in the United Nations has been formulated by Aureliu Cristescu, a United Nations special rapporteur. Cristescu argues that the term people denotes "a social entity possessing a clear identity and its own characteristics," and it implies a close "relationship with a territory."[480]

A third definition of "people" was adopted by the International Commission of Jurists, a non-governmental organization (NGO)[481] with consultative status at the United Nations.[482] This definition identifies the following characteristics of a people:

1. a common history;
2. racial or ethnic ties;
3. cultural or linguistic ties;
4. religious or ideological ties;

---

[478] The Greco-Roman "Communities," Collection of Advisory Opinions (Greece v. Bulgaria), 1930 P.C.I.J. (ser. B) No. 17, at 21 (July 31).

[480] A. Cristescu, [The Right to Self-Determination: Historical and Current Development on the Basis of United Nations Instruments, U.N. Doc. E/CN.4/Sub.2/404/Rev.1 (1981)] at ¶ 279.

[481] A non-governmental organization (NGO), according to the U.N., is any international organization not established by intergovernmental agreement. To qualify for consultative status at the U.N., an NGO must be of service in the Economic and Social Council's field of interest, act in the spirit of the U.N., be non-profit and possess the means to implement its objectives. E. Osmanczyk, *supra* note 447, at 565.

[482] International Commission of Jurists, The Events in East Pakistan, 1971 (A Report by the Secretariat) 70 (1972).

5. a common territory or geographical location;
6. a common economic base;
7. a sufficient number of people.

Most Indian groups qualify for status as a people under the three definitions offered above.

It is important from an international legal perspective to distinguish peoples from minorities, since they are granted different political status. A minority does not have the right to self-determination under international law, although some minority groups could conceivably fulfill the criteria of cultural and territorial ties set out in the definitions of a people discussed above. One way to distinguish peoples from minorities was suggested by the Mikmaq Nation in a 1982 submission to the U.N. Commission on Human Rights:

> The distinction therefore between a minority and a people, in our conception flows from the quality of *consent*. A people can become a minority, if it chooses. Minorities cannot be made by violence or oppression, however.[486]

The Mikmaq analysis of this issue focuses on whether a people has freely consented to incorporation into a state. If a people has been involuntarily subjected to alien political control, they retain their inherent right to self-determination as mandated by the U.N. declarations discussed above. The Mikmaq Nation's argument to the Human Rights Commission supports a definition of people that would include most American Indian nations since it emphasizes the importance of voluntary consent.

This legal distinction between peoples and minorities affects the status of American Indians, since categorization is a threshold issue in the argument that the right to self-determination should apply to Indians. While most Indian populations meet the criteria for a people, no formal international agreement or declaration specifically defines Indians as peoples.[489] But, according to the Indian Law Resource Center, a United Nations NGO, "[a]lmost all Indian representatives who have addressed international organizations during the past few years have urged the recognition of Indians as peoples and as nations, and some countries and non-governmental organizations have begun to give serious attention to this question of definition."[490]

In the final analysis, however, Indian efforts to assert their self-determination may be more important than legal definitions for promoting recognition of their status as distinct peoples. According to the Indian Law Resource Center:

---

[486] U.N. Doc. E/CN.4/1982/NGO/30/Rev.1. (emphasis supplied).

[489] *Id.* at 14. For example, in a recent study of indigenous rights in Nicaragua, the Organization of American States Inter-American Commission on Human Rights concluded that "at least under current international law" the Miskito Indians did not qualify as a people. Rather, they were defined as a Nicaraguan ethnic group. The Commission noted that "the right of self-determination was a limited one and needs to be harmonized with other principles such as equality under the law, sovereignty, territorial integrity, and political independence." S. Davis, Indigenous Peoples and Human Rights: The Emerging Role of the Inter-American Commission on Human Rights 19 (1984) (unpublished paper on file with Harvard Civil Rights-Civil Liberties Law Review). This argument demonstrates the continuing influence of the "blue water thesis" and the concern for territorial integrity, particularly among Latin American nations.

[490] Indian Law Resource Center, [Handbook for Indians on International Human Rights Complaint Procedures] 14 [1984].

History suggests that those who maintain and assert their self-government, their freedom from outside domination, and their own economic, social and cultural development are most likely to eventually gain international recognition as peoples who have the right to self-determination, regardless of formal rules.[491]

Cristescu makes the same point: "[W]henever in the course of history a people has become aware of being a people, all definitions have proved superfluous."[492] While existing international instruments also provide some limited protection specifically for minority groups, American Indians historically are distinct peoples who have never fully consented to the intrusive authority of the United States; therefore, they possess the broad right to self-determination enunciated in article 1 of the Human Rights Covenants.

4. *The International Labour Organisation Convention 107*

The only existing international instrument related specifically to indigenous peoples is the International Labour Organisation's (ILO) Convention 107. In its present form, the Convention is not a useful instrument for protecting indigenous rights, since its primary purpose is the assimilation of indigenous peoples into the dominant society. The ILO is, however, currently revising Convention 107 to make it more consistent with the interests and aspirations of indigenous peoples....

NOTES

1. "All Peoples Have the Right of Self-Determination": Indigenous peoples seeking to ground a right to self-determination in international law face many barriers. The United Nations Charter provisions referring to self-determination have been interpreted as applying only to colonies and not to indigenous groups treated as ethnic groups living within the boundaries of member states. The Human Rights Covenants have not been ratified by all states. Even states that have ratified the covenants can make the same argument regarding indigenous peoples' status as "peoples" within the meaning of article 1 of each covenant. As a result, only colonized peoples have a right to self-determination. Does this distinction make sense, logically or politically?

It is not surprising, then, that a struggle over semantics has ensued whenever documents on indigenous status are drafted. According to one commentator:

> Similar issues underlie the debate over the terms "peoples and "populations." In international contexts, the term "peoples" has sometimes been appropriated to mean only the whole population of a state or colonial territory, with other groups, including indigenous groups which make up less than the whole population of the state, being relegated to the status of "populations." The title of the Working Group on Indigenous Populations reflects this usage. Again the underlying difficulty is the assumption that particular claims — especially to self-determination or to control over natural resources — are implicitly conceded if the term "peoples" is conceded to be appropriate. That term is far from being a precise term of art, and it does not follow that a particular group which constitutes a "people" for the purpose of a certain claim or right does so for other purposes.

Crawford, *The Aborigine in Comparative Law*, 2 Law & Anthropology 5, 11 (Vienna 1987).

---

[491] [*Id.*] at 15.
[492] A. Cristescu, *supra* note [480], at ¶ 274.

The real question, as opposed to the semantic question, becomes: What is the substance of the right to self-determination? Perhaps the reluctance by the international legal community to treat indigenous peoples as entitled to self-determination is related to the fear that the term "self-determination" requires the granting of statehood to indigenous peoples with a concomitant destruction of the territorial integrity of the states within which they are located. Could or would any modern state accept the creation of new states within its boundaries with the power to enter into treaties with competing states and otherwise deal as equals in the international arena?

As Professor Anaya's article points out, one solution to this conundrum is a recognition that the notion of self-determination does not necessarily require statehood. According to Professor Howard Berman:

> Too often, the discussion of self-determination begins and ends with the issue of statehood. In my view, the central question is not statehood but rather the right of distinct peoples to determine their destinies free from alien domination. There are no inherent reasons why indigenous peoples uniquely should be excluded from this right....
> Fortunately, contemporary international law does offer some options for implementation. Self-determination may be effected by a spectrum of possibilities including statehood, free association, the creation of an internationalized territory, autonomy, or integration. The essence of the right is the ability of a people to choose its own political status within its territory free from external domination. In my experience, few indigenous peoples presently aspire to statehood.

Are Indigenous Populations Entitled to International Juridical Personality?, PROC. AM. SOC'Y INT'L L. 189, 192, 193 (April 1985) (Remarks by Howard Berman).

Recent standard-setting discussions have also emphasized redefining the notion of self-determination. For example, in a 1989 seminar organized by the United Nations Subcommission on Prevention of Discrimination and Protection of Minorities, the participants elected to call indigenous groups "peoples" but interpreted self-determination as the right of indigenous peoples to control their own destiny.

Under such a broad definition do United States Indian tribes already possess the right of self-determination? Clearly this is an issue upon which there is some division in the scholarly community as well as among tribal groups. See Professor Barsh's argument regarding IRA governments in Chapter 3, section B1, *supra*.

2. International Legal Protection for Land: Invoking international law to protect indigenous peoples' land is also problematic. Some international agreements, like ILO Convention No. 169, contain specific provisions protecting land to some extent. Groups in countries that have ratified these conventions can invoke them. Indigenous peoples can also rely on the anti-discrimination principle of various conventions such as the International Covenant on Political and Civil Rights and the International Convention on the Elimination of All Forms of Racial Discrimination (1966), 660 U.N.T.S. 195, art. 1 (4), if the state within which they are located accords their land differential treatment. Relying on the anti-discrimination principle creates its own problems, however, because this principle is concerned primarily with individual and not group rights, a problem arising with most of the human rights provisions.

In countries like the United States that have not ratified these agreements, indigenous groups could only argue that the principle of self-determination in the U.N. Charter requires recognition of the fact that preservation of territory is an essential prerequisite to exercise of self-determination. Of course, such an argument requires acceptance of indigenous groups as peoples within the meaning of the charter, an argument that has not yet been accepted in the international community.

Even if these arguments are successful, they could not be invoked to seek a remedy for takings of land that occurred before the effective dates of the relevant instruments, all in the latter half of the 20th century. A recent survey of the relevant provisions that could be invoked concluded: "[H]uman rights instruments alone are unsatisfactory as tools for returning Indian lands, as they provide no express remedies. While some human rights provisions are effective only if applied to past acts, it is not clear that this may be done with the issue of Indian land rights." Landman, *International Protections for American Indian Land Rights?*, 5 B.U. INT'L L.J. 59, 82 (1987).

3. Applying International Law in the Domestic Arena: International obligations are not automatically enforceable in the United States. For example, some courts in the United States have held that the U.N. Charter is not self-executing. *See, e.g., Sei Fujii v. California*, 38 Cal. 2d 718, 242 P.2d 617 (1952). Recent cases have cast some doubt on this approach, however, especially as it was partly based on a notion that the human rights provisions are too general to be made self-executing. Since the U.N. Charter was ratified, the declarations discussed in the excerpted materials and the international human rights covenants have given more specific content to the charter provisions and demonstrate an international consensus on the charter provisions' meanings.

Even a country adopting the official policy that these norms are not self-executing may be influenced by these norms in setting domestic policy regarding indigenous peoples, as Professor Anaya's article illustrates. For example, the Special Committee appointed by the Senate Select Committee on Indian Affairs in its Final Report acknowledged the influence of developing U.N. standards in its recommendations to strengthen tribal self-governments:

> Though based on uniquely American traditions, our call for tribal empowerment finds a resonant echo throughout the world. The United Nations has organized a Working Group to establish new international legal standards for native citizens "believing that indigenous peoples should be free to manage their own affairs to the greatest possible extent."

SPECIAL COMM. ON INVESTIGATIONS, SEN. SELECT COMM. ON INDIAN AFFAIRS, FINAL REPORT 22 (1989). In addition, a recent article in the *Navajo-Hopi Observer* reported that Senators McCain and DeConcini referred to U.N. human rights standards in arguing against forced relocation of Navajo or Hopi Indians as part of the government's attempt to settle the Navajo-Hopi dispute discussed in Chapter 5, section B3.

International customary law is applicable in United States courts. Although *The Paquete Habana*, 175 U.S. 677 (1900), is usually cited as the principal decision establishing that international law is part of United States law, Professor Anaya demonstrates that Chief Justice John Marshall's decisions in *Johnson v. M'Intosh* and *The Cherokee Cases* reflect an application of international customary law. According to the excerpted *Harvard Civil-Rights Civil-Liberties Comment*, some provisions of the human rights covenants have become part of the customary international law and thus could be given effect by United States courts. By what mechanism could an unratified international agreement become a part of international customary law? Instead of basing customary law on the covenants, a better tack might be taken by focusing on the declarations discussed in the comment and the Universal Declaration of Human Rights, G.A.

Res. 271A (III), U.N. Doc. A/180, at 71 (1948). The Universal Declaration, being unanimous, reflected an impressive international consensus. According to one of the drafters of the Declaration, it is now "part of the customary law of nations and therefore is binding on all states." Humphrey, *The International Bill of Rights: Scope and Implementation*, 17 WM. & MARY L. REV. 527, 529 (1976). For a comprehensive treatment of the use of international customary law, see LILLICH, INVOKING INTERNATIONAL HUMAN RIGHTS LAW IN DOMESTIC COURTS (1985) (ABA Standing Committee on World Order Under Law).

Arguing that international law can be invoked in U.S. courts does not answer the question of the scope and effect of international legal principles. For example, can a rule of customary law be applied as a rule of decision in a particular case or only to interpret and inform constitutional provisions, treaties and federal and state laws that would otherwise apply? *See* LILLICH, *supra*, at 16-18.

4. Remedies: Various procedures exist for bringing individual and group complaints regarding violations of human rights to the United Nations and other international organizations, such as the Organization of American States. *See generally* GUIDE TO INTERNATIONAL HUMAN RIGHTS PRACTICE (H. Hannum ed. 1984); INDIAN LAW RESOURCE CENTER, HANDBOOK FOR INDIANS ON INTERNATIONAL HUMAN RIGHTS COMPLAINT PROCEDURES (1984). The U.N. Economic and Social Council Resolution 1503 established a confidential procedure involving the submission of written communications. ECOSOC Res. 1503 (XLVIII), ECSOR Supp. (No. 1A), at 8-9, U.N. Doc. E/4832/Add.1 (1970). Upon review of a communication and response, the Human Rights Commission has the authority to conduct an on-site investigation and issue a report critical of the government's activities denying human rights.

A more informal procedure was established by Economic and Social Council Resolution No. 1235. ECOSOC Res. 1235 (XLII), 42 ESCOR Supp. (No. 1) at 17-18, U.N. Doc. E/4393 (1967). The 1235 procedure permits an oral presentation. Both resolutions authorize the Human Rights Commission of the Sub-Commission on Prevention of Discrimination and Protection of Minorities to hear these complaints. In addition, the Optional Protocol to the International Covenant on Civil and Political Rights sets up a procedure for individual complaints of violations of human rights.

The confidential written communication set forth in Resolution 1503 has been invoked by American Indian groups. In 1980, the Indian Law Resource Center invoked the 1503 Procedure to bring formal complaints on behalf of the traditional Seminoles, the Houdinousaunee (Six Nations Iroquois Confederacy), the Mohawk, the Hopi, the Western Shoshone, and the Lakota Nation. The communication alleged violations of equal protection and the right to be free of racial discrimination, but focused mainly on denial of self-determination and property rights. *March 11, 1980 Written Communications*, reprinted in NATIONAL LAWYERS GUILD, COMMITTEE ON NATIVE AMERICAN STRUGGLES, RETHINKING INDIAN LAW 139 (1982).

The communications alleging denial of self-determination involved both an IRA government and a state-recognized tribal government, which were attacked as puppet governments established without the true consent of the Hopi or Mohawk people. The communication on behalf of the traditional Hopi essentially attacked the legitimacy of the IRA government as imposed on the Hopi people without their true consent, thus subjecting them to "colonial rule." The communication on behalf of the Mohawk people made the same basic argument as to the state-recognized government.

The communications regarding property disputed the legitimacy of the United States laws permitting confiscation of tribal property without compensation (e.g., under the *Tee-Hit-Ton* and *Sioux Nation* rules). The communications also argued that even compensated takings violated human rights norms because of the destructive impact on Indian tribes' cultural and political integrity caused by loss of a land base. Each communication invoked the U.N. Charter provisions discussed in the excerpted material, as well as the Helsinki Final Act, to which the United States is a signatory. The Helsinki Final Act binds the signatory nations "to respect the equal rights of peoples and their self-determination." Conference on Security and Cooperation in Europe: Final Act, Aug. 1, 1975, 73 Dep't of State Bull. 323, 325 (1975) (art. 1(a)(VIII)).

The commission has taken no action on this communication, however — surely an indication by this date (1990) that no such action will be forthcoming. It is, thus, not surprising that other indigenous peoples have not invoked the 1503 Procedure. Moreover, the confidential nature of these proceedings prevents the complainants from publicizing the complaint. As a method for gaining international sympathy and support for the indigenous cause, the 1503 Procedure may not prove as useful as the more informal and public procedure permitted by Resolution 1235.

The 1503 and 1235 procedures can be invoked against any nation and not just those nations ratifying the civil and political rights covenants. The procedure invoked in the excerpt below can only be invoked against nations, like Canada, that executed the Covenants' Optional Protocol, however.

CASE OF SANDRA LOVELACE

Views of the Human Rights Committee under Article 5 (4)
of the Optional Protocol to the International Covenant
on Civil and Political Rights concerning
Communication No. R. 6/24

The Human Rights Committee, established under article 28 of the International Covenant of Civil and Political Rights, [having considered] Communication No. R.6/24 submitted to the Committee by Sandra Lovelace under the Optional Protocol to the International Covenant on Civil and Political Rights [and the state's response]; adopts the following:

Views Under Article 5 (4) of the Optional Protocol

1. [Sandra Lovelace] is a 32-year-old woman, living in Canada. She was born and registered as "Maliseet Indian" but has lost her rights and status as an Indian in accordance with section 12 (1) (b) of the Indian Act, after having married a non-Indian on 23 May 1970. Pointing out that an Indian man who marries a non-Indian woman does not lose his Indian status, she claims that the Act is discriminatory on the grounds of sex and contrary to articles 2 (1), 3, 23 (1) and (4), 26 and 27 of the Covenant. As to the admissibility of the communication, she contends that she was not required to exhaust local remedies since the Supreme Court of Canada, in *The Attorney-General of Canada v. Jeanette Lavalle, Richard Isaac et al. v. Ivonne Bidard* [1974] S.C.R. 1349, held that section 12 (1) (b) was fully operative, irrespective of its inconsistency with the Canadian Bill of Rights on account of discrimination based on sex.

2. By its decision of 18 July 1978 the Human Rights Committee transmitted the communication, under rule 91 of the provisional rules of procedure, to the State party concerned, requesting information [regarding the State's views on the relevancy and admissibility of the complaint. The State did not respond, and on August 14, 1979, the Committee decided the communication was admissible].

5. In its submission under article 4 (2) of the Optional Protocol concerning the merits of the case, dated 4 April 1980, the State party recognized that "many of the provisions of the ... Indian Act, including section 12 (1) (b), require serious reconsideration and reform." The Government further referred to an earlier public declaration to the effect that it intended to put a reform bill before the Canadian Parliament. It none the less stressed the necessity of the Indian Act as an instrument designed to protect the Indian minority in accordance with article 27 of the Covenant. A definition of the Indian was inevitable in view of the special privileges granted to the Indian communities, in particular their right to occupy reserve lands. Traditionally, patrilineal family relationships were taken into account for determining legal claims. Since, additionally, in the farming societies of the nineteenth century, reserve land was felt to be more threatened by non-Indian men than by non-Indian women, legal enactments as from 1869 provided that an Indian woman who married a non-Indian man would lose her status as an Indian. These reasons were still valid. A change in the law could only be sought in consultation with the Indians themselves who, however, were divided on the issue of equal rights. The Indian community should not [be] endangered by legislative changes. Therefore, although the Government was in principle committed to amending section 12 (1) (b) of the Indian Act, no quick and immediate legislative action could be expected.

6. The author of the communication, in her submission of 20 June 1980, disputes the contention that legal relationships within Indian families were traditionally patrilineal in nature. Her view is that the reasons put forward by the Canadian Government do not justify the discrimination against Indian women in section 12 (1) (b) of the Indian Act. She concludes that the Human Rights Committee should recommend the State party to amend the provisions in question.

7.1 In an *Interim decision*, adopted on 31 July 1980, the Human Rights Committee set out the issues of the case in the following considerations:

7.2 The Human Rights Committee recognized that the relevant provision of the Indian Act, although not legally restricting the right to marry as laid down in article 23 (2) of the Covenant, entails serious disadvantages on the part of the Indian woman who wants to marry a non-Indian man and may in fact cause her to live with her fiance in an unmarried relationship. There is thus a question as to whether the obligation of the State party under article 23 of the Covenant with regard to the protection of the family is complied with. Moreover, since only Indian women and not Indian men are subject to these disadvantages under the Act, the question arises whether Canada complies with its commitment under articles 2 and 3 to secure the rights under the Covenant without discrimination as to sex. On the other hand, article 27 of the Covenant requires States parties to accord protection to ethnic and linguistic minorities and the Committee must give due weight to this [duty].

7.3 In regard to the present communication, however, the Human Rights Committee must also take into account that the Covenant was entered into force in respect to Canada on 19 August 1976, several years after the marriage of Mrs. Lovelace. She consequently lost her status as an Indian at a time when Canada was not bound by the Covenant. The Human Rights Committee has held that it is empowered to consider a communication when the measures complained of, although they occurred before the entry into force of the Covenant, continued to have effects which themselves constitute a violation of the Covenant after that date. It is therefore relevant for the Committee to know whether the marriage of Mrs. Lovelace in 1970 has had any such effect.

7.4 Since the author of the communication is ethnically an Indian, some persisting effects of her loss of legal status as an Indian may, as from the entry into force of the Covenant for Canada, amount to a violation of rights protected by the Covenant. The Human Rights Committee has been informed that persons in her situation are denied the right to live on an Indian reserve with resultant separation from the Indian community and members of their families. Such prohibition may affect rights which the Covenant guarantees in articles 12 (1), 17, 23 (1), 24 and 27. There may [also be other effects].

9.2 It emerges from statistics provided by the State party that from 1965 to 1978, on an average, 510 Indian women married non-Indian men each year. Marriages between Indian women and Indian men of the same band during that period were 590 on the average each year; between Indian women and Indian men of a different band 422 on the average each year; and between Indian men and non-Indian women 448 on the average each year.

9.3 As to the legal basis of a prohibition to live on a reserve, the State party offers the following explanations:

"Section 14 of the Indian Act provides that '(an Indian) woman who is a member of a band ceases to be a member of that band if she marries a person who is not a member of that band.'[97] As such, she loses the right to the use and benefits, in common with other members of the band, of the land allotted to the band.[98] It should, however, be noted that 'when (an Indian woman) marries a member of another band, she thereupon becomes a member of the band of which her husband is a member.' As such, she is entitled to the use and benefit of lands allotted to her husband's band.

"An Indian (including a woman) who ceases to be a member of a band ceases to be entitled to reside by right on a reserve. None the less it is possible for an individual to reside on a reserve if his or her presence thereon is tolerated by a band or its members. It should be noted that under section 30 of the Indian Act, any person who trespasses on a reserve is guilty of an offence. In addition, section 31 of the Act provides that an Indian or a band (and of course its agent, the Band Council) may seek relief or remedy against any person, other than an Indian, who is or has been

"(a) unlawfully in occupation or possession of,
"(b) claiming adversely the right to occupation or possession of, or
"(c) trespassing upon

a reserve or part thereof."

---

[97] Mrs. Lovelace married a non-Indian. As such, she ceased to be a member of the Tobique band. In addition, by the application of subparagraph 12 (1) (b) of the Indian Act, she lost her Indian status.

[98] It should be noted that when an Indian ceases to be a member of a band, he is entitled, if he meets the conditions set out in sections 15 and 16 of the Indian Act, to compensation from Her Majesty for this loss of membership.

9.4 As to the reasons adduced to justify the denial of the right of abode on a reserve, the State party states that the provisions of the Indian Act which govern the right to reside on a reserve have been enacted to give effect to various treaty obligations reserving to the Indians exclusive use of certain lands.

9.5 With regard to the legislative proposals under consideration, the State party offers the following information:

"Legislative proposals are being considered which would ensure that no Indian person, male or female, would lose his or her status under any circumstances other than his or her own personal desire to renounce it.

"In addition, changes to the present sections under which the status of the Indian woman and minor children is dependent upon the status of her spouse are also being considered.

"Further recommendations are being considered which would give Band Councils powers to pass by-laws concerning membership in the band; such by-laws, however, would be required to be non-discriminatory in the areas of sex, religion and family affiliation...."

9.6 As to Mrs. Lovelace's place of abode prior to her marriage both parties confirm that she was at that time living on the Tobique Reserve with her parents. Sandra Lovelace adds that as a result of her marriage she was denied the right to live on an Indian reserve. As to her abode since then the State party observes:

"Since her marriage and following her divorce, Mrs. Lovelace has, from time to time, lived on the reserve in the home of her parents, and the Band Council has made no move to prevent her from doing so. However, Mrs. Lovelace wishes to live permanently on the reserve and to obtain a new house. To do so, she has to apply to the Band Council. Housing on reserves is provided with money set aside by Parliament for the benefit of registered Indians. The Council has not agreed to provide Mrs. Lovelace with a new house. It considers that in the provision of such housing priority is to be given to registered Indians."

9.7 In this connexion the following additional information has been submitted on behalf of Mrs. Lovelace:

"At the present time, Sandra Lovelace is living on the Tobique Indian Reserve, although she has no right to remain there. She has returned to the Reserve, with her children because her marriage has broken up and she has no other place to reside. She is able to remain on the reserve in violation of the law of the local Band Council because dissident members of the tribe who support her cause have threatened to resort to physical violence in her defense should the authorities attempt to remove her." ...

9.8 As to the other persisting effects of Mrs. Lovelace's loss of Indian status the State party submits the following:

"When Mrs. Lovelace lost her Indian status through marriage to a non-Indian, she also lost access to federal government programs for Indian people in areas such as education, housing, social assistance, etc. At the same time, however, she and her children became eligible to receive similar benefits from programs the provincial government provides for all residents of the province.

"Mrs. Lovelace is no longer a member of the Tobique band and no longer an Indian under the terms of the Indian Act. She however is enjoying all the rights recognized in the Covenant, in the same way as any other individual within the territory of Canada and subject to its jurisdiction."

10. The Human Rights Committee, in the examination of the communication before it, has to proceed from the basic fact that Sandra Lovelace married a non-Indian on 23 May 1970 and consequently lost her status as a Maliseet Indian under section 12 (1) (b) of the Indian Act. This provision was — and still is — based on a distinction *de jure* on the ground of sex. However, neither its application to her marriage as the cause of her loss of Indian status nor its effects could at that time amount to a violation of the Covenant, because this instrument did not come into force for Canada until 19 August 1976. Moreover, the Committee is not competent, as a rule, to examine allegations relating to events having taken place before the entry into force of the Covenant and the Optional Protocol. Therefore as regards Canada it can only consider alleged violations of human rights occurring on or after 19 August 1976. In the case of a particular individual claiming to be a victim of a violation, it cannot express its view on the law in the abstract, without regard to the date on which this law was applied to the alleged victim. In the case of Sandra Lovelace it follows that the Committee is not competent to express any view on the original cause of her loss of Indian status, i.e. the Indian Act as applied to her at the time of her marriage in 1970.

11. The Committee recognizes, however, that the situation may be different if the alleged violations, although relating to events occurring before 19 August 1976, continue, or have effects which themselves constitute violations, after that date. In examining the situation of Sandra Lovelace in this respect, the Committee must have regard to all relevant provisions of the Covenant. It has considered, in particular, the extent to which the general provisions in articles 2 and 3 as well as the rights in articles 12 (1), 17 (1), 24, 26 and 27, may be applicable to the facts of her present situation.

12. The Committee first observes that from 19 August 1976 Canada had undertaken under article 2(1) and (2) of the Covenant to respect and ensure to all individuals within its territory and subject to its jurisdiction, the rights recognized in the Covenant without distinction of any kind such as sex, and to adopt the necessary measures to give effect to these rights. Further, under article 3, Canada undertook to ensure the equal right of men and women to the enjoyment of these rights. These undertakings apply [to Sandra Lovelace].

13.1 The Committee considers that the essence of the present complaint concerns the continuing effect of the Indian Act, in denying Sandra Lovelace legal status as an Indian, in particular because she cannot for this reason claim legal right to reside where she wishes to, on the Tobique Reserve. This fact persists after the entry into force of the Covenant, and its effects have to be examined, without regard to their original cause. Among the effects referred to on behalf of the author, [most] relate to the Indian Act and other Canadian rules in fields which do not necessarily adversely affect the enjoyment of rights protected by the Covenant. In this respect the significant matter is her last claim, that "the major loss to a person ceasing to be an Indian is the loss of the cultural benefits of living in an Indian community, the emotional ties to home, family, friends and neighbours, and the loss of identity."

13.2 Although a number of provisions of the Covenant have been invoked by Sandra Lovelace, the Committee considers that the one which is most directly applicable to this complaint is article 27, which reads as follows:

"In those States in which ethnic, religious or linguistic minorities exist, persons belonging to such minorities shall not be denied the right, in community with the other members of their group, to enjoy their own culture, to profess and practise their own religion, or to use their own language."

It has to be considered whether Sandra Lovelace, because she is denied the legal right to reside on the Tobique Reserve, has by that fact been denied the right guaranteed by article 27 to persons belonging to minorities, to enjoy their own culture and to use their own language in community with other members of their group.

14. The rights under article 27 of the Covenant have to be secured to "persons belonging" to the minority. At present Sandra Lovelace does not qualify as an Indian under Canadian legislation. However, the Indian Act deals primarily with a number of privileges which, as stated above, do not as such come within the scope of the Covenant. Protection under the Indian Act and protection under article 27 of the Covenant therefore have to be distinguished. Persons who are born and brought up on a reserve, who have kept ties with their community and wish to maintain these ties must normally be considered as belonging to that minority with the meaning of the Covenant. Since Sandra Lovelace is ethnically a Maliseet Indian and has only been absent from her home reserve for a few years during the existence of her marriage, she is, in the opinion of the Committee, entitled to be regarded as "belonging" to this minority and to claim the benefits of article 27 of the Covenant. The question whether these benefits have been denied to her, depends on how far they extend.

15. The right to live on a reserve is not as such guaranteed by article 27 of the Covenant. Moreover, the Indian Act does not interfere directly with the functions which are expressly mentioned in that article. However, in the opinion of the Committee the right of Sandra Lovelace to access to her native culture and language "in community with the other members" of her group, has in fact been, and continues to be interfered with, because there is no place outside the Tobique Reserve where such a community exists. On the other hand, not every interference can be regarded as a denial of rights within the meaning of article 27. Restrictions on the right to residence, by way of national legislation, cannot be ruled out under article 27 of the Covenant. This also follows from the restrictions to article 12 (1) of the Covenant set out in article 12 (3). The Committee recognized the need to define the category of persons entitled to live on a reserve, for such purposes as those explained by the Government regarding protection of its resources and preservation of the identity of its people. However, the obligations which the Government has since undertaken under the Covenant must also be taken into account.

16. In this respect, the Committee is of the view that statutory restrictions affecting the right to residence on a reserve of a person belonging to the minority concerned, must have both a reasonable and objective justification and be consistent with the other provisions of the Covenant, read as a whole. Article 27 must be construed and applied in the light of the other provisions mentioned above, such as articles 12, 17 and 23 in so far as they may be relevant to the articles 2, 3 and 26, as the case may be. It is not necessary, however, to determine in any general manner which restrictions may be justified under the Cove-

nant, in particular as a result of marriage, because the circumstances are special in the present case.

17. The case of Sandra Lovelace should be considered in the light of the fact her marriage to a non-Indian has broken up. It is natural that in such a situation she wishes to return to the environment in which she was born, particularly as after the dissolution of her marriage her main cultural attachment again was to the Maliseet band. Whatever may be the merits of the Indian Act in other respect it does not seem to the Committee that to deny Sandra Lovelace the right to reside on the reserve is reasonable, or necessary to preserve the identity of the tribe. The Committee therefore concludes that to prevent her recognition as belonging to the band is an unjustifiable denial of her rights under article 27 of the Covenant, read in the context of the other provisions referred to.

18. In view of this finding, the Committee does not consider it necessary to examine whether the same facts also show separate breaches of the other rights invoked. The specific rights most directly applicable to her situation are those under article 27 of the Covenant. The rights to choose one's residence (article 12, and the rights aimed at protecting family life and children (articles 17, 23 and 24) are only indirectly at stake in the present case. The facts of the case do not seem to require further examination under those articles. The Committee's finding of a lack of reasonable justification for the interference with Sandra Lovelace's rights under article 27 of the Covenant also makes it unnecessary, as suggested above (paragraph 12), to examine the general provisions against discrimination (articles 2, 3 and 26) in the context of the present case, and in particular to determine their bearing upon inequalities predating the coming into force of the Covenant for Canada.

19. Accordingly, the Human Rights Committee, acting under article 5 (4) of the Optional Protocol to the International Covenant on Civil and Political Rights, is of the view that the facts of the present case, which establish that Sandra Lovelace has been denied the legal right to reside on the Tobique Reserve disclose a breach by Canada of article 27 of the Covenant.

NOTES

1. The Optional Protocol: Of the 87 parties to the Covenant, only 44 had adopted the Protocol as of 1989. Note that the opinion is termed an expression of the Committee's "view." This terminology expresses the fact that the Committee's opinion represents only a non-binding recommendation. In other words, the Committee's effectiveness depends on persuasion and the public embarrassment of being labeled a violator of human rights. Unfortunately, the Committee's decisions are not well publicized. The Committee does not issue any interim announcements regarding decisions on whether a communication is admissible. The Committee does issue a press release upon final resolution of a case, but the release states only the name of the communication and the fact that a decision has been reached. The opinion itself is published in the Committee's annual report to the Economic and Social Council. In Canada, very little publicity was given to the Committee's decision. *See* Bayefsky, *The Human Rights Committee and the Case of Sandra Lovelace*, 1982 CAN. Y.B. INT'L L. 244, 261. Although Canada's response to the Committee's view has been criticized, the offending provision was changed in 1985. For a comprehensive review of the

Optional Protocol decisions, see DeZayas, Möller, & Opsahl, *Application of the International Covenant on Civil and Political Rights Under the Optional Protocol by the Human Rights Committee*, 26 COMP. JUD'L R. 3 (1989).

2. **Lovelace and Equality:** Under the challenged provision, Indian men did not lose their status when they married non-Indian women. In fact, their non-Indian wives gained Indian status. What would be the rationale for granting Indian status to non-Indian wives? Evaluate Canada's argument that non-Indian men were more of a threat to Canadian tribes. Do you agree?

Why did the Committee decline to reach the question whether the Indian Act violated the nondiscrimination norms of the Covenant? The Committee has expressed the view that state laws discriminating based on gender violate the Covenant. In a 1978 case, the Committee found that state immigration laws that subjected foreign husbands of nationals to restrictions not imposed on foreign wives violated both article 23's right to protection of the family and articles 2, 3, and 26 as a discrimination based on gender. *Aumeeruddy-Cziffra v. Mauritius*, No. 35/1978, 1981 Human Rights Committee Report, Annex VII.

In 1985 Canada amended the Indian Act to provide that individual bands can determine membership instead of the central government. R.S.C. c. 27. The changes are described in note 4 after the Canadian materials in section A, *supra*. If a Band adopted a rigid patrilineal rule of membership, would such an action present any issue under the Covenants? Would your answer change if the Band's adoption of such a rule deviated from its traditional practice and was motivated by a perceived need to restrict eligibility for membership in order to keep down the members eligible for scarce national benefits?

3. **Lovelace and Community:** The Committee based its decision on Article 27, which provides "In those States in which ethnic, religious or linguistic minorities exist, persons belonging to such minorities shall not be denied the right, in community with the other members of their group, to enjoy their own culture, to profess and practise their own religion, or to use their own language." What was the rationale for the view that the Indian Act's membership provision violated Article 27? *Lovelace* is the first and, to date, only Committee decision interpreting Article 27. In what other contexts might an Indian tribe rely on Article 27? Could a tribe, for example, argue that compensation for a taking of tribal land must be in the form of comparable "in lieu" land on the theory that land is central to its ability to exist as a community?

3. DEVELOPING STANDARDS

CONVENTION ON INDIGENOUS AND TRIBAL PEOPLES IN INDEPENDENT COUNTRIES (No. 169)*

[Convention No. 169, designed to replace the assimilationist approach of Convention No. 107, is reprinted in Chapter 1, page 165.]

---

*Published in International Labour Conference, Report of the Committee on Convention 107 at 25/25-33, *Provisional Record*, No. 25, 76th Session (1989).

HURST HANNUM, NEW DEVELOPMENTS IN INDIGENOUS RIGHTS, 28 Virginia Journal of International Law, 657-62 (1988)*

II. *United Nations Involvement with the Question of Indigenous Peoples*

In 1949, Bolivia proposed establishing a sub-commission of the UN Social Commission to study "the situation of the aboriginal population of the American continent."[34] The resolution ultimately adopted, however, only called upon the Economic and Social Council to undertake a study on the situation of indigenous peoples. A number of countries, including the United States, Brazil, Chile, France, Peru, and Venezuela, objected to this decision, and a subsequent resolution effectively barred any such studies unless requested by affected member states. No requests were forthcoming, and this initiative was the last taken by the UN concerning the general problems of indigenous peoples for two decades.

In 1971, the UN Sub-Commission on Prevention of Discrimination and Protection of Minorities appointed a Special Rapporteur to study the problem of discrimination against indigenous populations. The Rapporteur's voluminous report, which was not completed until 1983, served as a vehicle for increasing international interest in indigenous problems and also prompted greater involvement by NGOs at the international level.

During the 1970s, international human rights standards and procedures also received increased attention. Indigenous peoples were victims of many of the worst human rights violations, and indigenous organizations and other NGOs were thus able to link their specific concerns regarding indigenous rights with more general human rights developments.

UN activities in the area of racial discrimination also highlighted the situation of indigenous peoples. A 1969 Sub-Commission study on racial discrimination included a chapter on indigenous peoples, and numerous state reports under the Convention on the Elimination of All Forms of Racial Discrimination[39] also contain references to the treatment of indigenous peoples. The concluding declaration of the 1978 World Conference to Combat Racism and Racial Discrimination refers specifically to both minorities and indigenous peoples.[41] The conference "endorses the right of indigenous peoples to maintain their traditional structure of economy and culture, including their own language, and also recognizes the special relationship of indigenous peoples to their land and stresses that their land, land rights and natural resources should not be taken away from them."[42]

---

* Copyright © 1988 Virginia Journal of International Law Association and Hurst Hannum. Reprinted by permission.

[34][UN Sub-Commission on Prevention of Discrimination and Protection of Minorities, Study of the Problem of Discrimination Against Indigenous Populations, U.N. Doc. E/CN.4/Sub.2/1986/7 & Adds.1-4 (1986) (Jose R. Martinez Cobo, Special Rapporteur),] at 25, originally released as E/CN.4/Sub.2/476/Add.4 at 25.

[39][International Convention on the Elimination of All Forms of Racial Discrimination, adopted Dec. 21, 1965, 660 U.N.T.S. 195.]

[41]Declaration of the World Conference to Combat Racism and Racial Discrimination, reprinted in 1 UN Indigenous Study, *supra* note [34], at 24-31-32, originally released as E/CN.4/Sub.2/476/Add.4 at 24, 31-32.

[42]*Id.* at 31, originally released as E/CN.4/Sub.2/476/Add.4 at 31.

The most significant international activity undertaken by NGOs has been the convening of several major conferences, which were notable because they were largely gatherings of indigenous peoples themselves and their representatives. Among the most important of these conferences were two Inuit Circumpolar Conferences,[44] three General Assemblies of the World Council of Indigenous Peoples,[45] the International NGO Conference on Discrimination against Indigenous Populations in the Americas,[46] the First Congress of Indian Movements of South America,[47] and the International NGO Conference on Indigenous Peoples and the Land.[48]

Partly in response to recommendations in the Sub-Commission study and the 1981 Geneva Conference on Indigenous Peoples and the Land, the UN Economic and Social Council approved creation of pre-sessional Working Group on Indigenous Populations ("Working Group") of the UN Sub-Commission on Prevention of Discrimination and Protection of Minorities. The Working Group held its first annual meeting in August 1982. Its mandate extends to the review of developments pertaining to the protection of the human rights of indigenous populations and to the development of international standards for indigenous rights.[51]

The Working Group has become the primary focus of international activities by both governments and nongovernmental organizations concerned with indigenous peoples. Its sessions are now held in the same large conference room at the UN headquarters in Geneva in which the Commission on Human Rights meets, a signal of the Group's growing importance. Its five members are drawn from different regions, according to standard UN practice, and all serve in their individual capacity, as do other members of the Sub-Commission.[52]

At its first session, the Working Group took the unprecedented step of allowing oral and written interventions from all indigenous organizations which wished to participate in its work, not limiting such participation to those with formal consultative status. Approximately 370 persons, including representatives from over 50 indigenous organizations and observers from 27 countries, took part in its fifth session in 1987.

As a result of this wide participation, the Working Group has provided a meaningful forum for the exchange of proposals regarding indigenous rights and for the exposition of indigenous reality throughout the world. While the Working Group reiterates at each session that it is not a "chamber of complaints" and has no authority to hear allegations of human rights violations, it has nevertheless permitted very direct criticisms of government practices by NGOs as a means of gathering data upon which standards will eventually be based.

---

[44]Alaska, 1977, and Greenland, 1980.

[45]Sweden, 1977, Australia, 1981, and Panama, 1984.

[46]Geneva, 1977.

[47]Peru, 1980.

[48]Geneva, 1981.

[51]E.S.C. Res. 34, U.N. ESCOR Supp. (No. 1) at 26-27, U.N. Doc. E./1982/82 (1982).

[52]Most subsidiary bodies such as the Working Group reflect the UN's membership through a practice of proportional geographic representation of the regional five groups of Africa, Asia, Latin America, Eastern Europe and the U.S.S.R., and Western Europe and others.

The early sessions of the Working Group were devoted largely to collecting data, which consisted of information from indigenous and other NGOs about the actual situation of indigenous peoples under assault from dominant societies in many parts of the world. The most common violations reported were arbitrary arrests, torture, and killings; dispossession of indigenous lands, either through settlement or pursuant to state-defined development projects, such as hydro-electric projects or large-scale mining or agricultural projects; and the attempted destruction of indigenous culture and identity through, *inter alia*, desecration or destruction of religious sites. The information submitted to the Working Group also made frequent references to the economic gap between indigenous and dominant populations, as illustrated by insufficient or unequal social services provided by governments and the exploitation of natural resources on indigenous lands without either indigenous consent or adequate compensation.

Although the review of developments related to the human rights of indigenous peoples continues to form an important segment of the Working Group's activity, since 1985 it has shifted its focus to preparing a draft declaration on the rights of indigenous populations. From the perspective of international law, this declaration will probably be the most significant development to date in the area of indigenous rights. Fourteen "draft principles" based on discussions during the Working Group's first five sessions represent initial steps towards development of this declaration.

The rapid progress at the Working Group's 1987 session and its decision to request its Chairman/Rapporteur to prepare a full draft declaration prior to the 1988 session are likely to lead to a discussion of the whole range of indigenous rights in the context of a specific text at the 1988 and subsequent sessions.

FIRST REVISED TEXT OF THE DRAFT UNIVERSAL DECLARATION ON THE RIGHTS OF INDIGENOUS PEOPLES

As Presented by
The Chairman/Rapporteur, Ms. Erica-Irene Daes, E/CN.4/Sub.2/1989/36/Annex II

The General Assembly,

Considering indigenous peoples born free and equal in dignity and rights in accordance with existing international standards while recognizing the right of all individuals and groups to be different, to consider themselves different and to be regarded as such,

Recognizing the specific need to promote and protect those rights and characteristics which stem from indigenous history, philosophy of life, traditions, culture and legal, social and economic structures, especially as these are tied to the lands which the groups have traditionally occupied,

Concerned that many indigenous peoples have been unable to enjoy and assert their inalienable human rights and fundamental freedoms, frequently resulting in insufficient land and resources, poverty and deprivation, which in turn may lead them to voice their grievances and to organize themselves in order to bring an end to all forms of discrimination and oppression which they face,

Convinced that all doctrines and practices of racial, ethnic or cultural superiority are legally wrong, morally condemnable and socially unjust,

Reaffirming that indigenous peoples in the exercise of their rights should be free from adverse distinction or discrimination of any kind,

Endorsing calls for the consolidation and strengthening of indigenous societies and their cultures and traditions through development based on their own needs and value systems and comprehensive participation in and consultation about all other relevant development efforts,

Emphasizing the need for special attention to the rights and skills of indigenous women and children,

Believing that indigenous peoples should be free to manage their own affairs to the greatest possible extent, while enjoying equal rights with other citizens in the political, economic and social life of States,

Bearing in mind that nothing in this declaration may be used as a justification for denying to any people, which otherwise satisfies the criteria generally established by human rights instruments and international law, its right to self-determination,

Calling on States to comply with and effectively implement all international human rights instruments as they apply to indigenous peoples,

Acknowledging the need for minimum standards taking account of the diverse realities of indigenous peoples in all parts of the world,

Solemnly proclaims the following declaration on rights of indigenous peoples and calls upon all States to take prompt and effective measures to implement the declaration in conjunction with the indigenous peoples.

PART I

1. The right to the full and effective enjoyment of all fundamental rights and freedoms, as well as the observance of the corresponding responsibilities, which are universally recognized in the Charter of the United Nations and in existing international human rights instruments.

2. The right to be free and equal to all the other human beings in dignity and rights and to be free from adverse distinction or discrimination of any kind.

PART II

3. The [collective] right to exist as distinct peoples and to be protected against genocide, as well as the [individual] rights to life, physical integrity, liberty and security of person.

4. The [collective] right to maintain and develop their ethnic and cultural characteristics and distinct identity, including the right of peoples and individuals to call themselves by their proper names.

5. The individual and collective right to protection against ethnocide. This protection shall include in particular, prevention of any act which has the air or effect of depriving them of their ethnic characteristics or cultural identity, or any form of forced assimilation or integration, of imposition of foreign lifestyles and of any propaganda derogating their dignity and diversity.

6. The right to preserve their cultural identity and traditions and to pursue their own cultural development. The rights to the manifestations of their cul-

tures, including archaeological sites, artefacts [*sic*], designs, technology and works of art, lie with the indigenous peoples or their members.

7. The right to require that States grant — within the resources available — the necessary assistance for the maintenance of their identity and their development.

8. The right to manifest, teach, practise and observe their own religious traditions and ceremonies, and to maintain, protect and have access to sacred sites and burial-grounds for these purposes.

9. The right to develop and promote their own languages, including an own literary language, and to use them for administrative, juridical, cultural and other purposes.

10. The right to all forms of education, including in particular the right of children to have access to education in their own languages, and to establish, structure, conduct and control their own educational systems and institutions.

11. The right to promote intercultural information and education, recognizing the dignity and diversity of their cultures, and the duty of States to take the necessary measures, among other sections of the national community, with the object of eliminating prejudices and of fostering understanding and good relations.

PART III

12. The right of collective and individual ownership, possession and use of the lands or resources which they have traditionally occupied or used. The lands may only be taken away from them with their free and informed consent as witnessed by a treaty or agreement.

13. The right to recognition of their own land-tenure systems for the protection and promotion of the use, enjoyment and occupancy of the land.

14. The right to special measures to ensure their ownership and control over surface and substances of resources pertaining to the territories they have traditionally occupied or otherwise used including flora and fauna, waters and ice sea.

15. The right to reclaim land and surface resources or where this is not possible, to seek just and fair compensation for the same, when the property has been taken away from them without consent, in particular, if such deprival has been based on theories such as those related to discovery, *terra nullius*, waste lands or idle lands. Compensation, if the parties agree, may take the form of land or resources of quality and legal status at least equal to that of the property previously owned by them.

16. The right to protection of their environment and in particular against any action or course of conduct which may result in the destruction, deterioration or pollution of their traditional habitat, land, air, water, sea ice, wildlife or other resources without free and informed consent of the indigenous peoples affected. The right to just and fair compensation for any such action or course of conduct.

17. The right to require that States consult with indigenous peoples and with both domestic and transnational corporations prior to the commencement of any large-scale projects, particularly natural resource projects or exploitation of

mineral and other subsoil resources in order to enhance the projects' benefits and to mitigate any adverse economic, social, environmental and cultural effect. Just and fair compensation shall be provided for any such activity or adverse consequence undertaken.

PART IV

18. The right to maintain and develop within their areas of lands or territories their traditional economic structures and ways of life, to be secure in the traditional economic structures and ways of life, to be secure in the enjoyment of their own traditional means of subsistence, and to engage freely in their traditional and other economic activities, including hunting, fresh- and salt-water fishing, herding, gathering, lumbering and cultivation, without adverse discrimination. In no case may an indigenous people be deprived of its means of subsistence. The right of just and fair compensation if they have been so deprived.

19. The right to special State measures for the immediate, effective and continuing improvement of their social and economic conditions, with their consent, that reflect their own priorities.

20. The right to determine, plan and implement all health, housing and other social and economic programmes affecting them, and as far as possible to develop, plan and implement such programmes through their own institutions.

PART V

21. The right to participate on an equal footing with all the other citizens and without adverse discrimination in the political, economic and social life of the State and to have their specific character duly reflected in the legal system and in political and socio-economic institutions, including in particular proper regard to and recognition of indigenous laws and customs.

22. The right to participate fully at the State level, through representatives chosen by themselves, in decision-making about and implementation of all national and international matters which may affect their life and destiny.

23. The [collective] right to autonomy in matters relating to their own internal and local affairs, including education, information, culture, religion, health, housing, social welfare, traditional and other economic activities, land and resources administration and the environment, as well as internal taxation for financing these autonomous functions.

24. The right to decide upon the structures of their autonomous institutions, to select the membership of such institutions, and to determine the membership of the indigenous people concerned for these purposes.

25. The right to determine the responsibilities of individuals to their own community, consistent with universally recognized human rights and fundamental freedoms.

26. The right to maintain and develop traditional contacts and co-operation, including cultural and social exchanges and trade, with their own kith and kin across State boundaries and the obligation of the State to adopt measures to facilitate such contacts.

27. The right to claim that States honour treaties and other agreements concluded with indigenous peoples.

PART VI

28. The individual and collective right to access to and prompt decision by mutually acceptable and fair procedures for resolving conflicts or disputes and any infringement, public or private, between States and indigenous peoples, groups or individuals. These procedures should include, as appropriate, negotiations, mediation, arbitration, national courts and international and regional human rights review and complaints mechanisms.

PART VII

29. These rights constitute the minimum standards for the survival and the well-being of the indigenous peoples of the world.

30. Nothing in this Declaration may be interpreted as implying for any State, group or individual any right to engage in any activity or to perform any act aimed at the destruction of any of the rights and freedoms set forth herein.

NOTES

1. The Relation of Convention No. 169 to Convention No. 107: Russel Barsh has described the relationship of the two conventions as follows:

> [T]he problem of indigenous populations can be viewed as either discrimination or assimilation, i.e., as lack of equality or forced equality with the population of the administering state. The International Labour Organisation took the first view in Convention No. 107 and encouraged states to remove all institutional obstacles to the complete integration of indigenous communities.

Barsh, *Indigenous Peoples: An Emerging Object of International Law*, 80 Am. J. Int'l L. 369, 377 (1986).* To what extent has Convention No. 169 been effective in changing the paternalistic and assimilationist tone of the earlier Convention?

Until Convention No. 169 is adopted, states that ratified No. 107 remain subject to the earlier convention. What factors might encourage a state to adopt the new Convention or, in the alternative, to cleave to Convention No. 107?

2. The Relation of ILO Convention No. 169 to the Draft Declaration: Are these two documents needlessly duplicative? The ILO has coordinated with the Working Group by, for example, sending representatives to the annual meetings and exchanging drafts and final reports and in collaborating on activities designed to gain assent to the objectives of the two documents by the international community. In light of this close collaboration, why do you suppose Convention No. 169 takes a more modest approach to the issues? For example, the Draft Declaration requires the consent of indigenous peoples before land can be developed, while Convention No. 169 requires only that a state consult with indigenous groups. Does the difference in character or legal effect between a convention and a draft declaration explain the differences in tone between the two documents?

---

*Copyright © 1986 American Journal of International Law and Russel Barsh. Reprinted with permission of the copyright holders.

3. The Draft Declaration: General Assembly Resolution 41/120 states that draft declarations should be written in clear and precise language and also be capable of engendering "broad international support." How well does the Draft Declaration fulfill these goals? As you read through the declaration, you might note language that either could be clarified or that might endanger the goal of gaining wide support. Understand that the draft may not become a final draft for several years. During the seventh session, the Working Group reviewed criticisms of the first revised text and charged the Chairman/Rapporteur, Ms. Erica-Irene A. Daes of Greece to prepare a second revised text. In addition, the Working Group called for "in-sessional and open-ended drafting groups" to meet and work on reaching agreement on draft principles to be recommended for change or adoption and called for governments and indigenous organizations to meet with the goal of agreeing on draft principles that can be submitted to future sessions of the working group. As always, in the international arena, the process focuses more on educating the participants, affected governments, and international opinion than on speed in reaching a consensus.

4. Collective Rights: A primary focus of the Draft Declaration is the protection of indigenous groups' right to exist and maintain their own culture. Note especially the strong statements against genocide (Art. 3) and ethnocide (Art. 5); the provisions regarding religious practices and artifacts (Arts. 6 and 8); the protections afforded to the development and promotion of indigenous languages (Arts. 9 and 10); and indigenous control of education (Art. 10). According to the chairman/rapporteur's report on the 1989 session, indigenous representatives "welcomed the emphasis of the draft declaration on collective rights," which "serves as a positive building force which would hopefully overcome the inadequacy of existing human rights norms aimed at the individual in the indigenous context." Report of the Working Group on Indigenous Populations on Its Seventh Session at 18, U.N. Doc. E/CN.4/Sub.2/199/36 (1989). Significantly, Convention No. 169 also protects group rights, especially in parts II and III, a radical departure from the approach of Convention No. 107. Under either document, could non-indigenous peoples argue that special measures taken to benefit indigenous peoples violate anti-discrimination norms? In addition, both documents guarantee freedom from discrimination, a concept focusing more on individual than group rights. How does each document accommodate anti-discrimination norms and the norm of indigenous control over membership determinations? Compare ILO Convention No. 169, article 8, § 2 and the Draft Declaration articles 24-25.

5. Protections for Tribal Land and Other Resource Issues: Contrast each document's treatment of tribal land. Neither document wholly prevents a national government from taking tribal land, but which enunciates stronger protections against confiscation? Is the approach taken by the Draft Declaration sufficiently strong? In contrast, is it too unrealistic? Would either approach permit a taking of aboriginal land without compensation on the theory that aboriginal property is not a compensable property right? Would either protect newly-acquired tribal land? Article 17 of the Draft Declaration requires states to consult with tribes before instituting large-scale projects. Those commenting on this draft language at the 1989 session of the Working Group criticized the general language of this draft provision. They argued that if the article intended to protect tribal lands from projects undertaken on all land it was unacceptably wide and if it was intended only to apply to projects undertaken on tribal land, the requirement for consultation was too weak. *See* 1989 Working Group report, *supra*, at 24.

Finally, do either of these documents go further than United States domestic law in protecting religious sites or tribal artifacts on private or publicly owned land?

6. Self-Determination: Note that both documents use the term "peoples." What is the meaning of article I-3 of Convention No. 169? In the 1989 session of the Working Group, indigenous representatives and working group members preferred the term "peoples," but some government representatives stated they could not support the use of the term without the sort of qualifier used in Convention 169, or at least a definition distinguishing between internal self-determination and self-determination within the meaning of the UN Charter and the 1960 Declaration on the Granting of Independence to Colonial Countries and Peoples. How do the two documents differ on the right to self-determination? Does either create a right that would permit indigenous peoples to secede? Note the emphasis on consultation with and participation by indigenous groups in the Convention, albeit with a stated goal of securing indigenous groups' consent to state actions affecting their welfare. By what mechanisms does the Draft Declaration seek to protect indigenous groups' right to autonomy? How would you apply article 23 of the Draft Declaration in a state that did not provide separate reserves for indigenous peoples?

7. Other Recent Initiatives: In recent years the world-wide indigenous rights movement has continued to build momentum. In addition to the conferences mentioned in the excerpts, a seminar was held in January 1989 in Geneva under the auspices of the UN Centre for Human Rights. Many delegates and the rapporteur were indigenous peoples, making this seminar the first event in which NGO's were both delegates and officers. *See* Report, The Effects of Racism and Racial Discrimination on the Social and Economic Relations Between Indigenous Peoples, E/CN.4/1989/22 *noted in* Current Developments, *United Nations Seminar on Indigenous Peoples and States*, 83 AM. J. INT'L L. 599 (1989) (Russel Barsh). The World Council of Churches met in Australia in May, 1989 and issued a strong declaration, the Darwin Declaration, in favor of protecting indigenous land rights. (The declaration is published as Annex III to the 1989 Working Group's report, at p. 36.) Finally, the General Assembly has scheduled a meeting on indigenous self-government in 1990 or 1991.

In its 1988-1989 Report, the Inter-American Commission on Human Rights of the Organization of American States proposed the adoption of a juridical instrument such as a declaration, an additional protocol to the American Convention on Human Rights, or even a separate convention on the rights of indigenous peoples to be adopted in 1992 as part of the OAS's planned celebration of the Discovery and Meeting of Two Worlds planned for that year. The report urged the adoption of standards that could receive the consent of the member states, noting, however:

> It should be kept in mind that as regards the issue of the rights of indigenous peoples, there has been a dichotomy between the resolutions that express the aspirations of the indigenous peoples themselves, usually adopted in congresses of indigenous peoples, and the incorporation of these rights into national or international law.

Inter-American Commission on Human Rights, Annual Report 1988-89 (Sept. 18, 1989).

The Commission asked the General Assembly to charge it with developing this instrument. On November 18, 1989, the General Assembly complied in a resolution requesting

... the Inter-American Commission on Human Rights to prepare a juridical instrument relative to the rights of indigenous peoples, for adoption in 1992.

OAS, General Assembly, Resolutions of November 18, 1989, Resolution No. 13.

Table of Cases

References are to page numbers. Principal cases and the pages where they appear are in italics.

A

A & A Concrete, Inc. v. White Mountain Apache Tribe, 420

Agua Caliente Tribal Council v. City of Palm Springs, 613

Ahuna v. Department of Hawaiian Home Lands, 1131

A.K. Mgt. Co. v. San Manuel Band of Mission Indians, 208, 1006

Alaska ex rel. Yukon Flats School Dist. v. Native Village of Venetie, 1097

Allstate Ins. Co. v. Hague, 351

Amoco Prod. Co. v. Village of Gambell, 231, 1074

Anderson v. Cumming, 971

Anderson v. O'Brien, 946

Andrus v. Glover Constr. Co., 231

Annis v. Dewey County Bank, 508

Antoine v. Washington, 231, 807, 836

Arizona v. California (Arizona I), 860, 863, 865, 868

Arizona v. California (Arizona II), 864

Arizona v. California (Arizona III), 865

Arizona v. California (Arizona IV), 873

Arizona v. San Carlos Apache Tribe, 873

Arizona ex rel. Merrill v. Turtle, 504, 514, 528

Armell v. Prairie Band of Potawatomi Indians, 413, 641

Assiniboine & Sioux Tribes v. Board of Oil & Gas Conserv., 252

Atkinson v. Haldane, 341

Attorney General v. Lavell, 1222

B

Bad Horse v. Bad Horse, 514

Badoni v. Higginson, 68

Baker v. Carr, 83, 198

Baker v. United States, 293

Baldwin v. Fish & Game Comm'n, 816

Barker v. Harvey, 679

Barona Group of Capitan Grande Band of Mission Indians v. American Mgt. & Amusement, Inc., 318, 1006

Barona Group of Capitan Grande Band of Mission Indians v. Duffy, 621

Barron v. Baltimore, 317

Barta v. Oglala Sioux Tribe, 318

Bates v. Clark, 108

Bear v. United States, 272

Black Hills Sioux Nation Treaty Council v. Stevens, 438

Black Spotted Horse v. Else, 271

Blake v. Arnett, 812

Blue Legs v. BIA, 342

Boe v. Ft. Belknap Indian Community, 342, 1100

Bottomly v. Passamaquoddy Tribe, 337, 1096, 1199

Bowen v. Roy, 45

Brendale v. Confederated Tribes & Bands of the Yakima Indian Nation, 461, 620, *1038*

Brown v. Babbitt Ford, Inc., 351

Brown v. United States, 386

B.R.T. v. Executive Dir. of Soc. Servs. Bd. of N.D., 658

Bryan v. Itasca County, 164, 232, 293, 418, *606,* 871, 808

Buck v. Kuykendall, 578

Burlington N.R.R. v. Ft. Peck Tribal Exec. Bd, 460, 762

Buttz v. Northern Pac. R.R., 762

C

California v. Cabazon Band of Mission Indians, 293, 296, 560, 613, *993,* 1033, 1167

California v. United States, 871

California State Bd. of Equalization v. Chemehuevi Tribe, 526, 992

Cape Fox Corp. v. United States, 253, 1063

Cappaert v. United States, 865

Carpenter v. Shaw, 229

Case of Sandra Lovelace, 1287

Catawba Indian Tribe v. South Carolina, 763

Cayuga Claims Case (Great Britain ex rel. Cayuga Indians in Canada v. United States), 179

Cayuga Indian Nation v. Cuomo, 763

Cayuga Indian Nation v. Cuomo II, 763

Central Machinery Co. v. Arizona State Tax Comm'n, 530

Chapoose v. Ute Indian Tribe, 439

Charrier v. Bell, 767

1305

Index

F

I

U

WATER RESOURCES AND RIGHTS—Cont'd
  Riverbeds.
    Eastern Oklahoma.
      Tribes in Eastern Oklahoma formerly the Indian Territory.
        Tribal riverbeds, pp. 1169 to 1173.
    Ownership.
      Conflicting state and tribal claims to ownership within reservations, pp. 765 to 767.
  Scope of Indian water rights, pp. 864, 865.
  State adjudication of Indian water rights.
    McCarran amendment, pp. 885 to 887.
    Arizona v. San Carlos Apache Tribe, pp. 873 to 885.
  Taking clause.
    Modification or abrogation of Indian water rights, pp. 871, 872.
  Trusteeship obligations.
    Federal government, pp. 255 to 273.
  Winters v. United States, pp. 859, 860.

WELFARE OF CHILDREN.
  Indian Child Welfare Act.
    Generally, pp. 622 to 665.
      See CHILD WELFARE.

WESTERN SHOSHONE TITLE LITIGATION.
  History, pp. 733 to 735.
  United States v. Dann, pp. 724 to 727.

WHEELER-HOWARD ACT.
  See INDIAN REORGANIZATION ACT.

Z

ZONING.
  State regulation of leased Indian land.
    Applicability of zoning ordinances to non-Indian lands.
      Brendale v. Confederated Tribes & Bands of The Yakima Indian Nation, p. 1038.
    Brendale v. Confederated Tribes & Bands of The Yakima Indian Nation.
      Applicability to non-Indian lands, p. 1038.
    Preemption of state and local laws.
      Note, pp. 1041, 1042.
    Sanitary landfills.
      Snohomish County v. Seattle Disposal Co., pp. 1038 to 1041.
    Snohomish County v. Seattle Disposal Co..
      Operation of sanitary landfill, pp. 1038 to 1041.
  Tribal governmental authority, pp. 461 to 476.